# THE COMPLETE ADVENTURES AND MEMOIRS OF SHERLOCK HOLMES

# THE ILLUSTRATED SHERLOCK HOLMES TREASURY

INCLUDING

## THE COMPLETE ADVENTURES AND MEMOIRS OF SHERLOCK HOLMES

## THE RETURN OF SHERLOCK HOLMES

## THE HOUND OF THE BASKERVILLES

## by Arthur Conan Doyle

*A facsimile of the original publications in*
STRAND MAGAZINE
1901-1905

WITH ALL THE ORIGINAL ILLUSTRATIONS
BY SIDNEY PAGET

AVENEL BOOKS
NEW YORK

ISBN: 0-517-205009
Copyright © MCMLXXVI by Crown Publishers, Inc.
Library of Congress Catalog Card Number: 76-40718
All rights reserved.
This edition is published by Avenel Books
a division of Barre Publishing, Inc.
h
Manufactured in the United States of America

# Contents

# INTRODUCTION

The deerstalker cap and cape-backed overcoat. The pipe. The grace of gaslit Victoriana. The clop clop of carriage and cobblestone. The fog rolling in from England's imperial seas. Baker Street.

Here is Sherlock Holmes in his original, classic setting: the pages of *The Strand Magazine*, the stage from which he made his debut in 1891, and from which Arthur Conan Doyle chose to lay him to rest—albeit temporarily—in 1893.

These are the most beloved of the Sherlock Holmes stories, the ones written in the first flush of Arthur Conan Doyle's genius. There are twenty-four stories here, and between "A Scandal in Bohemia" and "The Final Problem" there lie such masterpieces as "The Red-Headed League," "The Adventure of the Speckled Band," "The Five Orange Pips," "The Adventure of the Silver Blaze," and "The Adventure of the Musgrave Ritual."

The idea of writing a series of short stories around one central character was a new one in England. With the success of the first *Strand* story, "A Scandal in Bohemia," Doyle was encouraged to write a series of six, for which he agreed to be paid an average of $175 each. In a matter of days he had written the first series. Sherlock Holmes burst into tremendous popularity, and Doyle raised his price to $250 a story. He finished the next six in rapid time and wrote to his mother "I think of slaying Holmes in the last and winding him up for good. He takes my mind from better things."

*The Strand* continued to hound Conan Doyle for more about Holmes. The offer of much greater amounts of money disturbed the spiritual side of Conan Doyle as much as did his overexposure to Holmes. Doyle had found the perfect cliff from which to propel the detective, and did so in "The Final Problem." The resulting public outcry shocked him. Doyle was looked upon as an assassin; people wept; men wore mourning bands to their offices, and Doyle was called a brute by at least one outraged reader. It took eight years for Doyle to weaken in his resolve not to revive Sherlock Holmes. Finally, in an interview in *Harper's Weekly* in 1901, Conan Doyle allowed as how Dr. Watson's account of Holmes' death just *may* have been the result of hallucination. Holmes came back. As one reader put it, the fall may not have left him dead, but he seemed never to be quite the same. These early stories were never to be equalled.

The stories themselves have been translated into forty-one languages, including Basuto and shorthand. Ellery Queen contended that "more has been written about Sherlock Holmes than any other character in fiction."

Given a choice of three heroes of the printed word, the rare reader is one who would not place Sherlock Holmes among them. What other literary invention can boast a full-length biography, an immediately identifiable silhouette, or a name that, as a household word, reaches so far beyond class or nation as to be startlingly universal?

Sherlock Holmes is, said Sherlockian scholar Edgar W. Smith, "the personification of something in us that we have lost, or never had. For it is not Sherlock Holmes who sits in Baker Street, comfortable, competent and self-assured; it is ourselves who are there, full of a tremendous capacity for wisdom, complacent in the presence of our humble Watson, conscious of a warm well-being and a timeless, imperishable content. The easy chair in the room is drawn up to the hearthstone of our very hearts—it is *our* tobacco in the Persian slipper, and *our* violin lying so carelessly across the knees—it is *we* who hear the pounding on the stairs and the knock upon the door. The swirling fog without and the acrid smoke within bite deep indeed, for we taste them even now. And the time and place and all the great events are near and dear to us not because our memories call them forth in pure nostalgia, but because they are a part of us today.

"That is the Sherlock Holmes we love— the Holmes implicit and eternal in ourselves."

Sidney Paget, the illustrator for *The Strand* stories, was commissioned in error. The editors were under the mistaken impression that they were writing to his artist brother, Walter, who had made the drawings for Sir H. Rider Haggard's *King Solomon's Mines* and *She,* and was perhaps best known for his illustrations for *Robinson Crusoe,* and *Treasure Island.* Sidney Paget was successful as a painter, having shown two pictures at the Academy when he was only eighteen years old. He began painting portraits and small pictures at the same time as he was illustrating books and papers, chiefly war subjects of Egypt and the Sudan. Walter Paget, who lost the chance to be Holmes' *Strand* illustrator, did serve as model for his brother's successful attempts at bringing Holmes to life. Paget produced a total of 357 Sherlock Holmes drawings with Conan Doyle complaining that Paget had made Holmes far handsomer than his creator had ever intended him to be.

# Adventures of Sherlock Holmes.

## ADVENTURE I.—A SCANDAL IN BOHEMIA

### By A. Conan Doyle.

TO Sherlock Holmes she is always *the* woman. I have seldom heard him mention her under any other name. In his eyes she eclipses and predominates the whole of her sex. It was not that he felt any emotion akin to love for Irene Adler. All emotions, and that one particularly, were abhorrent to his cold, precise, but admirably balanced mind. He was, I take it, the most perfect reasoning and observing machine that the world has seen ; but, as a lover, he would have placed himself in a false position. He never spoke of the softer passions, save with a gibe and a sneer. They were admirable things for the observer —excellent for drawing the veil from men's motives and actions. But for the trained reasoner to admit such intrusions into his own delicate and finely adjusted temperament was to introduce a distracting factor which might throw a doubt upon all his mental results. Grit in a sensitive instrument, or a crack in one of his own high-power lenses, would not be more disturbing than a strong emotion in a nature such as his. And yet there was but one woman to him, and that woman was the late Irene Adler, of dubious and questionable memory.

I had seen little of Holmes lately. My marriage had drifted us away from each other. My own complete happiness, and the home-centred interests which rise up around the man who first finds himself master of his own establishment, were sufficient to absorb all my attention ; while Holmes, who loathed every form of society with his whole Bohemian soul, remained in our lodgings in Baker-street, buried among his old books, and alternating from week to week between cocaine and ambition, the drowsiness of the drug, and the fierce energy of his own keen nature. He was still, as ever, deeply attracted by the study of crime, and occupied his immense faculties and extraordinary powers of observation in following out those clues, and clearing up those mysteries, which had been abandoned as hopeless by the official police. From time to time I heard some vague account of his doings : of his summons to Odessa in the case of the Trepoff murder, of his clearing up of the singular tragedy of the Atkinson brothers at Trincomalee, and finally of the mission which he had accomplished so delicately and successfully for the reigning family of Holland. Beyond these signs of his activity, however, which I merely shared with all the readers of the daily press, I knew little of my former friend and companion.

One night—it was on the 20th of March, 1888—I was returning from a journey to a patient (for I had now returned to civil practice), when my way led me through Baker-street. As I passed the well-remembered door, which must always be associated in my mind with my wooing, and with the dark incidents of the Study in Scarlet, I was seized with a keen desire to see Holmes again, and to know how he was employing his extraordinary powers. His rooms were brilliantly lit, and, even as I looked up, I saw his tall spare figure pass twice in a dark silhouette against the blind. He was pacing the room swiftly, eagerly, with his head sunk upon his chest, and his hands clasped behind him. To me, who knew his every mood and habit, his attitude and manner told their own story. He was at work again. He had arisen out of his drug-created dreams, and was hot upon the scent of some new problem. I rang the bell, and was shown up to the chamber which had formerly been in part my own.

His manner was not effusive. It seldom was ; but he was glad, I think, to see me. With hardly a word spoken, but with a kindly eye, he waved me to an armchair, threw across his case of cigars, and indicated a spirit case and a gasogene in the corner. Then he stood before the fire, and looked me over in his singular introspective fashion.

"Wedlock suits you," he remarked. "I think, Watson, that you have put on seven and a half pounds since I saw you."

"Seven," I answered.

"Indeed, I should have thought a little more. Just a trifle more, I fancy, Watson. And in practice again, I observe. You did not tell me that you intended to go into harness."

"Then, how do you know ? "

"I see it, I deduce it. How do I know

that you have been getting yourself very wet lately, and that you have a most clumsy and careless servant girl?"

"My dear Holmes," said I, "this is too much. You would certainly have been burned, had you lived a few centuries ago. It is true that I had a country walk on Thursday and came home in a dreadful mess; but, as I have changed my clothes, I can't imagine how you deduce it. As to Mary Jane, she is incorrigible, and my wife has given her notice; but there again I fail to see how you work it out."

He chuckled to himself and rubbed his long nervous hands together.

"It is simplicity itself," said he; "my eyes tell me that on the inside of your left shoe, just where the firelight strikes it, the leather is scored by six almost parallel cuts. Obviously they have been caused by someone who has very carelessly scraped round the edges of the sole in order to remove crusted mud from it. Hence, you see, my double deduction that you had been out in vile

"THEN HE STOOD BEFORE THE FIRE."

weather, and that you had a particularly malignant boot-slitting specimen of the London slavey. As to your practice, if a gentleman walks into my rooms smelling of iodoform, with a black mark of nitrate of silver upon his right fore-finger, and a bulge on the side of his top-hat to show where he has secreted his stethoscope, I must be dull indeed, if I do not pronounce him to be an active member of the medical profession."

I could not help laughing at the ease with which he explained his process of deduction. "When I hear you give your reasons," I remarked, "the thing always appears to me to be so ridiculously simple that I could easily do it myself, though at each successive instance of your reasoning I am baffled, until you explain your process. And yet I believe that my eyes are as good as yours."

"Quite so," he answered, lighting a cigarette, and throwing himself down into an armchair. "You see, but you do not observe. The distinction is clear. For example, you have frequently seen the steps which lead up from the hall to this room."

"Frequently."

"How often?"

"Well, some hundreds of times."

"Then how many are there?"

"How many! I don't know."

"Quite so! You have not observed.

And yet you have seen. That is just my point. Now, I know that there are seventeen steps, because I have both seen and observed. By the way, since you are interested in these little problems, and since you are good enough to chronicle one or two of my trifling experiences, you may be interested in this." He threw over a sheet of thick pink-tinted notepaper which had been lying open upon the table. "It came by the last post," said he. "Read it aloud."

The note was undated, and without either signature or address.

"There will call upon you to-night, at a quarter to eight o'clock," it said, "a gentleman who desires to consult you upon a matter of the very deepest moment. Your recent services to one of the Royal Houses of Europe have shown that you are one who may safely be trusted with matters which are of an importance which can hardly be exaggerated. This account of you we have from all quarters received. Be in your chamber then at that hour, and do not take it amiss if your visitor wear a mask."

"This is indeed a

"I CAREFULLY EXAMINED THE WRITING."

mystery," I remarked. "What do you imagine that it means?"

"I have no data yet. It is a capital mistake to theorise before one has data. Insensibly one begins to twist facts to suit theories, instead of theories to suit facts. But the note itself. What do you deduce from it?"

I carefully examined the writing, and the paper upon which it was written.

"The man who wrote it was presumably well to do," I remarked, endeavouring to imitate my companion's processes. "Such paper could not be bought under half a crown a packet. It is peculiarly strong and stiff."

"Peculiar—that is the very word," said Holmes. "It is not an English paper at all. Hold it up to the light."

I did so, and saw a large E with a small g, a P, and a large G with a small t woven into the texture of the paper.

"What do you make of that?" asked Holmes.

"The name of the maker no doubt; or his monogram, rather."

"Not at all. The G with the small t stands for 'Gesellschaft,' which is the German for 'Company.' It is a customary contraction like our 'Co.' P, of course, stands for 'Papier.' Now for the Eg. Let us glance at our Continental Gazetteer." He took down a heavy brown volume from his shelves. "Eglow, Eglonitz—here we are, Egria. It is in a German - speaking country—in Bohemia, not far from Carlsbad. 'Remarkable as being the scene of the death of Wallenstein, and for its numerous glass factories and paper mills.' Ha, ha, my boy, what do you make of that?" His eyes sparkled, and he sent up a great blue triumphant cloud from his cigarette.

"The paper was made in Bohemia," I said.

"Precisely. And the man who wrote the note is a German. Do you note the peculiar construction of the sentence—'This account of you we have from all quarters received.' A Frenchman or Russian could not have written that. It is the German who is so uncourteous to his verbs. It only remains, therefore, to discover what is wanted by this German who writes upon Bohemian paper, and prefers wearing a mask to showing his face. And here he comes, if I am not mistaken, to resolve all our doubts."

As he spoke there was the sharp sound of horses' hoofs and grating wheels against the curb, foll wed by a sharp pull at the bell. Holmes whistled.

"A pair, by the sound," said he. "Yes," he continued, glancing out of the window. "A nice little brougham and a pair of beauties. A hundred and fifty guineas apiece. There's money in this case, Watson, if there is nothing else."

"I think that I had better go, Holmes."

"Not a bit, Doctor. Stay where you are. I am lost without my Boswell. And this promises to be interesting. It would be a pity to miss it."

"But your client ——"

"Never mind him. I may want your help, and so may he. Here he comes. Sit down in that armchair, Doctor, and give us your best attention."

A slow and heavy step, which had been heard upon the stairs and in the passage, paused immediately outside the door. Then there was a loud and authoritative tap.

"Come in!" said Holmes.

A man entered who could hardly have been less than six feet six inches in height, with the chest and limbs of a Hercules. His dress was rich with a richness which would, in England, be looked upon as akin to bad taste. Heavy bands of Astrakhan were lashed across the sleeves and fronts of his double-breasted coat, while the deep blue cloak which was thrown over his shoulders

"A MAN ENTERED."

was lined with flame-coloured silk, and secured at the neck with a brooch which consisted of a single flaming beryl. Boots which extended half way up his calves, and which were trimmed at the tops with rich brown fur, completed the impression of barbaric opulence which was suggested by his whole appearance. He carried a broadbrimmed hat in his hand, while he wore across the upper part of his face, extending down past the cheek-bones, a black vizard mask, which he had apparently adjusted that very moment, for his hand was still raised to it as he entered. From the lower part of the face he appeared to be a man of strong character, with a thick, hanging lip, and a long straight chin, suggestive of resolution pushed to the length of obstinacy.

"You had my note?" he asked, with a deep harsh voice and a strongly marked German accent. "I told you that I would call." He looked from one to the other of us, as if uncertain which to address.

"Pray take a seat," said Holmes. "This is my friend and colleague, Dr. Watson, who is occasionally good enough to help me in my cases. Whom have I the honour to address?"

"You may address me as the Count Von Kramm, a Bohemian nobleman. I understand that this gentleman, your friend, is a man of honour and discretion, whom I may trust with a matter of the most extreme importance. If not, I should much prefer to communicate with you alone."

I rose to go, but Holmes caught me by

the wrist and pushed me back into my chair. "It is both, or none," said he. "You may say before this gentleman anything which you may say to me."

The Count shrugged his broad shoulders. "Then I must begin," said he, " by binding you both to absolute secrecy for two years, at the end of that time the matter will be of no importance. At present it is not too much to say that it is of such weight that it may have an influence upon European history."

" I promise," said Holmes.

" And I."

" You will excuse this mask," continued our strange visitor. " The august person who employs me wishes his agent to be unknown to you, and I may confess at once that the title by which I have just called myself is not exactly my own."

" I was aware of it," said Holmes dryly.

" The circumstances are of great delicacy, and every precaution has to be taken to quench what might grow to be an immense scandal and seriously compromise one of the reigning families of Europe. To speak plainly, the matter implicates the great House of Ormstein, hereditary kings of Bohemia."

" I was also aware of that," murmured Holmes, settling himself down in his armchair, and closing his eyes.

Our visitor glanced with some apparent surprise at the languid, lounging figure of the man who had been no doubt depicted to him as the most incisive reasoner, and most energetic agent in Europe. Holmes slowly reopened his eyes, and looked impatiently at his gigantic client.

" If your Majesty would condescend to state your case," he remarked, " I should be better able to advise you."

The man sprang from his chair, and paced up and down the room in uncontrollable agitation. Then, with a gesture of

"HE TORE THE MASK FROM HIS FACE."

desperation, he tore the mask from his face and hurled it upon the ground. "You are right," he cried, " I am the King. Why should I attempt to conceal it ? "

" Why, indeed ? " murmured Holmes.

" Your Majesty had not spoken before I was aware that I was addressing Wilhelm Gottsreich Sigismond von Ormstein, Grand Duke of Cassel-Felstein, and hereditary King of Bohemia."

" But you can understand," said our strange visitor, sitting down once more and passing his hand over his high, white forehead, " you can understand that I am not accustomed to doing such business in my own person. Yet the matter was so delicate that I could not confide it to an agent without putting myself in his power. I have come *incognito* from Prague for the purpose of consulting you."

" Then, pray consult," said Holmes, shutting his eyes once more.

" The facts are briefly these : Some five years ago, during a lengthy visit to Warsaw, I made the acquaintance of the well-known adventuress Irene Adler. The name is no doubt familiar to you."

" Kindly look her up in my index, Doctor," murmured Holmes, without opening his eyes. For many years he had adopted a system of docketing all paragraphs concerning men and things, so that it was difficult to name a subject or a person on which he could not at once furnish information. In this case I found her biography sandwiched in between that of a Hebrew Rabbi and that of a staff-commander who had written a monograph upon the deep sea fishes.

"Let me see?" said Holmes. "Hum! Born in New Jersey in the year 1858. Contralto—hum! La Scala, hum! Prima donna Imperial Opera of Warsaw—Yes! Retired from operatic stage—ha! Living in London—quite so! Your Majesty, as I understand, became entangled with this young person, wrote her some compromising letters, and is now desirous of getting those letters back."

"Precisely so. But how——"

"Was there a secret marriage?"

"None."

"No legal papers or certificates?"

"None."

"Then I fail to follow your Majesty. If this young person should produce her letters for blackmailing or other purposes, how is she to prove their authenticity?"

"There is the writing."

"Pooh, pooh! Forgery."

"My private notepaper."

"Stolen."

"My own seal."

"Imitated."

"My photograph."

"Bought."

"We were both in the photograph."

"Oh dear! That is very bad! Your Majesty has indeed committed an indiscretion."

"I was mad—insane."

"You have compromised yourself seriously."

"I was only Crown Prince then. I was young. I am but thirty now."

"It must be recovered."

"We have tried and failed."

"Your Majesty must pay. It must be bought."

"She will not sell."

"Stolen, then."

"Five attempts have been made. Twice burglars in my pay ransacked her house. Once we diverted her luggage when she travelled. Twice she has been waylaid. There has been no result."

"No sign of it?"

"Absolutely none."

Holmes laughed. "It is quite a pretty little problem," said he.

"But a very serious one to me," returned the King, reproachfully.

"Very, indeed. And what does she propose to do with the photograph?"

"To ruin me."

"But how?"

"I am about to be married."

"So I have heard."

"To Clotilde Lothman von Saxe-Meningen, second daughter of the King of Scandinavia. You may know the strict principles of her family. She is herself the very soul of delicacy. A shadow of a doubt as to my conduct would bring the matter to an end."

"And Irene Adler?"

"Threatens to send them the photograph. And she will do it. I know that she will do it. You do not know her, but she has a soul of steel. She has the face of the most beautiful of women, and the mind of the most resolute of men. Rather than I should marry another woman, there are no lengths to which she would not go—none."

"You are sure that she has not sent it yet?"

"I am sure."

"And why?"

"Because she has said that she would send it on the day when the betrothal was publicly proclaimed. That will be next Monday."

"Oh, then, we have three days yet," said Holmes, with a yawn. "That is very fortunate, as I have one or two matters of importance to look into just at present. Your Majesty will, of course, stay in London for the present?"

"Certainly. You will find me at the Langham, under the name of the Count Von Kramm."

"Then I shall drop you a line to let you know how we progress."

"Pray do so. I shall be all anxiety."

"Then, as to money?"

"You have *carte blanche.*"

"Absolutely?"

"I tell you that I would give one of the provinces of my kingdom to have that photograph."

"And for present expenses?"

The king took a heavy chamois leather bag from under his cloak, and laid it on the table.

"There are three hundred pounds in gold, and seven hundred in notes," he said.

Holmes scribbled a receipt upon a sheet of his note-book, and handed it to him.

"And mademoiselle's address?" he asked.

"Is Briony Lodge, Serpentine-avenue, St. John's Wood."

Holmes took a note of it. "One other question," said he. "Was the photograph a cabinet?"

"It was."

"Then, good night, your Majesty, and I trust that we shall soon have some good news for you. And good night, Watson," he added, as the wheels of the Royal brougham rolled down the street. "If you will be good enough to call to-morrow afternoon, at three o'clock, I should like to chat this little matter over with you."

## II.

AT three o'clock precisely I was at Baker-street, but Holmes had not yet returned. The landlady informed me that he had left the house shortly after eight o'clock in the morning. I sat down beside the fire, however, with the intention of awaiting him, however long he might be. I was already deeply interested in his inquiry, for, though it was surrounded by none of the grim and strange features which were associated with the two crimes which I

"A DRUNKEN-LOOKING GROOM."

have already recorded, still, the nature of the case and the exalted station of his client gave it a character of its own. Indeed, apart from the nature of the investigation which my friend had on hand, there was something in his masterly grasp of a situation, and his keen, incisive reasoning, which made it a pleasure to me to study his system of work, and to follow the quick, subtle methods by which he disentangled the most inextricable mysteries. So accustomed was I to his invariable success that the very possibility of his failing had ceased to enter into my head.

It was close upon four before the door opened, and a drunken-looking groom, ill-kempt and side-whiskered, with an inflamed face and disreputable clothes, walked into the room. Accustomed as I was to my friend's amazing powers in the use of disguises, I had to look three times before I was certain that it was indeed he. With a nod he vanished into the bedroom, whence he emerged in five minutes tweed-suited and respectable, as of old. Putting his hands into his pockets, he stretched out his legs in front of the fire, and laughed heartily for some minutes.

"Well, really!" he cried, and then he choked; and laughed again until he was obliged to lie back, limp and helpless, in the chair.

"What is it?"

"It's quite too funny. I am sure you could never guess how I employed my morning, or what I ended by doing."

"I can't imagine. I suppose that you have been watching the habits, and perhaps the house, or Miss Irene Adler."

"Quite so, but the sequel was rather unusual. I will tell you, however. I left the house a little after eight o'clock this morning, in the character of a groom out of work. There is a wonderful sympathy and freemasonry among horsey men. Be one of them, and you will know all that there is to know. I soon found Briony Lodge. It is a *bijou* villa, with a garden at the back, but built out in front right up to the road, two stories. Chubb lock to the door. Large sitting-room on the right side, well furnished, with long windows almost to the floor, and those preposterous

English window fasteners which a child could open. Behind there was nothing remarkable, save that the passage window could be reached from the top of the coach-house. I walked round it and examined it closely from every point of view, but without noting anything else of interest.

"I then lounged down the street, and found, as I expected, that there was a mews in a lane which runs down by one wall of the garden. I lent the ostlers a hand in rubbing down their horses, and I received in exchange twopence, a glass of half-and-half, two fills of shag tobacco, and as much information as I could desire about Miss Adler, to say nothing of half a dozen other people in the neighbourhood in whom I was not in the least interested, but whose biographies I was compelled to listen to."

"And what of Irene Adler?" I asked.

"Oh, she has turned all the men's heads down in that part. She is the daintiest thing under a bonnet on this planet. So say the Serpentine-mews, to a man. She lives quietly, sings at concerts, drives out at five every day, and returns at seven sharp for dinner. Seldom goes out at other times, except when she sings. Has only one male visitor, but a good deal of him. He is dark, handsome, and dashing; never calls less than once a day, and often twice. He is a Mr. Godfrey Norton, of the Inner Temple. See the advantages of a cabman as a confidant. They had driven him home a dozen times from Serpentine-mews, and knew all about him. When I had listened to all that they had to tell, I began to walk up and down near Briony Lodge once more, and to think over my plan of campaign.

"This Godfrey Norton was evidently an important factor in the matter. He was a lawyer. That sounded ominous. What was the relation between them, and what the object of his repeated visits? Was she his client, his friend, or his mistress? If the former, she had probably transferred the photograph to his keeping. If the latter, it was less likely. On the issue of this question depended whether I should continue my work at Briony Lodge, or turn my attention to the gentleman's chambers in the Temple. It was a delicate point, and it widened the field of my inquiry. I fear that I bore you with these details, but I have to let you see my little difficulties, if you are to understand the situation."

"I am following you closely," I answered.

"I was still balancing the matter in my mind, when a hansom cab drove up to Briony Lodge, and a gentleman sprang out. He was a remarkably handsome man, dark, aquiline, and moustached—evidently the man of whom I had heard. He appeared to be in a great hurry, shouted to the cabman to wait, and brushed past the maid who opened the door with the air of a man who was thoroughly at home.

"He was in the house about half an hour, and I could catch glimpses of him, in the windows of the sitting-room, pacing up and down, talking excitedly and waving his arms. Of her I could see nothing. Presently he emerged, looking even more flurried than before. As he stepped up to the cab, he pulled a gold watch from his pocket and looked at it earnestly. 'Drive like the devil,' he shouted, 'first to Gross & Hankey's in Regent-street, and then to the church of St. Monica in the Edgware-road. Half a guinea if you do it in twenty minutes!'

"Away they went, and I was just wondering whether I should not do well to follow them, when up the lane came a neat little landau, the coachman with his coat only half buttoned, and his tie under his ear, while all the tags of his harness were sticking out of the buckles. It hadn't pulled up before she shot out of the hall door and into it. I only caught a glimpse of her at the moment, but she was a lovely woman, with a face that a man might die for.

"'The Church of St. Monica, John,' she cried, 'and half a sovereign if you reach it in twenty minutes.'

"This was quite too good to lose, Watson. I was just balancing whether I should run for it, or whether I should perch behind her landau, when a cab came through the street. The driver looked twice at such a shabby fare; but I jumped in before he could object. 'The Church of St. Monica,' said I, 'and half a sovereign if you reach it in twenty minutes.' It was twenty-five minutes to twelve, and of course it was clear enough what was in the wind.

"My cabby drove fast. I don't think I ever drove faster, but the others were there before us. The cab and the landau with their steaming horses were in front of the door when I arrived. I paid the man, and hurried into the church. There was not a soul there save the two whom I had followed and a surpliced clergyman, who seemed to be expostulating with them. They were all three standing in a knot in front of the altar. I lounged up the side aisle like any other idler who has dropped into a church. Suddenly, to my surprise, the three at the altar faced round to me, and Godfrey Norton came running as hard as he could towards me."

"Thank God!" he cried. "You'll do. Come! Come!"

"What then?" I asked.

"Come man, come, only three minutes, or it won't be legal."

"I FOUND MYSELF MUMBLING RESPONSES."

I was half dragged up to the altar, and, before I knew where I was, I found myself mumbling responses which were whispered in my ear, and vouching for things of which I knew nothing, and generally assisting in the secure tying up of Irene Adler, spinster, to Godfrey Norton, bachelor. It was all done in an instant, and there was the gentleman thanking me on the one side and the lady on the other, while the clergyman beamed on me in front. It was the most preposterous position in which I ever found myself in my life, and it was the thought of it that started me laughing just now. It seems that there had been some informality about their licence, that the clergyman absolutely refused to marry them without a witness of some sort, and that my lucky appearance saved the bridegroom from having to sally out into the streets in search of a best man. The bride gave me a sovereign, and I mean to wear it on my watch chain in memory of the occasion."

"This is a very unexpected turn of affairs," said I ; "and what then?"

"Well, I found my plans very seriously menaced. It looked as if the pair might take an immediate departure, and so necessitate very prompt and energetic measures on my part. At the church door, however, they separated, he driving back to the Temple, and she to her own house. 'I shall drive out in the Park at five as usual,' she said as she left him. I heard no more. They drove away in different directions, and I went off to make my own arrangements."

"Which are?"

"Some cold beef and a glass of beer," he answered, ringing the bell. "I have been too busy to think of food, and I am likely to be busier still this evening. By the way, Doctor, I shall want your co-operation."

"I shall be delighted."

"You don't mind breaking the law?"

"Not in the least."

"Nor running a chance of arrest?"

"Not in a good cause."

"Oh, the cause is excellent!"

"Then I am your man."

"I was sure that I might rely on you."

"But what is it you wish?"

"When Mrs. Turner has brought in the tray I will make it clear to you. Now," he said, as he turned hungrily on the simple fare that our landlady had provided, "I must discuss it while I eat, for I have not much time. It is nearly five now. In two hours we must be on the scene of action. Miss Irene, or Madame, rather, returns from her drive at seven. We must be at Briony Lodge to meet her."

"And what then?"

"You must leave that to me. I have already arranged what is to occur. There is only one point on which I must insist. You must not interfere, come what may. You understand?"

"I am to be neutral?"

"To do nothing whatever. There will probably be some small unpleasantness.

Do not join in it. It will end in my being conveyed into the house. Four or five minutes afterwards the sitting-room window will open. You are to station yourself close to that open window."

"Yes."

"You are to watch me, for I will be visible to you."

"Yes."

"And when I raise my hand—so—you will throw into the room what I give you to throw, and will, at the same time, raise the cry of fire. You quite follow me?"

"Entirely."

"It is nothing very formidable," he said, taking a long cigar-shaped roll from his pocket. "It is an ordinary plumber's smoke rocket, fitted with a cap at either end to make it self-lighting. Your task is confined to that. When you raise your cry of fire, it will be taken up by quite a number of people. You may then walk to the end of the street, and I will rejoin you in ten minutes. I hope that I have made myself clear?"

"I am to remain neutral, to get near the window, to watch you, and, at the signal, to throw in this object, then to raise the cry of fire, and to wait you at the corner of the street."

"Precisely."

"Then you may entirely rely on me."

"That is excellent. I think perhaps it is almost time that I prepared for the new *rôle* I have to play."

He disappeared into his bedroom, and returned in a few minutes in the character of an amiable and simple-minded Nonconformist clergyman. His broad black hat, his baggy trousers, his white tie, his sympathetic smile, and general look of peering and benevolent curiosity were such as Mr. John Hare alone could have equalled. It was not merely that Holmes changed his costume. His expression, his manner, his very soul seemed to vary with every fresh part that he assumed. The stage lost a fine actor, even as science lost an acute

"A SIMPLE MINDED CLERGYMAN.

reasoner, when he became a specialist in crime.

It was a quarter past six when we left Baker-street, and it still wanted ten minutes to the hour when we found ourselves in Serpentine-avenue. It was already dusk, and the lamps were just being lighted as we paced up and down in front of Briony Lodge, waiting for the coming of its occupant. The house was just such as I had pictured it from Sherlock Holmes' succinct description, but the locality appeared to be less private than I expected. On the contrary, for a small street in a quiet neighbourhood, it was remarkably animated. There was a group of shabbily-dressed men smoking and laughing in a corner, a scissors grinder with his wheel, two guardsmen who were flirting with a nurse-girl, and several well-dressed young men who were lounging up and down with cigars in their mouths.

"You see," remarked Holmes, as we paced to and fro in front of the house, "this marriage rather simplifies matters. The photograph becomes a double-edged weapon now. The chances are that she would be as averse to its being seen by Mr. Godfrey Norton, as our client is to its coming to the eyes of his Princess. Now the question is—Where are we to find the photograph?"

"Where, indeed?"

"It is most unlikely that she carries it about with her. It is cabinet size. Too large for easy concealment about a woman's dress. She knows that the King is capable of having her waylaid and searched. Two attempts of the sort have already been made. We may take it then that she does not carry it about with her."

"Where, then?"

"Her banker or her lawyer. There is that double possibility. But I am inclined to think neither. Women are naturally secretive, and they like to do their own secreting. Why should she hand it over to anyone else ? She could trust her own guardianship, but she could not tell what indirect or political influence might be brought to bear upon a business man. Besides, remember that she had resolved to use it within a few days. It must be where she can lay her hands upon it. It must be in her own house."

"But it has twice been burgled."

"Pshaw ! They did not know how to look."

"But how will you look ? "

"I will not look."

"What then ?"

"I will get her to show me."

"But she will refuse."

"She will not be able to. But I hear the rumble of wheels. It is her carriage. Now carry out my orders to the letter."

As he spoke the gleam of the sidelights of a carriage came round the curve of the avenue. It was a smart little landau which rattled up to the door of Briony Lodge. As it pulled up one of the loafing men at the corner dashed forward to open the door in the hope of earning a copper, but was elbowed away by another loafer who had rushed up with the same intention. A fierce quarrel broke out, which was increased by the two guardsmen, who took sides with one of the loungers, and by the scissors grinder, who was equally hot upon the other side. A blow was struck, and in an instant the lady, who had stepped from her carriage, was the centre of a little knot of flushed and struggling men who struck savagely at each other with their fists and sticks. Holmes dashed into the crowd to protect the lady ; but, just as he reached her, he gave a cry and dropped to the ground, with the blood running freely down his face. At his fall the guardsmen took to their heels in one direction and the loungers in the other, while a number of better dressed people who had watched the scuffle without taking part in it, crowded in to help the lady and to attend to the injured man. Irene Adler, as I will still call her, had hurried up the steps; but she stood at the top with her superb figure outlined against the lights of the hall, looking back into the street.

"Is the poor gentleman much hurt ? " she asked.

"He is dead," cried several voices.

"No, no, there's life in him," shouted another. "But he'll be gone before you can get him to hospital."

"He's a brave fellow," said a woman. "They would have had the lady's purse and watch if it hadn't been for him. They were a gang, and a rough one too. Ah, he's breathing now."

"He can't lie in the street. May we bring him in, marm ? "

"Surely. Bring him into the sitting-

"HE GAVE A CRY AND DROPPED."

room. There is a comfortable sofa. This way, please ! "

Slowly and solemnly he was borne into Briony Lodge, and laid out in the principal room, while I still observed the proceedings from my post by the window. The lamps had been lit, but the blinds had not been drawn, so that I could see Holmes as he lay upon the couch. I do not know whether he was seized with compunction at that moment for the part he was playing, but I know that I never felt more heartily ashamed of myself in my life than when I saw the beautiful creature against whom I was conspiring, or the grace and kindliness with which she waited upon the injured man. And yet it would be the blackest treachery to Holmes to draw back now from the part which he had entrusted to me. I hardened my heart, and took the smoke-rocket from under my ulster. After all, I thought, we are not injuring her. We are but preventing her from injuring another.

Holmes had sat up upon the couch, and I saw him motion like a man who is in need of air. A maid rushed across and threw open the window. At the same instant I saw him raise his hand, and at the signal I tossed my rocket into the room with a cry of " Fire." The word was no sooner out of my mouth than the whole crowd of spectators, well dressed and ill — gentlemen, ostlers, and servant maids — joined in a general shriek of " Fire." Thick clouds of smoke curled through the room, and out at the open window. I caught a glimpse of rushing figures, and a moment later the voice of Holmes from within, assuring them that it was a false alarm. Slipping through the shouting crowd I made my way to the corner of the street, and in ten minutes was rejoiced to find my friend's arm in mine, and to get away from the scene of uproar. He walked swiftly and in silence for some few minutes, until we had turned down one of the quiet streets which lead towards the Edgware-road.

" You did it very nicely, Doctor," he remarked. " Nothing could have been better. It is all right."

" You have the photograph ! "

" I know where it is."

" And how did you find out ? "

" She showed me, as I told you that she would "

" I am still in the dark."

" I do not wish to make a mystery," said he laughing. " The matter was perfectly simple. You, of course, saw that everyone in the street was an accomplice. They were all engaged for the evening."

" I guessed as much."

" Then, when the row broke out, I had a little moist red paint in the palm of my hand. I rushed forward, fell down, clapped my hand to my face, and became a piteous spectacle. It is an old trick."

" That also I could fathom."

" Then they carried me in. She was bound to have me in. What else could she do ? And into her sitting-room, which was the very room which I suspected. It lay between that and her bedroom, and I was determined to see which. They laid me on a couch, I motioned for air, they were compelled to open the window, and you had your chance."

" How did that help you ? "

" It was all-important. When a woman thinks that her house is on fire, her instinct is at once to rush to the thing which she values most. It is a perfectly overpowering impulse, and I have more than once taken advantage of it. In the case of the Darlington Substitution Scandal it was of use to me, and also in the Arnsworth Castle business. A married woman grabs at her baby—an unmarried one reaches for her jewel box. Now it was clear to me that our lady of to-day had nothing in the house more precious to her than what we are in quest of. She would rush to secure it. The alarm of fire was admirably done. The smoke and shouting were enough to shake nerves of steel. She responded beautifully. The photograph is in a recess behind a sliding panel just above the right bell pull. She was there in an instant, and I caught a glimpse of it as she half drew it out. When I cried out that it was a false alarm, she replaced it, glanced at the rocket, rushed from the room, and I have not seen her since. I rose, and, making my excuses, escaped from the house. I hesitated whether to attempt to secure the photograph at once ; but the coachman had come in, and, as he was watching me narrowly, it seemed safer to wait. A little over-precipitance may ruin all."

" And now ? " I asked.

" Our quest is practically finished. I shall call with the King to-morrow, and with you, if you care to come with us. We will be shown into the sitting-room to wait for the lady, but it is probable that when she comes she may find neither us nor the photograph. It might be a satisfaction to

His Majesty to regain it with his own hands."

"And when will you call ? "

"At eight in the morning. She will not be up, so that we shall have a clear field. Besides, we must be prompt, for this marriage may mean a complete change in her life and habits. I must wire to the King without delay."

We had reached Baker-street, and had stopped at the door. He was searching his pockets for the key, when someone passing said :—

"Good-night, Mister Sherlock Holmes."

There were several people on the pavement at the time, but the greeting appeared to come from a slim youth in an ulster who had hurried by.

"I've heard that voice before," said Holmes, staring down the dimly lit street. "Now, I wonder who the deuce that could have been."

### III.

I SLEPT at Baker-street that night, and we were engaged upon our toast and coffee in the morning when the King of Bohemia rushed into the room.

"You have really got it !" he cried, grasping Sherlock Holmes by either shoulder, and looking eagerly into his face.

"Not yet."

"But you have hopes ? "

"I have hopes."

"Then, come. I am all impatience to be gone."

"We must have a cab."

"No, my brougham is waiting."

"Then that will simplify matters." We descended, and started off once more for Briony Lodge.

"GOOD-NIGHT, MR. SHERLOCK HOLMES."

"Irene Adler is married," remarked Holmes.

"Married ! When ? "

"Yesterday."

"But to whom ? "

"To an English lawyer named Norton."

"But she could not love him ? "

"I am in hopes that she does."

"And why in hopes ? "

"Because it would spare your Majesty all fear of future annoyance. If the lady loves her husband, she does not love your Majesty. If she does not love your Majesty, there is no reason why she should interfere with your Majesty's plan."

"It is true. And yet— ! Well ! I wish she had been of my own station ! What a queen she would have made !" He relapsed into a moody silence which was not broken, until we drew up in Serpentine-avenue.

The door of Briony Lodge was open, and an elderly woman stood upon the steps. She watched us with a sardonic eye as we stepped from the brougham.

"Mr. Sherlock Holmes, I believe ? " said she.

"I am Mr. Holmes," answered my companion, looking at her with a questioning and rather startled gaze.

"Indeed ! My mistress told me that you were likely to call. She left this morning with her husband, by the 5.15 train from Charing-cross, for the Continent."

"What !" Sherlock Holmes staggered back, white with chagrin and surprise. "Do you mean that she has left England ?"

"Never to return."

"And the papers?" asked the King, hoarsely. "All is lost."

"We shall see." He pushed past the servant, and rushed into the drawing-room, followed by the King and myself. The furniture was scattered about in every direction, with dismantled shelves, and open drawers, as if the lady had hurriedly ransacked them before her flight. Holmes rushed at the bell-pull, tore back a small sliding shutter, and, plunging in his hand, pulled out a photograph and a letter. The photograph was of Irene Adler herself in evening dress, the letter was superscribed to "Sherlock Holmes, Esq. To be left till called for." My friend tore it open, and we all three read it together. It was dated at midnight of the preceding night, and ran in this way:—

"My Dear Mr. Sherlock Holmes,—You really did it very well. You took me in completely. Until after the alarm of fire, I had not a suspicion. But then, when I found how I had betrayed myself, I began to think. I had been warned against you months ago. I had been told that, if the King employed an agent, it would certainly be you. And your address had been given me. Yet, with all this, you made me reveal what you wanted to know. Even after I became suspicious, I found it hard to think evil of such a dear, kind old clergyman. But, you know, I have been trained as an actress myself. Male costume is nothing new to me. I often take advantage of the freedom which it gives. I sent John, the coachman, to watch you, ran upstairs, got into my walking clothes, as I call them, and came down just as you departed.

"Well, I followed you to your door, and so made sure that I was really an object of interest to the celebrated Mr. Sherlock Holmes. Then I, rather imprudently, wished you good night, and started for the Temple to see my husband.

"We both thought the best resource was flight, when pursued by so formidable an antagonist; so you will find the nest empty when you call to-morrow. As to the photograph, your client may rest in peace. I love and am loved by a better man than he. The King may do what he will without hindrance from one whom he has cruelly wronged. I keep it only to safeguard myself, and to preserve a weapon which will always secure me from any steps which he might take in the future. I leave a photograph which he might care to possess; and I remain, dear Mr. Sherlock Holmes, very truly yours,

"Irene Norton, *née* Adler."

"What a woman—oh, what a woman!" cried the King of Bohemia, when we had all three read this epistle. "Did I not tell you how quick and resolute she was? Would she not have made an admirable queen? Is it not a pity that she was not on my level?"

"From what I have seen of the lady, she seems, indeed, to be on a very different level to your Majesty," said Holmes, coldly. "I am sorry that I have not been able to

"THIS PHOTOGRAPH!"

bring your Majesty's business to a more successful conclusion."

"On the contrary, my dear sir," cried the King. "Nothing could be more successful. I know that her word is inviolate. The photograph is now as safe as if it were in the fire."

"I am glad to hear your Majesty say so."

"I am immensely indebted to you. Pray tell me in what way I can reward you. This ring——." He slipped an emerald snake ring from his finger, and held it out upon the palm of his hand.

"Your Majesty has something which I should value even more highly," said Holmes.

"You have but to name it."

"This photograph!"

The King stared at him in amazement.

"Irene's photograph!" he cried. "Certainly, if you wish it."

"I thank your Majesty. Then there is no more to be done in the matter. I have the honour to wish you a very good morning." He bowed, and, turning away without observing the hand which the King had stretched out to him, he set off in my company for his chambers.

And that was how a great scandal threatened to affect the kingdom of Bohemia, and how the best plans of Mr. Sherlock Holmes were beaten by a woman's wit. He used to make merry over the cleverness of women, but I have not heard him do it of late. And when he speaks of Irene Adler, or when he refers to her photograph, it is always under the honourable title of *the* woman.

## Adventures of Sherlock Holmes.

### ADVENTURE II.—THE RED-HEADED LEAGUE.

#### By A. Conan Doyle.

I HAD called upon my friend, Mr. Sherlock Holmes, one day in the autumn of last year, and found him in deep conversation with a very stout, florid-faced, elderly gentleman, with fiery red hair. With an apology for my intrusion, I was about to withdraw, when Holmes pulled me abruptly into the room, and closed the door behind me.

"You could not possibly have come at a better time, my dear Watson," he said cordially.

"I was afraid that you were engaged."

"So I am. Very much so."

"Then I can wait in the next room."

"Not at all. This gentleman, Mr. Wilson, has been my partner and helper in many of my most successful cases, and I have no doubt that he will be of the utmost use to me in yours also."

The stout gentleman half rose from his chair, and gave a bob of greeting, with a quick little questioning glance from his small, fat-encircled eyes.

"Try the settee," said Holmes, relapsing into his armchair, and putting his finger-tips together, as was his custom when in judicial moods. "I know, my dear Watson, that you share my love of all that is bizarre and outside the conventions and humdrum routine of every-day life. You have shown your relish for it by the enthusiasm which has prompted you to chronicle, and, if you will excuse my saying so, somewhat to embellish so many of my own little adventures."

"Your cases have indeed been of the greatest interest to me," I observed.

"You will remember that I remarked the other day, just before we went into the very simple problem presented by Miss Mary Sutherland, that for strange effects and extraordinary combinations we must go to life itself, which is always far more daring than any effort of the imagination."

"A proposition which I took the liberty of doubting."

"You did, Doctor, but none the less you must come round to my view, for otherwise I shall keep on piling fact upon fact on you, until your reason breaks down under them and acknowledges me to be right. Now, Mr. Jabez Wilson here has been good enough to call upon me this morning, and to begin a narrative which promises to be one of the most singular which I have listened to for some time. You have heard me remark that the strangest and most unique things are very often connected not with

MR. JABEZ WILSON.

the larger but with the smaller crimes, and occasionally, indeed, where there is room for doubt whether any positive crime has been committed. As far as I have heard, it is impossible for me to say whether the present case is an instance of crime or not, but the course of events is certainly among the most singular that I have ever listened to. Perhaps, Mr. Wilson, you would have the great kindness to recommence your narrative. I ask you, not merely because my friend Dr. Watson has not heard the opening part, but also because the peculiar nature of the story makes me anxious to have every possible detail from your lips. As a rule, when I have heard some slight indication of the course of events I am able to guide myself by the thousands of other similar cases which occur to my memory. In the present instance I am forced to admit that the facts are, to the best of my belief, unique."

The portly client puffed out his chest with an appearance of some little pride, and pulled a dirty and wrinkled newspaper from the inside pocket of his greatcoat. As he glanced down the advertisement column, with his head thrust forward, and the paper flattened out upon his knee, I took a good look at the man, and endeavoured after the fashion of my companion to read the indications which might be presented by his dress or appearance.

I did not gain very much, however, by my inspection. Our visitor bore every mark of being an average commonplace British tradesman, obese, pompous, and slow. He wore rather baggy grey shepherd's check trousers, a not overclean black frockcoat, unbuttoned in the front, and a drab waistcoat with a heavy brassy Albert chain, and a square pierced bit of metal dangling down as an ornament. A frayed top hat and a faded brown overcoat with a wrinkled velvet collar lay upon a chair beside him. Altogether, look as I would, there was nothing remarkable about the man save his blazing red head, and the expression of extreme chagrin and discontent upon his features.

Sherlock Holmes' quick eye took in my occupation, and he shook his head with a smile as he noticed my questioning glances. "Beyond the obvious facts that he has at some time done manual labour, that he takes snuff, that he is a Freemason, that he has been in China, and that he has done a considerable amount of writing lately, I can deduce nothing else."

Mr. Jabez Wilson started up in his chair, with his forefinger upon the paper, but his eyes upon my companion.

"How, in the name of good fortune, did you know all that, Mr. Holmes?" he asked. "How did you know, for example, that I did manual labour. It's as true as gospel, for I began as a ship's carpenter."

"Your hands, my dear sir. Your right hand is quite a size larger than your left. You have worked with it, and the muscles are more developed."

"Well, the snuff, then, and the Freemasonry?"

"I won't insult your intelligence by telling you how I read that, especially as, rather against the strict rules of your order, you use an arc and compass breastpin."

"Ah, of course, I forgot that. But the writing?"

"What else can be indicated by that right cuff so very shiney for five inches, and the left one with the smooth patch near the elbow where you rest it upon the desk."

"Well, but China?"

"The fish which you have tattooed immediately above your right wrist could only have been done in China. I have made a small study of tattoo marks, and have even contributed to the literature of the subject. That trick of staining the fishes' scales of a delicate pink is quite peculiar to China. When, in addition, I see a Chinese coin hanging from your watch-chain, the matter becomes even more simple."

Mr. Jabez Wilson laughed heavily. "Well, I never!" said he. "I thought at first that you had done something clever, but I see that there was nothing in it after all."

"I begin to think, Watson," said Holmes, "that I make a mistake in explaining. 'Omne ignotum pro magnifico,' you know, and my poor little reputation, such as it is, will suffer shipwreck if I am so candid. Can you not find the advertisement, Mr. Wilson?"

"Yes, I have got it now," he answered, with his thick, red finger planted half-way down the column. "Here it is. This is what began it all. You just read it for yourself, sir."

I took the paper from him, and read as follows:—

"To the Red-Headed League. On account of the bequest of the late Ezekiah Hopkins, of Lebanon, Penn., U.S.A., there is now another vacancy open which entitles a member of the League to a salary of four pounds a week for purely nominal services.

All red-headed men who are sound in body and mind, and above the age of twenty-one years, are eligible. Apply in person on Monday, at eleven o'clock, to Duncan Ross, at the offices of the League, 7, Pope's-court, Fleet-street."

"What on earth does this mean?" I ejaculated, after I had twice read over the extraordinary announcement.

"WHAT ON EARTH DOES THIS MEAN?"·

Holmes chuckled, and wriggled in his chair, as was his habit when in high spirits. "It is a little off the beaten track, isn't it?" said he. "And now, Mr. Wilson, off you go at scratch, and tell us all about yourself, your household, and the effect which this advertisement had upon your fortunes. You will first make a note, Doctor, of the paper and the date."

"It is *The Morning Chronicle*, of April 27, 1890. Just two months ago."

"Very good. Now, Mr. Wilson?"

"Well, it is just as I have been telling you, Mr. Sherlock Holmes," said Jabez Wilson, mopping his forehead, "I have a small pawnbroker's business at Coburg-square, near the City. It's not a very large affair, and of late years it has not done more than just give me a living. I used to be able to keep two assistants, but now I only keep one; and I would have a job to pay him, but that he is willing to come

for half wages, so as to learn the business."

"What is the name of this obliging youth?" asked Sherlock Holmes.

"His name is Vincent Spaulding, and he's not such a youth either. It's hard to say his age. I should not wish a smarter assistant, Mr. Holmes; and I know very well that he could better himself, and earn twice what I am able to give him. But after all, if he is satisfied, why should I put ideas in his head?"

"Why, indeed? You seem most fortunate in having an *employé* who comes under the full market price. It is not a common experience among employers in this age. I don't know that your assistant is not as remarkable as your advertisement."

"Oh, he has his faults, too," said Mr. Wilson. "Never was such a fellow for photography. Snapping away with a camera when he ought to be improving his mind, and then diving down into the cellar like a rabbit into its hole to develop his pictures. That is his main fault; but, on the whole, he's a good worker. There's no vice in him."

"He is still with you, I presume?"

"Yes, sir. He and a girl of fourteen, who does a bit of simple cooking, and keeps the place clean—that's all I have in the house, for I am a widower, and never had any family. We live very quietly, sir, the three of us; and we keep a roof over our heads, and pay our debts, if we do nothing more.

"The first thing that put us out was that advertisement. Spaulding, he came down into the office just this day eight weeks with this very paper in his hand, and he says:—

"'I wish to the Lord, Mr. Wilson, that I was a red-headed man.'

"'Why that?' I asks.

"'Why,' says he, 'here's another vacancy on the League of the Red-headed

Men. It's worth quite a little fortune to any man who gets it, and I understand that there are more vacancies than there are men, so that the trustees are at their wits' end what to do with the money. If my hair would only change colour, here's a nice little crib all ready for me to step into.'

" 'Why, what is it, then ? ' I asked. You see, Mr. Holmes, I am a very stay-at-home man, and, as my business came to me instead of my having to go to it, I was often weeks on end without putting my foot over the door-mat. In that way I didn't know much of what was going on outside, and I was always glad of a bit of news.

" 'Have you never heard of the League of the Red-headed Men ? ' he asked, with his eyes open.

" 'Never.'

" 'Why, I wonder at that, for you are eligible your-self for one of the vacan-cies.'

" ' And what are they worth ? ' I asked.

" 'Oh, merely a couple of hundred a year, but the work is slight, and it need not interfere very much with one's other occupations.'

"Well, you can easily think that that made me prick up my ears, for the business has not been over good for some years, and an extra couple of hundred would have been very handy.

" ' Tell me all about it,' said I.

" ' Well,' said he, show-ing me the advertisement, 'you can see for yourself that the League has a vacancy, and there is the address where you should apply for particulars. As far as I can make out, the League was founded by an American millionaire, Ezekiah Hopkins, who was very peculiar in his ways. He was himself red-headed, and he had a great sympathy for all red-headed men ; so, when he died, it was found that he had left his enormous fortune in the hands of trustees, with instructions to apply the interest to the providing of easy berths to men whose hair is of that colour. From all I hear it is splendid pay, and very little to do.'

" 'But,' said I, 'there would be millions of red-headed men who would apply.'

" 'Not so many as you might think,' he answered. 'You see it is really confined to Londoners, and to grown men. This American had started from London when he was young, and he wanted to do the old town a good turn. Then, again, I have heard it is no use your applying if your hair is light red, or dark red, or anything but real, bright, blazing, fiery red. Now, if you cared to apply, Mr. Wilson, you would just walk in ; but perhaps it would hardly be worth your while to put yourself out of the

"THE LEAGUE HAS A VACANCY."

way for the sake of a few hundred pounds."

" Now, it is a fact, gentlemen, as you may see for yourselves, that my hair is of a very full and rich tint, so that it seemed to me that, if there was to be any competi-tion in the matter, I stood as good a chance as any man that I had ever met. Vincent Spaulding seemed to know so much about it that I thought he might prove useful, so I just ordered him to put up the shutters for the day, and to come right away with me. He was very willing to have a holiday, so we shut the business up, and started off for the address that was given us in the advertisement.

"I never hope to see such a sight as that again, Mr. Holmes. From north, south, east, and west every man who had a shade of red in his hair had tramped into the City to answer the advertisement. Fleet-street was choked with red-headed folk, and Pope's-court looked like a coster's orange barrow. I should not have thought there were so many in the whole country as were brought together by that single advertisement. Every shade of colour they were—straw, lemon, orange, brick, Irish-setter, liver, clay; but, as Spaulding said, there were not many who had the real vivid flame-coloured tint. When I saw how many were waiting, I would have given it up in despair; but Spaulding would not hear of it. How he did it I could not imagine, but he pushed and pulled and butted until he got me through the crowd, and right up to the steps which led to the office. There was a double stream upon the stair, some going up in hope, and some coming back dejected; but we wedged in as well as we could, and soon found ourselves in the office."

"Your experience has been a most entertaining one," remarked Holmes, as his client paused and refreshed his memory with a huge pinch of snuff. "Pray continue your very interesting statement."

"There was nothing in the office but a couple of wooden chairs and a deal table, behind which sat a small man, with a head that was even redder than mine. He said a few words to each candidate as he came up, and then he always managed to find some fault in them which would disqualify them. Getting a vacancy did not seem to be such a very easy matter after all. However, when our turn came, the little man was much more favourable to me than to any of the others, and he closed the door as

"HE CONGRATULATED ME WARMLY."

we entered, so that he might have a private word with us.

"'This is Mr. Jabez Wilson,' said my assistant, 'and he is willing to fill a vacancy in the League.'

"'And he is admirably suited for it,' the other answered. 'He has every requirement. I cannot recall when I have seen anything so fine.' He took a step backwards, cocked his head on one side, and gazed at my hair until I felt quite bashful. Then suddenly he plunged forward, wrung my hand, and congratulated me warmly on my success.

"'It would be injustice to hesitate,' said he. 'You will, however, I am sure, excuse me for taking an obvious precaution.' With that he seized my hair in both his hands, and tugged until I yelled with the pain. 'There is water in your eyes,' said he, as he released me. 'I perceive that all is as it should be. But we have to be careful, for we have twice been deceived by wigs and once by paint. I could tell you tales of cobbler's wax which would disgust you with human nature.' He stepped over to the window, and shouted through it at the top of his voice that the vacancy was filled. A groan of disappointment came up from below, and the folk all trooped away in different directions, until there was not a red head to be seen except my own and that of the manager.

"'My name,' said he, 'is Mr. Duncan Ross, and I am myself one of the pensioners upon the fund left by our noble benefactor. Are you a married man, Mr. Wilson? Have you a family?'

"I answered that I had not.

"His face fell immediately.

"'Dear me!' he said, gravely, 'that is very serious indeed! I am sorry to hear you say that. The fund was, of course, for the propagation and spread of the red-heads as well as for their maintenance. It is exceedingly unfortunate that you should be a bachelor.'

"My face lengthened at this, Mr. Holmes, for I thought that I was not to have the vacancy after all; but, after thinking it over for a few minutes, he said that it would be all right.

"'In the case of another,' said he, 'the objection might be fatal, but we must stretch a point in favour of a man with such a head of hair as yours. When shall you be able to enter upon your new duties?'

"'Well, it is a little awkward, for I have a business already,' said I.

"'Oh, never mind about that, Mr. Wilson!' said Vincent Spaulding. 'I shall be able to look after that for you.'

"'What would be the hours?' I asked.

"'Ten to two.'

"Now a pawnbroker's business is mostly done of an evening, Mr. Holmes, especially Thursday and Friday evening, which is just before pay-day; so it would suit me very well to earn a little in the mornings. Besides, I knew that my assistant was a good man, and that he would see to anything that turned up.

"'That would suit me very well,' said I 'And the pay?'

"'Is four pounds a week.'

"'And the work?'

"'Is purely nominal.'

"'What do you call purely nominal?'

"'Well, you have to be in the office, or at least in the building, the whole time. If you leave, you forfeit your whole position for ever. The will is very clear upon that point. You don't comply with the conditions if you budge from the office during that time.'

"'It's only four hours a day, and I should not think of leaving,' said I.

"'No excuse will avail,' said Mr. Duncan Ross, 'neither sickness, nor business, nor anything else. There you must stay, or you lose your billet.'

"'And the work?'

"'Is to copy out the "Encyclopædia Britannica." There is the first volume of it in that press. You must find your own ink, pens, and blotting-paper, but we provide this table and chair. Will you be ready to-morrow?'

"'Certainly,' I answered.

"'Then, good-bye, Mr. Jabez Wilson, and let me congratulate you once more on the important position which you have been fortunate enough to gain.' He bowed me out of the room, and I went home with my assistant, hardly knowing what to say or do, I was so pleased at my own good fortune.

"Well, I thought over the matter all day, and by evening I was in low spirits again; for I had quite persuaded myself that the whole affair must be some great hoax or fraud, though what its object might be I could not imagine. It seemed altogether past belief that anyone could make such a will, or that they would pay such a sum for doing anything so simple as copying out the 'Encyclopædia Britannica.' Vincent Spaulding did what he could to cheer me up, but by bedtime I had reasoned myself out of the whole thing. However, in the morning I determined to have a look at it anyhow, so I bought a penny bottle of ink, and with a quill pen, and seven sheets of foolscap paper, I started off for Pope's-court.

"Well, to my surprise and delight everything was as right as possible. The table was set out ready for me, and Mr. Duncan Ross was there to see that I got fairly to work. He started me off upon the letter A, and then he left me; but he would drop in from time to time to see that all was right with me. At two o'clock he bade me good-day, complimented me upon the amount that I had written, and locked the door of the office after me.

"This went on day after day, Mr. Holmes, and on Saturday the manager came in and planked down four golden sovereigns for my week's work. It was the same next week, and the same the week after. Every morning I was there at ten, and every afternoon I left at two. By degrees Mr. Duncan Ross took to coming in only once of a morning, and then, after a time, he did not come in at all. Still, of course, I never dared to leave the room for an instant, for I was not sure when he might come, and the billet was such a good one, and suited me so well, that I would not risk the loss of it.

"Eight weeks passed away like this, and I had written about Abbots, and Archery, and Armour, and Architecture, and Attica, and hoped with diligence that I might get on to the Bs before very long. It cost me something in foolscap, and I had pretty nearly filled a shelf with my writings. And then suddenly the whole business came to an end."

" To an end ? "

" Yes, sir. And no later than this morning. I went to my work as usual at ten o'clock, but the door was shut and locked, with a little square of cardboard hammered on to the middle of the panel with a tack. Here it is, and you can read for yourself."

He held up a piece of white cardboard, about the size of a sheet of notepaper. It read in this fashion :—

" The Red-Headed League is Dissolved. Oct. 9, 1890."

Sherlock Holmes and I surveyed this curt announcement and the rueful face behind it, until the comical side of the affair so completely over-topped every other considera-tion that we both burst out into a roar of laughter.

THE DOOR WAS SHUT AND LOCKED."

" I cannot see that there is anything very funny," cried our client, flushing up to the roots of his flaming head. " If you can do nothing better than laugh at me, I can go elsewhere."

" No, no," cried Holmes, shoving him back into the chair from which he had half risen. " I really wouldn't miss your case for the world. It is most refreshingly unusual. But there is, if you will excuse my saying so, something just a little funny about it. Pray what steps did you take when you found the card upon the door ? "

" I was staggered, sir. I did not know what to do. Then I called at the offices round, but none of them seemed to know anything about it. Finally, I went to the landlord, who is an accountant living on the ground floor, and I asked him if he could tell me what had become of the Red-headed League. He said that he had never heard of any such body. Then I asked him who Mr. Duncan Ross was. He answered that the name was new to him."

" ' Well,' said I, ' the gentleman at No. 4.'

" ' What, the red-headed man ? '

" ' Yes.'

" ' Oh,' said he, ' his name was William Morris. He was a solicitor, and was using my room as a temporary con-venience until his new premises were ready. He moved out yester-day.'

" ' Where could I find him ? '

" ' Oh, at his new offices. He did tell me the address. Yes, 17, King Edward-street, near St. Paul's.' "

" I started off, Mr. Holmes, but when I got to that address it was a manufactory of artificial knee-caps, and no one in it had ever heard of either Mr. William Morris, or Mr. Duncan Ross."

" And what did you do then ? " asked Holmes.

" I went home to Saxe-Coburg-square, and I took the advice of my assistant. But he could not help me in any way. He could only say that if I waited I should hear by post. But that was not quite good enough, Mr. Holmes. I did not wish to lose such a place without a struggle, so, as I had heard that you were good enough to give advice to poor folk who were in need of it, I came right away to you."

" And you did very wisely," said Holmes. " Your case is an exceedingly remarkable one, and I shall be happy to look into it. From what you have told me I think that it is possible that graver issues hang from it than might at first sight appear."

"Grave enough!" said Mr. Jabez Wilson. "Why, I have lost four pound a week."

"As far as you are personally concerned," remarked Holmes, "I do not see that you have any grievance against this extraordinary league. On the contrary, you are, as I understand, richer by some thirty pounds, to say nothing of the minute knowledge which you have gained on every subject which comes under the letter A. You have lost nothing by them."

"No, sir. But I want to find out about them, and who they are, and what their object was in playing this prank—if it was a prank—upon me. It was a pretty expensive joke for them, for it cost them two and thirty pounds."

"We shall endeavour to clear up these points for you. And, first, one or two questions, Mr. Wilson. This assistant of yours who first called your attention to the advertisement—how long had he been with you?"

"About a month then."

"How did he come?"

"In answer to an advertisement."

"Was he the only applicant?"

"No, I had a dozen."

"Why did you pick him?"

"Because he was handy, and would come cheap."

"At half wages, in fact."

"Yes."

"What is he like, this Vincent Spaulding?"

"Small, stout-built, very quick in his ways, no hair on his face, though he's not short of thirty. Has a white splash of acid upon his forehead."

Holmes sat up in his chair in considerable excitement. "I thought as much," said he. "Have you ever observed that his ears are pierced for earrings?"

"Yes, sir. He told me that a gipsy had done it for him when he was a lad."

"Hum!" said Holmes, sinking back in deep thought. "He is still with you?"

"Oh yes, sir; I have only just left him."

"And has your business been attended to in your absence?"

"Nothing to complain of, sir. There's never very much to do of a morning."

"That will do, Mr. Wilson. I shall be happy to give you an opinion upon the subject in the course of a day or two. To-day is Saturday, and I hope that by Monday we may come to a conclusion."

"Well, Watson," said Holmes, when our visitor had left us, "what do you make of it all?"

"I make nothing of it," I answered, frankly. "It is a most mysterious business."

"As a rule," said Holmes, "the more bizarre a thing is the less mysterious it proves to be. It is your commonplace, featureless crimes which are really puzzling, just as a commonplace face is the most difficult to identify. But I must be prompt over this matter."

"What are you going to do then?" I asked.

"To smoke," he answered. "It is quite a three pipe problem, and I beg that you won't speak to me for fifty minutes." He curled himself up in his chair, with his thin knees drawn up to his hawk-like nose, and there he sat with his eyes closed and his black clay pipe thrusting out like the bill of some strange bird. I had come to the conclusion that he had dropped asleep, and indeed was nodding myself, when he suddenly sprang out of his chair with the gesture of a man who has made up his mind, and put his pipe down upon the mantelpiece.

"Sarasate plays at the St. James's Hall this afternoon," he remarked. "What do you think, Watson? Could your patients spare you for a few hours?"

"I have no thing to do

"HE CURLED HIMSELF UP IN HIS CHAIR."

to-day. My practice is never very absorbing."

"Then, put on your hat, and come. I am going through the City first, and we can have some lunch on the way. I observe that there is a good deal of German music on the programme, which is rather more to my taste than Italian or French. It is introspective, and I want to introspect. Come along !"

We travelled by the Underground as far as Aldersgate; and a short walk took us to Saxe-Coburg-square, the scene of the singular story which we had listened to in the morning. It was a pokey, little, shabby-genteel place, where four lines of dingy two-storied brick houses looked out into a small railed-in enclosure, where a lawn of weedy grass, and a few clumps of faded laurel bushes made a hard fight against a smoke-laden and uncongenial atmosphere. Three gilt balls and a brown board with "JABEZ WILSON" in white letters, upon a corner house, announced the place where our red-headed client carried on his business. Sherlock Holmes stopped in front of it with his head on one side, and looked it all over, with his eyes shining brightly between puckered lids. Then he walked slowly up the street, and then down again to the corner, still looking keenly at the houses. Finally he returned to the pawnbroker's, and, having thumped vigorously upon the pavement with his stick two or three times, he went up to the door and knocked. It was instantly opened by a bright-looking, clean-shaven young fellow, who asked him to step in.

"THE DOOR WAS INSTANTLY OPENED."

"Thank you," said Holmes, "I only wished to ask you how you would go from here to the Strand."

"Third right, fourth left," answered the assistant promptly, closing the door.

"Smart fellow, that," observed Holmes as we walked away. "He is, in my judgment, the fourth smartest man in London, and for daring I am not sure that he has not a claim to be third. I have known something of him before."

"Evidently," said I, "Mr. Wilson's assistant counts for a good deal in this mystery of the Red-headed League. I am sure that you inquired your way merely in order that you might see him."

"Not him."

"What then?"

"The knees of his trousers."

"And what did you see?"

"What I expected to see."

"Why did you beat the pavement?"

"My dear Doctor, this is a time for observation, not for talk. We are spies in an enemy's country. We know something of Saxe-Coburg-square. Let us now explore the parts which lie behind it."

The road in which we found ourselves as we turned round the corner from the retired Saxe-Coburg-square presented as great a contrast to it as the front of a picture does to the back. It was one of the main arteries which convey the traffic of the City to the north and west. The roadway was blocked with the immense stream of commerce flowing in a double tide inwards and outwards, while the footpaths were black with the hurrying swarm of pedestrians. It was difficult to realise as we looked at the line of fine shops and stately business premises that they really abutted on the other side upon the faded and stagnant square which we had just quitted.

"Let me see," said Holmes, standing at the corner, and glancing along the line, "I should like just to remember the order of the houses here. It is a hobby of mine to have an exact knowledge of London. There is Mortimer's, the tobacconist, the little newspaper shop, the Coburg branch of the City and Suburban Bank, the Vegetarian Restaurant, and McFarlane's carriage-building depôt. That carries us right on to the other block. And now, Doctor, we've done our work, so it's time we had some play. A sandwich, and a cup of coffee, and then off to violin-land, where all is sweetness, and delicacy, and harmony, and there are no red-headed clients to vex us with their conundrums."

My friend was an enthusiastic musician, being himself not only a very capable performer, but a composer of no ordinary merit. All the afternoon he sat in the stalls wrapped in the most perfect happiness, gently waving his long thin fingers in time to the music, while his gently smiling face and his languid dreamy eyes were as unlike those of Holmes the sleuth-hound; Holmes the relentless, keen-witted, ready-handed criminal agent, as it was possible to conceive. In his singular character the dual nature alternately asserted itself, and his extreme exactness and astuteness represented, as I have often thought, the reaction against the poetic and contemplative mood which occasionally predominated in him. The swing of his nature took him from extreme languor to devouring energy; and, as I knew well, he was never so truly formidable as when, for days on end, he had been lounging in his armchair amid his improvisations and his black-letter editions. Then it was that the lust of the chase would

"ALL AFTERNOON HE SAT IN THE STALLS."

suddenly come upon him, and that his brilliant reasoning power would rise to the level of intuition, until those who were unacquainted with his methods would look askance at him as on a man whose knowledge was not that of other mortals. When I saw him that afternoon so enwrapped in the music at St. James's Hall I felt that an evil time might be coming upon those whom he had set himself to hunt down.

"You want to go home, no doubt, Doctor," he remarked, as we emerged.

"Yes, it would be as well."

"And I have some business to do which will take some hours. This business at Coburg-square is serious."

"Why serious?"

"A considerable crime is in contemplation. I have every reason to believe that we shall be in time to stop it. But to-day being Saturday rather complicates matters. I shall want your help to-night."

"At what time?"

"Ten will be early enough."

"I shall be at Baker-street at ten."

"Very well. And, I say, Doctor! there may be some little danger, so kindly put your army revolver in your pocket." He waved his hand, turned on his heel, and disappeared in an instant among the crowd.

I trust that I am not more dense than my neighbours, but I was always oppressed with a sense of my own stupidity in my dealings with Sherlock Holmes. Here I had heard what he had heard, I had seen what he had seen, and yet from his words it was evident that he saw clearly not only what had happened, but what was about to happen, while to me the whole business was still confused and grotesque. As I drove home to my house in Kensington I thought over it all, from the extraordinary story of the red-headed copier of the "Encyclopædia" down to the visit to Saxe-Coburg-square, and the ominous words with which he had parted from me. What was this nocturnal expedition, and why should I go armed? Where were we going, and what were we to do? I had the hint from Holmes that this smooth-faced pawnbroker's assistant was a formidable man—a man who might play a deep game. I tried to puzzle it out, but gave it up in despair, and set the matter aside until night should bring an explanation.

It was a quarter past nine when I started from home and made my way across the Park, and so through Oxford-street to Baker-street. Two hansoms were standing at the door, and, as I entered the passage, I heard the sound of voices from above. On entering his room, I found Holmes in animated conversation with two men, one of whom I recognised as Peter Jones, the official police agent; while the other was a long, thin, sad-faced man, with a very shiny hat and oppressively respectable frock-coat.

"Ha! our party is complete," said Holmes, buttoning up his pea-jacket, and taking his heavy hunting crop from the rack. "Watson, I think you know Mr. Jones, of Scotland-yard? Let me introduce you to Mr. Merryweather, who is to be our companion in to-night's adventure."

"We're hunting in couples again, Doctor, you see," said Jones, in his consequential way. "Our friend here is a wonderful man for starting a chase. All he wants is an old dog to help him to do the running down."

"I hope a wild goose may not prove to be the end of our chase," observed Mr. Merryweather, gloomily.

"You may place considerable confidence in Mr. Holmes, sir," said the police agent, loftily. "He has his own little methods, which are, if he won't mind my saying so, just a little too theoretical and fantastic, but he has the makings of a detective in him. It is not too much to say that once or twice, as in that business of the Sholto murder and the Agra treasure, he has been more nearly correct than the official force."

"Oh, if you say so, Mr. Jones, it is all right!" said the stranger, with deference. "Still, I confess that I miss my rubber. It is the first Saturday night for seven-and-twenty years that I have not had my rubber."

"I think you will find," said Sherlock Holmes, "that you will play for a higher stake to-night than you have ever done yet, and that the play will be more exciting. For you, Mr. Merryweather, the stake will be some thirty thousand pounds; and for you, Jones, it will be the man upon whom you wish to lay your hands."

"John Clay, the murderer, thief, smasher and forger. He's a young man, Mr. Merryweather, but he is at the head of his profession, and I would rather have my bracelets on him than on any criminal in London. He's a remarkable man, is young John Clay. His grandfather was a Royal Duke, and he himself has been to Eton and Oxford. His brain is as cunning as his fingers, and though we meet signs of him at every turn, we never know where to find the man himself. He'll crack a crib in Scotland one week, and be raising money to build an orphanage in Cornwall the next. I've been on his track for years, and have never set eyes on him yet."

"I hope that I may have the pleasure of introducing you to-night. I've had one or two little turns also with Mr. John Clay, and I agree with you that he is at the head of his profession. It is past ten, however, and quite time that we started. If you two will take the first hansom, Watson and I will follow in the second."

Sherlock Holmes was not very communicative during the long drive, and lay back in the cab humming the tunes which he had heard in the afternoon. We rattled through an endless labyrinth of gas-lit streets until we emerged into Farringdon-street.

"We are close there now," my friend remarked. "This fellow Merryweather is a bank director and personally interested in the matter. I thought it as well to have Jones with us also. He is not a bad fellow, though an absolute imbecile in his profession. He has one positive virtue. He is as brave as a bulldog, and as tenacious as a lobster if he gets his claws upon anyone. Here we are, and they are waiting for us."

We had reached the same crowded thoroughfare in which we had found ourselves in the morning. Our cabs were dismissed, and, following the guidance of Mr. Merryweather, we passed down a narrow passage, and through a side door, which he opened for us. Within there was a small corridor, which ended in a very massive iron gate. This also was opened, and led down a flight of winding stone steps, which terminated at another formidable gate. Mr. Merryweather stopped to light a lantern, and then conducted us down a dark, earth-smelling passage, and so, after opening a third door, into a huge vault or cellar, which was piled all round with crates and massive boxes.

"You are not very vulnerable from above," Holmes remarked, as he held up the lantern, and gazed about him.

"Nor from below," said Mr. Merryweather, striking his stick upon the flags which lined the floor. "Why, dear me, it sounds quite hollow!" he remarked, looking up in surprise.

"I must really ask you to be a little more quiet," said Holmes, severely. "You have already imperilled the whole success of our expedition. Might I beg that you would have the goodness to sit down upon one of those boxes, and not to interfere?"

The solemn Mr. Merryweather perched himself upon a crate, with a very injured expression upon his face, while Holmes fell upon his knees upon the floor, and, with the lantern and a magnifying lens, began to examine minutely the cracks between the stones. A few seconds sufficed to satisfy him, for he sprang to his feet again, and put his glass in his pocket.

"We have at least an hour before us," he remarked, "for they can hardly take any steps until the good pawnbroker is safely in bed. Then they will not lose a minute, for the sooner they do their work the longer time they will have for their escape. We are at present, Doctor—as no doubt you have divined—in the cellar of the City branch of one of the principal London banks. Mr. Merryweather is the chairman of directors, and he will explain to you that there are reasons why the more daring criminals of London should take a considerable interest in this cellar at present."

"It is our French gold," whispered the director. "We have had several warnings that an attempt might be made upon it."

"Your French gold?"

"Yes. We had occasion some months ago to strengthen our resources, and borrowed, for that purpose, thirty thousand napoleons from the Bank of France. It has become known that we have never had occasion to unpack the money, and that it is still lying in our cellar. The crate upon which I sit contains two thousand napoleons packed between layers of lead foil. Our reserve of bullion is much larger at present than is usually kept in a single branch office, and the directors have had misgivings upon the subject."

"Which were very well justified," observed Holmes. "And now it is time that we arranged our little plans. I expect that within an hour matters will come to a head. In the meantime, Mr. Merryweather, we must put the screen over that dark lantern."

"And sit in the dark?"

"I am afraid so. I had brought a pack of cards in my pocket, and I thought that, as we were a *partie carrée*, you might have your rubber after all. But I see that the enemy's preparations have gone so far that we cannot risk the presence of a light.

"MR. MERRYWEATHER STOPPED TO LIGHT A LANTERN."

And, first of all, we must choose our positions. These are daring men, and, though we shall take them at a disadvantage they may do us some harm, unless we are careful. I shall stand behind this crate, and do you conceal yourselves behind those. Then, when I flash a light upon them, close in swiftly. If they fire, Watson, have no compunction about shooting them down."

I placed my revolver, cocked, upon the top of the wooden case behind which I crouched. Holmes shot the slide across the front of his lantern, and left us in pitch darkness—such an absolute darkness as I have never before experienced. The smell of hot metal remained to assure us that the light was still there, ready to flash out at a moment's notice. To me, with my nerves worked up to a pitch of expectancy, there was something depressing and subduing in the sudden gloom, and in the cold, dank air of the vault.

"They have but one retreat," whispered Holmes. "That is back through the house into Saxe-Coburg-square. I hope that you have done what I asked you, Jones?"

"I have an inspector and two officers waiting at the front door."

"Then we have stopped all the holes. And now we must be silent and wait."

What a time it seemed! From comparing notes afterwards it was but an hour and a quarter, yet it appeared to me that the night must have almost gone, and the dawn be breaking above us. My limbs were weary and stiff, for I feared to change my position, yet my nerves were worked up to the highest pitch of tension, and my hearing was so acute that I could not only hear the gentle breathing of my companions, but I could distinguish the deeper, heavier inbreath of the bulky Jones from the thin sighing note of the bank director. From my position I could look over the case in the direction of the floor. Suddenly my eyes caught the glint of a light.

At first it was but a lurid spark upon the stone pavement. Then it lengthened out until it became a yellow line, and then, without any warning or sound, a gash seemed to open and a hand appeared, a white, almost womanly hand, which felt about in the centre of the little area of light. For a minute or more the hand, with its writhing fingers, protruded out of the floor. Then it was withdrawn as suddenly as it appeared, and all was dark again save the single lurid spark, which marked a chink between the stones.

Its disappearance, however, was but momentary. With a rending, tearing sound, one of the broad, white stones turned over upon its side, and left a square, gaping hole, through which streamed the light of a lantern. Over the edge there peeped a clean-cut, boyish face, which looked keenly about it, and then, with a hand on either side of the aperture, drew itself shoulder high and waist high, until one knee rested upon the edge. In another instant he stood at the side of the hole, and was hauling after him a companion, lithe and small like himself, with a pale face and a shock of very red hair.

"It's all clear," he whispered. "Have you the chisel and the bags. Great Scott! Jump, Archie, jump, and I'll swing for it!"

Sherlock Holmes had sprung out and seized the intruder by the collar. The other dived down the hole, and I heard the sound of rending cloth as Jones clutched at his skirts. The light flashed upon the barrel of a revolver, but Holmes' hunting crop came down on the man's wrist, and the pistol clinked upon the stone floor.

"It's no use, John Clay," said Holmes blandly, "You have no chance at all."

"So I see," the other answered, with the utmost coolness. "I fancy that my pal is all right, though I see you have got his coat-tails."

"There are three men waiting for him at the door," said Holmes.

"Oh, indeed. You seem to have done the thing very completely. I must compliment you."

"And I you," Holmes answered. "Your red-headed idea was very new and effective."

"You'll see your pal again presently," said Jones. "He's quicker at climbing down holes than I am. Just hold out while I fix the derbies."

"I beg that you will not touch me with your filthy hands," remarked our prisoner, as the handcuffs clattered upon his wrists. "You may not be aware that I have royal blood in my veins. Have the goodness also when you address me always to say 'sir' and 'please.'"

"All right," said Jones, with a stare and a snigger. "Well, would you please, sir, march upstairs, where we can get a cab to carry your highness to the police-station."

"That is better," said John Clay, serenely. He made a sweeping bow to the three of us, and walked quietly off in the custody of the detective.

"Really, Mr. Holmes," said Mr. Merry-

"IT'S NO USE, JOHN CLAY."

the League, and the copying of the 'Encyclopædia,' must be to get this not over-bright pawnbroker out of the way for a number of hours every day. It was a curious way of managing it, but really it would be difficult to suggest a better. The method was no doubt suggested to Clay's ingenious mind by the colour of his accomplice's hair. The four pounds a week was a lure which must draw him, and what was it to them, who were playing for thousands? They put in the advertisement, one rogue has the temporary office, the other rogue incites the man to apply for it, and together they manage to secure his absence every morning in the week. From the time that I heard of the assistant having come for half wages, it was obvious to me that he had some strong motive for securing the situation."

"But how could you guess what the motive was?"

"Had there been women in the house, I should have suspected a mere vulgar intrigue. That, however, was out of the question. The man's business was a small one, and there was nothing in his house which could account for such elaborate preparations, and such an expenditure as they were at. It must then be something out of the house. What could it be? I thought of the assistant's fondness for photography, and his trick of vanishing into the cellar. The cellar! There was the end of this tangled clue. Then I made inquiries as to this mysterious assistant, and found that I had to deal with one of the coolest and most daring criminals in London. He was doing something in the cellar—something which took many hours a day for months on end. What could it be, once more? I could think of nothing save that he was running a tunnel to some other building.

"So far I had got when we went to visit the scene of action. I surprised you by beating upon the pavement with my stick. I was ascertaining whether the cellar stretched out in front or behind. It was

weather, as we followed them from the cellar, "I do not know how the bank can thank you or repay you. There is no doubt that you have detected and defeated in the most complete manner one of the most determined attempts at bank robbery that have ever come within my experience."

"I have had one or two little scores of my own to settle with Mr. John Clay," said Holmes, "I have been at some small expense over this matter, which I shall expect the bank to refund, but beyond that I am amply repaid by having had an experience which is in many ways unique, and by hearing the very remarkable narrative of the Red-headed League."

"You see, Watson," he explained, in the early hours of the morning, as we sat over a glass of whisky and soda in Baker-street, "it was perfectly obvious from the first that the only possible object of this rather fantastic business of the advertisement of

not in front. Then I rang the bell, and, as I hoped, the assistant answered it. We have had some skirmishes, but we had never set eyes upon each other before. I hardly looked at his face. His knees were what I wished to see. You must yourself have remarked how worn, wrinkled, and stained they were. They spoke of those hours of burrowing. The only remaining point was what they were burrowing for. I walked round the corner, saw that the City and Suburban Bank abutted on our friend's premises, and felt that I had solved my problem. When you drove home after the concert I called upon Scotland Yard, and upon the chairman of the bank directors, with the result that you have seen."

" And how could you tell that they would make their attempt to-night ? " I asked.

" Well, when they closed their League offices that was a sign that they cared no longer about Mr. Jabez Wilson's presence, in other words, that they had completed their tunnel. But it was essential that they should use it soon as it might be discovered, or the bullion might be removed. Saturday would suit them better than any other day, as it would give them two days for their escape. For all these reasons I expected them to come to-night."

" You reasoned it out beautifully," I exclaimed in unfeigned admiration. " It is so long a chain, and yet every link rings true."

" It saved me from ennui," he answered, yawning. " Alas ! I already feel it closing in upon me. My life is spent in one long effort to escape from the commonplaces of existence. These little problems help me to do so."

" And you are a benefactor of the race," said I.

He shrugged his shoulders. " Well, perhaps, after all, it is of some little use," he remarked. " ' L'homme c'est rien— l'œuvre c'est tout,' as Gustave Flaubert wrote to Georges Sand."

# Adventures of Sherlock Holmes.

## ADVENTURE III.—A CASE OF IDENTITY.

### BY A. CONAN DOYLE.

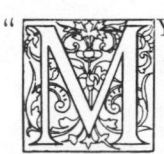

"MY dear fellow," said Sherlock Holmes, as we sat on either side of the fire in his lodgings at Baker-street, "life is infinitely stranger than anything which the mind of man could invent. We would not dare to conceive the things which are really mere commonplaces of existence. If we could fly out of that window hand in hand, hover over this great city, gently remove the roofs, and peep in at the queer things which are going on, the strange coincidences, the plannings, the cross-purposes, the wonderful chains of events, working through generations, and leading to the most *outré* results, it would make all fiction with its conventionalities and foreseen conclusions most stale and unprofitable."

"And yet I am not convinced of it," I answered. "The cases which come to light in the papers are, as a rule, bald enough, and vulgar enough. We have in our police reports realism pushed to its extreme limits, and yet the result is, it must be confessed, neither fascinating nor artistic."

"A certain selection and discretion must be used in producing a realistic effect," remarked Holmes. "This is wanting in the police report, where more stress is laid perhaps upon the platitudes of the magistrate than upon the details, which to an observer contain the vital essence of the whole matter. Depend upon it there is nothing so unnatural as the commonplace."

I smiled and shook my head. "I can quite understand you thinking so," I said. "Of course, in your position of unofficial adviser and helper to everybody who is absolutely puzzled, throughout three continents, you are brought in contact with all that is strange and bizarre. But here "—I picked up the morning paper from the ground—"let us put it to a practical test. Here is the first heading upon which I come. 'A husband's cruelty to his wife.' There is half a column of print, but I know without reading it that it is all perfectly familiar to me. There is, of course, the other woman, the drink, the push, the blow, the bruise, the sympathetic sister or landlady. The crudest of writers could invent nothing more crude."

"Indeed, your example is an unfortunate one for your argument," said Holmes, taking the paper, and glancing his eye down it. "This is the Dundas separation case, and, as it happens, I was engaged in clearing up some small points in connection with it. The husband was a teetotaler, there was no other woman, and the conduct complained of was that he had drifted into the habit of winding up every meal by taking out his false teeth and hurling them at his wife, which you will allow is not an action likely to occur to the imagination of the average story-teller. Take a pinch of snuff, doctor, and acknowledge that I have scored over you in your example."

He held out his snuffbox of old gold, with a great amethyst in the centre of the lid. Its splendour was in such contrast to his homely ways and simple life that I could not help commenting upon it.

"Ah," said he, "I forgot that I had not seen you for some weeks. It is a little souvenir from the King of Bohemia in return for my assistance in the case of the Irene Adler papers."

"And the ring?" I asked, glancing at a remarkable brilliant which sparked upon his finger.

"It was from the reigning family of Holland, though the matter in which I served them was of such delicacy that I cannot confide it even to you, who have been good enough to chronicle one or two of my little problems."

"And have you any on hand just now?" I asked with interest.

"Some ten or twelve, but none which present any feature of interest. They are important, you understand, without being interesting. Indeed, I have found that it is usually in unimportant matters that there is a field for the observation, and for the quick analysis of cause and effect which gives the charm to an investigation. The larger crimes are apt to be the simpler, for the bigger the crime, the more obvious, as a rule, is the motive. In these cases, save for one rather intricate matter which has been referred to me from Marseilles, there is nothing which presents any features of interest. It is possible, however, that I may have something better before very many minutes are over, for this is one of my clients, or I am much mistaken."

He had risen from his chair, and was standing between the parted blinds, gazing down into the dull, neutral-tinted London street. Looking over his shoulder I saw that on the pavement opposite there stood a large woman with a heavy fur boa round her neck, and a large curling red feather in a broad-brimmed hat which was tilted in a coquettish Duchess-of-Devonshire fashion over her ear. From under this great panoply she peeped up in a nervous, hesitating fashion at our windows, while her body oscillated backwards and forwards, and her fingers fidgetted with her glove buttons. Suddenly, with a plunge, as of the swimmer who leaves the bank, she hurried across the road, and we heard the sharp clang of the bell.

"I have seen those symptoms before," said Holmes, throwing his cigarette into the fire. "Oscillation upon the pavement always means an *affaire de cœur*. She would like advice, but is not sure that the matter is not too delicate for communication. And yet even here we may discriminate. When a woman has been seriously wronged by a man she no longer oscillates, and the usual symptom is a broken bell wire. Here we may take it that there is a love matter, but that the maiden is not so much angry as perplexed, or grieved. But here she comes in person to resolve our doubts."

As he spoke there was a tap at the door, and the boy in buttons entered to announce Miss Mary Sutherland, while the lady herself loomed behind his small black figure like a full-sailed merchant-

man behind a tiny pilot boat. Sherlock Holmes welcomed her with the easy courtesy for which he was remarkable, and having closed the door, and bowed her into an armchair, he looked her over in the minute, and yet abstracted fashion which was peculiar to him.

"Do you not find," he said, "that with your short sight it is a little trying to do so much typewriting?"

"I did at first," she answered, "but now I know where the letters are without looking." Then, suddenly realising the full purport of his words, she gave a violent start, and looked up with fear and astonishment upon her broad, good-humoured face. "You've heard about me, Mr. Holmes," she cried, "else how could you know all that?"

"Never mind," said Holmes, laughing, "It is my business to know things. Perhaps I have trained myself to see what others overlook. If not, why should you come to consult me?"

"SHERLOCK HOLMES WELCOMED HER."

"I came to you, sir, because I heard of you from Mrs. Etherege, whose husband you found so easy when the police and everyone had given him up for dead. Oh, Mr. Holmes, I wish you would do as much for me. I'm not rich, but still I have a hundred a year in my own right, besides the little that I make by the machine, and I would give it all to know what has become of Mr. Hosmer Angel."

"Why did you come away to consult me in such a hurry?" asked Sherlock Holmes, with his finger-tips together, and his eyes to the ceiling.

Again a startled look came over the somewhat vacuous face of Miss Mary Sutherland. "Yes, I did bang out of the house," she said, "for it made me angry to see the easy way in which Mr. Windibank —that is, my father—took it all. He would not go to the police, and he would not go to you, and so at last, as he would do nothing, and kept on saying that there was no harm done, it made me mad, and I just on with my things and came right away to you."

"Your father," said Holmes, "your stepfather, surely, since the name is different."

"Yes, my stepfather. I call him father, though it sounds funny, too, for he is only five years and two months older than myself."

"And your mother is alive?"

"Oh yes, mother is alive and well. I wasn't best pleased, Mr. Holmes, when she married again so soon after father's death, and a man who was nearly fifteen years younger than herself. Father was a plumber in the Tottenham Court-road, and he left a tidy business behind him, which mother carried on with Mr. Hardy, the foreman, but when Mr. Windibank came he made her sell the business, for he was very superior, being a traveller in wines. They got four thousand seven hundred for the goodwill and interest, which wasn't near as much as father could have got if he had been alive."

I had expected to see Sherlock Holmes impatient under this rambling and inconsequential narrative, but, on the contrary, he had listened with the greatest concentration of attention.

"Your own little income," he asked, "does it come out of the business?"

"Oh no, sir. It is quite separate, and was left me by my Uncle Ned in Auckland. It is in New Zealand Stock, paying 4½ per cent. Two thousand five hundred pounds was the amount, but I can only touch the interest."

"You interest me extremely," said Holmes. "And since you draw so large a sum as a hundred a year, with what you earn into the bargain, you no doubt travel a little, and indulge yourself in every way. I believe that a single lady can get on very nicely upon an income of about sixty pounds."

"I could do with much less than that, Mr. Holmes, but you understand that as long as I live at home I don't wish to be a burden to them, and so they have the use of the money just while I am staying with them. Of course that is only just for the time. Mr. Windibank draws my interest every quarter, and pays it over to mother, and I find that I can do pretty well with what I earn at typewriting. It brings me twopence a sheet, and I can often do from fifteen to twenty sheets in a day."

"You have made your position very clear to me," said Holmes. "This is my friend, Dr. Watson, before whom you can speak as freely as before myself. Kindly tell us now all about your connection with Mr. Hosmer Angel."

A flush stole over Miss Sutherland's face, and she picked nervously at the fringe of her jacket. "I met him first at the gas-fitters' ball," she said. "They used to send father tickets when he was alive, and then afterwards they remembered us, and sent them to mother. Mr. Windibank did not wish us to go. He never did wish us to go anywhere. He would get quite mad if I wanted so much as to join a Sunday-school treat. But this time I was set on going, and I would go, for what right had he to prevent? He said the folk were not fit for us to know, when all father's friends were to be there. And he said that I had nothing fit to wear, when I had my purple plush that I had never so much as taken out of the drawer. At last, when nothing else would do he went off to France upon the business of the firm, but we went, mother and I, with Mr. Hardy, who used to be our foreman, and it was there I met Mr. Hosmer Angel."

"I suppose," said Holmes, "that when Mr. Windibank came back from France, he was very annoyed at your having gone to the ball."

"Oh, well, he was very good about it. He laughed, I remember, and shrugged his shoulders, and said there was no use denying anything to a woman, for she would have her way."

"I see. Then at the gasfitters' ball you met, as I understand, a gentleman called Mr. Hosmer Angel."

"Yes, sir. I met him that night, and he

"AT THE GASFITTERS' BALL."

called next day to ask if we had got home all safe, and after that we met him—that is to say, Mr. Holmes, I met him twice for walks, but after that father came back again, and Mr. Hosmer Angel could not come to the house any more."

"No?"

"Well, you know, father didn't like anything of the sort He wouldn't have any visitors if he could help it, and he used to say that a woman should be happy in her own family circle. But then, as I used to say to mother, a woman wants her own circle to begin with, and I had not got mine yet."

"But how about Mr. Hosmer Angel? Did he make no attempt to see you?"

"Well, father was going off to France again in a week, and Hosmer wrote and

said that it would be safer and better not to see each other until he had gone. We could write in the meantime, and he used to write every day. I took the letters in in the morning, so there was no need for father to know."

"Were you engaged to the gentleman at this time?"

"Oh yes, Mr. Holmes. We were engaged after the first walk that we took. Hosmer —Mr. Angel—was a cashier in an office in Leadenhall-street—and—"

"What office?"

"That's the worst of it, Mr. Holmes, I don't know."

"Where did he live, then?"

"He slept on the premises."

"And you don't know his address?"

"No—except that it was Leadenhall-street."

"Where did you address your letters, then?"

"To the Leadenhall-street Post Office, to be left till called for. He said that if they were sent to the office he would be chaffed by all the other clerks about having letters from a lady, so I offered to typewrite them, like he did his, but he wouldn't have that, for he said that when I wrote them they seemed to come from me, but when they were typewritten he always felt that the machine had come between us. That will just show you how fond he was of me, Mr. Holmes, and the little things that he would think of."

"It was most suggestive," said Holmes, "It has long been an axiom of mine that the little things are infinitely the most important. Can you remember any other little things about Mr. Hosmer Angel?"

"He was a very shy man, Mr. Holmes. He would rather walk with me in the evening than in the daylight, for he said that he hated to be conspicuous. Very retiring and gentlemanly he was. Even his voice was gentle. He'd had the quinsy and swollen glands when he was young, he told me, and it had left him with a weak throat, and a hesitating, whispering fashion of speech. He was always well-dressed, very neat and plain, but his eyes were weak, just as mine are, and he wore tinted glasses against the glare."

"Well, and what happened when Mr. Windibank, your stepfather, returned to France?"

"Mr. Hosmer Angel came to the house again, and proposed that we should marry before father came back. He was in dreadful earnest, and made me swear, with my hands on the Testament, that whatever happened I would always be true to him. Mother said he was quite right to make me swear, and that it was a sign of his passion. Mother was all in his favour from the first, and was even fonder of him than I was. Then, when they talked of marrying within the week, I began to ask about father; but they both said never to mind about father, but just to tell him afterwards, and mother said she would make it all right with him. I didn't quite like that, Mr. Holmes. It seemed funny that I should ask his leave, as he was only a few years older than me; but I didn't want to do anything on the sly, so I wrote to father at Bordeaux, where the Company has its French offices, but the letter came back to me on the very morning of the wedding."

"It missed him, then?"

"Yes, sir, for he had started to England just before it arrived."

put us both into it, and stepped himself into a four-wheeler, which happened to be the only other cab in the street. We got to the church first, and when the four-wheeler drove up we waited for him to step out, but he never did, and when the cabman got down from the box and looked, there was no one there! The cabman said that he could not imagine what had become of him, for he had seen him get in with his own eyes. That was last Friday, Mr. Holmes, and I have never seen or heard anything since then to throw any light upon what became of him."

"It seems to me that you have been very shamefully treated," said Holmes.

"Oh no, sir! He was too good and kind to leave me so. Why, all the morning he was saying to me that, whatever happened, I was to be true; and that even if something quite unforeseen occurred to separate us, I was always to remember that I was pledged to him, and that he would claim his pledge

"THERE WAS NO ONE THERE."

"Ha! that was unfortunate. Your wedding was arranged, then, for the Friday. Was it to be in church?"

"Yes, sir, but very quietly. It was to be at St. Saviour's, near King's-cross, and we were to have breakfast afterwards at the St. Pancras Hotel. Hosmer came for us in a hansom, but as there were two of us, he

sooner or later. It seemed strange talk for a wedding morning, but what has happened since gives a meaning to it."

"Most certainly it does. Your own opinion is, then, that some unforeseen catastrophe has occurred to him?"

"Yes, sir. I believe that he foresaw some danger, or else he would not have talked so. And then I think that what he foresaw happened."

"But you have no notion as to what it could have been ? "

" None."

" One more question. How did your mother take the matter ? "

" She was angry, and said that I was never to speak of the matter again."

" And your father ?  Did you tell him ? "

" Yes, and he seemed to think, with me, that something had happened, and that I should hear of Hosmer again. As he said, what interest could anyone have in bringing me to the doors of the church, and then leaving me ? Now, if he had borrowed my money, or if he had married me and got my money settled on him, there might be some reason ; but Hosmer was very independent about money, and never would look at a shilling of mine. And yet what could have happened ? And why could he not write ? Oh, it drives me half mad to think of ! and I can't sleep a wink at night." She pulled a little handkerchief out of her muff, and began to sob heavily into it.

"SHE LAID A LITTLE BUNDLE UPON THE TABLE."

hands. I should like an accurate description of him, and any letters of his which you can spare."

" I advertised for him in last Saturday's *Chronicle*," said she. " Here is the slip, and here are four letters from him."

" Thank you.  And your address ? "

" 31, Lyon-place, Camberwell."

" Mr. Angel's address you never had, I understand.  Where is your father's place of business ? "

" He travels for Westhouse & Marbank, the great claret importers of Fenchurch-street."

" Thank you. You have made your statement very clearly. You will leave the papers here, and remember the advice which I have given you. Let the whole incident be a sealed book, and do not allow it to affect your life."

" You are very kind, Mr. Holmes, but I cannot do that. I shall be true to Hosmer. He shall find me ready when he comes back."

For all the preposterous hat and the vacuous face, there was something noble in the simple faith of our visitor which compelled our respect. She laid her little bundle of papers upon the table, and went her way, with a promise to come again whenever she might be summoned.

" I shall glance into the case for you," said Holmes, rising, " and I have no doubt that we shall reach some definite result. Let the weight of the matter rest upon me now, and do not let your mind dwell upon it further. Above all, try to let Mr. Hosmer Angel vanish from your memory, as he has done from your life."

" Then you don't think I'll see him again ? "

" I fear not."

" Then what has happened to him ? "

" You will leave that question in my

Sherlock Holmes sat silent for a few minutes with his finger tips still pressed together, his legs stretched out in front of him, and his gaze directed upwards to the ceiling. Then he took down from the rack the old and oily clay pipe, which was to him as a counsellor, and, having lit it, he leaned back in his chair, with the thick blue cloud-wreaths spinning up from him, and a look of infinite languor in his face.

" Quite an interesting study, that maiden,"

he observed. "I found her more interesting than her little problem, which, by the way, is rather a trite one. You will find parallel cases, if you consult my index, in Andover in '77, and there was something of the sort at the Hague last year. Old as is the idea, however, there were one or two details which were new to me. But the maiden herself was most instructive."

"You appeared to read a good deal upon her which was quite invisible to me," I remarked.

"Not invisible, but unnoticed, Watson. You did not know where to look, and so you missed all that was important. I can never bring you to realise the importance of sleeves, the suggestiveness of thumbnails, or the great issues that may hang from a bootlace. Now what did you gather from that woman's appearance? Describe it."

"Well, she had a slate-coloured, broadbrimmed straw hat, with a feather of a brickish red. Her jacket was black, with black beads sewn upon it, and a fringe of little black jet ornaments. Her dress was brown, rather darker than coffee colour, with a little purple plush at the neck and sleeves. Her gloves were greyish, and were worn through at the right forefinger. Her boots I didn't observe. She had small round, hanging gold earrings, and a general air of being fairly well to do, in a vulgar, comfortable, easy-going way."

Sherlock Holmes clapped his hands softly together and chuckled.

"'Pon my word, Watson, you are coming along wonderfully. You have really done very well indeed. It is true that you have missed everything of importance, but you have hit upon the method, and you have a quick eye for colour. Never trust to general impressions, my boy, but concentrate yourself upon details. My first glance is always at a woman's sleeve. In a man it is perhaps better first to take the knee of the trouser. As you observe, this woman had plush upon her sleeves, which is a most useful material for showing traces. The double line a little above the wrist, where the typewritist presses against the table, was beautifully defined. The sewing-machine, of the hand type, leaves a similar mark, but only on the left arm, and on the side of it farthest from the thumb, instead of being right across the broadest part, as this was. I then glanced at her face, and observing the dint of a pince-nez at either side of her nose, I ventured a remark upon

short sight and typewriting, which seemed to surprise her.

"It surprised me."

"But, surely, it was very obvious. I was then much surprised and interested on glancing down to observe that, though the boots which she was wearing were not unlike each other, they were really odd ones, the one having a slightly decorated toe-cap, and the other a plain one. One was buttoned only in the two lower buttons out of five, and the other at the first, third, and fifth. Now, when you see that a young lady, otherwise neatly dressed, has come away from home with odd boots, half-buttoned, it is no great deduction to say that she came away in a hurry."

"And what else?" I asked, keenly interested, as I always was, by my friend's incisive reasoning.

"I noted, in passing, that she had written a note before leaving home, but after being fully dressed. You observed that her right glove was torn at the forefinger, but you did not apparently see that both glove and finger were stained with violet ink. She had written in a hurry, and dipped her pen too deep. It must have been this morning, or the mark would not remain clear upon the finger. All this is amusing, though rather elementary, but I must go back to business, Watson. Would you mind reading me the advertised description of Mr. Hosmer Angel?"

I held the little printed slip to the light. "Missing," it said, "on the morning of the 14th, a gentleman named Hosmer Angel. About 5 ft. 7 in. in height; strongly built, sallow complexion, black hair, a little bald in the centre, bushy, black side whiskers and moustache; tinted glasses, slight infirmity of speech. Was dressed, when last seen, in black frock coat faced with silk, black waistcoat, gold Albert chain, and grey Harris tweed trousers, with brown gaiters over elastic-sided boots. Known to have been employed in an office in Leadenhall-street. Anybody bringing," &c., &c.

"That will do," said Holmes. "As to the letters," he continued, glancing over them, "they are very commonplace. Absolutely no clue in them to Mr. Angel, save that he quotes Balzac once. There is one remarkable point, however, which will no doubt strike you."

"They are typewritten," I remarked.

"Not only that, but the signature is typewritten. Look at the neat little 'Hosmer Angel' at the bottom. There is a date, you see, but no superscription except Leaden-hall-street, which is rather vague. The point about the signature is very suggestive—in fact, we may call it conclusive."

" Of what ? "

" My dear fellow, is it possible you do not see how strongly it bears upon the case."

" I cannot say that I do, unless it were that he wished to be able to deny his signature if an action for breach of promise were instituted."

" No, that was not the point. However, I shall write two letters which should settle the matter. One is to a firm in the City, the other is to the young lady's stepfather, Mr. Windibank, asking him whether he could meet us here at six o'clock to-morrow evening. It is just as well that we should do business with the male relatives. And now, doctor, we can do nothing until the answers to those letters come, so we may put our little problem upon the shelf for the interim."

I had had so many reasons to believe in my friend's subtle powers of reasoning, and extraordinary energy in action, that I felt that he must have some solid grounds for the assured and easy demeanour with which he treated the singular mystery which he had been called upon to fathom. Once only had I known him to fail, in the case of the King of Bohemia and of the Irene Adler photograph, but when I looked back to the weird business of the Sign of Four, and the extraordinary circumstances connected with the Study in Scarlet, I felt that it would be a strange tangle indeed which he could not unravel.

I left him then, still puffing at his black clay pipe, with the conviction that when I came again on the next evening I would find that he held in his hands all the clues which would lead up to the identity of the disappearing bridegroom of Miss Mary Sutherland.

A professional case of great gravity was engaging my own attention at the time, and the whole of next day I was busy at the bedside of the sufferer. It was not until close upon six o'clock that I found myself free, and was able to spring into a hansom

"I FOUND SHERLOCK HOLMES HALF."

and drive to Baker-street, half afraid that I might be too late to assist at the *dénouement* of the little mystery. I found Sherlock Holmes alone, however, half asleep, with his long, thin form curled up in the recesses of his armchair. A formidable array of bottles and test-tubes, with the pungent cleanly smell of hydro-chloric acid, told me that he had spent his day in the chemical work which was so dear to him.

" Well, have you solved it ? " I asked as I entered.

" Yes. It was the bisulphate of baryta."

" No, no, the mystery ! " I cried.

" Oh, that ! I thought of the salt that I have been working upon. There was never any mystery in the matter, though, as I said yesterday, some of the details are of interest. The only drawback is that there is no law, I fear, that can touch the scoundrel."

"Who was he, then, and what was his object in deserting Miss Sutherland ? "

The question was hardly out of my mouth, and Holmes had not yet opened his lips to reply, when we heard a heavy footfall in the passage, and a tap at the door.

"This is the girl's stepfather, Mr. James Windibank," said Holmes. "He has written to me to say that he would be here at six. Come in ! "

The man who entered was a sturdy middle-sized fellow, some thirty years of age, clean shaven, and sallow skinned, with a bland, insinuating manner, and a pair of wonderfully sharp and penetrating grey eyes. He shot a questioning glance at each of us, placed his shiny top hat upon the sideboard, and, with a slight bow, sidled down into the nearest chair.

"Good evening, Mr. James Windibank," said Holmes. "I think that this typewritten letter is from you, in which you made an appointment with me for six o'clock ? "

"Yes, sir. I am afraid that I am a little late, but I am not quite my own master, you know. I am sorry that Miss Sutherland has troubled you about this little matter, for I think it is far better not to wash linen of the sort in public. It was quite against my wishes that she came, but she is a very excitable, impulsive girl, as you may have noticed, and she is not easily controlled when she has made up her mind on a point. Of course, I did not mind you so much, as you are not connected with the official police, but it is not pleasant to have a family misfortune like this noised abroad. Besides it is a useless expense, for how could you possibly find this Hosmer Angel ? "

"On the contrary," said Holmes, quietly ; "I have every reason to believe that I will succeed in discovering Mr. Hosmer Angel."

Mr. Windibank gave a violent start, and dropped his gloves. "I am delighted to hear it," he said.

"It is a curious thing," remarked Holmes, "that a typewriter has really quite as much individuality as a man's handwriting. Unless they are quite new, no two of them write exactly alike. Some letters get more worn than others, and some wear only on one side. Now, you remark in this note of yours, Mr. Windibank, that in every case there is some little

slurring over of the ' e,' and a slight defect in the tail of the ' r.' There are fourteen other characteristics, but those are the more obvious."

"We do all our correspondence with this machine at the office, and no doubt it is a little worn," our visitor answered, glancing keenly at Holmes with his bright little eyes.

"And now I will show you what is really a very interesting study, Mr. Windibank," Holmes continued. "I think of writing another little monograph some of these days on the typewriter and its relation to crime. It is a subject to which I have devoted some little attention. I have here four letters which purport to come from the missing man. They are all typewritten. In each case, not only are the ' e's ' slurred and the ' r's ' tailless, but you will observe, if you care to use my magnifying lens, that the fourteen other characteristics to which I have alluded are there as well."

Mr. Windibank sprang out of his chair, and picked up his hat. "I cannot waste time over this sort of fantastic talk, Mr. Holmes," he said. "If you can catch the man, catch him, and let me know when you have done it."

"Certainly," said Holmes, stepping over and turning the key in the door. "I let you know, then, that I have caught him ! "

"What ! where ? " shouted Mr. Windibank, turning white to his lips, and glancing about him like a rat in a trap.

"Oh, it won't do—really it won't," said Holmes, suavely. "There is no possible getting out of it, Mr. Windibank. It is quite too transparent, and it was a very bad compliment when you said that it was impossible for me to solve so simple a question. That's right ! Sit down, and let us talk it over."

Our visitor collapsed into a chair, with a ghastly face, and a glitter of moisture on his brow. "It—it's not actionable," he stammered.

"I am very much afraid that it is not. But between ourselves, Windibank, it was as cruel, and selfish, and heartless a trick in a petty way as ever came before me. Now, let me just run over the course of events, and you will contradict me, if I go wrong."

The man sat huddled up in his chair, with his head sunk upon his breast, like one who is utterly crushed. Holmes stuck his feet up on the corner of the mantelpiece, and, leaning back with his hands in

"GLANCING ABOUT HIM LIKE A RAT IN A TRAP."

his pockets, began talking, rather to himself, as it seemed, than to us.

"The man married a woman very much older than himself for her money," said he, "and he enjoyed the use of the money of the daughter as long as she lived with them. It was a considerable sum, for people in their position, and the loss of it would have made a serious difference. It was worth an effort to preserve it. The daughter was of a good, amiable disposition, but affectionate and warm-hearted in her ways, so that it was evident that with her fair personal advantages, and her little income, she would not be allowed to remain single long. Now her marriage would mean, of course, the loss of a hundred a year, so what does her stepfather do to prevent it? He takes the obvious course of keeping her at home, and forbidding her to seek the company of people of her own age. But soon he found that that would not answer for ever. She became restive, insisted upon her rights, and finally announced her positive intention of going to a certain ball. What does her

clever stepfather do then? He conceives an idea more creditable to his head than to his heart. With the connivance and assistance of his wife he disguised himself, covered those keen eyes with tinted glasses, masked the face with a moustache and a pair of bushy whiskers, sunk that clear voice into an insinuating whisper, and doubly secure on account of the girl's short sight, he appears as Mr. Hosmer Angel, and keeps off other lovers by making love himself."

"It was only a joke at first," groaned our visitor. "We never thought that she would have been so carried away."

"Very likely not. However that may be, the young lady was very decidedly carried away, and having quite made up her mind that her stepfather was in France, the suspicion of treachery never for an instant entered her mind. She was flattered by the gentleman's attentions, and the effect was increased by the loudly expressed admiration of her mother. Then Mr. Angel began to call, for it was obvious that the matter should be pushed as far as it would go, if a real effect were to be produced. There were meetings, and an engagement, which would finally secure the girl's affections from turning towards anyone else. But the deception could not be kept up for ever. These pretended journeys to France were rather cumbrous. The thing to do was clearly to bring the business to an end in such a dramatic manner that it would leave a permanent impression upon the young lady's mind, and prevent her from looking upon any other suitor for some time to come. Hence those vows of fidelity exacted upon a Testament, and hence also the allusions to a possibility of something happening on the very morning of the wedding. James Windibank wished Miss Sutherland to be so bound to Hosmer Angel, and so uncertain as to his fate, that for ten years to come, at any rate, she would not listen to another man. As far as the church door he brought her, and then, as he could go no further, he conveniently vanished away by the old trick of stepping in at one door of a four-wheeler, and out at the other. I think that that was the chain of events, Mr. Windibank!"

Our visitor had recovered something of his assurance while Holmes had been talking, and he rose from his chair now with a cold sneer upon his pale face.

"It may be so, or it may not, Mr. Holmes," said he, " but if you are so very sharp you ought to be sharp enough to know that it is you who are breaking the law now, and not me. I have done nothing actionable from the first, but as long as you keep that door locked you lay yourself open to an action for assault and illegal constraint."

"The law cannot, as you say, touch you," said Holmes, unlocking

and throwing open the door, "yet there never was a man who deserved punishment more. If the young lady has a brother or a friend, he ought to lay a whip across your shoulders. By Jove!" he continued, flushing up at the sight of the bitter sneer upon the man's face, "it is not part of my duties to my client, but here's a hunting crop handy, and I think I shall just treat myself to——" He took two swift steps to the whip, but before he could grasp it there was a wild clatter of steps upon the stairs, the heavy hall door banged, and from the window we could see Mr. James Windibank running at the top of his speed down the road.

"There's a cold-blooded scoundrel!" said Holmes, laughing, as he threw himself down into his chair once more. "That fellow will rise from crime to crime until he does something very bad, and ends on a

" HE TOOK TWO SWIFT STEPS TO THE WHIP.'

gallows. The case has, in some respects, been not entirely devoid of interest."

"I cannot now entirely see all the steps of your reasoning," I remarked.

" Well, of course it was obvious from the first that this Mr. Hosmer Angel must have some strong object for his curious conduct, and it was equally clear that the only man who really profited by the incident, as far as we could see, was the stepfather. Then the fact that the two men were never together, but that the one always appeared when the other was away, was suggestive. So were the tinted spectacles and the curious voice, which both hinted at a disguise, as did the bushy whiskers. My suspicions were all confirmed by his peculiar action in typewriting his signature, which of course inferred that his handwriting was so familiar to her that she would recognise even the smallest sample of it. You see all these isolated facts, together with many minor ones, all pointed in the same direction."

" And how did you verify them ? "

" Having once spotted my man, it was easy to get corroboration. I knew the firm for which this man worked. Having taken the printed description, I eliminated every-thing from it which could be the result of a disguise—the whiskers, the glasses, the voice, and I sent it to the firm, with a re-quest that they would inform me whether it answered to the description of any of their travellers. I had already noticed the peculiarities of the typewriter, and I wrote to the man himself at his business address, asking him if he would come here. As I expected, his reply was typewritten, and revealed the same trivial but characteristic defects. The same post brought me a letter from Westhouse & Marbank, of Fenchurch-street, to say that the description tallied in every respect with that of their employé, James Windibank. *Voila tout !* "

" And Miss Sutherland ? "

" If I tell her she will not believe me. You may remember the old Persian saying, ' There is danger for him who taketh the tiger cub, and danger also for whoso snatches a delusion from a woman.' There is as much sense in Hafiz as in Horace, and as much knowledge of the world."

# Adventures of Sherlock Holmes.

## ADVENTURE IV.—THE BOSCOMBE VALLEY MYSTERY.

### By A. Conan Doyle.

WE were seated at breakfast one morning, my wife and I, when the maid brought in a telegram. It was from Sherlock Holmes, and ran in this way :

"Have you a couple of days to spare ? Have just been wired for from the West of England in connection with Boscombe Valley tragedy. Shall be glad if you will come with me. Air and scenery perfect. Leave Paddington by the 11.15."

"What do you say, dear ? " said my wife, looking across at me. "Will you go ? "

"I really don't know what to say. I have a fairly long list at present."

"Oh, Anstruther would do your work for you. You have been looking a little pale lately. I think that the change would do you good, and you are always so interested in Mr. Sherlock Holmes' cases."

"I should be ungrateful if I were not, seeing what I gained through one of them," I answered. "But if I am to go I must pack at once, for I have only half an hour."

My experience of camp life in Afghanistan had at least had the effect of making me a prompt and ready traveller. My wants were few and simple, so that in less than the time stated I was in a cab with my valise, rattling away to Paddington Station. Sherlock Holmes was pacing up and down the platform, his tall, gaunt figure made even gaunter and taller by his long grey travelling cloak, and close-fitting cloth cap.

"It is really very good of you to come, Watson," said he. "It makes a considerable difference to me, having someone with me on whom I can thoroughly rely. Local aid is always either worthless or else biassed. If you will keep the two corner seats I shall get the tickets."

We had the carriage to ourselves save for an immense litter of papers which Holmes had brought with him. Among these he rummaged and read, with intervals of note-taking and of meditation, until we were past Reading. Then he suddenly rolled them all into a gigantic ball, and tossed them up on to the rack.

"Have you heard anything of the case ? " he asked.

"Not a word. I have not seen a paper for some days."

"The London press has not had very full accounts. I have just been looking through all the recent papers in order to master the particulars. It seems, from what I gather, to be one of those simple cases which are so extremely difficult."

"WE HAD THE CARRIAGE TO OURSELVES."

F F

"That sounds a little paradoxical."

"But it is profoundly true. Singularity is almost invariably a clue. The more featureless and commonplace a crime is, the more difficult is it to bring it home. In this case, however, they have established a very serious case against the son of the murdered man."

"It is a murder, then?"

"Well, it is conjectured to be so. I shall take nothing for granted until I have the opportunity of looking personally into it. I will explain the state of things to you, as far as I have been able to understand it, in a very few words.

"Boscombe Valley is a country district not very far from Ross, in Herefordshire. The largest landed proprietor in that part is a Mr. John Turner, who made his money in Australia, and returned some years ago to the old country. One of the farms which he held, that of Hatherley, was let to Mr. Charles McCarthy, who was also an ex-Australian. The men had known each other in the Colonies, so that it was not unnatural that when they came to settle down they should do so as near each other as possible. Turner was apparently the richer man, so McCarthy became his tenant, but still remained, it seems, upon terms of perfect equality, as they were frequently together. McCarthy had one son, a lad of eighteen, and Turner had an only daughter of the same age, but neither of them had wives living. They appear to have avoided the society of the neighbouring English families, and to have led retired lives, though both the McCarthys were fond of sport, and were frequently seen at the race meetings of the neighbourhood. McCarthy kept two servants—a man and a girl. Turner had a considerable household, some half-dozen at the least. That is as much as I have been able to gather about the families. Now for the facts.

"On June 3, that is, on Monday last, McCarthy left his house at Hatherley about three in the afternoon, and walked down to the Boscombe Pool, which is a small lake formed by the spreading out of the stream which runs down the Boscombe Valley. He had been out with his serving-man in the morning at Ross, and he had told the man that he must hurry, as he had an appointment of importance to keep at three. From that appointment he never came back alive.

"From Hatherley Farmhouse to the Boscombe Pool is a quarter of a mile, and two people saw him as he passed over this ground. One was an old woman, whose name is not mentioned, and the other was William Crowder, a gamekeeper in the employ of Mr. Turner. Both these witnesses depose that Mr. McCarthy was walking alone. The gamekeeper adds that within a few minutes of his seeing Mr. McCarthy pass he had seen his son, Mr. James McCarthy, going the same way with a gun under his arm. To the best of his belief, the father was actually in sight at the time, and the son was following him. He thought no more of the matter until he heard in the evening of the tragedy that had occurred.

"The two McCarthys were seen after the time when William Crowder, the gamekeeper, lost sight of them. The Boscombe Pool is thickly wooded round, with just a fringe of grass and of reeds round the edge. A girl of fourteen, Patience Moran, who is the daughter of the lodge-keeper of the Boscombe Valley Estate, was in one of the woods picking flowers. She states that while she was there she saw, at the border of the wood and close by the lake, Mr. McCarthy and his son, and that they appeared to be having a violent quarrel. She heard Mr. McCarthy the elder using very strong language to his son, and she saw the latter raise up his hand as if to strike his father. She was so frightened by their violence that she ran away, and told her mother when she reached home that she had left the two McCarthys quarrelling near Boscombe Pool, and that she was afraid that they were going to fight. She had hardly said the words when young Mr. McCarthy came running up to the lodge to say that he had found his father dead in the wood, and to ask for the help of the lodge-keeper. He was much excited, without either his gun or his hat, and his right hand and sleeve were observed to be stained with fresh blood. On following him they found the dead body stretched out upon the grass beside the Pool. The head had been beaten in by repeated blows of some heavy and blunt weapon. The injuries were such as might very well have been inflicted by the butt-end of his son's gun, which was found lying on the grass within a few paces of the body. Under these circumstances the young man was instantly arrested, and a verdict of 'Wilful Murder' having been returned at the inquest on Tuesday, he was on Wednesday brought before the magistrates at Ross, who have referred the case to the next assizes. Those are the main facts of the case as they came out before the coroner and at the police-court."

"I could hardly imagine a more damning case," I remarked. "If ever circumstantial evidence pointed to a criminal it does so here."

"Circumstantial evidence is a very tricky thing," answered Holmes, thoughtfully. "It may seem to point very straight to one thing, but if you shift your own point of view a little, you may find it pointing in an equally uncompromising manner to something entirely different. It must be confessed, however, that the case looks exceedingly grave

"THEY FOUND THE BODY."

"Besides, we may chance to hit upon some other obvious facts which may have been by no means obvious to Mr. Lestrade. You know me too well to think that I am boasting when I say that I shall either confirm or destroy his theory by means which he is quite incapable of employing, or even of understanding. To take the first example to hand, I very clearly perceive that in your bedroom the window is upon the right-hand side, and yet I question whether Mr. Lestrade would have noted even so self-evident a thing as that."

"How on earth——!"

"My dear fellow, I know you well. I know the military neatness which characterises you. You shave every morning, and in this season you shave by the sunlight, but since your shaving is less and less complete as we get further back on the left side, until it becomes positively slovenly as we get round the angle of the jaw, it is surely very clear that that side is less well illuminated than the other. I could not imagine a man of your habits looking at himself in an equal light, and being satisfied with such a result. I only quote this as a trivial example of observation and inference. Therein lies my *métier*, and it is just possible that it may be of some service in the investigation which lies before us. There are one or two minor points which were brought out in the inquest, and which are worth considering."

"What are they?"

against the young man, and it is very possible that he is indeed the culprit. There are several people in the neighbourhood, however, and among them Miss Turner, the daughter of the neighbouring landowner, who believe in his innocence, and who have retained Lestrade, whom you may recollect in connection with the Study in Scarlet, to work out the case in his interest. Lestrade, being rather puzzled, has referred the case to me, and hence it is that two middle-aged gentlemen are flying westward at fifty miles an hour, instead of quietly digesting their breakfasts at home."

"I am afraid," said I, "that the facts are so obvious that you will find little credit to be gained out of this case."

"There is nothing more deceptive than an obvious fact," he answered, laughing.

" It appears that his arrest did not take place at once, but after the return to Hatherley Farm. On the inspector of constabulary informing him that he was a prisoner, he remarked that he was not surprised to hear it, and that it was no more than his deserts. This observation of his had the natural effect of removing any traces of doubt which might have remained in the minds of the coroner's jury."

" It was a confession," I ejaculated.

" No, for it was followed by a protestation of innocence."

" Coming on the top of such a damning series of events, it was at least a most suspicious remark."

" On the contrary," said Holmes, " it is the brightest rift which I can at present see in the clouds. However innocent he might be, he could not be such an absolute imbecile as not to see that the circumstances were very black against him. Had he appeared surprised at his own arrest, or feigned indignation at it, I should have looked upon it as highly suspicious, because such surprise or anger would not be natural under the circumstances, and yet might appear to be the best policy to a scheming man. His frank acceptance of the situation marks him as either an innocent man, or else as a man of considerable self-restraint and firmness. As to his remark about his deserts, it was also not unnatural if you consider that he stood beside the dead body of his father, and that there is no doubt that he had that very day so far forgotten his filial duty as to bandy words with him, and even, according to the little girl whose evidence is so important, to raise his hand as if to strike him. The self-reproach and contrition which are displayed in his remark appear to me to be the signs of a healthy mind, rather than of a guilty one."

I shook my head. " Many men have been hanged on far slighter evidence," I remarked.

" So they have. And many men have been wrongfully hanged."

" What is the young man's own account of the matter ? "

" It is, I am afraid, not very encouraging to his supporters, though there are one or two points in it which are suggestive. You will find it here, and may read it for yourself."

He picked out from his bundle a copy of the local Herefordshire paper, and having turned down the sheet, he pointed out the paragraph in which the unfortunate young man had given his own statement of what had occurred. I settled myself down in the corner of the carriage, and read it very carefully. It ran in this way :—

" Mr. James McCarthy, the only son of the deceased, was then called, and gave evidence as follows :—'I had been away from home for three days at Bristol, and had only just returned upon the morning of last Monday, the 3rd. My father was absent from home at the time of my arrival, and I was informed by the maid that he had driven over to Ross with John Cobb, the groom. Shortly after my return I heard the wheels of his trap in the yard, and, looking out of my window, I saw him get out and walk rapidly out of the yard, though I was not aware in which direction he was going. I then took my gun, and strolled out in the direction of the Boscombe Pool, with the intention of visiting the rabbit warren which is upon the other side. On my way I saw William Crowder, the gamekeeper, as he has stated in his evidence ; but he is mistaken in thinking that I was following my father. I had no idea that he was in front of me. When about a hundred yards from the Pool I heard a cry of " Cooee ! " which was a usual signal between my father and myself. I then hurried forward, and found him standing by the Pool. He appeared to be much surprised at seeing me, and asked me rather roughly what I was doing there. A conversation ensued, which led to high words, and almost to blows, for my father was a man of a very violent temper. Seeing that his passion was becoming ungovernable, I left him, and returned towards Hatherley Farm. I had not gone more than one hundred and fifty yards, however, when I heard a hideous outcry behind me, which caused me to run back again. I found my father expiring upon the ground, with his head terribly injured. I dropped my gun, and held him in my arms, but he almost instantly expired. I knelt besides him for some minutes, and then made my way to Mr. Turner's lodge-keeper, his house being the nearest, to ask for assistance. I saw no one near my father when I returned, and I have no idea how he came by his injuries. He was not a popular man, being somewhat cold and forbidding in his manners ; but he had, as far as I know, no active enemies. I know nothing further of the matter.'"

" The Coroner : Did your father make any statement to you before he died ?

"I HELD HIM IN MY ARMS."

"Witness : It was.

"The Coroner : How was it, then, that he uttered it before he saw you, and before he even knew that you had returned from Bristol ?

"Witness (with considerable confusion) : I do not know.

"A Juryman : Did you see nothing which aroused your suspicions when you returned on hearing the cry, and found your father fatally injured ?

"Witness : Nothing definite.

"The Coroner : What do you mean ?

"Witness : I was so disturbed and excited as I rushed out into the open, that I could think of nothing except of my father. Yet I have a vague impression that as I ran forward something lay upon the ground to the left of me. It seemed to me to be something grey in colour, a coat of some sort, or a plaid perhaps. When I rose from my father I looked round for it, but it was gone.

"'Do you mean that it disappeared before you went for help?'

"'Yes, it was gone.'

"'You cannot say what it was?'

"'No, I had a feeling something was there.'

"'How far from the body?'

"'A dozen yards or so.'

"'And how far from the edge of the wood?'

"'About the same.'

"'Then if it was removed it was while you were within a dozen yards of it?'

"'Yes, but with my back towards it.'

"This concluded the examination of the witness."

"Witness : He mumbled a few words, but I could only catch some allusion to a rat.

"The Coroner : What did you understand by that ?

"Witness : It conveyed no meaning to me. I thought that he was delirious.

"The Coroner : What was the point upon which you and your father had this final quarrel ?

"Witness : I should prefer not to answer.

"The Coroner : I am afraid that I must press it.

"Witness : It is really impossible for me to tell you. I can assure you that it has nothing to do with the sad tragedy which followed.

"The Coroner : That is for the Court to decide. I need not point out to you that your refusal to answer will prejudice your case considerably in any future proceedings which may arise.

"Witness : I must still refuse.

"The Coroner : I understand that the cry of 'Cooee' was a common signal between you and your father ?

"I see," said I, as I glanced down the column, "that the coroner in his concluding remarks was rather severe upon young McCarthy. He calls attention, and with reason, to the discrepancy about his father having signalled to him before seeing him, also to his refusal to give details of his conversation with his father, and his singular account of his father's dying words. They are all, as he remarks, very much against the son."

Holmes laughed softly to himself, and stretched himself out upon the cushioned seat. "Both you and the coroner have been at some pains," said he, "to single out the very strongest points in the young man's favour. Don't you see that you alternately give him credit for having too much imagination and too little? Too little, if he could not invent a cause of quarrel which would give him the sympathy of the jury; too much, if he evolved from his own inner consciousness anything so *outré* as a dying reference to a rat, and the incident of the vanishing cloth. No, sir, I shall approach this case from the point of view that what this young man says is true, and we shall see whither that hypothesis will lead us. And now here is my pocket Petrarch, and not another word shall I say of this case until we are on the scene of action. We lunch at Swindon, and I see that we shall be there in twenty minutes."

It was nearly four o'clock when we at last, after passing through the beautiful Stroud Valley, and over the broad gleaming Severn, found ourselves at the pretty little country town of Ross. A lean, ferret-like man, furtive and sly-looking, was waiting for us upon the platform. In spite of the light brown dustcoat and leather leggings which he wore in deference to his rustic surroundings, I had no difficulty in recognising Lestrade, of Scotland Yard. With him we drove to the "Hereford Arms," where a room had already been engaged for us.

"I have ordered a carriage," said Lestrade, as we sat over a cup of tea. "I knew your energetic nature, and that you would not be happy until you had been on the scene of the crime."

"It was very nice and complimentary of you," Holmes answered. "It is entirely a question of barometric pressure."

Lestrade looked startled. "I do not quite follow," he said.

"How is the glass? Twenty-nine, I see. No wind, and not a cloud in the sky. I have a caseful of cigarettes here which need smoking, and the sofa is very much superior to the usual country hotel abomination. I do not think that it is probable that I shall use the carriage to-night."

Lestrade laughed indulgently. "You have, no doubt, already formed your conclusions from the newspapers," he said. "The case is as plain as a pikestaff, and the more one

goes into it the plainer it becomes. Still, of course, one can't refuse a lady, and such a very positive one, too. She had heard of you, and would have your opinion, though I repeatedly told her that there was nothing which you could do which I had not already done. Why, bless my soul! here is her carriage at the door."

He had hardly spoken before there rushed into the room one of the most lovely young women that I have ever seen in my life. Her violet eyes shining, her lips parted, a pink flush upon her cheeks, all thought of her natural reserve lost in her overpowering excitement and concern.

"Oh, Mr. Sherlock Holmes!" she cried, glancing from one to the other of us, and finally, with a woman's quick intuition, fastening upon my companion, "I am so glad that you have come. I have driven down to tell you so. I know that James didn't do it. I know it, and I want you to start upon your work knowing it, too. Never let yourself doubt upon that point. We have know each other since we were little children, and I know his faults as no one else does; but he is too tender-hearted to hurt a fly. Such a charge is absurd to anyone who really knows him."

"I hope we may clear him, Miss Turner," said Sherlock Holmes. "You may rely upon my doing all that I can."

"But you have read the evidence. You have formed some conclusion? Do you not see some loophole, some flaw? Do you not yourself think that he is innocent?"

"I think that it is very probable."

"There now!" she cried, throwing back her head, and looking defiantly at Lestrade. "You hear! He gives me hopes."

Lestrade shrugged his shoulders. "I am afraid that my colleague has been a little quick in forming his conclusions," he said.

"But he is right. Oh! I know that he is right. James never did it. And about his quarrel with his father, I am sure that the reason why he would not speak about it to the coroner was because I was concerned in it."

"In what way?" asked Holmes.

"It is no time for me to hide anything. James and his father had many disagreements about me. Mr. McCarthy was very anxious that there should be a marriage between us. James and I have always loved each other as brother and sister, but of course he is young, and has seen very little

"LESTRADE SHRUGGED HIS SHOULDERS."

of life yet, and—and—well, he naturally did not wish to do anything like that yet. So there were quarrels, and this, I am sure, was one of them."

"And your father?" asked Holmes. "Was he in favour of such a union?"

"No, he was averse to it also. No one but Mr. McCarthy was in favour of it." A quick blush passed over her fresh young face as Holmes shot one of his keen, questioning glances at her.

"Thank you for this information," said he. "May I see your father if I call to-morrow?"

"I am afraid the doctor won't allow it."

"The doctor?"

"Yes, have you not heard? Poor father has never been strong for years back, but this has broken him down completely. He has taken to his bed, and Dr. Willows says that he is a wreck, and that his nervous system is shattered. Mr. McCarthy was the only man alive who had known dad in the old days in Victoria."

"Ha! In Victoria! That is important."

"Yes, at the mines."

"Quite so; at the gold mines, where, as I understand, Mr. Turner made his money."

"Yes, certainly."

"Thank you, Miss Turner. You have been of material assistance to me."

"You will tell me if you have any news to-morrow. No doubt you will go to the prison to see James. Oh, if you do, Mr. Holmes, do tell him that I know him to be innocent."

"I will, Miss Turner."

"I must go home now, for dad is very ill, and he misses me so if I leave him. Good-bye, and God help you in your undertaking." She hurried from the room as impulsively as she had entered, and we heard the wheels of her carriage rattle off down the street.

"I am ashamed of you, Holmes," said Lestrade with dignity, after a few minutes' silence. "Why should you raise up hopes which you are bound to disappoint? I am not over tender of heart, but I call it cruel."

"I think that I see my way to clearing James McCarthy," said Holmes. "Have you an order to see him in prison."

"Yes, but only for you and me."

"Then I shall reconsider my resolution about going out. We have still time to take a train to Hereford and see him to-night?"

"Ample."

"Then let us do so. Watson, I fear that you will find it very slow, but I shall only be away a couple of hours."

I walked down to the station with them, and then wandered through the streets of the little town, finally returning to the hotel, where I lay upon the sofa and tried to interest myself in a yellow-backed novel. The puny plot of the story was so thin, however, when compared to the deep mystery through which we were groping, and I found my attention wander so continually from the fiction to the fact, that I at last flung it across the room, and gave myself up entirely to a consideration of the events of the day. Supposing that this unhappy young man's story was absolutely true, then what hellish thing, what absolutely unforeseen and extraordinary calamity could have occurred between the time when he parted from his father, and the moment when, drawn back by his screams, he rushed into the glade? It was something terrible and deadly. What could it be? Might not the nature of the injuries reveal something to my medical instincts? I rang the bell, and called for the weekly county paper, which contained a verbatim account of the inquest. In the surgeon's deposition it was stated that the posterior third of the left parietal bone and the left half of the occi-

"I TRIED TO INTEREST MYSELF IN A YELLOW-BACKED NOVEL."

pital bone had been shattered by a heavy blow from a blunt weapon. I marked the spot upon my own head. Clearly such a blow must have been struck from behind. That was to some extent in favour of the accused, as when seen quarrelling he was face to face with his father. Still, it did not go for very much, for the older man might have turned his back before the blow fell. Still, it might be worth while to call Holmes' attention to it. Then there was the peculiar dying reference to a rat. What could that mean? It could not be delirium. A man dying from a sudden blow does not commonly become delirious. No, it was more likely to be an attempt to explain how he met his fate. But what could it indicate? I cudgelled my brains to find some possible

explanation. And then the incident of the grey cloth, seen by young McCarthy. If that were true, the murderer must have dropped some part of his dress, presumably his overcoat, in his flight, and must have had the hardihood to return and to carry it away at the instant when the son was kneeling with his back turned not a dozen paces off. What a tissue of mysteries and improbabilities the whole thing was! I did not wonder at Lestrade's opinion, and yet I had so much faith in Sherlock Holmes' insight that I could not lose hope as long as every fresh fact seemed to strengthen his conviction of young McCarthy's innocence.

It was late before Sherlock Holmes returned. He came back alone, for Lestrade was staying in lodgings in the town.

"The glass still keeps very high," he remarked, as he sat down. "It is of importance that it should not rain before we are able to go over the ground. On the other hand, a man should be at his very best and keenest for such nice work as that, and I did not wish to do it when fagged by a long journey. I have seen young McCarthy."

"And what did you learn from him?"

"Nothing."

"Could he throw no light?"

"None at all. I was inclined to think at one time that he knew who had done it, and was screening him or her, but I am convinced now that he is as puzzled as everyone else. He is not a very quick-witted youth, though comely to look at, and, I should think, sound at heart."

"I cannot admire his taste," I remarked, "if it is indeed a fact that he was averse to a marriage with so charming a young lady as this Miss Turner."

"Ah, thereby hangs a rather painful tale. This fellow is madly, insanely in love with her, but some two years ago, when he was only a lad, and before he really knew her, for she had been away five years at a boarding-school, what does the idiot do but get into the clutches of a barmaid in Bristol, and marry her at a registry office? No one knows a word of the matter, but you can imagine how maddening it must be to him to be upbraided for not doing what he would give his very eyes to do, but what he knows to be absolutely impossible. It was sheer frenzy of this sort which made him throw his hands up into the air when his father, at their last interview, was goading him on to propose to Miss Turner. On the other hand, he had no means of supporting himself, and his father, who was by all accounts a very hard man, would have thrown him over utterly had he known the truth. It was with his barmaid wife that he had spent the last three days in Bristol, and his father did not know where he was. Mark that point. It is of importance. Good has come out of evil, however, for the barmaid, finding from the papers that he is in serious trouble, and likely to be hanged, has thrown him over utterly, and has written to him to say that she has a husband already in the Bermuda Dockyard, so that there is really no tie between them. I think that that bit of news has consoled young McCarthy for all that he has suffered."

"But if he is innocent, who has done it?"

"Ah! who? I would call your attention very particularly to two points. One is that the murdered man had an appointment with someone at the Pool, and that the someone could not have been his son, for his son was away, and he did not know when he would return. The second is that the murdered man was heard to cry, 'Cooee!' before he knew that his son had returned. Those are the crucial points upon which the case depends. And now let us talk about George Meredith, if you please, and we shall leave all minor matters until to-morrow."

There was no rain, as Holmes had fore-told, and the morning broke bright and cloudless. At nine o'clock Lestrade called for us with the carriage, and we set off for Hatherley Farm and the Boscombe Pool.

"There is serious news this morning," Lestrade observed. "It is said that Mr. Turner, of the Hall, is so ill that his life is despaired of."

"An elderly man, I presume?" said Holmes.

"About sixty; but his constitution has been shattered by his life abroad, and he has been in failing health for some time. This business has had a very bad effect upon him. He was an old friend of McCarthy's, and, I may add, a great benefactor to him, for I have learned that he gave him Hatherley Farm rent free."

"Indeed! That is interesting," said Holmes.

"Oh, yes! In a hundred other ways he has helped him. Everybody about here speaks of his kindness to him."

"Really! Does it not strike you as a little singular that this McCarthy, who appears to have had little of his own, and to have been under such obligations to Turner, should still talk of marrying his son to Turner's daughter, who is, presumably, heiress to the estate, and that in such a very cocksure manner, as if it were merely a case of a proposal and all else would follow? It is the more strange, since we know that Turner himself was averse to the idea. The daughter told us as much. Do you not deduce something from that?"

"We have got to the deductions and the inferences," said Lestrade, winking at me. "I find it hard enough to tackle facts, Holmes, without flying away after theories and fancies."

"You are right," said Holmes, demurely; "you do find it very hard to tackle the facts."

"Anyhow, I have grasped one fact which you seem to find it difficult to get hold of," replied Lestrade, with some warmth.

"And that is?"

"That McCarthy, senior, met his death from McCarthy, junior, and that all theories to the contrary are the merest moonshine."

"Well, moonshine is a brighter thing than fog," said Holmes, laughing. "But I am very much mistaken if this is not Hatherley Farm upon the left."

"Yes, that is it." It was a widespread, comfortable-looking building, two-storied slate roofed, with great yellow blotches of lichen upon the grey walls. The drawn blinds and the smokeless chimneys, how-ever, gave it a stricken look, as though the weight of this horror still lay heavy upon it. We called at the door, when the maid at Holmes' request, showed us the boots which her master wore at the time of his death, and also a pair of the son's, though not the pair which he had then had. Hav-

"THE MAID SHOWED US THE BOOTS."

dead, and once he made quite a little *détour* into the meadow. Lestrade and I walked behind him, the detective indifferent and contemptuous, while I watched my friend with the interest which sprang from the conviction that every one of his actions was directed towards a definite end.

The Boscombe Pool, which is a little reed-girt sheet of water some fifty yards across, is situated at the boundary between the Hatherley Farm and the private park of the wealthy Mr. Turner. Above the woods which lined it upon the further side we could see the red jutting pinnacles which marked the site of the rich landowner's dwelling. On the Hatherley side of the Pool the woods grew very thick, and there was a narrow belt of sodden grass twenty paces across between the edge of the trees and the reeds which lined the lake. Lestrade showed us the exact spot at which the body had been found, and, indeed, so moist was the ground, that I could plainly see the traces which had been left by the fall of the stricken man. To Holmes, as I could see by his eager face and peering eyes, very many other things were to be read upon the trampled grass. He ran round, like a dog who is picking up a scent, and then turned upon my companion.

"What did you go into the Pool for?" he asked.

"I fished about with a rake. I thought there might be some weapon or other trace. But how on earth——?"

"Oh, tut, tut! I have no time! That left foot of yours with its inward twist is all over the place. A mole could trace it, and there it vanishes among the reeds. Oh, how simple it would all have been had I been here before they came like a herd of

ing measured these very carefully from seven or eight different points, Holmes desired to be led to the courtyard, from which we all followed the winding track which led to Boscombe Pool.

Sherlock Holmes was transformed when he was hot upon such a scent as this. Men who had only known the quiet thinker and logician of Baker-street would have failed to recognise him. His face flushed and darkened. His brows were drawn into two hard, black lines, while his eyes shone out from beneath them with a steely glitter. His face was bent downwards, his shoulders bowed, his lips compressed, and the veins stood out like whipcord in his long, sinewy neck. His nostrils seemed to dilate with a purely animal lust for the chase, and his mind was so absolutely concentrated upon the matter before him, that a question or remark fell unheeded upon his ears, or at the most, only provoked a quick, impatient snarl in reply. Swiftly and silently he made his way along the track which ran through the meadows, and so by way of the woods to the Boscombe Pool. It was damp, marshy ground, as is all that district, and there were marks of many feet, both upon the path, and amid the short grass which bounded it on either side. Sometimes Holmes would hurry on, sometimes stop

buffalo, and wallowed all over it. Here is where the party with the lodge-keeper came, and they have covered all tracks for six or eight feet round the body. But here are and this also he carefully examined and retained. Then he followed a pathway through the wood until he came to the high road, where all traces were lost.

" FOR A LONG TIME HE REMAINED THERE."

three separate tracks of the same feet." He drew out a lens, and lay down upon his waterproof to have a better view, talking all the time rather to himself than to us. "These are young McCarthy's feet. Twice he was walking, and once he ran swiftly so that the soles are deeply marked, and the heels hardly visible. That bears out his story. He ran when he saw his father on the ground. Then here are the father's feet as he paced up and down. What is this, then? It is the butt-end of the gun as the son stood listening. And this? Ha, ha! What have we here? Tip-toes! tip-toes! Square, too, quite unusual boots! They come, they go, they come again—of course that was for the cloak. Now where did they come from?" He ran up and down, sometimes losing, sometimes finding the track until we were well within the edge of the wood, and under the shadow of a great beech, the largest tree in the neighbourhood. Holmes traced his way to the further side of this, and lay down once more upon his face with a little cry of satisfaction. For a long time he remained there, turning over the leaves and dried sticks, gathering up what seemed to me to be dust into an envelope, and examining with his lens not only the ground, but even the bark of the tree as far as he could reach. A jagged stone was lying among the moss,

"It has been a case of considerable interest," he remarked, returning to his natural manner. "I fancy that this grey house on the right must be the lodge. I think that I will go in and have a word with Moran, and perhaps write a little note. Having done that, we may drive back to our luncheon. You may walk to the cab, and I shall be with you presently."

It was about ten minutes before we regained our cab, and drove back into Ross, Holmes still carrying with him the stone which he had picked up in the wood.

"This may interest you, Lestrade," he remarked, holding it out. "The murder was done with it."

"I see no marks."

"There are none."

"How do you know, then?"

"The grass was growing under it. It had only lain there a few days. There was no sign of a place whence it had been taken. It corresponds with the injuries. There is no sign of any other weapon."

"And the murderer?"

"Is a tall man, left-handed, limps with the right leg, wears thick-soled shooting boots and a grey cloak, smokes Indian cigars, uses a cigar-holder, and carries a blunt penknife in his pocket. There are several other indications, but these may be enough to aid us in our search."

Lestrade laughed. "I am afraid that I am still a sceptic," he said. "Theories are all very well, but we have to deal with a hard-headed British jury."

"*Nous verrons,*" answered Holmes, calmly. "You work your own method, and I shall work mine. I shall be busy this afternoon, and shall probably return to London by the evening train."

"And leave your case unfinished?"

"No, finished."

"But the mystery?"

"It is solved."

"Who was the criminal, then?"

"The gentleman I describe."

"But who is he?"

"Surely it would not be difficult to find out. This is not such a populous neighbourhood."

Lestrade shrugged his shoulders. "I am a practical man," he said, "and I really cannot undertake to go about the country looking for a left-handed gentleman with a game leg. I should become the laughing-stock of Scotland Yard."

"All right," said Holmes, quietly. "I have given you the chance. Here are your lodgings. Good-bye. I shall drop you a line before I leave."

Having left Lestrade at his rooms we drove to our hotel, where we found lunch upon the table. Holmes was silent and buried in thought with a pained expression upon his face, as one who finds himself in a perplexing position.

"Look here, Watson," he said, when the cloth was cleared; "just sit down in this chair and let me preach to you

"HE HAD STOOD BEHIND THAT TREE."

for a little. I don't quite know what to do, and I should value your advice. Light a cigar, and let me expound."

"Pray do so."

"Well, now, in considering this case there are two points about young McCarthy's narrative which struck us both instantly, although they impressed me in his favour and you against him. One was the fact that his father should, according to his account, cry 'Cooee!' before seeing him. The other was his singular dying reference to a rat. He mumbled several words, you understand, but that was all that caught the son's ear. Now from this double point our research must commence, and we will begin it by presuming that what the lad says is absolutely true."

"What of this 'Cooee!' then?"

"Well, obviously it could not have been meant for the son. The son, as far as he knew, was in Bristol. It was mere chance that he was within earshot. The 'Cooee!' was meant to attract the attention of whoever it was that he had the appointment with. But 'Cooee' is a distinctly Australian cry, and one which is used between Australians. There is a strong presumption that the person whom McCarthy expected to meet him at Boscombe Pool was someone who had been in Australia."

"What of the rat, then?"

Sherlock Holmes took a folded paper from his pocket and flattened it out on the table. "This is a map of the Colony of Victoria," he said. "I wired to Bristol for it last night." He put his hand over part of the map. "What do you read?" he asked.

"ARAT," I read.

"And now?" He raised his hand.

"BALLARAT."

"Quite so. That was the word the man uttered, and of which his son only caught the last two syllables. He was trying to utter the name of his murderer. So-and-so, of Ballarat."

"It is wonderful!" I exclaimed.

"It is obvious. And now, you see, I had narrowed the field down considerably. The possession of a grey garment was a third point which, granting the son's statement to be correct, was a certainty. We have come now out of mere vagueness to the definite conception of an Australian from Ballarat with a grey cloak."

"Certainly."

"And one who was at home in the district, for the Pool can only be approached by the farm or by the estate, where strangers could hardly wander."

"Quite so."

"Then comes our expedition of to-day. By an examination of the ground I gained the trifling details which I gave to that imbecile Lestrade, as to the personality of the criminal."

"But how did you gain them?"

"You know my method. It is founded upon the observance of trifles."

"His height I know that you might roughly judge from the length of his stride. His boots, too, might be told from their traces."

"Yes, they were peculiar boots."

"But his lameness?"

"The impression of his right foot was always less distinct than his left. He put less weight upon it. Why? Because he limped—he was lame."

"But his left-handedness."

"You were yourself struck by the nature of the injury as recorded by the surgeon at the inquest. The blow was struck from immediately behind, and yet was upon the left side. Now, how can that be unless it were by a left-handed man? He had stood behind that tree during the interview between the father and son. He had even smoked there. I found the ash of a cigar, which my special knowledge of tobacco ashes enabled me to pronounce as an Indian cigar. I have, as you know, devoted some attention to this, and written a little monograph on the ashes of 140 different varieties of pipe, cigar, and cigarette tobacco. Having

found the ash, I then looked round and discovered the stump among the moss where he had tossed it. It was an Indian cigar, of the variety which are rolled in Rotterdam."

"And the cigar-holder?"

"I could see that the end had not been in his mouth. Therefore he used a holder. The tip had been cut off, not bitten off, but the cut was not a clean one, so I deduced a blunt penknife."

"Holmes," I said, "you have drawn a net round this man from which he cannot escape, and you have saved an innocent human life as truly as if you had cut the cord which was hanging him. I see the direction in which all this points. The culprit is——"

"Mr. John Turner," cried the hotel waiter, opening the door of our sitting-room, and ushering in a visitor.

The man who entered was a strange and impressive figure. His slow, limping step and bowed shoulders gave the appearance of decrepitude, and yet his hard, deep-lined, craggy features, and his enormous limbs showed that he was possessed of unusual

"MR. JOHN TURNER," SAID THE WAITER.

strength of body and of character. His tangled beard, grizzled hair, and outstanding, drooping eyebrows combined to give an air of dignity and power to his appearance, but his face was of an ashen white, while his lips and the corners of his nostrils were tinged with a shade of blue. It was clear to me at a glance that he was in the grip of some deadly and chronic disease.

"Pray sit down on the sofa," said Holmes, gently. "You had my note?"

"Yes, the lodge-keeper brought it up. You said that you wished to see me here to avoid scandal."

"I thought people would talk if I went to the Hall."

"And why did you wish to see me?" He looked across at my companion with despair in his weary eyes, as though his question were already answered.

"Yes," said Holmes, answering the look rather than the words. "It is so. I know all about McCarthy."

The old man sank his face in his hands. "God help me!" he cried. "But I would not have let the young man come to harm. I give you my word that I would have spoken out if it went against him at the Assizes."

"I am glad to hear you say so," said Holmes, gravely.

"I would have spoken now had it not been for my dear girl. It would break her heart—it will break her heart when she hears that I am arrested."

"It may not come to that," said Holmes.

"What!"

"I am no official agent. I understand that it was your daughter who required my presence here, and I am acting in her interests. Young McCarthy must be got off, however."

"I am a dying man," said old Turner. "I have had diabetes for years. My doctor says it is a question whether I shall live a month. Yet I would rather die under my own roof than in a gaol."

Holmes rose and sat down at the table with his pen in his hand and a bundle of paper before him. "Just tell us the truth," he said. "I shall jot down the facts. You will sign it, and Watson here can witness it. Then I could produce your confession at the last extremity to save young McCarthy. I promise you that I shall not use it unless it is absolutely needed."

"It's as well," said the old man; "it's a question whether I shall live to the Assizes, so it matters little to me, but I should wish to spare Alice the shock. And now I will make the thing clear to you; it has been a long time in the acting, but will not take me long to tell.

"You didn't know this dead man, McCarthy. He was a devil incarnate. I tell you that. God keep you out of the clutches of such a man as he. His grip has been upon me these twenty years, and he has blasted my life. I'll tell you first how I came to be in his power.

"It was in the early sixties at the diggings. I was a young chap then, hot-blooded and reckless, ready to turn my hand to anything; I got among bad companions, took to drink, had no luck with my claim, took to the bush, and in a word became what you would call over here a highway robber. There were six of us, and we had a wild, free life of it, sticking up a station from time to time, or stopping the waggons on the road to the diggings. Black Jack of Ballarat was the name I went under, and our party is still remembered in the colony as the Ballarat Gang.

"One day a gold convoy came down from Ballarat to Melbourne, and we lay in wait for it and attacked it. There were six troopers and six of us, so it was a close thing, but we emptied four of their saddles at the first volley. Three of our boys were killed, however, before we got the swag. I put my pistol to the head of the waggon-driver, who was this very man McCarthy. I wish to the Lord that I had shot him then, but I spared him, though I saw his wicked little eyes fixed on my face, as though to remember every feature. We got away with the gold, became wealthy men, and made our way over to England without being suspected. There I parted from my old pals, and determined to settle down to a quiet and respectable life. I bought this estate which chanced to be in the market, and I set myself to do a little good with my money, to make up for the way in which I had earned it. I married, too, and though my wife died young, she left me my dear little Alice. Even when she was just a baby her wee hand seemed to lead me down the right path as nothing else had ever done. In a word, I turned over a new leaf, and did my best to make up for the past. All was going well when McCarthy laid his grip upon me.

"I had gone up to town about an investment, and I met him in Regent-street with hardly a coat to his back or a boot to his foot.

"'Here we are, Jack,' says he, touching me on the arm; 'we'll be as good as a family to you. There's two of us, me and my son, and you can have the keeping of us. If you don't—it's a fine, law-abiding country is England, and there's always a policeman within hail.'

"Well, down they came to the West country, there was no shaking them off, and there they have lived rent free on my best land ever since. There was no rest for me, no peace, no forgetfulness; turn where I would, there was his cunning, grinning face at my elbow. It grew worse as Alice grew up, for he soon saw I was more afraid of her knowing my past than of the police. Whatever he wanted he must have, and whatever it was I gave him without question, land, money, houses, until at last he asked a thing which I could not give. He asked for Alice.

"His son, you see, had grown up, and so had my girl, and as I was known to be in weak health, it seemed a fine stroke to him that his lad should step into the whole property. But there I was firm. I would not have his cursed stock mixed with mine; not that I had any dislike to the lad, but his blood was in him, and that was enough. I stood firm. McCarthy threatened. I braved him to do his worst. We were to meet at the Pool midway between our houses to talk it over.

"When I went down there I found him talking with his son, so I smoked a cigar, and waited behind a tree until he should be alone. But as I listened to his talk all that was black and bitter in me seemed to come uppermost. He was urging his son to marry my daughter with as little regard for what she

might think as if she were a slut from off the streets. It drove me mad to think that I and all that I held most dear should be in the power of such a man as this. Could I not snap the bond? I was already a dying and a desperate man. Though clear of mind and fairly strong of limb, I knew that my own fate was sealed. But my memory and my girl! Both could be saved, if I could but silence that foul tongue. I did it, Mr. Holmes. I would do it again. Deeply as I have sinned, I have led a life of martyrdom to atone for it. But that my girl should be entangled in the same meshes which held me was more than I could suffer. I struck him down with no more compunction than if he had been some foul and venomous beast. His cry brought back his son; but I had gained the cover of the wood, though I was forced to go back to fetch the cloak which I had dropped in my flight. That is the true story, gentlemen, of all that occurred."

"Well, it is not for me to judge you," said Holmes, as the old man signed the statement which had been drawn out. "I pray that we may never be exposed to such a temptation."

"I pray not, sir. And what do you intend to do?"

"In view of your health, nothing. You are yourself aware that you will soon have to answer for your deed at a higher Court than the assizes. I will keep your confession, and, if McCarthy is condemned, I shall be forced to use it. If not, it shall never be seen by mortal eye; and your secret, whether you be alive or dead, shall be safe with us."

"Farewell! then," said the old man, solemnly. "Your own death-beds, when they come, will be the easier for the thought of the peace which

"'FAREWELL, THEN,' SAID THE OLD MAN."

you have given to mine." Tottering and shaking in all his giant frame, he stumbled slowly from the room.

"God help us!" said Holmes. after a long silence. "Why does fate play such tricks with poor helpless worms? I never hear of such a case as this that I do not think of Baxter's words, and say, 'There, but for the grace of God, goes Sherlock Holmes.'"

James McCarthy was acquitted at the assizes, on the strength of a number of objections which had been drawn out by Holmes, and submitted to the defending counsel. Old Turner lived for seven months after our interview, but he is now dead; and there is every prospect that the son and daughter may come to live happily together, in ignorance of the black cloud which rests upon their past.

# Adventures of Sherlock Holmes.

## ADVENTURE V.—THE FIVE ORANGE PIPS.

### By A. Conan Doyle.

HEN I glance over my notes and records of the Sherlock Holmes cases between the years '82 and '90, I am faced by so many which present strange and interesting features, that it is no easy matter to know which to choose and which to leave. Some, however, have already gained publicity through the papers, and others have not offered a field for those peculiar qualities which my friend possessed in so high a degree, and which it is the object of these papers to illustrate. Some, too, have baffled his analytical skill, and would be, as narratives, beginnings without an ending, while others have been but partially cleared up, and have their explanations founded rather upon conjecture and surmise than on that absolute logical proof which was so dear to him. There is, however, one of these last which was so remarkable in its details and so startling in its results, that I am tempted to give some account of it, in spite of the fact that there are points in connection with it which never have been, and probably never will be, entirely cleared up.

The year '87 furnished us with a long series of cases of greater or less interest, of which I retain the records. Among my headings under this one twelve months, I find an account of the adventure of the Paradol Chamber, of the Amateur Mendicant Society, who held a luxurious club in the lower vault of a furniture warehouse, of the facts connected with the loss of the British barque *Sophy Anderson*, of the singular adventures of the Grice Patersons in the island of Uffa, and finally of the Camberwell poisoning case. In the latter, as may be remembered, Sherlock Holmes was able, by winding up the dead man's watch, to prove that it had been wound up two hours ago, and that therefore the deceased had gone to bed within that time—a deduction which was of the greatest importance in clearing up the case. All these I may sketch out at some future date, but none of them present such singular features as the strange train of circumstances which I have now taken up my pen to describe.

It was in the latter days of September, and the equinoctial gales had set in with exceptional violence. All day the wind had screamed and the rain had beaten against the windows, so that even here in the heart of great, hand-made London we were forced to raise our minds for the instant from the routine of life, and to recognise the presence of those great elemental forces which shriek at mankind through the bars of his civilisation, like untamed beasts in a cage. As evening drew in the storm grew higher and louder, and the wind cried and sobbed like a child in the chimney. Sherlock Holmes sat moodily at one side of the fireplace cross-indexing his records of crime, whilst I at the other was deep in one of Clark Russell's fine sea-stories, until the howl of the gale from without seemed to blend with the text, and the splash of the rain to lengthen out into the long swash of the sea waves. My wife was on a visit to her mother's, and for a few days I was a dweller once more in my old quarters at Baker-street.

"Why," said I, glancing up at my companion, "that was surely the bell. Who could come to-night? Some friend of yours, perhaps?"

"Except yourself I have none," he answered. "I do not encourage visitors."

"A client, then?"

"If so, it is a serious case. Nothing less would bring a man out on such a day, and at such an hour. But I take it that it is more likely to be some crony of the landlady's."

Sherlock Holmes was wrong in his conjecture, however, for there came a step in the passage, and a tapping at the door. He stretched out his long arm to turn the lamp away from himself and towards the vacant chair upon which a new-comer must sit. "Come in!" said he.

The man who entered was young, some two-and-twenty at the outside, well groomed and trimly clad, with something of refinement and delicacy in his bearing. The streaming umbrella which he held in his

M M

hand, and his long shining waterproof told of the fierce weather through which he had come. He looked about him anxiously in the glare of the lamp, and I could see that his face was pale and his eyes heavy, like those of a man who is weighed down with some great anxiety.

"I owe you an apology," he said, raising his golden *pince-nez* to his eyes. "I trust that I am not intruding. I fear that I have brought some traces of the storm and the rain into your snug chamber."

"Give me your coat and umbrella," said Holmes. "They may rest here on the hook, and will be dry presently. You have come up from the south-west, I see."

"Yes, from Horsham."

"That clay and chalk mixture which I see upon your toe-caps is quite distinctive."

"I have come for advice."

"That is easily got."

"And help."

"That is not always so easy."

"I have heard of you, Mr. Holmes. I heard from Major Prendergast how you saved him in the Tankerville Club Scandal."

"Ah, of course. He was wrongfully accused of cheating at cards."

"He said that you could solve anything."

"He said too much."

"That you are never beaten."

"I have been beaten four times—three times by men, and once by a woman."

"But what is that compared with the number of your successes?"

"It is true that I have been generally successful."

"Then you may be so with me."

"I beg that you will draw your chair up to the fire, and favour me with some details as to your case."

"It is no ordinary one."

"None of those which come to me are I am the last court of appeal."

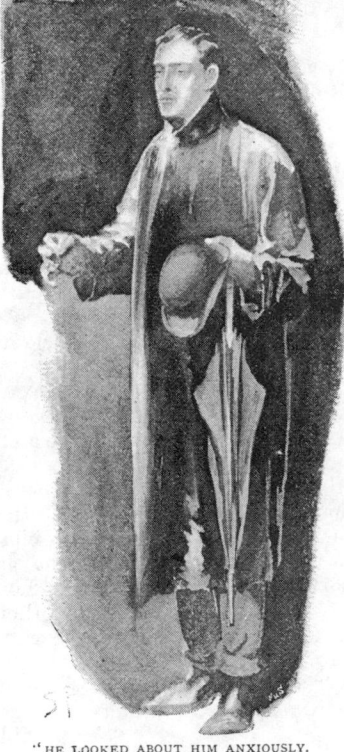

"HE LOOKED ABOUT HIM ANXIOUSLY."

"And yet I question, sir, whether, in all your experience, you have ever listened to a more mysterious and inexplicable chain of events than those which have happened in my own family."

"You fill me with interest," said Holmes. "Pray give us the essential facts from the commencement, and I can afterwards question you as to those details which seem to me to be most important."

The young man pulled his chair up, and pushed his wet feet out towards the blaze.

"My name," said he, "is John Openshaw, but my own affairs have, as far as I can understand it, little to do with this awful business. It is a hereditary matter, so in order to give you an idea of the facts, I must go back to the commencement of the affair.

"You must know that my grandfather had two sons—my uncle Elias and my father Joseph. My father had a small factory at Coventry, which he enlarged at the time of the invention of bicycling. He was the patentee of the Openshaw unbreakable tire, and his business met with such success that he was able to sell it, and to retire upon a handsome competence.

"My uncle Elias emigrated to America when he was a young man, and became a planter in Florida, where he was reported to have done very well. At the time of the war he fought in Jackson's army, and afterwards under Hood, where he rose to be a colonel. When Lee laid down his arms my uncle returned to his plantation, where he remained for three or four years. About 1869 or 1870 he came back to Europe, and took a small estate in Sussex, near Horsham. He had made a very considerable fortune in the States, and his reason for leaving them was his aversion to the negroes, and his dislike of the Republican policy in extending the franchise to them. He was a singular man, fierce and quick-tempered, very foul-mouthed when he was angry, and of a most retiring disposition. During all the years that he lived at Horsham I doubt if ever he set foot in the town. He had a garden and two or three fields round his house, and there he would take his exercise, though very often for weeks on end he would never leave his room. He drank a great deal of brandy, and smoked very heavily, but he would see no society, and did not want any friends, not even his own brother.

"He didn't mind me, in fact he took a fancy to me, for at the time when he saw me first I was a youngster of twelve or so. That would be in the year 1878, after he had been eight or nine years in England. He begged my father to let me live with him, and he was very kind to me in his way. When he was sober he used to be fond of playing backgammon and draughts with me, and he would make me his representative both with the servants and with the tradespeople, so that by the time that I was sixteen I was quite master of the house. I kept all the keys, and could go where I liked and do what I liked, so long as I did not disturb him in his privacy. There was one singular exception, however, for he had a single room, a lumber room up among the attics, which was invariably locked, and which he would never permit either me or anyone else to enter. With a boy's curiosity I have peeped through the keyhole, but I was never able to see more than such a collection of old trunks and bundles as would be expected in such a room.

"One day—it was in March, 1883—a letter with a foreign stamp lay upon the table in front of the Colonel's plate. It was not a common thing for him to receive letters, for his bills were all paid in ready money, and he had no friends of any sort. 'From India!' said he, as he took it up, 'Pondicherry postmark! What can this be?' Opening it hurriedly, out there jumped five little dried orange pips, which pattered down upon his plate. I began to laugh at this, but the laugh was struck from my lips at the sight of his face. His lip had fallen, his eyes were protruding, his skin the colour of putty, and he glared at the envelope which he still held in his trembling hand. 'K. K. K.' he shrieked, and then, 'My God, my God, my sins have overtaken me.'

"'What is it, uncle?' I cried.

"'Death,' said he, and rising from the table he retired to his room, leaving me palpitating with horror. I took up the envelope, and saw scrawled in red ink upon the inner flap, just above the gum, the letter K three times repeated. There was nothing else save the five dried pips. What could be the reason of his overpowering terror? I left the breakfast table, and as I ascended the stair I met him coming down with an old rusty key, which must have belonged to the attic, in one hand, and a small brass box, like a cash box, in the other.

"'They may do what they like, but I'll checkmate them still,' said he, with an oath. 'Tell Mary that I shall want a fire in my room to-day, and send down to Fordham, the Horsham lawyer.'

"I did as he ordered, and when the lawyer arrived I was asked to step up to the room. The fire was burning brightly, and in the grate there was a mass of black, fluffy ashes, as of burned paper, while the brass box stood open and empty beside it. As I glanced at the box I noticed, with a start, that upon the lid were printed the treble K which I had read in the morning upon the envelope.

"'I wish you, John,' said my uncle, 'to witness my will. I leave my estate, with all its advantages and all its disadvantages to my brother, your father, whence it will, no doubt, descend to you. If you can enjoy it in peace, well and good! If you find you cannot, take my advice, my boy, and leave it to your deadliest enemy. I am sorry to give you such a two-edged thing, but I can't say what turn things are going to take. Kindly sign the paper where Mr. Fordham shows you.'

"I signed the paper as directed, and the lawyer took it away with him. The singular incident made, as you may think, the deepest impression upon me, and I pondered over it, and turned it every way in my mind without being able to make anything of it. Yet I could not shake off the vague feeling of dread which it left behind it, though the sensation grew less keen as the weeks passed, and nothing happened to disturb the usual routine of our lives. I could see a change in my uncle, however. He drank more than ever, and he was less inclined for any sort of society. Most of his time he would spend in his room, with the door locked upon the inside, but sometimes he would emerge in a sort of drunken frenzy, and would burst out of the house and tear about the garden with a revolver in his hand, screaming out that he was afraid of no man, and that he was not to be cooped up, like a sheep in a pen, by man or devil. When these hot fits were over, however, he would rush tumultuously in at the door, and lock and bar it behind him, like a man who can brazen it out no longer against the terror which lies at the roots of his soul. At such times I have seen his face, even on a cold day, glisten with moisture as though it were new raised from a basin.

" Well, to come to an end of the matter, Mr. Holmes, and not to abuse your patience, there came a night when he made one of those drunken sallies from which he never came back. We found him, when we went to search for him, face downwards in a little green-scummed pool, which lay at the foot of the garden. There was no sign of any violence, and the water was but two feet deep, so that the jury, having regard to his known eccentricity, brought in a verdict of suicide. But I, who knew how he winced from the very thought of death, had much ado to persuade myself that he had gone out of his way to meet it. The matter passed, however, and my father entered into possession of the estate, and of some fourteen thousand

property, he, at my request, made a careful examination of the attic, which had been always locked up. We found the brass box there, although its contents had been destroyed. On the inside of the cover was a paper label, with the initials K. K. K. repeated upon it, and ' Letters, memoranda, receipts, and a register ' written beneath. These, we presume, indicated the nature of the papers which had been destroyed by Colonel Openshaw. For the rest, there was nothing of much importance in the attic, save a great many scattered papers and notebooks bearing upon my uncle's life in America. Some of them were of the war

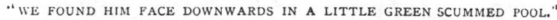

"WE FOUND HIM FACE DOWNWARDS IN A LITTLE GREEN SCUMMED POOL."

pounds, which lay to his credit at the bank."

"One moment," Holmes interposed. "Your statement is, I foresee, one of the most remarkable to which I have ever listened. Let me have the date of the reception by your uncle of the letter, and the date of his supposed suicide."

"The letter arrived on March the tenth, 1883. His death was seven weeks later, upon the night of the second of May."

"Thank you. Pray proceed."

"When my father took over the Horsham

time, and showed that he had done his duty well, and had borne the repute of being a brave soldier. Others were of a date during the reconstruction of the Southern States, and were mostly concerned with politics, for he had evidently taken a strong part in opposing the carpet-bag politicians who had been sent down from the North.

" Well, it was the beginning of '84 when my father came to live at Horsham, and all went as well as possible with us until the January of '85. On the fourth day after the New Year I heard my father give a sharp cry of surprise as we sat together at the breakfast table. There he was, sitting with a newly-opened envelope in one hand and five dried orange-pips in the outstretched palm of the other one. He had always laughed at what he called my cock-and-a-bull story about the Colonel, but he looked very scared and puzzled now that the same thing had come upon himself.

"'Why, what on earth does this mean, John?' he stammered.

"My heart had turned to lead. 'It is K. K. K.' said I.

"He looked inside the envelope. 'So it is,' he cried. 'Here are the very letters. But what is this written above them?'

"'Put the papers on the sun-dial,' I read, peeping over his shoulder.

"'What papers? What sun-dial?' he asked.

"'The sun-dial in the garden. There is no other,' said I; 'but the papers must be those that are destroyed.'

"'Pooh!' said he, gripping hard at his courage. 'We are in a civilised land here, and we can't have tomfoolery of this kind. Where does the thing come from?'

"'From Dundee,' I answered, glancing at the postmark.

"'Some preposterous practical joke,' said he. 'What have I to do with sun-dials and papers? I shall take no notice of such nonsense.'

"'I should certainly speak to the police,' I said.

"'And be laughed at for my pains. Nothing of the sort.'

"'Then let me do so?'

"'No, I forbid you. I won't have a fuss made about such nonsense.'

"It was in vain to argue with him, for he was a very obstinate man. I went about, however, with a heart which was full of forebodings.

"On the third day after the coming of the letter my father went from home to visit an old friend of his, Major Freebody, who is in command of one of the forts upon Portsdown Hill. I was glad that he should go, for it seemed to me that he was further from danger when he was away from home. In that, however, I was in error. Upon the second day of his absence I received a telegram from the Major, imploring me to come at once. My father had fallen over one of the deep chalk-pits which abound in the neighbourhood, and was lying senseless, with a shattered skull. I hurried to him, but he passed away without having ever recovered his consciousness. He had, as it appears, been returning from Fareham in the twilight, and as the country was unknown to him, and the chalk-pit unfenced, the jury had no hesitation in bringing in a verdict of 'Death from accidental causes.' Carefully as I examined every fact connected with his death, I was unable to find

'WHAT ON EARTH DOES THIS MEAN?'

anything which could suggest the idea of murder. There were no signs of violence, no footmarks, no robbery, no record of strangers having been seen upon the roads. And yet I need not tell you that my mind was far from at ease, and that I was well-nigh certain that some foul plot had been woven round him.

"In this sinister way I came into my inheritance. You will ask me why I did not dispose of it? I answer because I was well convinced that our troubles were in some way dependent upon an incident in my uncle's life, and that the danger would be as pressing in one house as in another.

"It was in January, '85, that my poor father met his end, and two years and eight months have elapsed since then. During that time I have lived happily at Horsham, and I had begun to hope that this curse had passed away from the family, and that it had ended with the last generation. I had begun to take comfort too soon, however ; yesterday morning the blow fell in the very shape in which it had come upon my father."

The young man took from his waistcoat a crumpled envelope, and, turning to the table, he shook out upon it five little dried orange pips.

"This is the envelope," he continued. "The postmark is London—eastern division. Within are the very words which were upon my father's last message. 'K. K. K.' ; and then 'Put the papers on the sun-dial.'"

"What have you done ?" asked Holmes.

"Nothing."

"Nothing ?"

"To tell the truth "—he sank his face into his thin, white hands— "I have felt helpless. I have felt like one of those poor rabbits when the snake is writhing towards it. I seem to be in the grasp of some resistless, inexorable evil, which no foresight and no precautions can guard against."

"Tut ! Tut !" cried Sherlock Holmes. "You must act, man, or you are lost. Nothing but energy can save you. This is no time for despair."

"I have seen the police."

"Ah ?"

"But they listened to my story with a smile. I am convinced that the inspector has formed the opinion that the letters are all practical jokes, and that the deaths of my relations were really accidents, as the jury stated, and were not to be connected with the warnings."

Holmes shook his clenched hands in the air. "Incredible imbecility !" he cried.

"They have, however, allowed me a policeman, who may remain in the house with me."

"Has he come with you to-night ? "

"No. His orders were to stay in the house."

Again Holmes raved in the air.

"Why did you come to me ?" he said ; "and, above all, why did you not come at once ?"

"I did not know. It was only to-day

that I spoke to Major Prendergast about my troubles, and was advised by him to come to you."

"It is really two days since you had the letter. We should have acted before this. You have no further evidence, I suppose, than that which you have placed before us—no suggestive detail which might help us ? "

"There is one thing," said John Openshaw. He rummaged in his coat pocket, and, drawing out a piece of discoloured, blue-tinted paper, he laid it out upon the table. "I have some remembrance," said

"SHOOK OUT FIVE LITTLE DRIED ORANGE PIPS."

he, "that on the day when my uncle burned the papers I observed that the small, unburned margins which lay amid the ashes were of this particular colour. I found this single sheet upon the floor of his room, and I am inclined to think that it may be one of the papers which has, perhaps, fluttered out from among the others, and in that way have escaped destruction. Beyond the mention of pips, I do not see that it helps us much. I think myself that it is a page from some private diary. The writing is undoubtedly my uncle's."

Holmes moved the lamp, and we both bent over the sheet of paper, which showed by its ragged edge that it had indeed been torn from a book. It was headed, " March,

1869," and beneath were the following enigmatical notices :—

"4th. Hudson came. Same old platform.

"7th. Set the pips on McCauley, Paramore, and John Swain of St. Augustine.

"9th. McCauley cleared.

"10th. John Swain cleared.

"12th. Visited Paramore. All well."

"Thank you!" said Holmes, folding up the paper, and returning it to our visitor. "And now you must on no account lose another instant. We cannot spare time even to discuss what you have told me. You must get home instantly, and act."

"What shall I do?"

"There is but one thing to do. It must be done at once. You must put this piece of paper which you have shown us into the brass box which you have described. You must also put in a note to say that all the other papers were burned by your uncle, and that this is the only one which remains. You must assert that in such words as will carry conviction with them. Having done this, you must at once put the box out upon the sun-dial, as directed. Do you understand?"

"Entirely."

"Do not think of revenge, or anything of the sort, at present. I think that we may gain that by means of the law; but we have our web to weave, while theirs is already woven. The first consideration is to remove the pressing danger which threatens you. The second is to clear up the mystery, and to punish the guilty parties."

"I thank you," said the young man, rising, and pulling on his overcoat. "You have given me fresh life and hope. I shall certainly do as you advise."

"Do not lose an instant. And, above all, take care of yourself in the meanwhile, for I do not think that there can be a doubt that you are threatened by a very real and imminent danger. How do you go back?"

"By train from Waterloo."

"It is not yet nine. The streets will be crowded, so I trust that you may be in safety. And yet you cannot guard yourself too closely."

"I am armed."

"That is well. To-morrow I shall set to work upon your case."

"I shall see you at Horsham, then?"

"No, your secret lies in London. It is there that I shall seek it."

"Then I shall call upon you in a day, or in two days, with news as to the box and the papers. I shall take your advice in every particular." He shook hands with us, and took his leave. Outside the wind still screamed, and the rain splashed and pattered against the windows. This strange, wild story seemed to have come to us from amid the mad elements—blown in upon us like a sheet of sea-weed in a gale—and now to have been reabsorbed by them once more.

Sherlock Holmes sat for some time in silence with his head sunk forward, and his eyes bent upon the red glow of the fire. Then he lit his pipe, and leaning back in his chair he watched the blue smoke rings as they chased each other up to the ceiling.

"I think, Watson," he remarked at last, "that of all our cases we have had none more fantastic than this."

"Save, perhaps, the Sign of Four."

"Well, yes. Save, perhaps, that. And yet this John Openshaw seems to me to be walking amid even greater perils than did the Sholtos."

"But have you," I asked, "formed any definite conception as to what these perils are?"

"There can be no question as to their nature," he answered.

"Then what are they? Who is this K. K. K., and why does he pursue this unhappy family?"

Sherlock Holmes closed his eyes, and placed his elbows upon the arms of his chair, with his finger-tips together. "The ideal reasoner," he remarked, "would, when he has once been shown a single fact in all its bearings, deduce from it not only all the chain of events which led up to it, but also all the results which would follow from it. As Cuvier could correctly describe a whole animal by the contemplation of a single bone, so the observer who has thoroughly understood one link in a series of incidents, should be able to accurately state all the other ones, both before and after. We have not yet grasped the results which the reason alone can attain to. Problems may be solved in the study which have baffled all those who have sought a solution by the aid of their senses. To carry the art, however, to its highest pitch, it is necessary that the reasoner should be able to utilise all the facts which have come to his knowledge, and this in itself implies, as you will readily see, a possession of all knowledge, which, even in these days of

" HIS EYES BENT UPON THE GLOW OF THE FIRE."

free education and encyclopædias, is a somewhat rare accomplishment. It is not so impossible, however, that a man should possess all knowledge which is likely to be useful to him in his work, and this I have endeavoured in my case to do. If I remember rightly, you on one occasion, in the early days of our friendship, defined my limits in a very precise fashion."

"Yes," I answered, laughing. "It was a singular document. Philosophy, Astronomy, and Politics were marked at zero, I remember. Botany variable, Geology profound as regards the mud-stains from any region within fifty miles of town, chemistry eccentric, anatomy unsystematic, sensational literature and crime records unique, violin player, boxer, swordsman, lawyer, and self-poisoner by cucaine and tobacco. Those, I think, were the main points of my analysis."

Holmes grinned at the last item. "Well," he said, "I say now, as I said then, that a man should keep his little brain attic stocked with all the furniture that he is likely to use, and the rest he can put away in the lumber room of his library, where he can get it if he wants it. Now, for such a case as the one which has been submitted to us to-night, we need certainly to muster

all our resources. Kindly hand me down the letter K of the American Encyclopædia which stands upon the shelf beside you. Thank you. Now let us consider the situation, and see what may be deduced from it. In the first place, we may start with a strong presumption that Colonel Openshaw had some very strong reason for leaving America. Men at his time of life do not change all their habits, and exchange willingly the charming climate of Florida for the lonely life of an English provincial town. His extreme love of solitude in England suggests the idea that he was in fear of someone or something, so we may assume as a working hypothesis that it was fear of someone or something which drove him from America. As to what it was he feared, we can only deduce that by considering the formidable letters which were received by himself and his successors. Did you remark the postmarks of those letters ? "

" The first was from Pondicherry, the second from Dundee, and the third from London."

" From East London. What do you deduce from that ? "

" They are all sea ports. That the writer was on board of a ship."

" Excellent. We have already a clue. There can be no doubt that the probability —the strong probability—is that the writer was on board of a ship. And now let us consider another point. In the case of Pondicherry seven weeks elapsed between the threat and its fulfilment, in Dundee it was only some three or four days. Does that suggest anything ?

" A greater distance to travel."

" But the letter had also a greater distance to come."

" Then I do not see the point."

" There is at least a presumption that the vessel in which the man or men are is a sailing ship. It looks as if they always sent their singular warning or token before them when starting upon their mission. You see how quickly the deed followed the sign when it came from Dundee. If they had come from Pondicherry in a steamer they would have arrived almost as soon as their letter. But as a matter of fact seven weeks elapsed. I think that those seven weeks represented the difference between the mail boat which brought the letter, and the sailing vessel which brought the writer."

" It is possible."

" More than that. It is probable. And now you see the deadly urgency of this new case, and why I urged young Openshaw to caution. The blow has always fallen at the end of the time which it would take the senders to travel the distance. But this one comes from London, and therefore we cannot count upon delay."

" Good God ! " I cried. " What can it mean, this relentless persecution ? "

" The papers which Openshaw carried are obviously of vital importance to the person or persons in the sailing ship. I think that it is quite clear that there must be more than one of them. A single man could not have carried out two deaths in such a way as to deceive a coroner's jury. There must have been several in it, and they must have been men of resource and determination. Their papers they mean to have, be the holder of them who it may. In this way you see K. K. K. ceases to be the initials of an individual, and becomes the badge of a society."

" But of what society ? "

" Have you never— " said Sherlock Holmes, bending forward and sinking his voice—" have you never heard of the Ku Klux Klan ? "

" I never have."

Holmes turned over the leaves of the book upon his knee. " Here it is," said he, presently, " Ku Klux Klan. A name derived from a fanciful resemblance to the sound produced by cocking a rifle. This terrible secret society was formed by some ex-Confederate soldiers in the Southern States after the Civil War, and it rapidly formed local branches in different parts of the country, notably in Tennessee, Louisiana, the Carolinas, Georgia, and Florida. Its power was used for political purposes, principally for the terrorising of the negro voters, and the murdering or driving from the country of those who were opposed to its views. Its outrages were usually preceded by a warning sent to the marked man in some fantastic but generally recognised shape—a sprig of oak-leaves in some parts, melon seeds or orange pips in others. On receiving this the victim might either openly abjure his former ways, or might fly from the country. If he braved the matter out, death would unfailingly come upon him, and usually in some strange and unforeseen manner. So perfect was the

organisation of the society, and so systematic its methods, that there is hardly a case upon record where any man succeeded in braving it with impunity, or in which any of its outrages were traced home to the perpetrators. For some years the organisation flourished, in spite of the efforts of the United States Government, and of the better classes of the community in the South. Eventually, in the year 1869, the movement rather suddenly collapsed, although there have been sporadic outbreaks of the same sort since that date."

" You will observe," said Holmes, laying down the volume, " that the sudden breaking up of the society was coincident with the disappearance of Openshaw from America with their papers. It may well have been cause and effect. It is no wonder that he and his family have some of the more implacable spirits upon their track. You can understand that this register and diary may implicate some of the first men in the South, and that there may be many who will not sleep easy at night until it is recovered."

" Then the page which we have seen—"

" Is such as we might expect. It ran, if I remember right, 'sent the pips to A, B, and C,'—that is, sent the society's warning to them. Then there are successive entries that A and B cleared, or left the country, and finally that C was visited, with, I fear, a sinister result for C. Well, I think, Doctor, that we may let some light into this dark place, and I believe that the only chance young Openshaw has in the meantime is to do what I have told him. There is nothing more to be said or to be done to-night, so hand me over my violin and let us try to forget for half an hour the miserable weather, and the still more miserable ways of our fellow men."

It had cleared in the morning, and the sun was shining with a subdued brightness through the dim veil which hangs over the great city. Sherlock Holmes was already at breakfast when I came down.

" You will excuse me for not waiting for you," said he ; " I have, I foresee, a very busy day before me in looking into this case of young Openshaw's."

" What steps will you take ? " I asked.

" It will very much depend upon the results of my first inquiries. I may have to go down to Horsham after all."

" You will not go there first ? "

" No, I shall commence with the City.

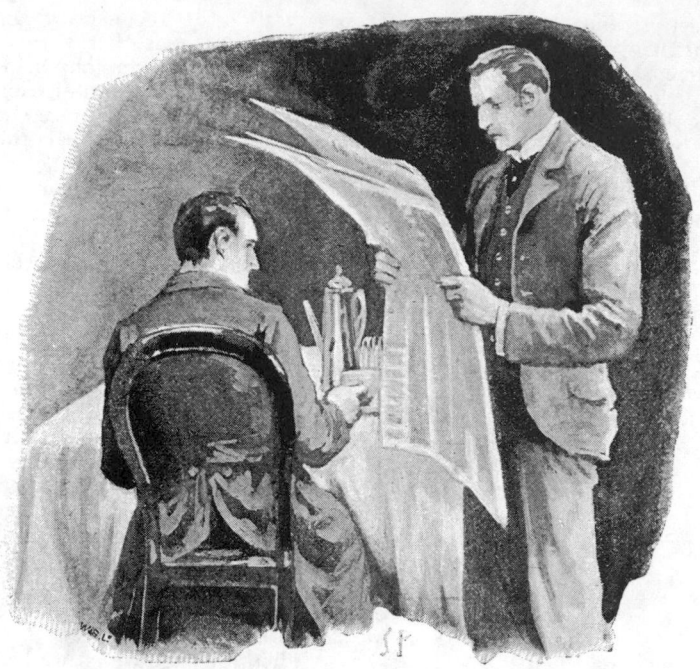

"HOLMES," I CRIED, "YOU ARE TOO LATE."

Just ring the bell and the maid will bring up your coffee."

As I waited, I lifted the unopened newspaper from the table and glanced my eye over it. It rested upon a heading which sent a chill to my heart.

"Holmes," I cried, "you are too late."

"Ah!" said he, laying down his cup, "I feared as much. How was it done?" He spoke calmly, but I could see that he was deeply moved.

"My eye caught the name of Openshaw, and the heading 'Tragedy near Waterloo Bridge.' Here is the account: 'Between nine and ten last night Police-constable Cooke, of the H Division, on duty near Waterloo Bridge, heard a cry for help and a splash in the water. The night, however, was extremely dark and stormy, so that, in spite of the help of several passers-by, it was quite impossible to effect a rescue. The alarm, however, was given, and, by the aid of the water police, the body was eventually recovered. It proved to be that of a young gentleman whose name, as it appears from an envelope which was found in his pocket, was John Openshaw, and whose residence is near Horsham. It is conjectured that he may have been hurrying down to catch the last train from

Waterloo Station, and that in his haste and the extreme darkness, he missed his path, and walked over the edge of one of the small landing-places for river steamboats. The body exhibited no traces of violence, and there can be no doubt that the deceased had been the victim of an unfortunate accident, which should have the effect of calling the attention of the authorities to the condition of the riverside landing stages."

We sat in silence for some minutes, Holmes more depressed and shaken than I had ever seen him.

"That hurts my pride, Watson," he said at last. "It is a petty feeling, no doubt, but it hurts my pride. It becomes a personal matter with me now, and, if God sends me health, I shall set my hand upon this gang. That he should come to me for help, and that I should send him away to his death—!" He sprang from his chair, and paced about the room in uncontrollable agitation, with a flush upon his sallow cheeks, and a nervous clasping and unclasping of his long, thin hands.

"They must be cunning devils," he exclaimed, at last. "How could they have decoyed him down there? The Embankment is not on the direct line to the station.

The bridge, no doubt, was too crowded, even on such a night, for their purpose. Well, Watson, we shall see who will win in the long run. I am going out now!"

"To the police?"

"No; I shall be my own police. When I have spun the web they may take the flies, but not before."

All day I was engaged in my professional work, and it was late in the evening before I returned to Baker-street. Sherlock Holmes had not come back yet. It was nearly ten o'clock before he entered, looking pale and worn. He walked up to the sideboard, and, tearing a piece from the loaf, he devoured it voraciously, washing it down with a long draught of water.

"You are hungry," I remarked.

"Starving. It had escaped my memory. I have had nothing since breakfast."

"Nothing?"

"Not a bite. I had no time to think of it."

"And how have you succeeded?"

"Well."

"You have a clue?"

"I have them in the hollow of my hand. Young Openshaw shall not long remain unavenged. Why, Watson, let us put their own devilish trade-mark upon them. It is well thought of!"

"What do you mean?"

He took an orange from the cupboard, and, tearing it to pieces, he squeezed out the pips upon the table. Of these he took five, and thrust them into an envelope. On the inside of the flap he wrote "S. H. for J. O." Then he sealed it and addressed it to "Captain James Calhoun, Barque *Lone Star*, Savannah, Georgia."

"That will await him when he enters port," said he, chuckling. "It may give him a sleepless night. He will find it as sure a precursor of his fate as Openshaw did before him."

"And who is this Captain Calhoun?"

"The leader of the gang. I shall have the others, but he first."

"How did you trace it, then?"

He took a large sheet of paper from his pocket, all covered with dates and names.

"I have spent the whole day," said he, "over Lloyd's registers and the files of the old papers, following the future career of every vessel which touched at Pondicherry in January and February in, '83. There were thirty-six ships of fair tonnage which were reported there during those months. Of these, one, the *Lone Star*, instantly attracted my attention, since, although it was reported as having cleared from London, the name is that which is given to one of the States of the Union."

"Texas, I think."

"I was not and am not sure which; but I knew that the ship must have an American origin."

"What then?"

"I searched the Dundee records, and when I found that the barque *Lone Star* was there in January, '85, my suspicion became a certainty. I then inquired as to the vessels which lay at present in the port of London."

"Yes?"

"The *Lone Star* had arrived here last week. I went down to the Albert Dock, and found that she had been taken down the river by the early tide this morning, homeward bound to Savannah. I wired to Gravesend, and learned that she had passed some time ago, and as the wind is easterly, I have no doubt that she is now past the Goodwins, and not very far from the Isle of Wight."

"What will you do, then?"

"Oh, I have my hand upon him. He and the two mates are, as I learn, the only native born Americans in the ship. The others are Finns and Germans. I know also that they were all three away from the ship last night. I had it from the stevedore who has been loading their cargo. By the time that their sailing ship reaches Savannah the mail-boat will have carried this letter, and the cable will have informed the police of Savannah that these three gentlemen are badly wanted here upon a charge of murder."

There is ever a flaw, however, in the best laid of human plans, and the murderers of John Openshaw were never to receive the orange pips which would show them that another, as cunning and as resolute as themselves, was upon their track. Very long and very severe were the equinoctial gales that year. We waited long for news of the *Lone Star* of Savannah, but none ever reached us. We did at last hear that somewhere far out in the Atlantic, a shattered sternpost of a boat was seen swinging in the trough of a wave, with the letters "L. S." carved upon it, and that is all which we shall ever know of the fate of the *Lone Star*.

# Adventures of Sherlock Holmes.

## ADVENTURE VI.—THE MAN WITH THE TWISTED LIP.

### By A. Conan Doyle.

SA WHITNEY, brother of the late Elias Whitney, D.D., Principal of the Theological College of St. George's, was much addicted to opium. The habit grew upon him, as I understand, from some foolish freak when he was at college, for having read De Quincey's description of his dreams and sensations, he had drenched his tobacco with laudanum in an attempt to produce the same effects. He found, as so many more have done, that the practice is easier to attain than to get rid of, and for many years he continued to be a slave to the drug, an object of mingled horror and pity to his friends and relatives. I can see him now, with yellow, pasty face, drooping lids and pin-point pupils, all huddled in a chair, the wreck and ruin of a noble man.

One night—it was in June, '89—there came a ring to my bell, about the hour when a man gives his first yawn, and glances at the clock. I sat up in my chair, and my wife laid her needlework down in her lap and made a little face of disappointment.

"A patient!" said she. "You'll have to go out."

I groaned, for I was newly come back from a weary day.

We heard the door open, a few hurried words, and then quick steps upon the linoleum. Our own door flew open, and a lady, clad in some dark-coloured stuff, with a black veil, entered the room.

"You will excuse my calling so late," she began, and then, suddenly losing her self-control, she ran forward, threw her arms about my wife's neck, and sobbed upon her shoulder. "Oh, I'm in such trouble!" she cried; "I do so want a little help."

"Why," said my wife, pulling up her veil, "it is Kate Whitney. How you startled me, Kate! I had not an idea who you were when you came in."

"I didn't know what to do, so I came straight to you." That was always the way. Folk who were in grief came to my wife like birds to a lighthouse.

"It was very sweet of you to come. Now, you must have some wine and water, and sit here comfortably and tell us all about it. Or should you rather that I sent James off to bed?"

"Oh, no, no. I want the Doctor's advice and help too. It's about Isa. He has not been home for two days. I am so frightened about him!"

It was not the first time that she had spoken to us of her husband's trouble, to me as a doctor, to my wife as an old friend and school companion. We soothed and comforted her by such words as we could find. Did she know where her husband was? Was it possible that we could bring him back to her?

It seemed that it was. She had the surest information that of late he had, when the fit was on him, made use of an opium den in the furthest east of the City. Hitherto his orgies had always been confined to one day, and he had come back, twitching and shattered, in the evening. But now the spell had been upon him eight and forty hours, and he lay there, doubtless among the dregs of the docks, breathing in the poison or sleeping off the effects. There he was to be found, she was sure of it, at the "Bar of Gold," in Upper Swandam-lane. But what was she to do? How could she, a young and timid woman, make her way into such a place, and pluck her husband out from among the ruffians who surrounded him?

There was the case, and of course there was but one way out of it. Might I not escort her to this place? And, then, as a second thought, why should she come at all? I was Isa Whitney's medical adviser, and as such I had influence over him. I could manage it better if I were alone. I promised her on my word that I would send him home in a cab within two hours if he were indeed at the address which she had given me. And so in ten minutes I had left my arm-chair and cheery sitting-room behind me, and was speeding eastward in a hansom on a strange errand, as it seemed to me at the time, though the future only could show how strange it was to be.

But there was no great difficulty in the first stage of my adventure. Upper Swandam-lane is a vile alley lurking behind the high wharves which line the north side of the river to the east of London Bridge. Between a slop shop and a gin shop, approached by a steep flight of steps leading down to a black gap like the mouth of a cave, I found the den of which I was in search. Or dering my cab to wait, I passed down the steps, worn hollow in the centre by the ceaseless tread of drunken feet, and by the light of a flickering oil lamp above the door I found the latch and made my way into a long, low room, thick and heavy with the brown opium smoke, and terraced with wooden berths, like the forecastle of an emigrant ship.

"STARING INTO THE FIRE."

Through the gloom one could dimly catch a glimpse of bodies lying in strange fantastic poses, bowed shoulders, bent knees, heads thrown back and chins pointing upwards, with here and there a dark, lacklustre eye turned upon the new comer. Out of the black shadows there glimmered little red circles of light, now bright, now faint, as the burning poison waxed or waned in the bowls of the metal pipes. The most lay silent but some muttered to themselves, and others talked together in a strange, low, monotonous voice, their conversation coming in gushes, and then suddenly tailing off into silence, each mumbling out his own thoughts, and paying little heed to the words of his neighbour. At the further end was a small brazier of burning charcoal, besides which on a three-legged wooden stool there sat a tall, thin old man with his jaw resting upon his two fists, and his elbows upon his knees, staring into the fire.

As I entered, a sallow Malay attendant had hurried up with a pipe for me and a supply of the drug, beckoning me to an empty berth.

"Thank you, I have not come to stay," said I. "There is a friend of mine here, Mr. Isa Whitney, and I wish to speak with him."

There was a movement and an exclamation from my right, and, peering through the gloom, I saw Whitney, pale, haggard, and unkempt, staring out at me.

"My God! It's Watson," said he. He was in a pitiable state of reaction, with every nerve in a twitter. "I say, Watson, what o'clock is it?"

"Nearly eleven."

"Of what day?"

"Of Friday, June 19."

"Good heavens! I thought it was Wednesday. It *is* Wednesday. What d'you want to frighten a chap for?" He sank his face on to his arms. and began to sob in a high treble key.

"I tell you that it is Friday, man. Your wife has been waiting this two days for you. You should be ashamed of yourself!"

"So I am. But you've got mixed, Watson, for I have only been here a few hours, three pipes, four pipes—I forget how many. But I'll go home with you. I wouldn't frighten Kate—poor little Kate. Give me your hand ! Have you a cab ? "

" Yes, I have one waiting."

" Then I shall go in it. But I must owe something. Find what I owe, Watson. I am all off colour. I can do nothing for myself."

I walked down the narrow passage between the double row of sleepers, holding my breath to keep out the vile, stupefying fumes of the drug, and looking about for the manager. As I passed the tall man who sat by the brazier I felt a sudden pluck at my skirt and a low voice whispered, " Walk past me, and then look back at me." The words fell quite distinctly upon my ear. I glanced down. They could only have come from the old man at my side, and yet he sat now as absorbed as ever, very thin, very wrinkled, bent with age, an opium

" HOLMES ! I WHISPERED."

pipe dangling down from between his knees, as though it had dropped in sheer lassitude from his fingers. I took two steps forward and looked back. It took all my self-control to prevent me from breaking out into a cry of astonishment. He had turned his back so that none could see him but I. His form had filled out, his wrinkles were gone, the dull eyes had regained their fire, and there, sitting by the fire, and grinning at my surprise, was none other than Sherlock Holmes. He made a slight motion to me to approach him, and instantly, as he turned his face half round to the company once more, subsided into a doddering, loose-lipped senility.

" Holmes ! " I whispered, " what on earth are you doing in this den ? "

" As low as you can," he answered, " I have excellent ears. If you would have the great kindness to get rid of that sottish friend of yours I should be exceedingly glad to have a little talk with you."

" I have a cab outside."

" Then pray send him home in it. You may safely trust him, for he appears to be too limp to get into any mischief. I should recommend you also to send a note by the cabman to your wife to say that you have thrown in your lot with me. If you will wait outside, I shall be with you in five minutes."

It was difficult to refuse any of Sherlock Holmes' requests, for they were always so exceedingly definite, and put forward with such a quiet air of mastery. I felt, however, that when Whitney was once confined in the cab, my mission was practically accomplished ; and for the rest, I could not wish anything better than to be associated with my friend in one of those singular adventures which were the normal condition of his existence. In a few minutes I had written my note, paid Whitney's bill, led him out to the cab, and seen him driven through the darkness. In a very short time a decrepit figure had emerged from the opium den, and I was walking down the street with Sherlock Holmes. For two streets he shuffled along with a bent back and an uncertain foot,

Then glancing quickly round, he straightened himself out and burst into a hearty fit of laughter.

"I suppose, Watson," said he, "that you imagine that I have added opium-smoking to cucaine injections and all the other little weaknesses on which you have favoured me with your medical views."

"I was certainly surprised to find you there."

"But not more so than I to find you."

"I came to-find a friend."

"And I to find an enemy."

"An enemy?"

"Yes, one of my natural enemies, or shall I say, my natural prey. Briefly, Watson, I am in the midst of a very remarkable inquiry, and I have hoped to find a clue in the incoherent ramblings of these sots, as I have done before now. Had I been recognised in that den my life would not have been worth an hour's purchase, for I have used it before now for my own purposes, and the rascally Lascar who runs it has sworn to have vengeance upon me. There is a trap-door at the back of that building, near the corner of Paul's Wharf, which could tell some strange tales of what has passed through it upon the moonless nights."

"What! You do not mean bodies?"

"Aye, bodies, Watson. We should be rich men if we had a thousand pounds for every poor devil who has been done to death in that den. It is the vilest murder-trap on the whole river-side, and I fear that Neville St. Clair has entered it never to leave it more. But our trap should be here!" He put his two fore-fingers between his teeth and whistled shrilly, a signal which was answered by a similar whistle from the distance, followed shortly by the rattle of wheels and the clink of horses' hoofs.

"Now, Watson," said Holmes, as a tall dog-cart dashed up through the gloom, throwing out two golden tunnels of yellow light from its side lanterns. "You'll come with me, won't you?"

"If I can be of use."

"Oh, a trusty comrade is always of use. And a chronicler still more so. My room at The Cedars is a double-bedded one."

"The Cedars?"

"Yes; that is Mr. St. Clair's house. I am staying there while I conduct the inquiry."

"Where is it, then?"

"Near Lee, in Kent. We have a seven-mile drive before us."

"But I am all in the dark."

"Of course you are. You'll know all about it presently. Jump up here! All right, John, we shall not need you. Here's half-a-crown. Look out for me to-morrow, about eleven. Give her her head! So long, then!"

He flicked the horse with his whip, and we dashed away through the endless succession of sombre and deserted streets, which widened gradually, until we were flying across a broad balustraded bridge, with the murky river flowing sluggishly beneath us. Beyond lay another dull wilderness of bricks and mortar, its silence broken only by the heavy, regular footfall of the policeman, or the songs and shouts of some belated party of revellers. A dull wrack was drifting slowly across the sky,

"HE FLICKED THE HORSE WITH HIS WHIP."

and a star or two twinkled dimly here and there through the rifts of the clouds. Holmes drove in silence, with his head sunk upon his breast, and the air of a man who is lost in thought, whilst I sat beside him, curious to learn what this new quest might be which seemed to tax his powers so sorely, and yet afraid to break in upon the current of his thoughts. We had driven several miles, and were beginning to get to the fringe of the belt of suburban villas, when he shook himself, shrugged his shoulders, and lit up his pipe with the air of a man who has satisfied himself that he is acting for the best.

"You have a grand gift of silence, Watson," said he. "It makes you quite invaluable as a companion. 'Pon my word, it is a great thing for me to have someone to talk to, for my own thoughts are not over pleasant. I was wondering what I should say to this dear little woman to-night when she meets me at the door."

"You forget that I know nothing about it."

"I shall just have time to tell you the facts of the case before we get to Lee. It seems absurdly simple, and yet, somehow, I can get nothing to go upon. There's plenty of thread, no doubt, but I can't get the end of it into my hand. Now, I'll state the case clearly and concisely to you, Watson, and maybe you may see a spark where all is dark to me."

"Proceed then."

"Some years ago—to be definite, in May, 1884—there came to Lee a gentleman, Neville St. Clair by name, who appeared to have plenty of money. He took a large villa, laid out the grounds very nicely, and lived generally in good style. By degrees he made friends in the neighbourhood, and in 1887 he married the daughter of a local brewer, by whom he has now had two children. He had no occupation, but was interested in several companies, and went into town as a rule in the morning, returning by the 5.14 from Cannon-street every night. Mr. St. Clair is now 37 years of age, is a man of temperate habits, a good husband, a very affectionate father, and a man who is popular with all who know him. I may add that his whole debts at the present moment, as far as we have been able to ascertain, amount to £88 10s., while he has £220 standing to his credit in the Capital and Counties Bank. There is no reason, therefore, to think that money troubles have been weighing upon his mind.

"Last Monday Mr. Neville St. Clair went into town rather earlier than usual, remarking before he started that he had two important commissions to perform, and that he would bring his little boy home a box of bricks. Now, by the merest chance his wife received a telegram upon this same Monday, very shortly after his departure, to the effect that a small parcel of considerable value which she had been expecting was waiting for her at the offices of the Aberdeen Shipping Company. Now, if you are well up in your London, you will know that the office of the company is in Fresno-street, which branches out of Upper Swandam-lane, where you found me to-night. Mrs. St. Clair had her lunch, started for the City, did some shopping, proceeded to the company's office, got her packet, and found herself exactly at 4.35 walking through Swandam-lane on her way back to the station. Have you followed me so far?"

"It is very clear."

"If you remember, Monday was an exceedingly hot day, and Mrs. St. Clair walked slowly, glancing about in the hope of seeing a cab, as she did not like the neighbourhood in which she found herself. While she walked in this way down Swandam-lane she suddenly heard an ejaculation or cry, and was struck cold to see her husband looking down at her, and, as it seemed to her, beckoning to her from a second-floor window. The window was open, and she distinctly saw his face, which she describes as being terribly agitated. He waved his hands frantically to her, and then vanished from the window so suddenly that it seemed to her that he had been plucked back by some irresistible force from behind, One singular point which struck her quick feminine eye was that, although he wore some dark coat, such as he had started to town in, he had on neither collar nor necktie.

"Convinced that something was amiss with him, she rushed down the steps—for the house was none other than the opium den in which you found me to-night—and, running through the front room, she attempted to ascend the stairs which led to the first floor. At the foot of the stairs, however, she met this Lascar scoundrel of whom I have spoken, who thrust her back, and, aided by a Dane, who acts as assistant there, pushed her out into the street. Filled with the most maddening doubts and fears, she rushed down the lane, and, by rare good fortune, met, in Fresno-street, a num-

"AT THE FOOT OF THE STAIRS SHE MET THIS LASCAR SCOUNDREL."

which lay upon the table, and tore the lid from it. Out there fell a cascade of children's bricks. It was the toy which he had promised to bring home.

"This discovery, and the evident confusion which the cripple showed, made the inspector realise that the matter was serious. The rooms were carefully examined, and results all pointed to an abominable crime. The front room was plainly furnished as a sitting-room, and led into a small bedroom, which looked out upon the back of one of the wharves. Between the wharf and the bedroom window is a narrow strip, which is dry at low tide, but is covered at high tide with at least four and a half feet of water. The bed-room window was a broad one, and opened from below. On examination traces of blood were to be seen upon the window sill, and several scattered drops were visible upon the wooden floor of the bedroom. Thrust away behind a curtain in the front room were all the clothes of Mr. Neville St. Clair, with the exception of his coat. His boots, his socks, his hat, and his watch—all were there. There were no signs of violence upon any of these garments, and there were no other traces of Mr. Neville St. Clair. Out of the window he must apparently have gone, for no other exit could be discovered, and the ominous bloodstains upon the sill gave little promise that he could save himself by swimming, for the tide was at its very highest at the moment of the tragedy.

"And now as to the villains who seemed to be immediately implicated in the matter. The Lascar was known to be a man of the vilest antecedents, but as by Mrs. St. Clair's story he was known to have been at the foot of the stair within a very few seconds of her husband's appearance at the window, he could hardly have been more than an accessory to the crime. His defence was one of absolute ignorance, and he protested that he had no knowledge as to the doings of Hugh Boone, his lodger, and that he could not account in any way for the presence of the missing gentleman's clothes.

"So much for the Lascar manager. Now

ber of constables with an inspector, all on their way to their beat. The inspector and two men accompanied her back, and, in spite of the continued resistance of the proprietor, they made their way to the room in which Mr. St. Clair had last been seen. There was no sign of him there. In fact, in the whole of that floor there was no one to be found, save a crippled wretch of hideous aspect, who, it seems, made his home there. Both he and the Lascar stoutly swore that no one else had been in the front room during the afternoon. So determined was their denial that the inspector was staggered, and had almost come to believe that Mrs. St. Clair had been deluded when, with a cry, she sprang at a small deal box

for the sinister cripple who lives upon the second floor of the opium den, and who was certainly the last human being whose eyes rested upon Neville St. Clair. His name is Hugh Boone, and his hideous face is one which is familiar to every man who goes much to the City. He is a professional beggar, though in order to avoid the police regulations he pretends to a small trade in wax vestas. Some little distance down Threadneedle-street upon the left hand side there is, as you may have remarked, a small angle in the wall. Here it is that the creature takes his daily seat, cross-legged, with his tiny stock of matches on his lap, and as he is a piteous spectacle a small rain of charity descends into the greasy leather cap which lies upon the pavement beside him. I have watched the fellow more than once, before ever I thought of making his professional acquaintance, and I have been surprised at the harvest which he has reaped in a short time. His appearance, you see, is so remarkable, that no one can pass

"HE IS A PROFESSIONAL BEGGAR."

him without observing him. A shock of orange hair, a pale face disfigured by a horrible scar, which, by its contraction, has turned up the outer edge of his upper lip, a bull-dog chin, and a pair of very penetrating dark eyes, which present a singular contrast to the colour of his hair, all mark him out from amid the common crowd of mendicants, and so, too, does his wit, for he is ever ready with a reply to any piece of chaff which may be thrown at him by the passers-by. This is the man whom we now learn to have been the lodger at the opium den,

and to have been the last man to see the gentleman of whom we are in quest."

"But a cripple !" said I. "What could he have done singlehanded against a man in the prime of life ?"

"He is a cripple in the sense that he walks with a limp ; but, in other respects, he appears to be a powerful and well-nurtured man. Surely your medical experience would tell you, Watson, that weakness in one limb is often compensated for by exceptional strength in the others."

"Pray continue your narrative."

"Mrs. St. Clair had fainted at the sight of the blood upon the window, and she was escorted home in a cab by the police, as her presence could be of no help to them in their investigations. Inspector Barton, who had charge of the case, made a very careful examination of the premises, but without finding anything which threw any light upon the matter. One mistake had been made in not arresting Boone instantly, as he was allowed some few minutes during which he might have communicated with his friend the Lascar, but this fault was soon remedied, and he was seized and searched, without anything being found which could incriminate him. There were, it is true, some bloodstains upon his right shirt-sleeve, but he pointed to his ring finger, which had been cut near the nail, and explained that the bleeding came from there, adding that he had been to the window not long before, and that the stains which had been observed there came doubtless from the same source. He denied strenuously having ever seen Mr. Neville St. Clair, and swore that the presence of the clothes in his room was as much a mystery to him as to the police. As to Mrs. St. Clair's assertion that she had actually seen her husband at the window, he declared that she must have been either mad or dreaming. He was removed, loudly protesting, to the police station, while the inspector remained upon the premises in the hope that the ebbing tide might afford some fresh clue.

"And it did, though they hardly found upon the mudbank what they had feared to find. It was Neville St. Clair's coat, and not Neville St. Clair, which lay uncovered as the tide receded. And what do you think they found in the pockets?"

"I cannot imagine."

"No, I don't think you would guess. Every pocket stuffed with pennies and halfpennies—four hundred and twenty-one pennies, and two hundred and seventy halfpennies. It was no wonder that it had not been swept away by the tide. But a human body is a different matter. There is a fierce eddy between the wharf and the house. It seemed likely enough that the weighted coat had remained when the stripped body had been sucked away into the river."

"But I understand that all the other clothes were found in the room. Would the body be dressed in a coat alone?"

"No, sir, but the facts might be met speciously enough. Suppose that this man Boone had thrust Neville St. Clair through the window, there is no human eye which could have seen the deed. What would he do then? It would of course instantly strike him that he must get rid of the tell-tale garments. He would seize the coat then, and be in the act of throwing it out when it would occur to him that it would swim and not sink. He has little time, for he has heard the scuffle downstairs when the wife tried to force her way up, and perhaps he has already heard from his Lascar confederate that the police are hurrying up the street. There is not an instant to be lost. He rushes to some secret horde, where he has accumulated the fruits of his beggary, and he stuffs all the coins upon which he can lay his hands into the pockets to make sure of the coat's sinking. He throws it out, and would have done the same with the other garments had not he heard the rush of steps below, and only just had time to close the window when the police appeared."

"It certainly sounds feasible."

"Well, we will take it as a working hypothesis for want of a better. Boone, as I have told you, was arrested and taken to the station, but it could not be shown that there had ever before been anything against him. He had for years been known as a professional beggar, but his life appeared to have been a very quiet and innocent one. There the matter stands at present, and the questions which have to be solved, what Neville St. Clair was doing in the opium den, what happened to him when there, where is he now, and what Hugh Boone had to do with his disappearance, are all as far from a solution as ever. I confess

"STUFFS ALL THE COINS INTO THE POCKETS."

that I cannot recall any case within my experience which looked at the first glance so simple, and yet which presented such difficulties."

Whilst Sherlock Holmes had been detailing this singular series of events we had been whirling through the outskirts of the great town until the last straggling houses had been left behind, and we rattled along with a country hedge upon either side of us. Just as he finished, however, we drove through two scattered villages, where a few lights still glimmered in the windows.

"We are on the outskirts of Lee," said my companion. "We have touched on three English counties in our short drive, starting in Middlesex, passing over an angle of Surrey, and ending in Kent. See that light among the trees? That is The Cedars, and beside that lamp sits a woman whose anxious ears have already, I have little doubt, caught the clink of our horse's feet."

"But why are you not conducting the case from Baker-street?" I asked.

"Because there are many inquiries which must be made out here. Mrs. St. Clair has most kindly put two rooms at my disposal, and you may rest assured that she will have nothing but a welcome for my friend and colleague. I hate to meet her, Watson, when I have no news of her husband. Here we are. Whoa, there, whoa!"

We had pulled up in front of a large villa which stood within its own grounds. A stable-boy had run out to the horse's head, and, springing down, I followed Holmes up the small, winding gravel drive which led to the house. As we approached, the door flew open, and a little blonde woman stood in the opening, clad in some sort of light mousseline de soie, with a touch of fluffy pink chiffon at her neck and wrists. She stood with her figure outlined against the flood of light, one hand upon the door, one half raised in her eagerness, her body slightly bent, her head and face protruded, with eager eyes and parted lips, a standing question.

"Well?" she cried, "well?" And then, seeing that there were two of us, she gave a cry of hope which sank into a groan as she saw that my companion shook his head and shrugged his shoulders.

"No good news?"

"None."

"No bad?"

"No."

"Thank God for that. But come in.

You must be weary, for you have had a long day."

"This is my friend, Dr. Watson. He has been of most vital use to me in several of my cases, and a lucky chance has made it possible for me to bring him out and associate him with this investigation."

"I am delighted to see you," said she, pressing my hand warmly. "You will, I am sure, forgive anything which may be wanting in our arrangements, when you consider the blow which has come so suddenly upon us."

"My dear madam," said I, "I am an old campaigner, and if I were not, I can very well see that no apology is needed. If I can be of any assistance, either to you or to my friend here, I shall be indeed happy."

"Now, Mr. Sherlock Holmes," said the lady, as we entered a well-lit dining-room, upon the table of which a cold supper had been laid out. "I should very much like to ask you one or two plain questions, to which I beg that you will give a plain answer."

"Certainly, madam."

"Do not trouble about my feelings. I am not hysterical, nor given to fainting. I simply wish to hear your real, real opinion."

"Upon what point?"

"In your heart of hearts do you think that Neville is alive?"

Sherlock Holmes seemed to be embarrassed by the question. "Frankly now!" she repeated, standing upon the rug, and looking keenly down at him, as he leaned back in a basket chair.

"Frankly then, madam, I do not."

"You think that he is dead?"

"I do."

"Murdered?"

"I don't say that. Perhaps."

"And on what day did he meet his death?"

"On Monday."

"Then perhaps, Mr. Holmes, you will be good enough to explain how it is that I have received a letter from him to-day."

Sherlock Holmes sprang out of his chair as if he had been galvanised.

"What!" he roared.

"Yes, to-day." She stood smiling, holding up a little slip of paper in the air.

"May I see it?"

"Certainly."

He snatched it from her in his eagerness, and, smoothing it out upon the table, he drew over the lamp, and examined it

"'FRANKLY, NOW,' SHE REPEATED."

"One of his hands."

"One?"

"His hand when he wrote hurriedly. It is very unlike his usual writing, and yet I know it well."

"'Dearest, do not be frightened. All will come well. There is a huge error which it may take some little time to rectify. Wait in patience. — Neville.' Written in pencil upon the fly-leaf of a book, octavo size, no watermark. Hum! Posted to-day in Gravesend by a man with a dirty thumb. Ha! And the flap has been gummed, if I am not very much in error, by a person who had been chewing tobacco. And you have no doubt that it is your husband's hand, madam?"

"None. Neville wrote those words."

"And they were posted to-day at Gravesend. Well, Mrs. St. Clair, the clouds lighten, though I should not venture to say that the danger is over."

"But he must be alive, Mr. Holmes."

"Unless this is a clever forgery to put us on the wrong scent. The ring, after all, proves nothing. It may have been taken from him."

"No, no; it is, it is, it is his very own writing!"

"Very well. It may, however, have been written on Monday, and only posted to-day."

"That is possible."

"If so, much may have happened between."

"Oh, you must not discourage me, Mr. Holmes. I know that all is well with him. There is so keen a sympathy between us that I should know if evil came upon him. On the very day that I saw him last he cut himself in the bedroom, and yet I in the dining-room rushed upstairs instantly with the utmost certainty that something had happened. Do you think that I would respond to such a trifle, and yet be ignorant of his death?"

intently. I had left my chair, and was gazing at it over his shoulder. The envelope was a very coarse one, and was stamped with the Gravesend post-mark, and with the date of that very day, or rather of the day before, for it was considerably after midnight.

"Coarse writing!" murmured Holmes. "Surely this is not your husband's writing, madam."

"No, but the enclosure is."

"I perceive also that whoever addressed the envelope had to go and inquire as to the address."

"How can you tell that?"

"The name, you see, is in perfectly black ink, which has dried itself. The rest is of the greyish colour which shows that blotting-paper has been used. If it had been written straight off, and then blotted, none would be of a deep black shade. This man has written the name, and there has then been a pause before he wrote the address, which can only mean that he was not familiar with it. It is, of course, a trifle, but there is nothing so important as trifles. Let us now see the letter! Ha! there has been an enclosure here!"

"Yes, there was a ring. His signet ring."

"And you are sure that this is your husband's hand?"

"I have seen too much not to know that the impression of a woman may be more valuable than the conclusion of an analytical reasoner. And in this letter you certainly have a very strong piece of evidence to corroborate your view. But if your husband is alive, and able to write letters, why should he remain away from you?"

"I cannot imagine. It is unthinkable."

"And on Monday he made no remarks before leaving you?"

"No."

"And you were surprised to see him in Swandam-lane?"

"Very much so."

"Was the window open?"

"Yes."

"Then he might have called to you?"

"He might."

"He only, as I understand, gave an inarticulate cry?"

"Yes."

"A call for help, you thought?"

"Yes. He waved his hands."

"But it might have been a cry of surprise. Astonishment at the unexpected sight of you might cause him to throw up his hands?"

"It is possible."

"And you thought he was pulled back?"

"He disappeared so suddenly."

"He might have leaped back. You did not see anyone else in the room?"

"No, but this horrible man confessed to having been there, and the Lascar was at the foot of the stairs."

"Quite so. Your husband, as far as you could see, had his ordinary clothes on?"

"But without his collar or tie. I distinctly saw his bare throat."

"Had he ever spoken of Swandam-lane?"

"Never."

"Had he ever shown any signs of having taken opium?"

"Never."

"Thank you, Mrs. St. Clair. Those are the principal points about which I wished to be absolutely clear. We shall now have a little supper and then retire, for we may have a very busy day to-morrow."

A large and comfortable double-bedded room had been placed at our disposal, and I was quickly between the sheets, for I was weary after my night of adventure. Sherlock Holmes was a man, however, who when he had an unsolved problem upon his mind would go for days, and even for a week, without rest, turning it over, rearranging his facts, looking at it from every point of view, until he had either fathomed it, or convinced himself that his data were insufficient. It was soon evident to me that he was now preparing for an all night sitting. He took off his coat and waistcoat, put on a large blue dressing gown, and then wandered about the room collecting pillows from his bed, and cushions from the sofa and arm-chairs. With these he constructed a sort of Eastern divan, upon which he perched himself cross-legged, with an ounce of shag tobacco and a box of matches laid out in front of him. In the dim light of the lamp I saw him sitting there, an old brier pipe between his lips, his eyes fixed vacantly upon the corner of the ceiling, the blue smoke curling up from him, silent, motionless, with the light shining upon his strong set aquiline features. So he sat as I dropped off to sleep, and so he sat when a sudden ejaculation caused me to wake up, and I found the summer sun shining into the apartment. The pipe was still between his lips, the smoke still curled upwards, and the room was full of a dense tobacco haze, but nothing remained of the heap of shag which I had seen upon the previous night.

"Awake, Watson?" he asked.

"Yes."

"Game for a morning drive?"

"Certainly."

"Then dress. No one is stirring yet, but I know where the stable boy sleeps, and we shall soon have the trap out." He chuckled to himself as he spoke, his eyes twinkled, and he seemed a different man to the sombre thinker of the previous night.

As I dressed I glanced at my watch. It was no wonder that no one was stirring. It was twenty-five minutes past four. I had hardly finished when Holmes returned with the news that the boy was putting in the horse.

"I want to test a little theory of mine," said he, pulling on his boots. "I think, Watson, that you are now standing in the presence of one of the most absolute fools in Europe. I deserve to be kicked from here to Charing-cross. But I think I have the key of the affair now."

"And where is it?" I asked, smiling.

"In the bath-room," he answered. "Oh, yes, I am not joking," he continued, seeing my look of incredulity. "I have just been there, and I have taken it out, and I have got it in this Gladstone bag. Come on, my boy, and we shall see whether it will not fit the lock."

We made our way downstairs as quietly

S.P

"THE PIPE WAS STILL BETWEEN HIS LIPS."

jacket. "I wish to have a quiet word with you, Bradstreet."

"Certainly, Mr. Holmes. Step into my room here."

It was a small office-like room, with a huge ledger upon the table, and a telephone projecting from the wall. The inspector sat down at his desk.

"What can I do for you, Mr. Holmes?"

"I called about that beggarman, Boone—the one who was charged with being concerned in the disappearance of Mr. Neville St. Clair, of Lee."

"Yes. He was brought up and remanded for further inquiries."

"So I heard. You have him here?"

"In the cells."

"Is he quiet?"

"Oh, he gives no trouble. But he is a dirty scoundrel."

"Dirty?"

"Yes, it is all we can do to make him wash his hands, and his face is as black as a tinker's. Well, when once his case has been settled he will have a regular prison bath; and I think, if you saw him, you would agree with me that he needed it."

"I should like to see him very much."

"Would you? That is easily done. Come this way. You can leave your bag."

"No, I think that I'll take it."

"Very good. Come this way, if you please." He led us down a passage, opened a barred door, passed down a winding stair, and brought us to a white-washed corridor with a line of doors on each side.

"The third on the right is his," said the inspector. "Here it is!" He quietly shot back a panel in the upper part of the door, and glanced through.

"He is asleep," said he. "You can see him very well."

We both put our eyes to the grating. The prisoner lay with his face towards us, in a very deep sleep, breathing slowly and heavily. He was a middle-sized man, coarsely clad as became his calling, with a coloured shirt protruding through the rents in his tattered coat. He was, as the inspector had said, extremely dirty, but the grime which covered his face could not con-

as possible, and out into the bright morning sunshine. In the road stood our horse and trap, with the half-clad stable boy waiting at the head. We both sprang in, and away we dashed down the London-road. A few country carts were stirring, bearing in vegetables to the metropolis, but the lines of villas on either side were as silent and lifeless as some city in a dream.

"It has been in some points a singular case," said Holmes, flicking the horse on into a gallop. "I confess that I have been as blind as a mole, but it is better to learn wisdom late, than never to learn it at all."

In town, the earliest risers were just beginning to look sleepily from their windows as we drove through the streets of the Surrey side. Passing down the Waterloo Bridge-road we crossed over the river, and dashing up Wellington-street wheeled sharply to the right, and found ourselves in Bow-street. Sherlock Holmes was well known to the Force, and the two constables at the door saluted him. One of them held the horse's head while the other led us in.

"Who is on duty?" asked Holmes.

"Inspector Bradstreet, sir."

"Ah, Bradstreet, how are you?" A tall, stout official had come down the stone-flagged passage, in a peaked cap and frogged

ceal its repulsive ugliness. A broad wheal from an old scar ran right across it from eye to chin, and by its contraction had turned up one side of the upper lip, so that three teeth were exposed in a perpetual snarl. A shock of very bright red hair grew low over his eyes and forehead.

"He's a beauty, isn't he?" said the inspector.

"He certainly needs a wash," remarked Holmes. "I had an idea that he might, and I took the liberty of bringing the tools with me." He opened his Gladstone bag as he spoke, and took out, to my astonishment, a very large bath sponge.

"He! he! You are a funny one," chuckled the inspector.

"Now, if you will have the great goodness to open that door very quietly, we will soon make him cut a much more respectable figure."

"Well, I don't know why not," said the inspector. "He doesn't look a credit to the Bow-street cells, does he?" He slipped his key into the lock, and we all very quietly entered the cell. The sleeper half turned, and then settled down once more into a deep slumber. Holmes stooped to the water jug, moistened his sponge, and then rubbed it twice vigorously across and down the prisoner's face.

"Let me introduce you," he shouted, "to Mr. Neville St. Clair, of Lee, in the county of Kent."

Never in my life have I seen such a sight. The man's face peeled off under the sponge like the bark from a tree. Gone was the

"HE TOOK OUT A VERY LARGE BATH SPONGE."

coarse brown tint! Gone, too, the horrid scar which had seamed it across, and the twisted lip which had given the repulsive sneer to the face! A twitch brought away the tangled red hair, and there, sitting up in his bed, was a pale, sad-faced, refined-looking man, black-haired and smooth-skinned, rubbing his eyes, and staring about him with sleepy bewilderment. Then suddenly realising the exposure, he broke into a scream, and threw himself down with his face to the pillow.

"Great heaven!" cried the inspector, "it is, indeed, the missing man. I know him from the photograph."

The prisoner turned with the reckless air of a man who abandons himself to his destiny. "Be it so," said he. "And pray, what am I charged with?"

"With making away with Mr. Neville St.—— Oh, come, you can't be charged with that, unless they make a case of attempted suicide of it," said the inspector, with a grin. "Well, I have been twenty-seven years in the force, but this really takes the cake."

"If I am Mr. Neville St. Clair, then it is obvious that no crime has been committed, and that, therefore, I am illegally detained."

"No crime, but a very great error has been committed," said Holmes. "You would have done better to have trusted your wife."

"It was not the wife, it was the children," groaned the prisoner. "God help me, I would not have them ashamed of their

"HE BROKE INTO A SCREAM."

father. My God! What an exposure! What can I do?"

Sherlock Holmes sat down beside him on the couch, and patted him kindly on the shoulder.

"If you leave it to a court of law to clear the matter up," said he, "of course you can hardly avoid publicity. On the other hand, if you convince the police authorities that there is no possible case against you, I do not know that there is any reason that the details should find their way into the papers. Inspector Bradstreet would, I am sure, make notes upon anything which you might tell us, and submit it to the proper authorities. The case would then never go into court at all."

"God bless you!" cried the prisoner, passionately. "I would have endured imprisonment, aye, even execution, rather than have left my miserable secret as a family blot to my children.

"You are the first who have ever heard my story. My father was a schoolmaster in Chesterfield, where I received an excellent education. I travelled in my youth, took to the stage, and finally became a reporter on an evening paper in London. One day my editor wished to have a series of articles upon begging in the metropolis, and I volunteered to supply them. There was the point from which all my adventures started. It was only by trying begging as an amateur that I could get the facts upon which to base my articles. When an actor I had, of course, learned all the secrets of making up, and had been famous in the green-room for my skill. I took advantage now of my attainments. I painted my face, and to make myself as pitiable as possible I made a good scar and fixed one side of my lip in a twist by the aid of a small slip of flesh-coloured plaster. Then with a red head of hair, and an appropriate dress, I took my station in the busiest part of the City, ostensibly as a match-seller, but really as a beggar. For seven hours I plied my trade, and when I returned home in the evening I found, to my surprise, that I had received no less than twenty-six shillings and fourpence.

"I wrote my articles, and thought little more of the matter until, some time later, I backed a bill for a friend, and had a writ served upon me for £25. I was at my wits' end where to get the money, but a sudden idea came to me. I begged a fortnight's grace from the creditor, asked for a holiday from my employers, and spent the time in begging in the City under my disguise. In ten days I had the money, and had paid the debt.

"Well, you can imagine how hard it was to settle down to arduous work at two pounds a week, when I knew that I could earn as much in a day by smearing my face with a little paint, laying my cap on the ground, and sitting still. It was a long fight between my pride and the money, but the dollars won at last, and I threw up reporting, and sat day after day in the corner which I had first chosen, inspiring pity by my ghastly face, and filling my pockets with coppers. Only one man knew my secret. He was the keeper of a low den in which I used to lodge in Swandam-lane, where I could every morning emerge as a squalid beggar, and in the evenings transform myself into a well-dressed man about town. This fellow, a Lascar, was well paid by me for his rooms, so that I knew that my secret was safe in his possession.

"Well, very soon I found that I was saving considerable sums of money. I do not mean that any beggar in the streets of London could earn seven hundred pounds a year—which is less than my average takings—but I had exceptional advantages in my power of making up, and also in a facility in repartee, which improved by practice, and made me quite a recognised character in the City. All day a stream of pennies, varied by silver, poured in upon me, and it was a very bad day upon which I failed to take two pounds.

"As I grew richer I grew more ambitious, took a house in the country, and eventually married, without anyone having a suspicion as to my real occupation. My dear wife knew that I had business in the City. She little knew what.

"Last Monday I had finished for the day, and was dressing in my room above the opium den, when I looked out of the window, and saw, to my horror and astonishment, that my wife was standing in the street, with her eyes fixed full upon me. I gave a cry of surprise, threw up my arms to cover my face, and, rushing to my confidant, the Lascar, entreated him to prevent anyone from coming up to me. I heard her voice downstairs, but I knew that she could not ascend. Swiftly I threw off my clothes, pulled on those of a beggar, and put on my pigments and wig. Even a wife's eyes could not pierce so complete a disguise. But then it occurred to me that there might be a search in the room, and that the clothes might betray me. I threw open the window, re-opening by my violence a small cut which I had inflicted upon myself in the bedroom that morning. Then I seized my coat, which was weighted by the coppers which I had just transferred to it from the leather bag in which I carried my takings. I hurled it out of the window, and it disappeared into the Thames. The other clothes would have followed, but at that moment there was a rush of constables up the stair, and a few minutes after I found, rather, I confess, to my relief, that instead of being identified as Mr. Neville St. Clair, I was arrested as his murderer.

"I do not know that there is anything else for me to explain. I was determined to preserve my disguise as long as possible, and hence my preference for a dirty face. Knowing that my wife would be terribly anxious, I slipped off my ring, and confided it to the Lascar at a moment when no constable was watching me, together with a hurried scrawl, telling her that she had no cause to fear."

"That note only reached her yesterday," said Holmes.

"Good God! What a week she must have spent."

"The police have watched this Lascar," said Inspector Bradstreet, "and I can quite understand that he might find it difficult to post a letter unobserved. Probably he handed it to some sailor customer of his, who forgot all about it for some days."

"That was it," said Holmes, nodding approvingly, "I have no doubt of it. But have you never been prosecuted for begging?"

"Many times; but what was a fine to me?"

"It must stop here, however," said Bradstreet. "If the police are to hush this thing up, there must be no more of Hugh Boone."

"I have sworn it by the most solemn oaths which a man can take."

"In that case I think that it is probable that no further steps may be taken. But if you are found again, then all must come out. I am sure, Mr. Holmes, that we are very much indebted to you for having cleared the matter up. I wish I knew how you reach your results."

"I reached this one," said my friend, "by sitting upon five pillows and consuming an ounce of shag. I think, Watson, that if we drive to Baker-street we shall just be in time for breakfast."

## VII.—THE ADVENTURE OF THE BLUE CARBUNCLE.

### By A. CONAN DOYLE.

I HAD called upon my friend Sherlock Holmes upon the second morning after Christmas, with the intention of wishing him the compliments of the season. He was lounging upon the sofa in a purple dressing-gown, a pipe-rack within his reach upon the right, and a pile of crumpled morning papers, evidently newly studied, near at hand. Beside the couch was a wooden chair, and on the angle of the back hung a very seedy and disreputable hard felt hat, much the worse for wear, and cracked in several places. A lens and a forceps lying upon the seat of the chair suggested that the hat had been suspended in this manner for the purpose of examination.

"You are engaged," said I; "perhaps I interrupt you."

"Not at all. I am glad to have a friend with whom I can discuss my results. The matter is a perfectly trivial one" (he jerked his thumb in the direction of the old hat), "but there are points in connection with it which are not entirely devoid of interest, and even of instruction."

I seated myself in his armchair, and warmed my hands before his crackling fire, for a sharp frost had set in, and the windows were thick with the ice crystals. "I suppose," I remarked, "that, homely as it looks, this thing has some deadly story linked on to it—that it is the clue which will guide you in the solution of some mystery, and the punishment of some crime."

"No, no. No crime," said Sherlock Holmes, laughing. "Only one of those whimsical little incidents which will happen when you have four million human beings all jostling each other within the space of a few square miles. Amid the action and reaction of so dense a swarm of humanity, every possible combination of events may be expected to take place, and many a little problem will be presented which may be striking and bizarre without being criminal. We have already had experience of such."

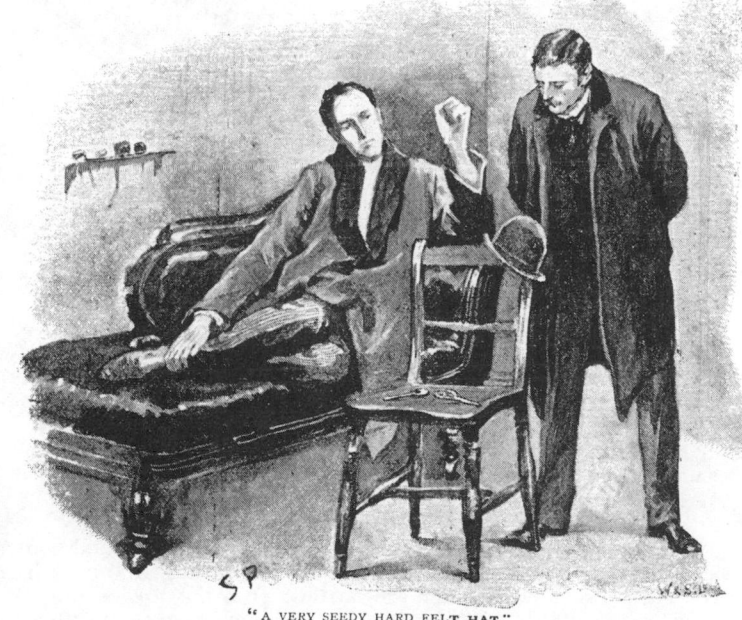

"A VERY SEEDY HARD FELT HAT."

"So much so," I remarked, "that, of the last six cases which I have added to my notes, three have been entirely free of any legal crime."

"Precisely. You allude to my attempt to recover the Irene Adler papers, to the singular case of Miss Mary Sutherland, and to the adventure of the man with the twisted lip. Well, I have no doubt that this small matter will fall into the same innocent category. You know Peterson, the commissionaire?"

"Yes."

"It is to him that this trophy belongs."

"It is his hat."

"No, no; he found it. Its owner is unknown. I beg that you will look upon it, not as a battered billycock, but as an intellectual problem. And, first, as to how it came here. It arrived upon Christmas morning, in company with a good fat goose, which is, I have no doubt, roasting at this moment in front of Peterson's fire. The facts are these. About four o'clock on Christmas morning, Peterson, who, as you know, is a very honest fellow, was returning from some small jollification, and was making his way homewards down Tottenham Court-road. In front of him he saw, in the gaslight, a tallish man, walking with a slight stagger, and carrying a white goose slung over his shoulder. As he reached the corner of Goodge-street, a row broke out between this stranger and a little knot of roughs. One of the latter knocked off the man's hat, on which he raised his stick to defend himself, and, swinging it over his head, smashed the shop window behind him. Peterson had rushed forward to protect the stranger from his assailants, but the man, shocked at having broken the

window, and seeing an official-looking person in uniform rushing towards him, dropped his goose, took to his heels, and vanished amid the labyrinth of small streets which lie at the back of Tottenham Court-road. The roughs had also fled at the appearance of Peterson, so that he was left in possession of the field of battle, and also of the spoils of victory in the shape of this

"THE ROUGHS HAD FLED AT THE APPEARANCE OF PETERSON."

battered hat and a most unimpeachable Christmas goose."

"Which surely he restored to their owner?"

"My dear fellow, there lies the problem. It is true that 'For Mrs. Henry Baker' was printed upon a small card which was tied to the bird's left leg, and it is also true that the initials 'H. B.' are legible upon the lining of this hat; but, as there are some thousands of Bakers, and some hundreds of Henry Bakers in this city of ours, it is not easy to restore lost property to any one of them."

"What, then, did Peterson do?"

"He brought round both hat and goose to me on Christmas morning, knowing that even the smallest problems are of interest to me. The goose we retained until this morning, when there were signs that, in spite of the slight frost, it would be well that it should be eaten without unnecessary delay. Its finder has carried it off, therefore, to fulfil the ultimate destiny of a goose, while I continue to retain the hat of the unknown gentleman who lost his Christmas dinner."

" Did he not advertise ? "

" No."

" Then, what clue could you have as to his identity ? "

" Only as much as we can deduce."

" From his hat ? "

" Precisely."

" But you are joking. What can you gather from this old battered felt ? "

" Here is my lens. You know my methods. What can you gather yourself as to the individuality of the man who has worn this article ? "

I took the tattered object in my hands, and turned it over rather ruefully. It was a very ordinary black hat of the usual round shape, hard, and much the worse for wear. The lining had been of red silk, but was a good deal discoloured. There was no maker's name ; but, as Holmes had remarked, the initials " H. B." were scrawled upon one side. It was pierced in the brim for a hat-securer, but the elastic was missing. For the rest, it was cracked, exceedingly dusty, and spotted in several places, although there seemed to have been some attempt to hide the discoloured patches by smearing them with ink.

" I can see nothing," said I, handing it back to my friend.

" On the contrary, Watson, you can see everything. You fail, however, to reason from what you see. You are too timid in drawing your inferences."

" Then, pray tell me what it is that you can infer from this hat ? "

He picked it up, and gazed at it in the peculiar introspective fashion which was characteristic of him. " It is perhaps less suggestive than it might have been," he remarked, " and yet there are a few inferences which are very distinct, and a few others which represent at least a strong balance of probability. That the man was highly intellectual is of course obvious upon the face of it, and also that he was fairly well-to-do within the last three years, although he has now fallen upon evil days. He had foresight, but has less now than formerly, pointing to a moral retrogression, which, when taken with the decline of his fortunes, seems to indicate some evil influence, probably drink, at work upon him. This may account also for the obvious fact that his wife has ceased to love him."

" My dear Holmes ! "

" He has, however, retained some degree of self-respect," he continued, disregarding my remonstrance. " He is a man who leads a sedentary life, goes out little, is out of training entirely, is middle-aged, has grizzled hair which he has had cut within the last few days, and which he anoints with lime-cream. These are the more patent facts which are to be deduced from his hat. Also, by the way, that it is extremely improbable that he has gas laid on in his house."

" You are certainly joking, Holmes."

" Not in the least. Is it possible that even now when I give you these results you are unable to see how they are attained ? "

" I have no doubt that I am very stupid ; but I must confess that I am unable to follow you. For example, how did you deduce that this man was intellectual ? "

For answer Holmes clapped the hat upon his head. It came right over the forehead and settled upon the bridge of his nose. " It is a question of cubic capacity," said he ; " a man with so large a brain must have something in it."

" The decline of his fortunes, then ? "

" This hat is three years old. These flat brims curled at the edge came in then. It is a hat of the very best quality. Look at the band of ribbed silk, and the excellent lining. If this man could afford to buy so expensive a hat three years ago, and has had no hat since, then he has assuredly gone down in the world."

" Well, that is clear enough, certainly. But how about the foresight, and the moral retrogression ? "

Sherlock Holmes laughed. " Here is the foresight," said he, putting his finger upon the little disc and loop of the hat-securer. " They are never sold upon hats. If this man ordered one, it is a sign of a certain amount of foresight, since he went out of his way to take this precaution against the wind. But since we see that he has broken the elastic, and has not troubled to replace it, it is obvious that he has less foresight now than formerly, which is a distinct proof of a weakening nature. On the other hand, he has endeavoured to conceal some of these stains upon the felt by daubing them with ink, which is a sign that he has not entirely lost his self-respect."

"Your reasoning is certainly plausible."

"The further points, that he is middle-aged, that his hair is grizzled, that it has been recently cut, and that he uses lime-cream, are all to be gathered from a close examination of the lower part of the lining. The lens discloses a large number of hair ends, clean cut by the scissors of the barber. They all appear to be adhesive, and there is a distinct odour of lime-cream. This dust, you will observe, is not the gritty, grey dust of the street, but the fluffy brown dust of the house, showing that it has been hung up indoors most of the time; while the marks of moisture upon the inside are proof positive that the wearer perspired very freely, and could, therefore, hardly be in the best of training."

"But his wife—you said that she had ceased to love him."

"This hat has not been brushed for weeks. When I see you, my dear Watson, with a week's accumulation of dust upon your hat, and when your wife allows you to go out in such a state, I shall fear that you also have been unfortunate enough to lose your wife's affection."

"But he might be a bachelor."

"Nay, he was bringing home the goose as a peace-offering to his wife. Remember the card upon the bird's leg."

"You have an answer to everything. But how on earth do you deduce that the gas is not laid on in his house?"

"One tallow stain, or even two, might come by chance; but, when I see no less than five, I think that there can be little doubt that the individual must be brought into frequent contact with burning tallow—walks upstairs at night probably with his hat in one hand and a guttering candle in the other. Anyhow, he never got tallow stains from a gas jet. Are you satisfied?"

"Well, it is very ingenious," said I,

laughing; "but, since, as you said just now, there has been no crime committed, and no harm done save the loss of a goose, all this seems to be rather a waste of energy."

Sherlock Holmes had opened his mouth to reply, when the door flew open, and Peterson the commissionaire rushed into the apartment with flushed cheeks and the face of a man who is dazed with astonishment.

"The goose, Mr. Holmes! The goose, sir!" he gasped.

"Eh? What of it, then? Has it returned to life, and flapped off through the kitchen window?" Holmes twisted himself round upon the sofa to get a fairer view of the man's excited face.

"SEE WHAT MY WIFE FOUND IN ITS CROP!"

"See here, sir! See what my wife found in its crop!" He held out his hand, and displayed upon the centre of the palm a brilliantly scintillating blue stone, rather smaller than a bean in size, but of such purity and radiance that it twinkled like an electric point in the dark hollow of his hand.

Sherlock Holmes sat up with a whistle. "By Jove, Peterson!" said he, "this is treasure trove indeed. I suppose you know what you have got?"

"A diamond, sir! A precious stone! It cuts into glass as though it were putty."

"It's more than a precious stone. It's *the* precious stone."

"Not the Countess of Morcar's blue carbuncle!" I ejaculated.

"Precisely so. I ought to know its size and shape, seeing that I have read the advertisement about it in *The Times* every day lately. It is absolutely unique, and its value can only be conjectured, but the reward offered of a thousand pounds is certainly not within a twentieth part of the market price."

"A thousand pounds! Great Lord of mercy!" The commissionaire plumped down into a chair, and stared from one to the other of us.

"That is the reward, and I have reason to know that there are sentimental considerations in the background which would induce the Countess to part with half her fortune, if she could but recover the gem."

"It was lost, if I remember aright, at the Hotel Cosmopolitan," I remarked.

"Precisely so, on the twenty-second of December, just five days ago. John Horner, a plumber, was accused of having abstracted it from the lady's jewel case. The evidence against him was so strong that the case has been referred to the Assizes. I have some account of the matter here, I believe." He rummaged amid his newspapers, glancing over the dates, until at last he smoothed one out, doubled it over, and read the following paragraph:—

"Hotel Cosmopolitan Jewel Robbery. John Horner, 26, plumber, was brought up upon the charge of having upon the 22nd inst. abstracted from the jewel case of the Countess of Morcar the valuable gem known as the blue carbuncle. James Ryder, upper-attendant at the hotel, gave his evidence to the effect that he had shown Horner up to the dressing-room of the Countess of Morcar upon the day of the robbery, in order that he might solder the second bar of the grate, which was loose. He had remained with Horner some little time, but had finally been called away. On returning, he found that Horner had disappeared, that the bureau had been forced open, and that the small morocco casket in which, as it afterwards transpired, the Countess was accustomed to keep her jewel was lying empty upon the dressing-table. Ryder instantly gave the alarm, and Horner was arrested the same evening; but the stone could not be found either upon his person or in his rooms. Catherine Cusack, maid to the Countess, deposed to having heard Ryder's cry of dismay on discovering the robbery,

and to having rushed into the room, where she found matters as described by the last witness. Inspector Bradstreet, B division, gave evidence as to the arrest of Horner, who struggled frantically, and protested his innocence in the strongest terms. Evidence of a previous conviction for robbery having been given against the prisoner, the magistrate refused to deal summarily with the offence, but referred it to the Assizes. Horner, who had shown signs of intense emotion during the proceedings, fainted away at the conclusion, and was carried out of court."

"Hum! So much for the police-court," said Holmes, thoughtfully, tossing aside the paper. "The question for us now to solve is the sequence of events leading from a rifled jewel case at one end to the crop of a goose in Tottenham Court-road at the other. You see, Watson, our little deductions have suddenly assumed a much more important and less innocent aspect. Here is the stone; the stone came from the goose, and the goose came from Mr. Henry Baker, the gentleman with the bad hat and all the other characteristics with which I have bored you. So now we must set ourselves very seriously to finding this gentleman, and ascertaining what part he has played in this little mystery. To do this, we must try the simplest means first, and these lie undoubtedly in an advertisement in all the evening papers. If this fail, I shall have recourse to other methods."

"What will you say?"

"Give me a pencil, and that slip of paper. Now, then: 'Found at the corner of Goodge-street, a goose and a black felt hat. Mr. Henry Baker can have the same by applying at 6.30 this evening at 221B, Baker-street.' That is clear and concise."

"Very. But will he see it?"

"Well, he is sure to keep an eye on the papers, since, to a poor man, the loss was a heavy one. He was clearly so scared by his mischance in breaking the window, and by the approach of Peterson, that he thought of nothing but flight; but since then he must have bitterly regretted the impulse which caused him to drop his bird. Then, again, the introduction of his name will cause him to see it, for everyone who knows him will direct his attention to it. Here you are, Peterson, run down to the advertising agency, and have this put in the evening papers."

"In which, sir."

"Oh, in the *Globe, Star, Pall Mall, St.*

*James's, Evening News, Standard, Echo,* and any others that occur to you."

"Very well, sir. And this stone?"

"Ah, yes, I shall keep the stone. Thank you. And, I say, Peterson, just buy a goose on your way back, and leave it here with me, for we must have one to give to this gentleman in place of the one which your family is now devouring."

When the commissionaire had gone, Holmes took up the stone and held it against the light. "It's a bonny thing," said he. "Just see how it glints and sparkles. Of course it is a nucleus and focus of crime. Every good stone is. They are the devil's pet baits. In the larger and older jewels every facet may stand for a bloody deed. This stone is not yet twenty years old. It was found in the banks of the Amoy River in Southern China, and is remarkable in having every characteristic of the carbuncle, save that it is blue in shade, instead of ruby red. In spite of its youth, it has already a sinister history. There have been two murders, a vitriol-throwing, a suicide, and several robberies brought about for the sake of this forty-grain weight of crystallised charcoal. Who would think that so pretty a toy would be a purveyor to the gallows and the prison? I'll lock it up in my strong box now, and drop a line to the Countess to say that we have it."

"Do you think that this man Horner is innocent?"

"I cannot tell."

"Well, then, do you imagine that this other one, Henry Baker, had anything to do with the matter?"

"It is, I think, much more likely that Henry Baker is an absolutely innocent man, who had no idea that the bird which he was carrying was of considerably more value than if it were made of solid gold. That, however, I shall determine by a very simple test, if we have an answer to our advertisement."

"And you can do nothing until then?"

"Nothing."

"In that case I shall continue my professional round. But I shall come back in the evening at the hour you have mentioned, for I should like to see the solution of so tangled a business."

"Very glad to see you. I dine at seven. There is a woodcock, I believe. By the way, in view of recent occurrences, perhaps I ought to ask Mrs. Hudson to examine its crop."

I had been delayed at a case, and it was a little after half-past six when I found myself in Baker-street once more. As I approached the house I saw a tall man in a Scotch bonnet, with a coat which was buttoned up to his chin, waiting outside in the bright semicircle which was thrown from the fanlight. Just as I arrived, the door was opened, and we were shown up together to Holmes' room.

"Mr. Henry Baker, I believe," said he, rising from his armchair, and greeting his visitor with the easy air of geniality which he could so readily assume. "Pray take this chair by the fire, Mr. Baker. It is a cold night, and I observe that your circulation is more adapted for summer than for winter. Ah, Watson, you have just come at the right time. Is that your hat, Mr. Baker?"

"Yes, sir, that is undoubtedly my hat."

He was a large man, with rounded shoulders, a massive head, and a broad, intelligent face, sloping down to a pointed beard of grizzled brown. A touch of red in nose and cheeks, with a slight tremor of his extended hand, recalled Holmes' surmise as to his habits. His rusty black frock coat was buttoned right up in front, with the collar turned up, and his lank wrists protruded from his sleeves without a sign of cuff or shirt. He spoke in a slow staccato fashion, choosing his words with care, and gave the impression generally of a man of learning and letters who had had ill-usage at the hands of fortune.

"We have retained these things for some days," said Holmes, "because we expected to see an advertisement from you giving your address. I am at a loss to know now why you did not advertise."

Our visitor gave a rather shame-faced laugh. "Shillings have not been so plentiful with me as they once were," he remarked. "I had no doubt that the gang of roughs who assaulted me had carried off both my hat and the bird. I did not care to spend more money in a hopeless attempt at recovering them."

"Very naturally. By the way, about the bird, we were compelled to eat it."

"To eat it!" Our visitor half rose from his chair in his excitement.

"Yes, it would have been no use to anyone had we not done so. But I presume that this other goose upon the sideboard, which is about the same weight and perfectly fresh, will answer your purpose equally well?"

"Oh, certainly, certainly!" answered Mr. Baker, with a sigh of relief.

"Of course, we still have the feathers, legs, crop, and so on of your own bird, so if you wish——"

The man burst into a hearty laugh. "They might be useful to me as relics of my adventure," said he, "but beyond that I can hardly see what use the *disjecta membra* of my late acquaintance are going to be to me. No, sir, I think that, with your permission, I will confine my attentions to the excellent bird which I perceive upon the sideboard."

Sherlock Holmes glanced sharply across at me with a slight shrug of his shoulders.

"There is your hat, then, and there your bird," said he. "By the way, would it bore you to tell me where you got the other one from? I am somewhat of a fowl fancier, and I have seldom seen a better-grown goose."

"Certainly, sir," said Baker, who had risen and tucked his newly-gained property under his arm. "There are a few of us who frequent the 'Alpha' Inn, near the Museum—we are to be found in the Museum itself during the day, you understand. This year our good host, Windigate by name, instituted a goose club, by which, on consideration of some few pence every week, we were each to receive a bird at Christmas. My pence were duly paid, and the rest is familiar to you. I am much

"HE BOWED SOLEMNLY TO BOTH OF US."

indebted to you, sir, for a Scotch bonnet is fitted neither to my years nor my gravity." With a comical pomposity of manner he bowed solemnly to both of us, and strode off upon his way.

"So much for Mr. Henry Baker," said Holmes, when he had closed the door behind him. "It is quite certain that he knows nothing whatever about the matter. Are you hungry, Watson?"

"Not particularly."

"Then I suggest that we turn our dinner into a supper, and follow up this clue while it is still hot."

"By all means."

It was a bitter night, so we drew on our ulsters and wrapped cravats about our throats. Outside, the stars were shining coldly in a cloudless sky, and the breath of the passers-by blew out into smoke like so many pistol shots. Our footfalls rang out crisply and loudly as we swung through the Doctors' quarter, Wimpole-street, Harley-street, and so through Wigmore-street into Oxford-street. In a quarter of an hour we were in Bloomsbury at the "Alpha" Inn, which is a small public-house at the corner of one of the streets which runs down into Holborn. Holmes pushed open the door of the private bar, and ordered two glasses of beer from the ruddy-faced, white-aproned landlord.

"Your beer should be excellent if it is as good as your geese," said he.

"My geese!" The man seemed surprised.

"Yes. I was speaking only half an hour ago to Mr. Henry Baker, who was a member of your goose-club."

"Ah! yes, I see. But you see, sir, them's not *our* geese."

"Indeed! Whose, then?"

"Well, I got the two dozen from a salesman in Covent Garden."

"Indeed! I know some of them. Which was it?"

"Breckinridge is his name."

"Ah! I don't know him. Well, here's your good health, landlord, and prosperity to your house. Good-night!"

"Now for Mr. Breckinridge," he continued, buttoning up his coat, as we came out into the frosty air. "Remember, Watson, that though we have so homely a thing as a goose at one end of this chain, we have at the other a man who will certainly get seven years' penal servitude, unless we can establish his innocence. It is possible that our inquiry may but confirm his guilt ; but, in any case, we have a line of investigation which has been missed by the police, and which a singular chance has placed in our hands. Let us follow it out to the bitter end. Faces to the south, then, and quick march ! "

We passed across Holborn, down Endell-street, and so through a zigzag of slums to Covent Garden Market. One of the largest stalls bore the name of Breckinridge upon it, and the proprietor, a horsey-looking man, with a sharp face and trim side-whiskers, was helping a boy to put up the shutters.

" Good evening. It's a cold night," said Holmes.

The salesman nodded, and shot a questioning glance at my companion.

" Sold out of geese, I see," continued Holmes, pointing at the bare slabs of marble.

" Let you have five hundred to-morrow morning."

" That's no good."

" Well, there are some on the stall with the gas flare."

" Ah, but I was recommended to you."

" Who by ? "

" The landlord of the ' Alpha.' "

" Oh, yes ; I sent him a couple of dozen."

" Fine birds they were, too. Now where did you get them from ? "

To my surprise the question provoked a burst of anger from the salesman.

" Now, then, mister," said he, with his head cocked and his arms akimbo, " what are you driving at ? Let's have it straight, now."

" It is straight enough. I should like to know who sold you the geese which you supplied to the ' Alpha.' "

" Well, then, I sha'n't tell you. So now ! "

" Oh, it is a matter of no importance ; but I don't know why you should be so warm over such a trifle."

" Warm ! You'd be as warm, maybe, if you were as pestered as I am. When I pay good money for a good article there should be an end of the business ; but it's ' Where are the geese ? ' and ' Who did you sell the geese to ? ' and ' What will you take for the geese ? ' One would think they were the only geese in the world, to hear the fuss that is made over them."

" Well, I have no connection with any other people who have been making inquiries," said Holmes, carelessly. " If you won't tell us the bet is off, that is all. But I'm always ready to back my opinion on a matter of fowls, and I have a fiver on it that the bird I ate is country bred."

" Well, then, you've lost your fiver, for it's town bred," snapped the salesman.

" It's nothing of the kind."

" I say it is."

" I don't believe it."

" D'you think you know more about fowls than I, who have handled them ever since I was a nipper ? I tell you, all those birds that went to the ' Alpha ' were town bred."

" You'll never persuade me to believe that."

" Will you bet, then ? "

" It's merely taking your money, for I know that I am right. But I'll have a sovereign on with you, just to teach you not to be obstinate."

The salesman chuckled grimly. " Bring me the books, Bill," said he.

The small boy brought round a small thin volume and a great greasy-backed one, laying them out together beneath the hanging lamp.

" Now then, Mr. Cocksure," said the salesman, " I thought that I was out of geese, but before I finish you'll find that there is still one left in my shop. You see this little book ? "

" Well ? "

" That's the list of the folk from whom I buy. D'you see ? Well, then, here on this page are the country folk, and the numbers after their names are where their accounts are in the big ledger. Now, then ! You see this other page in red ink ? Well, that is a list of my town suppliers. Now, look at that third name. Just read it out to me."

" Mrs. Oakshott, 117, Brixton-road—249," read Holmes.

" Quite so. Now turn that up in the ledger."

Holmes turned to the page indicated. " Here you are, ' Mrs. Oakshott, 117, Brixton-road, egg and poultry supplier.' "

" Now, then, what's the last entry ? "

" ' December 22. Twenty-four geese at 7s. 6d.' "

" Quite so. There you are. And underneath ? "

" ' Sold to Mr. Windigate of the " Alpha " at 12s.' "

" What have you to say now ? "

"JUST READ IT OUT TO ME."

Sherlock Holmes looked deeply chagrined. He drew a sovereign from his pocket and threw it down upon the slab, turning away with the air of a man whose disgust is too deep for words. A few yards off he stopped under a lamp-post, and laughed in the hearty, noiseless fashion which was peculiar to him.

"When you see a man with whiskers of that cut and the 'pink 'un' protruding out of his pocket, you can always draw him by a bet," said he. "I daresay that if I had put a hundred pounds down in front of him that man would not have given me such complete information as was drawn from him by the idea that he was doing me on a wager. Well, Watson, we are, I fancy, nearing the end of our quest, and the only point which remains to be determined is whether we should go on to this Mrs. Oakshott to-night, or whether we should reserve it for to-morrow. It is clear from what that surly fellow said that there are others besides ourselves who are anxious about the matter, and I should——"

His remarks were suddenly cut short by a loud hubbub which broke out from the stall which we had just left. Turning round we saw a little rat-faced fellow standing in the centre of the circle of yellow light which was thrown by the swinging lamp, while Breckinridge the salesman, framed in the door of his stall, was shaking his fists fiercely at the cringing figure.

"I've had enough of you and your geese," he shouted. "I wish you were all at the devil together. If you come pestering me any more with your silly talk I'll set the dog at you. You bring Mrs. Oakshott here and I'll answer her, but what have you to do with it? Did I buy the geese off you?"

"No; but one of them was mine all the same," whined the little man.

"Well, then, ask Mrs. Oakshott for it."

"She told me to ask you."

"Well, you can ask the King of Proosia for all I care. I've had enough of it. Get out of this!" He rushed fiercely forward, and the inquirer flitted away into the darkness.

"Ha, this may save us a visit to Brixton-road," whispered Holmes. "Come with me, and we will see what is to be made of this fellow." Striding through the scattered knots of people who lounged round the flaring stalls, my companion speedily overtook the little man and touched him upon the shoulder. He sprang round, and I could see in the gaslight that every vestige of colour had been driven from his face.

"Who are you, then? What do you want?" he asked in a quavering voice.

"You will excuse me," said Holmes

blandly, " but I could not help overhearing the questions which you put to the salesman just now. I think that I could be of assistance to you."

"You? Who are you? How could you know anything of the matter?"

"My name is Sherlock Holmes. It is my business to know what other people don't know."

"But you can know nothing of this?"

"Excuse me, I know everything of it. You are endeavouring to trace some geese which were sold by Mrs. Oakshott, of

"YOU ARE THE VERY MAN."

Brixton-road, to a salesman named Breckinridge, by him in turn to Mr. Windigate, of the ' Alpha,' and by him to his club, of which Mr. Henry Baker is a member."

"Oh, sir, you are the very man whom I have longed to meet," cried the little fellow, with outstretched hands and quivering fingers. " I can hardly explain to you how interested I am in this matter."

Sherlock Holmes hailed a four-wheeler

which was passing. " In that case we had better discuss it in a cosy room rather than in this windswept market-place," said he. " But pray tell me, before we go further, who it is that I have the pleasure of assisting."

The man hesitated for an instant. " My name is John Robinson," he answered, with a sidelong glance.

"No, no; the real name," said Holmes, sweetly. " It is always awkward doing business with an *alias*."

A flush sprang to the white cheeks of the stranger. " Well, then," said he, " my real name is James Ryder."

"Precisely so. Head attendant at the Hotel Cosmopolitan. Pray step into the cab, and I shall soon be able to tell you everything which you would wish to know."

The little man stood glancing from one to the other of us with half-frightened, half-hopeful eyes, as one who is not sure whether he is on the verge of a windfall or of a catastrophe. Then he stepped into the cab, and in half an hour we were back in the sitting-room at Baker-street. Nothing had been said during our drive, but the high thin breathing of our new companion, and the claspings and unclaspings of his hands spoke of the nervous tension within him.

"Here we are!" said Holmes, cheerily, as we filed into the room. " The fire looks very seasonable in this weather. You look cold, Mr. Ryder. Pray take the basket chair. I will just put on my slippers before we settle this little matter of yours. Now, then! You want to know what became of those geese?"

"Yes, sir."

"Or rather, I fancy, of that goose. It was one bird, I imagine, in which you were interested—white, with a black bar across the tail."

Ryder quivered with emotion. " Oh,

sir, he cried, "can you tell me where it went to?"

"It came here."

"Here?"

"Yes, and a most remarkable bird it proved. I don't wonder that you should take an interest in it. It laid an egg after it was dead—the bonniest, brightest little blue egg that ever was seen. I have it here in my museum."

Our visitor staggered to his feet, and clutched the mantelpiece with his right hand. Holmes unlocked his strong box, and held up the blue carbuncle, which shone out like a star, with a cold, brilliant, many-pointed radiance. Ryder stood glaring with a drawn face, uncertain whether to claim or to disown it.

"The game's up, Ryder," said Holmes, quietly. "Hold up, man, or you'll be into the fire. Give him an arm back into his chair, Watson. He's not got blood enough to go in for felony with impunity. Give him a dash of brandy. So! Now he looks a little more human. What a shrimp it is, to be sure!"

For a moment he had staggered and nearly fallen, but the brandy brought a tinge of colour into his cheeks, and he sat staring with frightened eyes at his accuser.

"I have almost every link in my hands, and all the proofs which I could possibly need, so there is little which you need tell me. Still that little may as well be cleared up to make the case complete. You had heard, Ryder, of this blue stone of the Countess of Morcar's?"

"It was Catherine Cusack who told me of it," said he, in a crackling voice.

"I see. Her ladyship's waiting maid. Well, the temptation of sudden wealth so easily acquired was too much for you, as it has been for better men before you; but you were not very scrupulous in the means you used. It seems to me, Ryder, that there is the making of a very pretty villain in you. You knew that this man Horner, the plumber, had been concerned in some such matter before, and that suspicion would rest the more readily upon him. What did you do, then? You made some small job in my lady's room—you and your confederate Cusack—and you managed that he should be the man sent for. Then, when he had left, you rifled the jewel case, raised the alarm, and had this unfortunate man arrested. You then——"

Ryder threw himself down suddenly upon the rug, and clutched at my companion's knees. "For God's sake, have mercy!" he shrieked. "Think of my father! Of my mother! It would break their hearts. I never went wrong before! I never will

again. I swear it. I'll swear it on a Bible. Oh, don't bring it into court ! For Christ's sake, don't ! "

"Get back into your chair ! " said Holmes, sternly. " It is very well to cringe and crawl now, but you thought little enough of this poor Horner in the dock for a crime of which he knew nothing."

" I will fly, Mr. Holmes. I will leave the country, sir. Then the charge against him will break down."

" Hum ! We will talk about that. And now let us hear a true account of the next act. How came the stone into the goose, and how came the goose into the open market ? Tell us the truth, for there lies your only hope of safety."

Ryder passed his tongue over his parched lips. " I will tell you it just as it happened, sir," said he. " When Horner had been arrested, it seemed to me that it would be best for me to get away with the stone at once, for I did not know at what moment the police might not take it into their heads to search me and my room. There was no place about the hotel where it would be safe. I went out, as if on some commission, and I made for my sister's house. She had married a man named Oakshott, and lived in Brixton-road, where she fattened fowls for the market. All the way there every man I met seemed to me to be a policeman or a detective, and for all that it was a cold night, the sweat was pouring down my face before I came to the Brixton-road. My sister asked me what was the matter, and why I was so pale ; but I told her that I had been upset by the jewel robbery at the hotel. Then I went into the back yard, and smoked a pipe, and wondered what it would be best to do.

" I had a friend once called Maudsley, who went to the bad, and has just been serving his time in Pentonville. One day he had met me, and fell into talk about the ways of thieves and how they could get rid of what they stole. I knew that he would be true to me, for I knew one or two things about him, so I made up my mind to go right on to Kilburn, where he lived, and take him into my confidence. He would show me how to turn the stone into money. But how to get to him in safety. I thought of the agonies I had gone through in coming from the hotel. I might at any moment be seized and searched, and there would be the stone in my waistcoat pocket. I was leaning against the wall at the time, and looking at the geese which were waddling about round my feet, and suddenly an idea came into my head which showed me how I could beat the best detective that ever lived.

" My sister had told me some weeks before that I might have the pick of her geese for a Christmas present, and I knew that she was always as good as her word. I would take my goose now, and in it I would carry my stone to Kilburn. There was a little shed in the yard, and behind this I drove one of the birds, a fine big one, white with a barred tail. I caught it, and, prizing its bill open, I thrust the stone down its throat as far as my finger could reach. The bird gave a gulp, and I felt the stone pass along its gullet and down into its crop. But the creature flapped and struggled, and out came my sister to know what was the matter. As I turned to speak to her the brute broke loose, and fluttered off among the others.

" ' Whatever were you doing with that bird, Jem ? ' says she.

" ' Well,' said I, ' you said you'd give me one for Christmas, and I was feeling which was the fattest.'

" Oh," says she, " we've set yours aside for you. Jem's bird, we call it. It's the big, white one over yonder. There's twenty-six of them, which makes one for you, and one for us, and two dozen for the market."

" Thank you, Maggie," says I ; " but if it is all the same to you I'd rather have that one I was handling just now."

" The other is a good three pound heavier," said she, " and we fattened it expressly for you."

" Never mind. I'll have the other, and I'll take it now," said I.

" Oh, just as you like," said she, a little huffed. " Which is it you want, then ? "

" That white one, with the barred tail, right in the middle of the flock."

" Oh, very well. Kill it and take it with you."

" Well, I did what she said, Mr. Holmes, and I carried the bird all the way to Kilburn. I told my pal what I had done, for he was a man that it was easy to tell a thing like that to. He laughed until he choked, and we got a knife and opened the goose. My heart turned to water, for there was no sign of the stone, and I knew that some terrible mistake had occurred. I left the bird, rushed back to my sister's, and hurried into the back yard. There was not a bird to be seen there.

" ' Where are they all, Maggie ? ' I cried.

" ' Gone to the dealer's, Jim.'

" ' Which dealer's ? '

" ' Breckinridge, of Covent Garden.'

" ' But was there another with a barred tail ? ' I asked, ' the same as the one I chose ? '

" ' Yes, Jem, there were two barred-tailed ones, and I could never tell them apart.'

" Well, then, of course, I saw it all, and I ran off as hard as my feet would carry me

" What, sir ! Oh, heaven bless you ! "

" No more words. Get out ! "

And no more words were needed. There was a rush, a clatter upon the stairs, the bang of a door, and the crisp rattle of running footfalls from the street.

" HE BURST INTO CONVULSIVE SOBBING."

to this man Breckinridge ; but he had sold the lot at once, and not one word would he tell me as to where they had gone. You heard him yourselves to-night. Well, he has always answered me like that. My sister thinks that I am going mad. Sometimes I think that I am myself. And now—and now I am myself a branded thief, without ever having touched the wealth for which I sold my character. God help me ! God help me ! " He burst into convulsive sobbing, with his face buried in his hands.

There was a long silence, broken only by his heavy breathing, and by the measured tapping of Sherlock Holmes' finger-tips upon the edge of the table. Then my friend rose, and threw open the door.

" Get out ! " said he.

" After all, Watson," said Holmes, reaching up his hand for his clay pipe, " I am not retained by the police to supply their deficiencies. If Horner were in danger it would be another thing, but this fellow will not appear against him, and the case must collapse. I suppose that I am commuting a felony, but it is just possible that I am saving a soul. This fellow will not go wrong again. He is too terribly frightened. Send him to gaol now, and you make him a gaol-bird for life. Besides, it is the season of forgiveness. Chance has put in our way a most singular and whimsical problem, and its solution is its own reward. If you will have the goodness to touch the bell, Doctor, we will begin another investigation, in which also a bird will be the chief feature."

# Adventures of Sherlock Holmes.

## VIII.—THE ADVENTURE OF THE SPECKLED BAND.

### By A. Conan Doyle.

IN glancing over my notes of the seventy odd cases in which I have during the last eight years studied the methods of my friend Sherlock Holmes, I find many tragic, some comic, a large number merely strange, but none commonplace ; for, working as he did rather for the love of his art than for the acquirement of wealth, he refused to associate himself with any investigation which did not tend towards the unusual, and even the fantastic. Of all these varied cases, however, I cannot recall any which presented more singular features than that which was associated with the well-known Surrey family of the Roylotts of Stoke Moran. The events in question occurred in the early days of my association with Holmes, when we were sharing rooms as bachelors, in Baker-street. It is possible that I might have placed them upon record before, but a promise of secrecy was made at the time, from which I have only been freed during the last month by the untimely death of the lady to whom the pledge was given. It is perhaps as well that the facts should now come to light, for I have reasons to know that there are widespread rumours as to the death of Dr. Grimesby Roylott which tend to make the matter even more terrible than the truth.

It was early in April in the year '83 that I woke one morning to find Sherlock Holmes standing, fully dressed, by the side of my bed. He was a late riser as a rule, and, as the clock on the mantelpiece showed me that it was only a quarter past seven, I blinked up at him in some surprise, and perhaps just a little resentment, for I was myself regular in my habits.

"Very sorry to knock you up, Watson," said he, "but it's the common lot this morning. Mrs. Hudson has been knocked up, she retorted upon me, and I on you."

"What is it, then ? A fire ?"

"No, a client. It seems that a young lady has arrived in a considerable state of excitement, who insists upon seeing me. She is waiting now in the sitting-room. Now, when young ladies wander about the Metropolis at this hour of the morning, and knock sleepy people up out of their beds, I presume that it is something very pressing which they have to communicate. Should it prove to be an interesting case, you would, I am sure, wish to follow it from the outset. I thought at any rate that I should call you, and give you the chance."

"My dear fellow, I would not miss it for anything."

I had no keener pleasure than in following Holmes in his professional investigations, and in admiring the rapid deductions, as swift as intuitions, and yet always founded on a logical basis, with which he unravelled the problems which were submitted to him. I rapidly threw on my clothes, and was ready in a few minutes to accompany my friend down to the sitting-room. A lady dressed in black and heavily veiled, who had been sitting in the window, rose as we entered.

"Good morning, madam," said Holmes, cheerily. "My name is Sherlock Holmes. This is my intimate friend and associate, Dr. Watson, before whom you can speak as freely as before myself. Ha, I am glad to see that Mrs. Hudson has had the good sense to light the fire. Pray draw up to it, and I shall order you a cup of hot coffee, for I observe that you are shivering."

"It is not cold which makes me shiver," said the woman in a low voice, changing her seat as requested.

"What then ?"

"It is fear, Mr. Holmes. It is terror." She raised her veil as she spoke, and we could see that she was indeed in a pitiable state of agitation, her face all drawn and grey, with restless, frightened eyes, like those of some hunted animal. Her features and figure were those of a woman of thirty,

"SHE RAISED HER VEIL.

poor fellow, can be of little aid. I have heard of you, Mr. Holmes; I have heard of you from Mrs. Farintosh, whom you helped in the hour of her sore need. It was from her that I had your address. Oh, sir, do you not think that you could help me too, and at least throw a little light through the dense darkness which surrounds me? At present it is out of my power to reward you for your services, but in a month or six weeks I shall be married, with the control of my own income, and then at least you shall not find me ungrateful."

Holmes turned to his desk, and unlocking it, drew out a small case-book which he consulted.

"Farintosh," said he. "Ah, yes, I recall the case; it was concerned with an opal tiara. I think it was before your time, Watson. I can only say, madam, that I shall be happy to devote the same care to your case as I did to that of your friend. As to reward, my profession is its own reward; but you are at liberty to defray whatever expenses I may be put to, at the time which suits you best. And now I beg that you will lay before us everything that may help us in forming an opinion upon the matter."

"Alas!" replied our visitor. "The very horror of my situation lies in the fact that my fears are so vague, and n.y suspicions depend so entirely upon small points, which might seem trivial to another, that even he to whom of all others I have a right to look for help and advice looks upon all that I tell him about it as the fancies of a nervous woman. He does not say so, but I can read it from his soothing answers and averted eyes. But I have heard, Mr. Holmes, that you can see deeply into the manifold wickedness of the human heart.

but her hair was shot with premature grey, and her expression was weary and haggard. Sherlock Holmes ran her over with one of his quick, all-comprehensive glances.

"You must not fear," said he, soothingly, bending forward and patting her forearm. "We shall soon set matters right, I have no doubt. You have come in by train this morning, I see."

"You know me, then?"

"No, but I observe the second half of a return ticket in the palm of your left glove. You must have started early, and yet you had a good drive in a dog-cart, along heavy roads, before you reached the station."

The lady gave a violent start, and stared in bewilderment at my companion.

"There is no mystery, my dear madam," said he, smiling. "The left arm of your jacket is spattered with mud in no less than seven places. The marks are perfectly fresh. There is no vehicle save a dog-cart which throws up mud in that way, and then only when you sit on the left hand side of the driver."

"Whatever your reasons may be, you are perfectly correct," said she. "I started from home before six, reached Leatherhead at twenty past, and came in by the first train to Waterloo. Sir, I can stand this strain no longer, I shall go mad if it continues. I have no one to turn to—none, save only one, who cares for me, and he,

You may advise me how to walk amid the dangers which encompass me."

"I am all attention, madam."

"My name is Helen Stoner, and I am living with my stepfather, who is the last survivor of one of the oldest Saxon families in England, the Roylotts of Stoke Moran, on the western border of Surrey."

Holmes nodded his head. "The name is familiar to me," said he.

"The family was at one time among the richest in England, and the estates extended over the borders into Berkshire in the north, and Hampshire in the west. In the last century, however, four successive heirs were of a dissolute and wasteful disposition, and the family ruin was eventually completed by a gambler in the days of the Regency. Nothing was left save a few acres of ground, and the two-hundred-year-old house, which is itself crushed under a heavy mortgage. The last squire dragged out his existence there, living the horrible life of an aristocratic pauper ; but his only son, my stepfather, seeing that he must adapt himself to the new conditions, obtained an advance from a relative, which enabled him to take a medical degree, and went out to Calcutta, where, by his professional skill and his force of character, he established a large practice. In a fit of anger, however, caused by some robberies which had been perpetrated in the house, he beat his native butler to death, and narrowly escaped a capital sentence. As it was, he suffered a long term of imprisonment, and afterwards returned to England a morose and disappointed man.

"When Dr. Roylott was in India he married my mother, Mrs. Stoner, the young widow of Major-General Stoner, of the Bengal Artillery. My sister Julia and I were twins, and we were only two years old at the time of my mother's remarriage. She had a considerable sum of money, not less than a thousand a year, and this she bequeathed to Dr. Roylott entirely whilst we resided with him, with a provision that a certain annual sum should be allowed to each of us in the event of our marriage. Shortly after our return to England my mother died—she was killed eight years ago in a railway accident near Crewe. Dr. Roylott then abandoned his attempts to establish himself in practice in London, and took us to live with him in the old ancestral house at Stoke Moran. The money which my mother had left

was enough for all our wants, and there seemed to be no obstacle to our happiness.

"But a terrible change came over our stepfather about this time. Instead of making friends and exchanging visits with our neighbours, who had at first been overjoyed to see a Roylott of Stoke Moran back in the old family seat, he shut himself up in his house, and seldom came out save to indulge in ferocious quarrels with whoever might cross his path. Violence of temper approaching to mania has been hereditary in the men of the family, and in my stepfather's case it had, I believe, been intensified by his long residence in the tropics. A series of disgraceful brawls took place, two of which ended in the police-court, until at last he became the terror of the village, and the folks would fly at his approach, for he is a man of immense strength, and absolutely uncontrollable in his anger.

"Last week he hurled the local blacksmith over a parapet into a stream, and it was only by paying over all the money which I could gather together that I was able to avert another public exposure. He had no friends at all save the wandering gipsies, and he would give these vagabonds leave to encamp upon the few acres of

"HE HURLED THE BLACKSMITH OVER A PARAPET."

bramble-covered land which represent the family estate, and would accept in return the hospitality of their tents, wandering away with them sometimes for weeks on end. He has a passion also for Indian animals, which are sent over to him by a correspondent, and he has at this moment a cheetah and a baboon, which wander freely over his grounds, and are feared by the villagers almost as much as their master.

"You can imagine from what I say that my poor sister Julia and I had no great pleasure in our lives. No servant would stay with us, and for a long time we did all the work of the house. She was but thirty at the time of her death, and yet her hair had already begun to whiten, even as mine has."

"Your sister is dead, then?"

"She died just two years ago, and it is of her death that I wish to speak to you. You can understand that, living the life which I have described, we were little likely to see anyone of our own age and position. We had, however, an aunt, my mother's maiden sister, Miss Honoria Westphail, who lives near Harrow, and we were occasionally allowed to pay short visits at this lady's house. Julia went there at Christmas two years ago, and met there a half-pay Major of Marines, to whom she became engaged. My stepfather learned of the engagement when my sister returned, and offered no objection to the marriage; but within a fortnight of the day which had been fixed for the wedding, the terrible event occurred which has deprived me of my only companion."

Sherlock Holmes had been leaning back in his chair with his eyes closed, and his head sunk in a cushion, but he half opened his lids now, and glanced across at his visitor.

"Pray be precise as to details," said he.

"It is easy for me to be so, for every event of that dreadful time is seared into my memory. The manor house is, as I have already said, very old, and only one wing is now inhabited. The bedrooms in this wing are on the ground floor, the sitting-rooms being in the central block of the buildings. Of these bedrooms the first is Dr. Roylott's, the second my sister's, and the third my own. There is no communication between them, but they all open out into the same corridor. Do I make myself plain?"

"Perfectly so."

"The windows of the three rooms open out upon the lawn. That fatal night Dr. Roylott had gone to his room early, though we knew that he had not retired to rest, for my sister was troubled by the smell of the strong Indian cigars which it was his custom to smoke. She left her room, therefore, and came into mine, where she sat for some time, chatting about her approaching wedding. At eleven o'clock she rose to leave me, but she paused at the door and looked back.

"'Tell me, Helen,' said she, 'have you ever heard anyone whistle in the dead of the night?'

"'Never,' said I.

"'I suppose that you could not possibly whistle yourself in your sleep?'

"'Certainly not. But why?'

"'Because during the last few nights I have always, about three in the morning, heard a low clear whistle. I am a light sleeper, and it has awakened me. I cannot tell where it came from—perhaps from the next room, perhaps from the lawn. I thought that I would just ask you whether you had heard it.'

"'No, I have not. It must be those wretched gipsies in the plantation.'

"'Very likely. And yet if it were on the lawn I wonder that you did not hear it also.'

"'Ah, but I sleep more heavily than you.'

"'Well, it is of no great consequence at any rate,' she smiled back at me, closed my door, and a few moments later I heard her key turn in the lock."

"Indeed," said Holmes. "Was it your custom always to lock yourselves in at night?"

"Always."

"And why?"

"I think that I mentioned to you that the Doctor kept a cheetah and a baboon. We had no feeling of security unless our doors were locked."

"Quite so. Pray proceed with your statement."

"I could not sleep that night. A vague feeling of impending misfortune impressed me. My sister and I, you will recollect, were twins, and you know how subtle are the links which bind two souls which are so closely allied. It was a wild night. The wind was howling outside, and the rain was beating and splashing against the windows. Suddenly, amidst all the hubbub of the gale, there burst forth the wild scream of a terrified woman. I knew that it was my sister's voice. I sprang from my bed, wrapped a shawl round me, and rushed into the corridor. As I opened my door I seemed to hear a low whistle, such as my sister described, and a few moments later a clanging sound, as if a mass of metal had fallen. As I ran down the passage my sister's door was unlocked, and revolved slowly upon its hinges. I stared at it horror-stricken, not knowing what was about to issue from it. By the light of the corridor lamp I saw my sister appear at the opening, her face blanched with terror, her hands groping for help, her whole figure swaying to and fro like that of a drunkard. I ran to her and threw my arms round her, but at that moment her knees seemed to give way and she fell to the ground. She writhed as one who is in terrible pain, and her limbs were dreadfully convulsed. At first I thought that she had not recognised me, but as I bent over her she suddenly

she was unconscious, and though he poured brandy down her throat, and sent for medical aid from the village, all efforts were in vain, for she slowly sank and died without having recovered her consciousness. Such was the dreadful end of my beloved sister."

"One moment," said Holmes ; "are you sure about this whistle and metallic sound ? Could you swear to it ? "

"That was what the county coroner asked me at the inquiry. It is my strong impression that I heard it, and yet among the crash of the gale, and the creaking of an old house, I may possibly have been deceived."

"Was your sister dressed ? "

"No, she was in her nightdress. In her right hand was found the charred stump of a match, and in her left a matchbox."

"HER FACE BLANCHED WITH TERROR."

shrieked out in a voice which I shall never forget, 'Oh, my God! Helen! It was the band! The speckled band!' There was something else which she would fain have said, and she stabbed with her finger into the air in the direction of the Doctor's room, but a fresh convulsion seized her and choked her words. I rushed out, calling loudly for my stepfather, and I met him hastening from his room in his dressing-gown. When he reached my sister's side

"Showing that she had struck a light and looked about her when the alarm took place. That is important. And what conclusions did the coroner come to ? "

"He investigated the case with great care, for Dr. Roylott's conduct had long been notorious in the county, but he was unable to find any satisfactory cause of death. My evidence showed that the door had been fastened upon the inner side, and the windows were blocked by old-fashioned shutters with broad iron bars, which were secured every night. The walls were carefully sounded, and were shown to be quite solid all round, and the flooring was also thoroughly examined, with the same result. The chimney is wide, but is barred up by four large staples. It is certain, therefore, that my sister was quite alone when she met her end. Besides, there were no marks of any violence upon her."

"How about poison?"

"The doctors examined her for it, but without success."

"What do you think that this unfortunate lady died of, then?"

"It is my belief that she died of pure fear and nervous shock, though what it was which frightened her I cannot imagine."

"Were there gipsies in the plantation at the time?"

"Yes, there are nearly always some there."

"Ah, and what did you gather from this allusion to a band—a speckled band?"

"Sometimes I have thought that it was merely the wild talk of delirium, sometimes that it may have referred to some band of people, perhaps to these very gipsies in the plantation. I do not know whether the spotted handkerchiefs which so many of them wear over their heads might have suggested the strange adjective which she used."

Holmes shook his head like a man who is far from being satisfied.

"These are very deep waters," said he; "pray go on with your narrative."

"Two years have passed since then, and my life has been until lately lonelier than ever. A month ago, however, a dear friend, whom I have known for many years, has done me the honour to ask my hand in marriage. His name is Armitage—Percy Armitage—the second son of Mr. Armitage, of Crane Water, near Reading. My stepfather has offered no opposition to the match, and we are to be married in the course of the spring. Two days ago some repairs were started in the west wing of the building, and my bedroom wall has been pierced, so that I have had to move into the chamber in which my sister died, and to sleep in the very bed in which she slept. Imagine, then, my thrill of terror when last night, as I lay awake, thinking over her terrible fate, I suddenly heard in the silence of the night the low whistle which had been the herald of her own death. I sprang up and lit the lamp, but nothing was to be seen in the room. I was too shaken to go to bed again, however, so I dressed, and as soon as it was daylight I slipped down, got a dog-cart at the 'Crown' inn, which is opposite, and drove to Leatherhead, from whence I have come on this morning with the one object of seeing you and asking your advice."

"You have done wisely," said my friend. "But have you told me all?"

"Yes, all."

"Miss Roylott, you have not. You are screening your stepfather."

"Why, what do you mean?"

For answer Holmes pushed back the frill of black lace which fringed the hand that lay upon our visitor's knee. Five little livid spots, the marks of four fingers and a thumb, were printed upon the white wrist.

"You have been cruelly used," said Holmes.

The lady coloured deeply, and covered over her injured wrist. "He is a hard man," she said, "and perhaps he hardly knows his own strength."

There was a long silence, during which Holmes leaned his chin upon his hands and stared into the crackling fire.

"This is a very deep business," he said at last. "There are a thousand details which I should desire to know before I decide upon our course of action. Yet we have not a moment to lose. If we were to come to Stoke Moran to-day, would it be possible for us to see over these rooms without the knowledge of your stepfather?"

"As it happens, he spoke of coming into town to-day upon some most important business. It is probable that he will be away all day, and that there would be nothing to disturb you. We have a housekeeper now, but she is old and foolish, and I could easily get her out of the way."

"Excellent. You are not averse to this trip, Watson?"

"By no means."

"Then we shall both come. What are you going to do yourself?"

"I have one or two things which I would wish to do now that I am in town. But I shall return by the twelve o'clock train, so as to be there in time for your coming."

"And you may expect us early in the afternoon. I have myself some small business matters to attend to. Will you not wait and breakfast?"

"No, I must go. My heart is lightened already since I have confided my trouble to you. I shall look forward to seeing you again this afternoon." She dropped her thick black veil over her face, and glided from the room.

"And what do you think of it all, Watson?" asked Sherlock Holmes, leaning back in his chair.

"It seems to me to be a most dark and sinister business."

"Dark enough, and sinister enough."

"Yet if the lady is correct in saying that the flooring and walls are sound, and that the door, window, and chimney are impassable, then her sister must have been undoubtedly alone when she met her mysterious end."

"What becomes, then, of these nocturnal whistles, and what of the very peculiar words of the dying woman?"

"I cannot think."

"When you combine the ideas of whistles at night, the presence of a band of gipsies who are on intimate terms with this old Doctor, the fact that we have every reason to believe that the Doctor has an interest in preventing his stepdaughter's marriage, the dying allusion to a band, and finally, the fact that Miss Helen Stoner heard a

"WHICH OF YOU IS HOLMES?"

metallic clang, which might have been caused by one of those metal bars which secured the shutters falling back into their place, I think that there is good ground to think that the mystery may be cleared along those lines."

"But what, then, did the gipsies do?"

"I cannot imagine."

"I see many objections to any such theory."

"And so do I. It is precisely for that reason that we are going to Stoke Moran this day. I want to see whether the objections are fatal, or if they may be explained away. But what, in the name of the devil!"

The ejaculation had been drawn from my companion by the fact that our door had been suddenly dashed open, and that a huge man had framed himself in the aperture. His costume was a peculiar mixture of the professional and of the agricultural, having a black top hat, a long frock coat, and a pair of high gaiters, with a hunting crop swinging in his hand. So tall was he that his hat actually brushed the cross bar of the doorway, and his breadth seemed to span it across from side to side. A large face, seared with a thousand wrinkles, burned yellow with the sun, and marked with every evil passion, was turned from one to the other of us, while his deep-set, bile-shot eyes, and his high thin fleshless nose, gave him somewhat the resemblance to a fierce old bird of prey.

"Which of you is Holmes?" asked this apparition.

"My name, sir, but you have the advantage of me," said my companion, quietly.

"I am Dr. Grimesby Roylott, of Stoke Moran."

"Indeed, Doctor," said Holmes, blandly. "Pray take a seat."

"I will do nothing of the kind. My stepdaughter has been here. I have traced her. What has she been saying to you?"

"It is a little cold for the time of the year," said Holmes.

"What has she been saying to you?" screamed the old man furiously.

"But I have heard that the crocuses promise well," continued my companion imperturbably.

"Ha! You put me off, do you?" said our new visitor, taking a step forward, and shaking his hunting crop. "I know you, you scoundrel! I have heard of you before. You are Holmes the meddler."

My friend smiled.

"Holmes the busybody!"

His smile broadened.

"Holmes the Scotland-yard Jack-in-office!"

Holmes chuckled heartily. "Your conversation is most entertaining," said he. "When you go out close the door, for there is a decided draught."

"I will go when I have said my say. Don't you dare to meddle with my affairs. I know that Miss Stoner has been here—I traced her! I am a dangerous man to fall foul of! See here." He stepped swiftly forward, seized the poker, and bent it into a curve with his huge brown hands.

"See that you keep yourself out of my grip," he snarled, and hurling the twisted poker into the fireplace, he strode out of the room.

"He seems a very amiable person," said Holmes, laughing. "I am not quite so bulky, but if he had remained I might have shown him that my grip was not much more feeble than his own." As he spoke he picked up the steel poker, and with a sudden effort straightened it out again.

"Fancy his having the insolence to confound me with the official detective force! This incident gives zest to our investigation, however, and I only trust that our little friend will not suffer from her imprudence in allowing this brute to trace her. And now, Watson, we shall order breakfast, and afterwards I shall walk down to Doctors' Commons, where I hope to get some data which may help us in this matter."

It was nearly one o'clock when Sherlock Holmes returned from his excursion. He held in his hand a sheet of blue paper, scrawled over with notes and figures.

"I have seen the will of the deceased wife," said he. "To determine its exact meaning I have been obliged to work out the present prices of the investments with which it is concerned. The total income, which at the time of the wife's death was little short of £1,100, is now through the fall in agricultural prices not more than £750. Each daughter can claim an income of £250, in case of marriage. It is evident, therefore, that if both girls had married

this beauty would have had a mere pittance, while even one of them would cripple him to a very serious extent. My morning's work has not been wasted, since it has proved that he has the very strongest motives for standing in the way of anything of the sort. And now, Watson, this is too serious for dawdling, especially as the old man is aware that we are interesting ourselves in his affairs, so if you are ready we shall call a cab and drive to Waterloo. I should be very much obliged if you would slip your revolver into your pocket. An Eley's No. 2 is an excellent argument with gentlemen who can twist steel pokers into knots. That and a tooth-brush are, I think, all that we need."

At Waterloo we were fortunate in catching a train for Leatherhead, where we hired a trap at the station inn, and drove for four or five miles through the lovely Surrey lanes. It was a perfect day, with a bright sun and a few fleecy clouds in the heavens. The trees and wayside hedges were just throwing out their first green shoots, and the air was full of the pleasant smell of the moist earth. To me at least there was a strange contrast between the sweet promise of the spring and this sinister quest upon which we were engaged. My companion sat in the front of the trap, his arms folded, his hat pulled down over his eyes, and his chin sunk upon his breast, buried in the deepest thought. Suddenly, however, he started, tapped me on the shoulder, and pointed over the meadows.

"Look there!" said he.

A heavily-timbered park stretched up in a gentle slope, thickening into a grove at the highest point. From amidst the branches there jutted out the grey gables and high roof-tree of a very old mansion.

"Stoke Moran?" said he.

"Yes, sir, that be the house of Dr. Grimesby Roylott," remarked the driver.

"There is some building going on there," said Holmes; "that is where we are going."

"There's the village," said the driver, pointing to a cluster of roofs some distance to the left; "but if you want to get to the house, you'll find it shorter to get over this stile, and so by the footpath over the fields. There it is, where the lady is walking."

"And the lady, I fancy, is Miss Stoner," observed Holmes, shading his eyes. "Yes, I think we had better do as you suggest."

We got off, paid our fare, and the trap rattled back on its way to Leatherhead.

"WE GOT OFF, PAID OUR FARE."

"I thought it as well," said Holmes, as we climbed the stile, "that this fellow should think we had come here as architects, or on some definite business. It may stop his gossip. Good afternoon, Miss Stoner. You see that we have been as good as our word."

Our client of the morning had hurried forward to meet us with a face which spoke her joy. "I have been waiting so eagerly for you," she cried, shaking hands with us warmly. "All has turned out splendidly. Dr. Roylott has gone to town, and it is unlikely that he will be back before evening."

"We have had the pleasure of making the Doctor's acquaintance," said Holmes, and in a few words he sketched out what had occurred. Miss Stoner turned white to the lips as she listened. "Good heavens!" she cried, "he has followed me, then."

"So it appears."

"He is so cunning that I never know when I am safe from him. What will he say when he returns?"

"He must guard himself, for he may find that there is someone more cunning than himself upon his track. You must lock yourself up from him to-night. If he is violent, we shall take you away to your aunt's at Harrow. Now, we must make the best use of our time, so kindly take us at once to the rooms which we are to examine."

The building was of grey, lichen-blotched stone, with a high central portion, and two curving wings, like the claws of a crab, thrown out on each side. In one of these wings the windows were broken, and blocked with wooden boards, while the roof was partly caved in, a picture of ruin. The central portion was in little better repair, but the right-hand block was comparatively modern, and the blinds in the windows, with the blue smoke curling up from the chimneys, showed that this was where the family resided. Some scaffolding had been erected against the end wall, and the stonework had been broken into, but there were no signs of any workmen at the moment of our visit. Holmes walked slowly up and down the ill-trimmed lawn, and examined with deep attention the outsides of the windows.

"This, I take it, belongs to the room in which you used to sleep, the centre one to your sister's, and the one next to the main building to Dr. Roylott's chamber?"

"Exactly so. But I am now sleeping in the middle one."

"Pending the alterations, as I understand. By the way, there does not seem to be any very pressing need for repairs at that end wall."

"There were none. I believe that it was an excuse to move me from my room."

"Ah! that is suggestive. Now, on the other side of this narrow wing runs the corridor from which these three rooms open. There are windows in it, of course?"

"Yes, but very small ones. Too narrow for anyone to pass through."

"As you both locked your doors at night your rooms were unapproachable from that side. Now, would you have the kindness to go into your room, and to bar your shutters."

Miss Stoner did so, and Holmes, after a careful examination through the open window, endeavoured in every way to force the shutter open, but without success. There was no slit through which a knife could be passed to raise the bar. Then with his lens he tested the hinges, but they were of solid iron, built firmly into the massive masonry. " Hum ! " said he, scratching his chin in some perplexity, " my theory certainly presents some difficulties. No one could pass these shutters if they were bolted. Well, we shall see if the inside throws any light upon the matter."

A small side door led into the white-washed corridor from which the three bed-rooms opened. Holmes refused to examine the third chamber, so we passed at once to the second, that in which Miss Stoner was now sleeping, and in which her sister had met with her fate. It was a homely little room, with a low ceiling and a gaping fire-place, after the fashion of old country houses. A brown chest of drawers stood in one corner, a narrow white-counterpaned bed in another, and a dressing-table on the left-hand side of the window. These articles, with two small wickerwork chairs, made up all the furniture in the room, save for a square of Wilton carpet in the centre. The boards round and the panelling of the walls were of brown, worm-eaten oak, so old and discoloured that it may have dated from the original building of the house. Holmes drew one of the chairs into a corner and sat silent, while his eyes travelled round and round and up and down, taking in every detail of the apartment.

" Where does that bell communicate with ? " he asked at last, pointing to a thick bell-rope which hung down beside the bed, the tassel actually lying upon the pillow.

" It goes to the housekeeper's room."

" It looks newer than the other things?"

" Yes, it was only put there a couple of years ago."

" Your sister asked for it, I suppose ? "

" No, I never heard of her using it. We used always to get what we wanted for ourselves."

" Indeed, it seemed unnecessary to put so nice a bell-pull there. You will excuse me for a few minutes while I satisfy myself as to this floor." He threw himself down upon his face with his lens in his hand, and crawled swiftly backwards and forwards, examining minutely the cracks between the boards. Then he did the same with the woodwork with which the chamber was

panelled. Finally he walked over to the bed and spent some time in staring at it, and in running his eye up and down the wall. Finally he took the bell-rope in his hand and gave it a brisk tug.

" Why, it's a dummy," said he.

" Won't it ring ? "

" No, it is not even attached to a wire. This is very interesting. You can see now that it is fastened to a hook just above where the little opening for the ventilator is."

" How very absurd ! I never noticed that before."

" Very strange ! " muttered Holmes, pulling at the rope. " There are one or two very singular points about this room. For example, what a fool a builder must be to open a ventilator into another room, when, with the same trouble, he might have communicated with the outside air ! "

" That is also quite modern," said the lady.

" Done about the same time as the bell-rope ? " remarked Holmes.

" Yes, there were several little changes carried out about that time."

" They seem to have been of a most interesting character—dummy bell-ropes, and ventilators which do not ventilate. With your permission, Miss Stoner, we shall now carry our researches into the inner apartment."

Dr. Grimesby Roylott's chamber was larger than that of his step-daughter, but was as plainly furnished. A camp bed, a small wooden shelf full of books, mostly of a technical character, an armchair beside the bed, a plain wooden chair against the wall, a round table, and a large iron safe were the principal things which met the eye. Holmes walked slowly round and examined each and all of them with the keenest interest.

" What's in here ? " he asked, tapping the safe.

" My stepfather's business papers."

" Oh ! you have seen inside, then ? "

" Only once, some years ago. I remember that it was full of papers."

" There isn't a cat in it, for example ? "

" No. What a strange idea ! "

" Well, look at this ! " He took up a small saucer of milk which stood on the top of it.

" No ; we don't keep a cat. But there is a cheetah and a baboon."

" Ah, yes, of course ! Well, a cheetah is just a big cat, and yet a saucer of milk does not go very far in satisfying its wants, I daresay. There is one point which I should wish to determine." He squatted down in front of the wooden chair, and examined the seat of it with the greatest attention.

"Thank you. That is quite settled," said he, rising and putting his lens in his pocket. "Hullo! here is something interesting!"

The object which had

"WELL, LOOK AT THIS."

caught his eye was a small dog lash hung on one corner of the bed. The lash, however, was curled upon itself, and tied so as to make a loop of whipcord.

"What do you make of that, Watson?"

"It's a common enough lash. But I don't know why it should be tied."

"That is not quite so common, is it? Ah, me! it's a wicked world, and when a clever man turns his brains to crime it is the worst of all. I think that I have seen enough now, Miss Stoner, and, with your permission, we shall walk out upon the lawn."

I had never seen my friend's face so grim, or his brow so dark, as it was when we turned from the scene of this investigation. We had walked several times up and down the lawn, neither Miss Stoner nor myself liking to break in upon his thoughts, before he roused himself from his reverie.

"It is very essential, Miss Stoner," said he, "that you should absolutely follow my advice in every respect."

"I shall most certainly do so."

"The matter is too serious for any hesitation. Your life may depend upon your compliance."

"I assure that I am in your hands."

"In the first place, both my friend and I must spend the night in your room."

Both Miss Stoner and I gazed at him in astonishment.

"Yes, it must be so. Let me explain. I believe that that is the village inn over there?"

"Yes, that is the 'Crown.'"

"Very good. Your windows would be visible from there?"

"Certainly."

"You must confine yourself to your room, on pretence of a headache, when your stepfather comes back. Then when you hear him retire for the night, you must open the shutters of your window, undo the hasp, put your lamp there as a signal to us, and then withdraw quietly with everything which you are likely to want into the room which you used to occupy. I have no doubt that, in spite of the repairs, you could manage there for one night."

"Oh, yes, easily."

"The rest you will leave in our hands."

"But what will you do?"

"We shall spend the night in your room, and we shall investigate the cause of this noise which has disturbed you."

"I believe, Mr. Holmes, that you have already made up your mind," said Miss Stoner, laying her hand upon my companion's sleeve.

"Perhaps I have."

"Then for pity's sake tell me what was the cause of my sister's death."

"I should prefer to have clearer proofs before I speak."

"You can at least tell me whether my own thought is correct, and if she died from some sudden fright."

"No, I do not think so. I think that there was probably some more tangible cause. And now, Miss Stoner, we must leave you, for if Dr. Roylott returned and

"GOOD-BYE, AND BE BRAVE."

The trap drove on, and a few minutes later we saw a sudden light spring up among the trees as the lamp was lit in one of the sitting-rooms.

"Do you know, Watson," said Holmes, as we sat together in the gathering darkness, "I have really some scruples as to taking you to-night. There is a distinct element of danger."

"Can I be of assistance?"

"Your presence might be invaluable."

"Then I shall certainly come."

"It is very kind of you."

"You speak of danger. You have evidently seen more in these rooms than was visible to me."

"No, but I fancy that I may have deduced a little more. I imagine that you saw all that I did."

"I saw nothing remarkable save the bell rope, and what purpose that could answer I confess is more than I can imagine."

"You saw the ventilator, too?"

"Yes, but I do not think that it is such a very unusual thing to have a small opening between two rooms. It was so small that a rat could hardly pass through."

"I knew that we should find a ventilator before ever we came to Stoke Moran."

"My dear Holmes!"

"Oh, yes, I did. You remember in her statement she said that her sister could smell Dr. Roylott's cigar. Now, of course that suggested at once that there must be a communication between the two rooms. It could only be a small one, or it would have been remarked upon at the Coroner's inquiry. I deduced a ventilator."

"But what harm can there be in that?"

"Well, there is at least a curious coincidence of dates. A ventilator is made, a cord is hung, and a lady who sleeps in the bed dies. Does not that strike you?"

"I cannot as yet see any connection."

"Did you observe anything very peculiar about that bed?"

"No."

"It was clamped to the floor. Did you ever see a bed fastened like that before?"

"I cannot say that I have."

saw us, our journey would be in vain. Good-bye, and be brave, for if you will do what I have told you, you may rest assured that we shall soon drive away the dangers that threaten you."

Sherlock Holmes and I had no difficulty in engaging a bedroom and sitting-room at the "Crown" Inn. They were on the upper floor, and from our window we could command a view of the avenue gate, and of the inhabited wing of Stoke Moran Manor House. At dusk we saw Dr. Grimesby Roylott drive past, his huge form looming up beside the little figure of the lad who drove him. The boy had some slight difficulty in undoing the heavy iron gates, and we heard the hoarse roar of the doctor's voice, and saw the fury with which he shook his clenched fists at him.

"The lady could not move her bed. It must always be in the same relative position to the ventilator and to the rope—for so we may call it, since it was clearly never meant for a bell-pull."

"Holmes," I cried, "I seem to see dimly what you are hinting at. We are only just in time to prevent some subtle and horrible crime."

"Subtle enough, and horrible enough. When a doctor does go wrong, he is the first of criminals. He has nerve and he has knowledge. Palmer and Pritchard were among the heads of their profession. This man strikes even deeper, but I think, Watson, that we shall be able to strike deeper still. But we shall have horrors enough before the night is over ; for goodness' sake let us have a quiet pipe, and turn our minds for a few hours to something more cheerful."

About nine o'clock the light among the trees was extinguished, and all was dark in the direction of the Manor House. Two hours passed slowly away, and then, suddenly, just at the stroke of eleven, a single bright light shone out right in front of us.

"That is our signal," said Holmes, springing to his feet ; "it comes from the middle window."

As we passed out he exchanged a few words with the landlord, explaining that we were going on a late visit to an acquaintance, and that it was possible that we might spend the night there. A moment later we were out on the dark road, a chill wind blowing in our faces, and one yellow light twinkling in front of us through the gloom to guide us on our sombre errand.

There was little difficulty in entering the grounds, for unrepaired breaches gaped in the old park wall. Making our way among the trees, we reached the lawn, crossed it, and were about to enter through the window, when out from a clump of laurel bushes there darted what seemed to be a hideous and distorted child, who threw itself upon the grass with writhing limbs, and then ran swiftly across the lawn into the darkness.

"My God !" I whispered ; "did you see it ?"

Holmes was for the moment as startled as I. His hand closed like a vice upon my wrist in his agitation. Then he broke into a low laugh, and put his lips to my ear.

"It is a nice household," he murmured. "That is the baboon."

I had forgotten the strange pets which the Doctor affected. There was a cheetah, too ; perhaps we might find it upon our shoulders at any moment. I confess that I felt easier in my mind when, after following Holmes' example and slipping off my shoes, I found myself inside the bedroom. My companion noiselessly closed the shutters, moved the lamp on to the table, and cast his eyes round the room. All was as we had seen it in the day-time. Then creeping up to me and making a trumpet of his hand, he whispered into my ear again so gently that it was all that I could do to distinguish the words.

"The least sound would be fatal to our plans."

I nodded to show that I had heard.

"We must sit without light. He would see it through the ventilator."

I nodded again.

"Do not go asleep ; your very life may depend upon it. Have your pistol ready in case we should need it. I will sit on the side of the bed, and you in that chair."

I took out my revolver and laid it on the corner of the table.

Holmes had brought up a long thin cane, and this he placed upon the bed beside him. By it he laid the box of matches and the stump of a candle. Then he turned down the lamp, and we were left in darkness.

How shall I ever forget that dreadful vigil ? I could not hear a sound, not even the drawing of a breath, and yet I knew that my companion sat open-eyed, within a few feet of me, in the same state of nervous tension in which I was myself. The shutters cut off the least ray of light, and we waited in absolute darkness. From outside came the occasional cry of a night bird, and once at our very window a long drawn, cat-like whine, which told us that the cheetah was indeed at liberty. Far away we could hear the deep tones of the parish clock, which boomed out every quarter of an hour. How long they seemed, those quarters ! Twelve struck, and one, and two, and three, and still we sat waiting silently for whatever might befall.

Suddenly there was the momentary gleam of a light up in the direction of the ventilator, which vanished immediately, but was succeeded by a strong smell of burning oil and heated metal. Someone in the next room had lit a dark lantern. I heard a gentle sound of movement, and then all was silent once more, though the

"HOLMES LASHED FURIOUSLY."

smell grew stronger. For half an hour I sat with straining ears. Then suddenly another sound became audible—a very gentle, soothing sound, like that of a small jet of steam escaping continually from a kettle. The instant that we heard it, Holmes sprang from the bed, struck a match, and lashed furiously with his cane at the bell-pull.

"You see it, Watson?" he yelled. "You see it?"

But I saw nothing. At the moment when Holmes struck the light I heard a low, clear whistle, but the sudden glare flashing into my weary eyes made it impossible for me to tell what it was at which my friend lashed so savagely. I could, however, see that his face was deadly pale, and filled with horror and loathing.

He had ceased to strike, and was gazing up at the ventilator, when suddenly there broke from the silence of the night the most horrible cry to which I have ever listened. It swelled up louder and louder, a hoarse yell of pain and fear and anger all mingled in the one dreadful shriek. They say that away down in the village, and even in the distant parsonage, that cry raised the sleepers from their beds. It struck cold to our hearts, and I stood gazing at Holmes, and

he at me, until the last echoes of it had died away into the silence from which it rose.

"What can it mean?" I gasped.

"It means that it is all over," Holmes answered. "And perhaps, after all, it is for the best. Take your pistol, and we shall enter Dr. Roylott's room."

With a grave face he lit the lamp, and led the way down the corridor. Twice he struck at the chamber door without any reply from within. Then he turned the handle and entered, I at his heels, with the cocked pistol in my hand.

It was a singular sight which met our eyes. On the table stood a dark lantern with the shutter half open, throwing a brilliant beam of light upon the iron safe, the door of which was ajar. Beside this table, on the wooden chair, sat Dr. Grimesby Roylott, clad in a long grey dressing-gown, his bare ankles protruding beneath, and his feet thrust into red heelless Turkish slippers. Across his lap lay the short stock with the long lash which we had noticed during the day. His chin was cocked upwards, and his eyes were fixed in a dreadful rigid stare at the corner of the ceiling. Round his brow he had a peculiar yellow band, with brownish speckles, which seemed to be bound tightly round his head. As we entered he made neither sound nor motion.

"The band! the speckled band!" whispered Holmes.

I took a step forward. In an instant his strange headgear began to move, and there reared itself from among his hair the squat diamond-shaped head and puffed neck of a loathsome serpent.

Dr. Grimesby Roylott, of Stoke Moran. It is not necessary that I should prolong a narrative which has already run to too great a length, by telling how we broke the sad news to the terrified girl, how we conveyed her by the morning train to the care of her good aunt at Harrow, of how the slow process of official inquiry came to the conclusion that the Doctor met his fate while indiscreetly playing with a dangerous

"HE MADE NEITHER SOUND NOR MOTION."

"It is a swamp adder!" cried Holmes— "the deadliest snake in India. He has died within ten seconds of being bitten. Violence does, in truth, recoil upon the violent, and the schemer falls into the pit which he digs for another. Let us thrust this creature back into its den, and we can then remove Miss Stoner to some place of shelter, and let the county police know what has happened."

As he spoke he drew the dog whip swiftly from the dead man's lap, and throwing the noose round the reptile's neck, he drew it from its horrid perch, and, carrying it at arm's length threw it into the iron safe, which he closed upon it.

Such are the true facts of the death of

pet. The little which I had yet to learn of the case was told me by Sherlock Holmes as we travelled back next day.

"I had," said he, "come to an entirely erroneous conclusion, which shows, my dear Watson, how dangerous it always is to reason from insufficient data. The presence of the gipsies, and the use of the word 'band,' which was used by the poor girl, no doubt, to explain the appearance which she had caught a hurried glimpse of by the light of her match, were sufficient to put me upon an entirely wrong scent. I can only claim the merit that I instantly reconsidered my position when, however, it became clear to me that whatever danger threatened an occupant of the room could not come either from the window or the door. My attention was speedily drawn, as I have already remarked to you, to this ventilator, and to the bell rope which hung down to the bed. The discovery that this was a dummy, and that the bed was clamped to the floor, instantly gave rise to the suspicion that the rope was there as a bridge for something passing through the hole, and coming to the bed. The idea of a snake instantly occurred to me, and when I coupled it with my knowledge that the Doctor was furnished with a supply of creatures from India, I felt that I was probably on the right track. The idea of using a form of poison which could not possibly be discovered by any chemical test was just such a one as would occur to a clever and ruthless man who had had an Eastern training. The rapidity with which such a poison would take effect would also, from his point of view, be an advantage. It would be a sharp-eyed coroner indeed who could distinguish the two little dark punctures which would show where the poison fangs had done their work. Then I thought of the whistle. Of course, he must recall the snake before the morning light revealed it to the victim. He had trained it, probably by the use of the milk which we saw, to return to him when summoned. He would put it through this ventilator at the hour that he thought best, with the certainty that it would crawl down the rope, and land on the bed. It might or might not bite the occupant, perhaps she might escape every night for a week, but sooner or later she must fall a victim.

" I had come to these conclusions before ever I had entered his room. An inspection of his chair showed me that he had been in the habit of standing on it, which, of course, would be necessary in order that he should reach the ventilator. The sight of the safe, the saucer of milk, and the loop of whipcord were enough to finally dispel any doubts which may have remained. The metallic clang heard by Miss Stoner was obviously caused by her father hastily closing the door of his safe upon its terrible occupant. Having once made up my mind, you know the steps which I took in order to put the matter to the proof. I heard the creature hiss, as I have no doubt that you did also, and I instantly lit the light and attacked it."

" With the result of driving it through the ventilator."

" And also with the result of causing it to turn upon its master at the other side. Some of the blows of my cane came home, and roused its snakish temper, so that it flew upon the first person it saw. In this way I am no doubt indirectly responsible for Dr. Grimesby Roylott's death, and I cannot say that it is likely to weigh very heavily upon my conscience."

# Adventures of Sherlock Holmes.

## IX.—THE ADVENTURE OF THE ENGINEER'S THUMB.

### By A. Conan Doyle.

F all the problems which have been submitted to my friend Mr. Sherlock Holmes for solution during the years of our intimacy, there were only two which I was the means of introducing to his notice, that of Mr. Hatherley's thumb and that of Colonel Warburton's madness. Of these the latter may have afforded a finer field for an acute and original observer, but the other was so strange in its inception and so dramatic in its details, that it may be the more worthy of being placed upon record, even if it gave my friend fewer openings for those deductive methods of reasoning by which he achieved such remarkable results. The story has, I believe, been told more than once in the newspapers, but, like all such narratives, its effect is much less striking when set forth *en bloc* in a single half-column of print than when the facts slowly evolve before your own eyes and the mystery clears gradually away as each new discovery furnishes a step which leads on to the complete truth. At the time the circumstances made a deep impression upon me, and the lapse of two years has hardly served to weaken the effect.

It was in the summer of '89, not long after my marriage, that the events occurred which I am now about to summarise. I had returned to civil practice, and had finally abandoned Holmes in his Baker-street rooms, although I continually visited him, and occasionally even persuaded him to forego his Bohemian habits so far as to come and visit us. My practice had steadily increased, and as I happened to live at no very great distance from Paddington Station, I got a few patients from among the officials. One of these whom I had cured of a painful and lingering disease, was never weary of advertising my virtues, and of endeavouring to send me on every sufferer over whom he might have any influence.

One morning, at a little before seven o'clock, I was awakened by the maid tapping at the door, to announce that two men had come from Paddington, and were waiting in the consulting room. I dressed hurriedly, for I knew by experience that railway cases were seldom trivial, and hastened downstairs. As I descended, my old ally, the guard, came out of the room, and closed the door tightly behind him.

"I've got him here," he whispered, jerking his thumb over his shoulder ; "he's all right."

"What is it, then ?" I asked, for his manner suggested that it was some strange creature which he had caged up in my room.

"It's a new patient," he whispered. "I thought I'd bring him round myself ; then he couldn't slip away. There he is, all safe and sound. I must go now, doctor, I have my dooties, just the same as you." And off he went, this trusty tout, without even giving me time to thank him.

I entered my consulting room, and found a gentleman seated by the table. He was quietly dressed in a suit of heather tweed, with a soft cloth cap, which he had laid down upon my books. Round one of his hands he had a handkerchief wrapped, which was mottled all over with bloodstains. He was young, not more than five-and-twenty, I should say, with a strong masculine face ; but he was exceedingly pale, and gave me the impression of a man who was suffering from some strong agitation, which it took all his strength of mind to control.

"I am sorry to knock you up so early, doctor," said he. "But I have had a very serious accident during the night. I came in by train this morning, and on inquiring at Paddington as to where I might find a doctor a worthy fellow very kindly escorted me here. I gave the maid a card, but I see that she has left it upon the side table."

I took it up and glanced at it. "Mr.

Victor Hatherley, hydraulic engineer, 16A, Victoria-street (3rd floor)." That was the name, style, and abode of my morning visitor. "I regret that I have kept you waiting," said I, sitting down in my library chair. "You are fresh from a night journey, I understand, which is in itself a monotonous occupation."

"Oh, my night could not be called monotonous," said he, and laughed. He laughed very heartily, with a high ringing note, leaning back in his chair, and shaking his sides. All my medical instincts rose up against that laugh.

"Stop it!" I cried. "Pull yourself together!" and I poured out some water from a caraffe.

It was useless, however. He was off in one of those hysterical outbursts which come upon a strong nature when some great crisis is over and gone. Presently he came to himself once more, very weary and blushing hotly.

"I have been making a fool of myself," he gasped.

"Not at all. Drink this!" I dashed some brandy into the water, and the colour began to come back to his bloodless cheeks.

"That's better!" said he. "And now, doctor, perhaps you would kindly attend to my thumb, or rather to the place where my thumb used to be."

He unwound the handkerchief and held out his hand. It gave even my hardened nerves a shudder to look at it. There were four protruding fingers and a horrid red spongy surface where the thumb should have been. It had been hacked or torn right out from the roots.

"Good heavens!" I cried, "this is a terrible injury. It must have bled considerably."

"Yes, it did. I fainted when it was done; and I think that I must have been senseless for a long time. When I came to, I found that it was still bleeding, so I tied one end of my handkerchief very tightly round the wrist, and braced it up with a twig."

"Excellent! You should have been a surgeon."

"It is a question of hydraulics, you see, and came within my own province."

"This has been done," said I, examining the wound, "by a very heavy and sharp instrument."

"A thing like a cleaver," said he.

"An accident, I presume?"

"By no means."

"What, a murderous attack!"

"Very murderous indeed."

"You horrify me."

I sponged the wound, cleaned it, dressed it; and, finally, covered it over with cotton wadding and carbolised bandages. He lay back without wincing, though he bit his lip from time to time.

"How is that?" I asked, when I had finished.

"Capital! Between your brandy and your bandage, I feel a new man. I was very weak, but I have had a good deal to go through."

"HE UNWOUND THE HANDKERCHIEF, AND HELD OUT HIS HAND."

"Perhaps you had better not speak of the matter. It is evidently trying to your nerves."

"Oh, no ; not now. I shall have to tell my tale to the police ; but, between ourselves, if it were not for the convincing evidence of this wound of mine, I should be surprised if they believed my statement, for it is a very extraordinary one, and I

"HE SETTLED OUR NEW ACQUAINTANCE ON THE SOFA.

have not much in the way of proof with which to back it up. And, even if they believe me, the clues which I can give them are so vague that it is a question whether justice will be done."

"Ha ! " cried I, " if it is anything in the nature of a problem which you desire to see solved, I should strongly recommend you to come to my friend Mr. Sherlock Holmes before you go to the official police."

"Oh, I have heard of that fellow," answered my visitor, "and I should be very glad if he would take the matter up, though of course I must use the official police as well. Would you give me an introduction to him ? "

"I'll do better. I'll take you round to him myself."

"I should be immensely obliged to you."

"We'll call a cab, and go together. We shall just be in time to have a little breakfast with him. Do you feel equal to it ? "

"Yes, I shall not feel easy until I have told my story."

"Then my servant will call a cab, and I shall be with you in an instant." I rushed upstairs, explained the matter shortly to my wife, and in five minutes was inside a hansom, driving with my new acquaintance to Baker-street.

Sherlock Holmes was, as I expected, lounging about his sitting-room in his dressing-gown, reading the agony column of *The Times*, and smoking his before-breakfast pipe, which was composed of all the plugs and dottels left from his smokes of the day before, all carefully dried and collected on the corner of the mantel-piece. He received us in his quietly genial fashion, ordered fresh rashers and eggs, and joined us in a hearty meal. When it was concluded he settled our new acquaintance upon the sofa, placed a pillow beneath his head, and laid a glass of brandy and water within his reach.

"It is easy to see that your experience has been no common one, Mr. Hatherley," said he. "Pray lie down there and make yourself absolutely at home. Tell us what you can, but stop when you are tired, and keep up your strength with a little stimulant."

"Thank you," said my patient, " but I have felt another man since the doctor bandaged me, and I think that your breakfast has completed the cure. I shall take up as little of your valuable time as possible, so I shall start at once upon my peculiar experiences."

Holmes sat in his big armchair with the weary, heavy-lidded expression which veiled his keen and eager nature, while I sat opposite to him, and we listened in silence to the strange story which our visitor detailed to us.

"You must know," said he, "that I am an orphan and a bachelor, residing alone in lodgings in London. By profession I am a hydraulic engineer, and I have had considerable experience of my work during the seven years that I was apprenticed to Venner and Matheson, the well-known firm, of Greenwich. Two years ago, having served my time, and having also come into a fair sum of money through my poor father's death, I determined to start in business for myself, and took professional chambers in Victoria-street.

"I suppose that everyone finds his first independent start in business a dreary experience. To me it has been exceptionally so. During two years I have had three consultations and one small job, and that is absolutely all that my profession has brought me. My gross takings amount to twenty-seven pounds ten. Every day, from nine in the morning until four in the afternoon, I waited in my little den, until at last my heart began to sink, and I came to believe that I should never have any practice at all.

"Yesterday, however, just as I was thinking of leaving the office, my clerk entered

"COLONEL LYSANDER STARK."

to say there was a gentleman waiting who wished to see me upon business. He brought up a card, too, with the name of "Colonel Lysander Stark" engraved upon it. Close at his heels came the Colonel himself, a man rather over the middle size but of an exceeding thinness. I do not think that I have ever seen so thin a man. His whole face sharpened away into nose and chin, and the skin of his cheeks was drawn quite tense over his outstanding bones. Yet this emaciation seemed to be his natural habit, and due to no disease, for his eye was bright, his step brisk, and his bearing assured. He was plainly but neatly dressed, and his age, I should judge, would be nearer forty than thirty.

"'Mr. Hatherley?' said he, with something of a German accent. 'You have been recommended to me, Mr. Hatherley, as being a man who is not only proficient in his profession, but is also discreet and capable of preserving a secret.'

"I bowed, feeling as flattered as any young man would at such an address. 'May I ask who it was who gave me so good a character?' I asked.

"'Well, perhaps it is better that I should not tell you that just at this moment. I have it from the same source that you are both an orphan and a bachelor, and are residing alone in London.'

"'That is quite correct,' I answered, 'but you will excuse me if I say that I cannot see how all this bears upon my professional qualifications. I understood that it was on a professional matter that you wished to speak to me?'

"'Undoubtedly so. But you will find that all I say is really to the point. I have a professional commission for you, but absolute secrecy is quite essential—*absolute* secrecy, you understand, and of course we may expect that more from a man who is alone than from one who lives in the bosom of his family.'

"'If I promise to keep a secret,' said I, 'you may absolutely depend upon my doing so.'

"He looked very hard at me as I spoke, and it seemed to me that I had never seen so suspicious and questioning an eye.

"'You do promise, then?' said he at last.

"'Yes, I promise.'

"'Absolute and complete silence, before, during, and after? No reference to the matter at all, either in word or writing?'

"'I have already given you my word.'

"'Very good.' He suddenly sprang up,

and darting like lightning across the room he flung open the door. The passage outside was empty.

"'That's all right,' said he, coming back. 'I know that clerks are sometimes curious as to their master's affairs. Now we can talk in safety.' He drew up his chair very close to mine, and began to stare at me again with the same questioning and thoughtful look.

"A feeling of repulsion, and of something akin to fear had begun to rise within me at the strange antics of this fleshless man. Even my dread of losing a client could not restrain me from showing my impatience.

"'I beg that you will state your business, sir,' said I; 'my time is of value.' Heaven forgive me for that last sentence, but the words came to my lips.

"'How would fifty guineas for a night's work suit you?' he asked.

"'Most admirably.'

"'I say a night's work, but an hour's would be nearer the mark. I simply want your opinion about a hydraulic stamping machine which has got out of gear. If you show us what is wrong we shall soon set it right ourselves. What do you think of such a commission as that?'

"'The work appears to be light, and the pay munificent.'

"'Precisely so. We shall want you to come to-night by the last train.'

"'Where to?'

"'To Eyford, in Berkshire. It is a little place near the borders of Oxfordshire, and within seven miles of Reading. There is a train from Paddington which would bring you in there at about eleven fifteen.'

"'Very good.'

"'I shall come down in a carriage to meet you.'

"'There is a drive, then?'

"'Yes, our little place is quite out in the country. It is a good seven miles from Eyford Station.'

"'Then we can hardly get there before midnight. I suppose there would be no chance of a train back. I should be compelled to stop the night.'

"'Yes, we could easily give you a shake-down.'

"'That is very awkward. Could I not come at some more convenient hour?'

"'We have judged it best that you should come late. It is to recompense you for any inconvenience that we are paying to you, a young and unknown man, a fee which would buy an opinion from the very heads of your profession. Still, of course, if you would like to draw out of the business, there is plenty of time to do so.'

"I thought of the fifty guineas, and of how very useful they would be to me. 'Not at all,' said I, 'I shall be very happy to accommodate myself to your wishes. I should like, however, to understand a little more clearly what it is that you wish me to do.'

"'Quite so. It is very natural that the pledge of secrecy which we have exacted from you should have aroused your curiosity. I have no wish to commit you to anything without your having it all laid before you. I suppose that we are absolutely safe from eavesdroppers?'

"'Entirely.'

"'Then the matter stands thus. You are probably aware that fuller's earth is a valuable product, and that it is only found in one or two places in England?'

"'I have heard so.'

"Some little time ago I bought a small place—a very small place—within ten miles of Reading. I was fortunate enough to discover that there was a deposit of fuller's earth in one of my fields. On examining it, however, I found that this deposit was a comparatively small one, and that it formed a link between two very much larger ones upon the right and the left—both of them, however, in the grounds of my neighbours. These good people were absolutely ignorant that their land contained that which was quite as valuable as a gold mine. Naturally, it was to my interest to buy their land before they discovered its true value; but, unfortunately, I had no capital by which I could do this. I took a few of my friends into the secret, however, and they suggested that we should quietly and secretly work our own little deposit, and that in this way we should earn the money which would enable us to buy the neighbouring fields. This we have now been doing for some time, and in order to help us in our operations we erected a hydraulic press. This press, as I have already explained, has got out of order, and we wish your advice upon the subject. We guard our secret very jealously, however, and if it once became known that we had hydraulic engineers coming to our little house, it would soon rouse inquiry, and then, if the facts came out, it would be good-bye to any chance of getting these fields and carrying out our plans. That is why I have made you promise me that you will not tell a human being that you are going to Eyford to-night. I hope that I make it all plain?'

"'I quite follow you,' said I. 'The only point which I could not quite understand, was what use you could make of a hydraulic press in excavating fuller's earth, which, as I understand, is dug out like gravel from a pit.'

"'Ah!' said he, carelessly, 'we have our own process. We compress the earth into bricks, so as to remove them without revealing what they are. But that is a mere detail. I have taken you fully into my confidence now, Mr. Hatherley, and I have shown you how I trust you.' He rose as he spoke. 'I shall expect you, then, at Eyford at 11.15.'

"'I shall certainly be there.'

"'NOT A WORD TO A SOUL!'"

"'And not a word to a soul.' He looked at me with a last long, questioning gaze, and then, pressing my hand in a cold, dank grasp, he hurried from the room.

"Well, when I came to think it all over in cool blood I was very much astonished, as you may both think, at this sudden commission which had been entrusted to me. On the one hand, of course, I was glad, for the fee was at least tenfold what I should have asked had I set a price upon my own services, and it was possible that this order might lead to other ones. On the other hand, the face and manner of my patron had made an unpleasant impression upon me, and I could not think that his explanation of the fuller's earth was sufficient to explain the necessity for my coming at midnight, and his extreme anxiety lest I should tell anyone of my errand. However, I threw all fears to the winds, ate a hearty supper, drove to Paddington, and started off, having obeyed to the letter the injunction as to holding my tongue.

"At Reading I had to change not only my carriage but my station. However, I was in time for the last train to Eyford, and I reached the little dim lit station after eleven o'clock. I was the only passenger who got out there, and there was no one upon the platform save a single sleepy porter with a lantern. As I passed out through the wicket gate, however, I found my acquaintance of the morning waiting in the shadow upon the other side. Without a word he grasped my arm and hurried me into a carriage, the door of which was standing open. He drew up the windows on either side, tapped on the woodwork, and away we went as hard as the horse could go."

"One horse?" interjected Holmes.

"Yes, only one."

"Did you observe the colour?"

U

" Yes, I saw it by the sidelights when I was stepping into the carriage. It was a chestnut."

" Tired-looking or fresh ? "

" Oh, fresh and glossy."

" Thank you. I am sorry to have interrupted you. Pray continue your most interesting statement."

" Away we went then, and we drove for at least an hour. Colonel Lysander Stark had said that it was only seven miles, but I should think, from the rate that we seemed to go, and from the time that we took, that it must have been nearer twelve. He sat at my side in silence all the time, and I was aware, more than once when I glanced in his direction, that he was looking at me with great intensity. The country roads seem to be not very good in that part of the world, for we lurched and jolted terribly. I tried to look out of the windows to see something of where we were, but they were made of frosted glass, and I could make out nothing save the occasional bright blurr of a passing light. Now and then I hazarded some remark to break the monotony of the journey, but the Colonel answered only in monosyllables, and the conversation soon flagged. At last, however, the bumping of the road was exchanged for the crisp smoothness of a gravel drive, and the carriage came to a stand. Colonel Lysander Stark sprang out, and, as I followed after him, pulled me swiftly into a porch which gaped in front of us. We stepped, as it were, right out of the carriage and into the hall, so that I failed to catch the most fleeting glance of the front of the house. The instant that I had crossed the threshold the door slammed heavily behind us, and I heard faintly the rattle of the wheels as the carriage drove away.

" It was pitch dark inside the house, and the Colonel fumbled about looking for matches, and muttering under his breath. Suddenly a door opened at the other end of the passage, and a long, golden bar of light shot out in our direction. It grew broader, and a woman appeared with a lamp in her hand, which she held above her head, pushing her face forward and peering at us. I could see that she was pretty, and from the gloss with which the light shone upon her dark dress I knew that it was a rich material. She spoke a few words in a foreign tongue in a tone as though asking a question, and when my companion answered in a gruff monosyllable she gave such a start that the lamp nearly fell from her

hand. Colonel Stark went up to her, whispered something in her ear, and then, pushing her back into the room from whence she had come, he walked towards me again with the lamp in his hand.

" ' Perhaps you will have the kindness to wait in this room for a few minutes,' said he, throwing open another door. It was a quiet little, plainly furnished room, with a round table in the centre, on which several German books were scattered. Colonel Stark laid down the lamp on the top of a harmonium beside the door. ' I shall not keep you waiting an instant,' said he, and vanished into the darkness.

" I glanced at the books upon the table, and in spite of my ignorance of German I could see that two of them were treatises on science, the others being volumes of poetry. Then I walked across to the window, hoping that I might catch some glimpse of the country side, but an oak shutter, heavily barred, was folded across it. It was a wonderfully silent house. There was an old clock ticking loudly somewhere in the passage, but otherwise everything was deadly still. A vague feeling of uneasiness began to steal over me. Who were these German people, and what were they doing, living in this strange, out-of-the-way place ? And where was the place ? I was ten miles or so from Eyford, that was all I knew, but whether north, south, east, or west I had no idea. For that matter, Reading, and possibly other large towns, were within that radius, so the place might not be so secluded after all. Yet it was quite certain from the absolute stillness that we were in the country. I paced up and down the room, humming a tune under my breath to keep up my spirits, and feeling that I was thoroughly earning my fifty-guinea fee.

" Suddenly, without any preliminary sound in the midst of the utter stillness, the door of my room swung slowly open. The woman was standing in the aperture, the darkness of the hall behind her, the yellow light from my lamp beating upon her eager and beautiful face. I could see at a glance that she was sick with fear, and the sight sent a chill to my own heart. She held up one shaking finger to warn me to be silent, and she shot a few whispered words of broken English at me, her eyes glancing back, like those of a frightened horse, into the gloom behind her.

" ' I would go,' said she, trying hard, as it seemed to me, to speak calmly ; ' I would go. I should not stay here. There is no good for you to do.'

" 'But, madam,' said I, 'I have not yet done what I came for. I cannot possibly leave until I have seen the machine.'

" 'It is not worth your while to wait,' she went on. 'You can pass through the door ; no one hinders.' And then, seeing that I smiled and shook my head, she suddenly threw aside her constraint, and made a step forward, with her hands wrung together. 'For the love of Heaven !' she

" 'GET AWAY FROM HERE BEFORE IT IS TOO LATE.' "

whispered, ' get away from here before it is too late !'

"But I am somewhat headstrong by nature, and the more ready to engage in an affair when there is some obstacle in the way. I thought of my fifty-guinea fee, of my wearisome journey, and of the unpleasant night which seemed to be before me. Was it all to go for nothing ? Why should I slink away without having carried out my commission, and without the payment which was my due ? This woman

might, for all I knew, be a monomaniac. With a stout bearing, therefore, though her manner had shaken me more than I cared to confess, I still shook my head, and declared my intention of remaining where I was. She was about to renew her entreaties when a door slammed overhead, and the sound of several footsteps were heard upon the stairs. She listened for an instant, threw up her hands with a despairing gesture, and vanished as suddenly and as noiselessly as she had come.

"The newcomers were Colonel Lysander Stark, and a short thick man with a chinchilla beard growing out of the creases of his double chin, who was introduced to me as Mr. Ferguson.

" 'This is my secretary and manager,' said the Colonel. 'By the way, I was under the impression that I left this door shut just now. I fear that you have felt the draught.'

" 'On the contrary,' said I, 'I opened the door myself, because I felt the room to be a little close.'

"He shot one of his suspicious glances at me. 'Perhaps we had better proceed to business, then,' said he. 'Mr. Ferguson and I will take you up to see the machine.'

" 'I had better put my hat on, I suppose.'

" 'Oh no, it is in the house.'

" 'What, you dig fuller's earth in the house ?'

" 'No, no. This is only where we compress it. But never mind that ! All we wish you to do is to examine the machine, and to let us know what is wrong with it.'

"We went upstairs together, the Colonel first with the lamp, the fat manager, and I behind him. It was a labyrinth of an old house, with corridors, passages, narrow winding staircases, and little low doors, the thresholds of which were hollowed out by the generations who had crossed them. There were no carpets, and no signs of any furniture above the ground floor, while the plaster was peeling off the walls, and the damp was breaking through in green, unhealthy blotches. I tried to put on as unconcerned an air as possible, but I had not forgotten the warnings of the lady, even though I disregarded them, and I kept a keen eye upon my two companions. Ferguson appeared to be a morose and silent man, but I could see from the little that he said that he was at least a fellow-countryman.

"Colonel Lysander Stark stopped at last before a low door, which he unlocked. Within was a small square room, in which the three of us could hardly get at one time. Ferguson remained outside, and the Colonel ushered me in.

"'We are now,' said he, 'actually within the hydraulic press, and it would be a particularly unpleasant thing for us if any-one were to turn it on. The ceiling of this small chamber is really the end of the descending piston, and it comes down with the force of many tons upon this metal floor. There are small lateral columns of water outside which receive the force, and which transmit and multiply it in the manner which is familiar to you. The machine goes readily enough, but there is some stiffness in the working of it, and it has lost a little of its force. Perhaps you will have the goodness to look it over, and to show us how we can set it right.'

"I took the lamp from him, and I examined the machine very thoroughly. It was indeed a gigantic one, and capable of exercising enormous pressure. When I passed outside, however, and pressed down the levers which controlled it, I knew at once by the whishing sound that there was a slight leakage, which allowed a regurgitation of water through one of the side cylinders. An examination showed that one of the indiarubber bands which was round the head of a driving rod had shrunk so as not quite to fill the socket along which it worked. This was clearly the cause of the loss of power, and I pointed it out to my companions, who followed my remarks very carefully, and asked several practical questions as to how they should proceed to set it right. When I had made it clear to them, I returned to the main chamber of the machine, and took a good look at it to satisfy my own curiosity. It was obvious at a glance that the story of the fuller's earth was the merest fabrication, for it would be absurd to suppose

that so powerful an engine could be designed for so inadequate a purpose. The walls were of wood, but the floor consisted of a large iron trough, and when I came to examine it I could see a crust of metallic deposit all over it. I had stooped and was scraping at this to see exactly what it was, when I heard a muttered exclamation in German, and saw the cadaverous face of the Colonel looking down at me.

"'What are you doing there?' he asked.

"I felt angry at having been tricked by so elaborate a story as that which he had told me. 'I was admiring your fuller's earth,' said I; 'I think that I should be better able to advise you as to your machine if I knew what the exact purpose was for which it was used.'

"The instant that I uttered the words I regretted the rashness of my speech. His face set hard, and a baleful light sprang up in his grey eyes.

"'Very well,' said he, 'you shall know all about the machine.' He took a step

"I RUSHED TO THE DOOR."

backward, slammed the little door, and turned the key in the lock. I rushed towards it and pulled at the handle, but it was quite secure, and did not give in the least to my kicks and shoves. 'Hullo!' I yelled. 'Hullo! Colonel! Let me out!'

"And then suddenly in the silence I heard a sound which sent my heart into my mouth. It was the clank of the levers, and the swish of the leaking cylinder. He had set the engine at work. The lamp still stood upon the floor where I had placed it when examining the trough. By its light I saw that the black ceiling was coming down upon me, slowly, jerkily, but, as none knew better than myself, with a force which must within a minute grind me to a shapeless pulp. I threw myself, scream-ing, against the door, and dragged with my nails at the lock. I implored the Colonel to let me out, but the remorseless clanking of the levers drowned my cries. The ceil-ing was only a foot or two above my head, and with my hand uplifted I could feel its hard, rough surface. Then it flashed through my mind that the pain of my death would depend very much upon the position in which I met it. If I lay on my face the weight would come upon my spine, and I shuddered to think of that dreadful snap. Easier the other way, perhaps, and yet had I the nerve to lie and look up at that deadly black shadow wavering down upon me? Already I was unable to stand erect, when my heart caught something which brought a gush of hope back to my heart.

"I have said that though floor and ceil-ing were of iron, the walls were of wood. As I gave a last hurried glance around, I saw a thin line of yellow light between two of the boards, which broadened and broad-ened as a small panel was pushed backwards. For an instant I could hardly believe that here was indeed a door which led away from death. The next I threw myself through, and lay half-fainting upon the other side. The panel had closed again behind me, but the crash of the lamp, and a few moments afterwards the clang of the two slabs of metal, told me how narrow had been my escape.

"I was recalled to myself by a frantic plucking at my wrist, and I found myself lying upon the stone floor of a narrow corridor, while a woman bent over me and tugged at me with her left hand, while she held a candle in her right. It was the same good friend whose warning I had so foolishly rejected.

"'Come! come!' she cried, breath-lessly. 'They will be here in a moment. They will see that you are not there. Oh, do not waste the so precious time, but come!'

"This time, at least, I did not scorn her advice. I staggered to my feet, and ran with her along the corridor and down a winding stair. The latter led to another broad passage, and, just as we reached it, we heard the sound of running feet, and the shouting of two voices—one answering the other—from the floor on which we were, and from the one beneath. My guide stopped, and looked about her like one who is at her wits' end. Then she threw open a door which led into a bedroom, through the window of which the moon was shining brightly.

"'It is your only chance,' said she. 'It is high, but it may be that you can jump it.'

"As she spoke a light sprang into view at the further end of the passage, and I saw the lean figure of Colonel Lysander Stark rushing forward with a lantern in one hand, and a weapon like a butcher's cleaver in the other. I rushed across the bedroom, flung open the window, and looked out. How quiet and sweet and wholesome the garden looked in the moonlight, and it could not be more than thirty feet down. I clambered out upon the sill, but I hesitated to jump, until I should have heard what passed between my saviour and the ruffian who pursued me. If she were ill-used, then at any risks I was determined to go back to her assistance. The thought had hardly flashed through my mind before he was at the door, pushing his way past her; but she threw her arms round him, and tried to hold him back.

"'Fritz! Fritz!' she cried in English, 'remember your promise after the last time. You said it should not be again. He will be silent! Oh, he will be silent!'

"'You are mad, Elise!' he shouted, struggling to break away from her. 'You will be the ruin of us. He has seen too much. Let me pass, I say!' He dashed her to one side, and, rushing to the win-dow, cut at me with his heavy weapon. I had let myself go, and was hanging by the hands to the sill, when his blow fell. I was conscious of a dull pain, my grip loosened, and I fell into the garden below.

"I was shaken, but not hurt by the fall; so I picked myself up, and rushed off among the bushes as hard as I could run, for I

"'HE CUT AT ME.'"

sprang to my feet with the feeling that I might hardly yet be safe from my pursuers. But, to my astonishment, when I came to look round me, neither house nor garden were to be seen. I had been lying in an angle of the hedge close by the high road, and just a little lower down was a long building, which proved, upon my approaching it, to be the very station at which I had arrived upon the previous night. Were it not for the ugly wound upon my hand, all that had passed during those dreadful hours might have been an evil dream.

"Half dazed, I went into the station, and asked about the morning train. There would be one to Reading in less than an hour. The same porter was on duty, I found, as had been there when I arrived. I inquired from him whether he had ever heard of Colonel Lysander Stark. The name was strange to him. Had he observed a carriage the night before waiting for me? No, he had not. Was there a police station anywhere near? There was one about three miles off.

"It was too far for me to go, weak and ill as I was. I determined to wait until I got back to town before telling my story to the police. It was a little past six when I arrived, so I went first to have my wound dressed, and then the doctor was kind enough to bring me along here. I put the case into your hands, and shall do exactly what you advise."

We both sat in silence for some little time after, listening to this extraordinary narrative. Then Sherlock Holmes pulled down from the shelf one of the ponderous commonplace books in which he placed his cuttings.

"Here is an advertisement which will interest you," said he. "It appeared in all the papers about a year ago. Listen to this :—'Lost, on the 9th inst., Mr. Jeremiah Hayling, aged 26, a hydraulic engineer. Left his lodgings at ten o'clock at night, and has not been heard of since. Was dressed in,' &c., &c. Ha! That represents the last time that the Colonel needed to have his machine overhauled, I fancy."

"Good heavens!" cried my patient. "Then that explains what the girl said."

understood that I was far from being out of danger yet. Suddenly, however, as I ran, a deadly dizziness and sickness came over me. I glanced down at my hand, which was throbbing painfully, and then, for the first time, saw that my thumb had been cut off, and that the blood was pouring from my wound. I endeavoured to tie my handkerchief round it, but there came a sudden buzzing in my ears, and next moment I fell in a dead faint among the rose-bushes.

"How long I remained unconscious I cannot tell. It must have been a very long time, for the moon had sunk, and a bright morning was breaking when I came to myself. My clothes were all sodden with dew, and my coat-sleeve was drenched with blood from my wounded thumb. The smarting of it recalled in an instant all the particulars of my night's adventure, and I

" Undoubtedly. It is quite clear that the Colonel was a cool and desperate man, who was absolutely determined that nothing should stand in the way of his little game, like those out-and-out pirates who will leave no survivor from a captured ship. Well, every moment now is precious, so, if you feel equal to it, we shall go down to Scotland Yard at once as a preliminary to starting for Eyford."

Some three hours or so afterwards we were all in the train together, bound from Reading to the little Berkshire village. There were Sherlock Holmes, the hydraulic engineer, Inspector Bradstreet of Scotland-yard, a plain-clothes man, and myself. Bradstreet had spread an ordnance map of the county out upon the seat, and was busy with his compasses drawing a circle with Eyford for its centre.

" There you are," said he. " That circle is drawn at a radius of ten miles from the village. The place we want must be somewhere near that line. You said ten miles, I think, sir ? "

" It was an hour's good drive."

" And you think that they brought you back all that way when you were unconscious ? "

" They must have done so. I have a confused memory, too, of having been lifted and conveyed somewhere."

" What I cannot understand," said I, " is why they should have spared you when they found you lying fainting in the garden. Perhaps the villain was softened by the woman's entreaties."

" I hardly think that likely. I never saw a more inexorable face in my life."

" Oh, we shall soon clear up all that," said Bradstreet. " Well, I have drawn my circle, and I only wish I knew at what point upon it the folk that we are in search of are to be found."

" I think I could lay my finger on it," said Holmes, quietly.

" Really, now ! " cried the Inspector, " you have formed your opinion ! Come now, we shall see who agrees with you. I say it is south, for the country is more deserted there."

" And I say east," said my patient.

" I am for west," remarked the plain-clothes man. " There are several quiet little villages up there."

" And I am for north," said I ; " because there are no hills there, and our friend says that he did not notice the carriage go up any."

" Come," cried the Inspector, laughing ;

" it's a very pretty diversity of opinion. We have boxed the compass among us. Who do you give your casting vote to ? "

" You are all wrong."

" But we can't *all* be."

" Oh yes, you can. This is my point," he placed his finger in the centre of the circle. " This is where we shall find them."

" But the twelve-mile drive ? " gasped Hatherley.

" Six out and six back. Nothing simpler. You say yourself that the horse was fresh and glossy when you got in. How could it be that, if it had gone twelve miles over heavy roads ? "

" Indeed it is a likely ruse enough," observed Bradstreet, thoughtfully. " Of course there can be no doubt as to the nature of this gang."

" None at all," said Holmes. " They are coiners on a large scale, and have used the machine to form the amalgam which has taken the place of silver."

" We have known for some time that a clever gang was at work," said the Inspector. " They have been turning out half-crowns by the thousand. We even traced them as far as Reading, but could get no further ; for they had covered their traces in a way that showed that they were very old hands. But now, thanks to this lucky chance, I think that we have got them right enough."

But the Inspector was mistaken, for those criminals were not destined to fall into the hands of justice. As we rolled into Eyford Station we saw a gigantic column of smoke which streamed up from behind a small clump of trees in the neighbourhood, and hung like an immense ostrich feather over the landscape.

" A house on fire ? " asked Bradstreet, as the train steamed off again on its way.

" Yes, sir ! " said the station-master.

" When did it break out ? "

" I hear that it was during the night, sir, but it has got worse, and the whole place is in a blaze."

" Whose house is it ? "

" Dr. Becher's."

" Tell me," broke in the engineer, " is Dr. Becher a German, very thin, with a long sharp nose ? "

The station-master laughed heartily. " No, sir, Dr. Becher is an Englishman, and there isn't a man in the parish who has a better-lined waistcoat. But he has a gentleman staying with him, a patient, as I understand, who is a foreigner, and he looks as if a little good Berkshire beef would do him no harm."

The station-master had not finished his speech before we were all hastening in the direction of the fire. The road topped a low hill, and there was a great widespread white-washed building in front of us, spouting fire at every chink and window, while in the garden in

"A HOUSE ON FIRE?"

front three fire-engines were vainly striving to keep the flames under.

"That's it!" cried Hatherley, in intense excitement. "There is the gravel drive, and there are the rose-bushes where I lay. That second window is the one that I jumped from."

"Well, at least," said Holmes, "you have had your revenge upon them. There can be no question that it was your oil lamp which, when it was crushed in the press, set fire to the wooden walls, though no doubt they were too excited in the chase after you to observe it at the time. Now keep your eyes open in this crowd for your friends of last night, though I very much fear that they are a good hundred miles off by now."

And Holmes' fears came to be realised, for from that day to this no word has ever been heard either of the beautiful woman, the sinister German, or the morose Englishman. Early that morning a peasant had

met a cart containing several people and some very bulky boxes driving rapidly in the direction of Reading, but there all traces of the fugitives disappeared, and even Holmes' ingenuity failed ever to discover the least clue as to their whereabouts.

The firemen had been much perturbed at the strange arrangements which they had found within, and still more so by discovering a newly severed human thumb upon a window-sill of the second floor. About sunset, however, their efforts were at last successful, and they subdued the flames, but not before the roof had fallen in, and the whole place been reduced to such absolute ruin that, save some twisted cylinders and iron piping, not a trace remained of the machinery which had cost our unfortunate acquaintance so dearly. Large masses of nickel and of tin were discovered stored in an outhouse, but no coins were to be found, which may have explained the presence of those bulky boxes which have been already referred to.

How our hydraulic engineer had been conveyed from the garden to the spot where he recovered his senses might have remained for ever a mystery were it not for the soft mould, which told us a very plain tale. He had evidently been carried down by two persons, one of whom had remarkably small feet and the other unusually large ones. On the whole, it was most probable that the silent Englishman, being less bold or less murderous than his companion, had assisted the woman to bear the unconscious man out of the way of danger.

"Well," said our engineer ruefully, as we took our seats to return once more to London, "it has been a pretty business for me! I have lost my thumb, and I have lost a fifty-guinea fee, and what have I gained?"

"Experience," said Holmes laughing. "Indirectly it may be of value, you know; you have only to put it into words to gain the reputation of being excellent company for the remainder of your existence."

# Adventures of Sherlock Holmes.

## X.—THE ADVENTURE OF THE NOBLE BACHELOR.

### By A. Conan Doyle.

THE Lord St. Simon marriage, and its curious termination, have long ceased to be a subject of interest in those exalted circles in which the unfortunate bridegroom moves. Fresh scandals have eclipsed it, and their more piquant details have drawn the gossips away from this four-year-old drama. As I have reason to believe, however, that the full facts have never been revealed to the general public, and as my friend Sherlock Holmes had a considerable share in clearing the matter up, I feel that no memoir of him would be complete without some little sketch of this remarkable episode.

It was a few weeks before my own marriage, during the days when I was still sharing rooms with Holmes in Baker-street, that he came home from an afternoon stroll to find a letter on the table waiting for him. I had remained indoors all day, for the weather had taken a sudden turn to rain, with high autumnal winds, and the jezail bullet which I had brought back in one of my limbs as a relic of my Afghan campaign, throbbed with dull persistency. With my body in one easy chair and my legs upon another, I had surrounded myself with a cloud of newspapers, until at last, saturated with the news of the day, I tossed them all aside and lay listless, watching the huge crest and monogram upon the envelope upon the table, and wondering lazily who my friend's noble correspondent could be.

"Here is a very fashionable epistle," I remarked as he entered. "Your morning letters, if I remember right, were from a fishmonger and a tide waiter."

"Yes, my correspondence has certainly the charm of variety," he answered, smiling, "and the humbler are usually the more interesting. This looks like one of those

"HE BROKE THE SEAL AND GLANCED OVER THE CONTENTS."

unwelcome social summonses which call
upon a man either to be bored or to lie."

He broke the seal, and glanced over the
contents.

"Oh, come, it may prove to be something of interest after all."

"Not social, then?"

"No, distinctly professional."

"And from a noble client?"

"One of the highest in England."

"My dear fellow, I congratulate you."

"I assure you, Watson, without affecta-
tion, that the status of my client is a
matter of less moment to me than the
interest of his case. It is just possible,
however, that that also may not be wanting
in this new investigation. You have been
reading the papers diligently of late, have
you not?"

"It looks like it," said I, ruefully, pointing to a huge bundle in the corner. "I
have had nothing else to do."

"It is fortunate, for you will perhaps be
able to post me up. I read nothing except
the criminal news and the agony column.
The latter is always instructive. But if you
have followed recent events so closely you
must have read about Lord St. Simon and
his wedding?"

"Oh, yes, with the deepest interest."

"That is well. The letter which I hold
in my hand is from Lord St. Simon. I
will read it to you, and in return you must
turn over these papers and let me have
whatever bears upon the matter. This is
what he says :—

"'My dear Mr. Sherlock Holmes,—Lord
Backwater tells me that I may place implicit
reliance upon your judgment and discretion. I have determined, therefore, to call
upon you, and to consult you in reference
to the very painful event which has occurred
in connection with my wedding. Mr.
Lestrade, of Scotland Yard, is acting
already in the matter, but he assures me
that he sees no objection to your co-operation, and that he even thinks that it might
be of some assistance. I will call at four
o'clock in the afternoon, and, should you
have any other engagement at that time, I
hope that you will postpone it, as this
matter is of paramount importance.—
Yours faithfully,            ST. SIMON.'

"It is dated from Grosvenor Mansions,
written with a quill pen, and the noble lord
has had the misfortune to get a smear of
ink upon the outer side of his right little
finger," remarked Holmes, as he folded up
the epistle.

"He says four o'clock. It is three now.
He will be here in an hour."

"Then I have just time, with your assistance, to get clear upon the subject. Turn
over those papers, and arrange the extracts
in their order of time, while I take a glance
as to who our client is." He picked a red-
covered volume from a line of books of
reference beside the mantelpiece. "Here
he is," said he, sitting down and flattening it
out upon his knee. "Lord Robert Walsing-
ham de Vere St. Simon, second son of the
Duke of Balmoral—Hum! Arms: Azure,
three caltrops in chief over a fess sable.
Born in 1846. He's forty-one years of age,
which is mature for marriage. Was Under-
Secretary for the Colonies in a late Administration. The Duke, his father, was at
one time Secretary for Foreign Affairs.
They inherit Plantagenet blood by direct
descent, and Tudor on the distaff side. Ha!
Well, there is nothing very instructive in
all this. I think that I must turn to you,
Watson, for something more solid."

"I have very little difficulty in finding
what I want," said I, "for the facts are
quite recent, and the matter struck me as
remarkable. I feared to refer them to you,
however, as I knew that you had an inquiry
on hand, and that you disliked the intrusion
of other matters."

"Oh, you mean the little problem of the
Grosvenor-square furniture van. That is
quite cleared up now—though, indeed, it
was obvious from the first. Pray give me
the results of your newspaper selections."

"Here is the first notice which I can
find. It is in the personal column of *The
Morning Post*, and dates, as you see, some
weeks back. 'A marriage has been arranged,'
it says, 'and will, if rumour is correct, very
shortly take place, between Lord Robert
St. Simon, second son of the Duke of
Balmoral, and Miss Hatty Doran, the only
daughter of Aloysius Doran, Esq., of San
Francisco, Cal., U.S.A.' That is all."

"Terse and to the point," remarked
Holmes, stretching his long, thin legs
towards the fire.

"There was a paragraph amplifying this
in one of the society papers of the same
week. Ah, here it is. 'There will soon
be a call for protection in the marriage
market, for the present free-trade principle
appears to tell heavily against our home
product. One by one the management of
the noble houses of Great Britain is passing
into the hands of our fair cousins from
across the Atlantic. An important addi-

tion has been made during the last week to the list of the prizes which have been borne away by these charming invaders. Lord St. Simon, who has shown himself for over twenty years proof against the little god's arrows, has now definitely announced his approaching marriage with Miss Hatty Doran, the fascinating daughter of a Californian millionaire. Miss Doran, whose graceful figure and striking face attracted much attention at the Westbury House festivities, is an only child, and it is currently reported that her dowry will run to considerably over the six figures, with expectancies for the future. As it is an open secret that the Duke of Balmoral has been compelled to sell his pictures within the last few years, and as Lord St. Simon has no property of his own, save the small estate of Birchmoor, it is obvious that the Californian heiress is not the only gainer by an alliance which will enable her to make the easy and common transition from a Republican lady to a British peeress.' "

"Anything else?" asked Holmes, yawning.

"Oh yes; plenty. Then there is another note in *The Morning Post* to say that the marriage would be an absolutely quiet one, that it would be at St. George's, Hanover-square, that only half a dozen intimate friends would be invited, and that the party would return to the furnished house at Lancaster-gate which has been taken by Mr. Aloysius Doran. Two days later— that is, on Wednesday last—there is a curt announcement that the wedding had taken place, and that the honeymoon would be passed at Lord Backwater's place, near Petersfield. Those are all the notices which appeared before the disappearance of the bride."

"Before the what?" asked Holmes, with a start.

"The vanishing of the lady."

"When did she vanish, then?"

"At the wedding breakfast."

"Indeed. This is more interesting than it promised to be; quite dramatic, in fact."

"Yes; it struck me as being a little out of the common."

"They often vanish before the ceremony, and occasionally during the honeymoon; but I cannot call to mind anything quite so prompt as this. Pray let me have the details."

"I warn you that they are very incomplete."

"Perhaps we may make them less so."

"Such as they are, they are set forth in a single article of a morning paper of yesterday, which I will read to you. It is headed, 'Singular Occurrence at a Fashionable Wedding':—

"'The family of Lord Robert St. Simon has been thrown into the greatest consternation by the strange and painful episodes which have taken place in connection with his wedding. The ceremony, as shortly announced in the papers of yesterday, occurred on the previous morning; but it is only now that it has been possible to confirm the strange rumours which have been so persistently floating about. In spite of the attempts of the friends to hush the matter up, so much public attention has now been drawn to it that no good purpose can be served by affecting to disregard what is a common subject for conversation.

"'The ceremony, which was performed at St. George's, Hanover-square, was a very quiet one, no one being present save the father of the bride, Mr. Aloysius Doran, the Duchess of Balmoral, Lord Backwater, Lord Eustace and Lady Clara St. Simon (the younger brother and sister of the bridegroom), and Lady Alicia Whittington. The whole party proceeded afterwards to the house of Mr. Aloysius Doran, at Lancaster Gate, where breakfast had been prepared. It appears that some little trouble was caused by a woman, whose name has not been ascertained, who endeavoured to force her way into the house after the bridal party, alleging that she had some claim upon Lord St. Simon. It was only after a painful and prolonged scene that she was ejected by the butler and the footman. The bride, who had fortunately entered the house before this unpleasant interruption, had sat down to breakfast with the rest, when she complained of a sudden indisposition, and retired to her room. Her prolonged absence having caused some comment, her father followed her; but learned from her maid that she had only come up to her chamber for an instant, caught up an ulster and bonnet, and hurried down to the passage. One of the footmen declared that he had seen a lady leave the house thus apparelled; but had refused to credit that it was his mistress, believing her to be with the company. On ascertaining that his daughter had disappeared, Mr. Aloysius Doran, in conjunction with the bridegroom, instantly put themselves into communication with the police, and very energetic inquiries are being made, which will pro-

"SHE WAS EJECTED BY THE BUTLER AND THE FOOTMAN."

she has known the bride-groom for some years. There are no further particulars, and the whole case is in your hands now —so far as it has been set forth in the public press."

"And an exceedingly interesting case it appears to be. I would not have missed it for worlds. But there is a ring at the bell, Watson, and as the clock makes it a few minutes after four, I have no doubt that this will prove to be our noble client. Do not dream of going, Watson, for I very much prefer having a witness, if only as a check to my own memory."

"Lord Robert St. Simon," announced our page boy, throwing open the door. A gentleman entered, with a pleasant, cultured face, high-nosed and pale, with something perhaps of petulance about the mouth, and with the steady, well-opened eye of a man whose pleasant lot it had ever been to com-mand and to be obeyed. His manner was brisk, and yet his general appearance gave an undue impression of age, for he had a slight forward stoop, and a little bend of the knees as he walked. His hair, too, as he swept off his very curly-brimmed hat, was grizzled round the edges, and thin upon the top. As to his dress, it was careful to the verge of foppishness, with high collar, black frock coat, white waistcoat, yellow gloves, patent-leather shoes, and light-coloured gaiters. He advanced slowly into the room, turning his head from left to right, and swinging in his right hand the cord which held his golden eye-glasses.

"Good day, Lord St. Simon," said Holmes, rising and bowing. "Pray take the basket chair. This is my friend and colleague, Dr. Watson. Draw up a little to the fire, and we shall talk this matter over."

"A most painful matter to me, as you can most readily imagine, Mr. Holmes. I have

bably result in a speedy clearing up of this very singular business. Up to a late hour last night, however, nothing had transpired as to the whereabouts of the missing lady. There are rumours of foul play in the matter, and it is said that the police have caused the arrest of the woman who had caused the original disturbance, in the belief that, from jealousy or some other motive, she may have been concerned in the strange disappearance of the bride.'"

"And is that all?"

"Only one little item in another of the morning papers, but it is a suggestive one."

"And it is?"

"That Miss Flora Millar, the lady who had caused the disturbance, has actually been arrested. It appears that she was formerly a *danseuse* at the Allegro, and that

been cut to the quick. I understand that you have already managed several delicate cases of this sort, sir, though I presume that they were hardly from the same class of society."

"No, I am descending."

"I beg pardon?"

"My last client of the sort was a king."

"Oh, really! I had no idea. And which king?"

"The King of Scandinavia."

"What! Had he lost his wife?"

"You can understand," said Holmes, suavely, "that I extend to the affairs of my other clients the same secrecy which I promise to you in yours."

"Of course! Very right! very right! I'm sure I beg pardon. As to my own case, I am ready to give you any information which may assist you in forming an opinion."

"Thank you. I have already learned all that is in the public prints, nothing more. I presume that I may take it as correct—this article, for example, as to the disappearance of the bride."

Lord St. Simon glanced over it. "Yes, it is correct, as far as it goes."

"But it needs a great deal of supplementing before anyone could offer an opinion. I think that I may arrive at my facts most directly by questioning you."

"Pray do so."

"When did you first meet Miss Hatty Doran?"

"In San Francisco, a year ago."

"You were travelling in the States?"

"Yes."

"Did you become engaged then?"

"No."

"But you were on a friendly footing?"

"I was amused by her society, and she could see that I was amused."

"LORD ROBERT ST. SIMON."

"Her father is very rich?"

"He is said to be the richest man on the Pacific slope."

"And how did he make his money?"

"In mining. He had nothing a few years ago. Then he struck gold, invested it, and came up by leaps and bounds."

"Now, what is your own impression as to the young lady's—your wife's character?"

The nobleman swung his glasses a little faster and stared down into the fire. "You see, Mr. Holmes," said he, "my wife was twenty before her father became a rich man. During that time she ran free in a mining camp, and wandered through woods or mountains, so that her education has come from Nature rather than from the schoolmaster. She is what we call in England a tomboy, with a strong nature, wild and free, unfettered by any sort of traditions. She is impetuous—volcanic, I was about to say. She is swift in making up her mind, and fearless in carrying out her resolutions. On the other hand, I would not have given her the name which I have the honour to bear" (he gave a little stately cough) "had I not thought her to be at bottom a noble woman. I believe that she is capable of heroic self-sacrifice, and that anything dishonourable would be repugnant to her."

"Have you her photograph?"

"I brought this with me." He opened a locket, and showed us the full face of a very lovely woman. It was not a photograph, but an ivory miniature, and the artist had brought out the full effect of the lustrous black hair, the large dark eyes, and the exquisite mouth. Holmes gazed long and earnestly at it. Then he closed the locket and handed it back to Lord St. Simon.

"The young lady came to London, then, and you renewed your acquaintance?"

"Yes, her father brought her over for this last London season. I met her several times, became engaged to her, and have now married her."

"She brought, I understand, a considerable dowry?"

"A fair dowry. Not more than is usual in my family."

"And this, of course, remains to you, since the marriage is a *fait accompli*?"

"I really have made no inquiries on the subject."

"Very naturally not. Did you see Miss Doran on the day before the wedding?"

"Yes."

"Was she in good spirits?"

"Never better. She kept talking of what we should do in our future lives."

"Indeed. That is very interesting. And on the morning of the wedding?"

"She was as bright as possible—at least, until after the ceremony."

"And did you observe any change in her then?"

"Well, to tell the truth, I saw then the first signs that I had ever seen that her temper was just a little sharp. The incident, however, was too trivial to relate, and can have no possible bearing upon the case."

"Pray let us have it, for all that."

"Oh, it is childish. She dropped her bouquet as we went towards the vestry. She was passing the front pew at the time, and it fell over into the pew. There was a moment's delay, but the gentleman in the pew handed it up to her again, and it did not appear to be the worse for the fall. Yet, when I spoke to her of the matter, she answered me abruptly; and in the carriage, on our way home, she seemed absurdly agitated over this trifling cause."

"Indeed. You say that there was a gentleman in the pew. Some of the general public were present, then?"

"Oh yes. It is impossible to exclude them when the church is open."

"This gentleman was not one of your wife's friends?"

"No, no; I call him a gentleman by courtesy, but he was quite a common-looking person. I hardly noticed his appearance. But really I think that we are wandering rather far from the point."

'THE GENTLEMAN IN THE PEW HANDED IT UP TO HER.'

"Lady St. Simon, then, returned from the wedding in a less cheerful frame of mind than she had gone to it. What did she do on re-entering her father's house?"

"I saw her in conversation with her maid."

"And who is her maid?"

"Alice is her name. She is an American, and came from California with her."

"A confidential servant?"

"A little too much so. It seemed to me that her mistress allowed her to take great liberties. Still, of course, in America they look upon these things in a different way."

"How long did she speak to this Alice ?"

"Oh, a few minutes. I had something else to think of."

"You did not overhear what they said ?"

"Lady St. Simon said something about 'jumping a claim.' She was accustomed to use slang of the kind. I have no idea what she meant."

"American slang is very expressive sometimes. And what did your wife do when she had finished speaking to her maid ?"

"She walked into the breakfast room."

"On your arm ?"

"No, alone. She was very independent in little matters like that. Then, after we had sat down for ten minutes or so, she rose hurriedly, muttered some words of apology, and left the room. She never came back."

"But this maid Alice, as I understand, deposes that she went to her room, covered her bride's dress with a long ulster, put on a bonnet, and went out."

"Quite so. And she was afterwards seen walking into Hyde-park in company with Flora Millar, a woman who is now in custody, and who had already made a disturbance at Mr. Doran's house that morning."

"Ah, yes. I should like a few particulars as to this young lady, and your relations to her."

Lord St. Simon shrugged his shoulders, and raised his eyebrows. "We have been on a friendly footing for some years—I may say on a *very* friendly footing. She used to be at the Allegro. I have not treated her ungenerously, and she has no just cause of complaint against me, but you know what women are, Mr. Holmes. Flora was a dear little thing, but exceedingly hot-headed, and devotedly attached to me. She wrote me dreadful letters when she heard that I was about to be married, and to tell the truth the reason why I had the marriage celebrated so quietly was that I feared lest there might be a scandal in the church. She came to Mr. Doran's door just after we returned, and she endeavoured to push her way in, uttering very abusive expressions towards my wife, and even threatening her, but I had foreseen the possibility of something of the sort, and I had two police fellows there in private clothes, who soon pushed her out again. She was quiet when she saw that there was no good in making a row."

"Did your wife hear all this ?"

"No, thank goodness, she did not."

"And she was seen walking with this very woman afterwards ?"

"Yes. That is what Mr. Lestrade, of Scotland Yard, looks upon as so serious. It is thought that Flora decoyed my wife out, and laid some terrible trap for her."

"Well, it is a possible supposition."

"You think so, too ?"

"I did not say a probable one. But you do not yourself look upon this as likely ?"

"I do not think Flora would hurt a fly."

"Still, jealousy is a strange transformer of characters. Pray what is your own theory as to what took place ?"

"Well, really, I came to seek a theory, not to propound one. I have given you all the facts. Since you ask me, however, I may say that it has occurred to me as possible that the excitement of this affair, the consciousness that she had made so immense a social stride, had the effect of causing some little nervous disturbance in my wife."

"In short, that she had become suddenly deranged ?"

"Well, really, when I consider that she has turned her back—I will not say upon me, but upon so much that many have aspired to without success—I can hardly explain it in any other fashion."

"Well, certainly that is also a conceivable hypothesis," said Holmes, smiling. "And now, Lord St. Simon, I think that I have nearly all my data. May I ask whether you were seated at the breakfast-table so that you could see out of the window ?"

"We could see the other side of the road, and the Park."

"Quite so. Then I do not think that I need detain you longer. I shall communicate with you."

"Should you be fortunate enough to solve this problem," said our client, rising.

"I have solved it."

"Eh ? What was that ?"

"I say that I have solved it."

"Where, then, is my wife ?"

"That is a detail which I shall speedily supply."

Lord St. Simon shook his head. "I am afraid that it will take wiser heads than yours or mine," he remarked, and bowing in a stately, old-fashioned manner, he departed.

"It is very good of Lord St. Simon to honour my head by putting it on a level with his own," said Sherlock Holmes, laughing. "I think that I shall have a whisky and soda and a cigar after all this cross-questioning. I had formed my conclusions as to the case before our client came into the room."

"My dear Holmes!"

"I have notes of several similar cases, though none, as I remarked before, which were quite as prompt. My whole examination served to turn my conjecture into a certainty. Circumstantial evidence is occasionally very convincing, as when you find a trout in the milk, to quote Thoreau's example."

"But I have heard all that you have heard."

"Without, however, the knowledge of pre-existing cases which serves me so well. There was a parallel instance in Aberdeen some years back, and something on very much the same lines at Munich the year after the Franco-Prussian war. It is one of these cases — but hullo, here is Lestrade! Good afternoon, Lestrade! You will find an extra tumbler upon the sideboard, and there are cigars in the box."

The official detective was attired in a pea-jacket and cravat, which gave him a decidedly nautical appearance, and he carried a black canvas bag in his hand. With a short greeting he seated himself, and lit the cigar which had been offered to him.

"What's up, then?" asked Holmes, with a twinkle in his eye. "You look dissatisfied."

"And I feel dissatisfied. It is this infernal St. Simon marriage case. I can make neither head nor tail of the business."

"Really! You surprise me."

"Who ever heard of such a mixed affair? Every clue seems to slip through my fingers. I have been at work upon it all day."

"And very wet it seems to have made you," said Holmes, laying his hand upon the arm of the pea-jacket.

"Yes, I have been dragging the Serpentine."

"In heaven's name, what for?"

"In search of the body of Lady St. Simon."

Sherlock Holmes leaned back in his chair and laughed heartily.

"Have you dragged the basin of the Trafalgar-square fountain?" he asked.

"Why? What do you mean?"

"Because you have just as good a chance of finding this lady in the one as in the other."

Lestrade shot an angry glance at my companion. "I suppose you know all about it," he snarled.

"Well, I have only just heard the facts, but my mind is made up."

"Oh, indeed! Then you think that the Serpentine plays no part in the matter?"

"'THERE,' SAID HE."

"I think it very unlikely."

"Then perhaps you will kindly explain how it is that we found this in it?" He opened his bag as he spoke, and tumbled on to the floor a wedding dress of watered silk, a pair of white satin shoes, and a bride's wreath and veil, all discoloured and soaked in water. "There," said he, putting a new wedding-ring upon the top of the pile. "There is a little nut for you to crack, Master Holmes."

"Oh, indeed," said my friend, blowing blue rings into the air. "You dragged them from the Serpentine?"

"No. They were found floating near the margin by a park-keeper. They have been identified as her clothes, and it seemed to me that if the clothes were there the body would not be far off."

"By the same brilliant reasoning, every man's body is to be found in the neighbourhood of his wardrobe. And pray what did you hope to arrive at through this?"

"At some evidence implicating Flora Millar in the disappearance."

"I am afraid that you will find it difficult."

"Are you indeed, now?" cried Lestrade, with some bitterness. "I am afraid, Holmes, that you are not very practical with your deductions and your inferences. You have made two blunders in as many minutes. This dress does implicate Miss Flora Millar."

"And how?"

"In the dress is a pocket. In the pocket is a card-case. In the card-case is a note. And here is the very note." He slapped it down upon the table in front of him. "Listen to this. 'You will see me when all is ready. Come at once. F. H. M.' Now my theory all along has been that Lady St. Simon was decoyed away by Flora Millar, and that she, with confederates no doubt, was responsible for her disappearance. Here, signed with her initials, is the very note which was no doubt quietly slipped into her hand at the door, and which lured her within their reach."

"Very good, Lestrade," said Holmes, laughing. "You really are very fine indeed. Let me see it." He took up the paper in a listless way, but his attention instantly became riveted, and he gave a little cry of satisfaction. "This is indeed important," said he.

"Ha, you find it so?"

"Extremely so. I congratulate you warmly."

Lestrade rose in his triumph and bent his head to look. "Why," he shrieked, "you're looking at the wrong side."

"On the contrary, this is the right side."

"The right side? You're mad! Here is the note written in pencil over here."

"And over here is what appears to be the fragment of a hotel bill, which interests me deeply."

"There's nothing in it. I looked at it before," said Lestrade, "'Oct. 4th, rooms 8s., breakfast 2s. 6d, cocktail 1s., lunch 2s. 6d., glass sherry, 8d.' I see nothing in that."

"Very likely not. It is most important all the same. As to the note, it is important also, or at least the initials are, so I congratulate you again."

"I've wasted time enough," said Lestrade, rising, "I believe in hard work, and not in sitting by the fire spinning fine theories. Good-day, Mr. Holmes, and we shall see which gets to the bottom of the matter first." He gathered up the garments, thrust them into the bag, and made for the door.

"Just one hint to you, Lestrade," drawled Holmes, before his rival vanished; "I will tell you the true solution of the matter. Lady St. Simon is a myth. There is not, and there never has been, any such person."

Lestrade looked sadly at my companion. Then he turned to me, tapped his forehead three times, shook his head solemnly, and hurried away.

He had hardly shut the door behind him when Holmes rose and put on his overcoat. "There is something in what the fellow says about outdoor work," he remarked, "so I think, Watson, that I must leave you to your papers for a little."

It was after five o'clock when Sherlock Holmes left me, but I had no time to be lonely, for within an hour there arrived a confectioner's man with a very large flat box. This he unpacked with the help of a youth whom he had brought with him, and presently, to my very great astonishment, a quite epicurean little cold supper began to be laid out upon our humble lodging-house mahogany. There were a couple of brace of cold woodcock, a pheasant, a *pâté de foie gras* pie, with a group of ancient and cobwebby bottles. Having laid out all these luxuries, my two visitors vanished away, like the genii of the Arabian Nights, with no explanation save that the things had been paid for, and were ordered to this address.

Just before nine o'clock Sherlock Holmes

stepped briskly into the room. His features were gravely set, but there was a light in his eye which made me think that he had not been disappointed in his conclusions.

"They have laid the supper, then," he said, rubbing his hands.

"You seem to expect company. They have laid for five."

"Yes, I fancy we may have some company dropping in," said he. "I am surprised that Lord St. Simon has not already arrived. Ha! I fancy that I hear his step now upon the stairs."

It was indeed our visitor of the morning who came bustling in, dangling his glasses more vigorously than ever, and with a very perturbed expression upon his aristocratic features.

"My messenger reached you, then?" asked Holmes.

"Yes, and I confess that the contents startled me beyond measure. Have you good authority for what you say?"

"The best possible."

Lord St. Simon sank into a chair, and passed his hand over his forehead.

"What will the duke say," he murmured, "when he hears that one of the family has been subjected to such a humiliation?"

"It is the purest accident. I cannot allow that there is any humiliation."

"Ah, you look on these things from another standpoint."

"I fail to see that anyone is to blame. I can hardly see how the lady could have acted otherwise, though her abrupt method of doing it was undoubtedly to be regretted. Having no mother she had no one to advise her at such a crisis."

"It was a slight, sir, a public slight," said Lord St. Simon, tapping his fingers upon the table.

"You must make allowance for this poor girl, placed in so unprecedented a position."

"I will make no allowance. I am very angry indeed, and I have been shamefully used."

"I think that I heard a ring," said Holmes. "Yes, there are steps on the landing. If I cannot persuade you to take a lenient view of the matter, Lord St. Simon, I have brought an advocate here who may be more successful." He opened the door and ushered in a lady and gentleman. "Lord St. Simon," said he, "allow me to introduce you to Mr. and Mrs. Francis Hay Moulton. The lady, I think, you have already met."

At the sight of these new-comers our client had sprung from his seat, and stood very erect, with his eyes cast down and his hand thrust into the breast of his frock coat, a picture of offended dignity. The lady had taken a quick step forward and had held out her hand to him, but he still refused

"A PICTURE OF OFFENDED DIGNITY."

to raise his eyes. It was as well for his resolution, perhaps, for her pleading face was one which it was hard to resist.

"You're angry, Robert," said she. "Well, I guess you have every cause to be."

"Pray make no apology to me," said Lord St. Simon, bitterly.

"Oh yes, I know that I treated you real bad, and that I should have spoken to you before I went ; but I was kind of rattled, and from the time when I saw Frank here again, I just didn't know what I was doing or saying. I only wonder I didn't fall down and do a faint right there before the altar."

"Perhaps, Mrs. Moulton, you would like my friend and me to leave the room while you explain this matter ?"

"If I may give an opinion," remarked the strange gentleman, "we've had just a little too much secrecy over this business already. For my part, I should like all Europe and America to hear the rights of it." He was a small, wiry, sunburned man, clean shaven, with a sharp face and alert manner.

"Then I'll tell our story right away," said the lady. "Frank here and I met in '84, in McQuire's camp, near the Rockies, where Pa was working a claim. We were engaged to each other, Frank and I ; but then one day father struck a rich pocket, and made a pile, while poor Frank here had a claim that petered out and came to nothing. The richer Pa grew, the poorer was Frank ; so at last Pa wouldn't hear of our engagement lasting any longer, and he took me away to 'Frisco. Frank wouldn't throw up his hand, though ; so he followed me there, and he saw me without Pa knowing anything about it. It would only have made him mad to know, so we just fixed it all up for ourselves. Frank said that he would go and make his pile, too, and never come back to claim me until he had as much as Pa. So then I promised to wait for him to the end of time, and pledged myself not to marry any-one else while he lived. 'Why shouldn't we be married right away, then,' said he, 'and then I will feel sure of you ; and I won't claim to be your husband until I come back.' Well, we talked it over, and he had fixed it all up so nicely, with a clergyman all ready in waiting, that we just did it right there ; and then Frank went off to seek his fortune, and I went back to Pa.

"The next that I heard of Frank was that he was in Montana, and then he went pro-specting into Arizona, and then I heard of him from New Mexico. After that came a long newspaper story about how a miners' camp had been attacked by Apache Indians, and there was my Frank's name among the killed. I fainted dead away, and I was very sick for months after. Pa thought I had a decline, and took me to half the doctors in 'Frisco. Not a word of news came for a year and more, so that I never doubted that Frank was really dead. Then Lord St. Simon came to 'Frisco, and we came to London, and a marriage was arranged, and Pa was very pleased, but I felt all the time that no man on this earth would ever take the place in my heart that had been given to my poor Frank.

"Still, if I had married Lord St. Simon, of course I'd have done my duty by him. We can't command our love, but we can our actions. I went to the altar with him with the intention that I would make him just as good a wife as it was in me to be. But you may imagine what I felt when, just as I came to the altar rails, I glanced back and saw Frank standing looking at me out of the first pew. I thought it was his ghost at first ; but, when I looked again, there he was still, with a kind of question in his eyes as if to ask me whether I were glad or sorry to see him. I wonder I didn't drop. I know that everything was turning round, and the words of the clergy-man were just like the buzz of a bee in my ear. I didn't know what to do. Should I stop the service and make a scene in the church ? I glanced at him again, and he seemed to know what I was thinking, for he raised his finger to his lips to tell me to to be still. Then I saw him scribble on a piece of paper, and I knew that he was writing me a note. As I passed his pew on the way out I dropped my bouquet over to him, and he slipped the note into my hand when he returned me the flowers. It was only a line asking me to join him when he made the sign to me to do so. Of course, I never doubted for a moment that my first duty now was to him, and I determined to do just whatever he might direct.

"When I got back I told my maid, who had known him in California, and had always been his friend. I ordered her to say nothing, but to get a few things packed and my ulster ready. I know I ought to have spoken to Lord St. Simon, but it was dreadful hard before his mother and all those great people. I just made up my mind to run away, and explain afterwards. I hadn't been at the table ten minutes before I saw Frank out of the window, at the other side of the road. He beckoned to me, and then began walking into the Park. I slipped out, put on my things, and followed him. Some woman came talking

"SOME WOMAN CAME TALKING ABOUT LORD ST. SIMON."

something or other about Lord St. Simon to me—seemed to me from the little I heard as if he had a little secret of his own before marriage also—but I managed to get away from her, and soon over took Frank. We got into a cab together, and away we drove to some lodgings he had taken in Gordon-square, and that was my true wedding after all those years of waiting. Frank had been a prisoner among the Apaches, had escaped, came on to 'Frisco, found that I had given him up for dead and had gone to England, followed me there, and had come upon me at last on the very morning of my second wedding."

"I saw it in a paper," explained the American. "It gave the name and the church, but not where the lady lived."

"Then we had a talk as to what we should do, and Frank was all for openness, but I was so ashamed of it all that I felt as if I would like to vanish away and never see any of them again, just sending a line to Pa, perhaps, to show him that I was alive. It was awful to me to think of all those lords and ladies sitting round that breakfast table, and waiting for me to come back. So Frank took my wedding clothes and things, and made a bundle of them so that I should not be traced, and dropped them away somewhere where no one should find them. It is likely that we should have gone on to Paris to-morrow, only that this good gentleman, Mr. Holmes, came round to us this evening, though how he found us is more than I can think, and he showed us very clearly and kindly that I was wrong and that Frank was right, and that we should put ourselves in the wrong if we were so secret. Then he offered to give us a chance of talking to Lord St. Simon alone, and so we came right away round to his rooms at once. Now, Robert, you have heard it all, and I am very sorry if I have given you pain, and I hope that you do not think very meanly of me."

Lord St. Simon had by no means relaxed his rigid attitude, but had listened with a frowning brow and a compressed lip to this long narrative.

"Excuse me," he said, "but it is not my custom to discuss my most intimate personal affairs in this public manner."

"Then you won't forgive me? You won't shake hands before I go?"

"Oh, certainly, if it would give you any pleasure." He put out his hand and coldly grasped that which she extended to him.

"I had hoped," suggested Holmes, "that you would have joined us in a friendly supper."

" I think that there you ask a little too much," responded his lordship. " I may be forced to acquiesce in these recent developments, but I can hardly be expected to make merry over them. I think that, with

obvious to me, the one that the lady had been quite willing to undergo the wedding ceremony, the other that she had repented of it within a few minutes of returning home. Obviously something had occurred

"'I WILL WISH YOU ALL A VERY GOOD NIGHT."

your permission, I will now wish you all a very good night." He included us all in a sweeping bow, and stalked out of the room.

"Then I trust that you at least will honour me with your company," said Sherlock Holmes. "It is always a joy to me to meet an American, Mr. Moulton, for I am one of those who believe that the folly of a monarch and the blundering of a Minister in far gone years will not prevent our children from being some day citizens of the same world-wide country under a flag which shall be a quartering of the Union Jack with the Stars and Stripes."

" The case has been an interesting one," remarked Holmes, when our visitors had left us, " because it serves to show very clearly how simple the explanation may be of an affair which at first sight seems to be almost inexplicable. Nothing could be more natural than the sequence of events as narrated by this lady, and nothing stranger than the result when viewed, for instance, by Mr. Lestrade of Scotland Yard."

" You were not yourself at fault at all, then ? "

" From the first, two facts were very

during the morning, then, to cause her to change her mind. What could that something be? She could not have spoken to anyone when she was out, for she had been in the company of the bridegroom. Had she seen someone, then ? If she had, it must be someone from America, because she had spent so short a time in this country that she could hardly have allowed anyone to acquire so deep an influence over her that the mere sight of him would induce her to change her plans so completely. You see we have already arrived, by a process of exclusion, at the idea that she might have seen an American. Then who could this American be, and why should he possess so much influence over her ? It might be a lover ; it might be a husband. Her young womanhood had, I knew, been spent in rough scenes, and under strange conditions. So far I had got before ever I heard Lord St. Simon's narrative. When he told us of a man in a pew, of the change in the bride's manner, of so transparent a device for obtaining a note as the dropping of a bouquet, of her resort to her confidential maid, and of her very significant allusion to claim-jumping, which in miners' parlance means taking possession of that which another person has a prior claim to, the whole situation became absolutely clear. She had gone off with a man, and the man was either a lover or was a previous husband, the chances being in favour of the latter."

"And how in the world did you find them?"

"It might have been difficult, but friend Lestrade held information in his hands the value of which he did not himself know. The initials were of course of the highest importance, but more valuable still was it to know that within a week he had settled his bill at one of the most select London hotels."

"How did you deduce the select?"

"By the select prices. Eight shillings for a bed and eightpence for a glass of sherry, pointed to one of the most expensive hotels. There are not many in London which charge at that rate. In the second one which I visited in Northumberland-avenue, I learned by an inspection of the book that Francis H. Moulton, an American gentleman, had left only the day before,

and on looking over the entries against him, I came upon the very items which I had seen in the duplicate bill. His letters were to be forwarded to 226, Gordon-square, so thither I travelled, and being fortunate enough to find the loving couple at home, I ventured to give them some paternal advice, and to point out to them that it would be better in every way that they should make their position a little clearer, both to the general public and to Lord St. Simon in particular. I invited them to meet him here, and as you see, I made him keep the appointment."

"But with no very good result," I remarked. "His conduct was certainly not very gracious."

"Ah! Watson," said Holmes, smiling, "perhaps you would not be very gracious either, if, after all the trouble of wooing and wedding, you found yourself deprived in an instant of wife and of fortune. I think that we may judge Lord St. Simon very mercifully, and thank our stars that we are never likely to find ourselves in the same position. Draw your chair up, and hand me my violin, for the only problem which we have still to solve is how to while away these bleak autumnal evenings."

## XI.—THE ADVENTURE OF THE BERYL CORONET.

"HOLMES," said I, as I stood one morning in our bow window looking down the street, "here is a madman coming along. It seems rather sad that his relatives should allow him to come out alone."

My friend rose lazily from his arm-chair, and stood with his hands in the pockets of his dressing gown, looking over my shoulder. It was a bright, crisp February morning, and the snow of the day before still lay deep upon the ground, shimmering brightly in the wintry sun. Down the centre of Baker-street it had been ploughed into a brown crumbly band by the traffic, but at either side and on the heaped-up edges of the footpaths it still lay as white as when it fell. The grey pavement had been cleaned and scraped, but was still dangerously slippery, so that there were fewer passengers than usual. Indeed, from the direction of the Metropolitan Station no one was coming save the single gentleman whose eccentric conduct had drawn my attention.

He was a man of about fifty, tall, portly, and imposing, with a massive, strongly marked face and a commanding figure. He was dressed in a sombre yet rich style, in black frock-coat, shining hat, neat brown gaiters, and well cut pearl grey trousers. Yet his actions were in absurd contrast to the dignity of his dress and features, for he was running hard, with occasional little springs, such as a weary man gives who is little accustomed to set any tax upon his legs. As he ran he jerked his hands up and down, waggled his head, and writhed his face into the most extraordinary contortions.

"What on earth can be the matter with him?" I asked. "He is looking up at the numbers of the houses."

"I believe that he is coming here," said Holmes, rubbing his hands.

"Here?"

"Yes; I rather think he is coming to consult me professionally. I think that I recognise the symptoms. Ha! did I not tell you?" As he spoke, the man, puffing and blowing, rushed at our door, and pulled at our bell until the whole house resounded with the clanging.

A few moments later he was in our room, still puffing, still gesticulating, but with so fixed a look of grief and despair in his eyes that our smiles were turned in an instant to horror and pity. For a while he could not get his words out, but swayed his body and plucked at his hair like one who has been driven to the extreme limits of his reason. Then, suddenly springing

"WITH A LOOK OF GRIEF AND DESPAIR."

to his feet, he beat his head against the wall with such force that we both rushed upon him, and tore him away to the centre of the room. Sherlock Holmes pushed him down into the easy-chair, and, sitting beside him, patted his hand, and chatted with him in the easy, soothing tones which he knew so well how to employ.

"You have come to me to tell your story, have you not?" said he. "You are fatigued with your haste. Pray wait until you have recovered yourself, and then I shall be most happy to look into any little problem which you may submit to me."

The man sat for a minute or more with a heaving chest, fighting against his emotion. Then he passed his handkerchief over his brow, set his lips tight, and turned his face towards us.

"No doubt you think me mad?" said he.

"I see that you have had some great trouble," responded Holmes.

"God knows I have!—a trouble which is enough to unseat my reason, so sudden and so terrible is it. Public disgrace I might have faced, although I am a man whose character has never yet borne a stain. Private affliction also is the lot of every man; but the two coming together, and in so frightful a form, have been enough to shake my very soul. Besides, it is not I alone. The very noblest in the land may suffer, unless some way be found out of this horrible affair."

"Pray compose yourself, sir," said Holmes, "and let me have a clear account of who you are, and what it is that has befallen you."

"My name," answered our visitor, "is probably familiar to your ears. I am Alexander Holder, of the banking firm of Holder & Stevenson, of Threadneedle-street."

The name was indeed well known to us, as belonging to the senior partner in the second largest private banking concern in the City of London. What could have happened, then, to bring one of the fore-most citizens of London to this most pitiable pass? We waited, all curiosity, until with another effort he braced himself to tell his story.

"I feel that time is of value," said he, "that is why I hastened here when the police inspector suggested that I should secure your co-operation. I came to Baker-street by the Undergound, and hurried from there on foot, for the cabs go slowly through this snow. That is why I was so out of breath, for I am a man who take very little exercise. I feel better now, and I will put the facts before you as shortly and yet as clearly as I can.

"It is, of course, well known to you that in a successful banking business as much depends upon our being able to find re-munerative investments for our funds, as upon our increasing our connection and the number of our depositors. One of our most lucrative means of laying out money is in the shape of loans, where the security is unimpeachable. We have done a good deal in this direction during the last few years, and there are many noble families to whom we have advanced large sums upon the security of their pictures, libraries, or plate.

"Yesterday morning I was seated in my office at the Bank, when a card was brought in to me by one of the clerks. I started when I saw the name, for it was that of none other than—— well, perhaps even to you I had better say no more than that it was a name which is a household word all over the earth—one of the highest, noblest, most exalted names in England. I was overwhelmed by the honour, and attempted, when he entered, to say so, but he plunged at once into business with the air of a man who wishes to hurry quickly through a disagreeable task.

"'Mr. Holder,' said he, 'I have been informed that you are in the habit of advancing money.'

"'The firm do so when the security is good,' I answered.

"'It is absolutely essential to me,' said he, 'that I should have fifty thousand pounds at once. I could of course borrow so trifling a sum ten times over from my friends, but I much prefer to make it a matter of business, and to carry out that business myself. In my position you can readily understand that it is unwise to place oneself under obligations.'

"'For how long, may I ask, do you want this sum?' I asked.

"'Next Monday I have a large sum due to me, and I shall then most certainly repay what you advance, with whatever interest you think it right to charge. But it is very essential to me that the money should be paid at once.'

"'I should be happy to advance it without further parley from my own private purse,' said I, 'were it not that the strain would be rather more than it could bear. If, on the other hand, I am to do it in the name of the firm, then in justice to my partner I must insist that, even in your case, every businesslike precaution should be taken.'

"'I should much prefer to have it so,' said he, raising up a square, black morocco case which he had laid beside his chair. 'You have doubtless heard of the Beryl coronet?'

"'One of the most precious public possessions of the Empire,' said I.

"'Precisely.' He opened the case, and there, embedded in soft, flesh-coloured velvet, lay the magnificent piece of jewellery which he had named. 'There are thirty-

"I TOOK THE PRECIOUS CASE."

nine enormous beryls,' said he, 'and the price of the gold chasing is incalculable. The lowest estimate would put the worth of the coronet at double the sum which I have asked. I am prepared to leave it with you as my security.'

"I took the precious case into my hands and looked in some perplexity from it to my illustrious client.

"'You doubt its value?' he asked.

"'Not at all. I only doubt——'

"'The propriety of my leaving it. You may set your mind at rest about that. I should not dream of doing so were it not

absolutely certain that I should be able in four days to reclaim it. It is a pure matter of form. Is the security sufficient?'

"'Ample.'

"'You understand, Mr. Holder, that I am giving you a strong proof of the confidence which I have in you, founded upon all that I have heard of you. I rely upon you not only to be discreet and to refrain from all gossip upon the matter, but, above all, to preserve this coronet with every possible precaution, because I need not say that a great public scandal would be caused if any harm were to befall it. Any injury to it would be almost as serious as its complete loss, for there are no beryls in the world to match these, and it would be impossible to replace them. I leave it with you, however, with every confidence, and I shall call for it in person on Monday morning.'

"Seeing that my client was anxious to leave, I said no more; but, calling for my cashier, I ordered him to pay over fifty thousand-pound notes. When I was alone once more, however, with the precious case lying upon the table in front of me, I could not but think with some misgivings of the immense responsibility which it entailed upon me. There could be no doubt that, as it was a national possession, a horrible scandal would ensue if any misfortune should occur to it. I already regretted having ever consented to take charge of it. However, it was too late to alter the matter now, so I locked it up in my private safe, and turned once more to my work.

"When evening came, I felt that it would be an imprudence to leave so precious a thing in the office behind me. Bankers' safes had been forced before now, and why should not mine be? If so, how terrible would be the position in which I should find myself! I determined, therefore, that for the next few days I would always carry the case backwards and forwards with me, so that it might never be really out of my reach. With this intention, I called a cab, and drove out to my house at Streatham, carrying the jewel with me. I did not breathe freely until I had taken it upstairs, and locked it in the bureau of my dressing-room.

"And now a word as to my household, Mr. Holmes, for I wish you to thoroughly understand the situation. My groom and my page sleep out of the house, and may be set aside altogether. I have three maid-servants who have been with me a number of years, and whose absolute reliability is quite above suspicion. Another, Lucy Parr, the second waiting-maid, has only been in my service a few months. She came with an excellent character, however, and has always given me satisfaction. She is a very pretty girl, and has attracted admirers who have occasionally hung about the place. That is the only drawback which we have found to her, but we believe her to be a thoroughly good girl in every way.

"So much for the servants. My family itself is so small that it will not take me long to describe it. I am a widower, and have an only son, Arthur. He has been a disappointment to me, Mr. Holmes—a grievous disappointment. I have no doubt that I am myself to blame. People tell me that I have spoiled him. Very likely I have. When my dear wife died I felt that he was all I had to love. I could not bear to see the smile fade even for a moment from his face. I have never denied him a wish. Perhaps it would have been better for both of us had I been sterner, but I meant it for the best.

"It was naturally my intention that he should succeed me in my business, but he was not of a business turn. He was wild, wayward, and, to speak the truth, I could not trust him in the handling of large sums of money. When he was young he became a member of an aristocratic club, and there, having charming manners, he was soon the intimate of a number of men with long purses and expensive habits. He learned to play heavily at cards and to squander money on the turf, until he had again and again to come to me and implore me to give him an advance upon his allowance, that he might settle his debts of honour. He tried more than once to break away from the dangerous company which he was keeping, but each time the influence of his friend Sir George Burnwell was enough to draw him back again.

"And, indeed, I could not wonder that such a man as Sir George Burnwell should gain an influence over him, for he has frequently brought him to my house, and I have found myself that I could hardly resist the fascination of his manner. He is older than Arthur, a man of the world to his finger-tips, one who had been everywhere, seen everything, a brilliant talker, and a man of great personal beauty. Yet when I think of him in cold blood, far away from the glamour of his presence, I am convinced from his cynical speech, and the look which I have caught in his eyes, that he is one who should be deeply distrusted. So I think, and so, too, thinks my little Mary, who has a woman's quick insight into character.

"And now there is only she to be described. She is my niece; but when my brother died five years ago and left her alone in the world I adopted her, and have looked upon her ever since as my daughter. She is a sunbeam in my house—sweet, loving, beautiful, a wonderful manager and housekeeper, yet as tender and quiet and gentle as a woman could be. She is my right hand. I do not know what I could do without her. In only one matter has she ever gone against my wishes. Twice my boy has asked her to marry him, for he loves her devotedly, but each time she has refused him. I think that if anyone could have drawn him into the right path it would have been she, and that his marriage might have changed his whole life; but now, alas! it is too late—for ever too late!

"Now, Mr. Holmes, you know the people who live under my roof, and I shall continue with my miserable story.

"When we were taking coffee in the drawing-room that night, after dinner, I told Arthur and Mary my experience, and of the precious treasure which we had under our roof, suppressing only the name of my client. Lucy Parr, who had brought in the coffee, had, I am sure, left the room; but I cannot swear that the door was closed. Mary and Arthur were much interested, and wished to see the famous coronet, but I thought it better not to disturb it.

"'Where have you put it?' asked Arthur.

"'In my own bureau.'

"'Well, I hope to goodness the house won't be burgled during the night,' said he.

"'It is locked up,' I answered.

"'Oh, any old key will fit that bureau. When I was a youngster I have opened it myself with the key of the box-room cupboard.'

"He often had a wild way of talking, so that I thought little of what he said. He

"OH, ANY OLD KEY WILL FIT THAT BUREAU."

followed me to my room, however, that night with a very grave face.

"'Look here, dad,' said he, with his eyes cast down. 'Can you let me have two hundred pounds?'

"'No, I cannot!' I answered, sharply. 'I have been far too generous with you in money matters.'

"'You have been very kind,' said he; 'but I must have this money, or else I can never show my face inside the club again.'

"'And a very good thing, too!' I cried.

"'Yes, but you would not have me leave it a dishonoured man,' said he. 'I could not bear the disgrace. I must raise the money in some way, and if you will not let me have it, then I must try other means.'

"I was very angry, for this was the third demand during the month. 'You shall not have a farthing from me,' I cried, on which he bowed and left the room without another word.

"When he was gone I unlocked my bureau, made sure that my treasure was safe, and locked it again. Then I started to go round the house to see that all was secure—a duty which I usually leave to Mary, but which I thought it well to perform myself that night. As I came down the stairs I saw Mary herself at the side window of the hall, which she closed and fastened as I approached.

"'Tell me, dad,' said she, looking, I thought, a little disturbed, 'did you give Lucy, the maid, leave to go out to-night?'

"'Certainly not.'

"'She came in just now by the back door. I have no doubt that she has only been to the side gate to see someone, but I think that it is hardly safe, and should be stopped.'

"'You must speak to her in the morning, or I will, if you prefer it. Are you sure that everything is fastened?'

"'Quite sure, dad.'

"'Then, good-night.' I kissed her, and went up to my bedroom again, where I was soon asleep.

"I am endeavouring to tell you everything, Mr. Holmes, which may have any bearing upon the case, but I beg that you will question me upon any point which I do not make clear."

"On the contrary, your statement is singularly lucid."

"I come to a part of my story now in which I should wish to be particularly so. I am not a very heavy sleeper, and the anxiety in my mind tended, no doubt, to make me even less so than usual. About two in the morning, then, I was awakened by some sound in the house. It had ceased ere I was wide awake, but it had left an impression behind it as though a window had gently closed somewhere. I lay listening with all my ears. Suddenly, to my horror, there was a distinct sound of footsteps moving softly in the next room. I slipped out of bed, all palpitating with fear, and peeped round the corner of my dressing-room door.

"'Arthur!' I screamed, 'you villain! you thief! How dare you touch that coronet?'

"AT MY CRY HE DROPPED IT."

"The gas was half up, as I had left it, and my unhappy boy, dressed only in his shirt and trousers, was standing beside the light, holding the coronet in his hands. He appeared to be wrenching at it, or bending it with all his strength. At my cry he dropped it from his grasp, and turned as pale as death. I snatched it up and examined it. One of the gold corners, with three of the beryls in it, was missing.

"'You blackguard!' I shouted, beside myself with rage. 'You have destroyed it! You have dishonoured me for ever! Where are the jewels which you have stolen?'

"'Stolen!' he cried.

"'Yes, you thief!' I roared, shaking him by the shoulder.

"'There are none missing. There cannot be any missing,' said he.

"'There are three missing. And you know where they are. Must I call you a liar as well as a thief? Did I not see you trying to tear off another piece?'

"'You have called me names enough,' said he, 'I will not stand it any longer. I shall not say another word about this business since you have chosen to insult me. I will leave your house in the morning, and make my own way in the world.'

"'You shall leave it in the hands of the police!' I cried, half mad with grief and rage. 'I shall have this matter probed to the bottom.'

"'You shall learn nothing from me,' said he, with a passion such as I should not have thought was in his nature. 'If you choose to call the police, let the police find what they can.'

"By this time the whole house was astir, for I had raised my voice in my anger. Mary was the first to rush into my room, and, at the sight of the coronet and of Arthur's face, she read the whole story, and, with a scream, fell down senseless on the ground. I sent the housemaid for the police, and put the investigation into their hands at once. When the inspector and a constable entered the house, Arthur, who had stood sullenly with his arms folded, asked me whether it was my intention to charge him with theft. I answered that it had ceased to be a private matter, but had become a public one, since the ruined coronet was national property. I was determined that the law should have its way in everything.

"'At least,' said he, 'you will not have me arrested at once. It would be to your advantage as well as mine if I might leave the house for five minutes.'

"'That you may get away, or perhaps that you may conceal what you have stolen,' said I. And then realising the dreadful position in which I was placed, I implored him to remember that not only my honour, but that of one who was far greater than I was at stake; and that he threatened to raise a scandal which would convulse the nation. He might avert it all if he would but tell me what he had done with the three missing stones.

"'You may as well face the matter,' said I; 'you have been caught in the act, and no confession could make your guilt more heinous. If you but make such reparation as is in your power, by telling us where the beryls are, all shall be forgiven and forgotten.'

"'Keep your forgiveness for those who ask for it,' he answered, turning away from me with a sneer. I saw that he was too hardened for any words of mine to influence him. There was but one way for it. I called in the inspector, and gave him into custody. A search was made at once, not only of his person, but of his room, and of every portion of the house where he could possibly have concealed the gems ; but no trace of them could be found, nor would the wretched boy open his mouth for all our persuasions and our threats. This morning he was removed to a cell, and I, after going through all the police formalities, have hurried round to you, to implore you to use your skill in unravelling the matter. The police have openly confessed that they can at present make nothing of it. You may go to any expense which you think necessary. I have already offered a reward of a thousand pounds. My God, what shall I do ! I have lost my honour, my gems, and my son in one night. Oh, what shall I do ! ''

He put a hand on either side of his head, and rocked himself to and fro, droning to himself like a child whose grief has got beyond words.

Sherlock Holmes sat silent for some few minutes, with his brows knitted and his eyes fixed upon the fire.

" Do you receive much company ? " he asked.

" None, save my partner with his family, and an occasional friend of Arthur's. Sir George Burnwell has been several times lately. No one else, I think."

" Do you go out much in society ? "

" Arthur does. Mary and I stay at home. We neither of us care for it."

" That is unusual in a young girl."

" She is of a quiet nature. Besides, she is not so very young. She is four and twenty."

" This matter, from what you say, seems to have been a shock to her also."

" Terrible ! She is even more affected than I."

" You have neither of you any doubt as to your son's guilt ? "

" How can we have, when I saw him with my own eyes with the coronet in his hands."

" I hardly consider that a conclusive proof. Was the remainder of the coronet at all injured ? "

" Yes, it was twisted."

" Do you not think, then, that he might have been trying to straighten it ? "

" God bless you ! You are doing what you can for him and for me. But it is too heavy a task. What was he doing there at all ? If his purpose were innocent, why did he not say so ? "

" Precisely. And if it were guilty, why did he not invent a lie? His silence appears to me to cut both ways. There are several singular points about the case. What did the police think of the noise which awoke you from your sleep ? "

" They considered that it might be caused by Arthur's closing his bedroom door."

" A likely story ! As if a man bent on felony would slam his door so as to wake a household. What did they say, then, of the disappearance of these gems ? "

" They are still sounding the planking, and probing the furniture in the hope of finding them."

" Have they thought of looking outside the house ? "

" Yes, they have shown extraordinary energy. The whole garden has already been minutely examined."

" Now, my dear sir," said Holmes, " is it not obvious to you now that this matter really strikes very much deeper than either you or the police were at first inclined to think ? It appeared to you to be a simple case ; to me it seems exceedingly complex. Consider what is involved by your theory. You suppose that your son came down from his bed, went, at great risk, to your dressing-room, opened your bureau, took out your coronet, broke off by main force a small portion of it, went off to some other place, concealed three gems out of the thirty-nine, with such skill that nobody can find them, and then returned with the other thirty-six into the room in which he exposed himself to the greatest danger of being discovered. I ask you now, is such a theory tenable ? "

" But what other is there ? " cried the banker with a gesture of despair. " If his motives were innocent, why does he not explain them ? "

" It is our task to find that out," replied Holmes, " so now, if you please, Mr. Holder, we wi'l set off for Streatham together, and devote an hour to glancing a little more closely into details."

My friend insisted upon my accompanying them in their expedition, which I was eager enough to do, for my curiosity and sympathy were deeply stirred by the story to which we had listened. I confess that the guilt of the banker's son appeared to me to be as obvious as it did to his unhappy father, but still I had such faith in Holmes' judgment that I felt that there must be some grounds for hope as long as he was dissatisfied with the accepted explanation. He hardly spoke a word the whole way out to the southern suburb, but sat with his chin upon his breast, and his hat drawn over his eyes, sunk in the deepest thought. Our client appeared to have taken fresh heart at the little glimpse of hope which had been presented to him, and he even broke into a desultory chat with me over his business affairs. A short railway journey, and a shorter walk, brought us to Fairbank, the modest residence of the great financier.

Fairbank was a good-sized square house of white stone, standing back a little from the road. A double carriage sweep, with a snowclad lawn, stretched down in front to the two large iron gates which closed the entrance. On the right side was a small wooden thicket which led into a narrow path between two neat hedges stretching from the road to the kitchen door, and forming the tradesmen's entrance. On the left ran a lane which led to the stables, and was not itself within the grounds at all, being a public, though little used, thoroughfare. Holmes left us standing at the door, and walked slowly all round the house, across the front, down the tradesmen's path, and so round by the garden behind into the stable lane. So long was he that Mr. Holder and I went into the dining-room, and waited

by the fire until he should return. We were sitting there in silence when the door opened, and a young lady came in. She was rather above the middle height, slim, with dark hair and eyes, which seemed the darker against the absolute pallor of her skin. I do not think that I have ever seen such deadly paleness in a woman's face. Her lips, too, were bloodless, but her eyes were flushed with crying. As she swept silently into the room she impressed me with a greater sense of grief than the banker had done in the morning, and it was the more striking in her as she was evidently a woman of strong character, with immense capacity for self-restraint. Disregarding my presence, she went straight to her uncle, and passed her hand over his head with a sweet womanly caress.

"You have given orders that Arthur should be liberated, have you not, dad?" she asked.

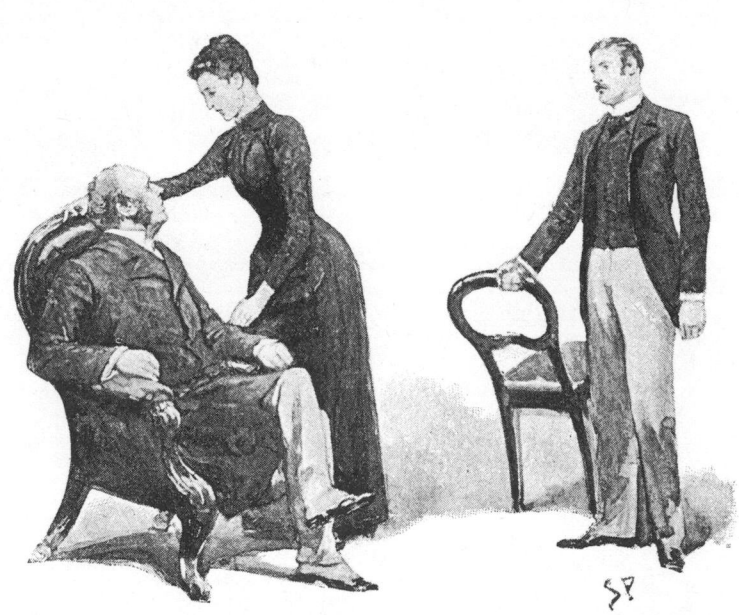

"SHE WENT STRAIGHT TO HER UNCLE."

"No, no, my girl, the matter must be probed to the bottom."

"But I am so sure that he is innocent. You know what women's instincts are. I know that he has done no harm, and that you will be sorry for having acted so harshly."

"Why is he silent, then, if he is innocent?"

"Who knows? Perhaps because he was so angry that you should suspect him."

"How could I help suspecting him, when I actually saw him with the coronet in his hand?"

"Oh, but he had only picked it up to look at it. Oh, do, do take my word for it that he is innocent. Let the matter drop, and say no more. It is so dreadful to think of our dear Arthur in prison!"

"I shall never let it drop until the gems are found—never, Mary! Your affection for Arthur blinds you as to the awful consequences to me. Far from hushing the thing up, I have brought a gentleman down from London to inquire more deeply into it."

"This gentleman?" she asked, facing round to me.

"No, his friend. He wished us to leave him alone. He is round in the stable lane now."

"The stable lane?" She raised her dark eyebrows. "What can he hope to find there! Ah! this, I suppose, is he. I trust, sir, that you will succeed in proving, what I feel sure is the truth, that my cousin Arthur is innocent of this crime."

"I fully share your opinion, and, I trust with you, that we may prove it," returned Holmes, going back to the mat to knock the snow from his shoes. "I believe I have the honour of addressing Miss Mary Holder. Might I ask you a question or two?"

"Pray do, sir, if it may help to clear this horrible affair up."

"You heard nothing yourself last night?"

"Nothing, until my uncle here began to speak loudly. I heard that, and I came down."

"You shut up the windows and doors the night before. Did you fasten all the windows?"

"Yes."

"Were they all fastened this morning?"

"Yes."

"You have a maid who has a sweetheart? I think that you remarked to your uncle last night that she had been out to see him?"

"Yes, and she was the girl who waited in the drawing-room, and who may have heard uncle's remarks about the coronet."

"I see. You infer that she may have gone out to tell her sweetheart, and that the two may have planned the robbery."

"But what is the good of all these vague theories," cried the banker, impatiently, "when I have told you that I saw Arthur with the coronet in his hands?"

"Wait a little, Mr. Holder. We must come back to that. About this girl, Miss Holder. You saw her return by the kitchen door, I presume?"

"Yes; when I went to see if the door was fastened for the night I met her slipping in. I saw the man, too, in the gloom."

"Do you know him?"

"Oh, yes; he is the greengrocer who brings our vegetables round. His name is Francis Prosper."

"He stood," said Holmes, "to the left of the door—that is to say, further up the path than is necessary to reach the door?"

"Yes, he did."

"And he is a man with a wooden leg?"

Something like fear sprang up in the young lady's expressive black eyes. "Why,

"SOMETHING LIKE FEAR SPRANG UP IN THE YOUNG LADY'S EYES."

you are like a magician," said she. "How do you know that?" She smiled, but there was no answering smile in Holmes' thin, eager face.

"I should be very glad now to go up-stairs," said he. "I shall probably wish to go over the outside of the house again. Perhaps I had better take a look at the lower windows before I go up."

He walked swiftly round from one to the other, pausing only at the large one which looked from the hall on to the stable lane. This he opened, and made a very careful examination of the sill with his powerful magnifying lens. "Now we shall go up-stairs," said he, at last.

The banker's dressing-room was a plainly furnished little chamber with a grey carpet, a large bureau, and a long mirror. Holmes went to the bureau first, and looked hard at the lock.

"Which key was used to open it?" he asked.

"That which my son himself indicated—that of the cupboard of the lumber-room."

"Have you it here?"

"That is it on the dressing-table."

Sherlock Holmes took it up and opened the bureau.

"It is a noiseless lock," said he. "It is no wonder that it did not wake you. This case, I presume, contains the coronet. We must have a look at it." He opened the case, and, taking out the diadem, he laid it upon the table. It was a magnificent specimen of the jeweller's art, and the thirty-six stones were the finest that I have ever seen. At one side of the coronet was a crooked cracked edge, where a corner holding three gems had been torn away.

"Now, Mr. Holder," said Holmes; "here is the corner which corresponds to that which has been so unfortunately lost. Might I beg that you will break it off."

The banker recoiled in horror. "I should not dream of trying," said he.

"Then I will." Holmes suddenly bent his strength upon it, but without result. "I feel it give a little," said he; "but, though I am exceptionally strong in the fingers, it would take me all my time to break it. An ordinary man could not do it. Now, what do you think would happen if I did break it, Mr. Holder? There would be a noise like a pistol shot. Do you tell me that all this happened within a few yards of your bed, and that you heard nothing of it?"

"I do not know what to think. It is all dark to me."

"But perhaps it may grow lighter as we go. What do you think, Miss Holder?"

"I confess that I still share my uncle's perplexity."

"Your son had no shoes or slippers on when you saw him?"

"He had nothing on save only his trousers and shirt."

"Thank you. We have certainly been favoured with extraordinary luck during this inquiry, and it will be entirely our own fault if we do not succeed in clearing the matter up. With your permission, Mr. Holder, I shall now continue my investigations outside."

He went alone, at his own request, for he explained that any unnecessary footmarks might make his task more difficult. For an hour or more he was at work, returning at last with his feet heavy with snow and his features as inscrutable as ever.

"I think that I have seen now all that there is to see, Mr. Holder," said he; "I can serve you best by returning to my rooms."

"But the gems, Mr. Holmes. Where are they?"

"I cannot tell."

The banker wrung his hands. "I shall never see them again!" he cried. "And my son? You give me hopes?"

"My opinion is in no way altered."

"Then for God's sake what was this dark business which was acted in my house last night?"

"If you can call upon me at my Baker-street rooms to-morrow morning between nine and ten I shall be happy to do what I can to make it clearer. I understand that you give me *carte blanche* to act for you, provided only that I get back the gems, and that you place no limit on the sum I may draw."

"I would give my fortune to have them back."

"Very good. I shall look into the matter between this and then. Good-bye, it is just possible that I may have to come over here again before evening."

It was obvious to me that my com-panion's mind was now made up about the case, although what his conclusions were was more than I could even dimly imagine. Several times during our homeward journey I endeavoured to sound him upon the point, but he always glided away to some other topic, until at last I gave it over in despair. It was not yet three when we found our-

"DRESSED AS A COMMON LOAFER."

I had just finished my tea when he returned, evidently in excellent spirits, swinging an old elastic-sided boot in his hand. He chucked it down into a corner and helped himself to a cup of tea.

"I only looked in as I passed," said he. "I am going right on."

"Where to?"

"Oh, to the other side of the West-end. It may be some time before I get back. Don't wait up for me in case I should be late."

"How are you getting on?"

"Oh, so so. Nothing to complain of. I have been out to Streatham since I saw you last, but I did not call at the house. It is a very sweet little problem, and I would not have missed it for a good deal. However, I must not sit gossiping here, but must get these disreputable clothes off and return to my highly respectable self."

I could see by his manner that he had stronger reasons for satisfaction than his words alone would imply. His eyes twinkled, and there was even a touch of colour upon his sallow cheeks. He hastened upstairs, and a few minutes later I heard the slam of the hall door, which told me that he was off once more upon his congenial hunt.

I waited until midnight, but there was no sign of his return, so I retired to my room. It was no uncommon thing for him to be away for days and nights on end when he was hot upon a scent, so that his lateness caused me no surprise. I do not know at what hour he came in, but when I came down to breakfast in the morning, there he was with a cup of coffee in one hand and the paper in the other, as fresh and trim as possible.

"You will excuse my beginning without you, Watson," said he; "but you remember that our client has rather an early appointment this morning."

"Why, it is after nine now," I answered. "I should not be surprised if that were he. I thought I heard a ring."

It was, indeed, our friend the financier. I was shocked by the change which had come over him, for his face, which was naturally of a broad and massive mould, was now pinched and fallen in, while his hair seemed to me at least a shade whiter. He entered with a weariness and lethargy which was even more painful than his violence of the morning before, and he dropped heavily into the arm-chair which I pushed forward for him.

selves in our room once more. He hurried to his chamber and was down again in a few minutes dressed as a common loafer. With his collar turned up, his shiny seedy coat, his red cravat, and his worn boots, he was a perfect sample of the class.

"I think that this should do," said he, glancing into the glass above the fireplace. "I only wish that you could come with me, Watson, but I fear that it won't do. I may be on the trail in this matter, or I may be following a will o' the wisp, but I shall soon know which it is. I hope that I may be back in a few hours." He cut a slice of beef from the joint upon the sideboard, sandwiched it between two rounds of bread, and, thrusting this rude meal into his pocket, he started off upon his expedition.

" I do not know what I have done to be so severely tried," said he. " Only two days ago I was a happy and prosperous man, without a care in the world. Now I am left to a lonely and dishonoured age. One sorrow comes close upon the heels of another. My niece, Mary, has deserted me."

" Deserted you ? "

" Yes. Her bed this morning had not been slept in, her room was empty, and a note lay for me upon the hall table. I had said to her last night, in sorrow and not in anger, that if she had married my boy all might have been well with him. Perhaps it was thoughtless of me to say so. It is to that remark that she refers in this note : ' My dearest Uncle,—I feel that I have brought trouble upon you, and that if I had acted differently this terrible misfortune might never have occurred. I cannot, with this thought in my mind, ever again be happy under your roof, and I feel that I must leave you for ever. Do not worry about my future, for that is provided for ; and, above all, do not search for me, for it will be fruitless labour, and an ill service to me. In life or in death, I am ever your loving,—MARY.' What could she mean by that note, Mr. Holmes ? Do you think it points to suicide ? "

" No, no, nothing of the kind. It is perhaps the best possible solution. I trust, Mr. Holder, that you are nearing the end of your troubles."

" Ha ! You say so ! You have heard something, Mr. Holmes ; you have learned something ! Where are the gems ? "

" You would not think a thousand pounds apiece an excessive sum for them ? "

" I would pay ten."

" That would be unnecessary. Three thousand will cover the matter. And there is a little reward, I fancy. Have you your cheque-book ? Here is a pen. Better make it out for four thousand pounds."

With a dazed face the banker made out the required cheque. Holmes walked over to his desk, took out a little triangular piece of gold with three gems in it, and threw it down upon the table.

With a shriek of joy our client clutched it up.

" You have it ! " he gasped. " I am saved ! I am saved ! "

The reaction of joy was as passionate as his grief had been, and he hugged his recovered gems to his bosom.

" There is one other thing you owe," said Sherlock Holmes, rather sternly.

" Owe ! " He caught up a pen. " Name the sum, and I will pay it."

" No, the debt is not to me. You owe a very humble apology to that noble lad, your son, who has carried himself in this matter as I should be proud to see my own son do, should I ever chance to have one."

" Then it was not Arthur who took them ? "

" I told you yesterday, and I repeat to-day, that it was not."

" You are sure of it ! Then let us hurry to him at once, to let him know that the truth is known."

" He knows it already. When I had cleared it all up I had an interview with him, and, finding that he would not tell me the story, I told it to him, on which he had to confess that I was right, and to add the very few details which were not yet quite clear to me. Your news of this morning, however, may open his lips."

" For Heaven's sake, tell me, then, what is this extraordinary mystery ! "

" I will do so, and I will show you the steps by which I reached it. And let me say to you, first, that which it is hardest for me to say and for you to hear. There has been an understanding between Sir George Burnwell and your niece Mary. They have now fled together."

" My Mary ? Impossible ! "

" It is, unfortunately, more than possible ; it is certain. Neither you nor your son knew the true character of this man when you admitted him into your family circle. He is one of the most dangerous men in England—a ruined gambler, an absolutely desperate villain ; a man without heart or conscience. Your niece knew nothing of such men. When he breathed his vows to her, as he had done to a hundred before her, she flattered herself that she alone had touched his heart. The devil knows best what he said, but at least she became his tool, and was in the habit of seeing him nearly every evening."

" I cannot, and I will not, believe it ! " cried the banker, with an ashen face.

" I will tell you, then, what occurred in your house last night. Your niece, when you had, as she thought, gone to your room, slipped down and talked to her lover through the window which leads into the stable lane. His footmarks had pressed right through the snow, so long had he stood there. She told him of the coronet. His wicked lust for gold kindled at the news, and he bent her to his will. I have no doubt that she loved you, but there are women in whom the love of a lover extinguishes all other loves, and I think that she must have been one. She had hardly listened to his instructions when she saw you coming down stairs, on which she closed the window rapidly, and told you about one of the servants' escapade with her wooden-legged lover, which was all perfectly true.

"Your boy, Arthur, went to bed after his interview with you, but he slept badly on account of his uneasiness about his club debts. In the middle of the night he heard a soft tread pass his door, so he rose, and looking out was surprised to see his cousin walking very stealthily along the passage, until she disappeared into your dressing-room. Petrified with astonishment the lad slipped on some clothes, and waited there in the dark to see what would come of this strange affair. Presently she emerged from the room again, and in the light of the passage lamp your son saw that she carried the precious coronet in her hands. She passed down the stairs, and he, thrilling with horror, ran along and slipped behind the curtain near your door, whence he could see what passed in the hall beneath. He saw her stealthily open the window, hand out the coronet to someone in the gloom, and then closing it once more hurry back to her room, passing quite close to where he stood hid behind the curtain.

"As long as she was on the scene he could not take any action without a horrible exposure of the woman whom he loved. But the instant that she was gone he realised how crushing a misfortune this would be for you, and how all-important it was to set it right. He rushed down, just as he was, in his bare feet, opened the window, sprang out into the snow, and ran down the lane, where he could see a dark

"ARTHUR CAUGHT HIM."

figure in the moonlight. Sir George Burnwell tried to get away, but Arthur caught him, and there was a struggle between them, your lad tugging at one side of the coronet, and his opponent at the other. In the scuffle, your son struck Sir George, and cut him over the eye. Then something suddenly snapped, and your son, finding that he had the coronet in his hands, rushed back, closed the window, ascended to your room, and had just observed that the coronet had been twisted in the struggle, and was endeavouring to straighten it, when you appeared upon the scene."

"Is it possible?" gasped the banker.

"You then roused his anger by calling him names at a moment when he felt that he had deserved your warmest thanks. He could not explain the true state of affairs without betraying one who certainly deserved little enough consideration at his hands. He took the more chivalrous view, however, and preserved her secret."

"And that was why she shrieked and fainted when she saw the coronet," cried Mr. Holder. "Oh, my God! what a blind fool I have been. And his asking to be allowed to go out for five minutes! The dear fellow wanted to see if the missing piece were at the scene of the struggle. How cruelly I have misjudged him!"

"When I arrived at the house," continued Holmes, "I at once went very carefully round it to observe if there were any traces in the snow which might help me. I knew that none had fallen since the evening before, and also that there had been a strong frost to preserve impressions. I passed along the tradesmen's path, but found it all trampled down and indistinguishable. Just beyond it, however, at the far side of the kitchen door, a woman had stood and talked with a man, whose round impressions on one side showed that he had a wooden leg. I could even tell that they had been disturbed, for the woman had run back swiftly to the door, as was shown by the deep toe and light heelmarks, while Wooden-leg had waited a little, and then had gone away. I thought at the time that this might be the maid and her sweetheart, of whom you had already spoken to me, and inquiry showed it was so. I passed round the garden without seeing anything more than random tracks, which I took to be the police; but when I got into the stable lane a very long and complex story was written in the snow in front of me.

"There was a double line of tracks of a booted man, and a second double line which I saw with delight belonged to a man with naked feet. I was at once convinced from what you had told me that the latter was your son. The first had walked both ways, but the other had run swiftly, and, as his tread was marked in places over the depression of the boot, it was obvious that he had passed after the other. I followed them up, and found that they led to the hall window, where Boots had worn all the snow away while waiting. Then I walked to the other end, which was a hundred yards or more down the lane. I saw where Boots had faced round, where the snow was cut up as though there had been a struggle, and, finally, where a few drops of blood had fallen, to show me that I was not mistaken. Boots had then run down

the lane, and another little smudge of blood showed that it was he who had been hurt. When he came to the high road at the other end, I found that the pavement had been cleared, so there was an end to that clue.

"On entering the house, however, I examined, as you remember, the sill and framework of the hall window with my lens, and I could at once see that someone had passed out. I could distinguish the outline of an instep where the wet foot had been placed in coming in. I was then beginning to be able to form an opinion as to what had occurred. A man had waited outside the window, someone had brought him the gems; the deed had been overseen by your son, he had pursued the thief, had struggled with him, they had each tugged at the coronet, their united strength causing injuries which neither alone could have effected. He had returned with the prize, but had left a fragment in the grasp of his opponent. So far I was clear. The question now was, who was the man, and who was it brought him the coronet?

"It is an old maxim of mine that when you have excluded the impossible, whatever remains, however improbable, must be the truth. Now, I knew that it was not you who had brought it down, so there only remained your niece and the maids. But if it were the maids, why should your son allow himself to be accused in their place? There could be no possible reason. As he loved his cousin, however, there was an excellent explanation why he should retain her secret—the more so as the secret was a disgraceful one. When I remembered that you had seen her at that window, and how she had fainted on seeing the coronet again, my conjecture became a certainty.

"And who could it be who was her confederate? A lover evidently, for who else could outweigh the love and gratitude which she must feel to you? I knew that you went out little, and that your circle of friends was a very limited one. But among them was Sir George Burnwell. I had heard of him before as being a man of evil reputation among women. It must have been he who wore those boots, and retained the missing gems. Even though he knew that Arthur had discovered him, he might still flatter himself that he was safe, for the lad could not say a word without compromising his own family.

"Well, your own good sense will suggest what measures I took next. I went in the shape of a loafer to Sir George's house, managed to pick up an acquaintance with his valet, learned that his master had cut his head the night before, and finally, at the expense of six shillings, made all sure by buying a pair of his cast-off shoes. With these I journeyed down to Streatham, and saw that they exactly fitted the tracks."

"I saw an ill-dressed vagabond in the lane yesterday evening," said Mr. Holder.

"Precisely. It was I. I found that I had my man, so I came home and changed my clothes. It was a delicate part which I had to play then, for I saw that a prosecution must be avoided to avert scandal, and I knew that so astute a villain would see that our hands were tied in the matter. I went and saw him. At first, of course, he denied everything. But when I gave him every particular that had occurred, he tried to bluster, and took down a life-preserver from the wall. I knew my man, however, and I clapped a pistol to his head before he could strike. Then he became a little more reasonable. I told him that we would give him a price for the stones he held—a thousand pounds apiece. That brought out the first signs of grief that he had shown.

"I CLAPPED A PISTOL TO HIS HEAD."

'Why, dash it all!' said he, 'I've let them go at six hundred for the three!' I soon managed to get the address of the receiver who had them, on promising him that there would be no prosecution. Off I set to him, and after much chaffering I got our stones at a thousand apiece. Then I looked in upon your son, told him that all was right, and eventually got to my bed about two o'clock, after what I may call a really hard day's work."

"A day which has saved England from a great public scandal," said the banker, rising. "Sir, I cannot find words to thank you, but you shall not find me ungrateful for what you have done. Your skill has indeed exceeded all that I have ever heard of it. And now I must fly to my dear boy to apologise to him for the wrong which I have done him. As to what you tell me of poor Mary, it goes to my very heart. Not even your skill can inform me where she is now."

"I think that we may safely say," returned Holmes, "that she is wherever Sir George Burnwell is. It is equally certain, too, that whatever her sins are, they will soon receive a more than sufficient punishment."

# Adventures of Sherlock Holmes.

## XII.—THE ADVENTURE OF THE COPPER BEECHES.

### By A. Conan Doyle.

"T O the man who loves art for its own sake," remarked Sherlock Holmes, tossing aside the advertisement sheet of *The Daily Telegraph*, "it is frequently in its least important and lowliest manifestations that the keenest pleasure is to be derived. It is pleasant to me to observe, Watson, that you have so far grasped this truth that in these little records of our cases which you have been good enough to draw up, and, I am bound to say, occasionally to embellish, you have given prominence not so much to the many *causes célèbres* and sensational trials in which I have figured, but rather to those incidents which may have been trivial in themselves, but which have given room for those faculties of deduction and of logical synthesis which I have made my special province."

"And yet," said I, smiling, "I cannot quite hold myself absolved from the charge of sensationalism which has been urged against my records."

"You have erred, perhaps," he observed, taking up a glowing cinder with the tongs, and lighting with it the long cherrywood pipe which was wont to replace his clay when he was in a disputatious, rather than a meditative mood—"you have erred perhaps in attempting to put colour and life into each of your statements, instead of confining yourself to the task of placing upon record that severe reasoning from cause to effect which is really the only notable feature about the thing."

"It seems to me that I have done you full justice in the matter," I remarked, with some coldness, for I was repelled by the egotism which I had more than once observed to be a strong factor in my friend's singular character.

"No, it is not selfishness or conceit," said he, answering, as was his wont, my thoughts rather than my words. "If I claim full justice for my art, it is because it is an impersonal thing—a thing beyond myself. Crime is common. Logic is rare. Therefore it is upon the logic rather than upon the crime that you should dwell. You have degraded what should have been a course of lectures into a series of tales."

It was a cold morning of the early spring, and we sat after breakfast on either side of a cheery fire in the old room at Baker-street. A thick fog rolled down between the lines of dun-coloured houses, and the opposing windows loomed like dark, shapeless blurs through the heavy yellow wreaths. Our gas was lit, and shone on the white cloth, and glimmer of china and metal, for the table had not been cleared yet. Sherlock Holmes had been

"TAKING UP A GLOWING CINDER WITH THE TONGS."

silent all the morning, dipping continuously into the advertisement columns of a succession of papers, until at last, having apparently given up his search, he had emerged in no very sweet temper to lecture me upon my literary shortcomings.

"At the same time," he remarked, after a pause, during which he had sat puffing at his long pipe and gazing down into the fire, "you can hardly be open to a charge of sensationalism, for out of these cases which you have been so kind as to interest yourself in, a fair proportion do not treat of crime, in its legal sense, at all. The small matter in which I endeavoured to help the King of Bohemia, the singular experience of Miss Mary Sutherland, the problem connected with the man with the twisted lip, and the incident of the noble bachelor, were all matters which are outside the pale of the law. But in avoiding the sensational, I fear that you may have bordered on the trivial."

"The end may have been so," I answered, "but the methods I hold to have been novel and of interest."

"Pshaw, my dear fellow, what do the public, the great unobservant public, who could hardly tell a weaver by his tooth or a compositor by his left thumb, care about the finer shades of analysis and deduction! But, indeed, if you are trivial, I cannot blame you, for the days of the great cases are past. Man, or at least criminal man, has lost all enterprise and originality. As to my own little practice, it seems to be degenerating into an agency for recovering lost lead pencils, and giving advice to young ladies from boarding-schools. I think that I have touched bottom at last, however. This note I had this morning marks my zero point, I fancy. Read it!" He tossed a crumpled letter across to me.

It was dated from Montague-place upon the preceding evening, and ran thus :—

"DEAR MR. HOLMES,—I am very anxious to consult you as to whether I should or should not accept a situation which has been offered to me as governess. I shall call at half-past ten to-morrow, if I do not inconvenience you.—Yours faithfully,

VIOLET HUNTER."

"Do you know the young lady?" I asked.

"Not I."

"It is half-past ten now."

"Yes, and I have no doubt that is her ring."

"It may turn out to be of more interest than you think. You remember that the affair of the blue carbuncle, which appeared to be a mere whim at first, developed into a serious investigation. It may be so in this case, also."

"Well, let us hope so! But our doubts will very soon be solved, for here, unless I am much mistaken, is the person in question."

As he spoke the door opened, and a young lady entered the room. She was plainly but neatly dressed, with a bright, quick face, freckled like a plover's egg, and with the brisk manner of a woman who has had her own way to make in the world.

"You will excuse my troubling you, I am sure," said she, as my companion rose to greet her; "but I have had a very strange experience, and as I have no parents or relations of any sort from whom I could ask advice, I thought that perhaps you would be kind enough to tell me what I should do."

"Pray take a seat, Miss Hunter. I shall be happy to do anything that I can to serve you."

I could see that Holmes was favourably impressed by the manner and speech of his new client. He looked her over in his searching fashion, and then composed himself with his lids drooping and his finger tips together to listen to her story.

"I have been a governess for five years," said she, "in the family of Colonel Spence Munro, but two months ago the Colonel received an appointment at Halifax, in Nova Scotia, and took his children over to America with him, so that I found myself without a situation. I advertised, and I answered advertisements, but without success. At last the little money which I had saved began to run short, and I was at my wit's end as to what I should do.

"There is a well-known agency for governesses in the West-end called Westaway's, and there I used to call about once a week in order to see whether anything had turned up which might suit me. Westaway was the name of the founder of the business, but it is really managed by Miss Stoper. She sits in her own little office, and the ladies who are seeking employment wait in an ante-room, and are then shown in one by one, when she consults her ledgers, and sees whether she has anything which would suit them.

"Well, when I called last week I was

shown into the little office as usual, but I found that Miss Stoper was not alone. A prodigiously stout man with a very smiling face, and a great heavy chin which rolled down in fold upon fold over his throat, sat at her elbow with a pair of glasses on his nose, looking very earnestly at the ladies who entered. As I came in he gave quite a jump in his chair, and turned quickly to Miss Stoper:

"'That will do," said he , 'I could not ask for anything better. Capital! capital!

French, a little German, music and drawing——'

"'Tut, tut!' he cried. 'This is all quite beside the question. The point is, have you or have you not the bearing and deportment of a lady? There it is in a nutshell. If you have not, you are not fitted for the rearing of a child who may some day play a considerable part in the history of the country. But if you have, why, then, how could any gentleman ask you to condescend to accept anything

"CAPITAL."

He seemed quite enthusiastic, and rubbed his hands together in the most genial fashion. He was such a comfortable-looking man that it was quite a pleasure to look at him.

"'You are looking for a situation, miss? he asked.

"'Yes, sir.'

"'As governess?

"'Yes, sir.'

"'And what salary do you ask?

"'I had four pounds a month in my last place with Colonel Spence Munro.'

"'Oh, tut, tut! sweating—rank sweating!' he cried, throwing his fat hands out into the air like a man who is in a boiling passion. 'How could anyone offer so pitiful a sum to a lady with such attractions and accomplishments?'

"'My accomplishments, sir, may be less than you imagine,' said I. 'A little

under the three figures? Your salary with me, madam, would commence at a hundred pounds a year.'

"You may imagine, Mr. Holmes, that to me, destitute as I was, such an offer seemed almost too good to be true. The gentleman, however, seeing perhaps the look of incredulity upon my face, opened a pocket-book and took out a note.

"'It is also my custom,' said he, smiling in the most pleasant fashion until his eyes were just two little shining slits, amid the white creases of his face, 'to advance to my young ladies half their salary beforehand, so that they may meet any little expenses or their journey and their wardrobe.'

"It seemed to me that I had never met so fascinating and so thoughtful a man. As I was already in debt to my tradesmen the advance was a great convenience, and yet there was something unnatural about the whole transaction which made me wish to know a little more before I quite committed myself.

"'May I ask where you live, sir?' said I.

"'Hampshire. Charming rural place. The Copper Beeches, five miles on the far side of Winchester. It is the most lovely country, my dear young lady, and the dearest old country house.'

"'And my duties, sir? I should be glad to know what they would be.'

"'One child—one dear little romper just six years old. Oh, if you could see him killing cockroaches with a slipper! Smack! smack! smack! Three gone before you could wink!' He leaned back in his chair and laughed his eyes into his head again.

"I was a little startled at the nature of the child's amusement, but the father's laughter made me think that perhaps he was joking.

"'My sole duties, then,' I asked, 'are to take charge of a single child?'

"'No, no, not the sole, not the sole, my dear young lady,' he cried. 'Your duty would be, as I am sure your good sense would suggest, to obey any little commands which my wife might give, provided always that they were such commands as a lady might with propriety obey. You see no difficulty, heh?'

"'I should be happy to make myself useful.'

"'Quite so. In dress now, for example! We are faddy people, you know—faddy but kind-hearted. If you were asked to wear any dress which we might give you, you would not object to our little whim. Heh?'

"'No,' said I, considerably astonished at his words.

"'Or to sit here, or sit there, that would not be offensive to you?'

"'Oh, no.'

"'Or to cut your hair quite short before you come to us.'

"I could hardly believe my ears. As you may observe, Mr. Holmes, my hair is somewhat luxuriant, and of a rather peculiar tint of chestnut. It has been considered artistic. I could not dream of sacrificing it in this offhand fashion.

"'I am afraid that that is quite impossible,' said I. He had been watching me eagerly out of his small eyes, and I could see a shadow pass over his face as I spoke.

"'I am afraid that it is quite essential,' said he. 'It is a little fancy of my wife's, and ladies' fancies, you know, madam, ladies'

fancies must be consulted. And so you won't cut your hair?'

"'No, sir, I really could not,' I answered firmly.

"'Ah, very well; then that quite settles the matter. It is a pity, because in other respects you would really have done very nicely. In that case, Miss Stoper, I had best inspect a few more of your young ladies.'

"The manageress had sat all this while busy with her papers without a word to either of us, but she glanced at me now with so much annoyance upon her face that I could not help suspecting that she had lost a handsome commission through my refusal.

"'Do you desire your name to be kept upon the books?' she asked.

"'If you please, Miss Stoper.'

"'Well, really, it seems rather useless, since you refuse the most excellent offers in this fashion,' said she sharply. 'You can hardly expect us to exert ourselves to find another such opening for you. Good day to you, Miss Hunter.' She struck a gong upon the table, and I was shown out by the page.

"Well, Mr. Holmes, when I got back to my lodgings and found little enough in the cupboard, and two or three bills upon the table, I began to ask myself whether I had not done a very foolish thing. After all, if these people had strange fads, and expected obedience on the most extraordinary matters, they were at least ready to pay for their eccentricity. Very few governesses in England are getting a hundred a year. Besides, what use was my hair to me? Many people are improved by wearing it short, and perhaps I should be among the number. Next day I was inclined to think that I had made a mistake, and by the day after I was sure of it. I had almost overcome my pride, so far as to go back to the agency and inquire whether the place was still open, when I received this letter from the gentleman himself. I have it here, and I will read it to you:—

"'The Copper Beeches, near Winchester.

"'DEAR MISS HUNTER,—Miss Stoper has very kindly given me your address, and I write from here to ask you whether you have reconsidered your decision. My wife is very anxious that you should come, for she has been much attracted by my description of you. We are willing to give thirty pounds a quarter, or £120 a year, so as to recompense you for any little inconvenience which our fads may cause you. They are not very exacting after all. My wife is fond of a particular shade of electric blue, and would like you to wear such a dress indoors in the morning. You need not, however, go to the expense of purchasing one, as we have one belonging to my dear daughter Alice (now in Philadelphia) which would, I should think, fit you very well. Then, as to sitting here or there, or amusing yourself in any manner indicated, that need cause you no inconvenience. As regards your hair, it is no doubt a pity, especially as I could not help remarking its beauty during our short interview, but I am afraid that I must remain firm upon this point, and I only hope that the increased salary may recompense you for the loss. Your duties, as far as the child is concerned, are very light. Now do try to come, and I shall meet you with the dogcart at Winchester. Let me know your train.—Yours faithfully,

JEPHRO RUCASTLE.'

"That is the letter which I have just received, Mr. Holmes, and my mind is made up that I will accept it. I thought, however, that before taking the final step, I should like to submit the whole matter to your consideration."

"Well, Miss Hunter, if your mind is made up, that settles the question," said Holmes, smiling.

"But you would not advise me to refuse?"

"I confess that it is not the situation which I should like to see a sister of mine apply for."

"What is the meaning of it all, Mr. Holmes?"

"Ah, I have no data. I cannot tell. Perhaps you have yourself formed some opinion?"

"Well, there seems to me to be only one possible solution. Mr. Rucastle seemed to be a very kind, good-natured man. Is it not possible that his wife is a lunatic, that he desires to keep the matter quiet for fear she should be taken to an asylum, and that he humours her fancies in every way in order to prevent an outbreak."

"That is a possible solution—in fact, as matters stand, it is the most probable one. But in any case it does not seem to be a nice household for a young lady."

"But the money, Mr. Holmes, the money!"

"Well, yes, of course the pay is good— too good. That is what makes me uneasy. Why should they give you £120 a year, when they could have their pick for £40? There must be some strong reason behind."

"I thought that if I told you the circumstances you would understand afterwards if I wanted your help. I should feel so much stronger if I felt that you were at the back of me."

"Oh, you may carry that feeling away with you. I assure you that your little problem promises to be the most interesting which has come my way for some months. There is something distinctly novel about some of the features. If you should find yourself in doubt or in danger——"

"Danger! What danger do you foresee?"

Holmes shook his head gravely. "It would cease to be a danger if we could define it," said he. "But at any time, day or night, a telegram would bring me down to your help."

"HOLMES SHOOK HIS HEAD GRAVELY."

"That is enough." She rose briskly from her chair with the anxiety all swept from her face. "I shall go down to Hampshire quite easy in my mind now. I shall write to Mr. Rucastle at once, sacrifice my poor hair to-night, and start for Winchester to morrow." With a few grateful words to Holmes she bade us both good-night and bustled off upon her way.

"At least," said I, as we heard her quick, firm step descending the stairs, "she seems to be a young lady who is very well able to take care of herself."

"And she would need to be," said Holmes, gravely ; "I am much mistaken if we do not hear from her before many days are past."

It was not very long before my friend's prediction was fulfilled. A fortnight went by, during which I frequently found my thoughts turning in her direction, and wondering what strange side-alley of human experience this lonely woman had strayed into. The unusual salary, the curious conditions, the light duties, all pointed to something abnormal, though whether a fad or a plot, or whether the man were a philanthropist or a villain, it was quite beyond my powers to determine. As to Holmes, I observed that he sat frequently for half an hour on end, with knitted brows and an abstracted air, but he swept the matter away with a wave of his hand when I mentioned it. "Data ! data ! data !" he cried impatiently. "I can't make bricks without clay." And yet he would always wind up by muttering that no sister of his should ever have accepted such a situation.

The telegram which we eventually received came late one night, just as I was thinking of turning in, and Holmes was settling down to one of those all-night chemical researches which he frequently indulged in, when I would leave him stooping over a retort and a test-tube at night, and find him in the same position when I came down to breakfast in the morning. He opened the yellow envelope, and then, glancing at the message, threw it across to me.

"Just look up the trains in Bradshaw," said he, and turned back to his chemical studies.

The summons was a brief and urgent one.

"Please be at the 'Black Swan' Hotel at Winchester at midday to-morrow," it said. "Do come ! I am at my wit's end.

"HUNTER."

"Will you come with me ? " asked Holmes, glancing up.

"I should wish to."

"Just look it up, then."

"There is a train at half-past nine," said I, glancing over my Bradshaw. "It is due at Winchester at 11.30."

"That will do very nicely. Then perhaps I had better postpone my analysis of the acetones, as we may need to be at our best in the morning."

By eleven o'clock the next day we were well upon our way to the old English capital. Holmes had been buried in the morning papers all the way down, but after we had passed the Hampshire border he threw them down, and began to admire the scenery. It was an ideal spring day, a light blue sky, flecked with little fleecy white clouds drifting across from west to east. The sun was shining very brightly, and yet there was an exhilarating nip in the air, which set an edge to a man's energy. All over the countryside, away to the rolling hills around Aldershot, the little red and grey roofs of the farm-steadings peeped out from amidst the light green of the new foliage.

"Are they not fresh and beautiful ? " I cried, with all the enthusiasm of a man fresh from the fogs of Baker-street.

But Holmes shook his head gravely.

"Do you know, Watson," said he, "that it is one of the curses of a mind with a turn like mine that I must look at everything with reference to my own special subject. You look at these scattered houses, and you are impressed by their beauty. I look at them, and the only thought which comes to me is a feeling of their isolation, and of the impunity with which crime may be committed there."

"Good heavens ! " I cried. "Who would associate crime with these dear old homesteads ? "

"They always fill me with a certain horror. It is my belief, Watson, founded upon my experience, that the lowest and vilest alleys in London do not present a more dreadful record of sin than does the smiling and beautiful countryside."

"You horrify me ! "

"But the reason is very obvious. The pressure of public opinion can do in the town what the law cannot accomplish. There is no lane so vile that the scream of a tortured child, or the thud of a drunkard's blow, does not beget sympathy and indignation among the neighbours, and then the whole machinery of justice is ever so close that a word of complaint can set it going, and there is but a step between the crime and the dock. But look at these lonely houses, each in its own fields, filled for the most part with poor ignorant folk who know little of the law. Think of the deeds of hellish cruelty, the hidden wickedness which may go on, year in, year out, in such places, and none the wiser. Had this lady who appeals to us for help gone to live in Winchester, I should never have had a fear for her. It is the five miles of country which makes the danger. Still, it is clear that she is not personally threatened."

"No. If she can come to Winchester to meet us she can get away."

"Quite so. She has her freedom."

"What *can* be the matter, then? Can you suggest no explanation?"

"I have devised seven separate explanations, each of which would cover the facts as far as we know them. But which of these is correct can only be determined by the fresh information which we shall no doubt find waiting for us. Well, there is the tower of the Cathedral, and we shall soon learn all that Miss Hunter has to tell."

The "Black Swan" is an inn of repute in the High-street, at no distance from the station, and there we found the young lady waiting for us. She had engaged a sitting-room, and our lunch awaited us upon the table.

"I am so delighted that you have come," she said, earnestly. "It is so very kind of you both; but indeed I do not know what I should do. Your advice will be altogether invaluable to me."

"Pray tell us what has happened to you."

"I will do so, and I must be quick, for I have promised Mr. Rucastle to be back before three. I got his leave to come into town this morning, though he little knew for what purpose."

"Let us have everything in its due

"I AM SO DELIGHTED THAT YOU HAVE COME.'

order." Holmes thrust his long thin legs out towards the fire, and composed himself to listen.

"In the first place, I may say that I have met, on the whole, with no actual ill-treatment from Mr. and Mrs. Rucastle. It is only fair to them to say that. But I cannot understand them, and I am not easy in my mind about them."

"What can you not understand?"

"Their reasons for their conduct. But you shall have it all just as it occurred. When I came down Mr. Rucastle met me here, and drove me in his dogcart to the Copper Beeches. It is, as he said, beautifully situated, but it is not beautiful in itself, for it is a large square block of a house, whitewashed, but all stained and streaked with damp and bad weather. There are grounds round it, woods on three sides, and on the fourth a field which slopes down to the Southampton high road, which curves past about a hundred yards from the front door. This ground in front belongs to the house, but the woods all round are part of Lord Southerton's preserves. A clump of copper beeches immediately in front of the hall door has given its name to the place.

"I was driven over by my employer, who was as amiable as ever, and was introduced by him that evening to his wife and the child. There was no truth, Mr. Holmes, in the conjecture which seemed to us to be probable in your rooms at Baker-street. Mrs. Rucastle is not mad. I found her to be a silent, pale-faced woman, much younger than her husband, not more than thirty, I should think, while he can hardly be less than forty-five. From their conversation I have gathered that they have been married about seven years, that he was a widower, and that his only child by the first wife was the daughter who has gone to Philadelphia. Mr. Rucastle told me in private that the reason why she had left them was that she had an unreasoning aversion to her step-mother. As the daughter could not have been less than twenty I can quite imagine that her position must have been uncomfortable with her father's young wife.

"Mrs. Rucastle seemed to me to be colourless in mind as well as in feature. She impressed me neither favourably nor the reverse. She was a nonentity. It was easy to see that she was passionately devoted both to her husband and to her little son. Her light grey eyes wandered continually from one to the other, noting every little want and forestalling it if possible. He was kind to her also in his bluff boisterous fashion, and on the whole they seemed to be a happy couple. And yet she had some secret sorrow, this woman. She would often be lost in deep thought, with the saddest look upon her face. More than once I have surprised her in tears. I have thought sometimes that it was the disposition of her child which weighed upon her mind, for I have never met so utterly spoilt and so ill-natured a little creature. He is small for his age, with a head which is quite disproportionately large. His whole life appears to be spent in an alternation between savage fits of passion, and gloomy intervals of sulking. Giving pain to any creature weaker than himself seems to be his one idea of amusement, and he shows quite remarkable talent in planning the capture of mice, little birds, and insects. But I

would rather not talk about the creature, Mr. Holmes, and, indeed, he has little to do with my story."

"I am glad of all details," remarked my friend, "whether they seem to you to be relevant or not."

"I shall try not to miss anything of importance. The one unpleasant thing about the house, which struck me at once, was the appearance and conduct of the servants. There are only two, a man and his wife. Toller, for that is his name, is a rough, uncouth man, with grizzled hair and whiskers, and a perpetual smell of drink. Twice since I have been with them he has been quite drunk, and yet Mr. Rucastle seemed to take no notice of it. His wife is a very tall and strong woman with a sour face, as silent as Mrs. Rucastle, and much less amiable. They are a most unpleasant couple, but fortunately I spend most of my time in the nursery and my own room, which are next to each other in one corner of the building.

"For two days after my arrival at the Copper Beeches my life was very quiet; on the third, Mrs. Rucastle came down just after breakfast and whispered something to her husband.

"'Oh yes,' said he, turning to me; 'we are very much obliged to you, Miss Hunter, for falling in with our whims so far as to cut your hair. I assure you that it has not detracted in the tiniest iota from your appearance. We shall now see how the electric blue dress will become you. You will find it laid out upon the bed in your room, and if you would be so good as to put it on we should both be extremely obliged.'

"The dress which I found waiting for me was of a peculiar shade of blue. It was of excellent material, a sort of beige, but it bore unmistakable signs of having been worn before. It could not have been a better fit if I had been measured for it. Both Mr. and Mrs. Rucastle expressed a delight at the look of it which seemed quite exaggerated in its vehemence. They were waiting for me in the drawing-room, which is a very large room, stretching along the entire front of the house, with three long windows reaching down to the floor. A chair had been placed close to the central window, with its back turned towards it. In this I was asked to sit, and then Mr. Rucastle, walking up and down on the other side of the room, began to tell me a series of the funniest stories that I have ever listened to. You cannot imagine how comical he was, and I laughed until I was quite weary. Mrs. Rucastle, however, who has evidently no sense of humour, never so much as smiled, but sat with her hands in her lap, and a sad, anxious look upon her face. After an hour or so, Mr. Rucastle suddenly remarked that it was time to commence the duties of the day, and that I might change my dress, and go to little Edward in the nursery.

"Two days later this same performance was gone through under exactly similar circumstances. Again I changed my dress, again I sat in the window, and again I laughed very heartily at the funny stories of which my employer had an immense *répertoire*, and which he told inimitably. Then he handed me a yellow-backed novel, and, moving my chair a little sideways, that my own shadow might not fall upon

"I READ FOR ABOUT TEN MINUTES."

the page, he begged me to read aloud to him. I read for about ten minutes, beginning in the heart of a chapter, and then suddenly, in the middle of a sentence, he

ordered me to cease and to change my dress.

"You can easily imagine, Mr. Holmes, how curious I became as to what the meaning of this extraordinary performance could possibly be. They were always very careful, I observed, to turn my face away from the window, so that I became consumed with the desire to see what was going on behind my back. At first it seemed to be impossible, but I soon devised a means. My hand mirror had been broken, so a happy thought seized me, and I concealed a piece of the glass in my handkerchief. On the next occasion, in the midst of my laughter, I put my handkerchief up to my eyes, and was able with a little management to see all that there was behind me. I confess that I was disappointed. There was nothing.

"At least, that was my first impression. At the second glance, however, I perceived that there was a man standing in the Southampton Road, a small bearded man in a grey suit, who seemed to be looking in my direction. The road is an important highway, and there are usually people there. This man, however, was leaning against the railings which bordered our field, and was looking earnestly up. I lowered my handkerchief, and glanced at Mrs. Rucastle to find her eyes fixed upon me with a most searching gaze. She said nothing, but I am convinced that she had divined that I had a mirror in my hand, and had seen what was behind me. She rose at once.

"'Jephro,' said she, 'there is an impertinent fellow upon the road there who stares up at Miss Hunter.'

"'No friend of yours, Miss Hunter?' he asked.

"'No; I know no one in these parts.'

"'Dear me! How very impertinent! Kindly turn round, and motion to him to go away!'

"'Surely it would be better to take no notice.'

"'No, no, we should have him loitering here always. Kindly turn round, and wave him away like that.'

"I did as I was told, and at the same instant Mrs. Rucastle drew down the blind. That was a week ago, and from that time I have not sat again in the window, nor have

I worn the blue dress, nor seen the man in the road."

"Pray continue," said Holmes. "Your narrative promises to be a most interesting one."

"You will find it rather disconnected, I fear, and there may prove to be little relation between the different incidents of which I speak. On the very first day that I was at the Copper Beeches, Mr. Rucastle took me to a small outhouse which stands near the kitchen door. As we approached it I heard the sharp rattling of a chain, and the sound as of a large animal moving about.

"'Look in here!' said Mr. Rucastle, showing me a slit between two planks. 'Is he not a beauty?'

"I looked through, and was conscious of two glowing eyes, and of a vague figure huddled up in the darkness.

"'Don't be frightened,' said my employer, laughing at the start which I had given. 'It's only Carlo, my mastiff. I call him mine, but really old Toller, my groom, is the only man who can do anything with him. We feed him once a day, and not too much then, so that he is always as keen as mustard. Toller lets him loose every night, and God help the trespasser whom he lays his fangs upon. For goodness' sake don't you ever on any pretext set your foot over the threshold at night, for it is as much as your life is worth.'

"The warning was no idle one, for two nights later I happened to look out of my bedroom window about two o'clock in the morning. It was a beautiful moonlight night, and the lawn in front of the house was silvered over and almost as bright as day. I was standing, wrapt in the peaceful beauty of the scene, when I was aware that something was moving under the shadow of the copper beeches. As it emerged into the moonshine I saw what it was. It was a giant dog, as large as a calf, tawny tinted, with hanging jowl, black muzzle, and huge projecting bones. It walked slowly across the lawn and vanished into the shadow upon the other side. That

dreadful silent sentinel sent a chill to my heart which I do not think that any burglar could have done.

"And now I have a very strange experience to tell you. I had, as you know, cut off my hair in London, and I had placed it in a great coil at the bottom of my trunk. One evening, after the child was in bed, I began to amuse myself by examining the furniture of my room, and by rearranging my own little things. There was an old chest of drawers in the room, the two upper ones empty and open, the lower one locked. I had filled the two first with my linen, and, as I had still much to pack away, I was naturally annoyed at not having the use of the third drawer. It struck me that it might have been fastened by a mere oversight, so I took out my bunch of keys and tried to open it. The very first key fitted to perfection, and I drew the drawer open. There was only one thing in it, but I am sure that you would never guess what it was. It was my coil of hair.

"I took it up and examined it. It was of the same peculiar tint, and the same thickness. But then the impossibility of the thing obtruded itself upon me. How *could* my hair have been locked in the drawer?

"I TOOK IT UP AND EXAMINED IT."

With trembling hands I undid my trunk turned out the contents, and drew from the bottom my own hair. I laid the two tresses together, and I assure you that they were identical. Was it not extraordinary? Puzzle as I would, I could make nothing at all of what it meant. I returned the strange hair to the drawer, and I said nothing of the matter to the Rucastles, as I felt that I had put myself in the wrong by opening a drawer which they had locked.

"I am naturally observant, as you may have remarked, Mr. Holmes, and I soon had a pretty good plan of the whole house in my head. There was one wing, however, which appeared not to be inhabited at all. A door which faced that which led into the quarters of the Tollers opened into this suite, but it was invariably locked. One day, however, as I ascended the stair, I met Mr. Rucastle coming out through this door, his keys in his hand, and a look on his face which made him a very different person to the round, jovial man to whom I was accustomed. His cheeks were red, his brow was all crinkled with anger, and the veins stood out at his temples with passion. He locked the door, and hurried past me without a word or a look.

"This aroused my curiosity; so when I went out for a walk in the grounds with my charge, I strolled round to the side from which I could see the windows of this part of the house. There were four of them in a row, three of which were simply dirty, while the fourth was shuttered up. They were evidently all deserted. As I strolled up and down, glancing at them occasionally, Mr. Rucastle came. out t me, looking as merry and jovial as ever.

"'Ah!' said he, 'you must not think me rude if I passed you without a word, my dear young lady. I was pre-occupied with business matters.'

"I assured him that I was not offended. 'By the way,' said I, you seem to have quite a suite of spare rooms up there, and one of them has the shutters up.'

"He looked surprised, and, as it seemed to me, a little startled at my remark.

"'Photography is one of my hobbies,' said he. 'I have made my dark room up there. But, dear me! what an observant young lady we have come upon. Who would have believed it? Who would have ever believed it?' He spoke in a jesting tone, but there was no jest in his eyes as he looked at me. I read suspicion there, and annoyance, but no jest.

"Well, Mr. Holmes, from the moment that I understood that there was something about that suite of rooms which I was not to know, I was all on fire to go over them. It was not mere curiosity, though I have my share of that. It was more a feeling of duty—a feeling that some good might come from my penetrating to this place. They talk of woman's instinct; perhaps it was woman's instinct which gave me that feeling. At any rate, it was there; and I was keenly on the look-out for any chance to pass the forbidden door.

"It was only yesterday that the chance came. I may tell you that, besides Mr. Rucastle, both Toller and his wife find something to do in these deserted rooms, and I once saw him carrying a large black linen bag with him through the door. Recently he has been drinking hard, and yesterday evening he was very drunk; and, when I came upstairs, there was the key in the door. I have no doubt at all that he had left it there. Mr. and Mrs. Rucastle were both downstairs, and the child was with them, so that I had an admirable opportunity. I turned the key gently in the lock, opened the door, and slipped through.

"There was a little passage in front of me, unpapered and uncarpeted, which turned at a right angle at the further end. Round this corner were three doors in a line, the first and third of which were open. They each led into an empty room, dusty and cheerless, with two windows in the one, and one in the other, so thick with dirt that the evening light glimmered dimly through them. The centre door was closed, and across the outside of it had been fastened one of the broad bars of an iron bed, padlocked at one end to a ring in the wall, and fastened at the other with stout cord. The door itself was locked as well, and the key was not there. This barricaded door corresponded clearly with the shuttered window outside, and yet I could see by the glimmer from beneath it that the room was not in darkness. Evidently there was a skylight which let in light from above. As I stood in the passage gazing at this sinister door, and wondering what secret it might veil, I suddenly heard the sound of steps within the room, and saw a shadow pass backwards and forwards against the little slit of dim light which shone out from under the door. A mad, unreasoning terror rose up in me at the sight, Mr. Holmes. My overstrung nerves failed me suddenly, and I turned and ran—ran as though some dreadful hand were behind me, clutching at the skirt of my dress. I rushed down the passage, through the door, and straight into the arms of Mr. Rucastle, who was waiting outside.

"'So,' said he, smiling, 'it was you, then. I thought that it must be when I saw the door open.'

"'Oh, I am so frightened!' I panted.

"'My dear young lady! my dear young lady!'—you cannot think how caressing and soothing his manner was—'and what has frightened you, my dear young lady?'

"But his voice was just a little too coaxing. He overdid it. I was keenly on my guard against him.

"'I was foolish enough to go into the empty wing,' I answered. 'But it is so lonely and eerie in this dim light that I was frightened and ran out again. Oh, it is so. dreadfully still in there!'

"'Only that?' said he, looking at me keenly.

"'OH! I AM SO FRIGHTENED!' I PANTED."

"'Why, what did you think?' I asked.

"'Why do you think that I lock this door?'

"'I am sure that I do not know.'

"'It is to keep people out who have no business there. Do you see?' He was still smiling in the most amiable manner.

"'I am sure if I had known—— '

"'Well, then, you know now. And if you ever put your foot over that threshold again—' here in an instant the smile hardened into a grin of rage, and he glared down at me with the face of a demon, 'I'll throw you to the mastiff.'

"I was so terrified that I do not know what I did. I suppose that I must have rushed past him into my room. I remember nothing until I found myself lying on my bed trembling all over. Then I thought of you, Mr. Holmes. I could not live there longer without some advice. I was frightened of the house, of the man, of the woman, of the servants, even of the child. They were all horrible to me. If I could only bring you down all would be well. Of course I might have fled from the house, but my curiosity was almost as strong as my fears. My mind was soon made up. I would send you a wire. I put on my hat and cloak, went down to the office, which is about half a mile from the house, and then returned, feeling very much easier. A horrible doubt came into my mind as I approached the door lest the dog might be loose, but I remembered that Toller had drunk himself into a state of insensibility that evening, and I knew that he was the only one in the household who had any influence with the savage creature, or who would venture to set him free. I slipped in in safety, and lay awake half the night in my joy at the thought of seeing you. I had no difficulty in getting leave to come into Winchester this morning, but I must be back before three o'clock, for Mr. and Mrs. Rucastle are going on a visit, and will be away all the evening, so that I must look after the child. Now I have told you all my adventures, Mr. Holmes, and I should be very glad if you could tell me what it all means, and, above all, what I should do."

Holmes and I had listened spell-bound to this extraordinary story.

My friend rose now, and paced up and down the room, his hands in his pockets, and an expression of the most profound gravity upon his face.

" Is Toller still drunk ? " he asked.

" Yes. I heard his wife tell Mrs. Rucastle that she could do nothing with him."

" That is well. And the Rucastles go out to-night ? "

" Yes."

" Is there a cellar with a good strong lock ? "

" Yes, the wine cellar."

" You seem to me to have acted all through this matter like a very brave and sensible girl, Miss Hunter. Do you think that you could perform one more feat ? I should not ask it of you if I did not think you a quite exceptional woman."

" I will try. What is it ? "

" We shall be at the Copper Beeches by seven o'clock, my friend and I. The Rucastles will be gone by that time, and Toller will, we hope, be incapable. There only remains Mrs. Toller, who might give the alarm. If you could send her into the cellar on some errand, and then turn the key upon her, you would facilitate matters immensely."

" I will do it."

" Excellent ! We shall then look thoroughly into the affair. Of course there is only one feasible explanation. You have been brought there to personate someone, and the real person is imprisoned in this chamber. That is obvious. As to who this prisoner is, I have no doubt that it is the daughter, Miss Alice Rucastle, if I remember right, who was said to have gone to America. You were chosen, doubtless, as resembling her in height, figure, and the colour of your hair. Hers had been cut off, very possibly in some illness through which she has passed, and so, of course, yours had to be sacrificed also. By a curious chance you came upon her tresses. The man in the road was, undoubtedly, some friend of hers—possibly her *fiancé*—and no doubt as you wore the girl's dress, and were so like her, he was convinced from your laughter, whenever he saw you, and afterwards from your gesture, that Miss Rucastle was perfectly happy, and that she no longer desired his attentions. The dog is let loose at night to prevent him from endeavouring to communicate with her. So much is fairly clear. The most serious point in the case is the disposition of the child."

" What on earth has that to do with it ? " I ejaculated.

" My dear Watson, you as a medical man are continually gaining light as to the tendencies of a child by the study of the parents. Don't you see that the converse is equally valid. I have frequently gained my first real insight into the character of parents by studying their children. This child's disposition is abnormally cruel, merely for cruelty's sake, and whether he derives this from his smiling father, as I should suspect, or from his mother, it bodes evil for the poor girl who is in their power."

" I am sure that you are right, Mr. Holmes," cried our client. " A thousand things come back to me which make me certain that you have hit it. Oh, let us lose not an instant in bringing help to this poor creature."

" We must be circumspect, for we are dealing with a very cunning man. We can do nothing until seven o'clock. At that hour we shall be with you, and it will not be long before we solve the mystery."

We were as good as our word, for it was just seven when we reached the Copper Beeches, having put up our trap at a wayside publichouse. The group of trees, with their dark leaves shining like burnished metal in the light of the setting sun, were sufficient to mark the house even had Miss Hunter not been standing smiling on the doorstep.

" Have you managed it ? " asked Holmes.

A loud thudding noise came from somewhere downstairs. " That is Mrs. Toller in the cellar," said she. " Her husband lies snoring on the kitchen rug. Here are his keys, which are the duplicates of Mr. Rucastle's."

" You have done well indeed ! " cried Holmes, with enthusiasm. " Now lead the way, and we shall soon see the end of this black business."

We passed up the stair, unlocked the door, followed on down a passage, and found ourselves in front of the barricade which Miss Hunter had described. Holmes cut the cord and removed the transverse bar. Then he tried the various keys in the lock, but without success. No sound came from within, and at the silence Holmes' face clouded over.

" I trust that we are not too late," said he. " I think, Miss Hunter, that we had better go in without you. Now, Watson, put your shoulder to it, and we shall see whether we cannot make our way in."

"It was an old rickety door, and gave at once before our united strength. Together we rushed into the room. It was empty. There was no furniture save a little pallet bed, a small table, and a basketful of linen. The skylight above was open, and the prisoner gone.

"There has been some villainy here," said Holmes, "this beauty has guessed Miss Hunter's intentions, and has carried his victim off."

"But how?"

"Through the skylight. We shall soon see how he managed it." He swung him-

heavy stick in his hand. Miss Hunter screamed and shrunk against the wall at the sight of him, but Sherlock Holmes sprang forward and confronted him.

"You villain!" said he, "where's your daughter?"

The fat man cast his eyes round, and then up at the open skylight.

"It is for me to ask you that," he shrieked, "you thieves! Spies and thieves! I have caught you, have I? You are in my power. I'll serve you!" He turned and clattered down the stairs as hard as he could go.

"'YOU VILLAIN!' SAID HE. 'WHERE'S YOUR DAUGHTER?'"

self up on to the roof. "Ah, yes," he cried, "here's the end of a long light ladder against the eaves. That is how he did it."

"But it is impossible," said Miss Hunter, "the ladder was not there when the Rucastles went away."

"He has come back and done it. I tell you that he is a clever and dangerous man. I should not be very much surprised if this were he whose step I hear now upon the stair. I think, Watson, that it would be as well for you to have your pistol ready."

The words were hardly out of his mouth before a man appeared at the door of the room, a very fat and burly man, with a

"He's gone for the dog!" cried Miss Hunter.

"I have my revolver," said I.

"Better close the front door," cried Holmes, and we all rushed down the stairs together. We had hardly reached the hall when we heard the baying of a hound, and then a scream of agony, with a horrible worrying sound which it was dreadful to listen to. An elderly man with a red face and shaking limbs came staggering out at a side door.

"My God!" he cried. "Some one has loosed the dog. It's not been fed for two days. Quick, quick, or it'll be too late!"

Holmes and I rushed out, and round the angle of the house, with Toller hurrying behind us. There was the huge famished brute, its black muzzle buried in Rucastle's throat, while he writhed and screamed upon the ground. Running up, I blew its brains out, and it fell over with its keen white teeth still meeting in the great creases of his neck. With much labour we separated them, and carried him, living but horribly mangled, into the house. We laid him upon the drawing-room sofa, and, having despatched the sobered Toller to bear the news to his wife, I did what I could to relieve his pain. We were all assembled

there's police-court business over this, you'll remember that I was the one that stood your friend, and that I was Miss Alice's friend too.

"She was never happy at home, Miss Alice wasn't, from the time that her father married again. She was slighted like, and had no say in anything; but it never really became bad for her until after she met Mr. Fowler at a friend's house. As well as I could learn, Miss Alice had rights of her own by will, but she was so quiet and patient, she was, that she never said a word about them, but just left everything in Mr. Rucastle's hands. He knew he was safe

'RUNNING UP, I BLEW ITS BRAINS OUT.'

round him when the door opened, and a tall, gaunt woman entered the room.

"Mrs. Toller!" cried Miss Hunter.

"Yes, miss. Mr. Rucastle let me out when he came back before he went up to you. Ah, miss, it is a pity you didn't let me know what you were planning, for I would have told you that your pains were wasted."

"Ha!" said Holmes, looking keenly at her. "It is clear that Mrs. Toller knows more about this matter than anyone else."

"Yes, sir, I do, and I am ready enough to tell what I know."

"Then, pray, sit down, and let us hear it, for there are several points on which I must confess that I am still in the dark."

"I will soon make it clear to you," said she; "and I'd have done so before now if I could ha' got out from the cellar. If

with her; but when there was a chance of a husband coming forward, who would ask for all that the law would give him, then her father thought it time to put a stop on it. He wanted her to sign a paper so that whether she married or not, he could use her money. When she wouldn't do it, he kept on worrying her until she got brain fever, and for six weeks was at death's door. Then she got better at last, all worn to a shadow, and with her beautiful hair cut off; but that didn't make no change in her young man, and he stuck to her as true as man could be.

"Ah," said Holmes, "I think that what you have been good enough to tell us makes the matter fairly clear, and that I can deduce all that remains. Mr. Rucastle then, I presume, took to this system of imprisonment?"

" Yes, sir."

" And brought Miss Hunter down from London in order to get rid of the disagreeable persistence of Mr. Fowler."

" That was it, sir."

" But Mr. Fowler being a persevering man, as a good seaman should be, blockaded the house, and, having met you, succeeded by certain arguments, metallic or otherwise, in convincing you that your interests were the same as his."

" Mr. Fowler was a very kind-spoken, free-handed gentleman," said Mrs. Toller serenely.

" And in this way he managed that your good man should have no want of drink, and that a ladder should be ready at the moment when your master had gone out."

" You have it, sir, just as it happened."

" I am sure we owe you an apology, Mrs. Toller," said Holmes, " for you have certainly cleared up everything which puzzled us. And here comes the country surgeon and Mrs. Rucastle, so I think, Watson, that we had best escort Miss Hunter back to Winchester, as it seems to me that our *locus standi* now is rather a questionable one."

And thus was solved the mystery of the sinister house with the copper beeches in front of the door. Mr. Rucastle survived, but was always a broken man, kept alive solely through the care of his devoted wife. They still live with their old servants, who probably know so much of Rucastle's past life that he finds it difficult to part from them. Mr. Fowler and Miss Rucastle were married, by special licence, in Southampton the day after their flight, and he is now the holder of a Government appointment in the Island of Mauritius. As to Miss Violet Hunter, my friend Holmes, rather to my disappointment, manifested no further interest in her when once she had ceased to be the centre of one of his problems, and she is now the head of a private school at Walsall, where I believe that she has met with considerable success.

## Adventures of Sherlock Holmes.*

### XIII.—THE ADVENTURE OF SILVER BLAZE

#### By A. Conan Doyle.

 "I AM afraid, Watson, that I shall have to go," said Holmes, as we sat down together to our breakfast one morning.

"Go! Where to?"

"To Dartmoor—to King's Pyland."

I was not surprised. Indeed, my only wonder was that he had not already been mixed up in this extraordinary case, which was the one topic of conversation through the length and breadth of England. For a whole day my companion had rambled about the room with his chin upon his chest and his brows knitted, charging and re-charging his pipe with the strongest black tobacco, and absolutely deaf to any of my questions or remarks. Fresh editions of every paper had been sent up by our newsagent only to be glanced over and tossed down into a corner. Yet, silent as he was, I knew perfectly well what it was, over which he was brooding. There was but one problem before the public which could challenge his powers of analysis, and that was the singular disappearance of the favourite for the Wessex Cup and the tragic murder of its trainer. When, therefore, he suddenly announced his intention of setting out for the scene of the drama, it was only what I had both expected and hoped for.

"I should be most happy to go down with you if I should not be in the way," said I.

"My dear Watson, you would confer a great favour upon me by coming. And I think that your time will not be mis-spent, for there are points about this case which promise to make it an absolutely unique one. We have, I think, just time to catch our train at Paddington, and I will go further into the matter upon our journey. You would oblige me by bringing with you your very excellent field-glass."

And so it happened that an hour or so later I found myself in the corner of a first-class carriage, flying along, en route for Exeter, while Sherlock Holmes, with his sharp, eager face framed in his earflapped travelling cap, dipped rapidly into the bundle of fresh papers which he had procured at Paddington. We had left Reading far behind us before he thrust the last of them under the seat, and offered me his cigar case.

"We are going well," said he, looking out of the window, and glancing at his watch. "Our rate at present is fifty-three and a half miles an hour."

"I have not observed the quarter-mile posts," said I.

"Nor have I. But the telegraph posts upon this line are sixty yards apart, and the calculation is a simple one. I presume that you have already looked into this matter of the murder of John Straker and the disappearance of Silver Blaze?"

"I have seen what the *Telegraph* and the *Chronicle* have to say."

"It is one of those cases where the art of the reasoner should be used rather for the sifting of details than for the acquiring of fresh evidence. The tragedy has been so uncommon, so complete, and of such personal importance to so many people that we are suffering from a plethora of surmise, conjecture, and hypothesis. The difficulty is to detach the framework of fact—of absolute, undeniable fact—from the embellishments of theorists and reporters. Then, having established ourselves upon this sound basis, it is our duty to see what inferences may be drawn, and which are the special points upon which the whole mystery turns. On Tuesday evening I received telegrams, both from Colonel Ross, the owner of the horse, and from Inspector Gregory, who is looking after the case, inviting my co-operation."

"Tuesday evening!" I exclaimed. "And this is Thursday morning. Why did you not go down yesterday?"

"Because I made a blunder, my dear Watson—which is, I am afraid, a more common occurrence than anyone would think who only knew me through your memoirs.

The fact is that I could not believe it possible that the most remarkable horse in England could long remain concealed, especially in so sparsely inhabited a place as the north of Dartmoor. From hour to hour yesterday I expected to hear that he had been found, and that his abductor was the murderer of John Straker. When, however, another morning had come and I found that, beyond the arrest of young Fitzroy Simpson, nothing had been done, I felt that it was time for me to take action. Yet in some ways I feel that yesterday has not been wasted."

"You have formed a theory then ?"

"At least I have got a grip of the essential facts of the case. I shall enumerate them to you, for nothing clears up a case so much as stating it to another person, and I can hardly expect your co-operation if I do not show you the position from which we start."

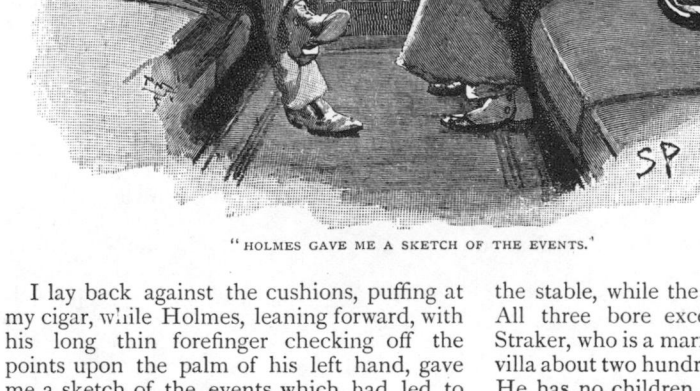

" HOLMES GAVE ME A SKETCH OF THE EVENTS.'

Isonomy stock, and holds as brilliant a record as his famous ancestor. He is now in his fifth year, and has brought in turn each of the prizes of the turf to Colonel Ross, his fortunate owner. Up to the time of the catastrophe he was first favourite for the Wessex Cup, the betting being three to one on. He has always, however, been a prime favourite with the racing public, and has never yet disappointed them, so that even at those odds enormous sums of money have been laid upon him. It is obvious, therefore, that there were many people who had the strongest interest in preventing Silver Blaze from being there at the fall of the flag, next Tuesday.

"This fact was, of course, appreciated at King's Pyland, where the Colonel's training stable is situated. Every precaution was taken to guard the favourite. The trainer, John Straker, is a retired jockey, who rode in Colonel Ross's colours before he became too heavy for the weighing chair. He has served the Colonel for five years as jockey, and for seven as trainer, and has always shown himself to be a zealous and honest servant. Under him were three lads, for the establishment was a small one, containing only four horses in all. One of these lads sat up each night in the stable, while the others slept in the loft. All three bore excellent characters. John Straker, who is a married man, lived in a small villa about two hundred yards from the stables. He has no children, keeps one maid-servant, and is comfortably off. The country round is very lonely, but about half a mile to

I lay back against the cushions, puffing at my cigar, while Holmes, leaning forward, with his long thin forefinger checking off the points upon the palm of his left hand, gave me a sketch of the events which had led to our journey.

"Silver Blaze," said he, "is from the

the north there is a small cluster of villas which have been built by a Tavistock contractor for the use of invalids and others who may wish to enjoy the pure Dartmoor air. Tavistock itself lies two miles to the west, while across the moor, also about two miles distant, is the larger training establishment of Mapleton, which belongs to Lord Backwater, and is managed by Silas Brown. In every other direction the moor is a complete wilderness, inhabited only by a few roaming gipsies. Such was the general situation last Monday night when the catastrophe occurred.

"On that evening the horses had been exercised and watered as usual, and the stables were locked up at nine o'clock. Two of the lads walked up to the trainer's house, where they had supper in the kitchen, while the third, Ned Hunter, remained on guard. At a few minutes after nine the maid, Edith Baxter, carried down to the stables his supper, which consisted of a dish of curried mutton. She took no liquid, as there was a water-tap in the stables, and it was the rule that the lad on duty should drink nothing else. The maid carried a lantern with her, as it was very dark, and the path ran across the open moor.

"A MAN APPEARED OUT OF THE DARKNESS."

"Edith Baxter was within thirty yards of the stables when a man appeared out of the darkness and called to her to stop. As he stepped into the circle of yellow light thrown by the lantern she saw that he was a person of gentlemanly bearing, dressed in a grey suit of tweed with a cloth cap. He wore gaiters, and carried a heavy stick with a knob to it. She was most impressed, however, by the extreme pallor of his face and by the nervousness of his manner. His age, she thought, would be rather over thirty than under it.

"'Can you tell me where I am?' he asked. 'I had almost made up my mind to sleep on the moor when I saw the light of your lantern.'

"'You are close to the King's Pyland training stables,' she said.

"'Oh, indeed! What a stroke of luck!' he cried. 'I understand that a stable boy sleeps there alone every night. Perhaps that is his supper which you are carrying to him. Now I am sure that you would not be too proud to earn the price of a new dress, would you?' He took a piece of white paper folded up out of his waistcoat pocket. 'See that the boy has this to-night, and you shall have the prettiest frock that money can buy.'

"She was frightened by the earnestness of his manner, and ran past him to the window through which she was accustomed to hand the meals. It was already open, and Hunter was seated at the small table inside. She had begun to tell him of what had happened, when the stranger came up again.

"'Good evening,' said he, looking through the window, 'I wanted to have a word with you.' The girl has sworn that as he spoke she noticed the corner of the little paper packet protruding from his closed hand.

"'What business have you here?' asked the lad.

"'It's business that may put something into your pocket,' said the other. 'You've two horses in for the Wessex Cup—Silver Blaze and Bayard. Let me have the straight tip, and you won't be a loser. Is it a fact that at the weights Bayard could give the other a hundred yards in five furlongs, and that the stable have put their money on him?'

"'So you're one of those damned touts,' cried the lad. 'I'll show you how we serve them in King's Pyland.' He sprang up and rushed across the stable to unloose the dog. The girl fled away to the house, but as she ran she looked back, and saw that the stranger was leaning through the window. A minute later, however, when Hunter rushed out with the hound he was gone, and though the lad ran all round the buildings he failed to find any trace of him."

"One moment!" I asked. "Did the stable-boy, when he ran out with the dog, leave the door unlocked behind him?"

"Excellent, Watson; excellent!" murmured my companion. "The importance of the point struck me so forcibly, that I sent a special wire to Dartmoor yesterday to clear the matter up. The boy locked the door before he left it. The window, I may add, was not large enough for a man to get through.

"Hunter waited until his fellow grooms had returned, when he sent a message up to the trainer and told him what had occurred. Straker was excited at hearing the account, although he does not seem to have quite realized its true significance. It left him, however, vaguely uneasy, and Mrs. Straker, waking at one in the morning, found that he was dressing. In reply to her inquiries, he said that he could not sleep on account of his anxiety about the horses, and that he intended to walk down to the stables to see that all was well. She begged him to remain at home, as she could hear the rain pattering against the windows, but in spite of her entreaties he pulled on his large mackintosh and left the house.

"Mrs. Straker awoke at seven in the morning, to find that her husband had not yet returned. She dressed herself hastily, called the maid, and set off for the stables. The door was open; inside, huddled together upon a chair, Hunter was sunk in a state of absolute stupor, the favourite's stall was empty, and there were no signs of his trainer.

"The two lads who slept in the chaff-cutting loft above the harness-room were quickly aroused. They had heard nothing during the night, for they are both sound sleepers. Hunter was obviously under the influence of some powerful drug; and, as no sense could be got out of him, he was left to sleep it off while the two lads and the two women ran out in search of the absentees. They still had hopes that the trainer had for some reason taken out the horse for early exercise, but on ascending the knoll near the house, from which all the neighbouring moors were visible, they not only could see no signs of the favourite, but they perceived something which warned them that they were in the presence of a tragedy.

"About a quarter of a mile from the stables, John Straker's overcoat was flapping from a

"THEY FOUND THE DEAD BODY OF THE UNFORTUNATE TRAINER.

furze bush. Immediately beyond there was a bowl-shaped depression in the moor, and at the bottom of this was found the dead body of the unfortunate trainer. His head had been shattered by a savage blow from some heavy weapon, and he was wounded in the thigh, where there was a long, clean cut, inflicted evidently by some very sharp instrument. It was clear, however, that Straker had defended himself vigorously against his assailants, for in his right hand he held a small knife, which was clotted with blood up to the handle, while in his left he grasped a red and black silk cravat, which was recognised by the maid as having been worn on the preceding evening by the stranger who had visited the stables.

"Hunter, on recovering from his stupor, was also quite positive as to the ownership of the cravat. He was equally certain that the same stranger had, while standing at the window, drugged his curried mutton, and so deprived the stables of their watchman.

"As to the missing horse, there were abundant proofs in the mud which lay at the bottom of the fatal hollow, that he had been there at the time of the struggle. But from that morning he has disappeared; and although a large reward has been offered, and all the gipsies of Dartmoor are on the alert, no news has come of him. Finally an analysis has shown that the remains of his supper, left by the stable lad, contain an appreciable quantity of powdered opium, while the people at the house partook of the same dish on the same night without any ill effect.

"Those are the main facts of the case, stripped of all surmise and stated as baldly as possible. I shall now recapitulate what the police have done in the matter.

"Inspector Gregory, to whom the case has been committed, is an extremely competent officer. Were he but gifted with imagination he might rise to great heights in his profession. On his arrival he promptly found and arrested the man upon whom suspicion naturally rested. There was little difficulty in finding him, for he inhabited one of those villas which I have mentioned. His name, it appears, was Fitzroy Simpson. He was a man of excellent birth and education, who had squandered a fortune upon the turf, and who lived now by doing a little quiet and genteel bookmaking in the sporting clubs of London. An examination of his betting-book shows that bets to the amount of five thousand pounds had been registered by him against the favourite.

"On being arrested he volunteered the statement that he had come down to Dartmoor in the hope of getting some information about the King's Pyland horses, and also about Desborough, the second favourite, which was in charge of Silas Brown, at the Mapleton stables. He did not attempt to deny that he had acted as described upon the evening before, but declared that he had no sinister designs, and had simply wished to obtain first-hand information. When confronted with his cravat he turned very pale, and was utterly unable to account for its presence in the hand of the murdered man. His wet clothing showed that he had been out in the storm of the night before, and his stick, which was a Penang lawyer, weighted with lead, was just such a weapon as might, by repeated blows, have inflicted the terrible injuries to which the trainer had succumbed.

"On the other hand, there was no wound upon his person, while the state of Straker's knife would show that one, at least, of his assailants must bear his mark upon him. There you have it all in a nutshell, Watson, and if you can give me any light I shall be infinitely obliged to you."

I had listened with the greatest interest to the statement which Holmes, with characteristic clearness, had laid before me. Though most of the facts were familiar to me, I had not sufficiently appreciated their relative importance, nor their connection to each other.

"Is it not possible," I suggested, "that the incised wound upon Straker may have been caused by his own knife in the convulsive struggles which follow any brain injury?"

"It is more than possible; it is probable," said Holmes. "In that case, one of the main points in favour of the accused disappears."

"And yet," said I, "even now I fail to understand what the theory of the police can be."

"I am afraid that whatever theory we state has very grave objections to it," returned my companion. "The police imagine, I take it, that this Fitzroy Simpson, having drugged the lad, and having in some way obtained a duplicate key, opened the stable door, and took out the horse, with the intention, apparently, of kidnapping him altogether. His bridle is missing, so that Simpson must have put this on. Then, having left the door open behind him, he was leading the horse away over the moor, when he was either met or overtaken by the trainer. A row naturally ensued, Simpson beat out the trainer's brains with his heavy stick without receiving any injury from the small knife which Straker used in self-defence, and then the thief either led the horse on to some secret hiding-place, or else it may have bolted during the struggle, and be now wandering out on the moors. That is the case as it appears to the police, and improbable as it is, all other explanations are more improbable still. However, I shall very quickly test the matter when I am once upon the spot, and until then I really cannot see how we can get much further than our present position."

It was evening before we reached the little town of Tavistock, which lies, like the boss of a shield, in the middle of the huge circle of Dartmoor. Two gentlemen were awaiting us at the station; the one a tall fair man with lion-like hair and beard, and curiously penetrating light blue eyes, the other a small alert person, very neat and dapper, in a frock-coat and gaiters, with trim little side-whiskers and an eye-glass. The latter was Colonel Ross, the well-known sportsman, the other Inspector Gregory, a man who was rapidly making his name in the English detective service.

"I am delighted that you have come down, Mr. Holmes," said the Colonel. "The Inspector here has done all that could possibly be suggested ; but I wish to leave no stone unturned in trying to avenge poor Straker, and in recovering my horse."

"Have there been any fresh developments?" asked Holmes.

"I am sorry to say that we have made very little progress," said the Inspector. "We have an open carriage outside, and as you would no doubt like to see the place before the light fails, we might talk it over as we drive."

A minute later we were all seated in a comfortable landau and were rattling through the quaint old Devonshire town. Inspector Gregory was full of his case, and poured out a stream of remarks, while Holmes threw in an occasional question or interjection. Colonel Ross leaned back with his arms folded and his hat tilted over his eyes, while I listened with interest to the dialogue of the two detectives. Gregory was formulating his theory, which was almost exactly what Holmes had foretold in the train.

"The net is drawn pretty close round Fitzroy Simpson," he remarked, "and I believe myself that he is our man. At the same time, I recognise that the evidence is purely circumstantial, and that some new development may upset it."

"How about Straker's knife?"

"We have quite come to the conclusion that he wounded himself in his fall."

"My friend Dr. Watson made that suggestion to me as we came down. If so, it would tell against this man Simpson."

"Undoubtedly. He has neither a knife nor any sign of a wound. The evidence against him is certainly very strong. He had a great interest in the

"I AM DELIGHTED THAT YOU HAVE COME DOWN, MR. HOLMES."

disappearance of the favourite, he lies under the suspicion of having poisoned the stable boy, he was undoubtedly out in the storm, he was armed with a heavy stick, and his cravat was found in the dead man's hand. I really think we have enough to go before a jury."

Holmes shook his head. "A clever counsel would tear it all to rags," said he. "Why should he take the horse out of the stable? If he wished to injure it, why could he not do it there? Has a duplicate key been found in his possession? What chemist sold him the powdered opium? Above all, where could he, a stranger to the district, hide a horse, and such a horse as this? What is his own explanation as to the paper which he wished the maid to give to the stable-boy?"

"He says that it was a ten-pound note. One was found in his purse. But your other difficulties are not so formidable as they seem. He is not a stranger to the district. He has twice lodged at Tavistock in the summer. The opium was probably brought from London. The key, having served its purpose, would be hurled away. The horse may lie at the bottom of one of the pits or old mines upon the moor."

"What does he say about the cravat?"

"He acknowledges that it is his, and declares that he had lost it. But a new element has been introduced into the case which may account for his leading the horse from the stable."

Holmes pricked up his ears.

"We have found traces which show that a party of gipsies encamped on Monday night within a mile of the spot where the murder took place. On Tuesday they were gone. Now, presuming that there was some understanding between Simpson and these gipsies, might he not have been leading the horse to them when he was overtaken, and may they not have him now?"

"It is certainly possible."

"The moor is being scoured for these gipsies. I have also examined every stable and outhouse in Tavistock, and for a radius of ten miles."

"There is another training stable quite close, I understand?"

"Yes, and that is a factor which we must certainly not neglect. As Desborough, their horse, was second in the betting, they had an interest in the disappearance of the favourite. Silas Brown, the trainer, is known to have had large bets upon the event, and he was no friend to poor Straker. We have, however, examined the stables, and there is nothing to connect him with the affair."

"And nothing to connect this man Simpson with the interests of the Mapleton stables?"

"Nothing at all."

Holmes leaned back in the carriage and the conversation ceased. A few minutes later our driver pulled up at a neat little red-brick villa with overhanging eaves, which stood by the road. Some distance off, across a paddock, lay a long grey-tiled out-building. In every other direction the low curves of the moor, bronze-coloured from the fading ferns, stretched away to the sky-line, broken only by the steeples of Tavistock, and by a cluster of houses away to the westward, which marked the Mapleton stables. We all sprang out with the exception of Holmes, who continued to lean back with his eyes fixed upon the sky in front of him, entirely absorbed in his own thoughts. It was only when I touched his arm that he roused himself with a violent start and stepped out of the carriage.

"Excuse me," said he, turning to Colonel Ross, who had looked at him in some surprise. "I was day-dreaming." There was a gleam in his eyes and a suppressed excitement in his manner which convinced me, used as I was to his ways, that his hand was upon a clue, though I could not imagine where he had found it.

"Perhaps you would prefer at once to go on to the scene of the crime, Mr. Holmes?" said Gregory.

"I think that I should prefer to stay here a little and go into one or two questions of detail. Straker was brought back here, I presume?"

"Yes, he lies upstairs. The inquest is to-morrow."

"He has been in your service some years, Colonel Ross?"

"I have always found him an excellent servant."

"I presume that you made an inventory of what he had in his pockets at the time of his death, Inspector?"

"I have the things themselves in the sitting-room if you would care to see them."

"I should be very glad."

We all filed into the front room and sat round the central table, while the Inspector unlocked a square tin box and laid a small heap of things before us. There was a box of vestas, two inches of tallow candle, an A.D.P. briar-root pipe, a pouch of sealskin with half an ounce of long-cut Cavendish, a silver watch with a gold chain, five sovereigns in gold, an aluminium pencil-case, a few papers, and an ivory-handled knife with a very delicate inflexible blade marked Weiss and Co., London.

"This is a very singular knife," said Holmes, lifting it up and examining it minutely. "I presume, as I see bloodstains upon it, that it is the one which was found in the dead man's grasp. Watson, this knife is surely in your line."

"It is what we call a cataract knife," said I.

"I thought so. A very delicate blade devised for very delicate work. A strange thing for a man to carry with him upon a rough expedition, especially as it would not shut in his pocket."

"The tip was guarded by a disc of cork which we found beside his body," said the Inspector. "His wife tells us that the knife had lain for some days upon the dressing-table, and that he had picked it up as he left the room. It was a poor weapon, but perhaps the best that he could lay his hand on at the moment."

"Very possibly. How about these papers?"

"Three of them are receipted hay-dealers' accounts. One of them is a letter of instructions from Colonel Ross. This other is a milliner's account for thirty-seven pounds fifteen, made out by Madame Lesurier, of Bond Street, to William Darbyshire. Mrs. Straker tells us that Darbyshire was a friend of her husband's, and that occasionally his letters were addressed here."

"Madame Darbyshire had somewhat expensive tastes," remarked Holmes, glancing down the account. "Twenty-two guineas is rather heavy for a single costume. However, there appears to be nothing more to learn, and we may now go down to the scene of the crime."

As we emerged from the sitting-room a woman who had been waiting in the passage took a step forward and laid her hand upon the Inspector's sleeve. Her face was haggard, and thin, and eager; stamped with the print of a recent horror.

"Have you got them? Have you found them?" she panted.

"No, Mrs. Straker; but Mr. Holmes, here, has come from London to help us, and we shall do all that is possible."

"Surely I met you in Plymouth, at a garden party, some little time ago, Mrs. Straker," said Holmes.

"No, sir; you are mistaken."

"HAVE YOU FOUND THEM?" SHE PANTED.

"Dear me; why, I could have sworn to it. You wore a costume of dove-coloured silk, with ostrich feather trimming."

"I never had such a dress, sir," answered the lady.

"Ah; that quite settles it," said Holmes; and, with an apology, he followed the Inspector outside. A short walk across the moor took us to the hollow in which the body had been found. At the brink of it was the furze bush upon which the coat had been hung.

"There was no wind that night, I understand," said Holmes.

"None ; but very heavy rain."

"In that case the overcoat was not blown against the furze bushes, but placed there."

"Yes, it was laid across the bush."

"You fill me with interest. I perceive that the ground has been trampled up a good deal. No doubt many feet have been there since Monday night."

"A piece of matting has been laid here at the side, and we have all stood upon that."

"Excellent."

"In this bag I have one of the boots which Straker wore, one of Fitzroy Simpson's shoes, and a cast horseshoe of Silver Blaze."

"My dear Inspector, you surpass yourself !" Holmes took the bag, and descending into the hollow he pushed the matting into a more central position. Then stretching himself upon his face and leaning his chin upon his hands he made a careful study of the trampled mud in front of him.

"Halloa !" said he, suddenly, "what's this ? "

It was a wax vesta, half burned, which was so coated with mud that it looked at first like a little chip of wood.

"I cannot think how I came to overlook it," said the Inspector, with an expression of annoyance.

"It was invisible, buried in the mud. I only saw it because I was looking for it."

"What ! You expected to find it ? "

"I thought it not unlikely." He took the boots from the bag and compared the impressions of each of them with marks upon the ground. Then he clambered up to the rim of the hollow and crawled about among the ferns and bushes.

"I am afraid that there are no more tracks," said the Inspector. "I have examined the ground very carefully for a hundred yards in each direction."

"Indeed !" said Holmes, rising, "I should not have the impertinence to do it again after what you say. But I should like to take a little walk over the moor before it grows dark, that I may know my ground to-morrow, and I think that I shall put this horseshoe into my pocket for luck."

Colonel Ross, who had shown some signs of impatience at my companion's quiet and systematic method of work, glanced at his watch.

"I wish you would come back with me, Inspector," said he. "There are several points on which I should like your advice, and especially as to whether we do not owe it to the public to remove our horse's name from the entries for the Cup."

"Certainly not," cried Holmes, with decision : "I should let the name stand."

The Colonel bowed. "I am very glad to have had your opinion, sir," said he. "You will find us at poor Straker's house when you have finished your walk, and we can drive together into Tavistock."

He turned back with the Inspector, while Holmes and I walked slowly across the moor. The sun was beginning to sink behind the stables of Mapleton, and the long sloping plain in front of us was tinged with gold, deepening into rich, ruddy brown where the faded ferns and brambles caught the evening light. But the glories of the landscape were all wasted upon my companion, who was sunk in the deepest thought.

"It's this way, Watson," he said at last. "We may leave the question of who killed John Straker for the instant, and confine ourselves to finding out what has become of the horse. Now, supposing that he broke away during or after the tragedy, where could he have gone to? The horse is a very gregarious creature. If left to himself his instincts would have been either to return to King's Pyland, or go over to Mapleton. Why should he run wild upon the moor ? He would surely have been seen by now. And why should gipsies kidnap him? These people always clear out when they hear of trouble, for they do not wish to be pestered by the police. They could not hope to sell such a horse. They would run a great risk and gain nothing by taking him. Surely that is clear."

"Where is he, then ? "

"I have already said that he must have gone to King's Pyland or to Mapleton. He is not at King's Pyland, therefore he is at Mapleton. Let us take that as a working hypothesis and see what it leads us to. This part of the moor, as the Inspector remarked, is very hard and dry. But it falls away towards Mapleton, and you can see from here that there is a long hollow over yonder, which must have been very wet on Monday night. If our supposition is correct, then the horse must have crossed that, and there is the point where we should look for his tracks."

We had been walking briskly during this conversation, and a few more minutes brought us to the hollow in question. At Holmes' request I walked down the bank to the right and he to the left, but I had not taken fifty paces before I heard him give a shout, and saw him waving his hand to me. The track of a horse was plainly outlined in the soft earth in front of him, and the shoe which he took from his pocket exactly fitted the impression.

"See the value of imagination," said Holmes. "It is the one quality which Gregory lacks. We imagined what might have happened, acted upon the supposition, and find ourselves justified. Let us proceed."

We crossed the marshy bottom and passed over a quarter of a mile of dry, hard turf. Again the ground sloped and again we came on the tracks. Then we lost them for half a mile, but only to pick them up once more quite close to Mapleton. It was Holmes who saw them first, and he stood pointing with a look of triumph upon his face. A man's track was visible beside the horse's.

"The horse was alone before," I cried.

"Quite so. It was alone before. Halloa, what is this?"

The double track turned sharp off and took the direction of King's Pyland. Holmes whistled, and we both followed along after it. His eyes were on the trail, but I happened to look a little to one side, and saw to my surprise the same tracks coming back again in the opposite direction.

"One for you, Watson," said Holmes, when I pointed it out; "you have saved us a long walk which would have brought us back on our own traces. Let us follow the return track."

We had not to go far. It ended at the paving of asphalt which led up to the gates of the Mapleton stables. As we approached a groom ran out from them.

"We don't want any loiterers about here," said he.

"I only wished to ask a question," said Holmes, with his finger and thumb in his waistcoat pocket. "Should I be too early to see your master, Mr. Silas Brown, if I were to call at five o'clock to-morrow morning?"

"Bless you, sir, if anyone is about he will be, for he is always the first stirring. But here he is, sir, to answer your questions for himself. No, sir, no; it's as much as my place is worth to let him see me touch your money. Afterwards, if you like."

As Sherlock Holmes replaced the half-crown which he had drawn from his pocket, a fierce-looking, elderly man strode out from the gate with a hunting-crop swinging in his hand.

"What's this, Dawson?" he cried. "No gossiping! Go about your business! And you—what the devil do you want here?"

"Ten minutes' talk with you, my good sir," said Holmes, in the sweetest of voices.

"I've no time to talk to every gadabout. We want no strangers here. Be off, or you may find a dog at your heels."

Holmes leaned forward and whispered

"BE OFF!"

something in the trainer's ear. He started violently and flushed to the temples.

"It's a lie!" he shouted. "An infernal lie!"

"Very good! Shall we argue about it here in public, or talk it over in your parlour?"

"Oh, come in if you wish to."

Holmes smiled. "I shall not keep you more than a few minutes, Watson," he said. "Now, Mr. Brown, I am quite at your disposal."

It was quite twenty minutes, and the reds had all faded into greys before Holmes and the trainer reappeared. Never have I seen such a change as had been brought about in Silas Brown in that short time. His face was ashy pale, beads of perspiration shone upon his brow, and his hands shook until the hunting-crop wagged like a branch in the wind. His bullying, overbearing manner was all gone too, and he cringed along at my companion's side like a dog with its master.

"Your instructions will be done. It shall be done," said he.

"There must be no mistake," said Holmes, looking round at him. The other winced as he read the menace in his eyes.

"Oh, no, there shall be no mistake. It shall be there. Should I change it first or not?"

Holmes thought a little and then burst out laughing. "No, don't," said he. "I shall write to you about it. No tricks now or——"

"Oh, you can trust me, you can trust me!"

"Yes, I think I can. Well, you shall hear from me to-morrow." He turned upon his heel, disregarding the trembling hand which the other held out to him, and we set off for King's Pyland.

"A more perfect compound of the bully, coward and sneak than Master Silas Brown I have seldom met with," remarked Holmes, as we trudged along together.

"He has the horse, then?"

"He tried to bluster out of it, but I described to him so exactly what his actions had been upon that morning, that he is convinced that I was watching him. Of course, you observed the peculiarly square toes in the impressions, and that his own boots exactly corresponded to them. Again, of course, no subordinate would have dared to have done such a thing. I described to him how, according to his custom, he was the first down, he perceived a strange horse wandering over the moor; how he went out to it, and his astonishment at recognising from the white forehead which has given the

favourite its name that chance had put in his power the only horse which could beat the one upon which he had put his money. Then I described how his first impulse had been to lead him back to King's Pyland, and how the devil had shown him how he could hide the horse until the race was over, and how he had led it back and concealed it at Mapleton. When I told him every detail he gave it up, and thought only of saving his own skin."

"But his stables had been searched."

"Oh, an old horse-faker like him has many a dodge."

"But are you not afraid to leave the horse in his power now, since he has every interest in injuring it?"

"My dear fellow, he will guard it as the apple of his eye. He knows that his only hope of mercy is to produce it safe."

"Colonel Ross did not impress me as a man who would be likely to show much mercy in any case."

"The matter does not rest with Colonel Ross. I follow my own methods, and tell as much or as little as I choose. That is the advantage of being unofficial. I don't know whether you observed it, Watson, but the Colonel's manner has been just a trifle cavalier to me. I am inclined now to have a little amusement at his expense. Say nothing to him about the horse."

"Certainly not, without your permission."

"And, of course, this is all quite a minor point compared to the question of who killed John Straker."

"And you will devote yourself to that?"

"On the contrary, we both go back to London by the night train."

I was thunderstruck by my friend's words. We had only been a few hours in Devonshire, and that he should give up an investigation which he had begun so brilliantly was quite incomprehensible to me. Not a word more could I draw from him until we were back at the trainer's house. The Colonel and the Inspector were awaiting us in the parlour.

"My friend and I return to town by the midnight express," said Holmes. "We have had a charming little breath of your beautiful Dartmoor air."

The Inspector opened his eyes, and the Colonel's lip curled in a sneer.

"So you despair of arresting the murderer of poor Straker," said he.

Holmes shrugged his shoulders. "There are certainly grave difficulties in the way," said he. "I have every hope, however, that your horse will start upon Tuesday, and I beg that you will have your jockey in readiness. Might I ask for a photograph of Mr. John Straker?"

The Inspector took one from an envelope in his pocket and handed it to him.

"My dear Gregory, you anticipate all my wants. If I might ask you to wait here for an instant, I have a question which I should like to put to the maid."

"I must say that I am rather disappointed in our London consultant," said Colonel Ross, bluntly, as my friend left the room. "I do not see that we are any further than when he came."

"At least, you have his assurance that your horse will run," said I.

"Yes, I have his assurance," said the Colonel, with a shrug of his shoulders. "I should prefer to have the horse."

I was about to make some reply in defence of my friend, when he entered the room again.

"Now, gentlemen," said he, "I am quite ready for Tavistock."

As we stepped into the carriage one of the stable-lads held the door open for us. A sudden idea seemed to occur to Holmes, for he leaned forward and touched the lad upon the sleeve.

"You have a few sheep in the paddock," he said. "Who attends to them?"

"I do, sir."

"Have you noticed anything amiss with them of late?"

"Well, sir, not of much account; but three of them have gone lame, sir."

I could see that Holmes was extremely pleased, for he chuckled and rubbed his hands together.

"A long shot, Watson; a very long shot!" said he, pinching my arm. "Gregory, let me recommend to your attention this singular epidemic among the sheep. Drive on, coachman!"

Colonel Ross still wore an expression which showed the poor opinion which he had formed of my companion's ability, but I saw by the Inspector's face that his attention had been keenly aroused.

"You consider that to be important?" he asked.

"Exceedingly so."

"Is there any other point to which you would wish to draw my attention?"

"HOLMES WAS EXTREMELY PLEASED."

"To the curious incident of the dog in the night-time."

"The dog did nothing in the night-time."

"That was the curious incident," remarked Sherlock Holmes.

Four days later Holmes and I were again in the train bound for Winchester, to see the race for the Wessex Cup. Colonel Ross met us, by appointment, outside the station, and we drove in his drag to the course beyond the town. His face was grave and his manner was cold in the extreme.

"I have seen nothing of my horse," said he.

"I suppose that you would know him when you saw him?" asked Holmes.

The Colonel was very angry. "I have been on the turf for twenty years, and never was asked such a question as that before," said he. "A child would know Silver Blaze with his white forehead and his mottled off fore leg."

"How is the betting?"

"Well, that is the curious part of it. You could have got fifteen to one yesterday, but the price has become shorter and shorter, until you can hardly get three to one now."

"Hum!" said Holmes. "Somebody knows something, that is clear!"

As the drag drew up in the inclosure near the grand stand, I glanced at the card to see the entries. It ran :—

Wessex Plate. 50 sovs. each, h ft, with 1,000 sovs. added, for four and five-year olds. Second £300. Third £200. New course (one mile and five furlongs).

1. Mr. Heath Newton's The Negro (red cap, cinnamon jacket).
2. Colonel Wardlaw's Pugilist (pink cap, blue and black jacket).
3. Lord Backwater's Desborough (yellow cap and sleeves).
4. Colonel Ross's Silver Blaze (black cap, red jacket).
5. Duke of Balmoral's Iris (yellow and black stripes).
6. Lord Singleford's Rasper (purple cap, black sleeves).

"We scratched our other one and put all hopes on your word," said the Colonel. "Why, what is that? Silver Blaze favourite?"

"Five to four against Silver Blaze!" roared the ring. "Five to four against Silver Blaze! Fifteen to five against Desborough! Five to four on the field!"

"There are the numbers up," I cried. "They are all six there."

"All six there! Then my horse is running," cried the Colonel, in great agitation. "But I don't see him. My colours have not passed."

"Only five have passed. This must be he."

As I spoke a powerful bay horse swept out from the weighing inclosure and cantered past us, bearing on its back the well-known black and red of the Colonel.

"That's not my horse," cried the owner. "That beast has not a white hair upon its body. What is this that you have done, Mr. Holmes?"

"Well, well, let us see how he gets on," said my friend, imperturbably. For a few minutes he gazed through my field-glass. "Capital! An excellent start!" he cried suddenly. "There they are, coming round the curve!"

From our drag we had a superb view as they came up the straight. The six horses were so close together that a carpet could have covered them, but half way up the yellow of the Mapleton stable showed to the front. Before they reached us, however, Desborough's bolt was shot, and the Colonel's horse, coming away with a rush, passed the post a good six lengths before its rival, the Duke of Balmoral's Iris making a bad third.

"It's my race anyhow," gasped the Colonel, passing his hand over his eyes. "I confess that I can make neither head nor tail of it. Don't you think that you have kept up your mystery long enough, Mr. Holmes?"

"Certainly, Colonel. You shall know everything. Let us all go round and have a look at the horse together. Here he is," he continued, as we made our way into the weighing inclosure where only owners and their friends find admittance. "You have only to wash his face and his leg in spirits of wine and you will find that he is the same old Silver Blaze as ever."

"You take my breath away!"

"I found him in the hands of a faker, and took the liberty of running him just as he was sent over."

"My dear sir, you have done wonders. The horse looks very fit and well. It never went better in its life. I owe you a thousand apologies for having doubted your ability. You have done me a great service by recovering my horse. You would do me a greater still if you could lay your hands on the murderer of John Straker."

"I have done so," said Holmes, quietly.

The Colonel and I stared at him in amazement. "You have got him! Where is he, then?"

"He is here."

"Here! Where?"

"In my company at the present moment."

The Colonel flushed angrily. "I quite recognise that I am under obligations to you, Mr. Holmes," said he, "but I must regard what you have just said as either a very bad joke or an insult."

Sherlock Holmes laughed. "I assure you that I have not associated you with the entirely unworthy of your confidence. But there goes the bell; and as I stand to win a little on this next race, I shall defer a more lengthy explanation until a more fitting time."

We had the corner of a Pullman car to

HE LAID HIS HAND UPON THE GLOSSY NECK.

crime, Colonel," said he; "the real murderer is standing immediately behind you!"

He stepped past and laid his hand upon the glossy neck of the thoroughbred.

"The horse!" cried both the Colonel and myself.

"Yes, the horse. And it may lessen his guilt if I say that it was done in self-defence, and that John Straker was a man who was entirely unworthy of your confidence. But ourselves that evening as we whirled back to London, and I fancy that the journey was a short one to Colonel Ross as well as to myself, as we listened to our companion's narrative of the events which had occurred at the Dartmoor training stables upon that Monday night, and the means by which he had unravelled them.

"I confess," said he, "that any theories

which I had formed from the newspaper reports were entirely erroneous. And yet there were indications there, had they not been overlaid by other details which concealed their true import. I went to Devonshire with the conviction that Fitzroy Simpson was the true culprit, although, of course, I saw that the evidence against him was by no means complete.

"It was while I was in the carriage, just as we reached the trainer's house, that the immense significance of the curried mutton occurred to me. You may remember that I was distrait, and remained sitting after you had all alighted. I was marvelling in my own mind how I could possibly have overlooked so obvious a clue."

"I confess," said the Colonel, "that even now I cannot see how it helps us."

"It was the first link in my chain of reasoning. Powdered opium is by no means tasteless. The flavour is not disagreeable, but it is perceptible. Were it mixed with any ordinary dish, the eater would undoubtedly detect it, and would probably eat no more. A curry was exactly the medium which would disguise this taste. By no possible supposition could this stranger, Fitzroy Simpson, have caused curry to be served in the trainer's family that night, and it is surely too monstrous a coincidence to suppose that he happened to come along with powdered opium upon the very night when a dish happened to be served which would disguise the flavour. That is unthinkable. Therefore Simpson becomes eliminated from the case and our attention centres upon Straker and his wife, the only two people who could have chosen curried mutton for supper that night. The opium was added after the dish was set aside for the stable-boy, for the others had the same for supper with no ill effects. Which of them, then, had access to that dish without the maid seeing them?

"Before deciding that question I had grasped the significance of the silence of the dog, for one true inference invariably suggests others. The Simpson incident had shown me that a dog was kept in the stables, and yet, though someone had been in and had fetched out a horse, he had not barked enough to arouse the two lads in the loft. Obviously the midnight visitor was someone whom the dog knew well.

"I was already convinced, or almost convinced, that John Straker went down to the stables in the dead of the night and took out Silver Blaze. For what purpose? For a dishonest one, obviously, or why should he drug his own stable-boy? And yet I was at a loss to know why. There have been cases before now where trainers have made sure of great sums of money by laying against their own horses, through agents, and then preventing them from winning by fraud. Sometimes it is a pulling jockey. Sometimes it is some surer and subtler means. What was it here? I hoped that the contents of his pockets might help me to form a conclusion.

"And they did so. You cannot have forgotten the singular knife which was found in the dead man's hand, a knife which certainly no sane man would choose for a weapon. It was, as Dr. Watson told us, a form of knife which is used for the most delicate operations known in surgery. And it was to be used for a delicate operation that night. You must know, with your wide experience of turf matters, Colonel Ross, that it is possible to make a slight nick upon the tendons of a horse's ham, and to do it subcutaneously so as to leave absolutely no trace. A horse so treated would develop a slight lameness which would be put down to a strain in exercise or a touch of rheumatism, but never to foul play."

"Villain! Scoundrel!" cried the Colonel.

"We have here the explanation of why John Straker wished to take the horse out on to the moor. So spirited a creature would have certainly roused the soundest of sleepers when it felt the prick of the knife. It was absolutely necessary to do it in the open air."

"I have been blind!" cried the Colonel. "Of course, that was why he needed the candle, and struck the match."

"Undoubtedly. But in examining his belongings, I was fortunate enough to discover, not only the method of the crime, but even its motives. As a man of the world, Colonel, you know that men do not carry other people's bills about in their pockets. We have most of us quite enough to do to settle our own. I at once concluded that Straker was leading a double life, and keeping a second establishment. The nature of the bill showed that there was a lady in the case, and one who had expensive tastes. Liberal as you are with your servants, one hardly expects that they can buy twenty-guinea walking dresses for their women. I questioned Mrs. Straker as to the dress without her knowing it, and having satisfied myself that it had never reached her, I made a note of the milliner's address, and felt that by calling there with Straker's photograph, I could easily dispose of the mythical Darbyshire.

"From that time on all was plain. Straker

had led out the horse to a hollow where his light would be invisible. Simpson, in his flight, had dropped his cravat, and Straker had picked it up with some idea, perhaps, that he might use it in securing the horse's leg. Once in the hollow he had got behind the horse, and had struck a light, but the creature, frightened at the sudden glare, and with the strange instinct of animals feeling that some mischief was intended, had lashed out, and the steel shoe had struck Straker full on the forehead. He had already, in spite of the rain, taken off his overcoat in order to do his delicate task, and so, as he fell, his knife gashed his thigh. Do I make it clear?"

"Wonderful!" cried the Colonel. "Wonderful! You might have been there."

"My final shot was, I confess, a very long one. It struck me that so astute a man as Straker would not undertake this delicate tendon-nicking without a little practice. What could he practise on? My eyes fell upon the sheep, and I asked a question which, rather to my surprise, showed that my surmise was correct."

"You have made it perfectly clear, Mr. Holmes."

"When I returned to London I called upon the milliner, who at once recognised Straker as an excellent customer, of the name of Darbyshire, who had a very dashing wife with a strong partiality for expensive dresses. I have no doubt that this woman had plunged him over head and ears in debt, and so led him into this miserable plot."

"You have explained all but one thing," cried the Colonel. "Where was the horse?"

"Ah, it bolted and was cared for by one of your neighbours. We must have an amnesty in that direction, I think. This is Clapham Junction, if I am not mistaken, and we shall be in Victoria in less than ten minutes. If you care to smoke a cigar in our rooms, Colonel, I shall be happy to give you any other details which might interest you."

SILVER BLAZE.

# The Adventures of Sherlock Holmes.

## XIV.—THE ADVENTURE OF THE CARDBOARD BOX.

### By Conan Doyle.

 IN choosing a few typical cases which illustrate the remarkable mental qualities of my friend, Sherlock Holmes, I have endeavoured, as far as possible, to select those which presented the minimum of sensationalism, while offering a fair field for his talents. It is, however, unfortunately, impossible to entirely separate the sensational from the criminal, and a chronicler is left in the dilemma that he must either sacrifice details which are essential to his statement, and so give a false impression of the problem, or he must use matter which chance, and not choice, has provided him with. With this short preface I shall turn to my notes of what proved to be a strange, though a peculiarly terrible, chain of events.

It was a blazing hot day in August. Baker Street was like an oven, and the glare of the sunlight upon the yellow brickwork of the houses across the road was painful to the eye. It was hard to believe that these were the same walls which loomed so gloomily through the fogs of winter. Our blinds were half-drawn, and Holmes lay curled upon the sofa, reading and re-reading a letter which he had received by the morning post. For myself, my term of service in India had trained me to stand heat better than cold, and a thermometer at 90 was no hardship. But the morning paper was uninteresting.

Parliament had risen. Everybody was out of town, and I yearned for the glades of the New Forest or the shingle of Southsea. A depleted bank account had caused me to postpone my holiday, and as to my companion, neither the country nor the sea presented the slightest attraction to him. He loved to lie in the very centre of five millions of people, with his filaments stretching out and running through them, responsive to every little rumour or suspicion of unsolved crime. Appreciation of Nature found no place among his many gifts, and his only change was when he turned his mind from the evil-doer of the town to track down his brother of the country.

Finding that Holmes was too absorbed for conversation I had tossed aside the barren paper and, leaning back in my chair, I fell into a brown study. Suddenly my companion's voice broke in upon my thoughts.

"You are right, Watson," said he. "It does seem a most preposterous way of settling a dispute."

"I FELL INTO A BROWN STUDY."

"Most preposterous!" I exclaimed, and then suddenly realizing how he had echoed the inmost thought of my soul, I sat up in my chair and stared at him in blank amazement.

"What is this, Holmes?" I cried. "This is beyond anything which I could have imagined."

He laughed heartily at my perplexity.

"You remember," said he, "that some little time ago when I read you the passage in one of Poe's sketches in which a close reasoner follows the unspoken thoughts of his companion, you were inclined to treat the matter as a mere *tour-de-force* of the author. On my remarking that I was constantly in the habit of doing the same thing you expressed incredulity."

"Oh, no!"

"Perhaps not with your tongue, my dear Watson, but certainly with your eyebrows. So when I saw you throw down your paper and enter upon a train of thought, I was very happy to have the opportunity of reading it off, and eventually of breaking into it, as a proof that I had been in rapport with you."

But I was still far from satisfied. "In the example which you read to me," said I, "the reasoner drew his conclusions from the actions of the man whom he observed. If I remember right, he stumbled over a heap of stones, looked up at the stars, and so on. But I have been seated quietly in my chair, and what clues can I have given you?"

"You do yourself an injustice. The features are given to man as the means by which he shall express his emotions, and yours are faithful servants."

"Do you mean to say that you read my train of thoughts from my features?"

"Your features, and especially your eyes. Perhaps you cannot yourself recall how your reverie commenced?"

"No, I cannot."

"Then I will tell you. After throwing down your paper, which was the action which drew my attention to you, you sat for half a minute with a vacant expression. Then your eyes fixed themselves upon your newly-framed picture of General Gordon, and I saw by the alteration in your face that a train of thought had been started. But it did not lead very far. Your eyes flashed across to the unframed portrait of Henry Ward Beecher which stands upon the top of your books. You then glanced up at the wall, and of course your meaning was obvious. You were thinking that if the portrait were framed, it would just cover that bare space and correspond with Gordon's picture over there."

"You have followed me wonderfully!" I exclaimed.

"So far I could hardly have gone astray. But now your thoughts went back to Beecher, and you looked hard across as if you were studying the character in his features. Then your eyes ceased to pucker, but you continued to look across, and your face was thoughtful. You were recalling the incidents of Beecher's career. I was well aware that you could not do this without thinking of the mission which he undertook on behalf of the North at the time of the Civil War, for I remember your expressing your passionate indignation at the way in which he was received by the more turbulent of our people. You felt so strongly about it, that I knew you could not think of Beecher without thinking of that also. When a moment later I saw your eyes wander away from the picture, I suspected that your mind had now turned to the Civil War, and when I observed that your lips set, your eyes sparkled, and your hands clenched, I was positive that you were indeed thinking of the gallantry which was shown by both sides in that desperate struggle. But then, again, your face grew sadder; you shook your head. You were dwelling upon the sadness and horror and useless waste of life. Your hand stole towards your own old wound and a smile quivered on your lips, which showed me that the ridiculous side of this method of settling international questions had forced itself upon your mind. At this point I agreed with you that it was preposterous, and was glad to find that all my deductions had been correct."

"Absolutely!" said I. "And now that you have explained it, I confess that I am as amazed as before."

"It was very superficial, my dear Watson, I assure you. I should not have intruded it upon your attention had you not shown some incredulity the other day. But I have in my hands here a little problem which may prove to be more difficult of solution than my small essay in thought reading. Have you observed in the paper a short paragraph referring to the remarkable contents of a packet sent through the post to Miss Susan Cushing, of Cross Street, Croydon?"

"No, I saw nothing."

"Ah! then you must have overlooked it. Just toss it over to me. Here it is, under the financial column. Perhaps you would be good enough to read it aloud."

I picked up the paper which he had

thrown back to me, and read the paragraph indicated. It was headed, "A Gruesome Packet."

"Miss Susan Cushing, living at Cross Street, Croydon, has been made the victim of what must be regarded as a peculiarly revolting practical joke, unless some more sinister meaning should prove to be attached to the incident. At two o'clock yesterday afternoon a small packet, wrapped in brown paper, was handed in by the postman. A cardboard box was inside, which was filled with coarse salt. On emptying this, Miss Cushing was horrified to find two human ears, apparently quite freshly severed. The box had been sent by parcel post from Belfast upon the morning before. There is no indication as to the sender, and the matter is the more mysterious as Miss Cushing, who is a maiden lady of fifty, has led a most retired life, and has so few acquaintances or correspondents that it is a rare event for her to receive anything through the post. Some years ago, however, when she resided at Penge, she let apartments in her house to three young medical students, whom she was obliged to get rid of on account of their noisy and irregular habits. The police are of opinion that this outrage may have been perpetrated upon Miss Cushing by these youths, who owed her a grudge, and who hoped to frighten her by sending her these relics of the dissecting-rooms. Some probability is lent to the theory by the fact that one of these students came from the north of Ireland, and, to the best of Miss Cushing's belief, from Belfast. In the meantime, the matter is being actively investigated, Mr. Lestrade, one of the very smartest of our detective officers, being in charge of the case."

"So much for the *Daily Chronicle*," said Holmes, as I finished reading. "Now for our friend Lestrade. I had a note from him this morning, in which

he says: 'I think that this case is very much in your line. We have every hope of clearing the matter up, but we find a little difficulty in getting anything to work upon. We have, of course, wired to the Belfast post-office, but a large number of parcels were handed in upon that day, and they have no means of identifying this particular one, or of remembering the sender. The box is a half-pound box of honeydew tobacco, and does not help us in any way. The medical student theory still appears to me to be the most feasible, but if you should have a few hours to spare, I should be very happy to see you out here. I shall be either at the house or in the police-station all day.' What say you, Watson? Can you rise superior to the heat, and run down to Croydon with me on the off chance of a case for your annals?"

"I was longing for something to do."

"You shall have it, then. Ring for our boots, and tell them to order a cab. I'll be back in a moment, when I have changed my dressing-gown and filled my cigar-case."

A shower of rain fell while we were in the train, and the heat was far less oppressive in Croydon than in town. Holmes had sent on a wire, so that Lestrade, as wiry, as dapper, and as ferret-like as ever, was waiting for us at the station. A walk of five minutes took us to Cross Street, where Miss Cushing resided.

"MISS CUSHING."

It was a very long street of two-story brick houses, neat and prim, with whitened stone steps and little groups of aproned women gossiping at the doors. Half-way down, Lestrade stopped and tapped at a door, which was opened by a small servant girl. Miss Cushing was sitting in the front room, into which we were ushered. She was a placid-faced woman with large, gentle eyes, and grizzled hair curving down over her temples on each side. A worked antimacassar lay upon her lap and a basket of coloured silks stood upon a stool beside her.

"They are in the outhouse, those dreadful things," said she, as Lestrade entered. "I wish that you would take them away altogether."

"So I shall, Miss Cushing. I only kept them here until my friend, Mr. Holmes, should have seen them in your presence."

"Why in my presence, sir?"

"In case he wished to ask any questions."

"What is the use of asking me questions, when I tell you that I know nothing whatever about it?"

"Quite so, madam," said Holmes, in his soothing way. "I have no doubt that you have been annoyed more than enough already over this business."

"Indeed, I have, sir. I am a quiet woman and live a retired life. It is something new for me to see my name in the papers and to find the police in my house. I won't have those things in here, Mr. Lestrade. If you wish to see them you must go to the outhouse."

It was a small shed in the narrow garden which ran down behind the house. Lestrade went in and brought out a yellow cardboard box, with a piece of brown paper and some string. There was a bench at the edge of the path, and we all sat down while Holmes examined, one by one, the articles which Lestrade had handed to him.

"The string is exceedingly interesting," he remarked, holding it up to the light and sniffing at it. "What do you make of this string, Lestrade?"

"It has been tarred."

"Precisely. It is a piece of tarred twine. You have also, no doubt, re-

marked that Miss Cushing has cut the cord with a scissors, as can be seen by the double fray on each side. This is of importance."

"I cannot see the importance," said Lestrade.

"The importance lies in the fact that the knot is left intact, and that this knot is of a peculiar character."

"It is very neatly tied. I had already made a note to that effect," said Lestrade, complacently.

"So much for the string then," said Holmes, smiling; "now for the box wrapper. Brown paper, with a distinct smell of coffee. What, you did not observe it? I think there can be no doubt of it. Address printed in rather straggling characters: 'Miss S. Cushing, Cross Street, Croydon.' Done with a broad pointed pen, probably a J, and with very inferior ink. The word Croydon has been spelt originally with an i, which has been changed to y. The parcel was directed, then, by a man—the printing is distinctly masculine—of limited education and unacquainted with the town of Croydon. So far, so good! The box is a yellow, half-pound honeydew box, with nothing distinctive save two thumb marks at the left bottom corner. It is filled with rough salt of the quality used for preserving hides and other of the coarser commercial purposes. And embedded in it are these very singular inclosures."

He took out the two ears as he spoke, and laying a board across his knees, he examined them minutely, while Lestrade and I, bending forward on each side of him, glanced

" HE EXAMINED THEM MINUTELY.'

alternately at these dreadful relics and at the thoughtful, eager face of our companion. Finally he returned them to the box once more, and sat for a while in deep thought.

"You have observed, of course," said he at last, "that the ears are not a pair."

"Yes, I have noticed that. But if this were the practical joke of some students from the dissecting-rooms, it would be as easy for them to send two odd ears as a pair."

"Precisely. But this is not a practical joke."

"You are sure of it?"

"The presumption is strongly against it. Bodies in the dissecting-rooms are injected with preservative fluid. These ears bear no signs of this. They are fresh, too. They have been cut off with a blunt instrument, which would hardly happen if a student had done it. Again, carbolic or rectified spirits would be the preservatives which would suggest themselves to the medical mind, certainly not rough salt. I repeat that there is no practical joke here, but that we are investigating a serious crime."

A vague thrill ran through me as I listened to my companion's words and saw the stern gravity which had hardened his features. This brutal preliminary seemed to shadow forth some strange and inexplicable horror in the background. Lestrade, however, shook his head like a man who is only half convinced.

"There are objections to the joke theory, no doubt," said he; "but there are much stronger reasons against the other. We know that this woman has led a most quiet and respectable life at Penge and here for the last twenty years. She has hardly been away from her home for a day during that time. Why on earth, then, should any criminal send her the proofs of his guilt, especially as, unless she is a most consummate actress, she understands quite as little of the matter as we do?"

"That is the problem which we have to solve," Holmes answered, "and for my part I shall set about it by presuming that my reasoning is correct, and that a double murder has been committed. One of these ears is a woman's, small, finely formed, and pierced for an earring. The other is a man's, sunburned, discoloured, and also pierced for an earring. These two people are presumably dead, or we should have heard their story before now. To-day is Friday. The packet was posted on Thursday morning. The tragedy, then, occurred on Wednesday or Tuesday, or earlier. If the two people were murdered, who but their murderer would have sent this sign of his work to Miss Cushing? We may take it that the sender of the packet is the man whom we want. But he must have some strong reason for sending Miss Cushing this packet. What reason, then? It must have been to tell her that the deed was done; or to pain her, perhaps. But in that case she knows who it is. Does she know? I doubt it. If she knew, why should she call the police in? She might have buried the ears, and no one would have been the wiser. That is what she would have done if she had wished to shield the criminal. But if she does not wish to shield him she would give his name. There is a tangle here which needs straightening out." He had been talking in a high, quick voice, staring blankly up over the garden fence, but now he sprang briskly to his feet and walked towards the house.

"I have a few questions to ask Miss Cushing," said he.

"In that case I may leave you here," said Lestrade, "for I have another small business on hand. I think that I have nothing further to learn from Miss Cushing. You will find me at the police-station."

"We shall look in on our way to the train," answered Holmes. A moment later he and I were back in the front room, where the impassive lady was still quietly working away at her antimacassar. She put it down on her lap as we entered, and looked at us with her frank, searching blue eyes.

"I am convinced, sir," she said, "that this matter is a mistake, and that the parcel was never meant for me at all. I have said this several times to the gentleman from Scotland Yard, but he simply laughs at me. I have not an enemy in the world, as far as I know, so why should anyone play me such a trick?"

"I am coming to be of the same opinion, Miss Cushing," said Holmes, taking a seat beside her. "I think that it is more than probable——" he paused, and I was surprised on glancing round to see that he was staring with singular intentness at the lady's profile. Surprise and satisfaction were both for an instant to be read upon his eager face, though when she glanced round to find out the cause of his silence he had become as demure as ever. I stared hard myself at her flat, grizzled hair, her trim cap, her little gilt earrings, her placid features; but I could see nothing which could account for my companion's evident excitement.

"There were one or two questions——"

"Oh, I am weary of questions!" cried Miss Cushing, impatiently.

" You have two sisters, I believe."

" How could you know that ? "

" I observed the very instant that I entered the room that you have a portrait group of three ladies upon the mantelpiece, one of whom is undoubtedly yourself, while the others are so exceedingly like you that there could be no doubt of the relationship."

" Yes, you are quite right. Those are my sisters, Sarah and Mary."

" And here at my elbow is another portrait, taken at Liverpool, of your younger sister, in the company of a man who appears to be a steward by his uniform. I observe that she was unmarried at the time."

" You are very quick at observing."

" That is my trade."

" Well, you are quite right. But she was married to Mr. Browner a few days afterwards. He was on the South American line when that was taken, but he was so fond of her that he couldn't abide to leave her for so long, and he got into the Liverpool and London boats."

" Ah, the *Conqueror*, perhaps ? "

" No, the *May Day*, when last I heard. Jim came down here to see me once. That was before he broke the pledge ; but afterwards he would always take drink when he was ashore, and a little drink would send him stark, staring mad. Ah ! it was a bad day that ever he took a glass in his hand again. First he dropped me, and then he quarrelled with Sarah, and now that Mary has stopped writing we don't know how things are going with them."

It was evident that Miss Cushing had come upon a subject on which she felt very deeply. Like most people who lead a lonely life, she was shy at first, but ended by becoming extremely communicative. She told us many details about her brother-in-law the steward, and then wandering off on to the subject of her former lodgers, the medical students, she gave us a long account of their delinquencies, with their names and those of their hospitals.

Holmes listened attentively to everything, throwing in a question from time to time.

" About your second sister, Sarah," said he. " I wonder, since you are both maiden ladies, that you do not keep house together."

" Ah ! you don't know Sarah's temper, or you would wonder no more. I tried it when I came to Croydon, and we kept on until about two months ago, when we had to part. I don't want to say a word against my own sister, but she was always meddlesome and hard to please, was Sarah."

" You say that she quarrelled with your Liverpool relations."

" Yes, and they were the best of friends at one time. Why, she went up there to live just in order to be near them. And now she has no word hard enough for Jim Browner. The last six months that she was here she would speak of nothing but his drinking and his ways. He had caught her meddling, I suspect, and given her a bit of his mind, and that was the start of it."

" Thank you, Miss Cushing," said Holmes, rising and bowing. " Your sister Sarah lives, I think you said, at New Street, Wallington ? Good-bye, and I am very sorry that you should have been troubled over a case with which, as you say, you have nothing whatever to do."

There was a cab passing as we came out, and Holmes hailed it.

" How far to Wallington ? " he asked.

" Only about a mile, sir."

" HOW FAR TO WALLINGTON ? "

"Very good. Jump in, Watson. We must strike while the iron is hot. Simple as the case is, there have been one or two very instructive details in connection with it. Just pull up at a telegraph office as you pass, cabby.'

Holmes sent off a short wire, and for the rest of the drive lay back in the cab with his hat tilted over his nose to keep the sun from his face. Our driver pulled up at a house which was not unlike the one which we had just quitted. My companion ordered him to wait, and had his hand upon the knocker, when the door opened and a grave young gentleman in black, with a very shiny hat, appeared on the step.

"Is Miss Sarah Cushing at home?" asked Holmes.

"Miss Sarah Cushing is extremely ill," said he. "She has been suffering since yesterday from brain symptoms of great severity. As her medical adviser, I cannot possibly take the responsibility of allowing anyone to see her. I should recommend you to call again in ten days." He drew on his gloves, closed the door, and marched off down the street.

"Well, if we can't, we can't," said Holmes, cheerfully.

"Perhaps she could not, or would not have told you much."

"I did not wish her to tell me anything. I only wanted to look at her. However, I think that I have got all that I want. Drive us to some decent hotel, cabby, where we may have some lunch, and afterwards we shall drop down upon friend Lestrade at the police-station."

We had a pleasant little meal together, during which Holmes would talk about nothing but violins, narrating with great exultation how he had purchased his own Stradivarius, which was worth at least five hundred guineas, at a Jew broker's in Tottenham Court Road for fifty-five shillings. This led him to Paganini, and we sat for an hour over a bottle of claret while he told me anecdote after anecdote of that extraordinary man. The afternoon was far advanced and the hot glare had softened into a mellow glow before we found ourselves at the police-station. Lestrade was waiting for us at the door.

"A telegram for you, Mr. Holmes," said he.

"Ha! It is the answer!" He tore it open, glanced his eyes over it, and crumpled it into his pocket. "That's all right," said he.

"Have you found out anything?"

"I have found out everything!"

"What!" Lestrade stared at him in amazement. "You are joking."

"I was never more serious in my life. A shocking crime has been committed, and I think that I have now laid bare every detail of it."

"And the criminal?"

Holmes scribbled a few words upon the back of one of his visiting cards and threw it over to Lestrade.

"That is it," he said; "you cannot effect an arrest until to-morrow night at the earliest. I should prefer that you would not mention my name at all in connection with the case, as I choose to be associated only with those crimes which present some difficulty in their solution. Come on, Watson." We strode off together to the station, leaving Lestrade still staring with a delighted face at the card which Holmes had thrown him.

"The case," said Sherlock Holmes, as we chatted over our cigars that night in our rooms at Baker Street, "is one where, as in the investigations which you have chronicled under the names of the 'Study in Scarlet' and of the 'Sign of Four,' we have been compelled to reason backward from effects to causes. I have written to Lestrade asking him to supply us with the details which are now wanting, and which he will only get after he has secured his man. That he may be safely trusted to do, for although he is absolutely devoid of reason, he is as tenacious as a bulldog when he once understands what he has to do, and indeed it is just this tenacity which has brought him to the top at Scotland Yard."

"Your case is not complete, then?" I asked.

"It is fairly complete in essentials. We know who the author of the revolting business is, although one of the victims still escapes us. Of course, you have formed your own conclusions."

"I presume that this Jim Browner, the steward of a Liverpool boat, is the man whom you suspect?"

"Oh! it is more than a suspicion."

"And yet I cannot see anything save very vague indications."

"On the contrary, to my mind nothing could be more clear. Let me run over the principal steps. We approached the case, you remember, with an absolutely blank mind, which is always an advantage. We had formed no theories. We were simply there to observe and to draw inferences from our observations. What did we see first?

A very placid and respectable lady, who seemed quite innocent of any secret, and a portrait which showed me that she had two younger sisters. It instantly flashed across my mind that the box might have been meant for one of these. I set the idea aside as one which could be disproved or confirmed at our leisure. Then we went to the garden, as you remember, and we saw the very singular contents of the little yellow box.

"The string was of the quality which is used by sail-makers aboard ship, and at once a whiff of the sea was perceptible in our investigation. When I observed that the knot was one which is popular with sailors, that the parcel had been posted at a port, and that the male ear was pierced for an earring which is so much more common among sailors than landsmen, I was quite certain that all the actors in the tragedy were to be found among our seafaring classes.

"When I came to examine the address of the packet I observed that it was to Miss S. Cushing. Now, the oldest sister would, of course, be Miss Cushing, and although her initial was 'S.,' it might belong to one of the others as well. In that case we should have to commence our investigation from a fresh basis altogether. I therefore went into the house with the intention of clearing up this point. I was about to assure Miss Cushing that I was convinced that a mistake had been made, when you may remember that I came suddenly to a stop. The fact was that I had just seen something which filled me with surprise, and at the same time narrowed the field of our inquiry immensely.

"As a medical man, you are aware, Watson, that there is no part of the body which varies so much as the human ear. Each ear is as a rule quite distinctive, and differs from all other ones. In last year's *Anthropological Journal* you will find two short monographs from my

"JIM BROWNER."

pen upon the subject. I had therefore examined the ears in the box with the eyes of an expert, and had carefully noted their anatomical peculiarities. Imagine my surprise then, when, on looking at Miss Cushing, I perceived that her ear corresponded exactly with the female ear which I had just inspected. The matter was entirely beyond coincidence. There was the same shortening of the pinna, the same broad curve of the upper lobe, the same convolution of the inner cartilage. In all essentials it was the same ear.

"Of course, I at once saw the enormous importance of the observation. It was evident that the victim was a blood relation, and probably a very close one. I began to talk to her about her family, and you remember that she at once gave us some exceedingly valuable details.

"In the first place, her sister's name was Sarah, and her address had, until recently, been the same, so that it was quite obvious how the mistake had occurred, and whom the packet was meant for. Then we heard of this steward, married to the third sister, and learned that he had at one time been so intimate with Miss Sarah that she had actually gone up to Liverpool to be near the Browners, but a quarrel had afterwards divided them. This quarrel had put a stop to all communications for some months, so that if Browner had occasion to address a packet to Miss Sarah, he would undoubtedly have done so to her old address.

"And now the matter had begun to straighten itself out wonderfully. We had learned of the existence of this steward, an impulsive man, of strong passions — you remember that he threw up what must have been a very superior berth, in order to be nearer to his wife — subject, too, to occasional fits of hard drinking. We had reason to believe that his wife had been murdered, and that a man — presumably a seafaring man

—had been murdered at the same time. Jealousy, of course, at once suggests itself as the motive for the crime. And why should these proofs of the deed be sent to Miss Sarah Cushing? Probably because during her residence in Liverpool she had some hand in bringing about the events which led to the tragedy. You will observe that this line of boats calls at Belfast, Dublin, and Waterford; so that, presuming that Browner had committed the deed, and had embarked at once upon his steamer, the *May Day*, Belfast would be the first place at which he could post his terrible packet.

"A second solution was at this stage obviously possible, and although I thought it exceedingly unlikely, I was determined to elucidate it before going further. An unsuccessful lover might have killed Mr. and Mrs. Browner, and the male ear might have belonged to the husband. There were many grave objections to this theory, but it was conceivable. I therefore sent off a telegram to my friend Algar, of the Liverpool force, and asked him to find out if Mrs. Browner were at home, and if Browner had departed in the *May Day*. Then we went on to Wallington to visit Miss Sarah.

"I was curious, in the first place, to see how far the family ear had been reproduced in her. Then, of course, she might give us very important information, but I was not sanguine that she would. She must have heard of the business the day before, since all Croydon was ringing with it, and she alone could have understood whom the packet was meant for. If she had been willing to help justice she would probably have communicated with the police already. However, it was clearly our duty to see her, so we went. We found that the news of the arrival of the packet—for her illness dated from that time—had such an effect upon her as to bring on brain fever. It was clearer than ever that she understood its full significance, but equally clear that we should have to wait some time for any assistance from her.

"However, we were really independent of her help. Our answers were waiting for us at the police-station, where I had directed Algar to send them. Nothing could be more conclusive. Mrs. Browner's house had been closed for more than three days, and the neighbours were of opinion that she had gone south to see her relatives. It had been ascertained at the shipping offices that Browner had left aboard of the *May Day*, and I calculate that she is due in the Thames tomorrow night. When he arrives he will be met by the obtuse but resolute Lestrade, and I have no doubt that we shall have all our details filled in."

Sherlock Holmes was not disappointed in his expectations. Two days later he received a bulky envelope, which contained a short note from the detective, and a type-written document, which covered several pages of foolscap.

"Lestrade has got him all right," said Holmes, glancing up at me. "Perhaps it would interest you to hear what he says."

"My dear Mr. Holmes,—In accordance with the scheme which we had formed in order to test our theories"—"the 'we' is rather fine, Watson, is it not?"—"I went down to the Albert Dock yesterday at 6 p.m., and boarded the ss. *May Day*, belonging to the Liverpool, Dublin, and London Steam Packet Company. On inquiry, I found that there was a steward on board of the name of James Browner, and that he had acted during the voyage in such an extraordinary manner that the captain had been compelled to relieve him of his duties. On descending to his berth, I found him seated upon a chest with his head sunk upon his hands, rocking himself to and fro. He is a big, powerful chap, clean-shaven, and very swarthy—something like Aldridge, who helped us in the bogus laundry affair. He jumped up when he heard my business, and I had my whistle to my lips to call a couple of river police, who were round the corner, but he seemed to have no heart in him, and he held out his hands quietly enough for the darbies. We brought him along to the cells, and his box as well, for we thought there might be something incriminating; but, bar a big sharp knife, such as most sailors have, we got nothing for our trouble. However, we find that we shall want no more evidence, for, on being brought before the inspector at the station, he asked leave to make a statement, which was, of course, taken down, just as he made it, by our shorthand man. We had three copies type-written, one of which I inclose. The affair proves, as I always thought it would, to be an extremely simple one, but I am obliged to you for assisting me in my investigation. With kind regards yours very truly,—G. LESTRADE."

"Hum! The investigation really was a very simple one," remarked Holmes; "but I don't think it struck him in that light when he first called us in. However, let us see what Jim Browner has to say for himself. This is his statement, as made before Inspector Mont-

"HE HELD OUT HIS HANDS QUIETLY."

mark in the mud than I did of her whole body and soul.

"There were three sisters altogether. The old one was just a good woman, the second was a devil, and the third was an angel. Sarah was thirty-three, and Mary was twenty-nine when I married. We were just as happy as the day was long when we set up house together, and in all Liverpool there was no better woman than my Mary. And then we asked Sarah up for a week, and the week grew into a month, and one thing led to ano-

gomery at the Shadwell Police Station, and it has the advantage of being verbatim."

"Have I anything to say? Yes, I have a deal to say. I have to make a clean breast of it all. You can hang me, or you can leave me alone. I don't care a plug which you do. I tell you I've not shut an eye in sleep since I did it, and I don't believe I ever will again until I get past all waking. Sometimes it's his face, but most generally it's hers. I'm never without one or the other before me. He looks frowning and black-like, but she has a kind o' surprise upon her face. Aye, the white lamb, she might well be surprised when she read death on a face that had seldom looked anything but love upon her before.

"But it was Sarah's fault, and may the curse of a broken man put a blight on her and set the blood rotting in her veins! It's not that I want to clear myself. I know that I went back to drink, like the beast that I was. But she would have forgiven me; she would have stuck as close to me as a rope to a block if that woman had never darkened our door. For Sarah Cushing loved me—that's the root of the business—she loved me, until all her love turned to poisonous hate when she knew that I thought more of my wife's foot-

ther, until she was just one of ourselves.

"I was blue ribbon at that time, and we were putting a little money by, and all was as bright as a new dollar. My God, whoever would have thought that it could have come to this? Whoever would have dreamed it?

"I used to be home for the week-ends very often, and sometimes if the ship were held back for cargo I would have a whole week at a time, and in this way I saw a deal of my sister-in-law, Sarah. She was a fine tall woman, black and quick and fierce, with a proud way of carrying her head, and a glint from her eye like the spark from a flint. But when little Mary was there I had never a thought for her, and that I swear as I hope for God's mercy.

"It had seemed to me sometimes that she liked to be alone with me, or to coax me out for a walk with her, but I had never thought anything of that. But one evening my eyes were opened. I had come up from the ship and found my wife out, but Sarah at home. 'Where's Mary?' I asked. 'Oh, she has gone to pay some accounts.' I was impatient and paced up and down the room. 'Can't you be happy for five minutes without Mary, Jim?' says she. 'It's a bad compliment to me that you can't be contented with my society for so short a time.' 'That's all right, my lass," said I, putting out my hand towards her in a kindly way, but she had it in both hers in an instant, and they burned as if they were in a fever. I looked into her eyes and I read it all there. There was no need for her to speak, nor for me either. I frowned and drew my hand away. Then she stood by my side in silence for a bit, and then put up her hand and patted me on the shoulder.

" 'THAT'S ALL RIGHT, MY LASS,' SAID I."

'Steady old Jim!' said she; and, with a kind o' mocking laugh, she ran out of the room.

"Well, from that time Sarah hated me with her whole heart and soul, and she is a woman who can hate, too. I was a fool to let her go on biding with us—a besotted fool —but I never said a word to Mary, for I knew it would grieve her. Things went on much as before, but after a time I began to find that there was a bit of a change in Mary herself. She had always been so trusting and so innocent, but now she became queer and suspicious, wanting to know where I had

been and what I had been doing, and whom my letters were from, and what I had in my pockets, and a thousand such follies. Day by day she grew queerer and more irritable, and we had causeless rows about nothing. I was fairly puzzled by it all. Sarah avoided me now, but she and Mary were just inseparable. I can see now how she was plotting and scheming and poisoning my wife's mind against me, but I was such a blind beetle that I could not understand it at the time. Then I broke my blue ribbon and began to drink again, but I think I should not have done it if Mary had been the same as ever. She had some reason to be disgusted with me now, and the gap between us began to be wider and wider. And then this Alec Fairbairn chipped in, and things became a thousand times blacker.

"It was to see Sarah that he came to my house first, but soon it was to see us, for he was a man with winning ways, and he made friends wherever he went. He was a dashing, swaggering chap, smart and curled, who had seen half the world, and could talk of what he had seen. He was good company, I won't deny it, and he had wonderful polite ways with him for a sailor man, so that I think there must have been a time when he knew more of the poop than the forecastle. For a month he was in and out of my house, and never once did it cross my mind that harm might come of his soft, tricky ways. And then at last something made me suspect, and from that day my peace was gone for ever.

"It was only a little thing, too. I had come into the parlour unexpected, and as I walked in at the door I saw a light of welcome on my wife's face. But as she saw who it was it faded again, and she turned away with a look of disappointment. That was enough for me. There was no one but Alec Fairbairn whose step she could have mistaken for mine. If I could have seen him then I should have killed him, for I have always been like a madman when my temper gets loose. Mary saw the devil's light in my eyes, and she ran forward with her hands on my sleeve. 'Don't, Jim, don't!' says she. 'Where's Sarah?' I asked. 'In the kitchen,' says she. 'Sarah,' says I, as I went in, 'this man Fairbairn is never to darken my door again.' 'Why not?' says she. 'Because I order it.' 'Oh!' says she, 'if my friends are not good enough for this house, then I am not good enough for it either.' 'You can do what you like,' says I, 'but if Fairbairn shows his face here again, I'll send you one of his ears for a keepsake.' She was frightened by my face, I think, for she never answered a word, and the same evening she left my house.

"Well, I don't know now whether it was pure devilry on the part of this woman, or whether she thought that she could turn me against my wife by encouraging her to misbehave. Anyway, she took a house just two streets off, and let lodgings to sailors. Fairbairn used to stay there, and Mary would go round to have tea with her sister and him. How often she went I don't know, but I followed her one day, and as I broke in at the door Fairbairn got away over the back garden wall, like the cowardly skunk that he was. I swore to my wife that I would kill her if I found her in his company again, and I led her back with me, sobbing and trembling, and as white as a piece of paper. There was no trace of love between us any longer. I could see that she hated me and feared me, and when the thought of it drove me to drink, then she despised me as well.

"Well, Sarah found that she could not make a living in Liverpool, so she went back, as I understand, to live with her sister in Croydon, and things jogged on much the same as ever at home. And then came this last week and all the misery and ruin.

"It was in this way. We had gone on the *May Day* for a round voyage of seven days, but a hogshead got loose and started one of our plates, so that we had to put back into port for twelve hours. I left the ship and came home, thinking what a surprise it would be for my wife, and hoping that maybe she would be glad to see me so soon. The thought was in my head as I turned into my own street, and at that moment a cab passed

me, and there she was, sitting by the side of Fairbairn, the two chatting and laughing, with never a thought for me as I stood watching them from the footpath.

"I tell you, and I give you my word on it, that from that moment I was not my own master, and it is all like a dim dream when I look back on it. I had been drinking hard of late, and the two things together fairly turned my brain. There's something throbbing in my head now, like a docker's hammer, but that morning I seemed to have all Niagara whizzing and buzzing in my ears.

"Well, I took to my heels, and I ran after the cab. I had a heavy oak stick in my hand, and I tell you that I saw red from the first; but as I ran I got cunning, too, and hung back a little to see them without being seen. They pulled up soon at the railway station. There was a good crowd round the booking-office, so I got quite close to them without being seen. They took tickets for New Brighton. So did I, but I got in three carriages behind them. When we reached it they walked along the Parade, and I was never more than a hundred yards from them. At last I saw them hire a boat and start for a row, for it was a very hot day, and they thought no doubt that it would be cooler on the water.

"It was just as if they had been given into my hands. There was a bit of a haze, and you could not see more than a few hundred yards. I hired a boat for myself, and I pulled after them. I could see the blur of their craft, but they were going nearly as fast as I, and they must have been a long mile from the shore before I caught them up. The haze was like a curtain all round us, and there were we three in the middle of it. My God, shall I ever forget their faces when they saw who was in the boat that was closing in upon them? She screamed out. He swore like a madman, and jabbed at me with an oar, for he must have seen death in my eyes. I got past it and got one in with my stick, that crushed his head like an egg. I would have spared her, perhaps, for all my madness, but she threw her arms round him, crying out to him, and calling him 'Alec.' I struck again, and she lay stretched beside him. I was like a wild beast then that had tasted blood. If Sarah had been there, by the Lord, she should have joined them. I pulled out my knife, and—well, there! I've said enough. It gave me a kind of savage joy when I thought how Sarah would feel when she had such signs as these of what her meddling had brought about. Then

I tied the bodies into the boat, stove a plank, and stood by until they had sunk. I knew very well that the owner would think that they had lost their bearings in the haze, and had drifted off out to sea. I cleaned myself up, got back to land, and joined my ship without a soul having a suspicion of what had passed. That night I made up the packet for Sarah Cushing, and next day I sent it from Belfast.

"There you have the whole truth of it. You can hang me, or do what you like with me, but you cannot punish me as I have been punished already. I cannot shut my eyes but I see those two faces staring at me —staring at me as they stared when my boat broke through the haze. I killed them quick, but they are killing me slow; and if I have another night of it I shall be either mad or dead before morning. You won't put me alone into a cell, sir? For pity's sake don't, and may you be treated in your day of agony as you treat me now."

"What is the meaning of it, Watson?" said Holmes, solemnly, as he laid down the paper. "What object is served by this circle of misery and violence and fear? It must tend to some end, or else our universe is ruled by chance, which is unthinkable. But what end? There is the great standing perennial problem to which human reason is as far from an answer as ever."

# The Adventures of Sherlock Holmes.

## XV.—THE ADVENTURE OF THE YELLOW FACE.

### By A. Conan Doyle.

IN publishing these short sketches, based upon the numerous cases which my companion's singular gifts have made me the listener to, and eventually the actor in some strange drama, it is only natural that I should dwell rather upon his successes than upon his failures. And this not so much for the sake of his reputation, for indeed it was when he was at his wits' end that his energy and his versatility were most admirable, but because where he failed it happened too often that no one else succeeded, and that the tale was left for ever without a conclusion. Now and again, however, it chanced that even when he erred the truth was still discovered. I have notes of some half-dozen cases of the kind of which "The Adventure of the Musgrave Ritual" and that which I am now about to recount are the two which present the strongest features of interest.

Sherlock Holmes was a man who seldom took exercise for exercise's sake. Few men were capable of greater muscular effort, and he was undoubtedly one of the finest boxers of his weight that I have ever seen, but he looked upon aimless bodily exertion as a waste of energy, and he seldom bestirred himself save where there was some professional object to be served. Then he was absolutely untiring and indefatigable. That he should have kept himself in training under such circumstances is remarkable, but his diet was usually of the sparest, and his habits were simple to the verge of austerity. Save for the occasional use of cocaine he had no vices, and he only turned to the drug as a protest against the monotony of existence when cases were scanty and the papers uninteresting.

One day in early spring he had so far relaxed as to go for a walk with me in the Park, where the first faint shoots of green were breaking out upon the elms, and the sticky spearheads of the chestnuts were just beginning to burst into their five-fold leaves. For two hours we rambled about together, in silence for the most part, as befits two men who know each other intimately. It was nearly five before we were back in Baker Street once more.

"Beg pardon, sir," said our page-boy, as he opened the door; "there's been a gentleman here asking for you, sir."

Holmes glanced reproachfully at me. "So much for afternoon walks!" said he. "Has this gentleman gone, then?"

"Yes, sir."

"Didn't you ask him in?"

"Yes, sir; he came in."

"How long did he wait?"

"Half an hour, sir. He was a very restless gentleman, sir, a-walkin' and a-stampin' all the time he was here. I was waitin' outside the door, sir, and I could hear him. At last he goes out into the passage and he cries: 'Is that man never goin' to come?' Those were his very words, sir. 'You'll only need to wait a little longer,' says I. 'Then I'll wait in the open air, for I feel half choked,' says he. 'I'll be back before long,' and with that he ups and he outs, and all I could say wouldn't hold him back."

"Well, well, you did your best," said Holmes, as we walked into our room. "It's very annoying though, Watson. I was badly in need of a case, and this looks, from the man's impatience, as if it were of importance. Halloa! that's not your pipe on the table! He must have left his behind him. A nice old briar, with a good long stem of what the tobacconists call amber. I wonder how many real amber mouthpieces there are in London. Some people think a fly in it is a sign. Why, it is quite a branch of trade the putting of sham flies into the sham amber. Well, he must have been disturbed in his mind to leave a pipe behind him which he evidently values highly."

"How do you know that he values it highly?" I asked.

"Well, I should put the original cost of the pipe at seven-and-sixpence. Now it has, you see, been twice mended: once in the wooden stem and once in the amber. Each of these mends, done, as you observe, with silver bands, must have cost more than the pipe did originally. The man must value the pipe highly when he prefers to patch it up rather than buy a new one with the same money."

"Anything else?" I asked, for Holmes

"HE HELD IT UP."

was turning the pipe about in his hand and staring at it in his peculiar, pensive way.

He held it up and tapped on it with his long, thin forefinger as a professor might who was lecturing on a bone.

"Pipes are occasionally of extraordinary interest," said he. "Nothing has more individuality save, perhaps, watches and boot-laces. The indications here, however, are neither very marked nor very important. The owner is obviously a muscular man, left-handed, with an excellent set of teeth, careless in his habits, and with no need to practise economy."

My friend threw out the information in a very off-hand way, but I saw that he cocked his eye at me to see if I had followed his reasoning.

"You think a man must be well-to-do if he smokes a seven-shilling pipe?" said I.

"This is Grosvenor mixture at eightpence an ounce," Holmes answered, knocking a little out on his palm. "As he might get an excellent smoke for half the price, he has no need to practise economy."

"And the other points?"

"He has been in the habit of lighting his pipe at lamps and gas-jets. You can see

that it is quite charred all down one side. Of course, a match could not have done that. Why should a man hold a match to the side of his pipe? But you cannot light it at a lamp without getting the bowl charred. And it is all on the right side of the pipe. From that I gather that he is a left-handed man. You hold your own pipe to the lamp, and see how naturally you, being right-handed, hold the left side to the flame. You might do it once the other way, but not as a constancy. This has always been held so. Then he has bitten through his amber. It takes a muscular, energetic fellow, and one with a good set of teeth to do that. But if I am not mistaken I hear him upon the stair, so we shall have something more interesting than his pipe to study."

An instant later our door opened, and a tall young man entered the room. He was well but quietly dressed in a dark-grey suit, and carried a brown wideawake in his hand. I should have put him at about thirty, though he was really some years older.

"I beg your pardon," said he, with some embarrassment; "I suppose I should have knocked. Yes, of course I should have knocked. The fact is that I am a little upset, and you must put it all down to that." He passed his hand over his forehead like a man who is half dazed, and then fell, rather than sat, down upon a chair.

"I can see that you have not slept for a night or two," said Holmes, in his easy, genial way. "That tries a man's nerves more than work, and more even than pleasure. May I ask how I can help you?"

"I wanted your advice, sir. I don't know what to do, and my whole life seems to have gone to pieces."

"You wish to employ me as a consulting detective?"

"Not that only. I want your opinion as a judicious man—as a man of the world. I want to know what I ought to do next. I hope to God you'll be able to tell me."

He spoke in little, sharp, jerky outbursts, and it seemed to me that to speak at all was very painful to him, and that his will all through was overriding his inclinations.

"It's a very delicate thing," said he. "One does not like to speak of one's domestic affairs to strangers. It seems dreadful to discuss the conduct of one's wife with two men whom I have never seen before. It's horrible to have to do it. But I've got to the end of my tether, and I must have advice."

"My dear Mr. Grant Munro ———" began Holmes.

Our visitor sprang from his chair. "What!" he cried. "You know my name?"

"If you wish to preserve your *incognito*," said Holmes, smiling, "I should suggest that you cease to write your name upon the lining of your hat, or else that you turn the crown towards the person whom you are addressing. I was about to say that my friend and I have listened to many strange secrets in this room, and that we have had the good fortune to bring peace to many troubled souls. I trust that we may do as much for you. Might I beg you, as time may prove to be of importance, to furnish me with the facts of your case without further delay?"

Our visitor again passed his hand over his forehead as if he found it bitterly hard. From every gesture and expression I could see that he was a reserved, self-contained man, with a dash of pride in his nature, more likely to hide his wounds than to expose them. Then suddenly with a fierce gesture of his closed hand, like one who throws reserve to the winds, he began.

"The facts are these, Mr. Holmes," said he. "I am a married man, and have been so

"OUR VISITOR SPRANG FROM HIS CHAIR."

for three years. During that time my wife and I have loved each other as fondly, and lived as happily, as any two that ever were joined. We have not had a difference, not one, in thought, or word, or deed. And now, since last Monday, there has suddenly sprung up a barrier between us, and I find that there is something in her life and in her thoughts of which I know as little as if she were the woman who brushes by me in the street. We are estranged, and I want to know why.

"Now there is one thing that I want to impress upon you before I go any further, Mr. Holmes. Effie loves me. Don't let there be any mistake about that. She loves me with her whole heart and soul, and never more than now. I know it—I feel it. I don't want to argue about that. A man can tell easily enough when a woman loves him. But there's this secret between us, and we can never be the same until it is cleared.

"Kindly let me have the facts, Mr. Munro," said Holmes, with some impatience.

"I'll tell you what I know about Effie's history. She was a widow when I met her first, though quite young—only twenty-five. Her name then was Mrs. Hebron. She went out to America when she was young and lived in the town of Atlanta, where she married this Hebron, who was a lawyer with a good practice. They had one child, but the yellow fever broke out badly in the place, and both husband and child died of it. I have seen his death certificate. This sickened her of America, and she came back to live with a maiden aunt at Pinner, in Middlesex. I may mention that her husband had left her comfortably off, and that she had a capital of about four thousand five hundred pounds, which had been so well invested by him that it returned an average of 7 per cent. She had only been six months at Pinner when I met her; we fell in love with each other, and we married a few weeks afterwards.

"I am a hop merchant myself, and as I have an income of seven or eight hundred, we found ourselves comfortably off, and took a nice eighty-pound-a-year villa at Norbury. Our little place was very countrified, considering that it is so close to town. We had an inn and two houses a little above us, and a single cottage at the other side of the field which faces us, and except those there were no houses until you got half-way to the station. My business took me into town at certain seasons, but in summer I had less to do, and then in our country home my wife and I were just as happy as could be wished. I tell you that there never was a shadow between us until this accursed affair began.

"There's one thing I ought to tell you before I go further. When we married, my wife made over all her property to me—rather against my will, for I saw how awkward it would be if my business affairs went wrong. However, she would have it so, and it was done. Well, about six weeks ago she came to me.

"'Jack,' said she, 'when you took my money you said that if ever I wanted any I was to ask you for it.'

"'Certainly,' said I, 'it's all your own.'

"'Well,' said she, 'I want a hundred pounds.'

"I was a bit staggered at this, for I had imagined it was simply a new dress or something of the kind that she was after.

"'What on earth for?' I asked.

"'Oh,' said she, in her playful way, 'you said that you were only my banker, and bankers never ask questions, you know.'

"'If you really mean it, of course you shall have the money,' said I.

"'Oh, yes, I really mean it.'

"'And you won't tell me what you want it for?'

"'Some day, perhaps, but not just at present, Jack.'

"So I had to be content with that, though it was the first time that there had ever been any secret between us. I gave her a cheque, and I never thought any more of the matter. It may have nothing to do with what came afterwards, but I thought it only right to mention it.

"Well, I told you just now that there is a cottage not far from our house. There is just a field between us, but to reach it you have to go along the road and then turn down a lane. Just beyond it is a nice little grove of Scotch firs, and I used to be very fond of strolling down there, for trees are always neighbourly kinds of things. The cottage had been standing empty this eight months, and it was a pity, for it was a pretty two-storied place, with an old-fashioned porch and honeysuckle about it. I have stood many a time and thought what a neat little homestead it would make.

"Well, last Monday evening I was taking a stroll down that way when I met an empty van coming up the lane, and saw a pile of carpets and things lying about on the grass-plot beside the porch. It was clear that the cottage had at last been let. I walked past it, and then stopping, as an idle man might, I ran my eye over it, and wondered what sort of folk they were who had come to live so near us. And as I looked I suddenly became aware that a face was watching me out of one of the upper windows.

"I don't know what there was about that face, Mr. Holmes, but it seemed to send a chill right down my back. I was some little way off, so that I could not make out the features, but there was something unnatural and inhuman about the face. That was the impression I had, and I moved quickly forwards to get a nearer view of the person who was watching me. But as I did so the face suddenly disappeared, so suddenly that it seemed to have been plucked away into the darkness of the room. I stood for five minutes thinking the business over, and trying to analyze my impressions. I could not tell if the face was that of a man or a woman. It had been too far from me for that. But its colour was what had impressed me most. It was of a livid, dead yellow, and with something set and rigid about it, which was shockingly unnatural. So disturbed was I, that I determined to see a little more of the new inmates of the cottage. I approached and knocked at the door, which was instantly opened by a tall, gaunt woman, with a harsh, forbidding face.

"'What may you be wantin'?' she asked, in a northern accent.

"'I am your neighbour over yonder,' said I, nodding towards my house. 'I see that you have only just moved in, so I thought that if I could be of any help to you in any——'

"'Aye, we'll just ask ye when we want ye,' said she, and shut the door in my face. Annoyed at the churlish rebuff, I turned my back and walked home. All the evening,

"WHAT MAY YOU BE WANTIN'?"

when suddenly my half-opened eyes fell upon her face, illuminated by the candle light, and astonishment held me dumb. She wore an expression such as I had never seen before—such as I should have thought her incapable of assuming. She was deadly pale, and breathing fast, glancing furtively towards the bed, as she fastened her mantle, to see if she had disturbed me. Then, thinking that I was still asleep, she slipped noiselessly from the room, and an instant later I heard a sharp creaking, which could only come from the hinges of the front door. I sat up in bed and rapped my knuckles against the rail to make certain that I was truly awake. Then I took my watch from under the pillow. It was three in the morning. What on this earth could my wife be doing out on the country road at three in the morning?

"I had sat for about twenty minutes turning the thing over in my mind and trying to find some possible explanation. The more I thought the more extraordinary and inexplicable did it appear. I was still puzzling over it when I heard the door gently close again and her footsteps coming up the stairs.

"'Where in the world have you been, Effie?' I asked, as she entered.

"She gave a violent start and a kind of gasping cry when I spoke, and that cry and start troubled me more than all the rest, for there was something indescribably guilty about them. My wife had always been a woman of a frank, open nature, and it gave me a chill to see her slinking into her own room, and crying out and wincing when her own husband spoke to her.

"'You awake, Jack?' she cried, with a nervous laugh. 'Why, I thought that nothing could awaken you.'

"'Where have you been?' I asked, more sternly.

"'I don't wonder that you are surprised,' said she, and I could see that her fingers were trembling as she undid the fastenings of her mantle. 'Why, I never remember having done such a thing in my life before. The fact is, that I felt as though I were choking, and had a perfect longing for a breath of fresh air. I really think that I should have fainted if I had not gone out. I stood at the door for a few minutes, and now I am quite myself again.'

"All the time that she was telling me this story she never once looked in my direction, and her voice was quite unlike her usual

though I tried to think of other things, my mind would still turn to the apparition at the window and the rudeness of the woman. I determined to say nothing about the former to my wife, for she is a nervous, highly-strung woman, and I had no wish that she should share the unpleasant impression which had been produced upon myself. I remarked to her, however, before I fell asleep that the cottage was now occupied, to which she returned no reply.

"I am usually an extremely sound sleeper. It has been a standing jest in the family that nothing could ever wake me during the night; and yet somehow on that particular night, whether it may have been the slight excitement produced by my little adventure or not, I know not, but I slept much more lightly than usual. Half in my dreams I was dimly conscious that something was going on in the room, and gradually became aware that my wife had dressed herself and was slipping on her mantle and her bonnet. My lips were parted to murmur out some sleepy words of surprise or remonstrance at this untimely preparation,

tones. It was evident to me that she was saying what was false. I said nothing in reply, but turned my face to the wall, sick at heart, with my mind filled with a thousand venomous doubts and suspicions. What was it that my wife was concealing from me? Where had she been during that strange expedition? I felt that I should have no peace until I knew, and yet I shrank from asking her again after once she had told me what was false. All the rest of the night I tossed and tumbled, framing theory after theory, each more unlikely than the last.

"I should have gone to the City that day, but I was too perturbed in my mind to be able to pay attention to business matters. My wife seemed to be as upset as myself, and I could see from the little questioning glances which she kept shooting at me, that she understood that I disbelieved her statement and that she was at her wits' ends what to do. We hardly exchanged a word during breakfast, and immediately afterwards I went out for a walk that I might think the matter out in the fresh morning air.

"'TRUST ME, JACK! SHE CRIED."

"I went as far as the Crystal Palace, spent an hour in the grounds, and was back in Norbury by one o'clock. It happened that my way took me past the cottage, and I stopped for an instant to look at the windows and to see if I could catch a glimpse of the strange face which had looked out at me on the day before. As I stood there, imagine my surprise, Mr. Holmes, when the door suddenly opened and my wife walked out!

"I was struck dumb with astonishment at the sight of her, but my emotions were nothing to those which showed themselves upon her face when our eyes met. She seemed for an instant to wish to shrink back inside the house again, and then, seeing how useless all concealment must be, she came forward with a very white face and frightened eyes which belied the smile upon her lips.

"'Oh, Jack!' she said, 'I have just been in to see if I can be of any assistance to our new neighbours. Why do you look at me like that, Jack? You are not angry with me?'

"'So,' said I, 'this is where you went during the night?'

"'What do you mean?' she cried.

"'You came here. I am sure of it. Who are these people that you should visit them at such an hour?'

"'I have not been here before.'

"'How can you tell me what you know is false?' I cried. 'Your very voice changes as you speak. When have I ever had a secret from you? I shall enter that cottage and I shall probe the matter to the bottom.'

"'No, no, Jack, for God's sake!' she gasped, in incontrollable emotion. Then as I approached the door she seized my sleeve and pulled me back with convulsive strength.

"'I implore you not to do this, Jack,' she cried. 'I swear that I will tell you everything some day, but nothing but misery can come of it if you enter that cottage.' Then, as I tried to shake her off, she clung to me in a frenzy of entreaty.

"'Trust me, Jack!' she cried. 'Trust me only this once. You will never have cause to regret it. You know that I would not have a secret from you if it were not for your own sake. Our whole lives are at stake on this. If you come home with me all will be well. If you force your way into that cottage, all is over between us.'

"There was such earnestness, such despair in her manner that her words arrested me, and I stood irresolute before the door.

"'I will trust you on one condition, and on one condition only,' said I at last. 'It is that this mystery comes to an end from now. You are at liberty to preserve your secret, but you must promise me that there shall be no more nightly visits, no more doings which are kept from my knowledge. I am willing to forget those which are passed if you will promise that there shall be no more in the future.'

"'I was sure that you would trust me,' she cried, with a great sigh of relief. 'It shall be just as you wish. Come away, oh, come away up to the house!' Still pulling at my sleeve she led me away from the cottage. As we went I glanced back, and there was that yellow livid face watching us out of the upper window. What link could there be between that creature and my wife? Or how could the coarse, rough woman whom I had seen the day before be connected with her? It was a strange puzzle, and yet I knew that my mind could never know ease again until I had solved it.

"For two days after this I stayed at home, and my wife appeared to abide loyally by our engagement, for, as far as I know, she never stirred out of the house. On the third day, however, I had ample evidence that her solemn promise was not enough to hold her back from this secret influence which drew her away from her husband and her duty.

"I had gone into town on that day, but I returned by the 2.40 instead of the 3.36, which is my usual train. As I entered the house the maid ran into the hall with a startled face.

"'Where is your mistress?' I asked.

"'I think that she has gone out for a walk,' she answered.

"My mind was instantly filled with suspicion. I rushed upstairs to make sure that she was not in the house. As I did so I happened to glance out of one of the upper windows, and saw the maid with whom I had just been speaking running across the field in the direction of the cottage. Then, of course, I saw exactly what it all meant. My wife had gone over there and had asked the servant to call her if I should return. Tingling with anger, I rushed down and hurried across, determined to end the matter once and for ever. I saw my wife and the maid hurrying back together along the lane, but I did not stop to speak with them. In the cottage lay the secret which was casting a shadow over my life. I vowed that, come what might, it should be a secret no longer. I did not even knock when I reached it, but turned the handle and rushed into the passage.

"It was all still and quiet upon the ground-floor. In the kitchen a kettle was singing on the fire, and a large black cat lay coiled up in a basket, but there was no sign of the woman whom I had seen before. I ran into the other room, but it was equally deserted. Then I rushed up the stairs, but only to find two other rooms empty and deserted at the top. There was no one at all in the whole house. The furniture and pictures were of the most common and vulgar description save in the one chamber at the window of which I had seen the strange face. That was comfortable and elegant, and all my suspicions rose into a fierce, bitter blaze when I saw that on the mantelpiece stood a full-length photograph of my wife, which had been taken at my request only three months ago.

"I stayed long enough to make certain that the house was absolutely empty. Then I left it, feeling a weight at my heart such as I had never had before. My wife came out into the hall as I entered my house, but I was too hurt and angry to speak with her, and pushing past her I made my way into my study. She followed me, however, before I could close the door.

"'I am sorry that I broke my promise, Jack,' said she, 'but if you knew all the circumstances I am sure that you would forgive me.'

"'Tell me everything, then,' said I.

"'I cannot, Jack, I cannot!' she cried.

"'Until you tell me who it is that has been living in that cottage, and who it is to whom you have given that photograph, there can never be any confidence between us,' said I, and breaking away from her I left the house. That was yesterday, Mr. Holmes, and I have not seen her since, nor do I know anything more about this strange business. It is the first shadow that has come between us, and it has so shaken me that I do not know what I should do for the best. Suddenly this morning it occurred to me that you were the man to advise me, so I have hurried to you now, and I place myself unreservedly in your hands. If there is any point which I have not made clear, pray question me about it. But above all tell me

"'TELL ME EVERYTHING,' SAID I."

"Did she ever talk of revisiting the place?"

"No."

"Or get letters from it?"

"Not to my knowledge."

"Thank you. I should like to think over the matter a little now. If the cottage is permanently deserted we may have some difficulty; if on the other hand, as I fancy is more likely, the inmates were warned of your coming, and left before you entered yesterday, then they may be back now, and we should clear it all up easily. Let me advise you, then, to return to Norbury and to examine the windows of the cottage again. If you have reason to believe that it is inhabited do not force your way in, but send a wire to my friend and me. We shall be with you within an hour of receiving it, and we shall then very soon get to the bottom of the business."

"And if it is still empty?"

"In that case I shall come out to-morrow and talk it over with you. Good-bye, and above all do not fret until you know that you really have a cause for it."

"I am afraid that this is a bad business, Watson," said my companion, as he returned after accompanying Mr. Grant Munro to the door. "What did you make of it?"

"It had an ugly sound," I answered.

"Yes. There's blackmail in it, or I am much mistaken."

"And who is the blackmailer?"

"Well, it must be this creature who lives in the only comfortable room in the place, and has her photograph above his fireplace. Upon my word, Watson, there is something very attractive about that livid face at the window, and I would not have missed the case for worlds."

"You have a theory?"

"Yes, a provisional one. But I shall be surprised if it does not turn out to be correct. This woman's first husband is in that cottage."

"Why do you think so?"

quickly what I have to do, for this misery is more than I can bear."

Holmes and I had listened with the utmost interest to this extraordinary statement, which had been delivered in the jerky, broken fashion of a man who is under the influence of extreme emotion. My companion sat silent now for some time, with his chin upon his hand, lost in thought.

"Tell me," said he at last, "could you swear that this was a man's face which you saw at the window?"

"Each time that I saw it I was some distance away from it, so that it is impossible for me to say."

"You appear, however, to have been disagreeably impressed by it."

"It seemed to be of an unnatural colour and to have a strange rigidity about the features. When I approached, it vanished with a jerk."

"How long is it since your wife asked you for a hundred pounds?"

"Nearly two months."

"Have you ever seen a photograph of her first husband?"

"No, there was a great fire at Atlanta very shortly after his death, and all her papers were destroyed."

"And yet she had a certificate of death. You say that you saw it?"

"Yes, she got a duplicate after the fire."

"Did you ever meet anyone who knew her in America?"

"No."

"How else can we explain her frenzied anxiety that her second one should not enter it? The facts, as I read them, are something like this: This woman was married in America. Her husband developed some hateful qualities, or, shall we say, that he contracted some loathsome disease, and became a leper or an imbecile. She fled from him at last, returned to England, changed her name, and started her life, as she thought, afresh. She had been married three years, and believed that her position was quite secure—having shown her husband the death certificate of some man, whose name she had assumed—when suddenly her whereabouts was discovered by her first husband, or, we may suppose, by some unscrupulous woman, who had attached herself to the invalid. They write to the wife and threaten to come and expose her. She asks for a hundred pounds and endeavours to buy them off. They come in spite of it, and when the husband mentions casually to the wife that there are new-comers in the cottage, she knows in some way that they are her pursuers. She waits until her husband is asleep, and then she rushes down to endeavour to persuade them to leave her in peace. Having no success, she goes again next morning, and her husband meets her, as he has told us, as she came out. She promises him then not to go there again, but two days afterwards, the hope of getting rid of those dreadful neighbours is too strong for her, and she makes another attempt, taking down with her the photograph which had probably been demanded from her. In the midst of this interview the maid rushes in to say that the master has come home, on which the wife, knowing that he would come straight down to the cottage, hurries the inmates out at the back door, into that grove of fir trees probably which was mentioned as standing near. In this way he finds the place deserted. I shall be very much surprised, however, if it is still so when he reconnoitres it this evening. What do you think of my theory?"

"It is all surmise."

"But at least it covers all the facts. When new facts come to our knowledge, which cannot be covered by it, it will be time enough to reconsider it. At present we can do nothing until we have a fresh message from our friend at Norbury."

But we had not very long to wait. It came just as we had finished our tea. "The cottage is still tenanted," it said. "Have seen the face again at the window. I'll meet the seven o'clock train, and take no steps until you arrive."

He was waiting on the platform when we stepped out, and we could see in the light of the station lamps that he was very pale, and quivering with agitation.

"They are still there, Mr. Holmes," said he, laying his hand upon my friend's sleeve. "I saw lights in the cottage as I came down. We shall settle it now, once and for all."

"What is your plan, then?" asked Holmes, as we walked down the dark, tree-lined road.

"I am going to force my way in, and see for myself who is in the house. I wish you both to be there as witnesses."

"You are quite determined to do this, in spite of your wife's warning that it was better that you should not solve the mystery?"

"Yes, I am determined."

"Well, I think that you are in the right. Any truth is better than indefinite doubt. We had better go up at once. Of course, legally we are putting ourselves hopelessly in the wrong, but I think that it is worth it."

It was a very dark night and a thin rain began to fall as we turned from the high road into a narrow lane, deeply rutted, with hedges on either side. Mr. Grant Munro pushed impatiently forward, however, and we stumbled after him as best we could.

"There are the lights of my house," he murmured, pointing to a glimmer among the trees, "and here is the cottage which I am going to enter."

We turned a corner in the lane as he spoke, and there was the building close beside us. A yellow bar falling across the black foreground showed that the door was not quite closed, and one window in the upper story was brightly illuminated. As we looked we saw a dark blurr moving across the blind.

"There is that creature," cried Grant Munro; "you can see for yourselves that someone is there. Now follow me, and we shall soon know all."

We approached the door, but suddenly a woman appeared out of the shadow and stood in the golden track of the lamp light. I could not see her face in the darkness, but her arms were thrown out in an attitude of entreaty.

"For God's sake, don't, Jack!" she cried. "I had a presentiment that you would come this evening. Think better of it, dear! Trust me again, and you will never have cause to regret it."

"I have trusted you too long, Effie!" he cried, sternly. "Leave go of me! I must pass you. My friends and I are going to settle this matter once and for ever." He pushed her to one side and we followed closely after him. As he threw the door open, an elderly woman ran out in front of him and tried to bar his passage, but he thrust her back, and an instant afterwards we were all upon the stairs. Grant Munro rushed into the lighted room at the top, and we entered it at his heels.

It was a cosy, well-furnished apartment, with two candles burning upon the table and two upon the mantelpiece. In the corner, stooping over a desk, there sat what appeared to be a little girl. Her face was turned away as we entered, but we could see that she was dressed in a red frock, and that she had long white gloves on. As she whisked round to us I gave a cry of surprise and horror. The face which she turned towards us was of the strangest livid tint, and the features were absolutely levoid of any expression. An instant later the mystery was explained. Holmes, with a laugh, passed his hand behind the child's ear, a mask peeled off from her countenance, and there was a little coal-black negress with all her white teeth flashing in amusement at our amazed faces. I burst out laughing out

"THERE WAS A LITTLE COAL-BLACK NEGRESS."

of sympathy with her merriment, but Grant Munro stood staring, with his hand clutching at his throat.

"My God!" he cried, "what can be the meaning of this?"

"I will tell you the meaning of it," cried the lady, sweeping into the room with a proud, set face. "You have forced me against my own judgment to tell you, and now we must both make the best of it. My husband died at Atlanta. My child survived."

"Your child!"

She drew a large silver locket from her bosom. "You have never seen this open."

"I understood that it did not open."

She touched a spring, and the front hinged back. There was a portrait within of a man, strikingly handsome and intelligent, but bearing unmistakable signs upon his features of his African descent.

"That is John Hebron, of Atlanta," said the lady, "and a nobler man never walked the earth. I cut myself off from my race in order to wed him; but never once while he lived did I for one instant regret it. It was our misfortune that our only child took after his people rather than mine. It is often so in such matches, and little Lucy is darker far than ever her father was. But, dark or fair, she is my own dear little girlie, and her mother's pet." The little creature ran across at the words and nestled up against the lady's dress.

"When I left her in America," she continued, "it was only because her health was weak, and the change might have done her harm. She was given to the care of a faithful Scotch-woman who had once been our servant. Never for an instant did I dream of disowning her as my child. But when chance threw you in my way, Jack, and I learned to love you, I feared to tell you about my child. God forgive me, I feared that I should lose you, and I had not the courage to tell you. I had to choose between you, and in my weakness I turned away from my own little girl. For three years I have kept her existence a secret from you, but I heard from the nurse, and I knew that all was well with her. At last, however, there came an overwhelming desire to see the child once more. I struggled against it, but in vain. Though I knew the danger I determined to have the child over, if it were but for a few weeks. I sent a hundred pounds to the nurse, and I gave her instructions about this cottage, so that she might come as a neighbour without my appearing to be in any way

child only just escaped from the back door as you rushed in at the front one. And now to-night you at last know all, and I ask you what is to become of us, my child and me?" She clasped her hands and waited for an answer.

It was a long two minutes before Grant Munro broke the silence, and when his answer came it was one of which I love to think. He lifted the little child, kissed her, and

"HE LIFTED THE LITTLE CHILD.'

connected with her. I pushed my precautions so far as to order her to keep the child in the house during the daytime, and to cover up her little face and hands, so that even those who might see her at the window should not gossip about there being a black child in the neighbourhood. If I had been less cautious I might have been more wise, but I was half crazy with fear lest you should learn the truth.

"It was you who told me first that the cottage was occupied. I should have waited for the morning, but I could not sleep for excitement, and so at last I slipped out, knowing how difficult it is to awaken you. But you saw me go, and that was the beginning of my troubles. Next day you had my secret at your mercy, but you nobly refrained from pursuing your advantage. Three days later, however, the nurse and

then, still carrying her, he held his other hand out to his wife and turned towards the door.

"We can talk it over more comfortably at home," said he. "I am not a very good man, Effie, but I think that I am a better one than you have given me credit for being."

Holmes and I followed them down to the lane, and my friend plucked at my sleeve as we came out. "I think," said he, "that we shall be of more use in London than in Norbury."

Not another word did he say of the case until late that night when he was turning away, with his lighted candle, for his bedroom.

"Watson," said he, "if it should ever strike you that I am getting a little over-confident in my powers, or giving less pains to a case than it deserves, kindly whisper 'Norbury' in my ear, and I shall be infinitely obliged to you."

# The Adventures of Sherlock Holmes.

## XVI.—THE ADVENTURE OF THE STOCKBROKER'S CLERK.

### By A. Conan Doyle.

HORTLY after my marriage I had bought a connection in the Paddington district. Old Mr. Farquhar, from whom I purchased it, had at one time an excellent general practice, but his age, and an affliction of the nature of St. Vitus' dance, from which he suffered, had very much thinned it. The public, not unnaturally, goes upon the principle that he who would heal others must himself be whole, and looks askance at the curative powers of the man whose own case is beyond the reach of his drugs. Thus, as my predecessor weakened, his practice declined, until when I purchased it from him it had sunk from twelve hundred to little more than three hundred a year. I had confidence, however, in my own youth and energy, and was convinced that in a very few years the concern would be as flourishing as ever.

For three months after taking over the practice I was kept very closely at work, and saw little of my friend Sherlock Holmes, for I was too busy to visit Baker Street, and I seldom went anywhere himself save upon professional business. I was surprised, therefore, when one morning in June, as I sat reading the *British Medical Journal* after breakfast, I heard a ring at the bell followed by the high, somewhat strident, tones of my old companion's voice.

"Ah, my dear Watson," said he, striding into the room. "I am very delighted to see you. I trust that Mrs. Watson has entirely recovered from all the little excitements connected with our adventure of the 'Sign of Four.'"

"Thank you, we are both very well," said I, shaking him warmly by the hand.

"And I hope also," he continued, sitting down in the rocking-chair, "that the cares of medical practice have not entirely obliterated the interest which you used to take in our little deductive problems."

"On the contrary," I answered; "it was only last night that I was looking over my old notes and classifying some of our past results."

"I trust that you don't consider your collection closed?"

"Not at all. I should wish nothing better than to have some more of such experiences."

"To-day, for example?"

"Yes; to-day, if you like."

"And as far off as Birmingham?"

"Certainly, if you wish it."

"And the practice?"

"I do my neighbour's when he goes. He is always ready to work off the debt."

"Ha! Nothing could be better!" said Holmes, leaning back in his chair and looking keenly at me from under his half-closed lids. "I perceive that you have been

"'NOTHING COULD BE BETTER,' SAID HOLMES."

unwell lately. Summer colds are always a little trying."

"I was confined to the house by a severe chill for three days last week. I thought, however, that I had cast off every trace of it."

"So you have. You look remarkably robust."

"How, then, did you know of it?"

"My dear fellow, you know my methods."

"You deduced it, then?"

"Certainly."

"And from what?"

"From your slippers."

I glanced down at the new patent leathers which I was wearing. "How on earth —— ?" I began, but Holmes answered my question before it was asked.

"Your slippers are new," he said. "You could not have had them more than a few weeks. The soles which you are at this moment presenting to me are slightly scorched. For a moment I thought they might have got wet and been burned in the drying. But near the instep there is a small circular wafer of paper with the shopman's hieroglyphics upon it. Damp would of course have removed this. You had then been sitting with your feet outstretched to the fire, which a man would hardly do even in so wet a June as this if he were in his full health."

Like all Holmes's reasoning the thing seemed simplicity itself when it was once explained. He read the thought upon my features, and his smile had a tinge of bitterness.

"I am afraid that I rather give myself away when I explain," said he. "Results without causes are much more impressive. You are ready to come to Birmingham, then?"

"Certainly. What is the case?"

"You shall hear it all in the train. My client is outside in a four-wheeler. Can you come at once?"

"In an instant." I scribbled a note to my neighbour, rushed upstairs to explain the matter to my wife, and joined Holmes upon the doorstep.

"Your neighbour is a doctor?" said he, nodding at the brass plate.

"Yes. He bought a practice as I did."

"An old-established one?"

"Just the same as mine. Both have been ever since the houses were built."

"Ah, then you got hold of the best of the two."

"I think I did. But how do you know?"

"By the steps, my boy. Yours are worn three inches deeper than his. But this gentleman in the cab is my client, Mr. Hall Pycroft. Allow me to introduce you to him. Whip your horse up, cabby, for we have only just time to catch our train."

The man whom I found myself facing was a well-built, fresh-complexioned young fellow with a frank, honest face and a slight, crisp, yellow moustache. He wore a very shiny top-hat and a neat suit of sober black, which made him look what he was—a smart young City man, of the class who have been labelled Cockneys, but who give us our crack Volunteer regiments, and who turn out more fine athletes and sportsmen than any body of men in these islands. His round, ruddy face was naturally full of cheeriness, but the corners of his mouth seemed to me to be pulled down in a half-comical distress. It was not, however, until we were all in a first-class carriage and well started upon our journey to Birmingham, that I was able to learn what the trouble was which had driven him to Sherlock Holmes.

"We have a clear run here of seventy minutes," Holmes remarked. "I want you, Mr. Hall Pycroft, to tell my friend your very interesting experience exactly as you have told it to me, or with more detail if possible. It will be of use to me to hear the succession of events again. It is a case, Watson, which may prove to have something in it, or may prove to have nothing, but which at least presents those unusual and *outré* features which are as dear to you as they are to me. Now, Mr. Pycroft, I shall not interrupt you again."

Our young companion looked at me with a twinkle in his eye.

"The worst of the story is," said he, "that I show myself up as such a confounded fool. Of course, it may work out all right, and I don't see that I could have done otherwise; but if I have lost my crib and get nothing in exchange, I shall feel what a soft Johnny I have been. I'm not very good at telling a story, Dr. Watson, but it is like this with me.

"I used to have a billet at Coxon and Woodhouse, of Drapers' Gardens, but they were let in early in the spring through the Venezuelan loan, as no doubt you remember, and came a nasty cropper. I had been with them five years, and old Coxon gave me a ripping good testimonial when the smash came; but, of course, we clerks were all turned adrift, the twenty-seven of us. I tried here and tried there, but there were lots of other chaps on the same lay as myself, and it was a perfect frost for a long time. I had been taking three pounds a week at Coxon's, and I had saved about seventy of them, but I soon worked my way through that and out at the other end. I was fairly at the end of my tether at last, and could hardly find the stamps to answer the advertisements or the envelopes to stick them to. I had worn out my boots padding up office stairs, and I seemed just as far from getting a billet as ever.

"At last I saw a vacancy at Mawson and Williams', the great stockbroking firm in Lombard Street. I daresay E.C. is not much in your line, but I can tell you that this is about the richest house in London. The advertisement was to be answered by letter only. I sent in my testimonial and application, but without the least hope of getting it. Back came an answer by return saying that if I would appear next Monday I might take over my new duties at once, provided that my appearance was satisfactory. No one knows how these things are worked. Some people say the manager just

"'MR. HALL PYCROFT, I BELIEVE?' SAID HE."

plunges his hand into the heap and takes the first that comes. Anyhow, it was my innings that time, and I don't ever wish to feel better pleased. The screw was a pound a week rise, and the duties just about the same as at Coxon's.

"And now I come to the queer part of the business. I was in diggings out Hampstead way—17, Potter's Terrace, was the address. Well, I was sitting doing a smoke that very evening after I had been promised the appointment, when up came my landlady with a card which had 'Arthur Pinner, financial agent,' printed upon it. I had never heard

the name before, and could not imagine what he wanted with me, but of course I asked her to show him up. In he walked—a middle-sized, dark-haired, dark-eyed, black-bearded man, with a touch of the sheeny about his nose. He had a brisk kind of way with him and spoke sharply, like a man that knew the value of time.

"'Mr. Hall Pycroft, I believe?' said he.

"'Yes, sir,' I answered, and pushed a chair towards him.

"'Lately engaged at Coxon and Woodhouse's?'

"'Yes, sir.'

"And now on the staff of Mawson's?'

"'Quite so.'

"'Well,' said he. 'The fact is that I have heard some really extraordinary stories about your financial ability. You remember Parker who used to be Coxon's manager? He can never say enough about it.'

"Of course I was pleased to hear this. I had always been pretty smart in the office, but I had never dreamed that I was talked about in the City in this fashion.

"'You have a good memory?' said he.

"'Pretty fair,' I answered, modestly.

"'Have you kept in touch with the market while you have been out of work?' he asked.

"'Yes; I read the Stock Exchange List every morning.'

"'Now, that shows real application!' he cried. 'That is the way to prosper! You won't mind my testing you, will you? Let me see! How are Ayrshires?'

"'One hundred and six and a quarter to one hundred and five and seven-eighths,' I answered.

"'And New Zealand Consolidated?'

"'A hundred and four.'

"'And British Broken Hills?'

"'Seven to seven and six.'

"'Wonderful!' he cried, with his hands up. 'This quite fits in with all that I had heard. My boy, my boy, you are very much too good to be a clerk at Mawson's!'

"This outburst rather astonished me, as you can think. 'Well,' said I, 'other people don't think quite so much of me as you seem to do, Mr. Pinner. I had a hard enough fight to get this berth, and I am very glad to have it.'

"'Pooh, man, you should soar above it. You are not in your true sphere. Now I'll tell you how it stands with me. What I have to offer is little enough when measured by your ability, but when compared with Mawson's it is light to dark. Let me see! When do you go to Mawson's?'

"'On Monday.'

"'Ha! ha! I think I would risk a little sporting flutter that you don't go there at all.'

"'Not go to Mawson's?'

"'No, sir. By that day you will be the business manager of the Franco-Midland Hardware Company, Limited, with one hundred and thirty-four branches in the towns and villages of France, not counting one in Brussels and one in San Remo.'

"This took my breath away. 'I never heard of it,' said I.

"'Very likely not. It has been kept very quiet, for the capital was all privately subscribed, and it is too good a thing to let the public into. My brother, Harry Pinner, is promoter, and joins the board after allotment as managing director. He knew that I was in the swim down here, and he asked me to pick up a good man cheap—a young, pushing man with plenty of snap about him. Parker spoke of you, and that brought me here to-night. We can only offer you a beggarly five hundred to start with——'

"'Five hundred a year!' I shouted.

"'Only that at the beginning, but you are to have an over-riding commission of 1 per cent. on all business done by your agents, and you may take my word for it that this will come to more than your salary.'

"'But I know nothing about hardware.'

"'Tut, my boy, you know about figures.'

"My head buzzed, and I could hardly sit still in the chair. But suddenly a little chill of doubt came over me.

"'I must be frank with you,' said I. 'Mawson only gives me two hundred, but Mawson is safe. Now, really, I know so little about your company that ——'

"'Ah, smart, smart!' he cried, in a kind of ecstasy of delight. 'You are the very man for us! You are not to be talked over, and quite right too. Now, here's a note for a hundred pounds; and if you think that we can do business you may just slip it into your pocket as an advance upon your salary.'

"'That is very handsome,' said I. 'When should I take over my new duties?'

"'Be in Birmingham to-morrow at one,' said he. 'I have a note in my pocket here which you will take to my brother. You will find him at 126B, Corporation Street, where the temporary offices of the company are situated. Of course he must confirm your engagement, but between ourselves it will be all right.'

"'Really, I hardly know how to express my gratitude, Mr. Pinner,' said I.

"'Not at all, my boy. You have only got your deserts. There are one or two small things—mere formalities—which I must arrange with you. You have a bit of paper beside you there. Kindly write upon it, "I am perfectly willing to act as business manager to the Franco-Midland Hardware Company, Limited, at a minimum salary of £500."'

"I did as he asked, and he put the paper in his pocket.

"'There is one other detail,' said he. 'What do you intend to do about Mawson's?'

"I had forgotten all about Mawson's in my joy.

"'I'll write and resign,' said I.

"'Precisely what I don't want you to do. I had a row over you with Mawson's manager. I had gone up to ask him about you, and he was very offensive—accused me of coaxing you away from the service of the firm, and that sort of thing. At last I fairly lost my temper. "If you want good men you should pay them a good price," said I. "He would rather have our small price than your big one," said he. "I'll lay you a fiver," said I, "that when he has my offer you will never so much as hear from him again." "Done!" said he. "We picked him out of the gutter, and he won't leave us so easily." Those were his very words.'

"'The impudent scoundrel!' I cried. 'I've never so much as seen him in my life. Why should I consider him in any way? I shall certainly not write if you would rather that I didn't.'

"'Good! That's a promise!' said he, rising from his chair. 'Well, I am delighted to have got so good a man for my brother.

Here is your advance of a hundred pounds, and here is the letter. Make a note of the address, 126B, Corporation Street, and remember that one o'clock to-morrow is your appointment. Good-night, and may you have all the fortune that you deserve.'

"That's just about all that passed between us as near as I can remember it. You can imagine, Dr. Watson, how pleased I was at such an extraordinary bit of good fortune. I sat up half the night hugging myself over it, and next day I was off to Birmingham in a train that would take me in plenty of time for my appointment. I took my things to an hotel in New Street, and then I made my way to the address which had been given me.

"It was a quarter of an hour before my time, but I thought that would make no difference. 126B was a passage between two large shops which led to a winding stone stair, from which there were many flats, let as offices to companies or professional men. The names of the occupants were painted up at the bottom on the wall, but there was no such name as the Franco-Midland Hardware Company, Limited. I stood for a few minutes with my heart in my boots, wondering whether the whole thing was an elaborate hoax or not, when up came a man and addressed me. He was very like the chap that I had seen the night before, the same figure and voice, but he was clean shaven and his hair was lighter.

"'Are you Mr. Hall Pycroft?' he asked.

"'Yes,' said I.

"'Ah! I was expecting you, but you are a trifle before your time. I had a note from my brother this morning, in which he sang your praises very loudly.'

"UP CAME A MAN AND ADDRESSED ME."

"'I was just looking for the offices when you came.'

"'We have not got our name up yet, for we only secured these temporary premises last week. Come up with me and we will talk the matter over.'

"I followed him to the top of a very lofty stair, and there right under the slates were a couple of empty and dusty little rooms, uncarpeted and uncurtained, into which he led me. I had thought of a great office with shining tables and rows of clerks such as I was used to, and I daresay I stared rather straight at the two deal chairs and one little table, which, with a ledger and a waste-paper basket, made up the whole furniture.

"'Don't be disheartened, Mr. Pycroft,' said my new acquaintance, seeing the length of my face. 'Rome was not built in a day, and we have lots of money at our backs, though we don't cut much dash yet in offices. Pray sit down and let me have your letter.'

"I gave it to him, and he read it over very carefully.

"'You seem to have made a vast impression upon my brother, Arthur,' said he, 'and I know that he is a pretty shrewd judge. He swears by London, you know, and I by Birmingham, but this time I shall follow his advice. Pray consider yourself definitely engaged.'

"'What are my duties?' I asked.

"'You will eventually manage the great depôt in Paris, which will pour a flood of English crockery into the shops of one hundred and thirty-four agents in France. The purchase will be completed in a week, and meanwhile you will remain in Birmingham and make yourself useful.'

"'How?'

"For answer he took a big red book out of a drawer. 'This is a directory of Paris,' said he, 'with the trades after the names of the people. I want you to take it home with you, and to mark off all the hardware sellers with their addresses. It would be of the greatest use to me to have them.'

"'Surely, there are classified lists?' I suggested.

"'Not reliable ones. Their system is different to ours. Stick at it and let me have the lists by Monday, at twelve. Good-day, Mr. Pycroft; if you continue to show zeal and intelligence, you will find the company a good master.'

"I went back to the hotel with the big book under my arm, and with very conflicting feelings in my breast. On the one hand I was definitely engaged, and had a hundred pounds in my pocket. On the other, the look of the offices, the absence of name on the wall, and other of the points which would strike a business man had left a bad impression as to the position of my employers. However, come what might, I had my money, so I settled down to my task. All Sunday I was kept hard at work, and yet by Monday I had only got as far as H. I went round to my employer, found him in the same dismantled kind of room, and was told to keep at it until Wednesday, and then come again. On Wednesday it was still unfinished, so I hammered away until Friday—that is, yesterday. Then I brought it round to Mr. Harry Pinner.

"'Thank you very much,' said he. 'I fear that I underrated the difficulty of the task. This list will be of very material assistance to me.'

"'It took some time,' said I.

"'And now,' said he, 'I want you to make a list of the furniture shops, for they all sell crockery.'

"'Very good.'

"'And you can come up to-morrow evening at seven, and let me know how you are getting on. Don't overwork yourself. A couple of hours at Day's Music-Hall in the evening would do you no harm after your labours.' He laughed as he spoke, and I saw with a thrill that his second tooth upon the left-hand side had been very badly stuffed with gold."

Sherlock Holmes rubbed his hands with delight, and I stared in astonishment at our client.

"You may well look surprised, Dr. Watson, but it is this way," said he. "When I was speaking to the other chap in London at the time that he laughed at my not going to Mawson's, I happened to notice that his tooth was stuffed in this very identical fashion. The glint of the gold in each case caught my eye, you see. When I put that with the voice and figure being the same, and only those things altered which might be changed by a razor or a wig, I could not doubt that it was the same man. Of course, you expect two brothers to be alike, but not that they should have the same tooth stuffed in the same way. He bowed me out and I found myself in the street, hardly knowing whether I was on my head or my heels. Back I went to my hotel, put my head in a basin of cold water, and tried to think it out. Why had he sent me from London to Birmingham; why had he got there before me; and why had he written a letter from himself to himself? It was altogether too much for me, and I could make no sense of it. And then suddenly it struck me that what was dark to me might be very light to Mr. Sherlock Holmes. I had just time to get up to town by the night train, to see him this morning, and to bring you both back with me to Birmingham."

There was a pause after the stockbroker's clerk had concluded his surprising experience. Then Sherlock Holmes cocked his eye at me, leaning back on the cushions with a pleased and yet critical face, like a connoisseur who had just taken his first sip of a comet vintage.

"Rather fine, Watson, is it not?" said he. "There are points in it which please me. I think you will agree with me that an interview with Mr. Arthur Harry Pinner in the temporary offices of the Franco-Midland Hardware Company, Limited, would be a rather interesting experience for both of us."

"But how can we do it?" I asked.

"Oh, easily enough," said Hall Pycroft, cheerily. "You are two friends of mine who are in want of a billet, and what could be more natural than that I should bring you both round to the managing director?"

"Quite so! Of course!" said Holmes. "I should like to have a look at the gentleman and see if I can make anything of his little game. What qualities have you, my friend, which would make your services so valuable? or is it possible that——" he began biting his nails and staring blankly out of the window, and we hardly drew another word from him until we were in New Street.

At seven o'clock that evening we were walking, the three of us, down Corporation Street to the company's offices.

"It is of no use our being at all before our time," said our client. "He only comes there to see me apparently, for the place is deserted up to the very hour he names."

"That is suggestive," remarked Holmes.

"By Jove, I told you so!" cried the clerk. "That's he walking ahead of us there."

He pointed to a smallish, blonde, well-dressed man, who was bustling along the other side of the road. As we watched him he looked across at a boy who was bawling out the latest edition of the evening paper, and, running over among the cabs and 'buses, he bought one from him. Then clutching it in his hand he vanished through a doorway.

"There he goes!" cried Hall Pycroft. "Those are the company's offices into which he has gone. Come with me and I'll fix it up as easily as possible."

Following his lead we ascended five stories, until we found ourselves outside a half-opened door, at which our client tapped. A voice within bade us "Come in," and we entered a bare, unfurnished room, such as Hall Pycroft had described. At the single table sat the man whom we had seen in the street, with his evening paper spread out in front of him, and as he looked up at us it seemed to me

dead white of a fish's belly, and his eyes were wild and staring. He looked at his clerk as though he failed to recognise him, and I could see, by the astonishment depicted upon our conductor's face, that this was by no means the usual appearance of his employer.

"You look ill, Mr. Pinner," he exclaimed.

"Yes, I am not very well," answered the other, making obvious efforts to pull himself together, and licking his dry lips before he spoke. "Who are these gentlemen whom you have brought with you?"

"One is Mr. Harris, of Bermondsey, and the other is Mr. Price, of this town," said our clerk, glibly. "They are friends of mine, and gentlemen of experience, but they have been out of a place for some little time, and they hoped that perhaps you might find an opening for them in the company's employment."

"Very possibly! Very possibly!" cried Mr. Pinner, with a ghastly smile. "Yes, I have no doubt that we shall be able to do something for you. What is your particular line, Mr. Harris?"

"I am an accountant," said Holmes.

"Ah, yes, we shall want something of the sort. And you, Mr. Price?"

"A clerk," said I.

"I have every hope that the company may accommodate you. I will let you know about it as soon as we come to any conclusion. And now I beg that you will go. For God's sake, leave me to myself!"

These last words were shot out of him, as though the constraint which he was evidently setting upon himself had suddenly and utterly burst asunder.

"HE LOOKED UP AT US."

that I had never looked upon a face which bore such marks of grief, and of something beyond grief—of a horror such as comes to few men in a lifetime. His brow glistened with perspiration, his cheeks were of the dull

self had suddenly and utterly burst asunder. Holmes and I glanced at each other, and Hall Pycroft took a step towards the table.

"You forget, Mr. Pinner, that I am here

by appointment to receive some directions from you," said he.

"Certainly, Mr. Pycroft, certainly," the other answered in a calmer tone. "You may wait here a moment, and there is no reason why your friends should not wait with you. I will be entirely at your service in three minutes, if I might trespass upon your patience so far." He rose with a very courteous air, and bowing to us he passed out through a door at the further end of the room, which he closed behind him.

"What now?" whispered Holmes. "Is he giving us the slip?"

"Impossible," answered Pycroft.

"Why so?"

"That door leads into an inner room."

"There is no exit?"

"None."

"Is it furnished?"

it was empty yesterday."

Then what on earth can he be doing? There is something which I don't understand in this matter. If ever a man was three parts mad with terror, that man's name is Pinner. What can have put the shivers on him?"

"He suspects that we are detectives," I suggested.

"That's it," said Pycroft.

Holmes shook his head. "He did not turn pale. He *was* pale when we entered the room," said he. "It is just possible that—"

His words were interrupted by a sharp rat-tat from the direction of the inner door.

"What the deuce is he knocking at his own door for?" cried the clerk.

Again and much louder came the rat-tat-tat. We all gazed expectantly at the closed door. Glancing at

Holmes I saw his face turn rigid, and he leaned forward in intense excitement. Then suddenly came a low gurgling, gargling sound and a brisk drumming upon woodwork. Holmes sprang frantically across the room and pushed at the door. It was fastened on the inner side. Following his example, we threw ourselves upon it with all our weight. One hinge snapped, then the other, and down came the door with a crash. Rushing over it we found ourselves in the inner room.

It was empty.

But it was only for a moment that we were at fault. At one corner, the corner nearest the room which we had left, there was a second door. Holmes sprang to it and pulled it open. A coat and waistcoat were lying on the floor, and from a hook behind the door, with his own braces round his neck, was hanging the managing director of the Franco-Midland Hardware Company. His knees were drawn up, his head hung at a dreadful angle to his body, and the clatter of his heels against the door made the noise which had broken in upon our conversation. In an instant I had caught him round the waist and held him up, while Holmes and Pycroft untied the elastic bands which had disappeared between the livid creases of skin. Then we carried him into the other room, where he lay with a clay-coloured face, puffing his purple lips in and out with every breath —a dreadful wreck of all that he had been but five minutes before.

"What do you think of him, Watson?" asked Holmes.

I stooped over him and examined him.

"WE FOUND OURSELVES IN THE INNER ROOM."

His pulse was feeble and intermittent, but his breathing grew longer, and there was a little shivering of his eyelids which showed a thin white slit of ball beneath.

"It has been touch and go with him," said I, "but he'll live now. Just open that window and hand me the water carafe." I undid his collar, poured the cold water over his face, and raised and sank his arms until he drew a long natural breath.

"It's only a question of time now," said I, as I turned away from him.

Holmes stood by the table with his hands deep in his trousers pockets and his chin upon his breast.

"I suppose we ought to call the police in now," said he; "and yet I confess that I like to give them a complete case when they come."

"It's a blessed mystery to me," cried Pycroft, scratching his head. "Whatever they wanted to bring me all the way up here for, and then——"

"Pooh! All that is clear enough," said Holmes, impatiently. "It is this last sudden move."

"You understand the rest, then?"

"I think that it is fairly obvious. What do you say, Watson?"

I shrugged my shoulders.

"I must confess that I am out of my depths," said I.

"Oh, surely, if you consider the events at first they can only point to one conclusion."

"What do you make of them?"

"Well, the whole thing hinges upon two points. The first is the making of Pycroft write a declaration by which he entered the service of this preposterous company. Do you not see how very suggestive that is?"

"I am afraid I miss the point."

"Well, why did they want him to do it? Not as a business matter, for these arrangements are usually verbal, and there was no earthly business reason why this should be an exception. Don't you see, my young friend, that they were very anxious to obtain a specimen of your handwriting, and had no other way of doing it?"

"And why?"

"Quite so. Why? When we answer that, we have made some progress with our little problem. Why? There can be only one adequate reason. Someone wanted to learn to imitate your writing, and had to procure a specimen of it first. And now if we pass on to the second point, we find that each throws light upon the other. That point is the request made by Pinner that you should not resign your place, but should leave the manager of this important business in the full expectation that a Mr. Hall Pycroft, whom he had never seen, was about to enter the office upon the Monday morning."

"My God!" cried our client, "what a blind beetle I have been!"

"Now you see the point about the handwriting. Suppose that someone turned up in your place who wrote a completely different hand from that in which you had applied for the vacancy, of course the game would have been up. But in the interval the rogue learnt to imitate you, and his position was therefore secure, as I presume that nobody in the office had ever set eyes upon you?"

"Not a soul," groaned Hall Pycroft.

"Very good. Of course, it was of the utmost importance to prevent you from thinking better of it, and also to keep you from coming into contact with anyone who might tell you that your double was at work in Mawson's office. Therefore they gave you a handsome advance on your salary, and ran you off to the Midlands, where they gave you enough work to do to prevent your going to London, where you might have burst their little game up. That is all plain enough."

"But why should this man pretend to be his own brother?"

"Well, that is pretty clear also. There are evidently only two of them in it. The other is personating you at the office. This one acted as your engager, and then found that he could not find you an employer without admitting a third person into his plot. That he was most unwilling to do. He changed his appearance as far as he could, and trusted that the likeness, which you could not fail to observe, would be put down to a family resemblance. But for the happy chance of the gold stuffing your suspicions would probably have never been aroused."

Hall Pycroft shook his clenched hands in the air. "Good Lord!" he cried. "While I have been fooled in this way, what has this other Hall Pycroft been doing at Mawson's? What should we do, Mr. Holmes? Tell me what to do!"

"We must wire to Mawson's."

"They shut at twelve on Saturdays."

"Never mind; there may be some doorkeeper or attendant——"

"Ah, yes; they keep a permanent guard there on account of the value of the securities that they hold. I remember hearing it talked of in the City."

"PYCROFT SHOOK HIS CLENCHED HANDS IN THE AIR."

"Very good, we shall wire to him, and see if all is well, and if a clerk of your name is working there. That is clear enough, but what is not so clear is why at sight of us one of the rogues should instantly walk out of the room and hang himself."

"The paper!" croaked a voice behind us. The man was sitting up, blanched and ghastly, with returning reason in his eyes, and hands which rubbed nervously at the broad red band which still encircled his throat.

"The paper! Of course!" yelled Holmes, in a paroxysm of excitement. "Idiot that I was! I thought so much of our visit that the paper never entered my head for an instant. To be sure the secret must lie there." He flattened it out upon the table, and a cry of triumph burst from his lips.

"Look at this, Watson!" he cried. "It is a London paper, an early edition of the *Evening Standard*. Here is what we want. Look at the headlines—'Crime in the City. Murder at Mawson and Williams'. Gigantic Attempted Robbery; Capture of the Criminal.'

Here, Watson, we are all equally anxious to hear it, so kindly read it aloud to us."

It appeared from its position in the paper to have been the one event of importance in town, and the account of it ran in this way:—

"A desperate attempt at robbery, culminating in the death of one man and the capture of the criminal, occurred this afternoon in the City. For some time back Mawson and Williams, the famous financial house, have been the guardians of securities which amount in the aggregate to a sum of considerably over a million sterling. So conscious was the manager of the responsibility which devolved upon him in consequence of the great interests at stake, that safes of the very latest construction have been employed, and an armed watchman has been left day and night in the building. It appears that last week a new clerk, named Hall Pycroft, was engaged by the firm. This person appears to have been none other than Beddington, the famous forger and cracksman, who, with his brother, has only recently emerged from a five years' spell of penal servitude. By some means, which are not yet clear, he succeeded in winning, under a false name, this official position in the office, which he utilized in order to obtain mouldings of various locks, and a thorough knowledge of the position of the strong room and the safes.

"It is customary at Mawson's for the clerks to leave at midday on Saturday. Sergeant Tuson, of the City Police, was somewhat surprised therefore to see a gentleman with a carpet bag come down the steps at twenty minutes past one. His suspicions being aroused, the sergeant followed the man, and with the aid of Constable Pollock succeeded, after a most desperate resistance, in arresting him. It was at once clear that a daring and gigantic robbery had been committed. Nearly a hundred thousand pounds worth of American railway bonds, with a large amount of scrip in other mines and companies, were discovered in the bag. On examining the premises the body of the unfortunate watchman was found doubled up and thrust into the largest of the safes, where it would not have been discovered until Monday morning had it not been for the prompt action of Sergeant Tuson. The man's skull had been shattered by a blow from a poker, delivered from behind. There at present be ascertained, although the police are making energetic inquiries as to his whereabouts."

"Well, we may save the police some little trouble in that direction," said Holmes, glancing at the haggard figure huddled up by the window. "Human nature is a strange mixture, Watson. You see that even a villain and a murderer can inspire

"GLANCING AT THE HAGGARD FIGURE."

could be no doubt that Beddington had obtained entrance by pretending that he had left something behind him, and having murdered the watchman, rapidly rifled the large safe, and then made off with his booty. His brother, who usually works with him, has not appeared in this job, so far as can such affection that his brother turns to suicide when he learns that his neck is forfeited. However, we have no choice as to our action. The doctor and I will remain on guard, Mr. Pycroft, if you will have the kindness to step out for the police,"

# The Adventures of Sherlock Holmes.

## XVII.—THE ADVENTURE OF THE "GLORIA SCOTT."

### By A. Conan Doyle.

"I HAVE some papers here," said my friend, Sherlock Holmes, as we sat one winter's night on either side of the fire, "which I really think, Watson, it would be worth your while to glance over. These are the documents in the extraordinary case of the *Gloria Scott*, and this is the message which struck Justice of the Peace Trevor dead with horror when he read it."

He had picked from a drawer a little tarnished cylinder, and, undoing the tape, he handed me a short note scrawled upon a half sheet of slate-grey paper.

"The supply of game for London is going steadily up," it ran. "Head-keeper Hudson, we believe, has been now told to receive all orders for fly-paper, and for preservation of your hen pheasant's life."

As I glanced up from reading this enigmatical message I saw Holmes chuckling at the expression upon my face.

"You look a little bewildered," said he.

"I cannot see how such a message as this could inspire horror. It seems to me to be rather grotesque than otherwise."

"Very likely. Yet the fact remains that the reader, who was a fine, robust old man, was knocked clean down by it, as if it had been the butt-end of a pistol."

"You arouse my curiosity," said I. "But why did you say just now that there were very particular reasons why I should study this case?"

"Because it was the first in which I was ever engaged."

I had often endeavoured to elicit from my companion what had first turned his mind in the direction of criminal research, but I had never caught him before in a communicative humour. Now he sat forward in his arm-chair, and spread out the documents upon his knees. Then he lit his pipe and sat for some time smoking and turning them over.

"You never heard me talk of Victor Trevor?" he asked. "He was the only friend I made during the two years that I was at college. I was never a very sociable fellow, Watson, always rather fond of moping in my rooms and working out my own little methods of thought, so that I never mixed much with the men of my year. Bar fencing and boxing I had few athletic tastes, and then my line of study was quite distinct from that of the other fellows, so that we had no points of contact at all. Trevor was the only man I knew, and that only through the accident of his bull-terrier freezing on to my ankle one morning as I went down to chapel.

"It was a prosaic way of forming a friendship, but it was effective. I was laid by the heels for ten days, and Trevor used to come in to inquire after me. At first it was only a minute's chat, but soon his visits lengthened, and before the end of the term we were close friends. He was a hearty, full-blooded fellow, full of spirits and energy, the very opposite to me in most respects; but we found we had some subjects in common, and it was a bond of union when I found that he was as friendless as I. Finally, he invited me down to his father's place at Donnithorpe, in Norfolk, and I accepted his hospitality for a month of the long vacation.

"Old Trevor was evidently a man of some wealth and consideration, a J.P. and a landed proprietor. Donnithorpe is a little hamlet just to the north of Langmere, in the country of the Broads. The house was an old-fashioned, wide-spread, oak-beamed, brick building, with a fine lime-lined avenue leading up to it. There was excellent wild duck shooting in the fens, remarkably good fishing, a small but select library, taken over, as I understood, from a former occupant, and a tolerable cook, so that it would be a fastidious man who could not put in a pleasant month there.

"Trevor senior was a widower, and my friend was his only son. There had been a daughter, I heard, but she had died of diphtheria while on a visit to Birmingham. The father interested me extremely. He was a man of little culture, but with a considerable amount of rude strength both physically and mentally. He knew hardly any books, but he had travelled far, had seen much of the world, and had remembered all that he had learned. In person he was a thick-set, burly man, with a shock of grizzled

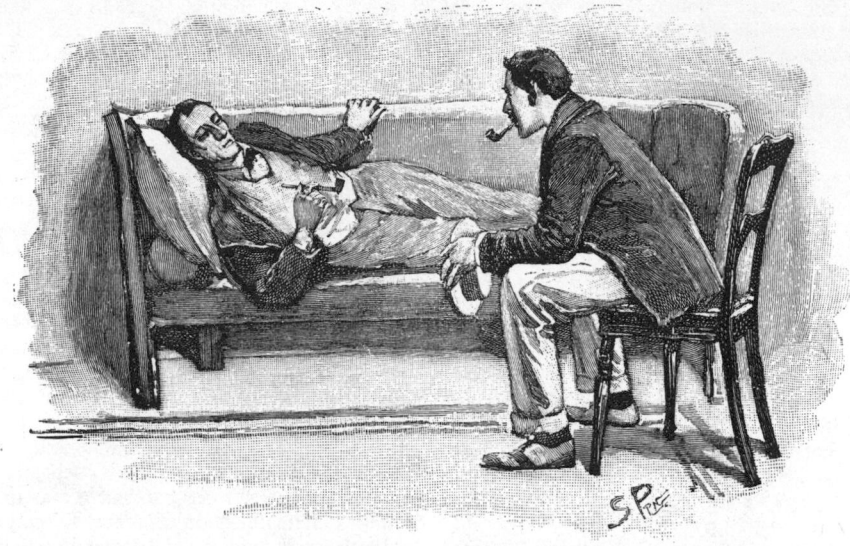

"TREVOR USED TO COME IN TO INQUIRE AFTER ME."

hair, a brown, weather-beaten face, and blue eyes which were keen to the verge of fierceness. Yet he had a reputation for kindness and charity on the country side, and was noted for the leniency of his sentences from the bench.

"One evening, shortly after my arrival, we were sitting over a glass of port after dinner, when young Trevor began to talk about those habits of observation and inference which I had already formed into a system, although I had not yet appreciated the part which they were to play in my life. The old man evidently thought that his son was exaggerating in his description of one or two trivial feats which I had performed.

"'Come now, Mr. Holmes,' said he, laughing good-humouredly, 'I'm an excellent subject, if you can deduce anything from me.'

"'I fear there is not very much,' I answered. 'I might suggest that you have gone about in fear of some personal attack within the last twelve months.'

"The laugh faded from his lips and he stared at me in great surprise.

"'Well, that's true enough,' said he. 'You know, Victor,' turning to his son, 'when we broke up that poaching gang, they swore to knife us ; and Sir Edward Hoby has actually been attacked. I've always been on my guard since then, though I have no idea how you know it.'

"'You have a very handsome stick,' I answered. 'By the inscription, I observed that you had not had it more than a year. But you have taken some pains to bore the head of it and pour melted lead into the hole, so as to make it a formidable weapon. I argued that you would not take such precautions unless you had some danger to fear.'

"'Anything else ?' he asked, smiling.

"'You have boxed a good deal in your youth.'

"'Right again. How did you know it ? Is my nose knocked a little out of the straight ?'

"'No,' said I. 'It is your ears. They have the peculiar flattening and thickening which marks the boxing man.'

"'Anything else ?'

"'You have done a great deal of digging, by your callosities.'

"'Made all my money at the gold-fields.'

"'You have been in New Zealand.'

"'Right again.'

"'You have visited Japan.'

"'Quite true.'

"'And you have been most intimately associated with someone whose initials were J. A., and whom you afterwards were eager to entirely forget.'

"Mr. Trevor stood slowly up, fixed his large blue eyes upon me with a strange, wild stare, and then pitched forward with his face among the nutshells which strewed the cloth, in a dead faint.

"You can imagine, Watson, how shocked both his son and I were. His attack did not last long, however, for when we undid his collar and sprinkled the water from one of the finger-glasses over his face, he gave a gasp or two and sat up.

"'Ah, boys!' said he, forcing a smile. 'I hope I haven't frightened you. Strong as I look, there is a weak place in my heart, and it does not take much to knock me over. I don't know how you manage this, Mr. Holmes, but it seems to me that all the detectives of fact and of fancy would be children in your hands. That's your line of life, sir, and you may take the word of a man who has seen something of the world.'

"And that recommendation, with the exaggerated estimate of my ability with which he prefaced it, was, if you will believe me, Watson, the very first thing which ever made me feel that a profession might be made out of what had up to that time been the merest hobby. At the moment, however, I was too much concerned at the sudden illness of my host to think of anything else.

"'I hope that I have said nothing to pain you,' said I.

"'Well, you certainly touched upon rather a tender point. Might I ask how you know and how much you know?' He spoke now in a half jesting fashion, but a look of terror still lurked at the back of his eyes.

"'It is simplicity itself,' said I. 'When you bared your arm to draw that fish into the boat I saw that "J. A." had been tattooed in the bend of the elbow. The letters were still legible, but it was perfectly clear from their blurred appearance, and from the staining of the skin round them, that efforts had been made to obliterate them. It was obvious, then, that those initials had once been very familiar to you, and that you had afterwards wished to forget them.'

"'What an eye you have!' he cried, with a sigh of relief. 'It is just as you say. But we won't talk of it. Of all ghosts, the ghosts of our old loves are the worst. Come into the billiard-room and have a quiet cigar.'

"From that day, amid all his cordiality, there was always a touch of suspicion in Mr. Trevor's manner towards me. Even his son remarked it. 'You've given the governor such a turn,' said he, 'that he'll never be sure again of what you know and what you don't know.' He did not mean to show it, I am sure, but it was so strongly in his mind that it peeped out at every action. At last I became so convinced that I was causing him uneasiness, that I drew my visit to a close. On the very day, however, before I left an incident occurred which proved in the sequel to be of importance.

"We were sitting out upon the lawn on garden chairs, the three of us, basking in the sun and admiring the view across the Broads, when the maid came out to say that there was a man at the door who wanted to see Mr. Trevor.

"'What is his name?' asked my host.

"'He would not give any.'

"'What does he want, then?'

"'He says that you know him, and that he only wants a moment's conversation.'

"'Show him round here.' An instant afterwards there appeared a little wizened fellow, with a cringing manner and a shambling style of walking. He wore an open jacket, with a splotch of tar on the sleeve, a red and black check shirt, dungaree trousers, and heavy boots badly worn. His face was thin and brown and crafty, with a perpetual smile upon it, which showed an irregular line of yellow teeth, and his crinkled hands were half-closed in a way that is distinctive of sailors. As he came slouching across the lawn I heard Mr. Trevor make a sort of hiccoughing noise in his throat, and, jumping out of his chair, he ran into the house. He was back in a moment, and I smelt a strong reek of brandy as he passed me.

"'Well, my man,' said he, 'what can I do for you?'

"The sailor stood looking at him with puckered eyes, and with the same loose-lipped smile upon his face.

"'You don't know me?' he asked.

"'Why, dear me, it is surely Hudson!' said Mr. Trevor, in a tone of surprise.

"'Hudson it is, sir,' said the seaman. 'Why, it's thirty year and more since I saw you last. Here you are in your house, and me still picking my salt meat out of the harness cask.'

"'Tut, you will find that I have not forgotten old times,' cried Mr. Trevor, and, walking towards the sailor, he said something in a low voice. 'Go into the kitchen,' he continued out loud, 'and you will get food and drink. I have no doubt that I shall find you a situation.'

"'Thank you, sir,' said the seaman, touching his forelock. 'I'm just off a two-yearer in an eight-knot tramp, short-handed at that, and I wants a rest. I thought I'd get it either with Mr. Beddoes or with you.'

"'Ah!' cried Mr. Trevor, 'you know where Mr. Beddoes is?'

"'Bless you, sir, I know where all my old friends are,' said the fellow, with a sinister smile, and slouched off after the maid to the

" 'HUDSON IT IS, SIR, SAID THE SEAMAN.

kitchen. Mr. Trevor mumbled something to us about having been shipmates with the man when he was going back to the diggings, and then, leaving us on the lawn, he went indoors. An hour later, when we entered the house we found him stretched dead drunk upon the dining - room sofa. The whole incident left a most ugly impression upon my mind, and I was not sorry next day to leave Donnithorpe behind me, for I felt that my presence must be a source of embarrassment to my friend.

"All this occurred during the first month of the long vacation. I went up to my London rooms, where I spent seven weeks working out a few experiments in organic chemistry. One day, however, when the autumn was far advanced and the vacation drawing to a close, I received a telegram from my friend imploring me to return to Donnithorpe, and saying that he was in great need of my advice and assistance. Of course I dropped everything, and set out for the north once more.

"He met me with the dog-cart at the station, and I saw at a glance that the last two months had been very trying ones for him. He had grown thin and careworn, and had lost the loud, cheery manner for which he had been remarkable.

" 'The governor is dying,' were the first words he said.

" 'Impossible!' I cried. 'What is the matter?'

" 'Apoplexy. Nervous shock. He's been on the verge all day. I doubt if we shall find him alive.'

"I was, as you may think, Watson, horrified at this unexpected news.

" 'What has caused it?' I asked.

" 'Ah, that is the point. Jump in, and we can talk it over while we drive. You remember that fellow who came upon the evening before you left us?'

" 'Perfectly.'

" 'Do you know who it was that we let into the house that day?'

" 'I have no idea.'

" 'It was the Devil, Holmes!' he cried.

"I stared at him in astonishment.

" 'Yes; it was the Devil himself. We have not had a peaceful hour since—not one. The governor has never held up his head from that evening, and now the life has been crushed out of him, and his heart broken all through this accursed Hudson.'

" 'What power had he, then?'

" 'Ah! that is what I would give so much to know. The kindly, charitable, good old governor! How could he have fallen into the clutches of such a ruffian? But I am so glad that you have come, Holmes. I trust very much to your judgment and discretion, and I know that you will advise me for the best.'

"We were dashing along the smooth, white country road, with the long stretch of the Broads in front of us glimmering in the red light of the setting sun. From a grove upon our left I could already see the high chimneys and the flag-staff which marked the squire's dwelling.

"'My father made the fellow gardener,' said my companion, 'and then, as that did not satisfy him, he was promoted to be butler. The house seemed to be at his mercy, and he wandered about and did what he chose in it. The maids complained of his drunken habits and his vile language. The dad raised their wages all round to recompense them for the annoyance. The fellow would take the boat and my father's best gun and treat himself to little shooting parties. And all this with such a sneering, leering, insolent face, that I would have knocked him down twenty times over if he had been a man of my own age. I tell you, Holmes, I have had to keep a tight hold upon myself all this time, and now I am asking myself whether, if I had let myself go a little more, I might not have been a wiser man.

"'Well, matters went from bad to worse with us, and this animal, Hudson, became more and more intrusive, until at last, on his making some insolent reply to my father in my presence one day, I took him by the shoulder and turned him out of the room. He slunk away with a livid face, and two venomous eyes which uttered more threats than his tongue could do. I don't know what passed between the poor dad and him after that, but the dad came to me next day and asked me whether I would mind apologizing to Hudson. I refused, as you can imagine, and asked my father how he could allow such a wretch to take such liberties with himself and his household.

"'Ah, my boy,' said he, 'it is all very well to talk, but you don't know how I am placed. But you shall know, Victor. I'll see that you shall know, come what may! You wouldn't believe harm of your poor old father, would you, lad?' He was very much moved, and shut himself up in the study all day, where I could see through the window that he was writing busily.

"'That evening there came what seemed to me to be a grand release, for Hudson told us that he was going to leave us. He walked into the dining-room as we sat after dinner, and announced his intention in the thick voice of a half-drunken man.

"'I've had enough of Norfolk,' said he. 'I'll run down to Mr. Beddoes, in Hampshire. He'll be as glad to see me as you were, I daresay.'

"'You're not going away in an unkind spirit, Hudson, I hope,' said my father, with a tameness which made my blood boil.

"'I've not had my 'pology," said he, sulkily, glancing in my direction.

"'Victor, you will acknowledge

"'I'VE NOT HAD MY 'POLOGY,' SAID HE, SULKILY."

that you have used this worthy fellow rather roughly?' said the dad, turning to me.

"'On the contrary, I think that we have

both shown extraordinary patience towards him,' I answered.

"'Oh, you do, do you?' he snarled. 'Very good, mate. We'll see about that!' He slouched out of the room, and half an hour afterwards left the house, leaving my father in a state of pitiable nervousness. Night after night I heard him pacing his room, and it was just as he was recovering his confidence that the blow did at last fall.

"'And how?' I asked, eagerly.

"'In a most extraordinary fashion. A letter arrived for my father yesterday evening, bearing the Fordingbridge postmark. My father read it, clapped both his hands to his head and began running round the room in little circles like a man who has been driven out of his senses. When I at last drew him down on to the sofa, his mouth and eyelids were all puckered on one side, and I saw that he had a stroke. Dr. Fordham came over at once, and we put him to bed; but the paralysis has spread, he has shown no sign of returning consciousness, and I think that we shall hardly find him alive.'

"'You horrify me, Trevor!' I cried. 'What, then, could have been in this letter to cause so dreadful a result?'

"'Nothing. There lies the inexplicable part of it. The message was absurd and trivial. Ah, my God, it is as I feared!'

"As he spoke we came round the curve of the avenue, and saw in the fading light that every blind in the house had been drawn down. As we dashed up to the door, my friend's face convulsed with grief, a gentleman in black emerged from it.

"'When did it happen, doctor?' asked Trevor.

"'Almost immediately after you left.'

"'Did he recover consciousness?'

"'For an instant before the end.'

"'Any message for me?'

"'Only that the papers were in the back drawer of the Japanese cabinet.'

"My friend ascended with the doctor to the chamber of death, while I remained in the study, turning the whole matter over and over in my head, and feeling as sombre as ever I had done in my life. What was the past of this Trevor: pugilist, traveller, and gold-digger; and how had he placed himself in the power of this acid-faced seaman? Why, too, should he faint at an allusion to the half-effaced initials upon his arm, and die of fright when he had a letter from Fordingbridge? Then I remembered that Fording-bridge was in Hampshire, and that this Mr. Beddoes, whom the seaman had gone to visit, and presumably to blackmail, had also been mentioned as living in Hampshire. The letter, then, might either come from Hudson, the seaman, saying that he had betrayed the guilty secret which appeared to exist, or it might come from Beddoes, warning an old confederate that such a betrayal was imminent. So far it seemed clear enough. But, then, how could the letter be trivial and grotesque, as described by the son? He must have misread it. If so, it must have been one of those ingenious secret codes which mean one thing while they seem to mean another. I must see this letter. If there were a hidden meaning in it, I was confident that I could pluck it forth. For an hour I sat pondering over it in the gloom, until at last a weeping maid brought in a lamp, and close at her heels came my friend Trevor, pale but composed, with these very papers which lie upon my knee held in his grasp. He sat down opposite to me, drew the lamp to the edge of the table, and handed me a short note scribbled, as you see, upon a single sheet of grey paper. 'The supply of game for London is going steadily up,' it ran. 'Head-keeper Hudson, we believe, has been now told to receive all orders for fly-paper and for preservation of your hen pheasant's life.'

"I daresay my face looked as bewildered as yours did just now when first I read this message. Then I re-read it very carefully. It was evidently as I had thought, and some second meaning must lie buried in this strange combination of words. Or could it be that there was a prearranged significance to such phrases as 'fly-paper' and 'hen pheasant'? Such a meaning would be arbitrary, and could not be deduced in any way. And yet I was loth to believe that this was the case, and the presence of the word 'Hudson' seemed to show that the subject of the message was as I had guessed, and that it was from Beddoes rather than the sailor. I tried it backwards, but the combination, 'Life pheasant's hen,' was not encouraging. Then I tried alternate words, but neither 'The of for' nor 'supply game London' promised to throw any light upon it. And then in an instant the key of the riddle was in my hands, and I saw that every third word beginning with the first would give a message which might well drive old Trevor to despair.

"It was short and terse, the warning, as I now read it to my companion :—

"THE KEY OF THE RIDDLE WAS IN MY HANDS."

" 'The game is up. Hudson has told all. Fly for your life.'

"Victor Trevor sank his face into his shaking hands. 'It must be that, I suppose,' said he. 'This is worse than death, for it means disgrace as well. But what is the meaning of these " head-keepers " and " hen pheasants " ?

" ' It means nothing to the message, but it might mean a good deal to us if we had no other means of discovering the sender. You see that he has begun by writing, " The . . . . . game . . . . . is," and so on. Afterwards he had, to fulfil the prearranged cipher, to fill in any two words in each space. He would naturally use the first words which came to his mind, and if there were so many which referred to sport among them, you may be tolerably sure that he is either an ardent shot or interested in breeding. Do you know anything of this Beddoes ? '

" 'Why, now that you mention it,' said he, 'I remember that my poor father used to have an invitation from him to shoot over his preserves every autumn.'

" ' Then it is undoubtedly from him that the note comes,' said I. 'It only remains for us to find out what this secret was which the sailor Hudson seems to have held over the heads of these two wealthy and respected men.'

" ' Alas, Holmes, I fear that it is one of sin and shame ! ' cried my friend. 'But from you I shall have no secrets. Here is the statement which was drawn up by my father when he knew that the danger from Hudson had become imminent. I found it in the Japanese cabinet, as he told the doctor. Take it and read it to me, for I have neither the strength nor the courage to do it myself.'

" These are the very papers, Watson, which he handed to me, and I will read them to you as I read them in the old study that night to him. They are indorsed outside, as you see : 'Some particulars of the voyage of the barque *Gloria Scott*, from her leaving Falmouth on the 8th October, 1855, to her destruction in N. lat. 15° 20', W. long. 25° 14', on November 6th.' It is in the form of a letter, and runs in this way :—

" My dear, dear son,—Now that approaching disgrace begins to darken the closing years of my life, I can write with all truth and honesty that it is not the terror of the law, it is not the loss of my position in the county, nor is it my fall in the eyes of all who have known me, which cuts me to the heart ; but it is the thought that you should come to blush for me—you who love me, and who have seldom, I hope, had reason to do other than respect me. But if the blow falls which is for ever hanging over me, then I should wish you to read this that you may know straight from me how far I have been to blame. On the other hand, if all should go well (which may kind God Almighty grant !), then if by any chance this paper should be still undestroyed, and should fall into your hands, I conjure you by all you hold sacred, by the memory of your dear mother, and by the love which has been between us, to hurl it into the fire, and to never give one thought to it again.

"If, then, your eye goes on to read this line, I know that I shall already have been exposed and dragged from my home, or, as is more likely—for you know that my heart is weak—be lying with my tongue sealed for ever in death. In either case the time for suppression is past, and every word which I tell you is the naked truth ; and this I swear as I hope for mercy.

" My name, dear lad, is not Trevor. I was James Armitage in my younger days, and you can understand now the shock that it was to me a few weeks ago when your college friend addressed me in words which seemed to imply that he had surmised my secret. As Armitage it was that I entered a London banking house, and as Armitage I was convicted of breaking my country's laws, and was sentenced to transportation. Do not think very harshly of me, laddie. It was a debt of honour, so-called, which I had to pay, and I used money which was not my own to do it, in the certainty that I could replace it before there could be any possibility of its being missed. But the most dreadful ill-luck pursued me. The money which I had reckoned upon never came to hand, and a premature examination of accounts exposed my deficit. The case might have been dealt leniently with, but the laws were more harshly administered thirty years ago than now, and on my twenty-third birthday I found myself chained as a felon with thirty-seven other convicts in the 'tween decks of the barque *Gloria Scott,* bound for Australia.

" It was the year '55, when the Crimean War was at its height, and the old convict ships had been largely used as transports in the Black Sea. The Government was compelled therefore to use smaller and less suitable vessels for sending out their prisoners. The *Gloria Scott* had been in the Chinese tea trade, but she was an old-fashioned, heavy-bowed, broad-beamed craft, and the new clippers had cut her out. She was a 500-ton boat, and besides her thirty-eight gaol-birds, she carried twenty-six of a crew, eighteen soldiers, a captain, three mates, a doctor, a chaplain, and four warders. Nearly a hundred souls were in her, all told, when we set sail from Falmouth.

" The partitions between the cells of the convicts, instead of being of thick oak, as is usual in convict ships, were quite thin and frail. The man next to me upon the aft side was one whom I had particularly noticed when we were led down the quay. He was a young man with a clear, hairless face, a long thin nose, and rather nutcracker jaws. He carried his head very jauntily in the air, had a swaggering style of walking, and was above all else remarkable for his extraordinary height. I don't think any of our heads would come up to his shoulder, and I am sure that he could not have measured less than six and a half feet. It was strange among so many sad and weary faces to see one which was full of energy and resolution. The sight of it was to me like a fire in a snowstorm. I was glad then to find that he was my neighbour, and gladder still when, in the dead of the night, I heard a whisper close to my ear, and found that he had managed to cut an opening in the board which separated us.

" ' Halloa, chummy !' said he, 'what's your name, and what are you here for ?'

" I answered him, and asked in turn who I was talking with.

" ' I'm Jack Prendergast,' said he, 'and, by God, you'll learn to bless my name before you've done with me !'

" I remembered hearing of his case, for it was one which had made an immense sensation throughout the country, some time before my own arrest. He was a man of good family and of great ability, but of incurably vicious habits, who had, by an ingenious system of fraud, obtained huge sums of money from the leading London merchants.

" ' Ah, ha ! You remember my case ?' said he, proudly.

" ' Very well indeed.'

" ' Then maybe you remember something queer about it ?'

" ' What was that, then ?'

" ' I'd had nearly a quarter of a million, hadn't I ?'

" ' So it was said.'

" ' But none was recovered, eh ?'

" ' No.'

" ' Well, where d'ye suppose the balance is ?' he asked.

" ' I have no idea,' said I.

" ' Right between my finger and thumb,' he cried. ' By God, I've got more pounds to my name than you have hairs on your head. And if you've money, my son, and know how to handle it and spread it, you can do *anything !* Now, you don't think it likely that a man who could do anything is going to wear his breeches out sitting in the stinking hold of a rat-gutted, beetle-ridden, mouldy old coffin of a China coaster? No, sir, such a man will look after himself, and will look after his chums. You may lay to that! You hold on to him, and you may kiss the Book that he'll haul you through.'

"That was his style of talk, and at first I thought it meant nothing, but after a while, when he had tested me and sworn me in with all possible solemnity, he let me understand that there really was a plot to gain command of the vessel. A dozen of the prisoners had hatched it before they came aboard; Prendergast was the leader, and his money was the motive power.

"'I'd a partner,' said he, 'a rare good man, as true as a stock to a barrel. He's got the dibbs, he has, and where do you think he is at this moment? Why, he's the chaplain of this ship — the chaplain, no less! He came aboard with a black coat and his papers right, and money enough in his box to buy the thing right up from keel to main-truck. The crew are his, body and soul. He could buy 'em at so much a gross with a cash discount, and he did it before ever they signed on. He's got two of the warders and Mercer the second mate, and he'd get the captain himself if he thought him worth it.'

"'What are we to do, then?' I asked.

"'What do you think?' said he. 'We'll make the coats of some of these soldiers redder than ever the tailor did.'

"'But they are armed,' said I.

"'And so shall we be, my boy. There's a brace of pistols for every mother's son of us, and if we can't carry this ship, with the crew at our back, it's time we were all sent to a young Miss's boarding school. You speak to

JACK PRENDERGAST.

your mate on the left to-night, and see if he is to be trusted.'

"I did so, and found my other neighbour to be a young fellow in much the same position as myself, whose crime had been forgery. His name was Evans, but he afterwards changed it, like myself, and he is now a rich and prosperous man in the South of England. He was ready enough to join the conspiracy, as the only means of saving ourselves, and before we had crossed the Bay there were only two of the prisoners who were not in the secret. One of these was of weak mind, and we did not dare to trust him, and the other was suffering from jaundice, and could not be of any use to us.

"From the beginning there was really nothing to prevent us taking possession of the ship. The crew were a set of ruffians, specially picked for the job. The sham chaplain came into our cells to exhort us, carrying a black bag, supposed to be full of tracts; and so often did he come that by the third day we had each stowed away at the foot of our bed a file, a brace of pistols, a pound of powder, and twenty slugs. Two of the warders were agents of Prendergast, and the second mate was his right-hand man. The captain, the two mates, two warders, Lieutenant Martin, his eighteen soldiers, and the doctor were all that we had against us. Yet, safe as it was, we determined to neglect no precaution, and to make our attack suddenly at night. It came, however, more quickly than we expected, and in this way:—

"One evening, about the third week after our start, the doctor had come down to see one of the prisoners, who was ill, and, putting his hand down on the bottom of his bunk, he felt the outline of the pistols. If he had been silent he might have blown the whole thing; but he was a nervous little chap, so he gave a cry of surprise and turned so pale, that the man knew what was up in an instant and seized him. He was gagged before he could give the alarm, and tied down upon the bed. He had unlocked the door that led to the deck, and we were through it in a rush. The two sentries were shot down, and so was a corporal who came running to see what was the matter. There were two more soldiers at the door of the state-room, and their muskets seemed not to be loaded, for they never fired upon us, and they were shot while trying to fix their bayonets. Then we rushed on into the captain's cabin, but as we pushed open the door there was an explosion from within, and there he lay with his head on the chart of the Atlantic, which was pinned upon the table, while the chaplain stood, with a smoking pistol in his hand,

more. There were lockers all round, and Wilson, the sham chaplain, knocked one of them in, and pulled out a dozen of brown sherry. We cracked off the necks of the bottles, poured the stuff out into tumblers, and were just tossing them off, when in an instant, without warning, there came the roar of muskets in our ears, and the saloon was so full of smoke that we could not see across the table. When it cleared again the place was a shambles. Wilson and eight others were wriggling on the top of each other on the floor, and the blood and the brown sherry on that table turn me sick now when I think of it. We were so cowed by the sight that I think we should have given the job up if it had not been for Prendergast. He bellowed like a bull, and rushed for the door with all that were left alive at his heels. Out we ran, and there on the poop were the lieutenant and ten of his men. The swing skylights above the saloon table had been a bit open, and they had fired on us through the slit. We got on them before they could load, and they stood to it like men, but we had the upper hand of them, and in five minutes it was all over. My God! was there ever a slaughter-house like that ship? Prendergast was like a raging devil, and he picked the soldiers up as if they had been children and threw them overboard, alive or dead. There was one sergeant that was horribly wounded, and yet kept on swimming for a surprising time, until someone in mercy blew out his brains.

"THE CHAPLAIN STOOD WITH A SMOKING PISTOL IN HIS HAND."

at his elbow. The two mates had both been seized by the crew, and the whole business seemed to be settled.

"The state-room was next the cabin, and we flocked in there and flopped down on the settees all speaking together, for we were just mad with the feeling that we were free once

When the fighting was over there was no one left of our enemies except just the warders, the mates, and the doctor.

"It was over them that the great quarrel arose. There were many of us who were glad enough to win back our freedom, and yet who had no wish to have murder on our souls. It was one thing to knock the soldiers over with their muskets in their hands, and it was another to stand by while men were being killed in cold blood. Eight of us, five convicts and three sailors, said that we would not see it done. But there was no moving Prendergast and those who were with him. Our only chance of safety lay in making a clean job of it, said he, and he would not leave a tongue with power to wag in a witness-box. It nearly came to our sharing the fate of the prisoners, but at last he said that if we wished we might take a boat and go. We jumped at the offer, for we were already sick of these bloodthirsty doings, and we saw that there would be worse before it was done. We were given a suit of sailors' togs each, a barrel of water, two casks, one of junk and one of biscuits, and a compass. Prendergast threw us over a chart, told us that we were shipwrecked mariners whose ship had foundered in lat. 15° N. and long. 25° W., and then cut the painter and let us go.

" And now I come to the most surprising part of my story, my dear son. The seamen had hauled the foreyard aback during the rising, but now as we left them they brought it square again, and, as there was a light wind from the north and east, the barque began to draw slowly away from us. Our boat lay, rising and falling, upon the long, smooth rollers, and Evans and I, who were the most educated of the party, were sitting in the sheets working out our position and planning what coast we should make for. It was a nice question, for the Cape de Verds were about 500 miles to the north of us, and the African coast about 700 miles to the east. On the whole, as the wind was coming round to north, we thought that Sierra Leone might be best, and turned our head in that direction, the barque being at that time nearly hull down on our starboard quarter. Suddenly as we looked at her we saw a dense black cloud of smoke shoot up from her, which hung like a monstrous tree upon the sky-line. A few seconds later a roar like thunder burst upon our ears, and as the smoke thinned away there was no sign left of the *Gloria Scott*. In an instant we swept the boat's head round again, and pulled with all our strength for the place where the haze, still trailing over the water, marked the scene of this catastrophe.

" It was a long hour before we reached it, and at first we feared that we had come too late to save anyone. A splintered boat and a number of crates and fragments of spars rising and falling on the waves showed us where the vessel had foundered, but there was no sign of life, and we had turned away in despair when we heard a cry for help, and saw at some distance a piece of wreckage with a man lying stretched across it. When we pulled him aboard the boat he proved to be a young seaman of the name of Hudson, who was so burned and exhausted that he could give us no account of what had happened until the following morning.

" It seemed that after we had left, Prendergast and his gang had proceeded to put to death the five remaining prisoners : the two warders had been shot and thrown overboard,

" WE PULLED HIM ABOARD THE BOAT."

and so also had the third mate. Prendergast then descended into the 'tween decks, and with his own hands cut the throat of the unfortunate surgeon. There only remained the first mate, who was a bold and active man. When he saw the convict approaching him with the bloody knife in his hand, he kicked off his bonds, which he had somehow contrived to loosen, and rushing down the deck he plunged into the after-hold.

"A dozen convicts who descended with their pistols in search of him found him with a match-box in his hand seated beside an open powder barrel, which was one of a hundred carried on board, and swearing that he would blow all hands up if he were in any way molested. An instant later the explosion occurred, though Hudson thought it was caused by the misdirected bullet of one of the convicts rather than the mate's match. Be the cause what it may, it was the end of the *Gloria Scott*, and of the rabble who held command of her.

"Such, in a few words, my dear boy, is the history of this terrible business in which I was involved. Next day we were picked up by the brig *Hotspur*, bound for Australia, whose captain found no difficulty in believing that we were the survivors of a passenger ship which had foundered. The transport ship, *Gloria Scott*, was set down by the Admiralty as being lost at sea, and no word has ever leaked out as to her true fate. After an excellent voyage the *Hotspur* landed us at Sydney, where Evans and I changed our names and made our way to the diggings, where, among the crowds who were gathered from all nations, we had no difficulty in losing our former identities.

"The rest I need not relate. We prospered, we travelled, we came back as rich Colonials to England, and we bought country estates. For more than twenty years we have led peaceful and useful lives, and we hoped that our past was for ever buried. Imagine, then, my feelings when in the seaman who came to us I recognised instantly the man who had been picked off the wreck! He had tracked us down somehow, and had set himself to live upon our fears. You will understand now how it was that I strove to keep peace with him, and you will in some measure sympathize with me in the fears which fill me, now that he has gone from me to his other victim with threats upon his tongue.

"Underneath is written, in a hand so shaky as to be hardly legible, 'Beddoes writes in cipher to say that H. has told all. Sweet Lord, have mercy on our souls!'

"That was the narrative which I read that night to young Trevor and I think, Watson, that under the circumstances it was a dramatic one. The good fellow was heartbroken at it, and went out to the Terai tea planting, where I hear that he is doing well. As to the sailor and Beddoes, neither of them was ever heard of again after that day on which the letter of warning was written. They both disappeared utterly and completely. No complaint had been lodged with the police, so that Beddoes had mistaken a threat for a deed. Hudson had been seen lurking about, and it was believed by the police that he had done away with Beddoes, and had fled. For myself, I believe that the truth was exactly the opposite. I think that it is most probable that Beddoes, pushed to desperation, and believing himself to have been already betrayed, had revenged himself upon Hudson, and had fled from the country with as much money as he could lay his hands on. Those are the facts of the case, Doctor, and if they are of any use to your collection, I am sure that they are very heartily at your service."

# The Adventures of Sherlock Holmes.

## XVIII.—THE ADVENTURE OF THE MUSGRAVE RITUAL

### By A. Conan Doyle.

AN anomaly which often struck me in the character of my friend Sherlock Holmes was that, although in his methods of thought he was the neatest and most method:cal of mankind, and although also he affected a certain quiet primness of dress, he was none the less in his personal habits one of the most untidy men that ever drove a fellow-lodger to distraction. Not that I am in the least conventional in that respect myself. The rough-and-tumble work in Afghanistan, coming on the top of a natural Bohemianism of disposition, has made me rather more lax than befits a medical man. But with me there is a limit, and when I find a man who keeps his cigars in the coal-scuttle, his tobacco in the toe end of a Persian slipper, and his unanswered correspondence transfixed by a jack-knife into the very centre of his wooden mantelpiece, then I begin to give myself virtuous airs. I have always held, too, that pistol practice should distinctly be an open-air pastime ; and when Holmes in one of his queer humours would sit in an arm-chair, with his hair-trigger and a hundred Boxer cartridges, and proceed to adorn the opposite wall with a patriotic V. R. done in bullet-pocks, I felt strongly that neither the atmosphere nor the appearance of our room was improved by it.

Our chambers were always full of chemicals and of criminal relics, which had a way of wandering into unlikely positions, and of turning up in the butter-dish, or in even less desirable places. But his papers were my great crux. He had a horror of destroying documents, especially those which were connected with his past cases, and yet it was only once in every year or two that he would muster energy to docket and arrange them, for as I have mentioned somewhere in these incoherent memoirs, the outbursts of passionate energy when he performed the remarkable feats with which his name is associated were followed by reactions of lethargy, during which he would lie about with his violin and his books, hardly moving,

save from the sofa to the table. Thus month after month his papers accumulated, until every corner of the room was stacked with bundles of manuscript which were on no account to be burned, and which could not be put away save by their owner.

One winter's night, as we sat together by the fire, I ventured to suggest to him that as he had finished pasting extracts into his commonplace book he might employ the next two hours in making our room a little more habitable. He could not deny the justice of my request, so with a rather rueful face he went off to his bedroom, from which he returned presently pulling a large tin box behind him. This he placed in the middle of the floor, and squatting down upon a stool in front of it he threw back the lid. I could see that it was already a third full of bundles of paper tied up with red tape into separate packages.

"There are cases enough here, Watson," said he, looking at me with mischievous eyes. "I think that if you knew all that I had in this box you would ask me to pull some out instead of putting others in."

"These are the records of your early work, then ? " I asked. "I have often wished that I had notes of those cases."

"Yes, my boy ; these were all done prematurely, before my biographer had come to glorify me." He lifted bundle after bundle in a tender, caressing sort of way. "They are not all successes, Watson," said he, "but there are some pretty little problems among them. Here's the record of the Tarleton murders, and the case of Vamberry, the wine merchant, and the adventure of the old Russian woman, and the singular affair of the aluminium crutch, as well as a full account of Ricoletti of the club foot and his abominable wife. And here—ah, now ! this really is something a little recherché."

He dived his arm down to the bottom of the chest, and brought up a small wooden box, with a sliding lid, such as children's toys are kept in. From within he produced a crumpled piece of paper, an old-fashioned brass key, a peg of wood with a ball of string

be glad that you should add this case to your annals, for there are points in it which make it quite unique in the criminal records of this or, I believe, of any other country. A collection of my trifling achievements would certainly be incomplete which contained no account of this very singular business.

"A CURIOUS COLLECTION."

attached to it, and three rusty old discs of metal.

"Well, my boy, what do you make of this lot?" he asked, smiling at my expression.

"It is a curious collection."

"Very curious, and the story that hangs round it will strike you as being more curious still."

"These relics have a history, then?"

"So much so that they *are* history."

"What do you mean by that?"

Sherlock Holmes picked them up one by one, and laid them along the edge of the table. Then he reseated himself in his chair, and looked them over with a gleam of satisfaction in his eyes.

"These," said he, "are all that I have left to remind me of 'The Adventure of the Musgrave Ritual.'"

I had heard him mention the case more than once, though I had never been able to gather the details.

"I should be so glad," said I, "if you would give me an account of it."

"And leave the litter as it is," he cried, mischievously. "Your tidiness won't bear much strain, after all, Watson. But I should

"You may remember how the affair of the *Gloria Scott*, and my conversation with the unhappy man whose fate I told you of, first turned my attention in the direction of the profession which has become my life's work. You see me now when my name has become known far and wide, and when I am generally recognised both by the public and by the official force as being a final court of appeal in doubtful cases. Even when you knew me first, at the time of the affair which you have commemorated in 'A Study in Scarlet,' I had already established a considerable, though not a very lucrative, connection. You can hardly realize, then, how difficult I found it at first, and how long I had to wait before I succeeded in making any headway.

"When I first came up to London I had rooms in Montague Street, just round the corner from the British Museum, and there I waited, filling in my too abundant leisure time by studying all those branches of science which might make me more efficient. Now and again cases came in my way, principally through the introduction of old fellow students, for during my last years at the university there was a good deal of talk there about myself and my methods. The third of these cases was that of the Musgrave Ritual, and it is to the interest which was aroused by that singular chain of events, and the large issues which proved to be at stake, that I trace my first stride towards the position which I now hold.

"Reginald Musgrave had been in the same college as myself, and I had some slight acquaintance with him. He was not generally popular among the undergraduates, though it always seemed to me that what was set down as pride was really an attempt to cover extreme natural diffidence. In appearance he was a man of an exceedingly aristocratic type, thin, high-nosed, and large-eyed, with languid and yet courtly manners. He was indeed a scion of one of the very oldest families in the kingdom, though his branch was a cadet one which had separated from the Northern Musgraves some time in the sixteenth century, and had established itself in Western Sussex, where the manor house of Hurlstone is perhaps the oldest inhabited building in the county. Something of his birthplace seemed to cling to the man, and I never looked at his pale, keen face, or the poise of his head without associating him with grey archways and mullioned windows and all the venerable wreckage of a feudal keep. Once or twice we drifted into talk, and I can remember that more than once he expressed a keen interest in my methods of observation and inference.

"For four years I had seen nothing of him, until one morning he walked into my room in Montague Street. He had changed little, was dressed like a young man of fashion—he was always a bit of a dandy—and preserved the same quiet, suave manner which had formerly distinguished him.

"'How has all gone with you, Musgrave?' I asked, after we had cordially shaken hands.

"'You probably heard of my poor father's death,' said he. 'He was carried off about two years ago. Since then I have, of course, had the Hurlstone estates to manage, and as

I am member for my district as well, my life has been a busy one; but I understand, Holmes, that you are turning to practical ends those powers with which you used to amaze us?'

"'Yes,' said I, 'I have taken to living by my wits.'

"'I am delighted to hear it, for your advice at present would be exceedingly valuable to me. We have had some very strange doings at Hurlstone, and the police have been able to throw no light upon the matter. It is really the most extraordinary and inexplicable business.'

REGINALD MUSGRAVE

"You can imagine with what eagerness I listened to him, Watson, for the very chance for which I had been panting during all those months of inaction seemed to have come within my reach. In my inmost heart I believed that I could succeed where others failed, and now I had the opportunity to test myself.

"'Pray let me have the details,' I cried.

"Reginald Musgrave sat down opposite to me, and lit the cigarette which I had pushed towards him.

"'You must know,' said he, 'that though I am a bachelor I have to keep up a considerable staff of servants at Hurlstone, for it is a rambling old place, and takes a good deal of looking after. I preserve, too, and in the pheasant months I usually have a house party, so that it would not do to be short-handed. Altogether there are eight maids, the cook, the butler, two footmen, and a boy. The garden and the stables, of course, have a separate staff.

" 'Of these servants the one who had been longest in our service was Brunton, the butler. He was a young schoolmaster out of place when he was first taken up by my father, but he was a man of great energy and character, and he soon became quite invaluable in the household. He was a well-grown, handsome man, with a splendid forehead, and though he has been with us for twenty years he cannot be more than forty now. With his personal advantages and his extraordinary gifts, for he can speak several languages and play nearly every musical instrument, it is wonderful that he should have been satisfied so long in such a position, but I suppose that he was comfortable and lacked energy to make any change. The butler of Hurlstone is always a thing that is remembered by all who visit us.

" 'But this paragon has one fault. He is a bit of a Don Juan, and you can imagine that for a man like him it is not a very difficult part to play in a quiet country district.

" 'When he was married it was all right, but since he has been a widower we have had no end of trouble with him. A few months ago we were in hopes that he was about to settle down again, for he became engaged to Rachel Howells, our second housemaid, but he has thrown her over since then and taken up with Janet Tregellis, the daughter of the head gamekeeper. Rachel, who is a very good girl, but of an excitable Welsh temperament, had a sharp touch of brain fever, and goes about the house now—or did until yesterday —like a black-eyed shadow of her former self. That was our first drama at Hurlstone, but a second one came to drive it from our minds, and it was prefaced by the disgrace and dismissal of butler Brunton.

" 'This is how it came about. I have said that the man was intelligent, and this very intelligence has caused his ruin, for it seems to have led to an insatiable curiosity about things which did not in the least concern him. I had no idea of the lengths to which this would carry him until the merest accident opened my eyes to it.

" 'I have said that the house is a rambling one. One night last week—on Thursday night, to be more exact—I found that I could not sleep, having foolishly taken a cup of strong *café noir* after my dinner. After struggling against it until two in the morning I felt that it was quite hopeless, so I rose and lit the candle with the intention of continuing a novel which I was reading. The book, however, had been left in the billiard-room, so I pulled on my dressing-gown and started off to get it.

" 'In order to reach the billiard-room I had to descend a flight of stairs, and then to cross the head of a passage which led to the library and the gun-room. You can imagine my surprise when as I looked down this corridor I saw a glimmer of light coming from the open door of the library. I had myself extinguished the lamp and closed the door before coming to bed. Naturally, my first thought was of burglars. The corridors at Hurlstone have their walls largely decorated with trophies of old weapons. From one of these I picked a battle-axe, and then, leaving my candle behind me, I crept on tip-toe down the passage and peeped in at the open door.

" 'Brunton, the butler, was in the library. He was sitting, fully dressed, in an easy chair, with a slip of paper, which looked like a map, upon his knee, and his forehead sunk forward upon his hand in deep thought. I stood, dumb with astonishment, watching him from the darkness. A small taper on the edge of the table shed a feeble light, which sufficed to show me that he was fully dressed. Suddenly, as I looked, he rose from his chair, and walking over to a bureau at the side he unlocked it and drew out one of the drawers. From this he took a paper, and, returning to his seat, he flattened it out beside the taper on the edge of the table, and began to study it with minute attention. My indignation at this calm examination of our family documents overcame me so far that I took a step forward, and Brunton looking up saw me standing in the doorway. He sprang to his feet, his face turned livid with fear, and he thrust into his breast the chart-like paper which he had been originally studying.

" ' So ! ' said I, 'this is how you repay the trust which we have reposed in you ! You will leave my service to-morrow.'

" ' He bowed with the look of a man who is utterly crushed, and slunk past me without a word. The taper was still on the table, and by its light I glanced to see what the paper was which Brunton had taken from the bureau. To my surprise it was nothing of

"HE SPRANG TO HIS FEET."

my station in life, and disgrace would kill me. My blood will be on your head, sir—it will, indeed—if you drive me to despair. If you cannot keep me after what has passed, then for God's sake let me give you notice and leave in a month, as if of my own free will. I could stand that, Mr. Musgrave, but not to be cast out before all the folk that I know so well.'

"'You don't deserve much consideration, Brunton,' I answered. 'Your conduct has been most infamous. However, as you have been a long time in the family, I have no wish to bring public disgrace upon you. A month, however, is too long. Take yourself away in a week, and give what reason you like for going.'

"'Only a week, sir?' he cried in a despairing voice. 'A fortnight—say at least a fortnight.'

"'A week,' I repeated, 'and you may consider yourself to have been very leniently dealt with.'

"'He crept away, his face sunk upon his breast, like a broken man, while I put out the light and returned to my room.

"'For two days after this Brunton was most assiduous in his attention to his duties. I made no allusion to what had passed, and waited with some curiosity to see how he would cover his disgrace. On the third morning, however, he did not appear, as was his custom, after breakfast to receive my instructions for the day. As I left the dining-room I happened to meet Rachel Howells, the maid. I have told you that she had only recently recovered from an illness, and was looking so wretchedly pale and wan that I remonstrated with her for being at work.

"'You should be in bed,' I said. 'Come back to your duties when you are stronger.'

"'She looked at me with so strange an expression that I began to suspect that her brain was affected.

"'I am strong enough, Mr. Musgrave,' said she.

"'We will see what the doctor says,' I answered. 'You must stop work now, and when you go downstairs just say that I wish to see Brunton.'

"'The butler is gone,' said she.

"'Gone! Gone where?'

any importance at all, but simply a copy of the questions and answers in the singular old observance called the Musgrave Ritual. It is a sort of ceremony peculiar to our family, which each Musgrave for centuries past has gone through upon his coming of age—a thing of private interest, and perhaps of some little importance to the archæologist, like our own blazonings and charges, but of no practical use whatever.'

"'We had better come back to the paper afterwards,' said I.

"'If you think it really necessary,' he answered, with some hesitation. 'To continue my statement, however, I re-locked the bureau, using the key which Brunton had left, and I had turned to go, when I was surprised to find that the butler had returned and was standing before me.

"'Mr. Musgrave, sir,' he cried, in a voice which was hoarse with emotion, 'I can't bear disgrace, sir. I've always been proud above

" 'He is gone. No one has seen him. He is not in his room. Oh, yes, he is gone—he is gone!' She fell back against the wall with shriek after shriek of laughter, while I, horrified at this sudden hysterical attack, rushed to the bell to summon help. The girl was taken to her room, still screaming and sobbing, while I made inquiries about Brunton. There was no doubt about it that he had disappeared. His bed had not been slept in ; he had been seen by no one since he had retired to his room the night before ; and yet it was difficult to see how he could have left the house, as both windows and doors were found to be fastened in the morning. His clothes, his watch, and even his money were in his room—but the black suit which he usually wore was missing. His slippers, too, were gone, but his boots were left behind. Where, then, could butler Brunton have gone in the night, and what could have become of him now ?

" 'Of course we searched the house from cellar to garret, but there was no trace of him. It is as I have said a labyrinth of an old house, especially the original wing, which is now practically uninhabited, but we ransacked every room and cellar without discovering the least sign of the missing man. It was incredible to me that he could have gone away leaving all his property behind him, and yet where could he be ? I called in the local police, but without success. Rain had fallen on the night before, and we examined the lawn and the paths all round the house, but in vain. Matters were in this state when a new development quite drew our attention away from the original mystery.

" 'For two days Rachel Howells had been so ill, sometimes delirious, sometimes hysterical, that a nurse had been employed to sit up with her at night. On the third night after Brunton's disappearance the nurse, finding her patient sleeping nicely, had dropped into a nap in the arm-chair, when she woke in the early morning to find the bed empty, the window open, and no signs of the invalid. I was instantly aroused, and with the two footmen started off at once in search of the missing girl. It was not difficult to tell the direction which she had taken, for, starting from under her window, we could follow her footmarks easily across the lawn to the edge of the mere, where they vanished, close to the gravel path which leads out of the grounds. The lake there is 8ft. deep, and you can imagine our feelings when we saw that the trail of the poor demented girl came to an end at the edge of it.

" 'Of course, we had the drags at once, and set to work to recover the remains ; but no trace of the body could we find. On the other hand, we brought to the surface an object of a most unexpected kind. It was a linen bag, which contained within it a mass of old rusted and discoloured metal and several dull-coloured pieces of pebble or glass. This strange find was all that we could get from the mere, and although we made every possible search and inquiry yesterday, we know nothing of the fate either of Rachel Howells or Richard Brunton. The county police are at their wits' end, and I have come up to you as a last resource.'

"You can imagine, Watson, with what eagerness I listened to this extraordinary sequence of events, and endeavoured to piece them together, and to devise some common thread upon which they might all hang.

"The butler was gone. The maid was gone. The maid had loved the butler, but had afterwards had cause to hate him. She was of Welsh blood, fiery and passionate. She had been terribly excited immediately after his disappearance. She had flung into the lake a bag containing some curious contents. These were all factors which had to be taken into consideration, and yet none of them got quite to the heart of the matter. What was the starting point of this chain of events ? There lay the end of this tangled line.

" 'I must see that paper, Musgrave,' said I, ' which this butler of yours thought it worth his while to consult, even at the risk of the loss of his place.'

" 'It is rather an absurd business, this Ritual of ours,' he answered, ' but it has at least the saving grace of antiquity to excuse it. I have a copy of the questions and answers here, if you care to run your eye over them.'

"He handed me the very paper which I have here, Watson, and this is the strange catechism to which each Musgrave had to submit when he came to man's estate. I will read you the questions and answers as they stand :—

" 'Whose was it ?

" 'His who is gone.

" 'Who shall have it ?

" 'He who will come.

" 'Where was the sun ?

" 'Over the oak.

" 'Where was the shadow ?

" 'Under the elm.

" 'How was it stepped ?

" 'North by ten and by ten, east by five

and by five, south by two and by two, west by one and by one, and so under.

"'What shall we give for it?

"'All that is ours.

"'Why should we give it?

"'For the sake of the trust.'

"'The original has no date, but is in the spelling of the middle of the seventeenth century,' remarked Musgrave. 'I am afraid, however, that it can be of little help to you in solving this mystery.'

"'At least,' said I, 'it gives us another mystery, and one which is even more interesting than the first. It may be that the solution of the one may prove to be the solution of the other. You will excuse me, Musgrave, if I say that your butler appears to me to have been a very clever man, and to have had a clearer insight than ten generations of his masters.'

"'I hardly follow you,' said Musgrave. 'The paper seems to me to be of no practical importance.'

"'But to me it seems immensely practical, and I fancy that Brunton took the same view. He had probably seen it before that night on which you caught him.'

"'It is very possible. We took no pains to hide it.'

"'He simply wished, I should imagine, to refresh his memory upon that last occasion. He had, as I understand, some sort of map or chart which he was comparing with the manuscript, and which he thrust into his pocket when you appeared?'

"'That is true. But what could he have to do with this old family custom of ours, and what does this rigmarole mean?'

"'I don't think that we should have much difficulty in determining that,' said I. 'With your permission we will take the first train down to Sussex and go a little more deeply into the matter upon the spot.'

"The same afternoon saw us both at Hurlstone. Possibly you have seen pictures and read descriptions of the famous old building, so I will confine my account of it to saying that it is built in the shape of an **L**, the long arm being the more modern portion, and the shorter the ancient nucleus from which the other has developed. Over the low, heavy-lintelled door, in the centre of this old part, is chiselled the date 1607, but experts are agreed that the beams and stonework are really much older than this. The enormously thick walls and tiny windows of this part had in the last century driven the family into building the new wing, and the old one was used now as a storehouse and a cellar when it was used at all. A splendid park, with fine old timber, surrounded the house, and the lake, to which my client had referred, lay close to the avenue, about two hundred yards from the building.

"I was already firmly convinced, Watson, that there were not three separate mysteries here, but one only, and that if I could read the Musgrave Ritual aright, I should hold in my hand the clue which would lead me to the truth concerning both the butler Brunton and the maid Howells. To that, then, I turned all my energies. Why should this servant be so anxious to master this old

"IT HAS A GIRTH OF TWENTY-THREE FEET."

formula? Evidently because he saw something in it which had escaped all those generations of country squires, and from which he expected some personal advantage. What was it, then, and how had it affected his fate?

"It was perfectly obvious to me on reading the Ritual that the measurements must refer to some spot to which the rest of the document alluded, and that if we could find that spot we should be in a fair way towards knowing what the secret was which the old Musgraves had thought it necessary to embalm in so curious a fashion. There were two guides given us to start with, an oak and an elm. As to the oak, there could be no question at all. Right in front of the house, upon the left-hand side of the drive, there stood a patriarch among oaks, one of the most magnificent trees that I have ever seen.

"'That was there when your Ritual was drawn up?' said I, as we drove past it.

"'It was there at the Norman Conquest, in all probability,' he answered. 'It has a girth of 23ft.'

"Here was one of my fixed points secured.

"'Have you any old elms?' I asked.

"'There used to be a very old one over yonder, but it was struck by lightning ten years ago, and we cut down the stump.'

"'You can see where it used to be?'

"'Oh, yes.'

"'There are no other elms?'

"'No old ones, but plenty of beeches.'

"'I should like to see where it grew.'

"'We had driven up in a dog-cart, and my client led me away at once, without our entering the house, to the scar on the lawn where the elm had stood. It was nearly midway between the oak and the house. My investigation seemed to be progressing.

"'I suppose it is impossible to find out how high the elm was?' I asked.

"'I can give you it at once. It was 64ft.'

"'How do you come to know it?' I asked in surprise.

"'When my old tutor used to give me an exercise in trigonometry it always took the shape of measuring heights. When I was a lad I worked out every tree and building on the estate.'

"This was an unexpected piece of luck. My data were coming more quickly than I could have reasonably hoped.

"'Tell me,' I asked, 'did your butler ever ask you such a question?'

"Reginald Musgrave looked at me in astonishment. 'Now that you call it to my mind,' he answered, 'Brunton did ask me about the height of the tree some months ago, in connection with some little argument with the groom.'

"This was excellent news, Watson, for it showed me that I was on the right road. I looked up at the sun. It was low in the heavens, and I calculated that in less than an hour it would lie just above the topmost branches of the old oak. One condition mentioned in the Ritual would then be fulfilled. And the shadow of the elm must mean the further end of the shadow, otherwise the trunk would have been chosen as the guide. I had then to find where the far end of the shadow would fall when the sun was just clear of the oak."

"That must have been difficult, Holmes, when the elm was no longer there."

"Well, at least, I knew that if Brunton could do it I could also. Besides, there was no real difficulty. I went with Musgrave to his study and whittled myself this peg, to which I tied this long string, with a knot at each yard. Then I took two lengths of a fishing-rod, which came to just six feet, and I went back with my client to where the elm had been. The sun was just grazing the top of the oak. I fastened the rod on end, marked out the direction of the shadow, and measured it. It was 9ft. in length.

"Of course, the calculation now was a simple one. If a rod of 6ft. threw a shadow of 9ft., a tree of 64ft. would throw one of 96ft., and the line of the one would of course be the line of the other. I measured out the distance, which brought me almost to the wall of the house, and I thrust a peg into the spot. You can imagine my exultation, Watson, when within 2in. of my peg I saw a conical depression in the ground. I knew that it was the mark made by Brunton in his measurements, and that I was still upon his trail.

"From this starting point I proceeded to step, having first taken the cardinal points by my pocket compass. Ten steps with each foot took me along parallel with the wall of the house, and again I marked my spot with a peg. Then I carefully paced off five to the east and two to the south. It brought me to the very threshold of the old door. Two steps to the west meant now that I was to go two paces down the stone-flagged passage, and this was the place indicated by the Ritual.

"Never have I felt such a cold chill of disappointment, Watson. For a moment it seemed to me that there must be some radical mistake in my calculations. The

"THIS WAS THE PLACE INDICATED."

"It had been used for the storage of wood, but the billets, which had evidently been littered over the floor, were now piled at the sides so as to leave a clear space in the middle. In this space lay a large and heavy flagstone, with a rusted iron ring in the centre, to which a thick shepherd's check muffler was attached.

"'By Jove!' cried my client, 'that's Brunton's muffler. I have seen it on him, and could swear to it. What has the villain been doing here?'

"At my suggestion a couple of the county police were summoned to be present, and I then endeavoured to raise the stone by pulling on the cravat. I could only move it slightly, and it was with the aid of one of the constables that I succeeded at last in carrying it to one side. A black hole yawned beneath, into which we all peered, while Musgrave, kneeling at the side, pushed down the lantern.

"A small chamber about 7ft. deep and 4ft. square lay open to us. At one side of this was a squat, brass-bound, wooden box, the lid of which was hinged upwards, with this curious, old-fashioned key projecting from the lock. It was furred outside by a thick layer of dust, and damp and worms had eaten through the wood so that a crop of livid fungi was growing on the inside of it. Several discs of metal—old coins apparently—such as I hold here, were scattered over the bottom of the box, but it contained nothing else.

"At the moment, however, we had no thought for the old chest, for our eyes were riveted upon that which crouched beside it. It was the figure of a man, clad in a suit of black, who squatted down upon his hams with his forehead sunk upon the edge of the box and his two arms thrown out on each side of it. The attitude had drawn all the stagnant blood to the face, and no man could have recognised that distorted, liver-coloured countenance; but his height, his dress, and his hair were all sufficient to show my client, when we had drawn the body up, that it was, indeed, his missing butler. He had been dead some days, but there was no wound or bruise upon his person to show how he had met his dreadful end. When his body had been carried from the cellar we found ourselves still confronted with a problem which was almost as formidable as that with which we had started.

setting sun shone full upon the passage floor, and I could see that the old foot-worn grey stones, with which it was paved, were firmly cemented together, and had certainly not been moved for many a long year. Brunton had not been at work here. I tapped upon the floor, but it sounded the same all over, and there was no sign of any crack or crevice. But fortunately, Musgrave, who had begun to appreciate the meaning of my proceedings, and who was now as excited as myself, took out his manuscript to check my calculations.

"'And under,' he cried: 'you have omitted the "and under."'

"I had thought that it meant that we were to dig, but now of course I saw at once that I was wrong. 'There is a cellar under this, then?' I cried.

"'Yes, and as old as the house. Down here, through this door.'

"We went down a winding stone stair, and my companion, striking a match, lit a large lantern which stood on a barrel in the corner. In an instant it was obvious that we had at last come upon the true place, and that we had not been the only people to visit the spot recently.

"IT WAS THE FIGURE OF A MAN."

"I confess that so far, Watson, I had been disappointed in my investigation. I had reckoned upon solving the matter when once I had found the place referred to in the Ritual ; but now I was there, and was apparently as far as ever from knowing what it was which the family had concealed with such elaborate precautions. It is true that I had thrown a light upon the fate of Brunton, but now I had to ascertain how that fate had come upon him, and what part had been played in the matter by the woman who had disappeared. I sat down upon a keg in the corner and thought the whole matter carefully over.

"You know my methods in such cases, Watson : I put myself in the man's place, and having first gauged his intelligence, I try to imagine how I should myself have proceeded under the same circumstances. In this case the matter was simplified by Brunton's intelligence being quite first rate, so that it was unnecessary to make any allowance for the personal equation, as the astronomers have dubbed it. He knew that something valuable was concealed. He had spotted the place. He found that the stone which covered it was just too heavy for a man to move unaided. What would he do next ? He could not get help from outside, even if he had someone whom he could trust, without the unbarring of doors, and considerable risk of detection. It was better, if he could, to have his helpmate inside the house. But whom could he ask ? This girl had been devoted to him. A man always finds it hard to realize that he may have finally lost a woman's love, however badly he may have treated her. He would try by a few attentions to make his peace with the girl Howells, and then would engage her as his accomplice. Together they would come at night to the cellar, and their united force would suffice to raise the stone. So far I could follow their actions as if I had actually seen them.

"But for two of them, and one a woman, it must have been heavy work, the raising of that stone. A burly Sussex policeman and I had found it no light job. What would they do to assist them ? Probably what I should have done myself. I rose and examined carefully the different billets of wood which were scattered round the floor. Almost at once I came upon what I expected. One piece, about 3ft. in length, had a marked indentation at one end, while several were flattened at the sides as if they had been compressed by some considerable weight. Evidently as they had dragged the stone up they had thrust the chunks of wood into the chink, until at last, when the opening was large enough to crawl through, they would hold it open by a billet placed lengthwise, which might very well become indented at the lower end, since the whole weight of the stone would press it down on to the edge of this other slab. So far I was still on safe ground.

"And now, how was I to proceed to reconstruct this midnight drama ? Clearly only one could get into the hole, and that one was Brunton. The girl must have waited above. Brunton then unlocked the box, handed up the contents, presumably—since they were not to be found—and then—and then what happened ?

"What smouldering fire of vengeance had suddenly sprung into flame in this passionate Celtic woman's soul when she saw the man who had wronged her—wronged her perhaps far more than we suspected—in her power? Was it a chance that the wood had slipped and that the stone had shut Brunton into what had become his sepulchre? Had she only been guilty of silence as to his fate? Or had some sudden blow from her hand dashed the support away and sent the slab crashing down into its place. Be that as it might, I seemed to see that woman's figure, still clutching at her treasure-trove, and flying wildly up the winding stair with her ears ringing perhaps with the muffled screams from behind her, and with the drumming of frenzied hands against the slab of stone which was choking her faithless lover's life out.

"Here was the secret of her blanched face, her shaken nerves, her peals of hysterical laughter on the next morning. But what had been in the box? What had she done with that? Of course, it must have been the old metal and pebbles which my client had dragged from the mere. She had thrown them in there at the first opportunity, to remove the last trace of her crime.

"For twenty minutes I had sat motionless thinking the matter out. Musgrave still stood with a very pale face swinging his lantern and peering down into the hole.

"'These are coins of Charles I.,' said he, holding out the few which had been left in the box. 'You see we were right in fixing our date for the Ritual.'

"'We may find something else of Charles I.,' I cried, as the probable meaning of the first two questions of the Ritual broke suddenly upon me. 'Let me see the contents of the bag which you fished from the mere.'

"We ascended to his study, and he laid the débris before me. I could understand his regarding it as of small importance when I looked at it, for the metal was almost black, and the stones lustreless and dull. I rubbed one of them on my sleeve, however, and it glowed afterwards like a spark, in the dark hollow of my hand. The metal-work was in the form of a double ring, but it had been bent and twisted out of its original shape.

"'You must bear in mind,' said I, 'that the Royal party made head in England even after the death of the King, and that when they at last fled they probably left many of their most precious possessions buried behind them, with the intention of returning for them in more peaceful times.'

"'My ancestor, Sir Ralph Musgrave, was a prominent Cavalier, and the right-hand man of Charles II. in his wanderings,' said my friend.

"'Ah, indeed!' I answered. 'Well, now, I think that really should give us the last link that we wanted. I must congratulate you on coming into the possession, though in rather a tragic manner, of a relic which is of great intrinsic value, but of even greater importance as an historical curiosity.'

"'What is it, then?' he gasped in astonishment.

"'It is nothing less than the ancient crown of the Kings of England.'

"'The crown!'

"'Precisely. Consider what the Ritual says. How does it run? "Whose was it?" "His who is gone." That was after the execution of Charles. Then, "Who shall have it?" "He who will come." That was Charles II., whose advent was already foreseen. There can I think be no doubt that this battered and shapeless diadem once encircled the brows of the Royal Stuarts.'

"'And how came it in the pond?'

"'Ah, that is a question which will take some time to answer,' and with that I sketched out to him the whole long chain of surmise and of proof which I had constructed. The twilight had closed in and the moon was shining brightly in the sky before my narrative was finished.

"'And how was it, then, that Charles did not get his crown when he returned?' asked Musgrave, pushing back the relic into its linen bag.

"'Ah, there you lay your finger upon the one point which we shall probably never be able to clear up. It is likely that the Musgrave who held the secret died in the interval, and by some oversight left this guide to his descendant without explaining the meaning of it. From that day to this it has been handed down from father to son, until at last it came within reach of a man who tore its secret out of it and lost his life in the venture.'

"And that's the story of the Musgrave Ritual, Watson. They have the crown down at Hurlstone—though they had some legal bother, and a considerable sum to pay before they were allowed to retain it. I am sure that if you mentioned my name they would be happy to show it to you. Of the woman nothing was ever heard, and the probability is that she got away out of England, and carried herself, and the memory of her crime, to some land beyond the seas."

# The Adventures of Sherlock Holmes.

## XIX.—THE ADVENTURE OF THE REIGATE SQUIRE.

### By A. Conan Doyle.

IT was some time before the health of my friend, Mr. Sherlock Holmes, recovered from the strain caused by his immense exertions in the spring of '87. The whole question of the Netherland-Sumatra Company and of the colossal schemes of Baron Maupertins are too recent in the minds of the public, and are too intimately concerned with politics and finance, to be fitting subjects for this series of sketches. They led, however, in an indirect fashion to a singular and complex problem, which gave my friend an opportunity of demonstrating the value of a fresh weapon among the many with which he waged his life-long battle against crime.

On referring to my notes, I see that it was upon the 14th of April that I received a telegram from Lyons, which informed me that Holmes was lying ill in the Hotel Dulong. Within twenty-four hours I was in his sick room, and was relieved to find that there was nothing formidable in his symptoms. His iron constitution, however, had broken down under the strain of an investigation which had extended over two months, during which period he had never worked less than fifteen hours a day, and had more than once, as he assured me, kept to his task for five days at a stretch. The triumphant issue of his labours could not save him from reaction after so terrible an exertion, and at a time when Europe was ringing with his name, and when his room was literally ankle-deep with congratulatory telegrams, I found him a prey to the blackest depression. Even the knowledge that he had succeeded where the police of three countries had failed, and that he had outmanœuvred at every point the most accomplished swindler in Europe, were insufficient to rouse him from his nervous prostration.

Three days later we were back in Baker Street together, but it was evident that my friend would be much the better for a change, and the thought of a week of spring-time in the country was full of attractions to me also.

My old friend Colonel Hayter, who had come under my professional care in Afghanistan, had now taken a house near Reigate, in Surrey, and had frequently asked me to come down to him upon a visit. On the last occasion he had remarked that if my friend would only come with me, he would be glad to extend his hospitality to him also. A little diplomacy was needed, but when Holmes understood that the establishment was a bachelor one, and that he would be allowed the fullest freedom, he fell in with my plans, and a week after our return from Lyons we were under the Colonel's roof. Hayter was a fine old soldier, who had seen much of the world, and he soon found, as I had expected, that Holmes and he had plenty in common.

On the evening of our arrival we were sitting in the Colonel's gun-room after dinner, Holmes stretched upon the sofa, while Hayter and I looked over his little armoury of fire-arms.

"By the way," said he, suddenly, "I think I'll take one of these pistols upstairs with me in case we have an alarm."

"An alarm!" said I.

"Yes, we've had a scare in this part lately. Old Acton, who is one of our county magnates, had his house broken into last Monday. No great damage done, but the fellows are still at large."

"No clue?" asked Holmes, cocking his eye at the Colonel.

"None as yet. But the affair is a petty one, one of our little country crimes, which must seem too small for your attention, Mr. Holmes, after this great international affair."

Holmes waved away the compliment, though his smile showed that it had pleased him.

"Was there any feature of interest?"

"I fancy not. The thieves ransacked the library and got very little for their pains. The whole place was turned upside down, drawers burst open and presses ransacked, with the result that an odd volume of Pope's 'Homer,' two plated candlesticks, an ivory letter-weight, a small oak barometer, and a ball of twine, are all that have vanished."

"What an extraordinary assortment!" I exclaimed.

"Oh, the fellows evidently grabbed hold of anything they could get."

Holmes grunted from the sofa.

"The country police ought to make something of that," said he. "Why, it is surely obvious that——"

But I held up a warning finger.

"Neither, sir. It was William, the coachman. Shot through the heart, sir, and never spoke again."

"Who shot him, then?"

"The burglar, sir. He was off like a shot and got clean away. He'd just broke in at the pantry window when William came on him and met his end in saving his master's property."

"I HELD UP A WARNING FINGER."

"You are here for a rest, my dear fellow. For Heaven's sake, don't get started on a new problem when your nerves are all in shreds."

Holmes shrugged his shoulders with a glance of comic resignation towards the Colonel, and the talk drifted away into less dangerous channels.

It was destined, however, that all my professional caution should be wasted, for next morning the problem obtruded itself upon us in such a way that it was impossible to ignore it, and our country visit took a turn which neither of us could have anticipated. We were at breakfast when the Colonel's butler rushed in with all his propriety shaken out of him.

"Have you heard the news, sir?" he gasped. "At the Cunningham's, sir!"

"Burglary!" cried the Colonel, with his coffee cup in mid air.

"Murder!"

The Colonel whistled. "By Jove!" said he, "who's killed, then? The J.P. or his son?"

"What time?"

"It was last night, sir, somewhere about twelve."

"Ah, then, we'll step over presently," said the Colonel, coolly settling down to his breakfast again. "It's a baddish business," he added, when the butler had gone. "He's our leading squire about here, is old Cunningham, and a very decent fellow too. He'll be cut up over this, for the man has been in his service for years, and was a good servant. It's evidently the same villains who broke into Acton's."

"And stole that very singular collection?" said Holmes, thoughtfully.

"Precisely."

"Hum! It may prove the simplest matter in the world; but, all the same, at first glance this is just a little curious, is it not? A gang of burglars acting in the country might be expected to vary the scene of their operations, and not to crack two cribs in the same district within a few days. When you spoke last night of taking precautions, I remember that it passed through my mind that this was probably the last parish in England to which the thief or thieves would be likely to turn their attention; which shows that I have still much to learn."

"I fancy it's some local practitioner," said the Colonel. "In that case, of course, Acton's and Cunningham's are just the places he would go for, since they are far the largest about here."

"And richest?"

"Well, they ought to be; but they've had a law-suit for some years which has sucked the blood out of both of them, I fancy. Old Acton has some claim on half Cunningham's estate, and the lawyers have been at it with both hands."

"If it's a local villain, there should not be much difficulty in running him down," said Holmes, with a yawn. "All right, Watson, I don't intend to meddle."

"Inspector Forrester, sir," said the butler, throwing open the door.

The official, a smart, keen-faced young fellow, stepped into the room. "Good morning, Colonel," said he. "I hope I don't intrude, but we hear that Mr. Holmes, of Baker Street, is here."

The Colonel waved his hand towards my friend, and the Inspector bowed.

"We thought that perhaps you would care to step across, Mr. Holmes."

"The Fates are against you, Watson," said he, laughing. "We were chatting about the matter when you came in, Inspector. Perhaps you can let us have a few details." As he leaned back in his chair in the familiar attitude, I knew that the case was hopeless.

"We had no clue in the Acton affair.

"INSPECTOR FORRESTER."

But here we have plenty to go on, and there's no doubt it is the same party in each case. The man was seen."

"Ah!"

"Yes, sir. But he was off like a deer after the shot that killed poor William Kirwan was fired. Mr. Cunningham saw him from the bedroom window, and Mr. Alec Cunningham saw him from the back passage. It was a quarter to twelve when the alarm broke out. Mr. Cunningham had just got into bed, and Mister Alec was smoking a pipe in his dressing-gown. They both heard William, the coachman, calling for help, and Mister Alec he ran down to see what was the matter. The back door was open, and as he came to the foot of the stairs he saw two men wrestling together outside. One of them fired a shot, the other dropped, and the murderer rushed across the garden and over the hedge. Mr. Cunningham, looking out of his bedroom window, saw the fellow as he gained the road, but lost sight of him at once. Mister Alec stopped to see if he could help the dying man, and so the villain got clean away. Beyond the fact that he was a middle-sized man, and dressed in some dark stuff, we have no personal clue, but we are making energetic inquiries, and if he is a stranger we shall soon find him out."

"What was this William doing there? Did he say anything before he died?"

"Not a word. He lives at the lodge with his mother, and as he was a very faithful fellow, we imagine that he walked up to the house with the intention of seeing that all was right there. Of course, this Acton business has put everyone on their guard.

The robber must have just burst open the door — the lock has been forced — when William came upon him."

" Did William say anything to his mother before going out ? "

" She is very old and deaf, and we can get no information from her. The shock has made her half-witted, but I understand that she was never very bright. There is one very important circumstance, however. Look at this ! "

He took a small piece of torn paper from a note-book and spread it out upon his knee.

" This was found between the finger and thumb of the dead man. It appears to be a fragment torn from a larger sheet. You will observe that the hour mentioned upon it is the very time at which the poor fellow met his fate. You see that his murderer might have torn the rest of the sheet from him or he might have taken this fragment from the murderer. It reads almost as though it was an appointment."

Holmes took up the scrap of paper, a facsimile of which is here reproduced :—

" Presuming that it is an appointment," continued the Inspector, " it is, of course, a conceivable theory that this William Kirwan, although he had the reputation of being an honest man, may have been in league with the thief. He may have met him there, may even have helped him to break in the door, and then they may have fallen out between themselves."

" This writing is of extraordinary interest," said Holmes, who had been examining it with intense concentration. " These are much deeper waters than I had thought." He sank his head upon his hands, while the Inspector smiled at the effect which his case had had upon the famous London specialist.

" Your last remark," said Holmes, presently, " as to the possibility of there being an under- standing between the burglar and the servant, and this being a note of appointment from one to the other, is an ingenious and not entirely an impossible supposition. But this writing opens up——" he sank his head into

his hands again and remained for some minutes in the deepest thought. When he raised his face again I was surprised to see that his cheek was tinged with colour and his eyes as bright as before his illness. He sprang to his feet with all his old energy.

" I'll tell you what!" said he. " I should like to have a quiet little glance into the details of this case. There is something in it which fascinates me extremely. If you will permit me, Colonel, I will leave my friend, Watson, and you, and I will step round with the Inspector to test the truth of one or two little fancies of mine. I will be with you again in half an hour."

An hour and a half had elapsed before the Inspector returned alone.

" Mr. Holmes is walking up and down in the field outside," said he. " He wants us all four to go up to the house together."

" To Mr. Cunningham's ? "

" Yes, sir."

" What for ? "

The Inspector shrugged his shoulders. " I don't quite know, sir. Between ourselves, I think Mr. Holmes has not quite got over his illness yet. He's been behaving very queerly, and he is very much excited."

" I don't think you need alarm yourself," said I. " I have usually found that there was method in his madness."

" Some folk might say there was mad- ness in his method," muttered the Inspector. " But he's all on fire to start, Colonel, so we had best go out, if you are ready."

We found Holmes pacing up and down in the field, his chin sunk upon his breast, and his hands thrust into his trouser pockets.

" The matter grows in interest," said he. " Watson, your country trip has been a distinct success. I have had a charming morning."

" You have been up to the scene of the crime, I understand ? " said the Colonel.

" Yes ; the Inspector and I have made quite a little reconnaissance together."

" Any success ? "

" Well, we have seen some very interesting things. I'll tell you what we did as we walk. First of all we saw the body of this unfortunate man. He certainly died from a revolver wound, as reported."

" Had you doubted it, then ? "

" Oh, it is as well to test everything. Our inspection was not wasted. We then had an interview with Mr. Cunningham and his son, who were able to point out the exact spot where the murderer had broken through the garden hedge in his flight. That was of great interest."

" Naturally."

" Then we had a look at this poor fellow's mother. We could get no information from her, however, as she is very old and feeble."

" And what is the result of your investigations ? "

" The conviction that the crime is a very peculiar one. Perhaps our visit now may do something to make it less obscure. I think that we are both agreed, Inspector, that the fragment of paper in the dead man's hand, bearing, as it does, the very hour of his death written upon it, is of extreme importance."

" It should give a clue, Mr. Holmes."

" It *does* give a clue. Whoever wrote that note was the man who brought William Kirwan out of his bed at that hour. But where is the rest of that sheet of paper ? "

" I examined the ground carefully in the hope of finding it," said the Inspector.

" It was torn out of the dead man's hand. Why was someone so anxious to get possession of it? Because it incriminated him. And what would he do with it? Thrust it into his pocket most likely, never noticing that a corner of it had been left in the grip of the corpse. If we could get the rest of that sheet, it is obvious that we should have gone a long way towards solving the mystery."

" Yes, but how can we get at the criminal's pocket before we catch the criminal ? "

" Well, well, it was worth thinking over. Then there is another obvious point. The note was sent to William. The man who wrote it could not have taken it, otherwise of course he might have delivered his own message by word of mouth. Who brought the note, then ? Or did it come through the post ? "

" I have made inquiries," said the Inspector. " William received a letter by the afternoon post yesterday. The envelope was destroyed by him."

" Excellent ! " cried Holmes, clapping the Inspector on the back. " You've seen the postman. It is a pleasure to work with you. Well, here is the lodge, and if you will come up, Colonel, I will show you the scene of the crime."

We passed the pretty cottage where the murdered man had lived, and walked up an oak-lined avenue to the fine old Queen Anne house, which bears the date of Malplaquet upon the lintel of the door. Holmes and the Inspector led us round it until we came to the side gate, which is separated by a stretch of garden from the hedge which lines the road. A constable was standing at the kitchen door.

" Throw the door open, officer," said Holmes. " Now it was on those stairs that young Mr. Cunningham stood and saw the two men struggling just where we are. Old Mr. Cunningham was at that window—the second on the left—and he saw the fellow get away just to the left of that bush. So did the son. They are both sure of it, on account of the bush. Then Mister Alec ran out and knelt beside the wounded man. The ground is very hard, you see, and there are no marks to guide us."

As he spoke two men came down the garden path, from round the angle of the house. The one was an elderly man, with a strong, deep-lined, heavy-eyed face ; the other a dashing young fellow, whose bright, smiling expression and showy dress were in strange contrast with the business which had brought us there.

" Still at it, then ? " said he to Holmes. " I thought you Londoners were never at fault. You don't seem to be so very quick, after all."

" Ah ! you must give us a little time," said Holmes, good-humouredly.

" You'll want it," said young Alec Cunningham. " Why, I don't see that we have any clue at all."

" There's only one," answered the Inspector. " We thought that if we could only find——Good heavens ! Mr. Holmes, what is the matter ? "

My poor friend's face had suddenly assumed the most dreadful expression. His eyes rolled upwards, his features writhed in agony, and with a suppressed groan he dropped on his face upon the ground. Horrified at the suddenness and severity of the attack, we carried him into the kitchen, where he lay back in a large chair and breathed heavily for some minutes. Finally, with a shamefaced apology for his weakness, he rose once more.

" Watson would tell you that I have only just recovered from a severe illness," he explained. " I am liable to these sudden nervous attacks."

" Shall I send you home in my trap ? " asked old Cunningham.

" Well, since I am here, there is one point on which I should like to feel sure. We can very easily verify it."

" What is it ? "

" Well, it seems to me that it is just possible that the arrival of this poor fellow William was not before but after the entrance of the burglar into the house. You appear to take it for granted that although the door was forced the robber never got in."

"GOOD HEAVENS ! WHAT IS THE MATTER ?"

"I fancy that is quite obvious," said Mr. Cunningham, gravely. "Why, my son Alec had not yet gone to bed, and he would certainly have heard anyone moving about."

"Where was he sitting ?"

"I was sitting smoking in my dressing-room."

"Which window is that ?"

"The last on the left, next my father's."

"Both your lamps were lit, of course ?"

"Undoubtedly."

"There are some very singular points here," said Holmes, smiling. "Is it not extraordinary that a burglar—and a burglar who had had some previous experience—should deliberately break into a house at a time when he could see from the lights that two of the family were still afoot ?"

"He must have been a cool hand."

"Well, of course, if the case were not an odd one we should not have been driven to ask you for an explanation," said Mister Alec. "But as to your idea that the man had robbed the house before William tackled him, I think it a most absurd notion. Shouldn't we have found the place disarranged and missed the things which he had taken ?"

"It depends on what the things were," said Holmes. "You must remember that we are dealing with a burglar who is a very peculiar fellow, and who appears to work on lines of his own. Look, for example, at the queer lot of things which he took from Acton's — what was it ?—a ball of string, a letter-weight, and I don't know what other odds and ends !"

"Well, we are quite in your hands, Mr. Holmes," said old Cunningham. "Anything which you or the Inspector may suggest will most certainly be done."

"In the first place," said Holmes, "I should like you to offer a reward — coming from yourself, for the officials may take a little time before they would agree upon the sum, and these things cannot be done too promptly. I have jotted down the form here, if you would not mind signing it. Fifty pounds was quite enough, I thought."

"I would willingly give five hundred," said the J.P., taking the slip of paper and the pencil which Holmes handed to him. "This is not quite correct, however," he added, glancing over the document.

"I wrote it rather hurriedly."

"You see you begin : 'Whereas, at about a quarter to one on Tuesday morning, an attempt was made '—and so on. It was at a quarter to twelve, as a matter of fact."

I was pained at the mistake, for I knew how keenly Holmes would feel any slip of the kind. It was his speciality to be accurate as to fact, but his recent illness had shaken him, and this one little incident was enough to show me that he was still far from being himself. He was obviously embarrassed for an instant, while the Inspector raised his eyebrows and Alec Cunningham burst into a laugh. The old gentleman corrected the mistake, however, and handed the paper back to Holmes.

"Get it printed as soon as possible," he said. "I think your idea is an excellent one."

Holmes put the slip of paper carefully away in his pocket-book.

"And now," said he, "it would really be a good thing that we should all go over the house together and make certain that this rather erratic burglar did not, after all, carry anything away with him."

Before entering, Holmes made an examination of the door which had been forced. It was evident that a chisel or strong knife had been thrust in, and the lock forced back with it. We could see the marks in the wood where it had been pushed in.

"You don't use bars, then?" he asked.

"We have never found it necessary."

"You don't keep a dog?"

"Yes; but he is chained on the other side of the house."

"When do the servants go to bed?"

"About ten."

"I understand that William was usually in bed also at that hour?"

"Yes."

"It is singular that on this particular night he should have been up. Now, I should be very glad if you would have the kindness to show us over the house, Mr. Cunningham."

A stone-flagged passage, with the kitchens branching away from it, led by a wooden staircase directly to the first floor of the house. It came out upon the landing opposite to a second more ornamental stair which led up from the front hall. Out of this landing opened the drawing-room and several bedrooms, including those of Mr. Cunningham and his son. Holmes walked slowly, taking keen note of the architecture of the house. I could tell from his expression that he was on a hot scent, and yet I could not in the least imagine in what direction his inferences were leading him.

"My good sir," said Mr. Cunningham, with some impatience, "this is surely very unnecessary. That is my room at the end of the stairs, and my son's is the one beyond it. I leave it to your judgment whether it was possible for the thief to have come up here without disturbing us."

"You must try round and get on a fresh scent, I fancy," said the son, with a rather malicious smile.

"Still, I must ask you to humour me a little further. I should like, for example, to see how far the windows of the bedrooms command the front. This, I understand, is your son's room"—he pushed

open the door—"and that, I presume, is the dressing-room in which he sat smoking when the alarm was given. Where does the window of that look out to?" He stepped across the bedroom, pushed open the door, and glanced round the other chamber.

"I hope you are satisfied now?" said Mr. Cunningham, testily.

"Thank you; I think I have seen all that I wished."

"Then, if it is really necessary, we can go into my room."

"If it is not too much trouble."

The J.P. shrugged his shoulders, and led the way into his own chamber, which was a plainly furnished and commonplace room. As we moved across it in the direction of the window, Holmes fell back until he and I were the last of the group. Near the foot of the bed was a small square table, on which stood a dish of oranges and a carafe of water. As we passed it, Holmes, to my unutterable astonishment, leaned over in front of me and deliberately knocked the whole thing over. The glass smashed into a thousand pieces, and the fruit rolled about into every corner of the room.

"You've done it now, Watson," said he,

" HE DELIBERATELY KNOCKED THE WHOLE THING OVER."

coolly. "A pretty mess you've made of the carpet."

I stooped in some confusion and began to pick up the fruit, understanding that for some reason my companion desired me to take the blame upon myself. The others did the same, and set the table on its legs again.

"Halloa!" cried the Inspector, "where's he got to?"

Holmes had disappeared.

"Wait here an instant," said young Alec Cunningham. "The fellow is off his head, in my opinion. Come with me, father, and see where he has got to!"

They rushed out of the room, leaving the Inspector, the Colonel, and me staring at each other.

"'Pon my word, I am inclined to agree with Mister Alec," said the official. "It may be the effect of this illness, but it seems to me that ——"

His words were cut short by a sudden scream of "Help! Help! Murder!" With a thrill I recognised the voice as that of my friend. I rushed madly from the room on to the landing. The cries, which had sunk down into a hoarse, inarticulate shouting, came from the room which we had first visited. I dashed in, and on into the dressing-room beyond. The two Cunninghams were bending over the prostrate figure of Sherlock Holmes, the younger clutching his throat with both hands, while the elder seemed to be twisting one of his wrists. In an instant the three of us had torn them away from him, and Holmes staggered to his feet, very pale, and evidently greatly exhausted.

"Arrest these men, Inspector," he gasped.

"On what charge?"

"That of murdering their coachman, William Kirwan!"

The Inspector stared about him in bewilderment. "Oh, come now, Mr. Holmes," said he at last; "I am sure you don't really mean to——"

"Tut, man; look at their faces!" cried Holmes, curtly.

Never, certainly, have I seen a plainer confession of guilt upon human countenances. The older man seemed numbed and dazed, with a heavy, sullen expression upon his strongly-marked face. The son, on the other hand, had dropped all that jaunty, dashing style which had characterized him, and the ferocity of a dangerous wild beast gleamed in his dark eyes and distorted his handsome features. The Inspector said nothing, but, stepping to the door, he blew his whistle. Two of his constables came at the call.

"I have no alternative, Mr. Cunningham," said he. "I trust that this may all prove to be an absurd mistake; but you can see that——Ah, would you? Drop it!" He struck out with his hand, and a revolver, which the younger man was in the act of cocking, clattered down upon the floor.

"BENDING OVER THE PROSTRATE FIGURE OF SHERLOCK HOLMES."

"Keep that," said Holmes, quickly putting his foot upon it. "You will find it useful at the trial. But this is what we really wanted." He held up a little crumpled piece of paper.

"The remainder of the sheet!" cried the Inspector.

"Precisely."

"And where was it?"

"Where I was sure it must be. I'll make the whole matter clear to you presently. I think, Colonel, that you and Watson might return now, and I will be with you again in an hour at the furthest. The Inspector and I must have a word with the prisoners; but you will certainly see me back at luncheon time."

Sherlock Holmes was as good as his word, for about one o'clock he rejoined us in the Colonel's smoking-room. He was accompanied by a little, elderly gentleman, who was introduced to me as the Mr. Acton whose house had been the scene of the original burglary.

"I wished Mr. Acton to be present while I demonstrated this small matter to you," said Holmes, "for it is natural that he should take a keen interest in the details. I am afraid, my dear Colonel, that you must regret the hour that you took in such a stormy petrel as I am."

"On the contrary," answered the Colonel, warmly, "I consider it the greatest privilege to have been permitted to study your methods of working. I confess that they quite surpass my expectations, and that I am utterly unable to account for your result. I have not yet seen the vestige of a clue."

"I am afraid that my explanation may disillusionize you, but it has always been my habit to hide none of my methods, either from my friend Watson or from anyone who might take an intelligent interest in them. But first, as I am rather shaken by the knocking about which I had in the dressing-room, I think that I shall help myself to a dash of your brandy, Colonel. My strength has been rather tried of late."

"I trust you had no more of those nervous attacks."

Sherlock Holmes laughed heartily. "We will come to that in its turn," said he. "I will lay an account of the case before you in its due order, showing you the various points which guided me in my de- cision. Pray interrupt me if there is any inference which is not perfectly clear to you.

"It is of the highest importance in the art of detection to be able to recognise out of a number of facts which are incidental and which vital. Otherwise your energy and attention must be dissipated instead of being concentrated. Now, in this case there was not the slightest doubt in my mind from the first that the key of the whole matter must be looked for in the scrap of paper in the dead man's hand.

"Before going into this I would draw your attention to the fact that if Alec Cunningham's narrative was correct, and if the assailant after shooting William Kirwan had *instantly* fled, then it obviously could not be he who tore the paper from the dead man's hand. But if it was not he, it must have been Alec Cunningham himself, for by the time that the old man had descended several servants were upon the scene. The point is a simple one, but the Inspector had overlooked it because he had started with the supposition that these county magnates had had nothing to do with the matter. Now, I make a point of never having any prejudices and of following docilely wherever fact may lead me, and so in the very first stage of the investigation I found myself looking a little askance at the part which had been played by Mr. Alec Cunningham.

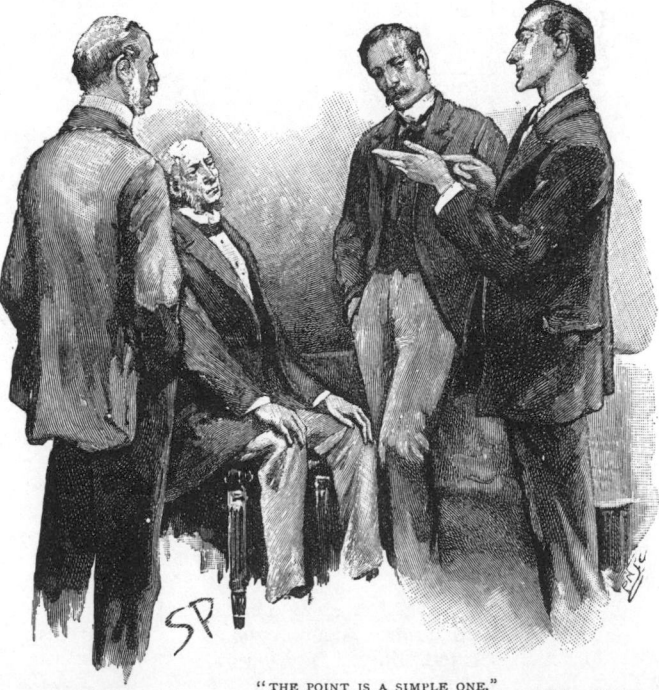

"THE POINT IS A SIMPLE ONE."

"And now I made a very careful examination of the corner of paper which the Inspector had submitted to us. It was at once clear to me that it formed part of a very remarkable document. Here it is. Do you not now observe something very suggestive about it?"

"It has a very irregular look," said the Colonel.

"My dear sir," cried Holmes, "there cannot be the least doubt in the world that it has been written by two persons doing alternate words. When I draw your attention to the strong t's of 'at' and 'to' and ask you to compare them with the weak ones of 'quarter' and 'twelve,' you will instantly recognise the fact. A very brief analysis of those four words would enable you to say with the utmost confidence that the 'learn' and the 'maybe' are written in the stronger hand, and the 'what' in the weaker."

"By Jove, it's as clear as day!" cried the Colonel. "Why on earth should two men write a letter in such a fashion?"

"Obviously the business was a bad one, and one of the men who distrusted the other was determined that, whatever was done, each should have an equal hand in it. Now, of the two men it is clear that the one who wrote the 'at' and 'to' was the ringleader."

"How do you get at that?"

"We might deduce it from the mere character of the one hand as compared with the other. But we have more assured reasons than that for supposing it. If you examine this scrap with attention you will come to the conclusion that the man with the stronger hand wrote all his words first, leaving blanks for the other to fill up. These blanks were not always sufficient, and you can see that the second man had a squeeze to fit his 'quarter' in between the 'at' and the 'to,' showing that the latter were already written. The man who wrote all his words first is undoubtedly the man who planned this affair."

"Excellent!" cried Mr. Acton.

"But very superficial," said Holmes. "We come now, however, to a point which is of importance. You may not be aware that the deduction of a man's age from his writing is one which has been brought to considerable accuracy by experts. In normal cases one can place a man in his true decade with tolerable confidence. I say normal cases, because ill-health and physical weakness reproduce the signs of old age, even when the invalid is a youth. In this case, looking at the bold, strong hand of the one, and the rather broken-backed appearance of the other, which still retains its legibility, although the t's have begun to lose their crossings, we can say that the one was a young man, and the other was advanced in years without being positively decrepit."

"Excellent!" cried Mr. Acton again.

"There is a further point, however, which is subtler and of greater interest. There is something in common between these hands. They belong to men who are blood-relatives. It may be most obvious to you in the Greek e's, but to me there are many small points which indicate the same thing. I have no doubt at all that a family mannerism can be traced in these two specimens of writing. I am only, of course, giving you the leading results now of my examination of the paper. There were twenty-three other deductions which would be of more interest to experts than to you. They all tended to deepen the impression upon my mind that the Cunninghams, father and son, had written this letter.

"Having got so far, my next step was, of course, to examine into the details of the crime and to see how far they would help us. I went up to the house with the Inspector, and saw all that was to be seen. The wound upon the dead man was, as I was able to determine with absolute confidence, fired from a revolver at the distance of something over four yards. There was no powder-blackening on the clothes. Evidently, therefore, Alec Cunningham had lied when he said that the two men were struggling when the shot was fired. Again, both father and son agreed as to the place where the man escaped into the road. At that point, however, as it happens, there is a broadish ditch, moist at the bottom. As there were no indications of boot-marks about this ditch, I was absolutely sure not only that the Cunninghams had again lied, but that there had never been any unknown man upon the scene at all.

"And now I had to consider the motive of this singular crime. To get at this I endeavoured first of all to solve the reason of the original burglary at Mr. Acton's. I understood from something which the Colonel told us that a law-suit had been going on between you, Mr. Acton, and the Cunninghams. Of course, it instantly occurred to me that they had broken into your library with the intention of getting at some document which might be of importance in the case."

"Precisely so," said Mr. Acton; "there

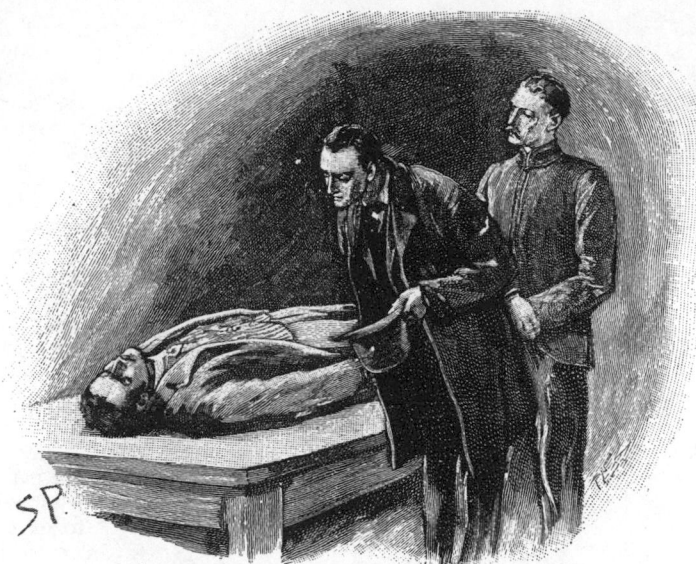

"THERE WAS NO POWDER-BLACKENING ON THE CLOTHES."

"Good heavens!" cried the Colonel, laughing. "Do you mean to say all our sympathy was wasted and your fit an imposture?"

"Speaking professionally, it was admirably done," cried I, looking in amazement at this man who was for ever confounding me with some new phase of his astuteness.

"It is an art which is often useful," said he. "When I recovered I managed by a device, which had, perhaps, some little merit of ingenuity, to get old Cunningham to write the word 'twelve,' so that I might compare it with the 'twelve' upon the paper."

"Oh, what an ass I have been!" I exclaimed.

"I could see that you were commiserating with me over my weakness," said Holmes, laughing. "I was sorry to cause you the sympathetic pain which I know that you felt. We then went upstairs together, and having entered the room and seen the dressing-gown hanging up behind the door, I contrived by upsetting a table to engage their attention for the moment and slipped back to examine the pockets. I had hardly got the paper, however, which was, as I had expected, in one of them, when the two Cunninghams were on me, and would, I verily believe, have murdered me then and there but for your prompt and friendly aid. As it is, I feel that young man's grip on my throat now, and the father has twisted my wrist round in the effort to get the paper out of my hand. They saw that I must know all about it, you see, and the sudden change from absolute security to complete despair made them perfectly desperate.

"I had a little talk with old Cunningham afterwards as to the motive of the crime. He was tractable enough, though his son was a perfect demon, ready to blow out his own or anybody else's brains if he could have got to his revolver. When Cunningham saw that the case against him was so strong he lost all heart, and made a clean breast of

can be no possible doubt as to their intentions. I have the clearest claim upon half their present estate, and if they could have found a single paper—which, fortunately, was in the strong box of my solicitors—they would undoubtedly have crippled our case."

"There you are!" said Holmes, smiling. "It was a dangerous, reckless attempt in which I seem to trace the influence of young Alec. Having found nothing, they tried to divert suspicion by making it appear to be an ordinary burglary, to which end they carried off whatever they could lay their hands upon. That is all clear enough, but there was much that was still obscure. What I wanted above all was to get the missing part of that note. I was certain that Alec had torn it out of the dead man's hand, and almost certain that he must have thrust it into the pocket of his dressing-gown. Where else could he have put it? The only question was whether it was still there. It was worth an effort to find out, and for that object we all went up to the house.

"The Cunninghams joined us, as you doubtless remember, outside the kitchen door. It was, of course, of the very first importance that they should not be reminded of the existence of this paper, otherwise they would naturally destroy it without delay. The Inspector was about to tell them the importance which we attached to it when, by the luckiest chance in the world, I tumbled down in a sort of fit and so changed the conversation."

everything. It seems that William had secretly followed his two masters on the night when they made their raid upon Mr. Acton's,

"And the note?" I asked.

Sherlock Holmes placed the subjoined paper before us :—

> If you will only come round at quarter to twelve to the east gate you will learn what will very much surprise you and maybe be of the greatest service to you and also to Annie Morrison But say nothing to anyone upon the matter

and, having thus got them into his power, proceeded under threats of exposure to levy blackmail upon them. Mister Alec, however, was a dangerous man to play games of that sort with. It was a stroke of positive genius on his part to see in the burglary scare, which was convulsing the country side, an opportunity of plausibly getting rid of the man whom he feared. William was decoyed up and shot ; and, had they only got the whole of the note, and paid a little more attention to detail in their accessories, it is very possible that suspicion might never have been aroused."

"It is very much the sort of thing that I expected," said he. "Of course, we do not yet know what the relations may have been between Alec Cunningham, William Kirwan, and Annie Morrison. The result shows that the trap was skilfully baited. I am sure that you cannot fail to be delighted with the traces of heredity shown in the p's and in the tails of the g's. The absence of the i-dots in the old man's writing is also most characteristic. Watson, I think our quiet rest in the country has been a distinct success, and I shall certainly return, much invigorated, to Baker Street to-morrow."

# The Adventures of Sherlock Holmes.

## XX.—THE ADVENTURE OF THE CROOKED MAN.

### By A. Conan Doyle.

ONE summer night, a few months after my marriage, I was seated by my own hearth smoking a last pipe and nodding over a novel, for my day's work had been an exhausting one. My wife had already gone upstairs, and the sound of the locking of the hall door some time before told me that the servants had also retired. I had risen from my seat and was knocking out the ashes of my pipe, when I suddenly heard the clang of the bell.

I looked at the clock. It was a quarter to twelve. This could not be a visitor at so late an hour. A patient, evidently, and possibly an all-night sitting. With a wry face I went out into the hall and opened the door. To my astonishment, it was Sherlock Holmes who stood upon my step.

"Ah, Watson," said he, "I hoped that I might not be too late to catch you."

"My dear fellow, pray come in."

"You look surprised, and no wonder! Relieved, too, I fancy! Hum! you still smoke the Arcadia mixture of your bachelor days, then! There's no mistaking that fluffy ash upon your coat. It's easy to tell that you've been accustomed to wear a uniform, Watson; you'll never pass as a pure-bred civilian as long as you keep that habit of carrying your handkerchief in your sleeve. Could you put me up to-night?"

"With pleasure."

"You told me that you had bachelor quarters for one, and I see that you have no gentleman visitor at present. Your hat-stand proclaims as much."

"I shall be delighted if you will stay."

"Thank you. I'll fill a vacant peg, then. Sorry to see that you've had the British workman in the house. He's a token of evil. Not the drains, I hope?"

"No, the gas."

"Ah! He has left two nail-marks from his boot upon your linoleum just where the light strikes it. No, thank you, I had some supper at Waterloo, but I'll smoke a pipe with you with pleasure."

I handed him my pouch, and he seated himself opposite to me, and smoked for some

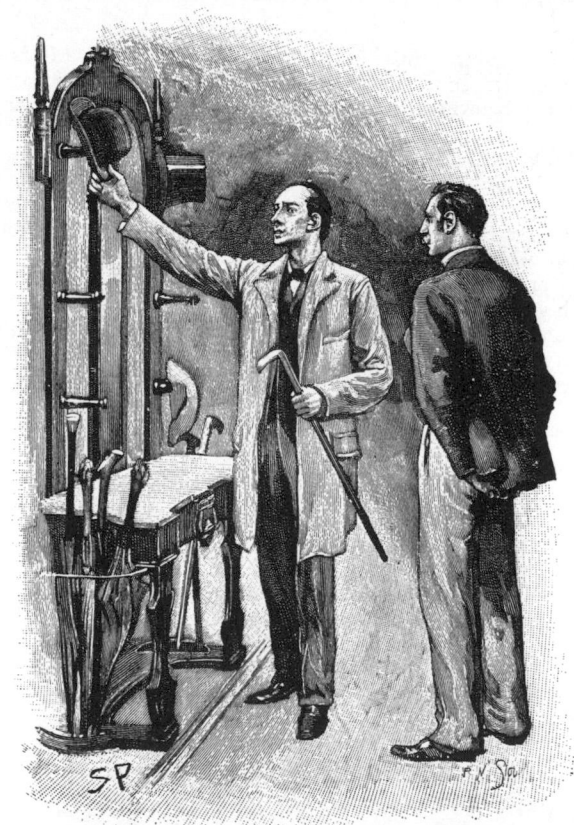

"I'LL FILL A VACANT PEG, THEN."

time in silence. I was well aware that nothing but business of importance could have brought him to me at such an hour, so I waited patiently until he should come round to it.

"I see that you are professionally rather busy just now," said he, glancing very keenly across at me.

"Yes, I've had a busy day," I answered. "It may seem very foolish in your eyes," I added, "but really I don't know how you deduced it."

Holmes chuckled to himself.

"I have the advantage of knowing your habits, my dear Watson," said he. "When your round is a short one you walk, and when it is a long one you use a hansom. As I perceive that your boots, although used, are by no means dirty, I cannot doubt that you are at present busy enough to justify the hansom."

"Excellent!" I cried.

"Elementary," said he. "It is one of those instances where the reasoner can produce an effect which seems remarkable to his neighbour, because the latter has missed the one little point which is the basis of the deduction. The same may be said, my dear fellow, for the effect of some of these little sketches of yours, which is entirely meretricious, depending as it does upon your retaining in your own hands some factors in the problem which are never imparted to the reader. Now, at present I am in the position of these same readers, for I hold in this hand several threads of one of the strangest cases which ever perplexed a man's brain, and yet I lack the one or two which are needful to complete my theory. But I'll have them, Watson, I'll have them!" His eyes kindled and a slight flush sprang into his thin cheeks. For an instant the veil had lifted upon his keen, intense nature, but for an instant only. When I glanced again his face had resumed that Red Indian composure which had made so many regard him as a machine rather than a man.

"The problem presents features of interest," said he; "I may even say very exceptional features of interest. I have already looked into the matter, and have come, as I think, within sight of my solution. If you could accompany me in that last step, you might be of considerable service to me."

"I should be delighted."

"Could you go as far as Aldershot to-morrow?"

"I have no doubt Jackson would take my practice."

"Very good. I want to start by the 11.10 from Waterloo."

"That would give me time."

"Then, if you are not too sleepy, I will give you a sketch of what has happened and of what remains to be done."

"I was sleepy before you came. I am quite wakeful now."

"I will compress the story as far as may be done without omitting anything vital to the case. It is conceivable that you may even have read some account of the matter. It is the supposed murder of Colonel Barclay, of the Royal Mallows, at Aldershot which I am investigating."

"I have heard nothing of it."

"It has not excited much attention yet, except locally. The facts are only two days old. Briefly they are these :—

"The Royal Mallows is, as you know, one of the most famous Irish regiments in the British Army. It did wonders both in the Crimea and the Mutiny, and has since that time distinguished itself upon every possible occasion. It was commanded up to Monday night by James Barclay, a gallant veteran, who started as a full private, was raised to commissioned rank for his bravery at the time of the Mutiny, and so lived to command the regiment in which he had once carried a musket.

"Colonel Barclay had married at the time when he was a sergeant, and his wife, whose maiden name was Miss Nancy Devoy, was the daughter of a former colour-sergeant in the same corps. There was therefore, as can be imagined, some little social friction when the young couple (for they were still young) found themselves in their new surroundings. They appear, however, to have quickly adapted themselves, and Mrs. Barclay has always, I understand, been as popular with the ladies of the regiment as her husband was with his brother officers. I may add that she was a woman of great beauty, and that even now, when she has been married for upwards of thirty years, she is still of a striking appearance.

"Colonel Barclay's family life appears to have been a uniformly happy one. Major Murphy, to whom I owe most of my facts, assures me that he has never heard of any misunderstanding between the pair. On the whole, he thinks that Barclay's devotion to his wife was greater than his wife's to Barclay. He was acutely uneasy if he were absent from her for a day. She, on the other hand, though devoted and faithful, was less obtrusively affectionate. But they were regarded in the regiment as the very model of a middle-aged couple. There was absolutely nothing in their mutual relations to prepare people for the tragedy which was to follow.

"Colonel Barclay himself seems to have had some singular traits in his character. He was a dashing, jovial old soldier in his usual mood, but there were occasions on which he seemed to show himself capable of considerable violence and vindictiveness. This side of his nature, however, appears never to have been turned towards his wife. Another fact which had struck Major Murphy, and three out of five of the other officers with whom I conversed, was the singular sort of depression which came upon him at times. As the Major expressed it, the smile had often been struck from his mouth, as if by some invisible hand, when he has been joining in the gaieties and chaff of the mess table. For days on end when the mood was on him he has been sunk in the deepest gloom. This and a certain tinge of superstition were the only unusual traits in his character which his brother officers had observed. The latter peculiarity took the form of a dislike to being left alone, especially after dark. This puerile feature in a nature which was conspicuously manly had often given rise to comment and conjecture.

"The first battalion of the Royal Mallows (which is the old 117th) has been stationed at Aldershot for some years. The married officers live out of barracks, and the Colonel has during all this time occupied a villa called Lachine, about half a mile from the North Camp. The house stands in its own grounds, but the west side of it is not more than thirty yards from the high road. A coachman and two maids form the staff of servants. These, with their master and mistress, were the sole occupants of Lachine, for the Barclays had no children, nor was it usual for them to have resident visitors.

"Now for the events at Lachine between nine and ten on the evening of last Monday.

"Mrs. Barclay was, it appears, a member of the Roman Catholic Church, and had interested herself very much in the establishment of the Guild of St. George, which was formed in connection with the Watt Street Chapel for the purpose of supplying the poor with cast-off clothing. A meeting of the Guild had been held that evening at eight, and Mrs. Barclay had hurried over her dinner in order to be present at it. When leaving the house, she was heard by the coachman to make some commonplace remark to her husband, and to assure him that she would be back before very long. She then called for Miss Morrison, a young lady who lives in the next villa, and the two went off together to their meeting. It lasted forty minutes, and at a quarter past nine Mrs. Barclay returned home, having left Miss Morrison at her door as she passed.

"There is a room which is used as a morning-room at Lachine. This faces the road and opens by a large glass folding door on to the lawn. The lawn is thirty yards across, and is only divided from the highway by a low wall with an iron rail above it. It was into this room that Mrs. Barclay went upon her return. The blinds were not down, for the room was seldom used in the evening, but Mrs. Barclay herself lit the lamp and then rang the bell, asking Jane Stewart, the housemaid, to bring her a cup of tea, which was quite contrary to her usual habits. The Colonel had been sitting in the dining-room, but hearing that his wife had returned, he joined her in the morning-room. The coachman saw him cross the hall, and enter it. He was never seen again alive.

"The tea which had been ordered was brought up at the end of ten minutes, but the maid, as she approached the door, was surprised to hear the voices of her master and mistress in furious altercation. She knocked without receiving any answer, and even turned the handle, but only to find that the door was locked upon the inside. Naturally enough, she ran down to tell the cook, and the two women with the coachman came up into the hall and listened to the dispute which was still raging. They all agree that only two voices were to be heard, those of Barclay and of his wife. Barclay's remarks were subdued and abrupt, so that none of them were audible to the listeners. The lady's, on the other hand, were most bitter, and, when she raised her voice, could be plainly heard. 'You coward!' she repeated over and over again. 'What can be done now? What can be done now? Give me back my life. I will never so much as breathe the same air as you again! You coward! You coward!' Those were scraps of her conversation, ending in a sudden dreadful cry in the man's voice, with a crash, and a piercing scream from the woman. Convinced that some tragedy had occurred, the coachman rushed to the door and strove to force it, while scream after scream issued from within. He was unable, however, to make his way in, and the maids were too distracted with fear to be of any assistance to him. A

"THE COACHMAN RUSHED TO THE DOOR."

sudden thought struck him, however, and he ran through the hall door and round to the lawn, upon which the long French windows open. One side of the window was open, which I understand was quite usual in the summer-time, and he passed without difficulty into the room. His mistress had ceased to scream, and was stretched insensible upon a couch, while with his feet tilted over the side of an arm-chair, and his head upon the ground near the corner of the fender, was lying the unfortunate soldier, stone dead, in a pool of his own blood.

"Naturally the coachman's first thought, on finding that he could do nothing for his master, was to open the door. But here an unexpected and singular difficulty presented itself. The key was not on the inner side of the door, nor could he find it anywhere in the room. He went out again, therefore, through the window, and having obtained the help of a policeman and of a medical man he returned. The lady, against whom

Vol. vi.—4.*

naturally the strongest suspicion rested, was removed to her room, still in a state of insensibility. The Colonel's body was then placed upon the sofa, and a careful examination made of the scene of the tragedy.

"The injury from which the unfortunate veteran was suffering was found to be a ragged cut, some two inches long, at the back part of his head, which had evidently been caused by a violent blow from a blunt weapon. Nor was it difficult to guess what that weapon may have been. Upon the floor, close to the body, was lying a singular club of hard carved wood with a bone handle. The Colonel possessed a varied collection of weapons brought from the different countries in which he had fought, and it is conjectured by the police that this club was among his trophies. The servants deny having seen it before, but among the numerous curiosities in the house it is possible that it may have been overlooked. Nothing else of importance was discovered in the room by the police, save the inexplicable fact that neither upon Mrs. Barclay's person, nor upon that of the victim, nor in any part of the room was the missing key to be found. The door had eventually to be opened by a locksmith from Aldershot.

"That was the state of things, Watson, when upon the Tuesday morning I, at the request of Major Murphy, went down to Aldershot to supplement the efforts of the police. I think you will acknowledge that the problem was already one of interest, but my observations soon made me realize that it was in truth much more extraordinary than would at first sight appear.

"Before examining the room I cross-questioned the servants, but only succeeded in eliciting the facts which I have already stated. One other detail of interest was remembered by Jane Stewart, the housemaid. You will remember that on hearing the sound of the quarrel she descended and returned with the other servants. On that first occasion, when she was alone, she says that the voices of her master and mistress were sunk so low that she could hear hardly anything, and judged by their tones, rather than their words, that they had fallen out. On my pressing her, however, she remembered that she heard the word 'David' uttered twice by the lady. The point is of the utmost importance as guiding us towards the reason of the sudden quarrel. The Colonel's name, you remember, was James.

"There was one thing in the case which had made the deepest impression both upon the servants and the police. This was the contortion of the Colonel's face. It had set, according to their account, into the most dreadful expression of fear and horror which a human countenance is capable of assuming. More than one person fainted at the mere sight of him, so terrible was the effect. It was quite certain that he had foreseen his fate, and that it had caused him the utmost horror. This, of course, fitted in well enough with the police theory, if the Colonel could have seen his wife making a murderous attack upon him. Nor was the fact of the wound being on the back of his head a fatal objection to this, as he might have turned to avoid the blow. No information could be got from the lady herself, who was temporarily insane from an acute attack of brain fever.

"From the police I learned that Miss Morrison, who, you remember, went out that evening with Mrs. Barclay, denied having any knowledge of what it was which had caused the ill-humour in which her companion had returned.

"Having gathered these facts, Watson, I smoked several pipes over them, trying to separate those which were crucial from others which were merely incidental. There could be no question that the most distinctive and suggestive point in the case was the singular disappearance of the door key. A most careful search had failed to discover it in the room. Therefore, it must have been taken from it. But neither the Colonel nor the Colonel's wife could have taken it. That was perfectly clear. Therefore a third person must have entered the room. And that third person could only have come in through the window. It seemed to me that a careful examination of the room and the lawn might possibly reveal some traces of this mysterious individual. You know my methods, Watson. There was not one of them which I did not apply to the inquiry. And it ended by my discovering traces, but very different ones from those which I had expected. There had been a man in the room, and he had crossed the lawn coming from the road. I was able to obtain five very clear impressions of his footmarks—one on the roadway itself, at the point where he had climbed the low wall, two on the lawn, and two very faint ones upon the stained boards near the window where he had entered. He had apparently rushed across the lawn, for his toe marks were much deeper than his heels. But it was not the man who surprised me. It was his companion."

"His companion!"

Holmes pulled a large sheet of tissue paper out of his pocket and carefully unfolded it upon his knee.

"What do you make of that?" he asked.

The paper was covered with tracings of the footmarks of some small animal. It

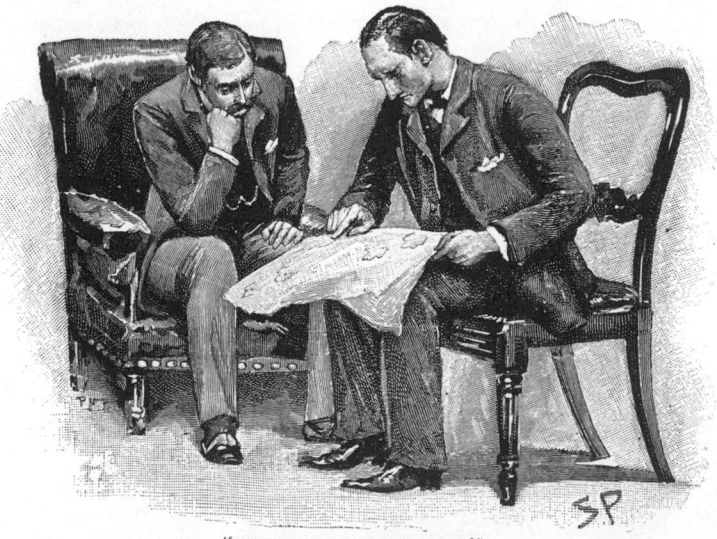

"WHAT DO YOU MAKE OF THAT?"

had five well-marked footpads, an indication of long nails, and the whole print might be nearly as large as a dessert spoon.

"It's a dog," said I.

"Did ever you hear of a dog running up a curtain? I found distinct traces that this creature had done so."

"A monkey, then?"

"But it is not the print of a monkey."

"What can it be, then?"

"Neither dog, nor cat, nor monkey, nor any creature that we are familiar with. I have tried to reconstruct it from the measurements. Here are four prints where the beast has been standing motionless. You see that it is no less than fifteen inches from fore foot to hind. Add to that the length of neck and head, and you get a creature not much less than two feet long—probably more if there is any tail. But now observe this other measurement. The animal has been moving, and we have the length of its stride. In each case it is only about three inches. You have an indication, you see, of a long body with very short legs attached to it. It has not been considerate enough to leave any of its hair behind it. But its general shape must be what I have indicated, and it can run up a curtain and is carnivorous."

"How do you deduce that?"

"Because it ran up the curtain. A canary's cage was hanging in the window, and its aim seems to have been to get at the bird."

"Then what was the beast?"

"Ah, if I could give it a name it might go a long way towards solving the case. On the whole it was probably some creature of the weasel and stoat tribe—and yet it is larger than any of these that I have seen."

"But what had it to do with the crime?"

"That also is still obscure. But we have learned a good deal, you perceive. We know that a man stood in the road looking at the quarrel between the Barclays—the blinds were up and the room lighted. We know also that he ran across the lawn, entered the room, accompanied by a strange animal, and that he either struck the Colonel, or, as is equally possible, that the Colonel fell down from sheer fright at the sight of him, and cut his head on the corner of the fender. Finally, we have the curious fact that the intruder carried away the key with him when he left."

"Your discoveries seem to have left the business more obscure than it was before," said I.

"Quite so. They undoubtedly showed that the affair was much deeper than was at first conjectured. I thought the matter over, and I came to the conclusion that I must approach the case from another aspect. But really, Watson, I am keeping you up, and I might just as well tell you all this on our way to Aldershot to-morrow."

"Thank you, you've gone rather too far to stop."

"It was quite certain that when Mrs. Barclay left the house at half-past seven she was on good terms with her husband. She was never, as I think I have said, ostentatiously affectionate, but she was heard by the coachman chatting with the Colonel in a friendly fashion. Now, it was equally certain that immediately on her return she had gone to the room in which she was least likely to see her husband, had flown to tea, as an agitated woman will, and, finally, on his coming in to her, had broken into violent recriminations. Therefore, something had occurred between seven-thirty and nine o'clock which had completely altered her feelings towards him. But Miss Morrison had been with her during the whole of that hour and a half. It was absolutely certain, therefore in spite of her denial, that she must know something of the matter.

"My first conjecture was that possibly there had been some passages between this young lady and the old soldier, which the former had now confessed to the wife. That would account for the angry return and also for the girl's denial that anything had occurred. Nor would it be entirely incompatible with most of the words overheard. But there was the reference to David, and there was the known affection of the Colonel for his wife to weigh against it, to say nothing of the tragic intrusion of this other man, which might of course be entirely disconnected with what had gone before. It was not easy to pick one's steps, but on the whole I was inclined to dismiss the idea that there had been anything between the Colonel and Miss Morrison, but more than ever convinced that the young lady held the clue as to what it was which had turned Mrs. Barclay to hatred of her husband. I took the obvious course therefore of calling upon Miss Morrison, of explaining to her that I was perfectly certain that she held the facts in her possession, and of assuring her that her friend, Mrs. Barclay, might find herself in the dock upon a capital charge unless the matter were cleared up.

"Miss Morrison is a little, ethereal slip of a girl, with timid eyes and blonde hair, but I found her by no means wanting in shrewdness and common sense. She sat thinking for some time after I had spoken, and then turning to me with a brisk air of resolution, she broke into a remarkable statement, which I will condense for your benefit.

"'I promised my friend that I would say nothing of the matter, and a promise is a promise,' said she. 'But if I can really help her when so serious a charge is made against her, and when her own mouth, poor darling, is closed by illness, then I think I am absolved from my promise. I will tell you exactly what happened upon Monday evening.

"'We were returning from the Watt Street Mission, about a quarter to nine o'clock. On our way we had to pass through Hudson Street, which·is a very quiet thoroughfare. There is only one lamp in it upon the left-hand side, and as we approached this lamp I saw a man coming towards us with his back very bent, and something like a box slung over one of his shoulders. He appeared to be deformed, for he carried his head low, and walked with his knees bent. We were passing him when he raised his face to look at us in the circle of light thrown by the lamp, and as he did so he stopped and screamed out in a dreadful voice, " My God, it's Nancy!" Mrs. Barclay turned as white as death, and would have fallen down had the dreadful-looking creature not caught hold of her. I was going to call for the police, but she, to my surprise, spoke quite civilly to the fellow.

"'I thought you had been dead this thirty years, Henry,' said she, in a shaking voice.

"'So I have,' said he, and it was awful to hear the tones that he said it in. He had a very dark, fearsome face, and a gleam in his eyes that comes back to me in my dreams. His hair and whiskers were shot with grey, and his face was all crinkled and puckered like a withered apple.

"'Just walk on a little way, dear,' said Mrs. Barclay. 'I want to have a word with this man. There is nothing to be afraid of.' She tried to speak boldly, but she was still deadly pale, and could hardly get her words out for the trembling of her lips.

"'I did as she asked me, and they talked together for a few minutes. Then she came down the street with her eyes blazing, and I saw the crippled wretch standing by the lamp-post and shaking his clenched fists in the air, as if he were mad with rage. She never said a word until we were at the door here, when she took me by the hand and begged me to tell no one what had happened. 'It is an old acquaintance of mine who has come down in the world,' said she. When I promised her that I would say nothing she kissed me, and I have never seen her since. I have told you now the whole truth, and if I withheld it from the police it is because I did not realize then the danger in which my dear friend stood. I know that it can only be to her advantage that everything should be known.'

"There was her statement, Watson, and to me, as you can imagine, it was like a light on a dark night. Everything which had been disconnected be-fore began at once to as-

"IT'S NANCY!"

sume its true place, and I had a shadowy presentment of the whole sequence of events. My next step obviously was to find the man who had produced such a remarkable impression upon Mrs. Barclay. If he were still in Aldershot it should not be a very difficult matter. There are not such a very great number of civilians, and a deformed man was sure to have attracted attention. I spent a day in the search, and by evening—this very evening, Watson—I had run him down. The man's name is Henry Wood, and he lives in lodgings in this same street in which the ladies met him. He has only been five days in the place. In the character of a registration agent I had a most interesting gossip with his landlady. The man is by trade a conjurer and performer, going round the canteens after nightfall, and giving a little entertainment at each. He carries some creature about with him in that box, about which the landlady seemed to be in considerable trepidation, for she had never seen an animal like it. He uses it in some of his tricks, according to her account. So much the woman was able to tell me, and also that it was a wonder the man lived, seeing how twisted he was, and that he spoke in a strange tongue sometimes, and that for the last two nights she had heard him groaning and weeping in his bedroom. He was all right as far as money went, but in his deposit he had given her what looked like a bad florin. She showed it to me, Watson, and it was an Indian rupee.

"So now, my dear fellow, you see exactly how we stand and why it is I want you. It is perfectly plain that after the ladies parted from this man he followed them at a distance, that he saw the quarrel between husband and wife through the window, that he rushed in, and that the creature which he carried in his box got loose. That is all very certain. But he is the only person in this world who can tell us exactly what happened in that room."

"And you intend to ask him?"

"Most certainly—but in the presence of a witness."

"And I am the witness?"

"If you will be so good. If he can clear the matter up, well and good. If he refuses, we have no alternative but to apply for a warrant."

"But how do you know he will be there when we return?"

"You may be sure that I took some precautions. I have one of my Baker Street boys mounting guard over him who would stick to him like a burr, go where he might. We shall find him in Hudson Street tomorrow, Watson; and meanwhile I should be the criminal myself if I kept you out of bed any longer."

It was midday when we found ourselves at the scene of the tragedy, and, under my companion's guidance, we made our way at once to Hudson Street. In spite of his capacity for concealing his emotions I could easily see that Holmes was in a state of suppressed excitement, while I was myself tingling with that half-sporting, half-intellectual pleasure which I invariably experienced when I associated myself with him in his investigations.

"This is the street," said he, as he turned into a short thoroughfare lined with plain two-storied brick houses—"Ah! here is Simpson to report."

"He's in all right, Mr. Holmes," cried a small street Arab, running up to us.

"Good, Simpson!" said Holmes, patting him on the head. "Come along, Watson. This is the house." He sent in his card with a message that he had come on important business, and a moment later we were face to face with the man whom we had come to see. In spite of the warm weather he was crouching over a fire, and the little room was like an oven. The man sat all twisted and huddled in his chair in a way which gave an indescribable impression of deformity, but the face which he turned towards us, though worn and swarthy, must at some time have been remarkable for its beauty. He looked suspiciously at us now out of yellow-shot bilious eyes, and, without speaking or rising, he waved towards two chairs.

"Mr. Henry Wood, late of India, I believe?" said Holmes, affably. "I've come over this little matter of Colonel Barclay's death."

"What should I know about that?"

"That's what I wanted to ascertain. You know, I suppose, that unless the matter is cleared up, Mrs. Barclay, who is an old friend of yours, will in all probability be tried for murder?"

The man gave a violent start.

"I don't know who you are," he cried, "nor how you come to know what you do know; but will you swear that this is true that you tell me?"

"Why, they are only waiting for her to come to her senses to arrest her."

"My God! Are you in the police yourself?"

"MR. HENRY WOOD, I BELIEVE?"

"No."

"What business is it of yours, then?"

"It's every man's business to see justice done."

"You can take my word that she is innocent."

"Then you are guilty?"

"No, I am not."

"Who killed Colonel James Barclay, then?"

"It was a just Providence that killed him. But, mind you this, that if I had knocked his brains out, as it was in my heart to do, he would have had no more than his due from my hands. If his own guilty conscience had not struck him down, it is likely enough that I might have had his blood upon my soul. You want me to tell the story. Well, I don't know why I shouldn't, for there's no cause for me to be ashamed of it.

"It was in this way, sir. You see me now with my back like a camel and my ribs all awry, but there was a time when Corporal Henry Wood was the smartest man in the 117th Foot. We were in India then, in cantonments, at a place we'll call Bhurtee. Barclay, who died the other day, was sergeant in the same company as myself, and the belle of the regiment—aye, and the finest girl that ever had the breath of life between her lips—was Nancy Devoy, the daughter of the colour-sergeant. There were two men who loved her, and one whom she loved; and you'll smile when you look at this poor thing huddled before the fire, and hear me say that it was for my good looks that she loved me.

"Well, though I had her heart, her father was set upon her marrying Barclay. I was a harum-scarum, reckless lad, and he had had an education, and was already marked for the sword belt. But the girl held true to me, and it seemed that I would have had her, when the Mutiny broke out, and all Hell was loose in the country.

"We were shut up in Bhurtee, the regiment of us with half a battery of artillery, a company of Sikhs, and a lot of civilians and women-folk. There were ten thousand rebels round us, and they were as keen as a set of terriers round a rat-cage. About the second week of it our water gave out, and it was a question whether we could communicate with General Neill's column, which was moving up country. It was our only chance, for we could not hope to fight our way out with all the women and children, so I volunteered to go out and warn General Neill of our danger. My offer was accepted, and I talked it over with Sergeant Barclay, who was supposed to know the ground better than any other man, and who drew up a route by which I might get through the rebel lines. At ten o'clock the same night I started off upon my journey. There were a thousand lives to save, but it was of only one that I was thinking when I dropped over the wall that night.

"My way ran down a dried-up watercourse which we hoped would screen me from the enemy's sentries, but as I crept round the corner of it I walked right into six of them, who were crouching down in the dark waiting for me. In an instant I was stunned with a blow, and bound hand and foot. But the real blow was to my heart and not to my

"I WALKED RIGHT INTO SIX OF THEM."

head, for as I came to and listened to as much as I could understand of their talk, I heard enough to tell me that my comrade, the very man who had arranged the way that I was to take, had betrayed me by means of a native servant into the hands of the enemy.

"Well, there's no need for me to dwell on that part of it. You know now what James Barclay was capable of. Bhurtee was relieved by Neill next day, but the rebels took me away with them in their retreat, and it was many a long year before ever I saw a white face again. I was tortured, and tried to get away, and was captured and tortured again. You can see for yourselves the state in which I was left. Some of them that fled into Nepaul took me with them, and then afterwards I was up past Darjeeling. The hill-folk up there murdered the rebels who had me, and I became their slave for a time until I escaped, but instead of going south I had to go north, until I found myself among the Afghans. There I wandered about for many a year, and at last came back to the Punjab, where I lived mostly among the natives, and picked up a living by the conjuring tricks that I had learned. What use was it for me, a wretched cripple, to go back to England, or to make myself known to my old comrades? Even my wish for revenge would not make me do that. I had

rather that Nancy and my old pals should think of Harry Wood as having died with a straight back, than see him living and crawling with a stick like a chimpanzee. They never doubted that I was dead, and I meant that they never should. I heard that Barclay had married Nancy, and that he was rising rapidly in the regiment, but even that did not make me speak.

"But when one gets old, one has a longing for home. For years I've been dreaming of the bright green fields and the hedges of England. At last I determined to see them before I died. I saved enough to bring me across, and then I came here where the soldiers are, for I know their ways, and how to amuse them, and so earn enough to keep me."

"Your narrative is most interesting," said Sherlock Holmes. "I have already heard of your meeting with Mrs. Barclay and your mutual recognition. You then, as I understand, followed her home and saw through the window an altercation between her husband and her, in which she doubtless cast his conduct to you in his teeth. Your own feelings overcame you and you ran across the lawn and broke in upon them."

"I did, sir, and at the sight of me he looked as I have never seen a man look before, and over he went with his head on the fender. But he was dead before he fell. I read death on his face as plain as I can read that text over the fire. The bare sight of me was like a bullet through his guilty heart."

"And then?"

"Then Nancy fainted, and I caught up the key of the door from her hand, intending to unlock it and get help. But as I was doing it it seemed to me better to leave it alone and get away, for the thing might look black against me, and any way my secret would be out if I were taken. In my haste I thrust the key into my pocket, and dropped my stick while I was chasing Teddy, who had run up the curtain. When I got him into his box, from which he had slipped, I was off as fast as I could run."

"Who's Teddy?" asked Holmes.

The man leaned over and pulled up the front of a kind of hutch in the corner. In an instant out there slipped a beautiful reddish-brown creature, thin and lithe, with the legs of a stoat, a long thin nose, and a pair of the finest red eyes that ever I saw in an animal's head.

"It's a mongoose!" I cried.

"Well, some call them that, and some call them ichneumon," said the man. "Snake catcher is what I call them, and Teddy is amazing quick on cobras. I have one here without the fangs, and Teddy catches it every night to please the folk in the canteen. Any other point, sir?"

"Well, we may have to apply to you again if Mrs. Barclay should prove to be in serious trouble."

"In that case, of course, I'd come forward."

"But if not, there is no object in raking up this scandal against a dead man, foully as he has acted. You have, at least, the satisfaction of knowing that for thirty years of his life his conscience bitterly reproached him for this wicked deed. Ah, there goes Major Murphy on the other side of the street. Good-bye, Wood; I want to learn if anything has happened since yesterday."

We were in time to overtake the Major before he reached the corner.

"Ah, Holmes," he said, "I suppose you have heard that all this fuss has come to nothing?"

"What, then?"

"The inquest is just over. The medical evidence showed conclusively that death was due to apoplexy. You see, it was quite a simple case after all."

"Oh, remarkably superficial," said Holmes, smiling. "Come, Watson, I don't think we shall be wanted in Aldershot any more."

"There's one thing," said I, as we walked down to the station, "if the husband's name was James, and the other was Henry, what was this talk about David?"

"IT WAS QUITE A SIMPLE CASE AFTER ALL."

"That one word, my dear Watson, should have told me the whole story had I been the ideal reasoner which you are so fond of depicting. It was evidently a term of reproach."

"Of reproach?"

"Yes, David strayed a little occasionally, you know, and on one occasion in the same direction as Sergeant James Barclay. You remember the small affair of Uriah and Bathsheba. My Biblical knowledge is a trifle rusty, I fear, but you will find the story in the first or second of Samuel."

# The Adventures of Sherlock Holmes.

## By A. Conan Doyle.

### XXI.—THE ADVENTURE OF THE RESIDENT PATIENT.

IN glancing over the somewhat incoherent series of memoirs with which I have endeavoured to illustrate a few of the mental peculiarities of my friend, Mr. Sherlock Holmes, I have been struck by the difficulty which I have experienced in picking out examples which shall in every way answer my purpose. For in those cases in which Holmes has performed some *tour-de-force* of analytical reasoning, and has demonstrated the value of his peculiar methods of investigation, the facts themselves have often been so slight or so commonplace that I could not feel justified in laying them before the public. On the other hand, it has frequently happened that he has been concerned in some research where the facts have been of the most remarkable and dramatic character, but where the share which he has himself taken in determining their causes has been less pronounced than I, as his biographer, could wish. The small matter which I have chronicled under the heading of "A Study in Scarlet," and that other later one connected with the loss of the *Gloria Scott*, may serve as examples of this Scylla and Charybdis which are for ever threatening his historian. It may be that, in the business of which I am now about to write, the part which my friend played is not sufficiently accentuated; and yet the whole train of circumstances is so remarkable that I cannot bring myself to omit it entirely from this series.

I cannot be sure of the exact date, for some of my memoranda upon the matter have been mislaid, but it must have been towards the end of the first year during which Holmes and I shared chambers in Baker Street. It was boisterous October weather, and we had both remained indoors all day, I because I feared with my shaken health to face the keen autumn wind, while he was deep in some of those abstruse chemical investigations which absorbed him utterly as long as he was engaged upon them. Towards evening, however, the breaking of a test-tube brought his research to a premature ending, and he sprang up from his chair with an exclamation of impatience and a clouded brow.

"A day's work ruined, Watson," said he, striding across to the window. "Ha! the stars are out and the wind has fallen. What do you say to a ramble through London?"

I was weary of our little sitting-room, and gladly acquiesced, muffling myself nose-high against the keen night air. For three hours we strolled about together, watching the ever-changing kaleidoscope of life as it ebbs and flows through Fleet Street and the Strand. Holmes had shaken off his temporary ill-humour, and his characteristic talk, with its keen observance of detail and subtle power of inference, held me amused and enthralled. It was ten o'clock before we reached Baker Street again. A brougham was waiting at our door.

"Hum! A doctor's—general practitioner, I perceive," said Holmes. "Not been long in practice, or had much to do. Come to consult us, I fancy! Lucky we came back!"

I was sufficiently conversant with Holmes's methods to be able to follow his reasoning, and to see that the nature and state of the various medical instruments in the wicker basket which hung in the lamp-light inside the brougham had given him the data for his swift deduction. The light in our window above showed that this late visit was indeed intended for us. With some curiosity as to what could have sent a brother medico to us at such an hour, I followed Holmes into our sanctum.

A pale, taper-faced man with sandy whiskers rose up from a chair by the fire as we entered. His age may not have been more than three or four and thirty, but his haggard expression and unhealthy hue told of a life which had sapped his strength and robbed him of his youth. His manner was nervous and shy, like that of a sensitive gentleman,

"WE STROLLED ABOUT TOGETHER."

and the thin white hand which he laid on the mantelpiece as he rose was that of an artist rather than of a surgeon. His dress was quiet and sombre, a black frock-coat, dark trousers, and a touch of colour about his necktie.

"Good evening, Doctor," said Holmes, cheerily; "I am glad to see that you have only been waiting a very few minutes."

"You spoke to my coachman, then?"

"No, it was the candle on the side-table that told me. Pray resume your seat and let me know how I can serve you."

"My name is Doctor Percy Trevelyan," said our visitor, "and I live at 403, Brook Street."

"Are you not the author of a monograph upon obscure nervous lesions?" I asked.

His pale cheeks flushed with pleasure at hearing that his work was known to me.

"I so seldom hear of the work that I thought it was quite dead," said he. "My publishers give me a most discouraging

account of its sale. You are yourself, I presume, a medical man?"

"A retired Army surgeon."

"My own hobby has always been nervous disease. I should wish to make it an absolute specialty, but, of course, a man must take what he can get at first. This, however, is beside the question, Mr. Sherlock Holmes, and I quite appreciate how valuable your time is. The fact is that a very singular train of events has occurred recently at my house in Brook Street, and to-night they came to such a head that I felt it was quite impossible for me to wait another hour before asking for your advice and assistance."

Sherlock Holmes sat down and lit his pipe. "You are very welcome to both," said he. "Pray let me have a detailed account of what the circumstances are which have disturbed you."

"One or two of them are so trivial," said Dr. Trevelyan, "that really I am almost ashamed to mention them. But the matter is so inexplicable, and the recent turn which it has taken is so elaborate, that I shall lay it all before you, and you shall judge what is essential and what is not.

"I am compelled, to begin with, to say something of my own college career. I am a London University man, you know, and I am sure you will not think that I am unduly singing my own praises if I say that my student career was considered by my professors to be a very promising one. After I had graduated I continued to devote myself to research, occupying a minor position in King's College Hospital, and I was fortunate enough to excite considerable interest by my research into the pathology of catalepsy, and finally to win the Bruce Pinkerton prize and medal by the monograph on nervous lesions to which your friend has just alluded. I should not go too far if I were to say that there was a general impression at that time that a distinguished career lay before me.

"But the one great stumbling-block lay in

my want of capital. As you will readily understand, a specialist who aims high is compelled to start in one of a dozen streets in the Cavendish Square quarter, all of which entail enormous rents and furnishing expenses. Besides this preliminary outlay, he must be prepared to keep himself for some years, and to hire a presentable carriage and horse. To do this was quite beyond my power, and I could only hope that by economy I might in ten years' time save enough to enable me to put up my plate. Suddenly, however, an unexpected incident opened up quite a new prospect to me.

"This was a visit from a gentleman of the name of Blessington, who was a complete stranger to me. He came up into my room one morning, and plunged into business in an instant.

"'You are the same Percy Trevelyan who has had so distinguished a career and won a great prize lately?' said he. I bowed.

"'Answer me frankly,' he continued, 'for you will find it to your interest to do so. You have all the cleverness which makes a successful man. Have you the tact?'

"I could not help smiling at the abruptness of the question.

"'I trust that I have my share,' I said.

"'Any bad habits? Not drawn towards drink, eh?'

"'Really, sir!' I cried.

"'Quite right! That's all right! But I was bound to ask. With all these qualities why are you not in practice?'

"I shrugged my shoulders.

"'Come, come!' said he, in his bustling way. 'It's the old story. More in your brains than in your pocket, eh? What would you say if I were to start you in Brook Street?'

"I stared at him in astonishment.

"'Oh, it's for my sake, not for yours,' he cried. 'I'll be perfectly frank with you, and if it suits you it will suit me very well. I have a few thousands to invest, d'ye see, and I think I'll sink them in you.'

"'But why?' I gasped.

"'Well, it's just like any other speculation, and safer than most.'

"'What am I to do, then?'

"'I'll tell you. I'll take the house, furnish it, pay the maids, and run the whole place. All you have to do is just to wear out your chair in the consulting-room. I'll let you have pocket-money and everything. Then you hand over to me three-quarters of what you earn and you keep the other quarter for yourself.'

"This was the strange proposal, Mr. Holmes, with which the man Blessington approached me. I won't weary you with the account of how we bargained and negotiated. It ended in my moving into the house next Lady Day and starting in practice on very much the same conditions as he had suggested. He came himself to live with me in the character of a resident patient. His heart was weak, it appears, and he needed constant medical supervision. He turned the two best rooms on the first floor into a sitting-room and bedroom for himself. He was a man of singular habits, shunning company and very seldom going out. His life was irregular, but in one respect he was regularity itself. Every evening at the same hour he walked into the consulting-room, examined the books, put down five and three-pence for every guinea that I had earned, and carried the rest off to the strong box in his own room.

"I STARED AT HIM IN ASTONISHMENT."

"I may say with confidence that he never had occasion to regret his speculation. From the first it was a success. A few good cases and the reputation which I had won in the hospital brought me rapidly to the front, and during the last few years I have made him a rich man.

"So much, Mr. Holmes, for my past history and for my relations with Mr. Blessington. It only remains for me now to tell you what has occurred to bring me here to-night.

"Some weeks ago Mr. Blessington came down to me in, as it seemed to me, a state of considerable agitation. He spoke of some burglary which, he said, had been committed in the West-end, and he appeared, I remember, to be quite unnecessarily excited about it, declaring that a day should not pass before we should add stronger bolts to our windows and doors. For a week he continued to be in quite a peculiar state of restlessness, peering continually out of the windows, and ceasing to take the short walk which had usually been the prelude to his dinner. From his manner it struck me that he was in mortal dread of something or somebody, but when I questioned him upon the point he became so offensive that I was compelled to drop the subject. Gradually as time passed his fears appeared to die away, and he had renewed his former habits, when a fresh event reduced him to the pitiable state of prostration in which he now lies.

"What happened was this. Two days ago I received the letter which I now read to you. Neither address nor date is attached to it.

"HELPED HIM TO A CHAIR."

"'A Russian nobleman who is now resident in England,' it runs, 'would be glad to avail himself of the professional assistance of Dr. Percy Trevelyan. He has been for some years a victim to cataleptic attacks, on which, as is well known, Dr. Trevelyan is an authority. He proposes to call at about a quarter-past six to-morrow evening, if Dr. Trevelyan will make it convenient to be at home.'

"This letter interested me deeply, because the chief difficulty in the study of catalepsy is the rareness of the disease. You may believe, then, that I was in my consulting-room when, at the appointed hour, the page showed in the patient.

"He was an elderly man, thin, demure, and commonplace—by no means the conception one forms of a Russian nobleman. I was much more struck by the appearance of his companion. This was a tall young man, surprisingly handsome, with a dark, fierce face, and the limbs and chest of a Hercules. He had his hand under the other's arm as they entered, and helped him to a chair with a tenderness which one would hardly have expected from his appearance.

"'You will excuse my coming in, Doctor,'

said he to me, speaking English with a slight lisp. 'This is my father, and his health is a matter of the most overwhelming importance to me.'

"I was touched by this filial anxiety. 'You would, perhaps, care to remain during the consultation,' said I.

"'Not for the world,' he cried, with a gesture of horror. 'It is more painful to me than I can express. If I were to see my father in one of those dreadful seizures, I am convinced that I should never survive it. My own nervous system is an exceptionally sensitive one. With your permission I will remain in the waiting-room while you go into my father's case.'

"To this, of course, I assented, and the young man withdrew. The patient and I then plunged into a discussion of his case, of which I took exhaustive notes. He was not remarkable for intelligence, and his answers were frequently obscure, which I attributed to his limited acquaintance with our language. Suddenly, however, as I sat writing he ceased to give any answer at all to my inquiries, and on my turning towards him I was shocked to see that he was sitting bolt upright in his chair, staring at me with a perfectly blank and rigid face. He was again in the grip of his mysterious malady.

"My first feeling, as I have just said, was one of pity and horror. My second, I fear, was rather one of professional satisfaction. I made notes of my patient's pulse and temperature, tested the rigidity of his muscles, and examined his reflexes. There was nothing markedly abnormal in any of these conditions, which harmonized with my former experiences. I had obtained good results in such cases by the inhalation of nitrite of amyl, and the present seemed an admirable opportunity of testing its virtues. The bottle was downstairs in my laboratory, so, leaving my patient seated in his chair, I ran down to get it. There was some little delay in finding it—five minutes, let us say—and then I returned. Imagine my amazement to find the room empty and the patient gone!

"Of course, my first act was to run into the waiting-room. The son had gone also. The hall door had been closed, but not shut. My page who admits patients is a new boy, and by no means quick. He waits downstairs, and runs up to show patients out when I ring the consulting-room bell. He had heard nothing, and the affair remained a complete mystery. Mr. Blessington came in from his walk shortly afterwards, but I did not say anything to him upon the subject, for,

to tell the truth, I have got in the way of late of holding as little communication with him as possible.

"Well, I never thought that I should see anything more of the Russian and his son, so you can imagine my amazement when at the very same hour this evening they both came marching into my consulting-room, just as they had done before.

"'I feel that I owe you a great many apologies for my abrupt departure yesterday, Doctor,' said my patient.

"'I confess that I was very much surprised at it,' said I.

"'Well, the fact is,' he remarked, 'that when I recover from these attacks my mind is always very clouded as to all that has gone before. I woke up in a strange room, as it seemed to me, and made my way out into the street in a sort of dazed way when you were absent.

"'And I,' said the son, 'seeing my father pass the door of the waiting-room, naturally thought that the consultation had come to an end. It was not until we had reached home that I began to realize the true state of affairs.'

"'Well,' said I, laughing, 'there is no harm done, except that you puzzled me terribly; so if you, sir, would kindly step into the waiting-room, I shall be happy to continue our consultation, which was brought to so abrupt an ending.'

"For half an hour or so I discussed the old gentleman's symptoms with him, and then, having prescribed for him, I saw him go off on the arm of his son.

"I have told you that Mr. Blessington generally chose this hour of the day for his exercise. He came in shortly afterwards and passed upstairs. An instant later I heard him running down, and he burst into my consulting-room like a man who is mad with panic.

"'Who has been in my room?' he cried.

"'No one,' said I.

"'It's a lie!' he yelled. 'Come up and look.'

"I passed over the grossness of his language, as he seemed half out of his mind with fear. When I went upstairs with him he pointed to several footprints upon the light carpet.

"'D'you mean to say those are mine?' he cried.

"They were certainly very much larger than any which he could have made, and were evidently quite fresh. It rained hard this afternoon, as you know, and my patients were the only people who called. It must have been the case, then, that the man in the

"HE BURST INTO MY CONSULTING-ROOM."

sombre, flat-faced houses which one associates with a West-end practice. A small page admitted us, and we began at once to ascend the broad, well-carpeted stair.

But a singular interruption brought us to a standstill. The light at the top was suddenly whisked out, and from the darkness came a reedy, quavering voice.

"I have a pistol," it cried; "I give you my word that I'll fire if you come any nearer."

"This really grows outrageous, Mr. Blessington," cried Dr. Trevelyan.

"Oh, then it is you, Doctor?" said the voice, with a great heave of relief. "But those other gentlemen, are they what they pretend to be?"

We were conscious of a long scrutiny out of the darkness.

"Yes, yes, it's all right," said the voice at last. "You can come up, and I am sorry if my precautions have annoyed you."

He re-lit the stair gas as he spoke, and we saw before us a singular-looking man, whose appearance, as well as his voice, testified to his jangled nerves. He was very fat, but had apparently at some time been much fatter, so that the skin hung about his face in loose pouches, like the cheeks of a bloodhound. He was of a sickly colour, and his thin sandy hair seemed to bristle up with the intensity of his emotion. In his hand he held a pistol, but he thrust it into his pocket as we advanced.

"Good evening, Mr. Holmes," said he; "I am sure I am very much obliged to you for coming round. No one ever needed your advice more than I do. I suppose that Dr. Trevelyan has told you of this most unwarrantable intrusion into my rooms."

"Quite so," said Holmes. "Who are these two men, Mr. Blessington, and why do they wish to molest you?"

"Well, well," said the resident patient, in a nervous fashion, "of course, it is hard to say

waiting-room had for some unknown reason, while I was busy with the other, ascended to the room of my resident patient. Nothing had been touched or taken, but there were the footprints to prove that the intrusion was an undoubted fact.

"Mr. Blessington seemed more excited over the matter than I should have thought possible, though, of course, it was enough to disturb anybody's peace of mind. He actually sat crying in an arm-chair, and I could hardly get him to speak coherently. It was his suggestion that I should come round to you, and of course I at once saw the propriety of it, for certainly the incident is a very singular one, though he appears to completely overrate its importance. If you would only come back with me in my brougham, you would at least be able to soothe him, though I can hardly hope that you will be able to explain this remarkable occurrence."

Sherlock Holmes had listened to this long narrative with an intentness which showed me that his interest was keenly aroused. His face was as impassive as ever, but his lids had drooped more heavily over his eyes, and his smoke had curled up more thickly from his pipe to emphasize each curious episode in the doctor's tale. As our visitor concluded Holmes sprang up without a word, handed me my hat, picked up his own from the table, and followed Dr. Trevelyan to the door. Within a quarter of an hour we had been dropped at the door of the physician's residence in Brook Street, one of those

"IN HIS HAND HE HELD A PISTOL."

that. You can hardly expect me to answer that, Mr. Holmes."

"Do you mean that you don't know?"

"Come in here, if you please. Just have the kindness to step in here."

He led the way into his bedroom, which was large and comfortably furnished.

"You see that," said he, pointing to a big black box at the end of his bed. "I have never been a very rich man, Mr. Holmes— never made but one investment in my life, as Dr. Trevelyan would tell you. But I don't believe in bankers. I would never trust a banker, Mr. Holmes. Between ourselves, what little I have is in that box, so you can understand what it means to me when unknown people force themselves into my rooms."

Holmes looked at Blessington in his questioning way, and shook his head.

"I cannot possibly advise you if you try to deceive me," said he.

"But I have told you everything."

Holmes turned on his heel with a gesture of disgust. "Good-night, Dr. Trevelyan," said he.

"And no advice for me?" cried Blessington, in a breaking voice.

"My advice to you, sir, is to speak the truth."

A minute later we were in the street and walking for home. We had crossed Oxford Street, and were half-way down Harley Street before I could get a word from my companion.

"Sorry to bring you out on such a fool's errand, Watson," he said at last. "It is an interesting case, too, at the bottom of it."

"I can make little of it," I confessed.

"Well, it is quite evident that there are two men—more, perhaps, but at least two— who are determined for some reason to get at this fellow Blessington. I have no doubt in my mind that both on the first and on the second occasion that young man penetrated to Blessington's room, while his confederate, by an ingenious device, kept the doctor from interfering."

"And the catalepsy!"

"A fraudulent imitation, Watson, though I should hardly dare to hint as much to our specialist. It is a very easy complaint to imitate. I have done it myself."

"And then?"

"By the purest chance Blessington was out on each occasion. Their reason for choosing so unusual an hour for a consultation was obviously to insure that there should be no other patient in the waiting-room. It just happened, however, that this hour coincided with Blessington's constitutional, which seems to show that they were not very well acquainted with his daily routine. Of course, if they had been merely after plunder they would at least have made some attempt to search for it. Besides, I can read in a man's eye when it is his own skin that he is frightened for. It is inconceivable that this fellow could have made two such vindictive enemies as these appear to be without knowing of it. I hold it, therefore, to be certain that he does know who these men are, and that for reasons of his own he suppresses it. It is just possible that to-morrow may find him in a more communicative mood."

"Is there not one alternative," I suggested, "grotesquely improbable, no doubt, but still just conceivable? Might the whole story of the cataleptic Russian and his son be a concoction of Dr. Trevelyan's, who has, for his own purposes, been in Blessington's rooms?"

I saw in the gaslight that Holmes wore an amused smile at this brilliant departure of mine.

"My dear fellow," said he, "it was one of the first solutions which occurred to me, but I was soon able to corroborate the doctor's tale. This young man has left prints upon the stair carpet which made it quite superfluous for me to ask to see those which he had made in the room. When I tell you that his shoes were square-toed, instead of being pointed like Blessington's, and were quite an inch and a third longer than the doctor's, you will acknowledge that there can be no doubt as to his individuality. But we may sleep on it now, for I shall be surprised if we do not hear something further from Brook Street in the morning."

Sherlock Holmes's prophecy was soon fulfilled, and in a dramatic fashion. At half-past seven next morning, in the first dim glimmer of daylight, I found him standing by my bedside in his dressing-gown.

"There's a brougham waiting for us, Watson," said he.

"What's the matter, then?"

"The Brook Street business."

"Any fresh news?"

"Tragic but ambiguous," said he, pulling up the blind. "Look at this—a sheet from a notebook with 'For God's sake, come at once—P. T.' scrawled upon it in pencil. Our friend the doctor was hard put to it when he wrote this. Come along, my dear fellow, for it's an urgent call."

In a quarter of an hour or so we were back at the physician's house. He came running out to meet us with a face of horror.

"Oh, such a business!" he cried, with his hands to his temples.

"What, then?"

"Blessington has committed suicide!"

Holmes whistled.

"Yes, he hanged himself during the night."

We had entered, and the doctor had preceded us into what was evidently his waiting-room.

"I really hardly know what I am doing," he cried. "The police are already upstairs. It has shaken me most dreadfully."

"When did you find it out?"

"He has a cup of tea taken in to him early every morning. When the maid entered about seven, there the unfortunate fellow was hanging in the middle of the room. He had tied his cord to the hook on which the heavy lamp used to hang, and he had jumped off from the top of the very box that he showed us yesterday."

Holmes stood for a moment in deep thought.

"With your permission," said he at last, "I should like to go upstairs and look into the matter." We both ascended, followed by the doctor.

It was a dreadful sight which met us as we entered the bedroom door. I have spoken of the impression of flabbiness which this man Blessington conveyed. As he dangled from the hook it was exaggerated and intensified until he was scarce human in his appearance. The neck was drawn out like a plucked chicken's, making the rest of him seem the more obese and unnatural by the contrast. He was clad only in his long night-dress, and his swollen ankles and ungainly feet protruded starkly from beneath it. Beside him stood a smart-looking police inspector, who was taking notes in a pocket-book.

"Ah, Mr. Holmes," said he, heartily, as my friend entered. "I am delighted to see you."

"Good morning, Lanner," answered Holmes. "You won't think me an intruder, I am sure. Have you heard of the events which led up to this affair?"

"Yes, I heard something of them."

"Have you formed any opinion?"

"As far as I can see, the man has been driven out of his senses by fright. The bed has been well slept in, you see. There's his impression deep enough. It's about five in the morning, you know, that suicides are most common. That would be about his time for hanging himself. It seems to have been a very deliberate affair."

"I should say that he has been dead about three hours, judging by the rigidity of the muscles," said I.

"Noticed anything peculiar about the room?" asked Holmes.

"Found a screwdriver and some screws on the wash-hand stand. Seems to have smoked heavily during the night, too. Here are four cigar ends that I picked out of the fireplace."

"Hum!" said Holmes. "Have you got his cigar-holder?"

"No, I have seen none."

"His cigar-case, then?"

"Yes, it was in his coat pocket."

Holmes opened it and smelled the single cigar which it contained.

"Oh, this is a Havana, and these others are cigars of the peculiar sort which are imported by the Dutch from their East Indian colonies. They are usually wrapped in straw, you know, and are thinner for their length than any other brand." He picked up the four ends and examined them with his pocket lens.

"Two of these have been smoked from a holder and two without," said he. "Two have been cut by a not very sharp knife, and two have had the ends bitten off by a set of excellent teeth. This is no suicide, Mr. Lanner. It is a very deeply-planned and cold-blooded murder."

"Impossible!" cried the inspector.

"And why?"

"Why should anyone murder a man in so clumsy a fashion as by hanging him?'

"That is what we have to find out."

"How could they get in?"

"Through the front door."

"It was barred in the morning."

"Then it was barred after them."

"How do you know?"

"I saw their traces. Excuse me a moment, and I may be able to give you some further information about it."

He went over to the door, and turning the lock he examined it in his methodical fashion. Then he took out the key, which was on the inside, and inspected that also.

"HOLMES OPENED IT AND SMELLED THE SINGLE CIGAR WHICH IT CONTAINED."

The bed, the carpet, the chairs, the mantelpiece, the dead body, and the rope were each in turn examined, until at last he professed himself satisfied, and with my aid and that of the inspector cut down the wretched object, and laid it reverently under a sheet.

"How about this rope?" he asked.

"It is cut off this," said Dr. Trevelyan, drawing a large coil from under the bed. "He was morbidly nervous of fire, and always kept this beside him, so that he might escape by the window in case the stairs were burning."

"That must have saved them trouble," said Holmes, thoughtfully. "Yes, the actual facts are very plain, and I shall be surprised if by the afternoon I cannot give you the reasons for them as well. I will take this photograph of Blessington which I see upon the mantelpiece, as it may help me in my inquiries."

"But you have told us nothing," cried the doctor.

"Oh, there can be no doubt as to the sequence of events," said Holmes. "There were three of them in it: the young man, the old man, and a third to whose identity I have no clue. The first two, I need hardly remark, are the same who masqueraded as the Russian Count and his son, so we can give a very full description of them. They were admitted by a confederate inside the house. If I might offer you a word of advice, Inspector, it would be to arrest the page, who, as I understand, has only recently come into your service, Doctor."

"The young imp cannot be found," said Dr. Trevelyan; "the maid and the cook have just been searching for him."

Holmes shrugged his shoulders.

"He has played a not unimportant part in this drama," said he. "The three men having ascended the stair, which they did on tiptoe, the elder man first, the younger man second, and the unknown man in the rear——"

"My dear Holmes!" I ejaculated.

"Oh, there could be no question as to the superimposing of the footmarks. I had the advantage of learning which was which last night. They ascended then to Mr. Blessington's room, the door of which they found to be locked. With the help of a wire, however, they forced round the key. Even without a lens, you will perceive by the scratches on this ward where the pressure was applied.

"On entering the room, their first proceeding must have been to gag Mr. Blessington. He may have been asleep, or he may have been so paralyzed with terror as to have been unable to cry out. These walls are thick, and it is conceivable that his shriek, if he had time to utter one, was unheard.

"Having secured him, it is evident to me that a consultation of some sort was held. Probably it was something in the nature of a judicial proceeding. It must have lasted for some time, for it was then that these cigars were smoked. The older man sat in that wicker chair: it was he who used the cigar-holder. The younger man sat over yonder: he knocked his ash off against the chest of drawers. The third fellow paced up and down. Blessington, I think, sat upright in the bed, but of that I cannot be absolutely certain.

"Well, it ended by their taking Blessington and hanging him. The matter was so prearranged that it is my belief that they brought with them some sort of block or pulley which might serve as a gallows. That screwdriver and those screws were, as I conceive, for fixing it up. Seeing the hook, however, they naturally

saved themselves the trouble. Having finished their work they made off, and the door was barred behind them by their confederate."

We had all listened with the deepest interest to this sketch of the night's doings, which Holmes had deduced from signs so subtle and minute, that even when he had pointed them out to us, we could scarcely follow him in his reasonings. The inspector hurried away on the instant to make inquiries about the page, while Holmes and I returned to Baker Street for breakfast.

"I'll be back by three," said he when we had finished our meal. "Both the inspector and the doctor will meet me here at that hour, and I hope by that time to have cleared up any little obscurity which the case may still present."

Our visitors arrived at the appointed time, but it was a quarter to four before my friend put in an appearance. From his expression as he entered, however, I could see that all had gone well with him.

"Any news, Inspector?"

"We have got the boy, sir."

"Excellent, and I have got the men."

"You have got them!" we cried all three.

"'YOU HAVE GOT THEM! WE CRIED.'"

"Well, at least I have got their identity. This so-called Blessington is, as I expected, well known at headquarters, and so are his assailants. Their names are Biddle, Hayward, and Moffat."

"The Worthingdon bank gang," cried the inspector.

"Precisely," said Holmes.

"Then Blessington must have been Sutton?"

"Exactly," said Holmes.

"Why, that makes it as clear as crystal," said the inspector.

But Trevelyan and I looked at each other in bewilderment.

"You must surely remember the great Worthingdon bank business," said Holmes; "five men were in it, these four and a fifth called Cartwright. Tobin, the caretaker, was murdered, and the thieves got away with seven thousand pounds. This was in 1875. They were all five arrested, but the evidence against them was by no means conclusive. This Blessington, or Sutton, who was the worst of the gang, turned informer. On his evidence, Cartwright was hanged and the other three got fifteen years apiece. When they got out the other day, which was some years before their full term, they set themselves, as you perceive, to hunt down the traitor and to avenge the death of their comrade upon him. Twice they tried to get at him and failed; a third time, you see, it came off. Is there any-thing further which I can explain, Dr. Trevelyan?"

"I think you have made it all remarkably clear," said the doctor. "No doubt the day on which he was so perturbed was the day when he had read of their release in the newspapers."

"Quite so. His talk about a burglary was the merest blind."

"But why could he not tell you this?"

"Well, my dear sir, knowing the vindictive character of his old associates, he was trying to hide his own identity from everybody as long as he could. His secret was a shameful one, and he could not bring himself to divulge it. However, wretch as he was, he was still living under the shield of British law, and I have no doubt, Inspector, that you will see that, though that shield may fail to guard, the sword of justice is still there to avenge."

Such were the singular circumstances in connection with the resident patient and the Brook Street doctor. From that night nothing has been seen of the three murderers by the police, and it is surmised at Scotland Yard that they were among the passengers of the ill-fated steamer *Norah Creina*, which was lost some years ago with all hands upon the Portuguese coast, some leagues to the north of Oporto. The proceedings against the page broke down for want of evidence, and the "Brook Street Mystery," as it was called, has never, until now, been fully dealt with in any public print.

# The Adventures of Sherlock Holmes.

## By A. Conan Doyle.

### XXII.—THE ADVENTURE OF THE GREEK INTERPRETER.

URING my long and intimate acquaintance with Mr. Sherlock Holmes I had never heard him refer to his relations, and hardly ever to his own early life. This reticence upon his part had increased the somewhat inhuman effect which he produced upon me, until sometimes I found myself regarding him as an isolated phenomenon, a brain without a heart, as deficient in human sympathy as he was pre-eminent in intelligence. His aversion to women, and his disinclination to form new friendships, were both typical of his unemotional character, but not more so than his complete suppression of every reference to his own people. I had come to believe that he was an orphan with no relatives living, but one day, to my very great surprise, he began to talk to me about his brother.

It was after tea on a summer evening, and the conversation, which had roamed in a desultory, spasmodic fashion from golf clubs to the causes of the change in the obliquity of the ecliptic, came round at last to the question of atavism and hereditary aptitudes. The point under discussion was how far any singular gift in an individual was due to his ancestry, and how far to his own early training.

"In your own case," said I, "from all that you have told me it seems obvious that your faculty of observation and your peculiar facility for deduction are due to your own systematic training."

"To some extent," he answered, thoughtfully. "My ancestors were country squires, who appear to have led much the same life, as is natural to their class. But, none the less, my turn that way is in my veins, and may have come with my grandmother, who was the sister of Vernet, the French artist. Art in the blood is liable to take the strangest forms."

"But how do you know that it is hereditary?"

"Because my brother Mycroft possesses it in a larger degree than I do."

This was news to me, indeed. If there were another man with such singular powers in England, how was it that neither police nor public had heard of him? I put the question, with a hint that it was my companion's modesty which made him acknowledge his brother as his superior. Holmes laughed at my suggestion.

"My dear Watson," said he, "I cannot agree with those who rank modesty among the virtues. To the logician all things should be seen exactly as they are, and to underestimate oneself is as much a departure from truth as to exaggerate one's own powers. When I say, therefore, that Mycroft has better powers of observation than I, you may take it that I am speaking the exact and literal truth."

"Is he your junior?"

"Seven years my senior."

"How comes it that he is unknown?"

"Oh, he is very well known in his own circle."

"Where, then?"

"Well, in the Diogenes Club, for example."

I had never heard of the institution, and my face must have proclaimed as much, for Sherlock Holmes pulled out his watch.

"The Diogenes Club is the queerest club in London, and Mycroft, one of the queerest men. He's always there from a quarter to five till twenty to eight. It's six now, so if you care for a stroll this beautiful evening I shall be very happy to introduce you to two curiosities."

Five minutes later we were in the street, walking towards Regent Circus.

"You wonder," said my companion, "why it is that Mycroft does not use his powers for detective work. He is incapable of it."

"But I thought you said——!"

"I said that he was my superior in observation and deduction. If the art of the detective began and ended in reasoning from an arm-chair, my brother would be the greatest criminal agent that ever lived. But

"Very likely not. There are many men in London, you know, who, some from shyness, some from misanthropy, have no wish for the company of their fellows. Yet they are not averse to comfortable chairs and the latest periodicals. It is for the convenience of these that the Diogenes Club was started, and it now contains the most unsociable and un-clubbable men in town. No member is permitted to take the least notice of any other one. Save in the Strangers' Room, no talking is, under any circumstances, permitted, and three offences, if brought to the notice of the committee, render the talker liable to ex-

"HOLMES PULLED OUT HIS WATCH."

he has no ambition and no energy. He will not even go out of his way to verify his own solutions, and would rather be considered wrong than take the trouble to prove himself right. Again and again I have taken a problem to him, and have received an explanation which has afterwards proved to be the correct one. And yet he was absolutely incapable of working out the practical points which must be gone into before a case could be laid before a judge or jury."

"It is not his profession, then?"

"By no means. What is to me a means of livelihood is to him the merest hobby of a dilettante. He has an extraordinary faculty for figures, and audits the books in some of the Government departments. Mycroft lodges in Pall Mall, and he walks round the corner into Whitehall every morning and back every evening. From year's end to year's end he takes no other exercise, and is seen nowhere else, except only in the Diogenes Club, which is just opposite his rooms."

"I cannot recall the name."

pulsion. My brother was one of the founders, and I have myself found it a very soothing atmosphere."

We had reached Pall Mall as we talked, and were walking down it from the St. James' end. Sherlock Holmes stopped at a door some little distance from the Carlton, and, cautioning me not to speak, he led the way into the hall. Through the glass panelling I caught a glimpse of a large and luxurious room in which a considerable number of men were sitting about and reading papers, each in his own little nook. Holmes showed me into a small chamber which looked out on to Pall Mall, and then, leaving me for a minute, he came back with a companion who I knew could only be his brother.

Mycroft Holmes was a much larger and stouter man than Sherlock. His body was absolutely corpulent, but his face, though massive, had preserved something of the sharpness of expression which was so remarkable in that of his brother. His eyes, which were of a peculiarly light watery grey, seemed to always retain that far-away, introspective look which I had only observed in Sherlock's when he was exerting his full powers.

"I am glad to meet you, sir," said he, putting out a broad, fat hand, like the flipper of a seal. "I hear of Sherlock everywhere since you became his chronicler. By the way, Sherlock, I expected to see you round last week to consult me over that Manor House case. I thought you might be a little out of your depth."

"No, I solved it," said my friend, smiling.

"It was Adams, of course?"

"Yes, it was Adams."

"I was sure of it from the first." The two sat down together in the bow-window of the club. "To anyone who wishes to study mankind this is the spot," said Mycroft. "Look at the magnificent types! Look at these two men who are coming towards us, for example."

"The billiard-marker and the other?"

"Precisely. What do you make of the other?"

The two men had stopped opposite the window. Some chalk marks over the waistcoat pocket were the only signs of billiards which I could see in one of them. The other was a very small dark fellow, with his hat pushed back and several packages under his arm.

"An old soldier, I perceive," said Sherlock.

"And very recently discharged," remarked the brother.

"Served in India, I see."

"And a non-commissioned officer."

"Royal Artillery, I fancy," said Sherlock.

"And a widower."

"But with a child."

"Children, my dear boy, children."

"Come," said I, laughing, "this is a little too much."

"Surely," answered Holmes, "it is not hard to say that a man with that bearing, expression of authority, and sun-baked skin is a soldier, is more than a private, and is not long from India."

MYCROFT HOLMES.

"That he has not left the service long is shown by his still wearing his 'ammunition boots,' as they are called," observed Mycroft.

"He has not the cavalry stride, yet he wore his hat on one side, as is shown by the lighter skin on that side of his brow. His weight is against his being a sapper. He is in the artillery."

"Then, of course, his complete mourning shows that he has lost someone very dear. The fact that he is doing his own shopping looks as though it were his wife. He has been buying things for children you perceive. There is a rattle, which shows that one of them is very young. The wife probably died in child-bed. The fact that he has a picture-book under his arm shows that there is another child to be thought of."

I began to understand what my friend meant when he said that his brother possessed even keener faculties than he did himself. He glanced across at me, and smiled. Mycroft took snuff from a tortoise-shell box, and brushed away the wandering grains from his coat front with a large, red silk handkerchief.

"By the way, Sherlock," said he, "I have had something quite after your own heart—a most singular problem—submitted to my judgment. I really had not the energy to follow it up, save in a very incomplete fashion, but it gave me a basis for some very pleasing speculations. If you would care to hear the facts——"

"My dear Mycroft, I should be delighted."

The brother scribbled a note upon a leaf of his pocket-book, and ringing the bell, he handed it to the waiter.

"I have asked Mr. Melas to step across," said he. "He lodges on the floor above me, and I have some slight acquaintance with him, which led him to come to me in his perplexity. Mr. Melas is a Greek by extraction, as I understand, and he is a remarkable linguist. He earns his living partly as interpreter in the law courts, and partly by acting as guide to any wealthy Orientals who may visit the Northumberland Avenue hotels. I think I will leave him to tell his very remarkable experience in his own fashion."

A few minutes later we were joined by a short, stout man, whose olive face and coal-black hair proclaimed his southern origin, though his speech was that of an educated Englishman. He shook hands eagerly with Sherlock Holmes, and his dark eyes sparkled with pleasure when he understood that the specialist was anxious to hear his story.

"I do not believe that the police credit me—on my word I do not," said he, in a wailing voice. "Just because they have never heard of it before, they think that such a thing cannot be. But I know that I shall never be easy in my mind until I know what has become of my poor man with the sticking-plaster upon his face."

"I am all attention," said Sherlock Holmes.

"This is Wednesday evening," said Mr. Melas; "well, then, it was on Monday night —only two days ago, you understand—that all this happened. I am an interpreter, as, perhaps, my neighbour there has told you. I interpret all languages—or nearly all—but as I am a Greek by birth, and with a Grecian name, it is with that particular tongue that I am principally associated. For many years I have been the chief Greek interpreter in London, and my name is very well known in the hotels.

"It happens, not unfrequently, that I am sent for at strange hours, by foreigners who get into difficulties, or by travellers who arrive late and wish my services. I was not surprised, therefore, on Monday night when a Mr. Latimer, a very fashionably-dressed young man, came up to my rooms and asked me to accompany him in a cab, which was waiting at the door. A Greek friend had come to see him upon business, he said, and, as he could speak nothing but his own tongue, the services of an interpreter were indispensable. He gave me to understand that his house was some little distance off, in Kensington, and he seemed to be in a great hurry, bustling me rapidly into the cab when we had descended to the street.

"I say into the cab, but I soon became doubtful as to whether it was not a carriage in which I found myself. It was certainly more roomy than the ordinary four-wheeled disgrace to London, and the fittings, though frayed, were of rich quality. Mr. Latimer seated himself opposite to me, and we started off through Charing Cross and up the Shaftesbury Avenue. We had come out upon Oxford Street, and I had ventured some remark as to this being a roundabout way to Kensington, when my words were arrested by the extraordinary conduct of my companion.

"He began by drawing a most formidable-looking bludgeon loaded with lead from his pocket, and switching it backwards and forwards several times, as if to test its weight and strength. Then he placed it, without a word, upon the seat beside him. Having done this he drew up the windows on each side, and I found to my astonishment that they were covered with paper so as to prevent my seeing through them.

"'I am sorry to cut off your view, Mr. Melas,' said he. 'The fact is that I have

"HE DREW UP THE WINDOWS."

no intention that you should see what the place is to which we are driving. It might possibly be inconvenient to me if you could find your way there again.'

"As you can imagine, I was utterly taken aback by such an address. My companion was a powerful, broad-shouldered young fellow, and, apart from the weapon, I should not have had the slightest chance in a struggle with him.

"'This is very extraordinary conduct, Mr. Latimer,' I stammered. 'You must be aware that what you are doing is quite illegal.'

"'It is somewhat of a liberty, no doubt,' said he, 'but we'll make it up to you. But I must warn you, however, Mr. Melas, that if at any time to-night you attempt to raise an alarm or do anything which is against my interests, you will find it a very serious thing. I beg you to remember that no one knows where you are, and that whether you are in this carriage or in my house, you are equally in my power.'

"His words were quiet, but he had a rasping way of saying them which was very menacing. I sat in silence, wondering what on earth could be his reason for kidnapping me in this extraordinary fashion. Whatever it might be, it was perfectly clear that there was no possible use in my resisting, and that I could only wait to see what might befall.

"For nearly two hours we drove without my having the least clue as to where we were going. Sometimes the rattle of the stones told of a paved causeway, and at others our smooth, silent course suggested asphalte, but save by this variation in sound there was nothing at all which could in the remotest way help me to form a guess as to where we were. The paper over each window was impenetrable to light, and a blue curtain was drawn across the glass-work in front. It was a quarter past seven when we left Pall Mall, and my watch showed me that it was ten minutes to nine when at last came to a standstill. My companion let down the window and I caught a glimpse of a low, arched doorway with a lamp burning above it. As I was hurried from the carriage it swung open, and I found myself inside the house, with a vague impression of a lawn and trees on each side of me as I entered. Whether these were private grounds, however, or *bonâ-fide* country was more than I could possibly venture to say.

"There was a coloured gas-lamp inside which was turned so low that I could see little save that the hall was of some size and hung with pictures. In the dim light I could make out that the person who had opened the door was a small, mean-looking, middle-aged man with rounded shoulders. As he turned towards us the glint of the light showed me that he was wearing glasses.

"'Is this Mr. Melas, Harold?' said he.

"'Yes.'

"'Well done! Well done! No ill-will, Mr. Melas, I hope, but we could not get on without you. If you deal fair with us you'll not regret it; but if you try any tricks, God help you!'

"He spoke in a jerky, nervous fashion, and with little giggling laughs in between, but somehow he impressed me with fear more than the other.

"'What do you want with me?' I asked.

"'Only to ask a few questions of a Greek gentleman who is visiting us, and to let us have the answers. But say no more than you are told to say, or'—here came the nervous giggle again—'you had better never have been born.'

"As he spoke he opened a door and showed the way into a room which appeared to be very richly furnished—but again the only light was afforded by a single lamp half turned down. The chamber was certainly large, and the way in which my feet sank into the carpet as I stepped across it told me of its richness. I caught glimpses of velvet chairs, a high, white marble mantelpiece and what seemed to be a suit of Japanese armour at one side of it. There was a chair just under the lamp, and the elderly man motioned that I should sit in it. The younger had left us, but he suddenly returned through another door, leading with him a gentleman clad in some sort of loose dressing-gown, who moved slowly towards us. As he came into the circle of dim light which enabled me to see him more clearly, I was thrilled with horror at his appearance. He was deadly pale and terribly emaciated, with the protruding, brilliant eyes of a man whose spirit is greater than his strength. But what shocked me more than any signs of physical weakness was that his face was grotesquely criss-crossed with sticking-plaster, and that one large pad of it was fastened over his mouth.

"'Have you the slate, Harold?' cried the older man, as this strange being fell rather than sat down into a chair. 'Are his hands loose? Now then, give him the pencil. You are to ask the questions, Mr. Melas, and he will write the answers. Ask him first of all whether he is prepared to sign the papers.'

"I WAS THRILLED WITH HORROR."

"'I care not. *I am a stranger in London.*'

"'Your fate will be on your own head. *How long have you been here?*'

"'Let it be so. *Three weeks.*'

"'The property can never be yours. *What ails you?*'

"'It shall not go to villains. *They are starving me.*'

"'You shall go free if you sign. *What house is this?*'

"'I will never sign. *I do not know.*'

"'You are not doing her any service. *What is your name?*'

"'Let me hear her say so. *Kratides.*'

"'You shall see her if you sign. *Where are you from?*'

"'Then I shall never see her. *Athens.*'

"Another five minutes, Mr. Holmes, and I should have wormed out the whole story under their very noses. My very next question might have cleared the matter up, but at that instant the door opened and a woman stepped into the room. I could not see her clearly enough to know more than that she was tall and graceful, with black hair, and clad in some sort of loose, white gown.

"'Harold!' said she, speaking English with a broken accent, 'I could not stay away longer. It is so lonely up there with only— oh, my God, it is Paul!'

"These last words were in Greek, and at the same instant the man, with a convulsive effort, tore the plaster from his lips, and screaming out 'Sophy! Sophy!' rushed into the woman's arms. Their embrace was but for an instant, however, for the younger man seized the woman and pushed her out of the room, while the elder easily overpowered his emaciated victim, and dragged him away through the other door. For a moment I was left alone in the room, and I sprang to my feet with some vague idea that I might in some way get a clue to what this house was in which I found myself. Fortunately, however, I took no steps, for, looking

"The man's eyes flashed fire.

"'Never,' he wrote in Greek upon the slate.

"'On no conditions?' I asked at the bidding of our tyrant.

"'Only if I see her married in my presence by a Greek priest whom I know.'

"The man giggled in his venomous way.

"'You know what awaits you then?'

"'I care nothing for myself.'

"These are samples of the questions and answers which made up our strange half-spoken, half-written conversation. Again and again I had to ask him whether he would give in and sign the document. Again and again I had the same indignant reply. But soon a happy thought came to me. I took to adding on little sentences of my own to each question—innocent ones at first to test whether either of our companions knew anything of the matter, and then, as I found that they showed no sign, I played a more dangerous game. Our conversation ran something like this:—

"'You can do no good by this obstinacy. *Who are you?*'

"SOPHY ! SOPHY !"

beard was thready and ill nourished. He pushed his face forward as he spoke, and his lips and eyelids were continually twitching like a man with St. Vitus's dance. I could not help thinking that his strange, catchy little laugh was also a symptom of some nervous malady. The terror of his face lay in his eyes, however, steel grey, and glistening coldly, with a malignant, inexorable cruelty in their depths.

"'We shall know if you speak of this,' said he. 'We have our own means of information. Now, you will find the carriage waiting, and my friend will see you on your way.'

"I was hurried through the hall, and into the vehicle, again obtaining that momentary glimpse of trees and a garden. Mr. Latimer followed closely at my heels, and took his place opposite to me without a word. In silence we again drove for an interminable distance, with the windows raised, until at last, just after midnight, the carriage pulled up.

"'You will get down here, Mr. Melas,' said my companion. 'I am sorry to leave you so far from your house, but there is no alternative. Any attempt upon your part to follow the carriage can only end in injury to yourself.'

"He opened the door as he spoke, and I had hardly time to spring out when the coachman lashed the horse, and the carriage rattled away. I looked round me in astonishment. I was on some sort of a heathy common, mottled over with dark clumps of furze bushes. Far away stretched a line of houses with a light here and there in the upper windows. On the other side I saw the red signal lamps of a railway.

"The carriage which had brought me was

up, I saw that the older man was standing in the doorway, with his eyes fixed upon me.

"'That will do, Mr. Melas,' said he. 'You perceive that we have taken you into our confidence over some very private business. We should not have troubled you only that our friend who speaks Greek and who began these negotiations has been forced to return to the East. It was quite necessary for us to find someone to take his place, and we were fortunate in hearing of your powers.'

"I bowed.

"'There are five sovereigns here,' said he, walking up to me, 'which will, I hope, be a sufficient fee. But remember,' he added, tapping me lightly on the chest and giggling, 'if you speak to a human soul about this— one human soul mind, well, may God have mercy upon your soul !'

"I cannot tell you the loathing and horror with which this insignificant-looking man inspired me. I could see him better now as the lamp-light shone upon him. His features were peaty and sallow, and his little, pointed

already out of sight. I stood gazing round and wondering where on earth I might be, when I saw someone coming towards me in the darkness. As he came up to me I made out that it was a railway porter.

" 'Can you tell me what place this is ? ' I asked.

" 'Wandsworth Common,' said he.

" 'Can I get a train into town ? '

" 'If you walk on a mile or so, to Clapham Junction,' said he, 'you'll just be in time for the last to Victoria.'

"So that was the end of my adventure, Mr. Holmes. I do not know where I was nor whom I spoke with, nor anything, save what I have told you. But I know that there is foul play going on, and I want to help that unhappy man if I can. I told the whole story to Mr. Mycroft Holmes next morning and, subsequently, to the police."

"I SAW SOMEONE COMING TOWARDS ME."

We all sat in silence for some little time after listening to this extraordinary narrative. Then Sherlock looked across at his brother.

"Any steps ? " he asked.

Mycroft picked up the *Daily News*, which was lying on a side table.

" 'Anybody supplying any information as to the whereabouts of a Greek gentleman named Paul Kratides, from Athens, who is unable to speak English, will be rewarded. A similar reward paid to anyone giving information about a Greek lady whose first name is Sophy. X 2473.' That was in all the dailies. No answer."

"How about the Greek Legation ? "

"I have inquired. They know nothing."

"A wire to the head of the Athens police, then."

"Sherlock has all the energy of the family,"

said Mycroft, turning to me. "Well, you take the case up by all means, and let me know if you do any good."

"Certainly," answered my friend, rising from his chair. "I'll let you know, and Mr. Melas also. In the meantime, Mr. Melas, I should certainly be on my guard, if I were you, for, of course, they must know through these advertisements that you have betrayed them."

As we walked home together Holmes stopped at a telegraph office and sent off several wires.

"You see, Watson," he remarked, "our evening has been by no means wasted. Some of my most interesting cases have come to me in this way through Mycroft. The problem which we have just listened to, although it can admit of but one explanation, has still some distinguishing features."

"You have hopes of solving it?"

"Well, knowing as much as we do, it will be singular indeed if we fail to discover the rest. You must yourself have formed some theory which will explain the facts to which we have listened."

"In a vague way, yes."

"What was your idea then ? "

"It seemed to me to be obvious that this Greek girl had been carried off by the young Englishman named Harold Latimer."

"Carried off from where ? "

"Athens, perhaps."

Sherlock Holmes shook his head. "This young man could not talk a word of Greek. The lady could talk English fairly well. Inference that she had been in England some little time, but he had not been in Greece."

"Well, then, we will presume that she had

come on a visit to England, and that this Harold had persuaded her to fly with him."

"That is the more probable."

"Then the brother—for that, I fancy, must be the relationship—comes over from Greece to interfere. He imprudently puts himself into the power of the young man and his older associate. They seize him and use violence towards him in order to make him sign some papers to make over the girl's fortune—of which he may be trustee—to them. This he refuses to do. In order to negotiate with him they have to get an interpreter, and they pitch upon this Mr. Melas, having used some other one before. The girl is not told of the arrival of her brother, and finds it out by the merest accident."

"Excellent, Watson," cried Holmes. "I really fancy that you are not far from the truth. You see that we hold all the cards, and we have only to fear some sudden act of violence on their part. If they give us time we must have them."

"But how can we find where this house lies?"

"Well, if our conjecture is correct, and the girl's name is, or was, Sophy Kratides, we should have no difficulty in tracing her. That must be our main hope, for the brother, of course, is a complete stranger. It is clear that some time has elapsed since this Harold established these relations with the girl—some weeks at any rate — since the brother in Greece has had time to hear of it and come across. If they have been living in the same place during this time, it is probable that we shall have some answer to Mycroft's advertisement."

We had reached our house in Baker Street whilst we had been talking. Holmes ascended the stairs first, and as he opened the door of our room he gave a start of surprise. Looking over his shoulder I was equally astonished. His brother Mycroft was sitting smoking in the arm-chair.

"Come in, Sherlock! Come in, sir," said he, blandly, smiling at our surprised faces. "You don't expect such energy from me, do you, Sherlock? But somehow this case attracts me."

"How did you get here?"

"I passed you in a hansom."

"There has been some new development?"

"I had an answer to my advertisement."

"Ah!"

"Yes; it came within a few minutes of your leaving."

"And to what effect?"

Mycroft Holmes took out a sheet of paper.

"Here it is," said he, "written with a J pen on royal cream paper by a middle-aged man with a weak constitution. 'Sir,' he says, 'in answer to your advertisement of to-day's date, I beg to inform you that I know the young lady in question very well. If you should care to call upon me, I could give you some particulars as to her painful history. She is living at present at The Myrtles, Beckenham. Yours faithfully, J. DAVENPORT."

"He writes from Lower Brixton," said Mycroft Holmes. "Do you not think that we might drive to him now, Sherlock, and learn these particulars?"

"' COME IN,' SAID HE, BLANDLY."

"My dear Mycroft, the brother's life is more valuable than the sister's story. I think we should call at Scotland Yard for Inspector Gregson, and go straight out to Beckenham. We know that a man is being done to death, and every hour may be vital."

"Better pick up Mr. Melas upon our way," I suggested; "we may need an interpreter."

"Excellent!" said Sherlock Holmes. "Send the boy for a four-wheeler, and we shall be off at once." He opened the table-drawer as he spoke, and I noticed that he slipped his revolver into his pocket. "Yes," said he, in answer to my glance, "I should say from what we have heard that we are dealing with a particularly dangerous gang."

It was almost dark before we found ourselves in Pall Mall, at the rooms of Mr. Melas. A gentleman had just called for him, and he was gone.

"Can you tell me where?" asked Mycroft Holmes.

"I don't know, sir," answered the woman who had opened the door. "I only know that he drove away with the gentleman in a carriage."

"Did the gentleman give a name?"

"No, sir."

"He wasn't a tall, handsome, dark young man?"

"Oh, no, sir. He was a little gentleman, with glasses, thin in the face, but very pleasant in his ways, for he was laughing all the time that he was talking."

"Come along!" cried Sherlock Holmes, abruptly. "This grows serious!" he observed, as we drove to Scotland Yard. "These men have got hold of Melas again. He is a man of no physical courage, as they are well aware from their experience the other night. This villain was able to terrorize him the instant that he got into his presence. No doubt they want his professional services; but, having used him, they may be inclined to punish him for what they will regard as his treachery."

Our hope was that by taking train we might get to Beckenham as soon as, or sooner, than the carriage. On reaching Scotland Yard, however, it was more than an hour before we could get Inspector Gregson and comply with the legal formalities which would enable us to enter the house. It was a quarter to ten before we reached London Bridge, and half-past before the four of us alighted on the Beckenham platform. A drive of half a mile brought us to the Myrtles—a large, dark house standing back from the road in its own grounds. Here we dismissed our cab, and made our way up the drive together.

"The windows are all dark," remarked the Inspector. "The house seems deserted."

"Our birds are flown and the nest empty," said Holmes.

"Why do you say so?"

"A carriage heavily loaded with luggage has passed out during the last hour."

The Inspector laughed. "I saw the wheel tracks in the light of the gate-lamp, but where does the luggage come in?"

"You may have observed the same wheel-tracks going the other way. But the outward-bound ones were very much deeper—so much so that we can say for a certainty that there was a very considerable weight on the carriage."

"You get a trifle beyond me there," said the Inspector, shrugging his shoulders. "It will not be an easy door to force. But we will try if we cannot make someone hear us."

He hammered loudly at the knocker and pulled at the bell, but without any success. Holmes had slipped away, but he came back in a few minutes.

"I have a window open," said he.

"It is a mercy that you are on the side of the force, and not against it, Mr. Holmes," remarked the Inspector, as he noted the clever way in which my friend had forced back the catch. "Well, I think that, under the circumstances, we may enter without waiting for an invitation."

One after the other we made our way into a large apartment, which was evidently that in which Mr. Melas had found himself. The Inspector had lit his lantern, and by its light we could see the two doors, the curtain, the lamp and the suit of Japanese mail as he had described them. On the table lay two glasses, an empty brandy bottle, and the remains of a meal.

"What is that?" asked Holmes, suddenly.

We all stood still and listened. A low, moaning sound was coming from somewhere above our heads. Holmes rushed to the door and out into the hall. The dismal noise came from upstairs. He dashed up, the Inspector and I at his heels, while his brother Mycroft, followed as quickly as his great bulk would permit.

Three doors faced us upon the second floor, and it was from the central of these that the sinister sounds were issuing, sinking sometimes into a dull mumble and rising again into a shrill whine. It was locked, but the key was on the outside. Holmes flung open the door and rushed in, but he was out again in an instant with his hand to his throat.

"It's charcoal," he cried. "Give it time. It will clear."

Peering in we could see that the only light in the room came from a dull, blue flame, which flickered from a small brass tripod in the centre. It threw a livid, unnatural circle upon the floor, while in the shadows beyond we saw the vague loom of two figures, which crouched against the wall. From the open door there reeked a horrible, poisonous exhalation, which set us gasping and coughing. Holmes rushed to the top of the stairs to draw in the fresh air, and then, dashing into the room, he threw up the window and hurled the brazen tripod out into the garden.

"We can enter in a minute," he gasped, darting out again. "Where is a candle? I doubt if we could strike a match in that atmosphere. Hold the light at the door and we shall get them out, Mycroft. Now!"

With a rush we got to the poisoned men and dragged them out on to the landing. Both of them were blue lipped and insensible, with swollen, congested faces and protruding eyes. Indeed, so distorted were their features that save for his black beard and stout figure we might have failed to recognise in one of them the Greek interpreter who had parted from us only a few hours before at the Diogenes Club. His hands and feet were securely strapped together, and he bore over one eye the mark of a violent blow. The other, who was secured in a similar fashion, was a tall man in the last stage of emaciation, with several strips of sticking-plaster arranged in a grotesque pattern over his face. He had ceased to moan as we laid him down, and a glance showed me that for him, at least, our aid had come too late. Mr. Melas, however, still lived, and in less than an hour, with the aid of ammonia and brandy, I had the satisfaction of seeing him open his eyes, and of knowing that my hand had drawn him back from the dark valley in which all paths meet.

It was a simple story which he had to tell,

"'IT'S CHARCOAL, HE CRIED.'"

and one which did but confirm our own deductions. His visitor on entering his rooms had drawn a life preserver from his sleeve, and had so impressed him with the fear of instant and inevitable death, that he had kidnapped him for the second time. Indeed, it was almost mesmeric the effect which this giggling ruffian had produced upon the unfortunate linguist, for he could not speak of him save with trembling hands and a blanched cheek. He had been taken swiftly to Beckenham, and had acted as interpreter in a second interview, even more dramatic than the first, in which the two Englishmen had menaced their prisoner with instant death if he did not comply with their demands. Finally, finding him proof against every threat, they had hurled him back into his prison, and after reproaching Melas with his treachery, which appeared from the newspaper advertisement, they had stunned him with a blow from a stick, and he remembered nothing more until he found us bending over him.

And this was the singular case of the

Grecian Interpreter, the explanation of which is still involved in some mystery. We were able to find out, by communicating with the gentleman who had answered the advertisement, that the unfortunate young lady came of a wealthy Grecian family, and that she had been on a visit to some friends in England. While there she had met a young man named Harold Latimer, who had acquired an ascendancy over her, and had eventually persuaded her to fly with him. Her friends, shocked at the event, had contented themselves with informing her brother at Athens, and had then washed their hands of the matter. The brother, on his arrival in England, had imprudently placed himself in the power of Latimer, and of his associate, whose name was Wilson Kemp—a man of the foulest antecedents. These two, finding that through his ignorance of the language he was helpless in their hands, had kept him a prisoner, and had endeavoured, by cruelty and starvation, to make him sign away his own and his sister's property. They had kept him in the house without the girl's knowledge, and the plaster over the face had been for the purpose of making recognition difficult in case she should ever catch a glimpse of him. Her feminine perceptions, however, had instantly seen through the disguise when, on the occasion of the interpreter's first visit, she had seen him for the first time. The poor girl, however, was herself a prisoner, for there was no one about the house except the man who acted as coachman, and his wife, both of whom were tools of the conspirators. Finding that their secret was out and that their prisoner was not to be coerced, the two villains, with the girl, had fled away at a few hours' notice from the furnished house which they had hired, having first, as they thought, taken vengeance both upon the man who had defied and the one who had betrayed them.

Months afterwards a curious newspaper cutting reached us from Buda-Pesth. It told how two Englishmen who had been travelling with a woman had met with a tragic end. They had each been stabbed, it seems, and the Hungarian police were of opinion that they had quarrelled and had inflicted mortal injuries upon each other. Holmes, however, is, I fancy, of a different way of thinking, and he holds to this day that if one could find the Grecian girl one might learn how the wrongs of herself and her brother came to be avenged.

# The Adventures of Sherlock Holmes.

## By A. Conan Doyle.

### XXIII.—THE ADVENTURE OF THE NAVAL TREATY.

THE July which immediately succeeded my marriage was made memorable by three cases of interest in which I had the privilege of being associated with Sherlock Holmes, and of studying his methods. I find them recorded in my notes under the headings of "The Adventure of the Second Stain," "The Adventure of the Naval Treaty," and "The Adventure of the Tired Captain." The first of these, however, deals with interests of such importance, and implicates so many of the first families in the kingdom, that for many years it will be impossible to make it public. No case, however, in which Holmes was ever engaged has illustrated the value of his analytical methods so clearly or has impressed those who were associated with him so deeply. I still retain an almost verbatim report of the interview in which he demonstrated the true facts of the case to Monsieur Dubuque, of the Paris police, and Fritz von Waldbaum, the well-known specialist of Dantzig, both of whom had wasted their energies upon what proved to be side issues. The new century will have come, however, before the story can be safely told. Meanwhile, I pass on to the second upon my list, which promised also, at one time, to be of national importance, and was marked by several incidents which give it a quite unique character.

During my school days I had been intimately associated with a lad named Percy Phelps, who was of much the same age as myself, though he was two classes ahead of me. He was a very brilliant boy, and carried away every prize which the school had to offer, finishing his exploits by winning a scholarship, which sent him on to continue his triumphant career at Cambridge. He was, I remember, extremely well connected, and even when we were all little boys together, we knew that his mother's brother was Lord Holdhurst, the great Conservative politician. This gaudy relationship did him little good at school; on the contrary, it seemed rather a piquant thing to us to chevy him about the playground and hit him over the shins with a wicket. But it was another thing when he came out into the world. I heard vaguely that his abilities and the influence which he commanded had won him a good position at the Foreign Office, and then he passed completely out of my mind until the following letter recalled his existence:—

"Briarbrae, Woking.

"MY DEAR WATSON,—I have no doubt that you can remember 'Tadpole' Phelps, who was in the fifth form when you were in the third. It is possible even that you may have heard that, through my uncle's influence, I obtained a good appointment at the Foreign Office, and that I was in a situation of trust and honour until a horrible misfortune came suddenly to blast my career.

"There is no use writing the details of that dreadful event. In the event of your acceding to my request, it is probable that I shall have to narrate them to you. I have only just recovered from nine weeks of brain fever, and am still exceedingly weak. Do you think that you could bring your friend, Mr. Holmes, down to see me? I should like to have his opinion of the case, though the authorities assure me that nothing more can be done. Do try to bring him down, and as soon as possible. Every minute seems an hour while I live in this state of horrible suspense. Assure him that if I have not asked his advice sooner it was not because I did not appreciate his talents, but because I have been off my head ever since the blow fell. Now I am clear again, though I dare not think of it too much for fear of a relapse. I am still so weak that I have to write, as you see, by dictating. Do try and bring him.

"Your old schoolfellow,

"PERCY PHELPS."

There was something that touched me as I read this letter, something pitiable in the reiterated appeals to bring Holmes. So moved was I that, even if it had been a difficult matter, I should have tried it; but of course I knew well that Holmes loved his art so, that he was ever as ready to bring his aid as his client could be to receive it. My wife agreed with me that not a moment should be lost in laying the matter before him, and so within an hour of breakfast time I found myself back once more in the old rooms in Baker Street.

" HOLMES WAS WORKING HARD OVER A CHEMICAL INVESTIGATION."

chair opposite, and drew up his knees until his fingers clasped round his long, thin shins.

"A very commonplace little murder," said he. "You've got something better, I fancy. You are the stormy petrel of crime, Watson. What is it?"

I handed him the letter, which he read with the most concentrated attention.

"It does not tell us very much, does it?" he remarked, as he handed it back to me.

"Hardly anything."

"And yet the writing is of interest."

"But the writing is not his own."

"Precisely. It is a woman's."

"A man's, surely!" I cried.

"No, a woman's; and a woman of rare character. You see, at the commencement of an investigation, it is something to know that your client is in close contact with someone who for good or evil has an exceptional nature. My interest is already awakened in the case. If you are ready, we will start at once for Woking and see this diplomatist who is in such evil case, and the lady to whom he dictates his letters."

We were fortunate enough to catch an early train at Waterloo, and in a little under an hour we found ourselves among the fir-woods and the heather of Woking. Briar-brae proved to be a large detached house standing in extensive grounds, within a few minutes' walk of the station. On sending in our cards we were shown into an elegantly-appointed drawing-room, where we were joined in a few minutes by a rather stout man, who received us with much hospitality. His age may have been nearer forty than thirty, but his cheeks were so ruddy and his eyes so merry, that he still conveyed the impression of a plump and mischievous boy.

"I am so glad that you have come," said he, shaking our hands with effusion. "Percy has been inquiring for you all the morning. Ah, poor old chap, he clings to any straw. His father and mother asked me to see you,

Holmes was seated at his side table clad in his dressing gown and working hard over a chemical investigation. A large curved retort was boiling furiously in the bluish flame of a Bunsen burner, and the distilled drops were condensing into a two-litre measure. My friend hardly glanced up as I entered, and I, seeing that his investigation must be of importance, seated myself in an armchair and waited. He dipped into this bottle or that, drawing out a few drops of each with his glass pipette, and finally brought a test-tube containing a solution over to the table. In his right hand he had a slip of litmus-paper.

"You come at a crisis, Watson," said he. "If this paper remains blue, all is well. If it turns red, it means a man's life." He dipped it into the test-tube and it flushed at once into a dull, dirty crimson. "Hum! I thought as much!" he cried. "I will be at your service in one instant, Watson. You will find tobacco in the Persian slipper." He turned to his desk and scribbled off several telegrams, which were handed over to the page-boy. Then he threw himself down in the

for the mere mention of the subject is very painful to them."

"We have had no details yet," observed Holmes. "I perceive that you are not yourself a member of the family."

Our acquaintance looked surprised, and then glancing down he began to laugh.

"Of course you saw the ' J. H.' monogram on my locket," said he. "For a moment I thought you had done something clever. Joseph Harrison is my name, and as Percy is to marry my sister Annie, I shall at least be a relation by marriage. You will find my sister in his room, for she has nursed him hand-and-foot this two months back. Perhaps we had better go in at once, for I know how impatient he is."

The chamber into which we were shown

He clutched her hand to detain her. "How are you, Watson?" said he, cordially. "I should never have known you under that moustache, and I daresay you would not be prepared to swear to me. This I presume is your celebrated friend, Mr. Sherlock Holmes?"

I introduced him in a few words, and we both sat down. The stout young man had left us, but his sister still remained, with her hand in that of the invalid. She was a striking-looking woman, a little short and thick for symmetry, but with a beautiful olive complexion, large, dark Italian eyes, and a wealth of deep black hair. Her rich tints made the white face of her companion the more worn and haggard by the contrast.

"I won't waste your time," said he, raising

"'I WON'T WASTE YOUR TIME,' SAID HE."

was on the same floor as the drawing-room. It was furnished partly as a sitting and partly as a bedroom, with flowers arranged daintily in every nook and corner. A young man, very pale and worn, was lying upon a sofa near the open window, through which came the rich scent of the garden and the balmy summer air. A woman was sitting beside him, and rose as we entered.

"Shall I leave, Percy?" she asked.

himself upon the sofa. "I'll plunge into the matter without further preamble. I was a happy and successful man, Mr. Holmes, and on the eve of being married, when a sudden and dreadful misfortune wrecked all my prospects in life.

"I was, as Watson may have told you, in the Foreign Office, and through the influence of my uncle, Lord Holdhurst, I rose rapidly to a responsible position. When my uncle became Foreign Minister in this Administration he gave me several missions of trust, and as I always brought them to a successful conclusion, he came at last to have the utmost confidence in my ability and tact.

"Nearly ten weeks ago—to be more accurate, on the 23rd of May—he called me into his private room and, after complimenting me upon the good work which I had done, he informed me that he had a new commission of trust for me to execute.

"'This,' said he, taking a grey roll of paper from his bureau, 'is the original of that secret treaty between England and Italy of which, I regret to say, some rumours have already got into the public Press. It is of enormous importance that nothing further should leak out. The French or Russian Embassies would pay an immense sum to learn the contents of these papers. They should not leave my bureau were it not that it is absolutely necessary to have them copied. You have a desk in your office?'

"'Yes, sir.'

"'Then take the treaty and lock it up there. I shall give directions that you may remain behind when the others go, so that

"THEN TAKE THE TREATY."

you may copy it at your leisure, without fear of being overlooked. When you have finished, re-lock both the original and the draft in the desk, and hand them over to me personally to-morrow morning.'

"I took the papers and—— "

"Excuse me an instant," said Holmes; "were you alone during this conversation?"

"Absolutely."

"In a large room?"

"Thirty feet each way."

"In the centre?"

"Yes, about it."

"And speaking low?"

"My uncle's voice is always remarkably low. I hardly spoke at all."

"Thank you," said Holmes, shutting his eyes; "pray go on."

"I did exactly what he had indicated, and waited until the other clerks had departed. One of them in my room, Charles Gorot, had some arrears of work to make up, so I left him there and went out to dine. When I returned he was gone. I was anxious to hurry my work, for I knew that Joseph, the Mr. Harrison whom you saw just now, was in town, and that he would travel down to Woking by the eleven o'clock train, and I wanted if possible to catch it.

"When I came to examine the treaty I saw at once that it was of such importance that my uncle had been guilty of no exaggeration in what he had said. Without going into details, I may say that it defined the position of Great Britain towards the Triple Alliance, and foreshadowed the policy which this country would pursue in the event of the French fleet gaining a complete ascendency over that of Italy in the Mediterranean. The questions treated in it were purely naval. At the end were the signatures of the high dignitaries who had signed it. I glanced my eyes over it, and then settled down to my task of copying.

"It was a long document, written in the French language, and containing twenty-six separate articles. I copied as quickly as I could, but at nine o'clock I had only done nine articles, and it seemed hopeless for me to attempt to catch my train. I was feeling drowsy and stupid, partly from my dinner and also from the effects of a long day's work. A cup of coffee would clear my brain. A commissionaire remains all night in a little lodge at the foot of the stairs, and is in the habit of making coffee at his spirit-lamp for any of the officials who may be working over-time. I rang the bell, therefore, to summon him.

"To my surprise, it was a woman who answered the summons, a large, coarse-faced, elderly woman, in an apron. She explained that she was the commissionaire's wife, who did the charing, and I gave her the order for the coffee.

"I wrote two more articles, and then, feeling more drowsy than ever, I rose and walked up and down the room to stretch my legs. My coffee had not yet come, and I wondered what the cause of the delay could be. Opening the door, I started down the corridor to find out. There was a straight passage dimly lighted which led from the room in which I had been working, and was the only exit from it. It ended in a curving staircase, with the commissionaire's lodge in the passage at the bottom. Half-way down this staircase is a small landing, with another passage running into it at right angles. This second one leads, by means of a second small stair, to a side door used by servants, and also as a short cut by clerks when coming from Charles Street. Here is a rough chart of the place."

"Thank you. I think that I quite follow you," said Sherlock Holmes.

"FAST ASLEEP IN HIS BOX."

"It is of the utmost importance that you should notice this point. I went down the stairs and into the hall, where I found the commissionaire fast asleep in his box, with the kettle boiling furiously upon the spirit-lamp, for the water was spurting over the floor. Then I put out my hand and was about to shake the man, who was still sleeping soundly, when a bell over his head rang loudly, and he woke with a start.

"'Mr. Phelps, sir!' said he, looking at me in bewilderment.

"'I came down to see if my coffee was ready.'

"'I was boiling the kettle when I fell asleep, sir.' He looked at me and then up at the still quivering bell, with an ever-growing astonishment upon his face.

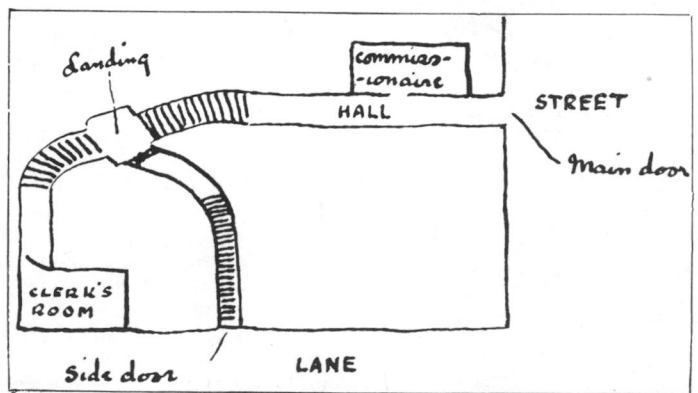

"HERE IS A ROUGH CHART OF THE PLACE,"

" 'If you was here, sir, then who rang the bell?' he asked.

" 'The bell!' I said. 'What bell is it?'

" 'It's the bell of the room you were working in.'

"A cold hand seemed to close round my heart. Someone, then, was in that room where my precious treaty lay upon the table. I ran frantically up the stairs and along the passage. There was no one in the corridors, Mr. Holmes. There was no one in the room. All was exactly as I left it, save only that the papers committed to my care had been taken from the desk on which they lay. The copy was there and the original was gone."

Holmes sat up in his chair and rubbed his hands. I could see that the problem was entirely to his heart. " Pray, what did you do then?" he murmured.

" I recognised in an instant that the thief must have come up the stairs from the side door. Of course, I must have met him if he had come the other way."

" You were satisfied that he could not have been concealed in the room all the time, or in the corridor which you have just described as dimly lighted?"

" It is absolutely impossible. A rat could not conceal himself either in the room or the corridor. There is no cover at all."

" Thank you. Pray proceed."

" The commissionaire, seeing by my pale face that something was to be feared, had followed me upstairs. Now we both rushed along the corridor and down the steep steps which led to Charles Street. The door at the bottom was closed but unlocked. We flung it open and rushed out. I can distinctly remember that as we did so there came three chimes from a neighbouring church. It was a quarter to ten."

" That is of enormous importance," said Holmes, making a note upon his shirt cuff.

" The night was very dark, and a thin, warm rain was falling. There was no one in Charles Street, but a great traffic was going on, as usual, in Whitehall at the extremity. We rushed along the pavement, bareheaded as we were, and at the far corner we found a policeman standing.

" 'A robbery has been committed,' I gasped. 'A document of immense value has been stolen from the Foreign Office. Has anyone passed this way?'

" 'I have been standing here for a quarter of an hour, sir,' said he; 'only one person has passed during that time—a woman, tall and elderly, with a Paisley shawl.'

" 'Ah, that is only my wife,' cried the commissionaire. 'Has no one else passed?'

" 'No one.'

" 'Then it must be the other way that the thief took,' cried the fellow, tugging at my sleeve.

" But I was not satisfied, and the attempts which he made to draw me away increased my suspicions.

" 'Which way did the woman go?' I cried.

" 'I don't know, sir. I noticed her pass, but I had no special reason for watching her. She seemed to be in a hurry.'

" 'How long ago was it?'

" 'Oh, not very many minutes.'

" 'Within the last five?'

" 'Well, it could not be more than five.'

" 'You're only wasting your time, sir, and every minute now is of importance,' cried the commissionaire. 'Take my word for it that my old woman has nothing to do with it, and come down to the other end of the street. Well, if you won't I will,' and with that he rushed off in the other direction.

" But I was after him in an instant and caught him by the sleeve.

" 'Where do you live?' said I.

" 'No. 16, Ivy Lane, Brixton,' he answered; ' but don't let yourself be drawn away upon a false scent, Mr. Phelps. Come to the other end of the street, and let us see if we can hear of anything.'

" Nothing was to be lost by following his advice. With the policeman we both hurried down, but only to find the street full of traffic, many people coming and going, but all only too eager to get to a place of safety upon so wet a night. There was no lounger who could tell us who had passed.

" Then we returned to the office, and searched the stairs and the passage without result. The corridor which led to the room was laid down with a kind of creamy linoleum which shows an impression very easily. We examined it very carefully, but found no outline of any footmark."

" Had it been raining all the evening?"

" Since about seven."

" How is it, then, that the woman who came into the room about nine left no traces with her muddy boots?"

" I am glad you raise the point. It occurred to me at the time. The charwomen are in the habit of taking off their boots at the commissionaire's office, and putting on list slippers."

" That is very clear. There were no marks, then, though the night was a wet one? The chain of events is certainly one of extraordinary interest. What did you do next?"

"We examined the room also. There is no possibility of a secret door, and the windows are quite thirty feet from the ground. Both of them were fastened on the inside. The carpet prevents any possibility of a trap-door, and the ceiling is of the ordinary white-washed kind. I will pledge my life that whoever stole my papers could only have come through the door."

"How about the fireplace?"

"They use none. There is a stove. The bell-rope hangs from the wire just to the right of my desk. Whoever rang it must have come right up to the desk to do it. But why should any criminal wish to ring the bell? It is a most insoluble mystery."

"Certainly the incident was unusual. What were your next steps? You examined the room, I presume, to see if the intruder had left any traces—any cigar end, or dropped glove, or hairpin, or other trifle?"

"There was nothing of the sort."

"No smell?"

"Well, we never thought of that."

"Ah, a scent of tobacco would have been worth a great deal to us in such an investigation."

"I never smoke myself, so I think I should have observed it if there had been any smell of tobacco. There was absolutely no clue of any kind. The only tangible fact was that the commissionaire's wife—Mrs. Tangey was the name—had hurried out of the place. He could give no explanation save that it was about the time when the woman always went home. The policeman and I agreed that our best plan would be to seize the woman before she could get rid of the papers, presuming that she had them.

"The alarm had reached Scotland Yard by this time, and Mr. Forbes, the detective, came round at once and took up the case with a great deal of energy. We hired a hansom, and in half an hour we were at the address which had been given to us. A young woman opened the door, who proved to be Mrs. Tangey's eldest daughter. Her mother had not come back yet, and we were shown into the front room to wait.

"About ten minutes later a knock came at the door, and here we made the one serious mistake for which I blame myself. Instead of opening the door ourselves we allowed the girl to do so. We heard her say, 'Mother, there are two men in the house waiting to see you,' and an instant afterwards we heard the patter of feet rushing down the passage. Forbes flung open the door, and we both ran into the back room or kitchen, but the woman had got there before us. She stared at us with defiant eyes, and then suddenly recognising me, an expres-

"WHY, IF IT ISN'T MR. PHELPS!"

sion of absolute astonishment came over her face.

"'Why, if it isn't Mr. Phelps, of the office!' she cried.

"'Come, come, who did you think we were when you ran away from us?' asked my companion.

"'I thought you were the brokers,' said she. 'We've had some trouble with a tradesman.'

"'That's not quite good enough,' answered Forbes. 'We have reason to believe that you have taken a paper of importance from the Foreign Office, and that you ran in here to dispose of it. You must come back with us to Scotland Yard to be searched.'

"It was in vain that she protested and resisted. A four-wheeler was brought, and we all three drove back in it. We had first made an examination of the kitchen, and especially of the kitchen fire, to see whether she might have made away with the papers during the instant that she was alone. There were no signs, however, of any ashes or scraps. When we reached Scotland Yard she was handed over at once to the female searcher. I waited in an agony of suspense until she came back with her report. There were no signs of the papers.

"Then, for the first time, the horror of my situation came in its full force upon me. Hitherto I had been acting, and action had numbed thought. I had been so confident of regaining the treaty at once that I had not dared to think of what would be the consequence if I failed to do so. But now there was nothing more to be done, and I had leisure to realize my position. It was horrible! Watson there would tell you that I was a nervous, sensitive boy at school. It is my nature. I thought of my uncle and of his colleagues in the Cabinet, of the shame which I had brought upon him upon myself, upon everyone connected with me. What though I was the victim of an extraordinary accident? No allowance is made for accidents where diplomatic interests are at stake. I was ruined; shamefully, hopelessly ruined. I don't know what I did. I fancy I must have made a scene. I have a dim recollection of a group of officials who crowded round me endeavouring to soothe me. One of them drove down with me to Waterloo and saw me into the Woking train. I believe that he would have come all the way had it not been that Dr. Ferrier, who lives near me, was going down by that very train. The doctor most kindly took charge of me, and it was well he did so, for I had a fit in the station, and before we reached home I was practically a raving maniac.

"You can imagine the state of things here when they were roused from their beds by the doctor's ringing, and found me in this condition. Poor Annie here and my mother were broken-hearted. Dr. Ferrier had just heard enough from the detective at the station to be able to give an idea of what had happened, and his story did not mend matters. It was evident to all that I was in for a long illness, so Joseph was bundled out of this cheery bedroom, and it was turned into a sick room for me. Here I have lain, Mr. Holmes, for over nine weeks, unconscious, and raving with brain fever. If it had not been for Miss Harrison here and for the doctor's care, I should not be speaking to you now. She has nursed me by day, and a hired nurse has looked after me by night, for in my mad fits I was capable of anything. Slowly my reason has cleared, but it is only during the last three days that my memory has quite returned. Sometimes I wish that it never had. The first thing that I did was to wire to Mr. Forbes, who had the case in hand. He came out and assured me that, though everything has been done, no trace of a clue has been discovered. The commissionaire and his wife have been examined in every way without any light being thrown upon the matter. The suspicions of the police then rested upon young Gorot, who, as you may remember, stayed overtime in the office that night. His remaining behind and his French name were really the only two points which could suggest suspicion; but as a matter of fact, I did not begin work until he had gone, and his people are of Huguenot extraction, but as English in sympathy and tradition as you and I are. Nothing was found to implicate him in any way, and there the matter dropped. I turn to you, Mr. Holmes, as absolutely my last hope. If you fail me, then my honour as well as my position are for ever forfeited."

The invalid sank back upon his cushions, tired out by this long recital, while his nurse poured him out a glass of some stimulating medicine. Holmes sat silently with his head thrown back and his eyes closed in an attitude which might seem listless to a stranger, but which I knew betokened the most intense absorption.

"Your statement has been so explicit," said he at last, "that you have really left me very few questions to ask. There is one of the very utmost importance, however. Did you tell anyone that you had this special task to perform?"

"No one."

"Not Miss Harrison here, for example?"

"No. I had not been back to Woking between getting the order and executing the commission."

"And none of your people had by chance been to see you?"

"None.".

"Did any of them know their way about in the office?"

"Oh, yes; all of them had been shown over it."

"Still, of course, if you said nothing to any one about the treaty, these inquiries are irrelevant."

"I said nothing."

"Do you know anything of the commissionaire?"

"Nothing, except that he is an old soldier."

"What regiment?"

"Oh, I have heard—Coldstream Guards."

"Thank you. I have no doubt I can get details from Forbes. The authorities are excellent at amassing facts, though they do not always use them to advantage. What a lovely thing a rose is!"

He walked past the couch to the open window, and held up the drooping stalk of a moss rose, looking down at the dainty blend of crimson and green. It was a new phase of his character to me, for I had never before seen him show any keen interest in natural objects.

"There is nothing in which deduction is so necessary as in religion," said he, leaning with his back against the shutters. "It can be built up as an exact science by the reasoner. Our highest assurance of the goodness of Providence seems to me to rest in the flowers. All other things, our powers, our desires, our food, are really necessary for our existence in the first instance. But this rose is an extra. Its smell and its colour are an embellishment of life, not a condition

"WHAT A LOVELY THING A ROSE IS.

of it. It is only goodness which gives extras, and so I say again that we have much to hope from the flowers."

Percy Phelps and his nurse looked at Holmes during this demonstration with surprise and a good deal of disappointment written upon their faces. He had fallen into a reverie, with the moss rose between his fingers. It had lasted some minutes before the young lady broke in upon it.

"Do you see any prospect of solving this mystery, Mr. Holmes?" she asked, with a touch of asperity in her voice.

"Oh, the mystery!" he answered, coming back with a start to the realities of life. "Well, it would be absurd to deny that the case is a very abstruse and complicated one; but I can promise you that I will look into the matter and let you know any points which may strike me."

"Do you see any clue?"

"You have furnished me with seven, but of course I must test them before I can pronounce upon their value."

"You suspect someone?"

"I suspect myself—"

"What?"

"Of coming to conclusions too rapidly."

"Then go to London and test your conclusions."

"Your advice is very excellent, Miss Harrison," said Holmes, rising. "I think, Watson, we cannot do better. Do not allow yourself to indulge in false hopes, Mr. Phelps. The affair is a very tangled one."

"I shall be in a fever until I see you again," cried the diplomatist.

"Well, I'll come out by the same train to-morrow, though it's more than likely that my report will be a negative one."

"God bless you for promising to come," cried our client. "It gives me fresh life to know that something is being done. By the way, I have had a letter from Lord Holdhurst."

"Ha, what did he say?"

"He was cold, but not harsh. I daresay my severe illness prevented him from being that. He repeated that the matter was of the utmost importance, and added that no steps would be taken about my future—by which he means, of course, my dismissal—until my health was restored and I had an opportunity of repairing my misfortune."

"Well, that was reasonable and considerate," said Holmes. "Come, Watson, for we have a good day's work before us in town."

Mr. Joseph Harrison drove us down to the station, and we were soon whirling up in a Portsmouth train. Holmes was sunk in profound thought, and hardly opened his mouth until we had passed Clapham Junction.

"It's a very cheering thing to come into London by any of these lines which run high and allow you to look down upon the houses like this."

I thought he was joking, for the view was sordid enough, but he soon explained himself.

"THE VIEW WAS SORDID ENOUGH."

"Look at those big, isolated clumps of building rising up above the slates, like brick islands in a lead-coloured sea."

"The Board schools."

"Lighthouses, my boy! Beacons of the future! Capsules, with hundreds of bright little seeds in each, out of which will spring the wiser, better England of the future. I suppose that man Phelps does not drink?"

"I should not think so."

"Nor should I. But we are bound to take every possibility into account. The poor devil has certainly got himself into very hot water, and it's a question whether we shall ever be able to get him ashore. What did you think of Miss Harrison?"

"A girl of strong character."

"Yes, but she is a good sort, or I am mistaken. She and her brother are the only children of an ironmaster somewhere up Northumberland way. He got engaged to her when travelling last winter, and she came down to be introduced to his people, with her brother as escort. Then came the smash, and she stayed on to nurse her lover, while brother Joseph, finding himself pretty snug, stayed on too. I've been making a few independent inquiries, you see. But to-day must be a day of inquiries."

"My practice——" I began.

"Oh, if you find your own cases more interesting than mine——" said Holmes, with some asperity.

"I was going to say that my practice could get along very well for a day or two, since it is the slackest time in the year."

"Excellent!" said he, recovering his good humour. "Then we'll look into this matter together. I think that we should begin by seeing Forbes. He can probably tell us all the details we want, until we know from what side the case is to be approached."

"You said you had a clue."

"Well, we have several, but we can only test their value by further inquiry. The most difficult crime to track is the one which is purposeless. Now, this is not purposeless. Who is it that profits by it? There is the

French Ambassador, there is the Russian, there is whoever might sell it to either of these, and there is Lord Holdhurst."

"Lord Holdhurst!"

"Well, it is just conceivable that a statesman might find himself in a position where he was not sorry to have such a document accidentally destroyed."

"Not a statesman with the honourable record of Lord Holdhurst."

"It is a possibility, and we cannot afford to disregard it. We shall see the noble lord to-day, and find out if he can tell us anything. Meanwhile, I have already set inquiries upon foot."

"Already?"

"Yes, I sent wires from Woking Station to every evening paper in London. This advertisement will appear in each of them."

He handed over a sheet torn from a note-book. On it was scribbled in pencil :—

"£10 Reward.—The number of the cab which dropped a fare at or about the door of the Foreign Office in Charles Street, at a quarter to ten in the evening of May 23rd. Apply 221B, Baker Street."

"You are confident that the thief came in a cab?"

"If not, there is no harm done. But if Mr. Phelps is correct in stating that there is no hiding-place either in the room or the corridors, then the person must have come from outside. If he came from outside on so wet a night, and yet left no trace of damp upon the linoleum which was examined within a few minutes of his passing, then it is exceedingly probable that he came in a cab. Yes, I think that we may safely deduce a cab."

"It sounds plausible."

"That is one of the clues of which I spoke. It may lead us to something. And then, of course, there is the bell—which is the most distinctive feature of the case. Why should the bell ring? Was it the thief that did it out of bravado? Or was it someone who was with the thief who did it in order to prevent the crime? Or was it an accident? Or was it —— ?" He sank back into the state of intense and silent thought from which he had emerged, but it seemed to me, accustomed as I was to

his every mood, that some new possibility had dawned suddenly upon him.

It was twenty past three when we reached our terminus, and after a hasty luncheon at the buffet we pushed on at once to Scotland Yard. Holmes had already wired to Forbes, and we found him waiting to receive us: a small, foxy man, with a sharp but by no means amiable expression. He was decidedly frigid in his manner to us, especially when he heard the errand upon which we had come.

"I've heard of your methods before now, Mr. Holmes," said he, tartly. "You are

"I'VE HEARD OF YOUR METHODS BEFORE NOW, MR. HOLMES."

ready enough to use all the information that the police can lay at your disposal, and then you try to finish the case yourself and bring discredit upon them."

"On the contrary," said Holmes; "out of my last fifty-three cases my name has only appeared in four, and the police have had all the credit in forty-nine. I don't blame you for not knowing this, for you are young and inexperienced; but if you wish to get on in your new duties you will work with me, and not against me."

"I'd be very glad of a hint or two," said the detective, changing his manner. "I've certainly had no credit from the case so far."

"What steps have you taken?"

"Tangey, the commissionaire, has been shadowed. He left the Guards with a good character, and we can find nothing against him. His wife is a bad lot, though. I fancy she knows more about this than appears."

"Have you shadowed her?"

"We have set one of our women on to her. Mrs. Tangey drinks, and our woman has been with her twice when she was well on, but she could get nothing out of her."

"I understand that they have had brokers in the house?"

"Yes, but they were paid off."

"Where did the money come from?"

"That was all right. His pension was due. They have not shown any sign of being in funds."

"What explanation did she give of having answered the bell when Mr. Phelps rang for the coffee?"

"She said that her husband was very tired and she wished to relieve him."

"Well, certainly that would agree with his being found, a little later, asleep in his chair. There is nothing against them, then, but the woman's character. Did you ask her why she hurried away that night? Her haste attracted the attention of the police constable."

"She was later than usual, and wanted to get home."

"Did you point out to her that you and Mr. Phelps, who started at least **twenty** minutes after her, got home before her?"

"She explains that by the difference between a 'bus and a hansom."

"Did she make it clear why, on reaching her house, she ran into the back kitchen?"

"Because she had the money there with which to pay off the brokers."

"She has at least an answer for everything. Did you ask her whether in leaving she met anyone or saw anyone loitering about Charles Street?"

"She saw no one but the constable."

"Well, you seem to have cross-examined her pretty thoroughly. What else have you done?"

"The clerk, Gorot, has been shadowed all these nine weeks, but without result. We can show nothing against him."

"Anything else?"

"Well, we have nothing else to go upon—no evidence of any kind."

"Have you formed any theory about how that bell rang?"

"Well, I must confess that it beats me. It was a cool hand, whoever it was, to go and give the alarm like that."

"Yes, it was a queer thing to do. Many thanks to you for what you have told me. If I can put the man into your hands you shall hear from me. Come along, Watson!"

"Where are we going to now?" I asked, as we left the office.

"We are now going to interview **Lord** Holdhurst, the Cabinet Minister and **future** Premier of England."

*(To be concluded next month.)*

# The Adventures of Sherlock Holmes.

## By A. Conan Doyle.

### XXIII.—THE ADVENTURE OF THE NAVAL TREATY.

*(Continued from page 403.)*

WE were fortunate in finding that Lord Holdhurst was still in his chambers at Downing Street, and on Holmes sending in his card we were instantly shown up. The statesman received us with that old-fashioned courtesy for which he is remarkable, and seated us on the two luxurious easy chairs on either side of the fireplace. Standing on the rug between us, with his slight, tall figure, his sharp-featured, thoughtful face, and his curling hair prematurely tinged with grey, he seemed to represent that not too common type, a nobleman who is in truth noble.

"Your name is very familiar to me, Mr. Holmes," said he, smiling. "And, of course, I cannot pretend to be ignorant of the object of your visit. There has only been one occurrence in these offices which could call for your attention. In whose interest are you acting, may I ask?"

"In that of Mr. Percy Phelps," answered Holmes.

"Ah, my unfortunate nephew! You can understand that our kinship makes it the more impossible for me to screen him in any way. I fear that the incident must have a very prejudicial effect upon his career."

"But if the document is found?"

"Ah, that, of course, would be different."

"I had one or two questions which I wished to ask you, Lord Holdhurst."

"A NOBLEMAN."

"I shall be happy to give you any information in my power."

"Was it in this room that you gave your

instructions as to the copying of the document?"

"It was."

"Then you could hardly have been overheard?"

"It is out of the question."

"Did you ever mention to anyone that it was your intention to give out the treaty to be copied?"

"Never."

"You are certain of that?"

"Absolutely."

"Well, since you never said so, and Mr. Phelps never said so, and nobody else knew anything of the matter, then the thief's presence in the room was purely accidental. He saw his chance and he took it."

The statesman smiled. "You take me out of my province there," said he.

Holmes considered for a moment. "There is another very important point which I wish to discuss with you," said he. "You feared, as I understand, that very grave results might follow from the details of this treaty becoming known?"

A shadow passed over the expressive face of the statesman. "Very grave results, indeed."

"And have they occurred?"

"Not yet."

"If the treaty had reached, let us say, the French or Russian Foreign Office, you would expect to hear of it?"

"I should," said Lord Holdhurst, with a wry face.

"Since nearly ten weeks have elapsed then, and nothing has been heard, it is not unfair to suppose that for some reason the treaty has not reached them?"

Lord Holdhurst shrugged his shoulders.

"We can hardly suppose, Mr. Holmes, that the thief took the treaty in order to frame it and hang it up."

"Perhaps he is waiting for a better price."

"If he waits a little longer he will get no price at all. The treaty will cease to be a secret in a few months."

"That is most important," said Holmes. "Of course it is a possible supposition that the thief has had a sudden illness——"

"An attack of brain fever, for example?" asked the statesman, flashing a swift glance at him.

"I did not say so," said Holmes, imperturbably. "And now, Lord Holdhurst, we have already taken up too much of your valuable time, and we shall wish you goodday."

"Every success to your investigation, be the criminal who it may," answered the nobleman, as he bowed us out at the door.

"He's a fine fellow," said Holmes, as we came out into Whitehall. "But he has a struggle to keep up his position. He is far from rich, and has many calls. You noticed, of course, that his boots had been re-soled? Now, Watson, I won't detain you from your legitimate work any longer. I shall do nothing more to-day, unless I have an answer to my cab advertisement. But I should be extremely obliged to you if you would come down with me to Woking to-morrow, by the same train which we took to-day."

I met him accordingly next morning, and we travelled down to Woking together. He had had no answer to his advertisement, he said, and no fresh light had been thrown upon the case. He had, when he so willed it, the utter immobility of countenance of a red Indian, and I could not gather from his appearance whether he was satisfied or not with the position of the case. His conversation, I remember, was about the Bertillon system of measurements, and he expressed his enthusiastic admiration of the French savant.

We found our client still under the charge of his devoted nurse, but looking considerably better than before. He rose from the sofa and greeted us without difficulty when we entered.

"Any news?" he asked, eagerly.

"My report, as I expected, is a negative one," said Holmes. "I have seen Forbes, and I have seen your uncle, and I have set one or two trains of inquiry upon foot which may lead to something."

"You have not lost heart, then?"

"By no means."

"God bless you for saying that!" cried Miss Harrison. "If we keep our courage and our patience, the truth must come out."

"We have more to tell you than you have for us," said Phelps, reseating himself upon the couch.

"I hoped you might have something."

"Yes, we have had an adventure during the night, and one which might have proved to be a serious one," his expression grew very grave as he spoke, and a look of something akin to fear sprang up in his eyes. "Do you know," said he, "that I begin to believe that I am the unconscious centre of some monstrous conspiracy, and that my life is aimed at as well as my honour?"

"Ah!" cried Holmes.

"It sounds incredible, for I have not, as

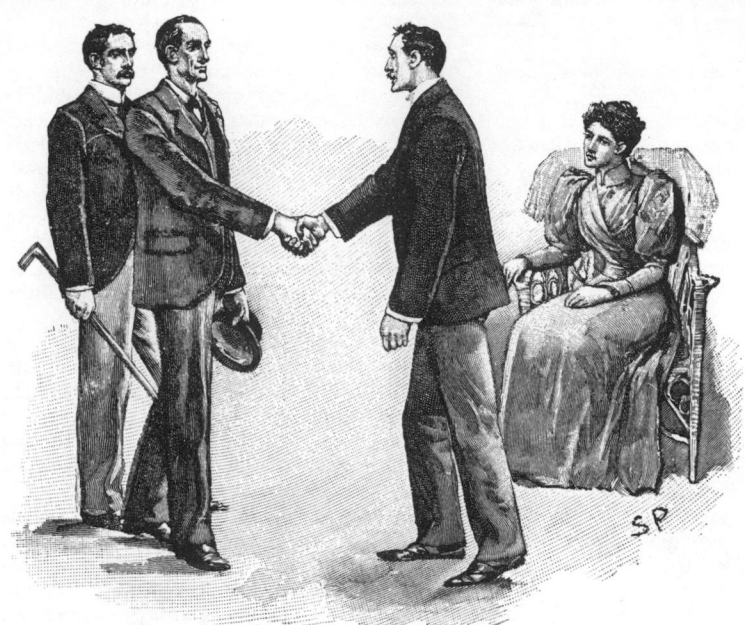

"'ANY NEWS?' HE ASKED."

shutters. A man was crouching at the window. I could see little of him, for he was gone like a flash. He was wrapped in some sort of cloak, which came across the lower part of his face. One thing only I am sure of, and that is that he had some weapon in his hand. It looked to me like a long knife. I distinctly saw the gleam of it as he turned to run."

"This is most interesting," said Holmes. "Pray, what did you do then?"

"I should have followed him through the open window if I had been stronger. As it was, I rang the bell and roused the house. It took me some little time, for the bell rings in the kitchen, and the servants all sleep upstairs. I shouted, however, and that brought Joseph down, and he roused the others. Joseph and the groom found marks on the flower-bed outside the window, but the weather has been so dry lately that they found it hopeless to follow the trail across the grass. There's a place, however, on the wooden fence which skirts the road which shows signs, they tell me, as if someone had got over and had snapped the top of the rail in doing so. I have said nothing to the local police yet, for I thought I had best have your opinion first."

This tale of our client's appeared to have an extraordinary effect upon Sherlock Holmes. He rose from his chair and paced about the room in incontrollable excitement.

"Misfortunes never come singly," said Phelps, smiling, though it was evident that his adventure had somewhat shaken him.

"You have certainly had your share," said Holmes. "Do you think you could walk round the house with me?"

"Oh, yes, I should like a little sunshine. Joseph will come too."

"And I also," said Miss Harrison.

far as I know, an enemy in the world. Yet from last night's experience I can come to no other conclusion."

"Pray let me hear it."

"You must know that last night was the very first night that I have ever slept without a nurse in the room. I was so much better that I thought I could dispense with one. I had a night-light burning, however. Well, about two in the morning I had sunk into a light sleep, when I was suddenly aroused by a slight noise. It was like the sound which a mouse makes when it is gnawing a plank, and I lay listening to it for some time, under the impression that it must come from that cause. Then it grew louder, and suddenly there came from the window a sharp metallic snick. I sat up in amazement. There could be no doubt what the sounds were now. The faint ones had been caused by someone forcing an instrument through the slit between the sashes, and the second by the catch being pressed back.

"There was a pause then for about ten minutes, as if the person were waiting to see whether the noise had awoken me. Then I heard a gentle creaking as the window was very slowly opened. I could stand it no longer, for my nerves are not what they used to be. I sprang out of bed and flung open the

"I am afraid not," said Holmes, shaking his head. "I think I must ask you to remain sitting exactly where you are."

The young lady resumed her seat with an air of displeasure. Her brother, however, had joined us, and we set off all four together. We passed round the lawn to the outside of the young diplomatist's window. There were, as he had said, marks upon the flower-bed, but they were hopelessly blurred and vague. Holmes stooped over them for an instant, and then rose, shrugging his shoulders.

"I don't think anyone could make much of this," said he. "Let us go round the house and see why this particular room was chosen by the burglar. I should have thought those larger windows of the drawing-room and dining-room would have had more attractions for him."

"They are more visible from the road," suggested Mr. Joseph Harrison.

"Ah, yes, of course. There is a door here which he might have attempted. What is it for?"

"It is the side entrance for tradespeople. Of course, it is locked at night."

"Have you ever had an alarm like this before?"

"Never," said our client.

"Do you keep plate in the house, or anything to attract burglars?"

"Nothing of value."

Holmes strolled round the house with his hands in his pockets, and a negligent air which was unusual with him.

"By the way," said he, to Joseph Harrison, "you found some place, I understand, where

"HOLMES EXAMINED IT CRITICALLY."

the fellow scaled the fence. Let us have a look at that."

The plump young man led us to a spot where the top of one of the wooden rails had been cracked. A small fragment of the wood was hanging down. Holmes pulled it off and examined it critically.

"Do you think that was done last night? It looks rather old, does it not?"

"Well, possibly so."

"There are no marks of anyone jumping down upon the other side. No, I fancy we shall get no help here. Let us go back to the bedroom and talk the matter over."

Percy Phelps was walking very slowly, leaning upon the arm of his future brother-in-law. Holmes walked swiftly across the lawn, and we were at the open window of the bedroom long before the others came up.

"Miss Harrison," said Holmes, speaking with the utmost intensity of manner. "You must stay where you are all day. Let nothing prevent you from staying where you are all day. It is of the utmost importance."

"Certainly, if you wish it, Mr. Holmes," said the girl, in astonishment.

"When you go to bed lock the door of this room on the outside and keep the key. Promise to do this."

"But Percy?"

"He will come to London with us."

"And I am to remain here?"

"It is for his sake. You can serve him! Quick! Promise!"

She gave a quick nod of assent just as the other two came up.

"Why do you sit moping there, Annie?" cried her brother. "Come out into the sunshine!"

"No, thank you, Joseph. I have a slight headache, and this room is deliciously cool and soothing."

"What do you propose now, Mr. Holmes?" asked our client.

"Well, in investigating this minor affair we must not lose sight of our main inquiry. It would be a very great help to me if you would come up to London with us."

"At once?"

"Well, as soon as you conveniently can. Say in an hour."

"I feel quite strong enough, if I can really be of any help."

"The greatest possible."

"Perhaps you would like me to stay there to-night?"

"I was just going to propose it."

"Then if my friend of the night comes to revisit me, he will find the bird flown. We are all in your hands, Mr. Holmes, and you must tell us exactly what you would like done. Perhaps you would prefer that Joseph came with us, so as to look after me?"

"Oh, no; my friend Watson is a medical man, you know, and he'll look after you. We'll have our lunch here, if you will permit us, and then we shall all three set off for town together."

It was arranged as he suggested, though Miss Harrison excused herself from leaving the bedroom, in accordance with Holmes's suggestion. What the object of my friend's manœuvres was I could not conceive, unless it were to keep the lady away from Phelps, who, rejoiced by his returning health and by the prospect of action, lunched with us in the dining-room. Holmes had a still more startling surprise for us, however, for after accompanying us down to the station and seeing us into our carriage, he calmly announced that he had no intention of leaving Woking.

"There are one or two small points which I should

desire to clear up before I go," said he. "Your absence, Mr. Phelps, will in some ways rather assist me. Watson, when you reach London you would oblige me by driving at once to Baker Street with our friend here, and remaining with him until I see you again. It is fortunate that you are old schoolfellows, as you must have much to talk over. Mr. Phelps can have the spare bedroom to-night, and I will be with you in time for breakfast, for there is a train which will take me into Waterloo at eight."

"But how about our investigation in London?" asked Phelps, ruefully.

"We can do that to-morrow. I think that just at present I can be of more immediate use here."

"You might tell them at Briarbrae that I hope to be back to-morrow night," cried Phelps, as we began to move from the platform.

"I hardly expect to go back to Briarbrae,"

I HARDLY EXPECT TO GO BACK TO BRIARBRAE.

answered Holmes, and waved his hand to us cheerily as we shot out from the station.

Phelps and I talked it over on our journey, but neither of us could devise a satisfactory reason for this new development.

"I suppose he wants to find out some clue as to the burglary last night, if a burglar it was. For myself, I don't believe it was an ordinary thief."

"What is your own idea, then?"

"Upon my word, you may put it down to my weak nerves or not, but I believe there is some deep political intrigue going on around me, and that, for some reason that passes my understanding, my life is aimed at by the conspirators. It sounds high-flown and absurd, but consider the facts! Why should a thief try to break in at a bedroom window, where there could be no hope of any plunder, and why should he come with a long knife in his hand?"

"You are sure it was not a housebreaker's jemmy?"

"Oh, no; it was a knife. I saw the flash of the blade quite distinctly."

"But why on earth should you be pursued with such animosity?"

"Ah, that is the question."

"Well, if Holmes takes the same view, that would account for his action, would it not? Presuming that your theory is correct, if he can lay his hands upon the man who threatened you last night, he will have gone a long way towards finding who took the naval treaty. It is absurd to suppose that you have two enemies, one of whom robs you while the other threatens your life."

"But Mr. Holmes said that he was not going to Briarbrae."

"I have known him for some time," said I, "but I never knew him do anything yet without a very good reason," and with that our conversation drifted off into other topics.

But it was a weary day for me. Phelps was still weak after his long illness, and his misfortunes made him querulous and nervous. In vain I endeavoured to interest him in Afghanistan, in India, in social questions, in anything which might take his mind out of the groove. He would always come back to his lost treaty; wondering, guessing, speculating as to what Holmes was doing, what steps Lord Holdhurst was taking, what news we should have in the morning. As the evening wore on, his excitement became quite painful.

"You have implicit faith in Holmes?" he asked.

"I have seen him do some remarkable things."

"But he never brought light into anything quite so dark as this?"

"Oh, yes; I have known him solve questions which presented fewer clues than yours."

"But not where such large interests are at stake?"

"I don't know that. To my certain knowledge he has acted on behalf of three of the reigning Houses of Europe in very vital matters."

"But you know him well, Watson. He is such an inscrutable fellow, that I never quite know what to make of him. Do you think he is hopeful? Do you think he expects to make a success of it?"

"He has said nothing."

"That is a bad sign."

"On the contrary, I have noticed that when he is off the trail he generally says so. It is when he is on a scent, and is not quite absolutely sure yet that it is the right one, that he is most taciturn. Now, my dear fellow, we can't help matters by making ourselves nervous about them, so let me implore you to go to bed, and so be fresh for whatever may await us to-morrow."

I was able at last to persuade my companion to take my advice, though I knew from his excited manner that there was not much hope of sleep for him. Indeed, his mood was infectious, for I lay tossing half the night myself, brooding over this strange problem, and inventing a hundred theories each of which was more impossible than the last. Why had Holmes remained at Woking? Why had he asked Miss Harrison to remain in the sick room all day? Why had he been so careful not to inform the people at Briarbrae that he intended to remain near them? I cudgelled my brains until I fell asleep in the endeavour to find some explanation which would cover all these facts.

It was seven o'clock when I awoke, and I set off at once for Phelps's room, to find him haggard and spent after a sleepless night. His first question was whether Holmes had arrived yet.

"He'll be here when he promised," said I, "and not an instant sooner or later."

And my words were true, for shortly after eight a hansom dashed up to the door and our friend got out of it. Standing in the window, we saw that his left hand was swathed in a bandage and that his face was very grim and pale. He entered the house, but it was some little time before he came upstairs.

"He looks like a beaten man," cried Phelps.

I was forced to confess that he was right. "After all," said I, "the clue of the matter lies probably here in town."

Phelps gave a groan.

"I don't know how it is," said he, "but I had hoped for so much from his return. But surely his hand was not tied up like that yesterday? What can be the matter?"

"You are not wounded, Holmes?" I asked, as my friend entered the room.

"Tut, it is only a scratch through my own clumsiness," he answered, nodding his good morning to us. "This case of yours, Mr. Phelps, is certainly one of the darkest which I have ever investigated."

said Holmes, uncovering a dish of curried chicken. "Her cuisine is a little limited, but she has as good an idea of breakfast as a Scotchwoman. What have you there, Watson?"

"Ham and eggs," I answered.

"Good! What are you going to take, Mr. Phelps: curried fowl, or eggs, or will you help yourself?"

"Thank you, I can eat nothing," said Phelps.

"Oh, come! Try the dish before you."

"Thank you, I would really rather not."

"Well, then," said Holmes, with a mischievous twinkle, "I suppose that you have no objection to helping me?"

Phelps raised the cover, and as he did so

"PHELPS RAISED THE COVER.

"I feared that you would find it beyond you."

"It has been a most remarkable experience."

"That bandage tells of adventures," said I. "Won't you tell us what has happened?"

"After breakfast, my dear Watson. Remember that I have breathed thirty miles of Surrey air this morning. I suppose there has been no answer from my cabman advertisement? Well, well, we cannot expect to score every time."

The table was all laid, and, just as I was about to ring, Mrs. Hudson entered with the tea and coffee. A few minutes later she brought in three covers, and we all drew up to the table, Holmes ravenous, I curious, and Phelps in the gloomiest state of depression.

"Mrs. Hudson has risen to the occasion,"

he uttered a scream and sat there staring with a face as white as the plate upon which he looked. Across the centre of it was lying a little cylinder of blue-grey paper. He caught it up, devoured it with his eyes, and then danced madly about the room, pressing it to his bosom and shrieking out in his delight. Then he fell back into an arm-chair, so limp and exhausted with his own emotions that we had to pour brandy down his throat to keep him from fainting.

"There! there!" said Holmes, soothingly, patting him upon the shoulder. "It was too bad to spring it on you like this; but Watson here will tell you that I never can resist a touch of the dramatic."

Phelps seized his hand and kissed it.

"God bless you!" he cried; "you have saved my honour."

"Well, my own was at stake, you know," said Holmes. "I assure you, it is just as hateful to me to fail in a case as it can be to you to blunder over a commission."

Phelps thrust away the precious document into the innermost pocket of his coat.

"I have not the heart to interrupt your breakfast any further, and yet I am dying to know how you got it and where it was."

Sherlock Holmes swallowed a cup of coffee and turned his attention to the ham and eggs. Then he rose, lit his pipe, and settled himself down into his chair.

"I'll tell you what I did first, and how I came to do it afterwards," said he. "After leaving you at the station I went for a charming walk through some admirable Surrey scenery to a pretty little village called Ripley, where I had my tea at an inn, and took the precaution of filling my flask and of putting a paper of sandwiches in my pocket. There I remained until evening, when I set off for Woking again, and found myself in the high road outside Briarbrae just after sunset.

"Well, I waited until the road was clear— it is never a very frequented one at any time, I fancy—and then I clambered over the fence into the grounds."

"Surely the gate was open?" ejaculated Phelps.

"Yes; but I have a peculiar taste in these matters. I chose the place where the three fir trees stand, and behind their screen I got over without the least chance of anyone in the house being able to see me. I crouched down among the bushes on the other side, and crawled from one to the other—witness the disreputable state of my trouser knees— until I had reached the clump of rhododendrons just opposite to your bedroom window. There I squatted down and awaited developments.

"The blind was not down in your room, and I could see Miss Harrison sitting there reading by the table. It was a quarter past ten when she closed her book, fastened the shutters, and retired. I heard her shut the door, and felt quite sure that she had turned the key in the lock."

"The key?" ejaculated Phelps.

"Yes, I had given Miss Harrison instructions to lock the door on the outside and take the key with her when she went to bed. She carried out every one of my injunctions to the letter, and certainly without her co-operation you would not have that paper in your coat pocket. She departed then and the lights went out, and I was left squatting in the rhododendron bush.

"The night was fine, but still it was a very weary vigil. Of course, it has the sort of excitement about it that the sportsman feels when he lies beside the water-course and waits for the big game. It was very long, though—almost as long, Watson, as when you and I waited in that deadly room when we looked into the little problem of the 'Speckled Band.' There was a church clock down at Woking which struck the quarters, and I thought more than once that it had stopped. At last, however, about two in the morning, I suddenly heard the gentle sound of a bolt being pushed back, and the creaking of a key. A moment later the servants' door was opened, and Mr. Joseph Harrison stepped out into the moonlight."

"JOSEPH HARRISON STEPPED OUT."

"Joseph!" ejaculated Phelps.

"He was bare-headed, but he had a black cloak thrown over his shoulder so that he could conceal his face in an instant, if there were any alarm. He walked on tip-toe under the shadow of the wall, and when he reached the window, he worked a long-bladed knife

through the sash and pushed back the catch.
Then he flung open the window and, putting his knife through the crack in the
shutters, he thrust the bar up and swung
them open.

" From where I lay I had a perfect view
of the inside of the room and of every one
of his movements. He lit the two candles
which stand upon the mantelpiece, and then
he proceeded to turn back the corner of the
carpet in the neigbourhood of the door. Presently he stooped and picked out a square
piece of board, such as is usually left to
enable plumbers to get at the joints of the
gas pipes. This one covered, as a matter of
fact, the T-joint which gives off the pipe
which supplies the kitchen underneath. Out
of this hiding-place he drew that little
cylinder of paper, pushed down the board,
rearranged the carpet, blew out the candles,
and walked straight into my arms as I stood
waiting for him outside the window.

" Well, he has rather more viciousness
than I gave him credit for, has Master
Joseph. He flew at me with his knife, and I
had to grass him twice, and got a cut over
the knuckles, before I had the upper hand of
him. He looked 'murder' out of the only
eye he could see with when we had finished,
but he listened to reason and gave up the
papers. Having got them I let my man go,
but I wired full particulars to Forbes this
morning. If he is quick enough to catch
his bird, well and good ! But if, as I
shrewdly suspect, he finds the nest empty
before he gets there, why, all the better
for the Government. I fancy that Lord
Holdhurst, for one, and Mr. Percy Phelps
for another, would very much rather that
the affair never got as far as a police-court."

" My God !" gasped our client. " Do you
tell me that during these long ten weeks of
agony, the stolen papers were within the very
room with me all the time?"

" So it was."

" And Joseph ! Joseph a villain and a
thief !"

" Hum ! I am afraid Joseph's character
is a rather deeper and more dangerous one
than one might judge from his appearance.
From what I have heard from him this
morning, I gather that he has lost heavily in
dabbling with stocks, and that he is ready to
do anything on earth to better his fortunes.
Being an absolutely selfish man, when a
chance presented itself he did not allow
either his sister's happiness or your reputation
to hold his hand."

Percy Phelps sank back in his chair.

" My head whirls," said he ; " your words
have dazed me."

" The principal difficulty in your case,"
remarked Holmes, in his didactic fashion,
" lay in the fact of there being too much
evidence. What was vital was overlaid and
hidden by what was irrelevant. Of all the
facts which were presented to us, we had to
pick just those which we deemed to be
essential, and then piece them together in
their order, so as to reconstruct this very
remarkable chain of events. I had already
begun to suspect Joseph, from the fact that
you had intended to travel home with him
that night, and that therefore it was a likely
enough thing that he should call for you—
knowing the Foreign Office well—upon his
way. When I heard that someone had been
so anxious to get into the bedroom, in which
no one but Joseph could have concealed anything—you told us in your narrative how you
had turned Joseph out when you arrived
with the doctor—my suspicions all changed
to certainties, especially as the attempt was
made on the first night upon which the nurse
was absent, showing that the intruder was
well acquainted with the ways of the house."

" How blind I have been !"

" The facts of the case, as far as I have
worked them out, are these : This Joseph
Harrison entered the office through the
Charles Street door, and knowing his way he
walked straight into your room the instant
after you left it. Finding no one there he
promptly rang the bell, and at the instant
that he did so his eyes caught the paper upon
the table. A glance showed him that chance
had put in his way a State document of immense value, and in an instant he had thrust
it into his pocket and was gone. A few
minutes elapsed, as you remember, before
the sleepy commissionaire drew your attention to the bell, and those were just enough
to give the thief time to make his escape.

" He made his way to Woking by the first
train, and, having examined his booty and
assured himself that it really was of immense
value, he concealed it in what he thought
was a very safe place, with the intention of
taking it out again in a day or two, and
carrying it to the French Embassy, or wherever
he thought that a long price was to be had.
Then came your sudden return. He, without
a moment's warning, was bundled out of his
room, and from that time onwards there were
always at least two of you there to prevent
him from regaining his treasure. The situation to him must have been a maddening
one. But at last he thought he saw his

chance. He tried to steal in, but was baffled by your wakefulness. You may remember that you did not take your usual draught that night."

" I remember."

" I fancy that he had taken steps to make that draught efficacious, and that he quite relied upon your being unconscious. Of course, I understood that he would repeat the attempt whenever it could be done with safety. Your leaving the room gave him the

therefore, from the hiding-place, and so saved myself an infinity of trouble. Is there any other point which I can make clear ? "

" Why did he try the window on the first occasion," I asked, " when he might have entered by the door ? "

" In reaching the door he would have to pass seven bedrooms. On the other hand, he could get out on to the lawn with ease. Anything else ? "

" IS THERE ANY OTHER POINT WHICH I CAN MAKE CLEAR ? "

chance he wanted. I kept Miss Harrison in it all day, so that he might not anticipate us. Then, having given him the idea that the coast was clear, I kept guard as I have described. I already knew that the papers were probably in the room, but I had no desire to rip up all the planking and skirting in search of them. I let him take them,

" You do not think," asked Phelps, " that he had any murderous intention ? The knife was only meant as a tool."

" It may be so," answered Holmes, shrugging his shoulders. " I can only say for certain that Mr. Joseph Harrison is a gentleman to whose mercy I should be extremely unwilling to trust."

THE DEATH OF SHERLOCK HOLMES.

# The Adventures of Sherlock Holmes.

### By A. Conan Doyle.

### XXIV.—THE ADVENTURE OF THE FINAL PROBLEM.

IT is with a heavy heart that I take up my pen to write these the last words in which I shall ever record the singular gifts by which my friend Mr. Sherlock Holmes was distinguished. In an incoherent and, as I deeply feel, an entirely inadequate fashion, I have endeavoured to give some account of my strange experiences in his company from the chance which first brought us together at the period of the "Study in Scarlet," up to the time of his interference in the matter of the "Naval Treaty"—an interference which had the unquestionable effect of preventing a serious international complication. It was my intention to have stopped there, and to have said nothing of that event which has created a void in my life which the lapse of two years has done little to fill. My hand has been forced, however, by the recent letters in which Colonel James Moriarty defends the memory of his brother, and I have no choice but to lay the facts before the public exactly as they occurred. I alone know the absolute truth of the matter, and I am satisfied that the time has come when no good purpose is to be served by its suppression. As far as I know, there have been only three accounts in the public Press: that in the *Journal de Genève* upon May 6th, 1891, the Reuter's despatch in the English papers upon May 7th, and finally the recent letters to which I have alluded. Of these the first and second were extremely condensed, while the last is, as I shall now show, an absolute perversion of the facts. It lies with me to tell for the first time what really took place between Professor Moriarty and Mr. Sherlock Holmes.

It may be remembered that after my marriage, and my subsequent start in private practice, the very intimate relations which had existed between Holmes and myself became to some extent modified. He still came to me from time to time when he desired a companion in his investigations, but these occasions grew more and more seldom, until I find that in the year 1890 there were only three cases of which I retain any record. During the winter of that year and the early spring of 1891, I saw in the papers that he had been engaged by the French Government upon a matter of supreme importance, and I received two notes from Holmes, dated

from Narbonne and from Nîmes, from which I gathered that his stay in France was likely to be a long one. It was with some surprise, therefore, that I saw him walk into my consulting-room upon the evening of the 24th of April. It struck me that he was looking even paler and thinner than usual.

"Yes, I have been using myself up rather too freely," he remarked, in answer to my look rather than to my words; "I have been a little pressed of late. Have you any objection to my closing your shutters?"

The only light in the room came from the lamp upon the table at which I had been reading. Holmes edged his way round the wall, and flinging the shutters together, he bolted them securely.

"You are afraid of something?" I asked.

"Well, I am."

"Of what?"

"Of air-guns."

"My dear Holmes, what do you mean?"

"I think that you know me well enough, Watson, to understand that I am by no means a nervous man. At the same time, it is stupidity rather than courage to refuse to recognise danger when it is close upon you. Might I trouble you for a match?" He drew in the smoke of his cigarette as if the soothing influence was grateful to him.

"I must apologize for calling so late," said he, "and I must further beg you to be so unconventional as to allow me to leave your house presently by scrambling over your back garden wall."

"But what does it all mean?" I asked.

He held out his hand, and I saw in the light of the lamp that two of his knuckles were burst and bleeding.

"It's not an airy nothing, you see," said he, smiling. "On the contrary, it is solid enough for a man to break his hand over. Is Mrs. Watson in?"

"She is away upon a visit."

"Indeed! You are alone?"

"Quite."

"Then it makes it the easier for me to propose that you should come away with me for a week on to the Continent."

"Where?"

"Oh, anywhere. It's all the same to me."

There was something very strange in all this. It was not Holmes's nature to take an

"TWO OF HIS KNUCKLES WERE BURST AND BLEEDING."

aimless holiday, and something about his pale, worn face told me that his nerves were at their highest tension. He saw the question in my eyes, and, putting his finger-tips together and his elbows upon his knees, he explained the situation.

"You have probably never heard of Professor Moriarty?" said he.

"Never."

"Aye, there's the genius and the wonder of the thing!" he cried. "The man pervades London, and no one has heard of him. That's what puts him on a pinnacle in the records of crime. I tell you, Watson, in all seriousness, that if I could beat that man, if I could free society of him, I should feel that my own career had reached its summit, and I should be prepared to turn to some more placid line in life. Between ourselves, the recent cases in which I have been of assistance to the Royal Family of Scandinavia, and to the French Republic, have left me in such a position that I could continue to live in the quiet fashion which is most congenial to me, and to concentrate my attention upon my chemical researches. But I could not rest, Watson, I could not sit quiet in my chair, if I thought that such a man as Professor Moriarty were walking the streets of London unchallenged."

"What has he done, then?"

"His career has been an extraordinary one. He is a man of good birth and excellent education, endowed by Nature with a phenomenal mathematical faculty. At the age of twenty-one he wrote a treatise upon the Binomial Theorem, which has had a European vogue. On the strength of it, he won the Mathematical Chair at one of our smaller Universities and had, to all appearance, a most brilliant career before him. But the man had hereditary tendencies of the most diabolical kind. A criminal strain ran in his blood, which, instead of being modified, was increased and rendered infinitely more dangerous by his extraordinary mental powers. Dark rumours gathered round him in the University town, and eventually he was compelled to resign his Chair and to come down to London, where he set up as an Army coach. So much is known to the world, but what I am telling you now is what I have myself discovered.

"As you are aware, Watson, there is no one who knows the higher criminal world of London so well as I do. For years past I have continually been conscious of some power behind the malefactor, some deep organizing power which for ever stands in the way of the law, and throws its shield over the wrong-doer. Again and again in cases of the most varying sorts—forgery cases, robberies, murders—I have felt the presence of this force, and I have deduced its action in many of those undiscovered crimes in which I have not been personally consulted. For years I have endeavoured to break through the veil which shrouded it, and at last the time came when I seized my thread and followed it, until it led me, after a thousand cunning windings, to ex-Professor Moriarty of mathematical celebrity.

"He is the Napoleon of crime, Watson. He is the organizer of half that is evil and of nearly all that is undetected in this great city. He is a genius, a philosopher, an abstract thinker. He has a brain of the first order. He sits motionless, like a spider in the centre of its web, but that web has a thousand radiations, and he knows well every quiver of each of them. He does little himself. He only plans. But his agents are numerous and splendidly organized. Is there a crime to be done, a paper to be abstracted, we will say, a house to be rifled, a man to be removed — the word is passed to the Professor, the matter is organized and carried out. The agent may be caught. In that case money is found for his bail or his defence. But the central power which uses the agent is never caught—never so much as suspected. This was the organization which I deduced, Watson, and which I devoted my whole energy to exposing and breaking up.

"But the Professor was fenced round with safeguards so cunningly devised that, do what I would, it seemed impossible to get evidence which could convict in a court of law. You know my powers, my dear Watson, and yet at the end of three months I was forced to confess that I had at last met an antagonist who was my

"PROFESSOR MORIARTY STOOD BEFORE ME."

intellectual equal. My horror at his crimes was lost in my admiration at his skill. But at last he made a trip—only a little, little trip—but it was more than he could afford, when I was so close upon him. I had my chance, and, starting from that point, I have woven my net round him until now it is all ready to close. In three days, that is to say on Monday next, matters will be ripe, and the Professor, with all the principal members of his gang, will be in the hands of the police. Then will come the greatest criminal trial of the century, the clearing up of over forty mysteries and the rope for all of them —but if we move at all prematurely, you understand, they may slip out of our hands even at the last moment.

"Now, if I could have done this without the knowledge of Professor Moriarty, all would have been well. But he was too wily for that. He saw every step which I took to draw my toils round him. Again and again he strove to break away, but I as often headed him off. I tell you, my friend, that if a detailed account of that silent contest could be written, it would take its place as the most brilliant bit of thrust-and-parry work in the history of detection. Never have I risen to such a height, and never have I been so hard pressed by an opponent. He cut deep, and yet I just undercut him. This morning the last steps were taken, and three days only were wanted to complete the business. I was sitting in my room thinking the matter over, when the door opened and Professor Moriarty stood before me.

"My nerves are fairly proof, Watson, but I must confess to a start when I saw the very man who had been so much in my thoughts standing there on my threshold. His appearance was quite familiar to me. He is extremely tall and thin, his forehead domes out in a white curve, and his two eyes are deeply sunken in his head. He is clean shaven, pale, and ascetic-looking, retaining something of the professor in his features. His shoulders are rounded from much study, and his face protrudes forward, and is for ever slowly oscillating from side to side in a curiously reptilian fashion. He peered at me with great curiosity in his puckered eyes.

"'You have less frontal development than I should have expected,' said he at last. 'It is a dangerous habit to finger loaded firearms in the pocket of one's dressing-gown.'

"The fact is that upon his entrance I had instantly recognised the extreme personal danger in which I lay. The only conceivable escape for him lay in silencing my tongue. In an instant I had slipped the revolver from the drawer into my pocket, and was covering him through the cloth. At his remark I drew the weapon out and laid it cocked upon the table. He still smiled and blinked, but there was something about his eyes which made me feel very glad that I had it there.

"'You evidently don't know me,' said he.

"'On the contrary,' I answered, 'I think it is fairly evident that I do. Pray take a chair. I can spare you five minutes if you have anything to say.'

"'All that I have to say has already crossed your mind,' said he.

"'Then possibly my answer has crossed yours,' I replied.

"'You stand fast?'

"'Absolutely.'

"He clapped his hand into his pocket, and I raised the pistol from the table. But he merely drew out a memorandum-book in which he had scribbled some dates.

"'You crossed my path on the 4th of January,' said he. 'On the 23rd you incommoded me; by the middle of February I was seriously inconvenienced by you; at the end of March I was absolutely hampered in my plans; and now, at the close of April, I find myself placed in such a position through your continual persecution that I am in positive danger of losing my liberty. The situation is becoming an impossible one.'

"'Have you any suggestion to make?' I asked.

"'You must drop it, Mr. Holmes,' said he, swaying his face about. 'You really must, you know.'

"'After Monday,' said I.

"'Tut, tut!' said he. 'I am quite sure that a man of your intelligence will see that there can be but one outcome to this affair. It is necessary that you should withdraw. You have worked things in such a fashion that we have only one resource left. It has been an intellectual treat to me to see the way in which you have grappled with this affair, and I say, unaffectedly, that it would be a grief to me to be forced to take any extreme measure. You smile, sir, but I assure you that it really would.'

"'Danger is part of my trade,' I remarked.

"'This is not danger,' said he. 'It is inevitable destruction. You stand in the way not merely of an individual, but of a mighty organization, the full extent of which you, with all your cleverness, have been unable to realize. You must stand clear, Mr. Holmes, or be trodden under foot.'

"'I am afraid,' said I, rising, 'that in the pleasure of this conversation I am neglecting business of importance which awaits me elsewhere.'

"He rose also and looked at me in silence, shaking his head sadly.

"'Well, well,' said he at last. 'It seems a pity, but I have done what I could. I know every move of your game. You can do nothing before Monday. It has been a duel between you and me, Mr. Holmes. You hope to place me in the dock. I tell you that I will never stand in the dock. You hope to beat me. I tell you that you will never beat me. If you are clever enough to bring destruction upon me, rest assured that I shall do as much to you.'

"'You have paid me several compliments, Mr. Moriarty,' said I. 'Let me pay you one in return when I say that if I were assured of the former eventuality I would, in the interests of the public, cheerfully accept the latter.'

"'I can promise you the one but not the other,' he snarled, and so turned his rounded back upon me and went peering and blinking out of the room.

"That was my singular interview with Professor Moriarty. I confess that it left an unpleasant effect upon my mind. His soft, precise fashion of speech leaves a conviction of sincerity which a mere bully could not produce. Of course, you will say: 'Why not take police precautions against him?' The reason is that I am well convinced that it is from his agents the blow would fall. I

"HE TURNED HIS ROUNDED BACK UPON ME."

the day. Now I have come round to you, and on my way I was attacked by a rough with a bludgeon. I knocked him down, and the police have him in custody; but I can tell you with the most absolute confidence that no possible connection will ever be traced between the gentleman upon whose front teeth I have barked my knuckles and the retiring mathematical coach, who is, I daresay, working out problems upon a blackboard ten miles away. You will not wonder, Watson, that my first act on entering your rooms was to close your shutters, and that I have been compelled to ask your permission to leave the house by some less conspicuous exit than the front door."

I had often admired my friend's courage, but never more than now, as he sat quietly checking off a series of incidents which must have combined to make up a day of horror.

"You will spend the night here?" I said.

"No, my friend, you might find me a dangerous guest. I have my plans laid, and all will be well. Matters have gone so far now that they can move without my help as far as the arrest goes, though my presence is necessary for a conviction. It is obvious, therefore, that I cannot do better than get away for the few days which remain before the police are at liberty to act. It would be a great pleasure to me, therefore, if you could come on to the Continent with me."

"The practice is quiet," said I, "and I have an accommodating neighbour. I should be glad to come."

"And to start to-morrow morning?"

"If necessary."

"Oh, yes, it is most necessary. Then these are your instructions, and I beg, my dear Watson, that you will obey them to the letter, for you are now playing a double-handed game with me against the cleverest

have the best of proofs that it would be so."

"You have already been assaulted?"

"My dear Watson, Professor Moriarty is not a man who lets the grass grow under his feet. I went out about midday to transact some business in Oxford Street. As I passed the corner which leads from Bentinck Street on to the Welbeck Street crossing a two-horse van furiously driven whizzed round and was on me like a flash. I sprang for the footpath and saved myself by the fraction of a second. The van dashed round by Marylebone Lane and was gone in an instant. I kept to the pavement after that, Watson, but as I walked down Vere Street a brick came down from the roof of one of the houses, and was shattered to fragments at my feet. I called the police and had the place examined. There were slates and bricks piled upon the roof preparatory to some repairs, and they would have me believe that the wind had toppled over one of these. Of course I knew better, but I could prove nothing. I took a cab after that and reached my brother's rooms in Pall Mall, where I spent

rogue and the most powerful syndicate of criminals in Europe. Now listen! You will dispatch whatever luggage you intend to take by a trusty messenger unaddressed to Victoria to-night. In the morning you will send for a hansom, desiring your man to take neither the first nor the second which may present itself. Into this hansom you will jump, and you will drive to the Strand end of the Lowther Arcade, handing the address to the cabman upon a slip of paper, with a request that he will not throw it away. Have your fare ready, and the instant that your cab stops, dash through the Arcade, timing yourself to reach the other side at a quarter-past nine. You will find a small brougham waiting close to the curb, driven by a fellow with a heavy black cloak tipped at the collar with red. Into this you will step, and you will reach Victoria in time for the Continental express."

"Where shall I meet you?"

"At the station. The second first-class carriage from the front will be reserved for us."

"The carriage is our rendezvous, then?"

"Yes."

It was in vain that I asked Holmes to remain for the evening. It was evident to me that he thought he might bring trouble to the roof he was under, and that that was the motive which impelled him to go. With a few hurried words as to our plans for the morrow he rose and came out with me into the garden, clambering over the wall which leads into Mortimer Street, and immediately whistling for a hansom, in which I heard him drive away.

In the morning I obeyed Holmes's injunctions to the letter. A hansom was procured with such precautions as would prevent its being one which was placed ready for us, and I drove immediately after breakfast to the Lowther Arcade, through which I hurried at the top of my speed. A brougham was waiting with a very massive driver wrapped in a dark cloak, who, the instant that I had stepped in, whipped up the horse and rattled off to Victoria Station. On my alighting there he turned the carriage, and dashed away again without so much as a look in my direction.

So far all had gone admirably. My luggage was waiting for me, and I had no difficulty in finding the carriage which Holmes had indicated, the less so as it was the only one in the train which was marked "Engaged." My only source of anxiety now was the non-appearance of Holmes. The station clock marked only seven minutes from the time when we were due to start. In vain I searched among the groups of travellers and leave-takers for the lithe figure of my friend. There was no sign of him. I spent a few minutes in assisting a venerable Italian priest, who was endeavouring to make a porter understand, in his broken English, that his luggage was to be booked through to Paris. Then, having taken another look round, I returned to my carriage, where I found that the porter, in spite of the ticket, had given me my decrepit Italian friend as a travelling companion. It was useless for me to explain to him that his presence was an intrusion, for my Italian was even more limited than his English, so I shrugged my shoulders resignedly, and continued to look out anxiously for my friend. A chill of fear had come over me, as I thought that his absence might mean that some blow had fallen during the night. Already the doors had all been shut and the whistle blown, when—

"My dear Watson," said a voice, "you have not even condescended to say good morning."

I turned in incontrollable astonishment. The aged ecclesiastic had turned his face towards me. For an instant the wrinkles were smoothed away, the nose drew away from the chin, the lower lip ceased to protrude and the mouth to mumble, the dull eyes regained their fire, the drooping figure expanded. The next the whole frame collapsed again, and Holmes had gone as quickly as he had come.

"Good heavens!" I cried. "How you startled me!"

"Every precaution is still necessary," he whispered. "I have reason to think that they are hot upon our trail. Ah, there is Moriarty himself."

The train had already begun to move as Holmes spoke. Glancing back I saw a tall man pushing his way furiously through the crowd and waving his hand as if he desired to have the train stopped. It was too late, however, for we were rapidly gathering momentum, and an instant later had shot clear of the station.

"With all our precautions, you see that we have cut it rather fine," said Holmes, laughing. He rose, and throwing off the black cassock and hat which had formed his disguise, he packed them away in a hand-bag.

"Have you seen the morning paper, Watson?"

"No."

SP

" MY DECREPIT ITALIAN FRIEND."

"Yes, it was waiting."

"Did you recognise your coachman?"

"No."

"It was my brother Mycroft. It is an advantage to get about in such a case without taking a mercenary into your confidence. But we must plan what we are to do about Moriarty now."

"As this is an express, and as the boat runs in connection with it, I should think we have shaken him off very effectively."

"My dear Watson, you evidently did not realize my meaning when I said that this man may be taken as being quite on the same intellectual plane as myself. You do not imagine that if I were the pursuer I should allow myself to be baffled by so slight an obstacle. Why, then, should you think so meanly of him?"

"What will he do?"

"What I should do."

"What would you do, then?"

"Engage a special."

"But it must be late."

"By no means. This train stops at Canterbury; and there is always at least a quarter of an hour's delay at the boat. He will catch us there."

"One would think that we were the criminals. Let us have him arrested on his arrival."

"It would be to ruin the work of three

"You haven't seen about Baker Street, then?"

"Baker Street?"

"They set fire to our rooms last night. No great harm was done."

"Good heavens, Holmes! This is intolerable."

"They must have lost my track completely after their bludgeon - man was arrested. Otherwise they could not have imagined that I had returned to my rooms. They have evidently taken the precaution of watching you, however, and that is what has brought Moriarty to Victoria. You could not have made any slip in coming?"

"I did exactly what you advised."

"Did you find your brougham?"

months. We should get the big fish, but the smaller would dart right and left out of the net. On Monday we should have them all. No, an arrest is inadmissible."

"What then?"

"We shall get out at Canterbury."

"And then?"

"Well, then we must make a cross-country journey to Newhaven, and so over to Dieppe. Moriarty will again do what I should do. He will get on to Paris, mark down our luggage, and wait for two days at the depôt. In the meantime we shall treat ourselves to a couple of carpet bags, encourage the manufactures of the countries through which we travel, and make our way at our leisure into Switzerland, viâ Luxembourg and Basle."

At Canterbury, therefore, we alighted, only to find that we should have to wait an hour before we could get a train to Newhaven.

I was still looking rather ruefully after the rapidly disappearing luggage van which contained my wardrobe, when Holmes pulled my sleeve and pointed up the line.

"Already, you see," said he.

Far away, from among the Kentish woods there rose a thin spray of smoke. A minute later a carriage and engine could be seen flying along the open curve which leads to the station. We had hardly time to take our place behind a pile of luggage when it passed with a rattle and a roar, beating a blast of hot air into our faces.

"There he goes," said Holmes, as we watched the carriage swing and rock over the points. "There are limits, you see, to our friend's intelligence. It would have been a *coup-de-maître* had he deduced what I would deduce and acted accordingly."

"And what would he have done had he overtaken us?"

"There cannot be the least doubt that he would have made a murderous attack upon me. It is, however, a game at which two

may play. The question now is whether we should take a premature lunch here, or run our chance of starving before we reach the buffet at Newhaven."

We made our way to Brussels that night and spent two days there, moving on upon the third day as far as Strasburg. On the Monday morning Holmes had telegraphed to the London police, and in the evening we found a reply waiting for us at our hotel. Holmes tore it open, and then with a bitter curse hurled it into the grate.

"'IT PASSED WITH A RATTLE AND A ROAR.'"

"I might have known it!" he groaned. "He has escaped!"

"Moriarty?"

"They have secured the whole gang with the exception of him. He has given them the slip. Of course, when I had left the country there was no one to cope with him. But I did think that I had put the game in their hands. I think that you had better return to England, Watson."

"Why?"

"Because you will find me a dangerous companion now. This man's occupation is gone. He is lost if he returns to London. If I read his character right he will devote his whole energies to revenging himself upon me. He said as much in our short interview, and I fancy that he meant it. I should certainly recommend you to return to your practice."

It was hardly an appeal to be successful with one who was an old campaigner as well as an old friend. We sat in the Strasburg *salle-à-manger* arguing the question for half an hour, but the same night we had resumed our journey and were well on our way to Geneva.

For a charming week we wandered up the Valley of the Rhone, and then, branching off at Leuk, we made our way over the Gemmi Pass, still deep in snow, and so, by way of Interlaken, to Meiringen. It was a lovely trip, the dainty green of the spring below, the virgin white of the winter above ; but it was clear to me that never for one instant did Holmes forget the shadow which lay across him. In the homely Alpine villages or in the lonely mountain passes, I could still tell by his quick glancing eyes and his sharp scrutiny of every face that passed us, that he was well convinced that, walk where we would, we could not walk ourselves clear of the danger which was dogging our footsteps.

Once, I remember, as we passed over the Gemmi, and walked along the border of the melancholy Daubensee, a large rock which had been dislodged from the ridge upon our right clattered down and roared into the lake behind us. In an instant Holmes had raced up on to the ridge, and, standing upon a lofty pinnacle, craned his neck in every direction. It was in vain that our guide assured him that a fall of stones was a common chance in the spring-time at that spot. He said nothing, but he smiled at me with the air of a man who sees the fulfilment of that which he had expected.

And yet for all his watchfulness he was never depressed. On the contrary, I can never recollect having seen him in such exuberant spirits. Again and again he recurred to the fact that if he could be assured that society was freed from

Professor Moriarty he would cheerfully bring his own career to a conclusion.

"I think that I may go so far as to say, Watson, that I have not lived wholly in vain," he remarked. "If my record were closed to-night I could still survey it with equanimity. The air of London is the sweeter for my presence. In over a thousand cases I am not aware that I have ever used my powers upon the wrong side. Of late I have been tempted to look into the problems furnished by Nature rather than those more superficial ones for which our artificial state of society is responsible. Your memoirs will draw to an end, Watson, upon the day that I crown my career by the capture or extinction of the most dangerous and capable criminal in Europe."

I shall be brief, and yet exact, in the little which remains for me to tell. It is not a subject on which I would willingly dwell, and yet I am conscious that a duty devolves upon me to omit no detail.

It was upon the 3rd of May that we reached the little village of Meiringen, where we put up at the Englischer Hof, then kept

"A LARGE ROCK CLATTERED DOWN."

by Peter Steiler the elder. Our landlord was an intelligent man, and spoke excellent English, having served for three years as waiter at the Grosvenor Hotel in London. At his advice, upon the afternoon of the 4th we set off together with the intention of crossing the hills and spending the night at the hamlet of Rosenlaui. We had strict injunctions, however, on no account to pass the falls of Reichenbach, which are about half-way up the hill, without making a small détour to see them.

It is, indeed, a fearful place. The torrent, swollen by the melting snow, plunges into a tremendous abyss, from which the spray rolls up like the smoke from a burning house. The shaft into which the river hurls itself is an immense chasm, lined by glistening, coal-black rock, and narrowing into a creaming, boiling pit of incalculable depth, which brims over and shoots the stream onward over its jagged lip. The long sweep of green water roaring for ever down, and the thick flickering curtain of spray hissing for ever upwards, turn a man giddy with their constant whirl and clamour. We stood near the edge peering down at the gleam of the breaking water far below us against the black rocks, and listening to the half-human shout which came booming up with the spray out of the abyss.

The path has been cut half-way round the fall to afford a complete view, but it ends abruptly, and the

traveller has to return as he came. We had turned to do so, when we saw a Swiss lad come running along it with a letter in his hand. It bore the mark of the hotel which we had just left, and was addressed to me by the landlord. It appeared that within a very few minutes of our leaving, an English lady had arrived who was in the last stage of consumption. She had wintered at Davos Platz, and was journeying now to join her friends at Lucerne, when a sudden hemorrhage had overtaken her. It was thought that she could hardly live a few hours, but it would be a great consolation to her to see an English doctor, and, if I would only return,

"I SAW HOLMES GAZING DOWN AT THE RUSH OF THE WATERS."

etc., etc. The good Steiler assured me in a postscript that he would himself look upon my compliance as a very great favour, since the lady absolutely refused to see a Swiss physician, and he could not but feel that he was incurring a great responsibility.

The appeal was one which could not be ignored. It was impossible to refuse the request of a fellow-countrywoman dying in a strange land. Yet I had my scruples about leaving Holmes. It was finally agreed, however, that he should retain the young Swiss messenger with him as guide and companion while I returned to Meiringen. My friend would stay some little time at the fall, he said, and would then walk slowly over the hill to Rosenlaui, where I was to rejoin him in the evening. As I turned away I saw Holmes, with his back against a rock and his arms folded, gazing down at the rush of the waters. It was the last that I was ever destined to see of him in this world.

When I was near the bottom of the descent I looked back. It was impossible, from that position, to see the fall, but I could see the curving path which winds over the shoulder of the hill and leads to it. Along this a man was, I remember, walking very rapidly.

I could see his black figure clearly outlined against the green behind him. I noted him, and the energy with which he walked, but he passed from my mind again as I hurried on upon my errand.

It may have been a little over an hour before I reached Meiringen. Old Steiler was standing at the porch of his hotel.

"Well,' said I, as I came hurrying up, " I trust that she is no worse ? "

A look of surprise passed over his face, and at the first quiver of his eyebrows my heart turned to lead in my breast.

"You did not write this ? " I said, pulling the letter from my pocket. " There is no sick Englishwoman in the hotel ? "

"Certainly not," he cried. " But it has the hotel mark upon it ! Ha, it must have been written by that tall Englishman who came in after you had gone. He said——"

But I waited for none of the landlord's explanations. In a tingle of fear I was already running down the village street, and making for the path which I had so lately descended. It had taken me an hour to come down. For all my efforts two more had passed before I found myself at the fall of Reichenbach once more. There was Holmes's Alpine-stock still leaning against the rock by which I had left him. But there was no sign of him, and it was in vain that I shouted. My only answer was my own voice reverberating in a rolling echo from the cliffs around me.

It was the sight of that Alpine-stock which turned me cold and sick. He had not gone to Rosenlaui, then. He had remained on that three-foot path, with sheer wall on one side and sheer drop upon the other, until his enemy had overtaken him. The young Swiss had gone too. He had probably been in the pay of Moriarty, and had left the two men together. And then what had happened? Who was to tell us what had happened then?

I stood for a minute or two to collect myself, for I was dazed with the horror of the thing. Then I began to think of Holmes's own methods and to try to practise them in reading this tragedy. It was, alas, only too easy to do. During our conversation we had not gone to the end of the path, and the Alpine-stock marked the place where we had stood. The blackish soil is kept for ever soft by the incessant drift of spray, and a bird would leave its tread upon it. Two lines of footmarks were clearly marked along the further end of the path, both leading away from me. There were none returning. A few yards from the end the soil was all ploughed up into a patch of mud, and the brambles and ferns which fringed the chasm were torn and bedraggled. I lay upon my face and peered over with the spray spouting up all around me. It had darkened since I left, and now I could only see here and there the glistening of moisture upon the black walls, and far away down at the end of the shaft the gleam of the broken water. I shouted; but only that same half-human cry of the fall was borne back to my ears.

But it was destined that I should after all have a last word of greeting from my friend and comrade. I have said that his Alpine-stock had been left leaning against a rock which jutted on to the path. From the top of this boulder the gleam of something bright caught my eye, and, raising my hand, I found that it came from the silver cigarette case which he used to carry. As I took it up a small square of paper upon which it had lain fluttered down on to the ground. Unfolding it I found that it consisted of three pages torn from his note-book and addressed to me. It was characteristic of the man that the direction was as precise, and the writing as firm and clear, as though it had been written in his study.

"A SMALL SQUARE OF PAPER FLUTTERED DOWN."

that the letter from Meiringen was a hoax, and I allowed you to depart on that errand under the persuasion that some development of this sort would follow. Tell Inspector Patterson that the papers which he needs to convict the gang are in pigeon-hole M., done up in a blue envelope and inscribed 'Moriarty.' I made every disposition of my property before leaving England, and handed it to my brother Mycroft. Pray give my greetings to Mrs. Watson, and believe me to be, my dear fellow,

"Very sincerely yours,
"SHERLOCK HOLMES."

A few words may suffice to tell the little that remains. An examination by experts leaves little doubt that a personal contest between the two men ended, as it could hardly fail to end in such a situation, in their reeling over, locked in each other's arms. Any attempt at recovering the bodies was absolutely hopeless, and there, deep down in that dreadful caldron of swirling water and seething foam, will lie for all time the most dangerous criminal and the foremost champion of the law of their generation. The Swiss youth was never found again, and there can be no doubt that he was one of the numerous agents whom Moriarty kept in his employ. As to the gang, it will be within the memory of the public how completely the evidence which Holmes had accumulated exposed their organization, and how heavily the hand of the dead man weighed upon them. Of their terrible chief few details came out during the proceedings, and if I have now been compelled to make a clear statement of his career, it is due to those injudicious champions who have endeavoured to clear his memory by attacks upon him whom I shall ever regard as the best and the wisest man whom I have ever known.

"My dear Watson," he said, "I write these few lines through the courtesy of Mr. Moriarty, who awaits my convenience for the final discussion of those questions which lie between us. He has been giving me a sketch of the methods by which he avoided the English police and kept himself informed of our movements. They certainly confirm the very high opinion which I had formed of his abilities. I am pleased to think that I shall be able to free society from any further effects of his presence, though I fear that it is at a cost which will give pain to my friends, and especially, my dear Watson, to you. I have already explained to you, however, that my career had in any case reached its crisis, and that no possible conclusion to it could be more congenial to me than this. Indeed, if I may make a full confession to you, I was quite convinced

# THE RETURN
# OF SHERLOCK HOLMES

INCLUDING

# THE HOUND OF THE BASKERVILLES

# Contents

# INTRODUCTION

"I couldn't revive him if I would, at least not for years, for I have had such an overdose of him that I feel towards him as I do towards *pâté-de-foie-gras,* of which I once ate too much. . . ."

So wrote Arthur Conan Doyle to a friend. Eight years later, in 1901, he published *The Hound of the Baskervilles* to a public so eagerly awaiting it that it stood in lines at the printer's and increased the circulation of *The Strand* by thirty thousand copies with the first installment. But, hedging a bit, Doyle explained *The Hound* as a reminiscence, not a resuscitation, dated as it is before Holmes' "death."

*The Strand* eagerly heralded the first installments of *The Hound of the Baskervilles,* with its eerie howling on the moor, strange deaths, superstitions, an escaped convict, a giant hound, heirs, property disputes and Moriarty. "Readers of to-day may also revel in the unexpected developments that follow in rapid succession as the 'man with eyes at the back of his head' discovers clue after clue of the mystery which enshrouds the gruesome legend of 'The Hound

of the Baskervilles,' " the magazine announced.

The overwhelming response on both sides of the Atlantic caused Conan Doyle to rethink his decision not to resurrect Holmes. In an interview in *Harper's Weekly* for August 31, 1901, he is reported to have said: "I know that my friend Dr. Watson is a most trustworthy man, and I gave the utmost credit to his story of the dreadful affair in Switzerland. He may have been mistaken, of course. It may not have been Mr. Holmes who fell from the ledge at all, or the whole affair might be the result of hallucination . . ."

Conan Doyle finally surrendered entirely to the demands of his audience when he published "The Adventure of the Empty House" in October, 1903. "I moved my head to look at the cabinet behind me. When I turned again Sherlock Holmes was standing smiling at me across my study table. I rose to my feet, stared at him for some seconds in utter amazement, and then it appears that I must have fainted for the first time and the last time in my life."

Sherlock Holmes was finally back.

# THE RETURN
## OF SHERLOCK HOLMES

# THE STRAND MAGAZINE.

Vol. xxvi.                    OCTOBER, 1903.                    No. 154.

# THE RETURN OF SHERLOCK HOLMES.

## By A. CONAN DOYLE.

### I.—The Adventure of the Empty House.

IT was in the spring of the year 1894 that all London was interested, and the fashionable world dismayed, by the murder of the Honourable Ronald Adair under most unusual and inexplicable circumstances. The public has already learned those particulars of the crime which came out in the police investigation ; but a good deal was suppressed upon that occasion, since the case for the prosecution was so overwhelmingly strong that it was not necessary to bring forward all the facts. Only now, at the end of nearly ten years, am I allowed to supply those missing links which make up the whole of that remarkable chain. The crime was of interest in itself, but that interest was as nothing to me compared to the inconceivable sequel, which afforded me the greatest shock and surprise of any event in my adventurous life. Even now, after this long interval, I find myself thrilling as I think of it, and feeling once more that sudden flood of joy, amazement, and incredulity which utterly submerged my mind. Let me say to that public which has shown some interest in those glimpses which I have occasionally given them of the thoughts and actions of a very remarkable man that they are not to blame me if I have not shared my knowledge with them, for I should have considered it my first duty to have done so had I not been barred by a positive prohibition from his own lips, which was only withdrawn upon the third of last month.

It can be imagined that my close intimacy with Sherlock Holmes had interested me deeply in crime, and that after his disappearance I never failed to read with care the various problems which came before the public, and I even attempted more than once for my own private satisfaction to employ his methods in their solution, though with indifferent success. There was none, however, which appealed to me like this tragedy of Ronald Adair. As I read the evidence at the inquest, which led up to a verdict of wilful murder against some person or persons unknown, I realized more clearly than I had ever done the loss which the community had sustained by the death of Sherlock Holmes. There were points about this strange business which would, I was sure, have specially appealed to him, and the efforts of the police would have been supplemented, or more probably anticipated, by the trained observation and the alert mind of the first criminal agent in Europe. All day as I drove upon my round I turned over the case in my mind, and found no explanation which appeared to me to be adequate. At the risk of telling a twice-told tale I will recapitulate the facts as they were known to the public at the conclusion of the inquest.

The Honourable Ronald Adair was the second son of the Earl of Maynooth, at that time Governor of one of the Australian Colonies. Adair's mother had returned from Australia to undergo the operation for cataract, and she, her son Ronald, and her daughter Hilda were living together at 427, Park Lane. The youth moved in the best society, had, so far as was known, no enemies, and no particular vices. He had been engaged to Miss Edith Woodley, of Carstairs, but the engagement had been broken off by mutual consent some months before, and there was no sign that it had left any very profound feeling behind it. For the rest the man's life moved in a narrow and conventional circle, for his habits were quiet and his nature unemotional. Yet it was upon this easy-going young aristocrat that death came in most strange and unexpected form between the hours of ten and eleven-twenty on the night of March 30th, 1894.

Ronald Adair was fond of cards, playing continually, but never for such stakes as would hurt him. He was a member of the Baldwin, the Cavendish, and the Bagatelle card clubs. It was shown that after dinner on the day of his death he had played a rubber of whist at the latter club. He had also played there in the afternoon. The evidence of those who had played with him —Mr. Murray, Sir John Hardy, and Colonel Moran—showed that the game was whist, and that there was a fairly equal fall of the cards. Adair might have lost five pounds, but not more. His fortune was a considerable one, and such a loss could not in any way affect him. He had played nearly every day at one club or other, but he was a cautious player, and usually rose a winner. It came out in evidence that in partnership with Colonel Moran he had actually won as much as four hundred and twenty pounds in a sitting some weeks before from Godfrey Milner and Lord Balmoral. So much for his recent history, as it came out at the inquest.

On the evening of the crime he returned from the club exactly at ten. His mother and sister were out spending the evening with a relation. The servant deposed that she heard him enter the front room on the second floor, generally used as his sitting-room. She had lit a fire there, and as it smoked she had opened the window. No sound was heard from the room until eleven-twenty, the hour of the return of Lady Maynooth and her daughter. Desiring to say good-night, she had attempted to enter her son's room. The door was locked on the inside, and no answer could be got to their cries and knocking. Help was obtained and the door forced. The unfortunate young man was found lying near the table. His head had been horribly mutilated by an expanding revolver bullet, but no weapon of any sort was to be found in the room. On the table lay two bank-notes for ten pounds each and seventeen pounds ten in silver and gold, the money arranged in little piles of varying amount. There were some figures also upon a sheet of paper with the names of some club friends opposite to them, from which it was conjectured that before his death he was endeavouring to make out his losses or winnings at cards.

A minute examination of the circumstances served only to make the case more complex. In the first place, no reason could be given why the young man should have fastened the door upon the inside. There was the possibility that the murderer had done this and had afterwards escaped by the window. The drop was at least twenty feet, however, and a bed of crocuses in full bloom lay beneath. Neither the flowers nor the earth showed any sign of having been disturbed, nor were there any marks upon the narrow strip of grass which separated the house from the road. Apparently, therefore, it was the young man himself who had fastened the door. But how did he come by his death? No one could have climbed up to the window without leaving traces. Suppose a man had fired through the window, it would indeed be a remarkable shot who could with a revolver inflict so deadly a wound. Again, Park Lane is a frequented thoroughfare, and there is a cab-stand within a hundred yards of the house. No one had heard a shot. And yet there was the dead man, and there the revolver bullet, which had mushroomed out, as soft-nosed bullets will, and so inflicted a wound which must have caused instantaneous death. Such were the circumstances of the Park Lane Mystery, which were further complicated by entire absence of motive, since, as I have said, young Adair was not known to have any enemy, and no attempt had been made to remove the money or valuables in the room.

All day I turned these facts over in my mind, endeavouring to hit upon some theory which could reconcile them all, and to find that line of least resistance which my poor friend had declared to be the starting-point of every investigation. I confess that I made little progress. In the evening I strolled across the Park, and found myself about six o'clock at the Oxford Street end of Park Lane. A group of loafers upon the pavements, all staring up at a particular window, directed me to the house which I had come to see. A tall, thin man with coloured glasses, whom I strongly suspected of being a plain-clothes detective, was pointing out some theory of his own, while the others crowded round to listen to what he said. I got as near him as I could, but his observations seemed to me to be absurd, so I withdrew again in some disgust. As I did so I struck against an elderly deformed man, who had been behind me, and I knocked down several books which he was carrying. I remember that as I picked them up I observed the title of one of them, "The Origin of Tree Worship," and it struck me that the fellow must be some poor bibliophile who, either as a trade or as a hobby, was a collector of obscure volumes. I endeavoured to apologize for the accident, but it was evident that these books which I had so unfortunately maltreated were very precious objects in the eyes of their owner. With a snarl of contempt he turned upon his heel, and I saw his curved back and white side-whiskers disappear among the throng.

My observations of No. 427, Park Lane, did little to clear up the problem in which I was interested. The house was separated from the street by a low wall and railing, the whole not more than five feet high. It was perfectly easy, therefore, for anyone to get into the garden, but the window was entirely inaccessible, since there was no water-pipe or anything which could help the most active man to climb it. More puzzled than ever I retraced my steps to Kensington. I had not been in my study five minutes when the maid entered to say that a person desired to see me. To my astonishment it was none other than my strange old book-collector, his sharp, wizened face peering out from a frame of white hair, and his precious volumes, a dozen of them at least, wedged under his right arm.

"You're surprised to see me, sir," said he, in a strange, croaking voice.

I acknowledged that I was.

"I KNOCKED DOWN SEVERAL BOOKS WHICH HE WAS CARRYING."

"Well, I've a conscience, sir, and when I chanced to see you go into this house, as I came hobbling after you, I thought to myself, I'll just step in and see that kind gentleman, and tell him that if I was a bit gruff in my manner there was not any harm meant, and that I am much obliged to him for picking up my books."

"You make too much of a trifle," said I. "May I ask how you knew who I was?"

"Well, sir, if it isn't too great a liberty, I am a neighbour of yours, for you'll find my little bookshop at the corner of Church Street, and very happy to see you, I am sure. Maybe you collect yourself, sir; here's 'British Birds,' and 'Catullus,' and 'The Holy War'—a bargain every one of them. With five volumes you could just fill that gap on that second shelf. It looks untidy, does it not, sir?"

I moved my head to look at the cabinet behind me. When I turned again Sherlock

tainly a grey mist swirled before my eyes, and when it cleared I found my collar-ends undone and the tingling after-taste of brandy upon my lips. Holmes was bending over my chair, his flask in his hand.

"My dear Watson," said the well-remembered voice, "I owe you a thousand apologies. I had no idea that you would be so affected."

I gripped him by the arm.

"Holmes!" I cried. "Is it really you? Can it indeed be that you are alive? Is it possible that you succeeded in climbing out of that awful abyss?"

"SHERLOCK HOLMES WAS STANDING SMILING AT ME ACROSS MY STUDY TABLE."

Holmes was standing smiling at me across my study table. I rose to my feet, stared at him for some seconds in utter amazement, and then it appears that I must have fainted for the first and the last time in my life. Cer-

"Wait a moment," said he. "Are you sure that you are really fit to discuss things? I have given you a serious shock by my unnecessarily dramatic reappearance."

"I am all right, but indeed, Holmes, I can

hardly believe my eyes. Good heavens, to think that you—you of all men—should be standing in my study!" Again I gripped him by the sleeve and felt the thin, sinewy arm beneath it. "Well, you're not a spirit, anyhow," said I. "My dear chap, I am overjoyed to see you. Sit down and tell me how you came alive out of that dreadful chasm."

He sat opposite to me and lit a cigarette in his old nonchalant manner. He was dressed in the seedy frock-coat of the book merchant, but the rest of that individual lay in a pile of white hair and old books upon the table. Holmes looked even thinner and keener than of old, but there was a dead-white tinge in his aquiline face which told me that his life recently had not been a healthy one.

"I am glad to stretch myself, Watson," said he. "It is no joke when a tall man has to take a foot off his stature for several hours on end. Now, my dear fellow, in the matter of these explanations we have, if I may ask for your co-operation, a hard and dangerous night's work in front of us. Perhaps it would be better if I gave you an account of the whole situation when that work is finished."

"I am full of curiosity. I should much prefer to hear now."

"You'll come with me to-night?"

"When you like and where you like."

"This is indeed like the old days. We shall have time for a mouthful of dinner before we need go. Well, then, about that chasm. I had no serious difficulty in getting out of it, for the very simple reason that I never was in it."

"You never were in it?"

"No, Watson, I never was in it. My note to you was absolutely genuine. I had little doubt that I had come to the end of my career when I perceived the somewhat sinister figure of the late Professor Moriarty standing upon the narrow pathway which led to safety. I read an inexorable purpose in his grey eyes. I exchanged some remarks with him, therefore, and obtained his courteous permission to write the short note which you afterwards received. I left it with my cigarette-box and my stick and I walked along the pathway, Moriarty still at my heels. When I reached the end I stood at bay. He drew no weapon, but he rushed at me and threw his long arms around me. He knew that his own game was up, and was only anxious to revenge himself upon me. We tottered together upon the brink of the fall. I have some knowledge, however, of baritsu, or the

Japanese system of wrestling, which has more than once been very useful to me. I slipped through his grip, and he with a horrible scream kicked madly for a few seconds and clawed the air with both his hands. But for all his efforts he could not get his balance, and over he went. With my face over the brink I saw him fall for a long way. Then he struck a rock, bounded off, and splashed into the water."

I listened with amazement to this explanation, which Holmes delivered between the puffs of his cigarette.

"But the tracks!" I cried. "I saw with my own eyes that two went down the path and none returned."

"It came about in this way. The instant that the Professor had disappeared it struck me what a really extraordinarily lucky chance Fate had placed in my way. I knew that Moriarty was not the only man who had sworn my death. There were at least three others whose desire for vengeance upon me would only be increased by the death of their leader. They were all most dangerous men. One or other would certainly get me. On the other hand, if all the world was convinced that I was dead they would take liberties, these men, they would lay themselves open, and sooner or later I could destroy them. Then it would be time for me to announce that I was still in the land of the living. So rapidly does the brain act that I believe I had thought this all out before Professor Moriarty had reached the bottom of the Reichenbach Fall.

"I stood up and examined the rocky wall behind me. In your picturesque account of the matter, which I read with great interest some months later, you assert that the wall was sheer. This was not literally true. A few small footholds presented themselves, and there was some indication of a ledge. The cliff is so high that to climb it all was an obvious impossibility, and it was equally impossible to make my way along the wet path without leaving some tracks. I might, it is true, have reversed my boots, as I have done on similar occasions, but the sight of three sets of tracks in one direction would certainly have suggested a deception. On the whole, then, it was best that I should risk the climb. It was not a pleasant business, Watson. The fall roared beneath me. I am not a fanciful person, but I give you my word that I seemed to hear Moriarty's voice screaming at me out of the abyss. A mistake would have been fatal. More than once, as tufts of grass came out in my hand or my foot slipped in the wet notches of the rock, I thought that I was gone. But I struggled upwards, and at last I reached a ledge several feet deep and covered with soft green moss, where I could lie unseen in the most perfect comfort. There I was stretched when you, my dear Watson, and all your following were investigating in the most sympathetic and inefficient manner the circumstances of my death.

"At last, when you had all formed your inevitable and totally erroneous conclusions, you departed for the hotel and I was left alone. I had imagined that I had reached the end of my adventures, but a very unexpected occurrence showed me that there were surprises still in store for me. A huge rock, falling from above, boomed past me, struck the path, and bounded over into the chasm. For an instant I thought that it was an accident; but a moment later, looking up, I saw a man's head against the darkening sky, and another stone struck the very ledge upon which I was stretched, within a foot of my head. Of course, the meaning of this was obvious. Moriarty had not been alone. A confederate—and even that one glance had told me how dangerous a man that confederate was—had kept guard while the Professor had attacked me. From a distance, unseen by me, he had been a witness of his friend's death and of my escape. He had waited, and then, making his way round to the top of the cliff, he had endeavoured to succeed where his comrade had failed.

"I did not take long to think about it, Watson. Again I saw that grim face look over the cliff, and I knew that it was the precursor of another stone. I scrambled down on to the path. I don't think I could have done it in cold blood. It was a hundred times more difficult than getting up. But I had no time to think of the danger, for another stone sang past me as I hung by my hands from the edge of the ledge. Half-way down I slipped, but by the blessing of God I landed, torn and bleeding, upon the path. I took to my heels, did ten miles over the mountains in the darkness, and a week later I found myself in Florence with the certainty that no one in the world knew what had become of me.

"I had only one confidant—my brother Mycroft. I owe you many apologies, my dear Watson, but it was all-important that it should be thought I was dead, and it is quite certain that you would not have written so convincing an account of my unhappy end

had you not yourself thought that it was true. Several times during the last three years I have taken up my pen to write to you, but always I feared lest your affectionate regard for me should tempt you to some indiscretion which would betray my secret. For that reason I turned away from you this evening when you upset my books, for I was in danger at the time, and any show of surprise and emotion upon your part might have drawn attention to my identity and led to the most deplorable and irreparable results. As to Mycroft, I had to confide in him in order to obtain the money which I needed. The course of events in London did not run so well as I had hoped, for the trial of the Moriarty gang left two of its most dangerous members, my own most vindictive enemies, at liberty. I travelled for two years in Tibet, therefore, and amused myself by visiting Lhassa and spending some days with the head Llama. You may have read of the remarkable explorations of a Norwegian named Sigerson, but I am sure that it never occurred to you that you were receiving news of your friend. I then passed through Persia, looked in at Mecca, and paid a short but interesting visit to the Khalifa at Khartoum, the results of which I have communicated to the Foreign Office. Returning to France I spent some months in a research into the coal-tar derivatives, which I conducted in a laboratory at Montpelier, in the South of France. Having concluded this to my satisfaction, and learning that only one of my enemies was now left in London, I was about to return when my movements were hastened by the news of this very remarkable Park Lane Mystery, which not only appealed to me by its own merits, but which seemed to offer some most peculiar personal opportunities. I came over at once to London, called in my own person at Baker Street, threw Mrs. Hudson into violent hysterics, and found that Mycroft had preserved my rooms and my papers exactly as they had always been. So it was, my dear Watson, that at two o'clock to-day I found myself in my old arm-chair in my own old room, and only wishing that I could have seen my old friend Watson in the other chair which he has so often adorned."

Such was the remarkable narrative to which I listened on that April evening—a narrative which would have been utterly incredible to me had it not been confirmed by the actual sight of the tall, spare figure and the keen, eager face, which I had never thought to see again. In some manner he had learned of my own sad bereavement, and his sympathy was shown in his manner rather than in his words. "Work is the best antidote to sorrow, my dear Watson," said he, "and I have a piece of work for us both to-night which, if we can bring it to a successful conclusion, will in itself justify a man's life on this planet." In vain I begged him to tell me more. "You will hear and see enough before morning," he answered. "We have three years of the past to discuss. Let that suffice until half-past nine, when we start upon the notable adventure of the empty house."

It was indeed like old times when, at that hour, I found myself seated beside him in a hansom, my revolver in my pocket and the thrill of adventure in my heart. Holmes was cold and stern and silent. As the gleam of the streetlamps flashed upon his austere features I saw that his brows were drawn down in thought and his thin lips compressed. I knew not what wild beast we were about to hunt down in the dark jungle of criminal London, but I was well assured from the bearing of this master huntsman that the adventure was a most grave one, while the sardonic smile which occasionally broke through his ascetic gloom boded little good for the object of our quest.

I had imagined that we were bound for Baker Street, but Holmes stopped the cab at the corner of Cavendish Square. I observed that as he stepped out he gave a most searching glance to right and left, and at every subsequent street corner he took the utmost pains to assure that he was not followed. Our route was certainly a singular one. Holmes's knowledge of the byways of London was extraordinary, and on this occasion he passed rapidly, and with

an assured step, through a network of mews and stables the very existence of which I had never known. We emerged at last into a small road, lined with old, gloomy houses, which led us into Manchester Street, and so to Blandford Street. Here he turned swiftly down a narrow passage, passed through a wooden gate into a deserted yard, and then opened with a key the back door of a house. We entered together and he closed it behind us.

The place was pitch-dark, but it was

"I CREPT FORWARD AND LOOKED ACROSS AT THE FAMILIAR WINDOW."

evident to me that it was an empty house. Our feet creaked and crackled over the bare planking, and my outstretched hand touched a wall from which the paper was hanging in ribbons. Holmes's cold, thin fingers closed round my wrist and led me forwards down a long hall, until I dimly saw the murky fan-light over the door. Here Holmes turned suddenly to the right, and we found ourselves in a large, square, empty room, heavily shadowed in the corners, but faintly lit in the centre from the lights of the street beyond. There was no lamp near and the window was thick with dust, so that we could only just discern each other's figures within. My companion put his hand upon my shoulder and his lips close to my ear.

"Do you know where we are?" he whispered.

"Surely that is Baker Street," I answered, staring through the dim window.

"Exactly. We are in Camden House, which stands opposite to our own old quarters."

"But why are we here?"

"Because it commands so excellent a view of that picturesque pile. Might I trouble you, my dear Watson, to draw a little nearer to the window, taking every precaution not to show yourself, and then to look up at our old rooms—the starting-point of so many of our little adventures? We will see if my three years of absence have entirely taken away my power to surprise you."

I crept forward and looked across at the familiar window. As my eyes fell upon it I gave a gasp and a cry of amazement. The blind was down and a strong light was burning in the room. The shadow of a man who was seated in a chair within was thrown in hard, black outline upon the luminous screen of the window. There was no mistaking the poise of the head, the square-ness of the shoulders, the sharpness of the features. The face was turned half-round, and the effect was that of one of those black silhouettes which our grandparents loved to frame. It was a perfect reproduction of Holmes. So amazed was I that I threw out my hand to make sure that the man himself was standing beside me. He was quivering with silent laughter.

"Well?" said he.

"Good heavens!" I cried. "It is marvellous."

"'I trust that age doth not wither nor custom stale my infinite variety,'" said he, and I recognised in his voice the joy and pride which the artist takes in his own creation. "It really is rather like me, is it not?"

"I should be prepared to swear that it was you."

"The credit of the execution is due to Monsieur Oscar Meunier, of Grenoble, who spent some days in doing the moulding. It is a bust in wax. The rest I arranged myself during my visit to Baker Street this afternoon."

"But why?"

"Because, my dear Watson, I had the strongest possible reason for wishing certain people to think that I was there when I was really elsewhere."

"And you thought the rooms were watched?"

"I *knew* that they were watched."

"By whom?"

"By my old enemies, Watson. By the charming society whose leader lies in the Reichenbach Fall. You must remember that they knew, and only they knew, that I was still alive. Sooner or later they believed that I should come back to my rooms. They watched them continuously, and this morning they saw me arrive."

"How do you know?"

"Because I recognised their sentinel when I glanced out of my window. He is a harmless enough fellow, Parker by name, a garroter by trade, and a remarkable per-former upon the Jew's harp. I cared nothing for him. But I cared a great deal for the much more formidable person who was behind him, the bosom friend of Moriarty, the man who dropped the rocks over the cliff, the most cunning and dangerous criminal in London. That is the man who is after me to-night, Watson, and that is the man who is quite unaware that we are after *him*."

My friend's plans were gradually reveal-ing themselves. From this convenient retreat the watchers were being watched and the trackers tracked. That angular shadow up yonder was the bait and we were the hunters. In silence we stood together in the darkness and watched the hurrying figures who passed and repassed in front of us. Holmes was silent and motionless; but I could tell that he was keenly alert, and that his eyes were fixed intently upon the stream of passers-by. It was a bleak and boisterous night, and the wind whistled shrilly down the long street. Many people were moving to and fro, most of them muffled in their coats and cravats. Once or twice it seemed to me that I had seen the same figure before, and I especially noticed two men who appeared to be sheltering themselves from the wind in the doorway of a house some distance up the street. I tried to draw my companion's attention to them, but he gave a little ejaculation of impatience and continued to stare into the street. More than once he fidgeted with his feet and tapped rapidly with his fingers upon the wall. It was evident to me that he was becoming uneasy and that his plans were not working out altogether as he had hoped. At last, as midnight approached and the street gradually cleared, he paced up and down the room in uncontrollable agitation. I was about to make some remark to him when I raised my eyes to the lighted window and again experienced almost as great a surprise as before. I clutched Holmes's arm and pointed upwards.

"The shadow has moved!" I cried.

It was, indeed, no longer the profile, but the back, which was turned towards us.

Three years had certainly not smoothed the asperities of his temper or his impatience with a less active intelligence than his own.

"Of course it has moved," said he. "Am I such a farcical bungler, Watson, that I should erect an obvious dummy and expect that some of the sharpest men in Europe would be deceived by it? We have been in this room two hours, and Mrs. Hudson has made some change in that figure eight times, or once in every quarter of an hour. She works it from the front so that her shadow may never be seen. Ah!" He drew in his breath with a shrill, excited intake. In the dim light I saw his head thrown forward, his whole attitude rigid with attention. Outside, the street was absolutely deserted. Those two men might still be crouching in the doorway, but I could no longer see them. All was still and dark, save only that brilliant yellow screen in front of us with the black figure outlined upon its centre. Again in the utter silence I heard that thin, sibilant note which spoke of intense suppressed excitement. An instant later he pulled me back into the blackest corner of the room, and I felt his warning hand upon my lips. The fingers which clutched me were quivering. Never had I known my friend more moved, and yet the dark street still stretched lonely and motionless before us.

But suddenly I was aware of that which his keener senses had already distinguished. A low, stealthy sound came to my ears, not from the direction of Baker Street, but from the back of the very house in which we lay concealed. A door opened and shut. An instant later steps crept down the passage— steps which were meant to be silent, but which reverberated harshly through the empty house. Holmes crouched back against the wall and I did the same, my hand closing upon the handle of my

"THE LIGHT OF THE STREET FELL FULL UPON HIS FACE."

revolver. Peering through the gloom, I saw the vague outline of a man, a shade blacker than the blackness of the open door. He stood for an instant, and then he crept forward, crouching, menacing, into the room. He was within three yards of us, this sinister figure, and I had braced myself to meet his spring, before I realized that he had no idea of our presence. He passed close beside us, stole over to the window, and very softly and noiselessly raised it for half a foot. As he sank to the level of this opening the light of the street, no longer dimmed by the dusty glass, fell full upon his face. The man seemed to be beside himself with excitement. His two eyes shone like stars and his features were working convulsively. He was an elderly man, with a thin, projecting nose, a high, bald forehead, and a huge grizzled moustache. An opera-hat was pushed to the back of his head, and an evening dress shirt-front gleamed out through his open overcoat. His face was gaunt and swarthy, scored with deep, savage lines. In his hand he carried what appeared to be a stick, but as he laid it down upon the floor it gave a metallic clang. Then from the pocket of his overcoat he drew a bulky object, and he busied himself in some task which ended with a loud, sharp click, as if a spring or bolt had fallen into its place. Still kneeling upon the floor he bent forward and threw all his weight and strength upon some lever, with the result that there came a long, whirling, grinding noise, ending once more in a powerful click. He straightened himself then, and I saw that what he held in his hand was a sort of a gun, with a curiously misshapen butt. He opened it at the breech, put something in, and snapped the breech-block. Then, crouching down, he rested the end of the barrel upon the ledge of the open window, and I saw his long moustache droop over the stock and his eye gleam as it peered along the sights. I heard a little sigh of satisfaction as he cuddled the butt into his shoulder, and saw that amazing target, the black man on the yellow ground, standing clear at the end of his fore sight. For an instant he was rigid and motionless. Then his finger tightened on the trigger. There was a strange, loud whiz and a long, silvery tinkle of broken glass. At that instant Holmes sprang like a tiger on to the marksman's back and hurled him flat upon his face. He was up again in a moment, and with convulsive strength he seized Holmes by the throat; but I struck him on the head with the butt of my revolver

and he dropped again upon the floor. I fell upon him, and as I held him my comrade blew a shrill call upon a whistle. There was the clatter of running feet upon the pavement and two policemen in uniform, with one plain, clothes detective, rushed through the front entrance and into the room.

"That you, Lestrade?" said Holmes.

"Yes, Mr. Holmes. I took the job myself. It's good to see you back in London, sir."

"I think you want a little unofficial help. Three undetected murders in one year won't do, Lestrade. But you handled the Molesey Mystery with less than your usual—that's to say, you handled it fairly well."

We had all risen to our feet, our prisoner breathing hard, with a stalwart constable on each side of him. Already a few loiterers had begun to collect in the street. Holmes stepped up to the window, closed it, and dropped the blinds. Lestrade had produced two candles and the policemen had uncovered their lanterns. I was able at last to have a good look at our prisoner.

It was a tremendously virile and yet sinister face which was turned towards us. With the brow of a philosopher above and the jaw of a sensualist below, the man must have started with great capacities for good or for evil. But one could not look upon his cruel blue eyes, with their drooping, cynical lids, or upon the fierce, aggressive nose and the threatening, deep-lined brow, without reading Nature's plainest danger-signals. He took no heed of any of us, but his eyes were fixed upon Holmes's face with an expression in which hatred and amazement were equally blended. "You fiend!" he kept on muttering; "you clever, clever fiend!"

"Ah, Colonel!" said Holmes, arranging his rumpled collar; "'journeys end in lovers' meetings,' as the old play says. I don't think I have had the pleasure of seeing you since you favoured me with those attentions as I lay on the ledge above the Reichenbach Fall."

The Colonel still stared at my friend like a man in a trance. "You cunning, cunning fiend!" was all that he could say.

"I have not introduced you yet," said Holmes. "This, gentlemen, is Colonel Sebastian Moran, once of Her Majesty's Indian Army, and the best heavy game shot that our Eastern Empire has ever produced. I believe I am correct, Colonel, in saying that your bag of tigers still remains unrivalled?"

The fierce old man said nothing, but still glared at my companion; with his savage eyes and bristling moustache he was wonderfully like a tiger himself.

"I wonder that my very simple stratagem could deceive so old a shikari," said Holmes. "It must be very familiar to you. Have you not tethered a young kid under a tree, lain above it with your rifle, and waited for the bait to bring up your tiger? This empty house is my tree and you are my tiger. You have possibly had other guns in reserve in case there should be several tigers, or in the unlikely supposition of your own aim failing you. These," he pointed around, "are my other guns. The parallel is exact."

Colonel Moran sprang forward, with a

pate that you would yourself make use of this empty house and this convenient front window. I had imagined you as operating from the street, where my friend Lestrade and his merry men were awaiting you. With that exception all has gone as I expected."

Colonel Moran turned to the official detective.

"You may or may not have just cause for arresting me," said he, "but at least there can be no reason why I should submit to the gibes of this person. If I am in the hands of the law let things be done in a legal way."

"Well, that's reasonable enough," said Lestrade. "Nothing further you have to say, Mr. Holmes, before we go?"

"COLONEL MORAN SPRANG FORWARD, WITH A SNARL OF RAGE."

snarl of rage, but the constables dragged him back. The fury upon his face was terrible to look at.

"I confess that you had one small surprise for me," said Holmes. "I did not antici-

Holmes had picked up the powerful air-gun from the floor and was examining its mechanism.

"An admirable and unique weapon," said he, "noiseless and of tremendous power. I knew Von Herder, the blind German mechanic, who constructed it to the order of the late Professor Moriarty. For years I have been aware of its existence, though I have never before had an opportunity of handling it. I commend it very specially to your attention, Lestrade, and also the bullets which fit it."

"You can trust us to look after that, Mr. Holmes," said Lestrade, as the whole party moved towards the door. "Anything further to say?"

"Only to ask what charge you intend to prefer?"

"What charge, sir? Why, of course, the attempted murder of Mr. Sherlock Holmes."

"Not so, Lestrade. I do not propose to appear in the matter at all. To you, and to you only, belongs the credit of the remarkable arrest which you have effected. Yes, Lestrade, I congratulate you! With your usual happy mixture of cunning and audacity you have got him."

"Got him! Got whom, Mr. Holmes?"

"The man that the whole force has been seeking in vain—Colonel Sebastian Moran, who shot the Honourable Ronald Adair with an expanding bullet from an air-gun through the open window of the second-floor front of No. 427, Park Lane, upon the 30th of last month. That's the charge, Lestrade. And now, Watson, if you can endure the draught from a broken window, I think that half an hour in my study over a cigar may afford you some profitable amusement."

Our old chambers had been left unchanged through the supervision of Mycroft Holmes and the immediate care of Mrs. Hudson. As I entered I saw, it is true, an unwonted tidiness, but the old landmarks were all in their place. There were the chemical corner and the acid-stained, deal-topped table. There upon a shelf was the row of formidable scrap-books and books of reference which many of our fellow-citizens would have been so glad to burn. The diagrams, the violin-case, and the pipe-rack—even the Persian slipper which contained the tobacco—all met my eyes as I glanced round me. There were two occupants of the room—one Mrs. Hudson, who beamed upon us both as we entered; the other the strange dummy which had played so important a part in the evening's adventures. It was a wax-coloured model of my friend, so admirably done that it was a perfect facsimile. It stood on a small pedestal table with an old dressing-gown of Holmes's so draped round it that

the illusion from the street was absolutely perfect.

"I hope you preserved all precautions, Mrs. Hudson?" said Holmes.

"I went to it on my knees, sir, just as you told me."

"Excellent. You carried the thing out very well. Did you observe where the bullet went?"

"Yes, sir. I'm afraid it has spoilt your beautiful bust, for it passed right through the head and flattened itself on the wall. I picked it up from the carpet. Here it is!"

Holmes held it out to me. "A soft revolver bullet, as you perceive, Watson. There's genius in that, for who would expect to find such a thing fired from an air-gun. All right, Mrs. Hudson, I am much obliged for your assistance. And now, Watson, let me see you in your old seat once more, for there are several points which I should like to discuss with you."

He had thrown off the seedy frock-coat, and now he was the Holmes of old in the mouse-coloured dressing-gown which he took from his effigy.

"The old shikari's nerves have not lost their steadiness nor his eyes their keenness," said he, with a laugh, as he inspected the shattered forehead of his bust.

"Plumb in the middle of the back of the head and smack through the brain. He was the best shot in India, and I expect that there are few better in London. Have you heard the name?"

"No, I have not."

"Well, well, such is fame! But, then, if I remember aright, you had not heard the name of Professor James Moriarty, who had one of the great brains of the century. Just give me down my index of biographies from the shelf."

He turned over the pages lazily, leaning back in his chair and blowing great clouds from his cigar.

"My collection of M's is a fine one," said he. "Moriarty himself is enough to make any letter illustrious, and here is Morgan the poisoner, and Merridew of abominable memory, and Mathews, who knocked out my left canine in the waiting-room at Charing Cross, and, finally, here is our friend of to-night."

He handed over the book, and I read: "*Moran, Sebastian, Colonel*. Unemployed. Formerly 1st Bengalore Pioneers. Born London, 1840. Son of Sir Augustus Moran, C.B., once British Minister to Persia. Educated Eton and Oxford. Served in Jowaki

Campaign, Afghan Campaign, Charasiab (despatches), Sherpur, and Cabul. Author of 'Heavy Game of the Western Himalayas,' 1881; 'Three Months in the Jungle,' 1884. Address: Conduit Street. Clubs: The Anglo-Indian, the Tankerville, the Bagatelle Card Club."

On the margin was written, in Holmes's precise hand: "The second most dangerous man in London."

"This is astonishing," said I, as I handed back the volume. "The man's career is that of an honourable soldier."

"It is true," Holmes answered. "Up to a certain point he did well. He was always a man of iron nerve, and the story is still told in India how he crawled down a drain after a wounded man-eating tiger.

"'MY COLLECTION OF M'S IS A FINE ONE,' SAID HE."

There are some trees, Watson, which grow to a certain height and then suddenly develop some unsightly eccentricity. You will see it often in humans. I have a theory that the individual represents in his development the whole procession of his ancestors, and that such a sudden turn to good or evil stands for some strong influence which came into the line of his pedigree. The person becomes, as it were, the epitome of the history of his own family."

"It is surely rather fanciful."

"Well, I don't insist upon it. Whatever the cause, Colonel Moran began to go wrong. Without any open scandal he still made India too hot to hold him. He retired, came to London, and again acquired an evil name. It was at this time that he was sought out by Professor Moriarty, to whom for a time he was chief of the staff. Moriarty supplied him liberally with money and used him only in one or two very high-class jobs which no ordinary criminal could have undertaken. You may have some recollection of the death of Mrs. Stewart, of Lauder, in 1887. Not? Well, I am sure Moran was at the bottom of it; but nothing could be proved. So cleverly was the Colonel concealed that even when the Moriarty gang was broken up we could not incriminate him. You remember at that date, when I called upon you in your rooms, how I put up the shutters for fear of air-guns? No doubt you thought me fanciful. I knew exactly what I was doing, for I knew of the existence of this remarkable gun, and I knew also that one of the best shots in the world would be behind it. When we were in Switzerland he followed us with Moriarty, and it was undoubtedly he who gave me that evil five minutes on the Reichenbach ledge.

"You may think that I read the papers with some attention during my sojourn in France, on the look-out for any chance of laying him by the heels. So long as he was free in London my life would really not have been worth living. Night and day the shadow would have been over me, and sooner or later his chance must have come. What could I do? I could not shoot him at sight, or I should myself be in the dock. There was no use appealing to a magistrate. They cannot interfere on the strength of what would appear to them to be a wild suspicion. So I could do nothing. But I watched the criminal news, knowing that sooner or later I should get him. Then came the death of this Ronald Adair. My chance had come at last! Knowing what I did, was it not certain that Colonel Moran had done it? He had played cards with the lad; he had followed him home from the club; he had shot him through the open window. There was not a doubt of it. The bullets alone are enough to put his head in a noose. I came over at once. I was seen by the sentinel, who would, I knew, direct the Colonel's attention to my presence. He could not fail to connect my sudden return with his crime and to be terribly alarmed. I was sure that he would make an attempt to get me out of the way *at once*, and would bring round his murderous weapon for that purpose. I left him an excellent mark in the window, and, having warned the police that they might be needed—by the way, Watson, you spotted their presence in that doorway with unerring accuracy—I took up what seemed to me to be a judicious post for observation, never dreaming that he would choose the same spot for his attack. Now, my dear Watson, does anything remain for me to explain?"

"Yes," said I. "You have not made it clear what was Colonel Moran's motive in murdering the Honourable Ronald Adair."

"Ah! my dear Watson, there we come into those realms of conjecture where the most logical mind may be at fault. Each may form his own hypothesis upon the present evidence, and yours is as likely to be correct as mine."

"You have formed one, then?"

"I think that it is not difficult to explain the facts. It came out in evidence that Colonel Moran and young Adair had between them won a considerable amount of money. Now, Moran undoubtedly played foul—of that I have long been aware. I believe that on the day of the murder Adair had discovered that Moran was cheating. Very likely he had spoken to him privately, and had threatened to expose him unless he voluntarily resigned his membership of the club and promised not to play cards again. It is unlikely that a youngster like Adair would at once make a hideous scandal by exposing a well-known man so much older than himself. Probably he acted as I suggest. The exclusion from his clubs would mean ruin to Moran, who lived by his ill-gotten card gains. He therefore murdered Adair, who at the time was endeavouring to work out how much money he should himself return, since he could not profit by his partner's foul play. He locked the door lest the ladies should surprise him and insist upon knowing what he was doing with these names and coins. Will it pass?"

"I have no doubt that you have hit upon the truth."

"It will be verified or disproved at the trial. Meanwhile, come what may, Colonel Moran will trouble us no more, the famous air-gun of Von Herder will embellish the Scotland Yard Museum, and once again Mr. Sherlock Holmes is free to devote his life to examining those interesting little problems which the complex life of London so plentifully presents."

"A LITTLE, WIZENED MAN DARTED OUT."

# THE STRAND MAGAZINE.

Vol. xxvi. NOVEMBER, 1903. No. 155.

# THE RETURN OF SHERLOCK HOLMES.

## By A. CONAN DOYLE.

### II.—The Adventure of the Norwood Builder.

"FROM the point of view of the criminal expert," said Mr. Sherlock Holmes, "London has become a singularly uninteresting city since the death of the late lamented Professor Moriarty."

"I can hardly think that you would find many decent citizens to agree with you," I answered.

"Well, well, I must not be selfish," said he, with a smile, as he pushed back his chair from the breakfast-table. "The community is certainly the gainer, and no one the loser, save the poor out-of-work specialist, whose occupation has gone. With that man in the field one's morning paper presented infinite possibilities. Often it was only the smallest trace, Watson, the faintest indication, and yet it was enough to tell me that the great malignant brain was there, as the gentlest tremors of the edges of the web remind one of the foul spider which lurks in the centre. Petty thefts, wanton assaults, purposeless outrage—to the man who held the clue all could be worked into one connected whole. To the scientific student of the higher criminal world no capital in Europe offered the advantages which London then possessed. But now——" He shrugged his shoulders in humorous deprecation of the state of things which he had himself done so much to produce.

At the time of which I speak Holmes had been back for some months, and I, at his request, had sold my practice and returned to share the old quarters in Baker Street. A young doctor, named Verner, had purchased my small Kensington practice, and given with astonishing little demur the highest price that I ventured to ask—an incident which only explained itself some years later when I found that Verner was a distant relation of Holmes's, and that it was my friend who had really found the money.

Our months of partnership had not been so uneventful as he had stated, for I find, on looking over my notes, that this period includes the case of the papers of Ex-President Murillo, and also the shocking affair of the Dutch steamship *Friesland*, which so nearly cost us both our lives. His cold and proud nature was always averse, however, to anything in the shape of public applause, and he bound me in the most stringent terms to say no further word of himself, his methods, or his successes—a prohibition which, as I have explained, has only now been removed.

Mr. Sherlock Holmes was leaning back in his chair after his whimsical protest, and was unfolding his morning paper in a leisurely fashion, when our attention was arrested by a tremendous ring at the bell, followed immediately by a hollow drumming sound, as if someone were beating on the outer door with his fist. As it opened there came a tumultuous rush into the hall, rapid feet clattered up the stair, and an instant later a wild-eyed and frantic young man, pale, dishevelled, and palpitating, burst into the room. He looked from one to the other of us, and under our gaze of inquiry he became conscious that some apology was needed for this unceremonious entry.

and the breathing which had prompted them. Our client, however, stared in amazement.

"Yes, I am all that, Mr. Holmes, and in addition I am the most unfortunate man at this moment in London. For Heaven's sake don't abandon me, Mr. Holmes! If they come to arrest me before I have finished my story, make them give me time so that I may tell you the whole truth. I could go to gaol happy if I knew that you were working for me outside."

"Arrest you!" said Holmes. "This is really most grati — most interesting. On what charge do you expect to be arrested?"

"A WILD-EYED AND FRANTIC YOUNG MAN BURST INTO THE ROOM."

"I'm sorry, Mr. Holmes," he cried. "You mustn't blame me. I am nearly mad. Mr. Holmes, I am the unhappy John Hector McFarlane."

He made the announcement as if the name alone would explain both his visit and its manner; but I could see by my companion's unresponsive face that it meant no more to him than to me.

"Have a cigarette, Mr. McFarlane," said he, pushing his case across. "I am sure that with your symptoms my friend Dr. Watson here would prescribe a sedative. The weather has been so very warm these last few days. Now, if you feel a little more composed, I should be glad if you would sit down in that chair and tell us very slowly and quietly who you are and what it is that you want. You mentioned your name as if I should recognise it, but I assure you that, beyond the obvious facts that you are a bachelor, a solicitor, a Freemason, and an asthmatic, I know nothing whatever about you."

Familiar as I was with my friend's methods, it was not difficult for me to follow his deductions, and to observe the untidiness of attire, the sheaf of legal papers, the watch-charm,

"Upon the charge of murdering Mr. Jonas Oldacre, of Lower Norwood."

My companion's expressive face showed a sympathy which was not, I am afraid, entirely unmixed with satisfaction.

"Dear me," said he; "it was only this moment at breakfast that I was saying to my friend, Dr. Watson, that sensational cases had disappeared out of our papers."

Our visitor stretched forward a quivering hand and picked up the *Daily Telegraph*, which still lay upon Holmes's knee.

"If you had looked at it, sir, you would have seen at a glance what the errand is on which I have come to you this morning. I feel as if my name and my misfortune must be in every man's mouth." He turned it over to expose the central page. "Here it is, and with your permission I will read it to you. Listen to this, Mr. Holmes. The head-lines are: 'Mysterious Affair at Lower Norwood. Disappearance of a Well-known Builder. Suspicion of Murder and Arson. A Clue to the Criminal.' That is the clue which they are already following, Mr. Holmes, and I know that it leads infallibly to me. I have been followed from London Bridge Station, and I am sure that they are only waiting for the warrant to arrest me. It will break my mother's heart—it will break her heart!" He wrung his hands in an agony of apprehension, and swayed backwards and forwards in his chair.

I looked with interest upon this man, who was accused of being the perpetrator of a crime of violence. He was flaxen-haired and handsome in a washed-out negative fashion, with frightened blue eyes and a clean-shaven face, with a weak, sensitive mouth. His age may have been about twenty-seven ; his dress and bearing that of a gentleman. From the pocket of his light summer overcoat protruded the bundle of endorsed papers which proclaimed his profession.

"We must use what time we have," said Holmes. "Watson, would you have the kindness to take the paper and to read me the paragraph in question ? "

Underneath the vigorous head-lines which our client had quoted I read the following suggestive narrative :—

Late last night, or early this morning, an incident occurred at Lower Norwood which points, it is feared, to a serious crime. Mr. Jonas Oldacre is a well-known resident of that suburb, where he has carried on his business as a builder for many years. Mr. Oldacre is a bachelor, fifty-two years of age, and lives in Deep Dene House, at the Sydenham end of the road of that name. He has had the reputation of being a man of eccentric habits, secretive and retiring. For some years he has practically withdrawn from the business, in which he is said to have amassed considerable wealth. A small timber-yard still exists, however, at the back of the house, and last night, about twelve o'clock, an alarm was given that one of the stacks was on fire. The engines were soon upon the spot, but the dry wood burned with great fury, and it was impossible to arrest the conflagration until the stack had been entirely consumed. Up to this point the incident bore the appearance of an ordinary accident, but fresh indications seem to point to serious crime. Surprise was expressed at the absence of the master of the establishment from the scene of the fire, and an inquiry followed, which showed that he had disappeared from the house. An examination of his room revealed that the bed had not been slept in, that a safe which stood in it was open, that a number of important papers were scattered about the room, and, finally, that there were signs of a murderous struggle, slight traces of blood being found within the room, and an oaken walking-stick, which also showed stains of blood upon the handle. It is known that Mr. Jonas Oldacre had received a late visitor in his bedroom upon that night, and the stick found has been identified as the property of this person, who is a young London solicitor named John Hector McFarlane, junior partner of Graham and McFarlane, of 426, Gresham Buildings, E.C. The police believe that they have evidence in their possession which supplies a very convincing motive for the crime, and altogether it cannot be doubted that sensational developments will follow.

LATER.—It is rumoured as we go to press that Mr. John Hector McFarlane has actually been arrested on the charge of the murder of Mr. Jonas Oldacre. It is at least certain that a warrant has been issued. There have been further and sinister developments in the investigation at Norwood. Besides the signs of a struggle in the room of the unfortunate builder it is now known that the French windows of his bedroom (which is on the ground floor) were found to be open, that there were marks as if some bulky object had been dragged across to the wood-pile, and, finally, it is asserted that charred remains have been found among the charcoal ashes of the fire. The police theory is that a most sensational crime has been committed, that the victim was clubbed to death in his own bedroom, his papers rifled, and his dead body dragged across to the wood-stack, which was then ignited so as to hide all traces of the crime. The conduct of the criminal investigation has been left in the experienced hands of Inspector Lestrade, of Scotland Yard, who is following up the clues with his accustomed energy and sagacity.

Sherlock Holmes listened with closed eyes and finger-tips together to this remarkable account.

"The case has certainly some points of interest," said he, in his languid fashion. "May I ask, in the first place, Mr. McFarlane, how it is that you are still at liberty, since there appears to be enough evidence to justify your arrest ? "

"I live at Torrington Lodge, Blackheath, with my parents, Mr. Holmes ; but last night, having to do business very late with Mr. Jonas Oldacre, I stayed at an hotel in Norwood, and came to my business from there. I knew nothing of this affair until I was in the train, when I read what you have just heard. I at once saw the horrible danger of my position, and I hurried to put the case into your hands. I have no doubt that I should have been arrested either at my City office or at my home. A man followed me from London Bridge Station, and I have no doubt —— Great Heaven, what is that ? "

It was a clang of the bell, followed instantly by heavy steps upon the stair. A moment later our old friend Lestrade appeared in the doorway. Over his shoulder I caught a glimpse of one or two uniformed policemen outside.

"Mr. John Hector McFarlane ? " said Lestrade.

Our unfortunate client rose with a ghastly face.

"I arrest you for the wilful murder of Mr. Jonas Oldacre, of Lower Norwood."

McFarlane turned to us with a gesture of despair, and sank into his chair once more like one who is crushed.

"One moment, Lestrade," said Holmes. "Half an hour more or less can make no difference to you, and the gentleman was about to give us an account of this very interesting affair, which might aid us in clearing it up."

"I think there will be no difficulty in clearing it up," said Lestrade, grimly.

"None the less, with your permission, I should be much interested to hear his account."

"Well, Mr. Holmes, it is difficult for me to refuse you anything, for you have been of use to the force once or twice in the past, and we owe you a good turn at Scotland Yard," said Lestrade. "At the same time I must remain with my prisoner, and I am bound to warn him that anything he may say will appear in evidence against him."

"I wish nothing better," said our client. "All I ask is that you should hear and recognise the absolute truth."

Lestrade looked at his watch. "I'll give you half an hour," said he.

"I must explain first," said McFarlane, "that I knew nothing of Mr. Jonas Oldacre. His name was familiar to me, for many years ago my parents were acquainted with him, but they drifted apart. I was very much surprised, therefore, when yesterday, about three o'clock in the afternoon, he walked into my office in the City. But I was still more astonished when he told me the object of his visit. He had in his hand several sheets of a note-book, covered with scribbled writing—here they are—and he laid them on my table.

"'Here is my will,' said he. 'I want you, Mr. McFarlane, to cast it into proper legal shape. I will sit here while you do so.'

"I set myself to copy it, and you can imagine my astonishment when I found that, with some reservations, he had left all his property to me. He was a strange little, ferret-like man, with white eyelashes, and when I looked up at him I found his keen grey eyes fixed upon me with an amused expression. I could hardly believe my own senses as I read the terms of the will; but he explained that he was a bachelor with hardly any living relation, that he had known my parents in his youth, and that he had always heard of me as a very deserving young man, and was assured that his money would be in worthy hands. Of course, I could only stammer out my thanks. The will was duly finished, signed, and witnessed by my clerk. This is it on the blue paper, and these

slips, as I have explained, are the rough draft. Mr. Jonas Oldacre then informed me that there were a number of documents—building leases, title-deeds, mortgages, scrip, and so forth—which it was necessary that I should see and understand. He said that his mind would not be easy until the whole thing was settled, and he begged me to come out to his house at Norwood that night, bringing the will with me, and to arrange matters. 'Remember, my boy, not one word to your parents about the affair until everything is settled. We will keep it as a little surprise for them.' He was very insistent upon this point, and made me promise it faithfully.

"You can imagine, Mr. Holmes, that I was not in a humour to refuse him anything that he might ask. He was my benefactor, and all my desire was to carry out his wishes in every particular. I sent a telegram home, therefore, to say that I had important business on hand, and that it was impossible for me to say how late I might be. Mr. Oldacre had told me that he would like me to have supper with him at nine, as he might not be home before that hour. I had some difficulty in finding his house, however, and it was nearly half-past before I reached it. I found him——"

"One moment!" said Holmes. "Who opened the door?"

"A middle-aged woman, who was, I suppose, his housekeeper."

"And it was she, I presume, who mentioned your name?"

"Exactly," said McFarlane.

"Pray proceed."

McFarlane wiped his damp brow and then continued his narrative:—

"I was shown by this woman into a sitting-room, where a frugal supper was laid out. Afterwards Mr. Jonas Oldacre led me into his bedroom, in which there stood a heavy safe. This he opened and took out a mass of documents, which we went over together. It was between eleven and twelve when we finished. He remarked that we must not disturb the housekeeper. He showed me out through his own French window, which had been open all this time."

"Was the blind down?" asked Holmes.

"I will not be sure, but I believe that it was only half down. Yes, I remember how he pulled it up in order to swing open the window. I could not find my stick, and he said, 'Never mind, my boy; I shall see a good deal of you now, I hope, and I will keep your stick until you come back to claim it.' I left him there, the safe open, and the papers made up in packets upon the table. It was so late that I could not get back to Blackheath, so I spent the night at the Anerley Arms, and I knew nothing more until I read of this horrible affair in the morning."

"Anything more that you would like to ask, Mr. Holmes?" said Lestrade, whose eyebrows had gone up once or twice during this remarkable explanation.

"Not until I have been to Blackheath."

man arose, and with a last beseeching glance at us he walked from the room. The officers conducted him to the cab, but Lestrade remained.

Holmes had picked up the pages which formed the rough draft of the will, and was looking at them with the keenest interest upon his face.

"There are some points about that document, Lestrade, are there not?" said he, pushing them over.

The official looked at them with a puzzled expression.

"THE WRETCHED YOUNG MAN AROSE."

"You mean to Norwood," said Lestrade.

"Oh, yes; no doubt that is what I must have meant," said Holmes, with his enigmatical smile. Lestrade had learned by more experiences than he would care to acknowledge that that razor-like brain could cut through that which was impenetrable to him. I saw him look curiously at my companion.

"I think I should like to have a word with you presently, Mr. Sherlock Holmes," said he. "Now, Mr. McFarlane, two of my constables are at the door and there is a four-wheeler waiting." The wretched young

"I can read the first few lines, and these in the middle of the second page, and one or two at the end. Those are as clear as print," said he; "but the writing in between is very bad, and there are three places where I cannot read it at all."

"What do you make of that?" said Holmes.

"Well, what do *you* make of it?"

"That it was written in a train; the good writing represents stations, the bad writing movement, and the very bad writing passing over points. A scientific expert would pronounce at once that this was drawn up on a suburban line, since nowhere save in the immediate vicinity of a great city could there be so quick a succession of points. Granting that his whole journey was occupied in drawing up the will, then the train was an express, only stopping once between Norwood and London Bridge."

Lestrade began to laugh.

"You are too many for me when you begin to get on your theories, Mr. Holmes," said he. "How does this bear on the case?"

"Well, it corroborates the young man's story to the extent that the will was drawn up by Jonas Oldacre in his journey yesterday. It is curious—is it not?—that a man should draw up so important a document in so haphazard a fashion. It suggests that he did not think it was going to be of much practical importance. If a man drew up a will which he did not intend ever to be effective he might do it so."

"Well, he drew up his own death-warrant at the same time," said Lestrade.

"Oh, you think so?"

"Don't you?"

"Well, it is quite possible; but the case is not clear to me yet."

"Not clear? Well, if that isn't clear, what *could* be clear? Here is a young man who learns suddenly that if a certain older man dies he will succeed to a fortune. What does he do? He says nothing to anyone, but he arranges that he shall go out on some pretext to see his client that night; he waits until the only other person in the house is in bed, and then in the solitude of the man's room he murders him, burns his body in the wood-pile, and departs to a neighbouring hotel. The blood-stains in the room and also on the stick are very slight. It is probable that he imagined his crime to be a bloodless one, and hoped that if the body were consumed it would hide all traces of the method of his death—traces which for some reason must have pointed to him. Is all this not obvious?"

"It strikes me, my good Lestrade, as being just a trifle too obvious," said Holmes. "You do not add imagination to your other great qualities; but if you could for one moment put yourself in the place of this young man, would you choose the very night after the will had been made to commit your crime? Would it not seem dangerous to you to make so very close a relation

between the two incidents? Again, would you choose an occasion when you are known to be in the house, when a servant has let you in? And, finally, would you take the great pains to conceal the body and yet leave your own stick as a sign that you were the criminal? Confess, Lestrade, that all this is very unlikely."

"As to the stick, Mr. Holmes, you know as well as I do that a criminal is often flurried and does things which a cool man would avoid. He was very likely afraid to go back to the room. Give me another theory that would fit the facts."

"I could very easily give you half-a-dozen," said Holmes. "Here, for example, is a very possible and even probable one. I make you a free present of it. The older man is showing documents which are of evident value. A passing tramp sees them through the window, the blind of which is only half down. Exit the solicitor. Enter the tramp! He seizes a stick, which he observes there, kills Oldacre, and departs after burning the body."

"Why should the tramp burn the body?"

"For the matter of that why should McFarlane?"

"To hide some evidence."

"Possibly the tramp wanted to hide that any murder at all had been committed."

"And why did the tramp take nothing?"

"Because they were papers that he could not negotiate."

Lestrade shook his head, though it seemed to me that his manner was less absolutely assured than before.

"Well, Mr. Sherlock Holmes, you may look for your tramp, and while you are finding him we will hold on to our man. The future will show which is right. Just notice this point, Mr. Holmes: that so far as we know none of the papers were removed, and that the prisoner is the one man in the world who had no reason for removing them, since he was heir-at-law and would come into them in any case."

My friend seemed struck by this remark.

"I don't mean to deny that the evidence is in some ways very strongly in favour of your theory," said he. "I only wish to point out that there are other theories possible. As you say, the future will decide. Good morning! I dare say that in the course of the day I shall drop in at Norwood and see how you are getting on."

When the detective departed my friend rose and made his preparations for the day's work with the alert air of a man who has a congenial task before him.

"My first movement, Watson," said he, as he bustled into his frock-coat, "must, as I said, be in the direction of Blackheath."

"And why not Norwood?"

"'MY FIRST MOVEMENT, WATSON,' SAID HE, 'MUST BE IN THE DIRECTION OF BLACKHEATH.'"

"Because we have in this case one singular incident coming close to the heels of another singular incident. The police are making the mistake of concentrating their attention upon the second, because it happens to be the one which is actually criminal. But it is evident to me that the logical way to approach the case is to begin by trying to throw some light upon the first incident—the curious will, so suddenly made, and to so unexpected an heir. It may do something to simplify what followed. No, my dear fellow, I don't think you can help me. There is no prospect of danger, or I should not dream of stirring out without you. I trust that when I see you in the evening I will be able to report that I have been able to do something for this unfortunate

youngster who has thrown himself upon my protection."

It was late when my friend returned, and I could see by a glance at his haggard and anxious face that the high hopes with which he had started had not been fulfilled. For an hour he droned away upon his violin, endeavouring to soothe his own ruffled spirits. At last he flung down the instrument and plunged into a detailed account of his misadventures.

"It's all going wrong, Watson—all as wrong as it can go. I kept a bold face before Lestrade, but, upon my soul, I believe that for once the fellow is on the right track and we are on the wrong. All my instincts are one way and all the facts are the other, and I much fear that British juries have not yet attained that pitch of intelligence when they will give the preference to my theories over Lestrade's facts."

"Did you go to Blackheath?"

"Yes, Watson, I went there, and I found very quickly that the late lamented Oldacre was a pretty considerable blackguard. The father was away in search of his son. The mother was at home —a little, fluffy, blue-eyed person, in a tremor of fear and indignation. Of course, she would not admit even the possibility of his guilt. But she would not express either surprise or regret over the fate of Oldacre. On the contrary, she spoke of him with such bitterness that she was unconsciously considerably strengthening the case of the police, for, of course, if her son had heard her speak of the man in this fashion it would predispose him towards hatred and violence. 'He was more like a malignant and cunning ape than a human being,' said she, 'and he always was, ever since he was a young man.'

"'You knew him at that time?' said I.

"'Yes, I knew him well; in fact, he was an old suitor of mine. Thank Heaven that I had the sense to turn away from him and to marry a better, if a poorer, man. I was engaged to him, Mr. Holmes, when I heard a shocking story of how he had turned a cat loose in an aviary, and I was so horrified at his brutal cruelty that I would have nothing more to do with him.' She rummaged in a bureau, and presently she produced a photograph of a woman, shamefully defaced and mutilated with a knife. 'That is my own photograph,' she said. 'He sent it to me in that state, with his curse, upon my wedding morning.'

"'Well,' said I, 'at least he has forgiven

"HE SENT IT TO ME IN THAT STATE, WITH HIS CURSE, UPON MY WEDDING MORNING."

you now, since he has left all his property to your son.'

"'Neither my son nor I want anything from Jonas Oldacre, dead or alive,' she cried, with a proper spirit. 'There is a God in Heaven, Mr. Holmes, and that same God who has punished that wicked man will show in His own good time that my son's hands are guiltless of his blood.'

"Well, I tried one or two leads, but could get at nothing which would help our hypothesis, and several points which would make against it. I gave it up at last and off I went to Norwood.

"This place, Deep Dene House, is a big modern villa of staring brick, standing back in its own grounds, with a laurel-clumped lawn in front of it. To the right and some distance back from the road was the timber-yard which had been the scene of the fire. Here's a rough plan on a leaf of my note-book. This window on the left is the one which opens into Oldacre's room. You can look into it from the road, you see. That is about the only bit of consolation I have had to-day. Lestrade was not there, but his head constable did the honours. They had just made a great treasure-trove. They had spent the morning raking among the ashes of the burned wood-pile, and besides the charred organic remains they had secured several discoloured metal discs. I examined them with care, and there was no doubt that they were trouser buttons. I even distinguished that one of them was marked with the name of 'Hyams,' who was Oldacre's tailor. I then worked the lawn very carefully for signs and traces, but this drought has made everything as hard as iron. Nothing was to be seen save that some body or bundle had been dragged through a low privet hedge which is in a line with the wood-pile. All that, of course, fits in with the official theory. I crawled about the lawn with an August sun on my back, but I got up at the end of an hour no wiser than before.

"Well, after this fiasco I went into the bedroom and examined that also. The blood-stains were very slight, mere smears and discolorations, but undoubtedly fresh. The stick had been removed, but there also the marks were slight. There is no doubt about the stick belonging to our client. He admits it.   Footmarks of both men could be made out on the carpet, but none of any third person, which again is a trick for the other side.   They were piling up their score all the time and we were at a standstill.

"Only one little gleam of hope did I get— and yet it amounted to nothing.   I examined the contents of the safe, most of which had been taken out and left on the table.   The papers had been made up into sealed envelopes, one or two of which had been opened by the police.   They were not, so far as I could judge, of any great value, nor did the bank-book show that Mr. Oldacre was in such very affluent circumstances.   But it seemed to me that all the papers were not there. There were allusions to some deeds—possibly the more valuable—which I could not find. This, of course, if we could definitely prove it, would turn Lestrade's argument against himself, for who would steal a thing if he knew that he would shortly inherit it?

"Finally, having drawn every other cover and picked up no scent, I tried my luck with the housekeeper.   Mrs. Lexington is her name, a little, dark, silent person, with suspicious and sidelong eyes.   She could tell us something if she would—I am convinced of it.   But she was as close as wax. Yes, she had let Mr. McFarlane in at half-past nine.   She wished her hand had withered before she had done so.   She had gone to bed at half-past ten.   Her room was at the other end of the house, and she could hear nothing of what passed. Mr. McFarlane had left his hat, and to the best of her belief his stick, in the hall. She had been awakened by the alarm of fire.   Her poor, dear master had certainly been murdered.   Had he any enemies?  Well, every man had enemies, but Mr. Oldacre kept himself very much to himself, and only met people in the way of business.   She had seen the buttons, and was sure that they belonged to the clothes which he had worn last night.   The wood-pile was very dry, for it had not rained for a month.   It burned like tinder, and by the time she reached the spot nothing could be seen but flames.   She and all the firemen smelled the burned flesh from inside it.   She knew nothing of the papers, nor of Mr. Oldacre's private affairs.

"So, my dear Watson, there's my report of a failure.   And yet—and yet——"—he clenched his thin hands in a paroxysm of conviction—"I *know* it's all wrong.   I feel it in my bones.   There is something that has not come out, and that housekeeper knows it,   There was a sort of sulky defiance in her

eyes, which only goes with guilty knowledge. However, there's no good talking any more about it, Watson; but unless some lucky chance comes our way I fear that the Norwood Disappearance Case will not figure in that chronicle of our successes which I foresee that a patient public will sooner or later have to endure."

"Surely," said I, "the man's appearance would go far with any jury?"

"That is a dangerous argument, my dear Watson.   You remember that terrible murderer, Bert Stevens, who wanted us to get him off in '87?   Was there ever a more mild-mannered, Sunday-school young man?"

"It is true."

"Unless we succeed in establishing an alternative theory this man is lost.   You can hardly find a flaw in the case which can now be presented against him, and all further investigation has served to strengthen it.   By the way, there is one curious little point about those papers which may serve us as the starting-point for an inquiry.   On looking over the bank-book I found that the low state of the balance was principally due to large cheques which have been made out during the last year to Mr. Cornelius.   I confess that I should be interested to know who this Mr. Cornelius may be with whom a retired builder has such very large transactions.   Is it possible that he has had a hand in the affair?   Cornelius might be a broker, but we have found no scrip to correspond with these large payments.   Failing any other indication my researches must now take the direction of an inquiry at the bank for the gentleman who has cashed these cheques.   But I fear, my dear fellow, that our case will end ingloriously by Lestrade hanging our client, which will certainly be a triumph for Scotland Yard."

I do not know how far Sherlock Holmes took any sleep that night, but when I came down to breakfast I found him pale and harassed, his bright eyes the brighter for the dark shadows round them.   The carpet round his chair was littered with cigarette-ends and with the early editions of the morning papers.   An open telegram lay upon the table.

"What do you think of this, Watson?" he asked, tossing it across.

It was from Norwood, and ran as follows:—

"IMPORTANT FRESH EVIDENCE TO HAND. MCFARLANE'S GUILT DEFINITELY ESTABLISHED. ADVISE YOU TO ABANDON CASE.—LESTRADE."

"This sounds serious," said I.

"It is Lestrade's little cock-a-doodle of

victory," Holmes answered, with a bitter smile. "And yet it may be premature to abandon the case. After all, important fresh evidence is a two-edged thing, and may possibly cut in a very different direction to that which Lestrade imagines. Take your breakfast, Watson, and we will go out together and see what we can do. I feel as if I shall need your company and your moral support to-day."

My friend had no breakfast himself, for it was one of his peculiarities that in his more intense moments he would permit himself no food, and I have known him presume upon his iron strength until he has fainted from pure inanition. "At present I cannot spare energy and nerve force for digestion," he would say, in answer to my medical remonstrances. I was not surprised, therefore, when this morning he left his untouched meal behind him and started with me for Norwood. A crowd of morbid sightseers were still gathered round Deep Dene House, which was just such a suburban villa as I had pictured. Within the gates Lestrade met us, his face flushed with victory, his manner grossly triumphant.

"Well, Mr. Holmes, have you proved us to be wrong yet? Have you found your tramp?" he cried.

"I have formed no conclusion whatever," my companion answered.

"But we formed ours yesterday, and now it proves to be correct; so you must acknowledge that we have been a little in front of you this time, Mr. Holmes."

"You certainly have the air of something unusual having occurred," said Holmes.

Lestrade laughed loudly.

"You don't like being beaten any more than the rest of us do," said he. "A man can't expect always to have it his own way, can he, Dr. Watson? Step this way, if you please, gentlemen, and I think I can convince you once for all that it was John McFarlane who did this crime."

He led us through the passage and out into a dark hall beyond.

"This is where young McFarlane must have come out to get his hat after the crime was done," said he. "Now, look at this." With dramatic suddenness he struck a match and by its light exposed a stain of blood upon the whitewashed wall. As he held the

"LOOK AT THAT WITH YOUR MAGNIFYING GLASS, MR. HOLMES."

match nearer I saw that it was more than a stain. It was the well-marked print of a thumb.

"Look at that with your magnifying glass, Mr. Holmes."

"Yes, I am doing so."

"You are aware that no two thumb marks are alike?"

"I have heard something of the kind."

"Well, then, will you please compare that print with this wax impression of young McFarlane's right thumb, taken by my orders this morning?"

As he held the waxen print close to the blood-stain it did not take a magnifying glass to see that the two were undoubtedly from the same thumb. It was evident to me that our unfortunate client was lost.

"That is final," said Lestrade.

"Yes, that is final," I involuntarily echoed.

"It is final," said Holmes.

Something in his tone caught my ear, and I turned to look at him. An extraordinary change had come over his face. It was writhing with inward merriment. His two eyes were shining like stars. It seemed to me that he was making desperate efforts to restrain a convulsive attack of laughter.

"Dear me! Dear me!" he said at last. "Well, now, who would have thought it? And how deceptive appearances may be, to be sure! Such a nice young man to look at! It is a lesson to us not to trust our own judgment, is it not, Lestrade?"

"Yes, some of us are a little too much inclined to be cocksure, Mr. Holmes," said Lestrade. The man's insolence was maddening, but we could not resent it.

"What a providential thing that this young man should press his right thumb against the wall in taking his hat from the peg! Such a very natural action, too, if you come to think of it." Holmes was outwardly calm, but his whole body gave a wriggle of suppressed excitement as he spoke. "By the way, Lestrade, who made this remarkable discovery?"

"It was the housekeeper, Mrs. Lexington, who drew the night constable's attention to it."

"Where was the night constable?"

"He remained on guard in the bedroom where the crime was committed, so as to see that nothing was touched."

"But why didn't the police see this mark yesterday?"

"Well, we had no particular reason to make a careful examination of the hall. Besides, it's not in a very prominent place, as you see."

"No, no, of course not. I suppose there is no doubt that the mark was there yesterday?"

Lestrade looked at Holmes as if he thought he was going out of his mind. I confess that I was myself surprised both at his hilarious manner and at his rather wild observation.

"I don't know whether you think that McFarlane came out of gaol in the dead of the night in order to strengthen the evidence against himself," said Lestrade. "I leave it to any expert in the world whether that is not the mark of his thumb."

"It is unquestionably the mark of his thumb."

"There, that's enough," said Lestrade. "I am a practical man, Mr. Holmes, and when I have got my evidence I come to my conclusions. If you have anything to say you will find me writing my report in the sitting-room."

Holmes had recovered his equanimity, though I still seemed to detect gleams of amusement in his expression.

"Dear me, this is a very sad development, Watson, is it not?" said he. "And yet there are singular points about it which hold out some hopes for our client."

"I am delighted to hear it," said I, heartily. "I was afraid it was all up with him."

"I would hardly go so far as to say that, my dear Watson. The fact is that there is one really serious flaw in this evidence to which our friend attaches so much importance."

"Indeed, Holmes! What is it?"

"Only this: that I *know* that that mark was not there when I examined the hall yesterday. And now, Watson, let us have a little stroll round in the sunshine."

With a confused brain, but with a heart into which some warmth of hope was returning, I accompanied my friend in a walk round the garden. Holmes took each face of the house in turn and examined it with great interest. He then led the way inside and went over the whole building from basement to attics. Most of the rooms were unfurnished, but none the less Holmes inspected them all minutely. Finally, on the top corridor, which ran outside three untenanted bedrooms, he again was seized with a spasm of merriment.

"There are really some very unique features about this case, Watson," said he. "I think it is time now that we took our friend Lestrade into our confidence. He has had his little smile at our expense, and perhaps we may do as much by him if my reading of this problem proves to be correct. Yes, yes; I think I see how we should approach it."

The Scotland Yard inspector was still writing in the parlour when Holmes interrupted him.

"I understood that you were writing a report of this case," said he.

"So I am."

"Don't you think it may be a little premature? I can't help thinking that your evidence is not complete."

Lestrade knew my friend too well to disregard his words. He laid down his pen and looked curiously at him.

"What do you mean, Mr. Holmes?"

"Only that there is an important witness whom you have not seen."

"Can you produce him?"

"I think I can."

"Then do so."

"I will do my best. How many constables have you?"

"There are three within call."

"Excellent!" said Holmes. "May I ask if they are all large, able-bodied men with powerful voices?"

"I have no doubt they are, though I fail to see what their voices have to do with it."

"Perhaps I can help you to see that and one or two other things as well," said Holmes. "Kindly summon your men, and I will try."

Five minutes later three policemen had assembled in the hall.

"In the outhouse you will find a considerable quantity of straw," said Holmes. "I will ask you to carry in two bundles of it. I think it will be of the greatest assistance in producing the witness whom I require. Thank you very much. I believe you have some matches in your pocket, Watson. Now, Mr. Lestrade, I will ask you all to accompany me to the top landing."

As I have said, there was a broad corridor there, which ran outside three empty bedrooms. At one end of the corridor we were all marshalled by Sherlock Holmes, the constables grinning and Lestrade staring at my friend with amazement, expectation, and derision chasing each other across his features. Holmes stood before us with the air of a conjurer who is performing a trick.

"Would you kindly send one of your constables for two buckets of water? Put the straw on the floor here, free from the wall on either side. Now I think that we are all ready."

Lestrade's face had begun to grow red and angry.

"I don't know whether you are playing a game with us, Mr. Sherlock Holmes," said he. "If you know anything, you can surely say it without all this tomfoolery."

"I assure you, my good Lestrade, that I have an excellent reason for everything that I do. You may possibly remember that you chaffed me a little some hours ago, when the sun seemed on your side of the hedge, so you must not grudge me a little pomp and ceremony now. Might I ask you, Watson, to open that window, and then to put a match to the edge of the straw?"

I did so, and, driven by the draught, a coil of grey smoke swirled down the corridor, while the dry straw crackled and flamed.

"Now we must see if we can find this witness for you, Lestrade. Might I ask you all to join in the cry of 'Fire!'? Now, then; one, two, three——"

"Fire!" we all yelled.

"Thank you. I will trouble you once again."

"Fire!"

"Just once more, gentlemen, and all together."

"Fire!" The shout must have rung over Norwood.

It had hardly died away when an amazing thing happened. A door suddenly flew open out of what appeared to be solid wall at the end of the corridor, and a little, wizened man darted out of it, like a rabbit out of its burrow.

"Capital!" said Holmes, calmly. "Watson, a bucket of water over the straw. That will do! Lestrade, allow me to present you with your principal missing witness, Mr. Jonas Oldacre."

The detective stared at the new-comer with blank amazement. The latter was blinking in the bright light of the corridor, and peering at us and at the smouldering fire. It was an odious face—crafty, vicious, malignant, with shifty, light-grey eyes and white eyelashes.

"What's this, then?" said Lestrade at last. "What have you been doing all this time, eh?"

Oldacre gave an uneasy laugh, shrinking back from the furious red face of the angry detective.

"I have done no harm."

"No harm? You have done your best to get an innocent man hanged. If it wasn't for this gentleman here, I am not sure that you would not have succeeded."

The wretched creature began to whimper.

"I am sure, sir, it was only my practical joke."

"Oh! a joke, was it? You won't find the laugh on your side, I promise you. Take him down and keep him in the sitting-room until I come. Mr. Holmes," he continued, when they had gone, "I could not speak before the constables, but I don't mind saying, in the presence of Dr. Watson, that this is the brightest thing that you have done yet, though it is a mystery to me how you did it. You have saved an innocent man's life, and you have prevented a very grave scandal, which would have ruined my reputation in the Force."

Holmes smiled and clapped Lestrade upon the shoulder.

"Instead of being ruined, my good sir, you will find that your reputation has been enormously enhanced. Just make a few

"HOLMES SMILED AND CLAPPED LESTRADE UPON THE SHOULDER."

A lath-and-plaster partition had been run across the passage six feet from the end, with a door cunningly concealed in it. It was lit within by slits under the eaves. A few articles of furniture and a supply of food and water were within, together with a number of books and papers.

"There's the advantage of being a builder," said Holmes, as we came out. "He was able to fix up his own little hiding-place without any confederate—save, of course, that precious housekeeper of his, whom I should lose no time in adding to your bag, Lestrade."

"I'll take your advice. But how did you know of this place, Mr. Holmes?"

"I made up my mind that the fellow was in hiding in the house. When I paced one corridor and found it six feet shorter than the corresponding one below, it was pretty clear where he was. I thought he had not the nerve to lie quiet before an alarm of fire. We could, of course, have gone in and taken him, but it amused me to make him reveal himself; besides, I owed you a little mystification, Lestrade, for your chaff in the morning."

"Well, sir, you certainly got equal with me on that. But how in the world did you know that he was in the house at all?"

"The thumb-mark, Lestrade. You said it was final; and so it was, in a very different sense. I knew it had not been there the day before. I pay a good deal of attention to matters of detail, as you may have observed, and I had examined the hall and was sure that the wall was clear. Therefore, it had been put on during the night."

"But how?"

"Very simply. When those packets were sealed up, Jonas Oldacre got McFarlane to secure one of the seals by putting his thumb upon the soft wax. It would be done so quickly and so naturally that I dare say the young man himself has no recollection of it.

alterations in that report which you were writing, and they will understand how hard it is to throw dust in the eyes of Inspector Lestrade."

"And you don't want your name to appear?"

"Not at all. The work is its own reward. Perhaps I shall get the credit also at some distant day when I permit my zealous historian to lay out his foolscap once more —eh, Watson? Well, now, let us see where this rat has been lurking."

Very likely it just so happened, and Oldacre had himself no notion of the use he would put it to. Brooding over the case in that den of his, it suddenly struck him what absolutely damning evidence he could make against McFarlane by using that thumb-mark. It was the simplest thing in the world for him to take a wax impression from the seal, to moisten it in as much blood as he could get from a pin-prick, and to put the mark upon the wall during the night, either with his own hand or with that of his house-keeper. If you examine among those documents which he took with him into his retreat I will lay you a wager that you find the seal with the thumb-mark upon it."

"Wonderful!" said Lestrade. "Wonderful! It's all as clear as crystal, as you put it. But what is the object of this deep deception, Mr. Holmes?"

It was amusing to me to see how the detective's overbearing manner had changed suddenly to that of a child asking questions of its teacher.

"Well, I don't think that is very hard to explain. A very deep, malicious, vindictive person is the gentleman who is now awaiting us downstairs. You know that he was once refused by McFarlane's mother? You don't! I told you that you should go to Blackheath first and Norwood afterwards. Well, this injury, as he would consider it, has rankled in his wicked, scheming brain, and all his life he has longed for vengeance, but never seen his chance. During the last year or two things have gone against him—secret speculation, I think—and he finds himself in a bad way. He determines to swindle his creditors, and for this purpose he pays large cheques to a certain Mr. Cornelius, who is, I imagine, himself under another name. I have not traced these cheques yet, but I have no doubt that they were banked under that name at some provincial town where Oldacre from time to time led a double existence. He intended to change his name altogether, draw this money, and vanish, starting life again elsewhere."

"Well, that's likely enough."

"It would strike him that in disappearing he might throw all pursuit off his track, and at the same time have an ample and crushing revenge upon his old sweetheart, if he could give the impression that he had been murdered by her only child. It was a masterpiece of villainy, and he carried it out like a master. The idea of the will, which would give an obvious motive for the crime, the secret visit unknown to his own parents, the retention of the stick, the blood, and the animal remains and buttons in the wood-pile, all were admirable. It was a net from which it seemed to me a few hours ago that there was no possible escape. But he had not that supreme gift of the artist, the knowledge of when to stop. He wished to improve that which was already perfect—to draw the rope tighter yet round the neck of his unfortunate victim—and so he ruined all. Let us descend, Lestrade. There are just one or two questions that I would ask him."

The malignant creature was seated in his own parlour with a policeman upon each side of him.

"It was a joke, my good sir, a practical joke, nothing more," he whined incessantly. "I assure you, sir, that I simply concealed myself in order to see the effect of my disappearance, and I am sure that you would not be so unjust as to imagine that I would have allowed any harm to befall poor young Mr. McFarlane."

"That's for a jury to decide," said Lestrade. "Anyhow, we shall have you on a charge of conspiracy, if not for attempted murder."

"And you'll probably find that your creditors will impound the banking account of Mr. Cornelius," said Holmes.

The little man started and turned his malignant eyes upon my friend.

"I have to thank you for a good deal," said he. "Perhaps I'll pay my debt some day."

Holmes smiled indulgently.

"I fancy that for some few years you will find your time very fully occupied," said he. "By the way, what was it you put into the wood-pile besides your old trousers? A dead dog, or rabbits, or what? You won't tell? Dear me, how very unkind of you! Well, well, I dare say that a couple of rabbits would account both for the blood and for the charred ashes. If ever you write an account, Watson, you can make rabbits serve your turn."

"HOLMES CLAPPED A PISTOL TO HIS HEAD AND MARTIN SLIPPED
THE HANDCUFFS OVER HIS WRISTS."

# THE STRAND MAGAZINE.

Vol. xxvi.    DECEMBER, 1903.    No. 156.

# THE RETURN OF SHERLOCK HOLMES.

## By A. CONAN DOYLE.

### III.—The Adventure of the Dancing Men.

HOLMES had been seated for some hours in silence with his long, thin back curved over a chemical vessel in which he was brewing a particularly malodorous product. His head was sunk upon his breast, and he looked from my point of view like a strange, lank bird, with dull grey plumage and a black top-knot.

"So, Watson," said he, suddenly, "you do not propose to invest in South African securities?"

I gave a start of astonishment. Accustomed as I was to Holmes's curious faculties, this sudden intrusion into my most intimate thoughts was utterly inexplicable.

"How on earth do you know that?" I asked.

He wheeled round upon his stool, with a steaming test-tube in his hand and a gleam of amusement in his deep-set eyes.

"Now, Watson, confess yourself utterly taken aback," said he.

"I am."

"I ought to make you sign a paper to that effect."

"Why?"

"Because in five minutes you will say that it is all so absurdly simple."

"I am sure that I shall say nothing of the kind."

"You see, my dear Watson"—he propped his test-tube in the rack and began to lecture with the air of a professor addressing his class—"it is not really difficult to construct a

series of inferences, each dependent upon its predecessor and each simple in itself. If, after doing so, one simply knocks out all the central inferences and presents one's audience with the starting-point and the conclusion, one may produce a startling, though possibly a meretricious, effect. Now, it was not really difficult, by an inspection of the groove between your left forefinger and thumb, to feel sure that you did *not* propose to invest your small capital in the goldfields."

"I see no connection."

"Very likely not; but I can quickly show you a close connection. Here are the missing links of the very simple chain: 1. You had chalk between your left finger and thumb when you returned from the club last night. 2. You put chalk there when you play billiards to steady the cue. 3. You never play billiards except with Thurston. 4. You told me four weeks ago that Thurston had an option on some South African property which would expire in a month, and which he desired you to share with him. 5. Your cheque-book is locked in my drawer, and you have not asked for the key. 6. You do not propose to invest your money in this manner."

"How absurdly simple!" I cried.

"Quite so!" said he, a little nettled. "Every problem becomes very childish when once it is explained to you. Here is an unexplained one. See what you can make of that, friend Watson." He tossed a sheet of paper upon the table and turned once more to his chemical analysis.

"HOLMES HELD UP THE PAPER."

which I had just examined and left upon the table.

"Well, Mr. Holmes, what do you make of these?" he cried. "They told me that you were fond of queer mysteries, and I don't think you can nnd a queerer one than that. I sent the paper on ahead so that you might have time to study it before I came."

"It is certainly rather a curious production," said Holmes. "At first sight it would appear to be some childish prank. It consists of a number of absurd little figures dancing across the paper upon which they are drawn. Why should you attribute any importance to so grotesque an object?"

"I never should, Mr. Holmes. But my wife does. It is frightening her to death. She says nothing, but I can see terror in her eyes. That's why I want to sift the matter to the bottom."

I looked with amazement at the absurd hieroglyphics upon the paper.

"Why, Holmes, it is a child's drawing," I cried.

"Oh, that's your idea!"

"What else should it be?"

"That is what Mr. Hilton Cubitt, of Riding Thorpe Manor, Norfolk, is very anxious to know. This little conundrum came by the first post, and he was to follow by the next train. There's a ring at the bell, Watson. I should not be very much surprised if this were he."

A heavy step was heard · upon the stairs, and an instant later there entered a tall, ruddy, clean-shaven gentleman, whose clear eyes and florid cheeks told of a life led far from the fogs of Baker Street. He seemed to bring a whiff of his strong, fresh, bracing, east-coast air with him as he entered. Having shaken hands with each of us, he was about to sit down when his eye rested upon the paper with the curious markings,

Holmes held up the paper so that the sunlight shone full upon it. It was a page torn from a note-book. The markings were done in pencil, and ran in this way :—

Holmes examined it for some time, and then, folding it carefully up, he placed it in his pocket-book.

"This promises to be a most interesting and unusual case," said he. "You gave me a few particulars in your letter, Mr. Hilton Cubitt, but I should be very much obliged if you would kindly go over it all again for the benefit of my friend, Dr. Watson."

"I'm not much of a story-teller," said our

visitor, nervously clasping and unclasping his great, strong hands. "You'll just ask me anything that I don't make clear. I'll begin at the time of my marriage last year; but I want to say first of all that, though I'm not a rich man, my people have been at Ridling Thorpe for a matter of five centuries, and there is no better-known family in the County of Norfolk. Last year I came up to London for the Jubilee, and I stopped at a boarding-house in Russell Square, because Parker, the vicar of our parish, was staying in it. There was an American young lady there—Patrick was the name—Elsie Patrick. In some way we became friends, until before my month was up I was as much in love as a man could be. We were quietly married at a registry office, and we returned to Norfolk a wedded couple. You'll think it very mad, Mr. Holmes, that a man of a good old family should marry a wife in this fashion, knowing nothing of her past or of her people; but if you saw her and knew her it would help you to understand.

"She was very straight about it, was Elsie. I can't say that she did not give me every chance of getting out of it if I wished to do so. 'I have had some very disagreeable associations in my life,' said she; 'I wish to forget all about them. I would rather never allude to the past, for it is very painful to me. If you take me, Hilton, you will take a woman who has nothing that she need be personally ashamed of; but you will have to be content with my word for it, and to allow me to be silent as to all that passed up to the time when I became yours. If these conditions are too hard, then go back to Norfolk and leave me to the lonely life in which you found me.' It was only the day before our wedding that she said those very words to me. I told her that I was content to take her on her own terms, and I have been as good as my word.

"Well, we have been married now for a year, and very happy we have been. But about a month ago, at the end of June, I saw for the first time signs of trouble. One day my wife received a letter from America. I saw the American stamp. She turned deadly white, read the letter, and threw it into the fire. She made no allusion to it afterwards, and I made none, for a promise is a promise; but she has never known an easy hour from that moment. There is always a look of fear upon her face—a look as if she were waiting and expecting. She would do better to trust me. She would find that I was her best friend. But until she speaks I can say nothing. Mind you, she is a truthful woman, Mr. Holmes, and whatever trouble there may have been in her past life it has been no fault of hers. I am only a simple Norfolk squire, but there is not a man in England who ranks his family honour more highly than I do. She knows it well, and she knew it well before she married me. She would never bring any stain upon it—of that I am sure.

"Well, now I come to the queer part of my story. About a week ago—it was the Tuesday of last week—I found on one of the window sills a number of absurd little dancing figures, like these upon the paper. They were scrawled with chalk. I thought that it was the stable-boy who had drawn them, but the lad swore he knew nothing about it. Anyhow, they had come there during the night. I had them washed out, and I only mentioned the matter to my wife afterwards. To my surprise she took it very seriously, and begged me if any more came to let her see them. None did come for a week, and then yesterday morning I found this paper lying on the sun-dial in the garden. I showed it to Elsie, and down she dropped in a dead faint. Since then she has looked like a woman in a dream, half dazed, and with terror always lurking in her eyes. It was then that I wrote and sent the paper to you, Mr. Holmes. It was not a thing that I could take to the police, for they would have laughed at me, but you will tell me what to do. I am not a rich man; but if there is any danger threatening my little woman I would spend my last copper to shield her."

He was a fine creature, this man of the old English soil, simple, straight, and gentle, with his great, earnest blue eyes and broad, comely face. His love for his wife and his trust in her shone in his features. Holmes had listened to his story with the utmost attention, and now he sat for some time in silent thought.

"Don't you think, Mr. Cubitt," said he, at last, "that your best plan would be to make a direct appeal to your wife, and to ask her to share her secret with you?"

Hilton Cubitt shook his massive head.

"A promise is a promise, Mr. Holmes. If Elsie wished to tell me she would. If not, it is not for me to force her confidence. But I am justified in taking my own line—and I will."

"Then I will help you with all my heart. In the first place, have you heard of any strangers being seen in your neighbourhood?"

"No."

"I presume that it is a very quiet place. Any fresh face would cause comment?"

"In the immediate neighbourhood, yes. But we have several small watering-places not very far away. And the farmers take in lodgers."

"These hieroglyphics have evidently a meaning. If it is a purely arbitrary one it may be impossible for us to solve it. If, on the other hand, it is systematic, I have no doubt that we shall get to the bottom of it. But this particular sample is so short that I can do nothing, and the facts which you have brought me are so indefinite that we have no basis for an investigation. I would suggest that you return to Norfolk, that you keep a keen look-out, and that you take an exact copy of any fresh dancing men which may appear. It is a thousand pities that we have not a reproduction of those which were done in chalk upon the window-sill. Make a discreet inquiry also as to any strangers in the neighbourhood. When you have collected some fresh evidence come to me again. That is the best advice which I can give you, Mr. Hilton Cubitt. If there are any pressing fresh developments I shall be always ready to run down and see you in your Norfolk home."

The interview left Sherlock Holmes very thoughtful, and several times in the next few days I saw him take his slip of paper from his note-book and look long and earnestly at the curious figures inscribed upon it. He made no allusion to the affair, however, until one afternoon a fortnight or so later. I was going out when he called me back.

"You had better stay here, Watson."

"Why?"

"Because I had a wire from Hilton Cubitt this morning—you remember Hilton Cubitt, of the dancing men? He was to reach Liverpool Street at one-twenty. He may be here at any moment. I gather from his wire that there have been some new incidents of importance."

We had not long to wait, for our Norfolk squire came straight from the station as fast as a hansom could bring him. He was looking worried and depressed, with tired eyes and a lined forehead.

"It's getting on my nerves, this business, Mr. Holmes," said he, as he sank, like a wearied man, into an arm-chair. "It's bad enough to feel that you are surrounded by unseen, unknown folk, who have some kind of design upon you; but when, in addition to that, you know that it is just killing your wife by inches, then it becomes as much as

flesh and blood can endure. She's wearing away under it—just wearing away before my eyes."

"Has she said anything yet?"

"No, Mr. Holmes, she has not. And yet there have been times when the poor girl has wanted to speak, and yet could not quite bring herself to take the plunge. I have tried to help her; but I dare say I did it clumsily, and scared her off from it. She has spoken about my old family, and our reputation in the county, and our pride in our unsullied honour, and I always felt it was leading to the point; but somehow it turned off before we got there."

"But you have found out something for yourself?"

"A good deal, Mr. Holmes. I have several fresh dancing men pictures for you to examine, and, what is more important, I have seen the fellow."

"What, the man who draws them?"

"Yes, I saw him at his work. But I will tell you everything in order. When I got back after my visit to you, the very first thing I saw next morning was a fresh crop of dancing men. They had been drawn in chalk upon the black wooden door of the tool-house, which stands beside the lawn in full view of the front windows. I took an exact copy, and here it is." He unfolded a paper and laid it upon the table. Here is a copy of the hieroglyphics:—

"Excellent!" said Holmes. "Excellent! Pray continue."

"When I had taken the copy I rubbed out the marks; but two mornings later a fresh inscription had appeared. I have a copy of it here":—

Holmes rubbed his hands and chuckled with delight.

"Our material is rapidly accumulating," said he.

"Three days later a message was left scrawled upon paper, and placed under a pebble upon the sun-dial. Here it is. The characters are, as you see, exactly the same as the last one. After that I determined to lie in wait; so I got out my revolver and I sat up in my study, which overlooks the lawn and garden. About two in the morning I was seated by the window, all being dark save for the moonlight outside, when I heard steps behind me, and there was my wife in her dressing-gown. She implored me to come to bed. I told her frankly that I wished to see who it was who played such absurd tricks upon us. She answered that it was some senseless practical joke, and that I should not take any notice of it.

"'If it really annoys you, Hilton, we might go and travel, you and I, and so avoid this nuisance.'

"'What, be driven out of our own house by a practical joker?' said I. 'Why, we should have the whole county laughing at us.'

"'Well, come to bed,' said she, 'and we can discuss it in the morning.'

"Suddenly, as she spoke, I saw her white face grow whiter yet in the moonlight, and her hand tightened upon my shoulder. Something was moving in the shadow of the tool-house. I saw a dark, creeping figure which crawled round the corner and squatted in front of the door. Seizing my pistol I was rushing out, when my wife threw her arms round me and held me with convulsive strength. I tried to throw her off, but she clung to me most desperately. At last I got clear, but by the time I had opened the door and reached the house the creature was gone. He had left a trace of his presence, however, for there on the door was the very same arrangement of dancing men which had already twice appeared, and which I have copied on that paper. There was no other sign of the fellow anywhere, though I ran all over the grounds. And yet the amazing thing is that he must have been there all the time, for when I examined the door again in the morning he had scrawled some more of his pictures under the line which I had already seen."

"Have you that fresh drawing?"

"Yes; it is very short, but I made a copy of it, and here it is."

Again he produced a paper. The new dance was in this form:—

"Tell me," said Holmes—and I could see by his eyes that he was much excited—"was this a mere addition to the first, or did it appear to be entirely separate?"

"It was on a different panel of the door."

"Excellent! This is far the most important of all for our purpose. It fills me with hopes. Now, Mr. Hilton Cubitt, please continue your most interesting statement."

"I have nothing more to say, Mr. Holmes, except that I was angry with my wife that night for having held me back when I might

"MY WIFE THREW HER ARMS ROUND ME."

have caught the skulking rascal. She said that she feared that I might come to harm. For an instant it had crossed my mind that perhaps what she really feared was that *he* might come to harm, for I could not doubt that she knew who this man was and what he meant by these strange signals. But there is a tone in my wife's voice, Mr. Holmes, and a look in her eyes which forbid doubt, and I am sure that it was indeed my own safety that was in her mind. There's the whole case, and now I want your advice as to what I ought to do. My own inclination is to put half-a-dozen of my farm lads in the shrubbery, and when this fellow comes again to give him such a hiding that he will leave us in peace for the future."

"I fear it is too deep a case for such simple remedies," said Holmes. "How long can you stay in London?"

"I must go back to-day. I would not leave my wife alone at night for anything. She is very nervous and begged me to come back."

"I dare say you are right. But if you could have stopped I might possibly have been able to return with you in a day or two. Meanwhile you will leave me these papers, and I think that it is very likely that I shall be able to pay you a visit shortly and to throw some light upon your case."

Sherlock Holmes preserved his calm professional manner until our visitor had left us, although it was easy for me, who knew him so well, to see that he was profoundly excited. The moment that Hilton Cubitt's broad back had disappeared through the door my comrade rushed to the table, laid out all the slips of paper containing dancing men in front of him, and threw himself into an intricate and elaborate calculation. For two hours I watched him as he covered sheet after sheet of paper with figures and letters, so completely absorbed in his task that he had evidently forgotten my presence. Sometimes he was making progress and whistled and sang at his work; sometimes he was puzzled, and would sit for long spells with a furrowed brow and a vacant eye. Finally he sprang from his chair with a cry of satisfaction, and walked up and down the room rubbing his hands together. Then he wrote a long telegram upon a cable form. "If my answer to this is as I hope, you will have a

very pretty case to add to your collection, Watson," said he. "I expect that we shall be able to go down to Norfolk to-morrow, and to take our friend some very definite news as to the secret of his annoyance."

I confess that I was filled with curiosity, but I was aware that Holmes liked to make his disclosures at his own time and in his own way; so I waited until it should suit him to take me into his confidence.

But there was a delay in that answering telegram, and two days of impatience followed, during which Holmes pricked up his ears at every ring of the bell. On the evening of the second there came a letter from Hilton Cubitt. All was quiet with him, save that a long inscription had appeared that morning upon the pedestal of the sun-dial. He enclosed a copy of it, which is here reproduced:—

Holmes bent over this grotesque frieze for some minutes, and then suddenly sprang to his feet with an exclamation of surprise and dismay. His face was haggard with anxiety.

"We have let this affair go far enough," said he. "Is there a train to North Walsham to-night?"

I turned up the time-table. The last had just gone.

"Then we shall breakfast early and take the very first in the morning," said Holmes. "Our presence is most urgently needed. Ah! here is our expected cablegram. One moment, Mrs. Hudson; there may be an answer. No, that is quite as I expected. This message makes it even more essential that we should not lose an hour in letting Hilton Cubitt know how matters stand, for it is a singular and a dangerous web in which our simple Norfolk squire is entangled."

So, indeed, it proved, and as I come to the dark conclusion of a story which had seemed to me to be only childish and bizarre I experience once again the dismay and horror with which I was filled. Would that I had some brighter ending to communicate to my readers, but these are the chronicles of fact, and I must follow to their dark crisis the strange chain of events which for some days made Ridling Thorpe Manor a household word through the length and breadth of England.

We had hardly alighted at North Walsham, and mentioned the name of our destination,

"'I SUPPOSE THAT YOU ARE THE DETECTIVES FROM LONDON?' SAID HE."

had been uneasy during all our journey from town, and I had observed that he had turned over the morning papers with anxious attention; but now this sudden realization of his worst fears left him in a blank melancholy. He leaned back in his seat, lost in gloomy speculation. Yet there was much around us to interest us, for we were passing through as singular a country-side as any in England, where a few scattered cottages represented the population of to-day, while on every hand enormous square-towered churches bristled up from the flat, green landscape and told of the glory and prosperity of old East Anglia. At last the violet rim of the German Ocean appeared over the green edge of the Norfolk coast, and the driver pointed with his whip to two old brick and timber gables which projected from a grove of trees. "That's Ridling Thorpe Manor," said he.

when the station-master hurried towards us. "I suppose that you are the detectives from London?" said he.

A look of annoyance passed over Holmes's face.

"What makes you think such a thing?"

"Because Inspector Martin from Norwich has just passed through. But maybe you are the surgeons. She's not dead—or wasn't by last accounts. You may be in time to save her yet—though it be for the gallows."

Holmes's brow was dark with anxiety.

"We are going to Ridling Thorpe Manor," said he, "but we have heard nothing of what has passed there."

"It's a terrible business," said the station-master. "They are shot, both Mr. Hilton Cubitt and his wife. She shot him and then herself—so the servants say. He's dead and her life is despaired of. Dear, dear, one of the oldest families in the County of Norfolk, and one of the most honoured."

Without a word Holmes hurried to a carriage, and during the long seven miles' drive he never opened his mouth. Seldom have I seen him so utterly despondent. He

As we drove up to the porticoed front door I observed in front of it, beside the tennis lawn, the black tool-house and the pedestalled sun-dial with which we had such strange associations. A dapper little man, with a quick, alert manner and a waxed moustache, had just descended from a high dog-cart. He introduced himself as Inspector Martin, of the Norfolk Constabulary, and he was considerably astonished when he heard the name of my companion.

"Why, Mr. Holmes, the crime was only committed at three this morning. How could you hear of it in London and get to the spot as soon as I?"

"I anticipated it. I came in the hope of preventing it."

"Then you must have important evidence

of which we are ignorant, for they were said to be a most united couple."

" I have only the evidence of the dancing men," said Holmes. " I will explain the matter to you later. Meanwhile, since it is too late to prevent this tragedy, I am very anxious that I should use the knowledge which I possess in order to ensure that justice be done. Will you associate me in your investigation, or will you prefer that I should act independently ? "

" I should be proud to feel that we were acting together, Mr. Holmes," said the inspector, earnestly.

" In that case I should be glad to hear the evidence and to examine the premises without an instant of unnecessary delay."

Inspector Martin had the good sense to allow my friend to do things in his own fashion, and contented himself with carefully noting the results. The local surgeon, an old, white-haired man, had just come down from Mrs. Hilton Cubitt's room, and he reported that her injuries were serious, but not necessarily fatal. The bullet had passed through the front of her brain, and it would probably be some time before she could regain consciousness. On the question of whether she had been shot or had shot herself he would not venture to express any decided opinion. Certainly the bullet had been discharged at very close quarters. There was only the one pistol found in the room, two barrels of which had been emptied. Mr. Hilton Cubitt had been shot through the heart. It was equally conceivable that he had shot her and then himself, or that she had been the criminal, for the revolver lay upon the floor midway between them.

" Has he been moved ? " asked Holmes.

" We have moved nothing except the lady. We could not leave her lying wounded upon the floor."

" How long have you been here, doctor ? "

" Since four o'clock."

" Anyone else ? "

" Yes, the constable here."

" And you have touched nothing ? "

" Nothing."

" You have acted with great discretion. Who sent for you ? "

" The housemaid, Saunders."

" Was it she who gave the alarm ? "

" She and Mrs. King, the cook."

" Where are they now ? "

" In the kitchen, I believe."

" Then I think we had better hear their story at once."

The old hall, oak-panelled and high-windowed, had been turned into a court of investigation. Holmes sat in a great, old-fashioned chair, his inexorable eyes gleaming out of his haggard face. I could read in them a set purpose to devote his life to this quest until the client whom he had failed to save should at last be avenged. The trim Inspector Martin, the old, grey-headed country doctor, myself, and a stolid village policeman made up the rest of that strange company.

The two women told their story clearly enough. They had been aroused from their sleep by the sound of an explosion, which had been followed a minute later by a second one. They slept in adjoining rooms, and Mrs. King had rushed in to Saunders. Together they had descended the stairs. The door of the study was open and a candle was burning upon the table. Their master lay upon his face in the centre of the room. He was quite dead. Near the window his wife was crouching, her head leaning against the wall. She was horribly wounded, and the side of her face was red with blood. She breathed heavily, but was incapable of saying anything. The passage, as well as the room, was full of smoke and the smell of powder. The window was certainly shut and fastened upon the inside. Both women were positive upon the point. They had at once sent for the doctor and for the constable. Then, with the aid of the groom and the stable-boy, they had conveyed their injured mistress to her room. Both she and her husband had occupied the bed. She was clad in her dress—he in his dressing-gown, over his night clothes. Nothing had been moved in the study. So far as they knew there had never been any quarrel between husband and wife. They had always looked upon them as a very united couple.

These were the main points of the servants' evidence. In answer to Inspector Martin they were clear that every door was fastened upon the inside, and that no one could have escaped from the house. In answer to Holmes they both remembered that they were conscious of the smell of powder from the moment that they ran out of their rooms upon the top floor. " I commend that fact very carefully to your attention," said Holmes to his professional colleague. " And now I think that we are in a position to undertake a thorough examination of the room."

The study proved to be a small chamber, lined on three sides with books, and with a

"THEY BOTH REMEMBERED THAT THEY WERE CONSCIOUS OF THE SMELL OF POWDER."

writing-table facing an ordinary window, which looked out upon the garden. Our first attention was given to the body of the unfortunate squire, whose huge frame lay stretched across the room. His disordered dress showed that he had been hastily aroused from sleep. The bullet had been fired at him from the front, and had remained in his body after penetrating the heart. His death had certainly been instantaneous and painless. There was no powder-marking either upon his dressing-gown or on his hands. According to the country surgeon the lady had stains upon her face, but none upon her hand.

"The absence of the latter means nothing, though its presence may mean everything," said Holmes. "Unless the powder from a badly-fitting cartridge happens to spurt backwards, one may fire many shots without leaving a sign. I would suggest that Mr. Cubitt's body may now be removed. I suppose, doctor, you have not recovered the bullet which wounded the lady?"

"A serious operation will be necessary before that can be done. But there are still four cartridges in the revolver. Two have been fired and two wounds inflicted, so that each bullet can be accounted for."

"So it would seem," said Holmes. "Perhaps you can account also for the bullet which has so obviously struck the edge of the window?"

He had turned suddenly, and his long, thin finger was pointing to a hole which had been drilled right through the lower window-sash about an inch above the bottom.

"By George!" cried the inspector. "How ever did you see that?"

"Because I looked for it."

"Wonderful!" said the country doctor. "You are certainly right, sir. Then a third shot has been fired, and therefore a third person must have been present. But who could that have been and how could he have got away?"

"That is the problem which we are now

about to solve," said Sherlock Holmes.
"You remember, Inspector Martin, when
the servants said that on leaving their
room they were at once conscious of a
smell of powder I remarked that the point
was an extremely important one?"

"Yes, sir; but I confess I did not quite
follow you."

"It suggested that at the time of the firing
the window as well as the door of the room
had been open. Otherwise the fumes of
powder could not have been blown so
rapidly through the house. A draught in
the room was necessary for that. Both door
and window were only open for a very short
time, however."

"How do you prove that?"

"Because the candle has not guttered."

"Capital!" cried the inspector. "Capital!"

"Feeling sure that the window had been
open at the time of the tragedy I conceived
that there might have been a third person in
the affair, who stood outside this opening and
fired through it. Any shot directed at this
person might hit the
sash. I looked, and
there, sure enough,
was the bullet mark!"

"But how came
the window to be shut
and fastened?"

"The woman's first
instinct would be to
shut and fasten the
window. But, halloa!
what is this?"

It was a lady's
hand-bag which stood
upon the study table
—a trim little hand-
bag of crocodile-skin
and silver. Holmes
opened it and turned
the contents out.
There were twenty
fifty-pound notes of
the Bank of England,
held together by an
india-rubber band—
nothing else.

"This must be
preserved, for it will
figure in the trial,"
said Holmes, as he
handed the bag with its contents to
the inspector. "It is now necessary
that we should try to throw some light
upon this third bullet, which has clearly,
from the splintering of the wood, been

fired from inside the room. I should like to
see Mrs. King, the cook, again. You said,
Mrs. King, that you were awakened by a *loud*
explosion. When you said that, did you
mean that it seemed to you to be louder than
the second one?"

"Well, sir, it wakened me from my sleep,
and so it is hard to judge. But it did seem
very loud."

"You don't think that it might have been
two shots fired almost at the same instant?"

"I am sure I couldn't say, sir."

"I believe that it was undoubtedly so. I
rather think, Inspector Martin, that we have
now exhausted all that this room can teach
us. If you will kindly step round with me,
we shall see what fresh evidence the garden
has to offer."

A flower-bed extended up to the study

"HE BENT FORWARD AND PICKED UP A LITTLE BRAZEN CYLINDER."

window, and we all broke into an exclamation as we approached it. The flowers were trampled down, and the soft soil was imprinted all over with footmarks. Large, masculine feet they were, with peculiarly long, sharp toes. Holmes hunted about among the grass and leaves like a retriever after a wounded bird. Then, with a cry of satisfaction, he bent forward and picked up a little brazen cylinder.

"I thought so," said he ; "the revolver had an ejector, and here is the third cartridge. I really think, Inspector Martin, that our case is almost complete."

The country inspector's face had shown his intense amazement at the rapid and masterful progress of Holmes's investigation. At first he had shown some disposition to assert his own position ; but now he was overcome with admiration and ready to follow without question wherever Holmes led.

"Whom do you suspect ? " he asked.

"I'll go into that later. There are several points in this problem which I have not been able to explain to you yet. Now that I have got so far I had best proceed on my own lines, and then clear the whole matter up once and for all."

"Just as you wish, Mr. Holmes, so long as we get our man."

"I have no desire to make mysteries, but it is impossible at the moment of action to enter into long and complex explanations. I have the threads of this affair all in my hand. Even if this lady should never recover consciousness we can still reconstruct the events of last night and ensure that justice be done. First of all I wish to know whether there is any inn in this neighbourhood known as ' Elrige's ' ? "

The servants were cross-questioned, but none of them had heard of such a place. The stable-boy threw a light upon the matter by remembering that a farmer of that name lived some miles off in the direction of East Ruston.

"Is it a lonely farm ? "

"Very lonely, sir."

"Perhaps they have not heard yet of all that happened here during the night ? "

"Maybe not, sir."

Holmes thought for a little and then a curious smile played over his face.

"Saddle a horse, my lad," said he. "I shall wish you to take a note to Elrige's Farm."

He took from his pocket the various slips of the dancing men. With these in front of him he worked for some time at the study-table. Finally he handed a note to the boy, with directions to put it into the hands of the person to whom it was addressed, and especially to answer no questions of any sort which might be put to him. I saw the outside of the note, addressed in straggling, irregular characters, very unlike Holmes's usual precise hand. It was consigned to Mr. Abe Slaney, Elrige's Farm, East Ruston, Norfolk.

"I think, inspector," Holmes remarked, "that you would do well to telegraph for an escort, as, if my calculations prove to be correct, you may have a particularly dangerous prisoner to convey to the county gaol. The boy who takes this note could no doubt forward your telegram. If there is an afternoon train to town, Watson, I think we should do well to take it, as I have a chemical analysis of some interest to finish, and this investigation draws rapidly to a close."

When the youth had been dispatched with the note, Sherlock Holmes gave his instructions to the servants. If any visitor were to call asking for Mrs. Hilton Cubitt no information should be given as to her condition, but he was to be shown at once into the drawing-room. He impressed these points upon them with the utmost earnestness. Finally he led the way into the drawing-room with the remark that the business was now out of our hands, and that we must while away the time as best we might until we could see what was in store for us. The doctor had departed to his patients, and only the inspector and myself remained.

"I think that I can help you to pass an hour in an interesting and profitable manner," said Holmes, drawing his chair up to the table and spreading out in front of him the various papers upon which were recorded the antics of the dancing men. "As to you, friend Watson, I owe you every atonement for having allowed your natural curiosity to remain so long unsatisfied. To you, inspector, the whole incident may appeal as a remarkable professional study. I must tell you first of all the interesting circumstances connected with the previous consultations which Mr. Hilton Cubitt has had with me in Baker Street." He then shortly recapitulated the facts which have already been recorded. "I have here in front of me these singular productions, at which one might smile had they not proved themselves to be the forerunners of so terrible a tragedy. I am fairly familiar with all forms of secret writings, and am myself the author of a trifling monograph upon the subject, in which I analyze one hundred and sixty separate ciphers; but I confess that this is entirely new to me. The object of those who invented the system has apparently been to conceal that these characters convey a message, and to give the idea that they are the mere random sketches of children.

"Having once recognised, however, that the symbols stood for letters, and having applied the rules which guide us in all forms of secret writings, the solution was easy enough. The first message submitted to me was so short that it was impossible for me to do more than to say with some confidence that the symbol

stood for E. As you are aware, E is the most common letter in the English alphabet, and it predominates to so marked an extent that even in a short sentence one would expect to find it most often. Out of fifteen symbols in the first message four were the same, so it was reasonable to set this down as E. It is true that in some cases the figure was bearing a flag and in some cases not, but it was probable from the way in which the flags were distributed that they were used to break the sentence up into words. I accepted this as a hypothesis, and noted that E was represented by

"But now came the real difficulty of the inquiry. The order of the English letters after E is by no means well marked, and any preponderance which may be shown in an average of a printed sheet may be reversed in a single short sentence. Speaking roughly, T, A, O, I, N, S, H, R, D, and L are the numerical order in which letters occur; but T, A, O, and I are very nearly abreast of each other, and it would be an endless task to try each combination until a meaning was arrived at. I, therefore, waited for fresh material. In my second interview with Mr. Hilton Cubitt he was able to give me two other short sentences and one message, which appeared—since there was no flag— to be a single word. Here are the symbols. Now, in the single word I have already got the two E's coming second and fourth in a word of five letters. It might be 'sever,' or 'lever,' or 'never.' There can be no question that the latter as a reply to an appeal is far the most probable, and the cir-

cumstances pointed to its being a reply written by the lady. Accepting it as correct, we are now able to say that the symbols

stand respectively for N, V, and R.

"Even now I was in considerable difficulty, but a happy thought put me in possession of several other letters. It occurred to me that if these appeals came, as I expected, from someone who had been intimate with the lady in her early life, a combination which contained two E's with three letters between might very well stand for the name 'ELSIE.' On examination I found that such a combination formed the termination of the message which was three times repeated. It was certainly some appeal to 'Elsie.' In this way I had got my L, S, and I. But what appeal could it be? There were only four letters in the word which preceded 'Elsie,' and it ended in E. Surely the word must be 'COME.' I tried all other four letters ending in E, but could find none to fit the case. So now I was in possession of C, O, and M, and I was in a position to attack the first message once more, dividing it into words and putting dots for each symbol which was still unknown. So treated it worked out in this fashion:—

   . M . ERE . . E SL . NE .

"Now the first letter *can* only be A, which is a most useful discovery, since it occurs no fewer than three times in this short sentence, and the H is also apparent in the second word. Now it becomes:—

   AM HERE A . E SLANE .

Or, filling in the obvious vacancies in the name:—

   AM HERE ABE SLANEY.

I had so many letters now that I could proceed with considerable confidence to the second message, which worked out in this fashion:—

   A . ELRI . ES.

Here I could only make sense by putting T and G for the missing letters, and supposing that the name was that of some house or inn at which the writer was staying."

Inspector Martin and I had listened with the utmost interest to the full and clear account of how my friend had produced results which had led to so complete a command over our difficulties.

"What did you do then, sir?" asked the inspector.

"I had every reason to suppose that this Abe Slaney was an American, since Abe is

an American contraction, and since a letter
from America had been the starting-point of
all the trouble. I had also every cause to
think that there was some criminal secret in
the matter. The lady's allusions to her past
and her refusal to take her husband into her
confidence both pointed in that direction.
I therefore cabled to my friend, Wilson
Hargreave, of the New York Police Bureau,
who has more than once made use of my
knowledge of London crime. I asked him
whether the name of Abe Slaney was known
to him. Here is his reply: 'The most
dangerous crook in Chicago.' On the very
evening upon which I had his answer Hilton
Cubitt sent me the last message from Slaney.
Working with known letters it took this
form :—
ELSIE . RE . ARE TO MEET THY GO .
The addition of a P and a D completed
a message which showed me that the rascal
was proceeding from persuasion to threats,
and my knowledge of the crooks of Chicago
prepared me to find that he might very
rapidly put his words into action. I at once
came to Norfolk with my friend and colleague, Dr. Watson, but, unhappily, only in
time to find that the worst
had already occurred."

"It is a privilege to be
associated with you in the
handling of a case," said the
inspector, warmly. "You
will excuse me, however, if
I speak frankly to you. You
are only answerable to yourself, but I have to answer
to my superiors. If this
Abe Slaney, living at Elrige's,
is indeed the murderer, and
if he has made his escape
while I am seated here, I
should certainly get into
serious trouble."

"You need not be un-
easy. He will not try to
escape."

" How do you know ? "

" To fly would be a con-
fession of guilt."

" Then let us go to arrest
him."

" I expect him here every
instant."

" But why should he
come ? "

" Because I have written
and asked him."

" But this is incredible,

Mr. Holmes ! Why should he come because
you have asked him ? Would not such a
request rather rouse his suspicions and cause
him to fly ? "

" I think I have known how to frame
the letter," said Sherlock Holmes. " In fact,
if I am not very much mistaken, here is
the gentleman himself coming up the
drive."

A man was striding up the path which led
to the door. He was a tall, handsome,
swarthy fellow, clad in a suit of grey flannel,
with a Panama hat, a bristling black beard,
and a great, aggressive hooked nose, and
flourishing a cane as he walked. He
swaggered up the path as if the place
belonged to him, and we heard his loud,
confident peal at the bell.

" I think, gentlemen," said Holmes, quietly,
" that we had best take up our position
behind the door. Every precaution is necessary when dealing with such a fellow. You
will need your handcuffs, inspector. You
can leave the talking to me."

We waited in silence for a minute—one
of those minutes which one can never forget.
Then the door opened and the man stepped

" HE BURIED HIS FACE IN HIS MANACLED HANDS."

in. In an instant Holmes clapped a pistol to his head and Martin slipped the handcuffs over his wrists. It was all done so swiftly and deftly that the fellow was helpless before he knew that he was attacked. He glared from one to the other of us with a pair of blazing black eyes. Then he burst into a bitter laugh.

"Well, gentlemen, you have the drop on me this time. I seem to have knocked up against something hard. But I came here in answer to a letter from Mrs. Hilton Cubitt. Don't tell me that she is in this? Don't tell me that she helped to set a trap for me?"

"Mrs. Hilton Cubitt was seriously injured and is at death's door."

The man gave a hoarse cry of grief which rang through the house.

"You're crazy!" he cried, fiercely. "It was he that was hurt, not she. Who would have hurt little Elsie? I may have threatened her, God forgive me, but I would not have touched a hair of her pretty head. Take it back—you! Say that she is not hurt!"

"She was found badly wounded by the side of her dead husband."

He sank with a deep groan on to the settee and buried his face in his manacled hands. For five minutes he was silent. Then he raised his face once more, and spoke with the cold composure of despair.

"I have nothing to hide from you, gentlemen," said he. "If I shot the man he had his shot at me, and there's no murder in that. But if you think I could have hurt that woman, then you don't know either me or her. I tell you there was never a man in this world loved a woman more than I loved her. I had a right to her. She was pledged to me years ago. Who was this Englishman that he should come between us? I tell you that I had the first right to her, and that I was only claiming my own."

"She broke away from your influence when she found the man that you are," said Holmes, sternly. "She fled from America to avoid you, and she married an honourable gentleman in England. You dogged her and followed her and made her life a misery to her in order to induce her to abandon the husband whom she loved and respected in order to fly with you, whom she feared and hated. You have ended by bringing about the death of a noble man and driving his wife to suicide. That is your record in this business, Mr. Abe Slaney, and you will answer for it to the law."

"If Elsie dies I care nothing what becomes of me," said the American. He opened one of his hands and looked at a note crumpled up in his palm. "See here, mister," he cried, with a gleam of suspicion in his eyes, "you're not trying to scare me over this, are you? If the lady is hurt as bad as you say, who was it that wrote this note?" He tossed it forwards on to the table.

"I wrote it to bring you here."

"You wrote it? There was no one on earth outside the Joint who knew the secret of the dancing men. How came you to write it?"

"What one man can invent another can discover," said Holmes. "There is a cab coming to convey you to Norwich, Mr. Slaney. But, meanwhile, you have time to make some small reparation for the injury you have wrought. Are you aware that Mrs. Hilton Cubitt has herself lain under grave suspicion of the murder of her husband, and that it was only my presence here and the knowledge which I happened to possess which has saved her from the accusation? The least that you owe her is to make it clear to the whole world that she was in no way, directly or indirectly, responsible for his tragic end."

"I ask nothing better," said the American. "I guess the very best case I can make for myself is the absolute naked truth."

"It is my duty to warn you that it will be used against you," cried the inspector, with the magnificent fair-play of the British criminal law.

Slaney shrugged his shoulders.

"I'll chance that," said he. "First of all, I want you gentlemen to understand that I have known this lady since she was a child. There were seven of us in a gang in Chicago, and Elsie's father was the boss of the Joint. He was a clever man, was old Patrick. It was he who invented that writing, which would pass as a child's scrawl unless you just happened to have the key to it. Well, Elsie learned some of our ways; but she couldn't stand the business, and she had a bit of honest money of her own, so she gave us all the slip and got away to London. She had been engaged to me, and she would have married me, I believe, if I had taken over another profession; but she would have nothing to do with anything on the cross. It was only after her marriage to this Englishman that I was able to find out where she was. I wrote to her, but got no answer. After that I came over, and, as letters were no use, I put my messages where she could read them.

"Well, I have been here a month now. I lived in that farm, where I had a room down below, and could get in and out every night, and no one the wiser. I tried all I could to coax Elsie away. I knew that she read the messages, for once she wrote an answer under one of them. Then my temper got the better of me, and I began to threaten her. She sent me a letter then, imploring me to go away and saying that it would break her heart if any scandal should come upon her husband. She said that she would

"No, she is not conscious. Mr. Sherlock Holmes, I only hope that if ever again I have an important case I shall have the good fortune to have you by my side."

We stood at the window and watched the cab drive away. As I turned back my eye caught the pellet of paper which the prisoner had tossed upon the table. It was the note with which Holmes had decoyed him.

"See if you can read it, Watson," said he, with a smile.

It contained no word, but this little line of dancing men :—

come down when her husband was asleep at three in the morning, and speak with me through the end window, if I would go away afterwards and leave her in peace. She came down and brought money with her, trying to bribe me to go. This made me mad, and I caught her arm and tried to pull her through the window. At that moment in rushed the husband with his revolver in his hand. Elsie had sunk down upon the floor, and we were face to face. I was heeled also, and I held up my gun to scare him off and let me get away. He fired and missed me. I pulled off almost at the same instant, and down he dropped. I made away across the garden, and as I went I heard the window shut behind me. That's God's truth, gentlemen, every word of it, and I heard no more about it until that lad came riding up with a note which made me walk in here, like a jay, and give myself into your hands."

A cab had driven up whilst the American had been talking. Two uniformed policemen sat inside. Inspector Martin rose and touched his prisoner on the shoulder.

"It is time for us to go."

"Can I see her first ?"

"If you use the code which I have explained," said Holmes, "you will find that it simply means 'Come here at once.' I was convinced that it was an invitation which he would not refuse, since he could never imagine that it could come from anyone but the lady. And so, my dear Watson, we have ended by turning the dancing men to good when they have so often been the agents of evil, and I think that I have fulfilled my promise of giving you something unusual for your note-book. Three-forty is our train, and I fancy we should be back in Baker Street for dinner.

Only one word of epilogue. The American, Abe Slaney, was condemned to death at the winter assizes at Norwich ; but his penalty was changed to penal servitude in consideration of mitigating circumstances, and the certainty that Hilton Cubitt had fired the first shot. Of Mrs. Hilton Cubitt I only know that I have heard she recovered entirely, and that she still remains a widow, devoting her whole life to the care of the poor and to the administration of her husband's estate.

"HE SPUN ROUND WITH A SCREAM AND FELL UPON HIS BACK."

# THE RETURN OF SHERLOCK HOLMES.

## By A. CONAN DOYLE.

### IV.—The Adventure of the Solitary Cyclist.

 ROM the years 1894 to 1901 inclusive Mr. Sherlock Holmes was a very busy man. It is safe to say that there was no public case of any difficulty in which he was not consulted during those eight years, and there were hundreds of private cases, some of them of the most intricate and extraordinary character, in which he played a prominent part. Many startling successes and a few unavoidable failures were the outcome of this long period of continuous work. As I have preserved very full notes of all these cases, and was myself personally engaged in many of them, it may be imagined that it is no easy task to know which I should select to lay before the public. I shall, however, preserve my former rule, and give the preference to those cases which derive their interest not so much from the brutality of the crime as from the ingenuity and dramatic quality of the solution. For this reason I will now lay before the reader the facts connected with Miss Violet Smith, the solitary cyclist of Charlington, and the curious sequel of our investigation, which culminated in unexpected tragedy. It is true that the circumstances did not admit of any striking illustration of those powers for which my friend was famous, but there were some points about the case which made it stand out in those long records of crime from which I gather the material for these little narratives.

On referring to my note-book for the year 1895 I find that it was upon Saturday, the 23rd of April, that we first heard of Miss Violet Smith. Her visit was, I remember, extremely unwelcome to Holmes, for he was immersed at the moment in a very abstruse and complicated problem concerning the peculiar persecution to which John Vincent Harden, the well-known tobacco millionaire, had been subjected. My friend, who loved above all things precision and concentration of thought, resented anything which distracted his attention from the matter in hand. And yet without a harshness which was foreign to his nature it was impossible to refuse to listen to the story of the young and beautiful woman, tall, graceful, and queenly, who presented herself at Baker Street late in the evening and implored his assistance and advice. It was vain to urge that his time was already fully occupied, for the young lady had come with the determination to tell her story, and it was evident that nothing short of force could get her out of the room until she had done so. With a resigned air and a somewhat weary smile, Holmes begged the beautiful intruder to take a seat and to inform us what it was that was troubling her.

"At least it cannot be your health," said he, as his keen eyes darted over her; "so ardent a bicyclist must be full of energy."

She glanced down in surprise at her own feet, and I observed the slight roughening of the side of the sole caused by the friction of the edge of the pedal.

"Yes, I bicycle a good deal, Mr. Holmes, and that has something to do with my visit to you to-day."

My friend took the lady's ungloved hand and examined it with as close an attention and as little sentiment as a scientist would show to a specimen.

"You will excuse me, I am sure. It is my business," said he, as he dropped it. "I nearly fell into the error of supposing that you were typewriting. Of course, it is

"MY FRIEND TOOK THE LADY'S UNGLOVED HAND AND EXAMINED IT."

obvious that it is music. You observe the spatulate finger-end, Watson, which is common to both professions? There is a spirituality about the face, however"—he gently turned it towards the light—"which the typewriter does not generate. This lady is a musician."

"Yes, Mr. Holmes, I teach music."

"In the country, I presume, from your complexion."

"Yes, sir; near Farnham, on the borders of Surrey."

"A beautiful neighbourhood and full of the most interesting associations. You remember, Watson, that it was near there that we took Archie Stamford, the forger. Now, Miss Violet, what has happened to you near Farnham, on the borders of Surrey?"

The young lady, with great clearness and composure, made the following curious statement:—

"My father is dead, Mr. Holmes. He was James Smith, who conducted the orchestra at the old Imperial Theatre. My mother and I were left without a relation in the world except one uncle, Ralph Smith, who went to Africa twenty-five years ago, and we have never had a word from him

since. When father died we were left very poor, but one day we were told that there was an advertisement in the *Times* inquiring for our whereabouts. You can imagine how excited we were, for we thought that someone had left us a fortune. We went at once to the lawyer whose name was given in the paper. There we met two gentlemen, Mr. Carruthers and Mr. Woodley, who were home on a visit from South Africa. They said that my uncle was a friend of theirs, that he died some months before in great poverty in Johannesburg, and that he had asked them with his last breath to hunt up his relations and see that they were in no want. It seemed strange to us that Uncle Ralph, who took no notice of us when he was alive, should be so careful to look after us when he was dead; but Mr. Carruthers explained that the reason was that my uncle had just heard of the death of his brother, and so felt responsible for our fate."

"Excuse me," said Holmes; "when was this interview?"

"Last December—four months ago."

"Pray proceed."

"Mr. Woodley seemed to me to be a most odious person. He was for ever making eyes at me—a coarse, puffy-faced, red-moustached young man, with his hair plastered down on each side of his forehead. I thought that he was perfectly hateful—and I was sure that Cyril would not wish to know such a person."

"Oh, Cyril is his name!" said Holmes, smiling.

The young lady blushed and laughed.

"Yes, Mr. Holmes; Cyril Morton, an electrical engineer, and we hope to be married at the end of the summer. Dear me, how *did* I get talking about him? What I wished to say was that Mr. Woodley was perfectly odious, but that Mr. Carruthers, who was a much older man, was more agreeable. He was a dark, sallow, clean-shaven, silent person ; but he had polite manners and a pleasant smile. He inquired how we were left, and on finding that we were very poor he suggested that I should come and teach music to his only daughter, aged ten. I said that I did not like to leave my mother, on which he suggested that I should go home to her every week-end, and he offered me a hundred a year, which was certainly splendid pay. So it ended by my accepting, and I went down to Chiltern Grange, about six miles from Farnham. Mr. Carruthers was a widower, but he had engaged a lady-housekeeper, a very respectable, elderly person, called Mrs. Dixon, to look after his establishment. The child was a dear, and everything promised well. Mr. Carruthers was very kind and very musical, and we had most pleasant evenings together. Every week-end I went home to my mother in town.

"The first flaw in my happiness was the arrival of the red-moustached Mr. Woodley. He came for a visit of a week, and oh, it seemed three months to me ! He was a dreadful person, a bully to everyone else, but to me something infinitely worse. He made odious love to me, boasted of his wealth, said that if I married him I would have the finest diamonds in London, and finally, when I would have nothing to do with him, he seized me in his arms one day after dinner—he was hideously strong—and he swore that he would not let me go until I had kissed him. Mr. Carruthers came in and tore him off from me, on which he turned upon his own host, knocking him down and cutting his face open. That was the end of his visit, as you can imagine. Mr. Carruthers apologized to me next day, and assured me that I should never be exposed to such an insult again. I have not seen Mr. Woodley since.

"And now, Mr. Holmes, I come at last to the special thing which has caused me to ask your advice to-day. You must know that every Saturday forenoon I ride on my bicycle to Farnham Station in order to get the 12.22 to town. The road from Chiltern Grange is a lonely one, and at one spot it is particularly so, for it lies for over a mile between Charlington Heath upon one side and the woods which lie round Charlington Hall upon the other. You could not find a more lonely tract of road anywhere, and it is quite rare to meet so much as a cart, or a peasant, until you reach the high road near Crooksbury Hill. Two weeks ago I was passing this place when I chanced to look back over my shoulder, and about two hundred yards behind me I saw a man, also on a bicycle. He seemed to be a middle-aged man, with a short, dark beard. I looked back before I reached Farnham, but the man was gone, so I thought no more about it. But you can imagine how surprised I was, Mr. Holmes, when on my return on the Monday I saw the same man on the same stretch of road. My astonishment was increased when the incident occurred again, exactly as before, on the following Saturday and Monday. He always kept his distance and did not molest me in any way, but still it certainly was very odd. I mentioned it to Mr. Carruthers, who seemed interested in what I said, and told me that he had ordered a horse and trap, so that in future I should not pass over these lonely roads without some companion.

"The horse and trap were to have come this week, but for some reason they were not delivered, and again I had to cycle to the station. That was this morning. You can think that I looked out when I came to Charlington Heath, and there, sure enough, was the man, exactly as he had been the two weeks before. He always kept so far from me that I could not clearly see his face, but it was certainly someone whom I did not know. He was dressed in a dark suit with a cloth cap. The only thing about his face that I could clearly see was his dark beard. To-day I was not alarmed, but I was filled with curiosity, and I determined to find out who he was and what he wanted. I slowed down my machine, but he slowed down his. Then I stopped altogether, but he stopped also. Then I laid a trap for him. There is a sharp turning of the road, and I pedalled very quickly round this, and then I stopped and waited. I expected him to shoot round and pass me before he could stop. But he never appeared. Then I went back and looked round the corner. I could see a mile of road, but he was not on it. To make it the more extraordinary, there was no side road at this point down which he could have gone."

Holmes chuckled and rubbed his hands. "This case certainly presents some features of its own," said he. "How much time elapsed between your turning the corner and your discovery that the road was clear ? "

"Two or three minutes."

"Then he could not have retreated down the road, and you say that there are no side roads ? "

"I SLOWED DOWN MY MACHINE."

"Oh, it may be a mere fancy of mine; but it has seemed to me sometimes that my employer, Mr. Carruthers, takes a great deal of interest in me. We are thrown rather together. I play his accompaniments in the evening. He has never said anything. He is a perfect gentleman. But a girl always knows."

"Ha!" Holmes looked grave. "What does he do for a living?"

"He is a rich man."

"No carriages or horses?"

"Well, at least he is fairly well-to-do. But he goes into the City two or three times a week. He is deeply interested in South African gold shares."

"None."

"Then he certainly took a footpath on one side or the other."

"It could not have been on the side of the heath or I should have seen him."

"So by the process of exclusion we arrive at the fact that he made his way towards Charlington Hall, which, as I understand, is situated in its own grounds on one side of the road. Anything else?"

"Nothing, Mr. Holmes, save that I was so perplexed that I felt I should not be happy until I had seen you and had your advice."

Holmes sat in silence for some little time.

"Where is the gentleman to whom you are engaged?" he asked, at last.

"He is in the Midland Electrical Company, at Coventry."

"He would not pay you a surprise visit?"

"Oh, Mr. Holmes! As if I should not know him!"

"Have you had any other admirers?"

"Several before I knew Cyril."

"And since?"

"There was this dreadful man, Woodley, if you can call him an admirer."

"No one else?"

Our fair client seemed a little confused.

"Who was he?" asked Holmes,

"You will let me know any fresh development, Miss Smith. I am very busy just now, but I will find time to make some inquiries into your case. In the meantime take no step without letting me know. Good-bye, and I trust that we shall have nothing but good news from you."

"It is part of the settled order of Nature that such a girl should have followers," said Holmes, as he pulled at his meditative pipe, "but for choice not on bicycles in lonely country roads. Some secretive lover, beyond all doubt. But there are curious and suggestive details about the case, Watson."

"That he should appear only at that point?"

"Exactly. Our first effort must be to find who are the tenants of Charlington Hall. Then, again, how about the connection between Carruthers and Woodley, since they appear to be men of such a different type? How came they both to be so keen upon looking up Ralph Smith's relations? One more point. What sort of a ménage is it which pays double the market price for a governess, but does not keep a horse although six miles from the station? Odd, Watson—very odd!"

"You will go down?"

"No, my dear fellow, *you* will go down. This may be some trifling intrigue, and I cannot break my other important research for the sake of it. On Monday you will arrive early at Farnham; you will conceal yourself near Charlington Heath; you will observe these facts for yourself, and act as your own judgment advises. Then, having inquired as to the occupants of the Hall, you will come back to me and report. And now, Watson, not another word of the matter until we have a few solid stepping-stones on which we may hope to get across to our solution."

We had ascertained from the lady that she went down upon the Monday by the train which leaves Waterloo at 9.50, so I started early and caught the 9.13. At Farnham Station I had no difficulty in being directed to Charlington Heath. It was impossible to mistake the scene of the young lady's adventure, for the road runs between the open heath on one side and an old yew hedge upon the other, surrounding a park which is studded with magnificent trees. There was a main gateway of lichen-studded stone, each side pillar surmounted by mouldering heraldic emblems; but besides this central carriage drive I observed several points where there were gaps in the hedge and paths leading through them. The house was invisible from the road, but the surroundings all spoke of gloom and decay.

The heath was covered with golden patches of flowering gorse, gleaming magnificently in the light of the bright spring sunshine. Behind one of these clumps I took up my position, so as to command both the gateway of the Hall and a long stretch of the road upon either side. It had been deserted when I left it, but now I saw a cyclist riding down it from the opposite direction to that in which I had come. He was clad in a dark suit, and I saw that he had a black beard. On reaching the end of the Charlington grounds he sprang from his machine and led it through a gap in the hedge, disappearing from my view.

A quarter of an hour passed and then a second cyclist appeared. This time it was the young lady coming from the station. I saw her look about her as she came to the Charlington hedge. An instant later the man emerged from his hiding-place, sprang upon his cycle, and followed her. In all the broad landscape those were the only moving figures, the graceful girl sitting very straight upon her machine, and the man behind her bending low over his handle-bar, with a curiously furtive suggestion in every movement. She looked back at him and slowed her pace. He slowed also. She stopped. He at once stopped too, keeping two hundred yards behind her. Her next movement was as unexpected as it was spirited. She suddenly whisked her wheels round and dashed straight at him! He was as quick as she, however, and darted off in desperate flight. Presently she came back up the road again, her head haughtily in the air, not deigning to take any further notice of her silent attendant. He had turned also, and still kept his distance until the curve of the road hid them from my sight.

I remained in my hiding-place, and it was well that I did so, for presently the man reappeared cycling slowly back. He turned in at the Hall gates and dismounted from his machine. For some few minutes I could see him standing among the trees. His hands were raised and he seemed to be settling his necktie. Then he mounted his cycle and rode away from me down the drive towards the Hall. I ran across the heath and peered through the trees. Far away I could catch glimpses of the old grey building with its bristling Tudor chimneys, but the drive ran through a dense shrubbery, and I saw no more of my man.

However, it seemed to me that I had done a fairly good morning's work, and I walked back in high spirits to Farnham. The local house-agent could tell me nothing about Charlington Hall, and referred me to a well-known firm in Pall Mall. There I halted on my way home, and met with courtesy from the representative. No, I could not have Charlington Hall for the summer. I was just too late. It had been let about a month ago. Mr. Williamson was the name of the tenant. He was a respectable elderly gentleman. The polite agent was afraid he could say no more, as the affairs of his clients were not matters which he could discuss.

Mr. Sherlock Holmes listened with attention to the long report which I was able to present to him that evening, but it did not elicit that word of curt praise which I had hoped for and should have valued. On the contrary, his austere face was even more severe than usual as he commented upon the things that I had done and the things that I had not.

"Your hiding-place, my dear Watson,

was very faulty. You should have been behind the hedge ; then you would have had a close view of this interesting person. As it is you were some hundreds of yards away, and can tell me even less than Miss Smith. She thinks she does not know the man ; I am convinced she does. Why, otherwise, should he be so desperately anxious that she should not get so near him as to see his features ? You describe him as bending over the handle-bar. Concealment again, you see. You really have done remarkably badly. He returns to the house and you want to find out who he is. You come to a London house-agent ! "

"What should I have done ? " I cried, with some heat.

"Gone to the nearest public-house. That is the centre of country gossip. They would have told you every name, from the master to the scullery-maid. Williamson ! It conveys nothing to my mind. If he is an elderly man he is not this active cyclist who sprints away from that athletic young lady's pursuit. What have we gained by your expedition ? The knowledge that the girl's story is true. I never doubted it. That there is a connection between the cyclist and the Hall. I never doubted that either. That the Hall is tenanted by Williamson. Who's the better for that ? Well, well, my dear sir, don't look so depressed. We can do little more until next Saturday, and in the meantime I may make one or two inquiries myself."

Next morning we had a note from Miss Smith, recounting shortly and accurately the very incidents which I had seen, but the pith of the letter lay in the postscript :—

"I am sure that you will respect my confidence, Mr. Holmes, when I tell you that my place here has become difficult owing to the fact that my employer has proposed marriage to me. I am convinced that his feelings are most deep and most honourable. At the same time my promise is, of course, given. He took my refusal very seriously, but also very gently. You can understand, however, that the situation is a little strained."

"Our young friend seems to be getting into deep waters," said Holmes, thought-fully, as he finished the letter. "The case certainly presents more features of interest and more possibility of development than I had originally thought. I should be none the worse for a quiet, peaceful day in the country, and I am inclined to run down this afternoon and test one or two theories which I have formed,"

Holmes's quiet day in the country had a singular termination, for he arrived at Baker Street late in the evening with a cut lip and a discoloured lump upon his forehead, besides a general air of dissipation which would have made his own person the fitting object of a Scotland Yard investigation. He was immensely tickled by his own adventures, and laughed heartily as he recounted them.

"I get so little active exercise that it is always a treat," said he. "You are aware that I have some proficiency in the good old British sport of boxing. Occasionally it is of service. To-day, for example, I should have come to very ignominious grief without it."

I begged him to tell me what had occurred.

"I found that country pub which I had already recommended to your notice, and there I made my discreet inquiries. I was in the bar, and a garrulous landlord was giving me all that I wanted. Williamson is a white-bearded man, and he lives alone with a small staff of servants at the Hall. There is some rumour that he is or has been a clergyman ; but one or two incidents of his short residence at the Hall struck me as peculiarly unecclesiastical. I have already made some inquiries at a clerical agency, and they tell me that there *was* a man of that name in orders whose career has been a singularly dark one. The landlord further informed me that there are usually week-end visitors—'a warm lot, sir '—at the Hall, and especially one gentleman with a red moustache, Mr. Woodley by name, who was always there. We had got as far as this when who should walk in but the gentleman himself, who had been drinking his beer in the tap-room and had heard the whole conversation. Who was I ? What did I want ? What did I mean by asking questions ? He had a fine flow of language, and his adjectives were very vigorous. He ended a string of abuse by a vicious back-hander which I failed to entirely avoid. The next few minutes were delicious. It was a straight left against a slogging ruffian. I emerged as you see me. Mr. Woodley went home in a cart. So ended my country trip, and it must be confessed that, however enjoyable, my day on the Surrey border has not been much more profitable than your own."

The Thursday brought us another letter from our client.

"You will not be surprised, Mr. Holmes," said she, "to hear that I am leaving Mr. Carruthers's employment. Even the high pay cannot reconcile me to the discomforts

"A STRAIGHT LEFT AGAINST A SLOGGING RUFFIAN."

Carruthers endure such a creature for a moment? However, all my troubles will be over on Saturday."

"So I trust, Watson; so I trust," said Holmes, gravely. "There is some deep intrigue going on round that little woman, and it is our duty to see that no one molests her upon that last journey. I think, Watson, that we must spare time to run down together on Saturday morning, and make sure that this curious and inconclusive investigation has no untoward ending."

I confess that I had not up to now taken a very serious view of the case, which had seemed to me rather grotesque and bizarre than dangerous. That a man should lie in wait for and follow a very handsome woman is no unheard of thing, and if he had so little audacity that he not only dared not address her, but even fled from her approach, he was not a very formidable assailant. The ruffian Woodley was a very different person, but, except on the one occasion, he had not molested our client, and now he visited the house of Carruthers without intruding upon her presence. The man on the bicycle was doubtless a member of those week-end parties at the Hall of which the publican had spoken; but who he was or what he wanted was as obscure as ever. It was the severity of Holmes's manner and the fact that he slipped a revolver into his pocket before leaving our rooms which impressed me with the feeling that tragedy might prove to lurk behind this curious train of events.

A rainy night had been followed by a glorious morning, and the heath-covered country-side with the glowing clumps of flowering gorse seemed all the more beautiful to eyes which were weary of the duns and drabs and slate-greys of London. Holmes and I walked along the broad, sandy road

of my situation. On Saturday I come up to town and I do not intend to return. Mr. Carruthers has got a trap, and so the dangers of the lonely road, if there ever were any dangers, are now over.

"As to the special cause of my leaving, it is not merely the strained situation with Mr. Carruthers, but it is the reappearance of that odious man, Mr. Woodley. He was always hideous, but he looks more awful than ever now, for he appears to have had an accident and he is much disfigured. I saw him out of the window, but I am glad to say I did not meet him. He had a long talk with Mr. Carruthers, who seemed much excited afterwards. Woodley must be staying in the neighbourhood, for he did not sleep here, and yet I caught a glimpse of him again this morning slinking about in the shrubbery. I would sooner have a savage wild animal loose about the place. I loathe and fear him more than I can say. How *can* Mr.

inhaling the fresh morning air, and rejoicing in the music of the birds and the fresh breath of the spring. From a rise of the road on the shoulder of Crooksbury Hill we could see the grim Hall bristling out from amidst the ancient oaks, which, old as they were, were still younger than the building which they surrounded. Holmes pointed down the long tract of road which wound, a reddish yellow band, between the brown of the heath and the budding green of the woods. Far away, a black dot, we could see a vehicle moving in our direction. Holmes gave an exclamation of impatience.

"I had given a margin of half an hour," said he. "If that is her trap she must be making for the earlier train. I fear, Watson, that she will be past Charlington before we can possibly meet her."

From the instant that we passed the rise we could no longer see the vehicle, but we hastened onwards at such a pace that my sedentary life began to tell upon me, and I was compelled to fall behind. Holmes, however, was always in training, for he had inexhaustible stores of nervous energy upon which to draw. His springy step never slowed until suddenly, when he was a hundred yards in front of me, he halted, and I saw him throw up his hand with a gesture of grief and despair. At the same instant an empty dog-cart, the horse cantering, the reins trailing, appeared round the curve of the road and rattled swiftly towards us.

"Too late, Watson; too late!" cried Holmes, as I ran panting to his side. "Fool that I was not to allow for that earlier train! It's abduction, Watson—abduction! Murder! Heaven knows what! Block the road! Stop the horse! That's right. Now, jump in, and let us see if I can repair the consequences of my own blunder."

We had sprung into the dog-cart, and Holmes, after turning the horse, gave it a sharp cut with the whip, and we flew back along the road. As we turned the curve the whole stretch of road between the Hall

and the heath was opened up. I grasped Holmes's arm.

"That's the man!" I gasped.

A solitary cyclist was coming towards us. His head was down and his shoulders rounded as he put every ounce of energy that he possessed on to the pedals. He was flying like a racer. Suddenly he raised his bearded face, saw us close to him, and pulled up, springing from his machine. That coal-black beard was in singular contrast to the pallor of his face, and his eyes were as bright as if he had a fever. He stared at us and at the dog-cart. Then a look of amazement came over his face.

"Halloa! Stop there!" he shouted, holding his bicycle to block our road. "Where did you get that dog-cart? Pull up, man!" he yelled, drawing a pistol from his side pocket. "Pull up, I say, or, by George, I'll put a bullet into your horse."

Holmes threw the reins into my lap and sprang down from the cart.

"'TOO LATE, WATSON;
TOO LATE!' CRIED HOLMES."

"You're the man we want to see. Where is Miss Violet Smith?" he said, in his quick, clear way.

"That's what I am asking you. You're in her dog-cart. You ought to know where she is."

"We met the dog-cart on the road. There was no one in it. We drove back to help the young lady."

"Good Lord! Good Lord! what shall I do?" cried the stranger, in an ecstasy of despair. "They've got her, that hellhound Woodley and the blackguard parson. Come, man, come, if you really are her friend. Stand by me and we'll save her, if I have to leave my carcass in Charlington Wood."

He ran distractedly, his pistol in his hand, towards a gap in the hedge. Holmes followed him, and I, leaving the horse grazing beside the road, followed Holmes.

"This is where they came through," said he, pointing to the marks of several feet upon the muddy path. "Halloa! Stop a minute! Who's this in the bush?"

It was a young fellow about seventeen, dressed like an ostler, with leather cords and gaiters. He lay upon his back, his knees drawn up, a terrible cut upon his head. He was insensible, but alive. A glance at his wound told me that it had not penetrated the bone.

"That's Peter, the groom," cried the stranger. "He drove her. The beasts have pulled him off and clubbed him. Let him lie; we can't do him any good, but we may save her from the worst fate that can befall a woman."

We ran frantically down the path, which wound among the trees. We had reached the shrubbery which surrounded the house when Holmes pulled up.

"They didn't go to the house. Here are their marks on the left—here, beside the laurel bushes! Ah, I said so!"

As he spoke a woman's shrill scream—a scream which vibrated with a frenzy of horror—burst from the thick green clump of bushes in front of us. It ended suddenly on its highest note with a choke and a gurgle.

"This way! This way! They are in the bowling alley," cried the stranger, darting through the bushes. "Ah, the cowardly dogs! Follow me, gentlemen! Too late! too late! by the living Jingo!"

We had broken suddenly into a lovely glade of greensward surrounded by ancient trees. On the farther side of it, under the shadow of a mighty oak, there stood a singular group of three people. One was a woman, our client, drooping and faint, a handkerchief round her mouth. Opposite her stood a brutal, heavy-faced, red-moustached young man, his gaitered legs parted wide, one arm akimbo, the other waving a riding-crop, his whole attitude suggestive of triumphant bravado. Between them an elderly, grey-bearded man, wearing a short surplice over a light tweed suit, had evidently just completed the wedding service, for he pocketed his prayer-book as we appeared and slapped the sinister bridegroom upon the back in jovial congratulation.

"They're married!" I gasped.

"Come on!" cried our guide; "come on!" He rushed across the glade, Holmes and I at his heels. As we approached, the lady staggered against the trunk of the tree for support. Williamson, the ex-clergyman, bowed to us with mock politeness, and the bully Woodley advanced with a shout of brutal and exultant laughter.

"You can take your beard off, Bob," said he. "I know you right enough. Well, you and your pals have just come in time for me to be able to introduce you to Mrs. Woodley."

Our guide's answer was a singular one. He snatched off the dark beard which had disguised him and threw it on the ground, disclosing a long, sallow, clean-shaven face below it. Then he raised his revolver and covered the young ruffian, who was advancing upon him with his dangerous riding-crop swinging in his hand.

"Yes," said our ally, "I *am* Bob Carruthers, and I'll see this woman righted if I have to swing for it. I told you what I'd do if you molested her, and, by the Lord, I'll be as good as my word!"

"You're too late. She's my wife!"

"No, she's your widow."

His revolver cracked, and I saw the blood spurt from the front of Woodley's waistcoat. He spun round with a scream and fell upon his back, his hideous red face turning suddenly to a dreadful mottled pallor. The old man, still clad in his surplice, burst into such a string of foul oaths as I have never heard, and pulled out a revolver of his own, but before he could raise it he was looking down the barrel of Holmes's weapon.

"Enough of this," said my friend, coldly. "Drop that pistol! Watson, pick it up! Hold it to his head! Thank you. You, Carruthers, give me that revolver. We'll have no more violence. Come, hand it over!"

"Who are you, then?"

"AS WE APPROACHED, THE LADY STAGGERED AGAINST THE TRUNK OF THE TREE."

"My name is Sherlock Holmes."

"Good Lord!"

"You have heard of me, I see. I will represent the official police until their arrival. Here, you!" he shouted to a frightened groom who had appeared at the edge of the glade. "Come here. Take this note as hard as you can ride to Farnham." He scribbled a few words upon a leaf from his note-book. "Give it to the superintendent at the police-station. Until he comes I must detain you all under my personal custody."

The strong, masterful personality of Holmes dominated the tragic scene, and all were equally puppets in his hands. Williamson and Carruthers found themselves carrying the wounded Woodley into the house, and I gave my arm to the frightened girl. The injured man was laid on his bed, and at Holmes's request I examined him. I carried my report to where he sat in the old tapestry-hung dining-room with his two prisoners before him.

"He will live," said I.

"What!" cried Carruthers, springing out of his chair. "I'll go upstairs and finish him first. Do you tell me that that girl, that angel, is to be tied to Roaring Jack Woodley for life?"

"You need not concern yourself about that," said Holmes. "There are two very good reasons why she should under no circumstances be his wife. In the first place, we are very safe in questioning Mr. Williamson's right to solemnize a marriage."

"I have been ordained," cried the old rascal.

"And also unfrocked."

"Once a clergyman, always a clergyman."

"I think not. How about the license?"

"We had a license for the marriage. I have it here in my pocket."

"Then you got it by a trick. But in any case a forced marriage is no marriage, but it is a very serious felony, as you will discover before you have finished. You'll have time to think the point out during the next ten years or so, unless I am mistaken. As to you, Carruthers, you would have done better to keep your pistol in your pocket."

"I begin to think so, Mr. Holmes; but when I thought of all the precaution I had taken to shield this girl—for I loved her, Mr. Holmes, and it is the only time that ever I knew what love was—it fairly drove me mad to think that she was in the power of the greatest brute and bully in South Africa, a man whose name is a holy terror from Kimberley to Johannesburg. Why, Mr. Holmes, you'll hardly believe it, but ever since that girl has been in my employment I never once let her go past this house, where I knew these rascals were lurking, without following her on my bicycle just to see that she came to no harm. I kept my distance from her, and I wore a beard so that she should not recognise me, for she is a good and high-spirited girl, and she wouldn't have stayed in my employment long if she had thought that I was following her about the country roads."

"Why didn't you tell her of her danger?"

"Because then, again, she would have left me, and I couldn't bear to face that. Even if she couldn't love me it was a great deal to me just to see her dainty form about the house, and to hear the sound of her voice."

"Well," said I, "you call that love, Mr. Carruthers, but I should call it selfishness."

"Maybe the two things go together. Anyhow, I couldn't let her go. Besides, with this crowd about, it was well that she should have someone near to look after her. Then when the cable came I knew they were bound to make a move."

"What cable?"

Carruthers took a telegram from his pocket.

"That's it," said he.

It was short and concise:—

"The old man is dead."

"Hum!" said Holmes. "I think I see how things worked, and I can understand how this message would, as you say, bring them to a head. But while we wait you might tell me what you can."

The old reprobate with the surplice burst into a volley of bad language.

"By Heaven," said he, "if you squeal on us, Bob Carruthers, I'll serve you as you served Jack Woodley. You can bleat about the girl to your heart's content, for that's your own affair, but if you round on your pals to this plain-clothes copper it will be the worst day's work that ever you did."

"Your reverence need not be excited," said Holmes, lighting a cigarette. "The case is clear enough against you, and all I ask is a few details for my private curiosity. However, if there's any difficulty in your telling me I'll do the talking, and then you will see how far you have a chance of holding back your secrets. In the first place, three of you came from South Africa on this game — you Williamson, you Carruthers, and Woodley."

"Lie number one," said the old man; "I never saw either of them until two months ago, and I have never been in Africa in my life, so you can put that in your pipe and smoke it, Mr. Busybody Holmes!"

"What he says is true," said Carruthers.

"Well, well, two of you came over. His

reverence is our own home-made article. You had known Ralph Smith in South Africa. You had reason to believe he would not live long. You found out that his niece would inherit his fortune. How's that—eh?"

Carruthers nodded and Williamson swore.

"She was next-of-kin, no doubt, and you were aware that the old fellow would make no will."

"Couldn't read or write," said Carruthers.

"So you came over, the two of you, and hunted up the girl. The idea was that one of you was to marry her and the other have a share of the plunder. For some reason Woodley was chosen as the husband. Why was that?"

"We played cards for her on the voyage. He won."

"I see. You got the young lady into your service, and there Woodley was to do the courting. She recognised the drunken brute that he was, and would have nothing to do with him. Meanwhile, your arrangement was rather upset by the fact that you had yourself fallen in love with the lady. You could no longer bear the idea of this ruffian owning her."

"No, by George, I couldn't!"

"There was a quarrel between you. He left you in a rage, and began to make his own plans independently of you."

"It strikes me, Williamson, there isn't very much that we can tell this gentleman," cried Carruthers, with a bitter laugh. "Yes, we quarrelled, and he knocked me down. I am level with him on that, anyhow. Then I lost sight of him. That was when he picked up with this cast padre here. I found that they had set up house-keeping together at this place on the line that she had to pass for the station. I kept my eye on her after that, for I knew there was some devilry in the wind. I saw them from time to time, for I was anxious to know what they were after. Two days ago Woodley came up to my house with this cable, which showed that Ralph Smith was dead. He asked me if I would stand by the bargain. I said I would not. He asked me if I would marry the girl myself and give him a share. I said I would willingly do so, but that she would not have me. He said, 'Let us get her married first, and after a week or two she may see things a bit different.' I said I would have nothing to do with violence. So he went off cursing, like the foul-mouthed blackguard that he was, and swearing that he would have her yet. She was leaving me this week-end, and I had got a trap to take her to the station, but I was so uneasy in my mind that I followed her on my bicycle. She had got a start, however, and before I could catch her the mischief was done. The first thing I knew about it was when I saw you two gentlemen driving back in her dog-cart."

Holmes rose and tossed the end of his cigarette into the grate. "I have been very obtuse, Watson," said he. "When in your report you said that you had seen the cyclist as you thought arrange his necktie in the shrubbery, that alone should have told me all. However, we may con- gratulate ourselves upon a curious and in some respects a unique case. I perceive three of the county constabulary in the drive, and I am glad to see that the little ostler is able to keep pace with them; so it is likely that neither he nor the interest- ing bridegroom will be permanently damaged by their morning's adventures. I think, Watson, that in your medical capacity you might wait upon Miss Smith and tell her that if she is sufficiently recovered we shall be happy to escort her to her mother's home. If she is not quite con- valescent you will find that a hint that we were about to telegraph to a young electrician in the Midlands would probably complete the cure. As to you, Mr. Car- ruthers, I think that you have done what you could to make amends for your share in an evil plot. There is my card, sir, and if my evidence can be of help to you in your trial it shall be at your disposal."

In the whirl of our incessant activity it has often been difficult for me, as the reader has probably observed, to round off my narratives, and to give those final details which the curious might expect. Each case has been the prelude to another, and the crisis once over the actors have passed for ever out of our busy lives. I find, however,

a short note at the end of my manuscripts dealing with this case, in which I have put it upon record that Miss Violet Smith did indeed inherit a large fortune, and that she is now the wife of Cyril Morton, the senior partner of Morton and Kennedy, the famous

"HOLMES TOSSED THE END OF HIS CIGARETTE INTO THE GRATE."

Westminster electricians. Williamson and Woodley were both tried for abduction and assault, the former getting seven years and the latter ten. Of the fate of Carruthers I have no record, but I am sure that his assault was not viewed very gravely by the Court, since Woodley had the reputation of being a most dangerous ruffian, and I think that a few months were sufficient to satisfy the demands of justice.

"I HEARD HIM CHUCKLE AS THE LIGHT FELL UPON A PATCHED DUNLOP TYRE."

# THE STRAND MAGAZINE.

Vol. xxvii.        FEBRUARY, 1904.        No. 158.

# THE RETURN OF SHERLOCK HOLMES.

## By A. CONAN DOYLE.

### V.—The Adventure of the Priory School.

E have had some dramatic entrances and exits upon our small stage at Baker Street, but I cannot recollect anything more sudden and startling than the first appearance of Dr. Thorneycroft Huxtable, M.A., Ph.D., etc. His card, which seemed too small to carry the weight of his academic distinctions, preceded him by a few seconds, and then he entered himself—so large, so pompous, and so dignified that he was the very embodiment of self-possession and solidity. And yet his first action when the door had closed behind him was to stagger against the table, whence he slipped down upon the floor, and there was that majestic figure prostrate and insensible upon our bearskin hearthrug.

We had sprung to our feet, and for a few moments we stared in silent amazement at this ponderous piece of wreckage, which told of some sudden and fatal storm far out on the ocean of life. Then Holmes hurried with a cushion for his head and I with brandy for his lips. The heavy white face was seamed with lines of trouble, the hanging pouches under the closed eyes were leaden in colour, the loose mouth drooped dolorously at the corners, the rolling chins were unshaven. Collar and shirt bore the grime of a long journey, and the hair bristled unkempt from the well-shaped head. It was a sorely-stricken man who lay before us.

"What is it, Watson?" asked Holmes.

"Absolute exhaustion — possibly mere hunger and fatigue," said I, with my finger on the thready pulse, where the stream of life trickled thin and small.

"Return ticket from Mackleton, in the North of England," said Holmes, drawing it from the watch-pocket. "It is not twelve o'clock yet. He has certainly been an early starter."

The puckered eyelids had begun to quiver, and now a pair of vacant, grey eyes looked up at us. An instant later the man had scrambled on to his feet, his face crimson with shame.

"Forgive this weakness, Mr. Holmes; I have been a little overwrought. Thank you, if I might have a glass of milk and a biscuit I have no doubt that I should be better. I came personally, Mr. Holmes, in order to ensure that you would return with me. I feared that no telegram would convince you of the absolute urgency of the case."

"When you are quite restored——"

"I am quite well again. I cannot imagine how I came to be so weak. I wish you, Mr. Holmes, to come to Mackleton with me by the next train."

My friend shook his head.

"My colleague, Dr. Watson, could tell you that we are very busy at present. I am retained in this case of the Ferrers Documents, and the Abergavenny murder is coming up for trial. Only a very important issue could call me from London at present."

"Important!" Our visitor threw up his hands. "Have you heard nothing of the abduction of the only son of the Duke of Holdernesse?"

"What! the late Cabinet Minister?"

"Exactly. We had tried to keep it out of the papers, but there was some rumour in the *Globe* last night. I thought it might have reached your ears."

Holmes shot out his long, thin arm and picked out Volume "H" in his encyclopædia of reference.

"'Holdernesse, 6th Duke, K.G., P.C.'— half the alphabet! 'Baron Beverley, Earl of

it happened, and, finally, what Dr. Thorney-croft Huxtable, of the Priory School, near Mackleton, has to do with the matter, and why he comes three days after an event—the state of your chin gives the date—to ask for my humble services."

Our visitor had consumed his milk and biscuits. The light had come back to his eyes and the colour to his cheeks as he set himself with great vigour and lucidity to explain the situation.

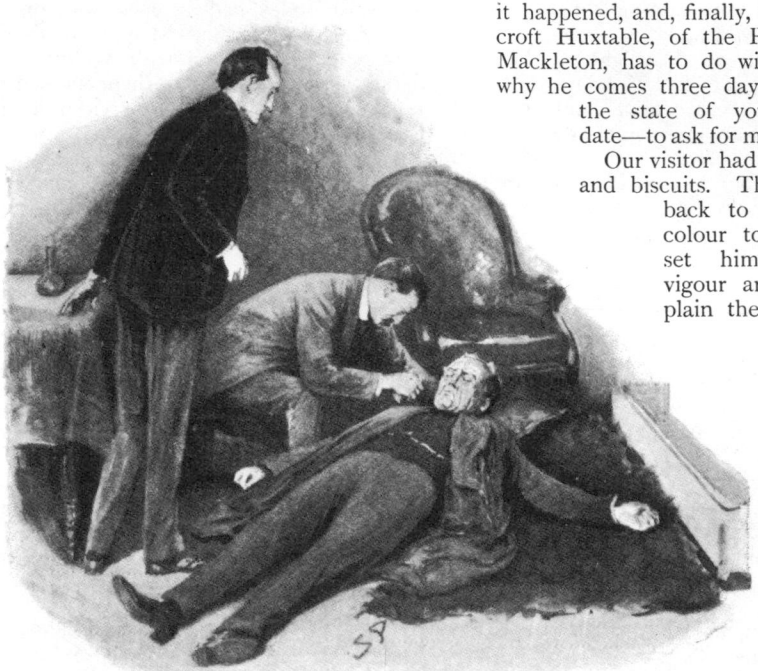

"THE HEAVY WHITE FACE WAS SEAMED WITH LINES OF TROUBLE."

"I must inform you, gentlemen, that the Priory is a preparatory school, of which I am the founder and principal. 'Huxtable's Sidelights on Horace' may possibly recall my name to your memories. The Priory is, without exception, the best and most select preparatory school in England. Lord Leverstoke, the Earl of Blackwater, Sir Cathcart Soames—they all have entrusted their sons to me. But I felt that my school had reached its zenith when, three weeks ago, the Duke of Holdernesse sent Mr. James Wilder, his secretary, with the intimation that young Lord Saltire, ten years old, his only son and heir, was about to be committed to my charge. Little did I think that this would be the prelude to the most crushing misfortune of my life.

"On May 1st the boy arrived, that being the beginning of the summer term. He was a charming youth, and he soon fell into our ways. I may tell you—I trust that I am not indiscreet, but half-confidences are absurd in such a case—that he was not entirely happy at home. It is an open secret that the Duke's married life had not been a peaceful one, and the matter had ended in a separation by mutual consent, the Duchess taking up her residence in the South of France. This had occurred very shortly before, and the boy's sympathies are known to have been strongly with his mother. He moped after her departure from Holdernesse Hall, and it was for this reason that the Duke desired to send him to my establishment. In a fort-

Carston'—dear me, what a list! 'Lord Lieutenant of Hallamshire since 1900. Married Edith, daughter of Sir Charles Appledore, 1888. Heir and only child, Lord Saltire. Owns about two hundred and fifty thousand acres. Minerals in Lancashire and Wales. Address: Carlton House Terrace; Holdernesse Hall, Hallamshire; Carston Castle, Bangor, Wales. Lord of the Admiralty, 1872; Chief Secretary of State for——' Well, well, this man is certainly one of the greatest subjects of the Crown!"

"The greatest and perhaps the wealthiest. I am aware, Mr. Holmes, that you take a very high line in professional matters, and that you are prepared to work for the work's sake. I may tell you, however, that his Grace has already intimated that a cheque for five thousand pounds will be handed over to the person who can tell him where his son is, and another thousand to him who can name the man, or men, who have taken him."

"It is a princely offer," said Holmes. "Watson, I think that we shall accompany Dr. Huxtable back to the North of England. And now, Dr. Huxtable, when you have consumed that milk you will kindly tell me what has happened, when it happened, how

night the boy was quite at home with us, and was apparently absolutely happy.

"He was last seen on the night of May 13th—that is, the night of last Monday. His room was on the second floor, and was approached through another larger room in which two boys were sleeping. These boys saw and heard nothing, so that it is certain that young Saltire did not pass out that way. His window was open, and there is a stout ivy plant leading to the ground. We could trace no footmarks below, but it is sure that this is the only possible exit.

"His absence was discovered at seven o'clock on Tuesday morning. His bed had been slept in. He had dressed himself fully before going off in his usual school suit of black Eton jacket and dark grey trousers. There were no signs that anyone had entered the room, and it is quite certain that anything in the nature of cries, or a struggle, would have been heard, since Caunter, the elder boy in the inner room, is a very light sleeper.

"When Lord Saltire's disappearance was discovered I at once called a roll of the whole establishment, boys, masters, and servants. It was then that we ascertained that Lord Saltire had not been alone in his flight. Heidegger, the German master, was missing. His room was on the second floor, at the farther end of the building, facing the same way as Lord Saltire's. His bed had also been slept in; but he had apparently gone away partly dressed, since his shirt and socks were lying on the floor. He had undoubtedly let himself down by the ivy, for we could see the marks of his feet where he had landed on the lawn. His bicycle was kept in a small shed beside this lawn, and it also was gone.

"He had been with me for two years, and came with the best references; but he was a silent, morose man, not very popular either with masters or boys. No trace could be found of the fugitives, and now on Thursday morning we are as ignorant as we were on Tuesday. Inquiry was, of course, made at once at Holdernesse Hall. It is only a few miles away, and we imagined that in some sudden attack of home-sickness he had gone back to his father; but nothing had been heard of him. The Duke is greatly agitated —and as to me, you have seen yourselves the state of nervous prostration to which the suspense and the responsibility have reduced me. Mr. Holmes, if ever you put forward your full powers, I implore you to do so now, for never in your life could you have a case which is more worthy of them."

Sherlock Holmes had listened with the utmost intentness to the statement of the unhappy schoolmaster. His drawn brows and the deep furrow between them showed that he needed no exhortation to concentrate all his attention upon a problem which, apart from the tremendous interests involved, must appeal so directly to his love of the complex and the unusual. He now drew out his note-book and jotted down one or two memoranda.

"You have been very remiss in not coming to me sooner," said he, severely. "You start me on my investigation with a very serious handicap. It is inconceivable, for example, that this ivy and this lawn would have yielded nothing to an expert observer."

"I am not to blame, Mr. Holmes. His Grace was extremely desirous to avoid all public scandal. He was afraid of his family unhappiness being dragged before the world. He has a deep horror of anything of the kind."

"But there has been some official investigation?"

"Yes, sir, and it has proved most disappointing. An apparent clue was at once obtained, since a boy and a young man were reported to have been seen leaving a neighbouring station by an early train. Only last night we had news that the couple had been hunted down in Liverpool, and they prove to have no connection whatever with the matter in hand. Then it was that in my despair and disappointment, after a sleepless night, I came straight to you by the early train."

"I suppose the local investigation was relaxed while this false clue was being followed up?"

"It was entirely dropped."

"So that three days have been wasted. The affair has been most deplorably handled."

"I feel it, and admit it."

"And yet the problem should be capable of ultimate solution. I shall be very happy to look into it. Have you been able to trace any connection between the missing boy and this German master?"

"None at all."

"Was he in the master's class?"

"No; he never exchanged a word with him so far as I know."

"That is certainly very singular. Had the boy a bicycle?"

"No."

"Was any other bicycle missing?"

"No."

"Is that certain?"

"Quite."

"Well, now, you do not mean to seriously suggest that this German rode off upon a bicycle in the dead of the night bearing the boy in his arms?"

"Certainly not."

"Then what is the theory in your mind?"

"The bicycle may have been a blind. It may have been hidden somewhere and the pair gone off on foot."

"Quite so; but it seems rather an absurd blind, does it not? Were there other bicycles in this shed?"

"Several."

"Would he not have hidden *a couple* had he desired to give the idea that they had gone off upon them?"

"I suppose he would."

"Of course he would. The blind theory won't do. But the incident is an admirable starting-point for an investigation. After all, a bicycle is not an easy thing to conceal or to destroy. One other question. Did anyone call to see the boy on the day before he disappeared?"

"No."

"Did he get any letters?"

"Yes; one letter."

"From whom?"

"From his father."

"Do you open the boys' letters?"

"No."

"How do you know it was from the father?"

"The coat of arms was on the envelope, and it was addressed in the Duke's peculiar stiff hand. Besides, the Duke remembers having written."

"When had he a letter before that?"

"Not for several days."

"Had he ever one from France?"

"No; never."

"You see the point of my questions, of course. Either the boy was carried off by

"WHAT IS THE THEORY IN YOUR MIND?"

force or he went of his own free will. In the latter case you would expect that some prompting from outside would be needed to make so young a lad do such a thing. If he has had no visitors, that prompting must have come in letters. Hence I try to find out who were his correspondents."

"I fear I cannot help you much. His only correspondent, so far as I know, was his own father."

"Who wrote to him on the very day of his disappearance. Were the relations between father and son very friendly?"

"His Grace is never very friendly with anyone. He is completely immersed in large public questions, and is rather inaccessible to all ordinary emotions. But he was always kind to the boy in his own way."

"But the sympathies of the latter were with the mother?"

"Yes."

"Did he say so?"

"No."

"The Duke, then?"

"Good heavens, no!"

"Then how could you know?"

"I have had some confidential talks with Mr. James Wilder, his Grace's secretary.

It was he who gave me the information about Lord Saltire's feelings."

" I see. By the way, that last letter of the Duke's—was it found in the boy's room after he was gone ? "

" No ; he had taken it with him. I think, Mr. Holmes, it is time that we were leaving for Euston."

" I will order a four-wheeler. In a quarter of an hour we shall be at your service. If you are telegraphing home, Mr. Huxtable, it would be well to allow the people in your neighbourhood to imagine that the inquiry is still going on in Liverpool, or wherever else that red herring led your pack. In the meantime I will do a little quiet work at your own doors, and perhaps the scent is not so cold but that two old hounds like Watson and myself may get a sniff of it."

That evening found us in the cold, bracing atmosphere of the Peak country, in which Dr. Huxtable's famous school is situated. It was already dark when we reached it. A card was lying on the hall table, and the butler whispered something to his master, who turned to us with agitation in every heavy feature.

" The Duke is here," said he. " The Duke and Mr. Wilder are in the study. Come, gentlemen, and I will introduce you."

I was, of course, familiar with the pictures of the famous statesman, but the man himself was very different from his representation. He was a tall and stately person, scrupulously dressed, with a drawn, thin face, and a nose which was grotesquely curved and long. His complexion was of a dead pallor, which was more startling by contrast with a long, dwindling beard of vivid red, which flowed down over his white waistcoat, with his watch-chain gleaming through its fringe. Such was the stately presence who looked stonily at us from the centre of Dr. Huxtable's hearthrug. Beside him stood a very young man, whom I understood to be Wilder, the private secretary. He was small, nervous, alert, with intelligent, light-blue eyes and mobile features. It was he who at once, in an incisive and positive tone, opened the conversation.

" I called this morning, Dr. Huxtable, too late to prevent you from starting for London. I learned that your object was to invite Mr. Sherlock Holmes to undertake the conduct of this case. His Grace is surprised, Dr. Huxtable, that you should have taken such a step without consulting him."

" When I learned that the police had failed——"

" His Grace is by no means convinced that the police have failed."

" But surely, Mr. Wilder——"

" You are well aware, Dr. Huxtable, that his Grace is particularly anxious to avoid all public scandal. He prefers to take as few people as possible into his confidence."

" The matter can be easily remedied," said the brow-beaten doctor ; " Mr. Sherlock Holmes can return to London by the morning train."

" Hardly that, doctor, hardly that," said Holmes, in his blandest voice. " This northern air is invigorating and pleasant, so I propose to spend a few days upon your moors, and to occupy my mind as best I may. Whether I have the shelter of your roof or of the village inn is, of course, for you to decide."

I could see that the unfortunate doctor was in the last stage of indecision, from which he was rescued by the deep, sonorous voice of the red-bearded Duke, which boomed out like a dinner-gong.

" I agree with Mr. Wilder, Dr. Huxtable, that you would have done wisely to consult me. But since Mr. Holmes has already been taken into your confidence, it would indeed be absurd that we should not avail ourselves of his services. Far from going to the inn, Mr. Holmes, I should be pleased if you would come and stay with me at Holdernesse Hall."

" I thank your Grace. For the purposes of my investigation I think that it would be wiser for me to remain at the scene of the mystery."

" Just as you like, Mr. Holmes. Any information which Mr. Wilder or I can give you is, of course, at your disposal."

" It will probably be necessary for me to see you at the Hall," said Holmes. " I would only ask you now, sir, whether you have formed any explanation in your own mind as to the mysterious disappearance of your son ? "

" No, sir, I have not."

" Excuse me if I allude to that which is painful to you, but I have no alternative. Do you think that the Duchess had anything to do with the matter ? "

The great Minister showed perceptible hesitation.

" I do not think so," he said, at last.

" The other most obvious explanation is that the child has been kidnapped for the purpose of levying ransom. You have not had any demand of the sort ? "

"No, sir."

"One more question, your Grace. I understand that you wrote to your son upon the day when this incident occurred."

"No ; I wrote upon the day before."

"Exactly. But he received it on that day?"

"Yes."

"Was there anything in your letter which might have unbalanced him or induced him to take such a step?"

"No, sir, certainly not."

"Did you post that letter yourself?"

The nobleman's reply was interrupted by his secretary, who broke in with some heat.

"His Grace is not in the habit of posting letters himself," said he. "This letter was laid with others upon the study table, and I myself put them in the post-bag."

"You are sure this one was among them?"

"Yes ; I observed it."

"How many letters did your Grace write that day?"

"Twenty or thirty. I have a large correspondence. But surely this is somewhat irrelevant?"

"Not entirely," said Holmes.

"For my own part," the Duke continued, "I have advised the police to turn their attention to the South of France. I have already said that I do not believe that the Duchess would encourage so monstrous an action, but the lad had the most wrong-headed opinions, and it is possible that he may have fled to her, aided and abetted by this German. I think, Dr. Huxtable, that we will now return to the Hall."

I could see that there were other questions which Holmes would have wished to put ;

"BESIDE HIM STOOD A VERY YOUNG MAN."

but the nobleman's abrupt manner showed that the interview was at an end. It was evident that to his intensely aristocratic nature this discussion of his intimate family affairs with a stranger was most abhorrent, and that he feared lest every fresh question would throw a fiercer light into the discreetly shadowed corners of his ducal history.

When the nobleman and his secretary had left, my friend flung himself at once with characteristic eagerness into the investigation.

The boy's chamber was carefully examined, and yielded nothing save the absolute conviction that it was only through the window that he could have escaped. The German master's room and effects gave no further clue. In his case a trailer of ivy had given way under his weight, and we saw by the light of a lantern the mark on the lawn where his heels had come down. That one dint in the short green grass was the only material witness left of this inexplicable nocturnal flight.

Sherlock Holmes left the house alone, and only returned after eleven. He had obtained a large ordnance map of the neighbourhood, and this he brought into my room, where he laid it out on the bed, and, having balanced the lamp in the middle of it, he began to smoke over it, and occasionally to point out objects of interest with the reeking amber of his pipe.

"This case grows upon me, Watson," said he. "There are decidedly some points of interest in connection with it. In this early stage I want you to realize those geographical features which may have a good deal to do with our investigation.

"Look at this map. This dark square is the Priory School. I'll put a pin in it. Now, this line is the main road. You see that it runs east and west past the school, and you see also that there is no side road for a mile either way. If these two folk passed away by road it was *this* road."

"Exactly."

"By a singular and happy chance we are able to some extent to check what passed along this road during the night in question. At this point, where my pipe is now resting, a country constable was on duty from twelve to six. It is, as you perceive, the first cross road on the east side. This man declares that he was not absent from his post for an instant, and he is positive that neither boy nor man could have gone that way unseen. I have spoken with this policeman to-night, and he appears to me to be a perfectly reliable person. That blocks this end. We have now to deal with the other. There is an inn here, the Red Bull, the landlady of which was ill. She had sent to Mackleton for a doctor, but he did not arrive until morning, being absent at another case. The people at the inn were alert all night, awaiting his coming, and one or other of them seems to have continually had an eye upon the road. They declare that no one passed. If their evidence is good, then we are fortunate enough to be able to block the west, and also to be able to say that the fugitives did *not* use the road at all."

"But the bicycle?" I objected.

"Quite so. We will come to the bicycle presently. To continue our reasoning: if these people did not go by the road, they must have traversed the country to the north of the house or to the south of the house. That is certain. Let us weigh the one against the other. On the south of the house is, as you perceive, a large district of arable land, cut up into small fields, with stone walls between them. There, I admit that a bicycle is impossible. We can dismiss the idea. We turn to the country on the north. Here there lies a grove of trees, marked as the 'Ragged Shaw,' and on the farther side stretches a great rolling moor, Lower Gill Moor, extending for ten miles and sloping gradually upwards. Here, at one side of this wilderness, is Holdernesse Hall, ten miles by road, but only six across the moor. It is a peculiarly desolate plain. A few moor farmers have small holdings, where they rear sheep and cattle. Except these, the plover and the curlew are the only inhabitants until you come to the Chesterfield

high road. There is a church there, you see, a few cottages, and an inn. Beyond that the hills become precipitous. Surely it is here to the north that our quest must lie."

"But the bicycle?" I persisted.

"Well, well!" said Holmes, impatiently. "A good cyclist does not need a high road. The moor is intersected with paths and the moon was at the full. Halloa! what is this?"

There was an agitated knock at the door, and an instant afterwards Dr. Huxtable was in the room. In his hand he held a blue cricket-cap, with a white chevron on the peak.

"At last we have a clue!" he cried. "Thank Heaven! at last we are on the dear boy's track! It is his cap."

"Where was it found?"

"In the van of the gipsies who camped on the moor. They left on Tuesday. To-day the police traced them down and examined their caravan. This was found."

"How do they account for it?"

"They shuffled and lied—said that they found it on the moor on Tuesday morning. They know where he is, the rascals! Thank goodness, they are all safe under lock and key. Either the fear of the law or the Duke's purse will certainly get out of them all that they know."

"So far, so good," said Holmes, when the doctor had at last left the room. "It at least bears out the theory that it is on the side of the Lower Gill Moor that we must hope for results. The police have really done nothing locally, save the arrest of these gipsies. Look here, Watson! There is a watercourse across the moor. You see it marked here in the map. In some parts it widens into a morass. This is particularly so in the region between Holdernesse Hall and the school. It is vain to look elsewhere for tracks in this dry weather; but at *that* point there is certainly a chance of some record being left. I will call you early to-morrow morning, and you and I will try if we can throw some little light upon the mystery."

The day was just breaking when I woke to find the long, thin form of Holmes by my bedside. He was fully dressed, and had apparently already been out.

"I have done the lawn and the bicycle shed," said he. "I have also had a ramble through the Ragged Shaw. Now, Watson, there is cocoa ready in the next room. I must beg you to hurry, for we have a great day before us."

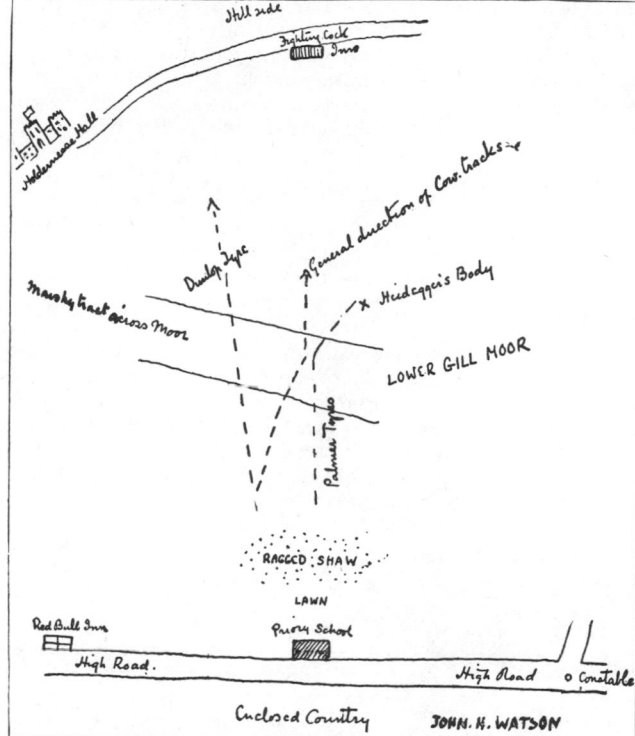

SKETCH MAP SHOWING THE LOCALITY

moor. "There is another morass down yonder and a narrow neck between. Halloa! halloa! halloa! what have we here?"

We had come on a small black ribbon of pathway. In the middle of it, clearly marked on the sodden soil, was the track of a bicycle.

"Hurrah!" I cried. "We have it."

But Holmes was shaking his head, and his face was puzzled and expectant rather than joyous.

"A bicycle certainly, but not *the* bicycle," said he. "I am familiar with forty-two different impressions left by tyres. This, as you perceive, is a Dunlop, with a patch upon the outer cover. Heidegger's tyres were Palmer's, leaving longitudinal stripes. Aveling, the mathematical master, was sure upon the point. Therefore, it is not Heidegger's track."

"The boy's, then?"

"Possibly, if we could prove a bicycle to have been in his possession. But this we have utterly failed to do. This track, as you perceive, was made by a rider who was going from the direction of the school."

"Or towards it?"

"No, no, my dear Watson. The more deeply sunk impression is, of course, the hind wheel, upon which the weight rests. You perceive several places where it has passed across and obliterated the more shallow mark of the front one. It was undoubtedly heading away from the school. It may or may not be connected with our inquiry, but we will follow it backwards before we go any farther."

We did so, and at the end of a few hundred yards lost the tracks as we emerged from the boggy portion of the moor. Following the path backwards, we picked out another spot, where a spring trickled across it. Here, once again, was the mark of the bicycle, though nearly obliterated by the hoofs of cows. After that there was no sign, but the path ran right on into Ragged Shaw, the wood which backed on to the school. From this wood the cycle must have

His eyes shone, and his cheek was flushed with the exhilaration of the master workman who sees his work lie ready before him. A very different Holmes, this active, alert man, from the introspective and pallid dreamer of Baker Street. I felt, as I looked upon that supple figure, alive with nervous energy, that it was indeed a strenuous day that awaited us.

And yet it opened in the blackest disappointment. With high hopes we struck across the peaty, russet moor, intersected with a thousand sheep paths, until we came to the broad, light-green belt which marked the morass between us and Holdernesse. Certainly, if the lad had gone homewards, he must have passed this, and he could not pass it without leaving his traces. But no sign of him or the German could be seen. With a darkening face my friend strode along the margin, eagerly observant of every muddy stain upon the mossy surface. Sheep-marks there were in profusion, and at one place, some miles down, cows had left their tracks. Nothing more.

"Check number one," said Holmes, looking gloomily over the rolling expanse of the

emerged. Holmes sat down on a boulder and rested his chin in his hands. I had smoked two cigarettes before he moved.

"Well, well," said he, at last. "It is, of course, possible that a cunning man might change the tyre of his bicycle in order to leave unfamiliar tracks. A criminal who was capable of such a thought is a man whom I should be proud to do business with. We will leave this question undecided and hark back to our morass again, for we have left a good deal unexplored."

We continued our systematic survey of the edge of the sodden portion of the moor, and soon our perseverance was gloriously rewarded. Right across the lower part of the bog lay a miry path. Holmes gave a cry of delight as he approached it. An impression like a fine bundle of telegraph wires ran down the centre of it. It was the Palmer tyre.

"AN IMPRESSION LIKE A FINE BUNDLE OF TELEGRAPH WIRES RAN DOWN THE CENTRE OF IT."

"Here is Herr Heidegger, sure enough!" cried Holmes, exultantly. "My reasoning seems to have been pretty sound, Watson."

"I congratulate you."

"But we have a long way still to go. Kindly walk clear of the path. Now let us follow the trail. I fear that it will not lead very far."

We found, however, as we advanced that this portion of the moor is intersected with soft patches, and, though we frequently lost sight of the track, we always succeeded in picking it up once more.

"Do you observe," said Holmes, "that the rider is now undoubtedly forcing the pace? There can be no doubt of it. Look at this impression, where you get both tyres clear. The one is as deep as the other. That can only mean that the rider is throwing his weight on to the handle-bar, as a man does when he is sprinting. By Jove! he has had a fall."

There was a broad, irregular smudge covering some yards of the track. Then there were a few footmarks, and the tyre reappeared once more.

"A side-slip," I suggested.

Holmes held up a crumpled branch of flowering gorse. To my horror I perceived that the yellow blossoms were all dabbled with crimson. On the path, too, and among the heather were dark stains of clotted blood.

"Bad!" said Holmes. "Bad! Stand clear, Watson! Not an unnecessary footstep! What do I read here? He fell wounded, he stood up, he remounted, he proceeded. But there is no other track. Cattle on this side path. He was surely not gored by a bull? Impossible! But I see no traces of anyone else. We must push on, Watson. Surely with stains as well as the track to guide us he cannot escape us now."

Our search was not a very long one. The tracks of the tyre began to curve fantastically upon the wet and shining path. Suddenly, as I looked ahead, the gleam of metal caught my eye from amid the thick gorse bushes. Out of them we dragged a bicycle, Palmer-tyred, one pedal bent, and the whole front of it horribly smeared and slobbered with blood. On the other side of the bushes a shoe was projecting. We ran round, and there lay the unfortunate rider. He was a tall man, full bearded, with spectacles, one glass of which had been knocked out. The cause of his death was a frightful blow upon the head,

"THERE LAY THE UNFORTUNATE RIDER."

which had crushed in part of his skull. That he could have gone on after receiving such an injury said much for the vitality and courage of the man. He wore shoes, but no socks, and his open coat disclosed a night-shirt beneath it. It was undoubtedly the German master.

Holmes turned the body over reverently, and examined it with great attention. He then sat in deep thought for a time, and I could see by his ruffled brow that this grim discovery had not, in his opinion, advanced us much in our inquiry.

"It is a little difficult to know what to do, Watson," said he, at last. "My own inclinations are to push this inquiry on, for we have already lost so much time that we cannot afford to waste another hour. On the other hand, we are bound to inform the police of the discovery, and to see that this poor fellow's body is looked after."

" I could take a note back."

" But I need your company and assistance. Wait a bit ! There is a fellow cutting peat up yonder. Bring him over here, and he will guide the police."

I brought the peasant across, and Holmes dispatched the frightened man with a note to Dr. Huxtable.

"Now, Watson," said he, "we have picked up two clues this morning. One is the bicycle with the Palmer tyre, and we see what that has led to. The other is the bicycle with the patched Dunlop. Before we start to investigate that, let us try to realize what we *do* know so as to make the most of it, and to separate the essential from the accidental.

"First of all I wish to impress upon you that the boy certainly left of his own free will. He got down from his window and he went off, either alone or with some-one. That is sure."

I assented.

"Well, now, let us turn to this unfortunate German master. The boy was fully dressed when he fled. Therefore, he foresaw what he would do. But the German went without his socks. He certainly acted on very short notice."

" Undoubtedly."

" Why did he go ? Because, from his bed-room window, he saw the flight of the boy. Because he wished to overtake him and bring him back. He seized his bicycle, pursued the lad, and in pursuing him met his death."

" So it would seem."

" Now I come to the critical part of my argument. The natural action of a man in pursuing a little boy would be to run after him. He would know that he could over-take him. But the German does not do so. He turns to his bicycle. I am told that he was an excellent cyclist. He would not do this if he did not see that the boy had some swift means of escape."

"The other bicycle."

"Let us continue our reconstruction. He meets his death five miles from the school—not by a bullet, mark you, which even a lad might conceivably discharge, but by a savage blow dealt by a vigorous arm. The lad, then, *had* a companion in his flight. And the flight was a swift one, since it took five miles before an expert cyclist could overtake them. Yet we survey the ground round the scene of the tragedy. What do we find? A few cattle tracks, nothing more. I took a wide sweep round, and there is no path within fifty yards. Another cyclist could have had nothing to do with the actual murder. Nor were there any human foot-marks."

"Holmes," I cried, "this is impossible."

"Admirable!" he said. "A most illumin-ating remark. It *is* impossible as I state it, and therefore I must in some respect have stated it wrong. Yet you saw for yourself. Can you suggest any fallacy?"

"He could not have fractured his skull in a fall?"

"In a morass, Watson?"

"I am at my wits' end."

"Tut, tut; we have solved some worse problems. At least we have plenty of mate-rial, if we can only use it. Come, then, and, having exhausted the Palmer, let us see what the Dunlop with the patched cover has to offer us."

We picked up the track and followed it onwards for some distance; but soon the moor rose into a long, heather-tufted curve, and we left the watercourse behind us. No further help from tracks could be hoped for. At the spot where we saw the last of the Dunlop tyre it might equally have led to Holdernesse Hall, the stately towers of which rose some miles to our left, or to a low, grey village which lay in front of us, and marked the position of the Chesterfield high road.

As we approached the forbidding and squalid inn, with the sign of a game-cock above the door, Holmes gave a sudden groan and clutched me by the shoulder to save himself from falling. He had had one of those violent strains of the ankle which leave a man helpless. With difficulty he limped up to the door, where a squat, dark, elderly man was smoking a black clay pipe.

"How are you, Mr. Reuben Hayes?" said Holmes.

"Who are you, and how do you get my name so pat?" the countryman answered, with a suspicious flash of a pair of cunning eyes.

"Well, it's printed on the board above your head. It's easy to see a man who is master of his own house. I suppose you haven't such a thing as a carriage in your stables?"

"No; I have not."

"I can hardly put my foot to the ground."

"Don't put it to the ground."

"But I can't walk."

"Well, then, hop."

Mr. Reuben Hayes's manner was far from gracious, but Holmes took it with admirable good-humour.

"Look here, my man," said he. "This is really rather an awkward fix for me. I don't mind how I get on."

"Neither do I," said the morose landlord.

"The matter is very important. I would offer you a sovereign for the use of a bicycle."

The landlord pricked up his ears.

"Where do you want to go?"

"To Holdernesse Hall."

"Pals of the Dook, I suppose?" said the landlord, surveying our mud-stained garments with ironical eyes.

Holmes laughed good-naturedly.

"He'll be glad to see us, anyhow."

"Why?"

"Because we bring him news of his lost son."

The landlord gave a very visible start.

"What, you're on his track?"

"He has been heard of in Liverpool. They expect to get him every hour."

Again a swift change passed over the heavy, unshaven face. His manner was suddenly genial.

"I've less reason to wish the Dook well than most men," said he, "for I was his head coachman once, and cruel bad he treated me. It was him that sacked me without a character on the word of a lying corn-chandler. But I'm glad to hear that the young lord was heard of in Liverpool, and I'll help you to take the news to the Hall."

"Thank you," said Holmes. "We'll have some food first. Then you can bring round the bicycle."

"I haven't got a bicycle."

Holmes held up a sovereign.

"I tell you, man, that I haven't got one. I'll let you have two horses as far as the Hall."

"WITH DIFFICULTY HE LIMPED UP TO THE DOOR."

"Yes, several."

"Where?"

"Well, everywhere. They were at the morass, and again on the path, and again near where poor Heidegger met his death."

"Exactly. Well, now, Watson, how many cows did you see on the moor?"

"I don't remember seeing any."

"Strange, Watson, that we should see tracks all along our line, but never a cow on the whole moor; very strange, Watson, eh?"

"Yes, it is strange."

"Now, Watson, make an effort; throw your mind back! Can you see those tracks upon the path?"

"Yes, I can."

"Can you recall that the tracks were sometimes like that, Watson"—he arranged a number of breadcrumbs in this fashion—: : : : : —"and sometimes like this"—: : : : : : · —"and occasionally like this"— . · · · · · "Can you remember that?"

"No, I cannot."

"But I can. I could swear to it. However, we will go back at our leisure and verify it. What a blind beetle I have been not to draw my conclusion!"

"And what is your conclusion?"

"Only that it is a remarkable cow which walks, canters, and gallops. By George, Watson, it was no brain of a country publican that thought out such a blind as that! The coast seems to be clear, save for that lad in the smithy. Let us slip out and see what we can see."

There were two rough-haired, unkempt horses in the tumble-down stable. Holmes raised the hind leg of one of them and laughed aloud.

"Old shoes, but newly shod—old shoes, but new nails. This case deserves to be a classic. Let us go across to the smithy."

The lad continued his work without regarding us. I saw Holmes's eye darting to right and left among the litter of iron and wood which was scattered about the floor. Suddenly, however, we heard a step behind us, and there was the landlord, his heavy eyebrows drawn down over his savage eyes, his swarthy features convulsed with passion.

"Well, well," said Holmes, "we'll talk about it when we've had something to eat."

When we were left alone in the stone-flagged kitchen it was astonishing how rapidly that sprained ankle recovered. It was nearly nightfall, and we had eaten nothing since early morning, so that we spent some time over our meal. Holmes was lost in thought, and once or twice he walked over to the window and stared earnestly out. It opened on to a squalid courtyard. In the far corner was a smithy, where a grimy lad was at work. On the other side were the stables. Holmes had sat down again after one of these excursions, when he suddenly sprang out of his chair with a loud exclamation.

"By Heaven, Watson, I believe that I've got it!" he cried. "Yes, yes, it must be so. Watson, do you remember seeing any cow-tracks to-day?"

He held a short, metal-headed stick in his hand, and he advanced in so menacing a fashion that I was right glad to feel the revolver in my pocket.

"You infernal spies!" the man cried. "What are you doing there?"

"Why, Mr. Reuben Hayes," said Holmes, coolly, "one might think that you were afraid of our finding something out."

The man mastered himself with a violent effort, and his grim mouth loosened into a false laugh, which was more menacing than his frown.

"You're welcome to all you can find out in my smithy," said he. "But look here, mister, I don't care for folk poking about my place without my leave, so the sooner you pay your score and get out of this the better I shall be pleased."

"All right, Mr. Hayes—no harm meant," said Holmes. "We have been having a look at your horses, but I think I'll walk after all. It's not far, I believe."

"Not more than two miles to the Hall gates. That's the road to the left." He watched us with sullen eyes until we had left his premises.

We did not go very far along the road, for Holmes stopped the instant that the curve hid us from the landlord's view.

"We were warm, as the children say, at that inn," said he. "I seem to grow colder every step that I take away from it. No, no; I can't possibly leave it."

"I am convinced," said I, "that this Reuben Hayes knows all about it. A more self-evident villain I never saw."

"Oh! he impressed you in that way, did he? There are the horses, there is the smithy. Yes, it is an interesting place, this Fighting Cock. I think we shall have another look at it in an unobtrusive way."

A long, sloping hillside, dotted with grey limestone boulders, stretched behind us. We had turned off the road, and were making our way up the hill, when, looking in the direction of Holdernesse Hall, I saw a cyclist coming swiftly along.

"Get down, Watson!" cried Holmes, with a heavy hand upon my shoulder. We had hardly sunk from view when the man flew past us on the road. Amid a rolling cloud of dust I caught a glimpse of a pale, agitated face—a face with horror in every lineament, the mouth open, the eyes staring wildly in front. It was like some strange caricature of the dapper James Wilder whom we had seen the night before.

"The Duke's secretary!" cried Holmes. "Come, Watson, let us see what he does."

We scrambled from rock to rock until in a few moments we had made our way to a point from which we could see the front door of the inn. Wilder's bicycle was leaning against the wall beside it. No one was moving about the house, nor could we catch a glimpse of any faces at the windows. Slowly the twilight crept down as the sun sank behind the high towers of Holdernesse Hall. Then in the gloom we saw the two side-lamps of a trap light up in the stable yard of the inn, and shortly afterwards heard the rattle of hoofs, as it wheeled out into the road and tore off at a furious pace in the direction of Chesterfield.

"What do you make of that, Watson?" Holmes whispered.

"It looks like a flight."

"A single man in a dog-cart, so far as I could see. Well, it certainly was not Mr. James Wilder, for there he is at the door."

A red square of light had sprung out of the darkness. In the middle of it was the black figure of the secretary, his head advanced, peering out into the night. It was evident that he was expecting someone. Then at last there were steps in the road, a second figure was visible for an instant against the light, the door shut, and all was black once more. Five minutes later a lamp was lit in a room upon the first floor.

"It seems to be a curious class of custom that is done by the Fighting Cock," said Holmes.

"The bar is on the other side."

"Quite so. These are what one may call the private guests. Now, what in the world is Mr. James Wilder doing in that den at this hour of night, and who is the companion who comes to meet him there? Come, Watson, we must really take a risk and try to investigate this a little more closely."

Together we stole down to the road and crept across to the door of the inn. The bicycle still leaned against the wall. Holmes struck a match and held it to the back wheel, and I heard him chuckle as the light fell upon a patched Dunlop tyre. Up above us was the lighted window.

"I must have a peep through that, Watson. If you bend your back and support yourself upon the wall, I think that I can manage."

An instant later his feet were on my shoulders. But he was hardly up before he was down again.

"THE MAN FLEW PAST US ON THE ROAD."

and I were walking up the famous yew avenue of Holdernesse Hall. We were ushered through the magnificent Elizabethan doorway and into his Grace's study. There we found Mr. James Wilder, demure and courtly, but with some trace of that wild terror of the night before still lurking in his furtive eyes and in his twitching features.

"You have come to see his Grace? I am sorry; but the fact is that the Duke is far from well. He has been very much upset by the tragic news. We received a telegram from Dr. Huxtable yesterday afternoon, which told us of your discovery."

"I must see the Duke, Mr. Wilder."

"But he is in his room."

"Then I must go to his room."

"I believe he is in his bed."

"I will see him there."

Holmes's cold and inexorable manner showed the secretary that it was useless to argue with him.

"Very good, Mr. Holmes; I will tell him that you are here."

After half an hour's delay the great nobleman appeared. His face was more cadaverous than ever, his shoulders had rounded, and he seemed to me to be an altogether older man than he had been the morning before. He greeted us with a stately courtesy and seated himself at his desk, his red beard streaming down on to the table.

"Well, Mr. Holmes?" said he.

But my friend's eyes were fixed upon the secretary, who stood by his master's chair.

"I think, your Grace, that I could speak more freely in Mr. Wilder's absence."

The man turned a shade paler and cast a malignant glance at Holmes.

"If your Grace wishes——"

"Yes, yes; you had better go. Now, Mr. Holmes, what have you to say?"

"Come, my friend," said he, "our day's work has been quite long enough. I think that we have gathered all that we can. It's a long walk to the school, and the sooner we get started the better."

He hardly opened his lips during that weary trudge across the moor, nor would he enter the school when he reached it, but went on to Mackleton Station, whence he could send some telegrams. Late at night I heard him consoling Dr. Huxtable, prostrated by the tragedy of his master's death, and later still he entered my room as alert and vigorous as he had been when he started in the morning. "All goes well, my friend," said he. "I promise that before to-morrow evening we shall have reached the solution of the mystery."

At eleven o'clock next morning my friend

My friend waited until the door had closed behind the retreating secretary.

"The fact is, your Grace," said he, "that my colleague, Dr. Watson, and myself had an assurance from Dr. Huxtable that a reward had been offered in this case. I should like to have this confirmed from your own lips."

"Certainly, Mr. Holmes."

"It amounted, if I am correctly informed, to five thousand pounds to anyone who will tell you where your son is?"

"Exactly."

"And another thousand to the man who will name the person or persons who keep him in custody?"

"Exactly."

"Under the latter heading is included, no doubt, not only those who may have taken him away, but also those who conspire to keep him in his present position?"

"Yes, yes," cried the Duke, impatiently. "If you do your work well, Mr. Sherlock Holmes, you will have no reason to complain of niggardly treatment."

My friend rubbed his thin hands together with an appearance of avidity which was a surprise to me, who knew his frugal tastes.

"I fancy that I see your Grace's cheque-book upon the table," said he. "I should be glad if you would make me out a cheque for six thousand pounds. It would be as well, perhaps, for you to cross it. The Capital and Counties Bank, Oxford Street branch, are my agents."

His Grace sat very stern and upright in his chair, and looked stonily at my friend.

"Is this a joke, Mr. Holmes? It is hardly a subject for pleasantry."

"Not at all, your Grace. I was never more earnest in my life."

"What do you mean, then?"

"I mean that I have earned the reward. I know where your son is, and I know some, at least, of those who are holding him."

The Duke's beard had turned more aggressively red than ever against his ghastly white face.

"Where is he?" he gasped.

"He is, or was last night, at the Fighting Cock Inn, about two miles from your park gate."

The Duke fell back in his chair.

"And whom do you accuse?"

Sherlock Holmes's answer was an astounding one. He stepped swiftly forward and touched the Duke upon the shoulder.

"I accuse *you*," said he. "And now, your Grace, I'll trouble you for that cheque."

Never shall I forget the Duke's appearance as he sprang up and clawed with his hands like one who is sinking into an abyss. Then, with an extraordinary effort of aristocratic self-command, he sat down and sank his face in his hands. It was some minutes before he spoke.

"How much do you know?" he asked at last, without raising his head.

"I saw you together last night."

"Does anyone else besides your friend know?"

"I have spoken to no one."

The Duke took a pen in his quivering fingers and opened his cheque-book.

"I shall be as good as my word, Mr. Holmes. I am about to write your cheque, however unwelcome the information which you have gained may be to me. When the offer was first made I little thought the turn which events might take. But you and your friend are men of discretion, Mr. Holmes?"

"I hardly understand your Grace."

"I must put it plainly, Mr. Holmes. If only you two know of this incident, there is no reason why it should go any farther. I think twelve thousand pounds is the sum that I owe you, is it not?"

But Holmes smiled and shook his head.

"I fear, your Grace, that matters can hardly be arranged so easily. There is the death of this schoolmaster to be accounted for."

"But James knew nothing of that. You cannot hold him responsible for that. It was the work of this brutal ruffian whom he had the misfortune to employ."

"I must take the view, your Grace, that when a man embarks upon a crime he is morally guilty of any other crime which may spring from it."

"Morally, Mr. Holmes. No doubt you are right. But surely not in the eyes of the law. A man cannot be condemned for a murder at which he was not present, and which he loathes and abhors as much as you do. The instant that he heard of it he made a complete confession to me, so filled was he with horror and remorse. He lost not an hour in breaking entirely with the murderer. Oh, Mr. Holmes, you must save him—you must save him! I tell you that you must save him!" The Duke had dropped the last attempt at self-command, and was pacing the room with a convulsed face and with his clenched hands raving in the air. At last he mastered himself and sat down once more at his desk. "I appreciate your conduct in coming here before you spoke to anyone

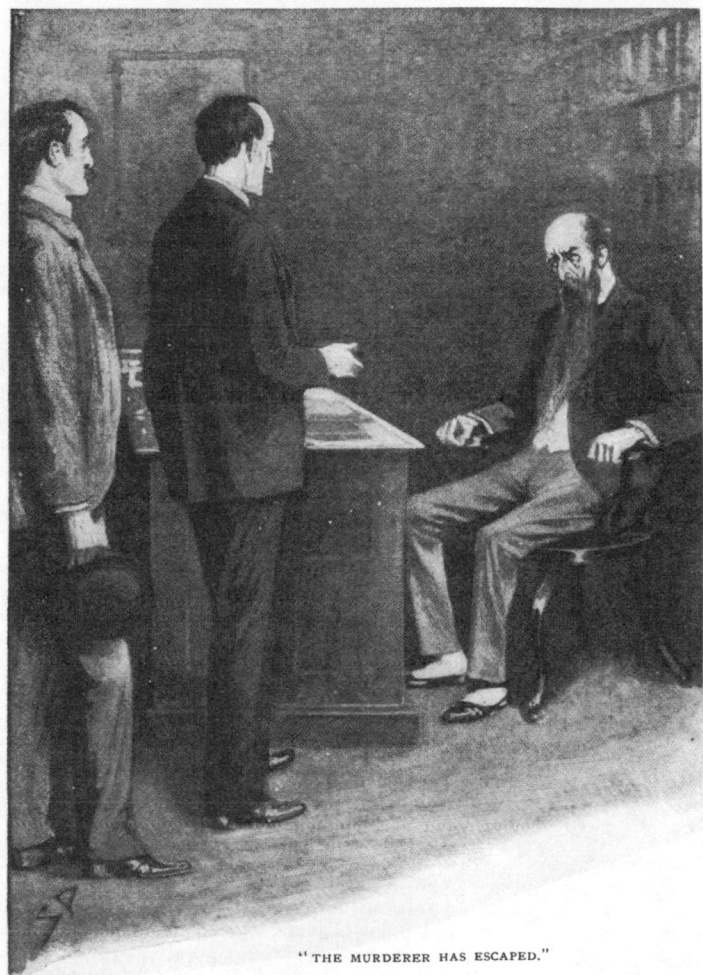

"THE MURDERER HAS ESCAPED."

else," said he. "At least we may take counsel how far we can minimize this hideous scandal."

"Exactly," said Holmes. "I think, your Grace, that this can only be done by absolute and complete frankness between us. I am disposed to help your Grace to the best of my ability; but in order to do so I must understand to the last detail how the matter stands. I realize that your words applied to Mr. James Wilder, and that he is not the murderer."

"No; the murderer has escaped."

Sherlock Holmes smiled demurely.

"Your Grace can hardly have heard of any small reputation which I possess, or you would not imagine that it is so easy to escape me. Mr. Reuben Hayes was arrested at Chesterfield on my information at eleven o'clock last night. I had a telegram from the head of the local police before I left the school this morning."

The Duke leaned back in his chair and stared with amazement at my friend.

"You seem to have powers that are hardly human," said he. "So Reuben Hayes is taken? I am right glad to hear it, if it will not react upon the fate of James."

"Your secretary?"

"No, sir; my son."

It was Holmes's turn to look astonished.

"I confess that this is entirely new to me, your Grace. I must beg you to be more explicit."

"I will conceal nothing from you. I agree with you that complete frankness, however painful it may be to me, is the best policy in this desperate situation to which James's folly and jealousy have reduced us. When I was a very young man, Mr. Holmes, I loved with such a love as comes only once in a lifetime. I offered the lady marriage, but she refused it on the grounds that such a match might mar my career. Had she lived I would certainly never have married anyone else. She died, and left this one child, whom for her sake I have cherished and cared for. I could not acknowledge the paternity to the world; but I gave him the best of educations, and since he came to manhood I have kept him near my person. He surprised my secret, and has presumed ever since upon the claim which he has upon me and upon his power of provoking a scandal, which would be abhorrent to me. His presence had something to do with the unhappy issue of my marriage. Above all, he hated my young legitimate heir from the first with a persistent hatred. You may well ask me why, under these circumstances, I still kept James under my roof. I answer that it was because I could see his mother's face in his, and that for her dear sake there was no end to my long-suffering. All her pretty ways, too — there was not one of them which he could not suggest and bring back to my memory. I *could* not send him away. But I feared so much lest he should do Arthur—that is, Lord Saltire—a mischief that I dispatched him for safety to Dr. Huxtable's school.

"James came into contact with this fellow Hayes because the man was a tenant of mine, and James acted as agent. The fellow was a rascal from the beginning; but in some extraordinary way James became intimate with him. He had always a taste for low company. When James determined to kidnap Lord Saltire it was of this man's service that he availed himself. You remember that I wrote to Arthur upon that last day. Well, James opened the letter and inserted a note asking Arthur to meet him in a little wood called the Ragged Shaw, which is near to the school. He used the Duchess's name, and in that way got the boy to come. That evening James bicycled over—I am telling you what he has himself confessed to me— and he told Arthur, whom he met in the wood, that his mother longed to see him, that she was awaiting him on the moor, and that if he would come back into the wood at midnight he would find a man with a horse, who would take him to her. Poor Arthur fell into the trap. He came to the appointment and found this fellow Hayes with a led pony. Arthur mounted, and they set off together. It appears—though this James only heard yesterday — that they were pursued, that Hayes struck the pursuer with his stick, and that the man died of his injuries. Hayes brought Arthur to his public-house, the Fighting Cock, where he was confined in an upper room, under the care of Mrs. Hayes, who is a kindly woman, but entirely under the control of her brutal husband.

"Well, Mr. Holmes, that was the state of affairs when I first saw you two days ago. I had no more idea of the truth than you. You will ask me what was James's motive in doing such a deed. I answer that there was a great deal which was unreasoning and fanatical in the hatred which he bore my heir. In his view he should himself have been heir of all my estates, and he deeply resented those social laws which made it impossible. At the same time he had a definite motive also. He was eager that I should break the entail, and he was of opinion that it lay in my power to do so. He intended to make a bargain with me—to restore Arthur if I would break the entail, and so make it possible for the estate to be left to him by will. He knew well that I should never willingly invoke the aid of the police against him. I say that he would have proposed such a bargain to me, but he did not actually do so, for events moved too quickly for him, and he had not time to put his plans into practice.

"What brought all his wicked scheme to wreck was your discovery of this man Heidegger's dead body. James was seized with horror at the news. It came to us yesterday as we sat together in this study. Dr. Huxtable had sent a telegram. James was so overwhelmed with grief and agitation that my suspicions, which had never been entirely absent, rose instantly to a certainty, and I taxed him with the deed. He made a complete voluntary confession. Then he implored me to keep his secret for three days longer, so as to give his wretched accomplice a chance of saving his guilty life. I yielded —as I have always yielded—to his prayers, and instantly James hurried off to the Fighting Cock to warn Hayes and give him the means of flight. I could not go there by daylight without provoking comment, but as soon as night fell I hurried off to see my dear Arthur. I found him safe and well, but horrified beyond expression by the dreadful deed he had witnessed. In deference to my promise, and much against my will, I consented to leave him there for three days under the charge of Mrs. Hayes, since it was evident that it was impossible to inform the police where he was without telling them also who was the murderer, and I could not see how that murderer could be punished without ruin to my unfortunate James. You asked for frankness, Mr. Holmes, and I have taken you at your word, for I have now told you everything without an attempt at circumlocution or concealment. Do you in your turn be as frank with me."

"I will," said Holmes "In the first place, your Grace, I am bound to tell you that you have placed yourself in a most serious position in the eyes of the law. You have condoned a felony and you have aided the escape of a murderer; for I cannot doubt that any money which was taken by James Wilder to aid his accomplice in his flight came from your Grace's purse."

The Duke bowed his assent.

"This is indeed a most serious matter. Even more culpable in my opinion, your Grace, is your attitude towards your younger son. You leave him in this den for three days."

"Under solemn promises——"

"What are promises to such people as these? You have no guarantee that he will not be spirited away again. To humour your guilty elder son you have exposed your innocent younger son to imminent and unnecessary danger. It was a most unjustifiable action."

The proud lord of Holdernesse was not accustomed to be so rated in his own ducal hall. The blood flushed into his high forehead, but his conscience held him dumb.

"I will help you, but on one condition only. It is that you ring for the footman and let me give such orders as I like."

Without a word the Duke pressed the electric bell. A servant entered.

"You will be glad to hear," said Holmes, "that your young master is found. It is the Duke's desire that the carriage shall go at once to the Fighting Cock Inn to bring Lord Saltire home.

"Now," said Holmes," when the rejoicing lackey had disappeared, "having secured the future, we can afford to be more lenient with the past. I am not in an official position, and there is no reason, so long as the ends of justice are served, why I should disclose all that I know. As to Hayes I say nothing. The gallows awaits him, and I would do nothing to save him from it. What he will divulge I cannot tell, but I have no doubt that your Grace could make him understand that it is to his interest to be silent. From the police point of view he will have kidnapped the boy for the purpose of ransom. If they do not themselves find it out I see no reason why I should prompt them to take a broader point of view. I would warn your Grace, however, that the continued presence of Mr. James Wilder in your household can only lead to misfortune."

"I understand that, Mr. Holmes, and it is already settled that he shall leave me for ever and go to seek his fortune in Australia."

"In that case, your Grace, since you have yourself stated that any unhappiness in your married life was caused by his presence, I would suggest that you make such amends as you can to the Duchess, and that you try to resume those relations which have been so unhappily interrupted."

"That also I have arranged, Mr. Holmes. I wrote to the Duchess this morning."

"In that case," said Holmes, rising, "I think that my friend and I can congratulate ourselves upon several most happy results from our little visit to the North. There is one other small point upon which I desire some light. This fellow Hayes had shod his horses with shoes which counterfeited the tracks of cows. Was it from Mr. Wilder that he learned so extraordinary a device?"

The Duke stood in thought for a moment, with a look of intense surprise on his face. Then he opened a door and showed us into a large room furnished as a museum. He led the way to a glass case in a corner, and pointed to the inscription.

"These shoes," it ran, "were dug up in the moat of Holdernesse Hall. They are for the use of horses; but they are shaped below with a cloven foot of iron, so as to throw pursuers off the track. They are supposed to have belonged to some of the marauding Barons of Holdernesse in the Middle Ages."

Holmes opened the case, and moistening his finger he passed it along the shoe. A thin film of recent mud was left upon his skin.

"Thank you," said he, as he replaced the glass. "It is the second most interesting object that I have seen in the North."

"And the first?"

Holmes folded up his cheque and placed it carefully in his note-book. "I am a poor man," said he, as he patted it affectionately and thrust it into the depths of his inner pocket.

"HE SANK DOWN UPON THE SEA-CHEST, AND LOOKED HELPLESSLY
FROM ONE OF US TO THE OTHER."

# THE RETURN OF
# SHERLOCK HOLMES.

## By A. CONAN DOYLE.

### VI.—The Adventure of Black Peter.

I HAVE never known my friend to be in better form, both mental and physical, than in the year '95. His increasing fame had brought with it an immense practice, and I should be guilty of an indiscretion if I were even to hint at the identity of some of the illustrious clients who crossed our humble threshold in Baker Street. Holmes, however, like all great artists, lived for his art's sake, and, save in the case of the Duke of Holdernesse, I have seldom known him claim any large reward for his inestimable services. So unworldly was he—or so capricious—that he frequently refused his help to the powerful and wealthy where the problem made no appeal to his sympathies, while he would devote weeks of most intense application to the affairs of some humble client whose case presented those strange and dramatic qualities which appealed to his imagination and challenged his ingenuity.

In this memorable year '95 a curious and incongruous succession of cases had engaged his attention, ranging from his famous investigation of the sudden death of Cardinal Tosca—an inquiry which was carried out by him at the express desire of His Holiness the Pope—down to his arrest of Wilson, the notorious canary-trainer, which removed a plague-spot from the East-end of London. Close on the heels of these two famous cases came the tragedy of Woodman's Lee, and the very obscure circumstances which surrounded the death of Captain Peter Carey. No record of the doings of Mr. Sherlock Holmes would be complete which did not include some account of this very unusual affair.

During the first week of July my friend had been absent so often and so long from our lodgings that I knew he had something on hand. The fact that several rough-looking men called during that time and inquired for Captain Basil made me understand that Holmes was working somewhere under one of the numerous disguises and names with which he concealed his own formidable identity. He had at least five small refuges in different parts of London in which he was able to change his personality. He said nothing of his business to me, and it was not my habit to force a confidence. The first positive sign which he gave me of the direction which his investigation was taking was an extraordinary one. He had gone out before breakfast, and I had sat down to mine, when he strode into the room, his hat upon his head and a huge barbed-headed spear tucked like an umbrella under his arm.

"Good gracious, Holmes!" I cried. "You don't mean to say that you have been walking about London with that thing?"

"I drove to the butcher's and back."

"The butcher's?"

"And I return with an excellent appetite. There can be no question, my dear Watson, of the value of exercise before breakfast. But I am prepared to bet that you will not guess the form that my exercise has taken."

"'GOOD GRACIOUS, HOLMES!' I CRIED. 'YOU DON'T MEAN TO SAY THAT YOU HAVE BEEN WALKING ABOUT
LONDON WITH THAT THING?'"

"I will not attempt it."

He chuckled as he poured out the coffee.

"If you could have looked into Allardyce's back shop you would have seen a dead pig swung from a hook in the ceiling, and a gentleman in his shirt-sleeves furiously stabbing at it with this weapon. I was that energetic person, and I have satisfied myself that by no exertion of my strength can I transfix the pig with a single blow. Perhaps you would care to try?"

"Not for worlds. But why were you doing this?"

"Because it seemed to me to have an indirect bearing upon the mystery of Woodman's Lee. Ah, Hopkins, I got your wire last night, and I have been expecting you. Come and join us."

Our visitor was an exceedingly alert man, thirty years of age, dressed in a quiet tweed suit, but retaining the erect bearing of one who was accustomed to official uniform. I recognised him at once as Stanley Hopkins, a young police inspector for whose future

Holmes had high hopes, while he in turn professed the admiration and respect of a pupil for the scientific methods of the famous amateur. Hopkins's brow was clouded, and he sat down with an air of deep dejection.

"No, thank you, sir. I breakfasted before I came round. I spent the night in town, for I came up yesterday to report."

"And what had you to report?"

"Failure, sir; absolute failure."

"You have made no progress?"

"None."

"Dear me! I must have a look at the matter."

"I wish to heavens that you would, Mr. Holmes. It's my first big chance, and I am at my wits' end. For goodness' sake come down and lend me a hand."

"Well, well, it just happens that I have already read all the available evidence, including the report of the inquest, with some care. By the way, what do you make of that tobacco-pouch found on the scene of the crime? Is there no clue there?"

Hopkins looked surprised.

"It was the man's own pouch, sir. His initials were inside it. And it was of seal-skin—and he an old sealer."

"But he had no pipe."

"No, sir, we could find no pipe; indeed, he smoked very little. And yet he might have kept some tobacco for his friends."

"No doubt. I only mention it because if I had been handling the case I should have been inclined to make that the starting-point of my investigation. However, my friend Dr. Watson knows nothing of this matter, and I should be none the worse for hearing the sequence of events once more. Just give us some short sketch of the essentials."

Stanley Hopkins drew a slip of paper from his pocket.

"I have a few dates here which will give you the career of the dead man, Captain Peter Carey. He was born in '45—fifty years of age. He was a most daring and successful seal and whale fisher. In 1883 he commanded the steam sealer *Sea Unicorn*, of Dundee. He had then had several successful voyages in succession, and in the following year, 1884, he retired. After that he travelled for some years, and finally he bought a small place called Woodman's Lee, near Forest Row, in Sussex. There he has lived for six years, and there he died just a week ago to-day.

"There were some most singular points about the man. In ordinary life he was a strict Puritan—a silent, gloomy fellow. His household consisted of his wife, his daughter, aged twenty, and two female servants. These last were continually changing, for it was never a very cheery situation, and sometimes it became past all bearing. The man was an intermittent drunkard, and when he had the fit on him he was a perfect fiend. He has been known to drive his wife and his daughter out of doors in the middle of the night, and flog them through the park until the whole village outside the gates was aroused by their screams.

"He was summoned once for a savage assault upon the old vicar, who had called upon him to remonstrate with him upon his conduct. In short, Mr. Holmes, you would go far before you found a more dangerous man than Peter Carey, and I have heard that he bore the same character when he commanded his ship. He was known in the trade as Black Peter, and the name was given him, not only on account of his swarthy features and the colour of his huge beard, but for the humours which were the terror of all around him. I need not say that he was loathed and avoided by every one of his neighbours, and that I have not heard one single word of sorrow about his terrible end.

"You must have read in the account of the inquest about the man's cabin, Mr. Holmes; but perhaps your friend here has not heard of it. He had built himself a wooden outhouse—he always called it 'the cabin'—a few hundred yards from his house, and it was here that he slept every night. It was a little, single-roomed hut, sixteen feet by ten. He kept the key in his pocket, made his own bed, cleaned it himself, and allowed no other foot to cross the threshold. There are small windows on each side, which were covered by curtains and never opened. One of these windows was turned towards the high road, and when the light burned in it at night the folk used to point it out to each other and wonder what Black Peter was doing in there. That's the window, Mr. Holmes, which gave us one of the few bits of positive evidence that came out at the inquest.

"You remember that a stonemason, named Slater, walking from Forest Row about one o'clock in the morning—two days before the murder — stopped as he passed the grounds and looked at the square of light still shining among the trees. He swears that the shadow of a man's head turned sideways was clearly visible on the blind, and that this shadow was certainly not that of Peter Carey, whom he knew well. It was that of a bearded man, but the beard was short and bristled forwards in a way very different from that of the captain. So he says, but he had been two hours in the public-house, and it is some distance from the road to the window. Besides, this refers to the Monday, and the crime was done upon the Wednesday.

"On the Tuesday Peter Carey was in one of his blackest moods, flushed with drink and as savage as a dangerous wild beast. He roamed about the house, and the women ran for it when they heard him coming. Late in the evening he went down to his own hut. About two o'clock the following morning his daughter, who slept with her window open, heard a most fearful yell from that direction, but it was no unusual thing for him to bawl and shout when he was in drink, so no notice was taken. On rising at seven one of the maids noticed that the door of the hut was open, but so great was the terror which the man caused that it was midday before anyone would venture down to see what had become of him. Peeping into the open door they saw a sight which sent them flying with white faces into the village. Within an hour I was on the spot and had taken over the case.

"Well, I have fairly steady nerves, as you know, Mr. Holmes, but I give you my word that I got a shake when I put my head into that little house. It was droning like a harmonium with the flies and bluebottles, and the floor and walls were like a slaughter-house. He had called it a cabin, and a cabin it was sure enough, for you would have thought that you were in a ship. There was a bunk at one end, a sea-chest, maps and charts, a picture of the *Sea Unicorn*, a line of log-books on a shelf, all exactly as one would expect to find it in a captain's room. And there in the middle of it was the man himself, his face twisted like a lost soul in torment, and his great brindled beard stuck upwards in his agony. Right through his broad breast a steel harpoon had been driven, and it had sunk deep into the wood of the wall behind him. He was pinned like a beetle on a card. Of course, he was quite dead, and had been so from the instant that he had uttered that last yell of agony.

"I know your methods, sir, and I applied them. Before I permitted anything to be moved I examined most carefully the ground outside, and also the floor of the room. There were no footmarks."

"Meaning that you saw none?"

"I assure you, sir, that there were none."

"My good Hopkins, I have investigated many crimes, but I have never yet seen one which was committed by a flying creature. As long as the criminal remains upon two legs so long must there be some indentation, some abrasion, some trifling displacement which can be detected by the scientific searcher. It is incredible that this blood-bespattered room contained no trace which could have aided us. I understand, however, from the inquest that there were some objects which you failed to overlook?"

The young inspector winced at my companion's ironical comments.

"I was a fool not to call you in at the time, Mr. Holmes. However, that's past praying for now. Yes, there were several objects in the room which called for special attention. One was the harpoon with which the deed was committed. It had been snatched down from a rack on the wall. Two others remained there, and there was a vacant place for the third. On the stock was engraved 'Ss. *Sea Unicorn*, Dundee.' This seemed to establish that the crime had been done in a

moment of fury, and that the murderer had seized the first weapon which came in his way. The fact that the crime was committed at two in the morning, and yet Peter Carey was fully dressed, suggested that he had an appointment with the murderer, which is borne out by the fact that a bottle of rum and two dirty glasses stood upon the table."

"Yes," said Holmes; "I think that both inferences are permissible. Was there any other spirit but rum in the room?"

"Yes; there was a tantalus containing brandy and whisky on the sea-chest. It is of no importance to us, however, since the decanters were full, and it had therefore not been used."

"For all that its presence has some significance," said Holmes. "However, let us hear some more about the objects which do seem to you to bear upon the case."

"There was this tobacco-pouch upon the table."

"What part of the table?"

"It lay in the middle. It was of coarse seal-skin—the straight-haired skin, with a leather thong to bind it. Inside was 'P. C.' on the flap. There was half an ounce of strong ship's tobacco in it."

"Excellent! What more?"

Stanley Hopkins drew from his pocket a drab-covered note-book. The outside was rough and worn, the leaves discoloured. On the first page were written the initials "J. H. N." and the date "1883." Holmes laid it on the table and examined it in his minute way, while Hopkins and I gazed over each shoulder. On the second page were the printed letters "C. P. R.," and then came several sheets of numbers. Another heading was Argentine, another Costa Rica, and another San Paulo, each with pages of signs and figures after it.

"What do you make of these?" asked Holmes.

"They appear to be lists of Stock Exchange securities. I thought that 'J. H. N.' were the initials of a broker, and that 'C. P. R.' may have been his client."

"Try Canadian Pacific Railway," said Holmes.

Stanley Hopkins swore between his teeth and struck his thigh with his clenched hand.

"What a fool I have been!" he cried. "Of course, it is as you say. Then 'J. H. N.' are the only initials we have to solve. I have already examined the old Stock Exchange lists, and I can find no one in 1883 either in the House or among the outside brokers whose initials correspond with these. Yet I feel that the clue is the most important one that I hold. You will admit, Mr. Holmes, that there is a possibility that these initials are those of the second person who was present—in other words, of the murderer. I would also urge that the

"Yes, sir, it is a blood-stain. I told you that I picked the book off the floor."

"Was the blood-stain above or below?"

"On the side next the boards."

"Which proves, of course, that the book was dropped after the crime was committed."

"Exactly, Mr. Holmes. I appreciated

"HOLMES EXAMINED IT IN HIS MINUTE WAY."

introduction into the case of a document relating to large masses of valuable securities gives us for the first time some indication of a motive for the crime."

Sherlock Holmes's face showed that he was thoroughly taken aback by this new development.

"I must admit both your points," said he. "I confess that this note-book, which did not appear at the inquest, modifies any views which I may have formed. I had come to a theory of the crime in which I can find no place for this. Have you endeavoured to trace any of the securities here mentioned?"

"Inquiries are now being made at the offices, but I fear that the complete register of the stockholders of these South American concerns is in South America, and that some weeks must elapse before we can trace the shares."

Holmes had been examining the cover of the note-book with his magnifying lens.

"Surely there is some discoloration here," said he,

that point, and I conjectured that it was dropped by the murderer in his hurried flight. It lay near the door."

"I suppose that none of these securities have been found among the property of the dead man?"

"No, sir."

"Have you any reason to suspect robbery?"

"No, sir. Nothing seemed to have been touched."

"Dear me, it is certainly a very interesting case. Then there was a knife, was there not?"

"A sheath-knife, still in its sheath. It lay at the feet of the dead man. Mrs. Carey has identified it as being her husband's property."

Holmes was lost in thought for some time.

"Well," said he, at last, "I suppose I shall have to come out and have a look at it."

Stanley Hopkins gave a cry of joy.

"Thank you, sir. That will indeed be a weight off my mind."

Holmes shook his finger at the inspector. "It would have been an easier task a week ago," said he. "But even now my visit may not be entirely fruitless. Watson, if you can spare the time I should be very glad of your company. If you will call a four-wheeler, Hopkins, we shall be ready to start for Forest Row in a quarter of an hour."

Alighting at the small wayside station, we drove for some miles through the remains of widespread woods, which were once part of that great forest which for so long held the Saxon invaders at bay—the impenetrable "weald," for sixty years the bulwark of Britain. Vast sections of it have been cleared, for this is the seat of the first iron-works of the country, and the trees have been felled to smelt the ore. Now the richer fields of the North have absorbed the trade, and nothing save these ravaged groves and great scars in the earth show the work of the past. Here in a clearing upon the green slope of a hill stood a long, low stone house, approached by a curving drive running through the fields. Nearer the road, and surrounded on three sides by bushes, was a small outhouse, one window and the door facing in our direction. It was the scene of the murder! Stanley Hopkins led us first to the house, where he introduced us to a haggard, grey-haired woman, the widow of

the murdered man, whose gaunt and deep-lined face, with the furtive look of terror in the depths of her red-rimmed eyes, told of the years of hardship and ill-usage which she had endured. With her was her daughter, a pale, fair-haired girl, whose eyes blazed defiantly at us as she told us that she was glad that her father was dead, and that she blessed the hand which had struck him down. It was a terrible household that Black Peter Carey had made for himself, and it was with a sense of relief that we found ourselves in the sunlight again and making our way along a path which had been worn across the fields by the feet of the dead man.

The outhouse was the simplest of dwellings, wooden-walled, shingle-roofed, one window beside the door and one on the farther side. Stanley Hopkins drew the

"'SOMEONE HAS BEEN TAMPERING WITH IT,' HE SAID."

key from his pocket, and had stooped to the lock, when he paused with a look of attention and surprise upon his face.

"Someone has been tampering with it," he said.

There could be no doubt of the fact. The woodwork was cut and the scratches showed white through the paint, as if they had been that instant done. Holmes had been examining the window.

"Someone has tried to force this also. Whoever it was has failed to make his way in. He must have been a very poor burglar."

"This is a most extraordinary thing," said the inspector; "I could swear that these marks were not here yesterday evening."

"Some curious person from the village, perhaps," I suggested.

"Very unlikely. Few of them would dare to set foot in the grounds, far less try to force their way into the cabin. What do you think of it, Mr. Holmes?"

"I think that fortune is very kind to us."

"You mean that the person will come again?"

"It is very probable. He came expecting to find the door open. He tried to get in with the blade of a very small penknife. He could not manage it. What would he do?"

"Come again next night with a more useful tool."

"So I should say. It will be our fault if we are not there to receive him. Meanwhile, let me see the inside of the cabin."

The traces of the tragedy had been removed, but the furniture within the little room still stood as it had been on the night of the crime. For two hours, with most intense concentration, Holmes examined every object in turn, but his face showed that his quest was not a successful one. Once only he paused in his patient investigation.

"Have you taken anything off this shelf, Hopkins?"

"No; I have moved nothing."

"Something has been taken. There is less dust in this corner of the shelf than elsewhere. It may have been a book lying on its side. It may have been a box. Well, well, I can do nothing more. Let us walk in these beautiful woods, Watson, and give a few hours to the birds and the flowers. We shall meet you here later, Hopkins, and see if we can come to closer quarters with the gentleman who has paid this visit in the night."

It was past eleven o'clock when we formed our little ambuscade. Hopkins was for leaving the door of the hut open, but Holmes was of opinion that this would rouse the suspicions of the stranger. The lock was a perfectly simple one, and only a strong blade was needed to push it back. Holmes also suggested that we should wait, not inside the hut, but outside it among the bushes which grew round the farther window. In this way we should be able to watch our man if he struck a light, and see what his object was in this stealthy nocturnal visit.

It was a long and melancholy vigil, and yet brought with it something of the thrill which the hunter feels when he lies beside the water pool and waits for the coming of the thirsty beast of prey. What savage creature was it which might steal upon us out of the darkness? Was it a fierce tiger of crime, which could only be taken fighting hard with flashing fang and claw, or would it prove to be some skulking jackal, dangerous only to the weak and unguarded?

In absolute silence we crouched amongst the bushes, waiting for whatever might come. At first the steps of a few belated villagers, or the sound of voices from the village, lightened our vigil; but one by one these interruptions died away and an absolute stillness fell upon us, save for the chimes of the distant church, which told us of the progress of the night, and for the rustle and whisper of a fine rain falling amid the foliage which roofed us in.

Half-past two had chimed, and it was the darkest hour which precedes the dawn, when we all started as a low but sharp click came from the direction of the gate. Someone had entered the drive. Again there was a long silence, and I had begun to fear that it was a false alarm, when a stealthy step was heard upon the other side of the hut, and a moment later a metallic scraping and clinking. The man was trying to force the lock! This time his skill was greater or his tool was better, for there was a sudden snap and the creak of the hinges. Then a match was struck, and next instant the steady light from a candle filled the interior of the hut. Through the gauze curtain our eyes were all riveted upon the scene within.

The nocturnal visitor was a young man, frail and thin, with a black moustache which intensified the deadly pallor of his face. He could not have been much above twenty years of age. I have never seen any human being who appeared to be in such a pitiable fright, for his teeth were visibly chattering and he was shaking in every limb. He was dressed like a gentleman, in Norfolk jacket and knickerbockers, with a cloth cap upon his head. We watched him staring round with frightened eyes. Then he laid the candle-end upon the table and disappeared from our view into one of the corners. He returned with a large book, one of the log-books which formed a line upon the shelves. Leaning on the table he rapidly turned over the leaves of this volume until he came to the entry which he sought. Then, with an angry gesture of his clenched hand, he closed the book, replaced it in the corner, and put out the light. He had hardly turned to leave the hut when Hopkins's hand was on the fellow's collar, and I heard his loud gasp of terror as he understood that he was taken. The candle was re-lit, and there was our wretched captive shivering and cowering in the grasp of the detective. He sank down upon the sea-chest, and looked helplessly from one of us to the other.

"HE RAPIDLY TURNED OVER THE LEAVES OF THIS VOLUME."

"Now, my fine fellow," said Stanley Hopkins, "who are you, and what do you want here?"

The man pulled himself together and faced us with an effort at self-composure.

"You are detectives, I suppose?" said he. "You imagine I am connected with the death of Captain Peter Carey. I assure you that I am innocent."

"We'll see about that," said Hopkins. "First of all, what is your name?"

"It is John Hopley Neligan."

I saw Holmes and Hopkins exchange a quick glance.

"What are you doing here?"

"Can I speak confidentially?"

"No, certainly not."

"Why should I tell you?"

"If you have no answer it may go badly with you at the trial."

The young man winced.

"Well, I will tell you," he said. "Why should I not? And yet I hate to think of this old scandal gaining a new lease of life. Did you ever hear of Dawson and Neligan?"

I could see from Hopkins's face that he never had; but Holmes was keenly interested.

"You mean the West-country bankers," said he. "They failed for a million, ruined half the county families of Cornwall, and Neligan disappeared."

"Exactly. Neligan was my father."

At last we were getting something positive, and yet it seemed a long gap between an absconding banker and Captain Peter Carey pinned against the wall with one of his own harpoons. We all listened intently to the young man's words.

"It was my father who was really concerned. Dawson had retired. I was only ten years of age at the time, but I was old enough to feel the shame and horror of it all. It has always been said that my father stole all the securities and fled. It is not true. It was his belief that if he were given time in which to realize them all would be well and every creditor paid in full. He started in his little yacht for Norway just before the warrant was issued for his arrest. I can remember that last night when he bade farewell to my mother. He left us a list of the securities he was taking, and he swore that he would come back with his honour cleared, and that none who had trusted him would suffer. Well, no word was ever heard from him again. Both the yacht and he vanished utterly. We believed, my mother and I, that he and it, with the securities that he had taken with him, were at the bottom of the sea. We had a faithful friend, however, who is a business man, and it was he who discovered some time ago that some of the securities which my father had with him have reappeared on the London market. You can imagine our amazement. I spent months in trying to trace them, and at last, after many doublings and difficulties, I discovered that the original seller had been Captain Peter Carey, the owner of this hut.

"Naturally, I made some inquiries about the man. I found that he had been in command of a whaler which was due to return from the Arctic seas at the very time when my father was crossing to Norway. The autumn of that year was a stormy one, and there was a long succession of southerly gales. My father's yacht may well have been blown to the north, and there met by Captain Peter Carey's ship. If that were so, what had become of my father? In any case, if I could prove from Peter Carey's evidence how these securities came on the market it would be a proof that my father had not sold them, and that he had no view to personal profit when he took them.

"I came down to Sussex with the intention of seeing the captain, but it was at this moment that his terrible death occurred. I read at the inquest a description of his cabin, in which it stated that the old log-books of his vessel were preserved in it. It struck me that if I could see what occurred in the month of August, 1883, on board the *Sea Unicorn*, I might settle the mystery of my father's fate. I tried last night to get at these log-books, but was unable to open the door. To-night I tried again, and succeeded; but I find that the pages which deal with that month have been torn from the book. It was at that moment I found myself a prisoner in your hands."

"Is that all?" asked Hopkins.

"Yes, that is all." His eyes shifted as he said it.

"You have nothing else to tell us?"

He hesitated.

"No; there is nothing."

"You have not been here before last night?"

"No."

"Then how do you account for *that?*" cried Hopkins, as he held up the damning note-book, with the initials of our prisoner on the first leaf and the blood-stain on the cover.

The wretched man collapsed. He sank his face in his hands and trembled all over.

"Where did you get it?" he groaned. "I did not know. I thought I had lost it at the hotel."

"That is enough," said Hopkins, sternly. "Whatever else you have to say you must say in court. You will walk down with me now to the police-station. Well, Mr. Holmes, I am very much obliged to you and to your friend for coming down to help me. As it turns out your presence was unnecessary, and I would have brought the case to this successful issue without you; but none the less I am very grateful. Rooms have been reserved for you at the Brambletye Hotel, so we can all walk down to the village together."

"Well, Watson, what do you think of it?" asked Holmes, as we travelled back next morning.

"I can see that you are not satisfied."

"Oh, yes, my dear Watson, I am perfectly satisfied. At the same time Stanley Hopkins's methods do not commend themselves to me. I am disappointed in Stanley Hopkins. I had hoped for better things from him. One should always look for a possible alternative and provide against it. It is the first rule of criminal investigation."

"What, then, is the alternative?"

"The line of investigation which I have myself been pursuing. It may give us nothing. I cannot tell. But at least I shall follow it to the end."

Several letters were waiting for Holmes at Baker Street. He snatched one of them up, opened it, and burst out into a triumphant chuckle of laughter.

"Excellent, Watson. The alternative develops. Have you telegraph forms? Just write a couple of messages for me: 'Sumner, Shipping Agent, Ratcliff Highway. Send three men on, to arrive ten to-morrow morning.—Basil.' That's my name in those parts. The other is: 'Inspector Stanley Hopkins, 46, Lord Street, Brixton. Come breakfast to-morrow at nine-thirty. Important. Wire if unable to come.—Sherlock Holmes.' There, Watson, this infernal case has haunted me for ten days. I hereby banish it completely from my presence. To-morrow I trust that we shall hear the last of it for ever."

Sharp at the hour named Inspector Stanley

Hopkins appeared, and we sat down together to the excellent breakfast which Mrs. Hudson had prepared. The young detective was in high spirits at his success.

"You really think that your solution must be correct?" asked Holmes.

"I could not imagine a more complete case."

"It did not seem to me conclusive."

"You astonish me, Mr. Holmes. What more could one ask for?"

"Does your explanation cover every point?"

"Undoubtedly. I find that young Neligan arrived at the Brambletye Hotel on the very day of the crime. He came on the pretence of playing golf. His room was on the ground-floor, and he could get out when he liked. That very night he went down to Woodman's Lee, saw Peter Carey at the hut, quarrelled with him, and killed him with the harpoon. Then, horrified by what he had done, he fled out of the hut, dropping the note-book which he had brought with him in order to question Peter Carey about these different securities. You may have observed that some of them were marked with ticks, and the others—the great majority—were not. Those which are ticked have been traced on the London market; but the others presumably were still in the possession of Carey, and young Neligan, according to his own account, was anxious to recover them in order to do the right thing by his father's creditors. After his flight he did not dare to approach the hut again for some time; but at last he forced himself to do so in order to obtain the information which he needed. Surely that is all simple and obvious?"

Holmes smiled and shook his head.

"It seems to me to have only one drawback, Hopkins, and that is that it is intrinsically impossible. Have you tried to drive a harpoon through a body? No? Tut, tut, my dear sir, you must really pay attention to these details. My friend Watson could tell you that I spent a whole morning in that exercise. It is no easy matter, and requires a strong and practised arm. But this blow was delivered with such violence that the head of the weapon sank deep into the wall. Do you imagine that this anæmic youth was capable of so frightful an assault? Is he the man who hobnobbed in rum and water with Black Peter in the dead of the night? Was it his profile that was seen on the blind two nights before? No, no, Hopkins; it is another and a more formidable person for whom we must seek."

The detective's face had grown longer and longer during Holmes's speech. His hopes and his ambitions were all crumbling about him. But he would not abandon his position without a struggle.

"You can't deny that Neligan was present that night, Mr. Holmes. The book will prove that. I fancy that I have evidence enough to satisfy a jury, even if you are able to pick a hole in it. Besides, Mr. Holmes, I have laid my hand upon *my* man. As to this terrible person of yours, where is he?"

"I rather fancy that he is on the stair," said Holmes, serenely. "I think, Watson, that you would do well to put that revolver where you can reach it." He rose, and laid a written paper upon a side-table. "Now we are ready," said he.

There had been some talking in gruff voices outside, and now Mrs. Hudson opened the door to say that there were three men inquiring for Captain Basil.

"Show them in one by one," said Holmes.

The first who entered was a little ribston-pippin of a man, with ruddy cheeks and fluffy white side-whiskers. Holmes had drawn a letter from his pocket.

"What name?" he asked.

"James Lancaster."

"I am sorry, Lancaster, but the berth is full. Here is half a sovereign for your trouble. Just step into this room and wait there for a few minutes."

The second man was a long, dried-up creature, with lank hair and sallow cheeks. His name was Hugh Pattins. He also received his dismissal, his half-sovereign, and the order to wait.

The third applicant was a man of remarkable appearance. A fierce, bull-dog face was framed in a tangle of hair and beard, and two bold dark eyes gleamed behind the cover of thick, tufted, overhung eyebrows. He saluted and stood sailor-fashion, turning his cap round in his hands.

"Your name?" asked Holmes.

"Patrick Cairns."

"Harpooner?"

"Yes, sir. Twenty-six voyages."

"Dundee, I suppose?"

"Yes, sir."

"And ready to start with an exploring ship?"

"Yes, sir."

"What wages?"

"Eight pounds a month."

"Could you start at once?"

"As soon as I get my kit."

"Have you your papers?"

"Yes, sir." He took a sheaf of worn and greasy forms from his pocket. Holmes glanced over them and returned them.

"You are just the man I want," said he. "Here's the agreement on the side-table. If you sign it the whole matter will be settled."

"'SHALL I SIGN HERE?' HE ASKED."

The seaman lurched across the room and took up the pen.

"Shall I sign here?" he asked, stooping over the table.

Holmes leaned over his shoulder and passed both hands over his neck.

"This will do," said he.

I heard a click of steel and a bellow like an enraged bull. The next instant Holmes

and the seaman were rolling on the ground together. He was a man of such gigantic strength that, even with the handcuffs which Holmes had so deftly fastened upon his wrists, he would have very quickly overpowered my friend had Hopkins and I not rushed to his rescue. Only when I pressed the cold muzzle of the revolver to his temple did he at last understand that resistance was vain. We lashed his ankles with cord and rose breathless from the struggle.

"I must really apologize, Hopkins," said Sherlock Holmes; "I fear that the scrambled eggs are cold. However, you will enjoy the rest of your breakfast all the better, will you not, for the thought that you have brought your case to a triumphant conclusion."

Stanley Hopkins was speechless with amazement.

"I don't know what to say, Mr. Holmes," he blurted out at last, with a very red face. "It seems to me that I have been making a fool of myself from the beginning. I understand now, what I should never have forgotten, that I am the pupil and you are the master. Even now I see what you have done, but I don't know how you did it, or what it signifies."

"Well, well," said Holmes, goodhumouredly. "We all learn by experience, and your lesson this time is that you should never lose sight of the alternative. You were so absorbed in young Neligan that you could not spare a thought to Patrick Cairns, the true murderer of Peter Carey."

The hoarse voice of the seaman broke in on our conversation.

"See here, mister," said he, "I make no complaint of being man-handled in this fashion, but I would have you call things by their right names. You say I murdered Peter Carey; I say I *killed* Peter Carey, and there's all the difference. Maybe you don't believe what I say. Maybe you think I am just slinging you a yarn."

"Not at all," said Holmes. "Let us hear what you have to say."

"It's soon told, and, by the Lord, every word of it is truth. I knew Black Peter, and when he pulled out his knife I whipped a harpoon through him sharp, for I knew that it was him or me. That's how he died. You can call it murder. Anyhow, I'd as soon die with a rope round my neck as with Black Peter's knife in my heart."

"How came you there?" asked Holmes.

"I'll tell it you from the beginning. Just sit me up a little so as I can speak easy. It was in '83 that it happened—August of that year. Peter Carey was master of the *Sea Unicorn*, and I was spare harpooner. We were coming out of the ice-pack on our way home, with head winds and a week's southerly gale, when we picked up a little craft that had been blown north. There was one man on her—a landsman. The crew had thought she would founder, and had made for the Norwegian coast in the dinghy. I guess they were all drowned. Well, we took him on board, this man, and he and the skipper had some long talks in the cabin. All the baggage we took off with him was one tin box. So far as I know, the man's name was never mentioned, and on the second night he disappeared as if he had never been. It was given out that he had either thrown himself overboard or fallen overboard in the heavy weather that we were having. Only one man knew what had happened to him, and that was me, for with my own eyes I saw the skipper tip up his heels and put him over the rail in the middle watch of a dark night, two days before we sighted the Shetland lights.

"Well, I kept my knowledge to myself and waited to see what would come of it. When we got back to Scotland it was easily hushed up, and nobody asked any questions. A stranger died by an accident, and it was nobody's business to inquire. Shortly after Peter Carey gave

up the sea, and it was long years before I could find where he was. I guessed that he had done the deed for the sake of what was in that tin box, and that he could afford now to pay me well for keeping my mouth shut.

"I found out where he was through a sailor man that had met him in London, and down I went to squeeze him. The first night he was reasonable enough, and was ready to give me what would make me free of the sea for life. We were to fix it all two nights later. When I came I found him three parts drunk and in a vile temper. We sat down and we drank and we yarned about old times, but the more he drank the less I liked the look on his face. I spotted that harpoon upon the wall, and I thought I might need it before I was through. Then at last he broke out at me, spitting and cursing, with murder in his eyes and a great clasp-knife in his hand. He had not time to get it from the sheath before I had the harpoon through him. Heavens! what a yell

"WE SAT DOWN AND WE DRANK AND WE YARNED ABOUT OLD TIMES."

he gave ; and his face gets between me and my sleep ! I stood there, with his blood splashing round me, and I waited for a bit ; but all was quiet, so I took heart once more. I looked round, and there was the tin box on a shelf. I had as much right to it as Peter Carey, anyhow, so I took it with me and left the hut. Like a fool I left my baccy-pouch upon the table.

" Now I'll tell you the queerest part of the whole story. I had hardly got outside the hut when I heard someone coming, and I hid among the bushes. A man came slinking along, went into the hut, gave a cry as if he had seen a ghost, and legged it as hard as he could run until he was out of sight. Who he was or what he wanted is more than I can tell. For my part, I walked ten miles, got a train at Tunbridge Wells, and so reached London, and no one the wiser.

" Well, when I came to examine the box I found there was no money in it, and nothing but papers that I would not dare to sell. I had lost my hold on Black Peter, and was stranded in London without a shilling. There was only my trade left. I saw these advertisements about harpooners and high wages, so I went to the shipping agents, and they sent me here. That's all I know, and I say again that if I killed Black Peter the law should give me thanks, for I saved them the price of a hempen rope."

" A very clear statement," said Holmes, rising and lighting his pipe. " I think, Hopkins, that you should lose no time in conveying your prisoner to a place of safety. This room is not well adapted for a cell, and Mr. Patrick Cairns occupies too large a proportion of our carpet."

" Mr. Holmes," said Hopkins, " I do not know how to express my gratitude. Even now I do not understand how you attained this result."

" Simply by having the good fortune to get the right clue from the beginning. It is very possible that if I had known about this note-book it might have led away my

thoughts, as it did yours. But all I heard pointed in the one direction. The amazing strength, the skill in the use of the harpoon, the rum and water, the seal-skin tobacco-pouch, with the coarse tobacco—all these pointed to a seaman, and one who had been a whaler. I was convinced that the initials ' P. C.' upon the pouch were a coincidence, and not those of Peter Carey, since he seldom smoked, and no pipe was found in his cabin. You remember that I asked whether whisky and brandy were in the cabin. You said they were. How many landsmen are there who would drink rum when they could get these other spirits ? Yes, I was certain it was a seaman."

" And how did you find him ? "

" My dear sir, the problem had become a very simple one. If it were a seaman, it could only be a seaman who had been with him on the *Sea Unicorn*. So far as I could learn he had sailed in no other ship. I spent three days in wiring to Dundee, and at the end of that time I had ascertained the names of the crew of the *Sea Unicorn* in 1883. When I found Patrick Cairns among the harpooners my research was nearing its end. I argued that the man was probably in London, and that he would desire to leave the country for a time. I therefore spent some days in the East-end, devised an Arctic expedition, put forward tempting terms for harpooners who would serve under Captain Basil—and behold the result ! "

" Wonderful ! " cried Hopkins. " Wonderful ! "

" You must obtain the release of young Neligan as soon as possible," said Holmes. " I confess that I think you owe him some apology. The tin box must be returned to him, but, of course, the securities which Peter Carey has sold are lost for ever. There's the cab, Hopkins, and you can remove your man. If you want me for the trial, my address and that of Watson will be somewhere in Norway—I'll send particulars later."

# THE RETURN OF SHERLOCK HOLMES.

## By A. CONAN DOYLE.

### VII.—The Adventure of Charles Augustus Milverton.

IT is years since the incidents of which I speak took place, and yet it is with diffidence that I allude to them. For a long time, even with the utmost discretion and reticence, it would have been impossible to make the facts public; but now the principal person concerned is beyond the reach of human law, and with due suppression the story may be told in such fashion as to injure no one. It records an absolutely unique experience in the career both of Mr. Sherlock Holmes and of myself. The reader will excuse me if I conceal the date or any other fact by which he might trace the actual occurrence.

We had been out for one of our evening rambles, Holmes and I, and had returned about six o'clock on a cold, frosty winter's evening. As Holmes turned up the lamp the light fell upon a card on the table. He glanced at it, and then, with an ejaculation of disgust, threw it on the floor. I picked it up and read:—

CHARLES AUGUSTUS MILVERTON,
APPLEDORE TOWERS,
AGENT.            HAMPSTEAD.

"Who is he?" I asked.

"The worst man in London," Holmes answered, as he sat down and stretched his legs before the fire. "Is anything on the back of the card?"

I turned it over.

"Will call at 6.30—C. A. M.," I read.

"Hum! He's about due. Do you feel a creeping, shrinking sensation, Watson, when you stand before the serpents in the Zoo and see the slithery, gliding, venomous creatures, with their deadly eyes and wicked, flattened faces? Well, that's how Milverton impresses me. I've had to do with fifty murderers in my career, but the worst of them never gave me the repulsion which I have for this fellow. And yet I can't get out of doing business

with him—indeed, he is here at my invitation."

"But who is he?"

"I'll tell you, Watson. He is the king of all the blackmailers. Heaven help the man, and still more the woman, whose secret and reputation come into the power of Milverton. With a smiling face and a heart of marble he will squeeze and squeeze until he has drained them dry. The fellow is a genius in his way, and would have made his mark in some more savoury trade. His method is as follows: He allows it to be known that he is prepared to pay very high sums for letters which compromise people of wealth or position. He receives these wares not only from treacherous valets or maids, but frequently from genteel ruffians who have gained the confidence and affection of trusting women. He deals with no niggard hand. I happen to know that he paid seven hundred pounds to a footman for a note two lines in length, and that the ruin of a noble family was the result. Everything which is in the market goes to Milverton, and there are hundreds in this great city who turn white at his name. No one knows where his grip may fall, for he is far too rich and far too cunning to work from hand to mouth. He will hold a card back for years in order to play it at the moment when the stake is best worth winning. I have said that he is the worst man in London, and I would ask you how could one compare the ruffian who in hot blood bludgeons his mate with this man, who methodically and at his leisure tortures the soul and wrings the nerves in order to add to his already swollen money-bags?"

I had seldom heard my friend speak with such intensity of feeling.

"But surely," said I, "the fellow must be within the grasp of the law?"

"Technically, no doubt, but practically not. What would it profit a woman, for example, to get him a few months' imprisonment if her own ruin must immediately follow? His victims dare not hit back. If ever he blackmailed an innocent person, then, indeed, we should have him ; but he is as cunning as the Evil One. No, no ; we must find other ways to fight him."

"And why is he here?"

"Because an illustrious client has placed her piteous case in my hands. It is the Lady Eva Brackwell, the most beautiful *débutante* of last season. She is to be married in a fortnight to the Earl of Dovercourt. This fiend has several imprudent letters — imprudent, Watson, nothing worse — which were written to an impecunious young squire in the country. They would suffice to break off the match. Milverton will send the letters to the Earl unless a large sum of money is paid him. I have been commissioned to meet him, and—to make the best terms I can."

"CHARLES AUGUSTUS MILVERTON."

At that instant there was a clatter and a rattle in the street below. Looking down I saw a stately carriage and pair, the brilliant lamps gleaming on the glossy haunches of the noble chestnuts. A footman opened the door, and a small, stout man in a shaggy astrachan overcoat descended. A minute later he was in the room. Charles Augustus Milverton was a man of fifty, with a large, intellectual head, a round, plump, hairless face, a perpetual frozen smile, and two keen grey eyes, which gleamed brightly from behind broad, golden-rimmed glasses. There was something of Mr. Pickwick's benevolence in his appearance, marred only by the insincerity of the fixed smile and by the hard glitter of those restless and penetrating eyes. His voice was as smooth and suave as his countenance, as he advanced with a plump little hand extended, murmuring his regret for having missed us at his first visit. Holmes disregarded the outstretched hand and looked at him with a face of granite. Milverton's smile broadened; he shrugged his shoulders, removed his overcoat, folded it with great deliberation over the back of a chair, and then took a seat.

"This gentleman?" said he, with a wave in my direction. "Is it discreet? Is it right?"

"Dr. Watson is my friend and partner."

"Very good, Mr. Holmes. It is only in your client's interests that I protested. The matter is so very delicate——"

"Dr. Watson has already heard of it."

"Then we can proceed to business. You say that you are acting for Lady Eva. Has she empowered you to accept my terms?"

"What are your terms?"

"Seven thousand pounds."

"And the alternative?"

"My dear sir, it is painful to me to discuss it ; but if the money is not paid on the 14th there certainly will be no marriage on the 18th." His insufferable smile was more complacent than ever,

Holmes thought for a little.

"You appear to me," he said, at last, "to be taking matters too much for granted. I am, of course, familiar with the contents of these letters. My client will certainly do what I may advise. I shall counsel her to tell her future husband the whole story and to trust to his generosity."

Milverton chuckled.

"You evidently do not know the Earl," said he.

From the baffled look upon Holmes's face I could clearly see that he did.

"What harm is there in the letters?" he asked.

"They are sprightly — very sprightly," Milverton answered. "The lady was a charming correspondent. But I can assure you that the Earl of Dovercourt would fail to appreciate them. However, since you think otherwise, we will let it rest at that. It is purely a matter of business. If you think that it is in the best interests of your client that these letters should be placed in the hands of the Earl, then you would indeed be foolish to pay so large a sum of money to regain them." He rose and seized his astrachan coat.

Holmes was grey with anger and mortification.

"Wait a little," he said. "You go too fast. We would certainly make every effort to avoid scandal in so delicate a matter."

Milverton relapsed into his chair.

"I was sure that you would see it in that light," he purred.

"At the same time," Holmes continued, "Lady Eva is not a wealthy woman. I assure you that two thousand pounds would be a drain upon her resources, and that the sum you name is utterly beyond her power. I beg therefore, that you will moderate your demands, and that you will return the letters at the price I indicate, which is, I assure you, the highest that you can get."

Milverton's smile broadened and his eyes twinkled humorously.

"I am aware that what you say is true about the lady's resources," said he. "At the same time, you must admit that the occasion of a lady's marriage is a very suitable time for her friends and relatives to make some little effort upon her behalf. They may hesitate as to an acceptable wedding present. Let me assure them that this little bundle of letters would give more joy than all the candelabra and butter-dishes in London."

"It is impossible," said Holmes,

"Dear me, dear me, how unfortunate!" cried Milverton, taking out a bulky pocket-book. "I cannot help thinking that ladies are ill-advised in not making an effort. Look at this!" He held up a little note with a coat-of-arms upon the envelope. "That belongs to—well, perhaps it is hardly fair to tell the name until to-morrow morning. But at that time it will be in the hands of the lady's husband. And all because she will not find a beggarly sum which she could get in an hour by turning her diamonds into paste. It is such a pity. Now, you remember the sudden end of the engagement between the Honourable Miss Miles and Colonel Dorking? Only two days before the wedding there was a paragraph in the *Morning Post* to say that it was all off. And why? It is almost incredible, but the absurd sum of twelve hundred pounds would have settled the whole question. Is it not pitiful? And here I find you, a man of sense, boggling about terms when your client's future and honour are at stake. You surprise me, Mr. Holmes."

"What I say is true," Holmes answered. "The money cannot be found. Surely it is better for you to take the substantial sum which I offer than to ruin this woman's career, which can profit you in no way?"

"There you make a mistake, Mr. Holmes. An exposure would profit me indirectly to a considerable extent. I have eight or ten similar cases maturing. If it was circulated among them that I had made a severe example of the Lady Eva I should find all of them much more open to reason. You see my point?"

Holmes sprang from his chair.

"Get behind him, Watson! Don't let him out! Now, sir, let us see the contents of that note-book."

Milverton had glided as quick as a rat to the side of the room, and stood with his back against the wall.

"Mr. Holmes, Mr. Holmes," he said, turning the front of his coat and exhibiting the butt of a large revolver, which projected from the inside pocket. "I have been expecting you to do something original. This has been done so often, and what good has ever come from it? I assure you that I am armed to the teeth, and I am perfectly prepared to use my weapons, knowing that the law will support me. Besides, your supposition that I would bring the letters here in a note-book is entirely mistaken. I would do nothing so foolish. And now, gentlemen, I have one or two little interviews this evening,

"EXHIBITING THE BUTT OF A LARGE REVOLVER, WHICH PROJECTED FROM THE INSIDE POCKET."

and it is a long drive to Hampstead." He stepped forward, took up his coat, laid his hand on his revolver, and turned to the door. I picked up a chair, but Holmes shook his head and I laid it down again. With a bow, a smile, and a twinkle Milverton was out of the room, and a few moments after we heard the slam of the carriage door and the rattle of the wheels as he drove away.

Holmes sat motionless by the fire, his hands buried deep in his trouser pockets, his chin sunk upon his breast, his eyes fixed upon the glowing embers. For half an hour he was silent and still. Then, with the gesture of a man who has taken his decision, he sprang to his feet and passed into his bedroom. A little later a rakish young workman with a goatee beard and a swagger lit his clay pipe at the lamp before descending into the street. "I'll be back some time, Watson," said he, and vanished into the night. I understood that he had opened his campaign against Charles Augustus Milverton ; but I little dreamed the strange shape which that campaign was destined to take.

For some days Holmes came and went at all hours in this attire, but beyond a remark that his time was spent at Hampstead, and that it was not wasted, I knew nothing of what he was doing. At last, however, on a wild, tempestuous evening, when the wind screamed and rattled against the windows, he returned from his last expedition, and having removed his disguise he sat before the fire and laughed heartily in his silent inward fashion.

"You would not call me a marrying man, Watson ? "

"No, indeed ! "

"You'll be interested to hear that I am engaged."

"My dear fellow ! I congrat——"

"To Milverton's housemaid."

"Good heavens, Holmes ! "

"I wanted information, Watson."

"Surely you have gone too far ? "

"It was a most necessary step. I am a plumber with a rising business, Escott by name. I have walked out with her each evening, and I have talked with her. Good heavens, those talks ! However, I have got all I wanted. I know Milverton's house as I know the palm of my hand."

"But the girl, Holmes ? "

He shrugged his shoulders.

"You can't help it, my dear Watson. You must play your cards as best you can when such a stake is on the table. However, I rejoice to say that I have a hated rival who will certainly cut me out the instant that my back is turned. What a splendid night it is!"

"You like this weather?"

"It suits my purpose. Watson, I mean to burgle Milverton's house to-night."

I had a catching of the breath, and my skin went cold at the words, which were slowly uttered in a tone of concentrated resolution. As a flash of lightning in the night shows up in an instant every detail of a wide landscape, so at one glance I seemed to see every possible result of such an action —the detection, the capture, the honoured career ending in irreparable failure and disgrace, my friend himself lying at the mercy of the odious Milverton.

"For Heaven's sake, Holmes, think what you are doing," I cried.

"My dear fellow, I have given it every consideration. I am never precipitate in my actions, nor would I adopt so energetic and indeed so dangerous a course if any other were possible. Let us look at the matter clearly and fairly. I suppose that you will admit that the action is morally justifiable, though technically criminal. To burgle his house is no more than to forcibly take his pocket-book—an action in which you were prepared to aid me."

I turned it over in my mind.

"Yes," I said; "it is morally justifiable so long as our object is to take no articles save those which are used for an illegal purpose."

"Exactly. Since it is morally justifiable I have only to consider the question of personal risk. Surely a gentleman should not lay much stress upon this when a lady is in most desperate need of his help?"

"You will be in such a false position."

"Well, that is part of the risk. There is no other possible way of regaining these letters. The unfortunate lady has not the money, and there are none of her people in whom she could confide. To-morrow is the last day of grace, and unless we can get the letters to-night this villain will be as good as his word and will bring about her ruin. I must, therefore, abandon my client to her fate or I must play this last card. Between ourselves, Watson, it's a sporting duel between this fellow Milverton and me. He had, as you saw, the best of the first exchanges; but my self-respect and my reputation are concerned to fight it to a finish."

"Well, I don't like it; but I suppose it must be," said I. "When do we start?"

"You are not coming."

"Then you are not going," said I. "I give you my word of honour—and I never broke it in my life—that I will take a cab straight to the police-station and give you away unless you let me share this adventure with you."

"You can't help me."

"How do you know that? You can't tell what may happen. Anyway, my resolution is taken. Other people beside you have self-respect and even reputations."

Holmes had looked annoyed, but his brow cleared, and he clapped me on the shoulder.

"Well, well, my dear fellow, be it so. We have shared the same room for some years, and it would be amusing if we ended by sharing the same cell. You know, Watson, I don't mind confessing to you that I have always had an idea that I would have made a highly efficient criminal. This is the chance of my lifetime in that direction. See here!" He took a neat little leather case out of a drawer, and opening it he exhibited a number of shining instruments. "This is a first-class, up-to-date burgling kit, with nickel-plated jemmy, diamond-tipped glass-cutter, adaptable keys, and every modern improvement which the march of civilization demands. Here, too, is my dark lantern. Everything is in order. Have you a pair of silent shoes?"

"I have rubber-soled tennis shoes."

"Excellent. And a mask?"

"I can make a couple out of black silk."

"I can see that you have a strong natural turn for this sort of thing. Very good; do you make the masks. We shall have some cold supper before we start. It is now nine-thirty. At eleven we shall drive as far as Church Row. It is a quarter of an hour's walk from there to Appledore Towers. We shall be at work before midnight. Milverton is a heavy sleeper and retires punctually at ten-thirty. With any luck we should be back here by two, with the Lady Eva's letters in my pocket."

Holmes and I put on our dress-clothes, so that we might appear to be two theatre-goers homeward bound. In Oxford Street we picked up a hansom and drove to an address in Hampstead. Here we paid off our cab, and with our great-coats buttoned up, for it was bitterly cold and the wind seemed to blow through us, we walked along the edge of the Heath.

"It's a business that needs delicate treatment," said Holmes. "These documents are contained in a safe in the fellow's study, and the study is the ante-room of his bed-chamber. On the other hand, like all these stout, little men who do themselves well, he is a plethoric sleeper. Agatha—that's my *fiancée*—says it is a joke in the servants' hall that it's impossible to wake the master. He has a secretary who is devoted to his interests and never budges from the study all day. That's why we are going at night. Then he has a beast of a dog which roams the garden. I met Agatha late the last two evenings, and she locks the brute up so as to give me a clear run. This is the house, this big one in its own grounds. Through the gate—now to the right among the laurels. We might put on our masks here, I think. You see, there is not a glimmer of light in any of the windows, and everything is working splendidly."

With our black silk face-coverings, which turned us into two of the most truculent figures in London, we stole up to the silent, gloomy house. A sort of tiled veranda extended along one side of it, lined by several windows and two doors.

"That's his bedroom," Holmes whispered. "This door opens straight into the study. It would suit us best, but it is bolted as well as locked, and we should make too much noise getting in. Come round here. There's a greenhouse which opens into the drawing-room."

The place was locked, but Holmes removed a circle of glass and turned the key from the inside. An instant afterwards he had closed the door behind us, and we had become felons in the eyes of the law. The thick, warm air of the conservatory and the rich, choking fragrance of exotic plants took us by the throat. He seized my hand in the darkness and led me swiftly past banks of shrubs which brushed against our faces. Holmes had remarkable powers, carefully cultivated, of seeing in the dark. Still holding my hand in one of his he opened a door, and I was vaguely conscious that we had entered a large room in which a cigar had been smoked not long before. He felt his way among the furniture, opened another door, and closed it behind us. Putting out my hand I felt several coats hanging from the wall, and I understood that I was in a passage. We passed along it, and Holmes very gently opened a door upon the right-hand side. Something rushed out at us and my heart sprang into my mouth, but I could have laughed when I realized that it was the cat. A fire was burning in this new room,

and again the air was heavy with tobacco smoke. Holmes entered on tiptoe, waited for me to follow, and then very gently closed the door. We were in Milverton's study, and a *portière* at the farther side showed the entrance to his bedroom.

It was a good fire, and the room was illuminated by it. Near the door I saw the gleam of an electric switch, but it was unnecessary, even if it had been safe, to turn it on. At one side of the fireplace was a heavy curtain, which covered the bay window we had seen from outside. On the other side was the door which communicated with the veranda. A desk stood in the centre, with a turning chair of shining red leather. Opposite was a large bookcase, with a marble bust of Athene on the top. In the corner between the bookcase and the wall there stood a tall green safe, the firelight flashing back from the polished brass knobs upon its face. Holmes stole across and looked at it. Then he crept to the door of the bedroom, and stood with slanting head listening intently. No sound came from within. Meanwhile it had struck me that it would be wise to secure our retreat through the outer door, so I examined it. To my amazement it was neither locked nor bolted! I touched Holmes on the arm, and he turned his masked face in that direction. I saw him start, and he was evidently as surprised as I.

"I don't like it," he whispered, putting his lips to my very ear. "I can't quite make it out. Anyhow, we have no time to lose."

"Can I do anything?"

"Yes; stand by the door. If you hear anyone come, bolt it on the inside, and we can get away as we came. If they come the other way, we can get through the door if our job is done, or hide behind these window curtains if it is not. Do you understand?"

I nodded and stood by the door. My first feeling of fear had passed away, and I thrilled now with a keener zest than I had ever enjoyed when we were the defenders of the law instead of its defiers. The high object of our mission, the consciousness that it was unselfish and chivalrous, the villainous character of our opponent, all added to the sporting interest of the adventure. Far from feeling guilty, I rejoiced and exulted in our dangers. With a glow of admiration I watched Holmes unrolling his case of instruments and choosing his tool with the calm, scientific accuracy of a surgeon who performs a delicate operation. I knew that the opening of safes was a particular hobby with him, and I understood the joy which it gave him to be

"HE STOOD WITH SLANTING HEAD LISTENING INTENTLY."

Holmes picked one out, but it was hard to read by the flickering fire, and he drew out his little dark lantern, for it was too dangerous, with Milverton in the next room, to switch on the electric light. Suddenly I saw him halt, listen intently, and then in an instant he had swung the door of the safe to, picked up his coat, stuffed his tools into the pockets, and darted behind the window curtain, motioning me to do the same.

It was only when I had joined him there that I heard what had alarmed his quicker senses. There was a noise somewhere within the house. A door slammed in the distance. Then a confused, dull murmur broke itself into the measured thud of heavy footsteps rapidly approaching. They were in the passage outside the room. They paused at the door. The door opened. There was a sharp snick as the electric light was turned on. The door closed once more, and the pungent reek of a strong cigar was borne to our nostrils. Then the footsteps continued backwards and forwards, backwards and forwards, within a few yards of us. Finally, there was a creak from a chair, and the footsteps ceased. Then a key clicked in a lock and I heard the rustle of papers.

confronted with this green and gold monster, the dragon which held in its maw the reputations of many fair ladies. Turning up the cuffs of his dress-coat—he had placed his overcoat on a chair—Holmes laid out two drills, a jemmy, and several skeleton keys. I stood at the centre door with my eyes glancing at each of the others, ready for any emergency ; though, indeed, my plans were somewhat vague as to what I should do if we were interrupted. For half an hour Holmes worked with concentrated energy, laying down one tool, picking up another, handling each with the strength and delicacy of the trained mechanic. Finally I heard a click, the broad green door swung open, and inside I had a glimpse of a number of paper packets, each tied, sealed, and inscribed.

So far I had not dared to look out, but now I gently parted the division of the curtains in front of me and peeped through. From the pressure of Holmes's shoulder against mine I knew that he was sharing my observations. Right in front of us, and almost within our reach, was the broad, rounded back of Milverton. It was evident that we had entirely miscalculated his movements, that he had never been to his bedroom, but that he had been sitting up in some smoking or billiard room in the farther wing of the house, the windows of which we had not seen. His broad, grizzled head, with its shining patch of baldness, was in the immediate foreground of our vision. He was leaning far back in the red leather chair, his legs outstretched, a long black cigar projecting at an angle from his mouth. He wore a semi-military smoking jacket, claret-coloured, with a black velvet collar. In his hand he held a long legal document, which he was reading in an indolent fashion, blowing rings of tobacco smoke from his lips as he did so. There was no promise of a speedy departure in his composed bearing and his comfortable attitude.

I felt Holmes's hand steal into mine and give me a reassuring shake, as if to say that the situation was within his powers and that he was easy in his mind. I was not sure whether he had seen what was only too obvious from my position, that the door of the safe was imperfectly closed, and that Milverton might at any moment observe it. In my own mind I had determined that if I were sure, from the rigidity of his gaze, that it had caught his eye, I would at once spring out, throw my great-coat over his head, pinion him, and leave the rest to Holmes. But Milverton never looked up. He was languidly interested by the papers in his hand, and page after page was turned as he followed the argument of the lawyer. At least, I thought, when he has finished the document and the cigar he will go to his room; but before he had reached the end of either there came a remarkable development which turned our thoughts into quite another channel.

Several times I had observed that Milverton looked at his watch, and once he had risen and sat down again, with a gesture of impatience. The idea, however, that he might have an appointment at so strange an hour never

occurred to me until a faint sound reached my ears from the veranda outside. Milverton dropped his papers and sat rigid in his chair. The sound was repeated, and then there came a gentle tap at the door. Milverton rose and opened it.

"Well," said he, curtly, "you are nearly half an hour late."

So this was the explanation of the unlocked door and of the nocturnal vigil of Milverton. There was the gentle rustle of a woman's dress. I had closed the slit between the curtains as Milverton's face had turned in our direction, but now I ventured very carefully to open it once more. He had resumed his seat, the cigar still projecting at an insolent angle from the corner of his mouth. In front of him, in the full glare of the electric light, there stood a tall, slim, dark woman, a veil over her face, a mantle drawn round her chin. Her breath came quick and fast, and every inch of the lithe figure was quivering with strong emotion.

"Well," said Milverton, "you've made me lose a good night's rest, my dear. I hope you'll prove worth it. You couldn't come any other time—eh?"

"YOU COULDN'T COME ANY OTHER TIME—EH?"

The woman shook her head.

"Well, if you couldn't you couldn't. If the Countess is a hard mistress you have your chance to get level with her now. Bless the girl, what are you shivering about? That's right! Pull yourself together! Now, let us get down to business." He took a note from the drawer of his desk. "You say that you have five letters which compromise the Countess d'Albert. You want to sell them. I want to buy them. So far so good. It only remains to fix a price. I should want to inspect the letters, of course. If they are really good specimens—— Great heavens, is it you?"

The woman without a word had raised her veil and dropped the mantle from her chin. It was a dark, handsome, clear-cut face which confronted Milverton, a face with a curved nose, strong, dark eyebrows shading hard, glittering eyes, and a straight, thin-lipped mouth set in a dangerous smile.

"It is I," she said; "the woman whose life you have ruined."

Milverton laughed, but fear vibrated in his voice. "You were so very obstinate," said he. "Why did you drive me to such extremities? I assure you I wouldn't hurt a fly of my own accord, but every man has his business, and what was I to do? I put the price well within your means. You would not pay."

"So you sent the letters to my husband, and he—the noblest gentleman that ever lived, a man whose boots I was never worthy to lace—he broke his gallant heart and died. You remember that last night when I came through that door I begged and prayed you for mercy, and you laughed in my face as you are trying to laugh now, only your coward heart cannot keep your lips from twitching? Yes, you never thought to see me here again, but it was that night which taught me how I could meet you face to face, and alone. Well, Charles Milverton, what have you to say?"

"Don't imagine that you can bully me," said he, rising to his feet. "I have only to raise my voice, and I could call my servants and have you arrested. But I will make allowance for your natural anger. Leave the room at once as you came, and I will say no more."

The woman stood with her hand buried in her bosom, and the same deadly smile on her thin lips.

"You will ruin no more lives as you ruined mine. You will wring no more hearts as you wrung mine. I will free the world of a poisonous thing. Take that, you hound, and that!—and that!—and that!—and that!"

She had drawn a little, gleaming revolver, and emptied barrel after barrel into Milverton's body, the muzzle within two feet of his shirt front. He shrank away and then fell forward upon the table, coughing furiously and clawing among the papers. Then he staggered to his feet, received another shot, and rolled upon the floor. "You've done me," he cried, and lay still. The woman looked at him intently and ground her heel into his upturned face. She looked again, but there was no sound or movement. I heard a sharp rustle, the night air blew into the heated room, and the avenger was gone.

No interference upon our part could have saved the man from his fate; but as the woman poured bullet after bullet into Milverton's shrinking body I was about to spring out, when I felt Holmes's cold, strong grasp upon my wrist. I understood the whole argument of that firm, restraining grip —that it was no affair of ours; that justice had overtaken a villain; that we had our own duties and our own objects which were not to be lost sight of. But hardly had the woman rushed from the room when Holmes, with swift, silent steps, was over at the other door. He turned the key in the lock. At the same instant we heard voices in the house and the sound of hurrying feet. The revolver shots had roused the household. With perfect coolness Holmes slipped across to the safe, filled his two arms with bundles of letters, and poured them all into the fire. Again and again he did it, until the safe was empty. Someone turned the handle and beat upon the outside of the door. Holmes looked swiftly round. The letter which had been the messenger of death for Milverton lay, all mottled with his blood, upon the table. Holmes tossed it in among the blazing papers. Then he drew the key from the outer door, passed through after me, and locked it on the outside. "This way, Watson," said he; "we can scale the garden wall in this direction."

I could not have believed that an alarm could have spread so swiftly. Looking back, the huge house was one blaze of light. The front door was open, and figures were rushing down the drive. The whole garden was alive with people, and one fellow raised a view-halloa as we emerged from the veranda and followed hard at our heels. Holmes seemed to know the ground perfectly, and he threaded his way swiftly among a plantation of small trees, I close at his heels, and our foremost pursuer panting behind us. It was a six-foot

"THEN HE STAGGERED TO HIS FEET AND RECEIVED ANOTHER SHOT."

wall which barred our path, but he sprang to the top and over. As I did the same I felt the hand of the man behind me grab at my ankle; but I kicked myself free and scrambled over a glass-strewn coping. I fell upon my face among some bushes; but Holmes had me on my feet in an instant, and together we dashed away across the huge expanse of Hampstead Heath. We had run two miles, I suppose, before Holmes at last halted and listened intently. All was absolute silence behind us. We had shaken off our pursuers and were safe.

We had breakfasted and were smoking our morning pipe on the day after the remarkable experience which I have recorded when Mr. Lestrade, of Scotland Yard, very solemn and impressive, was ushered into our modest sitting-room.

"Good morning, Mr. Holmes," said he; "good morning. May I ask if you are very busy just now?"

"Not too busy to listen to you."

"I thought that, perhaps, if you had nothing particular on hand, you might care to assist us in a most remarkable case which occurred only last night at Hampstead."

"Dear me!" said Holmes. "What was that?"

"A murder—a most dramatic and remarkable murder. I know how keen you are upon these things, and I would take it as a great favour if you would step down to Appledore Towers and give us the benefit of your advice. It is no ordinary crime. We have had our eyes upon this Mr. Milverton for some time, and, between ourselves, he was a bit of a villain. He is known to have held papers which he used for blackmailing purposes. These papers have all been burned by the murderers. No article of value was taken, as it is probable that the criminals were men of good position, whose sole object was to prevent social exposure."

"Criminals!" said Holmes. "Plural!"

"Yes, there were two of them. They were, as nearly as possible, captured red-handed. We have their foot-marks, we have their description; it's ten to one that we trace them. The first fellow was a bit too active, but the second was caught by the under-gardener and only got away after a struggle. He was a middle-sized, strongly-built man—square jaw, thick neck, moustache, a mask over his eyes."

"That's rather vague," said Sherlock Holmes. "Why, it might be a description of Watson!"

"It's true," said the inspector, with much amusement. "It might be a description of Watson."

"Well, I am afraid I can't help you, Lestrade," said Holmes. "The fact is that I knew this fellow Milverton, that I considered him one of the most dangerous men in London, and that I think there are certain crimes which the law cannot touch, and which therefore, to some extent, justify private revenge. No, it's no use arguing. I have made up my mind. My sympathies are with the criminals rather than with the victim, and I will not handle this case."

Holmes had not said one word to me about the tragedy which we had witnessed, but I observed all the morning that he was in his most thoughtful mood, and he gave me the impression, from his vacant eyes and his abstracted manner, of a man who is striving to recall something to his memory. We were in the middle of our lunch when he suddenly sprang to his feet. "By Jove, Watson; I've got it!" he cried. "Take your hat! Come with me!" He hurried at his top speed down Baker Street and along Oxford Street, until we had almost reached

Regent Circus. Here on the left hand there stands a shop window filled with photographs of the celebrities and beauties of the day. Holmes's eyes fixed themselves upon one of them, and following his gaze I saw the picture of a regal and stately lady in Court dress, with a high diamond tiara upon her noble head. I looked at that delicately-curved nose, at the marked eyebrows, at the straight mouth, and the strong little chin

"FOLLOWING HIS GAZE I SAW THE PICTURE OF A REGAL AND STATELY LADY IN COURT DRESS."

beneath it. Then I caught my breath as I read the time-honoured title of the great nobleman and statesman whose wife she had been. My eyes met those of Holmes, and he put his finger to his lips as we turned away from the window.

"WITH THE BOUND OF A TIGER HOLMES WAS ON HIS BACK."

# THE RETURN OF SHERLOCK HOLMES.

## By A. CONAN DOYLE.

### VIII.—The Adventure of the Six Napoleons.

IT was no very unusual thing for Mr. Lestrade, of Scotland Yard, to look in upon us of an evening, and his visits were welcome to Sherlock Holmes, for they enabled him to keep in touch with all that was going on at the police head-quarters. In return for the news which Lestrade would bring, Holmes was always ready to listen with attention to the details of any case upon which the detective was engaged, and was able occasionally, without any active interference, to give some hint or suggestion drawn from his own vast knowledge and experience.

On this particular evening Lestrade had spoken of the weather and the newspapers. Then he had fallen silent, puffing thoughtfully at his cigar. Holmes looked keenly at him.

"Anything remarkable on hand?" he asked.

"Oh, no, Mr. Holmes, nothing very particular."

"Then tell me about it."

Lestrade laughed.

"Well, Mr. Holmes, there is no use denying that there *is* something on my mind. And yet it is such an absurd business that I hesitated to bother you about it. On the other hand, although it is trivial, it is undoubtedly queer, and I know that you have a taste for all that is out of the common. But in my opinion it comes more in Dr. Watson's line than ours."

"Disease?" said I.

"Madness, anyhow. And a queer madness too! You wouldn't think there was anyone living at this time of day who had such a hatred of Napoleon the First that he would break any image of him that he could see."

Holmes sank back in his chair.

"That's no business of mine," said he.

"Exactly. That's what I said. But then, when the man commits burglary in order to break images which are not his own, that brings it away from the doctor and on to the policeman."

Holmes sat up again.

"Burglary! This is more interesting. Let me hear the details."

Lestrade took out his official note-book and refreshed his memory from its pages.

"The first case reported was four days ago," said he. "It was at the shop of Morse Hudson, who has a place for the sale of pictures and statues in the Kennington Road. The assistant had left the front shop for an instant when he heard a crash, and hurrying in he found a plaster bust of Napoleon, which stood with several other works of art upon the counter, lying shivered into fragments. He rushed out into the road, but, although several passers-by declared that they had noticed a man run out of the shop, he could neither see anyone nor could he find any means of identifying the rascal. It seemed to be one of those senseless acts of Hooliganism which occur from time to time, and it was reported to the constable on the beat as such. The plaster cast was not worth more than a few shillings, and the whole affair appeared to be too childish for any particular investigation.

"The second case, however, was more

"LESTRADE TOOK OUT HIS OFFICIAL NOTE-BOOK."

serious and also more singular. It occurred only last night.

"In Kennington Road, and within a few hundred yards of Morse Hudson's shop, there lives a well-known medical practitioner, named Dr. Barnicot, who has one of the largest practices upon the south side of the Thames. His residence and principal consulting-room is at Kennington Road, but he has a branch surgery and dispensary at Lower Brixton Road, two miles away. This Dr. Barnicot is an enthusiastic admirer of Napoleon, and his house is full of books, pictures, and relics of the French Emperor. Some little time ago he purchased from Morse Hudson two duplicate plaster casts of the famous head of Napoleon by the French sculptor, Devine. One of these he placed in his hall in the house at Kennington Road, and the other on the mantelpiece of the surgery at Lower Brixton. Well, when Dr. Barnicot came down this morning he was astonished to find that his house had been burgled during the night, but that nothing

had been taken save the plaster head from the hall. It had been carried out and had been dashed savagely against the garden wall, under which its splintered fragments were discovered."

Holmes rubbed his hands.

"This is certainly very novel," said he.

"I thought it would please you. But I have not got to the end yet. Dr. Barnicot was due at his surgery at twelve o'clock, and you can imagine his amazement when, on arriving there, he found that the window had been opened in the night, and that the broken pieces of his second bust were strewn all over the room. It had been smashed to atoms where it stood. In neither case were there any signs which could give us a clue as to the criminal or lunatic who had done the mischief. Now, Mr. Holmes, you have got the facts."

"They are singular, not to say grotesque," said Holmes. "May I ask whether the two busts smashed in Dr. Barnicot's rooms were the exact duplicates of the one which was destroyed in Morse Hudson's shop?"

"They were taken from the same mould."

"Such a fact must tell against the theory that the man who breaks them is influenced by any general hatred of Napoleon. Considering how many hundreds of statues of the great Emperor must exist in London, it is too much to suppose such a coincidence as that a promiscuous iconoclast should chance to begin upon three specimens of the same bust."

"Well, I thought as you do," said Lestrade. "On the other hand, this Morse Hudson is the purveyor of busts in that part of London, and these three were the only ones which had been in his shop for years. So, although, as you say, there are many hundreds of statues in London, it is very probable that these three were the only ones in that district. Therefore, a local fanatic would begin with them. What do you think, Dr. Watson?"

"There are no limits to the possibilities of monomania," I answered. "There is the condition which the modern French psychologists have called the 'idée fixe,' which may be trifling in character, and accompanied by complete sanity in every other way. A man who had read deeply about Napoleon, or who had possibly received some hereditary family injury through the great war, might conceivably form such an 'idée fixe' and under its influence be capable of any fantastic outrage."

"That won't do, my dear Watson," said Holmes, shaking his head; "for no amount of 'idée fixe' would enable your interesting monomaniac to find out where these busts were situated."

"Well, how do *you* explain it?"

"I don't attempt to do so. I would only observe that there is a certain method in the gentleman's eccentric proceedings. For example, in Dr. Barnicot's hall, where a sound might arouse the family, the bust was taken outside before being broken, whereas in the surgery, where there was less danger of an alarm, it was smashed where it stood. The affair seems absurdly trifling, and yet I dare call nothing trivial when I reflect that some of my most classic cases have had the least promising commencement. You will remember, Watson, how the dreadful business of the Abernetty family was first brought to my notice by the depth which the parsley had sunk into the butter upon a hot day. I can't afford, therefore, to smile at your three broken busts, Lestrade, and I shall be very much obliged to you if you will let me hear

of any fresh developments of so singular a chain of events."

The development for which my friend had asked came in a quicker and an infinitely more tragic form than he could have imagined. I was still dressing in my bedroom next morning when there was a tap at the door and Holmes entered, a telegram in his hand. He read it aloud:—

"Come instantly, 131, Pitt Street, Kensington.—Lestrade."

"What is it, then?" I asked.

"Don't know—may be anything. But I suspect it is the sequel of the story of the statues. In that case our friend, the image-breaker, has begun operations in another quarter of London. There's coffee on the table, Watson, and I have a cab at the door."

In half an hour we had reached Pitt Street, a quiet little backwater just beside one of the briskest currents of London life. No. 131 was one of a row, all flat-chested, respectable, and most unromantic dwellings. As we drove up we found the railings in front of the house lined by a curious crowd. Holmes whistled.

"By George! it's attempted murder at the least. Nothing less will hold the London message-boy. There's a deed of violence indicated in that fellow's round shoulders and outstretched neck. What's this, Watson? The top steps swilled down and the other ones dry. Footsteps enough, anyhow! Well, well, there's Lestrade at the front window, and we shall soon know all about it."

The official received us with a very grave face and showed us into a sitting-room, where an exceedingly unkempt and agitated elderly man, clad in a flannel dressing-gown, was pacing up and down. He was introduced to us as the owner of the house—Mr. Horace Harker, of the Central Press Syndicate.

"It's the Napoleon bust business again," said Lestrade. "You seemed interested last night, Mr. Holmes, so I thought perhaps you would be glad to be present now that the affair has taken a very much graver turn."

"What has it turned to, then?"

"To murder. Mr. Harker, will you tell these gentlemen exactly what has occurred?"

The man in the dressing-gown turned upon us with a most melancholy face.

"It's an extraordinary thing," said he, "that all my life I have been collecting other people's news, and now that a real piece of news has come my own way I am so confused and bothered that I can't put two

words together. If I had come in here as a
journalist I should have interviewed myself
and had two columns in every evening paper.
As it is I am giving away valuable copy by
telling my story over and over to a string of

came from outside. Then suddenly, about
five minutes later, there came a most horrible
yell—the most dreadful sound, Mr. Holmes,
that ever I heard. It will ring in my ears
as long as I live. I sat frozen with horror for

"HE WAS INTRODUCED TO US AS THE OWNER OF THE HOUSE—MR. HORACE HARKER."

different people, and I can make no use of it
myself. However, I've heard your name,
Mr. Sherlock Holmes, and if you'll only
explain this queer business I shall be paid for
my trouble in telling you the story."

Holmes sat down and listened.

"It all seems to centre round that bust of
Napoleon which I bought for this very room
about four months ago. I picked it up cheap
from Harding Brothers, two doors from the
High Street Station. A great deal of my
journalistic work is done at night, and I often
write until the early morning. So it was to-
day. I was sitting in my den, which is at the
back of the top of the house, about three
o'clock, when I was convinced that I heard
some sounds downstairs. I listened, but they
were not repeated, and I concluded that they

a minute or two. Then I seized the poker
and went downstairs. When I entered this
room I found the window wide open, and I
at once observed that the bust was gone from
the mantelpiece. Why any burglar should
take such a thing passes my understanding,
for it was only a plaster cast and of no real
value whatever.

"You can see for yourself that anyone
going out through that open window could
reach the front doorstep by taking a long
stride. This was clearly what the burglar
had done, so I went round and opened the
door. Stepping out into the dark I nearly
fell over a dead man who was lying there. I
ran back for a light, and there was the poor
fellow, a great gash in his throat and the
whole place swimming in blood. He lay on

his back, his knees drawn up, and his mouth horribly open. I shall see him in my dreams. I had just time to blow on my police-whistle, and then I must have fainted, for I knew nothing more until I found the policeman standing over me in the hall."

"Well, who was the murdered man?" asked Holmes.

"There's nothing to show who he was," said Lestrade. "You shall see the body at the mortuary, but we have made nothing of it up to now. He is a tall man, sunburned, very powerful, not more than thirty. He is poorly dressed, and yet does not appear to be a labourer. A horn-handled clasp knife was lying in a pool of blood beside him. Whether it was the weapon which did the deed, or whether it belonged to the dead man, I do not know. There was no name on his clothing, and nothing in his pockets save an apple, some string, a shilling map of London, and a photograph. Here it is."

It was evidently taken by a snap-shot from a small camera. It represented an alert, sharp-featured simian man with thick eyebrows, and a very peculiar projection of the lower part of the face like the muzzle of a baboon.

"And what became of the bust?" asked Holmes, after a careful study of this picture.

"We had news of it just before you came. It has been found in the front garden of an empty house in Campden House Road. It was broken into fragments. I am going round now to see it. Will you come?"

"Certainly. I must just take one look round." He examined the carpet and the window. "The fellow had either very long legs or was a most active man," said he. "With an area beneath, it was no mean feat to reach that window-ledge and open that window. Getting back was comparatively simple. Are you coming with us to see the remains of your bust, Mr. Harker?"

The disconsolate journalist had seated himself at a writing-table.

"I must try and make something of it," said he, "though I have no doubt that the first editions of the evening papers are out already with full details. It's like my luck! You remember when the stand fell at Doncaster? Well, I was the only journalist in the stand, and my journal the only one that had no account of it, for I was too shaken to write it. And now I'll be too late with a murder done on my own doorstep."

As we left the room we heard his pen travelling shrilly over the foolscap.

The spot where the fragments of the bust had been found was only a few hundred yards away. For the first time our eyes rested upon this presentment of the great Emperor, which seemed to raise such frantic and destructive hatred in the mind of the unknown. It lay scattered in splintered shards upon the grass. Holmes picked up several of them and examined them carefully. I was convinced from his intent face and his purposeful manner that at last he was upon a clue.

"Well?" asked Lestrade.

Holmes shrugged his shoulders.

"We have a long way to go yet," said he. "And yet—and yet—well, we have some suggestive facts to act upon. The possession of this trifling bust was worth more in the eyes of this strange criminal than a human life. That is one point. Then there is the singular fact that he did not break it in the house, or immediately outside the house, if to break it was his sole object."

"He was rattled and bustled by meeting this other fellow. He hardly knew what he was doing."

"Well, that's likely enough. But I wish to call your attention very particularly to the position of this house in the garden of which the bust was destroyed."

Lestrade looked about him.

"It was an empty house, and so he knew that he would not be disturbed in the garden."

"Yes, but there is another empty house farther up the street which he must have passed before he came to this one. Why did he not break it there, since it is evident that every yard that he carried it increased the risk of someone meeting him?"

"I give it up," said Lestrade.

Holmes pointed to the street lamp above our heads.

"He could see what he was doing here and he could not there. That was his reason."

"By Jove! that's true," said the detective. "Now that I come to think of it, Dr. Barnicot's bust was broken not far from his red lamp. Well, Mr. Holmes, what are we to do with that fact?"

"To remember it—to docket it. We may come on something later which will bear upon it. What steps do you propose to take now, Lestrade?"

"The most practical way of getting at it, in my opinion, is to identify the dead man. There should be no difficulty about that. When we have found who he is and who his associates are, we should have a good start in learning what he was doing in Pitt Street

"HOLMES POINTED TO THE STREET LAMP ABOVE OUR HEADS."

Lestrade stared.

"You don't seriously believe that?"

Holmes smiled.

"Don't I? Well, perhaps I don't. But I am sure that it will interest Mr. Horace Harker and the subscribers of the Central Press Syndicate. Now, Watson, I think that we shall find that we have a long and rather complex day's work before us. I should be glad, Lestrade, if you could make it convenient to meet us at Baker Street at six o'clock this evening. Until then I should like to keep this photograph found in the dead man's pocket. It is possible that I may have to ask your company and assistance upon a small expedition which will have to be undertaken to-night, if my chain of reasoning should prove to be correct. Until then, good-bye and good luck!"

Sherlock Holmes and I walked together to the High Street, where he stopped at the shop of Harding Brothers, whence the bust had been purchased. A young assistant informed us that Mr. Harding would be absent until after noon, and that he was himself a new-comer who could give us no information. Holmes's face showed his disappointment and annoyance.

"Well, well, we can't expect to have it all our own way, Watson," he said, at last. "We must come back in the afternoon if Mr. Harding will not be here until then. I am, as you have no doubt surmised, endeavouring to trace these busts to their source, in order to find if there is not something peculiar which may account for their remarkable fate. Let us make for Mr. Morse Hudson, of the Kennington Road, and see if he can throw any light upon the problem."

A drive of an hour brought us to the picture-dealer's establishment. He was a small, stout man with a red face and a peppery manner.

"Yes, sir. On my very counter, sir," said he. "What we pay rates and taxes for I don't know, when any ruffian can come in and break one's goods. Yes, sir, it was I

last night, and who it was who met him and killed him on the doorstep of Mr. Horace Harker. Don't you think so?"

"No doubt; and yet it is not quite the way in which I should approach the case."

"What would you do, then?"

"Oh, you must not let me influence you in any way! I suggest that you go on your line and I on mine. We can compare notes afterwards, and each will supplement the other."

"Very good," said Lestrade.

"If you are going back to Pitt Street you might see Mr. Horace Harker. Tell him from me that I have quite made up my mind, and that it is certain that a dangerous homicidal lunatic with Napoleonic delusions was in his house last night. It will be useful for his article."

who sold Dr. Barnicot his two statues. Disgraceful, sir! A Nihilist plot, that's what I make it. No one but an Anarchist would go about breaking statues. Red republicans, that's what I call 'em. Who did I get the statues from? I don't see what that has to do with it. Well, if you really want to know, I got them from Gelder and Co., in Church Street, Stepney. They are a well-known house in the trade, and have been this twenty years. How many had I? Three—two and one are three—two of Dr. Barnicot's and one smashed in broad daylight on my own counter. Do I know that photograph? No, I don't. Yes, I do, though. Why, it's Beppo. He was a kind of Italian piece-work man, who made himself useful in the shop. He could carve a bit and gild and frame, and do odd jobs. The fellow left me last week, and I've heard nothing of him since. No, I don't know where he came from nor where he went to. I have nothing against him while he was here. He was gone two days before the bust was smashed."

"Well, that's all we could reasonably expect to get from Morse Hudson,' said Holmes, as we emerged from the shop. " We have this Beppo as a common factor, both in Kennington and in Kensington, so that is worth a ten-mile drive. Now, Watson, let us make for Gelder and Co., of Stepney, the source and origin of busts. I shall be surprised if we don't get some help down there."

In rapid succession we passed through the fringe of fashionable London, hotel London, theatrical London, literary London, commercial London, and, finally, maritime London, till we came to a riverside city of a hundred thousand souls, where the tenement houses swelter and reek with the outcasts of Europe. Here, in a broad thoroughfare, once the abode of wealthy City merchants, we found the sculpture works for which we searched. Outside was a considerable yard full of monumental masonry. Inside was a large room in which fifty workers were carving or moulding. The manager, a big blonde German, received us civilly, and gave a clear answer to all Holmes's questions. A reference to his books showed that hundreds of casts had been taken from a marble copy of Devine's head of Napoleon, but that the three which had been sent to Morse Hudson a year or so before had been half of a batch of six, the other three being sent to Harding Brothers, of Kensington. There was no reason why those six should be different to any of the other casts. He could suggest no possible cause why anyone should wish

to destroy them—in fact, he laughed at the idea. Their wholesale price was six shillings, but the retailer would get twelve or more. The cast was taken in two moulds from each side of the face, and then these two profiles of plaster of Paris were joined together to make the complete bust. The work was usually done by Italians in the room we were in. When finished the busts were put on a table in the passage to dry, and afterwards stored. That was all he could tell us.

But the production of the photograph had a remarkable effect upon the manager. His face flushed with anger, and his brows knotted over his blue Teutonic eyes.

"Ah, the rascal!" he cried. "Yes, indeed, I know him very well. This has always been a respectable establishment, and the only time that we have ever had the police in it was over this very fellow. It was more than a year ago now. He knifed another Italian in the street, and then he came to the works with the police on his heels, and he was taken here. Beppo was his name—his second name I never knew. Serve me right for engaging a man with such a face. But he was a good workman, one of the best.''

"What did he get?"

"The man lived and he got off with a year. I have no doubt he is out now; but he has not dared to show his nose here. We have a cousin of his here, and I dare say he could tell you where he is."

"No, no," cried Holmes, "not a word to the cousin—not a word, I beg you. The matter is very important, and the farther I go with it the more important it seems to grow. When you referred in your ledger to the sale of those casts I observed that the date was June 3rd of last year. Could you give me the date when Beppo was arrested?"

"I could tell you roughly by the pay-list," the manager answered. "Yes," he continued, after some turning over of pages, "he was paid last on May 20th."

"Thank you," said Holmes. "I don't think that I need intrude upon your time and patience any more." With a last word of caution that he should say nothing as to our researches we turned our faces westward once more.

The afternoon was far advanced before we were able to snatch a hasty luncheon at a restaurant. A news-bill at the entrance announced "Kensington Outrage. Murder by a Madman," and the contents of the paper showed that Mr. Horace Harker had got his account into print after all. Two columns

"'AH, THE RASCAL!' HE CRIED."

were occupied with a highly sensational and flowery rendering of the whole incident. Holmes propped it against the cruet-stand and read it while he ate. Once or twice he chuckled.

"This is all right, Watson," said he. "Listen to this: 'It is satisfactory to know that there can be no difference of opinion upon this case, since Mr. Lestrade, one of the most experienced members of the official force, and Mr. Sherlock Holmes, the well-known consulting expert, have each come to the conclusion that the grotesque series of incidents, which have ended in so tragic a fashion, arise from lunacy rather than from deliberate crime. No explanation save mental aberration can cover the facts.' The Press, Watson, is a most valuable institution if you only know how to use it. And now, if you have quite finished, we will hark back to Kensington and see what the manager of Harding Brothers has to say to the matter."

The founder of that great emporium proved to be a brisk, crisp little person, very dapper and quick, with a clear head and a ready tongue.

"Yes, sir, I have already read the account in the evening papers. Mr. Horace Harker is a customer of ours. We supplied him with the bust some months ago. We ordered three busts of that sort from Gelder and Co., of Stepney. They are all sold now. To whom? Oh, I dare say by consulting our sales book we could very easily tell you. Yes, we have the entries here. One to Mr. Harker, you see, and one to Mr. Josiah Brown, of Laburnum Lodge, Laburnum Vale, Chiswick, and one to Mr. Sandeford, of Lower Grove Road, Reading. No, I have never seen this face which you show me in the photograph. You would hardly forget it, would you, sir, for I've seldom seen an uglier. Have we any Italians on the staff? Yes, sir, we have several among our workpeople and cleaners. I dare say they might get a peep at that sales book if they wanted to. There is no particular reason for keeping a watch upon that book. Well, well, it's a very strange business, and I hope that you'll let me know if anything comes of your inquiries."

Holmes had taken several notes during Mr. Harding's evidence, and I could see that he was thoroughly satisfied by the turn which affairs were taking. He made no remark, however, save that, unless we hurried, we should be late for our appointment with Lestrade. Sure enough, when we reached Baker Street the detective was already there, and we found him pacing up and down in a fever of impatience. His look of importance showed that his day's work had not been in vain.

"Well?" he asked. "What luck, Mr. Holmes?"

"We have had a very busy day, and not entirely a wasted one," my friend explained. "We have seen both the retailers and also the wholesale manufacturers. I can trace each of the busts now from the beginning."

"The busts!" cried Lestrade. "Well, well, you have your own methods, Mr. Sherlock Holmes, and it is not for me to say a word against them, but I think I have done a better day's work than you. I have identified the dead man."

"You don't say so?"

"And found a cause for the crime."

"Splendid!"

"We have an inspector who makes a speciality of Saffron Hill and the Italian quarter. Well, this dead man had some Catholic emblem round his neck, and that, along with his colour, made me think he was from the South. Inspector Hill knew him the moment he caught sight of him. His name is Pietro Venucci, from Naples, and he is one of the greatest cut-throats in London. He is connected with the Mafia, which, as you know, is a secret political society, enforcing its decrees by murder. Now you see how the affair begins to clear up. The other fellow is probably an Italian also, and a member of the Mafia. He has broken the rules in some fashion. Pietro is set upon his track. Probably the photograph we found in his pocket is the man himself, so that he may not knife the wrong person. He dogs the fellow, he sees him enter a house, he waits outside for him, and in the scuffle he receives his own death-wound. How is that, Mr. Sherlock Holmes?"

Holmes clapped his hands approvingly.

"Excellent, Lestrade, excellent!" he cried. "But I didn't quite follow your explanation of the destruction of the busts."

"The busts! You never can get those busts out of your head. After all, that is nothing; petty larceny, six months at the most. It is the murder that we are really investigating, and I tell you that I am gathering all the threads into my hands."

"And the next stage?"

"Is a very simple one. I shall go down with Hill to the Italian quarter, find the man whose photograph we have got, and arrest him on the charge of murder. Will you come with us?"

"I think not. I fancy we can attain our end in a simpler way. I can't say for certain, because it all depends—well, it all depends upon a factor which is completely outside our control. But I have great hopes—in fact, the betting is exactly two to one—that if you will come with us to-night I shall be able to help you to lay him by the heels."

"In the Italian quarter?"

"No; I fancy Chiswick is an address which is more likely to find him. If you will come with me to Chiswick to-night, Lestrade, I'll promise to go to the Italian quarter with you to-morrow, and no harm will be done by the delay. And now I think that a few hours' sleep would do us all good, for I do not propose to leave before eleven o'clock, and it is unlikely that we shall be back before morning. You'll dine with us, Lestrade, and then you are welcome to the sofa until it is time for us to start. In the meantime, Watson, I should be glad if you would ring for an express messenger, for I have a letter to send, and it is important that it should go at once."

Holmes spent the evening in rummaging among the files of the old daily papers with which one of our lumber-rooms was packed. When at last he descended it was with triumph in his eyes, but he said nothing to either of us as to the result of his researches. For my own part, I had followed step by step the methods by which he had traced the various windings of this complex case, and, though I could not yet perceive the goal which we would reach, I understood clearly that Holmes expected this grotesque criminal to make an attempt upon the two remaining busts, one of which, I remembered, was at Chiswick. No doubt the object of our journey was to catch him in the very act, and I could not but admire the cunning with which my friend had inserted a wrong clue in the evening paper, so as to give the fellow the idea that he could continue his scheme with impunity. I was not surprised when Holmes suggested that I should take my revolver with me. He had himself picked up the loaded hunting-crop which was his favourite weapon.

A four-wheeler was at the door at eleven, and in it we drove to a spot at the other side of Hammersmith Bridge. Here the cabman was directed to wait. A short walk brought us to a secluded road fringed with pleasant houses, each standing in its own grounds. In the light of a street lamp we read "Laburnum Villa" upon the gate-post of one of them. The occupants had evidently retired to rest, for all was dark save for a fanlight over the hall door, which shed a single blurred circle on to the garden path. The wooden fence which separated the grounds from the road threw a dense black shadow upon the inner side, and here it was that we crouched.

"I fear that you'll have a long wait," Holmes whispered. "We may thank our stars that it is not raining. I don't think we can even venture to smoke to pass the time. However, it's a two to one chance that we get something to pay us for our trouble."

It proved, however, that our vigil was not to be so long as Holmes had led us to fear, and it ended in a very sudden and singular fashion. In an instant, without the least sound to warn us of his coming, the garden gate swung open, and a lithe, dark figure, as swift and active as an ape, rushed up the garden path. We saw it whisk

"THE DOOR OPENED, AND THE OWNER OF THE HOUSE PRESENTED HIMSELF."

past the light thrown from over the door and disappear against the black shadow of the house. There was a long pause, during which we held our breath, and then a very gentle creaking sound came to our ears. The window was being opened. The noise ceased, and again there was a long silence.

The fellow was making his way into the house. We saw the sudden flash of a dark lantern inside the room. What he sought was evidently not there, for again we saw the flash through another blind, and then through another.

"Let us get to the open window. We will nab him as he climbs out," Lestrade whispered.

But before we could move the man had emerged again. As he came out into the glimmering patch of light we saw that he carried something white under his arm. He looked stealthily all round him. The silence of the deserted street reassured him. Turning his back upon us he laid down his burden, and the next instant there was the sound of a sharp tap, followed by a clatter and rattle. The man was so intent upon what he was doing that he never heard our steps as we stole across the grass plot. With the bound of a tiger Holmes was on his back, and an instant later Lestrade and I had him by either wrist and the handcuffs had been fastened. As we turned him over I saw a hideous, sallow face, with writhing, furious features, glaring up at us, and I knew that it was indeed the man of the photograph whom we had secured.

But it was not our prisoner to whom Holmes was giving his attention. Squatted on the doorstep, he was engaged in most carefully examining that which the man had brought from the house. It was a bust of

Napoleon like the one which we had seen that morning, and it had been broken into similar fragments. Carefully Holmes held each separate shard to the light, but in no way did it differ from any other shattered piece of plaster. He had just completed his examination when the hall lights flew up, the door opened, and the owner of the house, a jovial, rotund figure in shirt and trousers, presented himself.

"Mr. Josiah Brown, I suppose?" said Holmes.

"Yes, sir; and you, no doubt, are Mr. Sherlock Holmes? I had the note which you sent by the express messenger, and I did exactly what you told me. We locked every door on the inside and awaited developments. Well, I'm very glad to see that you have got the rascal. I hope, gentlemen, that you will come in and have some refreshment."

However, Lestrade was anxious to get his man into safe quarters, so within a few minutes our cab had been summoned and we were all four upon our way to London. Not a word would our captive say; but he glared at us from the shadow of his matted hair, and once, when my hand seemed within his reach, he snapped at it like a hungry wolf. We stayed long enough at the police-station to learn that a search of his clothing revealed nothing save a few shillings and a long sheath knife, the handle of which bore copious traces of recent blood.

"That's all right," said Lestrade, as we parted. "Hill knows all these gentry, and he will give a name to him. You'll find that my theory of the Mafia will work out all right. But I'm sure I am exceedingly obliged to you, Mr. Holmes, for the workmanlike way in which you laid hands upon him. I don't quite understand it all yet."

"I fear it is rather too late an hour for explanations," said Holmes. "Besides, there are one or two details which are not finished off, and it is one of those cases which are worth working out to the very end. If you will come round once more to my rooms at six o'clock to-morrow I think I shall be able to show you that even now you have not grasped the entire meaning of this business, which presents some features which make it absolutely original in the history of crime. If ever I permit you to chronicle any more of my little problems, Watson, I foresee that you will enliven your pages by an account of the singular adventure of the Napoleonic busts."

When we met again next evening Lestrade was furnished with much information concerning our prisoner. His name, it appeared, was Beppo, second name unknown. He was a well-known ne'er-do-well among the Italian colony. He had once been a skilful sculptor and had earned an honest living, but he had taken to evil courses and had twice already been in gaol—once for a petty theft and once, as we had already heard, for stabbing a fellow-countryman. He could talk English perfectly well. His reasons for destroying the busts were still unknown, and he refused to answer any questions upon the subject; but the police had discovered that these same busts might very well have been made by his own hands, since he was engaged in this class of work at the establishment of Gelder and Co. To all this information, much of which we already knew, Holmes listened with polite attention; but I, who knew him so well, could clearly see that his thoughts were elsewhere, and I detected a mixture of mingled uneasiness and expectation beneath that mask which he was wont to assume. At last he started in his chair and his eyes brightened. There had been a ring at the bell. A minute later we heard steps upon the stairs, and an elderly, red-faced man with grizzled side-whiskers was ushered in. In his right hand he carried an old-fashioned carpet-bag, which he placed upon the table.

"Is Mr. Sherlock Holmes here?"

My friend bowed and smiled. "Mr. Sandeford, of Reading, I suppose?" said he.

"Yes, sir, I fear that I am a little late; but the trains were awkward. You wrote to me about a bust that is in my possession."

"Exactly."

"I have your letter here. You said, 'I desire to possess a copy of Devine's Napoleon, and am prepared to pay you ten pounds for the one which is in your possession.' Is that right?"

"Certainly."

"I was very much surprised at your letter, for I could not imagine how you knew that I owned such a thing."

"Of course you must have been surprised, but the explanation is very simple. Mr. Harding, of Harding Brothers, said that they had sold you their last copy, and he gave me your address."

"Oh, that was it, was it? Did he tell you what I paid for it?"

"No, he did not."

"Well, I am an honest man, though not a very rich one. I only gave fifteen shillings for the bust, and I think you ought to know that before I take ten pounds from you."

"I am sure the scruple does you honour, Mr. Sandeford. But I have named that price, so I intend to stick to it."

"Well, it is very handsome of you, Mr. Holmes. I brought the bust up with me, as you asked me to do. Here it is!" He

"I BROUGHT THE BUST UP WITH ME, AS YOU ASKED ME TO DO."

opened his bag, and at last we saw placed upon our table a complete specimen of that bust which we had already seen more than once in fragments.

Holmes took a paper from his pocket and laid a ten-pound note upon the table.

"You will kindly sign that paper, Mr. Sandeford, in the presence of these witnesses. It is simply to say that you transfer every possible right that you ever had in the bust to me. I am a methodical man, you see, and you never know what turn events might take afterwards. Thank you, Mr. Sandeford; here is your money, and I wish you a very good evening."

When our visitor had disappeared Sherlock Holmes's movements were such as to rivet our attention. He began by taking a clean white cloth from a drawer and laying it over the table. Then he placed his newly-acquired bust in the centre of the cloth.

Finally, he picked up his hunting-crop and struck Napoleon a sharp blow on the top of the head. The figure broke into fragments, and Holmes bent eagerly over the shattered remains. Next instant, with a loud shout of triumph, he held up one splinter, in which a round, dark object was fixed like a plum in a pudding.

"Gentlemen," he cried, "let me introduce you to the famous black pearl of the Borgias."

Lestrade and I sat silent for a moment, and then, with a spontaneous impulse, we both broke out clapping as at the well-wrought crisis of a play. A flush of colour sprang to Holmes's pale cheeks, and he bowed to us like the master dramatist who receives the homage of his audience. It was at such moments that for an instant he ceased to be a reasoning machine, and betrayed his human love for admiration and applause. The same singularly proud and reserved nature which turned away with disdain from popular notoriety was capable of being moved to its depths by spontaneous wonder and praise from a friend.

"Yes, gentlemen," said he, "it is the most famous pearl now existing in the world, and it has been my good fortune, by a connected chain of inductive reasoning, to trace it from the Prince of Colonna's bedroom at the Dacre Hotel, where it was lost, to the interior of this, the last of the six busts of Napoleon which were manufactured by Gelder and Co., of Stepney. You will remember, Lestrade, the sensation caused by the disappearance of this valuable jewel, and the vain efforts of the London police to recover it. I was myself consulted upon the case; but I was unable to throw any light upon it. Suspicion fell upon the maid of the Princess, who was an Italian, and it was proved that she had a brother in London, but we failed to trace any connection between them. The maid's name was Lucretia Venucci, and there is no doubt in my mind that this Pietro who was murdered two nights ago was the brother. I have been looking up the dates in the old files of the paper, and I find that the disappearance of the pearl was exactly two days before the arrest of Beppo for some crime of violence, an event which took place in the factory of Gelder and Co., at the very moment when these busts were being made. Now you clearly see the sequence of events, though you see them, of course, in the inverse order to the way in which they presented themselves to me. Beppo had the pearl in his possession. He may have stolen it from Pietro, he may have been Pietro's confederate, he may have been the go-between of Pietro and his sister. It is of no consequence to us which is the correct solution. "The main fact is that he *had* the pearl, and at that moment, when it was on his person, he was pursued by the police. He made for the factory in which he worked, and he knew that he had only a few minutes in which to conceal this enormously valuable prize, which would otherwise be found on him when he was searched. Six plaster casts of Napoleon were drying in the passage. One of them was still soft. In an instant Beppo, a skilful workman, made a small hole in the wet plaster, dropped in the pearl, and with a few touches covered over the aperture once more. It was an admirable hiding-place. No one could possibly find it. But Beppo was condemned to a year's imprisonment, and in the meanwhile his six busts were scattered over London. He could not tell which contained his treasure. Only by breaking them could he see. Even shaking would tell him nothing, for as the plaster was wet it was probable that the pearl would adhere to it—as, in fact, it has done. Beppo did not despair, and he conducted his search with considerable ingenuity and perseverance. Through a cousin who works with Gelder he found out the retail firms who had bought the busts. He managed to find employment with Morse Hudson, and in that way tracked down three of them. The pearl was not there. Then, with the help of some Italian *employé*, he succeeded in finding out where the other three busts had gone. The first was at Harker's. There he was dogged by his confederate, who held Beppo

responsible for the loss of the pearl, and he stabbed him in the scuffle which followed."

"If he was his confederate why should he carry his photograph?" I asked.

"As a means of tracing him if he wished to inquire about him from any third person. That was the obvious reason. Well, after the murder I calculated that Beppo would probably hurry rather than delay his movements. He would fear that the police would read his secret, and so he hastened on before they should get ahead of him. Of course, I could not say that he had not found the pearl in Harker's bust. I had not even concluded for certain that it was the pearl; but it was evident to me that he was looking for something, since he carried the bust past the other houses in order to break it in the garden which had a lamp overlooking it. Since Harker's bust was one in three the chances were exactly as I told you, two to one against the pearl being inside it. There remained two busts, and it was obvious that he would go for the London one first. I warned the inmates of the house, so as to avoid a second tragedy, and we went down with the happiest results. By that time, of course, I knew for certain that it was the Borgia pearl that we were after. The name of the murdered man linked the one event with the other. There only remained a single bust—the Reading one—and the pearl must be there. I bought it in your presence from the owner—and there it lies."

We sat in silence for a moment.

"Well," said Lestrade, "I've seen you handle a good many cases, Mr. Holmes, but I don't know that I ever knew a more workmanlike one than that. We're not jealous of you at Scotland Yard. No, sir, we are very proud of you, and if you come down to-morrow there's not a man, from the oldest inspector to the youngest constable, who wouldn't be glad to shake you by the hand."

"Thank you!" said Holmes. "Thank you!" and as he turned away it seemed to me that he was more nearly moved by the softer human emotions than I had ever seen him. A moment later he was the cold and practical thinker once more. "Put the pearl in the safe, Watson," said he, "and get out the papers of the Conk-Singleton forgery case. Good-bye, Lestrade. If any little problem comes your way I shall be happy, if I can, to give you a hint or two as to its solution."

"'COME, COME,' SAID HOLMES, KINDLY, 'IT IS HUMAN TO ERR.'"

# THE RETURN OF SHERLOCK HOLMES.

## By A. CONAN DOYLE.

### IX.—The Adventure of the Three Students.

IT was in the year '95 that a combination of events, into which I need not enter, caused Mr. Sherlock Holmes and myself to spend some weeks in one of our great University towns, and it was during this time that the small but instructive adventure which I am about to relate befell us. It will be obvious that any details which would help the reader to exactly identify the college or the criminal would be injudicious and offensive. So painful a scandal may well be allowed to die out. With due discretion the incident itself may, however, be described, since it serves to illustrate some of those qualities for which my friend was remarkable. I will endeavour in my statement to avoid such terms as would serve to limit the events to any particular place, or give a clue as to the people concerned.

We were residing at the time in furnished lodgings close to a library where Sherlock Holmes was pursuing some laborious researches in early English charters — researches which led to results so striking that they may be the subject of one of my future narratives. Here it was that one evening we received a visit from an acquaintance, Mr. Hilton Soames, tutor and lecturer at the College of St. Luke's. Mr. Soames was a tall, spare man, of a nervous and excitable temperament. I had always known him to be restless in his manner, but on this particular occasion he was in such a state of uncontrollable agitation that it was clear something very unusual had occurred.

"I trust, Mr. Holmes, that you can spare me a few hours of your valuable time. We have had a very painful incident at St. Luke's, and really, but for the happy chance of your being in the town, I should have been at a loss what to do."

"I am very busy just now, and I desire no distractions," my friend answered. "I should much prefer that you called in the aid of the police."

"No, no, my dear sir; such a course is utterly impossible. When once the law is evoked it cannot be stayed again, and this is just one of those cases where, for the credit of the college, it is most essential to avoid scandal. Your discretion is as well known as your powers, and you are the one man in the world who can help me. I beg you, Mr. Holmes, to do what you can."

My friend's temper had not improved since he had been deprived of the congenial surroundings of Baker Street. Without his scrap-books, his chemicals, and his homely untidiness, he was an uncomfortable man. He shrugged his shoulders in ungracious acquiescence, while our visitor in hurried words and with much excitable gesticulation poured forth his story.

"I must explain to you, Mr. Holmes, that to-morrow is the first day of the examination for the Fortescue Scholarship. I am one of the examiners. My subject is Greek, and the first of the papers consists of a large passage of Greek translation which the candidate has not seen. This passage is printed on the examination paper, and it would naturally be an immense advantage if the candidate could prepare it in advance. For this reason great care is taken to keep the paper secret.

"To-day about three o'clock the proofs of this paper arrived from the printers. The exercise consists of half a chapter of Thucydides. I had to read it over carefully, as the text must be absolutely correct. At four-thirty my task was not yet completed. I had, however, promised to take tea in a friend's rooms, so I left the proof upon my desk. I was absent rather more than an hour.

"You are aware, Mr. Holmes, that our college doors are double—a green baize one within and a heavy oak one without. As I approached my outer door I was amazed to see a key in it. For an instant I imagined that I had left my own there, but on feeling in my pocket I found that it was all right. The only duplicate which existed, so far as I knew, was that which belonged to my servant, Bannister, a man who has looked after my room for ten years, and whose honesty is absolutely above suspicion. I found that the key was indeed his, that he had entered my room to know if I wanted tea, and that he had very carelessly left the key in the door when he came out. His visit to my room must have been within a very few minutes of my leaving it. His forgetfulness about the key would have mattered little upon any other occasion, but on this one day it has produced the most deplorable consequences.

"The moment I looked at my table I was aware that someone had rummaged among my papers. The proof was in three long slips. I had left them all together. Now I found that one of them was lying on the floor, one was on the side table near the window, and the third was where I had left it."

Holmes stirred for the first time.

"The first page on the floor, the second in the window, the third where you left it," said he.

"Exactly, Mr. Holmes. You amaze me. How could you possibly know that?"

"Pray continue your very interesting statement."

"For an instant I imagined that Bannister had taken the unpardonable liberty of examining my papers. He denied it, however, with the utmost earnestness, and I am convinced that he was speaking the truth. The alternative was that someone passing had observed the key in the door, had known that I was out, and had entered to look at the papers. A large sum of money is at stake, for the scholarship is a very valuable one, and an unscrupulous man might very well run a risk in order to gain an advantage over his fellows.

"Bannister was very much upset by the incident. He had nearly fainted when we found that the papers had undoubtedly been tampered with. I gave him a little brandy and left him collapsed in a chair while I made a most careful examination of the room. I soon saw that the intruder had left

" HOW COULD YOU POSSIBLY KNOW THAT?"

other traces of his presence besides the rumpled papers. On the table in the window were several shreds from a pencil which had been sharpened. A broken tip of lead was lying there also. Evidently the rascal had copied the paper in a great hurry, had broken his pencil, and had been compelled to put a fresh point to it."

"Excellent!" said Holmes, who was recovering his good-humour as his attention became more engrossed by the case. "Fortune has been your friend."

"This was not all. I have a new writing-table with a fine surface of red leather. I am prepared to swear, and so is Bannister, that it was smooth and unstained. Now I found a clean cut in it about three inches long—not a mere scratch, but a positive cut. Not only this, but on the table I found a small ball of black dough, or clay, with specks of something which looks like sawdust in it. I am convinced that these marks were left by the man who rifled the papers. There were no footmarks and no other evidence as to his identity. I was at my wits' ends, when suddenly the happy thought occurred to me that you were in the town, and I came straight round to put the matter into your hands. Do help me, Mr. Holmes! You see my dilemma. Either I must find the man or else the examination must be postponed until fresh papers are prepared, and since this cannot be done without explanation there will ensue a hideous scandal, which will throw a cloud not only on the college, but on the University. Above all things I desire to settle the matter quietly and discreetly."

"I shall be happy to look into it and to give you such advice as I can," said Holmes, rising and putting on his overcoat. "The case is not entirely devoid of interest. Had anyone visited you in your room after the papers came to you?"

"Yes ; young Daulat Ras, an Indian student who lives on the same stair, came in to ask me some particulars about the examination."

"For which he was entered?"

"Yes."

"And the papers were on your table?"

"To the best of my belief they were rolled up."

"But might be recognised as proofs?"

"Possibly."

"No one else in your room?"

"No."

"Did anyone know that these proofs would be there?"

"No one save the printer."

"Did this man Bannister know?"

"No, certainly not. No one knew."

"Where is Bannister now?"

"He was very ill, poor fellow. I left him collapsed in the chair. I was in such a hurry to come to you."

"You left your door open?"

"I locked up the papers first."

"Then it amounts to this, Mr. Soames, that unless the Indian student recognised the roll as being proofs, the man who tampered with them came upon them accidentally without knowing that they were there."

"So it seems to me."

Holmes gave an enigmatic smile.

"Well," said he, "let us go round. Not one of your cases, Watson—mental, not physical. All right ; come if you want to. Now, Mr. Soames—at your disposal ! "

The sitting-room of our client opened by a long, low, latticed window on to the ancient lichen-tinted court of the old college. A Gothic arched door led to a worn stone staircase. On the ground floor was the tutor's room. Above were three students, one on each story. It was already twilight when we reached the scene of our problem. Holmes halted and looked earnestly at the window. Then he approached it, and, standing on tiptoe with his neck craned, he looked into the room.

"He must have entered through the door. There is no opening except the one pane," said our learned guide.

"Dear me!" said Holmes, and he smiled in a singular way as he glanced at our companion. "Well, if there is nothing to be learned here we had best go inside."

The lecturer unlocked the outer door and ushered us into his room. We stood at the entrance while Holmes made an examination of the carpet.

"I am afraid there are no signs here," said he. "One could hardly hope for any upon so dry a day. Your servant seems to have quite recovered. You left him in a chair, you say ; which chair?"

"By the window there."

"I see. Near this little table. You can come in now. I have finished with the carpet. Let us take the little table first. Of course, what has happened is very clear. The man entered and took the papers, sheet by sheet, from the central table. He carried them over to the window table, because from there he could see if you came across the courtyard, and so could effect an escape."

"WITH HIS NECK CRANED, HE LOOKED INTO THE ROOM."

sharpen it again. This is of interest, Watson. The pencil was not an ordinary one. It was above the usual size, with a soft lead ; the outer colour was dark blue, the maker's name was printed in silver lettering, and the piece remaining is only about an inch and a half long. Look for such a pencil, Mr. Soames, and you have got your man. When I add that he possesses a large and very blunt knife, you have an additional aid."

Mr. Soames was somewhat overwhelmed by this flood of information. "I can follow the other points," said he, "but really in this matter of the length ——"

Holmes held out a small chip with the letters NN and a space of clear wood after them.

"You see?"

"No, I fear that even now——"

"Watson, I have always done you an injustice. There are others. What could this NN be? It is at the end of a word. You are aware that Johann Faber is the most common maker's name. Is it not clear that there is just as much of the pencil left as usually follows the Johann?" He held the small table sideways to the electric light. "I was hoping that if the paper on which he wrote was thin some trace of it might come through upon this polished surface. No, I see nothing. I don't think there is anything more to be learned here. Now for the central table. This small pellet is, I presume, the black, doughy mass you spoke of. Roughly pyramidal in shape and hollowed out, I perceive. As you say, there appear to be grains of sawdust in it. Dear me, this is very interesting. And the cut—a positive tear, I see. It began with a thin scratch and ended in a jagged hole. I am much indebted to you for directing my attention to this case, Mr. Soames. Where does that door lead to?"

"To my bedroom."

"As a matter of fact he could not," said Soames, "for I entered by the side door."

"Ah, that's good! Well, anyhow, that was in his mind. Let me see the three strips. No finger impressions—no! Well, he carried over this one first and he copied it. How long would it take him to do that, using every possible contraction? A quarter of an hour, not less. Then he tossed it down and seized the next. He was in the midst of that when your return caused him to make a very hurried retreat—*very* hurried, since he had not time to replace the papers which would tell you that he had been there. You were not aware of any hurrying feet on the stair as you entered the outer door?"

"No, I can't say I was."

"Well, he wrote so furiously that he broke his pencil, and had, as you observe, to

"Have you been in it since your adventure?"

"No; I came straight away for you."

"I should like to have a glance round. What a charming, old-fashioned room! Perhaps you will kindly wait a minute until I have examined the floor. No, I see nothing. What about this curtain? You hang your clothes behind it. If anyone were forced to conceal himself in this room he must do it there, since the bed is too low and the wardrobe too shallow. No one there, I suppose?"

As Holmes drew the curtain I was aware, from some little rigidity and alertness of his attitude, that he was prepared for an emergency. As a matter of fact the drawn curtain disclosed nothing but three or four suits of clothes hanging from a line of pegs. Holmes turned away and stooped suddenly to the floor.

"Halloa! What's this?" said he.

It was a small pyramid of black, putty-like stuff, exactly like the one upon the table of the study. Holmes held it out on his open palm in the glare of the electric light.

"Your visitor seems to have left traces in your bedroom as well as in your sitting-room, Mr. Soames."

"What could he have wanted there?"

"I think it is clear enough. You came back by an unexpected way, and so he had no warning until you were at the very door. What could he do? He caught up everything which would betray him and he rushed into your bedroom to conceal himself."

"Good gracious, Mr. Holmes, do you mean to tell me that all the time I was talking to Bannister in this room we had the man prisoner if we had only known it?"

"So I read it."

"Surely there is another alternative, Mr. Holmes. I don't know whether you observed my bedroom window?"

"Lattice-paned, lead framework, three separate windows, one swinging on hinge and large enough to admit a man."

"Exactly. And it looks out on an angle of the courtyard so as to be partly invisible. The man might have effected his entrance there, left traces as he passed through the bedroom, and, finally, finding the door open have escaped that way."

Holmes shook his head impatiently.

"Let us be practical," said he. "I understand you to say that there are three students who use this stair and are in the habit of passing your door?"

"Yes, there are."

"And they are all in for this examination?"

"Yes."

"Have you any reason to suspect any one of them more than the others?"

Soames hesitated.

"It is a very delicate question," said he. "One hardly likes to throw suspicion where there are no proofs."

"Let us hear the suspicions. I will look after the proofs."

"I will tell you, then, in a few words the character of the three men who inhabit these rooms. The lower of the three is Gilchrist, a fine scholar and athlete; plays in the Rugby team and the cricket team for the college, and got his Blue for the hurdles and the long jump. He is a fine, manly fellow. His father was the notorious Sir Jabez Gilchrist, who ruined himself on the turf. My scholar has been left very poor, but he is hard-working and industrious. He will do well.

"The second floor is inhabited by Daulat Ras, the Indian. He is a quiet, inscrutable fellow, as most of those Indians are. He is well up in his work, though his Greek is his weak subject. He is steady and methodical.

"The top floor belongs to Miles McLaren. He is a brilliant fellow when he chooses to work—one of the brightest intellects of the University, but he is wayward, dissipated, and unprincipled. He was nearly expelled over a card scandal in his first year. He has been idling all this term, and he must look forward with dread to the examination."

"Then it is he whom you suspect?"

"I dare not go so far as that. But of the three he is perhaps the least unlikely."

"Exactly. Now, Mr. Soames, let us have a look at your servant, Bannister."

He was a little, white-faced, clean-shaven, grizzly-haired fellow of fifty. He was still suffering from this sudden disturbance of the quiet routine of his life. His plump face was twitching with his nervousness, and his fingers could not keep still.

"We are investigating this unhappy business, Bannister," said his master.

"Yes, sir."

"I understand," said Holmes, "that you left your key in the door?"

"Yes, sir."

"Was it not very extraordinary that you should do this on the very day when there were these papers inside?"

"It was most unfortunate, sir. But I have occasionally done the same thing at other times."

"When did you enter the room?"

"It was about half-past ·four. That is Mr. Soames's tea time."

"How long did you stay?"

"When I saw that he was absent I withdrew at once."

"Did you look at these papers on the table?"

"No, sir; certainly not."

"HOW CAME YOU TO LEAVE THE KEY IN THE DOOR?"

"How came you to leave the key in the door?"

"I had the tea-tray in my hand. I thought I would come back for the key. Then I forgot."

"Has the outer door a spring lock?"

"No, sir."

"Then it was open all the time?"

"Yes, sir."

"Anyone in the room could get out?"

"Yes, sir."

"When Mr. Soames returned and called for you, you were very much disturbed?"

"Yes, sir. Such a thing has never happened during the many years that I have been here. I nearly fainted, sir."

"So I understand. Where were you when you began to feel bad?"

"Where was I, sir? Why, here, near the door."

"That is singular, because you sat down in that chair over yonder near the corner. Why did you pass these other chairs?"

"I don't know, sir. It didn't matter to me where I sat."

"I really don't think he knew much about it, Mr. Holmes. He was looking very bad—quite ghastly."

"You stayed here when your master left?"

"Only for a minute or so. Then I locked the door and went to my room."

"Whom do you suspect?"

"Oh, I would not venture to say, sir. I don't believe there is any gentleman in this University who is capable of profiting by such an action. No, sir, I'll not believe it."

"Thank you; that will do," said Holmes. "Oh, one more word. You have not mentioned to any of the three gentlemen whom you attend that anything is amiss?"

"No, sir; not a word."

"You haven't seen any of them?"

"No, sir."

"Very good. Now, Mr. Soames, we will take a walk in the quadrangle, if you please."

Three yellow squares of light shone above us in the gathering gloom."

"Your three birds are all in their nests," said Holmes, looking up. "Halloa! What's that? One of them seems restless enough."

It was the Indian, whose dark silhouette appeared suddenly upon his blind. He was pacing swiftly up and down his room.

"I should like to have a peep at each of them," said Holmes. "Is it possible?"

"No difficulty in the world," Soames answered. "This set of rooms is quite the oldest in the college, and it is not unusual for visitors to go over them. Come along, and I will personally conduct you."

"No names, please!" said Holmes, as we knocked at Gilchrist's door. A tall, flaxen-haired, slim young fellow opened it, and made us welcome when he understood our errand. There were some really curious pieces of mediæval domestic architecture within. Holmes was so charmed with one of them that he insisted on drawing it on his note-book, broke his pencil, had to borrow one from our host, and finally borrowed a knife to sharpen his own. The same curious accident happened to him in the rooms of the Indian—a silent, little, hook-nosed fellow, who eyed us askance and was obviously glad when Holmes's architectural studies had come to an end. I could not see that in either case Holmes had come upon the clue for which he was searching. Only at the third did our visit prove abortive. The outer door would not open to our knock, and nothing more substantial than a torrent of bad language came from behind it. "I don't care who you are. You can go to blazes!" roared the angry voice. "To-morrow's the exam., and I won't be drawn by anyone."

"A rude fellow," said our guide, flushing with anger as we withdrew down the stair. "Of course, he did not realize that it was I who was knocking, but none the less his conduct was very uncourteous, and, indeed, under the circumstances rather suspicious."

Holmes's response was a curious one.

"Can you tell me his exact height?" he asked.

"Really, Mr. Holmes, I cannot undertake to say. He is taller than the Indian, not so tall as Gilchrist. I suppose five foot six would be about it."

"That is very important," said Holmes. "And now, Mr. Soames, I wish you good-night."

Our guide cried aloud in his astonishment and dismay. "Good gracious, Mr. Holmes, you are surely not going to leave me in this

"HE INSISTED ON DRAWING IT IN HIS NOTE-BOOK."

abrupt fashion! You don't seem to realize the position. To-morrow is the examination. I must take some definite action to-night. I cannot allow the examination to be held if one of the papers has been tampered with. The situation must be faced."

"You must leave it as it is. I shall drop round early to-morrow morning and chat the matter over. It is possible that I may be in a position then to indicate some course of action. Meanwhile you change nothing—nothing at all."

"Very good, Mr. Holmes."

"You can be perfectly easy in your mind. We shall certainly find some way out of your difficulties. I will take the black clay with me, also the pencil cuttings. Good-bye."

When we were out in the darkness of the quadrangle we again looked up at the windows. The Indian still paced his room. The others were invisible.

"Well, Watson, what do you think of it?" Holmes asked, as we came out into the main street. "Quite a little parlour game—sort of three-card trick, is it not? There are your three men. It must be one of them. You take your choice. Which is yours?"

"The foul-mouthed fellow at the top. He is the one with the worst record. And yet that Indian was a sly fellow also. Why should he be pacing his room all the time?"

"There is nothing in that. Many men do it when they are trying to learn anything by heart."

"He looked at us in a queer way."

"So would you if a flock of strangers came in on you when you were preparing for an examination next day, and every moment was of value. No, I see nothing in that. Pencils, too, and knives—all was satisfactory. But that fellow *does* puzzle me."

"Who?"

"Why, Bannister, the servant. What's his game in the matter?"

"He impressed me as being a perfectly honest man."

"So he did me. That's the puzzling part. Why should a perfectly honest man—well, well, here's a large stationer's. We shall begin our researches here."

There were only four stationers of any consequence in the town, and at each Holmes produced his pencil chips and bid high for a duplicate. All were agreed that one could be ordered, but that it was not a usual size of pencil and that it was seldom kept in stock. My friend did not appear to be depressed by his failure, but shrugged his shoulders in half-humorous resignation.

"No good, my dear Watson. This, the best and only final clue, has run to nothing. But, indeed, I have little doubt that we can build up a sufficient case without it. By Jove! my dear fellow, it is nearly nine, and the landlady babbled of green peas at seven-thirty. What with your eternal tobacco, Watson, and your irregularity at meals, I expect that you will get notice to quit and that I shall share your downfall—not, however, before we have solved the problem of the nervous tutor, the careless servant, and the three enterprising students."

Holmes made no further allusion to the matter that day, though he sat lost in thought for a long time after our belated dinner. At eight in the morning he came into my room just as I finished my toilet.

"Well, Watson," said he, "it is time we went down to St. Luke's. Can you do without breakfast?"

"Certainly."

"Soames will be in a dreadful fidget until we are able to tell him something positive."

"Have you anything positive to tell him?"

"I think so."

"You have formed a conclusion?"

"Yes, my dear Watson; I have solved the mystery."

"But what fresh evidence could you have got?"

"Aha! It is not for nothing that I have turned myself out of bed at the untimely hour of six. I have put in two hours' hard work and covered at least five miles, with something to show for it. Look at that!"

He held out his hand. On the palm were three little pyramids of black, doughy clay.

"Why, Holmes, you had only two yesterday!"

"And one more this morning. It is a fair argument that wherever No. 3 came from is also the source of Nos. 1 and 2. Eh, Watson? Well, come along and put friend Soames out of his pain."

The unfortunate tutor was certainly in a state of pitiable agitation when we found him in his chambers. In a few hours the examinations would commence, and he was still in the dilemma between making the facts public and allowing the culprit to compete for the valuable scholarship. He could hardly stand still, so great was his mental agitation, and he ran towards Holmes with two eager hands outstretched.

"Thank Heaven that you have come! I feared that you had given it up in despair. What am I to do? Shall the examination proceed?"

"Yes; let it proceed by all means."

"But this rascal——?"

"He shall not compete."

"You know him?"

"I think so. If this matter is not to become public we must give ourselves certain powers, and resolve ourselves into a small private court-martial. You there, if you please, Soames! Watson, you here! I'll take the arm-chair in the middle. I think that we are now sufficiently imposing to strike terror into a guilty breast. Kindly ring the bell!"

Bannister entered, and shrunk back in evident surprise and fear at our judicial appearance.

"You will kindly close the door," said Holmes. "Now, Bannister, will you please tell us the truth about yesterday's incident?"

The man turned white to the roots of his hair.

"I have told you everything, sir."

"Nothing to add?"

"Nothing at all, sir."

"Well, then, I must make some suggestions to you. When you sat down on that chair yesterday, did you do so in order to conceal some object which would have shown who had been in the room?"

Bannister's face was ghastly.

"No, sir; certainly not."

"It is only a suggestion," said Holmes, suavely. "I frankly admit that I am unable to prove it. But it seems probable enough, since the moment that Mr. Soames's back was turned you released the man who was hiding in that bedroom."

Bannister licked his dry lips.

"There was no man, sir."

"Ah, that's a pity, Bannister. Up to now you may have spoken the truth, but now I know that you have lied."

The man's face set in sullen defiance.

"There was no man, sir."

"Come, come, Bannister!"

"No, sir; there was no one."

"In that case you can give us no further information. Would you please remain in the room? Stand over there near the bedroom door. Now, Soames, I am

going to ask you to have the great kindness to go up to the room of young Gilchrist, and to ask him to step down into yours."

An instant later the tutor returned, bringing with him the student. He was a fine figure of a man, tall, lithe, and agile, with a springy step and a pleasant, open face. His troubled blue eyes glanced at each of us, and finally rested with an expression of blank dismay upon Bannister in the farther corner.

"Just close the door," said Holmes. "Now, Mr. Gilchrist, we are all quite alone here, and no one need ever know one word of what passes between us. We can be perfectly frank with each other. We want to know, Mr. Gilchrist, how you, an honourable man, ever came to commit such an action as that of yesterday?"

The unfortunate young man staggered back and cast a look full of horror and reproach at Bannister.

"No, no, Mr. Gilchrist, sir; I never said a word—never one word!" cried the servant.

"No, but you have now," said Holmes. "Now, sir, you must see that after Bannister's words your position is hopeless, and that your only chance lies in a frank confession."

"AN INSTANT LATER THE TUTOR RETURNED, BRINGING WITH HIM THE STUDENT."

For a moment Gilchrist, with upraised hand, tried to control his writhing features. The next he had thrown himself on his knees beside the table and, burying his face in his hands, he had burst into a storm of passionate sobbing.

"Come, come," said Holmes, kindly; "it is human to err, and at least no one can accuse you of being a callous criminal. Perhaps it would be easier for you if I were to tell Mr. Soames what occurred, and you can check me where I am wrong. Shall I do so? Well, well, don't trouble to answer. Listen, and see that I do you no injustice.

"From the moment, Mr. Soames, that you said to me that no one, not even Bannister, could have told that the papers were in your room, the case began to take a definite shape in my mind. The printer one could, of course, dismiss. He could examine the papers in his own office. The Indian I also thought nothing of. If the proofs were in roll he could not possibly know what they were. On the other hand, it seemed an unthinkable coincidence that a man should dare to enter the room, and that by chance on that very day the papers were on the table. I dismissed that. The man who entered knew that the papers were there. How did he know?

"When I approached your room I examined the window. You amused me by supposing that I was contemplating the possibility of someone having in broad daylight, under the eyes of all these opposite rooms, forced himself through it. Such an idea was absurd. I was measuring how tall a man would need to be in order to see as he passed what papers were on the central table. I am six feet high, and I could do it with an effort. No one less than that would have a chance. Already you see I had reason to think that if one of your three students was a man of unusual height he was the most worth watching of the three.

"I entered and I took you into my confidence as to the suggestions of the side table. Of the centre table I could make nothing, until in your description of Gilchrist you mentioned that he was a long-distance jumper. Then the whole thing came to me in an instant, and I only needed certain corroborative proofs, which I speedily obtained.

"What happened was this. This young fellow had employed his afternoon at the athletic grounds, where he had been practising the jump. He returned carrying his jumping shoes, which are provided, as you are aware, with several sharp spikes. As he passed your window he saw, by means of his great height, these proofs upon your table, and conjectured what they were. No harm would have been done had it not been that as he passed your door he perceived the key which had been left by the carelessness of your servant. A sudden impulse came over him to enter and see if they were indeed the proofs. It was not a dangerous exploit, for he could always pretend that he had simply looked in to ask a question.

"Well, when he saw that they were indeed the proofs, it was then that he yielded to temptation. He put his shoes on the table. What was it you put on that chair near the window?"

"Gloves," said the young man.

Holmes looked triumphantly at Bannister. "He put his gloves on the chair, and he took the proofs, sheet by sheet, to copy them. He thought the tutor must return by the main gate, and that he would see him. As we know, he came back by the side gate. Suddenly he heard him at the very door. There was no possible escape. He forgot his gloves, but he caught up his shoes and darted into the bedroom. You observe that the scratch on that table is slight at one side, but deepens in the direction of the bedroom door. That in itself is enough to show us that the shoe had been drawn in that direction and that the culprit had taken refuge there. The earth round the spike had been left on the table, and a second sample was loosened and fell in the bedroom. I may add that I walked out to the athletic grounds this morning, saw that tenacious black clay is used in the jumping-pit, and carried away a specimen of it, together with some of the fine tan or sawdust which is strewn over it to prevent the athlete from slipping. Have I told the truth, Mr. Gilchrist?"

The student had drawn himself erect.

"Yes, sir, it is true," said he.

"Good heavens, have you nothing to add?" cried Soames.

"Yes, sir, I have, but the shock of this disgraceful exposure has bewildered me. I have a letter here, Mr. Soames, which I wrote to you early this morning in the middle of a restless night. It was before I knew that my sin had found me out. Here it is, sir. You will see that I have said, 'I have determined not to go in for the examination. I have been offered a commission in the Rhodesian Police,

"HERE IT IS, SIR."

and I am going out to South Africa at once."'

"I am indeed pleased to hear that you did not intend to profit by your unfair advantage," said Soames. "But why did you change your purpose?"

Gilchrist pointed to Bannister.

"There is the man who set me in the right path," said he.

"Come now, Bannister," said Holmes. "It will be clear to you from what I have said that only you could have let this young man out, since you were left in the room, and must have locked the door when you went out. As to his escaping by that window, it was incredible. Can you not clear up the last point in this mystery, and tell us the reasons for your action?"

"It was simple enough, sir, if you only had known; but with all your cleverness it was impossible that you could know. Time was, sir, when I was butler to old Sir Jabez Gilchrist, this young gentleman's father. When he was ruined I came to the college as servant, but I never forgot my old employer because he was down in the world. I watched his son all I could for the sake of the old days. Well, sir, when I came into this room yesterday when the alarm was given, the very first thing I saw was Mr. Gilchrist's tan gloves a-lying in that chair. I knew those gloves well, and I understood their message. If Mr. Soames saw them the game was up. I flopped down into that chair, and nothing would budge me until Mr. Soames he went for you. Then out came my poor young master, whom I had dandled on my knee, and confessed it all to me. Wasn't it natural, sir, that I should save him, and wasn't it natural also that I should try to speak to him as his dead father would have done, and make him understand that he could not profit by such a deed? Could you blame me, sir?"

"No, indeed," said Holmes, heartily, springing to his feet. "Well, Soames, I think we have cleared your little problem up, and our breakfast awaits us at home. Come, Watson! As to you, sir, I trust that a bright future awaits you in Rhodesia. For once you have fallen low. Let us see in the future how high you can rise."

"HOLMES HAD BOUNDED ACROSS THE ROOM AND HAD WRENCHED A
SMALL PHIAL FROM HER HAND."

# THE RETURN OF SHERLOCK HOLMES.

## By A. CONAN DOYLE.

### X.—The Adventure of the Golden Pince-Nez.

WHEN I look at the three massive manuscript volumes which contain our work for the year 1894 I confess that it is very difficult for me, out of such a wealth of material, to select the cases which are most interesting in themselves and at the same time most conducive to a display of those peculiar powers for which my friend was famous. As I turn over the pages I see my notes upon the repulsive story of the red leech and the terrible death of Crosby the banker. Here also I find an account of the Addleton tragedy and the singular contents of the ancient British barrow. The famous Smith-Mortimer succession case comes also within this period, and so does the tracking and arrest of Huret, the Boulevard assassin—an exploit which won for Holmes an autograph letter of thanks from the French President and the Order of the Legion of Honour. Each of these would furnish a narrative, but on the whole I am of opinion that none of them unite so many singular points of interest as the episode of Yoxley Old Place, which includes not only the lamentable death of young Willoughby Smith, but also those subsequent developments which threw so curious a light upon the causes of the crime.

It was a wild, tempestuous night towards the close of November. Holmes and I sat together in silence all the evening, he engaged with a powerful lens deciphering the remains of the original inscription upon a palimpsest, I deep in a recent treatise upon surgery. Outside the wind howled down Baker Street, while the rain beat fiercely against the windows. It was strange there in the very depths of the town, with ten miles of man's handiwork on every side of us, to feel the iron grip of Nature, and to be conscious that to the huge elemental forces all London was no more than the molehills that dot the fields. I walked to the window and looked out on the deserted street. The occasional lamps gleamed on the expanse of muddy road and shining pavement. A single cab was splashing its way from the Oxford Street end.

"Well, Watson, it's as well we have not to turn out to-night," said Holmes, laying aside his lens and rolling up the palimpsest. "I've done enough for one sitting. It is trying work for the eyes. So far as I can make out it is nothing more exciting than an Abbey's accounts dating from the second half of the fifteenth century. Halloa! halloa! halloa! What's this?"

Amid the droning of the wind there had come the stamping of a horse's hoofs and the long grind of a wheel as it rasped against the kerb. The cab which I had seen had pulled up at our door.

"What can he want?" I ejaculated, as a man stepped out of it.

"Want! He wants us. And we, my poor Watson, want overcoats and cravats and goloshes, and every aid that man ever invented to fight the weather. Wait a bit, though! There's the cab off again! There's hope yet. He'd have kept it if he had wanted us to come. Run down, my dear fellow, and open the door, for all virtuous folk have been long in bed."

When the light of the hall lamp fell upon

our midnight visitor I had no difficulty in recognising him. It was young Stanley Hopkins, a promising detective, in whose career Holmes had several times shown a very practical interest.

"Is he in?" he asked, eagerly.

"Come up, my dear sir," said Holmes's voice from above. "I hope you have no designs upon us on such a night as this."

The detective mounted the stairs, and our lamp gleamed upon his shining waterproof. I helped him out of it while Holmes knocked a blaze out of the logs in the grate.

"Now, my dear Hopkins, draw up and warm your toes," said he. "Here's a cigar, and the doctor has a prescription containing hot water and a lemon which is good medicine on a night like this. It must be something important which has brought you out in such a gale."

"It is indeed, Mr. Holmes. I've had a bustling afternoon, I promise you. Did you see anything of the Yoxley case in the latest editions?"

"I've seen nothing later than the fifteenth century to-day."

"Well, it was only a paragraph, and all wrong at that, so you have not missed anything. I haven't let the grass grow under my feet. It's down in Kent, seven miles from Chatham and three from the railway line. I was wired for at three-fifteen, reached Yoxley Old Place at five, conducted my investigation, was back at Charing Cross by the last train, and straight to you by cab."

"Which means, I suppose, that you are not quite clear about your case?"

"IT WAS YOUNG STANLEY HOPKINS, A PROMISING DETECTIVE."

"It means that I can make neither head nor tail of it. So far as I can see it is just as tangled a business as ever I handled, and yet at first it seemed so simple that one couldn't go wrong. There's no motive, Mr. Holmes. That's what bothers me—I can't put my hand on a motive. Here's a man dead—there's no denying that—but, so far as I can see, no reason on earth why anyone should wish him harm."

Holmes lit his cigar and leaned back in his chair.

"Let us hear about it," said he.

"I've got my facts pretty clear," said Stanley Hopkins. "All I want now is to know what they all mean. The story, so far as I can make it out, is like this. Some years ago this country house, Yoxley Old Place, was taken by an elderly man, who gave the name of Professor Coram. He was an invalid, keeping his bed half the time, and the other half hobbling round the house with a stick or being pushed about the grounds by the gardener in a bath-chair. He was well liked by the few neighbours who called upon him, and he has the reputation down there of being a very learned man. His household used to consist of an elderly housekeeper, Mrs. Marker, and of a maid, Susan Tarlton. These have both been with him since his arrival, and they seem to be women of excellent character. The Professor is writing a learned book, and he found it necessary about a year ago to engage a secretary. The first two that he tried were not successes; but the third, Mr. Willoughby Smith, a very young man straight from the University, seems to have been just what his employer wanted. His work consisted in writing all the morning to the Professor's dictation, and he usually spent the evening in hunting up references and passages which bore upon the next day's work. This Willoughby Smith has nothing against him either as a boy at Uppingham or as a young man at Cambridge. I have seen his testimonials, and from the first he was a decent, quiet, hardworking fellow, with no weak spot in him at all. And yet this is the lad who has met his death this morning in the Professor's study under circumstances which can point only to murder."

The wind howled and screamed at the windows. Holmes and I drew closer to the fire while the young inspector slowly and point by point developed his singular narrative.

"If you were to search all England," said he, "I don't suppose you could find a household more self-contained or free from outside influences. Whole weeks would pass and not one of them go past the garden gate. The Professor was buried in his work and existed for nothing else. Young Smith knew nobody in the neighbourhood, and lived very much as his employer did. The two women had nothing to take them from the house. Mortimer the gardener, who wheels the bath-chair, is an Army pensioner—an old Crimean man of excellent character. He does not live in the house, but in a three-roomed cottage at the other end of the garden. Those are the only people that you would find within the grounds of Yoxley Old Place. At the same time, the gate of the garden is a hundred yards from the main London to Chatham road. It opens with a latch, and there is nothing to prevent anyone from walking in.

"Now I will give you the evidence of Susan Tarlton, who is the only person who can say anything positive about the matter. It was in the forenoon, between eleven and twelve. She was engaged at the moment in hanging some curtains in the upstairs front bedroom. Professor Coram was still in bed, for when the weather is bad he seldom rises before midday. The housekeeper was busied with some work in the back of the house. Willoughby Smith had been in his bedroom, which he uses as a sitting-room ; but the maid heard him at that moment pass along the passage and descend to the study immediately below her. She did not see him, but she says that she could not be mistaken in his quick, firm tread. She did not hear the study door close, but a minute or so later

there was a dreadful cry in the room below. It was a wild, hoarse scream, so strange and unnatural that it might have come either from a man or a woman. At the same instant there was a heavy thud, which shook the old house, and then all was silence. The maid stood petrified for a moment, and then, recovering her courage, she ran downstairs. The study door was shut, and she opened it. Inside young Mr. Willoughby Smith was stretched upon the floor. At first she could see no injury, but as she tried to raise him she saw that blood was pouring from the underside of his neck. It was pierced by a very small but very deep wound, which had divided the carotid artery. The instrument with which the injury had been inflicted lay upon the carpet beside him. It was one of those small sealing-wax knives to be found on old-fashioned writing-tables, with an ivory handle and a stiff blade. It was part of the fittings of the Professor's own desk.

"At first the maid thought that young Smith was already dead, but on pouring some water from the carafe over his forehead he opened his eyes for an instant. 'The Professor,' he murmured — 'it was she.' The maid is prepared to swear that those were the exact words. He tried desperately to say something else, and he held his right hand up in the air. Then he fell back dead.

"In the meantime the housekeeper had also arrived upon the scene, but she was just too late to catch the young man's dying words. Leaving Susan with the body, she hurried to the Professor's room. He was sitting up in bed horribly agitated, for he had heard enough to convince him that something terrible had occurred. Mrs. Marker is prepared to swear that the Professor was still in his night-clothes, and, indeed, it was impossible for him to dress without the help of Mortimer, whose orders were to come at twelve o'clock. The Professor declares that he heard the distant cry, but that he knows nothing more. He can give no explanation of the young man's last words, 'The Professor—it was she,' but imagines that they were the outcome of delirium. He believes that Willoughby Smith had not an enemy in the world, and can give no reason for the crime. His first action was to send Mortimer the gardener for the local police. A little later the chief constable sent for me. Nothing was moved before I got there, and strict orders were given that no one should walk upon the paths leading to the house. It was a splendid chance of putting your theories into practice, Mr. Sherlock Holmes. There was really nothing wanting."

"Except Mr. Sherlock Holmes," said my companion, with a somewhat bitter smile. "Well, let us hear about it. What sort of job did you make of it?"

"I must ask you first, Mr. Holmes, to glance at this rough plan, which will give you a general idea of the position of the Professor's study and the various points of the case. It will help you in following my investigation."

He unfolded the rough chart, which I here reproduce, and he laid it across Holmes's knee. I rose, and, standing behind Holmes, I studied it over his shoulder.

"It is very rough, of course, and it only

There could be no question, however, that someone had passed along the grass border which lines the path, and that he had done so in order to avoid leaving a track. I could not find anything in the nature of a distinct impression, but the grass was trodden down and someone had undoubtedly passed. It could only have been the murderer, since neither the gardener nor anyone else had been there that morning and the rain had only begun during the night."

"One moment," said Holmes. "Where does this path lead to?"

"To the road."

"How long is it?"

"A hundred yards or so."

"At the point where the path passes through the gate you could surely pick up the tracks?"

"Unfortunately, the path was tiled at that point."

"Well, on the road itself?"

"No; it was all trodden into mire."

"Tut-tut! Well, then, these tracks upon the grass, were they coming or going?"

"It was impossible to say. There was never any outline."

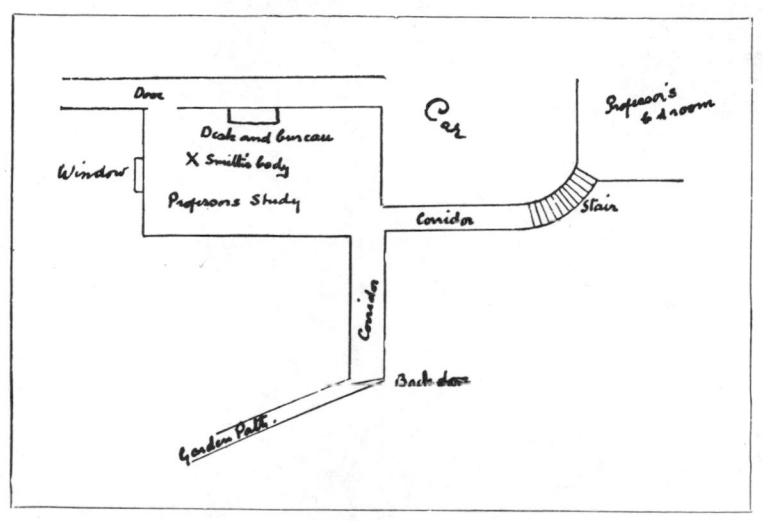

"A large foot or a small?"

"You could not distinguish."

Holmes gave an ejaculation of impatience.

"It has been pouring rain and blowing a hurricane ever since," said he. "It will be harder to read now than that palimpsest. Well, well, it can't be helped. What did you do, Hopkins, after you had made certain that you had made certain of nothing?"

"I think I made certain of a good deal, Mr. Holmes. I knew that someone had entered the house cautiously from without. I next examined the corridor. It is lined with cocoanut matting and had taken no impression of any kind. This brought me into the study itself. It is a scantily-furnished room. The main article is a large writing-table with a fixed bureau. This bureau consists of a double column of drawers with

deals with the points which seem to me to be essential. All the rest you will see later for yourself. Now, first of all, presuming that the assassin entered the house, how did he or she come in? Undoubtedly by the garden path and the back door, from which there is direct access to the study. Any other way would have been exceedingly complicated. The escape must have also been made along that line, for of the two other exits from the room one was blocked by Susan as she ran downstairs and the other leads straight to the Professor's bedroom. I therefore directed my attention at once to the garden path, which was saturated with recent rain and would certainly show any footmarks.

"My examination showed me that I was dealing with a cautious and expert criminal. No footmarks were to be found on the path.

a central small cupboard between them. The drawers were open, the cupboard locked. The drawers, it seems, were always open, and nothing of value was kept in them. There were some papers of importance in the cupboard, but there were no signs that this had been tampered with, and the Professor assures me that nothing was missing. It is certain that no robbery has been committed.

"I come now to the body of the young man. It was found near the bureau, and just to the left of it, as marked upon that chart.

important piece of evidence which was found clasped in the dead man's right hand."

From his pocket Stanley Hopkins drew a small paper packet. He unfolded it and disclosed a golden pince-nez, with two broken ends of black silk cord dangling from the end of it. "Willoughby Smith had excellent sight," he added. "There can be no question that this was snatched from the face or the person of the assassin."

Sherlock Holmes took the glasses into his hand and examined them with the utmost attention and interest. He held them on his

"THE BODY WAS FOUND NEAR THE BUREAU, AND JUST TO THE LEFT OF IT, AS MARKED UPON THAT CHART."

The stab was on the right side of the neck and from behind forwards, so that it is almost impossible that it could have been self-inflicted."

"Unless he fell upon the knife," said Holmes.

"Exactly. The idea crossed my mind. But we found the knife some feet away from the body, so that seems impossible. Then, of course, there are the man's own dying words. And, finally, there was this very

nose, endeavoured to read through them, went to the window and stared up the street with them, looked at them most minutely in the full light of the lamp, and finally, with a chuckle, seated himself at the table and wrote a few lines upon a sheet of paper, which he tossed across to Stanley Hopkins.

"That's the best I can do for you," said he. "It may prove to be of some use."

The astonished detective read the note aloud. It ran as follows:—

"HE ENDEAVOURED TO READ THROUGH THEM."

are too wide for your nose, show-ing that the lady's nose was very broad at the base. This sort of nose is usually a short and coarse one, but there are a sufficient number of exceptions to prevent me from being dogmatic or from insisting upon this point in my description. My own face is a narrow one, and yet I find that I cannot get my eyes into the centre, or near the centre, of these glasses. Therefore the lady's eyes are set very near to the sides of the nose. You will perceive, Watson, that the glasses are concave and of unusual strength. A lady whose vision has been so extremely contracted all her life is sure to have the physical characteristics of such vision, which are seen in the forehead, the eyelids, and the shoulders."

"Yes," I said, "I can follow each of your arguments. I con-fess, however, that I am unable to understand how you arrive at the double visit to the optician."

Holmes took the glasses into his hand.

"You will perceive," he said, "that the clips are lined with tiny bands of cork to soften the pressure upon the nose. One of these is discoloured and worn to some slight extent, but the other is new. Evidently one has fallen off and been replaced. I should judge that the older of them has not been there more than a few months. They exactly correspond, so I gather that the lady went back to the same establishment for the second."

"By George, it's marvellous!" cried Hopkins, in an ecstasy of admiration. "To think that I had all that evidence in my hand and never knew it! I had intended, however, to go the round of the London opticians."

"Of course you would. Meanwhile, have you anything more to tell us about the case?"

"Nothing, Mr. Holmes. I think that you know as much as I do now—probably more. We have had inquiries made as to any stranger seen on the country roads or at the railway station. We have heard of none. What beats me is the utter want of all object in the crime. Not a ghost of a motive can anyone suggest."

"Wanted, a woman of good address, attired like a lady. She has a remarkably thick nose, with eyes which are set close upon either side of it. She has a puckered forehead, a peering expression, and probably rounded shoulders. There are indications that she has had recourse to an optician at least twice during the last few months. As her glasses are of remarkable strength and as opticians are not very numerous, there should be no difficulty in tracing her."

Holmes smiled at the astonishment of Hopkins, which must have been reflected upon my features.

"Surely my deductions are simplicity itself," said he. "It would be difficult to name any articles which afford a finer field for inference than a pair of glasses, especially so remarkable a pair as these. That they belong to a woman I infer from their delicacy, and also, of course, from the last words of the dying man. As to her being a person of refinement and well dressed, they are, as you perceive, handsomely mounted in solid gold, and it is inconceivable that anyone who wore such glasses could be slatternly in other respects. You will find that the clips

"Ah! there I am not in a position to help you. But I suppose you want us to come out to-morrow?"

"If it is not asking too much, Mr. Holmes. There's a train from Charing Cross to Chatham at six in the morning, and we should be at Yoxley Old Place between eight and nine."

"Then we shall take it. Your case has certainly some features of great interest, and I shall be delighted to look into it. Well, it's nearly one, and we had best get a few hours' sleep. I dare say you can manage all right on the sofa in front of the fire. I'll light my spirit-lamp and give you a cup of coffee before we start."

The gale had blown itself out next day, but it was a bitter morning when we started upon our journey. We saw the cold winter sun rise over the dreary marshes of the Thames and the long, sullen reaches of the river, which I shall ever associate with our pursuit of the Andaman Islander in the earlier days of our career. After a long and weary journey we alighted at a small station some miles from Chatham. While a horse was being put into a trap at the local inn we snatched a hurried breakfast, and so we were all ready for business when we at last arrived at Yoxley Old Place. A constable met us at the garden gate.

"Well, Wilson, any news?"

"No, sir, nothing."

"No reports of any stranger seen?"

"No, sir. Down at the station they are certain that no stranger either came or went yesterday."

"Have you had inquiries made at inns and lodgings?"

"Yes, sir; there is no one that we cannot account for."

"Well, it's only a reasonable walk to Chatham. Anyone might stay there, or take a train without being observed. This is the garden path of which I spoke, Mr. Holmes. I'll pledge my word there was no mark on it yesterday."

"On which side were the marks on the grass?"

"This side, sir. This narrow margin of grass between the path and the flower-bed. I can't see the traces now, but they were clear to me then."

"Yes, yes; someone has passed along," said Holmes, stooping over the grass border. "Our lady must have picked her steps carefully, must she not, since on the one side she would leave a track on the path, and on the other an even clearer one on the soft bed."

"Yes, sir, she must have been a cool hand."

I saw an intent look pass over Holmes's face.

"You say that she must have come back this way?"

"Yes, sir; there is no other."

"On this strip of grass?"

"Certainly, Mr. Holmes."

"Hum! It was a very remarkable performance—very remarkable. Well, I think we have exhausted the path. Let us go farther. This garden door is usually kept open, I suppose? Then this visitor had nothing to do but to walk in. The idea of murder was not in her mind, or she would have provided herself with some sort of weapon, instead of having to pick this knife off the writing-table. She advanced along this corridor, leaving no traces upon the cocoanut matting. Then she found herself in this study. How long was she there? We have no means of judging."

"Not more than a few minutes, sir. I forgot to tell you that Mrs. Marker, the housekeeper, had been in there tidying not very long before—about a quarter of an hour, she says."

"Well, that gives us a limit. Our lady enters this room and what does she do? She goes over to the writing-table. What for? Not for anything in the drawers. If there had been anything worth her taking it would surely have been locked up. No; it was for something in that wooden bureau. Halloa! what is that scratch upon the face of it? Just hold a match, Watson. Why did you not tell me of this, Hopkins?"

The mark which he was examining began upon the brass work on the right-hand side of the keyhole, and extended for about four inches, where it had scratched the varnish from the surface.

"I noticed it, Mr. Holmes. But you'll always find scratches round a keyhole."

"This is recent, quite recent. See how the brass shines where it is cut. An old scratch would be the same colour as the surface. Look at it through my lens. There's the varnish, too, like earth on each side of a furrow. Is Mrs. Marker there?"

A sad-faced, elderly woman came into the room.

"Did you dust this bureau yesterday morning?"

"Yes, sir."

"Did you notice this scratch?"

"DID YOU DUST THIS BUREAU YESTERDAY MORNING?"

"No, sir, I did not."

"I am sure you did not, for a duster would have swept away these shreds of varnish. Who has the key of this bureau?"

"The Professor keeps it on his watch-chain."

"Is it a simple key?"

"No, sir; it is a Chubb's key."

"Very good. Mrs. Marker, you can go. Now we are making a little progress. Our lady enters the room, advances to the bureau, and either opens it or tries to do so. While she is thus engaged young Willoughby Smith enters the room. In her hurry to withdraw the key she makes this scratch upon the door. He seizes her, and she, snatching up the nearest object, which happens to be this knife, strikes at him in order to make him let go his hold. The blow is a fatal one. He falls and she escapes, either with or without the object for which she has come. Is Susan the maid there? Could anyone have got away through that door after the time that you heard the cry, Susan?"

"No, sir; it is impossible. Before I got down the stair I'd have seen anyone in the passage. Besides, the door never opened, for I would have heard it."

"That settles this exit. Then no doubt the lady went out the way she came. I understand that this other passage leads only to the Professor's room. There is no exit that way?"

"No, sir."

"We shall go down it and make the acquaintance of the Professor. Halloa, Hopkins! this is very important, very important indeed. The Professor's corridor is also lined with cocoa-nut matting."

"Well, sir, what of that?"

"Don't you see any bearing upon the case? Well, well, I don't insist upon it. No doubt I am wrong. And yet it seems to me to be suggestive. Come with me and introduce me."

We passed down the passage, which was of the same length as that which led to the garden. At the end was a short flight of steps ending in a door. Our guide knocked, and then ushered us into the Professor's bedroom.

It was a very large chamber, lined with innumerable volumes, which had overflowed from the shelves and lay in piles in the corners, or were stacked all round at the base of the cases. The bed was in the centre of the room, and in it, propped up with pillows, was the owner of the house. I have seldom seen a more remarkable-looking person. It was a gaunt, aquiline face which was turned towards us, with piercing dark eyes, which lurked in deep hollows under overhung and tufted brows. His hair and beard were white, save that the latter was curiously stained with yellow around his mouth. A cigarette glowed amid the tangle of white hair, and the air of the room was fetid with stale tobacco-smoke. As he held out his hand to Holmes I perceived that it also was stained yellow with nicotine.

"A smoker, Mr. Holmes?" said he, speaking well-chosen English with a curious little mincing accent. "Pray take a cigarette. And you, sir? I can recommend them, for I have them especially prepared by Ionides of Alexandria. He sends me a thousand at a time, and I grieve to say that I have to arrange for a fresh supply every fortnight. Bad, sir, very bad, but an old man has few pleasures. Tobacco and my work—that is all that is left to me."

Holmes had lit a cigarette, and was shooting little darting glances all over the room.

"Tobacco and my work, but now only tobacco," the old man exclaimed. "Alas! what a fatal interruption! Who could have foreseen such a terrible catastrophe? So estimable a young man! I assure you that after a few months' training he was an admirable assistant. What do you think of the matter, Mr. Holmes?"

"I have not yet made up my mind."

"I shall indeed be indebted to you if you can throw a light where all is so dark to us. To a poor bookworm and invalid like myself such a blow is paralyzing. I seem to have lost the faculty of thought. But you are a man of action—you are a man of affairs. It is part of the everyday routine of your life. You can preserve your balance in every emergency. We are fortunate indeed in having you at our side."

Holmes was pacing up and down one side of the room whilst the old Professor was talking. I observed that he was smoking with extraordinary rapidity. It was evident that he shared our host's liking for the fresh Alexandrian cigarettes.

"Yes, sir, it is a crushing blow," said the old man. "That is my *magnum opus*—the pile of papers on the side table yonder. It is my analysis of the documents found in the Coptic monasteries of Syria and Egypt, a work which will cut deep at the very foundations of revealed religion. With my enfeebled health I do not know whether I shall ever be able to complete it now that my assistant has been taken from me. Dear me, Mr. Holmes; why, you are even a quicker smoker than I am myself."

Holmes smiled.

"I am a connoisseur," said he, taking another cigarette from the box—his fourth—and lighting it from the stub of that which he had finished. "I will not trouble you with any lengthy cross-examination, Professor Coram, since I gather that you were in bed at the time of the crime and could know nothing about it. I would only ask this. What do you imagine that this poor fellow meant by his last words: 'The Professor—it was she'?"

The Professor shook his head.

"Susan is a country girl," said he, "and you know the incredible stupidity of that class. I fancy that the poor fellow murmured some incoherent delirious words, and that she twisted them into this meaningless message."

"I see. You have no explanation yourself of the tragedy?"

"Possibly an accident; possibly—I only breathe it among ourselves—a suicide. Young men have their hidden troubles—some affair of the heart, perhaps, which we have never known. It is a more probable supposition than murder."

"But the eye-glasses?"

"Ah! I am only a student—a man of dreams. I cannot explain the practical things of life. But still, we are aware, my friend, that love-gages may take strange shapes. By all means take another cigarette. It is a pleasure to see anyone appreciate them so. A fan, a glove, glasses—who knows what article may be carried as a token or treasured when a man puts an end to his life? This gentleman speaks of footsteps in the grass; but, after all, it is easy to be mistaken on such a point. As to the knife, it might well be thrown far from the unfortunate man as he fell. It is possible that I speak as a child, but to me it seems that Willoughby Smith has met his fate by his own hand."

Holmes seemed struck by the theory thus put forward, and he continued to walk up and down for some time, lost in thought and consuming cigarette after cigarette.

"Tell me, Professor Coram," he said, at last, "what is in that cupboard in the bureau?"

"Nothing that would help a thief. Family papers, letters from my poor wife, diplomas of Universities which have done me honour. Here is the key. You can look for yourself."

Holmes picked up the key and looked at it for an instant; then he handed it back.

"No; I hardly think that it would help me," said he. "I should prefer to go quietly down to your garden and turn the whole matter over in my head. There is something to be said for the theory of suicide which you have put forward. We must apologize

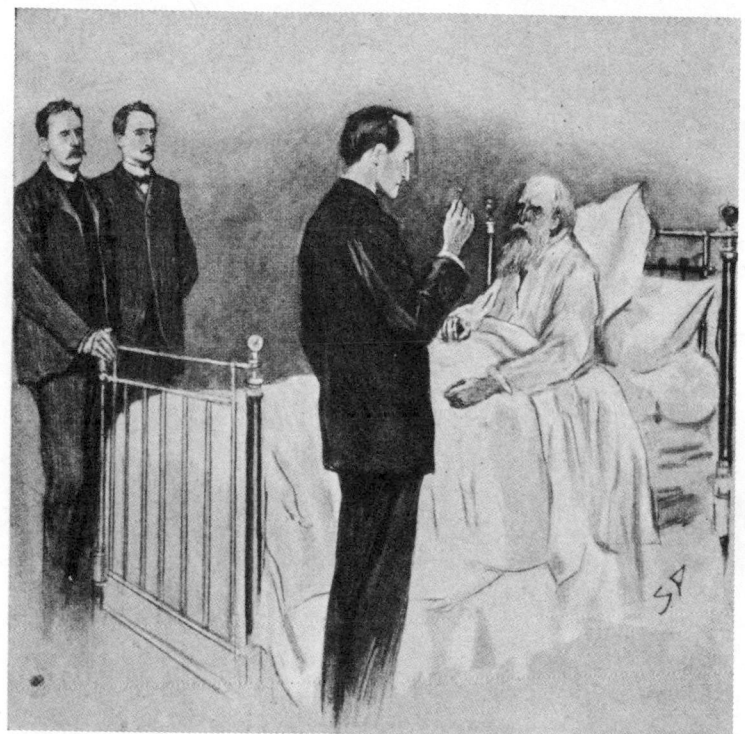

"HOLMES PICKED UP THE KEY AND LOOKED AT IT FOR AN INSTANT."

had captured the housekeeper's goodwill, and was chatting with her as if he had known her for years.

"Yes, Mr. Holmes, it is as you say, sir. He does smoke something terrible. All day and sometimes all night, sir. I've seen that room of a morning —well, sir, you'd have thought it was a London fog. Poor young Mr. Smith, he was a smoker also, but not as bad as the Professor. His health — well, I don't know that it's better nor worse for the smoking."

"Ah!" said Holmes, "but it kills the appetite."

"Well, I don't know about that, sir."

"I suppose the Professor eats hardly anything?"

"Well, he is variable. I'll say that for him."

"I'll wager he took no breakfast this morning, and won't face his lunch after all the cigarettes I saw him consume."

"Well, you're out there, sir, as it happens, for he ate a remarkable big breakfast this morning. I don't know when I've known him make a better one, and he's ordered a good dish of cutlets for his lunch. I'm surprised myself, for since I came into that room yesterday and saw young Mr. Smith lying there on the floor I couldn't bear to look at food. Well, it takes all sorts to make a world, and the Professor hasn't let it take his appetite away."

We loitered the morning away in the garden. Stanley Hopkins had gone down to the village to look into some rumours of a strange woman who had been seen by some children on the Chatham road the previous morning. As to my friend, all his usual energy seemed to have deserted him. I had never known him handle a case in such a

for having intruded upon you, Professor Coram, and I promise that we won't disturb you until after lunch. At two o'clock we will come again and report to you anything which may have happened in the interval."

Holmes was curiously distrait, and we walked up and down the garden path for some time in silence.

"Have you a clue?" I asked, at last.

"It depends upon those cigarettes that I smoked," said he. "It is possible that I am utterly mistaken. The cigarettes will show me."

"My dear Holmes," I exclaimed, "how on earth——"

"Well, well, you may see for yourself. If not, there's no harm done. Of course, we always have the optician clue to fall back upon, but I take a short cut when I can get it. Ah, here is the good Mrs. Marker! Let us enjoy five minutes of instructive conversation with her."

I may have remarked before that Holmes had, when he liked, a peculiarly ingratiating way with women, and that he very readily established terms of confidence with them. In half the time which he had named he

half-hearted fashion. Even the news brought back by Hopkins that he had found the children and that they had undoubtedly seen a woman exactly corresponding with Holmes's description, and wearing either spectacles or eye-glasses, failed to rouse any sign of keen interest. He was more attentive when Susan, who waited upon us at lunch, volunteered the information that she believed Mr. Smith had been out for a walk yesterday morning, and that he had only returned half an hour before the tragedy occurred. I could not myself see the bearing of this incident, but I clearly perceived that Holmes was weaving it into the general scheme which he had formed in his brain. Suddenly he sprang from his chair and glanced at his watch. "Two o'clock, gentlemen," said he. "We must go up and have it out with our friend the Professor."

The old man had just finished his lunch, and certainly his empty dish bore evidence to the good appetite with which his housekeeper had credited him. He was, indeed, a weird figure as he turned his white mane and his glowing eyes towards us. The eternal cigarette smouldered in his mouth. He had been dressed and was seated in an arm-chair by the fire.

"Well, Mr. Holmes, have you solved this mystery yet?" He shoved the large tin of cigarettes which stood on a table beside him towards my companion. Holmes stretched out his hand at the same moment, and between them they tipped the box over the edge. For a minute or two we were all on our knees retrieving stray cigarettes from impossible places. When we rose again I observed that Holmes's eyes were shining and his cheeks tinged with colour. Only at a crisis have I seen those battle-signals flying.

"Yes," said he, "I have solved it."

Stanley Hopkins and I stared in amazement. Something like a sneer quivered over the gaunt features of the old Professor.

"Indeed! In the garden?"

"No, here."

"Here! When?"

"This instant."

"You are surely joking, Mr. Sherlock Holmes. You compel me to tell you that this is too serious a matter to be treated in such a fashion."

"I have forged and tested every link of my chain, Professor Coram, and I am sure that it is sound. What your motives are or what exact part you play in this strange business I am not yet able to say. In a few minutes I shall probably hear it from your

own lips. Meanwhile I will reconstruct what is past for your benefit, so that you may know the information which I still require.

"A lady yesterday entered your study. She came with the intention of possessing herself of certain documents which were in your bureau. She had a key of her own. I have had an opportunity of examining yours, and I do not find that slight discoloration which the scratch made upon the varnish would have produced. You were not an accessory, therefore, and she came, so far as I can read the evidence, without your knowledge to rob you."

The Professor blew a cloud from his lips. "This is most interesting and instructive," said he. "Have you no more to add? Surely, having traced this lady so far, you can also say what has become of her."

"I will endeavour to do so. In the first place she was seized by your secretary, and stabbed him in order to escape. This catastrophe I am inclined to regard as an unhappy accident, for I am convinced that the lady had no intention of inflicting so grievous an injury. An assassin does not come unarmed. Horrified by what she had done she rushed wildly away from the scene of the tragedy. Unfortunately for her she had lost her glasses in the scuffle, and as she was extremely short-sighted she was really helpless without them. She ran down a corridor, which she imagined to be that by which she had come—both were lined with cocoanut matting—and it was only when it was too late that she understood that she had taken the wrong passage and that her retreat was cut off behind her. What was she to do? She could not go back. She could not remain where she was. She must go on. She went on. She mounted a stair, pushed open a door, and found herself in your room."

The old man sat with his mouth open staring wildly at Holmes. Amazement and fear were stamped upon his expressive features. Now, with an effort, he shrugged his shoulders and burst into insincere laughter.

"All very fine, Mr. Holmes," said he. "But there is one little flaw in your splendid theory. I was myself in my room, and I never left it during the day."

"I am aware of that, Professor Coram."

"And you mean to say that I could lie upon that bed and not be aware that a woman had entered my room?"

"I never said so. You *were* aware of it. You spoke with her. You recognised her. You aided her to escape."

Again the Professor burst into high-keyed laughter. He had risen to his feet and his eyes glowed like embers.

"You are mad!" he cried. "You are talking insanely. I helped her to escape? Where is she now?"

"She is there," said Holmes, and he pointed to a high bookcase in the corner of the room.

I saw the old man throw up his arms, a terrible convulsion passed over his grim face, and he fell back in his chair. At the same instant the bookcase at which Holmes pointed swung round upon a hinge, and a woman rushed out into the room. "You are right!" she cried, in a strange foreign voice. "You are right! I am here."

She was brown with the dust and draped with the cobwebs which had come from the walls of her hiding-place. Her face, too, was streaked with grime, and at the best she could never have been handsome, for she had the exact physical characteristics which Holmes had divined, with, in addition, a long and obstinate chin. What with her natural blindness, and what with the change from dark to light, she stood as one dazed,

"A WOMAN RUSHED OUT INTO THE ROOM."

blinking about her to see where and who we were. And yet, in spite of all these disadvantages, there was a certain nobility in the woman's bearing, a gallantry in the defiant chin and in the upraised head, which compelled something of respect and admiration. Stanley Hopkins had laid his hand upon her arm and claimed her as his prisoner, but she waved him aside gently, and yet with an overmastering dignity which compelled obedience. The old man lay back in his chair, with a twitching face, and stared at her with brooding eyes.

"Yes, sir, I am your prisoner," she said.

"From where I stood I could hear everything, and I know that you have learned the truth. I confess it all. It was I who killed the young man. But you are right, you who say that it was an accident. I did not even know that it was a knife which I held in my hand, for in my despair I snatched anything from the table and struck at him to make him let me go. It is the truth that I tell."

"Madam," said Holmes, "I am sure that it is the truth. I fear that you are far from well."

She had turned a dreadful colour, the more ghastly under the dark dust-streaks upon her face. She seated herself on the side of the bed; then she resumed.

"I have only a little time here," she said, "but I would have you to know the whole truth. I am this man's wife. He is not an Englishman. He is a Russian. His name I will not tell."

For the first time the old man stirred. "God bless you, Anna!" he cried. "God bless you!"

She cast a look of the deepest disdain in his direction. "Why should you cling so hard to that wretched life of yours, Sergius?" said she. "It has done harm to many and good to none —not even to yourself. However, it is not for me to cause the frail thread to be snapped before God's time. I have enough already upon my soul since I crossed the threshold of this cursed house. But I must speak or I shall be too late.

"I have said, gentlemen, that I am this man's wife. He was fifty and I a foolish girl of twenty when we married. It was in a city of Russia, a University—I will not name the place."

"God bless you, Anna!" murmured the old man again.

"We were reformers — revolutionists— Nihilists, you understand. He and I and many more. Then there came a time of trouble, a police officer was killed, many were arrested, evidence was wanted, and in order to save his own life and to earn a great reward my husband betrayed his own wife and his companions. Yes, we were all arrested upon his confession. Some of us found our way to the gallows and some to Siberia. I was among these last, but my term was not for life. My husband came to England with his ill-gotten gains, and has lived in quiet ever since, knowing well that if the Brotherhood knew where he was not a week would pass before justice would be done."

The old man reached out a trembling hand and helped himself to a cigarette. "I am in your hands, Anna," said he. "You were always good to me."

"I have not yet told you the height of his villainy," said she. "Among our comrades of the Order there was one who was the friend of my heart. He was noble, unselfish, loving — all that my husband was not. He hated violence. We were all guilty— if that is guilt —but he was not. He wrote for ever dissuading us from such a course. These letters would have saved him. So would my diary, in which from day to day I had entered both my feelings towards him and the view which each of us had taken. My husband found and kept both diary and letters. He hid them, and he tried hard to swear away the young man's life. In this he failed, but Alexis was sent a convict to Siberia, where now, at this moment, he works in a salt mine. Think of that, you villain, you villain ; now, now, at this very moment, Alexis, a man whose name you are not worthy to speak, works and lives like a slave, and yet I have your life in my hands and I let you go."

"You were always a noble woman, Anna," said the old man, puffing at his cigarette.

She had risen, but she fell back again with a little cry of pain.

"I must finish," she said. "When my term was over I set myself to get the diary and letters which, if sent to the Russian Government, would procure my friend's release. I knew that my husband had come to England. After months of searching I discovered where he was. I knew that he still had the diary, for when I was in Siberia I had a letter from him once reproaching me

"'I AM IN YOUR HANDS, ANNA,' SAID HE."

and quoting some passages from its pages. Yet I was sure that with his revengeful nature he would never give it to me of his own free will. I must get it for myself. With this object I engaged an agent from a private detective firm, who entered my husband's house as secretary—it was your second secretary, Sergius, the one who left you so hurriedly. He found that papers were kept in the cupboard, and he got an impression of the key. He would not go farther. He furnished me with a plan of the house, and he told me that in the forenoon the study was always empty, as the secretary was employed up here. So at last I took my courage in both hands and I came down to get the papers for myself. I succeeded, but at what a cost !

"I had just taken the papers and was locking the cupboard when the young man seized me. I had seen him already that morning. He had met me in the road and I had asked him to tell me where Professor Coram lived, not knowing that he was in his employ."

"Exactly ! exactly !" said Holmes. "The secretary came back and told his employer of the woman he had met. Then in his last breath he tried to send a message that it was she—the she whom he had just discussed with him."

"You must let me speak," said the woman, in an imperative voice, and her face contracted as if in pain. "When he had fallen I rushed from the room, chose the wrong door, and found myself in my husband's room. He spoke of giving me up. I showed him that if he did so his life was in my hands. If he gave me to the law I could give him to the Brotherhood. It was not that I wished to live for my own sake, but it was that I desired to accomplish my purpose. He knew that I would do what I said—that his own fate was involved in mine. For that reason and for no other he shielded me. He thrust me into that dark hiding-place, a relic of old days, known only to himself. He took his meals in his own room, and so was able to give me part of his food. It was agreed that when the police left the house I should slip away by night and come back no more. But in some way you have read our plans." She tore from the bosom of her dress a small packet. "These are my last words," said she ; "here is the packet which will save Alexis. I confide it to your honour and to your love of justice. Take it ! You will deliver it at the Russian Embassy. Now I have done my duty, and——"

"Stop her !" cried Holmes. He had bounded across the room and had wrenched a small phial from her hand.

"Too late !" she said, sinking back on the bed. "Too late ! I took the poison before I left my hiding-place. My head swims ! I am going ! I charge you, sir, to remember the packet."

"A simple case, and yet in some ways an instructive one," Holmes remarked, as we travelled back to town. "It hinged from the outset upon the pince-nez. But for the for-tunate chance of the dying man having seized these I am not sure that we could ever have reached our solution. It was clear to me from the strength of the glasses that the wearer must have been very blind and help-less when deprived of them. When you asked me to believe that she walked along a narrow strip of grass without once making a false step I remarked, as you may remember, that it was a noteworthy performance. In my mind I set it down as an impossible per-formance, save in the unlikely case that she had a second pair of glasses. I was forced, therefore, to seriously consider the hypothesis that she had remained within the house. On perceiving the similarity of the two corridors it became clear that she might very easily have made such a mistake, and in that case it was evident that she must have entered the Professor's room. I was keenly on the alert, therefore, for whatever would bear out this supposition, and I examined the room narrowly for anything in the shape of a hiding-place. The carpet seemed continuous and firmly nailed, so I dismissed the idea of a trap-door. There might well be a recess behind the books. As you are aware, such devices are common in old libraries. I observed that books were piled on the floor at all other points, but that one bookcase was left clear. This, then, might be the door. I could see no marks to guide me, but the carpet was of a dun colour, which lends itself very well to examination. I therefore smoked a great number of those excellent cigarettes, and I dropped the ash all over the space in front of the suspected bookcase. It was a simple trick, but exceedingly effective. I then went downstairs and I ascertained, in your presence, Watson, without your quite perceiving the drift of my remarks, that Professor Coram's consumption of food had increased—as one would expect when he is supplying a second person. We then ascended to the room again, when, by upsetting the cigarette-box, I obtained a very excellent view of the floor, and was able to see quite clearly, from the traces upon the cigarette ash, that the prisoner had, in our absence, come out from her retreat. Well, Hopkins, here we are at Charing Cross, and I congratulate you on having brought your case to a successful conclusion. You are going to head-quarters, no doubt. I think, Watson, you and I will drive together to the Russian Embassy."

"THE CARRIAGE RATTLED PAST."

# THE RETURN OF SHERLOCK HOLMES.

## By A. CONAN DOYLE.

### XI.—The Adventure of the Missing Three-Quarter.

E were fairly accustomed to receive weird telegrams at Baker Street, but I have a particular recollection of one which reached us on a gloomy February morning some seven or eight years ago and gave Mr. Sherlock Holmes a puzzled quarter of an hour. It was addressed to him, and ran thus:—

"Please await me. Terrible misfortune. Right wing three-quarter missing; indispensable to morrow.—OVERTON."

"Strand post-mark and dispatched ten-thirty-six," said Holmes, reading it over and over. "Mr. Overton was evidently considerably excited when he sent it, and somewhat incoherent in consequence. Well, well, he will be here, I dare say, by the time I have looked through the *Times*, and then we shall know all about it. Even the most insignificant problem would be welcome in these stagnant days."

Things had indeed been very slow with us, and I had learned to dread such periods of inaction, for I knew by experience that my companion's brain was so abnormally active that it was dangerous to leave it without material upon which to work. For years I had gradually weaned him from that drug mania which had threatened once to check his remarkable career. Now I knew that under ordinary conditions he no longer craved for this artificial stimulus, but I was well aware that the fiend was not dead, but sleeping; and I have known that the sleep was a light one and the waking near when in periods of idleness I have seen the drawn look upon Holmes's ascetic face, and the brooding of his deep-set and inscrutable eyes.

Therefore I blessed this Mr. Overton, whoever he might be, since he had come with his enigmatic message to break that dangerous calm which brought more peril to my friend than all the storms of his tempestuous life.

As we had expected, the telegram was soon followed by its sender, and the card of Mr. Cyril Overton, of Trinity College, Cambridge, announced the arrival of an enormous young man, sixteen stone of solid bone and muscle, who spanned the doorway with his broad shoulders and looked from one of us to the other with a comely face which was haggard with anxiety.

"Mr. Sherlock Holmes?"

My companion bowed.

"I've been down to Scotland Yard, Mr. Holmes. I saw Inspector Stanley Hopkins. He advised me to come to you. He said the case, so far as he could see, was more in your line than in that of the regular police."

"Pray sit down and tell me what is the matter."

"It's awful, Mr. Holmes, simply awful! I wonder my hair isn't grey. Godfrey Staunton—you've heard of him, of course? He's simply the hinge that the whole team turns on. I'd rather spare two from the pack and have Godfrey for my three-quarter line. Whether it's passing, or tackling, or dribbling, there's no one to touch him; and then, he's got the head and can hold us all together. What am I to do? That's what I ask you, Mr. Holmes. There's Moorhouse, first reserve, but he is trained as a half, and he always edges right in on to the scrum instead of keeping out on the touch-line. He's a fine place-kick, it's true, but, then, he has no judgment, and he can't sprint for nuts. Why, Morton or Johnson, the Oxford fliers, could romp round him. Stevenson is fast enough, but he couldn't drop from the twenty-five line, and a three-quarter who can't either punt or drop isn't worth a place

"Why, Mr. Holmes, I thought you knew things," said he. "I suppose, then, if you have never heard of Godfrey Staunton you don't know Cyril Overton either?"

Holmes shook his head good-humouredly.

"Great Scot!" cried the athlete. "Why,

"'WHY, MR. HOLMES, I THOUGHT YOU KNEW THINGS,' SAID HE."

for pace alone. No, Mr. Holmes, we are done unless you can help me to find Godfrey Staunton."

My friend had listened with amused surprise to this long speech, which was poured forth with extraordinary vigour and earnestness, every point being driven home by the slapping of a brawny hand upon the speaker's knee. When our visitor was silent Holmes stretched out his hand and took down letter "S" of his commonplace book. For once he dug in vain into that mine of varied information.

"There is Arthur H. Staunton, the rising young forger," said he, "and there was Henry Staunton, whom I helped to hang, but Godfrey Staunton is a new name to me."

It was our visitor's turn to look surprised.

I was first reserve for England against Wales, and I've skippered the 'Varsity all this year. But that's nothing! I didn't think there was a soul in England who didn't know Godfrey Staunton, the crack three-quarter, Cambridge, Blackheath, and five Internationals. Good Lord! Mr. Holmes, where *have* you lived?"

Holmes laughed at the young giant's naïve astonishment.

"You live in a different world to me, Mr. Overton, a sweeter and healthier one. My ramifications stretch out into many sections of society, but never, I am happy to say, into amateur sport, which is the best and soundest thing in England. However, your unexpected visit this morning shows me that even in that world of fresh air and fair play there may be work for me to do; so now, my good sir, I beg you to sit down and to tell me slowly and quietly exactly what it is that has occurred, and how you desire that I should help you."

Young Overton's face assumed the bothered look of the man who is more accustomed to using his muscles than his wits; but by degrees, with many repetitions and obscurities which I may omit from his narrative, he laid his strange story before us.

"It's this way, Mr. Holmes. As I have said, I am the skipper of the Rugger team of Cambridge 'Varsity, and Godfrey Staunton is my best man. To-morrow we play Oxford. Yesterday we all came up and we settled at Bentley's private hotel. At ten o'clock I went round and saw that all the fellows had gone to roost, for I believe in strict training and plenty of sleep to keep a team fit. I had a word or two with Godfrey before he turned in. He seemed to me to be pale and bothered. I asked him what was the matter. He said he was all right — just a touch of headache. I bade him good-night and left him. Half an hour later the porter tells me that a rough-looking man with a beard called with a note for Godfrey. He had not gone to bed and the note was taken to his room. Godfrey read it and fell back in a chair as if he had been pole-axed. The porter was so scared that he was going to fetch me, but Godfrey stopped him, had a drink of water, and pulled himself together. Then he went downstairs, said a few words to the man who was waiting in the hall, and the two of them went off together. The last that the porter saw of them, they were almost running down the street in the direction of the Strand. This morning Godfrey's room was empty, his bed had never been slept in, and his things were all just as I had seen them the night before. He had gone off at a moment's notice with this stranger, and no word has come from him since. I don't believe he will ever come back. He was a sportsman, was Godfrey, down to his marrow, and he wouldn't have stopped his training and let in his skipper if it were not for some cause that was too strong for him. No; I feel as if he were gone for good and we should never see him again."

Sherlock Holmes listened with the deepest attention to this singular narrative.

"What did you do?" he asked.

"I wired to Cambridge to learn if anything had been heard of him there. I have had an answer. No one has seen him."

"Could he have got back to Cambridge?"

"Yes, there is a late train—quarter-past eleven."

"But so far as you can ascertain he did not take it?"

"No, he has not been seen."

"What did you do next?"

"I wired to Lord Mount-James."

"Why to Lord Mount-James?"

"Godfrey is an orphan, and Lord Mount-James is his nearest relative—his uncle, I believe."

"Indeed. This throws new light upon the matter. Lord Mount-James is one of the richest men in England."

"So I've heard Godfrey say."

"And your friend was closely related?"

"Yes, he was his heir, and the old boy is nearly eighty—cram full of gout, too. They say he could chalk his billiard-cue with his knuckles. He never allowed Godfrey a shilling in his life, for he is an absolute miser, but it will all come to him right enough."

"Have you heard from Lord Mount-James?"

"No."

"What motive could your friend have in going to Lord Mount-James?"

"Well, something was worrying him the night before, and if it was to do with money it is possible that he would make for his nearest relative who had so much of it, though from all I have heard he would not have much chance of getting it. Godfrey was not fond of the old man. He would not go if he could help it."

"Well, we can soon determine that. If your friend was going to his relative, Lord Mount-James, you have then to explain the visit of this rough-looking fellow at so late an hour, and the agitation that was caused by his coming."

Cyril Overton pressed his hands to his head. "I can make nothing of it," said he.

"Well, well, I have a clear day, and I shall be happy to look into the matter," said Holmes. "I should strongly recommend you to make your preparations for your match without reference to this young gentleman. It must, as you say, have been an overpowering necessity which tore him away in such a fashion, and the same necessity is likely to hold him away. Let us step round together to this hotel, and see if the porter can throw any fresh light upon the matter."

Sherlock Holmes was a past-master in the art of putting a humble witness at his ease, and very soon, in the privacy of Godfrey

Staunton's abandoned room, he had extracted all that the porter had to tell. The visitor of the night before was not a gentleman, neither was he a working man. He was simply what the porter described as a "medium-looking chap"; a man of fifty, beard grizzled, pale face, quietly dressed. He seemed himself to be agitated. The porter had observed his hand trembling when he had held out the note. Godfrey Staunton had crammed the note into his pocket. Staunton had not shaken hands with the man in the hall. They had exchanged a few sentences, of which the porter had only distinguished the one word "time." Then they had hurried off in the manner described. It was just half-past ten by the hall clock.

"Let me see," said Holmes, seating himself on Staunton's bed. "You are the day porter, are you not?"

"Yes, sir; I go off duty at eleven."

"The night porter saw nothing, I suppose?"

"No, sir; one theatre party came in late. No one else."

"Were you on duty all day yesterday?"

"Yes, sir."

"Did you take any messages to Mr. Staunton?"

"Yes, sir; one telegram."

"Ah! that's interesting. What o'clock was this?"

"About six."

"Where was Mr. Staunton when he received it?"

"Here in his room."

"Were you present when he opened it?"

"Yes, sir; I waited to see if there was an answer."

"Well, was there?"

"Yes, sir. He wrote an answer."

"Did you take it?"

"No; he took it himself."

"But he wrote it in your presence?"

"Yes, sir. I was standing by the door, and he with his back turned at that table.

When he had written it he said, 'All right, porter, I will take this myself.'"

"What did he write it with?"

"A pen, sir."

"Was the telegraphic form one of these on the table?"

"Yes, sir; it was the top one."

Holmes rose. Taking the forms he carried them over to the window and carefully examined that which was uppermost.

"It is a pity he did not write in pencil," said he, throwing them down again with a shrug of disappointment. "As you have no doubt frequently observed, Watson, the

"DID YOU TAKE ANY MESSAGES TO MR. STAUNTON?"

impression usually goes through — a fact which has dissolved many a happy marriage. However, I can find no trace here. I rejoice, however, to perceive that he wrote with a broad-pointed quill pen, and I can hardly doubt that we will find some impression upon this blotting-pad.    Ah, yes, surely this is the very thing!"

He tore off a strip of the blotting-paper and turned towards us the following hiero-glyphic:—

Cyril Overton was much excited.    "Hold it to the glass!" he cried.

"That is unnecessary," said Holmes. "The paper is thin, and the reverse will give the message.    Here it is."    He turned it over and we read:—

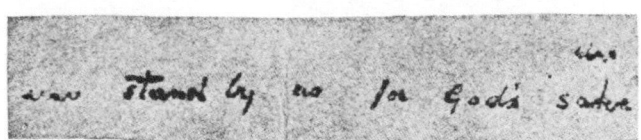

"So that is the tail end of the telegram which Godfrey Staunton dispatched within a few hours of his disappearance.    There are at least six words of the message which have escaped us; but what remains—'Stand by us for God's sake!'—proves that this young man saw a formidable danger which approached him, and from which someone else could protect him.    'Us,' mark you! Another person was involved.    Who should it be but the pale-faced, bearded man, who seemed himself in so nervous a state?    What, then, is the connection between Godfrey Staunton and the bearded man?    And what is the third source from which each of them sought for help against pressing danger? Our inquiry has already narrowed down to that."

"We have only to find to whom that telegram is addressed," I suggested.

"Exactly, my dear Watson.    Your reflec-tion, though profound, had already crossed my mind.    But I dare say it may have come to your notice that if you walk into a post-office and demand to see the counterfoil of another man's message there may be some disinclination on the part of the officials to oblige you.    There is so much red tape in these matters!    However, I have no doubt that with a little delicacy and finesse the end may be attained.    Meanwhile, I should like in your presence, Mr. Overton, to go through

these papers which have been left upon the table."

There were a number of letters, bills, and note-books, which Holmes turned over and examined with quick, nervous fingers and darting, penetrating eyes. "Nothing here," he said, at last. "By the way, I suppose your friend was a healthy young fellow—nothing amiss with him?"

"Sound as a bell."

"Have you ever known him ill?"

"Not a day.    He has been laid up with a hack, and once he slipped his knee-cap, but that was nothing."

"Perhaps he was not so strong as you suppose.    I should think he may have had some secret trouble.    With your assent I will put one or two of these papers in my pocket, in case they should bear upon our future inquiry."

"One moment! one moment!" cried a querul-ous voice, and we looked up to find a queer little old man, jerking and twitching in the doorway.    He was dressed in rusty black, with a very broad brimmed top-hat and a loose white necktie—the whole effect being that of a very rustic parson or of an under-taker's mute.    Yet, in spite of his shabby and even absurd appearance, his voice had a sharp crackle, and his manner a quick intensity which commanded atten-tion.

"Who are you, sir, and by what right do you touch this gentleman's papers?" he asked.

"I am a private detective, and I am endeavouring to explain his disappear-ance."

"Oh, you are, are you?    And who in-structed you, eh?"

"This gentleman, Mr. Staunton's friend, was referred to me by Scotland Yard."

"Who are you, sir?"

"I am Cyril Overton."

"Then it is you who sent me a telegram. My name is Lord Mount-James.    I came round as quickly as the Bayswater 'bus would bring me.    So you have instructed a detec-tive?"

"Yes, sir."

"And are you prepared to meet the cost?"

"I have no doubt, sir, that my friend

Godfrey, when we find him, will be prepared to do that."

"But if he is never found, eh? Answer me that!"

"In that case no doubt his family——"

"Nothing of the sort, sir!" screamed the little man. "Don't look to me for a penny—not a penny! You understand that, Mr. Detective! I am all the family that this young man has got, and I tell you that I am not responsible. If he has any expectations it is due to the fact that I have never wasted money, and I do not propose to begin to do so now. As to those papers with which you are making so free, I may tell you that in case there should be anything of any value among them you will be held strictly to account for what you do with them."

"Very good, sir," said Sherlock Holmes. "May I ask in the meanwhile whether you have yourself any theory to account for this young man's disappearance?"

"No, sir, I have not. He is big enough and old enough to look after himself, and if he is so foolish as to lose himself I entirely refuse to accept the responsibility of hunting for him."

"I quite understand your position," said Holmes, with a mischievous twinkle in his eyes. "Perhaps you don't quite understand mine. Godfrey Staunton appears to have been a poor man. If he has been kidnapped it could not have been for anything which he himself possesses. The fame of your wealth has gone abroad, Lord Mount-James, and it is entirely possible that a gang of thieves have secured your nephew in order to gain

"'ONE MOMENT, ONE MOMENT!' CRIED A QUERULOUS VOICE."

from him some information as to your house, your habits, and your treasure."

The face of our unpleasant little visitor turned as white as his neckcloth.

"Heavens, sir, what an idea! I never thought of such villainy! What inhuman rogues there are in the world! But Godfrey is a fine lad —a staunch lad. Nothing would induce him to give his old uncle away. I'll have the plate moved over to the bank this evening. In the meantime spare no pains, Mr. Detective! I beg you to leave no stone unturned to bring him safely back. As to money, well, so far as a fiver, or even a tenner, goes, you can always look to me."

Even in his chastened frame of mind the noble miser could give us no information which could help us, for he knew little of the private life of his nephew. Our only clue lay in the truncated telegram, and with a copy of this in his hand Holmes set forth to find a second link for his chain. We had shaken off Lord Mount-James, and Overton had gone to consult with the other members of his team over the misfortune which had befallen them.

There was a telegraph-office at a short distance from the hotel. We halted outside it.

"It's worth trying, Watson," said Holmes. "Of course, with a warrant we could demand to see the counterfoils, but we have not reached that stage yet. I don't suppose they remember faces in so busy a place. Let us venture it."

"I am sorry to trouble you," said he,

in his blandest manner, to the young woman behind the grating; "there is some small mistake about a telegram I sent yesterday. I have had no answer, and I very much fear that I must have omitted to put my name at the end. Could you tell me if this was so?"

The young woman turned over a sheaf of counterfoils.

"What o'clock was it?" she asked.

"A little after six."

"Whom was it to?"

Holmes put his finger to his lips and glanced at me. "The last words in it were 'for God's sake,'" he whispered, confidentially; "I am very anxious at getting no answer."

The young woman separated one of the forms.

"This is it. There is no name," said she, smoothing it out upon the counter.

"Then that, of course, accounts for my getting no answer," said Holmes. "Dear me, how very stupid of me, to be sure! Good morning, miss, and many thanks for having relieved my mind." He chuckled and rubbed his hands when we found ourselves in the street once more.

"Well?" I asked.

"We progress, my dear Watson, we progress. I had seven different schemes for getting a glimpse of that telegram, but I could hardly hope to succeed the very first time."

"And what have you gained?"

"A starting-point for our investigation." He hailed a cab. "King's Cross Station," said he.

"We have a journey, then?"

"Yes; I think we must run down to Cambridge together. All the indications seem to me to point in that direction."

"Tell me," I asked, as we rattled up Gray's Inn Road, "have you any suspicion yet as to the cause of the disappearance? I don't think that among all our cases I have known one where the motives are more obscure. Surely you don't really imagine that he may be kidnapped in order to give information against his wealthy uncle?"

"I confess, my dear Watson, that that does not appeal to me as a very probable explanation. It struck me, however, as being the one which was most likely to interest that exceedingly unpleasant old person."

"It certainly did that. But what are your alternatives?"

"I could mention several. You must admit that it is curious and suggestive that this incident should occur on the eve of this

important match, and should involve the only man whose presence seems essential to the success of the side. It may, of course, be coincidence, but it is interesting. Amateur sport is free from betting, but a good deal of outside betting goes on among the public, and it is possible that it might be worth someone's while to get at a player as the ruffians of the turf get at a race-horse. There is one explanation. A second very obvious one is that this young man really is the heir of a great property, however modest his means may at present be, and it is not impossible that a plot to hold him for ransom might be concocted."

"These theories take no account of the telegram."

"Quite true, Watson. The telegram still remains the only solid thing with which we have to deal, and we must not permit our attention to wander away from it. It is to gain light upon the purpose of this telegram that we are now upon our way to Cambridge. The path of our investigation is at present obscure, but I shall be very much surprised if before evening we have not cleared it up or made a considerable advance along it."

It was already dark when we reached the old University city. Holmes took a cab at the station, and ordered the man to drive to the house of Dr. Leslie Armstrong. A few minutes later we had stopped at a large mansion in the busiest thoroughfare. We were shown in, and after a long wait were at last admitted into the consulting-room, where we found the doctor seated behind his table.

It argues the degree in which I had lost touch with my profession that the name of Leslie Armstrong was unknown to me. Now I am aware that he is not only one of the heads of the medical school of the University, but a thinker of European reputation in more than one branch of science. Yet even without knowing his brilliant record one could not fail to be impressed by a mere glance at the man, the square, massive face, the brooding eyes under the thatched brows, the granite moulding of the inflexible jaw. A man of deep character, a man with an alert mind, grim, ascetic, self-contained, formidable —so I read Dr. Leslie Armstrong. He held my friend's card in his hand, and he looked up with no very pleased expression upon his dour features.

"I have heard your name, Mr. Sherlock Holmes, and I am aware of your profession, one of which I by no means approve."

"In that, doctor, you will find yourself in agreement with every criminal in the country," said my friend, quietly.

"So far as your efforts are directed towards the suppression of crime, sir, they must

"HE LOOKED UP WITH NO VERY PLEASED EXPRESSION ON HIS DOUR FEATURES."

blame, and that we are endeavouring to prevent anything like public exposure of private matters which must necessarily follow when once the case is fairly in the hands of the official police. You may look upon me simply as an irregular pioneer who goes in front of the regular forces of the country. I have come to ask you about Mr. Godfrey Staunton."

"What about him?"

"You know him, do you not?"

"He is an intimate friend of mine."

"You are aware that he has disappeared?"

"Ah, indeed!" There was no change of expression in the rugged features of the doctor.

"He left his hotel last night. He has not been heard of."

"No doubt he will return."

"To-morrow is the 'Varsity football match."

"I have no sympathy with these childish games. The young man's fate interests me deeply, since I know him and like him. The football match does not come within my horizon at all."

"I claim your sympathy, then, in my investigation of Mr. Staunton's fate. Do you know where he is?"

"Certainly not."

"You have not seen him since yesterday?"

"No, I have not."

"Was Mr. Staunton a healthy man?"

"Absolutely."

"Did you ever know him ill?"

"Never."

Holmes popped a sheet of paper before the doctor's eyes. "Then perhaps you will explain this receipted bill for thirteen guineas, paid by Mr. Godfrey Staunton last month to Dr. Leslie Armstrong of Cambridge. I

have the support of every reasonable member of the community, though I cannot doubt that the official machinery is amply sufficient for the purpose. Where your calling is more open to criticism is when you pry into the secrets of private individuals, when you rake up family matters which are better hidden, and when you incidentally waste the time of men who are more busy than yourself. At the present moment, for example, I should be writing a treatise instead of conversing with you."

"No doubt, doctor; and yet the conversation may prove more important than the treatise. Incidentally I may tell you that we are doing the reverse of what you very justly

picked it out from among the papers upon his desk."

The doctor flushed with anger.

"I do not feel that there is any reason why I should render an explanation to you, Mr. Holmes."

Holmes replaced the bill in his note-book. "If you prefer a public explanation it must come sooner or later," said he. "I have already told you that I can hush up that which others will be bound to publish, and you would really be wiser to take me into your complete confidence."

"I know nothing about it."

"Did you hear from Mr. Staunton in London?"

"Certainly not."

"Dear me, dear me; the post-office again!" Holmes sighed, wearily. "A most urgent telegram was dispatched to you from London by Godfrey Staunton at six-fifteen yesterday evening—a telegram which is undoubtedly associated with his disappearance—and yet you have not had it. It is most culpable. I shall certainly go down to the office here and register a complaint."

Dr. Leslie Armstrong sprang up from behind his desk, and his dark face was crimson with fury.

"I'll trouble you to walk out of my house, sir," said he. "You can tell your employer, Lord Mount-James, that I do not wish to have anything to do either with him or with his agents. No, sir, not another word!" He rang the bell furiously. "John, show these gentlemen out." A pompous butler ushered us severely to the door, and we found ourselves in the street. Holmes burst out laughing.

"Dr. Leslie Armstrong is certainly a man of energy and character," said he. "I have not seen a man who, if he turned his talents that way, was more calculated to fill the gap left by the illustrious Moriarty. And now, my poor Watson, here we are, stranded and friendless in this inhospitable town, which we cannot leave without abandoning our case. This little inn just opposite Armstrong's house is singularly adapted to our needs. If you would engage a front room and purchase the necessaries for the night, I may have time to make a few inquiries."

These few inquiries proved, however, to be a more lengthy proceeding than Holmes had imagined, for he did not return to the inn until nearly nine o'clock. He was pale and dejected, stained with dust, and exhausted with hunger and fatigue. A cold supper was ready upon the table, and when his needs were satisfied and his pipe alight he was ready to take that half comic and wholly philosophic view which was natural to him when his affairs were going awry. The sound of carriage wheels caused him to rise and glance out of the window. A brougham and pair of greys under the glare of a gas-lamp stood before the doctor's door.

"It's been out three hours," said Holmes; "started at half-past six, and here it is back again. That gives a radius of ten or twelve miles, and he does it once, or sometimes twice, a day."

"No unusual thing for a doctor in practice."

"But Armstrong is not really a doctor in practice. He is a lecturer and a consultant, but he does not care for general practice, which distracts him from his literary work. Why, then, does he make these long journeys, which must be exceedingly irksome to him, and who is it that he visits?"

"His coachman——"

"My dear Watson, can you doubt that it was to him that I first applied? I do not know whether it came from his own innate depravity or from the promptings of his master, but he was rude enough to set a dog at me. Neither dog nor man liked the look of my stick, however, and the matter fell through. Relations were strained after that, and further inquiries out of the question. All that I have learned I got from a friendly native in the yard of our own inn. It was he who told me of the doctor's habits and of his daily journey. At that instant, to give point to his words, the carriage came round to the door."

"Could you not follow it?"

"Excellent, Watson! You are scintillating this evening. The idea did cross my mind. There is, as you may have observed, a bicycle shop next to our inn. Into this I rushed, engaged a bicycle, and was able to get started before the carriage was quite out of sight. I rapidly overtook it, and then, keeping at a discreet distance of a hundred yards or so, I followed its lights until we were clear of the town. We had got well out on the country road when a somewhat mortifying incident occurred. The carriage stopped, the doctor alighted, walked swiftly back to where I had also halted, and told me in an excellent sardonic fashion that he feared the road was narrow, and that he hoped his carriage did not impede the passage of my bicycle. Nothing could have been more admirable than his way of putting it. I at once rode past the carriage, and, keeping to the main road, I went on for a few miles, and then halted in a convenient place to see if the carriage passed. There was no sign of it, however, and so it became evident that it had turned down one of several side roads which I had observed. I rode back, but again saw nothing of the carriage, and now, as you perceive, it has returned after me. Of course, I had at the outset no particular reason to connect these journeys with the disappearance of Godfrey Staunton, and was only inclined to investigate them on the general grounds that everything which concerns Dr. Armstrong is at present of interest to us ; but, now that I find he keeps so keen a look-out upon anyone who may follow him on these excursions, the affair appears more important, and I shall not be satisfied until I have made the matter clear."

"We can follow him to-morrow."

"Can we ? It is not so easy as you seem to think. You are not familiar with Cambridge-shire scenery, are you ? It does not lend itself to concealment. All this country that I passed over to-night is as flat and clean as the palm of your hand, and the man we are following is no fool, as he very clearly showed to-night. I have wired to Overton to let us know any fresh London developments at this address, and in the meantime we can only concentrate our attention upon Dr. Arm-strong, whose name the obliging young lady at the office allowed me to read upon the counterfoil of Staunton's urgent message. He knows where the young man is—to that I'll swear—and if he knows, then it must be our own fault if we cannot manage to know also. At present it must be admitted that the odd trick is in his possession, and, as you are aware, Watson, it is not my habit to leave the game in that condition."

And yet the next day brought us no nearer to the solution of the mystery. A note was handed in after breakfast, which Holmes passed across to me with a smile.

"Sir," it ran, "I can assure you that you are wasting your time in dogging my move-ments. I have, as you discovered last night, a window at the back of my brougham, and if you desire a twenty-mile ride which will lead you to the spot from which you started, you have only to follow me. Meanwhile, I can inform you that no spying upon me can in any way help Mr. Godfrey Staunton, and I am convinced that the best service you can do to that gentleman is to return at once to London and to report to your employer that

you are unable to trace him. Your time in Cambridge will certainly be wasted.

　　　　"Yours faithfully,
　　　　　　"LESLIE ARMSTRONG."

"An outspoken, honest antagonist is the doctor," said Holmes. "Well, well, he ex-cites my curiosity, and I must really know more before I leave him."

"His carriage is at his door now," said I. "There he is stepping into it. I saw him glance up at our window as he did so. Suppose I try my luck upon the bicycle ?"

"No, no, my dear Watson ! With all respect for your natural acumen I do not think that you are quite a match for the worthy doctor. I think that possibly I can attain our end by some independent ex-plorations of my own. I am afraid that I must leave you to your own devices, as the appearance of *two* inquiring strangers upon a sleepy countryside might excite more gossip than I care for. No doubt you will find some sights to amuse you in this venerable city, and I hope to bring back a more favourable report to you before evening."

Once more, however, my friend was destined to be disappointed. He came back at night weary and unsuccessful.

"I have had a blank day, Watson. Having got the doctor's general direction, I spent the day in visiting all the villages upon that side of Cambridge, and comparing notes with publicans and other local news agencies. I have covered some ground : Chesterton, Histon, Waterbeach, and Oakington have each been explored and have each proved disappointing. The daily appearance of a brougham and pair could hardly have been overlooked in such Sleepy Hollows. The doctor has scored once more. Is there a telegram for me ?"

"Yes ; I opened it. Here it is : ' Ask for Pompey from Jeremy Dixon, Trinity College.' I don't understand it."

"Oh, it is clear enough. It is from our friend Overton, and is in answer to a question from me. I'll just send round a note to Mr. Jeremy Dixon, and then I have no doubt that our luck will turn. By the way, is there any news of the match ?"

"Yes, the local evening paper has an excellent account in its last edition. Oxford won by a goal and two tries. The last sentences of the description say : ' The defeat of the Light Blues may be entirely attributed to the unfortunate absence of the crack International, Godfrey Staunton, whose want was felt at every instant of the game. The lack of combination in the three-quarter line and their weakness both in attack and defence more than neutralized the efforts of a heavy and hard-working pack.'"

"Then our friend Overton's forebodings have been justified," said Holmes. "Personally I am in agreement with Dr. Armstrong, and football does not come within my horizon. Early to bed to-night, Watson, for I foresee that to-morrow may be an eventful day."

I was horrified by my first glimpse of Holmes next morning, for he sat by the fire holding his tiny hypodermic syringe. I associated that instrument with the single weakness of his nature, and I feared the worst when I saw it glittering in his hand. He laughed at my expression of dismay, and laid it upon the table.

"No, no, my dear fellow, there is no cause for alarm. It is not upon this occasion the instrument of evil, but it will rather prove to be the key which will unlock our mystery. On this syringe I base all my hopes. I have just returned from a small scouting expedition and everything is favourable. Eat a good breakfast, Watson, for I propose to get upon Dr. Armstrong's trail to-day, and once on it I will not stop for rest or food until I run him to his burrow."

"In that case," said I, "we had best carry our breakfast with us, for he is making an early start. His carriage is at the door."

"Never mind. Let him go. He will be clever if he can drive where I cannot follow him. When you have finished come downstairs with me, and I will introduce you to a detective who is a very eminent specialist in the work that lies before us."

When we descended I followed Holmes into the stable yard, where

he opened the door of a loose-box and led out a squat, lop-eared, white-and-tan dog, something between a beagle and a foxhound.

"Let me introduce you to Pompey," said he. "Pompey is the pride of the local draghounds, no very great flier, as his build will show, but a staunch hound on a scent. Well, Pompey, you may not be fast, but I expect you will be too fast for a couple of middle-aged London gentlemen, so I will take the liberty of fastening this leather leash to your collar. Now, boy, come along, and show what you can do." He led him across to the doctor's door. The dog sniffed round for an instant, and then with a shrill whine of excitement started off down the street, tugging at his leash in his efforts to go faster. In half an hour we were clear of the town and hastening down a country road.

"What have you done, Holmes?" I asked.

"A threadbare and venerable device, but

"WE WERE CLEAR OF THE TOWN AND HASTENING DOWN A COUNTRY ROAD."

useful upon occasion. I walked into the doctor's yard this morning and shot my syringe full of aniseed over the hind wheel. A draghound will follow aniseed from here to John o' Groat's, and our friend Armstrong would have to drive through the Cam before he would shake Pompey off his trail. Oh, the cunning rascal! This is how he gave me the slip the other night."

The dog had suddenly turned out of the main road into a grass-grown lane. Half a mile farther this opened into another broad road, and the trail turned hard to the right in the direction of the town, which we had just quitted. The road took a sweep to the south of the town and continued in the opposite direction to that in which we started.

"This *détour* has been entirely for our benefit, then?" said Holmes. "No wonder that my inquiries among those villages led to nothing. The doctor has certainly played the game for all it is worth, and one would like to know the reason for such elaborate deception. This should be the village of Trumpington to the right of us. And, by Jove! here is the brougham coming round the corner. Quick, Watson, quick, or we are done!"

He sprang through a gate into a field, dragging the reluctant Pompey after him. We had hardly got under the shelter of the hedge when the carriage rattled past. I caught a glimpse of Dr. Armstrong within, his shoulders bowed, his head sunk on his hands, the very image of distress. I could tell by my companion's graver face that he also had seen.

"I fear there is some dark ending to our quest," said he. "It cannot be long before we know it. Come, Pompey! Ah, it is the cottage in the field!"

There could be no doubt that we had reached the end of our journey. Pompey ran about and whined eagerly outside the gate where the marks of the brougham's wheels were still to be seen. A footpath led across to the lonely cottage. Holmes tied the dog to the hedge, and we hastened onwards. My friend knocked at the little rustic door, and knocked again without response. And yet the cottage was not deserted, for a low sound came to our ears—a kind of drone of misery and despair, which was indescribably melancholy. Holmes paused irresolute, and then he glanced back at the road which we had just traversed. A brougham was coming down it, and there could be no mistaking those grey horses.

"By Jove, the doctor is coming back!" cried Holmes. "That settles it. We are bound to see what it means before he comes."

He opened the door and we stepped into the hall. The droning sound swelled louder upon our ears until it became one long, deep wail of distress. It came from upstairs. Holmes darted up and I followed him. He pushed open a half-closed door and we both stood appalled at the sight before us.

A woman, young and beautiful, was lying dead upon the bed. Her calm, pale face, with dim, wide-opened blue eyes, looked upwards from amid a great tangle of golden hair. At the foot of the bed, half sitting, half kneeling, his face buried in the clothes, was a young man, whose frame was racked by his sobs. So absorbed was he by his bitter grief that he never looked up until Holmes's hand was on his shoulder.

"Are you Mr. Godfrey Staunton?"

"Yes, yes; I am—but you are too late. She is dead."

The man was so dazed that he could not be made to understand that we were anything but doctors who had been sent to his assistance. Holmes was endeavouring to utter a few words of consolation, and to explain the alarm which had been caused to his friends by his sudden disappearance, when there was a step upon the stairs, and there was the heavy, stern, questioning face of Dr. Armstrong at the door.

"So, gentlemen," said he, "you have attained your end, and have certainly chosen a particularly delicate moment for your intrusion. I would not brawl in the presence of death, but I can assure you that if I were a younger man your monstrous conduct would not pass with impunity."

"Excuse me, Dr. Armstrong, I think we are a little at cross-purposes," said my friend, with dignity. "If you could step downstairs with us we may each be able to give some light to the other upon this miserable affair."

A minute later the grim doctor and ourselves were in the sitting-room below.

"Well, sir?" said he.

"I wish you to understand, in the first place, that I am not employed by Lord Mount-James, and that my sympathies in this matter are entirely against that nobleman. When a man is lost it is my duty to ascertain his fate, but having done so the matter ends so far as I am concerned; and so long as there is nothing criminal, I am much more anxious to hush up private scandals than to give them publicity. If, as

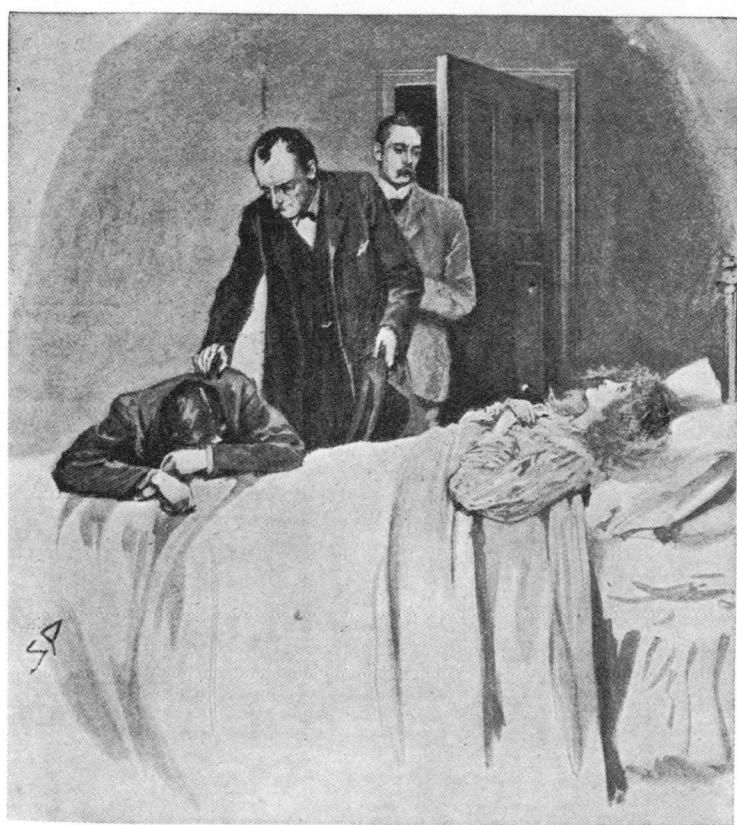

"HE NEVER LOOKED UP UNTIL HOLMES'S HAND WAS ON HIS SHOULDER."

him for his many excellent qualities. I did all I could to help him to keep things straight. We did our very best to keep the thing from everyone, for when once such a whisper gets about it is not long before everyone has heard it. Thanks to this lonely cottage and his own discretion, Godfrey has up to now succeeded. Their secret was known to no one save to me and to one excellent servant who has at present gone for assistance to Trumpington. But at last there came a terrible blow in the shape of dangerous illness to his wife. It was consumption of the most virulent kind. The poor boy was half crazed with grief, and yet he had to go to London to play this match, for he could not get out of it without explanations which would expose his secret. I tried to cheer him up by a wire, and he sent me one in reply imploring me to do all I could. This was the telegram which you appear in some inexplicable way to have seen. I did not tell him how urgent the danger was, for I knew that he could do no good here, but I sent the truth to the girl's father, and he very injudiciously communicated it to Godfrey. The result was that he came straight away in a state bordering on frenzy, and has remained in the same state, kneeling at the end of her bed, until this morning death put an end to her sufferings. That is all, Mr. Holmes, and I am sure that I can rely upon your discretion and that of your friend."

Holmes grasped the doctor's hand.

"Come, Watson," said he, and we passed from that house of grief into the pale sunlight of the winter day.

I imagine, there is no breach of the law in this matter, you can absolutely depend upon my discretion and my co-operation in keeping the facts out of the papers."

Dr. Armstrong took a quick step forward and wrung Holmes by the hand.

"You are a good fellow," said he. "I had misjudged you. I thank Heaven that my compunction at leaving poor Staunton all alone in this plight caused me to turn my carriage back, and so to make your acquaintance. Knowing as much as you do, the situation is very easily explained. A year ago Godfrey Staunton lodged in London for a time, and became passionately attached to his landlady's daughter, whom he married. She was as good as she was beautiful, and as intelligent as she was good. No man need be ashamed of such a wife. But Godfrey was the heir to this crabbed old nobleman, and it was quite certain that the news of his marriage would have been the end of his inheritance. I knew the lad well, and I loved

"IT WAS THE BODY OF A TALL, WELL-MADE MAN, ABOUT FORTY
YEARS OF AGE."

# THE RETURN OF SHERLOCK HOLMES.

## By A. CONAN DOYLE.

### XII.—The Adventure of the Abbey Grange.

 IT was on a bitterly cold and frosty morning during the winter of '97 that I was awakened by a tugging at my shoulder. It was Holmes. The candle in his hand shone upon his eager, stooping face and told me at a glance that something was amiss.

"Come, Watson, come!" he cried. "The game is afoot. Not a word! Into your clothes and come!"

Ten minutes later we were both in a cab and rattling through the silent streets on our way to Charing Cross Station. The first faint winter's dawn was beginning to appear, and we could dimly see the occasional figure of an early workman as he passed us, blurred and indistinct in the opalescent London reek. Holmes nestled in silence into his heavy coat, and I was glad to do the same, for the air was most bitter and neither of us had broken our fast. It was not until we had consumed some hot tea at the station, and taken our places in the Kentish train, that we were sufficiently thawed, he to speak and I to listen. Holmes drew a note from his pocket and read it aloud:—

"Abbey Grange, Marsham, Kent,
"3.30 a.m.

"MY DEAR MR. HOLMES,—I should be very glad of your immediate assistance in what promises to be a most remarkable case. It is something quite in your line. Except for releasing the lady I will see that everything is kept exactly as I have found it, but I beg you not to lose an instant, as it is difficult to leave Sir Eustace there.

"Yours faithfully, STANLEY HOPKINS."

"Hopkins has called me in seven times, and on each occasion his summons has been entirely justified," said Holmes. "I

"'COME, WATSON, COME!' HE CRIED. 'THE GAME IS AFOOT,'"

fancy that every one of his cases has found its way into your collection, and I must admit, Watson, that you have some power of selection which atones for much which I deplore in your narratives. Your fatal habit of looking at everything from the point of view of a story instead of as a scientific exercise has ruined what might have been an instructive and even classical series of demonstrations. You slur over work of the utmost finesse and delicacy in order to dwell upon sensational details which may excite, but cannot possibly instruct, the reader."

"Why do you not write them yourself?" I said, with some bitterness.

"I will, my dear Watson, I will. At present I am, as you know, fairly busy, but I propose to devote my declining years to the composition of a text-book which shall focus the whole art of detection into one volume. Our present research appears to be a case of murder."

"You think this Sir Eustace is dead, then?"

"I should say so. Hopkins's writing shows considerable agitation, and he is not an emotional man. Yes, I gather there has been violence, and that the body is left for our inspection. A mere suicide would not have caused him to send for me. As to the release of the lady, it would appear that she has been locked in her room during the tragedy. We are moving in high life, Watson; crackling paper, 'E.B.' monogram, coat-of-arms, picturesque address. I think that friend Hopkins will live up to his reputation and that we shall have an interesting morning. The crime was committed before twelve last night."

"How can you possibly tell?"

"By an inspection of the trains and by reckoning the time. The local police had to be called in, they had to communicate with Scotland Yard, Hopkins had to go out, and he in turn had to send for me. All that makes a fair night's work. Well, here we are at Chislehurst Station, and we shall soon set our doubts at rest."

A drive of a couple of miles through narrow country lanes brought us to a park gate, which was opened for us by an old lodge-keeper, whose haggard face bore the reflection of some great disaster. The avenue ran through a noble park, between lines of ancient elms, and ended in a low, widespread house, pillared in front after the fashion of Palladio. The central part was evidently of a great age and shrouded in ivy, but the large windows showed that modern changes had been carried out, and one wing of the house appeared to be entirely new. The youthful figure and alert, eager face of Inspector Stanley Hopkins confronted us in the open doorway.

"I'm very glad you have come, Mr. Holmes. And you too, Dr. Watson! But, indeed, if I had my time over again I should not have troubled you, for since the lady has come to herself she has given so clear an account of the affair that there is not much left for us to do. You remember that Lewisham gang of burglars?"

"What, the three Randalls?"

"Exactly; the father and two sons. It's their work. I have not a doubt of it. They did a job at Sydenham a fortnight ago, and were seen and described. Rather cool to do another so soon and so near, but it is they, beyond all doubt. It's a hanging matter this time."

"Sir Eustace is dead, then?"

"Yes; his head was knocked in with his own poker."

"Sir Eustace Brackenstall, the driver tells me."

"Exactly—one of the richest men in Kent. Lady Brackenstall is in the morning-room. Poor lady, she has had a most dreadful experience. She seemed half dead when I saw her first. I think you had best see her and hear her account of the facts. Then we will examine the dining-room together."

Lady Brackenstall was no ordinary person. Seldom have I seen so graceful a figure, so womanly a presence, and so beautiful a face. She was a blonde, golden-haired, blue-eyed, and would, no doubt, have had the perfect complexion which goes with such colouring had not her recent experience left her drawn and haggard. Her sufferings were physical as well as mental, for over one eye rose a hideous, plum-coloured swelling, which her maid, a tall, austere woman, was bathing assiduously with vinegar and water. The lady lay back exhausted upon a couch, but her quick, observant gaze as we entered the room, and the alert expression of her beautiful features, showed that neither her wits nor her courage had been shaken by her terrible experience. She was enveloped in a loose dressing-gown of blue and silver, but a black sequin-covered dinner-dress was hung upon the couch beside her.

"I have told you all that happened, Mr. Hopkins," she said, wearily; "could you not repeat it for me? Well, if you think it necessary, I will tell these gentlemen what occurred. Have they been in the dining-room yet?"

"I thought they had better hear your ladyship's story first."

"I shall be glad when you can arrange matters. It is horrible to me to think of him still lying there." She shuddered and buried her face for a moment in her hands. As she did so the loose gown fell back from her forearms. Holmes uttered an exclamation.

"You have other injuries, madam! What

conventional atmosphere of South Australia, and this English life, with its proprieties and its primness, is not congenial to me. But the main reason lies in the one fact which is notorious to everyone, and that is that Sir Eustace was a confirmed drunkard. To be with such a man for an hour is unpleasant. Can you imagine what it means for a sensitive and high-spirited woman to be tied to him for day and night? It is a sacrilege, a crime, a villainy to hold that such a marriage is binding. I say that these monstrous laws of yours will bring a curse upon the land—Heaven will not let such wickedness endure." For an instant she sat up, her cheeks flushed, and her eyes blazing from

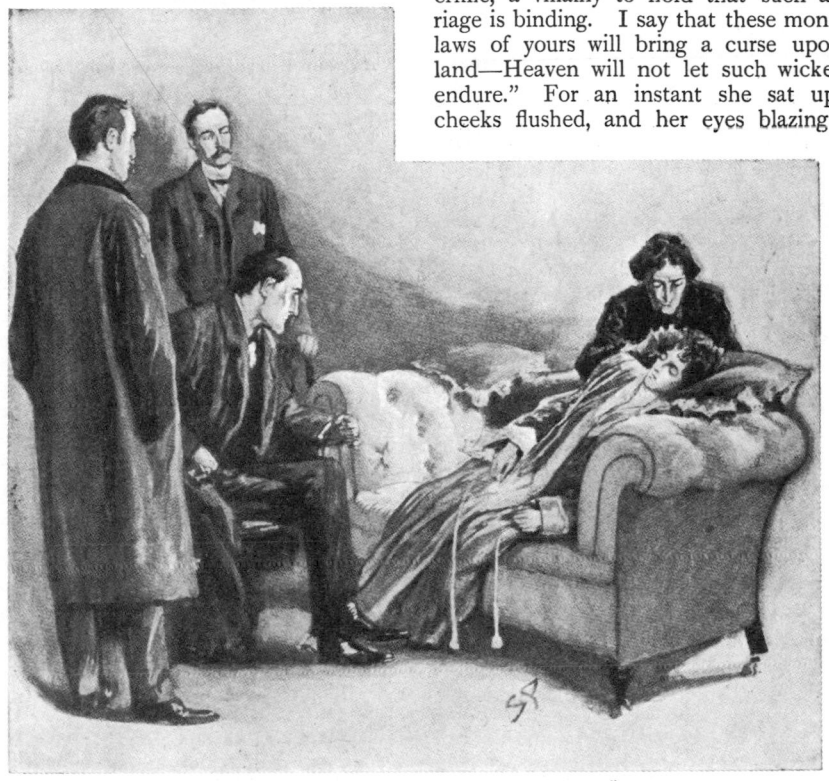

"I AM THE WIFE OF SIR EUSTACE BRACKENSTALL."

is this?" Two vivid red spots stood out on one of the white, round limbs. She hastily covered it.

"It is nothing. It has no connection with the hideous business of last night. If you and your friend will sit down I will tell you all I can.

"I am the wife of Sir Eustace Brackenstall. I have been married about a year. I suppose that it is no use my attempting to conceal that our marriage has not been a happy one. I fear that all our neighbours would tell you that, even if I were to attempt to deny it. Perhaps the fault may be partly mine. I was brought up in the freer, less

under the terrible mark upon her brow. Then the strong, soothing hand of the austere maid drew her head down on to the cushion, and the wild anger died away into passionate sobbing. At last she continued:—

"I will tell you about last night. You are aware, perhaps, that in this house all servants sleep in the modern wing. This central block is made up of the dwelling-rooms, with the kitchen behind and our bedroom above. My maid Theresa sleeps above my room. There is no one else, and no sound could alarm those who are in the farther wing. This must have been well known to the robbers, or they would not have acted as they did.

"Sir Eustace retired about half-past ten. The servants had already gone to their quarters. Only my maid was up, and she had remained in her room at the top of the house until I needed her services. I sat until after eleven in this room, absorbed in a book. Then I walked round to see that all was right before I went upstairs. It was my custom to do this myself, for, as I have explained, Sir Eustace was not always to be trusted. I went into the kitchen, the butler's pantry, the gun-room, the billiard-room, the drawing-room, and finally the dining-room. As I approached the window, which is covered with thick curtains, I suddenly felt the wind blow upon my face and realized that it was open. I flung the curtain aside and found myself face to face with a broad-shouldered, elderly man who had just stepped into the room. The window is a long French one, which really forms a door leading to the lawn. I held my bedroom candle lit in my hand, and, by its light, behind the first man I saw two others, who were in the act of entering. I stepped back, but the fellow was on me in an instant. He caught me first by the wrist and then by the throat. I opened my mouth to scream, but he struck me a savage blow with his fist over the eye, and felled me to the ground. I must have been unconscious for a few minutes, for when I came to myself I found that they had torn down the bell-rope and had secured me tightly to the oaken chair which stands at the head of the dining-room table. I was so firmly bound that I could not move, and a handkerchief round my mouth prevented me from uttering any sound. It was at this instant that my unfortunate husband entered the room. He had evidently heard some suspicious sounds, and he came prepared for such a scene as he found. He was dressed in his shirt and trousers, with his favourite blackthorn cudgel in his hand. He rushed at one of the burglars, but another—it was the elderly man—stooped, picked the poker out of the grate, and struck him a horrible blow as he passed. He fell without a groan, and never moved again. I fainted once more, but again it could only have been a very few minutes during which I was insensible. When I opened my eyes I found that they had collected the silver from the sideboard, and they had drawn a bottle of wine which stood there. Each of them had a glass in his hand. I have already told you, have I not, that one was elderly, with a beard, and the others young, hairless lads. They might have been a father with his two sons. They talked together in whispers. Then they came

over and made sure that I was still securely bound. Finally they withdrew, closing the window after them. It was quite a quarter of an hour before I got my mouth free. When I did so my screams brought the maid to my assistance. The other servants were soon alarmed, and we sent for the local police, who instantly communicated with London. That is really all I can tell you, gentlemen, and I trust that it will not be necessary for me to go over so painful a story again."

"Any questions, Mr. Holmes?" asked Hopkins.

"I will not impose any further tax upon Lady Brackenstall's patience and time," said Holmes. "Before I go into the dining-room I should be glad to hear your experience." He looked at the maid.

"I saw the men before ever they came into the house," said she. "As I sat by my bed-room window I saw three men in the moon-light down by the lodge gate yonder, but I thought nothing of it at the time. It was more than an hour after that I heard my mistress scream, and down I ran, to find her, poor lamb, just as she says, and him on the floor with his blood and brains over the room. It was enough to drive a woman out of her wits, tied there, and her very dress spotted with him; but she never wanted courage, did Miss Mary Fraser of Adelaide, and Lady Brackenstall of Abbey Grange hasn't learned new ways. You've questioned her long enough, you gentlemen, and now she is coming to her own room, just with her old Theresa, to get the rest that she badly needs."

With a motherly tenderness the gaunt woman put her arm round her mistress and led her from the room.

"She has been with her all her life," said Hopkins. "Nursed her as a baby, and came with her to England when they first left Australia eighteen months ago. Theresa Wright is her name, and the kind of maid you don't pick up nowadays. This way, Mr. Holmes, if you please!"

The keen interest had passed out of Holmes's expressive face, and I knew that with the mystery all the charm of the case had departed. There still remained an arrest to be effected, but what were these common-place rogues that he should soil his hands with them? An abstruse and learned specialist who finds that he has been called in for a case of measles would experience something of the annoyance which I read in my friend's eyes. Yet the scene in the dining-room of the Abbey Grange was sufficiently strange to arrest his attention and to recall his waning interest.

It was a very large and high chamber, with carved oak ceiling, oaken panelling, and a fine array of deer's heads and ancient weapons around the walls. At the farther end from the door was the high French window of which we had heard. Three smaller windows on the right-hand side filled the apartment with cold winter sunshine. On the left was a large, deep fireplace, with a massive overhanging oak mantelpiece. Beside the fireplace was a heavy oaken chair with arms and cross-bars at the bottom. In and out through the open woodwork was woven a crimson cord, which was secured at each side to the crosspiece below. In releasing the lady the cord had been slipped off her, but the knots with which it had been secured still remained. These details only struck our attention afterwards, for our thoughts were entirely absorbed by the terrible object which lay spread upon the tiger-skin hearthrug in front of the fire.

It was the body of a tall, well-made man, about forty years of age. He lay upon his back, his face upturned, with his white teeth grinning through his short black beard. His two clenched hands were raised above his head, and a heavy blackthorn stick lay across them. His dark, handsome, aquiline features were convulsed into a spasm of vindictive hatred, which had set his dead face in a terribly fiendish expression. He had evidently been in his bed when the alarm had broken out, for he wore a foppish embroidered night-shirt, and his bare feet projected from his trousers. His head was horribly injured, and the whole room bore witness to the savage ferocity of the blow which had struck him down. Beside him lay the heavy poker, bent into a curve by the concussion. Holmes examined both it and the indescribable wreck which it had wrought.

"He must be a powerful man, this elder Randall," he remarked.

"Yes," said Hopkins. "I have some record of the fellow, and he is a rough customer."

"You should have no difficulty in getting him."

"Not the slightest. We have been on the look-out for him, and there was some idea that he had got away to America. Now that we know the gang are here I don't see how they can escape. We have the news at every seaport already, and a reward will be offered before evening. What beats me is how they could have done so mad a thing, knowing that the lady could describe them, and that we could not fail to recognise the description."

"Exactly. One would have expected that they would have silenced Lady Brackenstall as well."

"HALLOA, HALLOA, WHAT IS THIS?"

"They may not have realized," I suggested, "that she had recovered from her faint."

"That is likely enough. If she seemed to be senseless they would not take her life. What about this poor fellow, Hopkins? I seem to have heard some queer stories about him."

"He was a good-hearted man when he was sober, but a perfect fiend when he was drunk, or rather when he was half drunk, for he seldom really went the whole way. The devil seemed to be in him at such times, and he was capable of anything. From what I hear, in spite of all his wealth and his title, he very nearly came our way once or twice. There was a scandal about his drenching a dog with petroleum and setting it on fire—her ladyship's dog, to make the matter worse—and that was only hushed up with difficulty. Then he threw a decanter at that maid, Theresa Wright; there was trouble about that. On the whole, and between ourselves, it will be a brighter house without him. What are you looking at now?"

Holmes was down on his knees examining with great attention the knots upon the red cord with which the lady had been secured. Then he carefully scrutinized the broken and frayed end where it had snapped off when the burglar had dragged it down.

"When this was pulled down the bell in the kitchen must have rung loudly," he remarked.

"No one could hear it. The kitchen stands right at the back of the house."

"How did the burglar know no one would hear it? How dared he pull at a bell-rope in that reckless fashion?"

"Exactly, Mr. Holmes, exactly. You put the very question which I have asked myself again and again. There can be no doubt that this fellow must have known the house and its habits. He must have perfectly understood that the servants would all be in bed at that comparatively early hour, and that no one could possibly hear a bell ring in the kitchen. Therefore he must have been in close league with one of the servants. Surely that is evident. But there are eight servants, and all of good character."

"Other things being equal," said Holmes, "one would suspect the one at whose head the master threw a decanter. And yet that would involve treachery towards the mistress to whom this woman seems so devoted. Well, well, the point is a minor one, and when you have Randall you will probably find no difficulty in securing his accomplice. The lady's story certainly seems to be corroborated, if it needed corroboration, by every detail which we see before us." He walked to the French window and threw it open. "There are no signs here, but the ground is iron hard, and one would not expect them. I see that these candles on the mantelpiece have been lighted."

"Yes; it was by their light and that of the lady's bedroom candle that the burglars saw their way about."

"And what did they take?"

"Well, they did not take much—only half-a-dozen articles of plate off the sideboard. Lady Brackenstall thinks that they were themselves so disturbed by the death of Sir Eustace that they did not ransack the house as they would otherwise have done."

"No doubt that is true. And yet they drank some wine, I understand."

"To steady their own nerves."

"Exactly. These three glasses upon the sideboard have been untouched, I suppose?"

"Yes; and the bottle stands as they left it."

"Let us look at it. Halloa! halloa! what is this?"

The three glasses were grouped together, all of them tinged with wine, and one of them containing some dregs of bees-wing. The bottle stood near them, two-thirds full, and beside it lay a long, deeply-stained cork. Its appearance and the dust upon the bottle showed that it was no common vintage which the murderers had enjoyed.

A change had come over Holmes's manner. He had lost his listless expression, and again I saw an alert light of interest in his keen, deep-set eyes. He raised the cork and examined it minutely.

"How did they draw it?" he asked.

Hopkins pointed to a half-opened drawer. In it lay some table linen and a large cork-screw.

"Did Lady Brackenstall say that screw was used?"

"No; you remember that she was senseless at the moment when the bottle was opened."

"Quite so. As a matter of fact that screw was *not* used. This bottle was opened by a pocket-screw, probably contained in a knife, and not more than an inch and a half long. If you examine the top of the cork you will observe that the screw was driven in three times before the cork was extracted. It has never been transfixed. This long screw would have transfixed it and drawn it with a single pull. When you catch this fellow you will find that he has one of these multiplex knives in his possession."

"Excellent!" said Hopkins.

"But these glasses do puzzle me, I confess. Lady Brackenstall actually *saw* the three men drinking, did she not?"

"Yes; she was clear about that."

"Then there is an end of it. What more is to be said? And yet you must admit that the three glasses are very remarkable, Hopkins. What, you see nothing remarkable! Well, well, let it pass. Perhaps when a man has special knowledge and special powers like my own it rather encourages him to seek a complex explanation when a simpler one is at hand. Of course, it must be a mere chance about the glasses. Well, good morning, Hopkins. I don't see that I can be of any use to you, and you appear to have your case very clear. You will let me know when Randall is arrested, and any further developments which may occur. I trust that I shall soon have to congratulate you upon a successful conclusion. Come, Watson, I fancy that we may employ ourselves more profitably at home."

During our return journey I could see by Holmes's face that he was much puzzled by something which he had observed. Every now and then, by an effort, he would throw off the impression and talk as if the matter were clear, but then his doubts would settle down upon him again, and his knitted brows and abstracted eyes would show that his thoughts had gone back once more to the great dining-room of the Abbey Grange in which this midnight tragedy had been enacted. At last, by a sudden impulse, just as our train was crawling out of a suburban station, he sprang on to the platform and pulled me out after him.

"Excuse me, my dear fellow," said he, as we watched the rear carriages of our train disappearing round a curve; "I am sorry to make you the victim of what may seem a mere whim, but on my life, Watson, I simply *can't* leave that case in this condition. Every instinct that I possess cries out against it. It's wrong — it's all wrong—I'll swear that it's wrong. And yet the lady's story was complete, the maid's corroboration was sufficient, the detail was fairly exact. What have I to put against that? Three wine-glasses, that is all. But if I had not taken things for granted, if I had examined everything with the care which I would have shown had we approached the case *de novo* and had no cut-and-dried story to warp my mind, would I not then have found some-

"I COULD SEE BY HOLMES'S FACE THAT HE WAS MUCH PUZZLED."

thing more definite to go upon? Of course I should. Sit down on this bench, Watson, until a train for Chislehurst arrives, and allow me to lay the evidence before you, imploring you in the first instance to dismiss from your mind the idea that anything which the maid or her mistress may have said must necessarily be true. The lady's charming personality must not be permitted to warp our judgment.

"Surely there are details in her story which,

if we looked at it in cold blood, would excite our suspicion. These burglars made a considerable haul at Sydenham a fortnight ago. Some account of them and of their appearance was in the papers, and would naturally occur to anyone who wished to invent a story in which imaginary robbers should play a part. As a matter of fact, burglars who have done a good stroke of business are, as a rule, only too glad to enjoy the proceeds in peace and quiet without embarking on another perilous undertaking. Again, it is unusual for burglars to operate at so early an hour ; it is unusual for burglars to strike a lady to prevent her screaming, since one would imagine that was the sure way to make her scream ; it is unusual for them to commit murder when their numbers are sufficient to overpower one man ; it is unusual for them to be content with a limited plunder when there is much more within their reach ; and finally I should say that it was very unusual for such men to leave a bottle half empty. How do all these unusuals strike you, Watson ? "

" Their cumulative effect is certainly considerable, and yet each of them is quite possible in itself. The most unusual thing of all, as it seems to me, is that the lady should be tied to the chair."

" Well, I am not so clear about that, Watson ; for it is evident that they must either kill her or else secure her in such a way that she could not give immediate notice of their escape. But at any rate I have shown, have I not, that there is a certain element of improbability about the lady's story ? And now on the top of this comes the incident of the wine-glasses."

" What about the wine-glasses ? "

" Can you see them in your mind's eye ? "

" I see them clearly."

" We are told that three men drank from them. Does that strike you as likely ? "

" Why not ? There was wine in each glass."

" Exactly ; but there was bees-wing only in one glass. You must have noticed that fact. What does that suggest to your mind ? "

" The last glass filled would be most likely to contain bees-wing."

" Not at all. The bottle was full of it, and it is inconceivable that the first two glasses were clear and the third heavily charged with it. There are two possible explanations, and only two. One is that after the second glass was filled the bottle was violently agitated, and so the third glass received the bees-wing. That does not appear probable. No, no ; I am sure that I am right."

" What, then, do you suppose ? "

" That only two glasses were used, and that the dregs of both were poured into a third glass, so as to give the false impression that three people had been here. In that way all the bees-wing would be in the last glass, would it not ? Yes, I am convinced that this is so. But if I have hit upon the true explanation of this one small phenomenon, then in an instant the case rises from the commonplace to the exceedingly remarkable, for it can only mean that Lady Brackenstall and her maid have deliberately lied to us, that not one word of their story is to be believed, that they have some very strong reason for covering the real criminal, and that we must construct our case for ourselves without any help from them. That is the mission which now lies before us, and here, Watson, is the Chislehurst train."

The household of the Abbey Grange were much surprised at our return, but Sherlock Holmes, finding that Stanley Hopkins had gone off to report to head-quarters, took possession of the dining-room, locked the door upon the inside, and devoted himself for two hours to one of those minute and laborious investigations which formed the solid basis on which his brilliant edifices of deduction were reared. Seated in a corner like an interested student who observes the demonstration of his professor, I followed every step of that remarkable research. The window, the curtains, the carpet, the chair, the rope—each in turn was minutely examined and duly pondered. The body of the unfortunate baronet had been removed, but all else remained as we had seen it in the morning. Then, to my astonishment, Holmes climbed up on to the massive mantelpiece. Far above his head hung the few inches of red cord which were still attached to the wire. For a long time he gazed upwards at it, and then in an attempt to get nearer to it he rested his knee upon a wooden bracket on the wall. This brought his hand within a few inches of the broken end of the rope, but it was not this so much as the bracket itself which seemed to engage his attention. Finally he sprang down with an ejaculation of satisfaction.

" It's all right, Watson," said he. " We have got our case—one of the most remarkable in our collection. But, dear me, how slow-witted I have been, and how nearly I have committed the blunder of my lifetime !

Now, I think that with a few missing links my chain is almost complete."

"You have got your men?"

"Man, Watson, man. Only one, but a very formidable person. Strong as a lion— witness the blow which bent that poker. Six foot three in height, active as a squirrel, dexterous with his fingers; finally, remarkably quick-witted, for this whole ingenious story is of his concoction. Yes, Watson, we have come upon the handiwork of a very remarkable individual. And yet in that bell-rope he has given us a clue which should not have left us a doubt."

"Where was the clue?"

"Well, if you were to pull down a bell-rope, Watson, where would you expect it to break? Surely at the spot where it is attached to the wire. Why should it break three inches from the top as this one has done?"

"Because it is frayed there?"

"Exactly. This end, which we can examine, is frayed. He was cunning enough to do that with his knife. But the other end is not frayed. You could not observe that from here, but if you were on the mantelpiece you would see that it is cut clean off without any mark of fraying whatever. You can reconstruct what occurred. The man needed the rope. He would not tear it down for fear of giving the alarm by ringing the bell. What did he do? He sprang up on the mantelpiece, could not quite reach it, put his knee on the bracket—you will see the impression in the dust—and so got his knife to bear upon the cord. I could not reach the place by at least three inches, from which I infer that he is at least three inches a bigger man than I. Look at that mark upon the seat of the oaken chair! What is it?"

"Blood."

"Undoubtedly it is blood. This alone puts the lady's story out of court. If she were seated on the chair when the crime was done, how comes that mark? No, no; she was placed in the chair *after* the death of her husband. I'll wager that the black dress shows a corresponding mark to this. We have not yet met our Waterloo, Watson, but this is our Marengo, for it begins in defeat and ends in victory. I should like now to have a few words with the nurse Theresa. We must be wary for awhile, if we are to get the information which we want."

She was an interesting person, this stern Australian nurse. Taciturn, suspicious, ungracious, it took some time before Holmes's pleasant manner and frank acceptance of all that she

"LOOK AT THAT MARK ON THE SEAT OF THE OAKEN CHAIR!"

said thawed her into a corresponding amiability. She did not attempt to conceal her hatred for her late employer.

"Yes, sir, it is true that he threw the decanter at me. I heard him call my mistress a name, and I told him that he would not dare to speak so if her brother had been there. Then it was that he threw it at me. He might have thrown a dozen if he had but left my bonny bird alone. He was for ever illtreating her, and she too proud to complain. She will not even tell me all that he has done to her. She never told me of those marks on her arm that you saw this morning, but I know very well that they come from a stab with a hat-pin. The sly fiend—Heaven forgive me that I should speak of him so, now that he is dead, but a fiend he was if ever one walked the earth. He was all honey when first we met him, only eighteen months ago, and we both feel as if it were eighteen years. She had only just arrived in London. Yes, it was her first voyage—she had never been from home before. He won her with his title and his money and his false London ways. If she made a mistake she has paid for it, if ever a woman did. What month did we meet him? Well, I tell you it was just after we arrived. We arrived in June, and it was July. They were married in January of last year. Yes, she is down in the morning-room again, and I have no doubt she will see you, but you must not ask too much of her, for she has gone through all that flesh and blood will stand."

Lady Brackenstall was reclining on the same couch, but looked brighter than before. The maid had entered with us, and began once more to foment the bruise upon her mistress's brow.

"I hope," said the lady, "that you have not come to cross-examine me again?"

"No," Holmes answered, in his gentlest voice, "I will not cause you any unnecessary trouble, Lady Brackenstall, and my whole desire is to make things easy for you, for I am convinced that you are a much-tried woman. If you will treat me as a friend and trust me you may find that I will justify your trust."

"What do you want me to do?"

"To tell me the truth."

"Mr. Holmes!"

"No, no, Lady Brackenstall, it is no use. You may have heard of any little reputation which I possess. I will stake it all on the fact that your story is an absolute fabrication."

Mistress and maid were both staring at Holmes with pale faces and frightened eyes.

"You are an impudent fellow!" cried Theresa. "Do you mean to say that my mistress has told a lie?"

Holmes rose from his chair.

"Have you nothing to tell me?"

"I have told you everything."

"Think once more, Lady Brackenstall. Would it not be better to be frank?"

For an instant there was hesitation in her beautiful face. Then some new strong thought caused it to set like a mask.

"I have told you all I know."

Holmes took his hat and shrugged his shoulders. "I am sorry," he said, and without another word we left the room and the house. There was a pond in the park, and to this my friend led the way. It was frozen over, but a single hole was left for the convenience of a solitary swan. Holmes gazed at it and then passed on to the lodge gate. There he scribbled a short note for Stanley Hopkins and left it with the lodge-keeper.

"It may be a hit or it may be a miss, but we are bound to do something for friend Hopkins, just to justify this second visit," said he. "I will not quite take him into my confidence yet. I think our next scene of operations must be the shipping office of the Adelaide-Southampton line, which stands at the end of Pall Mall, if I remember right. There is a second line of steamers which connect South Australia with England, but we will draw the larger cover first."

Holmes's card sent in to the manager ensured instant attention, and he was not long in acquiring all the information which he needed. In June of '95 only one of their line had reached a home port. It was the *Rock of Gibraltar*, their largest and best boat. A reference to the passenger list showed that Miss Fraser of Adelaide, with her maid, had made the voyage in her. The boat was now on her way to Australia, somewhere to the south of the Suez Canal. Her officers were the same as in '95, with one exception. The first officer, Mr. Jack Croker, had been made a captain, and was to take charge of their new ship, the *Bass Rock*, sailing in two days' time from Southampton. He lived at Sydenham, but he was likely to be in that morning for instructions, if we cared to wait for him.

No; Mr. Holmes had no desire to see him, but would be glad to know more about his record and character.

His record was magnificent. There was not an officer in the fleet to touch him. As to his character, he was reliable on duty, but a wild, desperate fellow off the deck of his ship, hot-headed, excitable, but loyal, honest, and kind-hearted. That was the pith of the information with which Holmes left the office of the Adelaide-Southampton company. Thence he drove to Scotland Yard, but instead of entering he sat in his cab with his brows drawn down, lost in profound thought. Finally he drove round to the Charing Cross telegraph office, sent off a message, and

"HOLMES GAZED AT IT AND THEN PASSED ON."

"I didn't know it."

"But you told me to examine it."

"You got it, then?"

"Yes, I got it."

"I am very glad if I have helped you."

"But you haven't helped me. You have made the affair far more difficult. What sort of burglars are they who steal silver and then throw it into the nearest pond?"

"It was certainly rather eccentric behaviour. I was merely going on the idea that if the silver had been taken by persons who did not want it, who merely took it for a blind as it were, then they would naturally be anxious to get rid of it."

"But why should such an idea cross your mind?"

then, at last, we made for Baker Street once more.

"No, I couldn't do it, Watson," said he, as we re-entered our room. "Once that warrant was made out nothing on earth would save him. Once or twice in my career I feel that I have done more real harm by my discovery of the criminal than ever he had done by his crime. I have learned caution now, and I had rather play tricks with the law of England than with my own conscience. Let us know a little more before we act."

Before evening we had a visit from Inspector Stanley Hopkins. Things were not going very well with him.

"I believe that you are a wizard, Mr. Holmes. I really do sometimes think that you have powers that are not human. Now, how on earth could you know that the stolen silver was at the bottom of that pond?"

"Well, I thought it was possible. When they came out through the French window there was the pond, with one tempting little hole in the ice, right in front of their noses. Could there be a better hiding-place?"

"Ah, a hiding-place—that is better!" cried Stanley Hopkins. "Yes, yes, I see it all now! It was early, there were folk upon the roads, they were afraid of being seen with the silver, so they sank it in the pond, intending to return for it when the coast was clear. Excellent, Mr. Holmes—that is better than your idea of a blind."

"Quite so; you have got an admirable theory. I have no doubt that my own ideas were quite wild, but you must admit that they have ended in discovering the silver."

"Yes, sir, yes. It was all your doing. But I have had a bad set-back."

"A set-back?"

"Yes, Mr. Holmes. The Randall gang were arrested in New York this morning."

"Dear me, Hopkins. That is certainly rather against your theory that they committed a murder in Kent last night."

"It is fatal, Mr. Holmes, absolutely fatal. Still, there are other gangs of three besides the Randalls, or it may be some new gang of which the police have never heard."

"Quite so ; it is perfectly possible. What, are you off ? "

"Yes, Mr. Holmes ; there is no rest for me until I have got to the bottom of the business. I suppose you have no hint to give me ? "

"I have given you one."

"Which ? "

"Well, I suggested a blind."

"But why, Mr. Holmes, why ? "

"Ah, that's the question, of course. But I commend the idea to your mind. You might possibly find that there was something in it. You won't stop for dinner? Well, good-bye, and let us know how you get on."

Dinner was over and the table cleared before Holmes alluded to the matter again. He had lit his pipe and held his slippered feet to the cheerful blaze of the fire. Suddenly he looked at his watch.

"I expect developments, Watson."

"When ? "

"Now—within a few minutes. I dare say you thought I acted rather badly to Stanley Hopkins just now ? "

"I trust your judgment."

"A very sensible reply, Watson. You must look at it this way : what I know is unofficial ; what he knows is official. I have the right to private judgment, but he has none. He must disclose all, or he is a traitor to his service. In a doubtful case I would not put him in so painful a position, and so I reserve my information until my own mind is clear upon the matter."

"But when will that be ? "

"The time has come. You will now be present at the last scene of a remarkable little drama."

There was a sound upon the stairs, and our door was opened to admit as fine a specimen of manhood as ever passed through it. He was a very tall young man, golden-moustached, blue-eyed, with a skin which had been burned by tropical suns, and a springy step which showed that the huge frame was as active as it was strong. He closed the door behind him, and then he stood with clenched hands and heaving breast, choking down some overmastering emotion.

"Sit down, Captain Croker. You got my telegram ? "

Our visitor sank into an arm-chair and looked from one to the other of us with questioning eyes.

"I got your telegram, and I came at the hour you said. I heard that you had been down to the office. There was no getting away from you. Let's hear the worst. What are you going to do with me ? Arrest me ? Speak out, man ! You can't sit there and play with me like a cat with a mouse."

"Give him a cigar," said Holmes. "Bite on that, Captain Croker, and don't let your nerves run away with you. I should not sit here smoking with you if I thought that you were a common criminal, you may be sure of that. Be frank with me, and we may do some good. Play tricks with me, and I'll crush you."

"What do you wish me to do ? "

"To give me a true account of all that happened at the Abbey Grange last night—a *true* account, mind you, with nothing added and nothing taken off. I know so much already that if you go one inch off the straight I'll blow this police whistle from my window and the affair goes out of my hands for ever."

The sailor thought for a little. Then he struck his leg with his great, sun-burned hand.

"I'll chance it," he cried. "I believe you are a man of your word, and a white man, and I'll tell you the whole story. But one thing I will say first. So far as I am concerned I regret nothing and I fear nothing, and I would do it all again and be proud of the job. Curse the beast, if he had as many lives as a cat he would owe them all to me ! But it's the lady, Mary—Mary Fraser—for never will I call her by that accursed name. When I think of getting her into trouble, I who would give my life just to bring one smile to her dear face, it's that that turns my soul into water. And yet—and yet—what less could I do? I'll tell you my story, gentlemen, and then I'll ask you as man to man what less could I do.

"I must go back a bit. You seem to know everything, so I expect that you know that I met her when she was a passenger and I was first officer of the *Rock of Gibraltar*. From the first day I met her she was the only woman to me. Every day of that voyage I loved her more, and many a time since have I kneeled down in the darkness of the night watch and kissed the deck of that ship

"THE DOOR WAS OPENED TO ADMIT AS FINE A SPECIMEN
OF MANHOOD AS EVER PASSED THROUGH IT."

because I knew her dear feet had trod it.
She was never engaged to me. She treated
me as fairly as ever a woman treated a man.
I have no complaint to make. It was all
love on my side, and all good comradeship
and friendship on hers. When we parted
she was a free woman, but I could never
again be a free man.

"Next time I came back from sea I heard
of her marriage. Well, why shouldn't she
marry whom she liked? Title and money
—who could carry them better than she?
She was born for all that is beautiful and
dainty. I didn't grieve over her marriage.
I was not such a selfish hound as that. I
just rejoiced that good luck had come her
way, and that she had not thrown herself
away on a penniless sailor. That's how I
loved Mary Fraser.

"Well, I never thought to see her again;
but last voyage I was promoted, and the new
boat was not yet launched, so I had to wait
for a couple of months with my people at
Sydenham. One day out in a country lane

I met Theresa Wright, her old maid. She
told me about her, about him, about everything. I tell you, gentlemen, it nearly drove
me mad. This drunken hound, that he
should dare to raise his hand to her
whose boots he was not worthy to lick!
I met Theresa again. Then I met Mary
herself—and met her again. Then she
would meet me no more. But the other
day I had a notice that I was to
start on my voyage within a week, and I
determined that I would see her once before
I left. Theresa was always my friend, for
she loved Mary and hated this villain almost
as much as I did. From her I learned the
ways of the house. Mary used to sit up
reading in her own little room downstairs. I
crept round there last night and scratched at
the window. At first she would not open to
me, but in her heart I know that now she
loves me, and she could not leave me in the
frosty night. She whispered to me to come
round to the big front window, and I found
it open before me so as to let me into the

dining-room. Again I heard from her own lips things that made my blood boil, and again I cursed this brute who mishandled the woman that I loved. Well, gentlemen, I was standing with her just inside the window, in all innocence, as Heaven is my judge, when he rushed like a madman into the room, called her the vilest name that a man could use to a woman, and welted her across the face with the stick he had in his hand. I had sprung for the poker, and it was a fair fight between us. See here on my arm where his first blow fell. Then it was my turn, and I went through him as if he had been a rotten pumpkin. Do you think I was sorry? Not I! It was his life or mine, but far more than that it was his life or hers, for how could I leave her in the power of this madman? That was how I killed him. Was I wrong? Well, then, what would either of you gentlemen have done if you had been in my position?

"She had screamed when he struck her, and that brought old Theresa down from the room above. There was a bottle of wine on the sideboard, and I opened it and poured a little between Mary's lips, for she was half dead with the shock. Then I took a drop myself. Theresa was as cool as ice, and it was her plot as much as mine. We must make it appear that burglars had done the thing. Theresa kept on repeating our story to her mistress, while I swarmed up and cut the rope of the bell. Then I lashed her in her chair, and frayed out the end of the rope to make it look natural, else they would wonder how in the world a burglar could have got up there to cut it. Then I gathered up a few plates and pots of silver, to carry out the idea of a robbery, and there I left them with orders to give the alarm when I had a quarter of an hour's start. I dropped the silver into the pond and made off for Sydenham, feeling that for once in my life I had done a real good night's work. And that's the truth and the whole truth, Mr. Holmes, if it costs me my neck."

Holmes smoked for some time in silence. Then he crossed the room and shook our visitor by the hand.

"That's what I think," said he. "I know that every word is true, for you have hardly said a word which I did not know. No one but an acrobat or a sailor could have got up to that bell-rope from the bracket, and no one but a sailor could have made the knots with which the cord was fastened to the chair. Only once had this lady been brought into contact with sailors, and that was on her voyage, and it was someone of her own class of life, since she was trying hard to shield him and so showing that she loved him. You see how easy it was for me to lay my hands upon you when once I had started upon the right trail."

"I thought the police never could have seen through our dodge."

"And the police haven't; nor will they, to the best of my belief. Now, look here, Captain Croker, this is a very serious matter, though I am willing to admit that you acted under the most extreme provocation to which any man could be subjected. I am not sure that in defence of your own life your action will not be pronounced legitimate. However, that is for a British jury to decide. Meanwhile I have so much sympathy for you that if you choose to disappear in the next twenty-four hours I will promise you that no one will hinder you."

"And then it will all come out?"

"Certainly it will come out."

The sailor flushed with anger.

"What sort of proposal is that to make to a man? I know enough of law to understand that Mary would be had as accomplice. Do you think I would leave her alone to face the music while I slunk away? No, sir; let them do their worst upon me, but for Heaven's sake, Mr. Holmes, find some way of keeping my poor Mary out of the courts."

Holmes for a second time held out his hand to the sailor.

"I was only testing you, and you ring true every time. Well, it is a great responsibility that I take upon myself, but I have given Hopkins an excellent hint, and if he can't avail himself of it I can do no more. See here, Captain Croker, we'll do this in due form of law. You are the prisoner. Watson, you are a British jury, and I never met a man who was more eminently fitted to represent one. I am the judge. Now, gentleman of the jury, you have heard the evidence. Do you find the prisoner guilty or not guilty?"

"Not guilty, my lord," said I.

"Vox populi, vox Dei. You are acquitted, Captain Croker. So long as the law does not find some other victim you are safe from me. Come back to this lady in a year, and may her future and yours justify us in the judgment which we have pronounced this night."

"IT HINGED BACK LIKE THE LID OF A BOX."

# THE RETURN OF SHERLOCK HOLMES.

## By A. CONAN DOYLE.

### XIII.—The Adventure of the Second Stain.

I HAD intended "The Adventure of the Abbey Grange" to be the last of those exploits of my friend, Mr. Sherlock Holmes, which I should ever communicate to the public. This resolution of mine was not due to any lack of material, since I have notes of many hundreds of cases to which I have never alluded, nor was it caused by any waning interest on the part of my readers in the singular personality and unique methods of this remarkable man. The real reason lay in the reluctance which Mr. Holmes has shown to the continued publication of his experiences. So long as he was in actual professional practice the records of his successes were of some practical value to him ; but since he has definitely retired from London and betaken himself to study and bee-farming on the Sussex Downs, notoriety has become hateful to him, and he has peremptorily requested that his wishes in this matter should be strictly observed. It was only upon my representing to him that I had given a promise that "The Adventure of the Second Stain" should be published when the times were ripe, and pointing out to him that it is only appropriate that this long series of episodes should culminate in the most important international case which he has ever been called upon to handle, that I at last succeeded in obtaining his consent that a carefully-guarded account of the incident should at last be laid before the public. If in telling the story I seem to be somewhat vague in certain details the public will readily understand that there is an excellent reason for my reticence.

It was, then, in a year, and even in a decade, that shall be nameless, that upon one Tuesday morning in autumn we found two visitors of European fame within the walls of our humble room in Baker Street. The one, austere, high-nosed, eagle-eyed, and dominant, was none other than the illustrious Lord Bellinger, twice Premier of Britain. The other, dark, clear-cut, and elegant, hardly yet of middle age, and endowed with every beauty of body and of mind, was the Right Honourable Trelawney Hope, Secretary for European Affairs, and the most rising statesman in the country. They sat side by side upon our paper-littered settee, and it was easy to see from their worn and anxious faces that it was business of the most pressing importance which had brought them. The Premier's thin, blue-veined hands were clasped tightly over the ivory head of his umbrella, and his gaunt, ascetic face looked gloomily from Holmes to me. The European Secretary pulled nervously at his moustache and fidgeted with the seals of his watch-chain.

"When I discovered my loss, Mr. Holmes, which was at eight o'clock this morning, I at once informed the Prime Minister. It was at his suggestion that we have both come to you."

"Have you informed the police ?"

"No, sir," said the Prime Minister, with the quick, decisive manner for which he was famous. "We have not done so, nor is it

"THEY SAT SIDE BY SIDE."

This morning it was gone. The despatch-box had stood beside the glass upon my dressing-table all night. I am a light sleeper, and so is my wife. We are both prepared to swear that no one could have entered the room during the night. And yet I repeat that the paper is gone."

"What time did you dine?"

"Half-past seven."

"How long was it before you went to bed?"

"My wife had gone to the theatre. I waited up for her. It was half-past eleven before we went to our room."

"Then for four hours the despatch-box had lain unguarded?"

"No one is ever permitted to enter that room save the housemaid in the morning, and my valet, or my wife's maid, during the rest of the day. They are both trusty servants who have been with us for some time. Besides, neither of them could possibly have known that there was anything more valuable than the ordinary departmental papers in my despatch-box."

"Who did know of the existence of that letter?"

"No one in the house."

"Surely your wife knew?"

"No, sir; I had said nothing to my wife until I missed the paper this morning."

The Premier nodded approvingly.

"I have long known, sir, how high is your sense of public duty," said he. "I am convinced that in the case of a secret of this importance it would rise superior to the most intimate domestic ties."

The European Secretary bowed.

"You do me no more than justice, sir. Until this morning I have never breathed one word to my wife upon this matter."

"Could she have guessed?"

"No, Mr. Holmes, she could not have guessed—nor could anyone have guessed."

"Have you lost any documents before?"

"No, sir."

"Who is there in England who did know of the existence of this letter?"

"Each member of the Cabinet was

possible that we should do so. To inform the police must, in the long run, mean to inform the public. This is what we particularly desire to avoid."

"And why, sir?"

"Because the document in question is of such immense importance that its publication might very easily—I might almost say probably—lead to European complications of the utmost moment. It is not too much to say that peace or war may hang upon the issue. Unless its recovery can be attended with the utmost secrecy, then it may as well not be recovered at all, for all that is aimed at by those who have taken it is that its contents should be generally known."

"I understand. Now, Mr. Trelawney Hope, I should be much obliged if you would tell me exactly the circumstances under which this document disappeared."

"That can be done in a very few words, Mr. Holmes. The letter—for it was a letter from a foreign potentate—was received six days ago. It was of such importance that I have never left it in my safe, but I have taken it across each evening to my house in Whitehall Terrace, and kept it in my bedroom in a locked despatch-box. It was there last night. Of that I am certain. I actually opened the box while I was dressing for dinner, and saw the document inside.

informed of it yesterday; but the pledge of secrecy which attends every Cabinet meeting was increased by the solemn warning which was given by the Prime Minister. Good heavens, to think that within a few hours I should myself have lost it!" His handsome face was distorted with a spasm of despair, and his hands tore at his hair. For a moment we caught a glimpse of the natural man, impulsive, ardent, keenly sensitive. The next the aristocratic mask was replaced, and the gentle voice had returned. "Besides the members of the Cabinet there are two, or possibly three, departmental officials who know of the letter. No one else in England, Mr. Holmes, I assure you."

"But abroad?"

"I believe that no one abroad has seen it save the man who wrote it. I am well convinced that his Ministers—that the usual official channels have not been employed."

Holmes considered for some little time.

"Now, sir, I must ask you more particularly what this document is, and why its disappearance should have such momentous consequences?"

The two statesmen exchanged a quick glance and the Premier's shaggy eyebrows gathered in a frown.

"Mr. Holmes, the envelope is a long, thin one of pale blue colour. There is a seal of red wax stamped with a crouching lion. It is addressed in large, bold handwriting to——"

"I fear, sir," said Holmes, "that, interesting and indeed essential as these details are, my inquiries must go more to the root of things. What *was* the letter?"

"That is a State secret of the utmost importance, and I fear that I cannot tell you, nor do I see that it is necessary. If by the aid of the powers which you are said to possess you can find such an envelope as I describe with its enclosure, you will have deserved well of your country, and earned any reward which it lies in our power to bestow."

Sherlock Holmes rose with a smile.

"You are two of the most busy men in the country," said he, "and in my own small way I have also a good many calls upon me. I regret exceedingly that I cannot help you in this matter, and any continuation of this interview would be a waste of time."

The Premier sprang to his feet with that quick, fierce gleam of his deep-set eyes before which a Cabinet has cowered. "I am not accustomed, sir——" he began, but

mastered his anger and resumed his seat. For a minute or more we all sat in silence. Then the old statesman shrugged his shoulders.

"We must accept your terms, Mr. Holmes. No doubt you are right, and it is unreasonable for us to expect you to act unless we give you our entire confidence."

"I agree with you, sir," said the younger statesman.

"Then I will tell you, relying entirely upon your honour and that of your colleague, Dr. Watson. I may appeal to your patriotism also, for I could not imagine a greater misfortune for the country than that this affair should come out."

"You may safely trust us."

"The letter, then, is from a certain foreign potentate who has been ruffled by some recent Colonial developments of this country. It has been written hurriedly and upon his own responsibility entirely. Inquiries have shown that his Ministers know nothing of the matter. At the same time it is couched in so unfortunate a manner, and certain phrases in it are of so provocative a character, that its publication would undoubtedly lead to a most dangerous state of feeling in this country. There would be such a ferment, sir, that I do not hesitate to say that within a week of the publication of that letter this country would be involved in a great war."

Holmes wrote a name upon a slip of paper and handed it to the Premier.

"Exactly. It was he. And it is this letter—this letter which may well mean the expenditure of a thousand millions and the lives of a hundred thousand men—which has become lost in this unaccountable fashion."

"Have you informed the sender?"

"Yes, sir, a cipher telegram has been dispatched."

"Perhaps he desires the publication of the letter."

"No, sir, we have strong reason to believe that he already understands that he has acted in an indiscreet and hot-headed manner. It would be a greater blow to him and to his country than to us if this letter were to come out."

"If this is so, whose interest is it that the letter should come out? Why should anyone desire to steal it or to publish it?"

"There, Mr. Holmes, you take me into regions of high international politics. But if you consider the European situation you will have no difficulty in perceiving the motive. The whole of Europe is an armed camp. There is a double league which makes a fair

"THE PREMIER SPRANG TO HIS FEET."

"I think it is very probable."

"Then, sir, prepare for war."

"That is a hard saying, Mr. Holmes."

"Consider the facts, sir. It is inconceivable that it was taken after eleven thirty at night, since I understand that Mr. Hope and his wife were both in the room from that hour until the loss was found out. It was taken, then, yesterday evening between seven-thirty and eleven-thirty, probably near the earlier hour, since whoever took it evidently knew that it was there, and would naturally secure it as early as possible. Now, sir, if a document of this importance were taken at that hour, where can it be now? No one has any reason to retain it. It has been passed rapidly on to those who need it. What chance have we now to overtake or even to trace it? It is beyond our reach."

The Prime Minister rose from the settee.

"What you say is perfectly logical, Mr. Holmes. I feel that the matter is indeed out of our hands."

"Let us presume, for argument's sake, that the document was taken by the maid or by the valet——"

"They are both old and tried servants."

"I understand you to say that your room is on the second floor, that there is no entrance from without, and that from within no one could go up unobserved. It must, then, be somebody in the house who has taken it. To whom would the thief take it? To one of several international spies and secret agents, whose names are tolerably familiar to me. There are three who may be said to be the heads of their profession. I will begin my research by going round and finding if each of them is at his post. If one is missing—especially if he has disappeared since last night—we will have some

balance of military power. Great Britain holds the scales. If Britain were driven into war with one confederacy, it would assure the supremacy of the other confederacy, whether they joined in the war or not. Do you follow?"

"Very clearly. It is then the interest of the enemies of this potentate to secure and publish this letter, so as to make a breach between his country and ours?"

"Yes, sir."

"And to whom would this document be sent if it fell into the hands of an enemy?"

"To any of the great Chancelleries of Europe. It is probably speeding on its way thither at the present instant as fast as steam can take it."

Mr. Trelawney Hope dropped his head on his chest and groaned aloud. The Premier placed his hand kindly upon his shoulder.

"It is your misfortune, my dear fellow. No one can blame you. There is no precaution which you have neglected. Now, Mr. Holmes, you are in full possession of the facts. What course do you recommend?"

Holmes shook his head mournfully.

"You think, sir, that unless this document is recovered there will be war?"

indication as to where the document has gone."

"Why should he be missing?" asked the European Secretary. "He would take the letter to an Embassy in London, as likely as not."

"I fancy not. These agents work independently, and their relations with the Embassies are often strained."

The Prime Minister nodded his acquiescence.

"I believe you are right, Mr. Holmes. He would take so valuable a prize to headquarters with his own hands. I think that your course of action is an excellent one. Meanwhile, Hope, we cannot neglect all our other duties on account of this one misfortune. Should there be any fresh developments during the day we shall communicate with you, and you will no doubt let us know the results of your own inquiries."

The two statesmen bowed and walked gravely from the room.

When our illustrious visitors had departed Holmes lit his pipe in silence, and sat for some time lost in the deepest thought. I had opened the morning paper and was immersed in a sensational crime which had occurred in London the night before, when my friend gave an exclamation, sprang to his feet, and laid his pipe down upon the mantelpiece.

"Yes," said he, "there is no better way of approaching it. The situation is desperate, but not hopeless. Even now, if we could be sure which of them has taken it, it is just possible that it has not yet passed out of his hands. After all, it is a question of money with these fellows, and I have the British Treasury behind me. If it's on the market I'll buy it—if it means another penny on the income-tax. It is conceivable that the fellow might hold it back to see what bids come from this side before he tries his luck on the other. There are only those three capable of playing so bold a game; there are Oberstein, La Rothiere, and Eduardo Lucas. I will see each of them."

I glanced at my morning paper.

"Is that Eduardo Lucas of Godolphin Street?"

"Yes."

"You will not see him."

"Why not?"

"He was murdered in his house last night."

My friend has so often astonished me in the course of our adventures that it was with a sense of exultation that I realized how completely I had astonished him. He stared in amazement, and then snatched the paper from my hands. This was the paragraph which I had been engaged in reading when he rose from his chair:—

## "MURDER IN WESTMINSTER.

"A crime of a mysterious character was committed last night at 16, Godolphin Street, one of the old-fashioned and secluded rows of eighteenth-century houses which lie between the river and the Abbey, almost in the shadow of the great Tower of the Houses of Parliament. This small but select mansion has been inhabited for some years by Mr. Eduardo Lucas, well known in society circles both on account of his charming personality and because he has the well-deserved reputation of being one of the best amateur tenors in the country. Mr. Lucas is an unmarried man, thirty-four years of age, and his establishment consists of Mrs. Pringle, an elderly housekeeper, and of Mitton, his valet. The former retires early and sleeps at the top of the house. The valet was out for the evening, visiting a friend at Hammersmith. From ten o'clock onwards Mr. Lucas had the house to himself. What occurred during that time has not yet transpired, but at a quarter to twelve Police-constable Barrett, passing along Godolphin Street, observed that the door of No. 16 was ajar. He knocked, but received no answer. Perceiving a light in the front room he advanced into the passage and again knocked, but without reply. He then pushed open the door and entered. The room was in a state of wild disorder, the furniture being all swept to one side, and one chair lying on its back in the centre. Beside this chair, and still grasping one of its legs, lay the unfortunate tenant of the house. He had been stabbed to the heart and must have died instantly. The knife with which the crime had been committed was a curved Indian dagger, plucked down from a trophy of Oriental arms which adorned one of the walls. Robbery does not appear to have been the motive of the crime, for there had been no attempt to remove the valuable contents of the room. Mr. Eduardo Lucas was so well known and popular that his violent and mysterious fate will arouse painful interest and intense sympathy in a widespread circle of friends."

"Well, Watson, what do you make of this?" asked Holmes, after a long pause.

"It is an amazing coincidence."

"A coincidence! Here is one of the three men whom we had named as possible actors in this drama, and he meets a violent death during the very hours when we know that that drama was being enacted. The odds are enormous against its being coincidence. No figures could express them. No, my dear Watson, the two events are connected — *must* be connected. It is for us to find the connection."

card upon her salver. Holmes glanced at it, raised his eyebrows, and handed it over to me.

"Ask Lady Hilda Trelawney Hope if she will be kind enough to step up," said he.

A moment later our modest apartment, already so distinguished that morning, was further honoured by the entrance of the most lovely woman in London. I had often heard of the beauty of the youngest daughter of the Duke of Belminster, but no description of it, and no contemplation of colourless photographs, had prepared me for the subtle, delicate charm and the beautiful colouring of that exquisite head. And yet as we saw it that autumn morning it was not its beauty which would be the first thing to impress the observer. The cheek was lovely, but it was paled with emotion; the eyes were

" MY DEAR WATSON, THE TWO EVENTS ARE CONNECTED—MUST BE CONNECTED."

"But now the official police must know all."

"Not at all. They know all they see at Godolphin Street. They know—and shall know—nothing of Whitehall Terrace. Only *we* know of both events, and can trace the relation between them. There is one obvious point which would, in any case, have turned my suspicions against Lucas. Godolphin Street, Westminster, is only a few minutes' walk from Whitehall Terrace. The other secret agents whom I have named live in the extreme West-end. It was easier, therefore, for Lucas than for the others to establish a connection or receive a message from the European Secretary's household — a small thing, and yet where events are compressed into a few hours it may prove essential. Halloa! what have we here?"

Mrs. Hudson had appeared with a lady's

bright, but it was the brightness of fever; the sensitive mouth was tight and drawn in an effort after self - command. Terror — not beauty—was what sprang first to the eye as our fair visitor stood framed for an instant in the open door.

"Has my husband been here, Mr. Holmes?"

"Yes, madam, he has been here."

"Mr. Holmes, I implore you not to tell him that I came here." Holmes bowed coldly, and motioned the lady to a chair.

"Your ladyship places me in a very delicate position. I beg that you will sit down and tell me what you desire; but I fear that I cannot make any unconditional promise."

She swept across the room and seated herself with her back to the window. It was a queenly presence—tall, graceful, and intensely womanly.

" Mr. Holmes," she said, and her white-gloved hands clasped and unclasped as she spoke—" I will speak frankly to you in the hope that it may induce you to speak frankly in return. There is complete confidence between my husband and me on all matters save one. That one is politics. On this his lips are sealed. He tells me nothing. Now, I am aware that there was a most deplorable occurrence in our house last night. I know that a paper has disappeared. But because the matter is political my husband refuses to take me into his complete confidence. Now it is essential—essential, I say—that I should thoroughly understand it. You are the only other person, save these politicians, who knows the true facts. I beg you, then, Mr. Holmes, to tell me exactly what has happened and what it will lead to. Tell me all, Mr. Holmes. Let no regard for your client's interests keep you silent, for I assure you that his interests, if he would only see it, would be best served by taking me into his complete confidence. What was this paper which was stolen?"

" Madam, what you ask me is really impossible."

She groaned and sank her face in her hands.

" You must see that this is so, madam. If your husband thinks fit to keep you in the dark over this matter, is it for me, who have only learned the true facts under the pledge of professional secrecy, to tell what he has withheld? It is not fair to ask it. It is him whom you must ask."

" I have asked him. I come to you as a last resource. But without your telling me anything definite, Mr. Holmes, you may do a great service if you would enlighten me on one point."

" What is it, madam?"

" Is my husband's political career likely to suffer through this incident?"

" Well, madam, unless it is set right it may certainly have a very unfortunate effect."

" Ah!" She drew in her breath sharply as one whose doubts are resolved.

" One more question, Mr. Holmes. From an expression which my husband dropped in the first shock of this disaster I understood that terrible public consequences might arise from the loss of this document."

" If he said so, I certainly cannot deny it."

" Of what nature are they?"

" Nay, madam, there again you ask me more than I can possibly answer."

" Then I will take up no more of your time. I cannot blame you, Mr. Holmes, for

having refused to speak more freely, and you on your side will not, I am sure, think the worse of me because I desire, even against his will, to share my husband's anxieties. Once more I beg that you will say nothing of my visit." She looked back at us from the door, and I had a last impression of that beautiful haunted face, the startled eyes, and the drawn mouth. Then she was gone.

" Now, Watson, the fair sex is your department," said Holmes, with a smile, when the dwindling frou-frou of skirts had ended in the slam of the front door. " What was the fair lady's game? What did she really want?"

" Surely her own statement is clear and her anxiety very natural."

" Hum! Think of her appearance, Watson—her manner, her suppressed excitement, her restlessness, her tenacity in asking questions. Remember that she comes of a caste who do not lightly show emotion."

" She was certainly much moved."

" Remember also the curious earnestness with which she assured us that it was best for her husband that she should know all. What did she mean by that? And you must have observed, Watson, how she manœuvred to have the light at her back. She did not wish us to read her expression."

" Yes; she chose the one chair in the room."

" And yet the motives of women are so inscrutable. You remember the woman at Margate whom I suspected for the same reason. No powder on her nose—that proved to be the correct solution. How can you build on such a quicksand? Their most trivial action may mean volumes, or their most extraordinary conduct may depend upon a hairpin or a curling-tongs. Good morning, Watson."

" You are off?"

" Yes; I will wile away the morning at Godolphin Street with our friends of the regular establishment. With Eduardo Lucas lies the solution of our problem, though I must admit that I have not an inkling as to what form it may take. It is a capital mistake to theorize in advance of the facts. Do you stay on guard, my good Watson, and receive any fresh visitors. I'll join you at lunch if I am able."

All that day and the next and the next Holmes was in a mood which his friends would call taciturn, and others morose. He ran out and ran in, smoked incessantly, played snatches on his violin, sank into reveries, devoured sandwiches at irregular hours, and hardly answered the casual questions which I put to him. It was evident to me that things were not going well with him or his quest. He would say nothing of the case, and it was from the papers that I learned the particulars of the inquest, and the arrest with the subsequent release of John Mitton, the valet of the deceased. The coroner's jury brought in the obvious "Wilful Murder," but the parties remained as unknown as ever. No motive was suggested. The room was full of articles of value, but none had been taken. The dead man's papers had not been tampered with. They were carefully examined, and showed that he was a keen student of international politics, an indefatigable gossip, a remarkable linguist, and an untiring letter-writer. He had been on intimate terms with the leading politicians of several countries. But nothing sensational was discovered among the documents which filled his drawers. As to his relations with women, they appeared to have been promiscuous but superficial. He had many acquaintances among them, but few friends, and no one whom he loved. His habits were regular, his conduct inoffensive. His death was an absolute mystery, and likely to remain so.

As to the arrest of John Mitton, the valet, it was a counsel of despair as an alternative to absolute inaction. But no case could be sustained against him. He had visited friends in Hammersmith that night. The

"SHE LOOKED BACK AT US FROM THE DOOR."

*alibi* was complete. It is true that he started home at an hour which should have brought him to Westminster before the time when the crime was discovered, but his own explanation that he had walked part of the way seemed probable enough in view of the fineness of the night. He had actually arrived at twelve o'clock, and appeared to be overwhelmed by the unexpected tragedy. He had always been on good terms with his master. Several of the dead man's possessions—notably a small case of razors—had been found in the valet's boxes, but he explained that they had been presents from the deceased, and the housekeeper was able to corroborate the story. Mitton had been in Lucas's employment for three years. It was noticeable that Lucas did not take Mitton on the Continent with him. Sometimes he visited Paris for three months on end, but Mitton was left in charge of the Godolphin Street house. As to the housekeeper, she had heard nothing on the night of the crime. If her master had a visitor he had himself admitted him.

So for three mornings the mystery remained, so far as I could follow it in the papers. If Holmes knew more he kept his own counsel, but, as he told me that Inspector Lestrade had taken him into his confidence in the case, I knew that he was in close touch with every development. Upon the fourth day there appeared a long telegram from Paris which seemed to solve the whole question.

" A discovery has just been made by the

Parisian police," said the *Daily Telegraph*, "which raises the veil which hung round the tragic fate of Mr. Eduardo Lucas, who met his death by violence last Monday night at Godolphin Street, Westminster. Our readers will remember that the deceased gentleman was found stabbed in his room, and that some suspicion attached to his valet, but that the case broke down on an *alibi*. Yesterday a lady, who has been known as Mme. Henri Fournaye, occupying a small villa in the Rue Austerlitz, was reported to the authorities by her servants as being insane. An examination showed that she had indeed developed mania of a dangerous and permanent form. On inquiry the police have discovered that Mme. Henri Fournaye only returned from a journey to London on Tuesday last, and there is evidence to connect her with the crime at Westminster. A comparison of photographs has proved conclusively that M. Henri Fournaye and Eduardo Lucas were really one and the same person, and that the deceased had for some reason lived a double life in London and Paris. Mme. Fournaye, who is of Creole origin, is of an extremely excitable nature, and has suffered in the past from attacks of jealousy which have amounted to frenzy. It is conjectured that it was in one of these that she committed the terrible crime which has caused such a sensation in London. Her movements upon the Monday night have not yet been traced, but it is undoubted that a woman answering to her description attracted much attention at Charing Cross Station on Tuesday morning by the wildness of her appearance and the violence of her gestures. It is probable, therefore, that the crime was either committed when insane, or that its immediate effect was to drive the unhappy woman out of her mind. At present she is unable to give any coherent account of the past, and the doctors hold out no hopes of the re-establishment of her reason. There is evidence that a woman, who might have been Mme. Fournaye, was seen for some hours on Monday night watching the house in Godolphin Street."

"What do you think of that, Holmes?" I had read the account aloud to him, while he finished his breakfast.

"My dear Watson," said he, as he rose from the table and paced up and down the room, "you are most long-suffering, but if I have told you nothing in the last three days it is because there is nothing to tell. Even now this report from Paris does not help us much."

"Surely it is final as regards the man's death."

"The man's death is a mere incident—a trivial episode—in comparison with our real task, which is to trace this document and save a European catastrophe. Only one important thing has happened in the last three days, and that is that nothing has happened. I get reports almost hourly from the Government, and it is certain that nowhere in Europe is there any sign of trouble. Now, if this letter were loose—no, it *can't* be loose—but if it isn't loose, where can it be? Who has it? Why is it held back? That's the question that beats in my brain like a hammer. Was it, indeed, a coincidence that Lucas should meet his death on the night when the letter disappeared? Did the letter ever reach him? If so, why is it not among his papers? Did this mad wife of his carry it off with her? If so, is it in her house in Paris? How could I search for it without the French police having their suspicions aroused? It is a case, my dear Watson, where the law is as dangerous to us as the criminals are. Every man's hand is against us, and yet the interests at stake are colossal. Should I bring it to a successful conclusion it will certainly represent the crowning glory of my career. Ah, here is my latest from the front!" He glanced hurriedly at the note which had been handed in. "Halloa! Lestrade seems to have observed something of interest. Put on your hat, Watson, and we will stroll down together to Westminster."

It was my first visit to the scene of the crime—a high, dingy, narrow-chested house, prim, formal, and solid, like the century which gave it birth. Lestrade's bulldog features gazed out at us from the front window, and he greeted us warmly when a big constable had opened the door and let us in. The room into which we were shown was that in which the crime had been committed, but no trace of it now remained, save an ugly, irregular stain upon the carpet. This carpet was a small square drugget in the centre of the room, surrounded by a broad expanse of beautiful, old-fashioned wood-flooring in square blocks highly polished. Over the fireplace was a magnificent trophy of weapons, one of which had been used on that tragic night. In the window was a sumptuous writing-desk, and every detail of the apartment, the pictures, the rugs, and the hangings, all pointed to a taste which was luxurious to the verge of effeminacy.

"Seen the Paris news?" asked Lestrade.

Holmes nodded.

"Our French friends seem to have touched the spot this time. No doubt it's just as they say. She knocked at the door—surprise visit, I guess, for he kept his life in water-tight compartments. He let her in—couldn't keep her in the street. She told him how she had traced him, reproached him, one thing led to another, and then with that dagger so handy the end soon came. It wasn't all done in an instant, though, for these chairs were all swept over yonder, and he had one in his hand as if he had tried to hold her off with it. We've got it all as clear as if we had seen it."

Holmes raised his eyebrows.

"And yet you have sent for me?"

"Ah, yes, that's another matter—a mere trifle, but the sort of thing you take an interest in—queer, you know, and what you might call freakish. It has nothing to do with the main fact—can't have, on the face of it."

"What is it, then?"

"Well, you know, after a crime of this sort we are very careful to keep things in their position. Nothing has been moved. Officer in charge here day and night. This morning, as the man was buried and the investigation over — so far as this room is concerned—we thought we could tidy up a bit. This carpet. You see, it is not fastened down; only just laid there. We had occasion to raise it. We found——"

"Yes? You found——"

Holmes's face grew tense with anxiety.

"Well, I'm sure you would never guess in a hundred years what we did find. You see that stain on the carpet? Well, a great deal must have soaked through, must it not?"

"Undoubtedly it must."

"Well, you will be surprised to hear that there is no stain on the white woodwork to correspond."

"No stain! But there must——"

"Yes; so you would say. But the fact remains that there isn't."

He took the corner of the carpet in his hand and, turning it over, he showed that it was indeed as he said.

"But the underside is as stained as the upper. It must have left a mark."

Lestrade chuckled with delight at having puzzled the famous expert.

"Now I'll show you the explanation. There *is* a second stain, but it does not correspond with the other. See for yourself." As he spoke he turned over another portion of the carpet, and there, sure enough, was a great crimson spill upon the square white facing of the old-fashioned floor. "What do you make of that, Mr. Holmes?"

"Why, it is simple enough. The two stains did correspond, but the carpet has

"HE TOOK THE CORNER OF THE CARPET IN HIS HAND."

been turned round. As it was square and unfastened it was easily done."

"The official police don't need you, Mr. Holmes, to tell them that the carpet must have been turned round. That's clear enough, for the stains lie above each other—if you lay it over this way. But what I want to know is, who shifted the carpet, and why?"

I could see from Holmes's rigid face that he was vibrating with inward excitement.

"Look here, Lestrade," said he, "has that constable in the passage been in charge of the place all the time?"

"Yes, he has."

"Well, take my advice. Examine him carefully. Don't do it before us. We'll wait here. You take him into the back room. You'll be more likely to get a confession out of him alone. Ask him how he dared to admit people and leave them alone in this room. Don't ask him if he has done it. Take it for granted. Tell him you *know* someone has been here. Press him. Tell him that a full confession is his only chance of forgiveness. Do exactly what I tell you!"

"By George, if he knows I'll have it out of him!" cried Lestrade. He darted into the hall, and a few moments later his bullying voice sounded from the back room.

"Now, Watson, now!" cried Holmes, with frenzied eagerness. All the demoniacal force of the man masked behind that listless manner burst out in a paroxysm of energy. He tore the drugget from the floor, and in an instant was down on his hands and knees clawing at each of the squares of wood beneath it. One turned sideways as he dug his nails into the edge of it. It hinged back like the lid of a box. A small black cavity opened beneath it. Holmes plunged his eager hand into it, and drew it out with a bitter snarl of anger and disappointment. It was empty.

"Quick, Watson, quick! Get it back again!" The wooden lid was replaced, and the drugget had only just been drawn straight when Lestrade's voice was heard in the passage. He found Holmes leaning languidly against the mantelpiece, resigned and patient, endeavouring to conceal his irrepressible yawns.

"Sorry to keep you waiting, Mr. Holmes. I can see that you are bored to death with the whole affair. Well, he has confessed, all right. Come in here, MacPherson. Let these gentlemen hear of your most inexcusable conduct."

The big constable, very hot and penitent, sidled into the room.

"I meant no harm, sir, I'm sure. The young woman came to the door last evening—mistook the house, she did. And then we got talking. It's lonesome, when you're on duty here all day."

"Well, what happened then?"

"She wanted to see where the crime was done—had read about it in the papers, she said. She was a very respectable, well-spoken young woman, sir, and I saw no harm in letting her have a peep. When she saw that mark on the carpet, down she dropped on the floor, and lay as if she were dead. I ran to the back and got some water, but I could not bring her to. Then I went round the corner to the Ivy Plant for some brandy, and by the time I had brought it back the young woman had recovered and was off—ashamed of herself, I dare say, and dared not face me."

"How about moving that drugget?"

"Well, sir, it was a bit rumpled, certainly, when I came back. You see, she fell on it, and it lies on a polished floor with nothing to keep it in place. I straightened it out afterwards."

"It's a lesson to you that you can't deceive me, Constable MacPherson," said Lestrade, with dignity. "No doubt you thought that your breach of duty could never be discovered, and yet a mere glance at that drugget was enough to convince me that someone had been admitted to the room. It's lucky for you, my man, that nothing is missing, or you would find yourself in Queer Street. I'm sorry to have called you down over such a petty business, Mr. Holmes, but I thought the point of the second stain not corresponding with the first would interest you."

"Certainly, it was most interesting. Has this woman only been here once, constable?"

"Yes, sir, only once."

"Who was she?"

"Don't know the name, sir. Was answering an advertisement about type-writing, and came to the wrong number—very pleasant, genteel young woman, sir."

"Tall? Handsome?"

"Yes, sir; she was a well-grown young woman. I suppose you might say she was handsome. Perhaps some would say she was very handsome. 'Oh, officer, do let me have a peep!' says she. She had pretty, coaxing ways, as you might say, and I thought there was no harm in letting her just put her head through the door."

"How was she dressed?"

"Quiet, sir—a long mantle down to her feet."

"What time was it?"

"It was just growing dusk at the time. They were lighting the lamps as I came back with the brandy,"

"Very good," said Holmes. "Come, Watson, I think that we have more important work elsewhere."

As we left the house Lestrade remained in the front room, while the repentant constable opened the door to let us out. Holmes turned on the step and held up something in his hand. The constable stared intently.

"Good Lord, sir!" he cried, with amazement on his face. Holmes put his finger on his lips, replaced his hand in his breast-pocket, and burst out laughing as we turned down the street. "Excellent!" said he. "Come, friend Watson, the curtain rings up for the last act. You will be relieved to hear that there will be no war, that the Right Honourable Trelawney Hope will suffer no set-back in his brilliant career, that the indiscreet Sovereign will receive no punishment for his indiscretion, that the Prime Minister will have no European complication to deal with, and that with a little tact and management upon our part nobody will be a penny the worse for what might have been a very ugly incident."

My mind filled with admiration for this extraordinary man.

"You have solved it!" I cried.

"Hardly that, Watson. There are some points which are as dark as ever. But we have so much that it will be our own fault if we cannot get the rest. We will go straight to Whitehall Terrace and bring the matter to a head."

When we arrived at the residence of the European Secretary it was for Lady Hilda Trelawney Hope that Sherlock Holmes inquired. We were shown into the morning-room.

"Mr. Holmes!" said the lady, and her face was pink with her indignation, "this is surely most unfair and ungenerous upon your part. I desired, as I have explained, to keep my visit to you a secret, lest my husband should think that I was intruding into his affairs. And yet you compromise me by coming here and so showing that there are business relations between us."

"Unfortunately, madam, I had no possible alternative. I have been commissioned to recover this immensely important paper. I must therefore ask you, madam, to be kind enough to place it in my hands."

The lady sprang to her feet, with the colour all dashed in an instant from her beautiful face. Her eyes glazed—she tottered—I thought that she would faint. Then with a grand effort she rallied from the shock, and a supreme astonishment and indignation chased every other expression from her features.

"You—you insult me, Mr. Holmes."

"YOU INSULT ME, MR. HOLMES."

"Come, come, madam, it is useless. Give up the letter."

She darted to the bell.

"The butler shall show you out."

"Do not ring, Lady Hilda. If you do, then all my earnest efforts to avoid a scandal will be frustrated. Give up the letter and all will be set right. If you will work with me I can arrange everything. If you work against me I must expose you."

She stood grandly defiant, a queenly figure, her eyes fixed upon his as if she would read his very soul. Her hand was on the bell, but she had forborne to ring it.

"You are trying to frighten me. It is not a very manly thing, Mr. Holmes, to come here and browbeat a woman. You say that you know something. What is it that you know?"

"Pray sit down, madam. You will hurt yourself there if you fall. I will not speak until you sit down. Thank you."

"I give you five minutes, Mr. Holmes."

"One is enough, Lady Hilda. I know of your visit to Eduardo Lucas, of your giving him this document, of your ingenious return to the room last night, and of the manner in which you took the letter from the hiding-place under the carpet."

She stared at him with an ashen face and gulped twice before she could speak.

"You are mad, Mr. Holmes—you are mad!" she cried, at last.

He drew a small piece of cardboard from his pocket. It was the face of a woman cut out of a portrait.

"I have carried this because I thought it might be useful," said he. "The policeman has recognised it."

She gave a gasp and her head dropped back in the chair.

"Come, Lady Hilda. You have the letter. The matter may still be adjusted. I have no desire to bring trouble to you. My duty ends when I have returned the lost letter to your husband. Take my advice and be frank with me; it is your only chance."

Her courage was admirable. Even now she would not own defeat.

"I tell you again, Mr. Holmes, that you are under some absurd illusion."

Holmes rose from his chair.

"I am sorry for you, Lady Hilda. I have done my best for you; I can see that it is all in vain."

He rang the bell. The butler entered.

"Is Mr. Trelawney Hope at home?"

"He will be home, sir, at a quarter to one."

Holmes glanced at his watch.

"Still a quarter of an hour," said he. "Very good, I shall wait."

The butler had hardly closed the door behind him when Lady Hilda was down on her knees at Holmes's feet, her hands outstretched, her beautiful face upturned and wet with her tears.

"Oh, spare me, Mr. Holmes! Spare me!" she pleaded, in a frenzy of supplication. "For Heaven's sake, don't tell him! I love him so! I would not bring one shadow on his life, and this I know would break his noble heart."

Holmes raised the lady. "I am thankful, madam, that you have come to your senses even at this last moment! There is not an instant to lose. Where is the letter?"

She darted across to a writing-desk, unlocked it, and drew out a long blue envelope.

"Here it is, Mr. Holmes. Would to Heaven I had never seen it!"

"How can we return it?" Holmes muttered. "Quick, quick, we must think of some way! Where is the despatch-box?"

"Still in his bedroom."

"What a stroke of luck! Quick, madam, bring it here!"

A moment later she had appeared with a red flat box in her hand.

"How did you open it before? You have a duplicate key? Yes, of course you have. Open it!"

From out of her bosom Lady Hilda had drawn a small key. The box flew open. It was stuffed with papers. Holmes thrust the blue envelope deep down into the heart of them, between the leaves of some other document. The box was shut, locked, and returned to the bedroom.

"Now we are ready for him," said Holmes; "we have still ten minutes. I am going far to screen you, Lady Hilda. In return you will spend the time in telling me frankly the real meaning of this extraordinary affair."

"Mr. Holmes, I will tell you everything," cried the lady. "Oh, Mr. Holmes, I would cut off my right hand before I gave him a moment of sorrow! There is no woman in all London who loves her husband as I do, and yet if he knew how I have acted—how I have been compelled to act—he would never forgive me. For his own honour stands so high that he could not forget or pardon a lapse in another. Help me, Mr. Holmes! My happiness, his happiness, our very lives are at stake!"

"Quick, madam, the time grows short!"

"It was a letter of mine, Mr. Holmes, an indiscreet letter written before my marriage

—a foolish letter, a letter of an impulsive, loving girl. I meant no harm, and yet he would have thought it criminal. Had he read that letter his confidence would have been for ever destroyed. It is years since I wrote it. I had thought that the whole matter was forgotten. Then at last I heard from this man, Lucas, that it had passed into his hands, and that he would lay it before my husband. I implored his mercy. He said that he would return my letter if I would bring him a certain document which he described in my husband's despatch-box. He had some spy in the office who had told him of its existence. He assured me that no harm could come to my husband. Put yourself in my position, Mr. Holmes! What was I to do?"

"Take your husband into your confidence."

"I could not, Mr. Holmes, I could not! On the one side seemed certain ruin; on the other, terrible as it seemed to take my husband's paper, still in a matter of politics I could not understand the consequences, while in a matter of love and trust they were only too clear to me. I did it, Mr. Holmes! I took an impression of his key; this man Lucas furnished a duplicate. I opened his despatch-box, took the paper, and conveyed it to Godolphin Street."

"What happened there, madam?"

"I tapped at the door as agreed. Lucas opened it. I followed him into his room, leaving the hall door ajar behind me, for I feared to be alone with the man. I remember that there was a woman outside as I entered. Our business was soon done. He had my letter on his desk; I handed him the document. He gave me the letter. At this instant there was a sound at the door. There were steps in the passage. Lucas quickly turned back the drugget, thrust the document into some hiding-place there, and covered it over.

"What happened after that is like some fearful dream. I have a vision of a dark, frantic face, of a woman's voice, which screamed in French, 'My waiting is not in vain. At last, at last I have found you with her!' There was a savage struggle. I saw him with a chair in his hand, a knife gleamed in hers. I rushed from the horrible scene, ran from the house, and only next morning in the paper did I learn the dreadful result. That night I was happy, for I had my letter, and I had not seen yet what the future would bring.

"It was next morning that I realized that I had only exchanged one trouble for another. My husband's anguish at the loss of his paper went to my heart. I could hardly prevent myself from there and then kneeling down at his feet and telling him what I had done. But that again would mean a confession of the past. I came to you that morning in order to understand the full enormity of my offence. From the instant that I grasped it my whole mind was turned to the one thought of getting back my husband's paper. It must still be where Lucas had placed it, for it was concealed before this dreadful woman entered the room. If it had not been for her coming, I should not have known where his hiding-place was. How was I to get into the room? For two days I watched the place, but the door was never left open. Last night I made a last attempt. What I did and how I succeeded, you have already learned. I brought the paper back with me, and thought of destroying it since I could see no way of returning it, without confessing my guilt to my husband. Heavens, I hear his step upon the stair!"

The European Secretary burst excitedly into the room.

"Any news, Mr. Holmes, any news?" he cried.

"I have some hopes."

"Ah, thank Heaven!" His face became radiant. "The Prime Minister is lunching with me. May he share your hopes? He has nerves of steel, and yet I know that he has hardly slept since this terrible event. Jacobs, will you ask the Prime Minister to come up? As to you, dear, I fear that this is a matter of politics. We will join you in a few minutes in the dining-room."

The Prime Minister's manner was subdued, but I could see by the gleam of his eyes and the twitchings of his bony hands that he shared the excitement of his young colleague.

"I understand that you have something to report, Mr. Holmes?"

"Purely negative as yet," my friend answered. "I have inquired at every point where it might be, and I am sure that there is no danger to be apprehended."

"But that is not enough, Mr. Holmes. We cannot live for ever on such a volcano. We must have something definite."

"I am in hopes of getting it. That is why I am here. The more I think of the matter the more convinced I am that the letter has never left this house."

"Mr. Holmes!"

"If it had it would certainly have been public by now."

"But why should anyone take it in order to keep it in this house?"

"I am not convinced that anyone did take it."

"Then how could it leave the despatch-box?"

"I am not convinced that it ever did leave the despatch-box."

"Mr. Holmes, this joking is very ill-timed. You have my assurance that it left the box."

"Have you examined the box since Tuesday morning?"

"No; it was not necessary."

"You may conceivably have overlooked it."

"Impossible, I say."

"But I am not convinced of it; I have known such things happen. I presume there are other papers there. Well, it may have got mixed with them."

"It was on the top."

"Someone may have shaken the box and displaced it."

"No, no; I had everything out."

"Surely it is easily decided, Hope," said the Premier. "Let us have the despatch-box brought in."

The Secretary rang the bell.

"Jacobs, bring down my despatch-box. This is a farcical waste of time, but still, if nothing else will satisfy you, it shall be done. Thank you, Jacobs; put it here. I have always had the key on my watch-chain. Here are the papers, you see. Letter from Lord Merrow, report from Sir Charles Hardy,

"THE PREMIER SNATCHED THE BLUE ENVELOPE FROM HIS HAND."

memorandum from Belgrade, note on the Russo-German grain taxes, letter from Madrid, note from Lord Flowers—good heavens! what is this? Lord Bellinger! Lord Bellinger!"

The Premier snatched the blue envelope from his hand.

"Yes, it is it—and the letter is intact. Hope, I congratulate you."

"Thank you! Thank you! What a weight from my heart. But this is inconceivable—impossible. Mr. Holmes, you are a wizard, a sorcerer! How did you know it was there?"

"Because I knew it was nowhere else."

"I cannot believe my eyes!" He ran wildly to the door. "Where is my wife? I must tell her that all is well. Hilda! Hilda!" we heard his voice on the stairs.

The Premier looked at Holmes with twinkling eyes.

"Come, sir," said he. "There is more in this than meets the eye. How came the letter back in the box?"

Holmes turned away smiling from the keen scrutiny of those wonderful eyes.

"We also have our diplomatic secrets," said he, and picking up his hat he turned to the door.

# THE HOUND
## OF THE BASKERVILLES

THE HOUND OF THE BASKERVILLES.

# THE STRAND MAGAZINE.

Vol. xxii.          AUGUST, 1901.          No. 128.

# The Hound of the Baskervilles.*

## ANOTHER ADVENTURE OF

# SHERLOCK HOLMES.

### By CONAN DOYLE.

### CHAPTER I.
#### MR. SHERLOCK HOLMES.

MR. SHERLOCK HOLMES, who was usually very late in the mornings, save upon those not infrequent occasions when he was up all night, was seated at the breakfast table. I stood upon the hearth-rug and picked up the stick which our visitor had left behind him the night before. It was a fine, thick piece of wood, bulbous-headed, of the sort which is known as a "Penang lawyer." Just under the head was a broad silver band, nearly an inch across. "To James Mortimer, M.R.C.S., from his friends of the C.C.H.," was engraved upon it, with the date "1884." It was just such a stick as the old-fashioned family practitioner used to carry—dignified, solid, and reassuring.

"Well, Watson, what do you make of it?"

Holmes was sitting with his back to me, and I had given him no sign of my occupation.

"How did you know what I was doing? I believe you have eyes in the back of your head."

"I have, at least, a well-polished silver-plated coffee-pot in front of me," said he. "But, tell me, Watson, what do you make of our visitor's stick? Since we have been so unfortunate as to miss him and have no notion of his errand, this accidental souvenir becomes of importance. Let me hear you reconstruct the man by an examination of it."

"I think," said I, following as far as I could the methods of my companion, "that Dr. Mortimer is a successful elderly medical man, well-esteemed, since those who know him give him this mark of their appreciation."

"Good!" said Holmes. "Excellent!"

"I think also that the probability is in favour of his being a country practitioner who does a great deal of his visiting on foot."

"Why so?"

"Because this stick, though originally a very handsome one, has been so knocked about that I can hardly imagine a town practitioner carrying it. The thick iron ferrule is worn down, so it is evident that he has done a great amount of walking with it."

"Perfectly sound!" said Holmes.

"And then again, there is the 'friends of the C.C.H.' I should guess that to be the Something Hunt, the local hunt to whose members he has possibly given some surgical assistance, and which has made him a small presentation in return."

"Really, Watson, you excel yourself," said Holmes, pushing back his chair and lighting a cigarette. "I am bound to say that in all the accounts which you have been so good as to give of my own small achievements you have habitually underrated your own abilities. It may be that you are not yourself luminous, but you are a conductor of light. Some people without possessing genius have a remarkable power of stimulating it. I confess, my dear fellow, that I am very much in your debt."

He had never said as much before, and I must admit that his words gave me keen pleasure, for I had often been piqued by his indifference to my admiration and to the attempts which I had made to give publicity to his methods. I was proud too to think that I had so far mastered his system as to apply it in a way which earned his approval. He now took the stick from my hands

---

*This story owes its inception to my friend, Mr. Fletcher Robinson, who has helped me both in the general plot and in the local details.—A. C. D.

and examined it for a few minutes with his naked eyes. Then with an expression of interest he laid down his cigarette and, carrying the cane to the window, he looked over it again with a convex lens.

"Interesting, though elementary," said he, as he returned to his favourite corner of the settee. "There are certainly one or two indications upon the stick. It gives us the basis for several deductions."

"Has anything escaped me?" I asked, with some self-importance. "I trust that there is nothing of consequence which I have overlooked?"

"I am afraid, my dear Watson, that most of your conclusions were erroneous. When I said that you stimulated me I meant, to be frank, that in noting your fallacies I was occasionally guided towards the truth. Not that you are entirely wrong in this instance. The man is certainly a country practitioner. And he walks a good deal."

"Then I was right."

"To that extent."

"But that was all."

"No, no, my dear Watson, not all—by no means all. I would suggest, for example, that a presentation to a doctor is more likely to come from an hospital than from a hunt, and that when the initials 'C.C.' are placed before that hospital the words 'Charing Cross' very naturally suggest themselves."

"You may be right."

"The probability lies in that direction. And if we take this as a working hypothesis we have a fresh basis from which to start our construction of this unknown visitor."

"Well, then, supposing that 'C.C.H.' does stand for 'Charing Cross Hospital,' what further inferences may we draw?"

"Do none suggest themselves? You know my methods. Apply them!"

"I can only think of the obvious conclusion that the man has practised in town before going to the country."

"HE LOOKED OVER IT AGAIN WITH A CONVEX LENS."

"I think that we might venture a little farther than this. Look at it in this light. On what occasion would it be most probable that such a presentation would be made? When would his friends unite to give him a pledge of their good will? Obviously at the moment when Dr. Mortimer withdrew from the service of the hospital in order to start in practice for himself. We know there has been a presentation. We believe there has been a change from a town hospital to a country practice. Is it, then, stretching our inference too far to say that the presentation was on the occasion of the change?"

"It certainly seems probable."

"Now, you will observe that he could not have been on the *staff* of the hospital, since only a man well-established in a London practice could hold such a position, and such a one would not drift into the country. What was he, then? If he was in the hospital and yet not on the staff he could only have been a house-surgeon or a house-physician—little more than a senior student. And he left five years ago —the date is on the stick. So your grave, middle-aged family practitioner vanishes into thin air, my dear Watson, and there emerges a young fellow under thirty, amiable, unambitious, absent-minded, and the possessor of a favourite dog, which I should describe roughly as being larger than a terrier and smaller than a mastiff."

I laughed incredulously as Sherlock Holmes leaned back in his settee and blew little wavering rings of smoke up to the ceiling.

"As to the latter part, I have no means of checking you," said I, "but at least it is not difficult to find out a few particulars about the man's age and professional career." From my small medical shelf I took down the Medical Directory and turned up the name. There were several

Mortimers, but only one who could be our visitor. I read his record aloud.

"Mortimer, James, M.R.C.S., 1882, Grimpen, Dartmoor, Devon. House surgeon, from 1882 to 1884, at Charing Cross Hospital. Winner of the Jackson prize for Comparative Pathology, with essay entitled 'Is Disease a Reversion?' Corresponding member of the Swedish Pathological Society. Author of 'Some Freaks of Atavism' (*Lancet*, 1882). 'Do We Progress?' (*Journal of Psychology*, March, 1883). Medical Officer for the parishes of Grimpen, Thorsley, and High Barrow."

"No mention of that local hunt, Watson," said Holmes, with a mischievous smile, "but a country doctor, as you very astutely observed. I think that I am fairly justified in my inferences. As to the adjectives, I said, if I remember right, amiable, unambitious, and absent-minded. It is my experience that it is only an amiable man in this world who receives testimonials, only an unambitious one who abandons a London career for the country, and only an absent-minded one who leaves his stick and not his visiting-card after waiting an hour in your room."

"And the dog?"

"Has been in the habit of carrying this stick behind his master. Being a heavy stick the dog has held it tightly by the middle, and the marks of his teeth are very plainly visible. The dog's jaw, as shown in the space between these marks, is too broad in my opinion for a terrier and not broad enough for a mastiff. It may have been—yes, by Jove, it *is* a curly-haired spaniel."

He had risen and paced the room as he spoke. Now he halted in the recess of the window. There was such a ring of conviction in his voice that I glanced up in surprise.

"My dear fellow, how can you possibly be so sure of that?"

"For the very simple reason that I see the dog himself on our very door-step, and there is the ring

of its owner. Don't move, I beg you, Watson. He is a professional brother of yours, and your presence may be of assistance to me. Now is the dramatic moment of fate, Watson, when you hear a step upon the stair which is walking into your life, and you know not whether for good or ill. What does Dr. James Mortimer, the man of science, ask of Sherlock Holmes, the specialist in crime? Come in!"

The appearance of our visitor was a surprise to me, since I had expected a typical country practitioner. He was a very tall, thin man, with a long nose like a beak, which jutted out between two keen, grey eyes, set closely together and sparkling brightly from behind a pair of gold-rimmed glasses. He was clad in a professional but rather slovenly fashion, for his frock-coat was dingy and his trousers frayed. Though young, his long back was already bowed, and he walked with a forward thrust of his head and a general air of peering benevolence. As he entered his eyes fell upon

"HIS EYES FELL UPON THE STICK IN HOLMES'S HAND."

the stick in Holmes's hand, and he ran towards it with an exclamation of joy. "I am so very glad," said he. "I was not sure whether I had left it here or in the Shipping Office. I would not lose that stick for the world."

"A presentation, I see," said Holmes.

"Yes, sir."

"From Charing Cross Hospital?"

"From one or two friends there on the occasion of my marriage."

"Dear, dear, that's bad!" said Holmes, shaking his head.

Dr. Mortimer blinked through his glasses in mild astonishment.

"Why was it bad?"

"Only that you have disarranged our little deductions. Your marriage, you say?"

"Yes, sir. I married, and so left the hospital, and with it all hopes of a consulting practice. It was necessary to make a home of my own."

"Come, come, we are not so far wrong after all," said Holmes. "And now, Dr. James Mortimer——"

"Mister, sir, Mister—a humble M.R.C.S."

"And a man of precise mind, evidently."

"A dabbler in science, Mr. Holmes, a picker up of shells on the shores of the great unknown ocean. I presume that it is Mr. Sherlock Holmes whom I am addressing and not——"

"No, this is my friend Dr. Watson."

"Glad to meet you, sir. I have heard your name mentioned in connection with that of your friend. You interest me very much, Mr. Holmes. I had hardly expected so dolichocephalic a skull or such well-marked supra-orbital development. Would you have any objection to my running my finger along your parietal fissure? A cast of your skull, sir, until the original is available, would be an ornament to any anthropological museum. It is not my intention to be fulsome, but I confess that I covet your skull."

Sherlock Holmes waved our strange visitor into a chair. "You are an enthusiast in your line of thought, I perceive, sir, as I am in mine," said he. "I observe from your fore-finger that you make your own cigarettes. Have no hesitation in lighting one."

The man drew out paper and tobacco and twirled the one up in the other with surprising dexterity. He had long, quivering fingers as agile and restless as the antennæ of an insect.

Holmes was silent, but his little darting glances showed me the interest which he took in our curious companion.

"I presume, sir," said he at last, "that it was not merely for the purpose of examining my skull that you have done me the honour to call here last night and again to-day?"

"No, sir, no; though I am happy to have had the opportunity of doing that as well. I came to you, Mr. Holmes, because I recognise that I am myself an unpractical man, and because I am suddenly confronted with a most serious and extraordinary problem. Recognising, as I do, that you are the second highest expert in Europe——"

"Indeed, sir! May I inquire who has the honour to be the first?" asked Holmes, with some asperity.

"To the man of precisely scientific mind the work of Monsieur Bertillon must always appeal strongly."

"Then had you not better consult him?"

"I said, sir, to the precisely scientific mind. But as a practical man of affairs it is acknowledged that you stand alone. I trust, sir, that I have not inadvertently——"

"Just a little," said Holmes. "I think, Dr. Mortimer, you would do wisely if without more ado you would kindly tell me plainly what the exact nature of the problem is in which you demand my assistance."

## CHAPTER II.
### THE CURSE OF THE BASKERVILLES.

"I HAVE in my pocket a manuscript," said Dr. James Mortimer.

"I observed it as you entered the room," said Holmes.

"It is an old manuscript."

"Early eighteenth century, unless it is a forgery."

"How can you say that, sir?"

"You have presented an inch or two of it to my examination all the time that you have been talking. It would be a poor expert who could not give the date of a document within a decade or so. You may possibly have read my little monograph upon the subject. I put that at 1730."

"The exact date is 1742." Dr. Mortimer drew it from his breast-pocket. "This family paper was committed to my care by Sir Charles Baskerville, whose sudden and tragic death some three months ago created so much excitement in Devonshire. I may say that I was his personal friend as well as his medical attendant. He was a strong-minded man, sir, shrewd, practical, and as unimaginative as I am myself. Yet he took this document very seriously, and his mind was prepared for just such an end as did eventually overtake him."

Holmes stretched out his hand for the manuscript and flattened it upon his knee.

"You will observe, Watson, the alternative use of the long *s* and the short. It is one of several indications which enabled me to fix the date."

I looked over his shoulder at the yellow paper and the faded script. At the head was written : "Baskerville Hall," and below, in large, scrawling figures : "1742."

his finger-tips together, and closed his eyes, with an air of resignation. Dr. Mortimer turned the manuscript to the light and read in a high, crackling voice the following curious, old-world narrative :—

"Of the origin of the Hound of the Baskervilles there have been many statements, yet as I come in a direct line from Hugo Baskerville, and as I had the story from my father, who also had it from his,

"DR. MORTIMER TURNED THE MANUSCRIPT TO THE LIGHT AND READ."

"It appears to be a statement of some sort."

"Yes, it is a statement of a certain legend which runs in the Baskerville family."

"But I understand that it is something more modern and practical upon which you wish to consult me?"

"Most modern. A most practical, pressing matter, which must be decided within twenty-four hours. But the manuscript is short and is intimately connected with the affair. With your permission I will read it to you."

Holmes leaned back in his chair, placed

I have set it down with all belief that it occurred even as is here set forth. And I would have you believe, my sons, that the same Justice which punishes sin may also most graciously forgive it, and that no ban is so heavy but that by prayer and repentance it may be removed. Learn then from this story not to fear the fruits of the past, but rather to be circumspect in the future, that those foul passions whereby our family has suffered so grievously may not again be loosed to our undoing.

"Know then that in the time of the Great Rebellion (the history of which by the learned

Lord Clarendon I most earnestly commend to your attention) this Manor of Baskerville was held by Hugo of that name, nor can it be gainsaid that he was a most wild, profane, and godless man. This, in truth, his neighbours might have pardoned, seeing that saints have never flourished in those parts, but there was in him a certain wanton and cruel humour which made his name a byword through the West. It chanced that this Hugo came to love (if, indeed, so dark a passion may be known under so bright a name) the daughter of a yeoman who held lands near the Baskerville estate. But the young maiden, being discreet and of good repute, would ever avoid him, for she feared his evil name. So it came to pass that one Michaelmas this Hugo, with five or six of his idle and wicked companions, stole down upon the farm and carried off the maiden, her father and brothers being from home, as he well knew. When they had brought her to the Hall the maiden was placed in an upper chamber, while Hugo and his friends sat down to a long carouse, as was their nightly custom. Now, the poor lass upstairs was like to have her wits turned at the singing and shouting and terrible oaths which came up to her from below, for they say that the words used by Hugo Baskerville, when he was in wine, were such as might blast the man who said them. At last in the stress of her fear she did that which might have daunted the bravest or most active man, for by the aid of the growth of ivy which covered (and still covers) the south wall she came down from under the eaves, and so homeward across the moor, there being three leagues betwixt the Hall and her father's farm.

"It chanced that some little time later Hugo left his guests to carry food and drink—with other worse things, perchance—to his captive, and so found the cage empty and the bird escaped. Then, as it would seem, he became as one that hath a devil, for, rushing down the stairs into the dining-hall, he sprang upon the great table, flagons and trenchers flying before him, and he cried aloud before all the company that he would that very night render his body and soul to the Powers of Evil if he might but overtake the wench. And while the revellers stood aghast at the fury of the man, one more wicked or, it may be, more drunken than the rest, cried out that they should put the hounds upon her. Whereat Hugo ran from the house, crying to his grooms that they should saddle his mare and unkennel the pack, and giving the hounds a kerchief of

the maid's, he swung them to the line, and so off full cry in the moonlight over the moor.

"Now, for some space the revellers stood agape, unable to understand all that had been done in such haste. But anon their bemused wits awoke to the nature of the deed which was like to be done upon the moorlands. Everything was now in an uproar, some calling for their pistols, some for their horses, and some for another flask of wine. But at length some sense came back to their crazed minds, and the whole of them, thirteen in number, took horse and started in pursuit. The moon shone clear above them, and they rode swiftly abreast, taking that course which the maid must needs have taken if she were to reach her own home.

"They had gone a mile or two when they passed one of the night shepherds upon the moorlands, and they cried to him to know if he had seen the hunt. And the man, as the story goes, was so crazed with fear that he could scarce speak, but at last he said that he had indeed seen the unhappy maiden, with the hounds upon her track. 'But I have seen more than that,' said he, 'for Hugo Baskerville passed me upon his black mare, and there ran mute behind him such a hound of hell as God forbid should ever be at my heels.' So the drunken squires cursed the shepherd and rode onwards. But soon their skins turned cold, for there came a galloping across the moor, and the black mare, dabbled with white froth, went past with trailing bridle and empty saddle. Then the revellers rode close together, for a great fear was on them, but they still followed over the moor, though each, had he been alone, would have been right glad to have turned his horse's head. Riding slowly in this fashion they came at last upon the hounds. These, though known for their valour and their breed, were whimpering in a cluster at the head of a deep dip or goyal, as we call it, upon the moor, some slinking away and some, with starting hackles and staring eyes, gazing down the narrow valley before them.

"The company had come to a halt, more sober men, as you may guess, than when they started. The most of them would by no means advance, but three of them, the boldest, or it may be the most drunken, rode forward down the goyal. Now, it opened into a broad space in which stood two of those great stones, still to be seen there, which were set by certain forgotten peoples in the days of old. The moon was shining bright upon the clearing, and there in the centre lay the unhappy maid where she had

"THERE IN THE CENTRE LAY THE UNHAPPY MAID WHERE SHE HAD FALLEN."

that many of the family have been unhappy in their deaths, which have been sudden, bloody, and mysterious. Yet may we shelter ourselves in the infinite goodness of Providence, which would not for ever punish the innocent beyond that third or fourth generation which is threatened in Holy Writ. To that Providence, my sons, I hereby commend you, and I counsel you by way of caution to forbear from crossing the moor in those dark hours when the powers of evil are exalted.

"[This from Hugo Baskerville to his sons Rodger and John, with instructions that they say nothing thereof to their sister Elizabeth.]"

When Dr. Mortimer had finished reading this singular narrative he pushed his spectacles up on his forehead and stared across at Mr. Sherlock Holmes. The latter yawned and tossed the end of his cigarette into the fire.

"Well?" said he.

"Do you not find it interesting?"

"To a collector of fairy tales."

Dr. Mortimer drew a folded newspaper out of his pocket.

"Now, Mr. Holmes, we will give you something a little more recent. This is the *Devon County Chronicle* of May 14th of this year. It is a short account of the facts elicited at the death of Sir Charles Baskerville which occurred a few days before that date."

My friend leaned a little forward and his expression became intent. Our visitor readjusted his glasses and began :—

"The recent sudden death of Sir Charles Baskerville, whose name has been mentioned as the probable Liberal candidate for Mid-Devon at the next election, has cast a gloom over the county. Though Sir Charles had resided at Baskerville Hall for a comparatively short period his amiability of character and extreme generosity had won the affection and respect of all who had been brought into contact with him. In these days of *nouveaux riches* it is refreshing to find a case where the scion of an old county family which has fallen upon evil days is able to make his own fortune and to bring it back

fallen, dead of fear and of fatigue. But it was not the sight of her body, nor yet was it that of the body of Hugo Baskerville lying near her, which raised the hair upon the heads of these three dare-devil roysterers, but it was that, standing over Hugo, and plucking at his throat, there stood a foul thing, a great, black beast, shaped like a hound, yet larger than any hound that ever mortal eye has rested upon. And even as they looked the thing tore the throat out of Hugo Baskerville, on which, as it turned its blazing eyes and dripping jaws upon them, the three shrieked with fear and rode for dear life, still screaming, across the moor. One, it is said, died that very night of what he had seen, and the other twain were but broken men for the rest of their days.

"Such is the tale, my sons, of the coming of the hound which is said to have plagued the family so sorely ever since. If I have set it down it is because that which is clearly known hath less terror than that which is but hinted at and guessed. Nor can it be denied

with him to restore the fallen grandeur of his line. Sir Charles, as is well known, made large sums of money in South African speculation. More wise than those who go on until the wheel turns against them, he realized his gains and returned to England with them. It is only two years since he took up his residence at Baskerville Hall, and it is common talk how large were those schemes of reconstruction and improvement which have been interrupted by his death. Being himself childless, it was his openly-expressed desire that the whole countryside should, within his own lifetime, profit by his good fortune, and many will have personal reasons for bewailing his untimely end. His generous donations to local and county charities have been frequently chronicled in these columns.

"The circumstances connected with the death of Sir Charles can-not be said to have been entirely cleared up by the inquest, but at least enough has been done to dis-pose of those rumours to which local superstition has given rise. There is no reason whatever to suspect foul play, or to imagine that death could be from any but natural causes. Sir Charles was a widower, and a man who may be said to have been in some ways of an eccen-tric habit of mind. In spite of his considerable wealth he was simple in his

"HIS BODY WAS DISCOVERED."

personal tastes, and his indoor servants at Baskerville Hall consisted of a married couple named Barrymore, the husband acting as butler and the wife as housekeeper. Their evidence, corroborated by that of several friends, tends to show that Sir Charles's health has for some time been impaired, and points especially to some affection of the heart, manifesting itself in changes of colour,

breathlessness, and acute attacks of nervous depression. Dr. James Mortimer, the friend and medical attendant of the deceased, has given evidence to the same effect.

"The facts of the case are simple. Sir Charles Baskerville was in the habit every night before going to bed of walking down the famous Yew Alley of Baskerville Hall. The evidence of the Barrymores shows that this had been his custom. On the 4th of May Sir Charles had declared his intention of starting next day for London, and had ordered Barrymore to prepare his luggage. That night he went out as usual for his nocturnal walk, in the course of which he was in the habit of smoking a cigar. He never returned. At twelve o'clock Barrymore, finding the hall door still open, became alarmed, and, lighting a lantern, went in search of his master. The day had been wet, and Sir Charles's footmarks were easily traced down the Alley. Half-way down this walk there is a gate which leads out on to the moor. There were indications that Sir Charles had stood for some little time here. He then proceeded down the Alley, and it was at the far end of it that his body was discovered. One fact which has not been explained is the statement of Barry-more that his master's footprints altered their character from the time that he passed the moor-gate, and that he appeared from thence onwards to have been walking upon his toes. One Murphy, a gipsy horse-dealer, was on the moor at no great distance at the time, but he appears by his own confession to have been the worse for drink. He declares that he heard cries, but is unable to state from what direction they came. No signs of violence were to be discovered upon Sir Charles's person, and though the doctor's evidence pointed to an almost incredible facial distortion—so great that Dr. Mortimer refused at first to believe that it was indeed his friend and patient who lay before him—it was explained that that is a symptom which is not unusual in cases of dyspnœa and death from cardiac exhaustion. This explanation was borne out by the post-mortem examination, which showed long-standing organic disease, and the coroner's jury returned a verdict in accordance with the medical evidence. It is well that this is so, for it is obviously of the utmost importance that Sir Charles's heir should settle at the Hall and continue the good work which has been so sadly interrupted. Had the prosaic finding of the coroner not finally put an end to the romantic stories which have been whispered in connection with the affair it might have been difficult to find a tenant for Baskerville Hall. It is understood that the next of kin is Mr. Henry Baskerville, if he be still alive, the son of Sir Charles Baskerville's younger brother. The young man when last heard of was in America, and inquiries are being instituted with a view to informing him of his good fortune."

Dr. Mortimer refolded his paper and replaced it in his pocket.

"Those are the public facts, Mr. Holmes, in connection with the death of Sir Charles Baskerville."

"I must thank you," said Sherlock Holmes, "for calling my attention to a case which certainly presents some features of interest. I had observed some newspaper comment at the time, but I was exceedingly preoccupied by that little affair of the Vatican cameos, and in my anxiety to oblige the Pope I lost touch with several interesting English cases. This article, you say, contains all the public facts?"

"It does."

"Then let me have the private ones." He leaned back, put his finger-tips together, and assumed his most impassive and judicial expression.

"In doing so," said Dr. Mortimer, who had begun to show signs of some strong emotion, "I am telling that which I have not confided to anyone. My motive for withholding it from the coroner's inquiry is that a man of science shrinks from placing himself in the public position of seeming to indorse a popular superstition. I had the further motive that Baskerville Hall, as the paper says, would certainly remain untenanted if anything were done to increase its already rather grim reputation. For both these reasons I thought that I was justified in telling rather less than I knew, since no practical good could result from it, but with you there is no reason why I should not be perfectly frank.

"The moor is very sparsely inhabited, and those who live near each other are thrown very much together. For this reason I saw a good deal of Sir Charles Baskerville. With the exception of Mr. Frankland, of Lafter Hall, and Mr. Stapleton, the naturalist, there are no other men of education within many miles. Sir Charles was a retiring man, but the chance of his illness brought us together, and a community of interests in science kept us so. He had brought back much scientific information from South Africa, and many a charming evening we have spent together discussing the comparative anatomy of the Bushman and the Hottentot.

"Within the last few months it became increasingly plain to me that Sir Charles's nervous system was strained to breaking point. He had taken this legend which I have read you exceedingly to heart—so much so that, although he would walk in his own grounds, nothing would induce him to go out upon the moor at night. Incredible as it may appear to you, Mr. Holmes, he was honestly convinced that a dreadful fate overhung his family, and certainly the records which he was able to give of his ancestors were not encouraging. The idea of some ghastly presence constantly haunted him, and on more than one occasion he has asked me whether I had on my medical journeys at night ever seen any strange creature or heard the baying of a hound. The latter question he put to me several times, and always with a voice which vibrated with excitement.

"I can well remember driving up to his house in the evening, some three weeks before the fatal event. He chanced to be at his hall door. I had descended from my gig and was standing in front of him, when I saw his eyes fix themselves over my shoulder, and stare past me with an expression of the most dreadful horror. I whisked round and had just time to catch a glimpse of something which I took to be a large black calf passing at the head of the drive. So excited and alarmed was he that I was compelled to

"I SAW HIS EYES FIX THEMSELVES OVER MY SHOULDER."

his health. I thought that a few months among the distractions of town would send him back a new man. Mr. Stapleton, a mutual friend who was much concerned at his state of health, was of the same opinion. At the last instant came this terrible catastrophe.

"On the night of Sir Charles's death Barrymore the butler, who made the discovery, sent Perkins the groom on horseback to me, and as I was sitting up late I was able to reach Baskerville Hall within an hour of the event. I checked and corroborated all the facts which were mentioned at the inquest. I followed the footsteps down the Yew Alley, I saw the spot at the moor-gate where he seemed to have waited, I remarked the change in the shape of the prints after that point, I noted that there were no other footsteps save those of Barrymore on the soft gravel, and finally I carefully examined the body, which had not been touched until my arrival. Sir Charles lay on his face, his arms out, his fingers dug into the ground, and his features convulsed with some strong emotion to such an extent that I could hardly have sworn to his identity. There was certainly no physical injury of any kind. But one false statement was made by Barrymore at the inquest. He said that there were no traces upon the ground round the body. He did not observe any. But I did—some little distance off, but fresh and clear."

"Footprints?"

"Footprints."

"A man's or a woman's?"

Dr. Mortimer looked strangely at us for an instant, and his voice sank almost to a whisper as he answered :—

"Mr. Holmes, they were the footprints of a gigantic hound!"

go down to the spot where the animal had been and look around for it. It was gone, however, and the incident appeared to make the worst impression upon his mind. I stayed with him all the evening, and it was on that occasion, to explain the emotion which he had shown, that he confided to my keeping that narrative which I read to you when first I came. I mention this small episode because it assumes some importance in view of the tragedy which followed, but I was convinced at the time that the matter was entirely trivial and that his excitement had no justification.

"It was at my advice that Sir Charles was about to go to London. His heart was, I knew, affected, and the constant anxiety in which he lived, however chimerical the cause of it might be, was evidently having a serious effect upon

*(To be continued.)*

"THERE'S OUR MAN, WATSON! COME ALONG."

# The Hound of the Baskervilles.

## ANOTHER ADVENTURE OF

# SHERLOCK HOLMES.

### By CONAN DOYLE.

## CHAPTER III.

### THE PROBLEM.

 CONFESS that at these words a shudder passed through me. There was a thrill in the doctor's voice which showed that he was himself deeply moved by that which he told us. Holmes leaned forward in his excitement and his eyes had the hard, dry glitter which shot from them when he was keenly interested.

"You saw this?"

"As clearly as I see you."

"And you said nothing?"

"What was the use?"

"How was it that no one else saw it?"

"The marks were some twenty yards from the body and no one gave them a thought. I don't suppose I should have done so had I not known this legend."

"There are many sheep-dogs on the moor?"

"No doubt, but this was no sheep-dog."

"You say it was large?"

"Enormous."

"But it had not approached the body?"

"No."

"What sort of night was it?"

"Damp and raw."

"But not actually raining?"

"No."

"What is the alley like?"

"There are two lines of old yew hedge, 12ft. high and impenetrable. The walk in the centre is about 8ft. across."

"Is there anything between the hedges and the walk?"

"Yes, there is a strip of grass about 6ft. broad on either side."

"I understand that the yew hedge is penetrated at one point by a gate?"

"Yes, the wicket-gate which leads on to the moor."

"Is there any other opening?"

"None."

"So that to reach the Yew Alley one either has to come down it from the house or else to enter it by the moor-gate?"

"There is an exit through a summer-house at the far end."

"Had Sir Charles reached this?"

"No; he lay about fifty yards from it."

"Now, tell me, Dr. Mortimer—and this is important—the marks which you saw were on the path and not on the grass?"

"No marks could show on the grass."

"Were they on the same side of the path as the moor-gate?"

"Yes; they were on the edge of the path on the same side as the moor-gate."

"You interest me exceedingly. Another point. Was the wicket-gate closed?"

"Closed and padlocked."

"How high was it?"

"About 4ft. high."

"Then anyone could have got over it?"

"Yes."

"And what marks did you see by the wicket-gate?"

"None in particular."

"Good Heaven! Did no one examine?"

"Yes, I examined myself."

"And found nothing?"

"It was all very confused. Sir Charles had evidently stood there for five or ten minutes."

"How do you know that?"

"Because the ash had twice dropped from his cigar."

Vol. xxii.—31.

"Excellent ! This is a colleague, Watson, after our own heart. But the marks ? "

"He had left his own marks all over that small patch of gravel. I could discern no others."

Sherlock Holmes struck his hand against his knee with an impatient gesture.

"If I had only been there ! " he cried. "It is evidently a case of extraordinary interest, and one which presented immense opportunities to the scientific expert. That gravel page upon which I might have read so much has been long ere this smudged by the rain and defaced by the clogs of curious peasants. Oh, Dr. Mortimer, Dr. Mortimer, to think that you should not have called me in ! You have indeed much to answer for."

and most experienced of detectives is helpless."

"You mean that the thing is supernatural ? "

"I did not positively say so."

"No, but you evidently think it."

"Since the tragedy, Mr. Holmes, there have come to my ears several incidents which are hard to reconcile with the settled order of Nature."

"For example ? "

"I find that before the terrible event occurred several people had seen a creature upon the moor which corresponds with this Baskerville demon, and which could not possibly be any animal known to science. They all agreed that it was a huge creature,

"YOU HAVE INDEED MUCH TO ANSWER FOR."

"I could not call you in, Mr. Holmes, without disclosing these facts to the world, and I have already given my reasons for not wishing to do so. Besides, besides——"

"Why do you hesitate ? "

"There is a realm in which the most acute

luminous, ghastly, and spectral. I have cross-examined these men, one of them a hard - headed countryman, one a farrier, and one a moorland farmer, who all tell the same story of this dreadful apparition, exactly corresponding to the hell-hound of the legend. I assure you that there is a reign of terror in the district and that it is a hardy man who will cross the moor at night."

"And you, a trained man of science, believe it to be supernatural?"

"I do not know what to believe."

Holmes shrugged his shoulders.

"I have hitherto confined my investigations to this world," said he. "In a modest way I have combated evil, but to take on the Father of Evil himself would, perhaps, be too ambitious a task. Yet you must admit that the footmark is material."

"The original hound was material enough to tug a man's throat out, and yet he was diabolical as well."

"I see that you have quite gone over to the supernaturalists. But now, Dr. Mortimer, tell me this. If you hold these views, why have you come to consult me at all? You tell me in the same breath that it is useless to investigate Sir Charles's death, and that you desire me to do it."

"I did not say that I desired you to do it."

"Then, how can I assist you?"

"By advising me as to what I should do with Sir Henry Baskerville, who arrives at Waterloo Station"—Dr. Mortimer looked at his watch—"in exactly one hour and a quarter."

"He being the heir?"

"Yes. On the death of Sir Charles we inquired for this young gentleman, and found that he had been farming in Canada. From the accounts which have reached us he is an excellent fellow in every way. I speak now not as a medical man but as a trustee and executor of Sir Charles's will."

"There is no other claimant, I presume?"

"None. The only other kinsman whom we have been able to trace was Rodger Baskerville, the youngest of three brothers of whom poor Sir Charles was the elder. The second brother, who died young, is the father of this lad Henry. The third, Rodger, was the black sheep of the family. He came of the old masterful Baskerville strain, and was the very image, they tell me, of the family picture of old Hugo. He made England too hot to hold him, fled to Central America, and died there in 1876 of yellow fever. Henry is the last of the Baskervilles. In one hour and five minutes I meet him at Waterloo Station. I have had a wire that he arrived at Southampton this morning. Now, Mr. Holmes, what would you advise me to do with him?"

"Why should he not go to the home of his fathers?"

"It seems natural, does it not? And yet, consider that every Baskerville who goes there meets with an evil fate. I feel sure that if Sir Charles could have spoken with me before his death he would have warned me against bringing this the last of the old race, and the heir to great wealth, to that deadly place. And yet it cannot be denied that the prosperity of the whole poor, bleak country-side depends upon his presence. All the good work which has been done by Sir Charles will crash to the ground if there is no tenant of the Hall. I fear lest I should be swayed too much by my own obvious interest in the matter, and that is why I bring the case before you and ask for your advice."

Holmes considered for a little time.

"Put into plain words, the matter is this," said he. "In your opinion there is a diabolical agency which makes Dartmoor an unsafe abode for a Baskerville—that is your opinion?"

"At least I might go the length of saying that there is some evidence that this may be so."

"Exactly. But surely, if your supernatural theory be correct, it could work the young man evil in London as easily as in Devonshire. A devil with merely local powers like a parish vestry would be too inconceivable a thing."

"You put the matter more flippantly, Mr. Holmes, than you would probably do if you were brought into personal contact with these things. Your advice, then, as I understand it, is that the young man will be as safe in Devonshire as in London. He comes in fifty minutes. What would you recommend?"

"I recommend, sir, that you take a cab, call off your spaniel who is scratching at my front door, and proceed to Waterloo to meet Sir Henry Baskerville."

"And then?"

"And then you will say nothing to him at all until I have made up my mind about the matter."

"How long will it take you to make up your mind?"

"Twenty-four hours. At ten o'clock to-morrow, Dr. Mortimer, I will be much obliged to you if you will call upon me here, and it will be of help to me in my plans for the future if you will bring Sir Henry Baskerville with you."

"I will do so, Mr. Holmes." He scribbled the appointment on his shirt cuff and hurried off in his strange, peering, absent-minded fashion. Holmes stopped him at the head of the stair.

"HE SCRIBBLED THE APPOINTMENT ON HIS SHIRT CUFF."

"Only one more question, Dr. Mortimer. You say that before Sir Charles Baskerville's death several people saw this apparition upon the moor?"

"Three people did."

"Did any see it after?"

"I have not heard of any."

"Thank you.  Good morning."

Holmes returned to his seat with that quiet look of inward satisfaction which meant that he had a congenial task before him.

"Going out, Watson?"

"Unless I can help you."

"No, my dear fellow, it is at the hour of action that I turn to you for aid.  But this is splendid, really unique from some points of view.  When you pass Bradley's would you ask him to send up a pound of the strongest shag tobacco?  Thank you.  It would be as well if you could make it convenient not to return before evening.  Then I should be very glad to compare impressions as to this most interesting problem which has been submitted to us this morning."

I knew that seclusion and solitude were very necessary for my friend in those hours of intense mental concentration during which he weighed every particle of evidence, constructed alternative theories, balanced one against the other, and made up his mind as to which points were essential and which immaterial.  I therefore spent the day at my club and did not return to Baker Street until evening. It was nearly nine o'clock when I found myself in the sitting-room once more.

My first impression as I opened the door was that a fire had broken out, for the room was so filled with smoke that the light of the lamp upon the table was blurred by it. As I entered, however, my fears were set at rest, for it was the acrid fumes of strong coarse tobacco which took me by the throat and set me coughing.  Through the haze I had a vague vision of Holmes in his dressing-gown coiled up in an arm-chair with his black clay pipe between his lips.  Several rolls of paper lay around him.

"Caught cold, Watson?" said he.

"No, it's this poisonous atmosphere."

"I suppose it *is* pretty thick, now that you mention it."

"Thick!  It is intolerable."

"Open the window, then!  You have been at your club all day, I perceive."

"My dear Holmes!"

"Am I right?"

"Certainly, but how——?"

He laughed at my bewildered expression.

"There is a delightful freshness about you, Watson, which makes it a pleasure to exercise any small powers which I possess at your expense.  A gentleman goes forth on a showery and miry day.  He returns immaculate in the evening with the gloss still on his hat and his boots.  He has been a fixture therefore all day.  He is not a man with intimate friends. Where, then, could he have been? Is it not obvious?"

"Well, it is rather obvious."

"The world is full of obvious things which nobody by any chance ever observes. Where do you think that I have been?"

"A fixture also."

"On the contrary, I have been to Devonshire."

"In spirit?"

"Exactly. My body has remained in this arm-chair, and has, I regret to observe, consumed in my absence two large

"THAT IS BASKERVILLE HALL IN THE MIDDLE."

pots of coffee and an incredible amount of tobacco. After you left I sent down to Stamford's for the Ordnance map of this portion of the moor, and my spirit has hovered over it all day. I flatter myself that I could find my way about."

"A large scale map, I presume?"

"Very large." He unrolled one section and held it over his knee. "Here you have the particular district which concerns us. That is Baskerville Hall in the middle."

"With a wood round it?"

"Exactly. I fancy the Yew Alley, though not marked under that name, must stretch along this line, with the moor, as you perceive, upon the right of it. This small clump of buildings here is the hamlet of Grimpen, where our friend Dr. Mortimer has his headquarters. Within a radius of five miles there are, as you see, only a very few scattered dwellings. Here is Lafter Hall, which was mentioned in the narrative. There is a house indicated here which may be the residence of the naturalist—Stapleton, if I remember right, was his name. Here are two moorland farmhouses, High Tor and Foulmire. Then fourteen miles away the great convict prison of Princetown. Between and around these scattered points extends the desolate, lifeless moor. This, then, is the stage upon which tragedy has been played, and upon which we may help to play it again."

"It must be a wild place."

"Yes, the setting is a worthy one. If the devil did desire to have a hand in the affairs of men——"

"Then you are yourself inclining to the supernatural explanation."

"The devil's agents may be of flesh and blood, may they not? There are two questions waiting for us at the outset. The one is whether any crime has been committed at all; the second is, what is the crime and how was it committed? Of course, if Dr. Mortimer's surmise should be correct, and we are dealing with forces outside the ordinary laws of Nature, there is an end of our investigation. But we are bound to exhaust all other hypotheses before falling back upon this one. I think we'll shut that window again, if you don't mind. It is a singular thing, but I find that a concentrated atmosphere helps a concentration of thought. I have not pushed it to the length of getting into a box to think, but that is the logical outcome of my convictions.

Have you turned the case over in your mind?"

"Yes, I have thought a good deal of it in the course of the day."

"What do you make of it?"

"It is very bewildering."

"It has certainly a character of its own. There are points of distinction about it. That change in the footprints, for example. What do you make of that?"

"Mortimer said that the man had walked on tiptoe down that portion of the alley."

"He only repeated what some fool had said at the inquest. Why should a man walk on tiptoe down the alley?"

"What then?"

"He was running, Watson—running desperately, running for his life, running until he burst his heart and fell dead upon his face."

"Running from what?"

"There lies our problem. There are indications that the man was crazed with fear before ever he began to run."

"How can you say that?"

"I am presuming that the cause of his fears came to him across the moor. If that were so, and it seems most probable, only a man who had lost his wits would have run *from* the house instead of towards it. If the gipsy's evidence may be taken. as true, he ran with cries for help in the direction where help was least likely to be. Then, again, whom was he waiting for that night, and why was he waiting for him in the Yew Alley rather than in his own house?"

"You think that he was waiting for someone?"

"The man was elderly and infirm. We can understand his taking an evening stroll, but the ground was damp and the night inclement. Is it natural that he should stand for five or ten minutes, as Dr. Mortimer, with

more practical sense than I should have given him credit for, deduced from the cigar ash?"

"But he went out every evening."

"I think it unlikely that he waited at the moor-gate every evening. On the contrary, the evidence is that he avoided the moor. That night he waited there. It was the night before he made his departure for London. The thing takes shape, Watson. It becomes coherent. Might I ask you to hand me my violin, and we will postpone all further thought upon this business until we have had the advantage of meeting Dr. Mortimer and Sir Henry Baskerville in the morning."

## CHAPTER IV.
### SIR HENRY BASKERVILLE.

OUR breakfast-table was cleared early, and Holmes waited in his dressing-gown for the promised interview. Our clients were punctual to their appointment, for the clock had just struck ten when Dr. Mortimer was shown up, followed by the young Baronet. The latter was a small, alert, dark-eyed man about thirty years of age, very sturdily built, with thick black eyebrows and a strong, pugnacious face. He wore a ruddy-tinted tweed suit, and had the weather-beaten appearance of one who has spent most of his time in the open air, and yet there was something in his steady eye and the quiet assurance of his bearing which indicated the gentleman.

"This is Sir Henry Baskerville," said Dr. Mortimer.

"Why, yes," said he, "and the strange thing is, Mr. Sherlock Holmes, that if my friend here had not proposed coming round to you this morning I should have come on my own. I understand that you think out little puzzles, and I've had one this morning which wants more thinking out than I am able to give to it."

SIR HENRY BASKERVILLE.

"Pray take a seat, Sir Henry. Do I understand you to say that you have yourself had some remarkable experience since you arrived in London?"

"Nothing of much importance, Mr. Holmes. Only a joke, as like as not. It was this letter, if you can call it a letter, which reached me this morning."

He laid an envelope upon the table, and we all bent over it. It was of common quality, greyish in colour. The address, "Sir Henry Baskerville, Northumberland Hotel," was printed in rough characters; the post-mark "Charing Cross," and the date of posting the preceding evening.

"Who knew that you were going to the Northumberland Hotel?" asked Holmes, glancing keenly across at our visitor.

"No one could have known. We only decided after I met Dr. Mortimer."

"But Dr. Mortimer was no doubt already stopping there?"

"No, I had been staying with a friend," said the doctor. "There was no possible indication that we intended to go to this hotel."

"Hum! Someone seems to be very deeply interested in your movements." Out of the envelope he took a half-sheet of foolscap paper folded into four. This he opened and spread flat upon the table. Across the middle of it a single sentence had been formed by the expedient of pasting printed words upon it. It ran: "as you value your life or your reason keep away from the moor." The word "moor" only was printed in ink.

"Now," said Sir Henry Baskerville, "perhaps you will tell me, Mr. Holmes, what in thunder is the meaning of that, and who it is that takes so much interest in my affairs?"

"What do you make of it, Dr. Mortimer? You must allow that there is nothing supernatural about this, at any rate?"

"No, sir, but it might very well come from someone who was convinced that the business is supernatural."

"What business?" asked Sir Henry, sharply. "It seems to me that all you gentlemen know a great deal more than I do about my own affairs."

"You shall share our knowledge before you leave this room, Sir Henry. I promise you that," said Sherlock Holmes. "We will confine ourselves for the present with your permission to this very interesting document, which must have been put together

"HE GLANCED SWIFTLY OVER IT."

and posted yesterday evening. Have you yesterday's *Times*, Watson?"

"It is here in the corner."

"Might I trouble you for it—the inside page, please, with the leading articles?" He glanced swiftly over it, running his eyes up and down the columns. "Capital article this on Free Trade. Permit me to give you an extract from it. 'You may be cajoled into imagining that your own special trade or your own industry will be encouraged by a protective tariff, but it stands to reason that such legislation must in the long run keep away wealth from the country, diminish the value of our imports, and lower the general conditions of life in this island.' What do you think of that, Watson?" cried Holmes, in high glee, rubbing his hands together with satisfaction. "Don't you think that is an admirable sentiment?"

Dr. Mortimer looked at Holmes with an air of professional interest, and Sir Henry Baskerville turned a pair of puzzled dark eyes upon me.

"I don't know much about the tariff and things of that kind," said he; "but it seems to me we've got a bit off the trail so far as that note is concerned."

"On the contrary, I think we are particularly hot upon the trail, Sir Henry. Watson here knows more about my methods than you do, but I fear that even he has not quite grasped the significance of this sentence."

"No, I confess that I see no connection."

"And yet, my dear Watson, there is so very close a connection that the one is extracted out of the other. 'You,' 'your,' 'your,' 'life,' 'reason,' 'value,' 'keep away,' 'from the.' Don't you see now whence these words have been taken?"

"By thunder, you're right! Well, if that isn't smart!" cried Sir Henry.

"If any possible doubt remained it is settled by the fact that 'keep away' and 'from the' are cut out in one piece."

"Well, now—so it is!"

"Really, Mr. Holmes, this exceeds anything which I could have imagined," said Dr. Mortimer, gazing at my friend in amazement. "I could understand anyone saying that the words were from a newspaper; but that you should name which, and add that it came from the leading article, is really one of the most remarkable things which I have ever known. How did you do it?"

"I presume, doctor, that you could tell the skull of a negro from that of an Esquimaux?"

"Most certainly."

"But how?"

"Because that is my special hobby. The differences are obvious. The supra-orbital crest, the facial angle, the maxillary curve, the——"

"But this is my special hobby, and the differences are equally obvious. There is as much difference to my eyes between the leaded bourgeois type of a *Times* article and the slovenly print of an evening halfpenny paper as there could be between your negro and your Esquimaux. The detection of types is one of the most elementary branches of knowledge to the special expert in crime, though I confess that once when I was very young I confused the *Leeds Mercury* with the *Western Morning News*. But a *Times* leader is entirely distinctive, and these words could have been taken from nothing else. As it was done yesterday the strong probability was that we should find the words in yesterday's issue."

"So far as I can follow you, then, Mr. Holmes," said Sir Henry Baskerville, "someone cut out this message with a scissors——"

"Nail-scissors," said Holmes. "You can see that it was a very short-bladed scissors, since the cutter had to take two snips over 'keep away.'"

"That is so. Someone, then, cut out the message with a pair of short-bladed scissors, pasted it with paste——"

"Gum," said Holmes.

"With gum on to the paper. But I want to know why the word 'moor' should have been written?"

"Because he could not find it in print. The other words were all simple and might be found in any issue, but 'moor' would be less common."

"Why, of course, that would explain it. Have you read anything else in this message, Mr. Holmes?"

"There are one or two indications, and yet the utmost pains have been taken to remove all clues. The address, you observe, is printed in rough characters. But the *Times* is a paper which is seldom found in any hands but those of the highly educated. We may take it, therefore, that the letter was composed by an educated man who wished to pose as an uneducated one, and his effort to conceal his own writing suggests that that writing might be known, or come to be known, by you. Again, you will observe that the words are not gummed on in an accurate line, but that some are much higher than others. 'Life,' for example, is quite out of its proper place. That may point to carelessness or it may point to agitation and hurry upon the part of the cutter. On the whole I incline to the latter view, since the matter was evidently important, and it is unlikely that the composer of such a letter would be careless. If he were in a hurry it opens up the interesting question why he should be in a hurry, since any letter posted up to early morning would reach Sir Henry before he would leave his hotel. Did the composer fear an interruption—and from whom?"

"We are coming now rather into the region of guess work," said Dr. Mortimer.

"Say, rather, into the region where we balance probabilities and choose the most likely. It is the scientific use of the imagination, but we have always some material basis on which to start our speculations. Now, you would call it a guess, no doubt, but I am almost certain that this address has been written in an hotel."

"How in the world can you say that?"

"If you examine it carefully you will see that both the pen and the ink have given the writer trouble. The pen has spluttered twice in a single word, and has run dry three times in a short address, showing that there was very little ink in the bottle. Now, a private pen or ink-bottle is seldom allowed to be in such a state, and the combination of the two must be quite rare. But you know the hotel ink and the hotel pen, where it is rare to get anything else. Yes, I have very little hesitation in saying that could we examine the waste-paper baskets of the hotels round Charing Cross until we found the remains of the mutilated *Times* leader we could lay our hands straight upon the person who sent this singular message. Halloa! Halloa! What's this?"

He was carefully examining the foolscap, upon which the words were pasted, holding it only an inch or two from his eyes.

"Well?"

"Nothing," said he, throwing it down. "It is a blank half-sheet of paper, without even

"HOLDING IT ONLY AN INCH OR TWO FROM HIS EYES."

a watermark upon it. I think we have drawn as much as we can from this curious letter; and now, Sir Henry, has anything else of interest happened to you since you have been in London?"

"Why, no, Mr. Holmes. I think not."

"You have not observed anyone follow or watch you?"

"I seem to have walked right into the thick of a dime novel," said our visitor. "Why in thunder should anyone follow or watch me?"

"We are coming to that. You have nothing else to report to us before we go into this matter?"

"Well, it depends upon what you think worth reporting."

"I think anything out of the ordinary routine of life well worth reporting."

Sir Henry smiled.

"I don't know much of British life yet, for I have spent nearly all my time in the States and in Canada. But I hope that to lose one of your boots is not part of the ordinary routine of life over here."

"You have lost one of your boots?"

"My dear sir," cried Dr. Mortimer, "it is only mislaid. You will find it when you return to the hotel. What is the use of troubling Mr. Holmes with trifles of this kind?"

"Well, he asked me for anything outside the ordinary routine."

"Exactly," said Holmes, "however foolish the incident may seem. You have lost one of your boots, you say?"

"Well, mislaid it, anyhow. I put them both outside my door last night, and there was only one in the morning. I could get no sense out of the chap who cleans them. The worst of it is that I only bought the pair last night in the Strand, and I have never had them on."

" If you have never worn them, why did you put them out to be cleaned ? "

" They were tan boots, and had never been varnished. That was why I put them out."

" Then I understand that on your arrival in London yesterday you went out at once and bought a pair of boots ? "

" I did a good deal of shopping. Dr. Mortimer here went round with me. You see, if I am to be squire down there I must dress the part, and it may be that I have got a little careless in my ways out West. Among other things I bought these brown boots—gave six dollars for them—and had one stolen before ever I had them on my feet."

" It seems a singularly useless thing to steal," said Sherlock Holmes. " I confess that I share Dr. Mortimer's belief that it will not be long before the missing boot is found."

" And, now, gentlemen," said the Baronet, with decision, " it seems to me that I have spoken quite enough about the little that I know. It is time that you kept your promise and gave me a full account of what we are all driving at."

" Your request is a very reasonable one," Holmes answered. " Dr. Mortimer, I think you could not do better than to tell your story as you told it to us."

Thus encouraged, our scientific friend drew his papers from his pocket, and presented the whole case as he had done upon the morning before. Sir Henry Baskerville listened with the deepest attention, and with an occasional exclamation of surprise.

" Well, I seem to have come into an inheritance with a vengeance," said he, when the long narrative was finished. " Of course, I've heard of the hound ever since I was in the nursery. It's the pet story of the family, though I never thought of taking it seriously before. But as to my uncle's death —well, it all seems boiling up in my head, and I can't get it clear yet. You don't seem quite to have made up your mind whether it's a case for a policeman or a clergyman."

" Precisely."

" And now there's this affair of the letter to me at the hotel. I suppose that fits into its place."

" It seems to show that someone knows more than we do about what goes on upon the moor," said Dr. Mortimer.

" And also," said Holmes, " that someone is not ill-disposed towards you, since they warn you of danger."

" Or it may be that they wish, for their own purposes, to scare me away."

" Well, of course, that is possible also. I am very much indebted to you, Dr. Mortimer, for introducing me to a problem which presents several interesting alternatives. But the practical point which we now have to decide, Sir Henry, is whether it is or is not advisable for you to go to Baskerville Hall."

" Why should I not go ? "

" There seems to be danger."

" Do you mean danger from this family fiend or do you mean danger from human beings ? "

" Well, that is what we have to find out."

" Which ever it is, my answer is fixed. There is no devil in hell, Mr. Holmes, and there is no man upon earth who can prevent me from going to the home of my own people, and you may take that to be my final answer." His dark brows knitted and his face flushed to a dusky red as he spoke. It was evident that the fiery temper of the Baskervilles was not extinct in this their last representative. " Meanwhile," said he, " I have hardly had time to think over all that you have told me. It's a big thing for a man to have to understand and to decide at one sitting. I should like to have a quiet hour by myself to make up my mind. Now, look here, Mr. Holmes, it's half-past eleven now and I am going back right away to my hotel. Suppose you and your friend, Dr. Watson, come round and lunch with us at two ? I'll be able to tell you more clearly then how this thing strikes me."

" Is that convenient to you, Watson ? "

" Perfectly."

" Then you may expect us. Shall I have a cab called ? "

" I'd prefer to walk, for this affair has flurried me rather."

" I'll join you in a walk, with pleasure," said his companion.

" Then we meet again at two o'clock. Au revoir, and good morning ! "

We heard the steps of our visitors descend the stair and the bang of the front door. In an instant Holmes had changed from the languid dreamer to the man of action.

" Your hat and boots, Watson, quick ! Not a moment to lose ! " He rushed into his room in his dressing-gown and was back again in a few seconds in a frock-coat. We hurried together down the stairs and into the street. Dr. Mortimer and Baskerville were still visible about two hundred yards ahead of us in the direction of Oxford Street.

" Shall I run on and stop them ? "

"Not for the world, my dear Watson. I am perfectly satisfied with your company if you will tolerate mine. Our friends are wise, for it is certainly a very fine morning for a walk."

He quickened his pace until we had decreased the distance which divided us by about half. Then, still keeping a hundred yards behind, we followed into Oxford Street and so down Regent Street. Once our friends stopped and stared into a shop window, upon which Holmes did the same. An instant afterwards he gave a little cry of satisfaction, and, following the direction of his eager eyes, I saw that a hansom cab with a man inside which had halted on the other side of the street was now walking slowly onwards again.

"There's our man, Watson! Come along! We'll have a good look at him, if we can do no more."

At that instant I was aware of a bushy black beard and a pair of piercing eyes turned upon us through the side window of the cab. Instantly the trap-door at the top flew up, something was screamed to the driver, and the cab flew madly off down Regent Street. Holmes looked eagerly round for another, but no empty one was in sight. Then he dashed in wild pursuit amid the stream of the traffic, but the start was too great, and already the cab was out of sight.

"There now!" said Holmes, bitterly, as he emerged panting and white with vexation from the tide of vehicles. "Was ever such bad luck and such bad management, too? Watson, Watson, if you are an honest man you will record this also and set it against my successes!"

"Who was the man?"

"I have not an idea."

"A spy?"

"Well, it was evident from what we have heard that Baskerville has been very closely shadowed by someone since he has been in town. How else could it be known so quickly that it was the Northumberland Hotel which he had chosen? If they had followed him the first day I argued that they would follow him also the second. You may have observed that I twice strolled over to the window while Dr. Mortimer was reading his legend."

"Yes, I remember."

"I was looking out for loiterers in the street, but I saw none. We are dealing with a clever man, Watson. This matter cuts very deep, and though I have not finally made up my mind whether it is a benevolent or a malevolent agency which is in touch with us, I am conscious always of power and design. When our friends left I at once

"HERE ARE THE NAMES OF TWENTY-THREE HOTELS."

followed them in the hopes of marking down their invisible attendant. So wily was he that he had not trusted himself upon foot, but he had availed himself of a cab, so that he could loiter behind or dash past them and so escape their notice. His method had the additional advantage that if they were to take a cab he was all ready to follow them. It has, however, one obvious disadvantage."

"It puts him in the power of the ,cabman."

"Exactly."

"What a pity we did not get the number!"

"My dear Watson, clumsy as I have been, you surely do not seriously imagine that I neglected to get the number? 2704 is our man. But that is no use to us for the moment."

"I fail to see how you could have done more."

"On observing the cab I should have instantly turned and walked in the other direction. I should then at my leisure have hired a second cab and followed the first at a respectful distance, or, better still, have driven to the Northumberland Hotel and waited there. When our unknown had followed Baskerville home we should have had the opportunity of playing his own game upon himself, and seeing where he made for. As it is, by an indiscreet eagerness, which was taken advantage of with extraordinary quickness and energy by our opponent, we have betrayed ourselves and lost our man."

We had been sauntering slowly down Regent Street during this conversation, and Dr. Mortimer, with his companion, had long vanished in front of us.

"There is no object in our following them," said Holmes. "The shadow has departed and will not return. We must see what further cards we have in our hands, and play them with decision. Could you swear to that man's face within the cab."

"I could swear only to the beard."

"And so could I—from which I gather that in all probability it was a false one. A clever man upon so delicate an errand has no use for a beard save to conceal his features. Come in here, Watson!"

He turned into one of the district messenger offices, where he was warmly greeted by the manager.

"Ah, Wilson, I see you have not forgotten the little case in which I had the good fortune to help you?"

"No, sir, indeed I have not. You saved my good name, and perhaps my life."

"My dear fellow, you exaggerate. I have some recollection, Wilson, that you had among your boys a lad named Cartwright, who showed some ability during the investigation."

"Yes, sir, he is still with us."

"Could you ring him up?—thank you! And I should be glad to have change of this five-pound note."

A lad of fourteen, with a bright, keen face, had obeyed the summons of the manager. He stood now gazing with great reverence at the famous detective.

"Let me have the Hotel Directory," said Holmes. "Thank you! Now, Cartwright, there are the names of twenty-three hotels here, all in the immediate neighbourhood of Charing Cross. Do you see?"

"Yes, sir."

"You will visit each of these in turn."

"Yes, sir."

"You will begin in each case by giving the outside porter one shilling. Here are twenty-three shillings."

"Yes, sir."

"You will tell him that you want to see the waste paper of yesterday. You will say that an important telegram has miscarried and that you are looking for it. You understand?"

"Yes, sir."

"But what you are really looking for is the centre page of the *Times* with some holes cut in it with scissors. Here is a copy of the *Times*. It is this page. You could easily recognise it, could you not?"

"Yes, sir."

"In each case the outside porter will send for the hall porter, to whom also you will give a shilling. Here are twenty-three shillings. You will then learn in possibly twenty cases out of the twenty-three that the waste of the day before has been burned or removed. In the three other cases you will be shown a heap of paper and you will look for this page of the *Times* among it. The odds are enormously against your finding it. There are ten shillings over in case of emergencies. Let me have a report by wire at Baker Street before evening. And now, Watson, it only remains for us to find out by wire the identity of the cabman, No. 2704, and then we will drop into one of the Bond Street picture galleries and fill in the time until we are due at the hotel."

*(To be continued.)*

"THE DRIVER POINTED WITH HIS WHIP—'BASKERVILLE HALL,' SAID HE."

# The Hound of the Baskervilles.

## ANOTHER ADVENTURE OF

# SHERLOCK HOLMES.

## By CONAN DOYLE.

### CHAPTER V.

#### THREE BROKEN THREADS.

SHERLOCK HOLMES had, in a very remarkable degree, the power of detaching his mind at will. For two hours the strange business in which we had been involved appeared to be forgotten, and he was entirely absorbed in the pictures of the modern Belgian masters. He would talk of nothing but art, of which he had the crudest ideas, from our leaving the gallery until we found ourselves at the Northumberland Hotel.

"Sir Henry Baskerville is upstairs expecting you," said the clerk. "He asked me to show you up at once when you came."

"Have you any objection to my looking at your register?" said Holmes.

"Not in the least."

The book showed that two names had been added after that of Baskerville. One was Theophilus Johnson and family, of Newcastle; the other Mrs. Oldmore and maid, of High Lodge, Alton.

"Surely that must be the same Johnson whom I used to know," said Holmes to the porter. "A lawyer, is he not, grey-headed, and walks with a limp?"

"No, sir, this is Mr. Johnson the coalowner, a very active gentleman, not older than yourself."

"Surely you are mistaken about his trade?"

"No, sir; he has used this hotel for many years, and he is very well known to us."

"Ah, that settles it. Mrs. Oldmore, too; I seem to remember the name. Excuse my curiosity, but often in calling upon one friend one finds another."

"She is an invalid lady, sir. Her husband was once Mayor of Gloucester. She always comes to us when she is in town."

"Thank you; I am afraid I cannot claim her acquaintance. We have established a most important fact by these questions, Watson," he continued, in a low voice, as we went upstairs together. "We know now that the people who are so interested in our friend have not settled down in his own hotel. That means that while they are, as we have seen, very anxious to watch him, they are equally anxious that he should not see them. Now, this is a most suggestive fact."

"What does it suggest?"

"It suggests—halloa, my dear fellow, what on earth is the matter?"

As we came round the top of the stairs we had run up against Sir Henry Baskerville himself. His face was flushed with anger, and he held an old and dusty boot in one of his hands. So furious was he that he was hardly articulate, and when he did speak it was in a much broader and more Western dialect than any which we had heard from him in the morning.

"Seems to me they are playing me for a sucker in this hotel," he cried. "They'll find they've started in to monkey with the wrong man unless they are careful. By thunder, if that chap can't find my missing boot there will be trouble. I can take a joke with the best, Mr. Holmes, but they've got a bit over the mark this time."

"Still looking for your boot?"

"Yes, sir, and mean to find it."

"But, surely, you said that it was a new brown boot?"

"So it was, sir. And now it's an old black one."

"What! you don't mean to say——?"

"That's just what I do mean to say. I

"HE HELD AN OLD AND DUSTY BOOT IN ONE OF HIS HANDS."

only had three pairs in the world—the new brown, the old black, and the patent leathers, which I am wearing. Last night they took one of my brown ones, and to-day they have sneaked one of the black. Well, have you got it? Speak out, man, and don't stand staring!"

An agitated German waiter had appeared upon the scene.

"No, sir; I have made inquiry all over the hotel, but I can hear no word of it."

"Well, either that boot comes back before sundown or I'll see the manager and tell him that I go right straight out of this hotel."

"It shall be found, sir—I promise you that if you will have a little patience it will be found."

"Mind it is, for it's the last thing of mine that I'll lose in this den of thieves. Well, well, Mr. Holmes, you'll excuse my troubling you about such a trifle——"

"I think it's well worth troubling about."

"Why, you look very serious over it."

"How do you explain it?"

"I just don't attempt to explain it. It seems the very maddest, queerest thing that ever happened to me."

"The queerest, perhaps," said Holmes, thoughtfully.

"What do you make of it yourself?"

"Well, I don't profess to understand it yet. This case of yours is very complex, Sir Henry. When taken in conjunction with your uncle's death I am not sure that of all the five hundred cases of capital importance which I have handled there is one which cuts so deep. But we hold several threads in our hands, and the odds are that one or other of them guides us to the truth. We may waste time in following the wrong one, but sooner or later we must come upon the right."

We had a pleasant luncheon in which little was said of the business which had brought us together It was in the private sitting-room to which we afterwards repaired that Holmes asked Baskerville what were his intentions.

"To go to Baskerville Hall."

"And when?"

"At the end of the week."

"On the whole," said Holmes, "I think that your decision is a wise one. I have ample evidence that you are being dogged in London, and amid the millions of this great city it is difficult to discover who these people are or what their object can be. If their intentions are evil they might do you a mischief, and we should be powerless to prevent it. You did not know, Dr. Mortimer, that you were followed this morning from my house?'

Dr. Mortimer started violently.

"Followed! By whom?"

"That, unfortunately, is what I cannot tell you. Have you among your neighbours or acquaintances on Dartmoor any man with a black, full beard?"

"No—or, let me see—why, yes. Barrymore, Sir Charles's butler, is a man with a full, black beard."

"Ha! Where is Barrymore?"

"He is in charge of the Hall."

"We had best ascertain if he is really there, or if by any possibility he might be in London."

"How can you do that?"

"Give me a telegraph form. 'Is all ready for Sir Henry?' That will do. Address to Mr. Barrymore, Baskerville Hall. Which is the nearest telegraph-office? Grimpen. Very good, we will send a second wire to the postmaster, Grimpen: 'Telegram to Mr. Barrymore, to be delivered into his own hand. If absent, please return wire to Sir Henry Baskerville, Northumberland Hotel.' That should let us know before evening whether Barrymore is at his post in Devonshire or not."

"That's so," said Baskerville. "By the way, Dr. Mortimer, who is this Barrymore, anyhow?"

"He is the son of the old caretaker, who is dead. They have looked after the Hall for four generations now. So far as I know, he and his wife are as respectable a couple as any in the county."

"At the same time," said Baskerville, "it's clear enough that so long as there are none of the family at the Hall these people have a mighty fine home and nothing to do."

"That is true."

"Did Barrymore profit at all by Sir Charles's will?" asked Holmes.

"He and his wife had five hundred pounds each."

"Ha! Did they know that they would receive this?"

"Yes; Sir Charles was very fond of talking about the provisions of his will."

"That is very interesting."

"I hope," said Dr. Mortimer, "that you do not look with suspicious eyes upon everyone who received a legacy from Sir Charles, for I also had a thousand pounds left to me."

"Indeed! And anyone else?"

"There were many insignificant sums to individuals and a large number of public charities. The residue all went to Sir Henry."

"And how much was the residue?"

"Seven hundred and forty thousand pounds."

Holmes raised his eyebrows in surprise. "I had no idea that so gigantic a sum was involved," said he.

"Sir Charles had the reputation of being rich, but we did not know how very rich he was until we came to examine his securities. The total value of the estate was close on to a million."

"Dear me! It is a stake for which a man might well play a desperate game. And one more question, Dr. Mortimer. Supposing that anything happened to our young friend here—you will forgive the unpleasant hypothesis!—who would inherit the estate?"

"Since Rodger Baskerville, Sir Charles's younger brother, died unmarried, the estate would descend to the Desmonds, who are distant cousins. James Desmond is an elderly clergyman in Westmorland."

"Thank you. These details are all of great interest. Have you met Mr. James Desmond?"

"Yes; he once came down to visit Sir Charles. He is a man of venerable appearance and of saintly life. I remember that he refused to accept any settlement from Sir Charles, though he pressed it upon him."

"And this man of simple tastes would be the heir to Sir Charles's thousands?"

"He would be the heir to the estate, because that is entailed. He would also be the heir to the money unless it were willed otherwise by the present owner, who can, of course, do what he likes with it."

"And have you made your will, Sir Henry?"

"No, Mr. Holmes, I have not. I've had no time, for it was only yesterday that I learned how matters stood. But in any case I feel that the money should go with the title and estate. That was my poor uncle's idea. How is the owner going to restore the glories of the Baskervilles if he has not money enough to keep up the property? House, land, and dollars must go together."

"Quite so. Well, Sir Henry, I am of one mind with you as to the advisability of your going down to Devonshire without delay. There is only one provision which I must make. You certainly must not go alone."

"Dr. Mortimer returns with me."

"But Dr. Mortimer has his practice to attend to, and his house is miles away from yours. With all the good will in the world, he may be unable to help you. No, Sir Henry, you must take with you someone, a trusty man, who will be always by your side."

"Is it possible that you could come yourself, Mr. Holmes?"

"If matters came to a crisis I should endeavour to be present in person; but you can understand that, with my extensive consulting practice and with the constant appeals which reach me from many quarters, it is impossible for me to be absent from London for an indefinite time. At the present instant one of the most revered names in England is being besmirched by a blackmailer, and only I can stop a disastrous scandal. You will see how impossible it is for me to go to Dartmoor."

"Whom would you recommend, then?"

Holmes laid his hand upon my arm.

"If my friend would undertake it there is no man who is better worth having at your side when you are in a tight place. No one can say so more confidently than I."

The proposition took me completely by

"THE PROPOSITION TOOK ME COMPLETELY BY SURPRISE."

as it will do, I will direct how you shall act. I suppose that by Saturday all might be ready?"

"Would that suit Dr. Watson?"

"Perfectly."

"Then on Saturday, unless you hear to the contrary, we shall meet at the 10.30 train from Paddington."

We had risen to depart when Baskerville gave a cry of triumph, and diving into one of the corners of the room he drew a brown boot from under a cabinet.

"My missing boot!" he cried.

"May all our difficulties vanish as easily!" said Sherlock Holmes.

"But it is a very singular thing," Dr. Mortimer remarked. "I searched this room carefully before lunch."

"And so did I," said Baskerville. "Every inch of it."

"There was certainly no boot in it then."

"In that case the waiter must have placed it there while we were lunching."

The German was sent for, but professed to know nothing of the matter, nor could any inquiry clear it up. Another item had been added to that constant and apparently purposeless series of small mysteries which had succeeded each other so rapidly. Setting aside the whole grim story of Sir Charles's death, we had a line of inexplicable incidents all within the limits of two days, which included the receipt of the printed letter, the black-bearded spy in the hansom, the loss of the new brown boot, the loss of the old black boot, and now the return of the new brown boot. Holmes sat in silence in the cab as we drove back to Baker Street, and I knew from his drawn brows and keen face that his mind, like my own, was busy in endeavouring to frame some scheme into which all these strange and apparently disconnected episodes could be fitted. All afternoon and late into the evening he sat lost in tobacco and thought.

Just before dinner two telegrams were handed in. The first ran:—

surprise, but before I had time to answer Baskerville seized me by the hand and wrung it heartily.

"Well, now, that is real kind of you, Dr. Watson," said he. "You see how it is with me, and you know just as much about the matter as I do. If you will come down to Baskerville Hall and see me through I'll never forget it."

The promise of adventure had always a fascination for me, and I was complimented by the words of Holmes and by the eagerness with which the Baronet hailed me as a companion.

"I will come, with pleasure," said I. "I do not know how I could employ my time better."

"And you will report very carefully to me," said Holmes. "When a crisis comes,

"Have just heard that Barrymore is at the Hall.—BASKERVILLE." The second:—

"Visited twenty-three hotels as directed, but sorry to report unable to trace cut sheet of *Times.*—CARTWRIGHT."

"There go two of my threads, Watson. There is nothing more stimulating than a case where everything goes against you. We must cast round for another scent."

"We have still the cabman who drove the spy."

"Exactly. I have wired to get his name and address from the Official Registry. I should not be surprised if this were an answer to my question."

The ring at the bell proved to be something even more satisfactory than an answer, however, for the door opened and a rough-looking fellow entered who was evidently the man himself.

"I got a message from the head office that a gent at this address had been inquiring for 2,704," said he. "I've driven my cab this seven years and never a word of complaint. I came here straight from the Yard to ask you to your face what you had against me."

"I have nothing in the world against you, my good man," said Holmes. "On the contrary, I have half a sovereign for you if you will give me a clear answer to my questions."

"Well, I've had a good day and no mistake," said the cabman, with a grin. "What was it you wanted to ask, sir?"

"First of all your name and address, in case I want you again."

"John Clayton, 3, Turpey Street, the Borough. My cab is out of Shipley's Yard, near Waterloo Station."

Sherlock Holmes made a note of it.

"Now, Clayton, tell me all about the fare who came and watched this house at ten o'clock this morning and afterwards followed the two gentlemen down Regent Street."

The man looked surprised and a little embarrassed. "Why, there's no good my telling you things, for you seem to know as much as I do already," said he. "The truth is that the gentleman told me that he was a detective and that I was to say nothing about him to anyone."

"My good fellow, this is a very serious business, and you may find yourself in a pretty bad position if you try to hide anything from me. You say that your fare told you that he was a detective?"

"Yes, he did."

"When did he say this?"

"When he left me."

"Did he say anything more?"

"He mentioned his name."

Holmes cast a swift glance of triumph at me. "Oh, he mentioned his name, did he? That was imprudent. What was the name that he mentioned?"

"His name," said the cabman, "was Mr. Sherlock Holmes."

Never have I seen my friend more completely taken aback than by the cabman's

"'HIS NAME,' SAID THE CABMAN, 'WAS MR. SHERLOCK HOLMES.'"

reply. For an instant he sat in silent amazement. Then he burst into a hearty laugh.

"A touch, Watson—an undeniable touch!" said he. "I feel a foil as quick and supple as my own. He got home upon me very prettily that time. So his name was Sherlock Holmes, was it?"

"Yes, sir, that was the gentleman's name."

"Excellent! Tell me where you picked him up and all that occurred."

"He hailed me at half-past nine in Trafalgar Square. He said that he was a detective, and he offered me two guineas if I would do exactly what he wanted all day and ask no questions. I was glad enough to agree. First we drove down to the Northumberland Hotel and waited there until two gentlemen came out and took a cab from the rank. We followed their cab until it pulled up somewhere near here."

"This very door," said Holmes.

"Well, I couldn't be sure of that, but I daresay my fare knew all about it. We pulled up half-way down the street and waited an hour and a half. Then the two gentlemen passed us, walking, and we followed down Baker Street and along——"

"I know," said Holmes.

"Until we got three-quarters down Regent Street. Then my gentleman threw up the trap, and he cried that I should drive right away to Waterloo Station as hard as I could go. I whipped up the mare and we were there under the ten minutes. Then he paid up his two guineas, like a good one, and away he went into the station. Only just as he was leaving he turned round and said: 'It might interest you to know that you have been driving Mr. Sherlock Holmes.' That's how I come to know the name."

"I see. And you saw no more of him?"

"Not after he went into the station."

"And how would you describe Mr. Sherlock Holmes?"

The cabman scratched his head. "Well, he wasn't altogether such an easy gentleman to describe. I'd put him at forty years of age, and he was of a middle height, two or three inches shorter than you, sir. He was dressed like a toff, and he had a black beard, cut square at the end, and a pale face. I don't know as I could say more than that."

"Colour of his eyes?"

"No, I can't say that."

"Nothing more that you can remember?"

"No, sir; nothing."

"Well, then, here is your half-sovereign. There's another one waiting for you if you can bring any more information. Good-night!"

"Good-night, sir, and thank you!"

John Clayton departed chuckling, and Holmes turned to me with a shrug of the shoulders and a rueful smile.

"Snap goes our third thread, and we end where we began," said he. "The cunning rascal! He knew our number, knew that Sir Henry Baskerville had consulted me, spotted who I was in Regent Street, conjectured that I had got the number of the cab and would lay my hands on the driver, and so sent back this audacious message. I tell you, Watson, this time we have got a foeman who is worthy of our steel. I've been checkmated in London. I can only wish you better luck in Devonshire. But I'm not easy in my mind about it."

"About what?"

"About sending you. It's an ugly business, Watson, an ugly, dangerous business, and the more I see of it the less I like it. Yes, my dear fellow, you may laugh, but I give you my word that I shall be very glad to have you back safe and sound in Baker Street once more."

## CHAPTER VI.
### BASKERVILLE HALL.

SIR HENRY BASKERVILLE and Dr. Mortimer were ready upon the appointed day, and we started as arranged for Devonshire. Mr. Sherlock Holmes drove with me to the station and gave me his last parting injunctions and advice.

"I will not bias your mind by suggesting theories or suspicions, Watson," said he; "I wish you simply to report facts in the fullest possible manner to me, and you can leave me to do the theorizing."

"What sort of facts?" I asked.

"Anything which may seem to have a bearing however indirect upon the case, and especially the relations between young Baskerville and his neighbours, or any fresh particulars concerning the death of Sir Charles. I have made some inquiries myself in the last few days, but the results have, I fear, been negative. One thing only appears to be certain, and that is that Mr. James Desmond, who is the next heir, is an elderly gentleman of a very amiable disposition, so that this persecution does not arise from him. I really think that we may eliminate him entirely from our calculations. There remain the people who will actually surround Sir Henry Baskerville upon the moor."

"Would it not be well in the first place to get rid of this Barrymore couple?"

"By no means. You could not make a

greater mistake. If they are innocent it would be a cruel injustice, and if they are guilty we should be giving up all chance of bringing it home to them. No, no, we will preserve them upon our list of suspects. Then there is a groom at the Hall, if I remember right. There are two moorland farmers. There is our friend Dr. Mortimer, whom I believe to be entirely honest, and there is his wife, of whom we know nothing. There is this naturalist Stapleton, and there is his sister, who is said to be a young lady of attractions. There is Mr. Frankland, of Lafter Hall, who is also an unknown factor, and there are one or two other neighbours. These are the folk who must be your very special study."

"I will do my best."

"You have arms, I suppose?"

"Yes, I thought it as well to take them."

"Most certainly. Keep your revolver near you night and day, and never relax your precautions."

Our friends had already secured a first-class carriage, and were waiting for us upon the platform.

"No, we have no news of any kind," said Dr. Mortimer, in answer to my friend's questions. "I can swear to one thing, and that is that we have not been shadowed during the last two days. We have never gone out without keeping a sharp watch, and no one could have escaped our notice."

"You have always kept together, I presume?"

"Except yesterday afternoon. I usually give up one day to pure amusement when I come to town, so I spent it at the Museum of the College of Surgeons."

"And I went to look at the folk in the park," said Baskerville. "But we had no trouble of any kind."

"It was imprudent, all the same," said Holmes, shaking his head and looking very grave. "I beg, Sir Henry, that you will not go about alone. Some great misfortune will befall you if you do. Did you get your other boot?"

"No, sir, it is gone for ever."

"Indeed. That is very interesting. Well, good-bye," he added, as the train began to

glide down the platform. "Bear in mind, Sir Henry, one of the phrases in that queer old legend which Dr. Mortimer has read to us, and avoid the moor in those hours of darkness when the powers of evil are exalted."

I looked back at the platform when we had left it far behind, and saw the tall, austere figure of Holmes standing motionless and gazing after us.

The journey was a swift and pleasant one,

"OUR FRIENDS WERE WAITING FOR US UPON THE PLATFORM."

and I spent it in making the more intimate acquaintance of my two companions and in playing with Dr. Mortimer's spaniel. In a very few hours the brown earth had become ruddy, the brick had changed to granite, and red cows grazed in well-hedged fields where the lush grasses and more luxuriant vegetation spoke of a richer, if a damper, climate. Young Baskerville stared eagerly out of the window, and cried aloud with delight as he recognised the familiar features of the Devon scenery.

"I've been over a good part of the world since I left it, Dr. Watson," said he; "but I have never seen a place to compare with it."

"I never saw a Devonshire man who did not swear by his county," I remarked.

"It depends upon the breed of men quite as much as on the county," said Dr. Mortimer. "A glance at our friend here reveals the rounded head of the Celt, which carries inside it the Celtic enthusiasm and power of attachment. Poor Sir Charles's head was of a very rare type, half Gaelic, half Ivernian in its characteristics. But you were very young when you last saw Baskerville Hall, were you not?"

"I was a boy in my teens at the time of my father's death, and had never seen the Hall, for he lived in a little cottage on the south coast. Thence I went straight to a friend in America. I tell you it is all as new to me as it is to Dr. Watson, and I'm as keen as possible to see the moor."

"Are you? Then your wish is easily granted, for there is your first sight of the moor," said Dr. Mortimer, pointing out of the carriage window.

Over the green squares of the fields and the low curve of a wood there rose in the distance a grey, melancholy hill, with a strange jagged summit, dim and vague in the distance, like some fantastic landscape in a dream. Baskerville sat for a long time, his eyes fixed upon it, and I read upon his eager face how much it meant to him, this first sight of that strange spot where the men of his blood had held sway so long and left their mark so deep. There he sat, with his tweed suit and his American accent, in the corner of a prosaic railway-carriage, and yet as I looked at his dark and expressive face I felt more than ever how true a descendant he was of that long line of high-blooded, fiery, and masterful men. There were pride, valour, and strength in his thick brows, his sensitive nostrils, and his large hazel eyes. If on that forbidding moor a difficult and dangerous quest should lie before us, this was at least a comrade for whom one might venture to take a risk with the certainty that he would bravely share it.

The train pulled up at a small wayside station and we all descended. Outside, beyond the low, white fence, a wagonette with a pair of cobs was waiting. Our coming was evidently a great event, for station-master and porters clustered round us to carry out our luggage. It was a sweet, simple country spot, but I was surprised to observe that by the gate there stood two soldierly men in dark uniforms, who leaned upon their short rifles and glanced keenly at us as we passed. The coachman, a hard-faced, gnarled little fellow, saluted Sir Henry Baskerville, and in a few minutes we were flying swiftly down the broad, white road. Rolling pasture lands curved upwards on either side of us, and old gabled houses peeped out from amid the thick green foliage, but behind the peaceful and sunlit country-side there rose ever, dark against the evening sky, the long, gloomy curve of the moor, broken by the jagged and sinister hills.

The wagonette swung round into a side road, and we curved upwards through deep lanes worn by centuries of wheels, high banks on either side, heavy with dripping moss and fleshy hart's-tongue ferns. Bronzing bracken and mottled bramble gleamed in the light of the sinking sun. Still steadily rising, we passed over a narrow granite bridge, and skirted a noisy stream which gushed swiftly down, foaming and roaring amid the grey boulders. Both road and stream wound up through a valley dense with scrub oak and fir. At every turning Baskerville gave an exclamation of delight, looking eagerly about him and asking countless questions. To his eyes all seemed beautiful, but to me a tinge of melancholy lay upon the country-side, which bore so clearly the mark of the waning year. Yellow leaves carpeted the lanes and fluttered down upon us as we passed. The rattle of our wheels died away as we drove through drifts of rotting vegetation—sad gifts, as it seemed to me, for Nature to throw before the carriage of the returning heir of the Baskervilles.

"Halloa!" cried Dr. Mortimer, "what is this?"

A steep curve of heath-clad land, an outlying spur of the moor, lay in front of us. On the summit, hard and clear like an equestrian statue upon its pedestal, was a mounted soldier, dark and stern, his rifle poised ready over his forearm. He was watching the road along which we travelled.

"What is this, Perkins?" asked Dr. Mortimer.

Our driver half turned in his seat.

"There's a convict escaped from Princetown, sir. He's been out three days now, and the warders watch every road and every station, but they've had no sight of him yet. The farmers about here don't like it, sir, and that's a fact."

"Well, I understand that they get five pounds if they can give information."

"Yes, sir, but the chance of five pounds is but a poor thing compared to the chance of having your throat cut. You see, it isn't like any ordinary convict. This is a man that would stick at nothing."

"Who is he, then?"

"It is Selden, the Notting Hill murderer."

I remembered the case well, for it was one in which Holmes had taken an interest on account of the peculiar ferocity of the crime and the wanton brutality which had marked all the actions of the assassin. The commutation of his death sentence had been due to some doubts as to his complete sanity, so atrocious was his conduct. Our wagonette had topped a rise and in front of us rose the huge expanse of the moor, mottled with gnarled and craggy cairns and tors. A cold wind swept down from it and set us shivering. Somewhere there, on that desolate plain, was lurking this fiendish man, hiding in a burrow like a wild beast, his heart full of malignancy against the whole race which had cast him out. It needed but this to complete the grim suggestiveness of the barren waste, the chilling wind, and the darkling sky. Even Baskerville fell silent and pulled his overcoat more closely around him.

We had left the fertile country behind and beneath us. We looked back on it now, the slanting rays of a low sun turning the streams to threads of gold and glowing on the red earth new turned by the plough and the broad tangle of the woodlands. The road in front of us grew bleaker and wilder over huge russet and olive slopes, sprinkled with giant boulders. Now and then we passed a moorland cottage, walled and roofed with stone, with no creeper to break its harsh outline. Suddenly we looked down into a cup-like depression, patched with stunted oaks and firs which had been twisted and bent by the fury of years of storm. Two high, narrow towers rose over the trees. The driver pointed with his whip.

"Baskerville Hall," said he.

Its master had risen and was staring with flushed cheeks and shining eyes. A few minutes later we had reached the lodge-gates, a maze of fantastic tracery in wrought iron, with weather-bitten pillars on either side, blotched with lichens, and surmounted by the boars' heads of the Baskervilles. The lodge was a ruin of black granite and bared ribs of rafters, but facing it was a new building, half constructed, the firstfruit of Sir Charles's South African gold.

Through the gateway we passed into the avenue, where the wheels were again hushed amid the leaves, and the old trees shot their branches in a sombre tunnel over our heads. Baskerville shuddered as he looked up the

"WELCOME, SIR HENRY!"

long, dark drive to where the house glimmered like a ghost at the farther end.

"Was it here?" he asked, in a low voice.

"No, no, the Yew Alley is on the other side."

The young heir glanced round with a gloomy face.

"It's no wonder my uncle felt as if trouble were coming on him in such a place as this," said he. "It's enough to scare any man. I'll have a row of electric lamps up here inside of six months, and you won't know it again, with a thousand candle-power Swan and Edison right here in front of the hall door."

The avenue opened into a broad expanse of turf, and the house lay before us. In the fading light I could see that the centre was a heavy block of building from which a porch projected. The whole front was draped in ivy, with a patch clipped bare here and there where a window or a coat-of-arms broke through the dark veil. From this central block rose the twin towers, ancient, crenellated, and pierced with many loopholes. To right and left of the turrets were more modern wings of black granite. A dull light shone through heavy mullioned windows, and from the high chimneys which rose from the steep, high-angled roof there sprang a single black column of smoke.

"Welcome, Sir Henry! Welcome, to Baskerville Hall!"

A tall man had stepped from the shadow of the porch to open the door of the wagonette. The figure of a woman was silhouetted against the yellow light of the hall. She came out and helped the man to hand down our bags.

"You don't mind my driving straight home, Sir Henry?" said Dr. Mortimer. "My wife is expecting me."

"Surely you will stay and have some dinner?"

"No, I must go. I shall probably find some work awaiting me. I would stay to show you over the house, but Barrymore will be a better guide than I. Good-bye, and never hesitate night or day to send for me if I can be of service."

The wheels died away down the drive while Sir Henry and I turned into the hall, and the door clanged heavily behind us. It was a fine apartment in which we found ourselves, large, lofty, and heavily raftered with huge balks of age-blackened oak. In the great old-fashioned fireplace behind the high iron dogs a log-fire crackled and snapped. Sir Henry and I held out our hands to it, for we were numb from our long drive. Then we gazed round us at the high, thin window of old stained glass, the oak panelling, the stags' heads, the coats-of-arms upon the walls, all dim and sombre in the subdued light of the central lamp.

"It's just as I imagined it," said Sir Henry. "Is it not the very picture of an old family home? To think that this should be the same hall in which for five hundred years my people have lived. It strikes me solemn to think of it."

I saw his dark face lit up with a boyish enthusiasm as he gazed about him. The light beat upon him where he stood, but long shadows trailed down the walls and hung like a black canopy above him. Barrymore had returned from taking our luggage to our rooms. He stood in front of us now with the subdued manner of a well-trained servant. He was a remarkable-looking man, tall, handsome, with a square black beard, and pale, distinguished features.

"Would you wish dinner to be served at once, sir?"

"Is it ready?"

"In a very few minutes, sir. You will find hot water in your rooms. My wife and I will be happy, Sir Henry, to stay with you until you have made your fresh arrangements, but you will understand that under the new conditions this house will require a considerable staff."

"What new conditions?"

"I only meant, sir, that Sir Charles led a very retired life, and we were able to look after his wants. You would, naturally, wish to have more company, and so you will need changes in your household."

"Do you mean that your wife and you wish to leave?"

"Only when it is quite convenient to you, sir."

"But your family have been with us for several generations, have they not? I should be sorry to begin my life here by breaking an old family connection."

I seemed to discern some signs of emotion upon the butler's white face.

"I feel that also sir, and so does my wife. But to tell the truth, sir, we were both very much attached to Sir Charles, and his death gave us a shock and made these surroundings very painful to us. I fear that we shall never again be easy in our minds at Baskerville Hall."

"But what do you intend to do?"

"I have no doubt, sir, that we shall succeed in establishing ourselves in some business. Sir Charles's generosity has given us the means to do so. And now, sir, perhaps I had best show you to your rooms."

A square balustraded gallery ran round

the. top of the old hall, approached by a double stair. From this central point two long corridors extended the whole length of the building, from which all the bedrooms opened. My own was in the same wing as Baskerville's and almost next door to it. These rooms appeared to be much more modern than the central part of the house, and the bright paper and numerous candles did something to remove the sombre impression which our arrival had left upon my mind.

But the dining-room which opened out of the hall was a place of shadow and gloom. It was a long chamber with a step separating the daïs where the family sat from the lower portion reserved for their dependents. At one end a minstrels' gallery overlooked it. Black beams shot across above our heads, with a smoke-darkened ceiling beyond them. With rows of flaring torches to light it up, and the colour and rude hilarity of an old-time banquet, it might have softened ; but now, when two black-clothed gentlemen sat in the little circle of light thrown by a shaded lamp, one's voice became hushed and one's spirit subdued. A dim line of ancestors, in every variety of dress, from the Elizabethan knight to the buck of the Regency, stared down upon us and daunted us by their silent company. We talked little, and I for one was glad when the meal was over and we were able to retire into the modern billiard-room and smoke a cigarette.

"My word, it isn't a very cheerful place," said Sir Henry. "I suppose one can tone down to it, but I feel a bit out of the picture at present. I don't wonder that my uncle got a little jumpy if he lived all alone in such a house as this. However, if it suits you, we will retire early to-night, and perhaps things may seem more cheerful in the morning."

I drew aside my curtains before I went to bed and looked out from my window. It opened upon the grassy space which lay in front of the hall door. Beyond, two copses of trees moaned and swung in a rising wind.

A half moon broke through the rifts of racing clouds. In its cold light I saw beyond the trees a broken fringe of rocks and the long, low curve of the melancholy moor. I closed the curtain, feeling that my last impression was in keeping with the rest.

"THE DINING-ROOM WAS A PLACE OF SHADOW AND GLOOM."

And yet it was not quite the last. I found myself weary and yet wakeful, tossing restlessly from side to side, seeking for the sleep which would not come. Far away a chiming clock struck out the quarters of the hours, but otherwise a deathly silence lay upon the old house. And then suddenly, in the very dead of the night, there came a sound to my ears, clear, resonant, and unmistakable. It was the sob of a woman, the muffled, strangling gasp of one who is torn by an uncontrollable sorrow. I sat up in bed and listened intently. The noise could not have been far away, and was certainly in the house. For half an hour I waited with every nerve on the alert, but there came no other sound save the chiming clock and the rustle of the ivy on the wall.

*( To be continued. )*

# The Hound of the Baskervilles.

## ANOTHER ADVENTURE OF
# SHERLOCK HOLMES.

### By CONAN DOYLE.

### CHAPTER VII.

#### THE STAPLETONS OF MERRIPIT HOUSE.

THE fresh beauty of the following morning did something to efface from our minds the grim and grey impression which had been left upon both of us by our first experience of Baskerville Hall. As Sir Henry and I sat at breakfast the sunlight flooded in through the high mullioned windows, throwing watery patches of colour from the coats of arms which covered them. The dark panelling glowed like bronze in the golden rays, and it was hard to realize that this was indeed the chamber which had struck such a gloom into our souls upon the evening before.

"I guess it is ourselves and not the house that we have to blame!" said the baronet. "We were tired with our journey and chilled by our drive, so we took a grey view of the place. Now we are fresh and well, so it is all cheerful once more."

"And yet it was not entirely a question of imagination," I answered. "Did you, for example, happen to hear someone, a woman I think, sobbing in the night?"

"That is curious, for I did when I was half asleep fancy that I heard something of the sort. I waited quite a time, but there was no more of it, so I concluded that it was all a dream."

"I heard it distinctly, and I am sure that it was really the sob of a woman."

"We must ask about this right away." He rang the bell and asked Barrymore whether he could account for our experience. It seemed to me that the pallid features of the butler turned a shade paler still as he listened to his master's question.

"There are only two women in the house, Sir Henry," he answered. "One is the scullery-maid, who sleeps in the other wing. The other is my wife, and I can answer for it that the sound could not have come from her."

And yet he lied as he said it, for it chanced that after breakfast I met Mrs. Barrymore in the long corridor with the sun full upon her face. She was a large, impassive, heavy-featured woman with a stern, set expression of mouth. But her tell-tale eyes were red and glanced at me from between swollen lids. It was she, then, who wept in the night, and if she did so her husband must know it. Yet he had taken the obvious risk of discovery in declaring that it was not so. Why had he done this? And why did she weep so bitterly? Already round this pale-faced, handsome, black-bearded man there was gathering an atmosphere of mystery and of gloom. It was he who had been the first to discover the body of Sir Charles, and we had only his word for all the circumstances which led up to the old man's death. Was it possible that it was Barrymore after all whom we had seen in the cab in Regent Street? The beard might well have been the same. The cabman had described a somewhat shorter man, but such an impression might easily have been erroneous. How could I settle the point for ever? Obviously the first thing to do was to see the Grimpen postmaster, and find whether the test telegram had really been placed in Barrymore's own hands. Be the answer what it might, I should at least have something to report to Sherlock Holmes.

Sir Henry had numerous papers to examine after breakfast, so that the time was propitious for my excursion. It was a pleasant walk of four miles along the edge of the moor, leading me at last to a small grey hamlet, in which two larger buildings, which proved to be the inn and the house of Dr. Mortimer, stood high above the rest. The postmaster, who was also the village grocer, had a clear recollection of the telegram.

"Certainly, sir," said he, "I had the telegram delivered to Mr. Barrymore exactly as directed."

"Who delivered it?"

"My boy here. James, you delivered that telegram to Mr. Barrymore at the Hall last week, did you not?"

"Yes, father, I delivered it."

"Into his own hands?" I asked.

"Well, he was up in the loft at the time, so that I could not put it into his own hands, but I gave it into Mrs. Barrymore's hands, and she promised to deliver it at once."

"Did you see Mr. Barrymore?"

"No, sir ; I tell you he was in the loft."

"If you didn't see him, how do you know he was in the loft?"

"Well, surely his own wife ought to know where he is," said the postmaster, testily. "Didn't he get the telegram? If there is any mistake it is for Mr. Barrymore himself to complain."

It seemed hopeless to pursue the inquiry any farther, but it was clear that in spite of Holmes's ruse we had no proof that Barrymore had not been in London all the time. Suppose that it were so — suppose that the same man had been the last who had seen Sir Charles alive, and the first to dog the new heir when he returned to England. What then? Was he the agent of others, or had he some sinister design of his own? What interest could he have in persecuting the Baskerville family? I thought of the strange warning clipped out of the leading article of the *Times*. Was that his work, or was it possibly the doing of someone who was bent upon counteracting his schemes? The only conceivable motive was that which had been suggested by Sir Henry, that if the family could be scared away a comfortable and permanent home would be secured for the Barrymores. But surely such an explanation as that would be quite inadequate to account for the deep and subtle scheming which seemed to be weaving an invisible net round the young baronet. Holmes himself had said that no more complex case had come to him in all the long series of his sensational investigations. I prayed, as I walked back along the grey, lonely road, that my friend might soon be freed from his preoccupations and able to come down to take this heavy burden of responsibility from my shoulders.

Suddenly my thoughts were interrupted by the sound of running feet behind me and by a voice which called me by name. I turned, expecting to see Dr. Mortimer, but to my surprise it was a stranger who was pursuing me. He was a small, slim, clean-shaven, prim-faced man, flaxen-haired and lean-jawed, between thirty and forty years of age, dressed in a grey suit and wearing a straw hat. A tin box for botanical specimens hung over his shoulder and he carried a green butterfly-net in one of his hands.

"IT WAS A STRANGER PURSUING ME."

"You will, I am sure, excuse my presumption, Dr. Watson," said he, as he came panting up to where I stood. "Here on the moor we are homely folk and do not wait for formal introductions. You may possibly have heard my name from our mutual friend, Mortimer. I am Stapleton, of Merripit House."

"Your net and box would have told me as much," said I, "for I knew that Mr. Stapleton was a naturalist. But how did you know me?"

"I have been calling on Mortimer, and he pointed you out to me from the window of his surgery as you passed. As our road lay the same way I thought that I would overtake you and introduce myself. I trust that Sir Henry is none the worse for his journey?"

"He is very well, thank you."

"We were all rather afraid that after the sad death of Sir Charles the new baronet might refuse to live here. It is asking much of a wealthy man to come down and bury himself in a place of this kind, but I need not tell you that it means a very great deal to the country-side. Sir Henry has, I suppose, no superstitious fears in the matter?"

"I do not think that it is likely."

"Of course you know the legend of the fiend dog which haunts the family?"

"I have heard it."

"It is extraordinary how credulous the peasants are about here! Any number of them are ready to swear that they have seen such a creature upon the moor." He spoke with a smile, but I seemed to read in his eyes that he took the matter more seriously. "The story took a great hold upon the imagination of Sir Charles, and I have no doubt that it led to his tragic end."

"But how?"

"His nerves were so worked up that the appearance of any dog might have had a fatal effect upon his diseased heart. I fancy that he really did see something of the kind upon that last night in the Yew Alley. I feared that some disaster might occur, for I was very fond of the old man, and I knew that his heart was weak."

"How did you know that?"

"My friend Mortimer told me."

"You think, then, that some dog pursued Sir Charles, and that he died of fright in consequence?"

"Have you any better explanation?"

"I have not come to any conclusion."

"Has Mr. Sherlock Holmes?"

The words took away my breath for an instant, but a glance at the placid face and steadfast eyes of my companion showed that no surprise was intended.

"It is useless for us to pretend that we do not know you, Dr. Watson," said he. "The records of your detective have reached us here, and you could not celebrate him without being known yourself. When Mortimer told me your name he could not deny your identity. If you are here, then it follows that Mr. Sherlock Holmes is interesting himself in the matter, and I am naturally curious to know what view he may take."

"I am afraid that I cannot answer that question."

"May I ask if he is going to honour us with a visit himself?"

"He cannot leave town at present. He has other cases which engage his attention."

"What a pity! He might throw some light on that which is so dark to us. But as to your own researches if there is any possible way in which I can be of service to you I trust that you will command me. If I had any indication of the nature of your suspicions, or how you propose to investigate the case, I might perhaps even now give you some aid or advice."

"I assure you that I am simply here upon a visit to my friend Sir Henry, and that I need no help of any kind."

"Excellent!" said Stapleton. "You are perfectly right to be wary and discreet. I am justly reproved for what I feel was an unjustifiable intrusion, and I promise you that I will not mention the matter again."

We had come to a point where a narrow grassy path struck off from the road and wound away across the moor. A steep, boulder-sprinkled hill lay upon the right which had in bygone days been cut into a granite quarry. The face which was turned towards us formed a dark cliff, with ferns and brambles growing in its niches. From over a distant rise there floated a grey plume of smoke.

"A moderate walk along this moor-path brings us to Merripit House," said he. "Perhaps you will spare an hour that I may have the pleasure of introducing you to my sister."

My first thought was that I should be by Sir Henry's side. But then I remembered the pile of papers and bills with which his study table was littered. It was certain that I could not help him with those. And Holmes had expressly said that I should study the neighbours upon the moor. I accepted Stapleton's invitation, and we turned together down the path.

"It is a wonderful place, the moor," said he, looking round over the undulating downs, long green rollers, with crests of jagged granite foaming up into fantastic surges. "You never tire of the moor. You cannot think the wonderful secrets which it contains. It is so vast, and so barren, and so mysterious."

"You know it well, then?"

"I have only been here two years. The residents would call me a new-comer. We came shortly after Sir Charles settled.

But my tastes led me to explore every part of the country round, and I should think that there are few men who know it better than I do."

" Is it so hard to know ? "

"Very hard. You see, for example, this great plain to the north here, with the queer hills breaking out of it. Do you observe anything remarkable about that ? "

" It would be a rare place for a gallop."

" You would naturally think so, and the thought has cost folk their lives before now. You notice those bright green spots scattered thickly over it ? "

" Yes, they seem more fertile than the rest."

Stapleton laughed.

" That is the great Grimpen Mire," said he. " A false step yonder means death to man or beast. Only yesterday I saw one of the moor ponies wander into it. He never

came out. I saw his head for quite a long time craning out of the bog-hole, but it sucked him down at last. Even in dry seasons it is a danger to cross it, but after these autumn rains it is an awful place. And yet I can find my way to the very heart of it and return alive. By George, there is another of those miserable ponies ! "

Something brown was rolling and tossing among the green sedges. Then a long, agonized, writhing neck shot upwards and a dreadful cry echoed over the moor. It turned me cold with horror, but my companion's nerves seemed to be stronger than mine.

" It's gone ! " said he. " The Mire has him. Two in two days, and many more, perhaps, for they get in the way of going there in the dry weather, and never know the difference until the Mire has them in its clutch. It's a bad place, the great Grimpen Mire."

" And you say you can penetrate it ? "

" Yes, there are one or two paths which a very active man can take. I have found them out."

" But why should you wish to go into so horrible a place ? "

" Well, you see the hills beyond ? They are really islands cut off on all sides by the impassable Mire, which has crawled round them in the course of years. That is where the rare plants and the butterflies are, if you have the wit to reach them."

" I shall try my luck some day."

He looked at me with a surprised face.

" For God's sake put such an idea out of your mind," said he. " Your blood would be upon my head. I assure you that there would not be the least chance of your coming back alive. It is only by remembering certain complex landmarks that I am able to do it."

" Halloa ! " I cried. " What is that ? "

A long, low moan, indescribably sad, swept over the moor. It filled the whole

" THAT IS THE GREAT GRIMPEN MIRE."

air, and yet it was impossible to say whence it came. From a dull murmur it swelled into a deep roar, and then sank back into a melancholy, throbbing murmur once again. Stapleton looked at me with a curious expression in his face.

"Queer place, the moor!" said he.

"But what is it?"

"The peasants say it is the Hound of the Baskervilles calling for its prey. I've heard it once or twice before, but never quite so loud."

I looked round, with a chill of fear in my heart, at the huge swelling plain, mottled with the green patches of rushes. Nothing stirred over the vast expanse save a pair of ravens, which croaked loudly from a tor behind us.

"You are an educated man. You don't believe such nonsense as that?" said I. "What do you think is the cause of so strange a sound?"

"Bogs make queer noises sometimes. It's the mud settling, or the water rising, or something."

"No, no, that was a living voice."

"Well, perhaps it was. Did you ever hear a bittern booming?"

"No, I never did."

"It's a very rare bird—practically extinct—in England now, but all things are possible upon the moor. Yes, I should not be surprised to learn that what we have heard is the cry of the last of the bitterns."

"It's the weirdest, strangest thing that ever I heard in my life."

"Yes, it's rather an uncanny place altogether. Look at the hill-side yonder. What do you make of those?"

The whole steep slope was covered with grey circular rings of stone, a score of them at least.

"What are they? Sheep-pens?"

"No, they are the homes of our worthy ancestors. Prehistoric man lived thickly on the moor, and as no one in particular has lived there since, we find all his little arrangements exactly as he left them. These are his wigwams with the roofs off. You can even see his hearth and his couch if you have the curiosity to go inside."

"But it is quite a town. When was it inhabited?"

"Neolithic man—no date."

"What did he do?"

"He grazed his cattle on these slopes, and he learned to dig for tin when the bronze sword began to supersede the stone axe.

Look at the great trench in the opposite hill. That is his mark. Yes, you will find some very singular points about the moor, Dr. Watson. Oh, excuse me an instant! It is surely Cyclopides."

A small fly or moth had fluttered across our path, and in an instant Stapleton was rushing with extraordinary energy and speed in pursuit of it. To my dismay the creature flew straight for the great Mire, but my acquaintance never paused for an instant, bounding from tuft to tuft behind it, his green net waving in the air. His grey clothes and jerky, zig-zag, irregular progress made him not unlike some huge moth himself. I was standing watching his pursuit with a mixture of admiration for his extraordinary activity and fear lest he should lose his footing in the treacherous Mire, when I heard the sound of steps, and turning round found a woman near me upon the path. She had come from the direction in which the plume of smoke indicated the position of Merripit House, but the dip of the moor had hid her until she was quite close.

I could not doubt that this was the Miss Stapleton of whom I had been told, since ladies of any sort must be few upon the moor, and I remembered that I had heard someone describe her as being a beauty. The woman who approached me was certainly that, and of a most uncommon type. There could not have been a greater contrast between brother and sister, for Stapleton was neutral tinted, with light hair and grey eyes, while she was darker than any brunette whom I have seen in England—slim, elegant, and tall. She had a proud, finely-cut face, so regular that it might have seemed impassive were it not for the sensitive mouth and the beautiful dark, eager eyes. With her perfect figure and elegant dress she was, indeed, a strange apparition upon a lonely moorland path. Her eyes were on her brother as I turned, and then she quickened her pace towards me. I had raised my hat, and was about to make some explanatory remark, when her own words turned all my thoughts into a new channel.

"Go back!" she said. "Go straight back to London, instantly."

I could only stare at her in stupid surprise. Her eyes blazed at me, and she tapped the ground impatiently with her foot.

"Why should I go back?" I asked.

"I cannot explain." She spoke in a low, eager voice, with a curious lisp in her utterance. "But for God's sake do what I

"'GO BACK!' SHE SAID."

ask you. Go back and never set foot upon the moor again."

"But I have only just come."

"Man, man!" she cried. "Can you not tell when a warning is for your own good? Go back to London! Start to-night! Get away from this place at all costs! Hush, my brother is coming! Not a word of what I have said. Would you mind getting that orchid for me among the mare's-tails yonder? We are very rich in orchids on the moor, though, of course, you are rather late to see the beauties of the place."

Stapleton had abandoned the chase and came back to us breathing hard and flushed with his exertions.

"Halloa, Beryl!" said he, and it seemed to me that the tone of his greeting was not altogether a cordial one.

"Well, Jack, you are very hot."

"Yes, I was chasing a Cyclopides. He is very rare, and seldom found in the late autumn. What a pity that I should have

missed him!" He spoke unconcernedly, but his small light eyes glanced incessantly from the girl to me.

"You have introduced yourselves, I can see."

"Yes. I was telling Sir Henry that it was rather late for him to see the true beauties of the moor."

"Why, who do you think this is?"

"I imagine that it must be Sir Henry Baskerville."

"No, no," said I. "Only a humble commoner, but his friend. My name is Dr. Watson."

A flush of vexation passed over her expressive face. "We have been talking at cross purposes," said she.

"Why, you had not very much time for talk," her brother remarked, with the same questioning eyes.

"I talked as if Dr. Watson were a resident instead of being merely a visitor," said she. "It cannot much matter to him whether it is early or late for the orchids. But you will come on, will you not, and see Merripit House?"

A short walk brought us to it, a bleak moorland house, once the farm of some grazier in the old prosperous days, but now put into repair and turned into a modern dwelling. An orchard surrounded it, but the trees, as is usual upon the moor, were stunted and nipped, and the effect of the whole place was mean and melancholy. We were admitted by a strange, wizened, rusty-coated old manservant, who seemed in keeping with the house. Inside, however, there were large rooms furnished with an elegance in which I seemed to recognise the taste of the lady. As I looked from their windows at the interminable granite-flecked moor rolling unbroken to the farthest horizon I could not but marvel at what could have brought this highly educated man and this beautiful woman to live in such a place.

"Queer spot to choose, is it not?" said he, as if in answer to my thought. "And yet we manage to make ourselves fairly happy, do we not, Beryl?"

"Quite happy," said she, but there was no ring of conviction in her words.

"I had a school," said Stapleton. "It was in the north country. The work to a man of my temperament was mechanical and uninteresting, but the privilege of living with youth, of helping to mould those young minds and of impressing them with one's own character and ideals, was very dear to me. However, the fates were against us. A serious epidemic broke out in the school and three of the boys died. It never recovered from the blow, and much of my capital was irretrievably swallowed up. And yet, if it were not for the loss of the charming companionship of the boys, I could rejoice over my own misfortune, for, with my strong tastes for botany and zoology, I find an unlimited field of work here, and my sister is as devoted to Nature as I am. All this, Dr. Watson, has been brought upon your head by your expression as you surveyed the moor out of our window."

"It certainly did cross my mind that it might be a little dull—less for you, perhaps, than for your sister."

"No, no, I am never dull," said she, quickly.

"We have books, we have our studies, and we have interesting neighbours. Dr. Mortimer is a most learned man in his own line. Poor Sir Charles was also an admirable companion. We knew him well, and miss him more than I can tell. Do you think that I should intrude if I were to call this afternoon and make the acquaintance of Sir Henry?"

"I am sure that he would be delighted."

"Then perhaps you would mention that I propose to do so. We may in our humble way do something to make things more easy for him until he becomes accustomed to his new surroundings. Will you come upstairs, Dr. Watson, and inspect my collection of lepidoptera? I think it is the most complete one in the south-west of England. By the time that you have looked through them lunch will be almost ready."

But I was eager to get back to my charge. The melancholy of the moor, the death of the unfortunate pony, the weird sound which had been associated with the grim legend of the Baskervilles, all these things tinged my thoughts with sadness. Then on the top of these more or less vague impressions there had come the definite and distinct warning of Miss Stapleton, delivered with such intense earnestness that I could not doubt that some grave and deep reason lay behind it. I resisted all pressure to stay for lunch, and I set off at once upon my return journey,

taking the grass-grown path by which we had come.

It seems, however, that there must have been some short cut for those who knew it, for before I had reached the road I was astounded to see Miss Stapleton sitting upon a rock by the side of the track. Her face was beautifully flushed with her exertions, and she held her hand to her side.

"I have run all the way in order to cut you off, Dr. Watson," said she. "I had not even time to put on my hat. I must not stop, or my brother may miss me. I wanted to say to you how sorry I am about the stupid mistake I made in thinking that you were Sir Henry. Please forget the words I said, which have no application whatever to you."

"But I can't forget them, Miss Stapleton," said I. "I am Sir Henry's friend, and his welfare is a very close concern of mine. Tell me why it was that you were so eager that Sir Henry should return to London."

"A woman's whim, Dr. Watson. When you know me better you will understand that I cannot always give reasons for what I say or do."

"No, no. I remember the thrill in your voice. I remember the look in your eyes. Please, please, be frank with me, Miss Stapleton, for ever since I have been here I have been conscious of shadows all round me. Life has become like that great Grimpen Mire, with little green patches everywhere into which one may sink and with no guide to point the track. Tell me then what it was that you meant, and I will promise to convey your warning to Sir Henry."

An expression of irresolution passed for an instant over her face, but her eyes had hardened again when she answered me.

"You make too much of it, Dr. Watson," said she. "My brother and I were very much shocked by the death of Sir Charles. We knew him very intimately, for his favourite walk was over the moor to our house. He was deeply impressed with the curse which hung over his family, and when this tragedy came I naturally felt that there must be some grounds for the fears which he had expressed. I was distressed therefore when another member of the family came down to live here, and I felt that he should be warned of the danger which he will run. That was all which I intended to convey."

"But what is the danger?"

"You know the story of the hound?"

"I do not believe in such nonsense."

"But I do. If you have any influence

"YOU KNOW THE STORY OF THE HOUND?"

he will miss me and suspect that I have seen you. Good-bye!" She turned, and had disappeared in a few minutes among the scattered boulders, while I, with my soul full of vague fears, pursued my way to Baskerville Hall.

## CHAPTER VIII.

### FIRST REPORT OF DR. WATSON.

FROM this point onwards I will follow the course of events by transcribing my own letters to Mr. Sherlock Holmes which lie before me on the table. One page is missing, but otherwise they are exactly as written, and show my feelings and sus-picions of the moment more accurately than my memory, clear as it is upon these tragic events, can possibly do.

BASKERVILLE HALL,
October 13th.

MY DEAR HOLMES, — My previous letters and telegrams have kept you pretty well up-to-date as to all that has occurred in this most God-forsaken corner of the world. The longer one stays here the more does the spirit of the moor sink into one's soul, its vast-ness, and also its grim charm. When you are once out upon its bosom you have left all traces of modern England behind you, but on the other hand you are conscious every-where of the homes and the work of the prehistoric people. On all sides of you as you walk are the houses of these forgotten folk, with their graves and the huge monoliths which are supposed to have marked their temples. As you look at their grey stone huts against the scarred hill-sides you leave your own age behind you, and if you were to see a skin-clad, hairy man crawl out from the low door, fitting a flint-tipped arrow on to the string of his bow, you would feel that his presence there was more natural than your own. The strange thing is that they should have lived so thickly on what must always have been most unfruitful soil. I am no antiquarian, but I could imagine that they were some unwarlike and harried race who were forced to accept that which none other would occupy.

All this, however, is foreign to the mission

with Sir Henry, take him away from a place which has always been fatal to his family. The world is wide. Why should he wish to live at the place of danger?"

"Because it *is* the place of danger. That is Sir Henry's nature. I fear that unless you can give me some more definite information than this it would be impossible to get him to move."

"I cannot say anything definite, for I do not know anything definite."

"I would ask you one more question, Miss Stapleton. If you meant no more than this when you first spoke to me, why should you not wish your brother to overhear what you said? There is nothing to which he, or anyone else, could object."

"My brother is very anxious to have the Hall inhabited, for he thinks that it is for the good of the poor folk upon the moor. He would be very angry if he knew that I had said anything which might induce Sir Henry to go away. But I have done my duty now and I will say no more. I must get back, or

on which you sent me, and will probably be very uninteresting to your severely practical mind. I can still remember your complete indifference as to whether the sun moved round the earth or the earth round the sun. Let me, therefore, return to the facts concerning Sir Henry Baskerville.

If you have not had any report within the last few days it is because up till to-day there was nothing of importance to relate. Then a very surprising circumstance occurred, which I shall tell you in due course. But, first of all, I must keep you in touch with some of the other factors in the situation.

One of these, concerning which I have said little, is the escaped convict upon the moor. There is strong reason now to believe that he has got right away, which is a considerable relief to the lonely householders of this district. A fortnight has passed since his flight, during which he has not been seen and nothing has been heard of him. It is surely inconceivable that he could have held out upon the moor during all that time. Of course, so far as his concealment goes there is no difficulty at all. Any one of these stone huts would give him a hiding-place. But there is nothing to eat unless he were to catch and slaughter one of the moor sheep. We think, therefore, that he has gone, and the outlying farmers sleep the better in consequence.

We are four able-bodied men in this household, so that we could take good care of ourselves, but I confess that I have had uneasy moments when I have thought of the Stapletons. They live miles from any help. There are one maid, an old manservant, the sister, and the brother, the latter not a very strong man. They would be helpless in the hands of a desperate fellow like this Notting Hill criminal, if he could once effect an entrance. Both Sir Henry and I were concerned at their situation, and it was suggested that Perkins the groom should go over to sleep there, but Stapleton would not hear of it.

The fact is that our friend the baronet begins to display a considerable interest in our fair neighbour. It is not to be wondered at, for time hangs heavily in this lonely spot to an active man like him, and she is a very fascinating and beautiful woman. There is something tropical and exotic about her which forms a singular contrast to her cool and unemotional brother. Yet he also gives the idea of hidden fires. He has certainly a very marked influence over her, for I have seen her continually glance at him as she talked as if seeking approbation for what she said. I trust that he is kind to her. There is a dry glitter in his eyes, and a firm set of his thin lips, which go with a positive and possibly a harsh nature. You would find him an interesting study.

He came over to call upon Baskerville on that first day, and the very next morning he took us both to show us the spot where the

"HE TOOK US TO SHOW US THE SPOT."

legend of the wicked Hugo is supposed to have had its origin. It was an excursion of some miles across the moor to a place which is so dismal that it might have suggested the story. We found a short valley between rugged tors which led to an open, grassy space flecked over with the white cotton grass. In the middle of it rose two great stones, worn and sharpened at the upper end, until they looked like the huge, corroding fangs of some monstrous beast. In every way it corresponded with the scene of the old tragedy. Sir Henry was much interested, and asked Stapleton more than once whether he did really believe in the possibility of the interference of the supernatural in the affairs of men. He spoke lightly, but it was evident that he was very much in earnest. Stapleton was guarded in his replies, but it was easy to see that he said less than he might, and that he would not express his whole opinion out of consideration for the feelings of the baronet. He told us of similar cases, where families had suffered from some evil influence, and he left us with the impression that he shared the popular view upon the matter.

On our way back we stayed for lunch at Merripit House, and it was there that Sir Henry made the acquaintance of Miss Stapleton. From the first moment that he saw her he appeared to be strongly attracted by her, and I am much mistaken if the feeling was not mutual. He referred to her again and again on our walk home, and since then hardly a day has passed that we have not seen something of the brother and sister. They dine here to-night, and there is some talk of our going to them next week. One would imagine that such a match would be very welcome to Stapleton, and yet I have more than once caught a look of the strongest disapprobation in his face when Sir Henry has been paying some attention to his sister. He is much attached to her, no doubt, and would lead a lonely life without her, but it would seem the height of selfishness if he were to stand in the way of her

making so brilliant a marriage. Yet I am certain that he does not wish their intimacy to ripen into love, and I have several times observed that he has taken pains to prevent them from being *tête-à-tête*. By the way, your instructions to me never to allow Sir Henry to go out alone will become very much more onerous if a love affair were to be added to our other difficulties. My popularity would soon suffer if I were to carry out your orders to the letter.

The other day—Thursday, to be more exact—Dr. Mortimer lunched with us. He has been excavating a barrow at Long Down, and has got a prehistoric skull which fills him with great joy. Never was there such a single-minded enthusiast as he ! The

"THE YEW ALLEY."

Stapletons came in afterwards, and the good doctor took us all to the Yew Alley, at Sir Henry's request, to show us exactly how everything occurred upon that fatal night. It is a long, dismal walk, the Yew Alley, between two high walls of clipped hedge, with a narrow band of grass upon either side. At the far end is an old, tumble-down summer-house. Half-way down is the moor-gate, where the old gentleman left his cigar-ash. It is a white wooden gate with a latch. Beyond it lies the wide moor. I remembered your theory of the affair and tried to picture all that had occurred. As the old man stood there he saw something coming across the moor, something which terrified him so that he lost his wits, and ran and ran until he died of sheer horror and exhaustion. There was the long, gloomy tunnel down which he fled. And from what? A sheep-dog of the moor? Or a spectral hound, black, silent, and monstrous? Was there a human agency in the matter? Did the pale, watchful Barrymore know more than he cared to say? It was all dim and vague, but always there is the dark shadow of crime behind it.

One other neighbour I have met since I wrote last. This is Mr. Frankland, of Lafter Hall, who lives some four miles to the south of us. He is an elderly man, red faced, white haired, and choleric. His passion is for the British law, and he has spent a large fortune in litigation. He fights for the mere pleasure of fighting, and is equally ready to take up either side of a question, so that it is no wonder that he has found it a costly amusement. Sometimes he will shut up a right of way and defy the parish to make him open it. At others he will with his own hands tear down some other man's gate and declare that a path has existed there from time immemorial, defying the owner to prosecute him for trespass. He is learned in old manorial and communal rights, and he applies his knowledge sometimes in favour of the villagers of Fernworthy and some-times against them, so that he is periodically either carried in triumph down the village street or else burned in effigy, according to his latest exploit. He is said to have about seven lawsuits upon his hands at present, which will probably swallow up the remainder of his fortune and so draw his sting and leave him harmless for the future. Apart from the law he seems a kindly, good-natured person, and I only mention him because you were particular that I should send some description of the people who surround us. He is curiously employed at present, for, being an amateur astronomer, he has an excellent telescope, with which he lies upon the roof of his own house and sweeps the moor all day in the hope of catching a glimpse of the escaped convict. If he would confine his energies to this all would be well, but there are rumours

that he intends to prosecute Dr. Mortimer for opening a grave without the consent of the next-of-kin, because he dug up the neolithic skull in the barrow on Long Down. He helps to keep our lives from being monotonous and gives a little comic relief where it is badly needed.

And now, having brought you up to date in the escaped convict, the Stapletons, Dr. Mortimer, and Frankland, of Lafter Hall, let me end on that which is most important and tell you more about the Barrymores, and especially about the surprising development of last night.

First of all about the test telegram, which you sent from London in order to make sure that Barrymore was really here. I have already explained that the testimony of the postmaster shows that the test was worthless and that we have no proof one way or the other. I told Sir Henry how the matter stood, and he at once, in his downright fashion, had Barrymore up and asked him whether he had received the telegram him-self. Barrymore said that he had.

" Did the boy deliver it into your own hands?" asked Sir Henry.

Barrymore looked surprised, and considered for a little time.

" No," said he, " I was in the box-room at the time, and my wife brought it up to me."

" Did you answer it yourself?"

" No; I told my wife what to answer and she went down to write it."

In the evening he recurred to the subject of his own accord.

" I could not quite understand the object of your questions this morning, Sir Henry," said he. " I trust that they do not mean that I have done anything to forfeit your confidence?"

Sir Henry had to assure him that it was not so and pacify him by giving him a con-siderable part of his old wardrobe, the London outfit having now all arrived.

Mrs. Barrymore is of interest to me. She is a heavy, solid person, very limited, in-tensely respectable, and inclined to be puri-tanical. You could hardly conceive a less emotional subject. Yet I have told you how, on the first night here, I heard her sobbing bitterly, and since then I have more than once observed traces of tears upon her face. Some deep sorrow gnaws ever at her heart. Sometimes I wonder if she has a guilty memory which haunts her, and sometimes I suspect Barrymore of being a domestic tyrant. I have always felt that there was something singular and questionable in this man's character, but the adventure of last night brings all my suspicions to a head.

And yet it may seem a small matter in itself. You are aware that I am not a very sound sleeper, and since I have been on guard in this house my slumbers have been lighter than ever. Last night, about two in the morning, I was aroused by a stealthy step passing my room. I rose, opened my door, and peeped out. A long black shadow was trailing down the corridor. It was thrown by a man who walked softly down the passage with a candle held in his hand. He was in shirt and trousers, with no covering to his feet. I could merely see the outline, but his height told me that it was Barrymore. He walked very slowly and circumspectly, and there was something indescribably guilty and furtive in his whole appearance.

I have told you that the corridor is broken by the balcony which runs round the hall, but that it is resumed upon the farther side. I waited until he had passed out of sight and then I followed him. When I came round the balcony he had reached the end of the farther corridor, and I could see from the glimmer of light through an open door that he had entered one of the rooms. Now, all these rooms are unfurnished and unoccupied, so that his expedition became more mysterious than ever. The light shone steadily as if he were standing motionless. I crept down the passage as noiselessly as I could and peeped round the corner of the door.

Barrymore was crouching at the window with the candle held against the glass. His profile was half turned towards me, and his face seemed to be rigid with expectation as he stared out into the blackness of the moor. For some minutes he stood watching intently. Then he gave a deep groan and with an impatient gesture he put out the light. Instantly I made my way back to my room, and very

"HE STARED OUT INTO THE BLACKNESS."

shortly came the stealthy steps passing once more upon their return journey. Long afterwards when I had fallen into a light sleep I heard a key turn somewhere in a lock, but I could not tell whence the sound came. What it all means I cannot guess, but there is some secret business going on in this house of gloom which sooner or later we shall get to the bottom of. I do not trouble you with my theories, for you asked me to furnish you only with facts. I have had a long talk with Sir Henry this morning, and we have made a plan of campaign founded upon my observations of last night. I will not speak about it just now, but it should make my next report interesting reading.

*( To be continued.)*

"OVER THE ROCKS WAS THRUST OUT AN EVIL YELLOW FACE."

# THE STRAND MAGAZINE.

Vol. xxii.        DECEMBER, 1901.        No. 132.

# The Hound of the Baskervilles.

## ANOTHER ADVENTURE OF

# SHERLOCK HOLMES.

### By CONAN DOYLE.

### CHAPTER IX.
### [SECOND REPORT OF DR. WATSON.]
#### THE LIGHT UPON THE MOOR.

Baskerville Hall, Oct. 15th.

MY DEAR HOLMES,—If I was compelled to leave you without much news during the early days of my mission you must acknowledge that I am making up for lost time, and that events are now crowding thick and fast upon us. In my last report I ended upon my top note with Barrymore at the window, and now I have quite a budget already which will, unless I am much mistaken, considerably surprise you. Things have taken a turn which I could not have anticipated. In some ways they have within the last forty-eight hours become much clearer and in some ways they have become more complicated. But I will tell you all and you shall judge for yourself.

Before breakfast on the morning following my adventure I went down the corridor and examined the room in which Barrymore had been on the night before. The western window through which he had stared so intently has, I noticed, one peculiarity above all other windows in the house—it commands the nearest outlook on to the moor. There is an opening between two trees which enables one from this point of view to look right down upon it, while from all the other windows it is only a distant glimpse which can be obtained. It follows, therefore, that Barrymore, since only this window would serve his purpose, must have been looking out for something or somebody upon the moor. The night was very dark, so that I can hardly imagine how he could have hoped to see anyone. It had struck me that it was possible that some love intrigue was on foot. That would have accounted for his stealthy movements and also for the uneasiness of his wife. The man is a striking-looking fellow, very well equipped to steal the heart of a country girl, so that this theory seemed to have something to support it. That opening of the door which I had heard after I had returned to my room might mean that he had gone out to keep some clandestine appointment. So I reasoned with myself in the morning, and I tell you the direction of my suspicions, however much the result may have shown that they were unfounded.

But whatever the true explanation of Barrymore's movements might be, I felt that the responsibility of keeping them to myself until I could explain them was more than I could bear. I had an interview with the baronet in his study after breakfast, and I told him all that I had seen. He was less surprised than I had expected.

"I knew that Barrymore walked about nights, and I had a mind to speak to him about it," said he. "Two or three times I have heard his steps in the passage, coming and going, just about the hour you name."

"Perhaps then he pays a visit every night to that particular window," I suggested.

"Perhaps he does. If so, we should be able to shadow him, and see what it is that he is after. I wonder what your friend Holmes would do if he were here?"

"I believe that he would do exactly what you now suggest," said I. "He would follow Barrymore and see what he did."

"Then we shall do it together."

"But surely he would hear us."

"The man is rather deaf, and in any case we must take our chance of that. We'll sit up in my room to-night, and wait until he passes." Sir Henry rubbed his hands with pleasure, and it was evident that he hailed the adventure as a relief to his somewhat quiet life upon the moor.

The baronet has been in communication with the architect who prepared the plans for Sir Charles, and with a contractor from London, so that we may expect great changes to begin here soon. There have been decorators and furnishers up from Plymouth, and it is evident that our friend has large ideas, and means to spare no pains or expense to restore the grandeur of his family. When the house is renovated and refurnished, all that he will need will be a wife to make it complete. Between ourselves there are pretty clear signs that this will not be wanting if the lady is willing, for I have seldom seen a man more infatuated with a woman than he is with our beautiful neighbour, Miss Stapleton. And yet the course of true love does not run quite as smoothly as one would under the circumstances · expect. To-day, for example, its surface was broken by a very unexpected ripple, which has caused our friend considerable perplexity and annoyance.

After the conversation which I have quoted about Barrymore Sir Henry put on his hat and prepared to go out. As a matter of course I did the same.

"What, are *you* coming, Watson?" he asked, looking at me in a curious way.

"That depends on whether you are going on the moor," said I.

"Yes, I am."

"Well, you know what my instructions are. I am sorry to intrude, but you heard how earnestly Holmes insisted that I should not leave you, and especially that you should not go alone upon the moor."

Sir Henry put his hand upon my shoulder, with a pleasant smile.

"My dear fellow," said he, "Holmes, with all his wisdom, did not foresee some things

which have happened since I have been on the moor. You understand me? I am sure that you are the last man in the world who would wish to be a spoil-sport. I must go out alone."

It put me in a most awkward position. I was at a loss what to say or what to do, and before I had made up my mind he picked up his cane and was gone.

But when I came to think the matter over my conscience reproached me bitterly for having on any pretext allowed him to go out of my sight. I imagined what my feelings would be if I had to return to you and to confess that some misfortune had occurred through my disregard for your instructions. I assure you my cheeks flushed at the very thought. It might not even now be too late

"SIR HENRY PUT HIS HAND UPON MY SHOULDER."

to overtake him, so I set off at once in the direction of Merripit House.

I hurried along the road at the top of my speed without seeing anything of Sir Henry, until I came to the point where the moor path branches off. There, fearing that perhaps I had come in the wrong direction after all, I mounted a hill from which I could command a view—the same hill which is cut into the dark quarry. Thence I saw him at once. He was on the moor path, about a quarter of a mile off, and a lady was by his side who could only be Miss Stapleton. It was clear that there was already an understanding between them and that they had met by appointment. They were walking slowly along in deep conversation, and I saw her making quick little movements of her hands as if she were very earnest in what she was saying, while he listened intently, and once or twice shook his head in strong dissent. I stood among the rocks watching them, very much puzzled as to what I should do next. To follow them and break into their intimate conversation seemed to be an outrage, and yet my clear duty was never for an instant to let him out of my sight. To act the spy upon a friend was a hateful task. Still, I could see no better course than to observe him from the hill, and to clear my conscience by confessing to him afterwards what I had done. It is true that if any sudden danger had threatened him I was too far away to be of use, and yet I am sure that you will agree with me that the position was very difficult, and that there was nothing more which I could do.

Our friend, Sir Henry, and the lady had halted on the path and were standing deeply absorbed in their conversation, when I was suddenly aware that I was not the only witness of their interview. A wisp of green floating in the air caught my eye, and another glance showed me that it was carried on a stick by a man who was moving among the broken ground. It was Stapleton with his butterfly-net. He was very much closer to the pair than I was, and he appeared to be moving in their direction. At this instant Sir Henry suddenly drew Miss Stapleton to his side. His arm was round her, but it seemed to me that she was straining away from him with her face averted. He stooped his head to hers, and she raised one hand as if in protest. Next moment I saw them spring apart and turn hurriedly round. Stapleton was the cause of the interruption. He was running wildly towards them, his absurd net dangling behind him. He gesticulated and almost danced with excitement in front of the lovers. What the scene meant I could not imagine, but it seemed to me that Stapleton was abusing Sir Henry, who offered explanations, which became more angry as the other refused to accept them. The lady stood by in haughty silence.

Finally Stapleton turned upon his heel and beckoned in a peremptory way to his sister, who, after an irresolute glance at Sir Henry, walked off by the side of her brother. The naturalist's angry gestures showed that the lady was included in his displeasure. The baronet stood for a minute looking after them, and then he walked slowly back the way that he had come, his head hanging, the very picture of dejection.

What all this meant I could not imagine, but I was deeply ashamed to have witnessed so intimate a scene without my friend's knowledge. I ran down the hill therefore and met the baronet at the bottom. His face was flushed with anger and his brows were wrinkled, like one who is at his wits' ends what to do.

"Halloa, Watson! Where have you dropped from?" said he. "You don't mean to say that you came after me in spite of all?"

I explained everything to him: how I had found it impossible to remain behind, how I had followed him, and how I had witnessed all that had occurred. For an instant his eyes blazed at me, but my frankness disarmed his anger, and he broke at last into a rather rueful laugh.

"You would have thought the middle of that prairie a fairly safe place for a man to be private," said he, "but, by thunder, the whole country-side seems to have been out to see me do my wooing—and a mighty poor wooing at that! Where had you engaged a seat?"

"I was on that hill."

"Quite in the back row, eh? But her brother was well up to the front. Did you see him come out on us?"

"Yes, I did."

"Did he ever strike you as being crazy—this brother of hers?"

"I can't say that he ever did."

"I daresay not. I always thought him sane enough until to-day, but you can take it from me that either he or I ought to be in a strait-jacket. What's the matter with me, anyhow? You've lived near me for some weeks, Watson. Tell me straight, now! Is there anything that would prevent me from making a good husband to a woman that I loved?"

"I should say not."

"He can't object to my worldly position, so it must be myself that he has this down on. What has he against me? I never hurt man or woman in my life that I know of. And yet he would not so much as let me touch the tips of her fingers."

"Did he say so?"

"That, and a deal more. I tell you, Watson, I've only known her these few weeks, but

"SIR HENRY SUDDENLY DREW MISS STAPLETON TO HIS SIDE."

from the first I just felt that she was made for me, and she, too—she was happy when she was with me, and that I'll swear. There's a light in a woman's eyes that speaks louder than words. But he has never let us get together, and it was only to-day for the first time that I saw a chance of having a few words with her alone. She was glad to meet me, but when she did it was not love that she would talk about, and she wouldn't have let me talk about it either if she could have stopped it. She kept coming back to it that this was a place of danger, and that she would never be happy until I had left it. I told her that since I had seen her I was in no hurry to leave it, and that if she really wanted me to go the only way to work it was for her to arrange to go with me. With that I offered in as many words to marry her,

but before she could answer down came this brother of hers, running at us with a face on him like a madman. He was just white with rage, and those light eyes of his were blazing with fury. What was I doing with the lady? How dared I offer her attentions which were distasteful to her? Did I think that because I was a baronet I could do what I liked? If he had not been her brother I should have known better how to answer him. As it was I told him that my feelings towards his sister were such as I was not ashamed of, and that I hoped that she might honour me by becoming my wife. That seemed to make the matter no better, so then I lost my temper too, and I answered him rather more hotly than I should perhaps, considering that she was standing by. So it ended by his going off with her, as you saw, and here am I as badly puzzled a man as any in this county. Just tell me what it all means, Watson, and I'll owe you more than ever I can hope to pay."

I tried one or two explanations, but, indeed, I was completely puzzled myself. Our friend's title, his fortune, his age, his character, and his appearance are all in his favour, and I know nothing against him, unless it be this dark fate which runs in his family. That his advances should be rejected so brusquely without any reference to the lady's own wishes, and that the lady should accept the situation without protest, is very amazing. However, our conjectures were set at rest by a visit from Stapleton himself that very afternoon. He had come to offer apologies for his rudeness of the morning, and after a long private interview with Sir Henry in his study the upshot of their conversation was that the breach is quite healed, and that we are to dine at Merripit House next Friday as a sign of it.

"I don't say now that he isn't a crazy man," said Sir Henry; "I can't forget the look in his eyes when he ran at me this morning, but I must allow that no man could make a more handsome apology than he has done."

"Did he give any explanation of his conduct?"

"His sister is everything in his life, he says. That is natural enough, and I am glad that he should understand her value. They have always been together, and according to his account he has been a very lonely man with only her as a companion, so that the thought of losing her was really terrible to him. He had not understood, he said, that I was becoming attached to her, but when he saw with his own eyes that it was really so, and that she might be taken away from him, it gave him such a shock that for a time he was not responsible for what he said or did. He was very sorry for all that had passed, and he recognised how foolish and how selfish it was that he should imagine that he could hold a beautiful woman like his sister to himself for her whole life. If she had to leave him he had rather it was to a neighbour like myself than to anyone else. But in any case it was a blow to him, and it would take him some time before he could prepare himself to meet it. He would withdraw all opposition upon his part if I would promise for three months to let the matter rest and to be content with cultivating the lady's friendship during that time without claiming her love. This I promised, and so the matter rests."

So there is one of our small mysteries cleared up. It is something to have touched bottom anywhere in this bog in which we are floundering. We know now why Stapleton looked with disfavour upon his sister's suitor—even when that suitor was so eligible a one as Sir Henry. And now I pass on to another thread which I have extricated out of the tangled skein, the mystery of the sobs in the night, of the tear-stained face of Mrs. Barrymore, of the secret journey of the butler to the western lattice window. Congratulate me, my dear Holmes, and tell me that I have not disappointed you as an agent—that you do not regret the confidence which you showed in me when you sent me down. All these things have by one night's work been thoroughly cleared.

I have said "by one night's work," but, in truth, it was by two nights' work, for on the first we drew entirely blank. I sat up with Sir Henry in his room until nearly three o'clock in the morning, but no sound of any sort did we hear except the chiming clock upon the stairs. It was a most melancholy vigil, and ended by each of us falling asleep in our chairs. Fortunately we were not discouraged, and we determined to try again. The next night we lowered the lamp and sat smoking cigarettes, without making the least sound. It was incredible how slowly the hours crawled by, and yet we were helped through it by the same sort of patient interest which the hunter must feel as he watches the trap into which he hopes the game may wander. One struck, and two, and we had almost for the second time given it up in despair, when in an instant we both sat bolt upright in our chairs, with all our weary senses keenly on the alert once more. We had heard the creak of a step in the passage.

Very stealthily we heard it pass along until it died away in the distance. Then the baronet gently opened his door and we set out in pursuit. Already our man had gone round the gallery, and the corridor was all in darkness. Softly we stole along until we had come into the other wing. We were just in time to catch a glimpse of the tall, black-bearded figure, his shoulders rounded, as he tip-toed down the passage. Then he passed through the same door as before, and the light of the candle framed it in the darkness and shot one single yellow beam across the gloom of the corridor. We shuffled cautiously towards it, trying every plank before we dared to put our whole weight upon it. We had taken the precaution of leaving our boots behind us, but, even so, the old boards snapped and creaked beneath our tread. Sometimes it seemed impossible that he should fail to hear our approach. However, the man is fortunately rather deaf, and he was entirely preoccupied in that which he was doing. When at last we reached the door and peeped through we found him crouching at the window, candle in hand, his white, intent face pressed against the pane, exactly as I had seen him two nights before.

We had arranged no plan of campaign, but the baronet is a man to whom the most direct way is always the most natural. He walked into the room, and as he did so Barrymore sprang up from the window with a sharp hiss of his breath, and stood, livid and trembling, before us. His dark eyes, glaring out of the white mask of his face, were full of horror and astonishment as he gazed from Sir Henry to me.

"What are you doing here, Barrymore?"

"Nothing, sir." His agitation was so great that he could hardly speak, and the shadows sprang up and down from the shaking of his candle. "It was the window, sir. I go round at night to see that they are fastened."

"On the second floor?"

"WHAT ARE YOU DOING HERE, BARRYMORE?"

"Yes, sir, all the windows."

"Look here, Barrymore," said Sir Henry, sternly; "we have made up our minds to have the truth out of you, so it will save you trouble to tell it sooner rather than later. Come, now! No lies! What were you doing at that window?"

The fellow looked at us in a helpless way, and he wrung his hands together like one who is in the last extremity of doubt and misery.

"I was doing no harm, sir. I was holding a candle to the window."

"And why were you holding a candle to the window?"

"Don't ask me, Sir Henry—don't ask me! I give you my word, sir, that it is not my secret, and that I cannot tell it. If it concerned no one but myself I would not try to keep it from you."

A sudden idea occurred to me, and I took the candle from the window-sill, where the butler had placed it.

"He must have been holding it as a signal," said I. "Let us see if there is any answer." I held it as he had done, and stared out into the darkness of the night. Vaguely I could discern the black bank of the trees and the lighter expanse of the moor, for the moon was behind the clouds. And then I gave a cry of exultation, for a tiny pin-point of yellow light had suddenly transfixed the dark veil, and glowed steadily in the centre of the black square framed by the window.

"There it is!" I cried.

"No, no, sir, it is nothing — nothing at all!" the butler broke in; "I assure you, sir——"

"Move your light across the window, Watson!" cried the baronet. "See, the other moves also! Now, you rascal, do you deny that it is a signal? Come, speak up! Who is your confederate out yonder, and what is this conspiracy that is going on?"

The man's face became openly defiant.

"It is my business, and not yours. I will not tell."

"Then you leave my employment right away."

"Very good, sir. If I must I must."

"And you go in disgrace. By thunder, you may well be ashamed of yourself. Your family has lived with mine for over a hundred years under this roof, and here I find you deep in some dark plot against me."

" No, no, sir ; no, not against you ! " It was a woman's voice, and Mrs. Barrymore, paler and more horror - struck than her husband, was standing at the door. Her bulky figure in a shawl and skirt might have been comic were it not for the intensity of feeling upon her face.

" We have to go, Eliza. This is the end of it. You can pack our things," said the butler.

" Oh, John, John, have I brought you to this ? It is my doing, Sir Henry—all mine. He has done nothing except for my sake, and because I asked him."

" Speak out, then ! What does it mean ? "

" My unhappy brother is starving on the moor. We cannot let him perish at our very gates. The light is a signal to him that food is ready for him, and his light out yonder is to show the spot to which to bring it."

" Then your brother is——"

" The escaped convict, sir—Selden, the criminal."

" That's the truth, sir," said Barrymore. " I said that it was not my secret and that I could not tell it to you. But now you have heard it, and you will see that if there was a plot it was not against you."

This, then, was the explanation of the stealthy expeditions at night and the light at the window. Sir Henry and I both stared at the woman in amazement. Was it possible that this stolidly respectable person was of the same blood as one of the most notorious criminals in the country ?

" Yes, sir, my name was Selden, and he is my younger brother. We humoured him too much when he was a lad, and gave him his own way in everything until he came to think that the world was made for his pleasure, and that he could do what he liked in it. Then, as he grew older, he met wicked companions, and the devil entered into him until he broke my mother's heart and dragged our name in the dirt. From crime to crime he sank lower and lower, until it is only the

mercy of God which has snatched him from the scaffold ; but to me, sir, he was always the little curly-headed boy that I had nursed and played with, as an elder sister would. That was why he broke prison, sir. He knew that I was here and that we could not refuse to help him. When he dragged himself here one night, weary and starving, with the warders hard at his heels, what could we do ? We took him in and fed him and cared for him. Then you returned, sir, and my brother thought he would be safer on the moor than

" 'THE ESCAPED CONVICT, SIR."

anywhere else until the hue and cry was over, so he lay in hiding there. But every second night we made sure if he was still there by putting a light in the window, and if there was an answer my husband took out some bread and meat to him. Every day we hoped that he was gone, but as long as he was there we could not desert him. That is the whole truth, as I am an honest Christian woman, and you will see that if there is blame in the matter it does not lie with my husband, but with me, for whose sake he has done all that he has."

The woman's words came with an intense earnestness which carried conviction with them.

" Is this true, Barrymore ? "

" Yes, Sir Henry. Every word of it."

" Well, I cannot blame you for standing by your own wife. Forget what I have said. Go to your room, you two, and we shall talk further about this matter in the morning."

When they were gone we looked out of the window again. Sir Henry had flung it open, and the cold night wind beat in upon our faces. Far away in the black distance there still glowed that one tiny point of yellow light.

" I wonder he dares," said Sir Henry.

" It may be so placed as to be only visible from here."

" Very likely. How far do you think it is ? "

" Out by the Cleft Tor, I think."

" Not more than a mile or two off."

" Hardly that."

" Well, it cannot be far if Barrymore had to carry out the food to it. And he is waiting, this villain, beside that candle. By thunder, Watson, I am going out to take that man ! "

The same thought had crossed my own mind. It was not as if the Barrymores had taken us into their confidence. Their secret had been forced from them. The man was a danger to the community, an unmitigated scoundrel for whom there was neither pity nor excuse. We were only doing our duty in taking this chance of putting him back where he could do no harm. With his brutal and violent nature, others would have to pay the price if we held our hands. Any night, for example, our neighbours the Stapletons might be attacked by him, and it may have been the thought of this which made Sir Henry so keen upon the adventure.

" I will come," said I.

" Then get your revolver and put on your boots. The sooner we start the better, as the fellow may put out his light and be off."

In five minutes we were outside the door, starting upon our expedition. We hurried through the dark shrubbery, amid the dull moaning of the autumn wind and the rustle of the falling leaves. The night air was heavy with the smell of damp and decay. Now and again the moon peeped out for an instant, but clouds were driving over the face of the sky, and just as we came out on the moor a thin rain began to fall. The light still burned steadily in front.

" Are you armed ? " I asked.

" I have a hunting-crop."

" We must close in on him rapidly, for he is said to be a desperate fellow. We shall take him by surprise and have him at our mercy before he can resist."

" I say, Watson," said the baronet, " what would Holmes say to this ? How about that hour of darkness in which the power of evil is exalted ? "

As if in answer to his words there rose suddenly out of the vast gloom of the moor that strange cry which I had already heard upon the borders of the great Grimpen Mire. It came with the wind through the silence of the night, a long, deep mutter, then a rising howl, and then the sad moan in which it died away. Again and again it sounded, the whole air throbbing with it, strident, wild, and menacing. The baronet caught my sleeve and his face glimmered white through the darkness.

" Good heavens, what's that, Watson ? "

" I don't know. It's a sound they have on the moor. I heard it once before."

It died away, and an absolute silence closed in upon us. We stood straining our ears, but nothing came.

" Watson," said the baronet, " it was the cry of a hound."

My blood ran cold in my veins, for there was a break in his voice which told of the sudden horror which had seized him.

" What do they call this sound ? " he asked.

" Who ? "

" The folk on the country-side."

" Oh, they are ignorant people. Why should you mind what they call it ? "

" Tell me, Watson. What do they say of it ? "

I hesitated, but could not escape the question.

" They say it is the cry of the Hound of the Baskervilles."

He groaned, and was silent for a few moments.

" A hound it was," he said, at last, " but it seemed to come from miles away, over yonder, I think."

" It was hard to say whence it came."

" It rose and fell with the wind. Isn't that the direction of the great Grimpen Mire ? "

" Yes, it is."

" Well, it was up there. Come now, Watson, didn't you think yourself that it was the cry of a hound ? I am not a child. You need not fear to speak the truth."

" Stapleton was with me when I heard it last. He said that it might be the calling of a strange bird."

" No, no, it was a hound. My God, can there be some truth in all these stories ? Is it possible that I am really in danger from so dark a cause? You don't believe it, do you, Watson?"

"No, no."

"And yet it was one thing to laugh about it in London, and it is another to stand out here in the darkness of the moor and to hear such a cry as that. And my uncle! There was the footprint of the hound beside him as he lay. It all fits together. I don't think that I am a coward, Watson, but that sound seemed to freeze my very blood. Feel my hand!"

It was as cold as a block of marble.

"You'll be all right to-morrow."

"I don't think I'll get that cry out of my head. What do you advise that we do now?"

"Shall we turn back?"

"No, by thunder; we have come out to get our man, and we will do it. We are after the convict, and a hell-hound, as likely as not, after us. Come on! We'll see it through if all the fiends of the pit were loose upon the moor."

We stumbled slowly along in the darkness, with the black loom of the craggy hills around us, and the yellow speck of light burning steadily in front. There is nothing so deceptive as the distance of a light upon a pitch-dark night, and sometimes the glimmer seemed to be far away upon the horizon and sometimes it might have been within a few yards of us. But at last we could see whence it came, and then we knew that we were indeed very close. A guttering candle was stuck in a crevice of the rocks which flanked it on each side so as to keep the wind from it, and also to prevent it from being visible, save in the direction of Baskerville Hall. A boulder of granite concealed our approach, and crouching behind it we gazed over it at the signal light. It was strange to see this single candle burning there in the middle of the moor, with no sign of life near it—just the one straight yellow flame and the gleam of the rock on each side of it.

"What shall we do now?" whispered Sir Henry.

"Wait here. He must be near his light. Let us see if we can get a glimpse of him."

The words were hardly out of my mouth when we both saw him. Over the rocks, in the crevice of which the candle burned, there was thrust out an evil yellow face, a terrible animal face, all seamed and scored with vile

"I SAW THE FIGURE OF A MAN UPON THE TOR."

passions. Foul with mire, with a bristling beard, and hung with matted hair, it might well have belonged to one of those old savages who dwelt in the burrows on the hill-sides. The light beneath him was reflected in his small, cunning eyes, which peered fiercely to right and left through the darkness, like a crafty and savage animal who has heard the steps of the hunters.

Something had evidently aroused his suspicions. It may have been that Barrymore had some private signal which we had neglected to give, or the fellow may have had some other reason for thinking that all was not well, but I could read his fears upon his wicked face. Any instant he might dash out the light and vanish in the darkness. I sprang forward therefore, and Sir Henry did the same. At the same moment the convict screamed out a curse at us and hurled a rock which splintered up against the boulder which had sheltered us. I caught one glimpse of his short, squat, strongly-built figure as he sprang to his feet and turned to run. At the same moment by a lucky chance the moon broke through the clouds. We rushed over the brow of the hill, and there was our man running with great speed down the other side, springing over the stones in his way with the activity of a mountain goat. A lucky long shot of my revolver might have crippled him, but I had brought it only to defend myself if attacked, and not to shoot an unarmed man who was running away.

We were both fair runners and in good condition, but we soon found that we had no chance of overtaking him. We saw him for a long time in the moonlight until he was only a small speck moving swiftly among the boulders upon the side of a distant hill. We ran and ran until we were completely blown, but the space between us grew ever wider. Finally we stopped and sat panting on two rocks, while we watched him disappearing in the distance.

And it was at this moment that there occurred a most strange and unexpected thing. We had risen from our rocks and were turning to go home, having abandoned the hopeless chase. The moon was low upon the right, and the jagged pinnacle of a granite tor stood up against the lower curve of its silver disc. There, outlined as black as an ebony statue on that shining background, I saw the figure of a man upon the tor. Do not think that it was a delusion, Holmes. I assure you that I have never in my life seen anything more clearly. As far as I could judge, the figure was that of a tall, thin man. He stood with his legs a little separated, his arms folded, his head bowed, as if he were brooding over that enormous

wilderness of peat and granite which lay before him. He might have been the very spirit of that terrible place. It was not the convict. This man was far from the place where the latter had disappeared. Besides, he was a much taller man. With a cry of surprise I pointed him out to the baronet, but in the instant during which I had turned to grasp his arm the man was gone. There was the sharp pinnacle of granite still cutting the lower edge of the moon, but its peak bore no trace of that silent and motionless figure.

I wished to go in that direction and to search the tor, but it was some distance away. The baronet's nerves were still quivering from that cry, which recalled the dark story of his family, and he was not in the mood for fresh adventures. He had not seen this lonely man upon the tor and could not feel the thrill which his strange presence and his commanding attitude had given to me. "A warder, no doubt," said he. "The moor has been thick with them since this fellow escaped." Well, perhaps his explanation may be the right one, but I should like to have some further proof of it. To-day we mean to communicate to the Princetown people where they should look for their missing man, but it is hard lines that we have not actually had the triumph of bringing him back as our own prisoner. Such are the adventures of last night, and you must acknowledge, my dear Holmes, that I have done you very well in the matter of a report. Much of what I tell you is no doubt quite irrelevant, but still I feel that it is best that I should let you have all the facts and leave you to select for yourself those which will be of most service to you in helping you to your conclusions. We are certainly making some progress. So far as the Barrymores go we have found the motive of their actions, and that has cleared up the situation very much. But the moor with its mysteries and its strange inhabitants remains as inscrutable as ever. Perhaps in my next I may be able to throw some light upon this also. Best of all would it be if if you could come down to us.

*( To be continued.)*

THE SHADOW OF SHERLOCK HOLMES.

# THE STRAND MAGAZINE.

Vol. xxiii.　　　　　JANUARY, 1902.　　　　　No. 133.

# The Hound of the Baskervilles.

## ANOTHER ADVENTURE OF

# SHERLOCK HOLMES.

## By CONAN DOYLE.

### CHAPTER X.

EXTRACT FROM THE DIARY OF DR. WATSON.

O far I have been able to quote from the reports which I have forwarded during these early days to Sherlock Holmes. Now, however, I have arrived at a point in my narrative where I am compelled to abandon this method and to trust once more to my recollections, aided by the diary which I kept at the time. A few extracts from the latter will carry me on to those scenes which are indelibly fixed in every detail upon my memory. I proceed, then, from the morning which followed our abortive chase of the convict and our other strange experiences upon the moor.

October 16th.—A dull and foggy day, with a drizzle of rain. The house is banked in with rolling clouds, which rise now and then to show the dreary curves of the moor, with thin, silver veins upon the sides of the hills, and the distant boulders gleaming where the light strikes upon their wet faces. It is melancholy outside and in. The baronet is in a black reaction after the excitements of the night. I am conscious myself of a weight at my heart and a feeling of impending danger —ever-present danger, which is the more terrible because I am unable to define it.

And have I not cause for such a feeling? Consider the long sequence of incidents which have all pointed to some sinister influence which is at work around us. There is the death of the last occupant of the Hall, fulfilling so exactly the conditions of the family legend, and there is the repeated reports from peasants of the appearance of a strange creature upon the moor. Twice I have with my own ears heard the sound which resembled the distant baying of a hound. It is incredible, impossible, that it should really be outside the ordinary laws of Nature. A spectral hound which leaves material footmarks and fills the air with its howling is surely not to be thought of. Stapleton may fall in with such a superstition, and Mortimer also; but if I have one quality upon earth it is common sense, and nothing will persuade me to believe in such a thing. To do so would be to descend to the level of these poor peasants who are not content with a mere fiend dog, but must needs describe him with hell-fire shooting from his mouth and eyes. Holmes would not listen to such fancies, and I am his agent. But facts are facts, and I have twice heard this crying upon the moor. Suppose that there were really some huge hound loose upon it; that would go far to explain everything. But where could such a hound lie concealed, where did it get its food, where did it come from, how was it that no one saw it by day? It must be confessed that the natural explanation offers almost as many difficulties as the other. And always, apart from the hound, there was the fact of the human agency in London, the man in the cab, and the letter which warned Sir Henry against the moor. This at least was real, but it might have been the work of a protecting friend as easily as an enemy. Where was that friend or enemy now? Had he remained in London, or had he followed us down here? Could he—could he be the stranger whom I had seen upon the Tor?

It is true that I have had only the one glance at him, and yet there are some things to which I am ready to swear. He is no one whom I have seen down here, and I have now met all the neighbours. The figure was far taller than that of Stapleton, far thinner than that of Frankland. Barrymore it might possibly have been, but we had left him behind us, and I am certain that he could not have followed us. A stranger then is still dogging us, just as a stranger had dogged us in London. We have never shaken him off. If I could lay my hands upon that man, then at last we might find ourselves at the end of all our difficulties. To this one purpose I must now devote all my energies.

My first impulse was to tell Sir Henry all my plans. My second and wisest one is to play my own game and speak as little as possible to anyone. He is silent and distrait. His nerves have been strangely shaken by that sound upon the moor. I will say nothing to add to his anxieties, but I will take my own steps to attain my own end.

We had a small scene this morning after breakfast. Barrymore asked leave to speak with Sir Henry, and they were closeted in his study some little time. Sitting in the billiard-room I more than once heard the sound of voices raised, and I had a pretty good idea what the point was which was under discussion. After a time the baronet opened his door and called for me.

"Barrymore considers that he has a grievance," he said. "He thinks that it was unfair on our part to hunt his brother-in-law down when he, of his own free will, had told us the secret."

The butler was standing, very pale but very collected, before us.

"I may have spoken too warmly, sir," said he, "and if I have I am sure that I beg your pardon. At the same time, I was very much surprised when I heard you two gentlemen come back this morning and learned that you had been chasing Selden. The poor fellow has enough to fight against without my putting more upon his track."

"If you had told us of your own free will

"THE BUTLER WAS STANDING,
VERY PALE BUT VERY COLLECTED,
BEFORE US."

it would have been a different thing," said the baronet. "You only told us, or rather your wife only told us, when it was forced from you and you could not help yourself."

"I didn't think you would have taken advantage of it, Sir Henry — indeed I didn't."

"The man is a public danger. There are lonely houses scattered over the moor, and he is a fellow who would stick at nothing. You only want to get a glimpse of his face to see that. Look at Mr. Stapleton's house, for example, with no one but himself to defend it. There's no safety for anyone until he is under lock and key."

"He'll break into no house, sir. I give you my solemn word upon that. But he will never trouble anyone in this country again. I assure you, Sir Henry, that in a very few days the necessary arrangements will have been made and he will be on his way to South America. For God's sake, sir, I beg of you not to let the police know that he is still on the moor. They have given up the chase there, and he can lie quiet until the ship is ready for him. You can't tell on him without getting my wife and me into trouble. I beg you, sir, to say nothing to the police."

"What do you say, Watson?"

I shrugged my shoulders. "If he were safely out of the country it would relieve the taxpayer of a burden."

"But how about the chance of his holding someone up before he goes?"

"He would not do anything so mad, sir. We have provided him with all that he can want. To commit a crime would be to show where he was hiding."

"That is true," said Sir Henry. "Well, Barrymore——"

"God bless you, sir, and thank you from my heart! It would have killed my poor wife had he been taken again."

"I guess we are aiding and abetting a felony, Watson? But, after what we have heard, I don't feel as if I could give the man up, so there is an end of it. All right, Barrymore, you can go."

With a few broken words of gratitude the man turned, but he hesitated and then came back.

"You've been so kind to us, sir, that I should like to do the best I can for you in return. I know something, Sir Henry, and perhaps I should have said it before, but it was long after the inquest that I found it out. I've never breathed a word about it yet to mortal man. It's about poor Sir Charles's death."

The baronet and I were both upon our feet. "Do you know how he died?"

"No, sir, I don't know that."

"What, then?"

"I know why he was at the gate at that hour. It was to meet a woman."

"To meet a woman! He?"

"Yes, sir."

"And the woman's name?"

"I can't give you the name, sir, but I can give you the initials. Her initials were L. L."

"How do you know this, Barrymore?"

"Well, Sir Henry, your uncle had a letter that morning. He had usually a great many letters, for he was a public man and well known for his kind heart, so that everyone who was in trouble was glad to turn to him. But that morning, as it chanced, there was only this one letter, so I took the more notice of it. It was from Coombe Tracey, and it was addressed in a woman's hand."

"Well?"

"Well, sir, I thought no more of the matter, and never would have done had it not been for my wife. Only a few weeks ago she was cleaning out Sir Charles's study— it had never been touched since his death— and she found the ashes of a burned letter in the back of the grate. The greater part of it was charred to pieces, but one little slip, the end of a page, hung together, and the writing could still be read, though it was grey on a black ground. It seemed to us to be a postscript at the end of the letter, and it said: 'Please, please, as you are a gentleman, burn this letter, and be at the gate by ten o'clock.' Beneath it were signed the initials L. L."

"Have you got that slip?"

"No, sir, it crumbled all to bits after we moved it."

"Had Sir Charles received any other letters in the same writing?"

"Well, sir, I took no particular notice of his letters. I should not have noticed this one only it happened to come alone."

"And you have no idea who L. L. is?"

"No, sir. No more than you have. But I expect if we could lay our hands upon that lady we should know more about Sir Charles's death."

"I cannot understand, Barrymore, how you came to conceal this important information."

"Well, sir, it was immediately after that our own trouble came to us. And then again, sir, we were both of us very fond of Sir Charles, as we well might be considering all that he has done for us. To rake this up couldn't help our poor master, and it's well to go carefully when there's a lady in the case. Even the best of us——"

"You thought it might injure his reputation?"

"Well, sir, I thought no good could come of it. But now you have been kind to us, and I feel as if it would be treating you unfairly not to tell you all that I know about the matter."

"Very good, Barrymore; you can go." When the butler had left us Sir Henry turned to me. "Well, Watson, what do you think of this new light?"

"It seems to leave the darkness rather blacker than before."

"So I think. But if we can only trace L. L. it should clear up the whole business. We have gained that much. We know that there is someone who has the facts if we can only find her. What do you think we should do?"

"Let Holmes know all about it at once. It will give him the clue for which he has been seeking. I am much mistaken if it does not bring him down."

I went at once to my room and drew up my report of the morning's conversation for Holmes. It was evident to me that he had been very busy of late, for the notes which I

ping from the eaves. I thought of the convict out upon the bleak, cold, shelterless moor. Poor fellow! Whatever his crimes, he has suffered something to atone for them. And then I thought of that other one—the face in the cab, the figure against the moon. Was he also out in that deluge—the unseen watcher, the man of darkness? In the

"FROM ITS CRAGGY SUMMIT I LOOKED OUT MYSELF ACROSS THE MELANCHOLY DOWNS."

had from Baker Street were few and short, with no comments upon the information which I had supplied, and hardly any reference to my mission. No doubt his blackmailing case is absorbing all his faculties. And yet this new factor must surely arrest his attention and renew his interest. I wish that he were here.

October 17th.—All day to-day the rain poured down, rustling on the ivy and drip-

evening I put on my waterproof and I walked far upon the sodden moor, full of dark imaginings, the rain beating upon my face and the wind whistling about my ears. God help those who wander into the Great Mire now, for even the firm uplands are becoming a morass. I found the black Tor upon which I had seen the solitary watcher, and from its craggy summit I looked out myself across the melancholy downs. Rain squalls drifted across their russet face, and the heavy, slate-coloured clouds hung low over the landscape, trailing in grey wreaths down the sides of the fantastic hills. In the distant hollow on the left, half hidden by the mist, the two thin towers of Baskerville Hall rose above the trees. They were the only signs of human life which I could see, save only those prehistoric huts which lay thickly upon the slopes of the hills. Nowhere was there any trace of that lonely man whom I had seen on the same spot two nights before.

As I walked back I was overtaken by Dr. Mortimer driving in his dog-cart over a rough moorland track, which led from the outlying farmhouse of Foulmire. He has been very attentive to us, and hardly a day has passed that he has not called at the Hall to see how we were getting on. He insisted upon my climbing into his dog-cart and he gave me a lift homewards. I found him much troubled over the disappearance of his little spaniel. It had wandered on to the moor and had never come back. I gave him such consolation as I might, but I thought of the pony on the Grimpen Mire, and I do not fancy that he will see his little dog again.

"By the way, Mortimer," said I, as we jolted along the rough road, "I suppose there are few people living within driving distance of this whom you do not know?"

"Hardly any, I think."

"Can you, then, tell me the name of any woman whose initials are L. L.?"

He thought for a few minutes. "No," said he. "There are a few gipsies and labouring folk for whom I can't answer, but among the farmers or gentry there is no one whose initials are those. Wait a bit, though," he added, after a pause. "There is Laura Lyons—her initials are L. L.—but she lives in Coombe Tracey."

"Who is she?" I asked.

"She is Frankland's daughter."

"What? Old Frankland the crank?"

"Exactly. She married an artist named Lyons, who came sketching on the moor. He proved to be a blackguard and deserted her. The fault from what I hear may not have been entirely on one side. Her father refused to have anything to do with her, because she had married without his consent, and perhaps for one or two other reasons as well. So, between the old sinner and the young one the girl has had a pretty bad time."

"How does she live?"

"I fancy old Frankland allows her a pittance, but it cannot be more, for his own affairs are considerably involved. Whatever she may have deserved one could not allow her to go hopelessly to the bad. Her story got about, and several of the people here did something to enable her to earn an honest living. Stapleton did for one, and Sir Charles for another. I gave a trifle myself. It was to set her up in a type-writing business."

He wanted to know the object of my inquiries, but I managed to satisfy his curiosity without telling him too much, for there is no reason why we should take any-one into our confidence. To-morrow morning I shall find my way to Coombe Tracey, and if I can see this Mrs. Laura Lyons, of equivocal reputation, a long step will have been made towards clearing one incident in this chain of mysteries. I am certainly developing the wisdom of the serpent, for when Mortimer pressed his questions to an inconvenient extent I asked him casually to what type Frankland's skull belonged, and so heard nothing but craniology for the rest of our drive. I have not lived for years with Sherlock Holmes for nothing.

I have only one other incident to record upon this tempestuous and melancholy day. This was my conversation with Barrymore just now, which gives me one more strong card which I can play in due time.

Mortimer had stayed to dinner, and he and the baronet played écarté afterwards. The butler brought me my coffee into the library, and I took the chance to ask him a few questions.

"Well," said I, "has this precious relation of yours departed, or is he still lurking out yonder?"

"I don't know, sir. I hope to Heaven that he has gone, for he has brought nothing but trouble here! I've not heard of him since I left out food for him last, and that was three days ago."

"Did you see him then?"

"No, sir, but the food was gone when next I went that way."

"Then he was certainly there?"

"So you would think, sir, unless it was the other man who took it."

I sat with my coffee-cup half-way to my lips and stared at Barrymore.

"You know that there is another man, then?"

"Yes, sir; there is another man upon the moor."

"Have you seen him?"

"No, sir."

"How do you know of him, then?"

"YOU KNOW THAT THERE IS ANOTHER MAN, THEN?"

"Look at Sir Charles's death! That was bad enough, for all that the coroner said. Look at the noises on the moor at night. There's not a man would cross it after sundown if he was paid for it. Look at this stranger hiding out yonder, and watching and waiting! What's he waiting for? What does it mean? It means no good to anyone of the name of Baskerville, and very glad I shall be to be quit of it all on the day that Sir Henry's new servants are ready to take over the Hall."

"But about this stranger," said I. "Can you tell me anything about him? What did Selden say? Did he find out where he hid, or what he was doing?"

"He saw him once or twice, but he is a deep one, and gives nothing away. At first he thought that he was the police, but soon he found that he had some lay of his own. A kind of gentleman he was, as far as he could see, but what he was doing he could not make out."

"And where did he say that he lived?"

"Among the old houses on the hillside—the stone huts where the old folk used to live."

"But how about his food?"

"Selden found out that he has got a lad who works for him and brings him all he needs. I daresay he goes to Coombe Tracey for what he wants."

"Very good, Barrymore. We may talk further of this some other time." When the butler had gone I walked over to the black window, and I looked through a blurred pane at the driving clouds and at the tossing outline of the wind-swept trees. It is a wild night indoors, and what must it be in a stone hut upon the moor? What passion of hatred can it be which leads a man to lurk in such a place at such a time? And what deep and earnest purpose can he have which calls for such a trial? There, in that hut upon the moor, seems to lie the very centre of that problem which has vexed me so sorely. I swear that another day shall not have passed before I have done all that man can do to reach the heart of the mystery.

"Selden told me of him, sir, a week ago or more. He's in hiding, too, but he's not a convict so far as I can make out. I don't like it, Dr. Watson—I tell you straight, sir, that I don't like it." He spoke with a sudden passion of earnestness.

"Now, listen to me, Barrymore! I have no interest in this matter but that of your master. I have come here with no object except to help him. Tell me, frankly, what it is that you don't like."

Barrymore hesitated for a moment, as if he regretted his outburst, or found it difficult to express his own feelings in words.

"It's all these goings-on, sir," he cried, at last, waving his hand towards the rain-lashed window which faced the moor. "There's foul play somewhere, and there's black villainy brewing, to that I'll swear! Very glad I should be, sir, to see Sir Henry on his way back to London again!"

"But what is it that alarms you?"

## CHAPTER XI.

### THE MAN ON THE TOR.

THE extract from my private diary which forms the last chapter has brought my narrative up to the 18th of October, a time when these strange events began to move swiftly towards their terrible conclusion. The incidents of the next few days are indelibly graven upon my recollection, and I can tell them without reference to the notes made at the time. I start, then, from the day which succeeded that upon which I had established two facts of great importance, the one that Mrs. Laura Lyons of Coombe Tracey had written to Sir Charles Baskerville and made an appointment with him at the very place and hour that he met his death, the other that the lurking man upon the moor was to be found among the stone huts upon the hillside. With these two facts in my possession I felt that either my intelligence or my courage must be deficient if I could not throw some further light upon these dark places.

I had no opportunity to tell the baronet what I had learned about Mrs. Lyons upon the evening before, for Dr. Mortimer remained with him at cards until it was very late. At breakfast, however, I informed him about my discovery, and asked him whether he would care to accompany me to Coombe Tracey. At first he was very eager to come, but on second thoughts it seemed to both of us that if I went alone the results might be better. The more formal we made the visit the less information we might obtain. I left Sir Henry behind, therefore, not without some prickings of conscience, and drove off upon my new quest.

When I reached Coombe Tracey I told Perkins to put up the horses, and I made inquiries for the lady whom I had come to interrogate. I had no difficulty in finding her rooms, which were central and well appointed. A maid showed me in without ceremony, and as I entered the sitting-room a lady, who was sitting before a Remington typewriter, sprang up with a pleasant smile of welcome. Her face fell, however, when she saw that I was a stranger, and she sat down again and asked me the object of my visit.

The first impression left by Mrs. Lyons was one of extreme beauty. Her eyes and hair were of the same rich hazel colour, and her cheeks, though considerably freckled, were flushed with the exquisite bloom of the brunette, the dainty pink which lurks at the heart of the sulphur rose. Admiration was, I repeat, the first impression. But the second

was criticism. There was something subtly wrong with the face, some coarseness of expression, some hardness, perhaps, of eye, some looseness of lip which marred its perfect beauty. But these, of course, are after-thoughts. At the moment I was simply conscious that I was in the presence of a very handsome woman, and that she was asking me the reasons for my visit. I had not quite understood until that instant how delicate my mission was.

"I have the pleasure," said I, "of knowing your father."

It was a clumsy introduction, and the lady made me feel it.

"There is nothing in common between my father and me," she said. "I owe him nothing, and his friends are not mine. If it were not for the late Sir Charles Baskerville and some other kind hearts I might have starved for all that my father cared."

"It was about the late Sir Charles Baskerville that I have come here to see you."

The freckles started out on the lady's face.

"What can I tell you about him?" she asked, and her fingers played nervously over the stops of her typewriter.

"You knew him, did you not?"

"I have already said that I owe a great deal to his kindness. If I am able to support myself it is largely due to the interest which he took in my unhappy situation."

"Did you correspond with him?"

The lady looked quickly up, with an angry gleam in her hazel eyes.

"What is the object of these questions?" she asked, sharply.

"The object is to avoid a public scandal. It is better that I should ask them here than that the matter should pass outside our control."

She was silent and her face was very pale. At last she looked up with something reckless and defiant in her manner.

"Well, I'll answer," she said. "What are your questions?"

"Did you correspond with Sir Charles?"

"I certainly wrote to him once or twice to acknowledge his delicacy and his generosity."

"Have you the dates of those letters?"

"No."

"Have you ever met him?"

"Yes, once or twice, when he came into Coombe Tracey. He was a very retiring man, and he preferred to do good by stealth."

"But if you saw him so seldom and wrote so seldom, how did he know enough about your affairs to be able to help you, as you say that he has done?"

She met my difficulty with the utmost readiness.

"There were several gentlemen who knew my sad history and united to help me. One was Mr. Stapleton, a neighbour and intimate friend of Sir Charles. He was exceedingly kind, and it was through him that Sir Charles learned about my affairs."

I knew already that Sir Charles Baskerville had made Stapleton his almoner upon several occasions, so the lady's statement bore the impress of truth upon it.

"Did you ever write to Sir Charles asking him to meet you?" I continued.

The flush had faded in an instant, and a deathly face was before me. Her dry lips could not speak the "No" which I saw rather than heard.

"Surely your memory deceives you," said I. "I could even quote a passage of your letter. It ran, ' Please, please, as you are a gentleman, burn this letter, and be at the gate by ten o'clock.' "

I thought that she had fainted, but she recovered herself by a supreme effort.

"Is there no such thing as a gentleman?" she gasped.

"You do Sir Charles an injustice. He

" REALLY, SIR, THIS IS A VERY EXTRAORDINARY QUESTION."

Mrs. Lyons flushed with anger again.

"Really, sir, this is a very extraordinary question."

"I am sorry, madam, but I must repeat it."

"Then I answer—certainly not."

"Not on the very day of Sir Charles's death?"

*did* burn the letter. But sometimes a letter may be legible even when burned. You acknowledge now that you wrote it?"

"Yes, I did write it," she cried, pouring out her soul in a torrent of words. "I did write it. Why should I deny it? I have no reason to be ashamed of it. I wished him to help me. I believed that if I had an interview I could gain his help, so I asked him to meet me."

"But why at such an hour?"

"Because I had only just learned that he was going to London next day and might be away for months. There were reasons why I could not get there earlier."

"But why a rendezvous in the garden instead of a visit to the house?"

"Do you think a woman could go alone at that hour to a bachelor's house?"

"Well, what happened when you did get there?"

"I never went."

"Mrs. Lyons!"

"No, I swear it to you on all I hold sacred. I never went. Something intervened to prevent my going."

"What was that?"

"That is a private matter. I cannot tell it."

"You acknowledge, then, that you made an appointment with Sir Charles at the very hour and place at which he met his death, but you deny that you kept the appointment?"

"That is the truth."

Again and again I cross-questioned her, but I could never get past that point.

"Mrs. Lyons," said I, as I rose from this long and inconclusive interview, "you are taking a very great responsibility and putting yourself in a very false position by not making an absolutely clean breast of all that you know. If I have to call in the aid of the police you will find how seriously you are compromised. If your position is innocent, why did you in the first instance deny having written to Sir Charles upon that date?"

"Because I feared that some false conclusion might be drawn from it, and that I might find myself involved in a scandal."

"And why were you so pressing that Sir Charles should destroy your letter?"

"If you have read the letter you will know."

"I did not say that I had read all the letter."

"You quoted some of it."

"I quoted the postscript. The letter had, as I said, been burned, and it was not all legible. I ask you once again why it was that you were so pressing that Sir Charles should destroy this letter which he received on the day of his death."

"The matter is a very private one."

"The more reason why you should avoid a public investigation."

"I will tell you, then. If you have heard anything of my unhappy history you will know that I made a rash marriage and had reason to regret it."

"I have heard so much."

"My life has been one incessant persecution from a husband whom I abhor. The law is upon his side, and every day I am faced by the possibility that he may force me to live with him. At the time that I wrote this letter to Sir Charles I had learned that there was a prospect of my regaining my freedom if certain expenses could be met. It meant everything to me—peace of mind, happiness, self-respect—everything. I knew Sir Charles's generosity, and I thought that if he heard the story from my own lips he would help me."

"Then how is it that you did not go?"

"Because I received help in the interval from another source."

"Why, then, did you not write to Sir Charles and explain this?"

"So I should have done had I not seen his death in the paper next morning."

The woman's story hung coherently together, and all my questions were unable to shake it. I could only check it by finding if she had, indeed, instituted divorce proceedings against her husband at or about the time of the tragedy.

It was unlikely that she would dare to say that she had not been to Baskerville Hall if she really had been, for a trap would be necessary to take her there, and could not have returned to Coombe Tracey until the early hours of the morning. Such an excursion could not be kept secret. The probability was, therefore, that she was telling the truth, or, at least, a part of the truth. I came away baffled and disheartened. Once again I had reached that dead wall which seemed to be built across every path by which I tried to get at the object of my mission. And yet the more I thought of the lady's face and of her manner the more I felt that something was being held back from me. Why should she turn so pale? Why should she fight against every admission until it was forced from her? Why should she have been so reticent at the time of the tragedy? Surely the explanation of all this could not be as innocent as she would have me believe. For the moment I could proceed no farther in that direction, but must turn back to that other clue which was to be sought for among the stone huts upon the moor.

And that was a most vague direction. I realized it as I drove back and noted how hill after hill showed traces of the ancient people. Barrymore's only indication had been that the stranger lived in one of these abandoned huts, and many hundreds of them are scattered throughout the length and breadth of the moor. But I had my own experience for a guide, since it had shown me the man himself standing upon the summit of the Black Tor. That, then, should be the centre of my search. From there I should explore every hut upon the moor until I lighted upon the right one. If this man were inside it I should find out from his own lips, at the point of my revolver if necessary, who he was and why he had dogged us so long. He might slip away from us in the crowd of Regent Street, but it would puzzle him to do so upon the lonely moor. On the other hand, if I should find the hut and its tenant should not be within it I must remain there, however long the vigil, until he returned. Holmes had missed him in London. It would indeed be a triumph for me if I could run him to earth where my master had failed.

Luck had been against us again and again in this inquiry, but now at last it came to my aid. And the messenger of good fortune was none other than Mr. Frankland, who was standing, grey-whiskered and red-faced, outside the gate of his garden, which opened on to the high road along which I travelled.

"Good-day, Dr. Watson," cried he, with unwonted good humour, "you must really give your horses a rest, and come in to have a glass of wine and to congratulate me."

My feelings towards him were far from being friendly after what I had heard of his treatment of his daughter, but I was anxious to send Perkins and the wagonette home, and the opportunity was a good one. I alighted and sent a message to Sir Henry that I should walk over in time for dinner. Then I followed Frankland into his dining-room.

"It is a great day for me, sir—one of the red-letter days of my life," he cried, with many chuckles. "I have brought off a double event. I mean to teach them in these parts that law is law, and that there is a man here who does not fear to invoke it. I have established a right of way through the centre of old Middleton's park, slap across it, sir, within a hundred yards of his own front door. What do you think of that? We'll teach these magnates that they cannot ride rough-shod over the rights of the commoners, confound them! And I've closed the wood where the Fernworthy folk used to picnic. These infernal people seem to think that there are no rights of property, and that they can swarm where they like with their papers and their bottles. Both cases decided, Dr.

"'GOOD-DAY, DR. WATSON,' HE CRIED."

Watson, and both in my favour. I haven't had such a day since I had Sir John Morland for trespass, because he shot in his own warren."

"How on earth did you do that?"

"Look it up in the books, sir. It will repay reading—Frankland v. Morland, Court of Queen's Bench. It cost me £200, but I got my verdict."

"Did it do you any good?"

"None, sir, none. I am proud to say that I had no interest in the matter. I act entirely from a sense of public duty. I have no doubt, for example, that the Fernworthy people will burn me in effigy to-night. I told the police last time they did it that they should stop these disgraceful exhibitions. The county constabulary is in a scandalous state, sir, and it has not afforded me the protection to which I am entitled. The case of Frankland v. Regina will bring the matter before the attention of the public. I told them that they would have occasion to regret their treatment of me, and already my words have come true."

"How so?" I asked.

The old man put on a very knowing expression.

"Because I could tell them what they are dying to know; but nothing would induce me to help the rascals in any way."

I had been casting round for some excuse by which I could get away from his gossip, but now I began to wish to hear more of it. I had seen enough of the contrary nature of the old sinner to understand that any strong sign of interest would be the surest way to stop his confidences.

"Some poaching case, no doubt?" said I, with an indifferent manner.

"Ha, ha, my boy, a very much more important matter than that! What about the convict on the moor?"

I started. "You don't mean that you know where he is?" said I.

"I may not know exactly where he is, but I am quite sure that I could help the police to lay their hands on him. Has it never struck you that the way to catch that man was to find out where he got his food, and so trace it to him?"

He certainly seemed to be getting uncomfortably near the truth. "No doubt," said I; "but how do you know that he is anywhere upon the moor?"

"I know it because I have seen with my own eyes the messenger who takes him his food."

My heart sank for Barrymore. It was a serious thing to be in the power of this spiteful old busybody. But his next remark took a weight from my mind.

"You'll be surprised to hear that his food is taken to him by a child. I see him every day through my telescope upon the roof. He passes along the same path at the same hour, and to whom should he be going except to the convict?"

Here was luck indeed! And yet I suppressed all appearance of interest. A child! Barrymore had said that our unknown was supplied by a boy. It was on his track, and not upon the convict's, that Frankland had stumbled. If I could get his knowledge it might save me a long and weary hunt. But incredulity and indifference were evidently my strongest cards.

"I should say that it was much more likely that it was the son of one of the moorland shepherds taking out his father's dinner."

The least appearance of opposition struck fire out of the old autocrat. His eyes looked malignantly at me, and his grey whiskers bristled like those of an angry cat.

"Indeed, sir!" said he, pointing out over the wide-stretching moor. "Do you see that Black Tor over yonder? Well, do you see the low hill beyond with the thorn-bush upon it? It is the stoniest part of the whole moor. Is that a place where a shepherd would be likely to take his station? Your suggestion, sir, is a most absurd one."

I meekly answered that I had spoken without knowing all the facts. My submission pleased him and led him to further confidences.

"You may be sure, sir, that I have very good grounds before I come to an opinion. I have seen the boy again and again with his bundle. Every day, and sometimes twice a day, I have been able—but wait a moment, Dr. Watson. Do my eyes deceive me, or is there at the present moment something moving upon that hillside?"

It was several miles off, but I could distinctly see a small dark dot against the dull green and grey.

"Come, sir, come!" cried Frankland, rushing upstairs. "You will see with your own eyes and judge for yourself."

The telescope, a formidable instrument mounted upon a tripod, stood upon the flat leads of the house. Frankland clapped his eye to it and gave a cry of satisfaction.

"Quick, Dr. Watson, quick, before he passes over the hill!"

There he was, sure enough, a small urchin with a little bundle upon his shoulder, toiling

"FRANKLAND CLAPPED HIS EYE TO IT AND GAVE A CRY OF SATISFACTION."

which these rascals burned at the stake. Surely you are not going! You will help me to empty the decanter in honour of this great occasion!"

But I resisted all his solicitations and succeeded in dissuading him from his announced intention of walking home with me. I kept the road as long as his eye was on me, and then I struck off across the moor and made for the stony hill over which the boy had disappeared. Everything was working in my favour, and I swore that it should not be through lack of energy or perseverance that I should miss the chance which Fortune had thrown in my way.

The sun was already sinking when I reached the summit of the hill, and the long slopes beneath me were all golden-green on one side and grey shadow on the other. A haze lay low upon the farthest sky-line, out of which jutted the fantastic shapes of Belliver and Vixen Tor. Over the wide expanse there was no sound and no movement. One great grey bird, a gull or curlew, soared aloft in the blue heaven. He and I seemed to be the only living things between the huge arch of the sky and the desert beneath it. The barren scene, the sense of loneliness, and the mystery and urgency of my task all struck a chill into my heart. The boy was nowhere to be seen. But down beneath me in a cleft of the hills there was a circle of the old stone huts, and in the middle of them there was one which retained sufficient roof to act as a screen against the weather. My heart leaped within me as I saw it. This must be the burrow where the stranger lurked. At last my foot was on the threshold of his hiding-place—his secret was within my grasp.

As I approached the hut, walking as warily as Stapleton would do when with poised net he drew near the settled butterfly, I satisfied myself that the place had indeed been used

slowly up the hill. When he reached the crest I saw the ragged, uncouth figure outlined for an instant against the cold blue sky. He looked round him, with a furtive and stealthy air, as one who dreads pursuit. Then he vanished over the hill.

"Well! Am I right?"

"Certainly, there is a boy who seems to have some secret errand."

"And what the errand is even a county constable could guess. But not one word shall they have from me, and I bind you to secrecy also, Dr. Watson. Not a word! You understand?"

"Just as you wish."

"They have treated me shamefully— shamefully. When the facts come out in Frankland *v.* Regina I venture to think that a thrill of indignation will run through the country. Nothing would induce me to help the police in any way. For all they cared it might have been me, instead of my effigy,

as a habitation. A vague pathway among the boulders led to the dilapidated opening which served as a door. All was silent within. The unknown might be lurking there, or he might be prowling on the moor. My nerves tingled with the sense of adventure. Throwing aside my cigarette I closed my hand upon the butt of my revolver and, walking swiftly up to the door, I looked in. The place was empty.

But there were ample signs that I had not come upon a false scent. This was certainly where the man lived. Some blankets rolled in a waterproof lay upon that very stone slab upon which neolithic man had once slumbered. The ashes of a fire were heaped in a rude grate. Beside it lay some cooking utensils and a bucket half-full of water. A litter of empty tins showed that the place had been occupied for some time, and I saw, as my eyes became accustomed to the chequered light, a pannikin and a half-full bottle of spirits standing in the corner. In the middle of the hut a flat stone served the purpose of a table, and upon this stood a small cloth bundle—the same, no doubt, which I had seen through the telescope upon the shoulder of the boy. It contained a loaf of bread, a tinned tongue, and two tins of preserved peaches. As I set it down again, after having examined it, my heart leaped to see that beneath it there lay a sheet of paper with writing upon it. I raised it, and this was what I read, roughly scrawled in pencil:—

"Dr. Watson has gone to Coombe Tracey."

For a minute I stood there with the paper in my hands thinking out the meaning of this curt message. It was I, then, and not Sir Henry, who was being dogged by this secret man. He had not followed me himself, but he had set an agent—the boy, perhaps—upon my track, and this was his report. Possibly I had taken no step since I had been upon the moor which had not been observed and repeated. Always there was this feeling of an unseen force, a fine net drawn round us with infinite skill and delicacy, holding us so lightly that it was only at some supreme moment that one

realized that one was indeed entangled in its meshes.

If there was one report there might be others, so I looked round the hut in search of them. There was no trace, however, of anything of the kind, nor could I discover any sign which might indicate the character or intentions of the man who lived in this singular place, save that he must be of Spartan habits, and cared little for the comforts of life. When I thought of the heavy rains and looked at the gaping roof I understood how strong and immutable must be the purpose which had kept him in that inhospitable abode. Was he our malignant enemy, or was he by chance our guardian angel? I swore that I would not leave the hut until I knew.

Outside the sun was sinking low and the west was blazing with scarlet and gold. Its reflection was shot back in ruddy patches by the distant pools which lay amid the Great Grimpen Mire. There were the two towers of Baskerville Hall, and there a distant blur of smoke which marked the village of Grimpen. Between the two, behind the hill, was the house of the Stapletons. All was sweet and mellow and peaceful in the golden evening light, and yet as I looked at them my soul shared none of the peace of Nature, but quivered at the vagueness and the terror of that interview which every instant was bringing nearer. With tingling nerves, but a fixed purpose, I sat in the dark recess of the hut and waited with sombre patience for the coming of its tenant.

And then at last I heard him. Far away came the sharp clink of a boot striking upon a stone. Then another and yet another, coming nearer and nearer. I shrank back into the darkest corner, and cocked the pistol in my pocket, determined not to discover myself until I had an opportunity of seeing something of the stranger. There was a long pause which showed that he had stopped. Then once more the footsteps approached and a shadow fell across the opening of the hut.

"It is a lovely evening, my dear Watson," said a well-known voice. "I really think that you will be more comfortable outside than in."

*(To be continued.)*

"IT WAS A PROSTRATE MAN FACE DOWNWARDS UPON THE GROUND."

# The Hound of the Baskervilles.

## ANOTHER ADVENTURE OF

# SHERLOCK HOLMES.

## By CONAN DOYLE.

### CHAPTER XII.

#### DEATH ON THE MOOR.

 FOR a moment or two I sat breathless, hardly able to believe my ears. Then my senses and my voice came back to me, while a crushing weight of responsibility seemed in an instant to be lifted from my soul. That cold, incisive, ironical voice could belong to but one man in all the world.

"Holmes!" I cried—"Holmes!"

"Come out," said he, "and please be careful with the revolver."

I stooped under the rude lintel, and there he sat upon a stone outside, his grey eyes dancing with amusement as they fell upon my astonished features. He was thin and worn, but clear and alert, his keen face bronzed by the sun and roughened by the wind. In his tweed suit and cloth cap he looked like any other tourist upon the moor, and he had contrived, with that cat-like love of personal cleanliness which was one of his characteristics, that his chin should be as smooth and his linen as perfect as if he were in Baker Street.

"I never was more glad to see anyone in my life," said I, as I wrung him by the hand.

"Or more astonished, eh?"

"Well, I must confess to it."

"The surprise was not all on one side, I assure you. I had no idea that you had found my occasional retreat, still less that you were inside it, until I was within twenty paces of the door."

"My footprint, I presume?"

"No, Watson; I fear that I could not undertake to recognise your footprint amid all the footprints of the world. If you seriously desire to deceive me you must change your tobacconist; for when I see the stub of a cigarette marked Bradley, Oxford Street, I know that my friend Watson is in the neighbourhood. You will see it there beside the path. You threw it down, no doubt, at that supreme moment when you charged into the empty hut."

"Exactly."

"I thought as much—and knowing your admirable tenacity I was convinced that you were sitting in ambush, a weapon within reach, waiting for the tenant to return. So you actually thought that I was the criminal?"

"I did not know who you were, but I was determined to find out."

"Excellent, Watson! And how did you localize me? You saw me, perhaps, on the night of the convict hunt, when I was so imprudent as to allow the moon to rise behind me?"

"Yes, I saw you then."

"And have, no doubt, searched all the huts until you came to this one?"

"No, your boy had been observed, and that gave me a guide where to look."

"The old gentleman with the telescope, no doubt. I could not make it out when first I saw the light flashing upon the lens." He rose and peeped into the hut. "Ha, I see that Cartwright has brought up some supplies. What's this paper? So you have been to Coombe Tracey, have you?"

"Yes."

"To see Mrs. Laura Lyons?"

"Exactly."

"Well done! Our researches have

"THERE HE SAT UPON A STONE."

which you ran which led me to come down and examine the matter for myself. Had I been with Sir Henry and you it is evident that my point of view would have been the same as yours, and my presence would have warned our very formidable opponents to be on their guard. As it is, I have been able to get about as I could not possibly have done had I been living at the Hall, and I remain an unknown factor in the business, ready to throw in all my weight at a critical moment."

"But why keep me in the dark?"

"For you to know could not have helped us, and might possibly have led to my discovery. You would have wished to tell me something, or in your kindness you would have brought me out some comfort or other, and so an unnecessary risk would be run. I brought Cartwright down with me—you remember the little chap at the Express office—and he has seen after my simple wants: a loaf of bread and a clean collar. What does man want more? He has given me an extra pair of eyes upon a very active pair of feet, and both have been invaluable."

"Then my reports have all been wasted!" My voice trembled as I recalled the pains and the pride with which I had composed them.

Holmes took a bundle of papers from his pocket.

"Here are your reports, my dear fellow, and very well thumbed, I assure you. I made excellent arrangements, and they are only delayed one day upon their way. I must compliment you exceedingly upon the zeal and the intelligence which you have shown over an extraordinarily difficult case."

I was still rather raw over the deception

evidently been running on parallel lines, and when we unite our results I expect we shall have a fairly full knowledge of the case."

"Well, I am glad from my heart that you are here, for indeed the responsibility and the mystery were both becoming too much for my nerves. But how in the name of wonder did you come here, and what have you been doing? I thought that you were in Baker Street working out that case of blackmailing."

"That was what I wished you to think."

"Then you use me, and yet do not trust me!" I cried, with some bitterness. "I think that I have deserved better at your hands, Holmes."

"My dear fellow, you have been invaluable to me in this as in many other cases, and I beg that you will forgive me if I have seemed to play a trick upon you. In truth, it was partly for your own sake that I did it, and it was my appreciation of the danger

which had been practised upon me, but the warmth of Holmes's praise drove my anger from my mind. I felt also in my heart that he was right in what he said, and that it was really best for our purpose that I should not have known that he was upon the moor.

"That's better," said he, seeing the shadow rise from my face. "And now tell me the result of your visit to Mrs. Laura Lyons—it was not difficult for me to guess that it was to see her that you had gone, for I am already aware that she is the one person in Coombe Tracey who might be of service to us in the matter. In fact, if you had not gone to-day it is exceedingly probable that I should have gone to-morrow."

The sun had set and dusk was settling over the moor. The air had turned chill, and we withdrew into the hut for warmth. There, sitting together in the twilight, I told Holmes of my conversation with the lady. So interested was he that I had to repeat some of it twice before he was satisfied.

"This is most important," said he, when I had concluded. "It fills up a gap which I had been unable to bridge, in this most complex affair. You are aware, perhaps, that a close intimacy exists between this lady and the man Stapleton?"

"I did not know of a close intimacy."

"There can be no doubt about the matter. They meet, they write, there is a complete understanding between them. Now, this puts a very powerful weapon into our hands. If I could only use it to detach his wife——"

"His wife?"

"I am giving you some information now, in return for all that you have given me. The lady who has passed here as Miss Stapleton is in reality his wife."

"Good heavens, Holmes! Are you sure of what you say? How could he have permitted Sir Henry to fall in love with her?"

"Sir Henry's falling in love could do no harm to anyone except Sir Henry. He took particular care that Sir Henry did not *make* love to her, as you have yourself observed. I repeat that the lady is his wife and not his sister."

"But why this elaborate deception?"

"Because he foresaw that she would be very much more useful to him in the character of a free woman."

All my unspoken instincts, my vague suspicions, suddenly took shape and centred upon the naturalist. In that impassive, colourless man, with his straw hat and his butterfly-net, I seemed to see something terrible—a creature of infinite patience and craft, with a smiling face and a murderous heart.

"It is he, then, who is our enemy—it is he who dogged us in London?"

"So I read the riddle."

"And the warning—it must have come from her!"

"Exactly."

The shape of some monstrous villainy, half seen, half guessed, loomed through the darkness which had girt me so long.

"But are you sure of this, Holmes? How do you know that the woman is his wife?"

"Because he so far forgot himself as to tell you a true piece of autobiography upon the occasion when he first met you, and I daresay he has many a time regretted it since. He *was* once a schoolmaster in the North of England. Now, there is no one more easy to trace than a schoolmaster. There are scholastic agencies by which one may identify any man who has been in the profession. A little investigation showed me that a school had come to grief under atrocious circumstances, and that the man who had owned it—the name was different—had disappeared with his wife. The descriptions agreed. When I learned that the missing man was devoted to entomology the identification was complete."

The darkness was rising, but much was still hidden by the shadows.

"If this woman is in truth his wife, where does Mrs. Laura Lyons come in?" I asked.

"That is one of the points upon which your own researches have shed a light. Your interview with the lady has cleared the situation very much. I did not know about a projected divorce between herself and her husband. In that case, regarding Stapleton as an unmarried man, she counted no doubt upon becoming his wife."

"And when she is undeceived?"

"Why, then we may find the lady of service. It must be our first duty to see her—both of us—to-morrow. Don't you think, Watson, that you are away from your charge rather long? Your place should be at Baskerville Hall."

The last red streaks had faded away in the west and night had settled upon the moor. A few faint stars were gleaming in a violet sky.

"One last question, Holmes," I said, as I rose. "Surely there is no need of secrecy between you and me. What is the meaning of it all? What is he after?"

Holmes's voice sank as he answered:—

"It is murder, Watson—refined, cold-blooded, deliberate murder. Do not ask me for particulars. My nets are closing upon him, even as his are upon Sir Henry, and with your help he is already almost at my mercy. There is but one danger which can threaten us. It is that he should strike before we are ready to do so. Another day —two at the most—and I have my case complete, but until then guard your charge as closely as ever a fond mother watched her ailing child. Your mission to-day has justified itself, and yet I could almost wish that you had not left his side—Hark!"

A terrible scream—a prolonged yell of horror and anguish burst out of the silence of the moor. That frightful cry turned the blood to ice in my veins.

"Oh, my God!" I gasped. "What is it? What does it mean?"

Holmes had sprung to his feet, and I saw his dark, athletic outline at the door of the hut, his shoulders stooping, his head thrust forward, his face peering into the darkness.

"Hush!" he whispered. "Hush!"

The cry had been loud on account of its vehemence, but it had pealed out from somewhere far off on the shadowy plain. Now it burst upon our ears, nearer, louder, more urgent than before.

"Where is it?" Holmes whispered; and I knew from the thrill of his voice that he, the man of iron, was shaken to the soul. "Where is it, Watson?"

"There, I think." I pointed into the darkness.

"No, there!"

Again the agonized cry swept through the silent night, louder and much nearer than ever. And a new sound mingled with it, a deep, muttered rumble, musical and yet menacing, rising and falling like the low, constant murmur of the sea.

"The hound!" cried Holmes. "Come, Watson, come! Great heavens, if we are too late!"

He had started running swiftly over the moor, and I had followed at his heels. But now from somewhere among the broken ground immediately in front of us there came one last despairing yell, and then a dull, heavy thud. We halted and listened. Not another sound broke the heavy silence of the windless night.

I saw Holmes put his hand to his forehead like a man distracted. He stamped his feet upon the ground.

"He has beaten us, Watson. We are too late."

"No, no, surely not!"

"Fool that I was to hold my hand. And you, Watson, see what comes of abandoning

your charge! But, by Heaven, if the worst has happened, we'll avenge him!"

Blindly we ran through the gloom, blundering against boulders, forcing our way through gorse bushes, panting up hills and rushing down slopes, heading always in the direction whence those dreadful sounds had come. At every rise Holmes looked eagerly round him, but the shadows were thick upon the moor and nothing moved upon its dreary face.

"Can you see anything?"

"Nothing."

"But, hark, what is that?"

A low moan had fallen upon our ears. There it was again upon our left! On that side a ridge of rocks ended in a sheer cliff which overlooked a stone-strewn slope. On its jagged face was spread-eagled some dark, irregular object. As we ran towards it the vague outline hardened into a definite shape. It was a prostrate man face downwards upon the ground, the head doubled under him at a horrible angle, the shoulders rounded and the body hunched together as if in the act of throwing a somersault. So grotesque was the attitude that I could not for the instant realize that that moan had been the passing of his soul. Not a whisper, not a rustle, rose now from the dark figure over which we stooped. Holmes laid his hand upon him, and held it up again, with an exclamation of horror. The gleam of the match which he struck shone upon his clotted fingers and upon the ghastly pool which widened slowly from the crushed skull of the victim. And it shone upon something else which turned our hearts sick and faint within us—the body of Sir Henry Baskerville!

There was no chance of either of us forgetting that peculiar ruddy tweed suit— the very one which he had worn on the first morning that we had seen him in Baker Street. We caught the one clear glimpse of it, and then the match flickered and went out, even as the hope had gone out of our souls. Holmes groaned, and his face glimmered white through the darkness.

"The brute! the brute!" I cried, with clenched hands. "Oh, Holmes, I shall never forgive myself for having left him to his fate."

"I am more to blame than you, Watson. In order to have my case well rounded and complete, I have thrown away the life of my client. It is the greatest blow which has befallen me in my career. But how could I know—how *could* I know—that he would risk his life alone upon the moor in the face of all my warnings?"

"That we should have heard his screams— my God, those screams!—and yet have been unable to save him! Where is this brute of a hound which drove him to his death? It may be lurking among these rocks at this instant. And Stapleton, where is he? He shall answer for this deed."

"He shall. I will see to that. Uncle and nephew have been murdered—the one frightened to death by the very sight of a beast which he thought to be supernatural, the other driven to his end in his wild flight to escape from it. But now we have to prove the connection between the man and the beast. Save from what we heard, we cannot even swear to the existence of the latter, since Sir Henry has evidently died from the fall. But, by heavens, cunning as he is, the fellow shall be in my power before another day is past!"

We stood with bitter hearts on either side of the mangled body, overwhelmed by this sudden and irrevocable disaster which had brought all our long and weary labours to so piteous an end. Then, as the moon rose, we climbed to the top of the rocks over which our poor friend had fallen, and from the summit we gazed out over the shadowy moor, half silver and half gloom. Far away, miles off, in the direction of Grimpen, a single steady yellow light was shining. It could only come from the lonely abode of the Stapletons. With a bitter curse I shook my fist at it as I gazed.

"Why should we not seize him at once?"

"Our case is not complete. The fellow is wary and cunning to the last degree. It is not what we know,

but what we can prove. If we make one false move the villain may escape us yet."

"What can we do?"

"There will be plenty for us to do to-morrow. To-night we can only perform the last offices to our poor friend."

Together we made our way down the precipitous slope and approached the body, black and clear against the silvered stones. The agony of those contorted limbs struck me with a spasm of pain and blurred my eyes with tears.

"We must send for help, Holmes! We cannot carry him all the way to the Hall. Good heavens, are you mad?"

He had uttered a cry and bent over the body. Now he was dancing and laughing and wringing my hand. Could this be my stern, self-contained friend? These were hidden fires, indeed!

"IT WAS THE FACE OF SELDEN, THE CRIMINAL."

"A beard! A beard! The man has a beard!"

"A beard?"

"It is not the Baronet—it is—why, it is my neighbour, the convict!"

With feverish haste we had turned the body over, and that dripping beard was pointing up to the cold, clear moon. There could be no doubt about the beetling forehead, the sunken animal eyes. It was, indeed, the same face which had glared upon me in the light of the candle from over the rock—the face of Selden, the criminal.

Then in an instant it was all clear to me. I remembered how the Baronet had told me that he had handed his old wardrobe to Barrymore. Barrymore had passed it on in order to help Selden in his escape. Boots, shirt, cap—it was all Sir Henry's. The tragedy was still black enough, but this man had at least deserved death by the laws of his country. I told Holmes how the matter stood, my heart bubbling over with thankfulness and joy.

"Then the clothes have been the poor fellow's death," said he. "It is clear enough that the hound has been laid on from some article of Sir Henry's—the boot which was abstracted in the hotel, in all probability—and so ran this man down. There is one very singular thing, however: How came Selden, in the darkness, to know that the hound was on his trail?"

"He heard him."

"To hear a hound upon the moor would not work a hard man like this convict into such a paroxysm of terror that he would risk recapture by screaming wildly for help. By his cries he must have run a long way after he knew the animal was on his track. How did he know?"

"A greater mystery to me is why this hound, presuming that all our conjectures are correct——"

"I presume nothing."

"Well, then, why this hound should be loose to-night. I suppose that it does not always run loose upon the moor. Stapleton would not let it go unless he had reason to think that Sir Henry would be there."

"My difficulty is the more formidable of the two, for I think that we shall very shortly get an explanation of yours, while mine may remain for ever a mystery. The question now is, what shall we do with this poor wretch's body? We cannot leave it here to the foxes and the ravens."

"I suggest that we put it in one of the huts until we can communicate with the police."

"Exactly. I have no doubt that you and I could carry it so far. Halloa, Watson, what's this? It's the man himself, by all that's wonderful and audacious! Not a word to show your suspicions—not a word, or my plans crumble to the ground."

A figure was approaching us over the moor, and I saw the dull red glow of a cigar. The moon shone upon him, and I could distinguish the dapper shape and jaunty walk of the naturalist. He stopped when he saw us, and then came on again.

"Why, Dr. Watson, that's not you, is it? You are the last man that I should have expected to see out on the moor at this time of night. But, dear me, what's this? Somebody hurt? Not—don't tell me that it is our friend Sir Henry!" He hurried past me and stooped over the dead man. I heard a sharp intake of his breath and the cigar fell from his fingers.

"Who—who's this?" he stammered.

"It is Selden, the man who escaped from Princetown."

Stapleton turned a ghastly face upon us, but by a supreme effort he had overcome his amazement and his disappointment. He looked sharply from Holmes to me.

"Dear me! What a very shocking affair! How did he die?"

"He appears to have broken his neck by falling over these rocks. My friend and I were strolling on the moor when we heard a cry."

"I heard a cry also. That was what brought me out. I was uneasy about Sir Henry."

"Why about Sir Henry in particular?" I could not help asking.

"Because I had suggested that he should come over. When he did not come I was surprised, and I naturally became alarmed for his safety when I heard cries upon the moor. By the way"—his eyes darted again from my face to Holmes's—"did you hear anything else besides a cry?"

"No," said Holmes; "did you?"

"No."

"What do you mean, then?"

"Oh, you know the stories that the peasants tell about a phantom hound, and so on. It is said to be heard at night upon the moor. I was wondering if there were any evidence of such a sound to-night."

"We heard nothing of the kind," said I.

"And what is your theory of this poor fellow's death?"

"I have no doubt that anxiety and exposure have driven him off his head. He

"'WHO—WHO'S THIS?' HE STAMMERED."

has rushed about the moor in a crazy state and eventually fallen over here and broken his neck."

"That seems the most reasonable theory," said Stapleton, and he gave a sigh which I took to indicate his relief. "What do you think about it, Mr. Sherlock Holmes?"

My friend bowed his compliments.

"You are quick at identification," said he.

"We have been expecting you in these parts since Dr. Watson came down. You are in time to see a tragedy."

"Yes, indeed. I have no doubt that my friend's explanation will cover the facts. I will take an unpleasant remembrance back to London with me to-morrow."

"Oh, you return to-morrow?"

"That is my intention."

"I hope your visit has cast some light

upon those occurrences which have puzzled us?"

Holmes shrugged his shoulders.

"One cannot always have the success for which one hopes. An investigator needs facts, and not legends or rumours. It has not been a satisfactory case."

My friend spoke in his frankest and most unconcerned manner. Stapleton still looked hard at him. Then he turned to me.

"I would suggest carrying this poor fellow to my house, but it would give my sister such a fright that I do not feel justified in doing it. I think that if we put something over his face he will be safe until morning."

And so it was arranged. Resisting Stapleton's offer of hospitality, Holmes and I set off to Baskerville Hall, leaving the naturalist to return alone. Looking back we saw the figure moving slowly away over the broad moor, and behind him that one black smudge on the silvered slope which showed where the man was lying who had come so horribly to his end.

"We're at close grips at last," said Holmes, as we walked together across the moor. "What a nerve the fellow has! How he pulled himself together in the face of what must have been a paralyzing shock when he found that the wrong man had fallen a victim to his plot. I told you in London, Watson, and I tell you now again, that we have never had a foeman more worthy of our steel."

"I am sorry that he has seen you."

"And so was I at first. But there was no getting out of it."

"What effect do you think it will have upon his plans, now that he knows you are here?"

"It may cause him to be more cautious, or it may drive him to desperate measures at once. Like most clever criminals, he may be too confident in his own cleverness and imagine that he has completely deceived us."

"Why should we not arrest him at once?"

"My dear Watson, you were born to be a man of action. Your instinct is always to do something energetic. But supposing, for argument's sake, that we had him arrested to-night, what on earth the better off should we be for that? We could prove nothing against him. There's the devilish cunning of it! If he were acting through a human agent we could get some evidence, but if we were to drag this great dog to the light of day it would not help us in putting a rope round the neck of its master."

"Surely we have a case."

"Not a shadow of one—only surmise and conjecture. We should be laughed out of court if we came with such a story and such evidence."

"There is Sir Charles's death."

"Found dead without a mark upon him.

You and I know that he died of sheer fright, and we know also what frightened him ; but how are we to get twelve stolid jurymen to know it? What signs are there of a hound? Where are the marks of its fangs? Of course, we know that a hound does not bite a dead body, and that Sir Charles was dead before ever the brute overtook him. But we have to *prove* all this, and we are not in a position to do it."

"Well, then, to-night?"

"We are not much better off to-night. Again, there was no direct connection between the hound and the man's death. We never saw the hound. We heard it : but we could not prove that it was running upon this man's trail. There is a complete absence of motive. No, my dear fellow ; we must reconcile ourselves to the fact that we have no case at present, and that it is worth our while to run any risk in order to establish one."

"And how do you propose to do so?"

"I have great hopes of what Mrs. Laura Lyons may do for us when the position of affairs is made clear to her. And I have my own plan as well. Sufficient for to-morrow is the evil thereof ; but I hope before the day is past to have the upper hand at last."

I could draw nothing farther from him, and he walked, lost in thought, as far as the Baskerville gates.

"Are you coming up?"

"Yes ; I see no reason for further concealment. But one last word, Watson. Say nothing of the hound to Sir Henry. Let him think that Selden's death was as Stapleton would have us believe. He will have a better nerve for the ordeal which he will have to undergo to-morrow, when he is engaged, if I remember your report aright, to dine with these people."

"And so am I."

"Then you must excuse yourself and he must go alone. That will be easily arranged. And now, if we are too late for dinner, I think that we are both ready for our suppers."

*(To be continued.)*

"THE HOUND OF THE BASKERVILLES."

# THE STRAND MAGAZINE.

Vol. xxiii.  MARCH, 1902.  No. 135.

# The Hound of the Baskervilles.

## ANOTHER ADVENTURE OF
# SHERLOCK HOLMES.

### By CONAN DOYLE.

## CHAPTER XIII.

### FIXING THE NETS.

IR HENRY was more pleased than surprised to see Sherlock Holmes, for he had for some days been expecting that recent events would bring him down from London. He did raise his eyebrows, however, when he found that my friend had neither any luggage nor any explanations for its absence. Between us we soon supplied his wants, and then over a belated supper we explained to the Baronet as much of our experience as it seemed desirable that he should know. But first I had the unpleasant duty of breaking the news of Selden's death to Barrymore and his wife. To him it may have been an unmitigated relief, but she wept bitterly in her apron. To all the world he was the man of violence, half animal and half demon; but to her he always remained the little wilful boy of her own girlhood, the child who had clung to her hand. Evil indeed is the man who has not one woman to mourn him.

"I've been moping in the house all day since Watson went off in the morning," said the Baronet. "I guess I should have some credit, for I have kept my promise. If I hadn't sworn not to go about alone I might have had a more lively evening, for I had a message from Stapleton asking me over there."

"I have no doubt that you would have had a more lively evening," said Holmes, drily. "By the way, I don't suppose you appreciate that we have been mourning over you as having broken your neck?"

Sir Henry opened his eyes. "How was that?"

"This poor wretch was dressed in your clothes. I fear your servant who gave them to him may get into trouble with the police."

"That is unlikely. There was no mark on any of them, so far as I know."

"That's lucky for him—in fact, it's lucky for all of you, since you are all on the wrong side of the law in this matter. I am not sure that as a conscientious detective my first duty is not to arrest the whole household. Watson's reports are most incriminating documents."

"But how about the case?" asked the Baronet. "Have you made anything out of the tangle? I don't know that Watson and I are much the wiser since we came down."

"I think that I shall be in a position to make the situation rather more clear to you before long. It has been an exceedingly difficult and most complicated business. There are several points upon which we still want light—but it is coming, all the same."

"We've had one experience, as Watson has no doubt told you. We heard the hound on the moor, so I can swear that it is not all empty superstition. I had something to do with dogs when I was out West, and I know one when I hear one. If you can muzzle that one and put him on a chain I'll be ready to swear you are the greatest detective of all time."

"I think I will muzzle him and chain him all right if you will give me your help."

"Whatever you tell me to do I will do."

"Very good; and I will ask you also to do it blindly, without always asking the reason."

"Just as you like."

"If you will do this I think the chances are that our little problem will soon be solved. I have no doubt——"

He stopped suddenly and stared fixedly up over my head into the air. The lamp beat upon his face, and so intent was it and so still that it might have been that of a clear-cut classical statue, a personification of alertness and expectation.

"What is it?" we both cried.

I could see as he looked down that he was repressing some internal emotion. His features were still composed, but his eyes shone with amused exultation.

"Excuse the admiration of a connoisseur," said he, as he waved his hand towards the line of portraits which covered the opposite wall. "Watson won't allow that I know anything of art, but that is mere jealousy, because our views upon the subject differ. Now, these are a really very fine series of portraits."

"Well, I'm glad to hear you say so," said Sir Henry, glancing with some surprise at my friend. "I don't pretend to know much about these things, and I'd be a better judge of a horse or a steer than of a picture. I didn't know that you found time for such things."

"I know what is good when I see it, and I see it now. That's a Kneller, I'll swear, that lady in the blue silk over yonder, and the stout gentleman with the wig ought to be a Reynolds. They are all family portraits, I presume?"

"HE STOPPED SUDDENLY AND STARED FIXEDLY
UP OVER MY HEAD INTO THE AIR."

"Every one."

"Do you know the names?"

"Barrymore has been coaching me in them, and I think I can say my lessons fairly well."

"Who is the gentleman with the telescope?"

"That is Rear-Admiral Baskerville, who served under Rodney in the West Indies. The man with the blue coat and the roll of paper is Sir William Baskerville, who was Chairman of Committees of the House of Commons under Pitt."

"And this Cavalier opposite to me—the one with the black velvet and the lace?"

"Ah, you have a right to know about him.

That is the cause of all the mischief, the wicked Hugo, who started the Hound of the Baskervilles. We're not likely to forget him."

I gazed with interest and some surprise upon the portrait.

"Dear me!" said Holmes, "he seems a quiet, meek-mannered man enough, but I daresay that there was a lurking devil in his eyes. I had pictured him as a more robust and ruffianly person."

"There's no doubt about the authenticity, for the name and the date, 1647, are on the back of the canvas."

Holmes said little more, but the picture of the old roysterer seemed to have a fascination for him, and his eyes were continually fixed upon it during supper. It was not until later, when Sir Henry had gone to his room, that I was able to follow the trend of his thoughts. He led me back into the banqueting-hall, his bedroom candle in his hand, and he held it up against the time-stained portrait on the wall.

"Do you see anything there?"

I looked at the broad plumed hat, the curling love-locks, the white lace collar, and the straight, severe face which was framed between them. It was not a brutal countenance, but it was prim, hard, and stern, with a firm-set, thin-lipped mouth, and a coldly intolerant eye.

"Is it like anyone you know?"

"There is something of Sir Henry about the jaw."

"Just a suggestion, perhaps. But wait an instant!" He stood upon a chair, and holding up the light in his left hand he curved his right arm over the broad hat and round the long ringlets.

"Good heavens!" I cried, in amazement.

The face of Stapleton had sprung out of the canvas.

"Ha, you see it now. My eyes have been trained to examine faces and not their trim-

"With designs upon the succession."

"Exactly. This chance of the picture has supplied us with one of our most obvious missing links. We have him, Watson, we have him, and I dare swear that before to-morrow night he will be fluttering in our net as helpless as one of his own butterflies. A

"'GOOD HEAVENS!' I CRIED, IN AMAZEMENT."

mings. It is the first quality of a criminal investigator that he should see through a disguise."

"But this is marvellous. It might be his portrait."

"Yes, it is an interesting instance of a throw-back, which appears to be both physical and spiritual. A study of family portraits is enough to convert a man to the doctrine of reincarnation. The fellow is a Baskerville—that is evident."

pin, a cork, and a card, and we add him to the Baker Street collection!" He burst into one of his rare fits of laughter as he turned away from the picture. I have not heard him laugh often, and it has always boded ill to somebody.

I was up betimes in the morning, but Holmes was afoot earlier still, for I saw him as I dressed coming up the drive.

"Yes, we should have a full day to-day," he remarked, and he rubbed his hands with the joy of action. "The nets are all in place, and the drag is about to begin. We'll know before the day is out whether we have caught our big, lean-jawed pike, or whether he has got through the meshes."

"Have you been on the moor already?"

"I have sent a report from Grimpen to Princetown as to the death of Selden. I think I can promise that none of you will be troubled in the matter. And I have also communicated with my faithful Cartwright, who would certainly have pined away at the door of my hut as a dog does at his master's grave if I had not set his mind at rest about my safety."

"What is the next move?"

"To see Sir Henry. Ah, here he is!"

"Good morning, Holmes," said the Baronet. "You look like a general who is planning a battle with his chief of the staff."

"That is the exact situation. Watson was asking for orders."

"And so do I."

"Very good. You are engaged, as I understand, to dine with our friends the Stapletons to-night."

"I hope that you will come also. They are very hospitable people, and I am sure that they would be very glad to see you."

"I fear that Watson and I must go to London."

"To London?"

"Yes, I think that we should be more useful there at the present juncture."

The Baronet's face perceptibly lengthened.

"I hoped that you were going to see me through this business. The Hall and the moor are not very pleasant places when one is alone."

"My dear fellow, you must trust me implicitly and do exactly what I tell you. You can tell your friends that we should have been happy to have come with you, but that urgent business required us to be in town. We hope very soon to return to Devonshire. Will you remember to give them that message?"

"If you insist upon it."

"There is no alternative, I assure you."

I saw by the Baronet's clouded brow that he was deeply hurt by what he regarded as our desertion.

"When do you desire to go?" he asked, coldly.

"Immediately after breakfast. We will drive in to Coombe Tracey, but Watson will leave his things as a pledge that he will come back to you. Watson, you will send a note

to Stapleton to tell him that you regret that you cannot come."

"I have a good mind to go to London with you," said the Baronet. "Why should I stay here alone?"

"Because it is your post of duty. Because you gave me your word that you would do as you were told, and I tell you to stay."

"All right, then, I'll stay."

"One more direction! I wish you to drive to Merripit House. Send back your trap, however, and let them know that you intend to walk home."

"To walk across the moor?"

"Yes."

"But that is the very thing which you have so often cautioned me not to do."

"This time you may do it with safety. If I had not every confidence in your nerve and courage I would not suggest it, but it is essential that you should do it."

"Then I will do it."

"And as you value your life do not go across the moor in any direction save along the straight path which leads from Merripit House to the Grimpen Road, and is your natural way home."

"I will do just what you say."

"Very good. I should be glad to get away as soon after breakfast as possible, so as to reach London in the afternoon."

I was much astounded by this programme, though I remembered that Holmes had said to Stapleton on the night before that his visit would terminate next day. It had not crossed my mind, however, that he would wish me to go with him, nor could I understand how we could both be absent at a moment which he himself declared to be critical. There was nothing for it, however, but implicit obedience; so we bade good-bye to our rueful friend, and a couple of hours afterwards we were at the station of Coombe Tracey and had dispatched the trap upon its return journey. A small boy was waiting upon the platform.

"Any orders, sir?"

"You will take this train to town, Cartwright. The moment you arrive you will send a wire to Sir Henry Baskerville, in my name, to say that if he finds the pocket-book which I have dropped he is to send it by registered post to Baker Street."

"Yes, sir."

"And ask at the station office if there is a message for me."

The boy returned with a telegram, which Holmes handed to me. It ran: "Wire received. Coming down with unsigned warrant. Arrive five-forty.—LESTRADE."

"That is in answer to mine of this morning. He is the best of the professionals, I think, and we may need his assistance. Now, Watson, I think that we cannot employ our time better than by calling upon your acquaintance, Mrs. Laura Lyons."

His plan of campaign was beginning to be evident. He would use the Baronet in order to convince the Stapletons that we were really gone, while we should actually return at the instant when we were likely to be needed. That telegram from London, if mentioned by Sir Henry to the Stapletons, must remove the last suspicions from their minds. Already I seemed to see our nets drawing closer round that lean-jawed pike.

Mrs. Laura Lyons was in her office, and Sherlock Holmes opened his interview with

you have communicated, and also of what you have withheld in connection with that matter."

"What have I withheld?" she asked, defiantly.

"You have confessed that you asked Sir Charles to be at the gate at ten o'clock. We know that that was the place and hour of his death. You have withheld what the connection is between these events."

"There is no connection."

"In that case the coincidence must indeed be an extraordinary one. But I think that we shall succeed in establishing a connection after all. I wish to be perfectly frank with you, Mrs. Lyons. We regard this case as one of murder, and the evidence may implicate not only your friend Mr. Stapleton, but his wife as well."

The lady sprang from her chair.

" THE LADY SPRANG FROM HER CHAIR."

a frankness and directness which considerably amazed her.

"I am investigating the circumstances which attended the death of the late Sir Charles Baskerville," said he. "My friend here, Dr. Watson, has informed me of what

"His wife!" she cried.

"The fact is no longer a secret. The person who has passed for his sister is really his wife."

Mrs. Lyons had resumed her seat. Her hands were grasping the arms of her chair, and I saw that the pink nails had turned white with the pressure of her grip.

" His wife ! " she said, again. " His wife ! He was not a married man."

Sherlock Holmes shrugged his shoulders.

" Prove it to me ! Prove it to me ! And if you can do so——! " The fierce flash of her eyes said more than any words.

" I have come prepared to do so," said Holmes, drawing several papers from his pocket. " Here is a photograph of the couple taken in York four years ago. It is indorsed ' Mr. and Mrs. Vandeleur,' but you will have no difficulty in recognising him, and her also, if you know her by sight. Here are three written descriptions by trustworthy witnesses of Mr. and Mrs. Vandeleur, who at that time kept St. Oliver's private school. Read them, and see if you can doubt the identity of these people."

She glanced at them, and then looked up at us with the set, rigid face of a desperate woman.

" Mr. Holmes," she said, " this man had offered me marriage on condition that I could get a divorce from my husband. He has lied to me, the villain, in every conceivable way. Not one word of truth has he ever told me. And why—why ? I imagined that all was for my own sake. But now I see that I was never anything but a tool in his hands. Why should I preserve faith with him who never kept any with me ? Why should I try to shield him from the consequences of his own wicked acts ? Ask me what you like, and there is nothing which I shall hold back. One thing I swear to you, and that is, that when I wrote the letter I never dreamed of any harm to the old gentleman, who had been my kindest friend."

" I entirely believe you, madam," said Sherlock Holmes. " The recital of these events must be very painful to you, and perhaps it will make it easier if I tell you what occurred, and you can check me if I make any material mistake. The sending of this letter was suggested to you by Stapleton ? "

" He dictated it."

" I presume that the reason he gave was that you would receive help from Sir Charles for the legal expenses connected with your divorce ? "

" Exactly."

" And then after you had sent the letter he dissuaded you from keeping the appointment ? "

" He told me that it would hurt his self-respect that any other man should find the money for such an object, and that though he was a poor man himself he would devote his last penny to removing the obstacles which divided us."

" He appears to be a very consistent character. And then you heard nothing until you read the reports of the death in the paper ? "

" No."

" And he made you swear to say nothing about your appointment with Sir Charles ? "

" He did. He said that the death was a very mysterious one, and that I should certainly be suspected if the facts came out. He frightened me into remaining silent."

" Quite so. But you had your suspicions ? "

She hesitated and looked down.

" I knew him," she said. " But if he had kept faith with me I should always have done so with him."

" I think that on the whole you have had a fortunate escape," said Sherlock Holmes. " You have had him in your power and he knew it, and yet you are alive. You have been walking for some months very near to the edge of a precipice. We must wish you good morning now, Mrs. Lyons, and it is probable that you will very shortly hear from us again."

" Our case becomes rounded off, and difficulty after difficulty thins away in front of us," said Holmes, as we stood waiting for the arrival of the express from town. " I shall soon be in the position of being able to put into a single connected narrative one of the most singular and sensational crimes of modern times. Students of criminology will remember the analogous incidents in Grodno, in Little Russia, in the year '66, and of course there are the Anderson murders in North Carolina, but this case possesses some features which are entirely its own. Even now we have no clear case against this very wily man. But I shall be very much surprised if it is not clear enough before we go to bed this night."

The London express came roaring into the station, and a small, wiry bulldog of a man had sprung from a first-class carriage. We all three shook hands, and I saw at once from the reverential way in which Lestrade gazed at my companion that he had learned a good deal since the days when they had first worked together. I could well remember the scorn which the theories of the reasoner used then to excite in the practical man.

" Anything good ? " he asked.

"The biggest thing for years," said Holmes. "We have two hours before we need think of starting. I think we might employ it in getting some dinner, and then, professional caution, which urged him never to take any chances. The result, however, was very trying for those who were acting as

" WE ALL THREE SHOOK HANDS."

employ it in getting some dinner, and then, Lestrade, we will take the London fog out of your throat by giving you a breath of the pure night air of Dartmoor. Never been there? Ah, well, I don't suppose you will forget your first visit."

## CHAPTER XIV.

### THE HOUND OF THE BASKERVILLES.

ONE of Sherlock Holmes's defects—if, indeed, one may call it a defect — was that he was exceedingly loth to communicate his full plans to any other person until the instant of their fulfilment. Partly it came no doubt from his own masterful nature, which loved to dominate and surprise those who were around him. Partly also from his

his agents and assistants. I had often suffered under it, but never more so than during that long drive in the darkness. The great ordeal was in front of us; at last we were about to make our final effort, and yet Holmes had said nothing, and I could only surmise what his course of action would be. My nerves thrilled with anticipation when at last the cold wind upon our faces and the dark, void spaces on either side of the narrow road told me that we were back upon the moor once again. Every stride of the horses and every turn of the wheels was taking us nearer to our supreme adventure.

Our conversation was hampered by the presence of the driver of the hired wagonette, so that we were forced to talk of trivial matters when our nerves were tense with emotion and anticipation. It was a relief to me, after that unnatural restraint, when we at last passed Frankland's house and knew that we were drawing near to the Hall and to the scene of action. We did not drive up to the door, but got down near the gate of the avenue. The wagonette was paid off and ordered to return to Temple Coombe forthwith, while we started to walk to Merripit House.

"Are you armed, Lestrade?"

The little detective smiled.

"As long as I have my trousers I have a

"I COULD LOOK STRAIGHT THROUGH THE
UNCURTAINED WINDOW."

hip-pocket, and as long as I have my hip-pocket I have something in it."

"Good! My friend and I are also ready for emergencies."

"You're mighty close about this affair, Mr. Holmes. What's the game now?"

"A waiting game."

"My word, it does not seem a very cheerful place," said the detective, with a shiver, glancing round him at the gloomy slopes of the hill and at the huge lake of fog which lay over the Grimpen Mire. "I see the lights of a house ahead of us."

"That is Merripit House and the end of our journey. I must request you to walk on tiptoe and not to talk above a whisper."

We moved cautiously along the track as if we were bound for the house, but Holmes halted us when we were about two hundred yards from it.

"This will do," said he. "These rocks upon the right make an admirable screen."

"We are to wait here?"

"Yes, we shall make our little ambush here. Get into this hollow, Lestrade. You have been inside the house, have you not, Watson? Can you tell the position of the rooms? What are those latticed windows at this end?"

"I think they are the kitchen windows."

"And the one beyond, which shines so brightly?"

"That is certainly the dining-room."

"The blinds are up. You know the lie of the land best. Creep forward quietly and see what they are doing—but for Heaven's sake don't let them know that they are watched!"

I tip-toed down the path and stooped behind the low wall which surrounded the stunted orchard. Creeping in its shadow I reached a point whence I could look straight through the uncurtained window.

There were only two men in the room, Sir Henry and Stapleton. They sat with their profiles towards me on either side of the round table. Both of them were smoking cigars, and coffee and wine were in front of them. Stapleton was talking with animation, but the Baronet looked pale and distrait. Perhaps the thought of that lonely walk across the ill-omened moor was weighing heavily upon his mind.

As I watched them Stapleton rose and left the room, while Sir Henry filled his glass again and leaned back in his chair, puffing at his cigar. I heard the creak of a door and the crisp sound of boots upon gravel. The steps passed along the path on the other side of the wall under which I crouched. Looking over, I saw the naturalist pause at the door of an out-house in the corner of the orchard. A key turned in a lock, and as he passed in there was a curious scuffling noise from within. He was only a minute or so inside, and then I heard the key turn once more and he passed me and re-entered the house. I saw him rejoin his guest, and I crept quietly back to where my companions were waiting to tell them what I had seen.

"You say, Watson, that the lady is not there?" Holmes asked, when I had finished my report.

"No."

"Where can she be, then, since there is no light in any other room except the kitchen?"

"I cannot think where she is."

I have said that over the great Grimpen Mire there hung a dense, white fog. It was drifting slowly in our direction and banked itself up like a wall on that side of us, low, but thick and well defined. The moon shone on it, and it looked like a great shimmering icefield, with the heads of the distant tors as rocks borne upon its surface. Holmes's face was turned towards it, and he muttered impatiently as he watched its sluggish drift.

"It's moving towards us, Watson."

"Is that serious?"

"Very serious, indeed — the one thing upon earth which could have disarranged my plans. He can't be very long, now. It is already ten o'clock. Our success and even his life may depend upon his coming out before the fog is over the path."

The night was clear and fine above us. The stars shone cold and bright, while a half-moon bathed the whole scene in a soft, uncertain light. Before us lay the dark bulk of the house, its serrated roof and bristling chimneys hard outlined against the silver-spangled sky. Broad bars of golden light from the lower windows stretched across the orchard and the moor. One of them was suddenly shut off. The servants had left the kitchen. There only remained the lamp in the dining-room where the two men, the murderous host and the unconscious guest, still chatted over their cigars.

Every minute that white woolly plain which covered one half of the moor was drifting closer and closer to the house. Already the first thin wisps of it were curling across the golden square of the lighted window. The farther wall of the orchard was already invisible, and the trees were standing out of a swirl of white vapour. As we watched it the fog-wreaths came crawling round both corners of the house and rolled slowly into one dense bank, on which the upper floor and the roof floated like a strange ship upon a shadowy sea. Holmes struck his hand passionately upon the rock in front of us, and stamped his feet in his impatience.

"If he isn't out in a quarter of an hour the path will be covered. In half an hour we won't be able to see our hands in front of us."

"Shall we move farther back upon higher ground?"

"Yes, I think it would be as well."

So as the fog-bank flowed onwards we fell back before it until we were half a mile from the house, and still that dense white sea, with the moon silvering its upper edge, swept slowly and inexorably on.

"We are going too far," said Holmes. "We dare not take the chance of his being overtaken before he can reach us. At all costs we must hold our ground where we are." He dropped on his knees and clapped his ear to the ground. "Thank Heaven, I think that I hear him coming."

A sound of quick steps broke the silence of the moor. Crouching among the stones we stared intently at the silver-tipped bank in front of us. The steps grew louder, and through the fog, as through a curtain, there stepped the man whom we were awaiting. He looked round him in surprise as he emerged into the clear, star-lit night. Then he came swiftly along the path, passed close to where we lay, and went on up the long slope behind us. As he walked he glanced continually over either shoulder, like a man who is ill at ease.

"Hist!" cried Holmes, and I heard the sharp click of a cocking pistol. "Look out! It's coming!"

There was a thin, crisp, continuous patter from somewhere in the heart of that crawling bank. The cloud was within fifty yards of where we lay, and we glared at it, all three, uncertain what horror was about to break from the heart of it. I was at Holmes's elbow, and I glanced for an instant at his face. It was pale and exultant, his eyes shining brightly in the moonlight. But suddenly they started forward in a rigid, fixed stare, and his lips parted in amazement. At the same instant Lestrade gave a yell of terror and threw himself face downwards upon the ground. I sprang to my feet, my have ever seen. Fire burst from its open mouth, its eyes glowed with a smouldering glare, its muzzle and hackles and dewlap were outlined in flickering flame. Never in the

" HE LOOKED ROUND HIM IN SURPRISE."

inert hand grasping my pistol, my mind paralyzed by the dreadful shape which had sprung out upon us from the shadows of the fog. A hound it was, an enormous coal-black hound, but not such a hound as mortal eyes delirious dream of a disordered brain could anything more savage, more appalling, more hellish be conceived than that dark form and savage face which broke upon us out of the wall of fog.

*(To be concluded.)*

"HOLMES EMPTIED FIVE BARRELS OF HIS REVOLVER INTO THE
CREATURE'S FLANK."

# THE STRAND MAGAZINE.

Vol. xxiii.                    APRIL, 1902.                    No. 136.

# The Hound of the Baskervilles.
## ANOTHER ADVENTURE OF
# SHERLOCK HOLMES.
### BY CONAN DOYLE.

### CHAPTER XIV. (*continued*).

 ITH long bounds the huge black creature was leaping down the track, following hard upon the footsteps of our friend. So paralyzed were we by the apparition that we allowed him to pass before we had recovered our nerve. Then Holmes and I both fired together, and the creature gave a hideous howl, which showed that one at least had hit him. He did not pause, however, but bounded onwards. Far away on the path we saw Sir Henry looking back, his face white in the moonlight, his hands raised in horror, glaring helplessly at the frightful thing which was hunting him down.

But that cry of pain from the hound had blown all our fears to the winds. If he was vulnerable he was mortal, and if we could wound him we could kill him. Never have I seen a man run as Holmes ran that night. I am reckoned fleet of foot, but he outpaced me as much as I outpaced the little professional. In front of us as we flew up the track we heard scream after scream from Sir Henry and the deep roar of the hound. I was in time to see the beast spring upon its victim, hurl him to the ground, and worry at his throat. But the next instant Holmes had emptied five barrels of his revolver into the creature's flank. With a last howl of agony and a vicious snap in the air it rolled upon its back, four feet pawing furiously, and then fell limp upon its side. I stooped, panting, and pressed my pistol to the dreadful, shimmering head, but it was useless to pull the trigger. The giant hound was dead.

Sir Henry lay insensible where he had fallen. We tore away his collar, and Holmes breathed a prayer of gratitude when we saw that there was no sign of a wound and that the rescue had been in time. Already our friend's eyelids shivered and he made a feeble effort to move. Lestrade thrust his brandy-flask between the Baronet's teeth, and two frightened eyes were looking up at us.

"My God!" he whispered. "What was it? What, in Heaven's name, was it?"

"It's dead, whatever it is," said Holmes. "We've laid the family ghost once and for ever."

In mere size and strength it was a terrible creature which was lying stretched before us. It was not a pure bloodhound and it was not a pure mastiff; but it appeared to be a combination of the two—gaunt, savage, and as large as a small lioness. Even now, in the stillness of death, the huge jaws seemed to be dripping with a bluish flame and the small, deep-set, cruel eyes were ringed with fire. I placed my hand upon the glowing muzzle, and as I held them up my own fingers smouldered and gleamed in the darkness.

"Phosphorus," I said.

"A cunning preparation of it," said Holmes, sniffing at the dead animal. "There is no smell which might have interfered with his power of scent. We owe you a deep apology, Sir Henry, for having exposed you to this fright. I was prepared for a hound, but not for such a creature as this. And the fog gave us little time to receive him."

"You have saved my life."

"Having first endangered it. Are you strong enough to stand?"

"Give me another mouthful of that brandy and I shall be ready for anything. So! Now, if you will help me up. What do you propose to do?"

"To leave you here. You are not fit for further adventures to-night. If you will wait, one or other of us will go back with you to the Hall."

He tried to stagger to his feet; but he was still ghastly pale and trembling in every limb. We helped him to a rock, where he sat shivering with his face buried in his hands.

"We must leave you now," said Holmes.

Vol. xxiii.—46.

"'PHOSPHORUS!' I SAID."

the house unexplored. No sign could we see of the man whom we were chasing. On the upper floor, however, one of the bedroom doors was locked.

"There's someone in here," cried Lestrade. "I can hear a movement. Open this door!"

A faint moaning and rustling came from within. Holmes struck the door just over the lock with the flat of his foot and it flew open. Pistol in hand, we all three rushed into the room.

But there was no sign within it of that desperate and defiant villain whom we expected to see. Instead we were faced by an object so strange and so unexpected that we stood for a moment staring at it in amazement.

The room had been fashioned into a small museum, and the walls were lined by a number of glass-topped cases full of that collection of butterflies and moths the formation of which had been the relaxation of this complex and dangerous man. In the centre of this room there was an upright beam,

"The rest of our work must be done, and every moment is of importance. We have our case, and now we only want our man.

"It's a thousand to one against our finding him at the house," he continued, as we retraced our steps swiftly down the path. "Those shots must have told him that the game was up."

"We were some distance off, and this fog may have deadened them."

"He followed the hound to call him off— of that you may be certain. No, no, he's gone by this time! But we'll search the house and make sure."

The front door was open, so we rushed in and hurried from room to room, to the amazement of a doddering old manservant, who met us in the passage. There was no light save in the dining-room, but Holmes caught up the lamp and left no corner of

which had been placed at some period as a support for the old, worm-eaten balk of timber which spanned the roof. To this post a figure was tied, so swathed and muffled in the sheets which had been used to secure it that one could not for the moment tell whether it was that of a man or a woman. One towel passed round the throat and was secured at the back of the pillar. Another covered the lower part of the face, and over it two dark eyes—eyes full of grief and shame and a dreadful questioning—stared back at us. In a minute we had torn off the gag, unswathed the bonds, and Mrs. Stapleton sank upon the floor in front of us. As her beautiful head fell upon her chest I saw the clear red weal of a whiplash across her neck.

"The brute!" cried Holmes. "Here, Lestrade, your brandy-bottle! Put her in the chair ! She has fainted from ill-usage and exhaustion."

She opened her eyes again.

" Is he safe ? " she asked. " Has he escaped ? "

" He cannot escape us, madam."

" No, no, I did not mean my husband. Sir Henry? Is he safe ? "

" Yes."

" And the hound ? "

" It is dead."

She gave a long sigh of satisfaction.

" Thank God ! Thank God ! Oh, this villain ! See how he has treated me ! " She shot her arms out from her sleeves, and we saw with horror that they were all mottled with bruises. " But this is nothing—nothing ! It is my mind and soul that he has tortured and defiled. I could endure it all, ill-usage, solitude, a life of deception, everything, as long as I could still cling to the hope that I had his love, but now I know that in this also I have been his dupe and his tool." She broke into passionate sobbing as she spoke.

" You bear him no good will, madam," said Holmes. " Tell us then where we shall find him. If you have ever aided him in evil, help us now and so atone."

" There is but one place where he can have fled," she answered. " There is an old tin mine on an island in the heart of the Mire. It was there that he kept his hound and there also he had made preparations so that he might have a refuge. That is where he would fly."

The fog-bank lay like white wool against the window. Holmes held the lamp towards it.

" See," said he. " No one could find his way into the Grimpen Mire to-night."

She laughed and clapped her hands. Her eyes and teeth gleamed with fierce merriment.

" He may find his way in, but never out," she cried. " How can he see the guiding wands to-night ? We planted them together, he and I, to mark the pathway through the

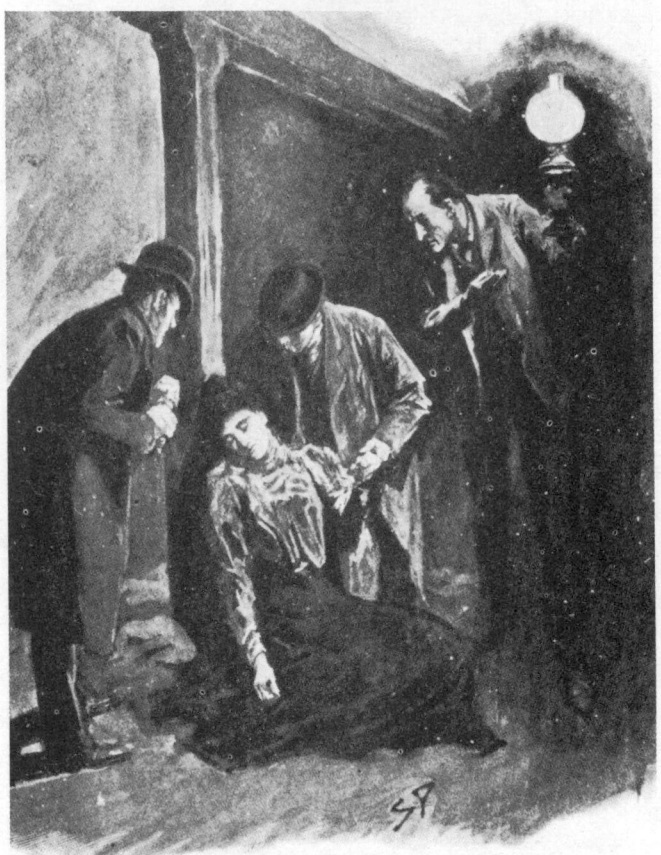

" MRS. STAPLETON SANK UPON THE FLOOR."

Mire. Oh, if I could only have plucked them out to-day. Then indeed you would have had him at your mercy ! "

It was evident to us that all pursuit was in vain until the fog had lifted. Meanwhile we left Lestrade in possession of the house while Holmes and I went back with the Baronet to Baskerville Hall. The story of the Stapletons could no longer be withheld from him, but he took the blow bravely when he learned the truth about the woman whom he had loved. But the shock of the night's adventures had shattered his nerves, and before morning he lay delirious in a high fever, under the care of Dr. Mortimer. The two of them were destined to travel together round the world before Sir Henry had become once more the hale, hearty man that he had been before he became master of that ill-omened estate.

And now I come rapidly to the conclusion of this singular narrative, in which I have tried to make the reader share those dark fears and vague surmises which clouded our lives so long, and ended in so tragic a manner. On the morning after the death of the hound the fog had lifted and we were guided by Mrs. Stapleton to the point where they had found a pathway through the bog. It helped us to realize the horror of this woman's life when we saw the eagerness and joy with which she laid us on her husband's track. We left her standing upon the thin peninsula of firm, peaty soil which tapered out into the widespread bog. From the end of it a small wand planted here and there showed where the path zig-zagged from tuft to tuft of rushes among those green scummed pits and foul quagmires which barred the way to the stranger. Rank reeds and lush, slimy water-plants sent an odour of decay and a heavy miasmatic vapour into our faces, while a false step plunged us more than once thigh-deep into the dark, quivering mire, which shook for yards in soft un-dulations around our feet. Its tenacious grip plucked at our heels as we walked, and when we sank into it it was as if some malignant hand were tugging us down into those obscene depths, so grim and purposeful was the clutch in which it held us. Once only we saw a trace that someone had passed that perilous way before us. From amid a tuft of cotton-grass which bore it up out of the slime some dark thing was projecting. Holmes sank to his waist as he stepped from the path to seize it, and had we not been there to drag him out he could never have set his foot upon firm land again. He held an old black boot in the air. "Meyers, Toronto," was printed on the leather inside.

"It is worth a mud bath," said he. "It is our friend Sir Henry's missing boot."

"Thrown there by Stapleton in his flight."

"Exactly. He retained it in his hand after using it to set the hound upon his track. He fled when he knew the game was up, still clutching it. And he hurled it away at this point of his flight. We know at least that he came so far in safety."

But more than that we were never destined to know, though there was much which we might surmise. There was no chance of finding footsteps in the mire, for the rising mud oozed swiftly in upon them, but as we at last reached firmer ground beyond the morass we all looked eagerly for them. But no slightest sign of them ever met our eyes. If the earth told a true story, then Stapleton never reached that island of refuge towards which he struggled through the fog upon that last night. Somewhere in the heart of the great Grimpen Mire, down in the foul slime of the huge morass which had sucked him in, this cold and cruel-hearted man is for ever buried.

Many traces we found of him in the bog-girt island where he had hid his savage ally. A huge driving-wheel and a shaft half-filled with rubbish showed the position of an abandoned mine.

"HE HELD AN OLD BLACK BOOT IN THE AIR."

Beside it were the crumbling remains of the cottages of the miners, driven away no doubt by the foul reek of the surrounding swamp. In one of these a staple and chain with a quantity of gnawed bones showed where the animal had been confined. A skeleton with a tangle of brown hair adhering to it lay among the *débris.*

"A dog!" said Holmes. "By Jove, a curly-haired spaniel. Poor Mortimer will never see his pet again. Well, I do not know that this place contains any secret which we have not already fathomed. He could hide his hound, but he could not hush its voice, and hence came those cries which even in daylight were not pleasant to hear. On an emergency he could keep the hound in the out-house at Merripit, but it was always a risk, and it was only on the supreme day, which he regarded as the end of all his efforts, that he dared to do it. This paste in the tin is no doubt the luminous mixture with which the creature was daubed. It was suggested, of course, by the story of the family hell-hound, and by the desire to frighten old Sir Charles to death. No wonder the poor wretch of a convict ran and screamed, even as our friend did, and as we ourselves might have done, when he saw such a creature bounding through the darkness of the moor upon his track. It was a cunning device, for, apart from the chance of driving your victim to his death, what peasant would venture to inquire too closely into such a creature should he get sight of it, as many have done, upon the moor? I said it in London, Watson, and I say it again now, that never yet have we helped to hunt down a more dangerous man than he who is lying yonder"—he swept his long arm towards the huge mottled expanse of green-splotched bog which stretched away until it merged into the russet slopes of the moor.

"WHERE THE ANIMAL HAD BEEN CONFINED."

## CHAPTER XV.

### A RETROSPECTION.

It was the end of November, and Holmes and I sat, upon a raw and foggy night, on either side of a blazing fire in our sitting-room in Baker Street. My friend was in excellent spirits over the success which had attended a succession of difficult and important cases, so that I was able to induce him to discuss the details of the Baskerville mystery. I had waited patiently for the opportunity, for I was aware that he would never permit cases to overlap, and that his clear and logical mind would not be drawn from its present work to dwell upon memories of the past. Sir Henry and Dr. Mortimer were, however, in London, on their way to that long voyage which had been recommended for the restoration of his shattered nerves. They had called upon us that very afternoon, so that it was natural that the subject should come up for discussion.

"The whole course of events," said Holmes, "from the point of view of the man who called himself Stapleton was simple and direct, although to us, who had no means in the beginning of knowing the motives of his actions and could only learn part of the facts, it all appeared exceedingly complex. I have had the advantage of two conversations with Mrs. Stapleton, and the case has now been so entirely cleared up that I am not aware that there is anything which has remained a secret to us. You will find a few notes upon the matter under the heading B in my indexed list of cases."

"Perhaps you would kindly give me a sketch of the course of events from memory."

"Certainly, though I cannot guarantee that I carry all the facts in my mind. Intense mental concentration has a curious way of blotting out what has passed. So far as the case of the Hound goes, however, I will give you the course of events as nearly as I can, and you will suggest anything which I may have forgotten.

"A RETROSPECTION."

"My inquiries show beyond all question that the family portrait did not lie, and that this fellow was indeed a Baskerville. He was a son of that Rodger Baskerville, the younger brother of Sir Charles, who fled with a sinister reputation to South America, where he was said to have died unmarried. He did, as a matter of fact, marry, and had one child, this fellow, whose real name is the same as his father. He married Beryl Garçia, one of the beauties of Costa Rica, and, having purloined a considerable sum of public money, he changed his name to Vandeleur and fled to England, where he established a school in the east of Yorkshire. His reason for attempting this special line of business was that he had struck up an acquaintance with a consumptive tutor upon the voyage home, and that he had used this man's ability to make the undertaking a success. Fraser, the tutor, died, however, and the school which had begun well sank from disrepute into infamy. The Vandeleurs found it convenient to change their name to Stapleton, and he brought the remains of his fortune, his schemes for the future, and his taste for entomology to the south of England. I learn at the British Museum that he was a recognised authority upon the subject, and that the name of Vandeleur has been permanently attached to a certain moth which he had, in his Yorkshire days, been the first to describe.

"We now come to that portion of his life which has proved to be of such intense interest to us. The fellow had evidently made inquiry, and found that only two lives intervened between him and a valuable estate. When he went to Devonshire his plans were, I believe, exceedingly hazy, but that he meant mischief from the first is evident from the way in which he took his wife with him in the character of his sister. The idea of using her as a decoy was clearly already in his mind, though he may not have been certain how the details of his plot were to be arranged. He meant in the end to have the estate, and he was ready to use any tool or run any risk for that end.   His first act was to establish himself as near to his ancestral home as he could, and his second was to cultivate a friendship with Sir Charles Baskerville and with the neighbours.

"The Baronet himself told him about the family hound, and so prepared the way for his own death.   Stapleton, as I will continue to call him, knew that the old man's heart was weak and that a shock would kill him. So much he had learned from Dr. Mortimer. He had heard also that Sir Charles was superstitious and had taken this grim legend very seriously.   His ingenious mind instantly suggested a way by which the Baronet could be done to death, and yet it would be hardly possible to bring home the guilt to the real murderer.

"Having conceived the idea he proceeded to carry it out with considerable finesse.   An ordinary schemer would have been content to work with a savage hound.   The use of artificial means to make the creature diabolical was a flash of genius upon his part.   The dog he bought in London from Ross and Mangles, the dealers in Fulham Road.   It was the strongest and most savage in their possession.   He brought it down by the North Devon line and walked a great distance over the moor so as to get it home without exciting any remarks.   He had already on his insect hunts learned to penetrate the Grimpen Mire, and so had found a safe hiding-place for the creature.   Here he kennelled it and waited his chance.

"But it was some time coming.   The old gentleman could not be decoyed outside of his grounds at night.   Several times Stapleton lurked about with his hound, but without avail.   It was during these fruitless quests that he, or rather his ally, was seen by peasants, and that the legend of the demon dog received a new confirmation.   He had hoped that his wife might lure Sir Charles to his ruin, but here she proved unexpectedly independent.   She would not endeavour to entangle the old gentleman in a sentimental attachment which might deliver him over to his enemy.   Threats and even, I am sorry to say, blows refused to move her.   She would have nothing to do with it, and for a time Stapleton was at a deadlock.

"He found a way out of his difficulties through the chance that Sir Charles, who had conceived a friendship for him, made him the minister of his charity in the case of this unfortunate woman, Mrs. Laura Lyons. By representing himself as a single man he acquired complete influence over her, and

he gave her to understand that in the event of her obtaining a divorce from her husband he would marry her.   His plans were suddenly brought to a head by his knowledge that Sir Charles was about to leave the Hall on the advice of Dr. Mortimer, with whose opinion he himself pretended to coincide.   He must act at once, or his victim might get beyond his power.   He therefore put pressure upon Mrs. Lyons to write this letter, imploring the old man to give her an interview on the evening before his departure for London. He then, by a specious argument, prevented her from going, and so had the chance for which he had waited.

"Driving back in the evening from Coombe Tracey he was in time to get his hound, to treat it with his infernal paint, and to bring the beast round to the gate at which he had reason to expect that he would find the old gentleman waiting.   The dog, incited by its master, sprang over the wicket-gate and pursued the unfortunate Baronet, who fled screaming down the Yew Alley.   In that gloomy tunnel it must indeed have been a dreadful sight to see that huge black creature, with its flaming jaws and blazing eyes, bounding after its victim.   He fell dead at the end of the alley from heart disease and terror.   The hound had kept upon the grassy border while the Baronet had run down the path, so that no track but the man's was visible.   On seeing him lying still the creature had probably approached to sniff at him, but finding him dead had turned away again.   It was then that it left the print which was actually observed by Dr. Mortimer. The hound was called off and hurried away to its lair in the Grimpen Mire, and a mystery was left which puzzled the authorities, alarmed the countryside, and finally brought the case within the scope of our observation.

"So much for the death of Sir Charles Baskerville.   You perceive the devilish cunning of it, for really it would be almost impossible to make a case against the real murderer.   His only accomplice was one who could never give him away, and the grotesque, inconceivable nature of the device only served to make it more effective.   Both of the women concerned in the case, Mrs. Stapleton and Mrs. Laura Lyons, were left with a strong suspicion against Stapleton. Mrs. Stapleton knew that he had designs upon the old man, and also of the existence of the hound.   Mrs. Lyons knew neither of these things, but had been impressed by the death occurring at the time of an uncancelled appointment which was only known to him. However, both of them were under his influence, and he had nothing to fear from them. The first half of his task was successfully accomplished, but the more difficult still remained.

"It is possible that Stapleton did not know of the existence of an heir in Canada. In any case he would very soon learn it from his friend Dr. Mortimer, and he was told by the latter all details about the arrival of Henry Baskerville. Stapleton's first idea was that this young stranger from Canada might possibly be done to death in London without coming down to Devonshire at all. He distrusted his wife ever since she had refused to help him in laying a trap for the old man, and he dared not leave her long out of his sight for fear he should lose his influence over her. It was for this reason that he took her to London with him. They lodged, I find, at the Mexborough Private Hotel, in Craven Street, which was actually one of those called upon by my agent in search of evidence. Here he kept his wife imprisoned in her room while he, disguised in a beard, followed Dr. Mortimer to Baker Street and afterwards to the station and to the Northumberland Hotel. His wife had some inkling of his plans; but she had such a fear of her husband — a fear founded upon brutal ill-treatment—that she dare not write to warn the man whom she knew to be in danger. If the letter should fall into Stapleton's hands her own life would not be safe. Eventually, as we know, she adopted the expedient of cutting out the words which would form the message, and addressing the letter in a disguised hand. It reached the Baronet, and gave him the first warning of his danger.

"It was very essential for Stapleton to get some article of Sir Henry's attire so that, in case he was driven to use the dog, he might always have the means of setting him upon his track. With characteristic promptness and audacity he set about this at once, and we cannot doubt that the boots or chambermaid of the hotel was well bribed to help him in his design. By chance, however, the first boot which was procured for him was a new one and, therefore, useless for his purpose. He then had it returned and obtained another—a most instructive incident, since it proved conclusively to my mind that we were dealing with a real hound, as no other supposition could explain this anxiety to obtain an old boot and this indifference to a new one. The more *outré* and grotesque an incident is the more carefully it deserves to be examined,

and the very point which appears to complicate a case is, when duly considered and scientifically handled, the one which is most likely to elucidate it.

"Then we had the visit from our friends next morning, shadowed always by Stapleton in the cab. From his knowledge of our rooms and of my appearance, as well as from his general conduct, I am inclined to think that Stapleton's career of crime has been by no means limited to this single Baskerville affair. It is suggestive that during the last three years there have been four considerable burglaries in the West Country, for none of which was any criminal ever arrested. The last of these, at Folkestone Court, in May, was remarkable for the cold-blooded pistolling of the page, who surprised the masked and solitary burglar. I cannot doubt that Stapleton recruited his waning resources in this fashion, and that for years he has been a desperate and dangerous man.

"We had an example of his readiness of resource that morning when he got away from us so successfully, and also of his audacity in sending back my own name to me through the cabman. From that moment he understood that I had taken over the case in London, and that therefore there was no chance for him there. He returned to Dartmoor and awaited the arrival of the Baronet."

"One moment!" said I. "You have, no doubt, described the sequence of events correctly, but there is one point which you have left unexplained. What became of the hound when its master was in London?"

"I have given some attention to this matter and it is undoubtedly of importance. There can be no question that Stapleton had a confidant, though it is unlikely that he ever placed himself in his power by sharing all his plans with him. There was an old manservant at Merripit House, whose name was Anthony. His connection with the Stapletons can be traced for several years, as far back as the schoolmastering days, so that he must have been aware that his master and mistress were really husband and wife. This man has disappeared and has escaped from the country. It is suggestive that Anthony is not a common name in England, while Antonio is so in all Spanish or Spanish-American countries. The man, like Mrs. Stapleton herself, spoke good English, but with a curious lisping accent. I have myself seen this old man cross the Grimpen Mire by the path which Stapleton had marked out. It is very probable, therefore, that in the absence of his master it was he who cared for the hound, though he may never have known the purpose for which the beast was used.

"The Stapletons then went down to Devonshire, whither they were soon followed by Sir Henry and you. One word now as to how I stood myself at that time. It may possibly recur to your memory that when I examined the paper upon which the printed words were fastened I made a close inspection for the water-mark. In doing so I held it within a few inches of my eyes, and was conscious of a faint smell of the scent known as white jessamine. There are seventy-five perfumes, which it is very necessary that a criminal expert should be able to distinguish from each other, and cases have more than once within my own experience depended upon their prompt recognition. The scent suggested the presence of a lady, and already my thoughts began to turn towards the Stapletons. Thus I had made certain of the hound, and had guessed at the criminal before ever we went to the West Country.

"It was my game to watch Stapleton. It was evident, however, that I could not do this if I were with you, since he would be keenly on his guard. I deceived everybody, therefore, yourself included, and I came down secretly when I was supposed to be in London. My hardships were not so great as you imagined, though such trifling details must never interfere with the investigation of a case. I stayed for the most part at Coombe Tracey, and only used the hut upon the moor when it was necessary to be near the scene of action. Cartwright had come down

with me, and in his disguise as a country boy he was of great assistance to me. I was dependent upon him for food and clean linen. When I was watching Stapleton Cartwright was frequently watching you, so that I was able to keep my hand upon all the strings.

"I have already told you that your reports reached me rapidly, being forwarded instantly from Baker Street to Coombe Tracey. They were of great service to me, and especially that one incidentally truthful piece of biography of Stapleton's. I was able to establish the identity of the man and the woman, and knew at last exactly how I stood. The case had been considerably complicated through the incident of the escaped convict and the relations between him and the Barrymores. This also you cleared up in a very effective way, though I had already come to the same conclusions from my own observations.

"By the time that you discovered me upon the moor I had a complete knowledge of the whole business, but I had not a case which could go to a jury. Even Stapleton's attempt upon Sir Henry that night which ended in the death of the unfortunate convict did not help us much in proving murder against our man. There seemed to be no alternative but to catch him red-handed, and to do so we had to use Sir Henry, alone and apparently unprotected, is a bait. We did so, and at the cost of a severe shock to our client we succeeded in completing our case and driving Stapleton to his destruction. That Sir Henry should have been exposed to this is, I must confess, a reproach to my management of the case, but we had no means of foreseeing the terrible and paralyzing spectacle which the beast presented, nor could we predict the fog which

" BE READY IN HALF AN HOUR."

enabled him to burst upon us at such short notice. We succeeded in our object at a cost which both the specialist and Dr. Mortimer assure me will be a temporary one. A long journey may enable our friend to recover not only from his shattered nerves, but also from his wounded feelings. His love for the lady was deep and sincere, and to him the saddest part of all this black business was that he should have been deceived by her.

"It only remains to indicate the part which she had played throughout. There can be no doubt that Stapleton exercised an influence over her which may have been love or may have been fear, or very possibly both, since they are by no means incompatible emotions. It was, at least, absolutely effective. At his command she consented to pass as his sister, though he found the limits of his power over her when he endeavoured to make her the direct accessory to murder. She was ready to warn Sir Henry so far as she could without implicating her husband, and again and again she tried to do so. Stapleton himself seems to have been capable of jealousy, and when he saw the Baronet paying court to the lady, even though it was part of his own plan, still he could not help interrupting with a passionate outburst that revealed the fiery soul which his self-contained manner so cleverly concealed. By encouraging the intimacy he made it certain that Sir Henry would frequently come to Merripit House and that he would sooner or later get the opportunity which he desired. On the day of the crisis, however, his wife turned suddenly against him. She had learned something of the death of the convict, and she knew that the hound was being kept in the out-house on the evening that Sir Henry was coming to dinner. She taxed her husband with his intended crime, and a furious scene followed, in which he showed her for the first time that she had a rival in his love. Her fidelity turned in an instant to bitter hatred and he saw that she would betray him. He tied her up, therefore, that she might have no chance of warning Sir Henry, and he hoped, no doubt, that when the whole countryside put down the Baronet's death to the curse of his family, as they certainly would do, he could win his wife back to accept an accomplished

fact and to keep silent upon what she knew. In this I fancy that in any case he made a miscalculation, and that, if we had not been there, his doom would none the less have been sealed. A woman of Spanish blood does not condone such an injury so lightly. And now, my dear Watson, without referring to my notes, I cannot give you a more detailed account of this curious case. I do not know that anything essential has been left unexplained."

"He could not hope to frighten Sir Henry to death as he had done the old uncle with his bogie hound."

"The beast was savage and half-starved. If its appearance did not frighten its victim to death, at least it would paralyze the resistance which might be offered."

"No doubt. There only remains one difficulty. If Stapleton came into the succession, how could he explain the fact that he, the heir, had been living unannounced under another name so close to the property? How could he claim it without causing suspicion and inquiry?"

"It is a formidable difficulty, and I fear that you ask too much when you expect me to solve it. The past and the present are within the field of my inquiry, but what a man may do in the future is a hard question to answer. Mrs. Stapleton has heard her husband discuss the problem on several occasions. There were three possible courses. He might claim the property from South America, establish his identity before the British authorities there, and so obtain the fortune without ever coming to England at all; or he might adopt an elaborate disguise during the short time that he need be in London; or, again, he might furnish an accomplice with the proofs and papers, putting him in as heir, and retaining a claim upon some proportion of his income. We cannot doubt from what we know of him that he would have found some way out of the difficulty. And now, my dear Watson, we have had some weeks of severe work, and for one evening, I think, we may turn our thoughts into more pleasant channels. I have a box for 'Les Huguenots.' Have you heard the De Reszkes? Might I trouble you then to be ready in half an hour, and we can stop at Marcini's for a little dinner on the way?"

THE END.

# INTERMEDIATE ACCOUNTING

**The Willard J. Graham Series in Accounting**

consulting editor
**Robert N. Anthony**   Harvard University

# INTERMEDIATE ACCOUNTING

**Glenn A. Welsch,** Ph.D., C.P.A.
*Professor of Accounting*

**Charles T. Zlatkovich,** Ph.D., C.P.A.
*Professor of Accounting*

**John Arch White,** Ph.D.
*Professor of Accounting, Emeritus*

*all of the*
*Graduate School of Business*
*University of Texas at Austin*

**Fourth Edition**     1976

**RICHARD D. IRWIN, INC.**   Homewood, Illinois   60430
Irwin-Dorsey Limited   Georgetown, Ontario   L7G 4B3

© RICHARD D. IRWIN, INC., 1963, 1968, 1972, and 1976

Fourth Edition

*First Printing, May 1976*
*Second Printing, August 1976*

ISBN 0-256-01817-0
Library of Congress Catalog Card No. 75–39360

*Printed in the United States of America*

LEARNING SYSTEMS COMPANY—
a division of Richard D. Irwin, Inc.—has developed a
PROGRAMMED LEARNING AID
to accompany texts in this subject area.
Copies can be purchased through your bookstore
or by writing PLAIDS.
1818 Ridge Road, Homewood, Illinois 60430.

# Preface

This fourth edition of our textbook is designed, as were the three previous editions, for students who have completed the study of two semesters or quarters of accounting principles. It is planned for a two-semester sequence, but with judicious selection of and emphasis on material the text is readily adaptable to shorter courses or to the needs of schools using the quarter plan. It is designed to complement a principles text having one of the same coauthors,[1] but may be used following any reasonably complete first-year text in accounting.

Accounting theory and concepts are emphasized throughout. Students are provided reasons for the various accounting practices and procedures presented; they will learn the more important "why" along with the "how" of current accounting practice. This edition continues the comprehensive features which gained wide recognition for the prior editions. Upon completion, the student should be well prepared for the theory and practice sections of the Uniform CPA Examination and for advanced courses in accounting. A salient feature of this book is that, rather than avoiding troublesome complexities, by omission or oversimplified exposition, it deals with them comprehensively and, where appropriate, alternative viewpoints are presented. Examination of the chapter contents will reveal that all important aspects of each topic are considered, consistent with the objectives of the book, despite the fact that this imposes on the text a comparatively high level of sophistication.

At the outset this edition provides a carefully designed review of the fundamentals. Next it introduces the concepts of present value and utilizes them throughout the remaining discussions. This feature is in line with the significant trend in the official pronouncements of the accounting profession to require application of these concepts in a wide range of accounting practices such as those dealing with debt and receivable transactions, amortization of discounts and premiums, leases, pensions, investments, and certain other related transactions. Experience by the authors and many others has confirmed that these

---

[1] Glenn A. Welsch and Robert N. Anthony, *Fundamentals of Financial Accounting* (Homewood, Ill.: Richard D. Irwin, Inc., 1974); or William W. Pyle and John Arch White, *Fundamental Accounting Principles* (Homewood, Ill.: Richard D. Irwin, Inc., 1975).

vii

concepts are not particularly troublesome to accounting students if introduced early in intermediate accounting and then applied throughout the course. Rather than using a less sophisticated (and inadequate) instructional content, this textbook reflects the increasing accounting sophistication in this area currently found in *APB Opinions,* FASB *Statements,* and the Uniform CPA Examinations.

Preferred accounting terminology is used throughout on a consistent basis. Citations and references to pronouncements of the APB, FASB, American Institute of Certified Public Accountants, the American Accounting Association, and the Securities and Exchange Commission permeate the 25 chapters. As a new and useful feature, this fourth edition includes an Appendix after the last chapter which lists all of the *Accounting Research Bulletins* (ARBs), *APB Opinions* and FASB *Statements* to date. The Appendix also indicates their current status and the chapters in which each is cited.

Recognizing that students learn much of their accounting at this point in their study by solving relevant assignment materials, the authors have supplied a wealth of questions, exercises, and problems for each chapter. The former policy of including both short exercises and longer comprehensive problems that are both relevant and challenging has been continued. Approximately 90 percent of these materials have been revised. An appropriate selection of materials from Uniform CPA Examinations is to be found in the assignment material. The professor is provided an unusually wide range of assignment materials of varying difficulty so that selections can be made that are suited to the student group.

This edition provides a unique variety of supplementary materials for the instructor and student. They include, in addition to the textbook, the following:

For the instructor:

1. A comprehensive teacher's manual including teaching suggestions and step-by-step computations.
2. An examination booklet classified by chapter.
3. A list of key figures.

For the student:

4. A study guide that incorporates for each chapter (*a*) study suggestions, (*b*) a study summary of important points with illustrations, (*c*) questions for self-evaluation and (*d*) answers to the questions for self-checkup.
5. A comprehensive *review* practice set designed to be used during the early part of the first semester. This practice set is included in the Study Guide (4 above); transaction narrative, forms, and selected key figures are provided therein. The complete solution is given in the Teacher's Manual (1 above).
6. A complete set of working papers that provides forms (with certain captions provided) for working the exercises and problems.

In addition, the prior policy of providing supplementary booklets, upon request and without cost, covering future FASB *Statements* will be continued by the authors and publisher.

Chapters are arranged in a teachable and logical sequence. They are grouped to facilitate rearrangement to suit individual preferences. The first two chapters set the stage for all that follows by presenting an integrating overview of the foundations of accounting theory. Following are three chapters that comprehensively review the principles of financial accounting and which carry the student somewhat beyond equivalent coverage in the traditional elementary accounting course.

Chapter 6 presents the concepts of present-value and actuarial mathematics and indicates their primary applications in financial accounting. This location significantly simplifies explanations, illustrations, and understandings in numerous instances throughout the course of intermediate instruction (and advanced courses as well). The authors also recognized the trend to include some instruction in present-value concepts in the better elementary accounting textbooks; the instruction should be continued on a higher level of sophistication at the intermediate level.

Chapters 1 through 14 are usually viewed as the first course in intermediate accounting. These chapters present a comprehensive treatment of assets and liabilities. Chapters 15 through 17 are devoted to corporations. Long-term investments in equity and debt securities are discussed in Chapters 18 and 19. The last six chapters are devoted, in order, to: special reporting problems, the Statement of Changes in Financial Position, pension plans, leases, statement analysis, and price-level accounting. Each of these chapters (as well as certain others) may be omitted in part or in whole, without significantly affecting the continuity of the course.

We are indebted to numerous colleagues and students from universities throughout the nation whose comments and suggestions led to many valuable improvements in this fourth edition. We appreciate the permission granted by the Financial Accounting Standards Board, the American Accounting Association and the American Institute of CPAs to quote from their various pronouncements. The latter organization also permitted us to make liberal use of materials adapted from the Uniform CPA Examinations.

We are especially appreciative of the many valuable suggestions provided by our colleagues and friends: David L. Wilson, Kermit D. Larson, Edward L. Summers, Fred Streuling, Larry A. Tomassini, Allen Bizzell, Lewis L. Davidson, and Charles H. Griffin. We also express thanks to graduate students at the University of Texas at Austin: Morley Lemon, Dewey Ward, Patti Smith, Scott Ikenberry, Richard Ratliff, Kathy Anderson, Charles Inman, Robert Sharp, Jacqueline Well, and Don Jones. Special gratitude is due Margaret Whatley, MPA candidate, for critiques, proofing, typing, and a host of other most helpful activities. Particularly valuable was a comprehensive critique of the textual and assignment materials provided by Phyllis Barker, Indiana State University, and many substantive suggestions by Kathryn C. Buckner, Georgia State University. We also express our thanks to numerous users of the prior editions for valuable suggestions in respect to content and arrangement.

Austin, Texas                    GLENN A. WELSCH
*April 1976*                     CHARLES T. ZLATKOVICH
                                 JOHN A. WHITE

# Contents

## 7. Cash, Short-Term Investments, and Receivables 267

Part A – Cash. Composition of Cash. Control of Cash: *Control of Cash Receipts. Control over Cash Disbursements. Petty Cash.* Cash Overage and Shortage. Reconciliation of Bank with Book Balance. Comprehensive Reconciliation. Part B – Short-Term Investments. Short-Term Investments Defined. Valuation of Short-Term Investments: *Lower of Cost or Market. Valuation at Cost. Market Value.* Identification of Units. Investment Revenue on Short-Term Investments. Part C – Receivables. Trade Receivables. Accounts Receivable: *Evaluation of Methods. Notes Receivable.* Special Receivables. Use of Receivables to Secure Immediate Cash: *Assignment. Factoring. Outright Sale of Accounts Receivable. Pledging.*

## 8. Inventories – General Problems 318

The Nature of Inventories. Classification of Inventories. The Dual Phase of the Inventory Problem. Identification of Goods (Items) That Should Be Included in Inventory. Measurement of Physical Quantities in Inventory: *Periodic Inventory System. Perpetual Inventory System.* Effect of Inventory Errors. Measuring the Accounting Value of Inventory. Content of Unit Cost: *Freight-In. Purchase Discounts.* Departures from the Cost Principle in Costing Inventory: *Lower of Cost or Market.* Accounting Problems in Applying Lower of Cost or Market: *Determination of Overall Inventory Valuation. Recording Lower of Cost or Market in the Accounts.* Net Realizable Value and Replacement Cost. Inventories Valued above Cost at Selling Price. Relative Sales Value Method. Losses on Purchase Commitments.

## 9. Inventories – Flow and Matching Procedures 364

Part A – Inventory Flow Methods. Specific Cost Identification. Average Cost: *Weighted Average. Moving Average.* First-In, First-Out. Last-In, First-Out: Lifo *Inventory Liquidation. Comparison of* Lifo *with* Fifo. Miscellaneous Inventory Flow Methods: *Next-In, First-Out. Cost-of-Last-Purchase. Base Stock Method.* Standard Costs for Inventory: *Variable or Direct Cost for Inventory.* Selection of a Flow Method. Part B – Complexities in Applying *Lifo.* Initial Adoption of *Lifo.* Continuing Application of *Lifo: Quantity of Goods* Lifo. *Changes in Items (Product Lines) in* Lifo *Inventory. Dollar-Value* Lifo. *Inventory Liquidation. Change in Product Mix. Indexing.* Lifo Applied to Interim Statements. *Lifo* Reserves. Summary.

## 10. Inventories – Special Valuation Procedures 415

Part A – Estimating Procedures for Inventories. Gross Margin Method. Retail Inventory Method. Markups and Markdowns. Application of the Retail Inventory Method: *Retail Method, Fifo Cost. Retail Method, Average Cost. Retail Method, Lower of Cost or Market (LCM). Special Items.* Inventories for Long-Term Construction Contracts: *Completed-Contract Method. Percentage-of-Completion Method. Comparative Results.* Part B – Dollar-Value, *Lifo*-Retail Method. Application of the Dollar-Value, *Lifo*-Retail Method: *Computation of Ending Inventory at* Lifo *Cost.* Changing to Dollar-Value, *Lifo*-Retail – Computation of Base Inventory.

Part A – Measuring, Recording, and Reporting Liabilities. Current Liabilities: *Current Liabilities Defined. Accounts and Notes Payable. Discounted Notes Payable. Dividends Payable. Advances and Returnable Deposits. Accrued Liabilities. Deferred Credits. Funds Collected for Third Parties. Payroll Taxes. Tax and Bonus Problems.* Long-Term Liabilities: *Unrealistic Interest Rates. Current Maturities of Long-Term Debt.* Estimated Liabilities: *Liability from Warranties. Liability from Premiums, Coupons, and Trading Stamps.* Contingencies: *Accrual of Estimated Contingency Losses. Disclosure of Estimated Contingency Losses. Contingency Gains. Appropriations and Reserves of Retained Earnings.* Part B – Accounting for Income Taxes. Interperiod Income Tax Allocation: *Tax Differences. Fundamental Concepts and Procedures.* Intraperiod Tax Allocation. A Comprehensive Illustration. Disclosure of Tax Allocation. Operating Losses and Tax Allocation: *Loss Carryback. Loss Carryforward.*

Capital and Revenue Expenditures. Principles Underlying Accounting for Property, Plant, and Equipment. Assets Acquired for Cash. Assets Acquired on Deferred Payment Plan. Assets Acquired in Exchange for Securities. Assets Acquired through Exchanges: *Similar versus Dissimilar Assets. Accounting Procedures for Exchanges.* Departures from Cost in Accounting for Tangible Assets. Donated Assets and Discovery Value: *Donated Assets. Discovery Value.* Write-Down of Operational Assets Based on Decreased Use Value. Outlays Subsequent to Acquisition but Prior to Use. Lump-Sum Purchases of Assets. Assets Constructed for Own Use: *General Overhead as a Cost of Construction. Excess Costs of Construction.* Interest during Construction Period. Acquisition Costs of Specific Property: *Land. Buildings. Machinery, Furniture, Fixtures, and Equipment. Patterns and Dies. Returnable Containers. Leasehold Improvements.* Cost Outlays Subsequent to Acquisition. Repairs and Maintenance: *Ordinary Repairs and Maintenance.* Extraordinary Repairs. Replacements and Betterments. Additions. Rearrangement of Assets. Retirement of Operational Assets.

Depreciation: *Depreciation and Dividends. Depreciation and Cash Flow. Depreciation Is an Estimate.* Depreciation Disclosures. Causes of Depreciation. Factors in Determining the Depreciation Charge. Recording Depreciation. Methods of Depreciation: *Straight-Line Method. Service-Hours Method. Productive-Output Method. Reducing-Charge Methods. Sum-of-the-Years'-Digits Method. Fixed-Percentage-on-Declining-Base Method. Double-Declining-Balance Method.* Depreciation Based on Investment Concepts. Fractional Year Depreciation. Special Depreciation Systems: *Inventory System. Retirement and Replacement Systems. Group and Composite-Life Systems.* Depreciation Policy. Changes and Correction of Depreciation. The Investment Tax Credit. Depletion: *Nature of Depletion.* Appendix – Annuity and Sinking Fund Methods of Depreciation. Annuity Method of Depreciation. Sinking Fund Method of Depreciation.

## 14. Intangible Assets       590

Accounting for Intangible Assets. Measuring and Recording Intangible Assets at Acquisition: *Classification of the Cost of Intangible Assets.* Amortization of the Cost of Intangible Assets. Disposition of Intangible Assets. Identifiable Intangible Assets: *Patents. Copyrights. Franchises.* Trademarks. Unidentifiable Intangible Assets: *Goodwill. Present Value Estimation of Goodwill.* Going Value. Deferred Charges: *Research and Development Costs. Organization Costs. Leaseholds.* Development Stage Companies. Insurance: *Liability Insurance. Casualty Insurance. Coinsurance. Blanket Policy. Accounting for a Casualty Loss. Life Insurance.* Reporting Intangibles.

## 15. Corporations – Formation and Contributed Capital       633

Classifications of Corporations. Nature of Capital Stock. Classes of Capital Stock: *Par-Value Stock. Nopar-Value Stock. Legal Capital. Common Stock. Preferred Stock. Cumulative Preferences on Preferred Stock. Participating Preferences on Preferred Stock.* Accounting for Issuance of Par-Value Stock: *Authorization. Stock Issued for Cash.* Accounting for Nopar Capital Stock: *Subscriptions.* Accounting for Stock Premium and Discount. Special Sales of Stock: *Noncash Sale of Stock.* Unrealized Capital Increment. Assessments on Shareholders. Incorporation of a Going Business.

## 16. Corporations – Retained Earnings and Dividends       664

Dividends: *Cash Dividends. Property Dividends. Liability Dividends. Liquidating Dividends. Stock Dividends.* Accumulated Dividends on Preferred Stock: *Fractional Share Warrants. Dividends and Treasury Stock.* Legality of Dividends. Appropriations of Retained Earnings. Appropriation Related to a Contractual Agreement. Appropriations as an Aspect of Financial Planning. Appropriation for Possible Future Losses. Reporting Retained Earnings. Quasi-Reorganizations.

## 17. Corporations – Contraction and Expansion of Corporate Capital after Formation; and Earnings per Share       700

Treasury Stock. Recording and Reporting Treasury Stock Transactions: *Cost Method. Par-Value Method.* Accounting for Nopar Treasury Stock. Treasury Stock Received through Donations. Retirement of Treasury Stock. Restriction of Retained Earnings for Treasury Stock. Retirement of Callable Stock. Convertible Stock. Changing Par Value. Stock Rights. Accounting for Stock Issued to Employees: *Theoretical Considerations. Practical Considerations. Accounting for Noncompensatory Plans. Accounting for Compensatory Plans. Illustrative Entries, Compensatory Plan, Measurement Date on Date of Grant. Illustrative Entries, Compensatory Plan, Measurement Date Subsequent to Date of Grant.* Earnings per Share: *Reporting Earnings per Share. Computing EPS with Complex Capital Structures. Computation of Earnings per Share, Complex Capital Structure. Antidilution.*

CONTENTS xvii

# Chapter *1*

## Introduction

### OBJECTIVES OF THE BOOK

This book focuses on financial accounting which provides financial information primarily for decision-makers outside the entity. This financial information is provided to external decision-makers primarily by means of general-purpose statements of operating results (i.e., the income statement), financial position (i.e., the balance sheet), and changes in financial position (i.e., statement of changes in financial position). Consistent with the broad objective of reporting to external parties, this book concentrates on the application of accounting theory, standards, principles, and procedures to accounting problems. The fundamental rationale for the various aspects of financial accounting are stressed. This book is designed especially for accounting majors, regardless of specialized interests in public, industrial, governmental, tax, or social accounting. Another objective is to prepare students for early entry into the real world of accounting; consequently, current financial accounting practices and trends are emphasized.

This book presumes that the student has studied a course in fundamentals of financial accounting.[1] Satisfactory completion of this text should prepare students for all advanced accounting courses. Emphasis throughout on theory, standards, and principles – the "why" of accounting – enables students to cope with new and complex accounting problems on a conceptual rather than a procedural (or memory) level.

### ACCOUNTING DEFINED

Accounting can be broadly defined as an information processing system designed to *capture* and *measure* the economic essence of events that affect an entity and to report their economic effects on that entity to

---

[1] Refer to books such as: G. A. Welsch and R. N. Anthony, *Fundamentals of Financial Accounting* (Homewood, Ill.: Richard D. Irwin, Inc., 1974).

1

decision-makers.[2] This broad definition serves the two broad groups of decision-makers: internal decision-makers and external decision-makers. These two groups have different information needs resulting from different relationships with the entity. *Internal* decision-makers are the managers responsible for planning the future of the entity, implementing the plans, and controlling operations on a day-to-day basis. Because of their internal relationship to the entity, they can command whatever financial data they may need or desire at dates of their choice. Further, the information is for their sole use and generally is not intended to be communicated to outsiders. The process of developing and reporting financial information to internal users is usually called *management accounting,* and the reports are referred to as internal management reports. Because of the confidential nature of internal management reports, and their focus on internal decision making, there is no requirement (other than as specified by the management) that they conform to generally accepted accounting standards. Clearly, internal management reports should be structured to conform to the particular decision-making needs of the management.

In contrast, the external decision-makers (i.e., the external users of financial information) make distinctly different types of decisions regarding the entity, such as, to invest or disinvest, to loan funds, and so on. External decision-makers comprise present and potential investors and creditors, investment analysts, governmental units, and the public at large. In view of the diverse range of external users of financial data, the accounting profession has developed *general-purpose financial statements* designed to meet their decision-making needs. These statements are developed in a phase of accounting known as *financial accounting.* Financial accounting may be broadly defined as information processing, beginning with transactions and other events affecting the entity, progressing through its accounting system, and reporting of their economic impact to external decision-makers. The external users, because of their detachment from the entity, cannot directly command specific financial information from the entity; therefore, they must rely primarily on general-purpose financial statements. The accounting profession, in order to serve external users, has developed a network of accounting theory, standards, principles, and procedures designed to assure that external financial reports are: (1) service oriented—basically they are designed to serve the decision-making needs of the external users; (2) credible—they are intended to be fair representations of the economic circumstances of the entity; and (3) accurate and free of bias—they must conform to specified standards of accounting and reporting.

---

[2] Another useful definition is: Accounting is a service activity. Its function is to provide quantitative information, primarily financial in nature, about economic entities that is intended to be useful in making economic decisions—in making reasoned choices among alternative courses of action. Accounting includes several branches, for example, financial accounting, managerial accounting, and governmental accounting (AICPA, *Statement of the Accounting Principles Board No. 4* [New York, October 1970], p. 17).

## OBJECTIVES OF EXTERNAL FINANCIAL STATEMENTS

Measurement of the economic effect of transactions and other events on an entity, and the communication of those economic effects, is the essence of financial accounting. Communication of the economic effect, by means of general-purpose financial statements, encompasses, as a minimum, the following:

1. Income statement—a periodic statement of the results of operations that reports revenues, expenses, extraordinary items, net income, and earnings per share.
2. Balance sheet—a periodic statement of financial position that reports assets, liabilities, and owners' equity.
3. Statement of changes in financial position—a periodic statement of the inflow of funds, outflow of funds, and net change in funds. This statement measures funds, in terms of either cash or working capital.
4. Supplementary information to assure full disclosure.

Because of the dynamic nature of the environment, general-purpose financial statements are in a constant state of evolution. The environment consists of the various aspects of a society: social, political, and economic. As the environment changes, the needs of external decision-makers change. Consequently, accounting measurements and reporting must evolve to meet those needs. Fundamentally, the basic objectives of external financial statements are:

(1) To provide information useful for making economic decisions.
(2) To serve primarily those users who have limited authority, ability, or resources to obtain information and who rely on financial statements as their principal source of information about an enterprise's economic activities.
(3) To provide information useful to investors and creditors for predicting, comparing, and evaluating potential cash flows in terms of amount, timing, and related uncertainty.
(4) To provide users with information for predicting, comparing, and evaluating enterprise earning power.
(5) To supply information useful in judging management's ability to use enterprise resources effectively in achieving the primary enterprise goal.
(6) To provide factual and interpretative information about transactions and other events which is useful for predicting, comparing, and evaluating enterprise earning power. Basic underlying assumptions with respect to matters subject to interpretation, evaluation, prediction, or estimation should be disclosed.[3]

We stress that the focus of financial accounting is on the *measurement* of economic effects and *communication* of the results to external decision-makers. The complexities of measurement, and the volume of

---

[3] AICPA, *Objectives of Financial Statements, Report of the Study Group on the Objectives of Financial Statements* (New York, October 1973), pp. 61–66 (adapted).

data processing encountered in an accounting system, are necessary to serve the end result—communication. We strongly emphasize this point because it is easy for the student to become immersed in the system and its procedures and to lose sight of the primary objective—reporting to the decision-maker.

## PROFESSIONAL ACCOUNTANTS

Accounting has a long and interesting history. Today professional accountants fulfill an important and unique role in society.[4] The professional accountant is usually a *certified public accountant* (CPA). As with lawyers, physicians, and engineers, accountants are engaged in a wide variety of endeavors. The primary endeavors are:

1. Public accounting—The independent certified public accountant offers services to the public in a manner similar to the doctor, lawyer, or architect. These services include: (*a*) auditing (the attest function), (*b*) tax planning and determination of tax liability, and (*c*) management advisory services (consulting). Certified public accountants in public practice have a unique relationship with their clients as an *independent* and impartial reviewer of the financial statements. Although *independent accountants* are paid by the client, the independence concept extends their responsibilities to third parties; that is, to users of the financial statements.

The primary service rendered by the independent certified public accountant is the audit or attest function. The result of this function is to provide the client with *audited* financial statements including an "auditors report" (see page 137). The auditor's report (1) states the scope of the audit examination of the accounts, and (2) expresses an "opinion" whether the financial report "presents fairly" in accordance with generally accepted accounting standards. The attest function is particularly important to external statement users because it is intended to protect them against outright misrepresentation and bias on the part of the reporting entity. The attest function lends credibility to the financial statements because the auditor must be independent of the client and responsive to the needs of the external users of the financial statements.

2. Industrial accounting—A large number of certified public accountants work in businesses where they serve as accountants, internal auditors, tax specialists, systems experts, controllers, financial vice presidents, and chief executives. In these capacities, their specialized interests typically focus on management, tax, and financial accounting. As an employee, they are not in the role of *independent* certified public accountants.

---

[4] A careful distinction should be made between an accountant and a bookkeeper. A bookkeeper is involved in the routine clerical phase of the accounting process, whereas an accountant is competent in transaction analysis, measurement of economic events, systems design, analytical and interpretative processes, financial evaluation, and the management process. (See Welsch and Anthony, *Fundamentals of Financial Accounting*, chap. 1.)

3. Governmental and nonprofit accounting—Certified public accountants serve at all levels of government and not-for-profit entities: local,
state, national, and international. In these capacities they are not in the
role of *independent* certified public accountants.

Since this is a book on financial accounting, it focuses on generally
accepted accounting principles and standards. These are the standards
that the *independent* certified public accountant must carefully interpret, apply, and enforce.

## ACCOUNTING ORGANIZATIONS AND LITERATURE

Because of the importance of external financial reports to investors,
creditors, government, and the public at large, there is widespread interest in generally accepted accounting standards and the way in which
they are established. In recent years interest in how the accounting profession answers its public-interest responsibility has increased dramati-
cally. Various aspects of the financial reports of major companies and
industries are reported by the news media almost every day.

The development of accounting theory and generally accepted accounting standards has been influenced by the financial community,
governmental regulations, laws, professional accounting organizations,
and accounting literature. Primary among the organizations are the
American Institute of Certified Public Accountants, Financial Accounting Standards Board, Securities and Exchange Commission, and the
American Accounting Association. The role of these organizations is
important in understanding the objectives, evolution, and complexities
of financial accounting.

Similarly, in your study of financial accounting, the accounting literature is important. Most of the organizations cited above support publications which are influential since they report the results of research, real-
life problems, and suggested changes in accounting standards. They are
rich sources for discussions of the major issues in accounting. Throughout this book numerous citations from the literature are provided. Early
in your study of accounting you should become familiar with the primary
accounting publications and use them to expand and enrich your comprehension of the major issues and the relevant alternatives being discussed for their resolution.

## AMERICAN INSTITUTE OF CERTIFIED PUBLIC ACCOUNTANTS (AICPA)

This is the professional organization of certified public accountants.
It is controlled by the CPAs in public practice; consequently, its primary
efforts and publications have focused on the practice of public accounting. Its primary publications relating to financial accounting are:

1. *The Journal of Accountancy*—a monthly magazine containing pronouncements, articles, and special sections of direct interest to the
   independent CPA.

2. *Accountants' Index* – an annual publication containing an index of the accounting literature published during the year.
3. *Accounting Trends and Techniques* – an annual publication containing a survey of the characteristics of the annual financial reports of 600 corporations. It presents tabulations, explanations, and illustrations of reporting procedures, policies, terminology, disclosures, and so on.
4. *Accounting Research Studies* – a series of monograms that focused on specific accounting problems. These studies provide background information, discussion of alternative solutions, and often recommendations.
5. *Statements on Auditing Procedures* – These statements are issued at various times and focus on specific auditing procedures to be followed by the independent CPA. These statements usually are studied comprehensively in the auditing courses offered at most colleges.
6. Statements that deal with specific accounting principles, standards, and procedures:[5]
   a. *Accounting Research Bulletins* – During the period 1938 through 1958, the AICPA had a *Committee on Accounting Procedure* which was responsible for "narrowing the areas of differences and inconsistencies" in accounting practice. To this end the Committee issued pronouncements dealing with accounting principles and procedures. The first 42 pronouncements were restated and revised as:

   *Accounting Research Bulletin* (ARB) *43,* "Restatement and Revision of Accounting Research Bulletins," June 1953.

   From 1953 to 1958, eight additional bulletins were issued; the last *Accounting Research Bulletin* was *No. 51.* In addition, during this period the AICPA Committee on Terminology issued eight terminology bulletins recommending improvements in accounting terminology. These were combined as *Accounting Terminology Bulletin No. 1,* "Review and Resumé, August 1953." Since they have been reaffirmed in many respects, they continue to exert some influence as recommendations.
   b. *Opinions of the Accounting Principles Board* – To provide more emphasis on the formulation of accounting principles, the AICPA established the *Accounting Principles Board* (APB) to replace the Committee on Accounting Procedure. The APB designated its pronouncements as *Opinions.* The *Opinions* prescribe specific accounting principles and procedures for designated types of trans-

---

[5] The contents of these statements, opinions, and bulletins are listed in the Appendix to this book with chapter citations used by your authors. Refer to the following sources for details:
   (a) AICPA Professional Standards, vol. 3, *Accounting – Current Text,* as of September 1, 1975, AICPA.
   (b) Original Pronouncements – *Opinions of the Accounting Principles Board* (Nos. 1–31 inclusive) and *Statements of the Financial Accounting Standards Board* (Nos. 1–12) as cited in the chapters to follow.

actions and other events. During its period of existence from 1959 to 1973, the Board issued 31 *Opinions*. In addition, the Board issued four *Statements*. In contrast to the *Opinions*, the *Statements* present recommendations, rather than requirements, which it was hoped would be followed with a consequent improvement in financial accounting and reporting to external decision-makers.

The *Accounting Research Bulletins* (ARBs), *Accounting Terminology Bulletins*, and the *Opinions of the Accounting Principles Board* are still in effect, as amended; therefore, they often will be cited in the chapters to follow.[6]

## FINANCIAL ACCOUNTING STANDARDS BOARD (FASB)

In the 1960s and early 1970s there were many complaints, within and outside the accounting profession, with respect to the establishment of accounting standards. These complaints focused on (a) lack of participation by organizations other than the AICPA, (b) "quality" of the opinions, (c) failure to develop a "broad statement of the objectives and principles" underlying external financial reports, and (d) insufficient output. Consequently, a committee was appointed to "study the issues and problems involved in setting accounting principles, and to make recommendations for improving the process and to make it more responsive to the needs of those who rely on financial statements." The "Wheat" Committee presented its report in March 1972.[7] Basically, the report recommended the following:

1. A Financial Accounting Foundation—composed of nine trustees appointed by the Board of Directors of the AICPA. Responsibilities: to appoint members of the Financial Accounting Standards Board; to appoint a Financial Accounting Standards Advisory Council; to raise funds to support the new structure; and to periodically review and revise the basic structure.
2. A Financial Accounting Standards Board (FASB)—composed of seven full-time members to establish standards of financial accounting and reporting. Four members would be CPAs drawn from public practice. The other three would not need to hold a CPA certificate but should possess extensive experience in the financial reporting field.
3. A Financial Accounting Standards Advisory Council—approximately 20 members; to work closely with the FASB, in an *advisory* capacity; to establish priorities, establish task forces, react to proposed standards; and whenever called upon.
4. Structure research activities with its objectives and needs clearly in mind.

The recommendations of the Committee were accepted by the AICPA.

---

[6] AICPA, *APB Accounting Principles*, vols. 1 and 2.

[7] *Establishing Financial Accounting Standards, Report of the Study on Establishment of Accounting Principles, American Institute of Certified Public Accountants*, March 1972, pp. 105 (chairman of the Committee, Francis M. Wheat).

Consequently, the APB was discontinued and the FASB became operational July 1, 1973. The first action of the FASB was a decision that the previous *Accounting Research Bulletins* approved by the APB, and the *Opinions* of the APB (as amended), would continue in force. To date the FASB has issued a number of pronouncements designated as:

1. Statements of Financial Accounting Standards – The FASB decided to issue *Statements of Standards* rather than *Opinions* used by the APB. They specify accounting principles and procedures (now called standards) on specific accounting issues. They have the same "force" as the *APB Opinions*.
2. Interpretations – These interpret prior *ARBs*, *APB Opinions*, and FASB *Statements of Financial Accounting Standards*.

Prior to issuing a *Statement* the FASB typically: (1) prepares and distributes a *Discussion Memorandum* which provides an analysis of the issue under consideration; (2) holds a *public hearing* on the issue; and (3) issues an *exposure draft* of the proposed statement. This process was designed to gain wide participation and full consideration of all relevant aspects of each accounting issue considered. After the process is completed, the FASB then makes a decision (*a*) whether to issue a statement, and (*b*), in case of issue, the standards of financial accounting and reporting to be prescribed. The FASB *Statements* and interpretations of the *Opinions* are cited in the text.

The Appendix after Chapter 25 lists the *ARBs*, *APB Opinions* and FASB *Statements* issued to date; chapter citations in this book also are cited.

## SECURITIES AND EXCHANGE COMMISSION (SEC)

A number of governmental regulatory agencies exert a continuing influence on accounting and reporting by businesses. Among these agencies are: Internal Revenue Service, Federal Power Commission, Interstate Commerce Commission, and the Securities and Exchange Commission. The SEC exerts a powerful influence on the development of accounting standards.

Because of the conditions reflected in the securities market at the beginning of the depression of the 1930s, Congress passed the Securities Act of 1933, the Securities Exchange Act of 1934, and the Public Utility Holding Company Act of 1935. The 1934 Act created the Securities and Exchange Commission and gave it broad authority to regulate the issuance and sale of securities in interstate commerce; that is, securities sold to the general public, including those listed on the stock exchanges. The Commission was given the authority to prescribe external financial reporting requirements for those companies under its jurisdiction. To obtain permission to sell an issue of securities, a company must obtain SEC approval of a *prospectus* which becomes a public record. The prospectus reports extensive information about the company, its officers, securities, and financial condition. The financial part of the prospectus must be audited by an independent CPA. After receiving permission to sell securities, the company must file with the Commission, as a matter of public record, audited financial statements each subsequent year and unaudited quarterly statements. The Commission requires more information in these annual financial statements than is typically included in the "published financial statements" furnished to the shareholders.

The SEC filing and reporting requirements are published as:

1. *Regulation S-X* — This is the original document issued by the Commission which prescribed the reporting requirement, including instructions and forms.
2. *Accounting Series Releases* — These releases are amendments, extensions, and additions to *Regulation S-X*. Over 159 *ASR*s have been issued to date.
3. Special SEC Releases.
4. Decisions on cases that come to the SEC.

Although the SEC has wide statutory authority to prescribe financial accounting and external reporting requirements, the Commission generally has relied on the accounting profession to set accounting standards, to enforce them, and to regulate the profession. The working relationship between the SEC and the accounting profession has been a positive one, and accounting regulation has remained largely in the private sector. However, there have been numerous occasions where the SEC has forced the accounting profession to move forward in tackling critical problems. These situations generally have been in areas where the SEC concluded that the public interest was not being fully served on a timely basis. In a few instances, the SEC has imposed certain accounting and reporting practices without waiting for the profession to act. Clearly, the SEC has exerted a significant influence on the establishment of accounting and reporting standards. This influence has increased in the last few years and is reflected in this book.

## PERSUASION VERSUS COMPULSION

Until 1964 the accounting profession, through the AICPA, followed a policy of persuasion. The pronouncements of the Accounting Procedures Committee and the Accounting Principles Board were viewed as recommendations of generally accepted accounting principles. They were not binding on the profession; there was no strict requirement for adherence.

Their force depended upon their "general acceptance" by the accounting profession. Acceptance was encouraged by persuasion; that is, by convincing the independent CPA that they represented the preferred solution to given accounting problems. By 1964, many leaders of the profession were convinced that persuasion alone was insufficient to reduce the wide range of differences and inconsistencies evident in accounting and reporting to external decision-makers. There were numerous instances where identical transactions could be accounted for by any one of several significantly different methods. Net income could be readily "doctored" by selecting a particular accounting approach from among several deemed "generally accepted."

Consequently, a particularly significant milestone in the development of accounting practice occurred in October 1964, when the Council of the AICPA adopted recommendations requiring that for fiscal periods beginning after December 31, 1965, *departures from accounting principles specified in APB Opinions and the preceding Accounting Research Bulletins be disclosed in footnotes to financial statements or in independent auditor's reports when the effects of any such departure on the financial statements was material.* This statement forced the independent CPA to follow the pronouncements or to assume the burden of proof that other principles applied were "generally accepted" and "fairly presented" the financial results. Because of this burden of proof, and the risk of liability to statement users, the pronouncements have been followed. Thus, the policy of persuasion gave way to *compulsion.* Most observers agree that the new policy has been more effective.

## AMERICAN ACCOUNTING ASSOCIATION (AAA)

The American Accounting Association is an organization dominated by accounting educators; however, its membership is open to practicing, industrial, and governmental accountants. Its broad objectives are the developing of accounting theory, encouraging and sponsoring accounting research, and improving education in accounting. The Association operates primarily through a series of committees and publishes monograms, committee reports, and a quarterly periodical, *The Accounting Review.* This periodical contains articles and sections that cover a wide range of subjects largely oriented toward research and accounting education.

Since 1936 the American Accounting Association, through its committees, has issued a series of statements on accounting theory. Starting in June 1936 with "A Tentative Statement of Accounting Principles Underlying Corporate Financial Statements," the Association carried on an active research program on accounting theory. These statements were issued as pamphlets and as articles in the *Accounting Review.* The 1936 statement was revised and supplemented three times; the latest revision was called "Accounting and Reporting Standards for Corporate Financial Statements, 1957 Revision." This statement, along with the preceding statements and nine supplements, was published in a single pamphlet by the Association in 1957. The latest statement, prepared by a special AAA committee, was published in 1966 and was entitled *A Statement of Basic Accounting Theory.* Like prior AAA statements, it dealt primarily with accounting theory, as opposed to accounting practice and procedures. The committee was more concerned with "what should be, as opposed to what was, or what is."[8] The statements relating to account-

---

[8] AAA, *A Statement of Basic Accounting Theory* (Evanston, Ill., 1966).

ing principles issued by the Association were *normative* rather than descriptive. That is, they tended to be more general, theoretical, and oriented toward future practice, whereas those issued by the AICPA primarily dealt with problems arising in current practice. Numerous references to these statements will be made throughout the discussions in this book.

## INCOME TAX LEGISLATION AND FINANCIAL ACCOUNTING

Income tax legislation and administration has a significant impact on financial accounting. The financial effects of income tax legislation must be recorded in the accounting system and reported on the financial statements. From another point of view, accounting maintains a careful distinction between financial accounting standards and practices and the legal provisions for determining tax liability. A primary objective of financial accounting is to measure and report net income (as defined by accounting standards), whereas the objective of income tax legislation is to assess a tax. The Congress, in devising tax legislation to generate revenue for the government, also seeks to encourage particular actions on the part of the taxpayers to serve certain social and fiscal policy ends. For example, accelerated depreciation, investment credit, exclusion from tax on the interest received on municipal bonds, deductibility of contributions to charitable organizations, statutory depletion, and so on, are favorable "tax breaks" to encourage the taxpayer to make certain choices that are believed to be in the public interest. Thus, tax legislation defines taxable income as something quite different than the amount designated as "accrual net income" by the accounting profession. Typically, taxable income and net income are two different amounts for a business.

Throughout your study of accounting, remember that the "income tax way" often is not in accord with the accounting way (see Chapter 20, Income Tax Allocation). Nevertheless, although income tax legislation and administration do not establish accounting principles and reporting standards, their indirect influence is substantial. For example, the inventory *Lifo* method often was frowned on by the accounting profession until it became an acceptable method for income tax purposes; the same was true for accelerated depreciation.

The accounting profession has vigorously opposed tax legislation and administration to limit tax alternatives (such as a choice among several acceptable depreciation methods) to the one used for financial accounting purposes. This policy is considered counterproductive by the accounting profession because it tends to encourage businesses to use, in the accounting system, the method most favorable for tax purposes with no regard as to whether it best measures accrual net income.

## CONCLUDING COMMENT

This chapter introduces the nature and objectives of financial accounting and reporting to external decision-makers. It presents a broad view of the accounting environment, the influential organizations affecting accounting, and the scope of the literature. It emphasizes that accounting must be responsive to the evolving needs of society; consequently, accounting principles and practices also are continually evolving. There are many forces in society that bear on, and determine, the general direction of the changes. In the next chapter, we will turn our attention to the foundations of financial accounting theory.

## QUESTIONS

1. Define accounting in a broad sense.

2. Explain the distinction between financial and management accounting. Does this distinction mean that a company should have two accounting systems? Explain.

3. What is meant by general purpose financial statements? What are their basic components?

4. What are the basic objectives of external financial statements?

5. Explain why the emphasis in financial accounting is on *measurement* and *communication*.

6. What are the primary endeavors of certified public accountants?

7. The independent certified public accountant fulfills a unique professional role. Explain the concept of independence and why it is important to society in general.

8. The following statements deal specifically with accounting principles, standards and procedures. For each, you are to explain their development and their current status generally:

   a. *Accounting Research Bulletins*
   b. *Accounting Terminology Bulletins*
   c. *Opinions* of the APB
   d. FASB *Statements of Financial Accounting Standards*
   e. FASB Interpretations

9. Explain the developments that led to the establishment of the FASB.

10. Briefly explain the role that the SEC has fulfilled in the establishment of accounting standards. What has been its relationship to the accounting profession in this role?

11. What is the AAA? What role has it fulfilled in the development of accounting theory and standards?

12. Briefly explain the relationship of income tax legislation to financial accounting standards.

13. Is an approach that is permitted for income tax purposes necessarily "generally accepted" for financial accounting purposes? Explain.

14. Why does the accounting profession oppose *conformity* between taxable income provisions and accrual accounting standards?

*Chapter* 2

# Theoretical Foundations of Financial Accounting and Reporting

The study of accounting can be approached on a theoretical or procedural basis, or a combination of the two. In this book, consistent with our objectives stated in Chapter 1, a combination approach is presented. At this level, the student interested in accounting should learn the basic accounting principles and procedures used to classify, analyze, and record transactions, and to report the summarized results to decision-makers. The procedural aspect of financial accounting involves the preparation of accounting entries, maintenance of accounts, and preparation of financial statements. However, of more importance, is a comprehension of the theoretical foundation that underlies financial accounting and reporting. This provides the rationale for the procedural aspects of accounting. We emphasize the conceptual foundation throughout this book.

A definition of theory, appropriate for accounting, is "a coherent set of hypothetical, conceptual, and pragmatic principles forming the general frame of reference for a field of inquiry."[1] Accounting theory is man-made to respond to the changing broad social and economic environment within which the accounting function operates.

Accounting theory is in a continuous process of evolution. The organizations, discussed in Chapter 1, have been influential in this continuing evolution. Accounting theory, as we know it today, is based upon both inductive and deductive reasoning, economic theory, experience, pragmatism, and general acceptability. Since accounting theory is pragmatic, it cannot be derived from, or proven by, the laws of nature as can be done in mathematics and the natural sciences.

At the present time, there is no single, agreed upon, statement of the broad structure of financial accounting theory. However, there does

---

[1] For those who desire to pursue in depth the subject of financial accounting theory, the authors recommend the following: Eldon S. Hendriksen, *Accounting Theory*, rev. ed. (Homewood, Ill.: Richard D. Irwin, Inc., 1970).

appear to be general agreement with respect to the basic theoretical foundations that underly financial accounting. The purpose of this chapter is to discuss those foundations.

## BROAD THEORETICAL STRUCTURE

In discussing accounting theory, one is confronted with a problem of terminology. Accounting literature makes numerous references to theory, assumptions, concepts, postulates, principles, standards, rules, procedures, and practices. Although each of these terms may be precisely defined, general usage by the profession has served to give them loose and overlapping meanings. To establish a basis for consistent terminology throughout this book we have designed the broad structure, and selected the terminology, presented in Exhibits 2–1 and 2–2. It is *descriptive*, since it describes present accounting, not prescriptive or normative (i.e., what accounting should be in the future). It represents *current* accounting theory and practice classified into the six basic components shown in Exhibit 2–1.

This frame of reference is easily understood and conforms to current usage. It will serve as a consistent and integrated theoretical structure

**EXHIBIT 2–1**
**Hierarchy of a Broad Structure of Financial Accounting and Reporting**

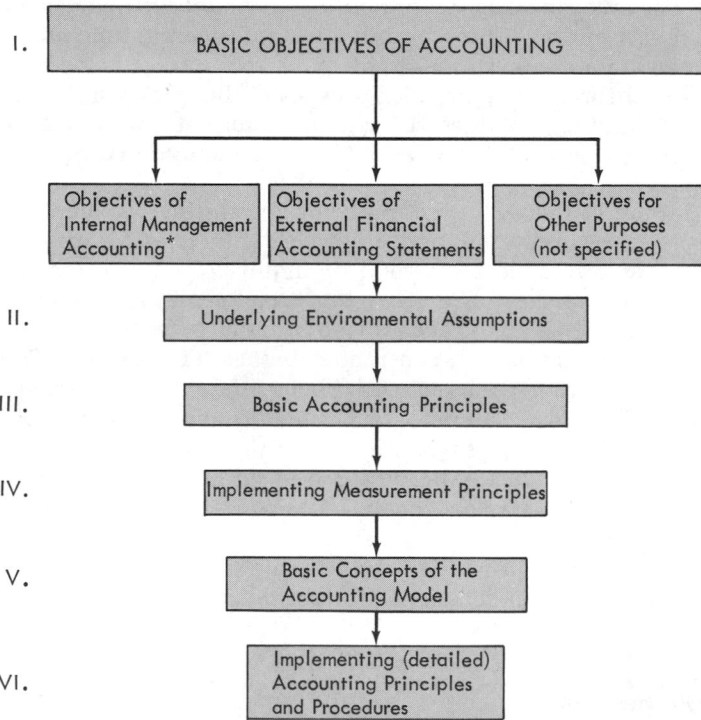

* Not focused on in this book; see books on management accounting.

for the readership of this textbook. Although not complete in every respect, it will serve as a valuable reference when later chapters discuss the rationale for the accounting and reporting treatment accorded the various accounting issues.

The structure outlined in Exhibits 2–1 and 2–2 is explained below. This structure is presented at the outset in order to provide the reader

**EXHIBIT 2–2**
**A Broad Structure of Financial Accounting and Reporting**

I. Basic Objectives of Accounting
   1. Objectives of internal management accounting
   2. Objectives of external financial accounting statements
   3. Objectives for other purposes (not yet specified)
II. Underlying Environmental Assumptions
   1. Separate-entity assumption
   2. Continuity assumption
   3. Unit-of-measure assumption
   4. Time-period assumption
III. Basic Accounting Principles
   1. Cost principle
   2. Revenue principle
   3. Matching principle
   4. Objectivity principle
   5. Consistency principle
   6. Financial reporting principle
   7. Modifying (or exception) principle
      *a.* Materiality
      *b.* Conservatism
      *c.* Industry peculiarities
IV. Implementing Measurement Principles
   1. Selection of the objects, activities, and events to be measured
   2. Identification and classification of the attributes of each object, activity, and event to be measured
   3. Assignment of quantitative amounts to the attributes
      *a.* Monetary
      *b.* Nonmonetary
   4. Modifying measurement principle
      *a.* Uncertainty
      *b.* Objectivity
      *c.* Limitations of monetary unit
      *d.* Cost effectiveness
V. Basic Concepts of the Accounting Model
   1. Financial position model: Assets = Liabilities + Owners' Equity
   2. Results of operations model: Revenues − Expenses = Net Income
   3. Changes in financial position model: Resource Inflows − Resource Outflows = Net Change in Resources
VI. Implementing (Detailed) Accounting Principles and Procedures
   1. Those related to determination of net income
   2. Those related to measurement of assets and liabilities
   3. Those related to presentation of accounting information
   4. Those related to how transactions and other events should be recorded, classified, and summarized
   5. Other accounting procedures

with a broad conceptual view that will be especially useful in understanding the subsequent chapters. In each chapter, we will refer explicitly to one or more of these concepts. Therefore, the student should return to this chapter often so that upon completion of the text there will be a keen understanding of the structure of current accounting theory and practice. An in-depth understanding of this foundation will (*a*) minimize the need to memorize procedures; and (*b*) help to resolve, on a logical basis, complex accounting issues not previously encountered.

Exhibit 2–1 presents the six basic components of the broad structure. The exhibit presents the *basic objectives of accounting* as the highest level in the hierarchy. As we move down the hierarchy, the theoretical focus shifts to the practices of *implementing* principles and procedures (the rules—how it is done!). Most of the *ARBs, APB Opinions,* and FASB *Standards* and interpretations are at this lower level.

Exhibit 2–2 presents an outline of the six basic components of the broad structure of financial accounting including the specific concepts. The remainder of this chapter will discuss, in order, each of the items listed in Exhibit 2–2.

## BASIC OBJECTIVES OF ACCOUNTING

The broad structure of accounting and reporting of financial information is based upon objectives. The basic objective of accounting is to provide relevant information to decision-makers. These decision-makers can be broadly classified as internal (i.e., the management of the entity) and external (i.e., the equity investors, creditors, government, and the general public).

Financial accounting focuses on *external* decision-makers. Governmental units have special requirements which are specified by law or by regulatory decree. Therefore, financial accounting objectives currently focus on reporting to equity investors, creditors, and the general public. Consequently, the broad objective of external financial accounting statements is to provide relevant information to equity investors, creditors, and the general public.

One of the major issues currently facing the accounting profession is whether the financial reporting objective should relate to the three groups, or to two of them, or only to one—the equity investors. A related issue is the problem of specifying in the objective (*a*) the assumed sophistication of the decision-maker (i.e., the statement user), and (*b*) the decision models the user should utilize. These issues remain unsettled. Clearly, greater specificity of the objectives of external financial accounting reports would significantly influence the broad structure of financial accounting.

## UNDERLYING ENVIRONMENTAL ASSUMPTIONS

The underlying environmental assumptions are broad aspects of the total *environment* in which accounting normally operates, and they directly affect the objectives of accounting. The underlying assumptions do not include all aspects of the environment but only those that directly affect the way in which a business entity operates. Accounting must conform to these environmental influences on the business entity. The underlying environmental assumptions—*separate entity, continuity, unit of measure,* and *time period*—suggest pervasive and accepted characteristics of the business environment that are broader even than accounting.

### Separate-Entity Assumption

Accounting is concerned with specific and separate entities. Thus each enterprise is considered as an *accounting unit* separate and apart from the owner or owners and from other entities. A corporation and the shareholders are separable entities for accounting purposes. Also partnerships and sole proprietorships are treated as separate and apart from the owners despite the fact that this distinction is not made in the legal sense.

Under the separate-entity concept the business entity is considered to own all resources committed to its purpose, subject to the rights and interests of creditors. The separate-entity assumption recognizes the fact that transactions of the business and those of the owners should be accounted for and reported separately. All records and reports are developed from the viewpoint of the particular entity. This viewpoint affects the analysis of transactions, accumulation and classification of data, and the resultant financial reporting. It provides a basis for clear-cut distinction in analyzing transactions between the enterprise and the owners. As an example, the personal residence of an individual owning an unincorporated business is not considered to be an appropriate item to report for the business, although there is a common owner. In this example the accounting entity makes a distinction that is not made in the legal sense; creditors may look to both the personal residence and the business assets for satisfaction of claims against the common owner. The accountant would be in an untenable situation from time to time if he or she did not have this basic concept to rely on in making distinctions between personal and business transactions. Pressures to overlook this distinction are encountered by accountants occasionally.

### Continuity Assumption

The continuity assumption is frequently referred to as the "going-concern" concept. It assumes indefinite continuance of the accounting entity; that is, the business is not expected to liquidate in the foreseeable future. The assumption does not imply that accountancy assumes permanent continuance; rather there is a presumption of stability and continuity for a period of time sufficient to carry out contemplated operations, contracts, and commitments. This concept establishes the rationale of acccounting on a *nonliquidation basis,* and thus provides the theoretical foundation for many of the valuations and allocations common in accounting. For example, depreciation and amortization procedures rely upon this concept. The estimates of remaining useful life and residual value are based upon the asset itself rather than upon an expectation of early liquidation of the entity.

This assumption generally underlies the decisions of investors to commit capital to the enterprise. Therefore, accounting for these commitments and the resulting incomes and losses must be based upon the assumption that the enterprise will continue to function in the contemplated manner, performing the business activities consistent with prior objectives including earning a return for the entrepreneur. The concept, as applied to accounting, holds that continuity of business activity is a reasonable expectation. If the particular entity should face serious loss and probable liquidation, conventional accounting based on the continuity assumption would not be appropriate for determining and reporting the true conditions. In such cases *liquidation* accounting is appropriate wherein all valuations immediately are accounted for at estimated realizable amounts.

Accountants are aware that no business entity will continue forever. To satisfy the continuity assumption, it is essential only that on the basis of *present facts* it appears that the business will continue so that its present resources are utilized according to plan without serious loss of capital investment. Only on the basis of this assumption can the accounting process remain stable and attain the objective of accurately recording and reporting on the capital commitments, the efficiency of management, and the financial status of the enterprise as a going concern.

### Unit-of-Measure Assumption

Some unit of exchange is essential to raise the level of commerce above that of barter. Similarly, some unit of measurement is necessary in accounting. With so many diverse assets and equities that must be recorded, analyzed, and reported, there must be a common denominator. Obviously, to be of maximum usefulness, accounting ideally should employ the same unit of measure as employed by the business community, that is, the monetary unit. Accounting may deal with some data in nonmonetary units; however the monetary unit predominates. Thus money is the common denominator—the yardstick—in the accounting process.

The unit-of-measure assumption asserts that accounting will measure and report the results of the economic activities of the entity in terms of money. It recognizes, as does society generally, that the monetary unit is the most effective means of communicating financial information. At this point we encounter a critical problem in accounting: unlike the yardstick which is always 36 inches long, the monetary unit (dollar) changes in value or purchasing power. Consequently, when there is inflation or deflation, dollars of different size (real value) are entered in the accounts over a period of time and dollars of cost are intermingled in the accounts as if they were of equal purchasing power. Because of this practice it is said that accounting either "assumes a stable monetary unit" or "changes in the value of money are not significant." However, in view of the relatively recent high rate of inflation, accounting has begun to reflect price-level effects. Accounting during periods of inflation and deflation is discussed in Chapter 25.

The unit-of-measure assumption has exerted a significant impact on the development of accounting. The basic theoretical concepts discussed in the next section of this chapter in part rest upon this assumption. Adherence to the cost principle (discussed below) and cost apportionments are related to this assumption. It is the basis in terms of *original* dollars of inflow and outflow. A subsequent section discusses the modifying measurement principle.

### Time-Period Assumption

Although the results of operations of a specific business enterprise cannot be known precisely until it has completed its life-span (i.e., final liquidation), short-term financial reports are necessary. Thus the environment—the business community and government—has imposed upon accounting a calendar constraint; that is, the necessity for assigning changes in wealth of a firm to a series of short time periods. These time periods vary; however, the year is the most common interval as a result of established business practice, tradition, and governmental requirements. For example, income tax laws require determination of income on an annual basis. Some firms adhere to the calendar year; however, more and more firms are changing to the fiscal or "natural" business year, the end of which is marked by the lowest point of business activity in each 12-month period. During the last few years, a number of leading companies have issued *interim* financial statements each quarter (a three-month period) which report summary information. Interim financial information "is essential to provide investors and others with timely information as to the progress of the enterprise."[2] Many companies also prepare *internal management* reports on a daily, weekly, or monthly basis.

The time-period assumption recognizes the need by the business community, and society in general, for short-term periodic financial statements. This assumption underlies the whole area of *accruals* and *deferrals* that distinguishes accrual basis accounting from cash basis accounting. If there were no need for periodic reports during the life-span of a business, accruals and deferrals of revenues and costs would be unnecessary. To illustrate, assume Company X was organized and $100,000 cash was invested in it. Assets were acquired, liabilities assumed, revenues earned, and costs paid for a five-year period at which time the business was liquidated (everything converted to cash) and the resulting cash of $175,000 returned to the investors. Assuming no return to the

---

[2] AICPA, *APB Opinion No. 28* (New York, May 1973), par. 9.

investors during the five-year period, we can report with certainty that the company earned $75,000 cash income. No accruals or deferrals (adjusting entries to the accountant) are necessary to determine the net income for the business. However, if the investors required a financial statement each year, accruals and deferrals for items such as unpaid wages, uncollected revenues, depreciation expense, and prepaid expenses would have to be made each period.

The continuity in business operations tends to obscure the results of the short-term "test readings" which accounting renders in the form of periodic financial statements. Many continuous and interrelated streams of data are arbitrarily severed in the preparation of annual financial statements. Despite these difficulties, short-term financial reports are of such significance to decision-makers that the accounting process must be designed to produce them. The time-period assumption recognizes this need despite the fact that precision is difficult to attain.

## BASIC ACCOUNTING PRINCIPLES

Seven basic accounting principles are listed in Exhibit 2–2. For our purposes, basic accounting principles are defined as broad standards or guidelines that rest upon the four fundamental underlying assumptions discussed above. These principles have evolved through experience to fulfill the primary objective of accounting – to provide relevant information to decision-makers (refer to page 3). They have been developed by the accounting profession and have stood the test of general acceptability. These basic principles do not include *detailed* principles and procedures.

### Cost Principle

This basic principle permeates the entire accounting process. It often is referred to as the "historical cost principle" as opposed to the fair market value or replacement cost theories. The cost principle holds that *cost* is the appropriate basis for initial accounting recognition (at date of the transaction) of all asset acquisitions, service acquisitions, expenses, liabilities, and owners' equity. It also holds that subsequent to acquisition, cost values are retained throughout the accounting process. The cost principle recognizes the basic subject matter of accounting as completed transactions which are to be translated into their financial effect on the entity in terms of the exchange price established at the date of the completed transaction. In applying the cost principle, the accountant frequently faces a serious problem of *measuring* cost, that is, where noncash considerations are involved. In determining cost the "cash bargained price" is utilized. Where considerations other than cash are involved, the cost measure is the cash equivalent of the consideration given up in the transaction or the cash equivalent of the asset or service acquired, whichever is the more clearly evident. Thus, where capital stock is issued to pay for land, the asset is recorded at the fair market value of the stock if that value is determinable; otherwise the fair market value of the land must be determined as objectively as possible. Another problem arises when noninterest-bearing debt is given for an asset. Cost is the *present value* of the future amount of cash to be paid *(APB Opinion No. 21)*. These two problems are discussed in detail in subsequent chapters.

The cost principle indicates that compared with other alternatives, the exchange price derived in an arm's-length transaction is the most useful for accounting and reporting. It is determinable, definite, and objective; it is not a matter of conjecture, opinion, or estimation. It is the basis used by the business community, taxing authorities, and society in general. As a result, users of financial statements know that a good portion of the information is based on objectively determined amounts. To illustrate the importance of these reasons, assume that instead of the cost principle, a "fair market value principle" is used. This principle would require that at each financial statement date (i.e., each year-end), all of the assets on the balance sheet be stated at their then fair market value. Appraisals and estimates would have to be made annually for receivables, investments, inventories, plant, equipment, land, patents, liabilities, and so on. The accountants may have one opinion, the management another opinion, and both may disagree with outside appraisers. The external statement user may have little confidence in these subjective judgments. The question would arise as to what should be included in net income. Assume a plant that cost $100,000 at the beginning of the year is appraised at $125,000 at year-end. Should the $25,000 increase in reported assets be reflected as an increase in net income for the year? Critics counter that the cost principle seriously distorts the financial statements in periods of significant inflation or deflation. Also some people believe that current market value, rather than original cost, better serves the external decision-maker. These issues are discussed in Chapter 25.

## Revenue Principle

The revenue principle *(a)* defines revenue, *(b)* specifies how revenue should be measured, and *(c)* pinpoints the timing of revenue recognition. Each of the three facets of the revenue principle presents difficult conceptual and operational problems.

*Revenue Defined.*  Revenue can be defined as "the creation of goods or services by an enterprise during a specific interval of time." Note that this definition does not dictate either the measurement (amount) or timing (date of recognition) of the revenue but is neutral in respect to them.[3] Another useful definition, from a different viewpoint, is: "Revenue . . . is the monetary expression of the aggregate of products or services transferred by an enterprise to its customers during a period of time."[4] The

---

[3] Adapted from Hendriksen, *Accounting Theory*, p. 161.

[4] AAA Committee on Accounting Concepts and Standards, *Accounting and Reporting Standards for Corporate Financial Statements and Preceding Statements and Supplements* (Columbus, Ohio, 1957), p. 5.

revenue principle holds that revenue should include all changes in the net assets of the firm other than those arising from owners' equity transactions. That is, revenue is the measure of new assets received for (a) the sale of goods and services; (b) interest, rents, royalties, and so on; (c) net gain on the sale of assets other than stock-in-trade; and (d) gain from advantageous settlement of liabilities. In applying the broad principle we will see in later chapters that adequate reporting (under the reporting principle) requires that revenue be reported in segments such as operating revenue and extraordinary gains.

*Measurement of Revenue.* The revenue principle dictates that revenue should be measured as the net cash equivalent price derived in an arm's-length exchange transaction. Thus, revenue is best measured by the net cash exchange value of the product, service, or other asset. This concept requires that all discounts be viewed as adjustments made to reach the true cash exchange value (i.e., sales and cash discounts should be deducted from sales revenues) and that in noncash transactions the fair market value of the consideration given or received, whichever is the more clearly determinable, should determine the revenue value.

*Timing Revenue Recognition.* This subprinciple generally is referred to as the revenue *realization* concept. The basic concept is that revenue is realized, and should be recorded as earned, when (a) there has been an exchange transaction involving a transfer of goods or services, and (b) the earning process is essentially complete. The realization concept is a pragmatic test for timing revenue recognition since it is characterized more by operational rather than by strict theoretical content. The primary test of revenue recognition is the point of sale. The point of sale generally is viewed as the time when ownership to the goods passes. For example, in the case of goods shipped f.o.b. shipping point, ownership passes at the time they are turned over to the shipper, hence revenue would be recognized at this point; whereas goods shipped f.o.b. destination give rise to revenue only upon delivery at destination.

Where services rather than goods are involved, revenue is considered realized, or earned, when the services are rendered. As a practical matter, the realization of revenue frequently is recognized when the service is completed and billed.

The timing of revenue recognition described above is often called the *sales basis.* It requires *accrual basis accounting* rather than cash basis accounting. For example, transactions for sales of goods or services on credit are recorded and reported in the period in which they occurred rather than in the period in which the cash is collected. The sales basis should be used where the following conditions exist: (a) the ultimate collection of the sales or service price in full is reasonably certain; and (b) the expenses related to the particular transaction appear to be determinable, with reasonable accuracy, in the period of sale or service. These conditions are essential to completion of the earning process.

Because of special circumstances in application of the realization concept there are four exceptions to its application. The exceptions are known as the cash, percentage-of-completion, production, and cost recovery approaches.

*Cash Approach.* Under this approach revenue is recognized on a cash basis. To illustrate, assume an installment sale of $600 that cost $360, and credit terms of $20 per month for 30 months. There is a potential gross margin of $240 or $8 per installment. Under the cash approach no revenue would be recognized at the date of sale; instead, $8 of revenue would be recognized as each collection is made. This is also known as the *installment method* of recognizing revenue. This method should be used where the sales basis is not appropriate due to the absence of reasonable assurance that ultimate collection will be made, or where the related and significant expenses and costs cannot yet be determined with a reasonable degree of accuracy. The existence of these conditions indicate that the earning process is not essentially completed at point of sale. The installment method has very limited application.

*Percentage-of-Completion Approach.* This approach is appropriate for certain long-term construction contracts. Revenue is recognized on the basis of progress of construction, although the earning process is not fully completed until delivery at the completion date. To illustrate, assume a construction company receives a $6,000,000 contract to construct a building that will require three years to build. Assume the estimated construction cost to the contractor is $5,700,000; therefore, a $300,000 profit over the three-year period is expected. At the end of the first year the building is one-third completed. Under this approach, the contractor may recognize $100,000 profit at the end of the first year. Contractors may, at their option, elect to use the percentage-of-completion approach or apply the revenue principle in the usual way and recognize no revenue until completion of the contract. Both approaches are widely used (see Chapter 10).

*Production Approach.* This approach is similar to percentage-of-completion approach. It is often applied in the case of cost-plus-fixed-fee contracts. Revenue is recognized as production progresses with a portion of the fixed fee recorded as earned.

*Cost Recovery Approach.* This approach is sometimes called the *sunk cost* approach. Under this approach all of the related costs incurred (i.e., the sunk costs) are recovered before any revenue is recognized. The cost recovery approach should be used for highly speculative transactions where the ultimate outcome is completely unpredictable. For example, an investor may have purchased bonds where the interest was in default for a number of years. The purchase price was at a fraction of the maturity value of the bonds because of the improbability of final collection. The transaction was highly speculative. Under the cost recovery approach, collections of interest would not be taken up as revenue until the original investment was recovered; collections subsequent to this point would be recognized as revenue.

Clearly the problem of determining when revenue should be recognized is a critical one. Due to diverse transactions involving revenue, no single theoretical concept can apply to all situations; therefore, accountants necessarily have developed the realistic guidelines explained above to determine when revenue should be recognized.

### The Matching Principle

The matching principle holds that for any period for which net income is to be reported, the revenues to be recognized should be determined according to the revenue principle; then the expenses incurred in generating that revenue should be determined and reported for that period. If revenue is carried over from a prior period or deferred to a future period in accordance with the revenue principle, all elements of expense related to that revenue likewise should be carried over from the prior period or deferred, as the case may be. This matching of expenses with revenue frequently is a difficult problem; however, careful matching is an essential function of accounting if there is to be a proper determination of periodic net income.

Many costs are deferred to the future by reporting them as assets because they have a future benefit or will aid in the generation of future revenues. Examples are inventories, prepaid expenses, and depreciable assets. Subsequently, they are recorded and reported as periodic expenses to *match* them with the future revenues. The deferral as assets, and subsequent write-off as periodic expenses in accordance with the matching principle, is generally based on *cause and effect*. Some are written off as expenses based on physical association (such as inventories and supplies used); some on a time basis (such as rent, interest, insurance, and depreciation); and some because there is no identifiable or measurable future benefit (such as advertising, donations to worthy causes, and research and development).

The matching principle requires that *accrual basis accounting,* as opposed to cash basis accounting, be used to record and report expenses. Thus, *adjusting entries* must be used to update expenses for the period. Examples are depreciation expense, supplies used, expired insurance, accrued (i.e., unpaid) expenses such as wages, warranty costs, and estimated bad debt expense. These often require the use of estimates. To illustrate, assume a home appliance is sold for cash during the last month of the current accounting period and it is guaranteed for a period of 12 months from date of sale. The sales revenue will be recognized as earned during the current accounting period. The expense of honoring the warranty also should be recognized in the current accounting period, although the actual warranty cost will not be known until the next year. Therefore, at the end of the current year, the amount of the warranty expense must be estimated, recorded, and reported. In this way the warranty expense is matched with the revenue of the period to which it is related.

### Objectivity Principle

This principle holds that to the fullest extent possible, accounting and reporting should be based on data that are (*a*) objectively determined, and *(b)* verifiable. *Objective determination* means that accounting should be based on completed arms'-length exchange transactions. An arms'-length transaction is characterized by an agreement between two or more parties that have adverse interests—the interest of the seller is a high price, whereas the interest of the buyer is a low price. Accountants recognize that many aspects of accounting are not based on factual data but necessarily involve estimates. For example, depreciation expense is based on *(a)* factual data—the cost of the asset, and *(b)* two estimates—useful life and residual value. The objectivity principle specifies that when estimates are necessary, they should be objectively determined by rational and systematic approaches including consideration of past experience and realistic expectations for the future.

*Verifiability* means that to the fullest extent possible, accounting data should be supported by verifiable business documents originating outside the business entity. Events recognized that do not result from transactions (such as periodic depreciation) must be supported by internally prepared documents that can be verified by the independent CPA. Thus, verifiability focuses on the adequacy of evidence to support the data processed in the accounting system and reported on the financial statements.

### Consistency Principle

This principle states that in recording and reporting economic events, there must be consistent application of accounting concepts, standards, and procedures from one accounting period to the next. Consistent application in accounting for an entity is essential so that the resulting financial statements for successive periods are comparable. Financial reports are more useful when prepared on a consistent basis because trends and other important relations are revealed. Inconsistent application of accounting standards often will materially affect reported net income and balance sheet amounts. For example, if a company used *Fifo* one year and *Lifo* the next year for inventory costing, and straight-line depreciation followed by accelerated depreciation, net income and asset amounts reported on the financial statements would become capricious. Inconsistency, if allowed, would open the door to manipulation of financial statements.

The consistency principle does not preclude an entity from changing to a different principle or procedure if it better measures economic reality. "Accounting Changes," *APB Opinion No. 20* (issued July 1971), specifies the conditions under which a change in accounting can be made and the disclosure requirements necessary to adequately explain the effect. The consistency principle, as implemented by *APB Opinion No. 20*, prevents repetitive and manipulative changes. This *Opinion* is discussed in a subsequent chapter.

The standard opinion given by the independent CPA, as a part of the audited financial statements, specifically recognizes the consistency principle as follows:

In our opinion the aforementioned financial statements present fairly the financial position of XYZ Company at December 31, 19—, and the results of its operations and the changes in its financial position for the year then ended, in conformity with generally accepted accounting principles applied on a basis *consistent with that of the preceding year*.[5]

### Financial Reporting Principle

This principle often is called the *full-disclosure* principle; however, it is a broader concept. The financial reporting principle maintains that financial statements should be designed and prepared to reasonably assure complete and understandable reporting of all significant information relating to the economic affairs of the accounting entity. The financial statements must be complete in the sense that all information reported is necessary for a "fair" presentation so that a "reasonably prudent investor" would not be misled; that is, sufficient information must be presented to permit a "knowledgeable" user to reach an informed decision. The principle is especially important for unusual events, major changes in expectations, and poststatement findings.

The financial reporting principle focuses on presentation of adequate and understandable information in the financial statements. It relates to the nature of the statements, information to be shown, classification of information on the statements, parenthetical information in the statements, and explanatory notes appended to the statements. *Full disclosure* emphasizes the necessity to include explanatory notes and parenthetical information to supplement the basic amounts reported in the financial statements. The standards of financial statement preparation developed by the accounting profession to implement the financial reporting principle are summarized in Exhibit 2–3. Application of these reporting standards will be discussed and illustrated throughout the remaining chapters.

### Modifying (or Exception) Principle

In a prior discussion the point was made that accounting principles are not principles of nature but are man-made. Further, accounting principles are subject to change when there is a change in the environment in which they operate, or in the related needs of financial statement users. Accounting principles are pragmatic and must be applied to a diverse set of facts and conditions. In view of these considerations some exceptions are to be expected. The modifying principle encompasses three fairly specific concepts which have been widely recognized and accepted in accounting as essential to accomplish the broad objectives of accounting. The three concepts that comprise the modifying principle are discussed below.

*Materiality.*    Although accounting rests upon a solid theoretical

---

[5] AICPA, "Codification of Auditing Standards and Procedures," *Statement on Auditing Standards No. 1* (New York, 1972), p. 81.

foundation, it must be pragmatic. Therefore, theory is applied realistically taking into account the nature of the economic event—the transaction—and the overall economic environment. Thus, the concept of materiality asserts that transactions and other events involving insignificant economic effects need not be accorded strict theoretical treatment because the economic effect is not *material* enough to affect the decision-maker. A less costly and timesaving approach may be used to account

**EXHIBIT 2-3**
**Financial Reporting Principle**
**Standards of Financial Statement Presentation**

1. Basic financial statements required:
    a. Balance sheet—statement of financial position.
    b. Income statement—statement of operations.
    c. Statement of changes in financial position—statement of inflows and outflows of funds.
    d. Supporting schedules essential for full disclosure.
2. Complete balance sheet—include all assets, liabilities, and classes of owners' equity (clearly identified).
3. Complete income statement—include all revenues, expenses, net income, infrequently occurring or unusual items, and earnings per share (clearly identified).
4. Classification and segregation—separate disclosure of the important components of the financial statements to make the information more useful.
5. Gains and losses—revenues and expenses other than sales of products, merchandise, or services should be separated from other revenue and expenses and the net effect disclosed as gains and losses.
6. Extraordinary items—extraordinary gains and losses (net of tax) should be presented separately from other revenue and expenses in the income statement.
7. Working capital—disclosure of components of working capital (current assets less current liabilities) is presumed to be useful in most enterprises.
8. Offsetting—assets and liabilities in the balance sheet should not be offset unless a legal right of setoff exists.
9. Consolidated statements—when one entity owns more than 50% of the outstanding voting stock of another entity consolidated statements are more meaningful.
10. Accounting period—basic time period for financial statements is one year; interim financial statements recommended for each quarter.
11. Foreign balances—financial information about foreign operations should be translated into U.S. dollars.
12. Accounting policies—accounting policies should be separately disclosed and explained.
13. Full disclosure—in addition to informative classifications and segregation of information, financial statements should disclose all additional information necessary for fair presentation. Notes and parenthetical information necessary for adequate disclosure are an integral part of the financial statements.

Adapted from: AICPA, "Basic Concepts and Accounting Principles Underlying Financial Statements," *Statement of the Accounting Principles Board No. 4* (New York, October 1970), pars. 188–201.

for *immaterial amounts.* In applying this modifying, or exception, concept, the accountant must weigh the worth of strict accuracy and compliance with accounting principles against the cost and time consumed in recordkeeping. Strict adherence to principles is not required when the accuracy of the financial report is not materially affected.

At the present time, the accounting profession has been unable to precisely define the line between a material and an immaterial amount. Materiality is a question of the effect on the user of the statements. Generally it is related to the more important financial amounts such as sales dollars, net income, total assets, total liabilities, and owners' equity. The *CPA Handbook* states:

> An item in relation to a financial statement would be considered material only if it would have a significant effect upon an important judgment based on that statement. Whether a particular item is material or significant cannot be determined by consideration only of the item itself. Its relationship to other items and to the surrounding circumstances have to be known before that judgment can be made.[6]

To illustrate, assume X Corporation purchased a pencil sharpener costing $5.98 that has an estimated useful life of three years. The assets on the balance sheet total approximately $100,000, and net income approximates $30,000. Theoretically, the pencil sharpener should be debited to an asset account and depreciated over three years at $2 per year. Clearly the $5.98 is immaterial to total assets, and the $2 is immaterial to net income. Under the materiality concept the rational accounting approach would be to debit the $5.98 to expense in the year of acquisition. No rational decision-maker would be influenced by these amounts in this particular situation. Observe that the materiality concept does not permit nonrecording and nonreporting of a transaction; it simply permits a pragmatic approach for handling immaterial amounts.

Some people assume that an amount that is 10% or less of a selected base amount is not material. This tendency should be avoided. The nature of the amount and its relative importance to other important amounts must be considered. For example, because of its size, 5% of revenue of $600 million probably should be considered material. It is important that each accounting entity establish uniform policies for implementing the materiality concept.

*Conservatism.* The concept of conservatism holds that where acceptable alternatives for an accounting determination are available, the alternative having the *least favorable immediate influence* on owners' equity should be selected. In recognizing assets where alternative valuations are acceptable, the lower should be selected, and the higher of two alternative liability amounts should be recorded. In recording expenses and revenues where there is reasonable doubt as to the appropriateness of alternative amounts, the one having the least favorable effect on net income should be chosen. Thus, where there is a choice among alternative valuations, accounting seeks to avoid favorable ex-

---

[6] *CPA Handbook,* vol. II, chap. 17, p. 24.

aggeration by relying on rational conservatism. Conservatism in accounting frequently results in an exception from theoretical treatment. For example, "lower of cost or market" as used in costing inventories is a departure from the cost principle.

Although the accounting profession has generally accepted the concept that profits should not be anticipated and that probable losses should be recognized as soon as the amounts are reasonably determinable, overconservatism usually results in misrepresentation. Reliance on conservatism should never be used to avoid the more laborious procedures to attain reasonable accuracy. Many errors in accounting have been committed under the guise of conservatism. A modified view of conservatism currently exerts an impact on accounting thought and practices.

The concept of conservatism is often misunderstood and criticized. It is essential because it is thought that when the "correct" amount is not determinable, the investment community usually is better served by understatement rather than overstatement of net income and assets. Accountants must make many accounting decisions based on judgment in selecting alternatives, making estimates, and applying accounting principles. These choices often affect net income, assets, and owners' equity; and they do not have a single answer that can be proven "correct." The concept of conservatism (a better word would be realism) provides a time-tested guideline for making these choices. Examples of the application of conservatism are: selecting an estimated useful life and residual value for depreciation purposes, the write-off of an asset of doubtful value, the write-off of an uncollectible account, application of the lower-of-cost or-market rule in valuing marketable equity securities and inventories, accruing anticipated losses, and using an accelerated depreciation method.

*Industry Peculiarities.* Because accounting focuses on usefulness, feasibility, and pragmatism, the peculiarities of an industry (such as the extractive industry) may warrant certain exceptions to accounting principles and practices. The modifying principle permits special accounting for specific items where there is a clear precedent in the industry based on uniqueness, rationale, and feasibility. It is appropriate also to note that some differences in accounting occur in response to legal requirements; this is especially true with respect to companies subject to regulatory controls.

## IMPLEMENTING MEASUREMENT PRINCIPLES

The information presented in external financial reports results from a wide range of accounting measurements. These measurements necessarily depend upon measurement principles, approaches, and techniques from other quantitative disciplines. The implementing measurement principles are those that have special application in accounting. Accounting measurement approaches and techniques generally rest upon the four broad implementing principles discussed below.

## Selection of the Objects, Activities, and Events to Be Measured

The first step in measurement is to determine what is to be measured. Fundamentally, accounting measures assets, liabilities, owners' equity, revenues, expenses, net income, resource inflows, and resource outflows. In measuring these broad classifications, *objects* must be selected and measured, such as inventory, plant and equipment, land, receivables, and obligations. Similarly, *activities* such as sales of goods and services, payment of dividends, and sale and issuance of equity securities must be identified for measurement. In addition, selected *events*, other than transactions, often must be measured. Examples of these events are casualty losses, price-level changes, depreciation, and certain "unrealized" gains and losses.

## Identification and Classification of Attributes

When an object, activity, or event has been selected for measurement, its specific attributes to be measured must be identified. For example, if goods held for resale (i.e., inventory) are selected for measurement, attributes such as units, description, condition, cost, net realizable value, replacement cost, and so on, can be measured. For measurement purposes, a choice must be made of the attributes to be measured that are relevant to the objectives of financial reports. As another example, assume an advertising *activity* is to be measured. Attributes such as description, number of ads, media used, cost, and effectiveness can be considered for measurement, and choices must be made. Measurement of the attributes of depreciation, such as cost basis depreciation, economic depreciation, and types of assets depreciated, are examples of *other events*. Because of relevance, time, and cost, the number of attributes measured generally are limited with respect to each object, activity, and other event. The attributes to be measured, to the extent feasible, must be classified to facilitate measurement and data processing. For example, one attribute classification pervading accounting is *historical cost*.

## Assignment of Quantitative Amounts

Accounting measurements of the selected attributes (of the things to be measured) are quantitative. Numerical values that can be aggregated must be assigned to the attributes of the objects, activities, and other events. For example, numerical values (such as number of units and dollar cost) must be assigned to each asset so that aggregate total asset amounts can be derived. The assignment of quantitative amounts for accounting purposes generally is in monetary terms. However, many numerical accounting measurements are not monetary, such as units of inventory, trends (i.e., indexes), shares of stock, and the number of employees, plants, and products.

### Modifying Measurement Principle

Since accounting measurements are made in an uncertain environment with limited data available, some adaptation of the basic measurement principle is necessary. This pragmatic aspect of accounting measurement not only affects the measurement process itself but influences accounting principles, procedures, and reports. For example, the inherent difficulties in measuring the "fair market value" of the multitudinous "parts" of a large complex business has been a significant argument for retaining the concept of historical cost as the valuation basis in accounting.

The modifying measurement principle has numerous facets; however, the major constraints are (a) uncertainty, (b) objectivity, (c) limitations of the monetary unit, and (d) cost effectiveness. *Uncertainty* arises because many measurements in accounting depend upon predictions. Primarily, these arise from the necessity to allocate values between past and future periods. Examples are depreciation expense, bad debt expense, warranty expense, deferred taxes, amortization of intangibles, and deferred revenue. The higher the degree of uncertainty, often the more complex the measurement.

Because of the importance attached to *objectivity* in accounting and financial reporting (see objectivity principle previously discussed), measurement adaptations are necessary to minimize bias. In addition, measurements must be based on verifiable and objective evidence. This constraint has had a strong influence on the selection and adaptation of measurement approaches and techniques used in accounting.

The *unit-of-measure assumption* (previously discussed) imposes a constraint on accounting measurements. There is general agreement that accounting measurements must use the monetary unit, although, over time, it is not a stable measuring unit. The instability of money as a measurement unit has been the basis for numerous proposals to modify both accounting principles and the selection of measurement approaches and techniques.

*Cost effectiveness* relates the value of information to the decision-maker to the cost of measuring and reporting that information. Measurement often is a costly effort; consequently, it must be adapted to meet the constraint of cost effectiveness. This often means that some accuracy and completeness in measurement are sacrificed.

## BASIC CONCEPTS OF THE ACCOUNTING MODEL

The accounting process broadly encompasses (a) collection of economic data affecting an accounting entity; (b) analysis of the economic effects of transactions and other events affecting the entity; (c) measuring, recording, and classifying the economic effects; and (d) reporting the summarized effects in periodic financial statements. This integrated process is built upon the fundamental assumptions, basic accounting principles and measurement principles, and the *accounting model.* This model comprises three submodels which parallel the three financial statements, viz:[7]

1. Financial position model—This is an economic model, expressed in algebraic format, that reflects the status of the resources (assets), obligations (liabilities), and residual equity (owners' equity) of the entity at specific points in time. Coupled with it, to facilitate data processing, is an arithmetical technique referred to as the debit-credit concept. This model, which reflects the basic content of a balance sheet (more appropriately, a statement of financial position), is:

| Basic Model → | **Assets** | = | **Liabilities** | + | **Owners' Equity** | |
|---|---|---|---|---|---|---|
| Debit-Credit Concept → | (Debit) Increase | (Credit) Decrease | (Debit) Decrease | (Credit) Increase | (Debit) Decrease | (Credit) Increase |
| | + | − | − | + | − | + |

2. Results of operations model—This model is reflected by the income statement, or more appropriately, the statement of operating results. The model is:

$$\text{Revenue} - \text{Expenses} = \text{Net Income}$$

3. Changes in financial position model—This model is reflected by the statement of changes in financial position. The model is:

$$\text{Funds Inflows} - \text{Funds Outflows} = \text{Net Change in Funds}$$

## DETAILED PRINCIPLES AND PROCEDURES

The fundamental underlying assumptions and the basic accounting principles, discussed in the preceding paragraphs, provide the broad foundation for the *detailed* principles and procedures that have been developed and accepted for financial accounting and reporting purposes. The detailed principles and procedures prescribe how transactions and other events should be recorded, classified, summarized, and reported. They are the means of implementing the underlying assumptions and the basic principles. Exhibits 2–1 and 2–2 present six categories of detailed principles and procedures; those relating to the financial reporting principle are summarized in Exhibit 2–3. The detailed principles and procedures are discussed and illustrated throughout the chapters to follow.

The term *generally accepted accounting principles* (often abbreviated as GAAP) is widely used in accounting. Although it is used in several contexts, it generally is used as defined in APB *Statement No. 4* (October 1970), par. 138:

---

[7] For a review of these basic concepts, see G. A. Welsch and R. N. Anthony, *Fundamentals of Financial Accounting* (Homewood, Ill.: Richard D. Irwin, Inc., 1974).

Generally accepted accounting principles therefore is a technical term in financial accounting. Generally accepted accounting principles encompass the conventions, rules, and procedures necessary to define accepted accounting practice at a particular time. The standard of "generally accepted accounting principles" includes not only broad guidelines of general application, but also detailed practices and procedures.

Therefore, it is consistent with the structure outlined in Exhibit 2–2.

## ACCOUNTING ON THE ACCRUAL BASIS VERSUS THE CASH BASIS

In the preceding discussion, we explained that generally accepted accounting principles require the accrual basis for accounting and reporting purposes. Nevertheless, some small sole proprietorships and partnerships use the cash basis because of its simplicity and because the financial reports are constructed only for the owners and perhaps the local banker. However, the banker may well have trouble in interpreting them, and they cannot be "certified" by an independent CPA.

When cash basis accounting is used, revenue is not recognized when the exchange transaction occurs, but rather only when the cash is collected. Similarly, expenses are not recognized when they are incurred as a result of an exchange transaction, but rather only when the cash payment is made. Therefore, net income (or loss) is essentially a cash concept. Cash basis accounting, since it is not in conformity with generally accepted accounting principles, is only briefly reviewed here to emphasize the characteristics of accrual basis accounting.

Accrual basis accounting is specified by the revenue and matching principles and is implicit in most of the other principles. Under the revenue principle, revenue is considered realized (i.e., earned), and is recognized in the accounts and reports, in the period in which the transaction occurs, regardless of the periods in which the related cash is collected. Similarly, under the matching principle, an expense is recognized, and matched with the revenue of the period to which it relates, regardless of when the related cash is expended. Therefore, net income determined in accordance with generally accepted accounting principles is not a cash concept; it is an approximation of income in the economic sense.

To illustrate the basic difference between accounting on the accrual basis versus on the cash basis, assume the following summarized data:

|  | Year 19A | Year 19B | Year 19C |
|---|---|---|---|
| Cash collections for sales: |  |  |  |
| On 19A sales | $80,000 | $15,000 | $ 5,000 |
| On 19B sales |  | 90,000 | 30,000 |
| Cash payments for expenses: |  |  |  |
| On 19A expenses | 50,000 | 7,000 | 3,000 |
| On 19B expenses | 6,000* | 50,000 | 14,000 |

* Prepayments of 19B expense.

The income statements would reflect the following:

|  | Year 19A | Year 19B |
|---|---|---|
| Cash basis: | | |
| Revenue | $ 80,000 | $105,000 |
| Expenses | 56,000 | 57,000 |
| Net income—cash basis | $ 24,000 | $ 48,000 |
| | | |
| Accrual basis: | | |
| Revenue | $100,000 | $120,000 |
| Expenses | 60,000 | 70,000 |
| Net income—accrual basis | $ 40,000 | $ 50,000 |

The misstatement of income on the cash basis is material in amount when there is a lag between the exchange transactions and the related cash-flow transactions.

## CONCLUSION

The discussion of the broad structure of financial accounting and reporting in this chapter is intended to provide the student with a frame of reference for study of subsequent chapters. Rather than presenting these concepts piecemeal throughout the text, the authors have chosen to present them briefly in this chapter. In studying the subject matter in subsequent chapters, these concepts will be reconsidered and related to the problem or practice at hand.

After studying this book we strongly recommend that the student return to this chapter for more critical study. Such an approach will help insure comprehension of a firm foundation of theory. We cannot overemphasize the importance of an understanding and appreciation of the foundations of accounting theory as opposed to a mere memorization of procedures and techniques. The accountant, whether in public practice or in industry, is faced continually with accounting problems that do not fit precisely what may have been encountered or considered previously; somehow many of them do not fit neatly into specific accounting practice and procedures. Consequently, many very practical judgments and decisions must be made by the accountant, and they should be resolved on the basis of sound theoretical analysis. For this approach there must be a logical and internally consistent structure of accounting theory. An accountant must have a deep understanding of the meaning and relevance of accounting theory to be successful as a professional. In this connection, we might repeat the hope, expressed earlier in this chapter, that there will emerge in the relatively near future an improved formulation of the foundations of accounting theory as contrasted with the implementing principles, procedures, and practices.

**QUESTIONS**

1. Define theory with special emphasis on accounting.

2. Explain briefly the characteristics of each of the following categories of the broad structure of financial accounting theory:
   a. Basic accounting objectives.
   b. Underlying environmental assumptions.
   c. Basic accounting principles.
   d. Implementing measurement principles.
   e. Basic concepts of the accounting model.
   f. Detailed principles and procedures.

3. Give the four underlying environmental assumptions and briefly explain each.

4. Complete the following:

| *Example* | *Underlying Environmental Assumptions* |
|---|---|
| a. The presentation of annual financial reports. | _____ |
| b. Measurement of assets, liabilities, and owners' equity in dollars. | _____ |
| c. Exclusion from the balance sheet of the personal assets of the owner. | _____ |
| d. Depreciation of a recently acquired fixed asset over an estimated life of 25 years when the youngest shareholder is 86 years of age. | _____ |

5. What is the basic problem created by the unit-of-measure assumption when there is significant inflation?

6. Explain why the time-period assumption gives rise to accruals and deferrals in accounting.

7. List the seven basic accounting principles. How are they different from the detailed principles and procedures?

8. Explain the cost principle. Why is it used in preference to fair market value or replacement cost?

9. How is cost measured in noncash transactions?

10. Define the revenue principle and explain each of its three aspects: (a) definition, (b) measurement, and (c) realization.

11. How is revenue measured in transactions involving noncash items (exclude credit situations)?

12. There are four exceptions to the revenue principle, briefly explain each: (a) cash, (b) percentage-of-completion, (c) production, and (d) cost recovery.

13. Explain the matching principle. What is meant by "the expense should follow the revenue"?

14. Explain why the matching principle usually necessitates the use of adjusting entries. Use depreciation expense, unpaid wages, and expired insurance as examples.

15. Relate the matching principle to the revenue and cost principles.

16. Explain the objectivity principle; focus on objectivity and verifiability.

17. Explain the consistency principle. Why is it important to the statement user?

18. Explain the financial reporting principle and relate it to the standards of financial statement presentation presented in Exhibit 2-3.

19. Why is a modifying, or exception, principle essential? Briefly explain each of the following: (a) materiality, (b) conservatism, and (c) industry peculiarities.

20. Complete the following:

| Example | Concepts of the Modifying Principle Applied |
|---|---|
| a. Banks do not separately report working capital. | _____ |
| b. An asset costs $100,000, the estimated residual value is $400 which was disregarded in computing depreciation. | _____ |
| c. Marketable securities that cost $75,000 were reported on the balance sheet at $62,000 which was the fair market value at balance sheet date. | _____ |

21. List and explain the four implementing measurement principles.

22. What are the four basic phases of the accounting process?

23. Give and briefly explain the three basic concepts of the accounting model.

24. Explain the nature of, and the need for, implementing (detailed) principles and procedures.

25. Briefly explain the technical term "generally accepted accounting principles" as used by the accounting profession.

## DECISION CASE 2-1

ABC Corporation, at the end of 1975, reported the following (summarized):

| Balance Sheet | | Income Statement | |
|---|---|---|---|
| Total assets | $400,000 | Sales revenue | $800,000 |
| Total liabilities | 100,000 | Expenses | 760,000 |
| Total owners' equity | 300,000 | Net income | 40,000 |

*Required:*

a. This problem focuses on the concept of materiality. For this particular company you are to present your own definition of what would be material. Make it as specific and precise as you can. Do not feel constrained by the definition in the chapter.

b. On the basis of *your definition,* use your best judgment to respond to each of the following examples. For each example make a choice as to materiality, then justify it.

1. At the end of the accounting year accrued wages are material if the amount is (check for "yes" response):

| | | | |
|---|---|---|---|
| _____ | $ 100 | _____ | $ 10,000 |
| _____ | 500 | _____ | 20,000 |
| _____ | 1,000 | _____ | 50,000 |
| _____ | 5,000 | _____ | 100,000 |

2. At the end of the accounting year unearned revenues (cash has been collected) are material if the amount is (check for "yes" response):

| | | | |
|---|---|---|---|
| _____ | $ 100 | _____ | $ 10,000 |
| _____ | 500 | _____ | 20,000 |
| _____ | 1,000 | _____ | 50,000 |
| _____ | 5,000 | _____ | 100,000 |

3. At the beginning of the accounting year a fixed asset, with an estimated useful life of five years and no residual value, was purchased. The transaction is material if the amount is (check for "yes" response):

| | | | |
|---|---|---|---|
| _____ | $ 100 | _____ | $ 10,000 |
| _____ | 500 | _____ | 20,000 |
| _____ | 1,000 | _____ | 50,000 |
| _____ | 5,000 | _____ | 100,000 |

## EXERCISES

### Exercise 2-1

Give the generally accepted principle(s) that establishes the dollar valuation in the balance sheet for each of the following items:

a. Accounts receivable.
b. Short-term (temporary) investments.
c. Inventory.
d. Plant and equipment.
e. Plant site (land).
f. Patent.

### Exercise 2-2

Explain how each of the following violates (if it does) the financial reporting principle.

a. Owners' equity reports only two amounts: capital stock, $100,000; and retained earnings, $80,000. The capital stock has a par value of $100,000 and originally sold for $150,000 cash.
b. Although sales amounted to $900,000 and cost of goods sold, $500,000, the first line on the income statement was revenues, $400,000.
c. No earnings per share amounts were reported.

*d.* Although current assets amounted to $200,000 and current liabilities $180,000, the balance sheet reported, under assets, the following: working capital, $20,000.

*e.* The income statement showed only the following classifications:

Gross revenues<br>
Costs<br>
Net profit

*f.* There was no comment or explanation of the fact that the company changed its inventory method from *Fifo* to *Lifo*.

## Exercise 2–3

On December 31, 1975, the balance sheet for ABC Corporation showed the following (summarized):

| | | | |
|---|---|---|---|
| Current assets* ......$ 60,000 | Current liabilities ...... | | $ 30,000 |
| Fixed assets ......... 135,000 | Long-term liabilities ... | | 20,000 |
| Patent .................. 5,000 | Contributed capital ...$100,000 | | |
| | Retained earnings ...... 50,000 | | 150,000 |
| $200,000 | | | $200,000 |

\* No cash

On this date the business (including all assets and liabilities) was sold to John Doe who paid $225,000 cash which included $35,000 for "goodwill." Assume generally accepted accounting principles were followed. Explain in terms of these principles why the selling price was still $40,000 higher than the sum of owners' equity shown on the balance sheet plus the goodwill.

## Exercise 2–4

Present accounting theory is based on the assumption that the "value of money" is relatively stable. If there is a significant change in the price level, or in the purchasing power of the dollar, problems arise in interpreting income data as determined under conventional accounting procedures.

*Required:*

State and explain briefly the nature of such problems as related to inventories and fixed assets. You need not attempt to offer specific solutions to these problems.

(AICPA adapted)

## Exercise 2–5

In making an audit of a corporation you find certain liabilities, such as taxes, which appear to be overstated. Also some semiobsolete inventory items seem to be undervalued, and the tendency is to expense rather than to capitalize as many items as possible.

In talking with the management about the policies, you are told that "the company has always taken a very conservative view of the business and its future prospects." Management suggests that they do not wish to weaken the company by reporting any more earnings or paying any more dividends than are absolutely necessary, since they do not expect business to continue to be good. They point out that the undervaluation of assets, and so on, does not lose anything for the company and creates reserves for "hard times."

*Required:*

You are to discuss fully whether the policies followed by the company are appropriate and comment on each of the arguments presented by management.

(AICPA adapted)

### Exercise 2–6

What is your understanding of the meaning of *consistency* in the application of accounting principles – for example, as used in the standard form of an independent public accountant's report?

(AICPA adapted)

### Exercise 2–7

Accountants frequently refer to a concept of "conservatism." Explain what is meant by conservatism in accounting. Discuss the question of the extent to which it is possible to follow accounting procedures which will result in consistently conservative financial statements over a considerable number of years. Give an example of an application of conservatism in accounting.

(AICPA adapted)

### Exercise 2–8

A financial statement included the following note: "During the current year, plant assets were written down by $2,000,000 because of economic conditions. This resulted in substantial savings to the company. Depreciation and other charges in the future years will be lower as a result; this will benefit the profits of future years." Appraise this statement in terms of (1) economic soundness, and (2) generally accepted accounting principles.

### Exercise 2–9

The following summarized data were taken from the records of XY Company at December 31, 1975, end of the accounting year:

1. Sales: 1975 cash sales, $300,000; 1975 credit sales, $100,000.
2. Cash collections during 1975: On 1974 credit sales, $30,000; on 1975 credit sales, $80,000; on 1976 sales (collected in advance), $20,000.
3. Expenses: 1975 cash expenses, $180,000; 1975 credit expenses, $70,000.
4. Cash payments during 1975: For 1974, credit expenses, $10,000; for 1975, credit expenses, $40,000; for 1976, expenses (paid in advance), $5,000.

*Required:*

Complete the following statements for 1975 as a basis for evaluating the difference between cash and accrual accounting.

|  | Cash Basis | Accrual Basis |
|---|---|---|
| Sales revenue | $_____ | $_____ |
| Expenses | _____ | _____ |
| Net Income | _____ | _____ |

**Exercise 2–10**

The general manager of the Cumberland Manufacturing Company received an income statement from the controller. The statement covered the calendar year. The general manager said to the controller, "This statement indicates that a net income of only $100,000 was earned last year. You know the value of the company is much more than it was this time last year."

"You're probably right," replied the controller. "You see, there are factors in accounting which sometimes keep reported operating results from reflecting the change in the fair market value of the company."

*Required:*

Present a detailed explanation of the accounting theories and principles to which the controller referred.

(AICPA adapted)

## PROBLEMS

### Problem 2–1

This problem focuses on the revenue principle. Respond to each of the following:

a. Define revenue in accordance with the revenue principle.
b. What should be the dollar amount of revenue recognized under the revenue principle in the case of (1) sales and services for cash, and (2) sales and services rendered in exchange for noncash considerations?
c. When should revenue be recognized in the case of long-term, low down payment sales and when collectibility is very uncertain.
d. When should revenue be recognized for long-term construction contracts?
e. When should revenue be recognized when there is a highly speculative transaction involving potential revenue?

### Problem 2–2

AD Corporation has been involved in a number of transactions necessitating careful interpretation of the revenue principle. For each of the following 1975 transactions specify (a) the amount of revenue that should be recognized during 1975, and (b) explain the basis for your determination.

a. Regular credit sales amounted to $600,000 of which two thirds was collected by the end of 1975; the balance will be collected in 1976.
b. Regular services were rendered on credit amounting to $100,000 of which three fourths will be collected in 1976.
c. A special item, that had been repossessed from the first purchaser, was sold again for $20,000. A $1,000 cash down payment was received in 1975; the balance is to be paid on a quarterly basis during 1976 and 1977. Repossession again would not be a surprise! The item has a cost of $14,000.
d. On January 1, 1974, the company purchased a $10,000 note. Because it was highly speculative whether the note was collectible, the company was able to acquire it for $1,000 cash. The note specifies 8% simple interest payable each year (disregard interest prior to 1974). The first collection on the note was $2,000 cash on December 31, 1975. Further collections are highly speculative.

## Problem 2–3

Appraise each of the following statements in terms of accounting principles and assumptions.

a. Lower of cost or market should be used in costing inventories.
b. The cost principle relates only to the income statement.
c. Revenue should be recognized when the cash is received.
d. Accruals and deferrals are necessary because of the separate-entity assumption.
e. Revenue should be recognized as early as possible and expenses as late as possible.
f. The accounting entity is considered to be separate and apart from the owners.
g. A transaction involving a very small amount may be disregarded because of materiality.
h. The monetary unit is not stable over time.
i. Revenues should be recognized sooner rather than later, and expenses should be recognized later rather than sooner.
j. Full disclosure requires the use of notes to the financial statements.

## Problem 2–4

Appraise the following items in financial statements in terms of generally accepted accounting principles. Indicate what principle(s) is violated and how it is violated with respect to each item.

a. Inventory is overstated by $8,000.
b. One old plant has been idle for six years; there is little likelihood that it will ever be opened. It has been depreciated at the regular amount, $10,000, each of the six years. It is reported on the current balance sheet at a book value of $140,000; estimated scrap value is $10,000.
c. The company sustained a $20,000 loss due to storm damage during the current year. The loss was reported as follows:
   Income statement: storm loss, $2,000.
   Balance sheet: deferred charge (under assets), $18,000.
d. Accounts receivable of $60,000 included amounts due from the company president amounting to $50,000.
e. Usual and ordinary repairs on fixed assets were recorded as follows: Debit: Fixed Assets, $8,000. Credit: Cash, $8,000.
f. Treasury stock (i.e., stock of the company that was sold and subsequently bought back from the shareholders) was reported on the balance sheet as an asset.
g. Depreciation expense was deducted directly from retained earnings.
h. Income tax expense was deducted directly from retained earnings.

## Problem 2–5

Cheatum Corporation was experiencing a bad year because they were operating at a loss. In order to minimize the loss they recorded certain transactions as indicated below. Determine for each transaction, what accounting principle was violated (if any) and explain the nature of the violation. Also in each instance indicate the correct accounting treatment.

a. Goods for resale (inventory) were being acquired for $1 per unit. However, the company located a good deal and acquired 10,000 units for $7,500 cash. They recorded the purchase as follows:

Inventory .................................................................... 10,000
    Cash ......................................................... 7,500
    Revenue.................................................... 2,500

b. At the beginning of the year a new machine costing $24,000 was purchased for cash for use in the business. The estimated useful life was ten years and a residual value of $4,000. The following depreciation entry was made at the end of the year:

Depreciation expense ......................................................... 1,000
    Accumulated depreciation (based on 20-year life)............ 1,000

c. A patent was being amortized over a 17-year useful life. The amortization entry made at the end of the current year was:

Retained earnings ................................................. 800
    Patent ............................................................. 800

d. Two delivery trucks were repaired (motor tune-up, new tires, brakes relined, front end realigned) at a cost of $350. The following entry was made:

Fixed asset—trucks................................................... 350
    Cash................................................................ 350

e. Although the bad debt loss rate did not change, no adjusting entry was made for the estimate of $450.

## Problem 2–6

The transactions summarized below were recorded as indicated during the current year. Determine, for each transaction, what accounting principle was violated (if any) and explain the nature of the violation. Also in each instance indicate how the transaction should have been recorded.

a. The company owns a plant that is located on a river that floods every few years. As a result, the company suffers a flood loss regularly. During the current year the flood was severe causing an uninsured loss of $4,800. The following entry was made for repair of the loss:

Retained earnings............................................................. 4,800
    Cash ......................................................... 4,800

b. The company originally sold and issued 50,000 shares of $100 par value common stock. During the current year 45,000 of these shares were outstanding and 5,000 were held by the company as treasury stock (they had been bought back from the shareholders in prior years). Near the end of the current year the board of directors declared and paid a cash dividend of $2 per share. The dividend was recorded as follows:

Retained earnings ......................................................... 100,000
    Cash ................................................................. 90,000
    Investment income.................................................. 10,000

c. The company needed a small structure for temporary storage. A contractor quoted a price of $60,000. The company decided to build it themselves. The cost was $50,000. The following entry was made:

```
Fixed assets—warehouse ............................................... 60,000
    Cash.................................................................         50,000
    Revenue ...........................................................         10,000
```

d. To construct the structure in (c) above the company borrowed $50,000 cash from the bank at 10% per annum. The loan was paid at the end of the year, and the following entry was made (12 months interest):

```
Note payable ............................................................. 50,000
Fixed assets—warehouse ............................................. 5,000
    Cash.................................................................         55,000
```

## Problem 2–7

Following is a series of transactions during 1976 for RS Corporation. Analyze each of them and then answer the questions.

a. The company engaged a local attorney to represent it in a dispute with respect to an accident involving a company vehicle. The attorney presented a bill for services for $1,500. Since the company was short of cash, the attorney agreed to accept ten shares of RS Corporation common stock (par $10 per share). The last sale of stock was for $17 per share three years earlier. The transaction to record settlement of the attorney's fee is under consideration.
   (1) What accounting principle should govern? Explain.
   (2) When should the fee be recognized as an expense? Explain.
   (3) What amount should be recorded as legal expense? Explain.
b. The corporation sold a large item of equipment which it stocked for sale. The sale was made on December 31, 1976, for $10,000 cash. It is estimated that because of a one-year guarantee on the equipment, during the following year $300 cash will be spent on the warranty. Recognition of the warranty expense is under consideration.
   (1) What accounting principle should govern? Explain.
   (2) When should the warranty expense be recognized? Explain.
   (3) What amount should be recorded as warranty expense in 1976? In 1977? Explain.
c. At December 31, 1976, there was an item in the inventory of goods for resale that cost $200. Because it had become obsolete it is estimated that it can be sold for $50 cash. Accounting for the obsolete item is under consideration.
   (1) What accounting principle should govern? Explain.
   (2) What amount should be used by the company for this item in the December 31, 1976, inventory? Explain.
d. The corporation acquired a special item of equipment that would be used in operations (a fixed asset). The suppliers catalog listed the item at $15,000. Since the corporation was short of cash it exchanged a small parcel of land that it had acquired ten years earlier at a cost of $8,000. The land was assessed for tax purposes at $12,000, and a recent appraisal by an independent appraiser showed a fair market value of $14,000. Accounting for the equipment is under consideration.
   (1) What accounting principle should govern at the date of acquisition? Explain.
   (2) What amount should be debited to the fixed asset account? Explain.
   (3) What accounting principle governs the recognition of depreciation on the asset? Explain.

**Problem 2–8**

The following summarized data were taken from the records of AC Corporation at the end of the annual accounting period, December 31, 1976:

Sales for cash ............................................................................$246,000
Sales on account.................................................................... 84,000
Cash purchases of merchandise for resale ..................................... 170,000
Credit purchases of merchandise for resale .................................. 40,000
Expenses paid in cash ................................................................ 71,000
Accounts receivable:
    Balance in the account on January 1, 1976.................................. 23,000
    Balance in the account on December 31, 1976 ........................... 30,000
Accounts payable:
    Balance in the account on January 1, 1976.................................. 14,000
    Balance in the account on December 31, 1976 ........................... 16,000
Merchandise inventory account:
    Beginning inventory, January 1, 1976 ...................................... 50,000
    Ending inventory, December 31, 1976 ....................................... 60,000
Accrued (unpaid) wages at December 31, 1976 (none at January 1,
    1976) ................................................................................. 2,000
Prepaid expenses at December 31, 1976 (none at January 1, 1976) ... 3,000
Fixed assets—equipment:
    Cost when acquired .............................................................. 100,000
    Annual depreciation ............................................................. 10,000

*Required:*

Based on the above data complete the following income statements for 1975 in order to evaluate the difference between cash and accrual basis:

|  | Cash Basis | Accrual Basis |
|---|---|---|
| Sales revenue | $_____ | $_____ |
| Less expenses: | | |
|     Cost of goods sold ............$_____ | $_____ | |
|     Depreciation expense......... _____ | _____ | |
|     Remaining expenses ......... _____ | _____ | |
|         Total Expenses............ _____ | _____ | |
| Pretax Income ..................... | $_____ | $_____ |

**Problem 2–9**

The general ledger of Enter-tane, Inc., a corporation engaged in the development and production of television programs for commercial sponsorship, contains the following accounts before amortization at the end of the current year:

| Account | Balance (debit) |
|---|---|
| Sealing Wax and Kings................................................................ | $51,000 |
| The Messenger ....................................................................... | 36,000 |
| The Desperado ....................................................................... | 17,500 |
| Shin Bone................................................................................ | 8,000 |
| Studio Rearrangement .............................................................. | 5,000 |

An examination of contracts and records revealed the following information:

a. The first two accounts listed above represent the total cost of completed programs that were televised during the accounting period just ended. Under the terms of an existing contract, Sealing Wax and Kings will be rerun during the next accounting period at a fee equal to 50% of the fee for the first televising of the program. The contract for the first run produced $300,000 of revenue. The contract with the sponsor of The Messenger provides that at the sponsor's option, the program can be rerun during the next season at a fee of 75% of the fee on the first televising of the program.

b. The balance in The Desperado account is the cost of a new program which has just been completed and is being considered by several companies for commercial sponsorship.

c. The balance in the Shin Bone account represents the cost of a partially completed program for a projected series that has been abandoned.

d. The balance of the Studio Rearrangement account consists of payments made to a firm of engineers which prepared a report relative to the more efficient utilization of existing studio space and equipment.

*Required:*

1. State the general principle (or principles) of accounting that are applicable to the first *four* accounts.
2. How would you report each of the first *four* accounts in the financial statements of Enter-tane, Inc.? Explain.
3. In what way, if at all, does the Studio Rearrangement account differ from the first four? Explain.

(AICPA adapted)

*Chapter* **3**

# Review—The Accounting Model and Information Processing

The broad objective of financial accounting is to provide relevant financial information to external decision makers. The information reported on periodic financial statements summarizes the economic impacts of a multitude of transactions and other events on an entity. Identification, analysis, recording, and classification of the impacts of transactions and other events require an efficient and sophisticated accounting information processing system. The larger the entity, the greater the number of transactions, and, consequently, the more complex the information processing system. The information processing system (i.e., the accounting system) must be designed effectively and economically to (1) collect and measure economic data, (2) classify and process the data, and (3) report the summarized economic effects to decision-makers. An accounting system must be tailored to the entity's characteristics such as size, nature of operations, organizational structure, management approaches, and the impact of government regulations. However, there is a fundamental structure, based upon the accounting model, that is common to most accounting systems.

We assume in this book that the reader has a sound knowledge of the *fundamentals* of financial accounting. Nevertheless, in this and the next two chapters, we shall review those fundamentals.[1] The purpose of this chapter is to review and illustrate the *sequential* accounting information processing cycle that is repeated each accounting period.

## THE ACCOUNTING MODEL

In Chapter 2 we outlined the fundamental accounting model on which accounting systems are based. This model is composed of three submodels, each of which represents one basic component of the peri-

---

[1] For a more comprehensive introductory discussion see: G. A. Welsch and R. N. Anthony, *Fundamentals of Financial Accounting* (Homewood, Ill.: Richard D. Irwin, Inc., 1974).

odic financial statement designed for external decision-makers. The three submodels are:

1. Financial position model: Assets = Liabilities + Owners' Equity (A = L + OE).
2. Results of operations model: Revenues − Expenses = Net Income (R − E = NI).
3. Funds flow model: Funds Inflow − Funds Outflow = Net Change in Funds (FI − FO = NCF).

Coupled with the accounting model is the debit-credit concept. This is a mathematical technique used to record increases and decreases in specific variables in the model – assets, liabilities, owners' equity, revenues, and expenses.

Fundamentally, all recognized accounting events are recorded in the accounting system in terms of the *financial position model:* A = L + OE. The debit-credit concept is superimposed on this basic model as follows:

| Basic Model | Assets | | = | Liabilities | + | Owners' Equity | |
|---|---|---|---|---|---|---|---|
| Debit-Credit Concept | Debit for Increases | Credit for Decreases | | Debit for Decreases | Credit for Increases | Debit for Decreases | Credit for Increases |

Since investments by owners and revenues *increase* owners' equity and since withdrawals by owners and expenses *decrease* owners' equity, the model can be expanded to include them as follows:

| Assets | | = | Liabilities | + | Owners' Equity | |
|---|---|---|---|---|---|---|
| Debit for increases | Credit for decreases | | Debit for decreases | Credit for increases | Debit for decreases: *a.* Withdrawals by owners'. *b.* Expenses. | Credit for increases: *a.* Investments by owners'. *b.* Revenues. |

Observe in the above diagram, that although the debits are *always* on the left and the credits on the right, the increases and decreases are opposite on each side of the equation. That is, debits represent increases to assets and decreases to liabilities and owners' equity; whereas credits represent decreases to assets and increases to liabilities and owners' equity. Expenses are recorded as debits and revenues as credits. This algebraic arrangement forces debits always to equal credits. Thus, the fundamental accounting model always maintains a dual balancing feature, viz:

1. Assets = Liabilities + Owners' Equity.
2. Debits = Credits.

Because of this dual feature, the accounting model is often referred to as a *double-entry system.* These two balancing features, in addition to

**EXHIBIT 3–1**
**Information Inputs in an Accounting System**

| Typical Transaction | Transaction Analysis | Entry into the Accounting System | | | Basic Accounting Model (cumulative balances) | | |
|---|---|---|---|---|---|---|---|
| | | Accounts | Debit | Credit | A = | L + | OE |
| 1. Service Corporation was organized; owners invested $100,000 cash and received nopar common stock. | Asset increased—cash, $100,000. Owners' equity increased—common stock, $100,000. Liabilities—no effect. | Cash ............... Common stock ... | 100,000 | 100,000 | + 100,000 _____ 100,000 | —0— _____ —0— | +100,000 _____ 100,000 |
| 2. Borrowed $50,000 on a note. | Asset increased—cash, $50,000. Liabilities increased—note payable, $50,000. Owners' equity—no effect. | Cash ............... Notes payable...... | 50,000 | 50,000 | + 50,000 _____ 150,000 | +50,000 _____ 50,000 | _____ 100,000 |
| 3. Purchased equipment for use in the business, $40,000; paid cash. | Asset increased—equipment, $40,000. Asset decreased—cash, $40,000. Liabilities—no effect. Owners' equity—no effect. | Equipment ........ Cash ............... | 40,000 | 40,000 | + 40,000 − 40,000 _____ 150,000 | _____ 50,000 | _____ 100,000 |

| Transaction | Analysis | Account | Debit | Credit | Assets | Liabilities | Owners' Equity |
|---|---|---|---|---|---|---|---|
| 4. Services rendered to clients, $20,000; of which $15,000 was collected in cash. | Assets increased—cash, $15,000; accounts receivable, $5,000. Revenue (owners' equity) increased $20,000. Liabilities—no effect. | Cash ............ Accounts receivable ......... Service revenue... | 15,000 5,000 |  20,000 | + 15,000 + 5,000  __170,000__ |  __50,000__ | + 20,000  __120,000__ |
| 5. Incurred operating expenses, $11,000; of which $8,000 was paid in cash. | Asset decreased—cash, $8,000. Liability increased— accounts payable, $3,000. Owners' equity (expense) decreased, $11,000. | Expenses........... Cash ......... Accounts payable........ | 11,000 |  8,000 3,000 | – 8,000  __162,000__ | + 3,000  __53,000__ | – 11,000  __109,000__ |
| 6. Paid $2,000 on accounts payable (5 above). | Asset decreased—cash, $2,000. Liability decreased— accounts payable, $2,000. Owners' equity—no effect. | Accounts payable........... Cash ....... | 2,000 |  2,000 | – 2,000  __160,000__ | – 2,000  __51,000__ | __109,000__ |
| 7. Depreciation for one year on equipment, estimated life ten years, no residual value. (3 above). | Asset decreased—ac- cumulated deprecia- tion, $4,000. Owners' equity de- creased—deprecia- tion expense, $4,000. Liabilities—no effect. | Depreciation ex- pense ......... Accumulated de- preciation, equipment ........ | 4,000 |  4,000 | – 4,000  __156,000__ | __51,000__ | – 4,000  __105,000__ |

other purposes, automatically call attention to many types of errors and add considerable reliability to the output of an accounting system.

Whether an accounting system is maintained manually, mechanically, or electronically, each entry is recorded in the basic accounting model. Thus, each entry entered in an accounting system, continuously maintains the dual-balancing feature. The fundamental information processing approach is reviewed in Exhibit 3-1. In particular, note the following: (1) transaction analysis in terms of the basic accounting model, (2) method of recording the increases and decreases, (3) $A = L + OE$ for each entry and cumulatively, and (4) debits equal credits for each entry and cumulatively.

## THE ACCOUNTING INFORMATION PROCESSING CYCLE

The accounting system provides a systematic approach for processing information from the capture of raw economic data that affect the entity to the end result, the periodic financial statements. Therefore, an accounting system incorporates an information processing cycle, often called the accounting cycle, that is repeated each accounting period. This cycle is common to all double-entry accounting systems; however, the larger the enterprise, the more complex its application. The accounting information processing cycle, diagrammed in Exhibit 3-2, reflects the primary phases in the *sequential order* in which they are usually accomplished. Each of these phases will be discussed and illustrated in order.

## COLLECTION OF RAW ECONOMIC DATA (PHASE 1)

The accounting system collects raw economic data about events affecting the entity that are to be recorded. There are two types of events that are recognized in an accounting system: (1) exchange transactions between the entity and one or more outside parties, such as the sale of goods, purchase of assets, sale of securities, and payment of wages; and (2) other events that are not transactions but which exert an economic impact on the enterprise and must be recorded. These events may be external such as casualties (i.e., floods, fires, hurricanes, etc.) and changes in currency exchange rates. Also they may be internal, which involves the conversion or use of resources such as depreciation of fixed assets and amortization of intangibles.[2]

Raw economic data are collected by means of *source documents*. Exchange transactions, since they involve external parties, almost always generate their own source documents – sale invoices, credit bills, freight bills, notes signed by debtors, purchase orders, deposit slips, checks, and so on. For recognized events that are not transactions, the entity itself must prepare the source documents. Examples are: depreciation computations, schedules of assets lost due to casualty, amorti-

---

[2] For convenience in exposition, the term *transactions* will be used broadly to include both transactions and the other events to be recognized.

**EXHIBIT 3–2**
**Diagram of the Accounting Information Processing Cycle**

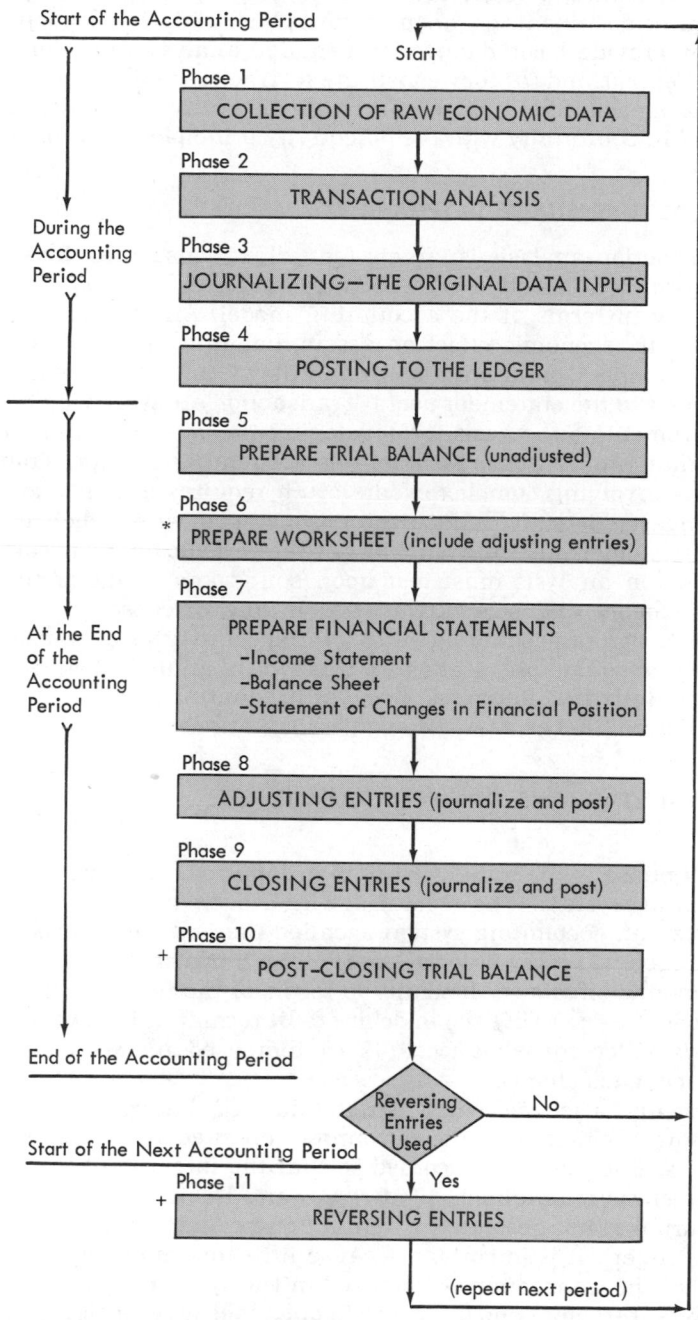

Note: See Exhibit 3–12 for complete summary.

* Worksheet is optional. If not used, prepare an *adjusted* trial balance after Phase 8 as a basis for preparing the financial statements.

+ Optional.

zation schedules, periodic inventory schedules, and issue requisitions. The source documents are an important phase of data collection because (a) they provide basic data for transaction analysis (and the resulting journal entry), and (b) they constitute a "track record" so that the event and the measurement of its effects on the entity can be subsequently *verified* in conformity with the objectivity principle (see Chapter 2).

### TRANSACTION ANALYSIS (PHASE 2)

Transaction analysis is largely mental. It constitutes the study and analysis of a transaction to identify and assess its economic impact on the entity in terms of the accounting model. An analysis is made to measure its economic effect on assets, liabilities, owners' equity, revenues, expenses, fund inflows, fund outflows, and other measurements of interest to the statement users. Transaction analysis, which includes measurement, is the basis for developing the *accounting entry*, or entries, that must be recorded in the accounting system. Transaction analysis involving complex events often requires a high degree of accounting sophistication since the competence with which it is done ultimately determines the reliability of the periodic financial statements. Transaction analysis must rest upon sound knowledge of the fundamental theory and structure of accounting discussed in Chapter 2. Memorization of accounting entries for specific types of transactions is wholly inadequate preparation for this type of analytical endeavor. This is particularly true in the real world of accounting because the accountant constantly faces new and complex situations.

### JOURNALIZING – THE ORIGINAL DATA INPUT (PHASE 3)

This phase is the initial, or original, input of economic data into an accounting system. The record in which each transaction is first recorded in an accounting system is called the *journal*. This is a chronological record (i.e., by order of date) of each transaction that expresses its economic effects on the entity in terms of the fundamental accounting model ($A = L + OE$) and in debit-credit format; it follows transaction analysis. It records what accounts are increased and decreased and the amount of each change.

Basically, a journal entry lists the date of the transaction, and the account(s) debited and the account(s) credited and their respective amounts. Each entry is recorded so that the integrity of the duality of the system is maintained: $A = L + OE$ and Debits = Credits. Although the journal is not absolutely essential (one could skip it and go directly to the ledger), it is important because it (a) maintains a chronological record of the transactions recognized in the system, which is useful for subsequent tracing; and (b) shows in one place all aspects of each transaction (i.e., all accounts affected and the amounts).

In an accounting system usually there are two types of journals:

(1) the general journal, and (2) several special journals. Each special journal is designed to accommodate like-kind transactions. The commonly used special journals are: credit sales, credit purchases, cash receipts, cash payments, and the voucher journal. Special journals are discussed and illustrated in Appendix A of this chapter. Most accounting systems use at least a general journal. A general journal will be used in the chapters to follow because of its value for instructional purposes. The general journal format, with a typical entry, is shown in Exhibit 3–3.

**EXHIBIT 3–3**
**General Journal and General Ledger Illustrated**

General Journal

Page J–16

| Date 1976 | Accounts and Explanation | Ledger Folio* | Amount Debit | Amount Credit |
|---|---|---|---|---|
| Jan. 2 | Equipment | 150 | 15,000 | |
| | Cash | 101 | | 5,000 |
| | Notes payable | 215 | | 10,000 |
| | Purchased equipment for use in the business. Paid $5,000 cash and gave a $10,000, one-year, 9% interest-bearing note. | | | |

\* The figures in this column indicate ,a. that the amount has been posted to the ledger, and ,b. the account number in the ledger to which posted.

General Ledger

| | Cash | | | | | Acct. 101 |
|---|---|---|---|---|---|---|
| 1976 Jan. 1 | Balance | 18,700 | 1976 Jan. 2 | J–16 † | | 5,000 |

| | Equipment | | | | Acct. 150 |
|---|---|---|---|---|---|
| 1976 Jan. 1 | Balance | 62,000 | | | |
| 2 | J–16 | 15,000 | | | |

| | Notes Payable | | | | Acct. 215 |
|---|---|---|---|---|---|
| | | | 1976 Jan. 2 | J–16 | 10,000 |

† This figure indicates the journal page from which the amount was posted.

## POSTING TO THE LEDGER (PHASE 4)

After the initial recording in the journal, the next step is to transfer the information to the ledger. The transfer process is called *posting* and is done at various times for all transactions. This transfer has the effect of reclassifying the information from a chronological format to an account classifications format in the *ledger*. Posting from the journal to the ledger is illustrated in Exhibit 3–3.

Recall that the ledger consists of a large number of separate accounts. There are accounts for each kind of asset (such as cash, accounts receivable, investments, fixed assets, and intangible assets), liability (such as accounts payable and bonds payable), owners' equity (such as capital stock and retained earnings), and the revenue and expense accounts. Posting amounts from the journal to the ledger results in reclassification of the data in ledger accounts which are compatible with the classifications of information in the financial statements.

### Real and Nominal Accounts

The accounts in the ledger often are classified as follows:

1. Real accounts – These are the balance sheet accounts; they are *permanent*, or real, in the sense that they are not closed at the end of the accounting period. They are the asset, liability, and owners' equity accounts.
2. Nominal accounts – These are the income statement accounts; they are *temporary*, or nominal, in the sense that they are closed at the end of the accounting period. They are the revenue and expense accounts.

Frequently an account, either real or nominal, will be *mixed* in the sense that its balance has both a real (i.e., balance sheet) component and a nominal (i.e., income statement) component. To illustrate, assume that on January 1 of the current year, a three-year insurance premium of $600 was paid and debited to an asset account, Prepaid Insurance. On December 31 of the current year, of the $600, the nominal component, Insurance Expense, is $200 and the real component, Prepaid Insurance, is $400 (an asset). An adjusting entry on December 31, debiting Insurance Expense and crediting Prepaid Insurance for $200, is necessary to "unmix" the Prepaid Insurance asset account by removing the expense component of $200.

### Subsidiary Ledgers and Control Accounts

Most companies use both a *general ledger* and one or more *subsidiary ledgers*. For each subsidiary ledger there is a related *control account* in the general ledger. The control account reflects summary information only whereas the subsidiary ledger reflects the details that support the control account. The general ledger contains the complete account structure for all assets, liabilities, owners' equity, revenues, and expenses.

Each subsidiary ledger is a device for keeping track of a multitude of details that relate to a particular *control account* in the general ledger. To illustrate, a department store may have 10,000 credit customers. A separate account receivable must be kept for each customer. Rather than 10,000 separate accounts receivable in the general ledger, one controlling account, Accounts Receivable Control, should be used. A separate accounts receivable subsidiary ledger composed of a separate account for each customer should also be maintained. Each credit sale would (*a*) be posted directly to the customer's account in the subsidiary ledger, and (*b*) the total of all credit sales would be posted to the Accounts Receivable Control account in the general ledger. Thus, at any time when posting is complete, the sum of the balances in the customer accounts in the subsidiary ledger would agree with the single balance in the Accounts Receivable Control account.

Subsidiary ledgers often are used for cash (when there are numerous cash accounts), accounts receivable, accounts payable, fixed assets, capital stock (the subsidiary ledger for this account is a record for each shareholder), revenue, and expense. Subsidiary ledgers and control accounts are discussed and illustrated in Appendix A to this chapter.

## PREPARE A TRIAL BALANCE—UNADJUSTED (PHASE 5)

At the end of the period after all of the regular entries have been journalized and posted to the ledger, a trial balance should be prepared. Since this trial balance is prepared before the adjusting entries are made, it is often called the *unadjusted trial balance*. A trial balance is simply a list of the accounts in the general ledger and their respective debit or credit balances. A trial balance, prepared after all of the regular entries, but before the adjusting entries, serves the following purposes:

1. It verifies that debits equal the credits.
2. It provides important information for the development of—
   *a.* A worksheet, and
   *b.* The end-of-the-period adjusting entries.

An unadjusted trial balance for Canby Retailers, Inc., is shown in Exhibit 3–4. This trial balance will be used to illustrate the discussions to follow.

## PREPARE WORKSHEET (PHASE 6)

As soon as the unadjusted trial balance is available, the following end-of-the-period procedures can be completed:

1. Develop the adjusting entries.
2. Journalize and post the adjusting and closing entries.

3. Develop an adjusted trial balance.
4. Develop the financial statements.

These procedures can be completed in the order listed above. Remember that the adjusting entries must be taken into consideration before the financial statements can be developed. However, accountants usually insert another step, preparation of two worksheets, viz: (1) one to facilitate development of the adjusting entries, the income statement, and the balance sheet; and (2) one to facilitate preparation of the statement of changes in financial position. These worksheets are simply *facilitating techniques*. They constitute an orderly and systematic approach to completing (*a*) the financial statements on a timely basis, and (*b*) the adjusting and closing entries. This is the only reason for using these worksheets.

A worksheet based on the trial balance given in Exhibit 3–4 is pre-

**EXHIBIT 3–4**

CANBY RETAILERS, INC.
Unadjusted Trial Balance
December 31, 1976

| Account | Debit | Credit |
|---|---:|---:|
| Cash | $ 55,300 | |
| Marketable securities (bonds) | 20,000 | |
| Accounts receivable | 45,000 | |
| Allowance for doubtful accounts | | $ 1,000 |
| Inventory of merchandise (periodic system) | 75,000 | |
| Prepaid insurance | 600 | |
| Accrued investment revenue receivable | | |
| Land | 8,000 | |
| Building | 160,000 | |
| Accumulated depreciation, building | | 90,000 |
| Equipment | 91,000 | |
| Accumulated depreciation, equipment | | 27,000 |
| Accounts payable | | 29,000 |
| Income taxes payable | | |
| Accrued bond interest payable | | |
| Prepaid rent revenue | | |
| Bonds payable, 6% | | 50,000 |
| Common stock, par $100 | | 150,000 |
| Contributed capital in excess of par | | 20,000 |
| Retained earnings | | 31,500 |
| Sales revenue | | 325,200 |
| Investment revenue | | 500 |
| Rent revenue | | 1,800 |
| Purchases | 130,000 | |
| Freight on purchases | 4,000 | |
| Purchase returns | | 2,000 |
| Selling expenses* | 104,000 | |
| General and administrative expenses* | 23,600 | |
| Interest expense | 2,500 | |
| Extraordinary loss | 9,000 | |
| Income tax expense | | |
| Totals | $728,000 | $728,000 |

* These broad categories of expense are used to conserve space.

sented in Exhibit 3-5. This worksheet provides data for the income statement and balance sheet.[3]

## Worksheet Techniques

The worksheet shown in Exhibit 3-5 was prepared as follows:

1. Enter the unadjusted trial balance (Exhibit 3-4) on the worksheet using the first pair of amount columns.
2. Develop the adjusting entries and record them in the second pair of columns.
3. Extend the unadjusted balances, plus and minus the adjustments, to the adjusted trial balance columns and check for balance.
4. Extend the adjusted amounts to the right, line by line, to the pair of columns under the financial statement on which they should be reported: income statement, statement of retained earnings (optional), and balance sheet.
5. Check each pair of columns for equality of debits and credits.

## Development of Adjusting Entries

Because of accrual basis accounting, numerous adjustments must be made to the account balances (as reflected in the unadjusted trial balance) at the end of each accounting period. These adjustments are necessary to restate (i.e., adjust) certain income statement and balance sheet accounts because (1) some accounts have a "mixed" balance which includes both real and nominal components, and (2) certain transactions have not yet been entered in the accounts. These adjustments may be classified as follows:

*Prepaid (Deferred) Items:*
   1. Prepaid expense – an expense paid but not yet incurred (i.e., not yet recognized).
   2. Prepaid revenue – a revenue collected but not yet earned (i.e., not yet realized); frequently called unearned rent revenue.

*Accrued Items:*
   3. Accrued expense – an expense incurred but not yet paid.
   4. Accrued revenue – a revenue earned but not yet collected.

*Other Items:*
   5. Estimated items.

*Prepaid Expenses.*  A prepaid expense occurs when a company has paid for services or supplies that are not used, or consumed, by the end of the accounting period. To illustrate, Canby Retailers, Inc., on January 1,

---

[3] Preparation of a worksheet for the statement of changes in financial position is discussed and illustrated in Chapter 21. It is more complex than one for the income statement and balance sheet. If you are not interested in the worksheet technique, study only the material captioned "Developing Adjusting Entries," and then move directly to the caption "Prepare Financial Statements."

**EXHIBIT 3–5**

## CANBY RETAILERS, INC.
### Worksheet for the Year Ended December 31, 1976

| Accounts | Unadjusted Trial Balance Debit | Unadjusted Trial Balance Credit | Adjusting Entries Debit | Adjusting Entries Credit | Adjusted Trial Balance Debit | Adjusted Trial Balance Credit | Income Statement Debit | Income Statement Credit | Retained Earnings Debit | Retained Earnings Credit | Balance Sheet Debit | Balance Sheet Credit |
|---|---|---|---|---|---|---|---|---|---|---|---|---|
| Cash | 55,300 | | | | 55,300 | | | | | | 55,300 | |
| Marketable securities (bonds) | 20,000 | | | | 20,000 | | | | | | 20,000 | |
| Accounts receivable | 45,000 | | | | 45,000 | | | | | | 45,000 | |
| Allowance for doubtful accounts | | 1,000 | | (e) 1,200 | | 2,200 | | | | | | 2,200 |
| Inventory (periodic system) | 75,000 | | | | 75,000 | | 75,000 | 90,000* | | | | |
| Prepaid insurance | 600 | | | (a) 200 | 400 | | | | | | 400 | |
| Accrued investment revenue receivable | | | (d) 100 | | 100 | | | | | | 100 | |
| Land | 8,000 | | | | 8,000 | | | | | | 8,000 | |
| Building | 160,000 | | | | 160,000 | | | | | | 160,000 | |
| Accumulated depreciation, building | | 90,000 | | (e) 10,000 | | 100,000 | | | | | | 100,000 |
| Equipment | 91,000 | | | | 91,000 | | | | | | 91,000 | |
| Accumulated depreciation, equipment | | 27,000 | | (e) 9,000 | | 36,000 | | | | | | 36,000 |
| Accounts payable | | 29,000 | | | | 29,000 | | | | | | 29,000 |
| Income taxes payable | | | | (g) 20,000 | | 20,000 | | | | | | 20,000 |

| Account | Trial Balance Dr | Trial Balance Cr | Adjustments Dr | Adjustments Cr | Adjusted Trial Balance Dr | Adjusted Trial Balance Cr | Income Statement Dr | Income Statement Cr | Retained Earnings Dr | Retained Earnings Cr | Balance Sheet Dr | Balance Sheet Cr |
|---|---|---|---|---|---|---|---|---|---|---|---|---|
| Accumulated bond interest payable | | | | (c) 500 | | 500 | | | | | | 500 |
| Prepaid rent revenue | | | | (b) 600 | | 600 | | | | | | 600 |
| Bonds payable, 6% | | 50,000 | | | | 50,000 | | | | | | 50,000 |
| Common stock, par $10 | | 150,000 | | | | 150,000 | | | | | | 150,000 |
| Contributed capital in excess of par | | 20,000 | | | | 20,000 | | | | | | 20,000 |
| Retained earnings | | 31,500 | | | | 31,500 | | | | 31,500 | | |
| Sales revenue | | 325,200 | | | | 325,200 | | 325,200 | | | | |
| Investment revenue | | 500 | | (d) 100 | | 600 | | 600 | | | | |
| Rent revenue | | 1,800 | (b) 600 | | | 1,200 | | 1,200 | | | | |
| Purchases | 130,000 | | | | 130,000 | | 130,000 | | | | | |
| Freight on purchases | 4,000 | | | | 4,000 | | 4,000 | | | | | |
| Purchase returns | | 2,000 | | | | 2,000 | | 2,000 | | | | |
| Selling expenses | 104,000 | | (e) 8,200 (f) 1,200 | | 113,400 | | 113,400 | | | | | |
| General and administrative expenses | 23,600 | | (a) 200 (e) 10,800 | | 34,600 | | 34,600 | | | | | |
| Interest expense | 2,500 | | (c) 500 | | 3,000 | | 3,000 | | | | | |
| Extraordinary loss | 9,000 | | | | 9,000 | | 9,000 | | | | | |
| Income tax expense | | | (g) 20,000 | | 20,000 | | 20,000 | | | | | |
| Net Income | | | | | | | 30,000 | | | 30,000 | | |
| Retained Earnings | | | | | | | | | 61,500 | | | 61,500 |
| Totals | 728,000 | 728,000 | 41,600 | 41,600 | 768,800 | 768,800 | 419,000 | 419,000 | 61,500 | 61,500 | 469,800 | 469,800 |

* This is only one of several techniques for entering the ending inventory on a worksheet.

1976, paid a three-year insurance premium in advance amounting to $600. At that date, the $600 payment was recorded as a debit to Prepaid Insurance and a credit to Cash. On the unadjusted trial balance of the worksheet, the $600 is reflected as the debit balance of an asset account, Prepaid Insurance. Since $200 of this service was "used" in 1976, there remains a $400 prepaid expense. Therefore, on December 31, 1976, an adjusting entry must be made as follows (the letter code to the left is used on the worksheet, Exhibit 3–5, for reference in study):

*a.* December 31, 1976:

| | | |
|---|---|---|
| Insurance expense (general and administrative expense) | 200 | |
| Prepaid insurance | | 200 |

The effects of this entry, which may be easily observed on the worksheet, are (1) to adjust the asset account to $400 on the balance sheet, and (2) to record the $200 expense component on the income statement.[4]

*Prepaid Revenues.* A prepaid revenue occurs when a company collects a revenue in advance and at the end of the accounting period some of it is not yet earned. Therefore, one account has a balance that must be separated into its income statement (nominal) and balance sheet (real) components by means of an adjusting entry. To illustrate, Canby Retailers, Inc., on January 1, 1976, leased to J. R. Jones a small office in their building that was not needed. At the start they collected, in advance, $1,800 cash for 18 months rent. At that time, the collection was recorded as a debit to Cash and a credit to Rent Revenue. On December 31, 1976, the $1,800 balance in the Rent Revenue account included $600 prepaid rent revenue. Therefore, the following adjusting entry was made (see Exhibit 3–5):

*b.* December 31, 1976:

| | | |
|---|---|---|
| Rent revenue | 600 | |
| Prepaid rent revenue | | 600 |

This entry leaves $1,200 in the Rent Revenue account and separates as a liability, the $600 prepaid rent revenue. The $600 is a liability on December 31, 1976, because Canby owes that amount of "occupancy" to Jones. In 1977 the $600 will be transferred to the Rent Revenue account.

*Accrued Expenses.* An accrued expense is an unpaid expense that has not been recorded in the accounts at the end of the accounting period. Therefore, at the end of the accounting period, an adjusting entry must be made to recognize it. To illustrate, Canby Retailers, Inc., has a liability for bonds payable of $50,000. These bonds require payment of 6% annual interest each October 30. Therefore, on December 31, 1976, there was accrued interest of $50,000 × .06 × 2/12 = $500.

---

[4] Sometimes a prepaid expense is initially debited to an expense account instead of an asset account. In this case, an adjusting entry also is required. To illustrate, assume the $600 was initially debited to *Insurance Expense;* the adjusting entry would be: debit, Prepaid Insurance, $400; credit, Insurance Expense, $400. In either case the net effect on the statements is the same.

This accrued interest must be recognized by the following adjusting entry (see Exhibit 3–5):

c. December 31, 1976:

```
Interest expense ................................................................. 500
     Accrued bond interest expense payable ...........................          500
```

This adjusting entry records (1) the expense for income statement purposes, and (2) the liability for balance sheet purposes.

*Accrued Revenues.* An accrued revenue is one that, although not yet recorded in the accounts, has been earned but not collected at the end of the accounting period. Therefore, an adjusting entry must be made to recognize it. To illustrate, Canby Retailers, Inc., owns marketable securities (bonds) that cost $20,000 (at par value). These bonds earn 6% annual interest which is received each November 30. Since there is accrued investment revenue earned for the month of December, an adjusting entry must be made as follows (see Exhibit 3–5):

d. December 31, 1976:

```
Accrued investment revenue receivable ....................................100
     Investment revenue ($20,000 × .06 × 1/12)...........................          100
```

This entry records (1) an asset, accrued investment revenue receivable, for balance sheet purposes; and (2) a revenue, for income statement purposes.

### Adjusting Entries for Estimated Items

Some adjusting entries must be based on *estimated amounts* because they depend upon future conditions and events. This means that some revenues and expenses for the current period will be determined by estimates. For example, depreciation expense, bad debt expense, and warranty (guarantee) expense must be based on estimates of future useful life, future collectibility, and future expenditures respectively.

*Depreciation Expense.* When certain assets, such as a machine, are acquired for use in operating a business (i.e., not for sale), they are "used up" over time through wear and obsolescence. The amount of this *use cost* is measured each accounting period and recorded as depreciation expense. Depreciation expense is always an estimate because the amount depends upon a known amount, the cost of the asset, and two estimates, useful life and residual (or scrap) value. To illustrate, Canby Retailers, Inc., has two assets on which depreciation is computed, viz:

$$\text{Building: } \frac{\text{Cost, \$160,000 — Residual Value, \$10,000}}{\text{Estimated Useful Life, 15 Years}} = \$10,000$$

$$\text{Equipment: } \frac{\text{Cost, \$91,000 — Residual Value, \$1,000}}{\text{Estimated Useful Life, Ten Years}} = 9,000$$

Total Depreciation Expense for the Year ...........$19,000

Based on these computations, an adjusting entry is necessary as follows (see Exhibit 3–5):

*e*. December 31, 1976:

```
Depreciation expense (selling)........................................... 8,000
Depreciation expense (general and administrative) ............11,000
    Accumulated depreciation, building ..........................     10,000
    Accumulated depreciation, equipment ......................      9,000
```

Depreciation expense was debited to two accounts because the company follows the policy of *allocating* it to the two categories of expense based upon the relative floor space used and the relative cost of the equipment used in operations and administration.

*Bad Debt Expense.* Credit sales and services almost always cause some losses due to uncollectible accounts receivable (i.e., bad debts). The fact that an account is uncollectible may be determined several periods subsequent to the period in which the credit was extended and the sale or service recognized as revenue in accordance with the revenue principle (see Chapter 2). The matching principle (see Chapter 2) requires that all *expenses* associated with sales and service revenue be recognized in the period in which the revenue was recorded. Since the actual amount of the revenue is recorded as earned for the period and the bad debt loss may not be known for several periods in the future, an estimation of bad debt expense must be recorded by means of an adjusting entry. To illustrate, Canby Retailers, Inc., extended credit on sales during 1976 amounting to $120,000. Experience by the company indicates an expected average bad debt loss rate of 1% of credit sales. Therefore, the following adjusting entry was needed (see Exhibit 3–5):

*f*. December 31, 1976:

```
Bad debt expense (selling)  ...............................................1,200
    Allowance for doubtful accounts....................................     1,200
```

The credit is made to an "allowance" account rather than directly to accounts receivable, because the identity of specific customers involved is not presently known. The allowance account is reported on the balance sheet as a deduction from accounts receivable (i.e., it is a contra asset account). When an account is subsequently determined to be bad, it is written off as a debit to the allowance account and a credit to Accounts Receivable; this will have no effect on expenses or on the book value of accounts receivable.

### Completion of the Worksheet

After the adjusting entries are entered on the worksheet (in the second pair of columns), it is completed by extending each account balance (i.e., the trial balance amount plus or minus any adjustments) to the next columns as illustrated in Exhibit 3–5. Two pairs of the columns shown on this exhibit are not essential: (1) the Adjusted Trial Balance columns, which are used to insure accuracy (i.e., a debits = credits check *after* the adjusting entries); and (2) the Retained Earnings column, which can be merged with the balance sheet. Observe in the extending that debits are always extended as debits and credits as credits.

There are three additional aspects of the worksheet that warrant some explanation:

1. Note that the *beginning* inventory amount, $75,000, is extended to the income statement as a debit and that the *ending* inventory is entered as a credit to the income statement and as a debit to the balance sheet.[5] This procedure results from the company's *periodic inventory system* (see Chapter 8). When a company uses the periodic inventory system, a Purchases account is used and the inventory account is unchanged during the period; it reflects the *beginning inventory* amount. Therefore, at the end of the accounting period, this balance must be closed out and the *ending* inventory amount, determined by physical count and valued at cost, must be recorded. In contrast, when a *perpetual inventory system* is used, purchases and issues are recorded directly in the inventory account on a continuing basis. Therefore, the inventory amount in the trial balance will reflect the ending inventory amount and no closing (or adjusting) entries will be needed for it on the worksheet. The inventory balance is extended directly to the Balance Sheet debit column. When the perpetual inventory system is used, there will be no purchases account; however, there will be a Cost of Goods Sold account on the worksheet. The Cost of Goods Sold account is extended directly to the Income Statement debit column as an expense.

2. When all of the amounts have been extended, the difference between the debits and credits under income statement will represent *pretax income*. This amount must be determined to compute income tax expense, for which an adjusting entry must be made. To illustrate, for Canby Retailers, Inc., the computation would be as follows, assuming an average 40% income tax rate:

Income Statement column totals (pretax):
Credit total............................................................$419,000
Debit total (before income taxes) ................................. 369,000
Pretax income ........................................................ 50,000
Income tax expense ($50,000 × .40) ............................... 20,000
Net Income ...........................................................$ 30,000

The adjusting entry would be:

g. December 31, 1976:

Income tax expense  .....................................20,000
    Income taxes payable.............................. 20,000

3. After the above adjusting entry is made, the extensions can be com-

---

[5] This approach views the two entries for the beginning and ending inventories as *closing* entries (see page 66). Another approach is to view them as *adjusting* entries. The technique used on the worksheet for inventories represents only one way; several other ways are widely used. The final result is precisely the same.

pleted. The amount of net income, $30,000, is entered on the worksheet as a debit to Income Statement and a credit to Retained Earnings. The ending balance of Retained Earnings is then extended to the balance sheet and the last two pairs of columns summed; in the absence of errors each pair of columns on the worksheet will balance. The worksheet can be used as a guide for the remaining phases in the cycle.

A worksheet for a manufacturing company, with explanatory comments, is shown in Appendix B to this chapter.

## PREPARE FINANCIAL STATEMENTS (PHASE 7)

The income statement, statement of retained earnings, and balance sheet can be prepared directly from the completed worksheet. An income statement and balance sheet, taken directly from the worksheet (Exhibit 3–5), are presented in Exhibits 3–6 and 3–7, respectively. Financial statements are discussed in Chapters 4 and 5.

**EXHIBIT 3–6**

CANBY RETAILERS, INC.
Income Statement*
For the Year Ended December 31, 1976

| | | |
|---|---:|---:|
| Revenues: | | |
| Sales | | $325,200 |
| Investments | | 600 |
| Rent | | 1,200 |
|     Total Revenue | | 327,000 |
| Expenses: | | |
| Cost of goods sold† | $117,000 | |
| Selling | 113,400 | |
| General and administrative | 34,600 | |
| Interest | 3,000 | |
|     Total Expenses (excluding income taxes) | | 268,000 |
| Pretax operating income | | 59,000 |
| Income taxes ($59,000 × .40) | | 23,600 |
| Income before extraordinary items | | 35,400 |
| Extraordinary loss | 9,000 | |
|     Less tax saving ($9,000 × .40) | 3,600 | 5,400 |
| Net Income | | $ 30,000 |

Earnings per share:
    Income before extraordinary items ($35,400 ÷ 15,000 shares) ..............$2.36
    Extraordinary loss ($5,400 ÷ 15,000 shares) .................................... (.36)
    Net Income ($30,000 ÷ 15,000 shares) ............................................ 2.00

  * This is a single-step income statement; various formats are discussed in Chapter 4.

  † Computation of cost of goods sold:

| | | |
|---|---:|---|
| Beginning inventory | $ 75,000 | |
| Purchases | 130,000 | |
| Freight-in | 4,000 | |
| Purchase returns | (2,000) | |
|     Total Goods Available for Sale | 207,000 | |
| Less ending inventory | 90,000 | |
|     Cost of Goods Sold | $117,000 | |

**EXHIBIT 3–7**

CANBY RETAILERS, INC.
Balance Sheet*
At December 31, 1976

### Assets

| | | |
|---|---:|---:|
| **Current Assets:** | | |
| Cash ............ | | $ 55,300 |
| Marketable securities ......... | | 20,000 |
| Accounts receivable .......... | $ 45,000 | |
| Allowance for doubtful accounts ....... | 2,200 | 42,800 |
| Inventory ........ | | 90,000 |
| Prepaid insurance.......... | | 400 |
| Investment revenue receivable ....... | | 100 |
|    Total Current Assets........ | | 208,600 |
| **Operational Assets:** | | |
| Land ......... | | 8,000 |
| Building ........ | 160,000 | |
| Accumulated depreciation, building ... | 100,000 | 60,000 |
| Equipment ......... | 91,000 | |
| Accumulated depreciation, equipment.. | 36,000 | 55,000 |
|    Total Operational Assets......... | | 123,000 |
| Total Assets ....... | | $331,600 |

### Liabilities

| | | |
|---|---:|---:|
| **Current Liabilities:** | | |
| Accounts payable ......... | | $ 29,000 |
| Income taxes payable ......... | | 20,000 |
| Bond interest payable ......... | | 500 |
| Prepaid rent revenue ......... | | 600 |
|    Total Current Liabilities ....... | | 50,100 |
| **Long-Term Liabilities:** | | |
| Bonds payable, 6% ......... | | 50,000 |
|    Total Liabilities ......... | | 100,100 |

### Stockholders' Equity

| | | |
|---|---:|---:|
| **Contributed Capital:** | | |
| Common stock, par $10, 15,000 shares | | |
|   outstanding......... | | $150,000 |
| Contributed capital in excess | | |
|   of par ......... | 20,000 | |
| Retained earnings......... | 61,500 | |
|    Total Stockholders' Equity...... | | 231,500 |
|    Total Liabilities and Stock- | | |
|      holders' Equity ......... | | $331,600 |

* Balance sheets and appropriate supplementary information are discussed in Chapter 5.

If a worksheet is not used, adjusting entries should be entered in the journal, posted to the ledger, and then an *adjusted trial balance,* taken from the ledger, will provide information for these statements.

The statement of changes in financial position requires a separate analysis, usually on a specially designed worksheet similar to those illustrated in Chapter 21.

## JOURNALIZING AND POSTING ADJUSTING ENTRIES (PHASE 8)

The adjusting entries should be entered in the general journal and posted to the general ledger, dated the last day of the accounting period. The adjusting entries *update* the ledger accounts by separating the "mixed" accounts into their real (i.e., balance sheet) and nominal (i.e., income statement) components. The adjusted nominal accounts are then ready to close.

If a worksheet, such as Exhibit 3–5, is developed, the adjusting entries can be taken directly from it. They are identical to those illustrated earlier. Recall that after the adjusting entries are posted to the general ledger, each account will then reflect the account balances shown in Exhibit 3–5, under the caption *Adjusted Trial Balance.*

## CLOSING ENTRIES (PHASE 9)

Recall that the balance sheet accounts are called *real* or *permanent accounts* in the sense that they are not closed out to a zero balance at the end of the accounting period. In contrast, the income statement accounts are called *nominal* or *temporary accounts* because at the end of each accounting period they are closed out to a zero balance. The income statement accounts are the *revenue* and *expense* accounts and are *subaccounts* to owners' equity. Revenues increase owners' equity, and expenses decrease owners' equity. These subaccounts are used each period to *classify* and *accumulate* revenue and expense information. At the end of the period, when they have served this information *classification* and *accumulation* purpose, each account is closed to Income Summary and in turn the net effect of their balances (i.e., net income or net loss) is transferred from Income Summary to Retained Earnings. The transferring process is called closing entries. The purpose is to close the nominal accounts to a zero balance so they will be ready for reuse the next period. A closing entry simply transfers a credit balance to another account as a credit, or it transfers a debit balance to another account. Generally, two *clearing,* or *suspense, accounts* called Cost of Goods Sold and Income Summary are used for convenience, although they are not essential. The nominal accounts are reopened the next period to record the revenues and expenses for that period.

The closing entries can be taken directly from the *adjusted trial balance;* or if a worksheet such as the one in Exhibit 3–5 is used, they can be taken directly from the Income Statement columns. To illustrate, the closing entries for Canby Retailers, Inc., would be as follows:[6]

December 31, 1976:

1. To close the revenue accounts to Income Summary:

| | | |
|---|---|---|
| Sales revenue | 325,200 | |
| Investment revenue | 600 | |
| Rent revenue | 1,200 | |
| Income summary | | 327,000 |

2. To close the purchases and beginning inventory accounts, to record the ending inventory, and to record cost of goods sold:[7]

| | | |
|---|---|---|
| Ending inventory (December 31, 1976) | 90,000 | |
| Purchase returns | 2,000 | |
| Cost of goods sold | 117,000 | |
| Purchases | | 130,000 |
| Freight on purchases | | 4,000 |
| Beginning inventory (January 1, 1976) | | 75,000 |

3. To close the expense accounts, including cost of goods sold, to Income Summary:

| | | |
|---|---|---|
| Income summary | 297,000 | |
| Cost of goods sold | | 117,000 |
| Selling expenses | | 113,400 |
| General and administrative expenses | | 34,600 |
| Interest expense | | 3,000 |
| Extraordinary loss | | 9,000 |
| Income tax expense | | 20,000 |

4. To close Income Summary account to Retained Earnings:

| | | |
|---|---|---|
| Income summary | 30,000 | |
| Retained earnings | | 30,000 |

For review purposes, the closing process is diagrammed in T-account form in Exhibit 3–8. Observe that after the closing process, each income

---

[6] The closing entries can be grouped in various ways, one of which is illustrated here. Alternatively, a separate closing entry can be made for each nominal account. Obviously, the net effect of the closing process would be the same.

[7] The Cost of Goods Sold account often is not used with a periodic inventory system. In this case, these accounts are closed directly to Income Summary. Also recall that when the periodic inventory system is used, the inventory accounts may be handled in the adjusting entries, in which case they would not be included in the closing entries; in either approach, the *beginning* inventory balance must be closed out and the *ending* inventory balance recorded. The net effect is the same.

To illustrate using the same data:

Adjusting entries (inventory):

| | | |
|---|---|---|
| Cost of goods sold | 75,000 | |
| Inventory (beginning) | | 75,000 |
| | | |
| Inventory (ending) | 90,000 | |
| Cost of goods sold | | 90,000 |

Closing entry for purchase accounts:

| | | |
|---|---|---|
| Purchase returns | 2,000 | |
| Cost of goods sold | 132,000 | |
| Purchases | | 130,000 |
| Freight on purchases | | 4,000 |

# EXHIBIT 3–8
## Closing Process Diagramed

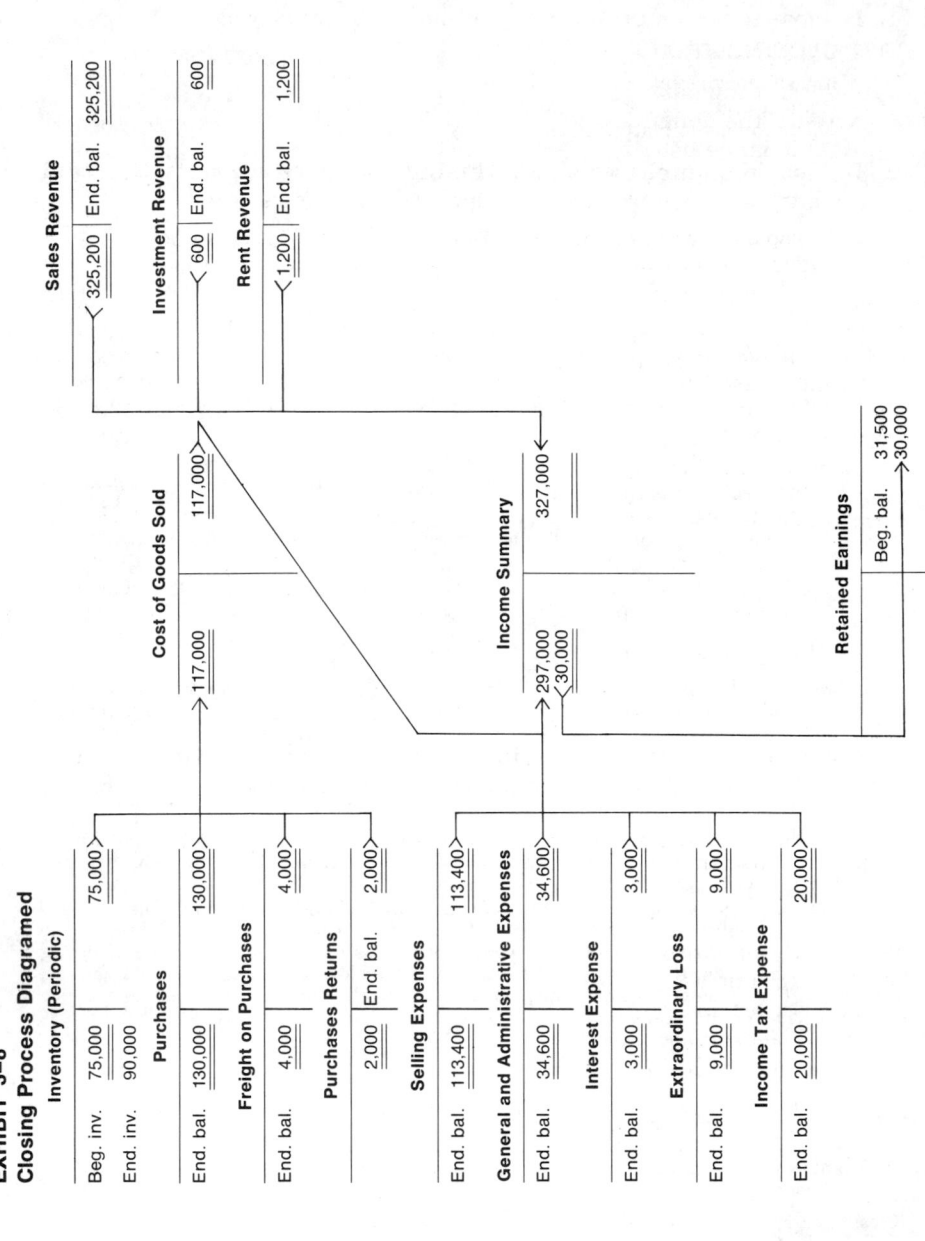

statement (i.e., nominal) account reflects a zero balance; therefore, they are ready to be used again during the next accounting period.

## POST-CLOSING TRIAL BALANCE (PHASE 10)

In a preceding paragraph, we defined a trial balance as a listing of the accounts in the general ledger along with their balances. The purposes of a trial balance usually are (a) to verify the equality of the debits and credits, and (b) to have the account balances handy for other uses. We have discussed two different trial balances up to this point: the *unadjusted* trial balance, taken immediately after the current entries are completed for the accounting period, but before the adjusting entries, and the *adjusted* trial balance which reflects the account balances after the adjusting entries. A third trial balance generally is taken after the closing entries have been posted. It is called the *post-closing trial balance* and is used to verify that the debits and credits are equal at the start of the next accounting period. It is usually done on an adding machine (or by computer) rather than by preparing a formal listing.

## REVERSING ENTRIES (PHASE 11)

After the adjusting and closing entries are journalized and posted to the general ledger, the accounts are ready for information inputs of the next period. Prior to starting the new information inputs, many companies make *reversing entries*. A reversing entry is dated the first day of the next period and simply reverses or "backs out" an adjusting entry that was made at the end of the period just ended. Reversing entries serve only one purpose; that is, to facilitate (i.e., simplify) a subsequent entry. Reversing entries are always optional; the same end results are attained whether or not they are used. If used, only a few of the adjusting entries usually are reversed.

The purpose and application of reversing entries are illustrated in Exhibit 3–9. In the exhibit, a series of entries related to accrued wages are analyzed under two options: (1) with a reversing entry, and (2) without a reversing entry. The exhibit demonstrates the *facilitating* feature of reversing entries. It also suggests the kinds of adjusting entries that are candidates for reversal. Although it is impossible to provide rigid rules for selecting adjusting entries to be reversed, some guidelines can be given.

1. Adjusting entries usually reversed—As a general rule, *only adjusting entries for accrued expenses and accrued revenues* should be reversed. Examples of accrued expenses are unpaid wages, interest, utilities, and other regularly recurring expenses that require subsequent cash disbursements. Examples of accrued revenues are uncollected interest, rent, and other recurring revenues that result in subsequent cash collections.
2. Adjusting entries not reversed—As a general rule, adjusting entries

**EXHIBIT 3–9**
**Reversing Entries Illustrated**

BOX CORPORATION
Annual Accounting Period Ends, December 31, 1976

| *With Reversing Entry* | *Without Reversing Entry* |
|---|---|

a. *Adjusting entry*—The last payroll was paid on December 28, 1976; the next payroll will be on January 5, 1977. Therefore, at December 31, 1976, accrued (unpaid) wages for three days amounted to $15,000. The following adjusting entry is required:

| December 31, 1976: | December 31, 1976: |
|---|---|
| Wage expense................................. 15,000<br>    Accrued wages payable ............       15,000 | Wage expense................................. 15,000<br>    Accrued wages payable ............       15,000 |

b. *Closing entry*—The revenue and expense accounts are closed to Income Summary.

| December 31, 1976: | December 31, 1976: |
|---|---|
| Income summary* ...........................215,000<br>    Wage expense...........................      215,000 | Income summary* ...........................215,000<br>    Wage expense...........................      215,000 |

c. At this point the adjusting and closing entries have been journalized and posted to the ledger. The information processing cycle for 1976 has been completed. At this point in time, January 1, 1977, the accountant must decide what adjusting entries are to be *reversed* (if any). *Question:* Would a reversing entry for accrued wages on January 1, 1977, simplify, or facilitate, making the next payroll entry on January 5, 1977?

| *Decision-reversing entry*, January 1, 1977: | *Decision*—no reversing entry to be made. |
|---|---|
| Accured wages payable .................. 15,000<br>    Wage expense...........................     15,000<br>(Note this reverses the adjusting<br>entry made above on December<br>31, 1976.) | |
| Effect: Accrued Wages Payable account now reflects a zero balance; Wage Expense reflects a *credit* balance of $15,000. | Effect: Accrued Wages Payable account continues to reflect a credit balance; Wage Expense reflects a zero balance. |

d. *Subsequent payroll entry*—Payment of $36,000 payroll on January 5, 1977. This amount includes the $15,000 liability (accrued wages) carried over from December 1976.

January 5, 1977, payroll entry (disregarding payroll taxes):

| Wage expense................................. 36,000<br>    Cash ......................................      36,000 | Accrued wages payable .................. 15,000<br>Wage expense................................. 21,000<br>    Cash ......................................      36,000 |
|---|---|

Did the reversing entry simplify this subsequent entry? The answer is yes; the last entry, on the left, required only one debit. However, after the last entry, under both methods, the Wage Expense account reflects a debit balance of $21,000 and Accrued Wages Payable reflects a zero balance. Without the reversing entry, the amount of unpaid wages must be identified which is troublesome when a number of such situations exist. Also when the payroll processing is computerized, a special routine must be written for the first payment entry which is different from the remaining 51 payroll entries during the year when no reversing entry is made.

* Includes $200,000 paid during the period.

for deferred expenses and deferred revenues are not reversed. Examples of deferred (i.e., prepaid) expenses are insurance premiums and unused supplies. Examples of deferred revenues are interest collected in advance, rent collected in advance, and subscriptions collected in advance.

3. Estimated adjusting entries not reversed—Adjusting entries based on estimates, where there is no subsequent cash inflow or outflow, are not reversed. Examples are depreciation and bad debt expense.

Alternatively, a guideline may be expressed as follows: adjusting entries should be reversed when they create or add to balances in *real* accounts. They should not be reversed when they create or add to balances in *nominal* accounts. There is an exception to the first sentence:

if the real account balance augmented is a valuation contra account (e.g., accumulated depreciation or allowance for doubtful accounts), then the adjusting entry ought not be reversed because to do so would undo the effects of having made it.

Although these guidelines may be helpful in deciding whether the reversal of a particular adjusting entry would be useful, one must consider (a) the original entry, (b) the adjusting entry, and (c) most important, the subsequent entry. The above rules cannot substitute for judgment.

## INFORMATION PROCESSING PROCEDURES

Information processing involves the ways and order of accomplishing the tasks necessary to collect raw economic data, record their economic

**EXHIBIT 3–10**
**Summary of the Accounting Information Processing Cycle**

| Phase (order) | Identification | Objective | Text Page |
|---|---|---|---|
| 1 | Collection of raw economic data. | To gather inputs to the accounting system. The inputs are supported by source documents as a basis for (a) transaction analysis, and (b) subsequent verifiability. | 50 |
| 2 | Transaction analysis. | To identify, assess, and measure the economic impact on the enterprise of each transaction recognized. To provide the basis for developing the accounting entry to be made in the journal. | 52 |
| 3 | Journalizing. | To provide a chronological record (i.e., by date) of the entries in the accounting system which reflect the increases and decreases in each account. | 52 |
| 4 | Posting. | To transfer the economic effects from the journal to the ledger; to reclassify and accumulate the economic effects for each asset, liability, owners' equity, revenue, and expense. | 54 |
| 5 | Prepare unadjusted trial balance. | To provide, in a convenient form, a listing of the accounts and their balances in the general ledger after all current entries have been posted. It serves to (a) check the debit-credit equality, and (b) provide data for use in developing the worksheet and the adjusting entries. | 55 |
| 6* | Prepare worksheets. | To provide an organized and systematic approach at the end of the accounting period for developing (a) the adjusting entries, (b) the financial statements, and (c) the closing entries. One worksheet suffices for the income statement and balance sheet. Another worksheet is needed to develop the statement of changes in financial position. | 55 |
| 7 | Prepare financial statements. | To provide a vehicle for communicating summarized financial information to external decision-makers. | 64 |
| 8 | Journalize and post adjusting entries. | To update the general ledger by separating the "mixed" accounts into their real (i.e., balance sheet) and nominal (i.e., income statement) components so they will be ready for the closing process. | 66 |
| 9 | Journalize and post closing entries. | To close the nominal accounts to retained earnings so they will be ready for reuse during the next period for accumulating and classifying revenues and expenses. | 66 |
| 10* | Prepare post-closing trial balance. | To verify the debit-credit accuracy of the general ledger after the closing entries are posted. | 69 |
| 11* | Reversing entries. | To facilitate subsequent entries by reversing certain adjusting entries. They are journalized and posted on the first day of the new period. | 69 |

* Optional.

effects on the entity, classify the information, and, finally, prepare the financial statements and supporting information. In most companies, a large amount of information must be processed daily. This work can be both time consuming and costly. Therefore, a well-designed information processing system is needed to provide a smooth, uninterrupted, and efficient flow of information from point of incurrence to the end result, the financial statements. Information processing may be done (1) manually, where the work is performed by hand; (2) mechanically, where the information is processed by the use of sorting equipment, tabulating machines, and so on; and (3) electronically, where electronic computers are used. Typically, an accounting system will use each of these approaches in varying degrees depending upon its complexity.

Consideration of these information approaches is not within the objectives of this book. For instructional purposes, the manual approach is used.

## SUMMARY OF THE INFORMATION PROCESSING CYCLE

An understanding of the information processing cycle will assist you in comprehending the chapters to follow. Each chapter considers various accounting problems, each of which is related to one or more steps in the cycle. It is especially helpful if you clearly understand how those problems relate to the broad area of information collection, transaction analysis, recording, classifying, and reporting. The sequence of the cycle is both logical and efficient. Exhibit 3-10 lists the major sequential phases of the cycle, summarizes the objective of each, and provides a cross-reference to the chapter.

# Appendix A. Control Accounts, Subsidiary Ledgers, and Special Journals

An accounting system usually includes application of the information processing techniques known as special journals, subsidiary ledgers, and control accounts. This Appendix discusses and illustrates these elements of the system.

## CONTROL ACCOUNTS AND SUBSIDIARY LEDGERS

The general ledger is the main ledger; it includes an account for each asset, liability, owners' equity, revenue, and expense. To facilitate recordkeeping for accounts that involve a large amount of detail, selected general ledger accounts are designated as *control accounts* to which only summary information is posted. The details related to each control account are maintained in a separate subsidiary ledger (one for each control account). Thus, each control account is supplemented by its specially designated subsidiary ledger. To illustrate, accounts receivable, because of the large number of credit customers, usually is designated as *accounts receivable control* in the general ledger and is supported by a separate *accounts receivable subsidiary ledger* which is composed of individual customer accounts. This arrangement will be illustrated below.

## JOURNALS

Both general and special journals are used in most accounting systems. Even when extensive use is made of special journals, there will be a need for a general journal in which to record those transactions that should not be recorded in the special journals. Exhibit 3–11 illustrates such an entry. These include nonrepetitive current transactions and the adjusting and closing journal entries. Occasionally there will be a complex entry with characteristics that would, in part, qualify for entry in a special journal, and in part in the general journal. Such entries may be entered only in the general journal or, alternatively, "split" between the general journal and a special journal.

### Special Journals

A special journal serves the same purpose as a general journal except that it is designed to handle *only* one type of transaction because of the large volume of transactions of a particular type. Each special journal, therefore, is designed specifically to simplify the data processing tasks involved in journalizing and posting a particular type of transaction. The format of each special journal and the number used depend upon the types of frequent transactions recorded by the entity. Commonly used special journals are:

**EXHIBIT 3–11**

| General Journal | | Page J–14 | | |
|---|---|---|---|---|
| Date 1976 | Accounts and Explanation | Ledger Folio | Amounts | |
| | | | Debit | Credit |
| Jan.2 | Equipment – trucks | 140 | 9,000 | |
| | Notes payable | 214 | | 9,000 |
| | Purchased truck for use in | | | |
| | the business. Gave $9,000, | | | |
| | 60-day, 10% interest-bearing | | | |
| | note. | | | |

1. Credit sales journal – designed for credit sales entries only.
2. Credit purchases journal – designed for credit purchases only.
3. Cash receipts journal – designed for all cash receipts.
4. Cash payments journal – designed for all cash payments.
5. Voucher system journals (replaces No. 4 when the voucher system is used) –
   a. Voucher register – designed to record payment vouchers only.
   b. Check register – designed to record all checks written in payment of vouchers.

*Special Journal for Credit Sales.* This journal is designed to accommodate entries for credit sales only. Therefore, it would handle only the following type of entry (cash sales would not be entered in this journal)[8]:

January 1, 1976:

|  | If Recorded at Net | | If Recorded at Gross | |
|---|---|---|---|---|
| Accounts receivable ..................... | 980 | | 1,000 | |
| Sales revenue ........................ | | 980 | | 1,000 |
| Credit sale to Adams Company; invoice price, $1,000; terms, 2/10, n/30. | | | | |

Credit sales may be recorded at net of discount or gross of discount as illustrated above. Theoretically, net of discount is preferable; however for practical reasons they often are recorded at gross of discount. To illustrate, in each approach the subsequent collection entry would be as follows:

Case A – Collection within the discount period:

|  | If Recorded at Net | | If Recorded at Gross | |
|---|---|---|---|---|
| Cash ................................................ | 980 | | 980 | |
| Sales discount ................................ | | | 20 | |
| Accounts receivable..................... | | 980 | | 1,000 |

Case B – Collection after the discount period:

|  | | | | |
|---|---|---|---|---|
| Cash ................................................ 1,000 | | | 1,000 | |
| Accounts receivable..................... | | 980 | | 1,000 |
| Interest revenue........................... | | 20 | | |

The theoretical basis for recording net of discount is (*a*) because of the high implicit interest rate (2% in 10 days), most customers pay within the discount period; (*b*) the net amount represents the cash equivalent sales price of the goods, hence the receivable should be measured at the net amount; (*c*) if a customer is extended credit and fails to pay within the discount period there is a charge (2% in this case) for use of the vendor's money, hence the vendor has earned interest revenue;

---

[8] Terms, 2/10, n/30, mean that if the account is paid within ten days after date of sale, a 2% discount is permitted to encourage early payment. If not paid within the 10-day discount period, the full amount is due at the end of 30 days.

EXHIBIT 3–12

| Special Journal — Credit Sales | | | | | | Page S-23 | |
|---|---|---|---|---|---|---|---|
| Date 1976 | Sales Invoice No. | Accounts Receivable (name) | Terms | Ledger Folio | Receivable and Sale Amount | Dept. Sales | |
| | | | | | | Dept. A | Dept. B |
| Jan. 2 | 93 | Adams Co. | 2/10, n/30 | 112.13 | 980 | | |
| 3 | 94 | Sayre Corp. | 2/10, n/30 | 112.80 | 490 | | |
| 11 | 95 | Cope & Day Co. | net | 112.27 | 5,734 | (Not illustrated — the | |
| 27 | 96 | XY Mfg. Co. | 2/10, n/30 | 112.91 | 1,960 | two totals below | |
| 30 | 97 | Miller, J. B. | 2/10, n/30 | 112.42 | 196 | would be posted to a sales | |
| 31 | — | Totals | — | — | 9,360 | subsidiary ledger.) | |
| 31 | — | Posting | — | — | (112/500) | | |

and (d) the $20 is revenue not a deduction from sales. The practical basis for recording gross is (a) precedent, (b) the amount of discount is not material in relation to total sales, (c) many customers do not pay within the discount period, and (d) sales discount is a reduction in sales price. However, on this latter point it often happens that the sale is in one period and the collection in a later period; this tends to mismatch the discount with the sale that caused it. On the other hand, the net method tends to record the interest revenue in the period earned. Either method is generally acceptable, primarily because the difference is not material (also see Chapter 8).

Exhibit 3–12 shows a typical special journal for credit sales for a business that has two sales departments. The general ledger contains an Accounts Receivable Control account. Observe that this special journal provides a convenient format to record all of the relevant data on each credit sale. Also, it can be designed to differentiate sales by department. Clearly, it is easier to enter a credit sale in this format than in the general journal. Sales can be entered at either net or gross of discount in the sales journal.

The mechanics of posting amounts from the special sales journal to the general and subsidiary ledgers also are simplified. There are two phases of posting a special journal, viz:

1. *Daily posting* — Daily the amount for each customer is posted to the individual account in the accounts receivable *subsidiary ledger*. Daily posting is essential so that each customer's account will be up-to-date when the customer pays. Posting is indicated by entering the account number in the folio column. For example, the number 112.13 entered in the folio column in Exhibit 3–12 is the account number assigned to Adams Company and signifies that $980 was posted as a debit to that account.
2. *Monthly posting* — At the end of each month, the amount column is summed. This total is posted to two accounts in the general ledger; that is, Account No. 112 denotes that $9,360 was posted (1) as a debit to Account No. 112 (Accounts Receivable Control), and (2) as a credit

**EXHIBIT 3–13**

| | | Purchases Journal | | Page _S-19_ | |
|---|---|---|---|---|---|
| Date 1976 | Purchase Order No. | Account Payable (name) | Terms | Ledger Folio | Amount |
| Jan. 3 | 41 | P. 2. Mfg. Co. | 1/20, n/30 | 210.61 | 990 |
| 7 | 42 | Able Suppliers, Inc. | net | 210.12 | 150 |
| 31 | — | Totals | — | — | 2,760 |
| 31 | — | Posting | — | — | (612/210) |

to Account No. 500 (Sales Revenue). The T-accounts shown in Exhibit 3–16 illustrate how these postings are reflected in the general ledger and the subsidiary ledger. Observe that the two ledgers show the *journal page* from which each amount was posted.

*Special Journal for Credit Purchases.* In situations where there are a large number of credit purchases, data processing may be facilitated by using a special journal designed only for this type of transaction, viz:

January 4, 1976:

```
Purchases ..................................................................................990
    Accounts payable (PT Mfg. Co.) ............................................     990
    Purchased merchandise for resale; invoice price, $1,000;
    terms, 1/20, n/60.
```

This transaction, rather than being entered in the general journal, would be entered in the purchases journal as in Exhibit 3–13. In this illustration the purchases are recorded at net of discount which is the theoretically correct approach. For practical reasons purchases also are recorded at gross of discount. Basically, the same practical and theoretical considerations apply that were discussed above for sales discount (see Chapter 8 for further discussion of this issue). During the month, each amount would be credited to the individual creditors' accounts in the *accounts payable subsidiary ledger.*

At the end of the month, the total of the amount column (i.e., $2,760) would be posted to the general ledger as (*a*) a debit to the Purchases account (No. 612), and (*b*) a credit to the Accounts Payable *Control* account (No. 210).

*Special Journal for Cash Receipts.* Since a large volume of transactions for cash receipts is typical, a special cash receipts journal is often used. This special journal is designed to accommodate *all* cash receipts. Therefore, it must have a column for *cash debit* and several credit columns, including a credit column for *sundry accounts.* Credit columns are designated for recurring credits, and a Sundry column accommodates infrequent credits. A typical special cash receipts journal is shown in Exhibit 3–14.

During the month, each amount in the Accounts Receivable column is posted as a credit to the individual customer accounts in the *accounts receivable subsidiary ledger.* At the end of the month, *(a)* the individual amounts in the Sundry column are posted as credits to the appropriate general ledger accounts, and *(b)* the totals are posted to the general ledger as indicated by the folio numbers, viz: Cash, debit; Accounts Receivable, credit; and Sales, credit. The total of the sundry accounts is not posted since the individual amounts have already been posted.

*Special Journal for Cash Payments.* Because of the large volume of cash disbursements, most companies use a special journal designed to accommodate *all* cash payments. The special journal must have a column for *cash credits* and a number of debit columns including one for sundry accounts. Debit columns are set up for frequently recurring

**EXHIBIT 3–14**

| Date 1976 | Explanation | Debits Cash | Account Title | Ledger Folio | Accounts Receivable | Sundry Accounts | Sales |
|---|---|---|---|---|---|---|---|
| | | | *Cash Receipts Journal* | Page CR-19 | | | |
| | | | | | Credits | | |
| Jan. 4 | Cash sales | 11,200 | — | | | | 11,200 |
| 7 | On acct. | 4,490 | Sayre Corp. | 112.80 | 4,490 | | |
| 8 | Sale of land | 10,000 | Land | 123 | | 4,000 | |
| | | | Gain on sale land | 510 | | 6,000 | |
| 10 | On acct. | 1,000 | Adams Co. | 112.13 | 1,000 | | |
| 19 | Cash sales | 43,600 | — | | | | 43,600 |
| 20 | On acct. | 5,734 | Cope & Day Co. | 112.27 | 5,734 | | |
| 31 | Totals | 116,224 | | | — | 11,224 | 34,000 | 71,000 |
| 31 | Posting | (101) | | | — | (112) | (NP)* | (500) |

* NP—Not posted.

**EXHIBIT 3–15**

| Date 1976 | Check No. | Explanation | Credits Cash | Account Name | Ledger Folio | Accounts Payable | Sundry Accounts | Cash Purchases |
|---|---|---|---|---|---|---|---|---|
| | | | | *Cash Payments Journal* | Page CP-31 | | | |
| | | | | | | Debits | | |
| Jan. 2 | 141 | Pur. mdse. | 3,000 | — | | | | 3,000 |
| 10 | 142 | On acct. | 990 | P. 2. Mfg. Co. | 210.61 | 990 | | |
| 15 | 143 | Jan. rent | 600 | Rent exp. | 612 | | 600 | |
| 16 | 144 | Pur. mdse. | 1,810 | — | | | | 1,810 |
| 31 | — | Totals | 98,400 | | | — | 5,820 | 1,600 | 34,700 |
| 31 | — | Posting | (101) | | | — | (210) | (NP) | (612) |

debits, and the Sundry column for infrequent debits. A typical special cash payments journal, with some common entries, is shown in Exhibit 3–15. Posting follows the same procedures explained above for the cash receipts special journal.

### Reconciling a Subsidiary Ledger

The sum of all accounts in a subsidiary ledger must agree with the overall balance reflected in the control account in the general ledger. To

**EXHIBIT 3–16**
**General Ledger and Subsidiary Ledger Illustrated**

General Ledger (partial)

| Cash | | | | | No. 101 |
|---|---|---|---|---|---|
| 1976 Jan. 1 31 | Balance | CR-19 | 18,000 116,224 | 1976 Jan. 31 CP-31 | 98,400 |

| Accounts Receivable Control | | | | | No. 112 |
|---|---|---|---|---|---|
| 1976 Jan. 1 31 | Balance | S-23 | 5,000 9,360 | 1976 Jan. 31 CR-19 | 11,224 |

| Equipment | | | | No. 140 |
|---|---|---|---|---|
| 1976 Jan. 2 | J-14 | 9,000 | | |

| Notes Payable | | | | No. 214 |
|---|---|---|---|---|
| | | 1976 Jan. 2 | J-14 | 9,000 |

| Sales Revenue | | | | |
|---|---|---|---|---|
| | | 1976 Jan. 31 31 | S-23 CR-19 | 9,360 71,000 |

Subsidiary Ledger – Accounts Receivable (Acct. No. 112)

| Adams Company | | | | | No. 112.13 |
|---|---|---|---|---|---|
| 1976 Jan. 1 11 | Balance | S-23 | 1,000 980 | 1976 Jan. 10 CR-19 | 1,000 |

| Cope & Day Company | | | | | No. 112.27 |
|---|---|---|---|---|---|
| 1976 Jan. 11 | | S-23 | 5,734 | 1976 Jan. 20 CR-19 | 5,734 |

| Miller, J. B. | | | | No. 112.42 |
|---|---|---|---|---|
| 1976 Jan. 31 | | S-23 | 196 | |

| Sayre Corporation | | | | | No. 112.80 |
|---|---|---|---|---|---|
| 1976 Jan. 1 3 | Balance | S-23 | 4,000 490 | 1976 Jan. 7 CR-19 | 4,490 |

| XY Manufacturing Company | | | | No. 112.91 |
|---|---|---|---|---|
| 1976 Jan. 27 | | S-23 | 1,960 | |

assure that this correspondence exists, frequent reconcilations should be made. Clearly, a reconciliation cannot be accomplished unless all posting is complete, both to the control account and to the subsidiary ledger. To illustrate, a reconciliation based upon the information in Exhibit 3–16 for *Accounts Receivable Control* and the *accounts receivable subsidiary ledger* would be as follows:

**Reconciliation of Accounts Receivable Subsidiary Ledger (at January 31, 1976)**

|  |  | *Amount* |
|---|---|---|
| Subsidiary ledger balances: | | |
| 112.13 | Adams Company | $   980 |
| 112.42 | Miller, J. B. | 196 |
| 112.91 | XY Manufacturing Company | 1,960 |
| | Total—per Balance in Accounts Receivable Control | |
| | ($14,360 − $11,224) | $3,136 |

The above discussion was intended to review the concepts underlying special journals, control accounts, and subsidiary ledgers. Their design and use depend upon the characteristics of the company. They do not require new accounting principles since they are only data processing techniques. The above discussion also serves to emphasize the four primary efficiencies that may result from their use, viz: (1) journalizing is simplified, (2) posting is simplified, (3) subdivision of work is simplified, and (4) a highly trained person is not needed to maintain a special journal or a subsidiary ledger that involves only one type of transaction.[9]

# Appendix B. Worksheet for a Manufacturing Company

A worksheet for a manufacturing company is somewhat different from that illustrated in Exhibit 3–5 for a merchandising company. Because of the cost accounting procedures generally used for the manufacturing activity, the worksheet should include a pair of columns for *manufacturing*. All of the manufacturing costs, including the raw materials and work in process inventories, are extended to manufacturing. A worksheet for a manufacturing situation is illustrated in Exhibit 3–17. The following information will be helpful in studying this worksheet:

---

[9] Voucher system journals are not discussed since they involve essentially the same procedures as illustrated. The voucher system journals are known as (a) the voucher register, and (b) the check register.

**EXHIBIT 3-17**

DUNCAN MANUFACTURING COMPANY
Worksheet for the Year Ended December 31, 1976

| Accounts | Unadjusted Trial Balance Debit | Credit | Adjustments Debit | Credit | Manufacturing Debit | Credit | Income Statement Debit | Credit | Balance Sheet Debit | Credit |
|---|---|---|---|---|---|---|---|---|---|---|
| Cash........................... | 32,000 | | | | | | | | 32,000 | |
| Inventory, January 1 (periodic system): | | | | | | | | | | |
| Raw materials ......... | 55,000 | | | | 55,000 | 62,000 | | | 62,000 | |
| Work in process ...... | 76,000 | | | | 76,000 | 81,000 | | | 81,000 | |
| Finished goods......... | 54,000 | | | | | | 54,000 | 52,000 | 52,000 | |
| Equipment (ten-year life) ..................... | 300,000 | | | | | | | | 300,000 | |
| Accumulated depreciation—equipment ... | | 90,000 | | (a) 10,000 | | | | | | 100,000 |
| Remaining assets......... | 13,000 | | | | | | | | 13,000 | |
| Accounts payable......... | | 15,000 | | | | | | | | 15,000 |
| Accumulated interest expense .............. | | | | (b)    800 | | | | | | 800 |
| Income taxes payable... | | | | (c) 36,000 | | | | | | 36,000 |
| Mortgage payable (8% each Nov. 1) ... | | 60,000 | | | | | | | | 60,000 |
| Common stock, par $10 .............. | | 200,000 | | | | | | | | 200,000 |
| Retained earnings ...... | | 74,200 | | | | | | | | 74,200 |
| Sales revenue ........... | | 474,800 | | | | | | 474,800 | | |
| Manufacturing costs: | | | | | | | | | | |
| Raw material purchases ........... | 70,000 | | | | 70,000 | | | | | |
| Direct labor ........... | 100,000 | | | | 100,000 | | | | | |
| Factory overhead ...... | 75,000 | | (a) 7,000 | | 82,000 | | | | | |
| Distribution expenses............... | 70,000 | | (a) 2,000 | | | | 72,000 | | | |
| General and administrative expenses... | 65,000 | | (a) 1,000 | | | | 66,000 | | | |
| Interest expense ......... | 4,000 | | (b)    800 | | | | 4,800 | | | |
| Income tax expense...... | | | (c) 36,000 | | | | 36,000 | | | |
| Cost of goods manufactured ...... | | | | | | 240,000 | 240,000 | | | |
| Net Income................. | | | | | | | 54,000 | | | 54,000 |
| Totals .............. | 914,000 | 914,000 | 46,800 | 46,800 | 383,000 | 383,000 | 526,800 | 526,800 | 540,000 | 540,000 |

a. Only representative accounts and adjusting entries are included.

b. There are columns for manufacturing; however, the columns for adjusted trial balance sheet and retained earnings have been omitted to demonstrate these simplifications. They were noted as optional in in the chapter.

c. Only three typical adjusting entries are included. Depreciation expense was allocated on a reasonable basis as follows: factory, 70%; distribution, 20%; and general, 10%. Interest was accrued for two months.

d. The current cost accounting entries for factory costs were:

```
Raw material purchases ........................................... 70,000
Direct labor ...........................................................100,000
     Cash ...............................................................        170,000

Factory overhead....................................................  65,000
     Various accounts.................................................       65,000
```

*e.* The ending inventories at December 31, 1976, were:

Raw materials ........................................................................62,000
Work in process .....................................................................81,000
Finished goods ......................................................................52,000

*f.* An average corporate income tax rate of 40% is assumed.

A cost of goods manufactured statement, taken directly from the manufacturing columns in the worksheet, would be as follows:

DUNCAN MANUFACTURING COMPANY
Statement of Cost of Goods Manufactured
For the Year Ended December 31, 1976

Materials:
Beginning inventory ................................................$ 55,000
Purchases ............................................................  70,000
   Total Materials Available...................................... 125,000
Less: Ending inventory ..........................................  62,000
   Cost of materials used............................................      $ 63,000
Direct labor................................................................     100,000
Factory overhead ......................................................      82,000
   Total Factory Costs .............................................     245,000
Add: Beginning work in process inventory .....................      76,000
        321,000
Less: Ending work in process inventory ........................      81,000
   Cost of Goods Manufactured................................     $240,000

Observe on the worksheet that the last amount ($240,000) was transferred from the Manufacturing columns to the Income Statement columns (a debit since it is a cost). In other respects the amounts are extended to the last four columns as explained and illustrated in the chapter (Exhibit 3–5).

## QUESTIONS

1. Explain why an accounting information processing system must be tailored to the characteristics of the entity.

2. What is the accounting model? Give the three submodels and briefly explain each.

3. Complete the following matrix by entering debit or credit in each cell.

| Item | Increase | Decrease |
|------|----------|----------|
| Liabilities | | |
| Revenues | | |
| Assets | | |
| Expenses | | |
| Owners' equity | | |

4. Explain the dual feature of the fundamental accounting model.

5. Broadly explain the purpose of the accounting information processing model.

6. With respect to the collection of raw economic data for the accounting system, why are source documents important? Give some examples of source documents.

7. Explain the nature and purpose of transaction analysis.

8. What kind of events are recorded in the accounting system? Explain.

9. What is meant by journalizing? What purpose does it serve?

10. What is meant by posting? What purpose does it serve?

11. Distinguish between mixed, real, and nominal accounts.

12. Classify the following accounts, before the adjusting entries, as mixed, real, or nominal (explain any assumptions you make):

| | |
|---|---|
| Accounts receivable | Prepaid insurance |
| Supplies inventory | Notes payable |
| Retained earnings | Interest revenue |
| Patents | Common stock |
| Interest expense | Property tax expense |

13. Distinguish between the general ledger, control accounts, and subsidiary ledgers. What is the basic purpose of each?

14. Explain the difference between the general journal and special journals. What is the basic purpose of each?

15. What is a trial balance? What are the two purposes of a trial balance? Distinguish between unadjusted, adjusted, and post-closing trial balances.

16. Why is a worksheet a facilitating technique? What does it facilitate? If a worksheet is strictly optional, as it is, why is it usually used?

17. What is the purpose and nature of an adjusting entry? Explain why they generally must be made. Explain why the adjusting entries must be considered prior to developing the financial statements.

18. Match the following:
    a. An expense incurred but not yet paid.        _____Prepaid expense
    b. A revenue collected but not yet earned.       _____Accrued expense
    c. A revenue earned but not yet collected.       _____Accrued revenue
    d. An expense paid but not yet incurred.         _____Prepaid revenue

19. Why are the adjusting entries journalized and posted?

20. What is the purpose and nature of the closing entries? Why are they journalized and posted?

21. What is the purpose and nature of reversing entries? Why are they journalized and posted?

22. X Company owes a $4,000, 9%, three-year, interest-bearing note payable. Interest is paid each November 30. Therefore, at the end of the accounting period, December 31, the following adjusting entry was made:

Interest expense.........................................................................30
      Accrued interest payable....................................................   30

Would you recommend that a reversing entry be used in this situation? Explain.

23. Number the following phases in the accounting information processing cycle to indicate their normal sequence of completion:

_____Reversing entries.

_____Posting.

_____Transaction analysis.

_____Collection of raw data.

_____Journalize and post adjusting entries.

_____Journalize and post closing entries.

_____Prepare financial statements.

_____Journalize current transactions.

_____Prepare post-closing trial balance.

_____Prepare worksheet.

_____Prepare unadjusted trial balance.

24. In posting a special journal, there are two phases: daily posting and periodic posting. Explain the purpose and nature of each.

25. What circumstances would suggest the need for special journals? Why?

26. What kind of entries are made in the following special journals?
    a. Purchases journal.
    b. Cash receipts journal.
    c. Sales journal.
    d. Cash payments journal.


## EXERCISES

### Exercise 3–1

Develop a diagram that shows that manner in which transactions are recorded in the accounting system in terms of the financial position model. Include the concept of debits and credits. Explain why expenses are increased with a debit and revenues are increased with a credit. Also explain the basis for the designation double-entry system.

### Exercise 3–2

The following selected transactions were completed during the current year by Clay Corporation:

a. Clay Corporation sold 50,000 shares of its own common stock, par $1 per share, for $60,000 cash.
b. Borrowed $30,000 cash on a one-year, 9%, interest-bearing note.
c. Purchased real estate for use in the business at a cash cost of $40,000, which consisted of a small building ($35,000) and the lot on which it was located ($5,000).
d. Purchased merchandise for resale at a cash cost of $8,600. Assume periodic inventory system.
e. Purchased merchandise for resale on credit; terms, 2/10, n/30. If paid within the ten days, the cash payment would be $490; however, if paid after ten days,

the payment would be $500. Since the company takes all discounts, credit purchases are recorded at net.

f. Sold merchandise for $9,600; collected one half in cash and the balance is due in 30 days.

g. Paid the balance due on the purchase in (e) within the ten day period.

*Required:*

Enter each of the above transactions in a general journal. Use the letter to the left to indicate the date.

**Exercise 3–3**

The 11 phases that compose the accounting information processing cycle are listed to the left in scrambled order. To the right is a brief statement of the objective of each phase, also in scrambled order. You are to present two responses.

*Required:*

(Use a separate sheet of paper.)

1. In the blanks to the left, number the phases in the usual sequence of completion.
2. In the blanks to the right, use the letters to match each phase with its objective.

| Sequence (order) | Phases | Matching (with objective) | Objective |
|---|---|---|---|
| _____ | Journalizing. | _____ | a. Verification after closing entries. |
| _____ | Reversing entries. | _____ | |
| _____ | Transaction analysis. | _____ | b. Communication to decision-makers. |
| _____ | Prepare financial statements. | _____ | c. Verification before adjusting entries. |
| _____ | Journalize and post closing entries. | _____ | d. Transfer from journal to ledger. |
| _____ | Collection of raw data. | _____ | e. Based on source documents. |
| _____ | Posting. | | |
| _____ | Journalize and post adjusting entries. | _____ | f. Update general ledger by separating "mixed" accounts. |
| _____ | Prepare worksheets. | _____ | g. Assess economic impact on each transaction. |
| _____ | Prepare unadjusted trial balance. | _____ | |
| _____ | Prepare post-closing trial balance. | _____ | h. Original input into the accounting system. |

i. To facilitate subsequent entries.

j. To obtain a zero balance in the revenue and expense accounts.

k. A logical and systematic technique for completing the end-of-the-period procedures.

**Exercise 3–4**

Frank Corporation completed the three transactions given below:

a. January 1, 1976 – sold 10,000 shares of its own unissued common stock, par $1 per share, for $18,000 cash.
b. January 3, 1976 – purchased a large machine costing $50,000. Payment was $10,000 cash down payment, a $15,000, one-year, 10% interest-bearing note payable, and a $25,000, three-year, 8%, interest-bearing note payable.
c. February 1, 1976 – sold two lots for $7,500, that would not be needed. Received $2,500 cash down payment and a $5,000, 90-day, 10% interest-bearing note. The two lots had a book value of $6,000.

*Required:*
1. Give the general journal entry to record each of the three transactions.
2. Set up T-accounts and post the entries in 1. Use a systematic numbering system for posting purposes.

**Exercise 3–5**

A clerk for Searls Company prepared the following unadjusted trial balance which the clerk was unable to balance:

|  | Debits | Credits |
|---|---|---|
| Cash | $ 33,563 | |
| Accounts receivable | 31,000 | |
| Allowance for doubtful accounts | (2,000) | |
| Inventory | | $ 18,000 |
| Equipment | 81,500 | |
| Accumulated depreciation | | 12,000 |
| Accounts payable | 18,000 | |
| Notes payable | | 25,000 |
| Common stock, par $10 | | 80,000 |
| Retained earnings | | 14,000 |
| Revenues | | 75,000 |
| Expenses | 60,000 | |
| Totals (out of balance by $1,937) | $222,063 | $224,000 |

Assume you are examining the accounts and have found the following errors:

a. Equipment purchased for $7,500 at year-end was debited to Expense.
b. Sales on account for $829 were debited to Accounts Receivable for $892 and credited to Revenues for $829.
c. A $6,000 collection on accounts receivable was debited to Cash and credited to Revenues.
d. The inventory amount is understated by $2,000.

*Required:*
Prepare a corrected trial balance. Show computations.

**Exercise 3-6**

Lyle Company adjusts and closes its accounts each December 31. The following are situations that require an adjusting entry at year-end. You are requested to prepare the adjusting entry in the general journal for each of the situations. Show computations.

a. A machine is to be depreciated for the full year. It cost $71,000, and the estimated useful life is 15 years with an estimated residual value of $11,000. Assume straight-line depreciation.

b. Credit sales for the current year amounted to $120,000. The estimated bad debt loss rate on credit sales is one half of 1%.

c. Property taxes for the current year have not been recorded or paid. A statement, for the calendar year, was received near the end of December for $2,400. The taxes are due and will be paid February 1 in the next year.

d. Supplies costing $800 were purchased for use in the offices during the year and debited to Office Supplies Expense. An inventory of these supplies at the end of the year reflected $150 on hand (unused).

e. Lyle rented an office in its building to an outsider for one year, starting on September 1. Rent for one year amounting to $1,800 was collected at that date. The total amount was credited to Rent Revenue.

f. Lyle holds a note receivable received from a customer dated November 1 of the current year. It is a $1,000, 9%, interest-bearing note, due in one year. At the maturity date, Lyle will collect the face value of the note plus interest for one year.

**Exercise 3-7**

For each of the following situations, you are to give, in general journal form, the adjusting entry required at the end of the annual accounting period, December 31. Show computations.

a. At the end of the year, unpaid and unrecorded salaries amounted to $2,500.

b. The company owns a building which is to be depreciated for the full year. It cost $254,000, has an estimated useful life of 20 years, and a residual value of $54,000. Accumulated depreciation at the beginning of the current year was $60,000.

c. The company rented some space in its building to an outsider on August 1 of the current year and collected $2,400 cash which was rent for one year in advance. Rent Revenue was credited for $2,400 on August 1.

d. The company paid a two-year insurance premium in advance on July 1 of the current year amounting to $900. The $900 was debited to Prepaid Insurance when paid.

e. Credit sales for the current year amounted to $90,000. The estimated bad debt loss rate is one half of 1% of credit sales.

f. On July 1 of the current year, the company received a $10,000, one-year, 8% interest-bearing note from a customer. At maturity date, the company will collect the face amount of $10,000 plus interest for one year.

**Exercise 3-8**

Piper Company adjusts and closes its accounts each December 31. Below are two typical situations involving adjusting entries.

*a.* During the current year, office supplies were purchased for cash, $650. At the end of the current year, an inventory showed $200 unused supplies still on hand.

*Required:*

Give the adjusting entry assuming at the time of the purchase that: Case A, the $650 was debited to Office Supplies Expense; Case B, the $650 was debited to Office Supplies Inventory.

*b.* On June 1, the company collected cash, $2,400, which was for rent collected in advance for the next 12 months.

Give the adjusting journal entry assuming at the time of the collection that: Case A, the $2,400 was credited to Rent Revenue; Case B, the $2,400 was credited to Rent Collected in Advance (i.e., Prepaid Rent Revenue).

## Exercise 3–9

1. On January 1, 1976, the Office Supplies Inventory account showed a balance on hand amounting to $350. During 1976, purchases of office supplies amounted to $800, which was debited to Office Supplies Inventory account. An inventory of office supplies on hand at December 31, 1976 reflected unused supplies amounting to $125. Give the adjusting journal entry that should be made on December 31, 1976.
2. On January 1, 1976, the Prepaid Insurance account showed a debit balance of $300, which was for coverage for the three months, January–March. On April 1, 1976, the company took out another policy covering a two-year period from that date. A two-year premium amounting to $3,600 was paid and debited to Prepaid Insurance. Give the adjusting journal entry that should be made on December 31, 1976.

## Exercise 3–10

Write a suitable explanation for each of the following journal entries:

| | | |
|---|---|---|
| *a.* Wage expense | 1,400 | |
| Accrued wages payable | | 1,400 |
| | | |
| *b.* Warranty (guarantee) expense | 950 | |
| Estimated warranty liability | | 950 |
| | | |
| *c.* Insurance expense | 600 | |
| Prepaid insurance | | 600 |
| | | |
| *d.* Interest expense | 1,200 | |
| Accrued bond interest expense | | 1,200 |
| | | |
| *e.* Interest receivable | 900 | |
| Interest revenue | | 900 |
| | | |
| *f.* Income summary | 5,000 | |
| Retained earnings | | 5,000 |
| | | |
| *g.* Rent revenue | 750 | |
| Deferred rent revenue | | 750 |

**Exercise 3–11**

The adjusted trial balance for Joy Company showed the following on December 31, 1976, which is the end of the annual accounting period:

| | | | |
|---|---|---|---|
| Sales revenue | $82,000 | Selling expenses | $23,000 |
| Interest revenue | 1,000 | Administrative expenses | 13,000 |
| Purchases | 44,000 | Interest expense | 400 |
| Purchase returns | 500 | Income tax expense | 1,000 |
| Freight-in | 1,500 | | |
| Beginning inventory | | Additional data: | |
| (periodic) | 17,800 | Ending inventory | 19,000 |

*Required:*

1. Set up T-accounts for each of the above items; enter the balances and diagram the closing entries. Use Cost of Goods Sold and Income Summary accounts.
2. Explain the manner in which you handled the inventory amounts. Explain an alternate approach.

**Exercise 3–12**

At the end of the annual accounting period, Jester Corporation made the following adjusting entries:

December 31, 1976:

| | | |
|---|---|---|
| *a.* Depreciation expense | 5,000 | |
| Accumulated depreciation | | 5,000 |
| | | |
| *b.* Wage expense | 2,000 | |
| Accrued wages payable | | 2,000 |
| | | |
| *c.* Bad debt expense | 400 | |
| Allowance for doubtful accounts | | 400 |
| | | |
| *d.* Income tax expense | 6,000 | |
| Income tax payable | | 6,000 |

*Required:*

1. Journalize the reversing entries that you think should be made on January 1, 1977.
2. Explain for each adjusting entry, the analysis you used to decide whether to reverse it.

**Exercise 3–13**

At the end of the annual accounting period, AB Corporation made the following adjusting entries:

December 31, 1976:

a. Property tax expense ...................................................... 800
        Property taxes payable .............................................        800
    (These are paid once each year.)

b. Rent receivable ..............................................................2,000
        Rent revenue ..............................................................        2,000
    (Rent revenue is collected each month.)

c. Patent amortization expense .............................................1,000
        Patents........................................................................        1,000

d. Warranty expense ............................................................ 600
        Estimated warranty liability ........................................        600

e. Salary expense ................................................................2,000
        Accrued salaries payable ...........................................        2,000

*Required:*

1. Journalize the reversing entries that you think should be made on January 1, 1977.
2. Explain, for each adjusting entry, the analysis you used to determine whether to reverse it.

### Exercise 3–14

Complete the following tabulations by entering the appropriate amount in each blank space:

1.

| | Owners' Equity at Start of Period | Additional Investment by Owner | Withdrawals by Owner | Owners' Equity at End of Period | Net Income or (Loss) |
|---|---|---|---|---|---|
| a. | $10,000 | $2,000 | $1,000 | $16,400 | $_____ |
| b. | 18,000 | 3,000 | _____ | 22,000 | 4,700 |
| c. | _____ | 1,200 | 800 | 30,000 | (2,200) |
| d. | 15,500 | 600 | _____ | 12,950 | (2,000) |
| e. | 18,000 | _____ | 2,700 | 22,000 | 4,700 |

2.

| | Sales | Finished Goods Initial Inventory | Cost of Goods Manu- factured | Finished Goods Ending Inventory | Cost of Goods Sold | Gross Margin | Expenses | Net Income |
|---|---|---|---|---|---|---|---|---|
| a. | $_____ | $15,000 | $60,000 | $_____ | $67,000 | $23,000 | $_____ | $1,000 |
| b. | 80,000 | _____ | 48,000 | 2,000 | _____ | 23,000 | 18,000 | _____ |
| c. | _____ | 20,000 | _____ | 36,000 | 59,000 | 18,000 | _____ | 8,000 |

### Exercise 3–15 (based on Appendix A)

Dow Company uses special journals for credit sales, credit purchases, cash receipts, and cash payments. For each of the following transactions, you are to indicate the appropriate journal.

| Transactions | Appropriate Journal |
|---|---|
| a. Sold common stock of Dow for cash. | _____ |
| b. Purchased merchandise for resale; terms, 2/10, n/60. | _____ |
| c. Borrowed $5,000 on 8% note. | _____ |
| d. Recorded depreciation expense. | _____ |
| e. Sold merchandise for cash. | _____ |
| f. Purchased merchandise for cash. | _____ |
| g. Purchased equipment for cash. | _____ |
| h. Sold fixed asset for cash. | _____ |
| i. Purchased machinery on credit. | _____ |
| j. Collected an account receivable. | _____ |
| k. Paid a note payable. | _____ |
| l. Recorded accrued wages. | _____ |
| m. Paid cash dividend on common stock. | _____ |
| n. Recorded estimated bad debt expense. | _____ |
| o. Recorded amortization expense on patent. | _____ |

### Exercise 3–16 (based on Appendix A)

Brown Retailers use special journals. Below is the special credit sales journal with several representative transactions:

| | | | | | | Dept. Sales | |
|---|---|---|---|---|---|---|---|
| | | Special Journal — Credit Sales | | | | Page S-9 | |
| Date 1976 | Sales Invoice No. | Account Receivable | Terms | Folio | Amount | A | B |
| 1 | 21 | Fly Corporation | 2/10, n/30 | | 98 | 40 | 58 |
| 5 | 22 | B. T. Company | " | | 490 | 290 | 200 |
| 7 | 23 | Easton Company | " | | 294 | 104 | 190 |
| 11 | 24 | Fly Corporation | " | | 588 | 288 | 300 |
| 13 | 25 | Wells Company | " | | 686 | 300 | 386 |
| 18 | 26 | Fly Corporation | " | | 147 | 100 | 47 |
| 21 | 27 | Easton Company | " | | 784 | 554 | 230 |
| 28 | 28 | B. T. Company | " | | 245 | 200 | 45 |
| 31 | 29 | Wells Company | " | | 637 | 407 | 230 |

*Required:*

1. Sum the above special journal and post it to the appropriate accounts in the general ledger and the two subsidiary ledgers. Use control accounts and subsidiary ledgers for sales and accounts receivable; assign systematic numbers to the accounts.
2. Prove the correctness of the two subsidiary ledgers.

## Exercise 3-17 (based on Appendix A)

Sorensen Retailers use special journals. Below is a special cash receipts journal with several selected transactions.

| | | Debits | Credits | | | | |
|---|---|---|---|---|---|---|---|
| Date 1976 | Explanation | Cash | Account Title | Folio | Accounts Receivables | Sundry Accounts | Sales |
| 1 | Cash sales | 30,000 | | | | | 30,000 |
| 2 | On account | 4,200 | Riley Corporation | | 4,200 | | |
| 5 | Cash sales | 10,000 | | | | | 10,000 |
| 6 | On account | 1,240 | Brown, Inc. | | 1,240 | | |
| 8 | Sale of temporary investment | 7,000 | Temporary investments Gain | | | 4,000 3,000 | |
| 11 | Cash sales | 41,000 | | | | | 41,000 |
| 12 | Borrowed cash | 10,000 | Notes payable | | | 10,000 | |
| 15 | On account | 5,500 | Watson Company | | 5,500 | | |
| 18 | Collected interest | 600 | Interest revenue | | | 600 | |
| 31 | Cash sales | 52,000 | | | | | 52,000 |

Cash Receipts Journal — Page CR-8

*Required:*

1. Sum the above special journal and post it to the appropriate accounts in the general ledger and subsidiary ledger. Use control account and subsidiary ledger for accounts receivable. Assign systematic numbers to the accounts. Assume beginning balances of Riley Corporation, $8,400; Brown, Inc., $1,240; and Watson, $10,000.
2. Prove the correctness of the subsidiary ledger.

## PROBLEMS

### Problem 3-1

The following selected transactions were completed during the current year by Botts Corporation:

a. Botts sold 10,000 shares of its own common stock, par $10 per share, for $12 per share and received cash in full.
b. Borrowed $40,000 cash on an 8%, one-year, interest-bearing note.
c. Purchased equipment for use in operating the business at a net cash cost of $35,000; paid in full.
d. Purchased merchandise for resale at a cash net cost of $20,500; paid cash. Assume a periodic inventory system.
e. Purchased merchandise for resale on credit terms 2/10, n/60. The merchandise will cost $9,800 if paid within ten days, after ten days, the payment will be $10,000. The company always takes the discount; therefore, such purchases are recorded at net.
f. Sold merchandise for $38,000; collected $30,000 cash, and the balance is due in one month.
g. Paid $9,000 cash for operating expenses.
h. Paid the balance for the merchandise purchased in (e), within the ten days.
i. Collected the balance due on the sales in (f).
j. Paid cash for an insurance premium, $500; the premium was for two years' coverage.

*Required:*

1. Enter each of the above transactions in a general journal. Use the letter to the left to indicate the date.
2. Post each entry to appropriate T-accounts (number them consecutively).
3. Prepare an unadjusted trial balance.


## Problem 3-2

The following selected transactions were completed during the current year by Grogan Corporation:

a. At date of organization, sold and issued 50,000 shares of its common stock, par $1 per share, for $75,000 cash.
b. Purchased a plant site for $100,000. The site included a building worth $82,000 and the land worth $18,000. Payment was made; $70,000 cash and a $30,000 one-year, 9%, interest-bearing note.
c. Borrowed $50,000 cash from the local bank; signed a 9% interest-bearing note due in six months.
d. Purchased equipment for use in the business for $12,000; paid cash.
e. Purchased goods for resale at a net cost of $80,000; paid $70,000 cash, balance on open account. Assume perpetual inventory system.
f. Sold goods for cash, $62,000.
g. Paid operating expenses, $31,000.
h. Sold goods for cash, $48,000.
i. Purchased goods for cash, $21,000.
j. Paid the $10,000 due from transaction (e).
k. Sold and issued 30,000 shares of its common stock for $60,000.
l. On due date, paid the local bank the note given in entry (c) in the amount of $50,000 plus the interest to maturity date.
m. Purchased a two-year insurance policy on the building and equipment. Paid the two-year premium amounting to $1,400.

*Required:*

1. Journalize the above transactions in a general journal. Use the letters to the left to indicate dates.
2. Set up T-accounts (number them starting with 101) as needed and post the entries from the journal. Use folio notations.
3. Prepare an unadjusted trial balance.


## Problem 3-3

Ring Company adjusts and closes its books each December 31. It is now December 31, 1976, and the adjusting entries are to be made. You are requested to prepare, in general journal format, the adjusting entry that should be made for each of the following items. Show computations.

a. Credit sales for the year amounted to $200,000. The estimated loss rate on bad debts is one fourth of 1%.
b. Unpaid and unrecorded wages at December 31 amounted to $1,950.
c. The company paid a two-year insurance premium in advance on April 1, 1976, amounting to $3,000 which was debited to Prepaid Insurance.
d. The worksheet is being completed, and pretax income has been computed to be $40,000. The applicable corporate tax rate is 22% on the first $25,000 income, plus 48% on all income above $25,000.

e. A machine that cost $33,700 is to be depreciated for the full year. The estimated useful life is ten years; and the residual value, $2,000. Assume straight-line depreciation.

f. The company rented a warehouse on June 1, 1976, for one year. They had to pay the full amount of rent one year in advance on June 1 amounting to $4,800, which was debited to Rent Expense.

g. The company received a 10%, interest-bearing note from a customer with a face amount of $6,000. The note was dated September 1, 1976; the principal plus the interest is payable one year later. Notes Receivable was debited, and Sales credited on September 1, 1976.

h. On December 30, 1976, the property tax bill was received in the amount of $1,700. This amount applied only to 1976 and had not been previously recorded. The taxes are due, and will be paid, on January 15, 1977.

i. On April 1, 1976, the company signed a $30,000, 8% interest-bearing note payable. On that date, Cash was debited and Notes Payable credited for $30,000. The note is payable on March 30, 1977, for the face amount plus interest for one year.

j. The company purchased a patent on January 1, 1976, at a cost of $5,950. On that date, Patent was debited and Cash credited for $5,950. The patent has an estimated useful life of 17 years and no residual value.

## Problem 3–4

Tracy Company adjusts and closes its accounts each December 31. It is December 31, 1976. You are requested to prepare, in general journal format, the adjusting entry that should be made for each of the following items. Show computations.

a. The company owns a building and the site on which it is situated. The Building account reflects a cost of $267,000, and the site, $20,000. The estimated useful life of the building is 20 years, and the residual value, $47,000. Accumulated depreciation to January 1, 1976, was $66,000. Assume straight-line depreciation.

b. Property taxes for the current year have not been recorded or paid. A tax statement was received near the end of December for $6,000. The taxes are due, and will be paid, on February 15, 1977.

c. The company received a $6,000, 10%, interest-bearing note from a customer on June 1, 1976. On this date, Notes Receivable was debited and Sales credited for $6,000. The face of the note plus interest for one year is payable on May 30, 1977.

d. At December 31, 1976, the Supplies Inventory account showed a debit balance of $1,350. An inventory of unused supplies taken at year-end reflected $380.

e. Sales for the year amounted to $1,500,000, of which $300,000 was on credit. The estimated bad debt loss rate, based on credit sales, was one third of 1% for the year.

f. On August 1, 1976, the company rented some space in its building to an outsider and collected $4,200 cash rent in advance. This was for the 12 months starting August 1, 1976, and was credited to Rent Revenue.

g. At December 31, 1976, unrecorded and unpaid salaries amounted to $8,000.

h. On April 1, 1976, the company borrowed $20,000 on a one-year, 9%, interest-bearing note. On that date, Cash was debited and Notes Payable credited for $20,000. On maturity date, the face amount plus interest for one year must be paid.

i. On January 1, 1976, the company purchased, with cash, a patent for use in the business at a cost of $2,550, which was debited to Patent. The patent has an estimated remaining economic life of 15 years and no residual value.

j. The company uses the periodic inventory system whereby the inventory is physically counted, then valued at unit cost at each year-end. The company prefers to consider the inventory amounts as adjusting entries. The beginning inventory amount was $38,000, and the ending inventory (December 31, 1976) was $44,500. You are to give the adjusting entry for each inventory amount assuming a Cost of Goods Sold account is used.

k. The worksheet is being completed; all of the above adjusting entries have been recorded on it. Pretax income has been computed to be $60,000. The applicable corporate tax rates are 22% on the first $25,000 income plus 48% on all income above $25,000.

## Problem 3–5

The following situations relate to the XY Corporation. The fiscal (accounting year) ends December 31. The situations relate to the year 1976. XY Corporation is a manufacturer rather than a retailer. The books are adjusted and closed each December 31.

In each instance, you are to give *only* the adjusting entry (or entries) that would be made on December 31, 1976, incident to adjusting and closing the books and preparation of the annual financial statements. State clearly any assumptions that you make. Give each adjusting entry in general journal format.

Situation 1: The company owns a machine that cost $87,000; it was purchased on July 1, 1973. It has an estimated useful life of 15 years and a residual value of $12,000. Straight-line depreciation is used. The machine is still being used.

Situation 2: Sales for 1976 amounted to $800,000, including $300,000 credit sales. It is estimated, based on past experience of the company, that bad debt losses will be one half of 1% of credit sales.

Situation 3: On January 1, 1975, the company purchased a patent that cost $15,300; at that time the estimated useful life remaining was 17 years. The patent is used in operations.

Situation 4: At the beginning of 1976, Office Supplies Inventory amounted to $200. During 1976, office supplies amounting to $4,100 were purchased which was debited to Office Supplies Expense. An inventory of office supplies at the end of 1976 showed $250 on the shelves. The January 1 balance of $200 is still reflected in the Office Supplies Inventory account.

Situation 5: On July 1, 1976, the company paid a three-year insurance premium amounting to $900; this amount was debited to Prepaid Insurance.

Situation 6: On October 1, 1976, the company paid rent on some leased office space. The payment of $3,000 cash was for the following 12 months. At the time of payment, Rent Expense was debited for the $3,000.

Situation 7: On July 1, 1976, the company borrowed $60,000 from the Sharpstown bank; the loan was for 12 months at 7% interest on the face of the note. Since it was a noninterest-bearing note, the interest was taken out of the proceeds at the date of the loan; hence, Cash was debited for $55,800; Interest Expense debited for $4,200, and Notes Payable was credited for $60,000.

Situation 8: Finished goods inventory on January 1, 1976, was $120,000; and on December 31, 1976, it was $135,000. Assume periodic inventory procedures and that inventory entries are viewed as adjusting entries.

Situation 9: The company owned some property (land) that was rented to Jack Joske on April 1, 1976, for 12 months for $3,600. On April 1, the entire annual rental of $3,600 was credited to Rent Revenue Collected in Advance and Cash was debited.

Situation 10: On December 31, 1976, wages earned by employees but not yet paid (nor recorded in the accounts) amounted to $7,500. Disregard payroll taxes.

Situation 11: On December 31, 1976, it was discovered that some raw material purchased on the preceding day, although not paid for, was included in the final inventory. A purchase had not been recorded. The cost was $950.

Situation 12: On September 1, 1976, the company loaned $12,000 to an outside party; the loan was at 9% per annum and was due in six months; interest is to be paid at maturity, as a consequence, Cash was credited for $12,000 and Notes Receivable debited for the same amount on September 1.

Situation 13: On January 1, 1976, factory supplies on hand amounted to $100. During 1976, factory supplies costing $1,800 were purchased and debited to Factory Supplies Inventory. At the end of 1976, a physical inventory count revealed that factory supplies on hand amounted to $300.

Situation 14: The company purchased a gravel pit on January 1, 1974, at a cost of $30,000; it was estimated that approximately 60,000 tons of gravel could be removed prior to exhaustion. It was also estimated that the company would utilize five years to exploit this natural resource. Tons of gravel removed were: 1974 — 2,000; 1975 — 7,000; 1976 — 5,000.

Situation 15: At the end of 1976, it was found that there were postage stamps costing $90 still on hand (in a "postage" box in the office). When the stamps were purchased, Miscellaneous Expense was debited and Cash credited.

Situation 16: At the end of 1976, property taxes for 1976 amounting to $2,300 had been assessed on property owned by the company. The taxes are due no later than February 1, 1977. The taxes had not been recorded on the books since payment had not been made.

Situation 17: The company borrowed $30,000 from the bank on December 1, 1976. A 60-day note payable was signed that called for 8% interest payable on the due date. As a consequence, on December 1, 1976, Cash was debited and Notes Payable credited for $30,000.

Situation 18: On July 1, 1976, the company paid the city a $500 license charge for the next 12 months. On that date, Cash was credited and License Expense debited for $500.

Situation 19: On March 1, 1976, the company made a loan to the company president and received a $12,000 noninterest-bearing note receivable. The loan was due in one year and called for 6% annual interest (or discount) with interest taken out in advance. As a consequence, Cash was credited for $11,280, Interest Revenue credited for $720, and Notes Receivable debited for $12,000.

Situation 20: The company owns three "company cars" used by the executives. A six-month maintenance contract on them was signed on October 1, 1976, whereby a local garage agreed to do "all the required maintenance." The payment was made for the following six months in advance. On October 1, 1976, Cash was credited and Maintenance Expense was debited for $1,800.

## Problem 3-6

The post-closing trial balance of the general ledger of Watkins Corporation at December 31, 1975, reflected the following:

| Account No. | Account | Debit | Credit |
|---|---|---|---|
| 101 | Cash ..................................................... | $28,000 | |
| 102 | Accounts receivable ............................... | 18,000 | |
| 103 | Allowance for doubtful accounts ................. | | $    400 |
| 104 | *Inventory (periodic) .................................... | 10,000 | |
| 105 | Equipment (20-year life; no residual value) ... | 20,000 | |
| 106 | Accumulated depreciation ......................... | | 6,000 |
| 200 | Accounts payable ..................................... | | 9,000 |
| 201 | Accrued wages payable ............................ | | |
| 202 | Income taxes payable .............................. | | |
| 300 | Common stock, par $1............................... | | 50,000 |
| 301 | Retained earnings.................................... | | 10,600 |
| 302 | Income summary ..................................... | | |
| 400 | Revenues................................................ | | |
| 500 | Operating expenses ................................. | | |
| 501 | Purchases ............................................. | | |
| 600 | Income tax expense ................................. | | |
| | | $76,000 | $76,000 |

*Ending inventory, $15,000 (at December 31, 1976).

The following is a summary of the transactions during 1976 (use the number to the left to indicate the date):

Date
1. Sold goods, $90,000, of which $20,000 was on credit.
2. Purchased goods, $40,000, of which $10,000 was on credit; assume periodic inventory.
3. Collected accounts receivable, $35,000.
4. Paid accounts payable, $17,000.
5. Paid operating expenses, $23,800.
6. Sold common stock of the company, 2,000 shares at par, collected cash in full.
7. On the last day of the year, purchased a new machine at a cost of $12,000, paid cash. Estimated useful life, ten years; residual value, $10,000.

*Required:*
1. Set up T-accounts in the general ledger for the accounts listed above; they are all you will need. Enter the beginning balances.
2. Journalize each of the above transactions in the general journal.
3. Post the journal entries; use folio notations.
4. Prepare an unadjusted trial balance.
5. Journalize and post the adjusting entries. Accrued (unpaid) wages at year-end amounted to $800. Bad debt expense is estimated to be 1% of credit sales for the period. Assume straight-line depreciation. Assume a flat 22% corporate income tax rate.
6. Prepare an adjusted trial balance.
7. Prepare an unclassified income statement and balance sheet.
8. Journalize and post the closing entries.
9. Prepare a post-closing trial balance.

**Problem 3–7**

The post-closing trial balance of the general ledger of Voss Corporation at December 31, 1975, reflected the following:

| Account No. | Accounts | Debit | Credit |
|---|---|---|---|
| 101 | Cash .................................................... | $ 27,000 | |
| 102 | Accounts receivable................................. | 21,000 | |
| 103 | Allowance for doubtful accounts.............. | | $ 1,000 |
| 104 | Inventory (periodic system)* .................... | 35,000 | |
| 105 | Prepaid insurance (20 months remaining) ......................................... | 900 | |
| 200 | Equipment (20-year estimated life; no residual value) ................................ | 50,000 | |
| 201 | Accumulated depreciation ........................ | | 22,500 |
| 300 | Accounts payable .................................... | | 7,500 |
| 301 | Accrued wages payable ........................... | | |
| 302 | Income taxes payable (for 1975) ............... | | 4,000 |
| 400 | Common stock, par $1 ........................... | | 80,000 |
| 401 | Retained earnings................................... | | 18,900 |
| 500 | Sales revenue......................................... | | |
| 600 | Purchases ............................................. | | |
| 601 | Operating expenses................................. | | |
| 602 | Income tax expense................................. | | |
| 700 | Income summary .................................... | | |
| | | $133,900 | $133,900 |

* Ending inventory, $45,000 (at December 31, 1976).

The following transactions occurred during 1976 in the order given (use the number at the left to indicate the date):

Date
1. Sold goods for $30,000 of which $10,000 was on credit.
2. Collected $17,000 on accounts receivable.
3. Paid income taxes payable (1975), $4,000.
4. Purchased merchandise $40,000, of which $8,000 was on credit.
5. Paid accounts payable, $6,000.
6. Sold goods for cash, $72,000.
7. Paid operating expenses, $19,000.
8. Sold and issued 1,000 shares of common stock, par $1, for $1,000 cash.
9. Purchased merchandise, $100,000, of which $27,000 was on credit.
10. Sold goods for $98,000, of which $30,000 was on credit.
11. Collected cash on accounts receivable, $26,000.
12. Paid cash on accounts payable, $28,000.
13. Paid various operating expenses in cash, $18,000.

*Required:*

1. Set up T-accounts in the general ledger for each of the accounts listed in the beginning trial balance and enter the beginning balances.
2. Journalize each of the transactions listed above for 1976. Use general journal only.
3. Post the journal entries; use folio notations.
4. Prepare an unadjusted trial balance.
5. Journalize the adjusting entries and post them to the ledger. Assume the bad debt rate is ½% of credit sales for the period and an average 40% corporate income tax rate. At December 31, 1976, accrued wages, $300. Assume straight-line depreciation.
6. Prepare an adjusted trial balance.
7. Prepare an unclassified income statement and balance sheet.
8. Journalize and post the closing entries. Do not use a Cost of Goods Sold account.
9. Prepare a post-closing trial balance.

## Problem 3-8

Young Corporation adjusts and closes its books each December 31. At December 31, 1976, the following unadjusted trial balance has been developed from the general ledger:

| Accounts | Balances (Unadjusted) Debits | Credits |
|---|---|---|
| Cash | $132,830 | |
| Accounts receivable | 34,000 | |
| Allowance for doubtful accounts | | $ 5,400 |
| Inventory (periodic system) | 62,000 | |
| Prepaid insurance (15 months remaining as of January 1, 1976) | 600 | |
| Long-term note receivable (7%) | 12,000 | |
| Investment revenue receivable | | |
| Land | 27,000 | |
| Building | 240,000 | |
| Accumulated depreciation, building | | 130,000 |
| Equipment | 90,000 | |
| Accumulated depreciation, equipment | | 50,000 |
| Accounts payable | | 23,000 |
| Accrued salaries payable | | |
| Income taxes payable | | |
| Accrued interest payable | | |
| Prepaid rent revenue | | |
| Bonds payable, 5% | | 120,000 |
| Common stock, par $10 | | 200,000 |
| Contributed capital in excess of par | | 10,000 |
| Retained earnings | | 27,900 |
| Sales revenue | | 290,000 |
| Investment revenue | | 630 |
| Rent revenue | | 6,000 |
| Purchases | 164,000 | |
| Purchase returns | | 4,000 |
| Selling expenses | 51,000 | |
| General and administrative expenses | 35,000 | |
| Interest expense | 3,500 | |
| Extraordinary loss (pretax) | 15,000 | |
| Income tax expense | | |
| | $866,930 | $866,930 |

Additional data for adjustments and other purposes:

a. Estimated bad debt loss rate is one half of 1% of credit sales. Ten percent of 1976 sales were on credit. Classify as a selling expense.

b. Ending inventory (December 31, 1976), $70,000.

c. Interest on the long-term note receivable was last collected on September 30, 1976.

d. Estimated useful life on the building was 20 years; residual value, $40,000. Allocate 10% to administrative. Assume straight-line depreciation.

e. Estimated useful life on the equipment was ten years; residual value, zero. Allocate 10% to administrative. Assume straight-line depreciation.

f. Unrecorded and unpaid sales salaries payable at December 31, 1976, was $7,500.

g. Interest on the bonds payable was paid last on July 31, 1976.

h. On August 1, 1976, the company rented some space in its building to an outsider and collected $6,000 for 12 months rent in advance which was credited to Rent Revenue.

i. Adjust for expired insurance. Assume selling expense.

j. Assume an average 40% corporate income tax rate on all items including the extraordinary loss.

*Required:*

1. Enter the above unadjusted trial balance on a worksheet similar to Exhibit 3-5.
2. Enter the adjusting entries on the worksheet and complete it (round to nearest dollar).
3. Prepare an unclassified income statement and a balance sheet.
4. Journalize the closing entries.

## Problem 3–9

Astro Corporation currently is completing the end-of-the-period accounting process. At December 31, 1976, and the following unadjusted trial balance has been developed from the general ledger:

| Accounts | Balances (Unadjusted) | |
| --- | --- | --- |
| | Debits | Credits |
| Cash | $    61,900 | |
| Accounts receivable | 38,000 | |
| Allowance for doubtful accounts | | $    2,000 |
| Inventory (periodic system) | 80,000 | |
| Office supplies inventory | 900 | |
| Long-term note receivable (7%) | 12,000 | |
| Equipment | 180,000 | |
| Accumulated depreciation, equipment | | 64,000 |
| Patent | 8,400 | |
| Accrued interest receivable | | |
| Accounts payable | | 23,000 |
| Accrued interest payable | | |
| Income taxes payable | | |
| Property taxes payable | | |
| Prepaid rent revenue | | |
| Mortgage payable, 8% | | 60,000 |
| Common stock, par $100 | | 100,000 |
| Contributed capital in excess of par | | 15,000 |
| Retained earnings | | 32,440 |
| Sales revenue | | 700,000 |
| Investment revenue | | 560 |
| Rent revenue | | 3,000 |
| Purchases | 400,000 | |
| Freight-in | 7,000 | |
| Purchase returns | | 2,000 |
| Selling expenses | 164,400 | |
| General and administrative expenses | 55,000 | |
| Interest expense | 4,400 | |
| Income tax expense | | |
| Extraordinary gain (pretax) | | 10,000 |
| | $1,012,000 | $1,012,000 |

Additional data for adjustments and other purposes:

a. Estimated bad debt loss rate is one fourth of 1% of credit sales. Credit sales for the year amounted to $200,000. This is a selling expense.
b. Ending inventory, December 31, 1976, $95,000.
c. Interest on the long-term note receivable was last collected August 31, 1976.
d. Estimated useful life of the equipment is ten years; residual value, $20,000. Allocate 10% to administrative expenses. Assume straight-line depreciation.
e. Estimated remaining economic life of the patent is 14 years (from January 1, 1976) and no residual value. Assume straight-line amortization to selling expense (used in sales promotion).
f. Interest on the mortgage payable was last paid on November 30, 1976.
g. On June 1, 1976, the company rented some office space to an outsider for one year and collected $3,000 rent in advance for the year which was credited to Rent Revenue.
h. On December 31, 1976, received a statement for calendar year 1976 unrecorded property taxes amounting to $1,300. The amount is due February 15, 1977. Assume it will be paid on that date and that it is a selling expense.
i. Office supplies on hand at December 31, 1976, amounted to $300 (selling expense).
j. Assume an average 40% corporate income tax rate on all items including the extraordinary gain.

*Required:*

1. Enter the above adjusted trial balance on a worksheet similar to Exhibit 3–5.
2. Enter the adjusting entries and complete the worksheet.
3. Prepare an unclassified income statement and balance sheet.
4. Journalize the closing entries.

## Problem 3–10

Write a suitable explanation for each of the following journals entries:

| | | |
|---|---:|---:|
| a. Sales revenue | 50,000 | |
| Rent revenue | 2,000 | |
| Interest revenue | 1,000 | |
| Sales returns | | 1,500 |
| Income summary | | 51,500 |
| | | |
| b. Salary expense | 7,000 | |
| Accrued salaries payable | | 7,000 |
| | | |
| c. Rent revenue | 800 | |
| Deferred rent revenue | | 800 |
| | | |
| d. Income summary | 10,000 | |
| Inventory | | 10,000 |
| | | |
| e. Inventory | 12,000 | |
| Income summary | | 12,000 |
| | | |
| f. Interest receivable | 900 | |
| Interest revenue | | 900 |
| | | |
| g. Supplies used expense | 400 | |
| Supplies inventory | | 400 |

h. Income summary............................................................39,000

|  |  |
|---|---|
| Operating expenses ............................................... | 21,000 |
| Administrative expenses ......................................... | 16,000 |
| Interest expense .................................................. | 2,000 |

i. Interest expense .........................................        750

| Accrued interest expense payable........................... | 750 |
|---|---|

j. Income summary.........................................        8,800

| Retained earnings ................................................. | 8,800 |
|---|---|

k. Investment revenue.......................................        600

| Deferred (unearned) investment revenue.................... | 600 |
|---|---|

l. Warranty (guarantee) expense  .......................        500

| Estimated warranty liability ...................................... | 500 |
|---|---|

m. Income tax expense  ....................................        3,700

| Income taxes payable  ............................................ | 3,700 |
|---|---|

n. Property tax expense.....................................        360

| Property taxes payable ........................................... | 360 |
|---|---|

o. Supplies inventory .......................................        440

| Supplies expense  ................................................ | 440 |
|---|---|

## Problem 3–11

The adjusted trial balance for Ransom Corporation reflected the following on December 31, 1976, end of the annual accounting period:

| | | |
|---|---|---|
| Cash ...............................................................................$ | 27,900 | |
| Inventory (periodic system)............................................. | 18,000 | |
| Accounts receivable ...................................................... | 32,000 | |
| Allowance for doubtful accounts...................................... | | $    500 |
| Prepaid insurance........................................................... | 600 | |
| Equipment ..................................................................... | 100,000 | |
| Accumulated depreciation, equipment ........................... | | 20,000 |
| Accounts payable .......................................................... | | 13,400 |
| Accrued wages .............................................................. | | 800 |
| Income taxes payable .................................................... | | 5,000 |
| Bonds payable .............................................................. | | 20,000 |
| Common stock, par $10 ................................................ | | 100,000 |
| Retained earnings.......................................................... | | 12,400 |
| Sales revenue................................................................ | | 126,000 |
| Interest revenue............................................................. | | 1,000 |
| Sales returns ................................................................ | 3,000 | |
| Purchases .................................................................... | 70,000 | |
| Freight-in....................................................................... | 2,500 | |
| Purchase returns ........................................................... | | 900 |
| Operating expenses....................................................... | 28,000 | |
| General expenses (including interest) ............................. | 13,000 | |
| Income tax expense....................................................... | 5,000 | |
| | $300,000 | $300,000 |

Inventory, December 31, 1976, $23,000.

*Required:*

1. Set up T-accounts only for the accounts to be closed and Retained Earnings.

Enter the balances. Diagram the closing entries. Use Cost of Goods Sold and Income Summary accounts.

2. Journalize the closing entries to agree with your diagram.
3. Explain the manner in which you handled the inventory amounts.
4. Did you use a Cost of Goods Sold account? Explain the alternate approach.

## Problem 3–12

The summarized adjusted trial balance for Exter Corporation reflected the following on December 31, 1976, end of the annual accounting period:

| | | |
|---|---:|---:|
| Cash | $ 60,700 | |
| Inventory (periodic system) | 12,000 | |
| Accounts receivable | 21,000 | |
| Allowance for doubtful accounts | | $    400 |
| Prepaid insurance | 300 | |
| Accounts payable | | 17,600 |
| Accrued wages payable | | 1,000 |
| Income taxes payable | | 2,000 |
| Common stock, par $10 | | 50,000 |
| Retained earnings | | 17,300 |
| Sales revenue | | 88,000 |
| Sales returns | 2,000 | |
| Purchases | 45,000 | |
| Freight-in | 1,000 | |
| Purchase returns | | 700 |
| Operating expenses | 18,400 | |
| General expenses (including interest) | 14,600 | |
| Income tax expense | 2,000 | |
| | $177,000 | $177,000 |

Inventory (ending), December 31, 1976, $18,800.

*Required:*

1. Set up T-accounts for Retained Earnings and those accounts that are to be closed. Enter the balances. Diagram the closing entries. Use an Income Summary account.
2. Journalize the closing entries to agree with your diagram.
3. Explain the manner in which you handled the inventory amounts. Explain an alternate approach.
4. Did you use a Cost of Goods Sold account? Explain an alternate approach to the one you used.

## Problem 3–13

At the end of the accounting period, Burke Corporation made the following adjusting entries:

December 31, 1976:

| | | |
|---|---:|---:|
| a. Depreciation expense | 7,000 | |
|     Accumulated depreciation | | 7,000 |
| b. Bad debt expense | 1,000 | |
|     Allowance for doubtful accounts | | 1,000 |
| c. Insurance expense | 600 | |
|     Prepaid insurance | | 600 |

| | | |
|---|---|---|
| d. Supplies used expense ....................................................2,000 | | |
| Supplies inventory .................................................... | | 2,000 |

| | | |
|---|---|---|
| e. Wage expense ................................................................5,000 | | |
| Accrued wages payable ............................................. | | 5,000 |

| | | |
|---|---|---|
| f. Rent receivable..................................................................3,000 | | |
| Rent revenue ............................................................. | | 3,000 |

| | | |
|---|---|---|
| g. Utilities (electric) expense ...................................................4,000 | | |
| Estimated utilities payable........................................... | | 4,000 |

| | | |
|---|---|---|
| h. Interest expense ............................................................ 900 | | |
| Accrued interest payable ............................................ | | 900 |

*Required:*

1. The first four adjusting entries given above generally are not viewed as candidates for reversal on January 1, 1977. Explain why each one is generally not a candidate.
2. The last four adjusting entries shown above generally are viewed as candidates for reversal on January 1, 1977. Give the reversing entry for each and explain why it may be desirable to reverse.
3. The last entry may, or may not, be reversed. In either event, the net effect is the same. Assume the next interest payment is March 31, 1977, for $1,200 (interest for the past 12 months). Prepare entries side by side under the captions "With Reversing Entry" and "Without Reversing Entry" and demonstrate that the net effects are the same.

### Problem 3–14 (based on Appendix A)

Boley Company uses special journals for credit sales and credit purchases. Below are listed some selected transactions involving purchases and sales. Amounts given for credit transactions are before any deduction of discount unless otherwise stated. Sales and purchases on credit are recorded net of discount. Assume periodic inventory.

a. Purchased merchandise for cash, $9,800, from X Corporation.
b. Sold merchandise on credit terms 2/10, n/30, $1,000, to AD Company.
c. Purchased merchandise, $3,000, terms, 2/10, n/30, from Benson Company.
d. Purchased equipment from Roy Company for use in the business for $10,000; paid cash.
e. Collected for merchandise sold in (b) within ten days.
f. Sold merchandise on credit terms 2/10, n/30, $2,000, to Z Company.
g. Purchased merchandise for cash, $15,000, from AK Company.
h. Sold merchandise for cash, $41,800, to AD Company.
i. Sold merchandise on credit terms 2/10, n/30, $4,000, BT Corporation.
j. Purchased merchandise from X Corporation, $1,500, credit terms 2/10, n/30.
k. Paid for merchandise purchased in (c) above within the discount period.
l. Sold merchandise to VEE Company, $3,300, credit terms 2/10, n/60.
m. Purchased merchandise from Benson Company, $4,000; terms, 2/10, n/30.

*Required:*

1. Design special journals for credit sales and credit purchases similar to those illustrated in the chapter.

2. Enter in the two special journals appropriate transactions from the above list. Enter the remaining entries in the general journal.
3. Set up ledger accounts for Sales, Purchases, Accounts Receivable Control, and Accounts Payable Control in the general ledger, and appropriate subsidiary ledgers for the two latter control accounts. Use T-account format. Post appropriate amounts to these records. Systematically number the accounts for posting purposes.
4. Prove the accuracy of the accounts receivable and accounts payable records.

### Problem 3–15 (based on Appendix A)

Thomas Company is a small department store. The accounting system is manually maintained. Control accounts and subsidiary ledgers are used. The following information was selected from the accounting system at January 1, 1976:

| Journals | Page No. to Be Used |
|---|---|
| General journal | J-27 |
| Special journals: | |
| Credit sales | S-13 |
| Credit purchases | P-9 |
| Cash receipts | CR-22 |
| Cash payments | CP-34 |

| General Ledger Accounts | Balance Jan. 1, 1977 | Account No. |
|---|---|---|
| Cash | $ 72,000 | 101 |
| Accounts receivable | 38,000 | 105 |
| Inventory (periodic system) | 45,000 | 110 |
| Equipment | 25,000 | 204 |
| Accounts payable | 21,000 | 303 |
| Notes payable | 10,000 | 305 |
| Common stock, par $10 | 100,000 | 400 |
| Contributed capital in excess of par | | 401 |
| Retained earnings | 49,000 | 410 |
| Sales revenue | | 500 |
| Sales returns | | 501 |
| Purchases | | 600 |
| Purchase returns | | 601 |
| Expenses | | 700 |

| Subsidiary Ledgers | | |
|---|---|---|
| Accounts receivable (No. 105): | | |
| Ames, C. P. | 7,000 | 105.1 |
| Graves Company | 16,000 | 105.2 |
| Mason Corporation | 5,000 | 105.3 |
| White Company | 10,000 | 105.4 |
| Accounts payable (No. 303): | | |
| Buford Wholesale Company | 11,000 | 303.1 |
| Dawn Suppliers, Inc. | 7,000 | 303.2 |
| Paul Wholesale Company | 3,000 | 303.3 |

The following transactions were completed during the month of January 1976:

Date
1. Purchased merchandise for cash, $18,000.
2. Paid $11,000 owed to Buford Wholesale Company within the discount period.

3. Sold merchandise for cash, $26,000.
4. Purchased a new truck for use in the business; paid cash, $4,200.
5. Sold merchandise to XY Corporation on credit; terms, 2/10, n/60; $9,800 if paid within ten days, otherwise $10,000 (record at net of discount).
6. Paid expenses $4,500.
7. Purchased merchandise on credit from Sauls Company; credit terms, 2/10, n/60; $20,000, if paid within ten days; otherwise add 2% charge.
8. Sold merchandise for cash, $37,000.
8. Collected on accounts receivable within the discount period as follows: Ames, $7,000; Graves, $16,000; and White, $10,000.
9. Purchased merchandise for cash, $21,000.
9. Collected in full from XY Corporation for the sale of January 5.
9. Paid accounts payable within the discount period: Dawn, $7,000; Paul $2,000.
10. Collected accounts receivable from Mason Corporation, $5,000, within the discount period.
10. Returned merchandise purchased from Paul Wholesale Company because its specifications were incorrect; received a credit for $1,000.
14. Paid expenses, $9,600.
15. Sold merchandise for cash, $11,400.
16. Paid balance due to Sauls within the discount period.
19. Borrowed $30,000 cash on a one-year, 8%, interest-bearing note.
22. Sold merchandise on credit terms, 2/10, n/30, as follows (net amount): Ames, $6,000; Graves, $13,000; Mason, $9,000; and White, $4,000.
23. A customer returned merchandise, purchased a few days earlier; since the correct size was unavailable, customer was given a cash refund of $175.
24. Collected the balance due from White Company within the discount period.
25. Returned damaged merchandise to a wholesale supplier and received a cash refund of $450.
26. Purchased merchandise on credit from Buford Wholesale Company; terms, 2/10, n/60; net amount, $35,000.
27. Purchased merchandise on credit from Dawn Suppliers, Inc.; terms, 2/10, n/60; net amount, $12,000.
28. Cash sales, $47,000.
29. Sold merchandise on credit to XY Corporation on the usual terms, net amount, $16,500.
30. Collected in full for the credit sale to Mason on January 22.
31. Sold common stock of Thomas Company to a new shareholder, 1,000 shares for $20,000 cash.

*Required:*

1. Set up a general journal and special journals for credit sales, credit purchases, cash receipts, and cash payments, similar to those illustrated in Appendix A. Sales and purchases on credit are recorded at net of discount.
2. Set up T-accounts for the general ledger and two subsidiary ledgers, accounts receivable and accounts payable. Enter the beginning balances in the T-accounts.
3. Journalize the above transactions in the appropriate journals.
4. Post to the subsidiary and general ledgers; use folio numbers.
5. Prepare reconciliation of the subsidiary ledgers.
6. Prepare a trial balance from the general ledger.

### Problem 3–16 (based on Appendix B)

Rose Manufacturing Corporation is in the process of completing the end-of-the-period accounting process. It is now December 31, 1976, and the following unadjusted trial balance has been developed from the general ledger:

| | Balance (Unadjusted) | |
| Accounts | Debits | Credits |
|---|---|---|
| Cash ............................................................... | $ 171,300 | |
| Inventory, January 1 (periodic system): | | |
|   Raw materials ..................................................... | 42,000 | |
|   Work in process .................................................. | 60,000 | |
|   Finished goods ................................................... | 38,000 | |
| Accounts receivable ............................................... | 18,000 | |
| Allowance for doubtful accounts ............................. | | $      450 |
| Factory supplies inventory ...................................... | 6,300 | |
| Plant and equipment.............................................. | 430,000 | |
| Accumulated depreciation ...................................... | | 180,000 |
| Remaining assets (not subject to depreciation)............ | 102,000 | |
| Accounts payable .................................................. | | 37,000 |
| Accrued wages payable ......................................... | | |
| Accrued interest payable......................................... | | |
| Income taxes payable ............................................ | | |
| Mortgage payable (9%, each August 31)..................... | | 40,000 |
| Common stock, par $100......................................... | | 500,000 |
| Retained earnings ................................................. | | 42,550 |
| Sales revenue ...................................................... | | 800,000 |
| Manufacturing costs: | | |
|   Raw materials purchases....................................... | 180,000 | |
|   Direct labor ....................................................... | 200,000 | |
|   Factory overhead ............................................... | 100,000 | |
| Distribution expenses ............................................ | 160,000 | |
| Administrative expenses ......................................... | 90,000 | |
| Interest expense................................................... | 2,400 | |
| Cost of goods manufactured ................................... | | |
| Income tax expense .............................................. | | |
| | $1,600,000 | $1,600,000 |

Additional data for adjustments and other purposes:

a. Ending inventories: raw materials, $45,000; work in process, $54,000; finished goods, $40,000.

b. Estimated bad debt loss rate is one third of 1% of credit sales. Credit sales for the period were $150,000 (distribution expense).

c. An inventory of factory supplies taken on December 31, 1976, showed unused supplies amounting to $4,800 (factory overhead).

d. Plant and equipment is depreciated over a 20-year life (estimated); residual value is $30,000 (debit Factory Overhead for depreciation).

e. Unrecorded and unpaid administrative wages at December 31 amounted to $3,500.

f. The last interest payment on the mortgage was on August 31, 1976.

g. Assume 40% corporate income tax rate.

*Required:*

1. Enter the above unadjusted trial balance on a worksheet similar to Exhibit 3–17.

2. Enter the adjusting entries on the worksheet and complete it; assume straight-line depreciation.

3. Prepare a manufacturing statement, single-step income statement, and an unclassified balance sheet.

4. Journalize the closing entries.

# Chapter *4*

## Review — The Income Statement and Retained Earnings

Periodic financial statements are the means by which information collected, recorded, and summarized in the accounting system is communicated to external decision-makers. Financial statements and the supplementary statements generally necessary for full disclosure are:

1. Income statement
   Supplementary — statement of retained earnings
2. Balance sheet
   Supplementary — statement of changes in stockholders' equity
3. Statement of changes in financial position
   Supplementary — changes in elements of working capital

The periodic financial statements present primarily *historical* information. They are *general-purpose* statements because they are designed primarily to serve several groups of decision-makers — investors, creditors, and the public at large. Also, they are summary in nature and are fundamentally related; that is, each statement is interrelated with the other statements. These relationships are illustrated in Exhibit 4–1.

In Exhibit 4–1, the income statement and the statement of changes in financial position are shown as the connecting links between the beginning and ending balance sheets. They are designed to explain, to the decision-maker, the causes of the changes in financial position during the period. The income statement explains the changes from *operations* (i.e., revenues and expenses), whereas the statement of changes in financial position explains the changes in financial position in terms of *fund* inflows and outflows during the period. The three statements are viewed by the accounting profession as the minimum requirement for reporting to external decision-makers.

This chapter discusses the income statement and the statement of retained earnings.

**EXHIBIT 4–1**

**Relationships between Financial Statements**

1975

Jan. 1, 1976

*Financial Position* (at start of period)

Reported on

**Balance Sheet**

(A statement of financial position at start of period—January 1, 1976)

Assets
Liabilities
Owners' Equity

1976

*Changes in Financial Position* (during the period)

Reported on

**Income Statement**

(A statement of changes during the period—January 1 to December 31, 1976—due to operations)

Revenues Minus Expenses

Net Income

**Statement of Changes in Financial Position**

(A statement of fund inflows and out-flows during the period—January 1 to December 31, 1976—due to financing and investing activities)

Fund Inflows Minus Fund Outflows

Increase or Decrease in Funds

Dec. 31, 1976

1977

*Financial Position* (at end of period)

Reported on

**Balance Sheet**

(A statement of financial position at end of period—December 31, 1976)

Assets
Liabilities
Owners' Equity

**CONCEPT OF INCOME**

Income is defined differently by economists and accountants. The economist broadly defines income as the change in real wealth between the beginning and end of a specified period; to state it another way, income is the net increase in real wealth that could be distributed to the owners of a business at the end of the period without reducing the real wealth of the entity from that at the start of the period. This concept requires careful measurement of the wealth at the beginning and end of each period. It provides no specific details for the causes of net income. Conceptually, wealth at each point in time should be measured as the *present value* of all expected future cash flows. Because of the difficulties in applying this concept, other ways of measuring wealth have been suggested, such as the current cash equivalent market value.

In contrast, the *accountant* defines net income on the basis of completed transactions that cause revenues and expenses. Income is defined as the difference between revenues and expenses arising from completed transactions. The economist's concept of income is impractical to apply; it is based upon subjective information and does not provide details required. Consequently, the accounting profession has evolved the *transactions approach* to define and measure net income. The transactions approach is pragmatic, provides details for continuous accounting, focuses on the stewardship function, and maintains a relatively high degree of objectivity.

The transactions approach used in accounting collects detailed data on each transaction and records the effects in terms of changes in assets, liabilities, and owners' equity (i.e., in terms of the basic accounting model). Basically, changes in assets, liabilities, and owners' equity are recognized if they are evidenced by *completed exchange transactions*. Changes in value generally are not recognized when they occur if they arise from changes in market valuations and changes in expectations; instead, they are recognized when exchange transactions occur. To illustrate, if an asset is acquired for $1,000 and subsequently increases in value to $1,200, the $200 accretion is not recognized as revenue. Should the asset later be sold for $1,300, a $300 gain would be recognized in the period of sale. The broad structure of accounting discussed in Chapter 2 explicitly requires the transactions approach. Since accounting defines income as the difference between total revenue and total expense, these two concepts require careful definition.

*Revenue* may be conceptually defined as the inflow of assets for the aggregate of products or services transferred (i.e., sold) by an enterprise during a specified period.[1] A pragmatic, though conceptually deficient, definition that more nearly expresses current practice is given in APB *Statement No. 4* as follows:

---

[1] Adapted from AAA Committee on Accounting Concepts and Standards, *Accounting and Reporting Standards for Corporate Financial Statements and Preceding Statements and Supplements* (Columbus, Ohio, 1957), p. 5.

> Revenue is a gross increase in assets or a gross decrease in liabilities recognized and measured in conformity with generally accepted accounting principles that results from those types of profit-directed activities of an enterprise that can change owners' equity. Revenue under present generally accepted accounting principles is derived from three general activities: (a) selling products, (b) rendering services and permitting others to use enterprise resources, which result in interest, rent, royalties, fees, and the like, and (c) disposing of resources other than products—for example, plant and equipment or investments in other entities. Revenue does not include receipt of assets purchased, proceeds of borrowing, investments by owners, or adjustments of revenue of prior periods.[2]

At this point it may be advisable to return to Chapter 2 for a review of the *revenue principle*, paying particular attention to when revenue is considered realized.

*Expense* may be defined conceptually as the use and consumption of goods and services in the process of obtaining revenues.[3] A pragmatic, though conceptually deficient, definition that more nearly expresses current practice is given in APB *Statement No. 4* as follows:

> Expenses are gross decreases in assets or gross increases in liabilities recognized and measured in conformity with generally accepted accounting principles that result from those types of profit-directed activities of an enterprise that can change owners' equity. Important classes of expenses are (1) cost of assets used to produce revenue (for example, cost of goods sold, selling and administrative expenses, and interest expense), (2) expense from nonreciprocal transfers and casualties (for example, taxes, fires and theft), (3) costs of other assets other than products (for example, plant and equipment or investments in other companies), disposed of, (4) costs incurred in unsuccessful efforts, and (5) declines in market prices of inventories held for sale. Expenses do not include repayments of borrowing, expenditures to acquire assets, distributions to owners (including acquisition of treasury stock), or adjustments of expenses of prior periods.[4]

At this point you should return to Chapter 2 and restudy the discussion of the cost principle (page 20).

## Terminology Problems

The terms revenue, income, gain, and earnings are often used rather loosely. The following distinctions will aid later discussions:

1. Revenue—resources received for goods sold (such as sales revenue) and services provided (such as services, rent, and interest revenue).
2. Income—a difference; that is, revenue minus expense.
3. Earnings—another term for income.

---

[2] AICPA, "Basic Concepts and Accounting Principles Underlying Financial Statements of Business Enterprises," *Statement of the Accounting Principles Board No. 4* (New York, 1960), pp. 58–60. This definition is conceptually deficient primarily because of circularity.

[3] Adapted from Eldon S. Hendrickson, *Accounting Theory*, rev. ed. (Homewood, Ill.: Richard D. Irwin, Inc., 1970), p. 177.

[4] AICPA, *Statement No. 4*, pp. 58–60.

4. Gain—a net revenue amount derived from transactions that are indirectly related to normal operations such as "gain from sale of fixed assets." In practice, gains generally are broadly classified as a revenue.

Similarly, the terms cost, expense, and loss are troublesome; the following distinctions are widely recognized:

1. Cost—the amount of resources given up to acquire goods and services which, at point of acquisition, are assets, such as prepaid insurance and fixed assets.
2. Expense—the use of assets and services in the creation of revenue; that is, an expired asset. Thus, most costs subsequently become expense. Cost and expense may be the same as in the case where office supplies are acquired and immediately used. In most instances, expense flows from cost, as in the case of office supplies acquired and subsequently used over two or more periods.
3. Loss—an unfavorable effect (asset reduction) not directly related to normal operations such as storm loss, loss on sale of fixed assets, and loss due to theft. In practice, losses are broadly classified as an expense.

## FORM OF INCOME STATEMENT

The accounting profession has not specified a particular format that must be used for the income statement because reasonable flexibility to fit various situations is considered more important than a standard format. A complete income statement is required that adequately reports all revenues and expenses. In addition, a number of *ARBs, APB Opinions,* and FASB *Statements* specify certain disclosure requirements that influence income statement presentation. Examples are presentation of extraordinary items, income tax expense, earnings per share, and items that are *either* unusual or occur infrequently.

Two different formats are widely used for the income statement, although there are numerous variations of each. These are generally referred to as the single-step and the multiple-step formats. A recent study of 600 major companies reported that 65% use the single-step and 35% use the multiple-step format.[5]

### Single-Step Format

The single-step format focuses on two classifications: revenues and expenses. These two classifications are viewed broadly as defined in APB *Statement No. 4* (see definitions on pages 109 and 110). A single-step income statement is illustrated in Exhibit 4–2. Observe the three basic categories: revenues, expenses, and extraordinary items. It is aptly

---

[5] AICPA, *Accounting Trends and Techniques, 1975* (New York, 1975), p. 247. This is an excellent reference for learning how various companies handle the multitude of different items on financial statements.

**EXHIBIT 4–2**
**Single-Step Income Statement**

ILLUSTRATIVE COMPANY
Income Statement
For the Year Ended December 31, 1976

Revenues:

| | | |
|---|---:|---:|
| Sales (less returns and allowances of $10,000) | | $540,000 |
| Services | | 130,000 |
| Rent | | 1,200 |
| Interest and dividends | | 4,800 |
| Gain on sale of fixed assets | | 6,000 |
| Total Revenues | | 682,000 |

Expenses:

| | | |
|---|---:|---:|
| *Cost of goods sold | $314,000 | |
| *Distribution | 153,500 | |
| *Administrative | 73,500 | |
| Depreciation | 54,000 | |
| Interest | 6,000 | |
| Loss on sale of investments | 5,000 | |
| Income taxes | 29,500 | |
| Total Expenses | | 635,500 |
| Income before extraordinary item | | 46,500 |

Extraordinary item:

| | | |
|---|---:|---:|
| Loss (specified) | 10,000 | |
| Less: Tax savings | 4,800 | 5,200 |
| Net Income | | $ 41,300 |

Earnings per share on common stock (20,000 shares outstanding):

| | |
|---|---:|
| Income before extraordinary item | $2.33 |
| Extraordinary loss | .26 |
| Net Income | $2.07 |

\* These items may be detailed in the statement, or separately in the notes to the financial statements, or as separate schedules.

called a single-step statement because there is only one step—income before extraordinary items—involving revenues and expenses. Exhibit 4–2 shows a "pure" single-step format; therefore, all revenues are grouped under one classification. This includes gains (other than extraordinary) such as the one illustrated. A gain is distinctly different from the other revenue items illustrated in that it reflects a net difference. That is, the $6,000 gain is the result of a transaction such as:

| | |
|---|---:|
| Cash received from sale of fixed asset | $15,000 |
| Less book value of the asset sold | 9,000 |
| Gain from sale of fixed asset | $ 6,000 |

In contrast, all other revenues are gross in the sense that the related expenses are deducted separately.

Consistent with the broad classification of revenues, all expenses are included under one broad category consistent with the definition quoted above from APB *Statement No. 4*. Included in the expenses illustrated is a *loss* which is distinctly different from the other expenses because it is a net difference as illustrated above for the gain.

There are numerous variations of the single-step format, such as:

1. Reporting income taxes separate from expenses (as a separate item immediately preceding income before extraordinary items).
2. Reporting one or more separate captions for certain revenues and expenses (such as, *financial items*—interest revenue and interest expense; *other revenues and expenses*—interest, dividends, gains and losses; and *other charges and credits*). When one of these three captions is used, it is located immediately above the caption, "income before extraordinary items."

The single-step format enjoys wide use because the broad classifications make it very flexible. Classification problems are minimized, and the presentation is simplified. On the other hand, some accountants feel that more intermediary differences, such as *gross margin on sales,* should be reported for the convenience of the decision-maker.

### Multiple-Step Format

This format focuses on multiple classifications, multiple intermediary differences, and relatively more detail. The multiple-step format is illustrated in Exhibit 4–3. Observe that the first major intermediary difference is gross margin on sales followed by income from operations, income before taxes and extraordinary items, income before extraordinary items, and finally, net income. There are no broad classifications for revenues and expenses; rather they are reported under several different classifications. Those who prefer the multiple-step format believe that the multiple classifications communicate better information to the user. Disadvantages often cited focus on relative inflexibility, as evidenced by these common complaints: (1) difficulty in naming and defining appropriate subcategories of revenues and expenses, (2) separation of revenues and expenses into several categories implies a priority that is hard to defend, and (3) difficulty of reporting service revenue when there is also sales revenue—inclusion of service revenue with sales revenue distorts the intermediary amount, gross margin on sales.

Like the single-step format, the multiple-step format has many variations. However, the differences are above the caption, "income before extraordinary items."

The diversity in income statement formats reflects the efforts of the entity to tailor the statement to the particular situation and reflects, in part, their conception of what should be communicated and how it should be communicated to the user. Income statements are presented in the Appendixes to this and the following chapter for your study.

*Manufacturing Situation.* An income statement of a manufacturing company differs from others in the presentation of manufacturing

**EXHIBIT 4–3**
**Multiple-Step Income Statement**

MELON COMPANY
Income Statement
For the Year Ended December 31, 1976

| | | | |
|---|---|---:|---:|
| Sales revenue | | | $600,000 |
| Less: Sales returns and allowances | | | 18,600 |
| Net Sales | | | 581,400 |
| Cost of goods sold: | | | |
| Beginning merchandise inventory | | $152,000 | |
| Merchandise purchases | $376,500 | | |
| Freight-in | 1,200 | | |
| Cost of purchases | 377,700 | | |
| Less: Purchase returns and allowances | 12,200 | 365,500 | |
| Total Goods Available for Sale | | 517,500 | |
| Less: Ending merchandise inventory | | 159,500 | |
| Cost of Goods Sold | | | 358,000 |
| Gross margin on sales | | | 223,400 |
| *Operating expenses: | | | |
| Distribution expenses | | 110,000 | |
| General and administrative expenses | | 43,000 | |
| Total Operating Expenses | | | 153,000 |
| Income from primary operations | | | 70,400 |
| Other revenues: | | | |
| Rent | 1,200 | | |
| Interest and dividends | 4,800 | | |
| Gain on sale of fixed assets | 12,000 | 18,000 | |
| Other expenses: | | | |
| Interest | 4,500 | | |
| Loss on sale of investments | 3,500 | 8,000 | 10,000 |
| Income before income taxes and extraordinary item | | | 80,400 |
| Income taxes | | | 32,090 |
| Income before extraordinary item | | | 48,310 |
| Extraordinary item: | | | |
| Loss due to earthquake | | 10,000 | |
| Less: Tax saving | | 4,800 | 5,200 |
| Net Income | | | $ 43,110 |

Earnings per share on common stock (20,000 shares outstanding):

| | |
|---|---:|
| Income before extraordinary item | $2.42 |
| Extraordinary loss | .26 |
| Net Income | $2.16 |

* These may be detailed on the statement or separately in the notes to the financial statements as separate schedules.

costs. In a trading company, goods are purchased ready for sale, but a manufacturing company makes its own goods for sale. In the latter case, "merchandise purchases" is replaced by "cost of goods manufactured," and a statement of cost of goods manufactured is often prepared as a supporting schedule to the income statement.

If the Melon Company manufactured the goods sold, the cost of goods sold section of the income statement in Exhibit 4–3 would appear as follows:

```
Cost of goods sold (for a manufacturing firm):
Finished goods inventory, January 1, 1976 ....................$152,000
Cost of goods manufactured (see manufacturing
   schedule)...............................................................  365,500
         Total Goods Available for Sale ............................  517,500
Less: Finished goods inventory, December 31, 1976.........  159,500
         Cost of Goods Sold ...........................................            $358,000
```

A supporting schedule of cost of goods manufactured details the costs of production generally as follows:

**Manufacturing Schedule**

MELON COMPANY
Cost of Goods Manufactured
For the Year Ended December 31, 1976

```
Raw material:
Inventory, January 1, 1976 ...........................  $ 28,000
Purchases...............................................$196,400
   Less: Returned purchases .......................      800    195,600
Freight-in ..................................................              900
Material available for issue ..........................           224,500
Inventory, December 31, 1976  .....................            31,000
Cost of material consumed...........................                            $193,500
Direct labor ..............................................                             106,200
Manufacturing expenses (factory overhead):
Depreciation — buildings ............................            2,200
Depreciation — machinery............................           15,100
Fuel.........................................................           20,900
Insurance — buildings and machinery ...........              480
Indirect labor ...........................................           16,100
Repairs — buildings....................................            1,920
Repairs — machinery ..................................            2,800
Taxes — plant and equipment ......................            1,600
                                                                                           61,100

Goods in process:
Inventory, January 1, 1976 ..........................           26,800
Inventory, December 31, 1976  .....................           22,100
Decrease .................................................                              4,700
         Cost of Goods Manufactured ..............                           $365,500
```

*Supporting Expense Schedules.*   Occasionally, it is desirable to provide detailed information with respect to the summarized amounts shown on an income statement. Generally, this is best done with one or more supplementary schedules. One such schedule was illustrated above for manufacturing costs. A detailed schedule of operating expenses to supplement the income statement given in Exhibit 4–3 could be as follows:

MELON COMPANY
Schedule of Operating Expenses
For the Year Ended December 31, 1976

Operating expenses:
  Distribution expenses:
    Advertising .......................................................$32,000
    Salaries ............................................................ 35,000
    Commissions ..................................................... 31,000
    Freight-out ........................................................ 3,000
    Insurance on inventory ............................................. 1,000
    Other selling expenses ............................................. 8,000   $110,000
  General and administrative expenses:
    Office expenses ................................................... 4,800
    Office payroll ..................................................... 32,100
    Depreciation of office equipment ............................... 1,100
    Rent............................................................... 2,000
    Bad debt expense ................................................. 3,000    43,000
    Total Operating Expenses ...................................    $153,000

## SPECIAL PROBLEMS AFFECTING THE INCOME STATEMENT

Until the 1930s the balance sheet, as a statement of financial position, was viewed by the business community as dominant because the assets owned and the liabilities owed were considered to be the most important indicator of the future potential of an enterprise. However, there was a gradual shift to recognizing the ability of the enterprise to generate income and cash which is more significant. Consequently, the income statement assumed a dominant role. Although the importance of cash flow has been largely overlooked in financial reporting, currently it is coming to the forefront.[6]

Because of the importance attached to the income statement for several decades, the accounting profession has focused on refining the concepts and accounting procedures for the measurement and reporting of net income. Consequently, the pronouncements by the several accounting groups, particularly the FASB, AICPA and the AAA, tend to focus on the income statement. In the remainder of this chapter, we will review the important income reporting issues on which the profession has taken a definite position.

## DISCLOSURE PROBLEMS

Recall the discussions of full disclosure under the reporting principle in Chapter 2. This broad principle encompasses all external financial reporting. With respect to the income statement, full disclosure is par-

---

[6] AICPA, *Objectives of Financial Statements* (New York, October 1973). This report, often referred to as the Trueblood Report, states on page 62: "Creditors and investors are concerned with the ability of the enterprise to generate cash flows to them and with their ability to predict, compare, and evaluate the amount, timing, and related uncertainty of these future cash flows. An objective of financial statements is to provide information to investors and creditors for predicting, comparing, and evaluating potential cash flows to them in terms of amount, timing, and related uncertainty." Cash flow is discussed in Chapter 21, Statement of Changes in Financial Position.

ticularly critical. There is a limit to the extent of disclosure possible in the income statement itself by way of titles, amounts, and parenthetical information. Therefore, the typical income statement refers to a number of *notes to the financial statements.* Typically, these notes include elaborations such as amounts, schedules, and written explanations. Their objective is a presentation of information, essential to full disclosure, that cannot be effectively communicated in another manner. Therefore, they must be viewed as an important supplement to the financial statements. Generally, pronouncements of the profession on reporting specific items specify that they may, or in some cases must, be disclosed in footnotes when it is impractical to adequately present the information in the statement itself.

## DEPRECIATION

*APB Opinion No. 12,* paragraph five, requires that (a) the amount of depreciation expense for the period, and (b) the method or methods of depreciation used, be disclosed either in the financial statements or in the notes thereto. This requirement was instituted because depreciation is a noncash expense; therefore, it must be considered in assessing the amount of cash outflow that was needed to meet expenses. Also, since the amount of depreciation expense reported depends upon internal decisions of management rather than on external transactions, it is subject to considerable latitude. Statement users need to know both the amount of depreciation expense and how it was determined (i.e., the method of depreciation used) in order to evaluate its impact on net income, assets, and cash flows.

Since 1967 all financial statements have reported depreciation expense. *Accounting Trends and Techniques, 1974* (AICPA), shows that of 600 major companies, 42% reported it in the income statement and 58% disclosed it in a footnote to the statement. In a manufacturing enterprise, one must remember that much of the depreciation expense may be included in the inventory and cost of goods sold amounts; therefore, reporting by footnote is characteristic of these kinds of companies.

## INCOME TAXES

Income taxes are assessed on profit-making corporations but not on sole proprietorships or partnerships. In contrast, the income of a sole proprietorship and partnership must be reported as income to the owners.[7] In turn, the stockholder must pay income taxes on dividends received; consequently, it is sometimes argued that corporate income is subject to double taxation.

Income taxes paid by corporations are viewed as an expense (as

---

[7] There are certain exceptions. For example, a corporation that qualifies under Subchapter S, Internal Revenue Code, is viewed, for income tax purposes, the same as a partnership. These are generally referred to as "Subchapter S Corporations."

opposed to a partial distribution of profits to the government); and because of their amount, they must meet the requirements of the full-disclosure principle. To meet these requirements, *APB Opinion No. 11* (1967) prescribed two types of income tax allocation procedures:

1. Intraperiod Tax Allocation—This requires that the income tax for the year be allocated within and between the income statement and the statement of retained earnings. It is an allocation of income tax expense within a single period.
2. Interperiod Tax Allocation—This requires that income tax *expense* for the period (for income statement purposes) and income taxes *payable* (for balance sheet purposes) be separately computed. Any difference is recorded as deferred income taxes. These situations arise when there is a revenue or expense on the income statement for the current year that appears on the income tax return either before or after the current year. This comes about because accounting principles and tax laws do not always agree as to the year in which the revenue or expense should fall. It is an allocation of income tax expense between periods. This type of allocation is discussed in Chapter 11 (liabilities).

## Intraperiod Tax Allocation

The need for allocation of income tax expense within and between the income statement, statement of retained earnings, and balance sheet is explained in *APB Opinion No. 11* as follows:

> The need for tax allocation within a period arises because items included in the determination of taxable income may be presented for accounting purposes as (*a*) extraordinary items, (*b*) adjustments of prior periods (or of the opening balance of retained earnings) or (*c*) as direct entries to other stockholders' accounts.[8]

The concept underlying intraperiod tax allocation is that on the financial statements for the period, *the income tax consequences should be reported along with the transaction that caused the tax expense.* Thus, total income tax expense for the period must be allocated to (1) income before extraordinary items, (2) extraordinary items, (3) prior period adjustments (retained earnings), and (4) direct entries to other stockholders' accounts to the extent that there are items in each category that affected total income tax expense for the period. Clearly, in most cases income tax expense for the period will be directly related to the first two categories—income before extraordinary items and extraordinary items. Seldom do the last two categories (prior period adjustments and other owners' equity accounts) affect income taxes.

Intraperiod tax allocation (sometimes called interstatement allocation) is not complicated or controversial. Exhibits 4-4, 4-5, and 4-6 illustrate application of the concept in three different situations. Note in

---

[8] AICPA, "Accounting for Income Taxes," *Accounting Principles Board Opinion No. 11,* (New York, 1967).

**EXHIBIT 4–4**
**Intraperiod Tax Allocation – with Extraordinary Gain**

*Situation*

A Corporation accounts for the period reflected the following:
1. Income before income taxes and before extraordinary items, $100,000.
2. Extraordinary gain (specified), $40,000.
3. Income tax expense, $60,700.*

A CORPORATION
Partial Income Statement

| | |
|---|---:|
| Income before income taxes and extraordinary items......... | $100,000 |
| Less: Applicable income taxes ................................... | 41,500 |
| Income before extraordinary items ............................... | 58,500 |
| Extraordinary items: | |
| Gain on extraordinary item (designated) ......................$40,000 | |
| Less: Applicable income tax ................................... 19,200 | |
| Extraordinary gain, net of applicable income tax ...... | 20,800 |
| Net Income ................................................................ | $ 79,300 |

| | | | |
|---|---|---|---|
| * Computation of tax allocation: | | Entry for income taxes: | |
| Tax on ordinary income: | | Income tax expense ............ 60,700 | |
| $25,000 × 22% = $ 5,500 | | Income taxes payable ...... | 60,700 |
| $75,000 × 48% = 36,000 | $41,500 | | |
| | | | |
| Tax on extraordinary item | | | |
| $40,000 × 48% = | 19,200 | | |
| Total Income Tax Allocated ........$60,700 | | | |

**EXHIBIT 4–5**
**Intraperiod Tax Allocation – with Extraordinary Loss**

*Situation*

B Corporation accounts for the period reflected the following:
1. Income before income taxes and before extraordinary items, $100,000.
2. Loss on earthquake damage, $40,000.
3. Income tax expense, $22,300.*

B CORPORATION
Partial Income Statement

| | |
|---|---:|
| Income before income taxes and extraordinary items......... | $100,000 |
| Less: Applicable income taxes ................................... | 41,500 |
| Income before extraordinary items ............................... | 58,500 |
| Extraordinary items: | |
| Extraordinary loss ...................................................$40,000 | |
| Less: Applicable tax saving ..................................... 19,200 | |
| Extraordinary loss, net of applicable income tax ...... | 20,800 |
| Net Income ................................................................ | $ 37,700 |

| | | | |
|---|---|---|---|
| * Computation of tax allocation: | | Entry for income taxes: | |
| Tax on ordinary income: | | Income tax expense ............... 22,300 | |
| $25,000 × 22% = $ 5,500 | | Income taxes payable ......... | 22,300 |
| $75,000 × 48% = 36,000 | $41,500 | | |
| Tax saving on extraordinary loss: | | | |
| $40,000 × 48% = | (19,200) | | |
| Total Income Tax Allocated........$22,300 | | | |

**EXHIBIT 4-6**
**Intraperiod Tax Allocation—Retained Earnings Affected**

*Situation*

C Corporation records for the period reflected the following:
1. Income before income taxes and before extraordinary items, $100,000.
2. Loss on earthquake damage, $40,000.
3. Income tax expense, $118,300.*
4. Claim for damages settled and collected (lawsuit), $200,000 (a prior period adjustment).
5. Balance retained earnings, beginning of period, $140,000.
6. Dividends paid during year, $20,000.

### C CORPORATION
#### Partial Income Statement

| | |
|---|---:|
| Income before income taxes and extraordinary items...... | $100,000 |
| Less: Applicable income tax....................................... | 41,500 |
| Income before extraordinary items............................... | 58,500 |
| Extraordinary items: | |
| Extraordinary loss ....................................................$ 40,000 | |
| Less: Applicable income tax saving ........................ 19,200 | |
| Extraordinary loss, net of applicable income tax ... | (20,800) |
| Net Income................................................................. | $ 37,700 |

### C CORPORATION
#### Statement of Retained Earnings

| | |
|---|---:|
| Retained earnings at beginning of period: | |
| As previously reported ............................................. | $140,000 |
| Add: Damages collected (lawsuit settled) .................$200,000 | |
| Less: Applicable income tax ............................... 96,000 | 104,000 |
| Beginning balance restated ......................................... | 244,000 |
| Add: Net income for period ........................................ | 37,700 |
| | 281,700 |
| Deduct: Dividends paid during period ........................ | 20,000 |
| Retained earnings, end of period ................................ | $261,700 |

---

* Computation of tax allocation:

| | | | | |
|---|---|---|---|---|
| Tax on ordinary loss: | | | Entry for income taxes: | |
| $25,000 × 22% = $ 5,500 | | | Income tax expense ............ | 22,300 |
| $75,000 × 48% = 36,000 | $ 41,500 | | Prior period adjustment | |
| | | | (income taxes) .................. | 96,000 |
| | | | Income taxes payable...... | 118,300 |
| Tax saving on extraordinary item: | | | | |
| $40,000 × 48% = | (19,200) | | | |
| Tax on retained earnings item: | | | | |
| $200,000 × 48% = | 96,000 | | | |
| Total Taxes Allocated .................$118,300 | | | | |

each exhibit that total income tax expense for the period is simply allocated to each of the four categories (listed above) so that the tax consequence follows the item that gives rise to the tax. You should particularly be aware in each illustration of the several amounts that would be incorrectly reported without intraperiod allocation of income tax expense. For example, in Exhibit 4–6, if one were to report total tax expense ($118,300) as a direct reduction from pretax income ($100,000) at least four amounts would be misstated: income before extraordinary items, net extraordinary loss, net income, and restated balance of retained earnings.

In computing the amount of income tax expense for each separate category, the assumption was made that the tax applies first to normal operations and then to the other items. Thus, in Exhibit 4–6, extraordinary items and prior period adjustments were taxed at the 48% rate. Another method of computing the interstatement tax allocation that has been widely used is based on an "average" tax rate for the period. Essentially this method involves computation of the average tax rate for the period then allocating income taxes to each classification on a proportional basis by utilizing this average. Since the issuance of *APB Opinion No. 11* in 1967 the averaging method has been used less frequently.

## EARNINGS PER SHARE

Earnings per share (EPS) is the relationship between reported income and outstanding shares of common stock (i.e., income ÷ average number shares of common stock outstanding). EPS is not computed on preferred stock. The reporting of EPS amounts has long been common in various information and press releases directed at investors and the financial community. Also, PE ratios are now reported daily in the news media. The practice has grown and, for accountants, has recently undergone a rapid evolution which has now proceeded to the point that reporting earnings per share on the face of the income statement, on which the accountant is expressing professional opinion, is mandatory.

Historically, reporting earnings per share on statements appearing in annual reports was optional prior to the issuance of *APB Opinion No. 9* in December 1966. In that *Opinion* the Accounting Principles Board stated "that earnings per share data are most useful when furnished in conjunction with a statement of income." Accordingly, the Board *strongly recommends* that earnings per share be disclosed in the statement of income. It is the Board's opinion that the reporting of per share data should disclose amounts for (a) income before extraordinary items; (b) extraordinary items, if any (less applicable income tax); and (c) net income—the total of (a) and (b). APB Opinion No. 15 issued in May 1969 changed the recommendation to a *requirement*. The latter *Opinion* calls for two presentations of earnings per share on the income statement: (a) primary earnings per share, and (b) fully diluted earnings per share. These terms are explained and discussed later in this section.

*APB Opinion No. 15* is a lengthy, complex document. Only its highlights will be presented here; it is not feasible to attempt a discussion of all of the details covered in its more than 60 pages of text and ex-

**EXHIBIT 4–7**
**Calculation of Earnings per Share under Increasingly Complex Cases**

| Assumptions | Calculation and Reporting EPS |
|---|---|
| **Case A**<br>Assumptions: 30,000 common shares outstanding throughout the year; net income for the year $96,000. | Net income .........................................$96,000<br>Earnings per common share ($96,000<br>  ÷ 30,000 shares)  ...............................  $3.20 |
| **Case B**<br>Assumptions: 30,000 common shares outstanding throughout the year; income before extraordinary items, $96,000, extraordinary loss less applicable tax saving $21,000; net income for year $75,000. | Income before extraordinary item  .........$96,000<br>Extraordinary loss less applicable<br>  tax saving  ....................................  21,000<br>Net Income .......................................$75,000<br>Earnings per common share:<br>  Income before extraordinary item  ......  $3.20<br>  Extraordinary loss.............................  .70<br>Net Income .......................................  $2.50<br><br>$96,000 ÷ 30,000 shares = $3.20<br>  21,000 ÷      ″        =   .70<br>  75,000 ÷      ″        =  2.50 |
| **Case C**<br>Assumptions: 30,000 common shares outstanding from January 1 through April 1, on which date an additional 10,000 common shares were sold; other data as in Case B. | Income before extraordinary item  .........$96,000<br>Extraordinary loss less applicable tax<br>  saving  .........................................  21,000<br>Net Income .......................................$75,000<br>Earnings per common share:<br>  Income before extraordinary item  ......  $2.56<br>  Extraordinary loss.............................  .56<br>Net Income .......................................  $2.00<br><br>Calculation of weighted average number of shares:<br><br>| Inclusive dates | Months | Shares | Product |<br>|---|---|---|---|<br>| Jan. 1–Apr. 1 | 3 | 30,000 | 90,000 |<br>| Apr. 1–Dec. 31 | 9 | 40,000 | 360,000 |<br>|  | 12 |  | 450,000 |<br><br>Average: 450,000 ÷ 12 = 37,500<br><br>$96,000 ÷ 37,500 shares = $2.56<br>  21,000 ÷      ″         =   .56<br>  75,000 ÷      ″         = $2.00 |
| **Case D**<br>Assumptions: 30,000 common shares outstanding from January 1 through April 1, on which date an additional 10,000 common shares were issued as a *stock dividend;* other data as in Case B (no additional shares were sold). | Income before extraordinary item  .........$96,000<br>Extraordinary loss less applicable tax<br>  saving  .........................................  21,000<br>Net Income .......................................$75,000<br>Earnings per common share:<br>  Income before extraordinary item  ......  $2.40<br>  Extraordinary loss.............................  .53<br>Net Income .......................................  $1.87<br><br>As provided in *APB Opinion No. 9*, when there is a stock dividend the divisor is the number of shares outstanding at year-end (in this case 40,000).<br><br>$96,000 ÷ 40,000 shares = $2.40<br>  21,000 ÷      ″        =   .53<br>  75,000 ÷      ″        =  1.87 |

hibits. Further, approximately a year after its publication *Opinion No. 15* was supplemented by an interpretive booklet of well over 100 pages.[9]

The simplest possible calculation of earnings per share in compliance with *Opinion No. 15* would involve a company with only common stock authorized, all of which had remained outstanding throughout its fiscal year. If such a company had only ordinary income, that is, no extraordinary items, calculation of its earnings per share for the year would merely involve dividing the net income by the number of shares. See Exhibit 4–7, Case A.

A slight advance in complexity would have the company experience an extraordinary gain or loss in arriving at its net income. In this case, earnings per share figures would be reported for income before extraordinary items and for net income. See Exhibit 4–7, Case B.

The next advance in complexity would involve a company with only common stock and had experienced an increase in the number of shares outstanding during the period due to the sale of common stock or the purchase of treasury shares. A material increase due to the sale of additional shares would call for the calculation of the weighted average of the number of shares outstanding. See Exhibit 4–7, Case C. However, a material increase due to a stock dividend or stock split would call for simply dividing by the number of shares outstanding at year-end.[10] See Exhibit 4–7, Case D.

The next level of complexity involve situations where there is both common and preferred stock; beyond those are situations where there are convertible securities (i.e., convertible preferred stock and convertible bonds) that may be converted into common stock. These complexities involve the concepts of common stock equivalents and fully diluted earnings per share. These situations are discussed in Chapter 17.

## EXTRAORDINARY ITEMS AND PRIOR PERIOD ADJUSTMENTS

Recall that extraordinary items are reported in a separate category on the income statement and prior period adjustments are reported on the statement of retained earnings (*APB Opinions No. 9* and *No. 30*). These two types of items have been controversial for a number of years because they are *a)* difficult to define precisely, and *b)* of different concepts of net income.

---

[9] AICPA, "Reporting the Results of Operations," *APB Opinion No. 9* (New York, 1966), p. 119 (emphasis supplied) *Opinion No. 15* requires EPS for (*a*) income before extraordinary items, and (*b*) net income. EPS on extraordinary items is recommended but not mandatory. Also, J T. Ball, *Computing Earnings per Share, Unofficial Interpretations of APB Opinion No. 15* (New York  AICPA, 1970).

[10] If the common shares change as a result of a stock dividend or split (or reverse split), the computations should give retroactive recognition to an appropriate equivalent change in capital structure for all periods presented in the case of comparative statements. Where such changes occur after the close of a fiscal period but before statements are issued, per share computations should be based on the new number of shares since readers' primary interests are presumably related to current capitalization. Disclosure should reflect the number of shares in the calculation.

### Concepts of Net Income

For a number of years, two different concepts of net income were prominent in accounting practice and literature. These concepts usually are referred to as the *current operating concept* and the *all-inclusive concept*.[11] Fundamentally, they differed with respect to whether unusual and infrequently occurring gains and losses should be included in net income and, consequently, reported on the income statement.

The *current operating concept* holds that in the measurement and reporting of net income, *only* the operating revenues and expenses should be included. Thus, the unusual, or nonoperating, and infrequently recurring gains and losses should be viewed as direct debits (decreases) and credits (increases) to Retained Earnings and reported on the statement of retained earnings. In contrast, the *all-inclusive concept* holds that in measuring and reporting net income, all operating revenues and expenses and all unusual and infrequently recurring gains and losses should be included. Under this concept, the statement of retained earnings would report only the net income, or loss, and dividends declared for the period. The two concepts in their pure form are compared in Exhibit 4–8. This exhibit emphasizes the point at issue—*what* should be included in net income? Observe that the current operating concept in this case shows a net income of $100,000 compared with $160,000 under the all-inclusive concept. From this, it is not difficult to perceive that it is an important issue.

It is generally correct to say that historically the AICPA favored the current operating concept whereas the AAA tended to favor the all-inclusive concept. With the issuance of *Opinion No. 9* in December 1966, the APB took a compromise position which leaned strongly toward the all-inclusive concept. That *Opinion* requires that all of the unusual, nonoperating, and infrequently recurring items be included in the computation of net income and reported separately on the income statement, except for a very limited range of items called prior period adjustments. The *Opinion* specified that the prior period adjustments should be reported on the statement of retained earnings and accounted for as direct debits and credits to Retained Earnings. *APB Opinion No. 9* set forth the basic principle as follows:

> Net income should reflect all items of profit and loss recognized during the period with the sole exception of the prior period adjustments described below. *Extraordinary items* should, however, be segregated from the results of ordinary operations and shown separately in the income statement, with disclosure of the nature and amounts thereof.

> Under this approach, the income statement should disclose the following elements:
> Income before extraordinary items
> Extraordinary items (less applicable income tax)
> Net Income[12]

---

[11] Some synonyms for *current operating performance* include "earnings power" and for *all-inclusive* "clean surplus" and "historical."

[12] AICPA, *APB Opinion No. 9*, pars. 17 and 20.

**EXHIBIT 4-8**
**Operating and All-Inclusive Concepts Compared**

Income Statement

| Operating Concept | | |
|---|---:|---:|
| Operating revenues | | $980,000 |
| Operating expenses | | (880,000) |
| Net Income | | $100,000 |

| All-Inclusive Concept | | |
|---|---:|---:|
| Operating revenues | | $980,000 |
| Operating expenses | | (880,000) |
| Unusual and infrequently occurring items: | | |
| Gain—expropriation of plant by foreign | | |
| government | | 30,000 |
| Loss—earthquake damages | | (10,000) |
| Gain—damages received in lawsuit | | 80,000 |
| Loss—additional assessment of income | | |
| taxes, prior years | | (40,000) |
| Net Income | | $160,000 |

Statement of Retained Earnings

| Operating Concept | | |
|---|---:|---:|
| Beginning balance | | $ 75,000 |
| Add net income | | 100,000 |
| Total | | 175,000 |
| Deduct: | | |
| Dividends | | (50,000) |
| Unusual and infrequently occurring items: | | |
| Gain—expropriation of plant by foreign | | |
| government | | 30,000 |
| Loss—earthquake damages | | (10,000) |
| Gain—damages received in lawsuit | | 80,000 |
| Loss—additional assessment of income | | |
| taxes, prior years | | (40,000) |
| Ending Balance | | $185,000 |

| All-Inclusive Concept | | |
|---|---:|---:|
| Beginning balance | | $ 75,000 |
| Add net income | | 160,000 |
| Total | | 235,000 |
| Deduct: | | |
| Dividends | | (50,000) |
| Ending Balance | | $185,000 |

## Extraordinary Items

Extraordinary items were defined in *APB Opinion No. 9;* however, the definition was imprecise, resulting in wide variation in application. It became a favorite way to "doctor" income before extraordinary items. Since investors are interested in a representative income amount useful for projecting future income potentials, the caption, "extraordinary items," became especially critical. Because of the dollar amount of the items under this caption, net income was often primarily composed of items which would not recur in the reasonable future and were not directly related to ongoing operations.

As a consequence, the APB issued *Opinion No. 30,* in June 1973. It was hoped that a redefinition of extraordinary items would correct the abuses. The definition of extraordinary items provided by *Opinion No. 30* is very restrictive, viz:

> Criteria for Extraordinary Items:
>
> Judgment is required to segregate in the income statement the effects of events or transactions that are extraordinary. . . . an event or transaction should be presumed to be an ordinary and usual activity of the reporting entity . . . unless the evidence clearly supports its classification as an extraordinary item as defined in this opinion.
>
> Extraordinary items are events and transactions that are distinguished by their unusual nature *and* by the infrequency of their occurrence. Thus, *both* of the following criteria should be met to classify an event or transaction as an extraordinary item:
>
> a. *Unusual nature* – The underlying event or transaction should possess a high degree of abnormality and be of a type clearly unrelated to, or only incidentally related to, the ordinary and typical activities of the entity, taking into account the environment in which the entity operates.
> b. *Infrequency of occurrence* – The underlying event or transaction should be of a type that would not reasonably be expected to recur in the foreseeable future, taking into account the environment in which the entity operates.[13]

There are two aspects of the above definitions that should be emphasized. First, both criteria must be met. Thus, an item that meets *either,* but not both, does not qualify as an extraordinary item. Obviously, there are not many such items. Secondly, in applying the two criteria, the *environment* in which the entity operates is often controlling. For example, earthquake damage usually would be extraordinary – it is certainly unusual and occurs infrequently in most parts of the world. However, if one were to locate a plant on a fault where earthquakes occur regularly, earthquake damage would be an ordinary item in that *particular environment;* the damage would be neither unusual nor

---

[13] AICPA, "Reporting the Results of Operations," *APB Opinion No. 30* (New York, 1973), pars. 19–20.

infrequent. Thus, whether an event or transaction is extraordinary ordinarily depends not on the type of event but rather *on the environment in which it occurs* (i.e., the situation). This basic point is overlooked in most discussions of extraordinary items; however, it is fully discussed in *Opinion No. 30*. The *Opinion* list only three different kinds of events that usually would be classified as extraordinary: (1) a major casualty, such as an earthquake; (2) expropriation by a foreign government; and (3) prohibition under a newly enacted law or regulation.

The *Opinion* specifically states that the following should not be considered as extraordinary items because they result from customary and continuing business activities:

> *a.* Write-down or write-off of receivables, inventories, equipment leased to others, or other intangible assets.
> *b.* Gains or losses from exchange or translation of foreign currencies, including those related to major devaluations or revaluations.
> *c.* Gains or losses on disposal of a segment of a business.
> *d.* Other gains or losses from sale of abandonment of property, plant, or equipment used in the business.
> *e.* Effects of a strike, including those against competitors and major suppliers.
> *f.* Adjustments of accruals on long-term contracts.

Because of the widespread misunderstanding of extraordinary items, as defined in *Opinion No. 30*, we have included some specific examples in Appendix A to this chapter.[14]

### Reporting Unusual or Infrequent Items

In the discussion above, we referred to items that are *either* unusual or infrequent, but not both. They do not qualify as extraordinary items; however, they should be called to the attention of the statement user to fulfill the *full-disclosure* requirement. Therefore, *APB Opinion No. 30* requires that they be reported separately on the income statement, viz:

> A material event or transaction that is unusual in nature or occurs infrequently, but not both, and therefore does not meet both criteria for classification as an extraordinary item, should be reported as a separate component of income from continuing operations. The nature and financial effects of each event and transaction should be disclosed on the face of the income statement, or alternatively, in notes to the financial statement.[15]

To illustrate, items that are *either* unusual or infrequent, but not both, should be reported along the following lines to meet the full-disclosure requirement:

---

[14] AICPA, "Accounting Interpretations, APB Opinion No. 30," *The Journal of Accountancy,* November 1973, pp. 82–84.

[15] AICPA, *APB Opinion No. 30,* par. 26.

Income Statement (Partial)

| | | |
|---|---|---|
| Pretax income from continuing operations...................... | | $112,000 |
| Unusual or infrequent items (see Note X): | | |
| Loss from disposal of long-term investment .................$43,000 | | |
| Gain on disposal of machinery ................................... 31,000 | | 12,000 |
| Total.......................................................... | | 100,000 |
| Income tax on operations and unusual or infrequent items ... | | 41,500 |
| Income before extraordinary item ................................... | | 58,500 |
| Extraordinary item: | | |
| Loss due to hurricane damage (less applicable tax saving); see Note Y................................................ | | 26,500 |
| Net Income ................................................................. | | $ 32,000 |
| | | |
| Earnings per share of common stock (20,000 shares outstanding): | | |
| Income before extraordinary item ............................... | | $2.93 |
| Extraordinary loss ..................................................... | | 1.33 |
| Net Income ........................................................... | | $1.60 |

Other formats can be devised to display the unusual or infrequent items in ways that meet the spirit of the above quotation from *Opinion No. 30*.

## Prior Period Adjustments

Since prior period adjustments never flow through the income statement but are direct debits or credits to Retained Earnings, they were defined very restrictively in *APB Opinion No. 9*. They are further removed from continuing operations than are extraordinary items. The *Opinion* specifies four criteria, all of which must be met, for an item to qualify for treatment as a prior period adjustment, viz:

1. Can be specifically identified with and directly related to the business activities of a particular prior period.
2. Are not attributable to economic events occurring subsequent to the date of the financial statement for the prior period.
3. Depend primarily on determinations by persons other than the management.
4. Were not susceptible to reasonable estimation prior to the current period.

This restrictive definition means that prior period adjustments are rare. Three examples, that often qualify, cited in the *Opinion* are: (1) nonrecurring adjustments or settlements of income taxes from prior years, (2) public utility settlements with regulatory bodies, and (3) settlement of court litigations. Reporting of prior period adjustments is illustrated in Exhibit 4–9.

A prior period adjustment is best recorded in the accounts in a special adjustment account, appropriately titled, rather than as a direct entry to Retained Earnings. Special adjustment accounts are closed to Retained

Earnings at the end of the period. Recall that this is the procedure usually used for dividends to shareholders; a *dividends* account is debited which is then closed to Retained Earnings at the end of the period. It is helpful to think of the accounts that are set up for closing to Retained Earnings as the same amounts that are reported on the statement of retained earnings. The same kind of correspondence can be attained with respect to the revenue and expense accounts. They are closed to Income Summary and are the accounts and amounts reported on the income statement.

## ACCOUNTING CHANGES

Accounting changes are discussed in detail in Chapter 20; however, it is necessary at this point to review some aspects of them. Accounting changes involve four distinctly different types of situations; and each requires a different accounting treatment. The four types of accounting changes specified in *APB Opinion No. 20* are:[16]

1. *Accounting errors.* The use of inappropriate accounting principles (including procedures) and unsupportable estimates, outright mathematical mistakes, oversights, and failure to properly reflect the economic essence of a transaction all constitute accounting errors.

2. *Changes in estimates.* The use of estimates (such as in determining depreciation or bad debt expense) is a natural consequence of the accounting process. From time to time, experience and additional information make it possible for estimates to be improved. For example, a fixed asset, after having been used (and depreciated) for 6 years, may realistically be changed from the original 10-year estimated life to a 15-year estimated life. Changes of this type are referred to as "changes in estimates" and are to be distinguished from an error or change in accounting principle.

3. *Changes in accounting principle.* Because of a change in circumstances, or the development of a new accounting principle, a change in the recordkeeping and financial reporting approach to one or more types of transactions may be desirable or necessary. For example, a change in circumstances may make it desirable, from the accounting point of view, to change from straight-line depreciation to sum-of-the-years'-digits depreciation. This would be a change in accounting principle, that is, a change from one acceptable principle to another acceptable principle.

4. *Change in the accounting entity* (see Chapter 20).

Now let's review briefly the accounting and reporting approach that is appropriate for the first two of these accounting changes. Type 3 and 4 changes will be discussed in subsequent chapters. You should observe in this brief discussion that each type of accounting change calls for a different approach to accommodate it appropriately.

---

[16] AICPA, "Accounting Changes," *APB Opinion No. 20* (New York, 1971).

## Treatment of Accounting Errors

Clearly, when an error in the accounting process is identified it should be corrected immediately in such a way as to reflect what the results would have been had the error not been committed. Thus, when an error is found that was committed in the *current year*, the accounts (and related schedules) should be corrected prior to preparation of the current financial reports. This normally can be best effected by reversing the incorrect entry and reentering the transaction correctly.

When an error is located during the current accounting period that was committed during some *prior period*, correction is more complex, especially where two or more past periods are affected. In this kind of situation a *correcting entry* must be made to reflect the correct current balances in the *real* accounts (i.e., the balance sheet accounts) and the *nominal* accounts (i.e., the income statement accounts). *APB Opinion No. 20* specifies the approach that should be used to correct this type of error. Often the correcting entry must include an "adjustment" amount; and the issue is whether this amount is to be treated as a normal operating item, an unusual or infrequent item, an extraordinary item, or a prior period adjustment. *Opinion No. 20* states: "The Board concludes that correction of an error in the financial statements of a prior period discovered subsequent to their issuance should be reported as a prior period adjustment." Thus, this type of error often requires recognition of a prior period adjustment in the accounts and on the statement of retained earnings.

To illustrate, assume a machine cost $10,000 (with a ten-year estimated useful life and no residual value), when purchased on January 1, 19A, was debited in full to an expense account. The error was discovered December 29, 19D. The following correcting entry would be required in 19D:

December 29, 19D:

```
Machinery ........................................................... 10,000
Depreciation expense (for 19D) ...........................  1,000
    Accumulated depreciation (A through D)..........................  4,000
    Prior period adjustment, error correction...........................  7,000
```

The Prior Period Adjustment, Error Correction account would be closed to Retained Earnings on December 31, 19D.


## Treatment of Changes in Estimates

These kind of changes are not considered errors; they are changes in estimates such as the useful life, residual value, loss rate on bad debts, and estimated warranty costs. As a company attains more experience in these areas, there is often a sound basis for revising a prior estimate. *APB Opinion No. 20* specifies that in such instances the *prior* accounting results are not to be disturbed; simply, the new estimate is to be used over the remaining periods including the current period. Thus, a change in estimate is made on a *prospective* basis.

To illustrate, assume a machine that cost $24,000 is being depreciated on a straight-line basis over a ten-year estimated useful life with no residual value. Near the end of the seventh year, on the basis of more experience with the machine, it is estimated that the useful life should have been 14 years. Thus, the remaining life is now eight years. This is a change in estimate and at the end of the current year would require the following *adjusting entry* only:

December 31, current year:

```
Depreciation expense ........................................................1,200
    Accumulated depreciation, machinery...............................          1,200
    Computations:
    Original cost ...........................................................$24,000
    Accumulated depreciation to date ($24,000 × 6/10) ...........   14,440
    Difference — to be depreciated over 8 years remaining life ...$ 9,600

    Annual depreciation over remaining life: $9,600 ÷ 8 years =       $ 1,200
```

## Treatment of Changes in Accounting Principles

These kinds of changes are the result of decisions by the management because the newly selected principle is more appropriate in reflecting net income and financial position. When an accounting principle is changed a "correction" is required to reflect the effect of the change over. For example a company had depreciated a machine $2,200 to date using the straight-line method. A change was made to sum-of-the-years'-digits depreciation; the amount of depreciation would have been $3,400, indicating a "correction" of $1,200. The entry for the change would be:

```
Change in accounting principle (closed to income summary)......1,200
    Accumulated depreciation ................................................          1,200
```

This topic is discussed comprehensively in Chapter 20.

## STATEMENT OF RETAINED EARNINGS

A statement of retained earnings usually is presented as a supplement to the income statement and balance sheet because it is needed to comply with the full-disclosure requirement. However, many companies are presenting a *statement of owners' equity* instead, which details all changes in owners' equity, not just retained earnings. The latter statement is discussed in Chapter 5 (see Exhibit 5–3).

The purpose of the statement of retained earnings is to report all changes in retained earnings during the year, to reconcile the beginning and ending balance of retained earnings, and to provide a connecting link between the income statement and the balance sheet. The ending balance of retained earnings is reported on the balance sheet as one element of owners' equity (see Exhibit 4–1) In accordance with *APB Opinion No. 9*, the major segments of a statement of retained earnings are (1) prior period adjustments, (2) net income or loss for the period, and

**EXHIBIT 4–9**
**Statement of Retained Earnings Illustrated**

ILLUSTRATIVE COMPANY
Statement of Retained Earnings
For the Year Ended December 31, 1976

| | |
|---|---:|
| Retained earnings, balance January 1, 1976 ..................................... | $ 77,400 |
| Prior period adjustments: | |
|   Additional income taxes assessed on income of prior years............ | (28,000) |
|   Damages collected from settlement of lawsuit (net of tax)............... | 15,000 |
|     Balance as adjusted ............................................................. | 64,400 |
| Add: Net income, 1976 (per income statement, Exhibit 4–2) ............... | 41,300 |
| | 105,700 |
| Deduct: Cash dividends paid in 1976 ($1.50 per share) ..................... | 30,000 |
| Retained Earnings, Balance December 31, 1976 (Note 7) ................. | $ 75,700 |

Note 7: Retained earnings—Of the $75,700 ending balance in retained earnings, $50,000 is restricted from dividend availability under the terms of the bond indenture. When the bonds are retired the restriction will be removed.

(3) dividends to stockholders. A typical statement of retained earnings is shown in Exhibit 4–9.

### Restrictions on Retained Earnings

Restrictions on retained earnings serve to limit retained earnings' availability for dividends to the unrestricted balance. Restrictions may arise because of *legal requirements*, as in the case of treasury stock held (in some states); by *contract*, as in the case of a bond indenture; or by *management decision*, as in the case of "retained earnings appropriated for future plant expansion." When a restriction is removed the amount then returns to dividend availability. *Accounting Trends and Techniques, 1975* (AICPA) revealed that 71% of the 600 companies surveyed reported restrictions imposed by debt agreements, capital expenditures, treasury stock purchases, or contracts with outside parties. In years past, restrictions sometimes were reported as separate items on the statement of retained earnings (or balance sheet); however, in recent years they generally are reported in notes to the financial statements as illustrated in Exhibit 4–9. Retained earnings is discussed in depth in Chapter 16.

### Combined Income Statement and Retained Earnings

The income statement and statement of retained earnings may be presented together in the form of a combined statement. *Accounting Trends and Techniques, 1975* (AICPA), reported that approximately 31% of the 600 leading companies studied followed this format. The primary advantage is that it brings together related and relevant information for the statement user. The following is a typical format at the bottom of the income statement:

Net income .............................................................................$41,300
Retained earnings, January 1, 1976................................................. 77,400
Prior period adjustments (Note 6)....................................................(13,000)
Cash dividends during 1976 ($1.50 per share) ...................................(30,000)
Retained Earnings, December 31, 1976 (Note 7) ...............................$75,700

Note 6: Prior period adjustments – During the year, the company was assessed additional income taxes from prior years in the amount of $28,000. Also during the year, a lawsuit, arising from an accident, was settled in favor of the company; damages amounting to $15,000 were collected (net of taxes).

Note 7: Restrictions – Of the $75,700 ending balance in retained earnings, $50,000 is restricted from dividend availability under the terms of the bond indenture. When the bonds are retired, the restriction will be removed.

## ACTUAL FINANCIAL STATEMENTS

Throughout this chapter, we have used illustrative examples for instructional purposes. To enable you to move easily to real-life financial statements, we have included Appendixes at the end of this and the following chapter which present recent financial statements for two well-known companies. We have selected representative statements that use typical format and terminology. One set uses a modified single-step format for income statements, and the other a modified multiple-step format. We suggest that you constructively, but critically, examine these examples and relate them to what you have learned at this point in your study.

# Appendix A. Characteristics and Examples of Extraordinary Items*

If it has been determined that the particular event or transaction is not a disposal of a segment of a business, then the criteria for extraordinary items classification should be considered. That is: Does the event or transaction meet both criteria of *unusual nature* and *infrequency of occurrence?*

*Discussion.* Paragraphs 19–22 of the *Opinion* discuss the criteria of unusual nature and infrequency of occurrence of events or transactions taking into account the environment in which the entity operates. Paragraph 23 specifies certain gains or losses which should not be reported as extraordinary unless they are the direct result of a major casualty, an

* Source: Excerpts from "Accounting Interpretations – APB Opinion 30," *Journal of Accountancy,* November 1973, pp. 82–84.

expropriation or a prohibition under a newly enacted law or regulation that clearly meets both criteria for extraordinary classification. Events or transactions which would meet both criteria in the circumstances described are:

10. A large portion of a tobacco manufacturer's crops are destroyed by a hail storm. Severe damage from hail storms in the locality where the manufacturer grows tobacco is rare.
11. A steel fabricating company sells the only land it owns. The land was acquired 10 years ago for future expansion, but shortly thereafter the company abandoned all plans for expansion and held the land for appreciation.
12. A company sells a block of common stock of a publicly traded company. The block of shares, which represents less than 10 percent of the publicly held company, is the only security investment the company has ever owned.
13. An earthquake destroys one of the oil refineries owned by a large multinational oil company.

   The following are illustrative of events or transactions which do not meet both criteria in the circumstances described and thus should not be reported as extraordinary items:

14. A citrus grower's Florida crop is damaged by frost. Frost damage is normally experienced every three or four years. The criterion of infrequency of occurrence taking into account the environment in which the company operates would not be met since the history of losses caused by frost damage provides evidence that such damage may reasonably be expected to recur in the foreseeable future.
15. A company which operates a chain of warehouses sells the excess land surrounding one of its warehouses. When the company buys property to establish a new warehouse, it usually buys more land than it expects to use for the warehouse with the expectation that the land will appreciate in value. In the past five years, there have been two instances in which the company sold such excess land. The criterion of infrequency of occurrence has not been met since past experience indicates that such sales may reasonably be expected to recur in the foreseeable future.
16. A large diversified company sells a block of shares from its portfolio of securities which it has acquired for investment purposes. This is the first sale from its portfolio of securities. Since the company owns several securities for investment purposes, it should be concluded that sales of such securities are related to its ordinary and typical activities in the environment in which it operates, and thus the criterion of unusual nature would not be met.
17. A textile manufacturer with only one plant moves to another location. It has not relocated a plant in 20 years and has no plans to do so in the foreseeable future. Notwithstanding the infrequency of occurrence of the event as it relates to this particular company, moving

from one location to another is an occurrence which is a consequence of customary and continuing business activities, some of
which are finding more favorable labor markets, more modern facilities and proximity to customers or suppliers. Therefore, the criterion
of unusual nature has not been met and the moving expenses (and
related gains and losses) should not be reported as an extraordinary
item. Another example of an event which is a consequence of customary and typical business activities (namely financing) is an unsuccessful public registration, the cost of which should not be reported as an extraordinary item. (For additional examples, see
Paragraph 23 of the *Opinion.*)

Disposals of part of a line of business, such as examples 5–9 of this
interpretation, should not be classified as extraordinary items. As discussed in Paragraph 13 of the *Opinion,* such disposals are incident to the
evolution of the entity's business, and therefore the criterion of unusual
nature would not be met.

*Question.* Paragraph 27 of the *Opinion* states that events and transactions that were reported as extraordinary items in statements of income for fiscal years ending before October 1, 1973, should not be
restated except that a statement of income including operations of discontinued segments of a business that meet the Paragraph 13 criteria
may be reclassified in comparative statements to conform with the provisions of Paragraphs 8 and 9 of the *Opinion.* If a gain or loss on such a
disposal in a prior year had been classified as an extraordinary item but
was not computed in the *manner* specified in Paragraphs 15–17 of the
*Opinion,* may the prior year income statements be reclassified and the
gain or loss adjusted to comply with the provisions of the *Opinion?*

*Interpretation.* The *Opinion* specifically uses the term "reclassified" in Paragraph 27 and makes direct reference to Paragraphs 8 and 9,
which describe the manner of reporting disposals of a segment of a business as defined in Paragraph 13. While such reclassification is optional
under the *Opinion,* there should not be a redetermination (restatement)
of net income using the measurement principles specified in Paragraphs
15–17. Since *Opinions* of the Board are not intended to be retroactive
unless otherwise stated, the method of computing the gain or loss on
disposals of a segment should not be retroactively applied if it results in
a change in net income of a prior year.

*Question.* Events or transactions which are not disposals of a segment of a business and are not extraordinary items may nevertheless be
required to be reported as a separate component of income from continuing operations under the provisions of Paragraph 26 of the *Opinion.*
If a company sells a portion of a line of business which does not meet the
definition of a segment of a business as defined in Paragraph 13 of the
*Opinion,* should the gain or loss be calculated using the measurement
principles for determination of gain or loss on disposal of a segment of a
business as prescribed in Paragraphs 15–17 of the *Opinion,* and how
should the financial effects of such sale be reported?

*Interpretation.* The gain or loss on a sale of a portion of a line of business which is not a segment of a business as defined in Paragraph 13 should be calculated using the same measurement principles as if it were a segment of a business (Paragraphs 15–17 of the *Opinion*). Under the provisions of Paragraph 26 of the *Opinion*, the amount of such gain or loss should be reported as a separate component of income from continuing operations. However, the gain or loss should not be reported on the face of the income statement net of income taxes or in any manner inconsistent with the provisions of Paragraphs 8 and 11 of the *Opinion* which may imply that it is a disposal of a segment of the business. In addition, the earnings per share effect should not be disclosed on the face of the income statement. Revenues and related costs and expenses of the portion of the line of business prior to the measurement date should not be segregated on the face of the income statement but may be disclosed in the notes to the financial statements, and such disclosure is encouraged. In addition, the notes to the financial statements should disclose, if known, those items specified in Paragraph 18 of the *Opinion*.

The foregoing examples are illustrative. It should be recognized that all attendant circumstances, which can vary from those above, need to be considered in making the judgments required by *APB Opinion No. 30*.

## Appendix B. Specimen Statements

**KOPPERS**

**Report of Certified Public Accountants**

ARTHUR YOUNG & COMPANY
CERTIFIED PUBLIC ACCOUNTANTS

The Board of Directors and Shareholders
Koppers Company, Inc.

We have examined the accompanying consolidated balance sheet of Koppers Company, Inc. and subsidiaries at December 31, 1974 and 1973 and the related consolidated statements of income, changes in financial position and shareholders' equity for the years then ended. Our examination was made in accordance with generally accepted auditing standards, and accordingly included such tests of the accounting records and such other auditing procedures as we considered necessary in the circumstances.

In our opinion, the statements mentioned above present fairly the consolidated financial position of Koppers Company, Inc. and subsidiaries at December 31, 1974 and 1973, the consolidated results of their operations and the consolidated changes in their financial position for the years then ended in conformity with generally accepted accounting principles applied on a consistent basis during the period except for the change in the method of valuing inventories in 1974, with which we concur, as described in the statement of accounting policies.

*Arthur Young & Company*

Pittsburgh, Pennsylvania
January 27, 1975

## Consolidated Statement of Income

Koppers Company, Inc. and Subsidiaries

Years ended December 31, 1974 and 1973
(See accompanying statement of accounting policies and notes to financial statements.)

|  | 1974 | 1973 |
|---|---|---|
| Net sales . . . . . . . . . . . . . . . . . . . . . . . . . . . . . . . . . . . . . . . . . . . . . . . . . . . . . | **$914,184,752** | $723,933,402 |
| Operating expenses (Notes 5 and 8): | | |
| Cost of sales . . . . . . . . . . . . . . . . . . . . . . . . . . . . . . . . . . . . . . . . . . . | **725,654,818** | 552,393,829 |
| Depreciation and depletion . . . . . . . . . . . . . . . . . . . . . . . . . . . . . . . . . . . . | **27,808,950** | 28,740,943 |
| Taxes, other than income taxes . . . . . . . . . . . . . . . . . . . . . . . . . . . . . . . | **16,502,384** | 14,898,696 |
| Selling, research, general and administrative expenses . . . . . . . . . . . . . . . . . . . | **71,219,080** | 69,948,274 |
| | **841,185,232** | 665,981,742 |
| Operating profit . . . . . . . . . . . . . . . . . . . . . . . . . . . . . . . . . . . . . . . . . . . . . . . | **72,999,520** | 57,951,660 |
| Other income (expense): | | |
| Dividends: | | |
| Affiliated company (Note 1) . . . . . . . . . . . . . . . . . . . . . . . . . . . . . . . | **12,961,985** | — |
| Other . . . . . . . . . . . . . . . . . . . . . . . . . . . . . . . . . . . . . . . . . . . . . | **616,526** | 520,561 |
| Interest income . . . . . . . . . . . . . . . . . . . . . . . . . . . . . . . . . . . . . . . . . . | **1,098,121** | 1,018,412 |
| Provision for possible decline in value of investments . . . . . . . . . . . . . . . . . . | **(1,626,000)** | (1,000,000) |
| Profit on sales of capital assets . . . . . . . . . . . . . . . . . . . . . . . . . . . . . . . | **870,599** | 1,193,426 |
| Equity in earnings of affiliates (dividends received: 1974—$335,366; 1973—$542,212) . . . . . . . . . . . . . . . . . . . . . . . . . . . . . . . . . . . . . . . . . . . | **1,701,023** | 1,382,023 |
| Miscellaneous . . . . . . . . . . . . . . . . . . . . . . . . . . . . . . . . . . . . . . . . . | **162,403** | 161,359 |
| | **15,784,657** | 3,275,781 |
| Interest expense: | | |
| Term debt (Note 6) . . . . . . . . . . . . . . . . . . . . . . . . . . . . . . . . . . . . . . . | **10,045,097** | 7,989,756 |
| Other . . . . . . . . . . . . . . . . . . . . . . . . . . . . . . . . . . . . . . . . . . . . . . . | **2,600,984** | 2,121,722 |
| | **12,646,081** | 10,111,478 |
| Income before provision for income taxes . . . . . . . . . . . . . . . . . . . . . . . . . . . | **76,138,096** | 51,115,963 |
| Provision for income taxes (Note 7) . . . . . . . . . . . . . . . . . . . . . . . . . . . . . . | **28,356,976** | 21,580,619 |
| Net income for the year . . . . . . . . . . . . . . . . . . . . . . . . . . . . . . . . . . . . . . | **$ 47,781,120** | $ 29,535,344 |
| Average number of shares of common stock outstanding during year . . . . . . . . . . . . . | **5,785,334** | 5,632,733 |
| Net earnings per share of common stock . . . . . . . . . . . . . . . . . . . . . . . . . . . . . | **$8.16** | $5.14 |

**Consolidated Balance Sheet**

**ASSETS**

Koppers Company, Inc. and Subsidiaries

December 31, 1974 and 1973
(See accompanying statement of accounting policies and notes to financial statements.)

| | 1974 | 1973 |
|---|---|---|
| Current assets: | | |
| Cash | $ 16,103,463 | $ 15,165,561 |
| Accounts receivable: | | |
| Due from affiliate (Note 1) | 11,899,000 | — |
| Trade, less allowance for doubtful accounts of $1,996,766 in 1974 and $1,836,173 in 1973 (Note 2) | 158,557,672 | 129,450,232 |
| Inventories: | | |
| Product inventories | 58,912,408 | 49,143,522 |
| Work in process | 51,116,772 | 28,692,899 |
| Raw materials and supplies | 35,909,807 | 26,637,611 |
| Prepaid expenses | 6,597,963 | 5,978,997 |
| Total current assets | 339,097,085 | 255,068,822 |
| Investments: | | |
| Common and preferred stock of affiliate, at cost (Note 1) | 55,265,264 | — |
| Affiliated companies, at equity (Note 3) | 12,197,647 | 10,181,448 |
| Other, at cost | 10,399,799 | 10,995,588 |
| | 77,862,710 | 21,177,036 |
| Less allowance for possible decline in value | 4,150,000 | 2,524,000 |
| | 73,712,710 | 18,653,036 |
| Notes and accounts receivable due after one year | 3,839,590 | 2,443,640 |
| Fixed assets, at cost: | | |
| Buildings | 45,496,798 | 52,768,643 |
| Machinery and equipment | 355,366,260 | 411,018,395 |
| | 400,863,058 | 463,787,038 |
| Less accumulated depreciation | 206,235,617 | 247,167,689 |
| | 194,627,441 | 216,619,349 |
| Depletable properties, less accumulated depletion | 19,363,244 | 12,629,091 |
| Land | 12,719,951 | 11,055,477 |
| | 226,710,636 | 240,303,917 |
| Intangible assets, net of amortization | 3,619,311 | 3,092,007 |
| Deferred charges | 925,866 | 667,045 |
| | $647,905,198 | $520,228,467 |

LIABILITIES AND SHAREHOLDERS' EQUITY

| | 1974 | 1973 |
|---|---:|---:|
| Current liabilities: | | |
| Federal income tax | $ 13,483,408 | $ 12,950,500 |
| Other taxes | 7,680,047 | 6,729,639 |
| Accounts payable, principally trade | 48,605,005 | 40,344,857 |
| Accrued pensions (Note 5) | 9,331,222 | 7,647,000 |
| Other accruals | 29,553,334 | 19,980,552 |
| Advance payments received on contracts | 30,337,549 | 16,844,015 |
| Debt due within one year including short-term borrowings of $2,401,000 in 1974 (Note 6) | 5,032,202 | 2,540,589 |
| Total current liabilities | 144,022,767 | 107,037,152 |
| Term debt due after one year (Note 6): | | |
| 6% notes due $3,000,000 annually commencing August 1, 1977 | 50,000,000 | 50,000,000 |
| Term loan payable to banks | 60,000,000 | 30,000,000 |
| Notes payable to banks | 33,000,000 | 10,000,000 |
| 5.8% promissory notes due $670,000 annually | 7,320,000 | 7,990,000 |
| Pollution control notes | 10,600,000 | 10,600,000 |
| Other | 5,725,960 | 4,167,568 |
| | 166,645,960 | 112,757,568 |
| Deferred compensation | 5,464,629 | 4,982,295 |
| Deferred income taxes | 18,765,718 | 20,565,869 |
| Deferred foreign exchange gain | 855,160 | 629,000 |
| Minority shareholders' interest in subsidiaries | 46,281 | 214,804 |
| Total liabilities | 335,800,515 | 246,186,688 |
| **SHAREHOLDERS' EQUITY** | | |
| Cumulative preferred stock, $100 par value: | | |
| Authorized 300,000 shares, issued 150,000 shares, 4% series | 15,000,000 | 15,000,000 |
| Preferred stock, no par value: | | |
| Authorized 1,000,000 shares, issued-none | — | — |
| Common stock, $5 par value, authorized 8,000,000 shares, issued and outstanding 5,799,955 in 1974 and 5,687,916 in 1973 | 28,999,775 | 28,439,580 |
| Capital in excess of par value | 62,933,097 | 61,289,033 |
| Earnings retained in the business (Notes 3 and 6) | 205,171,811 | 169,313,166 |
| Common shareholders' equity | 297,104,683 | 259,041,779 |
| Total preferred and common shareholders' equity | 312,104,683 | 274,041,779 |
| | $647,905,198 | $520,228,467 |

**Consolidated Statement of Changes in Financial Position**

Koppers Company, Inc. and Subsidiaries

Years ended December 31, 1974 and 1973
(See accompanying statement of accounting policies and notes to financial statements.)

| | 1974 | 1973 |
|---|---|---|
| Source of funds: | | |
| Operations: | | |
| Net income | $ 47,781,120 | $ 29,535,344 |
| Depreciation and depletion | 27,808,950 | 28,740,943 |
| Deferred income taxes and other expenses | (1,133,812) | 3,105,161 |
| Provision for possible decline in value of investments | 1,626,000 | 1,000,000 |
| Equity in earnings of affiliated companies, less dividends received | (1,365,657) | (839,811) |
| Funds provided from operations | 74,716,601 | 61,541,637 |
| Proceeds from term debt issued | 66,524,162 | 36,347,536 |
| Conversion of Sinclair-Koppers partnership fixed assets to investment in an affiliated company | 62,660,057 | — |
| Redemption of investment in an affiliated company | 25,219,200 | — |
| Common stock issued | 3,216,607 | 2,158,913 |
| Book value of fixed assets and other noncurrent assets disposed of or sold | 3,436,587 | 2,861,168 |
| | 235,773,214 | 102,909,254 |
| Disposition of funds: | | |
| Fixed assets purchased | 80,271,479 | 61,719,216 |
| Term debt retired | 12,635,770 | 44,386,760 |
| Dividends paid | 12,934,823 | 10,730,640 |
| Investment in an affiliated company | 80,668,057 | — |
| Other | 2,220,437 | 3,617,729 |
| | 188,730,566 | 120,454,345 |
| Increase (decrease) in working capital | $ 47,042,648 | $(17,545,091) |
| Changes in components of working capital: | | |
| Increase (decrease) in current assets: | | |
| Cash | $ 937,902 | $ 1,450,405 |
| Accounts receivable | 41,006,440 | 6,924,725 |
| Inventories | 41,464,955 | 11,294,978 |
| Prepaid expenses | 618,966 | (612,526) |
| | 84,028,263 | 19,057,582 |
| Increase (decrease) in current liabilities: | | |
| Federal income tax | 532,908 | 11,613,338 |
| Other taxes | 950,408 | 883,620 |
| Accounts payable | 8,260,148 | 3,882,896 |
| Accrued pensions | 1,684,222 | 2,782,278 |
| Other accruals | 9,572,782 | 8,175,715 |
| Advance payments received on contracts | 13,493,534 | 10,217,459 |
| Term debt due within one year, including short-term borrowings | 2,491,613 | (952,003) |
| | 36,985,615 | 36,602,673 |
| Increase (decrease) in working capital | $ 47,042,648 | $(17,545,091) |

**Consolidated Statement of Shareholders' Equity**

Koppers Company, Inc. and Subsidiaries

Years ended December 31, 1974 and 1973
(See accompanying statement of accounting policies and notes to financial statements.)

| | Cumulative Preferred Stock | Common Stock | Capital In Excess of Par Value | Earnings Retained in the Business | Total Preferred and Common Shareholders' Equity |
|---|---|---|---|---|---|
| **Balance at January 1, 1973** . . . . . . . . . . . . . . | $15,000,000 | $28,140,725 | $59,428,975 | $150,508,462 | $253,078,162 |
| Net income for the year 1973 . . . . . . . . . . . . . . | — | — | — | 29,535,344 | 29,535,344 |
| Cash dividends paid: | | | | | |
|   On preferred stock, $4.00 per share . . . . . . | — | — | — | (600,000) | (600,000) |
|   On common stock, $1.80 per share . . . . . . | — | — | — | (10,130,640) | (10,130,640) |
| Common stock issued (59,771 shares) for acquisitions . . . . . . . . . . . . . . . . . . . . . . . . . . . . | — | 298,855 | 1,860,058 | — | 2,158,913 |
| **Balance at December 31, 1973** . . . . . . . . . . . . | 15,000,000 | 28,439,580 | 61,289,033 | 169,313,166 | 274,041,779 |
| Net income for the year 1974 . . . . . . . . . . . . . . | — | — | — | 47,781,120 | 47,781,120 |
| Cash dividends paid: | | | | | |
|   On preferred stock, $4.00 per share . . . . . . | — | — | — | (600,000) | (600,000) |
|   On common stock, $2.14 per share . . . . . . | — | — | — | (12,334,823) | (12,334,823) |
| Common stock issued during 1974: | | | | | |
|   102,039 shares for acquisitions . . . . . . . . . | — | 510,195 | 1,299,064 | 1,012,348 | 2,821,607 |
|   10,000 shares for stock options exercised at $39.50 per share . . . . . . . . . . . . . . . . | — | 50,000 | 345,000 | — | 395,000 |
| **Balance at December 31, 1974** . . . . . . . . . . . . | $15,000,000 | $28,999,775 | $62,933,097 | $205,171,811 | $312,104,683 |

## Statement of Accounting Policies

Koppers Company, Inc. and Subsidiaries

The Company employs generally accepted accounting principles on a consistent basis to present fairly its financial position, results of operations and changes in financial position. The major accounting policies of the Company are set forth below. The word "Company" as used in this report includes consolidated entities as well as Koppers Company, Inc.

### Principles of Consolidation

The consolidated statements include the accounts of the Company and all of its subsidiaries. All intercompany transactions have been eliminated.

### Foreign Currency

The accounts of foreign subsidiaries maintained in foreign currencies have been converted to U.S. dollars on the following bases: current assets and current liabilities at year-end exchange rates; noncurrent assets, noncurrent liabilities and equity at rates of exchange in effect when acquired; and revenue and expense accounts at average rates of exchange in effect during the period, except for depreciation which is converted at rates of exchange which were in effect when the respective assets were acquired. Unrealized exchange gains are not recognized as income but are credited to unrealized exchange gain reserves. Unrealized exchange losses are charged against income to the extent that they exceed any unrealized exchange gain reserves established in prior years.

### Inventories

Inventories are valued at the lower of cost or market. Effective January 1, 1974, the Company adopted the LIFO (last-in, first-out) method of determining cost for substantially all domestic inventories of Koppers Company, Inc. This was done because the rapid increase in prices during the year would result in an overstatement of profits if use of the FIFO (first-in, first-out) method were continued, since inventories sold were replaced at substantially higher prices. This accounting change increased 1974 cost of goods sold by $34,038,000 and, accordingly, decreased net income by $16,638,000 ($2.88 per share). It is not possible under the LIFO method to determine the effect of this change on prior years. Cost for the remainder of the inventories represents average costs or standard costs which approximate actual on the first-in, first-out basis. Market is replacement cost for raw materials and net realizable value for work in process and finished goods.

### Investments

Companies owned 50% or less but more than 20% are accounted for on the equity method except for certain foreign investments, which are valued at cost because of repatriation regulations. Note 1 explains the accounting for a major investment in an affiliate.

### Fixed Assets

Buildings, machinery and equipment are depreciated on the straight-line method over their useful lives. All ordinary maintenance and repair expenses are charged to operations. Extraordinary repairs, which materially extend the life of property, are generally charged to accumulated depreciation. Timber and mineral properties are depleted on the basis of units produced.

When land, standing timber or property units are sold, the difference between selling price and cost, after recognition of accumulated depreciation and depletion, is reflected in Other Income.

### Intangible Assets

Patent costs are amortized over the lives of the patents. The excess of purchase price over net asset value of businesses acquired is amortized over the estimated useful lives of such assets not exceeding 40 years.

### Long-Term Contracts

Sales and income on long-term construction contracts are accounted for on the percentage-of-completion basis; losses are recognized as soon as they are determined.

### Research and Development

Research and development costs are expensed as incurred.

### Pension Plans

The Company has pension plans covering substantially all employees. The Company provides for amortization of unfunded prior service costs over periods up to 40 years and pays provisions for pension expense into trust funds.

### Income Taxes

Deferred income taxes are provided for timing differences between financial and tax reporting. Benefits from investment tax credits are reflected currently in income.

## Notes to Financial Statements

Koppers Company, Inc. and Subsidiaries

### 1. Reorganization of Sinclair-Koppers Company

The Company entered into an agreement effective January 1, 1974 with Atlantic Richfield Company to reorganize their Sinclair-Koppers partnership.

The business and net assets of the partnership were transferred to a new corporation (ARCO/Polymers, Inc.) in exchange for $100 (one hundred dollar) par value 12½% preferred stock and $1 (one dollar) par value common stock Class A and B. The Class A common stock was distributed to Atlantic Richfield, and all the 12½% nonvoting preferred stock and all of Class B common stock, which constitutes approximately 20% voting interest, was distributed to the Company. The securities received by the Company can be redeemed for cash at the option of ARCO/Polymers. Either the Company or ARCO/Polymers may cause to be redeemed by ARCO/Polymers in 1981 all the outstanding shares then held by the Company at contributed value.

All earnings of ARCO/Polymers are required to be distributed as dividends currently on its outstanding stock, first on the preferred stock and the balance on the common stock. Such dividends are declared and paid quarterly.

Prior to 1974, the Company's 50% interest in the income, expenses, assets and liabilities of the partnership had been included in the financial statements, while in 1974 the Company's interest is shown as an investment, and income is reported as dividends are earned. Therefore, the following important components of the Company's share of Sinclair-Koppers partnership included in the Company's consolidated financial statements at December 31, 1973 are furnished to facilitate comparison of 1974 and 1973:

| | |
|---|---:|
| Net working capital | $18,008,000 |
| Net fixed assets | $62,660,000 |
| Net sales | $81,066,000 |
| Depreciation | $ 6,185,000 |
| Operating profit | $12,052,000 |

### 2. Accounts Receivable

Receivables include the following amounts applicable to long-term construction contracts:

| | 1974 | 1973 |
|---|---:|---:|
| Billed | $29,027,000 | $22,131,000 |
| Retainage | 10,084,000 | 9,146,000 |

### 3. Investments in Affiliated Companies, at Equity

Consolidated earnings retained in the business include $9,080,000 in 1974 and $7,804,000 in 1973, representing the Company's equity in undistributed retained earnings of the affiliated companies less deferred taxes.

### 4. Foreign Operations

The Company's financial statements include the following amounts related to consolidated subsidiaries (all wholly owned) located outside of the United States at December 31, 1974 and 1973 and for the years then ended:

| | 1974 | 1973 |
|---|---:|---:|
| Assets | $49,825,000 | $44,352,000 |
| Liabilities | $26,350,000 | $12,855,000 |
| Sales | $56,638,000 | $48,143,000 |
| Net income | $ 1,390,000 | $ 4,677,000 |

### 5. Pensions

Total pension expense in 1974 was $9,754,000 as compared with $7,647,000 in 1973. In 1974, pension expense was increased as a result of recognition of a portion of the unrealized depreciation of investments held by the pension trusts.

The market value of these investments in 1973 did not necessitate the recognition of unrealized depreciation. The unfunded prior service costs under all plans at December 31, 1974 amounted to $28,332,000.

### 6. Debt

On April 1, 1974, the Company obtained an 8½%, $30,000,000 bank term loan of ten years with no repayments during the first seven years. Repayment provisions specify that 25% of the principal amount is to be paid in each of the eighth and ninth years, with 50% to be repaid in the tenth year. The $30,000,000 loan obtained February 1, 1973 has the same terms except that the interest rate is ¾ of 1% over the prime rate, with a maximum average annual interest cost during the first seven years of 7½%. Any interest payments in excess of this maximum will be refunded to the Company at the end of the seven-year period. The interest rate during the eighth, ninth and tenth years will be ¾ of 1% over the prime rate.

A bank credit agreement providing for up to $75,000,000 of 90-day renewable revolving credit loans became effective August 1, 1974. Interest on the loans is at the prime rate until July 31, 1977, at which time the notes are convertible at the option of the Company into term notes payable in eight equal semiannual installments commencing January 31, 1978 with interest at the prime rate plus ¼ of 1% through August 1, 1979 and at the prime rate plus ½ of 1% thereafter. During the renewable period, the Company is required to pay a commitment fee of ½ of 1% per annum on the unborrowed amount.

The Company has issued notes to provide funds for the construction of pollution control facilities at Company

Koppers Company, Inc. and Subsidiaries

plants. The notes bear interest at approximately 6%, payable semi-annually with principal payments commencing June 1, 1983 in annual installments over 16 years.

The aggregate term-debt maturity amounts for the years 1975 through 1979, respectively are $2,629,000; $2,394,000; $4,614,000; $12,533,000; and $12,352,000

The Company's term-debt agreements contain various restrictions as to dividend payments and incurrence of additional indebtedness. Under the most restrictive provisions at December 31, 1974, $54,846,000 of consolidated earnings retained in the business was available for cash dividends, and the Company could incur additional indebtedness of approximately $30,346,000.

The Company has additional agreements which make available $18,000,000 in short-term borrowings. The Company is not required to pay a commitment fee on the unborrowed funds under these agreements. At December 31, 1974, the Company had $2,401,000 of borrowings under these agreements.

The Company issues short-term promissory notes (commercial paper) to cover peak working capital requirements. The average amount of commercial paper outstanding during the year was $17,286,000 with a daily weighted averaged annual interest rate of 11.3%. The maximum amount of the commercial paper outstanding during the year was $30,000,000. No amounts were outstanding at the end of the year.

## 7. Income Taxes

Income tax expense has the following components:

| | Years ended December 31, | |
| | 1974 | 1973 |
|---|---|---|
| Federal: | | |
| Current .... | $25,487,482 | $13,839,707 |
| Deferred ... | (1,788,043) | 1,498,785 |
| | 23,699,439 | 15,338,492 |
| State ........ | 3,821,089 | 2,041,469 |
| Foreign: | | |
| Current .... | 1,548,294 | 3,534,658 |
| Deferred ... | (711,846) | 666,000 |
| | 836,448 | 4,200,658 |
| Total ........ | $28,356,976 | $21,580,619 |

Deferred taxes resulted from the following:

| | | |
|---|---|---|
| Excess of tax over book depreciation ......... | $ (365,000) | $3,171,000 |
| Items charged to expense on the books but not currently deductible for tax: | | |
| Incentive payments ... | 33,000 | (537,000) |
| Investment reserve ..... | (487,800) | (300,000) |
| Loss on foreign purchase commitments .. | (945,000) | — |
| Other—net .... | (735,089) | (169,215) |
| | $(2,499,889) | $2,164,785 |

The difference between the statutory and effective income tax rates is as follows:

| | Years ended December 31 | |
|---|---|---|
| | 1974 | 1973 |
| Statutory tax rate: | | |
| Federal .......... | 48.0% | 48.0% |
| State net of Federal tax benefit ....... | 2.6% | 2.5% |
| Foreign .......... | (0.1%) | (1.3%) |
| Investment tax credit .. | (2.9%) | (3.7%) |
| Effect of lower statutory tax rate applicable to dividends received from an affiliated company .......... | (8.5%) | — |
| Other—net .......... | (1.9%) | (3.3%) |
| | 37.2% | 42.2% |

The current provisions for Federal income taxes have been reduced by $2,201,000 and $1,909,000 in 1974 and 1973, respectively, for the investment tax credit.

## 8. Commitments and Contingencies

The total rental expense amounted to $10,622,000 in 1974 as compared with $9,927,000 in 1973.

At December 31, 1974, the minimum rental commitments under noncancelable leases with remaining terms of more than one year are as follows:

| | Financing Leases | Other Leases | Total |
|---|---|---|---|
| 1975... | $ 3,251,000 | $ 4,727,000 | $ 7,978,000 |
| 1976... | 2,985,000 | 2,925,000 | 5,910,000 |
| 1977... | 2,755,000 | 1,805,000 | 4,560,000 |
| 1978... | 2,145,000 | 1,279,000 | 3,424,000 |
| 1979... | 1,955,000 | 764,000 | 2,719,000 |
| 1980-1984.. | 2,689,000 | 930,000 | 3,619,000 |
| 1985-1989.. | 1,124,000 | 40,000 | 1,164,000 |
| 1990-1994.. | 422,000 | 1,000 | 423,000 |
| | $17,326,000 | $12,471,000 | $29,797,000 |

The Company has guaranteed $8,373,000 indebtedness of affiliated and other corporations.

## QUESTIONS

1. The income statement is a *general-purpose* statement. What does this mean?

2. Explain briefly how the income statement is a connecting link between the beginning and ending balance sheets.

3. Briefly explain the economist's definition of income. How does the accountant define income as reflected by the completed transactions approach?

4. Define revenue. Compare the conceptual view with the pragmatic definition provided by APB *Statement No. 4.*

5. Define expense. Compare the conceptual view with the pragmatic definition provided by APB *Statement No. 4.*

6. Distinguish between cost and expense. What is a loss?

7. Briefly explain the two "pure" formats used for income statements. Explain why actual income statements are usually somewhere between these two formats.

8. What is the basic difference between an income statement for a trading company and a manufacturing company?

9. Explain the reporting principle, including its full-disclosure aspect. (Refer to Chapter 2.)

10. Explain why the total amount of depreciation expense must be disclosed in the financial statement.

11. Briefly distinguish between intraperiod and interperiod tax allocation.

12. Define earnings per share. Why it is required as an integral part of the income statement? What amounts must be reported on the income statement?

13. Explain the difference between the all-inclusive and the operating concepts of income. Which concept do you prefer? Why?

14. Define an extraordinaly item. How should extraordinary items be reported on a (a) single-step, and (b) multiple-step income statement?

15. How are items that are either unusual or infrequent, but not both, reported on the income statement?

16. Define prior period adjustments; give the four criteria. How are prior period adjustments reported on the financial statements? Do you agree with this approach? Explain why.

17. What are the four types of accounting changes identified in APB *Opinion No. 20?* Define what is meant by a change due to (a) accounting error, and (b) change in estimate.

18. Explain the basic approach in accounting and reporting (a) accounting errors, and (b) changes in estimates.

19. What items are reported on a statement of retained earnings? Explain how it provides a link between the current income statement and the balance sheet.

20. What is meant by restrictions on retained earnings? How are they usually reported?

21. Explain why many companies prefer a combined statement of income and retained earnings.

## DECISION CASE 4-1

The president of Taylor School Supply Company, a wholesaler, presents you with a comparison of distribution costs for two salespersons and wants to know if you think their compensation plan is working to the detriment of the company. The president supplies you with the following data:

| | Salesperson | |
|---|---|---|
| | McKinney | Sim |
| Gross sales | $247,000 | $142,000 |
| Sales returns | 17,000 | 2,000 |
| Cost of goods sold | 180,000 | 100,000 |
| Reimbursed expenses (e.g., entertainment) | 5,500 | 2,100 |
| Other direct charges (e.g., samples distributed) | 4,000 | 450 |
| Commission rate on gross sales dollars | 5% | 5% |

*Required:*

1. A salesperson's compensation plan encourages one to work to increase the measure of performance to which compensation is related. List the questionable sales practices by a salesperson that might be encouraged by basing commissions on gross sales.
2. *a.* What evidence that the compensation plan may be working to the detriment of the company can be found in the data?
   *b.* What other information should the president obtain before reaching definite conclusions about this particular situation? Why?

(AICPA adapted)

## DECISION CASE 4-2

J. B. Jacobson opened a small retail cash-and-carry grocery business with an investment of $1,000 cash, $5,000 merchandise, and a lot and building valued at $18,000. Fixtures were obtained by signing a note payable in equal installments over a 36-month period. Cash is paid for all merchandise purchases, and Jacobson maintains no formal accounting records. When asked how one knew how well one was doing and where one stood, Jacobson made the following statement: "As long as I do not buy or sell anything except merchandise and that remains fairly constant, I can judge my profit or loss by the increase or decrease in my bank balance."

*Required:*

Evaluate Jacobson's statement in the light of the facts known.

## DECISION CASE 4-3

Generally accepted accounting principles define income as Revenue minus Expense equals Income. This model requires that revenue and expense be identified and carefully measured. Also, it requires a careful correspondence between revenue and expense.

*Required:*

1. What principle, or principles, govern identification and measurement of revenues?

2. What principle, or principles, govern identification and measurement of expenses?
3. Identify and explain some of the troublesome problems in applying the principles identified in 1 and 2.
4. What guidelines govern identification and measurement of extraordinary items? Do you agree with these guidelines? Explain.
5. What guidelines govern identification and measurement of prior period adjustments? Do you agree with these guidelines? Explain.
6. What guidelines govern reporting of items that are either unusual or infrequent, but not both? Do you agree with these guidelines? Explain.

## EXERCISES

### Exercise 4–1

For each of the following transactions, state when revenue and/or expense should be recognized; explain the basis for your decision. Assume the accounting period ends December 31.

a. On December 21, 1976, merchandise was sold for $3,000 cash. The buyer took possession of two thirds of the merchandise on that date. The balance will be picked up on January 3, 1977.
b. Services were rendered to a customer starting on December 27, 1976. The services will be completed around January 5, 1977, at which time cash in full will be collected. Assume eight working days are involved.
c. During 1976 the company sold ten TV sets and collected $4,000 cash in full. The company gives a one-year guarantee. It is estimated that the average cost per set under the guarantee is $15. Assume by the end of 1976, one half of the guarantees on the ten sets have been satisfied.
d. On December 31, 1976, a used truck was sold by the company that had been used in operating the business and had a book value of $300. The sales price was $500 which was payable six months from date of the sale plus 8% interest per annum.
e. On December 27, 1976, the company received an income tax refund of $1,000 after four years of negotiations with the Internal Revenue Service.

(*Hint:* Restudy the revenue, cost, and matching principles in Chapter 2.)

### Exercise 4–2

For each of the following transactions, state when revenue and/or expense should be recognized; explain the basis for your decision. Assume the accounting period ends December 31, 1976.

a. On December 30, 1976, sold $2,000 merchandise; terms, 2/10, n/30.
b. On December 29, 1976, paid $15,000 for advertising in the local paper. The ads related only to a clearance sale that would run from January 1–31, 1976.
c. Performed services each working day for a customer that extended from December 27, 1976, through January 5, 1977. Assume ten working days are involved. Cash collected was $2,000 (in full) on December 27, 1976.
d. Sold a used TV set for $100 on December 28, 1976, and collected $75 cash. The balance is due in six months; however, collection of the balance is very doubtful, and the set will not be worth repossessing again. It is now carried in the books at $60.

e. On December 1, 1976, borrowed $6,600 cash and gave a noninterest-bearing note payable; received cash, $6,000 (the face of the note less interest for one year deducted in advance).

(*Hint:* Restudy the revenue, cost, and matching principles in Chapter 2.)

## Exercise 4–3

The following items were taken from the adjusted trial balance of Blue Trading Corporation on December 31, 1976. Assume a flat 40% corporate tax rate on all items (including the casualty loss).

| | |
|---|---:|
| Sales | $640,000 |
| Rent collected | 2,400 |
| Interest revenue | 900 |
| Gain on sale of fixed assets (assume not qualified as a capital gain)... | 1,000 |
| Distribution expenses | 136,000 |
| General and administrative expenses | 110,000 |
| Interest expense | 1,500 |
| Depreciation for the period | 6,000 |
| Extraordinary item: Major casualty loss (pretax) | 20,000 |
| Common stock (par $10) | 100,000 |
| Cost of goods sold | 350,000 |

*Required:*

1. Prepare a single-step income statement (include EPS).
2. Prepare a multiple-step income statement (include EPS).
3. Which format do you prefer? Why?

## Exercise 4–4

The following items were taken from the adjusted trial balance of Slim Manufacturing Corporation at December 31, 1976:

| | |
|---|---:|
| Sales | $900,000 |
| Cost of goods manufactured | 550,000 |
| Dividends received on investment in stocks | 6,500 |
| Finished goods inventory, January 1, 1976 | 45,000 |
| Interest expense | 4,200 |
| Extraordinary item: Major fire loss (already reduced for tax savings)... | 33,000 |
| Distribution expenses | 135,300 |
| Common stock, par $20 | 200,000 |
| Administrative and general expenses | 113,000 |
| Interest revenue | 2,300 |
| Finished goods inventory, December 31, 1976 | 51,300 |
| Income taxes (excluding the extraordinary item); assume a flat 40% corporate tax rate | ? |

*Required:*

1. Prepare a single-step income statement (include EPS).
2. Prepare a multiple-step income statement (include EPS).
3. Which format do you prefer? Why?

**Exercise 4–5**

The following items were taken from the adjusted trial balance of Swenson Trading Corporation at December 31, 1976:

| | |
|---|---:|
| Sales revenue | $ 96,000 |
| Distribution expenses | 24,000 |
| Interest revenue | 600 |
| Cost of goods sold | 54,000 |
| Extraordinary item: Major casualty loss (already reduced for income tax savings) | 9,000 |
| Interest expense | 1,000 |
| Gain on sale of fixed assets (assume not taxed as a capital gain) | 3,000 |
| Common stock, par $10 | 100,000 |
| Income tax expense (excluding extraordinary item); assume a flat 22% corporate tax rate | ? |
| General and administrative expenses | 10,600 |

*Required:*

1. Prepare a single-step income statement (include EPS).
2. Prepare a multiple-step income statement (include EPS).
3. Which format do you prefer? Explain.

**Exercise 4–6**

The following pretax amounts were taken from the adjusted trial balance of Howe Company at December 31, 1976:

| | |
|---|---:|
| Balance, retained earnings, January 1, 1976 | $ 33,000 |
| Sales revenue | 120,000 |
| Cost of goods sold | 51,000 |
| Distribution expenses | 32,000 |
| Administrative expenses | 23,000 |
| Extraordinary loss (pretax) | 10,000 |
| Prior period adjustment, a gain (pretax) | 8,000 |
| Dividends paid | 6,000 |

Assume a flat 30% corporate tax rate on all items, including the extraordinary loss and prior period adjustment. Also assume common stock outstanding is 5,000 shares.

*Required:*

1. Prepare a single-step income statement and a statement of retained earnings including intraperiod tax allocation (include EPS).
2. Give the entry to record income taxes payable (assume none yet paid).

**Exercise 4–7**

The following pretax amounts were taken from the adjusted trial balance of White Corporation on December 31, 1976:

| | |
|---|---:|
| Balance, retained earnings, January 1, 1976 | $ 38,000 |
| Sales revenue | 200,000 |
| Cost of goods sold | 100,000 |
| Distribution expenses | 31,000 |

| | |
|---|---:|
| Administrative expenses | 29,000 |
| Extraordinary gain (pretax) | 10,000 |
| Prior period adjustment, a loss (pretax) | 20,000 |
| Dividends paid | 8,000 |

Assume the corporate income tax rates are 22% on the first $25,000 of net income and 48% on all income above that amount, including the extraordinary item and the prior period adjustment.

Common shares outstanding during the year were 10,000.

*Required:*

1. Prepare a multiple-step income statement with intraperiod tax allocation and EPS.
2. Prepare a statement of retained earnings with intraperiod tax allocation and EPS.
3. Give the entry to record income taxes payable (assume none yet paid).

## Exercise 4–8

The following pretax amounts were taken from the adjusted trial balance of Vinson Corporation at December 31, 1976:

| | |
|---|---:|
| Dividends paid | $ 30,000 |
| Sales revenue | 190,000 |
| Cost of goods sold | 100,000 |
| Operating expenses | 60,000 |
| Extraordinary loss (pretax) | 15,000 |
| Prior period adjustment, a gain (pretax) | 10,000 |
| Common stock (par $10) | 150,000 |
| Beginning retained earnings, January 1, 1976 | 45,000 |

*Required:*

1. Prepare a complete single-step income statement. Assume 22% rate for the first $25,000 of income and 48% on all amounts above $25,000. Show computations of earnings per share information.
2. Prepare a statement of retained earnings.
3. Give the entry to record income taxes payable (assume none yet paid).

## Exercise 4–9

The following pretax amounts were taken from the adjusted trial balance of Asher Corporation at December 31, 1976:

| | |
|---|---:|
| Sales revenue | $240,000 |
| Cost of goods sold | 110,000 |
| Operating expenses | 80,000 |
| Extraordinary gain (pretax) | 10,000 |
| Prior period adjustment, a loss (pretax) | 20,000 |

| Common stock (par $10): | Shares |
|---|---:|
| Outstanding January 1, 1976 | 15,000 |
| Sold and issued April 1, 1976 | 5,000 |
| Sold and issued October 1, 1976 | 8,000 |
| Outstanding December 31, 1976 | 28,000 |

*Required:*

Prepare a complete single-step income statement. Assume an average 30% corporate tax rate on all items. Show computations of earnings per share.

### Exercise 4-10

On December 31, 1976, the following pretax amounts were taken from the adjusted trial balance of Jackson Corporation:

| | |
|---|---:|
| Sales revenue | $190,000 |
| Cost of goods sold | 100,000 |
| Operating expenses | 45,000 |
| Extraordinary loss (pretax) | 20,000 |
| Prior period adjustment, loss (pretax) | 10,000 |

Assume an average 40% corporate tax rate on all items.

Common stock (par $10):
| | |
|---|---:|
| Shares outstanding, January 1, 1976 | 15,000 |
| Stock dividend, shares issued on July 1, 1976 | 5,000 |

*Required:*

Prepare a single-step income statement. Show computations for earnings per share.

### Exercise 4-11

The following pretax amounts were taken from the adjusted trial balance of Searles Corporation at December 31, 1976:

| | |
|---|---:|
| Revenues | $400,000 |
| Cost of goods sold | 220,000 |
| Operating expenses | 100,000 |
| Infrequent item, loss on disposal of long-term investment (pretax) | 10,000 |
| Extraordinary item, gain on expropriation of plant by foreign government (pretax) | 20,000 |
| Common stock (par $10), 10,000 shares outstanding. | |

Assume an average 40% corporate tax rate on all items.

*Required:*

Prepare a single-step income statement that meets the full-disclosure requirements with respect to infrequent items, extraordinary items, tax allocation, and earnings per share.

### Exercise 4-12

The following pretax amounts were taken from the adjusted trial balance of Youngblood Corporation at December 31, 1976:

| | |
|---|---:|
| Sales and service revenues | $200,000 |
| Cost of goods sold | 105,000 |
| Operating expenses | 65,000 |
| Unusual item, gain on sale of major fixed asset (pretax) | 10,000 |
| Extraordinary item, loss on major flood (pretax) | 25,000 |
| Prior period adjustment, damages paid from lawsuit (pretax) | 5,000 |
| Common stock (par $1), 50,000 shares outstanding. | |

Assume an average 40% corporate tax rate on all items.

*Required:*

Prepare a single-step income statement that meets the full-disclosure requirements with respect to unusual items, extraordinary items, tax allocation, and
earnings per share.

## Exercise 4–13

AB Company has a machine that cost $34,000 when acquired on January 1,
1971. The estimated useful life was 15 years and a residual value of $4,000.
Straight-line depreciation is used. On December 31, 1976, prior to the adjusting
entry, it was decided that the machine should have been depreciated over a 21-
year useful life, with no change in the residual value.

*Required:*

1. Give the adjusting entry at the end of 1976 for depreciation expense. Show
   computations.
2. Give the correcting entry required at the end of 1976. If none is required, so
   state and give the reasons.

## Exercise 4–14

It is December 31, 1976, and the SY Company is preparing adjusting entries at
the end of the year. The company owns two trucks of different types. The following situations confront the company accountant:

a. Truck No. 1 cost $6,500 on January 1, 1974. It is being depreciated on a
   straight line basis over an estimated useful life of ten years with a $500
   residual value. At December 31, 1976, it has been determined that the useful
   life should have been eight years instead of ten, with no changes in the residual
   value.
b. Truck No. 2 cost $4,550 on January 1, 1973. It is being depreciated on a
   straight-line basis over an estimated useful life of seven years with a $350
   residual value. At December 31, 1976, it was discovered that no depreciation
   had been recorded on this truck for 1973 and 1974.

*Required:*

1. For each truck, give the correct adjusting entry for depreciation expense at
   December 31, 1976. Show computations.
2. For each truck, if a correcting entry is required, provide it and show computations. If no correcting entry is needed, give the reasons.

**Exercise 4-15**

The following pretax amounts were taken from the accounts of Sauls Corporation at December 31, 1976:

| | |
|---|---|
| Cost of goods sold ..................................................................... | $60,000 |
| Sales revenue ........................................................................... | 95,000 |
| Operating expenses ................................................................... | 20,000 |
| Extraordinary item, loss due to expropriation of plant by a foreign government (pretax) ..................................................... | 10,000 |
| Prior period adjustment, damages collected on lawsuit (pretax).......... | 6,000 |
| Cash dividends ......................................................................... | 4,000 |
| Retained earnings balance, January 1, 1976.................................... | 25,000 |
| Common stock (par $10) outstanding, 10,000 shares. | |

Assume an average 30% corporate income tax rate on all items. Assume the expropriation and the damages collected are subject to tax.

*Required:*

Prepare a combined single-step income statement and statement of retained earnings including income tax allocation and earnings per share. Show computations.

**Exercise 4-16**

The following pretax amounts were taken from the accounts of Rawls Corporation at December 31, 1976:

| | |
|---|---|
| Sales revenue ........................................................................... | $140,000 |
| Cost of goods sold ..................................................................... | 80,000 |
| Distribution and administrative expenses ..................................... | 45,000 |
| Extraordinary item (gain from expropriation of foreign plant) ........... | 15,000 |
| Prior period adjustment (additional tax assessment on 1972 return) ... | 8,000 |
| Interest expense ....................................................................... | 600 |
| Cash dividends.......................................................................... | 5,000 |
| Retained earnings balance, January 1, 1976 ................................... | 30,000 |
| Common stock (par $5), 20,000 shares outstanding. | |

Assume an average 40% corporate tax rate on all items. Assume the expropriation is subject to tax.

*Required:*

Prepare a combined multiple-step income statement and statement of retained earnings, including income tax allocation and earnings per share. Show computations.

**PROBLEMS**

**Problem 4-1**

Below is listed a number of transactions and amounts that are reported on the annual financial statement. For each item, you are to indicate how it should be reported. A list of responses is given so you can indicate your response by *code letter.* Enter only one letter for each item. You should comment on doubtful items.

| Code | Classification |
|---|---|
| | Balance sheet, appropriately classified |
| A. | |
| | Income statement: |
| B. | Revenue |
| C. | Expense |
| D. | Unusual or infrequent, but not both |
| E. | Extraordinary item |
| | Statement of retained earnings: |
| F. | Prior period adjustment (as an addition or deduction) |
| G. | Addition to retained earnings |
| H. | Deduction to retained earnings |
| I. | Note to the financial statement only |

1. _B_ Total amount of cash and credit sales for the period. *contra to a/c*

2. _A_ Allowance for doubtful accounts.

3. _B or D_ Gain on sale of fixed asset. *area not conducive to hurrica... c otherwise on D*

4. _E_ Hurricane damages.

5. _C_ Depreciation expense for manufacturing company.

6. _F_ Payment of $30,000 additional income tax assessment (on prior year's income).

7. _E_ Earthquake damages. *H D*

8. _C_ Distribution expenses.

9. _A_ Estimated warranties payable. *Liability*

10. _B_ Gain on disposal of long-term investments in stocks.

11. _G_ Net income for the period. *G*

12. _E_ Insurance gain on major casualty (fire) — insurance proceeds exceeded the book value of the assets destroyed.

13. _H_ Cash dividends declared and paid.

14. _B_ Rent collected on office space rented temporarily.

15. _C_ Interest paid and interest accrued on liabilities. *A*

16. _B_ Dividends received on stocks held as an investment.

17. _E_ Damages paid as a result of a lawsuit by an individual injured while shopping in the store; the litigation covered three years.

18. _E_ Loss due to expropriation of a plant in a foreign country.

19. _C_ A $10,000 bad debt — the receivable had been outstanding for five years and the party cannot be located.

20. _F_ Adjustment due to correction of an error made two years earlier.

21. _A_ On December 31, of current year, paid rent expense in advance for the next two years.

22. _C_ Cost of goods sold.

23. _B_ Interest collected from a customer on a one-year note receivable.

24. _C_ Installment payment on a large machine, which included $1,000 *Exp* interest for the current year.

25. _C_ Year-end bonus of $50,000 paid to employees for performance during the year.

## Problem 4–2

During the current year, 1976, Ayr Company completed a number of transactions that posed questions as to when revenue and/or expense should be recognized. The end of the accounting period is December 31. For each of the following selected transactions, state when revenue and/or expense should be recognized and give the basis for your decision:

a. Merchandise was sold on the credit basis during the year. The terms were 25% down payment plus six monthly payments. The collection experience on such sales, although not as good as on regular credit sales (due at end of month of sale), has been quite satisfactory.

b. On December 24, 1976, the company sold a used TV set that had been repossessed and was set up in used goods inventory at $60. The sales price was $110. At the date of sale, $70 cash was collected; the balance due in six months. There is a high probability that collection will not be made and the TV set probably will not be worth repossessing again.

c. During 1976 the company sold 30 TV sets for a total of $6,000 and collected cash in full. The sets are guaranteed for 12 months from date of sale. It is estimated that the guarantee will cost the company, on the average, $15 per set. At year-end, it was estimated that one half of the guarantees were still outstanding.

d. On December 14, 1976, received a $20,000 income tax refund from prior years. The negotiations extended over a three-year period.

e. Services were rendered to a customer starting on December 28, 1976, and will be completed January 4, 1977. Cash in full ($3,000) will be collected at date of completion of the services. Assume eight working days.

f. On July 1, 1976, paid a two-year insurance premium in advance, $600.

g. On December 30, 1976, sold merchandise for $5,000; terms, 2/10, n/30.

h. On December 1, 1976, sold a customer merchandise for $1,000. Collected $600 cash and received a $400, 8%, interest-bearing note for the remainder, due in three months.

i. On November 15, 1976, the court assessed the company damages amounting to $25,000 cash. The suit was filed in 1974 as a result of an accident in the company store. Payment will be made on January 10, 1977.

j. On December 23, 1976, purchased merchandise for resale, $18,000; terms, 2/10, n/30.

(*Hint:* Restudy the revenue, cost, and matching principles in Chapter 2.)

## Problem 4-3

The following information was taken from the adjusted trial balance of Wonder Trading Corporation at December 31, 1976:

| | |
|---|---:|
| Merchandise inventory, January 1, 1976 | $ 70,000 |
| Purchases | 121,400 |
| Sales | 394,600 |
| Purchase returns | 3,400 |
| Sales returns | 5,200 |
| Common stock (par $10) | 200,000 |
| Depreciation expense (70% administrative; 30% distribution) | 50,000 |
| Rent revenue | 3,600 |
| Interest expense | 6,400 |
| Investment revenue | 2,500 |
| Distribution expenses (exclusive of depreciation) | 105,500 |
| General and administrative expenses (exclusive of depreciation) | 46,000 |
| Gain on sale of fixed assets (ordinary) | 5,000 |
| Loss on sale of long-term investments (ordinary) | 3,600 |
| Income tax expense (not including extraordinary item) | ? |
| Extraordinary item: Major flood loss (tax savings already deducted) | 20,000 |
| Freight paid on purchases | 1,000 |
| Merchandise inventory, December 31, 1976 | 90,000 |

Assume an average 40% corporate income tax rate on all items (including capital gains and losses and extraordinary items).

*Required:*
1. Prepare a single-step income statement and a schedule of cost of goods sold to support it.
2. Prepare a multiple-step income statement including EPS.
3. Explain the relative merits and disadvantages of each format.

## Problem 4–4

The following information was taken from the adjusted trial balance of Cox Manufacturing Corporation at December 31, 1976.

| | |
|---|---:|
| Sales .............................................................................. | $980,000 |
| Purchases ...................................................................... | 150,000 |
| Raw materials inventory, January 1, 1976 ........................................ | 30,000 |
| Work in process inventory, January 1, 1976 ..................................... | 40,000 |
| Finished goods inventory, January 1, 1976 ....................................... | 20,000 |
| Sales returns................................................................... | 5,000 |
| Purchase returns ............................................................... | 4,000 |
| Freight on purchases........................................................... | 7,500 |
| Distribution expenses.......................................................... | 140,000 |
| General and administrative expenses ............................................ | 92,300 |
| Rent revenue.................................................................. | 4,800 |
| Investment revenue............................................................. | 3,000 |
| Gain on sale of fixed assets (ordinary)......................................... | 8,000 |
| Interest expense .............................................................. | 9,000 |
| Extraordinary gain (expropriation of plant by foreign government; income tax effect already deducted) .................... | 40,000 |
| Loss on sale of long-term investments (ordinary)............................... | 10,000 |
| Manufacturing expenses: | |
| Direct labor .................................................................. | 230,000 |
| Factory overhead.............................................................. | 190,000 |
| Raw materials inventory, December 31, 1976................................... | 24,000 |
| Work in process inventory, December 31, 1976............................... | 38,000 |
| Finished goods inventory, December 31, 1976 ............................... | 22,000 |
| Income tax expense (not including extraordinary item) .................... | ? |

Assume an average 40% corporate income tax rate on all items.

*Required:*
1. Prepare a schedule of cost of goods manufactured to supplement the income statement.
2. Prepare a single-step income statement including EPS. Assume 20,000 shares of common stock outstanding.
3. Prepare a multiple-step income statement including EPS.
4. Discuss the relative merits and disadvantages of each format.

## Problem 4–5

The following pretax amounts were taken from the adjusted trial balance of Mason Company at December 31, 1976:

| | |
|---|---:|
| Revenues | $600,000 |
| Expenses | 480,000 |
| Extraordinary item, loss (pretax) | 30,000 |
| Prior period adjustment, gain (pretax) | 15,000 |
| Beginning balance, retained earnings | 55,000 |
| Dividends paid | 10,000 |

Common stock outstanding, 5,000 shares.

*Required:*

1. Prepare a single-step income statement and a statement of retained earnings with intraperiod tax allocation and EPS. Assume an average corporate income tax rate of 41.81% on all items.
2. Use the same data to complete the above requirement except assume a tax rate of 22% on the first $25,000 of income and 48% on all income above that amount (for all items). Compute intraperiod tax allocation in the following order: operating income, extraordinary items, and prior period adjustments (including EPS).
3. Give the entry to record income tax expense and income taxes payable under both requirements 1 and 2.
4. Assess the different results between 1 and 2.


## Problem 4–6

The following pretax amounts were taken from the adjusted trial balance of Thyme Corporation at December 31, 1976:

| | |
|---|---:|
| Balance retained earnings, January 1, 1976 | $ 48,000 |
| Sales revenue (net of return sales) | 200,000 |
| Cost of goods sold | 110,000 |
| Distribution expenses | 75,000 |
| Administration expenses | 25,000 |
| Extraordinary item, gain (pretax) | 30,000 |
| Prior period adjustment, gain (pretax) | 5,000 |
| Dividends | 6,000 |

Common stock outstanding, 10,000 shares.

Assume an average 30% corporate income tax rate on all items.

*Required:*

1. Prepare a single-step income statement and a statement of retained earnings with intraperiod tax allocation and EPS.
2. Assume net sales were $220,000 and that the prior period adjustment was a loss; all other amounts are the same as given. Prepare a single-step income statement and statement of retained earnings with intraperiod tax allocation and EPS.
3. Give the entry to record income taxes payable (assume none yet paid) for 1 and 2.


## Problem 4–7

The following pretax amounts were taken from the adjusted trial balances of Walden Corporation at December 31, 1975, and 1976:

|  | 1976 | 1975 |
|---|---|---|
| Sales and service revenue | $200,000 | $170,000 |
| Cost of goods sold | 80,000 | 70,000 |
| Operating expenses | 67,000 | 58,000 |
| Extraordinary item, major casualty loss (pretax) | 15,000 | -0- |
| Prior period adjustment, refund from 1971 income taxes... |  | 10,000 |
| Prior period adjustment, a loss (pretax) | 20,000 |  |
| Cash dividends | 36,000 | 4,000 |
| Stock dividends (July 1, 1975, see below) |  | 120,000* |
| Balance, retained earnings, January 1, 1975 |  | 160,000 |

Common stock (par $10) shares outstanding:

| | |
|---|---|
| January 1, 1975 | 15,000 |
| Stock dividends, July 1, 1975 | 5,000 |
| December 31, 1975 | 20,000 |
| October 1, 1976 sold and issued | 10,000 |
| December 31, 1976 | 30,000 |

* Amount debited to retained earnings.

Assume an average 40% corporate income tax rate on all items, including the casualty and prior period adjustment losses.

*Required:*

1. Prepare a comparative income statement, using single-step format, with columns for 1976 and 1975. Include earnings per share and intraperiod tax allocation. Show computations.
2. Prepare a comparative statement of retained earnings with columns for 1976 and 1975.
3. Give the entry for income taxes at the end of 1976; assume all 1975 taxes have been paid.

## Problem 4–8

The following pretax amounts were taken from the adjusted trial balances of Myers Corporation at December 31, 1975, and 1976:

|  | 1976 | 1975 |
|---|---|---|
| Sales revenue | $360,000 | $340,000 |
| Cost of goods sold | 190,000 | 175,000 |
| Distribution expenses | 70,000 | 64,000 |
| Administrative expenses | 54,000 | 51,000 |
| Extraordinary items (pretax): |  |  |
| Loss from major casualty | 20,000 |  |
| Gain from expropriation of plant by foreign government |  | 16,000 |
| Prior period adjustments (pretax): |  |  |
| Damages collected from lawsuit | 38,000 |  |
| Additional income taxes assessed on 1970 return |  | 9,000 |
| Dividends: |  |  |
| Common stock dividend (10,000 shares) |  | 150,000* |
| Cash | 5,000 | 4,000 |
| Balance retained earnings, January 1, 1975 |  | 275,000 |

Common stock outstanding (par $10):          *Shares*
   January 1, 1975 .........................................20,000
   July 1, 1975, common stock dividend ...........10,000
   December 31, 1975.....................................30,000
   July 1, 1976, sold and issued ...................... 6,000
   December 31, 1976....................................36,000
   *Amount debited to retained earnings.

Assume an average 40% corporate income tax rate on all items (including the casualty loss, expropriation, and damages).

*Required:*

1. Prepare a comparative income statement, using single-step format, with columns for 1976 and 1975. Include earnings per share and intraperiod tax allocation. Show computations.
2. Prepare a comparative statement of retained earnings with columns for 1976 and 1975.
3. Give the entry for income taxes at the end of 1976; assume all 1975 taxes and the 1970 assessment have been paid.

## Problem 4–9

Presented below are the comparative statements of consolidated income and retained earnings of the Sureal Corporation for the years ended December 31, 1975, and 1976, as prepared by the corporation's president.

SUREAL CORPORATION
Statements of Consolidated Income and Retained Earnings
Years Ended December 31

| | *1976* | *1975* |
|---|---|---|
| Revenues: | | |
| Sales......................................................................$275,000 | | $233,000 |
| Investment revenue .................................................... 10,000 | | 7,500 |
| Gain on sale of fixed assets (ordinary) .......................... | | 10,000 |
| Refund of income taxes from 1973 .............................. 13,750 | | |
|    Total Revenues ................................................ 298,750 | | 250,500 |
| Expenses: | | |
| Cost of goods sold ................................................. 115,000 | | 102,000 |
| Depreciation ............................................................ 17,000 | | 15,000 |
| Distribution expenses ............................................... 45,000 | | 49,000 |
| General and administrative expenses........................... 57,000 | | 54,000 |
| Loss on destruction of plant (assume extraordinary) ...... 12,000 | | |
| Interest expense ...................................................... 8,000 | | |
| Federal income tax expense ...................................... 15,500 | | 13,250 |
|    Total Expenses ............................................... 269,500 | | 233,250 |
| Net Income .............................................................$ 29,250 | | $ 17,250 |
| | | |
| Retained earnings, January 1 .....................................$ 14,225 | | $ 4,975 |
| Add net income........................................................ 29,250 | | 17,250 |
|    Total ............................................................... 43,475 | | 22,225 |
| Deduct cash dividends ............................................. 12,000 | | 8,000 |
| Retained Earnings, December 31..................................$ 31,475 | | $ 14,225 |

Assume the income tax amount is correct; the loss on destruction of plant is given net of tax. Assume the average number of shares of common stock outstanding were: 1975, 15,000; 1976, 18,000.

*Required:*

Recast the above combined statement of income (use a modified single-step format) and retained earnings. Make it complete in every respect. Comment on any doubtful items as well as preferred alternatives you selected. Include earnings per share.

### Problem 4-10

Brown Corporation is undergoing the annual audit by the independent CPA at December 31, 1976. During the audit, the following situations were found that needed attention:

*a.* Near the end of 1974, an asset that cost $1,200 was debited to operating expenses. The asset has a six-year estimated life and no residual value. The company uses straight-line depreciation.

*b.* During 1976 the company constructed a small warehouse using their own employees. The cost was $10,000. However, before the decision to build it themselves was made, they solicited a bid from a contractor; the bid was $15,000. Upon completion of the warehouse, they made the following entry in the accounts:

| | | |
|---|---|---|
| Warehouse (a fixed asset) ................................................15,000 | | |
| Cash......................................................................... | 10,000 | |
| Miscellaneous revenue ........................................... | 5,000 | |

*c.* Prior to recording depreciation expense for 1976, the management decided that a large machine that cost $128,000 should have been depreciated over a useful life of 16 years instead of 20 years. The machine was acquired January 2, 1971. Assume the residual value of $8,000 was not changed.

*d.* During December 1976 the company disposed of an old machine for $6,000 cash. Annual depreciation was $2,000 per year; at the beginning of 1976 the accounts reflect the following:

| | |
|---|---|
| Machine (cost) .......................................................$18,000 | |
| Accumulated depreciation ......................................... 13,000 | |

At date of disposal, the following entry was made:

| | |
|---|---|
| Cash ......................................................................$6,000 | |
| Machine ................................................................. | 6,000 |

*e.* A patent that cost $3,400 is being amortized over its legal life of 17 years at $200 per year. At the end of 1975, it had been amortized down to $800. At the end of 1976, it was determined, realistically, in view of a competitor's patent, that it will have no economic value to the company by the end of 1977. Straight-line amortization is used.

*Required:*

For each of the above situations, explain what should be done in the accounts. If a journal entry is needed to implement your decision in each case, provide it along with supporting computations.

## Problem 4–11

The following pretax amounts were taken from the accounts of Heinz Corporation at December 31, 1976:

| | |
|---|---:|
| Sales revenue | $540,000 |
| Cost of goods sold | 280,000 |
| Distribution expenses | 105,000 |
| Administration expenses | 70,000 |
| Interest revenue | 1,000 |
| Interest expense | 3,000 |
| Unusual item—gain on sale of major fixed asset | 19,000 |
| Extraordinary item—loss on expropriation of foreign plant (pretax) | 30,000 |
| Balance retained earnings, January 1, 1976 | 93,000 |
| Cash dividends | 15,000 |
| Prior period adjustment—additional taxes assessed on 1973 return | 8,000 |

Common stock (par $1), 50,000 shares outstanding.

Restriction on retained earnings amounting to $25,000 per indenture agreement on bonds payable.

Assume an average 45% corporate income tax rate on all items.

*Required:*

Prepare a combined multiple-step income statement and statement of retained earnings including tax allocation and earnings per share. Show computations.

## Problem 4–12

The following amounts were taken from the accounting records of Frumer Corporation at December 31, 1976:

| | |
|---|---:|
| Sales revenue | $240,000 |
| Service revenue | 60,000 |
| Cost of goods sold | 130,000 |
| Distribution and administrative expenses | 125,000 |
| Investment revenue | 6,000 |
| Interest expense | 4,000 |
| Infrequent item—loss on sale of long-term investment | 10,000 |
| Extraordinary item—earthquake loss (pretax) | 27,000 |
| Cash dividends | 8,000 |
| Prior period adjustment—tax refund on 1971 tax return | 12,000 |
| Balance retained earnings, January 1, 1976 | 78,000 |

Common stock (par $5), 30,000 shares outstanding.

Restriction on retained earnings, $50,000 per bond payable indenture.

Assume an average 45% corporate income tax rate on all items.

*Required:*

Prepare a combined single-step income statement and statement of retained earnings including tax allocation and earnings per share. Show computations.

**Problem 4–13**

The following financial statements have come to you for review:

BROWN PRODUCTION COMPANY
Profit and Loss Statement
December 31, 1976

Incomes:

| | | |
|---|---:|---:|
| Gross sales .............................................. | $256,800 | |
| Less: Sales returns ............................. | 5,120 | |
| Net sales ................................................ | | $251,680 |
| **Costs and expenses:** | | |
| Cost of goods sold: | | |
| Inventory, January 1 ............................... | 98,500 | |
| Purchases...............................................$132,600 | | |
| Less: Purchase returns.......................... 2,780 | 129,820 | |
| | 228,320 | |
| Inventory, December 31 .......................... | 102,300 | |
| Cost of goods sold............................... | | 126,020 |
| Gross profit ............................................. | | 125,660 |
| Operating costs: | | |
| Selling expenses..................................... | 38,000 | |
| General and administrative expenses: | | |
| General expenses .............................. 20,000 | | |
| Depreciation........................................ 8,800 | | |
| Bad debt expense .............................. 1,080 | 29,880 | |
| Total Operating Costs ........................ | | 67,880 |
| Income from operations ............................ | | 57,780 |
| Other income: | | |
| Interest income ...................................... | | 970 |
| Profit before federal income taxes ............... | | 58,750 |
| Less: Federal income taxes....................... | | 28,720 |
| Net Profit ................................................ | | $ 30,030 |

BROWN PRODUCTION COMPANY
Statement of Earned Surplus
December 31, 1976

| | | |
|---|---:|---:|
| Balance, January 1....................................... | | $287,600 |
| Corrections: | | |
| Additions: | | |
| Depreciation overstated ......................... | | 3,400 |
| Adjusted balance................................... | | 271,000 |
| Additions during current year: | | |
| Profit ........................................................$30,030 | | |
| Gain on sale of land .............................. 8,200 | | 38,230 |
| | | 309,230 |
| Deductions: | | |
| Dividends ............................................ 30,000 | | |
| Loss on sale of machinery ...................... 9,650 | | 39,650 |
| Earned Surplus Balance, December 31, 1976 (carried | | |
| to the balance sheet) ............................................ | | $269,580 |

*Required:*

Critically evaluate the above statements. What reporting concept appears to have been applied? Cite items to support your response. List and explain all of the aspects of the above statements that you would change in order to conform to appropriate reporting and terminology currently.

## Problem 4-14

The following income statement and statement of retained earnings were prepared by the bookkeeper for the Snow Corporation:

SNOW CORPORATION
Profit and Loss Statement
December 31, 1976

| | | |
|---|--:|--:|
| Sales income (net) | | $ 85,000 |
| Service income | | 46,000 |
| Total | | 131,000 |
| Cost of sales: | | |
| Inventory | $ 34,000 | |
| Purchases (net) | 71,000 | |
| Total | 105,000 | |
| Inventory | 40,000 | 65,000 |
| Gross profit on sales | | 66,000 |
| Expenses: | | |
| Salaries, wages etc. | 36,000 | |
| Depreciation and write-offs | 7,000 | |
| Rent | 3,000 | |
| Taxes | 500 | |
| Utilities | 2,100 | |
| Promotion | 900 | |
| Sundry | 6,700 | (55,200) |
| Special items: | | |
| Gain on asset sold | | 6,000 |
| Inventory theft | | (2,800) |
| Net Profit | | $ 14,000 |

SNOW CORPORATION
Earned Surplus Statement
December 31, 1976

| | | |
|---|--:|--:|
| Balance, December 31, 1975, earned surplus | | $27,000 |
| Add: Profit | | 14,000 |
| Correction of inventory error | | 5,000 |
| Total | | 46,000 |
| Deduct: Fire loss | $13,000 | |
| Dividends | 10,000 | |
| Earned surplus transferred to capital | 5,000 | 28,000 |
| Balance, December 31, 1976, Earned Surplus | | $18,000 |

*Required:*

List all aspects of the above statements that you consider to be wrong. Give your recommendations on each item.

**Problem 4–15**

The Appendix to this chapter gives an actual income statement and a statement of retained earnings. Examine them carefully and respond to the following questions:

a. Are they comparative statements? Explain.    *yes*
b. Are they consolidated statements? What do you understand this to mean?    *yes*
c. Is the income statement in single-step or multiple-step format? Explain any variations in format from those illustrated in this chapter. What title was used for the income statement?    *Consol. Statement of Income*
d. Is the combined income statement and statement of retained earnings used?    *no*
e. How many different kinds of revenue are reported? How many different kinds of expenses are reported?    *2     2*
f. Is this a trading or a manufacturing company? Explain.    *B.S. Points to W.P*
g. How is interest expense and interest revenue reported?    *in total, Separately*
h. Is the total amount of depreciation expense reported? How?    *total*
i. Are there any unusual or infrequently occurring (but not both) items reported? How?    *Provision for Insurance*
j. Is a discontinuance of a segment of the business reported? How? Is it net of tax?
k. Are any extraordinary items reported? What are they? Are they net of tax?
l. How are the expenses classified?
m. How are the revenues classified?
n. Was income taxes allocated? Explain.
o. How many earnings per share amounts were reported for the last year? Was there any explanation of the computation of EPS?
p. What "differences" were reported? Gross margin? Income from continuing operations? Income before extraordinary items? Net income? Others (list)?
q. What was the profit margin (net income divided by sales) for the last year?
r. List all unusual features of the income statement. What aspects of it would you criticize? Explain.
s. What title was used on the statement of retained earnings?
t. Were any prior period adjustments reported? Explain each. Were they net of tax?
u. Do you agree with their classification as prior period adjustments? Explain.
v. Were any dividends reported? What kind?
w. Did the auditor's report express any reservations about the income statement? Explain.
x. How many notes to the financial statements referred to the income statement? List the principal point at issue in each note. Overall, did the notes satisfy your full-disclosure expectations? Explain.
y. Were there any unusual features in the statement of retained earnings? Explain. What aspects of it would you criticize? Explain.
z. Overall, do you believe these two statements could be improved with respect to format and terminology? Explain each change that you would suggest for consideration.

**Problem 4–16**

The Appendix to Chapter 5 gives an actual income statement and statement of retained earnings. Examine them carefully and respond to the questions posed in Problem 4–15.

### Problem 4–17

Obtain an audited financial statement for the latest year for a company of your choice (from the library or other source) and use it as a basis for responding to each of the questions posed in Problem 4–15.

### Problem 4–18

The following income statement was developed by Hypothetical Company. It is unusual because all of the subclassifications of items are included.

HYPOTHETICAL COMPANY
Income Statement
For the Year Ended December 31, 1976

| | | | |
|---|---|---|---|
| Sales | | | $980,000 |
| Cost of goods sold | | | 420,000 |
| Gross margin | | | 560,000 |
| Operating expenses: | | | |
|   Distribution | $252,000 | | |
|   General and administrative | 78,000 | $330,000 | |
| Other revenue and expenses: | | | |
|   Interest expense | 7,000 | | |
|   Interest revenue | 3,000 | 4,000 | |
| Unusual or infrequent gains and losses: | | | |
|   Gain on sale of investment | 21,500 | | |
|   Losses from storm damage | 7,500 | (14,000) | |
|     Total Operating Expenses and | | | |
|     Unusual or Infrequent Items | | 320,000 | |
| Pretax income from continuing operations | | | |
|   and other items | | 240,000 | |
| Income taxes (46% average rate) | | 110,400 | |
| Income from continuing operations | | | |
|   and other items | | 129,600 | |
| Discontinuance of a segment of | | | |
|   the business (loss) | 60,000 | | |
|   Less: Income tax savings (46%) | 27,600 | 32,400 | |
| Income before extraordinary item | | 97,200 | |
| Extraordinary item: | | | |
|   Loss from earthquake | 40,000 | | |
|   Less: Income tax savings (46%) | 18,400 | 21,600 | |
| Net Income | | $ 75,600 | |

Earnings per share (50,000 shares common stock outstanding):
  Income before extraordinary item ($97,200 ÷ 50,000 shares) ...........$1.94
  Extraordinary item (loss) ($21,600 ÷ 50,000 shares) ....................... (0.43)
  Net income ($75,600 ÷ 50,000 shares) ...........................................$1.51

Entry for income taxes:
  Income tax expense ......................................................64,400
      Income taxes payable ($110,400 − $27,600 − $18,400 =
      $64,400)............................................................... 64,400

*Required:*

Critically review the format and captions used from the viewpoint of the statement user. Redraft the statement using the format and captions you believe should be used. Comment on any particular items you encounter.

# Chapter *5*

## Review — The Balance Sheet and Statement of Changes in Financial Position

The preceding chapter reviewed the income statement and statement of retained earnings. This chapter will review the two remaining statements required by generally accepted accounting principles—the balance sheet and the statement of changes in financial position. The relationships between the required statements were graphically presented in Exhibit 4–1. In Part A, we will discuss the balance sheet; and in Part B, the statement of changes in financial position.

### PART A—BALANCE SHEET

A balance sheet presents the assets, liabilities, and owners' equity of an enterprise, at a specific date, measured in conformity with generally accepted accounting principles. Because it is a presentation of the current *financial position* of an entity, it is often referred to as the *statement of financial position*. The designation, balance sheet, was adopted during the period when accounting first evolved; it refers to the fact that it balances in terms of the fundamental accounting model: Assets = Liabilities + Owners' Equity. It is unfortunate that this nondescriptive designation continues to be widely used today. Because of wide usage, we use it in this text, although reluctantly.

### CHARACTERISTICS OF THE BALANCE SHEET

The financial position of an enterprise is represented by the various assets owned, obligations owed, and claims of the owners at a designated date. For example, a balance sheet should be dated "At December 31, 19XX," in contrast with an income statement, which is dated "For the Year Ended December 31, 19XX." In APB *Statement No. 4*, financial position is defined as:

The *financial position* of an enterprise at a particular time comprises its assets, liabilities, and owners' equity and the relationship among them, plus contingencies, commitments, and other financial matters that pertain to the enterprise at that time. The financial position of an enterprise is presented in the *balance sheet* and in notes to the financial statements.[1]

Fundamentally a balance sheet reports (*a*) a listing of the assets, liabilities, and components of owners' equity; and (*b*) a quantitative measurement (valuation) of each item listed. First, let's look at the definitions of the three categories reported.

## Assets Defined

Assets can be defined at both a conceptual and a pragmatic level. At the conceptual level, two representative definitions are:

Assets are economic resources devoted to business purposes within a specific accounting entity; they are aggregates of service-potentials available for or beneficial to expected operations.[2]

Assets represent expected future economic benefits, rights to which have been acquired by the enterprise as a result of some current or past transaction.[3]

Hendricksen observes that these basic definitions require the following characteristics:

1. There must exist some specific right to future benefits or service potentials.
2. The rights must accrue to a specific individual or firm.
3. There must be a legally enforceable claim to the rights or services.[4]

In contrast, APB *Statement No. 4* provides a pragmatic definition that focuses on current accounting practice, viz:[5]

*Assets*—economic resources of an enterprise that are recognized and measured in conformity with generally accepted accounting principles. Assets also include certain deferred charges that are not resources but that are recognized and measured in conformity with generally accepted accounting principles.[6]

This definition defines assets in terms of generally accepted accounting principles; this approach has been subjected to criticism because of the implicit circularity.

---

[1] AICPA, "Basic Concepts and Accounting Principles Underlying Financial Statements," *Statement of the Accounting Principles Board No. 4* (New York, October 1970), pp. 49–50.

[2] AAA Committee on Accounting Concepts and Standards, *Accounting and Reporting Standards for Corporate Financial Statements and Preceding Statements and Supplements* (Columbus, Ohio, 1957), p. 3.

[3] Robert T Sprouse and Maurice Moonitz, "A Tentative Set of Broad Accounting Principles for Business Enterprises," *Accounting Research Study No. 3* (New York: AICPA, 1962), p. 20.

[4] Eldon S. Hendricksen, *Accounting Theory* (Homewood, Ill.: Richard D. Irwin, Inc., 1970), p. 253.

[5] AICPA, APB *Statement No. 4,* pp. 49–50.

[6] Deferred charges that are not resources include items such as "charges from income tax allocation." See also Chapter 11.

## Liabilities Defined

Liabilities may be conceptually defined as "obligations to convey assets or perform services, obligations resulting from past or current transactions and requiring settlement in the future."[7] APB *Statement No. 4* provides the following pragmatic definition that reflects current practice:

> *Liabilities* — economic obligations of an enterprise that are recognized and measured in conformity with generally accepted accounting principles. Liabilities also include certain deferred credits that are not obligations but that are recognized and measured in conformity with generally accepted accounting principles.[8]

## Owners' Equity Defined

Owners' equity is defined as the amount of the interest of the owners of an enterprise; it is the excess of the assets over the liabilities. It is also referred to as the *residual interest*. The owners' equity section of the balance sheet reports the various *sources* of capital provided by owners; that is, the amount of resources provided by owners (contributed capital) and the amount of internally generated resources retained by the entity (retained earnings).

## MEASUREMENTS (VALUATIONS) ON THE BALANCE SHEET

*Assets* as measured on the balance sheet rarely represent their market value at the date of the balance sheet. Rather, the assets are measured at what is often called *book value*. Book value is the result of applying the cost and matching principles (with certain exceptions); generally, it is acquisition cost less accumulated write-offs to date. Cash is reported at its current value, accounts receivable at expected net realizable value (amount of the receivables less the allowance for doubtful accounts), inventories and marketable equity securities usually are reported at lower of cost or market, and plant and equipment are reported at cost less accumulated depreciation.

*Liabilities* as measured on the balance sheet usually represent their current cash equivalent or discounted present value (which is generally the maturity amount of the debt).

Since *owners' equity* is a residual amount, it does not report the current fair market value of the business; rather, it is a measurement of the owners' interest that reflects the measurements used for the assets and liabilities, as determined in accordance with generally accepted accounting principles.

Throughout the remaining chapters of this book, we will identify and apply the accounting concepts, standards, and procedures used to derive the measurements that are reported on the financial statements of an enterprise.

---

[7] Sprouse and Moonitz, *Accounting Research Study No. 3*, p. 37.

[8] AICPA, APB *Statement No. 4*, pp. 49–50.

## IMPORTANCE OF THE BALANCE SHEET

The balance sheet generally is viewed as of less significance to decision-makers than the income statement. Nevertheless, sophisticated decision-makers consider each part of the overall financial statement essential to gaining a balanced view. This includes the income statement, balance sheet, statement of changes in financial position, supporting schedules, notes to the statements, and the auditor's report. To single out one of these parts for exclusive use often results in inadequate information and serious oversights. Regardless of what may be reported on a single statement, the *opinion* of the independent CPA (i.e., the auditor) is overriding. Similarly, the notes may report the single most important issue with respect to a particular decision. Because of the complexity of most enterprises and the varied economic ramifications, users of financial statements should focus on the totality of the financial statements rather than upon a single amount (such as EPS) or a single report, such as the income statement.

The balance sheet, as a part of the total financial statement, is important because it tells, at a specific date, the different assets held, the obligations by type and amount, and the sources and amounts of owners' equity. The balance sheet also provides subclassifications intended to aid the user. Various balance sheet amounts often are used in conjunction with amounts from other sources (such as the income statement) to analyze relationships, trends, and so on. Examples of relevant relationships are asset turnover, ratio of debt to owners' equity, earnings per share, and return on investment. Classification of liabilities as long term and short term often aids creditors and others in assessing the ability of the entity to meet its future obligations. All decision makers are interested in these issues as well as the composition of the assets and the capital structure.

Some decision-makers believe that the balance sheet has limited usefulness because the assets are not reported at their *current fair market value*. This is a basic problem facing the accounting profession because it poses critical measurement problems. Criticism is also directed to the fact that some balance sheet amounts (and other reported amounts) involve estimates, such as accumulated depreciation. Assuming the estimates are realistic, this criticism is not well founded. Of necessity, all decision making is surrounded by uncertainty; therefore it requires extensive use of estimates. Actual historical data provide the decision-maker only with a base from which to make realistic estimates or predictions.

## BALANCE SHEET FORMAT

The reporting principle requires that a full and complete balance sheet be presented as an integral part of the periodic financial statement. Although the format of the balance sheet is not specified, one of two different formats is almost always used. The *account form* was used by approximately 71% of the 600 companies reported in the *Accounting Trends and Techniques, 1975* (AICPA). The three major categories may be positioned either horizontally or vertically (the usual arrangement), viz:[9]

**1. Account Form—Horizontal Arrangement**

|  |  |
|---|---|
| *Assets* | *Liabilities* |
| Details ........................... | Details ........................... |
|  | Total Liabilities ......$300,000 |
|  | *Owners' Equity* |
|  | Details ........................... |
|  | Total Owners' Equity. 600,000 |
|  | Total Liabilities and Owners' |
| Total Assets ........$900,000 | Equity..............$900,000 |

**2. Report Forms—Vertical Arrangement**

**Or:**

| | |
|---|---|
| *Assets* | *Assets* |
| Details ........................... | Details ........................... |
| Total Assets ...........$900,000 | Total Assets ...........$900,000 |
| *Liabilities* | *Less Liabilities* |
| Details ........................... | Details ........................... |
| Total Liabilities ......$300,000 | Total Liabilities ...... 300,000 |
| *Owners' Equity* | *Owners' Equity* |
| Details ........................... | Details ........................... |
| Total Owners' Equity. 600,000 | Total Owners' Equity.$600,000 |
| Total Liabilities and Owners' | |
| Equity..............$900,000 | |

## CLASSIFICATIONS IN THE BALANCE SHEET

To help the decision-maker in analysis, interpretation, and evaluation of the wide range of financial information reported on a balance sheet, items are usually grouped according to common characteristics. The assets tend to be grouped in decreasing order of liquidity (i.e., nearness to cash), and the liabilities by time to due date, and owners' equity in decreasing order of permanency. Classifications of information used in a balance sheet, and the array of items under each classification, are influenced by the industry and type and size of the enterprise. For example, the balance sheet of a financial institution, such as a bank, will reflect quite different classifications than those for a manufacturing company. Variations in format and classification observed in actual statements generally are designed to comply with the reporting principle

---

[9] Another, the financial position format, is sometimes used. It is a vertical arrangement that shows noncurrent assets added to and noncurrent liabilities deducted from working capital to equal owners' equity.

since it specifies that reporting must be informative, fair, and not misleading. Therefore, flexibility in format and classifications is generally viewed as desirable. Nevertheless, there is a reasonable degree of uniformity. Insofar as it is feasible to generalize on balance sheet classifications, and in view of the variety of captions often used, the following classifications are representative of sound reporting practices:

*Assets*
   1. Current assets (including prepaid expenses).
   2. Investments and funds.
   3. Operational (or fixed) assets – tangible.
   4. Operational assets – intangible.
   5. Other assets.
   6. Deferred charges.

*Liabilities*
   1. Current liabilities (including short-term deferred credits).
   2. Long-term liabilities (including long-term deferred credits).

*Owners' Equity*
   1. Contributed capital:
       *a.* Capital stock.
       *b.* Contributed capital in excess of capital stock.
   2. Retained earnings.
   3. Unrealized capital increment.

Observe that the above classifications provide for the three major captions: assets, liabilities, and owners' equity. Under each major caption are several subclassifications, the designations of which tend to vary as explained above. Observe that we have included *deferred credits* in liabilities (some are current; others long term); however, a separate caption, "Deferred Credits," sometimes is reported between long-term liabilities and owners' equity. This poses an inconsistency since the fundamental accounting model represented by the balance sheet (Assets = Liabilities + Owners' Equity) does not include a separate category for deferred credits. Observe that *deferred charges* (i.e., long-term prepaid expenses) are included in the asset category. Following the same logic, deferred credits are properly classified as liabilities.

An illustrative balance sheet is shown in Exhibit 5–1 to supplement the discussions to follow.

## CURRENT ASSETS

Current assets are cash and other assets commonly identified as those which are *reasonably expected* to be realized in cash, or to be sold, or consumed during the *normal operating cycle* of the business or within one year from the balance sheet date, whichever is the longer. The normal operating cycle is defined as the average period of time between the expenditure of cash for goods and services and the date that those goods and services are reconverted to cash. It is the average length of time from cash expenditure, to inventory, to sale, to accounts receivable, and back to cash. For many businesses, the operating cycle is shorter than one year. However, there are certain businesses, particularly those manufacturing businesses with extended production processes, where the operating cycle extends beyond one year; examples include shipbuilding, distilleries, and logging. The length of the normal operating cycle is important to the classification of current assets when it extends beyond one year.

Current assets usually are presented on the balance sheet in order of decreasing liquidity (i.e., nearness to cash conversion). The major items comprising current assets, in order of liquidity, are: cash, short-term investments, receivables, inventories, and prepaid expenses. Items that are not current assets include: cash and claims to cash which are restricted for uses other than current operations, long-term investments, receivables which have an extended maturity date, land and natural resources, depreciable assets, and long-term prepayments of expenses.

Although the definition of current assets is reasonably clear-cut, problems are often encountered in implementation. In applying the definition of current assets, the phases "normal operating cycle" and "reasonably expected to be realized in cash" both involve judgment in application. Consequently, there is a tendency to incorrectly classify certain items as current assets because of their favorable effect on working capital. Recall that working capital is the difference between current assets and current liabilities. For example, marketable securities may be classified as a current or noncurrent asset depending upon the *stated intention* of the management as to the planned holding period. By a simple change in *intention* by the management, classification of the securities can be changed. Prepaid expenses is another area where there is considerable variation in classification. A short-term prepayment should be classified as a current asset (i.e., a prepaid expense), whereas a long-term prepayment should be classified as noncurrent (i.e., a deferred charge). Nevertheless, a three-year prepayment of an insurance premium usually is classified as a current asset, a procedure that can be justified only on the basis of materiality.

In some companies and industries, there is no basis for using a current asset category. For example, financial institutions, such as banks, do not report current assets because it would be pointless in view of the nature of their asset structure. Exhibit 5–1 illustrates how current assets should be reported. Observe the parenthetical information provided to satisfy the full-disclosure requirement.

## CURRENT LIABILITIES

The definition of current liabilities parallels the definition of current assets; that is, current liabilities are short-term liabilities "whose liquidation is reasonably expected to require the use of existing resources properly classified as current assets, or the creation of other liabilities."[10]

---

[10] AICPA, *Accounting Research and Terminology Bulletins, Final Edition,* (New York, 1961), p. 21.

**EXHIBIT 5–1**

AB CORPORATION
Statement of Financial Position (i.e., Balance Sheet)
At December 31, 1976

*Assets*

Current Assets:

| | | |
|---|---:|---:|
| Cash | | $ 34,000 |
| Short-term investments (current market value $21,000) | | 20,000 |
| Accounts receivable (trade) | $ 43,100 | |
| Less: Allowance for doubtful accounts | 1,300 | 41,800 |
| Merchandise inventory (*Fifo,* lower of cost or market) | | 120,000 |
| Prepaid expenses: | | |
| Supplies inventory | | 1,200 |
| Prepaid insurance | | 3,000 |
| Total Current Assets | | 220,000 |

Investments and Funds:

| | | |
|---|---:|---:|
| Investment in bonds of X Corporation (at cost) | 30,000 | |
| Investment in stock of Y Corporation (equity basis) | 70,000 | |
| Plant expansion fund | 50,000 | |
| Total Investments and Funds | | 150,000 |

Land, Building, and Equipment:

| | | | |
|---|---:|---:|---:|
| Land | | | 24,000 |
| Building | $200,000 | | |
| Less: Accumulated depreciation (straight line) | 80,000 | 120,000 | |
| Equipment and fixtures | 140,000 | | |
| Less: Accumulated depreciation (straight line) | 56,000 | 84,000 | |
| Total Land, Building and Equipment | | | 228,000 |

Intangible Assets:

| | | |
|---|---:|---:|
| Patent (cost, $17,000, less accumulated amortization, $8,000) | 9,000 | |
| Franchise (cost, $30,000, less accumulated amortization, $14,000) | 16,000 | |
| Total Intangible Assets | | 25,000 |

Other Assets:

| | |
|---|---:|
| Land held for future building site | 37,000 |

Deferred Charges:

| | |
|---|---:|
| Rearrangement costs | 8,000 |
| Total Assets | $668,000 |

Current liabilities include the following short-term items:

1. Accounts payable for goods and services that enter into the operating cycle of the business.
2. Special payables for nonoperating items and services.
3. Short-term notes payable.
4. Collections in advance for unearned revenue (such as rent revenue collected in advance).
5. Accrued expenses for wages, salaries, commissions, rentals, royalties, income, and other taxes.
6. Other obligations to be paid out of current assets such as serial maturities of long-term debts.

**EXHIBIT 5–1** *(continued)*

*Liabilities*

Current Liabilities:

| | |
|---|---:|
| Accounts payable (trade) ......................................... | $ 43,700 |
| Notes payable ..................................................... | 20,000 |
| Rent revenue collected in advance............................ | 1,800 |
| Accrued wages payable ........................................... | 2,000 |
| Current payment on long-term note .......................... | 20,000 |
| Income taxes payable.............................................. | 12,500 |
| Total Current Liabilities ..................................... | 100,000 |

Long-Term Liabilities:

| | | |
|---|---:|---:|
| Note payable, 9%, due 1977–78 ...............................$ 40,000 | | |
| Less 1977 current payment ................................... 20,000 | $ 20,000 | |
| Bonds payable, 6%, due 1985 ................................. 150,000 | | |
| Less unamortized discount ................................... 4,000 | 146,000 | |
| Total Long-Term Liabilities ............................. | | 166,000 |
| Total Liabilities .............................................. | | 266,000 |

*Stockholders' Equity*

Contributed Capital:

| | | |
|---|---:|---:|
| Preferred stock, 6% cumulative, nonparticipating, authorized 20,000 shares, par $10, issued and outstanding 5,000 shares ................................... | 50,000 | |
| Common stock, nopar, authorized 100,000 shares, issued and outstanding 75,000 shares .................. | 225,000 | |
| Total Stated Capital......................................... | 275,000 | |
| Additional contributed capital: | | |
| In excess of par value of preferred stock .................. | 45,000 | |
| Total Contributed Capital ............................... | 320,000 | |
| Retained earnings (Note A) ...................................... | 82,000 | |
| Total Stockholders' Equity................................ | | 402,000 |
| Total Liabilities and Stockholders' Equity......... | | $668,000 |

Note A. Under the terms of the bond indenture, an amount of retained earnings, determined by a formula, is restricted from dividend availability. The formula, computed for 1976, restricts retained earnings in the amount of $56,000. This amount will be increased each year as provided by the bond indenture formula. When the bonds are retired, the restriction will be automatically removed.

Items not properly classified as current liabilities include long-term notes, bonds, and obligations that will not be paid out of current assets. For example, a bond issue due during the coming year would not be classified as a current liability if it is to be paid out of a special cash fund classified under the caption "Investments and Funds." Similarly, a currently maturing bond issue that is to be refunded (i.e., paid off by issuing a new series of bonds) should not be classified as a current liability as specified in FASB *Statement Nos. 6 and 12.*

## WORKING CAPITAL

Working capital is defined as current assets minus current liabilities. Because it is an abstract concept, this does not define working capital; it simply tells how it is computed. If all of the current assets were converted to cash at their *book value* and all of the current liabilities paid, it would be the amount of cash remaining. Although the concept of working capital is widely used by accountants and security analysts, many investors have problems with it because of the abstraction. They understand cash, as it is definable and circulates freely; in contrast, no one ever handles, receives, or pays "working capital" as such. It is for this reason that many investors are more concerned with the items that comprise current assets and current liabilities than with the abstract difference between two opposites. A company may well report an excellent working capital position and at the same time have a serious cash deficiency. For these and other reasons, many accountants believe that cash flow statements are significantly more informative than are working capital statements (see Part B in this Chapter).

Nevertheless, the amount of working capital and the working capital ratio is widely viewed as a measure of liquidity; that is, the ability of the enterprise to meet its short-term obligations. To illustrate, AB Corporation, Exhibit 5–1, reported the following:

```
Current assets ............................................................................$220,000
Current liabilities...........................................................................  100,000
Difference—Working Capital  ....................................................$120,000
```

The amount of working capital is $120,000; and the working capital, or current, ratio is: $220,000 ÷ $100,000 = 2.2. The ratio indicates that the current assets are 2.2 times the current liabilities, or that for each $1 of current liabilities there is $2.20 in current assets. Because of the tendency of creditors and security analysts to view working capital as an index of liquidity, the independent auditor sometimes encounters attempts to misclassify some assets as current and some liabilities as noncurrent in order to report a better working capital position than actually exists.

Offsetting of current assets and liabilities is improper because this practice avoids full-disclosure and would permit a business to show a more favorable current ratio than actually exists. For example, a business whose current assets consist of cash of $20,000 and receivables of $25,000 and currently owing notes payable of $10,000 and accounts payable of $5,000 has a current ratio of 3 to 1. If the intent to use $10,000 of the cash to pay the notes is reflected in the balance sheet by offsetting, the current ratio would rise to 7 to 1. Offsetting is permissible only where a legal right of offset exists; thus, it would be proper to offset a $5,000 overdraft in one account with a bank against another account reflecting $8,000 on deposit in that same bank. Offsetting the two amounts where two different banks are involved is unacceptable.

## INVESTMENTS AND FUNDS

This caption is often labeled "Investments." It includes noncurrent assets, other than the operating assets, acquired for their financial or investment advantage, and funds set aside for future purposes. Items reported under this caption are long-term commitments; they include:

1. Long-term investments in securities, such as stocks, bonds, and long-term notes.
2. Investments in subsidiaries including long-term advances.
3. Long-term investments in tangible assets such as land and buildings which are not used in current operations.
4. Funds set aside for long-term future use such as bond sinking funds (to retire bonds payable), expansion funds, stock retirement funds, and long-term savings deposits.
5. Cash surrender value of life insurance policies.

The important distinctions are that the items (a) are nonoperational, and (b) management plans their long-term retention. The fact that an investment is currently marketable does not prevent its inclusion under this caption. Exhibit 5–1 illustrates typical reporting of this category of assets.

## OPERATIONAL ASSETS

Operational assets are defined as those assets used in carrying out the operations of the entity. Operational assets are distinguished from stock in trade (i.e., inventories of raw materials, work in process, finished goods, merchandise, and supplies). Historically, operational assets have been labeled as *fixed assets* because of their relative permanence or long-term nature. Operational assets are subclassified as follows:

1. Tangible – Those characterized by physical existence such as land, buildings, machinery, equipment, furniture, fixtures, tools, containers, and natural resources.
2. Intangible – Those having no physical existence but having value because of the rights their ownership confers. Examples are patents, copyrights, trademarks, brand names, leaseholds, formulas, processes, and goodwill.

### Operational Assets – Tangible

This group of operational assets is separately reported on the balance sheet under various captions depending upon the type of business. Manufacturing enterprises generally use captions such as *property, plant, and equipment;* and other enterprises use captions such as *property and equipment,* or simply *property.* Companies seldom use the older caption, *fixed assets.*

Tangible operational assets include items that are not subject to depreciation (land) and depreciable items, such as buildings, machinery, and fixtures. Land should be reported separately from depreciable assets. *APB Opinion No. 12* requires that the balance sheet report (a) balances of major classes of depreciable assets by nature or function; (b) accumulated depreciation, either by major classes of depreciable assets or in total; and (c) a general description of the methods used in computing depreciation for the major classes of operational assets. The word "reserve" should not be used to refer to accumulated depreciation. Exhibit 5-1 illustrates appropriate reporting of tangible operational assets.

### Operational Assets – Intangible

This classification (assets having no physical existence) is separately reported on the balance sheet under the title *intangible assets*. Major items should be separately listed; and the accumulated amount of amortization, if material in amount, should be disclosed. Seldom is the contra account, accumulated amortization, separately listed; this contrasts with the usual treatment given tangible operational assets (see Exhibit 5-1).

## OTHER ASSETS

"Other assets" are those which cannot be reasonably categorized under the usual asset classifications. Examples include cash in closed banks, stock subscriptions receivable (when demand for payment will not be made in the near future), and idle operational assets. Items should be analyzed carefully before being reported as other assets because often there is a logical basis for classifying them elsewhere. Items such as deferred strike losses and flood losses intended to be written off in time are sometimes reported as other assets. This treatment is unsupportable inasmuch as there is no element of future benefit associated with such losses; hence, there is no asset value.

## DEFERRED CHARGES

Deferred charges represent debit balances derived from expenditures not recognized as costs of operations of current or prior periods but involving a future benefit, and hence they are carried forward to be matched with future revenues. The everyday meaning of deferred is *delayed*, and charge is synonymous with *debit*; hence, these "delayed debits" have been held for matching against future revenues. Deferred charges are distinguished from prepaid expenses on the basis of the *time* over which they will be amortized; that is, they involve a longer period of time than do prepaid expenses. The following accounts typify those found under the "Deferred Charges" caption: Machinery Rearrangement Costs, Taxes (especially in connection with tax deferments such as discussed in Chapter 11), Organization Costs (alternatively shown under "intangibles"), Pension Costs Paid in Advance and Insurance Prepayments (long-term prepayments not classed as current), and start-up costs.

## LONG-TERM LIABILITIES

A long-term liability is an obligation that will not require the use of current assets during the upcoming normal operating cycle or during the next year, whichever is longer. All liabilities not appropriately classified as current liabilities are reported under this caption. Typical long-term liabilities are bonds payable, long-term notes payable, long-term lease obligations, and the noncurrent portion of deferred income taxes.

Bonds payable should be reported at their current debt equivalent, or their present value, at the date of the balance sheet. Therefore, when reporting bonds payable, any unamortized premium should be added to the amount of the bonds and any discount should be subtracted. To illustrate:

Bonds sold at a discount:

```
Long-Term Liabilities:
Bonds payable, 6%, due 19XX .....................................$100,000
Less: Unamortized bond discount .............................   7,000    $ 93,000
```

Bonds sold at a premium:

```
Long-Term Liabilities:
Bonds payable, 6%, due 19XX .....................................$100,000
Add: Unamortized bond premium ................................   7,000    $107,000
```

## DEFERRED CREDITS

Occasionally a company will include the caption "Deferred Credits," between long-term liabilities and owners' equity. Typical deferred credits are: long-term deferred income taxes, deferred revenues (i.e., revenues collected in advance), deferred investment tax credit, and deferred foreign currency translation gains. Admittedly, these items are difficult to classify, yet use of this caption is generally discouraged because these items are liabilities or an indication of a future liability. Practically all companies report them under the liability captions. More detailed discussion of deferred credits appears in Chapter 11 (also refer to footnote 6 of this chapter).

## OWNERS' EQUITY

Owners' equity represents the residual interests in a business; it is the difference between total assets and total liabilities. For a sole proprietorship, it usually is called proprietor's equity; for a partnership, partners' equity; and for a corporation, stockholders' or shareholders' equity. Owners' equity is subclassified to reflect sources; therefore, for a corporation, the following sources are reported:

1. Contributed capital:
   a. Capital stock.
   b. Contributed capital in excess of capital stock.
2. Retained earnings.
3. Unrealized capital.

## Capital Stock

This caption reports the *source* of owners' equity as represented by the stated or legal capital of the corporation as specified legally and in the Articles of Incorporation (i.e., the Charter) of the company. This source is the amount of legal capital provided by the stockholders. Each class of stock, common and preferred, must be reported at the par, or stated amount; or in the case of nopar stock, the total amount paid in (these matters vary depending on the law of the state of incorporation). Details of each class of capital stock should be set out separately, including title of each issue; number of shares authorized, issued, outstanding, and subscribed; conversion features; callability; preferences; and any other special features.

## Contributed Capital in Excess of Capital Stock

This is often called *additional paid in capital*. It reports the amounts received by the corporation in excess of the par or stated value of the capital stock outstanding. These amounts are received when the corporation sells its stock at a premium (sometimes called premium on capital stock) and from treasury stock transactions. This topic is discussed in detail in Chapters 15–17.

## Retained Earnings

Retained earnings (formerly called earned surplus) is the accumulated earnings of a corporation less losses and dividends to date. It reports the amount of resources (from undistributed earnings) that the corporation has retained for use in operations, expansion, and growth. In most corporations, in the long term, it is the major *source* of capital. In the long term, corporations tend to distribute dividends to the stockholders equivalent to considerably less than 50% of the earnings, thus establishing a continuing source of funds for internal use. Indirectly, retained earnings represent additional investments by the stockholders since they forego dividends equal to the balance of retained earnings. A negative balance in retained earnings is usually called a *deficit*.

Not infrequently, a portion of the total amount of retained earnings is *restricted* or *appropriated*. This means that during the period of restriction, the specified amount is not available for dividends. For example, AB Corporation (Exhibit 5–1) has total retained earnings of $82,000; however, $56,000 of that amount is restricted for a specific period of time. After the restriction is removed, the $56,000 again becomes available for dividends, subject to declaration by the board of directors of the corporation. A restriction may result from a legal requirement, as in the case where state law (in which the corporation is organized) imposes a restriction equal to the cost of any treasury stock held. Such laws are designed to protect the creditors of the corporation. Or, a restriction may be contractual, as in the case where the bond indenture carries such a stipulation. This situation is illustrated in Exhibit 5–1. Finally, the board of directors may decide to arbitrarily "appropriate" a portion of retained earnings, as in the case of "retained earnings appropriated for future plant expansion."

Restrictions or appropriations may be reflected in either of two ways. A few companies make an entry in the accounts to reflect the restriction or appropriation. For example, the $56,000 restriction on retained earnings reported by AB Corporation (Exhibit 5–1) could be recorded and reported as follows:

Entry in the accounts:

```
Retained earnings ................................................56,000
    Retained earnings restricted by bond indenture  ..........................56,000
```

Reporting on the balance sheet then could be as follows:

```
Retained earnings, unappropriated...................................$26,000
Retained earnings, restricted by bond indenture..................  56,000
    Total Retained Earnings...........................................        $82,000
```

In recent years, the above approach has practically disappeared. Instead, no formal entry is made in the accounts. Restrictions and appropriations are usually disclosed in the notes to the financial statements as illustrated in Exhibit 5–1.[11] Accounting for, and reporting of, retained earnings is discussed in detail in Chapter 16.

## UNREALIZED CAPITAL

This component of owners' equity has seldom been used in the past because of some unsettled accounting issues related to fair market valuations. However, the recent issuance of FASB *Statement No. 12* (December 31, 1975) will cause it to be used more often because the statement requires recognition of the "unrealized loss or gain" resulting from the application of the concept of lower of cost or market to long-term equity investments in capital stock (not bonds) accounted for on the cost basis (see Chapter 18 for the equity basis and consolidated statements). *Statement No. 12* requires the accumulated unrealized loss be accounted for and reported separately as an unrealized element of owners' equity.

To illustrate the use of unrealized capital, we will present an application of FASB *Statement No. 12*. The statement requires that long-term (i.e., noncurrent) investments in capital stock of another company be carried and reported at lower of cost or market. An "allowance" account must be used to accomplish this effect. The statement provides that, upon sale of a long-term investment, the difference between selling price and cost is a *realized* gain or loss. In contrast, at the end of the accounting period, an adjusting entry must be made to write down the portfolio to market (if it is lower than cost) and the recognition of an *unrealized* loss or gain. The following sequence of entries are illustrative:

---

[11] AICPA, *Accounting Trends and Techniques, 1975* (New York, 1975), pp. 212, 229–34.

January 1, 19A — Acquired as a long-term investment, 1,000 shares of X
        Corporation common stock @ $20.

Long-term investment, common stock, X Corp., (1,000
    shares) .................................................................... 20,000
        Cash ................................................................ 20,000

December 31, 19A — Adjusting entry to lower of cost or market ($15).

Unrealized loss on long-term investments in equity securities
    [1,000 × ($20 − $15)] .................................................... 5,000
        Allowance to reduce long-term investments in equity
            securities to market ............................................. 5,000

September 1, 19B — Sold 100 shares of X Corporation @ $18.

Cash (100 × $18)................................................................ 1,800
Realized loss on sale of long-term investment ..................... 200
    Long-term investment, common stock, X Corp. (100
        shares @ $20) ......................................................... 2,000

December 31, 19B — Adjusting entry to lower of cost or market ($19).

Allowance to reduce long-term investments in equity
    securities to market $5,000 − [900 shares × ($20 − $19)] ... 4,100
        Unrealized gain on long-term investments in equity
            securities .......................................................... 4,100

The financial statements for 19A and 19B would reflect the following:

|  | 19A | | 19B | |
|---|---|---|---|---|
| Income Statement: | | | | |
| Realized loss on sale of long-term investments ..................... | | | | $ 200 |
| Balance Sheet: | | | | |
| Funds and investments: | | | | |
| Investment, Common stock, X Corp., at cost ......................... | $20,000 | | $18,000 | |
| Less: Allowance to reduce to lower of cost or market ............ | 5,000 | $15,000 | 900 | $17,100 |
| Stockholders' Equity: | | | | |
| Unrealized capital: | | | | |
| Unrealized loss on long-term investments in equity securities............................... | | ($ 5,000) | | ($ 900) |

*Statement No. 12* specifies that should an investment in the capital
stock of another company be changed from a short-term to a long-term
investment or vice versa, the investment shall be transferred "at the
lower of its cost or market value at date of transfer and the difference
shall be accounted for as if it were a realized loss and included in the determination of net income." FASB *Statement No. 12* is discussed in
greater detail in Chapters 7 and 18.

Unrealized capital has been used in some situations to accomodate
the capital arising from the writing up of fixed assets (see Chapter 13).
The above discussion should not be understood to imply that writeups of
assets to fair market value are currently in accordance with generally

accepted accounting principles. However, there are a few exceptions as explained in Chapters 7, 13 and 25.

## PART B—STATEMENT OF CHANGES IN FINANCIAL POSITION

Since the issuance of *APB Opinion No. 19* (effective September 30, 1971), a statement of changes in financial position, in addition to the income statement and balance sheet, must be included in the annual financial statement. Although it evolved from the old funds statement (which was optional), it is significantly different in a number of respects. The statement of changes in financial position reports the *financing* and *investing* activities of a business enterprise during a specified period.

It is a *change statement*, as diagrammed in Exhibit 4–1, because the financing and investing activities serve to explain the causes of the changes between the beginning and ending balance sheets other than those explained by the income statement (which is also a change statement). Thus, it is dated the same as the income statement, "For the Year Ended (date)" Exhibit 5–2 presents a statement specially designed for instructional purposes.

The financing activities are represented as *inflows of funds* into the enterprise primarily from (*a*) operations (i.e., revenues less expenses), (*b*) issuance of capital stock, (*c*) borrowing, and (*d*) sale of assets owned by the entity (such as investments and operational assets). The investing activities are *outflows of funds* from the enterprise primarily for (*a*) acquisition of assets, (*b*) retirement of debt, and (*c*) payment of dividends. Thus, the statement reports all inflows and outflows of funds.

For purposes of the statement of changes in financial position, funds usually are defined as either (1) cash equivalents (cash plus short-term or temporary investments), or (2) working capital (current assets minus current liabilities). Consequently, when a statement of changes in financial position is used, the user should be alert to identify which of these two measures of funds was used in its preparation. *APB Opinion No. 19* permits either measure but requires that the identity be specified.

The statement of changes in financial position also must be based on an *all-resources concept*. This means that *all* financing and investing activities must be incorporated in it regardless of whether funds were directly affected. The word *all* is particularly important because it requires that direct exchanges (i.e., trades) be included even though neither cash nor working capital was affected. Examples of direct exchanges are the acquisition of property and paying for it by issuing capital stock, the conversion of bonds payable to common stock, and the trading of one asset, such as a tract of land, for a machine. In direct exchanges, there often is neither an inflow nor outflow of funds (of course, some exchanges do involve a cash difference). Nevertheless, transactions of this type must be included "as if" funds equal to the fair market value actually flowed in and out. This type of transaction is illustrated in Exhibit 5–2, as it should be reported in the statement and explained in a note. At the start of the period, the company had out-

**EXHIBIT 5–2**

ILLUSTRATIVE CORPORATION
Statement of Changes in Financial Position—Cash Equivalent Basis
For the Year Ended December 31, 1976

Sources of Cash (Inflow of Funds):

From operations:

| | | |
|---|---:|---:|
| Revenues (accrual basis) .......................................$850,000 | | |
| Add (deduct) adjustments to derive cash basis: | | |
| Increase in accounts receivable (trade) .............. | (10,000) | |
| Cash generated from revenues ....................... | | $840,000 |
| Expenses (accrual basis) ....................................... | 740,000 | |
| Add (deduct) adjustments to convert to cash basis: | | |
| Depreciation expense ...................................... | (30,000) | |
| Amortization of intangibles............................... | (1,000) | |
| Inventory increase ......................................... | 28,000 | |
| Accounts payable decrease (trade) ..................... | 12,000 | |
| Income taxes payable increase .......................... | (14,000) | |
| Loss on sale of operational assets.................... | (5,000) | |
| Cash disbursed for expenses........................... | | 730,000 |
| Total Cash Generated by Operations ........... | | 110,000 |
| From extraordinary item net of income tax .................. | | 20,000 |
| From other sources: | | |
| Sale of unissued preferred stock ............................ | 45,000 | |
| Sale of operational assets ................................... | 25,000 | |
| Common stock issued to retire convertible bonds | | |
| (Note A)................................................................ | 100,000 | |
| Total Cash Generated from Other Sources ...... | | 170,000 |
| Total Cash Generated from All Sources ......... | | 300,000 |

Uses of Cash (Outflow of Funds):

| | | |
|---|---:|---:|
| Payment of cash dividends....................................... | 40,000 | |
| Payment of long-term note payable............................ | 50,000 | |
| Acquisition of operational assets .............................. | 120,000 | |
| Purchase of long-term investment, stock | | |
| of X Corporation.................................................... | 30,000 | |
| Retirement of 5%, convertible bonds payable (Note A) ... | 100,000 | |
| Total Cash Expended for All Purposes ......... | | 340,000 |
| Net Increase (Decrease) in Cash and Cash Equivalents | | |
| during the Period ................................................. | | $ (40,000) |

Notes to the financial statements:

Note A. All of the outstanding 5% convertible bonds payable tendered to the Company for conversion to nopar common stock in accordance with the conversion provision in the bond indenture. Conversion required the issuance of 10,000 shares of nopar common stock; no cash was paid or received incidental to the conversion.

standing 5% convertible bonds payable with a maturity amount of $100,000. The bonds carried a conversion agreement which permitted the bondholders to turn them in during 1975 or 1976 and receive, in return, a specified number of shares of the nopar common stock of the company. During 1976, all of the bondholders tendered their bonds and received the requisite number of shares of stock. Thus, debt was retired by the issuance of common stock (a direct exchange of noncash items). Although no cash flowed in either direction, the transaction must be reported on the statement of changes in financial position "as if" cash was received for the stock and was then disbursed to retire the bonds. Therefore, the noncash exchange is reflected both as a source of cash and a use of cash, supplemented with an explanatory note to assure full disclosure. Without the all-resources requirement, direct exchanges would not be reported in the statement, thus often omitting significant financing and investing activities.

Observe in Exhibit 5–2 that cash flows related to operations are shown separately for revenues and expenses. In contrast, actual statements usually start with the difference, net income, and then report "adjustments" to derive "total cash generated by operations." The approach illustrated in Exhibit 5–2 generally is favored for instructional purposes (and often for communication purposes) because it does not imply that depreciation and amortization is a source of cash; rather, it emphasizes that they are adjustments to derive total cash outflows required for the expenses. Also, in this format, the "adjustments" are more easily understood. The net effect is the same regardless of the approach used.

The statement of changes in financial position is not difficult to understand and interpret, especially when prepared on a cash equivalent basis as in Exhibit 5–2. However, the adjustments in the section "from operations" sometimes are not readily understood. Exhibit 5–2 reports that sales recognized, on an accrual basis, amounted to $850,000; however, since $10,000 of that amount was not collected by the end of the year, the cash inflow from sales was $840,000. Alternatively, had accounts receivables *decreased*, the $10,000 would have been added, giving a cash inflow from sales of $860,000. In a similar manner, total expenses, determined on an accrual basis, must be adjusted to a strict cash basis. Depreciation expense and amortization expense of intangibles, since they were included in total expense but did not require cash expenditure, must be *deducted* from expenses. The inventory increase is added since additional cash (above cost of goods sold) was expended for this increase. Similarly, the *decrease* in accounts payable required the expenditure of additional cash above the amount of expenses recognized on the accrual basis. The increase in income taxes payable means that less cash (i.e., $14,000) was expended for this item than the amount of income tax expense reported. The loss on sale of operational assets, although included in total expenses, does not represent cash. The amount of cash from the sale of operational assets is reported under "other sources" as $25,000.[12]

Preparation and interpretation of the statement of changes in financial position on both the cash equivalent and the working capital basis are discussed in detail in Chapter 21.

---

[12] The entry to record the disposal of the operational assets was:

| | | |
|---|---:|---:|
| Cash (sales price) | 25,000 | |
| Loss on sale of operational assets | 5,000 | |
| Operational assets (book value) | | 30,000 |

## SOME SPECIAL REPORTING ISSUES

We will conclude the review of information processing and the financial statements with a brief discussion of several special reporting issues that are commonly encountered.

### Terminology

As in all professions, accounting has its own jargon. Often the same word or phrase is used to mean different things. We commented on some of these terminology problems in Chapter 2 — concepts, assumptions, principles, standards, and procedures. In preparing reports, accountants should refrain, as much as possible, from using vague and complex terminology. Generally, less technical terms can be used to better convey the message. Captions in statements and titles of items listed should be carefully selected, particularly since the statements will be used by a wide range of decision-makers, few of whom are trained in accounting. From time to time, pronouncements, such as the *ARBs*, *APB Opinions*, and FASB *Statements*, specifically recommend improved terminology.

For example, some years ago, the term "reserve" was used by accountants to refer to (*a*) a contra asset account for accumulated depreciation, such as "reserve for depreciation"; (*b*) an estimated liability for estimated warranty liability, such as "reserve for warranties"; and (*c*) an appropriation of retained earnings, such as "reserve for future expansion." *Accounting Terminology Bulletin No. 1* recommended that the term be restricted to the latter usage. However, many accountants do not use it even in that context. Similarly, the terminology bulletin recommended use of the terms *retained earnings* instead of earned surplus and *net income* instead of net profit. *APB Statement No. 19* recommended use of the title, *statement of changes in financial position,* instead of the older title, funds flow statement. Confusion of the terms cost and expense, discussed in Chapter 4, is another example of careless terminology. Throughout later chapters we will often discuss preferred terminology since effective communication is a primary objective of accounting.

### Comparative Statements

To evaluate the financial potentials of an enterprise, one should have available financial information for two or more periods. For prediction purposes, trends are usually much more revealing than information for only one period. In recognition of this fact, *ARB No. 43* states:

> The presentation of comparative financial statements in annual and other reports enhances the usefulness of such reports and brings out more clearly the nature and trends of current changes affecting the enterprise. Such presentation emphasizes the fact that statements for a series of periods are far more significant than those for a single period and that the accounts

for one period are but an installment of what is essentially a continuous history.[13]

Comparative statements for the current and prior year are now considered essential to meet the full-disclosure requirement. Of the 600 companies analyzed in *Accounting Trends and Techniques, 1974* (AICPA), all but one presented comparative statements. The actual statements shown in the appendixes at the end of Chapters 4 and 5 display comparative amounts. In addition to comparative statements, many companies present a special tabulation of especially relevant financial items for time spans of 5 to 20 or more years. Items often included are: total revenues, income before extraordinary items, net income, depreciation expense, earnings per share, dividends, total assets, total owners' equity, number of shares outstanding, and average stock price. These long-term summaries are particularly useful to external decision-makers.

## Rounding of Amounts

All major companies round amounts in their financial statements. According to *Accounting Trends and Techniques, 1975* (AICPA), of the 600 companies surveyed, 41% rounded to the nearest dollar, 57% to the nearest thousand dollars, and 2% to the nearest million dollars; none reported cents. Amounts not rounded often suggest greater accuracy than actually exists.

## Subsequent Events

Certain important events or transactions which occur subsequent to the balance sheet date but prior to the actual issuance of the financial statements (ordinarily one to three months) and which have a material affect on the financial statements are called *subsequent events*. Subsequent events must be reported because they involve important information that would influence the statement users' interpretation and evaluation of the future potentials of the enterprise. Auditing standards define these events and specify that they must be either (a) reflected in the statements, or (b) disclosed in notes to the statements, depending upon their nature.[14]

Subsequent events should be reflected *in the statements* if they (1) provide additional evidence about conditions that existed at balance sheet date, (2) affect estimates inherent in the process of preparing the financial statements, and (c) require adjustments to the financial statements resulting from the estimates. An example would be a material loss on an uncollectible receivable because of a customer's deteriorating financial condition. The deteriorating financial condition presumably

---

[13] AICPA, "Restatement and Revision of Accounting Research Bulletins," *Accounting Research Bulletin No. 43* (New York, 1953), chap. 2, sec. A.

[14] AICPA, *Statement on Auditing Standards No. 1* (New York, 1973), pp. 123–31.

was occurring at balance sheet date but recent information made it more evident.

Those subsequent events that should be *disclosed in notes* to the statements are characterized as (*a*) conditions that did not exist at balance sheet date but (*b*) arose subsequent to the balance sheet date and do not result in adjustment to the financial statements. Examples listed in *Auditing Standard No. 47* are: sale of a bond or capital stock issue, litigation based on an event subsequent to the balance sheet date, inventory losses due to casualty, and losses on receivables due to a condition that arose subsequent to balance sheet date (such as a fire or flood). The fire or flood did not "exist" at the balance sheet date.

This topic is considered in depth in auditing texts and courses (see also footnote 5).

## Full Disclosure

Full disclosure is a particularly important concept in the *reporting principle* discussed in Chapter 2. Full disclosure requires that there be complete and understandable reporting of all significant information relating to the economic affairs of the enterprise so that the financial statements will not be misleading. Full disclosure requires, in addition to the financial information reported in the body of the financial statements, additional information in notes to the financial statements, supporting schedules, cross-references, contra items, and parenthetical explanations. The accountant must exercise judgment in deciding the way in which each significant event or transaction should be reported to meet the full-disclosure requirement.

*Notes to the financial statements* is a singularly important part of the financial report because a note is often the only feasible way of adequately explaining and elaborating on certain critical events and situations. A particular note may refer to a single amount on one of the three basic statements or to several amounts on two or more of them, or to a situation that is not directly reflected on any of them. The guideline for deciding when a note is required, other than where specifically required, is simply judgmental within the framework of complete reporting, or alternatively, misleading inferences. Notes typically are a combination of narrative elaboration, additional amounts, and supplementary tables.

A number of *APB Opinions* and FASB *Statements* specifically require certain disclosures in the notes to the financial statements. For example, FASB *Statement of Accounting Standards No. 2*, "Accounting for Research and Development Costs" (October 1974) states:

> A government-regulated enterprise that defers research and development costs for financial accounting purposes in accordance with Addendum to APB Opinion No. 2, "Accounting for the Investment Credit," shall disclose the following additional information about its research and development costs:
>
> *a.* Accounting policy, including basis for amortization.

    *b.* Total research and development costs incurred each period for which an income statement is present and the amount of those costs that has been capitalized or deferred in each period.

Moreover, "Disclosure of Accounting Policies," *APB Opinion No. 22* (April 1972), specifically requires that information about *important* accounting policies adopted by the enterprise, including their identification and description must be disclosed "in a separate *Summary of Significant Accounting Policies* preceding the notes to the financial statements or as the initial note." At a minimum, the summary should include policies that involve (*a*) a selection from existing acceptable alternatives, (*b*) principles and methods peculiar to the industry, and (*c*) unusual or innovative applications of generally accepted accounting principles.

The actual statements presented in the Appendixes to Chapters 4 and 5 include typical notes.

*Supporting schedules* may be incorporated in the notes or presented separately. Supporting schedules are typical for large and complex companies, and in situations where a particular item involves a number of complex changes during the period. We mentioned in Chapter 4 that when there have been numerous changes in owners' equity, the statement of retained earnings often is replaced with a more comprehensive schedule. As an example, Exhibit 5–3 presents an actual supplementary schedule, *statement of stockholders' equity*, that often is used to disclose the detailed changes and balances of all elements of owners' equity.

*Parenthetical notes* are widely used to disclose information such as the method of inventory costing—Inventory (*Lifo;* applied on lower-of-cost-or-market basis). *Contra items*, such as accumulated depreciation and allowance for doubtful accounts, are reported as separate line deductions or parenthetically. *Cross-references* may provide expeditious and useful disclosures as in the case of mortgaged assets. Assets pledged as security for a loan may be identified parenthetically, and the related liability is cross-referenced to the pledged assets.

### Auditors' Report

The auditors' report is also called the accountants' report and the independent accountants' report. It usually follows the financial statements and the notes; however, many believe that it should be the first item because of the importance attached to it by some statement users and the heavy responsibility auditors assume in expressing their opinion on the credibility of the statements. The independent auditors' primary function is to express an *opinion* on the financial statements. Although the auditor has sole responsibility for his or her opinion expressed in the auditor's report, the primary responsibility for the statements and the supporting notes rests with the management of the enterprise. The statements are those of the management; the auditor affirms or disaffirms them in the *opinion*.

**EXHIBIT 5-3**
**Statement of Stockholders' Equity**

EMERSON ELECTRIC CO. (SEP)
Consolidated Statement of Stockholders' Equity
($ Thousands)

| | Preferred Stock | Common Stock | Additional Paid-in Capital | Retained Earnings | Treasury Stock | Total |
|---|---|---|---|---|---|---|
| **Year ended September 30, 1973:** | | | | | | |
| Balance at beginning of year | $8,275 | 47,283 | 12,637 | 337,134 | (5,241) | 400,088 |
| Add (deduct): | | | | | | |
| Net earnings | | | | 75,873 | | 75,873 |
| Stock options exercised | | 99 | 2,453 | | 128 | 2,680 |
| Preferred stock conversions | (4,789) | 2,682 | 2,107 | | | – |
| Expenses of common stock split | | | (153) | | | (153) |
| Stock issued by pooled companies prior to combination | | 66 | 574 | | | 640 |
| Cash dividends: | | | | | | |
| Preferred stock—$.90 per share | | | | (2,572) | | (2,572) |
| Common stock—$.62½ per share | | | | (29,498) | | (29,498) |
| By pooled companies prior to combination | | | | (379) | | (379) |
| Balance at End of Year | $3,486 | 50,130 | 17,618 | 380,558 | (5,113) | 446,679 |
| **Year ended September 30, 1972** | | | | | | |
| Balance at beginning of year: | | | | | | |
| As previously reported | 8,584 | 22,963 | 33,741 | 291,324 | (5,288) | 351,324 |
| Adjustments: | | | | | | |
| Common stock split | | 22,963 | (22,963) | | | – |
| Poolings of interests | | 1,119 | 174 | 9,676 | | 10,969 |
| As restated | 8,584 | 47,045 | 10,952 | 301,000 | (5,288) | 362,293 |
| Add (deduct): | | | | | | |
| Net earnings | | | | 66,867 | | 66,867 |
| Stock options exercised | | 65 | 1,549 | | 55 | 1,669 |
| Preferred stock conversions | (309) | 173 | 136 | | | – |
| Cash dividends: | | | | | | |
| Preferred stock—$.90 per share | | | | (3,014) | | (3,014) |
| Common stock—$.59½ per share | | | | (26,975) | | (26,975) |
| By pooled companies prior to combination | | | | (744) | | (744) |
| Treasury stock acquired | | | | | (8) | (8) |
| Balance at End of Year | $8,275 | 47,283 | 12,637 | 337,134 | (5,241) | 400,088 |

Source: AICPA, Accounting Trends and Techniques, 1974 (New York, 1974), p. 325.

The auditor's report includes (1) a *scope* paragraph, and (2) an *opinion* paragraph. The standard format of the auditors' report is as follows:

(Scope paragraph)

We have examined the balance sheet of X Company as of (at) December 31, 19XX, and the related statements of income, retained earnings and changes in financial position for the year then ended. Our examination was made in accordance with generally accepted auditing standards, and accordingly, included such tests of the accounting records and such other auditing procedures as we considered necessary in the circumstances.

(Opinion paragraph)

In our opinion, the financial statements referred to above present fairly the financial position of X Company as of (at) December 31, 19XX, and the results of its operations and the changes in its financial position for the year then ended, in conformity with generally accepted accounting principles applied on a basis consistent with that of the preceding year.[15]

There are eight key elements in the report that have special significance:

1. Date
2. Salutation
3. Identification of the statements examined
4. Statement of scope of the examination
5. Opinion introduction
6. Reference to fair presentation in conformity with generally accepted accounting principles
7. Reference to consistency
8. Signature[16]

Upon completion of the audit, the independent CPA is required to draft the opinion paragraph to clearly communicate his or her judgment for giving one of the following:

1. Unqualified opinion—An unqualified opinion is given when the CPA has formed the opinion that the statements (1) "fairly present" results of operations, financial position, and changes in financial position; (2) conform to generally accepted accounting principles, applied on a consistent basis; and (3) full-disclosure requirements are met so that the statements are not misleading.
2. Qualified opinion—A qualified opinion is given when there is an "exception" or "subject to" clause because all of the key requirements for an unqualified opinion are not fully met. A qualified opinion must clearly explain the nature of the "exception" or "subject to" and its effect on the financial statements.
3. Adverse opinion—An adverse opinion is given when the financial statements do not "fairly present" (see above). Also, material exceptions require an adverse opinion on the statements as a whole.
4. Disclaimer of opinion—When the auditor has not been able to obtain

---

[15] AICPA, *Statement on Auditing Standards No. 2* (New York, 1973), pp. 2–3.
[16] AICPA, *The Auditor's Report—Its Meaning and Significance* (New York, 1967), p. 2.

sufficient competent evidential matter to form an opinion, the auditor must state that he or she is unable to express an opinion (i.e., a disclaimer). The auditor must explain the reasons for not giving an opinion.

A comprehensive discussion of the responsibilities of the independent auditor is beyond the scope of this book. The above summary is provided to indicate the importance of the auditor's representations when an opinion is provided on whether the representations of the management in the financial statements fairly present, to all users of the statements, the company's financial position, statement of income, and changes in financial position. It is reasonable, therefore, to suggest that the auditors' report should be read prior to spending much time on the financial statements. If it is other than unqualified, one should proceed with caution.

## Appendix—Specimen Statements

**BETZ**

# FINANCIAL REPORT  Betz Laboratories, Inc. and Subsidiaries

DESIGN, TREATMENT AND CONTROL OF INDUSTRIAL, COMMERCIAL AND MUNICIPAL WATER, WASTEWATER AND PROCESS SYSTEMS. Betz produces and sells a wide range of specialty chemical products and associated feeding and control equipment used in the treatment of industrial water and industrial processes utilizing water, including the technical and laboratory services necessary to utilize Betz products effectively. Betz and its subsidiaries also manufacture control instruments for water and process systems and design water and waste distribution, waste treatment and water filtration plants for municipalities and industry.

Operations are conducted primarily in the United States and Canada and also in Mexico, Europe, Southeast Asia and the Caribbean. The Company employs approximately 2,100 persons.

## Sales of Products and Services

### By Company Groupings

| | 1974 | 1973 | Increase |
|---|---|---|---|
| U.S. SPECIALTY CHEMICAL OPERATIONS<br>Betz Laboratories, Inc. and Betz Entec, Inc. | $ 71,758,000 | $51,112,000 | 40% |
| INTERNATIONAL OPERATIONS<br>Betz International, Inc. and its foreign subsidiaries<br>and regions | 9,200,000 | 6,100,000 | 51 |
| CANADIAN OPERATIONS<br>Betz Laboratories, Ltd. | 6,128,000 | 4,385,000 | 40 |
| CONSULTING ENGINEERING<br>Betz Environmental Engineers, Inc. and its affiliates—<br>Johnson and Williams, Inc., William J. Murdoch Engineers,<br>Inc. and J.B. Converse & Co., Inc. | 10,510,000 | 6,624,000 | 59 |
| INSTRUMENTATION<br>Uniloc, Inc., Micro Sensors, Inc. and<br>Kay-Ray, Inc. | 9,620,000 | 6,713,000 | 43 |
| | 107,216,000 | 74,934,000 | |
| Less: sales to affiliated marketing companies for<br>subsequent resale to customers | (4,206,000) | (3,092,000) | |
| CONSOLIDATED SALES OF PRODUCTS<br>AND SERVICES | $103,010,000 | $71,842,000 | 43% |

### By Classes of Products and Services

| | Percentage of Consolidated Net Sales and Revenues | | | | |
|---|---|---|---|---|---|
| | 1970 | 1971 | 1972 | 1973 | 1974 |
| Specialty Chemicals and<br>Associated Products | 85.7 | 83.2 | 82.4 | 81.5 | 80.5 |
| Electronic systems and<br>instruments* | 7.3 | 8.2 | 9.1 | 9.3 | 9.3 |
| Consulting engineering<br>and design* | 7.0 | 8.6 | 8.5 | 9.2 | 10.2 |

*Includes sales of companies acquired in pooling of interests transactions.

## Accountants' Report

To the Shareholders and Board of Directors
Betz Laboratories, Inc.
Trevose, Pennsylvania

We have examined the consolidated balance sheets of Betz Laboratories, Inc. and subsidiaries as of December 31, 1974, and December 31, 1973, and the related consolidated statements of operations, shareholders' equity, and changes in financial position for the years then ended. Our examinations were made in accordance with generally accepted auditing standards and, accordingly, included such tests of the accounting records and such other auditing procedures as we considered necessary in the circumstances.

In our opinion, the financial statements referred to above present fairly the consolidated financial position of Betz Laboratories, Inc. and subsidiaries at December 31, 1974, and December 31, 1973, and the consolidated results of their operations and changes in their financial position for the years then ended, in conformity with generally accepted accounting principles consistently applied during the period except for the change, with which we concur, in the method of valuing inventories as described in Note 4 to the consolidated financial statements.

Philadelphia, Pennsylvania
January 31, 1975

*Ernst & Ernst*

## Consolidated Statements of Operations
BETZ LABORATORIES, INC. AND SUBSIDIARIES
Years ended December 31, 1974 and 1973

|  | 1974 | 1973 |
|---|---|---|
| Net sales and revenues | $103,009,768 | $71,841,501 |
| Other income | 369,686 | 514,651 |
|  | 103,379,454 | 72,356,152 |
| Costs and expenses: |  |  |
| Cost of products sold and services rendered | 48,859,158 | 32,870,406 |
| Selling, engineering, research, and administrative expenses | 37,641,151 | 27,939,686 |
| Interest expense | 330,340 | 147,262 |
|  | 86,830,649 | 60,957,354 |
| EARNINGS BEFORE INCOME TAXES | 16,548,805 | 11,398,798 |
| Income taxes—Note 7 | 8,202,000 | 5,461,000 |
| NET EARNINGS | $ 8,346,805 | $ 5,937,798 |
| Net earnings per share (after pooling of interests adjustment—Note 2—Acquisitions) | $ 1.04 | $ .74 |
| Average number of shares | 8,017,102 shares | 7,971,681 shares |

See notes to consolidated financial statements.

## Consolidated Balance Sheets

BETZ LABORATORIES, INC. AND SUBSIDIARIES
December 31, 1974 and 1973

| | 1974 | 1973 |
|---|---|---|
| **ASSETS** | | |
| **CURRENT ASSETS** | | |
| Cash | $ 2,295,294 | $ 2.251.973 |
| Short-term investments—at cost (approximating market) | 127,500 | 2.226.922 |
| Accounts receivable, less allowances: 1974—$274.043: 1973—$123.500: | | |
| Trade | 14,823,497 | 10.256.270 |
| Consulting engineering contracts—Note 3 | 7,037,517 | 6.058.853 |
| | 21,861,014 | 16.315.123 |
| Inventories—Note 4: | | |
| Finished products and goods purchased for resale | 4,439,269 | 2.911.209 |
| Raw materials | 8,563,792 | 4.877.857 |
| Consulting engineering contracts in process | 4,116,341 | 3.011.448 |
| | 17,119,402 | 10.800.514 |
| Prepaid expenses and sundry | 922,748 | 771.762 |
| TOTAL CURRENT ASSETS | 42,325,958 | 32.366.294 |
| **PROPERTY. PLANT. AND EQUIPMENT**—on the basis of cost | | |
| Buildings | 11,867,121 | 10.708.567 |
| Machinery and equipment | 16,036,928 | 13.241.202 |
| Allowance for depreciation (deduction) | ( 8,795,805) | ( 7.171.692) |
| | 19,108,244 | 16.778.077 |
| Land | 1,487,243 | 1.497.903 |
| Construction in progress (estimated cost to complete—$3.200.000) | 4,362,234 | 576.454 |
| | 24,957,721 | 18.852.434 |
| **INTANGIBLE ASSETS**—at cost, net of amortization | | |
| Cost in excess of net assets of businesses acquired | 821,985 | 738.750 |
| Deferred charges and patents | 717,565 | 519.169 |
| | 1,539,550 | 1.257.919 |
| | $68,823,229 | $52.476.647 |
| **LIABILITIES AND SHAREHOLDERS' EQUITY** | | |
| **CURRENT LIABILITIES** | | |
| Notes payable to banks | $ 1,303,869 | $ 76.685 |
| Trade accounts payable | 5,709,651 | 4.253.569 |
| Payroll and related taxes | 2,683,117 | 1.335.598 |
| Accrued vacation pay | 624,454 | 510.825 |
| Contributions due retirement plans | 947,916 | 134.405 |
| Other accrued expenses | 1,912,208 | 1.091.809 |
| Due seller of acquired company | — | 353.537 |
| Federal, foreign. and state income taxes—Note 7 | 5,583,525 | 2.984.334 |
| Current portion of long-term debt | 170,635 | 164.466 |
| TOTAL CURRENT LIABILITIES | 18,935,375 | 10.905.228 |
| **LONG-TERM DEBT**—Note 5 | 2,596,558 | 1.828.388 |
| **OTHER LIABILITIES** | | |
| Deferred compensation | 208,000 | 414.000 |
| Deferred federal income taxes—Note 7 | 1,482,998 | 1.293.515 |
| | 1,690,998 | 1.707.515 |
| **SHAREHOLDERS' EQUITY**—Note 6 | | |
| Preferred Shares. par value $.10 a share. Authorized 1,000,000 shares: issued—none | | |
| Common Shares. par value $.10 a share: | | |
| Authorized—35,000,000 shares | | |
| Issued and outstanding: 1974—8,034,479 shares: 1973—7,991,679 shares | 803,448 | 799.168 |
| Capital in excess of par value | 13,551,441 | 11.922.890 |
| Retained earnings | 31,993,949 | 25.313.458 |
| Unearned compensation (deduction) | ( 748,540) | — |
| TOTAL SHAREHOLDERS' EQUITY | 45,600,298 | 38.035.516 |
| **COMMITMENTS AND CONTINGENT LIABILITY**—Notes 8 and 9 | $68,823,229 | $52.476.647 |

See notes to consolidated financial statements.

## Consolidated Statements of Changes in Financial Position

BETZ LABORATORIES, INC. AND SUBSIDIARIES
Years ended December 31, 1974 and 1973

|  | 1974 | 1973 |
|---|---|---|
| SOURCE OF FUNDS | | |
| From operations: | | |
| Net earnings | $ 8,346,805 | $ 5.937,798 |
| Expenses not requiring outlay of funds: | | |
| Depreciation and amortization | 1,896,160 | 1,470,510 |
| Deferred compensation | 203,813 | 82,000 |
| Deferred income taxes | 524,826 | 475,572 |
| TOTAL FROM OPERATIONS | 10,971,604 | 7,965,880 |
| From financing activities: | | |
| Borrowings of long-term debt | 1,011,515 | 1,509,741 |
| Borrowings of short-term debt | 1,352,184 | 52,257 |
| Common Stock issued relating to stock options and acquisition of minority interests | 332,365 | 786,225 |
| Capital transaction of pooled company prior to acquisition | 290,000 | ( 144,000) |
| Other: | | |
| Accounts payable and accrued expenses | 6,461,451 | 2,194,426 |
| Tax benefit relating to employees' early disposition of stock acquired under stock options | 154,113 | 152,428 |
| TOTAL SOURCE OF FUNDS | 20,573,232 | 12,516,957 |
| DISPOSITION OF FUNDS | | |
| Invested in operations: | | |
| Accounts receivable | 5,545,891 | 2,329,701 |
| Inventories | 6,318,888 | 4,122,688 |
| Prepaid expenses and sundry | 150,986 | 250,858 |
| Property, plant, and equipment | 7,904,524 | 4,638,309 |
| Purchased companies: | | |
| Property, plant, and equipment | — | 68,405 |
| Cost in excess of net assets | — | 745,000 |
| Deferred charges | — | 369,741 |
| Deferred income taxes | — | ( 763,599) |
| TOTAL INVESTED IN OPERATIONS | 19,920,289 | 11,761,103 |
| Other: | | |
| Repayments of long-term debt | 237,176 | 111,290 |
| Repayments of short-term debt | 125,000 | — |
| Cash dividends paid | 1,666,314 | 1,539,678 |
| Deferred compensation paid | 302,000 | 12,000 |
| Acquisition of intangible assets | 378,554 | 2,958 |
| TOTAL DISPOSITION OF FUNDS | 22,629,333 | 13,427,029 |
| DECREASE IN CASH AND SHORT-TERM INVESTMENTS | ( 2,056,101) | ( 910,072) |
| Cash and short-term investments at beginning of period | 4,478,895 | 5,388,967 |
| CASH AND SHORT-TERM INVESTMENTS AT END OF PERIOD | $ 2,422,794 | $ 4,478,895 |

See notes to consolidated financial statements.

# Consolidated Statements of Shareholders' Equity

BETZ LABORATORIES, INC. AND SUBSIDIARIES
Years ended December 31, 1974 and 1973

|  | 1974 | 1973 |
|---|---|---|
| **COMMON SHARES** | | |
| Balance at beginning of year | $    799,168 | $    794,837 |
| Par value of shares sold under stock options—Note 6 | 1,190 | 4,331 |
| Par value of shares issued under Stock Incentive Plan—Note 6 | 2,389 | — |
| Par value of shares issued in connection with the purchase of minority interest—Note 2 | 701 | — |
| BALANCE AT END OF YEAR | $    803,448 | $    799,168 |
| **CAPITAL IN EXCESS OF PAR VALUE** | | |
| Balance at beginning of year | $11,922,890 | $10,992,886 |
| Tax benefit relating to employees' early disposition of stock acquired under stock options | 154,113 | 152,428 |
| Capital transaction of pooled companies prior to acquisition | 290,000 | (      4,318) |
| Proceeds in excess of par value of shares sold under stock options—Note 6 | 175,397 | 781,894 |
| Capital in excess of par value of shares issued under Stock Incentive Plan—Note 6 | 853,964 | — |
| Capital in excess of par value of shares issued in connection with the purchase of minority interest—Note 2 | 155,077 | — |
| BALANCE AT END OF YEAR | $13,551,441 | $11,922,890 |
| **RETAINED EARNINGS** | | |
| Balance at beginning of year | $25,313,458 | $21,055,020 |
| Net earnings for the year | 8,346,805 | 5,937,798 |
| Capital transaction of pooled company prior to acquisition | — | (    139,682) |
| Cash dividends paid (per share: 1974—$.21; 1973—$.195) (including $16,483 in 1974 and $28,899 in 1973 for pooled company prior to acquisition) | (  1,666,314) | (  1,539,678) |
| BALANCE AT END OF YEAR | $31,993,949 | $25,313,458 |

See notes to consolidated financial statements.

# Notes to Consolidated Financial Statements

Note 1—Summary of Significant Accounting Policies

*Principles of Consolidation*—The consolidated financial statements include the accounts of the Company and all subsidiaries. All significant intercompany items and transactions are eliminated from the consolidated statements.

*Foreign Operations*—Current assets and liabilities of foreign subsidiaries are translated at year-end rates of exchange. Long-term assets and liabilities are translated at rates in effect in the year of acquisition. Operations are translated at average rates prevailing during each year. Unrealized gains (losses) of approximately $81,000 for 1974 and ($29,000) for 1973, respectively, are included

in net earnings. If long-term debt had been translated at the year-end rates of exchange, the amount of that debt would have increased by approximately $49,000 and $43,000 for 1974 and 1973, respectively. The assets, liabilities, net sales, and net earnings of foreign subsidiaries are:

|  | 1974 | 1973 |
|---|---|---|
| Total assets at end of year | $11,386,619 | $6,827,132 |
| Total liabilities at end of year | 6,509,790 | 3,281,131 |
| Net sales for the year | 12,971,348 | 9,091,279 |
| Net earnings for the year | 1,187,036 | 864,486 |

*Inventories*—Finished products, goods purchased for resale, and raw materials inventories are stated at the lower of cost or market, cost being substantially determined by the last-in, first-out method in 1974, and by the first-in, first-out method in 1973 (see Note 4): Consulting engineering contracts in process represent the accumulated costs of engineers' time and expenses less costs billable, generally at the completion of significant phases of such contracts, and less allowances for estimated losses. The Company includes currently in income the excess of such billings over related accumulated contract cost.

*Depreciation*—For financial reporting purposes, depreciation is computed principally by the straight-line method over the estimated useful lives of the assets as follows: buildings—17 to 45 years; machinery and equipment—8 to 15 years; furniture and fixtures—10 years; automobiles and trucks—3 to 6 years.

*Research and Development*—All research and development costs are charged to expense as incurred. Total research and development costs amounted to $2,500,000 in 1974 and $2,000,000 in 1973.

*Patents*—The costs of patents purchased by the Company are amortized over their remaining lives.

*Income Taxes*—The Company files a consolidated federal return and provides for current taxes on that basis. Deferred taxes are provided on timing differences between financial and tax reporting (see Note 7). Investment tax credits are accounted for by the flow-through method as a reduction of the provision for federal income taxes. No provisions have been made for United States income taxes on the unremitted earnings of foreign subsidiaries because the Company plans to continue to finance foreign expansion and operating requirements by reinvestment of such undistributed earnings. Presently, no increase in income taxes would result from remittance of such earnings because of the foreign tax credits available.

*Retirement Plans*—The Company and its subsidiaries have pension plans covering substantially all of their employees. The policy is to fund pension costs accrued. The past service cost of the Company's plan is fully funded. Past service cost of one subsidiary's plan is being amortized over 30 years.

*Cost in Excess of Net Assets of Businesses Acquired*—These costs are being amortized ratably over ten and forty years according to the Company's estimate of the period benefited.

Note 2—Acquisitions

In November 1974 the Company acquired J. B. Converse & Co., Inc. in exchange for 157,460 shares of Common Stock in a pooling of interests transaction. The revenues and net earnings of Converse in 1974 for the

period prior to the acquisition amounted to $1,538,000 and $205,000, respectively. As previously reported, the consolidated revenues and net earnings for 1973 were $70,430,054 and $5,790,827 ($.74 per share), respectively.

In 1974 the Company acquired certain minority interests in subsidiary companies for $177,000, represented by 7,012 shares of Common Stock and $20,000 in cash. Of this amount, $116,000 was assigned to cost in excess of net assets acquired.

In August 1973 the Company acquired Kay-Ray, Inc. in exchange for 100,007 shares of Common Stock in a pooling of interests transaction. The sales and net earnings of Kay-Ray, Inc. in 1973 for the period prior to the acquisition amounted to $931,269 and $163,174, respectively.

In the latter half of 1973 a subsidiary purchased the assets and businesses of two consulting engineering companies for $1,522,318 in cash and notes, of which $745,000 was assigned to cost in excess of net assets acquired. Additionally, a noncompete agreement, having a present value of $369,741, was entered into with the owner of one of these companies. The revenues and earnings of these companies are not material in relation to the accompanying consolidated statement of operations.

Note 3—Accounts Receivable

The components of accounts receivable from consulting engineering contracts are as follows:

|  | 1974 | 1973 |
|---|---|---|
| Fees billed (1) | $2,431,532 | $1,580,602 |
| Fees earned but unbilled (2) | 4,605,985 | 4,478,251 |
|  | $7,037,517 | $6,058,853 |

(1) Fees billed include insignificant amounts of retainage which will be due upon completion of the contract and acceptance by the owners.

(2) These fees were unbilled because of the billing practices of J. B. Converse & Co., Inc., which, prior to the acquisition in a pooling of interests transaction in 1974, used the cash method of accounting. The Company intends to conform such billing practices to those followed by its other consulting engineering companies.

Note 4—Change in Accounting Method

In 1974, the Company changed its method of determining cost for substantially all of its chemical inventories from the first-in, first-out (FIFO) method to the last-in, first-out (LIFO) method. In adopting LIFO, management believes this method will more fairly present its results of operations by reducing the effect of inflationary cost increases in its chemical inventories and thus better match current costs with current revenues. It was not practical for international subsidiaries to change their method of valuing chemical inventories. The Company did not change to LIFO for other than chemical inventories because management does not believe LIFO provides an improved matching of costs and revenues for products and services whose results of operations are not significantly affected by inflationary cost increases in inventories. The effect of the change in 1974 was to reduce inventories by approximately $2,500,000 and net earnings by approximately $1,250,000 ($.16 per share). Inventories aggregating $7,200,000 at December 31, 1974, were stated at LIFO cost.

Note 5—Long-Term Debt

The Company obtained loans or issued long-term notes as follows:

| | 1974 | 1973 |
|---|---|---|
| Loans with foreign banks | $ 676,167 | $ 838,515 |
| Mortgage payable, 7¾%, payable in installments of principal and interest aggregating $988 per month | 81,301 | 86,630 |
| Notes payable to individuals, at ½% above prime rate, payable in monthly installments of $3,869 | 603,564 | 649,992 |
| Note payable relating to noncompete agreement (net of imputed interest at 8½% of $209,972 in 1974, and $239,576 in 1973) payable through 1987 | 355,478 | 370,524 |
| Construction financing arrangement with industrial development authority—interest at 70% of prime rate. Construction may be financed to a maximum of $2,600,000. The loan is payable in 120 equal monthly installments beginning no later than August, 1976. | 1,011,515 | — |
| Mortgage payable, 9%, payable in installments of principal and interest aggregating $996 per month | 39,168 | 47,193 |
| | 2,767,193 | 1,992,854 |
| Amount due within one year | 170,635 | 164,466 |
| | $2,596,558 | $1,828,388 |

Certain foreign subsidiaries are financing the construction of new plants with foreign bank loans which are guaranteed by the Company. One bank loan for $263,314 bears interest at 8.7 percent per annum and is repayable in eight annual installments approximating $38,000 which commenced in 1974. In connection with this loan, the Belgian Government has agreed to subsidize the subsidiary to the extent of 4 percent per annum of interest payable to 1976. Two other bank loans are payable in varying installments with $45,329 due by December 31, 1975. The larger loan ($365,775) bears interest at 2½ percent per annum above the Bank's base lending rate, but not less than 7%.

Note 6—Stock Option and Stock Incentive Plans

At December 31, 1974, the Company had reserved an aggregate of 300,292 shares of its Common Stock for issuance under its Qualified Stock Option and Employee Stock Incentive Plans. No effect is given to outstanding options in the computation of earnings per share, since the effect would be immaterial.

Options granted under the Qualified Stock Option plans are at the fair value at the date of grant and are exercisable at the time of the grant and for five years thereafter. No person may receive an option if he owns (or would own if his option were exercised) stock possessing 5 percent of the voting power or value of all classes of stock of the Company. Option activity is summarized as follows:

| | Number of Shares | Option Price Per Share |
|---|---|---|
| Outstanding at January 1, 1973 | 131,580 | $12.25 - $43.25 |
| Granted | 58,000 | 37.25 - 37.75 |
| Exercised | ( 29,300) | 12.25 - 33.50 |
| Outstanding at December 31, 1973 | 160,280 | 12.25 - 43.25 |
| Granted | 220,480 (1) | 22.625- 34.625 |
| Cancelled | (169,180) (1) | 18.125- 43.25 |
| Exercised | ( 11,900) | 12.25   23.00 |
| Outstanding at December 31, 1974 | 199,680 | 18.125- 37.75 |

(1) Includes options for 165,480 shares which were terminated and a like number of new options granted at $22.625 a share. These new options become exercisable 5 years after the date of grant of the original terminated options. At December 31, 1974, options for 32,800 shares were exercisable, and options for 21,500 shares were available for future grants.

In addition, apart from the Qualified Plan, options for 3,000 shares are outstanding at $22.625 and become exercisable in 1975. In 1973, 14,000 options were exercised at prices ranging from $18.125 to $21.875 apart from the Qualified Plan.

In 1974, the shareholders of the Company approved an Employee Stock Incentive Plan which provides that up to 100,000 shares of Common Stock may be granted to April 30, 1984, at the discretion of the Board to key employees. The Company granted 23,888 shares during 1974. Key employees receiving grants are entitled to receive dividends, but assumption of full beneficial ownership is contingent upon continuous employment for the period, usually four or five years, stipulated at the time of grant. In the event the employee does not remain in continuous employment for the periods stipulated, the shares are cancelled and revert to the Company for reissuance under the Plan.

The aggregate fair market value of the shares granted under this plan is considered unearned compensation at the time of grant and compensation is earned ratably over the stipulated period.

Note 7—Provision for Income Taxes

The provision for income taxes includes deferred taxes on timing differences as follows:

|  | 1974 | 1973 |
|---|---|---|
| Depreciation | $444.210 | $298.572 |
| Deferred compensation | (104.976) | ( 35,000) |
| Accrued revenues | 135.117 | 142,000 |
| DISC income | 50.475 | 70,000 |
|  | $524.826 | $475.572 |

Current taxes payable have been reduced in 1974 and 1973 by investment tax credits of $111,000 and $149,000, respectively. Federal income tax returns have been settled by the IRS through 1970.

A reconciliation of the effective income tax rate for 1974 and 1973 with the statutory federal income tax rate of 48% is as follows:

|  | 1974 | 1973 |
|---|---|---|
| Federal tax rate | 48.0% | 48.0% |
| State and local taxes, net of federal income taxes | 2.1 | 2.4 |
| Investment tax credits | ( .7) | ( 1.3) |
| Foreign tax credit | ( .9) | ( 1.0) |
| Other items | 1.1 | ( .2) |
| Effective income tax rate | 49.6% | 47.9% |

Note 8—Commitments

*Employee Retirement Plans*—Aggregate contributions to employee retirement plans of the Company and its subsidiaries were $554,124 in 1974 and $324,929 in

1973. The unfunded past service cost at July 1, 1974, of one subsidiary company's plan is $457,000. Aggregate amounts in the pension funds exceeded the actuarially computed value of the plans' vested benefits as of December 31, 1973, the latest valuation date. The Company does not anticipate any material changes in its pension costs as a result of the 1974 Pension Reform Act. In addition, the provision for the Stock Bonus Profit Sharing Plan amounted to $530.586 in 1974 and $179,404 in 1973. Contributions to this plan are determined at the discretion of the Board of Directors, and may be in cash or Common Stock of the Company at the equivalent fair market value.

*Other Plans*—The Company has a discretionary bonus plan for officers. The Board of Directors determines whether or not a bonus will be paid and sets the amount using the increase in consolidated earnings before income taxes as a guide. The amounts provided aggregated $298,662 and $91,996 for 1974 and 1973, respectively.

*Long-Term Leases*—Total rental expense for all leases amounted to $1,881,025 in 1974 and $1,294,537 in 1973.

The future rental commitments as of December 31, 1974 for all noncancelable leases are as follows:

|  | Total | Building Space | Equipment | Automobiles |
|---|---|---|---|---|
| 1975 | $957,651 | $479,959 | $34,070 | $443,622 |
| 1976 | 577,680 | 274,901 | 48,816 | 253,963 |
| 1977 | 136,353 | 64,778 | 47,835 | 23,740 |
| 1978 | 94,502 | 49,150 | 45,352 |  |
| 1979 | 42,133 | 90 | 42,043 |  |
| 1980-1984 | 79,726 | — | 79,726 |  |

As of December 31, 1974, there are no future commitments on present noncancelable leases after 1984.

Leases for substantially all of the building space may be renewed for periods varying from one to four years upon expiration of present leases.

Note 9—Contingent Liability

Prior to acquisition, action had been brought against J. B. Converse & Co., Inc. as an additional third-party defendant in which plaintiff is seeking aggregate damages of $2,300,000. No provision has been made for possible loss since management denies liability, and the Company's counsel believes that the claim is unreasonable and that there is no supportable legal basis for the subsidiary's liability.

## QUESTIONS

1. What is a balance sheet? Why is it dated differently than an income statement and a statement of changes in financial position?

2. Define assets. Contrast the conceptual and pragmatic definitions. Why are they different?

3. Define liabilities. Contrast the conceptual and pragmatic definitions. Why are they different?

4. Explain, in general terms, why the balance sheet is important to the decision-maker.

5. Explain why the balance sheet does not report the fair market value of a business.

6. Contrast the two balance sheet formats. Which one do you prefer? Explain.

7. Define current assets and current liabilities emphasizing their interrelationship.

8. Define working capital. What is the current ratio?

9. Distinguish between short-term investments and the investments classified as investments and funds. Under what conditions could an investment be moved from current assets to investments and funds and vice versa?

10. What are operational assets? Distinguish between tangible and intangible operational assets.

11. Why is it often necessary to use a caption "Other Assets?" Give two examples of items that might be reported under this classification.

12. Explain a deferred charge and contrast it with a prepaid expense.

13. Distinguish between current and noncurrent liabilities. Under what conditions would a noncurrent liability amount be reclassified as a current liability?

14. What is a deferred credit? Explain why this classification on a balance sheet is difficult to defend conceptually.

15. What is owners' equity? What are the main components of owners' equity?

16. What is a restriction on retained earnings? How are restrictions reported?

17. What is the purpose of the statement of changes in financial position? What is meant by all-resources concept?

18. Distinguish between a statement of changes in financial position prepared on (a) a cash equivalent basis, and (b) a working capital basis.

19. Explain the position of the accounting profession with respect to use of the terms reserves, surplus, and net profit. Why is care in selection of terminology used in financial statements important?

20. What is a comparative statement? Why are they important?

21. What is meant by subsequent events? Why are they reported? How are they reported?

22. In general, why are notes to the financial statements important? How does the accountant determine when a note should be included?

23. What is the auditors' report? Basically, what does it include? Why is it especially important to the statement user?

24. Are the financial statements representations of the management of the enterprise, the independent accountant, or both? Explain.

## DECISION CASE 5-1

A. McDougald & Sons is a family corporation operating a chain of seven retail clothing stores in the Southwest. The total owners' equity of $5 million (all shares are outstanding) is owned by A. McDougald, president and founder, and eight men and women in the McDougald family. Except for accounts payable, modest amounts of short-term bank credit, and the usual short-term liabilities, the entire resources of the enterprise came from contributed capital and retained earnings. The general reputation of the company is excellent, and there have never been complaints about slowness in paying its liabilities. The family now has an opportunity to undertake a profitable expansion from seven to ten stores and estimates that upwards of $2,500,000 would be required for the purpose. It will be necessary to borrow this sum, and the issuance of five- to eight-year mortgage notes is contemplated.

Because the business is closely held and has never borrowed to an extent that made issuance of financial statements to outsiders necessary, the only persons who have seen the corporation's statements are members of the family, a few top employees, and some governmental officials, chiefly tax agents. When A. McDougald was told by a prospective lender that detailed financial statements for the past five years and audited statements for the most recent year as a basis for considering the loan would have to be provided, McDougald's initial reaction was to "hit the ceiling." After consideration, however, McDougald became willing to have the audit made and to release balance sheets as of the end of the most recent five years. McDougald was, as yet, unwilling to release statements of income and changes in financial position, and a majority of the other owners agreed with this stand.

*Required:*

1. If these five balance sheets are quite detailed, what can prospective lenders ascertain from them?
2. In your opinion would the five balance sheets give enough information to warrant granting a $2,500,000 secured intermediate-term loan? Explain the basis for your response.
3. If you were the lending officer of the prospective creditor and sought a compromise in the form of getting some added financial facts without receiving the other statements, what added information would be most useful to you? Explain your reasons.

**EXERCISES**

### Exercise 5-1

To the left is a list of several different items from a typical balance sheet for a corporation. To the right is a list of brief statements of the valuations usually reported on the balance sheet for the different items.

*Required:*

Use the code letters to the right to indicate, for each balance sheet item listed, the *usual* valuation reported on the balance sheet. Feel free to comment on any doubtful items. Some code letters may be used more than once or not at all.

| *Balance Sheet Items* | *Valuations Reported* |
|---|---|
| _____Accounts receivable (trade). | a. Amount payable when due (usually no interest because short term). |
| _____Marketable (short-term) investments. | |
| _____Inventories (merchandise for sale). | b. Lower of cost or market. |
| | c. Original cost when acquired. |
| _____Long-term investment in bonds of another company (purchased at a discount). | d. Fair market value at date of the balance sheet whether it is above or below cost. |
| _____Plant site (in use). | e. Original cost less accumulated amortization over estimated economic life. |
| _____Plant and equipment (in use). | |
| _____Patent (in use). | |
| _____Accounts payable (trade). | f. Par value of the outstanding shares. |
| _____Bonds payable (sold at a premium). | g. Face amount of the obligation plus unamortized premium. |
| _____Common stock (par $10 per share). | h. Realizable value expected. |
| | i. Cost to acquire the asset plus discount amortization. |
| _____Contributed capital in excess of par. | j. Cost when acquired less accumulated depreciation. |
| _____Retained earnings. | k. Accumulated income less accumulated dividends. |
| _____Land (future plant site). | l. Excess of issue price over par value. |
| _____Idle plant (awaiting disposal). | m. No valuation reported (explain). |
| _____Natural resource. | n. Expected net disposal proceeds. |
| | o. Cost less depletion. |
| | p. None of the above (when this response is used, explain the valuation usually used). |

### Exercise 5-2

Following are listed, in scrambled order, the major and minor captions for a balance sheet and a statement of changes in financial position (cash equivalent basis). Terminology given in the chapter is used.

1. Owners' equity.
2. Sources of cash (inflows).
3. Contributed capital.
4. Add (deduct) adjustments to revenue to derive cash basis.
5. Retained earnings.
6. Expenses (accrual basis).
7. Current liabilities.
8. From extraordinary items (net of tax).
9. Uses of cash.
10. Unrealized capital increment.
11. Assets.
12. Total cash expended for all purposes.
13. Operational assets – tangible.
14. Cash generated from revenues.
15. Total cash generated from other sources.
16. Long-term liabilities.
17. Total assets.
18. Current assets.
19. Capital stock.
20. Cash from other sources.
21. Other assets.
22. From operations (cash inflow).
23. Revenues (accrual basis).
24. Contributed capital in excess of par.
25. Deferred charges.
26. Total cash generated by operations.
27. Total cash generated from all sources.
28. Liabilities.
29. Investments and funds.
30. Net increase (decrease) in cash equivalents during the period.
31. Operational assets – intangible.
32. Cash disbursed for expenses.
33. Total liabilities.
34. Total liabilities and owners' equity.
35. Total owners' equity.
36. Add (deduct) adjustments to expenses to derive cash basis.

*Required:*

Set up two captions: (*a*) Balance Sheet; (*b*) Statement of Changes in Financial Position. For each caption, list the numbers given above in the order that they normally would be reported on the statement (do not renumber). Example:

*a.* Balance Sheet: 11, 18, and so on.
*b.* Statement of Changes in Financial Position: 2, 22, and so on.

Comment on any doubtful items.

## Exercise 5–3

Indicate the best answer for each of the following (explain any qualifications):

1. Working capital means –
   *a.* Excess of current assets over current liabilities.
   *b.* Current assets.
   *c.* Capital contributed by stockholders.
   *d.* Capital contributed by stockholders plus retained earnings.
2. The distinction between current and noncurrent assets and liabilities is now based primarily on –
   *a.* One year; no exceptions.
   *b.* One year or operating cycle, whichever is shorter.
   *c.* One year or operating cycle, whichever is longer.
   *d.* Operating cycle; no exceptions.
3. Under current generally accepted accounting principles unexpired insurance is a –

    *a.* Noncurrent asset.

    *b.* Deferred charge.

    *c.* Prepaid expense.

    *d.* Short-term investment.

4. Which of the following is not a current asset?

    *a.* Office supplies inventory.

    *b.* Short-term investment.

    *c.* Petty cash (undeposited cash).

    *d.* Cash surrender value of life insurance policy.

5. Which of the following is not a current liability?

    *a.* Accrued interest on notes payable.

    *b.* Accrued interest on bonds payable.

    *c.* Rent revenue collected in advance.

    *d.* Premium on bonds payable (unamortized).

6. A deficit is synonymous with—

    *a.* A net loss for the current period.

    *b.* A cash overdraft at the bank.

    *c.* Negative working capital at the end of the period.

    *d.* A debit balance in retained earnings at the end of the period.

7. A balance sheet is an expression of the model—

    *a.* Assets = Liabilities + Owners' Equity.

    *b.* Assets = Liabilities − Owners' Equity.

    *c.* Assets + Liabilities = Owners' Equity.

    *d.* Working Capital + Operational Assets − Long-Term Liabilities = Contributed Capital.

8. Acceptable usage of the term *reserve* is reflected by—

    *a.* Deduction from an asset to reflect accumulated depreciation.

    *b.* Description of a known liability for which the amount is estimated.

    *c.* Restriction on retained earnings.

    *d.* Deduction on the income statement for an expected loss.

9. Which terminology essentially is synonymous with "balance sheet"?

    *a.* Operating statement.

    *b.* Statement of changes in financial position.

    *c.* Statement of financial value of the business.

    *d.* Statement of resources, obligations, and residual equity.

10. The "operating cycle concept"—

    *a.* Causes the distinction between current and noncurrent items to depend on whether they will affect cash within one year.

    *b.* Permits some assets to be classed as current even though they are more than one year removed from becoming cash.

    *c.* Is becoming obsolete.

    *d.* Affects the income statement but not the balance sheet.

## Exercise 5–4

A typical balance sheet has the following captions:

A. Current assets.

B. Investments and funds.

C. Operational assets (land, buildings, and equipment).

D. Intangible assets.
E. Other assets.
F. Deferred charges.
G. Current liabilities.
H. Long-term liabilities.
I. Capital stock.
J. Additional contributed capital.
K. Retained earnings.

Indicate by use of the above letters (use capitals and print) how each of the following items would be classified. When an item is a contra amount (i.e., a deduction) in a caption, place a minus before it.

1. Accounts payable (trade).
2. Prepaid interest revenue (on a note receivable).
3. Accumulated depreciation.
4. Investment in stock of X Company (long term).
5. Plant site (in use).
6. Restriction on retained earnings.
7. Office supplies inventory.
8. Loan to company president (collection not expected for two years).
9. Accumulated income less accumulated dividends.
10. Bond discount unamortized (on bonds payable).
11. Bond sinking fund (to retire long-term bonds).
12. Prepaid insurance.
13. Accounts receivable (trade).
14. Short-term investment.
15. Allowance for doubtful accounts.
16. Building (in use).
17. Common stock (par $10).
18. Accrued interest revenue.
19. Patent.
20. Land (speculative).

## Exercise 5-5

Typical balance sheet captions are listed in Exercise 5-4. Indicate, by use of the letters given there (use capitals and print), how each of the following items would be classified. When an item is a contra amount (i.e., a deduction) in a caption, place a minus before it.

1. Short-term investments.
2. Premium unamortized (on bonds payable).
3. Bonds payable (long term).
4. Cash dividends payable (within six months).
5. Prepaid rent revenue.
6. Accumulated depreciation.
7. Premium on common stock issued.
8. Idle plant held for final disposal.
9. Deferred costs being amortized over five years.
10. Inventory of supplies.
11. Preferred stock.
12. Discount unamortized on long-term investment in bonds of another company.
13. Installment payment due in six months on long-term note payable.
14. Accrued interest on note payable.
15. Rent revenue receivable.
16. Allowance for doubtful accounts.
17. Investment in bonds of another company (long term).
18. Undeposited cash (for making change).
19. Accounts receivable (trade).
20. Deficit.

**Exercise 5-6**

The following trial balance was prepared by Lowe Company as of December 31, 1976:

| | | |
|---|---:|---:|
| Cash ........................................................................ | $ 7,200 | |
| Accounts receivable ................................................. | 14,000 | |
| Merchandise inventories........................................... | 13,000 | |
| Equipment .............................................................. | 28,000 | |
| Land ....................................................................... | 6,000 | |
| Building ................................................................. | 8,000 | |
| Deferred charges .................................................... | 1,100 | |
| Accounts payable ................................................... | | $ 5,500 |
| Note payable — 6%.................................................. | | 8,000 |
| Capital stock (par $10)............................................ | | 43,000 |
| Earned surplus ....................................................... | | 20,800 |
| | $77,300 | $77,300 |

You ascertain that certain errors and omissions are reflected in the above, including the following:

1. The $14,000 balance in accounts receivable represents the entire amount owed to the company; of this sum, $12,500 is from trade customers, and 5% of that amount is estimated to be uncollectible. The remaining sum owed to the company represents a long-term advance to its president.
2. Inventories include $2,000 of goods incorrectly inventoried at double their cost (i.e., at $4,000). No correction has been recorded. Office supplies on hand of $400 are also included in the balance of inventories.
3. When the equipment and building were purchased new on January 1, 1972, they had, respectively, estimated lives of 10 and 25 years. They have been depreciated by the straight-line method on the assumption of zero salvage values, and depreciation has been credited directly to the asset accounts.
4. The balance of the Land account includes a $1,000 payment made as a deposit of earnest money on the purchase of an adjoining tract. The option to buy it has not yet been exercised and probably will not be exercised during the coming year.
5. The note matures March 31, 1977, having been drawn July 1, 1976. Interest on it has been ignored.
6. Common stock shares outstanding, 4,000.

*Required:*

Prepare a correct classified balance sheet using preferred terminology. Use whichever form is specified by your instructor; if not specified, use the format you prefer. Show computation of retained earnings.

**Exercise 5-7**

The following balance sheet has come to your attention:

DYER CORPORATION
Balance Sheet Statement
For Year Ended December 31, 1976

*Assets*

Liquid Assets:

| | | | |
|---|---|---|---|
| Cash | | $ 31,000 | |
| Receivables | $ 29,000 | | |
| Less: Reserve for bad debts | 700 | 28,300 | |
| Inventories | | 42,000 | |
| | | | $101,300 |

Investments and Funds:

| | | | |
|---|---|---|---|
| Petty cash fund | | 200 | |
| Sinking fund | | 70,000 | |
| | | | 70,200 |

Permanent Assets:

| | | | |
|---|---|---|---|
| Land and buildings | 140,000 | | |
| Less: Reserve for depreciation | 9,000 | 131,000 | |
| Equipment | 84,000 | | |
| Less: Reserve for depreciation | 29,000 | 55,000 | |
| | | | 186,000 |

Deferred Charges:

| | | | |
|---|---|---|---|
| Prepaid expenses | | 2,700 | |
| Accrued sinking fund income | | 600 | |
| | | | 3,300 |
| Total | | | $360,800 |

*Obligations*

Short term:

| | | | |
|---|---|---|---|
| Accrued interest on mortgage | | $ 700 | |
| Accounts payable | | 36,500 | |
| Reserve for income taxes | $ 13,000 | | |
| Less: U.S. government bonds | 8,000 | 5,000 | |
| | | | $ 42,200 |

Long term:

| | | | |
|---|---|---|---|
| Mortgage payable* | | | 74,000 |

*Net Worth*

| | | | |
|---|---|---|---|
| Capital stock | | 150,000 | |
| Earned surplus | | 52,400 | |
| Reserve for contingencies | | 66,400 | |
| | | 268,800 | |
| Less: Treasury stock | | 24,200 | |
| | | | 244,600 |
| Total | | | $360,800 |

\* The mortgage payable matures April 18, 1977, and is funded by the sinking fund.

*Required:*

Constructively criticize the above balance sheet. Set up your responses in the following format:

*Specific Criticism (list)*      *Explanation of Criticism*      *Correct Treatment*

1.

Etc.

## Exercise 5–8

The ledger of May Manufacturing Company reflects obsolete terminology but you find its books have been, on the whole, accurately kept. After the most recent closing of the books at December 31, 1976, the following accounts are submitted to you for the preparation of a balance sheet.

| | | | |
|---|---|---|---|
| Accounts payable | $ 2,700 | Raw materials | $ 9,600 |
| Accounts receivable | 9,800 | Reserve for bad debts | 500 |
| Accrued expenses | 800 | Reserve for depreciation | 9,000 |
| Bonds payable—7% | 25,000 | Rent paid in advance | |
| Capital stock ($100 par) | 100,000 | (a debit) | 4,000 |
| Cash | 18,200 | Sinking fund | 8,000 |
| Earned surplus | xx,xxx | Land | 15,000 |
| Factory equipment | 31,200 | Note receivable | 6,600 |
| Finished goods | 11,100 | Work in process | 18,300 |
| Investments | 13,700 | | |
| Office equipment | 9,500 | | |

You ascertain that two thirds of the depreciation relates to factory and one third to office equipment and that $4,000 of the balance in the Investments account will be converted to cash during the coming year; the remainder represents a long-term investment. Rent paid in advance is for the next year. The land was acquired as a future plant site. The note receivable is signed by the company president and is due in 1978. The sinking fund is being accumulated to retire the bonds at maturity.

*Required:*

1. Prepare a classified balance sheet using preferred terminology.
2. Compute (*a*) the amount of working capital, and (*b*) the current ratio.

## Exercise 5–9

Reed Corporation is preparing the balance sheet at December 31, 1976. The following items are at issue:

*a.* Notes payable, long term, $60,000. This note will be paid in installments. The first installment of $20,000 will be paid August 1, 1977.
*b.* Bonds payable, 6%, $200,000; at December 31, 1976, unamortized premium amounted to $6,000.
*c.* Bond sinking fund, $40,000; this fund is being accumulated to retire the bonds at maturity. There is a restriction on retained earnings required by the bond indenture equal to the balance in the bond sinking fund.
*d.* Rent revenue collected in advance for the first quarter of 1977, $6,000.
*e.* After the balance sheet date, but prior to issuance of the 1976 balance sheet, one third of the merchandise inventory was destroyed by flood (date January 13, 1977), estimated loss $150,000.

*Required:*

Show, by illustration, how each of these items should be reported, and disclosed, on the December 31, 1976, balance sheet.

### Exercise 5–10

Based upon the following information, prepare the stockholders' equity section of the balance sheet for Short Corporation, at December 31, 1976:

| | |
|---|---:|
| Retained earnings | $ 80,000 |
| Preferred stock, par $10, authorized 15,000 shares | 100,000 |
| Restriction on retained earnings as required by a special contract | 30,000 |
| Cash received above par of preferred stock | 15,000 |
| Common stock, nopar, 50,000 shares issued (75,000 shares authorized) | 175,000 |

### Exercise 5–11

The following adjusted trial balance was prepared by Cotton Corporation at December 31, 1976:

| *Debits* | | *Credits* | |
|---|---:|---|---:|
| Cost of goods sold | $270,000 | Sales revenue | $500,000 |
| Distribution and adminis- | | Accumulated depreciation, | |
| trative expenses | 130,000 | plant and equipment | 40,000 |
| Income tax expense | 41,500 | Accounts payable | 10,000 |
| Cash | 39,000 | Income taxes payable | 11,000 |
| Short-term investments | 12,000 | Bonds payable | 50,000 |
| Accounts receivable | 70,000 | Allowance for doubtful | |
| Merchandise inventory | 90,000 | accounts | 3,000 |
| Office supplies inventory | 2,000 | Premium on bonds payable | |
| Investment in bonds of X | | (unamortized) | 1,000 |
| Corporation (long term), | | Common stock, par $10 | |
| cost | 35,000 | (authorized 50,000 | |
| Land (plant site in use) | 10,000 | shares) | 200,000 |
| Plant and equipment | 100,000 | Excess of issue price over | |
| Franchise (less amorti- | | par on common stock | 18,000 |
| zation | 8,000 | Retained earnings, balance | |
| Rearrangement costs* | 15,000 | January 1, 1976 | 37,000 |
| Idle equipment held for | | | |
| disposal | 7,500 | | |
| Dividends paid during 1976 | 40,000 | | |
| | $870,000 | | $870,000 |

* Amortization period three years; this is the unamortized balance.

*Required:*

1. Prepare a single-step income statement.
2. Prepare a classified balance sheet.

**Exercise 5-12**

The following statement has just been prepared by Wilkerson Corporation:

WILKERSON CORPORATION
Statement of Changes in Financial Position
For the Year Ended December 31, 1976

Sources of Funds:

From operations:

| | | |
|---|---:|---:|
| Revenues................................................................$260,000 | | |
| Decrease in trade accounts receivable ..................... | 8,000 | |
| Total Funds from Revenues ............................. | | $268,000 |
| Expenses................................................................ | 220,000 | |
| Add (deduct) noncash expenses: | | |
| Depreciation ..................................................... | (17,000) | |
| Amortization of patent......................................... | (1,000) | |
| Inventory increase.............................................. | 7,000 | |
| Accounts payable decrease ................................ | 2,000 | |
| Income taxes payable increase............................. | (1,000) | |
| Loss on sale of machinery.................................... | (4,000) | |
| Total Funds for Expenses ............................. | | 206,000 |
| Funds generated by operations......................................... | | 62,000 |
| From other sources: | | |
| Sale of machinery.................................................... | 12,000 | |
| Long-term note payable ............................................. | 25,000 | |
| Issuance of capital stock for future plant site (Note A)...... | 30,000 | |
| Total Funds from Other Sources ........................... | | 67,000 |
| Total Funds Generated during the Year............ | | 129,000 |

Uses of Funds:

| | | |
|---|---:|---:|
| Retirement of mortgage note ........................................ | 20,000 | |
| Cash dividends ........................................................... | 24,000 | |
| Purchase of long-term investment (stock, X Corporation) ... | 15,000 | |
| Acquisition of machinery (operational asset) ................... | 11,000 | |
| Acquisition of land for future plant site (Note A)............... | 30,000 | |
| Total Funds Used during the Year ........................ | | 100,000 |
| Net Increase (Decrease) in Cash and Short-Term Investments during the Year .................................... | | $ 29,000 |

*Required:*

1. How are funds measured in this statement? Explain.
2. What was the net income for the year? How much did cash increase from operations? How did management generate more cash from operations than profit?
3. Explain the transaction "sale of machinery." Note that it is referred to twice.
4. Write footnote A with respect to the future plant site. Note that it is referred to twice.
5. Explain why depreciation expense and amortization of patent were deducted from total expenses. Why was the inventory change added to expenses?
6. Some changes in terminology are needed. Identify them and suggest preferable terminology.

**PROBLEMS**

## Problem 5–1

To the left are typical items from a balance sheet for a corporation. To the right is a list of brief statements of *valuations* usually reported on a balance sheet for different items.

*Required:*

Use the code letters to the right to indicate for each balance sheet item listed, the *usual* valuation reported on the balance sheet. Provide explanatory comments for each doubtful item. Some code letters may be used more than once or not at all.

| *Balance Sheet Item* | *Valuation Reported* |
|---|---|
| _t_ Cash. | a. Total amount paid in by stock-holders when issued. |
| _C_ Marketable investments (short term). | b. Face amount collectible at maturity. |
| _h_ Accounts receivable (trade). | c. Lower of cost or market. |
| _b_ Notes receivable (short term). | d. Cost to acquire the asset. |
| _c_ Inventories (merchandise for sale). | e. Excess of issue price over par value. |
| _j_ Prepaid expenses (such as insurance). | f. Accumulated income less accumulated dividends. |
| _m_ Long-term investment in bonds of another company (purchased at a premium). | g. Cost to acquire less amortization to date. |
| _c_ Long-term investment in stock of another company (less than 20% of the outstanding shares). | h. Estimated realizable value (amount billed less estimated loss due to uncollectibility). |
| _D_ Plant site (in use). | i. Par value of shares outstanding. |
| _q_ Plant equipment (in use). | j. Cost less expired or used portion. |
| _G_ Patent (used in operations). | k. Cost at date of investment. |
| _j_ Deferred charge. | l. Par value. |
| _o_ Accounts payable (trade). | m. Cost at date of investment ~~less~~ *plus* unamortized premium. |
| _o_ Income taxes payable. | n. Current market value. |
| _o_ Notes payable (short term). | o. Amount payable when due (short term). |
| _P_ Bonds payable (sold at a discount). | p. Face amount of the obligation less unamortized discount. |
| _A_ Common stock (nopar). | q. Cost to acquire less accumulated depreciation. |
| _I_ Preferred stock (par $10 per share). | r. Fair market value at the date of the balance sheet whether it is above or below cost. |
| _E_ Contributed capital in excess of par. | s. No valuation reported (explain). |
| _f_ Retained earnings. | t. Current value. |
| _D_ Land held for speculation. | u. None of the above (when this response is used, explain the valuation usually used). |
| _D_ Land held for a future plant site. | |
| _v_ Damaged merchandise (goods held for sale). | |

## Problem 5–2

Typical balance sheet classifications are as follows:

A. Current assets.
B. Investments and funds.
C. Operational assets (land, buildings, and equipment).
D. Intangible assets.
E. Other assets.
F. Deferred charges.
G. Current liabilities.
H. Long-term liabilities.
 I. Capital stock.
J. Additional contributed capital.
K. Retained earnings.

Indicate by use of the above letters (use capitals and print), how each of the following items would be classified. When it is a contra item (i.e., a deduction) in a caption, place a minus before it. Comment on doubtful items; and if an item is not reported on the balance sheet, write *none*.

1. Cash.
2. Cash set aside to meet long-term purchase commitment.
3. Land (used as plant site).
4. Accrued salaries.
5. Investment in subsidiary (long term; not a controlling interest).
6. Inventory of damaged goods.
7. Idle plant being held for disposal.
8. Investment in bonds of another company.
9. Cash surrender value of life insurance policy.
10. Goodwill.
11. Natural resource (timber track).
12. Allowance for doubtful accounts.
13. Stock subscriptions receivable (no plans to collect in near future).
14. Organization costs.
15. Discount on bonds payable.
16. Interest revenue collected in advance.
17. Accrued interest payable.
18. Accumulated amortization on patent.
19. Prepaid rent expense.
20. Short-term investment (common stock).
21. Rent revenue collected in advance.
22. Net of accumulated earnings and dividends.
23. Trade accounts payable.
24. Current maturity of long-term debt.
25. Land (held for speculation).
26. Notes payable (short term).
27. Special cash fund accumulated to build plant five years hence.
28. Bonds issued — to be paid within six months out of bond sinking fund.
29. Long-term investment in rental building.
30. Copyright.
31. Accumulated depreciation.
32. Deferred plant rearrangement costs.
33. Franchise.
34. Discount on long term investment costs.
35. Premium on bonds payable (unamortized).
36. Common stock (at par value).
37. Petty cash fund.
38. Deficit.
39. Contributed capital in excess of par.
40. Earnings retained in the business.

(AICPA adapted)

**Problem 5-3**

The president of Hill Manufacturing Company is a personal friend of yours and he tells you the company has never had an audit and is contemplating having one principally because it is suspected that the financial statements are not well prepared. As an example the president hands you the following balance sheet for review:

HILL MANUFACTURING CO., INC.
Balance Sheet
For the Year Ended December 31, 1976

*Assets*

| | |
|---|---:|
| Liquid Assets: | |
| Cash in banks.............................................................. | $12,000 |
| Receivables from various sources net of reserve | |
| for bad debts ............................................................. | 5,000 |
| Inventories ................................................................... | 6,000 |
| Cash for daily use ......................................................... | 500 |
| Total ................................................................. | 23,500 |
| Permanent Assets: | |
| Treasury stock ............................................................. | 5,000 |
| Fixed assets (net) ......................................................... | 26,000 |
| Grand Total........................................................ | $54,500 |

*Obligations and Net Worth*

| | | |
|---|---:|---:|
| Short Term: | | |
| Trade payables ............................................................. | | $ 3,000 |
| Salaries accrued ........................................................... | | 1,000 |
| Total ................................................................... | | 4,000 |
| Long Term: | | |
| Mortgage ...................................................................... | | 7,000 |
| Net Worth: | | |
| Capital stock ................................................................. | $30,000 | |
| Earned surplus ............................................................. | 13,500 | |
| Total ................................................................... | | 43,500 |
| Grand Total....................................................... | | $54,500 |

*Required:*

1. List and explain your criticisms of the above balance sheet; focus on all aspects of it.
2. Using the above data prepare a classified balance sheet that meets your specifications. Where amounts needed are missing use assumed, but realistic, amounts. *Hint:* Treasury stock is a reduction of stockholders' equity since it is the company's own stock reacquired by purchase.

**Problem 5–4**

The most recent balance sheet of Ray Corporation appears below.

RAY CORPORATION
Balance Sheet
For the Year Ended December 31, 1976

*Assets*

| | | |
|---|---:|---:|
| Current: | | |
| Cash ....................................................... | $ 5,000 | |
| Marketable securities...................................... | 10,000 | |
| Accounts receivable ...................................... | 30,000 | |
| Merchandise................................................ | 25,000 | |
| Supplies.................................................... | 5,000 | |
| Stock of subsidiary company (not a | | |
| controlling interest) ................................ | 17,000 | $ 92,000 |
| Investments: | | |
| Cash surrender value of life insurance ............ | 20,000 | |
| Treasury stock............................................. | 25,000 | 45,000 |
| Tangible: | | |
| Buildings and land.........................................$56,000 | | |
| Less: Reserve for depreciation ..................... 10,000 | 46,000 | |
| Equipment..................................................... 15,000 | | |
| Less: Reserve for depreciation ..................... 10,000 | 5,000 | 51,000 |
| Deferred: | | |
| Prepaid expenses ........................................ | 2,000 | |
| Discount on bonds payable............................ | 10,000 | 12,000 |
| Total ................................................. | | $200,000 |

*Liabilities and Capital*

| | | |
|---|---:|---:|
| Current: | | |
| Accounts payable ........................................ | $16,000 | |
| Reserve for income taxes............................... | 17,000 | |
| Customers' accounts with credit balance ......... | 100 | $ 33,100 |
| Long Term: | | |
| Bonds payable............................................. | 45,000 | |
| Mortgage ................................................. | 12,000 | 57,000 |
| Reserve for bad debts ................................... | | 900 |
| Capital: | | |
| Capital stock, par $10 ................................... | 75,000 | |
| Earned surplus ........................................... | 25,000 | |
| Capital surplus............................................. | 9,000 | 109,000 |
| Total ................................................. | | $200,000 |

*Required:*

1. List and explain your criticisms of the above balance sheet.
2. Prepare a correct classified balance sheet. *Hint:* The capital stock was sold above par. Deduct treasury stock from shareholders' equity.

**Problem 5–5**

The balance sheet shown below, which was submitted to you for review, has been prepared for inclusion in the published annual report of the XYZ Company for the year ended December 31, 1976:

XYZ COMPANY
Balance Sheet
December 31, 1976

*Assets*

Current Assets:

| | | |
|---|---:|---:|
| Cash..................................................................... | | $ 1,900,000 |
| Accounts receivable ...........................................$3,900,000 | | |
| Less: Reserve for bad debts................................ 50,000 | | 3,850,000 |
| Inventories—at the lower of cost (determined by the first-in, first-out method) or market .................. | | 3,500,000 |
| Total Current Assets .................................... | | 9,250,000 |

Fixed Assets:

| | | |
|---|---:|---:|
| Land—at cost ................................................. | 200,000 | |
| Buildings, machinery and equipment, furniture and fixtures—at cost ......$4,200,000 | | |
| Less: Reserves for depreciation ...... 1,490,000 | 2,710,000 | 2,910,000 |

Deferred Charges and Other Assets:

| | | |
|---|---:|---:|
| Cash surrender value of life insurance ..................... | 15,000 | |
| Unamortized discount on first-mortgage note ......... | 42,000 | |
| Prepaid expenses.................................................. | 40,000 | 97,000 |
| Total Assets ........................................... | | $12,257,000 |

*Liabilities*

Current Liabilities:

| | | |
|---|---:|---:|
| Notes payable to bank ......................................... | | $ 750,000 |
| Current maturities of first-mortgage note................. | | 600,000 |
| Accounts payable—trade ...................................... | | 1,900,000 |
| Reserve for income taxes for the year ended December 31, 1976 ......................................... | | 700,000 |
| Accrued expenses .............................................. | | 550,000 |
| | | 4,500,000 |

Funded Debt:

| | | |
|---|---:|---:|
| 4% first-mortgage note payable in quarterly installments of $150,000.................................$4,200,000 | | |
| Less: Current maturities..................................... 600,000 | | 3,600,000 |

Reserves:

| | | |
|---|---:|---:|
| Reserve for damages ......................................... | 50,000 | |
| Reserve for possible future inventory losses ........... | 300,000 | |
| Reserve for contingencies................................... | 500,000 | |
| Reserve for additional federal income taxes ........... | 100,000 | 950,000 |

Capital:

| | | |
|---|---:|---:|
| Capital stock—authorized, issued and outstanding 100,000 shares of $10 par value ...................... | 1,000,000 | |
| Capital surplus ................................................. | 300,000 | |
| Earned surplus ................................................. | 1,907,000 | 3,207,000 |
| Total Liabilities......................................... | | $12,257,000 |

Additional data:

1. Reserve for damages was set up by a charge against current fiscal year's income to cover damages possibly payable by the company as a defendant in a lawsuit in progress at the balance sheet date. Suit was subsequently compromised for $50,000 prior to issuance of the statement.
2. Reserve for possible future inventory losses was set up in prior years, by action of board of directors, by charges against earned surplus. No change occurred in the account during the current fiscal year.
3. Reserve for contingencies was set up by charges against earned surplus over a period of several years by the board of directors to provide for a possible future recession in general business conditions.
4. Reserve for federal income taxes was set up in a prior year and relates to additional taxes which the Internal Revenue Service contended that the company owed. The company has good evidence that settlement will be effected for the $100,000.
5. Capital surplus consists of the difference between the par value of $10 per share of capital stock and the price at which the stock was actually issued.

*Required:*

State what changes in classification or terminology you would advocate in the presentation of this balance sheet to make it conform with generally accepted accounting principles and with present-day terminology. State your reasons for your suggested changes.

(AICPA adapted)

**Problem 5–6**

The adjusted trial balance for Rollins Corporation, and other related data, at December 31, 1976, are given below in scrambled order. Although the company uses obsolete terminology, the amounts are correct. Assume perpetual inventory.

Additional information:

*a.* Market value of the short-term marketable securities is $47,300.
*b.* Merchandise inventory is based on *Fifo;* lower of cost or market.
*c.* Goodwill is being amortized (i.e., written off) over a 20-year period. The amortization for 1976 has already been recorded (as a direct credit to the Goodwill account). Amortization of other intangibles are recorded in this manner except for the patent (a contra-account is used for it).
*d.* Reserve for income taxes represents the estimated taxes payable at the end of 1976. Reserve for estimated damages was set up by debiting retained earnings during 1975. The $10,000 was the estimated amount of damages that would have to be paid as a result of a damage suit against the company; at December 31, 1976, the appeal was still pending. The $10,000 is an appropriation, or restriction, placed on retained earnings by management.

*e.* The cash advance from customer was for a special order that will not be completed and shipped until March 1977; the sales price has not been definitely established since it will be based on cost (no revenue should be recognized for 1976).

| | | | |
|---|---:|---|---:|
| Cash | $ 44,100 | Reserve for bad debts | $ 1,100 |
| Land (used for building | | Accounts payable (trade) | 15,000 |
| site) | 29,000 | Revenues | 200,000 |
| Cost of goods sold | 108,000 | Reserve for income taxes | 7,500 |
| Marketable securities (stock | | Note payable (short term) | 12,000 |
| of S Company, short | | Common stock, par $10, | |
| term) | 44,000 | authorized 50,000 | |
| Goodwill (unamortized | | shares | 100,000 |
| cost) | 12,000 | Reserve for depreciation, | |
| Merchandise inventory | 30,000 | building | 90,000 |
| Office supplies inventory | 1,000 | Retained earnings, | |
| Patent | 7,000 | January 1, 1976 | 48,000 |
| Operating expenses | 42,000 | Accrued wages | 2,100 |
| Income tax expense | 17,500 | Reserve for estimated | |
| Bond discount (unamor- | | damages | 10,000 |
| tized) | 7,500 | Premium on common | |
| Prepaid insurance | 900 | stock | 15,000 |
| Building (at cost) | 150,000 | Reserve for patent | |
| Land (held for speculation) | 31,000 | amortization | 4,000 |
| Accrued interest income | 300 | Cash advance from | |
| Accounts receivable | | customer | 3,000 |
| (trade) | 15,700 | Accrued property taxes | 1,300 |
| Note receivable, 10% | | Note payable (long term) | 16,000 |
| (long-term investment) | 20,000 | Precollected interest | |
| Cash surrender value of | | income | 1,000 |
| life insurance policy | 9,000 | Bonds payable, 6% | |
| Deferred store rearrange- | | ($25,000 due June 1, | |
| ment costs (assume a | | 1977) | 75,000 |
| deferred charge) | 6,000 | | |
| Dividends paid during 1976 | 10,000 | | |
| Prior period adjustment | | | |
| (tax assessment from | | | |
| prior year) | 16,000 | | |
| | $601,000 | | $601,000 |

*Required:*

1. Prepare a single-step income statement and a statement of retained earnings.
2. Prepare a classified balance sheet including appropriate disclosures. Use preferred terminology and format.

**Problem 5–7**

The adjusted trial balance for Nashville Manufacturing Corporation at December 31, 1976, is given below in scrambled order. Debits and credits are not indicated; all amounts are correct. Assume a normal balance situation in each account. Assume perpetual inventory system.

Work in process inventory...$ 24,000
Accrued interest on notes
   payable ....................... 1,000
Accrued interest receivable. 1,200
Accrued income on
   short-term investments ... 1,000
Common stock, nopar,
   authorized 20,000 shares,
   issued 10,000 ............... 150,000
Cash in bank ................. 40,000
Trademarks (unamortized
   cost) ........................... 1,400
Land held for speculation ... 17,000
Supplies inventory ............ 600
Goodwill (unamortized
   cost) ........................... 20,000
Raw material inventory ...... 13,000
Bond sinking fund ............ 10,000
Accrued property taxes...... 1,200
Accounts receivable (trade). 19,000
Accrued wages ............... 2,300
Mortgage payable (due in
   three years) ................. 10,000
Building........................... 130,000
Prepaid interest expense ... 1,700
Organization expenses
   (unamortized cost—
   assume deferred
   charge) ....................... 7,800
Deposits (cash by cus--
   tomers on sales orders
   to be delivered next
   quarter; no revenue yet
   recognized) ................. 1,000
Long-term investment
   in bonds of K Corpora-
   tion (at cost) ................. 60,000

Patents (unamortized cost) .$ 12,000
Reserve for bond sinking
   fund* ........................... 10,000
Reserve for depreciation,
   office equipment........... 1,600
Reserve for depreciation,
   building ....................... 5,000
Premium on preferred
   stock .......................... 8,000
Cash on hand for change... 400
Preferred stock, par $100,
   authorized 5,000 shares,
   5% noncumulative ......... 60,000
Precollected rent income... 900
Finished goods inventory... 42,000
Note receivable (short
   term) ........................... 4,000
Bonds payable, 6%, (due in
   15 years) .................... 50,000
Accounts payable (trade) ... 11,000
Reserve for bad debts ...... 1,400
Notes payable (short term). 7,000
Office equipment ............ 25,000
Land (used as building
   site)............................. 8,000
Short-term investments
   (at cost) ....................... 15,500
Retained earnings, unap-
   propriated (balance
   January 1, 1976) ............ 13,200
Cash dividends paid during
   1976 .......................... 20,000
Revenues during 1976 ...... 400,000
Cost of goods sold for
   1976 .......................... 210,000
Expenses for 1976 (in-
   cluding income taxes) ... 90,000
Income taxes payable ...... 40,000

* This is a restriction on retained earnings required by the bond indenture equal to the bond sinking fund which is being accumulated to retire the bonds.

Additional information:
Inventories are based on *Fifo;* lower of cost or market.

*Required:*
1. Prepare a single-step income statement. To compute earnings per share, deduct $3,000 of net income as an allocation to preferred stock.
2. Prepare a classified balance sheet; use preferred terminology and format. Comment on any items you consider doubtful with respect to classification.
3. Assume between December 31, 1976, and completion date, that a flood damaged the finished goods inventory in an amount estimated to be $17,000. Prepare an appropriate disclosure note to the balance sheet.

**Problem 5–8**

The following statement has just been prepared by Sutton Corporation:

SUTTON CORPORATION
Statement of Changes in Financial Position

| | | | |
|---|---|---:|---:|
| **Sources of Funds:** | | | |
| From operations: | | | |
|   Revenues | | $630,000 | |
|   Adjustments for nonfund items: | | | |
|     Accounts receivable decrease | | 15,000 | |
|       Total Funds from Revenues | | | $645,000 |
|   Expenses | | 550,000 | |
|   Adjustments for nonfund items (deductions): | | | |
|     Depreciation | | (30,000) | |
|     Inventory increase | | 17,000 | |
|     Accounts payable increase | | (11,000) | |
|     Income taxes payable decrease | | 4,000 | |
|     Loss on sale of long-term investment | | (3,000) | |
|       Total Funds Required for Expenses | | | 527,000 |
|   Funds generated by operations | | | 118,000 |
| From other sources: | | | |
|   Sale of long-term investment | | 21,000 | |
|   Disposal of land (Note A) | | 50,000 | |
|   Sale of unissued common stock | | 15,000 | |
|   Long-term note payable | | 20,000 | |
|     Total Funds from Other Sources | | | 106,000 |
|     Total Funds Generated | | | 224,000 |
| **Uses of Funds:** | | | |
| Dividends | | 40,000 | |
| Acquisition of machinery (Note A) | | 50,000 | |
| Payment on bonds payable | | 100,000 | |
|     Total Funds Used | | | 190,000 |
| Increase in Cash and Temporary Investments during the Year | | | $ 34,000 |

*Required:*

1. How are funds measured in this statement? Explain.
2. What was the net income for the year? How much cash was generated from operations? Explain how management generated more cash than profits.
3. What was the primary source of funds? What was the primary uses of funds? What sources and uses would you rely on for future predictions of funds flow in this company? Explain.
4. Explain the long-term investment transaction. Why is it reflected in two places?
5. Write Note A with respect to the machinery and land.
6. Explain why the accounts receivable decrease was added to revenues.
7. Explain the reason for the addition or deduction of each adjustment to total expenses.
8. Some changes in terminology would be helpful. Identify them and suggest preferable terminology.

## Problem 5-9

The following information was taken from the records of Adamson Corporation for the year ended December 31, 1976:

| | |
|---|---:|
| Net income (Revenues, $560,000 — Expenses, $500,000) | $60,000 |
| Depreciation expense | 12,000 |
| Accounts receivable increase | 3,000 |
| Accounts payable decrease | 4,000 |
| Purchase of operational assets (cash) | 23,000 |
| Merchandise inventory increase | 5,000 |
| Cash dividends paid | 23,000 |
| Loss on sale of operational asset (Cash, $18,000 — Book Value, $20,000) | 2,000 |
| Sold unissued common stock (cash) | 35,000 |
| Acquired future plant site; payment by issuance of 5,000 shares of common stock (fair market value) | 24,000 |
| Payment on bonds payable | 25,000 |
| Borrowed on long-term mortgage note | 40,000 |

*Required:*

1. Use the above information to prepare a statement of changes in financial position, cash equivalent basis.
2. Write the disclosure note with respect to the future plant site.

## Problem 5-10

The Appendix to this chapter gives an actual income statement and statement of changes in financial position. Examine them carefully and respond to the following questions. Respond for the latest year unless directed otherwise.

a. Are they comparative statements? Explain.
b. Are they consolidated statements? What do you understand this to mean?
c. What format was used for the balance sheet? Explain variations in format from those outlined in the chapter.
d. What title was used for the balance sheet and how was the statement dated?
e. How may different subclassifications were used for assets? For liabilities? For owners' equity? Explain variations from those suggested in the chapter.
f. What was total current assets? Total current liabilities? Amount of working capital? What was the current ratio?
g. How were short-term investments valued? Explain.
h. How were inventories costed? Explain.
i. What was the percent of the allowance for doubtful accounts to accounts receivable?
j. Were there any investments and funds? Explain the nature of each.
k. How were operational assets labeled and valued? Explain. What was the average percent of accumulated depreciation on each category of operational assets? From this, how would you characterize the operational assets as to remaining life?
l. Were any intangibles reported? Explain them.
m. Were any prepaid expenses reported? Were any deferred charges reported?

What were the deferred charges? Do you agree with the classification on this item? Explain.

n. Were any "other or miscellaneous" assets reported? List them.

o. How were liabilities classified? Do you agree with the classification of each liability? Explain why.

p. Was any unamortized bond premium or discount reported? If yes, how was it reported? Do you agree with the method of reporting? Explain.

q. Were there any convertible debt securities? What were the terms of conversion?

r. Do you agree with the subclassifications of stockholders' equity? Explain.

s. How many different classes of stock were there? What was the par per share of each? For each class, how many shares were (1) authorized, (2) issued, (3) held as treasury stock, and (4) outstanding?

t. Were there any restrictions on retained earnings? How were they reported?

u. What percent of total assets were provided by (1) creditors, and (2) owners?

v. What title and date was used on the statement of changes in financial position?

w. Was the statement of changes in financial position prepared on a working capital basis or a cash equivalent basis? How was this made known to you in the statement?

x. What percent of total fund inflows came from (1) operations, (2) extraordinary items, and (3) other sources?

y. How many notes to the statements referred to the balance sheet? The statement of changes in financial position? What was the important issue in each?

z. What was the scope of the independent auditors' examination? What kind of opinion did the auditor give? Explain.

aa. Were there any unusual features of the balance sheet and the statement of changes in financial position? What kind?

bb. Overall, do you believe these two statements could be improved with respect to format and terminology? Explain each change that you would recommend for consideration.

## Problem 5–11

The Appendix to Chapter 4 gives an actual income statement and statement of changes in financial position. Examine them carefully and respond to the questions posed in Problem 5–10. Respond for the latest year unless directed otherwise.

## Problem 5–12

Obtain an audited financial statement for the latest year for a company of your choice (from the library or other source) and use it as a basis for responding to each of the questions posed in Problem 5–10.

## Problem 5–13 (Review of Chapters 3, 4, and 5)

On January 1, 1976, Hays Company had the following trial balance:

|  |  | Debit | Credit |
|---|---|---|---|
| 101 | Cash .............................................................. | $ 96,000 | |
| 102 | Accounts receivable ............................................. | 45,000 | |
| 103 | Allowance for doubtful accounts .......................... | | $ 670 |
| 104 | Office supplies inventory....................................... | 800 | |
| 105 | Inventory (periodic system)* ............................... | 60,000 | |
| 106 | Short-term investments ........................................ | | |
| 107 | Investment revenue receivable ............................. | | |
| 108 | Fund to construct future plant ............................. | 30,000 | |
| 109 | Machinery........................................................... | 120,000 | |
| 110 | Accumulated depreciation, machinery..................... | | 72,000 |
| 111 | Land (future plant site)........................................ | 15,000 | |
| 112 | Patent................................................................. | 4,000 | |
| 113 | Other assets........................................................ | 55,000 | |
| 201 | Accounts payable ............................................... | | 35,000 |
| 202 | Accrued interest payable...................................... | | |
| 203 | Income taxes payable (1975) ................................ | | 12,330 |
| 204 | Long-term mortgage note .................................... | | |
| 301 | Common stock (par $10) ..................................... | | 150,000 |
| 302 | Contributed capital in excess of par ..................... | | 30,000 |
| 303 | Retained earnings ............................................... | | 125,800 |
| 400 | Income summary ................................................. | | |
| 500 | Sales revenue ..................................................... | | |
| 501 | Investment revenue ............................................. | | |
| 600 | Purchases............................................................ | | |
| 601 | Freight on purchases .......................................... | | |
| 602 | Purchase returns ................................................ | | |
| 700 | Selling expenses.................................................. | | |
| 701 | General and administrative expenses ..................... | | |
| 702 | Interest expense ................................................. | | |
| 703 | Depreciation expense .......................................... | | |
| 704 | Income tax expense ............................................. | | |
| 801 | Extraordinary items ............................................. | | |
| 802 | Prior period adjustments...................................... | | |
| | | $425,800 | $425,800 |

* Depending on the worksheet technique used, additional account for the ending inventory could be used

*1976 entries* (use number to left for date notations):

1. Paid 1975 income taxes payable on March 3, 1976, in full.
2. Purchases .......................................$350,000 (of whioh $50,000 wac on crodit)
   Purchase returns ............................    1,000 (on account)
   Freight on purchases ........................    2,000 (cash)
3. The following selling expenses were incurred and paid during 1976:
   Advertising .................................$  10,000
   Salaries ....................................   130,000
   Other selling ..............................    15,000
4. The following general and administrative expenses were incurred and paid during 1976:
   Salaries ....................................$ 100,000
   Office supplies ..........................        500 (debit Acct. #104)
   Rent expense..............................     24,000
5. A mortgage note was dated and signed on March 1, 1976, for $75,000; this amount of cash was received. Interest will be paid annually on this date; 8% interest.
6. A short-term investment was acquired for cash on June 1, 1976, at par, $20,000, 6%. The interest will be received annually thereafter on this date.

7. Suffered severe flood loss amounting to $40,000 (assume extraordinary item). (Credit cash because this was spent to restore the damages.)
8. Received damages (cash) of $30,000 from a court case which began in 1973.
9. At December 31, 1976, interest on the building fund amounting to $1,500 was added to the fund balance.
10. Cash collections on accounts receivable, $85,000.
11. Cash payments on accounts payable, $65,000.
12. Cash paid for dividends amounting to $2 per share (debit retained earnings).
13. Sales were $700,000 of which 15% was on credit.
14. Ending inventory was $70,000.

*Required:*

1. Set up a general journal and T-accounts (with account numbers). Enter beginning balances in the ledger accounts. All of the ledger accounts needed are listed in the above trial balance.
2. Journalize and post the current entries. Use posting notations.
3. Set up a worksheet with a minimum of eight columns (or more if you prefer). Develop the unadjusted trial balance from the ledger and enter it in the first two money columns of the worksheet.
4. Enter the following adjusting entries on the worksheet and complete it (label the adjusting entries with the letters to the left).
   *a.* Bad debt expense is 1% of total credit sales.
   *b.* Office supplies inventory at December 31, 1976, was determined by count to be $600.
   *c.* Accrue the investment revenue at 6% per year.
   *d.* The machinery had an estimated life of ten years, no salvage value; assume straight-line depreciation and a full year's depreciation for 1976.
   *e.* On January 1, 1976, the patent had eight years remaining life; assume straight-line amortization. General and administrative expense.
   *f.* Accrue interest on the mortgage note.
   *g.* Assume an average income tax rate of 40% on all items.
5. Prepare a single-step income statement and statement of retained earnings.
6. Prepare a classified balance sheet.
7. Journalize and post the adjusting entries.
8. Journalize and post the closing entries.
9. Prepare a post-closing trial balance.
10. Which adjusting entries would you reverse?

(Note: Unless directed otherwise by your instructor, to conserve time, you may substitute *account numbers* for account titles on completing any, or all, of the following requirements: 2, 3, 5, 6, 7, 8, and/or 9.)

## Chapter 6

# Concepts of Future and Present Value

## PURPOSE OF THE CHAPTER

This chapter focuses on the time value of money, commonly called interest. It is the cost of using money over time. Outflows for the time value of money are identified as interest expense, whereas inflows for the time value of money are identified as interest revenue. Entities at various times make decisions that involve either (a) receiving funds, goods, or services currently with a promise to make payments over one or more future periods; or (b) committing funds currently as an investment to obtain returns over one or more future periods. In both situations the time value of money is fundamental and important to the decision-making process and in subsequently measuring and reporting the financial effects of earlier decisions. Federal law now requires that the *true annual* rate of interest be specified on installment contracts and consumer loans. This often requires application of present value concepts.

Because of the time value of money (aside from inflation or deflation), a dollar has a different value today (often referred to as time zero) than at future or past dates. Therefore, dollar inflows and outflows that occur at significantly different dates cannot simply be aggregated in a meaningful way; rather they must be restated at a common date to reflect the time value of money by applying the concepts of present and/or future value. Restatement for the interest factor is essential in many situations: (a) when preparing information inputs for decision making (such as capital budgeting), and (b) for accounting measurement and reporting. Therefore, the accountant's knowledge necessarily must include an understanding of the concepts to be discussed in this chapter. Discussion of these concepts is presented early in this book because of their widespread use in accounting measurements, recording, and reporting as discussed and illustrated in later chapters. Some applications of future and present value concepts in accounting are:

1. Notes receivable and payable — Measuring and reporting those notes that either carry no stated rate of interest or a rate of interest that is not realistic in comparison with the "going" rates.

225

2. Leases—Measuring and reporting long-term leases.
3. Pensions—Measuring and reporting numerous aspects of pension plans.
4. Assets—Measuring and reporting assets acquired with long-term debt when the interest rate is unspecified or unrealistic.
5. Installment contracts—Measuring and reporting the effects of assets acquired or sold on long-term installment terms.
6. Sinking funds—Measuring and reporting resources (funds) set aside for specific uses in the future.
7. Depreciation—Measuring depreciation charges when the sinking fund or annuity methods are used.
8. Capital additions—Evaluation of the probable effects of alternative investments in capital assets.
9. Business combinations—Measuring and reporting of such items as receivables, debts, and accruals in a combination by purchase.
10. Premium and discount on certain receivables and payables—Measuring the amortization of bond premium and discount for both investments in bonds and bonds payable.
11. Future commitments of goods and/or services—Measuring and reporting future commitments to furnish or receive goods or services when the interest rate is unspecified or unrealistic.

The purpose of this chapter is to present the concepts of future and present value in a way that emphasizes their application in the accounting process—measuring, recording, and reporting. The basic concepts are presented and illustrated in a way that builds a solid foundation for their applications in subsequent chapters (and in more advanced accounting courses). The use of prepared tables, which are available from many sources, is emphasized. Part A discusses the amount and present value of 1, and Part B discusses annuities.

## CONCEPT OF INTEREST

Interest (i.e., the time value of money) represents the excess of resources (usually cash) received or paid over the amount of resources lent or borrowed at an earlier date. To illustrate, assume Entity A loaned Entity B $6,000 cash for one year with the stipulation that $6,600 cash would be repaid. The time value of money for this contract would be:

| | |
|---|---|
| Beginning of year, amount of resources committed .............. | $6,000 |
| End of year, amount of resources returned ......................... | 6,600 |
| Difference—time value of money per contract....................... | $ 600 |
| Analysis: | |
| Actual interest in dollars .................................................$600 | |
| Actual interest as a rate ($600 ÷ $6,000) ........................... | 10% |

### Simple Interest

In the above example the interest was based on the principal amount ($6,000), which would be the usual case in a loan covering one period only. However, had the loan covered two or more periods, a question would arise about the interest assumption.

## Simple versus Compound Interest

When a loan covers two or more periods, interest may be computed on either a simple or a compound interest basis. *Simple interest* is computed only on the principal amount. For example, assume the above loan contract was for two years with specified simple interest of 10% per year on the principal amount of $6,000. The amount of interest would be $600 × 2 = $1,200 (i.e., the simple interest amount). In contrast, *compound interest* is computed on the principal amount plus all interest that has accumulated on the principal. For example, assume the above loan contract was for two years with specified compound interest of 10% per year. The amount of compound interest would be computed as follows:

|  | Interest | Interest Basis | Resource Flows |
|---|---|---|---|
| Year 1: Principal (resources committed) ......... |  | $6,000 | $6,000 |
| Interest ($6,000 × .10) ........................$ | 600 |  |  |
| Year 2: Amount subject to interest.................. |  | 6,600 |  |
| Interest ($6,600 × .10) ........................ | 660 |  |  |
| Amount of resources returned ............ |  |  | 7,260 |
| Interest amount ...............................$1,260 |  |  | $1,260 |

Clearly, when a choice is available, the investor would always opt for compound interest. In the above example the investor would receive $60 ($1,260 − $1,200) more interest on a compound interest basis than on a simple interest basis. In contrast, the borrower would have to pay $60 more interest. Simple interest usually is applicable to short-term receivables and payables, and compound interest is used for long-term contracts.

## Interest Periods

Contracts which call for compound interest usually specify the interest rate on an *annual* basis. The interest periods—those intervals at which interest is accrued and added to the principal—may or may not be as much as one year apart. For example, a contract may call for "interest at 8% compounded annually," or for "interest at 8% compounded semiannually." In the first instance the rate is 8% for one interest period of a year; in the second instance the rate is 4% for each interest period of six months. If interest of 8% is compounded quarterly, the rate per period (quarter) is 2%, and there would be four interest periods per year. If an annual rate is stated and there is no mention of the frequency of compounding, interest is assumed to be compounded annually.[1]

### Summary of Concepts

The concepts of future and present value involve four basic values. These four concepts, discussed in the order listed below, may be briefly identified as:

*Part A—Amount and Present Value of 1:*

1. *Amount of 1*—the future value of $1 at the end of $n$ periods at $i$ compound interest rate.

$$a = (1 + i)^n \text{ (see Table 6-1)}$$

2. *Present value of 1*—the present value of $1 due $n$ periods hence, discounted at $i$ compound interest rate:

$$p = \frac{1}{(1 + i)^n} \text{ (see Table 6-2)}$$

*Part B—Annuities:*

3. *Amount of annuity of 1*—the future value of $n$ periodic contributions (rents) of $1 each plus accumulated compound interest at $i$ rate.

$$A_o = \frac{(1 + i)^n - 1}{i} \text{ (see Table 6-3)}$$

4. *Present value of annuity of 1*—the present value of $n$ periodic contributions (rents) of $1 each to be received, or paid, each period discounted at $i$ compound interest rate. Stated another way: The amount that must be invested today at $i$ compounded interest rate in order to receive $n$ periodic receipts in the future of $1 each.[2]

$$P_o = \frac{1 - \dfrac{1}{(1 + i)^n}}{i} \text{ (see Table 6-4)}$$

### PART A—AMOUNT AND PRESENT VALUE OF 1

In order to understand these two concepts, a clear distinction between an "amount" and "present value" is essential. Fundamentally, the difference is in the time assumption. "Amount" is a concept of *future* amounts, whereas "present value" is a concept of *present* amounts. This

---

[1] Throughout this chapter and in the problem materials, short-term periods and even interest rates usually are used to facilitate comprehension. Also amounts usually are rounded to even dollars. Obviously, in the real world these simplifications generally cannot be used.

[2] These are for *ordinary* annuities, not annuities due. Also the notations used vary considerably. For example, the symbol for an amount of annuity of 1 often used is $S_n$, and for present value of annuity of 1, $A_{n\,\overline{i}}$.

distinction can be graphically displayed. Note in particular the time
direction indicated by the arrows.

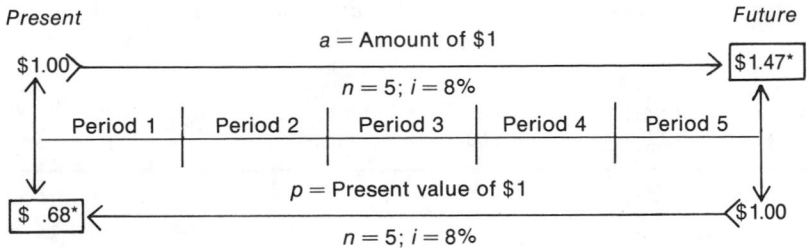

*Present*                                                          *Future*

$1.00 ————————— a = Amount of $1 —————————→ $1.47*

n = 5; i = 8%

| Period 1 | Period 2 | Period 3 | Period 4 | Period 5 |

$ .68* ←————————— p = Present value of $1 —————————— $1.00

n = 5; i = 8%

\* Rounded to even cents.

## AMOUNT OF 1

The concept of amount of 1 (the symbol is $a$) is often called compound
interest. The future amount is the principal at the start plus accumulated compound interest. For example, $1,000 deposited in a savings
account at 8% interest per year on January 1, 1976, would amount
(accumulate) to $1,469 at the end of the fifth year (December 31, 1980)
assuming annual compounding. The increase of $469 would be accumu-
lated compound interest during the five years.

### Calculation of Amount of 1

It is convenient and customary to use a base figure of 1 in compound
interest calculations. In the United States it would be natural to think of
1 as $1. The figure 1 could just as readily stand for one peso or one of
some other unit of currency.

We can determine how much an investment of $1 would be worth
after being left for a specified number of periods at a specified compounding rate per period by any one of several methods. To illustrate,
assume $1 is invested for five years at 8% compounded annually. The
total of principal and compound interest at the end of the five years may
be determined by any one of the following methods:

1. *By successive interest computations* – multiply the principal ($1)
by the interest rate (.08) and add the $.08 interest thus obtained for the
first period, and the sum ($1.08) is the amount ($a$) at the end of the first
period. This amount becomes the interest-bearing principal for the
second period. This sum is principal plus interest $(1 + i)$, which may then
be used as the multiplier in each succeeding period to secure the compound amount. Exhibit 6–1 uses this multiplier to secure the amount
($a$) at the end of each of the five periods.

2. *By formula* – substitute in a formula which states that for $n$ interest periods at $i$ rate of interest the amount of 1 is, $a = (1 + i)^n$.
Substituting, we would say $1 invested at 8% annual compound interest
for 5 years = ($1 + .08)^5$, or $1.47+. (Verifiable in Table 6–1.) Fifth-power

**EXHIBIT 6-1**

| Period | Balance at Start of Period | Multiplier $(1 + i)$ | Amount at End of Period | Alternate Computation at End $(1 + i)^n$ |
|---|---|---|---|---|
| 1 | $1 | 1.08 | $1.08 | $(1.08)^1$ |
| 2 | 1.08 | 1.08 | 1.1664 | $(1.08)^2$ |
| 3 | 1.1664 | 1.08 | 1.25971 | $(1.08)^3$ |
| 4 | 1.25971 | 1.08 | 1.36049 | $(1.08)^4$ |
| 5 | 1.36049 | 1.08 | 1.46933 | $(1.08)^5$ |

multiplication is a laborious process and would be especially so where the exponent is large. If a calculator is not available, one could employ logarithms to simplify the calculations. Exhibit 6-1 demonstrates that the formula for amount of 1 is: $a = (1 + i)^n$.

3. *By table* – Standard tables of the various future and present values may be obtained from numerous sources. Partial tables are presented in this chapter for your convenience. Table 6-1 is based on the formula $a = (1 + i)^n$; therefore it presents the amount of 1 values (for a limited number of periods and interest rates). Reference to Table 6-1, down the 8% column, and across on the five-period line, shows the amount of 1 to be 1.46933 (i.e., $1.47+, as computed above in Exhibit 6-1). Obviously, tables facilitate computation of future and present values. However, a word of caution is in order. Observe that Table 6-1 is entitled *Amount of 1* and the underlying formula is $a = (1 + i)^n$. The heading of the table (including the formula on which it is based) must be considered carefully since it is very easy to take an amount from the wrong table. Also, not infrequently tables show values carried to only two, three, or four decimal places. When the table value is to be applied to a large amount, rounding to this extent can cause a material error in the resulting amount computed. Observe that the tables presented in this chapter are carried to five places.

### Future Amount of a Specified Principal

Since the standard tables are based on $1 (for example, as in Table 6-1), amounts other than $1 are simply multiplied by appropriate table value. To illustrate, assume a company deposits $10,000 cash in a fund (or a savings account) that will earn 8% compounded annually for six years. How much will be in the fund at the end of the sixth year from the deposit date? We can readily compute this future amount by referring to Table 6-1, Amount of 1, as follows: $10,000 × $a_{n=6 \atop i=8\%}$ ; that is, $10,000 × 1.58687 = $15,869. The interest revenue earned would be $5,869.

As another example, assume another company deposits $50,000 cash in a building fund which will be needed at the end of ten years and that the fund will earn 8% interest per annum compounded semiannually. Since the interest periods are one-half year, there are 20 interest periods

and the compound interest rate is 4% per period. By reference to Table 6–1, the computation of the future amount is $50,000 × $a_{n=20}$; that is,
$i=4\%$
$50,000 × 2.19112 = $109,556$. Interest revenue earned over the ten-year period would be $59,556.

### Determination of Other Values Related to Amount of 1

In each of the two examples given above, *three* values were provided. To restate the first example: (*a*) principal, $10,000; (*b*) interest rate, 8%; and (*c*) periods, 6. A fourth value, the future amount $15,869, was computed. Obviously, if *any* three of these four values are known, the other one can be derived. Thus, there are three types of problems that may be encountered; viz:

1. To determine the future amount (discussed above – compound amount of a specified principal).
2. To determine the required interest rate (discussed below – determination of compound interest rate).
3. To determine the required number of interest periods (discussed below – determination of number of periods).

### Determination of the Compound Interest Rate

If the amount to which a given principal sum will accumulate (or is desired to accumulate) is known, and the number of periods is known, the required rate of compound interest can be calculated.

As an example, if it is desired to invest $5,000 at interest compounded annually for ten years so as to accumulate $10,795, what rate of interest is required? To find the rate the following steps may be taken:

1. $10,795 ÷ $5,000 = $2.159$, the amount to which $1 would accumulate at the unknown interest rate by the end of the ten-year period.
2. Referring to an amount of 1 table (Table 6–1) and reading across the ten-period line we find the amount of 2.15892 under the 8% column; thus, this is the required interest rate.

Often it is necessary to interpolate to derive the required rate. Suppose once again $5,000 is to be invested for ten years. In this case it is desired to accumulate $11,000. Here the rate of increase is the same as if $1 had grown to $11,000 ÷ $5,000 = 2.20. Referring to the ten-period line, we find the value under 8% is 2.15892; under the next higher rate, 9%, it is 2.36736. Therefore, the rate is between 8% and 9% – somewhat closer to the former – not quite one half of the way between them. We can conclude that the interest earned must be about 8¼%. Or more precisely,[3]

$$\left[ 8\% + \frac{2.20 - 2.15892}{2.36736 - 2.15892} (9 - 8) \right] = 8.20 + \%$$

---

[3] *Linear* interpolation was illustrated; calculus or methods of finite differences could have been used to give a more precise answer.

## Determination of Number of Periods

If the amount to which a given sum will accumulate is known, and the interest rate is known, the required number of periods can be calculated. To use the above example again, assume the following is known: (a) investment to be made $5,000; (b) accumulation desired $10,795; and (c) the desired interest rate to be 8%. To compute the required number of interest periods, the following steps may be taken:

1. $10,795 ÷ $5,000 = $2,159, the amount $1 would accumulate at 8% for the unknown number of interest periods.
2. Referring to an amount of 1 table (Table 6–1) and reading down the 8% column we find 2.159 (rounded) on the ten-year line, thus the required (implied) number of interest periods is ten.

## An Accounting Application of Amount of 1

Sonora Corporation, in order to assure funds for a planned future expansion, deposited $50,000 cash in a plant expansion fund on January 1, 1976. The bank, serving as trustee, will pay 7% interest compounded annually. The funds will be needed on January 1, 1979.

*Required:*

1. Compute the fund balance at December 31, 1978.
2. Prepare an accumulation table for the fund.
3. Give the accounting entries for the entire period including withdrawal on January 1, 1979.

*Solution:*

1. Fund balance at December 31, 1978:

$$\$50,000 \times a_{\substack{n=3 \\ i=7\%}} = \$50,000 \times 1.22504 = \underline{\$61,252}$$

2. Accumulation table, plant expansion fund:

| Date | Interest Revenue | Fund Balance |
|---|---|---|
| 1-1-76   deposit | | $50,000 |
| 12-31-76 | $50,000 × .07 = $3,500 | 53,500 |
| 12-31-77 | 53,500 × .07 =  3,745 | 57,245 |
| 12-31-78 | 57,245 × .07 =  4,007 | 61,252 |

3. Entries:

1-1-76 deposit of cash:

| | | |
|---|---|---|
| Plant expansion fund | 50,000 | |
| Cash | | 50,000 |

Each December 31 interest revenue earned:

| | 12-31-76 | | 12-31-77 | | 12-31-78 | |
|---|---|---|---|---|---|---|
| Plant expansion fund | 3,500 | | 3,745 | | 4,007 | |
| Investment revenue | | 3,500 | | 3,745 | | 4,007 |

1-1-79 withdrawal of fund:

Cash..............................................................................61,252
      Plant expansion fund ...............................................          61,252

## PRESENT VALUE OF 1

Present value is the present, or time zero, value of a sum of future dollars discounted back from a specified future date to the present date at a given rate of compound interest. It is a present, rather than a future, concept. Present value involves compound discounting, thus it can be said to be the inverse of the amount-of-1 concept of compound interest. Since a future amount is discounted, the present value will always be less than the future amount. For example, $1 discounted at 8% per annum for one year has a present value of $.9259, and discounted for two years has a present value of $.8573. The symbol usually used for present value of 1 is $p$.

We have seen that $1 invested at $i$ interest rate per period has a future value (amount of 1) of $(1 + i)^n$ dollars. It follows that $(1 + i)^n$ dollars has a present value that is less than $(1 + i)^n$ by an inverse or reciprocal relationship. To illustrate, assume $1, an interest rate of 8%, and 1 period:

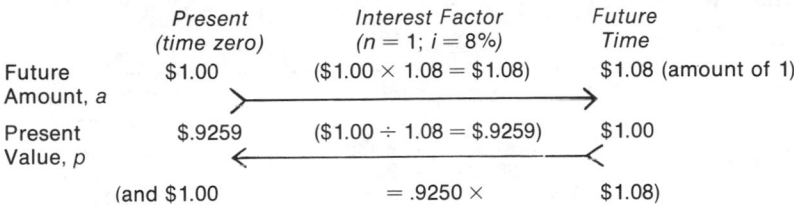

|  | Present (time zero) | Interest Factor ($n = 1; i = 8\%$) | Future Time |
|---|---|---|---|
| Future Amount, $a$ | $1.00 | ($1.00 × 1.08 = $1.08) | $1.08 (amount of 1) |
| Present Value, $p$ | $.9259 | ($1.00 ÷ 1.08 = $.9259) | $1.00 |
| (and $1.00 |  | = .9250 × | $1.08) |

The reciprocal relationship between the amount of 1 and the present value of 1 provides a symbolic expression of the computation of present value amounts, viz.:

$$\text{Amount of 1, } a = (1 + i)^n$$

Therefore; the reciprocal relationship is

$$\text{Present value of 1, } p = \frac{1}{(1 + i)^n}$$

This is the formula for computation of all present value of 1 amounts.

### Computation of Present Value of 1

Present value of 1 amounts can be laboriously computed through compound discounting inversely to that shown on Exhibit 6-1 for future amounts. Also, present value amounts can be computed by dividing the values given in Table 6-1, Amount of 1, into 1.00. For example, $p_{n=5 \atop i=8\%}$ can be computed as follows: $1.00 \div 1.46933$ (from Table 6-1) = .68058. However, a much more convenient approach is to use a standard table that discounts $1 at various *"n"* and *"i"* values. A *present value of 1* table for various interest rates and periods is shown as Table 6–2. (Carefully observe the table heading and the underlying formula.) Each value in this table is a reciprocal of the corresponding value in the amount of 1 table.

### An Accounting Application of Present Value of 1

To compute the present value of a future amount, the appropriate present value amount from Table 6–2 is multiplied by the specified future amount. To illustrate, assume Blue Corporation acquired a new machine on January 1, 1976. Because of a shortage of cash, the vendor agreed to let Blue Corporation pay for the machine at the end of the third year after purchase, that is, on December 31, 1978. The amount to be paid at that date is $50,000, which includes all interest charges. Assume the going compound interest rate is 8% per year. Question: Taking into account the interest, what was the cost of the machine, when acquired, in conformity with the cost principle? We must compute the present value of the future amount of $50,000 as follows: $50,000 \times p_{\substack{n=3 \\ i=8\%}} =$

$50,000 \times .79383$ (from Table 6–2) = $39,691. A *debt schedule* for this situation would be:

| Date | Interest Expense Incurred | Liability Balance |
|------|---------------------------|-------------------|
| 1-1-76 ...................... | | $39,691 |
| 12-31-76......................$39,691 × .08 = $3,175 | | 42,866 |
| 12-31-77...................... 42,866 × .08 = 3,429 | | 46,295 |
| 12-31-78...................... 46,295 × .08 = 3,705* | | 50,000 |

\* Adjusted for rounding error from using a five-place table.

It follows that the sequence of entries for this situation would be:

1-1-76 Acquisition of the machine:

| | | |
|---|---|---|
| Machine  ..................................................................................39,691 | | |
| Liability ................................................................................ | | 39,691 |

Each December 31, to record interest expense incurred:

| | 12-31-76 | 12-31-77 | 12-31-78 |
|---|---|---|---|
| Interest expense .........3,175 | | 3,429 | 3,705 |
| Liability ............... | 3,175 | 3,429 | 3,705 |

12-31-78 payment of the liability:

| | | |
|---|---|---|
| Liability...................................................................................50,000 | | |
| Cash  ................................................................................... | | 50,000 |

Other values can be computed for present value of 1 as illustrated above for amount of 1.

### PART B — ANNUITIES

Annuities involve the same concepts of future value and present value discussed in Part A. Annuities are identical to the amount of 1 and present value of 1 concepts except for one addition, concept of an *annuity*. The term annuity means a series of payments, or receipts, of *equal amounts* for a series of *equal time periods*. There is one equal amount (often called a rent) for each equal time period. In contrast, amount of 1 and present value of 1 involves a single amount only at the beginning (present) or at a future specified date. The monthly payments on an auto loan, for example, constitute an annuity; there is an equal cash payment each month by one party and an equal cash receipt each month by the other party. The future and present value of an annuity may be graphically displayed on a *time scale* as follows:

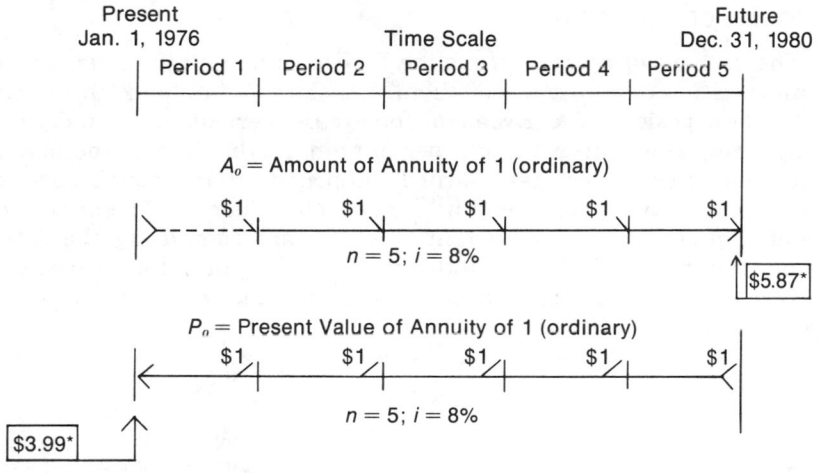

* Rounded to even cents.

The subscript "o" in $A_o$ and $P_o$ denotes an ordinary annuity.

In the above illustration observe that there are five *equal* rents in each instance (since $n = 5$) and the rents are at the *end* of each period. The *amount of annuity of 1* is a future concept, and the future amount of the five rents of $1 is $5.87. The future value will always be greater than the sum of the rents by the amount of the compound interest accumulation. Since the rents are assumed to be on the last day of each period, observe that for the amount of an annuity of 1, the future amount is calculated at the date of the last rent. This means that since there is no interest after the last rent, there is one more rent than *interest* periods.[4]

---

[4] The above illustration, and the discussion, assumes an *ordinary annuity* in each instance. The primary characteristic is that the rents are assumed to be at the *end* of each period as reflected in the graphic depiction. In contrast, an *annuity due* assumes the rents are at the *beginning* of each period. Annuities due will be discussed in a subsequent section.

The *present value of annuity of 1* is a present (i.e., time zero) concept. As shown in the above illustration, the present value of the five rents of $1 each is $3.99. The present value will always be less than the sum of the rents by the amount of the compound interest discounting. Note that the present value of annuity of 1, as shown above, is assumed to be at the *beginning* of the first period (i.e., time zero), or to state it another way, the rents are assumed to be at the end of each period. This means that there are the same number of interest discount periods as rents.

While the term annuity may imply equal *annual* rents to some people, we should note that equal rents over any series of equal time intervals, such as monthly, quarterly, semiannually, or annually, constitute an annuity. The accountant commonly encounters a variety of transactions involving annuities.

## AMOUNT OF AN ANNUITY

The *amount of an annuity* is the *future* sum of all its rents plus the compound interest on each of them. Consider a simple example. Suppose you deposit $100 per year for four years (periods) in a fund which earns compound interest at 6% per annum. At the date of the last deposit, the first rent will have earned compound interest for three years, the second for two years, the third for one year. There will be no interest accumulation on the fourth rent since we are computing the future amount on the date of deposit of this rent. Applying principles we learned in Part A on amount of 1, the accumulation at the *date of the last deposit* will be seen to consist of —

*Date of Deposit*

| | | |
|---|---|---|
| Year 1 | $100 \times (1.06)^3 =$ | $119.10 |
| Year 2 | $100 \times (1.06)^2 =$ | 112.36 |
| Year 3 | $100 \times (1.06)^1 =$ | 106.00 |
| Year 4 | $100 | 100.00 |
| Amount of Annuity (Ordinary) | | $437.46 |

The symbol often used to denote the amount of an annuity of 1 is A. The underlying formula to compute the amount of an annuity of 1 is based upon the formula for an amount of 1 (Table 6–1) since the amount of an annuity of 1, as illustrated above, is the sum of a series of computations of the amount of 1. Therefore, the underlying formula is:

$$A_o = \frac{(1 + i)^n - 1}{i}$$

Notice in the heading of Table 6–3 that this is the indicated formula for those table values. Observe that the notation "$n$" refers to the number of *periodic rents* and *not* to the number of interest periods; "$i$" refers to the interest rate per period (and not to the annual rate except when the periods are one year in length). The values given in Table 6–3 are at the *date of the last rent* (i.e., the rents are at the end of each period); therefore, it is called an ordinary annuity as is indicated in the title of the table.

### Use of Table of Amount of Annuity of 1

Tables of amount of annuity of 1 are commonly used to calculate the future amount of a series of rents at a specific rate of compound interest. In most situations the following are known: (1) the amount of the equal rents; (2) the number of rents, "$n$"; and (3) the interest rate per period, "$i$." To determine the future amount of a specific situation, the appropriate value from Table 6–3 is multiplied by the amount of the periodic rent.

To illustrate an accounting application, assume Hill Corporation plans to expand the office building three years from now. To assure sufficient cash for this purpose the company has decided to set up a building fund by making three equal annual contributions of $60,000 cash on each December 31, starting in 1976. The funds will be needed on December 31, 1978, the date of the last deposit. The fund will be deposited with a trustee and will earn 7% per year compounded annually.

*Required:*

1. What will be the balance of the fund on December 31, 1978; that is, immediately after the last deposit?
2. Prepare a fund accumulation table for this situation.
3. Prepare the accounting entries for the entire period.

*Solution:*

1. Balance in the fund on December 31, 1978 (ordinary annuity basis):

$$\$60,000 \times A_{o\,{n-3} \atop i=7\%} = \$60,000 \times 3.2149 \text{ (from Table 6–3)} = \underline{\$192,894}$$

2. Accumulation table – building fund, through December 31, 1978:

| Date | Cash Deposits | Interest Revenue Earned | Fund Increases | Fund Balance |
|---|---|---|---|---|
| 12-31-76......$60,000 | | | $60,000 | $ 60,000 |
| 12-30-77...... | | $ 60,000 × .07 = $4,200 | 4,200 | 64,200 |
| 12-31-77...... 60,000 | | | 60,000 | 124,200 |
| 12-30-78...... | | 124,200 × .07 = 8,694 | 8,694 | 132,894 |
| 12-31-78...... 60,000 | | | 60,000 | 192,894* |

\* Balance on date of last deposit (i.e., an ordinary annuity). Assume that interest is credited to the fund each December 30.

3. Required journal entries:

Deposits in the fund:

| | 12-31-76 | 12-31-77 | 12-31-78 |
|---|---|---|---|
| Building fund .........60,000 | | 60,000 | 60,000 |
| Cash .............. | 60,000 | 60,000 | 60,000 |

Interest revenue earned on the fund:

| | 12-30-77 | 12-30-78 |
|---|---|---|
| Building fund........................................4,200 | | 8,694 |
| Interest revenue .............................. | 4,200 | 8,694 |

### Determination of Other Values Related to Amount of Annuity

In the immediately preceding example, *three* values were given as follows: (1) periodic rents, $60,000; (2) number of rents, 3; and (3) the periodic interest rate, 7%. A fourth value, the future accumulation in a sinking fund, $192,894, was computed. Obviously, if any three of these four values are known, the other one can be derived. Thus, as was illustrated with respect to the amount of 1, there are four types of potential problems involving amount of an annuity of 1 that may be encountered; viz:

1. To determine the future annuity accumulation (value); discussed immediately above.
2. To determine an unknown interest rate.[5]
   *Example* (based on above data):
   Given:
      *a.* Periodic rents, $60,000.
      *b.* Rents, 3.
      *c.* Future accumulation desired, $192,894.
   To derive the required interest rate:
      *a.* $192,894 ÷ $60,000 = 3.2149 (table value for 3 rents at unknown interest rate).
      *b.* Reference to Table 6–3, *line* for 3 rents indicates the required interest rate to be 7%.
3. To determine an unknown number of periodic rents.
   *Example* (based on above data):
   Given:
      *a.* Periodic rents, $60,000.
      *b.* Future accumulation desired, $192,894.
      *c.* Interest rate, 7% per period.
   To derive the required number of rents:
      *a.* $192,894 ÷ $60,000 = 3.2149 (table value for $1 at 7% for unknown number of rents).
      *b.* Reference to Table 6–3, *column* for 7% interest indicates the required number of rents to be 3.

---

[5] In the following example, the data used above, with one "given" changed in each instance, is used in order to clearly demonstrate the correctness of the answer and the reasons for the computational approach.

4. To determine the unknown amount of each rent.
   *Example* (based on above data):
      Given:
         *a.* Number of rents, 3.
         *b.* Interest rate per period, 7%.
         *c.* Future accumulation desired, $192,894.
      To derive the unknown amount of each rent:
         *a.* Reference to Table 6–3, *column* for 7% and *line* for 3 rents
         gives the value 3.2149.
         *b.* $192,894 ÷ 3.2149 = $60,000 (the period rent required).

## PRESENT VALUE OF AN ANNUITY

The *present value of an annuity* is the equivalent value *now* (i.e., the present) of a series of future dollars (i.e., periodic rents) discounted back from a series of specific future dates (i.e., periods) to the present date at a specified rate of compound interest (i.e., compound discounting). Since it involves compound discounting instead of compound interest, it can be said to be the inverse of the amount of an annuity explained above. For example, $1 (the periodic rent) due at the end of each of three periods in the future (total sum due $3), when discounted back at 8% compound interest, has a present value of $2.58. Alternatively, $2.58 deposited today at 8% compound interest per period would pay back $1 at the end of each of the three future periods. Significantly, it should be noted that the rents on the present value of an ordinary annuity are assumed to be at the *end* of each period; hence, in contrast to the amount of an annuity of 1, there are the same number of interest periods as rents.[6]

The symbol often used to denote the present value of annuity of 1 is P. As before, "*n*" indicates the number of periodic rents, and "*i*" the rate of discounting each period. Table 6–4 gives the present values of annuity of 1 for a number of periods and interest rates. Observe the heading of the statement and the underlying formula, viz:

$$\frac{1 - \dfrac{1}{(1 + i)^n}}{i}$$

The values in Table 6–4 represent an *ordinary* annuity; therefore, they are at the *beginning of the period* of the first rent (see page 253). To illustrate a typical accounting application, assume Delphi Corporation is negotiating the purchase of a certain natural resource. It is estimated that the resource will produce a net cash inflow of $200,000 per year for the next three years. Assume the "going" rate of compound interest is 8% per year. *Question:* What is the maximum amount that should be paid today (i.e., at the present time) for the mine?

---

[6] In both instances an *ordinary* annuity is assumed; annuities due are discussed in the next section. The above amounts are rounded.

*Solution:*

This requires computation of the present value of the three future rents as follows:

$$\$200,000 \times P_{o_{\substack{n=3 \\ i=8\%}}} = \$200,000 \times 2.577 \text{ (from Table 6–4)} = \underline{\$515,420}$$

If purchased at this price the acquisition entry would be:

Natural resource (identified).........................................515,420
    Cash (and/or debt) ..................................................        515,420

## Determination of Other Values Related to Present Value of Annuity

In the immediately preceding example, *three* values were given as follows: (1) the periodic rent or contribution, $r$; (2) the number of periodic contributions, $n$; and (3) the periodic discounting rate, $i$. A fourth value, the present value, $P$ ($515,420) was computed. Obviously, if *any* three of these four values are known, the other one can be derived. Thus, as illustrated for the amount of an annuity of 1, there are four types of potential problems related to the present value of an annuity that may be encountered, viz:

1. To determine the present value of a series of future rents; discussed and illustrated immediately above.
2. To determine an unknown interest rate.
   *Example* (based on above data):
   Given:
     *a.* Periodic rents, $200,000.
     *b.* Number of periodic rents, 3.
     *c.* Present value of the future rents, $515,420.
   To derive the required interest rate:
     *a.* $515,420 ÷ $200,000 = 2.5771 (approximate table value for 3 rents at unknown interest rate).
     *b.* Reference to Table 6–4, *line* for 3 rents, indicates the required interest rate to be 8%.
3. To determine an unknown number of periodic rents.
   *Example* (based on above data):
   Given:
     *a.* Periodic rents, $200,000.
     *b.* Interest rate, 8%.
     *c.* Present value of the future rents, $515,420.
   To derive the unknown number of periodic rents:
     *a.* $515,420 ÷ $200,000 = 2.5771 (approximate table value at 8% at unknown number of rents).
     *b.* Reference to Table 6–4, *column* for 8%, indicates that 3 periodic rents are required.
4. To determine the unknown amount of each rent.
   *Example* (based on above data):
   Given:
     *a.* Number of periodic rents, 3.

b. Interest rate per period, 8%.
c. Present value of the future rents, $515,420.
To derive the amount of each rent:
    a. Table 6–4 value at 8%, 3 rents = 2.5771.
    b. $515,420 ÷ 2.5771 = $200,000 (the periodic rent).

To illustrate an accounting application similar to the last illustration, assume Voss Corporation purchased a fixed asset resulting in the incurrence of a $50,000 debt on January 1, 1976. The liability is to be paid in three equal installments on each December 31, starting at the end of 1976. The interest rate is 9 percent, and each installment is to include both interest and principal.

*Required:*

1. Compute the amount of each equal annual installment.
2. Prepare a debt amortization schedule for this situation.
3. Give the journal entries covering the period of the debt.

*Solution:*

1. $50,000 ÷ P_{o_{n=3 \atop i=9\%}}$ = $50,000 ÷ 2.53129 (from Table 6–4) = $\underline{\$19,753}$
    (the periodic rent)

2. A debt amortization schedule is a decumulation table that shows the reduction of the debt from $50,000 to zero over the three-year period. The debt amortization schedule showing interest expense and reduction of principal each period would be as follows:

**Debt Amortization Schedule**

| Date | Cash Payment | Interest Expense | Payment on Principal | Unpaid Principal |
|---|---|---|---|---|
| 1-1-76 ......... | | | | $50,000 |
| 12-31-76 .........$19,753 [a] | | $4,500 [b] | $15,253 [c] | 34,747 [d] |
| 12-31-77 ......... 19,753 | | 3,127 | 16,626 | 18,121 |
| 12-31-78 ......... 19,753 | | 1,632* | 18,121 | -0- |

[a] Computed above.        * Adjusted for rounding error.
Successive computations:
[b] $50,000 × .09 = $4,500.
[c] $19,753 − $4,500 = $15,253.
[d] $50,000 − $15,253 = $34,747.

3. Journal entries:

1-1-76 to record the debt:

Fixed asset.................................................................50,000
    Liability .............................................................        50,000

Each December 31 to record payment (per above schedule):

| | 12-31-76 | 12-31-77 | 12-31-78 |
|---|---|---|---|
| Interest expense ...... | 4,500 | 3,127 | 1,632 |
| Liability .................. | 15,253 | 16,626 | 18,121 |
| Cash .............. | 19,753 | 19,753 | 19,753 |

## ANNUITIES DUE

Discussion of annuities to this point has been confined to *ordinary annuities* since they represent the more or less "normal" situation encountered. It will be recalled that with respect to ordinary annuities, specific assumptions were noted in the preceding discussions relative to the *timing* of the rents and the interest periods. *Annuities due* involve different assumptions with respect to the timing of rents. The timing distinction is: For ordinary annuities, the rents are assumed to be paid or received at the *end* of each period; in contrast, for annuities due, the rents are assumed to be paid or received at the *beginning* of each period.

### Amount of Annuity Due

In the case of the amount of an ordinary annuity, the future amount is calculated as of the date of the last rent since the rents are assumed to be at the end of each period. In contrast, the amount of an annuity due is calculated at the end of the period of the last rent since the rents are assumed to be at the beginning of each period. The contrast between the two timing assumptions can be graphically shown as follows ($n = 4$; $i = 8\%$):[7]

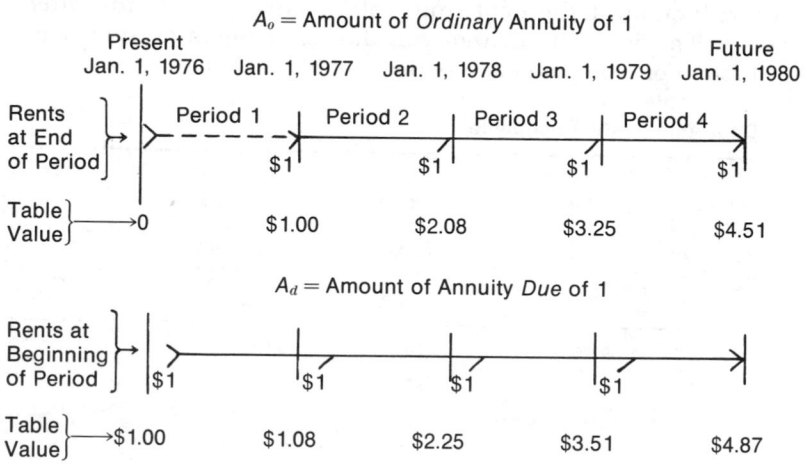

In the above diagram the following differences may be observed:

---

[7] The subscript "*o*" is an ordinary annuity and "*d*" an annuity due. The terms "ordinary" and "due" were coined by mathematicians; many accountants prefer more descriptive terminology:

1. Instead of "ordinary" – "end-of-the-period annuities."
2. Instead of "due" – "beginning-of-the-period annuities."

| | Type of Annuity | |
|---|---|---|
| Characteristic | $A_o$ – Ordinary | $A_d$ – Due |
| 1. Timing of each rent. | End of each period | Beginning of each period |
| 2. Number of rents. | Four | Four |
| 3. Number of interest periods. | Three | Four |
| 4. Point in time of the future amount (i.e., the table amount). | On date of last rent | At end of period following last rent |

The differences reflected in (3) and (4) are due solely to the different timing assumption for the rents. An understanding of the difference between an ordinary annuity and an annuity due is important in solving annuity problems. Care must be exercised to select the one that fits the specifications of the problem or situation. Ordinary annuity tables are found in various sources more often than annuity due tables. In situations where only an ordinary annuity table is available and an annuity due amount is needed, the conversion is simple and straightforward. Conversion from an ordinary annuity to an annuity due amount can be accomplished easily in either of two ways, viz:

1. Multiply the ordinary annuity amount by $(1 + i)$. That is, $A_d = A_o \times (1 + i)$. For example, the annuity due amounts shown in the graphic illustration on the previous page were computed as follows:

| Interest | Rents | Amount of Ordinary Annuity (Table 6–3) | Multiplier $\times (1 + i)$ | = Amount of Annuity Due |
|---|---|---|---|---|
| 8% | 1 | 1.00000 | (1.08) = | 1.08000 |
| 8% | 2 | 2.08000 | (1.08) = | 2.24640 |
| 8% | 3 | 3.24640 | (1.08) = | 3.50611 |
| 8% | 4 | 4.50611 | (1.08) = | 4.86660 |

Conversely, one could convert from an annuity due to an ordinary annuity by reversing the computations; that is, amount of annuity due, $n = 4$, $i = 8\%$, $4.86660 \div 1.08 = 4.50611$ (ordinary annuity).

2. Read the amount from an ordinary annuity table for *one greater* than the number of rents, then *subtract* the numeral 1 from it.[8] This has the effect of adding interest to the ordinary annuity amount for one period. To illustrate for $n = 3$; $i = 8\%$:

From Table 6–3 (amount of ordinary annuity), $n = 4$; $i = 8\%$ ............ 4.50611
Subtract the numeral 1.................................................................−1.00000
Difference – Amount of Annuity Due, $n = 3$; $i = 8\%$ ......................... 3.50611

---

[8] Frequently expressed as $(n + 1$ rents$) - 1$. Each method serves to increase the interest period by 1 for an annuity due and maintains the same number of rents.

In applying the concepts of future and present value, it is generally helpful to graphically analyze the situation, or problem, in a manner similar to the graphic illustrations in this chapter. This initial step will indicate the appropriate future or present value concept to apply. To illustrate, two examples are given below with explanation of the solution approaches. These focus on different situations requiring an amount of ordinary annuity and amount of annuity due.

*Situation A:* On January 1, 1976, Dawson Corporation entered into a contract with a foreign company that required Dawson to pay $50,000 cash on December 31, 1978. Because of disagreement over credit terms, it was agreed that Dawson would deposit three equal annual amounts in a Swiss bank starting December 31, 1976, so that the $50,000 would be available on December 31, 1978. On that date the bank will pay the foreign company in full. The bank agreed to add 6% annual compound interest to the fund each December 31.

*Required:*

1. Diagram the annuity required by the agreement to establish the debt payment fund with the bank.
2. What kind of annuity is indicated? Explain.
3. Compute the amount of the equal annual payments.

*Solution:*

1. Diagram of the annuity ($n = 3$; $i = 6\%$):

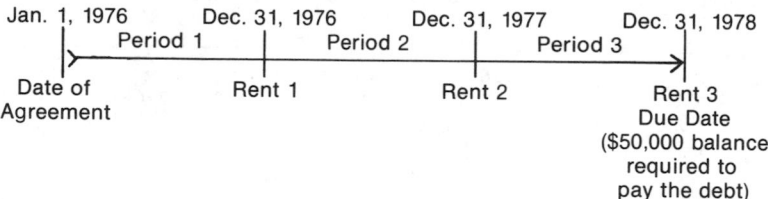

2. Since the rents are at the end of the period this is an *ordinary* annuity; that is, the future amount is at the date of the last rent.

3. $\text{Rent} = \dfrac{\text{Future Amount}}{A_{o_{\substack{n=3 \\ i=6\%}}}} = \dfrac{\$50,000}{3.1836 \text{ (Table 6–3)}} = \underline{\underline{\$15,705}}$

*Situation B:* On January 1, 1976, Cotter Corporation decided to create a plant expansion fund by making three annual deposits of $60,000 each on January 1, 1976, 1977, and 1978. The fund will be held by a trustee who will increase the fund on a 7% annual compound interest basis. The fund will be needed on December 31, 1978.

*Required:*

1. Diagram the annuity created in this situation. Identify dates.

2. What kind of annuity is indicated? Explain.
3. Compute the balance in the fund on December 31, 1978, and prepare a fund accumulation table.

*Solution:*

1. Diagram of the annuity ($n = 3$; $i = 7\%$):

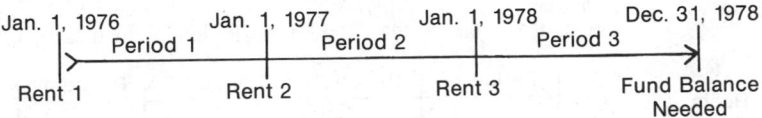

2. Since the rents are at the beginning of each period this is an annuity *due;* the amount desired in the fund is at the end of the period in which the last rent is contributed. Since the rents build a future amount it is an *amount of annuity due of 1.*
3. Fund balance at December 31, 1978:

Conversion:

$A_{d_{\substack{n=3 \\ i=7\%}}}$ = 3.2149 (Table 6–3) $\times$ 1.07 = 3.43994

Fund balance = \$60,000 $\times$ 3.43994
= \$206,396

The fund accumulation table for this amount of annuity due, $n = 3$; $i = 7\%$ would be:

| Date | Cash Deposits | Interest Revenue Earned | Fund Increases | Fund Balance |
|---|---|---|---|---|
| 1-1-76 ......| \$60,000 | | \$60,000 | \$ 60,000 |
| 12-31-76......| | \$ 60,000 $\times$ .07 = \$ 4,200 | 4,200 | 64,200 |
| 1-1-77 ...... | 60,000 | | 60,000 | 124,200 |
| 12-31-77......| | 124,200 $\times$ .07 = 8,694 | 8,694 | 132,894 |
| 1-1-78 ...... | 60,000 | | 60,000 | 192,894 |
| 12-31-78......| | 192,894 $\times$ .07 = 13,502 | 13,502 | 206,396 |

This accumulation table, prepared on an annuity due basis, may be compared with a similar set of facts, on an ordinary annuity basis, illustrated on page 237. Compare the timing difference for the rents and the resultant effects on the interest accumulations and fund balances.

### Present Value of Annuity Due

In the case of present value of an ordinary annuity the rents are assumed to be at the end of the period; therefore, the discount as calculated as of one period back from the first rent. In contrast, present value of an annuity due assumes the rents are at the beginning of each period; therefore, there is no discounting on the first rent. The contrast between the two timing assumptions for present value can be graphically shown as follows ($n = 4$; $i = 6\%$):

**$P_o$ = Present Value of *Ordinary* Annuity of 1**

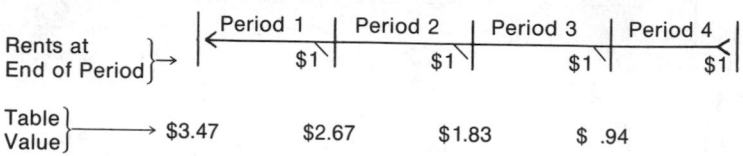

**$P_d$ = Present Value of Annuity *Due* of 1**

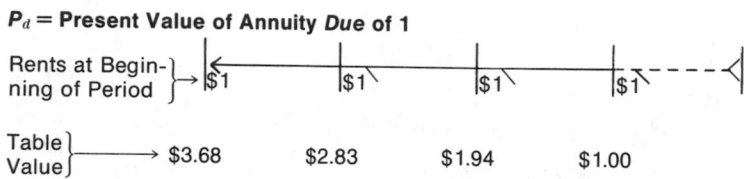

The above diagram shows that the *present value* of an ordinary annuity is calculated as of the beginning of the period even though the rents are at the end of each period (there are the same number of interest discount periods as rents). In contrast, the present value of an annuity due is computed at the date of the first rent (there is one less interest discount period than rents). Often an ordinary annuity table is available, but not an annuity due table. In such situations the present value of an ordinary annuity may be converted to the present value of an annuity due by either of two approaches, viz:

1. Multiply the present value ordinary annuity by $(1 + i)$. That is, $P_d = P_o \times (1 + i)$. For example, the present value of ordinary annuity for $n = 4$; $i = 6\%$ is 3.46511. The present value of an annuity due of 1 for $n = 4$; $i = 6\%$ is: $3.46511 \times 1.06 = 3.67301$.
2. Read the present value of an ordinary annuity of 1 table for *one less* than the number of rents, then *add* the numeral 1 to it.[9] To illustrate for $n = 4$; $i = 6\%$:

    From Table 6–4 (present value of ordinary annuity) $n = 3$; $i = 6\%$ ...2.67301
    Add the numeral 1 ....................................................................1.00000
    Summation—Present Value of Annuity Due, $n = 4$; $i = 6\%$...............3.67301

---

[9] Frequently expressed as $(n - 1$ rents$) + 1$. Either method serves to reduce the discount period by one for an annuity due and maintains the same number of rents.

Two situations presented below, with solutions, illustrate the different characteristics of present value of an ordinary annuity and annuity due. Careful attention to the timing of the rents is necessary in order to determine which type of annuity should be applied to each situation or problem.

*Situation C:* On January 1, 1976, Brown Corporation owes a $30,000 debt which is due. The creditor agreed to let Brown pay the debt in four equal annual payments on December 31, 1976, 1977, 1978, and 1979. Interest at 8% per year is to be paid on the unpaid principal. Each equal payment is to include interest and principal.

*Required:*
1. Diagram the annuity represented by the annual payments. Identify dates.
2. What kind of annuity is represented? Explain.
3. Compute the amount of the equal annual payments on the debt.

*Solution:*
1. Diagram of the annuity ($n = 4$; $i = 8\%$):

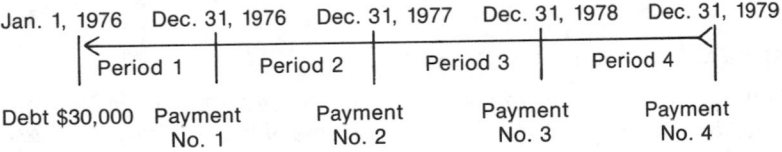

2. Since the payments are to be made at the end of each period, this is an ordinary annuity and the present value (i.e., the debt) is computed at the beginning of the first period.
3. The amount of each equal annual payment is computed as follows:

$$\text{Rent} = \frac{\text{Present Value}}{P_{o\,{n=4}\atop i=8\%}} = \frac{\$30,000}{3.31213 \text{ (Table 6-4)}} = \$9,058$$

*Situation D:* John Doe was seriously injured while working for X Corporation. On January 1, 1976, an agreement was reached whereby X Corporation would deposit $100,000 with the City Bank, as trustee. The bank agreed to pay 6% compound interest per year on the unused principal while making five equal annual payments to Doe. The payments are to be made on each January 1, starting immediately, until the fund, including all interest accumulations is fully expended.

*Required:*
1. Diagram the annuity represented by the payments. Identify dates.
2. What kind of annuity is represented? Explain.
3. Compute the amount of each equal annual payment.

*Solution:*

1. Diagram of annuity ($n = 5$; $i = 6\%$):

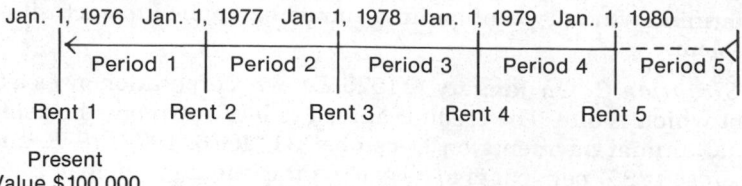

2. Since the rents are at the beginning of the period (the first one starts immediately), this is an annuity due. Since the $100,000 is deposited at the start, that amount represents the present value of the annuity on which the amount of the equal rents is based. The computation is:

3. $\text{Rent} = \dfrac{\text{Present Value}}{P_{d\,n=5 \atop i=6\%}} = \dfrac{\$100,000}{4.46511^*} = \underline{\underline{\$22,396}}.$

\* Conversion:
From Table 6–4, 4.21236 × 1.06 = 4.46511.

## USING MULTIPLE TABLE VALUES

Often situations are encountered where the analysis will require the use of two or more tables. These situations often involve annuities with uneven contributions (i.e., rents). Problems with these characteristics can be resolved readily if one understands the concepts underlying future amount and present value.

To illustrate, assume ST Construction Company is negotiating to purchase 40 acres of land with a deposit of gravel suitable for exploitation. The two parties are negotiating the price. ST Company has completed an extensive study that provided the following estimates:

Expected net cash revenues over the life of the resource:
Year 1 .................................................................................$ 5,000
Years 2–5 (per year) .................................................... 30,000
Years 6–9 (per year) ..................................................... 40,000
Year 10 (last year—resource exhausted) ...................................... 10,000
Estimated sales value of the 40 acres, after exploitation
    and net of land-leveling costs (end of tenth year) ...................... 2,000

*Required:*

Assuming the above estimates are realistic, compute how much ST Construction Company should offer for the land assuming they expect a 12% return on their investment. Assume all amounts are at year-end. Disregard income taxes.

*Solution:*

This requires computation of the present value of the future expected cash inflows as follows:

Year 1: $5,000 × $p_{n=1 \atop i=12\%}$  = $5,000 × .89286 =                              $ 4,464

Years 2–5: $30,000 × $P_{n=5-1 \atop i=12\%}$ = $30,000 × (3.60478 − .89286) =        81,358

Years 6–9: $40,000 × $P_{n=9-5 \atop i=12\%}$ = $40,000 × (5.32825 − 3.60478) =       68,939

Year 10: ($10,000 + $2,000) × $p_{n=10 \atop i=12\%}$  = $12,000 × .32197 =               3,864

Offering Price ...................................................................................$158,625

The solution involved the use of the two present value tables: present value of $1, and present value of ordinary annuity of $1. Alternatively, it can be solved by using only the former table in which case the discounting would have to be computed for each of the ten years separately and then summed. By using the annuity table for the periods 2–5 and 6–9, computational time was shortened; the results are the same.

## SUMMARY

This chapter has presented the concepts of compound interest and focuses on their relevance to certain accounting problems. At the beginning of the chapter the primary accounting applications were listed. These applications are required to conform to GAAP (generally accepted accounting principles). Because of the wide range of accounting applications accountants need a thorough understanding of them. In a related activity, they also have considerable relevance in financial analyses, capital budgeting, and alternative choice problems which accountants often encounter whether in public, private, or governmental accounting. Throughout the later chapters, and in subsequent advanced accounting courses, the concepts of compound interest will be used.

**TABLE 6-1**
**Amount of 1, $a = (1 + i)^n$**

| Periods | 2% | 2½% | 3% | 4% | 5% | 6% |
|---|---|---|---|---|---|---|
| 1 ........ | 1.02000 | 1.02500 | 1.03000 | 1.04000 | 1.05000 | 1.06000 |
| 2 ........ | 1.04040 | 1.05062 | 1.06090 | 1.08160 | 1.10250 | 1.12360 |
| 3 ........ | 1.06121 | 1.07689 | 1.09273 | 1.12486 | 1.15762 | 1.19102 |
| 4 ........ | 1.08243 | 1.10381 | 1.12551 | 1.16986 | 1.21551 | 1.26248 |
| 5 ........ | 1.10408 | 1.13141 | 1.15927 | 1.21665 | 1.27628 | 1.33823 |
| 6 ........ | 1.12616 | 1.15969 | 1.19405 | 1.26532 | 1.34010 | 1.41852 |
| 7 ........ | 1.14869 | 1.18869 | 1.22987 | 1.31593 | 1.40710 | 1.50363 |
| 8 ........ | 1.17166 | 1.21840 | 1.26677 | 1.36857 | 1.47746 | 1.59385 |
| 9 ........ | 1.19509 | 1.24886 | 1.30477 | 1.42331 | 1.55133 | 1.68948 |
| 10 ........ | 1.21899 | 1.28008 | 1.34392 | 1.48024 | 1.62889 | 1.79085 |
| 11 ........ | 1.24337 | 1.31209 | 1.38423 | 1.53945 | 1.71034 | 1.89830 |
| 12 ........ | 1.26824 | 1.34489 | 1.42576 | 1.60103 | 1.79586 | 2.01220 |
| 13 ........ | 1.29361 | 1.37851 | 1.46853 | 1.66507 | 1.88565 | 2.13293 |
| 14 ........ | 1.31948 | 1.41297 | 1.51259 | 1.73168 | 1.97993 | 2.26090 |
| 15 ........ | 1.34587 | 1.44830 | 1.55797 | 1.80094 | 2.07893 | 2.39656 |
| 16 ........ | 1.37279 | 1.48451 | 1.60471 | 1.87298 | 2.18287 | 2.54035 |
| 17 ........ | 1.40024 | 1.52162 | 1.65285 | 1.94790 | 2.29202 | 2.69277 |
| 18 ........ | 1.42825 | 1.55966 | 1.70243 | 2.02582 | 2.40662 | 2.85434 |
| 19 ........ | 1.45681 | 1.59865 | 1.75351 | 2.10685 | 2.52695 | 3.02560 |
| 20 ........ | 1.48595 | 1.63862 | 1.80611 | 2.19112 | 2.65330 | 3.20714 |
| 21 ........ | 1.51567 | 1.67958 | 1.86029 | 2.27877 | 2.78596 | 3.39956 |
| 22 ........ | 1.54598 | 1.72157 | 1.91610 | 2.36992 | 2.92526 | 3.60354 |
| 23 ........ | 1.57690 | 1.76461 | 1.97359 | 2.46472 | 3.07152 | 3.81975 |
| 24 ........ | 1.60844 | 1.80873 | 2.03279 | 2.56330 | 3.22510 | 4.04893 |
| 25 ........ | 1.64061 | 1.85394 | 2.09378 | 2.66584 | 3.38635 | 4.29187 |

| Periods | 7% | 8% | 9% | 10% | 11% | 12% |
|---|---|---|---|---|---|---|
| 1 ........ | 1.07000 | 1.08000 | 1.09000 | 1.10000 | 1.11000 | 1.12000 |
| 2 ........ | 1.14490 | 1.16640 | 1.18810 | 1.21000 | 1.23210 | 1.25440 |
| 3 ........ | 1.22504 | 1.25971 | 1.29503 | 1.33100 | 1.36763 | 1.40493 |
| 4 ........ | 1.31080 | 1.36049 | 1.41158 | 1.46410 | 1.51807 | 1.57352 |
| 5 ........ | 1.40255 | 1.46933 | 1.53862 | 1.61051 | 1.68506 | 1.76234 |
| 6 ........ | 1.50073 | 1.58687 | 1.67710 | 1.77156 | 1.87041 | 1.97382 |
| 7 ........ | 1.60578 | 1.71382 | 1.82804 | 1.94872 | 2.07616 | 2.21068 |
| 8 ........ | 1.71819 | 1.85093 | 1.99256 | 2.14359 | 2.30454 | 2.47596 |
| 9 ........ | 1.83846 | 1.99900 | 2.17189 | 2.35795 | 2.55804 | 2.77308 |
| 10 ........ | 1.96715 | 2.15892 | 2.36736 | 2.59374 | 2.83942 | 3.10585 |
| 11 ........ | 2.10485 | 2.33164 | 2.58043 | 2.85312 | 3.15176 | 3.47855 |
| 12 ........ | 2.25219 | 2.51817 | 2.81266 | 3.13843 | 3.49845 | 3.89598 |
| 13 ........ | 2.40985 | 2.71962 | 3.06580 | 3.45227 | 3.88328 | 4.36349 |
| 14 ........ | 2.57853 | 2.93719 | 3.34173 | 3.79750 | 4.31044 | 4.88711 |
| 15 ........ | 2.75903 | 3.17217 | 3.64248 | 4.17725 | 4.78459 | 5.47357 |
| 16 ........ | 2.95216 | 3.42594 | 3.97031 | 4.59497 | 5.31089 | 6.13039 |
| 17 ........ | 3.15882 | 3.70002 | 4.32763 | 5.05447 | 5.89509 | 6.86604 |
| 18 ........ | 3.37993 | 3.99602 | 4.71712 | 5.55992 | 6.54355 | 7.68997 |
| 19 ........ | 3.61653 | 4.31570 | 5.14166 | 6.11591 | 7.26334 | 8.61276 |
| 20 ........ | 3.86968 | 4.66096 | 5.60441 | 6.72750 | 8.06231 | 9.64629 |
| 21 ........ | 4.14056 | 5.03383 | 6.10881 | 7.40025 | 8.94917 | 10.80385 |
| 22 ........ | 4.43040 | 5.43654 | 6.65860 | 8.14027 | 9.93357 | 12.10031 |
| 23 ........ | 4.74053 | 5.87146 | 7.25787 | 8.95430 | 11.02627 | 13.55235 |
| 24 ........ | 5.07237 | 6.34118 | 7.91108 | 9.84973 | 12.23916 | 15.17863 |
| 25 ........ | 5.42743 | 6.84848 | 8.62308 | 10.83471 | 13.58546 | 17.00006 |

## TABLE 6-2

Present Value of 1, $p = \dfrac{1}{(1+i)^n}$

| Periods | 2% | 2½% | 3% | 4% | 5% | 6% |
|---|---|---|---|---|---|---|
| 1 ........ | .98039 | .97561 | .97087 | .96154 | .95238 | .94340 |
| 2 ........ | .96117 | .95181 | .94260 | .92456 | .90703 | .89000 |
| 3 ........ | .94232 | .92860 | .91514 | .88900 | .86384 | .83962 |
| 4 ........ | .92385 | .90595 | .88849 | .85480 | .82270 | .79209 |
| 5 ........ | .90573 | .88385 | .86261 | .82193 | .78353 | .74726 |
| 6 ........ | .88797 | .86230 | .83748 | .79031 | .74622 | .70496 |
| 7 ........ | .87056 | .84127 | .81309 | .75992 | .71068 | .66506 |
| 8 ........ | .85349 | .82075 | .78941 | .73069 | .67684 | .62741 |
| 9 ........ | .83676 | .80073 | .76642 | .70259 | .64461 | .59190 |
| 10 ........ | .82035 | .78120 | .74409 | .67556 | .61391 | .55839 |
| 11 ........ | .80426 | .76214 | .72242 | .64958 | .58468 | .52679 |
| 12 ........ | .78849 | .74356 | .70138 | .62460 | .55684 | .49697 |
| 13 ........ | .77303 | .72542 | .68095 | .60057 | .53032 | .46884 |
| 14 ........ | .75788 | .70773 | .66112 | .57748 | .50507 | .44230 |
| 15 ........ | .74301 | .69047 | .64186 | .55526 | .48102 | .41727 |
| 16 ........ | .72845 | .67362 | .62317 | .53391 | .45811 | .39365 |
| 17 ........ | .71416 | .65720 | .60502 | .51337 | .43630 | .37136 |
| 18 ........ | .70016 | .64117 | .58739 | .49363 | .41552 | .35034 |
| 19 ........ | .68643 | .62553 | .57029 | .47464 | .39573 | .33051 |
| 20 ........ | .67297 | .61027 | .55368 | .45639 | .37689 | .31180 |
| 21 ........ | .65978 | .59539 | .53755 | .43883 | .35894 | .29416 |
| 22 ........ | .64684 | .58086 | .52189 | .42196 | .34185 | .27751 |
| 23 ........ | .63416 | .56670 | .50669 | .40573 | .32557 | .26180 |
| 24 ........ | .62172 | .55288 | .49193 | .39012 | .31007 | .24698 |
| 25 ........ | .60953 | .53939 | .47761 | .37512 | .29530 | .23300 |

| Periods | 7% | 8% | 9% | 10% | 11% | 12% |
|---|---|---|---|---|---|---|
| 1 ........ | .93458 | .92593 | .91743 | .90909 | .90090 | .89286 |
| 2 ........ | .87344 | .85734 | .84168 | .82645 | .81162 | .79719 |
| 3 ........ | .81630 | .79383 | .77218 | .75131 | .73119 | .71178 |
| 4 ........ | .76290 | .73503 | .70843 | .68301 | .65873 | .63552 |
| 5 ........ | .71299 | .68058 | .64993 | .62092 | .59345 | .56743 |
| 6 ........ | .66634 | .63017 | .59627 | .56447 | .53464 | .50663 |
| 7 ........ | .62275 | .58349 | .54703 | .51316 | .48166 | .45235 |
| 8 ........ | .58201 | .54027 | .50187 | .46651 | .43393 | .40388 |
| 9 ........ | .54393 | .50025 | .46043 | .42410 | .39092 | .36061 |
| 10 ........ | .50835 | .46319 | .42241 | .38554 | .35218 | .32197 |
| 11 ........ | .47509 | .42888 | .38753 | .35049 | .31728 | .28748 |
| 12 ........ | .44401 | .39711 | .35553 | .31863 | .28584 | .25668 |
| 13 ........ | .41496 | .36770 | .32618 | .28966 | .25751 | .22917 |
| 14 ........ | .38782 | .34046 | .29925 | .26333 | .23199 | .20462 |
| 15 ........ | .36245 | .31524 | .27454 | .23939 | .20900 | .18270 |
| 16 ........ | .33873 | .29189 | .25187 | .21763 | .18829 | .16312 |
| 17 ........ | .31657 | .27027 | .23107 | .19784 | .16963 | .14564 |
| 18 ........ | .29586 | .25025 | .21199 | .17986 | .15282 | .13004 |
| 19 ........ | .27651 | .23171 | .19449 | .16351 | .13768 | .11611 |
| 20 ........ | .25842 | .21455 | .17843 | .14864 | .12403 | .10367 |
| 21 ........ | .24151 | .19866 | .16370 | .13513 | .11174 | .09256 |
| 22 ........ | .22571 | .18394 | .15018 | .12285 | .10067 | .08264 |
| 23 ........ | .21095 | .17032 | .13778 | .11168 | .09069 | .07379 |
| 24 ........ | .19715 | .15770 | .12640 | .10153 | .08170 | .06588 |
| 25 ........ | .18425 | .14602 | .11597 | .09230 | .07361 | .05882 |

## TABLE 6-3

## Amount of Annuity of 1 (Ordinary), $A_o = \dfrac{(1+i)^n - 1}{i}$

| Periodic Rents | 2% | 2½% | 3% | 4% | 5% | 6% |
|---|---|---|---|---|---|---|
| 1 ......... | 1.00000 | 1.00000 | 1.00000 | 1.00000 | 1.00000 | 1.00000 |
| 2 ......... | 2.02000 | 2.02500 | 2.03000 | 2.04000 | 2.05000 | 2.06000 |
| 3 ......... | 3.06040 | 3.07562 | 3.09090 | 3.12160 | 3.15250 | 3.18360 |
| 4 ......... | 4.12161 | 4.15252 | 4.18363 | 4.24646 | 4.31012 | 4.37462 |
| 5 ......... | 5.20404 | 5.25633 | 5.30914 | 5.41632 | 5.52563 | 5.63709 |
| 6 ......... | 6.30812 | 6.38774 | 6.46841 | 6.63298 | 6.80191 | 6.97532 |
| 7 ......... | 7.43428 | 7.54743 | 7.66246 | 7.89829 | 8.14201 | 8.39384 |
| 8 ......... | 8.58297 | 8.73612 | 8.89234 | 9.21423 | 9.54911 | 9.89747 |
| 9 ......... | 9.75463 | 9.95452 | 10.15911 | 10.58280 | 11.02656 | 11.49132 |
| 10 ......... | 10.94972 | 11.20338 | 11.46388 | 12.00611 | 12.57789 | 13.18079 |
| 11 ......... | 12.16872 | 12.48347 | 12.80780 | 13.48635 | 14.20679 | 14.97164 |
| 12 ......... | 13.41209 | 13.79555 | 14.19203 | 15.02581 | 15.91713 | 16.86994 |
| 13 ......... | 14.68033 | 15.14044 | 15.61779 | 16.62684 | 17.71298 | 18.88214 |
| 14 ......... | 15.97394 | 16.51895 | 17.08632 | 18.29191 | 19.59863 | 21.01507 |
| 15 ......... | 17.29342 | 17.93193 | 18.59891 | 20.02359 | 21.57856 | 23.27597 |
| 16 ......... | 18.63929 | 19.38022 | 20.15688 | 21.82453 | 23.65749 | 25.67253 |
| 17 ......... | 20.01207 | 20.86473 | 21.76159 | 23.69751 | 25.84037 | 28.21288 |
| 18 ......... | 21.41231 | 22.38635 | 23.41444 | 25.64541 | 28.13238 | 30.90565 |
| 19 ......... | 22.84056 | 23.94601 | 25.11687 | 27.67123 | 30.53900 | 33.75999 |
| 20 ......... | 24.29737 | 25.54466 | 26.87037 | 29.77808 | 33.06595 | 36.78559 |
| 21 ......... | 25.78332 | 27.18327 | 28.67649 | 31.96920 | 35.71925 | 39.99273 |
| 22 ......... | 27.29898 | 28.86286 | 30.53678 | 34.24797 | 38.50521 | 43.39229 |
| 23 ......... | 28.84496 | 30.58443 | 32.45288 | 36.61789 | 41.43048 | 46.99583 |
| 24 ......... | 30.42186 | 32.34904 | 34.42647 | 39.08260 | 44.50200 | 50.81558 |
| 25 ......... | 32.03030 | 34.15776 | 36.45926 | 41.64591 | 47.72710 | 54.86451 |

| Periodic Rents | 7% | 8% | 9% | 10% | 11% | 12% |
|---|---|---|---|---|---|---|
| 1 ......... | 1.00000 | 1.00000 | 1.00000 | 1.00000 | 1.00000 | 1.00000 |
| 2 ......... | 2.07000 | 2.08000 | 2.09000 | 2.10000 | 2.11000 | 2.12000 |
| 3 ......... | 3.21490 | 3.24640 | 3.27810 | 3.31000 | 3.34210 | 3.37440 |
| 4 ......... | 4.43994 | 4.50611 | 4.57313 | 4.64100 | 4.70973 | 4.77933 |
| 5 ......... | 5.75074 | 5.86660 | 5.98471 | 6.10510 | 6.22780 | 6.35285 |
| 6 ......... | 7.15329 | 7.33593 | 7.52333 | 7.71561 | 7.91286 | 8.11519 |
| 7 ......... | 8.65402 | 8.92280 | 9.20043 | 9.48717 | 9.78327 | 10.08901 |
| 8 ......... | 10.25980 | 10.63663 | 11.02847 | 11.43589 | 11.85943 | 12.29969 |
| 9 ......... | 11.97799 | 12.48756 | 13.02104 | 13.57948 | 14.16397 | 14.77566 |
| 10 ......... | 13.81645 | 14.48656 | 15.19293 | 15.93742 | 16.72201 | 17.54874 |
| 11 ......... | 15.78360 | 16.64549 | 17.56029 | 18.53117 | 19.56143 | 20.65458 |
| 12 ......... | 17.88845 | 18.97713 | 20.14072 | 21.38428 | 22.71319 | 24.13313 |
| 13 ......... | 20.14064 | 21.49530 | 22.95338 | 24.52271 | 26.21164 | 28.02911 |
| 14 ......... | 22.55049 | 24.21492 | 26.01919 | 27.97498 | 30.09492 | 32.39260 |
| 15 ......... | 25.12902 | 27.15211 | 29.36092 | 31.77248 | 34.40536 | 37.27971 |
| 16 ......... | 27.88805 | 30.32428 | 33.00340 | 35.94973 | 39.18995 | 42.75328 |
| 17 ......... | 30.84022 | 33.75023 | 36.97370 | 40.54470 | 44.50084 | 48.88367 |
| 18 ......... | 33.99903 | 37.45024 | 41.30134 | 45.59917 | 50.39594 | 55.74971 |
| 19 ......... | 37.37896 | 41.44626 | 46.01846 | 51.15909 | 56.93949 | 63.43968 |
| 20 ......... | 40.99549 | 45.76196 | 51.16012 | 57.27500 | 64.20283 | 72.05244 |
| 21 ......... | 44.86518 | 50.42292 | 56.76453 | 64.00250 | 72.26514 | 81.69874 |
| 22 ......... | 49.00574 | 55.45676 | 62.87334 | 71.40275 | 81.21431 | 92.50258 |
| 23 ......... | 53.43614 | 60.89330 | 69.53194 | 79.54302 | 91.14788 | 104.60289 |
| 24 ......... | 58.17667 | 66.76476 | 76.78981 | 88.49733 | 102.17415 | 118.15524 |
| 25 ......... | 63.24904 | 73.10594 | 84.70090 | 98.34706 | 114.41331 | 133.33387 |

**TABLE 6-4**

**Present Value of Annuity of 1 (Ordinary),** $P_o = \dfrac{1 - \dfrac{1}{(1+i)^n}}{i}$

| Periodic Rents | 2% | 2½% | 3% | 4% | 5% | 6% |
|---|---|---|---|---|---|---|
| 1 ......... | .98039 | .97561 | .97087 | .96154 | .95238 | .94340 |
| 2 ......... | 1.94156 | 1.92742 | 1.91347 | 1.88609 | 1.85941 | 1.83339 |
| 3 ......... | 2.88388 | 2.85602 | 2.82861 | 2.77509 | 2.72325 | 2.67301 |
| 4 ......... | 3.80773 | 3.76197 | 3.71710 | 3.62990 | 3.54595 | 3.46511 |
| 5 ......... | 4.71346 | 4.64583 | 4.57971 | 4.45182 | 4.32948 | 4.21236 |
| 6 ......... | 5.60143 | 5.50813 | 5.41719 | 5.24214 | 5.07569 | 4.91732 |
| 7 ......... | 6.47199 | 6.34939 | 6.23028 | 6.00205 | 5.78637 | 5.58238 |
| 8 ......... | 7.32548 | 7.17014 | 7.01969 | 6.73274 | 6.46321 | 6.20979 |
| 9 ......... | 8.16224 | 7.97087 | 7.78611 | 7.43533 | 7.10782 | 6.80169 |
| 10 ......... | 8.98259 | 8.75206 | 8.53020 | 8.11090 | 7.72173 | 7.36009 |
| 11 ......... | 9.78685 | 9.51421 | 9.25262 | 8.76048 | 8.30641 | 7.88687 |
| 12 ......... | 10.57534 | 10.25776 | 9.95400 | 9.38507 | 8.86325 | 8.38384 |
| 13 ......... | 11.34837 | 10.98318 | 10.63496 | 9.98565 | 9.39357 | 8.85268 |
| 14 ......... | 12.10625 | 11.69091 | 11.29607 | 10.56312 | 9.89864 | 9.29498 |
| 15 ......... | 12.84926 | 12.38138 | 11.93794 | 11.11839 | 10.37966 | 9.71225 |
| 16 ......... | 13.57771 | 13.05500 | 12.56110 | 11.65230 | 10.83777 | 10.10590 |
| 17 ......... | 14.29187 | 13.71220 | 13.16612 | 12.16567 | 11.27407 | 10.47726 |
| 18 ......... | 14.99203 | 14.35336 | 13.75351 | 12.65930 | 11.68959 | 10.82760 |
| 19 ......... | 15.67846 | 14.97889 | 14.32380 | 13.13394 | 12.08532 | 11.15812 |
| 20 ......... | 16.35143 | 15.58916 | 14.87747 | 13.59033 | 12.46221 | 11.46992 |
| 21 ......... | 17.01121 | 16.18455 | 15.41502 | 14.02916 | 12.82115 | 11.76408 |
| 22 ......... | 17.65805 | 16.76541 | 15.93692 | 14.45112 | 13.16300 | 12.04158 |
| 23 ......... | 18.29220 | 17.33211 | 16.44361 | 14.85684 | 13.48857 | 12.30338 |
| 24 ......... | 18.91393 | 17.88499 | 16.93554 | 15.24696 | 13.79864 | 12.55036 |
| 25 ......... | 19.52346 | 18.42438 | 17.41315 | 15.62208 | 14.09394 | 12.78336 |

| Periodic Rents | 7% | 8% | 9% | 10% | 11% | 12% |
|---|---|---|---|---|---|---|
| 1 ......... | .93458 | .92593 | .91743 | .90909 | .90090 | .89286 |
| 2 ......... | 1.80802 | 1.78326 | 1.75911 | 1.73554 | 1.71252 | 1.69005 |
| 3 ......... | 2.62432 | 2.57710 | 2.53129 | 2.48685 | 2.44371 | 2.40183 |
| 4 ......... | 3.38721 | 3.31213 | 3.23972 | 3.16987 | 3.10245 | 3.03735 |
| 5 ......... | 4.10020 | 3.99271 | 3.88965 | 3.79079 | 3.69590 | 3.60478 |
| 6 ......... | 4.76654 | 4.62288 | 4.48592 | 4.35526 | 4.23054 | 4.11141 |
| 7 ......... | 5.38929 | 5.20637 | 5.03295 | 4.86842 | 4.71220 | 4.56376 |
| 8 ......... | 5.97130 | 5.74664 | 5.53482 | 5.33493 | 5.14612 | 4.96764 |
| 9 ......... | 6.51523 | 6.24689 | 5.99525 | 5.75902 | 5.53705 | 5.32825 |
| 10 ......... | 7.02358 | 6.71008 | 6.41766 | 6.14457 | 5.88923 | 5.65022 |
| 11 ......... | 7.49867 | 7.13896 | 6.80519 | 6.49506 | 6.20652 | 5.93770 |
| 12 ......... | 7.94269 | 7.53608 | 7.16073 | 6.81369 | 6.49236 | 6.19437 |
| 13 ......... | 8.35765 | 7.90378 | 7.48690 | 7.10336 | 6.74987 | 6.42355 |
| 14 ......... | 8.74547 | 8.24424 | 7.78615 | 7.36669 | 6.98187 | 6.62817 |
| 15 ......... | 9.10791 | 8.55948 | 8.06069 | 7.60608 | 7.19087 | 6.81086 |
| 16 ......... | 9.44665 | 8.85137 | 8.31256 | 7.82371 | 7.37916 | 6.97399 |
| 17 ......... | 9.76322 | 9.12164 | 8.54363 | 8.02155 | 7.54879 | 7.11963 |
| 18 ......... | 10.05909 | 9.37189 | 8.75563 | 8.20141 | 7.70162 | 7.24967 |
| 19 ......... | 10.33560 | 9.60360 | 8.95011 | 8.36492 | 7.83929 | 7.36578 |
| 20 ......... | 10.59401 | 9.81815 | 9.12855 | 8.51356 | 7.96333 | 7.46944 |
| 21 ......... | 10.83553 | 10.01680 | 9.29224 | 8.64869 | 8.07507 | 7.56200 |
| 22 ......... | 11.06124 | 10.20074 | 9.44243 | 8.77154 | 8.17574 | 7.64465 |
| 23 ......... | 11.27219 | 10.37106 | 9.58021 | 8.88322 | 8.26643 | 7.71843 |
| 24 ......... | 11.46933 | 10.52876 | 9.70661 | 8.98474 | 8.34814 | 7.78432 |
| 25 ......... | 11.65358 | 10.67478 | 9.82258 | 9.07704 | 8.42174 | 7.84314 |

## QUESTIONS

1. Explain what is meant by the time value of money.

2. Fundamentally what is the difference between simple interest and compound interest?

3. Briefly explain each of the following:
   a. Amount of 1.
   b. Present value of 1.
   c. Amount of annuity of 1.
   d. Present value of annuity of 1.

4. Give the numerical values of $n$ and of $i$ in determining the compound amount of a sum for ten years for each of the following:
   a. 5% compounded annually.
   b. 5% compounded semiannually.
   c. 8% compounded quarterly.
   d. 6% compounded monthly.

5. Explain what is meant by the amount of 1. Relate it to the present value of 1.

6. If the table value for amount of 1 is known, how may it be converted to the table value for present value of 1?

7. Define an annuity in general terms. Explain rents and relate them to time periods and interest rates.

8. The table for amount of an annuity provides the value 3.09 (rounded) at 3% for three periods; explain the meaning of the table value.

9. What is meant by the present value of an annuity? Contrast it with the amount of an annuity.

10. Explain the fundamental difference between (a) amount of an ordinary annuity, and (b) amount of an annuity due.

11. Explain the fundamental difference between (a) present value of an ordinary annuity, and (b) present value of an annuity due.

12. Complete the following table of values assuming $n = 11$; $i = 10\%$:

|  | Annual Compounding | Semiannual Compounding |
|---|---|---|
| a. Amount of 1. | _____ | _____ |
| b. Present value of 1. | _____ | _____ |
| c. Amount of ordinary annuity of 1. | _____ | _____ |
| d. Amount of annuity due of 1. | _____ | _____ |
| e. Present value of ordinary annuity of 1. | _____ | _____ |
| f. Present value of annuity due of 1. | _____ | _____ |

## EXERCISES

### Exercise 6–1

Dowd Company plans to deposit $55,000 today in a special building fund which will be needed at the end of six years. They are looking for a financial institution (as trustee) that will pay them 8% interest on the fund balance.

*Required:*

How much will the fund total assuming (show computations):

Case A – Annual compounding?
Case B – Semiannual compounding?
Case C – Quarterly compounding?

## Exercise 6–2

Dustin Company, at the present date, has $33,000 which will be deposited in a savings account until needed. It is anticipated that $84,415 will be needed at the end of nine years to expand some manufacturing facilities. What rate of interest would be required to accumulate the $84,415 assuming compounding on an annual basis? Show computations.

## Exercise 6–3

Franklin Corporation is planning an addition to the office building as soon as adequate funds can be accumulated. The corporation has estimated that the addition will cost approximately $95,212. At the present time $60,000 cash is on hand that will not be needed in the near future. A local savings institution will pay 8% interest (compounded annually). How many periods would be required for the $60,000 to accumulate to $95,212? Show computations.

## Exercise 6–4

North Company has on hand $75,000 cash that will not be needed in the near future. However, the company will expand operations within the next three to five years. At the present date, the company has decided to establish a savings account locally which will earn 6% interest compounded annually. The interest will be added to the fund each year. Assuming the deposit of $75,000 is made on January 1, 1977, (a) compute the balance that will be in the fund at the end of the third year, and (b) prepare an accumulation table for the fund.

## Exercise 6–5

Samson Company will need $150,000 cash to renovate an old plant five years from now. Assume a financial institution will increase a fund at 6% interest. Compute the amount of cash that must be deposited now to meet this need assuming (show computations):

Case A – Annual compounding?
Case B – Semiannual compounding?

## Exercise 6–6

Brush Corporation has planned a plant expansion which will require approximately $160,000 at December 31, 1978. Since they have some idle cash on hand now, January 1, 1976, they desire to know how much they would have to invest as a lump sum now to accumulate the required amount assuming 6% annual compound interest is added to the fund each December 31.

*Required:*

1. Compute the amount that must be invested on January 1, 1976.
2. Prepare an accumulation table for plant expansion fund.

### Exercise 6–7

Dowdy Company purchased some additional equipment that was needed because of a new contract. The equipment was purchased on January 1, 1976. Because the contract would require three years to complete and Dowdy was short of cash, the vendor agreed to accept a down payment of $5,000 and a two-year noninterest-bearing note for $45,000 (this amount includes all interest charges) due December 31, 1977. Assume a 10% annual rate of interest.

*Required:*

1. Compute the cost of the equipment. Show computations.
2. Give the entry at date of acquisition of the equipment.
3. Prepare a debt schedule.

### Exercise 6–8

Storm Company, on January 1, 1976, has a contract whereby the company is due to receive $24,000 cash on December 31, 1981. The company is short of cash and desires to discount (sell) this claim. They are willing to accept a 12% annual discount (annual discounting). Under these conditions how much cash would Storm receive on January 1, 1976?'What would be the amount of interest paid by Storm? Show computations.

### Exercise 6–9

On January 1, 1976, Fawn Corporation, signed a $300,000 noninterest-bearing note which is due on December 31, 1980. According to the agreement they have the option to pay the $300,000 at maturity date or to pay the obligation in full on January 1, 1976, on an 8% compound interest discount basis. What would be the single amount of cash required on January 1, 1976, to settle the debt in full? Show computations. Assume this debt was incurred to purchase a fixed asset. What should be recorded as the cost of the asset? Explain.

### Exercise 6–10

S. Rath has a two-year-old child. Rath has decided to set up a fund to provide for the child's college education. A local financial institution will handle the fund and increase it each year on a 6% annual compound interest basis. Rath desires to make a single deposit on January 1, 1976, and specifies that the fund must have a $30,000 balance at the end of the 17th year. What amount of cash must be deposited on January 1, 1976. Show computations. Set up an accumulation table to cover the first two years

### Exercise 6–11

Strawn Company desires to accumulate a plant expansion fund over the next five years. The company will make equal deposits in the fund of $5,000 starting on December 31, 1976. The fund will be increased by the trustee by 8% interest. What will be the balance in the fund on December 31, 1980 (immediately after the last deposit), assuming:

1. Annual contributions and compounding?

2. Semiannual contributions and compounding?
3. Quarterly contributions and compounding?

### Exercise 6–12

Foster Corporation has decided to accumulate a debt retirement fund over the next three years by making equal annual deposits of $22,000 on December 31, starting at the end of 1976. Assume the fund will accumulate annual compound interest at 7% per year which will be added to the fund balance.

*Required:*

1. What will be the balance in the fund on December 31, 1978 (that is, immediately after the last deposit)?
2. Prepare an accumulation table for this fund.

### Exercise 6–13

Based upon the situation described in Exercise 6–12, prepare the journal entries for the period January 1, 1976, through December 31, 1978.

### Exercise 6–14

Stevens Company desires to accumulate a fund to retire a debt of $40,000. The debt is due on January 1, 1983. Equal annual contributions will be made to the fund by Stevens on each December 31, starting in 1976 and ending in 1982. The fund will be increased each year by 6% annual compound interest. Compute the amount of the equal annual contributions.

### Exercise 6–15

Eagle Corporation plans to establish a debt retirement fund, beginning December 31, 1976, amounting to $8,750 by making contributions of $2,000 to a trustee each December 31, so that the desired amount will be available on December 31, 1979, the date of the last rent. Compute the interest rate that must be applied to the fund on an annual compound basis to satisfy these requirements. Show your computations.

### Exercise 6–16

Sperry Corporation has decided to create a plant expansion fund by making equal annual deposits on each December 31 of $3,000. Interest at 7% compounded annually will be added to the fund balance. The company wants to know how many deposits will be required to build a fund of $75,390 (at the date of the last rent). Show your computations.

### Exercise 6–17

Alcan Company is considering purchasing a large used machine that is in excellent mechanical condition. The company plans to keep the machine for ten years at which time the residual value will be minimal. An analysis of the capacity of the machine and the costs of operating it (including materials used in production) provided an estimate that the machine would increase net revenue by approximately $8,500 per year. Compute the approximate amount that should be paid now for the machine assuming a 10% compound interest expectation. Assume also that the revenue is realized at each year-end. Show your computations and disregard income tax considerations.

## Exercise 6–18

On January 1, 1976, Dustin Corporation purchased a machine at a cost of $60,000. They paid $26,791 cash and incurred a debt for the difference. This debt is to be paid off in equal annual installments of $6,000 payable each December 31. The interest rate on the unpaid balance each period is 9% per annum. How many annual payments must be made? Show your computations.

## Exercise 6–19

On January 1, 1976, the Caster Company decided to create an expansion fund by making equal annual deposits of $66,000. The fund is required on December 31, 1980. Interest at 6% compounded annually will be added to the fund. Five deposits are planned. Two alternative dates are under consideration, viz:

Alternative A—Make the deposits on each December 31 starting in 1976.
Alternative B—Make the deposits on each January 1 starting in 1976.

*Required:*

Complete the following table:

| | | Balance in the Fund at End of 1980 | |
|---|---|---|---|
| Alternative | Type of Annuity | Computations | Amount |
| A | | | |
| B | | | |

## Exercise 6–20

Stans Company agreed on January 1, 1976, to deposit $120,000 cash with a trustee. The trustee will increase the fund on a 5% compound interest basis on the fund balance each successive year. The trustee is required to pay out the fund in equal annual installments to a former employee of Stans over a ten-year period so that the fund is completely exhausted at the end of that time. Two alternative payment dates are under consideration, viz:

Alternative A—Make the annual payments to the former employee each December 31 starting in 1976.
Alternative B—Make the annual payments to the former employee each January 1 starting in 1976.

*Required:*

Complete the following table:

| Alternative | Type of Annuity | Amount of the Equal Annual Payments | |
|---|---|---|---|
| | | Computations | Amount |
| A | | | |
| B | | | |

## PROBLEMS

### Problem 6-1

Gardner Company plans to deposit $20,000 in a special fund for future use as needed. The fund will accumulate 8% interest. The fund will be initiated on January 1, 1976.

*Required:*

*a.* Complete the following table by entering, in each cell, the balance in the fund:

| Compounding Assumption | Number of Years | | |
|---|---|---|---|
| | 2 | 4 | 6 |
| Annual | | | |
| Semiannual | | | |
| Quarterly | | | |

*b.* Prepare an accumulation table based on the first cell (annual only).
*c.* Give journal entries for the fund based on the first cell (annual only).

### Problem 6-2

*a.* An investor planned to deposit $5,000 in a savings account that would accumulate at 7% annual compound interest for three years. Compute the balance that would be in the savings account at the end of the third year. Prepare an accumulation table for this situation and verify the fund balance.

*b.* Another investor planned to deposit $5,000 in a savings account that would accumulate to $5,955 at the end of three years assuming annual compound interest. Compute the interest rate that would be necessary. Show computations. Prepare an accumulation table for this situation and verify the interest rate computed.

*c.* Another investor planned to deposit $5,000 in a savings account that would accumulate to $6,475 assuming 9% annual compound interest. Compute the number of periods that would be necessary. Show computations. Prepare an accumulation table for this situation and verify the number of periods computed.

**Problem 6–3**

a. An investor planned to deposit $40,000 in a savings account that would accumulate to $42,400 at the end of year 1. Assume the deposit was made at the beginning of year 1. What would be the balance in the fund at the end of the fifth year? The tenth year? The 20th year? Show computations.

b. Another investor planned to deposit $50,000 in a savings account that would accumulate to $89,542 at the end of the tenth year. What rate of annual compound interest would have to be earned on the fund to meet these specifications? Show computations.

c. Another investor planned to deposit $10,000 at annual compound interest. The investor desires to accumulate $20,000 over a ten-year period. What rate of interest would be required to meet these specifications? Show computations. Interpolation is required.

**Problem 6–4**

Constance Corporation decided to place $90,000 in a special expansion fund for use in the future as needed. The fund will accumulate at 6% annual compound interest. The fund will be established on March 1, 1976, and the interest will be added to the fund balance on an annual compound interest basis.

*Required:*

a. Compute the balance that will be in the fund at the end of three years, five years, and ten years respectively.

b. Prepare an accumulation table for three years (verify your first computation in [a]).

c. Give the journal entries for Constance Corporation for (b) the first three years. Disregard adjusting and closing entries.

d. What adjusting entry would be made on December 31, 1976 for (b) assuming this is the end of the accounting period for Constance Corporation.

**Problem 6–5**

Bennett Company anticipates that it will need $200,000 cash for an expansion in the next few years. Assume an interest rate of 8%. The company desires to set up a fund now, January 1, 1976, so $200,000 will be available when needed.

*Required:*

a. Complete the following table by entering, in each cell, the amount that must be deposited now to meet the above specifications:

| Compounding Assumption | Number of Years | | |
|---|---|---|---|
| | 2 | 3 | 5 |
| Annual | | | |
| Semiannual | | | |

b. Prepare an accumulation table based on the first cell.

c. Give journal entries for the fund based on the first cell.

## Problem 6–6

Sord Construction Company has just won a bid on a major contract. The contract will require the purchase of new equipment costing approximately $200,000. The vendor, X Company, requires $50,000 cash down payment and will accept a two-year $150,000 noninterest-bearing note (assume an interest rate on this type of note to be 9% per annum). The $150,000 includes all interest charges.

*Required:*

a. Compute the cost of the equipment on January 1, 1976. Show computations.

b. Give the entry by Sord on date of purchase to record the equipment and the related financing.

c. Prepare a debt schedule for the note that reflects the annual interest expense and the principal.

d. Give journal entries by Sord each year while the note is outstanding and for final payment of the note.

e. Assume that Sord is short of cash on the date of the purchase. To raise cash for the down payment Sord is considering the sale (discounting) of a $60,000 receivable owed to them by John Doe that is due on December 31, 1978 (i.e., three years hence). The receivable is evidenced by a noninterest-bearing note. Sord has located an individual that will buy this future claim at a 12% compound annual discount.

    Compute the amount that Sord would receive on January 1, 1976, the date of the sale of the future claim against John Doe. Show computations.

## Problem 6–7

Morley Company is trying to "clean up" some of its debts. On January 1, 1976, the company has savings accounts as follows:

| Date Established | Amount Deposited (a single deposit for each) | Annual Compound Interest Rate |
|---|---|---|
| Jan. 1, 1965 | ...........................$20,000 | 4% |
| Jan. 1, 1971 | ........................... 90,000 | 5 |

The outstanding debts to be paid off are as follows:

| Due Date | Type of Note | Face of Note |
|---|---|---|
| Dec. 31, 1978 | .....................Noninterest bearing | $ 60,000 |
| Dec. 31, 1985 | .....................Noninterest bearing | 200,000 |

*Required:*

a. Compute the amount of cash that can be obtained from the two savings accounts on January 1, 1976.

b. Compute the amount for which the two debts can be settled on January 1, 1976, assuming a going rate of interest of 9%.

c. How much extra cash additional to the savings accounts will be needed to settle the two debts on January 1, 1976 (in addition to the cash available from the savings accounts)?

**Problem 6-8**

a. Complete the following table assuming $n = 7$; $i = 9\%$:

| Concept | Usual Symbol | Table Formula | "Value" Based on $1 | Source |
|---|---|---|---|---|
| 1. Amount of 1. | ___ | ___ | ___ | ___ |
| 2. Present value of 1. | ___ | ___ | ___ | ___ |
| 3. Amount of ordinary annuity of 1. | ___ | ___ | ___ | ___ |
| 4. Present value of ordinary annuity of 1. | ___ | ___ | ___ | ___ |
| 5. Amount of annuity due of 1. | ___ | ___ | ___ | ___ |
| 6. Present value of annuity due of 1. | ___ | ___ | ___ | ___ |

b. Present a time scale similar to the illustrations in the chapter for each of the above concepts. Identify dates, periods, and amounts.

**Problem 6-9**

Bell Corporation is contemplating the accumulation of a special fund to be used for expanding sales activities into the western part of the country. It is January 1, 1976, and the fund will be needed at the beginning of 1979 according to present plans. The fund will earn 6% interest compounded annually. The company is considering two plans for accumulating the fund by December 31, 1978, viz:

> Plan A—Make three annual deposits of $50,000 each, starting on December 31, 1976.
>
> Plan B—Make three annual deposits of $50,000 each, starting on January 1, 1976.

*Required:*

a. What kind of annuity is involved for each plan? Compute the balance that will be in the special fund on December 31, 1978, under each plan. Show computations.
b. Prepare an accumulation table for each plan.
c. Tabulate the entries for each plan. Set up a tabulation with the following captions:

> Date      Fund, Debit      Cash, Credit      Interest Revenue, Credit

d. Explain why the fund has a different balance under each plan.

**Problem 6-10**

Freedom Company desires to build a special fund for future use in expanding into a foreign country by depositing an equal annual amount in the fund. The fund will be increased each year at 6% annual compounding. The company is considering two alternatives as follows:

> Alternative A—Deposit $50,000 annually December 31, 1976, through December 31, 1980.
>
> Alternative B—Deposit $50,000 annually on January 1, 1976, through January 1, 1980.

*Required:*

a. Compute the balance that will be in the fund for each alternative at December 30, 1980.

b. Prepare an accumulation table for Alternative B.

c. Give the entries indicated for Alternative B through December 31, 1980.


## Problem 6–11

Ross Corporation desires to build a special debt retirement fund amounting to $50,000. A trustee has agreed to handle the fund and to increase it on a 5% annual compound interest basis. Ross will make equal annual contributions of $11,600 at the end of each year, starting on December 31, 1976. Assume an ordinary annuity situation.

*Required:*

a. Determine the number of contributions that Ross must make to meet these specifications. Show computations.

b. Prepare an accumulation table for the fund.

c. Give the journal entries during the period the fund is being accumulated.


## Problem 6–12

Stickney Company agreed with its president, Jonas Smith, to set up a fund with a trustee that will pay Mr. Smith $40,000 per year for the three years following his retirement. Smith will retire on January 1, 1976, and the equal annual payments are to be made by the trustee each December 31 starting in 1976. The trustee will add to the fund, 5% annual compound interest on the fund balance each year-end. The fund is to have a zero balance on December 31, 1978, the date of the last payment.

*Required:*

a. Compute the single sum that must be deposited with the trustee on January 1, 1976, to meet these specifications.

b. Prepare a decumulation table through December 31, 1978. Set up table captions as follows: Date; Cash Payments; Interest Revenue Earned; Fund Decreases; and Fund Balance.


## Problem 6–13

Roller Construction Company can purchase a used crane that will be needed on a new job that will continue for approximately three years. It is January 1, 1976, and the crane is needed immediately. Because of a shortage of cash Roller has asked the vendor for credit terms with no down payment. The vendor expects 11% annual compound interest. The crane can be purchased under these terms by making three payments of $6,400 each on December 31, 1976, 1977, and 1978.

*Required:*

a. What should be the cash price of the crane on January 1, 1976?

b. Give the entry to record the purchase of the crane on the credit terms.

c. Prepare a debt amortization schedule using the following format:

| Date | Cash Payment | Interest Expense | Reduction on Principal | Liability Balance |
|------|--------------|------------------|------------------------|-------------------|

## Problem 6-14

Ronnie Student is considering the purchase of a Super Sail Boat which has a cash price of $6,500. Terms can be arranged for a $2,000 cash down payment and payment of the remaining $4,500, plus interest at 11% per annum, in three equal annual payments. Assume purchase on January 1, 1976, and each payment on each December 31 thereafter.

*Required:*

a. Compute the amount of each annual payment assuming annual compound interest.

b. What did the boat cost including interest? What was the interest amount?

c. Prepare a debt amortization schedule using the following format:

| Date | Cash Payment | Interest Expense | Reduction on Principal | Liability Balance |
|------|--------------|------------------|------------------------|-------------------|

## Problem 6-15

Complete the following table of future and present values based on $1, assuming 6 years and 12% interest:

| Concept | Symbol | Value Based on $1, Assuming Compounding | | |
|---------|--------|-----------------------------------------|---|---|
| | | Annual | Semiannual | Quarterly |
| 1. Amount of 1. | | | | |
| 2. Present value of 1. | | | | |
| 3. Amount of ordinary annuity of 1.* | | | | |
| 4. Amount of annuity due of 1.* | | | | |
| 5. Present value of ordinary annuity of 1.* | | | | |
| 6. Present value of annuity due of 1.* | | | | |

\* Assume one rent in each compound interest period.

Indicate sources, or show computations, of each value.

## Problem 6-16

Carson Company rents a warehouse for an annual rental of $2,000. They have some idle cash and have approached the owner with a proposal to pay three years' rent in advance. The owner has agreed to a compound discount rate of 10%.

*Required:*

a. Assume it is January 1, 1976, and that the three rents are due on January 1, 1976, 1977, and 1978. Compute the amount that Carson Company would have to pay as a single sum on January 1, 1976. What kind of annuity is this? Explain.

b. Assume it is January 1, 1976, and that the three rents are due on December

31, 1976, 1977, and 1978. Compute the amount that Carson Company would have to pay as a single sum on January 1, 1976. What kind of annuity is this? Explain.

c. Explain why the single sums to be paid computed under (1) and (2) are different.

## Problem 6–17

On January 1, 1976, Larson Company signed a three-year contract to rent some space that they needed immediately. The lease provided that Larson could pay annual rentals on each January 1 of $17,000, beginning in 1976, or alternatively, they can pay rent in advance at a 7% annual compound discount.

*Required:*

a. What sum would have to be paid by Larson on January 1, 1976, for the three annual rentals? What amount would be saved by advance payment?
b. What kind of annuity is this? Explain.

## Problem 6–18

On January 1, 1976, Cunard Company owes an $80,000 debt which is due. Since the company is short of cash they have reached an agreement with the creditor whereby the debt and interest is to be paid in equal annual installments on January 1, 1976, 1977, and 1978. Interest is 9% annual compounding.

*Required:*

a. What kind of annuity is this? Explain.
b. Compute the amount of the equal annual payments.
c. Prepare a debt amortization schedule, using the following format:

| Date | Cash Payment | Interest Expense | Reduction of Principal | Liability Balance |
|------|--------------|------------------|------------------------|-------------------|
| 1/1/76 | | | | $80,000 |

## Problem 6–19

Shakey Corporation is negotiating to purchase a plant from another company that will complement Shakey's operations. They have just completed a careful study of the plant and have developed the following estimates:

Expected net cash revenues:
| | |
|---|---|
| Years 1–5 (per year) | $44,000 |
| Years 6–10 (per year) | 34,000 |
| Year 11 | 20,000 |
| Year 12 | 10,000 |
| Expected net residual value at end of year 12 | 3,000 |

*Required:*

a. Compute the amount that Shakey should be willing to pay for the plant assuming an 11% return on the investment. Assume all amounts are at year-end; disregard income taxes.

Because Shakey is short of cash assume the down payment is $150,000. The bank will lend Shakey the balance at 9% per annum payable in equal annual payments (including interest and principal) over the first five years. The payments will be at each year-end, starting one year after the date of purchase.

b. Compute the amount of the equal annual payments on the loan. Compute the total interest that will be paid.

c. Give the entries (or entry) to record the purchase in (a) and the loan in (b) using the amounts you computed.

# Chapter 7

## Cash, Short-Term Investments, and Receivables

This chapter focuses on cash and near-cash items, often called quick assets. The three most liquid assets are cash, short-term investments, and current receivables (including short-term notes receivable). Their interchangeability and other similarities make it desirable to discuss them in a single integrated chapter. Planning, control, and accounting for this particular group of current assets involve common problems, concepts, and procedures. To facilitate discussion the chapter is divided into three parts.

### PART A—CASH

Cash is the medium of exchange and is used for most of the measurements in accounting. Because of its pervasive use by society the concept of cash is understood by most people; however, accounting for and reporting cash inflows and outflows presents some special problems. This part focuses on accounting for cash, including control; reporting cash flows is discussed in Chapter 21, Statement of Changes in Financial Position.

### COMPOSITION OF CASH

Two principal characteristics of cash are (1) its availability as a medium of exchange, and (2) its use as a measurement in accounting for the other items. Although its purchasing power may change, accountants make no effort to revalue cash. Some special measures which can be taken in conjunction with the effects of price-level changes on certain other financial statement items are discussed in Chapter 25. Cash includes coins, currency, and certain types of formal negotiable paper which are accepted by banks for deposit; but it excludes some items

267

commonly intermingled with cash. Examples of *exclusions* include postage stamps and cash-due memos. Cash-due memos or IOU's from officers, owners, or employees should be classified as special receivables, not as cash. Formal *negotiable* paper (i.e., transferable by endorsement) which is due on demand is classified as cash. Thus, bank drafts, cashier's checks, money orders, certified checks, and ordinary checks constitute cash for accounting purposes. Balances on deposit in commercial banks should be considered as cash if subject to immediate use. Balances in savings accounts generally are classed as short-term investments because the bank usually has a right to advance notice of withdrawal. Certificates of deposit are classed as cash; time certificates of deposit, depending on maturity dates and managerial intent, are classed as either short-term or long-term investments.

Deposits in foreign banks create two special problems, viz: (1) foreign currency units, such as pounds or pesos, first must be translated to dollars; and (2) it is not uncommon for the foreign deposits to be subject to restricted conversion and transfer to other countries. Discussion of conversion of deposits in foreign banks is beyond the scope of this book. Even when spendable immediately or in the near future, cash in foreign banks should be set out separately on the balance sheet.

Current assets were discussed in Chapter 5. The AICPA Committee on Accounting Procedure, in *Accounting Research Bulletin No. 43*, stated that such resources as "cash and claims to cash which are restricted as to withdrawal or use for other than current operations, are designated for expenditure in the acquisition or construction of noncurrent assets, or are segregated for the liquidation of long-term debts" should be excluded from current assets. The committee then added:

> Even though not actually set aside in special accounts, funds that are clearly to be used in the near future for the liquidation of long-term debts, payments to sinking funds, or for similar purposes should also, under this concept, be excluded from current assets. However, where such funds are considered to offset maturing debt which has properly been set up as a current liability, they may be included within the current asset classification.[1]

Petty cash funds and cash in the hands of branches or divisions should be included as cash because these ordinarily are used to meet current operating expenses and to liquidate current liabilities.

Checks drawn against a bank balance which have not been mailed or otherwise delivered to the payees by the end of the accounting period should not be deducted from the cash balance. The entry already made to record the check should be reversed before preparing the financial statements. An overdraft in a bank account should be shown as a current liability. However, where a depositor has overdrawn one account with Bank A but has positive balances in other accounts in that bank, it is appropriate to offset and show the net asset or liability on the

---

[1] AICPA, "Restatement and Revision of Accounting Research Bulletins," *Accounting Research Bulletin No. 43* (New York, 1961), p. 21.

balance sheet. It is improper to offset an overdraft in Bank A against a balance on deposit in Bank B.

## CONTROL OF CASH

The control of cash is critical in many businesses because (a) it is usually in short supply, or in some cases there is idle cash; and (b) it is easy to conceal and transport, and it is desired by everyone.

The control of cash involves careful planning of cash needs and control of expenditures and careful recordkeeping to assure that all cash is properly accounted for. Thus, control of cash generally requires the following:

1. A detailed cash budget that specifies planned cash inflows and outflows (not considered in this book).
2. Detailed cash control reports for internal management use to assure that cash is controlled as planned and as a basis for revising cash plans.
3. A system of internal control that incorporates careful delegation of authority for handling cash receipts, cash payments, and the related recordkeeping. The essential details of a system of internal control were discussed in Chapter 3.
4. Proper accounting for all cash receipts and cash disbursements including assurances that there are no unauthorized uses of cash receipts or improper cash disbursements. Chapter 3, Appendix A, discussed and illustrated the use of control and subsidiary accounts and special journals. These are important procedures in attaining adequate control of cash.
5. Adequate disclosure of cash inflows and outflows in the external financial statements provided to stockholders and others. This subject is discussed in Chapter 21, Statement of Changes in Financial Position, Cash Basis.

### Control of Cash Receipts

Cash inflows in most businesses come from numerous sources; therefore, the procedures that should be used to attain adequate control are varied. However, the following procedures are important in all situations:

1. Assign responsibilities and develop a system so there is a continuous and uninterrupted flow of cash from initial receipt to deposit in an authorized bank account. This requires (a) immediate counting of all cash received, (b) immediate recording of all cash received, and (c) timely deposit of all cash received.
2. Separation of all responsibilities for the cash-handling and cash-recording functions. In this manner an effective system of internal checks is implemented.
3. Continuous and close supervision of all cash-handling and record-keeping functions, including daily cash reports for internal use.

## Control over Cash Disbursements

The cash outflows in most businesses are for many purposes. Many of the cash defalcations happen in the disbursements process because they are relatively easy to cover up unless there is an effective system to control cash payments. In such situations, one or more of the fundamentals of internal control are missing. Although each control system should be tailored to the situation, there are several fundamentals that are indispensable; these are:

1. Make all cash disbursements by check. An exception can be made for small miscellaneous payments by use of a petty cash system.
2. Establish a petty cash system with tight controls and close supervision.
3. Prepare checks and sign them only when supported by adequate documentation and verification.
4. Separate responsibilities for cash disbursement documentation, check writing, check signing (and in some cases check mailing), and record-keeping.
5. Supervise continuously and closely all cash-disbursement and record-keeping functions including periodic internal reports.

## Petty Cash

The term petty cash, or *imprest cash*, refers to a systematic approach often used for making small expenditures that would be too impractical (too costly and time consuming) to make by check. Examples of typical payments are for the daily paper delivered to the office, express payments, local taxi fares, special postage charges on delivery, and minor office supplies. A petty cash system operates as follows:

1. A reliable employee is designated as the petty cash custodian. This person receives a single amount of cash for specified petty cash purposes, disburses the funds as needed, receives adequate documentation for each disbursement, maintains a running record of the cash on hand, and periodically reports the total amount spent supported by the documentation received for each disbursement. The record maintained, in addition to the documentation, often is referred to as the petty cash book.
2. When the petty cash held by the custodian runs low, a request for a resupply, supported by the documentation of prior expenditures, is submitted to the designated supervisor of company cash.
3. The initial amount to establish the petty cash fund, and resupply to the custodian, are provided by separate checks, made payable to petty cash, and processed in the normal manner.
4. Accounting—the initial check establishing the petty cash fund is recorded as a debit to Petty Cash and a credit to Cash. Checks to resupply the fund are recorded by debiting the expense accounts (or other accounts) for the expenditures reported by the custodian and by crediting Cash.

5. There should be close supervision and surprise audits of cash on hand and supporting documentation for expenditures.

To illustrate, assume a petty cash fund is established in the amount of $100 and employee X is designated as the custodian. At the end of the first two weeks the custodian requested a resupply of the $87 spent, supported by adequate documentation that reflected the following: postage, $18.50; office supplies bought, $23.60; taxi fares (local), $31; meals for employees, $10; and daily paper, $3.90. The indicated entries would be as follows:

To establish the petty cash fund:

| | | |
|---|---|---|
| Petty cash | 100.00 | |
|     Cash | | 100.00 |

To replenish the fund (at end of second week):

| | | |
|---|---|---|
| Postage expense | 18.50 | |
| Office supplies expense | 23.60 | |
| Administrative expense | 44.90 | |
|     Cash | | 87.00 |

The effect of the last entry is to increase the amount of cash held by the custodian to $100, the amount reflected in the Petty Cash account.

## CASH OVERAGE AND SHORTAGE

Cash is susceptible to theft, and it is inevitable that errors will be made in counting cash; therefore, cash overages and shortages must be expected. Cash overages and shortages, usually determined on a daily basis, should be recorded in an account entitled Cash Overages and Shortages with an offset to the regular Cash account. A debit balance in this account represents an operating expense and a credit represents a miscellaneous revenue. In the absence of theft, cash overages and shortages tend to balance out to zero over a period of time. In contrast, theft, when discovered and if material in amount, should be recorded as a credit to the regular Cash account and as a debit to (a) a receivable if recovery is expected from the individual involved or an insurance or bonding company, or (b) an extraordinary loss (on the presumption that it is unusual and infrequent), if there is no recovery probable.

## RECONCILIATION OF BANK WITH BOOK BALANCE

At the end of each month, the ending cash balance on deposit reported in the bank statement should be reconciled with the ending cash balance on deposit and on hand as reflected in the cash accounts of the business. Reconciliation of bank with book balances serves two important purposes: (1) control—it serves to check the accuracy of the records of both the bank and the company; and (2) accounting entries—it provides information for entries on the books of the company for items reflected on the bank statement that have not been recorded by the company (e.g., a bank service charge).

Reconciliation of the bank balance with the balance of the Cash account requires an analysis of the *monthly bank statement* and the cash records maintained by the company. Generally there will be a difference between the two cash balances. The usual causes of differences between the cash balance per the bank statement and the cash balance on the books of the company may be classified as follows:

A. Items already recorded as cash receipts in the books of the company but not yet added to the bank balance on the bank statement.

   *Examples:*

   1. Unrecorded deposits—deposits made up and deposited in the bank by the company but not reported by the bank on the current bank statement.
   2. Cash on hand including petty cash (i.e., not deposited).

B. Items already added to the bank balance but not recorded in the company books.

   *Examples:*

   1. Interest allowed the depositor by the bank but not yet recorded in the company books.
   2. Collections (and deposits) of notes and drafts by the bank for the depositor but not yet recorded on the company books.

C. Items already recorded as cash disbursements on the company books but not deducted by the bank from the bank balance.

   *Example:*

   1. Outstanding checks—checks written and properly recorded in the company books but not yet cleared through the bank.

D. Items already subtracted from the bank balance but not recorded in the company books:

   *Example:*

   1. Bank service charge.

It is possible to reconcile the bank and book balances by working from the bank balance to the book balance, or the opposite, or to reconcile both the book balance and bank balance to a common amount known as the correct or *true cash balance*. The "true balance" method is generally used.[2] The method is illustrated in Exhibit 7–1 based on the following data:

---

[2] The "true balance" method is preferable for the following reasons:

1. The reconciliation naturally falls into two parts (Books and Bank), and all the reconciling entries to be made in the books are grouped in the section devoted to the *book balance.*

2. It is less confusing. After the correctness of each item has been verified, the reconciliation merely involves placing such items under the appropriate part as an addition or deduction.

3. The reconciliation can be used as a schedule supporting the cash balance reported on the balance sheet; the last line on the reconciliation is reported on the balance sheet.

1. Bank statement, March 19A:

Balance carried forward from February .................................      $1,800
Deposits ...............................................................$6,550
Interest collected by the bank on a note for the company ......    20    6,570
     Total ........................................................      8,370
Charges:
    Checks cashed ........................................................    6,962
    Service charge by bank ...............................................      4    6,966
                                                   $1,404
Balance, March 31................................................................

2. Company records:

Cash account, March 19A:

Debits:
    Balance from February...................................................$1,600
    Cash receipts ................................................................   7,000
     Total .....................................................................   .$8,600
Credits:
    Checks written ............................................................     7,065
    Balance, March 31.........................................................    $1,535

3. An analysis of the bank statement compared with the company records revealed the following:

    a. A deposit made on March 31 for $450 was not included on the bank statement.

    b. Cash on hand in the company (hence, not deposited), $100.

    c. Checks written by the company and recorded in the accounts but not cleared (i.e., not deducted on the bank statement) by March 31:

         No. 401.........................................................................$150
         No. 403......................................................................... 200
         No. 412.........................................................................   53    $403

Using these data, the bank balance of $1,404 and the book balance of $1,535 are reconciled to the true cash balance, as computed on the reconciliation, $1,551 (Exhibit 7–1). The true balance would be reported as the cash balance on the balance sheet at March 31, 19A.

**EXHIBIT 7–1**
**Bank Reconciliation**

| Bank Balance | | | Book Balance | |
|---|---|---|---|---|
| Balance per bank...... | | $1,404 | Balance per books ...............$1,535 | |
| Additions: | | | Additions: | |
| Unrecorded | | | Interest collected by bank... | 20 |
| deposit...............$450 | | | | 1,555 |
| Cash on hand ......100 | | 550 | | |
| | | 1,954 | | |
| Deductions: | | | Deductions: | |
| Outstanding checks: | | | Bank charges ................... | 4 |
| No. 401............... 150 | | | | |
| No. 410............... 200 | | | | |
| No. 412............... 53 | 403 | | | |
| True Cash Balance ... | | $1,551 | True Cash Balance...............$1,551 | |

Entries to record items on the bank reconciliation which have not been recognized on the books previously may be taken directly from the bank reconciliation. If the method of reconciliation illustrated above is used, those items listed under the caption "book balance" constitute the amounts to be recognized. The entries necessary to reflect the correct cash balance in the books ($1,551 in the illustration) are as follows:

| | | |
|---|---:|---:|
| Cash | 20 | |
| Interest revenue | | 20 |
| | | |
| Expense—bank charges | 4 | |
| Cash | | 4 |

## COMPREHENSIVE RECONCILIATION

Comprehensive reconciliation or reconciliation of receipts and disbursements for a month (or an entire fiscal period) is usually undertaken by auditors and frequently by accountants. A comprehensive reconciliation has the advantages of (a) providing a complete reconciliation of the differences between the beginning and ending balances, (b) reflecting the detailed differences separately for the bank statement and the accounts, and (c) facilitating reconciliation in complex situations. Thus, comprehensive reconciliation is akin to a true balance reconciliation; however, it differs in that it also reconciles receipts and payments for the period under consideration and begins with a true balance type reconciliation (made as of the end of the prior period).

To illustrate the procedure, refer to the true balance reconciliation in Exhibit 7–1 completed on March 31, and assume the necessary entries to correct cash were reflected in the company's account as of that date. April transactions reflected on the bank statement and the company's Cash account are shown below. The reconciliation is shown in Exhibit 7–2.

Bank Statement, April 19A:*

| | | |
|---|---|---:|
| Mar. 31 | Balance forward | $ 1,404 |
| Apr. 1 | Deposit | 550 |
| | *The $450 unrecorded deposit + $100 undeposited cash as of March 31.* | |
| 2–29 | Deposits | 10,800 |
| | *Other April receipts deposited.* | |
| 30 | Note collected | 515 |
| | *$500 note + $15 interest collected by bank in behalf of company.* | |
| | Total Receipts | 11,865 |
| | Initial balance + receipts | 13,269 |
| Apr. 1 | Check Nos. 401 and 410 | 350 |
| | *March checks cleared in April.* | |
| 2–29 | Check Nos. 413–430 | 10,700 |
| | *April checks cleared in April.* | |
| 30 | April service charge | 10 |
| | Total April charges | 11,060 |
| 30 | Balance, April 30 | $ 2,209 |

Cash Account (per books), April 19A:

| | | |
|---|---|---:|
| Mar. 31 | Cash balance ..................................................... | $ 1,551 |
| | *Reflects entries called for by March 31 reconciliation.* | |
| Apr.  2–29 | Receipts ........................................................... | 10,800 |
| | *Receipts which were also deposited during April.* | |
| 30 | Receipts ............................................................ | 400 |
| | *Deposit in transit at April 30.* | |
| 30 | Receipts ............................................................ | 200 |
| | *Cash on hand at April 30.* | |
| | Total Receipts  ........................................... | 11,400 |
| | Initial balance + receipts  ...................................... | 12,951 |
| Apr.  2–29 | Check Nos. 413–430  .......................................... | 10,700 |
| | *April checks cleared in April.* | |
| 30 | Check No. 431  .................................................... | 100 |
| | *April check outstanding April 30.* | |
| | | 10,800 |
| 30 | Balance, April 30  ................................................ | $ 2,151 |

* Explanation in italics not part of the bank statement and Cash account.

**EXHIBIT 7–2**
**Comprehensive Reconciliation**

| | Balance March 31 | April Receipts | April Payments | Balance April 30 |
|---|---:|---:|---:|---:|
| Balances per bank .................. | $1,404 | $11,865 | $11,060 | $2,209 |
| Unrecorded deposits: | | | | |
| March 31............................. | 450 | (450) | | |
| April 30  ............................. | | 400 | | 400 |
| Undeposited cash: | | | | |
| March 31............................. | 100 | (100) | | |
| April 30  ............................. | | 200 | | 200 |
| Outstanding checks: | | | | |
| March 31, No. 401  .............. | (150) | | (150) | |
| No. 410  .............. | (200) | | (200) | |
| No. 412  .............. | (53) | | | (53) |
| April 30,   No. 431  .............. | | | 100 | (100) |
| Correct Balances ..................... | $1,551 | $11,915 | $10,810 | $2,656 |
| Balances per company's books... | $1,551 | $11,400 | $10,800 | $2,151 |
| April service charge.................. | | | 10 | (10) |
| Note and interest collected  ...... | | 515 | | 515 |
| Correct Balances .................... | $1,551 | $11,915 | $10,810 | $2,656 |

Observe that Check No. 412 for $53 which was outstanding at March 31 is still outstanding at April 30 and that payment on it has not been stopped.

Entries needed to record the correct cash balance as of April 30 are as follows:

| Cash | .515 | |
| Note receivable | | 500 |
| Interest revenue | | 15 |
| | | |
| Expense—bank charges | 10 | |
| Cash | | 10 |

The company should report a cash balance of $2,656 on its April 30 balance sheet.

## PART B—SHORT-TERM INVESTMENTS

Prior to a discussion of accounting for short-term investments, it is appropriate to describe briefly the nature and types of investments. Investments generally are classified for balance sheet purposes as either short-term investments (often called temporary investments) or long-term investments (often called permanent investments). This distinction is entirely one of accounting and not of law and arises out of the nature of the security and the purpose of the investment. Investment purposes may be outlined as follows:

A. Short-term investments:
   1. Funds set aside for emergency use on a current basis and invested in marketable securities.
   2. Investment of short-term excess cash.
B. Long-term investments:[3]
   1. Stocks, bonds, and similar securities of another company held on a long-term basis.
   2. Advances to affiliates or subsidiaries.
   3. Funds earmarked for a designated purpose such as retirement of a funded debt, replacement of plant and equipment, or payment of pensions.
   4. Cash value of life insurance on company executives.
   5. Major expenditures for certain types of memberships in associations and exchanges, such as a broker's "seat" on a stock exchange.
   6. Assets, other than investment securities, such as land not used in regular business operations.
   7. Funds invested in long-term assets not directly related to the primary operations of the company. For example, the National Laundry Machinery Company purchased a patent on a special pressing device, developed it for use in a field not in competition with its own operations, and secured regular royalties from its licensing. The cost of this patent should be accounted for as a long-term investment rather than as an intangible fixed asset.

## SHORT-TERM INVESTMENTS DEFINED

Short-term investments are reported on the balance sheet under the current asset caption. To be classified as a current asset a short-term investment must meet the following twofold test:

---

[3] Discussed in Chapters 18 and 19.

1. The security must be *readily marketable*. It must be a security which is regularly traded on a security exchange or for which there is an established market.
2. It must be the *intention* of the company's management to convert the security into cash in the short run and hence back into the normal operations for which working capital is used. This criterion has proven somewhat troublesome to auditors in practice. "Intentions" are elusive and prone to change from one period to the next.

## VALUATION OF SHORT-TERM INVESTMENTS

Short-term investments are recorded initially at cost in conformance with the cost principle. Subsequent to acquisition they may be accounted for at—

1. Lower of cost or market.
2. Cost.
3. Market.

### Lower of Cost or Market

FASB *Statement No. 12, Accounting for Certain Marketable Securities* (effective December 31, 1975), requires that investments in marketable equity securities be valued at each balance sheet date on a lower of cost or market basis.[4] The statement also applies to long-term investments in marketable equity securities. Long-term investments are discussed in Chapter 18; therefore, this chapter will focus only on short-term investments. Equity securities, as used in *Statement No. 12*, encompass all capital stock (including warrants, rights, and stock options) except preferred stock that, by its terms, must be redeemed either at the option of the issuer or the investor. Equity securities do not include bonds and other debt instruments since they are debt securities.

To apply lower of cost or market to investments in marketable equity securities, *Statement No. 12* specifies: "The carrying amount of a marketable equity securities portfolio shall be the lower of its aggregate cost or market value, determined at balance sheet date. The amount by which aggregate cost of the portfolio exceeds market value shall be accounted for as the valuation allowance."

In applying the concept of lower of cost or market, *Statement No. 12* makes a careful distinction between realized and unrealized gains and losses. A *realized* gain or loss is defined as the difference between the net proceeds received at sale and the cost of an equity security. In contrast, an *unrealized* gain or loss is defined as the difference between the aggregate market value and aggregate cost of the investment portfolio

---

[4] The provisions of FASB *Statement No. 12* do not apply to debt securities, to redeemable preferred stock (since it is similar to debt), or to long-term investments accounted for by the equity method (see Chapter 18). Also, that statement does not apply to industries having specialized practices with respect to marketable securities, including such financial organizations as insurance companies, investment companies, mutual funds, and securities dealers.

of marketable equity securities on a given date. Thus, realized gains and losses are recognized only when a security is disposed of. However, unrealized losses are recognized at the end of the accounting period when an adjusting entry is made to reflect lower of cost or market. In the accounts, an "allowance" account (a contra asset) is used to record the amount of the difference between aggregate market and aggregate cost when market is lower. On the other side of the entry, an unrealized gain/loss account is used. On the income statement, the unrealized gain or loss on short-term investments (but not long-term investments) is reported along with investment revenue. On the balance sheet, the allowance account balance is subtracted from the investment cost, thus reporting the portfolio at lower of cost or market. Dividends received on equity securities are credited to investment revenue.

To illustrate the accounting and reporting of short-term investments in marketable equity securities, the following transactions and responses are given.

**January 5, 19A—D** Company acquired the following short-term investments:

> Company E—Common stock (par $10), 5,000 shares at $20 per share.
> Company F—Common stock (nopar), 3,000 shares at $30 per share.
> Company G—Preferred stock (nonredeemable, par $20), 2,000 shares at $40 per share.

| | | |
|---|---|---|
| Short-term investments in equity securities ..................... | 270,000 | |
| Cash ................................................................ | | 270,000 |

**December 31, 19A—Adjusting** entry to record lower of cost or market valuation. Market values: E stock, $16; F stock, $31; G stock, $39.

| | | |
|---|---|---|
| Unrealized loss on short-term investments in equity securities* ................................................................ | 19,000 | |
|     Allowance to reduce short-term investments in equity securities to market ............................................. | | 19,000 |

\* Closed to income summary.

Computation:

| Company | Shares | Cost | Market | Unrealized Gain (loss) |
|---|---|---|---|---|
| E ......... | 5,000 | @ $20 = $100,000 | @ $16 = $ 80,000 | ($20,000) |
| F ......... | 3,000 | @ $30 = 90,000 | @ $31 = 93,000 | 3,000 |
| G ......... | 2,000 | @ $40 = 80,000 | @ $39 = 78,000 | (2,000) |
| Total | | $270,000 | $251,000 | ($19,000) |

**March 1, 19B—Received** cash dividends as follows: E stock, $1.00 per share; F stock, $.50 per share; G stock, none.

| | | |
|---|---|---|
| Cash ............................................................. | 6,500 | |
|     Investment revenue...................................................... | | 6,500 |

**December 31, 19B—Adjusting** entry to record lower of cost or market valuation. Market values: E stock, $18; F stock, $31; G stock, $42.

| | | |
|---|---|---|
| Allowance to reduce short-term investments in equity securities to market ................................................. | 16,000 | |
|     Unrealized gain on short-term investments in equity securities (closed to income summary) ..................... | | 16,000 |

Computation:

| Company | Shares | Cost | Market | Unrealized Gain (loss) |
|---------|--------|------|--------|------------------------|
| E | 5,000 | @ $20 = $100,000 | @ $18 = $ 90,000 | ($10,000) |
| F | 3,000 | @ $30 = 90,000 | @ $31 = 93,000 | 3,000 |
| G | 2,000 | @ $40 = 80,000 | @ $42 = 84,000 | 4,000 |
| Total | | $270,000 | $267,000 | ($ 3,000) |

| | |
|---|---|
| Balance in allowance account | $19,000 |
| Balance need in allowance account | 3,000 |
| Decrease in account (debit) | $16,000 |

Under the provisions of *Statement No. 12*, recoveries such as the $16,000 are permitted to be reflected in the accounts and reported on the income statement to the extent unrealized losses have previously been reported but the unrealized gains cannot exceed the previously recognized unrealized losses. Of course, *Statement No. 12* explicitly applies only to certain stocks; by inference, the same principle can be extended to other types of securities held as short-term investments.

October 10, 19C — Sale of the G Company stock at $44 per share.

| | | |
|---|---|---|
| Cash (2,000 shares × $44) | 88,000 | |
| Short-term investments in equity securities (2,000 shares × $40) | | 80,000 |
| Realized gain on sale of short-term investments* | | 8,000 |

* Closed to income summary.

Observe in the last entry that no cognizance was taken of the allowance account and the realized gain or loss is calculated in terms of recorded original cost.[5] The allowance account is adjusted only at the end of the period.

The financial statements at the end of 19A and 19B would reflect the following:

| | 19A | 19B |
|---|---|---|
| Income Statement: | | |
| Investment revenue | | $ 6,500 |
| Unrealized loss on equity securities | $ 19,000 | |
| Unrealized gain on equity securities | | 16,000 |
| Balance Sheet: | | |
| Current Assets: | | |
| Short-term investments in equity securities at cost | $270,000 | $270,000 |
| Less: Allowance to reduce equity securities to market | 19,000 | 3,000 |
| Marketable equity securities portfolio at lower of cost or market | $251,000 | $267,000 |

[5] Paragraph 23 of FASB *Statement No. 12* provides that unrealized gains and losses on marketable securities shall be considered as timing differences for income tax allocation purposes; however, that tax effects should be recognized on unrealized capital losses only when there exists assurance beyond a reasonable doubt that the benefit will be realized by an offset of the loss against capital gains. In the opinion of the authors; conservatism would normally mitigate against such tax allocation recognition (see Chapter 11).

Alternatively, the balance sheet may be as follows:

Current Assets:
Short-term investments in equity securities (cost
$270,000), at lower of cost or market ........................ $251,000

Disclosure requirements specified by FASB *Statement No. 12* are:

The following information with respect to marketable equity securities owned shall be disclosed either in the body of the financial statements or in the accompaning notes:

a. As of the date of each balance sheet presented, aggregate cost and market value (each segregated between current and noncurrent portfolios when a classified balance sheet is presented) with identification as to which is the carrying amount.

b. As of the date of the latest balance sheet presented, the following, segregated between current and noncurrent portfolios when a classified balance sheet is presented:

   i. Gross unrealized gains representing the excess of market value over cost for all marketable equity securities in the portfolio having such an excess.

   ii. Gross unrealized losses representing the excess of cost over market value for all marketable equity securities in the portfolio having such an excess.

c. For each period for which an income statement is presented:

   i. Net realized gain or loss included in the determination of net income.

   ii. The basis on which cost was determined in computing realized gain or loss (i.e., average cost or other method used).

   iii. The change in the valuation allowance(s) that has been included in the equity section of the balance sheet during the period and, when a classified balance sheet is presented, the amount of such change included in the determination of net income.

### Valuation at Cost

Short-term investments that are not covered by the provisions of FASB *Statement No. 12* (i.e., redeemable preferred stock and debt securities) are accounted for under the prior provisions of *ARB No. 43*, Chapter 3A which states: "In the case of maketable securities where market value is less than cost by a substantial amount and it is evident that the decline in market value is not due to a mere temporary condition, the amount to be included as a current asset should not exceed market value." Although lower of cost or market is specified, in actual practice short-term investments generally have been carried at cost in view of the "substantial" and "mere temporary condition" qualifiers. (Reference: *Accounting Trends and Techniques*, 1975, AICPA, p. 99).

When this basis of valuation is used, the short-term investment account remains unchanged except for acquisitions and dispositions. In view of the issuance of FASB *Statement No. 12*, the cost method is appropriate for nonstock short-term investments when the price change is "temporary" and when there has been no material drop in the market value of the securities compared to their cost. Cost includes brokerage costs, taxes, and all other legitimate and reasonable costs incurred in acquisition, as well as the agreed upon purchase price. In the case of bonds bought between interest dates, it does not include accrued interest purchased, which should be charged to Interest revenue.

To illustrate application of the cost method to *debt securities* acquired as a short-term investment, the following transactions and responses are given.

November 1, 19A—Purchased six $1,000 Baxter Company bonds at 104. Interest at 5% per annum is payable each March 1 and September 1. Accrued interest for September 1 to November 1 had to be purchased:

```
Short-term investments, bonds ($6,000 × 1.04)  .......................   6,240
Investment revenue ($6,000 × 5% × 2/12)...................................     50
    Cash  ..........................................................................           6,290
```

December 31, 19A—End of the accounting period. Adjusting entry for accured interest on Baxter bonds (September 1 to December 31):

```
Interest receivable.......................................................................   100
    Investment revenue ($6,000 × 5% × 4/12)................................           100
```

December 31, 19A—To close investment revenue account:

```
Investment revenue ($100 − $50) ..................................................    50
    Income summary  ................................................................            50
```

March 1, 19B—Collection of semiannual interest on Baxter bonds (assuming no reversing entry was made on January 1, 19B):

```
Cash ............................................................................................   150
    Interest receivable...............................................................           100
    Investment revenue  ...........................................................            50
```

April 30, 19B—Sold the Baxter bonds at 103¾ plus accrued interest March 1 to April 30):

```
Cash [($6,000 × 103¾) + ($6,000 × 5% × 2/12)]  .......................   6,275
Loss on sale of short-term investments  ...................................     15
    Short-term investments, bonds  .....................................                6,240
    Investment revenue ($6,000 × 5% × 2/12)  ..........................             50
```

December 31, 19B—To close investment revenue and loss on sale of investments:

```
Investment revenue ($50 + $50) ..................................................   100
    Loss on sale of short-term investments  ..............................            15
    Income summary .................................................................            85
```

## Market Value

As rising prices have accelerated and inflation has become a worldwide phenomenon, there has been an increasing clamor to depart from historical cost (i.e., the cost principle) as the basis for asset valuation.

The movement toward current or "fair value" has proceeded farther in other developed countries than in the United States.[6] This is partly because laws of some countries have permitted use of values other than cost for tax and other purposes, and also because in some instances their inflation rate has been extremely high by all standards. It seems safe to say that if the same certainty could attend the valuation of other assets as would apply to marketable securities, there would probably have been a greater impetus toward fair market values in accounting. Mutual funds and certain other types of financial entities often value and report their relatively vast investment portfolios at current market.

As to short-term investments, the primary arguments usually cited favoring current market as a valuation basis include:

1. Eliminating the present inconsistency inherent in use of lower of cost or market, wherein unrealized losses are recognized but unrealized gains are ignored.
2. Assigning to each period such gains or losses from holding investments which actually did occur during the period. Under the historical cost approach, much of the gain or loss that is finally recognized when the short-term investments are sold may have occurred in one or more earlier periods.
3. Reporting short-term investments at current market value is more informative to statement users than reporting at cost (which may be materially lower).
4. Eliminating the manipulation of periodic net income. For example, income can be artificially generated near the end of the period by selling securities from the portfolio that had a low cost and now have a high price. In the next period, the securities, or similar securities, are repurchased to maintain the portfolio. There have been occasional examples of this manipulation that changed a material loss to a net income amount.

Arguments against current market as a valuation basis are:

1. Market values often cannot be determined with reasonable certainty. A problem often arises because of a "thin market" with large blocks of securities and with securities that trade infrequently.
2. Market value at the balance sheet date may not be especially significant, particularly if there are no plans to sell them in the reasonably near future.
3. Recording market values will cause unrealized gains to be reported on the income statement.
4. Except for certain financial entities, market values are not permitted for income tax purposes.

Accounting and reporting marketable securities on the basis of market prices, instead of cost, poses two problems, viz: (1) determination of

---

[6] Fair value accounting is discussed in Chapter 25.

the appropriate fair market value of the securities at the end of each period, and (2) the method of recognizing the resulting market gain or loss (often called holding gains or losses). In accordance with present GAAP, the revenue realization principle does not permit the recognization of holding gains; however, holding losses are recognized by using the lower-of-cost-or-market approach.

To illustrate the issue of recognizing holding gains, assume a short-term investment in common stock is acquired at a cost of $10,000 at the beginning of 19A. Assume the fair market value of the stock at the end of 19A is $11,000. The indicated entries, assuming accounting on the basis of fair market value, would be:

At date of acquisition (record at cost):

```
Investments, short term ....................................................10,000
    Cash ...........................................................                    10,000
```

At end of period (market $11,000); to record market gain:

```
Investments, short term ...................................................  1,000
    Market gain on investments (or unrealized
       market gain on investments) .....................................        1,000
```

Some accountants feel strongly that the market gain of $1,000 should be reflected on the income statement for 19A; others feel equally strong that the gain is unrealized in 19A and should be reported on the balance sheet at the end of 19A as unrealized. They believe that it should be recognized on the income statement when the investment is finally sold. Of course, this latter approach inconsistently reports the investment on the balance sheet at market value, but reports net income on the basis of cost. To illustrate, assume the investment is sold during 19B for $11,500. The indicated entry would be:

a. Assuming market gain was considered as realized in 19A:

```
Cash..........................................................................11,500
    Investments, short term ..........................................            11,000
    Gain on sale of investments.....................................               500
```

b. Assuming the market gain was considered as unrealized in 19A:

```
Cash..........................................................................11,500
Unrealized market gain on investments  ..........................  1,000
    Investment, short term ...........................................            11,000
    Gain on sale of investment ....................................             1,500
```

A balance in the Unrealized Market Gain on Investments account (if used) would be classified, on the balance sheet, under owners' equity as "unrealized capital."

At this date, no definitive position for all businesses has been developed by the accounting profession in accounting for short-term investments on the basis of fair values (also see Chapter 25). Currently, generally accepted accounting principles require the use of cost or lower of cost or market as explained above.

## IDENTIFICATION OF UNITS

When short-term investments are sold, or otherwise disposed of, a question frequently is posed in respect to identification of unit cost. For example, assume three purchases of stock in XY Corporation as follows: purchase No. 1, 200 shares @ $80; purchase No. 2, 300 shares @ $100; and purchase No. 3, 100 shares @ $110. Now assume 100 shares are sold at $120; what is cost? For accounting purposes, *specific identification* of the particular shares sold is preferable; however, in cases where such identification is not feasible, *Fifo* or *average cost* flow may be assumed; the former appears to be more generally used. The Internal Revenue Service requires specific identification for tax purposes, and when it cannot be applied *Fifo* must be used.

## INVESTMENT REVENUE ON SHORT-TERM INVESTMENTS

Investment revenue from *capital stock* of other companies held as a short-term investment is recorded upon notification of the declaration of a cash dividend. Stock dividends received on such stock do not represent revenue, rather they serve to reduce the cost per share of the investment. Cash dividends on capital stock (common or preferred) held as an investment are not accrued prior to declaration.

Bonds purchased at a price above par are acquired at a premium; and if acquired below par, at a discount. In the case of short-term investments in bonds, the investment account is debited at cost and no premium or discount accounts are used. Any premium or discount on a bond held as a short-term investment is not amortized because, by definition, the investment will be converted to cash in the near future and the disposal date and price are unknown. This is in contrast to the accounting for bonds held as a long-term investment where amortization of premium and discount is required (see Chapter 19). Interest receivable on short-term investments in bonds is accrued at the end of the accounting period by means of an adjusting entry.

### PART C—RECEIVABLES

This section focuses on the classification, measurement, and accounting for receivables. Broadly speaking, the term *receivables* encompasses the entity's claims for money, goods, and services from other entities. For the most part, receivables consist of amounts due from customers and clients arising from normal operations; however, a variety of other receivables are encountered from time to time. The following aspects of receivables are discussed:

1. Trade receivables:
    *a.* Accounts receivable.
    *b.* Notes receivable.

2. Special receivables:
   a. Deposits.
   b. Claims against various parties.
   c. Advances to employees, officers, and stockholders.
3. Collection expectations:
   a. Current.
   b. Noncurrent.
4. Receivables used for borrowing:
   a. Accounts receivable assignment, factoring, sale, and pledging.
   b. Notes receivable discounting.

## TRADE RECEIVABLES

Trade receivables usually mark the first point in the sequence of merchandising and service transactions. The amounts *billed* as receivables are established by exchange credit transactions and usually are billed at the gross amount that can be realized in cash. The two principal classes of trade receivables are accounts receivable and notes receivable.

## ACCOUNTS RECEIVABLE

The term *accounts receivable* is commonly used to designate trade debtors' accounts. Other receivables are separately designated and recorded as special receivables. Considerable objection may be raised against the unqualified title "Accounts receivable." Strictly speaking, any claim for which no written statement of the obligation (such as a note) has been received by the creditor is an account receivable. The careless use of a title so broadly inclusive is not sufficiently descriptive to convey the true nature of the various assets included. It is preferable to employ more descriptive titles for the various classes of accounts receivable, such as "Accounts receivable—trade debtors" for accounts due for regular sales to customers. Such usage facilitates classification and interpretation of these assets on the balance sheet. Ordinarily accounts receivable are classified under the "Current asset" caption on the balance sheet, yet there are some special accounts receivable which should not be classified as current.

*Measurement of Bad Debt Expense and Accounts Receivable.* Valuation of accounts receivable poses the problem of estimating the amount which will be actually realized from the accounts through collection.[7] When credit is extended on a continuing basis, there are some inevitable losses due to uncollectibility. These losses are considered to be a normal expense of business. In accordance with the matching principle, this expense must be matched with the revenue of the period in which the

---

[7] Receivables arising from sales and services should be recorded at net of any trade discounts; see Chapter 8 for a complete discussion of accounting for cash discounts on receivables.

sales and service transactions occurred, rather than in later periods when the specific accounts receivable are found to be uncollectible. However, since these bad accounts cannot be known until future periods the expense must be estimated in advance, recorded in the accounts, and reported on the current financial statements.

The Accounts Receivable account reflects the amount collectible and a special valuation, or contra asset account, Allowance for Doubtful Accounts (or Allowance for Bad Debts), is used to record the estimates.

There are two common approaches used to estimate the loss due to uncollectible accounts; each approach has two adaptations as follows:

1. Estimating bad debt expense:
    a. On the basis of past experience the average percentage or ratio relationship for the company between actual losses from bad debts and *net credit sales* is ascertained. This percentage, adjusted for anticipated conditions, is then applied to the actual net credit sales of the period to determine both the current expense and concurrent addition to the allowance for doubtful accounts.
    b. Use the same procedure as in (a) except the percentage of bad debts to cash plus credit sales is used.
2. Estimating the net value of present receivables:
    a. Determine from past experience the average ratio or percentage of the amount uncollectible in accounts receivable to the total amount of outstanding accounts receivable. This percentage, adjusted for expected conditions, is then applied each period to the balance in accounts receivable. The balance in the allowance account is then adjusted so that its balance equals the total of the estimated uncollectible accounts.
    b. Age the accounts receivable and from the resulting analysis and other available information estimate the total uncollectible accounts. The balance in the allowance account is then adjusted so that its balance equals the total of the estimated uncollectible accounts.

The use of any of these approaches to estimate bad debts must take cognizance of changes in credit policy, changes in economic conditions, and any other external factors which might have a bearing upon the ability of customers to pay their debts. After a method is selected, it should be subjected to a more or less continuous review on the part of the accountant and the officers of the company so that rates may be revised or the approach changed to secure reliable results.

*Accounting for Bad Debt Expense.* The two methods of measuring bad debt expense outlined above affect the way in which the amount is determined for the adjusting entry to record estimated bad debt expense at the end of the period. In the first approach, estimation of bad debt expense, the amount estimated is recorded. In contrast, in the second approach, the allowance account is adjusted to the estimated balance needed.

To illustrate accounting for bad debt expense and uncollectible receivables, assume the following data for X Company:

```
Beginning balances:
  Accounts receivable (debit) .....................................................$100,000
  Allowance for doubtful accounts (credit)........................................  2,000

Transactions during the period:
  Credit sales  ..................................................................  500,000
  Cash sales.....................................................................  700,000
  Collections on accounts receivable  ...........................................  420,000
  Accounts written off as uncollectible .........................................    2,500
```

The indicated entries relating to bad debts are:

*a.* To write off the bad accounts:

```
Allowance for doubtful accounts .......................................2,500
        Accounts receivable (specific accounts)  ........................      2,500
```

The write-off of uncollectible accounts as bad normally would occur during the period and would precede the end-of-the-period adjusting entries. In some cases, as in this one, the allowance account has a temporary debit balance of $500.

The two different approaches for estimating the amount for the adjusting entry for bad debt expense are as follows:

*b.* Adjustment of the allowance by estimating bad debt expense (Method 1 above): Assume past experience has indicated that 1% of credit sales normally will not be collected and that this pattern is expected to continue.

```
Bad debt expense ($500,000 × 1%).....................................5,000
        Allowance for doubtful accounts...................................      5,000
    After posting this entry the allowance account will
    reflect a credit balance of $4,500.
```

*c.* Adjustment of allowance by estimating the net value of present receivables (Method 2 above): Assume it is estimated that 1.1% of the balance of accounts receivable eventually will be uncollectible.

```
Bad debt expense...............................    ................................2,453
        Allowance for doubtful accounts ...................................      2,453
    Computation:
      To adjust to the desired credit balance as follows:
        Desired balance (1.1% of $177,500) .........................$1,953
        Debit balance in allowance before adjustment ..........   500
        Amount of Credit Needed.....................................$2,453
```

A debit balance in the allowance account, should it occur after the adjusting entry, means that inadequate provision has been made in the past. If it is determined that the estimates have been too high or too low, the current and future rates should be adjusted accordingly. This would be a *change in estimate* as prescribed in "Accounting Changes," *APB Opinion No. 20* (see Chapters 2 and 20).

### Evaluation of Methods

Both methods of estimating bad debts are acceptable under generally accepted accounting principles. Each method has certain strengths and weaknesses. The first method discussed, *estimation of bad debt expense*, is generally preferable because it focuses on the matching principle by measuring current bad debt expense in relationship to the revenues of the current period that caused the bad accounts. Thus, it focuses on matching current expense with current revenue and emphasizes the income statement rather than the balance sheet. In respect to the use of credit sales or total sales, clearly the former is preferable because cash sales cannot cause credit losses.

The second method discussed, *estimation of net value of present receivables*, focuses on the balance sheet because it is essentially an evaluation of the net realizable value of all accounts receivable reflected in the accounts at the end of the current period. It only incidentally measures bad debt expense. It suffers from the probability that the bad debt expense reported on the income statement for the period may not be particularly related to the credit sales of the current period, thus violating the matching principle. It favors the balance sheet over the income statement. In applying this method, aging the accounts receivable (discussed below) at the end of each period is preferable to the use of a simple estimate as illustrated above.

*Aging Accounts Receivable.* Aging accounts receivables involves an analysis of each individual account to determine the amounts not yet due, moderately past due, and considerably past due. Classification of amounts by age (i.e., length of time uncollected) is deemed important because experience shows that the older an account the higher the probability of uncollectibility. Aging requires the preparation of an *aging schedule* similar to the illustration in Exhibit 7–3. In the absence

**EXHIBIT 7–3**

**Aging Schedule for Accounts Receivable (at December 31, 19XX)**

| Customer | Receivable Balance Dec. 31, 19XX | Not Past Due | Past Due 1–30 Days | Past Due 31–60 Days | Past Due Over 60 Days |
|---|---|---|---|---|---|
| Davis | $    500 | $    400 | $   100 | | |
| Evans | 900 | 900 | | | |
| Field | 1,650 | | 1,350 | $   300 | |
| Harris | 90 | | | 30 | $  60 |
| King | 800 | 700 | 60 | 40 | |
| Zilch | 250 | 250 | | | |
| Total | $32,500 | $26,000 | $4,200 | $2,000 | $300 |

of specific identification of collections, as related to several charges to an account, *Fifo* order is used in the aging schedule.

Upon completion of the aging schedule each past-due amount should be reviewed by credit department personnel to determine its probable collectibility. Sometimes such a procedure is prohibitively time consuming; therefore, the general approach used is to develop estimated loss percentages for each *age category* based on previous loss experience of the company. This approach to the aging schedule is shown in Exhibit 7–4.

**EXHIBIT 7–4**
**Estimating Allowance for Doubtful Accounts, Aging Approach**
**(at December 31, 19XX)**

| Status | Total Balances | Loss Experience Percentage | Estimated Amount to Be Lost |
|---|---|---|---|
| Not due | $26,000 | 1% | $   260 |
| 1–30 days past due | 4,200 | 8 | 336 |
| 31–60 days past due | 2,000 | 25 | 500 |
| Over 60 days past due | 300 | 50 | 150 |
| | $32,500 | | $1,246 |

At December 31, 19XX, the allowance for doubtful accounts would be adjusted to a credit balance of $1,246.

*Bad Debts Collected.* When an amount is collected from a customer whose account was previously written off as uncollectible, the customer's account should be recharged with that amount (or with the entire balance previously written off if it now appears collectible) and the allowance account should be credited for the same amount. This entry will cause the debtor's account to reflect a detailed record of the credit and related collections. Such information may be useful in future dealings with the customer.

*Customers' Credit Balances.* When individual customers' accounts have credit balances (from prepayments or overpayments), the amount may be deducted from the debit balances of the customers' accounts if immaterial in amount. If they are material in amount, separate disclosure as liabilities is preferable; "Credit balance of customers' accounts" is a suitable title.

### Notes Receivable

Notes receivable may consist of trade notes receivable, which arise from regular operations, and special notes receivable. Trade notes receivable are by far the most common. When material amounts are involved, trade notes and special notes should be accounted for and reported separately.

Notes receivable are unconditional written promises to pay the payee or holder of the note (i.e., a holder in due course) a specified sum. The payee ordinarily would be in possession of the note unless it has been endorsed to a subsequent holder in due course. Not all notes are negotiable (i.e., transferable by endorsement); hence separate classification of negotiable and nonnegotiable notes is required. Requisites for negotiability are a matter of law.

Notes may be designated as (a) interest-bearing or (b) noninterest-bearing; theoretically, however, all commercial notes are interest bearing. Interest-bearing notes require payment of the *face* amount of the note at maturity plus interest. In contrast, a noninterest-bearing note includes the interest in the face amount. Thus the present value of an interest-bearing note is the same as its maturity amount (i.e., its face value). In contrast, the present value of a noninterest-bearing note is less than its maturity amount.

Conceptually, a note receivable is recorded in the accounts and reported at its current present value (refer to Chapter 6). An interest-bearing note that specifies the going rate of interest will always have a current present value that is the same as its face amount.[8] However, when a note is noninterest-bearing or when the specified interest rate on an interest-bearing note is different from the going rate, the current present value and the maturity amounts will be different. In these two situations the current present value should be computed and reported as discussed and illustrated in Chapter 11 in respect to notes payable.

For purposes of this chapter a note receivable under two different assumptions (Case A, interest-bearing; and Case B, noninterest-bearing) will be illustrated.

Assume K Company sold merchandise for $2,000 on July 1, 19A, on credit and received a note receivable due in one year. The going rate of interest is 8%, and the accounting period ends on December 31. Assume two different situations, viz:

> Case A — Interest-bearing note, face amount $2,000. Payable at maturity, face amount plus interest at 8%, $160; total, $2,160.
>
> Case B — Noninterest-bearing note, face amount, $2,160, which includes 8% interest on the net amount of the sales price (rather than on the face amount of the note). The amount of the sale can be verified as: $2,160 ÷ 1.08 = $2,000.[9]

The entries for each separate case are:

---

[8] This can be demonstrated readily by using the appropriate table values given in Chapter 6 to discount from maturity to the present (a) the maturity amount, and (b) the interest payments required. These two discounted amounts when summed will always equal the face amount of the interest-bearing note.

[9] See Chapter 11, Liabilities, for discussion of the situation where the interest rate is applied to the face amount of the note.

| | Case A<br>Interest-Bearing<br>Note | | Case B<br>Noninterest-Bearing<br>Note | |
|---|---|---|---|---|
| July 1, 19A—to record note and sale: | | | | |
| Notes receivable...........................2,000 | | | 2,160 | |
| Unearned discount on notes receivable* ........................ | | | | 160 |
| Sales revenue........................ | | 2,000 | | 2,000 |
| * Alternative title, unearned interest revenue. | | | | |
| December 31, 19A—adjusting entry at end of accounting period: | | | | |
| Interest receivable ($2,000 × 8% × $^6/_{12}$)......................................... | 80 | | | |
| Unearned discount on notes receivable................................ | | | 80 | |
| Interest revenue...................... | | 80 | | 80 |
| June 30, 19B—collection of note (assuming no reversing entry on January 1, 19B): | | | | |
| Cash ...........................................2,160 | | | 2,160 | |
| Unearned discount on notes receivable................................ | | | 80 | |
| Interest receivable ................... | | 80 | | |
| Interest revenue ..................... | | 80 | | 80 |
| Notes receivable..................... | | 2,000 | | 2,160 |

On the December 31, 19A balance sheet, the balance in "Unearned discount on notes receivable" should be deducted from "Notes receivable" to reflect the then present value of the note.[10]

Though not all of the documents reported under the caption "notes receivable" technically are notes, the distinctions between them are seldom deemed vital enough to warrant the use of separate accounts for each type. For example, bills of exchange and trade acceptances usually are included in notes receivable. Drafts, trade acceptances, and other bills of exchange are written orders drawn by one party on a second party to pay a third party an amount of money under specified conditions.

The Notes Receivable account should include only commercial paper with trade debtors which is related to the operating cycle and not past due. All other notes, including those between the entity and its officers, employees, or stockholders, should be reported separately. Notes of affiliated companies also should be shown separately.

Balance sheet classification of notes receivable may be either current or noncurrent depending upon collection expectations.

*Provision for Losses on Notes.* Provision for uncollectible notes

---

[10] Alternatively, the noninterest-bearing note could have been recorded net of the discount (i.e., at $2,000) and the discount amortization entered in the note account so that the balance would be $2,160 at maturity date. The results are precisely the same.

from trade customers normally should be included in the provision credited to Allowance for Doubtful Accounts.

*Discounting of Notes Receivable.* If a note receivable is endorsed to another payee before maturity, the original payee receives money (through the discounting) before maturity, but may become *contingently liable* for payment of the note. This is generally called discounting a note receivable, and the contingent liability depends on whether or not the note was endorsed with or without recourse. Since the bank or other endorsee normally is unwilling to accept the note without recourse, most notes give rise to a contingent liability when discounted.

The interest cost of discounting a note receivable is computed as follows:

$$\text{Interest Cost (or discount)} = \text{Maturity Value of the Note} \times \text{Discount Rate} \times \text{Time to Be Held by the New Payee}$$

To illustrate, assume Company X has a 90-day, 10% interest-bearing note receivable, face amount, $3,000. It is discounted at the bank at 9% after being held 30 days from issue date. The proceeds and interest cost would be calculated as follows:

Maturity amount:

| | | |
|---|---:|---:|
| Face amount | $3,000 | |
| Interest to maturity ($3,000 × 10% × 3/12) | 75 | $3,075.00 |
| Interest cost (discount): | | |
| $3,075 × 9% × 2/12 | | 46.13 |
| Proceeds (Cash Received) upon Discounting | | $3,028.87 |

Company X, the endorser, would record the discounting transaction in either of the following ways:

| | Interest Expense and Revenue Recognized Separately | | Interest Expense and Revenue Recognized at Net |
|---|---|---|---|
| Cash | 3,028.87 | | 3,028.87 |
| Interest expense | 46.13 | | |
|    Notes receivable | | 3,000.00 | 3,000.00 |
|    Interest revenue | | 75.00 | 28.87 |

The first entry is preferable theoretically because it separately recognizes the expense and revenue elements. Also some accountants prefer to credit Notes Receivable Discounted for the face amount of the note; this account would be a contra account to Notes Receivable. It is one method of recording the contingent liability (also see Chapter 11).[11]

---

[11] A less conventional, though theoretically defensible, recording of the transaction would be:

| | | |
|---|---:|---:|
| Cash | 3,028.87 | |
|    Interest revenue (for 1 month) | | 25.00 |
|    Gain on discount of notes | | 3.87 |
|    Notes receivable | | 3,000.00 |

Often the refinements in recording discounted notes involve amounts (such as the $3.87) that are not material.

*Disclosure of the Contingent Liability on Discounted Notes.* Reporting contingencies, as specified in FASB *Statement No. 6*, is discussed and illustrated in Chapter 11. When a note receivable is discounted, the transfer by endorsement creates a contingent liability for the endorser, as defined in FASB *Statement No. 6*. Such a contingent liability usually is disclosed by a note to the financial statements such as the following: "The company is contingently liable for notes receivable discounted amounting to $3,000 should the maker default on due date. There is no reason to expect default at that date." Other methods sometimes used are:

1. Current Assets:
   Notes receivable (contingent liability for notes
       discounted, $3,000) ................................................ $7,000

2. Current Assets:
   Notes receivable.........................................................$10,000
       Less: Notes receivable discounted ...........................  3,000    7,000

*Dishonored Notes Receivable.* When a note receivable is not paid or renewed at maturity it is said to be dishonored. The accounting procedure for a dishonored note depends on whether or not the note has been discounted. If a dishonored note has been discounted, ordinarily it will be necessary for the original payee to pay it (unless he or she endorsed it without recourse).

To illustrate, assume the $3,000 interest-bearing note discounted by Company X was defaulted by the maker. Company X paid the bank the face amount of the note plus interest and a protest fee of $15. Company X would record the default as follows:

Special receivable—dishonored note .......................................3,090
    Cash ............................................................................    3,090

On the other hand, if this same note had not been discounted, upon dishonor the required entry by Company X would have been:

Special receivable—dishonored note .......................................3,075
    Notes receivable...............................................................    3,000
    Interest revenue ..............................................................    75
    To charge dishonored note to account of maker together with
    accrued interest to maturity date.

After dishonor, interest accrues on the maturity amount plus accrued interest and any protest fees at the *legal* rate of interest. However, if the note is uncollectible, the total claim should be written off as a bad debt.

Balance sheet presentation of dishonored notes would list a special receivable with adequate provision for the uncollectibility expectations. Footnote disclosure would be necessary for large notes in default.

## SPECIAL RECEIVABLES

Receivables, other than trade receivables, generally are classified as special receivables. They may be represented by open accounts or notes and may be current or noncurrent. Some of the usual types of special receivables are:

1. Deposits made to other parties to cover potential damages, and deposits as a guarantee of performance of a contract or payment of an expense.
2. Prepayments to others on contingent purchases and expense contracts.
3. Claims against creditors for damaged or lost or returned goods.
4. Claims against common carriers for lost or damaged goods.
5. Claims against the government for rebates.
6. Claims against officers and employees.
7. Claims against customers for return of containers (no deposit).
8. Advances to subsidiaries.
9. Advances to officers and employees.
10. Dividends receivable (declared but not yet paid by the issuing corporation).
11. Unexpended balances of working funds in the hands of agents.
12. Claims against insurance companies for losses sustained.
13. Claims in litigation.
14. Unpaid calls on stock subscriptions (subscriptions receivable).

Special receivables that are related to the operating cycle or are collectible within one year should be appropriately designated and reported in the current asset section of the balance sheet. Other special receivables normally are reported on the balance sheet under a noncurrent caption such as "Other assets." Thus, receivables from officers, employees, or affiliates, whether arising from cash advances or from sales, would be classed as noncurrent if not collectible on a current basis.

Special receivables should be evaluated independently, and a special allowance for doubtful accounts for this class of receivables should be established when warranted by the prevailing circumstances.

## USE OF RECEIVABLES TO SECURE IMMEDIATE CASH

Companies frequently utilize receivables to secure immediate cash prior to the regular collection date. The common methods of obtaining immediate cash on receivables are: (1) discounting of notes receivable (discussed above), (2) assignment of accounts receivable, (3) factoring of accounts receivable, (4) outright sale of accounts receivable, and (5) pledging accounts receivable. While detailed contractual arrangements vary, the following brief description generally typifies these transactions and their accounting.[12]

---

[12] Some of the following added details may be of interest. Accounts financed are commonly owed by other businesses rather than consumers. The volume and popularity of this kind of financing have increased markedly, especially since World War II. Contrary to popular belief, many very solvent businesses with excellent credit ratings use accounts receivable financing.

## Assignment

Accounts receivable financing frequently involves the assignment to a financing institution of receivables arising on open-account sales. Frequently, these assignments are made on a "with recourse, non-notification" basis. "With recourse" means that accounts becoming excessively delinquent or uncollectible must be repurchased by the seller or replaced with other accounts receivable of equivalent value. "Nonnotification" means debtors are not informed of the assignment, and hence remit to the seller in the usual way. As the seller collects on the invoices that have been assigned, the cash is transmitted to the finance company.

The cash advanced may range from 70% to 95% of the amount in the accounts. Annual interest rates charged may range as high as 18% to 20% where risks are greater and the low dollar volume per account causes high costs.

Assignment of receivables with recourse is akin to the discounting of notes receivable, and the accounting procedure is essentially parallel. An illustrative problem is presented to demonstrate the essential accounting for the assignment of accounts receivable.

*Illustrative Problem.* W Company assigned $40,000 of its receivables to Z Finance Company under a contract, including a promissory note, whereby the latter agreed to advance 85% of their amount.

Debtors remit directly to W since the assignment was "with recourse, nonnotification." The series of transactions and related entries are shown in Exhibit 7–5.

**EXHIBIT 7–5**
**Assignment of Accounts Receivable**

| Transaction | Entries on W's Books | | |
|---|---|---|---|
| Jan. 2: Assigned $40,000 accounts receivable; advance received 85%; gave note payable. | Accounts receivable assigned.........40,000 | | |
| | Accounts receivable .............. | | 40,000 |
| | Cash ($40,000 × 85%) .................34,000 | | |
| | Notes payable (Z Finance Co.)... | | 34,000 |
| Jan: Collected $30,000 of assigned accounts less cash discounts $300. Sales returns $500. | Cash ........................................29,700 | | |
| | Sales discounts .......................... | 300 | |
| | Sales returns ............................ | 500 | |
| | Accounts receivable assigned... | | 30,500 |
| Jan. 31: Remitted collections to finance company plus $350 interest. | Financing expense........................ | 350 | |
| | Notes payable (Z Finance Co.) .......29,700 | | |
| | Cash ................................... | | 30,050 |
| Feb: Collected balance of assigned accounts except $200 written off as uncollectible. | Cash ...................................... 9,300 | | |
| | Allowance for doubtful accounts ... | 200 | |
| | Accounts receivable assigned... | | 9,500 |
| Feb. 28: Remitted balance due to finance company plus $100 interest. | Financing expense........................ | 100 | |
| | Notes payable (Z Finance Co.) ....... 4,300 | | |
| | Cash ................................... | | 4,400 |

On January 31, the balance sheet would reflect the following:

Current Assets:
Accounts receivable ....................................... $150,000
Accounts receivable assigned..........................$9,500
Less: Note payable on assigned accounts ......... 4,300
Equity in accounts receivable assigned ............                 5,200
        Total Accounts Receivable .................... $155,200

Obviously, the details of a contract, such as the one illustrated above, will determine the appropriate accounting entries.

## Factoring

Accounts receivable may be sold on a *without recourse* basis to factors.[13] Customers whose accounts are sold are notified to pay directly to the factor who assumes the functions of billing, collecting, and so on.

Under a factoring contract, the factor controls the granting of credit for the client. As the latter sells to customers, copies of the sales invoices and supporting documents are sent to the factor. The client usually obtains cash immediately upon transferring the invoices. Gross amounts of the invoices less any discounts and allowances and less the factor's commission and a margin or reserve (factor's margin or reserve) to cover expected returns and claims is the measure of cash available. Interest (above the factor's commission) is charged only on cash drawn *prior* to the average due date of the factored invoices. Available money not drawn plus the amount reserved becomes available without interest cost on the average due date.

In addition to interest, factors charge commissions to compensate for their credit and collection services and the credit losses they must bear. Since cash needs are often seasonal, proportions of available cash drawn probably will vary throughout the term of the factoring contract.

## Outright Sale of Accounts Receivable

Occasionally accounts receivable are sold outright to a third party, usually without recourse. Outright sale involves a prohibitively high discount rate, varying from 15% to 50%, depending upon the circumstances. Outright sale occurs most frequently when a business is in serious financial difficulty. No unique accounting problems are involved; Cash is debited, the receivables sold and the related amount of the allowance for doubtful accounts are closed out, and the difference is recorded as the finance charge.

## Pledging

Loans are sometimes obtained from banks and other lenders by pledging accounts receivable as security. The borrower continues to collect

---

[13] Factors are financing organizations which buy trade receivables. Factoring is encountered in many lines of industry but is especially widespread in the textile industry.

the receivables and usually is required to apply collections to reduction of the loan. This method of lending on receivables is sometimes used because commercial banks may lack express or implied power to purchase accounts receivable. Disclosure of the fact that portions of the accounts receivable balance have been pledged should be accomplished by balance sheet footnotes or appropriate parenthetical notations. The accounting by the borrower is essentially the same as that illustrated above for assignment.

## QUESTIONS

1. Define cash in the accounting sense.

2. In what circumstances, if any, is it permissible to offset a bank overdraft against a positive balance in another bank account?

3. If you were called upon to establish a petty cash system that would be particularly effective from the standpoint of internal control, what important features would you incorporate in it?

4. Where (if at all) do items (a) through (g) belong in the following reconciliation?

```
Balance per bank statement, June 30 ........................................$x,xxx.xx
    Plus............................................................................_____
    Minus.........................................................................._____
        June 30 True Balance  .................................................$9,600.00

Balance per our ledger, June 30  ...........................................$x,xxx.xx
    Plus............................................................................_____
    Minus.........................................................................._____
        June 30 True Balance  .................................................$9,600.00
```

a. Note collected by bank for depositor on June 29; notification was received July 2 when the June 30 bank statement was delivered by the mail carrier.
b. Checks drawn in June which had not cleared bank by June 30.
c. Check of a depositor with a similar name which was returned with checks accompanying June 30 bank statement and which was charged to our account.
d. Bank service charge for which notification was received upon receipt of bank statement.
e. Deposit mailed June 30 which reached bank July 1.
f. Notification of charge for imprinting our name on blank checks was received with the June 30 bank statement.
g. Upon refooting cash receipts book, we discovered that one receipt was omitted in arriving at the total which was posted to the Cash account in the ledger.

5. Briefly describe a "comprehensive" bank reconciliation.

6. What criteria must a security meet to qualify as a short-term investment?

7. What is properly included in the cost of short-term investments?

8. In what ways, if any, does the accounting for investments in bonds differ if the securities are held as long-term investments instead of as short-term investments?

9. An investor bought 100 shares of PQ Company stock in January for $6,700 and another 100 in March for $7,000. In October, the investor sold 150 shares at 77. What is the amount of the gain or loss? Discuss briefly.

10. The account, Allowance to Reduce Short-Term Investments in Equity Securities to Market, may properly be debited or credited. Under what circumstances would this account be credited? Debited?

11. Briefly describe the basic approaches to estimating allowance for doubtful accounts in connection with trade receivables. Evaluate each approach.

12. It sometimes happens that a receivable which has been written off as uncollectible is subsequently collected. Describe the accounting procedures in such an event.

13. How should customer accounts that have credit balances be reported in the financial statements?

14. T Company received a $1,000 note from a customer which bore interest at 8% and matured in three months. After holding it one month, the note was discounted by T at the bank at 9%. Compute T's proceeds.

15. How should special receivables be reported on the balance sheet?

16. Aside from discounting notes receivable, by what other means can receivables be used to secure immediate cash?

## EXERCISES

## PART A: EXERCISES 1–7

### Exercise 7–1

The following items are on hand at the end of the period:

| | Exclude from Cash Balance | | |
| --- | --- | --- | --- |
| | Yes | No | Explanation |
| a. Postdated checks. | | | |
| b. Time deposits. | | | |
| c. Money advanced to officers. | | | |
| d. Postage stamps in cash drawer. | | | |
| e. Sight draft left with bank for collection. | | | |
| f. Deposit in foreign bank. | | | |
| g. Money orders. | | | |
| h. Cashiers' checks. | | | |
| i. Note receivable left with bank for collection. | | | |
| j. Time draft left with bank for collection. | | | |
| k. Check returned by bank, insufficient funds. | | | |

*Required:*

1. Complete the above tabulation to indicate what items should be excluded from the cash balance.
2. Provide an explanation of the basis for exclusion.

### Exercise 7–2

Indicate the amount (and how derived) which could be prcperly reported as Cash for each of the following independent cases:

*a.* Balance in general checking account, Bank H, $5,000; overdraft in special checking account, Bank H, $800; check held from company president for $400 received six weeks ago in settlement of advance to the president.
*b.* Balance in Bank P, $20,000; refundable deposit with state treasurer to guarantee performance of highway contract in progress, $10,000; balance in Banco de Sur America, $2,000 (foreign and restricted).
*c.* Cash on hand, $500; cash in Bank C, $9,000; cash held by salespersons as advances on expense accounts, $800; postage stamps on hand received from mail-order customers, $50.
*d.* Balance in checking account, $10,000; demand certificates of deposits, $5,000; deposit with bond sinking fund trustee, $15,000; cash on hand, $1,000.
*e.* Negotiable instruments in cash drawer on December 31:

| From | Date of Check | Other Data | |
|---|---|---|---|
| Customer W | Dec. 29 | On past-due account. | $500 |
| Customer X | Dec. 30 | In payment of $1,000 invoice of December 23. | 700 |
| Customer Y | Dec. 24 | Previously deposited and returned; insufficient funds. | 300 |
| Customer Z | Jan. 2 (next year) | In full payment of account. | 400 |
| J. T. Brown | Dec. 29 | American Express traveler check. | 100 |

### Exercise 7–3

As a part of their newly designed internal control system, the Mark Corporation established a petty cash fund. Operations for the first month were:

*a.* Wrote a check for $500 on August 1 and turned the cash over to the custodian.
*b.* Summary of the petty cash expenditures:

| | Aug. 1–15 | Aug. 16–31 |
|---|---|---|
| Postage | $ 48 | $ 46 |
| Supplies used | 230 | 220 |
| Delivery expense | 90 | 150 |
| Miscellaneous expenses | 20 | 30 |
| Total | $388 | $446 |

*c.* Fund replenished on August 16.
*d.* Fund replenished on August 31 and increased by $100.

*Required:*

Give all entries indicated through August.

## Exercise 7–4

Foster Company, as a matter of policy, deposits all receipts and makes all payments by check. The following data were taken from the cash records:

### Reconciliation at May 31

| | |
|---|---:|
| Balance per bank | $7,000 |
| Add: Outstanding deposits | 1,200 |
| | 8,200 |
| Deduct: Outstanding checks | 1,500 |
| Balance per Books | $6,700 |

### June Results

| | Per Bank | Per Books |
|---|---:|---:|
| Balance, June 30 | $ 4,090 | $ 5,100 |
| June deposits | 10,600 | 12,300 |
| June checks | 14,500 | 13,900 |
| June note collected | 1,000 | — |
| June bank charges | 10 | — |

*Required (for June):*

1. Compute the unrecorded deposits and outstanding checks.
2. Reconcile the bank account.
3. Give any correcting entries indicated.

## Exercise 7–5

Reconciliation of Darden Company's bank account at May 31 was as follows:

| | |
|---|---:|
| Balance per bank statement | $14,000 |
| Deposits outstanding | 800 |
| Checks outstanding | 150* |
| | $14,650 |
| Balance per books | $14,664 |
| Unrecorded service charge | 14* |
| | $14,650 |

 * Denotes deduction.

June data are as follows:

| | Bank | Books |
|---|---:|---:|
| Checks recorded | $11,500 | $11,800 |
| Deposits recorded | 10,100 | 11,000 |
| Service charges recorded | 12 | 14 |
| Collection by bank ($800 note plus interest) | 820 | — |
| NSF check returned with June 30 statement (will be redeposited; assumed to be good) | 50 | — |
| Balances June 30 | 13,358 | 13,850 |

*Required:*

1. Compute unrecorded deposits and outstanding checks at June 30.
2. Prepare a reconciliation for June.
3. Prepare entries needed at June 30.

## Exercise 7–6

Kay Company's cash transactions were made through its accounts at First National Bank. On April 30 the company reconciled its bank and book balances as follows:

| | | |
|---|---:|---:|
| Balance per bank statement | | $7,900 |
| Deduct outstanding checks: | | |
| No. 698 | $ 30 | |
| No. 699 | 80 | |
| No. 702 | 25 | 135 |
| | | 7,765 |
| Add: | | |
| Outstanding deposit | 150 | |
| April service charge | 3 | |
| May Company check charged to our account | 40 | 193 |
| April 30 Book Balance | | $7,958 |

In summary form, the Cash account on Kay Company's books for May is as below:

**Cash**

| | | | |
|---|---:|---|---:|
| April 30, balance | 7,958 | April service charge | 3 |
| May collections | 14,210 | Checks drawn | 13,812 |

At May 31 the following checks were outstanding: No. 702, $25; No. 735, $100; No. 738, $60; and No. 740, $20. The May 31 receipts amounting to $420 were mailed to the bank at the close of business that day. The May service charge of $5 was recorded by the bank only. The $40 item shown on the April 30 reconciliation was corrected by the bank during May. Assuming no errors by either the bank or Kay Company, the bank's records can be inferred on the basis of the foregoing.

*Required.*

Prepare a comprehensive reconciliation for May.

## Exercise 7–7

Wilson Company deposits all its receipts in the bank and makes all disbursements by check. Its February 28 bank reconciliation was as follows:

| | | |
|---|---:|---:|
| Balance, per bank | | $5,414 |
| Add: Outstanding deposits | $170 | |
| Unrecorded bank service charge | 6 | 176 |
| | | 5,590 |
| Deduct: Outstanding checks | | 390 |
| Balance per Books | | $5,200 |

March data are as follows:

|  | Per Bank | Per Books |
|---|---|---|
| Balance, March 31 | $6,024 | $3,994 |
| March deposits reflected | 4,760 | 4,900 |
| March checks reflected | 6,170* | 6,100 |
| Note collected (including $20 interest) | 2,020 | – |
| Service charge recorded | – | 6 |

\* Includes a check drawn by Dilson Company for $150.

## Required:

1. Determine apparent outstanding deposits and checks as of March 31.
2. Prepare a comprehensive reconciliation for March.
3. If March 31 were the end of Dilson's fiscal year, what entries would be needed on its books? Draft them.

## PART B: EXERCISES 8–11

## Exercise 7–8

At January 1, the short-term investments of Whitearch Company were:

| Number Held | Description | Par Value Each | Total Cost |
|---|---|---|---|
| 6 | Bonds, Day Co., 5% per annum (paid each April 1 and October 1)* | $1,000 | $5,850 |
| 100 | Shares, Knight Company, common stock | 50 | 8,300 |

\* Assume accrued interest reversed January 1.

The transactions below relate to the above short-term investments and those bought and sold during the year. All transactions are cash.

Feb. 2    Received $150 dividend from Knight Company.

Mar. 1    Sold four (4) Day Company bonds for a total consideration (including accrued interest) of $4,100.

Apr. 1    Collected semiannual interest on Day Company bonds.

May 1    Bought three bonds of King, Ltd. These 4%, $1,000 bonds pay interest each March 1 and September 1. Total consideration paid, $3,050.

June 1    For $2,100 sold the remaining Day Company bonds.

Aug. 2    Received $150 dividend from Knight Company.

Sept. 1    Collected semiannual interest on King, Ltd. bonds.

Dec. 31    Adjust and close books; recognize all accruals. At January 1, market value of marketable securities exceeded cost. However, at December 31, market prices on a per security basis were:

|  | Market Price |
|---|---|
| Knight Company common shares | 72¼ |
| King, Ltd. bonds | 102* |

\* Does not include accrued interest.

*Required:*

Journalize the foregoing transactions assuming lower-of-cost-or-market valuation on all short-term investments.

## Exercise 7-9

*Case A.* At December 31, 19A, the portfolio of short-term investments of Margo Company were comprised of the following items:

| Description | Quantity | Cost | Unit Market Prices |
|---|---|---|---|
| Hygro Corp. bonds, 7%, $1,000.................. | 5 | $5,200 | 101½ |
| Damon common stock............................ | 50 shares | 2,300 | 40⅝ |
| Martin common stock ........................... | 100 shares | 2,100 | 24 |

Assuming lower of cost or market is applied to all short-term investments:

a. At what value should the aggregate of short-term investments be reported on the December 31, 19A, balance sheet of Margo Company? Show computations.
b. One year later, the short-term investment portfolio of Margo consisted of —

| Description | Quantity | Cost | Unit Market Prices |
|---|---|---|---|
| Damon common stock.......................... | 20 shares | $ 920 | 37¼ |
| Martin common stock ......................... | 30 shares | 630 | 23 |
| Dries Corporation bonds, 8%, $1,000 ...... | 4 | 4,040 | 100½ |

During 19B, Margo had sold the 30 Damon shares at a gain of $200 and the 70 Martin shares at a gain of $140. At what value should the aggregate of short-term investments be reported on the December 31, 19B, balance sheet of Margo Company assuming lower of cost or market for all securities? Show computations.

*Case B.* Davis Company bought, as a short-term investment, seven of the $1,000 bonds of Massengill Corporation on April 1, 19A, at 102 plus accrued interest. These 9% bonds pay interest semiannually each May 1 and November 1. On December 1, 19A, four (4) of the bonds were sold at 101¼ plus accrued interest. Davis Company adjusts and closes books on December 31.

a. Journalize all events relating to the bonds for 19A, assuming the cost method.
b. If the bonds had been bought as a long-term or permanent investment, what added information would have been needed and why?

## Exercise 7-10

Prepare journal entries to record the following transactions relating to 8% bonds of Dial Corporation purchased as a short-term investment. These bonds pay interest each May 1 and November 1.

Aug. 1  Cash of $39,800 is disbursed for $40,000 par value bonds including interest.

Nov. 1 Collected interest.
Dec. 31 Adjust and close books for the year. The market value of the bonds is 98 excluding interest (assume LCM and use the cost method).
Jan. 1 Make any necessary reversing entries.
Feb. 1 Sold half of the bonds, receiving a check for $19,600, including accrued interest.
May 1 Collected interest.

## Exercise 7–11

On January 20, 19A, K Corporation acquired the following short-term investments in marketable equity securities:

Company L — 500 shares common stock (nopar) at $60 per share.
Company M — 300 shares preferred stock (par $10, nonredeemable) at $20 per share.
Additional data:

December 31, 19A Market values: L stock, $52; M stock, $24.
March 2, 19B Received cash dividends per share as follows: L stock, $1.00; M stock, $.50.
October 1, 19B Sold 100 of the Company M shares at $26 per share.
December 31, 19B Market values: L stock, $56; M stock, $25.

*Required:*

1. Give all entries indicated for K Corporation for the above short-term investments in marketable equity securities.
2. Show how the investments and related gains and losses would be reflected on the financial statements for K Corporation for 19A and 19B.

## PART C: EXERCISES 12–18

## Exercise 7–12

When examining the accounts of Hampton Company, you ascertain that balances relating to both receivables and payables are included in a single controlling account (called Receivables) which has a $44,100 debit balance. An analysis of the details of this account revealed the following:

|  | Debits | Credits |
|---|---|---|
| Accounts receivable — customers | $75,000 | |
| Accounts receivable — officers | 4,000 | |
| Debit balances — creditors | 900 | |
| Expense advances to salespersons | 2,000 | |
| Capital stock subscriptions receivable | 9,200 | |
| Accounts payable for merchandise | | $38,500 |
| Unpaid salaries | | 6,600 |
| Credit balances in customer accounts | | 1,000 |
| Payments received in advance for shipments not yet made | | 900 |

*Required:*

1. Give entry to reflect correct treatment of the above items and to clear the old receivables account.
2. How should the items be reported on Hampton Company's balance sheet?

### Exercise 7–13

An analysis of the receivables control account (debit balance, $81,600) of Elba Corporation at December 31 revealed the following:

a. Accounts from regular sales (current) ........................................$60,000
b. Accounts known to be uncollectible ............................................ 2,000
c. Dishonored notes charged back to customers ............................ 8,000
d. Credit balances in customer accounts ........................................ 400
e. Accounts of customers past due................................................. 6,000
f. Due from employees ................................................................. 6,000

The Allowance for Doubtful Accounts is adjusted each December 31. Its balance before adjustment on December 31 was a $1,600 debit. It was estimated that losses on receivables amounts at December would average as follows:

| Item | Loss % |
|---|---|
| a............................................. | 1 |
| c............................................. | 20 |
| e............................................. | 5 |

*Required:*

1. Give journal entries (*a*) to close the old receivables account, and (*b*) to reflect bad debt expense.
2. Indicate proper reporting on Elba Corporation's December 31 balance sheet. Assume all amounts to be material.

### Exercise 7–14

The following data are available concerning a company whose fiscal year is the calendar year:

Sales (of which $100,000 are on credit)................................$120,000
Accounts receivable, January 1........................................... 70,000
Accounts receivable, December 31....................................... 80,000
Allowance for doubtful accounts, January 1........................... 2,000 (credit)
Allowance for doubtful accounts, December 31*.................... 1,000 (debit)
     * Before making year-end adjusting entry for bad debt expense.

*Required:*

1. Assuming there were no recoveries of doubtful accounts previously charged off, what was the amount of receivables charged off as uncollectible during the year?
2. What was the amount of cash inflow from receivables during the year?
3. Give the year-end adjusting entry for bad debts under each of the following independent assumptions:
   a. Bad debts estimated to be 4% of credit sales.
   b. Bad debts estimated to be 3% of total sales.
   c. Bad debts estimated to be 5% of uncollected receivables.
   d. Bad debts estimated on basis of aging; the estimate is:
      (1) On receivables less than 60 days old ($20,000), 1%.
      (2) On receivables 60 to 120 days old ($50,000), 3½%.
      (3) On remaining receivables, 6%.

**Exercise 7–15**

Prasit Company has been in business three years and is being audited for the first time. Concerning accounts receivable, the auditor ascertained that the company has been charging off receivables as they finally proved uncollectible and treated them as expenses at the time of write-off. (Put another way, receivables were valued at 100 cents on the dollar.)

It is determined that receivables losses have approximated (and can be expected to approximate) 1½% of net sales. Down to the time of the audit, the company's sales and receivable write-off experience were as below:

| Year of Sales | Amount of Sales | Accounts Written Off in— | | |
|---|---|---|---|---|
| | | 19A | 19B | 19C |
| 19A | $ 800,000 | $2,000 | $7,500 | $1,000 |
| 19B | 700,000 | – | 3,000 | 6,500 |
| 19C | 1,000,000 | – | – | 3,500 |

*Required:*

1. Indicate the amount by which net income was understated or overstated (ignoring income tax effects) each year under the company's policy. Assume for purpose of this requirement that the old policy is to be in effect for 19C.
2. If Prasit Company were to switch over to a more acceptable basis of accounting for bad debts, assuming books were still open for 19C, what entry should be made at year-end, 19C?

**Exercise 7–16**

Eugenia Company accepted an interest-bearing note receivable for $3,000 from a customer whose account receivable had become due. In respect to the note, give the indicated journal entry for each of the following events; show computations. (Use months, not days.)

1. Received the note which matures in four months and bears interest at 8%.
2. Discounted the above note after two months at 9% interest. Make the entry under the two methods of recording.
3. The customer paid the note at maturity.
4. The customer defaulted on the note, and Eugenia Company paid the holder including a $15 protest fee.

**Exercise 7–17**

On November 1, 19A, Philip Company received from two customers two notes for merchandise sold to them. Each note was in settlement for a sale of goods for $9,000. Customer A gave an 8%, three-month, interest-bearing note. Customer B gave a three-month, noninterest-bearing note with an implied interest rate of 8% (i.e., 8% interest on the sales price was included in the face of the note).

*Required:*

1. Give all entries pertaining to the two notes on Philip Company's books from

date of receipt through time of payment assuming the company adjusts and closes its books at December 31, 19A.

2. Show how the notes should be reflected on the December 31, 19A, balance sheet.

### Exercise 7–18

A, Inc., assigned $50,000 of its receivables to Z Finance Company. The contract provided that Z would advance 80% of their gross value. A's debtors continued to remit directly to it with the checks being endorsed to Z immediately.

During the first month, customers owing $35,000 remitted $34,600 taking advantage of $400 cash discounts. Sales returns totaled $1,000. The finance charge paid after the first month was $300.

During the second month, remaining receivables were collected in full except for $200 written off as uncollectible. Final settlement was effected with the finance company, including payment of $100 added interest.

*Required:*

Give the journal entries needed to record the above assignment of accounts receivable. Closing entries are not necessary.

### PROBLEMS

### PART A: PROBLEMS 1–5

### Problem 7–1

The cash records for Voss Company provided the following data for the month of March:

|  | March 1 | March 31 |
|---|---|---|
| Balances per bank statement | $15,600.09 | $14,459.91 |
| Balances per company books | 14,375.00 | 13,409.00 |

Relevant items:

a. Outstanding checks March 31 (verified as correct) ...........................$1,400
b. Deposits in transit March 31 (verified as correct)............................ 800
c. Interest earned on bank balance (reported on bank statement) ........ 18
d. NSF check (customer check returned with bank statement).............. 50
e. Service charge by bank (reported on bank statement) .................... 7
f. Error in deposit for cash sales (deposit slip showed overage, corrected by bank)................................................................. 10
g. Error by bank (check for $10.89 cleared at $10.98) ......................... 109
h. Note collected by bank for us (including $30 interest) ................... 1,030
i. Deduction for church (per signed bank deduction form) ................. 20
j. Cash on hand ............................................................................. 500

*Required:*

1. Prepare a bank reconciliation in good form showing correct balance for the balance sheet. *Hint:* Be alert for a cash overage or shortage.
2. Prepare necessary entries at March 31.

## Problem 7–2

The records pertaining to cash for High Company provided the following data for May:

Bank statement:
- a. Balance, May 31 ............................................................$34,500
- b. Service charges for May....................................................... 5
- c. NSF check returned with May statement; customer gave this check, will redeposit next week, assumed to be good................. 50
- d. Note receivable ($5,000) collected for High by the bank and added to balance................................................................ 5,200
- e. Error from previous month in interest collected on another note receivable; bank credited High account in May for the amount ....................................................................... 100

Books:
- f. Balance, May 31 ................................................... 30,700
- g. Cash on hand ...................................................... 400
- h. Unrecorded deposit............................................... 3,700
- i. Outstanding checks................................................ 2,665

*Required:*

1. Prepare a bank reconciliation in good form. Assume all amounts provided above are correct. *Hint:* Be alert for a cash overage or shortage.
2. Give required entries for May 31.

## Problem 7–3

Tetzlaff Corporation began doing business with Fidelity Bank on October 1. On that date, the true cash balance was $4,000. All cash transactions are cleared through the bank account. Subsequent transactions during October and November relating to the Tetzlaff and Fidelity accounts are summarized below:

|  | Tetzlaff Company Books | Fidelity Bank Books |
|---|---|---|
| October deposits.......................................................... | $7,360 | $7,110 |
| October checks ............................................................ | 6,290 | 6,130 |
| October service charge.................................................. | — | 10 |
| October 31 balance...................................................... | 5,070 | 4,970 |
| November deposits (regular) ......................................... | 8,220 | 8,280 |
| November checks ......................................................... | 9,410 | 9,220 |
| November service charge.............................................. | — | 15 |
| Note collected by bank (includes $15 interest) ............... |  | 1,015 |
| October service charge.................................................. | 10 | — |
| November 30 balance.................................................... | 3,870 | 5,030 |

*Required:*

1. On the basis of the foregoing data, prepare a comprehensive bank reconciliation for November.
2. Assuming November 30 is the end of Tetzlaff's fiscal year, give entries that would be required by the bank reconciliation.

## Problem 7-4

You are examining the records of a client where internal control is found to be weak. Part of your work includes reconciliation of cash for December 19A. You have determined that the client's reconciliation as of November 30, 19A, is correct. The following information is available to you:

### Client's Reconciliation, November 30, 19A

| | |
|---|---:|
| Cash per general ledger | $2,631.74 |
| Less: Cash on hand | 210.89 |
| | 2,420.85 |
| Less: Bank service charge for November | 9.00 |
| | 2,411.85 |
| Add: Outstanding checks | 991.00 |
| Balance per Bank | $3,402.85 |

Cash receipts are summarized weekly; the cash receipts books for December appears below:

| Dec. | | |
|---|---|---:|
| 1 | Balance from Nov. 30 | $ 2,631.74 |
| 8 | Received on accounts | 25,774.80 |
| 15 | Received on accounts | 27,447.56 |
| 22 | Received on accounts | 4,659.82 |
| 29 | Received on accounts | 5,886.85 |
| | | $65,300.77 |

The cash payments record for December was as follows:

| Dec. | | |
|---|---|---:|
| 1 | November service charge | $ 9.00 |
| 3 | Checks | 5,236.50 |
| 5 | Checks | 3,645.21 |
| 8 | Checks | 16,394.89 |
| 10 | Checks | 15,873.42 |
| 12 | Checks | 4,848.89 |
| 19 | Checks | 3,622.83 |
| 22 | Checks | 3,692.09 |
| 31 | Checks | 7,657.70 |
| Balance—December 31 | | 4,311.24 |
| | | $65,300.77 |

Cash on hand December 31 amounted to $100. The transactions per the December bank statement, which are correctly recorded by the bank, show that deposits amounting to $62,870.92; checks paid amounted to $57,952.03; service charges for the month were $10; and a charge of $100 was made against the account because of the return unpaid of a customer's check. Neither the service charge nor the returned check were recorded on the client's books. The total of outstanding checks as of December 31 was found to be $4,110.50.

*Required:*

Prepare a comprehensive reconciliation for December together with a brief explanation of any items not self evident.

(AICPA adapted)

**Problem 7-5**

In connection with an audit of cash of Distributors, Inc., as at December 31, 19A, the following information has been obtained:

a. Balance per bank:
   11/30/19A ......................................................................... $  185,700
   12/31/19A ........................................................................      193,674
b. Balance per books:
   11/30/19A ........................................................................      154,826
   12/31/19A ........................................................................      167,598
c. Receipts for the month of December, 19A:
   Per bank...........................................................................    1,350,450
   Per books ........................................................................    2,335,445
d. Outstanding checks:
   11/30/19A ........................................................................       63,524
   12/31/19A ........................................................................       75,046
e. Dishonored checks are recorded as a reduction of cash receipts. Dishonored checks which are later redeposited are then recorded as a regular cash receipt. Dishonored checks returned by the bank and recorded by Distributors, Inc., amounted to $6,250 during the month of December 19A; according to the books, $5,000 were redeposited. Dishonored checks recorded on the bank statement but not on the books until the following months amounted to $250 at November 30, 19A, and $2,300 at December 31, 19A.
f. On December 31, 19A, a $2,323 check of the ABC Company was charged to the Distributors, Inc., account by the bank in error.
g. Proceeds of a note of the Able Company collected by the bank on December 10, 19A, were not entered on the books:

   Principal ..............................................................................$2,000
   Interest .................................................................................      20
                                                                                               2,020
   Less: Collection charge .............................................................       5
                                                                                             $2,015

h. The company has hypothecated (assigned) its accounts receivable with the bank under an agreement whereby the bank lends the company 80% on the hypothecated accounts receivable. Accounting for and collection of the accounts are performed by the company, and adjustments of the loan are made from daily sales reports and daily deposits.

The bank credits the Distributors, Inc., account and increases the amount of the loan for 80% of the reported sales. The loan agreement states specifically that the sales report must be accepted by the bank before Distributors, Inc., is credited. Sales reports are forwarded by Distributors, Inc., to the bank on the first day following the date of sales.

The bank allocates each deposit 80% to the payment of the loan and 20% to the Distributors, Inc., account.

Thus, only 80% of each day's sales and 20% of each collection are entered on the bank statement.

The Distributors, Inc., accountant records the hypothecation of new accounts receivable (80% of sales) as a debit to Cash and a credit to the bank loan as of the date of sales. One hundred percent of the collections on accounts receivable is recorded as a cash receipt; 80% of the collections is recorded in the cash disbursements book as a payment on the loan.

In connection with the hypothecation, the following facts were determined:

1. Included in the deposits in transit is cash from the hypothecation of accounts receivable. Sales were $40,500 on November 30, 19A, and $42,250 on December 31, 19A. The balance of the deposit in transit at December 31, 19A, was made up from collections of $32,110 which were entered on the books in the manner indicated above.
2. Collections on accounts receivable deposited in December other than deposits in transit totaled $1,200,000.
3. Sales for December totaled $1,450,000.

*i.* Interest on the bank loan for the month of December, charged by the bank but not recorded on the books, amounted to $6,140.

*Required:*

1. Prepare bank reconciliations as of November 30, 19A, and December 31, 19A, and reconciliations of cash receipts and disbursements per bank with cash receipts and disbursements per books for the month of December 19A. (Assume that you have satisfied yourself as to the propriety of the above information.) Show computations where applicable.
2. Prepare adjusting journal entries as required to correct the Cash account at December 31, 19A.

(AICPA adapted)

## PART B: PROBLEMS 6–9

### Problem 7–6

On January 1, 19A Scott Company acquired the following short-term investments in marketable equity securities:

| Company | Stock | Number of Shares | Cost per Share |
|---|---|---|---|
| T | Common (nopar) .............................. | 1,000 | $20 |
| U | Common (par $10)............................. | 600 | 15 |
| V | Preferred (par $20, nonredeemable)...... | 400 | 30 |

Data subsequent to the acquisition is as follows:

| | | |
|---|---|---|
| December 31, 19A | Market values: T stock, $16; U stock, $15; V stock, $34. |
| February 10, 19B | Cash dividends received per share: T stock, $1.50; U stock, $1.00; V stock, $.50. |
| November 1, 19B | Sold the share of V stock at $38 per share. |
| December 31, 19B | Market values: T stock, $18; U stock, $17; V stock, $33. |

*Required:*

1. Give all entries indicated for Scott Company for 19A and 19B.
2. Show how the income statement and balance sheet for Scott Company would reflect the short-term investments for 19A and 19B.

### Problem 7–7

Walsh Manufacturing Company's short-term investment portfolio included the following at December 31, 19A:

|                                                           | *Cost* |
|-----------------------------------------------------------|--------|
| AB Company, nine 8% bonds (face, $9,000) | $9,300 |
| BC Corporation common, 50 shares, nopar | 1,800 |
| CD Corporation, 4% preferred, 150 shares (par, $40) | 8,000 |

Transactions relating to the securities during 19B were as follows:

| Jan. 25 | Received semiannual dividend check on CD shares. |
|---------|---|
| Mar. 1 | Collected semiannual interest on AB bonds. |
| Apr. 15 | Sold 30 shares of BC Corporation stock for $1,020. |
| May 1 | Sold six of the AB bonds for a total consideration (including accrued interest) of $6,350. |
| June 20 | Purchased 50 shares of EF Corporation, common at 47 plus $30 brokerage fees. |
| July 25 | Received semiannual dividend check on CD shares. |
| Sept. 1 | Collected semiannual interest on AB bonds. |
| Oct. 1 | Purchased a $1,000 9% bond of DE, Inc., for total consideration of $1,100. Interest payment dates on this bond are February 1 and August 1. |
| Nov. 17 | Sold remaining BC Corporation shares for $700. |
| Dec. 2 | Received $60 dividend check from EF Corporation. |
| Dec. 31 | Preparatory to adjusting and closing the books for the year the following data as to current market values of securities held were obtained: |

| *Security* | *Market* |
|-----------|--------|
| AB bonds (ex-interest) | 103 |
| CD preferred | 54 |
| DE, Inc., bond (ex-interest) | 104 |
| EF common | 45 |

*Required:*

Journalize the foregoing transactions; adjust and close the books at December 31, 19B. Value the total portfolio of securities at market by means of an Allowance to Reduce Short-Term Investments to LCM account.

*Hint:* Do not overlook reversal of accrued interest adjustment on AB bonds on January 1, 19B.

## Problem 7–8

The DEF Manufacturing Company has followed the practice of valuing their short-term investments in marketable securities at the lower of cost or market. At December 31, 19B, their account, Investment in Marketable Securities, had a balance of $40,000; and the account, Allowance to Reduce Investments from Cost to Market, had a balance of $2,000. Analysis disclosed that on December 31, 19A, the facts relating to the securities were as follows:

| *Security* | *Cost* | *Market* | *Allowance Required* |
|-----------|--------|----------|----------------------|
| X Company bonds | $20,000 | $19,000 | $1,000 |
| Y Company bonds | 10,000 | 9,000 | 1,000 |
| Z Company bonds | 20,000 | 20,300 | 0 |
|  | $50,000 |  | $2,000 |

During 19B, the Y Company bonds were sold for $9,200; the difference between the $9,200 and the cost of $10,000 being charged to "Loss on Sale of Securities." The market price of the bonds on December 31, 19B, was X Company bonds, $19,200; Z Company bonds, $20,400.

*Required:*

1. What justification is there for the use of the lower of cost or market in valuing marketable securities?
2. Did the DEF Company properly apply this rule on December 31, 19A? Explain, including any alternative methods of application.
3. Are there any additional entries necessary for the DEF Company at December 31, 19B, to reflect the facts on the balance sheet and income statement in accordance with generally accepted accounting principles? Explain.

(AICPA adapted)

**Problem 7-9**

Check the best answer in each of the following and provide the basis (including computations where appropriate) to support your choice.

1. The June bank statement of Lucas Company showed a June 30 ending balance of $187,387. During June, the bank charged back NSF (i.e., insufficient funds) checks totaling $3,056, of which $1,856 had been redeposited by June 30. Deposits in transit on June 30 were $20,400. Outstanding checks on June 30 were $60,645, including a $10,000 check which the bank had certified on June 28. On June 14 the bank charged Lucas' account for a $2,300 item which should have been charged against the account of Luby Company; the bank did not detect the error. During June the bank collected foreign items for Lucas; the proceeds were $8,684, and bank charges for this service were $19. On June 30 the adjusted cash in bank of Lucas Company is:
   a. $149,442.
   b. $159,442.
   c. $147,142.
   d. $158,242.
   e. None of the above.
2. Which of the following items should never be included in the current sections of the balance sheet?
   a. Premium paid on short-term bond investment.
   b. Receivable from customer not collectible during coming year.
   c. Deferred income taxes resulting from interperiod income tax allocation.
   d. Funded serial bonds.
3. The test or marketability must be met before securities owned can be properly classified as—
   a. Debentures.
   b. Treasury stock.
   c. Long-term investments.
   d. Current assets.
4. How is the premium or discount on bonds purchased as a short-term investment generally reported in published financial statements?
   a. As an integral part of the cost of the asset acquired (investment) and amortized over a period of not less than 60 months.
   b. As an integral part of the cost of the asset acquired (investment) until such time as the investment is sold.
   c. As expense or revenue in the period the bonds are purchased.

     *d.* As an integral part of the cost of the asset acquired (investment) and amortized over the period the bonds are expected to be held.

5. Postage stamps and IOUs found in cash drawers should be reported as—
    *a.* Prepaid expense and receivables.
    *b.* Cash because they represent the equivalent of money.
    *c.* Petty cash.
    *d.* Investments.

6. George Company maintains two checking accounts. A special checking account is used for the weekly payroll only, and the general checking account is used for all other disbursements. Each week, a check for the aggregate amount of the payrolls is drawn on the general account and deposited in the Payroll account. Individual checks are drawn on the Payroll account. The company maintains a $5,000 minimum balance in the Payroll account. On a monthly bank reconciliation, the Payroll account should:
    *a.* Show a zero balance per the bank statement.
    *b.* Show a $5,000 balance per the bank statement.
    *c.* Reconcile to $5,000.
    *d.* Be reconciled jointly with the general account in a single reconciliation.

7. Which of the following is a current asset?
    *a.* Cash surrender value of a life insurance policy of which the company is the beneficiary.
    *b.* Investment in marketable securities for the purpose of continuing control of the issuing company.
    *c.* Cash designated for the purchase of tangible fixed assets.
    *d.* Trade installment receivables normally collectible in 18 months.

8. Which of the following should not be considered as a current asset?
    *a.* Installment notes receivable due over 18 months in accordance with normal trade practice.
    *b.* Prepaid property taxes.
    *c.* Marketable securities purchased as a short-term investment with cash provided by current operations.
    *d.* Cash surrender value of a life insurance policy carried by a corporation, the beneficiary, on its president.

                                             (AICPA adapted)

## PART C: PROBLEMS 10–14

### Problem 7–10

Records for Zarb Trading Company concerning receivables and recent sales history provided the following:

| | |
|---|---:|
| Cash sales for the period | $1,600,000 |
| Credit sales for the period | 1,000,000 |
| Balance in trade receivables, start of period | 200,000 |
| Balance in trade receivables, end of period | 240,000 |
| Balance in allowance for doubtful accounts, start of period | 4,000 (credit) |
| Accounts written off as uncollectible during period | 6,000 |

Recently Zarb's management has become concerned about various estimates used in their accounting process, including those relating to receivables and bad debts. The company is reviewing the various alternatives with a view to selecting the most appropriate one.

Assume the following simplified estimates:

1. Bad debt expense approximates three fifths of 1% of credit sales.
2. Bad debt expense approximates one fourth of 1% of net sales (cash plus credit sales).
3. As a rough estimate, 5% of the uncollected receivables will be bad at any one time.
4. Aging of the accounts at month-end indicated that three fourths of them would incur a 3% loss while the other one fourth would incur an 8% loss.

*Required:*

Four different approaches are being considered. Identify and briefly explain and give the advantages of each approach. After each explanation, give the adjusting entry based on the period data available.

## Problem 7–11

The Installment Jewelry Company has been in business for five years but has never had an audit made of its financial statements. Engaged to make an audit for 19E, you find that the company's balance sheet carries no allowance for doubtful accounts, uncollectible accounts having been expensed as written off, and recoveries credited to income as collected. The company's policy is to write off at December 31 of each year those accounts on which no collections have been received for three months. The installment contracts generally provide for uniform monthly collections over a time span of two years from date of sale.

Upon your recommendation the company agrees to revise its accounts for 19E in order to account for bad debts on the allowance basis. The allowance is to be based on a percentage of sales which is derived from the experience of prior years.

Statistics for the past five years are as follows:

| Year | Charge Sales | Accounts Written Off and Year of Sale | | | Recoveries and Year of Sale |
|---|---|---|---|---|---|
| 19A | $100,000 | (19A) $ 550 | | | |
| 19B | 250,000 | (19A) 1,500 | (19B) $1,000 | | (19A) $100 |
| 19C | 300,000 | (19A) 500 | (19B) 4,000 | (19C) $1,300 | (19B) 400 |
| 19D | 325,000 | (19B) 1,200 | (19C) 4,500 | (19D) 1,500 | (19C) 500 |
| 19E | 275,000 | (19C) 2,700 | (19D) 5,000 | (19E) 1,400 | (19D) 600 |

Accounts receivable at December 31, 19E, were as follows:

$$
\begin{array}{lr}
\text{19D sales} & \$ 15,000 \\
\text{19E sales} & 135,000 \\
\hline
& \$150,000 \\
\end{array}
$$

*Required:*

Prepare the adjusting journal entry or entries with appropriate explanations to set up the Allowance for Doubtful Accounts. (Support each item with organized computations; income tax implications should be ignored. The books have been adjusted but not closed at December 31, 19E.)

(AICPA adapted)

## Problem 7-12

Albert Company sold a building and the land on which it is located on January 1, 19A, receiving, as its consideration, a $100,000 note receivable payable in three years without interest. The sale was recorded as follows by Albert Company:

| | | |
|---|---:|---:|
| Note receivable ............................................................... 100,000 | | |
| Accumulated depreciation – building ................................. 100,000 | | |
| Building ................................................................ | 150,000 | |
| Land ..................................................................... | 25,000 | |
| Gain on sale of building ............................................. | 25,000 | |

It has been determined that 8% is a reasonable interest rate to impute to the note. You are recommending adjusting and correcting entries as of December 31, 19A (end of Albert Company's fiscal year). The books have not been adjusted or closed for 19A.

*Required:*

1. Give an entry to correct the sale entry and the adjustment for interest as of December 31, 19A. (Round to nearest dollar.)
2. Give entry to recognize interest earned at December 31, 19B.
3. Make entries at end of third year to (*a*) recognize interest earned, and (*b*) record collection of the note.
4. Aside from the correction in Requirement 1 for interest, do you see any other problem in the sale entry as originally made? Explain.

## Problem 7-13

Nabors Company has experienced a critical cash-flow problem largely occasioned by collection problems with certain customers. Consequently, it has become involved in a number of transactions relating to notes receivable. The following transactions occurred during a period ending December 31 (end of the accounting period):

| | | |
|---|---|---|
| May | 1 | Received a $10,000, 90-day, 9% interest-bearing note from E. M. Smith, a customer, in settlement of an account receivable for that amount. |
| May | 1 | Received a $15,000, six-month, 9% interest-bearing note from M. Johnson, a customer, in settlement of an account receivable for that amount. |
| Aug. | 1 | Discounted the Johnson note at the bank at 10%. |
| Aug. | 2 | Smith defaulted on the $10,000 note. |
| Sept. | 1 | Received a one-year, noninterest-bearing note from D. Karnes, a customer, in settlement of a $6,000 account receivable. The face of the note was $6,600, and the going rate of interest 10% (on the amount of the receivable). |
| Oct. | 1 | Received a $25,000, 90-day note from R. M. Cates, a customer. The note was in payment for goods purchased and was interest-bearing at 8%. |

Oct.   1   Collected the defaulted Smith note plus accrued interest to September 30 (10% per annum on the total amount due for three months).

Nov.   1   Johnson defaulted on the $15,000 note. Nabors Company paid the bank to total amount due plus a $25 protest fee.

Dec. 30   Collected Cates note in full. Collected from Johnson in full including interest on the full amount at 10% since default date.

Dec. 31   Accrued interest on outstanding notes.

*Required:*

1. Give the entry to record each of the above transactions. Show computations.
2. Show how the outstanding notes at December 31 would be reported on the balance sheet.

## Problem 7–14

Doe Company finances some of its current operations by assigning accounts receivable to a finance company. On July 1, 19A, it assigned, under guarantee, accounts amounting to $40,000, the finance company advancing to them 80% of the accounts assigned (20% of the total to be withheld until the finance company has made full recovery), less a commission charge of one half of 1% the total accounts assigned.

On July 31 the Doe Company received a statement that the finance company had collected $21,000 of these accounts, and had made an additional charge of one half of 1% of the total accounts outstanding as of July 31 – this charge to be deducted at the time of the first remittance due Doe Company from the finance company. On August 31 the Doe Company received a second statement from the finance company, together with a check for the amount due. The statement indicated that the finance company had collected an additional $16,000 and had made a further charge of one half of 1% of the balance outstanding as of August 31.

*Required (on books of Doe Company):*

1. Give the entry to record the assignment of the accounts on a notification basis (July 1).
2. Give entry to record the data from the first report from the finance company (July 31).
3. Reconstruct the report submitted by the finance company on August 31; show details to explain cash remitted and the uncollected accounts still held by the finance company.
4. Give the entry to record the data in the report of August 31.
5. Explain how the items should be reported on the financial statements of Doe Company at July 31 and August 31.

(AICPA adapted)

# Chapter 8

# Inventories — General Problems

The basic purpose in accounting for inventories is to aid in the determination of net income by matching appropriate inventory cost with revenue; a secondary purpose is to provide an inventory amount for the balance sheet. Inventories present problems of considerable magnitude for both the accountant and management. Both must seriously consider such inventory problems as measurement, control, safeguarding, and cost allocation. These problems are especially critical in view of the materiality of inventories in the typical business and the fact that inventories directly affect both the income statement and the balance sheet. These factors have caused the accounting profession to give particular attention to the problems related to inventories. This and the two following chapters present the principal accounting concepts and procedures relating to inventories.

## THE NATURE OF INVENTORIES

As an accounting category, *inventories* is an asset represented by goods owned by the business at a particular point in time and held for the purpose of future sale or for utilization in the manufacture of goods for sale. No other asset includes so great a variety of properties under a single heading, for practically all kinds of tangible goods and properties are found in the inventories of one business or another. Machinery and equipment are fixed assets of the business using them, but constituted at one time a part of the inventory of the manufacturer of such equipment. Even a building until finished and turned over to a buyer is an inventory item, a "contract in process," among the assets of the builder.

In many companies, inventories represent a significant portion of current assets or even total assets. Inventories generally represent an active asset in that there is constant usage and replacement. Although many inventory items are small, they frequently have considerable value; therefore, the problem of safeguarding inventories ranks next to protecting for cash. The advisability of adequate stocking of items for sale, coupled with the risk of loss and cost of overstocking, creates critical

318

management planning and control problems. Failure to control inventories adequately and to account for inventory quantities and costs might well lead to business failure.[1]

## CLASSIFICATION OF INVENTORIES

The major classifications of inventories relate to the types of business. A trading entity (i.e., wholesale and retail) acquires merchandise for resale, whereas a manufacturing concern acquires raw materials and component parts and manufactures finished products. The flow of inventory costs through these two types of entities may be diagrammed as follows:

*Trading entity:*

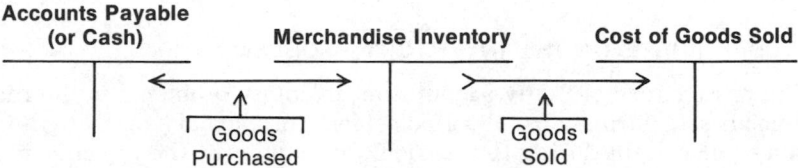

*Manufacturing entity:*

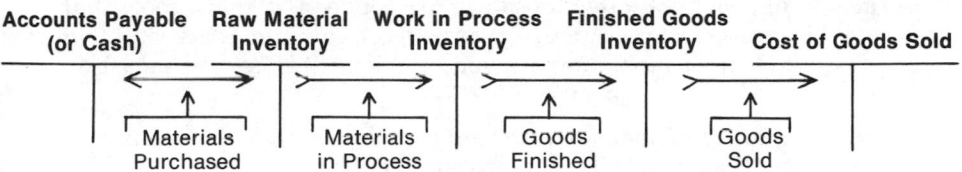

Inventories may be defined as follows:

1. Merchandise inventory – goods on hand purchased by a trading entity for resale. The physical form of the goods is not altered prior to resale.
2. Manufacturing inventory – the combined inventories of a manufacturing entity consisting of –
   a. Raw materials inventory – tangible goods purchased or obtained from natural sources and on hand principally for direct use in the manufacture of goods for resale. Parts or subassemblies manufactured prior to use are sometimes classified as raw materials; however, a preferable classification is *parts inventory*.
   b. Work in process inventory – goods partly processed and requiring further processing before sale. Work (goods) in process inventory normally is valued at the sum of *direct material, direct labor,* and *allocated manufacturing overhead costs* incurred to date of the inventory.

---

[1] For an introductory discussion of accounting for inventories refer to: G. A. Welsch and R. N. Anthony, *Fundamentals of Financial Accounting* (Homewood, Ill.: Richard D. Irwin, Inc., 1974), chap. 7.

   *c.* Finished goods inventory—manufactured articles completed and being held for sale. Finished goods inventory normally is valued at the sum of *direct material, direct labor,* and *allocated manufacturing overhead costs* related to their manufacture.

   *d.* Manufacturing supplies inventory—items on hand such as lube oils for the machinery, cleaning materials, and supply items which comprise an insignificant part of the finished product as, for example, the thread and glue used in binding this book.

3. Miscellaneous inventories—items such as office supplies, janitorial supplies, and shipping supplies. Inventories of this type normally are used in the near future and usually are charged to selling or general expense when used; consequently, these inventory amounts generally are reported as a prepaid expense (supplies inventory).

## THE DUAL PHASE OF THE INVENTORY PROBLEM

The basic cause of many accounting inventory problems is the fact that goods sold during a fiscal period seldom correspond exactly to those produced or bought during that period. Consequently, the typical situation is one where physical inventory increases or decreases. This increase or decrease in physical inventory necessitates a corresponding *allocation of the cost of goods available* for sale or use between (*a*) those goods that were sold or used, and (*b*) those that remain on hand. This situation creates two distinct problems in inventory identification and measurement, viz:

1. Identification and measurement of the *physical goods* (items and quantities) that should be included in inventory.
2. Measurement of the *accounting values* assigned to the physical goods included in inventory.

## IDENTIFICATION OF GOODS (ITEMS) THAT SHOULD BE INCLUDED IN INVENTORY

In identifying the physical goods to be included in inventory, accountants apply the general rule that all goods to which the concern has *ownership* at inventory date should be included, regardless of their location. The seller should include in inventory goods under contract for sale but not yet segregated and applied to the contract. Further, mere segregation does not create a "passage of ownership"—the terms of the contract itself must be determining. Since at the close of an accounting period, a business may (*a*) hold goods which it does not own or (*b*) own goods which it does not hold, care must be exercised in identifying the goods properly included in inventory.

Goods purchased, though not received, should be included in the inventory of the purchaser provided ownership to such goods has passed. Application of the "passage of ownership" rule requires the following: if the goods are shipped *f.o.b. destination,* ownership does not pass until the purchaser receives the goods from the common carrier; if the goods are shipped *f.o.b. shipping point,* ownership passes when the seller delivers them to the common carrier.[2]

Goods *out* on consignment, those held by agents, and those located at branches should be included in inventory. On the other hand, goods *held* (but owned by someone else) for sale on commission or consignment and those received from vendors but rejected and awaiting return for credit should be excluded from the inventory.[3]

In identifying items that should be included in inventory where there is a question as to whether ownership has passed, the accountant must exercise judgment in the light of the particular situation. Obviously the legal position should be followed; however, the accountant will face many situations where a strict legal determination is impractical. In such cases the intent of the sales agreement, policies of the parties involved, industry practices, and other available evidence of intent must be considered.

## MEASUREMENT OF PHYSICAL QUANTITIES IN INVENTORY

The physical quantities in inventory may be determined by means of (*a*) a *periodic (physical) inventory,* or (*b*) a *perpetual inventory.*

### Periodic Inventory System

When this system is used, an actual count of the goods on hand is taken at the end of each period for which financial statements are to be prepared. The goods are counted, weighed, or otherwise measured, then extended at *unit costs* to derive the inventory valuation. When a periodic inventory system is used, end-of-the-period entries are required for (*a*) adjusting or closing the beginning inventory, and (*b*) recording the ending inventory.

Under the periodic system cost of goods sold is a *residual amount* and cannot be independently verified. To illustrate:

```
Cost of goods sold:
  Beginning inventory (carried forward from last period)   $ 50,000
  Merchandise purchases (accumulated in the
      accounts).........................................   200,000
  Goods available for sale..............................   250,000
  Less: Ending inventory (determined by count)  ........    60,000
      Cost of Goods Sold (a residual amount)  ...........            $190,000
```

The accounting entries and external financial reporting, when the peri-

---

[2] Refer to Chapter 2, discussion of the revenue principle.

[3] Consignment is a special marketing arrangement whereby the consignor (the owner of the goods) ships merchandise to another party, known as a consignee, who is to act as a sales agent only. The consignee does not purchase the goods, but assumes responsibility for their care, and upon sale remits the proceeds (less expenses and a commission). Goods out on consignment, since they are owned by the consignor until sold, should be excluded from the inventory of the consignee and included in the inventory of the consignor.

odic inventory system is used, were discussed and illustrated in Chapters 3 and 4.

## Perpetual Inventory System

When this system is used, detailed subsidiary records are maintained for each item of inventory. An Inventory Control account is maintained on a current basis; consequently, the detailed inventory records for each different item will provide for recording (a) receipts, (b) issues, and (c) balances on hand, usually in both quantities and dollar amounts. Thus, the physical amount and valuation of goods on hand at any time are readily available from the accounting records; consequently, a physical inventory count is unnecessary except to check on the accuracy of the inventory records from time to time. Such checks (physical counts) are usually made at least annually or on a continuous rotation basis when large inventories are involved. When a discrepancy is found, the perpetual inventory records must be adjusted to the physical count. In such cases the inventory account is debited or credited as necessary for correction and an inventory adjustment account such as "Inventory Overages or Shortages" is used for the contra amount. The inventory adjustment account is closed to the Income Summary account at the end of the period.

A perpetual inventory system is particularly useful (a) to control and safeguard inventory, and (b) when monthly statements are prepared. A perpetual inventory is generally considered to be one of the essential characteristics of a good cost accounting system.

To briefly review and compare the accounting procedures for the periodic and the perpetual inventory systems, the following simplified data are used:

| | Units | Unit Amount |
|---|---|---|
| Merchandise inventory, beginning......................... | 500 | $4.00 |
| Merchandise purchases during the period ...........1,000 | | 4.00 |
| Total Goods Available for Sale ...................1,500 | | |
| Merchandise sold during the period ..................... | 900 | 6.00 (sales price) |
| Merchandise Inventory, Ending .................. | 600 | |

### Comparative Entries

*Periodic Inventory System*

a. Merchandise purchased for resale:

Purchases (1,000 @ $4)......4,000
    Cash .......................      4,000

b. Merchandise sold;

Cash (900 @ $6) ..............5,400
    Sales revenue ............      5,400

*Perpetual Inventory System*

a.

Merchandise inventory ...............4,000
    Cash .................................      4,000

b.

Cash ......................................5,400
    Sales revenue ......................      5,400

Cost of goods sold....................3,600
    Merchandise inventory
      (900 @ $4) ....................      3,600

c. Entries at end of the accounting period:

To close purchases account:

Income summary...............4,000
    Purchases ...................          4,000

None required since inventory and cost of goods sold account balances already up to date.

To close beginning inventory account:

Income summary...............2,000
    Inventory (beginning)...          2,000

To record ending inventory:

Inventory (ending) ............2,400
    Income summary.........          2,400

Income Statement (Partial):

| | | | |
|---|---|---|---|
| Sales revenue ... | | $5,400 | Sales revenue .....................$5,400 |
| Cost of goods sold: | | | |
| Beginning inventory... | $2,000 | | |
| Purchases ...... | 4,000 | | |
| Goods available for sale ......... | 6,000 | | |
| Ending inventory... | 2,400 | | |
| Cost of goods sold ......... | | 3,600 | Cost of goods sold............... 3,600 |
| Gross margin ... | | $1,800 | $1,800 |

Balance Sheet (Partial):

Current Assets:
Merchandise
    inventory......          $2,400          Merchandise inventory .........$2,400

A typical subsidiary inventory record (for Raw Material X) that would be maintained under the perpetual inventory system (but not under the periodic system) is shown in Exhibit 8–1.

## EFFECT OF INVENTORY ERRORS

Recall the effect of inventory errors on income, viz: The overstatement of final inventory overstates pretax income by the same amount, and an understatement of final inventory understates pretax income. Conversely, an overstatement of the beginning inventory understates pretax income by the same amount, and an understatement of the beginning inventory overstates pretax income. An overstatement of purchases alone, overstates cost of goods sold and understates pretax income.

Incorrect inclusion or exclusion of physical units for inventory purposes will result in errors in the financial statements. The following errors are not uncommon:[4]

Inclusion of items that should not be in final inventory:

---

[4] Some of the effects of these errors will differ depending on the inventory flow method used, that is, *Fifo, Lifo,* and so on.

**EXHIBIT 8-1**
**Perpetual Inventory Record**

## SUBSIDIARY LEDGER
### PERPETUAL INVENTORY RECORD

Article _Raw Material X_  Unit _lbs._  Maximum _1,600_  Verification Dates _____

Location _L-15_  Bin No. _32_  Minimum _800_

| Date | Ordered Order No. | Ordered Units | Received or Completed Order No. | Received or Completed Ref. | Received or Completed Units | Received or Completed Unit Cost | Received or Completed Total Cost | Issued or Sold Ref. | Issued or Sold Units | Issued or Sold Unit Cost | Issued or Sold Total Cost | Balance on Hand Units | Balance on Hand Unit Cost | Balance on Hand Total Cost |
|---|---|---|---|---|---|---|---|---|---|---|---|---|---|---|
| Jan. 1 | | | | | | | | | | | | 1,000 | $.40 | $400 |
| 10 | | | 17 | | 500 | $.40 | $200 | | | | | 1,500 | .40 | 600 |
| 18 | | | | | | | | | 600 | $.40 | $240 | 900 | .40 | 360 |
| 19 | 18 | 700 | | | | | | | | | | | | |
| | | | | | | | | | | | | | | |
| | | | | | | | | | | | | | | |

1. *Incorrect inclusion of items in inventory, and the purchase recorded.* These two errors result in an overstatement of inventory, purchases, and accounts payable. In this case pretax income will be correctly stated, since the errors in inventory and purchases will offset; however, the assets and liabilities on the balance sheet each will be overstated by the same amount.

2. *Incorrect inclusion of items in inventory, but purchase not recorded.* This error results in an overstatement of the final inventory, hence both pretax income and assets are overstated by the same amounts.

Exclusion of items that should be admitted to final inventory:

3. *Incorrect exclusion of items from inventory, but the purchase correctly recorded.* This error results in an understatement of the final inventory, hence an understatement of both pretax income and assets by the same amounts.

4. *Incorrect exclusion of items from inventory, and the purchase not recorded.* These two errors result in an understatement of inventory, purchases, and accounts payable. In this case pretax income will be correctly stated, since the errors in inventory and purchases will offset; however, the assets and liabilities on the balance sheet each will be understated by the same amount.

The effects of each situation are demonstrated in Exhibit 8-2.

Errors similar to those discussed above, which relate to purchases, may also arise when goods are sold. These errors not only cause the financial statements for the current period to be in error but also frequently cause future amounts to be wrong.

## MEASURING OF THE ACCOUNTING VALUE OF INVENTORY

At date of acquisition, inventory items are recorded at cost in harmony with the *cost principle;* subsequently when sold the cost is matched with revenue in accordance with the *matching principle.* Inventory items remaining on hand at the end of an accounting period are valued on the basis of the cost principle except when their value has been eroded through damage, obsolescence, erosion of replacement cost, and similar factors, in which case they are "valued" in accordance with the concept of *conservatism* (for example, by the lower-of-cost-or-market procedure). The discussions to follow in this and the next two chapters consider special inventory problems and procedures within the context of these broad theoretical requirements.

The *accounting value* of inventories represents an *acceptable* allocation of the total cost of goods or materials *available* between that portion used or sold (cost of goods sold) and that portion held as an asset for subsequent use or sale (inventory). The nature of the allocation is indicated in the following diagram (based on the example given on pages 322 and 323):

**EXHIBIT 8–2**
**Effects of Inventory Errors (pretax)**

| | Correct Amounts | Inventory Error Incorrectly Included $1,000 in Final Inventory | | Inventory Error Incorrectly Excluded $1,000 from Final Inventory | |
|---|---|---|---|---|---|
| | | (1) Purchases in Error (was recorded) | (2) Purchases Are Correct (was not recorded) | (3) Purchases Are Correct (was recorded) | (4) Purchases in Error (was not recorded) |
| **Income Statement:** | | | | | |
| Sales | $10,000 | $10,000 | $10,000 | $10,000 | $10,000 |
| Initial inventory | 3,000 | 3,000 | 3,000 | 3,000 | 3,000 |
| Purchases | 12,000 | 13,000† | 12,000 | 12,000 | 11,000* |
| Total | 15,000 | 16,000 | 15,000 | 15,000 | 14,000 |
| Final inventory | 8,000 | 9,000† | 9,000† | 7,000* | 7,000* |
| Cost of goods sold | 7,000 | 7,000 | 6,000 | 8,000 | 7,000 |
| Gross margin | 3,000 | 3,000 | 4,000 | 2,000 | 3,000 |
| Expenses | 1,000 | 1,000 | 1,000 | 1,000 | 1,000 |
| Income | $ 2,000 | $ 2,000 | $ 3,000† | $ 1,000* | $ 2,000 |
| **Balance Sheet:** | | | | | |
| Assets (inventory) | $ 8,000 | $ 9,000† | $ 9,000† | $ 7,000* | $ 7,000* |
| Liabilities (payables) | 12,000 | 13,000† | 12,000 | 12,000 | 11,000* |
| Retained earnings | 20,000 | 20,000 | 21,000† | 19,000* | 20,000 |

* Under.
† Over.

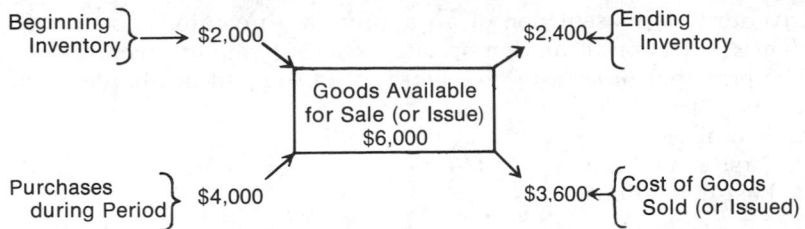

There are a number of procedures used for measuring the accounting value of inventories that satisfy the theoretical requirements. The acceptability of a number of procedures, as opposed to a single one, suggests the wide variation in inventory characteristics and conditions as related to particular situations and purposes. Basically the accounting values for inventories serve two somewhat opposing purposes. One purpose implies procedures that may not appear to be entirely appropriate for the other purpose. One is to develop a monetary value for the inventory reported on the *balance sheet*. There it is desirable to report this resource at cost or at its future utility to the business, whichever is lower. The other purpose, directed toward the *income statement*, is to measure the inventory value so there is a proper measurement of income between accounting periods. Conservatism with respect to inventory values in terms of one objective may not be conservative in terms of the other objective. In recent years the income measurement objective has predominated as indicated by the following quotation from *Accounting Research Bulletin No. 43:*

> In accounting for the goods in the inventory at any point of time, the major objective is the matching of appropriate costs against revenues in order that there may be a proper determination of the realized income. Thus, the inventory at any given date is the balance of costs applicable to goods on hand remaining after the matching of absorbed costs with concurrent revenues. This balance is appropriately carried to future periods provided it does not exceed an amount properly chargeable against the revenues expected to be obtained from ultimate disposition of the goods carried forward.[5]

Measurement of acceptable values for (1) inventory and (2) cost of goods sold, involves two distinct problems, viz:

1. Inventory unit cost – selection of an appropriate *unit cost* for valuation of the items in inventory. The principal bases or *inventory valuation methods* are:
   *a.* Cost basis.
   *b.* Departure from cost basis:
      1. Lower of cost or market.
      2. Net realizable value.
      3. Replacement cost.
      4. Selling price.

———————
[5] AICPA, "Restatement and Revision of Accounting Research Bulletins," *Accounting Research Bulletin No. 43* (New York, 1961).

2. Inventory flow — selection of an appropriate inventory flow method, that is, selection of an appropriate *assumed flow* of inventory costs. The principal *inventory flow methods* (discussed in Chapter 9) are:
   a. Specific cost.
   b. Average cost.
   c. First-in, first-out.
   d. Last-in, first-out.

## CONTENT OF UNIT COST

The cost principle provides the theoretical foundation for measurement of unit cost for inventory and cost of goods sold purposes, viz:

> The primary basis of accounting for inventories is cost, which has been defined generally as the price paid or consideration given to acquire an asset. As applied to inventories, cost means in principle the sum of the applicable expenditures and charges directly or indirectly incurred in bringing an article to its existing condition and location.[6]

Thus unit inventory cost is measured by the total outlay made to acquire the goods in question and to prepare them for the market. These costs include not only the purchase price but also those incidental costs such as excise and sales taxes, duties, freight, storage, insurance on the merchandise while in transit or in storage, and all other costs incurred on the goods up to the time they are ready for use or for sale to the customer. Some incidental costs, such as freight-in, frequently can be identified directly with specific goods, while other incidental costs may require a reasonable allocation to specific goods. As a practical matter many incidental costs, although theoretically a cost of goods purchased, frequently are not included in inventory valuation but reported as a separate expense; the cost of allocating may not be warranted by the slight increase in accuracy. In such cases *consistency* in application is particularly important.

General administrative and distribution expenses, often called *period expenses*, are not included in determining unit inventory costs because they are not directly related to the purchase or manufacture of goods for sale. They are called period expenses because they are deducted on the income statement for the period in which incurred.

### Freight-In

Freight and other incidental costs paid in connection with purchase of materials for use or merchandise for resale are additions to unit cost. Where such charges can be identified with specific goods, they should be charged to such goods. However, in some cases identification is impractical. Consequently, it is sometimes best to record transportation costs in a special account such as Freight-In and to report it as an addition to cost of goods sold in the case of a trading concern and to cost of

---

[6] Ibid., p. 28.

materials used in a manufacturing entity. However, in this case failure to add freight costs to the purchase price directly causes cost of goods sold to be overstated and inventory to be understated. Theoretically, freight-in should be apportioned to cost of goods sold and final inventory in proportion to the quantity of goods involved in each.

### Purchase Discounts

Cash discounts sometimes are given, as an element of credit purchases, to encourage early payment. Under the cost principle, the net cash equivalent paid is cost. Payments made for the extension of credit are accounted for as expenses. Theoretically, all cash discounts permitted, whether taken or not, should be omitted from cost upon payment of invoices. Discounts not taken constitute a financing expense. Since cash discounts are reductions in the cost of specific goods, they reduce both cost of purchases and inventory valuation. Therefore, credit purchases should be recorded at *net of discount* to reflect the *correct cost.* Alternatively, for practical reasons and because the cash discount often is immaterial, purchases may be recorded at the *gross amount.*

To illustrate each approach, assume merchandise is purchased for $1,000 on credit terms of 2/10, n/30. Assume further that three fourths of the charge is paid within the ten-day discount period.

|  *Net of Discount Approach*  |  *Gross Amount Approach*  |
| --- | --- |

To record the purchase (perpetual inventory system):

| | | | | |
| --- | --- | --- | --- | --- |
| Merchandise inventory ...................980 | | Merchandise inventory ...............1,000 | |
| Accounts payable (net) ............ | 980 | Accounts payable (gross)...... | 1,000 |

To record payment of three fourths of the liability within discount period:

| | | | | |
| --- | --- | --- | --- | --- |
| Accounts payable (net) ..................735 | | Accounts payable (gross)............ 750 | |
| Cash ...................................... | 735 | Cash ............................... | 735 |
| (980 × .75 = $735) | | Discount on purchases......... | 15 |

To record payment of one fourth of the liability after the discount period:

| | | | | |
| --- | --- | --- | --- | --- |
| Accounts payable (net) ..................245 | | Accounts payable (gross)............ 250 | |
| Interest expense* .......................... 5 | | Cash ............................... | 250 |
| Cash ...................................... | 250 | | |

\* Alternative title: Purchase discounts lost.

The net-of-discount approach correctly reflects the cost of the merchandise in conformity with the cost principle and also correctly states the amount of the liability since most companies take all discounts and pay only the net amount. Remember that 2% interest saved by paying within ten days is a significantly higher rate on an annual basis. This method also correctly allocates the discount effect between inventory and cost of goods sold. It follows the cost principle because the true costs of purchases, cost of goods sold, and inventory are recorded and reported. Similarly, accounts payable is recorded and reported at the amount that is usually paid. It does not violate the revenue principle by recording and reporting purchase discounts as "other income"; rather, it considers purchase discounts lost as expense.

When the gross method is used, purchase discounts taken are recorded separately in the Discount on Purchases account (as a credit). The amount often then is reported as financial revenue (similar to interest revenue). This violates the revenue principle; clearly, there is no financial revenue because there has been no earning process. The buyer is not lending money to the seller and thereby generating revenue; rather the buyer is paying a bill on time. To avoid this effect, the amount of discount taken sometimes is deducted in full from cost of goods sold. Of course, this understates cost of goods sold and overstates the ending inventory because all of the discount is deducted from cost of goods sold for the period. Thus, it is theoretically deficient. It has the advantage of simplicity, and the misstatement of amounts are often not material in relation to total purchases.[7]

## DEPARTURES FROM THE COST PRINCIPLE IN COSTING INVENTORY

Under certain prescribed conditions generally accepted accounting principles require departure from the cost principle in measuring the unit cost of inventory items. In most of these situations conservatism overrides the cost principle. The exceptions may be classified as follows:

1. Lower of cost or market.
2. Net realizable value.
3. Replacement cost.
4. Selling price.

### Lower of Cost or Market

Under the concept of conservatism, known losses, although not actually evidenced by a specific transaction, are recognized in the period of occurrence. In contrast, known gains not evidenced by a specific transaction are not recognized until realized. Therefore, under the lower-of-

---

[7] A variation of these two approaches sometimes is used; it attempts to attain the advantages of the net approach and avoid recording the liability at net. It is called the net-gross approach. To illustrate, the above transactions would be recorded as follows:

To record purchases at net and liability at gross:

| | | |
|---|---|---|
| Merchandise inventory (net) | 980 | |
| Allowance for purchase discounts | 20 | |
| Accounts payable | | 1,000 |

To record payment within the discount period:

| | | |
|---|---|---|
| Accounts payable | 750 | |
| Allowance for purchase discounts | | 15 |
| Cash | | 735 |

To record payment after discount period:

| | | |
|---|---|---|
| Accounts payable | 250 | |
| Interest expense (or discounts lost) | 5 | |
| Cash | | 250 |
| Allowance for purchase discounts | | 5 |

Any balance in the allowance account is reported as contra to the Accounts Payable account. Theoretically, this method is sound; due to its complexity, however, it is seldom used.

cost-or-market rule the unit cost used is the lower of (a) cost or (b) market at the end of the period. This position of conservatism has been accepted by the accounting profession on the basis of (a) the matching principle, that is, the utility of the goods on hand is less than original cost, hence there has been a loss which should be recognized for the period in which the decline in utility took place, and revenue should be matched with the replacement cost of goods sold; and (b) from the point of view of balance sheet conservatism the asset inventory should be reported at the lower figure. It is particularly important to realize also that there is an implicit assumption in the lower-of-cost-or-market rule that selling prices decrease in direct proportion to decreases in replacement cost. The position of the Committee on Accounting Procedure of the AICPA is expressed in *Accounting Research Bulletin No. 43* as:

> A departure from the cost basis of pricing the inventory is required when the utility of the goods is no longer as great as its cost. Where there is evidence that the utility of goods, in their disposal in the ordinary course of business, will be less than cost, whether due to physical deterioration, obsolescence, changes in price levels, or other causes, the difference should be recognized as a loss of the current period. This is generally accomplished by stating such goods at a lower level commonly designated as *market*.[8]

*Cost*, as used in this context, refers to the actual unit cost as defined in the preceding paragraphs and through application of an acceptable inventory flow method such as average, *Fifo*, or *Lifo* (see Chapter 9).

*Market*, as used in this context, by accountants and by the Treasury Department for income tax purposes, is defined as follows: "Under ordinary circumstances 'market' means the current bid price prevailing at the date of the inventory for the particular merchandise in the volume in which usually purchased by the taxpayer." In applying this definition the type of firm and the nature and condition of the items in inventory must be taken into account as follows:

1. For stock-in-trade, raw materials, and purchased parts, use purchase or replacement basis – *market* for the stock-in-trade of a trading concern is the current bid prices from the normal suppliers for the volume normally purchased, adjusted for regular transportation costs and other necessary expenses to secure the goods from the usual outlets.

2. For goods in process and finished goods, use reproduction basis – *market* for the goods in process and finished goods inventories for the manufacturer is based on the cost of manufacturing the items at the prevailing market prices for raw materials, labor, and other factory costs.

3. For damaged and deteriorated items use realization basis – *market* frequently must be interpreted in terms of the *condition* of the items in inventory. Damaged, obsolete, depreciated, used, and otherwise deteriorated items in inventory seldom will have a determinable replacement value in their current condition; therefore, accountants generally agree that such items should be valued for inventory purposes at their *net realizable value*. However, some accountants prefer net realizable value

---

[8] *Accounting Research Bulletin No. 43.*

*less an allowance for normal profit.* For example, the inventory under each of these concepts would be calculated as follows:

Final inventory, 1,000 units at estimated sales price...........................$1,000
    Less: Estimated distribution cost at $.40 per unit ............................ 400
Inventory at *net realizable value* ......................................................... 600
    Less: Allowance for normal profit (10% on sales) ............................ 100
Inventory at *Net Realizable Value Less Normal Profit* .........................$ 500

The deduction of distribution cost is necessary to prevent capitalization of the item at more than its current fair market value. In applying the lower-of-cost-or-market procedure, certain *exceptions* were recognized by the Committee on Accounting Procedure of the AICPA. "Judgment must always be exercised and no loss should be recognized unless the evidence indicates clearly that a loss has been sustained. There are, therefore, exceptions to such a standard." These exceptions were described as follows:

> As used in the phrase *lower of cost or market* the term *market* means current replacement cost (by purchase or by reproduction, as the case may be) except that:
>
> (1) Market should not exceed the net realizable value (i.e., estimated selling price in the ordinary course of business less reasonably predictable costs of completion and disposal); and
> (2) Market should not be less than net realizable value reduced by an allowance for an approximately normal profit margin.[9]

These exceptions in effect establish a "ceiling" and a "floor" for *market* in the comparison with original *cost* in applying the procedure. Exhibit 8–3 gives several independent situations under which the lower-of-cost-or-market rule is applied. The cost and other values are those of a single unit. Observe in the illustration that "market" results from a choice among current replacement cost, the ceiling (net realizable value), and the floor (net realizable value less normal profit). The "market" thus derived is compared with "cost" in order to determine the appropriate inventory valuation.

The limits (ceiling and floor) are necessary to measure properly the economic utility of the items in inventory. For example, in Case II in Exhibit 8–3, current replacement cost is $.65 and the net realizable value (ceiling) is $.60. To carry the $.65 forward in inventory, which is more than the net realizable value, would result in a charge against future sales greater than the economic utility of the goods, and a charge against current income for an amount less than the anticipated loss; hence the reported profit and inventory value of each period would be incorrect. In Case III, Exhibit 8–3, the net realizable value less normal profit (floor) is greater than current replacement cost, hence the floor value ($.50) should be carried forward in inventory. To carry forward a market value of $.45 would result in an understatement of the inventory since at $.50 a normal profit margin will be earned when the item is

---

[9] *Accounting Research Bulletin No. 43*, p. 31.

**EXHIBIT 8-3**
**Exceptions — Computation of Lower of Cost or Market**

| | Case | | | |
|---|---|---|---|---|
| | *I* | *II* | *III* | *IV* |
| a. Cost (per unit) | $1.00 | $1.00 | $1.00 | $.45 |
| b. Current replacement cost (per unit) | .55 | .65 | .45 | .40 |
| c. Ceiling (net realizable value–estimated sales price less predictable cost of completion and disposal)* | .60 | .60 | .60 | .60 |
| d. Floor (net realizable value less a normal profit margin)* | .50 | .50 | .50 | .50 |
| e. Market (selected from *b, c,* and *d* values) | .55 | .60 | .50 | .50 |
| f. Inventory valuation under lower-of-cost-or-market rule (selected from *a* and *e*) | .55 | .60 | .50 | .45 |

| * Additional data to verify ceiling and floor: | | | | |
|---|---|---|---|---|
| | *I* | *II* | *III* | *IV* |
| Estimated selling price | $.85 | $.90 | $.80 | $.75 |
| Less: Estimated cost to complete and sell | .25 | .30 | .20 | .15 |
| Net realizable value (ceiling) | $.60 | $.60 | $.60 | $.60 |
| Less: Estimated normal profit | .10 | .10 | .10 | .10 |
| Net Realizable Value Less Profit (Floor) | $.50 | $.50 | $.50 | $.50 |

sold. Therefore, if current replacement cost as the market value ($.45) were carried forward in this case, future profits on the inventory items would be overstated, and current period profits understated.

In applying the exceptions *Bulletin No. 43* states: "Because of the many variations of circumstances encountered in inventory pricing, Statement 6 (see above quotation) is intended as a guide rather than a literal rule. It should be applied realistically in light of the objectives expressed in this chapter and with due regard to the form, content, and composition of the inventory."

## ACCOUNTING PROBLEMS IN APPLYING LOWER OF COST OR MARKET

In applying the lower-of-cost-or-market procedure two primary accounting problems arise, viz:

1. How will the procedure be applied to determine the overall inventory valuation?
2. How will the resulting inventory valuation be recorded in the accounts?

### Determination of Overall Inventory Valuation

In applying the lower-of-cost-or-market procedure in determining the overall inventory valuation, three approaches have been suggested: (1) by comparison of cost and market separately for each item of inventory, (2) by comparison of cost and market separately for each *classification*

**EXHIBIT 8–4**
**Applying Lower of Cost or Market**

| | | | Lower of Cost or Market Applied by— | | |
|---|---|---|---|---|---|
| Commodity | Cost | Market | Individual Items | Classification | Total |
| Classification A: | | | | | |
| Item 1 ...................$10,000 | | $ 9,500 | $ 9,500 | | |
| Item 2 ................... 8,000 | | 9,000 | 8,000 | | |
| | 18,000 | 18,500 | | $18,000 | |
| Classification B: | | | | | |
| Item 3 ................... 21,000 | | 22,000 | 21,000 | | |
| Item 4 ................... 32,000 | | 29,000 | 29,000 | | |
| | 53,000 | 51,000 | | 51,000 | |
| Total............$71,000 | | $69,500 | | | $69,500 |
| Inventory Valuation... | | | $67,500 | $69,000 | $69,500 |

of inventory, and (3) by comparison of *total* cost with *total* market for the inventory. Exhibit 8–4 shows the application of each approach.

Generally, the lower-of-cost-or-market procedure applied to is by *individual items.* However, under certain circumstances, application of the procedure to classifications or totals may have greater significance for accounting purposes. For example, in applying the procedure to the raw materials inventory of a manufacturer producing only one major product and using several raw materials having common characteristics, the utility of the total stock of raw material may have more significance than the individual market prices of each raw material. Consistency in application is essential.

A particular problem arises when there are several unit costs with respect to a particular commodity to be compared with a single unit *market* price. This situation frequently arises when first-in, first-out (discussed in next chapter) and similar inventory flow procedures are used. In such cases the aggregate cost for the commodity should be compared with the aggregate market (see Exhibit 8–5).

With respect to departures from cost in inventory valuation, once an inventory item has been reduced to a value lower than cost, *subsequent*

**EXHIBIT 8–5**
**Lower of Cost or Market and *Fifo***

| | | Unit Prices | | | | Inventory Valuation | |
|---|---|---|---|---|---|---|---|
| Commodity | Units on Hand | Actual Cost | Current Market | Aggregate Cost | Aggregate Market | Unit | Total |
| A | 10,000 10,000 | $4.00⎫ 3.85⎭ | $3.90 | $ 78,500 | $ 78,000 | $3.90 | $78,000 |
| B | 10,000 10,000 | 7.70⎫ 8.00⎭ | 7.90 | 157,000 | 158,000 | ⎧7.70 ⎩8.00 | 77,000 80,000 |

*accounting* would consider the reduced value as "cost" for that particular item. Items once reduced for inventory valuation purposes should not be subsequently restored to their original cost.

### Recording Lower of Cost or Market in the Accounts

Recall that purchases are initially recorded at cost; therefore, if the inventories subsequently are reduced to *less than cost* (i.e., market when lower), two different *items* must be recognized: *(a)* the actual *cost* of goods used or sold, and *(b)* the *loss* due to decline in utility of the inventory (i.e., the difference between cost and market), frequently referred to as a *holding loss.* Proper accounting requires that these two different items — cost and loss — be accounted for and reported separately. Two methods of recording the results of the lower-of-cost-or-market rule in the accounts generally are found in practice:

1. Direct inventory reduction method wherein the actual cost of goods sold or used and the holding loss in inventory utility are *not* separately accounted for and reported.
2. Inventory allowance method wherein the cost and holding loss are separately accounted for and reported for *both* the beginning and ending inventories.

Recording in the accounts is further complicated by the fact that some firms employ a *periodic* inventory system, whereas other firms employ a *perpetual* inventory system.

In order to illustrate and compare the two methods outlined above, assume the following inventories for the years 19A and 19B:

| Inventory Date | At Original Cost | At Lower of Cost or Market | Difference (loss) |
|---|---|---|---|
| January 1, 19A | $75,000 | $75,000 | $ -0- |
| December 31, 19A | 80,000 | 70,000 | (10,000) |
| December 31, 19B | 60,000 | 56,000 | (4,000) |

The two methods are illustrated in Exhibit 8–6 for both perpetual and periodic inventory assumptions. The related income statements are compared in Exhibit 8–7 to show the effect of each method on the statement.

*Evaluation of the Two Approaches.* The effects on the income statement of each of the two methods of recording lower of cost or market are reflected in Exhibit 8–7. The two methods derive the same periodic net income amount and inventory valuation on the balance sheet each period. The difference is the manner in which the details are reported. The first approach includes the holding loss in cost of goods sold, whereas the second approach reports the holding loss separately. The first approach can be viewed as minimal disclosure, whereas the second approach represents maximum reporting. Regardless of the method

**EXHIBIT 8-6**
**Comparison of Methods of Recording Lower of Cost or Market in the Accounts**

| | Periodic Inventory System | | Perpetual Inventory System | |
|---|---|---|---|---|
| | 19A | 19B | 19A | 19B |
| **1. Direct inventory reduction method—holding loss not recognized separately:** | | | | |
| a. To close beginning inventory: | | | | |
| Income summary ........ | 75,000 | 70,000 | No comparable entry | |
| Inventory ........ | 75,000 | 70,000 | | |
| b. To record (or reduce) ending inventory to LCM basis: | | | | |
| Inventory ........ | 70,000 | 56,000 | 10,000 | 4,000 |
| Cost of goods sold ........ | | | | |
| Income summary ........ | 70,000 | 56,000 | | |
| Inventory ($80,000 − $70,000) and ($60,000 − $56,000) ........ | | | 10,000 | 4,000 |
| **2. Inventory allowance method—holding loss recognized separately for both beginning and ending inventory:** | | | | |
| a. To close beginning inventory: | | | | |
| Income summary ........ | 75,000 | 80,000 | No comparable entry | |
| Inventory ........ | 75,000 | 80,000 | | |
| b. To record (or reduce) ending inventory and holding loss: | | | | |
| Inventory ........ | 80,000 | 60,000 | 10,000 | 6,000 |
| *Holding loss (gain—credit) on inventory........ | 10,000 | 6,000 | | |
| Income summary ........ | 80,000 | 60,000 | | |
| Allowance to reduce inventory to market ($10,000 credit − $4,000 debit = $6,000 debit adjustment needed) ........ | | | 10,000 | 6,000 |

* Closed to Income Summary.

# EXHIBIT 8-7 Lower of Cost or Market—Reporting Inventory Holding Losses

|  | (1) Direct Inventory Reduction Method—Holding Loss Not Recognized Separately | (2) Inventory Allowance Method—Holding Loss Recognized Separately for Both Beginning and Ending Inventory |
|---|---|---|
| **Income Statement—Year Ended December 31, 19A:** | | |
| Sales | $200,000 | $200,000 |
| Cost of goods sold: | | |
| Beginning inventory | (cost) $ 75,000 | (cost) $ 75,000 |
| Purchases | 115,000 | 115,000 |
| Goods available for sale | 190,000 | 190,000 |
| Less: Ending inventory | (LCM) 70,000    120,000 | (cost) 80,000    110,000 |
| Gross margin | 80,000 | 90,000 |
| Less: Expenses | 60,000 | 60,000 |
|  | 20,000 | 30,000 |
| Less: Loss on inventory reduction to market | | 10,000 |
| Add: Gain on inventory adjustment to market | | |
| Net income | $ 20,000 | $ 20,000 |
| **Balance Sheet—December 31, 19A:** | | |
| Inventory | $ 70,000 | 80,000 |
| Less: Allowance for inventory reduction to market | | 10,000 |
|  | | $ 70,000 |
| **Income Statement—Year Ended December 31, 19B:** | | |
| Sales | $220,000 | $220,000 |
| Cost of goods sold: | | |
| Beginning inventory | (LCM) $ 70,000 | (cost) $ 80,000 |
| Purchases | 118,000 | 118,000 |
| Goods available for sale | 188,000 | 198,000 |
| Less: Ending inventory | (LCM) 56,000    132,000 | (cost) 60,000    138,000 |
| Gross margin | 88,000 | 82,000 |
| Less: Expenses | 66,000 | 66,000 |
|  | 22,000 | 16,000 |
| Less: Loss on inventory reduction to market | | |
| Add: Gain on inventory adjustment to market | | 6,000 |
| Net income | $ 22,000 | $ 22,000 |
| **Balance Sheet—December 31, 19B:** | | |
| Inventory | $ 56,000 | $ 60,000 |
| Less: Allowance for inventory reduction to market | | 4,000 |
|  | | $ 56,000 |

used, "when substantial and unusual losses result from the application of this rule it will frequently be desirable to disclose the amount of the loss in the income statement as a charge separately identified from the consumed inventory costs described as *cost of goods sold.*"[10]

In the second method illustrated, the credit balance in Allowance for Inventory Reduction should be shown on the balance sheet as a deduction from the related inventory, thus stating the inventory at market. This method is generally referred to as the allowance method, although it is sometimes inappropriately referred to as the "reserve" method.

The direct inventory reduction method (where the market loss is not recognized separately) has the practical advantage of simplicity. The primary disadvantages of this method are: (a) there is no distinction on the income statement between actual cost and market (holding) loss with a consequent overstatement of cost of goods sold and understatement of gross margin; and (b) the perpetual inventory subsidiary records must be adjusted to the reduced value.

With respect to balance sheet presentation when lower of cost or market is used, it is desirable that original cost be shown parenthetically or in some similar manner. Because of practical considerations, the parenthetical method is frequently used.

The allowance method is theoretically preferable because there is a distinction between actual cost and market loss on the income statement and balance sheet. Provision is made for reporting the inventory on the balance sheet at cost and subtracting the balance in the Allowance for Inventory Reduction to Market account. It is maintained that the effect of market fluctuations are correctly reported even though a *gain* may be recognized. For example, in Exhibit 8–7 the $6,000 *gain* for 19B is comprised of the $10,000 *loss* relating to the beginning inventory (recognized as a loss in the prior period), offset by the $4,000 *loss* relating to the 19B ending inventory. These two amounts offset to a *gain*, since the beginning inventory is *added* to cost and the ending inventory is *subtracted* as a cost in view of the computation of cost of goods sold in terms of original cost. In view of the current market value of $4,000 below cost, the position is taken that in terms of original cost and in recognition of the $10,000 loss previously recorded, there is a $6,000 gain that should be recognized in the current period.

The nature of the *gain* that frequently is reported may be seen more clearly by assuming that market is below cost at the end of one period and that there is no ending inventory at the end of the next period. The write-down in the prior period shifts cost (or rather a loss) from one period to the other. For example, assume the ending inventories are: Period 1—cost, $20,000, and market, $19,000; Period 2—no ending inventory (see Exhibit 8–8). The $1,000 market loss in Period 1 appears reasonable. The $1,000 market gain in Period 2 is in effect an adjustment of the initial inventory figure to $19,000. On the basis of actual cost the $1,000 must be added as income in the second period.

Another advantage frequently cited for the allowance method is that

---

[10] Ibid., p. 33.

when a company maintains a perpetual inventory system, the subsidiary inventory records need not be adjusted to a reduced value since the inventory control accounts remain at original cost. The position appears sound for a trading concern; however, there is a serious question as to whether it is equally sound for a manufacturing company, since failure to adjust the raw material inventory values to the reduced value might result in questionable costs for goods in process and finished goods inventories when the materials are issued. The primary disadvantages of the allowance method are (a) complexity, and (b) reporting a gain such as discussed above is impractical. However, this effect is implicit in the other methods, although not explicitly reported.[11]

**EXHIBIT 8-8**
**Effect of Inventory Holding Losses on Net Income**

| | Period 1—Final Inventory at Market Is $1,000 below Cost | | Period 2—No Final Inventory | |
| --- | --- | --- | --- | --- |
| | At Actual Cost | At Lower of Cost or Market (allowance method) | At Actual Cost | At Lower of Cost or Market (allowance method) |
| Sales.......................... | $100,000 | $100,000 | $200,000 | $200,000 |
| Beginning inventory...... | 10,000 | 10,000 | 20,000 | 20,000 |
| Purchases ................. | 70,000 | 70,000 | 100,000 | 100,000 |
| Total ................. | 80,000 | 80,000 | 120,000 | 120,000 |
| Ending inventory ......... | 20,000 | 20,000 | – | – |
| Cost of sales .............. | 60,000 | 60,000 | 120,000 | 120,000 |
| Gross margin .............. | 40,000 | 40,000 | 80,000 | 80,000 |
| Market loss (gain)......... | | 1,000 | | (1,000) |
| Net............................ | $ 40,000 | $ 39,000 | $ 80,000 | $ 81,000 |

## NET REALIZABLE VALUE AND REPLACEMENT COST

Many accountants believe that inventories should be reported at either net realizable value or replacement cost rather than at actual cost. They believe that inventories should be reported at these values whether they are *above* or below actual cost because "fair value" better serves the decision-maker using the financial statements.

Current generally accepted accounting principles limit the use of net

---

[11] A variation of the allowance method is sometimes used. It derives the same results; however, the allowance account is not used. To illustrate, the entries would be as follows (based on the data used in Exhibits 8–6 and 8–7):

| | 19A | | 19B | |
| --- | --- | --- | --- | --- |
| To close beginning inventory: | | | | |
| Income summary ..................................... | 75,000 | | 70,000 | |
| Inventory....................................... | | 75,000 | | 70,000 |
| To record ending inventory and holding loss: | | | | |
| Inventory.......................................... | 70,000 | | 56,000 | |
| Holding loss on inventory (gain) ................................. | 10,000 | | 4,000 | |
| Income summary ................................. | | 80,000 | | 60,000 |

realizable value and replacement cost to situations where specific inventory items were used or have become damaged, obsolete, or repossessed. Alternatively, the loss in value that is due to normal business operations, such as style changes, shop wear, change in local demand, and similar operational expectations, should be accounted for under the lower-of-cost-or-market procedure.

Goods subject to unusual changes in value and repossessed items should be valued at current replacement cost in their present condition. For example, assume X Appliance Store has on hand a repossessed TV set that cost $300. It was sold for $500 and was repossessed when $350 was owed on it by the customer. Assume further that similar used TV sets could be purchased for $290. The repossession should be recorded as follows:

```
Inventory—repossessed merchandise (replacement cost) ...............290
Loss on repossession*................................................................. 60
    Accounts receivable............................................................          350
```

> * If repossessions are normal in the situation, the allowance for doubtful accounts should be debited because the estimated rate would anticipate such losses.

Often replacement cost for used or damaged merchandise cannot be realistically or objectively determined. In this situation net realizable value may be used. To illustrate, assume the facts for X Appliance Store as above with the added assumptions that no replacement cost is available, the used TV set can be sold for $300, and that disposal (resale) costs will approximate 15% of the sales price. The repossession would be recorded as follows:

```
Inventory—repossessed merchandise (net realizable value) ............255
Loss on repossession ................................................................ 95
    Accounts receivable............................................................          350

Computation of inventory value:
    Estimated sales value.....................................................................$300
        Less: Estimated disposal costs (15%) ..........................................  45
    Net Realizable Value ...................................................................$255
```

Assume further that the TV set is subsequently sold for $310 cash. The entry would be:

```
Cash ...........................................................................................310
    Inventory—repossessed merchandise......................................          255
    Selling costs ......................................................          45
    Gain on sale of repossessed merchandise .............................          10
```

When repossessions are a recurring feature of operations, estimates of future losses should be made and recorded in the year of sale as a debit to expense and as a credit to an allowance account similar to Allowance for Doubtful Accounts. In this situation, when there is a repossession any loss determined at that subsequent date should be charged to the allowance account.

Damaged and obsolete goods should be reported at current replacement cost in their present condition, or alternatively, at net realizable value.

Inventory losses resulting from storm, fire, flood, and other unusual events, if material in amount, should be reported separately (a) as extraordinary items or (b) as a line item listed above income before extraordinary items in conformity with the criteria set forth in "Reporting the Results of Operations," APB Opinion No. 30 (see Chapter 4).

## INVENTORIES VALUED ABOVE COST AT SELLING PRICE

Under certain unusual circumstances an inventory item may be valued at selling price. The circumstances, to conform to generally accepted accounting principles are:

> It is generally recognized that income accrues only at the time of sale, and that gains may not be anticipated by reflecting assets at their current sales prices. For certain articles, however, exceptions are permissible. Inventories of gold and silver, when there is an effective government-controlled market at a fixed monetary value, are ordinarily reflected at selling prices. A similar treatment is not uncommon for inventories representing agricultural, mineral, and other products, units of which are interchangeable and have an immediate marketability at quoted prices and for which appropriate costs may be difficult to obtain. Where such inventories are stated at sales prices, they should of course be reduced by expenditures to be incurred in disposal, and the use of such basis should be fully disclosed in the financial statements.[12]

Under this method, when there is a decrease in selling price, a holding loss would be reported; conversely, when there is an increase in selling price, a holding gain would be reported. Thus, net income would include gross margin and the holding gain or loss for the period. This effect can be attained by valuing the inventory at selling price (also see Chapter 25 on fair value accounting). To illustrate, assume the following simplified data:

| Year | Sales | Purchases at Cost | Ending Inventory at Selling Price | Expenses |
|------|-------|-------------------|-----------------------------------|----------|
| 19A | $ -0- | $1,000 | $1,750 | $300 |
| 19B | 1,700 | -0- | -0- | 300 |

The comparative results would be:

| | Cost Basis | | Selling Price Basis | |
|------|------|------|------|------|
| | 19A | 19B | 19A | 19B |
| Income Statement: | | | | |
| Revenue | $ -0- | $1,700 | $750 | $1,700 |
| Cost of goods sold | -0- | (1,000) | -0- | (1,750) |
| Expenses | (300) | (300) | (300) | (300) |
| Gain (loss) | $(300) | $ 400 | $450 | $ (350) |
| Balance Sheet: | | | | |
| Inventory | $1,000 | $ -0- | $1,750 | $ -0- |

Illustrative of several pricing methods, a published financial statement recently reported the following inventory items:

---

[12] Accounting Research Bulletin No. 43.

Inventories:
  At market:
    Wheat and other grains, flour and meal............................................$xxxx
  At lower of cost (first-in, first-out) or market:
    Soybeans and other raw materials ............................................... xxxx
    Supplies .......................................................................................... xxxx
  At cost (last-in, first-out):
    Soybean, linseed, sperm, and crude fish oil.................................. xxxx

## RELATIVE SALES VALUE METHOD

When two or more items having different characteristics are purchased for a lump sum and a separate cost for each item is required for
accounting purposes, some method of apportioning the *joint cost* must
be used. The apportionment of the lump cost logically should be related
to the economic utility of each item and the quantities involved. Since
the *sales value* of a particular item may be a reasonable indication of its
relative utility, apportionment of the joint cost of "basket purchases" is
usually made on the basis of the *relative sales value* of the several items.
Also, when joint costs are incurred subsequent to purchase, such costs
frequently are allocated on the basis of relative sales value.

To illustrate, assume a packing plant purchases 1,000 bushels of
orchard-run apples (ungraded) for $1,000, and that after purchase the
apples are sorted into three grades at a cost of $35 with the following
results: Grade A, 200 bushels; Grade B, 300 bushels; and Grade C, 500
bushels. Assume further that sorted apples are selling at the following
prices: Grade A, $2; Grade B, $1.50; and Grade C, $.60. The cost appor-
tionment may be made as shown in Exhibit 8–9.

**EXHIBIT 8–9**
**Relative Sales Value Method**

| | | | | | Apportioned Cost | |
| Grade | Quantity (bushels) | Unit Sales Price | Total Sales Value | Multi- plier* | Total† | Per Bushel‡ |
|---|---|---|---|---|---|---|
| A ............... | 200 | $2.00 | $ 400 | .90 | $ 360 | $1.80 |
| B ............... | 300 | 1.50 | 450 | .90 | 405 | 1.35 |
| C ............... | 500 | .60 | 300 | .90 | 270 | .54 |
| | 1,000 | | $1,150 | | $1,035 | |

\* Total cost divided by total sales value, that is, $1,035 ÷ $1,150 = .90.
† Total sales value times multiplier.
‡ Unit sales price times multiplier.

Assuming a perpetual inventory system, the purchase would be recorded as follows:

Raw material inventory–apples Grade A (200 @ $1.80)  ...............360
Raw material inventory–apples Grade B (300 @ $1.35)  ...............405
Raw material inventory–apples Grade C (500 @ $.54) ..................270
  Cash ...................................................................................... 1,035

In cost allocations such as illustrated above, quantities lost due to shrinkage or spoilage should be ignored thereby resulting in a greater unit cost for the remaining units. In the case of real estate developments, improvements such as streets and parks may be apportioned in this manner to the cost of the salable areas. While the relative sales value method is frequently used, other bases, such as Btu's in petroleum products, are sometimes used.

## LOSSES ON PURCHASE COMMITMENTS

Occasionally a company will contract with a supplier for a specific *quantity* of materials during a specified future *period* at an agreed *unit cost*. Basically, such purchase commitments (contracts) may be (*a*) subject to revision or cancellation before the end of the specified period, or (*b*) not subject to revision or cancellation. Each of these situations requires different accounting and reporting procedures.

In the case of purchase contracts *subject to revision or cancellation,* where a future loss is possible, and if the amount of the commitment is material, full-disclosure requires a footnote. To illustrate, assume XY Company entered into a purchase contract during October 1976 that: "During 1977, 50,000 units of Material X will be purchased at $5 each. Upon 60 days notice, this contract is subject to revision or cancellation by either party." The following footnote should be included in the financial statements for 1976:

> Note 1. At the end of 1976 a purchase contract for a maximum of $250,000 for raw materials during 1977 was in effect. The contract can be revised or canceled upon 60 days notice by either party. At the end of 1976, the materials had a market price of $240,000.

Where purchase contracts are *not subject to revision or cancellation,* and when there is a high probability of loss which can be realistically measured, the loss should be recorded in the accounts and reported in the financial statements. In the above example, assume the $240,000 market price is realistically measured and does not appear to be a temporary situation. Therefore, the loss on the purchase commitment should be recorded as follows:

```
Estimated loss on purchase commitment ..............................10,000
     Liability—noncancellable purchase commitment...............        10,000
```

The estimated loss is reported on the 1976 income statement and the liability is reported on the balance sheet. When the goods are received in 1977, they are debited to merchandise inventory (or purchases) at their then current market value and the liability account is debited for the $10,000 estimated in 1976. To illustrate, assume the above raw materials have a market value at date of delivery of $235,000. The purchase entry would be:

```
Raw materials (or purchases)  ...........................................235,000
Liability—noncancellable purchase commitment  ..............  10,000
Loss on purchase contract................................................   5,000
     Cash .................................................................................        250,000
```

This is in accordance with *ARB No. 43*, Chapter 4, Statement 10 which reads: "Accrued net losses on firm purchase commitments for goods for inventory, measured in the same way as are inventory losses, should, if material, be recognized in the accounts and the amounts thereof separately disclosed in the income statement." FASB *Statement No. 5*, March 1975, requires this treatment.

## QUESTIONS

1. In general, why should the accountant and the management be concerned with inventories?

2. List and briefly explain the usual inventory classifications.

3. Why are inventories such as office supplies, janitorial supplies, and shipping supplies frequently reported as prepaid expenses rather than as inventory?

4. What general rule is applied by accountants in determining what goods should be included in inventory?

5. Assume you are in the process of adjusting and closing the books at the end of the fiscal year (for the purchaser), what treatment, for inventory purposes, would you accord the following goods in transit? (*a*) invoice received for $5,000, shipped f.o.b. shipping point; (*b*) invoice received for $10,000 shipped f.o.b. destination; and (*c*) invoice received for $1,000, shipped f.o.b. shipping point and delivery refused on the last day of the period due to damaged condition.

6. Complete the following:

|  | Include in Inventory | |
|---|---|---|
|  | Yes | No |
| a. Goods out on consignment. | ___ | ___ |
| b. Goods held on consignment. | ___ | ___ |
| c. Merchandise at our branch for sale. | ___ | ___ |
| d. Merchandise at conventions for display purposes. | ___ | ___ |
| e. Goods held by our agents for us. | ___ | ___ |
| f. Goods held by us for sale on commission. | ___ | ___ |
| g. Goods held by us but awaiting return to vendor due to damaged condition. | ___ | ___ |
| h. Goods returned to us from buyer, reason unknown to date. | ___ | ___ |

7. Explain the principal aspects of a periodic inventory system.

8. Why is cost of goods sold often a residual amount?

9. Explain the effect of each of the following errors in the final inventory of a trading business:
   a. Incorrectly included 100 units of Commodity A, valued at $1 per unit, in the final inventory; the purchase was recorded.
   b. Incorrectly included 200 units of Commodity B, valued at $2 per unit, in the final inventory; the purchase was not recorded.
   c. Incorrectly excluded 300 units of Commodity C, valued at $3 per unit, from the final inventory; the purchase was recorded.

    *d.* Incorrectly excluded 400 units of Commodity D, valued at $4 per unit, from the final inventory; the purchase was not recorded.

10. What is meant by the "accounting value" of inventory? What accounting principles predominate in measuring this value?

11. In determining *unit cost* for inventory purposes, how should the following items be treated?
    *a.* Freight on goods and materials purchased.
    *b.* Purchase returns.
    *c.* Purchase discounts.

12. Should purchase discounts be *(a)* deducted in total in the income statement for the period in which the discounts arose, or *(b)* deducted in part in the income statement and in part from inventory on the balance sheet? Explain.

13. Cost is the primary basis for inventory valuation. List the four exceptions to cost discussed in the chapter. Under what specified conditions is each generally acceptable?

14. Why is the concept of lower of cost or market applied to inventory valuation?

15. What is the nature and purpose of the Allowance for Inventory Reduction to Market account?

16. In what specific situations may inventories be valued at selling price even though it is above cost?

17. How should damaged, obsolete, and depreciated merchandise on hand at the end of the period be valued for inventory purposes?

18. What are the basic assumptions underlying the relative sales value method when used in allocating costs for inventory purposes?

19. Briefly outline the accounting and reporting of losses on purchase commitments when *(a)* the purchase contract is subject to revision or cancellation, and *(b)* it is noncancellable.

## DECISION CASE 8-1

Ward Manufacturing Company has been in operation since 1952 and has experienced satisfactory growth since that time. L. Ward, the organizer, was an experienced and skilled machinist having operated a small custom machine shop for years. In 1952, with the financial assistance of a friend, Ward organized the company to manufacture specially designed trailers for the transportation of horses. Most of the trailers manufactured were designed to haul one horse; consequently, they were built to meet the particular desires of each customer. These trailers varied from a standard type to super deluxe models in keeping with the horse-show tradition.

    In 1960 the company started making trailers for boats. Two standard models were developed for sale to sporting goods stores, and in addition trailers were made to meet the specifications of individual buyers. The company recently experienced an unexpected demand for boat trailers which was attributed to their quality, competitive price, and design. Ward is having considerable difficulty keeping up with this demand and hesitates to add capacity, workers, and materials needed, on the basis of expectations, rather than on the basis of firm orders.

As a consequence, the firm has lost some business. Customarily a 50% deposit is required on all custom-made trailers.

Ward has been particularly interested in the manufacturing side of the business, although the financial and management aspects appear to be a problem. Ward is not inclined to be the executive type. As a result of some income tax difficulties Ward engaged an outside CPA to set up records and help with the financial management of the company. One employee spends part time on the present recordkeeping which involves minimum records on cash, salaries, receivables, and wages.

The company regularly stocks 23 different items of raw materials and numerous small supplies such as bolts, screws, welding materials, and paint. The Company loses about two thirds of the available cash discounts on purchases through oversight. Customarily the company pays freight on the purchases. Finished goods, on the lot, usually consist of 8 to 15 horse trailers, 20 to 35 boat trailers, plus small quantities of eight other small items generally manufactured. Frequently, customers leave trailers on the lot a week or more before picking them up. Several kinds of raw material currently on hand are of such a nature that the replacement cost is less than the original cost. The company has always had difficulty with raw materials and supplies; frequently shortages hold up work on jobs for days. Frequently, substitutions of higher cost materials are necessary due to items out of stock. The raw materials are stored both outside and inside, and individual workmen select the material as they need it on a help-yourself basis. Ward feels that the company cannot afford an inventory clerk. Items are reordered from a notebook kept on Ward's desk where individual workers are instructed to write down any items that are low or out of stock. When raw materials are received they are moved to the storage area and placed wherever space is available. Space is a problem. No inventory records are maintained. No payments are made for raw materials unless the invoice is signed by the employee that checked in the goods. Theft is no problem for the company.

The CPA has decided to install a job-order cost system so that costs will be accumulated by job for direct material, direct labor, and manufacturing overhead; and it is recognized that in view of the smallness of the company, the overall system must be simple and easy to operate.

The CPA is concerned about the raw material and finished goods inventory situations in particular and has asked you to make recommendations relative to the inventory problem. The CPA has decided to employ *Fifo* and lower of cost or market. Specifically, the CPA wants your suggestions for the company relative to (1) determination of quantities in inventory, (2) treatment of freight-in and purchase discount, (3) the accounting treatment of lower of cost or market, and (4) recommendations for better control of inventory. Sound reasons are expected to support your suggestions.

*Required:*

Narrate your recommendations to the company giving particular attention to the raw materials and finished goods inventories. Give supporting reasons.

## EXERCISES

### Exercise 8–1

Listed below for the Adams Sales Company are items of inventory that are in question. The company stores a good portion of the merchandise in a separate warehouse and transfers damaged goods to a special inventory account. The company policy is "satisfied customers."

a. Items counted in warehouse by inventory crew ............................$30,000
b. Invoice received for goods ordered, goods shipped but not received (Adams pays the freight) .............................................. 400
c. Items shipped today, f.o.b. destination, invoice mailed to customer ...................................................................... 60
d. Items currently being used for window displays............................. 600
e. Items on counters for sale per inventory count (not in [a])............... 6,000
f. Items in shipping department, invoice not mailed to customer......... 140
g. Items in receiving department, refused by Adams because of damage ..................................................................................... 80
h. Items shipped today, f.o.b. shipping point, invoice mailed to customer ........................................................................ 300
i. Items included in warehouse count, damaged, not returnable ......... 120
j. Items included in warehouse count, specifically segregated for shipment to customer next period per sales contract ............... 200
k. Items in receiving department, returned by customer, no communication received from the customer ............................... 100
l. Items ordered and in the receiving department, invoice not received ................................................................................. 500

*Required:*

Complete the following tabulation to reflect the correct inventory:

| Item | Exclude or Include in Inventory | Amount | Explanation |
|---|---|---|---|
| a. Items counted in warehouse .........Include | | $30,000 | Items on hand |
| b. Etc.  ......................................... | | | |
| Total Inventory Valuation  ... | | $_____ | |

## Exercise 8-2

The records of X Company reflected the following data: sales revenue, $60,000; purchases, $45,900; net income to sales revenue, 4%; one inventory amount was $12,500; and expenses, $10,200.

*Required:*

1. Reconstruct the income statement. Assume a periodic inventory system.
2. Give entries at the end of the period for the inventories assuming: Case A, a periodic inventory system; and Case B, a perpetual inventory system.

## Exercise 8-3

The records for K Company at December 31, 19A, reflected the following:

| | Units | Unit Amount |
|---|---|---|
| Sales during the period .........................................| 10,000 | $11 |
| Inventory at beginning of period.............................. | 2,000 | 5 |
| Merchandise purchased during the period (for cash) ... | 18,400 | 5 |
| Purchase returns during the period (cash refund)...... | 100 | 5 |
| Inventory at end of the period ................................. | ? | |

*Required:*

In parallel columns, give entries for the above transactions, including entries at the end of the period assuming:

Case A – Periodic inventory system.
Case B – Perpetual inventory system.

Use the following format:

| *Accounts* | *Case A* | *Case B* |
| --- | --- | --- |

## Exercise 8-4

The independent CPA for Brown Company found the following errors in the records of the company:

a. Incorrect exclusion from the final inventory of items costing $3,000 for which the purchase was not recorded.
b. Inclusion in the final inventory of goods costing $5,000, although a purchase was not recorded. The goods in question were being held on consignment from Conley Company.
c. Incorrect exclusion of $2,000 from the inventory count at the end of the period. The goods were in transit (f.o.b. shipping point); the invoice had been received, and the purchase recorded.
d. Inclusion of items on the receiving dock that were being held for return to the vendor because of damage. In counting the goods in the receiving department, these items were incorrectly included. With respect to these goods, a purchase of $4,000 had been recorded.

The records (uncorrected) showed the following amounts: (*a*) purchases, $170,000; (*b*) pretax income, $15,000; (*c*) accounts payable, $20,000; and (*d*) inventory at the end of the period, $40,000.

*Required:*

Set up a table to reflect the uncorrected balances, changes occasioned by the errors, and the corrected balances for (1) purchases, (2) pretax income, (3) accounts payable, and (4) inventory.

## Exercise 8-5

The records of Smith Company reflected the following:

| | | |
| --- | --- | --- |
| Sales revenue | | $160,000 |
| Cost of goods sold: | | |
| Beginning inventory | $10,000 | |
| Purchases | 85,000 | |
| Goods available for sale | 95,000 | |
| Ending inventory | 25,000 | 70,000 |
| Gross margin | | 90,000 |
| Expenses | | 60,000 |
| Net Income (pretax) | | $ 30,000 |

The following errors were found that had not been corrected:

a. Accrued expenses not recognized, $6,000.
b. Prepaid revenues amounting to $4,000 are included in the sales revenue amount.

c. Goods costing $10,000 were incorrectly included in the ending inventory (they were being held on consignment from Blue Company). No purchase was recorded.
d. Goods costing $3,000 were correctly included in the ending inventory; however, no purchase was recorded (assume a credit purchase).

*Required:*

1. Recast the income statement on a correct basis.
2. What amounts would be incorrect on the balance sheet if the errors are not corrected?

### Exercise 8-6

Milam Company uses a perpetual inventory system. The items on hand are inventoried on a rotation basis throughout the year so that all items are checked twice each year. At the end of the year, the following data relating to goods on hand are available:

| Product | Per Perpetual Inventory Units | Unit Cost | Per Physical Count (units) |
|---------|-------|-----------|----------------------------|
| A | 200 | $ 1 | 180 |
| B | 1,500 | 2 | 1,520 |
| C | 2,000 | 3 | 1,900 |
| D | 8,000 | 1 | 8,000 |
| E | 13,000 | 2 | 12,800 |
| F | 500 | 20 | 480 |
| G | 9,400 | 5 | 9,495 |
| H | 11,000 | 2 | 11,200 |
| I | 4,000 | 21 | 3,990 |
| J | 5,000 | 10 | 4,995 |

*Required:*

Determine the amount of the inventory overage or shortage and give the indicated entry. Indicate the final disposition of any discrepancy that is recorded.

### Exercise 8-7

The recapitulation of inventory taken on December 31 was as follows for Noonan Company:

a. Merchandise in the store at 10% above cost...............................$330,000
b. Merchandise out on consignment at sales price (including markup of 60% on selling price) ......................... 9,600
c. Goods held on consignment from the Brown Electrical Company at sales price (sales commission, 20% of sales price included) ......................... 2,400
d. Goods purchased, in transit (shipped f.o.b. shipping point; estimated freight, not included, $600), invoice price ............ 5,000
e. Goods out on approval, sales price $1,500, cost, $1,000 ............... 1,500
    Total Inventory ......................... $348,500

*Required:*

Compute the correct final inventory. Show computations.

**Exercise 8-8**

Rose Company purchased 6,000 pounds of Commodity X at $5 per pound. In addition, the company paid $230 freight on the purchase. The company also purchased 20,000 pounds of Commodity Y at $2 per pound and 4,000 pounds of Commodity Z at $8 per pound. In connection with the two latter purchases, which were delivered simultaneously by the trucking line, a freight charge (not detailed by product) was paid amounting to $432. The company uses a perpetual inventory system.

*Required:*

1. Give the combined entry to record the purchases from a theoretical point of view.
2. From a practical point of view, how could the purchases be recorded?
3. If you suggested a different entry from the practical point of view, indicate the basis for your suggestion.

**Exercise 8-9**

Roberts Trading Company purchased merchandise on credit for $20,000; terms, 2/15, n/30. Payment for $15,000 of this amount was made during the discount period; the balance was paid after the discount period. The company uses a perpetual inventory system.

*Required:*

Give entries in parallel columns to record the purchase and payments on the liability assuming:

*a.* Net of discount approach is used for purchase discounts.
*b.* Gross amount approach is used for purchase discounts.

Which approach is preferable? Why?

**Exercise 8-10**

Economy Trading Company purchased merchandise on credit for $40,000; terms, 2/10, n/30. Payment was made within the discount period. At the end of the fiscal period, one fourth of this merchandise was unsold. Determine (1) the cost of goods sold that would be reported on the income statement, and (2) the final inventory valuation as regards this particular lot of merchandise assuming:

*a.* Purchases and accounts payable are recorded at gross, and purchase discounts are reported on the income statement as other income.
*b.* Purchases and accounts payable are recorded at gross, and purchase discounts are deducted in total from purchases on the income statement.
*c.* Purchases and accounts payable both are recorded at net.

Evaluate the several approaches. Which approach do you prefer? Why?

**Exercise 8-11**

HiFi Company, a large dealer in radio and television sets, buys large quantities of a television model which costs $400. The contract reads that if 100 or more are purchased during the year, a bonus or rebate of $15 per set will be made. On December 15, the records showed that 150 sets had been purchased and that 10 remained on hand in inventory. A claim for the rebate was made to the jobber, and a check was received on January 20 after the books were closed.

*Required:*

1. At what valuation should the inventory be shown on December 31? Why?
2. What entry should be made relative to the rebate on December 31? Why?
3. What entry would be made on January 20? Why?

## Exercise 8–12

Small Company had 1,000 units of Product A in inventory at the end of the fiscal period. The unit cost was $60; estimated distribution costs $3 per unit; and the "normal" profit is $4 per unit. Compute the unit valuation of the inventory under each separate case listed below. Apply the lower-of-cost-or-market procedure in accordance with the "exceptions" specified by the Committee on Accounting Procedure of the AICPA.

| Case | Anticipated Sales Price | Current Replacement Cost | Case | Anticipated Sales Price | Current Replacement Cost |
|------|------------------------|--------------------------|------|------------------------|--------------------------|
| a) | $65 | $61 | f) | $68 | $61 |
| b) | 70 | 62 | g) | 50 | 44 |
| c) | 60 | 58 | h) | 59 | 57 |
| d) | 58 | 50 | i) | 61 | 53 |
| e) | 66 | 57 | j) | 73 | 59 |

## Exercise 8–13

In the process of auditing the records of Ace Company, your client takes the position that under the lower-of-cost-or-market procedure the two items listed below should be reported in the final inventory at $12,000 (total). Do you agree? If not, indicate the correct inventory valuation by item. Show computations.

"Handyman" hedge clippers: 300 on hand; cost, $22 each; reproduction cost, $16; estimated sales price, $30; estimated distribution cost, $9 each; and normal profit, 10% on the sales price.

"Handyman" edgers: 200 on hand; cost, $40 each; reproduction cost, $36 each; estimated sales price, $90; estimated distribution cost, $28; and normal profit, 20% of sales.

## Exercise 8–14

The inventory records of the M Company showed the following data:

| Product | Units | Unit Basis Cost | Unit Basis Market |
|---------|-------|------|--------|
| A | 200 | $1.50 | $1.60 |
| B | 500 | 1.00 | .90 |
| C | 300 | 3.00 | 3.20 |
| D | 100 | 4.00 | 4.20 |

*Required:*

Determine the value of the inventory assuming the lower-of-cost-or-market procedure is applied—

*a.* To individual items.

*b.* To groups assuming A and B are in one group and C and D are in another group.

*c.* To totals.

## Exercise 8–15

The inventories for the years 19A and 19B are shown below for Ryan Retailers, Inc.:

| Inventory Date | Original Cost | Lower of Cost or Market | Difference |
|---|---|---|---|
| January 1, 19A .................... | $6,000 | $6,000 | $ -0- |
| December 31, 19A .............. | 7,000 | 6,500 | 500 |
| December 31, 19B .............. | 9,000 | 9,000 | -0- |

*Required:*

1. Give, in parallel columns, the journal entries to apply the lower-of-cost-or-market procedure to the inventories for 19A and 19B, assuming the company uses the direct inventory reduction method (where the holding loss is not separately recognized) under (*a*) periodic inventory procedures, and (*b*) perpetual inventory procedures.

2. What are the primary advantages and disadvantages of the direct inventory reduction method compared with other methods that could be used?

## Exercise 8–16

Utilizing the data given in Exercise 8–15, give, in parallel columns, the journal entries to apply the lower-of-cost-or-market procedure to the inventories for 19A and 19B, assuming the company utilizes the inventory allowance method where the holding losses in the beginning and ending inventories are separately recognized under (*a*) periodic inventory procedures, and (*b*) perpetual inventory procedures. What are the primary advantages and disadvantages of this method?

## Exercise 8–17

Snappy Canning Company purchased 1,910 bushels of ungraded apricots at $2 per bushel. The apricots were sorted as follows: Grade One, 600 bushels; Grade Two, 400 bushels; Grade Three, 900 bushels. Handling and sorting costs amounted to $500. The current market prices for graded apricots were: Grade One, $4 per bushel; Grade Two, $3 per bushel; and Grade Three, $1 per bushel. The company utilizes a perpetual inventory system. What entry would be made to record the purchase? Show computations of total and unit costs for each grade assuming the relative sales value method of cost allocation is used.

## Exercise 8–18

Community Development Corporation purchased a tract of land for development purposes. The tract was subdivided as follows: 30 lots to sell at $6,000 per lot, and 80 lots to sell at $9,000 per lot. The tract cost $200,000 and an additional $25,000 was spent in general development costs. Assuming cost allocation is based on the relative sales value method, give entries for (a) purchase of the tract and payment of the development costs, (b) sale of one $6,000 lot, and (c) sale of one $9,000 lot. Assume a perpetual inventory system.

### Exercise 8–19

Swift Realty Company purchased and subdivided a tract of land at a cost of $440,000. The subdivision was on the following basis:

20% used for streets, alleys, and parks.
30% divided into 100 lots to sell for $4,000 each.
40% divided into 200 lots to sell for $3,000 each.
10% divided into 50 lots to sell for $2,000 each.

*Required:*

1. Assuming the relative sales value method is used, compute the valuation of the inventory of lots at the end of the first year assuming 20, $4,000 lots; 50, $3,000 lots; and 10, $2,000 lots are on hand. (Ignore paving costs and other deferrable costs.) Assume a perpetual inventory system.
2. Record the purchase of the lots, reflect the cost allocation.
3. Record the sale of one $4,000 lot.

### Exercise 8–20

Sweet Candy Company purchased 1,000 bags of orchard-run pecans at a cost of $3,460. In addition, the company incurred $50 for transportation and grading. The pecans graded out as follows:

| Grade | Quantity | Current Market Price per Bag |
|-------|----------|------------------------------|
| A | 300 | $7.00 |
| B | 500 | 6.00 |
| C | 150 | 5.00 |
| Waste | 50 | |

*Required:*

Assuming the relative sales value method is used to allocate joint costs, give:

a. The entry for purchase assuming a perpetual inventory system (show computations).
b. Valuation of final inventory assuming the following quantities are on hand: Grade A, 100 bags; Grade B, 80 bags; and Grade C, 20 bags.
c. Sale of 20 bags of the Grade A pecans.

### Exercise 8–21

A fire damaged some of the merchandise held for sale by Thomas Appliance Company. Five television sets and six stereo sets were damaged. They will be repaired and sold as used sets. Data are as follows:

| | Per Set | |
|---|---|---|
| | Television | Stereo |
| Inventory (at cost) | $300 | $200 |
| Estimated cost to repair | 40 | 30 |
| Estimated cost to sell | 20 | 20 |
| Estimated sales price | 120 | 90 |
| Insurance recovery (cash) | 25 | 20 |

*Required:*

1. Compute the appropriate inventory value for each set.
2. Give the separate entries to record the damaged goods inventory for the television and stereo sets. Assume a perpetual inventory system.
3. Give the entries to record the subsequent repair of the television sets and the stereo sets. (Credit Cash.)
4. Give the entry to record sale for cash of one television set and one stereo set. (Credit Distribution Costs.)

### Exercise 8–22

Zakin Corporation, during 1975, signed a contract with Young Company to "purchase 20,000 subassemblies, at $30 each during 1976."

*Required:*

1. On December 31, 1975, end of the annual accounting period, the financial statements are to be prepared. Under what additional contractual and economic conditions should disclosure of the contract terms be made only by means of a note in the financial statements? Prepare an appropriate note. Assume the cost is dropping.
2. What additional contractual and economic conditions would require accrual of a loss? Give the accrual entry. Assume the cost has dropped.
3. Assume the subassemblies are received in 1976 when their cost was at the estimate you used in Requirement 2. The contract was paid in full. Give the required entry.

### PROBLEMS

### Problem 8–1

As the auditor for the year ended December 31, 19A, you found the following transactions occurred near the closing date for Adkins Company:

a. Merchandise received on January 6, 19B costing $800 was recorded on January 6, 19B. An invoice on hand showed the shipment was made f.o.b. supplier's warehouse on December 31, 19A. Since the merchandise was not on hand at December 31, 19A, it was not included in the inventory.
b. A sealed packing case containing a product costing $900 was in Adkins ship-

ping room when the physical inventory was taken. It was not included in the inventory because it was marked *"Hold for customer's shipping instructions."* Investigation revealed that the customer's order was dated December 18, 19A, but that the case was shipped and the customer billed on January 10, 19B. The product was a regular stock item.

c. A special machine, fabricated to order for a customer, was finished and in the shipping room on December 31, 19A. The customer had inspected it and was satisfied with it. The customer was billed in full for $1,000 on that date. The machine was excluded from inventory because it was shipped on January 1, 19B.

d. Merchandise costing $700 was received on December 28, 19A, and a purchase was not recorded. You located the related papers in the hands of the purchasing agent; they indicated *"on consignment from Baker Company."*

e. Merchandise costing $2,000 was received on January 3, 19B, and the related purchase invoice recorded January 5. The invoice showed the shipment was made on December 29, 19A, f.o.b. *destination.*

*Required:*

For each situation, state whether the merchandise should be included in the client's inventory. Give your reason for the decision on each item.

(AICPA adapted)

## Problem 8-2

Assume you are the independent auditor for the Cline Manufacturing Corporation. The final inventory for the year ended December 31, 19A, is under consideration. The following problems related to the final inventory have arisen, and the company accountant requests your advice on them:

| | Material A @ $3 | Material B @ $5 |
|---|---|---|
| Raw material inventory data on December 31, 19A (in units): | | |
| a. Items counted in bins Nos. 1–5 | 12,000 | 2,000 |
| b. Purchase invoice received, items not received (f.o.b. shipping point) | | 200 |
| c. Items counted in bin No. 2, set aside for return to vendor next period per agreement December 20, 19A; not up to specifications, shipped January 2, 19B | | 100 |
| d. Items counted in bin No. 3 that had been issued to factory and returned by them in damaged condition, not returnable to vendor | | 50 |
| e. Items counted in bin No. 4 from a shipment partly damaged when received, returnable to vendor per agreement; shipped January 3, 19B | | 40 |
| f. Items purchased, on receiving dock, refused because of damage | 50 | |
| g. Items purchased, on receiving dock, invoice not received | 100 | 300 |
| h. Items counted in bin No. 5, to be returned to vendor, rejected for incorrect specs | 200 | |
| i. Purchase invoice received, items not received (f.o.b. destination) | 20 | 100 |

|  | Product X @ $10 | Product Y @ $20 |
|---|---|---|
| Finished goods inventory data on December 31, 19A (in units): |  |  |
| j. Items counted in warehouse (excluding the items below) ...............................................................15,000 | | 10,000 |
| k. Items shipped to customer on January 1, 19B, invoice mailed December 31, 19A (f.o.b. shipping point) ...................................................... | | 500 |
| l. Items completed by factory, counted in the work in process inventory; not transported to warehouse ...... | 800 | |
| m. Items on receiving dock, returned by customer because of damage, notification from customer received ............................................................ | | 50 |
| n. Items on trucking company dock, invoice mailed to customer, buyer pays freight ............................. | 500 | |
| o. Items in damaged condition ................................. | 20 | 10 |
| p. Items in shipping department, invoice not mailed to customer................................................................ | 80 | |
| q. Items shipped December 31, 19A, f.o.b. destination; invoice mailed January 2, 19B ............................. | 100 | |
| r. Items on consignment to Brady Distributing Company ............................................................... | 400 | 700 |
| s. Items specifically segregated and crated for shipment to Cline Branch X .................................... | 100 | 100 |
| t. Items used for display purposes ............................. | 10 | 30 |
| u. Items specifically segregated and crated for shipment to customer early next period per signed sales contract ............................................. | | 500 |
| v. Items on receiving dock, returned by customer, no notification received (not damaged)..................... | 20 | |

*Required:*

Compute the valuation of the final inventory of raw materials and finished goods indicating specifically what items you would include and exclude. Give reasons you would present to the company relative to any doubtful items. The following format is recommended:

|  |  | Material A | | Material B | | |
|---|---|---|---|---|---|---|
| Item | Inventory Include/Exclude | Units | Amounts | Units | Amounts | Explanation |

## Problem 8–3

Foster Company's fiscal period ends on December 31, 19A. The company uses a periodic inventory system. An independent CPA was engaged after the end of the year to perform an audit. Therefore, the CPA did not observe the taking of the inventory. As a result, an examination was made of the inventory records, purchases, and sales.

The financial statements prepared by the company (uncorrected) showed the following: final inventory, $60,000; accounts receivable, $60,000; accounts payable, $20,000; sales, $400,000; purchases, $160,000; and pretax net income, $30,000.

The following data were found during the audit:

*a.* Merchandise that cost $10,000 and sold on December 31, 19A, for $14,000 was included in the final inventory. The sale was recorded. The goods were in transit; however, a clerk failed to note that the goods were shipped f.o.b. shipping point.

b. Merchandise that cost $6,000 was excluded from the final inventory and not recorded as a sale for $7,500 on December 26, 19A. The goods had been specifically segregated. According to the terms of the contract of sale, ownership did not pass until actual delivery.

c. Merchandise that cost $15,000 was included in the final inventory. The related purchase was not recorded. The goods had been shipped by the vendor f.o.b. destination; and the invoice, but not the goods, was received on December 30, 19A.

d. Merchandise in transit that cost $7,000 was excluded from inventory because it was not on hand. The shipment from the vendor was f.o.b. shipping point. The purchase was recorded on December 29, 19A, when the invoice was received.

e. Merchandise in transit that cost $11,000 was excluded from inventory because it had not arrived. The related purchase was not recorded by December 30, 19A. The merchandise was shipped by the vendor f.o.b. shipping point.

f. Merchandise that cost $8,000 was included in the final inventory since it was on hand. The merchandise had been rejected because of incorrect specifications and was being held for return to the vendor. The merchandise was recorded as a purchase on December 26, 19A.

g. Merchandise that cost $18,000 was excluded from the inventory, and the related sale for $23,000 was recorded. The goods had been segregated in the warehouse for shipment; there was no contract for sale; however, there was a purchase order from the customer.

h. Merchandise that cost $10,000 was out on consignment to the Goode Distributing Company and was excluded from the final inventory. The merchandise was recorded as a sale of $25,000 when shipped on December 2, 19A.

*Required:*

Prepare a schedule with one column for each of the six financial statement accounts (starting with the uncorrected balances) plus any other columns, deemed useful. Show the specific corrections to each balance and the corrected balances. Explain the basis for your decision on questionable items.


### Problem 8–4

Hiam Company completed the following selected transactions during 19A for Product A:

|                                              | Units  | Unit Amount |
|----------------------------------------------|--------|-------------|
| Beginning inventory                          | 5,000  | $18         |
| Purchases                                     | 20,000 | 18          |
| Purchase returns                              | 1,000  | 18          |
| Sales                                         | 18,000 | 35          |
| Sales returns                                 | 100    | 35          |
| Ending inventory per physical count           | 5,800  |             |
| Inventory shortage                            | ?      |             |
| Expenses (excluding income taxes), $258,900  |        |             |

*Required:*

1. In parallel columns, give entries for the above transactions including entries

at the end of the accounting period, December 31, 19A, for (assume cash transactions):

Case A—A periodic inventory system.
Case B—A perpetual inventory system.

2. Prepare a multiple-step income statement assuming a periodic inventory system, 10,000 shares of common stock outstanding, and a 40% income tax rate.
3. What amounts, if any, would be different on the income statement assuming a perpetual inventory system is used? Explain.

## Problem 8–5

Harris Company has completed the income statement and balance sheet (summarized and uncorrected shown below) at December 31, 19A. Subsequently, during the audit, the following items were discovered:

a. Expenses amounting to $3,000 were not accrued.
b. A conditional sale on credit for $9,000 was recorded on December 31, 19A. The goods, which cost $5,000, were included in the final inventory because they had not been shipped since the customer's address was not known and the credit had not been approved. Ownership had not passed.
c. Merchandise purchased on December 31, 19A, on credit for $6,000, was included in the final inventory because the goods were on hand. A purchase was not recorded because the accounting department had not received the invoice from the vendor.
d. The final inventory was overstated by $10,000 due to an addition error on the inventory sheet.
e. A sale return (on account) on December 31, 19A, was not recorded: sales amount, $15,000; cost, $8,000. The ending inventory did not include the goods returned.

|  | Uncorrected Amounts | Items for Correction | | | | | Corrected Amounts |
|---|---|---|---|---|---|---|---|
|  |  | (a) | (b) | (c) | (d) | (e) |  |
| **Income Statement:** |  |  |  |  |  |  |  |
| Sales revenue | $90,000 |  |  |  |  |  |  |
| Cost of goods sold | 50,000 |  |  |  |  |  |  |
| Gross margin | 40,000 |  |  |  |  |  |  |
| Expenses | 30,000 |  |  |  |  |  |  |
| Pretax income | $10,000 |  |  |  |  |  |  |
| **Balance Sheet:** |  |  |  |  |  |  |  |
| Accounts receivable | $32,000 |  |  |  |  |  |  |
| Inventory | 20,000 |  |  |  |  |  |  |
| Remaining assets | 40,000 |  |  |  |  |  |  |
| Accounts payable | 11,000 |  |  |  |  |  |  |
| Remaining liabilities | 6,000 |  |  |  |  |  |  |
| Common stock | 60,000 |  |  |  |  |  |  |
| Retained earnings | 15,000 |  |  |  |  |  |  |

*Required:*

Set up a schedule similar to the one above and derive the corrections. Indicate increases and decreases for each transaction. Explain any assumptions made with respect to doubtful items. Disregard income taxes.

## Problem 8–6

Pope Company purchased merchandise during 19A on credit for $63,000 (includes $3,000 freight charges paid in cash); terms, 2/10, n/30. All of the gross liability, except $10,000, was paid within the discount period; the remainder was paid within the 30-day term. At the end of the annual accounting period, December 31, 19A, 90% of the merchandise had been sold and 10% remained in inventory. The company uses a perpetual system.

*Required:*

1. Give entries, in parallel columns, for the purchase and the two payments on the liability assuming (a) purchases and accounts payable are recorded at gross, and (b) purchases and accounts payable are recorded at net.
2. What amounts would be reported for the final inventory and cost of goods sold under each method. Assume purchase discounts, under the gross method are reported as a deduction from cost of goods sold. Explain why the amounts are different between the two methods.
3. Which method do you prefer? Why?

## Problem 8–7

The information shown below relating to the final inventory was taken from the records of the Morris Publishing Company:

| | | Per Unit | |
|---|---|---|---|
| Inventory Classification | Quantity | Cost | Market |
| Newsprint: | | | |
| Stock A ................................200 | | $300 | $330 |
| B ................................. 60 | | 250 | 230 |
| Special stock (white): | | | |
| Stock H ................................. 20 | | 70 | 65 |
| I ................................. 10 | | 60 | 62 |
| Special stock (colored): | | | |
| Stock S ................................. 8 | | 75 | 70 |
| T ................................. 4 | | 90 | 80 |
| U ................................. 7 | | 100 | 110 |

*Required:*

1. Determine the valuation of the above inventory at cost and at lower of cost or market assuming application by (a) item by item, (b) classifications, and (c) total inventory.
2. Give the entry to record the ending inventory for each approach assuming periodic inventory and —
   a. Direct inventory reduction method.
   b. Allowance method.
3. Which method do you prefer? Why?

## Problem 8–8

The records of Waters Company provide the following data relating to inventories for the years 19A and 19B:

| Inventory Date | Original Cost | At Lower of Cost or Market |
|---|---|---|
| January 1, 19A | $40,000 | $40,000 |
| December 31, 19A | 50,000 | 46,000 |
| December 31, 19B | 40,000 | 37,000 |

Other data available are:

|  | 19A | 19B |
|---|---|---|
| Sales | $220,000 | $250,000 |
| Purchases | 135,000 | 150,000 |
| Administrative and selling expenses | 51,000 | 61,000 |

The company values inventories on the basis of lower of cost or market and uses the periodic inventory system. For problem purposes use only pretax amounts.

*Required:*

1. Give, in parallel columns, for 19A and 19B, the entries to apply the lower-of-cost-or-market procedure under each of the two methods: Case A—direct inventory reduction where the holding loss is not separately reported; and Case B—the allowance method. Set up a format similar to the following:

|  | Amounts | |
|---|---|---|
| Accounts | 19A | 19B |
| Case A: | | |
| Entries | | |
| Case B: | | |
| Entries | | |

2. Prepare an income statement and show the inventory amounts for the balance sheet for each case. Follow the format illustrated in the chapter.
3. Which method do you prefer? Why?

## Problem 8–9

The summarized income statements for the Ashton Company are shown below as developed by the company. The inventories are valued at cost.

|  | 19A | 19B |
|---|---|---|
| Sales | $104,000 | $97,000 |
| Cost of goods sold: | | |
| Beginning inventory | 25,000 | 20,000 |
| Purchases | 75,000 | 73,000 |
| Total | 100,000 | 93,000 |
| Ending inventory | 20,000 | 15,000 |
| Cost of goods sold | 80,000 | 78,000 |
| Gross margin | 24,000 | 19,000 |
| Less: Operating expenses | 14,000 | 12,000 |
| Pretax Income | $ 10,000 | $ 7,000 |

The inventories valued at lower of cost or market would have been at the beginning of 19A, $24,000; end of 19A, $17,000; and end of 19B, $13,000.

*Required:*

1. Restate the 19A and 19B income statements applying the lower-of-cost-or-market rule for each of the following procedures (use a format similar to that illustrated in the text). Disregard income taxes.
   a. Direct inventory reduction method where the inventory holding loss is not reported separately.
   b. Allowance method where the inventory holding losses in both beginning and ending inventories are reported separately.
2. Which procedure is preferable? Why?

## Problem 8–10

Fresh Fruit Company purchased a large quantity of mixed grapefruit for $34,300, which is sorted at a cost of $900 as indicated below. Sales (at the sales price indicated) and losses (frozen, theft, rotten, etc.) are also listed.

| Grade | Baskets Bought | Sales Price per Basket | Baskets Sold | Baskets Lost |
|---|---|---|---|---|
| A | 3,000 | $4.00 | 2,000 | 50 |
| B | 4,000 | 3.00 | 3,000 | 60 |
| C | 10,000 | 1.50 | 8,000 | 80 |
| D | 6,000 | .75 | 4,000 | |
| Culls | 1,000 | .50 | 900 | |
| Loss | 55 | | | |

*Required:*

1. Give entry for purchase assuming a perpetual inventory system. Show computations.
2. Give entries to record the sales and cost of goods sold.
3. Give entry relative to the losses assuming the losses are recorded separately from cost of sales.
4. Determine the valuation of the final inventory.
5. Compute the direct contribution for each grade of grapefruit. (Disregard operating, administrative, and selling expenses.)

## Problem 8–11

On May 1, 19A, Box and Carr invested $90,000 cash each for the purpose of purchasing and subdividing a tract of land for residential building purposes.

On June 1, they purchased 30 acres comprising the subdivision, at $5,000 per acre, paying $50,000 in cash and giving a one-year, 8% interest-bearing note (with mortgage) for the balance. Development costs amounted to $92,000.

The property was subdivided into 300 lots of equal size, 100 of which were to sell at $3,000 each and the balance at $4,000 each.

During June to December 19A the following sales were made for one-half cash and the balance on 9% interest-bearing notes, due in six months from date of sale.

_Lots_

Group A (sold at $4,000 each)..................30
Group B (sold at $3,000 each)..................20

Cash collections on the notes receivables up to December 31, 19A, amounted to $50,000 principal and $4,000 interest. Accrued interest recorded at December 31, 19A, amounted to $3,000.

Operating and selling expenses amounted to $95,000 by the end of December 19A. No payment was made on the note payable.

_Required:_

1. Journal entries for all of the above transactions. Disregard income taxes.
2. Statement of income for the months of June through December.
3. Compute the inventory of unsold lots on December 31, 19A.

**Problem 8–12**

Broome Appliance Company completed the following selected (and summarized) transactions during 19A:

a. Purchased merchandise for resale, quoted at $150,000, on credit terms, 2/10, n/30; immediately paid 80% of the cash cost.
b. Paid freight charges on purchases amounting to $6,000 cash.
c. Paid 60% of the accounts payable within the discount period. The remaining amount was unpaid at year-end; however, at year-end none was beyond the discount period.
d. Returned merchandise to a vendor because of damage in shipment and received a $1,980 cash refund.
e. Sold merchandise for $300,000, of which 10% was on end-of-the-month credit terms.
f. Repossessed a refrigerator abandoned by a customer who left town. The sales price was $400 of which $300 was unpaid. The refrigerator cost $320. Estimates are that the used refrigerator can be sold for $250 and that cost of repairs will be $30 and selling costs will be $10.
g. Operating expenses paid in cash, $90,000.
h. Paid $30 to repair the repossessed refrigerator.
i. The purchases amount given in (a) included a shipment, on credit, that had a quoted cost of $8,000 (terms, 2/10, n/30). The liability had not been paid. The shipment was in transit, f.o.b. destination, at December 31, 19A. The invoice had been received. It was not included in the ending inventory amount.
j. The beginning inventory was $70,000.
k. The ending inventory (excluding the repossessed refrigerator) was $78,000 at cost; at lower of cost or market, $73,000.

Accounting policies followed by the company are: (a) annual accounting period ends December 31; (b) purchases and accounts payable are recorded at net of cash discounts; (c) freight charges are allocated to the merchandise when purchased; (d) all cash discounts allowed are taken; (e) used and damaged merchandise carried in a separate inventory account; (f) inventories are reported at lower of cost or market and the loss on the ending inventory separately recognized (i.e., the allowance method).

*Required:*

1. Give entries for transactions (*a*) through (*h*) assuming periodic inventory system.
2. Give the end of the period entries (adjusting and closing).
3. Prepare a multiple-step income statement (19A). Assume 10,000 shares of common stock outstanding. Assume an income tax rate of 40%.
4. Show how the final inventory should be reported on the balance sheet at December 31, 19A.


**Problem 8–13**

Quillen Distributing Company completed the following selected (and summarized) transactions during 19A:

*a.* Merchandise inventory on hand January 1, 19A: $100,000 (already recorded).
*b.* Purchased merchandise for resale at quoted price of $200,000 on credit terms, 2/10, n/30. Immediately paid 85% of the cash cost.
*c.* Paid freight on merchandise purchased, $9,000 cash.
*d.* Paid 40% of the accounts payable within the discount period. The remaining payables were unpaid at the end of 19A and were still within the discount period.
*e.* Merchandise was returned to a supplier that had a quoted price of $3,000. A cash refund of $2,940 was received since the items were unsatisfactory.
*f.* Sold merchandise for $370,000 of which 10% was on credit terms, n/30.
*g.* A television set caught fire and was damaged internally; it was returned by the customer since it was guaranteed. The set was sold for $600 of which $200 remained unpaid. The set cost $420. Estimates are that the set, when repaired, can be sold for $240. Estimated repair costs are $50, and selling costs are estimated to be $10.
*h.* Operating expenses (administrative and distribution) paid in cash, $115,000.
*i.* Excluded from the purchase given in (*b*) and from the final inventory was a shipment for $7,000 (net of discount). This shipment was in transit, f.o.b. shipping point at December 31, 19A. The invoice was in hand.
*j.* Paid $50 cash to repair the damaged television set (see [*g*] above).
*k.* Sold the damaged television set for $245; selling costs allocated, $10.
*l.* The ending inventory was $110,000 at cost, and $102,000 at lower of cost or market. Assume an average income tax rate of 40%.

Accounting policies followed by the company are: (*a*) annual accounting period ends December 31; (*b*) purchases and accounts payable are recorded at net of cash discounts; (*c*) freight charges are allocated to merchandise when purchased; (*d*) all cash discounts are taken; (*e*) used and damaged merchandise carried in a separate inventory account; and (*f*) inventories are reported at lower of cost or market and the allowance method is used.

*Required:*

1. Give entries for transactions (*b*) through (*k*) assuming periodic inventory system.
2. Give the end of the period entries (adjusting and closing).
3. Prepare a multiple-step income statement (19A). Assume 10,000 shares of common stock outstanding.
4. Show how the final inventory should be reported on the balance sheet at December 31, 19A.

# Chapter 9

# Inventories—Flow
# and Matching Procedures

In Chapter 8 two pervasive inventory problems were identified—measurement of inventory *unit cost* and selection of an appropriate flow method. This chapter focuses on the latter problem; that is, the selection of an assumed inventory cost flow such as average cost, *Fifo*, or *Lifo*. To facilitate discussion and provide flexibility in the choice of materials, this chapter is divided into two parts: Part A—Inventory Flow Methods and Part B—Complexities in Application of *Lifo*.

## PART A—INVENTORY FLOW METHODS

When goods are purchased or manufactured there is an inflow of cost; when the goods are later sold or issued there is an outflow of cost. The net difference between these cost flows is represented by the amount remaining in inventory. During a period of time such as a month or year, items typically are manufactured or purchased at different unit costs. Upon issue or sale of the items where more than one unit cost is involved, the accountant is faced with the problem of selecting an appropriate unit cost for accounting purposes. Alternatively, the problem can be viewed as one of costing the units remaining on hand in inventory and of measuring the amount of cost of goods sold or used.

A definite policy on the assumed flow of costs for inventory and cost of goods sold (or cost of issues) is established when a particular inventory flow method is selected. Although some inventory flow methods may be essentially consistent with the physical flow of goods in a specific case, the methods focus on the flow of *costs* rather than on the flow of physical goods. *ARB No. 43* states:

Cost for inventory purposes may be determined under any one of several assumptions as to the flow of cost factors (such as first-in first-out, average, and last-in first-out); the major objective in selecting a method should be to choose the one which, under the circumstances, most clearly reflects periodic income.[1]

Each inventory flow method discussed in this chapter conforms to the *cost principle;* they do not involve departures from cost. The concept of *unit cost* discussed in Chapter 8 is applied; the central issue is the order in which these actual unit costs are assigned to inventory and cost of goods sold. Fundamentally, the selection of an inventory flow method reflects the manner in which the *matching principle* is to be applied to determine the cost of goods sold amount that is deducted from sales revenue for the period. Clearly, this affects net income and income taxes (a cash outflow). Generally accepted accounting principles state that the method selected should be the one that "most clearly reflects periodic income" in each particular situation. Of course, all of the methods give the same results if costs do not change, which is seldom the case.

The inventory flow methods discussed in this chapter are:

1. Specific cost identification.
2. Average cost.
3. First-in, first-out *(Fifo).*
4. Last-in, first-out *(Lifo).*
5. Miscellaneous methods.

For purposes of illustrating the various methods, the simplified data given in Exhibit 9–1 are used.

**EXHIBIT 9–1**

| | | Received | | | Units on |
| | Transactions | Units | Unit Cost | Units Issued | Hand |
|---|---|---|---|---|---|
| Jan. 1 | Inventory (@ $1) ............ | | | | 200 |
| 9 | Purchase ....................300 | | $1.10 | | 500 |
| 10 | Sale............................. | | | 400 | 100 |
| 15 | Purchase ....................400 | | 1.16 | | 500 |
| 18 | Sale............................. | | | 300 | 200 |
| 24 | Purchase ....................100 | | 1.26 | | 300 |

Using the data given in Exhibit 9–1, we can pinpoint, by diagram, the problem of selecting an assumed cost flow method for inventory and cost of goods sold purposes, viz:

---

[1] AICPA, "Restatement and Revision of Accounting Research Bulletins," *Accounting Research Bulletin No. 43* (New York, 1961), p. 29.

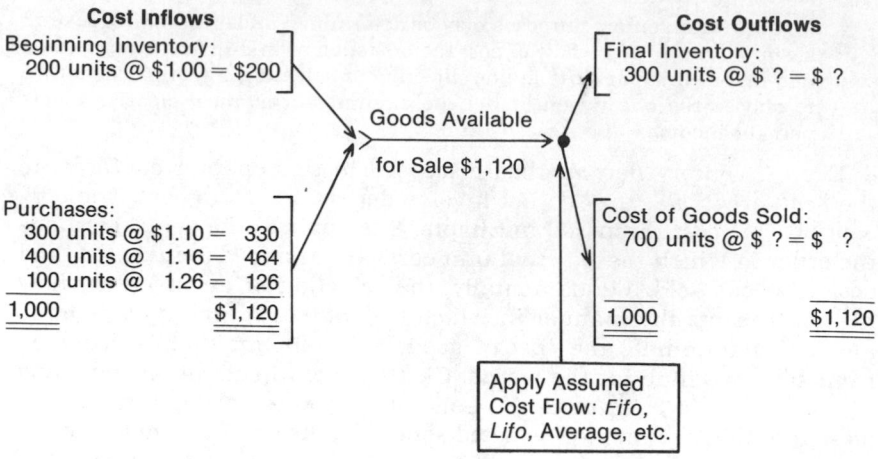

The application of the several inventory flow methods will usually vary somewhat depending on whether *periodic* or *perpetual* inventory procedures are utilized. The discussions to follow will distinguish between these procedures as they affect the application of the inventory flow method.

Recall that under periodic inventory procedures, the ending inventory is determined by a physical unit count; the unit costs (as defined in Chapter 8) are then applied by using one of the flow methods discussed in this chapter. Cost of goods sold (or used) is determined by subtracting the final inventory cost from the *goods available* amount. In contrast, under perpetual inventory procedures, all receipts and issues of inventory items are recorded so that an up-to-date or running inventory balance is continuously maintained directly in the records. As a consequence, the inventory records provide the amounts for inventory and cost of goods sold.

## SPECIFIC COST IDENTIFICATION

When the goods involved are relatively large or expensive and small quantities are handled, it may be feasible to tag or number each item when purchased or manufactured, as the case may be, so that the actual unit cost can be indicated on each item by code. This procedure makes it possible to easily identify the *unit cost* for each issue or sale and also for each item in inventory. The specific cost identification method identifies the *cost flow* with the specific flow of physical goods and may be applied with either periodic or perpetual inventory procedures. The specific cost method requires careful identification of each item; consequently, it is seldom used because of the practical limitation created by the detailed records involved, and because specific items remaining (as opposed to specific items issued) frequently are there more or less by accident. There is the possibility of profit manipulation by arbitrary selection of items. To illustrate, assume there are three identical stereo sets on the floor available for sale that cost $400, $420, and $426. One is sold for $600. In this instance, reported cost of goods sold (and gross margin) would depend upon the arbitrary selection between the three unit costs. The method lacks objectivity in application in many situations. However, the method is essential in certain situations such as dealers in automobiles and rare gems.

## AVERAGE COST

The average cost method is based on the concept that the best measure of inventory on the balance sheet and of cost of goods sold on the income statement is a representative unit cost for the period. The concept of average cost is applied in two ways depending upon the inventory system, viz: (a) periodic inventory system — weighted average unit cost for the period, and (b) perpetual inventory system — moving average unit cost.

### Weighted Average

Under this method, a weighted average unit cost is computed at the end of the period by using the unit purchase prices and the number of units in the beginning inventory and purchases for the period. The weighted unit price, thus computed, is applied to (a) the units in the final inventory, and (b) the units sold (to derive cost of goods sold). Exhibit 9–2 illustrates application of the weighted average method using the data given in Exhibit 9–1. Observe that the weighted average unit cost is derived by dividing the total amount for goods available for sale by the total number of units available.

**EXHIBIT 9–2**
**Inventory — Weighted Average Illustrated**

|  | Units | Unit Price | Total Cost |
|---|---|---|---|
| Goods available: |  |  |  |
| Jan.  1  Inventory.............. | 200 | $1.00 | $  200 |
| 9  Purchase.............. | 300 | 1.10 | 330 |
| 15  Purchase.............. | 400 | 1.16 | 464 |
| 24  Purchase.............. | 100 | 1.26 | 126 |
| Total.......................... | 1,000 | 1.12* | 1,120 |
| Cost of goods sold at weighted average cost: |  |  |  |
| Jan. 10 ............................ | 400 | 1.12 | 448 |
| 18 ............................ | 300 | 1.12 | 336 |
|  | 700 |  | 784 |
| Final inventory at weighted average cost: |  |  |  |
| Jan. 31 ............................ | 300 | 1.12 | $  336 |

* Weighted average unit cost ($1,120 ÷ 1,000 = $1.12).

The weighted average method is used frequently because it is theoretically and mathematically sound and is relatively easy to apply. Average cost minimizes the effect of extreme variations in purchase prices; on a rising market, weighted average cost will be lower than current cost, and on a declining market, it will be higher than current cost. The method is particularly sound because it is rational and systematic and it is not subject to manipulation. It is appropriate for periodic inventory procedures because (a) the inventory of physical units is not determined (counted) until the end of the period, and (b) the weighted average unit cost can be determined at that time. Thus, the measurements necessary to compute the amount of the final inventory and the amount of cost of goods sold are determined at the same point in time.

## Moving Average

When a perpetual inventory system is used, the weighted average approach cannot be used because the unit cost cannot be calculated until the end of the period. To overcome this problem, a moving weighted average unit cost may be used because it provides a new unit cost *after each purchase*. Thus, when goods are sold, or issued, the moving average unit cost is used at that point in time. Application of the moving average concept in a perpetual inventory system is shown in Exhibit 9–3 (based on data from Exhibit 9–1).

Note that the moving average unit cost is computed directly on the inventory card *after each purchase,* thus facilitating the current costing of issues during the period. On January 9 the $1.06 moving average cost was derived by dividing the total cost $530 by the total units 500; on January 15 the $1.14 moving average was derived by dividing $570

**EXHIBIT 9–3**
**Perpetual Inventory Record (moving average illustrated)**

| | Received | | | Issued | | | Balance | | |
|---|---|---|---|---|---|---|---|---|---|
| Date | Units | Unit Cost | Total Cost | Units | Unit Cost | Total Cost | Units | Unit Cost | Total Cost |
| Jan. 1 | | | | | | | 200 | $1.00 | $200 |
| 9 | 300 | $1.10 | $330 | | | | 500 | 1.06* | 530 |
| 10 | | | | 400 | $1.06 | $424 | 100 | 1.06 | 106 |
| 15 | 400 | 1.16 | 464 | | | | 500 | 1.14* | 570 |
| 18 | | | | 300 | 1.14 | 342 | 200 | 1.14 | 228 |
| 24 | 100 | 1.26 | 126 | | | | 300 | 1.18* | 354 |

* New average computed.

by 500 units; and on January 24, $354 divided by 300 units gave the $1.18 moving average. The ending inventory of 300 units is costed at the latest moving average unit cost of $1.18 (total $354). Cost of goods sold is the sum of the "Issued, Total Cost" column, $766.

The moving average is conceptually, mathematically, and practically sound. It is rational, consistent, not subject to manipulation, and is a representative average that is more current than the weighted average.

A practical problem with both the weighted and moving average methods is that the unit costs may not be even amounts. This problem usually is resolved by pricing the issues (cost of goods sold) so that the inventory unit costs are even.

In matching costs with revenues, the averaging methods do not match the latest unit cost with sales revenue. Rather, they generally provide inventory and cost of goods sold amounts between the *Lifo* and *Fifo* extremes. However, the amounts on the balance sheet (ending inventory) and on the income statement (cost of goods sold) are consistent as to valuation.

## FIRST-IN, FIRST-OUT

The first-in, first-out method *(Fifo)* is based upon the assumption that the first goods purchased, or manufactured, are the first costed out upon sale or issuance. Since the costs are "flowed out" in the same order that they flowed in, cost of goods sold (or issued) are costed at the *oldest* unit cost and the goods remaining in inventory are costed at the *newer* unit cost amounts. Application of *Fifo* requires the use of *inventory layers* for the different unit costs. The method may be used, without complexity, with either periodic or perpetual inventory systems.

Using the illustrative data in Exhibit 9–1, and a physical inventory count at the end of the period, *Fifo* results would be determined as follows:

***Fifo*—Periodic Inventory System**

| | | | |
|---|---|---|---|
| | Beginning inventory (200 units @ $1) | | $ 200 |
| | Add purchases during the period (computed above) | | 920 |
| | Goods available | | 1,120 |
| Inventory Computation | Deduct final inventory (300 units per physical inventory count): | | |
| | 100 units @ $1.26 (most recent purchase) | $126 | |
| | 200 units @ $1.16 (next most recent purchase) | 232 | |
| | Total Inventory | | 358 |
| | Cost of Goods Sold (or Issues) | | $ 762 |

The same data are used in Exhibit 9–4 to illustrate the application of *Fifo* with a perpetual inventory system. Note the maintenance of inventory layers throughout the period. This is necessary to cost out each issue.

**EXHIBIT 9–4**
**Perpetual Inventory Record (*Fifo* illustrated)**

| Date | Received Units | Received Unit Cost | Received Total Cost | Issued Units | Issued Unit Cost | Issued Total Cost | Balance Units | Balance Unit Cost | Balance Total Cost |
|------|------|------|------|------|------|------|------|------|------|
| Jan. 1 | | | | | | | 200 | $1.00 | $200 |
| 9 | 300 | $1.10 | $330 | | | | 200 300 | 1.00 1.10 | 200 330 |
| 10 | | | | 200 200 | $1.00 1.10 | $200 220 | 100 | 1.10 | 110 |
| 15 | 400 | 1.16 | 464 | | | | 100 400 | 1.10 1.16 | 110 464 |
| 18 | | | | 100 200 | 1.10 1.16 | 110 232 | 200 | 1.16 | 232 |
| 24 | 100 | 1.26 | 126 | | | | 200 100 | 1.16 1.26 | 232⎫ 126⎭ $358 |

In contrast with *Lifo*, discussed in the next section, *Fifo* gives the same results for the ending inventory and cost of goods sold (or issued) under the periodic and perpetual inventory systems. Also, under the perpetual inventory system, the issues on the inventory record may be costed out either (*a*) currently throughout the period (i.e., each time there is a withdrawal), or (*b*) all at the end of the period, with the same results. Again this is not the case with *Lifo*, as is illustrated in the next section. Because of the internal consistencies of *Fifo*, the final inventory derived under perpetual inventory procedures may be readily verified as follows (refer to Exhibit 9–4):

Most recent purchase (January 24) .....................100 @ $1.26 $126
Next most recent purchase (January 15)...............200 @ 1.16 232
Total Inventory (January 31) ....................300 $358

*Fifo* is widely used for inventory costing purposes because (*a*) it is easy to apply, (*b*) it is adaptable to either periodic or perpetual inventory procedures, (*c*) it produces an inventory amount for the balance sheet that approximates current replacement cost, (*d*) the flow of cost tends to be consistent with the physical flow of goods, (*e*) it is systematic and rational, and (*f*) it is not subject to manipulation. The fundamental weakness of *Fifo* is that it does not match *current cost* of goods sold with current revenues; rather the oldest unit costs are matched with the current sales revenue (also see Chapter 25). This means that when costs are rising (as is the case with inflation) reported net income will tend to be overstated; and, conversely, when prices are falling reported net income will tend to be understated. Some critics have said this tendency indirectly contributes to the severity of boom and bust conditions. The income tax implications also are serious—when prices are rising, pretax income tends to be overstated; and as a result, there is over-assessment of income taxes and a negative effect on cash flow. On a downswing the opposite prevails.

### LAST-IN, FIRST-OUT

The last-in, first-out *(Lifo)* method of inventory cost flow is based on the concept that the latest unit acquisition cost should be matched with current sales revenue. Consequently, under this method the cost outflows are inverse to the cost inflows. The units remaining in the ending inventory are costed at the oldest unit costs available, and the units in cost of goods sold, or issued, are costed at the newest unit costs available. *Lifo* application requires the use of inventory layers for the different unit costs.

Although the *Lifo* concept is simple, its application often is quite complex, because of the detailed recordkeeping required, the discipline (rules) necessary to prevent inconsistent results and manipulation, and a formidable array of tax regulations that must be followed.

This section will present the *Lifo* concept assuming a specific goods, single product situation.[2] Of course, this simple situation seldom exists in the real world of accounting; and to look at it alone, without consideration of the implementation problems, would give an oversimplified view of this complex subject. Therefore, Part B presents the primary complexities encountered in *Lifo* application.

*Lifo* may be applied with either a periodic or perpetual inventory system. Assuming a *periodic inventory system,* and a physical inventory of units at the end of the period, *Lifo* results would be determined as follows:

*Lifo*—Periodic Inventory System

|  |  |  |
|---|---|---|
| | Goods available (per above) ........................ | $1,120 |
| | Deduct final inventory (300 units per physical inventory count): | |
| Periodic Inventory Computation *(Lifo)* | 200 units @ $1 (oldest costs available; from January 1 inventory) .....................$200 | |
| | 100 units @ $1.10 (next oldest costs available; from January 9 purchase) ...... 110 | |
| | Total Inventory ................................. | 310 |
| | Cost of Goods Sold (or Issues) ............ | $ 810 |

When *Lifo* is applied with *perpetual* inventory procedures, the *issues*

---

[2] This is variously called the *quantity, specific goods,* or *unit Lifo* method of applying the *Lifo* concept; see Part B.

may be costed on the inventory card (*a*) currently throughout the period (i.e., each time there is a withdrawal), or (*b*) only at the end of the period. With respect to *Lifo* the timing of the costing of issues becomes important, since costing currently results in a different inventory valuation and cost of goods sold amount than costing at the end of a period. Costing at the end of the period will give the same results as periodic inventory procedures. The applications of *Lifo* under *perpetual inventory* procedures are shown in Exhibit 9–5 when the issues are costed currently throughout the period; and Exhibit 9–6 shows the issues costed at the end of the period. Note the maintenance of inventory layers for each different unit cost in the Balance column.

The items shown in italics in Exhibit 9–6 were entered at the end of the period. Note that Exhibit 9–6 (costed at end of period) provides the same inventory valuation ($310) as the previous periodic inventory computation. On the other hand, Exhibit 9–5 (costed currently) provides an inventory valuation of $342. The $32 difference occurs because the issues on January 10 and 18 were out of different inventory layers as a result of the difference in the timing in costing issues. The difference between the *cost of issues* on the two records is also $32. From this illustration it is apparent that the *Lifo* inventory valuation costed at the end of the period (but not when costed currently) may be verified readily by pricing the number of units in inventory out of the oldest unit costs.

### *Lifo* Inventory Liquidation

A serious problem under *Lifo* procedures occurs when a company fails to maintain the base year, or "normal" inventory position. This erosion of the base year inventory occurs when usage exceeds acquisitions of an inventory item subsequent to adoption of *Lifo* (i.e., the base year). To illustrate, assume the following:

|  | Units | Unit Cost | Total Cost |
|---|---|---|---|
| Beginning inventory (assumed to be the base year inventory) | 10,000 | $1.00 | $10,000 |
| Purchases | 40,000 | 1.50 | 60,000 |
| Total Available for Sale | 50,000 | | 70,000 |
| Sales (44,000 units, issues on *Lifo* basis) | { 40,000 | 1.50 | 60,000 |
|  | { 4,000 | 1.00 | 4,000 |
|  | 44,000 | | 64,000 |
| Final Inventory | 6,000 | 1.00 | $ 6,000 |

In the above example the company failed to maintain the base year inventory position by 4,000 units. This failure may have been due to—

*a.* Voluntary inventory liquidation. Management may have decided to reduce normal inventory quantity for some reason, such as shortage

**EXHIBIT 9–5**
**Perpetual Inventory Record (*Lifo* illustrated – costed currently)**

| Date | Received | | | Issued or Sold | | | Balance | | |
|------|-------|------|-------|-------|------|-------|-------|------|-------|
| | Units | Unit Cost | Total Cost | Units | Unit Cost | Total Cost | Units | Unit Cost | Total Cost |
| Jan. 1 | | | | | | | 200 | $1.00 | $200 |
| 9 | 300 | $1.10 | $330 | | | | 200 300 | 1.00 1.10 | 200 330 |
| 10 | | | | 300 100 | $1.10 1.00 | $330 100 | 100 | 1.00 | 100 |
| 15 | 400 | 1.16 | 464 | | | | 100 400 | 1.00 1.16 | 100 464 |
| 18 | | | | 300 | 1.16 | 348 | 100 100 | 1.00 1.16 | 100 116 |
| 24 | 100 | 1.26 | 126 | | | | 100 100 100 | 1.00 1.16 1.26 | 100 ⎫ 116 ⎬ 126 ⎭ $342 |

**EXHIBIT 9–6**
**Perpetual Inventory Record (*Lifo* illustrated – costed at end of period)**

| Date | Received | | | Issued or Sold | | | Balance | | |
|------|-------|------|-------|-------|------|-------|-------|------|-------|
| | Units | Unit Cost | Total Cost | Units | Unit Cost | Total Cost | Units | Unit Cost | Total Cost |
| Jan. 1 | | | | | | | 200 | $1.00 | $200 |
| 9 | 300 | $1.10 | $330 | | | | 500 | | |
| 10 | | | | 400* Detail: 100 300 | $1.26 1.16 | $126 348 | 100 | | |
| 15 | 400 | 1.16 | 464 | | | | 500 | | |
| 18 | | | | 300 Detail: 100 200 | 1.16 1.10 | 116 220 | 200 | | |
| 24 | 100 | 1.26 | 126 | | | | 300 Detail: 200 100 | 1.00 1.10 | 200 ⎫ 110 ⎭ $310 |

* Since pricing of issues is delayed until the end of the period, the first issue (400 units) is priced out of the last purchase (100 units at $1.26), and so on.

of liquid funds, anticipation of a decline in prices, or anticipation of an improvement in the product.[3]

b. Involuntary inventory liquidation. Noncontrollable causes such as shortages, strikes, delayed delivery dates, or unexpected demands may have forced the inventory reduction.

As a result of the liquidation of a part of the base inventory, cost of goods sold includes 4,000 units costed at an old cost ($1 per unit) which is matched against current revenue causing a distortion of reported net income. Assuming the inventory liquidation is temporary, should the 4,000 units be costed out at $1 per unit or at some other cost? The problem is further complicated if the 4,000 units are replaced in the next period, say at $1.60 per unit. Should the restoration of the base inventory position be at $1 per unit or at $1.60 per unit? One approach used, when the inventory liquidation is temporary, involves charging Cost of Goods Sold with the replacement cost, crediting Inventory at *Lifo* cost, and crediting the difference to a special account as follows (assuming perpetual inventory procedures):

Cost of goods sold (40,000 @ $1.50) + (4,000 @ $1.60)............66,400
    Inventory (40,000 @ $1.50) + (4,000 @ $1).......................      64,000
    Excess of replacement cost of *Lifo* inventory temporarily
      liquidated (4,000 @ $.60).............................................      2,400

When the liquidated inventory is replaced (base position restored) the following entry is made:

Inventory (4,000 @ $1) ........................................................4,000
Excess of replacement cost of *Lifo* inventory temporarily
    liquidated (4,000 @ $.60) ...................................................2,400
    Accounts payable (4,000 @ $1.60) .....................................      6,400

If the replacement occurs at a price other than $1.60, the inventory amount is affected by the difference. A balance (credit) in the Excess of Replacement Cost of *Lifo* Inventory Temporarily Liquidated should be reported as a special liability because it represents an amount which will have to be spent without a corresponding increase in inventory. There is disagreement on the theoretical validity of this procedure. Some accountants believe it is necessary to protect the integrity of the *Lifo* concept; others view it as income manipulation. As a practical matter, erosion of the base inventory seldom occurs because the IRS usually will disallow *Lifo* for tax purposes if it does occur.

Few companies use *Lifo* for *internal* accounting and control purposes. Most companies using *Lifo* have changed to it from another method for tax and external reporting purposes. Generally, for internal purposes they prefer to continue the method used in the past. For internal purposes, and in the accounts, most companies use either *Fifo*,

---

[3] A major criticism of *Lifo* is that it is subject to profit manipulation, for example, year-end purchasing policy can be used (1) to reduce reported profits by heavy buying, if prices have increased; and (2) to overstate profits by permitting inventories to decline and "old" low prices to be charged to cost of goods sold.

average, standard costs, or variable costing. These results are converted to *Lifo* for income tax purposes and for *external financial reporting*, external to the accounts. In some cases the results of the conversion to *Lifo* are entered in the accounts as a single amount by using an inventory allowance account (Allowance to Reduce Inventory to *Lifo* Basis). Unfortunately, this account is sometimes referred to as a *"Lifo* Reserve."

In those cases where *Lifo* is used for internal purposes and entered in the accounts throughout the period, the issues are almost always costed *currently* because the management cannot await until year-end for internal financial and control reports. Current costing minimizes the *Lifo* impact on inventory and cost of goods sold, whereas costing at the end of the year maximizes its impact. Consequently, the internal results generally are adjusted to an annual *Lifo* effect to attain the maximum tax benefit.

The Internal Revenue Code permits a company to use *Lifo* on the income tax return only if it is also used for its *external financial reports*. However, this does not require that *Lifo* must be used for internal purposes or entered into the accounts.

### Comparison of *Lifo* with *Fifo*

The significant effects of *Lifo* may be emphasized by comparing it with *Fifo*. As long as unit cost prices remain constant, the two methods give the same results; when unit cost prices change materially, the two methods provide significantly different effects on assets (inventories and cash) and net income (costs). Note that the comparative effect will depend upon the direction of the change in unit cost prices. With *rising* prices *Fifo* matches low costs (oldest costs) with increased sales revenue (inflated dollars) and provides an inventory valuation approximating higher current replacement cost, whereas *Lifo* matches high costs (newer costs) with increased sales revenue and provides an inventory valuation on a low-cost (oldest cost) basis. Conversely, with *declining* prices *Fifo* matches high costs (oldest costs) with decreased sales revenue and provides an inventory valuation approximating lower current replacement cost, whereas *Lifo* matches low costs (newer costs) with decreased sales revenue and provides an inventory valuation on a high-cost (oldest cost) basis.

With respect to the *cash flow* effects, when prices are rising *Lifo* results in a lower pretax net income amount and, consequently, less income tax; therefore, cash flow is greater than when *Fifo* is used. These effects can be observed in Exhibit 9–7. The data given in that exhibit assumes rising prices; note in particular the impact of *Lifo* on net income (a negative effect) and on cash inflow (a positive effect).

Because of a continuing worldwide inflationary trend and the pervasiveness of income taxes, an increasing number of companies are shifting to *Lifo*. The primary advantages of *Lifo* generally cited are: (1) it provides a better matching of current costs with current revenue;

**EXHIBIT 9–7**

*Lifo* Compared with *Fifo* — Prices Rising

Basic Data Assumed

Beginning cash balance.....................................$ 2,000
Beginning inventory balance, 5,000 units @.........     5 (base inventory)
Purchases during period,     5,000 units @.........     7
Sales,                       5,000 units @.........    18
Expenses (excluding income taxes) .................. 35,000
Income tax rate, 40%

Comparative Results

| | First-In, First-Out | | | Last-In, First-Out | | | Increase (Decrease) from |
|---|---|---|---|---|---|---|---|
| | Units | @ | Amount | Units | @ | Amount | Fifo to Lifo |
| Income Statement: | | | | | | | |
| Sales.............................. | 5,000 | $18 | $90,000 | 5,000 | $18 | $90,000 | $ -0- |
| Cost of goods sold ......... | 5,000 | 5 | 25,000 | 5,000 | 7 | 35,000 | 10,000 |
| Gross margin .................. | | | 65,000 | | | 55,000 | (10,000) |
| Expenses........................ | | | 35,000 | | | 35,000 | -0- |
| Pretax income .............. | | | 30,000 | | | 20,000 | (10,000) |
| Income taxes (@ 40%)...... | | | 12,000 | | | 8,000 | (4,000) |
| Net Income .................... | | | $18,000 | | | $12,000 | $ (6,000) |
| | | | | | | | |
| Balance Sheet (limited to above transactions): | | | | | | | |
| Cash (assuming all transactions were cash) ...... | | | $10,000 | | | $14,000 | $ 4,000 |
| Inventory ....................... | | | 35,000 | | | 25,000 | (10,000) |
| Net Effect (same as difference in net income) ........... | | | | | | | $ (6,000) |

(2) in periods of inflation, it results in lower income taxes, hence greater cash inflows; (3) it reflects the usual pricing policy of an enterprise to raise selling prices when replacement cost increases even though the goods already on hand are not yet sold; and (4) it is systematic.

The primary arguments generally cited against *Lifo* are: (1) it understates assets — the inventory on the balance sheet is costed at old, out-of-date cost; (2) it does not correctly match replacement cost with revenue; (3) it is subject to manipulation — profits can be manipulated by changing the usual purchasing patterns (voluntary inventory liquidation); (4) it is subject to involuntary inventory liquidation; (5) cost flows do not correspond to the physical flow of goods; and (6) it presents too many complexities and variations in application.

## MISCELLANEOUS INVENTORY FLOW METHODS

Numerous methods for determining the cost of inventory, in addition to those discussed above, have been proposed. Except in a few unique situations, none of these has been accepted under generally accepted accounting principles for external financial reporting purposes. However, some of them are used for *internal cost accounting* purposes. As background, several miscellaneous methods are briefly reviewed in this section.

### Next-In, First-Out

*Nifo* refers to the concept that cost of goods sold should be costed at the unit cost anticipated for the next purchase of a like volume. The concept attempts to precisely match cost of goods sold with the actual cost of replacing the goods sold. It is maintained that *Lifo* fails to precisely match replacement cost with current revenues since the method employs the cost of the latest purchase *prior* to the actual sale. *Nifo* has not received even limited general acceptance.

### Cost-of-Last-Purchase

*Colp*, as a method of inventory costing, has been proposed as a way to overcome the inherent lag in the usual *Lifo* procedures. Under this method *all issues* are priced at the last actual purchase price regardless of the number of units involved. Under certain conditions relating to price change and quantities, this method conceivably could produce a negative inventory value. For this and other obvious reasons it has received little attention.

### Base Stock Method

The base stock (or normal stock) method is generally viewed as the predecessor of the *Lifo* method. The method assumes that there is a normal or base stock of goods that should be maintained at all times. The base stock represents a permanent commitment of resources, similar to a fixed asset, that is costed at a normal price which is viewed as the original cost — usually the lowest cost experienced by the company. Maintenance of the base inventory at a constant amount is intended to avoid the problem of inventory profits. Goods must be acquired above the minimum base stock for operational purposes. These goods are viewed as temporary increments and are recorded at cost; issues should be costed out of the increment on a *Lifo* basis, although *Fifo* or average sometimes is used for practical reasons. The base stock method is illustrated in Exhibit 9–8.

The purpose of the base stock method is similar to that of last-in, first-out, that is, the matching of current costs with current revenues. The permanency assumed with respect to the base stock provides another avenue for justification. The method is not generally used because of the arbitrary nature of both the quantity and unit values of the assumed base stock; essentially similar results may be obtained under *Lifo;* it is subject to manipulation through selective purchasing; and it is not permitted for income tax purposes.

EXHIBIT 9-8
**Base Stock Inventory Method**

|  | Units | Unit Cost | Amount |
|---|---|---|---|
| Base stock............................................ | 10,000 | $1.00 | $10,000 |
| Extra stock............................................ | 2,000 | 1.20 | 2,400 |
| Total Beginning Inventory.............. | 12,000 |  | 12,400 |
| Purchases: |  |  |  |
| First..................................................... | 2,000 | 1.30 | 2,600 |
| Second ............................................... | 6,000 | 1.40 | 8,400 |
| Total Available ............................ | 20,000 |  | 23,400 |
| Ending inventory |  |  |  |
| (11,000 units per count): |  |  |  |
| Base stock......................................... | 10,000 | 1.00 | 10,000 |
| Extra stock......................................... | 1,000 | 1.20 | 1,200 |
| Total........................................... | 11,000 |  | 11,200 |
| Cost of Goods Sold........................ | 9,000 |  | $12,200 |

## STANDARD COSTS FOR INVENTORY

In manufacturing entities using a standard cost system, the inventories are valued, recorded, and reported for internal purposes on the basis of a standard unit cost. The standard cost approximates an ideal or expected cost; and its use prevents the inflation of inventory values by excluding losses and expenses due to inefficiency, waste, and abnormal conditions. Under this method the *differences* between actual cost and standard cost are recorded in separate variance accounts which are written off in the current period as a loss or *period cost* rather than being capitalized in inventory. Standard costs may be applied to raw materials, work in process, and finished goods inventories. To illustrate the utilization of standard costs for raw materials, assume a particular company has just adopted standard cost procedures and that the initial inventory is zero. During the current period the company makes two purchases and one issue and records them as follows:

1. To record the purchase of 10,000 units of raw material at $1.10 actual cost; standard cost has been established at $1:

```
Raw materials (10,000 units @ $1).....................................10,000
Raw materials purchase price variation
    (10,000 units @ $.10) .....................................................  1,000
        Accounts payable (10,000 units @ $1.10)....................          11,000
```

2. To record issuance of 8,000 units of raw material to factory for processing:

```
Material in process  .........................................................8,000
        Raw materials (8,000 units @ $1) ....................................          8,000
```

3. To record the purchase of 2,000 units of raw material at $.95:

```
Raw materials (2,000 units @ $1)  .......................................2,000
Raw materials purchase price variation
    (2,000 units @ $.05)....................................................              100
        Accounts payable (2,000 units @ $.95) .........................          1,900
```

Results for the period:

| | | | |
|---|---|---|---|
| Purchases at actual cost: | | | |
| 10,000 units @ $1.10 | $11,000 | | |
| 2,000 units @ .95 | 1,900 | | |
| Total | | $12,900 | |
| Issues at standard cost: | | | |
| 8,000 units @ $1 | $ 8,000 | | |
| Final inventory at standard cost: | | | |
| 4,000 units @ $1 | 4,000 | 12,000 | |
| Raw Materials Purchase Price Variation (debit — charged against current income as a *loss*) | | $ 900 | |

Under the procedures illustrated above for raw material there would be no need to consider inventory flow methods such as *Lifo, Fifo,* and average, since only one cost — the standard cost — appears in the records. In addition, perpetual inventory records could be maintained in *units only*, since all issues and inventory valuations are at the constant standard price. Clearly standard cost represents a departure from the cost principle as currently interpreted. We have included this brief discussion because for external reporting purposes, standard cost results generally are not used except in special circumstances. Therefore, the inventory is restated for external reports according to one of the generally accepted methods discussed above. Standard costs are widely used for *internal management* planning and control. A detailed discussion of standard cost procedures is beyond the scope of this book and can be found in any complete cost accounting textbook.

### Variable or Direct Cost for Inventory

For *internal management* planning and control purposes, the concept of variable or direct costing is often used in manufacturing companies. Under this concept, the fixed and variable costs are distinctly segregated. This separation is especially useful for internal management planning and control, particularly in manufacturing situations. One important aspect of this concept is that the cost of goods manufactured is measured as the sum of the variable costs only; that is, the sum of direct materials, direct labor, and variable manufacturing overhead. All fixed costs, including fixed manufacturing overhead, are treated as period costs; that is, they are deducted from revenues of the period rather than being capitalized and carried forward in inventory (and later reported as a part of cost of goods sold).

Valuation of inventories at only variable production costs, although highly useful for internal management purposes, is not generally acceptable for external financial reporting purposes nor can it be used for tax purposes except in special circumstances. Consequently, for external reporting and tax purposes, companies using variable costing for internal purposes convert the inventory and cost of goods sold to "actual" by using methods such as dollar-value *Lifo* (see Part B).

## SELECTION OF A FLOW METHOD

The trend in use of the several inventory cost flow methods, for external reporting and tax purposes, is indicated in the following tabulation taken from AICPA, *Accounting Trends and Techniques, 1975* (p. 114):

**Inventory Flow Methods (based on 600 companies)**

|  | 1974 | 1973 | 1972 | 1971 | 1970 |
|---|---|---|---|---|---|
| First-in, first-out | 375 | 394 | 377 | 333 | 292 |
| Average cost | 236 | 235 | 242 | 220 | 203 |
| Last-in, first-out | 303 | 150 | 150 | 144 | 146 |
| Standard costs | 49 | 52 | 54 | 36 | 30 |
| Retail method | 35 | 39 | 35 | 31 | 27 |
| Specific or "actual" cost | 24 | 23 | 26 | 15 | 17 |
| Accumulated production cost | 19 | 18 | 25 | 24 | 23 |
| Replacement or current cost | 9 | 10 | 8 | 13 | 16 |
| Other | 4 | 6 | 3 | 6 | 11 |
| Totals* | 1054 | 927 | 920 | 822 | 765 |

* Some companies use more than one method.

Selection of an inventory flow method, or whether to change from one method to another, presents a complex problem. Although income measurement should be the primary consideration, it is difficult to realistically avoid considering income tax effects. With respect to income measurement, it is also unrealistic to disregard the problem of inventory profits. In periods of rising prices, *Lifo* tends to minimize inventory profits whereas *Fifo* tends to maximize them. The tendency to emphasize the income statement, the relatively high inflation trend, and tax effects have prompted a number of companies in recent years to switch to *Lifo*. With respect to the favorable income tax effect of *Lifo* during periods of inflation, one must recognize that it would reverse with deflation. Because of the complexities involved and the potentials for manipulation, the Internal Revenue Code and Regulations pose a formidable array of rules governing *Lifo* for income tax purposes. On the other hand, the diverse economic impacts in the long run versus the short run and the negative impact of *Lifo* during periods of inflation on income, EPS, and certain other ratios, which may cause the price/earnings multiple to be less favorable than otherwise, has caused many companies to consider a switch to *Lifo* to be undesirable for them.

## PART B—COMPLEXITIES IN APPLYING *LIFO*

*Lifo* adheres to the cost principle. Major accounting firms consistently report that *Lifo* is generally viewed as a cost method for income tax and external reporting purposes and that most companies use either *Fifo* or average in their accounts for internal cost accounting and management purposes. The Internal Revenue Code (Section 472 c) dictates that any company using *Lifo* for tax purposes must also use it for *ex-*

*ternal reports.* This means that companies using other methods in the accounting system must convert those results to *Lifo* external to the accounts.[4] Application of *Lifo* often poses relatively complex conversion problems when there are diverse operations and numerous items in inventory. Particular problems also are encountered when a company decides to change to *Lifo* from another method for tax and financial reporting purposes.

*Lifo* application problems are discussed in the following order:

1. Initial adoption of *Lifo.*
2. Continuing application of *Lifo* after adoption.
   a. Quantity of goods method—
      (1) By single items.
      (2) By multiple inventory pools.
   b. Dollar-value method (for either single or multiple inventory pools).
      (1) Double extension.
      (2) Link chain.
   c. Indexing.
3. *Lifo* applied to interim statements.
4. *Lifo* reserves.

## INITIAL ADOPTION OF *LIFO*

Income tax regulations permit taxpayers to use *Lifo* for all or part of the total inventory of goods (i.e., for manufacturers and processors—raw materials, work in process, finished goods; for retailers and wholesalers —merchandise for sale). In the typical *Lifo* situation, the company has changed from some other method to *Lifo* for tax and external reporting purposes, although a few companies have changed in the opposite direction. The switch to *Lifo* involves a change in accounting method as described in *APB Opinion No. 20* ("Accounting Changes"). Paragraph 20 of that *Opinion* requires that the *cumulative* effect of a change in accounting principle be shown between the captions extraordinary items and net income. However, paragraph 26 of that *Opinion* specifically rules out measurement of the cumulative effect when the change is *to Lifo* (but not the reverse) because the prior period differences are almost always not determinable. The total effect of adopting *Lifo* is reported as an addition to *cost of goods sold* in the year of change. The following is a typical footnote for the year of change:

> At the beginning of the current year, the company changed its inventory measurement basis to cost applied on the last-in, first-out method. In prior years, inventories were measured on the first-in, first-out method, and stated at lower of cost or market. Had the *Fifo* method been used during the current year, inventory would have been $10,000,000 higher than reported in the attached statements for 1975. The net effect of the change in 1975 was to reduce net income (after tax) by approximately $4,800,000 ($.30 per

---

[4] Since *Lifo* at year-end is different than *Lifo* priced currently, conversion even in this case is usually done.

share). Proforma effects of retroactive application are not realistically determinable.

The management believes that the newly adopted inventory method will attain a better matching of current expenses with current revenues.[5]

When there is a change to *Lifo*, the *base year* is the year in which the change is made; and the *Lifo base cost* for the initial inventory, that is, the *base inventory*, at the start of the base year is the ending inventory (adjusted to cost regardless of the prior method used) carried over from the prior year (Reg. 1.472–2). This means that adjustments to the prior ending inventory, to lower of cost or market, must be restored (LCM is not applicable to *Lifo*) as well as any other write-downs.

For illustrative purposes throughout Part B, the inventory data for Tye Company given in Exhibit 9–9 will be used. In this example, the base year would be 19B and the base inventory amount would be $6,100 at the start of 19B. For the above reasons, no "adjustment" for this accounting change would be made in the accounts or reported on the financial statements for 19B.

**EXHIBIT 9–9**

**Tye Company — Illustrative Data (inventory change to *Lifo*)**

Situation: a. *Fifo* was used in prior years and through 19A for all purposes.
      b. *Lifo* was adopted at start of 19B for (1) income tax purposes and (2) external financial purposes.
      c. *Fifo* continued in the accounts and for internal management purposes.

Inventory Data per Accounts (*Fifo* basis)

| | Item A | | | Item B | | | Total Amount |
|---|---|---|---|---|---|---|---|
| | Units | Cost | Total | Units | Cost | Total | |
| Year 19A: | | | | | | | |
| Ending inventory: | | | | | | | |
| Layer 1 | 1,000 | $1.00 | $1,000 | 2,000 | $2.00 | $ 4,000 | |
| Layer 2 | | | | 500 | 2.20 | 1,100 | |
| | 1,000 | $1.00 | $1,000 | 2,500 | $2.04 | $ 5,100 | $6,100 |
| | | | | | | | |
| Year 19B: | | | | | | | |
| Purchases | 3,000 | $1.20 | $3,600 | 4,000 | $2.50 | $10,000 | |
| Sales | (2,800) | | | (3,500) | | | |
| Ending inventory: | | | | | | | |
| Fifo | 1,200 | 1.20 | 1,440 | 3,000 | 2.50 | 7,500 | $8,940 |
| | | | | | | | |
| Year 19C: | | | | | | | |
| Purchases | 3,300 | 1.30 | 4,290 | 4,200 | 2.60 | 10,920 | |
| Sales | (3,200) | | | (4,200) | | | |
| Ending inventory: | | | | | | | |
| Fifo | 1,300 | 1.30 | 1,690 | 3,000 | 2.60 | 7,800 | $9,490 |

---

[5] "Accounting Changes Related to the Cost of Inventory," FASB *Interpretation No. 1*, "In applying *APB Opinion No. 20*, preferability among accounting principles shall be determined on the basis of whether the new principle constitutes an improvement in financial reporting and not on the basis of the income tax effect alone."

Full-disclosure requirements, and limitations, in respect to the *initial adoption* of *Lifo* include:

1. Explanation of the change and the basis for the change.
2. Basis used for determining the inventory amounts.
3. Beginning and ending inventory amounts.
4. Excess of replacement or current cost over the *Lifo* amount.
5. For the base year *only*, and only by footnote, the dollar inventory difference between *Lifo* and the alternative method previously used and proforma income and earnings per share amounts for the method.

The IRS specified the last as a *constraint* because some companies, while taking the tax benefit, attempt to mitigate the adverse impact of *Lifo* on net income and earnings per share, by publishing and announcing results of the alternative inventory basis with a view to influencing investors. Violation of this constraint will result in disallowance of *Lifo* by the IRS; the objection is to the inconsistency in reporting on one inventory basis *(Lifo)* to the IRS and on another basis *(Fifo)* to the public.

## CONTINUING APPLICATION OF *LIFO*

After adopting *Lifo* for income tax and external reporting purposes, several methods of *Lifo* application are acceptable. These several methods make *Lifo* feasible for practically all taxpayers. Fundamentally, there are three *Lifo* application methods: (1) quantity of goods *Lifo*, (2) dollar-value *Lifo*, and (3) retail *Lifo* (discussed in Chapter 10).

### Quantity of Goods *Lifo*

This method (often called specific goods *Lifo* or unit *Lifo*) has two approaches known as (1) the single-item approach, and (2) the multiple pools approach.

*Single-Item Approach.* The single-item approach was illustrated in Part A of this chapter. It requires that the *quantity* of each item or product in the ending inventory be determined either by physical inventory count or from perpetual inventory records; then unit costs are applied in *Lifo* order, in the manner shown in Exhibit 9–6, to derive the *Lifo* inventory amount. Normally, the *Lifo* inventory amount will consist of a *base Lifo inventory* amount plus subsequent incremental *Lifo* layers for each new price. To illustrate, the *Lifo* ending inventories for Tye Company (data given in Exhibit 9–9) are shown in Exhibit 9–10.

The single-item approach is used in small businesses and in situations where there are a small number of different inventory items or products. In larger and more complex situations, the detailed recordkeeping usually is considered to be too burdensome, except in cases where only a few major items of inventory are on the *Lifo* basis.

*Multiple Pools Approach.* The multiple pools approach involves grouping of "substantially identical" items into inventory pools. Each

**EXHIBIT 9–10**

*Lifo*—Quantity of Goods Method, Single-Item Approach

Ending Inventory (*Lifo* basis)

| | Item A | | | Item B | | | |
|---|---|---|---|---|---|---|---|
| | Units | Cost | Amount | Units | Cost | Amount | Total Amount |
| **Year 19B:** | | | | | | | |
| Layer 1.................. | 1,000 | $1.00 | $1,000 | 2,000 | $2.00 | $4,000 | |
| Layer 2.................. | 200 | 1.20 | 240 | 500 | 2.20 | 1,100 | |
| Layer 3.................. | | | | 500 | 2.50 | 1,250 | |
| Total.............. | 1,200 | | $1,240 | 3,000 | | $6,350 | $7,590 |
| **Year 19C:** | | | | | | | |
| Layer 1.................. | 1,000 | 1.00 | $1,000 | 2,000 | 2.00 | $4,000 | |
| Layer 2.................. | 200 | 1.20 | 240 | 500 | 2.20 | 1,100 | |
| Layer 3.................. | 100 | 1.30 | 130 | 500 | 2.50 | 1,250 | |
| Total.............. | 1,300 | | $1,370 | 3,000 | | $6,350 | $7,720 |

pool then is treated as if it were a single inventory item. For the beginning inventory (the base layer when *Lifo* was adopted), the units in a pool are assumed to have been acquired at the same time so that the unit cost for the beginning inventory can be obtained by dividing the total number of units into the total inventory cost. The *ending Lifo inventory* each period, to the extent that the number of units do not exceed the beginning inventory, is obtained by multiplying the number of units remaining in inventory by the average unit cost at the start of the current period. The number of units in the ending inventory in excess of the number at the start (an inventory increment or layer) is valued by multiplying the excess number by (1) the average cost of purchases during the period; or (2) if the purchases during the current year are less than units sold, by price layers related to the units in order of acquisition (i.e., *Lifo* order). The ending inventory then is the base layer plus the incremental layers.

To illustrate, assume for Tye Company, Exhibit 9–9, that the two products are *substantially identical*. Therefore, under this assumption, the two items can be treated as an individual inventory pool. The ending inventories for this pool (let's call it Pool No. 1) would be computed as shown in Exhibit 9–11. Any remaining pools (such as Pool Nos. 2, 3, etc.) comprising the inventory, computed in this same manner, would be summed to determine the total amount of the ending *Lifo* inventory. Compared with the single-item approach, the multiple pools approach reduces the computations by approximately one half. This demonstrates the primary advantage of the multiple pools approach.

The multiple pools approach, although less burdensome clerically than the single-item approach, is not widely used because generally there are a number of pools with a consequent heavy clerical burden. Also, it does not resolve the problems of changes in the *mix* of items and products in the inventory.

**EXHIBIT 9–11**
*Lifo* — Quantity of Goods Method, Multiple Pools Approach

Ending Inventory (Lifo basis)

|  | Year 19B | | Year 19C | |
|---|---|---|---|---|
| Base layer ..........................a. | 3,500 @ $1.74 = $6,100 | | c. 3,500 @ $1.74 = $6,100 | |
| Incremental layer ..............b. | 700        1.94 =    1,360 | | 700        1.94 =    1,360 | |
|  | | | d.    100        2.03 =       203 | |
| Total Inventory............ | 4,200 | $7,460 | 4,300 | $7,663 |

Computations:

a. $6,100 ÷ 3,500 = $1.7429 (average).

b.  3,000 units @ $1.20 = $ 3,600
    4,000 units @   2.50 =  10,000
    ‾‾‾‾‾                ‾‾‾‾‾‾‾‾
    7,000                  $13,600

    $13,600 ÷ 7,000 = $1.9429 (average)

c. From 19A ending inventory.

d. 3,300 units @ $1.30 = $ 4,290
   4,200 units @  2.60 =  10,920
   ‾‾‾‾‾               ‾‾‾‾‾‾‾‾
   7,500                 $15,210

   $15,210 ÷ 7,500 = $2.03 (average)

## Changes in Items (Product Lines) in *Lifo* Inventory

Some industries commonly experience a constant change in the inventory mix — some products are dropped, others are added, and technological changes cause a continuing change in item or product mix content of the inventory over a period of years. In the quantity of goods method, the change in mix would cause the old *Lifo* inventory costs (usually low relative to current costs) to be moved out to cost of goods sold and replaced with later inventory costs which are usually much higher. To illustrate, a company may experience the following *Lifo* inventory situation over a five-year period:

| | | *Lifo* Inventory Unit Costs | | | |
|---|---|---|---|---|---|
| Product | 19A | 19B | 19C | 19D | 19E |
| A..............| $1.00 | $1.20 | Discontinued | | |
| B..............| 3.50 | 3.75 | $4.00 | Discontinued | |
| C..............| 2.80 | 2.90 | 3.00 | $3.15 | $3.30 |
| D..............| | *4.00 | 4.18 | 4.30 | 4.40 |
| E..............| | | *5.50 | 5.60 | 5.80 |

\* New products.

Clearly, with no change in quantity of goods, the *Lifo* inventory in dollars would have changed and the old (low) costs converted to more current (high) costs. The *quantity method* gives this result; however, the dollar-value method tends to overcome this problem, as explained later.

The quantity of goods *Lifo* method (including the single items and multiple pools approaches) is not widely used because (*a*) it is burdensome in complex situations, (*b*) the impact of change in technology and product mix is great, and (*c*) it lacks flexibility in avoiding the drastic impact of inventory invasions, particularly the base inventory.

**Dollar-Value** *Lifo*

This method was developed to overcome, as much as possible, the basic deficiencies of the quantity of goods method discussed above. Originally, only the quantity of goods method, single-item approach, was used for *Lifo;* however, because of its great clerical burden, the multiple pools approach evolved. Following that, dollar-value *Lifo* developed. Fundamentally, in the dollar-value *Lifo* method, the base inventory and any subsequent incremental layers are measured directly in terms of *dollars* rather than in quantities of *units*.

The dollar-value *Lifo* method uses the concepts of inventory pools and *index numbers*. This method has two approaches generally identified as (1) double-extension and (2) link-chain. These two approaches have common characteristics; their differences reflect adaptations to accommodate peculiarities in different situations. IRS regulations require that the double-extension approach be used in all cases except where it is clearly unrealistic. Use of the link-chain approach must be clearly preferable in the particular situation before it can be used. Consequently, dollar-value, double-extension *Lifo* is used in most situations.

Significantly, the dollar-value method enlarges the concept of an *inventory pool*. Recall that under the quantity of goods, multiple pools approach, an inventory pool could encompass *only* items that are *substantially identical*. In contrast, the dollar-value method permits an inventory pool to encompass all items that are characterized by *similarity*. Similarity is defined as a "natural business unit" pool which would consist of a product line, or related product lines, where raw materials, manufacturing, and sales distributions are integrated or related. Separate plants manufacturing similar products would constitute a natural business unit. A pool would include the raw materials, work in process, and finished goods inventories. Thus, the degree of inventory aggregation under the dollar-value method is very broad compared with the quantity of goods method. This aggregation of inventory pools significantly reduces the clerical burdens involved and, in addition, better copes with the disturbing impacts of changing product mix and technology. The level of aggregation thus provides a significant advantage of dollar-value *Lifo*.

Other than for computation of the index, the dollar-value method does not focus on inventory quantities of physical goods, but rather on inventory dollars; therefore, the computations require that each *Lifo* inventory pool be costed at both *base year dollar costs* and *current period dollar costs*. When the dollar total of the ending inventory at base year costs exceeds the dollar total of the beginning inventory at base costs, an inventory increment or layer has been added. If the difference is less, inventory *liquidation* has occurred. The inventory increment, stated at base year cost, must be converted, by using *appropriate index numbers*, to current year cost. If inventory is later decreased, the reductions are taken from the most recent increments or layers.

The index numbers used in dollar-value *Lifo* computations are critical because they materially affect the results. Tax regulations and generally accepted accounting principles require that a price index be used that is specific to the inventory pool as opposed to an external index or a general price index.[6] This means that an internal price index must be computed each period based upon the change in costs as reflected in the inventory and purchase records of the company. The internal price index is computed as follows:

$$\frac{\text{Ending Inventory for the Period at Current Year Costs}}{\text{Ending Inventory for the Period at Base Year Costs}} = \frac{\text{Price Index for}}{\text{the Current Year}}$$

This index number and the internal index numbers for prior years are used to convert the ending inventory to the *Lifo* basis.

Dollar-value *Lifo* computations are complicated because they involve two distinct phases that may be summarized as follows:

*Phase A*—Computation of an internal index for the current year that is specific to the inventory pool:

    Step 1. Determine the base year inventory in dollars; that is, the inventory value at the date of adoption of *Lifo*. This base inventory is maintained permanently if at all possible.

    Step 2. As the denominator for the index calculation, cost the ending inventory for the current period *at base year costs*.

    Step 3. As the numerator for the index calculation, cost the ending inventory for the current period at *current year costs*.

    Step 4. Compute the internal price index for the current year by dividing the results of step 3 by step 2.

*Phase B*—Computation of *Lifo* inventory by application of index numbers:

    Step 5. Convert the ending inventory layers, priced at base year costs, to the ending inventory layers at *Lifo* cost by applying the index number applicable to each layer.

These two phases are illustrated subsequently. They are applied with both the double-extension approach and the link-chain approach, on the basis of either:

a. *A single pool*—A single pool is used for the entire company when (1) the company is a manufacturer or processor, and (2) overall operations constitute a "natural business unit." Thus, an automobile manufacturer may use a single pool that would encompass raw materials, component parts, work in process, and finished goods (as if it were one big inventory item).

b. *Multiple pools*—Each pool encompasses a group of inventory items that are *similar* in respect to raw materials, manufacturing, and distribution. A separate inventory pool is formed which corresponds

---

[6] Two exceptions to this requirement are explained in a subsequent section—Indexing.

to the "natural business" *subunits* of the company. Manufacturers may use either single pool or multiple pools; however, retailers, wholesalers, and jobbers must use multiple pools. For example, a large department store may have separate inventory pools for mens clothing, ladies clothing, home appliances, and so on.

Obviously, single pool, because of the higher degree of aggregation, generally is preferred to multiple pools where there is a choice.

*Dollar-Value Method, Double-Extension Lifo Approach.* Double extension, as a designation, is based upon the fact that under dollar-value *Lifo*

**EXHIBIT 9–12**
*Lifo* **Inventory—Dollar-Value Method, Double-Extension Approach**

Phase A—Computation of Internal Index for Current Year

Step 1. Base inventory when *Lifo* adopted (at base year costs):
Beginning of base year (19B):

| | | | |
|---|---|---|---|
| Item A | 1,000 @ $1.00 | $1,000 |
| Item B | 2,500    2.04 | 5,100 |
| Total Base Inventory | | $6,100 |

Step 2. Ending inventory at base year costs:

| | Year End 19B | | Year End 19C | |
|---|---|---|---|---|
| Item A | 1,200 @ $1.00 | $1,200 | 1,300 @ $1.00 | $1,300 |
| Item B | 3,000    2.04 | 6,120 | 3,000    2.04 | 6,120 |
| Total Ending Inventory at Base Year Costs | | $7,320 | | $7,420 |

Step 3. Ending inventory at current year costs:

| | | |
|---|---|---|
| Item A ($3,600 ÷ 3,000 = $1.20) | 1,200 @ $1.20 | $1,440 |
| Item B ($10,000 ÷ 4,000 = $2.50) | 3,000    2.50 | 7,500 |
| 19B—Total Ending Inventory at Current Costs | | $8,940 |
| Item A ($4,290 ÷ 3,300 = $1.30) | 1,300 @ $1.30 | $1,690 |
| Item B ($10,920 ÷ 4,200 = $2.60) | 3,000    2.60 | 7,800 |
| 19C—Total Ending Inventory at Current Costs | | $9,490 |

Step 4. Current year index:
Current Year Costs ÷ Base Year Costs ......$8,940 ÷ $7,320 = 1.2213
$9,490 ÷ $7,420 = 1.278976

Phase B—Computation of Ending *Lifo* Inventory Amount

| Step 5. | Ending Inventory at Base Year Costs | Index (from Step 4) | Ending Inventory at Lifo Cost |
|---|---|---|---|
| End of 19B: | | | |
| Base year beginning inventory | $6,100 | 1.0000 | $6,100 |
| Incremental layer: 19B ($7,320 − $6,100) | 1,220 | 1.2213 | 1,490 |
| Ending inventory at *Lifo* | $7,320 | | $7,590 |
| End of 19C: | | | |
| Base year beginning inventory | $6,100 | 1.0000 | $6,100 |
| Incremental layers: 19B (from 19B) | 1,220 | 1.2213 | 1,490 |
| 19C ($7,420 − $7,320) | 100 | 1.278976 | 128 |
| Ending Inventory at *Lifo* | $7,420 | | $7,718 |

the ending inventory is double costed (or double priced); that is, in base year dollars and in current year dollars. This requires that an internal price index specific to the inventory be computed (Phase A computation in Exhibit 9–12). Double extension is the basic dollar-value approach; the link-chain approach is a short-cut adaptation suitable only for special situations.

Double extension, for a single pool, is illustrated and explained in Exhibit 9–12 for Tye Company (basic data given in Exhibit 9–9).

In Exhibit 9–12, an inventory incremental layer was added each year. The annual increment to the ending *Lifo* inventory was valued on the basis of the most recent purchase cost as reflected by the current year index. Alternatively, use of the earliest purchase or the average purchase cost during the current year is permitted for tax purposes.

### Inventory Liquidation

Frequently there will be full or partial *inventory liquidation* (or invasion) of one or more of the incremental layers. Liquidation should come from the most recent incremental layers. To illustrate, let's adapt the above illustration with the assumption that 19C sales for Item A were 3,500 units; this would leave 1,000 units of Item A in the 19C ending inventory — a liquidation of the inventory of the prior year by 200 units of Product A. In this situation, steps 2 through 4 for 19C would be as follows:

Steps 2, 3, and 4:

|  | *Step 2 — At Base Year Cost* | *Step 3 — At Current Period Cost* |
|---|---|---|
| Item A | 1,000 @ $1.00 = $1,000 | 1,000 @ $1.30 = $1,300 |
| Item B | 3,000      2.04 = 6,120 | 3,000      2.60 = 7,800 |
| Total | $7,120 | $9,100 |

Step 4 — index: $9,100 ÷ $7,120 = 1.278.

Step 5. Calculation of the ending *Lifo* inventory using the following indexes:

|  | *Ending Inventory at Base Year Cost* | *Index* | *Ending Inventory at Lifo Value* |
|---|---|---|---|
| Year 19C: | | | |
| Base cost (at base date) | $6,100 | 1.0000 | $6,100 |
| 19B increment ($1,220 − $200*) | 1,020 | 1.2213 | 1,246 |
|  | $7,120 | | $7,346 |

| * Liquidation: | 19B | $7,320 |
|---|---|---|
|  | 19C | 7,120 |
|  |  | $ 200 |

Observe that the liquidation is taken from the most recent layer and the index is applied for the year that the increment was added to inventory rather than the 19C index.

### Change in Product Mix

This problem was discussed previously (page 385). With the dollar-value method, when a new item is added to the product line (and hence to inventory), a *reconstructed* cost for it is established as the base cost at (a) what the item would have cost at the base date (based upon base year price lists, etc.); or (b) if the item did not exist at that date, the first cost after the base date that can be reconstructed; or (c) if no prior cost can be determined, then the cost at the date that the item was first stocked for use or sale. To illustrate, let's adapt the data for Tye Company for 19C. Assume Item A was completely sold and discontinued during 19C, that Item C was added to the line, and the following additional information:

Ending inventory, 19C:

| Item | Units | Current Unit Cost | Base Year Cost |
|------|-------|-------------------|----------------|
| A (discontinued) ............ | -0- | -0- | $1.00 |
| B (continued) .............. | 3,000 | $2.60 | 2.04 (as before) |
| C (new product) ............ | 2,000 | 1.10 | .80 (Reconstructed to base date) |

Steps 2 through 4, for this situation, would be (disregard the inventory liquidation example):

| Item | Step 2 — At Base Year Cost | Step 3 — At Current Period Cost |
|------|-----------------------------|----------------------------------|
| A (discontinued)... | | |
| B ..................... | 3,000 @ $2.04 = $6,120 | 3,000 @ $2.60 = $ 7,800 |
| C ..................... | 2,000 @ .80 = 1,600 | 2,000 @ 1.10 = 2,200 |
| | $7,720 | $10,000 |

Step 4. Index for 19C: $10,000 ÷ $7,720 = 1.295.

Step 5. Calculation of ending *Lifo* inventory using the indexes:

| | Ending Inventory at Base Year Cost | Index | Ending Inventory at Lifo Value |
|------|-------------------------------------|-------|--------------------------------|
| Year 19C: | | | |
| Base cost (at base date) ............ | $6,100 | 1.000 | $6,100 |
| 19B increment (as before) ......... | 1,220 | 1.2213 | 1,490 |
| 19C increment ($7,720 − $7,320)............................. | 400 | 1.295 | 518 |
| Total ............................... | $7,720 | | $8,108 |

The reconstructed base year cost prevents the adverse product-mix impact on the *Lifo* inventory amount. This is a distinct, and significant, advantage of the dollar-value method (for both the double-extension and link-chain approaches).

There are other problems such as damaged or obsolete goods and erosion of the base year inventory (which usually causes disallowance of the *Lifo* method by the IRS). However, the preceding discussions are intended to cover the basic application procedures. The dollar-value, double-extension approach, applied on a single-pool basis is extremely flexible and tends to maximize the *Lifo* impact.

Application of the dollar-value, multiple pools approach is identical with that illustrated above. The same procedures are applied to each separate pool, and the results of the separate computations are summed to derive the total *Lifo* inventory.

*Dollar-Value Method, Link-Chain Approach.* The link-chain approach was developed to better cope with the dual problems of (1) changes in items or product mix, and (2) rapid technological changes. These changes may exert a significant negative impact on *Lifo* inventory results. Although the double-extension approach partially adjusts for these changes, the link-chain approach goes farther in that direction. Application of the link-chain approach is illustrated in Exhibit 9–13.[7]

The link-chain approach involves the same two phases as illustrated above for the double-extension approach. However, the current year index is computed differently and a *cumulative index* is computed. The current year index is computed as follows:

$$\frac{\text{Ending Inventory for the Period at Current Year Costs}}{\text{Ending Inventory for the Period at Beginning of the Year Costs}} = \frac{\text{Index for the}}{\text{Current year}}$$

Thus, rather than being an index from the base year costs to current year costs (as is the case with the double-extension method) the index represents the change in costs for the current year only.

A cumulative index is used for converting the inventory to *Lifo;* the cumulative index is computed for each year by multiplying the index for the current year (above) by the cumulative index for the prior year. This linking together of the two ratios is the basis for the designation "link chain." Computation of the index for the current year and the cumulative index for the year is illustrated in Exhibit 9–13.

The ending inventory at current year prices is then divided by the cumulative index to convert that amount to *base cost* (Column E, Exhibit 9–13). The ending inventory for the current period, at base cost, is used in Phase B to calculate the incremental layer (or liquidation) of inventory during the current period (at base cost). The incremental layer, at base cost, is then multiplied by the cumulative index to derive the *Lifo amount.*

---

[7] This schedule could have been designed to parallel Exhibit 9–12; however, it has been rearranged to demonstrate variations that may attain greater efficiency in particular circumstances. The schedules are not unique.

**EXHIBIT 9-13**
*Lifo* Inventory—Dollar-Value, Method, Link-Chain Approach

### Phase A—Computation of Internal Index

| | (Step 2) Beginning of Year Cost (A) Note (a) | (Step 3) Current Year Cost (B) Note (b) | (Step 4) Current Year Index (C) (B ÷ A) | Cumulative Index (D) (prior D × current C) | Ending Inventory at Total Base Cost (E) (B ÷ D) |
|---|---|---|---|---|---|
| (Step 1) Beginning of base year (19B) ...... | $6,100 | $6,100 | 1.0000 | 1.0000 | $6,100 |
| End of 19B ................. | 7,320 | 8,940 | 1.2213 | 1.2213 | 7,320 |
| End of 19C ................. | 9,060 | 9,490 | 1.0475 | 1.2793 | 7,418 |

Note (a)—beginning cost:
19B: Item A—1,200 @ $1.00 = $1,200
     Item B—3,000 @ 2.04 = 6,120
                       $7,320

19C: Item A—1,300 @  1.20 = $1,560
     Item B—3,000 @ 2.50 = 7,500
                       $9,060

Note (b) current cost:
1,200 @ $1.20 = $1,440
3,000 @  2.50 =  7,500
            $8,940

1,300 @  1.30 = $1,690
3,000 @  2.60 =  7,800
            $9,490

### Phase B—Computation of *Lifo* Inventory Amount

| Step 5. | Ending Inventory at Total Base Cost (Col. E) | Cumulative Index (Col. D) | Ending Inventory at Lifo Cost |
|---|---|---|---|
| End of year 19B: | | | |
| Base year beginning inventory ................. | $6,100 | 1.0000 | $6,100 |
| Increment 19B ($7,320 − $6,100) ............... | 1,220 | 1.2213 | 1,490 |
| | $7,320 | | |
| Ending Inventory at *Lifo* ..................... | | | $7,590 |
| End of year 19C: | | | |
| Base year beginning inventory ................. | $6,100 | 1.0000 | $6,100 |
| Increment 19B......................................... | 1,220 | 1.2213 | 1,490 |
| Increment 19C ($7,418 − $7,320) .............. | 98 | 1.2793 | 125 |
| | $7,418 | | |
| Ending Inventory at *Lifo* ..................... | | | $7,715 |

For study convenience and for comparative analysis, the two phases, and five computational steps, summarized on page 387, were prominently identified in Exhibits 9–12 and 9–13.

The double-extension and link-chain methods will give the same results for the first year of application (19B in the illustration); in the periods following the results will be different, often by significant amounts. Link chain tends to give a lower ending inventory amount; however, this is not always the case.

The link-chain method represents a short-cut approach in applying the dollar-value method and is preferred where there are numerous changes in inventory items. For tax purposes, it is limited to those situations where the double-extension method can be shown to be impracticable or unsuitable to the situation because of product mix and technological impacts. The link-chain method provides maximum flexibility in application of the *Lifo* concept.

### Indexing

In the preceding discussions and illustrations of dollar-value *Lifo,* the indexes used were *internal indexes* since they were computed from the internal inventory data of the company; no externally computed indexes were used. Recall that computation of the internal index each period, under both methods (double extension and link chain), required that (*a*) unit cost data and (*b*) physical unit data for the ending inventory be available for each item in the inventory pool. In complex situations, this requirement for detailed data often poses a critical problem. As a consequence, there are two situations where the index might be derived in another way, viz:

1. Internal index derived on sampling basis—In situations where detailed unit and cost data for each item in the *entire* inventory pool is impractical (because of technological changes, extensive variety of items, or extreme fluctuations in the variety of items), the tax regulations state that an internal index may be computed by using a "representative portion of the inventory pool or by use, of other sound and consistent statistical methods." When this internal sampling approach is used, computation of the internal index is precisely the same as illustrated for the (*a*) double-extension approach in Exhibit 9–12, and (*b*) link-chain approach in Exhibit 9–13, except sampling data rather than total data are used.
2. External index—In situations where *neither* the entire ending inventory pool nor statistical sampling of the pool is feasible for computing an internal index, an *appropriate external price index* may be used. This is a rare situation because it is very difficult to justify in light of the IRS tax regulations. The selection of an external price index avoids the detailed index computations illustrated above (i.e., Phase A). Therefore, only Phase B computations are necessary. This phase simply involves costing the ending inventory base layer and incremental layers.[8] To illustrate the simplification, assume the following data for Tye Company:

> Inventory data:
> Base year inventory, end of 19A at 19A costs.................. $6,100
> 19B ending inventory, at 19B costs (*Fifo* basis)............... 8,940
>
> External price index selected:
> 19A............... 1.0000
> 19B............... 1.2213

---

[8] This is a widely used assumption in accounting literature for *Lifo* problems. It oversimplifies the dollar-value *Lifo* and gives no flavor of the real-life complexities encountered by all accountants. As explained earlier, the use of an external index is rarely permissible.

*Required:*

Compute the 19B ending inventory at *Lifo* value assuming the dollar-value, double-extension approach.

*Solution:*[9]

Computation of *Lifo* inventory amount (only Phase B needed):

|  | Ending Inventory Base Year Cost | Selected Index | Ending Inventory at Lifo Value |
|---|---|---|---|
| End of 19B: |  |  |  |
| Base year beginning inventory | $6,100 | 1.0000 | $6,100 |
| Increment, 19B | 1,220[b] | 1.2213 | 1,490 |
| Total Inventory at Base Year Cost | $7,320[a] |  | $7,590 |

Computations:

[a] 19B ending inventory at 19A cost, $8,940 ÷ 1.2213 = $7,320
    Less: Base inventory (19A ending inventory
    at 19A cost)............................................... 6,100
[b] Difference: Inventory Increase in 19B at 19A Cost... $1,220

## LIFO APPLIED TO INTERIM STATEMENTS

We have consistently stated that most companies using *Lifo* continue to maintain their accounts on *Fifo,* or some other basis, and make a conversion to *Lifo* inventory at year-end. This means that interim statements (quarterly) unless converted in some way, would be inconsistent with the annual report. *APB Opinion No. 28,* "Interim Reporting" (and the SEC as well), specifies that the consistency principle similarly applies to interim statements and the annual statements. Therefore, a company using *Lifo* for annual statements must also use it for interim statements. This often poses a critical problem because certain *Lifo* effects during the year may be changed before year-end. For example, there may be a liquidation of incremental layers, or even invasion of the base layer during the year, that may be replaced before year-end. Therefore, the company must forecast, at the end of the interim period, whether there will be replacement by the end of the year. Basically, the company must make a first quarter estimate of the inventory *quantity* expected to be on hand at year-end. This quantity is then used to compute the estimated dollar difference expected at year-end between *Lifo* and the inventory method used for operating purposes. This difference should be allocated to each interim period on some rational basis, such as the ratio of quarterly sales to estimated annual sales. *Fifo,* average, and specific identification costing methods do not pose this interim problem.

---

[9] We assumed an external index identical to the internal index computed in Exhibits 9–12 and 9–13 to demonstrate that there is no difference in application between the use of an internal index versus an external index except to the extent that the index values are different (and the index does not have to be computed which is the complex and burdensome phase).

## LIFO RESERVES

Companies using *Lifo* for tax and external reporting purposes and some other method, such as *Fifo*, for internal management and record-keeping purposes, sometimes employ a *Lifo* allowance account (often inappropriately called a *Lifo* reserve account) to reflect the difference between the two inventory amounts.

To illustrate, one company reported inventories as follows:

| | 1975 | 1974 |
|---|---|---|
| Current Assets: | | |
| Finished goods, work in process, and raw materials, *Lifo* basis (net of *Lifo* reserve of $3,200,000 in 1975 and $2,900,000 in 1974) | $8,000,000 | $6,500,000 |

Clearly, this reflects that the inventory method used for internal management purposes (*Fifo*) reflected ending inventory balances of $11,200,000 in 1975 and $9,400,000 in 1974. Although seldom formally entered in the accounts, the difference could be recognized in the accounts as follows:

1974 (first *Lifo* year):

| | | |
|---|---|---|
| Cost of goods sold | 2,900,000 | |
| Allowance to reduce inventory to *Lifo* basis | | 2,900,000 |

1975:

| | | |
|---|---|---|
| Cost of goods sold | 300,000 | |
| Allowance to reduce inventory to *Lifo* basis ($3,200,000 − $2,900,000) | | 300,000 |

## SUMMARY

The discussions in Part B have pinpointed the primary problems in *Lifo* application. Since the quantity, or specific unit, method of applying *Lifo* illustrated in Part A is seldom applied, for external purposes, its study alone imparts an oversimplification of the *Lifo* issue. In application, *Lifo* is comparatively complex and involves considerable clerical effort. Because of the wide range of opportunities for differences, and because it is subject to inventory manipulation, it has been accorded intensive attention by governmental regulatory agencies such as the SEC and the IRS. Similarly, the major accounting firms have devoted much research and study to *Lifo* because they generally view it as a conceptually and economically sound approach to the measurement of income. Also, accountants insist that the concept be applied in a conceptually sound, consistent, and realistic way in each diverse situation. *Lifo* is generally recommended in situations where:

1. Continuing price changes (inflation) can be projected realistically.
2. Income taxes will increase or remain high.
3. Inventory quantities (volume) will not decrease materially.
4. Shortages of items stocked are not expected.
5. Long-run trends in the business can be projected realistically.

## QUESTIONS

### PART A

1. What are the primary purposes to be served in selecting a particular inventory flow method? Why is the selection particularly important?

2. Briefly explain the differences between periodic and perpetual inventory procedures. Under what circumstances are each generally used?

3. Does the adoption of perpetual inventory procedures eliminate the need for physical count or measurement of inventories? Explain.

4. Explain the specific cost method and indicate the objections to it.

5. Distinguish between a weighted average and a moving average in determining unit cost. When is each generally used? Explain.

6. Explain the essential features of first-in, first-out. What are the primary advantages and disadvantages of *Fifo*? Explain the difference in the application of *Fifo* under (*a*) periodic inventory procedures, and (*b*) perpetual inventory procedures. In contrast with *Lifo*, how does it affect cash flow?

7. Explain the essential features of last-in, first-out. What are the primary advantages and disadvantages of *Lifo*? Explain the difference in application of *Lifo* under (*a*) periodic inventory procedures, and (*b*) perpetual inventory procedures.

8. Explain why *Lifo* costed currently and *Lifo* costed at the end of the month may give different results.

9. What is meant by inventory layers? Why are they significant with respect to the *Fifo, Lifo,* and base stock methods?

10. Assuming the *Lifo* method, what is meant by inventory liquidation? Why is it a serious problem for *Lifo* but not *Fifo*?

11. How is *Lifo* usually applied (*a*) in the accounts, (*b*) on the income tax return, and (*c*) the external financial reports.

12. Compare the balance sheet and income statement effects of *Fifo* versus *Lifo* (*a*) when prices are rising, and (*b*) when prices are declining.

### PART B

13. Why do the IRS regulations limit reporting to a footnote, for the base year only, of the impact on net income of two different inventory methods (and one of the methods is used for tax purposes)?

14. What is meant by the quantity of goods *Lifo* method? Identify and distinguish between the two approaches used to implement this method.

15. Explain how changes in the item or product mix of *Lifo* ending inventories over a period of several years will adversely affect the results of the quantity of goods approach.

16. What are the primary differences and limitations of the *Lifo* quantity method versus the dollar-value method?

17. Contrast the concept of a *Lifo* inventory pool as between the quantity method and the dollar-value method.

18. What are the basic features of the dollar-value *Lifo* method?

19. Contrast the dollar-value method, double-extension approach with the dollar-value method, link-chain approach, and indicate when each is appropriate.

20. What is indexing? When can an external price index be used?

21. Explain the problem that *Lifo* poses when interim statements are prepared. Why is this problem unique to *Lifo*?

## DECISION CASE 9–1

As a member of the controller's department of XYZ Corporation, you have been involved in an initial discussion with some other company executives concerning the merits of *Lifo* versus *Fifo* inventory procedures for the company. The following items were listed during the initial discussion:

| Items | Fifo | Lifo | Brief Explanation |
|---|---|---|---|
| | *Characteristic of —* | | |
| 1. Matches the actual physical flow of goods. | Yes | | |
| 2. Levels income. | | | |
| 3. Tends to cause income to vary with prices. | | | |
| 4. Matches old costs with new prices. | | | |
| 5. Costs inventory at approximate replacement cost. | | | |
| 6. Matches new costs with new prices. | | | |
| 7. Emphasizes the balance sheet. | | | |
| 8. Emphasizes the income statement. | | | |
| 9. Subject to profit manipulation. | | | |
| 10. Gives higher profits when prices rise. | | | |
| 11. Gives lower profits when prices fall. | | | |
| 12. Processes costs same order as incurred. | | | |
| 13. Matches current costs with current revenue. | | | |
| 14. Acceptable for income tax purposes. | | | |
| 15. Income figure more accurately reflects profits that are available to owners. | | | |

*Required:*

1. Complete the above tabulation.
2. Be prepared to discuss each item in detail.
3. Be prepared to explain and illustrate item 15.

**EXERCISES**

### PART A: Exercises 1–9

### Exercise 9–1

The perpetual inventory records of the North Company provided the following data for one item of merchandise for sale (assume the transactions in order of the number given).

|  | Units | Unit Cost | Amount |
|---|---|---|---|
| Goods available for sale: |  |  |  |
| Beginning inventory............... | 500 | $6.00 | $ 3,000 |
| Purchases: (1) ..................... | 600 | 6.10 | 3,660 |
| (3) ..................... | 600 | 6.20 | 3,720 |
| (5) ..................... | 400 | 6.30 | 2,520 |
|  | 2,100 |  | $12,900 |
| Sales: (2)............................. | 900 |  |  |
| (4)............................. | 500 |  |  |
| (6)............................. | 300 |  |  |

*Required:*

1. Complete the following (round unit costs to even cents and amounts to even dollars).

|  | Valuation | |
|---|---|---|
| *Costing Method* | *Final Inventory* | *Cost of Goods Sold* |
| a. Fifo...................................................... | $_____ | $_____ |
| b. Lifo (unit basis costed at end of period and assume base inventory is 400 units) ... | $_____ | $_____ |
| c. Weighted average ................................ | $_____ | $_____ |
| d. Base stock (base 300 units @ $1)............ | $_____ | $_____ |

2. Compute the amount of pretax net income and rank the methods in order of the amount of pretax net income (highest first) assuming *Fifo* net income is $30,000.
3. Which method would you prefer in this instance? Why?

### Exercise 9–2

The raw material records of the Star Manufacturing Corporation showed the following data relative to raw material K (assume the transactions occurred in the order given):

|  | Units | Unit Cost |
|---|---|---|
| 1. Inventory............... | 300 | $2.00 |
| 2. Purchase............... | 400 | 2.10 |
| 3. Issue..................... | 600 |  |
| 4. Purchase............... | 500 | 2.20 |
| 5. Issue..................... | 400 |  |
| 6. Purchase............... | 600 | 2.30 |

*Required:*

1. Compute the cost of issues for the period and the final inventory assuming (round unit costs to even cents):
   a. Weighted average method.

b. Moving average method.
c. *Fifo*.
d. *Lifo* (unit basis; costed at end; 300 units in base layer).
2. Under what general circumstances would each be preferable?

### Exercise 9–3

The inventory records of Goldstein Retailers showed the following data relative to a particular unit sold regularly (assume transactions in the order given):

|  | Units | Unit Cost |
|---|---|---|
| 1. Inventory | 2,000 | $4.00 |
| 2. Purchases | 18,000 | 4.50 |
| 3. Sales (@ $13 per unit) | 7,000 | |
| 4. Purchases | 6,000 | 4.60 |
| 5. Sales (@ $13.50 per unit) | 16,000 | |
| 6. Purchases | 4,000 | 4.70 |

*Required:*
1. Complete the following tabulation (round unit costs to even cents and keep unit costs of inventory even):

|  | Ending Inventory | Cost of Goods Sold | Gross Margin |
|---|---|---|---|
| a. *Fifo* | ——— | ——— | ——— |
| b. Weighted average | ——— | ——— | ——— |
| c. *Lifo* (unit basis, costed at end, 2,000 units in base layer) | ——— | ——— | ——— |
| d. Moving average (show computations) | ——— | ——— | ——— |

2. What method would be your first choice? Explain the basis for your choice.

### Exercise 9–4

Stockton Corporation manufactures three different products which are stocked for regular sale. The principal product is referred to as "Benders." The records of the company for the month of January provided the following data relative to Benders. The company maintains perpetual inventory records for finished goods. Assume the transactions in the order given.

| | |
|---|---|
| 1. In stock | 30 units @ $5.00 |
| 2. Received from factory | 10 units @ 5.30 |
| 3. Shipments | 20 units |
| 4. Received from factory | 40 units @ 5.20 |
| 5. Shipments | 50 units |
| 6. Received from factory | 20 units @ 5.40 |
| 7. Shipments | 12 units |

The company is using the weighted average method and periodic inventory procedures and is considering a change to *Fifo* or moving average for internal purposes because a perpetual inventory system will be used.

*Required:*
1. Which method would you prefer? Why?
2. Construct the perpetual inventory record for Benders using the method you

preferred in Requirement 1. (Round unit costs to even cents and keep inventory at even cents per unit.)

## Exercise 9-5

Simpson Company produced 40,000 units during the year. Sales were 50,000 units, and the beginning inventory was 30,000 units (base inventory, 10,000 units @ $5 = $50,000). The unit cost of production for the year was $10, and the initial inventory was carried at $210,000. Complete the following (round inventory unit costs to even cents):

| | Ending Inventory | | |
| | Computations | Amount | Pretax Income |
|---|---|---|---|
| a. First-in, first-out............... | | $_____ | $90,000 |
| b. Last-in, first-out (unit basis, costed at end)................. | | $_____ | $_____ |
| c. Weighted average ............ | | $_____ | $_____ |

## Exercise 9-6

Noonan Company uses *Lifo* (unit basis). The following data were available relative to the primary raw material for period 19A:

| | Units | Unit Cost |
|---|---|---|
| Beginning inventory (base inventory)............... | 5,000 | $3.00 |
| Beginning inventory (excess) ........................ | 1,000 | 3.10 |
| Purchases .................................................. | 19,000 | 3.40 |
| Issues ...................................................... | 22,000 | |

The first purchase in period 19B was 10,000 units at $3.70 per unit.

*Required:*

1. Compute the ending *Lifo* inventory and the cost of issues for period 19A.
2. Give the journal entries for purchases and issues, record the period 19A inventory invasion in the accounts (debit purchases to Inventory and issues to Work in Process).
3. Give the journal entry for the purchase in period 19B.
4. How should the inventory and any related accounts be reported on the balance sheet at the end of period 19A?

## Exercise 9-7

Lilly Company currently uses *Fifo* for all purposes. The inventory records for the period reflected the following for one major item sold regularly:

| | |
|---|---|
| Beginning inventory ..................................... | 10,000 units @ $ 8 |
| Purchases during the period ......................... | 40,000 units @  10 |
| Sales during the period (@ $30) .................. | 35,000 units |
| Expenses (excluding income taxes).............. | $40,000 |
| Beginning cash balance ............................. | $20,000 |
| Income tax average rate ............................. | 45% |

The company is considering a change to *Lifo* for all purposes. Assume the beginning inventory given above will be the *Lifo* base inventory.

*Required:*

1. Assuming all transactions are cash basis, compare *Lifo* and *Fifo* results by preparing for each: (*a*) an income statement, and (*b*) a partial balance sheet (limited to the above transactions). Include a column for *differences* and show computations of cash balances. Assume 100,000 shares of common stock outstanding.
2. In this situation, based on the data at hand, which inventory method would you recommend? Why?
3. Under what conditions would you recommend the other method?

### Exercise 9-8

Fisher Company records standard costs in the accounts. The finished goods inventory records are maintained at standard. When raw material is purchased, the difference between standard cost and actual cost is recorded in a separate variance account and reported as a *loss or gain* for the period in which the goods were purchased. The records relating to one item of raw material showed the following: standard cost per unit, $5; beginning inventory, 1,000 units; purchases during the period were No. 1–2,000 units at $5.10, No. 2–800 units at $4.95, and No. 3–1,200 units at $5; sales were 3,500 units at $12; expenses paid were $20,000.

*Required:*

1. Give journal entries for the purchases, sales, and expenses.
2. Prepare an income statement (disregard income taxes). Assume 3,000 shares of common stock outstanding.

### Exercise 9-9

Barber Manufacturing Company produces a single product in one plant that is distributed nationally. The plant is highly mechanized; therefore, fixed costs are relatively high. Full manufacturing cost and *Lifo* has been used for internal, external, and tax purposes. Because there is only one plant and wide distribution, a large inventory of finished goods is maintained. The controller is considering a variable (direct) costing system for internal purposes. *Lifo* (unit basis) will continue to be used for income tax purposes. The following year-end amounts were determined on a *Lifo* (full-cost) basis:

| | | |
|---|---|---|
| Sales (8,000 units @ $91). $728,000 | Beginning inventory, finished goods ............ | None |
| Cost of goods sold | | |
| (@ $46) ................... 368,000 | Manufacturing costs | |
| Gross margin................. 360,000 | (10,000 units): | |
| Expenses (fixed) ........... 160,000 | Direct material used ... | $ 55,000 |
| Pretax income .............. 200,000 | Direct labor incurred ... | 175,000 |
| Income taxes (@ 40%) ... 80,000 | Factory overhead— | |
| Net income.................... $120,000 | fixed..................... | 150,000 |
| | Factory overhead— | |
| | variable ............... | 80,000 |
| | Ending inventory, finished | |
| | goods (2,000 units) ... | (92,000) |
| | Cost of Goods Sold ......... | $368,000 |

*Required:*

1. Recast the above statements for internal purposes on a direct cost basis. Use the beginning inventory as given.

2. Which basis should be used for external reporting purposes? Explain.
3. Explain why net income is different between *Lifo* and direct costing? Use computations to demonstrate the difference.

## PART B: Exercises 10–14

### Exercise 9–10

On January 1, 19B, Foster Company changed from *Fifo* to *Lifo* for income tax and external reporting purposes. The ending inventory for 19A (*Fifo* basis) was $155,000 (this will be the base inventory amount for *Lifo*). At the end of 19B, the *Lifo* inventory amount, computed using the dollar-value, double-extension approach was $160,000; had the company continued using *Fifo,* this amount would have been $184,000. The average income tax rate is 46%.

*Required:*

1. Compute the difference in net income for 19B attributable to the change from *Fifo* to *Lifo*. Show computations.
2. Prepare an appropriate note to the financial statements for 19B.

### Exercise 9–11

Baker Wholesale Grocery Company uses the *Lifo* method for income tax and external reporting purposes. The ending inventory for 19A (*Lifo* basis) amounted to $260,000 (at base cost). The physical inventory taken at the end of 19B, at 19B costs, amounted to $336,000 (*Fifo* basis). An external price index indicated a 12% increase in prices during 19B. Assume this is a rare situation where an external price index can be used.

*Required:*

1. Use the external index to compute the *Lifo* inventory amount, assuming dollar-value, double-extension method.
2. Under what special conditions is the external index approach appropriate?

### Exercise 9–12

Stonewall Company uses *Lifo* for income tax and external reporting purposes. The *Lifo* base inventory (at end of 19A) for inventory Pool No. 1 amounted to $70,000. The periodic inventory of Pool No. 1 taken at the end of 19B, priced at 19B costs, amounted to $92,000. Analysis of a statistical sample of the inventory and related computations showed a price index for 19A of 100 and for 19B, 115.

*Required:*

1. Use the period internal indexes already derived to compute the 19B ending *Lifo* inventory amount assuming the dollar-value, double-extension method.
2. Under what conditions is the sampling index approach appropriate?

### Exercise 9–13

Kashin Company distributes quarterly interim reports to all shareholders. The annual accounting period ends on December 31. The first quarter interim report, dated March 31, 19B, is being prepared. The company uses *Lifo* for income tax and financial reporting purposes and *Fifo* for internal purposes.

The following data are available:

Actual amounts:
Base year *Lifo* inventory, January 1, 19B.............. $100,000
*Lifo* inventory, March 31, 19B............................ 110,000

Estimated amounts:
*Fifo* inventory, December 31, 19B ...................... 96,000
*Lifo* inventory, December 31, 19B ...................... 78,000

Sales for the first quarter were approximately 30% of the total sales budgeted for the year.

*Required:*

1. What should be the amount of the *Lifo* ending inventory at the end of the first quarter? Show computations.
2. Justify your answer.

## Exercise 9–14

At the end of the annual accounting period, the inventory records of Adams Company reflected the following:

|  | 19A | 19B |
|---|---|---|
| Ending inventory at *Fifo*............... | $350,000 | $390,000 |
| Ending inventory at *Lifo*............... | 340,000 | 320,000 |

The company uses *Fifo* for internal purposes and *Lifo* for income tax and external reporting purposes.

*Required:*

1. Assume the inventory difference is recognized in the accounts. Give the appropriate journal entry for each year.
2. Show how the inventories should be shown on the 19B comparative balance sheet.

## PROBLEMS

### PART A: Problems 1–10

### Problem 9–1

Stiles Company records showed the following transactions, in order of occurrence, relative to raw material W:

| | Units | Unit Cost |
|---|---|---|
| 1. Inventory.............. | 400 | $5.00 |
| 2. Purchase.............. | 600 | 5.50 |
| 3. Issue..................... | 700 | |
| 4. Purchase.............. | 900 | 5.60 |
| 5. Issue..................... | 800 | |
| 6. Purchase.............. | 200 | 5.80 |

*Required:*

Compute the cost of the issues and final inventory in each of the following completely independent situations (round unit costs to even cents and keep unit inventory cost at even cents; show computations):

| | Units and Amount | |
|---|---|---|
| *Assumption* | *Final Inventory* | *Issues* |
| a. Weighted average. · | | |
| b. Moving average. | | |
| c. Fifo. | | |
| d. Lifo costed currently (base inventory, 200 units). | | |
| e. Lifo costed at end of period. | | |
| f. Base stock (base stock, 100 units). | | |
| g. Standard cost (standard cost, $4.75). | | |

## Problem 9–2

The records of Smith Trading Company showed the following transactions, in the order given, relating to the major item sold:

| | *Units* | *Unit Cost* |
|---|---|---|
| 1. Inventory | 3,000 | $7.00 |
| 2. Purchase | 5,000 | 7.20 |
| 3. Sales (@ $15) | 4,000 | |
| 4. Purchase | 7,000 | 7.50 |
| 5. Sales (@ $15) | 9,000 | |
| 6. Purchase | 8,000 | 7.60 |
| 7. Sales (@ $16) | 9,000 | |
| 8. Purchase | 6,000 | 7.90 |

*Required:*

Complete the following tabulation for each independent assumption (round unit costs to even cents and keep inventory at even unit cost; show computations):

| | Units and Amount | | |
|---|---|---|---|
| *Assumption* | *Ending Inventory* | *Cost of Goods Sold* | *Gross Margin* |
| a. Fifo. | | | |
| b. Lifo costed at end of period (base inventory, 1,000 units). | | | |
| c. Lifo costed currently (base inventory, 1,000 units) – support with a perpetual inventory record. | | | |
| d. Weighted average. | | | |
| e. Moving average – support with a perpetual inventory record. | | | |

## Problem 9–3

The following purchases and sales of a major item, in the order given, were made by the Hoosier Company (beginning inventory was 800 units valued at $600):

| | Purchases | | Units Sold |
| | Units | Unit Cost | @ $3 Each |
|---|---|---|---|
| (1)............... | 500 | $.90 | |
| (2)............... | | | 800 |
| (3)............... | 1,600 | .85 | |
| (4)............... | | | 1,200 |
| (5)............... | 900 | .95 | |
| (6)............... | 600 | .90 | |
| (7)............... | | | 1,700 |
| (8)............... | 300 | .80 | |

*Required:*

Complete the following tabulation for each independent assumption (round to even unit costs and keep unit inventory cost to even cents). Show computations.

| | Units and Amount | | |
| *Assumption* | *Ending Inventory* | *Cost of Goods Sold* | *Gross Margin* |
|---|---|---|---|
| a. Fifo. | | | |
| b. Weighted average cost (round unit costs to three places). | | | |
| c. Lifo, costed currently (base inventory, 500 units). | | | |
| d. Lifo, costed at end of period. | | | |

## Problem 9–4

The records of Damon Company showed the following data relative to one of the major items being sold. Assume the transactions occurred in the order given.

| | Units | Unit Cost |
|---|---|---|
| Beginning inventory............... | 7,000 | $4.00 |
| Purchase No. 1 ...................... | 6,000 | 4.20 |
| Sale No. 1 (@ $10) ............... | 9,000 | |
| Purchase No. 2 ...................... | 8,000 | 4.50 |
| Sale No. 2 (@ $11) ............... | 4,000 | |

*Required:*

1. Compute the cost of goods sold, the valuation of the final inventory, and gross margin under each of the following independent assumptions (round unit costs to nearest cent):

| | Amount | |
| | *Inventory* | *Cost of Goods Sold* | *Gross Margin* |
|---|---|---|---|
| a. Weighted average cost with periodic inventory procedures. | | | |
| b. Fifo with perpetual inventory procedures. | | | |
| c. Lifo costed at end of period (base inventory, 7,000 units). | | | |
| d. Standard cost assuming the standard cost is $4. | | | |

2. Give all entries indicated by the above data assuming:

Case A—Weighted average cost ([a] above).
Case B—*Fifo* ([b] above).
Case C—Standard cost ([d] above).

## Problem 9–5

The records of Thomas Company showed the following data with respect to one raw material used in the manufacturing process. Assume the transactions occurred in the order given.

|  | Units | Unit Cost |
|---|---|---|
| Inventory | 4,000 | $7.00 |
| Purchase No. 1 | 3,000 | 7.60 |
| Issue No. 1 | 5,000 |  |
| Purchase No. 2 | 8,000 | 8.00 |
| Issue No. 2 | 7,000 |  |
| Purchase No. 3 | 3,000 | 8.20 |

*Required:*

1. Compute cost of goods issued (to work in process) and the valuation of the ending inventory for each of the following independent transactions (round unit costs to even cents and keep unit inventory costs to even cents; show computations):
   a. *Fifo.*
   b. *Lifo,* costed at end of period (base inventory, 4,000 units).
   c. Weighted average.
   d. Moving average.
   e. Standard cost (assuming a standard unit cost of $8).
2. In parallel columns, give all entries indicated for *Fifo* assuming—

   Case A—A Perpetual inventory system.
   Case B—A Periodic inventory system.

## Problem 9–6

Wilson Manufacturing Company manufactures one main product. Two raw materials are used in the manufacture of this product. The company uses standard costs in the accounts and carries the raw material, work in process, and finished goods inventories at standard. The records of the company showed the following:

|  | Material A | Material B |
|---|---|---|
| Beginning inventory (units) | 8,000 | 5,000 |
| Standard cost per unit | $2.00 | $7.00 |
| Purchases during the period: |  |  |
| No. 1 | 10,000 @ $2.00 | 7,000 @ $7.00 |
| No. 2 | 20,000 @  1.90 | 8,000 @  7.20 |
| Issues during the period (units) | 28,000 | 16,000 |
| Final inventory per physical count (units) | 10,000 | 3,900 |

*Required:*

1. Give all entries indicated relative to raw materials assuming standard costs.
2. Determine the value of the final inventory and cost issues for each raw material.
3. Accumulate the amount of the variations from standard for each raw material and explain or illustrate the reporting and accounting disposition of these amounts.

## Problem 9–7

Robins Corporation maintains perpetual inventory records on a *Fifo* basis for the three main products distributed by the company. A physical inventory is taken at the end of each six months in order to check the perpetual inventory records.

The following information relating to one of the products for the year was taken from the records of the company:

|  | Product A |
|---|---|
| Beginning inventory | 9,000 units @ $8.10 |
| Purchases and sales (in the order given): | |
| Purchase No. 11 | 5,000 units @ 8.15 |
| Sale No. 1 | 10,000 units |
| Purchase No. 12 | 16,000 units @ 8.20 |
| Sale No. 2 | 11,000 units |
| Purchase No. 13 | 4,000 units @ 8.30 |
| Purchase No. 14 | 7,000 units @ 8.20 |
| Sale No. 3 | 14,000 units |
| Purchase No. 15 | 5,000 units @ 8.10 |
| Ending inventory (per count) | 10,000 |
| Replacement cost (per unit) | $8.00 |

*Required:*

1. Reconstruct the perpetual inventory record for Product A.
2. Give all entries indicated by the above data assuming selling price is $18 per unit and that the company employs the direct inventory reduction method (holding losses not separately identified) in recognizing lower of cost or market.
3. Prepare the income statement for this product through gross margin.

## Problem 9–8

Watson Trading Company sells three main products. In the past, periodic inventory procedures have been employed on a *Fifo* basis. The records of the company showed the following information relating to one of the products:

| Beginning inventory | 500 units @ $3.00 |
|---|---|
| Purchases and sales (in the order given): | |
| Purchase No. 1 | 400 units @ 3.10 |
| Purchase No. 2 | 600 units @ 3.15 |
| Sale No. 1 | 1,000 units |
| Purchase No. 3 | 800 units @ 3.25 |
| Sale No. 2 | 700 units |
| Sale No. 3 | 500 units |
| Purchase No. 4 | 700 units @ 3.30 |

In considering a change in inventory policy, the following summary was prepared:

| | Illustration | | | |
| | --- | --- | --- | --- |
| | (1) | (2) | (3) | (4) |
| Sales ................................. | $15,400 | $15,400 | $15,400 | $15,400 |
| Cost of goods sold.............. | 6,911 | 7,110 | 6,996 | 6,905 |
| Gross margin .................... | $ 8,489 | $ 8,290 | $ 8,404 | $ 8,495 |

*Required:*

1. Identify the inventory flow method used for each illustration assuming the ending inventory only was affected.
2. What method would you recommend? Give its advantages and disadvantages.

## Problem 9–9

Stamford Company uses *Fifo* in costing the raw material inventory. During the first three years of operation, the inventory at the end of each year computed by different methods for comparative purposes was as follows:

| | Final Inventory | | |
| | --- | --- | --- |
| | 19A | 19B | 19C |
| Fifo ......................................... | $180,000 | $200,000 | $160,000 |
| Lifo ......................................... | 150,000 | 160,000 | 140,000 |
| Average cost (weighted) ............ | 170,000 | 210,000 | 150,000 |

*Required:*

Compute net income under each method. Results under *Fifo* method are given.

| | Net Income | | |
| | --- | --- | --- |
| | 19A | 19B | 19C |
| Fifo ......................................... | $40,000 | $70,000 | $30,000 |
| Lifo ......................................... | | | |
| Average cost (weighted).............. | | | |

## Problem 9–10

Foster Company uses *Fifo* for internal accounting and management purposes and *Lifo* for external reporting and income tax purposes. During a recent period, the *Fifo* inventory records reflected the following transactions, in the order given, for the main product:

| | | Units | Fifo Unit Cost |
| --- | --- | --- | --- |
| 1. | Beginning inventory.............. | 5,000 | $8.00 |
| 2. | Purchase ............................ | 4,000 | 8.20 |
| 3. | Sales (@ $20)...................... | 7,000 | |
| 4. | Purchase ............................ | 8,000 | 8.30 |
| 5. | Sales (@ $21)...................... | 6,000 | |

The purchasing officer has determined that the next purchase will cost $8.50 per unit.

*Required:*

1. Assume the *Lifo* base inventory is 5,000 units at $8. Complete a tabulation as follows:

|  | Fifo | Lifo |
|---|---|---|
| Sales revenue ...................... | | |
| Cost of goods sold ............... | | |
| Gross margin ..................... | | |

2. Give entries relating to the inventory invasion.
3. Explain and justify the way you handled the invasion of the *Lifo* base inventory.

## PART B: Problems 11–19

### Problem 9–11

Astro Company decided at the beginning of 19A to change from *Fifo* to *Lifo*. The records of the company showed the following data for 19A relative to one major item distributed:

|  | Units | Unit Cost |
|---|---|---|
| Beginning inventory (base inventory layers averaged) ................................... | 10,000 | $3.00 |
| Purchases and sales (in the order given): | | |
| 1 Purchase................................................. | 8,000 | 3.20 |
| 2 Sold (@ $8.00) ...................................... | 9,000 | |
| 3 Sold (@ $8.25) ...................................... | 5,000 | |
| 4 Purchase................................................. | 7,000 | 3.20 |
| 5 Purchase................................................. | 6,000 | 3.40 |
| 6 Sold (@ $8.75) ...................................... | 8,000 | |
| 7 Purchase................................................. | 3,000 | 3.50 |

Expenses (excluding income taxes), $40,000.

Average income tax rate, 40%.

*Required:*

1. Prepare an income statement for 19A, unit *Lifo* basis. Assume 10,000 shares of common stock outstanding.
2. Prepare an appropriate footnote, and any other required supporting data for the change in 19A from *Fifo* to *Lifo*.
3. What would be disclosed in 19B relative to the change? Why?

### Problem 9–12

Young Company changed from *Fifo* to *Lifo* for 19A and future periods. The records of the company pertaining to the main product provided the following data for 19A:

| | Units | Unit Cost |
|---|---|---|
| Beginning inventory (base inventory) ... | 5,000 | $6.00 |
| Purchases and sales (in order given): | | |
| First quarter: | | |
|   *a.* Purchase............................... | 4,000 | 6.20 |
|   *b.* Sale (@ $15.00) ....................... | 6,000 | |
| Second quarter: | | |
|   *a.* Purchase............................... | 8,000 | 6.50 |
|   *b.* Sale (@ $15.60)....................... | 6,000 | |
| Third quarter: | | |
|   *a.* Purchase............................... | 9,000 | 6.60 |
|   *b.* Sale (@ $15.60)....................... | 8,000 | |
| Fourth quarter: | | |
|   *a.* Purchase............................... | 3,000 | 6.80 |
|   *b.* Sale (@ $16.00) ....................... | 2,000 | |
| Expenses: | | |
|   Year ..................................... | $146,200 | |
|   First quarter ........................... | 40,000 | |
| Income tax rate, 40%. | | |

*Required:*

1. Prepare an income statement for 19A, unit *Lifo* basis. Assume 10,000 shares of common stock outstanding.
2. Prepare a note suitable for the 19A financial statements in view of the change from *Fifo* to *Lifo*.
3. Prepare an income statement for the first quarter of 19A only. Explain how you handled the invasion of the base inventory.
4. Prepare a note suitable for the first quarter financial statement.

## Problem 9–13

Storm Company uses *Lifo,* unit basis, to cost the ending inventory for income tax and external reporting purposes. Near the end of 19A, the records, and related estimates, provided the following annual data for one item sold regularly:

| | Units | Unit Cost |
|---|---|---|
| Beginning inventory: | | |
|   Base inventory ..................................... | 10,000 | $20 |
|   Increment No. 1...................................... | 5,000 | 30 |
| Purchases (actual) .................................... | 60,000 | 35 |
| * Sales (@ $50 per unit) ............................ | 65,000 | |
| * Expenses (excluding income taxes) $1,000,000 | | |
| Average income tax rate, 48%. | | |

    * Including estimates for remainder of 19A.

On December 26 the company has an opportunity to purchase 30,000 units of the above item at $33 (a special price). Delivery is immediate, and the offer will expire January 3, 19B. The question has been posed whether the purchase (and delivery) should be consummated in 19A or 19B.

*Required:*

1. What is your recommendation on the purchase date? Support your recommendation with reasons and proforma (as if) income statement and balance sheet data. Include computations suitable for presentation to the company president.

2. Explain why each of the following amounts are different: (a) purchases, (b) ending inventory, (c) gross margin, and (d) net income.
3. Would you suspect profit manipulation in this situation? Explain.

## Problem 9–14

Milliken Retailers, Incorporated, sells two main products regularly. The products are considered to be "substantially identical" for inventory purposes. The company used *Fifo* through 19A for all purposes. Starting in 19B, *Lifo* was adopted for external reporting and income tax purposes. The inventory pool at *Fifo* (the two products combined) records reflected the following:

|  | Purchases | | | Issues | | | Balance | | |
|---|---|---|---|---|---|---|---|---|---|
| 19A: Ending inventory ... | | | | | | | 400 | 1.00 | 400 |
| 19B: Purchase.............. | 700 | 1.20 | 840 | | | | 400 | 1.00 | 400 |
| | | | | | | | 700 | 1.20 | 840 |
| Sale (@ $3.00) ...... | | | | 400 | 1.00 | 400 | | | |
| | | | | 100 | 1.20 | 120 | 600 | 1.20 | 720 |
| 19C: Purchase.............. | 600 | 1.35 | 810 | | | | 600 | 1.20 | 720 |
| | | | | | | | 600 | 1.35 | 810 |
| Sale (@ $3.40) ...... | | | | 600 | 1.20 | 720 | | | |
| | | | | 200 | 1.35 | 270 | 400 | 1.35 | 540 |
| 19D: Purchase.............. | 500 | 1.50 | 750 | | | | 400 | 1.35 | 540 |
| | | | | | | | 500 | 1.50 | 750 |
| Sale (@ $3.75) ...... | | | | 400 | 1.35 | 540 | 500 | 1.50 | 750 |

*Required:*

1. Compute the ending inventory for years 19B, 19C, and 19D assuming the dollar-value method, double-extension approach is used.
2. Prepare a listing that compares the results for *Fifo* and *Lifo*. Which method should be used? Why?
3. Prepare a suitable footnote for the financial statements for 19B assuming *Lifo* is used.

## Problem 9–15

Use the data given in Problem 9–14 to complete the following requirements.

*Required:*

1. Compute the ending inventory for the years 19B, 19C, and 19D assuming the dollar-value method, link-chain approach is used.
2. Prepare a listing that compares *Fifo* and *Lifo* results. Which method should be used? Why?

## Problem 9–16

Stoey Distributing Company sells three main products regularly. The products are considered to be "substantially identical" for inventory purposes. The company used *Fifo* through 19A for all purposes. After 19A, *Fifo* was continued for internal management and accounting purposes; however, at the start of 19B,

*Lifo* was adopted for income tax and external reporting purposes. The following data, for the three products combined, from the records are for the three years after adoption of *Lifo*:

| | | Fifo Basis per Accounts | |
| --- | --- | --- | --- |
| | Units | Cost | Total |
| 19A: | | | |
| Ending inventory.............. | 2,000 | $3.00 | $ 6,000 |
| 19B: | | | |
| Purchases....................... | 6,000 | 3.30 | 19,800 |
| Sales (@ $8)..................... | 5,000 | | |
| Ending inventory.............. | 3,000 | 3.30 | 9,900 |
| 19C: | | | |
| Purchases....................... | 10,000 | 3.50 | 35,000 |
| Sales (@ $9)..................... | 6,000 | | |
| Ending inventory.............. | 7,000 | 3.50 | 24,500 |
| 19D: | | | |
| Purchases....................... | 3,000 | 4.00 | 12,000 |
| Sales (@ $9)..................... | 6,000 | | |
| Ending inventory | | | |
| Layer 1 ........................ | 1,000 | 3.50 | 3,500 |
| Layer 2 ........................ | 3,000 | 4.00 | 12,000 |
| Total .................... | 4,000 | | $15,500 |

*Required:*

1. Compute the ending inventory for the years 19B, 19C, and 19D assuming the dollar-value method, double-extension approach is used.
2. Prepare a listing that compares the results of the methods, *Fifo* and *Lifo*. Which method should be used? Why?
3. Prepare an appropriate footnote to the financial statements for 19B assuming double extension is used.

## Problem 9–17

Use the data given in Problem 9–16 to complete the following requirements.

*Required:*

1. Compute the ending inventory for the years 19B, 19C, and 19D assuming the dollar-value, link-chain approach is used.
2. Prepare a listing that compares the results of *Fifo* and *Lifo*. Which method should be used? Why?

## Problem 9–18

Thames Company sells two main products that have low volume but high cost. *Fifo*, with a perpetual inventory system, is used for internal cost accounting and management purposes. On January 1, 19B, the company adopted *Lifo* for external reporting and income tax purposes. The *Fifo* inventory records reflected the following:

| Product X | Purchases | | | Issues | | | Balance | | |
|---|---|---|---|---|---|---|---|---|---|
| December 31, 19A  ...... | | | | | | | 200 | 100 | 20,000 |
| 19B: Purchases............ | 400 | 130 | 52,000 | | | | 400 | 130 | 52,000 |
| Sales (@ $300)...... | | | | 200 | 100 | 20,000 | | | |
| | | | | 200 | 130 | 26,000 | 200 | 130 | 26,000 |
| | | | | | | | 200 | 130 | 26,000 |
| 19C: Purchases............ | 500 | 140 | 70,000 | | | | 500 | 140 | 70,000 |
| Sales (@ $300)...... | | | | 200 | 130 | 26,000 | 500 | 140 | 70,000 |
| | | | | | | | 500 | 140 | 70,000 |
| 19D: Purchases............ | 100 | 150 | 15,000 | | | | 100 | 150 | 15,000 |
| Sales (@ $325)...... | | | | 300 | 140 | 42,000 | 200 | 140 | 28,000 |
| | | | | | | | 100 | 150 | 15,000 |
| Product Y | | | | | | | | | |
| December 31, 19A  ...... | | | | | | | 300 | 90 | 27,000 |
| 19B: Purchases............ | 400 | 92 | 36,800 | | | | 400 | 92 | 36,800 |
| Sales (@ $275)...... | | | | 300 | 90 | 27,000 | 400 | 92 | 36,800 |
| | | | | | | | 400 | 92 | 36,800 |
| 19C: Purchases............ | 100 | 95 | 9,500 | | | | 100 | 95 | 9,500 |
| Sales (@ $275)...... | | | | 400 | 92 | 36,800 | 100 | 95 | 9,500 |
| | | | | | | | 100 | 95 | 9,500 |
| 19D: Purchases............ | 400 | 96 | 38,400 | | | | 400 | 96 | 38,400 |
| Sales (@ $295)...... | | | | 100 | 95 | 9,500 | 400 | 96 | 38,400 |

*Required:*

1. Assume the two products are "substantially identical" for inventory purposes. Compute the ending *Lifo* inventory assuming (show computations):

   Case A—Dollar-value method, double-extension approach.
   Case B—Dollar-value method, link-chain approach.

2. Prepare a listing that compares the results of *Fifo* and *Lifo* for Cases A and B. Which method should be used? Why?

3. Prepare a suitable footnote to the financial statements for 19B assuming double extension is used.

**Problem 9-19**

Wendt Company has been using *Fifo* for all internal and external reporting purposes. At the start of 19B, it adopted *Lifo* for external financial statement and income tax purposes. The *Fifo* inventory records reported the following for one inventory pool:

|  | Fifo Basis |
|---|---|
| 19A ending inventory............... | $100,000 |
| 19B ending inventory............... | 120,000 |
| 19C ending inventory............... | 130,000 |
| 19D ending inventory............... | 135,000 |

External price index selected: 19A—1.00; 19B—1.10; 19C—1.15; and 19D—1.21.

*Required:*

1. Compute the ending *Lifo* inventory amounts for 19B, 19C, and 19D assuming the dollar-value method, using an external price index. The external index selected is given above. Apply the index assuming double extension.
2. Prepare a tabulation comparing inventory amounts under *Fifo* and *Lifo* for 19B, 19C, and 19D. What method should be used? Why?
3. Prepare an appropriate footnote for the 19B financial statements assuming double-extension approach is used.

# Chapter 10

# Inventories — Special Valuation Procedures

There are numerous situations where the accountants must make estimates relating to inventories. As a result certain inventory estimating procedures have gained wide acceptance. Because of the technical complexities involved in applying the *Lifo* concept when the retail method of inventory is used, this chapter is divided into two parts as follows:

Part A — Estimating Procedures for Inventories
    1. Gross margin method
    2. Retail method of inventory
Part B — Dollar-Value, *Lifo*-Retail Method

## PART A — ESTIMATING PROCEDURES FOR INVENTORIES

### GROSS MARGIN METHOD

The gross margin[1] method represents an approach frequently used to approximate the valuation of an inventory independently of a physical count of the goods and as a check on the detailed inventory records in the case of perpetual inventory procedures. The method is based on the assumption that the short-run *rate of gross margin* (gross margin divided by sales) is approximately the same from one period to the next. The method involves computation of total goods *available* for sale in the normal manner based on data provided by the accounts. Next the estimated cost of goods sold is determined by applying the estimated gross margin rate to net sales and deducting this amount from sales to derive estimated cost of goods sold. Deduction of the estimated cost of goods sold from the cost of goods available for sale gives the ending inventory at estimated cost. For example, if the rate of gross margin for a business

---

[1] The method traditionally has been referred to as the gross profit method, nevertheless the descriptive modern terminology *gross margin* is used throughout these discussions. (Ref. AICPA *Terminology Bulletin No. 2.*)

has been uniformly 40% of sales, the final inventory may be approximated as follows:

| | Known Data | Computations | Order of Computations |
|---|---|---|---|
| Net sales ........................ | $10,000* | | |
| Cost of goods sold: | | | |
| Initial inventory ..............$ 5,000† | | | |
| Add: Purchases .............. 8,000* | | | |
| Goods available for sale ....................... 13,000 | | | |
| Less: Final inventory............................. ? | | ($13,000 − $6,000) = $7,000 | 3 |
| Cost of goods sold ......... | ? | ($10,000 − $4,000) = $6,000 | 2 |
| Gross Margin .................. 40%‡ | ? | ($10,000 × .40) = $4,000 | 1 |

\* From company records.
† Final inventory from prior period.
‡ Based on recent past performance.

A more comprehensive example where the data are rearranged to facilitate computation follows.

| | | |
|---|---|---|
| Cost of goods available for sale: | | |
| Beginning inventory..................................................... | | $ 50,000* |
| Purchases during period...............................................$160,400* | | |
| Freight-in.................................................................. 9,800* | | |
|    Total Purchases.................................................... 170,200 | | |
| Less: Purchase returns and allowances.......................... 200* | | |
| Net purchases ........................................................... | | 170,000 |
|    Cost of goods available for sale .......................... | | 220,000 |
| Deduct estimated cost of goods sold: | | |
| Sales........................................................................ 201,000* | | |
| Less: Sales returns and allowances .......................... 1,000* | | |
| Net sales ................................................................. 200,000 | | |
| Less: Estimated gross margin ($200,000 × .20†)............... 40,000 | | |
|    Estimated cost of goods sold ............................. | | 160,000 |
| Estimated Cost of Ending Inventory .............................. | | $ 60,000 |

   \* Data available from the records.
   † Based on recent past performance.

In some problems relating to the gross margin method, a *cost* percentage (cost of goods sold divided by sales) is given rather than the gross margin percentage (gross margin divided by sales). If either percentage is known the other percentage may be readily determined, since the two percentages must sum to 100%. In the above example, since the rate of gross margin is 20%, the cost percentage is 80% (100% − 20%). In the above example the gross margin rate, or markup, was given as a percent of sales (20% markup on sales); however, it could have been stated as 25% of the *cost of goods sold* (markup on cost). In the latter case a conversion of the rate on cost to a rate on sales would be desirable. Conversion of a rate on cost to a rate on sales or vice versa may be accomplished algebraically as follows:[2]

$$\text{Symbols:} \quad C = \text{Cost}$$
$$SP = \text{Selling price}$$

1. The markup on cost is 25%; determine the markup (gross margin rate) on sales:

$$C + .25C = SP; \text{ therefore, } C = \frac{1}{1.25} SP, \text{ or } C = .80SP$$

Markup on $SP = SP - .80SP$; therefore, <u>Markup on $SP = .20$</u>

2. The markup on sales is 20%; determine the markup on cost:

$$SP - .20SP = C; \text{ therefore, } C = .80SP, \text{ and } SP = 1.25C$$

Markup on $C = 1.25C - C$; therefore, <u>Markup on $C = .25$</u>

A more direct approach involves the use of fractions as illustrated below. Note that in all cases the numerator is the same; whereas when converting to a markup on sales, the denominator is the sum of the numerator and denominator of the cost fraction, and when converting to a markup on cost, the denominator is the difference between the numerator and the denominator of the sales fraction. Obviously the fraction or rate on sales must be smaller than the comparable fraction or rate on cost. Observe the relationship between the fractions on each line in the following example:

|  | Markup | |
|---|---|---|
|  | On Cost | On Sales |
| a. Markup is 25% on cost; determine the markup on sales | $1/4(25\%)$ | $1/5(20\%)$ |
| b. Markup is $33\frac{1}{3}\%$ on sales; determine the markup on cost | $1/2(50\%)$ | $1/3(33\frac{1}{3}\%)$ |
| c. Markup is $66\frac{2}{3}\%$ on cost; determine the markup on sales | $2/3(66\frac{2}{3}\%)$ | $2/5(40\%)$ |

The gross margin method frequently is employed in four different situations as follows:

1. By the auditor or others to test the reasonableness of an inventory valuation provided by some other person or determined by some other means, such as physical inventory, or perpetual inventory. To illustrate, assume the bookkeeper for the company referred to above

---

[2] An alternative computation (where markup is known on cost) giving the same results without a conversion to markup on sales could be made as follows:

| | |
|---|---|
| Cost of goods available for sale (per above) | $220,000 |
| Deduct estimated cost of goods sold: | |
| Sales reduced to estimated cost ($200,000 ÷ 1.25) | 160,000 |
| Estimated Cost of Ending Inventory | $ 60,000 |

submitted to the auditor an inventory valuation of $85,000. The gross margin method provides an approximation of $60,000, which would alert the auditor to investigate the inventory situation thoroughly.

2. To estimate the final inventory for internal financial statements (monthly statements for example) prepared during the year where the taking of interim physical inventories is impractical. The method finds fairly wide application for internal reporting purposes.

3. To estimate an inventory destroyed by a casualty such as fire or storm. Obviously, this application would be limited to those situations where the books of accounts are not destroyed since certain basic data from the accounts are essential. Valuation of inventory lost through casualty is necessary (a) to estimate the amount of loss, and (b) as a basis for settlement of insurance claims related to the inventory loss.

4. To develop budget estimates of cost of goods sold, gross margin, and inventory after a sales budget is developed.

In applying the gross margin method the accountant must bear in mind that a possibility of error exists because of (a) the assumption that the gross margin rate used from the past period(s) is realistic and reasonably accurate, and (b) the effect of using an *average* rate. In the usual situation a company will carry a number of different lines of merchandise each having a different markup or gross margin. Obviously, a change in markup on one or more lines, or a shift in the relative quantities of each line sold, will change the average gross margin rate (markup) thereby distorting the validity of the results derived by the method.

When the gross margin method is applied where significantly different markup rates are involved, computations should be developed for each separate class of merchandise if practicable.

## RETAIL INVENTORY METHOD

The retail method of inventory valuation is widely employed by retail stores, particularly department stores, which sell a great diversity of items. In such situations perpetual inventory procedures generally are impractical, and taking a complete physical inventory more often than annually is uncommon. Several features of department store operation make possible utilization of the retail inventory method. Particular features are (a) the departments are frequently homogeneous with respect to the markup on items sold within the departments, and (b) articles purchased are immediately priced for resale and displayed. The effect of this latter feature may be observed in the tendency by retailing establishments to relate markups, analyses, budgets, estimates, markdowns, and so on, to *sales price* rather than to cost price. Whereas those in nonretailing endeavors tend to think of markup as being on cost, the retailer traditionally thinks of markup on selling price. The retail inventory method provides a special approach to measure the ending inventory on a (1) *Fifo* basis, (2) average cost basis, (3) lower-of-cost-or-market basis, or (4) *Lifo* basis, depending on how the calculations are made.

The retail inventory method has been actively sponsored by the National Retail Merchants Association and approved by the Internal Revenue Service; consequently, it has become an important method of inventory determination. The accounting profession has accepted the method on its own merits as fundamentally sound where properly administered. It must be realized that the retail inventory method represents an approach in *estimating* the amount of the ending inventory to be used in computing cost of goods sold on the income statement and for reporting on the balance sheet.

Application of the retail method requires that records be kept which show the following data:

1. Beginning inventory valued at both cost and retail.
2. Purchases during the period valued at both cost and retail.
3. Adjustments to the original marked retail price such as additional markups, markup cancellations, markdowns, employee discounts, and markdown cancellations.
4. Data relating to other adjustments such as interdepartmental transfers, returns, breakage, and damaged goods.
5. Sales.

This method is similar to the gross margin method in that the inventory valuation is based on the ratio of cost to selling price. In contrast, the gross margin method uses a historical ratio, whereas the retail inventory method uses a ratio based on the current period relationships. Under the retail method records are maintained so that the ratio may be developed for the current period.

The retail method involves computation of the goods available for sale at both *cost* and *retail*. Total cost is divided by total retail to obtain the *cost ratio*. Sales are then deducted from goods available for sale (at retail); the result is the inventory at retail. Multiplication of the inventory at retail by the cost ratio provides the estimated inventory valuation at cost. Determination of the final inventory valuation employing the retail method is illustrated below with simplified data:

|  | At Cost | At Retail |
|---|---|---|
| Goods available for sale: |  |  |
| Beginning inventory (January 1) | $ 15,000* | $ 25,000* |
| Purchases during January | 195,000* | 275,000* |
| Cost of goods available for sale | $210,000 | 300,000 |
| Cost ratio: $210,000 ÷ $300,000 = .70 |  |  |
| Deduct January sales at retail |  | 260,000* |
| Ending inventory (January 31): |  |  |
| At retail |  | $ 40,000 |
| At cost ($40,000 × .70) | $ 28,000 |  |

\* Data available from the records.

Since the retail inventory method provides only an estimate of the final inventory, a physical inventory should be taken at least annually as a check on the accuracy of the estimates. Significant differences between the physical inventory and the retail inventory estimate should be carefully analyzed. Investigation may indicate (a) inventory shortages due to breakage, loss, or theft; (b) incorrect application of the retail method; (c) failure of departmental managers to report correctly markdowns, additional markups, or cancellations; (d) errors in the records; (e) errors in the physical inventory; or (f) inventory manipulation.

The primary uses of the retail method are as follows:

1. To provide estimated inventory valuations for interim periods (usually monthly) when physical inventories are impracticable. The method provides inventory valuations needed for monthly statements, analyses, and purchasing policy considerations.
2. To provide a means of converting a physical inventory, priced at retail, to a cost basis. To eliminate the necessity of marking the cost (in code) on the merchandise, or referring to invoices, many retail establishments, after physically counting the stock on hand, extend the inventory sheets at retail. The retail value is then converted to cost by applying the retail inventory method without reference to individual cost prices.
3. To provide a basis for interim control of inventory, purchases, theft, markdowns, and additional markups. Many department stores utilize the results of the retail inventory calculation by department for such interim control requirements.
4. To provide a basis for external financial reports.
5. To provide data for income tax purposes.

## MARKUPS AND MARKDOWNS

The preceding illustration assumed that there were no changes in the *original* marked selling price. The original selling price is frequently raised or lowered, particularly at the end of the selling season or when replacement costs are changing. The retail method requires that a careful record be kept of all adjustments to the *original* marked selling price since these adjustments must be taken into account in the computation. In order to apply this rule it is important to distinguish between the following terms:

Original sales price—the amount at which the merchandise is first marked for sale.

Markup—the original or initial amount that merchandise is marked up. Thus, it is the difference between cost and the original sales price. It may be expressed as a dollar amount or a percent of either cost or selling price. It is sometimes referred to as initial markup or markon.

Additional markup—an increase in the sales price above the original sales price. Note that the original sales price is the base from which additional markup is measured.

Additional markup cancellations—cancellation of an *additional* markup.

Additional markups less additional markup cancellations is usually called net additional markup.

Markdown — a reduction in selling price below the original sales price.

Markdown cancellation — after a reduction in the original selling price an increase in the selling price which does not exceed the original sales price (after that point an increase is an additional markup).

The definitions may be illustrated by assuming an item, that cost $8, is originally marked to sell at $10; subsequently marked to sell at $11, then finally reduced to sell at $7, viz:

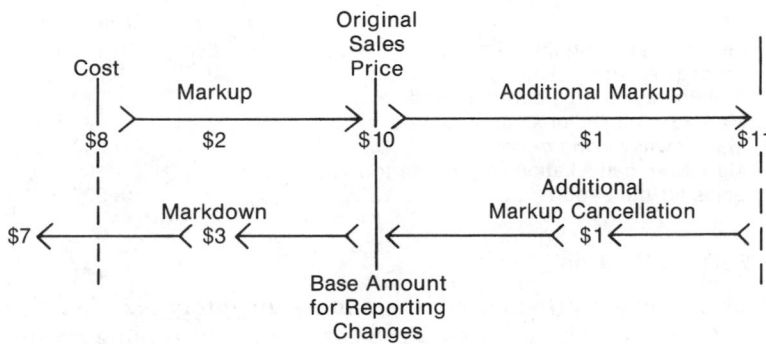

The validity of an inventory amount determined by using the retail inventory method depends largely upon the accuracy with which changes in the original selling price are reported by the merchandising personnel to the accounting department. To illustrate the reporting problem, assume the following additional data relating to the item illustrated immediately above:

| *Price Changes and Transactions* | | | *Price Change Information Reported to Accounting Department* | |
|---|---|---|---|---|
| Units acquired | 100 @ $ 8 | | | |
| Units sold | 60 @ 10 | | | |
| Increase in sales price | 40 @ 1 | ⟶ | Additional markups | $40 |
| Units sold | 30 @ 11 | | | |
| Decrease in sales price | 10 @ 1 | ⟶ | Additional markup cancellations | 10 |
| Units sold | 2 @ 10 | | | |
| Decrease in sales price | 8 @ 3 | ⟶ | Markdowns | 24 |
| Units sold | 8 @ 7 | | | |

## APPLICATION OF THE RETAIL INVENTORY METHOD

The basic concept and computations underlying the retail inventory method were illustrated above. However, the way in which the calculations are made determine the approximate valuations. The difference in calculations to derive a particular basis may be outlined as follows:

| Basis Desired | Computation of Cost Ratio |
|---|---|
| 1. *Fifo* cost. | Exclude beginning inventory from the computation of the cost ratio. |
| 2. Average cost. | Include beginning inventory in the computation of the cost ratio. |
| 3. Lower of cost or market. | Exclude net markdowns from the computation of the cost ratio; include them after the cost ratio is computed. |
| 4. *Lifo* cost. | Must use dollar-value approach (discussed in Part B). |

To illustrate the first three, the following data are assumed from the accounting records of KM Company at the end of the accounting period:

| | At Cost | At Retail |
|---|---|---|
| Inventory at beginning of period | $ 550 | $ 900 |
| Purchases during period | 6,290 | 8,900 |
| Additional markups during period | | 225 |
| Markup cancellations during period | | 25 |
| Markdowns during period | | 600 |
| Markdown cancellations during period | | 100 |
| Sales for the period | | 8,500 |

## Retail Method, *Fifo* Cost

Recall that when *Fifo* is used, the ending inventory is costed at the latest unit costs which means that the costs in the beginning inventory will be included in cost of goods sold for the period. Therefore, if the beginning inventory is excluded from the computation of the cost ratio, the result will approximate *Fifo*. The computations for KM Company would be:

### Retail Method—Approximate *Fifo* Cost

| | | At Cost | At Retail |
|---|---|---|---|
| Goods available for sale: | | | |
| Beginning inventory | | $ 550 | $ 900 |
| Purchases during the period | | 6,290 | 8,900 |
| Additional markups during the period | $225 | | |
| Less: Markup cancellations | 25 | | |
| Net additional markups | | | 200 |
| Deduct: | | | |
| Markdowns during the period | 600 | | |
| Less: Markdown cancellations | 100 | | |
| Net markdowns | | | (500) |
| Total Excluding Beginning Inventory | | 6,290 | 8,600 |
| Cost ratio: $6,290 ÷ $8,600 = .73 | | | |
| Total Including Beginning Inventory | | $6,840 | 9,500 |
| Deduct: | | | |
| Sales | | | 8,500 |
| Ending inventory: | | | |
| At retail | | | $1,000 |
| At approximate *Fifo* cost ($1,000 × .73) | | $ 730 | |

The markups and markdowns must be included as adjustments to the retail amounts because they represent changes in the marked selling prices. The cost ratio must express the relationship between sales value and cost.

### Retail Method, Average Cost

Recall that average cost is derived by dividing total goods available for sale in dollars of cost by total units available for sale; both totals include the beginning inventory. Therefore, if we calculate the cost ratio on the basis of totals, including the beginning inventory, the retail method derives approximate average cost. The computation for KM Company would be:

**Retail Method — Approximate Average Cost Basis**

|  | At Cost | At Retail |
|---|---|---|
| Total Including Beginning Inventory (from above) ...... | $6,840 | $9,500 |
| Cost ratio: $6,840 ÷ $9,500 = .72 |  |  |
| Deduct: |  |  |
| Sales ......................................................................... |  | 8,500 |
| Ending inventory: |  |  |
| At retail ......................................................................... |  | $1,000 |
| At approximate average cost ($1,000 × .72) ...................... | $   720 |  |

### Retail Method, Lower of Cost or Market (LCM)

Lower of cost or market is a conservative valuation method; it derives an inventory valuation that is less than *Fifo* or average. By excluding net markdowns from the computation of the cost ratio an approximate LCM valuation is derived. The LCM approach may be applied to either the *Fifo* or average computations illustrated above. To illustrate, it is applied to the *average* basis as follows:

**Retail Method — Average Cost Basis, Lower of Cost or Market**

|  |  | At Cost | At Retail |
|---|---|---|---|
| Goods available for sale: |  |  |  |
| Beginning inventory ............................................ |  | $  550 | $   900 |
| Purchases during period ...................................... |  | 6,290 | 8,900 |
| Additional markups .......................................... | $225 |  |  |
| Less: Markup cancellations .............................. | 25 |  |  |
| Net additional markups ................................ |  |  | 200 |
| Goods available for sale (Including |  |  |  |
| Beginning Inventory) ................................. |  | $6,840 | 10.000 |
| Cost ratio: $6,840 ÷ $10,000 = .684 |  |  |  |
| Deduct: |  |  |  |
| Sales ................................................................. |  |  | 8,500 |
| Remainder ................................................... |  |  | 1,500 |
| Markdowns ...................................................... | $600 |  |  |
| Less: Markdown cancellations ........................ | 100 |  |  |
| Net markdowns ......................................... |  |  | 500 |
| Ending inventory: |  |  |  |
| At retail ............................................................. |  |  | $ 1,000 |
| Average cost basis, lower of cost or market |  |  |  |
| ($1,000 × .684) ............................................. |  | $   684 |  |

## Special Items

Special discounts to employees and preferred customers, and known or estimated normal losses from spoilage or breakage, should be included in the computations in a manner similar to markdowns. Return purchases are deducted from purchases at both cost and retail; return sales are deducted from gross sales. Freight-in is added to purchase cost. These items are included in the illustration below:

### Retail Method—*Fifo* Basis, Lower of Cost or Market

|  | At Cost | At Retail |
|---|---|---|
| Goods available for sale: | | |
| Initial inventory .......................................... | $ 5,000 | $ 7,500 |
| Purchases ................................................. | 23,100 | 32,800 |
| Freight-in ................................................. | 500 | |
| Purchase returns......................................... | (600) | (840) |
| Net additional markups................................ | | 540 |
| Total Excluding Beginning Inventory ...... | 23,000 | 32,500 |
| Cost ratio: $23,000 ÷ $32,500 = .71 | | |
| Total Including Beginning Inventory......... | $28,000 | 40,000 |
| Deduct: | | |
| Sales (net of sales returns) ...........................$30,000 | | |
| Net markdowns ...................................... 3,000 | | |
| Employee discounts ................................... 2,000 | | 35,000 |
| Final inventory: | | |
| At retail .................................................. | | $ 5,000 |
| *Fifo* cost basis, lower of cost or market | | |
| ($5,000 × .71) ......................................... | $ 3,550 | |

The ending inventory is valued on the *Fifo* cost basis because the beginning inventory was excluded from the computation of the cost ratio. It is also at lower of cost or market because net markdowns were excluded from the cost ratio computation.

The preceding discussions of the retail inventory method presumed that the merchandise is similar in that (*a*) the markup was essentially the same for each kind of merchandise included, and (*b*) the relative proportion of the various kinds of merchandise in the ending inventory and in sales for the period was essentially the same. In individual departments, this is generally the case; however, on a storewide basis it often is not. Consequently, the essential data are accumulated in the accounting system, and the computations are made, on a departmental basis. The departmental inventories then are summed to derive the total inventory.

## INVENTORIES FOR LONG-TERM CONSTRUCTION CONTRACTS

A special inventory valuation problem arises for long-term construction contracts which are typical when buildings, bridges, ships, and dams are built. They are unique because the construction period often extends over two or more accounting periods. Directly related to the inventory valuation problem is one of *income recognition* during the construction period. For example, assume a 2½-year construction period;

should income be recognized as construction progresses (i.e., each period) or should income be recognized only at the end of the 2½ years?

The accounting profession and the income tax laws have recognized two distinctly different methods of accounting for long-term contracts. A business may select either; however, consistency is required once a selection is made. The two methods are generally identified as:

1. The completed-contract method – income recognized only upon completion.
2. The percentage-of-completion method – income recognized each period based upon progress; that is, on the basis of production (see discussion of the revenue principle in Chapter 2).

To illustrate the accounting for long-term construction contracts we will use the following data:

1. Ace Construction Company received a contract to erect a building for $1,500,000. Construction is to start February 1, 19A, and is to be completed in 2½ years from that date.
2. Progress billings are to be submitted at the end of each month based upon percentage-of-completion estimates developed by the independent architect as of the 15th of each month. The billings are payable to the contractor within ten days after the billing.
3. Data covering the entire construction period:

|  | Year 19A | Year 19B | Year 19C | Total |
|---|---|---|---|---|
| Contract price.................. |  |  |  | $1,500,000 |
| Costs incurred ...............$ | 350,000 | $550,000 | $465,000 | 1,365,000 |
| Estimated costs to complete (at year-end)... | 1,000,000 | 460,000 | -0- | -0- |
| Income .................. |  |  |  | $ 135,000 |
| Progress billings ............ | 300,000 | 575,000 | 625,000 | $1,500,000 |
| Collections on billings ...... | 270,000 | 555,000 | 675,000 | 1,500,000 |

### Completed-Contract Method

All costs incurred on the long-term construction contract are accumulated in a *Construction in Process Inventory* account. Since long-term construction contracts almost always provide for the contractor to bill the other party for progress payments (determined as agreed upon in the contract), the progress billings, as made, are debited to Accounts Receivable (construction contract billings) and credited to Billings on Contracts (long-term construction). The latter account is not a revenue account; it is an offset to the Construction in Process Inventory account on the balance sheet. If the net difference is a debit, it is usually reported as a current asset; if a credit, as a current liability. When the contract is completed, the income reported is the difference between the accumulated balances in the Billings on Contracts and the Construction in Process Inventory accounts. Under the completed-contract method, therefore, (1) the construction in process inventory is reported at the total cumulated costs to date, less the total progress billings to date; and (2) income on construction contracts ($135,000 in the example) is reported in the year of completion (19C). The entries in the accounts of Ace Construction Company, for this method, are illustrated in Exhibit 10–2, and the financial statement presentation for each year is shown in Exhibit 10–3.

### Percentage-of-Completion Method

Under this method, accounting for a long-term construction contract is the same as the completed-contract method explained above except that income is recognized each period during the construction time. Since the income on the contract will not be known until completion, an estimate must be made each period. The estimated amount of income is then apportioned to each period on the basis of percentage of completion of the contract represented by the work done during the period. Since progress billings usually are tied to percentage of completion, this can also be used at the end of the period to apportion the estimated amount of income to each period. Percentage of completion is usually derived as either (a) engineering and/or architectural estimates of the work performed to date to the total work necessary to complete the contract, or (b) the ratio of total costs incurred to date on the contract to the estimated total costs to be incurred on the contract. The estimated amount of income to be recognized each period is recorded by debiting Construction in Process and crediting Income on Construction (long-term contracts). The latter account is closed to Income Summary each period and reported on the income statement.

Computation of the amount of estimated income to be recognized each year by the Ace Construction Company is illustrated in Exhibit 10–1. Observe that the estimated total income of $135,000 is apportioned to each period on the basis of costs incurred to date to total costs to be incurred. The resulting entries in the accounts of Ace Construction Company are reflected in Exhibit 10–2, and the financial statement presentation for each period is shown in Exhibit 10–3.

### Comparative Results

The completed-contract and percentage-of-completion methods of accounting for long-term construction contracts are different approaches of measuring and reporting (a) periodic income from construction, and (b) the ending inventory (construction in process) during the period of construction. Exhibit 10–2 shows that the entries are identical each period under both methods except entry No. 4 (recognition of income from construction). Over the life of the construction period both methods recognize the same amount of total income. In this respect, the percentage of completion is deficient in that periodic income is recognized on the basis of estimates of remaining costs to complete; however, the total amount of income recognized over the life of a contract is the same for both methods. Alternatively, the completed-contract method, although more objective and more conservative, is generally viewed as deficient because recognition does not reflect current performance. Although most of the work may be completed prior to the last year, all of the income is recognized in the last year.

In respect to reporting on the balance sheet during the construction period, Exhibit 10–3 reflects that both methods derive the same results except for the amount of the ending inventory and retained earnings. Under the percentage-of-completion method the inventory is greater in amount by the accumulated amount of pretax income recognized in the current and prior periods. Thus, for Ace Manufacturing Company the ending inventory (i.e., costs in excess of billings) is greater by $38,889 at the end of 19A, and by $38,889 + $53,758 = $92,647 at the end of 19B. Recall that the estimated income recognized each year was debited to Construction in Process in the percentage of completion method.

Under either method, when there is a projected loss at any time, it must be recognized in the period in which a loss on the contract appears reasonably certain. The loss should be recognized by means of a debit to Loss on Construction Contract and a credit to Construction in Process. The credit removes from the inventory account the amount of costs in excess of expected recovery.

The accounting profession sanctioned the use of either method as follows:

> The committee believes that in general when estimates of costs to complete and extent of progress toward completion of long-term contracts are reasonably dependable, the percentage-of-completion method is preferable. When lack of dependable estimates or inherent hazards cause forecasts to be doubtful, the completed-contract method is preferable. Disclosure of the method followed should be made.[3]

**EXHIBIT 10–1**
**Apportionment of Estimated Income — Percentage-of-Completion Method**

| | Year 19A | Year 19B | Year 19C |
|---|---|---|---|
| Contract price ................................... | $1,500,000 | $1,500,000 | $1,500,000 |
| Less costs: | | | |
|   Actual cost to date ........................... | 350,000 | 900,000 | 1,365,000 |
|   Estimated cost to complete ............... | 1,000,000 | 460,000 | |
|   Estimated total costs ....................... | 1,350,000 | 1,360,000 | 1,365,000 |
|     Estimated Total Income ............... $ | 150,000 | $ 140,000 | $ 135,000 |
| Apportionment of total income: | | | |
|   19A: | | | |
|     $350,000/$1,350,000 × $150,000 ...... $ | 38,889 | | |
|   19B: | | | |
|     $900,000/$1,360,000 × $140,000 ...... | | $ 92,647 | |
|     Less income recognized to date ...... | | 38,889 | |
|       Income Recognized in 19B ......... | | $ 53,758 | |
|   19C: | | | |
|     Total income to be recognized | | | |
|       (actual)..................................... | | | $ 135,000 |
|     Less income recognized to date ...... | | | 92,647 |
|       Income Recognized in 19C ......... | | | $ 42,353 |

---

[3] AICPA, "Long-Term Construction-Type Contracts," *Accounting Research Bulletin No. 45* (New York, 1955), par. 15.

**EXHIBIT 10–2**
**Long-Term Construction Contracts**
**Completed-Contract and Percentage-of-Completion Methods Compared**

**Journal Entries**

| | Method | | | |
|---|---|---|---|---|
| | Completed Contract | | Percentage of Completion | |

*Year 19A:*

1. Costs of construction:

| | | | | |
|---|---|---|---|---|
| Construction in process ... | 350,000 | | 350,000 | |
| Cash, payables, etc. ... | | 350,000 | | 350,000 |

2. Progress billings:

| | | | | |
|---|---|---|---|---|
| Accounts receivable ......... | 300,000 | | 300,000 | |
| Billings on contracts... | | 300,000 | | 300,000 |

3. Collections on billings:

| | | | | |
|---|---|---|---|---|
| Cash ............................. | 270,000 | | 270,000 | |
| Accounts receivable ... | | 270,000 | | 270,000 |

4. Recognition of income:

| | | | | |
|---|---|---|---|---|
| Construction in process ... | (No income recognized | | 38,889 | |
| Income on | until completion) | | | |
| construction* | | | | 38,889 |

\* Closed to income summary.

*Year 19B:*

1. Costs of construction:

| | | | | |
|---|---|---|---|---|
| Construction in process ... | 550,000 | | 550,000 | |
| Cash, payables, etc. ... | | 550,000 | | 550,000 |

2. Progress billings:

| | | | | |
|---|---|---|---|---|
| Accounts receivable ......... | 575,000 | | 575,000 | |
| Billings on contracts... | | 575,000 | | 575,000 |

3. Collections on billings:

| | | | | |
|---|---|---|---|---|
| Cash ............................. | 555,000 | | 555,000 | |
| Accounts receivable ... | | 555,000 | | 555,000 |

4. Recognition of income:

| | | | | |
|---|---|---|---|---|
| Construction in process ... | (No income recognized | | 53,758 | |
| Income on | until completion) | | | |
| construction ......... | | | | 53,758 |

*Year 19C:*

1. Costs of construction:

| | | | | |
|---|---|---|---|---|
| Construction in process ... | 465,000 | | 465,000 | |
| Cash, payables, etc. ... | | 465,000 | | 465,000 |

2. Progress billings (final billing):

**EXHIBIT 10–2 (continued)**

### Journal Entries

*Method*

| | Completed Contract | | Percentage of Completion | |
|---|---|---|---|---|
| **Year 19C (continued)** | | | | |
| Accounts receivable ......... | 625,000 | | 625,000 | |
| Billings on contracts... | | 625,000 | | 625,000 |
| 3. Collections on billings (in full): | | | | |
| Cash ............................ | 675,000 | | 675,000 | |
| Accounts receivable ... | | 675,000 | | 675,000 |
| 4. Recognition of income (and to close the accumulated account balances): | | | | |
| Construction in process ... | | | 42,353 | |
| Billings on contracts.........1,500,000 | | | 1,500,000 | |
| Construction in process.................. | | 1,365,000 | | 1,500,000 |
| Income on construction ......... | | 135,000 | | 42,353 |

**EXHIBIT 10–3**
**Long-Term Construction Contracts**
**Completed-Contract and Percentage-of-Completion Methods Compared**

### Financial Statements

| | Year 19A | | Year 19B | | Year 19C | |
|---|---|---|---|---|---|---|
| | C.C.* | P.C.* | C.C. | P.C. | C.C. | P.C. |
| **Balance Sheet** | | | | | | |
| Current Assets: | | | | | | |
| Accounts receivable...| $ 30,000 | $ 30,000 | $ 50,000 | $ 50,000 | | |
| Inventory: | | | | | | |
| Construction in process ......... | 350,000 | 388,889 | 900,000 | 992,647 | | |
| Less: Billings on contracts......... | 300,000 | 300,000 | 875,000 | 875,000 | | |
| Costs in excess of billings ...... | 50,000 | 88,889 | 25,000 | 117,647 | | |
| **Income Statement** | | | | | | |
| Income on construction ......... | -0- | 38,889 | -0- | 53,758 | $135,000 | $ 42,353 |

\* C.C.—Completed-contract method.
  P.C.—Percentage-of-completion method.

## PART B—DOLLAR-VALUE, *LIFO*-RETAIL METHOD

Because of the income tax advantage of using *Lifo*, and the view of many accountants that *Lifo* provides a better matching of current costs with revenue, many retail and wholesale businesses have adopted dollar-value, *Lifo*-retail. When the retail method of inventory is used, *Lifo* results can be attained only by applying the dollar-value concept discussed in Chapter 9, Part B. Along with double extension, and link chain, *Lifo* retail is a variation of dollar-value *Lifo*. It meets the requirements of generally accepted accounting principles and can be used for income tax purposes (Reg. 1.471-8, 1.472-1). When *Lifo* results are desired, the retail inventory and the dollar-value concepts must be combined.

The *Lifo*-retail method requires that (*a*) a distinction be maintained between the base year inventory and subsequent incremental layers, and (*b*) the subsequent layers be measured by applying a price-level index to the results derived from the retail inventory approach. That is, at the end of each period, the retail inventory approach is used and the results are then converted to a *Lifo* basis using a price index.

Tax regulations specify that variety stores using the *Lifo*-retail method must use an *internally computed index* developed as discussed in Chapter 9, Part B. On the other hand, retailers that qualify as department stores (as defined for tax purposes) may use a published external index instead of an internally computed index. The published index used must be one prepared by the Bureau of Labor Statistics. In the discussions and illustrations to follow, we will assume a published index is used.

### APPLICATION OF THE DOLLAR-VALUE, *LIFO*-RETAIL METHOD

The dollar-value, *Lifo*-retail method, although conceptually simple, is somewhat complex in application. Basically, it involves an understanding of the use of price-level index numbers. Application of the dollar-value, *Lifo*-retail method involves three distinct phases, viz:

Phase 1—Computation or selection of an appropriate price index.
Phase 2—Computation of the ending inventory using the retail inventory method, *Fifo* basis (not lower of cost or market).
Phase 3—Computation of the ending inventory at *Lifo* cost by applying the index (Phase 1) to the results of Phase 2.

In Phases 2 and 3, a careful distinction must be maintained between the various inventory layers. Each period, the increase or decrease in ending inventory over the beginning inventory is computed; if there is an increase, a new incremental layer has been added during the period; if there is a decrease, there has been a partial or total liquidation of prior layers. A liquidation requires that the prior layers be liquidated in *Lifo* order; that is, the most recent layers must be liquidated first.

For dollar-value *Lifo*, two situations must be considered: (1) computation of the ending inventory on a *Lifo* cost basis at the end of each period (this is repeated each period), and (2) computation of the base inventory amount at the beginning of the base year (a one-time computation when *Lifo* is adopted). Each situation will be discussed and illustrated in this order.

## Computation of Ending Inventory at *Lifo* Cost

This process, accomplished at the end of each period, will be illustrated using the following data:

**WZ Company — Data from Company Records**

|  | 1977 | | 1978 | | 1979 | |
|---|---|---|---|---|---|---|
|  | At Cost | At Retail | At Cost | At Retail | At Cost | At Retail |
| Beginning (base) inventory ......... | $17,400 | $ 30,000 | | | | |
| Purchases ......... | 90,480 | 147,000 | $101,500 | $172,000 | $109,800 | $177,000 |
| Net additional markups ......... | | 8,800 | | 9,000 | | 7,000 |
| Net markdowns... | | 5,000 | | 6,000 | | 4,000 |
| Sales.................. | | 140,000 | | 162,800 | | 197,800 |
| Applicable price index (1976 = 100) .............. | | 102 | | 106 | | 110 |

Assume the company has been using the dollar-value, *Lifo*-retail method for external reporting and income tax purposes. The company uses a published index selected from an external source. A three-year period is used because a lesser span does not adequately illustrate the complexities.

*Required:*

Computation of the ending inventories for 1977, 1978, and 1979 on the *Lifo* cost basis. Show details of the computations.

*Solution with Explanatory Notes:*

The computations are shown in Exhibit 10–4 identified by Phase 1 (index), Phase 2 (retail inventory computation, *Fifo* basis), and Phase 3 (computation of the ending inventory at *Lifo* cost). We will focus on 1977 and explain the computations, viz:

Phase 1 — The computed, or selected index, is listed for convenience. These values are used *only* in the Phase 3 computations.[4]

Phase 2 — The ending inventory, on a *Fifo* basis, is computed exactly as illustrated in Part A. Lower of cost or market is not permitted when *Lifo* cost is used. The *Fifo* basis must be used in Phase 2

---

[4] When the index at the beginning of the base year is not 100, the current year index must be divided by the base index value to obtain the percentage or ratio index. To illustrate, assume the index value at the beginning of the base year is 1.05 and the index at the end of the year is 1.071. The index value to use at the end of 1977 would be: 1.071 ÷ 1.05 = 1.02 as above.

## EXHIBIT 10–4 Dollar-Value, *Lifo*-Retail Method

| | 1977 | | | 1978 | | | 1979 | | |
|---|---|---|---|---|---|---|---|---|---|
| | At Cost | At Retail | Cost Ratio | At Cost | At Retail | Cost Ratio | At Cost | At Retail | Cost Ratio |
| **Phase** | | | | | | | | | |
| **1** — Price index computed or selected (1976 = 100) ... | | 102 | | | 106 | | | 110 | |
| **2** — Computation of ending inventory at *Fifo* cost: | | | | | | | | | |
| Inventory, January 1 | $ 17,400 | $ 30,000 | | $ 24,480 | $ 40,800 | | $ 30,740 | $ 53,000 | |
| Purchases | 90,480 | 147,000 | | 101,500 | 172,000 | | 109,800 | 177,000 | |
| Net additional markups | | 8,800 | | | 9,000 | | | 7,000 | |
| Net markdowns | | (5,000) | | | (6,000) | | | (4,000) | |
| Total (excluding beginning inventory) ... | 90,480 | 150,800 | .60 | 101,500 | 175,000 | .58 | 109,800 | 180,000 | .61 |
| Total (including beginning inventory) ...... | $107,880 | 180,800 | | $125,980 | 215,800 | | $140,540 | 233,000 | |
| Sales | | 140,000 | | | 162,800 | | | 197,800 | |
| Ending Inventory | $ 24,480 | $ 40,800 | | $ 30,740 | $ 53,000 | | $ 21,472 | $ 35,200 | |
| **3** — Computation of ending inventory at *Lifo* cost: | | | | | | | | | |
| Ending inventory at retail deflated to base year retail prices: | | | | | | | | | |
| 1977: $40,800 ÷ 1.02 | | $ 40,000 | | | | | | | |
| 1978: 53,000 ÷ 1.06 | | | | | $ 50,000 | | | | |
| 1979: 35,200 ÷ 1.10 | | | | | | | | $ 32,000 | |
| Base layer: At base year costs | $ 17,400 | | | $ 17,400 | | | $ 17,400 | | |
| At base year retail prices | | (30,000) | | | (30,000) | | | (30,000) | |
| Incremental layers from prior years: 1977 | | | | 6,120 | (10,000) | | (b) | (10,000) | |
| 1978 | | | | | | | (b) | (10,000) | |
| Excess, new increments (or liquidations) at base year retail prices(a) | | $ 10,000 | | | $ 10,000 | | | $ (18,000) | |
| Increment (or liquidation) at current year retail prices: | | | | | | | | | |
| 1977: $10,000 × 1.02 | | $ 10,200 | | | | | | | |
| 1978: 10,000 × 1.06 | | | | | $ 10,600 | | | | |
| 1979: ($10,000 + $10,000) − $18,000 × 1.02(b) | | | | | | | | $ 2,040 | |
| Increment (or liquidation) at current year costs: | | | | | | | | | |
| 1977: $10,200 × .60 | 6,120 | | | | | | | | |
| 1978: 10,600 × .58 | | | | 6,148 | | | | | |
| 1979: 2,040 × .60 (1977 layer) (b) | | | | | | | 1,224 | | |
| Total Ending Inventory at *Lifo* Cost | $ 23,520 | | | $ 29,668 | | | $ 18,624 | | |

(a) When this difference is positive there is a new incremental layer; when it is negative there has been a partial liquidation of one or more prior layers. In 1979 there is a liquidation of the 1978 layer and part of the 1977 layer.

(b) The liquidation in 1979 must be taken from the most recent layers, in order, at the price index and cost ratio for the year in which the layers were added. In 1979 the liquidation left the base layer and $2,000 of the 1977 layer (at retail); that is, $2,000 × 1.02 × .60 = $1.224 at *Lifo* cost.

because separation of the "new costs" is necessary for the Phase 3 computations—the *cost ratio* must exclude the beginning inventory.

Phase 3—In Phase 3, the distinction between cost and retail must be maintained by layers. The inventory increase (increment) or decrease (liquidation) during the period is first measured at *base year* retail prices. First the *Fifo* inventory amount from Phase 2 is converted to base year retail prices by dividing that amount by the related price index given in Phase 1 (i.e., 1977: $40,800 \div 1.02 = \$40,000$). The difference between the ending inventory ($40,000) and the beginning inventory ($30,000), both at base year retail prices, gives the new increment or liquidation ($10,000 increment). This increment then is converted (*a*) to current year *retail* prices ($10,000 \times 1.02 = \$10,200$); and then (*b*) to *current year costs* ($10,200 \times .60 = \$6,120$). This is the *Lifo* cost for the new increment.

At the end of 1979, there is a slight complication because the ending inventory is less than the beginning inventory by $50,000 - \$32,000 = \$18,000$ at base year retail prices. This means that there was a partial liquidation of prior layers. The prior incremental layers must be used up in *Lifo* order; that is, in inverse chronological order. Also, the liquidation must be figured at the price index and cost ratio for the layers liquidated. The computations may be analyzed as follows:

| | |
|---|---:|
| Total inventory liquidated at base year retail prices | $18,000 |
| 1978 inventory layer liquidated at base year retail prices | 10,000 |
| Remainder at base year retail prices | 8,000 |
| 1977 inventory layer at base year retail prices | 10,000 |
| Difference—Remaining 1977 Inventory Layer | $ 2,000 |
| Conversion to *Lifo* Cost: $2,000 \times 1.02 \times .60 =$ | $ 1,224 |

## CHANGING TO DOLLAR-VALUE, *LIFO*-RETAIL—COMPUTATION OF BASE INVENTORY

In the discussions and illustrations above for WZ Company, the base inventory (at the beginning of the base year, 1977) was given as follows: at cost, $17,400; at retail, $30,000. These base year beginning inventory values would have been carried forward from the ending inventory of 1976 assuming the company was already on dollar-value, *Lifo* retail. However, *if the company had been on a method other than* Fifo (*such as average, or lower of cost or market), the ending inventory for 1976 would have to be restated at a* Fifo *cost basis.* The restatement usually is relatively simple.

To illustrate, assume WZ Company had been using the retail inventory method, average basis, and lower of cost or market. At the start of 1977, the company decided to change to the dollar-value, *Lifo*-retail method for tax and external reporting purposes. The retail method computation previously developed at the end of December 1976 (at *Fifo*, LCM) was:

|  | At Cost | At Retail |
|---|---|---|
| Inventory, January 1, 1976 | $ 5,700 | $ 10,000 |
| Purchases | 78,300 | 138,000 |
| Net additional markups | | 2,000 |
| Total | $84,000 | 150,000 |
| Cost ratio: $84,000 ÷ $150,000 = .56 | | |
| Net markdowns | | 5,000 |
| Remainder | | 145,000 |
| Sales | | 115,000 |
| Ending inventory, December 31, 1976: | | |
| At retail | | $ 30,000 |
| At average cost, lower of cost or market ($30,000 × .56)... | $16,800 | |

The computation to restate the beginning base year inventory (January 1, 1977) to a *Fifo* cost basis would be as shown below. Note the exclusion of the January 1, 1976, inventory and inclusion of both markups and markdowns to determine the cost ratio.

|  | At Cost | At Retail |
|---|---|---|
| Beginning inventory | $ 5,700 | $ 10,000 |
| Purchases | 78,300 | 138,000 |
| Net additional markups | | 2,000 |
| Net markdowns | | (5,000) |
| Total (excluding beginning inventory) | 78,300 | 135,000 |
| Total (including beginning inventory) | $84,000 | 145,000 |
| Cost ratio: *Fifo* cost basis: $78,300 ÷ $135,000 = .58 | | |
| Less: Sales | | 115,000 |
| Beginning base inventory, January 1, 1977: | | |
| At retail | | $ 30,000 |
| At cost ($30,000 × .58) | $17,400 | |

The two values, $30,000 and $17,400, represent the beginning base year inventory. Observe that they were used in Exhibit 10–4.

The entry to restate the January 1, 1977, inventory to base cost would be as follows:

Beginning inventory ($17,400 − $16,800) ................................... 600
　　Inventory adjustment due to adoption of *Lifo*-retail ............... 600

The inventory adjustment account would be closed to Income Summary and reported on the income statement as a gain during 1977.

This computation is needed only at the date of the change from some other method to dollar-value, *Lifo*-retail.

Because of the increasing use of dollar-value, *Lifo*-retail in the last few years, it has received increasing attention by public and industrial accountants. In applying the concept in the real world, a number of judgments must be made; and if used for tax purposes, the IRS Regulations and rulings must be carefully observed. Neither the accounting profession nor the taxing authorities have deemed it desirable to frame detailed and inflexible rules in this area because of the wide range of situations where it is used. Accounting students should be familiar with the method because of its increasing use.

## QUESTIONS

### PART A

1. What is the basic assumption implicit in the gross margin method?

2. Approximate the valuation of the ending inventory assuming the following data are available:

   Cost of goods available for sale ............................................. $100,000
   Net sales ............................................................................. 150,000
   Gross margin rate (on sales)................................................. 40%

3. Distinguish between (a) gross margin rate on sales, (b) gross margin percentage on cost of goods sold, (c) cost percentage, (d) markup on cost, and (e) markup on sales.

4. List the four principal uses of the gross margin method.

5. Why is it frequently desirable to apply the gross margin method by classes of merchandise?

6. Explain the basic approach in the retail method of estimating inventories. What data must be accumulated in order to apply the retail method?

7. The final inventory estimated by the retail inventory method was $40,000. A physical inventory of the merchandise on hand extended at retail showed $35,000. Suggest possible reasons for the discrepancy.

8. What are the primary uses of the retail method of estimating inventories?

9. Why are markdowns and markdown cancellations excluded in computing the cost ratio in the retail inventory method?

10. Explain the essential differences between (a) the completed-contract method and (b) the percentage-of-completion method of accounting for long-term construction contracts.

11. Why is the ending inventory of construction in process larger when the percentage-of-completion method is used compared with the completed-contract method? How much larger will the amount be?

12. As between the percentage-of-completion method and the completed-contract method, which would you usually prefer? Why? Do you believe that the accounting profession should continue to sanction the two alternative methods for the same set of facts? Why?

### PART B

13. Under what circumstances is the dollar-value, *Lifo*-retail method used?

14. Fundamentally, what is the basic distinction between the conventional retail inventory method and the dollar-value, *Lifo*-retail method?

15. Explain why the conventional retail inventory method must be slightly adapted when used in conjunction with the dollar-value, *Lifo*-retail method.

16. Explain why the conventional retail inventory method, as adapted, and the dollar-value, *Lifo*-retail method must be used in conbination to attain *Lifo*-retail results.

17. When *Lifo*-retail is adopted why must the ending inventory of the period prior to the base year be recomputed?

## EXERCISES

### PART A: EXERCISES 1–12

### Exercise 10–1

Income statement data for Bowen Company follows:

| | |
|---|---|
| Beginning inventory | $ 50,000 |
| Purchases | 475,000 |
| Sales | 725,000 |

*Required*:

Determine the ending inventory for each of the following independent assumptions:

*a.* Estimated gross margin on sales, 40%.
*b.* Estimated gross margin on cost, 120%.

### Exercise 10–2

Assume the following data for Taylor Company for a particular period:

| | |
|---|---|
| Sales | $120,000 |
| Initial inventory | 16,000 |
| Purchases | 80,000 |

For each of the separate situations below, estimate the final inventory:

*a.* Markup is 40% on sales.
*b.* Markup is one fourth on cost.
*c.* Markup is 60% on sales.
*d.* Markup is 50% on cost.
*e.* Markup is 57% on cost.

### Exercise 10–3

The books of Sutton Company provided the following information:

| | |
|---|---|
| Inventory, January 1 | $ 6,000 |
| Purchases to May 10 | 80,000 |
| Net sales to May 10 | 98,000 |

On May 11, the assets of the company were totally destroyed by fire. The insurance company adjuster found that the average rate of gross margin for the past few years had been 33⅓%.

*Required:*

What was the approximate value of the inventory destroyed assuming the gross margin percentage given was based on (a) sales, and (b) cost of goods sold?

## Exercise 10–4

You are engaged in the audit of the records of Storm Company. A physical inventory has been taken by the company under your observation, although the extensions have not been completed to determine the valuation of the inventory. The records of the company provide the following data: sales, $300,000; return sales, $4,000; purchases (gross), $155,000; beginning inventory, $50,000; freight-in, $5,000; and purchase returns and allowances, $2,000. The gross margin last period was 34% of net sales; you anticipate that it will be 35% for the year under audit. Estimate the value of the ending inventory. Show computations.

## Exercise 10–5

The records of Keller Company provided the following data for January for two products sold:

|  | Product A | Product B |
|---|---|---|
| Beginning inventory, January 1 | $ 40,000 | $ 60,000 |
| Purchases during January | 147,000 | 186,000 |
| Freight on purchases | 3,000 | 4,000 |
| Sales during January | 300,000 | 400,000 |

The gross margin rates on sales for the prior year were: company overall, 44%; Product A, 42%; and Product B, 49%.

*Required:*

1. Estimate the value of the ending inventory.
2. Under what conditions would your response to Requirement 1 be suspect?

## Exercise 10–6

Foster Retail Store uses the retail method of inventory. At the end of June, the records of the company reflected the following:

> Purchases during June: at cost, $265,000; at retail, $430,000.
> Sales during June: $380,000.
> Inventory, June 1: at cost, $40,000; at retail, $70,000.

Estimate the ending inventory for June assuming (a) average cost basis, and (b) *Fifo* cost basis. Show all computations.

## Exercise 10–7

The records of Popular Department Store showed the following data for Department 20 for January: beginning inventory at cost, $15,000, and $26,000 at selling price; purchases at cost, $160,000, and $297,000 at selling price; sales, $303,000; return sales, $6,000; purchase returns at cost, $4,000, and $7,000 at selling price and freight in $5,960. Determine the approximate valuation of the final inventory using the retail inventory method (a) at average cost, and (b) at *Fifo*. Show all computations.

**Exercise 10–8**

Use the retail inventory method(lower-of-cost-or-market basis) to estimate the ending inventory (*a*) at average cost and lower of cost or market, and (*b*) *Fifo* cost and lower of cost or market for Allan Retailers based on the following data:

|  | At Cost | At Retail |
|---|---|---|
| Beginning inventory | $ 84,000 | $142,000 |
| Purchases. | 330,000 | 561,000 |
| Purchases returned | 6,000 | 10,000 |
| Freight-in | 5,000 | |
| Additional markups | | 12,000 |
| Additional markup cancellations | | 5,000 |
| Markdowns | | 9,000 |
| Markdown cancellations | | 2,000 |
| Sales | | 560,000 |
| Sales returned. | | 4,000 |

**Exercise 10–9**

Waters Retail Store has just completed the annual physical inventory, which involved counting the goods on hand then pricing them at selling prices. The inventory valuation derived in this manner amounted to $96,000. The records of the company provide the following data: beginning inventory, $80,000 at retail and $52,120 at cost; purchases (including freight-in and returns), $750,000 at retail and $469,920 at cost; additional markups, $20,000; additional markup cancellations, $8,000; sales, $703,000; return sales, $9,000; and markdowns, $6,000.

*Required:*

1. Estimate the cost of the ending inventory assuming average cost and lower of cost or market.
2. Note any discrepancies and give possible reasons for them.

**Exercise 10–10**

The following data were available from the records of Swain's Retail Store with respect to a particular item sold:

|  | At Cost | At Retail |
|---|---|---|
| Purchases. | $3,310 | $5,250 |
| Additional markups | | 800 |
| Additional markup cancellations | | 50 |
| Sales | | 5,000 |
| Markdowns | | 850 |
| Markdown cancellations | | 300 |
| Initial inventory | 320 | |

*Required:*

1. Estimate the ending inventory valuations valued at (*a*) average cost and lower of cost or market, and (*b*) *Fifo* and lower of cost or market.
2. What conclusions can you draw from your answers to Requirement 1?

**Exercise 10–11**

Hood Construction Company contracted to build a plant for $500,000. Construction started in January 19A and was completed in November 19B. Data relating to the contract are summarized below:

|  | 19A | 19B |
|---|---|---|
| Cost incurred during the year | $290,000 | $135,000 |
| Estimated costs to complete | 145,000 | |
| Billings during the year | 230,000 | 270,000 |
| Cash collections during the year | 200,000 | 300,000 |

*Required:*

Give the journal entries for Hood, in parallel columns, assuming (a) the completed-contract method, and (b) the percentage-of-completion method (apportion on cost basis).

**Exercise 10–12**

Use the data given in Exercise 10–11 to complete a tabulation as follows:

|  | Completed-Contract Method | Percentage-Completion Method* |
|---|---|---|
| **Income Statement** | | |
| Income: | | |
| 19A | $_____ | $_____ |
| 19B | _____ | _____ |
| **Balance Sheet** | | |
| Receivables: | | |
| 19A | _____ | _____ |
| 19B | _____ | _____ |
| Inventory – construction in process, net of billings: | | |
| 19A | _____ | _____ |
| 19B | _____ | _____ |

* Apportion on a cost basis.

## PART D: EXERCISE 13–14

**Exercise 10–13**

Super Retailer's, Incorporated, uses the *Lifo*-retail inventory method for reporting and income tax purposes. The following data relates to 1977:

|  | At Cost | At Retail | Cost Ratio |
|---|---|---|---|
| January 1, 1977, base inventory (carried over from 1976) | $ 6,000 | $10,000 | .60 |
| Data during 1977: | | | |
| Sales | | 80,000 | |
| Purchases | 55,800 | 85,000 | |
| Net additional markups | | 7,000 | |
| Net markdowns | | 2,000 | |

*Required:*

Assume the index at January 1, 1977, was 100 and at December 31, 1977, 105. Prepare computations for 1977 to derive (*a*) the 1977 ending inventory at *Fifo* cost and (*b*) the 1977 ending inventory at *Lifo* cost. Use a format similar to Exhibit 10–4.

### Exercise 10–14

Finley's Retail Store has been using the traditional retail inventory method (lower-of-cost-or-market basis) for a number of years. On January 1, 1976, the management decided to use the *Lifo*-retail method. At the end of 1975, the traditional retail inventory method (LCM) computation was made:

|  | December 31, 1975 | |
| --- | --- | --- |
|  | At Cost | At Retail |
| Beginning inventory | $ 17,000 | $ 30,000 |
| Purchases (net) | 151,000 | 268,000 |
| Net additional markups | | 2,000 |
| Total | $168,000 | 300,000 |
| Cost ratio: $168,000 ÷ $300,000 = .56 | | |
| Sales (net) | | (275,000) |
| Net markdowns | | (5,000) |
| Inventory, December 31, 1975: | | |
| At retail | | $ 20,000 |
| At cost ($20,000 × .56) | $ 11,200 | |

*Required:*

1. Compute the values that should be used for the base year beginning inventory (January 1, 1976).
2. Explain why the December 31, 1975, inventory and the base inventory (January 1, 1976) are different.
3. Give the entry required on January 1, 1976, to restate the ending inventory of 1975 to the base inventory amount. Why is the entry made?

## PROBLEMS

### PART A: PROBLEMS 1–12

### Problem 10–1

The records of White Company revealed the following information on August 13, 19A:

| | |
| --- | --- |
| Inventory, January 1, 19A | $ 50,000 |
| Purchases, January 1 to August 13 | 300,000 |
| Sales, January 1 to August 13 | 400,000 |
| Purchase returns and allowances | 3,000 |
| Sales returns | 1,000 |
| Freight-in | 4,000 |

A fire completely destroyed the inventory on August 12, 19A, except for goods marked to sell at $6,000 which had an estimated salvage value of $4,000, and for goods in transit to which White Company had ownership; the purchase had been recorded. Invoices recorded on the latter show: merchandise cost, $2,000; and freight-in, $100. The average rate of gross margin on sales in recent years has been 25%.

*Required:*

1. Compute the inventory fire loss.
2. Under what conditions would your response to Requirement 1 be suspect? Explain.

## Problem 10-2

Amber Retail Company is developing a profit plan. The following planned data were developed for a three-month future period.

*a.* January 1 planned inventory, $90,000.
*h.* Planned average rate of gross margin on sales, 30%.

Complete the following profit plan:

| | January | February | March | Total |
|---|---|---|---|---|
| | | *Profit Plan Estimates* | | |
| Sales planned | $160,000 | $180,000 | $190,000 | $530,000 |
| Cost of goods sold: | | | | |
| Beginning inventory | ? | ? | ? | ? |
| Purchases budget | 110,000 | 130,000 | 160,000 | 400,000 |
| Total Goods Available | ? | ? | ? | ? |
| Less: Final inventory | ? | ? | ? | ? |
| Cost of goods sold | ? | ? | ? | ? |
| Gross Margin Planned | ? | ? | ? | ? |

## Problem 10-3

Davis Retail Store burned on March 19, 19D. The following information (up to the date of the fire) was taken from the records of the company which were stored in a safe: inventory, January 1, $28,000; sales, $140,000; purchases, $90,000; return sales, $3,000; purchase returns and allowances, $2,000; and freight-in, $4,000. The cost of goods sold and gross margins for the past three years were:

| | Cost of Goods Sold | Gross Margin |
|---|---|---|
| 19A | $468,000 | $122,000 |
| 19B | 435,000 | 130,000 |
| 19C | 472,000 | 127,000 |

*Required:*

1. Estimate the value of the inventory destroyed in the fire.
2. Under what conditions would your response to Requirement 1 be suspect?

3. The insurance company pays indemnity on "fair market value" at date of the fire. What amount would you recommend that Davis submit as an insurance claim? Explain.

## Problem 10–4

Dawson Company in the past valued inventories at cost. At the end of the current period, the inventory was valued at 45% of selling price as a matter of convenience. The current financial statements have been prepared and the inventory sheets destroyed; consequently, you find it impossible to reconstruct the final inventory at actual cost. The following data are available:

| | |
|---|---:|
| Sales | $300,000 |
| Final inventory (at 45% of selling price) | 22,500 |
| Cost of goods sold | 180,000 |
| Pretax income | 32,000 |
| Beginning inventory (at cost) | 20,000 |

*Required:*

Prepare a corrected multiple-step income statement. Show computations.

## Problem 10–5

The records of Stanford Department Store provided the following data for June:

| | | | | |
|---|---:|---|---|---:|
| Sales | $730,000 | | Purchase returns: | |
| Return sales | 2,000 | | At retail | $ 4,000 |
| Additional markups | 9,000 | | At cost | 3,900 |
| Additional markup cancellations | 5,000 | | Freight on purchases | 6,000 |
| Markdowns | 7,000 | | Beginning inventory: | |
| Purchases: | | | At cost | 51,000 |
| At retail | 749,000 | | At retail | 95,000 |
| At cost | 419,540 | | Employee discounts | 1,000 |
| | | | Markdown cancellations | 3,000 |

*Required:*

Estimate the valuation of the ending inventory using the retail inventory method assuming (*a*) average cost, and (*b*) *Fifo* cost (not lower of cost or market). Show computations.

## Problem 10–6

Snowden's Department Store uses the retail inventory method (LCM basis). Data for the year ended January 31, 1976, for one department appear below:

| | |
|---|---:|
| Inventory, January 31, 1975: | |
| Cost | $ 31,850 |
| Sales price | 54,000 |
| Purchases for the year ended January 31, 1976 (gross): | |
| Cost | 137,300 |
| Sales price | 245,000 |
| Sales for year (gross) | 250,000 |
| Freight on merchandise purchased | 6,000 |

Returns:
Purchases:
Cost ......................................................................... 1,150
Sales price ................................................................. 2,000
Sales......................................................................... 5,000
Additional markups ..................................................... 4,000
Additional markup cancellations ....................................... 1,000
Markdowns................................................................ 12,000
Markdown cancellations.................................................. 2,000
Employee discounts....................................................... 500

*Required:*

Estimate the January 31, 1976, inventory valuation using the retail inventory method assuming:

a. Average cost and lower of cost or market.
b. *Fifo* cost and lower of cost or market.
c. Average cost.
d. *Fifo* cost.

## Problem 10–7

The records of Austin Retailers provided the following data for the year:

|  | At Retail | At Cost |
|---|---|---|
| Inventory, January 1 ...................................... | $ 220,000 | $145,500 |
| Net purchases ............................................... | 1,573,000 | 973,500 |
| Freight-in ..................................................... |  | 15,000 |
| Additional markups ...................................... | 16,000 |  |
| Additional markup cancellations .................... | 9,000 |  |
| Markdowns ................................................... | 8,000 |  |
| Employee discounts ....................................... | 2,000 |  |
| Sales ........................................................... | 1,400,000 |  |
| Inventory December 31 (per physical count valued at retail) ......................................... | 370,000 |  |

*Required:*

1. Compute the final inventory at average cost and lower of cost or market.
2. Note any discrepancies that are indicated and suggest the possible reasons for them.
3. What accounting treatment should be accorded the discrepancy (if any)?

## Problem 10–8

The following monthly data relating to Department 5 were taken from the records of Dottie's, a ladies' ready-to-wear store: inventory March 1 at retail, $70,000, at cost, $47,600; sales, $768,900; return sales, $5,000; purchases at retail, $790,000, at cost, $520,600; freight on purchases, $12,000; special discounts on goods purchased by employees, $1,000; purchase returns at retail, $6,000, at cost, $4,000; additional markups, $14,000; additional markup cancellations, $8,000; markdowns, $7,000; markdown cancellations, $3,000; and loss of merchandise through spoilage and breakage, $1,100 (at retail). Estimate the cost of the final inventory for the department assuming average cost and lower of cost or market.

**Problem 10–9**

Master Builders, Incorporated, contracted to construct an office building for the Carson Company for $900,000. Construction began on January 15, 19A, and was completed on December 7, 19B. Master Builders' fiscal year ends December 31. Transactions by Master Builders relating to the contract are summarized below:

|  | 19A | 19B |
|---|---|---|
| Costs incurred to date ..................... | $500,000 | $800,000 |
| Estimated costs to complete............... | 320,000 |  |
| Progress billings to date ................. | 400,000 | 900,000 |
| Progress collections to date............... | 375,000 | 900,000 |

*Required:*

1. In parallel columns, give the entries on the contractor's books assuming (*a*) the completed-contract method, and (*b*) the percentage-of-completion method allocated on the basis of cost.
2. For each method, prepare the income statement and balance sheet presentations for this contract by year.
3. Which method would you recommend the contractor use? Why?

**Problem 10–10**

Chicago Construction Company contracted to build a dam for the city of Danville for $975,000. The contract provided for progress payments. Chicago Company closes the books each December 31. Work commenced under the contract on July 15, 19A, and was completed on September 30, 19C. Construction activities are summarized below by year:

19A—Construction costs incurred during the year, $180,000; estimated costs to complete, $630,000; progress billings to the city during the year, $153,000, and collections, $150,000.

19B—Construction costs incurred during the year, $450,000; estimated costs to complete, $190,000; progress billings to the city during the year, $382,500, and collections, $380,000.

19C—Construction costs incurred during the year, $195,000. Since the contract was completed, the remaining balance was billed and later collected in full per the contract.

*Required:*

1. Give the entries on the contractor's books assuming the percentage-of-completion method is used. Show computation of income apportionment on cost basis.
2. Prepare income statement and balance sheet presentations for this contract by year (percentage-of-completion basis).
3. Prepare income statement and balance sheet presentations by year assuming completed-contract method. For each amount that is different, explain the reason.
4. Which method would you recommend to this contractor? Why?

**Problem 10–11**

Richards Engineering Company contracted to build a bridge for $750,000. Payments were to be received on the basis of approved engineering estimates of costs as a basis for percentage of completion. The contract specified that 10% of each progress billing would be retained until final completion of the contract. Payment of a billing (less the 10%) is to be within five days after submission.

Transactions relating to the contract are summarized below:

19A—Construction costs incurred during the year, $200,000; estimated costs to complete, $400,000; progress billings, $190,000; and collections per the contract.

19B—Construction costs incurred during the year, $300,000; estimated costs to complete, $115,000; progress billings, $280,000; and collections per the contract.

19C—Construction costs incurred during the year, $110,000. The remaining billings were submitted by October 1 and final collections completed on November 30.

*Required:*

1. Complete a tabulation as follows:

| Date | Method | Income Recognized | Receivable Ending Balance | Construction in Process Ending Balance | Contracts in Excess of Billings Ending Balance |
|---|---|---|---|---|---|
| 19A | Completed contract | | | | |
| | Percentage completion* | | | | |
| 19B | Completed contract | | | | |
| | Percentage completion | | | | |
| 19C | Completed contract | | | | |
| | Percentage completion | | | | |

* Apportion on basis of costs.

2. Explain what causes the ending balance in construction in process to be different for the two methods.
3. Which method would you recommend for this contractor? Why?

### Problem 10–12

Superior Construction Company contracted to construct a building for $300,000. Construction commenced in 19A and was completed in 19C. Data relating to the contract are summarized below:

| | 19A | 19B | 19C |
|---|---|---|---|
| Cost incurred during the year............... | $ 80,000 | $120,000 | $ 40,000 |
| Estimated costs to complete ............... | 158,000 | 39,000 | |
| Billings during year............................. | 65,000 | 130,000 | 105,000 |
| Collections during year........................ | 60,000 | 128,000 | 110,000 |

*Required:*

Complete a tabulation as follows:

| Year | Method | Income Recognized | Receivable Ending Balance | Construction in Process Ending Balance | Contracts in Excess of Billings Ending Balance |
|------|--------|-------------------|---------------------------|----------------------------------------|------------------------------------------------|
| 19A | Completed contract | | | | |
| | Percentage completion* | | | | |
| 19B | Completed contract | | | | |
| | Percentage completion | | | | |
| 19C | Completed contract | | | | |
| | Percentage completion | | | | |

\* Apportion on basis of costs.

## PART B: PROBLEMS 13-15

### Problem 10-13

Midwest Retailers, Incorporated, uses the *Lifo*-retail inventory method. The base inventory at the start of 1976 was:

| | At Cost | At Retail | Cost Ratio |
|---|---------|-----------|------------|
| January 1, 1976, base inventory (carried over from 1975) ............... | $31,000 | $50,000 | .62 |

Data for 1976-78:

| | 1976 At Cost | 1976 At Retail | 1977 At Cost | 1977 At Retail | 1978 At Cost | 1978 At Retail |
|---|---|---|---|---|---|---|
| Sales (net) ........................ | | $130,000 | | $140,000 | | $155,000 |
| Purchases (net) ............... | $100,800 | 153,000 | $112,000 | 167,000 | $121,600 | 182,000 |
| Net markdowns ............... | | 2,000 | | 3,000 | | 2,000 |
| Net additional markups...... | | 9,000 | | 11,000 | | 10,000 |
| Applicable price index (1975 = 100) ................. | | 104 | | 107 | | 111 |

*Required:*

Prepare computations for 1976-78 to derive, for each year, (*a*) the ending inventory at *Fifo* cost, and (*b*) the ending inventory at *Lifo* cost. Use a format similar to Exhibit 10-4.

### Problem 10-14

Goode Department Store had been using the conventional retail inventory method (lower of cost or market) for some years. The management decided to continue the retail inventory method but on a last-in, first-out basis. After some investigation the decision was made to change as of January 1, 1976.

*a.* The 1975 retail records showed the following computations:

|  | At Cost | At Retail |
|---|---|---|
| Inventory, January 1, 1975 ........................ | $ 32,000 | $ 54,000 |
| Purchases (net) ..................................... | 493,400 | 680,000 |
| Net additional markups ......................... |  | 6,000 |
| Total ........................................ | $525,400 | 740,000 |
| Cost ratio: $525,400 ÷ $740,000 = .71 |  |  |
| Sales (net).............................................. |  | (670,000) |
| Net markdowns ..................................... |  | (10,000) |
| Inventory, December 31, 1975: |  |  |
| At retail................................................. |  | $ 60,000 |
| At LCM cost ($60,000 × .71) .................. | $ 42,600 |  |

*b.* Data for 1976–78:

| | 1976 | | 1977 | | 1978 | |
|---|---|---|---|---|---|---|
| | At Cost | At Retail | At Cost | At Retail | At Cost | At Retail |
| Purchases (net) ... | $501,120 | $689,000 | $497,000 | $711,000 | $529,250 | $722,000 |
| Net additional markups ......... | | 16,000 | | 10,000 | | 10,000 |
| Net markdowns ... | | 9,000 | | 11,000 | | 7,000 |
| Sales (net) ......... | | 683,900 | | 703,350 | | 732,470 |
| Applicable price index (1975 = 100)................. | | 103 | | 105 | | 108 |

*Required:*

1. Restate the December 31, 1975, inventory to base year cost for January 1, 1976. Give the entry to record the restatement on January 1, 1976 (include an explanation).
2. Prepare computations for 1976–78 to derive, for each year, (*a*) the ending inventory at *Fifo* cost, and (*b*) the ending inventory at *Lifo* cost. Use a format similar to Exhibit 10–4.

## Problem 10–15

Sewanee Department Store has used the conventional retail inventory method (LCM basis) for many years. The management decided to change to a *Lifo* cost basis effective January 1, 1976. Relevant data subject to the change follows:

*a.* Computation of retail inventory (LCM basis):

|  | At Cost | At Retail |
|---|---|---|
| Inventory, January 1, 1975 ........................ | $ 37,000 | $ 60,000 |
| Purchases, net........................................... | 227,000 | 413,000 |
| Net additional markups .......................... |  | 7,000 |
| Total ........................................ | $264,000 | 480,000 |
| Cost ratio: $264,000 ÷ $480,000 = .55 |  |  |
| Sales, net ..................................... |  | (416,000) |
| Net markdowns ...................................... |  | (14,000) |
| Inventory, December 31, 1975: |  |  |
| At retail................................................. |  | $ 50,000 |
| At LCM cost ($50,000 × .55) .................. | $ 27,500 |  |

*b.* Data for 1976–78:

| | 1976 | | 1977 | | 1978 | |
|---|---|---|---|---|---|---|
| | At Cost | At Retail | At Cost | At Retail | At Cost | At Retail |
| Purchases (net) ... | $231,000 | $400,000 | $262,200 | $450,000 | $271,600 | $470,000 |
| Net additional markups ......... | | 30,000 | | 17,000 | | 20,000 |
| Net markdowns ... | | 10,000 | | 7,000 | | 5,000 |
| Sales (net) ......... | | 380,000 | | 410,000 | | 485,000 |
| Applicable price index 1975 = 110 ................. | | 116.6 | | 122.1 | | 132.0 |

*Required:*

1. Restate the 1975 ending inventory to base year cost at January 1, 1976. Give the entry to record the restatement on January 1, 1976, and provide an explanation.
2. Prepare computations for 1976–78 to derive, for each year, (*a*) the ending inventory at *Fifo* cost, and (*b*) the ending inventory at *Lifo* cost. Use a format similar to Exhibit 10–4.

# Chapter 11

## Liabilities and Income Taxes — Measuring, Recording, and Reporting

This chapter focuses on liabilities of various types and accounting for income taxes. To facilitate discussion and study, Part A considers liabilities in general and Part B discusses accounting for income taxes.

### PART A—MEASURING, RECORDING, AND REPORTING LIABILITIES

In general, liabilities are obligations that result from past transactions to pay assets or render services in the future which are definite in amount, or subject to reasonable estimation, as stated or implied in oral or written contracts. The problems of identification and measurement are not as complex as those encountered with respect to assets.

Broadly, liabilities may be classified as (*a*) current and (*b*) long term. In accounting for liabilities, the primary problem is to make certain that no liabilities are omitted from the records and reports. The presence of an asset generally can be determined, whereas the existence of certain liabilities may be hard to ascertain. Accountants frequently see situations where it is to the advantage of management to overstate assets and understate liabilities. In particular, the accountant on occasion may find it almost impossible to learn of all liabilities, such as those owed to obscure parties in other states or regions. Once all liabilities are identified, there remains an important problem of *measurement* or *valuation*.

Conceptually, a liability is the *present value* of the future outlays it requires. Accounting practice generally measures, records, and reports current liabilities at their current cash equivalent amount which in most cases is substantially the same as their discounted present value.

Most liabilities are measured and reported at the maturity amount because (*a*) in the case of current liabilities, the difference between the maturity amount and the present value of the maturity amount is not

449

*material;* and (b) long-term debt that specifies the "going-rate" of interest will have identical maturity and present value amounts (see Chapters 6 and 19). Measurement of liabilities is in accordance with the *cost principle.* The amount of a liability usually is determined in an exchange transaction involving the acquisition of goods or services; the value of those goods and services, measured in accordance with the cost principle, in turn determines the amount of the liability.[1]

Although exchange transactions generally establish the definite amount and due date for a liability, there are situations where a definite liability is known to exist although the exact amount and/or the payment date are not known precisely. A section of the chapter is devoted to estimated liabilities.

## CURRENT LIABILITIES

Accounting for current liabilities involves the identification of certain types of items, such as short-term debts; accrued liabilities; deposits and advances received from customers, clients, and others; deferred credits; and implied contractual obligations. A particular problem of measurement arises because some of these liabilities are seldom shown in full in the accounts before some adjustment. For example, liabilities, such as wages payable, requiring periodic payments for services rendered continuously are seldom fully recorded in the accounts prior to end-of-the-period adjustments. Such liabilities frequently are not recorded in full except after an analysis has been made of certain financial facts preliminary to adjustments and other procedures have been performed preliminary to preparation of the financial statements. The identification, measurement, and reporting of these more or less fugitive liabilities often is of considerable significance. A primary objective of accounting for liabilities is to identify and measure them so that reporting will be in conformity with the *full-disclosure principle.* The amount and all other pertinent facts relative to liabilities must be identified and reported so that a company's financial condition may be evaluated.

### Current Liabilities Defined

Current liabilities for many years were defined as those obligations due within one year of balance sheet date. This definition was related to the older definition of current assets (liquidation within one year). It was recognized that these definitions were unrealistic for many concerns. As a consequence, the Committee on Accounting Procedure of the AICPA defined current liabilities as follows:

> The term *current liabilities* is used principally to designate obligations whose liquidation is reasonably expected to require the use of existing resources properly classifiable as current assets, or the creation of other current liabilities.

---

[1] These concepts are in conformity with *Statement of the Accounting Principles Board No. 4* and *APB Opinion Nos. 21 and 26,* and FASB *Statement No. 6.*

The committee further elaborated as follows:

> As a balance-sheet category, the classification is intended to include obligations for items which have entered into the operating cycle, such as payables incurred in the acquisition of materials and supplies to be used in the production of goods or in providing services to be offered for sale; collections received in advance of the delivery of goods or performance of services; and debts which arise from operations directly related to the operating cycle, such as accruals for wages, salaries, commissions, rentals, royalties, and income and other taxes. Other liabilities whose regular and ordinary liquidation is expected to occur within a relatively short period of time, usually 12 months, are also intended for inclusion, such as short-term debts arising from the acquisition of capital assets, serial maturities of long-term obligations, amounts required to be expended within one year under sinking fund provisions, and agency obligations arising from the collection or acceptance of cash or other assets for the account of third persons.

> This concept of current liabilities would include estimated or accrued amounts which are expected to be required to cover expenditures within the year for known obligations (a) the amount of which can be determined only approximately (as in the case of provisions for accruing bonus payments) or (b) where the specific person or persons to whom payment will be made cannot as yet be designated (as in the case of estimated costs to be incurred in connection with guaranteed servicing or repair of products already sold).[2]

This definition has gained wide acceptance particularly since it recognizes *operating cycles* of varying lengths in different industries.

The principal types of current liabilities are:

1. Known liabilities of a definite amount:
   a. Accounts payable.
   b. Short-term notes payable.
   c. Cash dividends payable.
   d. Advances and funds held as short-term deposits.
   e. Accrued liabilities.
   f. Deferred revenues (revenues collected in advance).
2. Known liabilities, amount dependent on operations:
   g. Taxes (income, sales, and social security).
   h. Bonus obligations.
   i. Accrued liabilities.
3. Known liabilities of an estimated amount:
   j. Guarantee and warranty obligations.
   k. Premium obligations.

Special accounting problems related to these types of current liabilities are discussed in the following sections. Normally each of the current liabilities listed above should be separately accounted for and separately reported on the balance sheet.

---

[2] AICPA, "Restatement and Revision of Accounting Research Bulletins," *Accounting Research Bulletin No. 43* (New York, 1961), pp. 21–22.

### Accounts and Notes Payable

Accounts payable and notes payable generally constitute the largest portion of current liabilities. Accounts payable as a designation is usually reserved for the recurring trade obligations of the business. This division in recording and reporting indicates the *source* of short-term funds and the *nature* of the obligation.

In determining the amount of accounts payable for goods purchased near the end of a specific period, careful attention should be given to goods that might be in transit. The purchase and liability should be recorded when *ownership passes*. In view of the fact that it is frequently difficult to determine precisely what goods are in transit, it is customary, for practical reasons, to record the liability for purchases when the goods are received. Frequently, goods are received during the last few days of the period; hence, there is a delay in checking the merchandise and the invoice may not be entered in the records. If the purchase is not recorded, liabilities are understated. Preferably the liability for goods purchased should be recorded net of cash discount allowed because that is the amount of liability that usually will be paid (see Chapter 8).

Short-term notes payable may be secured by collateral (pledged or mortgaged assets), or they may be unsecured. Secured notes should be reported separately, and the nature of the collateral should be reported both with respect to the notes and to the specific assets involved. One method is to report pledged assets in a footnote which refers both to the assets involved and the specific obligation. The preferable method is to report pledged assets parenthetically under both the asset and liability captions. To illustrate:

| | |
|---|---|
| Investment: | Current Liabilities: |
| Stock in X Corporation at cost (pledged for $1,000 note to "Y" Bank) ......... $5,000 | Notes payable (secured by stock in X Corporation) ... $3,000 |

### Discounted Notes Payable

A note payable may be either (*a*) interest bearing or (*b*) noninterest bearing (often called a discounted note). Despite these designations, all commercial notes require the borrower to pay interest. In theory, interest free loans do not exist because there is always a time cost of using money.

In the case of an *interest-bearing note* payable the borrower receives cash, or equivalent assets or services, for the *face amount* of the note; interest (in addition to the face of the note) is paid at one or more subsequent dates. To illustrate, assume X Company borrowed $3,000 cash and signed a one-year, 8% interest-bearing note, dated October 1, 19A. The borrowing transaction, accrual of interest at the end of the period, December 31, 19A, and repayment on September 30, 19B, would be recorded as follows:

October 1, 19A:

| | | |
|---|---|---|
| Cash ........................................................................ | 3,000 | |
|     Notes payable, short term............................................ | | 3,000 |

December 31, 19A:

| | | |
|---|---|---|
| Interest expense .................................................... | 60 | |
|     Accrued interest payable ($3,000 × .08 × 3/12) .................. | | 60 |

September 30, 19B: (assuming no reversing entry on January 1):

| | | |
|---|---|---|
| Accrued interest payable ................................................... | 60 | |
| Interest expense .................................................... | 180 | |
| Notes payable, short term................................................... | 3,000 | |
|     Cash ........................................................................ | | 3,240 |

In the case of a *noninterest-bearing note,* assuming the interest is based on the face amount of the note, the borrower would receive the face amount of the note less the interest deducted in advance (in the above example $3,000 − $240 = $2,760). In this situation the three entries would be as follows:

October 1, 19A:

| | | |
|---|---|---|
| Cash ........................................................................ | 2,760 | |
| Discount on note payable.................................................. | 240 | |
|     Notes payable, short term* ........................................... | | 3,000 |

December 31, 19A:

| | | |
|---|---|---|
| Interest expense .................................................... | 60 | |
|     Discount on note payable............................................... | | 60 |

September 30, 19B:

| | | |
|---|---|---|
| Interest expense .................................................... | 180 | |
| Notes payable, short term................................................... | 3,000 | |
|     Discount on note payable............................................... | | 180 |
|     Cash ........................................................................ | | 3,000 |

    * Alternatively, the note could be recorded at $2,760 and amortized up to $3,000 by the due date; see Chapter 19. The net results are the same.

At the end of 19A notes payable would be reported as follows:

Current Liabilities:

| | | |
|---|---|---|
| Notes payable ......................................... | $3,000 | |
|     Less: Discount on notes payable............... | 180 | $2,820 |

Observe that in the case of the interest-bearing note, the *effective* rate of interest was the same as the stated rate of interest, 8% per year. In the case of the noninterest-bearing note, the stated rate of interest was 8%; however, the effective rate of interest was $240 ÷ $2,760 = 8.6957%.

Alternatively, the interest terms may have specified that the 8% interest rate is to be applied to *cash proceeds.* The cash proceeds would be: $3,000 ÷ 1.08 = $2,778 (or $3,000 × .925926, from Table 6–2, = $2,778). On this basis the effective interest rate would be 8%, the same as the interest-bearing rate, and the entries would be the same as above for the discounted note except for the cash inflow and the interest amounts.

### Dividends Payable

Cash (or property) dividends payable (i.e., declared but not yet paid) should be reported as a current liability if there is an intention to pay them in the coming year or operating cycle. Stock dividends issuable are not reported as a current liability but as an element of stockholders' equity as explained in Chapter 16. Cash dividends payable are reported as a liability between date of declaration and date of payment on the legal basis that declaration is an enforceable contract that the corporation has assumed by virtue of formal authorization.

Liabilities are not recognized for undeclared dividends in arrears on preferred stock nor for any other dividends not yet declared formally by the board of directors. Scrip dividends payable (liability dividends) are reported as a current liability unless there is no intention to make payment within the near future.

### Advances and Returnable Deposits

A special type of liability arises when a company receives deposits from customers and employees. Deposits may be received from customers as guaranties to cover payment of obligations that may arise in the future or to guarantee performance of a contract or service. For example, when an order is taken, a company may require an advance payment to cover losses that would be incurred should the order be canceled. Such advances are liabilities of the company receiving the order until the underlying transaction is completed.

Deposits are frequently received from customers as guaranties for noncollection or for possible damage to property left with the customer. For example, deposits taken from customers by gas, water, light, and other public utilities are liabilities of such companies to their customers. Employees may make deposits for the return of keys and other company property, for locker privileges, and for club memberships. Some of the deposits are fairly permanent; others are current. Deposits should be reported as current or long-term liabilities depending upon the time involved between date of deposit and expected termination of the relationships. In cases where the advances or deposits are interest bearing, accrual of such interest costs is required.

### Accrued Liabilities

Accrued liabilities arise because accounting recognition must be given to expenses that have been incurred but not yet paid. Accrued liabilities usually are recognized in the accounts with adjusting entries at the end of the period. For example, property taxes usually are assessed near the end of the calendar year and are payable in the following year. The *matching principle* requires that such expenses and the related liabilities be estimated in advance, recognized in the accounts, and reported on the financial statements on an accrual basis. Determination of expense accruals may be made from an examination of the historical expense accounts and other supplementary records. In recording accrued liabilities it is especially important that appropriate account titles be used such as Wages Payable, Estimated Property Taxes Payable, and Interest Payable.

In respect to the accrual of property taxes the Committee on Accounting Procedure of the AICPA stated:

> Generally, the most acceptable basis of providing for property taxes is monthly accrual on the taxpayer's books during the fiscal period of the taxing authority for which the taxes are levied. The books will then show, at any closing date, the appropriate accrual or prepayment.[3]

For some liabilities established on an accrual basis, such as Property Taxes Payable, the amount actually paid and the amount accrued sometimes will differ. Such differences should be accounted for as an adjustment at the end of the period.

### Deferred Credits

A caption "deferred credits" or "deferred revenues" positioned after liabilities and before owners' equity sometimes is shown on published balance sheets. Usually one finds under this caption four types of items, viz:

1. Revenues collected in advance such as interest, rent, and advances received for services yet to be rendered. These items require that obligations, benefits, or services be rendered in the future before the revenue is realized.
2. Credits arising through certain external transactions that are difficult to classify. Examples are: premium on bonds payable, unearned deposit on royalties, discount on reacquired securities, and deferred income on installment sales.
3. Credits arising through certain internal transactions. Examples are: deferred repairs, allowance for rearrangement costs, and equities of minority interests (on consolidated statements).
4. Credits arising from income tax allocation procedures (deferred income taxes).

Rent collected in advance of being earned creates an obligation to render future occupancy (services). Such items are properly reported as liabilities until the services are furnished or there is a transfer of ownership to goods, as the case may be. For example, subscriptions collected in advance on magazines represent a liability to deliver a certain number of issues to the subscriber in the future. As the issues are delivered the liability, Subscriptions Collected in Advance, is reduced by a transfer to a revenue account, such as Subscription Revenue.

---

[3] Ibid., pp. 83–84.

Some of the items listed above are difficult to classify on the balance sheet. This reason underlies the wide usage of the vague balance sheet classification, Deferred credits. Observe that the classification, reported below liabilities and above owners' equity, is not consistent with the basic accounting model Assets = Liabilities + Owners' Equity, and it fails to identify clearly the true nature of the various items reported. Certain of these items are clearly in the nature of liabilities; others represent offsets or additions to related items. It is for these reasons that modern accounting theory and practice consider the deferred classification on the balance sheet to be objectionable. A sound basis for classification of the various items listed above is:

1. Classify as *current liabilities* (*a*) those items that represent a future claim against current assets whether or not there is an obligation to a specific individual or entity, and (*b*), those items that will represent revenue when the obligations for goods and services are met.
2. Classify as long-term or *other liabilities* all items that are consistent with (1) above, except that they are not *current*, that is, extended periods of time are involved.
3. Classify all other items according to their characteristics as asset offsets, owners' equity, or additions to regular liabilities.

On the above basis the following classifications are suggested:

| *Item* | *Classification* |
|---|---|
| Interest revenue collected in advance........ | Current liability |
| Rent revenue collected in advance............ | Current liability |
| Advances received for services to be rendered in the future.......................... | Current liability |
| Customer deposits, short term .............. | Current liability |
| Magazine subscriptions collected in advance ........................................... | Current liability |
| Deferred repairs ................................... | Current liability (represents a "claim" against current assets—may be long-term liability if related to several future periods) |
| Allowance for rearrangement costs ......... | Current liability |
| Premium on bonds payable..................... | Long-term liability (add to related bonds payable, see Chapter 19) |
| Equities of minority interests ................. | Owners' equity (special caption separate from controlling interest; see Chapter 18) |
| Long-term refundable deposits .............. | Long-term liability |
| Leasehold advances (leaseholds) ........... | Current or long-term liability |
| Deferred income taxes .......................... | Current or long-term liability depending upon the element of time involved. |

## Funds Collected for Third Parties

Numerous state and federal laws require businesses to collect taxes from customers and employees for remission to certain governmental agencies. Taxes collected, but not yet remitted, represent current liabilities. To illustrate, assume there is a 5% sales tax and that sales for the period were $400,000. The indicated entries are:

| | | |
|---|---|---|
| Cash and accounts receivable ...................................... | 420,000 | |
| Sales ................................................................ | | 400,000 |
| Sales taxes payable .............................................. | | 20,000 |
| | | |
| Sales taxes payable ..................................................... | 20,000 | |
| Cash ........................................................................ | | 20,000 |

## Payroll Taxes

Federal income tax laws require the employer to withhold from the pay of each employee an amount representing anticipated income taxes payable by the employee. The amount withheld depends upon the number of dependents and the level of income of the employee. Employers compute the amounts withheld according to a government-prescribed formula, or read them directly from withholding tax tables provided by the government. Income taxes withheld must be remitted to the Treasury through local depositaries (banks), and such amounts are current liabilities of the employer until remittance.

Social security legislation requires that the employer deduct a tax from the pay of each employee under specified conditions. In addition, the employer must match the contribution of the employee and remit the sum of both taxes to the Treasury along with income taxes withheld. Currently (1976–77) the tax amounts to 11.7%, one half of which is paid by the employee (5.85%) and one half by the employer.[4] The tax applies to the first $14,100 (subject to annual change by Congress) paid to each employee during the calendar year. Such taxes are referred to as F.I.C.A. taxes since the enabling act is the Federal Insurance Contributions Act. This tax is to provide survivor benefits, retirement pay, and so on.

Another social security tax levied by the federal government is to provide for *unemployment* insurance. This tax is required by the Federal Unemployment Tax Act and is generally referred to as F.U.T.A. taxes. This tax is paid wholly by the employer (of one or more persons) and amounts to a maximum of 3.2% on the first $4,200 in wages paid each employee. The law provides that 2.7% is payable to the state and .5% is payable to the federal Treasury.

Accounting for withholding taxes, F.I.C.A. taxes, and F.U.T.A. taxes may be illustrated simply. Assume salaries of $10,000 for the month of January and income tax withholdings of $1,100.

1. To record salaries and employee payroll taxes:

| | | |
|---|---|---|
| Salaries ......................................................... | 10,000 | |
| Withholding taxes payable ...................................... | | 1,100 |
| F.I.C.A. taxes payable—employees ($10,000 × 5.85%)... | | 585 |
| Cash ................................................................ | | 8,315 |

---

[4] The rate schedule for 1978–80 is 6.05%. These rates are changed by Congress from time to time.

2. To record employer payroll taxes:

| | | |
|---|---:|---:|
| Expense—payroll taxes................................................ | 905 | |
| F.I.C.A. taxes payable—employer ($10,000 × 5.85%) ... | | 585 |
| F.U.T.A. taxes payable—federal ($10,000 × .5%) ......... | | 50 |
| F.U.T.A. taxes payable—state ($10,000 × 2.7%)............ | | 270 |

When the taxes are remitted, Cash is credited and the current liability accounts established in the preceding entries are debited.

### Tax and Bonus Problems

It is not unusual to find employment contracts providing for the payment of a *bonus* to an officer, branch manager, or other employees of a corporation. A bonus should be treated as an operating expense and set up as a current liability when earned and pending payment. Bonus payments generally are deductible in computing taxable income under federal tax laws. Bonus contracts relating to income earned are usually one of two classes, viz:

1. The bonus is computed on the net income after deducting income taxes, but before deducting the bonus.
2. The bonus is computed after deducting both the bonus and the income taxes.

Since the tax is not determinable before the bonus is computed or vice versa, a special computation is required, based on simultaneous equations. To illustrate a typical situation, assume the Bryan Company reported income of $100,000 before deducting income taxes and before the bonus to the general manager. Assume the tax rate $T$ is 52%, and the bonus rate $B$ is 10%. Two situations are illustrated:

*Situation 1:* The bonus is based on income after deducting income taxes but before deducting the bonus.

$$B = .10(\$100,000 - T) \qquad (1)$$
$$T = .52(\$100,000 - B) \qquad (2)$$

Substitute value of $T$ in (2) for $T$ in (1):

$$B = .10[\$100,000 - .52(\$100,000 - B)] \qquad (3)$$
$$B = .10[\$100,000 - \$52,000 + .52B]$$
$$B = \$10,000 - \$5,200 + .052B$$
$$B - .052B = \$4,800$$
$$.948B = \$4,800$$
$$B = \underline{\$5,063}$$

Substitute value of $B$ in (2):

$$T = .52(\$100,000 - \$5,063)$$
$$T = \underline{\$49,367}$$

*Situation 2:* The bonus is based on net income after deducting both income taxes and the bonus.

$$B = .10(\$100,000 - B - T) \qquad (1)$$
$$T = .52(\$100,000 - B) \qquad (2)$$

Substitute value of $T$ in (2) for $T$ in (1):

$$B = .10[\$100,000 - B - .52(\$100,000 - B)] \qquad (3)$$
$$B = .10[\$100,000 - B - \$52,000 + .52B]$$
$$B = \$10,000 - .10B - \$5,200 + .052B$$
$$B + .10B - .052B = \$4,800$$
$$1.048B = \$4,800$$
$$B = \underline{\underline{\$4,580}}$$

Substitute value of $B$ in (2):

$$T = .52(\$100,000 - \$4,580)$$
$$T = \underline{\underline{\$49,618}}$$

**Proof of Computations**

|  | Situation 1 | Situation 2 |
|---|---|---|
| Computation of taxes: | | |
| Income before tax and bonus | $100,000 | $100,000 |
| Deduct bonus (as computed) | 5,063 | 4,580 |
| Taxable income | 94,937 | 95,420 |
| Multiply by tax rate | .52 | .62 |
| Tax | $ 49,367 | $ 49,618 |
| Computation of bonus: | | |
| Income before taxes and bonus | $100,000 | $100,000 |
| Taxes | 49,367 | 49,618 |
|  | 50,633 | 50,382 |
| Bonus (as computed) | | 4,580 |
| Income subject to bonus | 50,633 | 45,802 |
| Multiply by bonus rate | .10 | .10 |
| Bonus | $ 5,063 | $ 4,580 |

The entries to record the bonus and income taxes in Situation 2 would be as follows:

1. To record bonus:

| Expense—manager's bonus | 4,580 | |
|---|---|---|
| Bonus payable | | 4,580 |

2. To record income taxes:

| Expense—income taxes | 49,618 | |
|---|---|---|
| Income taxes payable | | 49,618 |

3. To record payment of bonus:

| Bonus payable | 4,580 | |
|---|---|---|
| Cash | | 4,580 |

## LONG-TERM LIABILITIES

All liabilities, not classified as current (as defined in the preceding section), usually are classified as long-term liabilities; however, some financial statements carry a second noncurrent category, *other liabilities*. Bonds payable and long-term notes and mortgages are often reported under long-term liabilities, and all other long-term obligations may be reported under the other liabilities category. Bonds payable are reported each period at their maturity amount plus any unamortized premium, or less any unamortized discount (also see Chapter 19).

### Unrealistic Interest Rates

A special measurement problem arises when long-term debt either (*a*) specifies an interest rate that is significantly below the going rate of interest, or (*b*) does not specify an interest rate. These situations complicate measurement of (*a*) the amount of the debt that should be reported on the balance sheet, and (*b*) the amount of interest expense that should be reported on the income statement. Prior to *APB Opinion No. 21,* "Interest on Receivables and Payables" (1971), this measurement problem tended to be overlooked in the accounting and reporting processes. The *Opinion* states:

> When a note is received or issued solely for cash and no other right or privilege is exchanged, it is presumed to have a present value at issuance measured by the cash proceeds exchanged. If cash and some other rights or privileges are exchanged for a note, the value of the rights or privileges should be given accounting recognition. . . .

> When a note is exchanged for property, goods, or services in a bargained transaction entered into at arm's length, there should be a general presumption that the rate of interest stipulated by the parties to the transaction represents fair and adequate compensation to the supplier for the use of the related funds. That presumption, however, must not permit the form of the transaction to prevail over its economic substance and thus would not apply when (1) interest is not stated, or (2) the stated interest rate is unreasonable, or (3) the stated face amount of the note is materially different from the current cash sales price for the same or similar items or from the market value of the note at the date of the transaction. In these circumstances, the note, the sales price, and the cost of the property, goods, or service exchanged for the note should be recorded at the fair value of the property, goods, or service or at an amount that reasonably approximates the market value of the note, whichever is the more clearly determinable. That amount may, or may not, be the same as its face amount, and any resulting discount or premium should be accounted for as an element of interest over the life of the note.

The two different situations will be illustrated.

*Situation 1:* Assume Company X acquires an asset (other than cash) and signs a three-year note for $10,000; the note does not specify interest. Assume the going rate of interest for this type of borrowing for this company is 9% payable annually. No fair market value for the asset is determinable.

*a.* The note and the asset, measured at the present value of the debt, would be recorded as follows:[5]

Asset acquired............................................................. 7,722
Discount on note payable................................................ 2,278
    Note payable, long term ............................................    10,000

   Computation: Since there are no periodic cash interest payments, only the maturity amount is discounted for "$n$" periods, at "$i$" interest rate to derive the present value of the note, viz: $10,000 $\times P_{n=3;\ i=9\%}$ = $10,000 $\times$ .772 (Table 6–2) = $7.722 (see Chapter 6).

*b.* At the end of the first year, the following adjusting entry for interest expense and discount amortization would be made assuming straight-line amortization (see footnote 6):

Interest expense .................................................... 759
    Discount on note payable..............................................    759

   Computation:
    Straight-line method (discussed below), $2,278 ÷ 3 years = $759.

At the end of the first year, the note would be reported on the balance sheet as follows:

Long-Term Liabilities:
Note payable, maturity amount ................................. $10,000
Less: Unamortized discount ($2,278 -- $759) ............... .  1,519   $8,481

*Situation 2:* Assume the same facts as Situation 1 above except that the note specifies an interest rate of 5%, payable at the end of each 12-month period. In this situation, the stated rate of interest is unreasonable; it is too low by 4%.

*a.* To measure and record the transaction at the present value of the debt:

Asset acquired............................................................. 8,988
Discount on note payable................................................ 1,012
    Note payable......................................................    10,000

   Computation–Since there are periodic cash interest payments, the maturity amounts and the amounts of the three interest payments must be discounted for "$n$" periods at "$i$" interest rate to derive the present value of the note, viz:
      $10,000 $\times P_{n=3,\ i=9\%}$ = (as in Situation 1) ............................ $7,722
      ($10,000 $\times$ .05) $\times P_{n=3,\ i=9\%}$ = $500 $\times$ 2.5313 (Table 6–4) .........    1,266
      Total Present Value ....................................................    $8,988

*b.* To record straight-line amortization of discount and interest expense at end of the first year:

Interest expense ................................................... 837
    Discount on note payable ($1,012 ÷ 3 years) ....................    337
    Cash ($10,000 $\times$ .05) ...................................................    500

The discount on note payable, Situations 1 and 2, was amortized using the straight-line method. This method, although not theoreti-

---

   [5] Alternatively, some accountants prefer to record the note at its present value of $7,722. Amortization of the discount would reflect a credit to Note Payable so that a maturity date the liability account would reflect $10,000. Both methods derive the same results.

cally sound, may be used when the amount is not material (see below).[6]

*APB Opinion No. 21*, par. 6, requires the interest method of amortization; however, if the difference in results between that method and the straight-line method is not material, the latter method may be used (see Chapter 19). Amortization each year using the interest method would be as follows:

| Year | Periodic Cash Interest Payments | Effective Interest | Amortization Amount | Debt Carrying Value |
|------|------|------|------|------|
| Situation 1: | | | | $ 7,722 |
| 1............... | $  0 | $7,722 × .09 = $695 | $695 | 8,417 |
| 2............... | 0 | 8,417 × .09 =  757 | 757 | 9,174 |
| 3............... | 0 | 9,174 × .09 =  826 | 826 | 10,000 |
| Situation 2: | | | | 8,988 |
| 1.........:..... | 500 | 8,988 × .09 =  809 | 309 | 9,297 |
| 2............... | 500 | 9,297 × .09 =  837 | 337 | 9,634 |
| 3............... | 500 | 9,634 × .09 =  866 | 366 | 10,000 |

Observe in Situation 2 that the asset is recorded at a higher cost ($8,988 − $7,722 = $1,266) than in Situation 1 because there was a different cash cost; in Situation 1 cash disbursed totaled $10,000 (at the end of the third year) whereas in Situation 2 cash disbursed was ($500 × 3) + $10,000 = $11,500. The difference in asset cost ($1,266) is not the same as the difference in total cash paid ($1,500) because the cash flows in Situation 2 were at different times (i.e., the time value of money caused the difference).

### Current Maturities of Long-Term Debt

On the balance sheet for the year preceding the maturity of a long-term debt, the amount to be paid during the upcoming current period, if payable out of current assets, should be reported as a current liability. FASB *Statement No. 7*, "Classification of Short-Term Obligations," specifies that this classification should not be used if the payment is to be made from a sinking fund, or the cash is to be derived from other noncurrent sources. To illustrate, the current payment of a *serial bond issue* would be reported as follows:

| | | |
|------|------|------|
| Current Liabilities: | | |
| Current payment on bond issue............... | | $100,000 |
| Long-Term Liabilities: | | |
| Bonds payable...................................... | $500,000 | |
| Less: Current payment ...................... | 100,000 | 400,000 |

---

[6] AICPA, "Interest on Receivables and Payables," *Accounting Principles Board Opinion No. 21* (New York 1971), par. 15.

Bonds payable are discussed in depth in Chapter 19 in conjunction with long-term investments in bonds.

## ESTIMATED LIABILITIES

Estimated liabilities are *known* liabilities that are *uncertain* in amount, and often as to due date at the time the financial statements are prepared. Estimated liabilities should be reported on the balance sheet as either current or long term rather than by footnote. The amount of each such liability should be estimated realistically on the basis of all available information. The account title should clearly indicate that the amount reported is an estimate. For example, appropriate titles are Estimated Income Taxes Payable and Estimated Warranty Liability. The term *reserve* should not be used in account titles for estimated liabilities, although this was common in the past.

There are numerous situations where known liabilities must be estimated as to amount at the balance sheet date. Several typical situations are discussed in the paragraphs to follow.

### Liability from Warranties

A warranty or guarantee is a promise by the seller to make good deficiencies in merchandise over a specified period after the sale. Sometimes they involve a formal written agreement; in other cases, only a verbal or implied promise. Since the expenditure of cash or other resources in the future is generally required, a liability exists from the date of sale to the end of the warranty period. This known liability, estimated in amount, should be recognized in the accounts by an accrual entry in the period that the merchandise was sold so that the expense is matched with the revenue of the period in accordance with the matching principle. The estimated amount of the expense is recorded as a debit to operating expense and as a credit to a liability (usually current). When actual resources are expended on the warranty, cash or other assets are credited and the warranty liability debited.

To illustrate, assume Company R sold merchandise for $200,000 cash during the period. Experience has indicated that warranty and guarantee costs will approximate one half of 1% of sales. The indicated entries are:

In year of sale:

| | | |
|---|---|---|
| Cash | 200,000 | |
| Sales revenue | | 200,000 |

| | | |
|---|---|---|
| Estimated warranty expense | 1,000 | |
| Estimated warranty liability | | 1,000 |

Subsequently during warranty period for actual expenditures:

| | | |
|---|---|---|
| Estimated warranty liability | 987 | |
| Cash (or other resources) | | 987 |

Clearly when warranty expense is immaterial in amount, a company would not accrue it as illustrated above; instead, they would account for it on a cash basis because, for practical reasons, the materiality concept is permitted to override the theoretical matching principle.

### Liability from Premiums, Coupons, and Trading Stamps

As a promotional device, many companies offer premiums of one kind or another to customers who turn in coupons, trading stamps, labels, box tops, wrappers, and so on, received when merchandise is purchased. At the end of each accounting period, a portion of these will be outstanding (unredeemed by the customers), some of which ultimately will be turned in for redemption. These outstanding claims for premiums represent a liability that must be recognized in the period of sale of the merchandise. The estimated cost of the premiums that will be given should be recorded as an estimated expense of the period of sale and an estimated liability credited.

To illustrate a typical situation, assume Baker Coffee Company offered to customers a premium – a silver coffee spoon (cost to Baker 75 cents each) upon the return of 20 coupons. One coupon is placed in each can of coffee when packed. The company estimated, on the basis of past experience, that only 70% of the coupons would ever be redeemed. The following additional data for two years are available:

|  | First Year | Second Year |
|---|---|---|
| Number of coffee spoons purchased @ $.75 | 6,000 | 4,000 |
| Number of coupons redeemed | 40,000 | 120,000 |
| Number of cans of coffee sold | 100,000 | 200,000 |

The indicated entries are as follows:

1. To record purchases of spoons:

|  | First Year | | Second Year | |
|---|---|---|---|---|
| Premiums – silverware | 4,500 | | 3,000 | |
| Cash | | 4,500 | | 3,000 |

2. To record estimated liability and premium expense on sales:

|  | | | | |
|---|---|---|---|---|
| Premium expense* | 2,625 | | 5,250 | |
| Estimated premium claims outstanding | | 2,625 | | 5,250 |

    * Computations:
       Year 1: $(100,000 \div 20) \times \$.75 \times .70 = \$2,625$.
       Year 2: $(200,000 \div 20) \times \$.75 \times .70 = \$5,250$.

3. To record redemption of coupons:

|  | | | | |
|---|---|---|---|---|
| Estimated premium claims outstanding* | 1,500 | | 4,500 | |
| Premiums – silverware | | 1,500 | | 4,500 |

    * Computations:

$$\frac{40,000}{20} \times \$.75 = \$1,500.$$

$$\frac{120,000}{20} \times \$.75 = \$4,500.$$

4. To close:

| | | |
|---|---|---|
| Income summary ................................... | 2,625 | 5,250 |
| Premium expense............................ | 2,625 | 5,250 |

Balances (ending) for financial statements:

Balance Sheet:

Premiums—silverware (inventory):

| | | |
|---|---|---|
| ($4,500 − $1,500) ........................................... | $3,000 | |
| ($3,000 + $3,000 − $4,500) ............................... | | $1,500 |

Estimated premium claims outstanding (liability):

| | | |
|---|---|---|
| ($2,625 − $1,500) ........................................... | 1,125 | |
| ($1,125 + $5,250 − $4,500) ............................... | | 1,875 |

Income Statement:

| | | |
|---|---|---|
| Premium expense (distribution expenses).............. | 2,625 | 5,250 |

The Premiums—Silverware account balance should be reported as a current asset. The balance in the Estimated Premium Claims Outstanding should be reported as a current liability.

In accounting for estimated expenses and liabilities, as illustrated above, not infrequently the actual amount often will vary from the estimate. In this situation, when the actual amount becomes known, an adjustment to the estimated liability account is necessary. Recall that under *APB Opinion No. 20*, this is a change in an estimate, and should be treated as a current item in the period of change; that is, on a prospective rather than on a retroactive basis (see Chapters 4 and 20).

## CONTINGENCIES

Prior to the issuance of FASB, *Statement of Financial Standards No. 5* "Accounting for Contingencies," (March 1975), as amended by FASB *Statement No. 11* (December 31, 1975), the reporting of contingencies was quite varied and most of the attention was focused only on *contingent liabilities. Statement No. 5* is much broader; it defines a contingency as:

> ... an existing condition, situation or set of circumstances involving uncertainty as to possible gain (a gain contingency) or loss (a loss contingency) to an enterprise that will ultimately be resolved when one or more future events occur or fail to occur. Resolution of the uncertainty may confirm the acquisition of an asset or the reduction of a liability or the loss or impairment of an asset or the incurrence of a liability.

Thus, a contingency is characterized by (a) an existing condition, (b) uncertainty as to the ultimate effect, and (c) its resolution depending on one or more future events. Examples of loss contingencies are: collectibility of receivables, warranty obligations, threatened or actual litigation, potential claims for damages, assessments, and guarantees of the debts of others.

The accounting and reporting requirements specified by FASB *State-*

*ment No.* 5 depend upon the seriousness of a contingency and hence the degree of certainty of loss or gain. To assess the range of certainty versus uncertainty, three terms are used in the *Statement* as follows:

*a.* Probable—The future event or events are or are not likely to occur.
*b.* Reasonably possible—The chance of the future event or events occuring (or not occurring) is more than remote but less than likely.
*c.* Remote—The chance of the future event or events occurring (or not occurring) is slight.

An estimated loss from a contingency may be *(a)* accrued in the accounts and reported in the financial statements and/or *(b)* disclosed in the notes to the financial statements.

A loss contingency *must be accrued* in the accounts and reported in the financial statements (as opposed to footnote only) if two conditions are met:

1. Information prior to issuance of the financial statements indicate that it is *probable* that an asset has been impaired or a liability has been incurred at the date of the financial statements. It is implicit in this condition that it must be probable that one or more future events will occur confirming the fact of the loss.
2. The amount of the loss can be reasonably estimated.

### Accrual of Estimated Contingency Losses

A contingency loss that meets both of the above criteria usually involves either *(a)* the reduction of an asset, or *(b)* the incurrence of a liability. Such losses must be accrued in the accounts and reported in the financial statements. A recurring and typical contingency loss arising from the *reduction of an asset* for bad debts (uncollectible receivables). Accounting for this type of contingency loss was explained in detail in Chapter 7. The loss is accrued since it clearly meets both of the above criteria. Recall that Bad Debt Expense is debited and the Allowance for Doubtful Accounts (a contra asset account) is credited for the estimated bad debt losses related to sales for the period. Accrual of this contingency loss has the effect of reducing income and assets by the amount of the estimated loss. It conforms to the matching principle.

A typical contingency loss arising from the *incurrence of a liability* is the obligation for product warranties and guarantees previously discussed. The estimated loss and related liability were accrued because both of the above criteria were met. Similar conditions may exist in the case of injury or damage caused by product defects (such as in drugs, toys, and automobiles).

In contrast, neither the absence of insurance on the assets of an enterprise, or the possibility of future injury to others meets both conditions for accrual of a contingency loss. In these situations, there is an existing condition, the absence of insurance. However, mere exposure to risk does not mean that an asset has been impaired nor that a liability has been incurred.

A contingency loss that is occurring with ever greater frequency is lawsuits for damages. In recent years, these suits have been particularly successful for the plaintiffs. These situations often fall into the *probable* category and, consequently, require *accrual* before the trials are terminated and the court decision rendered. To illustrate, assume XY Company is sued for $500,000 damages for a personal injury suffered by the plaintiff in a truck-auto accident. The truck was owned by XY Company. Although the trial has not been scheduled, the company counsel believes it is probable that the plaintiff will be successful against the company for approximately $100,000 (clearly, this often cannot be reasonably estimated). Therefore, XY Company is required by FASB *Statement No. 5* to make the following accrual entry prior to preparation of the financial statements:

```
Extraordinary loss — estimated damages from injury
   (Note A).........................................................     100,000
      Estimated liability — injury claim...............................           100,000
```

This contingency loss, reported on the income statement, created a contingent liability which is reported as a liability on the balance sheet.

In the case of a contingency loss which must be accrued, resulting in an asset reduction, the credit should be made to an "allowance" account which would be reported as a contra account to the asset involved.

### Disclosure of Estimated Contingency Losses

If a contingency loss meets one, but not both, of the criteria listed above, and as a result is not accrued, *disclosure by footnote* must be made when it is at least *reasonably possible* that there has been an impairment of assets or that a liability has been incurred. Disclosure must indicate the nature of the contingency and give an estimate of the *possible* loss, or it must state that a reasonable estimate cannot be made.

In the past this type of contingency loss generally was referred to as a *contingent liability*. For many years, the disclosure of contingent liabilities has been a part of generally accepted accounting principles. Some of the common contingent liabilities are: accommodation endorsements (cosigning a note for another party), purchase commitments, and lawsuit pending. *Statement No. 5* concludes that disclosure of contingent liabilities shall continue as before under generally accepted accounting principles.

However, all contingency losses, including contingent liabilities, now must be accounted for and reported in accordance with FASB *Statement No. 5* cited above. One particularly difficult area is determination of the appropriate accounting and reporting with respect to legal litigation, claims, and assessments, whether they are potential, pending, or in process. This area is complicated because many lawyers feel that presettlement disclosure may prejudice the outcome of the case. In these situations, FASB *Statement No. 5* states that "the opinions of legal counsel and other advisers, the experience of the enterprise in similar cases, the experience of other enterprises, and any decision of the enterprise's management as to how the enterprise intends to respond to the lawsuit, claim or assessment." It has been said that if the enterprise plans to forcefully contest the lawsuit, claim, or assessment, this is evidence that in their opinion a contingency loss is not *probable* (no accrual required) and may not even be *reasonably possible* (no accrual or disclosure required).

### Contingency Gains

A contingent gain exists when the three characteristics of a contingency exist (as defined above) and there is apt to be an increase in assets or a decrease in liabilities if the conditions materialize. Consistent with the concept of conservatism, contingency gains usually are not accrued; however, disclosure by footnote is permitted with certain constraints. FASB *Statement No. 5* reads:

a. Contingencies that might result in gains usually are not reflected in the accounts since to do so might be to recognize revenue prior to its realization.
b. Adequate disclosure shall be made of contingencies that might result in gains, but care shall be exercised to avoid misleading implications as to the likelihood of realization.

An example of a contingency gain would be the case where the company has sued another party for damages. Another case would be where expropriation (by a foreign government) of assets is probable and reimbursement will exceed book value.

### Appropriations and Reserves of Retained Earnings

The use of "reserves for general contingencies" and appropriations of retained earnings to record the *accrual of contingent losses* is not permitted by FASB *Statement No. 5*. The statement also asserts that if appropriations or reserves of retained earnings are recorded, the debit to create them must be to Retained Earnings, not to loss or expense, and the balances in these accounts must not be reported outside the stockholders' equity section of the balance sheet (also see Chapter 16).

### PART B—ACCOUNTING FOR INCOME TAXES

Chapter 4 briefly discussed income tax allocation. In that discussion, the concepts of intraperiod (i.e., interstatement) and interperiod income tax allocation were briefly introduced; here the topic is considered in more depth. *Intraperiod* refers to the allocation of income tax expense within the current period between certain subclassifications on the income statement and sometimes on the statement of retained earnings. *Interperiod* refers to the allocation of income tax expense as between two or more periods. Both types of income tax allocation have the primary purpose of reporting (or matching) income tax expense with operating income, extraordinary items, and prior period adjustments when they have a tax impact. First, interperiod tax allocation will be discussed, then intraperiod allocation.

## INTERPERIOD INCOME TAX ALLOCATION

Interperiod income tax allocation between accounting periods is necessary when some transactions (or items) affect the determination of *pretax accounting income* in one accounting period and affect the determination of *taxable income* in a different period. Fundamentally, this is due to differences between (1) the application of generally accepted accounting principles in recognizing revenues and expenses, and (2) the provisions of the income tax laws and related treasury regulations.

The first major pronouncement on income tax allocation was made in 1961 by the AICPA Committee on Accounting Procedure and stated:

> Income taxes are an expense that should be allocated, when necessary and practicable, to income and other accounts, as other expenses are allocated. What the income statements should reflect under this head, as under any other head, is the expense properly allocable to the income included in the income statement for the year.[7]

The next major pronouncement, and the one currently effective, was "Accounting for Income Taxes," *APB Opinion No. 11*, (December 1967). The discussions to follow conform with *Opinion No. 11*.

Federal income taxes are by far the most significant tax levied on the corporation both in respect to complexity and to the impact on decisions of management and on the resultant financial reports. In their early days, income taxes were levied primarily on a cash basis; since 1918 this approach has been modified to more generally conform to accrual accounting as reflected on the periodic financial reports. Despite this trend there are today many divergencies between *pretax accounting income* and *taxable income* for any given period. Clearly, the objectives of income taxation, in addition to raising revenues (presumably according to ability to pay), include: to control the economy, to promote full employment, to stimulate capital expenditures, and to attain certain social ends (i.e., tax deductibility of contributions to certain types of institutions).

### Tax Differences

The numerous differences between pretax accounting income and taxable income give rise to *differences;* for some, but not all, of these differences, the tax effect must be recognized in the accounts and in the financial statements. To illustrate, assume for the current year,

---

[7] AICPA, "Restatement and Revision of Accounting Research Bulletins," *Accounting Research Bulletin No. 43* (New York, 1961), p. 88.

19A, pretax accounting income of $40,000; taxable income, $35,000; and an average tax rate of 40%. There would be a difference of $5,000 and a *tax difference* of $5,000 × .40 = $2,000. The central question is the extent to which accounting recognition and reporting should be given to income tax differences. Accounting recognition of tax differences depends on the *type* of underlying difference; there are two distinct types: permanent differences and timing differences.

A number of *APB Opinions* and FASB *Statements* provide instructions on the tax allocation effects. For example, FASB *Statement No. 9* states: "interperiod tax allocation is required for intangible drilling costs and other costs associated with the exploration for and development of oil and gas reserves that enter into the determination of taxable income and pretax accounting income in different periods."

*Permanent Differences.* Income tax allocation is *never* applied to permanent differences because they will not be offset or reversed in the future; that is, they never "turn around" in the future. Permanent differences arise from (a) items that affect determination of pretax accounting income but never affect taxable income, and (b) items that affect determination of taxable income but never affect pretax accounting income. Common examples of the two categories are: tax exempt revenue on municipal bonds; the expense portion of premiums paid on life insurance policies carried by an enterprise on its officers; fines and expenses resulting from violations of the law; statutory depletion on natural resources; and amortization of goodwill. Since permanent differences are not subject to tax allocation procedures, our attention in the discussions to follow will focus only on timing differences.

*Timing Differences.* Income tax allocation procedures *always* are applied to timing differences because the tax effect will offset, reverse, or "turn around" in one or more periods in the future. They will turn around or reverse in the future because items that cause them will be included in the determination of both pretax accounting income and taxable income but in different periods. Four types of transactions cause timing differences, viz:

a. Revenues or gains which are included in taxable income one or more periods after they are included in pretax accounting income; for example, gross profit on installment sales.
b. Expenses or losses which are deducted in determining taxable income one or more periods after they are deducted in determining pretax accounting income; for example, estimated (accrued) warranty costs.
c. Revenues or gains which are included in taxable income before they are included in pretax accounting income; for example, rent revenue collected in advance.
d. Expenses or losses which are deducted in determining taxable income before they are deducted in determining pretax accounting income; for example, depreciation on an accelerated basis for tax purposes, but on a straight-line basis for accounting purposes.

## Fundamental Concepts and Procedures

The fundamental concepts and procedures of interperiod income tax allocation are not complex; however, the related recordkeeping can be somewhat burdensome in a complex situation. To illustrate tax allocation in a direct way, assume XY Corporation reported pretax accounting income of $40,000 in Year A and also in Year B and an average tax rate of 40%. Assume further that in Year A a $5,000 expense item was included on the income statement but was not allowable as a deduction on the income tax return until Year B. Thus, there was a timing tax difference of $5,000 × .40 = $2,000. The results for the two years would be as follows:

|                                                       | Year A   | Year B   |
|-------------------------------------------------------|----------|----------|
| Income taxes payable (per tax return):                |          |          |
| Year A: ($40,000 + $5,000) × .40................       | $18,000  |          |
| Year B: ($40,000 − $5,000) × .40...............        |          | $14,000  |
| Income Statement:                                     |          |          |
| Case A—with interperiod tax allocation (correct):     |          |          |
| Pretax operating income .......................       | $40,000  | $40,000  |
| Less: Income tax expense (allocated):                 |          |          |
| $40,000 × .40...............................           | 16,000   | 16,000   |
| Net Income .........................................  | $24,000  | $24,000  |
| Case B—without interperiod tax allocation (incorrect):|          |          |
| Pretax operating income .......................       | $40,000  | $40,000  |
| Less: Income tax expense (not allocated):             |          |          |
| Same as taxes payable .................               | 18,000   | 14,000   |
| Net Income ...........................................| $22,000  | $26,000  |

Observe that both total income tax expense and total income taxes payable are the same for the two years combined; however, each is different by year by the amount of the timing tax difference of $5,000 × .40 = $2,000.

Interperiod tax allocation has, as its purpose, the reporting of income tax expense on an accrual basis rather than on the tax return basis. Note that the timing difference in Year A reversed or turned around in Year B. Many accountants believe that failure to allocate tax differences between periods would cause net income to be incorrectly reported because expenses are not properly matched with revenues for the period.

The interperiod tax allocation reflected in the above example would be *accrued in the accounts* at each year-end as follows:

Year 19A:

| Income tax expense (per income statement).....................| 16,000 |        |
|---------------------------------------------------------------|--------|--------|
| Deferred income taxes ....................................     | 2,000  |        |
| Income taxes payable (per tax return) ........................ |        | 18,000 |

Year 19B:

| Income tax expense (per income statement) | 16,000 | |
|---|---|---|
| Deferred income taxes | | 2,000 |
| Income taxes payable (per tax return) | | 14,000 |

A more comprehensive example is shown in Exhibit 11–1. At the end of the year the balance in the deferred income tax account is reported on the balance sheet (a) if a debit, as a deferred charge; and (b) if a credit, as a liability. The current portion is reported as a current item, and the remainder is reported as a noncurrent item. "Accounting for Income Taxes," *APB Opinion No. 11,* reads:

> Deferred charges and deferred credits relating to timing differences represent the cumulative recognition given to their tax effects and as such do not represent receivables or payables in the usual sense. They should be classified in two categories—one for the net current amount and the other for the net noncurrent amount. This presentation is consistent with the customary distinction between current and noncurrent categories and also recognizes the close relationship among the various deferred tax accounts, all of which bear on the determination of income tax expense. The current portions of such deferred charges and credits should be those amounts which relate to assets and liabilities classified as current. Thus, if installment receivables are a current asset, the deferred credits representing the tax effects of uncollected installment sales should be a current item; if an estimated provision for warranties is a current liability, the deferred charge representing the tax effect of such provision should be a current item.[8]

## INTRAPERIOD TAX ALLOCATION

Intraperiod tax allocation sometimes called interstatement allocation, requires the allocation of income tax expense (as derived by application of interperiod tax allocation) within a period to certain subclassifications on the financial statements. The concept of intraperiod tax allocation is that the tax effect should be reported with the item that affected the tax. This means that income tax expense for the period must be allocated to (a) income from operations, (b) extraordinary items, and (c) prior period adjustments to the extent that each of these classifications reports items that affected total income tax expense for the period. This is strictly a *reporting allocation;* no entries are made in the accounts for the intraperiod allocation. The various items are reported *net of tax.* Exhibit 11–1 presents a rare situation where intraperiod tax allocation affects the balance sheet as well as the income statement and statement of retained earnings. The results are illustrated with and without allocation to demonstrate the misleading implications if intraperiod allocation is not followed. Observe that without intraperiod allocation net income is overstated by $12,000 (over 21%).

---

[8] AICPA, "Accounting for Income Taxes," *APB Opinion No. 11* (New York, December 1967), par. 57.

## A COMPREHENSIVE ILLUSTRATION

Interperiod and intraperiod tax allocation procedures were discussed separately above; however, they are interrelated. Interperiod allocation is accomplished first (and the effects recorded in the accounts); next income tax expense for the current period is allocated within the period for reporting purposes only. A comprehensive illustration is given in Exhibit 11–2.

## DISCLOSURE OF TAX ALLOCATION

Full disclosure of the components of income tax expense (including deferred income taxes) is required. In respect to the income statement *APB Opinion No. 11* states that "the components of income tax expense should be disclosed" on the income statement; that is, in addition to *intraperiod* allocation, taxes estimated to be payable and the tax effects of timing differences should be reported. The *Opinion* states that these amounts "may be presented as separate items in the income statement or, alternatively, as combined amounts with disclosure of the components parenthetically or in a note to the financial statements." An example of the footnote approach is shown in Exhibit 11–3.

**EXHIBIT 11–1**
**Intraperiod Tax Allocation**

1. Assumed income tax rate of 40% on all items.
2. Items subject to income taxes:
   a. Pretax operating income, $100,000.
   b. Extraordinary loss, $5,000.
   c. Prior period adjustment (decrease in retained earnings), $20,000 (example, damages paid).
   d. Decrease in owners' equity, $10,000 (example, effect of certain stock option plans).
3. Income tax expense, $26,000.

|  | Without Intraperiod Tax Allocation (incorrect) | With Intraperiod Tax Allocation (correct) | |
|---|---|---|---|
| Income Statement: | | | |
| Pretax operating income | $100,000 | | $100,000 |
| Less: Income tax expense | 26,000 | | 40,000 |
| Income before extraordinary item | 74,000 | | 60,000 |
| Extraordinary loss | (5,000) | $ 5,000 | |
| Less: Applicable tax saving | | 2,000 | (3,000) |
| Net Income | $ 69,000 | | $ 57,000 |
| Statement of Retained Earnings: | | | |
| Prior period adjustment (decrease) | $ 20,000 | 20,000 | |
| Less: Applicable tax saving | | 8,000 | $ 12,000 |
| Balance Sheet: | | | |
| Owners' equity (decrease) | $ 10,000 | 10,000 | |
| Less: Applicable tax saving | | 4,000 | $ 6,000 |

**EXHIBIT 11–2**

**Comprehensive Illustration – Interperiod and Intraperiod Tax Allocation**

Assumptions:

1. Income tax rates: first $25,000, 22%; above $25,000, 48%; capital gains, 25%.
2. Income on installment sales is included in the income tax return in period of collection rather than in period of sale. Collections on installment sales assumed to be in year following sale.
3. Data per accounts:

|  | 19A | 19B |
|---|---|---|
| Income on regular sales | $100,000 | $140,000 |
| Income on installment sales | 40,000 | -0- |
| Extraordinary gain | 9,600 | 9,600 |

Computations on income tax return:

|  | 19A | 19B |
|---|---|---|
| On regular sales: | $25,000 × 22% = $ 5,500 | $ 25,000 × 22% = $ 5,500 |
|  | 75,000 × 48% = 36,000 | 115,000 × 48% = 55,200 |
| On installment sales:* |  | 40,000 × 48% = 19,200 |
| On extraordinary gain: | 9,600 × 25% = 2,400 | 9,600 × 25% = 2,400 |
|  | $43,900 | $82,300 |

*Other assumptions are acceptable in respect of "order" of regular and installment sales. Also, the tax rates used are for illustrative purposes only.

**Partial Income Statement – with Interperiod and Intraperiod Tax Allocation**

|  | | 19A | | 19B |
|---|---|---|---|---|
| Income on regular sales | | $100,000 | | $140,000 |
| Income on installment sales | | 40,000 | |  |
| Total income before tax and extraordinary items | | 140,000 | | 140,000 |
| Less: Applicable income taxes* | | 60,700 | | 60,700 |
| Income before extraordinary items | | 79,300 | | 79,300 |
| Extraordinary items: |  |  |  |  |
| Gain | $9,600 | | $9,600 | |
| Less: Applicable income tax* | 2,400 | 7,200 | 2,400 | 7,200 |
| Net Income | | $ 86,500 | | $ 86,500 |

*Computation of income tax expense (accrual or allocation basis): Same for each year:

| $ 25,000 × 22% = $ 5,500 | |
|---|---|
| 115,000 × 48% = 55,200 | $60,700 |
| 9,600 × 25% = | 2,400 |
| Total Tax Expense ... | $63,100 |

Entries in the accounts to reflect the tax allocation

| 19A | | |
|---|---|---|
| Income tax expense (per income statement) | 63,100 | |
| Deferred income taxes | | 19,200 |
| Income taxes payable (per tax return) | | 43,900 |

| 19B | | |
|---|---|---|
| Income tax expense (per income statement) | 63,100 | |
| Deferred income taxes | 19,200 | |
| Income taxes payable (per tax return) | | 82,300 |

Note: For comparative purposes observe that, without income tax allocation, reported net income for 19A would have been $149,600 − $43,900 = $105,700 and for 19B, $149,600 − $82,300 = $67,300; each amount is materially different than that reported under allocation procedures.

Balance sheet disclosure requires (a) that income taxes payable be set out separately from deferred tax amounts, and (b) that deferred tax balances be reported in two amounts — a net *current* amount and a net *noncurrent* amount. The classification of the deferred amounts as current or noncurrent is made on the basis of the related assets and liabilities. For example, if a deferred tax credit arises as a result of installment receivables that are classified as current assets, then the tax credit would be classified as current. Reporting in this manner is reflected in Exhibit 11–3.

Disclosure of income taxes and the related interperiod and intraperiod tax allocations are illustrated in Exhibit 11–3.

**EXHIBIT 11–3**
**Disclosure of Income Tax Allocation**

B CORPORATION
Income Statement (partial)
For the Year Ended December 31, 19B

| | | |
|---|---|---|
| Income from operations | | $120,000 |
| Less: Income tax expense (Note A) | | 48,000* |
| Income before extraordinary items | | 72,000 |
| Extraordinary items: | | |
| Loss | $30,000 | |
| Less: Applicable income tax | 12,000 | 18,000 |
| Net Income | | $ 54,000 |

* An average tax rate of 40% is assumed on all items for illustrative purposes.

B CORPORATION
Balance Sheet (partial)
At December 31, 19B

Current Liabilities:
Income taxes payable (Note A) .............. $35,000
Deferred income taxes (Note B).............. 11,000

Long-Term Liabilities:
Deferred income taxes (Note B).............. 19,000

Notes to Financial Statement

A. Income tax payable was computed as follows:

| | |
|---|---|
| Income tax expense on current operations | $48,000 |
| Add decrease in current deferred tax credit | 2,000 |
| Deduct increase in noncurrent deferred tax credit | (3,000) |
| Income taxes payable on current operations | 47,000 |
| Deduct tax saving on extraordinary loss | 12,000 |
| Income Taxes Currently Payable | $35,000 |

B. The current portion of deferred income taxes is for gross profit on installment sales not yet taxed; the net decrease for the current year was $2,000. The noncurrent portion was for the excess tax credit for accelerated depreciation on the tax return over straight-line depreciation reflected on the income statement; the net increase for the year was $3,000.

## OPERATING LOSSES AND TAX ALLOCATION

Federal tax laws allow corporations which sustain losses to carry back and carry forward such losses under certain conditions. A corporation may secure refunds of income taxes paid in the three prior years, and if the loss is so large that after adjustment it is not absorbed fully when offset against the profitable years to which it is carried back, it can be carried forward for as many as five years, during which it may reduce taxes that would otherwise be owed on income in those years. The tax provision may be diagrammed as follows:

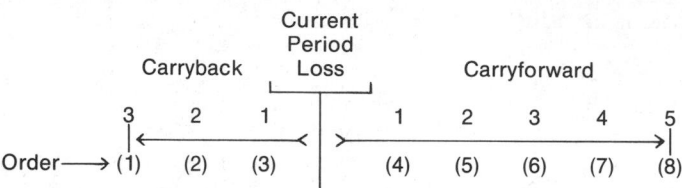

### Loss Carryback

In a period where an operating loss follows a period of net income sufficient to offset the loss, the resultant tax carryback will give rise to a refund of income taxes paid in the prior period. Since the refund is virtually certain, the *tax effect* should be recorded in the accounts and reflected in the financial statement for the loss period. *APB Opinion No. 11* states the following:

> The tax effects of any realizable loss carry*backs* should be recognized in the determination of net income (loss) of the loss periods. The tax loss gives rise to a refund (or claim for refund) of past taxes, which is both measurable and currently realizable; therefore the tax effect of the loss is properly recognizable in the determination of net income (loss) for the loss period. Appropriate adjustments of existing net deferred tax credits may also be necessary in the loss period.

To illustrate, assume AB Corporation reported net income before taxes of $80,000 in 19A, its first year of operations. Since the average tax rate was 40% (for illustrative purposes) and pretax accounting income and taxable income coincided, the corporation paid $32,000 in income tax. In 19B, due to a recession, the books showed a net pretax loss of $20,000, after certain technical adjustments. Under the carryback provision this entitled the company to an $8,000 refund of the taxes paid in 19A. Therefore, at the end of 19B the following entry would be made:

19B:

```
Receivable for refund of 19A income taxes............................. 8,000
     Income tax refund, loss carryback................................... 8,000
```

The bottom portion of the 19B income statement would show:

| | |
|---|---|
| Net loss before recognition of tax effect............... | $20,000 |
| Deduct estimated refund of prior year income tax due to loss carryback................................ | 8,000 |
| Net Loss........................................................... | $12,000 |

The above entry and the manner of reporting reflects the tax refund which has a high degree of certainty of materializing; its effect is to reduce the loss that otherwise would be reported for 19B. It should be reported in 19B because that is the year in which the refund was "earned."

### Loss Carryforward

In the situation where a company has experienced a net operating loss which cannot be offset through a carryback, it may be realized as a carryforward up to five years in the future. Where the years preceding a loss year have been profitable there can be little doubt that a carry*back* equal to or less than the profits of the years to which it can be applied will be fully realized. On the other hand, *uncertainty* necessarily attends the realizability of a carry*forward* since future profits are uncertain. On this point APB in *Opinion No. 11* stated:

> The tax effects of loss carry*forwards* also relate to the determination of net income (loss) of the loss periods. However, a significant question generally exists as to realization of the tax effects of the carry*forwards*, since realization is dependent upon future taxable income. Accordingly, the Board has concluded that the tax benefits of loss carry*forwards* should not be recognized until they are actually realized, except in unusual circumstances when realization is *assured beyond any reasonable doubt* at the time of the loss carry*forwards* arise. When the tax benefits of loss carry*forwards* are not recognized until realized in full or in part in subsequent periods, the tax benefits should be reported in the results of those periods as extraordinary items.

To illustrate the carryforward case, assume that Z Corporation sustained a $50,000 net operating loss during the first year of operations. Also assume for illustrative purposes, a 40% corporate average tax rate and that a potential loss carryforward of $20,000 arises. Whether or not Z Corporation will be able to avail itself of this as a *future* tax saving depends upon whether or not future income is earned. In view of the uncertainty of future income, appropriate accounting for the potential carryforward in the year of the loss is somewhat troublesome. Fundamentally, two alternative accounting approaches are available:

*Alternative 1:* Assured beyond any reasonable doubt—Recognize the tax carryforward as an asset (receivable for tax refund) and reduce the current operating loss by the amount of the tax carryforward. To illustrate:

Year of loss:

```
Receivable for tax refund (loss carryforward)....................... 20,000
    Income summary (income tax expense) .......................          20,000
```

```
    Income Statement:
    Pretax operating loss ............................................. $50,000
        Less: Tax loss carryforward ($50,000 × .40)..............  20,000
    Net Loss ..............................................................  $30,000
```

Succeeding year, assuming a pretax net operating profit of $80,000:

```
Income tax expense ....................................................... 32,000
    Receivable for tax refund (loss carryforward) ..............          20,000
    Income taxes payable ..............................................          12,000
```

```
    Income Statement:
    Pretax operating income .................. $80,000
        Less: Income tax expense..............  32,000
    Net Income.....................................  $48,000
```

*Alternative 2:* Not reasonably certain—Do not recognize the tax carryforward in the period of the loss; report the tax saving in the future period(s) when realized as an extraordinary item (correction of prior period loss). To illustrate:

Year of loss: no entry.

```
    Income Statement:
    Pretax operating loss ....................................... $50,000
    Income tax expense (loss carryforward)..............   -0-
    Net Loss ....................................................... $50,000
```

Succeeding year, assuming pretax operating income of $80,000:

```
Income tax expense ...................................................... 32,000
    Extraordinary item, tax loss carryforward .....................          20,000
    Income taxes payable ..............................................          12,000
```

```
    Income Statement:
    Pretax operating income ........................... $80,000
        Less: Income tax expense........................  32,000
    Income before extraordinary items..............  48,000
    Extraordinary item:
        Tax carryforward ..................................  20,000
    Net Income............................................  $68,000
```

Selection of the appropriate alternative depends upon the circumstances. Clearly, in the absence of *uncertainty*, Alternative 1 is used. Since the tax saving in the succeeding year was due solely to the loss in Year 1, the benefit should be reflected in the loss period. Seldom is the degree of certainty sufficient to justify Alternative 1.

The APB in *Opinion No. 11* stated that Alternative 1 was appropriate only when realization is assured, viz:

> Realization of the tax benefit of a loss carry*forward* would appear to be assured beyond any reasonable doubt when both of the following conditions exist: (*a*) the loss results from an identifiable, isolated and nonrecurring cause and the company either has been continuously profitable over a long period or has suffered occasional losses which were more than offset by taxable income in subsequent years, and (*b*) future taxable income is virtually certain to be large enough to offset the loss carry*forward* and will occur soon enough to provide realization during the carry*forward* period.

Since Alternative 1 is appropriate *only* when realization of the tax benefit of the loss carry*forward* is assured beyond reasonable doubt, Alternative 2 must be utilized for all other circumstances.

## QUESTIONS

### PART A

1. In evaluating a balance sheet for their purposes, bankers consistently report that the liability section is the most important part. What is the primary reason for their position on this point?

2. Most liabilities are reported at their maturity amount. In general, when should liabilities, prior to due date, be reported at less than their maturity amount?

3. How is the "cost principle" involved in accounting for current liabilities?

4. Define current liabilities.

5. Differentiate between secured and unsecured liabilities. Explain proper reporting procedures for each.

6. How are dividends declared, but not yet paid, classified on the balance sheet? Explain.

7. What are deferred revenues? What is the basis for classifying them as current liabilities?

8. Define a long-term liability.

9. When goods or services are acquired and a long-term note is given that either (*a*) specifies no interest, or (*b*) specifies an unrealistically low interest rate, how should the note be measured?

10. Basically, what is the accounting definition of a contingency? Why is the concept important?

11. How does the accountant measure the seriousness of a contingency? In general, how does this affect the accounting and reporting of contingencies?

12. Explain why loss contingencies are accounted for and reported differently than a gain contingency.

13. Under what circumstances would you consider appropriation of retained earnings with respect to a loss contingency?

14. How would each of the following items be reported on the balance sheet? Justify doubtful items.

a. Cash dividends payable.
b. Bonds payable.
c. Accommodation endorsement.
d. Lawsuit pending.
e. Stock dividend issuable.
f. Estimated taxes payable.
g. Unearned rent revenue.
h. Deferred interest revenue.

i. Customer deposits on containers.
j. Current payment on bonds payable.
k. Accounts payable.
l. Loans from officers.
m. Accrued wages.
n. Deferred repairs.

## PART B

15. Why is (a) interperiod, and (b) intraperiod tax allocation desirable?

16. In general terms, under what circumstances is income tax allocation appropriate on (a) an interperiod basis, and (b) an intraperiod basis?

17. Give four specific examples of *timing* differences. Under what circumstances is tax allocation required for each?

18. Interperiod income tax procedures are not appropriate when (check best answer):

a. An extraordinary loss will cause the amount of income tax expense to be less than the tax on ordinary net income.
b. An extraordinary gain will cause the amount of income tax expense to be greater than the tax on ordinary net income.
c. Differences between net income for tax purposes and financial reporting occur because tax laws and financial accounting principles do not concur on the items to be recognized as revenue and expense.
d. Differences between income for tax purposes and financial reporting occur because, even though financial accounting principles and tax laws concur on the items to be recognized as revenues and expenses, they do not concur on the timing of the recognition.

(AICPA adapted)

19. Briefly explain how deferred taxes should be reported on the financial statements.

20. Explain why interperiod tax allocation is both an accounting and reporting procedure, whereas intraperiod tax allocation is strictly a reporting procedure.

21. Explain the distinction between a loss carryback and a loss carryforward. In general, when does each apply?

22. Why is the accounting for a loss carryback different than for a loss carryforward?

## EXERCISES

### PART A: EXERCISES 1–11

**Exercise 11–1**

On September 1, 19A, B Company borrowed cash on a $4,000 note payable due in one year. Assume the going rate of interest was 9% per year on this type of note for this company. The accounting period ends December 31.

*Required:*

Complete a tabulation as follows (show computations):

|  | Assuming the Note Was— | |
| --- | --- | --- |
|  | Interest Bearing | Noninterest Bearing |
| a. Cash received (assuming interest is computed on the face amount of the note) ..................................... | $_____ | $_____ |
| b. Cash paid at due date ..................... | $_____ | $_____ |
| c. Total interest paid (cash)................. | $_____ | $_____ |
| d. Interest expense in 19A .................. | $_____ | $_____ |
| e. Interest expense in 19B .................. | $_____ | $_____ |
| f. Amount of liability to report on balance sheet at December 31, 19A (including any accrued interest) ...... | $_____ | $_____ |
| g. Effective rate of interest (%) ........... | $_____ | $_____ |

## Exercise 11–2

For each of the following, indicate the balance sheet classifications and pre-ferred title; include comments on doubtful items.

*a.* Accounts payable.

*b.* Deposits received from customer—trade.

*c.* Deferred interest revenue.

*d.* Accrued wages.

*e.* Accommodation endorsement.

*f.* Allowance for rearrangement costs.

*g.* Customer advances on orders received.

*h.* Sales taxes collected.

*i.* Bonds payable, one-third paid each year.

*j.* Advance on rent revenue.

*k.* Stock dividend declared.

*l.* Accrued property taxes.

*m.* Scrip dividends declared.

*n.* IOU to company president.

*o.* Accrued interest on note payable.

*p.* Prepaid interest revenue.

*q.* Cash dividends payable.

## Exercise 11–3

The records of the Rayburn Corporation provided the following information at December 31, 19A:

| | |
| --- | --- |
| a. Notes payable trade, short term (included a $4,000 note given on the purchase of equipment that cost $20,000; the assets were mortgaged in connection with the purchase)........................................................ | $30,000 |
| b. Bonds payable ($10,000 due each April 1) ......................................... | 80,000 |
| c. Accounts payable (including $10,000 owed to the president of the company)......................................................................................... | 40,000 |
| d. Accrued property taxes ............................................................... | 1,000 |
| e. Stock dividends issuable on March 1, 19B (at par value)........................ | 12,000 |
| f. Cash dividends payable, payable March 1, 19B .................................... | 20,000 |
| g. Long-term note payable, maturity amount ......................................... | 15,000 |
| h. Discount on the note (unamortized) ................................................ | 500 |

*Required:*

Assuming the fiscal year ends December 31, show how each of the above should be reported on the balance sheet at December 31, 19A.

### Exercise 11-4

Stopper Company paid salaries for the month amounting to $60,000. Of this amount, $10,000 was received by employees who had already been paid $14,100 (F.I.C.A.). In addition to the $10,000, another $4,000 was paid to employees who had already been paid $4,200 (F.U.T.A.). Withholding taxes amounted to $5,000, and $1,200 was withheld for investment in company stock per an agreement with certain employees. Use the rates given in the chapter.

*Required:*

Give entries to record (*a*) the salary payment including the deductions, (*b*) the employer payroll costs, and (*c*) remittance of the taxes.

### Exercise 11-5

Baker Company gives the general manager a bonus equal to 20% of net income after tax. The bonus is deductible for tax purposes. Assume an average tax rate of 40%. Net income prior to taxes and bonus was $80,000.

*Required:*

1. Compute the tax and the bonus.
2. Prove your computations.
3. Give entries to record the tax and the bonus.

### Exercise 11-6

Blue Company has an agreement to pay the president a bonus of 10% of net income, after deducting federal income taxes and after deducting an amount equal to 6% on the invested capital. Invested capital amounted to $300,000. Income before deductions for bonus and income taxes was $50,000. The bonus is deductible for tax purposes; assume an average income tax rate of 25%.

*Required:*

1. Compute the bonus, tax, and net income after deducting both bonus and tax.
2. Prove the computations.

### Exercise 11-7

On April 1, 19A, Garrison Company purchased a heavy machine for use in operations by paying $5,000 cash and signing a $24,000 (face amount) non-interest-bearing note due in two years (on March 31, 19C). The going rate of interest for Garrison on this type of note was 8½% payable annually. The company uses straight-line depreciation. The accounting period ends on December 31. Assume a five-year life for the machine and no residual value. The present value of 1 for 2 periods at 8½% is .849455.

*Required:*

1. Give the entries indicated on April 1, 19A, and December 31, 19A (assume straight-line amortization of the discount). Show computations of the cost of the machine.
2. Complete a tabulation as follows (show computations):
   *a.* Income Statement, 19A:

   Depreciation expense.................................................................. $_____
   Interest expense ..................................................................... $_____

b. Balance Sheet, 19A:

Fixed asset—machine ...................................................... $_____
Accumulated depreciation (disregard residual value).............. $_____
Current liability—accrued interest ....................................... $_____
Note payable............................................................................ $_____

3. When should the interest method, rather than the straight-line method, be used to amortize the discount on the note?

## Exercise 11-8

Stroble Company purchased a heavy-duty used truck (a fixed asset), on April 1, 19A, for $2,000 cash plus a $6,000, two-year note payable. The $6,000 face value was due on March 31, 19C, and specified 4% interest payable each March 31. Assume the going rate of interest for this type of debt for this company was 10%. The accounting period ends December 31.

*Required:*

1. Give the entry to record the purchase on April 1, 19A. Show computations.
2. Complete a tabulation as follows, include computations:
   a. Amount of cash interest payable each March 31 .................... $_____
   b. Total interest expense for the two-year period ....................... $_____
   c. Amount of interest reported on income statement for 19A ...... $_____
   d. Amount of liability reported on balance sheet at December 31, 19A (excluding accrued interest)............................................ $_____
   e. Depreciation expense for 19A assuming straight-line, even months, no residual value, and a four-year life ....................... $_____

## Exercise 11-9

Davis Corporation sells a line of products that carry a three-year warranty against defects. Based on past experience, the estimated warranty costs related to dollar sales are: first year after sale—1% of sales; second year after sale—3% of sales; and third year after sale—5%. Sales and actual warranty expenditures for a three-year period were:

| | Cash Sales | Actual Warranty Expenditures |
|---|---|---|
| 19A............... | $ 90,000 | $ 900 |
| 19D............... | 110,000 | 1,100 |
| 19C............... | 130,000 | 9,800 |

*Required:*

1. Give entries for the three years for the (a) sales, (b) estimated warranty costs, and (c) the actual expenditures.
2. What amount should be reported as a liability on the balance sheet at the end of each year?

## Exercise 11-10

Local Grocery has initiated a promotion program whereby customers are given coupons redeemable in U.S. savings bonds. One coupon is issued for each dollar of sales. On the surrender of 750 coupons, one $25 savings bond (cost $18.75) is given. It is estimated that 20% of the coupons issued will never be presented for redemption. Sales for the first period were $400,000, and the number of coupons redeemed totaled 225,000. Sales for the second period were $440,000, and the number of coupons redeemed totaled 405,000. The savings bonds are acquired as needed.

*Required:*

Prepare journal entries relative to the premium cost for the two periods including closing entries. Show ending balances and computations.

### Exercise 11–11

Sampson Company is preparing the annual financial statements at December 31, 19A. A customer fell on the escalator and has filed a lawsuit for $25,000 because of a claimed back injury. The lawyer employed by the company has carefully assessed all of the implications. If the suit is lost, the lawyer's opinion is that the $25,000 will be assessed by the court.

*Required:*

1. Assume the lawyer, the independent accountant, and the management have reluctantly concluded that it is probable that the suit will be successful. Show how this contingency should be reported on the financial statements for 19A. Also, give any entries that should be made in the accounts in 19A.
2. Assume instead that the conclusion is that it is reasonably possible that the company will be successful. In what way would your response to Requirement 1 be changed?

### PART B: EXERCISES 12–17

### Exercise 11–12

Income tax returns of Hill Corporation reflected the following:

|  | Years Ended Dec. 31 | | |
|---|---|---|---|
|  | 19A | 19B | 19C |
| Royalties | $ 50,000 | $ 70,000 | $ 40,000 |
| Investments | 30,000 | 10,000 | 20,000 |
| Rent | 60,000 |  |  |
| Total revenues | 140,000 | 80,000 | 60,000 |
| Deductible expenses | 80,000 | 60,000 | 50,000 |
| Taxable Income | $ 60,000 | $ 20,000 | $ 10,000 |

Assume the average income tax rate for each year was 40%.

The only differences between taxable income on the tax returns and the pretax accounting income relate to rent. On the tax return, the $60,000 rent collected October 1, 19A, relating to a 24-month period ending September 30, 19C, must be included in 19A taxable income. For accounting purposes, this rent revenue was recognized ratably over the period it covered.

*Required:*

1. Prepare income statements for each year reflecting tax allocation.

2. Give journal entries such as would appear at the end of each year to reflect income tax accrual and allocation.

## Exercise 11–13

Jackson Retailers, Inc., would have had identical net income before taxes on both its income tax returns and income statements for the years 19A through 19D were it not for the fact that for tax purposes fixed assets that cost $120,000 were depreciated by the sum-of-the-years'-digits method, whereas for accounting purposes, the straight-line method was used. These fixed assets have a four-year estimated life and zero residual value. Excess of revenue over expenses other than depreciation and income taxes for the years concerned were as follows:

|  | 19A | 19B | 19C | 19D |
|---|---|---|---|---|
| Pretax accounting income (excluding depreciation).............. | $60,000 | $80,000 | $70,000 | $70,000 |

Assume the average income tax rate for each year was 40%.

*Required:*

1. Prepare a partial income statement for each year to reflect tax allocation.
2. Give journal entries at the end of each year to record income taxes.

## Exercise 11–14

The actual tax liability of Z Corporation for each of three years was as follows: 19A, $60,000; 19B, $40,000; and 19C, $30,000.

Due to differences in timing of reporting of income for accounting purposes and tax purposes, the following variations existed in these three years:

19A—Pretax accounting income exceeded taxable income by $10,000.
19B—Taxable income exceeded pretax accounting income by   8,000.
19C—Pretax accounting income exceeded taxable income by   15,000.

*Required:*

Assuming these are timing differences, prepare the journal entry to record income taxes each year assuming an average tax rate of 40%.

## Exercise 11–15

The pretax income statements for R Corporation for two years (summarized) were:

|  | 19A | 19B |
|---|---|---|
| Revenues ..................... | $180,000 | $200,000 |
| Expenses ..................... | 150,000 | 165,000 |
| Pretax income.............. | $ 30,000 | $ 35,000 |

For tax purposes, the following differences existed:

a. An expense of $10,000 on above income statement for 19B will never be deductible for income tax purposes (it was goodwill amortization).
b. A revenue of $6,000 reported on the above income statement for 19B is taxable in 19A (it was unearned rent revenue).

c. An expense of $8,000 on the above income statement for 19A is not deductible for income tax purposes until 19B (it was estimated warranty costs).

*Required:*

1. Compute (a) income tax expense, and (b) income taxes payable for each period. Assume an average tax rate of 40%.
2. Give the entry to record income taxes for each period.
3. Recast the above income statements to include income taxes as allocated.

### Exercise 11-16

Larson Corporation reported pretax operating profit in 19A amounting to $80,000, the first year of operations. In 19B, the corporation experienced a $60,000 pretax operating loss. Assume an average income tax rate of 45%.

*Required:*

1. Compute the income tax consequences for each year.
2. Show how the tax consequences for each year would be reflected in the income statements for each year.
3. Give appropriate entries to record income tax effects for each year.

### Exercise 11-17

Wells Corporation experienced a $100,000 pretax operating loss for 19A, the first year of operations. Assume an average 40% tax rate.

*Required:*

1. Assume the loss resulted from an identifiable cause and that future taxable income over the next five years is virtually certain to be sufficient to offset the loss.
   a. Give entry and a partial income statement for 19A to reflect appropriate tax allocation consequences.
   b. Assume it is now the end of 19B and that a pretax operating profit in 19B is reported amounting to $150,000. Give entry and a partial income statement for 19B to reflect appropriate tax allocation consequences.
2. Assume that at the time of the loss there was no realistic basis to conclude that profits in the next five years would be sufficient to absorb the loss.
   a. Give entry and a partial income statement for 19A to reflect appropriate tax allocation consequences.
   b. Assume pretax operating incomes, following the year of loss, as follows: 19B, break even; 19C, $40,000; and 19D, $90,000. Give entry and a partial income statement for each of these three years to reflect appropriate tax allocation consequences.

### PROBLEMS

### PART A: PROBLEMS 1-11

### Problem 11-1

For each of the situations below indicate (1) correct title, (2) the correct balance sheet classification, (3) the amount to report, and (4) comment on classification. (Suggestion: Set up four columns for your response.)

a. Accounts payable (including $2,000 owed to the company president) .................................................... $30,000
b. Trade notes payable (including $9,000 for equipment note) ........................................................ 29,000
c. Long-term note payable (secured by stock in X Company) ............................................................ 10,000
d. Cash dividends payable ......................................... 12,000
e. Deposits by customers ......................................... 4,000
f. Prepaid rent revenue ............................................. 3,000
g. Premium on bonds payable ................................... 2,800
h. Bonds payable (annual payment $30,000).............. 90,000
i. Deferred repairs .................................................. 1,000
j. Prepaid lease revenue........................................... 2,000
k. Estimated taxes payable........................................ 7,000
l. Reserve for future contingencies........................... 15,000
m. Estimated future warranty liability ........................ 4,500
n. Accommodation endorsement .............................. 2,000

## Problem 11–2

Mason Corporation borrowed cash on August 1, 19A, and signed a $12,000 (face amount), one year, note payable, due on July 31, 19B. The accounting period ends December 31. Assume a going rate of interest of 10% for this company for this type of borrowing. Assume the interest rate is applied to the face amount of the note.

*Required:*

1. How much cash would Mason receive on the note assuming: Case A, an interest-bearing note; and, Case B, a noninterest-bearing note. What would be the effective rate of interest in each case? Show computations.
2. Give the following entries for each case:
   a. August 1, 19A, date of the loan.
   b. December 31, 19A, adjusting entry.
   c. July 31, 19B, payment of the note.
3. What liability amounts should be shown in each case on the December 31, 19A, balance sheet?
4. Compute the cash proceeds assuming the 10% interest rate is applied to the cash proceeds.

## Problem 11–3

On October 1, 19A, Wilson Company borrowed cash and signed a $27,000, 10%, one-year note payable, due on September 30, 19B. The accounting period ends on December 31.

*Required:*

1. Compute the amount of cash received on the note assuming (show computations):

   Case A – An interest-bearing note.
   Case B – A noninterest-bearing note, and the interest is based on the face amount of the note.

2. Give entries indicated for each case at October 1, 19A, December 31, 19A, and September 30, 19B.

3. Complete a tabulation as follows:

|  | Case A Interest Bearing | Case B Noninterest Bearing |
|---|---|---|
| a. Total cash received...................... | $_____ | $_____ |
| b. Total cash paid.......................... | $_____ | $_____ |
| c. Total interest paid .................... | $_____ | $_____ |
| d. Interest expense in 19A............... | $_____ | $_____ |
| e. Interest expense in 19B............... | $_____ | $_____ |
| f. Liability amounts on balance sheet, December 31, 19A: | | |
| (1) Note ................................. | $_____ | $_____ |
| (2) Accrued interest ............... | $_____ | $_____ |
| g. Effective rate of interest (%)......... | _____ | _____ |

4. What would the cash received have been assuming the interest is based on the cash proceeds?

## Problem 11-4

Thomas Corporation was formed for the purpose of constructing buildings. The first contract involved the construction of an office building. Since the corporation was short of ready cash, an agreement was made with the supervising engineer whereby compensation would be a share of the profits. The agreement provided that the supervising engineer would receive 20% of the profits on the contract after providing for federal income tax and after deducting the bonus.

Upon completion of the construction, the records of the corporation showed the following:

| | |
|---|---|
| Income before tax and before payment to the supervising engineer (assume a 40% tax rate) ............................................. | $450,000 |
| Costs already deducted from the net income, not allowable as deductions in computing income taxes but allowed as a deduction before computing the profit to be paid the supervising engineer ............................................................. | 10,000 |

Assume the compensation to the supervising engineer is deductible for income tax purposes.

*Required:*

1. Compute the amount of the compensation to the supervising engineer and the income taxes assuming the compensation is an expense in determining the basis for the compensation. Show proof of computations.
2. Give entries to record the compensation and taxes.

## Problem 11-5

For the purpose of stimulating sales, Black Coffee Company places a coupon in each can of coffee sold, the coupons being redeemable in chinaware. Each premium costs the company $.80. Ten coupons must be presented by the customers to receive one premium. The following data are available:

| Month | Cans of Coffee Sold | Premiums Purchased | Coupons Redeemed |
|---|---|---|---|
| January ............... | 650,000 | 25,000 | 220,000 |
| February.............. | 500,000 | 40,000 | 410,000 |
| March .................. | 560,000 | 35,000 | 300,000 |

It is estimated that only 70% of the coupons will be presented for redemption.

*Required:*

Compute the amount of the premium inventory, liability for premiums outstanding, and premium expense at the end of each month and give the related entries. *Hint:* Set up parallel columns for each period.

## Problem 11-6

Crunch Cereal Company gives a premium costing $.50 each for "five box tops received plus $.15 mailing costs." Actual mailing costs average $.10 per premium. Data covering three periods are as follows:

| | Period | | |
|---|---|---|---|
| | First | Second | Third |
| Premiums purchased........................ | 15,000 | 25,000 | 24,000 |
| Tops redeemed for premiums............ | 50,000 | 100,000 | 120,000 |
| Boxes of cereal sold at $.80 per box... | 220,000 | 250,000 | 280,000 |

It is estimated that 60% of the tops distributed will never be returned.

*Required:*

1. Give entries for each period to record sales, premium purchases, redemptions, adjustments, and closing entries. *Hint:* Set up parallel columns for the three periods.
2. Indicate how premiums and any related liabilities would be reported on the balance sheet at the end of each period.

## Problem 11-7

The following transactions were completed during the year (19A) just ended by Kelso Corporation:
a. Bonds payable dated February 1 with a maturity value of $100,000 were sold at par plus three months accrued interest on May 1. The bonds mature in ten years and bear 6% interest per annum payable on December 31.
b. Merchandise purchased on account amounted to $400,000. Cash payments were $340,000, a $3,000 one-year, 9% interest-bearing note, dated September 1, given to one creditor. Accounts carried over from the preceding year were $30,000.
c. Cosigned a $5,000 note payable for another party.
d. On June 1, the company borrowed cash and a $10,000, one-year, noninterest-bearing note was signed. Assume a going rate of interest of 9% and that interest is based on the face amount of the note.
e. Payroll records showed the following (assume amounts given are correct):

| | Employee | | | Employer | | |
|---|---|---|---|---|---|---|
| Gross Wages | With-holding | F.I.C.A. | Union Dues | F.I.C.A. | F.U.T.A. State | F.U.T.A. Federal |
| $30,000......... | $2,500 | $500 | $300 | $500 | $480 | $50 |
| 20,000......... | 1,800 | 470 | 200 | 470 | 450 | 45 |

Remittances were: union, $280; withholding taxes, $4,000; F.I.C.A., $1,900; F.U.T.A.–state, $750; and F.U.T.A.–federal, $95.

*f.* The company was sued for $25,000 damages. It appears a judgment against the company of about $10,000 is probable.

*g.* The company accrued $250 per month for "special repairs." At the end of the year only $2,000 had been spent for this purpose. It was decided to put off certain repairs until January, although they were definitely scheduled for December. The basic reason was that certain parts, although purchased, had not arrived by year-end.

*h.* Cash dividends declared, but not paid, $14,000.

*i.* On December 31, accrued interest on the bonds.

*j.* Accrue interest on notes.

*Required:*

1. Give the entry or entries for each of the above items.

2. Prepare a list (title and amount) of the resulting liabilities at December 31, 19A, assuming it is the end of the period. For each liability, indicate its appropriate classification on the balance sheet. *Hint:* Set up tabulations with three columns: title, amount, and classification.

## Problem 11-8

Handy Appliance Company provides a product warranty for defects on two lines of items sold. Line A carries a two-year warranty for all labor and service (but not parts). The company contracts with a local service establishment to provide the requirements of the warranty. The local service establishment charges a flat fee of $50 per unit payable at date of sale.

Line B carries a three-year warranty for labor and parts on service. Handy purchases the parts needed under the warranty and has service personnel who perform the work. On the basis of past experience, it is estimated that for Line B, the three-year warranty costs are 3% of dollar sales for parts and 7% for labor and overhead. Additional data available are:

| | Period | | |
|---|---|---|---|
| | 1 | 2 | 3 |
| Sales in units, Line A ............................ | 700 | 1,000 | |
| Sales price per unit, Line A .................... | $ 610 | $ 660 | |
| Sales in units, Line B ............................ | 600 | 800 | |
| Sales price per unit, Line B .................... | $ 700 | $ 750 | |
| Actual warranty costs on Line B: | | | |
| Parts................................................. | $3,000 | $ 9,600 | $12,000 |
| Labor and overhead............................ | $7,000 | $22,000 | $30,000 |

*Required:*

1. Give entries for period sales and costs identified by product. *Hint:* Set up parallel columns for the three periods.

2. Complete a tabulation as follows:

|  | Year End Amounts | | |
|---|---|---|---|
|  | Period 1 | Period 2 | Period 3 |
| a. Warranty expense (on the income statement).......................... | $_____ | $_____ | $_____ |
| b. Estimated warranty liability (on the balance sheet) .................... | $_____ | $_____ | $_____ |

## Problem 11-9

On September 1, 19A, Robbins Company acquired a badly needed machine (a fixed asset) by paying $5,000 cash and signing a two-year note that carried a face amount of $15,000 due at the end of the two years; the note did not specify interest. Assume the going rate of interest for this company for this type of loan was 8%. The accounting period ends December 31. Base interest calculations on the face of the note.

*Required:*

1. Give entries on September 1 and December 31, 19A, under (a) straight-line amortization of discount, and (b) the interest method of amortization.
2. Complete a tabulation as follows and show computations:

|  | Straight-Line Method | Interest Method |
|---|---|---|
| a. Cash paid at maturity ................................... | $_____ | $_____ |
| b. Total interest expense ...................................... | $_____ | $_____ |
| c. Interest expense on income statement for 19A ...................................................... | $_____ | $_____ |
| d. Amount of the liability reported on balance sheet at end of 19A ........................... | $_____ | $_____ |
| e. Depreciation expense for 19A (assume straight-line, even months, no residual value, and a useful life of four years) ............... | $_____ | $_____ |

## Problem 11-10

On August 1, 19A, Massie Company purchased a large used machine for operations. Payment was made by cash $6,000 and a $30,000 (face amount), two-year note payable (due on July 31, 19C). The note did not specify interest; however, for Massie, the going rate for this type of transaction was 8½%. Assume straight-line depreciation, a five-year life, and no residual value. The accounting period ends on December 31. The present value of 1 for two periods at 8½% is .84945.

*Required:*

1. Compute the cost of the machine.
2. Give entries indicated on August 1, 19A, and December 31, 19A. Assume straight-line amortization of note discount.
3. What items and amounts should be reported on the income statement and balance sheet for 19A (include the machine and depreciation).
4. Prepare an amortization schedule for the note assuming the interest method is used.
5. When should the interest method, rather than the straight-line method, be used to amortize the discount for the note?

**Problem 11–11**

Dollins Company is preparing the annual financial statements at December 31, 19A, and is concerned about application of FASB *Statement No. 5*, "Accounting for Contingencies." Four particular situations are under consideration, viz:

1. The company owns a small plant in a foreign country that has a book value of $3,000,000 and an estimated fair market value of $4,000,000. The foreign government has clearly indicated its intention to expropriate the plant during the coming year and to reimburse Dollins for 50% of the estimated fair market value.
2. An outside party has filed a claim against Dollins for $25,000 claiming that certain actions by Dollins caused them to lose a contract on which the estimated profit was this amount. In the opinion of the attorney hired by Dollins, the probability of the claim being successful is remote. They do not believe it will ever be brought to trial. If necessary, Dollins will defend itself in court.
3. During 19B, a third party (a potential customer) sued Dollins for $150,000 for a claimed injury that occurred on the premises owned by Dollins. No date for the trial has been set; however, the lawyer employed by Dollins has completed a thorough investigation. Although it can be proven that the third party did fall on the premises, the company lawyer believes it will be difficult for the plaintiff to prove injury and there is evidence that it was due to negligence by the plaintiff. Therefore, the attorney believes that it is not probable although it is reasonably possible that the suit will be successful (i.e., for the plaintiff).
4. Dollins had a $10,000, 8%, one-year note receivable from a customer. Dollins discounted the note, with recourse, at the bank to obtain cash before its due date (due on June 1, 19B). If the maker does not pay the bank on the note by due date, Dollins will have to pay it. The customer has an excellent credit rating (having never defaulted on a debt).

*Required:*

For each situation, respond to the following:

*a.* What accounting recognition (i.e., journal entries), if any, should be accorded each situation at the end of 19A? Explain why.
*b.* What should be reported on the income statement, balance sheet, and by footnote in each situation? Explain why.

## PART B: PROBLEMS 12–18

**Problem 11–12**

Speedy Construction Company has contracts for construction of three major projects. The percentage-of-completion method of accounting is used for accounting purposes while the completed contract method is used for the income tax returns. Data pertaining to these contracts are as follows:

| | Year | | Total Profit | Percentage Completion | | | |
|---|---|---|---|---|---|---|---|
| Project | Started | Completed | | 19A | 19B | 19C | 19D |
| A ............... | 19A | 19C | $ 70,000 | 40% | 50% | 10% | |
| B ............... | 19B | 19C | 90,000 | | 20 | 80 | |
| C ............... | 19B | 19D | 100,000 | | 10 | 70 | 20% |

*Required:*

1. For each year, compute (*a*) income tax expense, and (*b*) income taxes payable; assume an average tax rate of 45%.
2. Give the entry to record income taxes for each year.
3. Complete a tabulation as follows:

|  | 19A | 19B | 19C | 19D |
|---|---|---|---|---|
| **Income Statement:** | | | | |
| Pretax income ............ | $_____ | $_____ | $_____ | $_____ |
| Income taxes ............... | $_____ | $_____ | $_____ | $_____ |
| Net income.................. | $_____ | $_____ | $_____ | $_____ |
| **Balance Sheet:** | | | | |
| Income taxes payable ... | $_____ | $_____ | $_____ | $_____ |
| Deferred taxes (credit)... | $_____ | $_____ | $_____ | $_____ |

## Problem 11-13

Parson Company financial statements for a four-year period reflected the following pretax amounts:

|  | 19A | 19B | 19C | 19D |
|---|---|---|---|---|
| **Income Statement (summarized):** | | | | |
| Revenues............................... | $120,000 | $130,000 | $140,000 | $160,000 |
| Expenses............................... | (90,000) | (92,000) | (95,000) | (108,000) |
| Depreciation (straight line) ...... | ? | ? | ? | ? |
| Pretax income ....................... | $ ? | $ ? | $ ? | $ ? |
| **Balance Sheet (partial):** | | | | |
| Machine (four-year life, no residual value) ..................... | $ 40,000 | $ 40,000 | $ 40,000 | $ 40,000 |
| Income taxes payable ............... | ? | ? | ? | ? |
| Deferred taxes ........................ | ? | ? | ? | ? |

The company has an average tax rate of 40% and uses sum-of-the-years'-digits depreciation (no residual value) on the income tax return (for problem purposes, assume this method is acceptable for tax purposes in this situation) and straight line for accounting purposes.

*Required:*

1. Complete the above income statements incorporating income taxes appropriately allocated.
2. Compute income taxes payable for each year.
3. Give the entry for each year to record income taxes. Prove the deferred tax amount for each year.
4. Explain why tax allocation provides better financial statement amounts in this situation.

## Problem 11-14

Uvalde Company financial statements for a three-year period reflected the following pretax amounts:

| Income Statement (summarized): | 19A | 19B | 19C |
|---|---|---|---|
| Revenues | $190,000 | $200,000 | $215,000 |
| Expenses | (130,000) | (148,000) | (160,000) |
| Depreciation expense (straight line) | ? | ? | ? |
| Income before extraordinary items | ? | ? | ? |
| Extraordinary items, pretax (loss) | (20,000) | | 6,000 |
| Net Income, Pretax | $   ? | $   ? | $   ? |
| **Statement of Retained Earnings (partial):** | | | |
| Prior period adjustment, pretax (loss) | | | (30,000) |
| **Balance Sheet (partial):** | | | |
| Machine (three-year life, no residual value) | $ 60,000 | $ 60,000 | $ 60,000 |
| Income taxes payable | ? | ? | ? |
| Deferred taxes | ? | ? | ? |

Assume a 40% average tax rate on all items and double-declining depreciation (no residual value) for tax purposes (for problem purposes, assume this method is acceptable in this situation for tax purposes).

*Required:*

1. Restate the above financial statement amounts incorporating income taxes appropriately allocated.
2. Compute taxes payable for each year.
3. Give the entry each year to record income taxes. Prove the deferred tax amounts.
4. Explain why tax allocation derives better financial statement amounts in this situation.

## Problem 11–15

Assume the following data for X Corporation are available for a two-year period:

| | 19A | 19B |
|---|---|---|
| Operating income, pretax | $100,000 | $120,000 |
| Extraordinary losses, pretax | (15,000) | (17,000) |
| Prior period adjustment, gains, pretax | 7,000 | 8,000 |
| Timing differences included in above amounts: | | |
| a. Revenue on income statement, taxable following period | 5,000 | |
| b. Revenue on tax return, on income statement following period | 7,000 | |
| c. Expense on income statement, taxable following period | 9,000 | |
| d. Expense on tax return, on income statement following period | 6,000 | |
| e. Extraordinary loss on income statement, taxable following period | 10,000 | |
| f. Prior period gain on statement of retained earnings, taxable next period | 4,000 | |

Assume an average income tax rate of 40% on all items.

*Required:*

1. Compute income tax expense for each year that should be reflected on the income statement. Show operating income, extraordinary items, and prior period adjustments separately.
2. Compute income taxes payable for each year that should be reflected on the tax return. Show operating income, extraordinary items, and prior period adjustments separately.
3. Give the entry to record income taxes for each year.
4. Prepare a partial income statement and partial statement of retained earnings for each year to show how income tax expense should be reported. Include both interperiod and intraperiod allocation.

## Problem 11–16

Noonan Corporation pretax income statements for the first two years of operations reflected the following summarized amounts:

|  | 19A | 19B |
|---|---|---|
| Revenues | $250,000 | $280,000 |
| Expenses | 220,000 | 285,000 |
| Pretax Income (Loss) | $ 30,000 | $ (5,000) |

Assume an average tax rate of 30%.

*Required:*

1. Restate the income statements incorporating income tax effects and give the entries for each year in respect to income taxes. Show computations.
2. Assume the loss in year 19B was $35,000 instead of $5,000. Restate the income statements incorporating income tax effects and give the entries for each year in respect to income taxes. Explain the basis for your response. Show computations.

## Problem 11–17

Petty Corporation pretax financial statements for the first two years of operations reflected the following amounts:

|  | 19A | 19B |
|---|---|---|
| Revenues | $300,000 | $330,000 |
| Expenses | 320,000 | 315,000 |
| Pretax Income (Loss) | $ (20,000) | $ 15,000 |

Assume an average tax rate of 40%.

*Required:*

1. Assume future income during the next five years is unpredictable (i.e., uncertain):
   a. Restate the above financial statements incorporating the income tax effects appropriately allocated. Show computations.
   b. Give entries to record the income tax effects for each year. Explain the basis for your entries.

2. Assume future income is reasonably certain during the next five years. Complete Requirements 1 (a) and (b) above.


## Problem 11–18

Young Corporation's pretax financial statements for the first four years of operations reflected the following pretax amounts:

|                                   | 19A | 19B | 19C | 19D |
|-----------------------------------|-----|-----|-----|-----|
| Income Statement (summarized):    |     |     |     |     |
| Revenue.................................. | $125,000 | $155,000 | $180,000 | $230,000 |
| Expenses ............................. | 120,000 | 195,000 | 170,000 | 200,000 |
| Pretax Income (Loss)............... | $ 5,000 | $ (40,000) | $ 10,000 | $ 30,000 |

Assume an average income tax rate of 30% and that future incomes are uncertain at the end of each year.

*Required:*

1. Recast the above statement to incorporate the income tax effects appropriately allocated. Show computations.
2. Give entries to record the income tax effects for each year.

# Chapter 12

## Operational Assets:
## Property, Plant, and Equipment
## —Acquisition, Use, and Retirement

This chapter and the next two chapters focus on a broad category of assets that may be thought of as operational assets because they are used in the operations of the business and are not held for resale. Operational assets, also referred to as fixed assets, may be classified as follows for accounting purposes:

1. Tangible property, plant, and equipment—These operational assets are variously described by the terms *property, plant, and equipment; plant assets; capital assets;* or *tangible fixed assets.* The three classes of this group of assets are:
   a. Those subject to depreciation such as buildings, equipment, tools, and furniture.
   b. Those subject to depletion such as mineral deposits and timber tracts.
   c. Those not subject to depreciation or depletion such as land for plant site, farms, and ranches.
2. Intangibles—Those assets properly classified as fixed assets having no bodily substance; the value is represented by grants and business rights which confer some operating, financial, or income-producing advantages on the owner. They are amortized over their useful life in a manner that accords with the expiration of their economic value to the enterprise.

This chapter discusses property, plant, and equipment; Chapter 13 considers depreciation and depletion; and Chapter 14 focuses on intangibles.

Tangible property, plant, and equipment has five major characteristics: (1) actively used in operations, (2) not held as an investment or for resale, (3) relatively long lived, (4) have physical substance, and (5) provide measurable future benefits to the entity.

## CAPITAL AND REVENUE EXPENDITURES

Accounting for expenditures and obligations incident to the acquirement of property, plant, and equipment (tangible or intangible) necessitates classification of such outlays as either *capital expenditures* or as *revenue expenditures*. Capital expenditures relate to the acquirement of an asset, the benefit of which extends over one or more accounting periods beyond the current period; hence, they are recorded in appropriate asset accounts. Capital expenditures made for assets having a limited life are subsequently allocated to the periods benefitted through depreciation, amortization, or depletion. An expenditure that is debited to an asset account or to accumulated depreciation is said to be capitalized.

*Revenue expenditures* relate to the acquirement of property or benefits that do not extend beyond the current accounting period; hence, they are recorded in appropriate expense accounts for the current period.

In cases where (a) a capital expenditure is relatively small, or (b) the future benefit is insignificant, or (c) reasonable measurement of the future benefit is practically impossible, practical reasons suggest classification of the outlay as a revenue expenditure. Many companies have adopted a practical accounting policy in this respect to the effect that, for example, "expenditures under $50 will be classed as revenue expenditures; expenditures above this amount will be classified as capital expenditures only where there is clearly a significant and measurable benefit accruing to a future period."

## PRINCIPLES UNDERLYING ACCOUNTING FOR PROPERTY, PLANT, AND EQUIPMENT

The accounting for property, plant, and equipment fundamentally rests on the *cost and matching principles*. At date of acquisition, these assets are recorded in the accounts at cost. The acquisition cost of these assets is measured by the cash outlay made to acquire such assets; or if considerations other than cash are exchanged for the assets, the fair market value of such consideration at the time of the transaction is the measure of the cost of the assets so acquired. In the absence of a determinable fair market value for the consideration given, the asset is recorded at its fair market value. An asset is not "acquired" until it has been placed in the position where it is to be used and is ready for productivity in the broad business sense; thus all reasonable and legitimate costs incurred in placing an asset in this status are additions to the cost of the asset.

Subsequent to acquisition, items of property, plant, and equipment are carried in the accounts and reported at (a) cost (if unlimited life) or

(b) in the case of a limited life, at cost less accumulated depreciation, amortization, or depletion (reflecting continuing application of the matching principle.)

The following is an outline of the principal aspects influencing the accounting for property, plant, and equipment:

1. Acquisition cost of property, plant, and equipment when acquired:
   a. For cash.
   b. On a deferred payment plan.
   c. For stock or other securities.
   d. Through exchanges.
   e. Through mixed acquisitions at a lump cost.
2. Outlays subsequent to acquisition but before operational use:
   a. Installation costs.
   b. Reinstallation costs.
   c. Repairs and improvements prior to use.
   d. Razing old structures.
   e. Other incidental costs.
3. Assets constructed for own use.
4. Interest during the construction period.
5. Outlays subsequent to the beginning of operational use:
   a. Repairs and maintenance.
   b. Replacements and renewals.
   c. Betterments and improvements.
   d. Additions.
   e. Rearrangements of assets.

At this point we note that in accounting for these assets there are special circumstances where departure from the cost principle has been sanctioned by the accounting profession. These exceptions are discussed subsequently in this chapter.

## ASSETS ACQUIRED FOR CASH

If an operational asset is purchased for cash, any outlay that a prudent buyer would make for the asset in an arm's-length transaction, including costs of installation and making ready to use, should be capitalized. The capitalizable costs include the invoice price (less discounts), plus incidental costs such as insurance during transit, freight, duties, ownership searching, ownership registration, installation, and breaking-in costs. All available discounts, *whether taken or not*, should be deducted from the invoice cost. Discounts not taken should be recorded as discounts lost and treated as a current financial expense.

## ASSETS ACQUIRED ON DEFERRED PAYMENT PLAN

Assets acquired on a deferred or long-term payment plan (on credit) should be recorded at the cash equivalent price excluding all interest and financing charges. Actual and implied interest and other finance charges should be charged to financing expense and not to the fixed asset account. If the contract of purchase does not specify interest and financing charges, such charges, nevertheless, should be deducted in determining the cost of the asset. If a current cash price for the asset is determinable, the excess charged under the deferred payment contract should be treated as expense apportioned over the period covered by the purchase contract. If no cash price is determinable for the asset, a realistic interest charge should be recognized in recording the purchase. Although sound in theory these latter distinctions are not always observed in practice, since the amounts involved may not be *material*.

To illustrate the purchase of an asset on credit, assume a machine was purchased under a contract that required equal payments of $3,951 at the end of each of three years when the going interest rate was 9% per annum. To record the asset purchased at $11,853 (i.e., $3,951 × 3) would include in the asset account the interest cost implicit in the contract. Rather the asset account should be debited for the *present value* of the three payments discounted at 9% as follows:

$$PV = \text{Annual Payment} \times P \text{ (Table 6–4)}$$
$$= \$3,951 \times 2.53129 \text{ (present value of annuity of 1 at 9\% for 3 periods)}$$
$$= \$10,000 \text{ (rounded)}$$

Therefore, the indicated entries are as follows.

At date of purchase:[1]

| | | |
|---|---:|---:|
| Asset—machinery ..................................................... | 10,000 | |
|     Installments payable—machinery contract.................... | | 10,000 |

At payment dates (amounts rounded):

| | 1st Year | 2d Year | 3d Year |
|---|---:|---:|---:|
| Interest expense .................. | 900 | 625 | 328 |
| Installments payable— | | | |
|   machinery contract........... | 3,051 | 3,326 | 3,623 |
|     Cash ......................... | 3,951 | 3,951 | 3,951 |

A table of debt amortization and interest expense follows (see Chapters 6 and 11):

---

[1] Alternatively this entry could be made as follows:

| | | |
|---|---:|---:|
| Asset—machinery...................................................................... | 10,000 | |
| Deferred interest cost ................................................................ | 1,853 | |
|     Installments payable—machinery contract ............................ | | 11,853 |

The payment entries would be revised accordingly; the net effect would be the same in all respects. The first payment entry would be:

| | | |
|---|---:|---:|
| Interest expense ..................................................................... | 900 | |
| Installments payable—machinery contract .................................... | 3,951 | |
|     Deferred interest cost ............................................................. | | 900 |
|     Cash ................................................................................ | | 3,951 |

| Period | Annual Payment (cash credit) | Interest Expense (debit) | | Payment on Liability (debit) | Unpaid Principal |
|--------|---------|---------|---------|---------|---------|
| Start............ | | | | | $10,000 |
| 1............... | $ 3,951 | $10,000 × 9% $ | 900 | $ 3,051 | 6,949 |
| 2............... | 3,951 | 6,949 × 9% | 625 | 3,326 | 3,623 |
| 3............... | 3,951 | 3,623 × 9% | 328 | 3,623* | -0- |
| | $11,853 | | $1,853 | $10,000 | |

\* Rounding error $2.

## ASSETS ACQUIRED IN EXCHANGE FOR SECURITIES

The proper valuation of operational assets received in exchange for bonds and stocks of the acquiring company frequently is difficult to determine for numerous reasons, some of which are:

1. There may be no readily determinable fair market value for the securities or the assets involved.
2. The absence of an arm's-length bargaining with respect to the exchange.
3. The nature of the assets generally involved, such as unexplored or unproven mineral deposits, manufacturing rights, patents, chemical formulas, mining claims, and the like, may make value estimates difficult.
4. The current quoted market price of the security may be based upon a market volume far below the volume of shares involved in the exchange (i.e., a thin market).
5. The vagaries of the stock market, involving as it does wide fluctuations in stock prices over short periods of time, generally casts significant doubt on the relevance of the price per share at a specific time.

The general principle is that assets acquired should be recorded at their then current cash equivalent cost. Lacking this amount, the cost of assets acquired through exchange of securities should be measured as follows:

1. Determine the current fair market value of the consideration given, that is, the securities. Where the securities have an established market price, it should be used assuming there are sound reasons for the presumption that the current price is indicative that the market would absorb the volume of securities involved at that price.
2. If the fair market value of the securities in the volume exchanged cannot be determined, the current fair market value of the assets acquired should be estimated. In the absence of an actual cash-basis sale of the assets involved in the immediate past, an independent appraisal of them by a professionally recognized appraiser may be recorded as the cost of the assets acquired.
3. If a fair market value for either the securities or the assets received cannot be determined objectively, values established by the directors

of the corporation may be used. The law generally allows the directors considerable discretion in establishing values in this situation, except in cases where fraudulent intent on the part of the directors can be shown.

When assets are acquired by exchange of securities, any actual or implied discounts or premiums on the securities should be accounted for in the normal manner. Since bonds have a definite and legally enforceable maturity value and interest charge, problems of valuation of assets received in exchange for them generally are not as critical as in the case where capital stock is involved. Assets acquired in exchange for bonds payable should be recorded at the current cash value of the bonds. If there is no currently established market price for the bonds, the cost of the asset can be computed as the *present value* of the bond principal plus the present value of the interest payments, at the going rate of interest (see Chapters 6 and 19).

Operational assets acquired for cash *and* securities combined should be capitalized at the sum of the cash, and the fair market value of the securities determined in accordance with the standards discussed above. When property is financed through notes, care should be taken so that financing expenses are not charged as a part of the cost of the fixed asset.

## ASSETS ACQUIRED THROUGH EXCHANGES

Items of property, plant, and equipment frequently are acquired by trading in an old asset in full, or part payment, for another asset. In some transactions, there is an exchange of two or more noncash assets; in other cases, an asset is acquired by exchanging another asset plus a payment or receipt of cash (often referred to as boot). Prior to the issuance of *APB Opinion No. 29*, "Accounting for Nonmonetary Transactions," (effective September 30, 1973), exchanges were recorded by debiting the asset account for the item acquired at either (1) its quoted list price, (2) the cash paid plus the book value of the old asset exchanged, or (3) at its current fair market value. These three alternatives were widely used in financial accounting.

*APB Opinion No. 29* specifies the accounting approach for a wide range of nonmonetary transactions, including those involving the acquisition of operational assets through exchanges. The basic principle established in the *Opinion* is:

> Accounting for nonmonetary transactions should be based on the fair values of the assets (or services) involved which is the same as that used in monetary transactions. This is a *fair market value concept* because realization is assumed to have occurred (i.e., a purchase/sales transaction).

Thus, under the basic principle, the cost of an operational asset acquired in exchange for another nonmonetary asset is the fair market value of the asset surrendered to obtain it, and a gain or loss on the disposition of the old asset should be recognized in accounting for the exchange. The fair market value of the asset acquired should be used to measure its cost only if it is more clearly determinable than the fair market value of the asset surrendered. However, the *Opinion* specifies several exceptions to the basic principle and also covers exchanges where cash (i.e., boot) is paid or received in the exchange.

## Similar versus Dissimilar Assets

In respect to the exchange of operational assets, the *Opinion* specifies that the accounting will depend on whether the assets exchanged are *similar* or *dissimilar*. Similar productive assets are defined as "assets that are of the same general type, that perform the same function, or that are employed in the same line of business." All other productive assets would be classified as dissimilar. For example, the trading in of an old truck on a new truck would involve similar assets; however, the trading in of a tract of land on a new truck would involve dissimilar assets.

## Accounting Procedures for Exchanges

In exchanges of dissimilar assets, whether or not there is a cash difference (boot) paid or received, both parties record the transaction on a *fair market value* basis. Fair market value, when there is no cash difference, is the fair market value of the asset surrendered (if this is not determinable the fair market value of the asset received is used). When there is a cash difference, fair market value is the cash paid plus the fair market value of the asset surrendered. If the latter is not determinable the fair market value of the asset received is used.

In contrast, when similar assets are exchanged, and no cash difference (boot) is paid or received, both parties reflect a *book value* basis. When a cash difference is received or paid, and the assets are similar, the latter guideline is altered as illustrated in (c) below. Therefore, the accounting prescribed by the *Opinion* for the exchange of similar and dissimilar operational assets is as follows:

1. Dissimilar assets—Use the fair market value concept; record the asset acquired at the fair market value of the asset surrendered and recognize a gain or loss on the old asset.

   *Example:* Company A has an old crane that cost $50,000; accumulated depreciation to date of $45,000 (i.e., a carrying value of $5,000). It is exchanged with Company B for a tract of land; cash boot of $12,000 was paid. The fair market value for the old crane is determined to be $13,000.

   To record the exchange by Company A:

   | | | |
   |---|---:|---:|
   | Land ($13,000 + $12,000) | 25,000 | |
   | Accumulated depreciation (old crane) | 45,000 | |
   |     Machinery—old crane | | 50,000 |
   |     Cash | | 12,000 |
   |     Gain on disposal of machinery* | | 8,000 |

   * Fair market value recognized, $13,000 − book value, $5,000 = $8,000.

2. Similar assets—In this situation, a book value concept is prescribed by *APB Opinion No. 29* because it is assumed that nonmonetary exchange transactions are not essentially the culmination of an earnings process.

The procedure for recording an exchange of similar assets depends on whether a monetary consideration (usually cash boot) was also paid or received in the exchange. Accounting for the three situations is prescribed as follows:

a. Similar assets exchanged and *no* monetary consideration (boot) paid or received—the cost of the asset acquired is recorded at the carrying (book) value of the asset surrendered.

*Example:* Company A exchanged an old crane that cost $50,000, accumulated depreciation to date, $45,000, for another much smaller crane having a current cash price of $8,000. No cash difference was paid or received by Company A in this exchange of similar assets. The exchange would be recorded as follows:

| | | |
|---|---|---|
| Machinery, new crane (at book value of old crane)...... | 5,000* | |
| Accumulated depreciation, old crane ........................ | 45,000 | |
|    Machinery, old crane.......................................... | | 50,000 |

\* Cannot exceed fair market value.

b. Similar assets exchanged and a monetary consideration (boot) is paid—In this situation, the asset acquired is recorded at the sum of the cash paid plus the book value of the old asset surrendered. As in all cases, the asset acquired cannot be recorded at more than its current fair market value. Therefore, no gain can be recorded; however, if the fair market value of the asset received is less than the sum of the cash paid plus the book value of the old asset, a loss must be recorded.

*Example:* Company A exchanged the old crane that cost $50,000, accumulated depreciation, $45,000, for the new smaller crane having a current cash price of $8,000, and *paid* $1,000 cash boot. The transaction would be recorded as follows:

| | | |
|---|---|---|
| Machinery, new crane ($1,000 + $5,000).................... | 6,000 | |
| Accumulated depreciation, old crane ........................ | 45,000 | |
|    Machinery, old crane.......................................... | | 50,000 |
|    Cash ............................................................... | | 1,000 |

c. Similar assets exchanged and a monetary consideration (boot) is received—In this situation, *APB Opinion No. 29* specifies that a gain shall be recognized on the asset given up "to the extent that the amount of the monetary receipt exceeds a proportionate share of the recorded amount of the asset surrendered." Thus, when a cash difference is *received*, the assumption is a part sale and a part exchange of the asset surrendered. In this case, a gain on that part sold for cash may be recognized. The asset acquired is recorded as a proportionate part of the book value of the asset surrendered. Thus, this transaction is treated in part at fair market value and in part at book value.

*Example:* Company A exchanged the old crane that cost $50,000, accumulated depreciation, $45,000, for a new smaller crane having a current cash price of $8,000, and *received* a cash difference of $2,000. The transaction would be recorded as follows:

| | | |
|---|---|---|
| Cash ............................................................ | 2,000 | |
| Machinery, new crane[1] ......................................... | 4,000 | |
| Accumulated depreciation, old crane ....................... | 45,000 | |
|     Machinery, old crane......................................... | | 50,000 |
|     Gain on disposal of old machinery[2] ..................... | | 1,000 |

Computations:

1. Cost of new crane — Book value of old crane less the proportion of book value sold:

   Book value, old crane ($50,000 − $45,000) ............................................................... $5,000

   Proportion of book value sold for cash:

   $$\text{Book value, old} \times \frac{\text{Cash}}{\text{Cash} + \text{FMV of asset acquired}}$$

   $5,000 \times \dfrac{\$2,000}{\$2,000 + \$8,000} =$ ................................................................. 1,000

   Difference — cost of asset acquired.................................................................. $4,000

2. Gain on disposal of asset surrendered — Cash received less portion sold of book value of asset surrendered:

   Cash received ............................................................................................. $2,000

   Proportion of book value sold (per above) ................................................................ 1,000

   Difference — gain on asset surrendered................................................................... $1,000

Alternatively, in case of a loss, the *Opinion* requires that the full amount of such loss be recognized. To illustrate, assume in the preceding example that the accumulated depreciation was $39,000. The transaction would be recorded as follows:

| | | |
|---|---|---|
| Cash ............................................................... | 2,000 | |
| Accumulated depreciation, old crane ............................. | 39,000 | |
| Loss on disposal of old machinery ...................................... | 1,000 | |
| Machinery, new crane ................................................... | 8,000 | |
|     Machinery, old crane ................................................. | | 50,000 |

Observe that the full loss is recognized because the asset acquired cannot be recorded in excess of its fair market value. Thus, there is no calculation of the proportionate part sold. A loss is reported because the book or carrying value of the asset is greater than its fair market value as reflected in the exchange transaction. Under generally accepted accounting principles, the carrying value of the asset is rarely greater than is fair market value.

The *Opinion* does not recognize the quoted list price as the cost of an operational asset in any situation unless that price is the actual cash equivalent price (current market value). List prices often are merely a basis for bargaining rather than a genuine cash cost. To determine fair value in exchanges of operational assets, *Opinion No. 29* states that fair values should be determined by referring to "quoted market prices, independent appraisals, estimated fair values of assets or services received in exchange and other available evidence."[2]

---

[2] Under generally accepted accounting principles, no asset, irrespective of its characteristics, should be recorded at acquisition at more than its then fair market value. This is the definition of cost under the cost principle.

## DEPARTURES FROM COST IN ACCOUNTING FOR TANGIBLE ASSETS

Although accounting for assets fundamentally is based upon the cost principle, there are special circumstances where departure from that principle is sanctioned. These exceptions are:

1. Write-up to appraisal value above cost.
2. Write-up due to donation of assets to the company.
3. Write-up due to high and unexpected discovery value.
4. Write-down due to significant and permanent decrease in use value to the company.
5. Revaluations due to quasi-reorganization (discussed in Chapter 16).

Items 2, 3, and 4 are discussed in the paragraphs to follow.

## DONATED ASSETS AND DISCOVERY VALUE

### Donated Assets

Assets occasionally are donated to a corporation by stockholders for various reasons, and by municipalities, or local nonprofit organizations, as an inducement to locate a plant or other facilities in the area. Frequently, such gifts are conditional upon some particular performance on the part of the corporation such as the employment of a certain number of individuals by a given date.

Strict adherence to the cost principle would involve recording donated assets at the amount of incidental costs incurred in acceptance of the gift and in fulfilling the related agreements. Accountability for the resources of an enterprise and measurement of enterprise earning power require that every economic facility employed, regardless of origin, be entered on the books at acquisition at the current cash equivalent price or some other equivalent value. In the case of donated assets, an independent and realistic appraisal of the current market value of the donated asset should be recorded, provided the donation is unconditional. Should the donor impose restrictions, however, any "negative values" arising from such conditions should be considered in determination of the valuation to be recorded. *APB Opinion No. 29* states that "a nonmonetary asset received in a *nonreciprocal transfer* should be recorded at the fair market value of the asset received." A donated asset would represent a nonreciprocal (one-way) transfer. To illustrate, assume a building, including the land on which it is located, is given by a city to the XYZ Corporation as an inducement to establish a plant therein. The related transactions may be recorded as follows:[3]

1. To record the fair market value, per appraisal at date of donation:

---

[3] Some have argued, rather illogically, that the value recorded for assets donated by nonshareholders also should be credited to a special revenue account and reported on the current income statement, while donations by shareholders should be credited to contributed capital as illustrated. Present GAAP do not permit revenue recognition for the value of donated assets.

| Plant building | 8,000 | |
| Plant land | 4,000 | |
| Contributed capital—donated plant | | 12,000 |

2. At date of transfer and payment of transfer costs:

| Contributed capital—donated plant (basis: the fair market value already recognized implicitly includes this cost) | 900 | |
| Cash | | 900 |

3. To record depreciation for first year assuming a ten-year life and no residual value:

| Depreciation expense | 800 | |
| Accumulated depreciation—plant building | | 800 |

If the donation is contingent upon the fulfillment in the future of some contractual obligation on the part of the recipient, most accountants agree that the asset should be treated as a contingent asset until such time that the contingent condition has been met. If the contractual obligation has not been undertaken or if there is some doubt that it will be fulfilled, the donated asset should be disclosed by a note to the financial statements. When the obligation is essentially met, or upon conditional transfer of ownership, the asset may be recognized in the accounts on a contingent basis. To illustrate, assume the city donated a plant site having a fair market value of $25,000 to a corporation subject to a provision that ownership would transfer one year after the beginning of operations. A conditional ownership transfer was executed. The transactions may be recorded as follows:

1. At date of agreement:

| Contingent asset—donated plant site | 25,000 | |
| Contingent contributed capital—donated plant site | | 25,000 |

2. At date of transfer of ownership and incidental costs of $100:

| Plant site | 25,000 | |
| Contingent contributed capital—donated plant site | 25,000 | |
| Contingent asset—donated plant site | | 25,000 |
| Cash | | 100 |
| Contributed capital—donated plant site | | 24,900 |

Depreciable assets received by donation should be depreciated in the normal manner on the basis of the fair market value recorded in the accounts. A contingent asset (as recorded in entry No. 1 above), if depreciable in nature, should be depreciated on the basis of the fair market value from date of initial recognition (or initial use, depending upon the circumstances) as a contingent asset.

### Discovery Value

Property owned by a company may increase in value substantially as a result of the *discovery* of valuable mineral or other natural resources. In such cases the original cost of the property may not provide a suitable basis for accountability. In the case of discovery value the accounting profession recognizes another exception to the cost principle. The fair market value of the property, in consideration of the valuable natural resource, should be realistically estimated, usually by appraisal, and recorded in the accounts. The resulting credit should be to Unrealized Capital Increment—Discovery Value. Depletion should be recognized on the basis of the increased value. To illustrate, assume a tract of land was purchased in 1954 for $2,000 and that in 1976 a valuable gravel deposit (that will be commercially exploited) was discovered on it. Related entries are:

1. To record purchase in 1954:

Land ...................................................................... 2,000
    Cash .................................................................     2,000

2. To record discovery value (estimated total quantity exploitable, 100,000 tons; appraised at $25,000 exclusive of residual land value) in 1976:[4]

Land—appraisal increment (gravel deposit) .................... 25,000
    Unrealized capital increment (gravel deposit) ............     25,000

3. To record depletion for first year based on depletion rate of $.25 per ton; 10,000 tons mined during first year:

Depletion expense ...................................................... 2,500
    Land—appraisal increment (gravel deposit) ..............     2,500

## WRITE-DOWN OF OPERATIONAL ASSETS BASED ON DECREASED USE VALUE

If an operational asset loses its operational value by a *material amount*, it should be written down or written off as the circumstances warrant. Thus, for example, a plant may become idle due to factors such as continuing decline in demand, the obsolescence of its products, or inadequate transportation facilities, so that it has little or no resale value and its decreased value, if any, can only be realized as salvage. In such cases, accounting standards *require* an immediate write-down to net realizable value and recognition of the related loss for the period. Normally the write-down should be accomplished through a credit to the accumulated depreciation account (in recognition of obsolescence) and a debit to a nonrecurring loss. The loss would be extraordinary if it is (*a*) unusual and (*b*) occurs infrequently (*APB Opinion No. 30*). As a general principle it can be said that operational assets should not be carried at a book value in excess of their fair market value in use.

## OUTLAYS SUBSEQUENT TO ACQUISITION BUT PRIOR TO USE

Outlays subsequent to acquisition but prior to operational use of a fixed asset, made to improve the asset and to bring it up to operational condition, should be capitalized as a part of the cost of the asset.

---

[4] The accounting profession has sanctioned, but not required, this procedure.

Prior to operational use, a secondhand asset frequently will require considerable outlays for repairs, reconditioning, remodeling, and installation, all of which should be capitalized. Reinstallation and rearrangement costs of machinery, rearrangement of partitions, renovation of buildings, and similar outlays on operational assets purchased in a used condition should be capitalized as a part of the cost. Overhead items such as insurance, taxes, supervisory salaries, and similar incidental expenditures directly related to the asset during a period of renovation also should be capitalized. Depreciation should not be recorded prior to the period of use.

## LUMP-SUM PURCHASES OF ASSETS

It is not unusual for a business to acquire several dissimilar assets for a lump sum. This type of acquisition, frequently referred to as a basket purchase, poses the problem of apportioning the lump-sum cost to the several assets acquired, some of which may be depreciable and others nondepreciable. The apportionment should be based upon some realistic indicator of the relative values of the several assets involved, such as appraised values, tax assessment, cost savings, or the present value of estimated future earnings.

To illustrate, assume that $90,000 was paid for property that included land, a building, and some machinery. Assume further that an independent appraisal showed appraised values of land, $30,000; building, $50,000; and machinery, $20,000. The cost apportionment and entry to record the transaction are shown below.

| Asset | Appraised Value | Multiplier* | Apportioned Cost |
|---|---|---|---|
| Land........................ | $ 30,000 | .9 | $27,000 |
| Building ................... | 50,000 | .9 | 45,000 |
| Machinery ............... | 20,000 | .9 | 18,000 |
| Total............... | $100,000 | | $90,000 |

* Multiplier    ₵00,000 ∶ ₵100,000 − .0

Entry to record the purchase:

| | | |
|---|---|---|
| Land ........................................................................... | 27,000 | |
| Building ..................................................................... | 45,000 | |
| Machinery ................................................................. | 18,000 | |
| Cash ..................................................................... | | 90,000 |

## ASSETS CONSTRUCTED FOR OWN USE

Companies may construct buildings, plants, equipment, furniture, and fixtures on occasion for their own use. Operational assets may be constructed rather than acquired from the outside in order to utilize idle facilities and personnel, to effect an expected cost saving, or to satisfy a need that outsiders cannot meet in the desired time. In the case of assets constructed for a company's own use, several problems arise relative to measurement of the amount that should be capitalized as the cost of the asset. Obviously, all material, labor, and overhead costs *directly* identifiable with the construction should be capitalized. Capitalizable costs during the construction period also should include charges for licenses, permits and fees, taxes, insurance, and similar charges relating to the assets being constructed. Aside from the directly identifiable costs of construction that should be capitalized, there are two problems that require further consideration, viz:

1. General company overhead as a cost of assets constructed for own use.
2. Excess costs on assets constructed for own use.

### General Overhead as a Cost of Construction

Assets may be constructed by a company for its own use under two different operating circumstances.

First, there is the case where for all practical purposes the plant is operating at capacity in producing goods for sale and the management decides to construct some asset to be used rather than sold. Management might make such a decision when the item otherwise is unavailable at the time required. In this case production of regular goods for sale is reduced. Clearly, in this situation the asset should be charged for all direct costs incurred in construction including (a) *additional* overhead costs caused by the construction, and (b) a fair share of *general factory overhead* allocated on the same basis as that applied to goods manufactured for sale.

Second, there is the instance where the plant is operating at less than capacity in producing regular goods for sale. In this case idle plant capacity, or a part of such capacity, is utilized in manufacturing an asset for own use and production of goods for sale is unaffected. In this case the asset should be charged with all direct costs incurred in such construction including *additional* overhead costs caused by the construction. At this point the question arises as to whether any of the *general factory overhead* also should be allocated to the asset constructed for own use. On this specific point some accountants take the position that the general factory overhead should be apportioned to the asset on the same basis as it is apportioned to the production for sale; others take the opposite position that none of the general factory overhead should be assigned to the asset constructed.

When idle plant capacity is used, it is argued in support of assigning a ratable portion of general factory overhead to the asset being constructed that (a) such assets should be accorded the same treatment as regular products; (b) the full cost of the asset should include general factory overhead (otherwise loss from idle capacity is overstated); (c) a future benefit is involved, hence such costs should be deferred; (d) no special favor should be accorded such assets; (e) normal operations should not be penalized by carrying such overhead costs; and (f) in conformance with the cost principle, an allocation is essential if the true cost of both the asset being constructed and the concurrent production for sale is to be assigned.

On the other hand, it is argued in support of not assigning a portion of the general factory overhead to the asset being constructed that (a) such allocation would be reflected as an increase in income due to construction rather than as a result of production and sale of goods; (b) the full cost of the asset should not include overhead that would be incurred even in the absence of such construction; (c) the cost of production for sale should not be influenced by such construction; and (d) management should not consider the general factory overhead in making the decision to construct the fixed asset.

Although there are persuasive arguments for both positions, the authors are of the opinion that in theory it is preferable to capitalize a portion of general factory overhead when idle plant capacity is used in the construction of assets for a firm's own use.

When assets are diverted from inventory and put into use as property, plant, and equipment, the carrying values they had as inventory should be transferred to the plant account.

## Excess Costs of Construction

Ordinarily when management has made a decision to construct assets for own use, the full cost should be capitalized on the basis that the alternative cost of outside producers is not now available as an alternative. However, when construction costs of such assets are materially in excess of their fair value, the excess cost should be recorded as a period loss, as opposed to a capitalization. Construction costs materially in excess of those of an independent producer may be an indication that the full construction cost is an unwarranted charge to future operations through capitalization.

## INTEREST DURING CONSTRUCTION PERIOD

Traditionally, public utilities have capitalized interest costs during construction on funds used to finance construction of fixed assets as part of the cost of those assets. Governmental regulatory agencies responsible for regulating the rates charged by utilities have allowed (but not required) interest during construction as a cost of the asset rather than as a current expense. This has the effect of deferring the impact of interest cost on utility rates to the period of usage of the fixed assets. The future impact will be greater because the utility rate base is higher by the amount of interest capitalized.

Historically, interest has been viewed as a cost of borrowing funds rather than as a cost of the asset acquired with those funds. Therefore, capitalization of interest during the construction period generally has been viewed as not theoretically sound from the accounting point of view. Obviously, if interest during construction is capitalized, any premium or discount related to the borrowing should be accorded the same treatment.

Capitalization of interest during construction outside the public utility industry was not a widespread practice but became a growing one in the early 1970s. However, its spread has been halted, temporarily at least for most companies, by issuance of SEC *Accounting Series Release No. 163.* Under provisions of this release (after June 21, 1974), only electric, gas, water, and telephone utilities plus, in certain situations, those companies covered by provisions of two AICPA industry guides can capitalize interest.[5] In addition, companies that, prior to June 21, 1974, had publicly disclosed an accounting policy of capitalizing interest may continue interest capitalization but may not extend it to new types of assets. On all financial statements filed after January 1, 1975, the amount of interest capitalized must be reported. In the case of nonutility companies, the basis for capitalizing interest and the method of determining capitalized interest must be disclosed.

The issue is under serious study by the FASB, SEC, and the accounting profession because it poses some critical theoretical and practical questions, such as:

1. Should interest on all funds, or only borrowed funds, be capitalized?
2. On what basis are internally generated and borrowed funds separately identified?
3. What rate of interest should be used? Typically, there are several borrowing rates. What rate should be used on general funds used?
4. What assets should qualify for capitalization of interest?
5. What should be the credit entry to offset the debit to the asset for interest capitalized? Should interest on borrowed or internally generated funds be permitted to increase net income during the construction period? For example, some utilities have experienced their highest earnings during construction and a significant drop when the plant goes on stream.

## ACQUISITION COSTS OF SPECIFIC PROPERTY

In determining the acquisition cost of an operational asset, the general principles discussed heretofore are applicable; however, certain items of property give rise to special problems in applying the general principles. These special problems are considered in the immediately succeeding paragraphs.

### Land

The acquisition cost of land should be recorded in an account captioned Land or Real Estate. Some of the specific elements of land cost include the following:

---

[5] *Audits of Savings and Loan Associations,* an AICPA industry audit guide (1973); and *Accounting for Retail Land Sales,* an AICPA industry accounting guide (1973).

1. Original contract price.
2. Brokers' commissions.
3. Legal fees for examining and recording ownership.
4. Cost of ownership guarantee insurance policies.
5. Cost of real estate surveys.
6. Cost of an option when it is exercised.
7. Special paving assessments.
8. Cost of razing an old building (net of any salvage).
9. Cost of cancellation of an unexpired lease.
10. Payment of noncurrent taxes accrued on the land at date of purchase if payable by the purchaser.

On the other hand, the cost of land does not include: fees for surveying, ownership searches, geological opinions, legal and other expert services on land not purchased, expenditures in connection with disposal of refuse, costs of easements or rights of way which are limited as to time, assessments for repairs to roads and sidewalks, and repairs to other improvements.[6]

Costs incurred subsequent to acquisition to *permanently* improve the land for the purpose acquired, such as draining, clearing, landscaping, grading, and subdividing costs, are proper additions to the capitalized cost of the land.

A special problem arises concerning the treatment of taxes and carrying charges in respect to real estate held for investment or for future use. From a conservative point of view such charges should be recorded as current expenses. However, accounting theory tends to hold that in view of the fact that the asset is not producing income against which the charges may be offset, the carrying charges should be capitalized, particularly when the fair market value of the property is increasing. If the real estate is producing income, through rent for example, or is declining in value, there are sound reasons for treating the carrying costs as a current expense. Such charges may be either capitalized or expensed for income tax purposes.

### Buildings

Specific cost elements of buildings include:

1. Original contract price or cost of construction.
2. Expenses incurred in remodeling, reconditioning, or altering a purchased building to make it available for the purpose for which it was acquired.
3. Cost of excavation or grading or filling of land for the specific building.
4. Expenses incurred for the preparation of plans, specifications, blueprints, and so on.
5. Cost of building permits.

---

[6] *Fixed Asset Accounting: The Capitalization of Costs* (New York: NAA, 1972), pp. 9–10.

6. Payment of noncurrent taxes accrued on the building at date of purchase if payable by purchaser.
7. Architects' and engineers' fees for design and supervision.
8. Other costs, such as temporary buildings used during the construction period.
9. Unanticipated expenditures such as rock blasting, piling, or relocation of the channel of an underground stream.

On the other hand, the cost of building should not include: extraordinary costs incidental to the erection of a building, such as those due to a strike, flood, fire, or other casualty, and the cost of abandoned construction.[7]

Removable building equipment may have a shorter life than the building and may be subject to replacement without impairment of the integrity of the building, in which case it should be separately recorded as building equipment and be separately depreciated. Razing costs of a building that has been used by an entity should be identified with the retirement of the old building.

### Machinery, Furniture, Fixtures, and Equipment

Specific cost elements of machinery, furniture, fixtures, and equipment include:

1. Original contract or invoice cost.
2. Freight- and drayage-in, cartage, import duties, handling and storage costs.
3. Specific in-transit insurance charges.
4. Sales, use, and other taxes imposed on the acquisition.
5. Costs of preparation of foundations, protective apparatus, and other costs in connection with making a proper situs for the asset.
6. Installation charges including company overhead on the same basis as it is charged to inventory.
7. Charges for testing and preparation for use.
8. Costs for reconditioning used items when purchased.[8]

Since machine and hand tools are relatively low in cost per unit, are frequently lost or broken, and thus have a short service life, they normally are not accorded the same treatment as other tangible fixed assets; rather they are accounted for in one of three ways, viz:

1. Capitalized at date of purchase, periodically inventoried, and the asset account adjusted to the inventory value, thereby charging the losses due to breakage, theft, or disappearance to current expense.
2. Capitalized as an asset at a conservative valuation for the ordinary or normal stock; all subsequent tool purchases are then charged to current expense.
3. Expensed as acquired (see Chapter 13).

---

[7] Ibid., pp. 10–11.
[8] Ibid.

### Patterns and Dies

Patterns and dies are used in the fabrication of many manufactured items such as automobile bodies. Patterns and dies used for regular production over a period of time should be recorded in a fixed asset account, Patterns and Dies, and depreciated over their estimated service life. Patterns and dies that are purchased or constructed for a particular job or order should be charged directly to the cost of that job.

### Returnable Containers

Products are frequently sold in containers that have a relatively high value, hence are returnable for reuse. Gas cylinders, oil drums, and steel tanks generally can be returned by the purchaser for value. In some cases the purchaser is charged a deposit for the container and will receive a credit or refund when it is returned. In such cases, until returned, the containers should be carried in the vendor's accounts as a fixed asset and depreciated over their estimated useful life. Containers not returned within a reasonable time are accounted for as retired by sale; the deposit becomes the sales price. In contrast some companies do not bill the customer for the container, although the customer is expected to hold the container available for pickup. In such cases the vendor may account for the containers as operating supplies rather than as fixed assets and the loss determined by inventory similar to the procedure described for tools.

### Leasehold Improvements

Improvements on *leased* property such as buildings, walks, landscaping, and certain types of permanent equipment, unless specifically exempted in the lease agreement, revert to the owner of the property upon termination of the lease. Improvements on leased property of this nature are referred to as *leasehold improvements*. The cost of such improvements should be capitalized by the lessee in a tangible fixed asset account entitled Leasehold Improvements (considered by some to be an intangible asset). The cost of the leasehold improvements should be depreciated over the term of the lease or the service life of the improvement, whichever is the shorter. Renewal provisions in the lease agreement normally are disregarded in depreciating leasehold improvements.

## COST OUTLAYS SUBSEQUENT TO ACQUISITION

### REPAIRS AND MAINTENANCE

After acquisition cost has been measured and recorded, numerous costs related to *utilization* of plant and equipment assets are incurred such as repairs, maintenance, betterments, and replacements. What outlays should be charged to an asset account, to the accumulated depreciation account, to Retained Earnings, to expense, or to some combination of these accounts? The problem is particularly critical as a result of the difficulty in distinguishing between the several classifications of outlay, such as ordinary repairs as opposed to extraordinary repairs, each of which requires different treatment in the accounts and financial reports.

*Maintenance costs* are those costs, such as lubrication, cleaning, adjustment, and painting, which are incurred to keep equipment in normal usable condition. *Ordinary repairs* (as distinguished from major repairs) are outlays for parts, labor, and other related costs which are necessary to keep the equipment in normal operating condition but do not add materially to the use value of the asset, nor prolong its life appreciably. Ordinary repairs are recurring and normally involve relatively small expenditures. Examples of ordinary repairs are fixing a broken chain or electrical circuit, and replacing spark plugs. Since maintenance costs and ordinary repairs are similar in many respects and accounted for in the same way, they usually are combined for accounting purposes.

### Ordinary Repairs and Maintenance

Maintenance and ordinary repair costs may be accounted for using either of two approaches:

1. As revenue expenditures — an appropriate expense account is debited for each outlay as incurred. The effect of this procedure is to recognize expenses when the repairs and maintenance actually happen. Since use precedes repairs, it is sometimes argued that the matching principle is not adequately implemented. However, materiality and the short-term gap involved are compensating factors.

2. Allowance procedure — in the case of a new asset, the maintenance and repair costs initially will be low, increasing in amount each year as the asset is utilized. Repair costs also follow use and tend to vary during the year. Rather than charging operating expense as the repairs are incurred, it is sometimes preferable to use the allowance procedure. The allowance procedure requires an estimate of the total cost of ordinary repairs and maintenance during (*a*) the life of the asset, or (*b*) during the year, depending on the choice of period over which apportionment is desired. The amount of estimated repairs is allocated to each interim period on the basis of time (an equal amount each month or year as the case may be) or on the basis of production or output. Repair and Maintenance Expense is debited, and an allowance account is credited for the estimated amount. Actual expenditures for maintenance and ordinary repairs are then debited to the allowance account when incurred. To illustrate, assume ordinary repairs and maintenance for the year have been estimated at $1,800 and that this amount is to be apportioned on a time basis (an equal amount each month). Assume that the actual repairs and maintenance costs incurred for the first month amounted to $110. The entries would be:

1. To record the estimated maintenance and ordinary repair cost for the month:

    Repairs and maintenance expense ....................................... 150
        Allowance for maintenance and repairs ...........................       150

2. To record actual outlays for the month for ordinary repairs and maintenance:

    Allowance for maintenance and repairs ................................ 110
        Cash or payables............................................................       110

The income statement would report repairs and maintenance expense of $150 for the month. The $40 credit balance in the allowance account would be reported on the interim balance sheet as a current liability because it reflects a future demand on current assets. In this example, at the end of the year any balance in the allowance account would be closed to the related repair expense account.

The allowance procedure for maintenance and ordinary repairs has been accorded general acceptability by the accounting profession. The procedure is justifiable for apportioning an expense where there is a sound basis for doing so; it is not acceptable simply as a means of equalizing profits as between several periods. It is used on either an annual basis, or to cover the entire life of the asset. In the latter case, the ending balance in the allowance account, each year, is reported on the balance sheet as a special liability (a claim against future assets) or as a contra to the related asset account similar to accumulated depreciation. The allowance method is not acceptable for federal income tax purposes.

## EXTRAORDINARY REPAIRS

Extraordinary or major repairs involve relatively large amounts, are not recurring in nature, and tend to increase the *use value* (efficiency and use utility) or the service life of the asset beyond what it was originally. There are two acceptable alternative approaches in accounting for extraordinary repairs:

1. Capitalize—If the expenditure serves primarily to increase the use value, the cost is debited to the related asset account.
2. Reduce accumulated depreciation—If the expenditure serves primarily to increase the service life of the asset (and perhaps the residual value), the cost is debited to the related accumulated depreciation account.

Examples of extraordinary repairs are major overhauls, major improvements in the electrical system, and strengthening the foundation of a building.

Because of the difficulty in making a realistic distinction between increase in utility and increase in useful life as a result of extraordinary repairs, and because the two methods give the same net results (with the same set of facts) both are widely used. Often the depreciation rate must be revised.

## REPLACEMENTS AND BETTERMENTS

*Replacements* involve the removal of a major part or component of plant or equipment and the substitution of a new part or component of essentially the *same type and performance capabilities*. Replacement may involve specific subunits or a number of major items similar in many respects to an extraordinary repair. In fact, the line between replacements and extraordinary repairs often is difficult to draw.

In contrast, *betterments,* or improvements, constitute the removal of a major part or component of plant or equipment and the substitution of a different part or component having significantly *improved and superior* performance capabilities. The result of the improved substitute serves to increase the overall efficiency and tends to increase the useful life of the primary asset. The replacing of an old shingle roof with a modern fireproof tile roof, installing a more powerful engine in a shrimp boat, and replacement of an improved electrical system in a building, are illustrations of betterments.

Because of the difference in circumstances in which replacements and betterments are made, three different approaches are used, viz:

1. Capitalize—The cost of the replacement or betterment is debited to the primary asset in conformance with the cost principle. The primary asset is improved as to performance and perhaps remaining life. In this approach, the cost and accumulated depreciation on the unit replaced are not removed from the accounts because they are not realistically determinable. Often the depreciation rate must be revised. This approach is used when the old costs and related accumulated depreciation amounts are not known and when the primary effect is to increase efficiency (rather than to lengthen the life of the basic asset). Because of the difficulty in making this distinction in practice, this approach and the next one are generally viewed as full-fledged alternatives.

2. Reduce accumulated depreciation—The cost of the replacement or betterment is debited to the related accumulated depreciation account on the basis that it is a recovery of past depreciation and that the life of the primary asset is lengthened. This approach is recommended when the primary effect is to lengthen the remaining life of the related asset; however, it is used as a full-fledged alternative to capitalization in the asset account. Often the depreciation rate must be revised.

3. Substitution—Conceptually this method assumes that there has been a disposal of the old unit and acquisition of a new unit. Therefore, these two separate events are recorded as follows:

   a. The cost of the old unit replaced is removed from the asset account, the accumulated depreciation on the old unit is removed, and a gain or loss on disposal recognized.

   b. The new replacement unit is debited to the asset account.

To illustrate, assume the old shingle roof on Plant A, original cost $20,000, 80% depreciated, is replaced with a new fireproof tile roof that cost $60,000. The two entries (which could be combined) are:

*a.* To remove old roof from the accounts:

Accumulated depreciation, old roof ($20,000 × 80%) ... 16,000
Loss on disposal of plant assets ............................ 4,000
    Plant assets (old roof) ...................................... 20,000

*b.* To record acquisition of new roof:

Plant assets (new roof)........................................... 60,000
    Cash .......................................................... 60,000

Theoretically, the third method is sound in every respect. However, it can be applied only when the cost of the old subunit, and the related accumulated depreciation, are known or can be realistically estimated. The loss would not be extraordinary as prescribed by *APB Opinion No. 30* ("Reporting the Results of Operations").[9]

## ADDITIONS

Additions are extensions, enlargements, or expansions made to an existing asset. An extra wing or room added to a building and the addition of a production unit to an existing machine are examples of additions. An addition represents a capital expenditure and should be recorded in the fixed asset accounts at the full acquisition cost determined under the principles discussed above for acquisition cost of the original asset. Work done on the existing structure such as the shoring up of the foundation to accommodate the addition or the cutting of an entranceway through an existing wall should be regarded as a part of the cost of the addition and capitalized. The cost of an addition, less any estimated residual value, normally should be depreciated over its own service life or the remaining life of the original asset of which it is a part, whichever period is the shorter.

Pollution control devices have recently been added or are now being added by large numbers of entities either voluntarily or in compliance with laws or court or administrative orders. Sometimes, either because the original assets (which are the source of the pollution) were acquired when prices were low or because of stringency of the control regulations, the antipollution devices are quite costly in relation to the original assets. The devices themselves are capitalizable as plant additions. A question arises as to the accounting dispostion of fines, damages, or penalties which are sometimes assessed in connection with pollution which has been caused. Some have argued such costs should be charged to the current period; others believe that the proper treatment is a prior period adjustment; still others contend the costs should be capitalized and amortized over future periods. The authors prefer the first of the three alternatives. Whatever case can be made for the second alternative would have to rest on the notion that the penalty was assessed to correct damage resulting from production of prior periods and thus the costs of

---

[9] Some accountants believe that this is a change in estimate (*APB Opinion No. 20*, "Accounting Changes"); therefore, the loss should not be separately recognized but should be debited to accumulated depreciation and thereby spread prospectively, over the remaining life of the primary asset.

those periods was understated; some of the criteria for a prior period adjustment may well be met. Accounting for the costs as a capitalizable item to be amortized in the future has to rest on the notion that if the assessment is not paid, the entity will not get to operate in the future; therefore, there is a measurable future benefit.

## REARRANGEMENT OF ASSETS

The cost of reinstallation, rerouting, or rearrangement of factory machinery for the purpose of securing greater efficiency in production or reduced production costs in the future should be capitalized if material in amount and if the benefits of the rearrangement definitely will extend beyond the current accounting period. Such costs should be capitalized as a deferred charge and amortized over the ensuing periods benefiting from the rearrangement.

## RETIREMENT OF OPERATIONAL ASSETS

Operational assets may be retired voluntarily through disposal by sale, trade, or abandonment—or involuntarily lost as a result of casualty such as fire or storm. Irrespective of the cause of retirement, if the asset is subject to depreciation, it should be depreciated to date of such retirement. Likewise, taxes, insurance premium costs, and similar costs should be accrued up to the date of retirement. At date of retirement the cost of the asset and its related accumulated depreciation should be removed from the accounts. To illustrate, assume a truck costing $3,200 on February 1, 1972, is sold on July 1, 1976, for $650. Straight-line depreciation has been recorded on the basis of an estimated service life of five years and an estimated residual value of $200. The company closes its books on December 31 of each year. The entries at date of sale would be as follows:

1. Depreciation expense ....................................................... 300
      Accumulated depreciation—equipment ........................ 300
    To record 6 months' depreciation for 1976 at $50 per month computed as follows:
    Amount to be depreciated ($3,200 − $200) ... $3,000
    Service life—5 years or 60 months.
    Monthly depreciation ($3,000/60 months)...... $  50

2. Cash .............................................................................. 650
    Accumulated depreciation—equipment ............................ 2,650
      Delivery equipment ................................................. 3,200
      Gain on sale of equipment* ..................................... 100
    To record retirement of old truck by sale.

| | | | |
|---|---|---|---|
| * Sales price ............................................... | | | $650 |
| Less book value of asset sold: | | | |
| Original cost............................................. | | $3,200 | |
| Accumulated depreciation: | | | |
| 1972—11 months ............................. | $550 | | |
| 1973—12 months ............................. | 600 | | |
| 1974—12 months ............................. | 600 | | |
| 1975—12 months ............................. | 600 | | |
| 1976— 6 months ............................. | 300 | 2,650 | 550 |
| Gain on Sale....................................... | | | $100 |

The gain on sale of equipment is closed to the Income Summary account.

The accounting entries for an exchange were discussed and illustrated earlier in the chapter. In case an operational asset is abandoned or disposed of because it has no value, the cost and accumulated depreciation amounts should be removed from the accounts and any loss on abandonment, including costs of disposal, recognized.

Outlays made to restore and repair uninsured assets damaged through fire, storm, or other casualty should be recorded as losses and closed to the Income Summary account. Outlays made where the properties are improved beyond their approximate operating condition prior to the casualty should be apportioned between losses and the asset.[10] Damaged assets not restored should be reduced to a carrying value consistent with the decrease in going-concern utility. Accounting for *insured* casualty losses is discussed in Chapter 14.

## QUESTIONS

1. Operational assets used in day-to-day business operations can be classed as tangible or intangible; distinguish between the two, giving examples. Under what balance sheet caption are tangible operational assets reported? Give at least one synonym for whatever title you specify.

2. Distinguish between capital and revenue expenditures. What accounting implications are involved?

3. Relate the *cost principle* to the acquisition of operational assets. Relate the *matching principle* to operational asset accounting.

4. How is asset acquisition cost determined when the consideration given is securities?

5. Define book value with respect to (a) assets having no limited service life, and (b) assets having a limited service life.

6. Explain the relationship between book value and fair market value of an operational asset.

7. In determining the cost of an operational asset how should the following items be treated: (a) invoice price, (b) freight, (c) discounts, (d) ownership costs, (e) installation costs, (f) breaking-in costs, and (g) cost of major overhaul before operational use?

8. A machine is purchased on the following terms: cash, $10,000, plus ten semiannual payments of $3,000 each. How should the acquisition cost of the machine be recorded? Explain.

9. Basically, how are assets acquired recorded when payment includes the trading in of an old asset (refer to *APB Opinion No. 29*)?

10. Where several assets are bought for a single lump-sum consideration, a cost apportionment procedure is usually employed. Explain the procedure. Why is apportionment necessary?

---

[10] In instances where the casualty loss is both (a) unusual and (b) occurs infrequently, as defined in *APB Opinion No. 30*, it must be reported as an extraordinary item.

11. Some businesses self-construct plant assets. What costs should be capitalized? In connection with self-construction of assets, explain what to do with (a) general company overhead, and (b) any excess costs incurred.

12. Capitalization of interest during the period operational assets were under construction has been a widespread practice in one industry. Identify the industry; explain why interest capitalization was practiced.

13. Distinguish between maintenance, ordinary repairs, and extraordinary repairs.

14. Explain the accounting for (a) extraordinary repairs, (b) replacements and renewals, and (c) betterments and improvements.

15. The XY Corporation added a new wing at a cost of $50,000, plus $1,000 spent in making passageways through the walls of an old structure to the existing plant. The plant was 10 years old and was being depreciated an equal amount each year over a 30-year life. Discuss the implications in determining the depreciation of the new wing.

16. What are leasehold improvements? How should they be accounted for?

17. Outline the accounting steps related to the disposition of an operational asset.

## DECISION CASE 12-1

One of your clients, a savings bank with several local branches, recently acquired ownership to a lot and building located in a historical part of the city. The building was in a dilapidated condition, unsuitable for human habitation. The bank, at the time, thought it was, in essence, acquiring a site for a new branch. Although a firm of architects recommended demolition, the city council, in whose discretion such activity rests, refused consent in view of the building's historical and architectural value.

In order to comply with safety requirements and to make the building suitable for use as a branch location, the bank spent $125,000 restoring and altering the old building. It had paid $25,000 for the building and lot and had contemplated spending $80,000 on a new building after demolishing the old structure. Somewhat similar old buildings in less run-down condition could have been bought in the same area for about the same $25,000 price. It is possible, even likely, that some of these which were not so old could have been demolished without governmental intervention, and the bank could have carried out its original plan.

Now that the restoration has been completed and the bank is making final plans to open its newest branch in the restored building, the bank has been informed by the State Historical Commission that the building qualifies for and will receive a plaque designating it as a historical site. This designation will be of some value in attracting traffic to the site, will probably result in the building being pointed out when tours of the city visit the area, and so on. Under present laws, receipt of the designation may well mean that the bank can never demolish the structure as long as it is the owner and has obligations to preserve it even if the property is later vacated.

*Required:*

a. Discuss the pros and cons of capitalizing the entire $125,000 spent on restoration of the building.

b. How should the $25,000 original expenditure be treated? What would have been the cost of the site if the bank had been able to carry out its original plans?

c. Sooner or later, your client is likely to seek advice as to proper accounting of subsequent costs—repairs, depreciation, possible improvements, and so on. What advice will you give?

## DECISION CASE 12-2

Elmo Company operates several plants at which limestone is processed into quicklime and hydrated lime. The Bland plant, where most of the equipment was installed many years ago, continually deposits a dusty white substance over the surrounding countryside. Citing the unsanitary condition of the neighboring community of Adeltown, the pollution of the Adel River, and the high incidence of lung disease among workers at Bland, the state's Pollution Control Agency has ordered the installation of air pollution control equipment. Also, the Agency has assessed a substantial penalty, which will be used to clean up Adeltown. After considering the costs involved (which could not have been reasonably estimated prior to the Agency's action), Elmo decides to comply with the Agency's orders, the alternative being to cease operations at Bland at the end of the current year. The officers of Elmo agree that the air pollution control equipment should be capitalized and depreciated over its useful life, but they disagree over the period(s) to which the penalty should be charged.

*Required:*

Discuss the conceptual merits and reporting requirements of accounting for the penalty as a—

*a.* Charge to the current period.
*b.* Correction of prior periods.
*c.* Capitalizable item to be amortized over future periods.

(AICPA adapted)

## EXERCISES

### Exercise 12-1

When examining the accounts of a new corporate client, you encounter the following items:

| *Identity* | *Description or Added Data* | *Valuation Data* |
|---|---|---|
| *a.* Franchise | Acquired as perpetual franchise. | Cost, $12,000 |
| *b.* Land | Purchased last year for future plant site. | Cost, $ 6,000 |
| *c.* Building | Purchased 12 years ago for warehouse. (Being depreciated over 45-year life by straight-line method; no salvage value.) | Cost, $90,000 |
| *d.* Patent | Purchased three years ago. (Half of useful life has elapsed and is reflected by amortization recorded.) | Cost, $15,000 |
| *e.* Fixtures | Purchased at start of current year. | Cost, $30,000 |
| *f.* Returnable Containers | Bought three years ago. (Being depreciated on basis of ten-year life by straight-line method; 20% are expected not to be returned.) | Cost, $30,000 |
| *g.* Goodwill | Arose when business acquired a division in 1971 which has since been merged in as integral part of client corporation. | Remaining unamortized balance $9,000 |
| *h.* Land | Bought for speculative purposes last year. | Cost, $25,000 |
| *i.* Hand tools | Bought at various times. | Remaining balance is value at date of examination, $8,000. |

*Required:*

Indicate the balance sheet classification and amount for each of the foregoing items.

## Exercise 12-2

What is the proper cost to use for recording the land in each of the following independent cases? Give reasons in support of your answer.

Case A — Issued 15,000 shares (par value per share $1) par value capital stock with a "market value" of $1.50 per share (based upon a recent sale of ten shares) for the land. The land was recently appraised at $17,000 by competent appraisers.

Case B — Rejected an offer two years ago by the vendor to sell the land for $7,500 cash. Issued 1,000 shares of capital stock for the land (market value of the stock based on several recent transactions, $7 average volume, sold 2,000 shares).

Case C — At the middle of the current year gave a check for $5,000 for the land and assumed the liability for unpaid taxes: taxes in arrears last year, $100; assessed for current year, $80.

Case D — Issued 1,000 shares of capital stock for the land. The par value of the stock was $50 per share; the market value (stock sells daily with an average daily volume of 5,000 shares) was $63 per share at time of purchase of land. Vendor offered to sell the land for $62,000 cash. Competent appraisers valued the land at $64,000.

## Exercise 12-3

a. Delivery equipment was purchased having a list price of $6,000; terms were 2/10, n/30. Payment was made within the discount period.

b. Delivery equipment was purchased having a list price of $4,000; terms were 2/10, n/30. Payment was made after the discount period.

c. Delivery equipment listed at $10,000 was purchased and invoiced at 2/10, n/30. In order to take advantage of the discount, the company borrowed $8,000 of the purchase price by issuance of a 60-day, 9% note which was repaid with interest at maturity.

*Required:*

Give entries in each separate situation for costs, borrowing, and any expenses involved.

## Exercise 12-4

Franklin Company purchased a machine, having an estimated ten-year useful life, on a time payment plan. The cash price of the machine was $28,771. Terms were $3,000 cash down payment plus three equal annual payments to include interest on the unpaid balance at 8% per annum.

*Required:*

(Round to even dollars).

a. Give entry to reflect the purchase.

b. Give entry for depreciation at the end of one year assuming straight-line depreciation and no residual value.

c. Compute the amount of the annual payments.

d. Prepare a table to reflect the accounting entries for each of the four payments.

### Exercise 12–5

For each of the following numbered items, indicate, by using one of the five lettered choices listed below, which accounting treatment is correct. Explain questionable items and assumptions you make. Each cost, identified as a numbered item, was incurred by a corporation incident to acquisition of a new machine.

*Lettered Choices:*

a. Increases or decreases Machinery account.

b. Debit an expense account for current period.

c. Debit Prepaid Expense or Deferred Charge and amortize separately from machinery.

d. Debit Plant, Property, and Equipment account other than machinery.

e. An accounting treatment other than the four choices above. Explain.

1. Invoice price of the machinery, before discount.
2. Cash discount for prompt payment of foregoing invoice, not taken.
3. Cost of moving machinery into place.
4. Cost of removing old machine which this machinery replaced.
5. Sales tax based on purchase price of new machinery.
6. Special electrical wiring required to connect new machine.
7. Enlargement of electrical system of plant to accommodate new machine and provide for some expected future needs.
8. Service contract paid in full covering first two years' operation of the machine.
9. Cost of materials used while testing new machine.
10. Payment to technicians who assisted with break-in of new machine.
11. Cost of training three of our employees who will operate machine.
12. Charge to machine which was offset by credit to "Miscellaneous Revenue" amounting to anticipated first years' savings from use of new machine.
13. Insurance premium paid covering first year of protection of new machine against hazards to which it will be exposed.
14. Repair charges incurred during first year of operations.
15. Cost of installing sound insulation so new machine will not disturb those who work near it.

### Exercise 12–6

Strong Company purchased a tract of land on which was located a warehouse and an office building. The cash purchase price was $128,650 plus $350 fees in connection with the purchase. The following data were collected concerning the property:

|  | Tax Assessment | Vendor's Book Value | Original Cost |
|---|---|---|---|
| Land | $10,000 | $10,000 | $10,000 |
| Warehouse | 20,000 | 15,000 | 30,000 |
| Office building | 30,000 | 25,000 | 60,000 |

*Required:*

Journalize the purchase; show computations.

## Exercise 12–7

Marshal Company bought a machine on a time payment plan. The cash purchase price was $23,936. Terms were $7,000 cash down payment plus four equal annual payments of $5,000 which includes interest on the unpaid balance at 7% per annum.

*Required:*

1. Give entry to record the purchase. Show computations (round to even dollars).
2. Give entry to record depreciation at the end of the first full year assuming straight-line depreciation, an eight-year life and no residual value.
3. Prepare a table to reflect the accounting entries for each of the four installment payments.

## Exercise 12–8

Charmaine Company manufactured a new machine for its own use. The ledger account below reflects charges and credits made during the year to the Machinery account incidental to the project.

### Machinery (new)

| | | | | |
|---|---:|---|---:|
| Cost of dismantling old machine replaced | 1,200 | Cash proceeds from sale of old machine | 300 |
| Labor charges | 22,000 | | |
| Raw materials used | 24,000 | | |
| Installation charges | 3,000 | | |
| Materials spoiled | 800 | | |
| Profit on construction | 5,000 | | |
| Spare parts | 4,500 | | |
| Auxiliary tools | 3,000 | | |

Your investigation revealed the following additional facts:

1. The old machine that was removed had originally cost $30,000; accumulated depreciation was $29,600.
2. The manufacturing overhead account balance is $200,000; you determine that 96% of this relates to ordinary manufacture and the rest to the self-construction.
3. Cash discounts average 2% on all raw material purchases; the entire amount of discounts taken was recorded as Purchase Discounts.
4. The installation charges represent a payment to outsiders for technical assistance during the break-in period of the machine.
5. Materials spoiled represent the cost of materials used during the testing and break-in period.
6. Profit on construction was credited to an account of that title. Charmaine Company estimates it saved at least $5,000 by self-constructing the machinery instead of purchasing it.
7. The charge for spare parts represents the cost of parts purchased and set aside to cover breakdowns and maintenance during the first two years of normal use of the machine.

8. Auxiliary tools are items used in conjunction with the machine which have an estimated useful life of five years. The machine is expected to last from 10 to 12 years.

*Required:*

Prepare journal entries to correct the machinery account and other accounts of Charmaine Company. Insofar as possible, key your entries to the numbers identifying data above.

**Exercise 12–9**

Select the best answer for each of the following. Briefly justify your choice for each item.

1. If the present value of a note issued in exchange for a plant asset is less than its face amount, the difference should be —
   a. Included in the cost of the asset.
   b. Amortized as interest expense over the life of the note.
   c. Amortized as interest expense over the life of the asset.
   d. Included in interest expense in the year of issuance.
2. When a closely held corporation issues preferred stock for land, the land should be recorded at the —
   a. Total par value of the stock issued.
   b. Total book value of the stock issued.
   c. Appraised value of the land.
   d. Total liquidating value of the stock issued.
3. The debit for a sales tax levied and paid on the purchase of machinery preferably would be a charge to —
   a. The Machinery account.
   b. A separate Deferred Charge account.
   c. Miscellaneous Tax Expense (which includes all taxes other than those on income).
   d. Accumulated Depreciation — Machinery.
4. The Wise Corporation purchased a new machine on October 31, 19A. A $250 down payment was made, and three monthly installments of $800 each are to be made beginning on November 30, 19A. The cash price would have been $2,500. Wise paid no installation charges under the monthly payment plan but a $50 installation charge would have been incurred with a cash purchase. The amount to be capitalized as the cost of the machine during 19A would be —
   a. $2,700.
   b. $2,650.
   c. $2,550.
   d. $1,850.
   e. None of the above.
5. If a corporation purchased a lot and building and subsequently demolished the building and now uses the property as a parking lot, the accounting treatment of the cost of the building at acquisition would depend on —
   a. The significance of the cost allocated to the building in relation to the combined cost of the lot and building.
   b. The length of time for which the building was held prior to its demolition.
   c. The contemplated future use of the parking lot.
   d. The intention of management for the property when the building was acquired.

6. Property, plant, and equipment may properly include:
   a. Cash paid on machinery purchased but not yet received.
   b. Idle equipment awaiting sale.
   c. Property held for investment purposes.
   d. Land held for possible future plant site.
   e. None of the above.

   (AICPA adapted)

### Exercise 12–10

Morris Company has some old equipment that cost $11,500; accumulated depreciation, $7,200. This equipment was traded in on a new machine that had a list price of $14,000; however, it could be purchased without a trade-in for $13,700 cash. The difference is to be paid as cash boot.

*Required:*

Give the entry to record the acquisition of the new machine under each of the following independent cases:

Case A – The new machine was purchased for cash with no trade-in.
Case B – The equipment and the machine are dissimilar. The old machine is traded in and $9,000 cash boot is paid.
Case C – Same as Case B except that the equipment and the machine are similar.

### Exercise 12–11

Frank Company operates two separate plants. In Plant A, the accounting policy is to consider all ordinary (minor) repairs as revenue expenditures when incurred. In contrast, in Plant B, the accounting policy is to use the allowance procedure that charges repairs equally each period. Selected data for 19A are:

|  | Plant A | Plant B |
|---|---|---|
| Estimated repair costs budgeted for the year............ | $3,000 | $3,600 |
| Actual repair costs incurred and paid: |  |  |
| First quarter ..................................................... | 150 | 400 |
| Second quarter................................................... | 1,400 | 700 |
| Third quarter...................................................... | 900 | 2,100 |
| Fourth quarter ................................................... | 550 | 500 |

*Required:*

1. Give the entries in parallel columns for each plant for each of the four quarters.
2. Would you recommend any changes in the accounting policies? Explain and justify your response.

### Exercise 12–12

Steele Company operates one plant which is adjacent to its relatively modest office building. The plant building is old and demands continuous maintenance and repairs. The accounts reflect the cost of the plant building to be $125,000, and accumulated depreciation is $100,000. During the current year, the following expenditures relating to the plant building were made:

a. Continuing, frequent, and low-cost repairs ................................. $13,000
b. Complete overhaul of the plumbing system (old
   costs not known) ...................................................................... 8,500
c. Added a new storage shed attached to the building,
   estimated physical life of eight years ......................................... 24,000
d. Removed the original roof, original cost, $16,000, and replaced
   it with a new modern roof that was guaranteed ......................... 30,000
e. Unusual, infrequent, and costly repairs ...................................... 4,000

*Required:*

Give the journal entry to record each of the above items. Explain the basis for your treatment of each item.

## PROBLEMS

### Problem 12–1

An examination of the Property, Plant, and Equipment account of Phillips Company disclosed the following transactions:

a. Bought a delivery truck for which the list price was $4,500; paid cash $1,500 and gave a one-year noninterest-bearing note payable for the balance. The current interest rate for this type of note was 7%.
b. Contracted for a building at a price of $400,000. Settlement was effected with the contractor by transferring $400,000, 20-year, 8% company bonds payable, at which time financial consultants advised that the bonds would sell at 96.
c. Purchased a new machine having a list price of $20,000. Failed to take a 1% cash discount available upon full payment of the invoice within ten days. Shipping costs paid by the vendor amounted to $100. Installation costs amounted to $250, including $100 which represented 10% of the monthly salary of the factory superintendent (installation period two days). A wall was torn out and replaced (moved two feet) at a cost of $500 to make room for the machine.
d. Purchased an automatic counter to be attached to a machine in use. The counter cost $560. The estimated useful life of the counter was seven years, whereas the estimated life of the machine was ten years.
e. During the first month of operations the machine became inoperative due to a defect in manufacture. The vendor repaired the machine at no cost; however, the specially trained operator was idle during the two weeks the machine was inoperative. The operator was paid the regular wages ($540) during the period, although the only work performed was to observe the repair by the factory representative.
f. After one year of use, exchanged the electric motor on the machine for a heavier motor at an exchange cost of $400. The new motor had a list price of $1,250. The parts list indicated a list price for the original motor of $900.

*Required:*

Prepare entries to record each of the above transactions. Explain and justify your decision on questionable items.

**Problem 12-2**

Kraus Construction Company entered into a contract to buy five Master Loaders, agreeing to make five equal annual payments of $6,800 each at the end of each of the next five years. Master Loaders have a list price of $5,576 each, an estimated service life of eight years, and zero salvage value.

*Required:*

(Round to nearest dollar.)

1. Determine the implied interest rate of the contract and give appropriate entries to record the transaction at the date of the contract.
2. Assuming the first payment date coincides with the close of Kraus' fiscal year, make all appropriate entries if the payment is made.
3. Give entries for the fifth year.

**Problem 12-3**

Murphy Corporation bought equipment on July 1, 19A, for which its entries throughout the first year and one half of ownership were as below:

July 1, 19A:

| | | |
|---|---|---|
| Equipment..................................................................... | 25,000 | |
|     Installment note payable ........................................... | | 25,000 |

December 31, 19A:

| | | |
|---|---|---|
| Depreciation expense (½ year) ....................................... | 1,250 | |
|     Accumulated depreciation ........................................ | | 1,250 |

July 1, 19B:

| | | |
|---|---|---|
| Installment note payable ................................................. | 5,000 | |
|     Cash ........................................................................ | | 5,000 |

December 31, 19B:

| | | |
|---|---|---|
| Depreciation expense ................................................... | 2,500 | |
|     Accumulated depreciation ........................................ | | 2,500 |

As can be inferred from the foregoing, the equipment is being depreciated on a straight-line basis with an assumed ten-year life and zero salvage value. The $25,000 installment note is payable in five equal annual installments which includes interest. Assume 8% is a reasonable interest rate to impute.

*Required:*

1. Prepare a table to reflect the entries for the note. The present value of an annuity of 1 for five periods at 8% is 3.99271.
2. Give the journal entry or entries to correct Murphy Corporation's books as of December 31, 19B, on the basis that the books are still open as of that date.

**Problem 12-4**

MW Corporation acquired a new machine by trading in an old machine and paying $35,000 cash. The old machine originally cost $40,000 and had accumulated depreciation at the date of exchange of $30,000. This transaction could be recorded by either of the two following methods:

|                                      | Method 1 |        | Method 2 |        |
|--------------------------------------|----------|--------|----------|--------|
| Machinery (new)....................................... | 42,500 |        | 45,000 |        |
| Accumulated depreciation (old)............... | 30,000 |        | 30,000 |        |
| Loss on disposal of machinery ............... | 2,500 |        |          |        |
| Cash  ............................................ |          | 35,000 |          | 35,000 |
| Machinery (old)  ............................ |          | 40,000 |          | 40,000 |

*Required:*

1. Identify and discuss the reasons for recording the above transaction using Method 1.
2. Identify and discuss the reasons for recording the above transaction using Method 2.
3. Suppose the fair value of the used machine traded in was $18,000 at the time of the exchange, how would the exchange be recorded in accordance with today's accounting principles? (Assume the same amount of cash boot as above, $35,000.)

(AICPA adapted)

### Problem 12-5

The city of Rockdale entered into an agreement with Watt Manufacturing Company whereby the city would donate to Watt Company a tract of land near the city on which was located a vacant building suitable for manufacturing operations. The agreement provided that ownership would transfer to the company at the end of five years (from January 1, 19A) if a plant was put in operation for not less than three years and that the company would employ on the average of 300 or more employees. Watt Company entered into the agreement on January 1, 19A, and started operations on November 1, 19A, on a reduced scale; by the end of 19B the plant was in full production and 325 persons were on the payroll.

Just prior to signing the agreement the city had hired a competent appraiser to appraise the property with the following results: plant site, $30,000; and building, $85,000. The appraiser estimated the remaining useful life for the building at 20 years. Watt Company spent $150 in connection with the ownership of the site and $23,000 on renovating the building.

*Required:*

1. Give entries to record the donation, incidental costs, renovating costs, depreciation for 19A and 19B (if any), and to record the transfer of ownership. Disregard residual values.
2. Give entries assuming that Watt Company did not complete the agreement and abandoned the plant in January 19C.

### Problem 12-6

Max Company utilized its own facilities to construct a small addition to their office building. Construction began on March 1 and was completed on June 30 of the same year. Prior to the decision to construct the asset with its own facilities, the company accepted bids from outside contracts; the lowest bid was $240,000. Detailed costs accumulated during the construction period are summarized as follows:

| | |
|---|---|
| Materials used (including $120,000 for normal production) ............ | $180,000 |
| Direct labor (including $300,000 for normal production)................. | 450,000 |
| General supplies used on construction........................................... | 8,000 |
| Rent paid on construction machinery ............................................ | 3,000 |
| Insurance premiums on construction............................................. | 700 |
| Supervisory salary on construction................................................ | 5,000 |
| Total general administrative overhead for the year ....................... | 115,000 |
| Total factory overhead for the year: | |
| Fixed ($10,000 due to construction) ........................................ | 100,000 |
| Variable ................................................................................. | 60,000 |
| Direct labor hours (including 100,000 for normal production) ......... | 150,000 |

The company allocates factory overhead to normal production on the basis of direct labor cost.

*Required:*

Compute the amounts that might be capitalized—

a. Assuming the plant capacity to be 150,000 direct labor hours and that the construction displaced production for sale to the extent indicated.

b. Assuming the plant capacity to be 200,000 direct labor hours and that idle capacity was utilized for the construction.

*Hint:* Use overhead rates for factory overhead.

### Problem 12–7

Prepare journal entries to record the following transactions related to the acquisition of fixed assets. Justify your position on doubtful items.

a. Purchased a tract of land for $20,000, assumed taxes already assessed amounting to $180. Paid title fees, $50, and attorney fees of $300 in connection with the purchase. Payments were in cash.

b. Purchased property which included land and buildings for $78,900 cash. The purchase price included an offset of $300 for unpaid taxes. Purchaser borrowed $30,000 at 7% interest (principal and interest due one year from date) from the bank to help make the cash payment. The property was appraised for taxes as follows: land, $22,000; and building, $44,000.

c. Prior to use of the property purchased in (b) above the following expenditures were made:

| | |
|---|---|
| Repair and renovation of building ................................................. | $7,000 |
| Installation of 220-volt electrical wiring........................................... | 4,000 |
| Removal of separate shed of no use (sold scrap lumber for $50)......... | 300 |
| Construction of a new driveway ..................................................... | 1,000 |
| Repair of existing driveways.......................................................... | 600 |
| Deposits with utilities for connections ........................................... | 50 |
| Painting the company name on two sides of the building .................. | 400 |
| Installation of wire fence around property ...................................... | 2,500 |

d. The land purchased in (a) above was leveled and two retaining walls built to stop erosion that had created two rather large gulleys across the property. Total cash cost of the work was $4,500. The property is being held as a future plant site.

e. Purchased a used machine at a cash cost of $12,500. Subsequent to purchase the following expenditures were made:

| | |
|---|---:|
| General overhaul prior to use | $1,500 |
| Installation of machine | 500 |
| Cost of moving the machine | 150 |
| Cost of removing two small machines to make way for the larger machine purchased | 100 |
| Cost of reinforcing the floor prior to installation | 140 |
| Testing costs prior to operation | 60 |
| Cost of tool kit (new) essential to adjustment of machine for various types of work | 170 |

## Problem 12–8

The books of Braley Manufacturing Company had never been audited prior to 1976. In auditing the books for the year ended December 31, 1976, the auditor found the following account for the plant:

### Plant and Equipment

| 1973 | | 1973 | |
|---|---:|---|---:|
| Plant purchased | 90,000 | Sale of scrap | 300 |
| Repairs | 5,300 | Depreciation (5%) | 5,000 |
| Legal | 600 | 1974 | |
| Title fees | 50 | Depreciation (5%) | 6,700 |
| Insurance | 3,000 | | |
| Taxes | 1,200 | 1975 | |
| 1974 | | Cash proceeds from old machine | 1,150 |
| Addition to plant | 15,000 | Depreciation (5%) | 6,800 |
| Write-up | 20,000 | | |
| Interest expense | 1,500 | 1976 | |
| Repairs | 500 | Depreciation (5%) | 7,100 |
| Machinery for new addition | 2,000 | | |
| 1975 | | | |
| New machine | 3,000 | | |
| Installation | 600 | | |
| 1976 | | | |
| Machinery overhaul | 1,350 | | |
| Replaced roof | 900 | | |
| Fence | 3,400 | | |

(Balance $121,350)

Additional data relating to plant and equipment developed during the audit follow:

a. The plant was purchased during January 1973. At that time the tax assessment listed the plant as follows: plant site at $10,000, the building at $20,000, and the machinery therein at $30,000. The estimated life of the plant and machinery was 20 years.

b. During the first six months of 1973 the company expended the amounts listed in the account for the year in getting the plant ready for operation; operations began July 1. The repairs pertain to both the building and machinery. No breakdown was available. The legal fees were incurred in connection with the plant purchase and applied to all components of it. The $3,000 insurance premium represented a one-year policy on the plant and equipment, dated January 10, 1973 ($1,000 of the premium applied to the machinery). The property tax rate for the year was 2%. The scrap was accumulated during the "repair period."

c. In 1974 a plant addition was completed costing $15,000, at which time the company was paying 10% on some funds borrowed. The addition was under construction for four months. During the year $1,500 was spent for ordinary repairs, of which one third was capitalized. Machine costing $2,000 was purchased. The asset account was written up by $20,000 to bring it in line with the bank's security allowance on loans (Paid-In Surplus credited).

d. During 1975 a new machine was purchased (July 1) for $3,000 plus installation costs of $600; an old machine costing an estimated $2,100 was sold for $1,150. The old machine was acquired when the plant was acquired.

e. During 1976 several items of equipment were completely reconditioned at a cost of $1,350. Minor repairs were charged to expense during the year. The roof was replaced on one wing of the plant. A fence was constructed around the plant to keep unauthorized personnel out; it is estimated that the fence will have the same remaining life as the plant.

*Required:*

1. Set up a worksheet to compute the correct balances for the following accounts: (suggested top captions) Land, Buildings, Machinery, Land Improvements, and Accumulated Depreciation (assume 5% straight-line depreciation on ending balances; disregard residual value and round to even dollars.) Suggested side captions: list each item by year. Justify any assumptions that you make.
2. Give entry to correct the accounts assuming the books are closed for 1976.

### Problem 12-9

Ellford Corporation received a $400,000 low bid from a reputable manufacturer for the construction of special production equipment needed by Ellford in an expansion program. Because the company's own plant was not operating at capacity, Ellford decided to construct the equipment there and recorded the following production costs related to the construction:

| | |
|---|---:|
| Services of consulting engineer | $ 10,000 |
| Work subcontracted | 20,000 |
| Materials | 200,000 |
| Plant labor normally assigned to production | 65,000 |
| Plant labor normally assigned to maintenance | 100,000 |
| Total | $395,000 |

Management prefers to record the cost of the equipment under the incremental cost method. Approximately 40% of the corporation is devoted to government supply contracts which are all based in some way on cost. The contracts require that any self-constructed equipment be allocated its full share of all costs related to the construction.

The following information is also available:

a. The above production labor was for partial fabrication of the equipment in the plant. Skilled personnel were required and were assigned from other projects.

The maintenance labor would have been idle time of nonproduction plant employees who would have been retained on the payroll whether or not their services were utilized.

b. Payroll taxes and employee fringe benefits are approximately 30% of labor cost and are included in manufacturing overhead cost. Total manufacturing overhead for the year was $5,630,000.

c. Manufacturing overhead is approximately 50% variable and is applied on the basis of production labor cost. Production labor cost for the corporation's normal products totaled $6,810,000.

d. General and administrative expenses include $22,500 of executive salary cost and $10,500 of postage, telephone, supplies, and miscellaneous expenses identifiable with this equipment construction.

*Required:*

1. Prepare a schedule computing the amount which should be reported as the full cost of the constructed equipment to meet the requirements of the government contracts. Any supporting computations should be in good form.
2. Prepare a schedule computing the incremental cost of the constructed equipment.
3. What is the greatest amount that should be capitalized as the cost of the equipment? Why?

(AICPA adapted)

## Problem 12–10

Valley Manufacturing Company was incorporated on January 2, 19A, but was unable to begin manufacturing activities until July 1, 19A, because new factory facilities were not completed until that date.

The Land and Building account at December 31, 19A, was as follows:

| Date | Item | Amount |
|---|---|---|
| Jan. 31, 19A | Land and building | $ 98,000 |
| Feb. 28, 19A | Cost of removal of building | 1,500 |
| May 1, 19A | Partial payment of new construction | 35,000 |
| May 1, 19A | Legal fees paid | 2,000 |
| June 1, 19A | Second payment on new construction | 30,000 |
| June 1, 19A | Insurance premium | 1,800 |
| June 1, 19A | Special tax assessment | 2,500 |
| June 30, 19A | General expenses | 12,000 |
| July 1, 19A | Final payment on new construction | 35,000 |
| Dec. 31, 19A | Asset write-up | 12,500 |
| | | $230,300 |
| Dec. 31, 19A | Depreciation — 19A at 1% | 2,300 |
| | Account balance | $228,000 |

The following additional information is to be considered:

a. To acquire land and building the company paid $48,000 cash and 500 shares of its 5% cumulative preferred stock, par value $100 per share.

b. Cost of removal of old buildings amounted to $1,500 with the demolition company retaining all materials of the building.

c. Legal fees covered the following:

| Cost of organization | $ 500 |
|---|---|
| Examination of title covering purchase of land | 1,000 |
| Legal work in connection with construction work | 500 |
| | $2,000 |

d. Insurance premium covered premiums for three-year term beginning May 1, 19A.

e. General expenses covered the following for the period from January 2, 19A, to June 30, 19A:

| President's salary | $ 6,000 |
|---|---|
| Plant superintendent covering supervision on new building | 5,000 |
| Office salaries | 1,000 |
| | $12,000 |

f. The special tax assessment covered street improvements.

g. Because of a general increase in construction costs after entering into the building contract, the board of directors increased the value of the building $12,500, believing such increase justified to reflect current market at the time the building was completed. Retained Earnings was credited for this amount.

h. Estimated life of building—50 years.

Write-off for 19A—1% of asset value (1% of $230,300 = $2,300).

*Required:*

1. Prepare entries to reflect correct land, and building and depreciation allowance accounts at December 31, 19A.
2. Show the proper presentation of land, building and depreciation allowance on the balance sheet at December 31, 19A.

(AICPA adapted)


**Problem 12–11**

Equipment which cost $12,800 on January 1, 19A, was sold for $4,000 on June 30, 19F. It had been depreciated over a ten-year life by the straight-line method on the assumption its salvage value would be $800.

A warehouse that cost $110,000, residual value $5,000, was being depreciated over 35 years by the straight-line method. When the structure was 20 years old, an additional wing was constructed at a cost of $36,000. The estimated life of the wing considered separately was 25 years, and its residual value is $1,000. The accounting period ends December 31.

*Required:*

1. Give entries (and show computations) to record:
   a. The sale of the equipment. Accrue current depreciation in the sale entry.
   b. The addition; cash was paid.
   c. Depreciation for the warehouse and its addition after the latter has been in use for one year.
2. Show how the structures would be reported on a balance sheet prepared immediately after entry (c).

**Problem 12-12**

Sampler Company, a manufacturer, operates three plants in different locations. This problem focuses on Plant No. 1. The plant asset records reflected the following at the beginning of the current year, January 1, 19A:

| | |
|---|---:|
| Plant building (residual value, $20,000; | |
|     estimated useful life, 30 years) ........................ | $120,000 |
| Accumulated depreciation ................................. | 75,000 |
| Machinery (residual value, $35,000; | |
|     estimated useful life, 15 years) ........................ | 200,000 |
| Accumulated depreciation ............................... | 110,000 |

During the current year ending December 31, 19A, the following transactions (summarized) relating to the above accounts were completed:

a. Expenditures for nonrecurring, relatively large repairs
    that tend to increase the use value of the assets:
      Plant building........................................................................ $32,000
      Machinery ............................................................................ 19,000
b. Replacement of the original electrical wiring system of
    the plant building (original cost, $21,000)................................ 42,000
c. Additions:
    Plant building — added a small wing to the plant
      building to accommodate new equipment acquired.
      The wing has a useful life of 15 years and no
      residual value......................................................................... 45,000
    Machinery — added special protection devices to ten
      machines. These devices are attached to the
      machines and will have to be replaced every five
      years (no residual value)...................................................... 2,000
d. Outlays for maintenance parts, labor, and so on to keep
    the assets in normal working condition:

| Quarter | Plant Building | Machinery |
|---|---|---|
| 1.................. | 1,700 | 2,000 |
| 2.................. | 1,500 | 6,000 |
| 3.................. | 1,800 | 1,000 |
| 4.................. | 2,000 | 10,000 |

*Required:*

1. Give appropriate entries to record transactions (*a*) through (*c*). Explain the basis underlying your decisions.
2. Give appropriate entries by quarter, in parallel columns, for transaction (*d*) assuming: (*a*) the accounting policy is to record all ordinary repairs incurred as revenue expenditures, and (*b*) to use an allowance procedure. The annual budgeted amounts for this item were: plant building, $7,500; machinery, $18,000.
3. Which method used in Requirement 2 do you prefer? Explain.

**Problem 12-13**

On July 15, 19E, Joseph Doan, your client, sold his apartment house to John Ames. The escrow statement follows:

| | Joseph Doan, Seller | | John Ames, Buyer | |
| --- | --- | --- | --- | --- |
| | Charges | Credits | Charges | Credits |
| Sales price | | $250,000 | $250,000 | |
| Paid directly to seller .....................$ | 10,000 | | | $ 10,000 |
| First mortgage assumed by buyer ...... | 106,000 | | | 106,000 |
| Purchase money mortgage ............... | 84,000 | | | 84,000 |
| Prorations: | | | | |
|   Real estate taxes ......................... | | 250 | 250 | |
|   Insurance adjustment ................... | | 200 | 200 | |
|   Interest....................................... | | 300 | 300 | |
| Fees: | | | | |
|   Escrow....................................... | 100 | | 100 | |
|   Title insurance ........................... | | | 790 | |
|   Recording ................................... | 5 | | 10 | |
|   Attorney .................................... | 35 | | 50 | |
|   Revenue stamps ........................... | | | 550 | |
| Funds deposited in escrow account: | | | | |
|   July 14, 19E ............................... | | | | 52,250 |
| Items paid from escrow account: | | | | |
|   Commission to Lion Reality | | | | |
|     Company.................................... | 15,000 | | | |
| Remit: | | | | |
|   Joseph Doan ............................... | 35,610 | | | |
| | $250,750 | $250,750 | $252,250 | $252,250 |

Doan's accounting records are maintained on the cash basis method. When you undertake the September 30, 19E, quarterly audit for your client, the following information is available to you:

1. A "Suspense" account was opened for money received in connection with the sale of the property.
2. The apartment building and land were purchased on July 1, 19A, for $225,000. The building was being depreciated over a 40-year life by the straight-line method for the purposes of both reporting and income taxes. Accumulated depreciation at December 31, 19D, was $17,500. A half year's depreciation has been consistently recorded on Doan's books for assets purchased or sold during the year. No depreciation has been recorded on the books for 19E.
3. The contract of sale stated that the price for the land on which the building was built was $25,000; the cost recorded on Doan's books.
4. The purchase money mortgage payments are $1,000 per month plus accrued interest. The first payment was due on August 1, 19E.

*Required:*

Prepare the adjusting journal entries to record the sale on Doan's books.

(AICPA adapted)

### Problem 12–14

You are the accountant for the White Corporation and receive a telephone call from their bookkeeper informing you that the corporation has sold a storage building and land. You have submitted a list of annual adjusting entries for this client as of December 31 each year. The sale of the property took place as of June 30, 19D, and the bookkeeper requests that you advise her how to record the transaction. You advise her to open an account called "Sale of Property" and credit the account with the proceeds and charge same with expenses paid in connection with the sale, if any, and you will complete the recording when you make your next audit.

The escrow statements were as follows:

### Seller's Statement

| | | |
|---|---:|---:|
| Selling price ................................... | | $34,000.00 |
| Cash due from— | | |
|     Bank ........................................... | $14,740.27 | |
|     Buyer........................................... | 6,725.75 | $21,466.02 |
| Purchase money from second | | |
|     mortgage.................................... | | 12,000.00 |
| Balance 19C taxes to be paid by bank... | | 166.53 |
| Tax adjustment for 19D: | | |
|     Credit to buyer—6 months............... | | 354.75 |
| Revenue stamps ........................... | | 35.20 |
| Insurance adjustment— | | |
|     credit to seller .......................... | | 22.50 |
| | $34,022.50 | $34,022.50 |

### Buyer's Statement

| | | |
|---|---:|---:|
| Purchase price ............................... | $34,000.00 | |
| Cash due to seller............................. | | $ 6,725.75 |
| Insurance adjustment ......................... | 22.50 | |
| Title fee and recording ...................... | 58.00 | |
| Tax adjustment for 19D ...................... | | 354.75 |
| First mortgage to bank ..................... | | 15,000.00 |
| Purchase money for second | | |
|     mortgage.................................... | | 12,000.00 |
| | $34,080.50 | $34,080.50 |

Note: The bank will deduct from the $15,000 (first mortgage) the following items:

| | | |
|---|---:|---:|
| | | $15,000.00 |
| 19C taxes ...................................... | $166.53 | |
| Revenue stamps ........................... | 35.20 | |
| Title fee and recording ................... | 58.00 | 259.73 |
| Net due from bank ........................ | | 14,740.27 |
| Net due from buyer........................ | | 6,725.75 |
|     Total Due Seller ................. | | $21,466.02 |

Property taxes are assessed on December 31 of each year and are payable either in full the following September or the first of four quarterly installments is due on that date. Included in the accrued tax account are:

| | |
|---|---:|
| 1. The balance of the 19C taxes .................. | $166.53 |
| 2. One half of the 19D assessment............... | 354.75* |
|     Total........................................... | $521.28 |

* This represents the estimated tax expense applicable to the first six months of 19D.

During your subsequent quarterly audit, you find the following facts:

*a.* The property was purchased January 1, 19A, at a total cost of $32,000, $30,000 for the building and $2,000 for the land.

b. Depreciation is booked annually at 2½%, and the accumulated depreciation at December 31, 19C, is $2,250.

c. The account, Sale of Property, contains a credit of $21,466.02 (funds received from sale) and a debit of $500 which is a commission paid to an individual who obtained the buyer.

*Required:*

1. Give journal entries to complete the recording of the transaction on White Corporation's books.
2. Prepare a schedule showing the gain or loss.

(AICPA adapted)

### Problem 12–15

Part 1 – Company X had an old machine that originally cost $10,000 and has depreciation to date of $7,500. The old machine was exchanged for a new similar machine that had a firm cash price of $4,500. Two independent cases are assumed:

    Case A – There was a direct exchange (no cash difference was paid or received).

    Case B – Company X exchanged the old machine for the new machine and paid a cash difference of $2,100.

Part 2 – Company Y had an old machine that originally cost $12,000 and has accumulated depreciation to date of $8,000. The old machine was exchanged for a new similar machine that had a firm cash price of $3,000. Two independent cases are assumed:

    Case C – There was a direct exchange (no cash difference was paid or received).

    Case D – Company Y exchanged the old machine for the new machine and received a cash difference of $500.

*Required:*

1. Give the entries to record the exchange of similar assets in Cases A, B, C and D.
2. Give the entries for each case assuming the assets were dissimilar.

### Problem 12–16

Two dissimilar operational assets were exchanged when the accounts of the two companies involved reflected the following:

| Account | Company A (designate as Asset A) | Company B (designate as Asset B) |
|---|---|---|
| Operational asset | $5,000 | $8,000 |
| Accumulated depreciation | 3,000 | 5,300 |

The fair market value of Asset A was realistically determined to be $2,500; no realistic estimate could be made for Asset B.

*Required:*

1. Give the exchange entry for each company assuming no cash difference was involved.
2. Give the exchange entry for both companies assuming a cash difference of $100 was paid by Company A to Company B.

**Problem 12–17**

Two similar operational assets were exchanged when the accounts of the two companies involved reflected the following:

| Account | Company A (designate as Asset A) | Company B (designate as Asset B) |
|---|---|---|
| Operational asset | $5,000 | $8,000 |
| Accumulated depreciation | 3,000 | 5,300 |

The fair market value of Asset A was realistically determined to be $2,500; no realistic estimate could be made for Asset B.

*Required:*

1. Give the exchange entry for each company assuming no cash difference is involved.
2. Give the exchange entry for each company assuming a cash difference of $500 was paid by Company A to Company B.

# Chapter 13

# Property, Plant, and Equipment —
# Depreciation and Depletion

At the outset of the preceding chapter we defined the several classes of assets acquired for operational purposes rather than for sale; that is, they are acquired and utilized because of their *future* revenue-generating potentials to the enterprise. Thus, they can be viewed by the enterprise as comprising a store of economic-service values that will expire as they are utilized in the revenue-generating process. Therefore, as these economic-service values are utilized in generating revenue, a portion of their total cost periodically must be matched with (allocated against) the period revenues generated in order to fulfill the requirements of income measurement. The process of periodically allocating a portion of the total cost of property, plant, and equipment against the revenue generated must be applied to most operational assets (land is an exception). This entails application of allocation procedures to three distinct classes of assets; the accounting terminology commonly utilized in this respect is:

1. Depreciation. The accounting process of allocating against periodic revenue the cost expiration of *tangible* property, plant, and equipment.
2. Depletion. The accounting process of allocating against periodic revenue the cost expiration of an asset represented by a *natural resource* such as mineral deposits, gravel deposits, and timber stands.
3. Amortization. The accounting process of allocating against periodic revenue the cost expiration of *intangibles* represented by *special rights* or benefits such as patents, copyrights, and leaseholds.

This chapter discusses depreciation and depletion; Chapter 14 considers the amortization of intangibles.

Clearly, the three processes just described are similar conceptually; each focuses on a different class of assets. Conceptually they represent the process of cost allocation as opposed to asset valuation. They constitute an application of the *matching principle*.

In a sense, the cost of property, plant, and equipment may be compared with a prepaid expense; the cost is prepaid (in advance of utilization of the asset), hence is recorded as an asset; as the economic service life of the asset expires with the passage of time and through use, the cost thereof must be systematically allocated to operations as a current cost. Operational assets, like goods and services represented by current expenditures for operating costs, contribute measurable future benefits to the enterprise.

In accounting for operational assets the underlying principles are: (a) at acquisition, the assets are recorded at cost on the basis of the *cost principle*; (b) subsequent to acquisition, those assets that have a determinable limited life are reported at the cost recognized at acquisition less the accumulated allocations of such costs (depreciation amortization and depletion); and (c) periodic allocations of acquisition cost, made on a systematic and rational basis, are recognized as current expense in conformance with the *matching principle*.

## DEPRECIATION

Now let's turn our attention specifically to depreciation as defined above. In order to understand fully the nature of depreciation accounting it is necessary to examine its effects on (a) the income statement, (b) retained earnings and dividends, (c) cash flow, and (d) balance sheet presentation.

Depreciation is recognized on the income statement as selling, administrative, or manufacturing expenses, depending upon the nature and use of the assets involved. The periodic depreciation charge may affect the income statement in two ways. That portion of the depreciation charge in a period classified as selling expense and administrative expense directly reduces pretax income by the amount involved. That part of the depreciation charge classified as factory cost is reported as a part of the cost of goods manufactured. The goods sold during the current period carry to cost of goods sold a portion of the depreciation charge allocated to manufacturing cost. Such depreciation costs likewise decrease reported income where the goods are sold. On the other hand, that portion of depreciation charge remaining in the valuation of goods on hand at the end of the period is reported as an *asset* (inventory) and deferred until the goods are sold. It follows that income of a given period is reduced by depreciation initially charged to inventory only to the extent that such goods are sold during that period.

### Depreciation and Dividends

Since the depreciation charge reduces reported pretax income, the amount of retained earnings is likewise reduced. This effect reduces the reported amount of retained earnings available for dividends; consequently, over the life of the operational asset an amount equivalent to the cost of the tangible fixed asset recognized at acquisition (less any residual value) is "held back" from retained earnings and dividend availability. Thus one of the results of depreciation accounting is to prevent the impairment of capital through dividends based upon overstated earnings. Failure to recognize depreciation causes overstatement of income with an attendant possible dissipation of capital through liquidating dividends.

### Depreciation and Cash Flow

Depreciation accounting attempts to measure a cost and to charge it against income. Where revenue is sufficient, depreciation like other expenses is recovered. It should be apparent, however, that the mere booking of depreciation can have no effect upon the amount of assets coming into the business through sales of product. But if a business can sell its product for enough to cover all operating costs including depreciation, the assets received from customers (cash and receivables) will exceed other expense outlays by at least the amount of the depreciation. Since dividends normally are paid only out of net income, net assets equal to the amount of the depreciation charged off will be retained in the business which operates at a profit or merely at break even.[1]

In view of the above discussion it is important to realize that although the depreciation provision does hold back assets from dividends equivalent to the provision, it does not provide or "hold back" cash specifically. The relationship of depreciation and cash flow is simply that although most costs and expenses require cash when incurred, the depreciation charge is a noncash reduction of net income; the cash was disbursed when the fixed asset was acquired. Therefore, the *cash generated by net income is greater* than reported net income by the amount of noncash expenses (less noncash revenues) reported on the income statement. Obviously, the fact that depreciation has been recognized does not mean that cash (or even other assets) necessarily will be available to replace the assets when their service life expires. The assets retained as a result of deducting from income a provision for depreciation before making the dividend distribution are not automatically segregated into a fund for replacements. On the contrary, the retained funds will probably find uses in paying off liabilities and in purchasing of new and different types of assets; therefore, such funds seldom are available for actual replacements when old assets reach the end of their service life. Any specific fund for replacement must be the result of planned appropriation of cash or other liquid assets from period to period.

### Depreciation Is an Estimate

The importance of depreciation as an expense may be seen readily upon examination of the operating statements of any business with a

---

[1] Different methods of depreciation have different effects on cash flow. For example, accelerated depreciation in the early years will give a higher depreciation expense amount than will straight line; consequently, income taxes would be lower. This would result in a saving of cash paid for income taxes during the early periods. See Chapter 21 for discussion of cash flows.

relatively large investment in property, plant, and equipment. The importance of depreciation varies with the nature of the business and the degree of mechanization or automation involved. Significantly, reported net income is no more accurate than the estimate of the periodic depreciation figure. Since periodic depreciation expense as well as certain other expenses are estimates, reported net income reflects such estimates. In view of these considerations any attempt to compute and report the depreciation provision to even pennies, for example, implies a degree of accuracy that does not exist. With respect to accounting, rounding of the periodic charge should be consistent with the probable margin of error involved in the estimate.

## DEPRECIATION DISCLOSURES

Because of the significant effects of the depreciation methods used, on both financial position and the results of operations, the APB in *Opinion No. 12* reaffirmed an earlier ARB that the following disclosures should be made in the financial statements or accompanying notes:

a. Depreciation expense for the period.
b. Balances of major classes of depreciable assets, by nature or function, at the balance sheet date.
c. Accumulated depreciation, either by major classes of depreciable assets or in total, at the balance sheet date.
d. A general description of the methods used in computing depreciation on major classes of depreciable assets.

This was augmented in *APB Opinion No. 22*, "Disclosure of Accounting Policies" (April 1973), where depreciation methods and amortization policies were cited as examples of disclosure which would be commonly required.

## CAUSES OF DEPRECIATION

The causes of depreciation may be classified as follows:

| *Physical Factors* | *Functional Factors* |
|---|---|
| 1. Wear and tear from operation. | 1. Inadequacy. |
| 2. Action of time and other elements. | 2. Supersession and |
| 3. Deterioration and decay. | obsolescence. |

Significantly, a *change in market value* is not recognized as one of the causes of depreciation in the accounting sense.[2] The three physical factors, as they affect the service life of a tangible fixed asset, are self-explanatory. Inadequacy is brought about by expansion of a business,

---

[2] Depreciation is not caused by changes in the market value of an operational asset; however, when the carrying value is significantly above the use value to the entity, in terms of fair value (such as an idle plant), the asset must be written down to reflect the loss (this is not depreciation expense). See Chapter 12.

the fixed asset becoming unequal to the increased service required, although still in good condition and quite capable of the service originally expected of it. Supersession results when an asset is superseded by another asset which operates more efficiently. Supersession is brought about when inventions give rise to new assets which may be operated more cheaply in rendering the same or an improved service. In such cases it may be desirable to discard the old asset. Obsolescence may arise from inadequacy, supersession, and other causes. Obsolescence of an operational asset may arise as a result of the outmoding of the product being produced or the service being rendered.

Depreciation accounting takes into account all predictable factors that tend to limit the economic usefulness of an operational asset to the enterprise. The periodic apportionment of cost through depreciation must be based upon both the physical and functional causes of depreciation. Generally those factors that operate more or less continuously are given recognition in depreciation accounting, whereas sudden and unexpected factors such as storms, floods, sudden change in demand, and radical outmoding of the asset must be accorded special treatment with respect to the fixed assets involved. One of these special treatments, for example, might result in the immediate removal of an asset from the accounts and the related recording of a loss.

The useful life of an operational asset generally is influenced directly by the repair and maintenance policies of the firm. Low standards of maintenance and repairs may reduce costs temporarily; however, the useful life of the asset will be shortened considerably thereby increasing the periodic depreciation expense. Although some have contended that depreciation should include both amortization of the original cost and current repair costs, accountants have viewed repairs and depreciation (as previously defined) as separate cost elements.

In the case of facilities temporarily idle or being held for possible future use, depreciation should continue since the physical and functional causes, which tend to reduce the ultimate economic usefulness of the asset to the firm, continue. Operational assets that will not be returned to service should be reduced to their fair market value in anticipation of disposal. Special accounts normally should be established in accounting for idle facilities.

## FACTORS IN DETERMINING THE DEPRECIATION CHARGE

The periodic depreciation expense should represent the allocation of the original cost (less the estimated residual value) of the asset to operations in proportion to the economic benefit received from the asset. The factors which must be considered in calculating the periodic depreciation charge are:

1. Actual cost (as defined in the preceding chapter).
2. Estimated residual (scrap) value.
3. Estimated service life.

Clearly, determination of depreciation is based on one "actual" and two "estimated" factors. The residual value is the estimated amount which may be recovered through sale, trade-in allowance, or by other means when the asset is finally retired from service. In estimating the residual value, allowance must be made for the costs of dismantling and disposal of the retired asset. For example, assume it is estimated that upon retirement the asset can be sold for $250 and that the costs of dismantling and selling are estimated at $50. In this case the residual value would be $200. In practice, recovery value and dismantling and selling costs are frequently disregarded entirely – a procedure which is acceptable when the recovery and disposal costs may offset, when the amounts involved are immaterial, or when the estimates involve a wide margin of error.

In estimating the service life of an asset for accounting purposes it is important to realize that service life implies (a) use of the asset by the owner, (b) use of the asset for the purpose for which acquired, and (c) a definite repair and maintenance policy over the life of the asset. Allocation of depreciation charges should be representative of the expiration of the "economic-service values" of the asset to the enterprise. Thus, the service life should be measured in terms that are most representative of the expiration of such values. Accordingly, service life may be measured in terms of (a) definite time periods such as months or years, (b) units of output, or (c) hours of operating time. Selection of the appropriate measure of service life should depend upon the nature of the asset involved and the primary causes of depreciation.

## RECORDING DEPRECIATION

The periodic depreciation amount is recorded as a debit to an expense account or a cost of manufacturing account (factory overhead) and a credit to an asset contra account entitled Accumulated Depreciation. Rather than a direct credit to the related asset account, a special contra account traditionally has been credited in order to maintain a separation of the original cost and the amount of that cost expired through depreciation. The contra account should not be labeled as a "reserve" for depreciation, but as Accumulated Depreciation.

In the subsidiary asset records, the periodic depreciation charges and accumulated depreciation are recorded for each individual asset or group of assets.

## METHODS OF DEPRECIATION

Methods of depreciation focus on computation of the amount of depreciation expense that should be recorded each period. A number of methods have been developed, each of which provides a somewhat different pattern of depreciation charges over the life of the tangible asset. The methods may be classified as follows:

a. Based on time:
   1. Straight line.

b. Based on output:
    2. Service hours.
    3. Units of output.
c. Reducing depreciation charge:
    4. Sum-of-the-years' digits.
    5. Fixed percentage on declining base amount.
    6. Declining rate on cost.
    7. Double-declining balance.
d. Based on investment and interest concepts (discussed in Chapter 6):
    8. Annuity.
    9. Sinking fund.

To illustrate these methods the following symbols and simplified amounts are used:

| Item | Symbol | Illustrative Figures |
|---|---|---|
| Acquisition cost | C | $ 100 |
| Scrap or residual value | S | 10 |
| Estimated service life | n | |
| Years | | 3 |
| Service hours | | 6,000 |
| Productive output in units | | 9,000 |
| Depreciation rate (per year, per service hour, or per unit of productive output) | r | |
| Dollar amount of depreciation per period | D | |

## Straight-Line Method

The straight-line method has been used widely because of its simplicity. This method relates depreciation directly to the passage of time rather than to specific use. It is called straight line because it results in an equal charge for depreciation in each of the periods of the service life of the asset; thus, when graphed against time, both the accumulated depreciation and the undepreciated asset cost are indicated by straight lines. The use of the formula for computing the periodic depreciation charge (annual in this case) is illustrated below.

$$D = \frac{C - S}{n} \quad \text{or} \quad D = \frac{\$100 - \$10}{3} = \$30 \text{ per period}$$

Depreciation frequently is expressed as a *rate*. For the illustrative figures that the periodic (annual) rate $(r)$ may be expressed as either (a) $33\frac{1}{3}\%$ on net depreciable value ($\$90 \times 33\frac{1}{3}\% = \$30$) or (b) 30% on cost ($\$100 \times 30\%$)[3]; the percent on cost generally is used.

Exhibit 13–1 illustrates application of straight-line depreciation over the life of the illustrative asset and the accounting entries involved.

---

[3] Many accountants prefer to express the rate as a percent of depreciable value, viz, $\$30 \div (\$100 - \$10) = 33\frac{1}{3}\%$. In this case, to compute the periodic charge, the "net to be depreciated" is multiplied by the rate.

**EXHIBIT 13–1**
**Depreciation Table and Entries, Straight-Line Method (life three years)**

| Year | Depreciation Expense (debit) | Accumulated Depreciation (credit) | Balance Accumulated Depreciation | Undepreciated Asset Balance (book value) |
|------|------------------------------|-----------------------------------|----------------------------------|------------------------------------------|
| 0............ |        |      |      | $100 |
| 1............ | $30    | $30  | $30  | 70 |
| 2............ | 30     | 30   | 60   | 40 |
| 3............ | 30     | 30   | 90   | 10 (residual value) |
|      | $90    | $90  |      | |

The straight-line method is simple, easy to understand, and is widely used. It meets the criterion of being "systematic and rational" (*ARB No. 44*, revised, par. 2). It is theoretically acceptable when the following conditions prevail:

1. The decline in economic-service potential of the asset is approximately the same each period.
2. The decline in economic-service potential of the asset is related to the passage of time rather than to use.
3. Use of the asset is consistent from period to period.
4. Repairs and maintenance are essentially the same each period.

Straight-line depreciation is deficient in that (*a*) depreciation is considered a function of time rather than a function of use, which often is not the case; (*b*) it may not effectively match expense with revenue; and (*c*) it causes a distortion in certain rate of return computations.

The latter effect occurs because depreciation expense remains constant each period (and affects the rate of return, numerator, net income, in this way) whereas the asset (and total assets, the denominator) reduces each year. Of course, similar effects occur for all depreciation methods except in the case where depreciation expense changes each period inversely and in proportion to changes in the carrying value of the depreciable assets.

### Service-Hours Method

The service-hours method is based upon the assumption that the decrease in service life is conditioned primarily by the actual running time of the asset rather than by the mere passage of time. Rather than an equal periodic charge for depreciation, this method results in a periodic charge which correlates with the amount of time the asset operated. If a machine is operated twice as much in the current period as in the prior period, the depreciation charge for the current period will be twice as much as that of the last period. In utilizing this method the service life of the asset must be estimated in terms of total probable service or working hours prior to retirement; then a rate per service hour is computed.

Assuming a 6,000-hour estimated useful life, the formula for the depreciation rate would be:

$$r = \frac{C - S}{n} \quad \text{or} \quad r = \frac{\$100 - \$10}{6,000} = \$.015 \text{ per service hour}$$

Assuming 3,000 actual hours of running time the first year, depreciation expense would be:

$$D = r \times \text{Service Hours Current Period}$$

or

$$D = \$.015 \times 3,000 = \$45$$

Exhibit 13–2 illustrates application of the service-hours method over the life of the illustrative asset.

**EXHIBIT 13–2**
**Depreciation Table and Entries, Service-Hours Method (life 6,000 hours)**

| Year | Service Hours Worked* | Depreciation Expense (debit) | | Accumulated Depreciation (credit) | Balance Accumulated Depreciation | Undepreciated Asset Balance (book value) |
|------|------------------------|-------------------------------|------|-----------------------------------|----------------------------------|-------------------------------------------|
| 0............ | | | | | | $100 |
| 1............ | 3,000 | (3,000 × $.015) | $45 | $45 | $45 | 55 |
| 2............ | 2,000 | (2,000 × $.015) | 30 | 30 | 75 | 25 |
| 3............ | 1,000 | (1,000 × $.015) | 15 | 15 | 90 | 10 (residual value) |
| | 6,000 | | $90 | $90 | | |

* It is assumed that the asset was actually used in this manner and that the original estimate of useful life was confirmed.

The service-hours method satisfies the criterion of "rational and systematic" and would tend to insure a logical matching of cost and revenue on the assumption that the asset loses service potential on the basis of running time. Under this method the amount of cost allocated would tend to vary with the productive output of the asset. However, to the extent that there was running time without productive output, this relationship would not prevail. Where obsolescence is not a primary factor and where the economic-service potentials of the asset to the company are used up primarily by running time, the service-hours method would seem appropriate. Also wide variations in use from period to period would suggest application of the service-hours method. Obviously, relative to many assets, such as buildings, furniture, and typewriters, it would be impracticable, if not impossible, to apply the service-hours method. In contrast, it would be appropriate for vehicles.

### Productive-Output Method

Under this method the service life of the asset is estimated in terms of the number of *units* of output. A proportionate part of the total cost to be depreciated (cost less scrap value) is charged to each unit of output as a cost of production; consequently, depreciation charges fluctuate periodically with changes in the volume of production or output. Each unit of output is charged with a constant amount of depreciation, in contrast to the straight-line method where each unit of output will be charged with a different amount of depreciation if output varies from period to period.

The cost to be depreciated over the life of the asset is divided by the service life in units to derive a depreciation rate per unit of output; multiplication of this rate times the output for the period gives the periodic depreciation charge. Thus computation of the rate, assuming an estimated productive life of 9,000 units of output, would be:

$$r = \frac{C - S}{n}$$

or

$$r = \frac{\$100 - \$10}{9,000} = \$.01 \text{ per unit of output}$$

Assuming 4,000 units of actual output during the first year, the depreciation charge would be:

$$D = r \times \text{Units of Output Current Period}$$

or

$$D = \$.01 \times 4,000 = \$40$$

Exhibit 13–3 illustrates an application of the productive-output method over the life of the asset.

**EXHIBIT 13–3**
**Depreciation Table and Entries, Productive-Output Method (life 9,000 units)**

| Year | Units of Output* | Depreciation Expense (debit) | | Accumulated Depreciation (credit) | Balance Accumulated Depreciation | Undepreciated Asset Balance (book value) |
|---|---|---|---|---|---|---|
| 0............. | | | | | | $100 |
| 1............. | 4,000 | (4,000 × $.01) | $40 | $40 | $40 | 60 |
| 2............. | 3,000 | (3,000 × $.01) | 30 | 30 | 70 | 30 |
| 3............. | 2,000 | (2,000 × $.01) | 20 | 20 | 90 | 10 (residual value) |
| | 9,000 | | $90 | $90 | | |

* It is assumed that the asset was actually used in this manner.

The productive-output method and the service-hours method both recognize the fact that some assets, such as trucks and machinery, depreciate more rapidly with higher usage than with lower usage. These methods relate more closely the benefit derived from the use of the asset and the depreciation cost allocated than do other methods. The productive-output method is particularly appropriate where obsolescence is not a major factor, where actual output can be realistically measured, and where the service life in units of output can be reasonably estimated.

The differences between the periodic depreciation in the service-hours method and the productive-output method in the illustrative problem are due to a change in the efficiency of operations—the asset was used more efficiently in some periods than others. This observation would lead to the conclusion that in situations where either method could be applied, the productive-output method generally would be preferable.

It is important to recognize the effect the different methods have on *total cost of products* and on *unit product cost.* The straight-line method reports depreciation as a *fixed cost in total,* but *variable per unit* of output. In contrast, the service-hours method and productive-output method reports depreciation as *variable in total,* but *fixed per unit of output.* To illustrate assume an asset costing $600 (no residual value) with an estimated life of five years or 500 units of output. Assume further that output was: Year 1—90; Year 2—100; Year 3—110; Year 4—120; and Year 5—80. The comparative depreciation charges and unit cost figures for the straight-line and output methods are compared below:

| Year | Units of Output | Output Depreciation | | Straight-Line Depreciation | |
|---|---|---|---|---|---|
| | | Amount | Unit Cost | Amount | Unit Cost |
| 1............ | 90 | $108 | $1.20 | $120 | $1.33 |
| 2............ | 100 | 120 | 1.20 | 120 | 1.20 |
| 3............ | 110 | 132 | 1.20 | 120 | 1.09 |
| 4............ | 120 | 144 | 1.20 | 120 | 1.00 |
| 5............ | 80 | 96 | 1.20 | 120 | 1.50 |
| | 500 | $600 | | $600 | |

These distinctions are particularly important in cost analyses for managerial pricing, control, and decision-making considerations. These relative effects should be considered carefully in selecting a method of depreciation.

## Reducing-Charge Methods

The reducing-charge methods are designed to allocate the cost to be depreciated in such a manner that periodic depreciation expense charges are higher in the early years and lower in the later years of the life of the operational asset. The reducing-charge methods are based upon the theory that new assets are more efficient than old assets; therefore, the economic-service potentials rendered by the asset are greater during the early life of the asset. If the cost of these greater values being con-sumed through utilization of the asset is to be matched with the result-ing revenue, some form of reducing-charge depreciation (frequently referred to as accelerated depreciation) is theoretically desirable. The reducing-charge methods are also defended on the grounds that the annual depreciation charge should decrease as repair costs on the asset increase, thus resulting in a more equitable charge to the operating periods for the use of the operational asset.

Numerous procedures have been proposed for computing a reducing depreciation charge from period to period over the life of an asset; however, the principal methods currently being used are:

1. Sum-of-the-years'-digits.
2. Fixed-percentage-on-declining-base.
3. Declining rate on cost.
4. Double-declining balance.

## Sum-of-the-Years'-Digits Method

This method (usually referred to as the SYD method) applies to a decreasing fraction each succeeding period during the life of the asset to the cost to be depreciated. The fractions are determined by using as the denominator the sum-of-the-years'-digits for the life of the asset. The numerator, which changes each period, is the years' digits in in-verse order (same as the remaining life including the current period). For example, the asset in the illustration, having an estimated service life of three years, would be depreciated as follows:

> Denominator:  Sum-of-the-years'-digits; $1 + 2 + 3 = 6$.
> Numerators:   Digits in inverse order; 3, 2, and 1.
> Fractions:    First period, $3/6$.
>               Second period, $2/6$.
>               Third period, $1/6$.

Exhibit 13–4 illustrates an application of the method for the illustra-tive asset.

**EXHIBIT 13–4**
**Depreciation Table and Entries — Sum-of-the-Years'-Digits Method**
**(life three years)**

| Year | Depreciation Expense (debit) | | Accumulated Depreciation (credit) | Balance Accumulated Depreciation | Undepreciated Asset Balance (book value) |
|---|---|---|---|---|---|
| 0............ | | | | | $100 |
| 1............ | $(3/6 \times \$90)$ | $45 | $45 | $45 | 55 |
| 2............ | $(2/6 \times \$90)$ | 30 | 30 | 75 | 25 |
| 3............ | $(1/6 \times \$90)$ | 15 | 15 | 90 | 10 (residual value) |
| | | $90 | $90 | | |

Note that the reducing fraction is multiplied by the cost to be depreciated (cost less residual value) in each period. When the life of the asset is relatively long, the denominator (sum of the digits) can be readily computed by using the following formula and a 25-year assumed life:

$$\text{SYD} = n\left(\frac{n+1}{2}\right) \quad \text{or} \quad \text{SYD} = 25\left(\frac{25+1}{2}\right) = 325$$

## Fixed-Percentage-on-Declining-Base Method

To apply this method the book value of the asset (undepreciated asset balance) is multiplied by a constant percentage rate. Since a constant rate is applied to a *declining base*, each subsequent periodic depreciation charge will be less. The rate must be computed taking into account the cost, estimated life, and residual value; consequently, the rate will automatically provide for the residual value at the end of the service life of the asset. The depreciation rate (the fixed percentage) and its application is illustrated below:

$$r = 1 - \sqrt[n]{\frac{S}{C}} \quad \text{or} \quad r = 1 - \sqrt[3]{\frac{\$10}{\$100}} = .536, \text{ or } 53.6\%$$

Calculation of $\sqrt[n]{\frac{S}{C}}$ is readily achieved by use of logarithms or some pocket calculators.

**EXHIBIT 13-5**
**Depreciation Table and Entries—Fixed-Percentage-on-Declining-Base Method**

| Year | Depreciation Expense (debit) | | Accumulated Depreciation (credit) | Balance Accumulated Depreciation | Undepreciated Asset Balance (book value) |
|---|---|---|---|---|---|
| 0............... | | | | | $100.00 |
| 1............... | (53.6% × $100) | $53.60 | $53.60 | $53.60 | 46.40 |
| 2............... | (53.6% × $46.40) | 24.87 | 24.87 | 78.47 | 21.53 |
| 3............... | (53.6% × $21.53) | 11.53 | 11.53 | 90.00 | 10.00 (residual value) |
| | | $90.00 | $90.00 | | |

Observe in Exhibit 13-5 that the book value at the end of the service life is precisely the estimated scrap value. It should be pointed out that where the asset has no scrap value the formula given above for calculation of the depreciation percentage or rate cannot be used unless a nominal scrap value of, say, $1, is assumed. As a matter of practical application it is usually desirable to round the rate to an even percentage.

*Declining-Rate-on-Cost Method.* This method is not based on a particular formula; the depreciation rate is different each period, since it is selected arbitrarily for each period. A series of decreasing percentages are selected to provide the desired reduction in the periodic depreciation charge. The residual or scrap value, as a percent of cost, is provided for by excluding it from the periodic rates. The total of the periodic rates plus the scrap percent must total 100%. Application of the declining-rate-on-cost method is shown in Exhibit 13–6, assuming the declining rates selected are those indicated in the second column.

**EXHIBIT 13–6**
**Depreciation Table and Entries – Declining-Rate-on-Cost Method**
**(estimated life three years)**

| Year | Declining Rates | Depreciation Expense (debit) | | Allowance for Depreciation (credit) | Balance Accumulated Depreciation | Undepreciated Asset Balance (book value) |
|---|---|---|---|---|---|---|
| 0 ............ | | | | | | $100 |
| 1 ............ | 55% | (55% × $100) | $55 | $55 | $55 | 45 |
| 2 ............ | 25 | (25% × $100) | 25 | 25 | 80 | 20 |
| 3 ............ | 10 | (10% × $100) | 10 | 10 | 90 | 10 (residual value) |
| | 90% | | $90 | $90 | | |
| Scrap % | 10 | | | | | |
| | 100% | | | | | |

A primary weakness of the declining-rate-on-cost method is that the periodic rates, being *arbitrarily* selected, lack objectivity and may not be representative of the actual expiration of service values throughout the life of the asset. The method also has a serious flaw in that it cannot be classed as "rational and systematic," and therefore is not in accordance with GAAP.

## Double-Declining-Balance Method

Reducing-charge depreciation is acceptable for federal income tax purposes, except the regulations provide that the amount of depreciation must not be more than double the amount that would result under the straight-line method when the residual value is ignored.[4] This provision gave rise to the double-declining-balance method. Under this method the fixed percentage used is simply double the straight-line rate; residual value is ignored. This rate is multiplied each year by the declining book value. Based on the above data the rate would be 67% (i.e., 33⅓% × 2). The depreciation would be:

---

[4] For income tax purposes there are numerous restrictions on the double-declining-balance method. Double the straight-line rate may be used only on certain types of new property acquired within certain range dates. Used property, certain types of new property, and property acquired before 1954 may be depreciated at 150% of the straight-line rate. Although residual is ignored, an asset may not be depreciated below a reasonable residual value.

**Double-Declining-Balance Depreciation**

| Year | Book Value | | Rate | | Depreciation* |
|---|---|---|---|---|---|
| 1.......................................... | $100 | × | 67% | = | $ 67 |
| 2.......................................... | 33 | × | 67 | = | 22 |
| 3.......................................... | 11 | × | 67 | = | 1 |
| | | | | | 90 |
| Implicit residual value............ | | | | | 10 |
| | | | | | $100 |

* Illustrative only—the present time double-declining depreciation may be used for tax purposes only when the life is three years or more.

The reducing-charge methods discussed above can be classed as rational and systematic, except for the declining rate on cost. They are not difficult to apply. For all practical purposes the sum-of-the-years'-digits and double-declining-balance methods are the only reducing-charge methods used. The important criterion to apply is whether they properly match periodic depreciation expense with periodic revenue.

With respect to acceptability of the reducing-charge approach, the Committee on Accounting Procedure of the AICPA stated in *Accounting Research Bulletin No. 44* that

> The declining-balance method is one of those which meets the requirements of being "systematic and rational." In those cases where the expected productivity or revenue-earning power of the asset is relatively greater during the earlier years of its life, or where maintenance charges tend to increase during the later years, the declining-balance method may well provide the most satisfactory allocation of cost. The conclusions of this bulletin also apply to other methods, including the "sum-of-the-years'-digits" method, which produce substantially similar results.

## DEPRECIATION BASED ON INVESTMENT CONCEPTS

The preceding paragraphs discussed depreciation approaches that provided: (1) a *constant* depreciation charge (expense) per period, (2) a *decreasing* depreciation charge per period, or (3) a *varying* depreciation charge per period (output methods). The *compound interest methods* represent a distinctly different approach since they provide an *increasing periodic* expense effect. The other approaches to depreciation have been criticized because, among other things, they ignore the investment characteristics of the ownership of property, plant, and equipment. Depreciation based on investment concepts view an investment in property, plant, and equipment, and the return on that investment, in the same manner as if an annuity investment was made. Implicit is the concept that the subsequent periodic returns received over the life of the annuity comprises both principal and interest. Therefore, the total depreciation expense amount each period would be offset by two credits: (1) the recovery of principal is credited to accumulated depreciation, and (2) the remainder is credited to an account for *imputed interest revenue*. The effect of this entry each period, since the principal amount increases each period and the interest amount decreases, is an increasing reduction in net income because of depreciation. Currently, generally accepted accounting standards do not accept these methods except in a very few limited situations. The two methods — annuity and sinking fund — give the same net effect on income; they are briefly illustrated in the Appendix to this chapter.

## FRACTIONAL YEAR DEPRECIATION

Implicit in the preceding illustrations has been the assumption that the asset year and the company's fiscal year coincide; however, assets seldom are purchased on the first day of a fiscal period and are seldom retired at the end of the fiscal year. Therefore, depreciation often must be computed for fractional parts of the year. An accounting policy should be established so that consistent and realistic amounts of depreciation are recorded for fractional parts of the year. Most companies do not count days because depreciation is an estimate and such precision would be irrelevant. Policies widely used are:

1. Compute depreciation on the basis of even months.
2. Depreciate from the first of the month all assets acquired on or before the 15th of the month; if acquired after the 15th, do not depreciate for the partial month. Assets disposed of on or before the 15th of the month are not depreciated for the partial month; if disposed after the 15th, record a full month's depreciation.
3. To determine the monthly depreciation amount, divide the annual amount by $1/12$ regardless of the method of depreciation used.
4. For methods other than straight-line depreciation, when the asset year and the fiscal year do not coincide, compute partial depreciation on the basis of the months for each of the partial years of the asset life and sum the results.

To illustrate implementation of the latter policy, assume the asset used in the preceding illustration was acquired on May 5, Year 1, and was retired on April 25, Year 4. The fiscal year ends on December 31. Using sum-of-the-years'-digits depreciation, as given in Exhibit 13–4, the computations and results would be as follows:

| Year | Annual Depreciation (Exhibit 13–4) | Months | Computation | Depreciation Expense |
|------|-----|------|-----|-----|
| 1 | $45 | 8 | ($45 × $8/12$) | $30 |
| 2 | 30 | 12 | ($45 × $4/12$) + ($30 × $8/12$) | 35 |
| 3 | 15 | 12 | ($30 × $4/12$) + ($15 × $8/12$) | 20 |
| 4 | | 4 | ($15 × $4/12$) | 5 |
| | $90 | 36 | | $90 |

Other viable alternatives include (1) depreciation computed on the balance in the asset account at the beginning of the year; (2) depreciation computed on the balance in the asset account at the end of the year; (3) depreciation computed only on assets acquired during the first half of the year, and no depreciation on assets disposed of during the first half of the year; and (4) depreciation computed on a semiannual basis.

## SPECIAL DEPRECIATION SYSTEMS

Special problems confronting the firm, due to both internal and external factors, frequently require adaptations of the *depreciation methods* of cost allocation discussed above. The primary adaptations, generally referred to as "systems," are discussed in this section under the captions:

1. Inventory (or appraisal) system.
2. Retirement system.
3. Replacement system.
4. Composite life system.
5. Group system.

### Inventory System

Under this system, sometimes referred to as the appraisal system, purchases of depreciable assets are debited to an appropriate asset account in the usual manner, and allocations of cost representing depreciation are credited to the same account. The amount recorded as depreciation for the period is determined by estimating the "value" of the asset on hand in its present condition; the asset account then is reduced to this amount and depreciation expense is charged. Salvage recovery serves to reduce depreciation expense for the period. The value of the asset on hand is determined by inventory procedures and an estimate of its cost, taking into account its present condition.

To illustrate, assume the Hand Tools account showed a balance of $680; an inventory of the tools on hand at the end of the period, valued at cost and adjusted for present condition, indicated a value of $560. The broken and obsolete tools were sold for $10. The entry to record the periodic depreciation is:

```
Cash .................................................................................    10
Depreciation expense—hand tools ($120 − $10) ...........................   110
    Hand tools ($680 − $560).....................................................         120
```

The inventory system should be used only in situations where the asset account represents numerous asset items of a small unit cost, such as hand tools, machine tools, patterns, and dies. Even in these cases the system should be used only when the usual methods are impractical with respect to the specific asset.

In applying the inventory system care must be exercised to exclude changes in value due to changes in the price level or other market fluctuations, otherwise the depreciation charge will include noncost elements such as unrealized (holding) market gains and losses. A conventional matching of expired cost and periodic revenues requires that the items be valued at original cost adjusted for present condition.

## Retirement and Replacement Systems

The retirement and replacement systems of depreciation frequently are used by public utilities because of the peculiar problems often encountered with respect to certain assets such as poles and other line items. They are also used in accounting for low-cost items such as hand tools. Under both systems, no periodic entry is made for depreciation in the normal manner; instead depreciation is recognized at the *time of replacement* of the asset. The basic distinction between them is that under the *retirement* system, the cost of the *old* asset (less its residual value) is charged to depreciation expense when it is replaced, whereas under the *replacement* system the cost of the *new* asset (less residual value of the *old* asset) is charged to depreciation expense when it replaces the old asset. To illustrate both systems assume the Hi-Power Utility Company replaced ten utility poles at a cost of $100 each. The old poles replaced originally cost $50 each and have a salvage value of $10 each.

*Retirement System*

1. To record the retirement of the old poles:

| | | |
|---|---|---|
| Depreciation expense ..................................................... | 400 | |
| Salvage inventory (residual value, old poles) ..................... | 100 | |
|     Plant assets (cost of old poles)................................... | | 500 |

2. To record the new asset:

| | | |
|---|---|---|
| Plant asset (cost of new poles)........................................ | 1,000 | |
|     Cash (or inventory) ................................................. | | 1,000 |

*Replacement System*

| | | |
|---|---|---|
| Depreciation expense ..................................................... | 900 | |
| Salvage inventory (residual value, old poles) ..................... | 100 | |
|     Cash (cost of new poles) ......................................... | | 1,000 |

From this example it should be clear that the retirement system represents a *Fifo* approach whereas the replacement system represents a *Lifo* system in allocating the asset cost to depreciation. The retirement system provides depreciation charges based on older costs and reports the operational asset at newer costs, whereas the replacement system provides depreciation charges based on newer costs and reports the operational asset at the older cost. Neither system adequately matches cost with revenue particularly in the early and late life of the business, inasmuch as depreciation is recognized when assets are being replaced. Once the company has reached a relatively stable level of growth and replacement, the resulting periodic depreciation charges may approximate cost depreciation. Neither of these systems provides a "systematic and rational" allocation of operational asset costs. The systems have been used in the utility field because of the practical difficulty in depreciating large numbers of relatively low-cost items such as poles, cross-members, brackets, and conduits at many locations. In such situations the distinction between ordinary repairs and capitalizable replacements is difficult to establish and apply on a practical basis. Although lacking theoretical justification, the retirement system in particular has practical justification under certain conditions.

### Group and Composite-Life Systems

The discussions up to this point have assumed that each item of property will be depreciated as a separate unit. In actual practice, many companies group certain fixed assets for depreciation purposes. For example, all of the one-ton trucks may be grouped, or an entire operating assembly such as a refinery may be depreciated as a single unit. In such cases an *average depreciation* rate is applied to the group or assembly. Where an average rate of depreciation is applied to a number of *homogeneous* assets having similar characteristics and service lives, such as the trucks mentioned above, the procedure is referred to as *group depreciation*. Where an average rate of depreciation is applied to a number of *heterogeneous* assets having dissimilar characteristics and service lives, such as the refinery mentioned above, the procedure is referred to as *composite depreciation*. Many accountants view composite depreciation as a special variation of group depreciation. It is difficult to draw a definite distinction between the two on the basis of characteristics and service lives. From the accounting standpoint there is no difference in mechanical application of the average rate nor in the resulting journal entries as between the two systems.[5]

Under the group system, all of the assets in the group are recorded in one asset account, and one accumulated depreciation account is established for the entire group; consequently, it would be incorrect to consider that any one item in the group has a "book value"—the book value appearing in the account applies to the entire group and not to individual items. Subsequent acquisitions of items belonging to the group are similarly charged to the group asset account at cost. Depreciation is computed by multiplying an *average depreciation rate* times the balance in the group asset account regardless of the age of the individual assets represented therein. The rate may be computed and applied to cost or cost less salvage value, as desired. The depreciation entry is made by charging Depreciation Expense and crediting Accumulated Depreciation for the periodic amount of depreciation thus computed. Upon retirement of a unit which is a part of the group, the group asset account is credited for the *original cost* of the item and the Accumulated Depreciation account is debited for the *same amount less*

---

[5] Eugene L. Grant and Paul T. Norton, Jr., *Depreciation* (New York: The Ronald Press Co., 1955), chap. vii.

*any salvage recovery.* The system, therefore, does not recognize "losses or gains" on retirement of group assets.[6]

To illustrate the group system, assume the Derden Wholesale Corporation purchased ten panel trucks for delivery purposes, each costing $2,400. Each truck has an estimated residual value of $400 at the end of the estimated service life of five years. The company desires to depreciate the trucks on a group basis. Assuming depreciation is recognized on the ending balance in the asset account, typical entries under the group system are indicated below:

1. To record the initial purchase of ten trucks at $2,400 each:

| | | |
|---|---|---|
| Trucks | 24,000 | |
| Cash | | 24,000 |

2. To record group depreciation at the end of the first year:

| | | |
|---|---|---|
| Depreciation expense ($24,000 × 16⅔%) | 4,000 | |
| Accumulated depreciation | | 4,000 |

Computation:

| | |
|---|---|
| Cost | $24,000 |
| Estimated residual value | 4,000 |
| To be depreciated over 5 years | $20,000 |
| Depreciation per year ($20,000 ÷ 5) | $ 4,000 |
| Depreciation rate on asset balance ($4,000 ÷ $24,000) | 16⅔% |

3. To record retirement of one truck at the end of the second year due to wreck; amount received from insurance, $1,500:

| | | |
|---|---|---|
| Cash | 1,500 | |
| Accumulated depreciation (cost less residual recovery) | 900 | |
| Trucks | | 2,400 |

4. To record purchase of two additional trucks at $2,500 each:

| | | |
|---|---|---|
| Trucks | 5,000 | |
| Cash | | 5,000 |

5. To record the retirement of a truck that has been used for 5½ years, and then sold to a salvage yard for $150, original cost, $2,400:

| | | |
|---|---|---|
| Cash | 150 | |
| Accumulated depreciation | 2,250 | |
| Trucks | | 2,400 |

In applying the group system it may be necessary to approximate the "book value" of a specific unit that is a part of the group. For example, when a unit is transferred from one group account to another group account, as might be done when the asset is moved from one organizational division of the company to another, it is desirable that the original acquisition cost and accumulated depreciation to date be transferred in the accounts. In such cases the accumulated depreciation under the group system may be approximated as follows:

$$\frac{\text{Present Age}}{\text{Service Life}} \times (\text{Acquisition Cost} - \text{Residual Value})$$

---

[6] Ibid.

To illustrate, assume a machine is being transferred from Plant A to Plant B; the machine originally cost $5,300 and has been in operation six years. Its estimated service life is 15 years, and the estimated salvage value, $300. The machine has been depreciated on a group basis, the *average* group rate being used is 8%. The entry to record the transfer might be:

```
Machinery—Plant B  .....................................................  5,300
Accumulated depreciation—machinery—Plant A*.....................  2,000
     Machinery—Plant A  ..................................................         5,300
     Accumulated depreciation—machinery—Plant B*..............         2,000
```

\* Computation: $\frac{6}{15} \times (\$5,300 - \$300) = \underline{\$2,000}$

Under the *composite system* the units making up the operating unit or assembly may have a fairly wide range of service lives. Because of this condition, composite-life depreciation is subject to theoretical objections. In establishing the average rate under composite depreciation, both the *composite life* and *composite rate* may be computed. Composite life is the average life of the various units which go to make up an operating unit or assembly, and the composite rate is the ratio of the periodic depreciation to the acquisition cost of all components of the operating unit, as illustrated in Exhibit 13–7.

**EXHIBIT 13–7**
**Composite Depreciation—Operating Assembly XY**

| Component Item | Original Cost | Residual Value | Amount to Be Depreciated | Estimated Service Life (years) | Annual Depreciation |
|---|---|---|---|---|---|
| A............... | $50,000 | $5,000 | $45,000 | 15 | $3,000 |
| B............... | 20,000 | 4,000 | 16,000 | 10 | 1,600 |
| C............... | 7,000 | 600 | 6,400 | 8 | 800 |
| D............... | 3,000 | -0- | 3,000 | 3 | 1,000 |
| | $80,000 | $9,600 | $70,400 | | $6,400* |

\* Composite life: $70,400 ÷ $6,400 = 11 years.
Composite depreciation rate:
$6,400 ÷ $80,000 = 8% on cost.

Depreciation first period:
Depreciation expense ($80,000 × 8%). 6,400
  Accumulated depreciation  ......      6,400

If there are no changes in the asset account, the assembly will be depreciated to the residual value (at the end of the 11th year in the above example). However, when replacements of component parts are made, the debit to the asset account for the replacement and the credit to the asset account for the cost of the old component (the compensating entry is a debit to Accumulated Depreciation for this same amount, less any salvage recovery) would tend to spread the total cost of utilizing the asset over the actual service life. This service life would be determined in large part by the repair and replacement policy.

The group and composite methods are easier to apply than the unit method and would therefore result in savings on recordkeeping costs for many entities. Of course, for those entities using computers this factor likely becomes insignificant. Group and composite methods recognize that depreciation estimates are based on averages and that gains or losses on disposition of single assets are of minor significance.

The chief disadvantage of the group and composite methods is that it is possible for them to conceal faulty estimates for long periods; and through their failure to recognize gains or losses, not correct for changes in asset usage or for other errors. Unit methods are simple and theoretically they facilitate computation of gains or losses on retirements of particular assets. In case portions of the assets should become idle, depreciation on those could be more readily isolated under unit methods.

## DEPRECIATION POLICY

With the possible exception of inventories, no single area of accounting offers as much potential variety of practice or choice as does depreciation accounting. About the only "constant" is the starting point, which usually is historical cost; there are not many variables in the calculation of cost, though such matters as capitalizing or not capitalizing interest during construction, determining fair values in some cases, and treatment of overhead on self-construction afford examples of how identical assets acquired at the same time can begin with different costs. During the life of an asset there are often many judgmental decisions on whether a related expenditure is to be capitalized or expensed. As to capitalized balances (original cost plus post acquisition expenditures), we have seen there are many patterns and formulas which can be adopted for depreciation expense. It is necessary to determine in advance such uncertain elements as life in years, output or hours of use, and rate of return. It is also usually necessary to estimate salvage value; sometimes it is necessary to anticipate costs of dismantling or of restoration incident to retirement of a plant asset. Small wonder, then, that great variability attends depreciation accounting.

For larger companies, it is easier to report their depreciation practices than to assess whether these practices conform to theoretical ideals. To judge whether a particular company's depreciation policies are rational requires an intimate knowledge of maintenance policies, particulars about obsolescence, plans for replacement, and financial considerations, among other things. Only a limited segment of the management of most entities is privy to such data or sophisticated enough to appreciate its implications. The financial statement reader, even if knowledgeable is probably able to make only limited judgments about what is reported concerning depreciation.

*Accounting Trends and Techniques, 1975,* the AICPA annual survey of practices of 600 large industrial corporations, indicates that in annual reports, the straight-line method is used more than the other methods accounting for 70% of the total, and its popularity is growing.

Accelerated depreciation account for almost 25% of the total, while unit of production methods accounted for almost 5%.[7] Details from the 1975 survey covering the four preceding years are set out in Exhibit 13–8.

EXHIBIT 13–8
Depreciation and Depletion Policy*

| Method used: | 1974 | 1973 | 1972 | 1971 |
|---|---|---|---|---|
| Straight line | 563 | 568 | 565 | 545 |
| Declining balance | 71 | 74 | 73 | 77 |
| Sum-of-the-years' digits | 45 | 47 | 52 | 51 |
| Accelerated method — not specified | 74 | 76 | 80 | 74 |
| Unit of production | 35 | 40 | 38 | 36 |
| Other methods | 1 | 1 | 1 | 1 |
| Total Disclosures | 789 | 806 | 809 | 784 |

* AICPA, *Accounting Trends and Techniques, 1975* (New York, 1975), p. 287.

The same study indicates that approximately 83% of the companies used different depreciation methods on their income tax returns than they did for financial reporting purposes. For the most part, accelerated methods were used for tax purposes while straight line was used for financial reporting. This, of course, would require interperiod income tax allocation. In a substantial number of instances, the use of different depreciation methods was disclosed but the nature of the differences was not.

The effects of inflation on depreciation is a critical problem facing the accounting profession. Chapter 25 discusses this problem and illustrates certain price-level adjustments.

## CHANGES AND CORRECTION OF DEPRECIATION

Occasionally a business will change the method of depreciation used, change estimates of service life or residual value, or locate prior errors. *APB Opinion No. 20*, "Accounting Changes" (July 1971), carefully specifies how each of these three different situations should be accounted for and reported. The provisions of the *Opinion*, as they relate to depreciation, may be summarized as follows:

1. Changes in accounting principle—A change from one generally accepted method to another generally accepted method (such as from SYD to straight line). Changes of this type require an adjustment for the differences in accumulated depreciation to date between the old

---

[7] The depreciation practices of small companies for financial reporting companies are known only on a piecemeal basis. Those public accountants who have large numbers of small clients and those banks which receive large numbers of reports from small customers can tell what *their* clientele's practices are, but overall data on small business at large are woefully inadequate.

and new methods. This difference is recorded as a depreciation adjustment which is reported on the income statement for the period of change between the captions "extraordinary items" and "net income."

To illustrate, assume XY Corporation has a machine that cost $150,000, having an estimated life of five years and no residual value. After the end of Year 2, the company decided to change from SYD to straight-line depreciation. Computation of the adjustment, the change entry, and reporting on the income statement are illustrated below:

*a.* Computation of adjustment:

| Year | Prior Method—SYD | | New Method— Straight Line | Difference to Date |
|---|---|---|---|---|
| | SYD | Amount | | |
| 1 ......................... | 5/15 | $50,000 | $30,000 | $20,000 |
| 2 ......................... | 4/15 | 40,000 | 30,000 | 10,000 |
| Total.............. | | $90,000 | $60,000 | $30,000 |

*b.* Change entry at start of Year 3:

Accumulated depreciation ...................................... 30,000
    Depreciation adjustment, change in accounting
      method ..................................................... 30,000

*c.* Reporting on the current income statement:

Income before extraordinary items....................................... $60,000
Extraordinary items (detailed) ........................................... (10,000)
Adjustment due to accounting charge (depreciation) ......... 30,000*
Net Income........................................................................ $80,000

    * Appropriate footnote.

This treatment is theoretically sound since it does not permit the adjustment to be reflected as an operating item, documents the item, does not permit it to "bypass" the income statement, and establishes better values for future financial reports.

2. Change in estimate—A change in either, or both, the estimated useful life and residual value. Changes of this type are made prospectively. This means that the undepreciated balance is apportioned to the new remaining life taking into account the new residual value (if changed).

To illustrate, assume XY Corporation has another machine that cost $160,000, with an estimated useful life of five years, no residual value, and straight-line depreciation. At the start of the fourth year, it is decided that an eight-year estimated life would be more realistic with no change in the residual value. Computation of annual depreciation for the remaining life of five years and the adjusting entry for the fourth year follows:

a. Computation of depreciation expense:

Undepreciated balance: $160,000 × ²/₅ = $64,000.
Annual depreciation, straight line: $64,000 ÷ 5 years = $12,800.

b. Adjusting entry for depreciation expense end of fourth year:

| | | |
|---|---|---|
| Depreciation expense ........................................... | 12,800 | |
| Accumulated depreciation ............................... | | 12,800 |

3. Accounting error—Errors in depreciation recorded in prior years should be corrected when found. A correcting entry is required which reflects a *prior period adjustment* (reported on the statement of retained earnings) for the net effect of the error. To illustrate, assume that a machine that cost $10,000, estimated service life of five years, no residual value, was incorrectly debited to expense when acquired. The error was discovered at the end of the third year after acquisition. The correcting and adjusting entries for the third year follow:

a. Correcting entry at end of third year:

| | | |
|---|---|---|
| Machine ................................................................ | 10,000 | |
| Accumulated depreciation ($10,000 × ²/₅)............... | | 4,000 |
| Prior period adjustment—error correction ............ | | 6,000 |

b. Adjusting entry for depreciation expense, end of third year:

| | | |
|---|---|---|
| Depreciation expense ($10,000 ÷ 5) .......................... | 2,000 | |
| Accumulated depreciation.................................. | | 2,000 |

Accounting changes, as prescribed in *APB Opinion No. 20*, are discussed more comprehensively in Chapter 20.

## THE INVESTMENT TAX CREDIT

From time to time Congress has included in the income tax laws provisions designed to encourage certain kinds of investments. The *investment tax credit* which relates to investment in productive facilities is such a provision. Details concerning the investment credit have changed from time to time.[8] The most recent changes provide that taxpayers who acquire qualified property after January 21, 1975, and place it in service before January 1, 1977, receive a 10% investment credit. The tax effect of the investment credit is to reduce by the amount of the credit the amount of taxes that would otherwise have to be paid. To illustrate the essential nature of the investment credit, assume data pertaining to X Corporation for 1976 as follows:

---

[8] The first investment credit was provided by the Revenue Act of 1962; it was revised by the 1964 Act, suspended in 1966, and restored in 1967. The Tax Reform Act of 1969 again repealed the credit, but its provisions remained effective for property bought as late as 1975. When effective prior to 1975, the rate was 7% for most entities; it is now 10%.

a. Equipment bought early in 1976 that qualified for the
investment credit (ten-year life, zero salvage value) .................. $200,000
b. Straight-line depreciation on equipment for 1976 ..................... 20,000
c. Income subject to tax for 1976 (after deducting $20,000
depreciation on equipment)..................................................... 60,000
d. Income tax before investment credit....................................... 24,000*

* Assuming a flat 40% rate for illustrative purposes.

The effect of the investment credit would be as follows:

Income taxes for 1976 before investment credit............... $24,000
Less investment credit (10% of $200,000)....................... 20,000
Amount of tax to be paid ............................................. $4,000

In the above example the significant reduction in income taxes, as a result of the investment credit, obviously would be viewed with considerable interest by the taxpayer and surely would influence some of his or her investment decisions. With respect to proper accounting, the question is posed as to how the $20,000 tax credit should be recorded and reported. Fundamentally, two distinctly different accounting approaches have been vigorously debated by the accounting profession. In these discussions the nature of the investment credit has been viewed as:

a. A reduction in income taxes. The proponents of this view feel that since the investment credit was made available by the Revenue Act, it is in substance a selective reduction in taxes related to the taxable income of the year in which the credit arises. They feel that it is a "tax item"; to view it as a reduction of the cost of the asset would permit identical items purchased from the same supplier, at the same cost, to be recorded at different costs depending on the respective tax problems of several purchasers and not upon the conditions existing between the buyer and seller of the equipment. They note that various tax consequences as well as the investment credit affect a whole host of managerial decisions. They feel that the investment credit, as an adjustment to income taxes, should affect the net income (after taxes) only in the year in which the tax credit arises. This frequently is referred to as the "flow-through" method.

b. Cost reduction or deferral method. Proponents for this position argue that it is the *use*, not the *purchase*, of the asset that gives rise to the benefits to be received from the investment credit. Strong support for this argument is found in the fact that if the property which gave rise to the credit is not retained, part or all of the credit will be lost. It can also be noted that shorter lived property receives a smaller credit. The original tax provision, although later revised, required that the credit be treated for tax purposes as a reduction of asset cost.

The effects of these two diverse positions may now be emphasized by comparing the accounting entries that would result from the illustrative data given above. Entries in 1976 would be as follows:

|  *Investment Credit Treated as a Reduction in Income Taxes (flow-through method)* | *Investment Credit Treated as a Cost Reduction (deferral)* |
|---|---|

a. To record purchase of equipment early in 1976 for $200,000:

| Equipment ..................... 200,000 | | Equipment...................... 200,000 | |
|---|---|---|---|
| Cash ........................ | 200,000 | Cash ........................ | 200,000 |

b. To record income taxes for 1976:

| Income tax expense ......... 4,000 | | Income tax expense ......... 24,000 | |
|---|---|---|---|
| Income tax payable ... | 4,000 | Income tax payable ... | 4,000 |
| | | Deferred investment credit ..................... | 20,000 |
| | | | |
| | | Deferred investment credit .......................... | 2,000 |
| | | Income tax expense (¹/₁₀ of $20,000) ...... | 2,000 |

c. Depreciation on equipment for 1976 (ten-year life):

| Depreciation expense ...... 20,000 | | Depreciation expense ...... 20,000 | |
|---|---|---|---|
| Accumulated depreciation .................. | 20,000 | Accumulated depreciation .................. | 20,000 |

The above tabulation of entries clearly reveals that when the investment credit is treated as a reduction in income taxes, its effects flow through the income statement and balance sheet in a single year. In contrast, under the deferral method, with a ten-year asset only one tenth of the benefit is recognized in the first year and similarly (assuming the asset is retained) in each subsequent year another one tenth of the tax reduction benefit increases net income. The credit balance in the Deferred Investment Credit account is a contra account on the balance sheet to the related asset account; however, it is sometimes illogically reported as a liability.

Either procedure may be followed at the present time under generally accepted accounting principles as specified in *APB Opinion Nos. 2* and *4*. This not altogether ideal state of affairs is the result of some early indecision on the part of the Accounting Principles Board. To the Board's credit, however, it should be pointed out that it moved to correct the situation in 1971 by issuing an exposure draft of an *Opinion* which would have allowed only the deferral method. The Board lost the battle in the political arena when business executives pressured Congress to insert a provision in the Revenue Act of 1971 which legally permitted choice of either method of accounting for the investment credit. Whichever method is adopted it must be used consistently and disclosed.

## DEPLETION

### Nature of Depletion

Depletion in the accounting sense represents allocation against revenue of the cost of a natural resource (wasting asset) that is being exploited. Examples of such resources are ore, oil, coal, timber, and gravel. In accounting for such assets, the original cost is recorded in harmony with the *cost principle* and subsequently amortized over the total production economically available. Allocation between periods, consistent with the *matching principle*, usually is accomplished by dividing the cost of the asset (less any residual value) by the estimated number of units that can be withdrawn economically; the *unit depletion rate* thus computed is multiplied by the actual units withdrawn during the period to determine the depletion charge for the period. As with other tangible assets, three factors are involved: (1) cost, including all development costs that can be related to the resource, (2) estimated residual value of the property upon exhaustion of the natural resource, and (3) the estimated production over the life of the resource. To illustrate, assume that it is estimated by competent reserve geologists that a given mineral lease has a potential production of two million units, and that the total cost of the lease, including development costs, is $160,000 with no residual value. The depletion rate per unit of mineral produced and its application would be computed as follows:

Depletion rate: $160,000 ÷ 2,000,000 = $.08 per unit
Production for period: 10,000 units
Depletion charge for period: 10,000 × $.08 = $800

This method generally is used for financial and cost accounting purposes. For federal income tax purposes, other depletion methods may be employed in accordance with the Internal Revenue Code. For example, the Code permits the taxpayer to elect *statutory* or *percentage depletion* rather than cost depletion illustrated above. Under statutory depletion a stated percentage of gross income may be taken as the depletion deduction on the tax return. The percentage varies from 5% on some deposits to 22% on others. Some of the more common depletion percentages follow:

| | |
|---|---|
| Sulphur and uranium; and, if from deposits in the United States, asbestos, lead, zinc, nickel, and certain others | 22% |
| Oil and gas* | 22% |
| Gold, silver, copper, iron ore, and oil shale | 15% |
| Coal and sodium chloride | 10% |
| Clay and shale used for certain purposes | 7½% |
| Other clay | 5% |
| Most other minerals and metallic ores | 14% |

* For many years the percentage rate on oil and gas was 27½%; it was cut to 22%. Recently it was eliminated for larger oil producers but still has applicability on a greatly reduced scale.

Under the Code the sum of the statutory depletion charges allowed may (and in practice frequently does) exceed the original cost of the resource.

Original acquisition costs, development costs, and tangible property costs associated with a natural resource should be set up in separate accounts. If any of such facilities is likely to have a shorter life than the natural resource, its cost should be amortized over the shorter period. When buildings and similar improvements are constructed in connection with the exploitation of the specific resource, their lives may be limited by the duration of the resource. In such cases costs should be amortized on the same basis as the other costs related to the resource.

In view of the difficulties in estimating underground deposits of minerals, the evaluation of additional information derived through further developmental work and the additional costs incident thereto, the depletion rate must be changed from time to time. The new rate is determined by dividing the unamortized cost plus any additional development costs by the *remaining* estimated reserves. Past depletion charges are not revised.

Dividends sometimes are paid by companies exploiting natural resources equivalent to accumulated net income plus the accumulated depletion charge. State laws generally permit such dividends. This practice is common where there are no plans to replace the natural resource in kind and operations are to cease upon exhaustion of the deposit. In such cases, the stockholders should be informed of the portion of each dividend that represents a return of capital (i.e., the depletion charge). To illustrate, assume the Tex Oil Company accounts showed the following (summarized):

| | |
|---|---:|
| Assets | $1,000,000 |
| Accumulated depreciation | (200,000) |
| Allowance for depletion | (100,000) |
| | $ 700,000 |
| Liabilities | $ 150,000 |
| Capital stock | 500,000 |
| Retained earnings | 50,000 |
| | $ 700,000 |

The board of directors could declare a dividend of $150,000 which would be recorded as follows:

| | | |
|---|---:|---:|
| Retained earnings | 50,000 | |
| Return of capital to stockholders | 100,000 | |
|    Cash | | 150,000 |

The return of capital to stockholders would be reported as a deduction in the owners' equity section of the balance sheet.

# Appendix. Annuity and Sinking Fund Methods of Depreciation

The annuity and sinking fund methods of depreciation are based on the same concepts that underlie an annuity investment. In this situation an investment is made and subsequently returns are received, usually each period. Each return is viewed as comprising two elements:

(a) a return of principal, and (b) investment revenue. Each period, assuming a constant amount received, the principal element is larger (this represents depreciation) and the interest element is smaller. The annuity and sinking fund methods derive the same overall effect on the income statement and balance sheet; their differences relate to depreciation expense and imputed interest revenue reported on the income statement.

To illustrate the annuity and sinking fund methods of depreciation, assume the following simplified data:

Investment in plant item at cost at beginning of Year 1 ............ $100
Residual or scrap value estimated at end of Year 3 .................. $ 10
Estimated useful life of the plant item...................................... 3 years
Average cost of capital........................................................... 5%
Present value of 1 for 3 periods at 5% (from Table 6–2) ........... .863838
Present value of annuity of 1 for 3 periods at 5% (from Table 6–4)... 2.723248

## ANNUITY METHOD OF DEPRECIATION

To apply this method the annual depreciation charge is computed on an annuity basis. The amount of the annual return on the investment is assumed to represent depreciation expense; accumulated depreciation is credited for the portion that represents return of principal, and the difference is credited to imputed interest revenue.

To illustrate, the periodic charge to depreciation expense would be computed as follows:

$$\text{Depreciation Expense} = \frac{CV - (SV \times p)}{P} = \frac{\$100 - (\$10 \times .863838)}{2.723248} = \$33.55$$

With this value we can construct a depreciation table reflecting the entries for depreciation and the periodic carrying value of the asset from acquisition to retirement. The table would be as follows:

**Depreciation Table and Journal Entries — Annuity Method**

| Year | Depreciation Expense Dr. (a) | Accumulated Depreciation Cr. (b) | Interest Revenue Cr. (c) | Unamortized Asset Balance (d) |
|---|---|---|---|---|
| 0 .............. | — | — | — | $100.00 |
| 1 .............. | $ 33.55 | $28.55 | $ 5.00 | 71.45 |
| 2 .............. | 33.55 | 29.98 | 3.57 | 41.47 |
| 3 .............. | 33.55 | 31.47 | 2.08 | 10.00 |
|  | $100.65 | $90.00 | $10.65 | |

(a) Constant amount from formula as computed above.
(b) (a) minus (c).
(c) Previous unamortized asset balance times .05.
(d) Previous balance minus current (b).

Observe that the above table is identical with an annuity amortization table (Chapter 6) except for the column captions. Also observe the following characteristics of the annuity method, as revealed by the entries in the above table, viz:

1. Depreciation Expense is debited each period for a *constant* amount.
2. Accumulated Depreciation is credited for an *increasing* amount each period.
3. Interest Revenue (this is imputed interest) is credited for a *decreasing* amount each period.
4. Because of the net effect of Depreciation Expense and Interest Revenue, there is an *increasing expense* effect on the income statement. It is the same as the credit to accumulated depreciation each period.
5. The carrying value of the asset decreases each period by a continuously increasing amount.

## SINKING FUND METHOD OF DEPRECIATION

The sinking fund and annuity methods are closely akin. Their chief difference is that under the sinking fund method interest is reflected in the periodic depreciation charge but is not separately recorded and reported, while under the annuity method imputed interest is accorded separate recognition. It should be pointed out that while a sinking fund to replace the asset being depreciated might be maintained, most companies would prefer to invest in other productive assets and that formal sinking funds (asset replacement funds) are quite rare. The journal entries, assuming depreciation only and no sinking fund, for the two methods are as follows:

**Annuity and Sinking Fund Depreciation Methods Compared**

|  | Annuity Method | | Sinking Fund Method | |
|---|---|---|---|---|
| Year 1: |  |  |  |  |
| Depreciation expense | 33.55 |  | 28.55 |  |
| Accumulated depreciation |  | 28.55 |  | 28.55 |
| Interest revenue |  | 5.00 |  |  |
| Year 2: |  |  |  |  |
| Depreciation expense | 33.55 |  | 29.98 |  |
| Accumulated depreciation |  | 29.98 |  | 29.98 |
| Interest revenue |  | 3.57 |  |  |
| Year 3: |  |  |  |  |
| Depreciation expense | 33.55 |  | 31.47 |  |
| Accumulated depreciation |  | 31.47 |  | 31.47 |
| Interest revenue |  | 2.08 |  |  |

Observe in the illustration that the sum of the three annual amounts of depreciation under the sinking fund method is $90 (enough to replace the asset if its replacement cost does not rise and if the $10 estimated salvage value is realized). Also observe that if a series of three payments of $28.55 were made to a sinking fund earning 5%, $90 would accumulate at the end of three years. The above entries reveal the basic difference between the two methods; the sinking fund method does not report imputed interest revenue; otherwise, we see the same effects on the income statement and balance sheet.

The compound interest methods have been criticized on several counts. Some claim that they are not "rational" since an increasing charge for depreciation over the life of the asset is inconsistent with the fact that ownership costs based on value tend to decrease in later years. Also a part of the depreciation charge under the *annuity method* is for imputed or theoretical interest; the offsetting credit for this element is made to Interest Revenue and therefore affects the income or loss of the period in which the depreciation is recorded. If the assets being depreciated are used in the production of goods for inventory, the consequence may be that an element of imputed interest will be found in an asset balance rather than in an expense balance at the close of the period.

For a combination of reasons the compound interest methods have been used relatively little in practice. Many entities, for reasons already cited, prefer to adopt depreciation methods which result in a somewhat opposite pattern of depreciation charges. The complexity and extra calculation effort of the compound interest methods may also be a deterrent to their adoption. The limited extent to which the methods have been used seems to be confined largely to public utilities. There is some theoretical justification for their use by regulated businesses where a precalculated rate of return on investment is contemplated and revenues and rates are theoretically set on the basis of rate of return on invested capital.

## QUESTIONS

1. Distinguish between amortization, depletion, and depreciation.

2. Explain the effects of depreciation on (a) the income statement, and (b) the balance sheet.

3. Explain the relationship of depreciation to (a) cash flow, and (b) assets.

4. What is the relationship of depreciation to replacement of the assets being depreciated?

5. What are the primary causes of depreciation? What effect do changes in the market value of the asset being depreciated have on the depreciation estimates?

6. List and briefly explain the three factors which must be considered in allocating the cost of an operational asset.

7. What is meant by reducing-charge methods of depreciation? Under what circumstances would these methods generally be appropriate?

8. What accounting policy problems arise when the entity's fiscal year and the

asset year do not coincide? In other words, if a company closes books on June 30 but has bought a depreciable asset on January 1.

9. Briefly explain the inventory system of depreciation. Under what circumstances is such a system appropriate?

10. Compare the retirement and replacement depreciation systems.

11. Wherein are composite-life depreciation and group depreciation similar? Explain.

12. There are three categories in respect to change and correction of depreciation. Briefly explain each and outline the accounting involved as specified in *APB Opinion No. 20*.

13. What is the investment credit? What are the accepted ways of accounting for it?

14. Define depletion. How is depletion generally computed for financial and cost accounting purposes?

## DECISION CASE 13–1

Two symbols of modern technology which comprise costly, if not principal, depreciable assets owned by some companies are computers and jet airplanes. They pose interesting depreciation problems. Consider the following items abstracted from news stories in *The Wall Street Journal*.

*Part A — Computers.* In computer circles, Gordon Berg is fondly known as "the king of the IBM 7074." Mr. Berg, who buys computers for Pacific Telephone & Telegraph Company, has, in recent years, accumulated 13 of the six-foot tall International Business Machines Corporations computers to tabulate customer bills. "On a cost-performance basis, they (IBM 7074s) can't be beat," he says. That's because Mr. Berg buys them used. Four 7074's he purchased last year cost Pacific Telephone something under $20,000 each — a nifty savings over the nearly $1 million IBM charged until it stopped making 7074's four years ago. Nor does Mr. Berg just buy used 7074's. A quarter of all Pacific Telephone's dozens of computers were purchased used (February 7, 1974).

And adapted from the same issue, another story — Dearborn-Storm Corporation said it agreed in principle to sell its System 360 computers for $17 million in cash to a group of private investors here. The company said it expects the transaction to be closed within 30 days. The effect of the sale will be reflected in the company's results for the fiscal year ended October 31, 1973, and will result in a loss, including phase-out costs, of about $9 million after tax benefits of about $4.2 million. For the nine months ended last July 31, the company reported a loss of $315,000 after a new charge of $4.5 million for additional depreciation on the leased computers. This compared with a profit of $3.6 million, or $1.32 per share, in the year-earlier period.

*Part B — Jet Airplanes.* In late 1974 and early 1975, several items appeared in *The Wall Street Journal* detailing how various airlines were dealing with their surplus jet capacity during the energy crisis and a period when passenger demand was well below their ability to transport passengers. Excerpts adapted from this story, dated February 3, 1975, are representative.

Trans World Airlines announced the near conclusion of arrangements to sell six 747 jumbo jets to Iran for $99 million. At $16.5 million per plane, TWA was in a position to underbid Pan Am (which had also been interested in selling off surplus 747's). At this price, TWA was selling below its book value, said to average $17 to $18 million (exact figures would vary with the age of each plane). Pan Am was barred by conditions of its debt arrangements from selling aircraft at less than book value; TWA was aware of this restriction and took advantage of the restriction in setting its price.

On the other hand, consider the following excerpts adapted from the February 27, 1975, issue concerning another type of plane—the DC3. Douglas Aircraft division of McDonnell Douglas Corporation began producing the DC3 in 1935, subsequently turned out 10,928 military and commercial versions of the plane. Douglas estimates 2,500 to 3,000 DC3's are still flying. Some 159 commercial companies owned or operated 512 of the venerable workhorses as recently as last June. Douglas continues to make money from the DC3, selling something on the order of $50,000 of parts a year. But International Engine Parts, Incorporated, does better, selling about $100,000 annually to repair shops and foreign governments. "This business will continue on for another ten years or so," says Verne Morand, sales manager. "It's a phenomenally good aircraft." "What's a DC3 worth?" says one New York aircraft dealer, "I suppose you could buy one for $25,000 to $30,000."

Added information (not from *The Wall Street Journal*): For income tax purposes, depreciable lives used for new computers appear to range from five to seven years and for aircraft, from four to six years. Although the stories cited deal with three specific situations, Pacific Telephone, Dearborn-Storm, and TWA and a widespread phenomena (the DC3), other similar evidence to bolster what was cited could be adduced.

*Required:*

1. Discuss the problems of properly depreciating and valuing computers and aircraft when purchased new in the light of what was recited.
2. Do buyers of used assets, of the types cited at bargain prices, have special problems in respect to depreciation? Discuss.

## EXERCISES

### Exercise 13-1

In order to demonstrate the mechanical computations involved in several methods of depreciation the following simplified situation is presented:

| | |
|---|---|
| Acquisition cost | $ 6,400 |
| Scrap or residual value | $ 400 |
| Estimated service life: | |
| Years | 4 |
| Service hours | 10,000 |
| Productive output | 24,000 |

*Required:*

Compute the annual depreciation under each of the following situations (show computations and round to even dollars):

1. Straight-line depreciation; compute the depreciation charge and rate for each year.
2. Service-hours method; compute the depreciation rate and charge for the first year assuming 3,000 service hours of actual operation.

3. Productive-output method of depreciation; compute the depreciation rate and charge for the first year assuming 7,000 units of output.
4. Sum-of-the-years'-digits method; compute the depreciation charge for each year.
5. Double-declining-balance method; compute the depreciation charge for each year.

### Exercise 13-2

Equipment which cost Davis Company $12,000 will be depreciated on the assumption it will last eight years and have an $800 residual value. Several possible methods of depreciation are under consideration.

*Required:*

1. Prepare a schedule which shows annual depreciation expense, accumulated depreciation, and book values for the *first two* years assuming (show computations and round to even dollars):
   a. Fixed percentage on declining base method. The eighth root of .06667 is .71283.
   b. Productive output method. Estimated output is a total of 84,000 units, of which 9,000 will be produced the first year; 12,000 for each of the next three years; 15,000 the fourth year; 9,000 the fifth, sixth, and seventh years; and 6,000 the final year.
   c. Sum-of-the-years'-digits method.
2. What criteria would you consider in selecting a method?

### Exercise 13-3

A depreciable asset acquired by Ute Company cost $4,800 and is estimated to have a useful life of four years and a residual value of $400.

*Required:*

1. Prepare a depreciation table covering the life of the asset assuming (show computations and round to even dollars):
   a. Straight-line method.
   b. Sum-of-the-years'-digits method.
   c. Double-declining-balance method.
2. What criteria should be considered in selecting a method?

### Exercise 13-4

A machine is to be depreciated which cost $8,000, has an estimated service life of four years, and a residual value of $600.

*Required:*

1. Prepare a depreciation table covering the life of the machine assuming (show computations and round to even dollars):
   a. Sum-of-the-years'-digits method.
   b. Productive output method. Total output is estimated at 36,000 units. Actual output from start to end, in order, was 11,000, 8,000, 7,000, and 10,000 units.
   c. Double-declining-balance method.

2. Facts are the same as requirement 1(*a*) except that in the fourth year, after ten months, the machine was sold for $600. Give the entry to record the sale.
3. What criteria should be considered in selecting a method?

## Exercise 13–5

Ellen Company bought equipment on January 1, 19A, for $22,000 for which the expected life is ten years and residual value is $2,000. Under three popular depreciation methods, the annual depreciation expense and cumulative balance of accumulated depreciation at the end of 19A and 19B are shown below:

|  | Method A | | Method B | | Method C | |
|---|---|---|---|---|---|---|
| Year | Annual Expense | Accumu- lated Amount | Annual Expense | Accumu- lated Amount | Annual Expense | Accumu- lated Amount |
| 19A | $4,400 | $4,400 | $2,000 | $2,000 | $3,636 | $3,636 |
| 19B | 3,520 | 7,920 | 2,000 | 4,000 | 3,272 | 6,908 |

*Required:*
1. Identify the depreciation method used in each instance.
2. Project continued use of the same method through years 19C and 19D and determine the annual depreciation expense and accumulated depreciation amount for each year under each method.

## Exercise 13–6

Taylor Utility Company purchased 500 poles at $120 per pole; the debit being to the Inventory—Poles P-113 account. Subsequent to the purchase, 100 of the new poles were used to replace an equal number of old poles (Poles M-101) which were carried in the tangible fixed asset account, Poles—Austin Line. The old poles originally cost $30 each and had an estimated salvage value of $10 per pole.

*Required:*
1. Give all indicated entries (*a*) assuming the retirement system is employed, and (*b*) assuming the replacement system is used.
2. Compare the effect on the periodic depreciation charge and the asset accounts as between the two systems.

## Exercise 13–7

Milton Company owned a power plant which consisted of the following, all acquired on January 1, 1973:

|  | Cost | Estimated Scrap Value | Estimated Life (years) |
|---|---|---|---|
| Building | $450,000 | None | 15 |
| Machinery, etc. | 180,000 | $18,000 | 10 |
| Other equipment | 150,000 | 10,000 | 5 |

*Required:*

1. Compute the total straight-line depreciation for 1976 on all items combined.
2. Compute the composite depreciation rate on the plant.
3. Determine the composite life of the plant.

## Exercise 13–8

Mannix Company depreciates its spot welders on a straight-line basis. Transactions relative to spot welders in Plant A were:

*a.* January 2, 19A: Bought six spot welders for an aggregate price of $16,500, paying cash.
*b.* December 31, 19A: On the assumption the salvage value of the group would total 10% of original cost and their useful life was five years, recorded depreciation at year-end.
*c.* Recorded depreciation at year-end, December 31, 19B.
*d.* January 2, 19C: One unit which performed unsatisfactorily was sold for $1,250 cash.
*e.* Two additional spot welders were bought January 10, 19C, at the same unit price as the original elements of the group and added to the group.
*f.* Recorded depreciation at December 31, 19C, for full year for all units in group.
*g.* Transferred one spot welder to Plant C on January 2, 19D.

*Required:*

Give entries for each transaction in general journal form. Show computations; closing entries are not required.

## Exercise 13–9

Clara Company's records show the following property acquisitions and retirements during the first two years of operations:

| Year | Cost of Property Acquired | Estimated Useful Life (years) | Sales or Retirements Year of Acquisition | Amount |
|---|---|---|---|---|
| 19A.............. | $50,000 | 10 | — | — |
| 19B.............. | 20,000 | 10 | 19A | $7,000 |

Property is depreciated one half in the year of acquisition. Retired property is to be depreciated for the full year in its year of retirement. Assume zero salvage values.

*Required:*

Determine depreciation expense for 19A and for 19B and the balances of the Property account and related Accumulated Depreciation at the end of each year under the following depreciation methods (show computations and round to even dollars):

*a.* Straight-line method.
*b.* Sum-of-the-years'-digits method.

(AICPA adapted)

## Exercise 13–10

Downs Company owned ten warehouses of a similar type except for varying size. The group system is applied to the ten warehouses, the rate being 8% per year on cost. At the end of the tenth year the asset account Warehouses showed a balance of $530,000 (residual value $30,000), and the Accumulated Depreciation account showed a balance of $240,000. Shortly after the end of the tenth year, Warehouse No. 65, costing $60,000, was retired and demolished. Materials of $5,000 were sold, and $1,500 was spent in demolition.

*Required:*

Give entries to record (*a*) depreciation for the 10th year, (*b*) retirement of the warehouse, and (*c*) depreciation for the 11th year.

## Exercise 13–11

Brown Corporation purchased a machine (which qualified for the 10% investment credit) on January 1, 19A, at a cost of $60,000; having an estimated useful life of 12 years and no residual value. The company uses straight-line depreciation and has an average tax rate of 35%. Income (after deducting depreciation expense) subject to tax was: 19A, $40,000; and 19B, $45,000.

*Required:*

Give the entries for income taxes and depreciation at December 31, 19A, and December 31, 19B, end of the fiscal period, assuming the—

*a.* Flow-through method.
*b.* Deferral method.

## Exercise 13–12

XT Company's investment in a gravel quarry amounted to $400,000, of which $40,000 could be ascribed to land value after the gravel has been removed. Geologists were engaged to estimate the economically removable gravel reported originally that three million cubic yards (units) could be extracted. In the first year 600,000 units were extracted and 550,000 units were sold. In the second year 400,000 units were extracted and sales were 450,000 units.

At the start of the third year management of XT Company had the quarry examined again, at which time it was determined the remaining economically removable gravel was 1.5 million units. Production and sales for the third year amounted to 300,000 units. In the fourth year production was 500,000 units while sales amounted to 450,000 units.

*Required:*

1. Calculate the depletion deduction to be reported on XT's income statement for each of the four years. Show supporting computations.
2. Show how the gravel deposit would be reported on XT's balance sheet at the end of the fourth year. Assume an accumulated account is used.

## Exercise 13–13

Rankin Minerals, Inc., paid $1,700,000 for property with removable ore estimated at 2,000,000 tons. The property has an estimated value of $100,000 after the ore has been extracted. Before any ore could be removed it was necessary to incur $400,000 of developmental costs. In the first year 200,000 tons were removed and 175,000 tons of ore were sold; in the second year 300,000 tons were removed and 325,000 tons were sold. In the course of the second year's production, discoveries were made which indicated that if an added $300,000 is spent on developmental costs, future removable ore will total 2,700,000 tons. After incurring these added costs, production and sales for the third year amount to 540,000 tons.

*Required:*

1. Calculate the depletion deduction to be reported on Rankin's income statement for each of the three years. Show supporting computations.
2. Show how the resource would be reported on Rankin's balance sheet at the end of the third year. Assume an accumulated account is used.
3. Give the journal entry to record depletion expense at the end of the first year.

## PROBLEMS

### Problem 13-1

Depreciation continues to be one of the most controversial, difficult, and important problem areas in accounting.

*Required:*

1. *a.* Explain the conventional accounting concept of depreciation accounting.
   *b.* Discuss its conceptual merit with respect to (*a*) the value of the asset, (*b*) the charge(s) to expense, and (*c*) the discretion of management in selecting the method.
2. *a.* Explain the factors that should be considered when applying the conventional concept of depreciation to the determination of how the value of a newly acquired computer system should be assigned to expense for financial reporting purposes. (Ignore income tax considerations.)
   *b.* What depreciation methods might be used for the computer system?

(AICPA adapted)

### Problem 13-2

Scott Company purchased a special machine at a cost of $45,500. It was estimated that the machine would have a net resale value at the end of its useful life for the company of $3,500. Statistics relating to the machine over its service life were as follows:

Estimated service life:
Years ....................... 5
Output, units.............. 6,000

Actual operations:

| Year | Units of Output |
|------|------|
| 1.............................. | 1,400 |
| 2.............................. | 1,300 |
| 3.............................. | 1,000 |
| 4.............................. | 1,100 |
| 5.............................. | 1,200 |

*Required:*

Prepare a depreciation table for each assumption below indicating entries for the asset over the useful life under the following methods: (a) straight line, (b) output, (c) sum-of-the-years'-digits, (d) fixed percentage of 40% on declining base, and (e) double-declining balance. Show computations and round to even dollars.


## Problem 13-3

Royal Company purchased a piece of special factory equipment on January 1, 19A, costing $51,000. In view of pending technological developments it is estimated that the machine will have a resale value upon disposal in four years of $15,500 and that disposal cost will be $4,500.

Data relating to the equipment follows:

Estimated service life:
Years ........................ 4
Service hours.............. 20,000

Actual operations:

| Calendar Year | Service Hours |
|---|---|
| 19A ........................ | 5,500 |
| 19B ........................ | 5,000 |
| 19C ........................ | 4,800 |
| 19D ........................ | 4,600 |

*Required:*

(Round to even dollars and show computations):

1. Prepare a depreciation table for the service-hours method assuming the books are closed each December 31.
2. Compute depreciation expense for the first and second years assuming: (a) straight line, (b) sum-of-the-years'-digits, (c) fixed percent on declining base (30% rate), and (d) double-declining balance.


## Problem 13-4

Machinery which cost Karen Corporation $10,000 is expected to last ten years and have a $500 residual value. Several depreciation methods in common use were applied to these data. The results in terms of annual charges covering the Year 2 and Year 3 are set out below:

| Year | Method A | Method B | Method C | Method D |
|---|---|---|---|---|
| 1.............. | ? | ? | ? | ? |
| 2.............. | $1,924 | $1,600 | $1,555 | $950 |
| 3.............. | 1,424 | 1,280 | 1,382 | 950 |

*Required:*

1. Identify the method used to get the results for each method; show computations to support your response. Round to even dollars.

2. In connection with Methods C and D, suppose that after the completion of Year 3, it is determined the total remaining life of the machinery is five instead of seven years. Determine the annual charge and the balance of Accumulated Depreciation at the end of Year 4 and Year 5.

## Problem 13–5

BK Manufacturing Company utilizes a number of small machine tools in their operations. Although there are numerous variations in the tools, they cost approximately the same and have similar useful lives. The company carries a Machine Tools account in the records; the account showed a balance of $1,600 (200 tools) at the end of 19A. Acquisitions, retirements, and other data for a period of two years are given below:

|  | 19B | 19C |
|---|---|---|
| Acquisitions ..................... | 100 @ $7.50 | 120 @ $7.75 |
| Retirements: | | |
|    Number .................... | 150 | 80 |
|    Salvage proceeds.............. | $ 40 | $ 20 |
| Inventory............................ | 150 @ $5.20 | 190 @ $5.40 |

*Required:*

1. Give entries for each of the two years assuming (round to even dollars and show computations):
   *a.* The inventory system is used.
   *b.* The retirement system is used.
   *c.* The replacement system is used.
2. Prepare a tabulation covering the two years to present for the annual depreciation charge and the balance in the Machine Tools account under each system.

## Problem 13–6

Davis Company utilizes a large number of identical small tools in operations. On January 1, 19A, the first year of operations, 1,000 of these tools were purchased at a cost of $4 each. On December 31, 19A, 200 of the tools were scrapped, the estimated salvage value being $40 ($.20 each). During the year the 200 were replaced at a cost of $4.20 each. On December 31, 19B, 300 of the tools were scrapped, having an estimated salvage value of $.25 each and replaced at a cost of $4.50 each. On December 31, 19C, 140 of the tools were scrapped (salvage value $.25 each) each being replaced at a cost of $3.60.

*Required:*

1. Compute the annual depreciation charge for 19A, 19B, and 19C and the balance at the end of each year in the Tools account, assuming the company employed the (*a*) retirement system, and (*b*) the replacement system.
2. Compare the results.

## Problem 13–7

One set of plant assets depreciated by Sonntag Company on a composite basis is identified as Group No. 16, components of which are as follows:

| Component | Cost | Estimated Residual Value | Estimated Life (years) |
|---|---|---|---|
| A.............. | $29,800 | $1,800 | 10 |
| B.............. | 14,000 | 0 | 7 |
| C.............. | 38,000 | 8,000 | 15 |
| D.............. | 6,200 | 200 | 5 |
| E.............. | 12,000 | 2,000 | 5 |

*Required:*

1. Calculate the composite life and annual composite depreciation for Group No. 16. Record depreciation after one full year of use.
2. During the second year it became necessary to replace component B which was sold for $8,000. The replacement component cost $16,000 and has an estimated salvage value of $2,600 at the end of its estimated six-year useful life. Record the retirement and substitution which was a cash acquisition.
3. Record depreciation at the end of the second full year.

## Problem 13–8

The accounts for Trucks and Accumulated Depreciation on the books of Dacy Hardware Store are as shown below:

### Trucks

| | | | | | |
|---|---|---|---|---|---|
| 1/1/19A Trucks No. 1 and 2 | 7,200 | | 1/1/19C Truck No. 1 scrapped | 3,600 | |
| 1/1/19C Truck No. 3 | 3,780 | | 1/1/19D Truck No. 2 scrapped | 3,600 | |
| 1/1/19D Truck No. 4 | 3,840 | | | | |
| 7/1/19D New tires, Truck 3 | 600 | | | | |

### Accumulated Depreciation

| | | | | |
|---|---|---|---|---|
| 1/1/19C Truck No. 1 scrapped ($1,500 received as salvage) | 2,400 | 12/31/19A Depreciation | 2,400 | |
| | | 12/31/19B Depreciation | 2,400 | |
| | | 12/31/19C Depreciation | 2,460 | |
| 1/1/19D Truck No. 2 scrapped ($300 received as salvage) | 3,300 | 12/31/19D Depreciation | 2,460 | |
| | | 12/31/19E Depreciation | 1,905 | |

*Required:*

1. Prepare a depreciation schedule showing correct account balances and depreciation by year, assuming the estimated lives of Trucks No. 3 and No. 4 were changed from three to four years on January 1, 19E. Suggested captions: Date, Truck No., Trucks (debit-credit*), Correct Depreciation by Year (five columns), and Accumulated Depreciation (debit-credit*).
2. Journal entry or entries to correct the books as of December 31, 19E, assuming they were not yet closed for 19E. The schedule prepared for Requirement 1 should provide the data needed.

## Problem 13–9

The Machinery account as of December 31, 19F, on the books of the Darwin Company was as follows:

**Machinery**

| | | | | |
|---|---|---|---|---|
| 1/1/A Purchase | $50,000 | 12/31/A Depreciation | $ 5,000 |
| 7/1/B Purchase | 10,000 | 9/ 1/B Machinery sold | 2,000 |
| 11/1/C Purchase | 30,000 | 12/31/C Depreciation | 6,200 |
| | | 12/31/D Depreciation | 7,200 |
| | | 7/ 1/E Machinery sold | 1,000 |
| | | 12/31/E Depreciation | 7,200 |
| | | 12/31/F Depreciation | 8,700 |

Additional data:

Machinery sold September 1, 19B, cost $3,600 on January 1, 19A; machinery sold July 1, 19E, cost $2,500 on January 1, 19A. Machinery costing $2,000, which was purchased on July 1, 19B, was destroyed on July 1, 19F and was a total loss.

*Required:*

1. A depreciation schedule showing correct annual depreciation and account balances. Assume ten-year life on all items, straight line and no residual value. Suggested captions: Date, Machinery (debit-credit*), Correct Depreciation by Year (six columns), and Accumulated Depreciation (debit-credit*).
2. Journal entry or entries to correct the books on December 31, 19F, assuming the books are not closed for 19F.

### Problem 13-10

Thompson Corporation, a manufacturer of steel products, began operations on October 1, 19A. The accounting department of Thompson has started the fixed asset and depreciation schedule presented on page 585. You have been asked to assist in completing this schedule. In addition to ascertaining that the data already on the schedule are correct, you have obtained the following information from the company's records and personnel:

a. Depreciation is computed from the first of the month of acquisition to the first of the month of disposition.
b. Land A and Building A were acquired from a predecessor corporation. Thompson paid $812,500 for the land and building together. At the time of acquisition, the land had an appraised value of $72,000 and the building had an appraised value of $828,000.
c. Land B was acquired on October 2, 19A, in exchange for 3,000 newly issued shares of Thompson's common stock. At the date of acquisition, the stock had a par value of $5 per share and a fair value of $25 per share. During October 19A, Thompson paid $10,400 to demolish an existing building on this land so it could construct a new building.
d. Construction of Building B on the newly acquired land began on October 1, 19B. By September 30, 19C, Thompson had paid $210,000 of the estimated total construction costs of $300,000. Estimated completion and occupancy date is July 19D.
e. Certain equipment was donated to the corporation by a local university. An independent appraisal of the equipment when donated placed the fair value at $16,000 and the salvage value at $2,000.
f. Machinery A's total cost of $110,000 includes installation expense of $550 and normal repairs and maintenance of $11,000. Salvage value is estimated as $5,500. Machinery A was sold on February 1, 19C.

THOMPSON CORPORATION
Fixed Asset and Depreciation Schedule
For Fiscal Years Ended September 30, 19A, 19B, and September 30, 19C

| Assets | Acquisition Date | Cost | Salvage | Depreciation Method | Estimated Life in Years | Depreciation Expense Year Ended September 30, | |
|---|---|---|---|---|---|---|---|
| | | | | | | 19B | 19C |
| Land A............ | October 1, 19A | $ (1) | N/A | N/A | N/A | N/A | N/A |
| Building A......... | October 1, 19A | (2) | $47,500 | Straight line | (3) | $14,000 | $ (4) |
| Land B............ | October 2, 19A | (5) | N/A | N/A | N/A | N/A | N/A |
| Building B ........ | Under construction | 210,000 to date | – | Straight line | Thirty | – | (6) |
| Donated equipment....... | October 2, 19A | (7) | 2,000 | 150% declining balance | Ten | (8) | (9) |
| Machinery A ...... | October 2, 19A | (10) | 5,500 | Sum-of-the-years'-digits | Ten | (11) | (12) |
| Machinery B ...... | October 1, 19B | (13) | – | Straight line | Fifteen | – | (14) |

N/A—Not applicable.

*g.* On October 1, 19B, Machinery B was acquired with a down payment of $4,000 and the remaining payments to be made in ten annual installments of $4,000 each beginning October 1, 19C. The prevailing interest rate was 8%. The following data were abstracted from present-value tables:

|  | *Present Value of $1 at 8%* | *Present Value of Annuity of $1 in Arrears at 8%* |
|---|---|---|
| 10 years | .463 | 6.710 |
| 11 years | .429 | 7.139 |
| 15 years | .315 | 8.559 |

*Required:*

Number your answer sheet from 1 to 14. For each numbered item on the preceding schedule, supply the correct amount next to the corresponding number on your answer sheet. Round each answer to the nearest dollar. *Do not recopy the schedule.* Show supporting computations in good form.

(AICPA adapted)

## Problem 13-11

Hotstrike Minerals Company bought mineral-bearing land for $90,000 which engineers say will yield 200,000 tons of economically removable ore; the land will have a value of $20,000 after the ore is removed.

To work the property, the company built structures and sheds on the site which cost $30,000; these will last 12 years and, because their use is confined to mining and it would be expensive to dismantle and move them, they will have no salvage value. Machinery which cost $30,000 was installed at the mine and added cost for installation was $6,000. This machinery should last 15 years; like the structures, usefulness of the machinery is confined to mines. Dismantling and removal costs when the property has been fully worked will approximately equal the value of the machinery at that time.

In the first year, Hotstrike removed only 10,000 tons of ore; however, production was doubled in the second year. It is expected that all of the removable ore will be extracted within eight years from the start of operations.

*Required:*

1. Prepare a schedule showing unit and total depletion and depreciation and book value for the first and second year of operation.
2. On the assumption that in the first year 90% of production was sold, and in the second year, the inventory carried over from the first year plus 90% of the second year's production was sold, give entries to record accumulated depreciation and depletion. To show the affect of these costs, make the offsetting debits to goods sold and inventory. Use accumulated accounts.

## Problem 13-12 (reviews Chapters 12 and 13)

For each of the following situations, (*a*) select the best response from those given, and (*b*) explain the basis for your choice showing computations where appropriate.

On July 1, 19A, Miller Mining, a calendar-year corporation, purchased the rights to a copper mine. Of the total purchase price, $2,800,000 was allocable to the copper. Estimated reserves were 800,000 tons of copper. Miller expects to extract and sell 10,000 tons of copper each month. Production began immediately.

The selling price is $25 per ton. Miller uses percentage depletion (15%) for tax purposes.

To aid production, Miller also purchased some new equipment on July 1, 19A. The equipment cost $76,000 and had an estimated useful life of eight years. However, after all the copper is removed from this mine, the equipment will be of no use to Miller and will be sold for an estimated $4,000. Use straight line depreciation.

1. If sales and production conform to expectations, what is Miller's depletion expense on this mine for financial accounting purposes for the calendar year, 19A?

   a. $105,000.                    c. $225,000.
   b. $210,000.                    d. $420,000.

2. If sales and production conform to expectations, what is Miller's depreciation expense on the new equipment for financial accounting purposes for the calendar year 19A?

   a. $4,500.                      c. $9,000.
   b. $5,400.                      d. $10,800.

3. Willard, Inc., purchased some equipment on January 2, 19A, for $24,000 (no salvage). Willard used straight-line depreciation based on a ten-year estimated life. During 19D, Willard decided that this equipment would be used only three more years and then replaced with a technologically superior model. What entry, if any, should Willard make as of January 1, 19D, to reflect this change?

   a. No entry.
   b. Debit an extraordinary item for $4,800 and credit accumulated depreciation for $4,800.
   c. Debit a prior period adjustment for $4,800 and credit accumulated depreciation for $4,800.
   d. Debit depreciation expense for $4,800 and credit accumulated depreciation for $4,800.

4. Gorch Company sold an item of plant equipment. Gorch received a noninterest-bearing note to be paid $1,000 per year for ten years. A fair rate of interest for this transaction is 8%. What discount should Gorch reflect on this transaction?

   a. Zero.                        c. $4,630.
   b. $3,290.                      d. $6,710.

5. Blacker Company exchanged a business car for a new car. The old car had an original cost of $3,500, an undepreciated cost of $1,600, and a market value of $2,000 when exchanged. In addition, Blacker paid $2,200 cash for the new car. The list price of the new car was $4,300. At what amount should the new car be recorded for financial accounting purposes?

   a. $3,500.                      c. $4,200.
   b. $3,800.                      d. $4,300.

Items 6 and 7 are based on the following information: On January 2, 19A, Kirk Manufacturing Company acquired some equipment from Quarter Corporation. The sale contract requires Kirk to make annual payments of $10,800 at the start of each year. The first payment was made on January 2, 19A, and no deposit was required. The equipment has an estimated useful life of 12 years with no anticipated salvage value. The prevailing interest rate for Kirk in similar financing arrangements is 8%.

6. At what amount should Kirk have capitalized this equipment?

   a. $77,100.                     c. $103,720.
   b. $81,390.                     d. $106,040.

7. If the equipment was capitalized at $80,000 and all other facts remain as originally stated, how much interest expense should Kirk have recorded in 19A?

a. Zero.                                           c. $7,200.
b. $6,400.                                         d. $9,600.

(AICPA adapted)

## Problem 13–13

Rocky Gravel Company mines and processes rock and gravel. It started in business on January 1, 19A, when it purchased the assets of another company. You have examined its financial statements at December 31, 19A, and have been requested to assist in planning and projecting operations for 19B. The company also wants to know the maximum amount by which notes payable to officers can be reduced at December 31, 19B.

The adjusted trial balance on December 31, 19A, was:

| | | |
|---|---:|---:|
| Cash | $ 17,000 | |
| Accounts receivable | 24,000 | |
| Mining properties | 60,000 | |
| Accumulated depletion | | $  3,000 |
| Equipment | 150,000 | |
| Accumulated depreciation | | 10,000 |
| Organization expense | 5,000 | |
| Accumulated amortization | | 1,000 |
| Accounts payable | | 12,000 |
| Federal income taxes payable | | 22,000 |
| Notes payable to officers | | 40,000 |
| Capital stock | | 100,000 |
| Premium on capital stock | | 34,000 |
| Sales | | 300,000 |
| Production costs (including depreciation and depletion) | 184,000 | |
| Administrative expense (including amortization and interest) | 60,000 | |
| Provision for federal income taxes | 22,000 | |
| | $522,000 | $522,000 |

You are able to develop the following information:

1. The total yards of material sold is expected to increase 10% in 19B, and the average sales price per cubic yard will be increased from $1.50 to $1.60.
2. The estimated recoverable reserves of rock and gravel were 4,000,000 cubic yards when the properties were purchased.
3. Production costs include direct labor of $110,000 of which $10,000 was attributed to inefficiencies in the early stages of operation. The union contract calls for 5% increases in hourly rates effective January 1, 19B. Production costs, other than depreciation, depletion and direct labor, will increase 4% in 19B.
4. Administrative expense, other than amortization and interest, will increase $8,000 in 19B.
5. The company has contracted for additional movable equipment costing $60,000 to be in production on July 1, 19B. This equipment will result in a direct labor hour savings of 8% as compared with the last half of 19A. The

new equipment will have a life of 20 years. All depreciation is computed on the straight-line method. The old equipment will continue in use.

6. The new equipment will be financed by a 20% down payment and a 6% three-year chattel mortgage. Interest and principal payments are due semiannually on June 30 and December 31, beginning December 31, 19B. The notes payable to officers are demand notes dated January 1, 19A, on which 6% interest is provided for and was paid on December 31, 19A.

7. Accounts receivable will increase in proportion to sales. No bad debts are anticipated. Accounts payable will remain substantially the same.

8. Percentage depletion allowable on rock and gravel is to be computed at 5% of gross income and is limited to 50% of net income before depletion.

9. It is customary in the rock and gravel business not to place any value on stockpiles of processed material which are awaiting sale.

10. Assume an income tax rate of 50%.

11. The company has decided to maintain a minimum cash balance of $20,000.

12. The client understands that the ethical considerations involved in preparing the following statements will be taken care of by your letter accompanying the statements. (Do not prepare the letter.)

*Required:*

1. Prepare a statement showing the net income projection for 19B.
2. Prepare a statement which will show cash flow projection for 19B and will indicate the amount that notes payable to officers can be reduced at December 31, 19B.
   Note: Round all amounts to the nearest $100. If the amount to be rounded is exactly $50, round to the next highest $100.

(AICPA adapted)

### Problem 13–14 (based on Appendix)

Equipment costing $100,000 has an estimated five-year life and $20,000 salvage value.

*Required:*

Using an 8% rate, prepare a depreciation table covering the entire life of the equipment assuming:

1. Annuity method.
2. Sinking fund method.

### Problem 13–15 (based on Appendix)

Machinery with an estimated life of ten years and a salvage value of 15% was acquired for $10,000. Using a 7% rate, what depreciation entries would be made at the end of each of the first two years assuming (*a*) the annuity method, and (*b*) the sinking fund method.

# Chapter 14

# Intangible Assets

In the broad sense, intangible assets are those properties, *without physical substance*, which are useful to an entity because of the special *rights* their ownership confers. The accounting classification of assets reports some intangibles as (*a*) current assets, such as cash, receivables, short-term investments and prepaid insurance; (*b*) funds and investments, such as bond sinking funds; bond investments, and equity securities; (*c*) other assets, such as noncurrent claims to cash; (*d*) operational or fixed assets, such as patents, franchises, and goodwill; and (*e*) deferred charges (i.e., long-term expense prepayments).

Since a number of different kinds of intangibles have been discussed in prior chapters, this chapter focuses on three different kinds of intangible assets, viz: (1) intangible operational assets, (2) deferred charges, and (3) cash surrender value of insurance and premium prepayments. Each will be considered separately.

The intangibles used in operating a business are generally classified for accounting purposes as *intangible* assets; other titles used are intangible fixed assets, intangible operational assets, or simply, intangibles. This classification includes intangible long-lived assets such as patents, copyrights, franchises, trademarks, trade names, secret processes, and goodwill. The primary characteristics of these intangible assets are (*a*) they are purchased from external sources or developed internally, (*b*) their ownership confers some exclusive rights, (*c*) they provide future benefits to operations, and (*d*) they are relatively long-lived. For example, a company that owns a patent used in making one of its products has a valuable intangible asset.[1]

Intangible assets may be further classified on the basis of—

1. Identifiability—separate indentifiability, such as a patent, or un-identifiability, such as goodwill.
2. Manner of acquisition—acquired from external sources by purchase,

---

[1] A patent held for speculative rather than for operational purposes would be classified as a noncurrent investment or other asset.

such as the purchase of a patent, or internally created, such as the development of a patent by the company research department.
3. Expected period of benefit—limited by law, contract, or economic factors, such as the 17-year legal life of a patent or indeterminate life, such as company goodwill.
4. Separability from the entire enterprise—salable without title, such as a trademark, or inseparable from the entity, such as goodwill.[2]

## ACCOUNTING FOR INTANGIBLE ASSETS

Accounting for intangible assets involves essentially the same problems, accounting principles, and procedures as for tangible property, plant, and equipment (discussed in Chapters 12 and 13); that is:

1. At acquisition—measuring and recording acquisition cost.
2. During period of use—measuring, recording, and reporting for expiration of the acquisition cost over the period of benefit. This process is usually referred to as *amortization*. In contrast, the process when applied to property, plant, and equipment is called depreciation; and when applied to natural resources, it is called depletion.
3. At disposition—recording and reporting disposition at sale, exchange, or end of economic useful life.

Accounting and reporting for intangible assets acquired after October 1970 is prescribed by *APB Opinion No. 17*, "Intangible Assets." Accounting for intangible assets acquired on or before October 30, 1970, may be accounted for in accordance with *APB Opinion No. 17* or *ARB No. 43*, Chapter 5 (otherwise this *ARB* was superseded by the *Opinion*).

Prior to *APB Opinion No. 17*, intangible assets were accounted for on the basis of *life expectancy*. Intangible assets having limited lives were identified as *Type A;* they were amortized over their estimated period of future use. Intangible assets having indeterminate lives were identified as *Type B;* and were not amortized until a realistic determination of useful life could be made. Often this determination was never made; hence, many Type B intangibles were carried indefinitely as assets. *Opinion No. 17*, among other things, stopped this practice by providing that:

> ... the value of intangible assets at any one date eventually disappears and that the recorded costs of intangible assets should be amortized by systematic charges to income over the periods estimated to be benefited. ... The cost of each type of intangible should be amortized on the basis of the estimated life of that specific asset. ... The period of amortization should not, however, exceed 40 years.

## MEASURING AND RECORDING INTANGIBLE ASSETS
## AT ACQUISITION

Intangible assets should be recorded at acquisition at their cash equivalent cost in conformity with the cost principle. When an intangible

---

[2] AICPA, "Intangible Assets," *APB Opinion No. 17* (New York, 1970), par. 10.

asset is acquired for some consideration other than cash, cost is determined by either the market value of the consideration given or by the fair market value of the right acquired, whichever is the more clearly evident. For example, if a patent is acquired by the issuance of capital stock, the cost of the patent may be determined as the fair market value of the shares of stock issued; or if the shares issued do not have an established market value consistent with the volume issued, then evidence of the fair market value of the patent should be sought as the measurement of cost in the transaction. If there is evidence of a definite cash offer to sell the patent, this offering price might be acceptable as a measure of the cost of the intangible asset. Supporting evidence of fair market value should be rather conclusive if the cost measured thereby is to be accepted as valid.

### Classification of the Cost of Intangible Assets

With intangibles, as in the case of property, plant, and equipment, costs must be carefully classified in the accounts to facilitate subsequent accounting. Proper accounting for cost requires that where two or more intangible assets are acquired at a single lump-sum purchase price, an allocation of the joint cost should be made to determine the cost basis of each intangible involved. Allocation of the cost of intangibles acquired in a "basket purchase" may be made by using the methods described for tangible assets, such as the relative sales value method.

## AMORTIZATION OF THE COST OF INTANGIBLE ASSETS

The cost of intangible assets should be *amortized* by systematic charges to expense over the estimated periods of useful life, just as the cost of tangible assets having a limited period of usefulness is depreciated. Capricious and arbitrary determination of the amount to be charged as expense from period to period distorts income and violates the *matching principle*. Neither is it desirable from the standpoint of income determination to accelerate the amortization process and write off the cost of intangibles substantially before the end of their usefulness. In the past, overconservatism frequently resulted in inappropriate accounting in these respects. Intangible assets normally are amortized by a direct credit to the asset account and a debit to expense.

In estimating the future useful life of an intangible asset the following factors should be considered:[3]

*a.* Legal, regulatory, or contractual provisions may limit the maximum useful life.

*b.* Provisions for renewal or extension may alter a specified limit on useful life.

---

[3] AICPA, "Intangible Assets," *APB Opinion No. 17* (New York, 1970), par. 27.

c. Effects of obsolescence, demand, competition, and other economic factors may reduce a useful life.

d. A useful life may parallel the service life expectancies of individuals or groups of employees.

e. Expected actions of competitors and others may restrict present competitive advantages.

f. An apparently unlimited useful life may in fact be indefinite and benefits cannot be reasonably projected.

g. An intangible asset may be a composite of many individual factors with varying effective lives.

The method of amortization should be systematic and should reflect over time the decline in economic service value of the intangible. Thus, straight-line, declining-balance charges, or increasing balance charges, may be appropriate. Perhaps reflecting precedent rather than economic realities, *APB Opinion No. 17* states that "the straight-line method of amortization—equal annual amounts—should be applied unless a company demonstrates that another systematic method is more appropriate." The *Opinion* also states that changes in amortization rates should be *prospective;* that is, the remaining unamortized cost should be amortized over the remaining life, but not to exceed 40 years after acquisition. Intangibles seldom, if ever, have a residual value.

## DISPOSITION OF INTANGIBLE ASSETS

When an intangible asset is sold, exchanged, or otherwise retired, the unamortized cost (or cost and accumulated amortization if separately recorded) must be removed from the accounts and a loss or gain recorded.

Because analysts often viewed intangibles as of questionable asset value and because of overconservatism, accounting practice in the past tended to encourage their arbitrary write-down to a nominal amount, either by lump sum in one period or over an unrealistically short estimated life. Contemporary accounting principles and practice do not support this arbitrary practice because it misstates net income and financial position. On this point, *APB Opinion No. 17* states that intangible assets "should not be written off in the period of acquisition" and "analysis of all factors should result in a reasonable estimate of the useful life. . . ."

On the other hand, in common with all assets, during the period of use, an estimate of value and future benefits of an intangible asset may indicate that the unamortized cost is above current fair value. Therefore, the unamortized cost should be significantly reduced in determining net income. In these unusual circumstances, an intangible asset should be written down to a realistic value and that value amortized over the estimated remaining useful life, not to exceed 40 years from date of acquisition (see *APB Opinion No. 17,* par. 31). Full disclosure is required by a note to the financial statement.

## IDENTIFIABLE INTANGIBLE ASSETS

Identifiable intangible assets are so designated because they can be specifically and separately identified from the enterprise itself. Examples are patents, copyrights, franchises, and trademarks (but not goodwill). They may be (a) acquired by purchase, or (b) developed internally. In either instance, they are recorded initially at cost, in conformance with the cost principle and amortized, as used, in conformance with the matching principle.

Because of the wide range of intangible assets, the procedures tend to vary somewhat in applying the foregoing principles and guidelines. In the next few paragraphs, we will discuss the specifically identifiable intangible assets commonly encountered in accounting.

### Patents

A patent is an exclusive grant by the U.S. Patent Office that enables the holder to use, manufacture, sell, and control the patent without interference or infringement by others. In reality the registration of the patent with the Patent Office is no guarantee of protection. Therefore, the patent is not conclusive until it has been successfully defended in court. For this reason it is generally held that the cost of *successful* court tests should be capitalized as a part of the cost of the patent.

The cost of a patent acquired by purchase is determined according to the *cost principle*, that is, cost is the cash or cash-equivalent value of the consideration given. Where the patent is produced in the company's own experimental laboratory, it must be accounted for as specified by FASB *Statement No. 2* as discussed on page 603.

Patents are granted for a period of 17 years. The useful life of most patents is for a shorter period due to new patents, improved models, substitutes, and general technological progress. Patent costs should be amortized over the useful life or legal life, whichever is shorter.

Patent amortizations may be credited directly to the Patent account or to an Accumulated Patent Amortization account; the former is the more common practice.

### Copyrights

A copyright is an exclusive right granted by the federal government to reproduce, publish, sell, and control a literary product or artistic work. The right is for a term of 28 years with provision for renewal for another 28 years. Many copyrights have value for a much shorter term, and their costs should be amortized over the shorter period. Often these costs are nominal and are written off in the period of expenditure.

### Franchises

A common type of franchise is a grant by some governmental unit for the use of public properties (or a monopoly to furnish services such as the telephone company) in a manner beneficial to the public. Franchises normally involve rights for a specified period; therefore, the cost of acquiring them should be amortized over that period.

In recent years another type of franchise has become rather common; that is, the granting of a right, by one company to another entity, to utilize a specific designation (such as Colonel Sanders Fried Chicken) subject to certain obligations agreed to by each party. The consideration paid for such a franchise should be recorded by the franchisee as an intangible asset and amortized over its expected useful life. When the era of franchising was in its heyday and fast food chains, motels, and similar franchised type businesses were expanding rapidly, there were some rather optimistic accounting practices adopted by some franchisors (i.e., grantors of franchises) to recognize revenue. Due to action by the practicing profession and the issuance of an AICPA publication, the abuses have been substantially curbed.[4]

## TRADEMARKS

Trademarks can be registered with the federal patent office to help prove ownership. Thus, names, symbols, or other devices providing distinctive identity for a product are afforded a degree of legal protection. Amounts paid or incurred directly in the acquisition, protection, expansion, registration, or defense of a trademark or trade name should be capitalized. Such capitalized balances are subject to amortization. Since they are amortizable for income tax purposes over periods of not less than five years, it is likely that many entities will use a similar amortization period for financial accounting purposes.

## UNIDENTIFIABLE INTANGIBLE ASSETS

Unidentifiable intangible assets are so designated because they result from a number of economic factors and cannot be separately identified from the enterprise. Examples are goodwill and going value. Unidentifiable intangible assets can be (a) purchased externally through the acquisition of a going business (not purchased singly), or (b) developed internally by excellent business practices, providing superior goods and services, promotion, and so on, all of which builds long-range customer appeal.

In contrast to identifiable intangible assets, unidentifiable intangibles are recorded and reported *only when acquired by purchase.* In this situation, the cost of unidentifiable intangibles usually can be realistically measured. *APB Opinion No. 17* states:

> The cost of unidentifiable intangible assets is measured by the difference between the cost of the group of assets or enterprise acquired and the sum of the assigned costs of individual tangible and identifiable intangible assets acquired less liabilities assumed.

---

[4] AICPA, *Accounting for Franchise Fee Revenue* (New York, 1973).

To illustrate, assume X Company purchased Y Company with the following results:

| | | |
|---|---:|---:|
| Purchase price ..................................................... | | $900,000 |
| Assets acquired from Y Company (at fair market value): | | |
| Tangible assets ................................................... | $890,000 | |
| Identifiable intangibles: | | |
| Patent ........................................................... | 14,000 | |
| Franchise ........................................................ | 16,000 | |
| Total ............................................................. | 920,000 | |
| Less: Liabilities of Y Company assumed ...................... | 120,000 | |
| Net tangible fair market values acquired ..................... | | 800,000 |
| Difference — unidentifiable intangibles (i.e., goodwill) ... | | $100,000 |

In contrast, unidentifiable intangibles developed internally by the company are *not* capitalized under generally accepted accounting principles because the efforts and continuing expenditures (i.e., promotion, cost of superior service, etc.) ordinarily are not distinguishable from the current expenses of operations. *APB Opinion No. 17* states that the costs of developing, maintaining, or restoring unidentifiable intangible assets "inherent in a continuing business and related to the enterprise as a whole — such as goodwill — should be deducted from income when incurred."

### Goodwill

Goodwill represents the potential of a business to earn above "normal" profits. Goodwill arises as a result of such factors as customer acceptance, efficiency of operation, reputation for dependability, quality of products, location, internal competences, and financial standing. The cost of goodwill represents a valuation placed upon the *above-normal earning capacity* of the firm. Conceptually, goodwill is the *present value* of the expected future excess earnings. Above-normal or excess earning capacity is the earning power of a firm above what is considered normal for the industry. For example, a firm consistently earning, say, 15% on total assets in an industry averaging a 10% return would have an excess earning capacity of 5%. The basic principle in accounting for goodwill initially is that it should be recorded at cost in conformance with the cost principle. In implementing this principle, goodwill should be recognized only when *actually paid for* in an arm's-length transaction. Consequently, goodwill should be recorded only when a business is purchased (or part of the business is purchased, as in the admission of a new partner) and the price paid exceeds the fair market value of all other tangible and identifiable intangible assets acquired less any debts assumed. Goodwill is recognized in the accounts only under these limited conditions so that an objective accounting will result and misrepresentation in financial statements will not occur. In the normal process of building up a business over time, an element of goodwill is developed.

This is frequently referred to as "internally developed goodwill," and in contrast to purchased goodwill is not properly reflected as an asset for two fundamental reasons: (1) directly there has been no disbursement of assets for it as is the case of other assets such as equipment; and (2) to the extent that expenses have been incurred that may have indirectly contributed to goodwill (such as promotion expenditures), they have been reflected in past income statements as expenses and any attempt to separate them out would be quite arbitrary.

*Amortization of Goodwill.* Accounting for purchased goodwill is controversial. One view is that it should not be amortized but should be reported as an intangible asset until there is definite evidence of its demise (such as failure to earn profits). Another view is that it should be deducted in full from capital at date of acquisition. Still another view is that it should be amortized over a realistic period during which the above-normal or superior earnings contemplated in the purchase decision are being realized.[5]

Some argue that there should be no amortization so long as profits are high since it is a permanent asset that has resale value. It is also argued that future profits and earnings per share should not be "penalized" because of a "good deal"; to amortize would penalize the excess profits which justified recording the goodwill in the first instance. The logical extension of this argument would be (*a*) to write it off directly to capital, or (*b*) to amortize goodwill only when profits fail to materialize.

The argument in favor of amortization is that purchased goodwill, like any other fixed asset, was acquired to generate earnings and, like other assets, should be amortized against those earnings. Thus, the conclusion is that goodwill should be amortized when the superior earnings are being realized. The argument continues that the purchase decision contemplated a specific amount of goodwill at the date of purchase which had already been developed. The purchaser envisioned a particularly profitable period in the future for which a price would be paid; that is, the cost of the *original goodwill purchased.* Acquired goodwill should be amortized over the approximate period of excess earnings contemplated in the purchase decision. Obviously, a competent management will continue to build *new* layers of internally generated goodwill the cost of which will flow through the income statements as current operating expenses. Thus, there is the concept that purchased goodwill

---

[5] It is sometimes alleged that goodwill can be negative. Cases cited are when the book value of assets purchased are in excess of the purchase price, or alternatively where the fair market value of the individual assets is in excess of the purchase price. In the opinion of the authors this reasoning flies in the face of both reality and concept. In the first instance book value has no relationship to market value, and in the second instance the fair value of a package of assets is the cash consideration given (or its equivalent). It is difficult to perceive, as a practical matter, an informed seller disposing of a group of assets for an amount substantially less than he could derive for them piecemeal. The instances cited usually make an absurd assumption or there is an obvious breakdown in the measurement process. There are situations where a credit may emerge; however, it should be identified for what it is and not carelessly labeled "negative goodwill." *APB Opinion No. 17* requires revaluation of the tangible and intangible identifiable assets acquired so that no negative goodwill will be recognized.

represents an established layer; the purchase cost of it should be allocated to the revenues generated by that particular layer.

These arguments were resolved, as far as current practice is concerned, by *APB Opinion No. 17*. It requires that goodwill be amortized by systematic charges each period, using the straight-line method, "unless a company demonstrates that another systematic method is more appropriate." The amortization period must be the estimated useful life, but not more than 40 years from date of purchase.

Amortization of goodwill is not permitted for income tax purposes – it does not cause a tax timing difference; therefore, allocation of income taxes is inappropriate.

*Estimating Goodwill.* In negotiations relating to the purchase or sale of a business the accountant may be requested to assist in valuing goodwill. *However, in such circumstances goodwill obviously is the result of bargaining between the purchaser and seller.* Computations based upon an analysis of asset values and income potentials frequently are useful in such negotiations since goodwill relates to the excess earning capacity of the business. In such analyses it must be emphasized that *future earning potentials* rather than past earnings are significant. Past earnings, properly adjusted, may provide a sound basis for estimating future potentials. In estimating future earnings, the earnings history of the firm should be studied. As a basis for estimating future earnings the following steps may be suggested:

1. Select for study a series of past years' earnings which appears to be most representative of usual operations and indicative of future expectations. A period of five years frequently is used. The period of years should be long enough to reveal the pattern of earnings fluctuations experienced by the company.
2. Adjust these past earnings (a) by eliminating all extraneous and nonrecurring gains and losses; (b) for changes in accounting, such as depreciation estimates and methods; (c) for changes which are expected to occur in salaries; and (d) for any other changes in costs, expenses, and revenue which are expected to occur in the future.
3. Analyze the trend and uniformity of past earnings. Even though past earnings have been above normal, any observed downward trend in the immediate past may indicate the disappearance of above-normal earning capacity. Such a downward trend would largely negate any basis for goodwill value.
4. On the basis of the above analysis project the future earnings and assets.

Within the above framework several approaches in *estimating* the value of goodwill are discussed below. To illustrate, assume that on January 1, 1977, it is desired to estimate the goodwill for Company X and that the data in Exhibit 14–1 are available.

Assume after careful analysis of the data in Exhibit 14–1, appraisal of the assets, and other pertinent factors the following estimates are derived:

**EXHIBIT 14-1**
**Estimation of Goodwill**

| Year | Net Income (adjusted for nonrecurring items) | Book Values | | |
|---|---|---|---|---|
| | | Total Assets | Liabili-ties | Owners' Equity |
| 1972 | $18,000 | $162,000 | $ 82,000 | $ 80,000 |
| 1973 | 17,000 | 172,000 | 90,000 | 82,000 |
| 1974 | 19,000 | 190,000 | 105,000 | 85,000 |
| 1975 | 19,000 | 187,000 | 90,000 | 97,000 |
| 1976 | 21,000 | 200,000 | 98,000 | 102,000 |
| Total | $94,000 | $911,000 | $465,000 | $446,000 |
| Five-year average | $18,800 | $182,200 | $ 93,000 | $ 89,200 |

Average annual earnings expected................................................. $ 20,000
Estimated average future value of net assets (exclusive of
goodwill) at appraised values less liabilities to be assumed ......... 100,000

We will illustrate four rather unsophisticated methods followed by a conceptually sound one.

CAPITALIZATION OF EARNINGS.  The expected earnings may be capitalized at a "normal" rate of return for the industry in order to estimate the total asset value. The difference between this value (total asset value implied) and the average assets expected (exclusive of goodwill) may be considered as an unsophisticated representation of goodwill. To illustrate, assuming a "normal" rate of return of 12%, goodwill for Company X may be computed as follows:

Average annual earnings expected.............................. $20,000
Normal rate of return for the industry .......................... 12%
Total asset value implied ($20,000 ÷ 12%) ..................... $166,667
Average assets expected (exclusive of goodwill) ........... 100,000
Estimated goodwill ...................................... $ 66,667

    Total Valuation Including Goodwill ($100,000 +
    $66,667) ...................................................... $166,667

CAPITALIZATION OF EXCESS EARNINGS.  The preceding method may be deficient in that it does not recognize excess earnings as a special factor. Capitalization of excess earnings requires the selection of a special rate to be applied to such earnings. The special capitalization rate should represent the planned annual rate of recovery of investment in the intangible as a result of excess earnings. The special rate should be higher than the normal rate because of the greater risk of not earning above the "normal" rate. Obviously, the greater the risk the higher the rate should be.

To illustrate the computation for Company X, assume a normal rate on assets of 12% and a capitalization rate for the excess earnings of 20%.

| | |
|---|---:|
| Average annual earnings expected................................ | $20,000 |
| Return on average assets expected (exclusive of goodwill) at the normal rate ($100,000 × 12%) ......................... | 12,000 |
| Excess earnings ............................................. | $ 8,000 |
| Goodwill: Excess earnings capitalized at 20% ($8,000 ÷ 20%)........................................................... | $ 40,000 |
| Total Valuation Including Goodwill ($100,000 + $40,000) ..................................................... | $140,000 |

YEAR'S PURCHASE OF AVERAGE EXCESS EARNINGS. The goodwill may be estimated more directly by multiplying the estimated excess earnings by the number of years over which the investor expects to recover his or her investment in goodwill from the above-normal earnings of the business. To illustrate, assume the expected period of recovery is six years:

| | |
|---|---:|
| Excess earnings (computed above) ........................... | $ 8,000 |
| Expected period of recovery..................................... | 6 years |
| Estimated goodwill ................................................. | $ 48,000 |
| Total Valuation Including Goodwill ($100,000 + $48,000)......... | $148,000 |

Obviously, there is implicit in this method an amortization period for goodwill of six years.

OTHER UNSOPHISTICATED METHODS OF ESTIMATING GOODWILL VALUE. Other methods are used in estimating goodwill value. Generally, any method which does not take into account the expectation of above-normal earnings is not recommended. For example, the following method is sometimes used:

**Years' Purchase of Average Earnings**

| | |
|---|---:|
| Average annual earnings expected............................... | $ 20,000 |
| Four years' purchase (multiply by 4) ........................... | × 4 |
| Estimated goodwill ................................................. | $ 80,000 |
| Total Valuation Including Goodwill ($100,000 + $80,000)......... | $180,000 |

Under this method some goodwill would be estimated even though below-normal earnings were experienced. For example, if average annual earnings expected were $7,000, an estimated goodwill of $28,000 would result despite the fact that annual earnings were $5,000 *below* normal.

**Present Value Estimation of Goodwill**

A conceptually sound approach to estimating (and amortizing) goodwill is to determine the *present value of the future excess earnings*

*purchased.* To illustrate, assume for the above example that the negotiations implied the purchase of future excess earnings for ten years in
addition to the identifiable assets and that the expected earnings rate
was 8%. Computation of the implied goodwill would be as follows:

| | | |
|---|---|---|
| Average annual expected earnings purchased | | |
| (estimated for ten years) ..................................... | $20,000 | |
| Average assets expected (at fair value).......................... | | $100,000 |
| Normal expected annual earnings expected | | |
| ($100,000 × 8%) ..................................... | 8,000 | |
| Excess annual earnings for ten years ..................... | $12,000 | |
| Goodwill: | | |
| Present value of future earnings for $n = 10$, $i = 8\%$: | | |
| $12,000 × $P_{n=10,i=8}$ (from Table 6–4) | | |
| $12,000 × 6,7101 = | | 80,521 |
| Total Valuation Including Goodwill ................ | | $180,521 |

The *purchase* at $180,521 would be recorded as follows:

| | | |
|---|---|---|
| Identifiable assets (detailed)....................................... | 100,000* | |
| Goodwill ................................................................. | 80,521 | |
| Cash (or other consideration) ............................. | | 180,521 |
| * At fair value. | | |

Conceptually, the goodwill would then be amortized over the ten years
as shown in Exhibit 14–2.

Of course, straight-line amortization over the ten-year period could be
utilized; however, the present value approach as illustrated above conceptually is in harmony with the nature of goodwill.

The recording and reporting of purchased goodwill and its amortization is a central issue in mergers and consolidations; a topic discussed
in Chapter 18.

**EXHIBIT 14–2**
**Goodwill Amortized on Present Value Basis**

| Year | Annual Excess Earnings (a) | (8%) Return on Goodwill Investment (b) | Goodwill Amortization | | Goodwill Investment Carrying Value (e) |
|---|---|---|---|---|---|
| | | | Expense (dr) (c) | Goodwill (cr) (d) | |
| Start | | | | | $80,521 |
| 1......... | $12,000 | $6,442 | $ 5,558 | $ 5,558 | 74,963 |
| 2......... | 12,000 | 5,997 | 6,003 | 6,003 | 68,960 |
| 3......... | 12,000 | 5,517 | 6,483 | 6,483 | 62,477 |
| 4......... | 12,000 | 4,998 | 7,002 | 7,002 | 55,475 |
| 5......... | 12,000 | 4,438 | 7,562 | 7,562 | 47,913 |
| 6......... | 12,000 | 3,833 | 8,167 | 8,167 | 39,746 |
| 7......... | 12,000 | 3,180 | 8,820 | 8,820 | 30,926 |
| 8......... | 12,000 | 2,474 | 9,526 | 9,526 | 21,400 |
| 9......... | 12,000 | 1,712 | 10,288 | 10,288 | 11,112 |
| 10......... | 12,000 | 888* | 11,112 | 11,112 | -0- |

* Rounding error—$1.
(a) Projected annual excess earnings.
(b) 8% of previous goodwill balance ($80,521 × 8% = $6,440, etc.).
(c) and (d)  Column (a) minus column (b).
(e) Previous balance minus column (d).

## GOING VALUE

Going value (also known as going-concern value) is closely akin to goodwill but does not appear as such on the financial records of businesses.[6] It has greater importance in the income tax field than in financial reporting. Despite the fact that it does not appear on the financial statement, it constitutes a substantial asset that should be considered in negotiating the price of a business to be bought or sold. Going value's chief distinction from goodwill is that the latter is associated with unusual profitability, whereas going value is associated with the value of the effort and cost to start a business. An ordinary profitable business (or even one temporarily reporting losses) may have going value.

Like goodwill, going value is an intangible asset. It may be reflected in the financial statements as part of a lump-sum amount representing the excess of a purchase price over the values of the underlying tangible and intangible assets acquired (i.e., as a part designated as goodwill). As an alternative to buying a going business, persons planning to enter a line of activity have the alternative of starting a new entity from scratch, thus incurring numerous start-up costs. Leading authorities on engineering valuation have presented methods of estimating going value based on (1) revenues, costs, and net operating losses; and (2) return on investment foregone during a representative start-up period. These costs and economic losses would be required to bring the same or a similar new business from start-up status to a stage where the business would earn the same rate of return as the industry average.

Several recent court decisions have taken cognizance of going value; one held that the buyer of a going business must recognize the element of going value as an intangible asset and assign to it a portion of the lump-sum purchase price. The Tax Court allowed a deduction for the loss of the tax basis for going-concern value at the time that one plant was closed and manufacturing operations were transferred to another plant.

## DEFERRED CHARGES

Deferred charges are intangibles and are closely related to intangible assets as defined in the preceding section of this chapter. Whereas intangible assets derive value based on *rights,* deferred charges derive asset value because they are long-term prepayments of expenses that will contribute to the production of future revenues. Also, deferred charges are akin to prepaid expenses (a short-term intangible reported as a current asset). Examples of deferred charges are bond issue costs, organization costs, machinery rearrangement costs, long-term prepaid insurance premiums, and prepaid leasehold costs.

A special item, debit balances, arising from interperiod income tax allocation are reported under this classification.

Deferred charges are amortized over the future period that they will

---

[6] See the subsequent discussion of organization costs which is a related issue.

contribute to the generation of future revenues. The 40-year rule, specified in *APB Opinion No. 17*, does not apply to deferred charges; however, they seldom, if ever, have lives that long.

In the next few paragraphs we will discuss the deferred charges usually encountered in accounting.

## Research and Development Costs

Research and development costs, commonly called R & D, have become an increasingly important factor in modern industry. R & D departments are responsible for the development of new products, improvement of present products, testing of competitors' products, development of new or improved manufacturing methods, and similar functions.

Accounting practice for to R & D costs became quite varied over the years. Some businesses expensed all R & D expenditures in the period they were incurred. At an opposite extreme, others capitalized practically all R & D expenditures, followed by their amortization. In between were various practices, including selective capitalization of costs related to successful projects with subsequent amortization at varying rates. This hodge-podge practice received the early attention of the Financial Accounting Standards Board and resulted in the issuance of FASB *Statement No. 2* (October 1974), titled "Accounting for Research and Development Costs."

The main provisions of this *Statement* are as follows:

1. All R & D costs covered by the statement shall be charged to expense when incurred.[7] Stated another way, R & D expenditures (except for item 3 below) must not be capitalized.
2. Financial statements must disclose *total* R & D costs charged to expense in each period for which an income statement is presented.
3. It does not apply to R & D costs where work is done for others under contract. Also, exceptions were made for certain government-regulated entities. In other words, in these areas, R & D costs can be charged to an asset account when incurred.
4. The *Statement* became effective for fiscal years beginning on or after January 1, 1975. Those entities who had capitalized R & D costs on that date are to clear their books by means of prior period adjustments.

The statement represents a practical solution to a critical problem.

---

[7] In the context of the standard, *research* is planned activities aimed at discovery of new knowledge with the hope it will be useful in developing new products, processes, or services, or in bringing about significant improvement to existing products or processes. *Development* is the translation of research findings into a plan or design for a new product or process or for a significant improvement to an existing one, whether intended for sale or use. It includes conceptual formulation, design, and testing of product alternatives, construction of prototypes, and operation of pilot plants. It excludes routine or periodic alterations to existing products, manufacturing processes, and other on-going operations, even though these alterations may represent improvements. It also excludes market research and testing activities.

Careful study indicated that it was difficult to establish criteria for deferment of R & D costs and that companies were reporting their R & D expenditures in a variety of ways (the majority expensing them).[8]

One of the chief aims of the FASB and its predecessors and of the SEC is to reduce the variety of ways in which essentially similar factual situations can be reported. By mandating that all R & D costs be expensed when incurred, the FASB swept away the wide range of alternatives in this area. From an income statement standpoint, long-run implementation of the standard sometimes makes little difference. The amount of R & D expense will be about the same whether there is immediate expensing or temporary deferment of some costs and subsequent amortization of them.

Critics of the standard argue that while its long-run income statement effects are often minimal, from a balance sheet standpoint it is hard to defend. In essence the standard requires companies to report that none of their R & D expenditures has future benefit since no intangible asset related to R & D costs can appear on the balance sheet. For successful companies operating in high-technology industries such as electronics, chemicals, and aero-space, to name but a few, this means that some of their most valuable assets (from an intrinsic if not from a cost standpoint) are not even reported. Whether this could be corrected, since the assets do not appear on the basic statements, if current value statements were to be prepared is a good question. Defenders of the standard rejoin that informed analysts and others are well aware that successful, high-technology companies have assets resulting from R & D and that the standard was not aimed at such companies; it was aimed at companies inclined to exaggerate the value of assets associated with their R & D efforts. Regardless of who has the better side of the argument, the standard is operational and seemingly has the strong support of the practicing profession.

## Organization Costs

Expenditures incurred in the original incorporation and promotion of a business enterprise, such as legal fees, state incorporation fees, stock certificate costs, stamp taxes, reasonable underwriting costs, and office expenses incident to organizing, are capitalized as organization costs on the theory that such costs benefit each succeeding year; hence, to charge them off as a cost in the first year of operation would result in an incorrect matching of cost and revenue. Since the life of a corporation generally is indefinite, the length of the period which will receive the benefits of this cost is usually indeterminate. For this reason, and because the recognition of organization costs as a business asset depends entirely upon intangible values presumably attached to the corporate form of organization for the particular business, organization expenses generally are amortized over an arbitrarily selected short period. This practice

---

[8] Oscar S. Gellein and Maurice S. Newman, "Accounting for R & D Expenditures" *Accounting Research Study No. 14* (New York: AICPA, 1973).

is encouraged by the tax rules which permit the corporation to amortize most organization costs ratably over such period as the company desires as long as that period is not less than five years.

A troublesome problem is posed in respect to *stock issue costs;* that is, the costs of printing stock certificates, attorney fees related directly to the issue, commissions paid for sale, and accountants' fees (such as the cost of filing with the SEC). Three approaches in accounting for these particular costs are found in practice:

1. *Charge such costs to organization costs.* Although this is a fairly common practice, many accountants feel that it is conceptually deficient.
2. *Offset such costs against the sales price of the stock.* Under this practice they would be included in the determination of stock discount or premium. In this alternative such costs would not be amortized against revenue. It is conceptually deficient since it may create a recorded discount on stock that does not agree with the amount paid in by the shareholder. This approach appears to be the most widely used primarily because (*a*) frequently the costs are not separable from the issue transaction, and (*b*) such costs benefit the entire life of the corporation.
3. *Charge such costs to a deferred charge and amortize them similar to organization costs.* This approach is conceptually sound providing such costs are amortized over the useful life of the "asset." As a practical matter they generally are amortized over a short period similar to organization costs.

## Leaseholds

The right of a lessee to use real property under the terms of a lease agreement is known as a *leasehold.*[9] A lease agreement calls for periodic rent and may require, in addition, the down payment of a lump sum. The lump sum is a deferred charge (leasehold) which should be amortized over the life of the lease. Amortization may be (*a*) on a straight-line basis or preferably (*b*) on a present value basis. The amortization period is the life of the lease; options to renew the lease are usually disregarded in determining the amortization period. Procedurally, the down payment should be debited to a deferred charge account labeled Leaseholds; the amortization is recorded as a credit to this account and as a debit to Rental Expense.

To illustrate, assume a property owner is leasing a building for $8,000 per year payable at the start of each year. As a result of bargaining between the lessor (owner) and lessee (tenant), instead of annual rentals, a lump-sum payment at the start of the upcoming year of $40,801.60 would constitute the total rent for six years. This arrangement could be accounted for by each party on a *straight-line* amortization basis as follows:

---

[9] These discussions assume operating leases; other types of leases are discussed in Chapter 23.

| *Lessor* | *Lessee* |
|---|---|

1. At date of prepayment:

| | | | | |
|---|---|---|---|---|
| Cash .................. | 40,801.60 | Prepaid rent expense | | |
| Prepaid rent | | (or leasehold) ............ | 40,801.60 | |
| revenue ...... | 40,801.60 | Cash........................ | | 40,801.60 |

2. Amortization each year for six years (straight line):

| | | | | |
|---|---|---|---|---|
| Prepaid rent | | Rent expense ............... | 6,800.27 | |
| revenue ............ | 6,800.27 | Prepaid rent | | |
| Rent | | expense ............... | | 6,800.27 |
| revenue ...... | 6,800.27 | | | |
| ($40,801.60 ÷ 6 = $6,800.27) | | | | |

The straight-line approach does not consider the time value of money; hence, the rent revenue (or expense) is misstated and interest as a factor is not recognized. Theoretically, the leasehold and the amortization (on both sets of books) should be accounted for on a present value basis. The advance payment represents the present value of an annuity of $8,000 for six periods. Since the first payment (rent) is due immediately there is an *annuity due* which may be schematically demonstrated as follows:

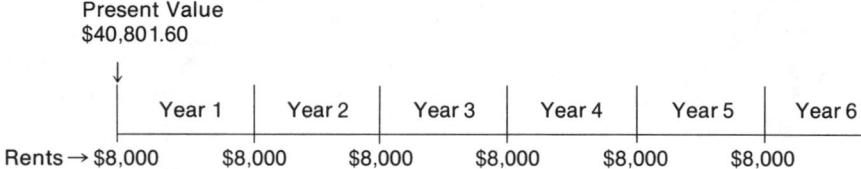

The agreed rate of interest between the parties was 7%; therefore, the advance payment was computed as follows:

Present value of annuity due for six rents at 7%:
That is, an annuity due is equivalent to the $(n - 1$ rents$)$ +
1 value for an ordinary annuity Table 6–4, 7%, 5 rents

|  |  |
|---|---:|
| = 4.1002 + 1 = | 5.1002 |
| Multiply by annual rental ....................................................... | × $8,000 |
| Lump-Sum Payment, (if made now) ........................................... | $40,801.60 |

Determination of (1) the periodic amortization using the present value approach, and (2) the related accounting entries are best accomplished for either the lessor or lessee by development of an amortization table as shown in Exhibit 14–3. Since the annual rent is due at the beginning of each period, you should observe that there would be no interest in the sixth year as reflected in the above schematic for the annuity due.

The interest computations in Exhibit 14–3 reflect the characteristics of an annuity due, that is, the *rents* are assumed to be paid at the beginning of each period.

Amortization entries for the lessor and lessee for the first, second, and

**EXHIBIT 14–3**
**Leasehold Amortization Table (present value basis) at $8,000 Annual Rental\***

| Year-End | Rent | Computation of Interest | Leasehold Amortization | Leasehold Balance |
|---|---|---|---|---|
| | | | | $40,801.60† |
| 1 ...... | $8,000 | $(40,801.60−$8,000)7% = $2,296.11 | $5,703.89‡ | 35,097.71§ |
| 2 ...... | 8,000 | (35,097.71− 8,000)7% = 1,896.84 | 6,103.16 | 28,994.55 |
| 3 ...... | 8,000 | (28,994.55− 8,000)7% = 1,469.62 | 6,530.38 | 22,464.17 |
| 4 ...... | 8,000 | (22,464.17− 8,000)7% = 1,012.49 | 6,987.51 | 15,476.66 |
| 5 ...... | 8,000 | (15,476.66− 8,000)7% = 523.34 | 7,476.66 | 8,000.00 |
| 6 ...... | 8,000 | | 8,000.00 | -0- |

†Present value of future rents as computed above.
‡$8,000.00 − $2,296.11 = $5,703.89.
§$40,801.60 − $5,703.89 = $35,097.71.
* Alternatively the table could have been started as follows with the same results:

| Period | Rent | Interest | Amortization | Balance |
|---|---|---|---|---|
| Balance ........................ | | | | $40,801.60 |
| Start ............................. | 8,000 | | | 32,801.60 |
| 1.................................... | 8,000 | $32,801.60 × 7% = $2,296.11 | $5,703.89 | 27,097.71 |
| 2.................................... | 8,000 | 27,097.71 × 7% = 1,896.84 | 6,103.16 | 20,994.55 |
| Etc. ............................. | | | | |

sixth years are shown in the tabulation below assuming the fiscal and lease years coincide. Entries for the years not shown would be made in accordance with the amortization table shown in Exhibit 14–3.

|  | *Lessor* | | *Lessee* | |
|---|---|---|---|---|
| **Year 1:** | | | | |

**At start of lease:**

| | Lessor | | Lessee | |
|---|---|---|---|---|
| Cash.................. | 40,801.60 | | Leasehold ............... 40,801.60 | |
| Deferred | | | Cash.................. | 40,801.60 |
| rent | | | | |
| revenue ... | | 40,801.60 | | |

**At end of first year:**

| | | | | |
|---|---|---|---|---|
| Deferred rent | | | Rent expense ......... 8,000.00* | |
| revenue ......... | 5,703.89 | | Interest | |
| Interest | | | revenue ......... | 2,296.11* |
| expense ......... | 2,296.11 | | Leasehold .... | 5,703.89 |
| Rent | | | | |
| revenue ... | | 8,000.00* | | |

**Year 2:**

| | | | | |
|---|---|---|---|---|
| Deferred rent | | | Rent expense ......... 8,000.00 | |
| revenue ......... | 6,103.16 | | Interest | |
| Interest | | | revenue ......... | 1,896.84 |
| expense ......... | 1,896.84 | | Leasehold ......... | 6,103.16 |
| Rent | | | | |
| revenue ... | | 8,000.00 | | |

**Year 6:**

| | | | | |
|---|---|---|---|---|
| Deferred rent | | | Rent expense ......... 8,000.00 | |
| revenue ......... | 8,000.00 | | Interest | |
| Interest | | | revenue ......... | -0- |
| expense ......... | -0- | | Leasehold ......... | 8,000.00 |
| Rent | | | | |
| revenue ... | | 8,000.00 | | |

* These two amounts generally are offset for practical reasons.

Clearly the present value (scientific) approach provides more realistic values for the balance sheet and the income statement than does the straight-line approach. The present value approach derives rental and interest values that represent the economic essence of the lease contract. Obviously, the difference between the present value of $40,801.60 and the $48,000.00 that would have been paid is due to the time value of money agreed to by the two parties.

## DEVELOPMENT STAGE COMPANIES

The subject of accounting for companies in the development stage is closely akin to deferred charges because such companies in the past deferred a wide range of costs. This was done because, during the development stage, they incur high start-up costs and generally have little or no revenues against which they can be matched.

Because of the lack of guidelines and the wide variety of practices, the FASB issued *Statement of Financial Accounting Standards No. 7,* "Accounting and Reporting by Development Stage Companies" (June 1975).

The *Statement* defines development stage companies essentially as follows:

> An enterprise shall be considered to be in the development stage if it is devoting substantially all of its efforts to establishing a new business and either of the following conditions exists: (a) planned principal operations have not commenced, or (b) planned principal operations have commenced but there has been no significant revenue therefrom. A development stage enterprise will typically be devoting most of its efforts to activities such as financial planning; raising capital; exploring for natural resources; developing natural resources; research and development; establishing sources of supply; acquiring property, plant, or other operating assets, such as mineral rights; recruiting and training personnel; developing markets; and starting up production.

Prior to the issuance of *Statement No. 7,* the accounting practices of development stage companies included the following which many accountants felt did not accord with generally accepted accounting principles: (*a*) deferral of various types of costs without regard to their recoverability; (*b*) issuance of special types of statements, including statements of assets and unrecovered preoperating costs; and (*c*) other practices, in the view of many far outside the purview of generally accepted accounting principles.

To correct these abuses, *Statement No. 7* requires development stage companies to present financial statements prepared on the same basis as other businesses; special reporting formats are unacceptable. Capitalization and deferral of costs is subject to the same assessment of future benefit and recoverability applicable to established businesses. Thus, the statement specifies that a development stage company is required to prepare basic statements and provide additional disclosure as follows:

> a. A balance sheet, including any cumulative net losses reported with a

descriptive caption such as "deficit accumulated during the development stage" in the owners' equity section.

b. An income statement, showing amounts of revenue and expenses for each period covered by the income statement and, in addition, cumulative amounts from the enterprise's inception.

c. A statement of changes in financial position, showing the sources and uses of financial resources for each period for which an income statement is presented and, in addition, cumulative amounts from the enterprise's inception.

d. A statement of stockholders' equity, showing from the enterprise's inception for each issuance:
   1. date and number of shares issued for cash or other consideration.
   2. dollar amounts (per share or other equity unit) assigned to consideration received for securities.
   3. where there is noncash consideration, its nature and the basis of determining amounts.[10]

The *Statement* also requires that the financial statements be *specifically identified* as those of a development stage enterprise and include a description of the nature of the development stage in which the enterprise is engaged.

## INSURANCE

Practically all businesses carry one or more kinds of insurance. Insurance requires prepayment of the premium, at which time an asset having intangible characteristics is created. Depending on the type and length of time covered, the prepaid premium may represent (a) a current asset (i.e., short-term prepayments), (b) a long-term investment (i.e., cash surrender value of life insurance policies), or (c) a deferred charge (i.e., long-term prepayments).

Although there are many different kinds of insurance, the usual kinds carried by businesses include (a) liability insurance, (b) casualty insurance, and (c) life insurance on key executives.

### Liability Insurance

Liability insurance involves a contract whereby the insurance company, in consideration of a specified premium, assumes an obligation to assume liabilities to third parties that arise from specified events such as damages sought by a customer for injuries in an accident on company premises. The premium typically is paid in advance for periods of one to five years—the longer the period, the less the prorated premium. Prepaid premiums represent an intangible asset. To illustrate, assume on January 1, 19A, that Company B paid a $2,500 five-year premium for a liability insurance contract. The accounting and reporting for 19A would be as follows:

---

[10] Adapted from FASB *Statement of Financial Accounting Standards No. 7*, "Accounting and Reporting by Development Stage Enterprises" (Stanford, Conn.: FASB, June 1975), par. 11.

*Entries:*

January 1, 19A – insurance premium paid:

| | | |
|---|---|---|
| Prepaid insurance | 2,500 | |
|     Cash | | 2,500 |

December 31, 19A – adjusting entry:

| | | |
|---|---|---|
| Insurance expense | 500 | |
|     Prepaid insurance | | 500 |

*Reporting at December 31, 19A:*

Income Statement:

| | |
|---|---|
|     Insurance expense | 500 |

Balance Sheet:

| | |
|---|---|
| Current Assets: | |
|     Prepaid insurance | 500 |
| Deferred Charges: | |
|     Prepaid insurance, long term | 1,500 |

## Casualty Insurance

Casualty insurance involves a contract whereby the insurance company in consideration for a premium payment assumes an obligation under certain circumstances to reimburse the policyholder an amount not exceeding the *fair market value* (at date of loss) of the property lost due to storm, fire, and so on, as specified in the policy. The indemnity in no case exceeds the amount stipulated in the contract, that is, the *face* of the policy.

The great diversity in the forms of policies and the legal status of their provisions in the past caused most states to adopt a standard policy. The companies are allowed a certain degree of flexibility in varying the terms of the standard policy by attaching "riders" (standardized paragraphs).

The premium, a charge per $100 of insurance carried, is usually computed on a standard basis, depending upon the nature of the asset insured. For example, in the case of insurance on a building, the premium is adjusted for such things as type of construction, kind of roof, types of flues, occupancy by owner or tenant, space rented, office in the building, and location.

When a policy is canceled at the request of the insurance company, the insured is entitled to a refund of a pro rata portion of the premium, which covers the unexpired time. If the cancellation is requested by the insured, the premium to be returned is computed by reference to a short-rate table which refunds less than the pro rata portion of the premium. For example, one state's schedule provides that the insured who pays 2½ times the annual rate for a three-year policy may recover 60% of the premium if he or she has the policy canceled at the end of one year.

## Coinsurance

To encourage adequate insurance coverage many policies carry a *coinsurance clause* which provides that if the property is insured for less than a stated percentage (often 80%) of its fair market value at the time of a loss, the insured is a *coinsurer* with the insurance company. As a coinsurer the insured must stand a share of any loss. The share of a loss, when there is a coinsurance clause, is determined by application of the policy provision that the insurance company will pay the *lower* of the three following amounts:

1. Face of the policy.
2. Fair market value of the loss.
3. Coinsurance indemnity (determined by formula).

To illustrate the effect of a coinsurance clause, assume the following for Company C:

1. Policy on casualties – face, $7,000; coinsurance clause, 80%.
2. Casualty – fire, fair market value of the loss at date of fire (there was a partial loss of the property), $5,680.
3. Fair market value of the property immediately prior to the fire, $10,000.

Computation of the coinsurance indemnity (by formula):

$$\frac{\text{Face of Policy}}{.80 \times \text{Fair Market Value of Property at Date of Casualty}} \times \begin{array}{l}\text{Fair market} \\ \text{Value of the} \\ \text{Loss}\end{array} = \text{Coinsurance Indemnity}$$

$$\frac{\$7,000}{.80 \times \$10,000} \times \$5,680 = \$4,970$$

Thus, the insurance company would reimburse the insured for $4,970 because it is lower than either the face of the policy ($7,000) and the amount of the loss ($5,680).

Application of this rule is further illustrated by the cases shown in Exhibit 14–4 (assuming in each case that the policy contains an 80% coinsurance clause).

**EXHIBIT 14–4**
**Indemnity under Coinsurance**

|  | Case 1 (when formula is lowest) | Case 2 (when loss is lowest) | Case 3 (when policy is lowest) |
|---|---|---|---|
| Fair market value of property at date of loss | $10,000 | $10,000 | $10,000 |
| Face of policy carried by insured | 7,000 | 8,800 | 6,000 |
| Fair market value of loss | 5,680 | 6,000 | 10,000 |
| Maximum indemnity (formula) | 4,970* | 6,600† | 7,500‡ |
| Actual indemnity payable | 4,970 | 6,000 | 6,000 |

\* Computed above.

† $\dfrac{8,800}{.80 \times \$10,000} \times \$6,000 = \$6,600.$

‡ $\dfrac{\$6,000}{.80 \times \$10,000} \times \$10,000 = \$7,500.$

## Blanket Policy

When a company takes out a fire insurance policy covering several items of property (frequently called a blanket policy), the policy usually includes an "average" clause, which provides that the protection shall attach to each item of property in such proportion as each property bears to the entire value (fair market value at time of loss) of the property insured. For example, assume that a blanket policy for $9,000, containing the 80% coinsurance clause, insured two buildings—A having a fair market value at the date of the fire of $10,000 and B of $5,000. The face of the policy would be allocated as $6,000 on A and $3,000 on B. If a fire loss of $2,000 occurred in B, the maximum indemnity would be:

$$\frac{\$3,000}{.80 \times \$5,000} \times \$2,000 = \$1,500$$

Since $1,500 is less than either the loss ($2,000) or the effective policy ($3,000), the actual indemnity would be $1,500, the maximum set by the formula.

## Accounting for a Casualty Loss

When there is a casualty loss, prepaid insurance must be adjusted accordingly. To illustrate the nature of the adjustment we will utilize a *fire loss*. When a fire has occurred, an orderly accounting procedure is essential for *separately reporting the loss* and for proper matching of operating expense and revenue. In accounting for a fire loss, certain procedures should be followed, viz:

1. Determine to what extent the accounting records have been damaged or destroyed. Take steps to supplement damaged records, or to reconstruct them if they have been destroyed.
2. Adjust the books to the date of the fire for all operating items affected by the fire. Make all necessary adjusting entries for depreciation, amortization, accrued and prepaid expense, and income items affected by the fire.
3. Determine the *book value* of all assets destroyed by the fire.
4. Open a Fire Loss account in the general ledger and transfer to it the book value of all assets destroyed. Charge the Fire Loss account with any unexpired insurance premium on that portion of the policy which is paid by the insurance company as a result of the casualty, and with any expenses incurred in connection with the fire and the settlement. When a policy is paid in full, the entire adjusted unexpired premium should be charged to Fire Loss. If 60% of the potential indemnity were collected, 60% of the adjusted unexpired premium should be changed to Fire Loss. The remainder of the policy amount could be continued in force as insurance on what was not damaged or, if the policy is cancelled, could become the basis of a refund. These provisions tend to vary according to the policy provisions.
5. Determine the amounts recoverable (this determination is made through negotiations with the adjuster appointed by the insurance

company) under the insurance policies in force. Credit the Fire Loss account with these amounts, and with any proceeds from the sale of damaged assets or merchandise whose cost has been charged to Fire Loss.

6. Close the balance of the Fire Loss account to Income Summary. It is advisable to close the books as at year-end when the fire is of major proportions.

In determining the book value of assets destroyed, cognizance must be taken not only of the estimated depreciation recorded for past periods but also of the depreciation to be accrued for the elapsed portion of the present period to date of loss. The portion of the insurance premium to be charged to the Fire Loss account is the unexpired portion at the date of the fire if the full amount of the policy is paid. If only a portion of the policy is paid, then the amount of the payment is endorsed on the policy and the remainder continues in force. In this case, that portion of the unexpired premium which the endorsement bears to the face of the policy is taken out of Prepaid Insurance and charged to Fire Loss. If the policy is continued, the remainder is left in the Prepaid Insurance account; if canceled, this remainder is a cash refund.[11]

If a perpetual inventory system is used, and if the records are not destroyed, the amount of the merchandise on hand at the time of the fire can be determined from the records. In the absence of such records, the amount of the inventory may be estimated by the "gross margin" method as described in Chapter 10.

*Accounting for Fire Loss Illustrated.* Assume the Fire Alarm Company suffered a fire loss on July 1 of the current year; the relevant values were:

a. Fair market values at date of the fire (July 1):
   Inventory (same as cost), 100% loss ..................................... $ 3,000
   Furniture and equipment, 100% loss...................................... 1,000
   Building—total fair market value ....................................... 26,250
   Building—amount of loss at fair market value, ²/₃ loss ............ 17,500

b. Insurance coverage:
   Inventory—none.
   Furniture and equipment, insured—face of policy $2,400 (no
      coinsurance clause). Unexpired insurance on January 1
      of current year (30 months unexpired)............................ 50
   Building, insured—face of policy $16,800 (includes an 80%
      coinsurance clause). Unexpired insurance on January 1
      of current year (24 months unexpired)............................ 320

c. Account balances January 1 of current year:
   Prepaid insurance ($50 + $320) ......................................... 370
   Inventory (at cost) ....................................................... 1,500
   Furniture and equipment (at cost)....................................... 2,400
      Accumulated depreciation, furniture and equipment
      (depreciation rate, 25% on cost)..................................... 1,200
   Building (at cost)......................................................... 30,000
      Accumulated depreciation, building (depreciation
      rate, 3¹/₃% on cost)................................................... 10,000

---

[11] These tend to vary depending upon the specific provisions of the insurance contract.

The entries to adjust the books to the date of the fire, to record the fire loss, and to record the settlement with the insurance company follow with explanations and computations.

1. Entries to adjust the books to the date of the fire for operating items affected:

| | | |
|---|---:|---:|
| Fire loss (goods destroyed) ......................................... | 3,000 | |
|    Goods burned (inventory destroyed) ........................ | | 3,000 |

To set up inventory of unsold merchandise destroyed by fire. (Note: Goods Burned is closed to Income Summary at regular closing. This amount offsets the charges to regular income from the beginning inventory and purchases, part of which was burned).*

  * An alternative treatment would be to credit the beginning inventory and purchases to the extent of the loss and to debit the Fire Loss account.

| | | |
|---|---:|---:|
| Depreciation on furniture and equipment........................ | 300 | |
|    Accumulated depreciation on furniture and | | |
|      equipment ......................................................... | | 300 |

To record depreciation, at a rate of 25% per year, from January 1 to July 1 ($2,400 × 25% × $^6/_{12}$).

| | | |
|---|---:|---:|
| Depreciation on building ........................................... | 500 | |
|    Accumulated depreciation on building .................... | | 500 |

To record depreciation, from January 1 to July 1 ($30,000 × 3$^1/_3$% × $^6/_{12}$ = $500).

| | | |
|---|---:|---:|
| Insurance expense ..................................................... | 90 | |
|    Prepaid insurance................................................. | | 90 |

To record the expired insurance premium from January 1 to July 1, as follows:

| | |
|---|---:|
|    Furniture and equipment ($50 × $^6/_{30}$)................. | 10 |
|    Building ($320 × $^6/_{24}$) ..................................... | 80 |

2. Entries to close the book value of assets destroyed to the Fire Loss account:

| | | |
|---|---:|---:|
| Fire loss ................................................................. | 900 | |
| Accumulated depreciation on furniture and equipment ... | 1,500 | |
|    Furniture and equipment ..................................... | | 2,400 |

To close the accumulated depreciation and the asset account into the Fire Loss account.

| | | |
|---|---:|---:|
| Fire loss ................................................................. | 13,000 | |
| Accumulated depreciation on building ......................... | 7,000 | |
|    Building ............................................................. | | 20,000 |

To close two thirds of the accumulated depreciation and of the asset account into the Fire Loss account ($10,000 + $500) × $^2/_3$ = $7,000.

3. Entry to record the settlement with the insurance company:

| | | |
|---|---:|---:|
| Cash ...................................................................... | 15,000 | |
|    Fire loss ........................................................... | | 15,000 |

To record the payment received from the insurance company, computed as follows: furniture and equipment,

$1,000 (full settlement): building, per formula [$16,800 ÷
($26,250 × 80%)] × $17,500 = $14,000 (which is less than
face of policy or fair market value of the loss). No insurance or inventory loss.

4. To adjust balance in Prepaid Insurance:

*If Policies Continued*

| | | |
|---|---|---|
| Fire loss ................................. | 217 | |
| Prepaid insurance.............. | | 217 |

*If Policies Not Continued*

| | | |
|---|---|---|
| Fire loss ................................. | 217 | |
| Cash ....................................... | 63 | |
| Prepaid insurance.............. | | 280 |

Analysis of prepaid insurance:

| | Furniture and Fixtures | Building | Total |
|---|---|---|---|
| Unexpired January 1..................................... | $50 | $320 | $370 |
| Amortized to July 1 ................................... | 10 | 80 | 90 |
| Unexpired July 1........................................ | 40 | 240 | 280 |
| Amount related to indemnity: | | | |
| $1,000/$2,400 × $40 = | 17 | | 17 |
| $14,000/$16,800 × $240 = | | 200 | 200 |
| Unexpired after fire loss (or cash refund) ...... | $23 | $ 40 | $ 63 |

The Fire Loss account is closed to Income Summary.

## Life Insurance

Life insurance companies sell insurance contracts that call for a stipulated payment (indemnity) in case of death, receiving in return compensation in the form of premiums. In an *ordinary life* policy, the premiums are paid until the death of the insured at which time the stipulated
benefit is paid to the beneficiary. During the period the policy is in force
it has both a cash surrender value and a loan value. In a *limited payment* policy, the premiums are paid for a stated number of periods or
until the death of the insured (if prior to the end of the stipulated period)
and the benefit is paid at death or after a stipulated date as an endow-
ment. As with the ordinary life policy there is a cash surrender value and
a loan value. In *term insurance,* the premium payments are made for
a stated number of periods or until death (if prior to the end of the
stipulated period); the benefit is paid only if death occurs within the
stated number of periods. In term insurance, there is no cash surrender
or loan values and the policy must be renewed at the end of the stipulated period; otherwise it lapses. At renewal, a new premium scale is
effective based on the advanced age. As most of the characteristics are

involved in ordinary life policies, the discussion to follow will be limited to this type.

The law and insurance companies have long recognized that a company has an insurable interest in certain of its *executives*. Thus, it is not uncommon for a company to insure the life of certain key executives; the proceeds are payable to the company to compensate for the loss incurred in replacing a deceased executive.

In accounting for a life insurance contract of this type, premiums paid (cash paid less any dividends) and the related asset (intangible) must be recorded and reported.

*Cash Surrender and Loan Value.* The cash surrender value of a policy is the sum payable upon the cancellation of the policy at the request of the insured. The loan value of a policy is the sum the insurance company will loan on a policy maintained in force. The cash surrender value is computed as of the end of the year; the loan value is computed as of the beginning of the year. Each policy carries a table that indicates the cash surrender value and the loan value for specific policy years. At any given time the loan value is somewhat less than the cash surrender value. Since the policy could be canceled and a portion of the premiums which have been paid out be returned in the form of the cash surrender value, not all of the premiums paid constitute an expense but only the excess of the total premiums paid over the cash surrender value.[12]

The portion of premiums paid equal to the cash surrender value is an asset and should be shown as such on the balance sheet under the caption Investments and Funds.

To illustrate one sequence of entries, assume the following data taken from an insurance policy having an indemnity of $25,000.

| Year | Premium (beginning of year) | Cash Surrender Value (end of year) |
|------|------------------------------|-------------------------------------|
| 1 | $720 | -0- |
| 2 | 720 | -0- |
| 3 | 720 | $1,140 |
| 4 | 720 | 1,480 |
| 5 | (Etc., as specified in the policy) | |

Indicated entries:

Year 1:  Life insurance expense ........................................... 720
         Cash ................................................................. 720

Year 2:  Life insurance expense ........................................... 720
         Cash ................................................................. 720

----

[12] In mutual companies the stated premium is reduced by a dividend credit.

Year 3: Life insurance expense ............................................. 720

　　　　　Cash ................................................................. 　　　　720

At year-end:

Cash surrender value of life insurance ........................ 1,140

　　Life insurance expense ($1/3 \times \$1,140$) .................... 　　　　380

　　Nonrecurring adjustment—prior year

　　　($2/3 \times \$1,140$) ................................................. 　　　　760*

Year 4: Life insurance expense ............................................. 720

　　　　　Cash ................................................................. 　　　　720

At year-end:

Cash surrender value of life insurance

　($1,480 - $1,140) ................................................. 340

　　Life insurance expense ....................................... 　　　　340

* Another alternative would be to "allocate" the third-year cash surrender value to the first three years on some basis (say, equally) at the time the annual entry for premium is made.

Each year thereafter the Cash surrender value of life insurance account would be debited for the increase in the cash surrender value as shown by the table in the policy. The above example was simplified by assuming the policy year and the accounting year coincided. If they do not coincide, as is the normal case, an adjusting entry at the end of each accounting period would be required for the prepaid amount of insurance expense.

The following entry would be made when the face of policy is paid at the death of the president, assuming the cash surrender value of the policy at date of death was $3,500 and that three months' premium is to be refunded in accordance with the insurance contract whereby premiums paid beyond date of death are refunded.

Cash [$25,000 + ($3/12 \times \$720$)] ............................................. 25,180

　　Life insurance expense ($3/12 \times \$720$) ............................ 　　　180

　　Cash surrender value of life insurance.......................... 　　3,500

　　Gain on settlement of life insurance indemnity.............. 　21,500

The gain normally would be extraordinary.

## REPORTING INTANGIBLES

Noncurrent assets that characteristically are properly classified as intangibles are variously reported under the balance sheet captions (or similar captions): "Intangibles," "Deferred charges," and "Other assets." Although reasonably precise definitions have been provided in this chapter, in the practical world of accounting, there are no comparable authoritative distinctions between the three captions. Therefore, considerable variation between companies can be observed in the balance sheet reporting of noncurrent intangibles. Usually each intangible is descriptively titled in the statement and then noted so that the statement user will not be misled.

**QUESTIONS**

1. What distinguishes intangibles from other assets traditionally reported outside the current asset category? How are intangibles reported on the balance sheet?

2. What factors should determine whether or not an intangible asset is amortized and over what span of time?

3. What outlays are properly considered part of the cost of an intangible asset?

4. Explain the conceptual nature of goodwill and the basis on which goodwill is amortized.

5. What is the proper role of the accountant in valuation of goodwill?

6. Briefly describe going value. How can it be distinguished from goodwill?

7. What is the nature of a franchise? Of a trademark?

8. There are different kinds of deferred charges. What are they? Give one or more examples of the different kinds.

9. Define a deferred charge. Is it an intangible?

10. How are deferred charges distinguished from prepaid expenses? Give examples of each.

11. What are the chief provisions of the FASB accounting statement on accounting for research and development costs?

12. What items are properly chargeable to organization costs? Should organization costs be amortized? Explain.

13. What is a leasehold? What are the primary accounting aspects of a leasehold?

14. Some casualty policies have coinsurance clauses. What is the purpose of such a clause? Does its presence in a policy affect the indemnity which the insured can collect if the insured property is totally destroyed?

15. When a casualty occurs for which insurance is in force, certain accounting steps should be taken. What are these accounting measures?

16. What is the relationship between cash surrender value and loan value of a life insurance policy? Which one affects accounting entries? How?

17. For what reasons do some companies insure the lives of executives and name the companies as beneficiaries?

**DECISION CASE 14-1**

A new corporation was organized in 19A with a capital of $10,000,000 to manufacture a new type of sports car.

In 19A and 19B, it invested $4,000,000 in a plant, machinery, and tools and expended $2,000,000 for materials, labor, advertising, and overhead expenses in connection with perfecting a first experimental model. There was no income from sales or other sources in those years. Management charged the expenses of $2,000,000 to a Development and Experimental Expense account which appeared among "Deferred charges" on the December 31, 19A balance sheet.

In January 19C its model was pronounced a success and its factory was ready to produce at the rate of 100 cars per year, to be sold for $10,000 per car. However, because of labor, material, and other problems, only five cars were produced and only three cars were sold. In 19C its total sales were $30,000; purchases of material and supplies were $200,000; factory labor was $80,000; and advertising, clerical, and overhead costs were $150,000. Management charged the net loss for the year 19C to Developmental and Experimental Expense which was reported on the balance sheet under "Deferred charges."

During 19D, management forecast the production and sale of 100 units. However, 80 were produced and only 20 were sold. The net operating loss for the year was $400,000, which management suggests deferring.

*Required:*

1. If 19A through 19D were years shortly before 1975 and you were the auditor of the company, discuss the acceptability of the accounting treatment, the disclosures, if any, you would make and the opinion you wound render as of—
   a. December 31, 19B.
   b. December 31, 19C.
   c. December 31, 19D.
2. If instead the years 19C and 19D were calendar years 1976 and 1977 (or later), what about the acceptability of the accounting treatment, disclosures, and so on, as of—
   a. December 31, 19C.
   b. December 31, 19D.

(AICPA adapted)

## EXERCISES

### Exercise 14–1

The data below pertain to two separate intangible assets:

|  | Asset X | Asset Y |
|---|---|---|
| Cost | $7,200 | $8,400 |
| Estimated economic life | Indefinite | 14 years |

*Required:*

1. Give annual entry for amortization, if any, for each asset. (Assume both were acquired in 1971 or later.)
2. If after Asset Y has been in use for eight full years, it is determined at the start of the ninth year that its remaining life will be four years, make any entry then that is appropriate. Give the amortization entry for Asset Y at the end of its ninth year.

### Exercise 14–2

Check the best answer in each of the following and indicate the basis for your choice.

1. On January 15, 19A, a corporation was granted a patent on a product. On January 2, 19J, to protect its patent, the corporation purchased a patent on a competing product that originally was issued on January 10, 19F. Because of its

unique plant, the corporation does not feel the competing patent can be used in producing a product. The cost of the competing patent should be—
  a. Amortized over a maximum period of 17 years.
  b. Amortized over a maximum period of 13 years.
  c. Amortized over a maximum period of 8 years.
  d. Expensed in 19J.

2. Goodwill should be written off—
  a. As soon as possible against retained earnings.
  b. As soon as possible as an extraordinary item.
  c. By systematic charges against retained earnings over the period benefited, but not more than 40 years.
  d. By systematic charges to expense over the period benefited, but not more than 40 years.

3. A large publicly held company has developed and registered a trademark during 19A. How should the cost of developing and registering the trademark be accounted for?
  a. Charged to an asset account that should not be amortized.
  b. Expensed as incurred.
  c. Amortized over 25 years if in accordance with management's evaluation.
  d. Amortized over its useful life or 17 years, whichever is shorter.

4. A deferred charge should be—
  a. Expensed as incurred.
  b. Capitalized and not amortized until it clearly has no value.
  c. Capitalized and amortized over the estimated future benefited.
  d. Capitalized and amortized over the estimated period benefited but not exceeding 40 years.

5. The cost of purchasing patent rights for a product that might otherwise have seriously competed with one of the purchaser's patented products should be—
  a. Charged off in the current period.
  b. Amortized over the legal life of the purchased patent.
  c. Added to factory overhead and allocated to production of the purchaser's product.
  d. Amortized over the remaining estimated life of the patent for the product whose market would have been impaired by competition from the newly patented product.

6. Research and development costs incurred after 1975 should be—
  a. Capitalized on a selective basis, then amortized.
  b. Capitalized, then amortized over 40 years.
  c. Expensed in the year in which they are incurred.
  d. Charged directly to retained earnings.

7. Goodwill is most closely akin to—
  a. Going value.
  b. Franchises.
  c. Trademarks.
  d. Copyrights.

(Items 1–3, 5 AICPA adapted)


**Exercise 14–3**

For the past five years, the total assets of Day Brothers Store have averaged $700,000 while average liabilities amounted to $150,000. Cumulative total earnings for the five-year period have been $280,000. Included in the latter figure are extraordinary gains of $45,000 and nonrecurring losses of $30,000. An 8% return on investment is considered normal for the industry. In calculating goodwill where a transfer of the business to new interests is contemplated, the parties agree that excess earnings should be capitalized at 15%.

*Required:*

In the light of the foregoing, calculate the implied goodwill. Show computations.

## Exercise 14-4

A quarry which is available for purchase can be expected to produce for the next three years; it will be exhausted at that time and have a zero salvage value due to restoration cost obligations. Best estimates place its net receipts at $35,000 for the first year; thereafter, there will be an annual $10,000 drop in net receipts.

*Required:*

Using an assumed 9% return rate and assuming net receipts occur at year-end, calculate the goodwill implicit in an offer of $67,750 for the property. Round calculations to the nearest dollar.

## Exercise 14-5

The following projections were developed as a basis for estimating goodwill:

Budgeted average annual expected earnings ................................. $ 9,000
Budgeted average future value of assets (excluding goodwill) ......... 66,000

*Required:*

Estimate goodwill under each independent approach below:

a. Goodwill equal to earnings capitalized at 12½% (normal rate for industry) over budgeted average assets.
b. Goodwill equal to excess earnings capitalized at 20%; normal rate for industry, 10%.
c. Goodwill equal to six years of excess earnings; normal earnings rate for industry, 10%.
d. Goodwill based on present value of excess earnings as computed in b at an 8% expected earnings rate for five years. Prove your answer.

## Exercise 14-6

New Corporation is negotiating with the Old Company with a view to purchasing the entire assets and liabilities of the latter. You have been asked to help evaluate the "goodwill on the basis of the latest concepts." Accordingly, you decide to utilize the present value approach. The following data have been assembled on Old Company:

|  | Fair Market Value | Book Value |
|---|---|---|
| Total identifiable assets (exclusive of goodwill) ...... | $8,000,000 | $5,000,000 |
| Liabilities......................................................... | 3,000,000 | 3,000,000 |
| Average annual earnings expected (next five years)................................................. | 520,000 | |

*Required:*

(Round to even dollars.)

1. Compute goodwill assuming a 9% expected earnings rate.
2. Assume the deal is consummated; New's offer, as accepted, was cash equal to the fair market value of the net identifiable assets plus the goodwill computed in (1). Give entry on New's books to record the transaction.
3. Prepare an amortization table that is conceptually consistent with your computations in (1).

### Exercise 14-7

Sanders Company signed a contract on January 1 whereby the company was to pay $6,000 cash plus $600 per month rent for an office building. The contract covered a ten-year period and was renewable at the end of that time for an additional ten years at a rental not to exceed 10% of that specified for the prior period. The management has no definite ideas as to whether the renewal option will be exercised.

Prior to occupancy the Sanders Company spent $2,000 in renovation costs. In addition, a large garage was built upon the property costing $15,000. It is estimated that the garage has a 15-year life with no significant residual value. Give all entries on Sanders' books for the first year of the lease; assume straight-line accounting procedures.

### Exercise 14-8

In lieu of paying six $7,000 rentals at six-month intervals with each payment due in advance, a lessor and lessee agree upon a single lump-sum advance payment of $38,162.74 which covers the entire lease period. This reflects recognition of interest at an annual rate of 8% throughout the lease period.

*Required:*

1. Show how the lump-sum figure was calculated and prepare an amortization table covering the entire term of the lease.
2. Give the entry by the lessee to record the initial payment under the lease and the entries at end of the first year assuming the lease year and the lessee's fiscal year coincide.

### Exercise 14-9

After extended negotiations, a lessor and lessee agree that instead of paying $6,000 annual rental over a four-year term with each rental payable in advance, a single lump-sum payment of $21,187.74 at the start of the lease should be paid. This amount was arrived at through use of a 9% interest rate.

*Required:*

1. Show how the initial amount was calculated.
2. Prepare an appropriate leasehold amortization schedule using the 9% rate. Make journal entries for the first year for both the lessor and lessee, assuming their fiscal years and the lease year coincide.

### Exercise 14-10

Select the best answer in each of the following and indicate the basis for your choice (show computations if appropriate).

1. Inger Company bought a patent in January 19A for $6,800. For the first four years, it was amortized on the assumption that the total useful life would be eight years. At the start of the fifth year, it was determined six years would be the probable total life. Amortization at the end of the fifth year should be—
   a. $1,133.                              c. $850.
   b. $1,700.                              d. None of the foregoing.

2. XY Company has a lease on a site which does not expire for 25 years. With the land owner's permission, XY erected a building on the site which will last 50 years. XY should recognize expense in connection with the building's cost—
   a. One fortieth each year.
   b. One twenty-fifth each year.
   c. In totality as soon as it is completed.
   d. One fiftieth each year.

3. Where there is an 80% coinsurance clause, the fair value of the insured property is $30,000 and the amount of loss and of the face of the policy are respectively $15,000 and $12,000, indemnity collectible would be—
   a. $7,500.                              c. $15,000.
   b. $12,000.                             d. $30,000.

4. Where the policy has an 80% coinsurance clause, if the fair value of the property is $10,000, the amount of loss is $8,500, and insurance carried is $7,000, the indemnity collectible would be—
   a. $10,000.                             d. $7,000.
   b. $8,500.                              e. None of the foregoing.
   c. $8,000.

5. Suppose the facts are as in 4 above except that the amount of the loss is $7,000, then the indemnity collectible would be—
   a. $10,000.                             d. $6,000.
   b. $8,000.                              e. None of the foregoing.
   c. $7,000.

6. Which of the following is not properly reported as a deferred charge?
   a. Bond issue costs.                    c. Organization costs.
   b. Discount on bonds payable.           d. Deferred income taxes.

7. Prepaid expenses and deferred charges are alike in that they are both—
   a. Reported as current assets on a classified balance sheet.
   b. Destined to be charged to expense in some subsequent period in harmony with the matching principle.
   c. Reported as other assets.
   d. Applicable to the fiscal period immediately following the balance sheet on which they appear

## Exercise 14–11

Assuming that all policies contain an 80% coinsurance clause, show what the insurance company would pay under each of the following cases:

|                              | Case A   | Case B   | Case C   |
|------------------------------|----------|----------|----------|
| Fair market value of property | $25,000 | $15,000  | $10,000  |
| Amount of loss               | 24,000   | 3,000    | 3,200    |
| Face of policy               | 22,500   | 12,500   | 2,500    |

### Exercise 14–12

On January 1, a store had $120 unexpired premiums on an 80% coinsurance fire policy, which ran one year, for $15,000 on its merchandise. On January 1, the inventory was $20,000. January purchases were $44,000, and January sales were $60,000. A fire on February 1 destroyed the entire stock on hand. The insurance policy is canceled upon payment of the indemnity, and any unexpired premium after the fire was refunded.

*Required:*

Give journal entries to record the estimated inventory and the fire loss assuming a 30% gross margin rate on sales.

### Exercise 14–13

ABC Company sustained a fire loss on February 28. The following data were available (fiscal year ends December 31):

a. Sixty percent of the inventory burned; cost and fair market value of loss was $1,800 (assume periodic inventory procedures).
b. Furniture and fixtures: depreciation $20 per month; fair market value of the item burned, $3,600 (original cost, $3,000; accumulated depreciation to January 1, $480).
c. Insurance premium $60 per year paid on last January 1 for one year; payment of the indemnity canceled the policy and the unexpired premium after the fire was refunded in cash.
d. Settled with insurance company; face of policy, $5,000, 90% coinsurance clause; fair market value of property insured, $7,500. Close Fire Loss account.

*Required:*

Give indicated journal entries.

### Exercise 14–14

On January 1, Wilkins Company purchased a $100,000 ordinary life insurance policy on its president. The following data relate to the first five years:

| Year | Annual Advance Premium | Cash Surrender Value (Year-End) | |
| | | Increase | Cumulative |
|---|---|---|---|
| 1 | $2,000 | -0- | -0- |
| 2 | 2,000 | -0- | -0- |
| 3 | 2,000 | $2,100 | $2,100 |
| 4 | 2,000 | 720 | 2,820 |
| 5 | 2,000 | 750 | 3,570 |
| 6 | Etc. | Etc. | Etc. |

*Required:*

1. Give all entries indicated up to death of the president on July 2 of the fifth year.
2. Give entry to record insurance settlement upon death of the president. The premium unexpired was refunded. Assume the policy year and accounting year agree; also there are no dividends since the company is not a mutual.

## PROBLEMS

### Problem 14-1

*Case A.* One of your corporate clients bought all of the assets of another company whose operations were compatible with those of the client and continued to operate the business of the acquired entity as a separate division. The purchase price paid included an excess consideration for such items as cutomers' lists, going concern value, and goodwill, aside from what was paid for identifiable tangibles and intangibles. Under terms of the original contract, if the division (i.e., the acquired unit) proves sufficiently profitable, an added payment will become due. This added payment is almost certain to materialize and will approximately equal what was already paid for customer lists, going concern value, and goodwill. These intangibles have been amortized since acquisition over a more or less arbitrary eight-year total life. The client has inquired whether the added payment, which is clearly related, can be amortized over 12 years from the date the payment is to be made. If this were to be done, vestiges of the balance related to the new payment would remain on the books as much as seven years after the last of the first payment had been fully amortized.

*Case B.* Another corporate client is in a regulated industry and has franchise rights granted by a federal commission. The rights are worth considerably more than the cost of obtaining them; they can be transferred with the permission of the commission (which usually is not difficult to obtain). The rights do not lapse as long as the client is a going concern, although they could be revoked. Revocation of such rights has rarely occurred. The client's management contends there is no need to amortize the franchise rights over 40 years, much less a shorter period. Indeed, some of the managers feel they should be written up in value.

*Required:*

Draft memoranda setting forth your recommendations concerning the above situations. Support whatever positions you take.

### Problem 14-2

The Tiger Corporation, a retail farm implements dealer, has increased its annual sales volume to a level three times greater than the annual sales of a dealer purchased eight years ago in order to begin operations.

The board of directors of Tiger Corporation recently received an offer to negotiate the sale of Tiger Corporation to a large competitor. As a result, the majority of the board wants to increase the stated value of goodwill on the balance sheet to reflect the larger sales volume developed through intensive promotion and the current market prices of the company's products. However, a few of the company's board members would prefer to eliminate goodwill altogether from the balance sheet in order to prevent "possible misinterpretations." Goodwill was properly recorded when the business was acquired eight years ago.

*Required:*

1. *a.* Discuss the meaning of the term "goodwill." Do not discuss goodwill arising from consolidated statements or the conditions under which goodwill is recorded.
   *b.* List the techniques used to calculate the tentative value of goodwill in negotiations to purchase a going concern.

2. Why are the book and market values of the goodwill of Tiger Corporation different?
3. Discuss the propriety of —
   a. Increasing the stated value of goodwill prior to the negotiations.
   b. Eliminating goodwill completely from the balance sheet prior to negotiations.

(AICPA adapted)

## Problem 14–3

After considerable analysis the following projections were derived as a basis for estimating the potential value of goodwill in anticipation of negotiations for the sale of the business:

Average annual earnings projected ...................................... $ 40,000
Average fair value of net assets expected............................... 350,000
"Normal" rate of return for the industry, 8½%.
Rate of return expected on excess profits, 10%.
Expected recovery period for excess earnings, five years.
Years' purchase of average annual earnings, three.

Estimate the value of goodwill under five different approaches (including a present value determination at 8½%). Present value amounts for five periods at 8½% annually: PV of 1 is .665045; PV of annuity of 1 is 3.940642.

## Problem 14–4

On June 30, 19A your client, Vandiver Corporation, was granted two patents covering plastic cartons that it has been producing and marketing profitably for the past three years. One patent covers the manufacturing process, and the other covers the related products.

Vandiver executives tell you that these patents represent the most significant breakthrough in the industry in the past 30 years. The products have been marketed under the registered trademarks Safetainer, Duratainer and Sealrite. Licenses under the patents have already been granted by your client to other manufacturers in the United States and abroad and are producing substantial royalties.

On July 1, Vandiver commenced patent infringement actions against several companies whose names you recognize as those of substantial and prominent competitors. Vandiver's management is optimistic that these suits will result in a permanent injunction against the manufacture and sale of the infringing products and collection of damages for loss of profits caused by the alleged infringement.

The financial vice president has suggested that the patents be recorded at the discounted value of expected net royalty receipts.

*Required:*

1. What is an intangible asset? Explain.
2. a. What is the meaning of "discounted value of expected net receipts?" Explain.
   b. How would such a value be calculated for net royalty receipts?
3. What basis of valuation for Vandiver's patents would be generally accepted in accounting? Give supporting reasons for this basis.

4. *a.* Assuming no practical problems of implementation and ignoring generally accepted accounting principles, what is the preferable basis of evaluation for patents? Explain.

   *b.* What would be the preferable theoretical basis of amortization? Explain.

5. What recognition, if any, should be made of the infringement litigation in the financial statements for the year ending September 30, 19A? Discuss.

(AICPA adapted)

## Problem 14–5

Your new client, PQR Company, is being audited for the first time. In the course of your examination, you encounter in the ledger, an account titled "Intangibles" which is essentially as below:

### Intangibles

| | | | | | |
|---|---|---|---|---|---|
| June 30, 19A | Goodwill | 5,000 | Dec. 31, 19B | Amortization | 480 |
| Dec. 31, 19A | R & D | 10,700 | Dec. 31, 19C | Amortization | 1,200 |
| Apr.  1, 19B | Goodwill | 11,400 | | | |
| June 30, 19B | Patent | 9,600 | | | |
| Dec. 31, 19B | R & D | 13,900 | | | |
| June  1, 19C | Goodwill | 16,500 | | | |
| July  1, 19C | Bond discount | 4,800 | | | |
| Dec. 31, 19C | R & D | 17,100 | | | |

By tracing entries to the journal and other supporting documents, you ascertain the following facts:

*a.* The June 30, 19A, entry was made when, somewhat surprisingly, the first six months' operations were profitable; a loss had been anticipated. At the direction of the company president, and with the approval of the board of directors, an entry was made charging Intangibles and crediting Retained earnings for $5,000.

*b.* All debit entries dated December 31 pertaining to R & D arise from the fact that the company has continuously engaged in an extensive research and development program to keep its products competitive and to develop new products. The charges represent half of the costs of the R & D program transferred at year-end from the R & D expense account.

*c.* The April 1, 19B, entry was made after an extensive advertising campaign had seemingly proved particularly successful. Sales rose 8% after the campaign and never dropped again to within 4% increase over their former level. The charge represents the cost of the campaign.

*d.* The $9,600 charge on June 30, 19B represents the purchase price of a patent bought because the company feared if it fell into other hands, it would damage the company's products competitively.

*e.* The June 1, 19C, charge was made after PQR acquired a division of another profitable company. The price represented an excess payment of $16,500 over the fair values of identifiable assets acquired and was based on an expectation of continued high profitability.

*f.* The July 1, 19C, charge for $4,800 represents discount on a ten-year $100,000 bond issue marketed by the company on that date. (Since the amount is relatively immaterial, use of straight-line amortization need not be changed.)

*g.* The credits to the intangibles account represent an attempt by the company bookkeeper to amortize the year-end balances 10% each year (subject to the policy described below). When you question the bookkeeper and company officials, you learn the company's policy is to amortize those intangibles it regards as having limited lives over ten years. For this purpose, acquisitions and retirements are accounted for in terms of the most proximate quarter in which they entered or were removed from the books. All items are regarded as amortizable except R & D and Goodwill. You concur with the judgment as to the ten-year life of those intangibles properly subject to amortization.

*Required:*

Make journal entries to correct PQR's books as of December 31, 19C, on the assumption the books have been adjusted but not closed for the year as of that date. (Although years such as 19A and 19B have not been specifically identified as particular calendar years, for purposes of your solution, assume all events of the problem have occurred recently and that the current pronouncements of authoritative bodies reflected in the text apply to the various items.)

It is suggested you key your entries to the letter, identifying the items in the problem. Explain each correcting entry. For the most part, compound entries should be avoided unless elements of the entry are closely related.

## Problem 14-6

During an examination of the financial statements of the Fendo Company, your assistant calls attention to significant costs incurred in the development of EDP programs (i.e., software) for major segments of the sales and production scheduling systems.

The EDP program development costs will benefit future periods to the extent that the systems change slowly and the program instructions are compatible with new equipment acquired at three- to six-year intervals. The service value of the EDP programs is affected almost entirely by changes in the technology of systems and EDP equipment and does not decline with the number of times the program is used. Since many system changes are minor, program instructions frequently can be modified with only minor losses in program 'efficiency. The frequency of such changes tends to increase with the passage of time.

*Required:*

1. Discuss the propriety of classifying the unamortized EDP program development costs as—
    *a.* A prepaid expense.
    *b.* An intangible fixed asset with limited life.
    *c.* An operational asset.
2. Numerous methods are available for amortizing assets that benefit future periods. Each method (like a model) presumes that certain conditions exist and, hence, is most appropriate under those conditions. Discuss the propriety of amortizing the EDP program development costs with—
    *a.* The straight-line method.
    *b.* An increasing-charge method (e.g., the annuity method).
    *c.* A decreasing-charge method (e.g., the sum-of-the-years'-digits method).
    *d.* A variable-charge method (e.g., the units-of-production method).

(AICPA adapted)

## Problem 14-7

On January 1, 19A, Charmes Company negotiated a five-year lease with Box Realty Company whereby in lieu of payment of annual rents (at the beginning of the year) of $10,000, the lessor and lessee agreed upon a single lump-sum payment discounted at 8% per annum.

*Required:*

1. Determine the amount of the lump-sum payment per the agreement.
2. Box Realty Company (lessor) closes the books on December 31 and intends to utilize present value accounting for the lease. Develop an amortization table and give entries for the first two, and the last, years.
3. The tenant (lessee) also closed the books on December 31 but had adopted straight-line accounting procedures for the lease. Give entries for the first two, and the last, years.
4. Which party has adopted the more realistic approach? Explain.

## Problem 14-8

Marsalles Mercantile Company operates retail branches in various cities. Branches in four cities are served out of Warehouse No. 16 which sustained fire damage on April 10.

Between January 1 and April 10 recorded shipments from Warehouse No. 16 to its four stores were as below:

| Branch | Shipments |
|--------|-----------|
| W | $80,500 |
| X | 92,000 |
| Y | 69,000 |
| X | 23,000 |

Shipments to branches are marked up 15% above cost as reflected in the foregoing amounts. The January 1 inventory at Warehouse No. 16 was $43,100; purchases between January 1 and April 10 totaled $220,100; freight-in was $7,300; purchase returns were $4,700.

To arrive at the April 10 inventory for insurance settlement purposes it was agreed to deduct 5% for goods shopworn and damaged prior to the fire as goods are determined based on the foregoing data.

A compromise agreement between the insurance adjuster and Marsalles Company management set the amount of inventory lost in the fire at $20,950.

*Required:*

1. Estimate the amount of inventory in the warehouse at April 10.
2. Determine the indemnity claim if the warehouse contents were insured by a single $20,000 policy having an 80% coinsurance clause. Calculate to nearest dollar.

## Problem 14-9

The records of Company X showed at date of fire (all merchandise destroyed): sales, $240,000; initial inventory, $15,000; purchases, $205,000; insurance (one-year policy for $12,000 with 80% coinsurance clause) premium, $200; sales-persons' salaries, $15,000; and general expense, $13,000. The fire occurred six months after the premium was paid; payment of the indemnity canceled the insurance policy, hence any unexpired insurance premium was refunded. It was agreed that the gross margin percentage based on sales was 16⅔%.

*Required:*

1. Compute the indemnity to be received from the insurance company.
2. Give entries relating to the fire loss.
3. Prepare a classified income statement for the period ending on a date immediately following the fire.

**Problem 14-10**

Estimate the amount of insurance collectible on each of the following assets assuming the policies include an 80% coinsurance clause:

| Asset | Fair Market Value | Loss Suffered | Insurance Carried |
|---|---|---|---|
| Buildings .......................... | $80,000 | $40,000 | $65,000 |
| Furniture ......................... | 20,000 | 18,000 | 15,000 |
| Delivery equipment.............. | 9,000 | 4,000 | 5,000 |
| Merchandise....................... | ? | 60% | 10,000 |

To find the value of the merchandise destroyed, the following facts are submitted from which to select the significant data:

| | |
|---|---|
| The gross margin averages 30% of sales. | |
| The fair market value of the inventory is the same as its cost. | |
| Purchases for the period ................................................. | $60,000 |
| Beginning inventory ...................................................... | 23,400 |
| Return purchases ......................................................... | 2,000 |
| Salespersons' commission and advertising ...................... | 8,000 |
| Interest revenue ......................................................... | 200 |
| Postage and stationery ................................................. | 1,000 |
| Sales ........................................................................ | 84,000 |
| Credit department expense ............................................ | 700 |
| Sales returns ............................................................. | 2,000 |

**Problem 14-11**

Prince Company operates in a leased building; it adjusts and closes books each December 31. On April 30 a fire seriously damaged its inventory and fixtures. Inventory was totally destroyed; fixtures were half destroyed. Different insurance policies cover the assets, but both have a common feature providing they are canceled for future or remaining coverage to whatever extent a portion of the total potential indemnity is collected.

The company uses a periodic inventory system, and the accounting records were saved; these reveal that in the past three years gross margin has averaged 38% of sales price. The January 1 inventory was $73,280. Between January 1 and April 30 purchases and sales were respectively $116,320 and $206,500. Inventory was insured by a $65,000 policy with no coinsurance clause. The latest premium payment covering a one-year period from September 1 of last year amounted to $720.

When the books were closed last December 31, the fixtures were two and one-half years old. Accounts related to the fixtures and their insurance policy are set forth below.

| Fixtures | Accumulated Depreciation | Prepaid Insurance |
|---|---|---|
| Balance 20,000 | Year 1   900<br>Year 2 1,800<br>Year 3 1,800 | Policy A   42<br>Policy B 480 |

Policy A expired February 28 of the current year. Policy B was immediately put in force to replace it and covers a two-year period. It is for $10,000 maximum coverage, provides for indemnity on the basis of market value of any loss, and has an 80% coinsurance clause. It is determined that the fair value of the fixtures when the fire occurred was $15,000 and that the damage amounted to a loss of half their value.

*Required:*

1. Adjust the books to April 30 and reflect the inventory as of that date.
2. Open a Fire Loss account; set up the indemnities collectible as a receivable due from the Insurance Company.
3. Transfer the net balance in Fire Loss to Income Summary.

## Problem 14-12

On April 1, 19A, Clara Company insured the life of its president, Ray Cox, for $60,000, naming itself as beneficiary. Annual premiums paid each April 1 are $2,400. As a result of the third premium payment and at the end of the third year, the policy has a cash surrender value of $1,200. One year later this will increase to $1,620. It is decided to "anticipate" recognition of the cash surrender value and subsequent increments by recording the amounts at the time the premium payments are made which assure the values will materialize.

Clara Company adjusts and closes its books on December 31 and charges premium payments to Prepaid Insurance. All premiums are paid when due. Mr. Cox died July 1, 19D. No refund of unexpired premiums as of date of death is provided for in the policy.

*Required:*

Make all entries related to the policy through July 1, 19D, including adjusting and closing entries at the end of each year the policy is in force.

## Problem 14-13

One of your corporate clients is somewhat "insurance minded" and maintains in force, several life insurance policies which have a cash surrender value feature on which the corporation is beneficiary. Several questions have arisen concerning the accounting presentation or treatment of these policies and their cash surrender value aspects.

a. One policy is on the life of the company president (who is not a stockholder). A substantially high proportion of what could be borrowed against this policy has been borrowed; the loan amounts to 88% of the cash surrender value at balance sheet date. One reason for borrowing this way is that the interest rate is about half the rate at which other loans could be obtained. You are asked for advice as to how to report the loan on the company's balance sheet and whether the fact that there may be a current liability against the policy changes the classification of cash surrender value.

b. Most of the stock of the corporation is held by a few large stockholders. To retain control within a limited group, your client has bought policies on the lives of these principal stockholders which will provide for repurchase of their stock in the event of a stockholder's death. The cash surrender value of these policies has been reported on the balance sheet. You are asked whether further disclosure is necessary.

c. Looking to the future and possible repayment of the loan on the policy mentioned, especially if interest rates should fall, a hypothetical question is posed.

Assuming the loan is repaid, would it be mandatory to report cash surrender value on this policy since the insurance is carried to cover the loss it is anticipated would be sustained as the result of the death of a key official?

d. For a time, another officer of the corporation (who also is not a stockholder) personally owned and paid premiums on a substantial life insurance policy on which his wife was beneficiary. For business reasons, your client bought the policy from him at a price equal to his past premium payments ($80,000). The corporation became beneficiary of the policy and beneficial owner of its cash surrender value ($45,000); the latter amount was recorded on the accounts as an asset. The $35,000 difference is being amortized over the life expectancy of the insured as disclosed on a mortality table. You are asked for your concurrence or disagreement with this accounting treatment.

### Required:

Draft a reply responding to the above questions. Give reasons to support whatever positions you take.

# Chapter *15*

## Corporations — Formation
## and Contributed Capital

The corporate form of business organization has become a dominant one in the United States. This particular form gained widespread use primarily as a result of the legal foundations upon which it is built. A corporation is, in the eyes of the law, an entity separate and apart from the owners. Limited liability of corporate owners, provision for succession of ownership, facility for capital accumulation, separation of management from ownership, and the legal right to act in the same capacity as an individual in the transaction of authorized business are five important factors contributing to the growth of the corporate form of business. In view of the unique features of the corporate form and its extensive use, accountants have considerable concern with respect to the special accounting problems encountered. This chapter and the next two consider these special accounting problems.

Unique problems are encountered in accounting for a corporation in respect to the *owners' equity.* In other respects the accounting treatment of transactions is largely unaffected by the form of business organization. At the outset it is well to realize that there is not complete agreement in the accounting profession on a number of the issues related to accounting for owners' equity. In a sole proprietorship, owners' equity usually is represented by a single equity account and in a partnership by separate equity accounts for each partner. In contrast, accounting for a corporation generally requires a number of owners' equity accounts.

In accounting for corporate proprietary equities, accountants adhere to the concept of *source of capital.* In order to apply this concept, owners' equity accounts are established so that the *sources* of the capital used in the enterprise are clearly segregated. In accounting by *source,* aside from the funds supplied by creditors (liabilities), the primary sources of corporate capital are *(a)* contributions by the owners, and *(b)* earnings retained in the business. The term capital has long been used to refer to the resources provided by owners; that is, the shareholders. It

633

includes contributions by owners plus retained earnings. In recent years it has been more often called shareholders' or stockholders' equity. The accountant should be familiar with the four following classes of equities and capital:

1. *Total equity (enterprise capital)*. Total equity represents the total interests of all lenders and owners of a particular corporation in the properties of that business; it is the sum of the creditors' equity and the owners' equity.
2. *Proprietary equity (owners' equity)*. Proprietary equity represents the total equity at a given time of the legal owners of the enterprise; it is the total of contributed capital and all subsequent accretions in the form of additional contributions and retained earnings.
3. *Contributed capital*. Contributed capital is the investment made by the owners; in a corporation it is the total amount paid in by all parties other than creditors. It does not include retained earnings.
4. *Legal or stated capital*. Legal capital is that portion of corporate capital that is required by statute to be retained in the business for the protection of creditors.

## CLASSIFICATIONS OF CORPORATIONS

The laws of each state provide for the formation and operation of corporations. Although state laws relating to corporations vary in many respects, there is much similarity in basic provisions. The statutes of all states provide for the existence of a separate entity and for the basic capital structure (capital stock). Corporations are brought into legal existence by submitting an application (articles of incorporation) for a charter to the secretary of state; if approved, a charter is issued which specifies the detailed conditions under which the corporation may operate such as what business activities are permitted, types of capital stock to be issued, and the method of electing officers. The charter is supplemented with bylaws which are adopted by the stockholders.

Corporations may be classified as follows:

By Ownership:

1. Public corporations, when they relate to governmental units or business operations owned by governmental units.
2. Private corporations, when they are privately owned. Such corporations may be nonstock (nonprofit organizations such as colleges and churches) or stock (usually organized for profit making).

By Nationality:

3. Domestic corporations, when operating in the state in which incorporated.
4. Foreign corporations, when operating in states other than the one in which incorporated.

By Availability of Ownership Interests:

5. Open corporations, when the stock is available for purchase. The stock is usually widely held.
6. Closed corporations, when the stock is not available for purchase and is generally held by a few shareholders.

## NATURE OF CAPITAL STOCK

Shares of capital stock, represented by stock certificates, evidence ownership in a corporation. Shares may be transferred freely by shareholders unless there is an enforceable agreement not to do so. Ownership of shares entitles the holder to certain basic rights. These rights are:

1. The right to participate in the *management* of the corporation through participating and voting in stockholder meetings.
2. The right to participate in the *profits* of the corporation through dividends declared by the board of directors.
3. The right to share in the distribution of *assets* of the corporation at liquidation or through liquidating dividends.
4. The right to purchase shares of stock on a *pro rata basis* in the corporation when such shares represent additional capital stock issues. This right is designed to protect the proportional interests of each shareholder in the ownership.

These rights are shared equitably and proportionately by all stockholders unless the charter or bylaws (and stock certificates) specifically provide otherwise. In the case of one class of stock, all holders enjoy equal rights; in the case of two or more classes of stock, the holders of one class of stock may have rights that have been withheld from the others.

In order to comprehend clearly the nature of capital stock, and to account for it correctly, the accountant must understand the following terms:

1. Authorized capital stock – the number of shares of stock that can be issued legally as specified in the charter.
2. Issued capital stock – the number of shares of authorized stock that have been issued to date.
3. Unissued capital stock – the number of shares of authorized capital stock that have *never* been issued.
4. Outstanding capital stock – the number of shares of stock that have been issued and are being held by shareholders at a given date.
5. Treasury stock – those shares once issued and later reacquired by the corporation, that is, the difference between issued shares and outstanding shares.
6. Subscribed stock – unissued shares of stock set aside to meet subscription contracts. Subscribed stock usually is not issued until the subscription price is paid in full.

In accounting for stockholders' equity descriptive terms have been evolved by the accounting profession. Although in practice there is some variation in such categories and in terminology, the following appears to represent current trends:[1]

1. Contributed capital (sometimes referred to as paid-in capital):
   a. Capital stock:
      (1) Preferred stock.
      (2) Common stock.
   b. Other contributed capital (an obsolete term, capital surplus, is sometimes used):
      (1) From owners:
          Contributed capital in excess of par or stated value (sometimes called premium on capital stock).
      (2) From outsiders:
          Donation of assets.
2. Retained earnings (an obsolete term, earned surplus, is sometimes used).
   a. Appropriated (frequently referred to as reserves).
   b. Unappropriated.
3. Unrealized capital increment.

The above classifications of stockholders' equity are used in well-designed balance sheets. To illustrate, the stockholders' equity section of a balance sheet may be reported as shown in Exhibit 15–1.

Although in practice one frequently observes different terms and arrangements of the various subclassifications of stockholders' equity shown in Exhibit 15–1, emphasis should be on *source, clarity of presentation,* and *avoidance of needless technical terminology.*

## CLASSES OF CAPITAL STOCK

Corporations tend to use several different types of capital stock, which give the respective shareholders various privileges, restrictions, and responsibilities. Some of these restrictions may result from provisions of state statutes, the charter, or the bylaws of the corporation, and are made operative by contract between the corporation and the shareholders. The two primary classifications of capital stock are (a) par-value and nopar-value stock, and (b) common and preferred stock.

### Par-Value Stock

The laws of each state provide for the issuance of par-value stock; that is, shares of stock with a designated dollar "value" per share as provided for in the articles of incorporation and as printed on the face

---

[1] In AICPA *Accounting Terminology Bulletin No. 1,* "Review and Résumé," the Committee on Terminology recommended: "The use of the term *surplus* (whether standing alone or in such combination as *capital surplus, paid-in surplus, earned surplus, appraisal surplus,* etc.) be discontinued."

**EXHIBIT 15-1**
**Stockholders' Equity Section of a Balance Sheet**

Stockholders' Equity

Contributed Capital:

Capital stock:

| | | |
|---|---:|---:|
| Preferred stock, 6%, par $10, cumulative and nonparticipating, 20,000 shares authorized, 15,000 issued ... | $150,000 | |
| Preferred stock subscribed, 100 shares .................... | 1,000 | |
| Total ......................................................... | 151,000 | |
| Common stock, nopar value, authorized 10,000 shares, issued and outstanding 8,000 shares, stated value, $5 ............................................................... | 40,000 | $191,000 |

Other Contributed Capital:

| | | |
|---|---:|---:|
| In excess of par value, preferred stock ..................... | 12,000 | |
| In excess of stated value, common stock ................. | 3,000 | |
| Donation of plant site ............................................ | 5,000 | 20,000 |
| Total Contributed Capital ............................... | | 211,000 |

Retained Earnings:

Appropriated:

| | | |
|---|---:|---:|
| Reserve for bond sinking fund .............................. | 50,000 | |
| Unappropriated .......................................................... | 70,000 | |
| Total Retained Earnings .................................... | | 120,000 |
| Unrealized increment, discovery value of natural resource ........................................................... | | 50,000 |
| Total Stockholders' Equity ............................ | | $381,000 |

of the stock certificates. Par-value stock may be either common or preferred. In the early history of corporations in the United States, only par-value stock was authorized. Since the owners of a corporation were not liable to creditors (beyond the assets of the corporation), statutes provided for a par value to afford some measure of protection to creditors. In this respect the courts tended to hold that shareholders who had paid *less* than par value for their stock could be assessed for an amount equal to the discount to satisfy creditors' claims. Par-value stock sold initially at less than par is said to have been issued at a discount, whereas par-value stock sold above par is said to have been issued at a premium. Today the issuance of stock at a discount is illegal in most, if not all, states. Subsequent to issue, par value has no particular relationship to market value. Today par value has significance in most states in that (1) it represents the minimum amount that must be paid in at initial sale of the stock, (2) it establishes the maximum liability of a holder of a share of stock in case of insolvency or liquidation, and (3) it establishes the minimum amount of owners' equity that must be maintained.

In order to avoid a real or implied discount, most new corporations, and those distributing new issues, use a very low par value, such as $1, and offer the stock at a much higher price such as $10, $20, or even $100 per share.

### Nopar-Value Stock

True nopar stock does not carry a designated or assigned value per share—nor is such provided for in the articles of incorporation. However, the laws of most states authorize the issuance of nopar stock with a *stated* or *assigned* value. The stated or assigned value is established by the corporate directors or the bylaws of the corporation. Nopar stock with a stated or assigned value is encountered more frequently than is true nopar stock. The use of an assigned or stated value serves to place the nopar stock on practically the same basis as par-value stock for accounting purposes. Both common and preferred stock may be represented by nopar shares. Nopar stock was first permitted by statute in New York in 1912; since that date the authorization of stock without par value has become so generally accepted that today practically all states permit its issuance. The chief advantages claimed for this type of stock are as follows:

1. It avoids a contingent liability of stockholders to creditors for stock discount.
2. It places the investor on guard to determine the true value of the stock rather than blindly to assume it to be worth the par value.
3. It facilitates the accounting for capital in that the total amount paid in generally is credited to the capital stock account.
4. It does away with the dubious expediency, frequently encountered in par-value stock, of overvaluing assets received for stock in order to report such stock fully paid. The use of nopar stock is particularly advantageous in connection with issuance for property such as patents, leaseholds, manufacturing rights, goodwill, and other intangibles, the true worth of which has not been proved.

The disadvantages of nopar stock result from excessive franchise and other taxes levied by some jurisdictions and the opportunity to manipulate part of the proceeds of the issue to give the appearance of excessive paid-in capital upon organization. Conversely, in some jurisdictions there is less tax on nopar shares.

### Legal Capital

The distinction between par and nopar capital stock may be more fully appreciated by a consideration of legal capital. The total proprietary equity in a corporation is represented by capital contributed by owners, capital contributed by outsiders, retained earnings, and unrealized capital increments. *Legal capital* is defined by the laws of each state somewhat differently. Recall that the stockholders in a corporation have limited liability; that is, they cannot be held legally liable for the debts of the corporation. In order to afford some measure of protection to creditors, state laws designate some minimum investment in the corporation to be identified specifically as legal capital. This legal capital usually cannot be returned to the owners through dividends or by purchase of shares held by them, unless creditor claims are first satisfied.

When par-value stock is issued, most states specify that the par value of all outstanding shares constitutes legal capital. In the case of nopar stock the legal capital generally is regarded as the stated or assigned value per share. In the case of true nopar stock most states require that the full proceeds from the sale of nopar stock be treated as legal capital. In case the legal capital is impaired through dividend payments or purchase of the corporation's own shares (treasury stock), the courts generally have held that creditors may obtain payment from the shareholders for claims to the extent of such impairment.

The concept of legal capital is particularly important in accounting for corporate ownership equities. The capital accounts should be maintained so that sources are known, thereby providing appropriate data for determination of legal capital in conformance with the statutes of the particular state in which incorporated. Since state statutes define legal capital and there is considerable variation as between states, careful accounting for corporate capital is essential.

The amount of legal capital should be entered in the capital stock account, and investments in excess of legal capital should be recorded in other appropriately designated capital accounts.

## Common Stock

Common stock represents the basic issue of shares and normally carries all of the basic rights listed in a preceding paragraph. When there is only one class of stock all of the shares are common stock.

## Preferred Stock

Preferred stock is so designated because it has some preference or priority over the common stock. The preference or priority may relate to:

1. Dividends.
    a. Cumulative or noncumulative.
    b. Fully participating, partially participating, or nonparticipating.
2. Assets.
3. Redemption.
4. Convertibility.

Since the right to vote is a basic right, preferred shareholders have full voting rights unless specifically prohibited in the charter. Likewise, all the other basic rights listed in a preceding paragraph apply to preferred stock unless specifically stated otherwise in the charter.

Preferred stock is usually par-value stock, in which case the dividend preference is expressed as a percentage. For example, 6% preferred stock would carry a dividend preference of 6% of the *par value* of each share. In the case of nopar preferred stock a dividend preference is expressed as a specific dollar *amount* per share. Occasionally a corporation may issue two or more classes of preferred stock each having different preferences.

In order to identify correctly the preferences relating to preferred stock, corporations must indicate on the stock certificate the exact nature of the preferences; that is, whether the stock is cumulative, participating, callable, or convertible.[2]

## Cumulative Preferences on Preferred Stock

Noncumulative preferred stock provides that dividends not declared (i.e., dividends passed or in arrears) for any year or series of years are lost permanently as far as the preferred shareholder is concerned. As a result the noncumulative restriction generally is viewed as an undesirable feature by potential investors.

Cumulative preferred stock provides that dividends in arrears for any year or series of years accumulate and must be paid to the preferred shareholders when dividends are declared, before the common stockholders may receive a dividend. If only a part of the preference is met for any one year, then the balance of the preference is in arrears. Cumulative preferred stock does not carry the right, in liquidation of the corporation, to dividends in arrears if there are no retained earnings. However, express provisions may be made in the charter and stock specifications concerning dividends in arrears in such situations. At common law, where the charter is silent as to the cumulative feature, preferred stock is considered to be cumulative.

*APB Opinion No. 9*, paragraph 35, requires disclosure on the financial statements of "the aggregate and per share amounts of arrearages in cumulative preferred dividends."

## Participating Preferences on Preferred Stock

Preferred stock is *fully* participating when the preferred shareholders are entitled to extra dividends on a pro rata basis (based on par or stated value) with the holders of common stock. In this case the preference relates to a prior claim to dividends up to a stated percent of par (the preferential rate), after which both classes of stock share ratably (including the preference).

Preferred stock is nonparticipating when the dividends on such stock for any one year are limited in the charter to a specified preferential rate. *Partially* participating preferred stock provides that the shareholders thereof participate above the preferential rate with the common stockholders, but only up to an additional rate which is specified in the charter and on the stock certificate. For example, a corporation may issue 6% preferred stock, with participation up to a total of 8%, in which case participation privileges with the common shareholders would be limited to an additional 2%.

---

[2] In some cases the distinction between common and preferred stock represents restrictions or negative features. For example, noncumulative, nonparticipating, and nonvoting are negative features.

In the absence of an expressed stipulation most courts have taken the view that preferred stock has no right to participate with the common stock, unless this preference is stated expressly in the preferred stock specifications in the charter.

Since accountants frequently are called upon to advise management with respect to dividend declarations, it is important that computation of dividends be clearly understood. To illustrate dividend computations, assume the following:

Preferred stock, 5% ($100 par value per share — 1,000 shares) ... $100,000
Common stock ($100 par value per share — 2,000 shares) ...... 200,000

| | Preferred | Common |
|---|---|---|
| *Illustration No. 1:* Preferred stock is cumulative, nonparticipating; dividends two years in arrears; dividends declared, $28,000. | | |
| Step 1 — Preferred in arrears .................................... | $10,000 | |
| Step 2 — Preferred, current (at 5%) ........................... | 5,000 | |
| Step 3 — Common (balance) .................................... | | $13,000 |
| | $15,000 | $13,000 |
| *Illustration No. 2:* Preferred stock is cumulative, fully participating; dividends two years in arrears; dividends declared, $28,000. | | |
| Step 1 — Preferred in arrears .................................... | $10,000 | |
| Step 2 — Preferred, current (at 5%) ........................... | 5,000 | |
| Step 3 — Common, current (to match preferred at 5%) ...... | | $10,000 |
| Step 4 — Balance (ratably with par) ........................... | 1,000 | 2,000 |
| | $16,000 | $12,000 |
| *Illustration No. 3:* Preferred stock is noncumulative, partially participating up to 7%; dividends declared, $28,000. | | |
| Step 1 — Preferred, current (at 5%) ........................... | $ 5,000 | |
| Step 2 — Common, current (to match preferred at 5%) ... | | $10,000 |
| Step 3 — Preferred, partial participation, additional 2% ... | 2,000 | |
| Step 4 — Common (balance) .................................... | | 11,000 |
| | $ 7,000 | $21,000 |
| *Illustration No. 4:* Preferred stock is noncumulative; partially participating up to 7%; dividends declared, $16,000. | | |
| Step 1 — Preferred, current at 5% ............................... | $ 5,000 | |
| Step 2 — Common, current (to match preferred at 5%) ... | | $10,000 |
| Step 3 — {Preferred, partial participation...................... | 333 | |
| {Common..................................................... | | 667 |
| | $ 5,333 | $10,667 |

Preferred stock that is *preferred as to assets* (i.e., a liquidation preference) provides that the holders, in case of corporate dissolution, have a priority up to par value or other stated amount per share over common shareholders. Once the priority for the preferred is satisfied, the remainder of the assets are distributed to the common shareholders.

*APB Opinion No. 10,* paragraph 10, states that "the liquidation preference of the preferred stock be disclosed in the equity section of the balance sheet in the aggregate, either parenthetically or 'in short' rather than on a per share basis or by disclosure in notes."

Preferred stock having *redemption* privileges (redeemable stock), provides that the shareholder, at his or her option, may, under the conditions specified, turn in the shares owned to the corporation at a specified price per share.

Preferred stock may carry a provision of *convertibility* (convertible stock), at the option of the holder, for other securities such as common stock. Conversion privileges frequently turn out to be particularly valuable and, hence, are favored by investors.

Preferred stock may be *callable;* that is, the corporation may, at its option, call the stock (purchase it) for cancellation under specified conditions of time and price.

*APB Opinion No. 10,* paragraph 11, states that there should be disclosure "on the face of the balance sheet or in notes pertaining thereto: the aggregate or per share amounts at which preferred shares may be called or subject to redemption through sinking fund operations or otherwise."

## ACCOUNTING FOR ISSUANCE OF PAR-VALUE STOCK

In accounting for stockholders' equity, recall that *source* is particularly important; accordingly, if a corporation has more than one class of stock, separate accounts must be maintained for each class. In case there is only one class of stock, an account "Capital Stock" is usually employed. In cases where there are two or more classes of stock, titles such as "Common Stock," "Preferred Stock, 5%," and "Common Stock, Nopar" are appropriate. The complete sequence of transactions related to issuance of stock is (a) authorization of shares, (b) subscriptions, (c) collections on subscriptions, and (d) issuance of the shares.

### Authorization

The authorization in the charter to issue a specified number of shares may be recorded (a) by notation or (b) by a formal journal entry. To illustrate, under the first method the notation for the journal and the ledger account heading may be as follows:

Common Stock—Par Value $100 per Share
(authorized 5,000 shares)

In case a formal journal entry is made, it would be as follows:

```
Unissued common stock  ..........................................  500,000
    Common stock (5,000 shares, par $100)  ...............        500,000
    To record authorization of 5,000 shares of common
    stock, par value $100 per share.
```

Observe that these two accounts are offsetting. The notation approach is preferred by most accountants.

## Stock Issued for Cash

In most situations capital stock is sold and issued for cash rather than on a subscription basis. Using the above example and assuming the sale of 1,000 shares at $102 per share, the issue entry would be:

1. Notation method:

| | | |
|---|---:|---:|
| Cash | 102,000 | |
|     Common stock (1,000 shares, par $100) | | 100,000 |
|     Contributed capital in excess of par, common | | 2,000 |

2. Unissued capital stock method:

| | | |
|---|---:|---:|
| Cash | 102,000 | |
|     Unissued common stock (1,000 shares, par $100)... | | 100,000 |
|     Contributed capital in excess of par, common | | 2,000 |

The capital stock account is credited for the par value of the stock times the number of shares issued, and the excess over par is credited to a descriptively named contributed capital account to record *source* in detail.

## ACCOUNTING FOR NOPAR CAPITAL STOCK

Because the statutes in many states permit two types of nopar stock — true nopar stock and stated value nopar stock — there is some variation in accounting. Nopar-value stock with a stated value is accounted for as discussed above for par-value stock since the stated value places the nopar stock on practically the same basis as par-value stock. Amounts received in excess of stated value should be credited to an account with a descriptive title such as Contributed Capital in Excess of Stated Value, Nopar Common Stock.

In the case of *true* nopar stock, no entry can be made for the authorization; instead, notation may be made in the journal and in the ledger account heading such as:

Common Stock — Nopar Value
(authorized 10,000 shares)

With respect to nopar stock, most states require that the total number of shares authorized, as well as the number of shares represented by the individual stock certificate, be shown on the face of each such certificate. It is important to note that entries to record true nopar stock should indicate the *number of shares* as well as the dollar amounts. In the case of true nopar stock the accounting treatment should follow the applicable legal requirements. If the statutes provide that all proceeds represent legal capital, then the capital stock account should be credited for the full amount received so that no "excess" amount need be recorded separately. If the statutes establish a minimum amount per share, then at least this amount should be credited to the capital stock account. In the absence of legal requirements, the total amount received normally should be credited to the capital stock account.

**EXHIBIT 15–2**
**Entries for Nopar Stock**

|  | Stated Value Method | | True Nopar Value Method | |
|---|---|---|---|---|
| 1. To record authorization of nopar stock: | | | | |
| Notation— 10,000 shares of nopar common stock authorized. | (Stated value, $5)* | | (No stated value) | |
| 2. To record sale of 5,000 shares @ $6: | | | | |
| Cash ............................................................... | 30,000 | | 30,000 | |
| Common stock, nopar, stated value $5 ......... | | 25,000 | | |
| Common stock, nopar ................................. | | | | 30,000 |
| Contributed capital in excess of stated value, nopar common stock ............................. | | 5,000 | | |
| 3. To record sale of 5,000 shares @ $6; 20% paid in cash: | | | | |
| Cash ............................................................... | 6,000 | | 6,000 | |
| Subscriptions receivable—nopar common stock... | 24,000 | | 24,000 | |
| Nopar common stock subscribed (5,000 shares) ................................................. | | 25,000 | | 30,000 |
| Contributed capital in excess of stated value, nopar common stock ............................. | | 5,000 | | |
| 4. To record collection of subscription and issuance of stock: | | | | |
| Cash ............................................................... | 24,000 | | 24,000 | |
| Subscriptions receivable—nopar common stock .................................................... | | 24,000 | | 24,000 |
| Nopar common stock subscribed........................ | 25,000 | | 30,000 | |
| Common stock, nopar, stated value $5 (5,000 shares) ......................................... | | 25,000 | | |
| Common stock, nopar (5,000 shares) ........... | | | | 30,000 |

* Note: This could take the form of a journal entry as illustrated above for par-value stock.

The entries in Exhibit 15–2 show the accounting for nopar stock, assuming that the corporation is authorized to issue 10,000 shares of nopar common stock.

### Subscriptions

Prospective stockholders may sign a contract to purchase a specified number of shares with payment to be made at one or more stated dates in the future. Such a contract is known as a *stock subscription*. Since a legal contract is involved, accounting recognition must be given to this transaction. The purchase price is debited to Stock Subscriptions Receivable, Common Stock Subscribed is credited for the par, stated, or assigned amount per share, and the difference is credited to Contributed Capital in Excess of Par (or Stated Value).

To illustrate, assume 1,000 are subscribed for at $102; the entry would be:

| Stock subscriptions receivable—common stock ............... | 102,000 | |
| Common stock subscribed (1,000 shares).................. | | 100,000 |
| Contributed capital in excess of par, common............ | | 2,000 |

Observe that the premium is recorded when the subscription is recorded rather than later when the cash is collected. The Common Stock Subscribed account recognizes the corporation's obligation to issue the 1,000 shares upon fulfillment of the terms of the agreement by the subscribers. This account is reported on the balance sheet in a manner similar to the related capital stock account (see Exhibit 15-1). Subscriptions receivable is classified as a current asset if the corporation expects current collection. If there are no plans for collection, subscriptions receivable cannot be considered a realizable asset and therefore should be offset against capital stock subscribed in the owners' equity section of the balance sheet. In some cases subscription contracts call for installment payments. In such cases separate "call" accounts may be set up for each installment. If there are a number of subscriptions it is usually desirable to maintain a *subscribers' ledger* as a subsidiary record to the subscriptions receivable account in a manner similar to that maintained for regular accounts receivable.

Collections on stock subscriptions may be in cash, property, or services. The appropriate account is debited, and subscriptions receivable is credited. If a service or property is received, the *amount* recorded would result from an agreement between the individual and the corporate officials as to the value of the property or services.

Stock certificates usually are not issued until the subscription price is paid in full.[3] Therefore, the last collection often requires two entries. To illustrate, assume the last collection on the above subscription (for $102,000) was $25,000; the entries would be:

To record collection:

| Cash ..................................................................... | 25,000 | |
| Stock subscriptions receivable—common stock ......... | | 25,000 |

To record issuance of the stock:

| Common stock subscribed ........................................... | 100,000 | |
| Common stock (1,000 shares) ............................... | | 100,000 |

Accounting for nopar stock, including stock subscriptions is illustrated in Exhibit 15-2.

In order to issue the stock, a *stock certificate* is prepared for each shareholder specifying the number of shares represented. An entry for each shareholder would be made in the *stockholder ledger* which is a subsidiary ledger to the capital stock account.

When a subscriber *defaults* after fulfilling a part of the subscription contract, certain complexities arise. In case of default, the corporation simply may decide to (1) return to the subscriber all payments made, or

---

[3] Although the shares are not issued, the subscriber is accorded all the privileges of a stockholder unless the subscription contract specifies otherwise.

(2) issue shares equivalent to the number paid for in full, rather than the total number contracted. These two options obviously involve no disadvantage to the subscriber, although the corporation may incur a resultant loss. The laws of most states cover the contingency where the corporation does not elect either of these alternatives. Such laws vary considerably; two contrasting provisions follow —

a. The stock is *forfeited,* and all payments made by the defaulting subscriber are lost to the subscriber; hence, they become a source of contributed capital to the corporation. Further, the corporation is free to sell the shares again. Obviously, provisions of this type favor the corporation.

b. The stock is forfeited, and the corporation must resell the stock under a *lien,* whereby the original subscriber must be reimbursed for the amount that the total receipts for the stock (his or her payments plus the later sale proceeds), less the costs incurred by the corporation in making the second sale, exceed the original subscription price. The reimbursement to the defaulting subscriber cannot exceed the amount paid by the subscriber to the date of default.

## ACCOUNTING FOR STOCK PREMIUM AND DISCOUNT

In the preceding discussions and illustrations, amounts received in excess of par value were credited to an appropriately designated stock premium account. Similarly, amounts received less than par are debited to an appropriately titled stock discount account. Premium constitutes an increase in total corporate capital, whereas stock discount serves to reduce total corporate capital. In view of the advent of nopar stock and the passage of laws in many states forbidding the sale of stock at a discount, accountants seldom encounter the problem of stock discount.

Contributed capital in excess of par value is classified as contributed or paid-in capital and should remain in the accounts until retirement of the stock. Upon retirement of the stock the related premium should be removed from the accounts. Some states allow such contributed capital to be used for stock dividends; a few allow charges to such accounts for cash dividends as well. When state laws allow these charges, the shareholders receiving the dividends should be informed that they represent a return of original investment (i.e., a liquidating dividend) rather than a distribution of earnings.

Separate premium and discount accounts should be established for each class of stock. Premium and discount should not be offset against each other. Discount can be disposed of by additional collections (stock assessments) from shareholders or through retirement of the related stock. Discount is reported on the balance sheet (a) preferably as a negative item directly under the particular class of stock to which it relates, or (b) secondarily as a negative item under the "other contributed" capital. See Chapter 14 for a discussion of stock issue costs.

## SPECIAL SALES OF STOCK

A corporation may sell each class of stock separately as assumed in the preceding discussions or it may sell two or more classes of securities for one lump sum. Further, a corporation may sell stock for services or property rather than for cash. Each of these situations presents special accounting problems.

In the situation where two or more classes of securities are sold for a single lump sum, the proceeds must be allocated between the several classes of securities on some logical basis. Two methods available for such situations are (a) the proportional method, where the lump sum received is allocated proportionally between the classes of stock such as on the relative fair market value of each security related to the units involved, and (b) the incremental method, where the market value of one security is used as a basis for that security and the remainder of the lump sum is allocated to the other class of security. Selection of an appropriate method should depend upon the information available. To illustrate several situations, assume 100 shares of common stock (par value $100 per share) and 50 shares of preferred stock (par value $80 per share) are sold for a lump sum of $15,000.

*Assumption 1:* The common stock is selling at 104, and the preferred stock at 101 — apportionment on basis of relative fair market values.

| | | |
|---|---:|---:|
| Cash ............................................................................ | 15,000 | |
|     Common stock (100 shares, par $100) .......................... | | 10,000 |
|     Preferred stock (50 shares, par $80)............................. | | 4,000 |
|     Contributed capital in excess of par, common .............. | | 100 |
|     Contributed capital in excess of par, preferred.............. | | 900 |

Computations (rounded):

Common: $\frac{\$10,400}{\$15,450} \times \$15,000 = \$10,100$     $\$10,100 - \$10,000 = \$100$

Preferred: $\frac{\$5,050}{\$15,450} \times \$15,000 = \frac{4,900}{\$15,000}$     $\$ 4,900 - \$ 4,000 = \$900$

*Assumption 2:* The common stock is selling at 104; no market has been established for the preferred stock — apportionment on basis of fair market value of one class of shares.

| | | |
|---|---:|---:|
| Cash ............................................................................ | 15,000 | |
|     Common stock (100 shares, par $100)......................... | | 10,000 |
|     Preferred stock (50 shares, par $80)............................. | | 4,000 |
|     Contributed capital in excess of par, common | | |
|       ($4 per share) ....................................................... | | 400 |
|     Contributed capital in excess of par, preferred.............. | | 600 |

*Assumption 3:* No current market value is determinable for either class of stock. In this case an arbitrary allocation is the only alternative. In the absence of any other logical basis, a temporary allocation may be made on the basis of relative par values. Should a market value be estab-

lished for one of the securities in the relatively near future, a correcting entry based on such value would be appropriate. The entry to record the arbitary allocation would be:

```
Cash ........................................................................... 15,000
        Common stock (100 shares, par $100)........................         10,000
        Preferred stock (50 shares, par $80).............................          4,000
        Contributed capital in excess of par, common ..............            714
        Contributed capital in excess of par, preferred..............            286
    Computations:
```

$$\frac{\$10,000}{\$14,000} \times \$15,000 = \$10,714 \qquad \$10,714 - \$10,000 = \$714$$

$$\frac{\$4,000}{\$14,000} \times \$15,000 = \$4,286 \qquad \$4,286 - \$4,000 = \$286$$

## Noncash Sale of Stock

When a corporation issues stock as payment for assets or services, the question of stock valuation for accounting purposes arises. The values to apply in this situation, in determination of the proceeds, are as follows, in order of preference:

1. Current fair market value of the assets or services.
2. Current fair market value of the stock issued.
3. Appraised value of the assets or services.
4. Valuation of the assets or services established by the board of directors.

The exchange of noncash assets for stock has given rise to many abuses over the years through improper valuation of the assets received. Overvalued assets create an overstatement of corporate capital — a condition frequently referred to as *watered stock*. On the other hand, undervaluation of assets creates an understatement of corporate capital giving rise to what is frequently referred to as *secret reserves*. Secret reserves also may be created by depreciating or amortizing assets over a period substantially less than their useful life.

## UNREALIZED CAPITAL INCREMENT

Unrealized capital increment, as a category of stockholders' equity, is not widely used in practice. It arises when assets are written up above cost; thus, it violates the cost principle. Because of adherence to the cost principle and the concept of conservatism, assets rarely are written up from cost to fair market value (sometimes called appraisal increases). The most common example of such write-ups involve *discovery value* of natural resources. Other examples are to be found in a few industries such as the insurance industry. Typically, in the insurance and mutual fund industries the investment portfolio is adjusted to fair market value at the end of each period. An adjustment upward of the asset account requires an offsetting credit to either revenue or unrealized capital increment. There are a number of unsettled issues such as (*a*) measurement of fair market value, (b) classification of the credit, and (c) adequate disclosure. As the profession moves toward "fair value accounting" these issues will necessarily come into greater focus and demand definitive solutions.

The write-up of fixed assets to appraisal value was briefly discussed in Chapter 13. Other examples are briefly discussed in subsequent chapters. However, except in limited situations, current GAAP does not permit the write-up of assets to fair market value. However, when the fair market value of an asset has dropped significantly below its carrying value in the accounts, it is written down and a loss recognized. Examples are lower of cost or market for inventories and short-term investments, and idle plants.

FASB *Statement No. 12*, "Accounting for Certain Marketable Securities," (December, 1975) requires the recording of an "Unrealized Loss on Long-term Investments in Equity Securities." This *negative* unrealized capital item is discussed in Chapter 18, Part A.

## ASSESSMENTS ON SHAREHOLDERS

Some states permit the issuance of *assessable stock,* providing the charter includes such a provision. Also in some states, under certain conditions, stockholders may be assessed a certain amount per share, although the stock held is not identified as assessable stock. A stock assessment involves the collection of cash from the stockholders in proportion to the shares held without the issuance of additional stock. Stock assessments are used only when the corporation is in dire need of cash or when the stock originally was issued at a discount. If the stock was issued originally at a discount, the assessment (up to the amount of the discount) is credited to the discount account. If no stock discount is carried in the accounts, the credit is to a contributed capital account with an appropriate title such as Contributed Capital, Stock Assessments.

## INCORPORATION OF A GOING BUSINESS

The owner, or owners, of a sole proprietorship or partnership may decide to incorporate, or a corporation may acquire another business in exchange for shares of stock.[4] Certain accounting problems arise in such situations, particularly with respect to (a) the values to be placed on the assets received for shares of stock, and (b) the entries to record the exchange.

In accounting for assets in the situation where an unincorporated business is selling its assets, the cost principle requires that the assets be recorded by the acquirer at their fair market value as of the date of the exchange. If this is not determinable, the fair market value of the stock issued for the assets should be used. In many situations neither of these values can be determined; in such cases the responsible parties

---

[4] See Chapter 18 on business combinations.

involved must be relied upon to establish a realistic estimate of fair market value. It is not unusual, in the case of a going business, for the parties to agree to an exchange value in excess of the total fair market value of the tangible assets acquired because of the recognition of goodwill. In cases where goodwill is paid for, it should be recorded as an intangible asset at the purchased price.

In situations where the only change is in the form of organization; that is, the ownership and management is continuous, as where a partnership is simply incorporated, a case can be made for carrying forward the book values and no recognition of goodwill.

The entries to record the exchange of a going business for shares of stock will depend upon whether the original books of the acquired business will be continued or whether new books will be opened for the corporation, and any adjustments to fair market values.

If the *original books* are retained, two basic steps are required assuming the cost principle applies:

1. Entries must be made to revalue the assets (and any other items agreed upon) in accordance with the cost principle.
2. Entries must be made to close out the old owners' equity accounts, and to replace them with corporate capital accounts.

If *new books* are to be started the old books must be closed and new books for the corporation opened. Entries should be made on the *old books* to—

1. Revalue the assets (and any other items agreed upon) in accordance with the cost principle.
2. Record the transfer of the assets.
3. Record receipt of the stock and its distribution.

Entries must be made on the *new books* to—

1. Record the stock authorization.
2. Record the receipt of the assets.
3. Record issuance of the stock.

To illustrate each situation, assume the books for the AB Partnership showed the following:

| | | | |
|---|---|---|---|
| Cash | $ 2,000 | Accounts payable | $ 5,000 |
| Accounts receivable | 10,000 | Notes payable | 2,000 |
| Allowance for doubtful accounts | (1,000) | A, capital | 30,000 |
| Inventory | 21,000 | B, capital | 20,000 |
| Fixed assets | 40,000 | | |
| Accumulated depreciation | (15,000) | | |
| | $57,000 | | $57,000 |

The XYZ Corporation is formed with 20,000 shares of common stock authorized (par value $5 per share); 12,000 of the shares are issued in exchange for the assets, except the cash; the liabilities are assumed by the corporation. It was agreed that the inventory should be written down to $16,000 and that the accumulated depreciation should be $14,000. The book value of the remaining assets essentially represented fair market value at the time of transfer to XYZ Corporation. The 12,000 shares and the $2,000 cash are to be divided between A and B according to their capital balances after the above adjustments. The partners had divided profits and losses equally. The remaining 8,000 shares were sold to the public at $5.10 per share.

*Assumption 1:* The old books are to be retained.

1. To record the adjustments:

| | | |
|---|---|---|
| Accumulated depreciation | 1,000 | |
| Adjustment account | 4,000 | |
| Inventory | | 5,000 |

2. To record goodwill:[5]

| | | |
|---|---|---|
| Goodwill* | 17,200 | |
| Adjustment account | | 17,200 |

* Computation:

| | |
|---|---|
| Value of shares exchanged (12,000 at $5.10) | $61,200 |
| Value of net assets (after adjustment and excluding cash) | 44,000 |
| Goodwill | $17,200 |

3. To close Adjustment account to partners' capital accounts:

| | | |
|---|---|---|
| Adjustment account | 13,200 | |
| A, capital | | 6,600 |
| B, capital | | 6,600 |

4. Notation: Capital stock authorized, 20,000 shares, par $5 per share.
5. To record distribution of $2,000 cash and issuance of 12,000 shares of stock to the partners for the other assets (net):

| | | |
|---|---|---|
| A, capital ($30,000 + $6,600) | 36,600 | |
| B, capital ($20,000 + $6,600) | 26,600 | |
| Cash | | 2,000 |
| Common stock (12,000 shares, par $5) | | 60,000 |
| Contributed capital in excess of par | | 1,200 |

6. To record sale of 8,000 shares at $5.10 per share:

| | | |
|---|---|---|
| Cash | 40,800 | |
| Common stock (8,000 shares, par $5) | | 40,000 |
| Contributed capital in excess of par | | 800 |

*Assumption 2:* New books are opened and the old books closed. See Exhibit 15–3.

For tax purposes, if control is continued by the original owners (at least 80% of the voting stock), no loss or gain is recognized and the valuation basis for tax purposes remains unchanged.

---

[5] See Chapter 14 for discussion of amortization of goodwill.

**EXHIBIT 15–3**
**Incorporation of a Partnership**

| Entries on New Books | | Entries on Old Books | |
|---|---|---|---|
| 1. To record authorization of capital stock: | | | |
| Notation: Common stock authorized, 20,000 shares, $5. | | | |
| par value per share. | | | |
| 2. To record adjustments agreed upon: | | | |
| | | Accumulated depreciation ............... 1,000 | |
| | | Adjustment account ........................... 4,000 | |
| | | Inventory ................................... | 5,000 |
| 3. To record goodwill (as computed in Assumption 1): | | | |
| | | Goodwill............................................ 17,200 | |
| | | Adjustment account ..................... | 17,200 |
| 4. To close Adjustment account to capital accounts: | | | |
| | | Adjustment account ........................... 13,200 | |
| | | A, capital ............................... | 6,600 |
| | | B, capital ............................... | 6,600 |
| 5. To record transfer of assets and liabilities as adjusted: | | | |
| Accounts receivable ........................... 10,000 | | Allowance for doubtful accounts ......... 1,000 | |
| Inventory ....................................... 16,000 | | Accumulated depreciation .................. 14,000 | |
| Fixed assets .................................... 40,000 | | Accounts payable ............................. 5,000 | |
| Goodwill............................................ 17,200 | | Notes payable .................................. 2,000 | |
| Allowance for doubtful accounts ... | 1,000 | Receivable from XY Corporation ......... 61,200 | |
| Accumulated depreciation ........... | 14,000 | Accounts receivable ..................... | 10,000 |
| Accounts payable ....................... | 5,000 | Inventory ................................... | 16,000 |
| Notes payable ............................ | 2,000 | Fixed assets ................................ | 40,000 |
| Payable to AB partnership ........... | 61,200 | Goodwill...................................... | 17,200 |
| 6. To record transfer of stock: | | | |
| Payable to AB Partnership .................. 61,200 | | Stock in XY Corporation ..................... 61,200 | |
| Common stock............................ | 60,000 | Receivable from XY Corporation ... | 61,200 |
| Contributed capital in excess | | | |
| of par ..................................... | 1,200 | | |
| 7. Distribution of stock and cash: | | | |
| | | A, capital .......................................... 36,600 | |
| | | B, capital .......................................... 26,600 | |
| | | Stock in XY Corporation .............. | 61,200 |
| | | Cash .......................................... | 2,000 |
| 8. To record sale of 8,000 shares at $5.10 per share: | | | |
| Cash ............................................... 40,800 | | | |
| Common stock............................ | 40,000 | | |
| Contributed capital in excess | | | |
| of par ..................................... | 800 | | |

## QUESTIONS

1. Explain the meaning of each of the following: total equity, contributed capital, proprietary equity, and legal capital.

2. Distinguish between public, private, domestic, foreign, open, and closed corporations.

3. What are the four basic rights of shareholders? How may one or more of these rights be withheld from the shareholder?

4. Explain each of the following: authorized capital stock, issued capital stock, unissued capital stock, outstanding capital stock, subscribed stock, and treasury stock.

5. In accounting for corporate capital why is *source* particularly important?

6. Distinguish between par and nopar stock.

7. Distinguish between common and preferred stock.

8. Explain the difference between cumulative and noncumulative stock.

9. Explain the difference between nonparticipating, partially participating, and fully participating stock.

10. Under what circumstances should stock subscriptions receivable be reported (*a*) as a current asset, (*b*) as a noncurrent asset, and (*c*) as a deduction in the corporate capital section of the balance sheet?

11. What is a liquidating dividend? Why is it important that a liquidating dividend be identified separately?

12. Explain and illustrate "secret reserves" and "watered stock."

13. How should premium and discount on capital stock be accounted for and reported?

14. Indicate the priorities for stock valuation when assets other than cash are received in payment thereof.

15. What is a stock assessment?


## DECISION CASE 15–1

C. Banfield, an engineer, developed a special device to be installed in backyard swimming pools that would set off an alarm should anything fall into the water. Over a two-year period Banfield's spare time was spent developing and testing the device. After receiving a patent, three of Banfield's friends, including a lawyer, considered plans to market the device. Accordingly, a charter was obtained which authorized 25,000 shares of $10 par-value stock. Each of the four organizers contributed $1,000, and each received in return 100 shares of stock. They agreed that each would receive 500 additional shares. The remaining shares were to be held as unissued stock. Each organizer made a proposal as to how the additional 500 shares would be paid for. These individual proposals were made independently; then the group considered them as a package. The four proposals were:

BANFIELD: The patent would be turned over to the corporation as payment for the 500 shares.

LAWYER: One hundred shares to be received for legal fees already rendered during organization, 100 shares to be received as advance payment for legal retainer fees for the next three years, and the balance to be paid for in cash at par.

FRIEND No. 3: A small building, suitable for operations, would be turned over to the corporation plus $750 cash, in payment for 500 shares. It was estimated that $750 would be needed for renovation. The owner estimates that the fair value of the property is $25,000 and there is an $18,000 loan on it to be assumed by the corporation.

FRIEND No. 4: To pay $1,000 cash on the stock and to give a noninterest-bearing note for $4,000 to be paid out of dividends over the next five years.

*Required:*

You have been engaged as an independent CPA to advise the group. Specifically, you have been asked the following questions:

1. How would the above proposals be recorded in the accounts? Criticize the valuation basis for each.
2. What are your recommendations for an agreement that would be equitable to each organizer; explain the basis for such recommendations?

## EXERCISES

### Exercise 15–1

Burke Corporation received a charter authorizing 50,000 shares of stock, par value $10 per share. During the course of the first year, 30,000 shares were sold at $15 per share. One hundred additional shares were issued in payment for legal fees. At the end of the first year, reported net income was $20,000. Dividends of $6,000 were paid as of the last day of the year. Liabilities at the year-end amounted to $10,000.

*Required:*

Complete the following tabulation (show calculations):

| Item | Amount | Assumptions |
|------|--------|-------------|
| a. Total equities | $ | |
| b. Owners' equity | $ | |
| c. Contributed capital | $ | |
| d. Legal capital | $ | |
| e. Issued capital stock | $ | |
| f. Outstanding capital stock | $ | |
| g. Unissued capital stock | $ | |
| h. Treasury stock | $ | |

### Exercise 15–2

Texas Corporation charter authorized 50,000 shares of common stock, nopar value, and 20,000 shares of 6%, cumulative and nonparticipating preferred stock, par value, $10 per share. Stock issued to date: 30,000 shares of common sold at $150,000 and 10,000 shares of preferred stock sold at $18 per share. Subscriptions for 1,000 shares of preferred have been taken, and 30% of the purchase price of $18 has been collected. The stock will be issued upon collection in full. The Retained earnings balance is $60,000.

*Required:*

Prepare the stockholders' equity section of the balance sheet in good form.

### Exercise 15–3

Prepare, in good form, the stockholders' equity section of the balance sheet for AB Manufacturing Company.

| | |
|---|---|
| Retained earnings | $ 60,000 |
| Premium on common stock | 32,000 |
| Preferred stock subscribed (1,000 shares) | 10,000 |
| Preferred stock, 6%, par $10, authorized 25,000 shares | 140,000 (issued) |
| Common stock, par $20, authorized 50,000 shares | 160,000 (issued) |
| Stock subscriptions receivable, preferred | 4,000 |
| Donation of plant site | 12,000 |
| Premium on preferred stock | 30,000 |

## Exercise 15–4

The following data were provided by the accounts of Askew Corporation at December 31, 19A:

| | |
|---|---|
| Subscriptions receivable | $ 4,000 |
| Retained earnings | 150,000 |
| Capital stock, par ?, authorized 100,000 shares | 600,000 |
| Future site for office donated | 15,000 |
| Capital stock subscribed, 1,000 shares (to be issued upon collection in full) | 10,000 |
| Premium on capital stock | 315,000 |
| Subscriptions receivable, capital stock (due in three months) | 2,000 |
| Bonds payable | 100,000 |
| Net income for 19A (included in retained earnings above) | 120,000 |

*Required:*

1. Respond to the following (state any assumptions made):

| | |
|---|---|
| a. Total retained earnings is | $_____ |
| b. Retained earnings on January 1, 19A was | $_____ |
| c. The number of shares outstanding is | _____shares |
| d. Legal capital is | $_____ |
| e. Total stockholders' equity is | $_____ |
| f. Earnings per share for 19A was | $_____ |
| g. Number of shares issued is | _____shares |
| h. The selling price per share was | $_____ |
| i. The number of shares sold was | _____shares |
| j. The par value per share is | $_____ |

2. Prepare the stockholders' equity section of the balance sheet at December 31, 19A. Use good form and complete with respect to details.

## Exercise 15–5

Troy Corporation has the following stock outstanding:
Common, $50 par value — 6,000 shares
Preferred, 6%, $100 par value — 1,000 shares

*Required:*

Compute the amount of dividends payable in total and per share on the common and preferred for each separate case:

Case A — Preferred is noncumulative and nonparticipating; dividends declared, $15,000.

Case B – Preferred is cumulative and nonparticipating; three years in arrears; dividends declared, $36,000.

Case C – Preferred is noncumulative and fully participating; dividends declared, $24,000.

Case D – Preferred is noncumulative and fully participating; dividends declared, $33,000.

Case E – Preferred is cumulative and participating up to an additional 3%; three years in arrears; dividends declared, $60,000.

Case F – Preferred is cumulative and fully participating; three years in arrears; dividends declared, $60,000.

## Exercise 15–6

Baker Corporation reported net income during four successive years as follows: $1,000; $2,000; $1,000; and $20,000.

The capital stock consisted of $70,000 common (par $20 per share) and $30,000 of 5% preferred (par $10 per share).

*Required:*

If net income in full were declared and paid as dividends each year, determine the amount to be paid on each class of stock for each of the four years assuming:

Case A – Preferred is noncumulative and nonparticipating.
Case B – Preferred is cumulative and nonparticipating.
Case C – Preferred is noncumulative and fully participating.
Case D – Preferred is cumulative and fully participating.

## Exercise 15–7

Tavis Corporation received a charter authorizing the issuance of 100,000 shares of common stock. Give the journal entries in parallel columns for the following transactions during the first year assuming: Case A – par value of $5 per share; and Case B – true nopar stock.

*a.* To record authorization.
*b.* Sold 50,000 shares at $6; collected in full and issued shares.
*c.* Received subscriptions for 10,000 shares at $6 per share; collected 60% of the subscription price. The stock will not be issued until collection in full.
*d.* Issued 100 shares to attorney in payment for legal fees.
*e.* Issued 8,000 shares and paid cash $50,000 in payment for a building.
*f.* Collected balance on subscriptions receivable in (*c*).

State and justify any assumptions you made.

## Exercise 15–8

Story Manufacturing Company's charter authorized the issuance of 50,000 shares of nopar common stock. Give journal entries for the following transactions assuming: Case A – the board of directors set a stated value of $6 per share; Case B – the stock is true nopar. Set up two columns so that Case A is to the left and Case B is to the right. Explain and justify any assumptions you make.

*a.* Authorization recognized.
*b.* Sold 30,000 shares at $7 and collected in full; shares were issued.
*c.* Received subscriptions for 10,000 shares at $7 per share; collected 40% of the subscription price. The shares will be issued upon collection in full.

*d.* Issued 100 shares for legal services.

*e.* Issued 2,000 shares and paid $10,000 cash for some used machinery.

*f.* Collected balance of subscriptions in (*c*).

## Exercise 15–9

Morley Corporation charter authorized 100,000 shares of $10 par-value stock. A. B. Cook subscribed to 500 shares at $25 per share, paying $2,500 down, the balance to be paid $1,000 per month. The stock will not be issued until collection in full. After paying for three months, Cook defaulted. Subsequently, the corporation sold the stock for $30 per share and at that time made a full refund to Cook.

*Required:*

Give all entries relative to the 500 shares originally subscribed for by Cook. State and justify any assumptions you made.

## Exercise 15–10

The charter for Kork Manufacturing Company authorized 50,000 shares of common stock ($100 par value) and 10,000 shares of preferred stock ($50 par value). The company issued 100 shares of common and 50 shares of preferred for used machinery.

*Required:*

For each separate situation, give the entry to record the purchase of the machinery assuming: Case A – the common stock currently is selling at $120 and the preferred at $60; Case B – the common stock has been selling at $120 and there have been no recent sales of the preferred stock; Case C – there is no current market price for either class of stock, however, the machinery has been appraised at $14,000.

State and justify any assumptions made.

## Exercise 15–11

RT Corporation charter authorized 10,000 shares of $20 par value common stock and 10,000 shares of $10 preferred stock. The following transactions were completed. Assume each is completely independent.

*a.* Sold 200 shares of common and 100 shares of preferred for a lump sum amounting to $6,000. The common had been selling at $25 and the preferred at $12.

*b.* Issued 40 shares of common stock for some used equipment. The equipment had been appraised at $1,100; the book value shown by the seller was $600.

*c.* A 10% assessment on par was voted on both the common and preferred when 6,000 shares of common and 4,000 shares of preferred were outstanding. The assessment was collected in full.

*d.* Sold 300 shares of common and 200 shares of preferred to one person for a total cash price of $10,000. The common recently had been selling at $26; there were no recent sales of the preferred.

*Required:*

Give the journal entries for each transaction. State and justify any assumptions you made.

**Exercise 15-12**

Model Corporation was incorporated with 250 shares of capital stock, par $100; 210 of the shares were issued for the equity in the Brown and Black partnership. The remaining 40 shares were sold at par. The balance in the accounts for the partnership were as follows:

| | | | |
|---|---:|---|---:|
| Cash | $ 1,000 | Accounts payable | $10,000 |
| Notes receivable | 3,000 | Allowance for doubtful | |
| Accounts receivable | 7,000 | accounts | 1,000 |
| Inventory | 6,000 | Accumulated depreciation | 2,000 |
| Fixed assets | 15,000 | Brown, capital | 10,000 |
| | | Black, capital | 9,000 |
| | $32,000 | | $32,000 |

The following adjustments were to be made prior to the exchange: decrease inventory to $4,000 and increase accumulated depreciation to $3,000. The partners shared profits equally.

*Required:*

Give entries assuming the old books are to be continued (compute goodwill assuming the fair market value of the stock issued was $100 per share).

## PROBLEMS

### Problem 15-1

Using appropriate data from the information given below, prepare, in good form, the stockholders' equity section of a balance sheet for the Miller Corporation.

| | |
|---|---:|
| Stock subscriptions receivable, preferred stock | $ 8,000 |
| Reserve for bond sinking fund | 60,000 |
| Unrealized capital increment per appraisal of natural resources (discovery value) | 45,000 |
| Preferred stock, 6%, authorized 1,000 shares, par $100 per share, cumulative and participating | 60,000 |
| Bonds payable, 7% | 125,000 |
| Common stock, nopar, 5,000 shares authorized and outstanding | 250,000 |
| Donation of future plant site | 6,000 |
| Premium on preferred stock | 12,000 |
| Discount on bonds payable | 1,000 |
| Retained earnings, unappropriated | 50,000 |
| Preferred stock subscribed (to be issued upon collection in full) | 10,000 |

### Problem 15-2

Moore Corporation was granted a charter authorizing 10,000 shares of 6% preferred stock, par value $10 per share, and 50,000 shares of common stock, nopar value. No stated or assigned value was identified with the common stock. During the first year, the following transactions occurred:

a. 20,000 shares of common stock were sold for cash at $5 per share.
b. 1,000 shares of preferred stock sold for cash at $15 per share.
c. Subscriptions were received for 1,000 shares of preferred stock at $15 per share;

40% was received as a down payment, and the balance in two equal install-ments. The shares will be issued upon collection in full.

d. 5,000 shares of common stock, 500 shares of preferred stock, and $15,500 cash were given as payment for a small plant that the company needed. This plant originally cost $40,000 and had a depreciated value on the books of the selling company of $20,000.

e. The first installment on the preferred subscriptions was collected.

*Required:*

1. Give journal entries to record the above transactions. State and justify any assumptions you made.
2. Prepare the stockholders' equity section of the balance sheet at year-end. Re-tained earnings at the end of the year amounted to $17,000.

## Problem 15-3

Fisher Corporation received a charter to conduct a manufacturing business. It was authorized to issue common stock 50,000 shares, nopar value; and 6% preferred stock 10,000 shares, cumulative and nonparticipating and par value per share of $10. During the first year, the following transactions occurred:

a. Each of the six incorporators subscribed to 1,000 shares of the common at $15 per share and 500 shares of the preferred, at par. One half of the subscrip-tion price was paid and one half of the subscribed shares issued.

b. Another individual purchased 500 shares of common and 100 shares of pre-ferred stock paying $9,010 cash.

c. One of the incorporators purchased a used machine for $40,000 and imme-diately transferred to the Fisher Corporation for 2,000 shares of common stock, 200 shares of preferred stock, and a one year interest-bearing note for $8,000.

d. The investors paid the subscriptions, and the remaining stock was issued.

*Required:*

1. Give all entries indicated for the Fisher Corporation.
2. Prepare the stockholders' equity section of the balance sheet. Assume Retained earnings of $23,000 at year-end.

## Problem 15-4

Grayson Corporation received a charter that authorized 100,000 shares of cap-ital stock. During the first year, the following transactions affecting stockholders' equity were completed:

a. Sold 60,000 shares at $25 per share for cash.

b. Received a subscription for 1,000 shares at $25 per share, collected 60% cash, balance due within one year. The stock will be issued upon collection in full.

c. Issued 500 shares for a used machine that would be used in operations. The machine had cost $20,000 new and was carried by the seller at a book value of $11,000. It was recently appraised at $13,000.

d. Collected one half of the unpaid subscriptions in (b).

*Required:*

1. Give entries for each of the above transactions, assuming: Case A—the stock has a par value of $10 per share; Case B—the stock is true nopar value; Case C—the stock is nopar; however, it is assigned a stated value of $5 per share.

Set up parallel columns for each case. State and justify any assumptions you make.
2. Prepare the stockholders' equity section of the balance sheet at the end of the first year for each case. Use good form. Assume a balance in Retained earnings of $124,000.

## Problem 15–5

The charter for Jackson Corporation authorized 500,000 shares of capital stock. During the first year of operations, the following transactions were completed that affected stockholders' equity:

a. Sold 400,000 shares of capital stock at $10 per share; collected cash.
b. Sold 10,000 shares of capital stock to one individual at $10 per share. Collected 40% of the subscription and the balance is due at the end of one year. The shares will be issued upon collection in full.
c. Exchanged 6,000 shares of capital stock for a plant site. The site was carried on the books of the seller at $25,000, and it had been appraised within the past year at $65,000.
d. Collected $12,000 on the subscription in (b).

*Required:*
1. Give entries for the above transactions assuming:

Case A – Par-value stock; $2 par value per share.
Case B – True nopar-value stock.
Case C – Nopar-value stock with a stated value of $1 per share.

Set up parallel columns for each case. State and justify any assumptions you make.
2. Prepare the stockholders' equity section of the balance sheet at the end of the first year for each case. Use good form. Assume a $119,000 ending balance in Retained earnings and, in addition, a reserve for bond sinking fund of $10,000.

## Problem 15–6

The charter of Peerless Corporation authorized the issuance of 20,000 shares of 6% cumulative, nonparticipating preferred stock, par $10 per share, and 100,000 shares of common stock, nopar value. During the first year of operations, the following transactions affecting stockholders' equity were completed:

a. The promoters sold 9,000 shares of the preferred stock at par; the stock was issued.
b. Subscriptions were received for an additional 1,000 shares of preferred stock at $10.50 per share; 20% was collected, the balance is to be paid in three equal installments, at which time the stock will be issued.
c. Each of the three promoters was issued 1,000 shares of common stock (only the common stock carried voting privileges) at $20 per share, each paid one fifth in cash, the remainder was considered to be reimbursement for promotional activities; the shares were issued. Debit Organization expense.
d. An individual purchased 100 shares of preferred and 100 shares of common stock and paid a single sum of $3,300. The stock was issued. Assume a current market price of $20 for the preferred stock and no current market for the common.
e. Collected cash from the promoters (b above) for 10% of the receivable.

*f.* Issued 5,000 shares of common stock for a used plant. The plant had been appraised during the past month at $110,000 and was carried by the seller at a book value of $60,000.

*Required:*

1. Prepare journal entries to record the foregoing transactions. State and justify any assumptions you make.
2. Prepare the stockholders' equity section of the balance sheet assuming retained earnings at year-end of $131,000.

## Problem 15–7

The stockholders' equity section of the balance sheet for the Day Metals Corporation at the end of its first fiscal year was reported as follows:

*Stockholders' Equity*

Contributed Capital:

Capital stock:

| | | |
|---|---:|---:|
| Preferred 6% cumulative, $100 par value, redeemable at $125 per share, authorized 5,000 shares, issued and outstanding 4,185 .......................... | $  418,500 | |
| Preferred stock subscribed, 465 shares .............. | 46,500 | $  465,000 |
| Common stock, stated value $8 per share, authorized 1,500,000 shares, issued and outstanding 954,000 shares............................................. | 7,632,000 | |
| Common stock subscribed, 106,000 shares ......... | 848,000 | 8,480,000 |
| Other contributed capital: | | |
| Excess of par, preferred stock ......................... | 15,000 | |
| In excess of stated value, common stock ........... | 21,200 | 36,200 |
| Retained earnings ............................................... | | 110,000 |
| Total Stockholders' Equity .......................... | | $9,091,200 |

*Required:*

Prepare journal entries during the first year as indicated by the above report. Use unissued stock accounts and assume that all stock was purchased through subscriptions under terms of 60% down and 40% six months later. Also assume that 90% of the subscriptions were collected in full by year-end. The shares are issued upon collection in full.

## Problem 15–8

Tobias Corporation reported net income during five successive years as follows: $20,000; $30,000; $9,000; $5,000; and $60,000. The capital stock consisted of $300,000, $20 par value common and $200,000, $10 par value, 6% preferred.

*Required:*

For each separate case, prepare a computation showing the amount each class of stock would receive in dividends (1) if the entire net income was distributed each year, and (2) if 60% of the earnings were distributed each year.

Case A — Preferred stock is noncumulative and nonparticipating.
Case B — Preferred stock is cumulative and nonparticipating.
Case C — Preferred stock is cumulative and fully participating.

## Problem 15–9

The charter for Hillary Corporation authorized 5,000 shares of 6% preferred stock, par value $20 per share, and 8,000 shares of common stock, par value of $50 per share, all of which have been issued. In a five-year period, total dividends paid were $4,000; $40,000; $32,000; $5,000; and $40,000.

*Required:*

Compute the amount of dividends paid to each class of stock for each year under the following separate cases:

Case A – Preferred stock is noncumulative and nonparticipating.
Case B – Preferred stock is cumulative and nonparticipating.
Case C – Preferred stock is noncumulative and fully participating.
Case D – Preferred stock is cumulative and fully participating.
Case E – Preferred stock is cumulative and partially participating up to an additional 2%.

## Problem 15–10

Town Corporation was formed with 5,000 shares of capital stock authorized. The shares were to be issued as follows:

*a.* 400 shares for $40,800 cash.
*b.* 800 shares for the equity in the RT Partnership which reported the following balance sheet at "appraised fair market value."

| | | | |
|---|---|---|---|
| Accounts receivable | $ 13,000 | Notes payable | $ 20,000 |
| Inventory | 22,000 | R, capital | 40,000 |
| Fixed assets | 65,000 | T, capital | 40,000 |
| | $100,000 | | $100,000 |

*Required:*

Give entries for the acquisition of the partnership on (1) the partnership books and (2) the corporation books (new books are opened) in each separate case below, assuming profits are divided equally:

Case A – The capital stock has a par value of $50, and the implied goodwill is recognized.
Case B – The capital stock is nopar value with a stated value of $40 per share. The goodwill is to be recognized.
Case C – The capital stock is nopar value and is to be recorded on a consideration-received basis. The goodwill is to be recognized.

*Hint:* Set up six columns across the top; that is, a debit and credit column for each case. List entries down the left side. Do not use unissued and subscription accounts. State and justify any assumptions you make.

## Problem 15–11

National Corporation was formed to take over the partnership of Brown and Smith. The charter authorized 10,000 shares of capital stock, par value $100 per share. The balance sheet as of June 30 for Brown and Smith was as follows (at book value):

### BROWN & SMITH PARTNERSHIP

| Assets | | Liabilities and Proprietorship | |
|---|---:|---|---:|
| Cash | $ 10,000 | Accounts payable | $ 29,000 |
| Accounts receivable | 13,000 | Accrued expenses | 4,000 |
| Allowance for doubtful | | Brown, proprietorship | 60,000 |
| accounts | (1,000) | Smith, proprietorship | 40,000 |
| Prepaid expenses | 1,000 | | |
| Buildings | 90,000 | | |
| Accumulated | | | |
| depreciation | (20,000) | | |
| Equipment | 60,000 | | |
| Accumulated | | | |
| depreciation | (30,000) | | |
| Land | 10,000 | | |
| | $133,000 | | $133,000 |

The partnership profits and losses were divided 70% to Brown and 30% to Smith. Incorporators were Brown, Smith, Franks, Box, and Cane. The latter three purchased 2,000 shares each at $102. According to the agreement, 1,500 shares will be issued to Brown and Smith, based upon their capital balances, in payment for the business (including the liabilities), except for cash $10,000 which will be distributed 60% to Brown and 40% to Smith (i.e., in their capital ratios prior to adjustment). The following adjustments to the appraised fair market value, prior to the exchange, were agreed upon:

a. Allowance for doubtful accounts increased to $3,000.
b. Accumulated depreciation, buildings decreased to $7,000.
c. Land revalued to $20,000.
d. Goodwill recognition based on the "appraised fair market values."

*Required:*

1. Prepare entries for National Corporation assuming the old partnership books are to be continued by the corporation. The partnership will go out of existence.
2. Prepare an unclassified balance sheet immediately after the above entries.

# Chapter 16

# Corporations – Retained Earnings and Dividends

In Chapter 15, the three major categories of corporate capital were identified as contributed capital, retained earnings, and unrealized capital increment. Contributed capital was discussed there; this chapter focuses on retained earnings and dividends.

Retained earnings represent the accumulated gains and losses of a corporation to date reduced by dividend distributions to shareholders and amounts transferred to permanent capital accounts. *Gains* and *losses* may come from regular operations, nonrecurring or unusual transactions, extraordinary items, and prior period adjustments. If the accumulated losses and distributions of retained earnings exceed the accumulated gains, a *deficit* in retained earnings exists and must be reported.

Some variation in terminology with respect to retained earnings may be noted in practice. In prior years the term *earned surplus* was commonly used to denote what has been defined above as retained earnings. More descriptive terminology is much preferred since the basic concept involved is strongly implied, whereas the older term is quite inappropriate since there is no "surplus." On this point the AICPA Committee on Terminology recommended:

> The use of the term *surplus* (whether standing alone or in such combinations as *capital surplus, paid-in surplus, earned surplus, appraisal surplus,* etc.) be discontinued. . . .
>
> The term *earned surplus* be replaced by terms which will indicate source, such as *retained income, retained earnings, accumulated earnings* or *earnings retained for use in the business.*[1]

In accounting for stockholders' equity careful distinction is maintained between contributed capital (comprised of the capital stock and other contributed capital accounts) and retained earnings.

---

[1] AICPA, "Review and Résumé," *Accounting Terminology Bulletin No. 1* (New York, 1961), pp. 30–31.

It is reemphasized that in accounting for retained earnings, as with other elements of corporate capital, reporting in terms of *source* is paramount.

In accounting for *total* retained earnings, often more than one account is involved. Total retained earnings at a given date may be represented in two categories of accounts. The Retained Earnings account (undesignated otherwise) represents that portion of retained earnings not appropriated or set aside by the management for specific purposes. The second category is often called appropriated retained earnings, and the accounts comprising it are given special designations such as Retained Earnings Appropriated for Bond Sinking Fund (or, Reserve for Bond Sinking Fund). This category is discussed in a subsequent section. The usual debits and credits to the Retained Earnings account are as follows:

Retained Earnings

| *Debits* | *Credits* |
|---|---|
| Net losses (including extraordinary losses) | Net income (including extraordinary gains) |
| Prior period adjustments | Prior period adjustments |
| Cash dividends | |
| Stock dividends | |

Particularly observe that no debits or credits are included that occur as a result of the sale, issuance, purchase (as treasury stock), or exchanges of capital stock. These items are accounted for as elements of contributed capital.

## DIVIDENDS

Dividends consist of distributions to the corporation's stockholders in proportion to the number of shares of each class of stock held. In most cases such distributions take place at regular intervals; however, on occasion, extraordinary dividends may be distributed. The term *dividends* used alone usually refers to cash dividends. When dividends in a form other than cash are distributed, they should be labeled according to the form of disbursement. The following types of dividends are encountered with some frequency by accountants:

1. Cash dividends.
2. Property dividends.
3. Liability or scrip dividends.
4. Liquidating dividends.
5. Stock dividends.

Distributions to stockholders may involve:

1. The distribution of corporate assets and a decrease in *total* corporate capital as in the case of cash, property, or liquidating dividends.
2. The creation of a liability and a decrease in *total* corporate capital

as in the case of liability dividends or a cash dividend declared but not yet paid.

3. No change in assets, liabilities, or *total* corporate capital, but only a change in the internal categories of corporate capital as in the case of a stock dividend.

The question always arises on the "use" of retained earnings for dividends. Obviously, dividends are not *paid* with retained earnings but are paid with cash or some other asset (except in the case of a stock dividend). More appropriately, dividends generally reduce both retained earnings and assets. Cash or property dividends cannot be paid without this dual effect. As noted above, assets other than cash, and even liabilities, may be involved in dividend distributions. Similarly other elements of corporate capital may be affected rather than retained earnings. The laws of all states allow retained earnings to be used as a basis for dividends, although some states place restrictions even here, such as a provision that dividends in any one year may not exceed the earnings for the preceding year. Some states permit debits to certain contributed capital accounts, such as stock premium, as a basis for cash dividends, providing creditor interests are not jeopardized.[2] Generally statutes are much more liberal with respect to stock dividends since no assets are disbursed. The statutes of the particular state are controlling; however, in the absence of any statement or information to the contrary one should assume a debit to Retained Earnings when dividend distributions are recorded.

In accounting for dividends three dates are important: (1) date of declaration, (2) date of record, and (3) date of payment. Prior to payment, dividends must be formally *declared* by the board of directors of the corporation. Stockholders normally cannot force a dividend declaration; the courts have consistently held that dividend declaration is a matter of prudent management to be decided upon by the duly elected board of directors. Of course, the board must meet all statutory, charter, and by-law requirements, act in good faith, and protect the interests of all parties involved. In deciding whether to declare a dividend (and of what type), the board of directors should consider the financial impact on the company, including the adequacy of cash and retained earnings, and financial expectations for the future including corporate growth and expansion needs.

On the *date of declaration* the board formally announces the dividend declaration. In the case of a cash or property dividend, the declaration is recorded on this date by debiting Retained Earnings and crediting Dividends Payable. In the absence of fraud or illegality,[3] the courts have held that formal announcement of the declaration of a cash, property, or liability dividend constitutes an enforceable contract (i.e., a nonrevocable declaration) between the corporation and the shareholders. In view of the irrevocability of this action, the liability is recorded on

---

[2] A liquidating dividend may be involved; see subsequent section on liquidating dividends.
[3] Questions of legality should be referred to an attorney.

declaration date. In the case of *stock dividends,* no assets are involved, directly or indirectly, as far as the corporation is concerned; therefore, the courts generally have held that a stock dividend declaration is revocable. Consequently, no formal entry is made on declaration date in the case of a stock dividend.[4]

The *date of record* is selected by the board and is stated in the announcement of the declaration. The date of record is the date on which the list of stockholders of record is prepared. Individuals holding stock at this date receive the dividend, regardless of sales or purchases of stock after this date. No formal dividend entry is made in the records on this date.

The *date of payment* is also determined by the board and generally is stated in the announcement of the declaration. At the date of payment, in the case of cash or property dividends, the liability recorded at date of declaration is debited, and the appropriate asset account is credited. A stock dividend distribution is recorded on this date as illustrated in a subsequent section.

Dividends on par-value stock may be stated as a certain percent of the par value, but dividends on nopar stock must be stated as a dollar amount per share.

## Cash Dividends

The usual form of distributions to stockholders involves cash dividends. The declaration must meet the preferences of the preferred stockholders and then may extend to the common stockholders. In declaring a cash dividend the board of directors should be careful that the cash position for the coming months is not jeopardized and the retained earnings balance is sufficient. The cash problem may be met, in part, by careful selection of the *payment* date.

To illustrate a cash dividend, assume the following announcement is made: The board of directors of the Bass Company, at their meeting on January 20, 19A, declared a dividend of $.50 per share, payable March 20, 19A, to shareholders of record as of March 1, 19A. Assume further that 10,000 shares of stock, par value $10 per share, are outstanding.

At date of declaration (January 20, 19A):[5]

Retained earnings (or dividends paid) ................................... 5,000
    Cash dividends payable................................................... 5,000

At date of record (March 1, 19A):

No entry. The stockholders' record is "closed," and the list of dividend recipients is prepared.

---

[4] A few accountants prefer to make a formal entry at this date. See subsequent section on stock dividends. Also, in the case of cash dividends, if the declaration date and payment date are in the same accounting period there would be no reason to make an entry in the accounts on the declaration date.

[5] Sometimes a temporary account, Dividends Paid, is debited at this date and subsequently closed to Retained Earnings.

At date of payment (March 20, 19A):

| | | |
|---|---|---|
| Cash dividends payable........................................................ | 5,000 | |
| Cash ............................................................................ | | 5,000 |

Cash Dividends Payable is reported on the balance sheet as a current liability.

## Property Dividends

Corporations occasionally pay dividends in a form of assets other than cash. Such dividends are known as property dividends. The property may be in the form of securities of other companies held by the corporation, real estate, merchandise, or any other asset designated by the board of directors. Property received by the stockholder as a dividend is subject to income tax at its fair market value.

A property dividend should be recorded at the fair market value of the assets transferred. On this point *APB Opinion No. 29* (May 1973), "Accounting for Nonmonetary Transactions," states:

> A transfer of a nonmonetary asset to a stockholder or to another entity in a nonreciprocal transfer should be recorded at the fair value of the asset transferred, and a gain or loss should be recognized on disposition of the asset.

Most property dividends are paid with the securities of other companies. Among other advantages, this avoids the problem of indivisibility of units as would be the case with most assets other than cash.

To illustrate a sequence of entries for a property dividend, assume a $10,000 balance in the account "Investment in X Company Stock (at cost)" and a fair market value of $15,000. Assume further that a $15,000 property dividend is declared and that this stock is to be used for payment. The transactions would be recorded as follows:

| | | |
|---|---|---|
| 1. Investment in X Company stock ..................................... | 5,000 | |
|     Gain on disposal of stock investment......................... | | 5,000 |
| 2. Retained earnings...................................................... | 15,000 | |
|     Property dividends payable (stock of X Company) ...... | | 15,000 |
| 3. Property dividends payable (stock of X Company)............. | 15,000 | |
|     Investment in X Company stock ............................... | | 15,000 |

## Liability Dividends

Strictly speaking, any dividend involving the distribution of assets is a liability dividend between the declaration date and the date of payment. Nevertheless, liability or *scrip* dividends refer to instances where the board of directors declares a dividend and issues promissory notes, bonds, or scrip to the stockholders. In most cases scrip dividends are declared when a corporation has sufficient retained earnings to serve as a basis for dividends but is short of cash  The stockholder may hold the scrip until due date and collect the dividend or possibly may discount it to obtain immediate cash. When bonds or notes are involved, the due date and rate of interest are specified. Scrip may or may not be interest bearing and is usually payable at a specified date; however, in some cases the maturity date is indefinite, being left to the option of the issuing corporation. The immediate effect of a scrip or liability dividend is a charge to Retained Earnings and a credit to a liability account such as Scrip Dividends Payable or Notes Payable to Stockholders. Upon payment, Cash is credited and the liability account debited. A liability dividend is in effect a cash dividend with a considerable time lapsing between declaration date and payment date. Since interest paid on a liability dividend is not a part of the dividend itself, such payments should be charged to interest expense.

## Liquidating Dividends

Distributions that constitute a *return of capital* rather than earnings are known as liquidating dividends. Liquidating dividends may be either intentional or unintentional. Intentional liquidating dividends occur when the board of directors knowingly declares dividends which will, in effect, represent a return of investment to the shareholders, as in the case when a corporation is discontinuing operations or when there is excessive capitalization.

Mining companies may pay dividends on the basis of earnings prior to a deduction for depletion. In such cases there is an intentional liquidating dividend equal to the depletion not deducted. Stockholders should be informed of the portion of any dividend that represents a return of capital. Such dividends are not taxable to the shareholder as income but serve to reduce the cost basis of his or her stock.

In accounting for liquidating dividends, contributed capital rather than retained earnings should be charged since a portion of stockholder investment is returned. Rather than debiting the capital stock accounts, as would be done if shares were being retired, other contributed capital accounts such as premium accounts may be charged. In some cases it may be desirable to set up a special account, Capital Repayment, which would be treated as a deduction in the corporate capital section of the balance sheet.

Unintentional liquidating dividends may occur when net income, and hence retained earnings, is overstated because of errors and inappropriate accounting. The omission or understatement of depreciation charges, amortizations, and depletion charges would cause retained earnings to be overstated. In such cases if reported retained earnings (prior to correction) were used in full as a basis for dividends, part of the resulting dividend would represent a return of contributed capital.

## Stock Dividends

A stock dividend is a distribution of additional shares, without cost, to the shareholders in proportion to their prior stock holdings. A stock dividend may be in the form of treasury stock or unissued stock; and common or preferred shares may be issued. When the stock dividend is of the same class as that held by the recipients, there is an *ordinary* stock dividend; on the other hand, when a different class of stock is issued, it is a *special* stock dividend. It was noted in a preceding section that state laws vary as to the availability of various classes of corporate capital for stock dividends. Some states permit the use of certain *contributed* capital, such as stock premium and unrealized capital increment. All states permit retained earnings to be used as a basis for stock dividends. In the absence of information to the contrary it should be assumed that the charge is to Retained Earnings. The entry to record a stock dividend should be made on the date of issuance (not date of declaration); the credit is to the respective contributed capital accounts for the shares issued.

There are a number of circumstances and reasons that might make a stock dividend advisable. The principal reasons are:

1. To permanently retain profits in the business by *capitalizing* a portion of the retained earnings. The effect of a stock dividend, through a charge to Retained Earnings and an offsetting credit to permanent capital, is to raise the contributed (and legal) capital.
2. To continue dividends without distributing assets needed for expansion and working capital. This action may be motivated by a desire to pacify stockholders, since many shareholders are willing to accept a stock dividend representing accumulated profits almost as readily as a cash dividend. Ordinary stock dividends are not subject to income tax; they serve instead to reduce the cost per share to the holder.
3. To increase the number of shares outstanding, thus reducing the market price per share. An indirect effect of a stock dividend may cause increased trading of the shares in the market.

It is especially important that the exact nature of a stock dividend be understood and that it be clearly differentiated from a *stock split*. A stock dividend does not require the distribution of assets or the creation of a liability. It does not change *total* corporate capital. Rather, a stock dividend is no more than an interequity transaction. Normally, the only effect on the issuing corporation's balance sheet is a transfer of part of the retained earnings to contributed capital and an increase in the number of shares outstanding. A stock dividend does not affect the par value per share. Thus, a stock dividend does not affect the assets, liabilities, or total capital, but only the internal content of corporate capital.

In contrast, a *stock split* increases the number of shares and at the same time it involves a *pro rata reduction in the par value per share*. A stock split is accomplished by replacing the old shares with a greater number of new shares which have a smaller par value per share; total par value outstanding remains the same after a stock split. A stock split does not cause a transfer of retained earnings to contributed capital; neither is changed. In the case of stock split only the content (number of shares, but not the dollar amount) of contributed capital is changed, whereas in a stock dividend the dollar amount of contributed capital is changed. To illustrate, assume X Corporation had authorized 40,000 shares of common stock, par $100, of which 10,000 shares were sold at par, and $1,600,000 in retained earnings. The effects of a 100% stock dividend versus a stock split may be summarized as follows:

|  | Prior to Change | After Stock Dividend | After Stock Split |
|---|---|---|---|
| Stock outstanding: |  |  |  |
| 10,000 shares, par $100 ............ | $1,000,000 |  |  |
| 20,000 shares, par $100 ............ |  | $2,000,000 |  |
| 20,000 shares, par $50 .............. |  |  | $1,000,000 |
| Retained earnings ..................... | 1,600,000 | 600,000 | 1,600,000 |
| Total Capital........................ | $2,600,000 | $2,600,000 | $2,600,000 |

Since a stock dividend requires capitalization of retained earnings, the question arises as to the amount of retained earnings to be capitalized (transferred to contributed capital) for the additional shares issued. The *statutory minimum* in most states is par value.[6] In the case of preferred stock it may be the liquidating value. However, the amount transferred from retained earnings to contributed capital should not necessarily be limited to the statutory minimum. The Committee on Accounting Procedure of the AICPA has stated a definite position on this matter. The committee recognized two distinct situations and indicated a different accounting procedure for each, viz:

*Situation 1 — A Small Stock Dividend:* The proportion of additional shares is *small* in relation to the total shares previously outstanding. In this situation the *fair market value* of the additional shares should be capitalized. The committee stated:

> ... many recipients of stock dividends look upon them as distributions of corporate earnings and usually in an amount equivalent to the fair value of the additional shares received. Furthermore, it is to be presumed that such views of recipients are materially strengthened in those instances, which are by far the most numerous, where the issuances are so small in comparison with the shares previously outstanding that they do not have any apparent effect upon the share market price and, consequently, the market value of the shares previously held remains substantially unchanged. The committee therefore believes that where these circumstances exist the corporation should in the public interest account for the transaction by transferring from retained earnings to the category of permanent capitalization ... an amount equal to the fair value of the additional shares issued (i.e., the fair market value immediately after issuance.).[7]

This position is further buttressed by the fact that the market price per share, in the case of a small stock dividend, does not drop proportionately to the increased number of shares outstanding after the dividend. Thus, the shareholders received a real value increase in their holdings.

---

[6] Most of the states specify as the legal minimum either the par value, stated value, or average price per share originally paid in.

[7] AICPA, "Restatement and Revision of Accounting Research Bulletins," *Accounting Research Bulletin No. 43* (New York, 1961), p. 51. (Words in parentheses supplied.)

*Situation 2—A Large Stock Dividend:* The proportion of additional shares is *large* in relation to the total shares previously outstanding. In this situation the legal minimum (generally par value) should be capitalized, as the committee stated:

> Where the number of additional shares issued as a stock dividend is so great that it has, or may reasonably be expected to have, the effect of materially reducing the share market value, the committee believes that the implications and possible constructions discussed in the preceding paragraph are not likely to exist. . . . Consequently, the committee considers that under such circumstances there is no need to capitalize earned surplus (retained earnings), other than to the extent occasioned by legal requirements.[8]

The dividing line between the two situations described above (a small versus a large stock dividend) is often difficult to draw. The significant distinction is the effect of the additional shares on the market price rather than the exact proportion between the new and old shares. The market price per share will depend upon a number of factors such as the economic characteristics of the company, the vagaries of the market, the general condition of the economy, and the number of additional shares issued. In considering this problem the committee further stated: "It would appear that there would be few instances involving the issuance of additional shares of less than, say, 20% or 25% of the number previously outstanding where the effect would not be such as to call for the procedure" for a small stock dividend outlined above as *Situation 1.*

As explained, there is a minimum amount per share (the legal amount required) that should be capitalized in some situations and a preferred higher amount per share (fair market value) that should be capitalized in other situations. In the past many corporate managements have elected to capitalize an amount between these two extremes, frequently using the *average* contributed capital per share on the old shares. It may be noted further that the above discussions are particularly applicable to *ordinary* stock dividends. In the case of special stock dividends, such as a stock dividend in preferred stock issued to common shareholders, theoretical considerations would suggest that fair market value be capitalized in all cases.

In order to illustrate several situations involving stock dividends, assume the following for Z Corporation:

| | | |
|---|---:|---:|
| Preferred stock, par value $20, 10,000 shares authorized, 5,000 shares outstanding | $100,000 | |
| Common stock, par value $10, 20,000 shares authorized, 10,000 shares outstanding | 100,000 | |
| Contributed capital in excess of par, preferred stock ... | 10,000 | |
| Contributed capital in excess of par, common stock | 15,000 | |
| Retained earnings | 150,000 | |
| Total Stockholders' Equity | | $375,000 |
| Market price per share immediately after issuance: | | |
| Preferred | $25 | |
| Common | 11 | |

---

[8] Ibid., p. 52.

*Illustration 1—A Small Stock Dividend:* A 10% common stock dividend (i.e., one additional share is issued for each ten shares held) is declared on the common stock.

At date of issuance:[9]

```
Retained earnings (1,000 shares at market $11) .................  11,000
    Common stock (1,000 shares)....................................          10,000
    Contributed capital in excess of par, common stock ......           1,000
```

*Illustration 2—A Large Stock Dividend:* A 50% common stock dividend (i.e., one additional share for each two shares held) is declared. The market value per share drops to $7.50.

At issue date:

```
Retained earnings (5,000 shares at par, $10) .......................  50,000
    Common stock (5,000 shares)....................................          50,000
```

*Situation 3—A Large Stock Dividend:* A 50% common stock dividend is declared. The market value drops to $7.50 per share. Management decides to capitalize on the basis of the average paid in.

At issue date:

```
Retained earnings (5,000 shares at $11.50) ........................  57,500
    Common stock (5,000 shares)....................................          50,000
    Contributed capital in excess of par, common stock ......           7,500
    Computation: ($100,000 + $15,000) ÷ 10,000 shares = $11.50.
```

*Situation 4—A Small Stock Dividend:* A 20% common stock dividend (i.e., one additional share for each five shares held) is issued to both common and preferred shareholders. The market price per share does not change appreciably.

At issue date:

```
Retained earnings (3,000 shares at $11) .............................  33,000
    Common stock (3,000 shares)....................................          30,000
    Contributed capital in excess of par, common stock ......           3,000
    Computation: (10,000 + 5,000) × .20 = 3,000 shares.
```

## ACCUMULATED DIVIDENDS ON PREFERRED STOCK

Dividends in arrears on *cumulative* preferred stock, prior to formal declaration of such dividends, do not constitute a liability to the corporation. However, full disclosure requires that cumulative dividends in

---

[9] A few accountants prefer to make an entry on declaration date and another entry on issue date by using a temporary contributed capital account entitled Stock Dividend Distributable. The two entries would be:

Declaration date:

```
Retained earnings ...........................................................  11,000
    Stock dividends distributable ...................................          10,000
    Contributed capital in excess of par, common stock ....           1,000
```

Payment date:

```
Stock dividends distributable .........................................  10,000
    Common stock....................................................          10,000
```

arrears be reported. Preferably a footnote should be used to indicate the years and amounts of dividends in arrears. An alternative method is to report the years and amount of dividends in arrears separately from the unappropriated retained earnings figure. For example, retained earnings may be reported as follows:[10]

```
Retained earnings:
    Amount equal to preferred dividends in arrears  ...........  $10,000
    Unappropriated balance  .........................................   20,000    $30,000
```

### Fractional Share Warrants

Stock warrants, often called stock rights, are agreements issued to shareholders that entitles them to purchase a particular class of stock from the corporation under specified conditions. Usually warrants provide for purchase of stock under favorable conditions compared to purchase in the open market. Subject to the conditions, one or more warrants may be required as a basis for acquiring one share of stock.

When a stock dividend is issued (except when it is 100%; i.e., one for one), *fractional share warrants* often must be issued. For example, if a one for five (i.e., 20%) stock dividend is declared, a holder of 13 shares of stock would receive two additional shares and three fractional share warrants. To get another share the shareholder must obtain two additional fractional share warrants in the marketplace. Soon after issuance, stock warrants generally are freely traded on the market (also see Chapter 17).

To illustrate the accounting for fractional share warrants, assume Z Corporation (page 672) declared a 20% stock dividend whereby each shareholder receives one share of common stock, par $10, for each five shares held. Assume further that 1,730 shares of common stock and 1,350 fractional share warrants were issued to various shareholders calling for 270 shares (1,350 ÷ 5). Each fractional share warrant qualifies for one fifth of a share of stock. In order to obtain a share, five such warrants have to be presented. The resulting entries would be:

1. At date of issuance (assumed to be a small stock dividend):

```
Retained earnings (2,000 shares at market, $11)  ...........  22,000
    Common stock (1,730 shares at par) .......................           17,300
    Stock warrants outstanding, common (1,350 warrants
        requiring 270 shares of common stock)  ..............            2,700
    Contributed capital in excess of par, common
        (2,000 shares at $1) ...........................................            2,000
```

2. Receipt of the 1,350 stock warrants:

```
Stock warrants outstanding, common (1,350).................   2,700
    Common stock (270 shares at par).........................            2,700
```

---

[10] *APB Opinion No. 10* states that "the liquidation preference of the stock be disclosed in the equity section of the balance sheet in the aggregate, either parenthetically or 'in short' rather than on a per share basis or by disclosure in notes"; and *APB Opinion No. 9*, par. 35, specifies that amounts in arrearages in cumulative preferred also should be disclosed.

3. Alternatively, assume 90% of the warrants are turned in and the remainder lapse:

| | | |
|---|---|---|
| Stock warrants outstanding, common (1,350) | | 2,700 |
| Common stock (243 shares at par) | | 2,430 |
| Contributed capital, lapse of stock warrants (for 27 shares)* | | 270 |

\* An alternative would be to reverse that portion of the entry that relates to 27 shares.

If a balance sheet for Z Corporation is prepared between the date of the issuance of the stock warrants and their receipt later, the outstanding warrants would be reported as follows:

**Z CORPORATION**
Stockholders' Equity

| | | | |
|---|---|---:|---:|
| Contributed Capital: | | | |
| Capital stock: | | | |
| Preferred stock, $20 par value, 10,000 shares authorized, 5,000 shares outstanding | | | $100,000 |
| Common stock, $10 par value, 20,000 shares authorized, 11,730 shares outstanding | | $117,300 | |
| Common stock warrants outstanding (for 270 shares) | | 2,700 | 120,000 |
| Total Capital Stock | | | 220,000 |
| Other contributed capital: | | | |
| Contributed capital in excess of par, preferred | | 10,000 | |
| Contributed capital in excess of par, common | | 17,000 | 27,000 |
| Total Contributed Capital | | | 247,000 |
| Retained Earnings: | | | |
| Unappropriated | | | 128,000 |
| Total Stockholders' Equity | | | $375,000 |

Observe that stock warrants outstanding are reported next to the related stock account. This reports the obligation to issue the requisite number of shares.

### Dividends and Treasury Stock

Dividends are not paid on treasury stock. However, treasury stock occasionally is used to pay a stock dividend. If treasury stock is used for this purpose, it should be recorded as having been issued at its fair market value (also see discussion of treasury stock in Chapter 17).

To illustrate a stock dividend from treasury stock, assume a corporation issued 6,000 shares of $20 par-value common stock at $22 per share of which 5,000 shares are currently outstanding and 1,000 shares are held as treasury stock acquired (and recorded) at $21 per share. The board of directors declared a stock dividend whereby one share of treasury stock would be transferred for each five shares of stock held. The current market value per share remained essentially unchanged at

$23 per share. The indicated entry assuming a small stock dividend is:

```
Retained earnings (1,000 shares at market of $23) ..............  23,000
     Treasury stock (1,000 shares at cost of $21) .................           21,000
     Contributed capital, treasury stock transactions ...........            2,000
```

## LEGALITY OF DIVIDENDS

The availability of retained earnings and certain elements of contributed capital as a basis for dividends was mentioned in the first section of this chapter. To attempt to define just what elements of corporate capital are available as a basis for cash, property, and stock dividends would require a minute and detailed study of the laws of each state. Manifestly, such a study is beyond the scope of this text; further, questions of law rather than accounting are involved. There are at least two limitations which appear uniform, namely, that dividends may not be paid from *legal capital* (usually represented by the capital stock accounts) and that unappropriated retained earnings are available for dividends.[11] Between these two limits there are numerous variations, depending upon the respective state statutes, such as:

1. All contributed capital, other than legal capital, is available for dividends.
2. Specified items of contributed capital, other than legal capital, are available for dividends.
3. Contributed capital, other than legal capital, is available for dividends on preferred stock but not on common stock.
4. Unrealized capital increment is not available for dividends.
5. Unrealized capital increment is available for stock dividends only.
6. Capital losses and deficits must be restored before payment of any dividends.
7. Dividends from retained earnings must not reduce the retained earnings balance below the cost of treasury stock held.

The accountant has a responsibility in circumstances where the propriety and legality of dividends are at issue to (*a*) insure that such matters are referred to an attorney, and (*b*) ascertain that the financial statements fully disclose all known and material facts concerning such dividends.

## APPROPRIATIONS OF RETAINED EARNINGS

Income and losses from operations and extraordinary gains and losses are transferred to the Retained Earnings account. This account is also charged for dividends in the manner explained previously. From time to time *appropriations* of retained earnings may be made as a result of management action, by contract, or by law. Appropriations of

---

[11] Some states permit the payment of dividends from current earnings even though the corporation has an accumulated deficit in retained earnings.

retained earnings constitute a *restriction* on a specified portion of accumulated earnings for specific purposes. Such specific appropriations nevertheless represent a part of *total* retained earnings. Thus, retained earnings is comprised of two subcategories: (1) appropriated retained earnings, and (2) unappropriated retained earnings.

Although retained earnings fundamentally may be appropriated to indicate that such amounts are not available as a basis for dividends, thereby protecting the working capital position of the corporation, such restrictions arise from a number of situations, the primary reasons are:

1. To fulfill a *legal requirement,* as in the case of a restriction on retained earnings equivalent to the cost of treasury stock held as required by the law of the specific state.
2. To fulfill a *contractual agreement,* as in the case of a bond issue where the bond indenture requires a sinking fund and carries a stipulation providing for a restriction on retained earnings. Such agreements have been used less in recent years.
3. To record formally a discretionary action by the board of directors to restrict a portion of retained earnings as an aspect of *financial planning.*
4. To record formally a discretionary action by the board of directors to restrict a portion of retained earnings in anticipation of *possible future losses.*

Since item (1) in the above list will be discussed in Chapter 17, the remaining items will be discussed below. Preliminary to the discussions to follow, observe that the appropriation of retained earnings fundamentally has no direct effect upon the composition of the assets. The appropriation is a "clerical" identification and does not set aside specific assets; this latter effect would occur only if a separate fund, such as a Bond Sinking Fund, also is set aside.

Appropriations of retained earnings may be accounted for and reported using either of two approaches, viz:

1. Make no formal entries in the accounts. Report the appropriations or restrictions either parenthetically on the balance sheet (or statement of retained earnings) or by footnote to the statements.
2. Make formal entries in the accounts and report the appropriations as a subclassification of retained earnings.

Some years ago the second approach was used almost exclusively; however, in recent years the first approach has been used by an increasing number of companies. Both approaches will be discussed in the paragraphs to follow. Sometimes it is desirable to supplement the reporting under the second approach with footnote disclosure.

When an appropriation ceases, as a result of either management action or by time expiration, the restriction is no longer reported; and prior entries recording the restriction (if the second approach is used) are reversed.

When the second approach is used, the restriction is formally entered in the accounts as a debit to the Retained Earnings account (i.e., unappropriated retained earnings) and as a credit to an appropriately designated appropriated account, such as Retained Earnings Appropriated for Bond Sinking Fund, or simply, Reserve for Bond Sinking Fund.[12] Under this approach the basic principle is that an appropriation account is *never* debited for a loss, or for any other reason, except to return the balance to the original source; that is the Retained Earnings account. Even in the case of a stock dividend (which requires a debit to Retained Earnings) or when a new appropriation is established as the consequence of closing another such account, balances of any appropriated Retained Earnings accounts should be returned first to the regular Retained Earnings account, and the new restriction should be recorded in the normal manner. On this point FASB *Statement No. 5* states:

> Some enterprises have classified a portion of retained earnings as "appropriated" for loss contingencies. In some cases, the appropriation has been shown outside the stockholders' equity section of the balance sheet. Appropriation of retained earnings is not prohibited by this Statement provided that it is shown within the stockholders' equity section of the balance sheet and is clearly identified as appropriation of retained earnings. Costs or losses shall not be charged to an appropriation of retained earnings, and no part of the appropriation shall be transferred to income.[13]

Exhibit 16–1 illustrates the second approach used in reporting appropriations of retained earnings.

## APPROPRIATION RELATED TO A CONTRACTUAL AGREEMENT

To offer more security to purchasers of a bond issue, the bond indenture may include various provisions favorable to the bondholders (also see Chapter 19). One such provision, generally referred to as a bond sinking or redemption fund, might call for the periodic deposit of a specified amount of cash in a fund, held by a trustee, to be used to pay the bonds at maturity. A second provision might also call for the periodic *appropriation* of a specific amount of retained earnings. The amount to be appropriated may or may not be the same as the cash contributed to the fund. Or in some cases there may be an appropriation agreement without a fund provision. This situation is frequently true for serial bonds. The appropriation of retained earnings related to a bond sinking fund has two purposes: (1) to inform statement users of the planned use of assets (derived from earnings) to retire the fixed liability, and (2) to assure creditors (bondholders) that assets received from revenue are being held back to meet the drain occasioned by the bond liability requirement.

To illustrate, assume a $1 million bond issue, sold at par, with the provisions that (*a*) $100,000 per year for ten years shall be deposited in a

---

[12] Recall the discussion of *reserves* in Chapter 5. The term reserve should be limited in usage to appropriations of retained earnings (AICPA, "Review and Résumé," *Accounting Terminology Bulletin No. 1* (New York, 1961), p. 27.

[13] FASB, "Accounting for Contingencies," *Statement of Financial Accounting Standards No. 5* (March 1975), par. 15.

special fund, and (b) that an equal amount shall be set aside as an appropriation of retained earnings. Assuming the appropriation is to be recorded in the accounts (the second approach above), the entries would be:

1. At date of sale of bonds:

| | | |
|---|---|---|
| Cash ........................................................... | 1,000,000 | |
|    Bonds payable ............................................ | | 1,000,000 |

2. At end of each of the ten years:[14]

| | | |
|---|---|---|
| Bond redemption fund (or bond sinking fund)......... | 100,000 | |
|    Cash ...................................................... | | 100,000 |
| | | |
| Retained earnings............................................. | 100,000 | |
|    Retained earnings appropriated for bond | | |
|    redemption fund (or reserve for bond sinking | | |
|    fund) ..................................................... | | 100,000 |

3. At date of maturity:

| | | |
|---|---|---|
| Bonds payable ................................................ | 1,000,000 | |
|    Bond redemption fund................................... | | 1,000,000 |
| | | |
| Retained earnings appropriated for bond | | |
|    redemption fund ......................................... | 1,000,000 | |
|    Retained earnings........................................ | | 1,000,000 |

Since the original proceeds of the bond issue may have been used to acquire fixed assets, upon payment of the bonds the management may desire to reappropriate the $1,000,000 or to "capitalize" it through a stock dividend. To illustrate each situation:

1. The board of directors voted that $1,000,000 be reappropriated in view of investment in plant:

| | | |
|---|---|---|
| Retained earnings............................................. | 1,000,000 | |
|    Retained earnings appropriated for investment | | |
|    in plant.................................................... | | 1,000,000 |

2. The board of directors declared and issued a $1,000,000 stock dividend (to be capitalized at par value):

| | | |
|---|---|---|
| Retained earnings............................................. | 1,000,000 | |
|    Capital stock ............................................. | | 1,000,000 |

Similar contractual appropriations may relate to agreements such as the purchase of specific assets, retirement of preferred stock and payment of various obligations.

If the appropriation is not recorded in the accounts (approach 1), a footnote is used to report the restriction. However, under any event the entries relating to the *fund* (but not to the appropriation) would be necessary.

---

[14] Interest revenue on the fund balance is revenue disregarded in this example. Interest normally is recorded as a credit to interest revenue and a debit to the sinking fund. This serves to reduce the amount of cash transferred to the sinking fund each year (see Chapters 11 and 19).

## APPROPRIATIONS AS AN ASPECT OF FINANCIAL PLANNING

Many corporations began with a small initial capital investment and have grown large through earnings; that is, a good portion of the earnings have been retained in the business in order to expand, purchase fixed assets, and increase working capital. In such circumstances a portion of accumulated earnings may be permanently capitalized through stock dividends (or increases in par values); or instead, the management, at least temporarily, may set aside a portion of accumulated earnings in one or more appropriation accounts such as the following:

> Retained Earnings Appropriated for Investment in Plant
> Retained Earnings Appropriated for Working Capital
> Retained Earnings Invested in Fixed Assets

Appropriations of this type serve only to inform statement users that (a) the retained earnings, in part, are represented in the asset structure as more or less permanent committments, and (b) there is a limitation on retained earnings for dividend availability.

These appropriated accounts are established through a debit to the regular Retained Earnings account (unappropriated) and are returned to this account when the purpose has been served. Obviously, they represent only a restriction on retained earnings and do not relate to *specific* earnings or assets since accounting does not identify assets with specific items of corporate capital or vice versa. In many cases upon return of the appropriation to the regular Retained Earnings account (unappropriated), a stock dividend for the same amount is declared and issued as was illustrated above for the bond transactions.


## APPROPRIATION FOR POSSIBLE FUTURE LOSSES

In anticipation of possible future losses often the board of directors will direct that a portion of accumulated earnings be appropriated and specifically identified with titles such as the following:

Retained Earnings Appropriated for Contingencies
Retained Earnings Appropriated for Possible Storm Damage
Retained Earnings Appropriated for Possible Future Inventory
    Cost Declines
Retained Earnings Appropriated for Possible Loss in Pending Lawsuit
Retained Earnings Appropriated for Self-insurance

Appropriations of this type are reported on the financial statements, or by footnote, and often are recorded in the accounts. When recorded in the accounts they are established through a debit to the Unappropriated Retained Earnings account and are subsequently returned to this same account. As stated earlier, even though the anticipated contingency does materialize, any actual loss arising therefrom should be charged to operations or to the regular Retained Earnings account as would be done when there is no related appropriation account; such losses are not properly charged to the appropriation account. If the balance of an appropriation account needs adjustment, such changes should directly involve the Unappropriated Retained Earnings account.

An appropriation for possible future inventory cost decline is not the same account discussed in Chapter 8 which related to the valuation of inventory at lower of cost or market (Allowance to Reduce Inventory to Lower of Cost or Market). That account was related to a cost decline that had *already* materialized, whereas the appropriation account relates to a possible cost decline in the future, that is, one that has not yet materialized and may not ever materialize but the possibility does exist.

The use of this type of appropriation is subject to specific constraints given in FASB *Statement No. 5*, "Accounting for Contingencies." This FASB *Statement* is discussed in detail in Chapter 20.

## REPORTING RETAINED EARNINGS

The statement of retained earnings was discussed in Chapter 4; illustrative examples were given in Chapters 4 and 5. Within recent years there has been considerable diversity of views as to what should be reported on the income statement versus the statement of retained earnings. The issue tended to focus on reporting extraordinary items and prior period adjustments. *APB Opinion Nos. 9, 12,* and *30* largely resolved these issues. Those *Opinions* require that extraordinary items be reported on the income statement and prior period adjustments on the statement of retained earnings.

*APB Opinion No. 30* revised the definition of extraordinary items previously given in *Opinion No. 9. APB Opinion No. 30* is much more restrictive; it specifies that extraordinary items must meet two criteria: (*a*) unusual in nature, and (*b*) infrequent in occurrence (see Chapter 4). Extraordinary items are not permitted on the statement of retained earnings.

*APB Opinion No. 9* carefully defines prior period adjustments which are reported on the statement of retained earnings as follows:

> Adjustments related to prior periods—and thus excluded in the determination of net income for the current period—are limited to those material adjustments which (a) can be specifically identified with and directly related to the business activities of particular prior periods, and (b) are not attributable to economic events occurring subsequent to the date of the financial statements for the prior period, and (c) depend primarily on determinations by persons other than management and (d) were not susceptible of reasonable estimation prior to such determination. Such adjustments are rare in modern financial accounting. . . .

Thus, to be accounted for and reported as a prior period adjustment, all four criteria listed in the above definition must be met. In recording prior period adjustments in the accounts, specially designated accounts are used which are closed directly to the Retained Earnings account. A typical example would be: Prior Period Adjustment, Damages Paid from Lawsuit.

*APB Opinion No. 9* also specifies a full-disclosure requirement for prior period adjustments as follows:

> When financial statements for a single period only are presented, this disclosure should indicate the effects of such restatement on the balance of retained earnings at the beginning of the period. When financial statements for more than one period are presented, which is ordinarily the preferable procedure, the disclosure should include the effects for each of the periods included in the statements. Such disclosures should include the amounts of income tax applicable to the prior period adjustments.

Under generally accepted accounting principles, as specified in these and other pronouncements, the statement of retained earnings should report the following:

1. Beginning balance.
2. Prior period adjustments.
3. Net income or loss for the period.
4. Dividends.
5. Appropriations of retained earnings.
6. Adjustments made pursuant to a quasi-reorganization.
7. Ending balance.

To illustrate the reporting of retained earnings, the following data from the records of Model Stores, Incorporated, are used:

For Year Ended December 31, 1976

| | | |
|---|---:|---:|
| Sales | | $520,000 |
| Cost of goods sold | | 300,000 |
| Expenses | | 120,000 |
| Income taxes on ordinary income | | 52,000 |
| Extraordinary gain | | 25,000 |
| Extraordinary loss | | 15,000 |
| Income taxes on extraordinary items | | 6,000 |
| Balance in retained earnings, January 1, 1976: | | |
| Unappropriated | $120,000 | |
| Appropriation for bond sinking fund | 40,000 | |
| Appropriation for plant expansion | 60,000 | 220,000 |
| Refund from overpayment of 1974 income taxes | | 27,000 |
| Damages from 1973 lawsuit (paid this year) | 15,000 | |
| Less: Related income tax adjustment | 7,000 | 8,000 |
| Dividends for current year | | 30,000 |
| Appropriation of retained earnings for bond sinking fund for current year | | 10,000 |

The income statement and statement of retained earnings for Model Stores are shown in Exhibit 16–1.

When the statement of retained earnings is not complex it is sometimes included with the income statement in a combined income and

**EXHIBIT 16–1**
**Income Statement and Statement of Retained Earnings Illustrated**

MODEL STORES, INCORPORATED
Income Statement
For the Year Ended December 31, 1976

| | | |
|---|---:|---:|
| Sales | | $520,000 |
| Less: Cost of goods sold | | 300,000 |
| Gross margin | | 220,000 |
| Less: Expenses | $120,000 | |
| Income taxes | 52,000 | 172,000 |
| Income before extraordinary items | | 48,000 |
| Extraordinary items: | | |
| Gain (designated) | 25,000 | |
| Loss (designated) | (15,000) | |
| | 10,000 | |
| Less: Applicable income tax | 6,000 | |
| Total Extraordinary Items | | 4,000 |
| Net Income | | $ 52,000 |

Earnings per share (not illustrated)


MODEL STORES, INCORPORATED
Statement of Retained Earnings
For the Year Ended December 31, 1976

| | | | |
|---|---:|---:|---:|
| Unappropriated Retained Earnings: | | | |
| Unappropriated balance, January 1, 1976 | | $120,000 | |
| Adjustments applicable to prior periods: | | | |
| Refund of 1974 income taxes | $27,000 | | |
| Damages paid from lawsuit (1973) ...... $15,000 | | | |
| Less: Tax adjustment    7,000 | 8,000 | 19,000 | |
| Corrected balance | | 139,000 | |
| Add: Net income for current year | | 52,000 | |
| | | 191,000 | |
| Deductions and appropriations: | | | |
| Dividends | 30,000 | | |
| Appropriation to reserve for bond sinking fund ... | 10,000 | 40,000 | |
| Unappropriated balance, December 31, 1976 | | | $151,000 |
| Appropriated Retained Earnings: | | | |
| Reserve for bond sinking fund, balance January 1, 1976 | 40,000 | | |
| Addition for current year | 10,000 | | |
| Reserve for bond sinking fund, balance December 31, 1976 | | 50,000 | |
| Appropriation for plant expansion | | 60,000 | |
| Appropriated balance, December 31, 1976... | | | 110,000 |
| Total Appropriated and Unappropriated, Balance December 31, 1976 | | | $261,000 |

retained earnings statement. In complex situations, full disclosure will necessitate the use of notes to the statement of retained earnings.

*APB Opinion No. 12* ("Omnibus Opinion," 1967) also has had an impact on the reporting of retained earnings; paragraph 10 of the *Opinion* states:

> When both financial position and results of operations are presented, disclosure of changes in the separate accounts comprising stockholders' equity (in addition to retained earnings) and of the changes in the number of shares of equity securities during at least the most recent annual fiscal period and any subsequent interim period presented is required to make the financial statements sufficiently informative. Disclosure of such changes may take the form of separate statements or may be made in the basic financial statements or notes thereto.

Consequently, in recent years there has been widespread use of comprehensive supplementary statements of all changes in owners' equity similar to that illustrated in Chapter 5, Exhibit 5–3.

## QUASI-REORGANIZATIONS

When a corporation has sustained heavy losses over a period of time so that there is a significant deficit in Retained Earnings and a related *overstatement* of the carrying value of certain assets, a quasi-reorganization may be desirable from the prudent management and the accounting points of view.

A quasi-reorganization refers to a procedure whereby a corporation may, without formal court proceedings of dissolution, establish a new basis for accounting for assets and corporate capital. In effect, a quasi-reorganization is an accounting reorganization in which a "fresh start" is effected in the accounts with respect to certain assets, legal capital, and retained earnings.

The Committee on Accounting Procedure of the AICPA recognized the procedure, provided it is properly safeguarded.[15] The Securities and Exchange Commission listed certain safeguards or conditions with respect to a quasi-reorganization. These conditions are summarized below:

1. Retained earnings after the quasi-reorganization must be zero.
2. Upon completion of the quasi-reorganization no deficit shall remain in any corporate capital account.
3. The effects of the whole procedure shall be made known to all stockholders entitled to vote and appropriate approval in advance obtained from them.
4. A fair and conservative balance sheet shall be presented as of the date of the reorganization and the readjustment of values should be reasonably complete, in order to obviate as far as possible future readjustments of like nature.[16]

Characteristics of a quasi-reorganization are: (*a*) the recorded values

---

[15] *Accounting Research Bulletin No. 43*, pp. 45–47.

[16] Securities and Exchange Commission, *Accounting Series Release No. 25*.

relating to appropriately selected assets are restated downward; (b) the capital accounts are restated, and the Retained Earnings account is restated to a zero balance; (c) the Retained Earnings account is "dated" for a period of time (five to ten years) following the reorganization (illustrated below); (d) full disclosure of the procedure and the effects thereof are reported on the financial statements; and (e) the corporate entity is unchanged.[17]

To illustrate the accounting for a quasi-reorganization, assume the following simplified balance sheet at January 1, 19A:

| | | | |
|---|---:|---|---:|
| Current assets | $ 200,000 | Capital stock | $1,500,000 |
| | | Premium on stock | 100,000 |
| Fixed assets | 1,000,000 | Retained earnings | (400,000) |
| | $1,200,000 | | $1,200,000 |

Assume that it is determined that the inventories are overvalued by $50,000 and that the fixed asset carrying value should be reduced by $250,000 if a realistic accounting is to be made in the future.

Under these conditions the company would consider two alternatives. First, the corporation may be dissolved and a new corporation formed. The new corporation would receive the assets, record them at $900,000, and report the same amount as corporate capital. Second, the corporation may undergo a quasi-reorganization (without dissolution) which would be less cumbersome and less expensive than legal reorganization. By complying with the conditions set forth above, including stockholder approval, the quasi-reorganization may be effected through the following entries, assuming capital stock is to be reduced to $900,000:

1. To write down assets:

| | | |
|---|---:|---:|
| Clearance — quasi-reorganization | 300,000 | |
| Current assets (inventories) | | 50,000 |
| Fixed assets | | 250,000 |

2. To eliminate the deficit in retained earnings:

| | | |
|---|---:|---:|
| Clearance — quasi-reorganization | 400,000 | |
| Retained earnings | | 400,000 |

3. To write off premium:

| | | |
|---|---:|---:|
| Premium on stock | 100,000 | |
| Clearance — quasi-reorganization | | 100,000 |

4. To reduce legal capital from $1,500,000 to $900,000:

| | | |
|---|---:|---:|
| Capital stock | 600,000 | |
| Clearance — quasi-reorganization | | 600,000 |

The balance sheet, including the dating of retained earnings, after the quasi-reorganization would be:

[17] For a detailed treatment of quasi-reorganization see: James S. Schindler, *Quasi-Reorganization* (Michigan Business Studies, vol. XIII, no. 5) (Ann Arbor: Bureau of Business Research, University of Michigan, 1958).

| | | | |
|---|---|---|---|
| Current assets | $150,000 | Capital stock | $900,000 |
| Fixed assets | 750,000 | Retained earnings (Note 1) | – |
| | $900,000 | | $900,000 |

Note 1. Retained earnings represents accumulations since January 1, 19A, at which time a $400,000 deficit was eliminated as the result of a quasi-reorganization.

In general, a quasi-reorganization is justified when (a) a large deficit from operations exists, (b) it is approved by the stockholders and creditors, (c) the cost basis of accounting for fixed assets becomes unrealistic in terms of going-concern values, (d) a break in continuity of the historical cost basis is clearly needed so that realistic financial reporting is possible, (e) the retained earnings balances are totally inadequate to absorb an obvious decrease in going-concern asset values, and (f) a "fresh start," in the accounting sense, appears to be desirable or advantageous to all parties properly concerned with the corporation.

## QUESTIONS

1. What are the principal sources and dispositions of retained earnings?

2. Differentiate between total retained earnings and the balance of the Retained Earnings account.

3. What is the position of the accounting profession on use of the word *surplus*? What is the basis for this position?

4. What are the three important dates relative to accounting for dividends? Explain the importance of each.

5. Distinguish between cash dividends, property dividends, and liability dividends.

6. What is a liquidating dividend? What are the responsibilities of the accountant with respect to such dividends?

7. Explain the difference between intentional and unintentional liquidating dividends.

8. Basically what is the difference between a cash or property dividend and a stock dividend?

9. Distinguish between a stock dividend and a stock split.

10. What are the reasons for appropriations of retained earnings?

11. Explain the distinction between (a) a bond sinking fund and (b) an appropriation of retained earnings for bond sinking fund.

12. What items are properly reported on the statement of retained earnings?

13. Is the following statement correct? "Retained earnings was reduced by $10,000 appropriated for plant expansion." Explain.

14. What is a quasi-reorganization? Under what conditions is it acceptable?

## DECISION CASE 16-1

Bland Plastics, Incorporated, was formed in 1969 to manufacture a wide range of plastic products from three basic components. The company was originally owned by 23 shareholders; however, five years after formation the capital structure was expanded considerably at which time preferred stock was issued for the first time. At the present time there are over 250 holders of preferred and common stock. The preferred is nonvoting, cumulative, 6% stock. The company had experienced a substantial growth in business over the years. This growth was due to two principal factors: (a) the dynamic management, and (b) geographical location. The firm served a rapidly expanding area with relatively few regionally situated competitors.

The last audited balance sheet showed the following (summarized):

### Balance Sheet, December 31, 1976

| | |
|---|---:|
| Cash | $ 11,000 |
| Other current assets | 76,000 |
| Investment in K Company stock (at cost) | 30,000 |
| Plant and equipment (net) | 310,000 |
| Intangible assets | 15,000 |
| Other assets | 8,000 |
| | $450,000 |
| | |
| Current liabilities | $ 38,000 |
| Long-term loans | 60,000 |
| Preferred stock, par value $100* | 50,000 |
| Common stock, $15 par value (10,000 shares)* | 150,000 |
| Premium on preferred stock | 2,000 |
| Retained earnings | 25,000 |
| Profits invested in plant | 125,000 |
| | $450,000 |

* Authorized shares — preferred, 2,000; common, 20,000.

The board of directors had not declared a dividend since organization; instead, the profits were used to expand the company. This decision was based on the facts that the original capital was small and there was a decision to limit the number of shareholders. At the present time the common stock is held by slightly fewer than 50 individuals. Each of these individuals also owns preferred shares; their total holdings approximate 46% of the outstanding preferred. The preferred was issued at the time of the expansion of capital.

The board of directors had been planning to declare a dividend during the early part of 1977, payable June 30. However, the cash position as shown by the balance sheet had raised serious doubts as to the advisability of a dividend in 1977. The president had explained that most of the cash was temporarily tied up in inventory and plant.

The company has a chief accountant, but no controller. The board relies on an outside CPA for advice concerning financial management. The CPA was asked to advise about the contemplated dividend declaration. Four of the seven members of the board felt very strongly that some kind of dividend must be declared so that all shareholders will get something.

### Required:

You have been asked to analyze the situation and make whatever dividend proposals that appear to be worthy of consideration by the board. Present figures to support your recommendations in a form suitable for consideration by the board in reaching a decision. Provide the basis for your proposals and indicate any preferences that you may have.

## EXERCISES

### Exercise 16–1

Ace Corporation's books on January 1 showed the following balances (summarized):

| | | | |
|---|---|---|---|
| Cash | $ 25,000 | Current liabilities | $ 20,000 |
| Other current assets | 25,000 | Long-term liabilities | 60,000 |
| Fixed assets (net) | 250,000 | Capital stock 2,000 shares | 200,000 |
| Other assets | 50,000 | Premium on stock | 10,000 |
| | | Retained earnings | 60,000 |
| | $350,000 | | $350,000 |

The board of directors is considering a cash dividend, and you have been requested to provide certain assistance as the independent CPA. The following matters have been referred to you:

1. What is the maximum amount of dividends that can be paid? Explain.
2. What amount of dividends would you recommend based upon the data from the accounts? Explain.
3. What entries would be made assuming a $15,000 cash dividend is declared with the following dates specified: (a) declaration date; (b) date of record; and (c) date of payment.
4. Assuming a balance sheet is prepared between declaration date and payment date, how would the dividend declaration be reported?

### Exercise 16–2

White Manufacturing Corporation had outstanding 12,000 shares of capital stock, par value $10 per share. The shares were held by ten stockholders, each having an equal number of shares. The Retained Earnings account showed a balance of $60,000, although the company was short of cash. The company owned 1,000 shares of stock in AB Company that had been purchased for $7,000. The current market value is $15 per share. The board of directors of White Corporation declared a dividend of $2 per share "to be paid with AB stock within 30 days after declaration date and scrip to be issued for the difference. The scrip will be payable at the end of 12 months from issue date and will earn 6% interest per annum."

*Required:*

1. Give all entries indicated through date of payment of the scrip.
2. What items related to the dividend declaration would be reported on the balance sheet prior to payment of the scrip?

**Exercise 16–3**

The board of directors of GT Mining Company declared a maximum dividend. There were 60 stockholders, each holding 200 shares of stock having a par value of $5 per share. The laws of the state provide that "dividends may be paid equal to accumulated profits prior to depletion charges." The Retained Earnings account showed a balance of $8,000; accumulated depletion charges amounted to $10,000. The dividend was payable within 60 days of declaration date.

*Required:*

1. What entries are indicated?
2. What special notification, if any, should be given the shareholders?
3. What items related to the dividend declaration would be reported on the balance sheet between declaration date and payment date?

**Exercise 16–4**

The records of Mason Corporation showed the following balances on November 1, 19A:

| | |
|---|---|
| Capital stock authorized, par $10 ................. | $500,000 |
| Capital stock unissued ............................... | 225,000 |
| Contributed capital in excess of par.............. | 82,500 |
| Retained earnings ..................................... | 95,000 |

On November 5, 19A, the board of directors declared a stock dividend (from unissued stock) of one additional share for each five shares outstanding; issue date January 10, 19B. The market value of the stock immediately after the declaration was $18 per share.

*Required:*

1. Give entries in parallel columns for the stock dividend assuming (a) fair market value is capitalized, (b) par value is capitalized, and (c) average paid in is capitalized.
2. Explain when each should be used.
3. What should be reported on the balance sheet at December 31, 19A assuming no intervening transactions?

**Exercise 16–5**

The records of Aiken Corporation showed the following:

| | |
|---|---|
| Preferred stock, 6% cumulative, nonparticipating, par $20 ......... | $200,000 |
| Common stock, nopar value, 50,000 shares issued..................... | 240,000 |
| Contributed capital in excess of par, preferred......................... | 30,000 |
| Retained earnings ............................................................. | 125,000 |
| Investment in stock of X Corporation | |
| (500 shares at cost) ......................................................... | 10,000 |

The preferred stock has dividends in arrears for the past two years. The board of directors has just passed the following resolution: "The current year dividend shall be 6% on the preferred and $.90 per share on the common; the dividends in arrears are to be paid by issuing a property dividend using the requisite amount of X Corporation stock." Currently the stock of X Corporation is selling at $60 per share.

*Required:*

1. Compute the amount of the dividends to be paid to each class of shareholders, including the number of shares of X Corporation stock required and the amount of cash.
2. Give journal entries to record all aspects of the dividend declaration and payment at a later date.

### Exercise 16-6

Owens Manufacturing Company's books carried an account entitled "Reserve for Profits Invested in Fixed Assets, $450,000" and another account entitled "Reserve for General Contingencies, $80,000." Capital stock outstanding, par value $20, amounted to $400,000.

The company also had bonds outstanding of $200,000. The following accounts were carried also: Bond Sinking Fund, $90,000; Bond Sinking Fund Reserve, $90,000.

The board of directors voted a 50% stock dividend and directed that the fair market value of the stock, $30 per share, be capitalized using as a basis "the general reserves" to the extent possible.

*Required:*

Give entries for the following using preferable titles:

a. To originally establish the reserves related to fixed assets and general contingencies.
b. To record the issuance of the stock dividend.
c. To originally establish the bond sinking fund.
d. To originally establish the reserve for bond sinking fund.
e. To record payment of the bonds assuming the bond sinking fund and the reserve each have a $160,000 balance at retirement date.

### Exercise 16-7

Using the simplified data below construct (1) a single-step income statement, and (2) a statement of retained earnings. Assume all amounts are material and annual data:

Current items:

| | | |
|---|---|---|
| a. Sales revenue | | $400,000 |
| b. Cost of goods sold | | 160,000 |
| c. Expenses | | 120,000 |
| d. Extraordinary loss | | 20,000 |
| e. Prior period adjustment—Damages paid (arising from lawsuit instituted in prior year) | | 4,000 |
| f. Appropriation to reserve for bond sinking fund | | 10,000 |
| g. Dividends paid | | 40,000 |
| Balances—beginning of period: | | |
| h. Retained earnings | | 110,000 |
| i. Reserve for bond sinking fund | | 60,000 |

Income taxes — assume a 40% average rate on all items including extraordinary items and prior period adjustments.

### Exercise 16–8

Using the simplified data below construct comparative statements of (1) income (single step), and (2) retained earnings for 19A and 19B. Assume all amounts are material, annual data, and an average tax rate of 40% on all items.

| Current items: | 19A | 19B |
|---|---|---|
| a. Sales................................................................... | $110,000 | $120,000 |
| b. Cost of goods sold ............................................. | 45,000 | 50,000 |
| c. Expenses.......................................................... | 25,000 | 29,000 |
| d. Extraordinary gain ............................................ | 3,000 | |
| e. Extraordinary loss ............................................. | | 6,000 |
| f. Dividends paid .................................................. | 12,000 | 10,000 |
| g. Appropriation for profits invested in fixed assets ... | 40,000 | |
| h. Prior period adjustment — Prior to 19A the corporation was sued for $10,000 damages; the suit was settled in 19A requiring the payment of $4,000 damages; this caused a reduction in income taxes. | | |
| i. Prior period adjustment — Correction of accounting error made in prior period (no tax effect)............... | | 2,000 (credit) |
| Beginning balances: | | |
| Unappropriated retained earnings .......................... | $130,000 | ? |
| Appropriation for profits invested in fixed assets ...... | -0- | ? |

### Exercise 16–9

AB Company had experienced a net loss for a number of years. Recently a new president was hired. The board of directors agreed to a quasi-reorganization and to restate certain items in the accounts as outlined by the new president, subject to stockholder approval. Prior to the restatement the balance sheet reported the following (summarized at July 1, 19A):

| | | | |
|---|---|---|---|
| Cash and receivables ... | $ 21,000 | Current liabilities ............... | $ 50,000 |
| Inventories ................. | 210,000 | Fixed liabilities .................. | 85,000 |
| Fixed assets (net) ......... | 560,000 | Capital stock (8,000 | |
| Other assets................. | 44,000 | shares) ............................ | 800,000 |
| | | Premium on stock .............. | 40,000 |
| | | Retained earnings .............. | (150,000) |
| | | Reserve for contingencies ... | 10,000 |
| | $835,000 | | $835,000 |

The stockholders approved the quasi-reorganization which carried the following provisions:

a. The inventories to be reduced to a lower-of-cost-or-market value of $140,000.
b. Receivables of $3,000 to be written off as worthless.
c. The fixed assets to be reduced to a net carrying value of $400,000.

*d.* The capital structure to be adjusted so that the deficit will be eliminated and the capital reduced by the net adjustment made to assets.

*Required:*

1. Give entries to record the quasi-reorganization as approved by the stockholders.
2. Prepare a balance sheet after the quasi-reorganization.

## PROBLEMS

### Problem 16–1

The balance sheet for Ward Manufacturing Company is shown below in summary:

| | | | |
|---|---|---|---|
| Cash ............................ | $ 28,000 | Current liabilities............... | $ 26,000 |
| Receivables ..................... | 36,000 | Bonds payable.................. | 50,000 |
| Inventory ........................ | 110,000 | Preferred stock .............. | 20,000 |
| Investments—4,000 shares | | Common stock (5,000 | |
| of Taylor stock at cost ... | 6,000 | shares, nopar .............. | 100,000 |
| Fixed assets (net) ............ | 80,000 | Premium on preferred ...... | 5,000 |
| Other assets..................... | 10,000 | Retained earnings ........... | 69,000 |
| | $270,000 | | $270,000 |

The preferred stock is 6%, $100 par value and cumulative. Dividends are three years in arrears (excluding the current year).

The investment in stock of Taylor Company has been held for a number of years; that stock is now selling for $5 per share.

On October 1, 19A the board of directors of Ward declared dividends as follows:

*a.* Preferred stock, all dividends in arrears plus current year dividend; payment to be made by transferring the requisite number of shares of Taylor stock at $5 per share.

*b.* Common stock, $4 per share for the current year, payment to be made by transferring the remainder of the Taylor stock and issuing a scrip dividend for the balance. The scrip will earn 8% annual interest and will be paid at the end of six months from date of declaration.

*Required:*

1. Compute the amount of dividends payable to each class of shareholder, indicate the amount of the scrip dividend.
2. Give entries to record the transfer of the Taylor stock and the issuance of the scrip dividend (assume declaration and payment date are the same). Make separate entries for the common and preferred stock.
3. Give the adjusting entry at December 31, 19A, for the interest on the scrip dividend.
4. Give the entry to record payment of the scrip dividend and interest on March 31, 19B.
5. Prepare the stockholders' equity section of the balance sheet as of December 31, 19A. Assume reported net income of $20,000 for 19A (including the interest on the scrip dividend).

## Problem 16-2

Bay Corporation's board of directors declared a stock dividend whereby each holder of common stock is to receive one share of common for each five shares held and a cash dividend on the preferred stock for the one year in arrears and for the current year. The average originally paid in per share of common will be capitalized for the stock dividend. At this date the records of the corporation showed:

| | |
|---|---:|
| Preferred stock, 6%, $10 par value, authorized 20,000 shares, 10,000 outstanding | $100,000 |
| Common stock, nopar, stated value $5, authorized 50,000, issued 30,000 shares | 150,000 |
| Contributed capital – excess over stated value, preferred | 20,000 |
| Contributed capital – excess over stated value, common | 30,000 |
| Retained earnings | 160,000 |

Upon issuance of the stock dividend, stock warrants were distributed for 1,000 shares of stock; subsequently warrants for 900 of the shares were exercised. The remaining warrants are outstanding to date.

*Required:*

1. Give entries to record the issuance of the stock dividend and payment of the cash dividend.
2. Prepare the stockholders' equity section of the balance sheet after giving effect to the entries in (1) above.

## Problem 16-3

The accounts for Scott Corporation showed the following balances:

*Stockholders' Equity*

| | |
|---|---:|
| Preferred stock, 6%, par value $25, 10,000 shares authorized, 8,000 shares outstanding | $200,000 |
| Common stock, nopar value, assigned value $10, authorized 20,000 shares, issued 12,000 shares | 120,000 |
| Contributed capital in excess of par, preferred | 15,000 |
| Contributed capital in excess of assigned value, common | 30,000 |
| Retained earnings | 175,000 |

During the subsequent year the following sequential transactions were recorded relating to the capital accounts:

a. A stock dividend was issued whereby each holder of ten preferred shares received one share of common stock, and each holder of six shares of common stock received one share of common. The board directed that the "average originally paid in per share of common" be capitalized. In issuing the stock dividend, warrants were issued for 100 shares.
b. All of the warrants were redeemed except those for ten shares which remained outstanding.
c. A 6% cash dividend on the preferred shares and $.50 per share on the common shares were declared and paid.
d. Reported net income was $60,000.

*Required:*

1. Prepare journal entries for the above transactions.
2. Prepare the stockholders' equity section of the balance sheet.

## Problem 16–4

The records for Jones Corporation showed the following balances at the end of 19A:

| | | | | |
|---|---:|---|---:|---|
| Current assets | $ 165,000 | Current liabilities | $ 60,000 |
| Fixed assets | 960,000 | Long-term liabilities | 100,000 |
| Other assets | 300,000 | Preferred stock | 300,000 |
| Investment in X | | Common stock, 100,000 | |
|   Corporation stock | |   shares | 800,000 |
|   (5,000 shares at cost) | 5,000 | Premium on preferred | 12,000 |
| | | Retained earnings | 158,000 |
| | $1,430,000 | | $1,430,000 |

To date 3,000 shares of preferred stock (6%, $100 par value, cumulative) have been issued. Authorized shares were: common, 200,000; and preferred, 3,000. No dividends were declared for the preceding year. During the subsequent two years the following transactions affected stockholders' equity:

19B:

a. Declared and immediately issued one share of X Corporation stock to each shareholder of preferred stock as a property dividend. The current market value of $2 per share is to be recognized in the dividend. In addition, a cash dividend was paid to complete payment of the dividends in arrears.
b. Declared and immediately issued scrip dividends amounting to 6% on the preferred and $.80 per share on the common stock. Interest on the scrip is 7% per year.
c. Reported net income $150,000 including any effects of the above transactions.

19C:

d. Paid the scrip dividends including 7% per annum interest for 12 months.
e. Declared and issued a stock dividend, payable in common stock to holders of both preferred and common stock. The preferred holders to receive "value" equivalent to 6%, and the common holders to receive one share for each five shares held. The value and the amount capitalized per share shall be the fair market value. The current price per share on the common stock is $1.50.

    Issued the stock dividend except for 500 shares for which stock warrants were issued; of these, 100 warrants related to the preferred.
f. Warrants for 300 shares were honored. The remaining warrants are outstanding.
g. Reported net income $87,000 including any effects of the above transactions.

*Required:*

1. Prepare journal entries for each of the foregoing transactions (round amounts to even dollars).
2. Prepare the stockholders' equity section of the balance sheet after giving recognition to the foregoing transactions.

**Problem 16–5**

Stone Manufacturing Company was organized with an authorization for 50,000 shares of $10 par-value stock. During the first five years of operations the following transactions affected stockholders' equity. Assume they occurred in the order given.

19A:

a. Received subscriptions for 20,000 shares of stock at $15 per share; 50% was collected from each subscriber as a down payment; the stock is not issued until fully paid.
b. Balance was collected on all shares except 1,500.
c. Reported net income was $5,000.

19B:

d. The balance was collected on 1,400 of the subscribed shares. Subscriptions for the other 100 shares were defaulted. The subscriber was refunded the amount paid in less 20% of the purchase price per agreement. Issued the 1,400 shares.
e. Reported net income was $7,000.

19C:

f. Declared and paid cash dividend amounting to $.50 per share on the shares outstanding.
g. Reported net income was $18,000.

19D:

h. Sold 5,000 shares of stock at $18; collected cash and issued stock.
i. Reported net income, $20,000.

19E:

j. Declared a 10% stock dividend on the shares outstanding. The board of directors voted that the "average paid in to date per share" be capitalized. Immediately issued the stock dividend and stock warrants for 200 of the shares.
k. Stock warrants for 190 shares received and stock issued; the balance lapsed.
l. Declared a $.50 per share dividend — one half payable in cash, balance in scrip payable in six months with interest at 7% per annum.
m. Accrued two months' interest on the scrip dividends.
n. Reported net income $18,000 (includes the interest on the scrip).

*Required:*

1. Prepare entries for the foregoing transactions.
2. Prepare the stockholders' equity section of the balance sheet after giving effect to the foregoing entries.

**Problem 16–6**

The following annual data were taken from the records of Barstow Corporation at the end of the current year (assume all amounts material; the items in parentheses are credit balances):

Current items:

a. Sales ................................................................................ $(400,000)
b. Cost of goods sold .......................................................... 230,000
c. Expenses ........................................................................ 85,000
d. Extraordinary loss........................................................... 20,000
e. An expense incorrectly charged to a nondepreciable asset
   in a prior year.................................................................. 3,000
f. Stock dividend issued ...................................................... 40,000
g. Cash dividend paid .......................................................... 9,000
h. Prior period adjustment—income tax renegotiation
   (refund of prior year taxes)................................................ (12,000)
i. Prior period adjustment—damages paid from lawsuit
   (pending for past three years) ........................................... 10,000
j. Current appropriation to reserve for bond sinking fund ........... 10,000
k. Current appropriation to reserve for plant expansion .............. 40,000

Income taxes:

Assume an average tax rate of 40% on all items including extraordinary items and prior period adjustments.

Beginning balances:

l. Unappropriated retained earnings ....................................... (80,000)
m. Reserve for bond sinking fund............................................ (50,000)
n. Reserve for plant expansion ............................................... (60,000)

*Required:*

1. Prepare a single-step income statement.
2. Prepare a statement of retained earnings.

**Problem 16–7**

Cooper Corporation records provided the following annual data for the years 19A and 19B. (Assume all amounts to be material):

Current items:

|  | 19A | 19B |
|---|---|---|
| a. Sales ................................................. | $240,000 | $260,000 |
| b. Cost of goods sold ............................... | 134,000 | 143,000 |
| c. Expenses ........................................... | 71,000 | 77,000 |
| d. Extraordinary loss ................................ | 7,000 | 2,000 |
| e. Cash dividend paid................................ | 20,000 |  |
| f. Stock dividend issued ............................ |  | 30,000 |
| g. Appropriation to reserve for bond sinking fund ...... | 10,000 | 10,000 |
| h. Increase in bond sinking fund.................... | 10,000 | 10,000 |
| i. Prior period adjustment—error correction (debit)...... | 6,000 |  |
| j. Income taxes—assume an average rate of 46% on all items including extraordinary items and prior period adjustments. |  |  |

Beginning balances:

|  | | |
|---|---|---|
| k. Reserve for bond sinking fund ........................... | 70,000 | ? |
| l. Unappropriated retained earnings......................... | 160,000 | ? |
| m. Reserve for plant expansion ................................. | 100,000 | ? |
| n. Bond sinking fund ............................................... | 70,000 | |
| o. Bonds payable.................................................... | 100,000 | |

*Required:*

1. Prepare a single-step comparative income statement for the years 19A and 19B.

2. Prepare comparative statements of retained earnings, in good form.

## Problem 16–8

King Corporation records provided the following unclassified data at year-end:

a. Appropriation during the year of retained earnings for reserve for bond sinking fund, $15,000; the prior balance was $75,000.
b. Balance in Retained Earnings, Unappropriated, account per books at end of prior year, $90,000.
c. Dividends declared on preferred stock December 31 of the year just ended, payable the following January 15 amounting to $10,000.
d. Declared and issued a small stock dividend on common stock July 1 of year just ended; par, $20,000, and fair market value, $30,000.
e. Preferred stock sold during year just ended 200 shares, par, $100, and market, $130.
f. Income statement data for current year: sales, $340,000; cost of goods sold, $160,000; expenses, $80,000.
g. Additional assessment during year just ended by Internal Revenue Service for prior years' income taxes, $4,000 (a prior period adjustment).
h. Damages paid on prior year lawsuit, $8,000 (a prior period adjustment).
i. Income taxes — assume an average rate of 45% on all items including extraordinary items and the damages paid (item h).

*Required:*
1. Prepare a single-step income statement.
2. Prepare a statement of retained earnings.

## Problem 16–9

Jackson Corporation is undergoing an audit. The books show an account entitled Surplus which is reproduced below covering a five-year period, January 1, 1972, to December 31, 1976.

### Credits

| | | |
|---|---|---:|
| 1972–75 | Net income carried to surplus | $ 800,000 |
| 1972 | By debit to goodwill — authorized by board | 50,000 |
| 12/31/73 | Premium on capital stock sold | 6,000 |
| 1/1/74 | Correction of prior accounting error | 2,000 |
| 1/1/74 | Donation to company — fixed asset | 5,000 |
| 12/31/74 | Refund of prior years' income taxes | 9,000 |
| 7/1/75 | Reduction in capital stock from par value $100 to par value $50 with no change in the number of shares outstanding (10,000); approved by shareholders | 500,000 |
| 12/31/76 | Net income, 1976 | 70,000 |
| | | $1,442,000 |

### Debits

| | | |
|---|---|---:|
| 1972–76 | Cash dividends paid | $ 600,000 |
| 1/1/72 | To reserve for bond sinking fund (annually) | 20,000 |
| 12/31/74 | Reserve for bond sinking fund | 20,000 |
| 12/31/75 | Reserve for bond sinking fund | 20,000 |
| 9/1/76 | Fifty percent stock dividend | 250,000 |
| | | $ 910,000 |

Assume the net income amounts are correct.

*Required:*

1. The above account is to be closed and replaced with appropriate accounts. Complete a worksheet analysis of the above account to reflect the correct account balances and the corrections needed. It is suggested that the worksheet carry the following columns: (*a*) surplus account per books, (*b*) corrected net income, 1976, (*c*) unappropriated retained earnings, and (*d*) columns for any other specific accounts needed.
2. Give the appropriate entry or entries to close this account and to set up appropriate accounts in its place.

## Problem 16–10

During the last five years, Hanson Corporation has experienced severe losses. A new president has been tentatively employed who is confident the company can be saved from going into bankruptcy (and dissolution). Working with an independent CPA, the new president has proposed a quasi-reorganization with the condition that it must be approved by the stockholders before the position is accepted. The board approved the proposal and submitted it to a vote of the stockholders.

Prior to reorganization, the balance sheet (summarized) reflected the following:

| | | | |
|---|---:|---|---:|
| Cash | $ 20,000 | Current liabilities | $150,000 |
| Accounts receivable | 94,000 | Long-term liabilities | 240,000 |
| Allowance for doubtful | | Common stock, par $50 | 500,000 |
| accounts | (4,000) | Preferred stock, par $100 | 100,000 |
| Inventory | 150,000 | Premium on preferred | |
| Fixed assets | 800,000 | stock | 30,000 |
| Accumulated | | Retained earnings | (220,000) |
| depreciation | (300,000) | | |
| Deferred charges | 40,000 | | |
| | $800,000 | | $800,000 |

The reorganization proposal, as approved by the stockholders, provided the following:

*a.* To adequately provide for probable losses on accounts receivable, increase the allowance by $6,000.
*b.* Write down the inventory to $100,000 because of obsolete and damaged goods.
*c.* Reduce the book value of the fixed assets to $400,000 by increasing accumulated depreciation.
*d.* By agreement of the creditors, reduce all liabilities by 5%.
*e.* Reduce the par value of the preferred shares to $60.
*f.* Change the common stock to nopar and reduce the balance to leave a zero balance in retained earnings.
*g.* Close all capital balances, other than the preferred and common stock accounts.

*Required:*

1. Give a separate entry for each of the above changes.
2. Prepare a balance sheet immediately after the quasi-reorganization.

**Problem 16–11**

Weston Corporation, a medium-sized manufacturer, has experienced losses for the past five years. Although operations for the year ended resulted in a loss, several important changes resulted in a profitable fourth quarter; and as a result, future operations of the company are expected to be profitable.

The treasurer suggested a quasi-reorganization to (a) eliminate the accumulated deficit of $423,620, (b) write up the $493,100 cost of operating land and buildings to their fair value, and (c) set up an asset of $203,337 representing the estimated future tax benefit of the losses accumulated to date.

*Required:*

1. What are the characteristics of a quasi-reorganization? That is, of what does it consist?
2. List the conditions under which a quasi-reorganization generally would be justified.
3. Discuss the propriety of the treasurer's proposals to:
   a. Eliminate the deficit of $423,620.
   b. Write up the value of the operating land and buildings of $493,100 to their fair value.
   c. Set up an asset of $203,337 representing the future tax benefit of the losses accumulated to date.

(AICPA adapted)

# Chapter *17*

## Corporations — Contraction and Expansion of Corporate Capital after Formation; and Earnings per Share

Once the corporate charter is granted and the bylaws are approved, provisions governing corporate capital are established; however, this does not mean that such provisions may not be changed. Aside from the sale of unissued shares already authorized, a corporation may obtain authorization for additional classes of stock, expansion of the number of shares of currently authorized stock, or change the par or stated values. Or it may contract and expand corporate capital by purchasing and selling its own shares in the marketplace. Callable and redeemable shares may be acquired and convertible shares exchanged. The corporation may undergo a corporate reorganization involving a significant change in the entire capital structure; or it may combine with other entities. These changes are controlled in various manners: by state laws, by charter and bylaw provisions, or by the shareholders themselves. Obviously, upon approval of the shareholders the bylaws may be changed and even a new or amended charter obtained. In the long-term the primary source of expansion of stockholders' equity is net income not distributed as cash or property dividends.

Retained earnings frequently is capitalized by means of stock dividends (see Chapter 16) or through certain other forms of capital changes.

This chapter focuses on changes after initial formation, particularly treasury stock, stock conversion, expansion of legal and contributed capital, and stock rights. Earnings per share of common stock also is discussed.

In accounting and reporting changes in corporate capital, other than as a result of net income and prior period adjustments, five basic principles have general applicability, viz:

700

1. Sources of capital are separately recorded and reported.
2. Information must be accumulated and reported to meet the requirements of the accounting profession and the prevailing laws.
3. A corporation cannot recognize, as income or as increases in retained earnings, gains that result from capital transactions between itself and its owners; accounting recognition of increases resulting from transactions relating to the corporation's own stock are recorded as changes in contributed capital rather than as gains.
4. Increases in authorized shares, authorized legal capital, changes in par or stated values, or exchanges of its own equity shares (such as its own preferred shares for its own common shares) do not create income, losses, or retained earnings.
5. Certain payments (of assets) by a corporation for its own shares above the contributed capital per share may be considered to be a form of cash (or property) dividends which would be charged to retained earnings.

## TREASURY STOCK

Expansion and contraction in contributed capital after formation frequently arise as a result of treasury stock transactions. The statutes of most states permit a corporation to purchase its own stock subject to certain limitations. *Treasury stock* is a corporation's own stock (preferred or common) that (*a*) has been issued; (*b*) is subsequently reacquired by the issuing corporation; and (*c*) after acquisition has not been sold or formally retired. Treasury shares may be subsequently sold and reclassified as outstanding shares. The courts generally have held that a discount liability does not apply to treasury stock resold (see Chapter 15), assuming the second purchaser did not have knowledge of any prior discount liability. The purchase of a corporation's own stock serves to contract both assets and corporate capital, whereas a sale of treasury stock serves to expand both assets and corporate capital. Treasury shares may be obtained by purchase, by settlement of an obligation, or through donation. Obviously, treasury stock does not carry voting, dividend, or liquidation privileges. Although the acquisition of treasury stock involves the disbursement of assets, or the cancellation of an obligation, it is not an asset since a corporation cannot own itself. Also treasury stock is generally viewed as similar to unissued stock, which by no stretch of the imagination can be viewed as an asset; it must be sold before any assets arise.

In contrast to treasury stock, a corporation may reacquire its own shares because they were issued as either callable or redeemable shares (see Chapter 15). Callable or redeemable shares received are not classified as treasury stock since their acquisition usually entails their immediate cancellation and they are not available for subsequent resale.

Treasury stock may be acquired for the following reasons: (1) the corporation has ready cash and the stock is considered to be unrealistically underpriced; (2) to use for employee stock options, bonus plans, and direct sale to employees; (3) to use in exchange for other securities or assets; (4) to pay a stock dividend; (5) to settle debts; (6) to increase earnings per share; (7) to buy out one or more particular stockholders; and (8) to support the market price of the stock.

## RECORDING AND REPORTING TREASURY STOCK TRANSACTIONS

There are several prevailing views as to the approach that should be used in accounting for treasury stock. These views may be grouped broadly under two methods, viz:

1. Cost method (one-transaction concept).
2. Par-value method (dual-transaction concept).

Both of these methods are generally accepted; however, they derive different results for certain individual items in the stockholders' equity section of the balance sheet. Total stockholders' equity is the same under both methods.

### Cost Method

This method sometimes is referred to as the one-transaction concept because the purchase and subsequent sale of treasury stock is viewed as one transaction rather than two. At acquisition, the *cost* of the treasury stock is debited to a "holding" account called Treasury Stock. Under this concept the cost is "held" until subsequent sale at which time the effect of the various components of stockholders' equity can be determined and recorded. Thus, at date of subsequent sale, any difference between cost and resale price is accounted for in the appropriate manner.

Separate treasury stock accounts should be established for each class of stock. Where treasury shares have been acquired at different costs, specific shares should be identified; otherwise a *Fifo* or average cost per share must be used to credit the Treasury Stock account at resale date.

Under the cost method the balance in the Treasury Stock account at the end of the accounting period is viewed as an *unallocated reduction* of total stockholders' equity (illustrated subsequently).

The following entries illustrate the accounting for treasury stock assuming the *cost method* is used:

#### Recording Treasury Stock—Cost Method

1. To record the initial sale and issuance of 10,000 shares of capital stock, par $25, at $26 per share:

    | | | |
    |---|---|---|
    | Cash ................................................................... | 260,000 | |
    |     Contributed capital in excess of par .................. | | 10,000 |
    |     Capital stock (10,000 shares, par $25).................. | | 250,000 |

2. To record a purchase of 2,000 shares of treasury stock at cost ($28):

| Treasury stock (by type of stock) | 56,000 | |
| Cash | | 56,000 |

3a. To record a sale of 500 of the shares of treasury stock at $28 per share (same as the purchase price):

| Cash | 14,000 | |
| Treasury stock (500 shares @ $28) | | 14,000 |

b. Now assume instead a sale of the 500 shares at $30 per share (i.e., $2 per share above the purchase price):

| Cash (500 shares @ $30) | 15,000 | |
| Contributed capital, from sale of treasury stock | | |
| (500 shares @ $2) | | 1,000 |
| Treasury stock (500 shares @ $28) | | 14,000 |

4. To record a sale of another 500 shares at $22 per share (i.e., $6 per share below the purchase price; also below par):

| Cash | 11,000 | |
| Contributed capital, from sale of treasury stock | 1,000 | |
| Retained earnings | 2,000 | |
| Treasury stock (500 shares @ $28) | | 14,000 |

Under the cost method when treasury stock is sold at a price in excess of its cost, the "gain" should be recorded as contributed capital, as in transaction 3b above, and not as a credit to Income or Retained Earnings.

Alternatively, when treasury stock is sold at less than cost, the "loss" should be charged to contributed capital "to the extent that previous net 'gains' from the sales or retirements of the same class of stock are included therein, otherwise to retained earnings."[1] For example, in transaction 4 above, had there been no balance in the account, Contributed Capital from Sale of Treasury Stock, the entire $3,000 would have been debited to Retained Earnings; alternatively had the balance in the contributed account been in excess of $3,000, there would have been no charge to Retained Earnings. The debit to Retained Earnings may be viewed as a "dividend" to the stockholder from whom the shares were purchased, or, alternatively, as the capitalization of a portion of retained earnings.[2]

When the cost method is used, treasury stock is reported as an *unallocated reduction* of stockholders' equity reported as follows (assuming transaction 3a and a beginning balance in retained earnings of $40,000):

---

[1] AICPA, "Status of Accounting Research Bulletins," *APB Opinion No. 6* (New York, 1965), par. 12.

[2] A minor variation of the above method of recording the "loss" charges contributed capital with a pro rata amount per share of any premium that was recorded when that class of stock was originally sold; any remaining amount is charged to Retained Earnings. For example, transaction 4 illustrated above would be recorded as follows:

| Cash | 11,000 | |
| Contributed capital in excess of par ($1 per share) | 500 | |
| Retained earnings | 2,500 | |
| Treasury stock | | 14,000 |

Stockholders' Equity
(cost method for treasury stock)

Contributed capital:

Capital stock, par $25, authorized 50,000 shares, issued
  10,000 shares of which 1,000 are held as treasury stock.............. $250,000
Contributed capital in excess of par ........................................... 10,000

    Total Contributed Capital ................................................. 260,000
Retained earnings........................................................................ 38,000

    Total Contributed Capital and Retained Earnings .............. 298,000
Less: Treasury stock, 1,000 shares at cost ................................... 28,000

    Total Stockholders' Equity............................................... $270,000

The cost method is frequently used because of its simplicity. It may avoid the necessity of developing specific data concerning the original premiums, discounts, and so on, relating to the specific stock involved. It can be defended largely on practical grounds; theoretical justification is difficult even if no "gain" or "loss" is involved. The primary objection from the point of view of theory is that the *sources* of the various components of capital are not maintained. Under this procedure the actual capital contributed (after the treasury stock transactions are recorded) for the outstanding stock is not specifically identified in the accounts.

### Par-Value Method

This method is sometimes referred to as the dual-transaction concept because it views the purchase and sale of treasury stock as completely independent and unrelated. The objectives of the par-value method are:

1. At date of purchase of treasury stock—to make a final accounting with the retiring stockholder and to adjust the capital accounts accordingly.
2. At date of sale of treasury stock—to record it in the same way as the sale and issuance of unissued stock.

To accomplish these purposes the Treasury Stock account is carried at the par or stated value per share; hence, the designation par-value method.

The final accounting with the retiring stockholder (at date of purchase of the treasury shares) involves comparing the amount withdrawn (price paid for the treasury shares) with the amount originally invested by the stockholder (computed on an average basis for all shares issued). If the amount withdrawn exceeds the original investment, the excess is charged to Retained Earnings as a form of dividend to the retiring stockholder. If the original investment exceeds the amount withdrawn, the difference is credited to an appropriately designated contributed capital account.

When the treasury stock is sold, the entire proceeds are viewed as an investment by the new stockholder. The Treasury Stock account is credited for par, and any excess over par or stated value is credited to Contributed Capital in Excess of Par (or Stated Value) in the same manner as for unissued shares. If, as rarely occurs, the treasury stock is sold for less than par (or stated value) the difference between the selling price and par should be debited to Retained Earnings since no discount liability is associated with treasury stock sold at less than par.

The preceding example is used to illustrate the accounting for treasury stock assuming the *par-value method* is used:

### Recording Treasury Stock — Par-Value Method

1. To record the initial sale and issuance of 10,000 shares of capital stock, par $25, at $26 per share:

| | | |
|---|---|---|
| Cash ..................................................................... | 260,000 | |
| Capital stock (10,000 shares, par $25) ............... | | 250,000 |
| Contributed capital in excess of par .................. | | 10,000 |

2. To record a purchase of 2,000 shares of treasury stock at $28 per share:

| | | |
|---|---|---|
| Treasury stock (2,000 shares at par) ........................ | 50,000 | |
| Contributed capital in excess of par ........................ | 2,000 | |
| Retained earnings................................................... | 4,000 | |
| Cash ............................................................... | | 56,000 |

3a. To record a sale of 500 shares of treasury stock at $28 per share (same as the purchase price; $3 above par):

| | | |
|---|---|---|
| Cash ...................................................................... | 14,000 | |
| Treasury stock (500 shares at par) ..................... | | 12,500 |
| Contributed capital in excess of par, from treasury stock transactions* .......................... | | 1,500 |
| * The separate designation "from treasury stock transactions" often is not used. | | |

b. Now assume instead a sale of 500 shares of treasury stock at $30 per share ($5 per share above par):

| | | |
|---|---|---|
| Cash (500 shares @ $30)......................................... | 15,000 | |
| Treasury stock (500 shares at par) ..................... | | 12,500 |
| Contributed capital in excess of par, from treasury stock transactions* .......................... | | 2,500 |
| * The separate designation "from treasury stock transactions" often is not used. | | |

4. To record a sale of another 500 shares at $22 per share ($3 per share below par):

| | | |
|---|---|---|
| Cash (500 shares @ $22).......................................... | 11,000 | |
| Retained earnings ($25 − $22) × 500 shares.............. | 1,500* | |
| Treasury stock (500 shares at par, $25) .............. | | 12,500 |
| * Discount on stock is not debited since a discount liability is not created. | | |

When the par-value method is used, treasury stock is reported as a deduction, at its par or stated value, from the capital stock to which it relates. Stockholders' equity, using the above illustrative data would be reported as follows:

Stockholders' Equity
(par-value method for treasury stock)

Contributed capital:

| | |
|---|---:|
| Capital stock, par $25, authorized 50,000 shares, issued 10,000 shares | $250,000 |
| Less: Treasury stock, 1,000 shares at par | 25,000 |
| Total Capital Stock Outstanding, 9,000 Shares | 225,000 |
| Contributed capital in excess of par | 10,500 |
| Total Contributed Capital | 235,500 |
| Retained earnings | 34,500 |
| Total Stockholders' Equity | $270,000 |

Observe that total stockholders' equity reported under the cost method and par-value method is the same; the basic difference between the two methods is reflected in the capital stock and retained earnings subclassifications.

The dual-transaction concept, (i.e., the par-value method) theoretically is sound in that the *sources* of capital are maintained intact. An exact record of capital received on all outstanding stock is maintained. The principal disadvantage is the problem of identifying the various components of contributed capital with the specific shares involved.

In overall perspective the par-value method is considered to be theoretically preferable, and it is consistent with the concept of accounting and reporting by source. However, because of its simplicity the cost method is widely used.

## ACCOUNTING FOR NOPAR TREASURY STOCK

Nopar stock having a *stated* or *assigned* value per share when purchased, is accounted for in exactly the same manner as illustrated above for par-value treasury stock under the two methods. The stated or assigned value per share is treated as if it were par value in all of the entries. However, if *true* nopar stock is purchased as treasury stock (no stated or assigned value per share), the transactions would be recorded somewhat differently as illustrated below.

If the cost method (i.e., the one-transaction concept) is used, the Treasury Stock account reflects the cost per share in the same manner as illustrated above for par-value stock. If the dual-transaction concept is used the Treasury Stock account reflects the average original issue price per share (i.e., the average amount per share credited to the Capital Stock account). To illustrate the accounting entries for true nopar stock, we will adapt the preceding example by assuming that the Nopar Capital Stock account was credited for the issue price originally.

**Recording Treasury Stock – True Nopar Stock**

| | Cost Method | | Par-Value Method | |
|---|---|---|---|---|
| 1. To record sale and issuance of 10,000 shares of nopar capital stock at $26 per share: | | | | |
| Cash .............................................. | 260,000 | | 260,000 | |
| Capital stock, nopar (10,000 shares @ $26) ........................ | | 260,000 | | 260,000 |
| 2. To record purchase of 2,000 shares of treasury stock at $28 per share: | | | | |
| Treasury stock (2,000 shares @ $28) ... | 56,000 | | | |
| Treasury stock (2,000 shares @ $26) ... | | | 52,000 | |
| Retained earnings .......................... | | | 4,000 | |
| Cash ...................................... | | 56,000 | | 56,000 |
| 3. To record the sale of 500 shares of treasury stock at $30 per share: | | | | |
| Cash .............................................. | 15,000 | | 15,000 | |
| Treasury stock (500 shares @ $28) ............................... | | 14,000 | | |
| Treasury stock (500 shares @ $26) ............................... | | | | 13,000 |
| Contributed capital, from treasury stock transactions ................... | | 1,000 | | 2,000 |
| 4. To record sale of 500 shares of treasury stock at $22 per share: | | | | |
| Cash .............................................. | 11,000 | | 11,000 | |
| Contributed capital, from treasury stock transactions ....................... | 1,000 | | 2,000 | |
| Retained earnings ........................... | 2,000 | | | |
| Treasury stock........................... | | 14,000 | | 13,000 |

## TREASURY STOCK RECEIVED THROUGH DONATIONS

Shareholders may donate shares of stock back to the corporation. Such donations may (a) be to raise needed working capital through resale of donated stock, (b) represent the return of the stock in recognition of an overvaluation of assets originally given in exchange for the stock. Stock received by donation is classified as treasury stock. Neither total assets nor *total* equity is changed by the donation of treasury stock. Three methods have been employed in recording the receipt of donated treasury stock, viz:

1. When the donated stock is received, charge the Treasury Stock account with the fair market value of the stock and credit Contributed Capital, Donated Treasury Stock for the same amount. Upon subsequent sale any "gains" or "losses" would be accounted for as illustrated above for the cost method.
2. When the donated stock is received, charge the Treasury Stock ac-

count with the par, stated or, in the case of true nopar stock, average paid in and credit an appropriately designated donated capital account. Subsequent sale would be recorded as illustrated above for the par-value method.

3. When the donated stock is received, a memorandum entry is made on the basis that there was no cost. Subsequent sales would be credited to contributed capital for the full sales price.[3]

The first approach is theoretically preferable and is consistent with the thrust of *APB Opinion No. 29,* "Accounting for Nonmonetary Transactions" (however, the *Opinion* does not specifically cover this transaction). When the cost method is used this approach should be applied.

The second approach is internally consistent and is generally used with the par-value method. The third approach has very little merit; and although used in earlier years, it appears to be seldom used at the present time.[4]

## RETIREMENT OF TREASURY STOCK

Subject to stockholder approval (in most jurisdictions) and in conformance with all legal requirements, including the protection of creditors, a corporation may decide to formally retire treasury shares and have them revert to unissued status. When treasury stock is retired in this manner, all capital account balances related to the treasury shares are closed out on a proportional basis and the net effect is charged to contributed capital (if a credit) or to retained earnings (if a debit).

To illustrate, we will continue the preceding example assuming par value stock. Recall that the capital balances, after the illustrative entries reflected the following (refer to the balance sheet examples):

|  | Cost Method | Par-Value Method |
|---|---|---|
| Capital stock, par $25, 10,000 shares issued ... | $250,000 | $250,000 |
| Contributed capital in excess of par ............ | 10,000 | 10,500 |
| Treasury stock (1,000 shares): |  |  |
| At cost ................................................ | (28,000) |  |
| At par value ....................................... |  | (25,000) |
| Retained earnings, unappropriated............... | 38,000 | 34,500 |
| Total Stockholders' Equity.................. | $270,000 | $270,000 |

---

[3] In some cases donated stock may involve a "treasury stock subterfuge." This situation involves a collusive agreement to issue an excess number of shares for properties (when valued at fair market value) followed by a donation back to the corporation of a part of such shares. In some jurisdictions the donated shares have then been sold at a discount with no assumed discount liability since such liability normally attaches only to the *first* issuance. Recent court decisions have tended to hold this to be illegal; and because par values tend to be set very low, it rarely occurs today.

[4] At the present time the FASB has the topic of corporate capital on its agenda. It is anticipated that this and related issues will be definitively treated and the array of alternatives narrowed.

The entry to record retirement of the 1,000 shares of treasury stock would be:

|  | Cost Method | Par-Value Method |
|---|---|---|
| Capital stock (1,000 shares × $25 par) .... | 25,000 | 25,000 |
| Contributed capital in excess of par: | | |
| ($10,000 ÷ 10,000 shares) × 1,000 | | |
| shares......................................... | 1,000 | |
| ($10,500 ÷ 10,000 shares) × 1,000 | | |
| shares......................................... | | 1,050 |
| Retained earnings ........................... | 2,000 | |
| Treasury stock: | | |
| At cost  .................................. | 28,000 | |
| At par...................................... | | 25,000 |
| Contributed capital, from retirement | | |
| of treasury shares .................. | | 1,050 |

Had there been a balance in Contributed Capital from Treasury Stock Transactions it would have also been closed out in the above entry.

## RESTRICTION OF RETAINED EARNINGS FOR TREASURY STOCK

In Chapter 15 legal capital was discussed and the point was made that the laws frequently attempt to protect creditor interests through the maintenance of legal capital requirements and restriction of dividends. When treasury stock is purchased, assets of the corporation are disbursed to the owners of the shares purchased. Should a corporation have a completely free hand in this matter, it is not difficult to perceive how creditor interests (or the interests of another class of shareholders) may be jeopardized through the distribution of corporate assets via treasury stock purchases, even though legal capital may be "reported intact." To prevent this situation many states have laws limiting the amount of treasury stock that may be held at any one time to some amount such as the total retained earnings. This provision has the effect of (a) requiring restriction of retained earnings equivalent to the cost of treasury stock, and (b) reducing the amount of retained earnings that may be used for dividends until the treasury shares are resold.[5] To illustrate, assume a corporation reports the following stockholders' equity:

| | |
|---|---|
| Capital stock, par $25, 10,000 shares issued............... | $250,000 |
| Contributed capital in excess of par.......................... | 10,000 |
| Retained earnings, unappropriated .......................... | 38,000 |

---

[5] In most states the restriction applies to retained earnings; on the other hand, some states permit the purchase of treasury stock equivalent in cost to other capital items such as premium. Throughout these discussions we will assume that the cost of treasury stock held cannot exceed the balance of retained earnings.   •

Assuming a statutory limitation that the cost of treasury stock held cannot exceed the balance of retained earnings, the corporation could purchase treasury stock costing $38,000; if it did, no dividends could be declared. Should the corporation purchase treasury stock with a cost of $30,000, dividends up to $8,000 could be declared. The restriction on retained earnings would be removed (a) by sale of the treasury shares, or (b) by their formal retirement. The restriction on retained earnings is reported either as a line item on the balance sheet or as a footnote as explained and illustrated in Chapter 16.

## RETIREMENT OF CALLABLE STOCK

Corporations frequently issue callable preferred stock that provides that the corporation, at its option after a certain date, can call in the shares at a specified price for retirement. The call price is at or above the par value and is usually above the original issuance price.[6] Thus, callable shares are not classified as treasury stock.

When callable stock is acquired and immediately retired, all capital balances relating to the specific shares are removed from the accounts, any "loss" is charged to Retained Earnings as a form of dividends and any "gain" is recorded in a contributed capital account appropriately designated. If the stock is cumulative preferred and there are dividends in arrears, such dividends are paid and charged to Retained Earnings in the normal manner. To illustrate several typical situations, assume a corporation had 2,500 shares of callable preferred stock (par value $100) outstanding, $250,000; contributed capital in excess of par, preferred stock, $10,000; contributed capital from other sources, $5,000; and retained earnings, $45,000. Now assume the corporation called and retired 1,000 shares of the preferred stock. Three different assumptions as to the call and retirement are illustrated below:

*Assumption 1:* The preferred stock is callable at the original issue price of $104 per share.

| | | |
|---|---|---|
| Preferred stock (1,000 shares at par) ............................. | 100,000 | |
| Contributed capital in excess of par ($4 per share)............ | 4,000 | |
| Cash ................................................................. | | 104,000 |

*Assumption 2:* The preferred stock is callable at $110 per share— $6 per share above the original issue price of $104.

| | | |
|---|---|---|
| Preferred stock (1,000 shares at par) ............................. | 100,000 | |
| Contributed capital in excess of par ($4 per share)............ | 4,000 | |
| Retained earnings ..................................................... | 6,000 | |
| Cash ................................................................. | | 110,000 |

*Assumption 3:* The preferred stock is 5% cumulative; three years'

---

[6] *APB Opinion No. 10* recommends that "the liquidation preference of the stock be disclosed in the equity section of the balance sheet in the aggregate, either parenthetically or 'in short' rather than on a per share basis or by disclosure in notes." Amounts of arrearages on cumulative preferred dividends also should be disclosed.

dividends are in arrears. The stock is callable at 101 plus the dividends in arrears.

| | | |
|---|---:|---:|
| Retained earnings ($100,000 × 5% × 3 years) ................ | 15,000 | |
| Cash ................................................................. | | 15,000 |

Note: The remaining preferred shares are not considered in this entry; cumulative dividends on them also would be paid and recorded at this time.

| | | |
|---|---:|---:|
| Preferred stock (1,000 shares at par) ............................ | 100,000 | |
| Contributed capital in excess of par ($4 per share)........... | 4,000 | |
| Contributed capital from retirement of preferred stock ................................................................... | | 3,000 |
| Cash ................................................................. | | 101,000 |

If true nopar stock is retired, the average price per share originally credited to the stock account is removed and the "loss" or "gain" is accounted for as illustrated above. If nopar stock with a stated or assigned value is retired, the procedures illustrated above for par-value stock are appropriate.

## CONVERTIBLE STOCK

Corporations frequently issue *convertible* stock which give the shareholder an option, within a specified time period, to exchange convertible shares currently held for other classes of capital stock (or bonds) at a specified rate. The convertible shares then are usually retired when received by the corporation. Conversion privileges require the issuing corporation to set aside a sufficient number of shares to fulfill the conversion rights until they are exercised or expire.

At date of conversion, all account balances related to the convertible shares are removed and the new shares issued are recorded at their par or stated value; any difference, if a credit, is recorded in an appropriately designated contributed capital account; if a debit, Retained Earnings is charged. To illustrate three typical situations, assume the following data:

| | |
|---|---:|
| Preferred convertible stock, par $2, 100,000 shares outstanding ...... | $200,000 |
| Contributed capital in excess of par, preferred stock ..................... | 20,000 |
| Common stock, par $1, 500,000 shares authorized, 150,000 shares outstanding ................................................................ | 150,000 |
| Contributed capital in excess of par, common stock ..................... | 50,000 |

*Situation 1:* The conversion privilege specifies one share of common stock for each share of preferred stock converted. Shareholders turn in 10,000 shares of preferred stock for conversion.

| | | |
|---|---:|---:|
| Preferred stock (10,000 shares at par) ................................ | 20,000 | |
| Contributed capital in excess of par, preferred stock ($.20 per share) ........................................................... | 2,000 | |
| Common stock (10,000 shares at par) ......................... | | 10,000 |
| Contributed capital from conversion of preferred stock... | | 12,000 |

*Situation 2:* The conversion privilege specifies two shares of common stock for each share of preferred stock converted. Shareholders turn in 10,000 shares of preferred stock for conversion.

| | | |
|---|---:|---:|
| Preferred stock (10,000 shares at par) | 20,000 | |
| Contributed capital in excess of par, preferred stock | 2,000 | |
| Common stock (20,000 shares) | | 20,000 |
| Contributed capital from conversion of preferred stock... | | 2,000 |

*Situation 3:* The conversion privilege specifies three shares of common stock for each share of preferred stock converted. Shareholders turn in 10,000 shares of preferred stock for conversion.

| | | |
|---|---:|---:|
| Preferred stock (10,000 shares) | 20,000 | |
| Contributed capital in excess of par, preferred stock | 2,000 | |
| Retained earnings | 8,000 | |
| Common stock (30,000 shares) | | 30,000 |

Conversion of bonds for capital stock is discussed in Chapters 11 and 19.

## CHANGING PAR VALUE

A corporation, if it conforms with the applicable state laws, may amend the charter and bylaws to change the par value of one or more classes of authorized stock. Par-value stock may be called in and replaced with nopar stock or stock of a different par value; conversely, nopar stock may be replaced with par-value stock.[7]

The entries to record changes in par value follow the principles enunciated at the beginning of this chapter and illustrated in the preceding paragraphs. To illustrate several typical situations, assume the following data:

| | |
|---|---:|
| Capital stock, par $2, 50,000 shares outstanding | $100,000 |
| Contributed capital in excess of par | 20,000 |
| Retained earnings | 30,000 |

*Situation 1:* The shares are changed from par value to an equal number of true nopar shares.

| | | |
|---|---:|---:|
| Capital stock, par $2 (50,000 shares) | 100,000 | |
| Contributed capital in excess of par | 20,000 | |
| Capital stock, nopar, (50,000 shares) | | 120,000 |

*Situation 2:* The shares are changed from par value to an equal number of nopar shares with a stated value of $1 per share.

---

[7] Stock splits are discussed in Chapter 16. In a stock split the par value is reduced and the number of shares outstanding is increased proportionately; therefore, the balance in the capital stock account is unchanged. Only a memorandum entry in the original stock account is needed to reflect the new par value per share and the number of shares outstanding after the split.

Capital stock, par $2 (50,000 shares) ............................ 100,000
Contributed capital in excess of par ............................ 20,000
    Capital stock, nopar, stated value $1 (50,000 shares)...    50,000
    Contributed capital from change to nopar stock.........    70,000

*Situation 3:* The shares are changed from par value to an equal number of nopar shares with a stated value of $2.50 per share.

Capital stock, par $2 (50,000 shares) ............................ 100,000
Contributed capital in excess of par ............................ 20,000
Retained earnings ...................................................... 5,000
    Capital stock, nopar, stated value $2.50
    (50,000 shares) .................................................    125,000

*Situation 4:* The original shares were true nopar, and the capital stock account reflected a credit balance of $120,000. The true nopar shares are changed to an equal number of shares with a par value of $2.

Capital stock, nopar (50,000 shares) ............................ 120,000
    Capital stock, par $2 (50,000 shares) .......................    100,000
    Contributed capital from conversion of nopar shares ...    20,000

## STOCK RIGHTS

A corporation may extend rights to acquire shares of stock under specified conditions. A certificate, known as a *stock warrant*, is issued by the corporation which conveys to the holder one or more *stock rights;* such warrants allow the holder to acquire shares of a specified stock issued by the corporation when certain conditions are met. A warrant specifies (*a*) the option price for the specified security, (*b*) the number of rights required to obtain each share of the specified security, (*c*) the expiration date of the right, and (*d*) instructions for exercise of the right.

Each stock right is a privilege extended by the corporation to acquire a fractional share or a specified number of shares of its capital stock. For example, X Corporation issued to the holder of each share of its common stock one stock right. According to the specified conditions a share of new preferred stock could be purchased for $40 upon the presentation of five of the stock rights within a specified time period. The warrants would have value to the extent that the $40 per share option price is below the expected future price of the new shares during the option period. In the absence of a restriction, stock rights may be bought and sold on the market similar to shares of stock. The market value of a stock right at issuance will approximate the difference between the then current market price of the stock ex rights (i.e., without rights) and the option price specified on the stock warrant, divided by the number of rights needed to purchase one share of stock. For example, if the market price of X Corporation preferred stock was $45 on the date the rights were issued, they would have an approximate market value immediately of [($45 − $40) ÷ 5 rights] = $1 per right.

Situations where stock rights often are issued include:

1. A special concession to present shareholders to encourage them to purchase additional shares that are to be sold to raise additional capital.
2. As a means of handling fractional shares needed when a stock dividend is declared and issued (see Chapter 16).
3. As a means of enhancing the marketability of other securities issued by the corporation, such as bonds payable and preferred stock.
4. As compensation to outsiders (such as underwriters, promoters, and professionals) for rendering services to the corporation.
5. As additional compensation to corporate officers and other employees. In this situation, the stock rights are generally referred to as *stock options*.

The issuance of stock rights pose accounting problems for both the recipient and the issuing corporation. Accounting for stock rights received by an investor is discussed in Chapter 18.

In respect to the *issuing corporation,* at least a memorandum entry must be made at date of issuance of stock rights because the balance sheet, or notes to the statements, must disclose the number of stock rights outstanding by class of stock. However, accounting entries usually are made in the accounts for the last four situations listed above. Fractional share warrants with stock dividends are illustrated in Chapter 16, and the issuance of bonds payable with detachable stock warrants is illustrated in Chapter 19. In the case of items 4 and 5 above, the compensation must be recorded at the fair market value of the compensation or the fair market value of the stock rights, whichever is the more clearly determinable.

For example, if 500 stock rights are issued to an attorney for legal services when the rights are selling at $1 on the market, the entry by the issuing corporation, assuming five rights and $40 will acquire one share of stock, would be:

```
Expenses—legal services .......................................................  500
     Stock rights outstanding (for 100 shares of stock).................       500
```

When the rights are exercised, the Stock Rights Outstanding account is debited. During the period the rights are outstanding, the account is reported along with the capital stock account to which it relates.

## ACCOUNTING FOR STOCK ISSUED TO EMPLOYEES

Corporations often establish plans whereby shares of stock in the company are issued to employees. The purposes of stock plans are quite varied, ranging from a desire to encourage ownership in the company by the employees, to raising equity capital, and to provide additional compensation to one or more employees. Often stock rights are given because shares are to be issued to the employees or a particular group of employees (such as top executives) at some future date. Consequently, stock warrants, or stock options, are often issued when an employee meets the certain specified conditions. In these instances, the stock rights generally are specified as *nontransferable;* the shares received, through exercise of the rights, are *transferable.*

Plans for the issuance of stock to employees are designated with a variety of terms, none of which has been accorded a uniform definition. Typical terms used are: stock purchase plans, stock option plans, stock bonus plans, stock award plans, stock thrift plans, and stock savings plans. One must carefully examine the specifications of a plan in order to determine the rights and obligations of the issuing corporation (sometimes called the grantor) and of the recipient of the shares (sometimes called the grantee). It is important that the accountant carefully examine the specifications of a plan to issue stock to employees because those specifications determine the appropriate accounting, reporting, and disclosures.

Fundamentally, there are two basic characteristics of a stock issue plan that the accountant must consider, viz:

1. Cost to the corporation — In some stock plans, such as a stock purchase plan, the corporation sets up a purchase plan (often by payroll deduction) whereby employees, at their option, can purchase shares directly from the company and thereby save certain marketing costs. These plans involve no cost to the company (and no additional compensation to the employee). In other stock plans, the company pays a part of the cost of the shares purchased. In these situations, there is a cost to the company for their part of the purchase price, and some additional compensation to the employee.

   In still other cases, the stock is given to the employee without cost when certain specified conditions are met. This is the case with many executive stock options; such stock serves as additional compensation to the employee. A stock plan is said to be *compensatory* if additional compensation is involved and *noncompensatory* if no additional compensation is involved.

2. Income tax effects — There are two income tax effects that are important: the tax implications for the company and for the employee. These are related because, as a general proposition, the tax laws permit a tax deduction for the corporation (when there is additional compensation to the employee) only when the employee (the grantee) is subject to income taxes on the options or shares received. In this regard, a plan is said to be a *qualified plan* if there is no tax to the recipient initially, and the shares, when sold, qualify as a long-term capital gain; if such is not the case, and the options are taxed as income to the employee, the plan is said to be a *nonqualified plan.*

The income tax requirements and effects may be summarized in general terms as follows:

| Feature | Qualified Plan | Nonqualified Plan |
|---------|---------------|-------------------|
| 1. Option price. | Not less than the fair market value of the stock at date of grant. | Can be set at any price. |
| 2. Holding period by grantee. | Shares received must be held at least three years from issue date to qualify as a long-term capital gain. | No special constraints. |
| 3. Expiration period for stock rights. | Options (rights) must expire within five years from date of grant. | Can be effective for any number of years. |
| 4. Option granting period. | Options must be granted within ten years of approval of plan by the stockholders. | No limit on granting period. |
| 5. Tax effects: a. Grantee. | Long-term capital gain when stock is sold; no tax at date of grant. | Taxable as earned income when option is granted. |
| b. Issuer. | Additional compensation expense not deductible for tax purposes. | Additional compensation expense (equivalent to amount taxed to grantee) deductible for tax purposes. |

Fundamentally, the accounting, reporting, and disclosure requirements for all plans whereby stock is, or will be, issued to employees is determined by whether the plan is compensatory or noncompensatory. Within these two broad categories, certain accounting differences, though less fundamental, exist. Because of the numerous differences between plans, this discussion will focus only on the broad issues.

The accounting, reporting, and disclosure requirements, with respect to plans for the issuance of stock directly to employees, must be in conformity with *Accounting Research Bulletin (ARB) No. 43*, Chapter 13B, as amended and supplemented by *APB Opinion No. 25*, "Accounting for Stock Issued to Employees" (October 1972). The discussions to follow conform to these two pronouncements.

### Theoretical Considerations

Historically, and continuing to date, there has been considerable controversy over the appropriate accounting for *compensatory plans*. There is a theoretical answer, upon which most informed accountants tend to agree, and a practical answer (provided by *ARB No. 43* and *APB Opinion*

*No.* 25) designed to cope with the real-world complexities caused by the wide variations in plans and the problems of measurement. The basic issues can best be pinpointed by illustration. For this purpose, assume the following continuing situation:

1. AB Corporation—executive stock option plan:
   Options approved for each designated top executive:
   *a.* Five thousand shares of common stock, par $5.
   *b.* Nontransferable, exercisable three years after grant and prior to expiration date (five years from date of grant) providing continuing employment.
   *c.* Option price, $20 per share.
2. On January 1, 1976, Executive Z was granted an option for 5,000 shares:
   *a.* For services rendered 1976 through 1980 (approximately equal each year).
   *b.* At January 1, 1976, the quoted market price was $30 per share.
   *c.* The option was exercised by Executive Z in December 1980 when the quoted market price per share was $70.

The fundamental question for the accountant is to determine the appropriate accounting, reporting, and disclosure procedures during the period 1976 through 1980. To answer this question, the detailed specifications of the plan must be carefully examined in light of the two aforementioned pronouncements. The following questions must be answered:

1. Is the plan compensatory?
   *a.* If no, there are no unique accounting problems.
   *b.* If yes, then:
2. At what date should the compensation be measured?
3. What is the total amount of the compensation?
4. To what accounting periods should the compensation, as measured, be assigned?

The theoretical response to these questions is not complicated. The issuance of stock to employees at less than cost, or no cost, (other than for services to be rendered) involves a cost to the corporation; therefore this constitutes a compensatory plan. The compensation should be measured *at the date the grant is made to the employee;* that is, the point when the corporation foregoes the principal alternative use of the shares. This is usually identified as the date on which the option is granted to a specific individual. The total amount of the compensation should be measured as the *fair market value* of the *stock rights* (not the shares themselves) at the date of the grant to the specific individual. The total amount of compensation, thus measured, should be assigned to the accounting periods in which the services are rendered. This serves to match the additional compensation expense with the related revenues in conformity with the matching principle.

### Practical Considerations

The accounting profession, despite continued efforts, has not been able to attain the theoretical positions to the satisfaction of many accountants. The primary problem is one of measurement. Let's review the practical guidelines provided by *ARB No. 43* and *APB Opinion No. 25.* We will consider each of the questions listed above separately.

*Is the plan compensatory?* Because the decision on this point fundamentally affects the accounting, reporting, and disclosure procedures to be followed, and because the precise lines of distinction are not obvious in many plans, *APB Opinion No. 25,* paragraph 7, carefully defines a *noncompensatory* plan as follows:

> . . . at least four characteristics are essential in a noncompensatory plan: (a) substantially all full-time employees meeting limited employment qualifications may participate (employees owning a specified percent of the outstanding stock and executives may be excluded), (b) stock is offered to eligible employees equally or based on a uniform percentage of salary or wages (the plan may limit the number of shares of stock that an employee may purchase through the plan), (c) the time permitted for exercise of an option or purchase right is limited to a reasonable period, and (d) the discount from the market price of the stock is no greater than would be reasonable in an offer of stock to stockholders or others. An example of a noncompensatory plan is the "statutory" employee stock purchase plan that qualifies under Section 423 of the Internal Revenue Code.

All other plans are classified as compensatory.

### Accounting for Noncompensatory Plans

Since noncompensatory plans do not involve compensation expense and are stock purchase plans, there are no unique accounting problems involved. To illustrate, assume Company Y has a stock purchase plan whereby employees may acquire stock from the company either by direct purchase or through payroll deduction. The price of the stock is 10% below the quoted market price. Assuming payroll deductions, typical entries would be:

1. To record the monthly payroll and related deductions:

| | | |
|---|---|---|
| Salary and wage expense | 90,000 | |
| Income taxes withheld | | 5,500 |
| Payroll taxes withheld (F.I.C.A., F.U.T.A., etc.) | | 1,500 |
| Union dues | | 440 |
| Liability—employee stock purchase plan* | | 7,560 |
| Cash (or salary and wages payable) | | 75,000 |

\* Per payroll deductions authorized by employees.

2. To record issuance of shares to employees (market price, $12):

| | | |
|---|---|---|
| Liability—employee stock purchase plan | 7,560 | |
| Capital stock, par $10 (700 shares) | | 7,000 |
| Contributed capital in excess of par | | 560 |

($7,560 ÷ .90) ÷ $12 = 700 shares.

## Accounting for Compensatory Plans

Since accounting for compensatory plans involves measurement of the amount of *additional compensation,* and its recognition in appropriate periods, the complexities are significantly increased. To discuss these complexities, we will proceed to the remaining questions posed above and, for illustrative purposes, return to the data given above for AB Corporation.

*When Should the Compensation Be Measured?*  In a compensatory plan, the amount of additional compensation is measured at a *measurement date* specified in *APB Opinion No. 25,* paragraph 10, as follows:

> The *measurement date* for determining compensation cost in stock option, purchase, and award plans is the first date on which are known both (1) the number of shares that an individual employee is entitled to receive and (2) the option or purchase price, if any.

The measurement date may be either:

a. At the date the option is granted to the individual employee. This is the usual case because both the number of shares and the purchase price generally are set at that date.

b. At a date subsequent to date of the grant; that is, the earliest subsequent date when both the number of shares and the purchase price are known. This situation occurs, for example, when either the number of shares or the purchase price are contingent upon future earnings of the company or upon future prices of the stock. Acceptance of this later date, rather than the date of the grant, is a concession to the measurement problem — additional compensation must be measured when both the purchase price and the number of shares to which the employee is entitled are known.

In respect to AB Corporation, the measurement date is the date of grant because, in this case, both the *(a)* number of shares, and *(b)* purchase or option price are known at that date.

*What Is the Total Amount of the Compensation?*  On this measurement problem, the *Opinion* states that the total additional compensation:

> . . . for services that a corporation receives as consideration for stock issued through employee stock option, purchase, and award plan should be measured by the quoted market price of the stock at the measurement date less the amount, if any, that the employee is required to pay.

The difference between the quoted market price of the stock at measurement date and the option price is used as a surrogate for *fair market value* of the rights. The *Opinion* also states that "If a quoted market price is unavailable, the best estimate of the market value of the stock should be used to measure compensation."

In respect to the plan outlined above for AB Corporation, total additional compensation, which is measurable in this instance on the date of the grant, January 1, 1976, is $30 - $20 = $10 per share, or $50,000 for Executive Z. This particular measurement rule is subject to severe and justified criticism because it does not measure the fair market value of the stock rights involved; that is, fair market value cannot be determined because there will be no established market (since the rights are nontransferable). Typically, companies set the option price at the current market price of the shares in which case the total additional compensation would be measured, under this rule, as zero. Recall that a *qualified* plan does not permit an option price less than the current market price of the stock.[8]

When the measurement date is at a date subsequent to the date of the grant, the number of shares, the option price, and market price generally must be *estimated* for the measurement of the compensation because *accruals* of estimated annual compensation expense must be recorded between the date of grant and the measurement date (when the dates are different). Total *actual* compensation expense then is measured and recorded as a deferred expense on measurement date. Annual compensation expense is recorded for the remaining periods prior to expiration or exercise date.[9]

*To What Accounting Periods Should the Measured Compensation Be Assigned?* The total amount of additional compensation expense must be assigned to the periods in which the services are rendered so that compensation expense is matched with the related revenues. This generally requires accrual, and/or deferral, of the additional compensation expense. On this point, *APB Opinion No. 25* states (italics added):

> 12. *Accruing Compensation Cost.* Compensation cost in stock option, purchase, and award plans should be recognized as an expense of one or more periods in which an employee performs services and also as part or all of the consideration received for stock issued to the employee through a plan. The grant or award may specify the period or periods during which the employee performs services, or the period or periods may be inferred from the terms or from the past pattern of grants or awards (ARB No. 43, Chapter 13B, paragraph 14; APB Opinion No. 12, *Omnibus Opinion-1967*, paragraph 6).
>
> 13. An employee may perform services in several periods before an employer corporation issues stock to him for those services. The employer corporation should *accrue* compensation expense in each period in which the services are performed. If the measurement date is later than the date of grant or award, an employer corporation should record the compensation expense *each period from date of grant or award to date of measurement based on the quoted market price of the stock at the end of each period.*
>
> 14. If stock is issued in a plan before some or all of the services are performed, part of the consideration recorded for the stock issued is unearned compensation and should be shown as a *separate reduction of stockholders' equity.* The unearned compensation should be accounted for as expense of the period or periods in which the employee performs service.

---

[8] Some accountants believe that sophisticated measurement models are currently available that can cope effectively with this measurement problem.

[9] If the grantee exercises the option prior to the end of the expiration date, the amount of total compensation not assigned to specific periods usually is assigned to the period in which exercise occurs.

15. Accruing compensation expense may require estimates, and adjustment of those estimates in later periods may be necessary (APB Opinion No. 20, *Accounting Changes*, paragraphs 31 to 33). For example, if a stock option is not exercised (or awarded stock is returned to the corporation) because an employee fails to fulfill an obligation, the estimate of compensation expense recorded in previous periods should be adjusted by decreasing compensation expense in the period of forfeiture.

Thus, the *Opinion* specifies precise guidelines for accrual and deferral of total additional compensation when the measurement date is (*a*) at the date of grant, or (*b*) at a date subsequent to the date of grant. Observe that the phrase in italics in paragraph 13 is significant because it excludes service in *prior* periods.

With respect to AB Corporation, the total compensation expense of $50,000 should be assigned equally to the five-year period, 1976–80.

### Illustrative Entries, Compensatory Plan, Measurement Date on Date of Grant

Using the example for AB Corporation, we have determined (in accordance with *ARB No. 43*, Chapter 13B, and *APB Opinion No. 25*) that:

1. The company plan is compensatory.
2. The measurement date is the date of the grant, January 1, 1976.
3. The total additional compensation for Executive Z is $50,000.
4. The total additional compensation expense should be assigned equally to the five years 1976 through 1980 (date of retirement or expiration).

Therefore, the employer, AB Corporation, should make the following entries with respect to participation by Executive Z in the executive stock option plan:

*a.* January 1, 1976 — date of grant; to record total deferred compensation expense and stock rights outstanding:

| | | |
|---|---|---|
| Deferred compensation expense............................... | 50,000 | |
|     Executive stock options outstanding (for 5,000 | | |
|       shares of common stock) ..........  .............. | | 50,000 |

($30 − $20) × 5,000 shares = $50,000.

*b.* December 31, 1976, through 1980 — to record annual apportionment of compensation expense:

| | | |
|---|---|---|
| Executive compensation expense ............................. | 10,000 | |
|     Deferred compensation expense......................... | | 10,000 |

$50,000 ÷ 5 years = $10,000 per year.

*c.* December 31, 1980 — exercise date, to record the stock warrants tendered by Executive Z and issuance of the shares:

| | | |
|---|---|---|
| Cash (5,000 shares @ $20 option price) ..................... | 100,000 | |
| Executive stock options outstanding (for 5,000 shares) ... | 50,000 | |
|     Common stock, par $5 (5,000 shares) .................. | | 25,000 |
|     Contributed capital in excess of par ..................... | | 125,000 |

Compensation expense ($10,000) is reported on the income statement each period as a normal operating expense. Stock options outstanding and deferred compensation are reported on the balance sheet (December 31, 1976) as follows:

*Stockholders' Equity*

Contributed Capital:

| | | |
|---|---|---|
| Common stock, par $5, authorized 500,000 shares, outstanding 200,000 shares .............. | | $1,000,000 |
| Executive stock options outstanding (for 5,000 shares)............................................. | $50,000 | |
| Less: Deferred compensation expense............... | 40,000 | 10,000 |
| Other contributed capital (etc.) ....................... | (not illustrated) | |

In addition, *ARB No. 43*, Chapter 13, paragraph 15, requires disclosure of —

    *a.* The status of the option plan at the end of the period.
    *b.* The number of shares under option.
    *c.* The option price.
    *d.* The number of shares to which options were exercisable.
    *e.* The number of shares exercised during the period and the option price thereof.

### Illustrative Entries, Compensatory Plan, Measurement Date Subsequent to Date of Grant

When the measurement date is subsequent to date of grant, because both the number of shares and option price are unknown, the entries are slightly more complex. To illustrate, the data for AB Corporation are adapted as follows:

1. The number of shares and option price are not known on the date of grant, January 1, 1976, since the plan defers their determination to the end of 1978 (the measurement date).
2. The number of shares and option price are based on the increase in net income from the date of grant to the *third* year following date of grant.
3. Estimated and actual data:

| | Estimate Made on January 1, 1976 of What the Amount Will Be on December 31, 1978 | Actual Amount on December 31, 1978 |
|---|---|---|
| Number of shares optioned ............ | 5,000 | 5,000 |
| Option price ................................ | $23 | $22 |
| Market price per share (a relatively steady increase each year) ................................ | $34 | $32.50 |

Entries:

*a.* January 1, 1976 — date of grant:

> No entry — measurement and recording of total compensation cost occurs on subsequent measurement date.

*b.* December 31, 1976, and 1977 — end of period; to record accrual of *estimated* annual compensation expense:

|  | 1976 | 1977 |
|---|---|---|
| Compensation expense ..................... | 11,000 | 11,000 |
| Accrued compensation expense (stock options) ....................... |  11,000 |  11,000 |

Computations:
Total estimated compensation expense: ($34 − $23) × 5,000 shares = $55,000.
Assignment to periods: $55,000 ÷ 5 years = $11,000.

*c.* December 31, 1978 — measurement date; to record actual total compensation cost:

| Accrued compensation expense ($11,000 × 2) ............ | 22,000 |  |
| Deferred compensation expense ($52,500 − $22,000) ... | 30,500 |  |
| Executive stock options outstanding (for 5,000 shares) ............................................. |  | 52,500 |

Computation of total compensation expense:
($32.50 − $22) × 5,000 shares = $52,500.

*d.* December 31, 1978, 1979, and 1980 — end of period; to record annual compensation expense:

| Compensation expense ............................................. | 10,167 |  |
| Deferred compensation expense.......................... |  | 10,167 |

$30,500 ÷ 3 years = $10,167.

*e.* December, 1980 — exercise date; to record issuance of the 5,000 shares:

| Cash ($23 × 5,000 shares) ........................................ | 115,000 |  |
| Executive stock options outstanding (for 5,000 shares) ... | 52,500 |  |
| Common stock, par $5 (5,000 shares) .................... |  | 25,000 |
| Contributed capital in excess of par .................... |  | 142,500 |

A decision tree is shown in Exhibit 17–1 which summarizes the decisions and sequence of entries for:

1. Noncompensatory plans.
2. Compensatory plans:
    *a.* Measurement date on date of grant.
    *b.* Measurement date subsequent to date of grant.

## EARNINGS PER SHARE

Earnings per share was briefly discussed in Chapter 4. The comments and illustrations in that section should be reviewed at this point. Earnings per share is computed and reported as prescribed in *APB Opinion No. 15,* "Earnings Per Share" (May 1969). It is a complex opinion that

**EXHIBIT 17–1**

**Decision Tree—Stock Issued to Employees**

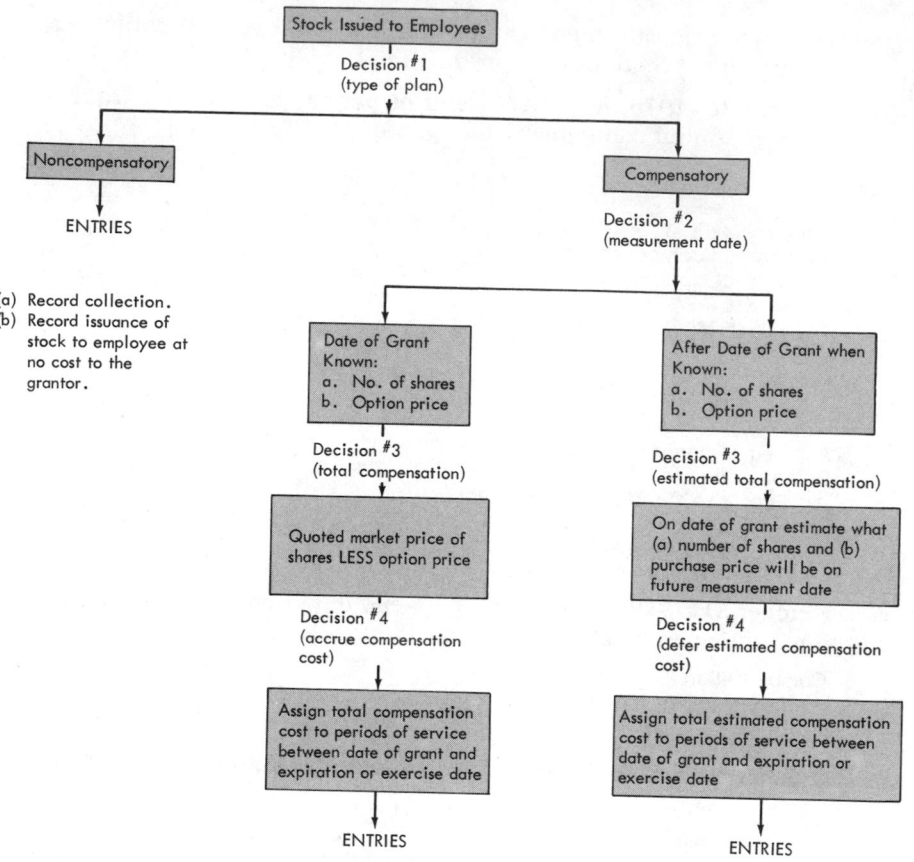

Stock Issued to Employees

Decision #1
(type of plan)

**Noncompensatory**

ENTRIES

(a) Record collection.
(b) Record issuance of
stock to employee at
no cost to the
grantor.

**Compensatory**

Decision #2
(measurement date)

Date of Grant
Known:
a. No. of shares
b. Option price

Decision #3
(total compensation)

Quoted market price of
shares LESS option price

Decision #4
(accrue compensation
cost)

Assign total compensation
cost to periods of service
between date of grant and
expiration or exercise date

ENTRIES

a. Date of grant—Record
accrued compensation
cost and issuance of
stock rights.
b. Each year—Assign portion
of total compensation
cost to year.
c. Exercise date—Record
issuance of shares
and cancellation of
stock rights outstanding

After Date of Grant when
Known:
a. No. of shares
b. Option price

Decision #3
(estimated total compensation)

On date of grant estimate what
(a) number of shares and (b)
purchase price will be on
future measurement date

Decision #4
(defer estimated compensation
cost)

Assign total estimated compensation
cost to periods of service between
date of grant and expiration or
exercise date

ENTRIES

a. Date of grant—No entry; measurement
and recording of total compensation
will be on subsequent measurement
date.
b. Each year from date of grant to
measurement date —Accrue annual
compensation expense based on
estimates of number of shares,
option price and market price per
share.
c. Measurement date—Record total
compensation expense and close
accrued compensation expense
from prior periods.
d. Each year from measurement date
to expiration date—Record annual
apportionment of compensation
expense.
e. Exercise date—Record issuance of
shares and cancellation of stock
rights outstanding.

was supplemented with an interpretation of 186 pages.[10] It would be totally unrealistic to attempt to discuss all of the complexities in this book. Therefore, this discussion is intended to explain and illustrate, in a general way, only the major concepts involved in computing EPS.

## Reporting Earnings per Share

*APB Opinion No. 15* requires that earnings per share amounts (for common stock only) be reported on the income statement for each year financial information is presented. Computation of EPS and the reporting requirements depend on the capital structure of the corporation, viz:

1. Simple capital structure — the case where the stockholders' equity either consists of only common stock or it does not include convertible securities, stock warrants, or other rights convertible to common stock.[11] In the case of a simple capital structure, a single presentation of the basic EPS amounts for common stock is required. In Chapter 4, several cases were presented that illustrated EPS with simple capital structures. We will add one more example, a simple capital structure where there is *nonconvertible* preferred stock. Assume the following data for MW Corporation:

```
Common stock, par $10, authorized 200,000 shares:
   Outstanding at beginning of year, 90,000 shares.................... $900,000
   Issued during the year, on May 1, 6,000 shares  ....................   96,000
Preferred stock, par $20, 6% nonconvertible, authorized
   5,000 shares, outstanding at end of the year,
   2,500 shares........................................................   50,000
Income before extraordinary items  .....................................  120,000
Extraordinary loss (net of 45% tax rate) ...............................  (10,000)
Net income  ............................................................  110,000
```

To compute earnings per share in this situation (a simple capital structure), two preliminary computations must be made because (*a*) income, the numerator, must be reduced by the dividend claim of the preferred stock; and (*b*) the denominator must be the *average* shares outstanding during the year, viz:

a. Portion of net income (dividend claim) applicable to preferred stock (whether declared or not):

$$\$50,000 \times .06 = \underline{\underline{\$3,000}}$$

---

[10] J. T. Ball, *Computing Earnings per Share — Unofficial Accounting Interpretations of APB Opinion No. 15*, (New York, AICPA, 1970).

[11] Convertible securities that do not affect EPS by more than 3% may be disregarded on the basis of materiality. Also, a simple capital structure may include preferred stock if it is not convertible to common stock.

*b.* Average shares outstanding during the year:[12]

| | Months | No. of Shares | Product |
|---|---|---|---|
| January 1 to April 30 ..................... | 4 | 90,000 | 360,000 |
| May 1 to December 31 ................. | 8 | 96,000 | 768,000 |
| Totals .............................. | 12 | | 1,128,000 |

Average shares outstanding: 1,128,000 ÷ 12 = 94,000 shares

Earnings per share on common stock:

| | |
|---|---|
| Income before extraordinary items ($120,000 − $3,000) ÷ 94,000 shares = | $1.25 |
| Extraordinary loss $10,000 ÷ 94,000 shares = | ( .11) |
| Net Income ($110,000 − $3,000) ÷ 94,000 shares = | $1.14 |

2. Complex capital structure—Capital that do not qualify as simple structures are classified as complex by *APB Opinion No. 15*. Such capital structures include securities such as convertible bonds, convertible preferred stock warrants, stock options, and stock rights. In the case of a complex capital structure, two sets of EPS amounts must be presented, viz:

    *a.* Primary EPS—Based on common stock plus common stock equivalents (defined below).[13]

    *b.* Fully diluted EPS—Based on common stock outstanding plus common stock equivalents and any other shares of common stock that would be issued assuming *all* stock purchase contracts and convertible securities are converted to common stock. This represents maximum dilution of EPS. Fully diluted EPS amounts will be less than (or equal to) primary EPS amounts because of convertible securities (i.e., convertible debt and preferred stock) that do not qualify as common stock equivalents.

The discussions and illustrations to follow will focus only on complex capital structures.

### Computing EPS with Complex Capital Structures

Fundamentally, the difference between primary and fully diluted EPS is determination of whether or not the various convertible securities

---

[12] In computing the average, reacquired shares are included in the weighted average only for the time they were outstanding. Stock dividends and stock splits are always assumed to be at year-end; that is, the average is computed and then the additional shares are added.

[13] Primary EPS amounts in a complex capital structure would be identical with the basic EPS amount in a simple capital structure when there are no common stock equivalents.

and stock options outstanding represent common stock equivalents, viz:

a. Primary EPS — Based on the average number of common shares outstanding during the period *plus all common stock equivalents.*

b. Fully diluted EPS — Based on the average number of common shares outstanding during the period plus all common stock equivalents and *plus all other shares of common stock that potentially may be issued because of conversion privileges.*

Thus, the definition and identification of common stock equivalents are critical.

A *common stock equivalent* is defined in *Opinion No. 15* as: "A security which, because of its terms or the circumstances under which it was issued, is in substance equivalent to common stock." In form, it is not common stock; however, it enables its holder to acquire common stock under specified conditions.

Neither conversion nor the imminence of conversion is necessary to classify a security as a common stock equivalent for EPS purposes. Classification of a convertible security that is convertible to common stock, as to whether it is a common stock equivalent should be made "only at time of issuance and should not be changed thereafter so long as the security remains outstanding."

In determining when a security is a common stock equivalent and in computing *number of equivalent* shares for EPS computation, separate consideration must be given to (a) stock options, warrants, rights, and other stock purchase contracts; and (b) convertible securities composed of bonds and preferred stock convertible to common stock. These two categories must be considered separately because they have different characteristics; therefore, the computations are quite different. Each will be discussed and illustrated separately.

*Stock Options, Warrants, Rights, and Other Stock Purchase Contracts.* These items, although not designated as convertible securities, when exercised cause the issuance of common stock. Thus, they compose one category of common stock equivalents. Since exercise would cause a cash inflow, which would earn a return, some method of reflecting this "as if" situation is needed. *APB Opinion No. 15* prescribes the *treasury stock method* for this purpose. Basically, the method computes common stock equivalents as the number of shares that would be issued upon exercise of the stock rights (at the option price) less the number of those shares that could be bought back as treasury stock (at the average market price for the period). Thus, the method assumes that any cash proceeds from the issuance of common shares, should the options, warrants, rights, or other contracts be exercised, will be used immediately to purchase treasury stock.[14]

---

[14] If the number of common shares issuable exceeds 20% of the number of common shares outstanding at the end of the period, the treasury stock method, as illustrated above, must be modified to include both repurchase of stock and to reduce debt. Also the market price used for treasury stock calculations for fully diluted EPS is at the end of the current period (rather than the average price used for primary EPS).

Application of the treasury stock method to compute the number of equivalent shares may be illustrated as follows:

Basic data (MW Corporation):

| | |
|---|---|
| Common stock warrants outstanding.................... | 2,000 (for 2,000 shares) |
| Option or exercise price per share ....................... | $20 |
| Average market price of the shares for the period of issuance of the warrants ........................... | $25 |

Computation of common stock equivalents:

| | Shares |
|---|---|
| Shares that would be issued upon exercise of the warrants ............ | 2,000 |
| Cash proceeds that would be realized, $20 × 2,000 shares = $40,000 | |
| Treasury stock that could be purchased, $40,000 ÷ $25 = | 1,600 |
| Difference—common stock equivalents (i.e., incremental shares that would be outstanding)................................................. | 400 |

Thus, to complete both primary and fully diluted EPS the 400 common stock equivalents (not the 2,000 shares) would be added to the average number of common shares actually outstanding during the year.[15]

*Convertible Securities.* Bonds payable and preferred stock which are convertible to common stock are referred to as convertible securities. They may or may not represent a second category of common stock equivalents. Determination of whether a convertible security represents common stock equivalents depends upon the relationship between their *cash yield* rate (stated interest or dividend rate) and "normal" *interest rates* at the time of issuance. The *Opinion* states: "convertible securities should be considered common stock equivalents if the cash yield to the holder at time of issuance is significantly below what would be a comparable rate for a similar security of the issuer without the conversions option." The *Opinion* sets up an arbitrary *prime rate test* (as the "normal" rate) to make this distinction: "a convertible security should be considered as a common stock equivalent at the time of issuance if, based on its market price, it has a cash yield less that 66⅔% of the then current bank prime interest rate."[16] If this test is met, such dilutive common stock warrants are included in the computation of primary EPS. Alternatively, they are included in fully diluted EPS computations even though they do not meet this test.

From a realistic point of view, a security bought to yield less than two thirds of the prime rate obviously was acquired for potential appreciation and not for current yield; therefore, its conversion feature was an important element in the total consideration paid for it. Consequently, a test, such as this one, was necessary for primary EPS calculations be-

---

[15] An opposite effect occurs when the option price is greater than the current market price. In this case, the security would be antidilutive and the common stock equivalents excluded; see subsequent discussion of this concept.

[16] The current bank prime interest rate is the rate the banks locally are charging on short-term loans to borrowers with the best credit risk.

cause convertible securities may never be converted because of the relative earnings compared with the common stock. The prime rate test is an arbitrary method of determining whether, in fact, convertible securities are substantially common stock equivalents.

Application of the prime rate test may be illustrated as follows:

Basic data (MW Corporation):
  Convertible bonds payable, 6%, $100,000
  Conversion rate: Each $1,000 bond is convertible to 40 shares of common
                 stock.
  Annual interest expense, net of tax: $6,000 × (1.00 − .45) = $3,300
  At issuance date: Bond price, 120
               Prime bank interest rate, 7%

Prime rate test:
  Shares issuable at conversion ($100,000 ÷ $1,000) × 40 = 4,000 shares
  Comparison of rates:

$$\frac{\text{Cash Yield (Interest) per Year}}{\text{Market Price at Issuance}} = \frac{\$6,000}{\$120,000} = 5.00\% \text{ Cash Yield Rate}$$

Bond prime rate: 7% × 66⅔% = 4.67% adjusted prime rate

Interpretation: Since the cash yield rate is greater than the adjusted prime rate, the convertible bonds representing 4,000 shares of common stock would *not* be classified as common stock equivalents for primary EPS computations. They would be included in computing fully diluted EPS.

## Computation of Earnings per Share, Complex Capital Structure

When there is a complex capital structure, primary and fully diluted EPS amounts are computed for (1) income before extraordinary items, (2) extraordinary items (optional), and (3) net income. The computation of each amount may be summarized as follows.[17]

### Primary Earnings per Share*

| Numerator | Denominator |
|---|---|
| 1. Income before extraordinary items:<br>Income before extraordinary items minus claims of nonconvertible preferred stock and plus interest (net of tax) on convertible debt classified as common stock equivalents. | Weighted average number of shares outstanding plus common stock equivalents. |
| 2. Extraordinary items:<br>Extraordinary gain or loss (net of tax). | Same. |
| 3. Net income:<br>Same as (1) plus or minus extraordinary items. | Same. |

---

[17] This summary does not specify the numerous exceptions and certain detailed computations which would serve to confuse the broader issues. It is not feasible to cover all of the complexities, and memorization of them would be fruitless. As stated earlier our objective is to focus on the broad issues.

**Fully Diluted Earnings per Share***

| *Numerator* | *Denominator* |
|---|---|
| 1. Income before extraordinary items: | |
| Income before extraordinary items minus claims of nonconvertible preferred stock plus interest expense (net of tax) on convertible debt. | Weighted average number of shares outstanding plus common stock equivalents and plus all *other common shares that would be issued on convertible securities.* |
| 2. Extraordinary items: | |
| Extraordinary gain or loss (net of tax). | Same. |
| 3. Net income: | |
| Same as (1) plus or minus extraordinary items. | Same. |

* Excluding all antidilutive securities.

Computation of earnings per share, assuming a complex capital structure, is illustrated below for MW Corporation (adapted) and the prior illustrations of common stock equivalents and convertible debt.

*Primary earnings per share* (include common stock equivalents):

Income before extraordinary items: $\dfrac{\$120,000 - \$3,000}{94,000 + 400^*} = \$1.24$

Extraordinary loss: $\dfrac{\$10,000}{94,400} = (.11)$

Net income: $\dfrac{\$110,000 - \$3,000}{94,400} = \underline{\$1.13}$

* See page 728.

*Fully diluted earnings per share* (include all potential issuances):

Income before extraordinary items: $\dfrac{\$120,000 - \$3,000 + \$3,300^*}{94,000 + 400 + 4,000^*} = \$1.22$

Extraordinary loss: $\dfrac{\$10,000}{98,400} = (.10)$

Net income: $\dfrac{\$110,000 - \$3,000 + \$3,300}{98,400} = \underline{\$1.12}$

* See page 729.

In the case of a complex capital structure, *Opinion No. 15* requires additional disclosures: "a description, in summary form, sufficient to explain the pertinent rights and privileges of the various securities outstanding."

## Antidilution

A reduction in earnings per share amounts resulting from common stock equivalents, and convertible securities that do not represent common stock equivalents, is known as *dilution,* and the stock purchase contracts and convertible securities that cause this effect are called *dilutive securities.*

*Antidilution,* caused by *antidilutive* stock purchase contracts and convertible securities, is the opposite effect. Antidilution causes an increase in earnings per share amounts above the amounts that would otherwise be reported. To attain the maximum dilutive effect on EPS (because of conservatism), all antidilutive securities are excluded in computing both primary and fully diluted earnings per share amounts. To repeat, antidilution may arise from either stock purchase contracts (options, warrants, rights, etc.) or convertible securities (convertible debt or preferred stock). For example, if the option price on common stock warrants outstanding is greater than the market price, those common stock equivalents would increase EPS; hence, they would be antidilutive and thus are excluded from the computations. Similarly, if the conversion of bonds payable in the above illustration had been 20 shares of stock per $1,000 bond (instead of 40 shares), the convertible bonds would have been antidilutive; in this case they would have been excluded from the computation of EPS amounts.

Antidilutive effects can be illustrated as follows:

1. Stock rights, warrants, options, and other stock purchase contracts: Was the option or exercise price *above* the average market price of the optioned stock? If yes, the common stock equivalents would be antidilutive and would not be included in the EPS calculations (see footnote 14).

Illustration for WZ Corporation:

   a. Dilutive—option price *below* market price:

   As illustrated above—option price $20; market price $25.
   Computation: 2,000 shares − ($40,000 ÷ $25) = +400, positive common stock equivalents. Clearly, this positive amount in the denominator would cause it to increase, which would serve to *decrease* all of the EPS amounts below what they would be without the rights, warrants, and options. Thus, they are *dilutive*.

   b. Antidilutive—option price *above* market price:

   Assumption—option price $20; market price $18.
   Computation: 2,000 shares − ($40,000 ÷ $18) = −222, negative common stock equivalents. Clearly, this negative amount would decrease the denominator, which would serve to *increase* all of the EPS amounts above what they would be without the rights, warrants, and options. Thus, they are *antidilutive*.

2. Convertible debt and convertible preferred stock: Does the interest (or preferred dividends) added to the numerator, divided by the shares added to the denominator, exceed the EPS amounts that would be reported excluding the conversion assumptions? If yes, the common stock equivalents would be antidilutive and would not be included in the EPS calculations.

Illustration for WZ Corporation:

   a. Dilutive—EPS amounts *decreased* because of conversion:

   Assumption—Conversion ratio 20 shares per bond (as illustrated above).

$$\text{EPS without Conversion} = \frac{\$120,000 - \$3,000}{94,000 + 400} = \$1.24$$

$$\text{EPS with Conversion} = \frac{\$120,000 - \$3,000 + \$3,300}{94,000 + 400 + 4,000} = \$1.22$$

Since the conversion feature *decreased* EPS, it was dilutive and would be included in the EPS computations.

b. Antidilutive—EPS amounts *increased* because of conversion: Assumption—conversion ratio 40 shares per bond.

$$\text{EPS without Conversion} = \frac{\$120,000 - \$3,000}{94,000 + 400} = \$1.24$$

$$\text{EPS with Conversion} = \frac{\$120,000 - \$3,000 + \$3,300}{94,000 + 400 + 2,000} = \$1.25$$

Since the conversion feature *increased* EPS, it was antidilutive and would not be included in the EPS computations.

## QUESTIONS

1. Define treasury stock.

2. Explain the basic difference in theory between the one-transaction concept and the dual-transaction concept in accounting for treasury stock.

3. In comparing the recording of treasury stock at cost with recording at par "total capital is unaffected, however subdivisions thereof are affected." Explain this statement.

4. Why have many states limited purchases of treasury stock to the amount reported as retained earnings? How may the restriction on retained earnings be removed?

5. In recording treasury stock transactions why are "gains" recorded in a contributed capital account, whereas "losses" debited to retained earnings?

6. How is treasury stock reported on the balance sheet (a) under the cost method, and (b) under the par-value method?

7. How is the restriction on retained earnings, equal to the cost of treasury stock held, reported on the balance sheet?

8. How is stock donated back to the corporation recorded? Indicate any preference.

9. What are stock rights? In what situations are stock warrants frequently issued?

10. Distinguish between a compensatory and a noncompensatory stock option plan.

11. What is meant by the measurement date? When is it later than the date of grant?

12. Theoretically what is the amount of total compensation in a stock bonus plan?

13. Why are estimates necessary when the measurement date is later than the date of the grant of a stock option that is compensatory?

14. What is the basic impact on earnings per share computations and reporting as between a simple capital structure and a complex capital structure?

15. What is a common stock equivalent? How do common stock equivalents affect earning per share computations?

16. Contrast primary earnings per share and fully diluted earnings per share.

17. What is the difference between a dilutive security and an antidilutive security? Why is the distinction important in earnings per share considerations?

## DECISION CASE 17-1

The Unknown Corporation purchased $144,000 of equipment in 1976 for $90,000 cash and a promise to deliver an indeterminate number of treasury shares of its $5 par common stock, with a market value of $15,000 on January 1 of each year for the next four years. Hence $60,000 in "market value" of treasury shares will be required to discharge the $54,000 balance due on the equipment.

The corporation then acquired 5,000 shares of its own stock in the expectation that the market value of the stock would increase substantially before the delivery dates.

*Required:*

1. Discuss the propriety of recording the equipment at—
   a. $90,000 (the cash payment).
   b. $144,000 (the cash price of the equipment).
   c. $150,000 (the $90,000 cash payment + the $60,000 market value of treasury stock that must be transferred to the vendor in order to settle the obligation according to the terms of the agreement).
2. Discuss the arguments *for* treating the balance due as—
   a. A liability.
   b. Treasury stock subscribed.
3. Assuming that legal requirements do not affect the decision, discuss the arguments *for* treating the corporation's treasury shares as—
   a. An asset awaiting ultimate disposition.
   b. A capital element awaiting ultimate disposition.

(AICPA adapted)

## EXERCISES

### Exercise 17-1

Young Corporation had 5,000 shares of $20 par-value common stock outstanding, originally sold at $50 per share. On January 15, Young purchased 20 shares of its own stock at $55 per share. On March 1, 12 of the treasury shares were sold at $58. The balance in retained earnings was $25,000 prior to these transactions.

*Required:*

1. Give all entries indicated in parallel columns, assuming (a) the cost method, and (b) the par-value method.

2. What would be the resulting balances in the stockholders' equity accounts for each method?

## Exercise 17–2

Kyle Corporation had the following stock outstanding:

Common stock, nopar, 10,000 shares sold at $15 .............. $150,000
Preferred stock, par $10, 5,000 shares sold at $25.............. 50,000

The following treasury stock transactions were completed:

a. Purchased 20 shares of the common stock at $17 per share.
b. Purchased ten shares of the preferred stock at $27.
c. Sold 15 shares of the common stock at $14.
d. Sold five shares of the preferred stock at $30.

*Required:*

1. Give entries for all of the above stock transactions, assume the par-value method is used.
2. Give resulting balances in the stockholders' equity accounts; assume a starting balance in retained earnings of $20,000.

## Exercise 17–3

Baker Corporation had outstanding 5,000 shares of preferred stock, par value $10, and 10,000 shares of nopar common stock sold initially for $20 per share. Contributed capital in excess of par on the preferred stock amounted to $25,000; and retained earnings balance is $30,000. The corporation purchased 200 shares of preferred at $18 per share and 300 shares of common stock at $24 per share. Subsequently, 100 shares of the common treasury stock was sold for $19 per share.

*Required:*

1. Give entries to record the treasury stock transactions assuming the cost method is used.
2. Prepare the resulting stockholders' equity section of the balance sheet.

## Exercise 17–4

At January 1, 19A, the records of Adams Corporation showed the following:

Capital stock, par $10, 50,000 shares outstanding............... $500,000
Contributed capital in excess of par ................................. 250,000
Retained earnings ...................................................... 150,000

During the year, the following transactions affecting stockholders' equity were recorded:

a. Purchased 500 shares of treasury stock at $20 per share.
b. Purchased 500 shares of treasury stock at $22 per share.
c. Sold 600 shares of treasury stock at $25.
d. Net income was $40,000.

The state law places a restriction on retained earnings equal to the cost of treasury stock held.

*Required:*

1. Give entries for the above transactions, in parallel columns, assuming (a) the cost method, and (b) the par-value method. Establish an appropriation of retained earnings.
2. Prepare the stockholders' section of the balance sheet for each method. Include any required disclosure related to the treasury stock.


**Exercise 17–5**

The balance sheet for Allison Corporation at December 31, 19A, showed the following:

| | |
|---|---:|
| Assets ......................................................... | $126,000 |
| Liabilities ..................................................... | 20,000 |
| Stockholders' equity: | |
|    Capital stock, par $10, 7,000 shares .............. | 70,000 |
|    Treasury stock, 1,000 shares (at cost)............. | 17,000 |
|    Contributed capital in excess of par .............. | 14,000 |
|    Retained earnings........................................ | 39,000 |

*Required:*

Prepare a balance sheet for the corporation with special emphasis on the stockholders' equity section assuming the state law places a restriction on retained earnings equal to the cost of treasury stock held. Assume (a) the cost method, and (b) the par-value method. Include all required disclosures related to the treasury stock.


**Exercise 17–6**

AB Corporation had 30,000 shares of $10 par-value capital stock authorized, of which 20,000 shares were issued three years ago at $15 per share. During the current year, the corporation received 500 shares of the capital stock as a bequest from a deceased shareholder; in addition, 1,000 shares were purchased at $14 per share. State law places a restriction on retained earnings equal to the cost of treasury stock held. At the end of the year, a cash dividend of $.50 per share was paid; prior to the dividend, retained earnings amounted to $40,000.

*Required:*

1. Prepare entries to record all of the transactions assuming the cost method for recording treasury stock is used. Record the donated stock at its fair market value.
2. Prepare the stockholders' equity section of the balance sheet at year-end and include all required disclosures related to the treasury stock.


**Exercise 17–7**

The records for XY Corporation reflected the following data on stockholders' equity:

a. Preferred stock, par $50, issued 2,000 shares.

b. Preferred treasury stock, 200 shares (cost $54 per share).
c. Premium on preferred stock at original issue was $1 per share.
d. Common stock, par $100, issued 3,000 shares.
e. Common treasury stock, 300 shares (cost $98 per share).
f. Premium on common stock at original issue was $2 per share.
g. Retained earnings, unappropriated, $110,000.
h. Retained earnings appropriated for cost of treasury stock, $40,200. The state law places a restriction on retained earnings equal to the cost of treasury stock held.

The shareholders voted to retire all of the treasury stock forthwith and another 400 shares of common stock that could be purchased immediately at $101 per share.

*Required:*

Give the following entries, in parallel columns, assuming the (a) cost method, and (b) par-value method:

1. Purchase of the 400 additional treasury shares for retirement.
2. To retire all of the treasury shares. Give separate entries for the preferred and common.

## Exercise 17–8

The records of Erwin Corporation reflected the following:

Preferred stock, 1,000 shares outstanding, par $100 ............... $100,000
Common stock, 1,000 shares outstanding, par $50.................. 50,000
Contributed capital in excess of par, preferred stock.............. 5,000
Contributed capital in excess of par, common stock .............. 2,000
Retained earnings ............................................................ 50,000

The preferred stock is convertible into common stock. Give entry, or entries, required in each of the following cases:

Case A – The preferred shares are converted to common stock on a par-for-par basis; that is, two shares of common are issued for each share of preferred.
Case B – The preferred shares are converted to common share for share.
Case C – The preferred shares are converted to common stock on a one-for-three basis; that is, three shares of common are issued for each share of preferred.
Case D – The preferred shares are converted for a new class of stock known as Common Class B, nopar share for share.

## Exercise 17–9

Swisher Corporation has a stock savings plan with the following provisions:

Each full-time employee, with a minimum of one year's service, may acquire common stock, par $5, in the company through payroll deductions at 4% below the market price on the date selected by the employee for stock purchase.

Employee Jones signed a payroll deduction form on January 1, 1976, for $40 per month. At that date, the market price of the stock was $27. Assume a monthly salary of $1,000 and other payroll deductions in the aggregate of 12%. At the end of 1976, Jones requested that stock be purchased equal to the amount accumulated to his credit. At that date, the market price of the stock was $25.

*Required:*

1. Is this a compensatory plan? Explain.
2. What is the total additional compensation to Jones? Explain.
3. How many shares is Jones entitled to? Show computations.
4. Give entries to record (a) the monthly payroll, and (b) issuance of the shares.

## Exercise 17–10

Stiger Corporation is authorized to issue 300,000 shares of common stock, par $1; to date 140,000 shares have been issued. The corporation initiated a stock bonus plan during 1976 for designated managers. Each manager will receive stock rights to purchase 1,000 shares of common stock; if still employed by the company, any time after two years from the date of the grant, January 1, 1976. The rights are nontransferable and expire on December 31, 1980. The option price is $15 per share; the market price on date of grant was $20. The services will be rendered approximately equally over the five-year period.

*Required:*

1. Is this a noncompensatory plan? Explain.
2. What is the measurement date? Explain.
3. What is the amount of total compensation for each manager?
4. Over what period should this compensation expense be assigned? How much should be assigned to 1976? To 1977? Explain.
5. What entry should be made on the date of the grant (for one manager)?
6. What entry should be made on December 31, 1976?

## Exercise 17–11

The records for Voss Corporation, at year-end, reflected the following:

Stockholders' Equity:

| | |
|---|---:|
| Common stock, nopar, authorized shares 500,000: | |
| Outstanding at beginning of year, 100,000 shares | $175,000 |
| Issued during the year, September 1, 3,000 shares | 6,000 |
| Preferred stock, 6%, par $10, nonconvertible, authorized 20,000 shares. | |
| Outstanding during the year, 6,000 shares | 60,000 |
| Contributed capital in excess of par, preferred stock | 3,000 |
| Retained earnings | 50,000 |

Liabilities:

| | |
|---|---:|
| Bonds payable, 6½%, nonconvertible | 100,000 |
| Income before extraordinary items | 90,000 |
| Extraordinary loss (net of tax) | (20,000) |
| Net income | 70,000 |

*Required:*

1. Is this a simple or complex capital structure? Explain.
2. What kinds of EPS presentation is required? Explain.
3. Compute the required EPS amounts (show all computations).

**Exercise 17-12**

The records of Sterling Corporation provided the following data; assuming a complex capital structure; at year-end (assume all amounts are correct):

| | |
|---|---|
| Average common shares outstanding during the year, 50,000 shares, par $2 ................ | $100,000 |
| Preferred stock, 6½, par $5 nonconvertible, shares outstanding during the year, 3,000 ... | 15,000 |
| Common stock equivalents (based on stock warrants outstanding), 10,000 shares | |
| Additional shares that would be issued assuming full dilution, 5,000 shares (based on $30,000, 6% convertible bonds outstanding). | |
| Retained earnings ...................................... | 40,000 |
| Income before extraordinary items .............. | 60,000 |
| Extraordinary loss (net of tax)...................... | (8,000) |
| Net income ............................................... | 52,000 |

*Required:*

1. What characteristics of the capital structure supports the assumption of a complex capital structure?
2. What kind of EPS presentation is required? Explain.
3. Compute the required EPS amounts (show all computations). Assume a 40% tax rate.

**Exercise 17-13**

Fisher Corporation is computing the EPS amounts at December 31, 19A. It is complicated because the capital structure is properly classified as complex. Two problems are yet to be resolved, viz:

a. Average common shares outstanding:
   Relevant data available:
   | | |
   |---|---|
   | Common stock, nopar, shares outstanding at beginning of year ...................................................... | 75,000 |
   | Shares sold and issued on April 1, 19A ............................ | 10,000 |
   | Shares acquired as treasury stock on October 1, 19A............ | 3,000 |

b. Common stock equivalents:
   Common stock options outstanding for 1,500 shares.
   Average market price of the common stock, $18 per share.
   Option price, $15 per share.

*Required:*

1. What kind of EPS presentation is required? Explain.
2. Compute the average number of shares outstanding (show computations).
3. Are there any common stock equivalents? Provide computations to support your response.
4. Under what conditions would the common stock options outstanding be omitted from the EPS computations?

**Exercise 17-14**

Jackson Corporation has a complex capital structure. At the end of 19A, the EPS presentation is to be developed. At issue is the proper treatment of the outstanding bonds, viz:

Bonds payable, 8%, convertible.............. $150,000
Conversion ratio: 30 shares of common
   stock for each $1,000 bond.
Bond issuance price: 112.
Prime bank interest rate: 7½%.

*Required:*

1. Present an analysis to determine whether the bonds represent common stock equivalents (show computations).
2. How many additional shares, because of the bonds, should be included in the computation of the (a) primary EPS amount, and (b) fully diluted EPS amount? Explain.
3. Under what circumstances would the effect of the bonds payable be omitted from the EPS computations?

## PROBLEMS

### Problem 17-1

Martin Corporation reported the following summarized data:

| | | | |
|---|---|---|---|
| Assets .......................... | $655,000 | Stockholders' Equity: | |
| Less: Liabilities............... | 100,000 | Preferred stock, $10 par... | $300,000 |
| | | Common stock, $5 par | |
| | | value, 30,000 shares ... | 150,000 |
| | | Contributed capital in ex- | |
| | | cess of par, preferred... | 30,000 |
| | | Retained earnings ......... | 75,000 |
| | $555,000 | | $555,000 |

The state law places a restriction on retained earnings equal to the cost of treasury stock held.

The following transactions affecting stockholders' equity were recorded:

a. Purchased preferred treasury stock, 500 shares at $14.
b. Purchased common treasury stock, 1,000 shares at $20.
c. Sold preferred treasury stock, 100 shares at $15.
d. Sold common treasury stock, 400 shares at $18.

*Required:*

1. Give entries in parallel columns for the treasury stock transactions assuming (a) the cost method, and (b) the par-value method is used.
2. Prepare the resulting balance sheet (unclassified) for each method.

### Problem 17-2

Sadler Corporation reported the following data:

| | |
|---|---|
| Common stock, $5 par value, 50,000 shares outstanding............... | $250,000 |
| Preferred stock, 6%, $10 par value, 10,000 shares | |
|    authorized, 6,000 issued ................................................ | 60,000 |
| Contributed capital in excess of par, common stock ................. | 62,500 |
| Contributed capital in excess of par, preferred stock................. | 6,000 |
| Retained earnings ........................................................ | 200,000 |

Subsequent to this date, the following transactions affecting stockholders' equity were recorded:

a. Purchased 2,000 shares of common treasury stock at $20 per share.
b. Purchased 1,000 shares of preferred treasury stock at $10.50 per share.
c. Sold 1,000 shares of the common treasury stock for $22 per share.
d. Transferred 20 shares of preferred treasury stock to A. K. Jones in payment for professional services rendered the corporation.

The state law places a restriction on retained earnings equal to the cost of treasury stock held.

*Required:*

1. Give the entries, in parallel columns, for the treasury stock transactions assuming (a) the cost method, and (b) the par-value method.
2. Prepare the resulting stockholders' equity section of the balance sheet for each method. Give all required disclosures with respect to the treasury stock.

## Problem 17–3

Sala Corporation had authorized and outstanding 5,000 shares of common stock, par value $50 per share. The stockholders approved the recall of the old stock and the exchange for each share of old stock two shares of new common stock. The new authorization was for 15,000 shares of stock.

*Required:*

Prepare entries to record the change under each of the following separate cases (assume a sufficient balance in retained earnings):

Case A – The old stock originally was sold at a premium of $2 per share and the new stock was $25 par-value common stock.

Case B – The old stock was sold at a premium of $3 per share, and the new stock was nopar-value stock with no stated or assigned value.

Case C – The old stock was sold at a premium of $1 per share, and the new stock was nopar-value stock with no stated or assigned value.

Case D – The old stock was sold at par, and the new stock was nopar-value stock with no stated or assigned value.

Case E – The old stock was sold at a premium of $2 per share, and the new stock was nopar-value stock with a stated value of $20 per share.

Case F – The old stock was sold at a premium of $5 per share, and the new stock was nopar-value stock with a stated value of $30 per share.

Case G – The old stock was sold at par, and the new stock was nopar-value stock with a stated value of $27.50 per share.

## Problem 17–4

The following account balances were shown on the books of SW Corporation at December 31:

| | |
|---|---|
| Cumulative preferred stock, par $100, 6% 2,000 shares | $200,000 |
| Common stock, par $50, 5,000 shares | 250,000 |
| Retained earnings (deficit) | (45,000) |

At a stockholders' meeting (including holders of preferred shares) the following quasi-reorganization was decided on:

a. That an amendment to the charter be obtained authorizing a total issue of 5,000 shares of noncumulative 8% preferred, par $100 per share, and 40,000 shares of nopar common stock.
b. That all outstanding stock be returned in exchange for new stock as follows:
   (1) For each share of old preferred, one share of new preferred. Purchased for cash at par 20 shares of old preferred stock from a dissatisfied stockholder.
   (2) For each share of old common, two shares of new common; the credit to the nopar stock account shall be at an amount, in contributed capital from conversion, sufficient to exactly provide for the deficit in retained earnings.
c. That the past operating deficit be written off against the credit created by the conversion of the common stock.

During the ensuing year the following transactions were effected:

d. Sold 200 shares of the new preferred stock at $105 per share.
e. The company issued 1,200 shares of nopar common in payment for a patent tentatively valued by the seller at $20,000. (The market value of a share was $15).
f. The company sold 50 shares of nopar common at $19 per share, receiving cash, and at the same time issued 100, $1,000 bonds at 102; one share of common stock, as a bonus, was given with each bond.
g. At the end of the year the board of directors met and was informed that the net income before deductions for bonuses to officers was $100,000. The directors took the following actions:
   (1) Ordered that 500 shares of nopar common stock (from authorized but unissued shares) be issued to officers as a bonus. The market price of a nopar common share on this date was $16.
   (2) Declared and paid dividends (for one year) on the preferred stock outstanding.

*Required:*

1. Prepare journal entries to record the above transactions.
2. Prepare the stockholders' equity section of the balance sheet after giving effect to the above transactions.


### Problem 17–5 (a review problem)

The following condensed trial balance was taken from the books of the LaRue Corporation at December 31:

| | | |
|---|---:|---:|
| Assets .................................................. | $584,000 | |
| Liabilities ............................................... | | $ 60,000 |
| Common stock, $10 par value (100,000 shares authorized; 40,000 shares issued).............. | | 400,000 |
| Contributed capital in excess of par.............. | | 4,000 |
| Retained earnings ..................................... | | 120,000 |
| | $584,000 | $584,000 |

During the year the following transactions were completed:

a. Subscriptions were received for 10,000 shares of common stock at $11 per share; 40% of the subscription price was collected. The shares will not be issued until the full price is collected.

b. A patent was acquired in exchange for 5,000 shares of common stock. The owner valued the patent at $60,000. Common stock was selling at $11.

c. An original stockholder desired to get money back from the corporation for 1,000 shares purchased at $10.10 per share. The corporation purchased the shares paying $10.50 per share. The par-value method is used for treasury stock.

d. The balance on subscriptions (a) was collected; the stock was issued.

e. Machinery costing $34,000 was purchased; 50% was paid down, the balance due in one year.

f. The charter was amended authorizing 200,000 shares of nopar common stock (to replace the par-value common stock) and 5,000 shares of preferred stock, par $100.

g. The old common stock (54,000 shares outstanding) was exchanged for the new nopar stock; two shares of the new stock were issued for each share of old stock. The 1,000 shares of old treasury stock were canceled.

h. 1,000 shares of the preferred stock were sold at $105.

i. 200 shares of common were reacquired as treasury stock at $12; and 100 shares of preferred at $105.

j. Net income for the period was $40,000 (debit assets).

k. A 3% dividend was declared on the preferred, and $.50 per share was declared on the common stock.

*Required:*

1. Set up a worksheet with debit and credit columns for (a) starting balances, (b) interim entries, and (c) ending balances (six money columns). Enter the beginning balances as given, record the transactions, and compute the ending balances. Key the entries. Do not detail assets and liabilities; set up one account for assets and one for liabilities. Since the problem focuses on stockholders' equity it should be detailed.

2. Prepare the resulting balance sheet that reflects appropriate detail in the stockholders' section. Include all disclosures relating to treasury stock. Assume the state law places a restriction on retained earnings equal to the cost of treasury stock held.

## Problem 17-6

You have just commenced your audit of Shaky Company for the year ended December 31, 19B. The president advises you that the company is insolvent and must declare bankruptcy unless a large loan can be obtained immediately. A lender who is willing to advance $450,000 to the company has been located, but will only make the loan subject to the following conditions:

1. A $450,000, 8% mortgage payable over 15 years on the land and buildings will be given as security on a new loan (cash received $450,000).

2. A new issue of 500 shares of $100 par-value, 5%, noncumulative, nonparticipating preferred stock will replace 500 outstanding shares of $100 par-value, 7%, cumulative, participating preferred stock. Preferred stockholders will repudiate all claims to $21,000 of dividends in arrears. The company has never formally declared the dividends.

3. A new issue of 600 shares of $50 par-value, class A common stock will replace 600 outstanding shares of $100 par-value, class A common stock.

4. A new issue of 650 shares of $40 par-value, class B common stock will replace 650 outstanding shares of $100 par-value, class B common stock.
5. A $600,000, 6% mortgage payable on the company's land and buildings held by a major stockholder will be canceled along with four months' accrued interest already recorded. The mortgage will be replaced by 5,000 shares of $100 par-value, 6%, cumulative if earned, nonparticipating preferred stock.
6. On May 1, 19A, the company's trade creditors had accepted $360,000 in notes payable on demand at 6% interest in settlement of all past-due accounts. No payment has been made to date on the accrued interest or principal. The company will offer to settle these liabilities at $.75 per $1 owed or to replace the notes payable on demand with new notes payable for full indebtedness over five years at 6% interest. It is estimated that $200,000 of the demand notes and the accrued interest thereon will be exchanged for the longer term notes and that the balance will accept the offer of a reduced cash settlement.

The president of the Shaky Company requests that you determine the effect of the foregoing on the company and furnishes the following condensed account balances (incomplete), which you believe are correct:

| | |
|---|---:|
| Bank overdraft | $ 15,000 |
| Other current assets | 410,000 |
| Fixed assets | 840,000 |
| Trade accounts payable | 235,000 |
| Other current liabilities | 85,000 |
| Contributed capital in excess of par value | 125,000 |
| Retained earnings deficit | 345,000 |

*Required:*

1. Prepare pro forma journal entries that you would suggest to give effect to the foregoing as of January 1, 19C. Entries should be keyed to numbered information in order.
2. Prepare a pro forma balance sheet for the Shaky Company at January 1, 19C, as if the recapitalization had been consummated.

(AICPA adapted)

**Problem 17-7**

Coulson Corporation is authorized to issue 100,000 shares of common stock, par $25; of which 60,000 is outstanding. During 1976, the company initiated a stock bonus plan for certain top managers. The plan provides for each qualified executive to receive an option for 1,000 shares of the common stock. Subject to continued employment, the option is exercisable at any time after three years and, prior to expiration, five years from the date of grant. The option is nontransferable and the specified option price is $60 per share. The option is considered to be additional compensation, prorated equally, for the year of the grant and the following four years. On January 1, 1976, E. R. Smalley, the company president, was granted an option under the plan when the market price of the stock was $66. Assume Smalley exercised the grant during the latter part of 1980 when the market price of the stock was $90 per share.

*Required:*

1. Is this a compensatory plan? Explain.
2. What is the measurement date? Explain.
3. What is the amount of the total compensation?

4. Over what period should this compensation be assigned as expense? How much should be assigned to 1976? to 1977? Explain.
5. Give appropriate entries on the following dates (if none, explain why):
   a. Date of grant.
   b. Measurement date.
   c. End of each year, starting on December 31, 1976.
   d. Exercise date.
6. Illustrate how the option would affect the income statement and balance sheet at the end of 1976 and 1977.

## Problem 17–8

Foster Corporation has a stock option plan for the top managers that includes the following provisions:

a. Each manager that qualifies will receive an option to acquire 10,000 shares of Foster common stock, par $1, at an option price of $10 per share.
b. The option is nontransferable and, if not exercised, expires five years from date of grant.
c. The option cannot be exercised prior to the end of two years from date of grant and requires continued employment in a covered position.
d. The stock option is for additional compensation for the year of the grant and the following four years; approximately equal each year.

An option was granted to the top executive on January 1, 1976, at which time the common stock was selling at $16 per share. Assume the option is exercised on December 31, 1980, when the stock is quoted at $30 per share.

At January 1, 1976, common stock, par $1, authorized was 150,000 shares of which 90,000 was outstanding.

*Required:*
1. Is this a compensatory plan? Explain.
2. What is the measurement date? Explain.
3. Compute the total compensation expense.
4. Over what period of time should this total compensation be assigned as expense? Explain.
5. Give appropriate entries for the following dates (if none, explain why):
   a. Date of grant.
   b. Measurement date.
   c. End of each year, starting on December 31, 1976.
   d. Exercise date.
6. Illustrate how the option would affect the income statement and balance sheet at the end of 1976 and 1977.

## Problem 17–9

Goodson Corporation has 100,000 shares of common stock, par $20, authorized, of which 40,000 shares are outstanding. The company has a stock option plan that provides the following:

a. Each qualified manager shall receive on January 1, a computed number of shares of common stock at a computed option price per share. The computation of each amount shall be made two years after the option is granted and will be related to the percentage increase in net income over that period.

b. The options are nontransferable and must be exercised, not earlier than two years and not later than five years, from date of grant. Affiliation with the company is required to the exercise date.

On January 1, 1976, an option was granted to A. B. Cox, the controller. At that date, the common stock was quoted on the market at $50 per share. Assume Cox exercised the option near the end of 1980.

| | Estimates Made on January 1, 1976, of What the Amount Would Be on December 31, 1977 | Actual Amount on December 31, 1977 |
|---|---|---|
| Number of shares optioned | 500 | 510 |
| Option price | $60 | $62 |
| Market price per share (a relatively steady increase each year) | $70 | $73 |

*Required:*

1. Is this a compensatory plan? Explain.
2. When is the measurement date? Explain.
3. Over what period should total compensation expense be assigned?
4. Give appropriate entries for the following dates (if none, explain why):
   a. Date of grant.
   b. End of 1976 and 1977.
   c. Measurement date.
   d. End of 1978, 1979, and 1980.
   e. Exercise date.

## Problem 17–10

Frost Corporation is authorized to issue 200,000 shares of common stock, par $10; to date 75,000 shares have been issued. During 1976, the corporation initiated a stock option plan for the three top managers. The plan provides that each manager will receive an option to purchase, two years from date of grant, 2,000 shares of the common stock at a base option price of $48, adjusted for changes in earnings per share, and providing continued employment. The option price is to be established on December 31, 1977, and will be based on changes in earnings per share. EPS for 1975 was $2. The option price will be established at the end of 1977 as follows:

The option price per share will be the base option price of $48 adjusted proportionately upward or downward in inverse relationship to changes in EPS from 1975 to 1977.

The options are nontransferable and expire five years from date of grant. The stock was quoted at $45 per share on the market on January 1, 1976. The management has made, what they consider to be, realistic estimates that earnings per share would increase steadily to $3.20 at December 31, 1977, and that the stock would increase steadily to $46 per share on that date. EPS on December 31, 1977, actually turned out to be $3, and the market price, $50.

The president received the options with the option price unknown at January

1, 1976. Assume the president exercised the option, the last day possible, on January 1, 1981.

*Required:*

1. Is this a compensatory plan? Explain.
2. What is the measurement date? Explain.
3. Over what period should this total compensation expense be assigned?
4. Give appropriate entries on the following dates (if none, explain why):
   *a.* Date of grant.
   *b.* End of 1976 and 1977.
   *c.* Measurement date.
   *d.* End of 1978, 1979, and 1980.
   *e.* Exercise date.

### Problem 17–11

Beame Corporation is developing the EPS presentation at December 31, 19A. The records of the company provide the following information:

Liabilities:

| | |
|---|---|
| Convertible bonds payable, 7% (each $1,000 bond is convertible to 20 shares of common stock) | $200,000 |

Stockholders' Equity:

| | |
|---|---|
| Common stock, nopar, authorized 100,000 shares: | |
| Outstanding January 1, 19A, 59,000 shares | 300,000 |
| Issued 10,000 shares on April 1, 19A | 60,000 |
| Common stock warrants outstanding (for 4,000 shares of common stock) | 16,000 |
| Preferred stock, 6%, par $10, nonconvertible, authorized 20,000 shares, outstanding during 19A, 5,000 shares | 50,000 |
| Contributed capital in excess of par, preferred stock | 10,000 |
| Retained earnings | 80,000 |
| Income before extraordinary items | 150,000 |
| Extraordinary loss (net of tax) | (20,000) |
| Net income | 130,000 |

Other data:

*a.* Stock warrants—option price $4 per share; market price of the common stock at date of issuance of the warrants, $6.
*b.* Convertible bonds—issue price, 115; prime interest rate at date of issuance was 8%.
*c.* Average income tax rate of 45%.

*Required:*

1. Is this a simple, or a complex, capital structure? Explain.
2. What kind of EPS presentation is required? Explain.
3. Prepare the required EPS presentation for 19A. Show all computations.
4. Were there any antidilutive securities? How was this determined?
5. How should antidilutive securities be treated in the computations of EPS? Why?

## Problem 17–12

The records of Indus Corporation reflected the following data at the end of 19A:

Liabilities:
Bonds payable, 7½%, convertible (each $1,000 bond is converted
  to 30 shares of common stock) ............................................ $150,000

Stockholders' Equity:
Common stock, par $2, authorized 300,000 shares:
  Outstanding January 1, 19A, 150,000 shares ........................... 300,000
  Issued on October 1, 19A, 20,000 shares ................................. 40,000
Common stock warrants outstanding (for 6,000 shares) ................. 18,000
Preferred stock, 6%, par $5, authorized 100,000 shares,
  outstanding during 19A, 20,000 shares ................................. 100,000
Contributed capital in excess of par, common ........................... 340,000
Contributed capital in excess of par, preferred .......................... 60,000
Retained earnings ...................................................... 110,000
Income before extraordinary items............................................. 170,000
Extraordinary loss (net of tax) ...................................... (20,000)
Net income........................................................................ 150,000

Other data:

a. Stock warrants—option price, $3 per share; market price of common stock, $3.60 per share.
b. Convertible bonds—issue price, 125; prime interest rate at date of issuance of the bonds was 8½%.
c. Average income tax rate of 40%.

*Required:*

1. Is this a simple, or a complex, capital structure? Explain.
2. What kind of EPS presentation is required? Explain.
3. Prepare the required EPS presentation for 19A. Show all computations.
4. Were there any antidilutive securities? How was this determined?
5. How should antidilutive securities be treated in EPS computations? Why?

# Chapter *18*

## Long-Term Investments in
## Equity Securities

A company may invest in another company by acquiring either (*a*) debt securities (i.e., notes, mortgages, and bonds) or (*b*) equity securities (i.e., common and preferred stock). The investments may be acquired with the intention of holding them on a short-term or long-term basis. Short-term investments (also called temporary investments) were discussed in Chapter 7. Investments are classified as current assets when they meet the dual test of (1) ready *marketability* and (2) a clear *intention* by management to convert them to cash during the upcoming year or normal operating cycle, whichever is the longer. All investments not clearly meeting both of these criteria are classified as noncurrent assets on the balance sheet under the caption "Investments and Funds" (see Chapter 5). Investments classified under this category are referred to as long-term or permanent investments. They include both debt and equity securities and may or may not meet the test of ready marketability; however, the intention of management must be to retain them in the long-term.

The purpose of this chapter is to discuss the measuring, accounting, and reporting of long-term investments in equity securities. Long-term investments in debt securities are discussed in Chapter 19. To accomplish this purpose, the chapter is divided into two parts: Part A — Cost, Equity, and Market Value Methods; and Part B — Consolidated Statements. There is a general discussion at the start of the chapter, and Part B is followed by a discussion of some special problems.[1]

---

[1] Subdivision of the chapter provides flexibility should consideration of consolidated statements be deferred to a more advanced course. Alternatively, this topic is included because surveys have consistently indicated that a good percentage of accounting majors do not take an advanced course in consolidations and mergers.

## RECORDING LONG-TERM INVESTMENTS AT DATE OF ACQUISITION

At date of acquisition of a long-term investment, an appropriately designated investment account is debited with the full cost, in accordance with the cost principle. Shares of stock may be acquired on various security markets. At date of purchase, full cost includes the basic cost of the security plus brokerage fees, excise taxes, and any other transfer costs incurred by the purchaser. Stocks may be purchased for cash, "on margin," or on a subscription basis. When stock is acquired on margin, only part of the purchase price is paid initially, and the balance is borrowed. The stock should be recorded at its full cost, and the liability to the lender recognized. A stock subscription or agreement to buy the stock of another corporation creates an asset represented by the stock investment and a liability for the amount to be paid. Interest paid on a subscription contract, or on funds borrowed to purchase the investment, should be recorded as interest expense and not capitalized as part of the cost of the investment.

When noncash considerations (property or services) are given for long-term investments, the cost assigned to the securities should be (1) the fair market value of the consideration given or (2) the fair market value of the securities received, whichever is more definitely determinable. Determination of either value in the case of unlisted or closely held securities being exchanged for property for which no established market value exists may force resort to appraisals or estimates.

Securities frequently are purchased between regular interest or dividend dates. Under generally accepted accounting principles, interest is accrued on debt securities but dividends are rarely accrued. In the case of a purchase of cumulative preferred stock on which the issuing corporation has been regularly paying dividends, the correct treatment is debatable. The authors would not accrue dividends (even in this case) because dividends legally do not accrue.[2]

To illustrate, assume that on October 1, 1976, X Corporation purchased 500 shares of the common stock of Y Corporation, par $5, at $20 per share. Dividends are paid regularly around July 1 of each year; the last dividend was $.50 per share. The investment would be recorded as follows:

Long-term investment, Y Corporation common stock
  (500 shares) .................................................................. 10,000
    Cash ...................................................................... 10,000
  (Note: No dividends are accrued.)

Alternatively, assume that on October 1, 1976, X Corporation pur-

---

[2] Theoretically, dividends should be recognized when stock is purchased between the declaration date and record date (ex-dividend date).

The price of a listed stock (especially preferred) tends to rise as the regular dividend date approaches and to decline by approximately the amount of the dividend as soon as the stock goes "ex dividends." Prices of stocks are, however, subject to many variables which may obscure these pre- and post-dividend movements.

chased a $10,000, 6% bond (interest payable each July 1) of Y Corporation for $10,000 plus accrued interest. The acquisition of this long-term investment in *debt securities* would be recorded as follows:

Long-term investment, Y Corporation bond (at cost) ........... 10,000
Accrued investment revenue ($10,000 × .06 × 3/12) .............. 150
    Cash ..................................................................... 10,150
    <small>(Note: Interest accrued to date of purchase—discussed in detail in the next chapter.)</small>

## Special Cost Problems

A purchase of two or more classes of securities for a single lump sum (sometimes called a basket purchase) necessitates allocation of the total cost to each class of securities based upon their relative fair market value. For example, if a block of Security A purchased alone would cost $1,000 and a block of Security B purchased separately would cost $2,000, one third of the total lump-sum cost would be allocated to A and two thirds to B whether the combined cost was $3,000 or some other amount. In case one class of securities has a known market value and the other does not, the known market value is used for that class and the remainder of the lump-sum price is allocated to the others. If neither has a known market value it is better to defer any apportionment until evidence of at least one value becomes sufficiently clear.

Securities sometimes are acquired in exchange for other securities. The securities acquired should be recorded at their fair market value or at the fair market value of those given up at the time of the exchange, whichever is more clearly determinable. To illustrate an exchange of securities, assume that each holder of a share of $100 par value preferred stock in AB Corporation becomes entitled to receive in exchange five shares of nopar common stock of the company. An investor who had paid $6,000 for 50 shares of preferred stock makes the exchange. At the time of the exchange the nopar common shares were selling at $27. The exchange would be recorded as follows:[3]

Investment in nopar common stock of AB Corporation
($27 × 250 shares) ......................................................... 6,750
    Investment in preferred stock of AB Corporation .............. 6,000
    Gain on conversion of stock investment ......................... 750

In accounting for investments, generally, it is necessary to maintain an identification of each security acquired. Usually, this can be done by using the stock or bond certificate number. In effect, this requires the maintenance of inventory records with respect to securities in order that they may be "costed out" upon disposition. For example, if 10 shares of X Corporation stock are purchased at $150 per share and later an additional 30 shares are purchased at $200 per share, the subsequent sale of 5 shares at $180 per share would pose a cost identification problem. If the five shares can be identified by certificate number as a part of the

---

[3] A more extended discussion of the exchange of securities is presented in Chapter 19; an alternate treatment whereby no gain or loss is recognized also is presented. The authors are of the opinion that the treatment illustrated here is preferable, assuming materiality.

first purchase, a gain of $30 per share should be recognized. Alternatively, if they are identified with the second purchase, a loss of $20 per share should be recognized. If an averaging procedure were applied, the result would be a loss of $7.50 per share computed as follows:

| First purchase | ............ | 10 shares @ $150 = $1,500 |
|---|---|---|
| Second purchase | ......... | 30 shares @ $200 = 6,000 |
| Total | ................ | 40 $7,500 |

| Average cost per share $7,500 ÷ 40 shares = | $187.50 |
|---|---|
| Sales price per share | = 180.00 |
| Loss per Share ........................... | $ 7.50 |

Identification of shares sold ordinarily is not difficult. However, where blocks of shares have been transferred through an estate, or where the issuing corporation has exchanged substitute securities for those originally purchased, an identification problem can arise. Federal tax laws require use of "first-in, first-out" where specific identification cannot be made. Use of either *Fifo* or an *average cost* procedure is acceptable from the standpoint of accounting theory.

## ACCOUNTING AND REPORTING FOR STOCK INVESTMENTS SUBSEQUENT TO ACQUISITION

In accounting for long-term investments in stock subsequent to acquisition date, a careful distinction is maintained between (a) voting common stock and nonvoting stock, such as nonvoting preferred stock; and (b) the proportion of voting shares owned to the total shares outstanding (i.e., the level of ownership of the voting shares).[4]

Fundamentally, there are three different methods of accounting and reporting stock investments, viz: (1) cost method, (2) equity method, and (3) fair market value method. Each of these methods is used under certain specified conditions. In addition, when one company owns a controlling interest in the voting stock of another company, the controlling company must prepare *consolidated financial statements* (discussed in Part B of this chapter).

In accounting for long-term investments, a careful distinction must be maintained between *voting common stock* and nonvoting stock because the former permits the owner to exercise some influence or control through voting on the operating and financial policies of the other company. The degree of influence or control depends upon the proportion of voting shares owned as an investment (usually the common stock) to the total of such shares outstanding. Therefore, in accounting and reporting for long-term investments in the voting capital stock of

---

[4] Level of ownership refers to the proportion of shares owned to the total shares outstanding. To illustrate, assume Company X purchased 20,000 shares of common stock of Company Y when there were 100,000 total shares outstanding. The level of ownership by Company X in Company Y would be: 20,000 ÷ 100,000 = 20%. Ownership of exactly 50% of the voting shares may fit the "significant influence" category or the controlling interest category depending on other factors.

another company, *APB Opinion No. 18*, "Equity Method for Investments in Common Stock" (March 1971), defined two important concepts, "significant influence" and "control," as follows:

1. Significant influence—the ability of the investor company to affect, in an important degree, the operating and financing policies of another company because of ownership of a sufficient number of shares of its voting stock. Ability to exercise significant influence also may be indicated in several other ways, such as representation on the board of directors, participation in policy making processes, material intercompany transactions, interchange of managerial personnel, or technological dependency. In order to achieve a reasonable degree of uniformity, the APB provided an operational rule that an investment of 20% or more of the voting stock should lead to the presumption that in the absence of evidence to the contrary, an investor has the ability to exercise significant influence over the other company.

2. Controlling interest—a controlling interest exists when the investing company owns enough of the voting stock of the other company to effectively control its operating and financing policies. Ownership of over 50% of the outstanding voting stock usually would assure control; however, there are situations where this may not be the case (discussed in Part B). On the other hand, circumstances sometimes exist where ownership of something less than 50% may create a controlling interest. Factors such as number of shares outstanding, number of shareholders, and shareholder participation in voting bear on the point at which a controlling interest is attained. The accounting profession has found it very difficult to develop an operational definition of control based on 50% or less of the voting stock. As a consequence, the presumption is that a controlling interest is represented by over 50% of the voting stock.

The issuance of *APB Opinion No. 18* had a significant impact on the accounting for long-term investments in capital stock. In accordance with certain prior pronouncements and *Opinion No. 18*, accounting for long-term investments in stock may be outlined as follows:

**Accounting for Long-Term Equity Investments**

| Investment Characteristics | Level of Ownership | Reporting Method |
|---|---|---|
| A. No significant influence or control: | | |
| 1. Nonvoting stock owned. | All levels | Cost |
| 2. Voting stock owned. | Less than 20% | Cost |
| B. Significant influence but not control: | | |
| 3. Voting stock owned. | 20% up to 50% | Equity |
| C. Controlling interest: | | |
| 4. Voting stock owned, but for special reasons not appropriate to consolidate. | Over 50% | Equity |
| 5. Voting stock owned, appropriate to consolidate. | Over 50% | Consolidated statement basis |

Part A of this chapter will discuss and illustrate categories (1) through (4); Part B will discuss the accounting and reporting where there is a controlling interest and when *consolidated statements* are required, that is, category (5).

## PART A—COST, EQUITY, AND MARKET VALUE METHODS

### COST METHOD

Under the cost method, a long-term investment in equity securities is recorded in the accounts at cost. Subsequently, it is reflected in the accounts and reported on the balance sheet at lower of cost or market. On this point, FASB *Statement No. 12* (December 31, 1975) states:

> The carrying value of a marketable equity securities portfolio shall be the lower of its aggregate cost or market value, determined at the balance sheet date. The amount by which aggregate cost of the portfolio exceeds market value shall be accounted for as the valuation allowance.
>
> Marketable equity securities owned by an entity shall, in the case of a classified balance sheet, be grouped into separate portfolios according to the current or noncurrent classification of the securities for the purpose of comparing aggregate cost and market value to determine carrying amount. In the case of an unclassified balance sheet, marketable equity securities shall for the purposes of this Statement be considered as noncurrent assets.

Equity securities, as used in *Statement No. 12*, encompasses all capital stock (including warrants, rights, and stock options) except preferred stock that by its terms either must be redeemed by the issuing enterprise or is redeemable at the option of the investor. Treasury stock and convertible bonds are excluded.

To apply the lower-of-cost-or-market concept, *Statement No. 12* defines *cost* after acquisition as the original cost of the equity security except when a *new cost basis* is established after acquisition; *(a)* when a marketable equity security is transferred between current and noncurrent classification and *(b)* when an individual marketable security (rather than the portfolio) has been written down to cost to reflect a permanent, as opposed to a temporary, decline in market value. These two situations are discussed later.

*Statement No. 12* makes a careful distinction between realized and unrealized losses and gains on marketable equity securities. A *realized* loss or gain represents the difference between the net proceeds received and the investment cost of an equity security at date of sale. In contrast, an *unrealized* gain or loss on a marketable equity security represents the difference between the aggregate market value and aggregate cost of the long-term investment portfolio on a given date. Realized gains and losses on a marketable equity security are recognized only when securities are sold (or written down because of a permanent decline) whereas, unrealized gains and losses are recognized only at the end of the accounting period when the adjusting entry is made to apply the lower-of-cost-or-market concept to the portfolio.

In the adjusting entry, an allowance account (an asset contra account) is used to record the difference between cost and market, and an unrealized loss or gain account is used for the other side of the entry. On the balance sheet, the allowance account balance is subtracted from the cost of the portfolio and the accumulated unrealized loss amount is reported under the owners' equity caption as unrealized capital. In contrast, recall from Chapter 7 that, for marketable securities classified as *current assets*, both the unrealized and realized gains and losses are reported on the income statement. Under no circumstances can the cumulative unrealized gain exceed the unrealized losses on the long-term portfolio of equity securities.

Under the cost method, cash dividends received are recorded as investment revenue. Dividends are usually recorded as revenue when the cash is received; however if the accounting period ends between the declaration date and payment date, they should be recorded in the period of declaration. A cash dividend would be recorded as follows:

```
Cash ............................................................................. 7,500
    Investment revenue......................................................          7,500
```

Occasionally, an investor receives a dividend that is entirely, or in part, a *liquidating dividend* (see Chapter 16). Dividends received in excess of earnings accumulated since the acquisition date are considered liquidating dividends. In such instances, the investor should reduce the investment account for the amount of the liquidating dividend. Dividends received in noncash assets should be recorded at the fair market value of the assets received.

To illustrate application of the cost method for long-term investments in equity securities, the following series of transactions and entries for X Corporation are presented:

January 5, 19A—Purchased the following equity securities as a long-term investment (less than 20% of the outstanding shares in each case):

Y Corporation, common stock (par $5), 5,000 shares at $12
Z Corporation, preferred stock (par $10, nonredeemable), 4,000 shares at $20

```
Long-term investments in equity securities ..................... 140,000
    Cash (5,000 × $12) + (4,000 × $20) .........................          140,000
```

December 31, 19A—Adjusting entry to lower of cost or market; Market value: Y stock, $10; Z stock, $21.

```
Unrealized loss on long-term investments in equity securities... 6,000
    Allowance to reduce long-term investments in equity
        securities to market  ...............................................          6,000
```

Computation:

| Security | Shares | Cost | Market | Unrealized Gain (Loss) |
|---|---|---|---|---|
| Y.................. | 5,000 | @ $12 = $ 60,000 | @ $10 = $ 50,000 | ($10,000) |
| Z.................. | 4,000 | @ $20 = 80,000 | @ $21 = 84,000 | 4,000 |
| Total .............. | | $140,000 | $134,000 | ($ 6,000) |

August 10, 19B—Unexpectedly sold 1,000 shares of the Z Corporation stock at $24.

Cash (1,000 × $24) ............................................................... 24,000
    Long-term investments in equity securities (1,000 × $20) ...       20,000
    Realized gain on sale of long-term investments* ...........       4,000
    * Closed to income summary

### December 31, 19B – Adjusting entry to lower of cost or market; Market value: Y stock, $10.50; Z stock, $21.50.

Allowance to reduce long-term investment in equity securities
    to market ................................................................... 3,000
    Unrealized gain on long-term investment in equity
       securities ............................................................       3,000

Computation:

| Security | Shares | Cost | Market | Unrealized Gain (Loss) |
|---|---|---|---|---|
| Y .................. | 5,000 | @ $12 = $ 60,000 | @ $10.50 = $ 52,500 | ($7,500) |
| Z .................. | 3,000 | @ $20 = 60,000 | @ $21.50 = 64,500 | 4,500 |
| Total .............. | | $120,000 | $117,000 | ($3,000) |

Balance in allowance account........................... $6,000
Balance needed in allowance account ............... 3,000
       Adjustment needed (debit) ..................... $3,000

The financial statements for X Corporation would reflect the following:

| | 19A | 19B |
|---|---|---|
| **Income Statement:** | | |
| Realized gain on long-term investment .......................... | $ 4,000 | |
| **Balance Sheet:** | | |
| Funds & Investments: | | |
| Investments in equity securities, at cost ............................. | $140,000 | $120,000 |
| Less: Allowance to reduce equity investments to market ............................. | 6,000 | 3,000 |
| Investment portfolio at lower of cost or market ............... | $134,000 | $117,000 |
| **Stockholders' Equity:** | | |
| Unrealized capital: | | |
| Unrealized loss on investment in equity securities.............. | (6,000) | (3,000) |

In the case of a *permanent decline* (as opposed to a temporary decline) in the value of a long-term marketable equity security, the *individual* security (separate from the portfolio) must be written down to market. This reduced valuation thereafter is considered to be *cost;* the amount of the writedown is accounted for as a *realized* loss and is reported on the current income statement.

To illustrate, refer to the above example. Assume Y Corporation stock was selling at $5.00 per share at the end of 19B and that the drop in value was clearly not temporary. This situation would be recorded as follows:

December 31, 19B — To record permanent decline in value of Y Corporation common stock.

```
Realized loss, permanent decline in valuation of equity
   security ....................................................................... 35,000
      Long-term investment in equity securities [5,000 ×
      ($12 − $5)]..............................................................          35,000
```

In the case of a change in *classification* between short-term (current) and long-term (noncurrent) of an individual security, the security must be transferred at the lower-of-cost-or-market value at date of transfer. This value than becomes cost for subsequent periods. If market is below cost, the difference must be accounted for as a realized loss and reported on the income statement.

To illustrate, refer to the example above. Assume Y Corporation stock was reclassified at the end of 19B when the market value was $10.50 (cost was $12). This change in classification would be recorded as follows:

December 31, 19B — To record reclassification of Y Corporation stock.

```
Short-term investment in equity securities (at market) ............ 52,500
Realized loss on marketable equity securities*  ...................... 7,500
      Long-term investment in equity securities (at cost)  .........          60,000
   * Closed to income summary
```

The cost method is relatively simple and limits the recognition of revenue to the receipt of dividends since the investor is presumed to have no ability to significantly influence or control the other company. Disclosure requirements are given in Chapter 7.


## EQUITY METHOD

The equity method is more complex and is significantly different from the cost method. It is based on the presumption that the investor owns a sufficient number of the outstanding voting shares of the other company (usually called the investee company) to exercise significant influence (although not control) over the operating and financial policies of the other company. An important element is influence over the *dividend policy* of the investee. This presumption changes the basis for recognition of *investment revenue* from that used in the cost method.

*APB Opinion No. 18* states that investors should use the equity method in accounting for "investments in common stock of all unconsolidated subsidiaries (foreign as well as domestic)" and also for all investments in common stock where the "investment in voting stock gives it the ability to exercise significant influence over operating and financial policies of an investee even though the investor holds 50% or less of the voting stock." The *Opinion* also states that "an investment (direct or indirect) of 20% or more of the voting stock of an investee should lead to a presumption that in absence of evidence to the contrary an investor has the ability to exercise significant influence over an investee."[5] *Opinion No. 18* sets forth procedures for applying the equity method; among them are the following:

    a. Intercompany profits and losses should be eliminated until realized by the investor or investee as if a subsidiary, corporate joint venture or investee company were consolidated.

    b. A difference between the cost of an investment and the amount of underlying equity in net assets of an investee should be accounted for as if the investee were a consolidated subsidiary.

    c. The investment(s) in common stock should be shown in the balance sheet of an investor as a single amount, and the investor's share of earnings or losses of an investee(s) should ordinarily be shown in the income statement as a single amount except for the extraordinary items as specified in (d) below.

    d. The investor's share of extraordinary items and its share of prior-period adjustments reported in the financial statements of the investee in accordance with *APB Opinions Nos. 9* and *30* should be classified in a similar manner unless they are immaterial in the income statement of the investor.

    e. A transaction of an investee of a capital nature that affects the investor's share of stockholders' equity of the investee should be accounted for as if the investee were a consolidated subsidiary.

    f. Sales of stock of an investee by an investor should be accounted for as gains or losses equal to the difference at the time of sale between selling price and carrying amount of the stock sold.

Thus, under the equity method the accounting procedure may be outlined as follows:

1. At acquisition of the investment, the investor records the stock purchase at cost.
2. Subsequent to acquisition, each period the investor—
       *a.* Records the proportionate share of the investee's reported profits by debiting the investment account and crediting Investment Revenue. For a loss the investment account would be credited and Investment Loss debited.
       *b.* Records the proportionate share of dividends received as a debit to Cash and a credit to the investment account.
       *c.* Records *depreciation* on any increase in the depreciable assets for the proportionate share of the difference between their fair market value at date of acquisition of the investment and the carrying value reported by the investee. The depreciation amount is debited to Investment Revenue and credited to the investment account.

---

[5] The equity method gives the same net results on the financial statements as would consolidation procedures discussed in Part B; as a consequence it is frequently referred to as "one-line consolidation." Recognition and amortization of goodwill as well as intercompany transactions must be accounted for. Explanations and illustrations of the equity method often assume that the stock was purchased at its book value. This oversimplification rarely occurs and gives misleading knowledge of the concept and essence of the equity method.

d. Records amortization of any *purchased goodwill* resulting from the acquisition transaction. Investment Revenue is debited and the investment account is credited.

3. If all or a part of the investment is subsequently sold, a gain or loss is reported for the difference between the sales price and the then carrying value of the investment (as reflected in the investment account).

Since the equity method is based upon the concept of *significant influence,* (*a*) the investment account is adjusted each period to reflect the proportionate increase or decrease in the ownership of the investee company, and (*b*) investment revenue is recognized by the investor on the basis of the proportionate share of the earnings of the investee (adjusted for additional depreciation and goodwill amortization based on market values).

To illustrate application of the equity method in a relatively simple situation, assume that on January 1, 19A, Company R (the investor) purchased 1,800 shares (representing 20%) of the outstanding voting common stock of Company E (the investee company) for $300,000 cash. Assume on date of acquisition the following values relating to Company E were assembled by Company R:

|  | Data on Company E | |
| --- | --- | --- |
|  | Book Values Reported by Co. E | Fair Market Values |
| Assets not subject to depreciation ................. | $ 550,000 | $ 570,000 |
| Assets subject to depreciation (net of accumulated depreciation; remaining life, ten years) ................................................ | 500,000 | 700,000 |
| Total Assets....................................... | $1,050,000 | $1,270,000 |
| Liabilities .................................................... | $ 50,000 | |
| Common stock (9,000 shares, par $100) ................................... $900,000 | | |
| Retained earnings .......................... 100,000 | 1,000,000 | |
| Total Liabilities and Shareholders' Equity............ | $1,050,000 | |

The *equity method* must be applied in this situation because Company R owns 20% of the outstanding stock of Company E as a long-term investment. The purchase of this investment would be recorded by Company R, the investor, as follows:

*a.* January 1, 19A — Purchase of 1,800 shares of Company E stock (20% ownership) as a long-term investment:

Investment, Company E common stock (1,800 shares)... 300,000
    Cash................................................................. 300,000

Assume further that at the end of 19A Company E reported the following:

1. Income before extraordinary items ..................... $ 80,000
   Extraordinary gain (net of tax) .......................... 30,000
   Net Income ..................................................... $110,000
2. Total Cash Dividends Declared and Paid.............. $ 50,000

To apply the equity method, the first step is to compute the *goodwill purchased*, which is the difference between the purchase price and the identifiable net assets of the investee company valued at *fair market value*, viz:[6]

**Computation of Purchased Goodwill**

| | | |
|---|---:|---:|
| Purchase price (for 20% ownership interest) .................. | | $300,000 |
| Purchased book value ($1,000,000 × .20)....................... | | 200,000 |
| Excess of purchase price over book value purchased... | | 100,000 |
| Adjustments to market values: | | |
| Increase on assets not subject to depreciation<br>($570,000 − $550,000) × .20 .................................... | $ 4,000 | |
| Increase on assets subject to depreciation<br>($700,000 − $500,000) × .20 .................................... | 40,000 | 44,000 |
| Difference—Goodwill Purchased................................... | | $ 56,000 |

The entries to reflect the effects in the accounts of investor Company R at the end of 19A would be as follows:

*b.* End of 19A – To recognize revenue and an increase in the investment account, based on the proportionate share of net income reported by Company E.

Investment, Company E common stock ........................ 22,000
    Investment revenue (ordinary) ................................ 16,000
    Extraordinary gain (on stock investment).................. 6,000

Computations:
    Ordinary:       $80,000 × .20 = $16,000
    Extraordinary:  30,000 × .20 =   6,000

*c.* End of 19A – To record cash dividend received on Company E stock.

Cash....................................................................... 10,000
    Investment, Company E common stock .................. 10,000

Computation: $50,000 × .20 = $10,000.
(Note: A cash dividend, under the equity method, is viewed as a "collection" of a part of the investment since revenue is recognized on net income of the investee and not on dividends.)

*d.* End of 19A – To record depreciation on the $40,000 *increase* in depreciable assets implicit in the purchase.

---

[6] Recall the discussion of goodwill in Chapter 14. Purchased goodwill is the difference between the total purchase price of a business and the fair market value of the net assets of that business. The net assets must be reduced to agree with the proportionate share of the business purchased. Under generally accepted accounting principles, goodwill is recorded only when purchased. *APB Opinion No. 17* requires that all intangibles, including goodwill, be amortized over a reasonable period not exceeding 40 years.

Investment revenue (ordinary) ..................................... 4,000

    Investment, Company E common stock .................. 4,000

Computation: $40,000 ÷ 10 years = $4,000.

(Note: This amount of depreciation is, in effect, a decrease in the revenue recognized in entry *(b)* above since it is additional expense above that included in the computation of net income reported by Company E.)

*e.* End of 19A — To record periodic amortization of the $56,000 goodwill purchased (as computed above). Assume straight-line amortization over 40 years (maximum permitted by *APB Opinion No. 17*):

Investment revenue (ordinary) ..................................... 1,400

    Investment, Company E common stock...................... 1,400

Computation: $56,000 ÷ 40 years = $1,400.

(Note: This entry is made for the same reason as the prior entry. It represents a decrease in the revenue recognized in entry *(b)* because it is an additional expense that was not included in the computation of net income reported by Company E.)

Careful study of the above illustration will emphasize the concepts of the equity method. They may be summarized as follows:

1. Investment amount — Record original acquisition at cost in the investment account. Subsequently, increase the investment account for the proportionate share of the income of the investee company; decrease the investment account for dividends paid, additional depreciation, and additional amortization of goodwill. Thus, the investment account in the above illustration was as follows:

**Investment, Company E Common Stock (2,000 Shares; 20%)**

| | | | |
|---|---|---|---|
| *a.* Acquisition (cost) | 300,000 | *c.* Dividends received | 10,000 |
| *b.* Proportionate share of | | *d.* Additional depreciation | 4,000 |
|    income of investee | 22,000 | *e.* Amortization of goodwill | 1,400 |

(Ending debit balance — $306,600)

The ending balance represents the 20% ownership interest of the investor, Company R, in the net assets of the investee, Company E.

2. Revenue recognition — Recognize revenue based upon a proportionate share of net income reported by the investee company, Company E. Reduce the revenue recognized by additional expenses — depreciation and amortization of goodwill. Separately record ordinary and extraordinary gains and losses. Thus, the two revenue accounts in the above illustration were as follows:

**Investment Revenue (Ordinary)**

| | | | |
|---|---|---|---|
| *d.* Depreciation | 4,000 | *b.* Reported income | 16,000 |
| *e.* Amortization | 1,400 | | |

(Ending credit balance
to income summary, $10,600)

**Extraordinary Gain (Stock Investment)**

| | | |
|---|---|---|
| | *b.* Reported gain | 6,000 |

(Ending credit balance
to income summary, $6,000)

For the investor, the equity method has significant conceptual and measurement differences from the cost method because it is based upon different concepts of (1) investment valuation, and (2) revenue recognition. To illustrate the differences:

|  | | Amount | Difference |
|---|---|---|---|
| Investment valuation: | | | |
| Cost method (remains at original cost) ... | | $300,000 | |
| Equity method (adjusted to proportionate | | | |
| share of net assets) ....................... | | 306,600 | $6,600 |
| Revenue recognition: | | | |
| Cost method (limited to | | | |
| dividends received): | | | |
| Ordinary............................................ | | 10,000 | |
| Equity method (proportionate share of | | | |
| net income, adjusted): | | | |
| Ordinary............................................ | $10,600 | | |
| Extraordinary ................................... | 6,000 | 16,600 | 6,600 |

The two differences ($6,600) are the same because, under the equity method, the investment account is adjusted from the cost basis to the parent's share of the net income of the subsidiary, less dividends received. Similarly, investment revenue is different by the proportionate share of the income of the subsidiary after taking into account that dividends received were recognized as revenue under the cost method but not under the equity method.

## MARKET VALUE METHOD

The market value method of accounting for, and reporting, long-term investments is based upon a fundamental concept that is entirely different from those underlying the other methods. The market value method is based upon the concept of *fair value accounting;* that is, the investment should be revalued at each balance sheet date to the then current market price of the stocks held. Thus, *investment valuation* is at current market value and *investment revenue* for the period is comprised of dividends received plus or minus the change in the market value of the securities held during the period.

Many accountants believe strongly that all marketable securities, whether short term or long term, should be accounted for using the market value method because the results (a) meet more closely the objective of reporting the economic consequences of holding the investment, and (b) are more useful to decision-makers in projecting future economic potentials and cash flows.

At the present time, the market value method is not in accordance with generally accepted accounting principles. However, the method is currently used in special circumstances.[7] Its use in special circumstances is permitted under the modifying principle – industry peculiari-

---

[7] AICPA, *APB Opinion No. 18,* March 1971, par. 9. Also see Chapter 25.

ties (see Chapter 2, page 26). The market value method is widely used today by insurance companies and mutual funds in accounting for their portfolios. The method is applied in those situations only to marketable securities (i.e., those readily marketable); other methods are used for "nonmarketable" securities. The market value method may be outlined as follows:

1. At date of acquisition, investments are recorded at full cost in accordance with the cost principle.
2. Subsequent to acquisition, the investment account periodically is adjusted to the then current market value of the securities held. The adjusted amount then becomes the "carrying value" for subsequent accounting.
3. Revenue recognized each period includes:
   a. All cash or property dividends received during the period.
   b. The increase (or decrease) in the market value of the portfolio during the period. This is often referred to as the *market* or *holding gain or loss.*
4. At disposition of the investment, the difference between carrying value and sales price is recognized as a gain or loss.

To illustrate the market value method, assume Company A purchased 3,000 shares (10%) of the outstanding common stock of Company B for $50 per share. The events and related journal entries for Company A, for a three-year period, are given below for the *market value method:*

a. Year 1 – purchased 3,000 shares of common stock of Company B at $50 per share.

| Investment in Company B, common stock | | |
|---|---|---|
| (3,000 shares) | 150,000 | |
| Cash | | 150,000 |

b. End of Year 1 – Company B reported net income, $20,000.

No entry on books of Company A.

c. End of Year 1 – market price per share on Company B common stock, $55.

| Investment in Company B, common stock | 15,000 | |
|---|---|---|
| Investment revenue (holding gain on stock | | |
| investment) | | 15,000 |

($55 − $50) × 3,000 shares = $15,000.

d. End of Year 2 – Company B reported net income, $22,000.

No entry on books of Company A.

e. End of Year 2 – Company B paid a cash dividend of $.25 per share.

| Cash (3,000 shares × $.25) | 750 | |
|---|---|---|
| Investment revenue (dividends) | | 750 |

f. End of Year 2 – market price of Company B common stock, $55.

No entry on books of Company A since market price is unchanged.

*g.* Year 3 — sold 1,000 shares of the Company B stock at $54 per share.

| | | |
|---|---|---|
| Cash.................................................................... | 54,000 | |
| Loss on sale of stock investment .............................. | 1,000 | |
|     Investment in Company B (1,000 shares × $55)......... | | 55,000 |

The market value method poses several critical problems in application; among them are the following:

1. Determination of fair market value. In the case of a thin market, a large block of stock may be overvalued if the price per share prevailing at a given time is simply multiplied by the number of shares held. Additionally, many accountants seriously question the realism of using a price per share on a given day (last day of the period). Strong arguments have been made for use of some form of average price per share.

2. Reporting the market gain or loss. Many take the position that the market gain or loss should be viewed as "unrealized" and reported as an unrealized increment (or decrease) in owners' equity. The gain or loss would later be reported through the income statement as "realized" upon disposal of the investment. In contrast, logic and theory suggest that market gains and losses should be reported on the income statement in the period in which they occur. In the illustration immediately above, this position was assumed. In contrast, if the market changes are accounted for as unrealized, the above entries would be changed as follows:

Entry (*c*):

| | | |
|---|---|---|
| Investment in Company B, common stock.......................... | 15,000 | |
|     Unrealized market gain on investments (owners'<br>    equity) ................................................................ | | 15,000 |

Entry (*g*):

| | | |
|---|---|---|
| Cash ................................................................... | 54,000 | |
| Unrealized market gain on investments ............................ | 5,000 | |
|     Investment in Company B, common stock.................... | | 55,000 |
|     Gain on sale of stock investment .............................. | | 1,000 |

Numerous arguments have been advanced in favor of and against the valuation of marketable securities at fair market value. The principal arguments cited against it are: (*a*) it violates the cost principle and places on the balance sheet questionable and transitory values that tend to mislead the user, (*b*) it introduces another variance between book and tax amounts, (*c*) it violates the realization principle since revenue is recognized on market changes rather than on sale, and (*d*) because of the typical vagaries of stock prices it introduces a possible "Yo-Yo" effect on net income. In contrast, the proponents disagree with the first two points and argue that (*a*) market values are much more relevant information for decision making by the user; (*b*) it avoids "managed" earnings through the sale of selected securities held that have a low original cost and a high current market value; (*c*) stock yield including both dividends and holding gains and losses should be reported on the income statement each period since that best reflects what is happening to the investment; and *(d)* investors make decisions on the basis of present and future values and cash flows as opposed to historical costs.

## PART B—CONSOLIDATED STATEMENTS

### PURPOSE OF PART B

The purpose of Part B is to present the fundamental concepts underlying consolidated statements. Therefore, the numerous complexities involved are deferred to more advanced books.

### CONCEPT OF A CONTROLLING INTEREST

When an investor company owns over 50% of the outstanding voting stock of another company, in the absence of overriding constraints, a controlling interest is deemed to exist. The investor company is often designated as the *parent* company, and the other company is known as a *subsidiary*. In a parent-subsidiary relationship, both corporations continue as separate legal entities; consequently, they are separate accounting entities (refer to separate-entity assumption, Chapter 2, page 17). As separate entities, they have separate accounting systems and separate financial statements. Because of their special ownership relationship, the *parent company* (but not the subsidiary) is required to prepare *consolidated financial statements* which view the parent and the subsidiary (or subsidiaries) as a single economic entity. To accomplish consolidation, the separate financial statements of the parent and the subsidiary are combined each period by the parent company into one overall set of financial statements as if they were one single entity. The income statement, balance sheet, and statement of changes in financial position are consolidated in this manner.

Consolidated financial statements are not always prepared when over 50% of the stock of another corporation is owned because certain constraints may preclude the exercise of a controlling interest. To qualify for consolidation as a single economic entity, two basic elements must exist, viz:

1. Control of voting rights—this is presumed to exist when over 50% of the outstanding voting stock of another entity is owned by the investor. Nonvoting stock is excluded because it does not provide an avenue for control by vote. However, control may not exist even though over 50% of the voting stock is owned as in the case of a foreign subsidiary where the restrictions imposed by the foreign country are such that effective control cannot be exercised by the parent company. In such situations, the subsidiary would not qualify for consolidation. These are commonly called *unconsolidated subsidiaries* and must be accounted for under the equity method.

2. Economic compatibility—this means that the operations of the parent and the subsidiary are complementary (i.e., they are related operationally and possess similar economic characteristics). For example,

a parent company manufacturing a major product and a subsidiary manufacturing a component part for that product would have economic compatibility. In contrast, a manufacturing company and a bank would lack economic compatibility. In the latter case, the statements would not be consolidated; the subsidiary would be accounted for as an unconsolidated subsidiary.

In applying these two basic elements, the criteria for including a subsidiary in consolidated statements generally are stated as follows:[8]

1. The parent corporation must have the ability to govern, or effectively regulate, the subsidiary corporation's managerial decisions.
2. The parent must be so related to the subsidiary that the economic results of the subsidiary will accrue to the parent (allowing for allocations to the minority shareholders of the subsidiary).
3. The expectation of continuity of control.
4. The degree of existing restrictions upon the availability of earnings of the subsidiary to the parent (frequently a problem with foreign subsidiaries).
5. The general coincidence of accounting periods.
6. The degree of heterogeneity in the operations of the parent and the subsidiary.

Although each affiliate (parent and subsidiaries) keeps separate books and prepares separate financial statements, these individualized statements do not present a comprehensive report of the *economic unit* as a whole. Since the entire economic unit is under one management (and one group of stockholders), a financial report for that unit is essential to meet the needs of owners, creditors, and management. When a subsidiary is less than 100% owned, there is a group of minority shareholders (minority interest) to be recognized in the consolidated financial statements.

## ACQUIRING A CONTROLLING INTEREST

There are often a number of economic, legal, and operational advantages to a parent-subsidiary relationship. One company may acquire a controlling interest in the voting stock of another in two basic ways, viz:

1. Pooling of interests.   The voting stock of an existing corporation is acquired by the parent by exchanging shares of its own capital stock for the acquired shares of the subsidiary. In this situation, the parent disburses no cash or other resources.
2. Purchase.   The voting stock of an existing corporation is acquired by the parent with cash, noncash assets, or debt, for the acquired shares of the subsidiary. In this situation, the parent disburses a significant amount of resources.

---

[8] Adapted from: Charles H. Griffin, Thomas H. Williams, and Kermit D. Larson, *Advanced Accounting*, rev. ed. (Homewood, Ill.: Richard D. Irwin, Inc., 1971).

## ACCOUNTING AND REPORTING PROBLEMS

Generally accepted accounting principles require that each subsidiary prepare its own financial statements in the usual manner. However, the parent company is required to prepare *consolidated* financial statements which include all subsidiaries, except those designated unconsolidated subsidiaries as described above. In consolidated financial statements, there is an item by item combination (aggregation) of the parent and subsidiary statements. For example, the amount of cash shown on a consolidated statement would be the sum of the amounts of cash shown on the separate statements of the parent and the subsidiaries.

Emphasis in accounting for a controlling interest is on the consolidated financial statements. Either the cost or equity method may be used by the parent company in its accounts; however, the resulting consolidated financial statements must be the same irrespective of the accounting method used in the accounts.[9] Therefore, this part of the chapter will focus on the *preparation* of consolidated financial statements.

In preparing consolidated financial statements, the method of acquistion — pooling of interests versus purchase — has a significant impact both on the parent company and the resultant consolidated statements.

Consolidated financial statements are prepared by means of a worksheet, and the results are not entered in the accounts. In practically all situations, a special worksheet approach is essential. The essential steps on a worksheet can be summarized as follows:[10]

1. The assets and liabilities of the subsidiary are substituted for the investment account as reflected on the books of the parent. This is accomplished by "eliminating" the owner equity accounts of the subsidiary against the investment account of the parent.
2. Elimination of intercompany receivables and payables.
3. Elimination of intercompany revenues, expenses, gains, and losses.
4. Elimination of other intercompany items.
5. Adjustments on the worksheet are made to reflect certain acquisition effects that differ from the book values.

---

[9] In the case of a controlling interest, the investment account may be carried on either the cost or equity basis. The cost basis is often used because the parent company does not desire to formally enter into its accounts the income, dividend offset, depreciation, amortization, and so on, required by the equity method. Also, the accounting periods may be different, and changes in percentage of ownership complicate the formal approach. Not infrequently, a company, when it moves from the equity approach range (i.e., 20%–50%) to a controlling interest range (over 50%), will adjust the accounts from the equity basis to the cost basis for these reasons. Since consolidation is a *reporting* approach, as opposed to an accounts approach, a worksheet is used, and the accounts of the parent are unaffected by the consolidation procedures. Under either method, the consolidation procedures are adapted on the worksheet so that the consolidated results are precisely the same whether the cost or equity method is used in the accounts. The cost method is used in the discussions in this chapter primarily for instructional convenience. When a parent company prepares unconsolidated statements for special purposes, all subsidiaries and other stock investments that qualify must be reported on the equity basis.

[10] It is important to realize that these steps refer to worksheet entries and to the resultant financial statements and not to the books of accounts of the respective entities which are continued as the records of separate legal entities.

6. The remaining revenues and expenses of the parent and subsidiary are combined to derive a consolidated income statement.
7. The assets and liabilities of the parent and subsidiary are combined to derive a consolidated balance sheet.
8. Utilize similar procedures to develop other desired financial statements on a consolidated basis.

Consolidated financial statements are commonly prepared (a) at the date of acquisition of a controlling interest (balance sheet only), and (b) for each accounting period subsequent to acquisition (income statement, balance sheet, and statement of changes in financial position).

## COMBINATION BY POOLING OF INTERESTS

The acquisition of a controlling interest by one company (the parent company) in the stock of another company (the subsidiary company) by an exchange of shares of stock often occurs because the combination can be effected without the disbursement of cash or other resources by the parent company. The exchange of shares is viewed as the *uniting of ownership interests* and not as a purchase/sale transaction between two companies and their shareholders. As a consequence, the recorded assets, liabilities, revenues, expenses, and so forth, for both entities are combined for consolidated statement purposes, at their *recorded* or book amounts. The net income of the parent and its subsidiaries are combined and restated as consolidated net income. Since a purchase/sale transaction is not presumed for the exchange, fair market values of the assets of the subsidary are not considered in consolidation.

*APB Opinion No. 16* specifies that "The combining of existing voting common stock interests by the exchange of stock is the essence of a business combination accounted for by the pooling of interests method." However, the *Opinion* specifies 12 conditions that must be met in order to apply the method; and if they are met, the pooling of interests method *must be used*. All combinations not meeting all of these twelve specifications *must* use the purchase method. Not all stock exchanges will meet the criteria for pooling of interests.

The general characteristics of the pooling of interests method of preparing consolidated statements may be summarized as follows:

1. The assets and liabilities of the combining companies are reported at the previously established *book values* of each. Although adjustments may be made to reflect consistent applications of accounting principles, the current fair values at the time of the combination are not used as a substitute for the book values at that date.
2. No goodwill results from the combination.
3. The retained earnings balances of the combining companies are added to determine the retained earnings balance of the combined companies at date of acquisition.
4. After combination, financial statements which pertain to precombination periods must be restated to reflect the data that would have

been reported had the firms been combined throughout the pre-combination periods being reflected.

We stated earlier that at date of acquisition, a consolidated balance sheet usually is prepared by the parent company; and at the end of each subsequent period, a consolidated income statement, balance sheet, and a statement of changes in financial position are prepared. At this point, we will illustrate preparation of a consolidated balance sheet at date of acquisition, *pooling of interests basis.*

Assume that Company P (parent) acquired 90% of the outstanding voting stock of Company S (subsidiary); therefore, minority share-holders own the remaining 10%. Prior to the exchange, their respective balance sheets reflected the following:

**Amounts Immediately Prior to Acquisition**

| | Company P Book Value | Company S Book Value | Company S Fair Value (appraised) |
|---|---|---|---|
| Cash | $610,000 | $ 20,000 | $ 20,000 |
| Inventories | 20,000 | 30,000 | 25,000 |
| Accounts receivable (net) | 10,000* | 40,000 | 40,000 |
| Plant and equipment (net) | 200,000 | 110,000 | 151,000 |
| Patents (net) | 20,000 | 10,000 | 14,000 |
| | $860,000 | $210,000 | $250,000 |
| Current liabilities | $ 10,000 | $ 20,000* | |
| Long-term liabilities | 50,000 | 40,000 | |
| Common stock (par $100) | 600,000 | 100,000 | |
| Retained earnings | 200,000 | 50,000 | |
| | $860,000 | $210,000 | |

* At date of acquisition, Company S owed Company P $5,000 accounts payable.

Company P issued 900 shares of its $100 par common stock to the shareholders of Company S for 900 shares of the outstanding $100 par common stock of Company S. This is an exchange of shares (a continuity of ownership), and we will assume that it meets the 12 criteria for pooling of interests (one of the criteria requires at least 90% ownership). Company S will continue as a separate legal entity, and as a 90% subsidiary of Company P. The exchange would not affect the books of Company S; however, Company P would make the following entry at date of acquisition:[11]

---

[11] Since this entry is not considered under the pooling of interests concept to be a purchase/sale transaction, it is generally recorded at par value of the stock issued or the proportionate share acquired of the subsidiary's contributed capital. Some accountants prefer to use average contributed capital per share; others prefer market value of the stock issued. This is an unsettled issue; however, in any case, the elimination entry is adapted to attain the pooling of interests result. Par value equal to the proportionate share of the subsidiary's contributed capital is used in this discussion because of its instructional convenience. Consideration of the broader issue is beyond the objective of this chapter (refer to *Advanced Accounting* of this series).

Investment in Company S, common stock (90% ownership)...  90,000
   Common stock (900 shares at $100 par)  ........................  90,000

Now, assume that Company P prepares a consolidated balance sheet immediately after the acquisition; the worksheet used, on a pooling of interests basis, is shown in Exhibit 18–1.

**EXHIBIT 18–1**

Consolidation Worksheet to Develop Balance Sheet (at date of acquisition)
Company P and Its Subsidiary, Company S (90% interest)
Pooling of Interests Basis

|  | Balance Sheet per Books | | Eliminations | | Consolidated Balance Sheet |
|---|---|---|---|---|---|
|  | Company P | Company S | Debit | Credit |  |
| Cash | 610,000 | 20,000 |  |  | 630,000 |
| Inventories | 20,000 | 30,000 |  |  | 50,000 |
| Accounts receivable | 10,000 | 40,000 |  | (b)  5,000 | 45,000 |
| Investment in |  |  |  |  |  |
|   Company S | 90,000* |  |  | (a) 90,000 |  |
| Plant and equipment | 200,000 | 110,000 |  |  | 310,000 |
| Patents | 20,000 | 10,000 |  |  | 30,000 |
|  | 950,000 | 210,000 |  |  | 1,065,000 |
| Current liabilities | 10,000 | 20,000 | (b)  5,000 |  | 25,000 |
| Long-term liabilities | 50,000 | 40,000 |  |  | 90,000 |
| Common stock (par $100): |  |  |  |  |  |
|   Parent | 690,000* |  |  |  | 690,000 |
|   Subsidiary |  | 100,000 | (a) 90,000 |  | 10,000M |
| Retained earnings: |  |  |  |  |  |
|   Parent | 200,000 |  |  |  | 200,000 |
|   Subsidiary |  | 50,000 |  |  | 40,000 |
|  |  |  |  |  | 10,000M |
|  | 950,000 | 210,000 |  |  | 1,065,000 |

M—minority shareholders' 10% interest in Company S.
* Includes effects of acquisition entry.
Eliminations:
  (a) To eliminate the investment account balance against the stockholders' equity (90%) of the subsidiary.
  (b) To eliminate the intercompany debt of $5,000.

The worksheet is started by entering the two separate balance sheets, using *book values* for each company immediately *after* the acquisition entry. Observe, that two accounts on Company P balance sheet have been changed to reflect the above acquisition entry. The worksheet is designed to provide an orderly procedure for combining the two separate statements into a consolidated statement (the last column). The pair of columns for *eliminations* is used to prevent double counting of reciprocal items (i.e., items that are strictly between the two companies). In this instance, there are two such items that must be eliminated, viz:

a. The investment account balance reflected on the balance sheet of Company P ($90,000) must be eliminated because in its place the various assets and liabilities of Company S will be added to those of the parent. Similarly, 90% of the common stock reflected by Company S must be offset because it is owned now by the parent. Thus, entry (a) on the worksheet offsets the investment account balance on the balance sheet of the parent against the stock account reflected on the balance sheet of the subsidiary.

b. Intercompany debt—Included in current liabilities of Company S is a $5,000 debt owed to Company P; therefore, accounts receivable on the balance sheet of Company P also includes this amount. When the two balance sheets are combined, this intercompany debt must be eliminated since there is no debt or receivable involving the combined entity and outsiders. Entry (b) on the worksheet effects this offset.

After the elimination entries for all intercompany items are recorded on the worksheet, the two balance sheets are aggregated horizontally line by line. The 10% interest of the *minority shareholders* of Company S represented by their proportionate share of the owners' equity is set out separately (denoted as M). The last column provides all the data needed to prepare a formal consolidated balance sheet. Note that the *book value* of Company S is added to the book values of Company P; the fair market values given in the data above do not affect a combination by pooling of interests.

## COMBINATION BY PURCHASE

The acquisition of a controlling interest by purchase occurs when the combination does not meet all of the criteria for a pooling of interests. Typically, an acquisition by purchase occurs when the parent company acquires a controlling interest in the subsidiary company by purchasing the voting stock with cash or other resources. This situation is viewed as a purchase/sale exchange transaction and the *fair market values* related to the subsidiary must be introduced into the consolidation procedures in accordance with the cost principle. *APB Opinion No. 16* states: "Accounting for a business combination by the purchase method follows the principles normally applicable under historical cost accounting to recording acquisitions of assets and issuances of stock and to accounting for assets and liabilities after acquisition." This means that the parent company must debit the investment account for the fair market value of the shares of the subsidiary acquired. The significant implication of this requirement is that in preparing consolidated statements, the assets of the subsidiary (including any purchased goodwill) must be valued at their *fair market value at date of acquisition* before being aggregated with the *book values* of the assets of the parent company. Recall that in a pooling of interests, book values rather than fair market values of the subsidiary are used in consolidation.

Although there are numerous complexities in application of the purchase method, the general characteristics may be outlined as follows:

1. The assets and liabilities of the subsidiary are reported by the parent

company at cost at date of acquisition in conformity with the cost principle. Cost is the price paid for the stock of the subsidiary (cash equivalent cost) and is the *fair market value* at that date.

2. Individual assets of the subsidiary are reported at their individual fair values at date of acquisition. This includes all identifiable tangible and intangible assets (land, equipment, patents, etc.). Liabilities of the subsidiary are reported at their present "debt" value.

3. The difference between the total purchase cost and the fair value of the identifiable assets acquired (less the liabilities acquired) is reported as "goodwill from acquisition."[12] Goodwill from acquisition is subsequently amortized as an income statement charge.

4. At date of combination, the retained earnings balance of the combined entity is defined as the retained earnings balance of the parent company; that is, the retained earnings balance of the subsidiary is eliminated (not carried forward).

5. After the combination, financial statements which pertain to precombination periods must depict the historical data of the parent company only.

To illustrate preparation of a consolidated balance sheet immediately after acquisition *by purchase,* we will again use the data given for Company P and Company S on page 768. Assume Company P purchases, in the open market, 90% of the 1,000 shares of outstanding stock of Company S for $211,000 cash. Company S will not make an entry to recognize this sale of stock by its stockholders; however, Company P will record the purchase, at cost, as follows:

| | | |
|---|---|---|
| Investment in Company S, common stock, 900 shares | | |
| (90% ownership, at cost) ............................................. | 211,000 | |
| Cash ......................................................................... | | 211,000 |

Assume that Company P prepares a consolidated balance sheet immediately after acquisition and the purchase method must be used. The first step is to determine the amount of *goodwill purchased* in consideration of the fair market values as follows:

| | | |
|---|---|---|
| Purchase price for an 90% interest in Company S ......... | | $211,000 |
| Book value of Company S purchased ($150,000 × .90) ... | | 135,000 |
| Differential ..................................................... | | 76,000 |
| Adjustments to fair market value (see page 768): | | |
| Inventories ($25,000 − $30,000) × .90..................... | $ (4,500) | |
| Plant and equipment ($151,000 − $110,000) × .90... | 36,900 | |
| Patents ($14,000 − $10,000) × .90 ...................... | 3,600 | |
| Total Adjustments ..................................... | | 36,000 |
| Difference − Goodwill Purchased............................... | | $ 40,000 |

The purchase basis worksheet shown in Exhibit 18–2 is used to de-

---

[12] If total purchase cost is less than the summed fair market values of individual assets and liabilities, the difference is applied to reduce the valuations of the identifiable tangible and intangible assets.

**EXHIBIT 18–2**

Consolidation Worksheet to Develop Balance Sheet (at date of acquisition)
Company P and Its Subsidiary, Company S (90% ownership)
Purchase Basis

| | Balance Sheet per Books | | Eliminations and Adjustments | | Consolidated Balance Sheet |
|---|---|---|---|---|---|
| | Company P | Company S | Debit | Credit | |
| Cash | 399,000* | 20,000 | | | 419,000 |
| Inventories | 20,000 | 30,000 | | (b) 4,500 | 45,500 |
| Accounts receivable | 10,000 | 40,000 | | (c) 5,000 | 45,000 |
| Investment in Company S | 211,000* | | | (a) 211,000 | |
| Plant and equipment (net) | 200,000 | 110,000 | (b) 36,900 | | 346,900 |
| Patents | 20,000 | 10,000 | (b) 3,600 | | 33,600 |
| Goodwill | | | (b) 40,000 | | 40,000 |
| | 860,000 | 210,000 | | | 930,000 |
| Differential | | | (a) 76,000 | (b) 76,000 | |
| Current liabilities | 10,000 | 20,000 | (c) 5,000 | | 25,000 |
| Long-term liabilities | 50,000 | 40,000 | | | 90,000 |
| Common stock: | | | | | |
|   Company P | 600,000 | | | | 600,000 |
|   Company S | | 100,000 | (a) 90,000 | | 10,000M |
| Retained earnings: | | | | | |
|   Company P | 200,000 | | | | 200,000 |
|   Company S | | 50,000 | (a) 45,000 | | 5,000M |
| | 860,000 | 210,000 | | | 930,000 |

M—minority shareholders' 10% interest in Company S.

* Includes effects of the acquisition entry.

Adjustments and eliminations:

  (a) To eliminate investment account balance against stockholders' equity (90% ownership) and to enter the differential of $76,000 (see prior computation of goodwill).

  (b) To apportion the differential and to convert the assets of Company S from book value to fair market value (see prior computation of goodwill).

  (c) To eliminate the intercompany debt.

velop the consolidated balance sheet. The worksheet is started by entering the two balance sheets, using amounts immediately after the acquisition entry. Observe that two accounts (i.e., cash and investments) on Company P balance sheets have been changed to reflect the acquisition entry. Also, the middle pair of columns are headed "eliminations and adjustments" because (a) the eliminating entries must be made, and (b) the assets of Company S must be *adjusted* from book value to fair market value. In respect to the latter, the above computation of goodwill reflects that inventories must be reduced by $4,500, plant and equipment increased by $36,900, patents increased by $3,600, and goodwill recorded as $40,000. These eliminations and adjustments are explained below the worksheet. The worksheet is completed by extending each item horizontally, taking into consideration the eliminations and adjustments. The last column provides all of the data needed to prepare a formal consolidated balance sheet, on the purchase basis.

In summary, a comparison of Exhibit 18–1 with Exhibit 18–2 reflects the following underlying conceptual difference: in pooling of interests the book values of the subsidiary are added to the book values of the parent, whereas in a purchase the market values of the subsidiary at acquisition are added to the book values of the parent. In the illustrations of consolidation to follow, this basic difference will be maintained in the combined statements for subsequent periods.

## PREPARING CONSOLIDATED STATEMENTS SUBSEQUENT TO ACQUISITION

At the end of each accounting period subsequent to acquisition of a controlling interest in another company, the parent company must prepare consolidated statements of income, balance sheet, and changes in financial position. The worksheet illustrated above can be expanded to develop a consolidated balance sheet and income statement. A separate worksheet usually is needed to develop a consolidated statement of changes in financial position.

In this section, an expanded worksheet to develop a consolidated balance sheet and income statement subsequent to acquisition will be illustrated assuming (a) pooling of interests, and (b) purchase. The same data will be used for both illustrations. The section will conclude with an illustration of the formal consolidated statements (purchase basis).

### Pooling of Interests Basis

For illustrative purposes, assume that Company P acquired a 90% interest in Company S on January 1, 19A. Company P issued 9,000 shares of its own common stock (par $10) in exchange for 9,000 shares of Company S stock (par $10) which represented 90% of the 10,000 shares outstanding. Assume this acquisition meets the 12 criteria for pooling of interests. Consequently, at acquisition date, Company P recorded the acquisition on a pooling of interests basis as follows:

January 1, 19A:

| | | |
|---|---|---|
| Investment in Company S, common stock (9,000 shares; 90% interest) | 90,000 | |
| Common stock (9,000 shares) | | 90,000 |

Assume one year later, at December 31, 19A, the separate income statements and balance sheets prepared by Companies P and S reflected the following:

At December 31, 19A

|  | Company P | Company S |
|---|---|---|
| **Income Statement:** | | |
| Sales | $520,000 | $105,000 [a] |
| Cost of goods sold | 300,000 [a] | 53,000 |
| Depreciation | 20,000 | 4,000 |
| Other expenses | 140,000 | 36,000 |
| Total | 460,000 | 93,000 |
| Net Income | $ 60,000 | $ 12,000 |
| **Balance Sheet:** | | |
| Current assets | $387,000 [b] | $ 86,000 |
| Investment in Company S (90%) | 80,000 [c] | |
| Fixed assets, net | 480,000 | 76,000 |
| Total | $947,000 | $162,000 |
| Liabilities | $ 97,000 | $ 40,000 [b] |
| Common stock | 680,000 (par $10) | 100,000 (par $10) |
| Retained earnings | 170,000 [d] | 22,000 [d] |
| Total | $947,000 | $162,000 |

[a] Includes intercompany sales of $7,000 (transferred at cost).
[b] Includes intercompany debt of $3,000.
[c] Pooling of interests basis.
[d] Retained earnings balance at date of acquisition: Company P, $110,000; Company S, $10,000.

The expanded consolidation worksheet is shown in Exhibit 18–3 (on a pooling of interests basis). Note that it is the same as the worksheet shown in Exhibit 18–1 (consolidated balance sheet at acquisition) with the addition of the income statement. The reported amounts from the separate statements are entered directly on the worksheet. For worksheet convenience, and to facilitate understanding, common stock, retained earnings at date of acquisition, and income since acquisition are set out separately. The worksheet involves only one item not previously discussed – the $7,000 intercompany sales. During the year, Company S transferred to Company P goods with a cost of $7,000. Company S recorded this as a sale, and Company P recorded it as a purchase (cost of goods sold). This is an intercompany item that must be eliminated to prevent double counting – when Company P sold the goods to outsiders, a sale was recorded at that time.[13] The eliminations are explained at the bottom of the worksheet. Since the consolidated statements are prepared on a pooling of interests basis, the *book values* of the two companies are aggregated item by item. Note that consolidated income is the sum of the net income amounts reported by the companies separately; the same is true with respect to consolidated retained earnings.

---

[13] The elimination of intercompany sales of $7,000 assumed the goods were transferred at cost. If (a) the transfer price included an element of profit for the selling entity, and (b) the goods were still held by the purchasing entity, the profit residue (unrealized intercompany inventory profit) would be eliminated by debiting Sales for the sales price, crediting Cost of Goods Sold for the cost price, and crediting Ending Inventory for the markup.

**EXHIBIT 18–3**

Worksheet to Develop Consolidated Income Statement and Balance Sheet
Company P and Its Subsidiary, Company S (90% ownership) at December 31, 19A
Pooling of Interests Basis

| | Reported Amounts | | Eliminations | | Consolidated Statements |
|---|---|---|---|---|---|
| | Company P | Company S | Debit | Credit | |
| Income Statement: | | | | | |
| Sales | 520,000 | 105,000 | (c)  7,000 | | 618,000 |
| Cost of goods sold | 300,000 | 53,000 | | (c)  7,000 | 346,000 |
| Depreciation | 20,000 | 4,000 | | | 24,000 |
| Other expenses | 140,000 | 36,000 | | | 176,000 |
| Total | 460,000 | 93,000 | | | 546,000 |
| Income (carried down) | 60,000 | 12,000 | | | 72,000 |
| Apportioned for consolidation: | | | | | |
| Minority interest (.10 × $12,000) | | | | | 1,200M |
| Parent interest | | | | | 70,800 |
| | | | | | |
| Balance Sheet: | | | | | |
| Current assets | 387,000 | 86,000 | (b)  3,000 | | 470,000 |
| Investment in Company S | 90,000* | | | (a) 90,000 | |
| Fixed assets (net) | 480,000 | 76,000 | | | 556,000 |
| Total | 957,000 | 162,000 | | | 1,026,000 |
| Liabilities: | 97,000 | 40,000 | (b)  3,000 | | 134,000 |
| Common stock: | | | | | |
| Company P (par $10) | 690,000* | | | | 690,000 |
| Company S (par $10) | | 100,000 | (a) 90,000 | | 10,000M |
| Retained earnings (at acquisition): | | | | | |
| Company P | 110,000 | | | | 110,000 |
| Company S | | 10,000 | | | 9,000 |
| | | | | | 1,000M |
| Income (from above) | 60,000 | 12,000 | | | 70,800 |
| | | | | | 1,200M |
| Total | 957,000 | 162,000 | | | 1,026,000 |

M—minority interests' share in Company S (10%).

* Includes effects of the acquisition entry.

Eliminations:
(a)  To eliminate investment account balance against stockholders' equity (90% ownership) of the subsidiary.
(b)  To eliminate intercompany debt, $3,000.
(c)  To eliminate intercompany sales, $7,000 (at cost).

**Purchase Basis**

Assume the same facts for Company P and Company S as given on page 768 except that the acquisition was effected by purchase. Assume at date of acquisition, that Company P purchased 90% of the outstanding stock of Company S for $124,000 cash. Also assume that the fixed assets of Company S had a *fair market value* of $10,000 greater than their then book value (as reflected on the books of Company S at acquisition date); the current assets of Company S essentially reflect fair market value. On date of acquisition, Company P recorded the purchase of the 90% interest as follows:[14]

January 1, 19A:

Investment in Company S, common stock (9,000 shares,
at cost) ................................................................... 124,000
    Cash .................................................................           124,000

The analysis of the purchase to determine purchased goodwill at acquisition date:

Purchase price for 90% interest in Company S ........................ $124,000
Book value of Company S purchased ($110,000 × 90) ..............   99,000
    Differential ...............................................................   25,000
Adjustments to fair market value:
    Fixed assets ($10,000 × .90) .............................................    9,000
Difference — Goodwill Purchased........................................... $  16,000

Assume the fixed assets have a 10-year remaining life (straight-line depreciation) and that goodwill will be amortized over 40 years.

The expanded consolidation worksheet is shown in Exhibit 18–4 on the purchase basis. Note that it follows the format shown in Exhibit 18–2 (consolidated balance sheet at date of acquisition) with the addition of the income statement. Recall that on the worksheet (Exhibit 18–2) there are (a) adjustments of the assets of Company S to fair market value, and (b) eliminations of intercompany reciprocal items. Exhibit 18–4 includes one additional concept not previously discussed; that is, the write-up of Company S assets, including goodwill, necessitates *adjustments* for additional depreciation and the amortization of goodwill for the period (adjustment [c]). The eliminations and adjustments are explained below the worksheet.

The consolidated income statement and balance sheet for Company P are shown in Exhibit 18–5. Note in particular the presentation of the 10% interest in Company S owned by the minority shareholders; alternatively it may be shown as a separate caption in shareholders' equity. Also, the balance sheet uses a more appropriate title for goodwill, cost of investment in excess of fair value of identifiable net assets of subsidiary.

---

[14] This entry changes two amounts on the balance sheet of Company P, viz:

Investment account (at cost)..................................................... $124,000
Current assets (i.e., cash) $387,000 − $124,000 ..........................  263,000

**EXHIBIT 18–4**

Worksheet to Develop Consolidated Income Statement and Balance Sheet
Company P and Its Subsidiary, Company S (90% ownership), at December 31, 19A
Purchase Basis

| | Reported Amounts | | Eliminations | | Consolidated Statements |
|---|---|---|---|---|---|
| | Company P | Company S | Debit | Credit | |
| Income Statement: | | | | | |
| Sales | 520,000 | 105,000 | *(d)* 7,000 | | 618,000 |
| Cost of goods sold | 300,000 | 53,000 | | *(d)* 7,000 | 346,000 |
| Depreciation | 20,000 | 4,000 | *(c)* 900 | | 24,900 |
| Other expenses | 140,000 | 36,000 | | | 176,000 |
| Amortization goodwill | | | *(c)* 400 | | 400 |
| Total | 460,000 | 93,000 | | | 547,300 |
| Income (carried down) | 60,000 | 12,000 | | | 70,700 |
| Minority interest (.10 × $12,000) | | | | | 1,200M |
| Parent interest | | | | | 69,500 |
| Differential | | | *(a)* 25,000 | *(b)* 25,000 | |
| | | | | | |
| Balance Sheet: | | | | | |
| Current assets | 263,000* | 86,000 | | *(e)* 3,000 | 346,000 |
| Investment in Company S | 124,000* | | | *(a)* 124,000 | |
| Fixed assets (net) | 480,000 | 76,000 | *(b)* 9,000 | *(c)* 900 | 564,100 |
| Goodwill | | | *(b)* 16,000 | *(c)* 400 | 15,600 |
| Total | 867,000 | 162,000 | | | 925,700 |
| Liabilities | 97,000 | 40,000 | *(e)* 3,000 | | 134,000 |
| Common stock: | | | | | |
| Company P (par $10) | 600,000 | | | | 600,000 |
| Company S (par $10) | | 100,000 | *(a)* 90,000 | | 10,000M |
| Retained earnings at acquisition): | | | | | |
| Company P | 110,000 | | | | 110,000 |
| Company S | | 10,000 | *(a)* 9,000 | | 1,000M |
| Income (from above) | 60,000 | 12,000 | | | 1,200M |
| | | | | | 69,500 |
| Total | 867,000 | 162,000 | | | 925,700 |

M—minority interest share in Company S (10%).

* Includes effects of acquisition entry (purchase basis).

Adjustments and eliminations:
*(a)* Elimination of investment account balance against stockholders' equity of Company S (90%) and to enter the differential of $25,000 (see prior computation of goodwill).
*(b)* To apportion the differential as an adjustment of the fixed assets of Company S to their fair market value at date of acquisition (see prior computation of goodwill).
*(c)* To record additional depreciation on fixed assets and amortization of goodwill for one year.
*(d)* To eliminate intercompany sales, $7,000 (at cost).
*(e)* To eliminate intercompany debt outstanding at December 31, 19A, $3,000.

**EXHIBIT 18–5**

COMPANY P AND SUBSIDIARY, COMPANY S
Consolidated Income Statement (unclassified)
For the Year Ended December 31, 19A

| | | |
|---|---:|---:|
| Sales | | $618,000 |
| Expenses: | | |
| Cost of goods sold | $346,000 | |
| Depreciation | 24,900 | |
| Other expenses | 176,000 | |
| Amortization of goodwill | 400 | 547,300 |
| Consolidated net income | | 70,700 |
| Minority interest in net income (10%) | | 1,200 |
| Controlling Interest in Net Income | | $ 69,500 |

Consolidated Balance Sheet (unclassified), December 31, 19A

*Assets*

| | | |
|---|---:|---:|
| Current assets | | $346,000 |
| Fixed assets (net) | | 564,100 |
| Cost of investment in subsidiary in excess of fair value of identifiable net assets of subsidiary (goodwill) | | 15,600 |
| Total Assets | | $925,700 |

*Liabilities and Shareholders' Equity*

| | | |
|---|---:|---:|
| Liabilities | | $134,000 |
| Minority interest in Company S (10%): | | |
| Common stock | $ 10,000 | |
| Retained earnings | 2,200 | 12,200 |
| Shareholders' Equity: | | |
| Common stock, par $10, 60,000 shares outstanding | 600,000 | |
| Retained earnings | 179,500 | 779,500 |
| Total Liabilities and Shareholders' Equity | | $925,700 |

Most *published* financial statements are consolidated statements involving one or a number of subsidiaries. Full disclosure on consolidated statements normally requires extensive use of notes to the statements as illustrated in the Appendixes to Chapters 4 and 5.

In summary, we can compare the results of pooling of interests with purchase as reflected in the common situation used in Exhibits 18–3 and 18–4, viz:

| | Basis | | Difference— |
|---|---|---|---|
| | | | Pooling |
| | Pooling | Purchase | over Purchase |
| Net income: | | | |
| Parent interest | $ 70,800 | $ 69,500 | $ 1,300 |
| Minority interest | 1,200 | 1,200 | -0- |
| Current assets (i.e., cash) | 470,000 | 346,000 | 124,000 |
| Fixed assets (net) | 556,000 | 564,100 | (8,100) |
| Goodwill | -0- | 15,600 | (15,600) |
| Liabilities | 134,000 | 134,000 | -0- |
| Capital stock | 690,000 | 600,000 | 90,000 |
| Retained earnings: | | | |
| Parent interest | 189,800 | 179,500 | 10,300 |
| Minority interest | 2,200 | 2,200 | -0- |

Net income is lower under the purchase basis because that approach requires that the assets of the subsidiary be adjusted to fair market value and that goodwill be recognized, each of which must be allocated on an annual basis to expense ($900 + $400 = $1,300). Cash and capital stock are lower under the purchase basis because, at acquisition, cash rather than capital stock is used to acquire the controlling interest. Purchase basis requires recognition of fair market values (for subsidiary assets) and purchased goodwill which caused the $15,600 difference. Retained earnings are higher under pooling of interests because it is the sum of the parent and subsidiary amounts, whereas when the purchase method is used, retained earnings of the subsidiary is eliminated. The minority interest in net income and retained earnings is the same under both methods.

Principally because of the (a) effect on cash and (b) accounting effects on net income and retained earnings, companies prefer pooling of interests. On the other hand, the stockholders of the acquired company often prefer cash to stock in the parent company. In respect to the accounting aspects, and the opportunity to manipulate reported earnings, the APB in *Opinion No. 16* placed severe restrictions (12 in number) on use of the pooling of interests approach. Also, in conformity with the full-disclosure concept, *Opinion No. 16*, paragraphs 64 and 95, specifies a number of items that must be explained in the notes to the consolidated financial statements; these vary somewhat between pooling of interests and purchase.

## SOME SPECIAL PROBLEMS IN ACCOUNTING FOR STOCK INVESTMENTS

Several problems relating to the acquisition, holding, and sale of stock investments are discussed in the remaining paragraphs.

### Stock Dividends on Investment Shares

In order to conserve cash and yet make a distribution to shareholders, a corporation may issue a dividend using its own shares of stock as payment. Such a dividend is referred to as a stock dividend. When a stock dividend is issued, the distributing corporation debits Retained Earnings and credits the appropriate capital stock accounts (see Chapter 16). The effect of a stock dividend as far as the issuing corporation is concerned is to "capitalize" a part of retained earnings; significantly, a stock dividend does not decrease the assets of the issuing corporation.

From the investor's point of view, the nature of a stock dividend is suggested by the effect on the issuing corporation. In effect, the investor does not receive assets or revenue from the corporation; neither does he or she own more of the issuing corporation. The investor does have more shares to represent the same prior proportional ownership. Thus, the receipt of a stock dividend in the same class of shares as already owned results, from the standpoint of the investor's records, in more shares but no increase in the cost (carrying value) of the holdings. Since such a dividend involves no distribution of corporate assets and does not affect the proportional interest of the stockholder in the assets of the corporation whose stock is held, the investor should make no entry for revenue nor change the investment account other than to record a memorandum entry for the number of shares received. In case of a sale of any of the shares, a new cost per share is computed by adding the new shares to the old and dividing this sum into the carrying value. To illustrate, assume X purchased 100 shares of stock at $90 and subsequently received a 50% dividend payable in identical stock, and later sold 20 shares at $85. A schedule showing the gain or loss on the sale and the balance remaining in the investment account (cost method) follows:[15]

|  | Shares | Cost per Share | Total Cost Price | Sales Price | Gain (Loss) |
|---|---|---|---|---|---|
| Purchase .............. | 100 | $90 | $9,000 |  |  |
| Stock dividend ...... | 50 |  | 0 |  |  |
| Total ............ | 150 | 60 | 9,000 |  |  |
| Sold ..................... | 20 | 60 | 1,200 | $1,700 | $500 |
| Ending Balance ...... | 130 | 60 | $7,800 |  |  |

If the stock dividend is of a different class of stock than that on which the dividend is declared, such as preferred stock received as a dividend on common stock, three methods of accounting for the dividend have been suggested:

1. Record the new stock in terms of shares only, and when it is sold recognize the total sales price as a gain.
2. Record the new stock at an amount determined by apportioning the carrying value of the old stock between the new stock and the old stock on the basis of the fair market value of the different classes of stock *after* issuance of the dividend.
3. Do not change the carrying value of the old stock but record the new stock on the books at its market value upon receipt with an offsetting credit to dividend revenue. This method is predicated on the assumption that stock of a different class received as a dividend is no different from a property dividend.

Of these three methods the first is the most conservative, the second is theoretically sound and more in keeping with generally accepted accounting principles, while the third is the least logical. To illustrate the second method, assume an investor purchased 50 shares of X Company common stock for $7,500. When the market value of the common stock was $10,000 the industry received a stock dividend of 20 shares of

---

[15] Under the Internal Revenue Code stock dividends are exempt from taxation except (a) where the shareholder can elect to take cash rather than stock for the dividend, and (b) when stock dividends satisfy dividend preference requirements.

X preferred stock having a fair market value of $2,500. Using the relative sales value method the cost may be apportioned as follows:

$$\text{Apportioned Cost} - \text{Common} = \$7,500 \times \frac{\$10,000}{\$12,500} = \$6,000$$

$$\text{Apportioned Cost} - \text{Preferred} = \$7,500 \times \frac{\$2,500}{\$12,500} = \underline{\quad 1,500}$$

$$\$7,500$$

Indicated entry:

| | | |
|---|---|---|
| Investment in preferred stock of X Company........................... | 1,500 | |
|    Investment in common stock of X Company ..................... | | 1,500 |

## Stock Split of Investment Shares

A stock split is effected when a corporation issues new or additional shares without "capitalizing" (debiting) retained earnings or otherwise adding to the dollar amount of *legal capital*. In a stock split the number of shares outstanding is increased, accompanied by a proportionate decrease in the par or stated value per share of stock (refer to Chapters 16 and 17). Thus, a stock split is essentially different from a stock dividend from the point of view of the issuer but very similar from the point of view of the investor. To the latter a stock dividend is not income. A two-for-one stock split means, for example, that the holder of shares at the date of the split will receive two shares in place of each old share held; concurrently, the par or stated value per share of stock is halved. To the investor this merely means that he or she has twice as many shares after the split to represent the same total cost as was had before. The accounting for investment shares where there is a stock split simply involves a memorandum entry for the number of shares received; the resulting "cost per share" is reduced proportionately.

## Convertible Securities

In recent years there has been a significant increase in the use of convertible securities. An enterprise may invest in preferred stock or bonds that are convertible into common stock under specified conditions. An accounting measurement problem arises at the time of conversion since the cost or book value of the convertible securities generally is different from the market value of the common stock received at the time of conversion. Two alternative views are held on this point:

1. At date of conversion record the book value of the convertible security given up as the cost of the new security received, thus no gain or loss upon conversion would be recognized. This position is supported by the arguments that (a) the original transaction is continuing to materialize; prearranged conversion does not constitute a distinct exchange transaction, (b) conversion usually is at the option of the investor, and (c) most conversions do not give rise to a taxable gain or loss.

2. At date of conversion record the new security received at its fair market value and recognize a gain or loss on conversion. This position is supported by the arguments that (a) a distinct and separate exchange transaction has occurred, (b) market value is objective evidence of the "value received," and (c) this is similar to the exchange of any other asset and should be accounted for accordingly.

The former view tends to prevail in practice although the latter appears to be theoretically preferable. Also see Chapter 19.

### Stock Rights on Investment Shares

The privilege accorded stockholders (investors) of purchasing additional shares of stock from the issuing corporation at a specific price and by a specified future date commonly is known as a *stock right*. The term *stock right* is usually interpreted to mean the right related to *each share of old stock*. Therefore, a holder of ten shares of stock who receives the rights to subscribe for five new shares is said to own ten stock rights rather than five; that is, there is one right per old share irrespective of the "new" share arrangement. Rights have value when the holder can buy added shares through *exercise* of his or her rights at a lower price per share than can persons buying similar shares on the market without rights. As the spread between the privileged subscription price and the market price of shares bought without rights changes subsequent to issuance of the rights, the value of the rights will change.

When the intention to issue stock rights is declared, obviously the stock will start selling in the market "rights on"; that is, purchasers have time to "register" newly bought shares in their names so as to secure the rights when issued. Therefore, the market price of the share sold "rights on" is the price of a share and a right. After the rights are issued the shares will sell in the market "ex rights." After issuance, rights usually will have as ready a market as the related stock and thus will be quoted at a specific market price.

The accounting problems surrounding stock rights are important since some stockholders prefer to sell their rights rather than to exercise them, in which event any gain on rights sold must be determined and entries made to reflect allocation of the cost of the old shares between the rights and the stock. After rights are received the investor has shares of stock and stock rights, both arising out of the single original cost commitment. To determine the gain or loss on the sale of either stock or rights, it is necessary to apportion the total cost of the investment between the stock and the rights. This is done by the use of the relative sales value method; that is, the total cost of the old shares is divided between the old stock and the rights in proportion to their respective market values at the time that the rights are issued.

### Illustrative Problem

A comprehensive illustration is presented to indicate the entries which would be made in the case of stock rights. Assume an investor purchased 500 shares of stock in the XY Corporation at $93 per share, and later by reason of the ownership of such stock received 500 stock rights entitling the investor to subscribe to 100 additional shares at $100 per share. Upon the issuance of the rights, each share of stock on which the rights were issued had a fair market value of $120 (ex rights), and the rights had a fair market value of $4 each when issued.

Case A—Assume that instead of subscribing for the additional shares, the investor later sold the rights at $4.50 each.

Case B—Assume the investor exercised his or her rights to subscribe to the additional shares and later sold one of the new shares for $140.

*Solution:*

### Case A—Investor's Entries

a. Investment—stock of XY Corporation............................ 46,500
    Cash .................................................................     46,500
    For purchase of 500 shares at $93 = $46,500.

b. Investment—stock rights XY Corporation* ..................... 1,500
    Investment—stock of XY Corporation........................     1,500

    Allocation:
    Shares: $\frac{\$120}{\$124} \times \$46,500 = \$45,000$

    Rights: $\frac{\$4}{\$124} \times \$46,500 =$   1,500
        Total Cost ......... $46,500

c. Cash ................................................................. 2,250
    Investment—stock rights XY Corporation .................     1,500
    Gain on sale of stock rights ...................................     750
    For sale of the 500 stock rights at $4.50 each.

### Case B—Investor's Entries

a. Investment—stock of XY Corporation—first purchase ...... 46,500
    Cash .................................................................     46,500
    To record purchase of 500 shares at $93 = $46,500.

b. Investment—stock rights XY Corporation ........................ 1,500
    Investment stock of XY Corporation—first purchase...     1,500
    To allocate cost of 500 rights as computed in Case A.

c. Investment—stock of XY Corporation—second
    purchase ............................................................. 11,500
    Investment—stock rights XY Corporation .................     1,500
    Cash .................................................................     10,000
    To record exercise of rights and receipt of 100 new shares of stock.

d. Cash ................................................................. 140
    Investment—stock of XY Corporation—second
    purchase .........................................................     115
    Gain on sale of stock investment.............................     25
    To record sale of one new share; cost,
    $11,500 ÷ 100 = $115.

In the unlikely event the rights are not sold or exercised, they will lapse. In this situation, theoretically a loss equivalent to the allocated cost of the rights should be recognized. However, as a practical matter, the allocation entry usually is simply reversed.

## SPECIAL-PURPOSE FUNDS

Companies often set aside cash, and sometimes other assets, in special funds to be used in the future for a specific purpose. Funds may be set aside by contract, as in the case of a bond sinking fund, or voluntarily, as in the case of a plant expansion fund. Special-purpose funds may be either a current asset, as in the case of short-term investments, or a noncurrent asset, when they are not directly related to current operations. The latter are classified under the caption "Long-term Investments and Funds" (see Chapter 5). Typical long-term funds are:

1. Funds set aside to retire a specific long-term liability, such as bonds payable, mortgages payable, long-term notes payable (see Chapters 6 and 11).
2. Funds set aside to retire preferred stock (see Chapter 6).
3. Funds set aside to purchase major assets, such as land, buildings, and plant (see Chapters 6 and 13).

Typically, special-purpose funds are deposited with a *trustee*, such as a financial institution. In this situation, arrangements usually are agreed to whereby a specific rate of interest will be earned each period on the balance in the fund. Usually, the return earned on the fund each period is added to the fund balance. Depending upon the agreement, a fund increases (a) on a compound interest basis at an agreed rate, or (b) by the actual amount earned on the fund.

A special-purpose fund may be created (a) by making a single contribution at the start (an amount of 1 situation), or (b) by making equal periodic contributions (an annuity of 1 situation). The concepts, fund accumulation tables, and related accounting entries were comprehensively discussed and illustrated in Chapter 6. Liability funds were discussed in Chapter 11, and future asset acquisition funds in Chapter 13.

## QUESTIONS

1. Distinguish between debt and equity securities; also between short-term and long-term investments.

2. What accounting principle is applied in recording the acquisition of an investment? Explain its applications in cash and noncash acquisitions.

3. Explain why interest revenue is accrued on investments but dividend revenue is not accrued.

4. In accounting under the cost method, no distinction is made between voting and nonvoting stock, alternatively, the distinction is important with respect to the equity and consolidation approaches. Explain.

5. Briefly define and distinguish between (a) controlling interest, (b) significant influence but not control, and (c) neither control nor significant influence. Briefly explain the effect of each situation on accounting for long-term investments.

6. Explain when the cost method of accounting for equity investments is applicable.

7. Explain the application of the lower-of-cost-or-market concept to long-term investments to equity securities.

8. Explain the basic features of the equity method of accounting for long-term investments. When is it applicable? In an overall perspective, what method is it most closely related to (cost, market value, pooling of interests, purchase)? Explain.

9. Assume Company R acquired, as a long-term investment, 30% of the outstanding voting common stock of Company S at a cash cost of $100,000. At date of acquisition, the balance sheet of Company S showed total shareholders' equity of $250,000. The fair market value of the assets of Company S was $20,000 greater than their book value at date of acquisition. Compute goodwill purchased. What accounting method should be used? Explain why.

10. Assume the same facts as given in Question 9, with the additional data that the net assets have a remaining estimated life of 10 years and goodwill will be amortized over 20 years (assume no residual values and straight line). How much additional depreciation and amortization expense should be reflected by the investor, Company R, each year in accounting for this long-term investment?

11. The equity method of accounting for a long-term investment usually will reflect a larger amount of investment revenue than would the cost method under the same circumstances. Explain why.

12. Explain the basic features of the market value method of accounting for investments. Is it a generally accepted method? Explain the basis for your response.

13. How would the market value method of accounting for investments, in contrast to the cost method, tend to prevent "managed" earnings?

14. When does a parent/subsidiary relationship exist? Identify and briefly explain the two basic elements that must be present as a basis for preparing consolidated financial statements.

15. Outline the characteristics of an acquisition transaction of a long-term investment that would generally indicate (a) a pooling of interests, and (b) a purchase situation.

16. Contrast the primary effects on the balance sheet and income statement of a pooling of interests versus a purchase. Why are the effects different?

17. Explain why fair market values are used in the purchase method but not in the pooling of interests method.

18. Explain why goodwill is recognized in a purchase but not in a pooling of interests.

19. What are intercompany items? Why must they be eliminated in preparing consolidated financial statements?

20. What is meant by minority interest in consolidated statements? How is this interest reported on (a) the income statement, and (b) the balance sheet?

21. Explain the basic reasons why many companies, other things being equal, would prefer the pooling of interests method over the purchase method of accounting for parent/subsidiary relationships.

22. Fundamentally, the investor accounts for a stock dividend and a stock split in the same way. Briefly, explain the accounting that should be followed by the investor in these situations.

23. What is a convertible security? Assume an investor has a convertible security with a book value of $200,000 which is turned in to the issuer for conversion. The investor receives, in conformance with the conversion, common stock with a current fair market value of $225,000. Explain how the investor should account for the conversion of this long-term investment.

24. What is a stock right (or warrant)? If they have a market value, briefly how would the investor account for the receipt of stock rights?

## DECISION CASE 18-1

May Corporation is currently negotiating a combination with Nott Corporation, a successful enterprise that would complement the operations of May. An important factor in the negotiations has been the potential effects of the merger on May's financial statements. Accordingly, May management has requested that pro forma (i.e., as if) financial statements be prepared under two assumptions.

The balance sheets for the two corporations for the year just ended (prior to combination) is shown in the following table:

| | May Corporation | Nott Corporation Book Value | Nott Corporation Appraised Value |
|---|---|---|---|
| Balance Sheet: | | | |
| Cash | $   485,000 | $    15,000 | |
| Receivables (net) | 30,000 | 65,000 | $  50,000 |
| Inventories | 85,000 | 70,000 | 70,000 |
| Land | 50,000 | | |
| Plant | 600,000 | 100,000 | 230,000 |
| Patents | 10,000 | 30,000 | 40,000 |
| | $1,260,000 | $  280,000 | |
| Current liabilities | $    40,000 | $    15,000 | |
| Long-term liabilities | 110,000 | 25,000 | |
| Common stock (par $100) | 1,000,000 | 200,000 | |
| Retained earnings | 110,000 | 40,000 | |
| | $1,260,000 | $  280,000 | |
| Income Statement: | | | |
| Sales | $6,000,000 | $1,000,000 | |
| Costs and expenses (excluding depreciation and amortization) | 5,754,000 | 967,000 | |
| Depreciation | 65,000 | 10,000 | |
| Amortization of patents | 1,000 | 3,000 | |
| Income | 180,000 | 20,000 | |

At year-end Nott Corporation owed a $10,000 current liability to May Corporation. For case purposes, assume that all depreciable assets and intangible assets have a remaining useful life of ten years from date of combination.

*Required:*

1. Assume that May will purchase all of the outstanding stock of Nott for a cash consideration of $460,000.
   a. Give the pro forma entry for the investment.
   b. Prepare a pro forma balance sheet on a purchase basis (or if you prefer, present a pro forma consolidation worksheet).
2. Assume instead that May obtained all of the outstanding shares of Nott by exchanging stock on a share for share basis.
   a. Give the pro forma entry for the exchange.
   b. Prepare a pro forma balance sheet (or worksheet) on a pooling of interests basis.
3. Identify the amounts on the two balance sheets that will be different between (1) and (2) above and explain the reasons for each. Identify and explain the amounts that would be different on the income statements for the next period as between (1) and (2).
4. Which alternative would you recommend to the management of May Corporation? Why?

## EXERCISES

### Exercise 18-1

On September 1, 1976, Thomas Company acquired, on a cash basis, the two securities listed below as long-term investments:

a. Bond payable of Dawson Company, maturity value, $20,000, 6% interest payable each August 31; purchased at par value.
b. Preferred stock of Castor Company, par $20, shares purchased, 1,000 at par. The preferred is 6% cumulative; and in the past, annual dividends have been paid during the latter part of August.

*Required:*

1. Give the entry to record each investment.
2. Assume it is December 31, 1976, end of the accounting period. Give any adjusting entries that should be made in respect to the two investments. Explain the basis for your response for each investment and show any computations.

### Exercise 18-2

During 19A Franklin Company purchased shares in two corporations, as indicated below, with the intention of holding them as long-term investments; purchases were in the following order:

a. Purchased 100 shares of the 10,000 shares outstanding of common stock of M Corporation at $31 per share plus a 5% brokerage fee and transfer cost of $45.
b. Purchased 200 shares of preferred stock (nonvoting) of N Corporation at $78 per share plus a 3% brokerage fee and transfer costs of $42.

c. Purchased 20 shares of common stock of M Corporation at $35 per share plus a 5% brokerage fee and transfer costs of $5.
d. Received $.20 per share cash dividend on the N Corporation stock (out of earnings since acquisition).

*Required:*

1. Give the indicated entries in the accounts of Franklin Company for transactions (a), (b), (c), and (d). Assume the cost method is appropriate.
2. The market value of the shares held at the end of 19A were: M stock, $34; N stock, $75. Give the appropriate adjusting entry for Franklin Company; show computations.
3. The market value of the shares held at the end of 19B were: M stock, $36; N stock, $77. Give the appropriate adjusting entry with computations.
4. Show how the income statement and balance sheet for Franklin Company would reflect the long-term investments for 19A and 19B.

## Exercise 18-3

Adams Company purchased common stock (par value $50) of the Baker Corporation as a long-term investment. Transactions related to this investment were as follows and in the order given.

a. Purchased 500 shares of the common stock at $90 per share (designated as lot No. 1).
b. Purchased 2,000 shares of the common stock at $95 per share (designated as lot No. 2).
c. At the end of the first year, Baker Corporation reported a net income of $52,000.
d. Baker Corporation paid a cash dividend on the common stock of $2 per share.
e. After reporting a net income of $5,000 for the second year, Baker Corporation issued a stock dividend whereby each stockholder received one additional share for each two shares owned. At the time of the stock dividend the stock was selling at $85.
f. Baker Corporation revised its charter to provide for a stock split. The par value was reduced to $25. The "old" common stock was turned in, and the holders received in exchange two shares of the new stock for each old share owned.

*Required:*

Give the entries for each transaction as they should be made in the accounts of Adams Company. Show computations. Assume the cost method and less than 20% ownership throughout.

## Exercise 18-4

On January 1, 1975, Smith Company purchased 300 of the 1,000 outstanding shares of common stock of Rankin Corporation for $23,200. At that date, the balance sheet of Rankin showed the following book values:

| | |
|---|---|
| Assets not subject to depreciation | $40,000 |
| Assets subject to depreciation (net) | 26,000* |
| Liabilities | 6,000 |
| Common stock (par $50) | 50,000 |
| Retained earnings | 10,000 |

*Fair market value, $30,000; the assets have a ten-year remaining life (straight-line depreciation).

*Required:*

1. Assuming the equity method is appropriate, give the entry by Smith to record the acquisition at a cost of $23,200. Assume a long-term investment.
2. Show the computation of goodwill purchased at acquisition.
3. Assume at December 31, 1975 (end of the accounting period), Rankin Corporation reported a net income of $12,000. Assume goodwill amortization over a ten-year period. Give all entries indicated on the records of Smith Company.
4. In February 1976, Rankin Corporation paid a $2 cash dividend. Give the necessary entry.

**Exercise 18–5**

On January 1, 1975, Kyle Corporation purchased 2,000 of the 8,000 outstanding shares of common stock of Low Corporation for $20,000 cash. At that date, Low's balance sheet reflected the following book values:

| | |
|---|---|
| Assets not subject to depreciation ............... | $35,000 |
| Assets subject to depreciation (net)............... | 30,000* |
| Liabilities .................................................. | 5,000 |
| Common stock (par $5) ............................. | 40,000 |
| Retained earnings ....................................... | 10,000 |

　　　* Fair market value, $38,000; estimated remaining life of ten years (straight-line depreciation).

*Required:*

1. Assuming the equity method is appropriate, show the computation of goodwill purchased at acquisition.
2. At the end of 1975, Low reported income before extraordinary items, $19,000, extraordinary loss, $2,000, and net income, $17,000. In March 1976, Low Corporation paid a $1 per share cash dividend. Reconstruct the following accounts (use T-account format) for Kyle Corporation: Cash, Investment in Low Corporation Stock, Investment Revenue – Ordinary, Investment Revenue – Extraordinary. Assume the equity method is appropriate and straight-line amortization of goodwill is over a ten-year period. Date and identify all amounts entered in the accounts.

**Exercise 18–6**

On January 3, 1975, Bloomington Company purchased 2,000 shares of the 10,000 outstanding shares of common stock of Kokomo Corporation for $14,600 cash. At that date, the balance sheet of Kokomo reflected total shareholders' equity of $60,000. In addition, the fair market value of the assets, subject to depreciation, was $3,000 in excess of their book value reported on the balance sheet. Assume a ten-year remaining life (straight-line depreciation) and amortization of goodwill over ten years.

*Required:*

Set up captions as follows and enter the indicated information (show computations):

| Information – Bloomington Accounts | Assuming Cost Method Appropriate | Assuming Equity Method Appropriate |
|---|---|---|
| a. Entry at date of acquisition. | | |
| b. Goodwill purchased–computation only. | | |
| c. Entry on December 31, 1975, to record $15,000 net income reported by Kokomo. | | |
| d. Entry on December 31, 1975, for additional depreciation expense. | | |
| e. Entry on December 31, 1975, for amortization of goodwill. | | |
| f. Entry on March 3, 1976, for a cash dividend of $1 per share paid by Kokomo. | | |

## Exercise 18–7

On January 10, 19A, Company X purchased as a long-term investment 12% of the 10,000 shares of the outstanding common stock of Company Y (par value $40 per share) at $50 per share. During 19A, 19B, and 19C the following additional data were available:

| | 19A | 19B |
|---|---|---|
| Reported net income by Company Y at year-end............... | $30,000 | $35,000 |
| Cash dividends by Company Y at year-end ..................... | 10,000 | 15,000 |
| Quoted market price per share of Company Y stock at year-end ......................................................... | 57 | 55 |

On January 2, 19C, Company X sold 100 shares of the Company Y shares at $56 per share.

*Required:*

1. Assuming the market value method is used, give all entries indicated in the accounts of Company X assuming market changes are considered as "realized."
2. Prepare a tabulation to show the investment revenue of Company X and the balance in the investment account for the years 19A, 19B, and 19C.

## Exercise 18–8

On January 1, 19A, Company R purchased, as a long-term investment, 6% of the 50,000 (par $10) shares of the outstanding common stock of Company S at $11 per share. During the years 19A, 19B, and 19C the following additional data were available:

| | Company S |
|---|---|
| End of 19A: | |
| Reported net income ............................. | $30,000 |
| Cash dividends paid ............................. | 20,000 |
| Market value per share .......................... | 15 |
| End of 19B: | |
| Reported net income ............................. | 25,000 |
| Cash dividends paid ............................. | 15,000 |
| Market value per share .......................... | 14 |
| January 10, 19C: | |
| Company R sold 200 shares of the Company S stock at $17.50 per share. | |

*Required:*

1. Assuming the market value method is used, give all entries related to the investment for Company R assuming:
   *a.* Market changes are considered "realized."
   *b.* Market changes are considered "unrealized."
2. In parallel columns for each assumption, show the (*a*) balance of the investment account at each year-end, (*b*) the balance in the "unrealized" account at each year-end, and (*c*) revenue from the investment for each period.

**Exercise 18–9**

During January 19A, Company A purchased 20% of the 5,000 shares of outstanding common stock of Company B at $20 per share. At that date, the following data were available:

|  | Company B | |
| --- | --- | --- |
|  | At Book Value | Market Value per Appraisal |
| Assets not subject to depreciation............... | $ 60,000 | $63,000 |
| Assets subject to depreciation (ten-year remaining life) ....................................... | 40,000 | 45,000 |
|  | $100,000 | |
| Liabilities ................................................ | $ 20,000 | 20,000 |
| Common stock (par value $10) ................... | 50,000 | |
| Retained earnings ..................................... | 30,000 | |
|  | $100,000 | |

At the end of 19A, Company B reported a net income of $15,000 and paid cash dividends of $5,000. At the end of 19A, Company B common stock was quoted on the market at $22 per share.

In January 19B, Company A sold 100 of the shares of Company B at $23 per share.

*Required:*

In parallel columns prepare entries for the accounts of Company A from the date of the purchase of the long-term investment through date of sale of the 100 shares assuming: Case A—the cost method is used; Case B—the equity method is used; and Case C—the market value method is used (market changes are treated as realized). Assume goodwill is amortized over a 20-year period.

**Exercise 18–10**

On January 1, 19A, Company P acquired all of the outstanding shares of Company S common stock by exchanging, on a share for share basis, 4,000 shares of its own stock. The balance sheets reflected the following summarized data:

|  | Company P | Company S |
|---|---|---|
| Assets not subject to depreciation ............... | $180,000 | $40,000* |
| Assets subject to depreciation (ten-year remaining life)......................................... | 120,000 | 25,000 |
|  | $300,000 | $65,000 |
| Liabilities ................................................. | $ 20,000* | $ 5,000 |
| Common stock (par $10)............................. | 200,000 | 40,000 |
| Retained earnings ..................................... | 80,000 | 20,000 |
|  | $300,000 | $65,000 |

\* Includes a $4,000 debt owed by Company P to Company S.

*Required:*

1. Give entry in the accounts of Company P for the acquisition of this long-term investment on a pooling of interests basis.
2. Prepare a consolidation worksheet at date of acquisition (assume the pooling of interests method).

## Exercise 18–11

Refer to the balance sheets at the date of acquisition for Companies P and S as given in Exercise 18–10.

Assume the same requirements and facts except that Company P exchanged, on a share for share basis, 3,600 shares of its own stock for a 90% interest in Company S.

## Exercise 18–12

In January 19A, Company P purchased, for $149,000 cash, all of the 10,000 outstanding voting shares of the common stock of Company S. At that date, the following additional summarized data were available:

|  |  | Company S | |
|---|---|---|---|
|  | Company P Book Value | Book Value | Fair Value (appraised) |
| Assets not subject to depreciation ... | $410,000 | $ 80,000* | $ 85,000 |
| Assets subject to depreciation ......... | 200,000 | 60,000 | 67,000† |
| Total ................................. | $610,000 | $140,000 | $152,000 |
| Liabilities ...................................... | $ 40,000 | $ 10,000 | |
| Common stock (par $10) ................. | 500,000 | 100,000 | |
| Retained earnings .......................... | 70,000 | 30,000 | |
| Total ................................. | $610,000 | $140,000 | |

\* Includes a $12,000 debt owed by Company P to Company S.
† Estimated remaining life, ten years (straight-line depreciation).

*Required:*

1. Give entry in the accounts of Company P to record acquisition of this long-term investment assuming the purchase method.
2. Compute the amount of goodwill purchased.
3. Prepare a consolidation worksheet at date of acquisition using the purchase method.
4. How much additional depreciation expense and goodwill amortization (assume a 20-year amortization period) will be reflected on the consolidated income statement each year after the acquisition?

**Exercise 18-13**

Refer to the balance sheets at date of acquisition for Companies P and S given in Exercise 18–12. Assume the same facts except that Company P purchased 60% of the outstanding shares of Company S for $146,200 cash.

*Required:*

1. Give entry in the accounts of Company P to record acquisition of this long-term investment assuming the purchase method.
2. Compute the amount of goodwill purchased.
3. Prepare a consolidated worksheet at acquisition using the purchase method.
4. How much additional depreciation expense and goodwill amortization (assume a 20-year amortization period) will be reflected on the consolidated income statement each year after the acquisition?

**Exercise 18-14**

On January 1, 19A, Par Company purchased a 80% interest in Sub Company for $116,400. At date of acquisition, the goodwill purchased was computed as follows:

| | |
|---|---:|
| Purchase price for 80% interest in Sub Company ........................... | $116,400 |
| Book value of Sub Company purchased ($128,000 × .80) .............. | 102,400 |
| Differential ...................................................................... | 14,000 |
| Adjustments to market value: | |
| Increase fixed assets to fair market value | |
| ($104,000 − $99,000) × .80..................................................... | 4,000 |
| Difference—goodwill purchased ......................................... | $ 10,000 |

At the end of 19A, the financial statements reflected the following (summarized):

| | *Reported at End of Year 19A* | |
|---|---|---|
| | *Par Company* | *Sub Company* |
| Income Statement: | | |
| Sales............................................... | $360,000 | $ 80,000 |
| Interest revenue................................ | | 400 |
| | 360,000 | 80,400 |
| Cost of goods sold ........................... | 150,000 | 42,000 |
| Other operating expenses ................. | 109,600 | 26,300 |
| Interest expense ............................ | 400 | 100 |
| | 260,000 | 60,400 |
| Net Income ..................................... | $100,000 | $ 12,000 |
| Balance Sheet: | | |
| Current assets ............................... | $172,000 | $ 80,000 |
| Investment in Sub Company .............. | 116,400 | |
| Fixed assets (net) ........................... | 400,000 | 90,000 |
| | $688,400 | $170,000 |
| Current liabilities ............................ | $ 50,000 | $ 30,000 |
| Common stock ............................... | 500,000 | 100,000 |
| Retained earnings............................ | 138,400 | 40,000* |
| | $688,400 | $170,000 |

* At acquisition, the balance was $28,000.

Intercompany items at year-end were:

a. Par Company sold Sub Company goods (at cost) during the year amounting to $5,000.
b. Par Company paid Sub Company $400 interest during the year.
c. Par Company owed Sub Company $3,000 at the end of the year.

*Required:*

Prepare a worksheet to develop a consolidated income statement and balance sheet at the end of 19A assuming the purchase method. Assume the fixed assets have a 10-year remaining life and goodwill will be amortized over 20 years.

**Exercise 18–15**

On January 1, 19A, X Company purchased 80% of the outstanding common stock of Y Company at a cost of $137,200. At date of acquisition, the goodwill purchased was computed as follows:

| | |
|---|---:|
| Purchase price for 80% interest in Y Company ........................ | $137,200 |
| Book value of Y Company purchased ($159,000 × .80)............... | 127,200 |
| Differential ................................................................. | 10,000 |
| Adjustments to fair market value: | |
| Current assets ($1,250 × .80)............................................. | (1,000) |
| Fixed assets ($6,250 × .80).................................................. | (5,000) |
| Difference—goodwill purchased .................................... | $    4,000 |

After one year of operations, each company prepared a balance sheet and income statement as follows (summarized):

| | Reported at End of Year 19A | |
|---|---:|---:|
| | X Company | Y Company |
| Income Statement: | | |
| Sales................................................. | $340,000 | $ 90,000 |
| Cost of goods sold ........................... | 190,000 | 46,000 |
| Depreciation ..................................... | 32,000 | 15,000 |
| Other operating expenses ................. | 72,000 | 17,000 |
| Interest expense  ............................. | 2,000 | 1,000 |
| Total ...................................... | 296,000 | 79,000 |
| Net Income....................................... | $ 44,000 | $ 11,000 |
| | | |
| Balance Sheet: | | |
| Current assets  ................................. | $170,800 | $ 40,000 |
| Investment in Y Company ................. | 137,200 | |
| Fixed assets (net)............................. | 330,000 | 160,000 |
| | $638,000 | $200,000 |
| | | |
| Liabilities.......................................... | $138,000 | $ 30,000 |
| Common stock .................................. | 400,000 | 150,000 |
| Retained earnings  ........................... | 100,000 | 20,000* |
| | $638,000 | $200,000 |

* Balance at date of acquisition, $9,000.

Intercompany items at year-end were determined to be:

a. Sales of X Company to Y Company during the year were $15,000 (at cost).
b. Depreciation on fixed assets; assume a ten-year remaining life.
c. Amortization of any goodwill; assume a 20-year amortization period.

*Required:*

Prepare a worksheet to develop a consolidated income statement and balance sheet at the end of 19A assuming the purchase method.

## Exercise 18–16

Brown Company purchased, for a lump sum of $104,070, the three different stocks listed below:

| Company and Stock | Number of Shares |
|---|---|
| X Corporation, common stock, par $10 .................. | 200 |
| Y Corporation, preferred stock, par $100 .............. | 400 |
| Z Corporation, common stock, no par .................. | 500 |

In addition, Brown paid transfer fees and other costs related to the acquisition amounting to $790. At the time of purchase, the stocks were quoted on the local market at the following prices per share: X common, $70; Y preferred, $120; and Z common, $90.

*Required:*

Give entry to record the purchase of these long-term investments and payment of the transfer fees. Show computations. Record each stock in a separate account.

## Exercise 18–17

Each of the following situations are completely independent; however, both of them relate to the receipt of a stock dividend by an investor.

*Case A:* Corporation K had 20,000 shares of $50 par value stock outstanding at which time the board of directors voted to issue a 25% stock dividend (i.e., one additional share for each four [4] shares owned).

*Required:*

Company L owns 2,000 shares of the Corporation K stock (a long-term investment) acquired at a cost of $65 per share. After receiving the stock dividend, Company L sold 200 of the additional stock received at $70 per share. Give the entries for Company L to record (1) acquisition of the 2,000 shares, (2) receipt of the stock dividend, and (3) sale of the 200 shares. Assume the cost method.

*Case B:* During the course of an audit, you find accounts as follows:

**Investments – Stock in A Company ($100 par per share)**

*Debits*

| | |
|---|---|
| Jan. 1 Cost of 100 shares .................................................... | $17,500 |
| Feb. 1 50 shares received as a stock dividend (at par).............. | 5,000 |

*Credits*

| | |
|---|---|
| July 1 25 shares of dividend stock sold at 125 ....................... | 3,125 |

**Income Summary**

*Credits*

Feb. 1 Stock dividend on A Company stock ........................... $ 5,000
July 1 Cash dividend on A Company stock............................    3,000

*Required:*

Assuming the cost method, restate these accounts on a correct basis. Give reasons for each change.

### Exercise 18–18

Box Corporation issued one stock right for each share of common stock owned by investors. The rights provided that for each six rights held a share of new preferred stock could be purchased for $100 cash (par of the preferred was $80 per share). When the rights were issued they had a market value of $7 each and the common stock was selling at $142 per share (ex rights). Roy Company owned 300 shares of Box common stock, acquired as a long-term investment at a cost of $22,350. Assume the cost method.

*Required:*

1. How many rights did Roy Company receive?
2. Determine the cost of the stock rights to Roy Company and give any entry that should be made upon receipt of the rights.
3. Assume Roy Company exercised the rights, determine the cost of the new stock and give the entry to record the exercise of the rights.
4. Assuming that Roy Company sold its rights for $7.40 each. Give entry to record the sale.

### Exercise 18–19

Give entries in the accounts of XY Corporation under the cost method for the following transactions which occurred over a period of time and in the chronological order shown:

a. XY Corporation purchased 100 shares of Bell Corporation common stock at $99 per share as a long-term investment.
b. Bell Corporation issued a 10% stock dividend in additional common shares.
c. Bell Corporation issued rights to present common stockholders entitling each holder of five old shares to buy one additional share of new common stock at 95. At the time the rights sold for $4 per right and the shares outstanding sold for $116 each (ex rights). Make an allocation to the rights.
d. XY Corporation exercised its rights and bought new shares.
e. XY Corporation sold 120 shares of Bell stock for $12,000 failing to identify the specific shares disposed of. (Use *Fifo* procedures.)

### Exercise 18–20

Clay Company purchased 100 shares of X Corporation's common stock paying $90 per share. Shortly thereafter, Clay Company received stock rights entitling it to purchase one additional share of stock for $65 for each ten rights tendered. At the time the rights were issued, the common stock was selling at $115 per share (ex rights) and the rights were selling at $5 each.

*Required:*

1. Give entry to record the purchase of the investment assuming the cost method.
2. Give the entry to record the receipt of the rights by Clay Company (make an allocation).
3. Give entry assuming the investor sold 20 rights at $5.50 each.
4. Give entry assuming the investor exercised the remaining rights.

## PROBLEMS

### Problem 18–1

On January 1, 19A, Freeze Company purchased 4,000 shares of the 20,000 shares outstanding of common stock (par $10) of Gray Corporation for $64,000 cash and 3,000 shares of the 100,000 shares outstanding of common stock (nopar) of Hobbs Corporation for $14,000 cash as a long-term investment. The accounting periods for the companies end on December 31.

Subsequent information was as follows:

December 31, 19A:

|  | Freeze | Hobbs |
|---|---|---|
| Income reported for 19A | $40,000 | $20,000 |
| Cash dividend per share paid at the end of 19A | $1.50 | None |
| Market price per share of stock | $12 | $8 |

October 20, 19B:
Sold 1,000 shares of the Hobbs stock at $10 per share.

December 31, 19B:

|  | Freeze | Hobbs |
|---|---|---|
| Income reported for 19B | $50,000 | $26,000 |
| Cash dividends per share paid at the end of 19B | $1.00 | $.50 |
| Market price per share of stock | $14 | $11 |

Reclassified Hobbs stock as a current asset (short-term investment).

*Required:*

1. Assuming the cost method, give all entries indicated for Freeze Company for 19A and 19B.
2. Show how the investments in equity securities would be reported on the financial statements of Freeze Company at the end of each year.

### Problem 18–2

On January 1, 19B, Abel Company purchased 3,000 shares of the 15,000 outstanding shares of common stock of Briggs Corporation for $80,000 cash as a long-term investment. At that date, the balance sheet of Briggs Company showed the following book values (summarized):

| | |
|---|---|
| Assets not subject to depreciation | $140,000[a] |
| Assets subject to depreciation (net) | 100,000[b] |
| Liabilities | 40,000 |
| Common stock (par $10) | 150,000 |
| Retained earnings | 50,000 |

[a] Fair market value, $150,000.

[b] Fair market value, $140,000, estimated remaining life, ten years. Assume straight-line depreciation and amortization of goodwill over 20 years.

Additional subsequent data on Briggs Corporation:

| | 19B | 19C |
|---|---|---|
| Income before extraordinary items | $25,000 | $26,000 |
| Extraordinary item—gain | | 5,000 |
| Cash dividends paid | 10,000 | 12,000 |
| Market value per share | 25 | 26 |

*Required:*

1. Set up captions as follows and enter the indicated information (show computations):

| Information (Abel's accounts) | Assuming Cost Method Is Appropriate | Assuming Equity Method Is Appropriate |
|---|---|---|
| a. Entry at date of acquisition. | | |
| b. Amount of goodwill purchased. | | |
| c. Entries at December 31, 19B. | | |
| (1) Investment revenue and dividends. | | |
| (2) Additional depreciation expense. | | |
| (3) Amortization of goodwill. | | |
| d. Entries at December 31, 19C. | | |
| (1) Investment revenue and dividends. | | |
| (2) Additional depreciation expense. | | |
| (3) Amortization of goodwill. | | |

2. Reconstruct the investment account for each assumption; also include the "allowance" and "unrealized" accounts.
3. Explain why the investment account balance is different between the cost and equity methods.

### Problem 18–3

During January 19A, Riley Company purchased 1,000 shares of the 10,000 shares of the outstanding common stock (par $20) of Swanson Corporation for $36,000 cash, as a long-term investment. During 19A, 19B, and 19C, the following additional data were available:

|                                                          | 19A      | 19B      |
|----------------------------------------------------------|----------|----------|
| Net income reported by Swanson at year-end               | $15,000  | $20,000  |
| Cash dividends paid by Swanson at year-end               | 10,000   | 12,000   |
| Market price per share                                   | 40       | 37       |

On January 2, 19C, Riley sold 100 shares of the Swanson stock at $38 per share.

*Required:*

(Suggestion – Set up a three-column tabulation for Requirements 1–3.)

1. Give all entries indicated in the accounts of Riley Company assuming the cost method is used.
2. Give all entries indicated in the accounts of Riley Company assuming the market value method is used and that market value changes are considered "realized."
3. Give all entries indicated in the accounts of Riley Company assuming the market value is used and that market changes are considered "unrealized."
4. Explain why the investment account balance is different between Requirements 1 and 2.
5. Assuming you could make the choice, which of the three methods would you prefer? Explain the basis of your choice and why you rejected the other two methods.

## Problem 18–4

In January 19A, Bricker Company purchased 10% of the 100,000 outstanding common shares of Core Company at $6 per share as a long-term investment. During the years 19A and 19B, the following additional data were available:

|                              | Core Company    |
|------------------------------|-----------------|
| End 19A:                     |                 |
|     Reported net income   | $30,000         |
|     Cash dividends paid    | 15,000          |
|     Market value per share | 9               |
| End 19B:                     |                 |
|     Reported net income   | $ (8,000) loss  |
|     Cash dividends paid    | 10,000          |
|     Market value per share | 7               |

*Required:*

(Suggestion: Set up a three-column tabulation for Requirements 1–3.)

1. Give all entries indicated in the accounts of Bricker Company assuming the cost method is used.
2. Give all entries indicated assuming that the market value method is used and that market changes are considered as "realized."
3. Give all entries indicated assuming that the market value method is used and that market changes are considered as "unrealized."
4. Prepare a tabulation to reflect by years, for each of the above requirements, (*a*) the balance in the investment account at each year-end, (*b*) the balance in any "unrealized" accounts, and (*c*) investment revenue for Bricker Company.
5. Give entry assuming 1,000 of the shares of Core Company were sold by Bricker early in 19C at $8 per share.

**Problem 18–5**

During January, 19A, Company P purchased 20% of the 30,000 outstanding common shares of Company S at $16 per share as a long-term investment. At date of acquisition of the shares, the following data in respect to Company S had been assembled by Company P:

| | Company S | |
| --- | --- | --- |
| | At Book Value | At Estimated Value |
| Assets not subject to depreciation ................ | $250,000 | $260,000 |
| Assets subject to depreciation (ten-year remaining life; straight line) .................... | 200,000 | 220,000 |
| | $450,000 | |
| Liabilities .................................................... | $ 50,000 | |
| Common stock (par $10)............................... | 300,000 | |
| Retained earnings......................................... | 100,000 | |
| | $450,000 | |

Selected data available at year-end:

| | 19A | 19B |
| --- | --- | --- |
| Reported net income, Company S: | | |
| Income before extraordinary items ................ | $20,000 | $(10,000) loss |
| Extraordinary items ..................................... | 10,000 | |
| Cash dividends paid: | | |
| Company S................................................. | 8,000 | 5,000 |
| Quoted market price per share, Company S ...... | 21 | 15 |

*Required:*

1. In parallel columns, prepare all entries for Company P in respect to the investment assuming (a) the cost method is appropriate, (b) the equity method is appropriate (amortize any goodwill over 20 years straight line), and (c) the market value method is used, market value changes are considered as "realized."
2. Prepare a tabulation for each assumption in Requirement 1 to reflect (a) the balance in the investment account at each year-end, (b) investment revenue for each period, and (c) the allowance accounts.

**Problem 18–6**

In January, 19A, Company P acquired, as a long-term investment, 9,000 of the 10,000 outstanding common stock shares of Company S (par $20) by issuing 18,000 shares of its own common stock (par $10). Just prior to acquisition, the balance sheets reflected the following (summarized):

|  | Company P Book Value | Company S Book Value | Company S Fair Market Value (appraisal) |
|---|---|---|---|
| Cash................................ | $290,000 | $ 70,000 | $ 70,000 |
| Inventories........................ | 237,000 | 170,000 | 160,000 |
| Receivables (net) .............. | 63,000† | 36,000 | 33,000 |
| Fixed assets (net).............. | 260,000 | 100,000 | 150,000* |
| Patents (net) ..................... |  | 14,000 | 10,000* |
| Total....................... | $850,000 | $390,000 | $423,000 |
| Current liabilities............... | $ 60,000 | $ 10,000† |  |
| Long-term liabilities ......... | 150,000 | 140,000 |  |
| Common stock.................. | 514,000 | 200,000 |  |
| Retained earnings ............ | 126,000 | 40,000 |  |
| Total....................... | $850,000 | $390,000 |  |

*Estimated useful life: fixed assets, ten years; patent, five years. Assume purchased goodwill recognized will be amortized over 20 years.
†Includes a $4,000 debt owed by Company S to Company P.

*Required:*

1. Assume the acquisition meets all of the criteria for the pooling of interests method.
   a. Give the entry to record the stock exchange in the accounts of Company P at date of acquisition.
   b. Prepare a consolidation worksheet for the balance sheet immediately after acquisition.
2. Assume the same facts as above except that, instead of the exchange of shares, Company P paid $286,700 cash for the 9,000 shares of Company S. Also assume the acquisition qualifies as a purchase.
   a. Give the entry to record the acquisition in the accounts of Company P.
   b. Compute the amount of goodwill purchased (show computations).
   c. Prepare a consolidation worksheet for the balance sheet immediately after acquisition.
3. To compare the two methods, pooling of interests versus purchase, complete the tabulation as follows:

| Item (consolidated) | Consolidated Amounts the Same | Explanation of Reasons |
|---|---|---|
| 1. Current assets |  |  |
| 2. Investment account balances |  |  |
| 3. Liabilities |  |  |
| 4. Common stock balance |  |  |
| 5. Retained earnings balance |  |  |
| 6. Minority interest amount |  |  |
| 7. Future net income |  |  |

**Problem 18-7**

On January 1, 19A, P Company acquired 90% of the common stock of S Company by issuing 13,500 shares of its own common stock to the shareholders of S Company for an equal number of S Company shares. After one year of operations, each company prepared an income statement and balance sheet as follows (summarized):

|  | Reported at End of Year 19A | |
|---|---|---|
|  | P Company | S Company |
| **Income Statement:** | | |
| Sales ................................................................. | $620,000 | $140,000 |
| Interest revenue ................................................ | 700 | |
| Total ......................................................... | 620,700 | 140,000 |
| Cost of goods sold ........................................... | 370,000 | 75,000 |
| Depreciation expense ....................................... | 40,000 | 15,000 |
| Other operating expenses ................................. | 132,700 | 36,300 |
| Interest expense............................................... | 1,000 | 700 |
| Total ......................................................... | 543,700 | 127,000 |
| Net Income ....................................................... | $ 77,000 | $ 13,000 |
| **Balance Sheet:** | | |
| Current assets................................................... | $335,000 | $101,000 |
| Investment in S Company ................................. | 135,000 | |
| Fixed assets (net—remaining life, ten years)........... | 330,000 | 149,000 |
| Total ......................................................... | $800,000 | $250,000 |
| Liabilities ......................................................... | $ 80,000 | $ 40,000 |
| Common stock (par $10)..................................... | 600,000 | 150,000 |
| Retained earnings ............................................. | 120,000 | 60,000* |
| Total ......................................................... | $800,000 | $250,000 |

* Balance at acquisition date, $47,000.

Intercompany items and adjustments for 19A:

a. S Company sold $17,000 worth of goods (at cost) to P Company during the year.
b. S Company paid P Company $700 interest during the year.
c. At the end of 19A, S Company owed P Company $20,000.

*Required:*

1. Prepare a worksheet for 19A to develop a consolidated income statement and balance sheet. Use the pooling of interests basis. Assume straight-line depreciation.
2. Prepare a classified income statement and balance sheet clearly identifying the minority interest.

## Problem 18–8

Refer to the balance sheets for Companies P and S given in Problem 18–7. Assume the same facts except that Company P purchased 13,500 shares (90%) of the common stock of Company S at a cash cost of $226,000. At date of acquisition, the fixed assets, at fair market value, were $43,000 above book value.

The purchase method changes the trial balance for Company P given in Problem 18–7 as follows (new balances):

| | |
|---|---|
| Current assets ................................. | $109,000 |
| Investment account (at cost)............... | 226,000 |
| Common stock (par $10) ................... | 465,000 |

*Required:*

1. Compute the purchased goodwill at date of acquisition. Show computations.
2. Prepare a worksheet for 19A to develop a consolidated balance sheet and income statement. Use the purchase basis. Use straight-line depreciation and amortize goodwill over 20 years.

## Problem 18–9

On January 1, 19A, Company A purchased for cash, in the market, 80% of the outstanding common stock of Company B at a cost of $188,000. At date of acquisition, based upon an appraisal of Company B assets for consolidation purposes, the fixed assets had a fair market value of $10,000 above their book value and the current assets had a fair market value of $7,500 less than their book value.

After one year of operations, each company prepared an income statement and balance sheet as follows (summarized):

|  | Reported at End of Year 19A | |
|---|---|---|
|  | Company A | Company B |
| Income Statement: |  |  |
| Sales................................................... | $630,000 | $180,000 |
| Interest revenue ................................. | 1,000 |  |
| Total..................................................... | 631,000 | 180,000 |
| Cost of goods sold ............................. | 370,000 | 98,000 |
| Depreciation expense........................... | 37,000 | 16,000 |
| Other operating expenses..................... | 140,000 | 45,000 |
| Interest expense ................................ | 4,000 | 1,000 |
| Total............................................. | 551,000 | 160,000 |
| Net Income.......................................... | $ 80,000 | $ 20,000 |
| Balance Sheet: |  |  |
| Current assets ................................... | $372,000 | $110,000 |
| Investment in Company B (at cost)............... | 188,000 |  |
| Fixed assets (net)................................. | 360,000 | 160,000 |
| Total............................................. | $920,000 | $270,000 |
| Current liabilities ............................... | $ 70,000 | $ 30,000 |
| Common stock (par $10) .......................... | 760,000 | 200,000 |
| Retained earnings ................................ | 90,000 | 40,000* |
| Total............................................. | $920,000 | $270,000 |

* Balance at date of acquisition, $20,000.

Data relating to 19A eliminations and adjustments:

a. During the year, Company A sold merchandise to Company B for $35,000 (at cost).
b. During 19A, Company B paid Company A $1,000 interest on loans.
c. At the end of 19A, Company B owed Company A $20,000.
d. The assets of Company B have an estimated remaining life of ten years (no residual value, straight-line depreciation).
e. Goodwill is to be amortized over a 20-year life.

*Required:*

1. Compute the goodwill purchased at date of acquisition; show computations.
2. Prepare a worksheet to develop a consolidated income statement and balance sheet on the purchase basis.

### Problem 18–10

Refer to the balance sheets for Companies A and B given in Problem 18–9. Assume the same facts except that Company A acquired the 90% interest in Company B by exchanging 18,000 shares of its own common stock for an equal number of shares in Company B.

The pooling of interests method changes the trial balance given for Company A in Problem 18–9 as follows:

| | |
|---|---:|
| Current assets ........................... | $560,000 |
| Investment account ..................... | 180,000 |
| Common stock (par $10).............. | 940,000 |

*Required:*

1. Prepare a worksheet for 19A to develop a consolidated income statement and balance sheet. Use the pooling of interest basis.
2. Prepare an unclassified income statement and balance sheet clearly identifying the minority interest.

### Problem 18–11

Foster Corporation completed the following transactions, in the order given, relative to their portfolio of stocks held as long-term investments:

*a.* Purchased 200 shares of common stock (par value $50) of M Corporation at $70 per share plus a brokerage commission of 4% and transfer costs of $20.
*b.* Purchased, for a lump sum of $96,000, the following stocks of N Corporation:

| Stocks | Number of Shares | Market Price at Date of Purchase |
|---|---|---|
| Class A, common, par value $100 ........................ | 200 | $ 50 |
| Preferred, par value $50 ................................... | 300 | 100 |
| Class B, nopar value stock (stated value, $100)  ... | 400 | 150 |

*c.* Purchased 300 shares of common stock of M Corporation common at $80 per share plus a brokerage commission of 4% and transfer costs of $60.
*d.* Received a stock dividend on the M Corporation stock; for each share held, an additional share was received.
*e.* Sold 100 shares of M Corporation stock at $45 per share (from Lot 1).
*f.* Received a two-for-one stock split on the Class A common stock of the N Corporation (the number of shares doubled).
*g.* Received cash dividends as follows:
   M Corporation common stock – $5 per share
   N, Class A, common stock – $3 per share
   N preferred – 6%
   N, Class B, nopar value stock – $1.50 per share.

*Required:*

1. Give entries for Foster Corporation for the above transactions assuming the cost method is appropriate. Show calculations and assume *Fifo* order when shares are sold.
2. Prepare an inventory of the long-term investment portfolio; include number of shares and balance sheet valuations after giving effect to the above transactions.

## Problem 18–12

Hay Company owns the following long-term investments:

a. 100 shares of Ajax Corporation common stock acquired in 1954 at $100 per share. No dividends have ever been received. In recent years, the stock has been selling around $6 per share.
b. 600 shares of Preston Mines, Inc., stock acquired in 1955 at $7 per share. In recent years a portion of each dividend has been designated as a liquidating dividend. Dividends have been received as follows:

| | Revenue | Return of Capital | Total |
|---|---|---|---|
| 1973............... | $3.00 | $4.00 | $7.00 |
| 1974............... | 2.00 | 3.00 | 5.00 |
| 1975............... | 2.00 | 1.00 | 3.00 |
| 1976............... | 1.00 | | 1.00 |

c. 2,000 shares of Brown, Inc., common stock acquired in 1968 at $150 per share; the current market price recently has been $210 per share. The stock regularly pays dividends. A two-for-one stock split has just been issued (the number of shares doubled).
d. 200 shares of common stock (par $30) and 400 shares of preferred stock (par $75) of the Sky Corporation. These shares were purchased as a package in 1975 at a lump sum of $48,500; at the time they were selling at common, $50, and preferred, $100, per share. During 1976, one-for-one stock dividend was received on the common shares (the number of shares doubled).

*Required:*

For Hay Company give *all* entries indicated since 1954; show computations with respect to each lot of shares. Explain any assumptions made. Also compute the carrying value and cost per share of each lot of shares at the end of 1976. Use the cost method.

## Problem 18–13

Foster Corporation has long-range plans to build a new plant on the West Coast in approximately five years. To provide some of the funds, Foster management has decided to establish a future plant expansion fund. The funds will be deposited with a trustee and will earn 6% annual compound interest. The interest accumulations each year will be added to the fund balance.

Case A—Assume Foster makes only one contribution of $500,000 on January 1, 19A.

　　　*a.* Compute the balance that will be in the fund at the end of the fifth year. Show computations.

　　　*b.* Prepare a fund accumulation table for the five years. (*Hint:* Refer to Chapters 6 and 13.)

　　　*c.* Prepare journal entries for Foster through January 1, 19B.

Case B—Assume instead that Foster decides to make five equal annual contributions of $100,000 on each January 1, starting January 1, 19A.

　　　*a.* Compute the balance that will be in the fund immediately after the fifth and last contribution. Show computations.

　　　*b.* Prepare a fund accumulation table for the five contributions. (*Hint:* Refer to Chapters 6 and 13.)

　　　*c.* Give entries for Foster through January 1, 19B.

Explain why there is a different balance in the fund between the two cases at the end.

# Chapter *19*

## Accounting for Bonds
## as Long-Term Liabilities
## and Investments

The preceding chapter discussed long-term investments in equity securities (i.e., capital stock), and Chapter 11 discussed short-term and long-term liabilities. Because of their unique characteristics, discussion of bonds was deferred to this chapter. This chapter analyzes bonds from the viewpoints of (*a*) the issuer (i.e., the borrower) and (*b*) the investor (i.e., the lender). This dual approach is logical because the accounting and reporting concepts and procedures for the issuer and the investor are essentially the same. Bonds represent a long-term liability for the issuer and usually a long-term investment for the lender.[1] The usual time from issuance date to maturity date of bonds is 10 to 20 years.

The chapter is divided into three parts: Part A—Accounting for the Issuer and Investor Compared; Part B—Special Problems in Accounting for Bonds; and Part C—Serial Bonds.

### NATURE OF BONDS

Bonds, evidenced by outstanding bond certificates, are contractual representations that a debt is owed by one party, the issuer, to one or more other parties, the investors. A bond certificate indicates the principal amount, specified interest dates (usually semiannual), the nominal rate of interest based upon the principal amount, and any other special agreements. Thus, a bond may be defined as a formal (i.e., written) promise to pay a specified principal at a designated date in the future

---

[1] Bonds are sometimes held as short-term investments, in which case they are accounted for in the manner discussed in Chapter 7. They are recorded at cost, and subsequently, at lower of cost or market. Any premium or discount generally is not amortized in view of the short holding period (i.e., the operating cycle or one year, whichever is the longer). This chapter focuses on long-term investments in bonds.

and, in addition, periodic interest on the principal at a specified rate per period.

Bonds are used to borrow a large amount from the investment community, including individuals, by dividing the total long-term debt into a number of small units, usually in denominations of $10,000 and $1,000 (sometimes $100). The total amount to be borrowed, evidenced by the bond certificates, is usually referred to as a *bond issue*. A bond issue requires the preparation of a *bond indenture*, which is the basic contract between the borrower and the investors who acquire the bonds. The bond indenture usually includes provision for an outside *independent trustee* who is given the authority to protect the rights of both the investors and the lender. A bond indenture specifies the following information which is particularly important in accounting and reporting (1) the liability for the issuer and (2) the investment for the investor:

1. Maturity date.
2. Interest payments—dates and nominal rate of interest.
3. Denominations of principal.
4. Call and/or conversion provisions.
5. Security (i.e., whether supported by pledged assets or not).
6. The trustee, including certification of the bonds.
7. Repayment plans, such as a bond sinking fund.
8. Special provisions such as restrictions on retained earnings of the issuer and the maintenance of certain minimum ratios (such as the rate of debt to owners' equity).

## CLASSES OF BONDS

Bonds are classified in various ways as follows:

1. Character of issuing corporation. The borrower may be a private corporation issuing *industrial* bonds or a public entity issuing *municipal* or *government* bonds.

2. Character of security. Secured bonds are supported by a lien, or mortgage, on specific assets, whereas unsecured bonds have no such support. Unsecured bonds are frequently called *debenture bonds*. *Guaranty security bonds* are those which, in case of default, will be paid as to principal and interest by the guarantor. For example, a parent corporation may guarantee payment of the bonds issued by its subsidiary companies. *Lien security bonds* are secured by a lien on property consisting of securities (collateral trust bonds), rolling stock (car trust and equipment bonds), or a lien on realty (real estate bonds).

3. Purpose of issue. *Purchase money bonds* are issued in full or part payment for property. *Refunding bonds* are issued to retire current obligations and may have the same security as the redeemed debt. *Consolidated bonds* replace several prior issues and unite the securities for the retired issues.

4. Payment of interest. *Income bonds* differ from ordinary bonds in

that the payment of interest each period on income bonds depends on the earning of net income by the issuer. *Participating bonds* have a specified minimum rate of interest plus a stated participation in the income of the issuer; they may have a specified limited participation or an unlimited participation.

*Registered bonds* are recorded in the name of the investor, and the periodic interest payments are sent only to that person; therefore, a sale or transfer by the investor must be reported to the issuer, trustee, or other party designated for this purpose. In contrast, *coupon bonds* have a coupon attached for each periodic interest payment. At each coupon due date, the holder of the bond simply detaches the appropriate coupon, signs it, and cashes it as if it were a check. The sale of a coupon bond does not require registration of title transfer.

5. Maturity of principal. Bonds maturing at a specified date are called *straight* (or ordinary) *bonds;* that is, the entire bond issue matures at a single date. Bonds maturing at stated installment dates, say one fifth each year, are called *serial bonds* (see Part C). *Callable bonds* give the *issuer* the option to retire them at a stated price before the obligatory maturity date. *Redeemable bonds* give the *investor* the option to turn them in for a stated redemption price prior to maturity. *Convertible bonds* give the *investor* the option to turn them in and to receive, in exchange, other specified securities of the borrower (usually common stock).

## FINANCIAL AND MARKETING CONDITIONS

In going to the money market, a borrower needing a large amount of funds must make the fundamental decision as whether to use debt or capital stock, or a combination. This decision depends on a number of factors, some peculiar to the company and some based on the vagaries of the money market. Long-term debt has the advantage that interest payments are deductible as an expense for income tax purposes; thus, an 8% interest rate and a 45% tax bracket reduces the net interest rate (i.e., after tax) to 4.4%. In contrast, dividends paid on funds acquired from the sale of capital stock are not deductible for tax purposes. The periodic interest payments are fixed legal obligations that must be paid in cash each interest period. In contrast, dividends on capital stock are paid only when there are sufficient earnings (and cash). Debt has a fixed maturity date, whereas most capital stock does not.

From the *investor's* point of view, the guaranteed fixed interest rate and maturity amount must be balanced against the potential for dividends (that tend to vary with the earnings of the company) and accretion in the value of the stock. Generally speaking, equity investments are considered to be a better hedge against inflation than debt investments. Both interest revenue (except for tax-free municipal bonds) and dividend revenue are subject to income tax to the investor.

Bonds may be marketed initially by the borrower several ways. Typically, an entire bond issue is sold to one or more investment bankers who *underwrite* them at a specified price and then market them at a higher price to individual investors (and thus realize underwriter's compensation). Alternatively, the investment banker may agree to act as a selling agent for the borrower for an agreed commission; the selling price less the costs of selling is remitted to the issuer. Occasionally, the issuer may sell the bonds privately to financial institutions and individual investors.

Often, where there is no underwriter, the issuer may choose not to sell the entire bond issue if the bonds do not have sufficient appeal in the market. In these situations, unissued bonds should be disclosed in the financial statements, either parenthetically, or by note.

## PART A—ACCOUNTING FOR THE BORROWER AND THE INVESTOR COMPARED

### ILLUSTRATIVE DATA FOR BONDS

For convenience in illustration in Part A, a common set of facts will be used. Typically, bonds specify a long term from date of issuance to date of maturity (i.e., 10, 20, or more years), fractional interest rates, and semiannual interest payments. However, to simplify and shorten the illustrations at the outset, we will use a five-year term, even interest rates and annual rather than semiannual interest. These simplifications will not affect the basic concepts and accounting procedures.[2] The common set of facts used in this section are:

| | |
|---|---|
| Issuer (i.e., the borrower): | X Corporation |
| Investor (i.e., the lender): | Y Corporation |

Terms of the bond indenture:

| | |
|---|---|
| a. Maturity amount of the bonds. | $100,000 (in $10,000 and $1,000 denominations). |
| b. Date of the bonds. | January 1, 1976. |
| c. Maturity date. | December 31, 1980 (term, five years). |
| d. Stated interest rate. | 7% per year. |
| e. Interest payments (cash). | Annually each December 31 (amount, $100,000 × .07 = $7,000). |
| f. Date sold. | January 1, 1976 (unless otherwise stated). |
| g. Price or effective interest rate. | As specified in the examples to follow. |

End of the accounting period—December 31 for both companies (unless otherwise specified).

---

[2] Subsequent to the introductory illustrations, semiannual interest is assumed in the chapter.

To facilitate study, analysis, and problem solving, it is often quite helpful to prepare a *time scale* of a bond issue (or investment) that details important data such as issue date, interest dates, maturity date, period outstanding, and interest rates. A time scale for the above bond issue would appear as follows:

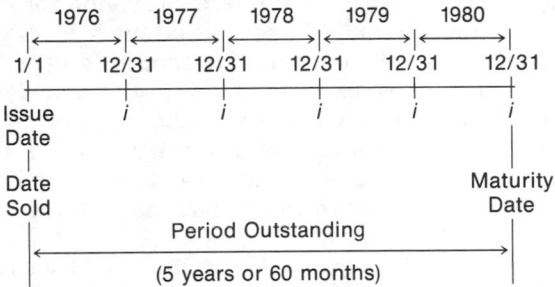

**Time Scale (amount $100,000; stated interest 7%)**

## BOND INTEREST AND PRICES

Because bonds have fixed maturity values, definite maturity dates, and specified interest payments, they tend to fluctuate less in price than do stocks. As a class of securities, the market price of bonds fluctuates inversely with changes in the market interest rates. When the market rate of interest rises, the market price of outstanding bonds falls; when the market rate of interest falls, the market price of bonds rises. These market fluctuations adjust the fixed-dollar interest return specified on the bonds to the prevailing *yield rate* in the particular market. The price of individual bonds tends to move with the interest market; however, the price also is influenced by changes in the issuer's financial standing and the approach of maturity (when the market value and maturity amount normally will coincide).

The bond indenture, and the face of each bond certificate, will always specify a *nominal*[3] interest rate which is applied to the principal amount of the bond to determine the amount of *cash interest* that will be paid each period. For example, each bond certificate of X Corporation (see data above) will specify a nominal rate of 7% per year. Thus, each of the $10,000 bonds will always pay $700 cash interest each annual interest period (December 31), and a $1,000 denomination bond will always pay $70 cash, regardless of its issue price. In the case of semiannual interest payments, the bonds of X Corporation, would pay 3.5% nominal interest each six months (refer to Chapter 6 for discussion of interest calculations).

---

[3] The nominal rate also is often referred to as the contract, stated, or coupon rate of interest. The principal also often is referred to as the face, maturity, or par amount.

In contrast to the nominal rate of interest, the *yield* or *effective* rate is the true rate of interest paid by the issuer and earned by the investor after taking into account the issue (or purchase) price of the bond.[4] Because the money market may establish a rate of interest on the bonds different than the nominal rate, bonds may sell at more or less than their face or par amount.

A bond sold at *par* will incur interest expense for the issuer at the stated rate of interest and will earn interest revenue for the investor at the same rate of interest. Only in this situation, will the nominal and the yield rates of interest be the same. A bond sold at a *discount* (less than par) will incur interest expense for the issuer at a yield rate higher than the nominal rate, and it will earn for the investor the higher effective rate. Conversely, a bond sold at a *premium* (more than par) will incur interest expense for the issuer at a yield rate which is lower than the nominal rate and will earn interest revenue for the investor the lower yield rate.[5]

Investment houses often quote bonds on a yield basis. A 7% bond quoted at 7–50 can be bought at a price that will yield 7.5% on the price of the bond each year from date of sale to maturity date. Thus, a $1,000 bond with a nominal rate of 7%, payable 3.5% semiannually, sold on a 7.50% basis (yield rate) five years before maturity date would have a price of $979.47. The $20.53 discount is an adjustment of the nominal interest rate to the higher yield rate. Sometimes bonds are quoted in relation to their par or maturity amount. For example, a $1,000 bond quoted at 100 is selling for $1,000 (i.e., at par); if quoted at 97, it is selling at $970 (i.e., at a discount of $30); and if quoted at 103, it is selling at $1,030 (i.e., at a premium of $30).

### Determination of Bond Prices

When bonds are marketed, investors make purchase offers tending to establish the yield rate of interest. Given the provisions of the bond indenture and the yield rate of interest, the price of a bond can be readily computed. Of course, if the yield rate is the same as the nominal rate, the price of the bond is par; that is, the face or maturity amount. Alternatively, when the yield rate established is different than the nominal rate, the *bond price* (sometimes called the bond valuation) is the *present value* of the future cash flows (i.e., principal plus all interest payments) at the yield rate of interest.

The *bond price* may be determined by either of two ways:

1. Compute the present value of (*a*) the future cash principal due (i.e.,

---

[4] The effective rate is also called the yield, true, or market rate.

[5] This discussion assumes that the issuer sells the bonds direct to the investors with no bond issue costs. Bond issue costs will be discussed in a later section.

the face amount) plus (b) the present value of the future *cash* interest payments.

To illustrate, assume the $100,000, 7% (annual interest payments), five-year bonds were sold by X Corporation to Y Corporation at an effective rate of 8% (see page 810).

Computation of the bond price:
    Present value of the future principal:
      $100,000 × $p_{n=5;i=8\%}$ (Table 6-2) = $100,000 × .68058 =         $68,058
    Present value of future annual interest payments:
      $7,000 × $P_{n=5;i=8\%}$ (Table 6-4) = $7,000 × 3.99271   =        27,949

    Bond price ............................................................................  $96,007

Since the yield rate (8%) was higher than the nominal rate (7%), the bond issue was sold at a *discount* of $100,000 − $96,007 = $3,993.

To illustrate a premium, assume instead that the bonds were sold at a yield rate of 6%.

Computation of the bond price:
    $100,000 × $p_{n=5;i=6\%}$ (Table 6-2) = $100,000 × .74726 =    $ 74,726
    $7,000 × $P_{n=5;i=6\%}$ (Table 6-4) = $7,000 × 4.21236   =    29,486
    Bond price ...........................................................................  $104,212

Amount of premium: $104,212 − $100,000 = $4,212.

2. Refer to a *bond table* that gives bond prices for various nominal rates, yield rates, and time to maturity date. Exhibit 19-1 shows excerpts from three typical bond tables. The bond prices computed above can be verified by referring to Exhibit 19-1, Table A.

### ACCOUNTING FOR, AND REPORTING, BONDS (BORROWER AND INVESTOR)

The cost principle governs the initial recording of a bond in the accounts. The issuer records the cash amount received for a bond and the present value of the liability (i.e., the maturity amount minus or plus any discount or premium). Similarly, the investor records the cash amount paid for the bond investment. It is important to note that a bond sold (or purchased) at par has a present value identical to the par or maturity amount. In contrast, a bond sold (or purchased) at a discount has a present value *less* than par or maturity amount (by the amount of the discount); a bond sold (or purchased) at a premium has a present value *higher* than par or maturity amount (by the amount of the premium).

To illustrate these three situations, the above data for X and Y Corporations and the computations of bond prices are used. Assume the entire issue, $100,000, was sold by X Corporation to Y Corporation on January 1, 1976 (date of the bonds):

**EXHIBIT 19–1**
**Excerpts from Three Typical Bond Tables**

Table A—Face of Bond $100,000; Nominal
Interest 7% Payable Annually

| Yield | 3 Years | 4 Years | 5 Years |
|---|---|---|---|
| 6.00 .............. | 102,673.01 | 103,465.11 | 104,212.37 |
| 6.50 .............. | 101,324.24 | 101,712.90 | 102,077.84 |
| 7.00 .............. | 100,000.00 | 100,000.00 | 100,000.00 |
| 7.50 .............. | 98,699.74 | 98,325.33 | 97,977.05 |
| 8.00 .............. | 97,422.90 | 96,687.88 | 96,007.29 |

Table B—Face of Bond $100,000; Nominal Interest 7% Payable Semiannually

| Yield | 3 Years | 3½ Years | 4 Years | 4½ Years | 5 Years |
|---|---|---|---|---|---|
| 6.00 .............. | 102,708.60 | 103,115.14 | 103,508.92 | 103,893.11 | 104,265.00 |
| 6.50 .............. | 101,343.17 | 101,543.00 | 101,736.56 | 101,924.03 | 102,105.58 |
| 7.00 .............. | 100,000.00 | 100,000.00 | 100,000.00 | 100,000.00 | 100,000.00 |
| 7.50 .............. | 98,678.75 | 98,486.55 | 98,299.29 | 98,119.78 | 97,946.76 |
| 8.00 .............. | 97,378.93 | 96,998.97 | 96,633.63 | 96,282.33 | 95,944.57 |

Table C—Face of Bond $100; Nominal Interest 8% Payable Semiannually*

| Time to Maturity | | Yield Rates | | | | |
|---|---|---|---|---|---|---|
| Years + Months | | 7% | 7.5% | 8.0% | 8.5% | 9.0% |
| 2 | Even | 101.836540 | 100.912846 | 100.000000 | 99.097848 | 98.206237 |
| 2 | 1 | 101.899336 | 100.938290 | 100.000000 | 99.050970 | 98.124359 |
| 2 | 2 | 101.959145 | 100.964777 | 100.000000 | 99.013029 | 98.055281 |
| 2 | 3 | 102.028761 | 100.997959 | 100.000000 | 98.975859 | 97.984160 |
| 2 | 4 | 102.099515 | 101.033906 | 100.000000 | 98.944696 | 97.920657 |
| 2 | 5 | 102.176104 | 101.074992 | 100.000000 | 98.917427 | 97.860498 |
| 2 | 6 | 102.253567 | 101.118541 | 100.000000 | 98.895778 | 97.807526 |
| 2 | 7 | 102.314867 | 101.143701 | 100.000000 | 98.851452 | 97.729809 |
| 2 | 8 | 102.378644 | 101.171736 | 100.000000 | 98.810866 | 97.656296 |
| 2 | 9 | 102.443779 | 101.202734 | 100.000000 | 98.776419 | 97.590496 |
| 2 | 10 | 102.514595 | 101.238737 | 100.000000 | 98.745780 | 97.527980 |
| 2 | 11 | 102.586503 | 101.277397 | 100.000000 | 98.720893 | 97.472743 |
| 3 | Even | 102.664277 | 101.321268 | 100.000000 | 98.700065 | 97.421064 |
| 3 | 1 | 102.722250 | 101.344166 | 100.000000 | 98.655990 | 97.345035 |
| 3 | 2 | 102.777727 | 101.368367 | 100.000000 | 98.620563 | 97.281201 |
| 3 | 3 | 102.842574 | 101.399033 | 100.000000 | 98.586158 | 97.215846 |
| 3 | 4 | 102.908739 | 101.432560 | 100.000000 | 98.557652 | 97.157883 |
| 3 | 5 | 102.980613 | 101.471160 | 100.000000 | 98.533110 | 97.103406 |
| 3 | 6 | 103.053539 | 101.512319 | 100.000000 | 98.514082 | 97.055892 |
| 3 | 7 | 103.110178 | 101.535025 | 100.000000 | 98.472445 | 96.983774 |
| 3 | 8 | 103.169321 | 101.560621 | 100.000000 | 98.434528 | 96.915819 |
| 3 | 9 | 103.229997 | 101.589273 | 100.000000 | 98.402648 | 96.855356 |
| 3 | 10 | 103.296232 | 101.622865 | 100.000000 | 98.374642 | 96.798317 |
| 3 | 11 | 103.363732 | 101.659208 | 100.000000 | 98.352286 | 96.748341 |
| 4 | Even | 103.436978 | 101.700699 | 100.000000 | 98.334055 | 96.702057 |
| 4 | 6 | 103.800321 | 101.878147 | 100.000000 | 98.162873 | 96.367598 |
| 5 | Even | 104.158303 | 102.053197 | 100.000000 | 97.997278 | 96.043641 |

*This table is more precise than the traditional one established in the 1800s because when the bond is priced between interest dates the actual number of days in the month is used in the calculation instead of the traditional one that assumes 30 days in each month. The first month is January; in certain other situations a slight difference beyond the third decimal point may exist. This is close enough for instructional purposes.

*Borrower's Books — X Corporation          Investor's Books — Y Corporation*

Case A — The bond issue was sold (and purchased) at par, $100,000:

| | | |
|---|---|---|
| Cash .......................... | 100,000 | |
|    Bonds payable......... | | 100,000 |

| | | |
|---|---|---|
| Bond investment (at cost)... | 100,000 | |
|    Cash ....................... | | 100,000 |

Case B — The bond issue was sold (and purchased) at a discount, $96,007:

| | | |
|---|---|---|
| Cash .......................... | 96,007 | |
| Discount on bonds | | |
|    payable .................... | 3,993 | |
|    Bonds payable......... | | 100,000 |

| | | |
|---|---|---|
| Bond investment.............. | 100,000 | |
| Discount on bonds | | |
|    investment ........... | | 3,993 |
|    Cash ....................... | | 96,007 |

Case C — The bond issue was sold (and purchased) at a premium, $104,212:*

| | | |
|---|---|---|
| Cash .......................... | 104,212 | |
| Premium on bonds | | |
|    payable .............. | | 4,212 |
|    Bonds payable......... | | 100,000 |

| | | |
|---|---|---|
| Bond investment.............. | 100,000 | |
| Premium on bond | | |
|    investment ................. | 4,212 | |
|    Cash ....................... | | 104,212 |

* Some accountants do not record the discount and premium in separate contra accounts. Under this approach, the entries would be:

Case B:

| Borrower | | |
|---|---|---|
| Cash .......................... | 96,007 | |
|    Bonds payable......... | | 96,007 |

| Investor | | |
|---|---|---|
| Bond investment.............. | 96,007 | |
|    Cash ....................... | | 96,007 |

Case C:

| | | |
|---|---|---|
| Cash .......................... | 104,212 | |
|    Bonds payable......... | | 104,212 |

| | | |
|---|---|---|
| Bond investment.............. | 104,212 | |
|    Cash ....................... | | 104,212 |

This approach records the liability and the investment at the net amount that would be reported on the balance sheet. It also simplifies the amortization of premium and discount since the periodic amortization entries are made directly to the liability and investment accounts so that at maturity date, they both reflect the maturity amount. Either approach derives precisely the same results on the periodic financial statements.

## Amortization of Discount and Premium

Bond discount or premium affects the amounts of interest expense for the issuer and interest revenue for the investor. For example, the interest effects in each of the three cases given above can be summarized as follows:

| | Case A (sold at par) | Case B (sold at discount) | Case C (sold at premium) |
|---|---|---|---|
| Price of the bonds (cash) ........................... | $100,000 | $ 96,007 | $104,212 |
| Payment of principal at maturity (cash) ...... | (100,000) | (100,000) | (100,000) |
| Payment of periodic interest ($7,000 × 5) ...... | (35,000) | (35,000) | (35,000) |
| Difference — Total Interest.......................... | $ 35,000 | $ 38,993 | $ 30,788 |
| Average interest per period (÷ 5) .............. | $ 7,000 | $ 7,799 | $ 6,158 |

When sold at par, the total interest expense of $35,000 reflects both a nominal and yield rate of 7%. In contrast, the total interest in Case B is greater than $35,000 by the amount of the discount ($3,993), since the price reflects a yield rate of 8%; in Case C, the total interest is less than $35,000 by the amount of the premium ($4,212), since the price reflects a yield rate of 6%. Thus, we see that bond discount and premium affect (a) balance sheet investment or liability amounts, and (b) interest revenue or expense on the income statement. To record and report these effects in accordance with the matching principle, bond discount and premium must be *amortized* as interest over the *period outstanding; that is, the period from date of sale to maturity date.* The two amortization methods used are (1) the *straight-line* method, and (2) the *interest* method.

   *Straight-Line Amortization.*   Under this method, an *equal dollar amount* of the discount or premium is amortized each period over the life of the bonds. To illustrate for Cases B and C above, the amortization each period for the five-year life of the bonds would be recorded as follows:

   *Borrower's Books — X Corporation*          *Investor's Books — Y Corporation*
   December 31, annual interest and amortization (each year for five years):

   Case B — bonds sold at a discount (straight-line amortization):

   | | | | | | |
   |---|---|---|---|---|---|
   | Bond interest expense ......... | 7,799* | | Cash .................................... | 7,000 | |
   | Discount on bonds | | | Discount on bond investment... | 799 | |
   | payable .................... | | 799 | Bond interest revenue ...... | | 7,799 |
   | Cash .......................... | | 7,000 | | | |

   Case C — bonds sold at a premium (straight-line amortization):

   | | | | | | |
   |---|---|---|---|---|---|
   | Bond interest expense ......... | 6,158 | | Cash .................................... | 7,000 | |
   | Premium on bonds payable... | 842† | | Premium on bond in- | | |
   | Cash .......................... | | 7,000 | vestment........................ | | 842 |
   | | | | Bond interest revenue ...... | | 6,158 |

   Computations:
   * Cash: $100,000 × .07 = $7,000.
   Amortization: $3,993 ÷ 5 yrs. = $799.
   † Amortization: $4,212 ÷ 5 yrs. = $842.

   The straight-line method of amortization, illustrated above, gives a constant *amount* of interest each period rather than a constant *rate* each period. It can be used under generally accepted accounting principles *only* when the results obtained are not material in comparison with the interest method results (refer to modifying principle, materiality, Chapter 2, page 26). This has been the case since the issuance of *APB Opinion No. 21* (August, 1971), which reads:

   > . . . the difference between the present value and the face amount should be treated as discount or premium and amortized as interest expense or income over the life of the note in such a way as to result in a constant rate of interest when applied to the amount outstanding at the beginning of any given period. This is the "interest" method. . . . However, other methods of amortization may be used if the results obtained are not materially different from those which would result from the "interest" method.

When the results are not materially different from the interest method, straight-line amortization may be used because of its simplicity. It is a practical approach, although not theoretically sound.

   *Interest Method of Amortization.*   The interest method is also called present value amortization. As explained in the preceding paragraph, it is required by *APB Opinion No. 21* (unless the results of another approach used are not materially different). The interest method is based upon the concept of an annuity (see Chapter 6) because (*a*) changes in both interest and carrying value are recognized each period, and (*b*) periodic interest expense (i.e., the effective interest amount) is computed as a *constant rate* applied to the book value or carrying amount of the bonds. The constant rate is the yield rate of interest as illustrated in Exhibits 19–2 (8%) and 19–3 (6%). Because Exhibit 19–2 is based on a *discount*, the effective interest amount (column [b]) *increases* each period because the carrying value in column (e) is increasing. In contrast, since Exhibit 19–3 is based on a *premium*, the effective interest amount (column [b]) *decreases* each period, because the carrying value in column (e) is decreasing.

**EXHIBIT 19–2**
**Bond Interest and Discount Amortization Interest Method—Annual Interest Payments**
**(face amount—$100,000)**

| Date | Cash Interest (7% annual) | Effective Interest (8% annual) | Discount Amortization | Balance Unamortized Discount | Carrying Value of Bonds |
|---|---|---|---|---|---|
| 1/1/76 starting date | | | | 3,993 | 96,007 |
| 12/31/76 | 7,000(a) | 7,681(b) | 681(c) | 3,312(d) | 96,688(e) |
| 12/31/77 | 7,000 | 7,735 | 735 | 2,577 | 97,423 |
| 12/31/78 | 7,000 | 7,794 | 794 | 1,783 | 98,217 |
| 12/31/79 | 7,000 | 7,857 | 857 | 926 | 99,074 |
| 12/31/80 | 7,000 | 7,926 | 926 | -0- | 100,000 |

(a) $100,000 × .07 = $7,000 (based on nominal rate).
(b) $96,007 × .08 = $7,681 (based on yield rate of interest).
(c) $7,681 − $7,000 = $681.
(d) $3,993 − $681 = $3,312.
(e) $96,007 + $681 = $96,688 (or $100,000 − $3,312 = $96,688).

**EXHIBIT 19–3**
**Bond Interest and Premium Amortization Interest Method—Annual Interest Payments**
**(face amount—$100,000)**

| Date | Cash Interest (7% annual) | Effective Interest (6% annual) | Premium Amortization | Balance Unamortized Premium | Carrying Value of Bonds |
|---|---|---|---|---|---|
| 1/1/76 starting date | | | | 4,212 | 104,212 |
| 12/31/76 | 7,000(a) | 6,253(b) | 747(c) | 3,465(d) | 103,465(e) |
| 12/31/77 | 7,000 | 6,208 | 792 | 2,673 | 102,673 |
| 12/31/78 | 7,000 | 6,160 | 840 | 1,833 | 101,833 |
| 12/31/79 | 7,000 | 6,110 | 890 | 943 | 100,943 |
| 12/31/80 | 7,000 | 6,057 | 943 | -0- | 100,000 |

(a) $100,000 × .07 = $7,000 (based on nominal rate).
(b) $104,212 × .06 = $6,253 (based on yield rate of interest).
(c) $7,000 − $6,253 = $747.
(d) $4,212 − $747 = $3,465.
(e) $104,212 − $747 = $103,465 (or $100,000 + $3,465 = $103,465).

When the interest method is used, it is convenient to prepare an *amortization schedule* such as those illustrated in Exhibits 19–2 and 19–3. The entries for both the issuer and the investor, for the periodic interest and amortization of premium or discount, can be taken directly from the schedule. To illustrate, the entries at the end of the first year would be:

*Borrower's Books — X Corporation*          *Investor's Books — Y Corporation*

December 31, 1976, annual interest and amortization:

Case B — Bonds sold at a discount (interest method amortization):

| | | | | | |
|---|---|---|---|---|---|
| Bond interest expense ......... 7,681 | | | Cash ................................... | 7,000 | |
| Discount on bonds | | | Discount on bond investment... | 681 | |
| payable ...................... | 681 | | Bond interest revenue ...... | | 7,681 |
| Cash .......................... | | 7,000 | | | |

Computations: Exhibit 19–2.

Case C — Bonds sold at a premium (interest method amortization):

| | | | | | |
|---|---|---|---|---|---|
| Bond interest expense ......... 6,253 | | | Cash ................................... | 7,000 | |
| Premium on bonds payable... 747 | | | Premium on bond in- | | |
| Cash .......................... | | 7,000 | vestment....................... | | 747 |
| | | | Bond interest revenue ............ | | 6,253 |

Computations: Exhibit 19–3.

A comparison of the results of straight-line amortization (page 816) and the interest method (Exhibits 19–2 and 3) clearly demonstrates the conceptual and practical differences between the two methods.[6]

## REPORTING BONDS ON THE FINANCIAL STATEMENTS

If the unamortized bond discount or premium is separately recorded, as illustrated above, it should be reported as a direct deduction from or addition to the basic account balance.

### Reporting by the Borrower

Bonds payable should be reported under the balance sheet caption Long-term Liabilities. The issuer should deduct unamortized bonds discount (a debit balance) from the face amount of the related bonds payable whereas unamortized bond premium (a credit balance) should be added to the face amount of the bonds. *APB Opinion No. 21* specifically states that bond discount or premium "should not be classified as a deferred charge or deferred credit." To assure full disclosure, the *Opinion* also states that the face of the note (i.e., the principal) and the yield rate of interest should be disclosed in the financial statements or in the notes to the statements.[7] To illustrate, the long-term liability for bonds payable should be reported essentially as follows (refer to Exhibit 19–2):

X CORPORATION
Balance Sheet (partial)
At December 31, 1976

Long-Term Liabilities:

| | | |
|---|---|---|
| Bonds payable, maturity amount (due December 31, 1980, 7% interest, payable annually) .......................... | $100,000 | |
| Less unamortized discount (based on 8% effective interest) ............................................................... | 3,312 | |
| Bonds payable less unamortized discount ..................... | | $96,688 |

---

[6] If separate accounts are not used to record discount or premium, the amortization entry would be made directly to the respective liability or investment accounts. See footnote* to the tabulation of entries on page 815.

[7] *APB Opinion No. 21*, August 1971, Appendix, par. 19. Observe that the provisions of FASB *Statement No. 12* do not apply to long-term investments in debt securities and that the lower-of-cost-or-market concept is not applied to them.

**Reporting by the Investor**

Long-term investments in bonds should be reported under the balance sheet caption, Investments and Funds. The amount reported should include cost, plus or minus any unamortized discount or premium. In addition, the current market value, if determinable and materially different from the carrying value, and the yield rate of interest used for amortization purposes, should be reported to assure full disclosure. For example, the long-term investment analyzed in Exhibit 19–2 would be reported as follows:

Y CORPORATION
Balance Sheet (partial)
At December 31, 1976

Investments and Funds:
Investment in 6% bonds of X Corporation (amortized cost
   based on 8% effective interest, due December 31, 1980) .............. $96,688

The maturity amount ($100,000), the unamortized discount ($3,312), and the difference ($96,688) could be shown separately; however, as a matter of practice, this is seldom done.

## ACCOUNTING FOR SEMIANNUAL INTEREST PAYMENTS

Most bonds specify an annual interest rate with semiannual interest payments. In this situation, the semiannual rate used is one half the annual rate and the number of interest periods is double the number of years (see Chapter 6).

To illustrate the accounting process when interest is paid semiannually, assume the bonds issued on January 1, 19A, by X Corporation specified semiannual interest payments on June 30 and December 31. The *nominal* semiannual interest rate would be 3.5%, the number of semiannual *interest periods* would be 10; if sold at an effective annual rate of 8%, the semiannual *effective rate* would be 4%. The price of this bond issue on January 1, 1976, would be computed as follows:

Present value of future principal:
   $100,000 \times p_{n=10;\,i=4\%}$ (Table 6–2) = $100,000 \times .67556 =$        $67,556
Present value of future semiannual interest payments:
   $3,500 \times P_{n=10;\,i=4\%}$ (Table 6–4) = $3,500 \times 8.11089$    =      28,388
Bond Price (semiannual interest payments assumed)....................... $95,944*

   * In Exhibit 19–1, Table A, this shown to be $95,944.57; the difference is due to table rounding.

The bond amortization table for this situation is presented in Exhibit 19–4. The entries for the issuer and the investor for this example are the same as previously illustrated except that (*a*) an interest entry must be made for each semiannual interest date, and (*b*) the amounts of cash, interest, and discount amortization will be as reflected in Exhibit 19–4.

**EXHIBIT 19–4**

**Bond Interest and Discount Amortization Interest Method—Semiannual Interest Payments (face amount—$100,000)**

| Date | Cash Interest (3½% semi-annual) | Effective Interest (4% semi-annual) | Discount Amortization | Balance Unamortized Discount | Carrying Value of Bonds |
|------|------|------|------|------|------|
| 1/1/76 starting date | | | | 4,056 | 95,944 |
| 6/30/76 | 3,500(a) | 3,838(b) | 338(c) | 3,718(d) | 96,282(e) |
| 12/31/76 | 3,500 | 3,851 | 351 | 3,367 | 96,633 |
| 6/30/77 | 3,500 | 3,865 | 365 | 3,002 | 96,998 |
| 12/31/77 | 3,500 | 3,880 | 380 | 2,622 | 97,378 |
| 6/30/78 | 3,500 | 3,895 | 395 | 2,227 | 97,773 |
| 12/31/78 | 3,500 | 3,911 | 411 | 1,816 | 98,184 |
| 6/30/79 | 3,500 | 3,927 | 427 | 1,389 | 98,611 |
| 12/31/79 | 3,500 | 3,944 | 444 | 945 | 99,055 |
| 6/30/80 | 3,500 | 3,962 | 462 | 483 | 99,517 |
| 12/31/80 | 3,500 | 3,983 | 483 | -0- | 100,000 |

(a) $100,000 × .035 = $3,500 (based on nominal interest rate).
(b) $95,944 × .04 = $3,838 (based on effective rate).
(c) $3,838 − $3,500 = $338.
(d) $4,056 − $338 = $3,718.
(e) $95,944 + $338 = $96,282 (or $100,000 − $3,718 = $96,282).

## PART B—SPECIAL PROBLEMS IN ACCOUNTING FOR BONDS

In Part A, certain complexities were excluded in order to provide a sound understanding of the fundamentals in accounting for and reporting bonds for both the issuer and the investor. A number of special problems often occur in accounting for and reporting bonds; however, they do not change the fundamentals discussed in Part A. These special problems will be discussed in this part of the chapter.

For illustrative purposes, a different fact situation will be used. Semiannual interest payments will be assumed; and an early maturity and even interest rates again will be used to shorten the illustrations. The common set of facts are:

Issuer:   Cox Corporation
Investor:  Day Corporation

Terms of the bond indenture:

a. Maturity amount of the bonds.    $200,000 ($10,000 and $1,000 denominations).

b. Date of the bonds.    January 1, 1976.

c. Maturity date.    December 31, 1978 (3 years).

d. Nominal interest rate.    8%, payable 4% semiannually.

e. Interest payments (cash).    $8,000 each June 30 and December 31.

f. Date sold.    As specified in each example to follow.

g. Yield interest rate and bond price.    7% (3½% semiannually); price, $205,329.

h. Amortization schedule (interest method):

| Date | Cash Interest (4% semi-annual) | Effective Interest (3½% semi-annual) | Premium Amortization | Balance Unamortized Premium | Carrying Value of Bonds |
|------|------|------|------|------|------|
| 1/1/76 starting date ... | | | | 5,329 | 205,329 |
| 6/30/76 ................. | 8,000(a) | 7,186(b) | 814(c) | 4,515(d) | 204,515(e) |
| 12/31/76 ................. | 8,000 | 7,158 | 842 | 3,673 | 203,673 |
| 6/30/77 ................. | 8,000 | 7,129 | 871 | 2,802 | 202,802 |
| 12/31/77 ................. | 8,000 | 7,098 | 902 | 1,900 | 201,900 |
| 6/30/78 ................. | 8,000 | 7,066 | 934 | 966 | 200,966 |
| 12/31/78 ................. | 8,000 | 7,034 | 966 | -0- | 200,000 |

(a) $200,000 × .04 = $8,000 (based on nominal rate).
(b) $205,329 × .035 = $7,186 (based on effective rate).
(c) $8,000 − $7,186 = $814.
(d) $5,329 − $814 = $4,515.
(e) $200,000 + $4,515 = $204,515 (or $205,329 − $814 = $204,515).

## BONDS SOLD, AND PURCHASED, BETWEEN INTEREST DATES

Bonds often are sold and purchased at dates other than an interest date specified on the bonds. This situation necessitates recognition, in the accounts, of accrued interest from the *last interest date* to the date of the transaction. The amount of cash is increased by the amount of the accrued interest for the same period. Accrued interest arises because of a particular characteristic of bonds. That is, the *full amount* of the specified periodic *nominal interest* on a bond will be paid in cash on each interest date after sale, regardless of its sale date. Therefore, when a bond is sold between interest dates, the amount paid by the investor will be (*a*) the price of the bond plus (*b*) any accrued interest from the last interest date.

### Bonds Sold between Interest Dates at Par

To illustrate when bonds are sold at par between interest dates, assume Cox Corporation sold the $200,000, 8% bonds, dated January 1, 1976, to Day Corporation on November 1, 1976, at par plus the four months accrued interest. This situation can be reflected on a time scale as follows:

**TIME SCALE**

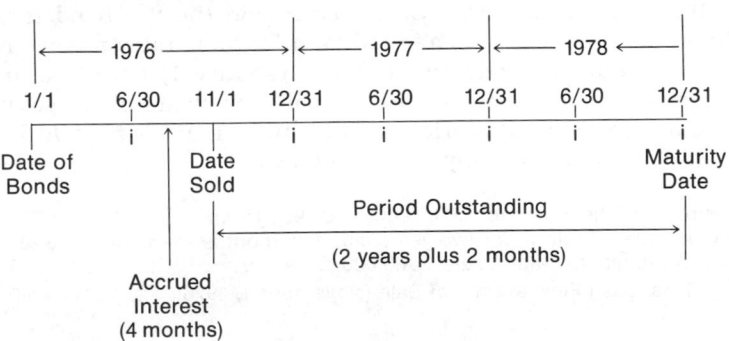

The amount of cash flowing from the investor to the issuer can be computed as follows:

```
Sales price of the bond issue on 11/1/76 (at par) .......................... $200,000
Add: Accrued interest since last interest date (June 30
    to November 1—$200,000 × .04 × 4/6) ..................................    5,333
        Total Cash Paid on Date of Sale/Purchase Transaction ......... $205,333
```

The borrower and the investor would make the following entries in 1976:

*Cox Corporation—Borrower*                *Day Corporation—Investor*

November 1, 1976—To record sale and purchase of the bonds (including four months accrued interest):

```
Cash ........................... 205,333        Investment in bonds ......... 200,000
    Bonds payable.........          200,000     Bond interest revenue ......   5,333
    Bond interest                                   Cash ........................        205,333
        expense..............          5,333
```

December 31, 1976—To record payment of nominal semiannual interest:

```
Bond interest expense ...   8,000               Cash ............................   8,000
    Cash ($200,000 ×                                Bond interest revenue.             8,000
        .04) .....................    8,000
```

If the purchase/sale transaction date is in one accounting period and the next interest date is in the following accounting period, most accountants use accrued interest expense and accrued interest revenue, respectively, in these two entries. Both approaches derive the same ultimate net effect. See Exhibits 19–6 and 19–7.

After posting both entries, the respective interest expense and interest revenue accounts will stand at \$2,667 (i.e., \$8,000 — \$5,333) which represents interest for the two months outstanding (\$200,000 × .04 × $2/6$ = \$2,667). Similarly, bond transactions between *individual investors,* when not on an interest date, necessitates recognition of accrued interest by both parties.

## Bonds Sold between Interest Dates at a Discount or Premium

When a bond is sold or purchased between interest dates at a *discount* or *premium,* the accounting illustrated immediately above is followed except that the discount or premium must be recorded and amortized over the *period outstanding; that is, the period from the date of sale (not the date of the bond) to the maturity date.*

To illustrate, assume Cox Corporation sold the 8% bond issue, reflected on the time scale on page 821, at a 7% yield rate on November 1, 1976. Recall that the bonds were dated January 1, 1976, and mature on December 31, 1978; thus they are sold two years plus two months before maturity. The sales price on November 1, 1976, to yield 7%, and the cash flow would be computed as follows:

```
Sales price of the 8% bonds: $200,000 × 101.959 (from
    Exhibit 19–1, Table C, for two years plus two months at 7%) =  ... $203,918
Accrued interest to date of sale: $200,000 × .04 × 4/6 = .................    5,333
        Total Cash Flow at Date of Sale (November 1, 1976) ........... $209,251
```

The borrower and investor would record the transaction as follows:

*Borrower*                                    *Investor*

November 1, 1976 — to record sale/purchase of bond issue:

| Cash ........................ 209,251 | | Bond investment ........... 200,000 | |
| Bond interest | | Bond interest revenue ...... 5,333 | |
| expense ........... | 5,333 | Premium on bond | |
| Premium on bonds | | investment ................. | 3,918 |
| payable............... | 3,918 | Cash ...................... | 209,251 |
| Bonds payable ...... | 200,000 | | |

The premium must be amortized over the total period outstanding (26 months); therefore, assuming the amortization amounts are not material, the straight-line method can be used. On the next interest date, the nominal interest (cash) for the full six months and amortization of premium for the two months since date of sale would be recorded as follows:[8]

*Borrower*                                    *Investor*

December 31, 1976 — to record semiannual interest payment using straight-line amortization:

| Bond interest expense ......... 7,698 | | Cash .................................. 8,000 | |
| Premium on bonds | | Premium on bond | |
| payable .......................... | 302 | investment.................... | 302 |
| Cash ($200,000 × .04)...... | 8,000 | Bond interest revenue ...... | 7,698 |

Amortization: $3,918 ÷ 26 (total months outstanding) = $151 per month (rounded)
$151 × 2 (months outstanding this period) = $302

After the above entries are posted, the respective interest expense and revenue accounts will reflect net interest amounts for two months (i.e., the period outstanding since the date of sale).

Alternatively, amortization based on the *interest method* would be as reflected in Exhibit 19–5. When the transaction is between interest dates, as in this illustration (two months before next interest date), the amortization amount at the first interest date after acquisition must be uniquely determined. It is computed as the difference between the sales price at transaction date (November 1, 1976, in the example) and the sales price at the next interest date (i.e., December 31, 1976). This computation is shown in Exhibit 19–5. Entries to reflect the semiannual interest and premium amortization also are reflected in that exhibit. This is an important example because typically bonds are bought and sold between interest dates, at a discount or premium, and the interest method should be used.

---

[8] These entries assume amortization on interest dates; amortization often is delayed until the end of the accounting period; see Exhibits 19–7 and 19–8. These entries also assume discount and premium are recorded in separate accounts. If the approach shown in footnote* to the tabulation of entries on page 815 is followed, the amount amortized would be recorded directly in the liability and investment accounts respectively.

**EXHIBIT 19-5**

**Bond Interest and Discount Amortization between Interest Dates—Interest Method (semiannual interest payments)**

| Date | Cash Interest (4% semiannual) | Effective Interest (3½% semiannual) | Premium Amortization | Balance Unamortized Premium | Carrying Value of Bonds |
|---|---|---|---|---|---|
| 11/1/76 starting date ... | | | | 3,918 | 203,918 |
| 12/31/76 ........... | 8,000(b) | 7,755(b) | 245(a) | 3,673 | 203,673 |
| 6/30/77 ........... | 8,000 | 7,129 | 871 | 2,802 | 202,802 |
| 12/31/77 ........... | 8,000 | 7,098 | 902 | 1,900 | 201,900 |
| 6/30/78 ........... | 8,000 | 7,066 | 934 | 966 | 200,966 |
| 12/31/78 ........... | 8,000 | 7,034 | 966 | -0- | 200,000 |

Computations:

(a) Bond price at date of sale (November 1, 1976), Exhibit 19-1, Table C, for
   two years plus two months at 7%; $200,000 × 101.959 = ............................................. $203,918
   Bond price at next interest date (December 31, 1976), Exhibit 19-1, Table
   C, for two years even at 7%; $200,000 × 101.83654 = ..................................... 203,673
   Difference—Amortization for First Interest Period (two months) ..................... $    245

(b) Semiannual cash interest on December 31, 1976, $200,000 × .04 = ..................... $  8,000
   Premium amortization first period as above ......................................................... 245
   Effective Interest (before accrual of interest at acquisition) ...................... $  7,755

Net interest expense for 1976:
   Effective interest as computed above ............................................................... $  7,755
   Less accrued interest at date of bond transaction (see issue transaction on
   November 1, 1976, given on page 823) ............................................................. 5,333
   Net Interest Cost for the Two-Month Holding Period during 1976................................ $  2,422

Alternatively: ($200,000 × .04 × ²/₆) − $245 = $2,422.

## ACCOUNTING WHEN THE INTEREST DATE AND END OF THE ACCOUNTING PERIOD DO NOT COINCIDE

Typically, the interest date on bonds (and other debt securities) does not coincide with the end of the accounting period. In this situation, a borrower must *accrue* interest expense on the debt from the last interest date to the end of the accounting period. Similarly, an investor must accrue interest revenue on the bond investment.

In respect to bonds sold (or purchased) at a discount or premium, there must be an accrual at the end of the accounting period of a portion of the unamortized amount. Each year the amount of discount or premium amortized must be equivalent to the portion of the year the bonds were outstanding (or held as an investment).

To illustrate, assume (for this example only) that the accounting periods for Cox Corporation and Day Corporation ends on March 31 and that the bonds were sold on January 1, 1976. At the end of the accounting period, the following adjusting entries would be made:[9]

---

[9] These entries assume amortization on interest dates; amortization often is delayed until the end of the accounting period; see Exhibits 19-7 and 19-8. These entries also assume discount and premium are recorded in separate accounts. If the approach shown in footnote* to the tabulation of entries on page 815 is followed, the amount amortized would be recorded directly in the liability and investment accounts respectively.

March 31, 1976 – Adjusting entry for accrued bond interest and premium amortization for the three months, January–March (computations based on data from the amortization schedule shown on page 821):

Borrower – Cox Corporation:

| | | |
|---|---|---|
| Bond interest expense ($7,186 × ³⁄₆) | 3,593 | |
| Premium on bonds payable ($814 × ³⁄₆) | 407 | |
|    Accrued bond interest payable ($200,000 × .04 × ³⁄₆) | | 4,000 |

(Note: Assuming the straight-line method, the amortization would be $5,329 × ³⁄₃₆ = $444).

Investor – Day Corporation:

| | | |
|---|---|---|
| Accrued bond interest receivable | 4,000 | |
|    Premium on bond investment | | 407 |
|    Bond interest revenue | | 3,593 |

These entries are candidates for reversing entries (see Chapter 3). If reversed, the entry on the next entry date would be affected; whether reversed or not, the net results would be the same (see Exhibits 19–7 and 19–8 for a complete sequence of entries including reversing entries).

## BOND ISSUE COSTS

There are numerous material expenditures incurred in preparing and selling a bond issue. Bond issue costs include legal, accounting, other professional fees, commissions, engraving, printing, registration, and promotion costs. Generally accepted accounting principles treat these expenditures collectively as a *deferred charge* rather than as an element of bond discount or premium.[10] As a deferred charge, the total amount should be amortized (usually on a straight-line basis) over the period outstanding between the sale date and the maturity date, because it is assumed that there will be related future revenue benefits flowing from the proceeds of the financing. Theoretically, bond issue costs should be amortized using the interest method; however, the straight-line method often is used because they are not material in amount. In some situations, these costs are immaterial in amount; in other cases where an underwriter handles the planning, issue, and sale of the bonds, it may be difficult to distinguish issue costs from the discount or premium.

To illustrate, assume W Corporation sold $100,000, 7¹⁄₂%, ten-year bonds at 101 on January 1, 19A (also date of the bonds). Bond issue costs were $300, and the bond interest is payable annually each December 31.

*a.* January 1, 19A – to record sale:

| | | |
|---|---|---|
| Cash | 100,700 | |
| Bond issue costs deferred | 300 | |
|    Premium on bonds payable | | 1,000 |
|    Bonds payable | | 100,000 |

---

[10] *APB Opinion No. 21*, August 1971, par. 16.

*b.* December 31, 19A—to record interest and amortization of premium and bond issue costs (straight-line basis):

| | | |
|---|---:|---:|
| Bond interest expense ......................................... | 7,430 | |
| Premium on bonds payable ($1,000 ÷ 10 years)............ | 100 | |
| Bond issue costs deferred ($300 ÷ 10 years) ........ | | 30 |
| Cash........................................................... | | 7,500 |

## COMPREHENSIVE ILLUSTRATION—AMORTIZATION AT YEAR-END VERSUS AT INTEREST DATES

The preceding discussion and illustrations focused on specific concepts and problems. At this point, a comprehensive illustration is presented to tie together the various elements of accounting for bonds. Additionally, bond discount or premium may be amortized either (*a*) at year-end only, or (*b*) at each interest date. Both approaches give the same results, and it is largely a matter of personal choice between them.

To provide a comprehensive illustration from date of sale to maturity date, assume the following facts:

> Issuer: Z Corporation.
> Maturity amount of the bonds: $10,000 (in $1,000 denominations).
> Date of the bonds: April 1, 1975.
> Issue date (date sold): April 1, 1975.
> Maturity date: April 1, 1977 (two-year term).
> Stated interest rate: 7%, payable 3½% semiannually.
> Interest dates (cash): $350 each April 1 and October 1.
> Price: $10,185.85 (i.e., a premium of $185.85).
> Yield rate of interest: 6%.
> Accounting period ends on December 31.

Exhibits 19–6, 19–7, and 19–8 illustrate entries for sale, interest payments, adjustments, reversals, closing entries, and debt payment at maturity.

An amortization table, using the interest method, is shown in Exhibit 19–6. Amortization on each *interest date* is illustrated in Exhibit 19–7. In contrast, amortization only at *year-end* is illustrated in Exhibit 19–8.

**EXHIBIT 19–6**
**Amortization Bond Premium—Interest Method**

| Date | Cash Cr. | Bond Interest Expense Dr. | Bond Premium Dr. | Balance Unamortized Premium | Liability Carrying Value |
|---|---|---|---|---|---|
| 4/1/75.......... | (issuance) | | | 185.85 | 10,185.85 |
| 10/1/75.......... | 350.00[a] | 305.58[b] | 44.42[c] | 141.43[d] | 10,141.43[e] |
| 4/1/76.......... | 350.00 | 304.24 | 45.76 | 95.67 | 10,095.67 |
| 10/1/76.......... | 350.00 | 302.87 | 47.13 | 48.54 | 10,048.54 |
| 4/1/77.......... | 350.00 | 301.46 | 48.54 | -0- | 10,000.00 |

(a) $10,000 × .07 × 6/12 = $350.00 (at nominal rate, 7%).
(b) $10,185.85 × .06 × 6/12 = $305.58 (at effective rate, 6%).
(c) Column (a) minus column (b).
(d) $185.85 − $44.42 = $141.43.
(e) $10,185.85 − $44.42 = $10,141.43.

**EXHIBIT 19–7**
**Bonds Payable, Semiannual Interest—Amortization on Interest Dates (interest method)**

| Date | Explanation | Cash Dr., Cr.* | Bonds Payable Dr., Cr.* | Bond Interest Expense Dr., Cr.* | Accrued Bond Interest Dr., Cr.* | Income Summary Dr., Cr.* | Bond Premium Dr., Cr.* |
|---|---|---|---|---|---|---|---|
| 4/1/75......... | Sale of bonds | 10,185.85 | 10,000.00* | | | | 185.85* |
| 10/1/75......... | Interest payment and amortization | 350.00* | | 305.58 | | | 44.42 |
| 12/31/75......... | Adjusting entry | | | 152.12 | 175.00* | | 22.88(a) |
| 12/31/75......... | Closing entry | | | 457.70* | | 457.70 | |
| 1/1/76......... | Reversing entry | | | 152.12* | 175.00 | | 22.88* |
| 4/1/76......... | Interest payment and amortization | 350.00* | | 304.24 | | | 45.76 |
| 10/1/76......... | Interest payment and amortization | 350.00* | | 302.87 | | | 47.13 |
| 12/31/76......... | Adjusting entry | | | 150.73 | 175.00* | | 24.27(b) |
| 12/31/76......... | Closing entry | | | 605.72* | | 605.72 | |
| 1/1/77......... | Reversing entry | | | 150.73* | 175.00 | | 24.27* |
| 4/1/77......... | Interest payment and amortization | 350.00* | | 301.46 | | | 48.54 |
| 4/1/77......... | Payment of bonds | 10,000.00* | 10,000.00 | | | | |
| 12/31/77......... | Closing entry | | | 150.73* | | 150.73 | |
| | | 1,214.15 | | | | 1,214.15 | |

Refer to Exhibit 19–6:
(a) $45.76 × 3/6 = $22.88
(b) $48.54 × 3/6 = $24.27

**EXHIBIT 19–8**
**Bonds Payable, Semiannual Interest—Amortization Only at Year-End (interest method)**

| Date | Explanation | Cash Dr., Cr.* | Bonds Payable Dr., Cr.* | Bond Interest Expense Dr., Cr.* | Accrued Bond Interest Dr., Cr.* | Income Summary Dr., Cr.* | Bond Premium Dr., Cr.* |
|---|---|---|---|---|---|---|---|
| 4/1/75 | Sale of bonds | 10,185.85 | 10,000.00* | | | | 185.85* |
| 10/1/75 | Interest payment | 350.00* | | 350.00 | | | |
| 12/31/75 | Adjusting entry | | | 175.00 | 175.00* | | |
| 12/31/75 | Premium amortization | | | 67.30* | | | 67.30 [a] |
| 12/31/75 | Closing entry | | | 457.70* | | 457.70 | |
| 1/1/76 | Reversing of accrued interest | | | 175.00* | 175.00 | | |
| 4/1/76 | Interest payment | 350.00* | | 350.00 | | | |
| 10/1/76 | Interest payment | 350.00* | | 350.00 | | | |
| 12/31/76 | Adjusting entry | | | 175.00 | 175.00* | | |
| 12/31/76 | Premium amortization | | | 94.28* | | | 94.28 [b] |
| 12/31/76 | Closing entry | | | 605.72* | | 605.72 | |
| 1/1/77 | Reversing of accrued interest | | | 175.00* | 175.00 | | |
| 4/1/77 | Interest payment | 350.00* | | 350.00 | | | |
| 4/1/77 | Payment of bonds | 10,000.00* | 10,000.00 | | | | |
| 12/31/77 | Premium amortization | | | 24.27* | | | 24.27 [c] |
| 12/31/77 | Closing entry | | | 150.73* | | 150.73 | |
| | | 1,214.15 | | | | 1,214.15 | |

Refer to Exhibit 19–7:
(a) $44.42 + ($45.76 × 3/6) = $67.30.
(b) ($45.76 × 3/6) + $47.13 + ($48.54 × 3/6) = $94.28.
(c) ($48.54 × 3/6) = $24.27.

Observe in particular computations of the amortization amounts for the adjusting entries. The net results are the same in both exhibits as reflected in (a) the amount of interest expense each period (compare the closing entries), and (b) the carrying value of the bonds (face amount plus the unamortized premium) at the end of each accounting period.

## EARLY EXTINGUISHMENT OF DEBT

Bonds and certain other debt instruments frequently carry a *call provision* stating that at the option of the *borrower,* the debt may be called for payment prior to the obligatory maturity date. Call provisions, including time limits and the call or reacquisition price, are specified in the bond indenture and are printed on each bond certificate. Obviously, bonds without a call provision may be reacquired by purchase in the market. Early extinguishment by exercise of a call normally is made on an interest date, in which case the amortization of any discount or premium and bond issue costs will be up-to-date; thus there will be no accrued interest. Early extinguishment by purchase in the market often is not at an interest date in which case accruals must be brought up to date prior to recording the extinguishment transaction.

In early extinguishment of debt, the difference between *reacquisition price* and *net carrying amount* of the debt is a "gain or loss on early extinguishment of debt." The net carrying amount is the net of the par, unamortized discount, premium and bond issue costs, related to the debt paid off.

*APB Opinion No. 26,* "Early Extinguishment of Debt" (October 1972), specifies the appropriate accounting for early extinguishment of debt. Prior to that opinion, four different alternatives were used to account for the gain or loss on early extinguishment of debt: it was (1) amortized over what would have been the remaining life of the old debt; (2) recorded as an *ordinary* item on the income statement in the year of recall; (3) reported as an *extraordinary* item on the income statement in the year of recall; and (4) amortized over the life of any new debt that was created to obtain funds to pay off the old debt. To attain uniformity and realistic reporting on the income statement, *Opinion No. 26* states: "A difference between the reacquisition price and the net carrying amount of the extinguished debt should be recognized currently in income of the period of extinguishment as losses or gains and identified as a separate item." Under the restrictive criteria given in *APB Opinion No. 30* (June 1973) for extraordinary items (see page 126), the gain or loss was reported as an ordinary item. Because early extinguishment was quickly used to generate a large credit (an ordinary gain) on the income statement, the FASB in *Statement No. 4* specified that the gain or loss on early extinguishment of debt be reported on the *income statement as an extraordinary item.*[11]

To illustrate early extinguishment of debt, assume the bonds issued by X Corporation (data on page 810A) had a call provision that they could

---

[11] FASB, *Statement of Financial Accounting Standards No. 4,* March 1975, par. 8.

be called at a reacquisition price of 102 at any time on or after December 31, 1978. At that date, assume the accounts of X Corporation reflected the balances shown in Exhibit 19–2 and, in addition, unamortized bond issue costs were $400. If all of the bonds are recalled, the reacquisition entry (after the entry to record interest and discount amortization on that date) would be:

December 31, 1978:

| | | |
|---|---:|---:|
| Bonds payable........................................................ | 100,000 | |
| Extraordinary loss—early extinguishment of bonds ......... | 4,183 | |
| Discount on bonds payable (unamortized)................. | | 1,783 |
| Bond issue costs (unamortized) ........................... | | 400 |
| Cash (at 102) ....................................................... | | 102,000 |

## Refunding Bonds Payable

When debt (usually an old bond issue) is extinguished early and the necessary cash is obtained by issuing a new bond series, it is usually referred to as *refunding*. Refunding generally is advantageous (*a*) when the new series has a lower interest rate than the old series, or (*b*) when the old series can be reacquired in the market at a "deep" discount. The issuing corporation must consider factors before making a refunding decision, such as future interest costs including present value effects. The basic question should be: Can future costs be reduced by refunding? For example, in view of the current high interest rates, one company with an old $50,000,000, 4.75% bond issue outstanding could extinguish that issue by purchasing them at 82 in the market (i.e., for $41,000,000). The result would be a $9,000,000 gain in the year of extinguishment. In most situations, a large portion of the cash would be obtained by a *refunding issue* at interest rates about 8%. Several factors, in addition to present value analysis, entered into the decisions; such as the immediate effect of the $9,000,000 gain on the income statement. Accounting for refunding situations is the same as illustrated in the preceding paragraph.

Because of inappropriate *balance sheet reporting* practices, FASB *Statement No. 6*, "Classification of Short-Term Obligations Expected to Be Refunded," was issued in 1975. This statement affirms prior GAAP that "short-term obligations arising from transactions in the normal course of business that are due in customary terms shall be classified as current liabilities." The statement permits the exclusion from *current liabilities*, currently maturing debt that the enterprise intends to *refinance on a long-term basis*. The intention must be supported either by (*a*) long-term refinancing prior to issuance of the financial statements, or (*b*) an enforceable long-term financing agreement.

## CONVERTIBLE BONDS

A convertible bond is a debt security which may be converted to capital stock (usually common stock) of the issuer, at the option of the *holder*, under specified conditions. Typically, convertible securities also are *callable* at a specified redemption or call price at the option of the *issuer* and are subordinated to nonconvertible debt. Subordinated means a lower class; that is, the convertible debt ranks below nonconvertible debt as a claim against assets. In case of insolvency, the nonconvertible debt would be paid first. Generally, convertible bonds can be sold at an interest rate lower than it would be for nonconvertible bonds because investors impute a value to the conversion privilege. Convertible securities also have a conversion ratio and a conversion price specified in the bond indenture. The *conversion ratio* is the number of shares of common stock the holder of a convertible bond will receive when tendered for conversion. In contrast, the *conversion price* is the relationship between the face amount of the convertible bond and the number of shares of common stock to be received upon conversion.

To illustrate, assume AB Corporation issued $1,000 convertible bonds, each of which could be converted, at the option of the holder at any time after the second year from issuance, for ten shares of AB Corporation common stock. The conversion ratio for each bond would be 10 (shares of stock) to 1 (bond); the conversion price would be $1,000 ÷ 10 shares = $100.

Convertible bonds offer certain advantages to both the issuer and the investor. The primary advantages to the issuer are (*a*) a lower rate of interest, and (*b*) a means of securing equity (stockholder) financing in the long run (after conversion, this is the net effect since the debt is not paid in cash). The call option usually is used by the issuer to force conversion when the aggregate price of the stock to be received on conversion is greater than the call price; in this case, only a foolish investor would take cash in lieu of the stock.

The primary advantages of convertible bonds to the investor are (*a*) an option to receive either the face of the bond at maturity or common stock of the issuer, (*b*) a guaranteed rate of interest up to conversion date or maturity, and (*c*) benefits of appreciation in the price of the common stock of the issuer.

### Accounting for the Issuance of Convertible Bonds

Since convertible bonds specify a lower rate of interest than would nonconvertible debt for the same company, and since they can be converted to common stock, there is the basic question upon issuance as to what portion of the sales price should relate to *debt* and what portion should be allocated to *equity* (stockholders' equity). To illustrate the problem, assume AB Corporation issued $100,000, 7%, ten-year *nonconvertible* bonds payable which were sold for $96,000. The transaction would be recorded as follows:

| | | |
|---|---|---|
| Cash............................................................................ | 96,000 | |
| Discount on bonds payable .......................................... | 4,000 | |
|     Bonds payable, 7% (nonconvertible) ......................... | | 100,000 |

Now assume instead, that each $1,000 bond (without detachable stock warrants) was convertible after the second year, at the option of the holder, to ten shares of common stock (par $75) of AB Corporation. Because of this feature, the bonds specified an interest rate of 5% (as opposed to the prior 7% rate) and would sell for $106,000. How should this transaction be recorded? There are two alternatives:

Alternative 1 — View the transaction as debt only:

| | | |
|---|---:|---:|
| Cash ............................................................................... | 106,000 | |
|     Premium on bonds payable ..................................... | | 6,000 |
|     Bonds payable, 5% (convertible) ............................. | | 100,000 |

Alternative 2 — View the transaction as part debt and part equity:

| | | |
|---|---:|---:|
| Cash ............................................................................... | 106,000 | |
| Discount on bonds payable ($106,000 — $96,000) ............ | 10,000 | |
|     Bonds payable, 5% (convertible) ............................. | | 100,000 |
|     Contributed capital — bond conversion option ............ | | 16,000 |

Reflecting the differing views and implementation problems, *APB Opinion No. 10* (1966) required the second alternative; the following year, *APB Opinion No. 12* (1967) suspended this requirement. Finally, *APB Opinion No. 14* (1969) specified the *current requirement* to be *Alternative 1*, except when there are detachable stock warrants (discussed below). The principal reasons for selecting Alternative 1 when the bonds do not have detachable stock warrants are (*a*) the inseparability of the debt and the conversion option, and (*b*) difficulty in implementation–in the absence of separate transferability for the two portions the amounts that should be assigned separately to debt and equity cannot be derived from the market. Therefore, because an objective assignment of separate values to debt and equity is impossible, Alternative 1, although not conceptually preferable, was considered more realistic.

The *investor* would record a $1,000 convertible bond of AB Corporation acquired as a long-term investment as follows:

| | | |
|---|---:|---:|
| Bond investment (convertible bonds) ................................... | 1,000 | |
| Premium on bond investment.............................................. | 60 | |
|     Cash ................................................................................ | | 1,060 |

### Accounting for Conversion by the Borrower

When convertible bonds are tendered by the investor to the issuer for conversion to common stock in accordance with the conversion privilege, the carrying value of the bonds must be removed from the accounts and issuance of the common stock recorded. Prior to recording the conversion transaction, all account balances related to the bonds should be brought up to the current status. If the conversion is made on an interest date, these items will be on a current basis; if not, bond discount or premium and accrued interest from the last interest date to date of conversion must be recorded.

In recording the conversion transaction, an accounting issue arises as to whether (*a*) market value of the bonds or the stock, whichever is the more clearly determinable, or (b) book value of the bonds should prevail. To illustrate, refer to AB Corporation, Alternative 1 above. Assume an AB Corporation bondholder tenders a $1,000 bond for conversion (to ten shares of common stock, par $75) when the bond accounts reflected the following:

| | |
|---|---:|
| Bonds payable, 5% (convertible)............... | $100,000 |
| Bond premium (unamortized) ................. | 3,000 |

Assume further that at date of conversion, AB common stock was selling at $95 per share. There are two alternatives for recording conversion of the $1,000 bond:

Alternative 1 — Use market value:

| | | |
|---|---:|---:|
| Bonds payable, 5% (convertible) ............................................. | 1,000 | |
| Premium on bonds payable..................................................... | 30 | |
|     Common stock (ten shares @ $75 par) ............................. | | 750 |
|     Contributed capital in excess of par (ten shares @ $20) ...... | | 200 |
|     Gain on redemption of convertible bonds ........................... | | 80 |

Alternative 2 — Use book value of the bonds:

| | | |
|---|---:|---:|
| Bonds payable, 5% (convertible) ............................................. | 1,000 | |
| Bond premium......................................................................... | 30 | |
|     Common stock (ten shares @ $75) .................................... | | 750 |
|     Contributed capital in excess of par.................................. | | 280 |

Alternative 1, market value, is generally viewed as theoretically preferable on the basis that the exchange completes the transaction cycle for the bonds and starts a new cycle for the stock. Additionally, market value is theoretically preferable because it recognizes changes in market valuations which have been occurring and it subordinates a consideration determined some time in the past when the bonds were issued.

Despite this theoretical argument, *current practice* generally uses Alternative 2 because (a) in some situations, the market value of the stock or the bonds is not determinable; (b) the transaction is viewed merely as an exchange of two securities that have some characteristics in common; (c) there is no "earning process"; and (d) transactions in a corporation's own stock should not cause recognition of gains and losses.

The *investor* would record the conversion on an interest date of a $1,000 bond of AB Corporation, acquired as a long-term investment (see page 832) as follows (assuming the same rate of amortization as the issuer):

| | | |
|---|---:|---:|
| Investment in common stock (ten shares, AB Corporation) ...... | 1,030 | |
|     Bond investment........................................................... | | 1,000 |
|     Premium on bond investment (unamortized).................... | | 30 |

Convertible bonds that are reacquired by exercise of the *call provision*, rather than by conversion, should be accounted for under the provisions of *APB Opinion No. 26,* and reported in accordance with FASB *Statement No. 4,* "Reporting Gains and Losses from Early Extinguishment of Debt," and FASB *Statement No. 6* as discussed and illustrated on page 829.

## DEBT WITH DETACHABLE STOCK WARRANTS

Debt securities, usually bonds, sometimes are issued with *stock warrants* attached. A stock warrant gives the holder the option, within a specified time period, to purchase from the issuer a specified number of shares of common stock at a specified price per share. Detachable stock warrants are often "attached" to bonds to enhance the marketability of the bonds. As with convertible bonds, the bonds usually carry a lower interest rate and tend to sell for a higher market price on the market. Detachable warrants can be separated from the bonds and traded on the market; that is, they are *equity* instruments that are *separable* from the debt instrument. Because of this separability, *APB Opinion No. 14* states that: "the portion of the proceeds of debt securities issued with detachable stock purchase warrants which is allocable to the warrants should be accounted for as paid-in capital. The allocation should be based on the relative fair values of the two securities at time of issuance." When no fair market value can be determined, the fair market value of either of the elements must be used. To illustrate, assume AB Corporation issued $100,000, 5%, ten-year, *nonconvertible bonds with detachable stock warrants*. Each $1,000 bond carried ten detachable warrants; each warrant was for one share of common stock, par $10, at a specified option price of $15 per share. The bonds, including the warrants, sold at $105,000; and shortly after issuance, the warrants were quoted on the market for $4 each. No market value can be determined for the bonds above. The bond issuance would be recorded as follows:

Borrower:

| | | |
|---|---:|---:|
| Cash | 105,000 | |
|     Bonds payable, 5% (with detachable stock warrants)... | | 100,000 |
|     Premium on bonds payable | | 1,000 |
|     Detachable stock warrants outstanding (1,000 | | |
|         warrants @ $4) | | 4,000 |

Investor:

| | | |
|---|---:|---:|
| Bond investment | 100,000 | |
| Premium on bond investment | 1,000 | |
| Investment—detachable stock warrants (1,000 | | |
|     warrants @ $4) | 4,000 | |
|     Cash | | 105,000 |

Subsequently, tender of the 1,000 detachable stock warrants would be recorded as follows:

Borrower:

| | | |
|---|---:|---:|
| Cash (1,000 × $15) | 15,000 | |
| Detachable stock warrants outstanding | 4,000 | |
|     Common stock, 1,000 shares, par $10 | | 10,000 |
|     Contributed capital in excess of par | | 9,000 |

Investor:

| | | |
|---|---:|---:|
| Investment in common stock, 1,000 shares | 19,000 | |
|     Investment—detachable stock warrants | | 4,000 |
|     Cash (1,000 × $15) | | 15,000 |

### PART C—SERIAL BONDS

## CHARACTERISTICS OF SERIAL BONDS

An issue of bonds with provision for repayment of principal in a series of *installments* is called a serial bond issue. Serial bond issue are especially attractive since they avoid the need for a sinking fund. Serial bonds are well adapted for use by school districts and other taxing authorities which borrow money upon agreement that a special tax will be levied to pay off the obligation. As the taxes are collected, the money so raised can best be utilized by paying off a part of the indebtedness. This may be done by having a part of the bond issue mature each year.

## DETERMINING SELLING PRICE OF SERIAL BONDS

The selling price of serial bonds may be derived by computing the selling price for each series separately in the same way that a straight bond issue is valued and then totaling the prices of the several series. For example, assume that serial bonds carrying 7% interest payable $3\frac{1}{2}\%$ semiannually are sold to yield 5% with the following maturity dates: $10,000 at end of 12 months, $20,000 at end of 18 months, and $30,000 at end of 24 months. The selling price of each of the three series, as well as that of the whole issue, may be (a) derived from a bond table (similar to Exhibit 19–1) or (b) computed as follows (see page 814)[12]

|  | Bond Price | Premium |
|---|---|---|
| Series No. 1 (due in 12 months—2 interest periods): |  |  |
| Principal: $10,000 × .9518144* | $ 9,518.14 |  |
| Interest payments: $350 × 1.9274242† | 674.60 |  |
|  | 10,192.74 | $   192.74 |
| Series No. 2 (due in 18 months—3 interest periods): |  |  |
| Principal: $20,000 × .9285994 | 18,571.99 |  |
| Interest payments: $700 × 2.8560236 | 1,999.21 |  |
|  | 20,571.20 | 571.20 |
| Series No. 3 (due in 24 months—4 interest periods): |  |  |
| Principal: $30,000 × .9059506 | 27,178.52 |  |
| Interest payments: $1,050 × 3.7619742 | 3,950.07 |  |
|  | 31,128.59 | 1,128.59 |
| Total Price of All Series | $61,892.53 |  |
| Total Premium on All Series |  | $1,892.53 |

* Table 6–2—$p_{n=2}$
         $i=2\frac{1}{2}\%$

† Table 6–4—$P_{n=2}$
         $i=2\frac{1}{2}\%$

---

[12] Although not realistic, a short time span is used to simplify the computations.

**EXHIBIT 19-9**

**Amortization of Premium on Serial Bonds—Straight Line**

| Serial No. (a) | Months Outstanding (b) | Par Value (c) | Sales Price (d) | Total Premium to Be Amortized (e) | Amortization of Premium—Straight Line | | | |
|---|---|---|---|---|---|---|---|---|
| | | | | | At End of 6 Months (f) | At End of 12 Months (g) | At End of 18 Months (h) | At End of 24 Months (i) |
| 1 | 12 | $10,000 | $10,192.74 | $ 192.74 | $ 96.37 | $ 96.37 | | |
| 2 | 18 | 20,000 | 20,571.20 | 571.20 | 190.40 | 190.40 | $190.40 | |
| 3 | 24 | 30,000 | 31,128.59 | 1,128.59 | 282.15 | 282.15 | 282.15 | $282.14 |
| Total Amortization per Period | | | | $1,892.53 | $568.92 | $568.92 | $472.55 | $282.14 |

## AMORTIZATION OF PREMIUM AND DISCOUNT ON SERIAL BONDS

Amortization of premium or discount on serial bonds is identical with that on ordinary bonds; however, the computations involve more arithmetic. When the results are *not* materially different from the interest method, the straight-line method may be used; otherwise, the interest method must be used. In both methods, the amount of periodic amortization must be related to the amount of bonds *outstanding* during the period. Therefore the amount of periodic amortization of premium or discount will decrease as each serial is paid off at its maturity date.

*Straight-line amortization* of the $1,892.53 premium from the above example is computed for each period in Exhibit 19–9. Observe that the premium on each serial is simply apportioned to the number of periods it is outstanding.[13]

The entries for the foregoing example are given below, with the added assumption that $5,000 par of the Serial No. 3 bonds, which were to mature at the end of 24 months, were purchased for $5,100 and retired at the end of 12 months.

1. To record sale of the bonds:

| | | |
|---|---|---|
| Cash | 61,892.53 | |
| Premium on bonds payable | | 1,892.53 |
| Bonds payable | | 60,000.00 |

2. To record payment of interest and straight-line amortization of premium at the end of six months:

| | | |
|---|---|---|
| Bond interest expense | 1,531.08 | |
| Premium on bonds payable | 568.92 | |
| Cash | | 2,100.00 |

3. To record payment of interest and amortization of premium at end of 12 months:

| | | |
|---|---|---|
| Bond interest expense | 1,531.08 | |
| Premium on bonds payable | 568.92 | |
| Cash | | 2,100.00 |

---

[13] Occasionally problems are given that do not provide a basis for determining the amount of premium or discount applicable to each series. In this situation, an approximation, known as the dollar-periods allocation, is used. It is appropriate only for the straight-line method. To illustrate, the $1,892.53 total premium could be allocated as follows:

| Serial | Par | Periods Outstanding (semiannual) | Dollar Periods | Allocation Fraction | Allocation to Serials | |
|---|---|---|---|---|---|---|
| 1 | $10,000 | 2 | $ 20,000 | 20/200 | × $1,892.53 = $ | 189.25 |
| 2 | 20,000 | 3 | 60,000 | 60/200 | × $1,892.53 = | 567.76 |
| 3 | 30,000 | 4 | 120,000 | 120/200 | × $1,892.53 = | 1,135.52 |
| | | | $200,000 | | | $1,892.53 |

The amounts in the last column are then allocated to each period on a straight-line basis as illustrated in Exhibit 19–9.

4. To record payment of Serial No. 1 bonds at the end of 12 months:

```
Bonds payable (Serial No. 1) ...............................   10,000.00
    Cash ......................................................                10,000.00
```

5. To record retirement of $5,000 of Serial No. 3 bonds at end of 12 months for $5,100 cash:

```
Bonds payable  ...........................................   5,000.00
Bond premium  ...........................................     94.05*
Loss on bonds retired .............................          5.95
    Cash .....................................................                 5,100.00
        * ($5,000/$30,000) × ($282.15 + $282.14) = $94.05.
```

6. To pay interest, amortize premium, and pay off Serial No. 2 bonds at end of 18 months:

```
Bond interest ...........................................       1,149.47
Bond premium [$190.40 + (⁵⁄₆ × $282.15)] .................     425.53
    Cash .......................................................               1,575.00

Bonds payable  ...............................................  20,000.00
    Cash .......................................................               20,000.00
```

7. To pay interest, amortize premium, and pay off Serial No. 3 bonds at end of 24 months:

```
Bond interest ......................................          639.88
Bond premium (⁵⁄₆ × $282.14)  .............................     235.12
    Cash .......................................................                875.00

Bonds payable  ...............................................  25,000.00
    Cash .......................................................               25,000.00
```

*Interest method amortization,* used when the amounts are material, requires that the yield rate of interest and the selling price must be known. When serial bonds are involved, an amortization table should be prepared in the same manner as the amortization table for ordinary (nonserial) bonds, except that the maturity values of each installment must be deducted from the "carrying value" figures when the installments are paid. An amortization table showing present value amortization of the premium and payment of the three serial installments on the serial bond issue illustrated in the preceding section is given in Exhibit 19–10. In that example, it will be recalled that the sales price was $61,892.53 and the yield rate was 2½% semiannually. In Exhibit 19–10, observe that the computations are identical to those previously illustrated for nonserial bonds (Exhibit 19–3) except for the payments on principal as each serial matures.

When the interest method is used and some portion of a serial is retired before maturity, the carrying value at the date of early extinguishment must be reduced by the present value of the portion retired. To illustrate, assume $5,000 par of Serial No. 3 bonds are purchased for retirement at the end of 12 months (i.e., two interest periods before maturity date); the reduction in carrying value would be:

Principal: $5,000 × .951814 (i.e., $p_{n=2}$ — Table 6–2)        = $4,759.07
                  $i=.025$

Interest payments: $175 × 1.927424 (i.e., $P_{n=2}$ — Table 6–4) =    337.30
                      $i=.025$

Present value retired (including premium retired, $96.37) ......$5,096.37

The retirement, using the present value computed above, is reflected in Exhibit 19–11, which is a continuation of Exhibit 19–10 starting with line 4. Observe that the first line of Exhibit 19–11 reflects the entry for early extinguishment. The loss, if material in amount, would be reported as an extraordinary item in conformance with FASB *Statement No. 4* (see page 829).

The straight-line method appears to be used much less than in prior years in view of the APB and FASB pronouncements and the ease with which the interest method calculations can be made on the computer (pocket or otherwise).

**EXHIBIT 19–10**
**Serial Bond Entries Tabulated — Interest Method Amortization**

| Date | Cash Cr. | Bond Interest Expense Dr. | Bond Premium Dr. | Bonds Payable Dr. | Carrying Value |
|---|---|---|---|---|---|
| At issue ..................... | – | – | – | – | 61,892.53 |
| End 6 months ........... | 2,100.00 | 1,547.31* | 552.69 | – | 61,339.84 |
| End 12 months ........... | 2,100.00 | 1,533.50 | 566.50 | – | 60,773.34 |
| End 12 months ........... | 10,000.00 | – | – | 10,000.00 | 50,773.34 |
| End 18 months ........... | 1,750.00 | 1,269.33 | 480.67 | – | 50,292.67 |
| End 18 months ........... | 20,000.00 | – | – | 20,000.00 | 30,292.67 |
| End 24 months ........... | 1,050.00 | 757.33 | 292.67 | – | 30,000.00 |
| End 24 months ........... | 30,000.00 | – | – | 30,000.00 | – |
| | 67,000.00 | 5,107.47 | 1,892.53 | 60,000.00 | |

* $61,892.53 × .025 = $1,547.31.

**EXHIBIT 19–11**
**Serial Bond Entries Tabulated — Interest Method Amortization**

| Date | Cash Cr. | Bond Interest Expense Dr. | Bond Premium Dr. | Bonds Payable Dr. | Loss on Retirement Dr. | Carrying Value |
|---|---|---|---|---|---|---|
| Balance end 12 months ......... | – | – | – | – | – | 50,773.34* |
| End 12 months...... | 5,100.00 | – | 96.37 | 5,000.00 | 3.63 | 45,676.97 |
| End 18 months...... | 1,575.00 | 1,141.92 | 433.08 | – | – | 45,243.89 |
| End 18 months...... | 20,000.00 | – | – | 20,000.00 | – | 25,243.89 |
| End 24 months...... | 875.00 | 631.11 | 243.89 | – | – | 25,000.00 |
| End 24 months...... | 25,000.00 | – | – | 25,000.00 | – | – |

* From Exhibit 19–10, line 4.

## QUESTIONS

1. What are the primary characteristics of a bond? What distinguishes it from capital stock?

2. Distinguish between each of the following classes of bonds: (a) industrial versus governmental, (b) secured versus unsecured, (c) ordinary versus income, (d) ordinary versus serial, (e) callable versus convertible, and (f) registered versus coupon.

3. What are the principal advantages, and disadvantages, of bonds versus common stock for (a) the borrower, and (b) the investor?

4. Explain the nominal and effective (or yield) rates of interest on a bond. What causes them to be different on a particular bond?

5. Distinguish between the face amount and the price of a bond. When are they the same? When different? Explain.

6. Explain the significance of bond discount and bond premium to (a) the borrower, and (b) the investor.

7. Assume a $1,000, 6%, payable semiannually, ten-year bond is sold at an effective rate of 8%. Explain two approaches for determining the sales price.

8. Conceptually, in terms of cash flows and interest rates, what is the current price of a bond?

9. What accounting principle governs in recording a bond sale/purchase transaction for (a) the borrower, and (b) the investor? Briefly, explain the application for each party.

10. Explain why, and how, bond discount and bond premium affects (a) the balance sheet of the borrower and the investor, and (b) the income statement of each.

11. Conceptually, what is the basic difference between the straight-line and interest methods of amortizing bond discount and premium?

12. Under generally accepted accounting principles, when is it appropriate to use (a) straight-line, and (b) interest method amortization for bond discount or premium?

13. When the end of the accounting period of the borrower (or the investor) is not on the bond interest date, adjusting entries must be made for (a) accrued interest, and (b) discount or premium amortization. Explain in general terms, the amount for each.

14. When bonds are sold (or purchased) between interest dates, accrued interest must be recognized. Explain why.

15. Bond discount or premium can be amortized either (a) at each interest date, or (b) at year-end. Which would you generally prefer? Why?

16. What is meant by early extinguishment of debt? How should any resultant gain or loss be reported?

17. What is meant by refunding? When would it generally be advantageous to the issuer?

18. What is a convertible bond? What are the primary reasons for their use?

19. Why is the accounting different for convertible bonds with detachable stock warrants and those without detachable stock warrants?

## EXERCISES

### PART A: EXERCISES 1-5

#### Exercise 19-1

BA Corporation has just issued $500,000, 8% (payable 4% semiannually) ten-year bonds payable. The bonds were dated January 1, 19A; interest dates are June 30 and December 31.

Assume four different cases with respect to the sale of the bonds:

Case A—Sold on January 1, 19A, at par.
Case B—Sold on January 1, 19A, at 102.
Case C—Sold on January 1, 19A, at 98.
Case D—Sold on March 1, 19A, at par.

*Required:*

1. For each case, what amount of interest (cash) will be paid on the first interest date, June 30, 19A?
2. In what cases is the nominal rate of interest not 4% each semiannual period?
3. In what cases will the effective rate of interest be (a) the same, (b) higher, or (c) lower than the nominal rate?
4. After sale of the bonds, in what cases will the carrying or book value of the bonds (as reported on the balance sheet) be (a) the same, (b) higher, or (c) lower than the maturity or face amount?
5. After the sale of the bonds, in Cases A, B, and C, which case will report bond interest expense (as reported on the income statement) (a) the same, (b) higher, or (c) lower than the amount of interest paid (in cash)?

#### Exercise 19-2

A $10,000 bond, 8% (payable 4% semiannually), ten-year (remaining period outstanding), was sold by A to B, on an interest date, at an effective rate of 10%. The bond price was computed as follows: $3,769 + $4,985 = $8,754.

*Required:*

Explain in detail, using values for "*i*" and "*n*" how each of the two dollar amounts was computed. Explain why the computation correctly derives the bond price.

#### Exercise 19-3

Determine the bond price for each of the following situations:

a. A ten-year $1,000 bond; annual interest at 7% (payable 3½% semiannually) purchased to yield 6% effective interest.
b. An eight-year $1,000 bond; annual interest at 6% (payable annually) purchased to yield 7% effective interest.

*c.* A 12-year $1,000 bond; annual interest at 8% (payable 4% semiannually) purchased to yield 7% effective interest. Present value amounts for 24 periods at 3½% interest per semiannual period: PV of 1, .43795; PV of annuity of 1, 16.058367.

### Exercise 19–4

B Corporation sold to C Corporation a $20,000, 8% (payable 4% semiannually on June 30 and December 31) ten-year bond dated and sold on January 1, 19A. Assumptions: Case A – sold at par; Case B – sold at 103; and Case C – sold at 97.

*Required:*

In parallel columns for the issuer and the investor (as a long-term investment) for each case, give the appropriate journal entries on (1) January 1, 19A, and (2) June 30, 19A. Assume the amortization amount is not material, therefore, use straight line.

### Exercise 19–5

Foster Corporation sold to Gray Corporation a $10,000, 8% (payable 4% semiannually on June 30 and December 31) ten-year bond, dated and sold on January 1, 19A. The bond was sold at a 6% effective rate (3% semiannually).

*Required:*

1. Compute the price of the bond.
2. In parallel columns for the issuer and the investor (as a long-term investment), give the appropriate journal entries on (*a*) January 1, 19A, and (*b*) June 30, 19A. Assume the amortization amount is material, therefore, use the interest method.

## PART B: EXERCISES 6–15

### Exercise 19–6

On September 1, 19A Royal Company sold Suber Company $30,000, five-year, 9% (payable 4½% semiannually) bonds for $32,320 plus accrued interest. The bonds were dated July 1, 19A, and interest is payable each June 30 and December 31. The accounting period for each company ends on December 31.

*Required:*

In parallel columns, give entries on the books of the borrower and investor (as a long-term investment) for the following dates: September 1, 19A, December 31, 19A, January 1, 19B, and June 30, 19B. Assume the amortization amounts are not material; and use straight-line amortization.

### Exercise 19–7

XY Corporation sold $150,000, three-year, 8% (payable 4% semiannually) bonds payable for $156,400 plus accrued interest. Interest is payable each February 28 and August 31. The bonds were dated March 1, 19A, and were sold on July 1, 19A. The accounting period ends on December 31.

*Required:*

1. How much accrued interest should be recognized at date of sale?
2. How long is the amortization period?
3. Give entries for XY Corporation through February, 19B. Use straight-line method of amortization.
4. Would the above accounts also be recorded by the investor? Explain.

### Exercise 19–8

Boston Corporation sold Charles Corporation (as a long-term investment) $50,000, four-year, 8% bonds on September 1, 1976. Interest is payable (4% semi-annually) on August 31 and February 28. The bonds mature on August 31, 1980, and were sold to yield 7% effective interest. The accounting period for both companies ends on December 31. Present value amounts for 8 periods at 3½% per semiannual period: PV of 1, .75941; PV of annuity of 1, 6.87396.

*Required:*

1. Compute the price of the bond (show computations).
2. In parallel columns, give all entries required through February 1977 in the accounts of the borrower and the investor. Assume the amortization amounts are not material; therefore use straight-line amortization.

### Exercise 19–9

Assume the same fact situation and requirements in Exercise 19–8, except that the amortization amounts are material. Therefore, use the interest method of amortization.

### Exercise 19–10

Goodson Company sold Hobson Company $30,000, three-year, 8% bonds dated June 1, 19A. Interest is payable 4% semiannually on May 31 and November 30. The bonds were sold on September 1, 19A, for $29,277 plus accrued interest. The accounting period ends on December 31 for both companies. The effective interest rate was 9%.

*Required:*

In parallel columns, give the entries for the borrower and the investor (as a long-term investment) for the following dates: September 1, 19A, November 30, 10A, January 1, 19B, and May 31, 19B. Use straight-line amortization.

### Exercise 19–11

Assume the same facts and requirements as in Exercise 19–10 except that the amortization amounts are material; therefore, the interest method must be used. Refer to Exhibit 19–1 for appropriate value.

### Exercise 19–12

XY Corporation, on January 1, 1971, issued $400,000, 6%, ten-year bonds payable at 103. The bonds are callable at the option of the issuer at 104. Since the amortization amounts are not material, the company uses the straight-line method of amortization.

On December 31, 1976, the bonds were selling at 92 because of the rise in interest rates. Since XY had available cash, they purchased $100,000 of the bonds in the open market at 92.

*Required:*

1. Give the entry by XY Corporation to record the issuance of the bonds on January 1, 1971.
2. Give the entry by XY Corporation to record the reacquisition on December 31, 1976.
3. Explain how any loss or gain on the reacquisition should be reported in the financial statements for 1976 and thereafter.

### Exercise 19-13

Capps Corporation issued $200,000, 4½%, ten-year bonds on January 1, 1972. The issuer could call them at any time after 1975 at 104. The bonds were originally sold at 98. The amortization amounts are not material; therefore, straight-line amortization is used.

Due to a significant increase in interest rates, the bonds were being sold during 1976 at 90. In view of this situation, Capps decided to issue a new series of bonds (a refunding issue) in the amount of $150,000 (8½%, ten-year) on December 31, 1976. They have cash on hand sufficient for the remaining cost of retirement of the old bonds.

*Required:*

1. Give the entry to record the sale and issuance on January 1, 1972.
2. Assume the refunding issue is sold at par; give the required entry for Capps.
3. Assume the old bonds are purchased in the open market at 90 on December 31, 1976; give the required entry for Capps.
4. Explain how any loss or gain on retirement of the old bonds should be reported in the financial statements for 1976 and thereafter. What *APB Opinion* is controlling?

### Exercise 19-14

Walters Corporation issued $40,000, 5%, ten-year convertible bonds (without detachable stock warrants). Each $1,000 bond was (*a*) callable at 103, and (*b*) convertible to ten shares of common stock (par $50) of Walters Corporation three years after issuance. At date of issuance of the bonds, the common stock was selling at $60 per share. The bonds were sold at 105 to Young Corporation as a long-term investment.

*Required:*

1. Give entry for the borrower and investor at the date of issuance.
2. Give entries for the borrower and investor assuming the call privilege is subsequently exercised by Walters Corporation on an interest date. Assume 10% of any premium or discount has been amortized.
3. Give entries for the borrower and investor assuming instead that the conversion privilege is subsequently exercised by Young Corporation. Assume 10% of any premium or discount has been amortized and that at date of conversion, the common stock was selling at $125 per share.

**Exercise 19-15**

Yates Corporation issued $150,000, 6%, ten-year bonds (nonconvertible) with detachable stock warrants. Each $1,000 bond carried 20 detachable warrants, each of which was for one share of Yates common stock, par $20, with a specified option price of $60. The bonds sold at 102 and at date of issuance, the common stock was selling at $40 per share and the warrants for $4.

The entire issue was acquired by Zinn Company as a long-term investment.

*Required:*

1. Give entries for the borrower and the investor at date of acquisition of the bonds.
2. Give entry for the investor assuming subsequent sale of all of the warrants to another investor at $5.50 each.
3. Give entries for the borrower and investor assuming subsequent tender of all of the warrants by the investor for exercise at the specified option price. At this date the stock was selling at $75 per share.

## PART C: EXERCISES 16-17

**Exercise 19-16**

A serial bond issue was dated and sold on January 1, 1976, with the following maturities: December 31, 1976, $10,000; December 31, 1977, $15,000; and December 31, 1978, $25,000. The bonds carried a nominal interest rate of 7%, payable 3½% each June 30 and December 31. They were sold to yield 8% (4% semi-annually). Compute the price on the bond issue on January 1, 1976; show computations.

**Exercise 19-17**

Stone Corporation sold a small bond issue that carried a 8% annual interest rate, payable annually, with a total maturity value of $60,000. The bonds were sold for $54,000 on the date of the indenture. The bonds were to be paid as follows:

| Serial | At End of Year | Maturity Value |
|--------|--------|--------|
| A | 2 | $10,000 |
| B | 3 | 20,000 |
| C | 4 | 30,000 |

*Required:*

1. Set up an amortization table using straight-line amortization to show the amortization by serial, by year. Assume the discount for each serial is as follows: A, $600; B, $1,800; and C, $3,600 (allocation on dollar-periods method).
2. Give entry to pay off one third of Serial C, at par, assuming it is paid one year before maturity, that is, at the end of the third year.

## PROBLEMS

### PART A: PROBLEMS 1–4

### Problem 19–1

X Corporation needs $500,000 cash to implement current expansion plans. Two alternatives are under consideration: Alternative A, issue ten-year, 8% (payable 4% semiannually) bonds; and Alternative B, issue 20,000 shares of common stock (par $10) expected to sell at $25 per share. Average common stock data for the past three years: 30,000 shares outstanding; earnings per share, $2.60; dividends per share, $1.00.

*Required:*

Based on the data given, which alternative would you recommend? Explain the basis for your recommendation. Assume an income tax rate of 48% and that the bonds would probably sell at 98.

### Problem 19–2

Able Corporation sold Baker Corporation (as a long-term investment) a $20,000, 7%, ten-year bond. The bond was dated January 1, 19A, and interest is payable annually each December 31. Assume the accounting periods end December 31. Assume four different cases in respect to the sale of the bond:

    Case A – sold on January 1, 19A, at 7% yield.
    Case B – sold on January 1, 19A, at 6% yield.
    Case C – sold on January 1, 19A, at 8% yield.
    Case D – sold on March 31, 19A, at 6% yield.

*Required:*

1. For each case, compute the amount of interest that will be paid (i.e., cash) on the first interest date, December 31, 19A.
2. Identify what cases sold at (a) par, (b) a discount, and (c) a premium.
3. For each case, indicate (a) the nominal interest rate, and (b) the effective rate of interest.
4. Excluding Case D, identify those cases where the amount of cash paid and received for the bond was (a) the same as par, (b) greater than par, and (c) less than par.
5. Subsequent to the transaction, in what cases will the respective balance sheets report the bonds at (a) par, (b) more than par, and (c) less than par?
6. Subsequent to the transaction, in Cases A, B, and C, which will report interest expense and interest revenue (on the respective income statements) at more or less than the amount of interest paid in cash?
7. Identify those cases where the book or carrying value of the bond liability (or bond investment) will be (a) the same, (b) higher, or (c) lower than the maturity amount.
8. Can straight-line amortization be used in each case? Explain.
9. Can the interest method of amortization be used in each case? Explain.
10. What is the effect of periodic amortization of bond premium and discount on (a) interest expense (as reported on the income statement), and (b) bond carrying value (as reported on the balance sheet).

## Problem 19-3

Franklin Corporation sold Golden Corporation $200,000, 8% (payable 4% semi-annually on June 30 and December 31), three-year bonds. The bonds were dated and sold on January 1, 19A, at an effective rate of 9%. The accounting period for each company ends on December 31. Present value amounts for six periods at $4\frac{1}{2}$% per semiannual period: PV of 1, .76789; PV of annuity of 1, 5.15787.

*Required:*

1. Compute the price of the bonds.
2. Prepare an amortization table for the life of the bonds assuming the amounts involved are material.
3. Prepare in parallel columns, entries for the borrower and the investor (as a long-term investment) through June 30, 19B.
4. Show how the issuer and the investor would report the bonds on their respective balance sheets at December 31, 19A.
5. What would be reported on the income statement for each party for the year ended December 31, 19A?

## Problem 19-4

Park Corporation sold to King Corporation, $40,000, 7% (payable $3\frac{1}{2}$% semi-annually on June 30 and December 31) four-year bonds dated January 1, 19A. The bonds were sold on January 1, 19A, at an effective rate of 6%.

*Required:*

1. Compute the price of the bonds.
2. Prepare an amortization table over the life of the bonds assuming material amounts.
3. In parallel columns for the issuer and investor (as a long-term investment) give all journal entries from issuance to retirement. Assume the accounting period for each company ends on December 31.
4. Show how the issuer and the investor should report the bonds on their respective balance sheets on December 31, 19A.
5. What would be reported on the income statement for each party for the year ended December 31, 19A?

## PART B: PROBLEMS 5-17

## Problem 19-5

Jackson Company sold King Company $50,000 bonds on June 1, 1976, for $51,320 plus accrued interest. The bond indenture provided the following information:

| | |
|---|---|
| Maturity amount | $50,000 |
| Date of bonds | April 1, 1976 |
| Maturity date | March 31, 1978 (2 years) |
| Nominal interest rate | $6\frac{1}{2}$%, payable $3\frac{1}{4}$% semiannually |
| Interest payments | $1,625 each March 31 and September 30 |

*Required:*

1. In parallel columns, give entries for the borrower and investor (as a long-term investment) from date of sale to maturity. Assume the amortization amounts

are not material; therefore, use straight-line amortization. Also assume the accounting period ends December 31.

2. Show how the bonds would be reported on the balance sheet of the two companies at December 31, 1976.

3. What would be reported on the income statement for each party for the year ended December 31, 1976?

## Problem 19-6

Mason Corporation has completed all arrangements for a bond issue with the following provisions:

| | |
|---|---|
| Maturity amount | $300,000 ($1,000 denominations) |
| Date of bonds | June 1, 1976 |
| Maturity date | May 31, 1979 (3 years) |
| Nominal interest rate | 7½%, payable 3¾% semiannually |
| Interest payments (cash) | $11,250 each May 31 and November 30 |

On September 1, 1976, Nash Corporation purchased $10,000 of the bonds from Mason for $9,604 plus accrued interest (as a long-term investment).

*Required:*

1. In parallel columns, give entries for the borrower and investor through May 31, 1977. Assume the amortization amounts are not material; therefore, use straight-line amortization. The accounting period for each corporation ends on December 31.

2. Show how these bonds would be reported on the balance sheets of the two corporations at December 31, 1976.

3. What would be reported on the income statement for each party for the year ended December 31, 1976?

## Problem 19-7

R Corporation sold to S Corporation bonds payable having a maturity value of $120,000. The bonds were due in ten years from March 1, 1976, and carried a nominal interest rate of 7% payable 3½% each February 28 and August 31. S Corporation purchased the bonds on March 1, 1976, at an effective rate of 6½%. Present value amounts for 20 periods at 3¼% interest per semiannual period: PV of 1, .527471; PV of annuity of 1, 14.539346.

*Required:*

1. Compute the price of the bond issue.

2. Assuming straight-line amortization, give in parallel columns, entries for the borrower and the investor through March 1, 1977. Assume both parties close their books on December 31.

3. Show how the bonds should be reported on the balance sheets of the borrower and the investor at December 31, 1976.

4. What should be reported on the income statements for the year ended December 31, 1976, for the borrower and the investor?

## Problem 19-8

Owens Corporation has completed all arrangements for a bond issue with the following provisions:

| Maturity amount | $80,000 |
| Date of bonds | May 1, 1976 |
| Maturity date | April 30, 1979 (3 years) |
| Nominal interest rate | 7½%, payable 3¾% semiannually |
| Interest payments (cash) | $3,000 each April 30 and October 31 |
| Date sold | May 1, 1976 |
| Effective interest rate | 8% (semiannual basis) |

*Required:*

1. Compute the price of the bonds.
2. Prepare an amortization schedule assuming the straight-line method.
3. In parallel columns, give entries for the borrower and the investor (as a long-term investment) through May 1, 1977. Assume the accounting period ends December 31.
4. Show how the bonds should be reported on the balance sheets of the borrower and investor at December 31, 1976.
5. What should be shown on the income statements for the borrower and the investor for the year ended December 31, 1976?

**Problem 19–9**

Use the data given in Problem 19–8 and complete the following requirements:

1. Compute the price of the bonds.
2. Prepare an amortization table assuming the interest method.
3. Prepare a tabulation of entries for the borrower similar to Exhibit 19–7 for the life of the bonds (amortization on interest dates).
4. Show how the bonds and the interest should be reported on the balance sheet and income statement for each party for the statements prepared at the end of 1976?

**Problem 19–10**

B Corporation issued bonds, face amount $100,000, three-year, 8% (payable 4% semiannually on June 30 and December 31). The bonds were dated January 1, 1976, and were sold on November 1, 1976, to yield 9% interest. The bonds mature on December 31, 1978. The bonds were purchased as a long-term investment by I Corporation. Refer to Exhibit 19–1 for appropriate table values.

*Required:*

1. Construct a time scale that depicts the important dates for this bond issue.
2. Determine (a) the price of the bond issue on the date of sale, and (b) the total cash paid by I Corporation.
3. In parallel columns, give the entries at November 1, 1976, for the borrower and the investor.
4. Prepare a bond amortization table from date of sale to maturity date using the interest method.
5. In parallel columns, give the entries for interest and amortization at the interest date, December 31, 1976.
6. Determine and verify the balance in the interest accounts of the two parties to the transaction immediately after Requirement 5.
7. Assume the accounting period for each party ends on February 28. In parallel columns, give the adjusting entries for each party on February 28, 1977. Assume the interest method of amortization.

8. Compute the amount of amortization per month for each party assuming straight-line amortization is appropriate (i.e., amounts are not material).

## Problem 19-11

Bliss Corporation issued $200,000, 8% (payable each February 28 and August 31), four-year bonds. The bonds were dated March 1, 1976, and mature on February 28, 1980. They were sold on August 1, 1976, to yield 8½% interest. The bonds were purchased by Ivy Corporation as a long-term investment. The accounting period for both companies ends on December 31. Refer to Exhibit 19-1 for appropriate table values.

### Required:

1. Diagram a time scale depicting the important dates for this bond issue.
2. Determine (a) the price of the bond issue on the date of sale, and (b) the total cash paid by Ivy Corporation.
3. Prepare an amortization table from date of sale to the maturity date using the interest method of amortization.
4. In parallel columns, give entries for the borrower and the investor from date of sale through February 28, 1977. Base amortization on Requirement 3.
5. Compute the amount of amortization per month for each party assuming the straight-line method is appropriate (i.e., amounts are not material).

## Problem 19-12

Anderson Corporation, on July 1, 1971, issued $500,000, 4¾%, ten-year bonds. Interest is paid each June 30 and December 31. The bonds are callable at the option of the issuer at 102. The bonds were issued at 97 and issue costs were $1,400. The amortization amounts are not material; therefore, straight-line amortization is used for both the discount and issue costs.

Due to the increase in interest costs, these bonds were selling in the market during 1976 at 90. Since the company had available cash, $100,000 of the bonds were purchased in the market at 90 on December 31, 1976. The accounting period ends December 31.

### Required:

1. Give the entry by Anderson Corporation to record the issuance of the old bonds on July 1, 1971.
2. Give the entry to record the reacquisition on December 31, 1976.
3. Explain how any gain or loss on the acquisition should be reported on the financial statements for 1976 and thereafter. What APB Opinion and FASB Statements are controlling?

## Problem 19-13

Assume the same fact situation as given in Problem 19-12 for Anderson Corporation except that Anderson Corporation is short of cash, needing funds, and issues a new series of bonds (a refunding) to obtain the needed cash. The new issue is $500,000, 8%, six-year bonds. They were sold (and dated) October 1, 1976, at par, and issue costs were $2,880 (assume no accrued interest).

### Required:

1. Give the entry for Anderson Corporation to record the issuance of the old bonds on July 1, 1971.

2. Give the entry by Anderson Corporation to record the issuance of the new refunding bonds during October 1976.
3. Give the entry by Anderson Corporation to record the reacquisition of all of the old bonds at 90 on December 31, 1976.
4. Explain how any gain or loss on the acquisition should be reported on the financial statements for 1976 and thereafter. What *APB Opinion* and FASB *Statements* are controlling?

## Problem 19-14

On January 1, 1974, Brown Corporation issued $50,000, 5%, five-year convertible/callable bonds with the provisions that (a) Brown could recall the bonds at any time after 1975 at 102 and (b) the holder of each $1,000 bond can tender it for conversion to 15 shares of Brown common stock, par $50, at any time after 1975. The Company estimated that nonconvertible bonds would have to carry an interest rate of 7½% to sell at par. The bonds were sold for $54,000. On July 1, 1976, the stock was selling at $110 per share. Assume straight-line amortization.

*Required:*

1. Assume the bonds do not have detachable stock warrants. Give the entries for Brown at—
   a. Date of issuance—January 1, 1974.
   b. Date of conversion—July 1, 1976, assuming all bonds were turned in for conversion.
2. Assume Cooper Corporation acquired all of the bonds. Give entries by Cooper at (a) date of acquisition, and (b) date of conversion.
3. Explain the basis for the value recognized at date of conversion.

## Problem 19-15

Assume the same situation given in Problem 19-14 except that instead of being convertible, each $1,000 bond had 15 detachable stock warrants. Each warrant was for one share of common stock at a specified price of $60 per share. Immediately after issuance of the bonds on January 1, 1974, the warrants sold on the market at $2.

*Required:*

1. Give entry by Brown Corporation at date of issuance, January 1, 1974.
2. Give entries for Cooper Corporation at date of acquisition (as a long-term investment) on January 1, 1974.
3. Explain the basis for the values recognized in Requirements 1 and 2.
4. Assume 100 of the detachable stock warrants are tendered on July 1, 1976. At that date the stock was selling at $70 per share. Give entry for (a) Brown Corporation, and (b) Cooper Corporation.

## Problem 19-16

Myers Corporation issued $500,000, 6%, nonconvertible bonds with detachable stock warrants. Each $1,000 bond carried 20 detachable stock warrants, each of which called for one share of Myers common stock, par $50, at a specified option price of $60 per share. The bonds sold at 106, and shortly thereafter the warrants were quoted at $1 each on the market.

Nabors Company purchased the entire issue as a long-term investment.

*Required:*

1. Give the following entries for Myers Corporation (the borrower):
   a. To record the issuance of the bonds.
   b. To record the subsequent exercise by investor of the 10,000 stock warrants.
2. Give the following entries for Nabors Company (the investor):
   a. Acquisition of the bonds (including the warrants).
   b. Subsequent sale to another investor of one half of the stock warrants at $1.50 each.
   c. Subsequent exercise of the remaining one half of the stock warrants (by tendering them to Myers Corporation.)

## Problem 19–17

Zakin Company recently issued $1 million face value, 5%, 30-year subordinated convertible debentures (i.e., bonds) at 97. The debentures are also callable at 103 upon demand by the issuer at any date upon 30 days' notice ten years after the issue. The debentures are convertible into $10 par value common stock of the company at the conversion price of $12.50 per share for each $500 or multiple thereof of the principal amount of the debentures.

*Required:*

1. Explain how the conversion feature of convertible debt has a value to the (*a*) issuer, and (*b*) purchaser.
2. Management of Zakin Company has suggested that in recording the issuance of the debentures a portion of the proceeds should be assigned to the conversion feature.
   a. What are the arguments for according separate accounting recognition to the conversion feature of the debentures?
   b. What are the arguments supporting accounting for the convertible debentures as a single element?
3. Assume that no value is assigned to the conversion feature upon issue of the debentures. Assume further that five years after issue, debentures with a face value of $100,000 and book value of $97,500 are tendered for conversion on an interest payment date when the market price of the debentures is 104 and the common stock is selling at $14 per share and that the company records the conversion as follows:

| | | |
|---|---|---|
| Bonds payable | 100,000 | |
| Bond discount | | 2,500 |
| Common stock | | 80,000 |
| Premium on common stock | | 17,500 |

Discuss the propriety of the above accounting treatment.

(AICPA adapted)

## PART C: PROBLEMS 18–19

## Problem 19–18

A serial issue of $700,000 of bonds dated April 1, 1976, was sold on that date for $707,600. The interest rate is 8%, payable 4% semiannually on March 31 and September 30. Scheduled maturities are as follows:

| Serial | Date Due | Amount |
|--------|----------|--------|
| A............... | March 31, 1977 | $100,000 |
| B............... | March 31, 1978 | 200,000 |
| C............... | March 31, 1979 | 200,000 |
| D............... | March 31, 1980 | 200,000 |

*Required:*

1. Prepare an amortization table; use straight-line and dollars-period allocation.
2. Give all entries relating to the bonds including closing entries through March 31, 1977. The company adjusts and closes its books each December 31. Use straight-line amortization.


**Problem 19-19**

On January 1, 1976, ABC Corporation sold serial bonds (dated January 1, 1976) due as follows: Series A, $10,000, December 31, 1980; Series B, $15,000, December 31, 1981; and Series C, $25,000, December 31, 1982. The bonds carried a 3% coupon (nominal) interest rate per semiannual period (each June 30 and December 31) and were sold to yield 4% interest per semiannual period.

*Required:*

1. Compute the selling price of the bond issue.
2. Prepare a table of amortization for the life of the bond issue assuming the interest method is used.
3. Give entry to record retirement of one half of Series C at 99½ on June 30, 1982. Assume the accounting period ends December 31.

# Chapter 20

# Accounting Changes, Error Correction, and Incomplete Records

Whether in public practice or in industrial accounting, situations are frequently encountered where changes in accounting methods and estimates and error corrections must be made. Similarly, situations are encountered, particularly in very small businesses, where the records maintained are incomplete in many respects. In recognition of these two problems, this chapter is divided into two parts: Part A is concerned with accounting changes and error correction. Part B is concerned with the preparation of financial statements from single-entry and other incomplete records.

In view of the nature of the two problems considered in this chapter there are no new accounting principles and concepts introduced; rather, the chapter deals exclusively with guidelines and techniques designed for orderly resolution of the two specific types of problems. The techniques presented herein have been developed and tested over many years and have been found to be efficient for problem-solving purposes whether for the student, the independent CPA, or the accountant in government or private industry.

## PART A—ACCOUNTING CHANGES AND ERROR CORRECTION

Current practices and procedures for accommodating accounting changes and errors evolved gradually, and no authoritative body such as the APB dealt with them comprehensively prior to *APB Opinion No. 20*, "Accounting Changes" (August 1971). As a consequence there existed a diverse range of accounting approaches for recording and reporting their effects. These approaches were conceptually inconsistent and lacking in forthright disclosures in some cases. Prior to *Opinion No. 20* it was not unusual for changes in accounting, depending on how they were recorded and reported, to result in a particular amount of revenue or expense over time (*a*) "passing through" the income statement twice (or even three times in a few cases), or (*b*) completely missing the income statement. Accounting changes were widely used for "doctoring" net income, or loss. *APB Opinion No. 20* significantly narrowed the alternatives available; more consistent application will benefit the statement user. Those familiar with the earlier practices in this area are quite aware of the importance of the new direction provided by the *Opinion*.

## TYPES OF ACCOUNTING CHANGES AND ERRORS

Because of the diversity of accounting changes and errors, *Opinion No. 20*, as a basis for specifying the accounting and reporting requirements, provides the following classifications:

A. Accounting Changes
   1. Change in accounting principle. When the enterprise adopts a different generally accepted accounting principle or procedure from the one previously used. An example would be: A change from straight-line depreciation to double-declining-balance depreciation.
   2. Change in accounting estimate. As more current and improved data are obtained in respect to accounting determinations based on estimates, the prior estimate may be changed. An example would be: Based on new information it is decided to depreciate Asset X over 12 years rather than on the 10-year life currently being utilized.
   3. Change in reporting entity. Because of changes in the reporting entity, such as including or excluding financial statements of subsidiaries in consolidated statements, accounting applications may be affected.
B. Error Correction
   4. Correction due to discovery of an error. An error is defined as a misapplication (i.e., incorrect recording) of the facts existing at the time of the exchange transaction; the misapplication may have been unintentional or intentional. An example would be charging expense for the cost of an operational asset when acquired that should have been capitalized and depreciated over its useful life.

## METHODS FOR RECORDING AND REPORTING ACCOUNTING CHANGES AND ERROR CORRECTIONS

*APB Opinion No. 20* recognizes that there are three fundamental ways in which accounting changes and error corrections can be reflected in the accounts and reported on the financial statements. They are:

1. Retroactively—The cumulative effect of the accounting change or error correction is determined. The "adjustment" for this amount is recorded in the accounts, usually as a prior period adjustment, and is reported in the same manner on the financial statements.

2. Currently—The cumulative effect of the accounting change or error correction is determined. The "adjustment" for this amount is recorded in the accounts as a special item (similar to extraordinary items) and is reported in the same manner on the current financial statements.

3. Prospectively—The cumulative effect of the accounting change or error correction is not determined. No "adjustment" is recognized or reported; rather, the change effect is spread over the current and future periods.

Because of the different characteristics of the three accounting changes and error correction listed above, the *Opinion* relies on each of these fundamental approaches. Basically, the *Opinion* prescribes the following (with certain exceptions and adaptations explained later):

| Type of Change | Basic Method |
|---|---|
| 1. Change in accounting principle | Currently |
| 2. Change in accounting estimate | Prospectively |
| 3. Change in accounting entity | Retroactively |
| 4. Error correction | Retroactively |

These relationships may be diagrammed as follows:

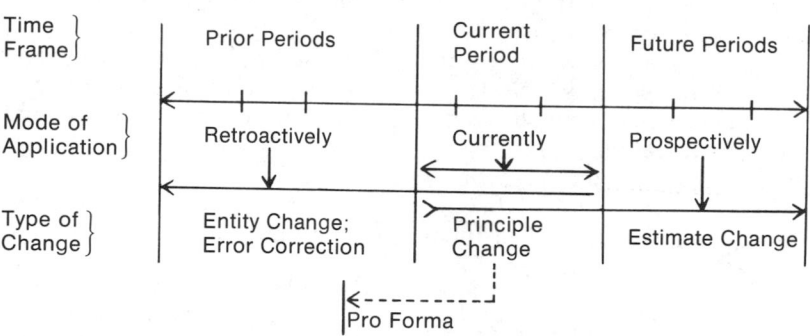

With these fundamentals in mind we can now proceed to a detailed discussion of each of the accounting changes and error correction. In the discussions to follow we will focus on (1) the appropriate entry in the accounts, and (2) appropriate reporting on the *comparative* financial statements affected.

## CHANGE IN ACCOUNTING PRINCIPLE

A change in accounting principle occurs when a company adopts a generally accepted accounting principle different from a previously used one that *also* was generally accepted at the time adopted. The *Opinion* states that the term accounting principle includes "not only accounting principles and practices but also the methods of applying them." It excludes the adoption of a principle occasioned by events occurring for the first time or that were previously immaterial in their effect. Examples of a change in accounting principle are:

1. A change from straight line to some other acceptable method of depreciation.
2. A change in inventory cost flow such as *Fifo* to average.
3. A change in accounting for long-term construction contracts from completed contract basis to percentage of completion.

The *Opinion* states that *most* changes in accounting principle should be recognized by including the cumulative effect "in net income of the period of the change," but that a *few* specific changes in accounting principles "should be reported by restating the financial statements of prior periods" (i.e., retroactively). This latter quota is an exception to the basic rule; examples are (1) a change from *Lifo* inventory to another method, (2) a change in the method of accounting for long-term construction contracts, and (3) a change from "full cost" to another method in the extractive industries. These exceptions were deemed advisable to prevent income manipulation; observe that they generally give rise to credits (which would serve to increase net income materially in the year of change).

The cumulative effect is computed to the beginning of the period of change since the financial statements for the period of change must reflect the newly adopted principle. The amount of the cumulative effect should be shown separately between "income before extraordinary items" and "net income." The *Opinion* states that it is "not an extraordinary item but should be shown in a manner similar to an extraordinary item." Per share amounts should be shown for the cumulative amount reported.

The *Opinion* also requires that income before extraordinary items and net income be shown on a *pro forma* basis on the "face of the income statements for all periods presented as if the newly adopted accounting principle had been applied during all periods affected." This requirement is to satisfy the full-disclosure principle.[1]

To illustrate *a change in accounting principle*, assume Company M has been depreciating an asset for two years which cost $200,000, on a straight-line basis over ten years and no residual value. Starting in the third year the decision was made to adopt double-declining-balance depreciation.[2]

The accounting and reporting would be as follows:

---

[1] *Pro forma* is defined in *Webster's Dictionary* as "for the sake of or as a matter of form." Pro forma statements are "as if" statements; the "as if" assumptions should be clearly stated.

[2] This illustration disregards the tax effects; depending upon the circumstances deferred taxes should be taken into account.

*a.* To compute the cumulative effect to beginning of year of change:

Depreciation based on new method—double declining:

| | |
|---|---|
| Year 1—$200,000 × 20% .......................................... | $40,000 |
| Year 2—($200,000 − $40,000) × 20% ....................... | 32,000 |
| Amount that should be reflected in accumulated depreciation ............................ | $72,000 |

Depreciation recorded to date—straight-line method:

| | |
|---|---|
| Years 1 and 2 — $200,000 × $\frac{1}{10}$ × 2 ......................... | 40,000 |
| Cumulative effect of change (catch-up adjustment, increase in accumulated depreciation balance required) ................................ | .$32,000 |

*b.* Accounting—To record the catch-up adjustment in Year 3:

| | | |
|---|---|---|
| Adjustment due to change in accounting principle (depreciation) ..................................................... | 32,000 | |
| Accumulated Depreciation ................................. | | 32,000 |

*c.* Reporting—Comparative income statement presentation at end of Year 3:

| | Year 2 | Year 3 |
|---|---|---|
| Depreciation expense ............................................. | $ 20,000 | |
| ($200,000 − $40,000 − $32,000) × 20% = $25,600 ...... | | $ 25,600 |
| Income before extraordinary items ............................ | $100,000 | $110,000 |
| Extraordinary item (loss) ........................................ | (6,000) | 10,000 |
| Accounting change effect* ...................................... | | (32,000) |
| Net Income ......................................................... | $ 94,000 | $ 88,000 |
| Earnings per share (100,000 shares outstanding): | | |
| Income before extraordinary items and changes........ | $1.00 | $1.10 |
| Extraordinary items ............................................. | (.06) | .10 |
| Change in accounting principle ............................. | — | (.32) |
| Net income ......................................................... | $ .94 | $ .88 |
| Pro forma net income, assuming retroactive application of accounting change‡ ........................ | $ 82,000 | $120,000 |
| Pro forma EPS assuming retroactive application of accounting chage:† | | |
| Income before extraordinary items‡ ....................... | $ .88 | $ 1.10 |
| Net Income‡ ....................................................... | .82 | 1.20 |

* Appropriate footnote.

† The pro forma share amounts represent what "would have been" had the new method been used from the beginning. *APB Opinion No. 15* recommends, but does not require, earnings per share amounts for the extraordinary items.

| ‡Computations: | Year 2 | Year 3 |
|---|---|---|
| Income before extraordinary items, as reported ........................ | $100,000 | $110,000 |
| Add back straight-line depreciation ......................................... | 20,000 | |
| Deduct double-declining depreciation....................................... | (32,000) | (already deducted) |
| Income before extraordinary items ......................................... | 88,000 | 110,000 |
| Extraordinary item .............................................................. | (6,000) | 10,000 |
| Net Income ........................................................................ | $ 82,000 | $120,000 |

*Opinion No. 20* states that a change to another principle can be made only if the enterprise justifies the change "on the basis that it is prefer-able." The *Opinion* did not specify the criteria for determining when another principle is "preferable."

## CHANGE IN ACCOUNTING ESTIMATE

Accounting necessarily requires the use of estimates because future developments and events cannot be perceived with certainty. For ex-ample, the periodic depreciation charge is the result of one known (cost) and two estimates (residual value and useful life). Estimates result from judgments which are based on specific assumptions and projections con-cerning future events. As the anticipated event, or events, approach reality in time, it is generally possible to improve on the accuracy of the estimates. As a consequence, the accountant is frequently faced with the problem of what to do about improved estimates. For example, during the first few years' life of a firm the estimated loss rate due to uncollect-ible accounts necessarily may have a relatively wide range of error due to the lack of historical experience on collections; as time progresses the rate is refined as a result of additional information. Thus, changes in accounting estimates are a *natural consequence* of the accounting process. A change in an accounting estimate is quite different in cause than is a change in accounting principle or an accounting error. Ex-amples of changes in accounting estimates are:

1. Change in the residual value or estimated useful life of an asset sub-ject to depreciation, amortization, or depletion.
2. Change in the estimated loss rate on receivables.
3. Change in the expected recovery of a deferred charge.
4. Change in the expected realization of a revenue collected in advance.
5. Change in the expected warranty cost on goods sold under guarantee.

When a change in an estimate has been decided upon, the accountant is faced with the dual problem of (*a*) how to reflect the change on the comparative financial statements, and (*b*) how to record the effect of the change of estimate in the accounts. The accountant presumes that a change in an accounting estimate will be made only when there are sound reasons for doing so as opposed to intent to manipulate reported net income.[3]

Generally accepted accounting principles tend to recognize that changes in estimates are occasioned primarily by uncertainties that are influenced by external conditions. As a consequence, changes in ac-counting estimates generally are accounted for *prospectively*. On this point *APB Opinion No. 20* states:

---

[3] This definition of a change in estimates assumes that the original estimate and the new estimate both represent realistic and good faith determinations based upon the information available at the time the respective estimates were made. Changes in estimates not meeting these criteria must be classified as an "accounting error" as defined and discussed in the next section of this chapter.

The Board concludes that the effect of a change in accounting estimate should be recognized in (a) the period of change if the change affects that period only, or (b) the period of change and future periods if the change affects both.

Since there is no change or catch-up adjustment to be made, the only additional disclosure required by the *Opinion* is "The effect on income before extraordinary items, net income and related per share amounts of the current period should be disclosed."

In some situations a change in accounting principle and a change in estimate for the same item are made concurrently. When the effects of each can be separated, two changes should be reflected. However, when the two are indistinguishable, the one that is clearly dominant should be used; if neither is clearly dominant, a change in estimate should be reflected.

To illustrate a *change* in *estimate* assume assets that cost $120,000 (no residual value) are being depreciated over a 10-year life; on the basis of new information after 5 years' use, a 15-year life appears to be more realistic. The change in the depreciation estimate, starting in the sixth year, would be recognized as follows:

*a.* To compute annual depreciation for the current and subsequent years (no catch-up adjustment to be made):

| | |
|---|---:|
| Original cost | $120,000 |
| Accumulated depreciation to date of change in estimate ($120,000 × $5/10$) | 60,000 |
| Undepreciated balance at beginning of year of change in estimate | $ 60,000 |

Annual depreciation after change, $60,000 ÷ (15 − 5 years) = $6,000

*b.* Accounting — no catch-up adjustment.

To record depreciation for Year 6:

| | | |
|---|---:|---:|
| Depreciation expense | 6,000 | |
| Accumulated depreciation | | 6,000 |

*c.* Reporting — income statement for year of change, Year 6:

| | |
|---|---:|
| Depreciation expense | $6,000 |

Disclosure by note: Starting in Year 6 the company changed the estimated lives of certain tangible assets from 10 years to 15 years. This change in estimate increased net income by $3,600 (net of income taxes). Per share amounts were increased by $.036.

## CHANGE IN REPORTING ENTITY

Changes in reporting entity are to be effected and reported through retroactive restatement; that is, "they should be reported by restating the financial statements of all prior periods presented in order to show financial information for the new reporting entity for all periods." *APB Opinion No. 20* also defines this type of accounting change as follows:

One type of accounting change results in financial statements which, in effect, are those of a different reporting entity. This type is limited mainly to (a) presenting consolidated or combined statements in place of statements of individual companies, (b) changing specific subsidiaries comprising the group of companies for which consolidated statements are presented and (c) changing the companies included in combined financial statements. A different group of companies comprise the reporting entity after each change.

This type of change is discussed in detail in another book in this series.[4]

## CORRECTION OF ERRORS

Accounting errors are of two basic types: (1) those that occur and are discovered in the same accounting period, and (2) those that occur in one accounting period and are discovered in a later accounting period. The accountant frequently must deal with these types of errors. When an accounting error is discovered it should be corrected immediately. The former type of error is not difficult to deal with since the accounts have not been closed and the financial statements have not been issued. This type of error can be readily corrected either (a) by reversing the incorrect entry and then entering the correct entry, or (b) by making a single correcting entry designed to directly correct the account balances.

APB Opinion No. 20 deals with the second type of error; those discovered in a subsequent period. Obviously, such errors must be corrected prior to issuance of the financial statements to which the CPA certifies. Seldom is an error discovered in statements on which the independent CPA has expressed an opinion. Accounting errors usually are inadvertent and reflect a lack of sophistication; at the same time, the auditor must be alert for intentional errors designed to manipulate income or financial position or to conceal fraud.

An accounting error is specifically defined as the *misapplication* of facts existing at the time the exchange transaction is recorded or when some other related effects are recorded or reported. The following are examples of accounting errors as distinguished from changes in accounting principle or changes in estimates:

a. Use of an inappropriate or unacceptable accounting principle. Thus a change from an unacceptable accounting principle to a generally accepted one would require the correction of an error (not a change in accounting principle).

b. Use of an unrealistic accounting estimate, that is, the misapplication of known information at the date of the decision in respect to the estimate. Thus, the adoption of a clearly unrealistic depreciation rate would require the correction of an error (not a change in accounting estimate).

---

[4] C. H. Griffin, T. H. William, and K. L. Larson, *Advanced Accounting* (Homewood, Ill.: Richard D. Irwin, Inc., 1971.

c. Misstatement of an accounting value, such as for inventory, a deferred charge or credit, liabilities, or owners' equity.
d. Failure to recognize accruals and deferrals.
e. Incorrect classification of an expenditure as between expense and asset.
f. Incorrect or unrealistic allocations of accounting values.
g. Failure to record a completed transaction.

Errors discovered in the current period that were made in a prior period require that all of the cumulative effects be computed and a correcting entry be made on a retroactive basis. The correcting entry should be made so as to correct all account balances affected; the amount of adjustment for correction of the total net incomes of the prior periods should be entered in an account Prior Period Adjustment – Correction of Accounting Error. This account is closed to Retained Earnings and serves to correct the balance of that account.

The prior period adjustment, in accordance with *APB Opinion No. 9* (par. 18), is reported on the statement of retained earnings as a retroactive adjustment of the beginning balance. As to disclosure, *Opinion No. 20* states: "The nature of an error in previously issued financial statements and the effect of its correction on income before extraordinary items, net income, and the related per share amounts should be disclosed in the period in which the error was discovered and corrected. Financial statements of subsequent periods need not repeat the disclosures."

To illustrate the correction of an accounting error, assume that a $6,000 expenditure for an asset, having a six-year estimated life (no residual value), was recorded in January 19A as an expense. Assume it is now 19C, and in the process of preparing the 19C year-end financial statement, the error was discovered. Net income originally reported in 19A was $14,000 and in 19B, $19,000. Accounting and reporting recognition of the error at the end of 19C, assuming straight-line depreciation and a 40% average income tax rate, would be as follows:

a. Accounting – at end of Year 19C:

To correct the accounts (assume no income tax adjustment):

| | | |
|---|---|---|
| Asset (designated) | 6,000 | |
|     Accumulated depreciation ($6,000 × $\frac{2}{6}$) | | 2,000 |
|     Prior period adjustment – correction of | | |
|       accounting error | | 4,000 |

To record depreciation for 19C:

| | | |
|---|---|---|
| Depreciation expense | 1,000 | |
|     Accumulated depreciation | | 1,000 |

Closing entries at end of 19C:

| | | |
|---|---|---|
| Income summary | 1,000 | |
|     Depreciation expense | | 1,000 |
| Prior period adjustment – correction of | | |
|     accounting error | 4,000 | |
|     Retained earnings | | 4,000 |

*b.* Reporting—at end of 19C (comparative statements):

|  | 19B | 19C |
|---|---|---|
| **Balance Sheet:** | | |
| Asset | $ 6,000 | $ 6,000 |
| Less: Allowance for depreciation | 2,000 | 3,000 |
|  | $ 4,000 | $ 3,000 |
| **Income Statement:** | | |
| Depreciation expense | $ 1,000 | $ 1,000 |
| Net income (Note 1) | 18,000 | 21,000 |
| **Statement of Retained Earnings:** | | |
| Beginning balance | 70,000 | 93,000 |
| Prior period adjustment—depreciation correction (Note 1) | 5,000 | |
| Adjusted balance | 75,000 | 93,000 |
| Net income | 18,000 | 21,000 |
| Ending Balance | $93,000 | $114,000 |

Note 1. Appropriate explanation.

Observe that because these were comparative statements, the amounts are not the same as indicated in the above entries in two respects, viz: (1) net income for 19B was reduced from $19,000 to $18,000 which is the correct amount that would have been reported had the error not been made, and (2) the prior period adjustment is reflected as $5,000 instead of $4,000 since the beginning balance for 19B (rather than 19C) must be corrected in the comparative statement. Had the error been found during 19B the prior period adjustment would have been, $6,000 −$1,000=$5,000.

The above illustration assumed that income tax expense each year was correct; however, this may well not be the case. If not, the above entries and reports would have to reflect net of tax effects. To illustrate, assume the error was carried to the income tax return each year and that a tax penalty of $352 is assessed. The correcting entry would be as follows:

| | | |
|---|---|---|
| Asset (designated) | 6,000 | |
| Accumulated depreciation | | 2,000 |
| Taxes payable—prior years | | 1,952 |
| Prior period adjustment—correction of accounting error | | 2,048 |

Computations:

Taxes payable:

| | | |
|---|---|---|
| 19A − ($6,000 − $1,000) × .40 = | $2,000 | |
| 19B − $1,000 × .40          = | (400) | $1,600 |
| Add penalty | | 352 |
| Total | | $1,952 |

Prior period adjustment:

| | | |
|---|---|---|
| Pretax − ($6,000 − $2,000) | $4,000 | |
| Deduct tax plus penalty | 1,952 | $2,048 |

The remaining entries and the financial reports would reflect these net of tax amounts.

In overall perspective, we can observe that the four types of *changes* discussed are diverse in situation, characteristics, and accounting treatment. This is another area where the judgment and professional responsibility of the independent accountant is paramount. The distinctions discussed and illustrated in the preceding paragraphs focus on one central issue, that is, the distinction between changes occasioned by change in circumstances (change in principle, change in estimate, and change in entity) that provide a good faith and logical basis for change, and those occasioned either by lack of good faith or unsophistication (accounting errors). The accounting treatments that appear most appropriate are related to these circumstances and are designed to best serve the statement user through accuracy, full disclosure, and the absence of misleading inferences.

## ANALYTICAL PROCEDURES FOR CORRECTING ERRORS

In many situations the accountant needs to use efficient analytical procedures for dealing with accounting changes whether they are due to principles, estimates, or errors. Changes and correcting entries must be determined, and previously prepared financial statements frequently must be revised. This section presents some analytical techniques that are useful for these purposes as well as for problem-solving purposes for students, CPA candidates, and others.

Errors may be classified according to which financial statements are affected. Some may affect only the balance sheet. For example, a credit to Retained Earnings instead of Contributed Capital would affect only the balance sheet. Correction would involve a transfer from one real account to another real account. In this case, balance sheets for future periods would be in error until correction of the respective account balances. Other changes affect only the income statement. For example, a credit to the Sales account instead of Interest Revenue would affect only the income statement. Correction of this error would involve a transfer from one nominal account to another nominal account. In this case financial reports of future periods would be unaffected whether or not the error is corrected.

A third type of error affects both the balance sheet and the income statement. This type may be further classified on the basis of the effect on the current and future financial statements as follows:

1. *Counterbalancing errors.* This kind of error results from failure to allocate properly an expense or revenue item between two consecutive accounting periods. There is no discernible effect upon the balance sheet at the end of the second period, since the total revenue and total expense to that date are correct; no error would be left in Retained Earnings or other balance sheet accounts. Examples of counterbalancing errors are:

*a.* Errors in adjusting for prepaid expenses, accrued expenses, prepaid revenues, or accrued (uncollected) revenues. Such errors cause an incorrect income statement in the period in which the error was made with an equal misstatement in the opposite direction on the income statement for the following period. To illustrate, assume accrued wages were not recognized in 19A. The effect of this error is as follows:

19A income statement — Wage expense understated
— Income overstated
19A balance sheet      — Current liabilities understated
— Retained earnings overstated
19B income statement — Wage expense overstated
— Income understated
19B balance sheet      — No misstatements

b. Errors in the merchandise inventory. Errors of this type are counterbalancing because the final inventory of the current period is the beginning inventory of the next period and the beginning and ending inventories have an opposite effect on income. To illustrate, assume the final inventory for 19A is understated. The effect of this error is as follows:

19A income statement — Ending inventory understated
— Cost of goods sold overstated
— Income understated
19A balance sheet      — Assets (inventory) understated
— Retained earnings understated
19B income statement — Beginning inventory understated
— Cost of goods sold understated
— Income overstated
19B balance sheet      — No misstatements

2. *Noncounterbalancing errors.* This kind of error continues to affect account balances until corrected; hence, one or more balance sheet accounts continue to be reported inaccurately. Examples of noncounterbalancing errors are:

a. Over- or understatement of the depreciation charge; the accumulated depreciation and retained earnings balances are in error until corrected or the asset is disposed of. The income statements are inaccurate for the periods in which the incorrect charges were recorded.

b. Recognition of a capital expenditure as an expense, or vice versa, results in incorrect asset balances, depreciation charges, and retained earnings.

### Preparing Correcting Entries for Errors

Correcting entries will vary depending on whether the error is counterbalancing (i.e., self correcting) and the period of time lapsed since the error was made. To illustrate, the following situations involving both counterbalancing and noncounterbalancing errors are analyzed and corrected at two different points in time. Recall that when an error made in a prior period is corrected, the cumulative misstatement of prior years' net income is reflected in the period of correction as a *prior period adjustment.* Since prior period adjustments are closed to Retained Earnings, this serves to correct the balance of that account.

*Situation 1:* Error in merchandise inventory. Assume that the final inventory for 19A was understated by $1,000.

Case A—The error was found at the end of 19B (before books were closed).

Analysis: Net income for 19A was understated by $1,000; hence retained earnings at the start of 19B is understated by this amount. Beginning inventory for 19B is understated by $1,000.

Correcting entry in 19B:

Inventory, beginning...................................................... 1,000
    Prior period adjustment, error correction .................... 1,000

Case B—The error was found during 19C.

Analysis: Counterbalanced; net income for 19A was understated by $1,000 and 19B overstated by the same amount. No correcting entry is needed in 19C. Restate 19A and 19B financial statements for all subsequent reporting purposes.

*Situation 2:* Error in both purchases and inventory. Assume that a $2,000 purchase in 19A was not recorded until 19B and the goods were not included in the 19A ending inventory.

Case A—The two errors were discovered in 19B (before books were closed).

Analysis: In 19A both purchases and ending inventory were understated by the same amounts; therefore, since they have opposite effects on income, that amount for 19A was correct. However, on the balance sheet for 19A both inventory and payables were understated by $2,000. In 19B both inventory (beginning) and purchases are in error.

Correcting entry in 19B:

Inventory, beginning....................................................... 2,000
    Purchases ............................................................. 2,000

Case B—The two errors were discovered in 19C.

Analysis: Both errors counterbalanced in 19B. No correcting entry is needed in 19C. Restate 19A and 19B financial statements for all subsequent reporting purposes.

*Situation 3:* Error in prepaid expense. Assume that a five-year fire insurance policy was acquired on January 1, 19A; the five-year premium of $500 was paid and charged to insurance expense in 19A.

Case A—The error was discovered at the end of 19B (before books were closed).

Analysis: In 19A insurance expense was overstated and income understated by $400. Also in 19A prepaid insurance and retained earnings were understated by $400. No insurance expense for 19B has been recorded.

Correcting entry in 19B:

Prepaid insurance ..................................................................... 400
　　　Prior period adjustment, error correction............................　　　　400
(An adjusting entry for $100 expired insurance must also be
made for 19B.)

Case B—The error was discovered in 19C.

Correcting entry at end of 19C:

Prepaid insurance ..................................................................... 300
　　　Prior period adjustment, error correction............................　　　　300
(An adjusting entry for $100 expired insurance also must
be made for 19C.)

*Situation 4:* Error in accrued expense. Assume accrued property taxes for $100 at the end of 19A were not recorded. They were paid early in 19B.

Case A—The error was found at the end of 19B (before books were closed).

Analysis: In 19A tax expense was understated and income overstated. Also liabilities were understated and retained earnings overstated by $100. Tax expense for 19B is overstated by $100 because of the payment entry.

Correcting entry at end of 19B:

Prior period adjustment, error correction ............................. 100
　　　Tax expense ................................................................　　　　100

Case B—The error was found during 19C.

Analysis: The error counterbalanced in 19B because 19A income was overstated and 19B income understated by $100. No correcting entry is needed for 19C. Restate 19A and 19B financial statements for all subsequent reporting purposes.

*Situation 5:* Error in revenue earned but not yet collected. Assume interest receivable of $75 at the end of 19A was not recorded. The interest was collected in 19B.

Case A—The error was found at the end of 19B (before books were closed).

Analysis: In 19A interest revenue was understated and income was understated. On the balance sheet receivables and retained earnings were understated. In 19B interest revenue is overstated because of the collection entry.

Correcting entry at end of 19B:

Interest revenue......................................................................... 75
　　　Prior period adjustment, error correction .............................　　　　75

Case B—The error was discovered during 19C.

Analysis: The error counterbalanced in 19B because 19A income was understated and 19B income overstated. No correcting entry is needed in 19C. Restate 19A and 19B financial statements for all subsequent reporting purposes.

*Situation 6:* Expense capitalized. Assume that on January 1, 19A, $500 was expended for ordinary repairs; the $500 was debited to the Machinery account which was being depreciated 10% per year.

Case A—The error was discovered at the end of 19B (before books were closed).

Analysis: For 19A repair expense was understated, depreciation expense overstated, and income incorrect by the difference. On the balance sheet assets were overstated and retained earnings overstated by $500 × .90 = $450.

Correcting entry at end of 19B:

| | | |
|---|---:|---:|
| Accumulated depreciation (for 19A) | 50 | |
| Prior period adjustment, error correction | 450 | |
| Machinery | | 500 |

Case B—The error was discovered during 19C (before the adjustment for depreciation expense was made for 19C).

Correcting entry at end of 19C:

| | | |
|---|---:|---:|
| Accumulated depreciation (for 19A and 19B) | 100 | |
| Prior period adjustment, error correction | 400 | |
| Machinery | | 500 |

These illustrations should be sufficient to indicate the care that must be taken in analyzing and correcting errors. Fundamental to the analysis are the following: (1) a clear understanding of how the incorrect entry was made, (2) a determination of what the correct entry should have been, and (3) development of correcting entry to bring (1) in conformity with (2) by taking into account the effects between the date of the error and the date of the correction.

## Worksheet Techniques for Correcting Errors

Usually errors can be analyzed and appropriate accounting developed without a worksheet. However, when errors are numerous and complicated a worksheet approach often is helpful. An efficient worksheet usually can be designed easily to meet the needs of the particular situation. Of necessity, the worksheet will be unique to the situation; therefore, the accountant should develop an ability to design efficient worksheets for specific problems when they arise.[5] In the remainder of this part two different worksheets often used will be presented.

---

[5] A reasonable skill in worksheet design often is quite helpful in tackling problems on the CPA examination.

## Worksheet to Correct Net Income and Provide Correcting Entries

A type of problem sometimes encountered is where there have been a number of errors in income. Usually the situation requires (a) determination of correct income for a series of periods, and (b) preparation of a correcting entry (or entries) at the time the errors are discovered.

To illustrate, assume the following data have been developed for Company A:

| | 19A | 19B | 19C |
|---|---|---|---|
| Reported income (uncorrected) .......................... | $5,000 | $7,000 | $6,000 |
| Errors made in the records and reports: | | | |
| a) Prepaid expenses not recognized.................. | 100 | 200 | 400 |
| b) Prepaid revenue (collected in advance, not recognized) ............................................... | 300 | 500 | 100 |
| c) Accrued expenses not recognized.................. | 600 | 800 | 500 |
| d) Accrued revene (revenue earned but not yet collected, not recognized) ...................... | 500 | 400 | 600 |
| e) Depreciation understated............................. | 200 | 200 | 200 |

*Required:*

1. Determine correct income for each year.
2. Give the correcting entries needed assuming:

> Case A—the errors were discovered at the end of 19C (before the adjusting and closing entries were made).
>
> Case B—the errors were discovered during 19D (before the adjusting and closing entries were made).

A worksheet, designed to meet Requirement 1 is shown in Exhibit 20–1. Observe that the worksheet starts with the uncorrected amounts and (a) provides for correction of income for each year, and (b) identifies account balances that are incorrect at the end of 19C. To explain the mechanics of the worksheet, observe prepaid expenses. Since prepaid expenses of $100 were not recognized in 19A, expenses were overstated and income understated for that year by $100. In the following year the opposite effect occurred because of this item. Therefore, income for 19A is increased and for 19B decreased on the worksheet by $100. At the end of 19C the $400 prepaid expense has not counterbalanced; that amount should be reflected as a debit in prepaid expenses (to be reported on the 19C balance sheet). The remaining entries on the worksheet follow this pattern. You should carefully study each item on the worksheet.

Requirement 2, Case A—the errors were discovered at the end of 19C (books were not closed). Based on data provided in Exhibit 20–1.

| | | |
|---|---|---|
| a. Prepaid expense ...................................................... | 400 | |
| Expense, 19C ($400 – $200) ............................................. | | 200 |
| Prior period adjustment, error correction........................... | | 200 |
| | | |
| b. Prior period adjustment, error correction................................. | 500 | |
| Revenue, 19C ($500 – $100) ............................................. | | 400 |
| Revenue collected in advance (prepaid revenue) .............. | | 100 |

c. Prior period adjustment, error correction.............................. 800
       Expense, 19C ($800 — $500) ...........................................      300
       Accrued expenses payable  ..........................................      500

d. Revenue earned but not collected (accrued revenue) .............. 600
       Revenue, 19C ($600 — $400) ...........................................      200
       Prior period adjustment, error correction..........................      400

e. Depreciation expense, 19C ....................................................... 200
       Prior period adjustment, error correction......................... 400
       Accumulated depreciation................................................      600

Observe that each of the above entries could be made in two separate entries; for example, entry (a) could be as follows:

a–1. Prepaid expense ............................................................... 400
       Expense, 19C....................................................................      400

a–2. Expense, 19C..................................................................... 200
       Prior period adjustment, error correction.........................      200

Requirement 2, Case B — the errors were discovered in 19D (prior to adjusting and closing entries). See Exhibit 20–1 for data.

a. Prepaid expense ............................................................... 400
       Prior period adjustment, error correction..........................      400

b. Prior period adjustment, error correction................................. 100
       Revenue collected in advance (prepaid revenue) ..............      100

**EXHIBIT 20–1**
**Worksheet to Correct Income and Provide Data for Correcting Entry**
**At End of Year 19C**

| Particulars | 19A | 19B | 19C | Corrections | |
|---|---|---|---|---|---|
| | | | | Amount | Account |
| Reported income (loss) | 5,000 | 7,000 | 6,000 | 18,000* | Balancing |
| Corrections: | | | | | |
| a. Prepaid expenses — 19A | 100 | 100* | | | |
|     (not recognized)    19B | | 200 | 200* | | |
|                19C | | | 400 | 400* | Prepaid expenses |
| b. Prepaid revenue   — 19A | 300* | 300 | | | |
|     (not recognized)    19B | | 500* | 500 | | |
|                19C | | | 100* | 100 | Prepaid revenue |
| c. Accrued expenses — 19A | 600* | 600 | | | |
|     (not recognized)    19B | | 800* | 800 | | |
|                19C | | | 500* | 500 | Accrued expenses |
| d. Accrued revenue  — 19A | 500 | 500* | | | |
|     (not recognized)    19B | | 400 | 400* | | |
|                19C | | | 600 | 600* | Accrued revenue |
| e. Depreciation      — 19A | 200* | | | | |
|     (understated)      19B | | 200* | | 600 | Accumulated |
|                19C | | | 200* | | depreciation |
| Correct income (loss) | 4,500 | 6,400 | 6,900 | 17,800* | Balancing |

Note: As an arithmetic check note that the last line and last column sum to the same total.
* Denotes debit.

| | | |
|---|---|---|
| c. Prior period adjustment, error correction............................... | 500 | |
| Accrued expenses payable ........................................... | | 500 |
| | | |
| d. Revenue earned but not collected (accrued revenue) .............. | 600 | |
| Prior period adjustment, error correction......................... | | 600 |
| | | |
| e. Prior period adjustment, error correction............................... | 600 | |
| Accumulated depreciation............................................. | | 600 |

## Worksheets to Recast Financial Statements

Another group of problems commonly require that the income state-ment, balance sheet, and statement of retained earnings be recast on a correct basis. To demonstrate adaptation of the *interim worksheet* to problems where an uncorrected trial balance is available and the re-quirement is to provide correct statements of income, retained earn-ings, and assets and equities, the following illustrative problem is presented. To simplify, income tax effects are disregarded.

## ILLUSTRATIVE PROBLEM

1. Uncorrected and unadjusted trial balance at December 31, 19B – As shown in the first two columns of Exhibit 20–2.
2. Additional data:

   a. Merchandise inventory December 31, 19A, overstated $4,000.
   b. Prepaid advertising of $2,000 at December 31, 19B, not recorded.
   c. Prepaid insurance of $2,000 at December 31, 19B, not recorded; the entire premium paid on June 1, 19B, was debited to general expense.
   d. Accrued sales salaries of $1,000 at December 31, 19A, not recorded.
   e. Accrued rent expense of $1,000 at December 31, 19B, not recorded; treated as general expense.
   f. No provision was made for doubtful accounts. The following esti-mates have been made: 19A, $1,000; 19B, $3,000. Treated as gen-eral expense.
   g. No provision was made for depreciation. The following amounts have been computed: prior to 19B, $15,000; 19B, $5,000. Treated as general expense.
   h. Dividends paid and properly recorded in 19B, $8,000. (Note: Trans-actions occurring during the current year and affecting retained earnings may be entered on the worksheet so that the worksheet will provide detail concerning all changes in retained earnings.)
   i. Cash shortage, $1,000 at end of 19B.
   j. Correction for premium on capital stock (7,500 shares, par $10 per share).
   k. The inventory was $32,000 at the end of 19B.

*Required:*

Complete a worksheet to provide corrected amounts for 19C income statement, statement of retained earnings, and balance sheet. Key all entries on the worksheet to the data given.

## EXHIBIT 20-2
### Worksheet to Correct Financial Statements — December 31, 19B

| | Trial Balance Debit | Trial Balance Credit | Entries Debit | Entries Credit | Income Summary Debit | Income Summary Credit | Retained Earnings Debit | Retained Earnings Credit | Balance Sheet Debit | Balance Sheet Credit |
|---|---|---|---|---|---|---|---|---|---|---|
| Cash | 9,000 | | | (i) 1,000 | | | | | 8,000 | |
| Receivables | 20,000 | | | | | | | | 20,000 | |
| Allowance for doubtful accounts | | | | (f) 4,000 | | | | | | 4,000 |
| Inventory, beginning | 30,000 | | | (a) 4,000 | 26,000 | | | | | |
| Equipment | 60,000 | | | | | | | | 60,000 | |
| Accumulated depreciation | | | | (g) 20,000 | | | | | | 20,000 |
| Accounts payable | | 5,000 | | | | | | | | 5,000 |
| Capital stock, par $10, 7,500 shares outstanding | | 76,000 | (j) 1,000 | | | | | | | 75,000 |
| Retained earnings | | 25,000 | | (h) 8,000 | | | | 33,000 | | |
| Prior period adjustments: | | | | | | | | | | |
| Inventory correction | | | (a) 4,000 | | | | 4,000 | | | |
| Salaries correction | | | (d) 1,000 | | | | 1,000 | | | |
| Bad debt correction | | | (f) 1,000 | | | | 1,000 | | | |
| Depreciation correction | | | (g) 15,000 | | | | 15,000 | | | |
| Sales | | 130,000 | | | | 130,000 | | | | |
| Purchases | 90,000 | | | | 90,000 | | | | | |
| Selling expenses | 17,000 | | | (b) 2,000 (d) 1,000 | 14,000 | | | | | |
| General expenses | 10,000 | | (e) 1,000 (f) 3,000 (g) 5,000 (i) 1,000 | (c) 2,000 | 18,000 | | | | | |
| | 236,000 | 236,000 | | | | | | | | |
| Prepaid advertising | | | (b) 2,000 | | | | | | 2,000 | |
| Prepaid insurance | | | (c) 2,000 | | | | | | 2,000 | |
| Accrued rent expense | | | | (e) 1,000 | | | | | | 1,000 |
| Dividends paid 19B | | | (h) 8,000 | | | | 8,000 | | | |
| Inventory, ending | | | | | | 32,000 | | | 32,000 | |
| Premium on capital stock | | | | (j) 1,000 | | | | | | 1,000 |
| Net income | | | | | 14,000 | | | 14,000 | | |
| Retained earnings balance | | | | | | | 18,000 | | | 18,000 |
| | | | 44,000 | 44,000 | 162,000 | 162,000 | 47,000 | 47,000 | 124,000 | 124,000 |

Exhibit 20–2 shows an efficient worksheet that meets all of the requirements of this situation. Observe that it is similar to the worksheets illustrated in Chapter 3. The entries include both (a) current adjusting entries, and (b) correcting entries. You should follow each item through the worksheet. The required financial statements, on a corrected basis, can be readily prepared from the worksheet.

This type of worksheet is especially important throughout accounting because (1) it can be adapted to many different problem situations, and (2) its built-in debit/credit feature assures a degree of accuracy and completeness not otherwise attainable.

## PART B—STATEMENTS FROM SINGLE-ENTRY AND OTHER INCOMPLETE RECORDS

Most businesses maintain a reasonably complete record of all transactions directly affecting the firm. Usually complete records are best accomplished through a systematic model based on (a) the double-entry concept and (b) the accounting model. However, a small entity, especially if a sole proprietorship, may maintain only a single-entry system that records just the "bare essentials." The proprietor may maintain the records and may not be familiar with effective recordkeeping procedures nor appreciate the importance of good records to sound management.

Single-entry recordkeeping includes all those records, whether kept systematically or not, deemed necessary by the proprietor but which do not attempt to record the *dual effect* of each transaction on both assets and equities as expressed in the accounting model. In some cases only records of cash, accounts receivable, accounts payable, and taxes paid may be maintained. No record may be kept, except perhaps in memorandum form, of fixed assets, inventories, expenses, revenues, and other elements usually considered essential in an accounting system. However, the incomplete data, plus other information that often can be assembled, generally can be analyzed sufficiently to provide a reasonably accurate income statement and balance sheet.

### Preparation of Balance Sheet from Single-Entry Records

Since single-entry records usually provide sparse information about assets other than cash and accounts receivable, preparation of the balance sheet involves inventorying, counting, and verification procedures to determine the nature and amount of most of the assets and liabilities. The cost of the fixed assets must be determined from such data as are available. Canceled checks, receipts, bills of sale, deeds, papers transferring title to real estate, and other similar records provide much of the needed data. Once the cost of the fixed assets is determined, depreciation can be computed. The amount of merchandise, supplies, and other inventories on hand are obtained by actual count. The original cost of these items must be determined in order to cost the inventory. If

**EXHIBIT 20-3**

### A. A. BROWN COMPANY
Balance Sheet, At December 31, 19A

*Assets*

| | | |
|---|---:|---:|
| Current Assets: | | |
| Cash .................................................................... | | $2,345 |
| Accounts receivable ................................................ | | 90 |
| Notes receivable, trade........................................... | | 50 |
| Merchandise inventory.............................................. | | 1,550 |
|     Total Current Assets ........................................ | | 4,035 |
| Property and Equipment: | | |
| Office and store fixtures ........................................... | $500 | |
| Less accumulated depreciation.................................. | 25 | 475 |
|     Total Assets .................................................... | | $4,510 |

*Liabilities*

| | |
|---|---:|
| Current Liabilities: | |
| Accounts payable .................................................... | $  240 |
| Long-Term Liabilities ............................................... | None |
|     Total Liabilities ........................................... | 240 |

*Owner's Equity*

| | |
|---|---:|
| A. A. Brown, proprietorship ($4,510 − $240) ................. | 4,270 |
|     Total Liabilities and Owner's Equity............... | $4,510 |

original cost cannot be obtained, merchandise and supplies can be priced at current replacement cost.

Similarly, notes payable and other liabilities (except accounts payable for which there is generally a record) must be obtained from memoranda, correspondence, and even by consultation with creditors. Usually in this manner a fairly reliable balance sheet can be developed.

To illustrate preparation of a balance sheet from single-entry records, assume the following data has been gathered for the sole proprietorship, A. A. Brown Company for 19A:

a. Cash on hand and on deposit, $2,345 – from count of cash and bank statement.

b. Merchandise inventory, $1,550 – Count made by Brown, costed at current replacement cost since purchase invoices were not available.

c. Store and office equipment acquired on January 1, 19A, $500 – from invoice found in the files.

d. Brown agreed that a depreciation rate of 5% per annum, with no material amount of residual value, was reasonable.

e. Interest-bearing note, dated December 31, 19A, $50 – This note, signed by a customer for goods purchased, was in the files.

f. Accounts receivable, $90 – Brown maintained a "Charge Book" which listed four customers as owing a total of $90; Brown was positive that the bills were outstanding. You called the customers for verification.

g. Accounts payable, $240 – The "unpaid invoices" file contained two invoices that totaled to this amount; Brown assured you that they had not been paid.

A balance sheet prepared from the above data is shown in Exhibit 20–3. Owner's equity was determined by subtracting total liabilities from total assets.

## Computation of Income

The computation of income where single-entry records are kept may be based on an analysis of the changes in owner's equity for the period. For example, if it is determined that the only change in owner's equity for Brown Company resulted from a gain or loss from operations, the summary income statement in Exhibit 20–4 may be prepared (proprietorship, January 1, 19A, taken from balance sheet for prior period).

If there had been additional investments or withdrawals during the period, these must be considered in the computation of income or loss. The following equation indicates the procedure when there have been investments or withdrawals during the period:

Income = Ending Owner's Equity − Beginning Owner's
Equity + Withdrawals − Additional Investments

The two examples of the single-entry income statement computations shown in Exhibit 20–5 indicate the procedure when there have been investments and withdrawals during the period.

### EXHIBIT 20–4

A. A. BROWN COMPANY
Computation of Net Loss
For the Year Ended December 31, 19A

| | |
|---|---:|
| Owner's equity, January 1, 19A ................. | $4,500 |
| Owner's equity, December 31, 19A.............. | 4,270 |
| Net Loss for Period................................... | $ 230 |

### EXHIBIT 20–5
### Income Determination — Single Entry

| | Computation Where There Was— | |
|---|---:|---:|
| | An Income | A Loss |
| Owner's equity, end of period................................. | $8,000 | $5,500 |
| Owner's equity, beginning of period........................ | 7,100 | 6,300 |
| Change (increase) ................................................ | 900 | |
| (decrease) ................................................ | | (800) |
| Add: Withdrawals during period............................. | 1,200 | 1,000 |
| | 2,100 | 200 |
| Deduct: Additional investments during period ......... | 500 | 400 |
| Income for Period ................................................ | $1,600 | |
| Loss for Period ................................................... | | $ (200) |

## PREPARATION OF A DETAILED INCOME STATEMENT FROM INCOMPLETE DATA

Computation of the amount of income or loss can be accomplished as shown in the preceding section. However, knowing only the amount of income or loss does not meet the internal needs of management for information about operations nor does it meet the needs of other interested parties. Banks and other credit grantors usually request a statement setting out the details of operations. The Internal Revenue Service requires a detailed statement of revenues and expenses for income tax purposes.

An itemized income statement in the conventional form may be prepared from single-entry records and supplemental data without converting the records to double-entry form. By analyzing the cash receipts and disbursements, much of the needed detail may be obtained. The preparation of an income statement from single-entry data may be simply illustrated as follows:

The following information was obtained from the single-entry records of John Mercer Company. Balance sheets as of January 1 and December 31 and an income statement for 19A are to be prepared:

|  | 19A | |
| --- | --- | --- |
|  | January 1 | December 31 |
| Accounts and trade notes receivable (no doubtful accounts) | $35,000 | $48,000 |
| Inventory (per physical count) | 6,900 | 8,700 |
| Building and equipment (appraised at estimated cost less depreciation) | 17,000 | 17,400 |
| Prepaid expenses (per memoranda) | 100 | 110 |
| Accounts payable (per files) | 8,100 | 9,200 |
| Notes payable (for equipment per files) |  | 500 |
| Cash on hand (register) | 60 | 110 |
| Accrued expenses (per memoranda) | 120 | 150 |
| Salaries | | 7,000 |

An analysis of the bank statements indicated deposits and disbursements as follows:

| | |
| --- | --- |
| Bank overdraft, January 1, 19A | $ 2,800 |
| Deposits during year: | |
| Collections on account | 42,000 |
| Additional capital contributions by owner | 10,000 |
| Checks drawn during year: | |
| Purchases | 26,000 |
| Expenses | 6,000 |
| Salaries of employees | 7,000 |
| Withdrawals by owner | 3,000 |
| Purchase of equipment | 340 |

## Balance Sheet Preparation

In preparing the balance sheets, cash in the bank on December 31, 19A, must be computed; there was an overdraft on January 1, 19A. Total deposits of $52,000 less the January 1 overdraft of $2,800 and total checks drawn of $42,340 indicates a December 31, 19A, balance of $6,860. The balance sheets would be as shown in Exhibit 20-6.

**EXHIBIT 20-6**

JOHN MERCER COMPANY
Balance Sheets

|  | 19A | |
|---|---|---|
|  | *January 1* | *December 31* |
| *Assets* | | |
| Cash in bank ........................................ | $ — | $. 6,860 |
| Cash in register .................................... | 60 | 110 |
| Accounts and notes receivable.............. | 35,000 | 48,000 |
| Inventory ............................................. | 6,900 | 8,700 |
| Prepaid expenses ................................ | 100 | 110 |
| Buildings and equipment ..................... | 17,000 | 17,400 |
|  | $59,060 | $81,180 |
| *Liabilities* | | |
| Notes payable....................................... | $ — | $ 500 |
| Bank overdraft ..................................... | 2,800 | — |
| Accounts payable ................................. | 8,100 | 9,200 |
| Accrued expenses payable.................... | 120 | 150 |
|  | 11,020 | 9,850 |
| *Owner's Equity (difference)* | | |
| John Mercer, proprietorship ................. | $48,040 | $71,330 |

## Computation of Net Income

Using the single-entry method, net income may be computed by analysis of the change in proprietorship as follows:

| | |
|---|---|
| Owner's equity, December 31, 19A ........................ | $71,330 |
| Owners' equity, January 1, 19A ............................ | 48,040 |
| Increase in owner's equity ................................... | 23,290 |
| Add withdrawals during year ............................... | 3,000 |
| | 26,290 |
| Deduct additional investments during year.............. | 10,000 |
| Net Income, 19A ................................................. | $16,290 |

*Analysis of Revenue and Expenses.* To prepare a detailed income statement, each item of revenue and expense to be included thereon must be determined. Such a determination may be made by summarizing all the transactions in debit and credit form, which in effect would involve conversion to double-entry procedures. This approach is subsequently illustrated (in worksheet form) in this chapter. Alternatively, the desired figures may be derived directly by analyzing the respective items as illustrated below.

*Computation of Sales.* Cash and credit sales combined may be determined by analyzing cash receipts and changes in accounts receivable and trade notes receivable as follows:

Schedule 1

| | |
|---|---:|
| Accounts and trade notes receivable, December 31, 19A............... | $48,000 |
| Cash collected from customers and deposited .......................... | 42,000 |
| Increase in cash on hand ..................................................... | 50 |
| | 90,050 |
| Less: Accounts and trade notes receivable, | |
| January 1, 19A .................................................................. | 35,000 |
| Sales for the Period, 19A ..................................................... | $55,050 |

Alternatively, to determine the sales for the period, you may prefer simply to reconstruct the T-accounts for the *accounts receivable* and *sales* accounts as follows:

| **Accounts Receivable** | | | | **Sales** | |
|---|---|---|---|---|---|
| Beg. bal. (Jan. 1) | 35,000 | Cash collections (deposited) | 42,000 | (A) | 55,050 |
| (A) Sales (amount necessary to complete account) | 55,050 | Cash collections (on hand) | 50 | | |
| | | End balance (Dec. 31) | 48,000 | | |
| | 90,050 | | 90,050 | | |
| Balance carried forward | 48,000 | | | | |

Many people find the T-account approach preferable to the schedule in that the problem of whether to add or subtract a given amount is easily resolved by making the normal entries; also there is a built-in self-check. The items are simply entered in the account in the normal manner and the missing amount (sales in the above case) is the "plug" figure. Note that the *ending* balance is always entered on the "opposite side" for balancing purposes in reconstructing the account as is done in the normal year-end closing of accounts with balances to be carried forward.

Note that the increase of cash on hand is assumed to represent collections from customers. If there had been data relative to cash discounts on sales, returned sales, or accounts charged off as uncollectible, both the sales discounts and the bad debts written off should be added to the total in Schedule 1. In such cases if the T-account analysis is used, it would appear advisable to reconstruct the following accounts: Accounts Receivable, Allowance for Doubtful Accounts, Loss from Doubtful Accounts, Sales Discounts, Sales Returns, and Sales.

## Computation of Purchases

The amount of purchases may be determined by the analysis of cash disbursements and changes in both accounts payable and trade notes payable.

*Schedule 2*

| | |
|---|---:|
| Accounts and trade notes payable, December 31, 19A | $ 9,200 |
| Payments to creditors | 26,000 |
| | 35,200 |
| Less: Accounts and trade notes payable, | |
| January 1, 19A | 8,100 |
| Purchases for the Period, 19A | $27,100 |

It should be noted that cash discounts may have been taken. If this is the case, such discounts should be added in the schedule (or included in the T-account analysis) to derive gross purchases.

## Computation of Depreciation

The building and equipment were valued at appraised cost less depreciation. The decrease in the net book value of the asset, taking into account additions and dispositions of equipment during the period, is the amount of depreciation for the period as computed below:

*Schedule 3*

| | |
|---|---:|
| Net balance of buildings and equipment, January 1, 19A | $17,000 |
| Purchases of equipment during 19A: | |
| By issue of note payable | 500 |
| By cash payment | 340 |
| Balance before depreciation | 17,840 |
| Less: Net balance on December 31, 19A (after | |
| current depreciation) | 17,400 |
| Depreciation for the Period, 19A | $    440 |

## Computation of Expenses

The expenses paid in cash, determined from an analysis of cash disbursements, must be adjusted for prepaid and accrued items at the beginning and at the end of the period as follows:

*Schedule 4*

| | | |
|---|---:|---:|
| Expenses paid in cash during 19A | | $6,000 |
| Add: Expenses accrued on December 31, 19A | | 150 |
| Prepaid expenses on January 1, 19A | | 100 |
| | | 6,250 |
| Deduct: Accrued expenses, January 1, 19A | $120 | |
| Prepaid expenses, December 31, 19A | 110 | 230 |
| Expenses for the Period, 19A | | $6,020 |

Again, you may find it easier to analyze the more involved situations, such as this one, by reconstructing the related accounts in the following manner:

| Prepaid Expenses | | | | Accrued Expenses | |
|---|---|---|---|---|---|
| Beginning balance (Jan. 1) 100 | (A) Transfer to expense | 100 | (B) Transfer to expense | 120 | Beginning balance (Jan. 1) 120 |
| (C) To record final balance (Dec. 31)      110 | | | | | (D) To record final balance (Dec. 31)      150 |

**Expenses**

| | | | |
|---|---|---|---|
| Paid in cash during 19A | 6,000 | (B) Transfer from accrued | 120 |
| (A) Transfer from prepaid | 100 | (C) Final balance prepaid | 110 |
| (D) Final balance accrued | 150 | | |

(Expenses for 19A — account balance, $6,020.)

Note again that the beginning balances are entered, then the "normal" accounting entries are made in the accounts.

The information does not reveal any adjustments to salary expense; therefore, that expense is $7,000 as given.

### Preparation of the Income Statement

All information needed to prepare the income statement has now been determined. That statement would appear as shown in Exhibit 20–7.

**EXHIBIT 20–7**

JOHN MERCER COMPANY
Income Statement
For Year Ended December 31, 19A

| | | | |
|---|---|---|---|
| Sales (Schedule 1) | | | $55,050 |
| Cost of goods sold: | | | |
| Inventory, January 1, 19A (given) | | $ 6,900 | |
| Purchases (Schedule 2) | | 27,100 | |
| Goods available for sale | | 34,000 | |
| Less: Inventory, December 31, 19A (given) | | 8,700 | |
| Cost of Goods Sold | | | 25,300 |
| Gross margin on sales | | | 29,750 |
| Less: Expenses: | | | |
| Depreciation (Schedule 3) | | 440 | |
| Expenses (Schedule 4) | | 6,020 | |
| Salaries. (given) | | 7,000 | 13,460 |
| Net Income | | | $16,290 |

## WORKSHEETS FOR PROBLEMS FROM SINGLE-ENTRY AND OTHER INCOMPLETE RECORDS

The preceding example, although simplified, demonstrates the need for a worksheet approach to reduce clerical work and minimize the possibility of errors and omissions. In problem-solving situations, whether in study or in practice, the *interim worksheet* again is particularly useful. The interim worksheet provides for several internal checks on accuracy and recognizes each group of transactions in their debit and credit effects. In order to provide a "track record" such worksheets should be accompanied by explanations and computations of the analyses involved.

The following illustrative problem is presented to demonstrate adaptation and use of the interim worksheet in solving problems involving incomplete data:

J. C. Main had been in business two years and had not maintained double-entry records. A financial statement was prepared by an accountant at the end of last year, 19A. This balance sheet (balances at January 1, 19B) and one developed at the end of the current year (dated December 31, 19B) are presented in Exhibit 20–8. They were developed by "inventorying" all assets and liabilities.

The following additional information for 19B was developed:

a. Main kept no record of cash receipts and disbursements, but an analysis of canceled checks showed the following payments: accounts payable, $71,000; expenses, $20,700; and purchase of equipment, $3,700. No checks appeared to be outstanding.

b. Main stated that $100 cash was withdrawn regularly each week from the cash register for personal use. No record was made of these personal withdrawals.

c. The bank loan was for one year, the note was discounted by the bank at 6% on July 1, 19B.

**EXHIBIT 20–8**

### J. C. MAIN COMPANY
### Balance Sheets

|  | 19B | |
| --- | --- | --- |
|  | January 1 | December 31 |
| Cash | $ 10,000 | $ 22,000 |
| Notes receivable | 5,000 | 3,000 |
| Accounts receivable | 61,000 | 68,000 |
| Inventories | 25,000 | 27,000 |
| Prepaid expenses | 500 | 200 |
| Furniture and equipment (net) | 10,600 | 12,400 |
|  | $112,100 | $132,600 |
| Bank loan | $ — | $ 5,000 |
| Accounts payable | 30,000 | 36,000 |
| Accrued expenses | 800 | 650 |
| J. C. Main, proprietorship | 81,300 | 90,950 |
|  | $112,100 | $132,600 |

# EXHIBIT 20-9

## J. C. MAIN COMPANY
### Worksheet for Year Ended December 31, 19B

| | Beginning Balances January 1, 19B | Interim Entries Debit | Interim Entries Credit | Income Statement | Ending Balances December 31, 19B |
|---|---|---|---|---|---|
| **Debit accounts:** | | | | | |
| Cash | 10,000 | (c) 4,700<br>(d) 620<br>(e) 4,000<br>(h) 103,280<br>(g) 2,400 | (a) 95,400<br>(b) 5,200 | | 22,000 |
| Notes receivable | 5,000 | | (e) 4,000<br>(f) 400 | | 3,000 |
| Accounts receivable | 61,000 | (i) 112,680 | (g) 2,400<br>(h) 103,280 | | 68,000 |
| Inventories | 25,000 | (j) 27,000 | (j) 25,000 | | 27,000 |
| Prepaid expenses | 500 | (c) 150<br>(k) 50 | (k) 500 | | 200 |
| Furniture and equipment (net) | 10,600 | (a) 3,700 | (d) 900<br>(l) 1,000 | | 12,400 |
| Expenses | | (a) 20,700<br>(k) 500<br>(n) 650 | (k) 50<br>(n) 800 | 21,000 | |
| Interest expense | | (c) 150 | | 150 | |
| Loss on sale of equipment | | (d) 280 | | 280 | |
| Loss on worthless note | | (f) 400 | | 400 | |
| Depreciation | | (l) 1,000 | | 1,000 | |
| Purchases | | (m) 77,000 | | 77,000 | |
| Net income | | (o) 14,850 | | 14,850 | |
| | 112,100 | | | 114,680 | 132,600 |
| **Credit accounts:** | | | | | |
| Bank loan | | | (c) 5,000 | | 5,000 |
| Accounts payable | 30,000 | (a) 71,000 | (m) 77,000 | | 36,000 |
| Accrued expenses | 800 | (n) 800 | (n) 650 | | 650 |
| J. C. Main, proprietorship | 81,300 | (b) 5,200 | (o) 14,850 | | 90,950 |
| Sales | | | (i) 112,680 | 112,680 | |
| Income summary (inventory change) | | (j) 25,000 | (j) 27,000 | 2,000 | |
| | 112,100 | 476,110 | 476,110 | 114,680 | 132,600 |

*d.* Main stated that equipment listed in the January 1 balance sheet at $900 was sold for $620 cash.

*e.* The bank reported that it had credited Main with $4,000 during the year for customers' notes left for collection.

*f.* One $400 note on hand December 31, 19B, was past due and appeared to be worthless. Therefore, this note was not included in the $3,000 notes receivable listed in the December 31 balance sheet. Assume no allowance for doubtful accounts; bad debts are written off directly to expense because of immateriality.

Main needs a detailed income statement for the current year, 19B.

*Solution.* An eight-column or five-column interim worksheet may be adapted for this problem. A five-colum worksheet is shown in Exhibit 20-9. Note that a five-column worksheet is achieved by placing "debits over credits." Columns are set up for beginning balances, interim entries (debit and credit), income statement, and ending balances.

The beginning and ending balances, taken from the two balance sheets, are entered directly on the worksheet as illustrated with sufficient line spacing for the anticipated entries. Next the interim entries for all transactions are reconstructed (as explained below) to account for all changes in each account during the period. Last, all items not listed in the column "ending balances" are carried as debits or credits to the column headed "Income Statement." At this point in the solution the *net income* (or loss) is the difference between the debits and credits in the Income Statement column. Particular attention should be called to the fact that considerable data needed for reconstruction of the entries are missing; therefore, care must be exercised as to sequence of developing the entries. Note that all of the data available are used first (entries [a] through [f]) then subsequent entries are developed by computing the "missing data" as illustrated in entry (g) and following. Problems such as this one are frequently referred to as missing data problems.

*Explanation of Entries on the Worksheet:*

*a.* To record payments shown by analysis of canceled checks.

*b.* To record Main's cash withdrawals of $100 per week for 52 weeks.

*c.* To record bank loan of $5,000 less $300 interest of which $150 was prepaid as of December 31, 19B.

*d.* To record sale of equipment, cost less depreciation, $900, for $620 cash.

*e.* To record $4,000 notes receivable collected by bank.

*f.* To record charge-off of bad note, $400.

*g.* To record notes from customers, computed as follows (data taken directly from worksheet):

| | |
|---|---:|
| Notes collected............................................ | $4,000 |
| Note written off ........................................ | 400 |
| Notes on hand December 31, 19B................. | 3,000 |
| | 7,400 |
| Less: Notes on hand January 1, 19B.............. | 5,000 |
| New Notes Receivable ................................ | $2,400 |

h. Cash collected from customers (observe that it does not matter whether the collection was at time of sale or on account) is computed as follows from data shown in the Cash account on the worksheet:

| | |
|---|---:|
| Cash paid out ($95,400 + $5,200) | $100,600 |
| Cash balance, December 31, 19B | 22,000 |
| | 122,600 |
| Cash collected from all sources other than from customers: | |
| ($4,700 + $620 + $4,000) | 9,320 |
| | 113,280 |
| Less: Cash balance, January 1, 19B | 10,000 |
| Cash Collected from Customers | $103,280 |

i. Sales are computed by finding the only entry missing on the worksheet in accounts receivable, which entry is for sales on account. (Balance in notes receivable has been already reconciled on the worksheet.)

| | |
|---|---:|
| Notes received on account | $ 2,400 |
| Cash collected from customers | 103,280 |
| Final balance of accounts receivable | 68,000 |
| Total credits and balance | 173,680 |
| Less: January 1 balance | 61,000 |
| Total Debits for the Year (Sales) | $112,680 |

j. To close the January 1 inventory and to record the December 31 inventory (to income summary).

k. To close the January 1 balance of prepaid expenses and to increase the prepaid expense balance as of December 31 to $200 as given.

l. To set up the depreciation allowance for the period. All entries have been made in the Furniture and Equipment accounts on the worksheet except the depreciation credit. Depreciation is computed as follows:

| | |
|---|---:|
| Furniture and equipment, January 1, 19B | $10,600 |
| Equipment purchased | 3,700 |
| | 14,300 |
| Less: Equipment sold | 900 |
| | 13,400 |
| Less: Balance of furniture and equipment, | |
| December 31, 19B | 12,400 |
| Depreciation for the Period | $ 1,000 |

m. Purchases are computed by finding the missing entry in accounts payable on the worksheet as follows:

| | |
|---|---:|
| Payments on accounts payable | $ 71,000 |
| Balance of accounts payable, December 31, 19B | 36,000 |
| | 107,000 |
| Less: Accounts payable, January 1, 19B | 30,000 |
| Purchases for the Period | $ 77,000 |

*n.* To close the January 1 balance of accrued expenses and to record accrued expenses as of December 31.

*o.* To close net income to proprietorship. The net income may be computed by analyzing the changes in capital from January 1 to December 31, 19B, as illustrated previously or by extending nominal accounts balances to the column "Income Statement" and then computing the difference between the debits and credits. Obviously, one computation would serve as a check on the other.

The resulting income statement taken directly from the worksheet is shown in Exhibit 20–10.

**EXHIBIT 20–10**

J. C. MAIN COMPANY
Income Statement
For Year Ended December 31, 19B

| | | |
|---|---:|---:|
| Revenues: | | |
| Sales | | $112,680 |
| Costs and expenses: | | |
| Cost of goods sold: | | |
| Beginning inventory, January 1, 19B | $ 25,000 | |
| Purchases | 77,000 | |
| Total Goods Available for Sale | 102,000 | |
| Less: Final inventory, December 31, 19B | 27,000 | 75,000 |
| Gross margin on sales | | 37,680 |
| Less: Expenses: | | |
| Expenses | 21,000 | |
| Depreciation | 1,000 | |
| Loss on worthless note | 400 | 22,400 |
| Operating income | | 15,280 |
| Less: Other costs and losses: | | |
| Interest expense | 150 | |
| Loss on sale of equipment | 280 | 430 |
| Net Income | | $ 14,850 |

## LIMITATIONS OF SINGLE-ENTRY RECORDKEEPING

Single-entry recordkeeping is employed by a large number of particularly small businesses, by nonprofit organizations, by persons acting in a fiduciary capacity as administrators or executors of estates, and by many individuals relative to their personal affairs. Even some regular systems of recordkeeping recommended for retail outlets by trade associations and by manufacturers are based on single entry. For example, one such system is used by a large number of small retail druggists. Single-entry systems are used in the interest of simplicity and generally are less expensive to maintain than double-entry records since they do not require the services of a trained person. In fact, more often than not, single-entry records are maintained by the proprietor or someone closely associated with the activities being recorded.

Single-entry recordkeeping is generally inadequate except where operations are especially simple and the volume of activity is small. Some of the more important disadvantages of single-entry systems are:

1. Data are not available to the management for effectively planning and controlling the business.
2. Lack of systematic and precise recordkeeping may lead to inefficiency in administration and control over the affairs of the business.
3. They do not provide a check against clerical errors, as does a double-entry system. This is one of the most serious of the defects of single entry.
4. They seldom make provision for recording all transactions. Many internal transactions (i.e., those normally reflected through adjusting entries) in particular are not recorded.
5. Since no accounts are provided for many of the items appearing in both the balance sheet and income statement, omission of important data is always a possibility.
6. In the absence of detailed records of all assets, lax administration of those assets is quite likely.
7. Theft and other losses are less likely to be known.

## QUESTIONS

1. Briefly distinguish between the following: (a) change in principle, (b) change in estimate, (c) change in entity, and (d) accounting error.

2. What are the three basic alternatives for reflecting the effects of accounting changes and error corrections?

3. Complete the following matrix:

|  | Method of Reflecting the Effect* | | |
|---|---|---|---|
|  | (1)_____ | (2)_____ | (3)_____ |
| a. Change in estimate | _____ | _____ | _____ |
| b. Change in principle | _____ | _____ | _____ |
| c. Correction of error | _____ | _____ | _____ |

\* Identify these three captions; then enter appropriate check on each line.

4. What is a pro forma statement? Why are they used in respect to some accounting changes?

5. What is the difference between a counterbalancing and a noncounterbalancing error? Basically, why is the distinction significant in the analysis of errors?

6. Complete the following matrix by entering a plus to indicate overstatement and a minus to indicate understatement:

|  | Effect of Error on— | | | |
|  | Net Income | Assets | Liabilities | Owners' Equity |
|---|---|---|---|---|
| a. Ending inventory for 19A understated: | | | | |
|    19A financial statements ............................. | —— | —— | —— | —— |
|    19B financial statements ............................. | —— | —— | —— | —— |
| b. Ending inventory for 19B overstated: | | | | |
|    19A financial statements ............................. | —— | —— | —— | —— |
|    19B financial statements ............................. | —— | —— | —— | —— |
| c. Failed to record depreciation in 19A: | | | | |
|    19A financial statements ............................. | —— | —— | —— | —— |
|    19B financial statements ............................. | —— | —— | —— | —— |
| d. Failed to record revenue collected in advance at end of 19A: | | | | |
|    19A financial statements ............................. | —— | —— | —— | —— |
|    19B financial statements ............................. | —— | —— | —— | —— |

7. Give two examples of each of the following types of errors:
   a. Affects income statement only.
   b. Affects balance sheet only.
   c. Affects both income statement and balance sheet.

8. Briefly explain the differences between a double-entry and a single-entry system.

9. What are the primary shortcomings of a single-entry system? What are the advantages?

## EXERCISES

### PART A: EXERCISES 1–7

### Exercise 20–1

Lyle Corporation has been depreciating Machine A over a ten-year life on sum-of-the-years'-digits basis. The machine cost $68,000 and has an estimated residual value of $13,000. On the basis of an engineering study of its economic potential to the company, completed during the fifth year (19B), the management decided to change to straight-line depreciation with no change in the estimated useful life or the residual value. The annual financial statements are prepared on a comparative basis (two years presented). Net incomes (no extraordinary items) prior to giving effect to this change (i.e., on the old basis) were: 19A, $50,000; 19B, $51,000. Shares of stock outstanding, 100,000. Disregard income tax considerations.

*Required:*

1. Identify the type of accounting change involved and analyze the effects of the change.
2. Prepare the entry, or entries, to appropriately reflect the change in the accounts in 19B (fifth year), the year of the change.
3. Illustrate how the change should be reflected on the 19B financial statement which includes 19A results for comparative purposes.

### Exercise 20-2

Lyle Corporation has been depreciating Machine B over a ten-year life on a straight-line basis. The machine cost $24,000 and has an estimated residual value of $6,000. On the basis of experience since acquisition (four years prior to 19B) the management has decided to depreciate it over a total life of 14 years instead of 10, and no change in the estimated residual value. The annual financial statements are prepared on a comparative basis (two years presented). Net incomes (no extraordinary items) on the old basis were: 19A, $50,000; 19B, $51,000. Shares of stock outstanding, 100,000. Disregard income tax considerations.

*Required:*

1. Identify the type of accounting change involved and analyze the effects of the change.
2. Prepare entry, or entries, to appropriately reflect the change in the accounts for 19B (fifth year), the year of the change.
3. Illustrate how the change should be reflected on the 19B financial statement which includes 19A results for comparative purposes.

### Exercise 20-3

AB Corporation has never had an audit prior to 19D, the current year. Prior to the arrival of the auditor the company accountant had prepared a comparative financial statement with 19C and 19D shown thereon for comparative purposes. The books for 19D have not been closed. During the audit it was discovered that an invoice dated January 19A for $9,000 (paid in cash at that time) was debited to operating expenses, although it was for the purchase of Machine X. Machine X has an estimated useful life of ten years and no residual value.

Reported income reflected on the comparative financial statement prepared by the company auditor (prior to discovery of the error) was: 19C, $30,000; 19D, $33,000. Shares of stock outstanding, 100,000. Disregard income tax considerations.

*Required:*

1. Identify the type of accounting change involved and analyze the effects of the change.
2. Prepare entry, or entries, to appropriately reflect the change in the accounts for 19D, the year of the change.
3. Illustrate how the change should be reflected on the 19D financial statement which includes 19C results for comparative purposes.

### Exercise 20-4

Give journal entries to correct the accounts, and the subsequent adjusting entry, for each of the errors listed below assuming (1) the errors were discovered on December 31, 19B, before the books were adjusted and closed, and (2) the errors were discovered in January 19C (after the books for 19B were adjusted and closed). Assume each item is material. Disregard income tax considerations.

a. Merchandise costing $6,000 was received on December 28, 19A, and was included in the final inventory of 19A, but the purchase was not recorded in the purchases journal until January 3, 19B.
b. An entry was made on December 30, 19B, for write-off of organization expense as follows (assume only one year's amortization was justified through 19B; amortization per year $1,000):

| General expense | 5,000 | |
| Deferred organization expense | | 5,000 |

c. Discount of $3,300 on a long-term bond investment purchased on May 1, 19A, was written off to retained earnings on that date. These bonds mature on July 1, 19J. Use straight-line amortization.

d. Machinery costing $900 was purchased and charged to repair expense on June 30, 19A. The depreciation rate on machinery is 10% per year.

## Exercise 20–5

You are in the process of auditing the accounts of Zero Manufacturing Corporation for the year ended December 31, 19B. You discover that the adjustments made on the previous audit for the year 19A were not entered in the accounts; therefore, the accounts are not in agreement with the audited amounts as of December 31, 19A. The following adjustments were included in the 19A audit report:

a. Invoices for merchandise purchased in December 19A, not entered on the books until January 19B and not included in the December 31, 19A inventory, $6,000.

b. Invoices for merchandise received in December 19A were not recorded in the accounts; the goods were included in the 19A ending inventory, $9,000.

c. Provision for doubtful accounts for 19A understated by $1,000.

d. Factory expense for 19A not entered in the accounts until January 19B, $2,500.

e. Accrued payroll at December 31, 19A, not recorded at that date, $2,000.

f. Prepaid insurance at December 31, 19A, $300 not recorded.

g. Property taxes for year ended December 31, 19A, not entered in the accounts until January 19B, $1,200.

h. Depreciation not recorded prior to January 19A, $3,000; for year ended December 31, 19A, $1,500.

*Required:*

Assume you have the uncorrected and unadjusted trial balance dated December 31, 19B. Give the journal entry for each of the above items that should be made to the trial balance before using it for further audit purposes. Show computations. Disregard income tax implications.

## Exercise 20–6

Dawson Company has made several accounting changes with a view to improving the matching of expenses with revenue. Assume it is at the end of 19C and that the accounting period ends on December 31. The books have not been adjusted and closed at the end of 19C. Among the changes were the following:

a. Machinery that cost $25,000, estimated useful life ten years, residual value $3,000. The company has been using sum-of-the-years'-digits depreciation. Early in the eighth year (19C), it was decided to change to straight-line depreciation (with no change in residual value or estimated life).

b. A patent that cost $8,500 is being depreciated over the legal life of 17 years. Early in the 6th year (19C), it was decided that the economic benefits would not last longer than 13 years from date of acquisition.

c. During 19A and 19B all repair expenditures have been debited to the Machinery account. The repair expenditures capitalized amounted to $7,000 and $11,000 during the two years respectively. The machinery was being depreciated 12% per year on cost. It is now the third year (19C), and the error has been discovered.

*Required:*

1. For each of the above situations, identify the type of accounting change or error that was involved and briefly explain how it should be accounted for.
2. Give the appropriate entry to reflect the change and the 19C adjusting entry in each instance. Show computations and disregard income tax considerations. If no entry is required in a particular instance, explain why.

### Exercise 20-7

RB Company failed to recognize accruals and prepayments since organization three years previously. The net income, accruals, and prepayments at year-end are given below:

|  | 19A | 19B | 19C |
|---|---|---|---|
| Reported income ............................................... | $4,000 | $1,000* | $5,000 |
| Items not recognized at year-end: |  |  |  |
| a. Prepaid expenses ...................................... | 200 | 280 | 109 |
| b. Accrued expenses ..................................... | 250 | 225 | 247 |
| c. Revenue collected in advance ..................... | 325 | 360 | 293 |
| d. Revenue earned but not yet collected ............ | 275 | 230 | 196 |

* Net loss.

*Required:*

1. Compute the correct net income for each year (disregard income tax effects).
2. Give entry to correct each item assuming the errors were discovered at year-end 19C (books were not closed).
3. Give entry to correct each item assuming the errors were discovered during 19D prior to the 19D adjusting and closing entries.

### PART B: EXERCISES 8-13

### Exercise 20-8

During the year ended December 31, 19A, M. Lane, a retail merchant who had started a business January 2, 19A, paid trade creditors $49,062 in cash, and final inventory per count (*Fifo* basis) was $9,563. Balances available on December 31, 19A, were the following: accounts payable, $16,125; expenses, $2,450; capital (representing total investment in cash January 2, 19A), $45,000; accounts receivable, $13,188; and sales, $50,000. There were no withdrawals. All sales and purchases were on credit.

*Required:*

1. Develop a worksheet and complete it to provide information for a corrected income statement and balance sheet. *Hint:* Set up columns for interim entries, income statement, and balance sheet.
2. Prepare a statement of cash inflows and outflows for the year ended December 31, 19A.

### Exercise 20-9

On January 1, 19A, A. B. Cline invested $5,000 cash in a television repair shop. Memoranda revealed that $50 per week was withdrawn for living expenses. Cline's personal automobile, having a fair market value of $2,500 at that time, was invested in the business for use as a service car. The shop then paid $500 for body changes on the car to make it suitable for its needs; this amount was capitalized. On January 1, 19A, F. Frye also invested as a partner. Frye invested equipment valued at $3,000 and $1,000 cash. It was agreed that the partners would share profits equally after January 1, 19A. Frye withdrew $800 cash during the year.

On December 31, 19A, the following assets and liabilities were determined from memoranda and incomplete records: cash, $4,810; equipment (less depreciation), $4,600; receivables, $1,200; car-truck (less depreciation), $2,250; notes payable, $1,000.

### Required:

Prepare a balance sheet showing capital balances for each partner and a separate computation of net income.

### Exercise 20–10

Make the computations needed for the 19B income statement from the following data (each item is independent):

a. Wages: amount paid, $15,000; accrued on December 31, 19A, $1,000; accrued on December 31, 19B, $2,000.
b. Rent revenue: amount collected, $8,000; prepaid $500 on December 31, 19A, and $300 on December 31, 19B; accrued rental, $200 on December 31, 19A, and $600 on December 31, 19B.
c. Total sales: Cash account, balance, December 31, 19A, $26,000; balance, December 31, 19B, $33,000; total disbursements for 19B, $39,000. All cash receipts were from customers. Accounts receivable: balance, December 31, 19A, $40,160; balance, December 31, 19B, $59,000. Accounts written off during 19B as uncollectible, $960.
d. Purchases (before discounts): accounts payable balance on December 31, 19A, $28,320, and on December 31, 19B, $33,000; payments made on accounts during 19B, $46,000; cash discounts taken, $820.

### Exercise 20–11

Give the journal entry to account for the missing amount in each of the following situations:

a. Prepaid Insurance: starting balance, $1,400; final balance, $1,900; amount expired, $1,200.
b. Allowance for Doubtful Accounts: starting balance, $5,000; final balance, $6,000; bad debts written off, $2,700.
c. Sinking Fund: starting balance, $90,000; final balance, $102,000; current payment to sinking fund, $20,000.
d. Premium on Bonds Payable: starting balance, $6,000; final balance, $4,500.
e. Capital Stock: starting balance, $200,000; final balance, $250,000; stock sold at par during the year, $30,000.
f. Retained Earnings: starting balance, $34,000 (credit); appropriation to reserve for bond sinking fund, $10,000; charge for stock dividend, $20,000; net income, $42,000; final balance, $36,000 (credit).
g. Accounts Receivable: starting balance, $25,000; collections on accounts, $27,000; bad accounts written off, $1,200; sales returns on account, $900; notes received on accounts, $3,000; final balance, $25,900.
h. Accounts Payable: starting balance, $17,300; cash paid on accounts, $30,200; cash discounts taken, $600; final balance, $15,500.

### Exercise 20–12

For each account indicate the amount that should be reported on the income statement. Show computations.

| | Beginning of Period | End of Period |
|---|---|---|
| a. Deferred (prepaid) interest revenue | $    50 | $    75 |
| Uncollected interest revenue earned | 65 | 20 |
| Interest collected during period, $200. | | |
| Interest revenue should be reported as $_____. | | |
| b. Accrued wages | $ 1,000 | $ 1,800 |
| Prepaid wages | 400 | 200 |
| Wages paid during period, $12,000. | | |
| Wages should be reported as $_____. | | |
| c. Accounts receivable | $10,000 | $14,000 |
| Notes receivable | 2,000 | 1,000 |
| Cash sales | $120,000 | |
| Collections on accounts | 40,000 | |
| Return sales (on account) | 2,000 | |
| Collection on trade notes | 5,000 | |
| Accounts written off as bad | 500 | |
| Discounts given (on account) | 600 | |
| Gross sales should be reported as $_____. | | |
| d. Accounts payable | $ 5,000 | $ 7,000 |
| Notes payable (trade) | 10,000 | 6,000 |
| Payments on accounts | $ 40,000 | |
| Cash purchases | 100,000 | |
| Discounts taken on credit purchases | 1,000 | |
| Purchase returns (on account) | 1,500 | |
| Payments on trade notes | 8,000 | |
| Gross purchases should be reported as $_____. | | |

### Exercise 20–13

M. F. Sharp operated a hat shop but had not kept careful business records. The following data were secured from various memoranda and records:

An analysis of canceled checks revealed the following cash expenditures: expenses, $4,800; accounts payable, $9,200. Sharp stated that money was withdrawn from time to time from the cash register for personal living expenses. These withdrawals were estimated to total $3,600. All other receipts were deposited in the bank.

A list of assets and liabilities that was developed follows:

| | Jan. 1, 19A | Dec. 31, 19A |
|---|---|---|
| Cash | $ 1,200 | $    900 |
| Accounts receivable | 1,000 | 1,500 |
| Inventories | 3,900 | 4,600 |
| Prepaid expenses | 100 | 60 |
| Equipment (net) | 4,200 | 3,800 |
| | 10,400 | 10,860 |
| Accounts payable | 1,100 | 1,300 |
| Proprietorship | $ 9,300 | $ 9,560 |

*Required:*

Prepare a worksheet to develop the income statement and balance sheet.

## PROBLEMS

### PART A: PROBLEMS 1–6

**Problem 20–1**

Franklin Corporation initiated several accounting changes during the year and discovered some errors. The changes and errors are given below. Assume the current year is 19C and that the accounting period ends December 31. The books have not been adjusted or closed at the end of 19C. Disregard income tax considerations.

a. The merchandise inventory at December 31, 19B, was overstated by $10,000.

b. During January 19A, extraordinary repairs on machinery was debited to repair expense; the $15,000 should have been debited to machinery which is being depreciated 15% per year on cost (no residual value).

c. A patent that cost $9,350 has been amortized for the past 7 years (excluding 19C) over its legal life of 17 years. It is now clear that its economic life will not be more than 12 years from acquisition date.

d. At the end of 19B revenue collected in advance of $3,000 was included in revenue. It is earned in 19C.

e. A machine that cost $8,000, acquired during January 19A was debited to Operating Expense. It has an estimated life of five years and a residual value of $3,000. Assume straight-line depreciation.

f. The rate for bad debts used has been ½ of 1% which has proven to be too low; therefore, for 19C and thereafter the rate is to be 1% of credit sales. The amount of the adjustment under the old rate was: 19A, $800; 19B, $1,000; and 19C, $1,100 (the amount for 19C has not been entered in the accounts since the adjusting entries have not been made).

g. During January 19A, a five-year insurance premium of $750 was paid which was debited to Insurance Expense.

h. At the end of 19B, accrued wages payable of $1,800 were not recorded; they were paid early in 19C.

*Required:*

1. For each of the above situations, identify the type of accounting change or error that was involved and briefly explain how each should be accounted for.

2. Give the appropriate entry to record the change and any subsequent adjusting entry in each instance at the end of 19C. Show computations. If no entry is needed, explain why.

**Problem 20–2**

On January 3, 19A, Cooper Company purchased a machine that cost $15,000. Although the machine has an estimated useful life of ten years and estimated residual value of $3,000, it was debited to expense when acquired. It is now December 19D, and the error was discovered. The average income tax rate is 45% and straight-line depreciation is used.

*Required:*

1. Give the entry to correct the accounts at the end of 19D and a second entry for depreciation for 19D. Assume the income tax return was correct; therefore, disregard income taxes.

2. Assume instead that the income tax return also was incorrect because of this error; therefore, additional taxes will have to be paid including an 8% penalty

per annum (for three years) on the amount of the tax underpayments. Give the entry to correct the accounts at the end of 19D and a second entry for depreciation for 19D.

## Problem 20–3

The accounting department of Virginia Corporation had completed the comparative financial reports for the period ending 19C prior to the initiation of the first audit by an outside certified public accountant. This problem relates specifically to two changes recommended by the CPA after the statements were prepared by the company.

The statements have been summarized for problem purposes; details are provided only in respect to the recommended changes; the statements were:

|  | 19A | 19B | 19C |
|---|---|---|---|
| **Balance Sheet:** | | | |
| **Assets:** | | | |
| Machinery | $ 300,000 | $ 300,000 | $ 300,000 |
| Accumulated depreciation | (80,000) | (100,000) | (120,000) |
| Remaining assets | 2,280,000 | 2,290,000 | 2,420,000 |
| Total | $2,500,000 | $2,490,000 | $2,600,000 |
| Liabilities | $ 373,000 | $ 349,000 | $ 410,000 |
| Capital stock (200,000 shares) | 2,000,000 | 2,000,000 | 2,000,000 |
| Retained earnings | 127,000 | 141,000 | 190,000 |
| Total | $2,500,000 | $2,490,000 | $2,600,000 |
| **Income Statement:** | | | |
| Sales (all on credit) | $1,000,000 | $1,100,000 | $1,200,000 |
| Cost of goods sold | 600,000 | 650,000 | 700,000 |
| Gross margin | 400,000 | 450,000 | 500,000 |
| Operating expenses | 300,000 | 330,000 | 360,000 |
| Income taxes (assume 50%) | 50,000 | 60,000 | 70,000 |
| Income before extraordinary items | 50,000 | 60,000 | 70,000 |
| Extraordinary items | 10,000 | (20,000) | 14,000 |
| Less income tax effect | (3,000) | 4,000 | (5,000) |
| Net Income | $ 57,000 | $ 44,000 | $ 79,000 |
| **Earnings per share data:** | | | |
| Income before extraordinary items | .250 | .300 | .350 |
| Net income | .285 | .220 | .395 |
| **Statement of Retained Earnings:** | | | |
| Beginning balance | $ 100,000 | $ 127,000 | $ 141,000 |
| Net income | 57,000 | 44,000 | 79,000 |
| Dividends | (30,000) | (30,000) | (30,000) |
| Ending Balance | $ 127,000 | $ 141,000 | $ 190,000 |

On the basis of the examination the auditor insisted on the following changes:

1. Starting with 19C, change the loss experience rate on credit sales from one half of 1% to one fourth of 1%. This change was dictated by collection experi-

ence and losses during the past two years. These analyses indicate a drop in expected losses due to bad debts. The company has initiated a tight control on credit granting and stepped up collection efforts.

2. On January 1, 19A, a machine costing $20,000 (ten-year life, no residual value) was inadvertently debited to Operating Expense at that time. The error was discovered by the CPA at the end of 19C; the machine has seven more years of useful life (after 19C). Assume a 6% per annum tax penalty on net tax deficiencies for 19A and 19B only.

*Required:*

a. Analyze the nature of each of the changes.
b. Determine the effects on the financial statements assuming they are to be reported on comparative statements covering the three years.
c. Give the entry to effect the change including the correction of 19C entries. The books for 19C have been adjusted but not closed.
d. Compute the correct amounts for those items that would be affected for each of the three years.

## Problem 20-4

Landon Company failed to recognize accruals and deferrals in the accounts. In addition, numerous other errors were made in computing net income. The net incomes for the past three years are given below along with a list of the items that were not recognized in the recordkeeping.

You are to set up a worksheet to correct net income for each year. Set up columns for the following: particulars, 19A, 19B, 19C, and accounts to be corrected. Key and briefly identify the errors under the "particulars" column and enter amounts under the respective years as plus or minus so that the last line will report corrected net income. Maintain equality of balances in the worksheet. Assume that all items are material. Disregard income tax effects.

| | 19A | 19B | 19C |
|---|---|---|---|
| a. Reported income | $4,000 | $(3,500) | $10,000 |
| Items not recognized at each year-end: | | | |
| b. Accrued expenses | 400 | 250 | 300 |
| c. Revenue collected in advance | 100 | | 200 |
| d. Prepaid expenses | 320 | 410 | 120 |
| e. Revenue earned but not collected | 170 | 140 | |
| f. Annual depreciation overstated (not cumulative) | | 1,000 | 1,200 |
| g. Annual provision for doubtful accounts understated | 170 | 200 | 190 |
| h. Goods purchased on December 31, included in ending inventory; not recorded until following year | 460 | 210 | 150 |
| i. Sales on December 31 not recorded until following year; the goods were not included in final inventory | 290 | 770 | 390 |
| j. Ending inventory overstated | 130 | 240 | 290 |
| k. Checks written and mailed on December 31 as payment on accounts payable; not recorded until next year | 1,100 | 1,500 | 1,400 |
| l. Bad debts not written off to allowance for doubtful accounts by year-end | 800 | 950 | 1,170 |

## Problem 20-5

R. Waters established a retail business in 19A. Early in 19D Waters entered into negotiations with J. Jones with a view to forming a partnership. You have been asked by Waters and Jones to check Waters' books for the past three years and to compute correct net income for each year.

The profits per clients' statements were as follows:

| | Year Ending 12/31 | | |
|---|---|---|---|
| | 19A | 19B | 19C |
| Net Income.............. | $9,000 | $10,109 | $8,840 |

During the audit, you found the following:

| | | Year Ending 12/31 | | |
|---|---|---|---|---|
| | | 19A | 19B | 19C |
| | Omissions from the books: | | | |
| *Item* | | | | |
| A | Accrued expenses at end of year........................ | $2,160 | $2,094 | $4,624 |
| B | Accrued (uncollected) revenue at end of year ...... | 200 | – | |
| C | Prepaid expenses at end of year ........................ | 902 | 1,210 | 1,406 |
| D | Deferred revenue at end of year ........................ | – | 610 | – |
| | Goods in transit at end of year omitted from inventory: | | | |
| E | For which purchase entry had been made ......... | – | 2,610 | – |
| F | For which purchase entry had not been made...... | – | – | 1,710 |
| | Other points requiring consideration: | | | |
| G | Depreciation on equipment had been recorded monthly by a charge to expense and a credit to an allowance for depreciation account at a blanket rate of 1% of end-of-month balances of equipment accounts. However, the sale during December 19B of certain equipment was entered as a debit to Cash and a credit to the asset account for the sale price of............................................. | – | 5,000 | – |
| | (This equipment was purchased in July 19A at a cost of $6,000.) | | | |
| H | No allowance had been set up for uncollectible accounts. It is decided to set up one for the estimated probable losses as of December 31, 19C, for: | | | |
| | 19B accounts ............................................. | – | – | 700 |
| | 19C accounts ............................................. | – | – | 1,500 |
| | and to correct the charge against each year so that it will show the losses (actual and estimated) relating to that year's sales. | | | |
| | Accounts had been written off to expense as follows: | | | |
| | 19A accounts ............................................. | 1,000 | 1,200 | – |
| | 19B accounts ............................................. | – | 400 | 2,000 |
| | 19C accounts ............................................. | – | – | 1,600 |

(AICPA adapted)

## Problem 20-6

The records of AB Corporation have never been audited. At the end company prepared the following financial statements (summarized).

Income Statement:

| | |
|---|---:|
| Sales and service revenue | $600,0 |
| Expenses: | |
| Cost of goods sold | (050,0( |
| Distribution expenses | (100,0( |
| Administrative expenses | (60,00 |
| Pretax income | 70,00 |
| Income taxes | 21,50 |
| Net Income | $ 48,50( |

Balance Sheet:

Assets:

| | |
|---|---:|
| Cash | $ 23,000 |
| Accounts receivable (net) | 40,000 |
| Inventory (periodic system) | 110,000 |
| Property, plant, and equipment (net) | 160,000 |
| Patent | 8,000 |
| Other assets | 9,000 |
| Total Assets | $350,000 |

Liabilities:

| | |
|---|---:|
| Accounts payable | $ 80,000 |
| Income taxes payable | 15,000 |
| Notes payable, long term (6%) | 40,000 |
| Total Liabilities | 135,000 |

Stockholders' Equity:

| | |
|---|---:|
| Common stock, par $10 (12,000 shares) | 145,000 |
| Retained earnings | 80,000 |
| Dividends paid | (10,000) |
| Total Stockholders' Equity | 215,000 |
| Total Liabilities and Stockholders' Equity | $350,000 |

The company is in the process of negotiating a large loan for expansion purposes. The bank has requested that an audit be performed. During the course of the audit, the following facts were determined:

a. The inventory at December 31, 19B, was overstated by $10,000.

b. The inventory at December 31, 19C, was overstated by $20,000.

c. The property, plant, and equipment was underdepreciated in 19B by $9,000 and in 19C by $12,000.

d. A three-year insurance premium of $900 paid on January 3, 19B, was debited to expense at that time.

e. Accrued wages were not recorded as follows: 19B, $800; 19C, $1,000.

f. The patent which originally cost $17,000 has been amortized to administrative expense over a 17-year life (including 19C). Evidence clearly indicates that its economic life will approximate 14 years from date of acquisition.

g. Service revenue earned but not yet collected were not recognized as follows: 19B, $5,000; 19C, $7,500.

h. A special delivery truck purchased January 19C at a cost of $13,000, was debited to Distribution Expense at that time. The truck has an estimated useful life of ten years and an estimated residual value of $2,000. The company uses straight-line depreciation.

*i*. Bad debts amounting to $7,500 have not been written off.

*Required:*

1. Set up a worksheet to develop corrected amounts for the income statement and balance sheet. Complete the worksheet and key your entries. Assume the income tax expense amount is correct despite the above items.
2. Prepare a corrected income statement and balance sheet.

## PART B: PROBLEMS 7–10

### Problem 20–7

Cooper Hat Shop maintained incomplete records. After investigation you found the following assets and liabilities:

### Assets

|  | Jan. 1, 19A | Dec. 31, 19A |
|---|---|---|
| Cash on hand ..................................... | $    90 | $    160 |
| Cash in bank........................................ | 1,250 | 870 |
| Accounts receivable ............................ | 6,700 | 6,830 |
| Inventory ............................................. | 3,100 | 3,800 |
| Equipment (net of depreciation)............... | 5,200 | 5,600 |
| Prepaid insurance ................................ | 120 | 60 |
|  | 16,460 | 17,320 |

### Liabilities

|  | | |
|---|---|---|
| Accounts payable ................................. | 1,000 | 2,200 |
| Bank loan ............................................. |  | 3,000 |
| Accrued expenses payable .................... | 90 | 50 |
|  | 1,090 | 5,250 |
| Owner's Equity.............................. | $15,370 | $12,070 |

An analysis of bank deposits and disbursements showed:

Deposits:
    Collections from customers ........................ $8,900
    Proceeds of bank loan................................. 3,000
    Additional investment by proprietor............... 1,200
Checks and charges:
    Payments to creditors ................................. 6,100
    Expenses .................................................... 4,500
    Refunds on sales (allowances) ..................... 350
    Proprietor's withdrawals .............................. 1,500
    Interest on bank loan .................................. 30
Purchase of equipment .................................. 1,000

*Required:*

1. Compute the net income or loss by analyzing the changes in proprietorship.

2. Prepare a detailed income schedule including computation schedules.


## Problem 20–8

Harper Company has maintained incomplete records. In applying for a loan that was very important to the company, a financial statement was needed. An analysis of the records provided the following data:

| | |
|---|---:|
| Cash receipts: | |
|    Cash sales .................................................................... | $130,000 |
|    Collections on credit sales ............................................ | 43,000 |
|    Collections on trade notes ........................................... | 1,000 |
|    Purchase allowances ................................................... | 1,500 |
|    Miscellaneous............................................................... | 250 |
| Cash payments: | |
|    Cash purchases ............................................................ | 84,500 |
|    Payments to trade creditors ......................................... | 34,100 |
|    Payment on mortgage plus annual interest ..................... | 4,020 |
|    Sales commissions ....................................................... | 7,200 |
|    Rent expense ............................................................... | 2,400 |
|    General expenses ......................................................... | 14,590 |
|    Other operating expenses ............................................. | 29,800 |
|    Sales returns ($3,000 of which $1,000 was cash).............. | 1,000 |
|    Insurance (renewal three-year premium, April 1).............. | 468 |
|    Fixed assets purchased ................................................ | 1,500 |

|  | Balances | |
|---|---|---|
| | Jan. 1, 19A | Dec. 31, 19A |
| Cash ...................................................... | $14,100 | $10,172 |
| Accounts receivable ................................... | 13,000 | 18,000 |
| Trade notes receivable ............................... | 2,000 | 1,500 |
| Inventory ................................................ | 10,000 | 18,400 |
| Unexpired insurance ................................... | 39 | ? |
| Prepaid interest expense ............................ | 600 | 510 |
| Trade accounts payable ............................. | 26,500 | 23,800 |
| Income taxes payable ................................ | | 1,984 |
| Accrued operating expenses ........................ | 600 | 400 |
| Fixed assets (net) .................................... | 35,400 | 33,290 |
| Other assets.............................................. | 11,861 | 11,861 |
| Capital stock .......................................... | 40,000 | 40,000 |
| Mortgage payable (6% dated July 1).............. | 20,000 | ? |

No fixed assets were sold during the year.


### Required:

Prepare a worksheet that will provide data for a detailed income statement for the year and a balance sheet for 19A. Show computations.


## Problem 20–9

The following data were taken from the incomplete records of Baker's Sporting Goods Store:

|  | Balances | |
|---|---|---|
|  | Jan. 1, 19A | Dec. 31, 19A |
| Accounts receivable ................................... | $ 2,300 | $ 3,900 |
| Notes receivable (trade) ............................ | 1,500 | 2,000 |
| Accrued interest on notes receivable ........... | 90 | 70 |
| Prepaid interest on notes payable................. | 75 | 60 |
| Inventory ............................................... | 9,255 | 10,400 |
| Prepaid expenses (operating)....................... | 100 | 130 |
| Store equipment (net) .............................. | 8,500 | 8,600 |
| Other assets............................................ | – | 500 |
| Accounts payable .................................... | 1,700 | 1,900 |
| Notes payable (trade)................................. | 11,000 | 11,500 |
| Notes payable (equipment) ......................... | – | 500 |
| Accrued interest payable ............................ | 40 | 30 |
| Accrued expenses (operating) .................... | 170 | 210 |
| Prepaid interest revenue ............................ | 30 | 40 |

An analysis of the checkbook, canceled checks, deposit slips, and bank statements provided the following summary for the year:

| Balance, January 1, 19A ..................................... | | $4,200 |
|---|---|---|
| Cash receipts: | | |
| Cash sales.................................................... | $23,000 | |
| On accounts receivable.................................... | 7,600 | |
| On notes receivable ...................................... | 1,000 | |
| Interest revenue ........................................... | 160 | |
| Cash disbursements: | | |
| Cash purchases .......................................... | 11,800 | |
| On accounts payable...................................... | 2,400 | |
| On notes payable (trade) ............................... | 500 | |
| Interest expense .......................................... | 560 | |
| Operating expenses ...................................... | 14,130 | |
| Miscellaneous nonoperating expenses............... | 970 | |
| Other assets purchased................................. | 500 | |
| Withdrawals by H. Baker ............................... | 2,400 | |
| Balance, December 31, 19A............................... | | $2,700 |

*Required:*

1. Compute the net income by analyzing the changes in the capital account.
2. Prepare a detailed income statement with supporting schedules; show computations.

**Problem 20–10**

Kelley-Thomas Company is a partnership that has not maintained adequate accounting records because it has been unable to employ a competent bookkeeper. The company sells hardware items to the retail trade and also wholesales to builders and contractors. As the company's CPA, you have been asked to prepare the company's financial statements as of June 30, 19B.

Your work papers provide the following post-closing trial balance at December 31, 19A:

Post-Closing Trial Balance
December 31, 19A

|                                                    | Debit    | Credit   |
|----------------------------------------------------|----------|----------|
| Cash                                               | $10,000  |          |
| Accounts receivable                                | 8,000    |          |
| Allowance for bad debts                            |          | $   600  |
| Merchandise inventory                              | 35,000   |          |
| Prepaid insurance                                  | 150      |          |
| Automobiles                                        | 7,800    |          |
| Accumulated depreciation – automobiles             |          | 4,250    |
| Furniture and fixtures                             | 2,200    |          |
| Accumulated depreciation – furniture and fixtures  |          | 650      |
| Accounts payable                                   |          | 13,800   |
| Bank loan payable                                  |          | 8,000    |
| Accrued expenses                                   |          | 200      |
| Kelley, capital                                    |          | 17,500   |
| Thomas, capital                                    |          | 18,150   |
| Total                                              | $63,150  | $63,150  |

You are able to collect the following information at June 30, 19B:

a. Your analysis of cash transactions, derived from the company's bank statements and checkbook stubs, is as follows:

Deposits:

| | |
|---|---|
| Cash receipts from customers | $65,000 |
| ($40,000 of this amount represents collections on receivables including deposited protested checks totaling $600) | |
| Bank loan, 1/2/19B (due 5/1/19B, 5%, face $8,000) | 7,867 |
| Bank loan, 5/1/19B (due 9/1/19B, 5%, face $9,000) | 8,850 |
| Sale of old automobile used by the business | 20 |
| Total Deposits | $81,737 |

Disbursements:

| | |
|---|---|
| Payments to merchandise creditors | $45,000 |
| Payment to Internal Revenue Service on Thomas' 19B declaration of estimated income taxes | 3,000 |
| General expenses | 7,000 |
| Bank loan, 1/2/19B | 8,000 |
| Bank loan, 5/2/19B | 8,000 |
| Payment for new automobile for the business | 2,400 |
| Protested checks | 900 |
| Kelley withdrawals | 5,000 |
| Thomas withdrawals | 2,500 |
| Total Disbursements | $81,800 |

b. The protested checks, amounting to $900, include customers' checks totaling $600 that were redeposited and a $300 check from an employee that is still on hand.

c. Accounts receivable from customers for merchandise sales amounts to $18,000 on June 30, 19B, and includes accounts totaling $800 that have been placed with an attorney for collection. Correspondence with the client's attorney reveals that one of the accounts for $175 is uncollectible. Experience indicates that 1% of credit sales will prove uncollectible.

d. On April 1, 19B a new automobile was purchased. The list price of the automobile was $2,700, and $300 was allowed for the trade-in of an old automobile, even though the dealer stated that its condition was so poor that it could not be used. The old automobile cost $1,800 and was fully depreciated at December 31, 19A.

e. Depreciation is recorded by the straight-line method and is computed on acquisitions to the nearest full month. The estimated life for furniture and fixtures is ten years and for automobiles three years. [Salvage value is to be ignored in computing depreciation. No asset other than the car in item (d) was fully depreciated prior to June 30, 19B.]

f. Other data as of June 30, 19B, include the following:

> Merchandise inventory............... $37,500
> Prepaid insurance ....................      80
> Accrued expenses....................     166

g. Accounts payable to merchandise vendors total $18,750 on June 30, 19B. There is on hand a $750 credit memorandum from a merchandise vendor for returned merchandise; the company will apply the credit to July merchandise purchases. Neither the credit memorandum nor the return of the merchandise had been recorded on the books nor included in the June 30 inventory.

h. Profits and losses are divided equally between the partners.

*Required:*

Prepare a worksheet that provides, on the accrual basis, information regarding transactions for the six months ended June 30, 19B, the results of the partnership operations for the period, and the financial position of the partnership at June 30, 19B. (No need to prepare formal financial statements or formal journal entries.)

(AICPA adapted)

# Chapter *21*

# The Statement of Changes
# in Financial Position

Throughout the preceding chapters, references have been made to the statement of changes in financial position. Since the issuance of *APB Opinion No. 19*, "Reporting Changes in Financial Position" (March 1971), this statement has been required along with the income statement and balance sheet. The APB made it mandatory in the following terms:

> The Board concludes that information concerning the financing and investing activities of a business enterprise and the changes in its financial position for a period is essential for financial statement users, particularly owners and creditors, in making economic decisions. When financial statements purporting to present both financial position (balance sheet) and results of operations (statement of income and retained earnings) are issued, a statement summarizing changes in financial position should also be presented as a basic financial statement for each period for which an income statement is presented. These conclusions apply to all profit-oriented business entities, whether or not the reporting entity normally classifies its assets and liabilities as current and noncurrent.

*Opinion No. 19* is particularly noteworthy in that it *(a)* made the statement mandatory, *(b)* required that it be developed on an *all-resources* basis, and *(c)* strongly recommended the title, statement of changes in financial position. This title is now used almost exclusively. The significance of the statement, as prescribed by *Opinion No. 19,* is that it requires the reporting of comprehensive information on the financing and investing activities of the business. The *financing activities* result in inflows of resources, and the *investing activities* result in outflows of resources.

The words "changes in financial position" are descriptive of the report because the inflows and outflows of resources are reflected in

903

the changes in the asset, liability, and owners' equity accounts during the period. The statement focuses on reporting these changes.

The balance sheet reports the financial position at a *specific point in time;* consequently, it is not a change statement. In contrast, the income statement is a change statement; it reports the change in retained earnings *during* a specified period due to operations and extraordinary items. The details on the income statement serve to explain comprehensively specific factors that underlie net income. Similarly, the statement of retained earnings is a change statement; it explains, in detail, all of the changes in retained earnings *during* the specified period. Observe, that neither of these two change statements report the *causes* of the changes in assets, liabilities, and owners' equity (other than retained earnings). The statement of changes in financial position has the objective of filling this gap by reporting the other changes *during* the specified period. To do this, it reports changes in asset, liability, and owners' equity accounts measured in terms of *funds flow.*

This chapter discusses and illustrates development of the statement of changes in financial position in conformity with *APB Opinion No. 19.*

## BASIC CHARACTERISTICS OF THE STATEMENT OF CHANGES IN FINANCIAL POSITION

The statement of changes in financial position measures the changes in assets, liabilities, and owners' equity during a specified period in terms of the inflows and outflows of funds. The key concept is that assets, liabilities, and owners' equity increase and decrease during a period only because funds are generated and used. For example, the disposition of an asset or incurrence of a liability generates an inflow of funds, and the acquisition of an asset or the payment of a liability causes an outflow or use of funds. The generation or inflows of resources is called *financing activities,* and the use or outflow of resources is called *investing activities.*

The statement of changes in financial position, as prescribed in *APB Opinion No. 19,* must be based on an *all-resources concept,* viz: "... the statement summarizing changes in financial position should be based on a broad concept embracing all changes in financial position" and "each reporting entity should disclose all important aspects of its financial and investing activities regardless of whether cash or other elements of working capital are directly affected." This means that the statement also must include all direct exchanges of nonfund items; that is, those transactions that involve neither the direct inflow or outflow of funds. For example, if a business acquires a machine (an asset acquisition) and pays for it in full by issuing its own capital stock to the vendor, there has been no inflow or outflow of funds. Under *Opinion No. 19,* transactions of this type must be reported as (a) an inflow of funds (from the issuance of the stock), and (b) an outflow of funds (due to acquisition of the asset).[1] This means that the statement must report:

1. The inflows of all funds during the period and an identification of these inflows with changes in assets, liabilities, and owners' equity.
2. The outflows of all funds during the period and an identification of these outflows with changes in assets, liabilities, and owners' equity.
3. The net increase or decrease in funds during the period.

In the preceding paragraphs, the terms "funds" and "resources" have been used interchangeably. The inflows and outflows reported on the statement of changes in financial position are measured in dollars of "funds." For measurement purposes, we must be precise in defining what is meant by "funds." This general term is used throughout financial and accounting literature with diverse meanings.[2] Because of this diversity, and the need for precise measurement, APB Opinion No. 19 stated:

> The Statement may be in balanced form or in a form expressing the changes in financial position in terms of cash, or cash and temporary investments combined, of all quick assets, or of working capital.

Basically, this means that the inflows and outflows of funds may be measured in terms of either:

1. Cash (or cash plus near-cash items), or
2. Working capital (i.e., current assets minus current liabilities).

In elaboration of these two bases for measurement, the Opinion states:

> a. If the format shows the flow of cash, changes in other elements of working capital (e.g., in receivables, inventories, and payables) constitute sources and uses of cash and should accordingly be disclosed in appropriate detail in the body of the statement.
> b. If the format shows the flow of working capital and two-year comparative balance sheets are presented, the changes in each element of working capital for the current period (but not for earlier periods) can be computed by the user of the statements. Nevertheless, the Board believes that the objectives of the Statement usually require that the net change in working capital be analyzed in appropriate detail in a tabulation accompanying the Statement, and accordingly this detail should be furnished.

Because of these specifications, the statement of changes in financial position takes the following general formats:

---

[1] Prior to APB Opinion No. 19, these types of transactions were not reported on the old "funds flow statements." This was a significant improvement in meeting the requirements of the full-disclosure principle.

[2] Funds is a particularly troublesome term because of the wide diversity of use. It is sometimes viewed as cash only, cash plus near-cash items (such as short-term investments), working capital (i.e., current assets minus current liabilities), assets set aside for a specific purpose (such as a bond sinking fund), and it has yet another special meaning in governmental accounting.

| (a) Funds Measured on Cash, or Cash plus Near-Cash Basis | (b) Funds Measured on Working Capital Basis* |
|---|---|
| 1. Sources of cash, or cash plus near-cash items (inflows). | Part A—Sources and Uses of Working Capital |
| 2. Uses of cash, or cash plus near-cash items (outflows). | 1. Sources of working capital (inflows). |
| 3. Net increase or decrease in cash, or cash plus near-cash items. | 2. Uses of working capital (outflows). |
| | 3. Net increase or decrease in working capital. |
| | Part B—Changes in Working Capital Accounts |
| | 4. Net Change in current asset accounts. |
| | 5. Net change in current liability accounts. |
| | 6. Net increase or decrease in working capital. |

* The designations "Part A and Part B" are not specifically reflected on the statement; they are used here to facilitate explanation.

The *Opinion* permits the use of either approach; however, the specific basis used must be clearly disclosed; for example, "Cash Provided from Operations" or "Working Capital Provided from Operations."[3]

In order to establish a clear-cut delineation between the two approaches to measure "funds" and to facilitate discussion, this chapter discusses, separately, changes in financial position, working capital basis; and, changes in financial position, cash (or cash plus near-cash) basis.

### Illustration of Cash Flows versus Working Capital Flows

The statement of changes in financial position reports significant differences in results when the flow of funds is measured on a cash flow basis rather than a working capital basis. The distinction between the cash flow and working capital bases is important in understanding the analyses and discussions in this chapter.

Exhibits 21–1 and 21–2 present analyses of a series of situations to illustrate the distinction between the cash and working capital bases. The resulting statement of changes in financial position is summarized in Exhibit 21–3. These exhibits should be studied carefully.

In Exhibit 21–1, observe that more cash than working capital was generated in each of the four situations. In item (d), note that total sales caused an increase in working capital, whereas only cash sales caused an increase in cash. Expenses, whether paid or accrued as a current liability, caused a decrease in working capital, whereas only

---

[3] Since cash flows are generally viewed as more critical than working capital flows, and the latter often are larger in amount, there have been cases where an entity, by vague terminology, has led users to believe working capital amounts to be cash flow. The *Opinion* recognized this problem by stating: "Terms referring to 'cash' should not be used to describe amounts provided from operations unless all non-cash items have been appropriately adjusted."

cash expenses caused a decrease in cash. Depreciation expense does not affect either working capital or cash flow.

In transactions (a), (b), and (c), the differences between working capital and cash flows resulted from the short-term (current) receivables and payables; long-term receivables and payables have the same affect on both cash and working capital flows.

In transactions (b) and (d), the $2,000 gain on sale of plant assets did not generate cash or working capital; rather cash was increased by the amount of the sales price collected during the period and working capital was increased by the amount of the sales price "collected" in cash plus the short-term receivable recorded during the period. These situations will be discussed in detail subsequently.

### Criteria for the Statement of Changes in Financial Position

In view of the wide diversity in the old funds statements, *APB Opinion No. 19* specifies certain criteria that should be satisfied in developing a statement of changes in financial position; these criteria may be summarized as follows:

1. The statement should be presented as a basic financial statement for each period in which an income statement is prepared.
2. The statement applies to all profit-oriented business entities whether or not there is a classification of assets and liabilities between current and noncurrent.
3. The statement should be based on a broad concept embracing all changes in financial position (not limited to working capital or cash). The statement should disclose all important changes in financial position for the period.
4. The statement should begin with the income or loss before extraordinary items, if any, and add back (or deduct) items recognized in determining income (or loss) which did not use (or provide) working capital or cash during the period.[4]
5. The items to be added back (or deleted) in 4 above should be clearly presented to avoid the interpretation that they provided funds (e.g., "Add—Expenses not requiring outlay of working capital in the current period.")
6. The effects of extraordinary items should be reported separately from the effects of normal operating items.
7. The effects of all financing and investing activities, as well as working capital or cash, should be *individually* disclosed.
8. If the format shows the flow of working capital and two-year comparative balance sheets are presented, the detailed changes in working capital accounts nevertheless must be presented.

---

[4] An acceptable alternative procedure, which gives the same result, starts with revenues that generated working capital or cash during the period and deducts therefrom operating expenses that required the outflow of working capital or cash. This approach has the advantage of not suggesting that "adjustments" to net income, such as depreciation, generated working capital or cash.

**EXHIBIT 21–1**

**Inflows of Cash and Working Capital Compared**

| Transaction | | | Cash Generated | Working Capital Generated |
|---|---|---|---|---|
| a. Sold 1,000 shares of common stock during the period resulting in the following entry: | | | | |
| Cash ...................................... | 3,000 | | $ 3,000 | $ 3,000 |
| Special receivable (current)......... | 4,000 | | | 4,000 |
| Special receivable (noncurrent) ... | 5,000 | | | |
| Common stock (par $10) ...... | | 10,000 | | |
| Contributed capital in excess of par ................................ | | 2,000 | | |
| Total Generated .............. | | | 3,000 | 7,000 |

Observe that working capital was generated by the amount of current assets received and not by the selling price, the par value of the stock, or the noncurrent receivable.

| | | | | |
|---|---|---|---|---|
| b. Sold a plant asset during the period resulting in the following entry: | | | | |
| Cash ...................................... | 4,000 | | 4,000 | 4,000 |
| Notes receivable, short term ...... | 5,000 | | | 5,000 |
| Mortgage receivable, long term ... | 14,000 | | | |
| Accumulated depreciation ......... | 10,000 | | | |
| Plant asset.......................... | | 31,000 | | |
| Gain on sale of plant asset ... | | 2,000 | | |
| Total Generated .............. | | | 4,000 | 9,000 |

Observe that working capital generated was the sum of cash and current receivables recognized and not the amount of the sales price, the gain recognized on the sale, or the noncurrent receivable.

| | | | | |
|---|---|---|---|---|
| c. Borrowed from the bank resulting in the following entry: | | | | |
| Cash ...................................... | 30,000 | | 30,000 | +30,000 |
| Notes payable, short term...... | | 20,000 | | −20,000 |
| Notes payable, long term ...... | | 10,000 | | |
| Total Generated .............. | | | 30,000 | 10,000 |

Observe that, although there was an inflow of cash of $30,000, working capital increased by only $10,000. This was because the increase in current liabilities for the short-term debt "offset" $20,000 of the inflow. Thus, working capital was increased by the amount of the increase in long-term debt.

| | | | | |
|---|---|---|---|---|
| d. Net income for the period was as follows: | | | | |
| Sales: Cash.................................... | $40,000 | | +40,000 | +40,000 |
| On account........................... | 10,000 | $50,000 | | +10,000 |
| Cost of goods sold: | | | | |
| Goods purchased for cash............ | 18,000 | | −18,000 | −18,000 |
| Goods purchased on account ...... | 7,000 | | | − 7,000 |
| Reduction in inventory................. | 3,000 | 28,000 | | − 3,000 |
| Gross margin ........................ | | 22,000 | | |
| Expenses: | | | | |
| Paid in cash ............................ | 10,000 | | −10,000 | −10,000 |
| Accrued (liability) ....................... | 2,000 | | | − 2,000 |
| Depreciation ............................ | 4,000 | 16,000 | | |
| Income from operations ................. | | 6,000 | | |
| Gain on sale of plant asset........... | | 2,000 | | |
| Net Income .................................. | | $ 8,000 | | |
| Total Generated from Operations*..................... | | | 12,000 | 10,000 |
| Total Generated for the Period (all transactions) ..................... | | | $49,000 | $36,000 |

* The results of this analysis are: (a) Net income on accrual basis of $8,000 converted to a working capital basis is $10,000, and (b) Net income on accrual basis of $8,000 converted to a cash basis is $12,000.

**EXHIBIT 21–2**

**Outflows of Cash and Working Capital Compared**

| Transaction | | Cash Applied | Working Capital Applied |
|---|---|---|---|
| a. Purchased a plant asset during the period resulting in the following entry: | | | |
| Plant asset ........................... | 30,000 | | |
| Cash ............................. | 3,000 | $ 3,000 | $ 3,000 |
| Note payable, short term ... | 7,000 | | 7,000 |
| Mortgage payable, long term ....................... | 20,000 | | |
| Total Applied ............... | | 3,000 | 10,000 |

Observe that working capital applied was the sum of the cash paid plus the current liability recognized, not the purchase price or the long-term debt incurred.

| | | Cash Applied | Working Capital Applied |
|---|---|---|---|
| b. Cash dividends declared, or paid, resulted in the following entry: | | | |
| Retained earnings .................. | 12,000 | | |
| Cash ............................. | 8,000 | 8,000 | 8,000 |
| Dividends payable (current) .................. | 4,000 | | 4,000 |
| Total Applied ............... | | 8,000 | 12,000 |

| | | Cash Applied | Working Capital Applied |
|---|---|---|---|
| c. Payments on debts during the period resulted in the following entry: | | | |
| Accounts payable .................. | 15,000 | | −15,000 |
| Notes payable, long term......... | 25,000 | | |
| Cash ............................. | 40,000 | 40,000 | 40,000 |
| Total Applied ............... | | 40,000 | 25,000 |

Observe that although $40,000 cash (and working capital) was disbursed, the decrease in net working capital was only $25,000. This was because the $15,000 paid on a working capital debt constituted an "offset." Thus the working capital applied was equivalent to the decrease in long-term debt only.

| | | Cash Applied | Working Capital Applied |
|---|---|---|---|
| d. Treasury stock purchased during the period resulted in the following entry: | | | |
| Treasury stock (at cost) ......... | 8,000 | | |
| Cash ............................. | 5,000 | 5,000 | 5,000 |
| Special payable, short term ....................... | 3,000 | | 3,000 |
| Total Applied ............... | | 5,000 | 8,000 |
| Total Applied for the Period (all transactions) | | $56,000 | $55,000 |

**EXHIBIT 21–3**

Statement of Changes in Financial Position (summarized)*
For the Year Ended December 31, 19XX

| | Cash Basis | Working Capital Basis |
|---|---|---|
| Resources generated (inflows): | | |
| From operations ............................. | $12,000 | $ 10,000 |
| Sale of common stock........................ | 3,000 | 7,000 |
| Sale of plant assets .......................... | 4,000 | 9,000 |
| Borrowing ...................................... | 30,000 | 10,000 |
| Total Resources Generated ......... | 49,000 | 36,000 |
| Resources applied (outflows): | | |
| Purchase of plant assets.................... | 3,000 | 10,000 |
| Dividends........................................ | 8,000 | 12,000 |
| Debt retirement ................................ | 40,000 | 25,000 |
| Acquisition of treasury stock.............. | 5,000 | 8,000 |
| Total Resources Applied............... | 56,000 | 55,000 |
| Net increase (decrease) in resources during period: | | |
| Cash ........................................... | $ (7,000) | |
| Working Capital........................... | | $(19,000) |

* This summarized statement omits some details required for full disclosure. It is summarized in this manner for instructional purposes; detailed statements will be presented subsequently.

9. Working capital or cash provided from (or used) should be appropriately described.
10. If the format shows the flow of cash, detailed changes in other working capital accounts should be disclosed in the body of the statement.
11. Terms referring to cash should not be used unless all noncash items have been appropriately adjusted.
12. There should be flexibility in form, content, and terminology in the statement; flexibility should be used to develop the presentation that is most informative in the circumstances.
13. It is strongly recommended that isolated statistics of working capital and cash, especially on a per-share basis, not be presented.

Next we discuss and illustrate the development of the statement of changes in financial position on the working capital basis in Part A and on the cash basis in Part B.

### PART A—STATEMENT OF CHANGES IN FINANCIAL POSITION, WORKING CAPITAL BASIS

Working capital is composed of positive current items (cash, short-term investments, short-term receivables, inventories, prepaid expenses, etc.) and a series of negative current items (accounts payable, short-term notes payable, accrued liabilities, etc.); the difference represents a "liquid pool" of net working resources. In a transaction where there is a net increase in working capital, it is said that working capital has been generated, or provided; where there is a net decrease in working capital, it is said that working capital has been applied or used. Thus, transactions such as the payment of a current liability, the collection of a current receivable, or the purchase of inventory for cash will neither generate or use working capital; they merely rearrange the internal *content* of working capital. In contrast, certain other transactions, such as the purchase of a noncurrent asset for cash or the payment of a long-term debt, will cause both the *content* and the *amount* of net working capital to change.

A statement of changes in financial position, working capital basis, necessitates considerable analysis, except in very simple situations because the accounts do not directly provide the required data. Recall from the discussions above that the inflows and outflows of working capital are the result of changes in assets, liabilities, and owners' equity. Thus, the key to developing the statement of changes in financial position is an analysis of the transactions that affected these three groups of accounts. Clearly, in most situations, this will involve a rigorous analytical process. Since the statement summarizes the changes in assets, liabilities, and owners' equity *during* the period, the basic data needed for analytical purposes can be taken from the comparative balance sheets, the income statement, the statement of retained earnings, and other records concerning certain transactions.

On page 906, the statement of changes in financial position, working capital basis, was outlined; two distinct parts were identified: Part A—sources and uses of working capital and Part B—changes in working capital accounts. A statement for the Adamson Company detailed in this way is shown in Exhibit 21–5. This statement was developed from the comparative balance sheets and other data given in Exhibit 21–4.

The statement for Adamson Company (Exhibit 21–5) has four sig-

**EXHIBIT 21–4**

ADAMSON COMPANY
Summarized Data for the Year Ended December 31, 1976

|  | Dec. 31, 1976 | Dec. 31, 1975 |
|---|---|---|
| **1. Balance Sheet:** | | |
| Cash | $ 45,000 | $ 30,000 |
| Accounts receivable (net) | 38,000 | 40,000 |
| Inventory | 67,000 | 60,000 |
| Long-term investments | 162,000 | 200,000 |
| Land | 128,000 | 100,000 |
| Building (net) | 98,000 | |
| Total | $538,000 | $430,000 |
| Accounts payable | $ 36,000 | $ 40,000 |
| Notes payable, short term (nontrade) | 24,000 | 30,000 |
| Bonds payable | 35,000 | 50,000 |
| Mortgage payable | 100,000 | |
| Common stock | 295,000 | 270,000 |
| Retained earnings | 48,000 | 40,000 |
| Total | $538,000 | $430,000 |
| **2. Income Statement:** | | |
| Sales | $100,000 | |
| Cost of goods sold | 51,000 | |
| Expenses (including interest and taxes) | 16,000 | |
| Total | 67,000 | |
| Net Income | $ 33,000 | |

3. Summary of transactions for 1976:
   a. Net income, $33,000.
   b. Purchases, $58,000, on account.
   c. Increase in inventory, $7,000.
   d. All sales were on credit.
   e. Expenses, $14,000, cash.
   f. Collection on accounts receivable, $102,000.
   g. Paid on accounts payable, $62,000.
   h. Sold bonds payable, $10,000, for cash at par value.
   i. Purchased land, $28,000 cash.
   j. Paid cash dividend, $25,000.
   k. Paid short-term notes payable, $6,000 (nontrade).
   l. Sold long-term investment for cash, $38,000 (sold at book value). Assume this is an extraordinary item for illustrative purposes.
   m. Retired $25,000 bonds payable by issuing common stock. The bonds retired were equivalent to the market value of the $25,000 stock issued.
   n. A new building was completed on the land in January 1976 at a cost of $100,000; gave an interest-bearing mortgage for the full amount. The building had an estimated life of 50 years and no residual value; straight-line depreciation.
   o. Depreciation expense, $2,000.

nificant captions, viz: (1) working capital generated (inflows of working capital), (2) working capital applied (outflows of working capital), (3) financing and investing activities that did not affect (flow through) working capital, and (4) a detailed report of changes in the internal content of working capital. This statement was designed to meet the *minimum* criteria specified in *APB Opinion No. 19.*

## THE WORKSHEET APPROACH

In simple situations, such as the hypothetical Adamson Company, it would be possible to develop the statement of changes in financial position by inspection of the data or in a more rational way by using the elementary T-account approach. However, for more complex and typical situations, one would find the use of a worksheet more convenient if not essential. Practically, a worksheet is necessary to handle the large quantities of data and the complex transactions found in extensive problems frequently encountered by students and in real-life situations. Exhibit 21–6 presents an efficient worksheet that has been designed for analysis of the *nonworking capital accounts* and to sort out the data needed for each major classification on the statement of changes in financial position. In contrast to some worksheets (which involve complex reversing and reclassifying entries), this one simply requires summary restatement of the former entries without change of format or direction. The interim entries are keyed to the list of transactions given in Exhibit 21–4.

It is significant to observe that this worksheet is built around the fact that the *causes* of the changes in working capital and nonworking capital financing and investing activities can be found only in an analysis of the *nonworking capital accounts*. In contrast, an analysis of *only* the working capital accounts will divulge only changes in the *content* of working capital; observe that the worksheet does not deal with the content of working capital.

The worksheet is set up with four amount columns and five major side captions. The first column (beginning balance) and last column (ending balance) are taken from the two consecutive balance sheets; the two interim columns (debit and credit) are provided for "reconciling through analysis" the beginning and ending balances for each account listed. The five side captions may be explained as follows.

*Basic Data:*
1. Working Capital. This is the net working capital at the beginning and ending dates; it is entered on the worksheet only for balancing purposes since the worksheet does not deal with an analysis of the content of working capital accounts themselves.
2. Nonworking Capital Accounts. These are the accounts to be analyzed in detail; they are grouped by debit and credit balances only for convenience. The amounts are taken directly from the two consecutive balance sheets; sufficient space should be provided for accounts that may have had high activity during the period.

*Data to be Elicited and Grouped from the Analysis:*

3. Working Capital Generated.   This section, paralleling the statement to be developed, provides for listing the various sources of working capital inflow. The amounts under this section normally will be reflected on the worksheet as debits.
4. Working Capital Applied.   This section parallels the statement to be developed and the amounts normally will be reflected as credits.
5. Financing and Investing Activities Not Affecting Working Capital. This section parallels the statement and will reflect each direct exchange as both a debit and credit. This effect is due to the fact that the direct exchanges analyzed in this section, represent simultaneous financing and investing activities.

Completion of the worksheet involves an analysis of the transactions that affected a *nonworking capital account* (transactions that affect working capital *only* are not entered on the worksheet) and entering them on the worksheet in the debit-credit format used when they were originally recorded in the accounts; all debits and credits to working capital accounts (such accounts are not on the worksheet) are reflected under the third and fourth captions on the worksheet. Transactions that did not directly affect (flow through) working capital result in debits and credits under the fifth caption (financing and investing activities not affecting working capital). The following is a step-by-step approach to be used in completing the worksheet (Exhibit 21–6) for Adamson Company.

Step 1: Set up the four amount columns and the five major side captions.

Step 2: Enter the original data from the beginning and ending balance sheets for (*a*) working capital and (*b*) each nonworking capital account.

Step 3: Analyze each account; enter on the worksheet under "analysis of interim entries" only those transactions that affected one or more *nonworking capital accounts* so that all differences between the beginning and ending balances are finally accounted for. The analysis may be explained as follows (the entries are keyed to the transactions listed in Exhibit 21–4).

|  | Original Entry | Worksheet Entry |
|---|---|---|
| *a.* Net income for the period: | | |
| Income summary .......................... 33,000 | | |
| Working capital generated, | | |
| net income ............................. | | 33,000 |
| Retained earnings .................. | 33,000 | 33,000 |

Analysis: Net income for the period (*a*) generated working capital, and (*b*) affected a noncurrent account (Retained Earnings). The worksheet entry repeats the original entry except for the debit; on the worksheet this debit reflects the generation of working capital.

**EXHIBIT 21–5**

ADAMSON COMPANY
Statement of Changes in Financial Position, Working Capital Basis
For the Year Ended December 31, 1976

Part A — Sources and Uses of Working Capital

Working Capital Generated:

From operations:

Net income before extraordinary items.............................. $33,000
    Add expenses not requiring working capital in
    the current period:

    Depreciation ..................................................... 2,000

Total working capital generated by operations (exclusive
    of extraordinary items) .................................................. $ 35,000

Extraordinary items generating working capital:

Long-term investments sold................................................. 38,000

Other sources of working capital:

    Bonds payable issued....................................................... 10,000

        Total Working Capital Generated ............................. 83,000

Working Capital Applied:

Land purchased ................................................................. $28,000

Cash dividends paid ........................................................... 25,000

        Total Working Capital Applied...................................... 53,000

Net Increase in Working Capital during the Period ................. $ 30,000

Financing and Investing Activities Not Affecting
    Working Capital:

Bonds retired by issuing common stock .............................. $ 25,000

Building acquired in exchange for long-term mortgage payable... 100,000

        Total......................................................................... $125,000

Part B — Changes in Working Capital Accounts

|  | Balances December 31 | | Working Capital Increase (decrease) |
|---|---|---|---|
|  | 1976 | 1975 |  |
| Current Assets: | | | |
| Cash .............................................. | $ 45,000 | $ 30,000 | $15,000 |
| Accounts receivable (net) ................. | 38,000 | 40,000 | (2,000) |
| Inventory ....................................... | 67,000 | 60,000 | 7,000 |
| Total Current Assets .................. | 150,000 | 130,000 | |
| Current Liabilities: | | | |
| Accounts payable ............................. | $ 36,000 | $ 40,000 | 4,000 |
| Notes payable — short term (nontrade)... | 24,000 | 30,000 | 6,000 |
| Total Current Liabilities ............ | 60,000 | 70,000 | |
| Working Capital .................... | $ 90,000 | $ 60,000 | $30,000 |

$$WC = CA - CL \qquad CA - CL = WC$$
$$\Delta WC = 42 - 41$$

# EXHIBIT 21-6

**ADAMSON COMPANY**
Worksheet to Develop Statement of Changes in Financial Position, Working Capital Basis
For the Year Ended December 31, 1976

| | Beginning Balance Dec. 31, 1975 | Analysis of Interim Entries Debit | Analysis of Interim Entries Credit | Ending Balance Dec. 31, 1976 |
|---|---|---|---|---|
| **Debits** | | | | |
| 1. Working Capital | 60,000 | (p) 30,000 | | 90,000 |
| 2. Nonworking Capital Accounts: | | | | |
| Long-term investments | 200,000 | | (l) $ 38,000 | 162,000 |
| Land | 100,000 | (i) 28,000 | | 128,000 |
| Building (net) | | (n − 1) 100,000 | (o) 2,000 | 98,000 |
| | 360,000 | | | 478,000 |
| **Credits** | | | | |
| Bonds payable | 50,000 | (m − 1) 25,000 | (h) 10,000 | 35,000 |
| Mortgage payable | | | (n − 2) 100,000 | 100,000 |
| Common stock | 270,000 | | (m − 2) 25,000 | 295,000 |
| Retained earnings | 40,000 | (j) 25,000 | (a) 33,000 | 48,000 |
| | 360,000 | 208,000 | 208,000 | 478,000 |
| 3. Working Capital Generated: | | | | |
| From operations: | | | | |
| Net income | | (a) 33,000 | | |
| Adjustments for nonworking capital items: | | | | |
| Depreciation | | (o) 2,000 | | |
| Extraordinary items generating working capital: | | | | |
| Long-term investments sold | | (l) 38,000 | | |
| Other sources of working capital: | | | | |
| Bonds payable issued | | (h) 10,000 | | |
| 4. Working Capital Applied: | | | | |
| Land purchased | | | (i) 28,000 | |
| Cash dividends paid | | | (j) 25,000 | |
| 5. Financing and Investing Activities not Affecting Working Capital: | | | | |
| Bonds retired by issuing common stock | | (m − 2) 25,000 | (m − 1) 25,000 | |
| Building purchased; gave long-term mortgage | | (n − 2) 100,000 | (n − 1) 100,000 | |
| Increase in net working capital for the period | | | (p) 30,000 | |
| | | 208,000 | 208,000 | |

Source of data: Exhibit 21-4.

The following transactions are not entered on the worksheet since each one did not affect a noncurrent account: (b) purchases on account; (c) inventory increase; (d) sales on account; (e) expenses paid in cash; (f) collection on accounts receivable; (g) payment on accounts payable; and (k) payment on short-term notes payable.

| | Original Entry | Worksheet Entry |
|---|---|---|
| h. Sold bonds payable for cash: | | |
| Cash ........................................ 10,000 | | |
| Working capital generated, | | |
|     Other sources ........................... | | 10,000 |
|     Bonds payable ..................... | 10,000 | 10,000 |

Analysis: This worksheet entry corresponds to the original entry except that the original debit to a working capital account (Cash) is reflected in the lower part of the worksheet as a debit to Working Capital Generated, Other Sources. The original debit to Cash (a working capital account) cannot be entered as such on the worksheet since no working capital accounts are listed; this is a built-in safety feature.

| | Original Entry | Worksheet Entry |
|---|---|---|
| i. Purchased land for cash: | | |
| Land ........................................ 28,000 | | 28,000 |
|     Cash ................................. | 28,000 | |
|     Working capital applied ......... | | 28,000 |

Analysis: This transaction used working capital; a nonworking capital account, Land, was affected. This worksheet entry corresponds to the original entry except for the original credit to working capital (Cash); on the worksheet this is reflected as a credit under Working Capital Applied.

| | Original Entry | Worksheet Entry |
|---|---|---|
| j. Paid cash dividend: | | |
| Retained earnings ....................... 25,000 | | 25,000 |
|     Cash ................................. | 25,000 | |
|     Working capital applied ......... | | 25,000 |

Analysis: This transaction used working capital; a noncurrent account, Retained Earnings, was affected. The worksheet entry reflects the original credit to Cash as a credit under Working Capital Applied.

k. Paid short-term notes payable: Not entered on the worksheet since noncurrent accounts were not affected.

| | Original Entry | Worksheet Entry |
|---|---|---|
| l. Sold long-term investment for cash: | | |
| Cash ........................................ 38,000 | | |
| Working capital generated, | | |
|     Other sources ....................... | | 38,000 |
|     Long-term investments.................. | 38,000 | 38,000 |

Analysis: This transaction generated working capital; a noncurrent account, Long-Term Investments, was affected. Since the investment was sold at book value there was no gain or loss. The worksheet entry reflects the original debit (to Cash) under working capital generated as a debit.

|  | Original Entry | Worksheet Entry |
|---|---|---|

*m.* Retired bonds payable by issuing common stock:

Bonds payable ........................ 25,000      25,000
*(m − 1)*

    Common stock ................. 25,000      25,000
*(m − 2)*

Financing and investing activities not affecting working
    capital ...............................      25,000    25,000
     *(m − 2)*   *(m − 1)*

Analysis: This transaction is a *direct exchange,* and as such it (1) did not affect working capital, and (2) affected only noncurrent accounts, yet it constituted both a financing and an investing activity. It must be reflected on the statement of changes in financial position; therefore, it must be entered on the worksheet under the caption Financing and Investing Activities Not Affecting Working Capital. Obviously, if one were to simply repeat the original entry on the worksheet this aspect would be omitted. As a consequence, it is desirable to reflect on the worksheet two interrelated and concurrent entries as shown above. The view is that entry $(m-1)$ reflects payment of a debt (the debit) and an outflow for that purpose (the credit), and entry $(m-2)$ reflects the issuance of common stock (the credit) and an inflow from that source (the debit). This is what is sometimes called an "in and out" item of financing and investing. At this point you should follow this entry through the worksheet and back to the statement (Exhibit 21–5).

*n.* Purchased new building; gave long-term mortgage note for purchase price:

Building ................................ 100,000      100,000
*(n − 1)*

    Mortgage payable............... 100,000      100,000
*(n − 2)*

Financing and investing activities not affecting working
    capital ...............................      100,000    100,000
     *(n − 2)*   *(n − 1)*

Analysis: This transaction is a direct exchange; it is the same type as analyzed in *(m)* above. This transaction (1) did not affect working capital, and (2) affected only noncurrent accounts; yet it constituted a financing and investing activity. It is reflected on the worksheet as an "in and out" item as explained immediately above.

*o.* Depreciation expense for the period:

Expenses, depreciation ............ 2,000
Working capital generated,
    net income (adjustment).........      2,000
    Accumulated depreciation ... 2,000      2,000

Analysis: This transaction did not generate working capital, yet it affected a noncurrent account—Accumulated Depreciation. Since depreciation is an expense it was deducted from net income; however, it did not require the use of working capital in the period of recognition, in contrast to other expenses that are either paid in the period or recognized as a current liability (accrual). Significantly, we see an item that reduced net income but did not require working capital; as a consequence, to determine the amount of working capital generated from operations, depreciation must be added back. The worksheet entry (a debit to Working Capital Generated, Net Income) reflects this effect. At this point you should follow this item through the worksheet and back to the statement.

> *p.* Entry *(p)* does not represent a transaction; it is an optional entry that may be made simply to balance the worksheet. After this entry is made, two internal checks for accuracy and completeness can be made, viz:
>
> 1. Check each line on the worksheet horizontally to be sure that the interim entries clear out all differences between the beginning and ending balances.
> 2. Total the debit and credit columns under "Analysis of Interim Entries" at two levels on the worksheet as illustrated; the worksheet debits and credits in these columns must balance at these two levels.

One of the special features of this worksheet is that the formal statement of changes in financial position (Exhibit 21–5) can be copied directly from the lower portion of the worksheet, adding thereto the last section wherein the *content* of the working capital accounts is presented. The last section (Part B in Exhibit 21–5) is copied directly from the balance sheet.[5]

For examination and problem-solving purposes by students, this worksheet generally will suffice without the added clerical burden of preparing a formal statement of changes in financial position.

### Some Special Problems

In developing the worksheet the following special situations may require careful attention.

1. Transactions that affect only owners' equity accounts. Generally, such changes (e.g., a common stock dividend on common stock) are not reported on the statement of changes in financial position. However, *APB Opinion No. 19* specifies that the statement should disclose: "Conversion of long-term debt or preferred to common stock." This is interpreted to mean that basic changes in owners' equity should be reported. The exchange of preferred stock for common stock would be reflected on the worksheet and on the statement as an "in and out" item similar to that previously illustrated for the exchange of debt for stock.

2. Amortization of long-term items. Long-term (noncurrent) amortizations (either debits or credits) reduce or increase reported net income, although they do not require or provide working capital during the current period. Examples of this type of item are discount and premium on bonds. To illustrate, assume $1,000 discount on bonds payable is being amortized over a ten-year period on a straight-line basis. The annual amortization of $100 would appear on the income statement as

---

[5] For this reason some accountants consider Part B to be redundant; however, it is required by *APB Opinion No. 19.*

an increase in bond interest expense, although it would not require the application of working capital during the current period. Therefore, the worksheet entry would be a debit to "Net Income – Adjustment" similar to depreciation and a credit to Discount on Bonds Payable.

3. Reclassification of a long-term liability. When a long-term liability is payable within the upcoming year it is usually reclassified as a current liability. The reclassification has the effect of decreasing working capital; therefore, there should be recognition on the worksheet and in the statement of a working capital application. The entry on the worksheet would be a debit to Long-Term Liabilities and a credit to Working Capital Applied.

## COMPREHENSIVE ILLUSTRATION

The comprehensive illustration that follows for F. P. Corporation presents a situation where the data are more complex and the analysis more involved than those shown in the previous example. The illustration includes the following:

Exhibit 21–7 – Basic data for illustration
Exhibit 21–8 – Worksheet to develop statement of changes in financial
　　　　　　　position, working capital basis
Exhibit 21–9 – Statement of changes in financial position, working
　　　　　　　capital basis

The analysis of transactions and the related entries on the worksheet (Exhibit 21–8) are explained below; the discussions and entries are keyed to the basic data given in Exhibit 21–7. Only those transactions that represent situations different from those explained above for Adamson Company are discussed.

| | Original Entry | Worksheet Entry |
|---|---|---|
| *h.* Common stock dividend issued: | | |
| Retained earnings ........................ 10,000 | | 10,000 |
| Common stock ..................... | 10,000 | 10,000 |

Analysis: This transaction *(a)* did not affect working capital and *(b)* did not represent a financing or investing activity, although two noncurrent accounts were affected. It merely represents a transfer of one equity account to another and is generally considered not to be encompassed in the provisions of *APB Opinion No. 19*. The worksheet entry, identical to the original entry, must be made for clearing purposes.

| | Original Entry | Worksheet Entry |
|---|---|---|
| *j.* Sold land for cash at a gain: | | |
| Cash ........................................ 53,000 | | |
| Working capital generated, extraordinary item ..................... | | 53,000 |
| Land .................................... | 35,000 | 35,000 |
| Gain on sale of land (assumed to be an extraordinary item)... | 18,000 | |
| Working capital generated, net income (adjustment) ...... | | 18,000 |

**EXHIBIT 21-7**

F. P. CORPORATION
Basic Data for Illustration

Comparative Balance Sheet Data:

|  | Amounts Reported at— | |
|---|---|---|
| *Debits* | 12/31/19A | 12/31/19B |
| Cash | $ 30,000 | $ 84,000 |
| Short-term investments (X Company stock) | 10,000 | 8,000 |
| Accounts receivable (net) | 50,000 | 80,000 |
| Inventory | 20,000 | 30,000 |
| Prepaid expenses | | 2,000 |
| Land | 60,000 | 25,000 |
| Machinery | 80,000 | 90,000 |
| Accumulated depreciation | (20,000) | (27,900) |
| Other assets | 29,000 | 39,000 |
| Discount on bonds payable | 1,000 | 900 |
| Total debits | $260,000 | $331,000 |
| *Credits* | | |
| Accounts payable | $ 40,000 | $ 55,000 |
| Dividends payable | | 15,000 |
| Bonds payable | 70,000 | 55,000 |
| Common stock, nopar | 100,000 | 131,000 |
| Preferred stock, nopar | 20,000 | 30,000 |
| Retained earnings | 30,000 | 45,000 |
| Total Credits | $260,000 | $331,000 |

| Income Statement Data: | 12/31/19B |
|---|---|
| Sales | $180,000 |
| Cost of goods sold | 90,000 |
| Expenses | 55,000 |
| Depreciation | 7,900 |
| Amortization of discount on bonds payable | 100 |
| Total Expenses | 153,000 |
| Income before extraordinary items | 27,000 |
| Extraordinary items: | |
| Gain on special sale of land (net of tax) | 18,000 |
| Loss on bond retirement | (1,000) |
| Net Income | $ 44,000 |

Additional data; summary of selected transactions for the year:

a. Sales (on account), $180,000.
b. Purchases (on account), $100,000.
c. Inventory increase, $10,000.
d. Expenses, $55,000 (including income taxes).
e. Depreciation, $7,900.
f. Prepaid expenses increased $2,000 during the year.
g. Cash dividend declared, $15,000.
h. Common stock dividend issued; retained earnings debited for $10,000.
i. Issued bonds payable for cash, $5,000.
j. Sold land for $53,000 cash; book value, $35,000 (net of tax); for illustrative purposes, assumed to be an extraordinary item.
k. Purchased machinery for $10,000 cash.
l. Purchased short-term investments, $2,000 cash.
m. Paid dividend on preferred stock with short-term investments, $4,000.
n. Retired $20,000 bonds payable by issuing common stock; the common stock had a fair market value of $21,000 (assumed to be extraordinary for illustrative purposes).
o. Collected cash on accounts receivables, $150,000.
p. Paid cash on accounts payable, $85,000.
q. Acquired other assets for $10,000 by issuing preferred stock.
r. Amortization of discount on bonds payable, $100.

Analysis: This transaction generated working capital by the amount of cash received ($53,000) rather than by the amount of the gain ($18,000). Since net income included the gain, it must be *removed from the net income amount* through an adjustment (credit on the worksheet). This has the effect of restoring net income to the amount de-

**EXHIBIT 21–8**

F. P. CORPORATION
Worksheet to Develop Statement of Changes in Financial Position, Working Capital Basis
For the Year Ended December 31, 19B

| Debits | Balance Dec. 31, 19A | Analysis of Interim Entries Debit | | Analysis of Interim Entries Credit | | Balance Dec. 31, 19B |
|---|---|---|---|---|---|---|
| Working Capital | 70,000 | (s) | 64,000 | | | 134,000 |
| Nonworking Capital Accounts: | | | | | | |
| Land | 60,000 | | | (j) | 35,000 | 25,000 |
| Machinery | 80,000 | (k) | 10,000 | | | 90,000 |
| Other assets | 29,000 | (q − 1) | 10,000 | | | 39,000 |
| Discount on bonds payable | 1,000 | | | (r) | 100 | 900 |
| Total | 240,000 | | | | | 288,900 |
| | | | | | | |
| Credits | | | | | | |
| Accumulated depreciation | 20,000 | | | (e) | 7,900 | 27,900 |
| Bonds payable | 70,000 | (n − 2) | 20,000 | | | 55,000 |
| | | | | (i) | 5,000 | |
| Common stock | 100,000 | | | (h) | 10,000 | 131,000 |
| | | | | (n − 1) | 21,000 | |
| Preferred stock | 20,000 | | | (q − 2) | 10,000 | 30,000 |
| Retained earnings | 30,000 | (g) | 15,000 | (a) | 44,000 | 45,000 |
| | | (h) | 10,000 | | | |
| | | (m) | 4,000 | | | |
| Total | 240,000 | | 133,000 | | 133,000 | 288,900 |
| Working Capital Generated: | | | | | | |
| Net income | | (a) | 44,000 | | | |
| To remove gain on land | | | | (j) | 18,000 | |
| To remove loss on bonds | | (n − 2) | 1,000 | | | |
| Adjustments: | | | | | | |
| Depreciation expense | | (e) | 7,900 | | | |
| Amortization of bond discount | | (r) | 100 | | | |
| Extraordinary items: | | | | | | |
| Land sold | | (j) | 53,000 | | | |
| Other sources of working capital: | | | | | | |
| Bonds payable sold | | (i) | 5,000 | | | |
| *Nonworking capital resources generated: | | | | | | |
| Common stock issued to retire bonds | | (n − 1) | 21,000 | | | |
| Preferred stock issued for other assets | | (q − 2) | 10,000 | | | |
| Working Capital Applied: | | | | | | |
| Dividends declared | | | | (g) | 15,000 | |
| Machinery purchased | | | | (k) | 10,000 | |
| Dividends on preferred stock, paid with short-term investments | | | | (m) | 4,000 | |
| *Nonworking capital resources applied: | | | | | | |
| Bonds payable retired by issuing common stock | | | | (n − 2) | 21,000 | |
| Other assets acquired by issuing preferred stock | | | | (q − 1) | 10,000 | |
| Increase in net working capital for the period | | | | (s) | 64,000 | |
| | | | 142,000 | | 142,000 | |

*On this worksheet these two captions are illustrative of a variation in format; observe that these two captions were combined in Exhibit 21–6.

sired—income before extraordinary items. This transaction should be traced through the worksheet and then to the statement of changes in financial position.

| | Original Entry | Worksheet Entry |
|---|---|---|
| *m.* Paid dividends with short-term investments (X Company stock): | | |
| Retained earnings | 4,000 | 4,000 |
| Investments, short term | 4,000 | |
| Working capital applied | | 4,000 |

Analysis: This transaction used working capital (short-term investments) and affected a nonworking capital account.

|  | Original Entry | Worksheet Entry |
|---|---|---|

n. Retired bonds payable by issuing common stock:

| | | |
|---|---|---|
| Bonds payable ........................... 20,000 | | 20,000 |
| | | $(n-2)$ |
| Extraordinary loss on bond | | |
| retirement ............................. 1,000 | | 1,000 |
| | | $(n-2)$ |
| Common stock ..................... | 21,000 | 21,000 |
| | | $(n-1)$ |
| Financing and investing | | |
| activities not affecting | | |
| working capital.................. | | 21,000     21,000 |
| | | $(n-1)$    $(n-2)$ |

Analysis: This transaction was a direct exchange that affected two nonworking capital accounts but did not affect working capital; it is an in and out item that must be reported on the statement (see prior discussion). Since common stock with a market value of $21,000 was issued to retire bonds payable with a carrying value of $20,000, a $1,000 loss on retirement was recognized (as required by APB Opinion No. 29) and classified as an extraordinary item (as required by FASB Statement No. 4).[6]

q. Acquired other assets by issuing preferred stock:

| | | |
|---|---|---|
| Other assets ........................... 10,000 | | 10,000 |
| | | $(q-1)$ |
| Preferred stock..................... | 10,000 | 10,000 |
| | | $(q-2)$ |
| Financing and investing | | |
| activities not affecting | | |
| working capital.................. | | 10,000     10,000 |
| | | $(q-2)$    $(q-1)$ |

Analysis: This transaction is a direct exchange that did not affect working capital; it affected two nonworking capital accounts. It is an "in and out" item that represents a financing and investing activity; hence it must be recognized on the worksheet (see prior discussion of direct exchanges).

r. Amortization of discount on bonds payable:

| | | |
|---|---|---|
| Expenses, amortization of bond | | |
| discount ............................. 100 | | |
| Working capital generated, net | | |
| income (adjustment).................. | | 100 |
| Discount on bonds payable ..... | 100 | 100 |

Analysis: This transaction did not affect working capital; it affected

---

[6] APB Opinion No. 29, "Accounting for Nonmonetary Transactions" (May 1973), specifies with certain exceptions that direct exchanges shall be recorded to recognize fair market value. FASB Statement of Financial Accounting Standards No. 4 (March 1975) specifies that loss or gain on early extinguishment of debt shall be reported as an extraordinary item (if material in amount), net of tax. The above amounts are assumed to be net of tax.

a nonworking capital account—Discount on Bonds Payable—and reported net income. Since it was deducted from net income, but did not affect working capital, it must be *added back to net income as a nonworking capital charge.* This item is similar in effect to depreciation expense for the period previously discussed.

The following transactions were not entered on the worksheet since they affected only working capital accounts: *(a), (b), (c), (d), (f), (l), (o),* and *(p).* Entry *(s)* is an optional balancing entry on the worksheet.

### STATEMENT FORMAT

*APB Opinion No. 19* stated that "Provided that these guides are met, the statement may take whatever form gives the most useful portrayal of the financing and investing activities and the changes in financial position of the reporting entity." In the light of this statement there is a range of variation in the forms developed by industry. Clearly, numerous variations of form can meet the criteria specified in *Opinion No. 19* (see list of criteria on page 907).

In Exhibit 21–5, and at the end of Chapters 4, 5, and 24, various statement formats are illustrated. A statement of changes in financial position for F. P. Corporation is presented in Exhibit 21–9 that maximizes explanation and disclosure, and uses some variation in terminology. Note in particular the manner of reporting the direct-exchange transactions. In Exhibit 21–9 for F. P. Corporation, the effects of direct exchanges are reported twice, under working capital generated and under working capital used. In contrast, direct exchanges in Exhibit 21–4 for Adamson Company are reported once under a separate caption. These are mere reporting differences and do not suggest substantive differences in the concept of analyzing and reporting direct exchanges.

### PART B—STATEMENT OF CHANGES IN FINANCIAL POSITION, CASH BASIS (AND CASH PLUS NEAR CASH)

The critical problems of cash planning and cash control create a serious need by internal management for meaningful statements of cash inflows and outflows coupled with the other financing and investing activities. Similarly, in decision making the external investor has a critical need for relevant information on the ability of the enterprise to generate cash inflows, the cash requirements, and the related noncash financing and investing activities. Although a statement of changes in financial position prepared on a working capital basis, as discussed in the first part of this chapter, serves useful purposes, similar statements prepared on a cash flow basis are more relevant both for internal management and the investor. Clearly, cash, as opposed to the concept of working capital, is understood by the investor. Also, working capital problems tend to be reflected first in the cash position. A statement of changes in financial position prepared on the cash basis would preclude the need for a similar statement on the working capital basis, although the opposite is not the case.

In view of the greater relevance of cash-based statements, one may

**EXHIBIT 21-9**

### F. P. CORPORATION
Statement of Changes in Financial Position, Working Capital Basis
For the Year Ended December 31, 19B

Financial Resources Generated:

Working capital generated:

| | | |
|---|---|---|
| Income before extraordinary items ($44,000 − $18,000)... | $26,000 | |
| Add: Expenses not requiring working capital in the current period: | | |
| Loss on bonds ................................................. | 1,000 | |
| Depreciation expense........................................ | 7,900 | |
| Amortization of bond discount ........................... | 100 | |
| Working capital generated by operations exclusive of extraordinary items............................................ | | $ 35,000 |
| Extraordinary items: | | |
| Land sold ...................................................... | | 53,000 |
| Other sources of working capital: | | |
| Bonds payable sold.......................................... | | 5,000 |
| Total Working Capital Generated ...................... | | 93,000 |
| Financial resources generated not affecting working capital: | | |
| Common stock issued to retire bonds payable ............ | 21,000 | |
| Preferred stock issued to acquire other assets ........... | 10,000 | |
| Total......................................................... | | 31,000 |
| Total Financial Resources Generated ............... | | $124,000 |

Financial Resources Applied:

Working capital applied:

| | | |
|---|---|---|
| Cash dividends declared ........................................ | $15,000 | |
| Machinery purchased............................................. | 10,000 | |
| Dividends paid on preferred stock with short-term investments ..................................................... | 4,000 | |
| Total Working Capital Applied............................. | | $ 29,000 |
| Financial resources applied not affecting working capital: | | |
| Bonds payable retired by issuing common stock ......... | 21,000 | |
| Other assets acquired by issuing preferred stock ......... | 10,000 | |
| Total........................................................... | | 31,000 |
| Increase in net working capital during the period......... | | 64,000 |
| Total Financial Resources Applied.................... | | $124,000 |

Changes in Working Capital Accounts:

| | Account Balances | | Working Capital Increase (decrease) |
|---|---|---|---|
| | 12/31/19B | 12/31/19A | |
| Current Assets: | | | |
| Cash ......................................... | $ 84,000 | $ 30,000 | $54,000 |
| Short-term investments .............. | 8,000 | 10,000 | (2,000) |
| Accounts receivable (net) ........... | 80,000 | 50,000 | 30,000 |
| Inventory.................................... | 30,000 | 20,000 | 10,000 |
| Prepaid expenses....................... | 2,000 | | 2,000 |
| Total Current Assets............ | 204,000 | 110,000 | |
| Current Liabilities: | | | |
| Accounts payable........................ | 55,000 | 40,000 | (15,000) |
| Dividends payable....................... | 15,000 | | (15,000) |
| Total Current Liabilities ...... | 70,000 | 40,000 | |
| Working Capital............... | $134,000 | $ 70,000 | $64,000 |

ask the question as to why working-capital-based statements have tended to dominate in published financial statements (although not in internal managerial accounting reports). The answer probably lies in the facts that working capital based statements (a) developed first in external reports, (b) are easier to prepare, (c) divulge less about the critical financing strengths and weakness of the enterprise, (d) have been given more attention in textbooks on financial accounting, and (e) represent precedent (which is difficult to change). In Opinion No. 19 the APB specified that the statement of changes in financial position could be presented either on a working capital or cash basis. Unfortunately the APB did not specifically recognize the greater relevance of the cash flow approach.[7] However, a major concession to the cash flow approach is evidenced in the Opinion by the requirement, under the working capital approach, that: "Whether or not working capital flow is presented in the Statement, net changes in each element of working capital (as customarily defined) should be appropriately disclosed for at least the current period, either in the Statement or in a related tabulation." In contrast, in respect to the cash flow approach the Opinion states: "If the format shows the flow of cash, changes in other elements of working capital (e.g., in receivables, inventories, and payables) constitute sources and uses of cash and should accordingly be disclosed in appropriate detail in the body of the Statement" (italics supplied). The difference in reporting on a cash basis versus a working capital basis can be observed by comparing the illustrations in this chapter in Parts A and B since identical data (for Adamson Company and F. P. Corporation) are used in both parts.

Changing from the working capital basis to the cash basis is not difficult; the latter simply requires the additional analysis of the non-cash working capital items. Thus, more transactions must be analyzed and reported. In respect to the cash basis statement, a separate schedule of the changes in working capital accounts (Part B of the statement illustrated in Exhibit 21–5) is not required because the cash flow analysis incorporates these data in the basic report.

The statement of changes in financial position on a cash basis can be developed by measuring funds as (a) cash only, or (b) cash plus near-cash items. The total of cash plus short-term investments is generally used because this is consistent with the definition of short-term marketable securities. Cash only will be illustrated for the Adamson Company, and cash plus short-term investments for the F. P. Corporation.[8]

---

[7] There are a few situations where the cash basis is required, such as in the land development industry and for companies that do not classify assets and liabilities as current (primarily financial institutions). The Trueblood Committee Report on the objectives of financial statements took a strong stand for cash flow reports on the grounds that users are more concerned with cash flows.

[8] It is sometimes suggested that either a summary of the Cash account, or a conversion of the income statement to a cash basis, adequately reports cash flows for the period. Both of these approaches are superficial, incomplete, and are apt to be misleading. In contrast, a statement of changes in financial position, cash basis, focuses on the changes in assets, liabilities, and owners' equity, on an all-resources basis, that is measured in terms of cash. Conceptually, it is the same as the working capital basis except that funds are measured as cash rather than as working capital.

In Exhibits 21-1 and 21-2, a series of transactions were analyzed to compare the cash flow and working capital effects. The resulting statement of changes in financial position (summarized) for each basis were presented in Exhibit 21-3. You should return to those illustrations and the related discussions for restudy at this point. Observe that cash generated *from net income* was $12,000. Alternatively, this amount could have been derived by starting with reported net income and adding and deducting the noncash items that are reflected either directly or indirectly on the income statement. In effect, this would convert accrual basis, net income as reported on the income statement, to a cash flow basis. Using the data in Exhibit 21-1, the alternative computation is:

| | |
|---|---:|
| Net income reported (accrual basis).............. | $ 8,000 |
| Add (deduct) noncash items affecting the income statement: | |
| Trade receivables increase ........................ | (10,000) |
| Trade payables increase ........................... | 7,000 |
| Inventory decrease................................... | 3,000 |
| Depreciation expense ............................... | 4,000 |
| Accrued expense increase ......................... | 2,000 |
| Gain on sale of fixed asset ........................ | (2,000) |
| Cash Generated from Operations .................. | $12,000 |

In Exhibit 21-3, you can observe the fundamental distinctions between a statement developed on a cash basis versus a working capital basis. With these concepts and distinctions in mind, we can proceed directly to the development of the statement of changes in financial position on a cash basis and a cash plus near-cash basis in more complex situations.

## WORKSHEET TO DEVELOP STATEMENT OF CHANGES IN FINANCIAL POSITION, CASH BASIS

Development of a statement of changes in financial position, cash basis, except in the simplest of situations, requires an organized approach to analyzing the transactions for the period. For complex situations and those involving a large number of transactions, the worksheet approach is necessary. Since the general format of the statement of changes in financial position is the same under either the working capital or cash approaches, we can utilize the same worksheet approach for each. In order to simplify the illustrations in this part of the chapter we have decided to parallel the worksheet format shown in Exhibit 21-8 with a few changes in terminology (essentially from the words *working capital to cash*). For the first example, we will utilize the data for Adamson Company given in Exhibit 21-4. The cash basis worksheet for these data is shown in Exhibit 21-10. In preparing the worksheet the summarized transactions are analyzed and entered in debit-credit format under the pair of columns headed "Analysis of Interim Entries." Observe that similar to the working capital basis, the original entries are repeated with adaptation and entry at the bottom of the worksheet for the original debits and credits to Cash. Fundamentally the worksheet reflects the following major side captions:

Cash — Entered on the worksheet simply as a balancing feature.

Noncash Accounts — All of the noncash accounts from the beginning and ending balance sheets are entered on the worksheet for analysis and reconciliation. It is in the analysis of the noncash accounts that we find the sources and applications of cash; or to state it another way, to identify the *causes* of the changes in cash during the period. As with the working capital approach, we are also able to identify and "pull out" the effects of the "in and out" items. Recall that these are noncash investing and financing activities that did not affect (flow through) cash.

Cash Generated — This major caption is subdivided for net income, extraordinary items, other sources of cash, and finally for the noncash financing activities.

Cash Used or Applied — This major caption is subdivided for cash applied for nonoperating items and for noncash resources applied.

Net Increase (Decrease) in Cash for the Period.

In developing the worksheet (and the related statement) on a working capital basis, *net income* and other amounts are converted from an accrual basis amount to a working capital basis (i.e., working capital generated by operations exclusive of extraordinary items). This concept is carried over to the cash basis worksheet (and the related statement); that is, net income, and other amounts, on an accrual basis are converted to a *cash basis* (i.e., cash generated by operations exclusive of extraordinary items). Therefore, in Exhibit 21–10, cash basis worksheet, and Exhibit 21–11, cash basis statement, you will observe that the "adjustments" to net income are for all *noncash charges and credits* reported on the income statement.[9]

In studying the worksheet for Adamson Company you are urged to compare it with the respective worksheet under the working capital basis shown in Exhibit 21–6. The interim entries reflected on the cash basis worksheet are identical with those entered on the working capital basis worksheet, except for the following:

|  | Original Entry | Worksheet Entry |
|---|---|---|
| c. Inventory increase of $7,000: | | |
| Inventory ...................................... | 7,000 | 7,000 |
|     Cost of goods sold ................. | 7,000 | |
|     Cash generated, net income | | |
|       (adjustment)......................... | | 7,000 |

---

[9] General practice is to start with net income and add (or deduct) the noncash items to derive the cash or working capital generated from operations. Alternatively, many accountants prefer to use a gross rather than a net approach. This approach gives precisely the same cash or working capital generated by operations. On this point *APB Opinion No. 19* states: "An acceptable alternative procedure, which gives the same result, is to begin with total revenue that provided working capital or cash during the period and deduct operating costs and expenses that required the outlay of working capital or cash during the period. In either case the resulting amount of working capital or cash should be appropriately described, e.g., 'Working capital provided from [used in] operations for the period, exclusive of extraordinary items.' This total should be immediately followed by working capital or cash provided or used by income or loss from extraordinary items, if any; extraordinary income or loss should be similarly adjusted for items recognized that did not provide or use working capital or cash during the period."

Analysis: This change in a noncash account must be reconciled. Cash Generated, Net Income account is credited as an adjustment to net income since this item represents a noncash credit to cost of goods sold through the inventory increase.

| | Original Entry | Worksheet Entry |
|---|---|---|

b & g. Decrease in accounts payable, $4,000:

| | Original Entry | Worksheet Entry |
|---|---|---|
| Accounts payable .................... | 4,000 | 4,000 |
| Cash .............................. | 4,000 | |
| Cash generated, net income (adjustment)................... | | 4,000 |

**EXHIBIT 21–10**

ADAMSON COMPANY
Worksheet to Develop Statement of Changes in Financial Position, Cash Basis
For the Year Ended December 31, 1976

| Debits | Balance Dec. 31, 1975 | Analysis of Interim Entries Debit | | Analysis of Interim Entries Credit | | Balance Dec. 31, 1976 |
|---|---|---|---|---|---|---|
| Cash | 30,000 | (p) | 15,000 | | | 45,000 |
| Noncash Accounts: | | | | | | |
| Accounts receivable (net) | 40,000 | | | (d & f) | 2,000 | 38,000 |
| Inventory | 60,000 | (c) | 7,000 | | | 67,000 |
| Long-term investments | 200,000 | | | (l) | 38,000 | 162,000 |
| Land | 100,000 | (i) | 28,000 | | | 128,000 |
| Building (net) | | (n − 1) | 100,000 | (o) | 2,000 | 98,000 |
| Total | 430,000 | | | | | 538,000 |
| **Credits** | | | | | | |
| Accounts payable | 40,000 | (b & g) | 4,000 | | | 36,000 |
| Notes payable, short term (nontrade) | 30,000 | (k) | 6,000 | | | 24,000 |
| Bonds payable | 50,000 | (m − 1) | 25,000 | (h) | 10,000 | 35,000 |
| Mortgage payable | | | | (n − 2) | 100,000 | 100,000 |
| Common stock | 270,000 | | | (m − 2) | 25,000 | 295,000 |
| Retained earnings | 40,000 | (j) | 25,000 | (a) | 33,000 | 48,000 |
| Total | 430,000 | | 210,000 | | 210,000 | 538,000 |
| Cash Generated: | | | | | | |
| Net income | | (a) | 33,000 | | | |
| Adjustments for noncash items: | | | | | | |
| Inventory increase | | | | (c) | 7,000 | |
| Accounts payable decrease | | | | (b & g) | 4,000 | |
| Accounts receivable decrease | | (d & f) | 2,000 | | | |
| Depreciation expense | | (o) | 2,000 | | | |
| Extraordinary items generating cash: | | | | | | |
| Long-term investment sold | | (l) | 38,000 | | | |
| Cash from other sources: | | | | | | |
| Bonds payable sold | | (h) | 10,000 | | | |
| Noncash financing activities: | | | | | | |
| Common stock issued to retire bonds payable | | (m − 2) | 25,000 | | | |
| Mortgage payable issued for building | | (n − 2) | 100,000 | | | |
| Cash Applied: | | | | | | |
| For nonoperating items: | | | | | | |
| Land purchased | | | | (i) | 28,000 | |
| Dividends paid | | | | (j) | 25,000 | |
| Notes paid, short term (nontrade) | | | | (k) | 6,000 | |
| Noncash resources applied: | | | | | | |
| Bonds payable retired by issuing common stock | | | | (m − 1) | 25,000 | |
| Building acquired, gave long-term mortgage | | | | (n − 1) | 100,000 | |
| Net increase in cash for the period | | | | (p) | 15,000 | |
| | | | 210,000 | | 210,000 | |

Analysis: This is the net effect of two entries: (b) purchases of goods on account, $58,000, and (g) payment on accounts, $62,000. They could be represented on the worksheet as two entries; however, it is convenient to combine them for the net effect. The decrease in accounts payable affects one noncash account that must be reconciled. Cash Generated, Net Income account is credited as an adjustment to net income since this item represents a noncash credit through cost of goods sold.

|  | Original Entry | Worksheet Entry |
|---|---|---|
| d & f. Decrease in accounts receivable $2,000: |  |  |
| Cash | 2,000 |  |
| Cash generated, net income (adjustment) |  | 2,000 |
| Accounts receivable | 2,000 | 2,000 |

Analysis: This is the net effect of two entries: (d) sales on account of $100,000, and (f) collections on receivables, $102,000. They could be represented on the worksheet as two entries; however, it is convenient to combine them for the net effect. Cash Generated, Net Income account is debited as an adjustment to net income since this item represents a noncash debit to income (sales).

**EXHIBIT 21-11**

ADAMSON COMPANY
Statement of Changes in Financial Position, Cash Basis
For the Year Ended December 31, 1976

| | | |
|---|---|---|
| Cash Generated: | | |
| Income before extraordinary items | $33,000 | |
| Add (deduct) items not requiring, or generating, cash during the current period: | | |
| Inventory increase | (7,000) | |
| Trade payables decrease | (4,000) | |
| Trade receivables decrease | 2,000 | |
| Depreciation expense | 2,000 | |
| Total Cash Generated by Operations Exclusive of Extraordinary Items | | $ 26,000 |
| Extraordinary items generating cash: | | |
| Long-term investment sold | | 38,000 |
| Other sources of cash: | | |
| Bonds payable sold | | 10,000 |
| Total Cash Generated | | 74,000 |
| | | |
| Cash Applied: | | |
| Land purchased | $28,000 | |
| Dividends paid | 25,000 | |
| Notes—short term (nontrade) paid | 6,000 | |
| Total Cash Applied | | 59,000 |
| Increase in Cash for the Period | | $ 15,000 |
| | | |
| Financing and Investing Activities Not Affecting Cash: | | |
| Bonds payable retired by issuing common stock | | $ 25,000 |
| Building acquired, gave long-term mortgage payable | | 100,000 |
| Total | | $125,000 |

**EXHIBIT 21–12**

F. P. CORPORATION
Worksheet to Develop a Statement of Changes in Financial Position, Cash Plus Near-Cash Basis
For the Year Ended December 31, 19B

| Debits | Balance Dec. 31, 19A | Analysis of Interim Entries Debit | | Analysis of Interim Entries Credit | | Balance Dec. 31, 19B |
|---|---|---|---|---|---|---|
| Cash plus short-term investments | 40,000 | (s) | 52,000 | | | 92,000 |
| Noncash Accounts: | | | | | | |
| Accounts receivable (net) | 50,000 | (a & o) | 30,000 | | | 80,000 |
| Inventory | 20,000 | (c) | 10,000 | | | 30,000 |
| Prepaid expenses | | (f) | 2,000 | | | 2,000 |
| Land | 60,000 | | | (j) | 35,000 | 25,000 |
| Machinery | 80,000 | (k) | 10,000 | | | 90,000 |
| Other assets | 29,000 | (q − 1) | 10,000 | | | 39,000 |
| Discount on bonds payable | 1,000 | | | (r) | 100 | 900 |
| Total | 280,000 | | | | | 358,900 |
| Credits | | | | | | |
| Accumulated depreciation | 20,000 | | | (e) | 7,900 | 27,900 |
| Accounts payable | 40,000 | | | (b & p) | 15,000 | 55,000 |
| Dividends payable | | | | (g − 2) | 15,000 | 15,000 |
| Bonds payable | 70,000 | (n − 2) | 20,000 | | | 55,000 |
| | | | | (i) | 5,000 | |
| Common stock | 100,000 | | | (h) | 10,000 | 131,000 |
| | | | | (n − 1) | 21,000 | |
| Preferred stock | 20,000 | | | (q − 2) | 10,000 | 30,000 |
| Retained earnings | 30,000 | (g) | 15,000 | (a) | 44,000 | 45,000 |
| | | (h) | 10,000 | | | |
| | | (m) | 4,000 | | | |
| | 280,000 | | 163,000 | | 163,000 | 358,900 |
| Financial Resources Generated: | | | | | | |
| Cash generated: | | | | | | |
| Net income | | (a) | 44,000 | | | |
| To remove gain on land | | | | (j) | 18,000 | |
| To remove loss on bonds | | (n − 2) | 1,000 | | | |
| Adjustments for noncash items: | | | | | | |
| Depreciation expense | | (e) | 7,900 | | | |
| Amortization of bond discount | | (r) | 100 | | | |
| Inventory increase | | | | (c) | 10,000 | |
| Prepaid expenses increase | | | | (f) | 2,000 | |
| Accounts receivable increase | | | | (a & o) | 30,000 | |
| Accounts payable increase | | (b & p) | 15,000 | | | |
| Extraordinary items generating cash: | | | | | | |
| Land sold | | (j) | 53,000 | | | |
| Cash from other sources: | | | | | | |
| Bonds payable sold | | (i) | 5,000 | | | |
| Noncash financing activities: | | | | | | |
| Liability for dividends declared | | (g − 2) | 15,000 | | | |
| Common stock issued to retire bonds | | (n − 1) | 21,000 | | | |
| Preferred stock issued for other assets | | (q − 2) | 10,000 | | | |
| Financial Resources Applied: | | | | | | |
| Cash applied for nonoperating items: | | | | | | |
| Machinery purchased | | | | (k) | 10,000 | |
| Noncash resources applied: | | | | | | |
| Dividends declared but not paid | | | | (g − 1) | 15,000 | |
| Bonds retired by issuing common stock | | | | (n − 2) | 21,000 | |
| Dividends on preferred stock paid with short-term investments | | | | (m) | 4,000 | |
| Other assets acquired by issuing preferred stock | | | | (q − 1) | 10,000 | |
| Net increase in cash during the period | | | | (s) | 52,000 | |
| | | | 172,000 | | 172,000 | |

**EXHIBIT 21–13**

F. P. CORPORATION
Statement of Changes in Financial Position, Cash Plus Near-Cash Basis
For the Year Ended December 31, 19B

Financial Resources Generated:

Cash generated:

| | | |
|---|---:|---:|
| Net income before extraordinary items....................... | $27,000 | |
| Add (deduct) items not requiring, or generating, cash during the current period: | | |
| Depreciation expense......................................... | 7,900 | |
| Amortization of discount on bonds payable ......... | 100 | |
| Inventory increase ........................................... | (10,000) | |
| Prepaid expenses increase ............................... | (2,000) | |
| Trade accounts receivable increase .................... | (30,000) | |
| Trade accounts payable increase ....................... | 15,000 | |
| Total Cash Generated by Operations Exclusive of Extraordinary Items ................................. | | $   8,000 |
| Extraordinary items generating cash: | | |
| Land sold ........................................................... | | 53,000 |
| Total Cash Generated by Operations............... | | 61,000 |
| Other sources of cash: | | |
| Bonds issued.................................................... | | 5,000 |
| Total Cash Generated.................................... | | 66,000 |
| Financial resources generated not affecting cash: | | |
| Liability for dividends declared but not paid .............. | 15,000 | |
| Common stock issued to retire bonds payable ............ | 21,000 | |
| Preferred stock issued for other assets  ..................... | 10,000 | |
| Total...................................................... | | 46,000 |
| Total Financial Resources Generated  ......... | | $112,000 |

Financial Resources Applied:

Cash applied:

| | | |
|---|---:|---:|
| Machinery purchased.............................................. | 10,000 | |
| Dividends on preferred stock paid with short-term investments ......................................... | 4,000 | |
| Total....................................................... | | 14,000 |
| Financial resources applied not affecting cash: | | |
| Cash dividends declared but not paid ......................... | 15,000 | |
| Bonds payable retired by issuing common stock ......... | 21,000 | |
| Other assets acquired by issuing preferred stock ......... | 10,000 | |
| Total................................................................ | | 46,000 |
| Increase in cash during the period.............................. | | 52,000 |
| Total Financial Resources Applied.................. | | $112,000 |

|  | Original Entry | Worksheet Entry |
|---|---|---|
| *k.* Paid short term notes payable (nontrade) $6,000: | | |
| Notes payable—short term (nontrade) | 6,000 | 6,000 |
| Cash | 6,000 | |
| Cash applied for nonoperating items | | 6,000 |

Analysis: This item affected a noncash account and represented the use of cash for an item not related to the income statement. Note—It did not appear on the working capital analysis since the transaction did not affect a nonworking capital account.

Since the worksheet involves an analysis of all noncash accounts, it is obvious that all transactions as summarized (except the rare cash to cash transaction) would be reflected on the worksheet. Entry *(p)* is an optional "balancing" entry. Observe, the arithmetic checks at two levels on the worksheet.

## PREPARING THE STATEMENT OF CHANGES IN FINANCIAL POSITION (CASH BASIS)

The completed worksheet in Exhibit 21–10 provides all of the details needed to prepare the statement of changes in financial position on a cash basis in conformity with the criteria of *APB Opinion No. 19.* Observe on the cash basis statement, in contrast to the working capital basis statement, that it is not necessary to include a section comparable to "Changes in Working Capital Accounts." As was discussed in respect to the working capital basis, the statement on a cash basis may be prepared under flexible guidelines. The formal statement is illustrated in Exhibit 21–11.

## COMPREHENSIVE ILLUSTRATION, CASH PLUS NEAR-CASH BASIS

The data for F. P. Corporation provided in Exhibit 21–7 are used to illustrate some of the complexities omitted from the previous illustration. The cash basis worksheet is reflected in Exhibit 21–12, and the resultant statement of changes in financial position, cash basis, is shown in Exhibit 21–13. You are urged to follow each transaction through the worksheet, remembering the principles and concepts previously discussed. In this respect it should be helpful to compare this worksheet and statement with those for the F. P. Corporation on a working capital basis as reflected in Exhibits 21–8 and 21–9.

A comparison of the statement of financial position, cash basis, for Adamson Company with that for F. P. Corporation, as well as those presented at the end of Chapters 4, 5, and 24, will reflect the flexibility in format and terminology permitted by *APB Opinion No. 19*. No single format can said to be the best because of the differing characteristics of each situation. However, reasonable uniformity as to terminology and format will better serve the statement users.

## QUESTIONS

1. Briefly explain the objectives and significance of the statement of changes in financial position.

2. Distinguish between an investing activity and a financing activity.

3. Explain the all-resource concept as applied to the statement of changes in financial position.

4. Explain the basic measurement distinction between the cash basis and the working capital basis for the statement of changes in financial position.

5. Why is it necessary that the changes in the noncurrent accounts rather than the changes in the current accounts be analyzed in developing the statement of changes in financial position, working capital basis?

6. The income statement for X Company reported a net income of $10,000. The statement also showed a deduction for depreciation of $5,000 and an increase in accounts receivable of $8,000. Give the (a) cash and (b) working capital generated by operations and explain why each is different from net income.

7. The income statement for Y Company reported a net loss of $7,000. The statement also showed a deduction for depreciation of $6,000 and amortization of patents of $3,000. In addition, the statement showed amortization of premium on bonds payable of $1,000. Compute the working capital generated by operations and explain why it is different from the net loss.

8. There are two "parts" to the statement of changes in financial position, working capital basis, and only one part for the cash basis statement. Explain.

9. Give an example of working capital generated involving (a) noncurrent assets, (b) noncurrent liabilities, (c) capital stock, and (d) retained earnings.

10. Give an example of working capital applied involving (a) noncurrent assets, (b) noncurrent liabilities, (c) capital stock, and (d) retained earnings.

11. Assume the sale of a fixed asset that cost $50,000, one half depreciated, for $5,000 cash plus a $15,000 one-year, interest-bearing note. How much cash was generated? How much working capital was generated? Explain why an adjustment to the net income for the loss or gain on this transaction is necessary to determine the amount of cash or working capital generated from operations.

12. Explain why net income is adjusted for the depreciation amount but not for the estimated bad debt amount in determining working capital generated. How do they affect cash flow?

13. Why is the cash basis often more relevant than the working capital basis for evaluating the financing and investing activities of an enterprise?

**DECISION CASE 21-1**

The following statement was prepared by the controller of the Clovis Company. The controller indicated that this statement was prepared under the "all financial resources" concept of funds, which is the broadest concept of funds and includes all financing and investing activities.

CLOVIS COMPANY
Statement of Source and Application of Funds
December 31, 19B

Funds were provided by:

| | |
|---|---:|
| Contribution of plant site by the city of Camden (Note 1) .............. | $115,000 |
| Net income after extraordinary items per income statement (Note 2) ................................................................................. | 75,000 |
| Issuance of note payable—due 19F ........................................... | 60,000 |
| Depreciation and amortization.................................................... | 50,000 |
| Deferred income taxes relating to accelerated depreciation ............ | 10,000 |
| Sale of equipment—book value (Note 3) ...................................... | 5,000 |
| Total Funds Provided ........................................................... | $315,000 |

Funds were applied to:

| | |
|---|---:|
| Acquisition of future plant site (Note 1)........................................... | $250,000 |
| Increase in working capital ......................................................... | 30,000 |
| Cash dividends declared but not paid ......................................... | 20,000 |
| Acquisition of equipment ........................................................... | 15,000 |
| Total Funds Applied................................................................ | $315,000 |

Notes to Financial Statement

1. The city of Camden donated a plant site to Clovis Company valued by the board of directors at $115,000. The company purchased adjoining property for $135,000.
2. Research and development expenditures of $25,000 incurred in 19B were expensed.
3. Equipment with a book value of $5,000 was sold for $8,000. The gain was included as an extraordinary item on the income statement.

*Required:*

1. Why is it considered desirable to present a statement similar to the above in the financial reports?
2. Define and discuss the relative merits of the following three concepts used in funds flow analysis in terms of their measurement accuracy and freedom from manipulation (window dressing) in one accounting period:
   a. Cash concept of funds.
   b. Net monetary assets (quick assets) concept of funds.
   c. Working capital concept of funds.
3. In view of *APB Opinion No. 19,* identify and discuss the weaknesses in presentation and disclosure in the above statement for Clovis Company. Your discussion should explain why you consider them to be weaknesses and what you consider the proper treatment of the items to be. Do not prepare a revised statement.

(AICPA adapted)

**EXERCISES**

### Exercise 21-1

The balance sheets for TS Company showed the following information.

|  | December 31 | |
|  | 19A | 19B |
| --- | --- | --- |
| Cash | $ 4,000 | $17,000 |
| Accounts receivable (net) | 5,000 | 9,000 |
| Inventory | 10,000 | 12,000 |
| Long-term investment | 2,000 | |
| Fixed assets | 30,000 | 47,000 |
| Total Debits | $51,000 | $85,000 |
| Accumulated depreciation | $ 5,000 | $ 7,000 |
| Accounts payable | 3,000 | 5,000 |
| Notes payable, short term (nontrade) | 4,000 | 3,000 |
| Long-term notes payable | 10,000 | 18,000 |
| Common stock | 25,000 | 40,000 |
| Retained earnings | 4,000 | 12,000 |
| Total Credits | $51,000 | $85,000 |

Additional data concerning changes in the noncurrent accounts:

a. Net income for the year 19B, $26,000.
b. Depreciation on fixed assets for the year, $2,000.
c. Sold the long-term investment at cost.
d. Paid dividends of $7,000.
e. Purchased fixed assets costing $5,000; paid cash.
f. Purchased fixed assets and gave a $12,000 long-term note payable.
g. Paid a $4,000 long-term note payable by issuing common stock.
h. Issued a stock dividend; $11,000 debited to Retained Earnings and credited to Capital Stock.

*Required:*

1. Prepare a statement of changes in financial position, working capital basis, without the benefit of a worksheet.
2. Prepare a statement of changes in financial position, cash basis, without the benefit of a worksheet.

### Exercise 21-2

During the year ended December 31, 19A, AC Corporation completed the following transactions:

a. Sold 2,000 shares of common stock, par $10, for $20 per share, collected cash.
b. Borrowed $10,000 on a one-year, 9%, interest-bearing note; the note was dated June 1.

c. On December 31, 19A, purchased machinery that cost $25,000; paid $5,000 cash and signed two notes: (1) a 60-day, 8%, interest-bearing note, face $15,000; and (2) a 1-year, 7%, interest-bearing note, face $5,000.

d. Purchased merchandise for resale at a cost of $40,000; paid $30,000 cash, balance credited to Accounts Payable.

e. Declared a cash dividend of $6,000; paid $2,000 in December 19A, the balance will be paid March 1, 19B.

f. Income statement:

| | | |
|---|---:|---:|
| Sales: Cash | $55,000 | |
| On credit | 20,000 | $75,000 |
| Cost of goods sold: | | |
| Purchases (d) above | 40,000 | |
| Less: ending inventory | 10,000 | (30,000) |
| Expenses (including income taxes): | | |
| Paid in cash | 10,000 | |
| Accrued (unpaid) | 17,000 | |
| Depreciation | 2,000 | (29,000) |
| Net Income | | $16.000 |

*Required:*

1. Set up a tabulation to derive the fund flows for each item on a (a) cash basis, and (b) working capital basis. Use parallel columns.
2. Prepare a summarized statement of changes in financial position (similar to Exhibit 21–3).

### Exercise 21–3

Use the data given below to compute (a) total cash generated by operations, and (b) total working capital generated by operations.

| Transaction | Cash Basis | Working Capital Basis |
|---|---:|---:|
| Net income reported (accrual basis)* | $50,000 | $50,000 |
| Depreciation expense, $6,000 | _____ | _____ |
| Increase in accrued wages payable, $1,000 | _____ | _____ |
| Increase in trade accounts receivable, $1,800 | _____ | _____ |
| Decrease in merchandise inventory, $2,300 | _____ | _____ |
| Amortization of patent, $200 | _____ | _____ |
| Decrease in long-term liabilities, $10,000 | _____ | _____ |
| Sale of capital stock for cash, $25,000 | _____ | _____ |
| Amortization of bond discount, $300 | _____ | _____ |
| Total Cash Generated by Operations | _____ | |
| Total Working Capital Generated by Operations | | _____ |

* Revenues, $190,000; expenses, $140,000.

**Exercise 21-4**

The following worksheet has been set up; you are to complete it in every respect on a working capital basis:

DOLLEY CORPORATION
Worksheet, Statement of Changes in Financial Position, Working Capital Basis
For the Year Ended December 31, 19B

| Debits | Balances Dec. 31, 19A | Analysis Debit | Analysis Credit | Balances Dec. 31, 19B |
|---|---|---|---|---|
| Working Capital | 30,000 | | | 29,800 |
| Nonworking Capital Accounts: | | | | |
| Investments, long-term | | | | 10,000 |
| Fixed assets (net) | 60,000 | | | 59,000 |
| Patent (net) | 3,000 | | | 2,700 |
| Other assets | 7,000 | | | 7,000 |
| | 100,000 | | | 108,500 |
| **Credits** | | | | |
| Bonds payable | 40,000 | | | 20,000 |
| Capital stock, par $10 | 35,000 | | | 40,000 |
| Contributed capital in excess of par | | | | 4,500 |
| Retained earnings | 25,000 | | | 44,000 |
| | 100,000 | | | 108,500 |
| Sources of Working Capital: | | | | |
| Uses of Working Capital: | | | | |
| Change in Working Capital: | | | | |

Additional data:

a. Net income, $23,000 (after tax).
b. Payment on bonds payable (on principal), $20,000.
c. Amortization of patent, $300.
d. Purchased long-term investment, $10,000.
e. Purchased fixed asset, paid cash, $7,000.
f. Purchased short-term investment, $3,000.
g. Depreciation expense, $8,000.
h. Paid cash dividend, $4,000.
i. Sold unissued stock, 500 shares at $19 per share.

**Exercise 21–5**

The records of K Company reflected the following data.

Balance Sheet Data

|  | December 31 | |
|---|---|---|
|  | *19A* | *19B* |
| Cash | $ 34,000 | $ 33,500 |
| Accounts receivable (net) | 12,000 | 17,000 |
| Inventory | 16,000 | 14,000 |
| Long-term investments | 6,000 |  |
| Fixed assets | 80,000 | 98,000 |
| Treasury stock |  | 11,500 |
| Total Debits | $148,000 | $174,000 |
| | | |
| Accumulated depreciation | $ 48,000 | $ 39,000 |
| Accounts payable | 19,000 | 12,000 |
| Bonds payable | 10,000 | 30,000 |
| Common stock, nopar | 50,000 | 65,000 |
| Retained earnings | 21,000 | 28,000 |
| Total Credits | $148,000 | $174,000 |

Additional data for the period January 1, 19B, through December 31, 19B:

a. Sales on account, $70,000.
b. Purchases on account, $40,000.
c. Depreciation, $5,000.
d. Expenses paid in cash, $18,000.
e. Decrease in inventory, $2,000.
f. Sold fixed assets for $6,000 cash; cost $21,000 and two-thirds depreciated (assume loss or gain is not an extraordinary item).
g. Purchased fixed assets for cash, $9,000.
h. Purchased fixed assets; exchanged unissued bonds payable of $30,000 in payment.
i. Sold the long-term investments for $9,000 cash (assume this is an extraordinary item).
j. Purchased treasury stock for cash, $11,500.
k. Retired bonds payable by issuing common stock, $10,000.
l. Collections on accounts receivable, $65,000.
m. Payments on accounts payable, $47,000.
n. Sold unissued common stock for cash, $5,000.

*Required:*

Prepare a worksheet to develop a statement of changes in financial position, working capital basis.

**Exercise 21–6**

The records of DK Company showed the following information relating to the balance sheet accounts.

Balance Sheet Data

| | December 31 | |
| --- | --- | --- |
| Debits | 19A | 19B |
| Cash ......................................................... | $ 15,000 | $ 20,000 |
| Accounts receivable (net) ............................ | 14,000 | 19,000 |
| Inventory ................................................... | 53,000 | 51,000 |
| Prepaid expenses ........................................ | 3,000 | 4,000 |
| Long-term investments.................................. | 10,000 | |
| Buildings ................................................... | 90,000 | 120,000 |
| Machinery.................................................... | 40,000 | 67,000 |
| Patents ..................................................... | 5,000 | 4,000 |
| | $230,000 | $285,000 |

| Credits | | |
| --- | --- | --- |
| Accounts payable ........................................ | $ 13,000 | $  9,000 |
| Notes payable—short term (nontrade).............. | 9,000 | 13,000 |
| Accrued wages ........................................... | 3,000 | 2,000 |
| Accumulated depreciation ............................. | 40,000 | 38,000 |
| Notes payable—long term .............................. | 30,000 | 35,000 |
| Common stock, nopar ................................... | 120,000 | 155,000 |
| Retained earnings ....................................... | 15,000 | 33,000 |
| | $230,000 | $285,000 |

Additional data relating to the noncurrent accounts:

a. Net income for the year was $28,000.
b. Depreciation recorded on fixed assets was $7,000.
c. Amortization of patents amounted to $1,000.
d. Purchased machinery costing $15,000; paid one third in cash and gave a five-year interest-bearing note for the balance.
e. Purchased machinery costing $30,000 which was paid for by issuing common stock.
f. Sold old machinery for $7,000 that originally cost $18,000 (one-half depreciated); loss (or gain) reported on income statement as ordinary item.
g. Made addition to building costing $30,000; paid cash.
h. Paid a $5,000 long-term note by issuing common stock.
i. Sold the long-term investments for $12,000 cash (assume this is an extra-ordinary item).
j. Paid cash dividends.
k. Sales of $120,000 on account.
l. Collections on accounts receivable, $115,000.

*Required:*

Prepare a worksheet to determine changes in financial position, working capital basis.

**Exercise 21–7**

The following worksheet has been set up; you are to complete it in every respect on a cash flow basis:

| | Balances Dec. 31, 19A | Analysis | | Balances Dec. 31, 19B |
|---|---|---|---|---|
| Debits | | Debit | Credit | |
| Cash plus short-term investments | 19,500 | | | 32,200 |
| Accounts receivable (net) | 34,000 | | | 34,000 |
| Merchandise inventory | 78,000 | | | 85,000 |
| Investments, long term | | | | 10,000 |
| Fixed assets | 168,500 | | | 180,500 |
| | 300,000 | | | 341,700 |
| Credits | | | | |
| Accumulated depreciation | 44,000 | | | 34,000 |
| Accounts payable | 21,000 | | | 19,000 |
| Accrued expenses | 1,500 | | | 500 |
| Income taxes payable | 2,000 | | | 3,500 |
| Bonds payable | 100,000 | | | 100,000 |
| Premium on bonds payable | 4,000 | | | 3,700 |
| Capital stock, nopar | 120,000 | | | 155,500 |
| Retained earnings | 7,500 | | | 25,500 |
| | 300,000 | | | 341,700 |
| Sources of Cash: | | | | |
| Uses of Cash: | | | | |

Additional data:

a. Net income (after tax), $28,000.
b. Acquisition of fixed asset, $30,000; issued 1,000 shares of capital stock in full payment.
c. Depreciation expense, $6,000.
d. Increase in merchandise inventory, $7,000.
e. Decrease in accounts payable, $2,000.
f. Amortization of bond premium, $300.
g. Purchased long-term investment, $10,000.
h. Increase in income taxes payable, $1,500.
i. Decrease in accrued expenses, $1,000.
j. Declared and paid cash dividend, $10,000.
k. Sold fixed assets for $5,000 that cost $18,000; accumulated depreciation, $16,000 (not an extraordinary items).
l. Sold 500 shares of capital stock at $11 per share.

### Exercise 21–8 ´

Use the data given in Exercise 21–5 to prepare a worksheet to develop a statement of changes in financial position, cash basis.

## Exercise 21-9

Use the data given in Exercise 21–6 to prepare a worksheet to develop a statement of changes in financial position, cash basis.

## PROBLEMS

### Problem 21-1

The following worksheet has been set up; you are to complete it in every respect on a working capital basis:

| Debits | Balances Dec. 31, 19A | Analysis Debit | Analysis Credit | Balances Dec. 31, 19B |
|---|---|---|---|---|
| Cash plus short-term investments | 40,000 | | | 44,900 |
| Accounts receivable (net) | 60,000 | | | 52,500 |
| Merchandise inventory | 180,000 | | | 141,600 |
| Prepaid insurance | 2,400 | | | 1,200 |
| Investments, long term | 30,000 | | | |
| Land | 10,000 | | | 38,400 |
| Fixed assets | 250,000 | | | 259,000 |
| Patent (net) | 1,600 | | | 1,400 |
| Total Debits | 574,000 | | | 539,000 |
| | | | | |
| Credits | | | | |
| Accumulated depreciation | 65,000 | | | 79,000 |
| Accounts payable | 50,000 | | | 53,000 |
| Accrued wages payable | 2,000 | | | 1,500 |
| Income taxes payable | 9,000 | | | 13,400 |
| Bonds payable | 100,000 | | | 50,000 |
| Premium on bonds payable | 5,000 | | | 1,700 |
| Capital stock, par $10 | 300,000 | | | 306,000 |
| Contributed capital in excess of par | 15,000 | | | 18,000 |
| Retained earnings | 28,000 | | | 16,400 |
| | 574,000 | | | 539,000 |
| Sources of Working Capital: | | | | |
| Uses of Working Capital: | | | | |

Additional data:

a. Revenues, $400,000 − expenses (including income taxes), $375,000 = $25,000.
b. Depreciation expense, $14,000.
c. Cash dividends declared and paid, $30,000.
d. Increase in income taxes payable, $4,400.
e. Amortization of patent, $200.
f. Purchased fixed asset, cost $9,000; payment by issuing 600 shares of stock.
g. Decrease in accrued wages payable, $500.

h. Payment on bonds payable, principal, $50,000.
i. Sold the long-term investments for $40,000 after tax (assume this is an extraordinary item).
j. Decrease in accounts receivable (net), $7,500.
k. Decrease in prepaid insurance, $1,200.
i. Decrease in merchandise inventory, $38,400.
m. Increase in accounts payable, $3,000.
n. Amortization of bond premium, $3,300.
o. Payment of additional assessment on prior years' income taxes (a prior period adjustment), $6,600.
p. Purchased land, $28,400, paid cash.

## Problem 21-2

The balance sheets of Murray Company provided the information shown below.

|  | December 31 | |
|---|---|---|
|  | *19A* | *19B* |
| Cash | $ 4,000 | $ 11,000 |
| Accounts receivable (net) | 9,000 | 12,000 |
| Inventory | 8,000 | 5,000 |
| Long-term investments | 2,000 | |
| Plant | 30,000 | 30,000 |
| Equipment | 20,000 | 22,000 |
| Land | 10,000 | 40,000 |
| Patents | 8,000 | 7,000 |
|  | $91,000 | $127,000 |
|  |  |  |
| Accumulated depreciation—plant | $ 7,000 | $ 10,000 |
| Accumulated depreciation—equipment | 10,000 | 8,000 |
| Accounts payable | 8,000 | 2,000 |
| Accrued wages payable | 1,000 | |
| Notes payable, long term | 10,000 | 19,000 |
| Common stock, par $10 | 50,000 | 75,000 |
| Retained earnings | 5,000 | 13,000 |
|  | $91,000 | $127,000 |

Additional data:

a. Net income for the year, $12,000.
b. Depreciation on plant for the year, $3,000.
c. Depreciation on equipment for the year, $2,000.
d. Amortization of patents for the year, $1,000.
e. Sales on account, $67,000.
f. Purchases on account, $35,000.
g. Expenses paid in cash (including accrued wages), $15,000.
h. At the end of the year sold equipment costing $8,000 (50% depreciated) for $3,000 cash (assume this was not an extraordinary item).
i. Purchased land costing $10,000; paid $2,000 cash, gave long-term note for the balance.
j. Paid $4,000 on long-term notes.
k. Sold $10,000 capital stock at par.
l. Purchased equipment costing $10,000; paid one-half cash, balance due in three years (interest-bearing note).

*m.* Issued 1,500 shares common stock (at par) for land that cost $20,000, balance in cash.

*n.* Collections on accounts receivable, $64,000.

*o.* Payment on accounts payable, $41,000.

*p.* Sold the long-term investments for $8,000 cash (assume this was an extraordinary item).

*q.* Paid dividends, $4,000.

*Required:*

1. Prepare a worksheet to develop a statement of changes in financial position, working capital basis, for 19B. Key your entries.
2. Prepare a statement of changes in financial position unless directed otherwise by your instructor.

## Problem 21–3

The records of Mills Trading Company provided the following summaries and data:

1. Income statement for the month of April 19A:

| | | |
|---|---:|---:|
| Sales | | $ 80,000 |
| Less: Purchases | $ 40,000 | |
| Increase in inventory | 5,000 | 35,000 |
| | | 45,000 |
| Expenses: | | |
| Depreciation | $ 5,000 | |
| Allowance for doubtful accounts | 1,000 | |
| Insurance | 1,000 | |
| Interest expense | 2,000 | |
| Salaries and wages | 12,000 | |
| Other expenses (including income taxes) | 16,000 | |
| Loss on sale of fixed assets | 2,000 | |
| Total Expenses | | 39,000 |
| Net Income | | $ 6,000 |

2. Balance sheets (unclassified):

| | March 31, 19A | April 30, 19A |
|---|---:|---:|
| Cash | $ 15,000 | $ 31,000 |
| Accounts receivable | 30,000 | 28,500 |
| Allowance for doubtful accounts | 1,500* | 2,000* |
| Inventory | 10,000 | 15,000 |
| Prepaid insurance | 2,400 | 1,400 |
| Fixed assets | 80,000 | 81,000 |
| Accumulated depreciation | 20,000* | 16,000* |
| Land | 40,100 | 81,100 |
| Total | $156,000 | $220,000 |
| Accounts payable | $ 10,000 | $ 11,000 |
| Wages payable | 2,000 | 1,000 |
| Accrued interest payable | | 1,000 |
| Notes payable, long term | 20,000 | 46,000 |
| Common stock, nopar | 100,000 | 136,000 |
| Retained earnings | 24,000 | 25,000 |
| Total | $156,000 | $220,000 |

* Deductions.

3. Cash account:

| Debits | | Credits | |
|---|---|---|---|
| Balance | $15,000 | Purchases | $10,000 |
| Sales | 20,000 | Salaries and wages | 5,000 |
| Fixed assets | 4,000 | Accounts payable | 4,000 |
| Sales | 15,000 | Salaries and wages | 2,000 |
| Notes payable | 20,000 | Purchases | 5,000 |
| Sales | 15,000 | Expenses | 6,000 |
| Accounts receivable | 31,000 | Dividends | 5,000 |
| Common stock | 5,000 | Purchases | 5,000 |
| | | Expenses | 10,000 |
| | | Accounts payable | 6,000 |
| | *125000* | Land | 20,000 |
| | | Accounts payable | 9,000 |
| | | Wages | 6,000 |
| | | Interest | 1,000 |

*85000*

4. Retained Earnings account showed a debit for dividends, $5,000.
5. Wrote off $500 accounts receivable as uncollectible.
6. Acquired land for common stock issued.
7. Acquired fixed assets costing $16,000; gave three-year, interest-bearing note.
8. Paid a $10,000 long-term note by issuing the creditor common stock.

*Required:*

1. Prepare a worksheet to develop a statement of changes in financial position, working capital basis.
2. Prepare the statement of changes in financial position (unless directed otherwise by your instructor).

## Problem 21–4

The comparative balance sheets for Hall Corporation reflected a significant increase in current assets, a relatively minor increase in current liabilities, and a low net income. The executive committee of the corporation has requested a report that shows the detailed financing and investing activities for the year 19B. You have been provided the incomplete data below.

### Balance Sheet Data

| | December 31 | |
|---|---|---|
| | 19A | 19B |
| Cash | $ 2,000 | $ 11,510 |
| Investments, short term | | 2,000 |
| Accounts receivable | 7,000 | 8,300 |
| Inventory | 39,000 | 43,500 |
| Prepaid property insurance | 250 | 225 |
| Office supplies inventory | 75 | 80 |
| Sinking fund | | 300 |
| Delivery equipment | 5,000 | 20,250 |
| Office equipment | 2,000 | 1,900 |
| Organization expense (unamortized) | 600 | 400 |
| Discount on Series A bonds | 100 | |
| Patents | 1,000 | 800 |
| Cash surrender value of life insurance policies | 1,000 | 1,100 |
| Land | | 20,000 |
| | $58,025 | $110,365 |

| | December 31 | |
| --- | --- | --- |
| | 19A | 19B |
| Notes payable, short term (nontrade)............................. | $    300 | $    250 |
| Accounts payable...................................................... | 2,000 | 2,590 |
| Cash dividends payable .............................................. | | 1,500 |
| Bonds payable, Series A  ......................................... | 2,000 | |
| Bonds payable, Series B  ......................................... | | 25,000 |
| Premium on Series B bonds........................................ | | 700 |
| Allowance for doubtful accounts  .............................. | 700 | 900 |
| Accumulated depreciation – delivery equipment............... | 2,500 | 3,050 |
| Accumulated depreciation – office equipment  ............... | 400 | 520 |
| Preferred stock, par $10............................................ | 3,500 | |
| Common stock, par $20.............................................. | 40,000 | 46,000 |
| Retained earnings  .................................................. | 6,625 | 4,055 |
| Contributed capital in excess of par, common  .............. | | 25,500 |
| Reserve for bond sinking fund...................................... | | 300 |
| | $58,025 | $110,365 |

Selected additional data:

a. Net income for 19B was $7,040.
b. Preferred stock, par value $500, purchased at 110 and canceled. The premium paid was debited to Retained Earnings.
c. Sold 50 shares of common stock at $105 per share.
d. Office equipment costing $100, recorded depreciation $80, was sold for $15. The gain or loss was reported on income statement as an ordinary item.
e. Delivery equipment costing $500, recorded depreciation $450, sold for $30. The gain or loss was reported as ordinary item.
f. Depreciation for the year: delivery equipment, $1,000; office equipment, $200.
g. Discount on the Series A bonds was written off as follows: July 1 amortized $25 to interest expense; July 2 by recording the retirement of the issue before maturity by payment of $1,775 cash.
h. Amortized $200 organization expense.
i. Paid $100 legal costs in defense of the patent rights which was capitalized. Amortized $300 patent costs.
j. Paid cash dividends on preferred stock, $260.
k. Declared $1,500 cash dividends on common stock, payable January 15 next year.
l. Sold $5,000 of the Series B bonds at 115 on July 1 and amortized $50 of the premium to expense.
m. Paid premium on life insurance on certain executives, $500; the cash value increased $100.
n. Bad debts written off during the period totaled $1,000; bad debt expense recorded for the period was $1,200.
o. Office supplies of $250 costing were purchased during the year.
p. U.S. bonds were purchased on August 1 as a short-term investment, $2,000.
q. Property insurance premiums paid totaled $150; expired premiums totaled $175.
r. Retired the preferred stock (par $3,000) by issuing 100 shares of the common stock. The common stock was selling at $105.
s. Issued Series B bonds at par value for land, $20,000.
t. Acquired delivery equipment by issuing 150 shares of common stock. The common stock was selling at $105.

The Retained Earnings account reflected the following changes:

| Balance December 31, 19A ........................ | $6,625 |
| Net income................................................. | 7,040 |
| Preferred stock purchased........................... | (50) |
| Dividends, preferred.................................... | (260) |
| Dividends, common...................................... | (1,500) |
| Preferred stock retired .............................. | (7,500) |
| Appropriated to bond sinking fund............... | (300) |
| Balance, December 31, 19B ....................... | $4,055 |

*Required:*

1. Prepare a worksheet to develop a statement of changes in financial position, working capital basis.
2. Unless directed otherwise by your instructor, prepare a formal statement of changes in financial position, working capital basis suitable for presentation to the executive committee.

### Problem 21–5

Use the data given in Problem 21–1.

*Required:*

1. Prepare a worksheet to develop a statement of changes in financial position, cash basis.
2. Unless directed otherwise by your instructor, prepare a statement of changes in financial position, cash basis.

### Problem 21–6

Use the data given in Problem 21–2.

*Required:*

1. Prepare a worksheet to develop a statement of changes in financial position, cash basis.
2. Unless directed otherwise by your instructor, prepare a statement of changes in financial position, cash basis.

### Problem 21–7

Use the data given in Problem 21–3.

*Required:*

1. Prepare a worksheet to develop a statement of changes in financial position, cash basis.
2. Unless directed otherwise by your instructor, prepare a statement of changes in financial position, cash basis.

### Problem 21–8

Use the data provided in Problem 21–4

*Required:*

1. Prepare a worksheet to develop a statement of changes in financial position, cash basis.
2. Unless directed otherwise by your instructor, prepare a statement of changes in financial position, cash basis for the executive committee.

# Chapter 22

# Accounting for Pension Costs

Pension plans sponsored by business enterprises have become quite pervasive and important, and the assets dedicated to pension purposes now account for a staggering sum of wealth. Half of today's work force in commerce and industry is now covered by some form of retirement plan other than social security, whereas 35 years ago, fewer than 20% of a much smaller work force was so covered.[1]

Not surprisingly, with so many persons affected and with vast amounts of wealth involved, the federal government is vitally interested in the subject. Late in 1974, comprehensive legislation regulating many aspects of employee pension plans was enacted. The law, officially known as The Employee Retirement Income Security Act of 1974 (ERISA) is often referred to as the Pension Reform Act of 1974. The full accounting impact of its lengthy, complex provisions is not yet altogether determined, but seemingly it is relatively slight.

## PENSION PLAN FUNDAMENTALS

The primary purpose of pension plans is to provide retirement income to employees. This goal can be accomplished in various ways. Insofar as employers having large numbers of employees are concerned, the goal is attained by establishing a *defined benefit plan* which is funded either by purchase of investments whose income will hopefully provide wherewithal for the benefits, or by purchase of annuity contracts.

Defined benefit plans state the amount of benefits or the method of determining the benefits to be received by employees after retirement. In plans for hourly paid employees, the benefit is ordinarily a specified amount per month based upon years of credited service. In plans for

---

[1] *Journal of Accountancy*, February 1975, p. 52, citing in turn, *Life Insurance Fact Book 1973*. According to these sources, in 1940, assets of private plans were below $3 billion; they now exceed $150 billion and are expected to rise to $250 billion by the end of the decade. A source quoted in *The Wall Street Journal*, September 2, 1975, predicts pension plan assets of around $400 billion in 1980 (p. 23).

salaried employees, benefits are usually related to their compensation (for example, a percent of the highest five years' earnings). Other types of plans are not specific in this respect; rather they provide that whatever the accumulated contributions (plus interest earned) will purchase at the time of retirement will comprise the benefits.

A preponderance of pension benefits payable under defined benefit plans are related to length of service rendered by the employee who is to receive a pension. In general, it can be said that an hourly paid employee who worked in covered employment 20 years is likely to draw about twice as large periodic pension benefits as one who worked in covered employment only 10 years.

Because pension benefits are related to length of employment, a unique problem often arises in connection with pension plans. Most pension plans were adopted after substantial numbers of employees had already been on their employers' payrolls for some time. It would have been inequitable to put these experienced employees on the same footing with respect to their future pension benefits as employees who were hired at about the time or after the pension plan was adopted. If from the date a pension plan is adopted two employees, A and B, work 20 years for the same employer in the same kind of employment, then retire, but A has worked there 15 years before the plan was adopted but B did not, it is hardly fair to A that their pension benefits should be equal. Providing A benefits for the 15 years worked before adoption of the plan causes the employer to incur *past service costs.*

Most pension plans are formally established through a "retirement plan" that meets Internal Revenue Code qualifications so that:

1. Contributions paid by the employer are deductible for income tax purposes.
2. Earnings of the pension fund are not subject to income tax.
3. Employer contributions in behalf of employees are not taxable to the employees at the time the contributions are made.

Prior to passage of the 1974 Pension Reform Act, employers with defined benefit plans had the option of funding or not funding past service costs connected with their plans. Funding meant paying currently for the past service costs. Funding was accomplished by periodically remitting to a trustee (who administered the pension plan and its assets and payments in behalf of the employer and employees) a series of annual cash payments which would, with interest, cover the total lump sum past service cost liability "inherited" at the time a pension plan was adopted. Funding seldom was completed in less than ten years (partly because of income tax provisions) and sometimes was done even more slowly. As will be seen later in the chapter, some companies did not reduce their liability for past service costs but simply funded the accrued interest on the liability. The option to fund or not to fund past service costs no longer exists; the only option the law has left pertains to the date a defined benefit plan began. For plans which existed on January 1, 1974, the funding of past service cost must now be accomplished in 40 years or less. Past service liabilities which arise after January 1, 1974, must be funded in 30 years or less.

Similarly, prior to the 1974 Pension Reform Act, employers had the option of funding or not funding the normal pension costs and the vesting costs. The act now requires that these continuing pension costs also be funded.

A pension plan may be contributory, where the employees bear part of the cost, or noncontributory, where the employer bears the entire cost. An employee's right to receive a present or future pension benefit is said to *vest* when his or her right to eventually receive the benefit is no longer contingent upon remaining an employee of the company. Vesting occurs when the employee retires, but may occur prior to that date. For example, a benefit may vest after a specified number of years of service or at a specified age.[2]

Actuarial determinations and estimates are an integral part of pension plans since *pension costs* are related to a number of significant uncertainties concerning future events, such as: retirement age, mortality (the average life expectancy of employees both before and after retirement), employee turnover, interest rates, gains and losses of fund investments, administrative requirements, future salary levels, pension benefits, and vesting provisions.

A pension plan may be initiated under one of two quite different circumstances which would have significant effects on pension costs, funding requirements, and accounting, viz:

1. A pension plan may be initiated when the company is organized, in which case persons upon initial employment would qualify for the pension plan. Subsequent to inception of the plan only *normal pension costs* would be incurred (each year) by the company.

2. A pension plan may be initiated some years after the company was organized. In this case *present* employees, as well as new employees subsequently hired, would qualify for the plan. *Normal* pension costs would be incurred (each year) by the company for both groups of employees. However, in this case an additional pension cost also would be incurred at date of inception of the pension plan. All employees working for the enterprise at date of the inception of the pension plan generally are given past service credits under the plan for prior years' employment with the company. Thus, the company must bear a one-time pension cost (in addition to the normal pension cost incurred on a year-to-year basis) to provide for the "catch-up" for prior employees; this cost generally is referred to as *past service pension cost.*

---

[2] The 1974 act has imposed stringent safeguards in behalf of employees concerning their vesting rights. An employee must now be at least 25% vested in accrued benefits derived from employer contributions after five years of covered service. By the time an employee has 15 years of covered service, the vesting must have risen (according to a table in the law) to 100%. Under another provision an employee with five years of covered service must be at least 50% vested in the accrued benefit from employer contributions when the sum of the employee's age and years of covered service totals 45.

Past service cost (just defined) is often called *initial past service cost* because it is a cost that comes into existence at the date of adoption of a pension plan. In contrast, *prior service cost* arises when the pension plan is amended or assumptions relating to it are changed with the result that the liabilities related to the past are changed. Prior service cost sometimes is used in the broad sense to include the entire past cost; this includes *initial* past service cost plus the effect of the changes that relate to all service before the amendment date. Examples of these changes are fluctuations in earnings and values of securities held by the pension plan trustee, and changes in the benefits and rates of employee turnover which would affect the actuarial calculations of the fund requirements.[3]

## PENSION PLAN ACCOUNTING

Since most pension plans are funded, accounting for pension plans focuses on *(a)* accounting for the costs of the plan to the employer, and *(b)* accounting for the funding. Most business prefer to keep these two phases in harmony to the extent possible.[4]

There are two basic types of pension costs that must be recorded each period (assuming past services are involved); they are:

1. Normal pension costs — the amount of expense, on an accrual basis, that should be assigned each period to the pension plan for current services by the employees. It is determined by actuarial calculations, for the service credits earned by the employees during the current period.
2. Prior (including past) service costs — the amount of expense, on an accrual basis, assigned for service credits earned by the employees of the entity *prior* to the inception of the pension plan. It includes initial past service cost plus prior service cost (as defined above). Thus, prior service cost exists when *(a)* an established company has instituted a pension plan which recognizes past service credits, and *(b)* when the pension plan or assumptions are changed which relate to past service credits.[5]

Each period these two costs are charged to *pension expense* which is reported on the income statement as an ordinary expense of the business.

The amount of pension expense recorded each period will be affected

---

[3] The distinction drawn here between past and prior service cost is one that has been made in authoritative accounting literature. The 1974 act refers to what accountants call *past service cost* as *initial past service cost* and to what they call *prior service cost* as *past service cost*.

[4] Ernest L. Hicks and René A. Miller, "Pension Cost" in Sidney Davidson, ed., *Handbook of Modern Accounting* (New York: McGraw-Hill Book Co., 1970), 25:17–22.

[5] Although the actuary normally computes the cost of a vesting provision separately, it usually is added to the normal and past service costs respectively for accounting purposes. Separate accounting for it would present no special problem.

by the extent to which the prior service costs have been funded, or are being funded during the current period.

*APB Opinion No. 8*, "Accounting for the Cost of Pension Plans" (December 1966), provides the current guidelines for accounting for pension plans. It was largely based on *Accounting Research Study No. 8*, "Accounting for the Cost of Pension Plans," published by the AICPA in 1965. The discussions to follow are consistent with *Opinion No. 8*.

In accounting for pension plans, all costs, including fund gains and losses, must be identified, recorded, and reported in a manner consistent with the long-term characteristics of a pension plan; on this point *APB Opinion No. 8* states:

> In the absence of convincing evidence that the company will reduce or discontinue the benefits called for in a pension plan, the cost of the plan should be accounted for on the assumption that the company will continue to provide such benefits. This assumption implies a long-term undertaking, the cost of which should be recognized annually whether or not funded. . . . The entire cost of benefit payments ultimately to be made should be charged against income subsequent to the adoption or amendment of a plan and that no portion of such cost should be charged directly against retained earnings.

In accounting for pension plans it is essential that a careful distinction be made between *pension costs* and *pension funding*. In the discussions and illustrations to follow, however, you will observe that they are intimately related.

In respect to *funding* a pension plan, the company must disburse cash for each of the two types of pension costs, viz:

1. For normal pension costs, the company disburses cash (to the fund trustee or funding agency) each period in an amount sufficient to satisfy the *normal* pension credits being earned currently by the employees.

2. For past service pension cost (a one-time cost), the company may elect to disburse cash at date of inception of the plan sufficient to satisfy this obligation, or, as is the usual case, to spread the payments over a selected number of periods in the future (say ten) from date of inception of the plan. The latter choice, obviously, is tantamount to paying a currently due debt on an installment basis which would give rise to an interest charge.

Past service pension costs represent a "catch-up" obligation and the question as to when it should be reflected in the accounts and the manner of reflecting it has been the concern of the accounting pronouncements mentioned above. Obviously, since it is a one-time and generally significant amount that relates to past service of the employees, this has caused it to be somewhat controversial. All accountants agree that it must be given recognition at date of inception of the plan; however, there is a difference of opinion as to whether past service cost should be reflected as (1) an adjustment to prior period earnings (retained earnings), (2) an extraordinary item on the income statement in the year of inception of the plan, or (3) spread over a selected number of years (as a current cost) in the future (after inception of the plan). The quotation above from *APB Opinion No. 8* clearly requires the latter. The details of the *Opinion* state, in effect, that past service cost must be amortized after date of inception of the plan as a part of total pension cost each year; the period of amortization is variable, being subject to the particular circumstances. The following quotation from *APB Opinion No. 8* applies:

> To be acceptable for determining cost for accounting purposes, an actuarial cost method should be rational and systematic and should be consistently applied so that it results in a reasonable measure of pension cost from year to year. Therefore, in applying an actuarial cost method that separately assigns a portion of cost as prior service cost, any amortization of such portion should be based on a rational and systematic plan and generally should result in reasonable stable annual amounts.

For analytical and problem-solving purposes it is sometimes helpful to diagram a pension plan along the following lines:

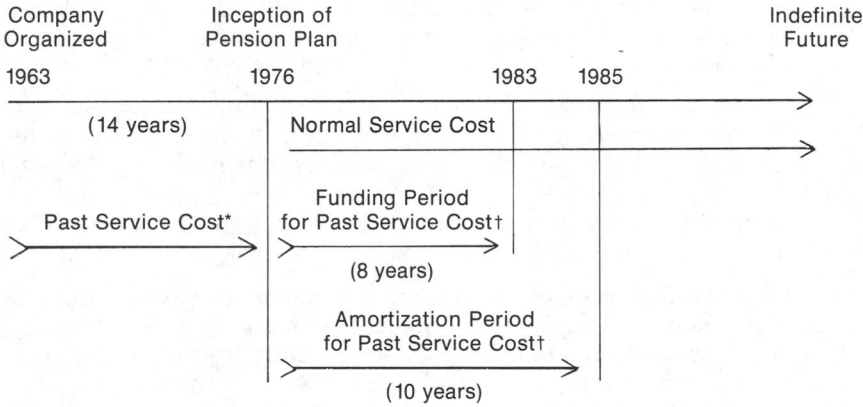

* $70,000 (present value)
† Must be on present value basis; see Case II pages 956–57.

The accounting entries for a pension plan are not complex; however computations of the amounts of (*a*) normal pension cost for the period, (*b*) prior service cost and its amortization, and (*c*) funding and its earnings, often are complex. *APB Opinion No. 8* specifies that actuarial determinations and the application of *present value* concepts are necessary both with respect to the amortization of prior pension cost and to the funding.

However, to introduce the entries we will first use a simple situation employing "straight-line" relationships and disregarding interest. Bear in mind that this is only for instructional purposes; present value applications will be introduced in the next illustration as required by the *Opinion.* Four separate cases will be presented.

Case A – A new company is formed and a pension plan is initiated immediately, hence there are no past service costs. The pension cost is fully funded each year.

To record the normal pension cost, and funding, appropriately determined at the end of the first two years:

|  | Year 1 | Year 2 |
|---|---|---|
| Pension expense | 10,000 | 12,000 |
| Cash (paid to trustee) | 10,000 | 12,000 |

No entry would be made for subsequent payments to retired employees; payment would be made to the retired employees by the funding agency (trustee).

Case B — An established company initiates a funded pension plan. Past service costs are appropriately determined to be $70,000; normal pension costs as in Case A.

To record the normal pension cost, amortization of past service costs over a ten-year future period, and a ten-year funding period for the past service costs.

|  | Year 1 | | Year 2 | |
|---|---|---|---|---|
| Pension expense | 17,000 | | 19,000 | |
| Cash (paid to trustee) | | 17,000 | | 19,000 |
|  | Cost | Funding | Cost | Funding |
| Computation: |  |  |  |  |
| Normal pension cost | $10,000 | $10,000 | $12,000 | $12,000 |
| Past pension cost amortization (ten years) | 7,000 | | 7,000 | |
| Annual funding (ten years) | | 7,000 | | 7,000 |
| Total | $17,000 | $17,000 | $19,000 | $19,000 |

Case C — Same as Case B except that the funding is over a 15-year period for the past service costs. Therefore, the funding each year is: $70,000 ÷ 15 years = $4,667.

|  | Year 1 | | Year 2 | |
|---|---|---|---|---|
| Pension expense | 17,000 | | 19,000 | |
| Liability — pension costs in excess |  |  |  |  |
| of funding | | 2,333 | | 2,333 |
| Cash (paid to trustee) | | 14,667 | | 16,667 |
|  | Cost | Funding | Cost | Funding |
| Computation: |  |  |  |  |
| Normal pension cost | $10,000 | $10,000 | $12,000 | $12,000 |
| Past pension cost amortization | 7,000 | | 7,000 | |
| Annual funding (15 years) | | 4,667 | | 4,667 |
| Total | $17,000 | $14,667 | $19,000 | $16,667 |

Case D — Same as Case B except that the funding is over an eight-year period for the past service costs. The funding each year is: $70,000 ÷ 8 years = $8,750.

|  | Year 1 | | Year 2 | |
|---|---|---|---|---|
| Pension expense | 17,000 | | 19,000 | |
| Deferred charge — funding in excess |  |  |  |  |
| of pension costs | 1,750 | | 1,750 | |
| Cash (paid to trustee) | | 18,750 | | 20,750 |

## Measuring the Amount of Pension Cost

The preceding illustrations and discussions emphasized that the critical aspects of accounting for pension plans are determination (estimation) of *(a)* the periodic pension cost for accounting purposes and *(b)* the funding required each period (in the case of funded plans). Accountants generally agree that pension costs should be accounted for on an accrual basis; however, there is not general agreement as to the precise nature of periodic pension costs (expense) in relationship to the future (prospective) benefits that will have to be paid. Clearly, interest earned on funds set aside many years before disbursement as benefits will significantly affect certain accounting values to be recorded. *Opinion No. 8*, as quoted above, clearly specifies that both "normal" and "past service" costs should be included in the periodic charge (pension cost). The board also stated in *Opinion No. 8* that the annual provision for pension cost should be based on an *accounting method* that uses an acceptable *"actuarial cost method"* (as defined below).[6]

The *actuarial cost methods* are approaches that have been developed primarily as funding techniques in that they provide the specific amounts for periodic payments to be made to the funding agency (funded plans) such as insurance companies or trustees (trust agreements). Since determination of the funding requirements explicitly requires estimation of the underlying pension costs for several of the actuarial cost methods they are also useful in determining pension costs for accounting purposes. Although these methods are alike in that they utilize present value concepts and rest on actuarial assumptions, they differ significantly in their approach and can produce quite different results for the same situation.

We noted above that, in accordance with *APB Opinion No. 8*, the *accounting method* utilized in accounting for pension plans must use an acceptable *actuarial cost method*. The *Opinion* states:

> (1) Accrued Benefit Cost Method (Unit Credit Method)—under the unit credit method, future service benefits are funded as they accrue—that is, each employee works out the service period involved. The past service cost is the present value at the plan's inception date of the units of future benefit credited to employees for service prior to inception of the plan. Thus, the annual contribution (and cost) comprises primarily *(a)* the normal cost and *(b)* the past service cost.

> (2) Projected Benefit Cost Methods—There are four methods in this group; entry age normal, individual level premium, aggregate, and attained age normal methods. The amount assigned (for funding) to the current year usually represents a level or constant amount that will provide for the estimated projected retirement benefits over the service lives of either the individual employees or the employee group, depending on the method selected. Pension cost projected under these methods tends to be stable or decline year by year, depending on the method selected.

---

[6] The minimum amortization period for past service costs is ten years; to minimize computations shorter periods are utilized in the chapter and in the exercises and problems. This simplification for instructional purposes does no violence to the concepts involved.

Although the APB, in *Opinion No. 8*, listed these methods as acceptable it recognized that other methods may be acceptable if they conform to the guidelines established in the *Opinion*. It is important to understand that the above methods are applied by the actuary that determines the appropriate funding requirements each year for the company. *They provide both the amounts needed by the accountant to record pension costs and funding requirements as illustrated below.*

## ILLUSTRATION OF RECORDING OF PENSION COSTS AND FUNDING

Now that we have identified the basic approaches utilized by actuaries in determining funding requirements, normal pension costs, and past service costs, the essential steps leading to development of the periodic accounting entries may be listed as follows:

1. Determination of *past service cost* by the actuary. This involves a complicated actuarial estimate derived by applying an acceptable actuarial method taking into account factors such as those listed on page 949. The actuary develops the present obligation (present value) of the cost of credits for services prior to the inception of the pension plan.

2. Determination of normal pension cost for the period by the actuary. This involves a complicated determination based upon service credits for the current year. There must be a separate determination for each year as it occurs. Obviously, the number of employees, salaries, and terms of the plan must underlie this actuarial determination for each period.

3. When there are past service costs, develop a present value amortization schedule for the period of amortization (at an appropriate interest rate). Develop a funding schedule for the funding period (at an appropriate interest rate). The two schedules may be combined in one table as shown in Exhibit 22-1.

4. Based upon *(a)* the normal pension cost for the period, *(b)* the amortization schedule, and *(c)* the funding schedule, develop the accounting entries for the period.

To illustrate, assume the AB Corporation, having been in operation for 14 years, decided in 1976 to adopt a funded pension plan for its employees. A trust agreement has been entered into with a bank (trustee) whereby the required payments to the fund will be made each year. The pension plan provides for vesting after 20 years of service by each eligible employee; it is noncontributory. An actuary was engaged on a consultation basis to develop the normal and past service costs and fund contributions each period. The management decided to utilize the "unit credit method." After an extended analysis, and based upon certain actuarial assumptions, the actuary developed the following:

1. Normal pension cost for 1976, $10,000.
2. Present value of the past service cost at date of inception of the pension plan (January 1, 1976), $70,000.

The management, upon recommendation of the actuary, decided to assume a 4% interest rate and to amortize the past service costs over a ten-year period.[7]

Three cases will be illustrated in respect to *funding* of the past service costs (funding payments to be made at the end of each year):

Case I. Past service costs to be funded over a ten-year period (same as the amortization period).

Case II. Past service costs to be funded over an eight-year period (two years less than the amortization period; see diagram on page 952).

Case III. Past service costs to be funded over a 12-year period (two years more than the amortization period).

*Case I.* The next step is to compute the periodic *amortization* and *funding* for the *past service costs*. In this case the amortization and funding periods are identical; therefore, the two schedules (periodic amounts) are the same; that is, we have two questions and they have identical responses:

1. Assuming a present obligation of $70,000 to be paid in equal installments over ten years, at 4%, what is the periodic payment?
2. Assuming a $70,000 value (cost) to be amortized over ten equal periods (years) on a present value basis, at 4%, what is the periodic amortization?

*Computation:*
Periodic Funding Payment
(and amortization) = $70,000 ÷ Present Value of Annuity of 1 for
                            Ten Rents at 4% (Table 6–4)
            = $70,000 ÷ 8.11090
            = $  8,630.37

Indicated entries for the pension costs and funding at year-end:

1976:

| Pension expense (normal) | 10,000.00 | |
| Pension expense (amortization of past service cost)* ... | 8,630.37 | |
| Cash (paid to trustee) | | 18,630.37 |

1977 (assuming normal pension cost of $12,000):

| Pension expense (normal) | 12,000.00 | |
| Pension expense (amortization of past service cost)* ... | 8,630.37 | |
| Cash (paid to trustee) | | 20,630.37 |

* Observe that these amounts implicitly include an interest factor that decreases each period.

Clearly, after the tenth year the past service costs, and the related funding, would drop out and only the normal costs and normal funding would be recognized thereafter.

*Case II.* This case introduces another complexity; that is, the amor-

---

[7] This interest rate is net of all administration costs and charges by the trustee; hence, it represents a net return.

tization period is ten years whereas the funding period is eight years. Clearly, in this situation we must compute the amortization schedule on one basis and the funding schedule on another basis. Since funds will be disbursed at a greater rate than the cost accrual we also must adjust the *amortization* schedule for the interest differential. A special table is essential to this determination (Exhibit 22–1).

In respect to the distinctive features of Exhibit 22–1 you should observe the following:

1. This table relates only to past service costs (not normal pension costs).
2. The periodic amortization of past service costs (column [a]) is *reduced* by the interest on the funding paid in *excess* of the periodic amortization; this causes a decreasing periodic amortization (column [c]).
3. The periodic funding payments cease at the end of Year 8 (1983).
4. Payments to the fund are constant each year.
5. The amortization of past service costs terminates at the end of the tenth year (1985).

**EXHIBIT 22–1**
**Schedule of Past Service Pension Costs and Related Funding†**
**(amortization period ten years; funding period eight years)**

| Year | Amortization of Past Service Cost— 10 Years | | | Funding— 8 Years | Balance Sheet— Deferred Charge | |
|---|---|---|---|---|---|---|
| | 10-Year Accrual Factor (a) | Reduction for Interest (b) | Past Pension Cost (Debit) (c) | Cash (Credit) (d) | Debit/ Credit* (e) | Account Balance (f) |
| 1976 ............ | $8,630.37‡ | | $ 8,630.37 | $10,396.95§ | $1,766.58 | $ 1,766.58 |
| 1977 ............ | 8,630.37 | $ 70.66 | 8,559.71 | 10,396.95 | 1,837.24 | 3,603.82 |
| 1978 ............ | 8,630.37 | 144.15 | 8,486.22 | 10,396.95 | 1,910.73 | 5,514.55 |
| 1979 ............ | 8,630.37 | 220.58 | 8,409.79 | 10,396.95 | 1,987.16 | 7,501.71 |
| 1980 ............ | 8,630.37 | 300.07 | 8,330.30 | 10,396.95 | 2,066.65 | 9,568.36 |
| 1981 ............ | 8,630.37 | 382.73 | 8,247.64 | 10,396.95 | 2,149.31 | 11,717.67 |
| 1982 ............ | 8,630.37 | 468.71 | 8,161.66 | 10,396.95 | 2,235.29 | 13,952.96 |
| 1983 ............ | 8,630.37 | 558.12 | 8,072.25 | 10,396.95 | 2,324.70 | 16,277.66 |
| 1984 ............ | 8,630.37 | 651.11 | 7,979.26 | -0- | 7,979.26* | 8,298.40 |
| 1985 ............ | 8,630.37 | 331.97 | 8,298.40 | -0- | 8,298.40* | -0- |
| | | | $83,175.60 | $83,175.60 | | |

† It may be observed that this table assumes (1) amortization at end of the period (year), (2) the present value of the past service cost is at the beginning of the period, and (3) the funding payments are made at the end of each period. Other viable assumptions are possible.

‡ Amortization: (10 periods, @ 4%):
  Periodic amortization = $70,000 ÷ 8.1109 (Table 6–4)
                = $ 8,630.37 to column (a)

§ Funding: (8 periods, @ 4%):
  Periodic payment = $70,000 ÷ 6.73274 (Table 6–4)
              = $10,396.95 to column (d)

(a) Independently computed above.
(b) 4% of the preceding balance of column (f).
(c) Column (a) less column (b).
(d) Independently computed above.
(e) Column (d) minus column (c).
(f) Preceding balance plus (or minus) column (e).

6. Total past pension costs (column [c]) and total fund payments (column [d]) are equal ($83,175.60) although their timing is different.
7. The deferred charge (column [f]) to be reported on the balance sheet is due to the fact that funding payments exceed amortization; however, at the end of the amortization period the deferred charge balance is zero.
8. Total funding payments are comprised of two elements; principal (past service cost), $70,000, and interest (on unpaid principal), $13,175.60.
9. Accounting entries are indicated by the table but do not include normal pension costs.

Entries for pension costs and funding at year-end:

1976:

| | | |
|---|---:|---:|
| Pension expense (normal) | 10,000.00 | |
| Pension expense (amortization of past service cost) ... | 8,630.37 | |
| Deferred charge—funding in excess of pension costs... | 1,766.58 | |
| Cash (paid to trustee) | | 20,396.95 |

1977:

| | | |
|---|---:|---:|
| Pension expense (normal) | 12,000.00 | |
| Pension expense (amortization of past service cost) ... | 8,559.71 | |
| Deferred charge—funding in excess of pension costs... | 1,837.24 | |
| Cash (paid to trustee) | | 22,396.95 |

*Case III.* This is the same as Case II except that the amortization period for past service costs is two years less than the funding period. As a consequence, the Schedule of Past Pension Costs and Related Funding (as shown in Exhibit 22–1) obviously must be changed in two respects: (1) in the amortization portion the interest differential must be added (rather than deducted), and (2) in the balance sheet column a *liability* (rather than a deferred charge) must be reflected. Exhibit 22–2 reflects these differences.

The entries indicated in Exhibit 22–2 are:

1976:

| | | |
|---|---:|---:|
| Pension expense (normal) | 10,000.00 | |
| Pension expense (amortization of past service cost) ... | 8,630.37 | |
| Liability—pension cost in excess of funding | | 1,171.72 |
| Cash (paid to trustee) | | 17,458.65 |

1977:

| | | |
|---|---:|---:|
| Pension expense (normal) | 12,000.00 | |
| Pension expense (amortization of past service cost) ... | 8,677.24 | |
| Liability—pension cost in excess of funding | | 1,218.59 |
| Cash (paid to trustee) | | 19,458.65 |

For instructional purposes we have recorded normal and past service costs separately. In practice these two amounts usually are recorded in one expense account since there is no requirement that they be separately recorded and reported. Pension expense is classified as an ordinary business expense.

**EXHIBIT 22–2**
**Schedule of Past Service Pension Costs and Related Funding**
**(amortization period 10 years; funding period 12 years)**

| Year | Amortization of Past Service Cost— 10 Years | | | Funding— 12 Years | Balance Sheet— Liability | |
| | 10-Year Accrual Factor (a) | Addition for Interest (b) | Past Pension Cost (Debit) (c) | Cash (Credit) (d) | Credit Debit* (e) | Account Balance (f) |
|---|---|---|---|---|---|---|
| 1976 ............ | $8,630.37† | | $ 8,630.37 | $ 7,458.65‡ | $1,171.72 | $1,171.72 |
| 1977 ............ | 8,630.37 | $ 46.87 | 8,677.24 | 7,458.65 | 1,218.59 | 2,390.31 |
| 1978 ............ | 8,630.37 | 95.61 | 8,725.98 | 7,458.65 | 1,267.33 | 3,657.64 |
| 1979 ............ | 8,630.37 | 146.31 | 8,776.68 | 7,458.65 | 1,318.03 | 4,975.67 |
| 1980 ............ | 8,630.37 | 199.03 | 8,829.40 | 7,458.65 | 1,370.75 | 6,346.42 |
| 1981 ............ | 8,630.37 | 253.86 | 8,884.23 | 7,458.65 | 1,425.58 | 7,772.00 |
| 1982 ............ | 8,630.37 | 310.88 | 8,941.25 | 7,458.65 | 1,482.60 | 9,254.60 |
| 1983 ............ | 8,630.37 | 370.18 | 9,000.55 | 7,458.65 | 1,541.90 | 10,796.50 |
| 1984 ............ | 8,630.37 | 431.86 | 9,062.23 | 7,458.65 | 1,603.58 | 12,400.08 |
| 1985 ............ | 8,630.37 | 496.00 | 9,126.37 | 7,458.65 | 1,667.72 | 14,067.80 |
| 1986 ............ | -0- | 562.71 | 562.71 | 7,458.65 | 6,895.94* | 7,171.86 |
| 1987 ............ | -0- | 286.79 | 286.79 | 7,458.65 | 7,171.86* | -0- |
| | | | $89,503.80 | $89,503.80 | | |

† Periodic amortization = $70,000 ÷ 8.11090 (Table 6–4)
               = $ 8,630.37 To column (a)

‡ Periodic funding = $70,000 ÷ 9.38507 (Table 6–4)
              = $ 7,458.65 To column (d)

(a) Independently computed above.
(b) 4% of the preceding balance of column (f).
(c) Column (a) plus column (b).
(d) Independently computed above.
(e) Column (c) less column (d).
(f) Preceding balance plus (or minus) column (e).

## MAXIMUM AND MINIMUM PROVISION FOR PAST SERVICE COSTS

Recall from the prior discussion and illustrations that the periodic debit to pension expense is comprised of (a) normal pension cost plus (b) an amortized amount of prior pension cost. Recall also that the funding provisions affect the determination of the amount of past service cost amortized for the period (because of the interest effect); the accounting does not affect the funding provision.

APB *Opinion No. 8* specifies a maximum and minimum provision for pension expense; this means that the debit to pension expense for the period should not be less than the minimum nor more than the maximum. The maximum and minimum for pension expense is different only because of the amortization of prior service cost and the interest effect of any unfunded past service cost. The maximum and minimum provisions specified in *Opinion No. 8* essentially read as follows:

Minimum. The provision for pension cost should not be less than the *total* of:

1. Normal cost.
2. An amount equivalent to interest on any unfunded prior service cost.
3. If indicated – a provision for vested benefits.

Maximum. The annual provision for pension cost should not be greater than the *total* of:

1. Normal cost.
2. Ten percent of the past service cost (i.e., at least a ten year amortization period).
3. Ten percent of the amounts of any increases or decreases in prior service costs arising on amendments of the plan (until fully amortized); in effect, a ten-year minimum period.
4. Interest equivalents on the difference between provisions (pension costs) and amounts funded.

The maximum provision includes normal service cost for the period plus the amortization of past service cost including the effect of interest on any unfunded past service cost. In contrast, the minimum provision includes normal service cost for the period plus interest only on any unfunded prior service cost. Clearly, the minimum provision is very difficult to justify.

The accounting illustrated above, Exhibits 22–1 and 22–2, reflect *maximum* pension expense since amortization of past service cost and the interest effect is included. Application of the maximum and minimum provisions for these two situations is shown in Exhibit 22–3 (for the first two years only).

Significantly, the maximum and minimum provisions are no longer important since the 1974 Pension Reform Act, for all practical purposes, requires that the maximum amount be used for pension expense.[8]

**EXHIBIT 22–3**
**Application of Maximum and Minimum Limits on Pension Expense**

| | Normal Cost (a) | Ten Percent Unamortized Prior Service Cost* (b) | Vested Cost (c) | Interest on Unfunded Past Service† (d) | Total Pension Expense Maximum (a + b + c) | Minimum (a + c + d) |
|---|---|---|---|---|---|---|
| Exhibit 22–1: | | | | | | |
| 1976 ............ | $10,000 | $8,630.37 | -0- | $ -0- | $18,630.37 | $10,000.00 |
| 1977 ............ | 12,000 | 8,559.71 | -0- | 70.66 | 20,559.71 | 12,070.66 |
| Exhibit 22–2: | | | | | | |
| 1976 ............ | 10,000 | 8,630.37 | -0- | -0- | 18,630.37 | 10,000.00 |
| 1977 ............ | 12,000 | 8,677.24 | -0- | 46.87 | 20,677.24 | 12,046.87 |

\* From Column *(c)* on prior exhibits.
† From Column *(b)* on prior exhibits; assuming funding.

---

[8] As this is being written the FASB has revision of *Opinion No. 8* on its agenda. It will undoubtedly be made to conform to the requirements of the new act in all respects.

## EXPERIENCE GAINS AND LOSSES

Recall that the entries presented in Cases I, II, and III presumed that the interest rate (4% net) materialized and that the determinations of past service cost would not change over time. Obviously, actuaries must deal with many uncertainties in making such estimates. Regardless of the degree of competence, it is likely that some of these determinations will subsequently have to be revised. The effects on actuarially calculated pension costs of (a) changes in the underlying assumptions, and (b) deviations between planned and actual results have, in the past, been called actuarial gains and losses. The Pension Reform Act of 1974 refers to such deviations as *experience gains and losses* — terminology which is considerably more descriptive. Adjustments for experience gains and losses may be needed annually to reflect actual experience or from time to time to reflect a revision in the underlying assumptions. There are two related questions: (a) determination of the experience gain or loss, and (b) timing of its recognition in the accounts. In practice three methods are to be found: immediate recognition, spreading on a prospective basis, and averaging. On this point *Opinion No. 8* states:

> Actuarial gains and losses, including realized investment gains and losses, should be given effect in the provision for pension cost in a consistent manner that reflects the long-range nature of pension cost. . . . Accordingly, (with certain exceptions) actuarial gains and losses should be spread over the current year and future years or recognized on the basis of an average.

The Pension Reform Act of 1974 provides that under the required funding rules, *experience losses* are to be amortized over a period of not more than 15 years from the time that an experience deficiency is determined. Similarly, *experience gains* are to be amortized over a period of up to 15 years. The losses would increase amounts employers must contribute to meet funding requirements, while the gains would decrease such amounts.

## DISCLOSURE

According to *APB Opinion No. 8*, the following disclosures should be made in financial statements or their notes:

1. A statement that such plans exist, identifying or describing the employee groups covered.
2. A statement of the company's accounting and funding policies.
3. The provision for pension cost for the period.
4. The excess, if any, of the actuarially computed value of vested benefits over the total of the pension fund and any balance sheet pension accruals, less any pension repayments or deferred charges.
5. Nature and effect of significant matters affecting comparability for all periods presented, such as changes in accounting methods (actuarial cost method, amortization of past and prior service cost, treatment of actuarial gains and losses, etc.), changes in circumstances (actuarial assumptions, etc.), or adoption or amendment of a plan.

## PENSION PLAN DISCLOSURE REQUIREMENTS OF 1974 ACT

The 1974 act has imposed disclosure requirements for pension plans which treat the plans as separate entities. Plan administrators must publish a comprehensive plan description and a summary plan description; the latter must be so written that participants can understand it. Both of these descriptions must be filed with the Secretary of Labor.

Plan administrators must publish annual reports on plans within 210 days after the close of the plan year in accordance with forms prescribed by the Secretary of Labor. These annual reports must contain:

1. Statements of the pension plan assets and liabilities.
2. Statements of changes in net assets available for plan benefits which shall include details of revenues and expenses and other changes aggregated by general source and application.
3. Schedules of investment assets.
4. Schedules of transactions involving known "parties in interest" (e.g., officer, fiduciary, or counsel of the plan).
5. Schedules of loans in default or uncollectible and other loans exceeding 3% of the value of the plan as well as loans to "parties in interest."
6. When fund assets are held in a common trust or separate trust by a bank or similar institution, a statement of the assets and liabilities of that trustee must be filed.
7. Schedules of each transaction involving amounts exceeding 3% of the value of the fund.
8. Detailed statements of salaries, fees, and commissions charged to the plan.
9. Identity of each plan fiduciary and an indication of his or her relationship to the employer or employee organization and any position held with "parties in interest."
10. Number of employees covered by the plan.
11. An actuarial report. (A full actuarial report is required only every third plan year.)
12. Information concerning items 8, 9, and 10 plus an explanation of any changes of trustee, actuary, independent accountant, administrator, investment manager, custodian, or insurance carrier.
13. If any benefits are purchased from an insurance carrier, a statement from the carrier enumerating premiums and benefits paid, administrative expense charged, commissions, and amount held to pay future benefits.

The act requires plan administrators to engage qualified independent public accountants to conduct examinations of plan financial statements of sufficient scope as the accountants deem necessary to express an opinion on the items enumerated above.[9]

---

[9] Under certain circumstances, item 6 is an exception.

## FUTURE DEVELOPMENTS

Further developments in the realm of pension accounting and reporting can be expected as the FASB and their task forces progress with studies which have been launched, as experience is gained under the 1974 act, and as federal administrators issue detailed regulations for implementation of the act. Meanwhile, the FASB has issued one interpretation as an outgrowth of the 1974 act.[10] Some principal provisions of that interpretation are summarized below.

1. No change in the minimum and maximum limits for the annual provision for pension cost set forth in *APB Opinion No. 8* is required as a result of the 1974 act.[11]

2. If, prior to the date a plan becomes subject to the act's participation, vesting, and funding requirements, it appears likely that compliance will have a significant effect in the future on the entity's (a) periodic pension expense, (b) periodic pension funding, or (c) unfunded vested benefits, this fact and an estimate of the effect shall be disclosed in notes to the financial statements.

3. With but two exceptions, the FASB does not believe that the act creates legal obligations for unfunded pension costs that warrant accounting recognition as a liability. (a) There are minimum funding requirements (unless a waiver is obtained); in the absence of a waiver, the amount currently required to be funded shall be recognized as a liability by a charge to pension expense for the period, by a deferred charge, or by a combination of the two as appropriate. (b) In the event of termination of a pension plan, the act imposes a liability on an enterprise. In the face of strong evidence a plan will be terminated and that the liability on termination will exceed fund assets and related prior accruals, the excess liability shall be accrued. Where the amount cannot be reasonably determined, disclosure of the circumstances and an estimate of the possible range of the liability shall appear in notes to the financial statements.[12]

---

[10] FASB *Interpretation No. 3*, "An Interpretation of APB Opinion No. 8" (High Ridge, Conn.: FASB, 1974).

[11] The interpretation points out, however, that *APB Opinion No. 8* requires that "the entire cost of benefit payments ultimate to be made should be charged against income subsequent to the adoption or amendment of a plan." Consistent with that requirement, and within the minimum and maximum provisions of the *Opinion*, any change in pension cost resulting from compliance with the act shall enter into determination of periodic provisions for pension expense *subsequent* to the date a plan becomes subject to the act's participation, vesting, and funding requirements. That date will be determined either by dates prescribed by the act or by an election of earlier compliance with its provisions.

[12] "A Flood of Pension Plan Terminations," *Business Week*, September 1, 1975 (p. 42). Although the legislation is still quite new and there has been very little time for companies to decide whether or not to terminate their pension plans under the option provided in the 1974 act, early experience indicates a very brisk rate of terminations. In its first five months of existence the newly created federal Pension Benefit Guaranty Corporation received notifications of termination of 4,000 plans—four times as many as had been expected. Most terminated plans have been small and relatively new; most of the assets that have come in to PBGC have come from large plans that have failed.

## QUESTIONS

1. What does the acronym ERISA stand for? By what other identification is the same thing known? Thus far has accounting been greatly affected by it?

2. What is vesting?

3. In connection with pension plans, explain the meaning of (a) normal service cost, (b) past service cost, and (c) prior service cost.

4. Under *APB Opinion No. 8* certain guidelines as to the *minimum* and *maximum* annual provision for pension cost are set out. What are they?

5. In respect to pension plans, what are actuarial gains and losses? By what term are these referred to in the 1974 act?

6. Under *APB Opinion No. 8* guidelines for pension plan accounting, what disclosures should be made in financial statements or their related notes?

7. If accounting charges for past service costs exceed funding payments, what kind of account arises and how should it be reported in financial statements? Suppose the reverse is true, that is, payments exceed charges, what then?

8. What statements and schedules of a financial character are required to be included in the annual report of a pension plan filed annually with the Secretary of Labor?

9. What are the principal provisions of the FASB *Interpretation* issued in connection with pension plan accounting?


## EXERCISES

### Exercise 22–1

Welzee Company initiated a pension plan on a funded, noncontributory basis several years after the company began operations. Its consulting actuary determined that at inception of the plan the past service cost amounted to $338,721.

*Required:*

1. Using a 7% interest table, prepare a schedule that reflects amortization of the past service cost over a four-year period and funding over a three-year period. Round to nearest dollar.
2. Give journal entries relating to the pension plan covering its first two years of operations based upon funding in accordance with the table developed in compliance with Requirement 1 and on the assumptions that the plan year and the fiscal year coincided and normal costs for the first two years were Year 1, $50,000, and Year 2, $53,000.


### Exercise 22–2

The independent actuary engaged by Martin Company determined that should it adopt the type of pension plan contemplated, its unfunded past service cost would amount to $331,213.

*Required:*

1. Prepare a schedule that reflects amortization of the past service cost over a four-year period and funding over a six-year period based on 8% annual interest rates. Round to nearest dollar.
2. Assuming the actuary determined the normal pension cost to be Year 1, $120,000, and Year 2, $132,000, journalize pension expense for both years.
3. Indicate what would be reported on Martin Company's income statement and balance sheet for each of the two years.

## Exercise 22-3

Cisco Corporation initiated a funded pension plan and gave employees credit for past service. The actuary estimated the past service cost at inception at $50,000.

*Required:*

(Round calculations to the nearest dollar.)

1. Using a 5% annual rate calculate the periodic amortization factor and periodic funding payment assuming:
    Case A—Funding and amortization are over three years.
    Case B—Funding is over four years; amortization is over three.
    Case C—Funding is over two years; amortization is over three.
2. Prepare an amortization and funding schedule for the past service cost for Case C.
3. Give entries for four years for Case C if the normal costs for the years are respectively: $12,000, $14,000, $18,000, and $22,000.
4. Indicate the amounts that would be reflected on the income statement and the balance sheet under Case C for the four years.

## Exercise 22-4

Check the best answer in each of the following and explain the basis for your choice.

1. When pension plan costs are presented in a statement of income and retained earnings, past and current service costs—
    a. Must be shown separately in computing income before extraordinary items.
    b. Must be separated so that past service costs can be treated as a prior period adjustment.
    c. Must be separated so that past service costs can be treated as an extraordinary item.
    d. May be either combined or shown separately in computing income before extraordinary items.
2. In accounting for a pension plan any difference between the pension cost charged to expense and payments into the found should be reported as—
    a. An offset to the liability for past service cost.
    b. Accrued or prepaid pension cost.
    c. An operating expense in this period.
    d. An accrued actuarial liability.
3. A company in accounting properly for pension cost—
    a. Allocates total pension costs systematically and rationally.

b. Records fluctuating gains and losses on pension fund investments as they occur.

c. Gives recognition to all pension costs for which legal liability exists.

d. Establishes a positive relationship between contributions to the fund and the recorded provision.

4. Benefits under a pension plan that are not contingent upon an employee's continuing service are—

a. Granted under a plan of defined contribution.

b. Based upon terminal funding.

c. Actuarially unsound.

d. Vested.

5. When an established company adopts a pension plan, the costs related to past services of employees should be charged to—

a. Operations of current and future periods.

b. Operations of prior periods.

c. Operations of the current period.

d. Retained earnings.

(AICPA adapted)

### Exercise 22–5

Set forth below is an amortization table of a company which adopted a pension plan at a time when its past service cost amounted to $1,000,000. This past service cost is being funded in a lesser number of years than it is being amortized.

| (a) | (b) | (c) | (d) | (e) | (f) | (g) |
|---|---|---|---|---|---|---|
| 1...... | $123,290.94 | — | $123,290.94 | $148,527.83 | $ 25,236.89 | $ 25,236.89 |
| 2...... | 123,290.94 | $1,009.48 | 122,281.46 | 148,527.83 | 26,246.37 | 51,483.26 |
| 3...... | 123,290.94 | 2,059.33 | 121,231.61 | 148,527.83 | 27,296.22 | 78,779.48 |
| 4...... | 123,290.94 | 3,151.18 | 120,139.76 | 148,527.83 | 28,338.07 | 107,167.55 |
| 5...... | 123,290.94 | 4,286.70 | 119,004.24 | 148,527.83 | 29,523.59 | 136,691.14 |
| 6...... | 123,290.94 | 5,467.65 | 117,823.29 | 148,527.83 | 30,704.54 | 167,395.68 |
| 7...... | 123,290.94 | 6,695.83 | 116,595.11 | 148,527.83 | 31,932.72 | 199,328.40 |
| 8...... | 123,290.94 | 7,973.14 | 115,317.80 | 148,527.83 | 33,210.03 | 232,538.43 |
| 9...... | 123,290.94 | 9,301.54 | 113,989.40 | — | 113,989.40* | 118,549.03 |
| 10...... | 123,290.94 | 4,741.91* | 118,549.03 | — | 118,549.03* | — |

* Reflects rounding.

*Required:*

1. What interest rate was assumed in making the amortization and funding calculations? Show how you arrived at your results.

2. Supply appropriate titles for columns (a) through (g) of the table.

3. If the normal costs in Years 1, 2, and 3 were respectively $90,000, $100,000, and $110,000, what were (a) total disbursements for pensions for these three years, and (b) total pension plan expenses for these three years?

4. What balance sheet amounts would be shown by this company in respect to its pension plan at the end of Years 7, 8, and 9 and what is the nature of the account under which the amounts would be reported?

## PROBLEMS

### Problem 22–1

After having been in business a number of years without a pension plan, Dean Corporation adopted a funded, noncontributory plan. For simplicity, the number of periods dealt with will be limited and the first year of the pension plan will be designated as 19A. Amounts will be kept small. Past service costs as of January 1, 19A, amounted to $60,000. Normal costs for 19A were $9,000; in the four succeeding years they were $9,500, $10,000, $10,400, and $10,900.

*Required:*

1. Using 8% interest rate and assuming year-end funding, prepare schedules of amortization and funding for each of the following sets of assumptions as to years over which amortization and funding of past service is to occur:

|  | Periods | |
|---|---|---|
|  | Amortization | Funding |
| Case A............... | 4 | 4 |
| Case B............... | 3 | 4 |
| Case C............... | 4 | 3 |
| Case D............... | 4 | 1 |

2. Give journal entries related to pension costs and cash payments for 19A, 19D, and 19E (round all computations to nearest dollar). Use present value, not straight line.
3. Indicate amounts that would be reported on the income statement and balance sheet for 19A, 19D, and 19E concerning the pension plan.

### Problem 22–2

Mannix Company initiated a funded, noncontributory pension plan effective January 1, 1976. This was several years after the company began operations so there was an initial past service cost of $30,000. Because the company has an excess of investable cash it was decided to fund the past service cost fully as of year-end, 1976, and to amortize the cost over a four-year term. In connection with the latter, a 7% rate will be assumed. Payments will be made to an independent pension fund trustee.

*Required:*

1. Prepare a schedule of amortization and funding of the past service cost. Round all amounts to the nearest dollar.
2. Assuming that normal costs are as follows: 1976, $9,000; 1977, $9,400; 1978, $10,000; and 1979, $10,500, give journal entries related to pension costs and cash payments for each year.
3. Suppose the first eligible employee retired late in 1978 and was paid first benefits amounting to $500 late that year. Give any entries indicated. Explain.
4. Indicate amounts that would be reported on the income statement and balance sheet for 1976, 1977, and 1978.

# Schedule of Amortization of Past Service Costs and Related Funding

| Year | Amortization Past Pension Cost – 10 Years | | | 12-Year Funding | Balance Sheet – Liability | |
| --- | --- | --- | --- | --- | --- | --- |
| | 10-Year Accrual Factor | Addition for 6% Interest | Past Pension Cost (a) + (b) | | Credit Debit* | Account Balance |
| 1 | $135,867.96(a) | $   — | $135,867.96(b) | $119,277.03 | $ 16,590.93(c) | $ 16,590.93 |
| 2 | 135,867.96 | $    995.46(d) | 136,863.42 | 119,277.03 | 17,586.39 | 34,177.32 |
| 3 | 135,867.96 | 2,050.64 | 137,918.60 | 119,277.03 | 18,641.57 | 52,818.89 |
| 4 | 135,867.96 | 3,169.13 | 139,037.09 | 119,277.03 | 19,760.06 | 72,578.95 |
| 5 | 135,867.96 | 4,354.74 | 140,222.70 | 119,277.03 | 20,945.67 | 93,524.62 |
| 6 | 135,867.96 | 5,611.48 | 141,479.44 | 119,277.03 | 22,202.41 | 115,727.03 |
| 7 | 135,867.96 | 6,943.62 | 142,811.58 | 119,277.03 | 23,534.55 | 139,261.58 |
| 8 | 135,867.96 | 8,355.69 | 144,223.65 | 119,277.03 | 24,946.62 | 164,208.20 |
| 9 | 135,867.96 | 9,852.49 | 145,720.45 | 119,277.03 | 26,443.42 | 190,651.62 |
| 10 | 135,867.96 | 11,439.10 | 147,307.06 | 119,277.03 | 28,030.03 | 218,681.65 |
| 11 | — | 13,120.90 | 13,120.90 | 119,277.03 | 106,156.13* | 112,525.52 |
| 12 | — | 6,751.51† | 6,751.51 | 119,277.03 | 112,525.52* | — |

† Reflects rounding of 2 cents.

Computations:

(a) Amortization (10 years, 6%):
$1,000.000 ÷ 7.3600871 = $135,867.96.

(b) Funding (12 years, 6%):
$1,000.000 ÷ 8.3838439 = $119,277.03.

(c) $135,867.96 − $119,277.03 = $16,590.93.

(d) $16,590.93 × 6% = $995.46.

**Problem 22–3**

Set forth opposite is an amortization and funding table for a company whose past service cost was determined to be $1,000,000 when its pension plan was adopted. If the company were to amortize this amount of past service cost over a 10-year period and to fund it over a 12-year period, using a 6% rate the table would apply.

*Required:*

(Make all computations and entries rounded to nearest dollar.)

1. If the company's normal cost for pensions for Years 1 and 2 respectively amounted to $140,000 and $148,000 and the management had decided initially to postpone funding of the past service cost rather than to implement, what is the *minimum* pension expense the company could report under provisions of *APB Opinion No. 8*? Show computations. (Assume there are no vesting requirements.)
2. If the company instead decided to implement the funding and amortization as reflected on the foregoing table, what is the *maximum* pension expense the company could report for Years 1 and 2 if normal costs are as given in Requirement 1?
3. Again assume the normal costs for the first two years are the same as in Requirement 1. In this instance the company management decides to amortize the $100,000 past service cost over ten years but to fund it in eight years and to use a 5% annual rate in connection with past service cost. Calculate the ten-year accrual factor and the eight-year funding factor; prepare a partial table (through the first two years) and indicate the *maximum* allowed pension expense under provisions of *APB Opinion No. 8*.

**Problem 22–4**

The TP Company decided to initiate a funded pension plan and to give employees credit for prior employment. The plan is noncontributory, and the benefits vest at age 60. The actuary estimated the past service cost at date of inception of the plan to be $50,000. To keep the problem short assume the past service cost is to be amortized over three years and that the interest rate is 5%.

*Required:*

1. Compute the periodic amortization *factor* and the periodic funding payment assuming:

   Case A – Funding is over a three-year period.
   Case B – Funding is over a four-year period.
   Case C – Funding is over a two-year period.

2. Prepare an amortization and funding schedule for the past service cost for Case C.
3. Give entries for the four years for Case C assuming the actuarially determined normal pension costs to be: Year 1, $15,000; Year 2, $18,000; Year 3, $20,000; and Year 4, $24,000.
4. Indicate the amounts that would be reflected on the income statement and the balance sheet under Case C for the four years.

## Problem 22–5

Simpson Company was organized in 1964. The decision was made to initiate a funded, noncontributory pension plan starting January 1, 1976. The First Security Bank will be the funding agency. The actuary determined the past service cost at date of inception of the plan (as of January 1, 1976) to be $30,000 and the normal pension cost for the year 1976 to be $10,000. Since the company had an excess of ready cash, it was decided to completely fund the past pension cost at the end of 1976. Past pension cost will be amortized over four years; a 6% rate of interest will be assumed.

*Required:*

1. Prepare a schedule of funding and amortization of past service costs.
2. Give all entries indicated for 1976.
3. Give entries for 1977–81 assuming the following normal pension costs: 1977, $11,000; 1978, $12,000; 1979, $13,000; 1980, $14,000; and 1981, $15,000.
4. Assume a long-time employee retired during 1981 and was paid a first monthly pension benefit of $300. Give any entries indicated. Explain.
5. What would be reported on the income statement and balance sheet for each period 1976–81 inclusive?

## Problem 22–6

Rake Corporation has been in business for approximately 25 years. Recently the management made a decision to institute a funded, noncontributory pension plan. A trustee has been selected to receive and disburse the pension funds in accordance with the plan. To shorten this problem the amounts are relatively small and the number of periods limited. Assume that the program started on January 1, 1976, and that estimates through 1980 made by the actuary were:

1. Past service costs at the beginning of 1976, $60,000.
2. Normal service costs: 1976, $8,000; 1977, $8,400; 1978, $9,000; 1979, $9,500; and 1980, $10,200.
3. Interest rate, 5%.

In respect to amortization of past service costs and their funding there are four separate cases:

| | Periods | |
|---|---|---|
| Case | Amortization | Funding |
| A | 4 | 4 |
| B | 3 | 4 |
| C | 4 | 3 |
| D | 4 | 1 |

*Required:*

For each case, show computations.

1. Schedule of amortization and funding (assume funding at year-end).
2. Journal entries for years 1976, 1979, and 1980.
3. Balances to be reported on financial statements for 1976, 1979, and 1980.

**Problem 22–7**

Sims Distributing Company began operations a number of years ago. Recently its management decided to add pensions as a fringe benefit for the employees. The actuary employed determined that as of the year the pension plan was to begin, past service costs amounted to $800,000. A decision was made to amortize these costs over eight years and to fund them over six years. Star Trust Company will serve as trustee of the noncontributory pension trust; a 7% interest rate has been assumed.

*Required:*

1. Prepare a schedule of amortization and funding for the past service cost. Round all calculations to the nearest dollar.
2. Give journal entries for Years 1, 3, 6, and 7 if normal costs paid for these years are, respectively, $80,000, $85,000, $95,000, and $110,000, and other payments are in accordance with the table developed in Requirement 1.
3. Give any necessary entry to record payments in Year 6 to long-time employee Smith who retired in that year and who drew pension benefits that year amounting to $1,300. Explain.
4. What would be reflected on the income statement and balance sheet of Sims Distributing Company for Years 1, 3, 6, and 7 in respect to its pension plan?

**Problem 22–8**

The Tudor Corporation adopted a qualified profit-sharing plan for its employees on January 1, 1966. The trust agreement contains the following provisions:

1. For each year in which the amount of eligible net earnings equals or exceeds the profit-sharing base for that year, the corporation shall remit to the trustee an amount equal to 5% of the profit-sharing base for the year plus 10% of any eligible net earnings for the year in excess of the base.
2. "Eligible net earnings" with respect to any year shall be net income for the year after deducting the payment to the trustee and the provision for federal income taxes.
3. An employee shall be eligible to participate in the plan on January 1 of the year following the completion of one full year of employment.
4. The annual payment to the trustee shall be allocated to the interests of the participants according to the following unit system:
   a. For each full calendar year of employment under the plan each participant shall be entitled to eight units.
   b. For each $10 of average weekly pay earned in the current year, based on a 52-week year, the employee shall be entitled to one unit.
5. Ten percent of a participant's total interest is vested for each full year of his participation in the plan.
6. Forfeitures and investment income will be distributed to the remaining participants at the end of each year in proportion to their interests in the plan at the beginning of the year.

In the course of your audit of Tudor Corporation as of December 31, 1975, you find that the trustee has submitted the trial balance below but that the corporation's 1975 contribution to the trust has not been computed and allocated to the participants.

PROFIT-SHARING TRUST
Trial Balance
December 31, 1975

|  | Debit | Credit |
|---|---|---|
| Cash ............................................... | $ 500 | |
| Investment, 1/1/75 .......................... | 26,000 | |
| R. Johnson's interest, 1/1/75............... | | $ 6,512 |
| K. Kegler's interest, 1/1/75................. | | 5,984 |
| J. Wright's interest, 1/1/75................. | | 7,500 |
| M. Penny's interest, 1/1/75................. | | 5,104 |
| Investment income for 1975 .............. | | 1,400 |
| | $26,500 | $26,500 |

The following information also is available.

| Employee | Date Employed | Date Terminated | 1975 Salary |
|---|---|---|---|
| R. Johnson | 12/8/65 | | $ 8,320 |
| K. Kegler | 7/1/66 | | 7,280 |
| J. Wright | 11/20/66 | 8/1/75 | 6,200 |
| M. Penny | 9/15/71 | | 5,200 |
| J. Rawlings | 8/20/74 | 12/26/75 | 800 |
| A. Morris | 5/5/74 | | 1,100 |
| | | | $28,900 |

The 1975 net income for Tudor Corporation before deducting the payment to the trustee and the provision for federal income taxes is $88,500.

*Required:*

a. Assume that the profit-sharing base for 1975 is $30,000 and the income tax rate is 50%. Compute the corporation's 1975 contribution to the trust.
b. Assume that the answer to Requirement (a) is $4,000. Prepare a schedule allocating the 1975 contribution to the various participants.
c. Prepare a schedule allocating the amount of any forfeitures and investment income to the remaining participants.

(AICPA adapted)

### Problem 22-9

C & L Printers, Inc., was organized over a decade ago. Four years ago the company established a formal pension plan to provide retirement benefits for all employments. The plan is noncontributory and funded through a trustee, X Bank, which pays all benefits as they become due. Original past service cost of $110,000 is being amortized over 15 years and funded over 10 years. C & L also funds an amount equal to current normal cost net of actuarial gains and losses. There have been no plan amendments since inception. Portions of the independent actuary's report covering the latest year appear below.

I. Current Year's Funding and Pension Cost:

| | | |
|---|---:|---:|
| Normal cost (before adjustment for actuarial gains) computed under the entry-age-normal method .............. | | $34,150 |
| Actuarial gains: | | |
| Investment gains (losses): | | |
| Excess of expected dividend income over actual dividend income ......... | | (350) |
| Gain on sale of investments ............ | | 4,050 |
| Gains in actuarial assumptions for: | | |
| Mortality ................................... | | 3,400 |
| Employee turnover .................... | | 5,050 |
| Reduction in pension cost from closing of plant .......................... | | 8,000 |
| Net actuarial gains .................. | | 20,150 |
| Normal cost (funded currently)............... | $ 14,000 | 14,000 |
| Past service costs: | | |
| Funding ....................................... | 14,245 | |
| Amortization ................................... | | 10,597 |
| Total Funded .......................... | $ 28,245 | |
| Total Pension Cost for Financial-Statement Purposes ........................... | | $24,597 |

II. Fund Assets:

| | |
|---|---:|
| Cash ................................................. | $ 4,200 |
| Dividends receivable .......................... | 1,525 |
| Investment in common stocks, at cost (market value, $177,800) ................... | 162,750 |
| | $168,475 |

*Required:*

1. Comment on (*a*) treatment of actuarial gains and losses, and (*b*) computation of pension cost for financial-statement purposes on the basis of requirements for accounting for pension plan costs.
2. What interest rate is being used in connection with the past service cost amortization and funding? Support your findings.

(AICPA adapted)

# Chapter 23

## Accounting for Leases

Lease accounting can best be described as "state of the art" account-ing. It has been evolving since 1949 when *Accounting Research Bulletin No. 38* appeared.[1] The highlights of what is regarded currently as proper lease accounting and reporting will be discussed. It is safe to predict that new forms of lease contracts will emerge and that new accounting principles and procedures will be developed as a result.

Some material in this chapter is based upon provisions of an exposure draft of an FASB *Statement on Lease Accounting* which was to have become effective January 1, 1976. Shortly before the statement was to become operational it was withdrawn for further study. Since that ex-posure draft represents the latest authoritative expression of what lease accounting should be (even though it has not become effective in March, 1976) we have chosen to present it as a model of modern lease account-ing.

A lease is a contract between an owner (the lessor) and another party (the lessee) which conveys to the lessee the right to use the lessor's property in return for a consideration, usually periodic rental payments. Broadly, there are two principal types of leases – operating leases and financing or capital leases.

Under an *operating lease,* the lessor, while giving the lessee use of the leased property, retains practically all of the risks and rewards of ownership (e.g., early obsolescence and appreciation of value). Oper-ating leases characteristically are of shorter duration than financing leases. Rentals of apartments, space in shopping centers, and automo-biles typify operating leases.

In contrast, *financing leases* almost invariably are long term; they transfer most of the ownership risks and rewards to the lessee, usually are noncancellable, and obligate the lessee to pay taxes, insurance, and maintenance on the property.[2] Often the lessee has the option to buy the

---

[1] AICPA, "Disclosure of Long-Term Leases in Financial Statements of Lessees," *ARB No. 38* (New York, 1949).

[2] The same lease identified as a *financing lease* by a lessor is called a *capital lease* by the lessee.

974

property for a nominal sum when the financing lease expires. The lessor is primarily interested in a rate of return on his or her investment in the property, not in its appreciation or longevity. The distinctions between an operating and a financing lease may be summarized as follows:

| Usual Lease Characteristics | Type of Lease | |
| --- | --- | --- |
| | Operating | Financing |
| a. Duration of lease | Short term | Long term |
| b. Cancellation of lease prior to termination date | Cancellable or non-cancellable | Noncancellable |
| c. Composition of periodic rental payments | Includes return on investment and most ownership costs (maintenance, taxes, depreciation, obsolescence, casualty losses, etc.) | Includes return on investment but little or no ownership costs |
| d. Termination options | None | Asset may be acquired at no cost or a nominal cost |
| e. Special property rights | None transferred | Substantially transferred |
| f. Financing characteristics | Short term, and lessor does not tend to assume role of financial institution. | Substantial and usually long term. Lessor tends to assume role of financing institution. |

Some contracts are called leases when in fact they are nothing more than long-term installment sales contracts; in these cases, the accountant has to look beyond the form and account for the substance of the transaction. A fairly recent development is the three-party or *leverage lease*.[3]

Before studying the details of lease accounting the different situations, it may be helpful to study Exhibit 23–1 which presents an overview of current accounting for leases.

## ACCOUNTING FOR OPERATING LEASES

The two broad classifications of leases defined above (operating leases and financing leases) have influenced the development of accounting concepts and procedures for lease agreements. In the discussions to follow operating leases will be accounted for under the following methods:[4]

---

[3] Leveraged leases are discussed in the Appendix to the chapter.

[4] John H. Meyers, "Reporting Leases in Financial Statements," *Accounting Research Study No. 4* (New York: AICPA, 1962). FASB Exposure Draft, "Accounting for Leases, Financial Accounting Standards Board" (Stamford, Conn., 1975).

**EXHIBIT 23–1**
**Accounting for Leases Summarized**

| | Lessor Accounting | Lessee Accounting |
|---|---|---|
| **Operating Leases:** | | |
| 1. Accounting method | Operating (or rental) method | Noncapitalization (or expense) method |
| 2. Conceptual basis | Ownership of leased property not transferred | Ownership of leased property not acquired |
| 3. Leased asset | Accounted for as a *tangible* asset | Not accounted for as an asset |
| 4. Debt | No receivable for the rent contract recorded | No liability for the rent contract recorded |
| 5. Depreciation | Recorded in normal manner | Not recorded |
| 6. Maintenance costs | Recorded in normal manner | Not paid or recorded |
| 7. Rental payments | Recorded as revenue | Recorded as expense |
| **Financing Leases:** | | |
| 1. Accounting method | Financing (sale) method | Financing (capitalization or purchase) method |
| 2. Conceptual basis | Ownership of leased property is transferred (as a sale) | Ownership of leased property is acquired (as a purchase) |
| 3. Leased asset | Cost removed from the tangible asset accounts (as in a sale) | Cost recorded in a capitalized lease asset account (an intangible asset) |
| 4. Debt | Record present value of lease payments as a receivable | Record present value of lease payments as a liability |
| 5. Depreciation | Not recorded | No depreciation; however, amortize the intangible asset |
| 6. Maintenance costs | Not paid or recorded | Paid and recorded as expense |
| 7. Rental payments | Collection on receivable (plus interest revenue) | Payment on liability (plus interest expense) |

Lessor—operating (or rental) method

Lessee—noncapitalization (or expense) method

These methods are consistent in that both sides of the lease agreement, as represented by the lessor and the lessee, recognize revenue, expense, and amortization on the same conceptual basis. Both methods focus on determination of net income by recognizing revenues and expenses on an accrual basis; they ignore *future* rights, obligations, and commitments (because such rights normally do not exist in an operating lease situation).

An example of a simple operating lease situation is presented in Exhibit 23–2. A owns a small office building, part of which is rented to B for an annual rental of $1,200 payable in advance each January 1. It is assumed that the fiscal period of each party ends October 31. This is an operating lease since the lessor retains all the normal risks of ownership and the lessee gains no special property or purchase rights, but only temporary and cancellable occupancy rights.

**EXHIBIT 23–2**
**Simple Operating Lease Situation—Accounting by Lessor and Lessee**

| Lessor A (operating method) | Lessee B (noncapitalization method) |
|---|---|

January 1, 19A:

To record annual rental payments:

| | | | | | |
|---|---|---|---|---|---|
| Cash | 1,200 | | Rent expense | 1,200 | |
| Rent revenue | | 1,200 | Cash | | 1,200 |

October 10, 19A:

To record payment of property taxes:

| | | | |
|---|---|---|---|
| Expense | 60 | | No entry. |
| Cash | | 60 | |

October 13, 19A:

To report payment of monthly telephone bill:

| | | | | |
|---|---|---|---|---|
| No entry. | | Expense | 15 | |
| | | Cash | | 15 |

October 31, 19A:

To record adjusting entry (two months' rent unexpired):

| | | | | |
|---|---|---|---|---|
| Rent revenue | 200 | | Prepaid rent expense | 200 | |
| Unearned rent revenue | | 200 | Rent expense | | 200 |

**Prepaid Rent**

An operating lease becomes slightly more complex when, in addition to the annual rental, there is a payment made in advance (a downpayment). In this situation the additional payment must be allocated (amortized) over the life of the lease on a realistic basis. Two amortization methods are commonly used, viz:

1. Straight-line method—a constant *dollar amount* of the prepayment is allocated to each period covered by the lease.[5]
2. Present value (or interest) method—a constant *rate* of allocation is utilized as determined by application of the annuity concept to the prepayment. This method necessitates utilization of the present value of an annuity (Table 6–4).

This type of situation, including both methods of amortization of the prepayment, is presented in Exhibit 23–3. This illustration is identical with the preceding one, Exhibit 23–2, with the additional provision that (a) there is a three-year lease agreement, (b) there is an advance payment of $3,000 (in addition to the $1,200 annual rental), and (c) the fiscal year for both parties ends on December 31. A 6% annual interest rate is assumed.

As the unamortized balance of Leasehold or Prepaid Rent diminishes, so also does periodic rent revenue or expense.

In summary, we may observe that the lessor under the operating method did not recognize any transfers of rights or property, or any "purchase" agreements. The lessor recognized the prepayment of a revenue and then amortized it to derive a periodic credit to revenue. The lessee, under the noncapitalization method, did not capitalize any property rights or recognize any "purchase" agreements. The prepayment was capitalized as an intangible asset which was then amortized to derive a periodic charge to expense.

## EVOLUTION OF ACCOUNTING FOR FINANCING LEASES

For many years practically all leases were accounted for as operating leases. However, accounting theorists contended that long-term leases that reflected primarily the characteristics of a financing transaction (and hence were called financing leases) should be recorded by the lessor as a sale involving recognition of a long-term receivable. Consistent accounting for the lessee conceptually would require capitalization of the leased asset and recognition of a long-term liability. While many thought this was conceptually sound, relatively few entities accounted for leases in this way, and it was not required by generally accepted accounting principles. An increasing amount of footnote disclosure about lease terms and obligations occurred during this period.

Because of the rapid increase in leasing and the wide array of accounting alternatives used by both the lessee and lessor, the APB issued *Opinion No.* 5, "Reporting of Leases in Financial Statements of Lessee" (September 1964), and *Opinion No.* 7, "Accounting for Leases in Financial Statements of Lessors" (May 1966). Each of these opinions specified conditions under which a lease should be accounted for as a financing

---

[5] The FASB has expressed a preference for use of the straight-line method by lessees on operating leases. The FASB Exposure Draft, "Accounting for Leases," states: "Normally, rent on an operating lease shall be charged to expense over the lease term as it becomes payable. If rental payments are not made on a straight-line basis, rental expense nevertheless shall be recognized on a straight-line basis unless another systematic and rational basis is justified by the circumstances."

**EXHIBIT 23-3**
**Operating Lease with Amortization—Accounting by Lessor and Lessee**

| *Lessor A* | *Lessee B* |
|---|---|
| *(operating method)* | *(noncapitalization method)* |

**January 1, 19A:**

To record prepayment of rent:

| Cash.................. 3,000 | | Leasehold (prepaid rent) | |
|---|---|---|---|
| Prepaid rent | | expense ..................... 3,000 | |
| revenue ... | 3,000 | Cash........................ | 3,000 |

To record annual rental:

| Cash.................. 1,200 | | Rent expense ............... 1,200 | |
|---|---|---|---|
| Rent revenue. | 1,200 | Cash........................ | 1,200 |

**December 31, 19A:**

To record amortization of advance rental payment (for 12 months):

*Case A—Straight-line method:*

| Prepaid rent | | Rent expense ............... 1,000 | |
|---|---|---|---|
| revenue ......... 1,000 | | Leasehold ............... | 1,000 |
| Rent revenue. | 1,000 | | |
| * Computation: | | | |
| $3,000 \times {}^{12}/_{36} = \$1,000$ | | | |

*Case B—Present value method (see computations below):*

| Prepaid rent | | Rent expense................. 1,122.33 | |
|---|---|---|---|
| revenue ......... 942.33 | | Interest revenue ...... | 180.00 |
| Interest expense . 180.00 | | Leasehold ............... | 942.33 |
| Rent revenue. | 1,122.33 | | |

**December 31, 19A:**

Closing entry (Case B):

| Rent revenue...... 2,322.33 | | Income summary .................. 2,142.33 | |
|---|---|---|---|
| Interest ex- | | Interest revenue ............ 180.00 | |
| pense ...... | 180.00 | Rent expense ......... | 2,322.33 |
| Income | | | |
| summary... | 2,142.33 | | |

Computations:

**Schedule of Amortization (see note)**

| Period | Periodic Rent | Interest (6%) | Amortization of Prepayment | Unamortized Balance |
|---|---|---|---|---|
| 1-1-19A | | | | $3,000.00 |
| 12-31-19A ............ | $1,122.33* | $180.00† | $ 942.33‡ | 2,057.67§ |
| 12-31-19B ............ | 1,122.33 | 123.46 | 998.87 | 1,058.80 |
| 12-31-19C ............ | 1,122.33 | 63.53 | 1,058.80 | -0- |

* Implied periodic rent = $3,000 ÷ Present value of ordinary annuity (3 rents, 6%)
　　　　　　　　　　 = $3,000 ÷ 2.6730120 (Table 6-4)
　　　　　　　　　　 = $1,122.33

† $3,000 × 6% = $180.00

‡ $1,122.33 − $180.00 = $942.33

§ $3,000.00 − $942.33 = $2,057.67

Note: An ordinary annuity is assumed; that is, that the advance payment represents the present value of three equal year-end amounts of $1,122.33 each. Alternatively, an annuity due could have been assumed; that is, that the three payments would be at the *beginning* of each period. In this case the Table 6-4 value would be $(n - 1) + 1$. An annuity due for advance rentals was illustrated in Chapter 14, under the caption "Leaseholds."

lease; all leases not classifiable as financing leases were accounted for as operating leases. These two *Opinions* were inconsistent in that different criteria for identifying financing leases were specified for the lessee and the lessor. *APB Opinion No. 27*, "Accounting for Lease Transactions by Manufacturer or Dealer Lessors (November 1972), was issued in response to questions concerning a special type of lease involving "manufacturer's or dealer's profit" and "third party" leases. To enhance full disclosure, *APB Opinion No. 31*, "Disclosure of Lease Commitments by Lessees" (June 1973), was issued. These *Opinions* represented a significant move in the direction of theoretical correctness in accounting for leases. However, for a variety of reasons they still presented a number of theoretical and practical problems.

The latest step in the development of lease accounting and reporting is the issuance of an FASB Exposure Draft of a proposed Statement, "Accounting for Leases." This statement is planned to supercede the four APB *Opinions* cited above *(Nos. 5, 7, 27, and 31)* and establish new criteria and reporting requirements for both the lessee and the lessor. Leases meeting the criteria must be accounted for as financing leases, and all other must be accounted for as operating leases.

## CRITERIA FOR IDENTIFYING TYPES OF LEASES

The FASB Exposure Draft has provided two sets of criteria for distinguishing different types of leases. From the standpoint of the *lessee*, if a lease meets any one of the five criteria set out in Column A below, it shall be classed as a *capital* (synonymous with "financing") *lease*; otherwise, it shall be classed as an *operating lease*. From the standpoint of the *lessor*, if a lease meets any one of the five criteria from Column A and *both* of the criteria in Column B, it shall be classed as a *financing lease*; otherwise, it shall be classed as an operating lease.

**Criteria for Classifying Leases**

| Column A | Column B |
|---|---|
| 1. Transfers title to property to lessee by end of lease term. | 1. Collectibility of payments required from the lessee is reasonably predictable. |
| 2. Contains a bargain purchase option.* | 2. No important uncertainties surround the amount of costs yet to be incurred by the lessor under the lease. |
| 3. Lease term is equal to 75% or more of the estimated economic life of the property. | |
| 4. Estimated residual value of leased property is less than 25% of property's fair value at inception of lease. | |
| 5. Leased property as a whole is specially designed for the needs of the lessee. | |

* A bargain purchase option is a provision which allows the lessee, at his or her option, to buy the leased property for a price that at the inception of the lease is expected to be substantially less than the fair value of the property when the option becomes exercisable.

The FASB proposed statement identifies two types of financing leases for the lessor and one type for the lessee, viz:

*Lessor:*

1. Direct financing leases—leases that do not give rise to manufacturer's or dealer's profit (or loss) to the lessor that meets one or more of the criteria in Column A above and both of the criteria in Column B above.
2. Sales-type leases—leases that give rise to manufacturer's or dealer's profit (or loss) to the lessor that meets one or more of the criteria in Column A above and both of the criteria in Column B above.

*Lessee:*

1. Capital leases—leases that meet one or more of the criteria in Column A above. Thus, both types of financing leases for the lessor qualify as capital leases to the lessee.

Clearly, the key distinction for the lessor between a direct financing lease and a sales-type lease is whether there is a manufacturer's or dealer's profit (or loss). Manufacturer's profit relates to the situation where the lessor is a manufacturer, and dealer's profit relates to the situation where the lessor is not a manufacturer. Manufacturer's or dealer's profit arises when the sum of the future lease payments required by the lease (selling price) is greater than the cost of the leased equipment. In contrast, there is no manufacturer's or dealer's profit when the present value of the future lease payments are equal to the cost of the leased equipment. To illustrate—

|  | Type of Financing Lease—Lessor Company | | |
|---|---|---|---|
|  | Direct Financing | | Sales Type |
| Sum of the required lease payments ($47,479.28 × 5) | $237,396.40 | | $237,396.40 |
| Present value of the rental payments (page 983) | 200,000.00 | | |
| Sales price: | | | |
| Cost (assumed) | | $180,000 | |
| Manufacturer's or dealer's profit ... | | 20,000 | 200,000.00 |
| Lease Revenue (interest) | $ 37,396.40 | | $ 37,396.40 |

## ACCOUNTING FOR FINANCING LEASES

The discussions to follow will relate to much more complex lease arrangements than operating leases. Financing leases have become rather common in recent years, and they represent a fairly wide range of contractual specifications. They are commonly referred to as financing leases in view of their dominant characteristic as a form of major financing; the lessor primarily is in the business of providing financing and the lessee is using the lease as a source of financing.

Frequently, the primary business activities of the lessor-owner are providing financing by lending money and by leasing assets such as equipment and buildings. Basically, the lessor-owner has money to invest for a return and may choose to invest it in property acquired for rental purposes and thus gain a return on the investments through rents. In these circumstances the lessor-owner may offer lease contracts that give rise to *special property rights* for the lessee. On the other side, by renting under these conditions, the lessee basically is using this approach as one means of major financing of the business. The lessor provides the capital through the assets leased and the lessee makes "installment" payments in the form of rent. These payments include both principal and interest; generally they are deductible for tax purposes by the lessee. Thus, in accounting for leases of this type the underlying concept is that the *special* property rights and related liabilities (and receivables) should be measured, accounted for, and reported in the financial statements of the two parties to the transaction.

The underlying accounting concept for *financing leases* as they relate to the lessor-owner and the lessee as outlined in Exhibit 23–1 may be detailed as follows:

| Party | Accounting Method | Characteristics |
|---|---|---|
| Lessor | Financing (sale) method | Underlying concept—in essence the lessor is providing financing for the lessee by purchasing assets which are conveyed to the lessee, and the latter assumes the risks of ownership without a formal transfer of title. |
|  |  | Accounting—recognizes *(a)* a receivable from the lessee for the life of the lease; *(b)* a "sale" of the leased asset; and *(c)* an unearned lease and/or interest revenue. The receivable and unearned revenue, recognized at inception of the lease, should be amortized over the life of the lease on a present value (interest) basis as the periodic rentals are collected. |
| Lessee | Financing (capitalization or purchase) method | Underlying concept—in essence the lessee is obtaining major financing by contracting for *special* property rights on a noncancellable basis. As a consequence, over the life of the property rented, the rental payments to the lessor constitute a payment of principal plus interest. The ordinary costs of ownership will be paid by the lessee; hence they must be recognized as current expenses as paid (or accrued). |
|  |  | Accounting—recognizes *(a)* an intangible asset "lease-rights" for the life of the lease; *(b)* a payable "lease obligation" to the lessor extending over the life of the lease; *(c)* rental payments as reductions of the payable to the lessor; *(d)* the interest should be amortized over the life of the lease on a present value (interest) basis; and *(e)* amortization of the intangible asset over the life of the lease (or if acquired finally, over its useful life). |

Accounting by the lessor and lessee using the financing method will now be illustrated separately with a common set of facts.

### Illustration of Financing Method (Lessor)

There is one difference in accounting for a direct financing lease and a sales-type lease; that is, whether there is manufacturer's or dealer's profit. First we will discuss and illustrate direct financing leases.

*Direct Financing Leases.* Recall that this type of lease does not involve a manufacturer's or dealer's profit. The gain to the lessor is composed only of *interest* on the investment in the asset leased. To illustrate accounting for direct financing leases by the *lessor,* assume that the Lessor Company is primarily engaged in leasing out heavy construction equipment. Among the equipment that the company has available for leasing is a newly acquired package of machines that cost $200,000 with an estimated useful life of five years and no residual value. Lessor Company has been negotiating with Lessee Company in respect to the capital needs of the latter. As a result of these negotiations a lease agreement was signed on January 1, 19A, by the two parties with the essential provisions that: *(a)* Lessor Company would provide a package of new machines on a five-year contract; *(b)* Lessee Company would pay an equal annual rent at the *end* of each year amounting to $47,479.28; *(c)* the contract is noncancellable; *(d)* Lessee Company would assume (pay directly in addition to the rent) all of the normal ownership costs such as taxes, maintenance, and insurance; and *(e)* at the termination of the lease the equipment reverts to the lessor unless the lessee elects to pay $1,000 for it. These conditions meet the criteria for a *direct financing* lease, and there is no manufacturer's or dealer's profit (see page 981). On January 1, 19A, the effective date of the agreement, the equipment was turned over to Lessee Company. Using these data we will illustrate accounting by the lessor; the next section will consider accounting by the lessee.

Lessor Company established the annual rental amount quoted to Lessee Company (and incorporated in the lease agreement) on the basis that it had an investment with a present value of $200,000 and expected a 6% return on that investment. The resultant computations were:

Annual Rent = $200,000      ÷ Present Value of an Ordinary Annuity
                                (5 periods @ 6%) (Table 6–4)
           = $200,000      ÷ 4.2123638
           = $  47,479.28

The following amortization schedule for the life of the lease (investment) was developed as a basis for the accounting entries for the lessor:

**Lessor—Schedule of Lease Amortization and Related Accounting Entries (direct financing method)**

| Date | Annual Rental (a) | Interest on Unrecovered Investment (b) | Investment Recovery (c) | Unrecovered Investment (d) |
|---|---|---|---|---|
| Jan. 1, 19A ........ | | | | $200,000.00 |
| Dec. 31, 19A ........ | $ 47,479.28 | $12,000.00 | $ 35,479.28 | 164,520.72 |
| Dec. 31, 19B ........ | 47,479.28 | 9,871.24 | 37,608.04 | 126,912.68 |
| Dec. 31, 19C ........ | 47,479.28 | 7,614.76 | 39,864.52 | 87,048.16 |
| Dec. 31, 19D ........ | 47,479.28 | 5,222.89 | 42,256.39 | 44,791.77 |
| Dec. 31, 19E ........ | 47,479.28 | 2,687.51 | 44,791.77 | -0- |
| | $237,396.40 | $37,396.40 | $200,000.00 | -0- |

(a) Computed directly per above.
(b) Preceding balance in columns (d) times 6%.
(c) Column (a) minus column (b).
(d) Preceding balance minus column (c).

Based on the amortization schedule, the lessor would make the following accounting entries under the financing method:

January 1, 19A:

To record the inception of the lease by recognizing the receivable, the "constructive" sale of the asset, and the unearned lease (interest) revenue:

Receivables—lease contracts ............................... 237,396.40*
    Equipment.................................................... 200,000.00
    Unearned interest revenue ............................ 37,396.40*

\* Obviously, these two amounts could be recorded "net" in the receivables account, thus the balance in the receivables account would accord with column (d) in the above tabulation from period to period. The net effect on the financial statements would be the same.

December 31, 19A:

To record first rental collection and to recognize the interest revenue earned (per above schedule):

Cash ............................................................. 47,479.28
    Receivables—lease contracts .......................... 47,479.28

Unearned interest revenue ................................. 12,000.00
    Interest earned (or lease revenue).................... 12,000.00

December 31, 19B:

To record second rental and to recognize revenue earned:

Cash ............................................................. 47,479.28
    Receivables—lease contracts .......................... 47,479.28

Unearned interest revenue ................................. 9,871.24
    Interest earned............................................. 9,871.24

Entries for the remaining periods of the lease would follow the pattern established above. Obviously, after the December 31, 19E entries, each account established in the initial entry on January 1, 19A, would have a zero balance and the Cash account of the lessor would have been increased by the investment ($200,000) plus the interest earned ($37,396.40); and if not purchased by the lessee for the $1,000 nominal amount, the lessor would reclaim the worn-out equipment which has little value. Alternatively, should the lessor sell the worn-out equipment, say as scrap, at an amount in excess of the cost of disposal, a "gain on sale of scrap" would be recorded. You should note that the lessor recorded no depreciation on the machinery; the recovery of principal was included in the rental collections which served to reduce the receivable from the lessor.

In respect to reporting and disclosure on the periodic financial statements, during the life of the lease the lease revenue earned would be reported as an operating revenue by the Lessor Company. On the balance sheet the debit balance in the receivables account would be reduced by the credit balance in the Unearned Lease Revenue account. The current portion would be reported as a current asset and the remainder under a noncurrent receivable or "other" asset caption. To illustrate, the Lessor Company would report at December 31, 19B, as follows (refer to the above amortization schedule for source of amounts):

December 31, 19B*

Income Statement:
Interest revenue ...................................... $ 9,871.24
Balance Sheet:
Current Assets:
   Receivables — lease contracts .................. 47,479.28
   Less: Unearned interest revenue........... 7,614.76    $39,864.52
Other Assets:
   Receivables — lease contracts ................. 94,958.56
   Less: Unearned interest revenue.............. 7,910.40    87,048.16

Appropriate footnote.
* Alternatively, some accountants believe that the balance sheet amounts should be:

Current Assets:
   Receivables — lease contracts ................. $47,479.28
   Less: Unearned interest revenue.............. 2,687.51    $44,791.77
Other Assets:
   Receivables — lease contracts ................. 94,958.56
   Less: Unearned interest revenue.............. 12,837.65    82,120.91

*Sales-Type Financing Leases.* Recall that this type of financing lease, for the *lessor*, includes a manufacturer's or dealer's profit. The profit is the difference between the sum of the required lease payments and the sum of the cost of the leased equipment plus the required interest payments (see computation on page 981).

In the case of sales-type financing leases, the manufacturer's or dealer's profit is recognized in the period of the sale (i.e., period in which the lease is signed). Accounting for interest revenue and lease rental payments is the same as illustrated above for direct financing leases.

To illustrate, a sales-type financing lease we will adopt the above example for Lessor and Lessee Companies. Assume the following change in the basic data for Lessor Company:

| | |
|---|---:|
| Cost of equipment | $180,000 |
| Manufacturer's or dealer's normal profit | 20,000 |
| Normal Sales Price of the Equipment | $200,000 |

The lease rental payments and the amortization table would be based on the $200,000 normal sales price since this is the amount Lessor Company expects from the transaction *plus* interest on the long-term receivable. The lessor would make the following entries:

January 1, 19A:

| | | |
|---|---:|---:|
| Receivables—lease contracts | 237,396.40 | |
|     Equipment (cost or carrying value) | | 180,000.00 |
|     Revenue (manufacturer's profit) interest | | 20,000.00 |
|     Unearned interest revenue (see page 981) | | 37,396.40 |

To record the lease including manufacturer's or dealer's profit and unearned interest revenue (often called unearned lease revenue).

December 31 and subsequent entries would be as those shown on page 984. The lessee's entries would be unaffected; they would be as shown on page 988.

In respect to disclosure by the lessor, the FASB Exposure Draft calls for presentation of the following information in the lessor's financial statements or footnotes thereto:

1. For direct financing and sales-type leases:
   a. Minimum rents receivable as of the date of the latest balance sheet presented, in the aggregate and for each of the succeeding five fiscal years, with separate deductions for—
      (1) Unearned interest and lease revenue.
      (2) Accumulated allowance for uncollectible rentals.
      (3) Amounts representing executory expenses included in the minimum rentals (these include taxes, maintenance, and insurance to be paid by lessor).
   b. Minimum rents receivable and estimated residual values, separately, by major property categories as of the date of the latest balance sheet presented.
   c. Total contingent rentals included in income for each period for which an income statement is presented.
2. For operating leases:
   a. Cost of property on lease (included in 3 below).
   b. Minimum future rents on noncancellable leases in the aggregate and for each of the give succeeding years.
   c. Total contingent rentals included in income for each period for which an income statement is presented.
3. Cost of property on operating leases and cost of that held for leasing purposes by major property categories as of the date of the latest

balance sheet presented. Amounts of accumulated depreciation shall also be disclosed by major property categories.

4. A general description of the lessor's leasing arrangements.

The proposed FASB statement illustrates the balance sheet presentation by the lessor as follows:

**Lessor's Disclosure (other than for leveraged leases)**

COMPANY X
Balance Sheet

|  | December 31, | |
|---|---|---|
| *Assets* | *1975* | *1974* |
| Current Receivables: | | |
| Receivables under sales-type leases and direct financing leases (net of accumulated allowance for uncollectibles of $XXX and $XXX and unearned income of $XXX and $XXX for 1975 and 1974, respectively) (Note 2) | XXX | XXX |
| Long-Term Receivables: | | |
| Receivables under sales-type leases and direct financing leases (net of accumulated allowance for uncollectibles of $XXX and $XXX and unearned income of $XXX and $XXX for 1975 and 1974, respectively) (Note 2) | XXX | XXX |
| Property, Plant, and Equipment: | | |
| Property on operating leases (net of accumulated depreciation of $XXX and $XXX for 1975 and 1974, respectively) (Note 4) | XXX | XXX |
| Property held for lease (net of accumulated depreciation of $XXX and $XXX for 1975 and 1974, respectively) (Note 4) | XXX | XXX |
| Estimated residual values of leased property (Note 3) | XXX | XXX |

(Appropriate disclosure notes, not illustrated)

## Illustration of Financing Method (Lessee)

For this purpose we will utilize the preceding example with no changes thus enabling you to compare the two methods. You should observe that they are internally consistent conceptually. Upon signing the five-year lease, which called for five equal rentals of $47,479.28, payable annually at *year-end*, Lessee Company should debit an asset account for the *present value* of the special property rights accruing under the lease agreement and credit a liability to Lessor Company for the total amount of the obligation—the difference is the interest factor. To determine the capitalizable value of the special rights the Lessor Company would make the following computation:

Present Value of the Special
Property Rights = $ 47,479.28 × Present Value of an Ordinary Annuity (5 periods @ 6%) (Table 6–4)

= 47,479.28 × 4.2123638

= $200,000

The Lessee Company would then develop the following schedule of amortization and related entries for the period covered by the lease:

**Lessee—Schedule of Lease or Amortization and Related Accounting Entries (financing or capital lease method)**

| Date | Annual Rental (a) | Interest on Unpaid Liability (b) | Payment on Principal (c) | Unpaid Principal (d) |
|---|---|---|---|---|
| Jan. 1, 19A...... | | | | $200,000.00 |
| Dec. 31, 19A...... | $ 47,479.28 | $12,000.00 | $ 35,479.28 | 164,520.72 |
| Dec. 31, 19B...... | 47,479.28 | 9,871.24 | 37,608.04 | 126,912.68 |
| Dec. 31, 19C...... | 47,479.28 | 7,614.76 | 39,864.52 | 87,048.16 |
| Dec. 31, 19D...... | 47,479.28 | 5,222.89 | 42,256.39 | 44,791.77 |
| Dec. 31, 19E...... | 47,479.28 | 2,687.51 | 44,791.77 | -0- |
| | $237,396.40 | $37,396.40 | $200,000.00 | -0- |

(a) Annual payment per lease contract.
(b) Preceding balance in column (d) times 6%.
(c) Column (a) minus column (b).
(d) Preceding balance minus column (c).

Based on the amortization schedule, the lessee would make the following accounting entries under the capital lease method:

**January 1, 19A:**

To record the inception of the lease by capitalizing the present value of the special property rights; to recognize the liability and the interest:

| | | |
|---|---|---|
| Asset—leasehold rights (equipment)....................... | 200,000.00 | |
| Discount on lease contracts ............................... | 37,396.40* | |
| Liability—lease contracts ................................ | | 237,396.40* |

\* Obviously these two amounts could be recorded "net" in the liability account, thus the balance therein from period to period would accord with column (d) of the above tabulation. The net effect on the financial statements would be the same.

**December 31, 19A:**

To record payment of the first rental (per above schedule):

| | | |
|---|---|---|
| Liability—lease contracts ...................................... | 47,479.28 | |
| Cash ......................................................... | | 47,479.28 |

To record interest expense (per above schedule):

| | | |
|---|---|---|
| Interest expense (or lease expense) ....................... | 12,000.00 | |
| Discount on lease contracts .......................... | | 12,000.00 |

To record amortization of asset—leasehold rights (straight line):

| | | |
|---|---|---|
| Expense—amortization of property rights (equipment) .................................................... | 40,000.00 | |
| Asset—leasehold rights (equipment)................. | | 40,000.00 |

Note: Frequently the interest expense and amortization expense is reported on the income statement as one expense item; also these three entries generally are combined.

October 15, 19B:

To pay a cost of ownership such as repairs:

| | | |
|---|---|---|
| Repair expense ............................................... | 600.00 | |
| Cash ......................................................... | | 600.00 |

December 31, 19B:

To record payment of the second rental:

| | | |
|---|---|---|
| Liability—lease contracts ..................................... | 47,479.28 | |
| Cash ......................................................... | | 47,479.28 |

To record interest expense (per above schedule):

| | | |
|---|---|---|
| Interest expense ............................................... | 9,871.24 | |
| Discount on lease contracts ........................... | | 9,871.24 |

To record amortization of asset—leasehold rights (straight line):

| | | |
|---|---|---|
| Expense—amortization of property rights (equipment) .................................................... | 40,000.00 | |
| Asset—leasehold rights (equipment).................. | | 40,000.00 |

Observe in the above tabulation that two distinctly separate series of entries are involved, viz:

1. Recording the equal annual payments on the liability; each rental constitutes in part a payment on the principal and in part a payment of interest for the period. Since the principal is reduced each period by a progressively greater amount, the interest is less each period. This reflects the economic essence of installment payments on debt.[6]

2. Recording periodic amortization (or depreciation) of the asset, leasehold rights. The FASB Exposure Draft states that "the asset shall be amortized in a manner consistent with the lessee's normal depreciation policy." The lessee should amortize the asset following conventional approaches: straight line, decreasing charge, and so on. Alternatively, a strong conceptual argument can be made for amortizing leasehold rights on a present value basis in view of the financing characteristics of the leasing arrangement. In this instance the periodic amortization would accord with column (c) in the above schedule; this approach would be comparable to depreciation by the sinking fund method discussed in a prior chapter. Obviously, the lessee has no residual value to consider.

Entries for the remaining periods would follow the pattern established above. Obviously, after the December 31, 19E, entries, the balances in the asset, liability, and discount accounts, established at the inception of the lease, would be zero. If not purchased, the worn-out equipment would be returned to the lessor and no further entries would be needed. Note that the lessee, by virtue of the lease agreement, received $200,000 financing which was repaid over a five-year period plus 6% interest (total interest expense, $37,396.40).

---

[6] Although conceptually unsound in every respect a few have argued for "straight-line" recognition of the interest expense.

In respect to reporting and disclosure on the periodic financial statements, during the life of the lease, the expense (amortization and interest) would be reflected as an operating item by the Lessee Company. On the balance sheet the asset "Leasehold rights" would be reported as an intangible asset; the payable, less the unamortized discount, would be reported under liabilities appropriately classified as to current and noncurrent. To illustrate, the balance sheet for Lessee Company on December 31, 19B, should reflect the following (refer to above amortization schedule for source of amounts; also see footnote * to table on page 988):

Intangible Assets:
Leasehold rights capitalized
    ($200,000–$80,000) ........................ $120,000.00

Current Liabilities:
Liability — lease contracts ..................... 47,479.28
    Less: Unamortized discount* ............... 7,614.76    $39,864.52

Long-Term Liabilities:
Liability — lease contracts ..................... 94,958.56
    Less: Unamortized discount* ............... 7,910.40    87,048.16

    * A less desirable alternative would be to report this as a deferred charge; also some accountants prefer to report the leasehold rights under fixed assets.

## LEASE DISCLOSURES BY THE LESSEE

The following information with respect to leases shall be disclosed in the lessee's financial statements or related footnotes:

1. For capital leases:
    a. The gross amount of assets recorded under capital leases with separate identification of lease-related assets. Amounts of additions for major categories such as real estate, office equipment, trucks, and so on, between balance sheet dates. The amount of accumulated amortization shall be disclosed in total.
    b. Minimum future payments required as of the date of the latest balance sheet presented, in the aggregate and for each of the succeeding five fiscal years.
    c. The range of rates used to reduce the net minimum future payments in (b) above to present value and the weighted average of those rates.
    d. The total of minimum sublease rents due in the future under noncancellable subleases as of the date of the latest balance sheet.
    e. Total contingent rents actually incurred for each period for which an income statement is presented.
2. For operating leases (where the initial or remaining noncancellable terms exceeds one year):
    a. Minimum future rents in the aggregate and for each of the five succeeding fiscal years, with a deduction from the total for imputed interest to reduce the rents to present value.

    *b.* The range of rates used in *(a)* above and the weighted average of those rates.

    *c.* The present value of minimum future rents by major property categories.

    *d.* The total of minimum rents due in the future under noncancellable subleases as of the date of the latest balance sheet presented.

3. For all operating leases:

    *a.* Rental expense for each period for which an income statement is presented, with separate amounts for minimum rentals, contingent rentals, and sublease rentals.

In addition, there shall be a description of the lessee's leasing arrangements including, but not limited to, the following: (1) basis on which contingent rents are determined; (2) existence and terms of renewal or purchase options and escalation clauses; and (3) restrictions imposed by lease agreements (e.g., on dividends, additional debt, etc.).

The FASB Exposure Draft illustrates the balance sheet presentation by the lessee as follows:

**Lessee's Disclosure**

COMPANY X
Balance Sheet

| Assets | *December 31,* 1975 | 1974 | Liabilities | *December 31,* 1975 | 1974 |
|---|---|---|---|---|---|
| Leased property: | | | Current: | | |
| Capital leases, less accumulated amortization (Note 2) | XXX | XXX | Obligations under capital leases (Note 2) | XXX | XXX |
| | | | Long term: | | |
| Operating leases ($XXX and $XXX for 1975 and 1974, respectively) (Note 3) | | | Obligations under capital leases (Note 2) | XXX | XXX |
| | | | Commitments under operating leases ($XXX and $XXX for 1975 and 1974, respectively) (Note 3) | | |

(Appropriate notes, not illustrated)

## SALE AND LEASEBACK

A typical sale and leaseback arrangement involves the sale of real estate or other long-lived property to a financial institution and immediately leasing it back from that institution. Such a contract can provide important tax advantages. Ownership of the property would have entitled its original owner to a deduction for depreciation, but under the sale and leaseback contract the entire rental payments can be deducted.

Since the latter will include interest and amortization of the cost of both *the land* and the building, a substantially larger tax deduction results, expecially if the building had already been partly depreciated.

When the lease contract meets the criteria for treatment as a capital lease (see Column A, page 980), the seller-lessee should account for the lease as a capital lease as previously described. Any profit on the sale must be deferred and then amortized over the lease term in proportion to the amortization of the leased asset. Whereas any deferred profit must be deducted in the balance sheet from the asset reported under the capital leases, any loss on the sale shall be recognized in full at the time of the transaction. Suppose property with a book value of $250,000 is sold for $285,000 under a sale and leaseback contract which meets the criteria for treatment as a capital lease. Immediately after the sale and before it was subject to any form of amortization it would be reported on the balance sheet as follows:

| | | |
|---|---:|---:|
| Right to use property transferred under sale leaseback contract............................................. | $285,000 | |
| Less: Deferred profit on contract ............................. | 35,000 | $250,000 |

Instead, if the same property had been sold for $220,000, it would be reported at that amount and the $30,000 loss would be recognized in the period of sale.

In case the lease contract does not meet the criteria for treatment as a capital lease and the sales price of the asset exceeds its cost to the seller-lessee, a fair rental value for the property shall be determined. If this fair rental value for the lease term equals or exceeds the amount of the rental called for under the lease, the seller-lessee shall recognize the excess of the sales price over cost as income at the time of the sale. On the other hand, if the fair rental value is less than the amount of the rental called for under the lease, the seller-lessee shall record, as an obligation, the amount of the difference, calculated over the lease term, not to be greater than the excess of the sales price over cost. Any excess remaining after deducting the obligation shall be recognized as income at the time of the sale. A proportionate share of each rent must be recorded as a reduction of the obligation over the lease term. The remainder of each rental payment shall be recognized as rent expense.

When the lease fails to meet the criteria for treatment as a capital lease and the cost of the asset to the seller-lessee is in excess of sales price, the difference shall be recognized as a loss at the time of sale. When the lease meets the criteria for treatment as a direct financing lease, the purchaser-lessor must record the transaction as a purchase and a direct financing lease; otherwise, the transaction should be recorded as a purchase and an operating lease.

## Appendix.   Leveraged Leases

The leveraged lease is a relative newcomer to the field of leasing. It is a three-party lease involving a *lender* in addition to the usual lessor and lessee. The lender typically is a financial institution who supplies from 50% to 80% of the purchase price of the leased asset.[7] A dominant characteristic of the leveraged lease is the unique pattern of cash flows to the lessor. After making the initial investment in the asset (for the portion not financed by the long-term creditor), the lessor ordinarily receives an early substantial net cash inflow consisting of lease rentals, an investment tax credit based on the total cost of the property, plus other income tax benefits such as depreciation on the total cost of the property (often on an accelerated basis), interest expense on the debt, and possibly others.

A leveraged lease is designated in this way because loans coupled with income tax advantages are used to provide a particularly favorable return on the *equity participation* by the lessor. Analysis of the merits of a leveraged lease is made on a cash flow basis.

### ILLUSTRATION OF LEVERAGED LEASE ACCOUNTING

The essential characteristics of a leveraged lease can be illustrated with a simple example. While the periodic cash flows might occur more frequently than in the example, and while the useful life of the asset and the lease would often be longer, nothing would be gained in illustrating the concepts and procedures by having a vast array of figures.

*Data:* Assume the lessor has an average income tax rate of 40% over the lease term, and that the investment credit and accelerated depreciation are acceptable for income tax purposes. At the start of Year 1, the lessor acquired property costing $1,000,000 and immediately leased it for $216,315 annually payable at the end of each of the next six years (the interest rate is 8%). At the end of the sixth year, the property will be fully depreciated and the residual value, zero. The lessor provides $200,000 (called the equity participation) of the purchase price of the property and finances the remainder by borrowing $800,000 (called the leverage) at 9% interest; the loan is to be repaid in six equal annual installments, at the end of each year, of $178,336 (i.e., $800,000 principal plus $270,015 interest). For income tax purposes, the property will be depreciated by the lessor over a four-year term using the double-declin-

---

[7] Ordinarily the loan is nonrecourse to the general credit of the lessor and is secured by a mortgage on the leased property plus an assignment of the lease and lease payments; the lessee may also guarantee the debt. If the property is realty, the percentage of the loan may exceed 80% of the total cost.

**EXHIBIT 23-4**

**Leveraged Lease—Cash Flow Analysis by Years for the Lessor**

| Year | (1) Cash Lease Rentals (as given) | (2) Depreciation (double-declining for tax purposes) (a) | (3) Cash Interest Payments (b) | (4) Taxable Income (loss) (Cols. 1 − 2 − 3) | (5) Income Tax Credits (charges) (Col. 4 × 40%) | (6) Cash Payments on Loan Principal (b) | (7) Annual Cash Flow (Cols. 1 − 3 + 5 − 6) | (8) Cumulative Cash Flow |
|---|---|---|---|---|---|---|---|---|
| Initial investment by lessor | | | | | | | (200,000) | (200,000) |
| Investment tax credit | | | | | | | 70,000 | (130,000) |
| 1 ... | 216,315 | 500,000 | 72,000 | (355,685) | 142,274 | 106,336 | 180,253 | 50,253 |
| 2 ... | 216,315 | 250,000 | 62,430 | (96,115) | 38,446 | 115,906 | 76,425 | 126,678 |
| 3 ... | 216,315 | 125,000 | 51,998 | 39,317 | (15,727) | 126,338 | 22,252 | 148,930 |
| 4 ... | 216,315 | 125,000 | 40,628 | 50,687 | (20,275) | 137,708 | 17,704 | 166,634 |
| 5 ... | 216,315 | — | 28,234 | 188,081 | (75,232) | 150,102 | (37,253) | 129,381 |
| 6 ... | 216,317 | — | 14,275 | 201,592 | (80,637) | 163,610 | (42,655) | 86,726 |
| | 1,297,892 | 1,000,000 | 270,015 | 27,877 | (11,151) | 800,000 | 86,726 | |

(a) $1,000,000 × 50% = $500,000 (etc.)

(b) Equal period payment on bank loan ............ $178,336

Interest payment on unpaid principal,
$800,000 × 9% ............................... 72,000

Payment on Loan Principal ............... $106,336 (etc.)

**EXHIBIT 23-5**

**Leveraged Lease—Income Statement Reporting by Lessor Financing Lease**

| Year | (1) Unrecovered Investment (a) | (2) Lease Revenue (Col. 1 × 8%) | (3) Interest Expense (b) | (4) Income before Tax (Col. 2 − 3) | (5) Income after 40% Taxes (Col. 4 × 60%) | (6) Investment Credit (c) | (7) Net Income (Col. 5 + 6) |
|---|---|---|---|---|---|---|---|
| 1 | 1,000,000 | 80,000 | 72,000 | 8,000 | 4,800 | 18,798 | 23,598 |
| 2 | 863,685 | 69,095 | 62,430 | 6,665 | 3,999 | 16,236 | 20,235 |
| 3 | 716,465 | 57,317 | 51,998 | 5,319 | 3,191 | 13,469 | 16,660 |
| 6 | 557,467 | 44,597 | 40,628 | 3,969 | 2,381 | 10,480 | 12,861 |
| 5 | 385,749 | 30,860 | 28,234 | 2,626 | 1,576 | 7,252 | 8,828 |
| 6 | 200,294 | 16,023 | 14,725 | 1,298 | 779 | 3,765 | 4,544 |
| | | 297,892 | 270,015 | 27,877 | 16,726 | 70,000 | 86,726 |

Computations:

(a) Prior unrecorded balance ............ $1,000,000

    Less: Lease rental ............ $216,315

    Deduct Column 2 amount.......... 80,000

    Recovery of investment............ 136,315

    New Balance ............ $ 863,685 (etc.)

(b) Interest on unpaid principal on bank loan, $800,000 × 9% = $72,000 (etc.)

(c) Proration on basis of Column 1: $70,000 × $80,000/$297,892 = $18,798 (etc.)

ing-balance method.[8] At the time the property was acquired, the investment credit was 7%; this was recognized by the lessor for tax purposes in the year of acquisition but was deferred for financial accounting purposes.

The *lessor's* cash flow analysis is set out in Exhibit 23–4. All amounts have been rounded to the nearest dollar. Column 2, Depreciation, reflects double-declining-balance depreciation of a $1,000,000 asset over a four-year life. Column 3, Cash Interest Payments, reflects interest at 9% on the unpaid debt principal for any given year. For each period, the loan principal payment (Column 6) is the difference between the $178,336 equal periodic payments on the loan and the period interest.

Exhibit 23–5 summarizes the income statement for each year of the lease assuming the lease agreement qualifies as a *financing lease*. Recall that the annual rent of $216,315, for a $1,000,000 cost, indicates an annual interest rate or return of 8%; that is, $1,000,000 ÷ 4.62288 (from Table 6–4, $n=6$, $i=8\%$) = $216,315. This ignores the investment credit because it is realized immediately and will be separately considered (Exhibit 23–5, Column 6).

On Exhibit 23–5, the investment of $1,000,000 is recovered on an annuity basis as reflected in the computation below the table. The investment credit, although realized in Year 1 as a cash inflow (i.e., a reduction in income taxes payable), is prorated or amortized on a rational basis each year; the basis used is lease revenue (Column 2) as indicated in the computations below the table in Exhibit 23–5. The remaining computations are indicated on the exhibit.

The underlying concepts may be better understood by studying the entries that would be made by the lessor for the first year. Two cases will be assumed:

Case A – The lease transaction qualifies as a financing lease.
Case B – The lease transaction qualifies as an operating lease.

Case A – Year 1 entries assuming financing lease:

*a.* January 1 – asset acquired:

| | | |
|---|---:|---:|
| Asset – property | 1,000,000 | |
| Cash | | 200,000 |
| Liability – bank loan, 9% | | 800,000 |

*b.* January 1 – lease contract (financing lease):

| | | |
|---|---:|---:|
| Receivable, lease contract | 1,297,892 | |
| Asset – property | | 1,000,000 |
| Unearned lease revenue | | 297,892 |

*c.* January 1 – investment credit deferred:

| | | |
|---|---:|---:|
| Income taxes payable (debit balance) | 70,000 | |
| Investment credit deferred (unamortized) | | 70,000 |

---

[8] Because of flexible tax provisions, the lessor is permitted to depreciate property for tax purposes, although it is a financing lease.

*d.* December 31 — payment on bank loan:

| | | |
|---|---:|---:|
| Liability — bank loan, 9% (Exhibit 23–5, Column 6) ... | 106,336 | |
| Interest expense (Exhibit 23–5, Column 3) ............ | 72,000 | |
| Cash (per loan agreement)................................ | | 178,336 |

*e.* December 31 — collection of rental:

| | | |
|---|---:|---:|
| Cash (per lease agreement) ................................. | 216,315 | |
| Receivable, lease contract ............................. | | 216,315 |

*f.* December 31 — lease revenue earned:

| | | |
|---|---:|---:|
| Unearned lease revenue ...................................... | 80,000 | |
| Lease revenue (Exhibit 23–5, Column 2) ......... | | 80,000 |

*g.* December 31 — amortize investment credit:

| | | |
|---|---:|---:|
| Investment credit deferred (unamortized) .............. | 18,798 | |
| Investment credit realized, revenue | | |
| (Exhibit 23–5, Column 6)............................. | | 18,798 |

*h.* December 31 — income taxes:

| | | |
|---|---:|---:|
| Income tax expense ($8,000 × .40) ........................ | 3,200 | |
| Income taxes payable ..................................... | | 3,200 |

The resultant unclassified balance sheet relating solely to the leveraged lease would be:

| | | |
|---|---:|---:|
| Cash ............................................................... | | $ 37,979 |
| Taxes payable (debit balance) .................................. | | 66,800 |
| Receivable, lease contracts........................................ | $1,081,577 | |
| Less: Unearned lease revenue ................................. | 217,892 | 863,685 |
| Total Assets ................................................ | | $968,464 |
| Liability — bank loan, 9% ......................................... | | $693,664 |
| Investment credit, deferred ...................................... | | 51,202 |
| Capital (original investment) .................................... | | 200,000 |
| Retained earnings (Year 1 net income) .................... | | 23,598 |
| Total Liabilities and Stockholders' Equity ......... | | $968,464 |

## Case B — Year 1 entries assuming an operating lease:

*a.* January 1 — asset acquired:

| | | |
|---|---:|---:|
| Asset — property................................................... | 1,000,000 | |
| Cash ........................................................... | | 200,000 |
| Liability — bank loan ......................................... | | 800,000 |

*b.* January 1 — investment credit:

| | | |
|---|---:|---:|
| Income taxes payable ........................................... | 70,000 | |
| Income tax expense........................................... | | 70,000 |

*c.* December 31 — annual depreciation (double declining, Exhibit 23–5):

| | | |
|---|---:|---:|
| Depreciation expense ........................................... | 500,000 | |
| Accumulated depreciation ................................. | | 500,000 |

*d.* December 31 — payment on loan:

| | | |
|---|---:|---:|
| Liability — bank loan ............................................. | 106,336 | |
| Interest expense ................................................. | 72,000 | |
| Cash ........................................................... | | 178,336 |

*e.* December 31 — collection of annual rent:

| | | |
|---|---|---|
| Cash | 216,315 | |
|     Lease revenue | | 216,315 |

*f.* December 31 — income taxes:

| | | |
|---|---|---|
| Income tax expense | 3,200 | |
|     Income taxes payable | | 3,200 |

The economics of a typical leveraged lease are reflected in Exhibits 23–4 and 23–5. The cash flows and net income results are significantly different; however, at the termination of the lease, they total to the same amount ($86,726). The cumulative cash flow and cumulative net income are shown graphically in Exhibit 23–6. The graph shows that the

**EXHIBIT 23–6**
**Leveraged Lease — Graph of Lessor's Cash Flow and Net Income Compared**

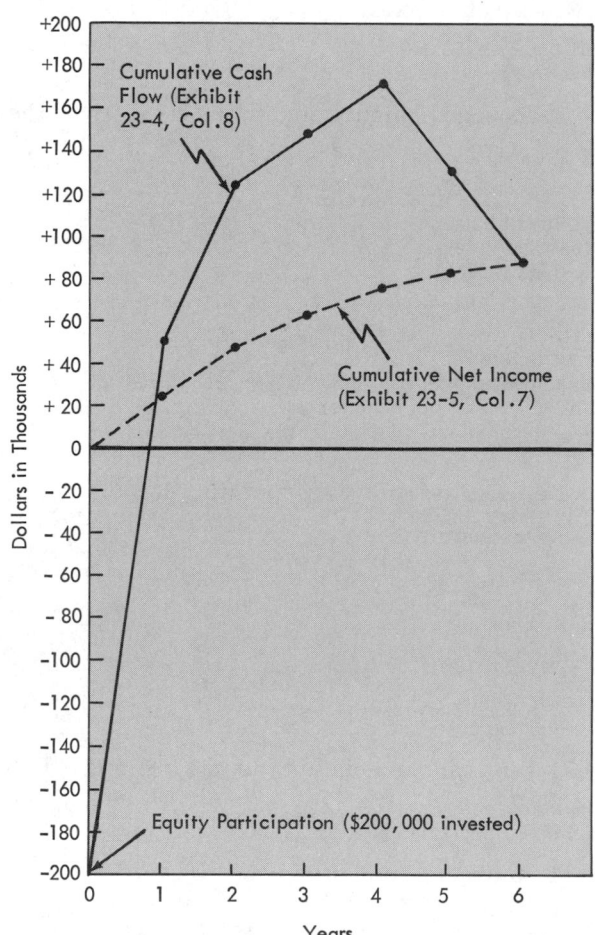

cumulative cash received by the lessor during the positive cash inflow period exceeded both the total net income and the equity participation ($200,000). The excess cash inflow rises quickly but reverses slowly. The reversal is due to the termination of the tax advantage of depreciation expense at the end of the fourth year. In leveraged leases, a relatively small equity investment, 20% in this case, and a high leverage loan, 80% in this case, provides a significant tax advantage. The tax advantages in respect to (1) interest on the loan is a tax deductible expense, and (2) high depreciation at an accelerated rate, on the total investment, makes leveraged leases excellent investments for those in a high tax bracket. The graph shown in Exhibit 23–6 reflects these advantages and also the importance of cash flow analysis as well as accrual accounting analysis.

The lease illustrated above is typical, except that the time span has been capsuled to a shorter period than normal for a typical leveraged lease, also the cash flow is somewhat accelerated. Typically, the equity participation is recovered in the first or second year. These simplifications do not alter the analytical and accounting approaches.

## QUESTIONS

1. Match the numbered items below with the lettered items at the right.

   1. Lessor.
   2. Leveraged lease.
   3. Operating lease.
   4. Lessee.

   a. Comparatively new type of contract in which owner puts up relatively small portion of cost of the property to be leased.
   b. Lender in a lease contract transaction.
   c. Tenant in a lease contract transaction.
   d. Property owner in a lease contract transaction.
   e. Type of lease which transfers most of risks of ownership to the tenant.
   f. Type of lease in which owner retains most of usual rewards and risks of ownership.

2. Distinguish between operating leases and financing leases.

3. Give highlights of generally accepted accounting methods for (a) operating leases, and (b) financing leases.

4. Often advance rental payments are received under operating lease contracts which extend well beyond a single fiscal year. Outline possible accounting procedures to be followed in respect to such payments.

5. By what criteria can financing or capital leases be distinguished from operating leases according to the FASB?

6. In some sale and leaseback transactions the seller-leasee realizes a profit on sale of the asset; in others, a loss is realized. Briefly describe proper accounting treatment of gains and losses related to sale and leaseback transactions.

7. XYZ Company operates retail stores in numerous cities; for the most part leased locations are used. Most of the leases are noncancelable; their average life is 9 years (some run as long as 16 years). Quite a number of the leases are

in shopping centers in which part of the rent may be dependent on the volume of business transacted. Some of the leases contain renewal option clauses; virtually none give XYZ an option to buy the properties involved, nor do they involve the company in guarantees, dividend restrictions, and so on. What disclosures should XYZ make in its current financial statements in respect to the leases?

8. What distinguishes a leveraged lease from other leases? What pattern of cash flow usually attends a leveraged lease insofar as the lessor is concerned?

## DECISION CASE 23-1

The practice of obtaining the right to use property by noncancellable leases is becoming more prevalent.

*Required:*

1. Assets acquired under noncancellable leases that are in substance installment purchases should be capitalized in the accounts of the lessee in order to show the facts properly. List the defects in the lessee's balance sheet and income statement that would result from *not* recording assets acquired under such contracts.
2. Other noncancellable leases that give the lessee essentially all the rights and obligations of ownership are not installment purchases in substance.
   a. Discuss the case *against* recording assets acquired by such leases.
   b. The case for recording assets acquired by such leases rests primarily on the belief that the opportunity to exercise the right of use creates an asset that should be recognized in the accounts with its related liability. Discuss the arguments that *support* this belief.

(AICPA adapted)

## EXERCISES

### Exercise 23-1

Lessors engage in leasing activies for diverse reasons.

*Required:*

1. What factors should a lessor consider in choosing a method of assigning revenues and expenses to lease periods?
2. For what types of leasing activities should lessors utilize the—
   a. Financing method?
   b. Operating (or rental) method?
3. Under the operating method, lessors report gross rentals as revenues over the life of the lease.
   a. How should the investment be classified?
   b. What should be disclosed?

(AICPA adapted)

### Exercise 23-2

Margo Company paid $7,000 on January 1, 19A, to Dexter Properties as a lease bonus to secure a three-year lease on premises it will occupy starting from that date. Additionally, $6,000 per annum paid on each December 31 throughout the term of the lease will be paid as rent. There is no specific renewal agreement. Margo adjusts and closes its books each December 31. Dexter will maintain the property, pay taxes, and other ownership costs.

*Required:*

1. What type of lease contract is involved?
2. What are Margo's alternatives as to treatment of the $7,000? Develop an amortization table using an 8% rate.
3. What is Margo's total occupancy cost for 19B under each alternative given in your response to Requirement 2?
4. What should Margo's financial statements reflect as of December 31, 19A, if the amortization table developed in Requirement 2 is used?

**Exercise 23-3**

Delta Leasing Company agreed with Wilson Corporation to provide the latter equipment under lease for a four-year period. The equipment cost Delta $18,500 and will have no salvage value when the lease term ends. Wilson has agreed to pay all normal ownership costs throughout the lease period including taxes, maintenance, and insurance. On January 1, 19A, the equipment was delivered. Delta expects a 9% return; the four equal annual rents are payable in advance starting January 1, 19A.

*Required:*

1. Assuming this is a financing lease, for both parties, prepare an amortization table suitable for use by either party.
2. On the assumption both companies adjust and close books each December 31, give journal entries relating to the lease for both companies through December 31, 19A, based on data derived in the amortization table. Assume straight-line amortization.

**Exercise 23-4**

Select the best answer in each of the following and give your basis for selecting it.

1. Where the balance sheet for the lessor indicates that a portion of property, plant, and equipment and of the related accumulated depreciation pertains to equipment leased to customers, it is evident that the—
   a. Operating method of accounting is used for these leases.
   b. Financing method of accounting is used for these leases.
   c. Lessor has violated generally accepted accounting principles.
   d. Lessor is using the income tax method of accounting for these leases.
2. Under the provisions of authoritative pronouncements, when leases are treated as installment purchases, the method of amortization used by the lessee should be appropriate to the nature and use of the asset and should be chosen—
   a. To result in a level annual pattern of charges to expense over the useful life of the property.
   b. To result in a level annual rate of return on the capitalized amount over the useful life of the property.
   c. To result in an annual pattern of charges to expense based on the annual change in the present value of the related obligation.

    *d.* Without reference to the period over which the related obligation is discharged.

3. Iden Company leased a warehouse from Jarrold, Inc., on January 2, 19A, for five years for a fixed annual rental payment. On April 1, 19A, Iden subleased the same warehouse to Walter Company for a substantially larger yearly rental for the four years and nine months remaining on the lease. Walter is a well-established company with an excellent credit rating and earnings history. How should Iden disclose the lease and sublease on its financial statements at December 31, 19A?

    *a.* By means of a footnote to the financial statements only.

    *b.* No disclosure is needed in the balance sheet or in the footnotes because Iden's earnings statement should show rental revenue received from Walter and rental expense paid to Jarrold.

    *c.* Iden should capitalize the lease payments to be made to Jarrold and amortize the balance over the five years of the lease. No disclosure needs to be made for the sublease.

    *d.* Iden's statement of financial position should include an asset and a liability each for the present value of the difference between the amount to be received from the sublease and the amount to be paid for the lease.

4. On June 30, 19A, the Ingalls Corporation sold equipment for $420,000 which had a net book value of $400,000 and a remaining life of ten years. That same day, the equipment was leased back at $1,000 per month for five years with no option to renew the lease or repurchase the equipment. Ingall's rent expense for this equipment for the six months ended December 31, 19A, would be—

    *a.* $5,000.               *c.* $6,000.

    *b.* $4,000.               *d.* ($14,000).

5. Property under construction to be sold and leased back for operating use under a leasing arrangement, which in substance is a purchase, should be reported by the lessee on a classified balance sheet under the caption—

    *a.* Long-term investments.

    *b.* Deferred charges.

    *c.* Property, plant, and equipment.

    *d.* Short-term investment.

6. Material gains resulting from sale-and-leaseback transactions usually should be accounted for—

    *a.* As an ordinary gain in the period of the transaction.

    *b.* As an extraordinary gain in the period of the transaction.

    *c.* By amortizing the gain over the life of the lease.

    *d.* By crediting the gain to the cost of the related property.

7. Manufacturers and dealer lessors sometimes sell or assign leases to third parties, usually independent financing companies. Where such a lease sale or assignment has occurred—

    *a.* The lease cannot qualify for treatment as a sale even though it would have met the criteria for sale accounting treatment if only the lessor and the lessee had been involved.

    *b.* Involvement of the independent financing company does not disqualify the lease from sale accounting treatment if it otherwise qualifies for this treatment.

    *c.* The operating method of accounting for lease transactions becomes mandatory.

    *d.* The financing method of accounting for lease transactions becomes mandatory.

(Items 4 through 7 AICPA adapted)

**Exercise 23-5**

Select the best answer in each of the following and explain the basis for your choice.

1. In accounting for a lease, the account(s) that should appear on the balance sheet of a lessor using the financing method but not using the operating method would be the —
   a. Investment in Leased Property account.
   b. Property, Plant, and Equipment account.
   c. Receivable — Equipment Rentals and Property, Plant, and Equipment accounts.
   d. Receivable — Equipment Rentals account.
2. Under the financing method of accounting for leases, the excess of the present value of the aggregate rentals over the cost of leased property should be recognized as revenue by the lessor —
   a. In increasing amounts during the term of the lease.
   b. In constant amounts during the term of the lease.
   c. In decreasing amounts during the term of the lease.
   d. After the cost of the leased property has been fully recovered through rentals.
3. A company sold property at a price which exceeded book value and then leased back the property for ten years. The gain resulting from the sale should be recognized by the company —
   a. In the year of sale.
   b. At the end of the ten-year period or termination of the lease, whichever is earlier.
   c. Over the term of the lease.
   d. As a prior period adjustment.
4. When measuring the present value of future rentals to be capitalized as part of the purchase price in a lease that is to be accounted for as a financing lease, identifiable payments to be made by the lessee to cover taxes, insurance, and maintenance should be —
   a. Included with the future rentals to be capitalized.
   b. Excluded from future rentals to be capitalized.
   c. Capitalized but at a different discount rate and recorded in a different account than future rental payments.
   d. Capitalized but at a different discount rate and for a relevant period that tends to be different than for the future rental payments.
5. On January 1, 19A, Ramos Company signed a ten-year noncancelable lease for certain machinery. The terms of the lease call for payments of $10,000 per year to be made by Ramos for ten years. The machinery has a 20 year life and no salvage value. Ramos uses the straight-line depreciation method on all depreciable assets.

   Assume that, in substance, this lease is an installment purchase of the machinery by Ramos, and accordingly should be capitalized (i.e., a financing lease). Assuming a 10% discount rate, the lease payments have a present value of $61,440.

   Relative to the capitalized lease described above, Ramos' 19A income statement should include —
   a. Interest expense of $10,000 and depreciation expense of $3,072.
   b. Interest expense of $10,000 only.
   c. Interest expense of $6,144 and depreciation expense of $3,072.
   d. Interest expense of $6,298 and depreciation expense of $3,072.

6. On December 31, 19A T Company entered into an agreement to lease a piece of machinery from Y Company. Lease payments are $1,000 per month for ten years. The lease is in substance an installment purchase of the machinery by T Company, and so the machinery and related lease obligations must be capitalized (i.e., a financing lease). This means that on T Company's balance sheet as of December 31, 19A, the leased machinery will be carried at—
   a. Some amount greater than $120,000.
   b. Some amount less than $120,000.
   c. Cannot determine whether the amount should be more or less than $120,000 from the information given.
   d. Exactly $120,000.

(AICPA adapted)

### Exercise 23–6

*Case A:* XYZ Company leases computers to various lessees and uses the financing method. The average length of its lease contracts is 42 months. For balance sheet purposes, describe how its receivables should be classified, valued, and characterized.

*Case B:* Your client, DEF Corporation, recently concluded an arm's-length sale and leaseback of all of its plant, property, and equipment. The transaction resulted in a gain of $600,000 in terms of book value which the client wants to pick up as extraordinary gain in financial statements of the current year. Can you, as DEF's independent CPA, accept this proposal? If not, what alternatives can you offer?

*Case C:* Another client (a lessee) intends to lease a material amount of machinery under terms of a lease which calls for the client to be responsible for and pay directly (not included in the rental) maintenance, taxes, insurance, and other expenses related to the property while used by the lessee. At the termination of the noncancellable lease, your client would have the option to buy the machinery at a nominal salvage value. The duration of the lease and expected life of the machinery are about the same. How would you advise your client to account for this lease transaction and its related payments?

### Exercise 23–7 (based on the Appendix)

LR Company leased from LE Leasing Company, for a four-year period, equipment with an estimated four-year life and zero salvage value. The equipment cost the LE Company $125,000. LE Company paid $25,000 cash and borrowed the remainder at 9% interest under a loan which provided for repayment by four equal annual installments of $30,867 payable at the end of each of the four years.

LR agreed to pay the lessor four equal annual rents of $39,434. On this basis, the lessor will earn 10% before taxes (aside from the investment credit) since the rents are due at the end of each of the four years. Assume the equipment will be depreciated by the sum-of-the-years'-digits method and that a 7% investment credit can be fully realized in the year the equipment is acquired; assume also that the investor will remain in a 40% income tax bracket throughout the term of the lease, and that the lease transaction qualifies as a financing lease.

*Required:*

Prepare for the lessor an anticipated cash flow schedule covering the entire four-year lease period similar to Exhibit 23–4. Round all amounts to the nearest dollar.

### Exercise 23–8 (based on the Appendix)

Brand Company leased to Neville, Inc., for a four-year period, equipment which cost Brand $600,000. Brand obtained the equipment by paying $100,000 cash and signing a note calling for four equal annual payments at the end of the four years $150,960 (due to rounding, raise the last payment by $1). On this basis, the $500,000 loan bears interest at 8%.

Neville agreed to pay Brand four equal annual rents of $189,282 at the end of each of the four years. The leased property has an estimated zero value at the termination of the lease. It will qualify for a 7% investment credit. Brand will depreciate the property by the sum-of-the-years'-digits method. The rents will yield the lessor 10% return before taxes ignoring the investment credit. Assume the transaction qualifies as a financing lease.

*Required:*

Prepare for Brand an anticipated cash flow schedule covering the entire four-year lease period similar to Exhibit 23–4. Assume Brand's income will be taxed throughout the period at 40%. Round all amounts to the nearest dollar.

## PROBLEMS

### Problem 23–1

Dix Corporation leased some space to Menn Company under a three-year contract starting January 1, 19A. Terms of the contract required an annual rental of $8,000 starting January 1, 19A, plus an advance payment of $6,000 on January 1, 19A. There is no provision for renewal; and Dix is to pay insurance, taxes, and maintenance expenses. Both companies adjust and close books annually on December 31.

*Required:*

1. Indicate the type of lease involved and explain. What accounting approach should be used by each company? Indicate any alternatives.
2. Develop an amortization table (interest method) suitable for use by either party using 7% interest.
3. What would be the annual amortization assuming the straight-line method is adopted?
4. Give all entries related to the lease contract for 19A and 19B for the lessor and lessee in parallel columns using present value (interest) amortization.
5. What should be reflected on the income statement and balance sheet of both parties at December 31, 19A, and December 31, 19B?

### Problem 23–2

On January 1, 19A, Company A rented an office to Company B for an annual rental of $1,200 payable each January 1. In addition, an advance payment of $3,000 was required. The lease was for three-year period. The advance payment represented three annual rentals that would have been payable each January 1;

the $3,000 was somewhat less than the sum of the three annual payments that would have been made in addition to the normal rent of $1,200. This is an operating lease as to both parties.

*Required:*

1. Give all entries, including closing entries, for both the lessor and lessee assuming (*a*) both parties' fiscal year ends December 31, and (*b*) a 6% interest rate for amortization purposes. Utilize present value amortization and present the two sets of entries in parallel columns. Show all computations.
2. Show amounts that would be reported on the income statement and balance sheet for each year for both the lessor and lessee.

### Problem 23-3

During 19A, Amx Finance Company began leasing equipment to small manufacturers. Information regarding leasing arrangements follows:

*a.* Amx Finance Company leases equipment with terms from three to five years depending upon the useful life of the equipment. At the expiration of the lease, the equipment will be sold to the lessee at 10% of the lessor's cost, the expected salvage value of the equipment.
*b.* The amount of the lessee's monthly payment is computed by multiplying the lessor's cost of the equipment by the payment factor applicable to the term of the lease.

| Term of Lease | Payment Factor |
|---|---|
| Three years | 3.32% |
| Four years | 2.63 |
| Five years | 2.22 |

*c.* The excess of the gross contract receivable for equipment rentals over the cost (reduced by the estimated salvage value at the termination of the lease) is recognized as revenue over the term of the lease under the sum-of-the-years'-digits method computed on a monthly basis.
*d.* The following leases were entered into during 19A:

| Machine | Dates of Lease | Period of Lease | Machine Cost |
|---|---|---|---|
| Die | 7/1/19A–6/30/19E | 4 years | $45,000 |
| Press | 9/1/19A–8/31/19D | 3 years | 30,000 |

*Required:*

1. Prepare a schedule of gross contracts receivable for equipment rentals at the dates of the lease for the die and press machines.
2. Prepare a schedule of unearned lease revenue at December 31, 19A, for each machine lease.
3. Prepare a schedule computing the present value of contracts receivable for equipment rentals at December 31, 19A. (The present value of the "contracts receivable for equipment rentals" is the outstanding amount of the gross contracts receivable less the unearned lease income included therein.) Without prejudice to your solution to Requirement 2, assume that the unearned lease revenue at December 31, 19A, was $14,500.

(AICPA adapted)

**Problem 23-4**

Stokes Leasing Corporation is a newly formed dealer lessor. Stokes will be engaged in leasing a basic machine that costs $50,000 each and has a six-year life and no residual value at the end of its useful life. Stokes started operations with ten of the machines; its equities consist of a $150,000 note due in three years which bears 5% interest payable each December 31 and $350,000 capital stock. The fiscal year ends on December 31. The machines will be rented under six-year contracts whereby annual rentals are paid at year-end; 6% return on the investment is expected. The lessee assumes all risks and costs of normal ownership, and the lease is noncancellable. The machines revert to the lessor at the termination of the lease. Assume a financing lease for both the lessor and lessee.

*Required:*

1. Show how the lessor would compute the annual rent on a machine.
2. Show how the lessee would compute the present value of the special property rights.
3. Prepare an amortization table that would be suitable for either the lessor or lessee.
4. Give journal entries for the lessor for the following transactions; you may use abbreviated account titles.

    Jan.   1, 19A—Concluded leases on all ten machines with various lessors.
    Dec. 31, 19A—Collected lease rentals due; paid salaries and other expenses, $20,000; paid interest due on the note.
    Dec. 31, 19A—Adjust the lease accounts and accrue income taxes at 20%; closing entries not required.

5. Prepare a classified balance sheet for the lessor as of December 31, 19A.
6. Give journal entries for a lessee who leased one of the machines on January 1, 19A, for the following: (*a*) to record the lease, and (*b*) to record payment of first rental and adjustment of lease accounts (present value amortization of the asset).

**Problem 23-5**

Lessor Company and Lessee Company entered into a financing type of lease on January 1, 19A. The lease was for new construction equipment which cost the Lessor Company $200,000 (useful life five years, no residual value). Lessor Company expects 6% return over the five-year period of the lease. The lease calls for five annual rentals payable each January 1, that is, at the *beginning* of each year starting on January 1, 10A. Lessee Company is to assume all the risks and normal costs of ownership and the machines revert to the lessor at the termination of the lease.

*Required:*

1. Show how the Lessor Company would compute the annual rental amount. How would the Lessee Company compute the present value of the lease rights?
2. Prepare an amortization table that would be suitable for each party (straight-line amortization).
3. Give the entries for both the lessor and lessee, in parallel columns, for the years 19A and 19B. You may use abbreviated account titles.
4. Show the items and amounts that would be reported on the income statement and balance sheet at the end of 19B for both the lessor and lessee.

**Problem 23-6**

James Leasing Company rented a new machine to Conway Contractors that cost $18,000; having a four-year life and no residual value at that time. The lease was signed on January 1, 19A, and the lessee was to assume all normal risks and costs of ownership; the lease was noncancellable. The James Company computed the rent on the basis of a 7% return and the lessee utilized this same rate for accounting for the lease. The property will revert to the lessor at termination of the lease.

*Required:*

1. Assuming the annual rentals are payable at the end of each year complete the following: (a) lessor computation of periodic rental payments; (b) lessee computation of the present value of the special property rights under the lease; and (c) an amortization table that would be suitable for both the lessor and lessee.
2. Assuming the annual rentals are payable at the start of each year complete the same three items required in Requirement 1.
3. Give the entries for the lessor and lessee, in parallel columns, for Requirement 2 throughout 19A. You may utilize abbreviated account titles (straight-line amortization).
4. Indicate the asset and liability amounts that would be reported on the balance sheets at December 31, 19A, by the lessor and lessee.

**Problem 23-7 (based on the Appendix)**

Barnes Company, needing a new special trailer, seeks one under lease. Kandu Corporation, a company which specializes in providing such equipment, agreed to furnish a trailer to Barnes' specifications. Kandu acquired the $100,000 trailer by paying $25,000 from its own funds and borrowed the remaining $75,000 on a loan which requires seven equal annual loan payments of $14,902 (due to rounding, the last payment is $2 less). The interest rate is 9%, and the payments are due at the end of each year.

The lease term is for seven years, and Barnes is to pay Kandu $18,555 at the end of each year. The trailer is expected to have a residual value of $6,000 at the end of the seven years; it is to be depreciated initially by the double-declining-balance method for both tax and book purposes; however, in the last two years, straight-line depreciation is to be applied to the remaining book value.* The asset qualifies for the 7% investment credit which is recognized in the first year. Assume that Kandu is subject to an income tax rate of 40% throughout the term of the lease and that the company has other taxable income of substantial amounts.

*Required:*

1. Develop for Kandu a schedule showing annual and cumulative cash flow effects of this lease contract for the seven years. Round all amounts to the nearest dollar. Assume the $6,000 residual value of the property is realized as cash when the lease is terminated.
2. Prepare journal entries for Kandu's books to reflect the lease transactions for the first and second years. This includes acquisition of the leased property, the loan, closing entries, and so on. Assume the operating method of accounting for the lease is used.

* *Hint:* Use .28571 as the depreciation rate.

## Problem 23–8 (based on the Appendix)

Refer to the data in Problem 23–8. Although figures were not given, Kandu's yield rate on the lease, if it were treated as a financing lease (before income taxes and ignoring the investment credit), is 7%.

*Required:*

1. Prepare a schedule to reflect net income for each year (similar to Exhibit 23–5).
2. Prepare journal entries for Kandu's books for all transactions relating to the leased property and the lease for the first two years if the lease were treated as a financing lease. Round all computations to the nearest dollar.

## Problem 23–9 (based on the Appendix)

Lessor Company leased a large machine to Lessee Company for a five-year period, starting on January 1, 19A. Lessor Company acquired the machine especially for Lessee Company at a cost of $250,000, paying cash, $50,000, and borrowing the difference from a bank on a 8% note which provides for four equal annual year-end payments starting on December 31, 19A.

Lessee Company is required to pay five equal annual rental payments determined on the basis of a 9% return to the lessor, not considering the investment credit. The rental payments are to be made each December 31. The lease essentially transfers all of the risks and rewards of ownership to Lessee Company; therefore, it is a financing lease for both parties. However, for tax purposes, the Lessor will realize the 10% investment credit and depreciation over a five-year estimated life, on a straight-line basis with no residual value. Lessor Company has extensive income from other leases; therefore, its average tax rate for the life of this lease is 45%.

*Required:*

(Round all amounts to the nearest dollar.)

1. Compute the amount of the equal annual payments to be made by Lessor Company on the bank loan and prepare a loan amortization schedule.
2. Compute the amount of the equal annual rental payments to be made by Lessee Company.
3. Prepare an estimated cash flow schedule for the Lessor Company covering the life of the lease.
4. Prepare a five-year summary of the income statement effects of this lease for Lessor Company.
5. Prepare the journal entries for 19A to reflect the amounts shown in the income statement prepared in Requirement 4.
6. Prepare an unclassified balance sheet giving the effects of this single lease.

# Chapter 24

# Analysis of Financial Statements

Throughout this book, the focus is on financial reporting to external parties—stockholders, potential investors, financial analysts, creditors, other interested individuals and groups, and the public at large. External financial reports are designed to serve a wide range of users with quite different levels of financial sophistication. In contrast, the management of an enterprise has access to a variety of detailed and summary internal reports—daily, weekly, monthly, quarterly, and annually—to serve their diverse and continuing decision-making needs. Basically, the external reports are not designed to meet the decision-making needs of the management of the enterprise.

Because of the diversity of external users of financial statements, analytical techniques are important. They can be applied to help meet the particular needs of external decision-makers. The accountant is often involved in the analysis, interpretation, and evaluation of financial statements, as well as in the process of their development.

The purpose of this chapter is to discuss and illustrate analytical approaches by which accounting information may be better understood, interpreted, and evaluated for decision-making purposes. However, no single approach can be devised that would be wholly appropriate for all situations.

To add a practical focus an Appendix to the chapter is included which presents a specially selected actual case for study.

## CHARACTERISTICS OF THE ANALYSIS OF FINANCIAL STATEMENTS

Analysis of financial statements focuses on the data reported plus supplementary information from other sources such as the company management, investment advisors, business periodicals, and other materials distributed by the company. These latter sources are often particularly important because many of the strengths and weaknesses of a company may not be reflected directly in the financial statements. For example, the most important element in evaluating the future potentials of a company often is the quality of the management. This kind of information obviously is very difficult to obtain; hence, as an indirect measure of management quality, one is forced to rely largely on the past track record of earnings, financial position, and funds flow as reported in the financial statements. A particularly important aspect of the analysis of financial statements is to identify *major changes* (i.e., turning points) in trends, amounts, and relationships and then to investigate the reasons underlying those changes. Often a *turning point* may provide an early warning of a significant change in the future success or failure of the business.

In analyzing and interpreting financial statements, one should recognize that financial statements necessarily are *organized summaries* of an extensive mass of detailed financial information. For example, the published financial statements of a large corporation, such as General Motors, Exxon, or IBM, usually fills from five to ten printed pages including the supporting notes. It is difficult to imagine the number of transactions, the critical accounting decisions, and the mass of detail summarized in these few pages. It is also difficult to imagine, although it is often true, that amounts of $5 million or more may be immaterial because it is less than 5% of the total base amount of which it is a part. Summarization presents serious communication problems. On the other hand, excessive detail has been found to be undesirable because most statement users experience such constraints as time, motivation, or understanding.

## ANALYTICAL APPROACHES AND TECHNIQUES

The analysis of financial statements is much broader than the mere computation of a few ratios. More importantly, it involves an organized approach to glean from the totality of the statements the maximum amount of interpretative and evaluative information. Often investors look at the net income, EPS, and total asset amounts and then sign off. Important steps in the interpretation and evaluation of financial statements are:

1. Examine the auditors' report.
2. Analyze the statement of accounting policies.
3. Examine the overall financial statements, including notes and supporting schedules.
4. Apply analytical techniques:
   *a.* Comparative statements.
   *b.* Horizontal and vertical percentage analyses.
   *c.* Proportionate (or ratio) analyses.
5. Search for important supplemental information not provided by the financial statements.

## EXAMINE THE AUDITORS' REPORT

Expert financial analysts consistently report that in evaluating a financial statement, the first basic step is careful examination of the auditors' report (often called the accountants' report). Of course, this presumes that the financial statements are audited—if they are not, one should usually give very little, if any, credibility to them. The auditors' report is important because it provides the analyst with information concerning the "fairness" of the representations in the financial statements and calls attention to all major concerns of the auditor that came to light as a result of the auditor's intensive examination.

The auditors' report was discussed in Chapter 5 and it would be advisable to restudy those discussions. Examples of unqualified auditors' opinions were given there and at the end of Chapter 4. Also the Appendix presents an auditors' report and the statements to which it relates. Of particular importance is the possibility that instead of an *unqualified opinion*, the auditor may give *(a)* a qualified opinion, *(b)* an adverse opinion, or *(c)* a disclaimer of opinion. Each of these unfavorable opinions must include an explanation by the auditor of the underlying factors. These serve to alert the statement user to major problem areas that should be carefully investigated. Throughout the process of statement analysis, these problem areas should be kept to the forefront. Often they are so significant that the company will go to great lengths to satisfy the requirements for an unqualified opinion. An unfavorable auditors' opinion generally causes an immediate and significant adverse impact on the market price of the company's stock, on the credit standing, and perhaps even on their general reputation—depending of course on the nature and magnitude of the problem cited.

Below is a qualified opinion (and related matters) illustrating the kind of information frequently cited by an auditor.[1] Observe in this situation that the qualification is related to an expropriation by a foreign government, an action over which the management of the company had no control. Nevertheless, the action will have a significant adverse affect on the earnings and financial position of the company for a number of years, although this is not reflected in the historical financial information, up to an including the financial statements to which this opinion relates. Clearly, this is the single most important bit of information in the financial statements for this particular situation.

To the Board of Directors and Shareholders
The Anaconda Company

We have examined the consolidated balance sheets of The Anaconda Company as of December 31, 1973 and 1972 and the related statements of consolidated income and retained earnings and of changes in consolidated financial position for the years then ended. Our examinations were made

---

[1] Anaconda Company, Annual Report, 1973. Extracted from AICPA *Accounting Trends and Techniques*, 28th ed. (New York, 1975) pp. 411–12.

in accordance with generally accepted auditing standards and accordingly included such tests of the accounting records and such other auditing procedures as we considered necessary in the circumstances.

The current status of the company's efforts to obtain compensation for the 1971 loss, through expropriation, of its Chilean investments is reported on page 23 of this Annual Report. The net amount the company may realize as indemnification for its expropriated investments from Chile, Overseas Private Investment Corporation, or through court actions, is not subject to final determination at this time.

In our opinion, subject to the effect of the ultimate resolution of the uncertainties referred to in the preceding paragraph, the accompanying consolidated financial statements present fairly the consolidated financial position of The Anaconda Company and its consolidated subsidiaries at December 31, 1973 and 1972 and the results of their operations and the changes in financial position for the years then ended, in conformity with generally accepted accounting principles. These principles have been consistently applied during the period subsequent to the change, with which we concur, made as of January 1, 1972 in the method of translating foreign currency obligations as described on page 26 of this Annual Report.
— *Report of Independent Accountants.*

*Financial Review*

*Current Status of Chilean Expropriation Loss* — During the year Anaconda continued its efforts to recover losses resulting from the expropriation of its investments in Chile by the Chilean government in 1971.

The government of President Allende, which expropriated the investments, was deposed by Chilean military forces on September 11, 1973 and was replaced by a military government. The new government is taking steps to restore the productivity of the mines and to reestablish credit relationships throughout the world.

Representatives of the new government have advised the company that they expect to initate negotiations on the issues of the payment of compensation for the expropriated investments and the possible role of Anaconda in the development and operation of Chile's copper properties. Anaconda has indicated its willingness to participate in such negotiations and preliminary meetings have been held. The government has publicly stated that the mines will not be returned to the former owners.

Anaconda is preserving its rights to pursue other remedies, including the following:

Ligitation is still pending in New York on suits brought against Corporacion del Cobre and Corporacion de Fomento de la Produccion, Chilean public corporations, for unpaid principal and interest due on promissory notes issued at the end of 1969 in connection with the sale of a 51% interest in Anaconda's major properties in Chile.

Included in the Consolidated Balance Sheet at December 31, 1973 and 1972 is the aggregate amount of the claims pending against Overseas Private Investment Corporation (OPIC) as a result of the expropriation of investments in the Chuquicamata and El Salvador properties. In 1972 OPIC formally rejected these claims. The company continues to believe that it is entitled to payment, and has submitted the claims to binding arbitration as provided in the OPIC insurance contracts. Proceedings before the arbitration panel are expected to take place in 1974.

## ANALYZE THE STATEMENT OF ACCOUNTING POLICIES

Accounting is man-made and must accommodate a wide variety of circumstances. Although accounting principles and their implementation are largely prescribed by the *ARBs*, *APB Opinions*, FASB *Statements*, and by precedent, there is considerable room for judgment by the reporting entity and by the independent accountant. Also, in numerous areas of accounting, several alternatives are acceptable, such as the completed-contract and percentage-of-completion methods of recognizing revenue on long-term construction contracts (see Chapter 11). The range of judgments and alternatives permitted place the statement user in a literal "no-man's land" if the major judgments made and alternatives used by the company are not clearly communicated.

In response to the *full-disclosure* principle, *APB Opinion No. 22* (April 1972) states that "information about the accounting policies adopted by a reporting entity is essential for financial statement users." Accounting policies are the specific accounting principles and methods of application that have been adopted by a company for preparation of its financial statements. The *Opinion* requires that a statement of these policies be clearly enunciated either in the notes, or preferably "in a separate *Summary of Significant Accounting Policies* preceding the notes to the financial statements or as the initial note." The statement must disclose all important accounting policies including (a) selections from acceptable alternatives, (b) accounting policies used that are peculiar to the industry, and (c) unusual or innovative applications of generally accepted accounting principles. Examples include the basis for consolidated statements, depreciation and amortization methods, inventory pricing, translation of foreign currencies, revenue recognition on long-term construction contracts, franchising, and leasing.

An comprehensive statement of accounting policies for a well-known company follows:

SHELL OIL COMPANY (DEC)
*Accounting Policies*
This summary of the major accounting policies of Shell Oil Company and its consolidated subsidiaries (hereinafter referred to as "Shell") is presented to assist the reader in evaluating Shell's financial statements and other data contained in this report. In all material respects, Shell has consistently followed these policies for the ten year period covered by this annual report and originally reported net income has not been revised or restated. As noted below, in 1973 Shell changed its method of valuing inventories of oils and chemicals.
*Principles of Consolidation* — The financial statements include the accounts of Shell Oil Company (hereinafter referred to as "Company") and all of its wholly owned subsidiaries. All companies acquired have consistently been accounted for as purchases; goodwill, if any, is amortized over a period of benefit which has not exceeded ten years.
The only subsidiary of Shell not wholly owned is Butte Pipe Line Company (51% owned), and the investment therein, plus the investments in less than majority owned companies in which Shell has a voting stock interest of 20% or more, are carried at equity in underlying net assets. Investments

in less than 20% owned companies are carried at cost with dividends recorded in income as received.

*Short Term Securities* – Short term securities are carried at cost which approximates market. Interest is accrued and reflected in dividends, interest and other income.

*Inventories* – In 1973 the Company adopted as its cost basis the last-in-first-out method of valuing inventories of oils and chemicals. Prior to 1973 inventories of oils and chemicals were carried at the lower of market or of the average cost resulting from charging to costs the highest of inventory carrying value, current cost of production or purchases. Materials and supplies inventories are carried at average cost or less, as in the past.

The new method, which was adopted to achieve a better matching of current costs against current income and to conform more closely to U.S. petroleum industry practice, had no material effect on 1973 net income.

*Mineral Leasehold Costs* – Direct cost of acquiring undeveloped acreage, generally called lease bonus, is capitalized. Amortization from date of acquisition is based upon experience of the Company in order to fully amortize over the holding period those leases that may be unproductive. The cost of leases which become productive is transferred to a producing property account.

*Exploratory Costs* Exploratory expenses, including geological and geophysical expenses, annual delay rentals on oil and gas leases and all exploratory and development dry hole costs are charged to income as incurred.

*Research* – Expenditures for research, except for land, buildings and standard items of equipment which extend beyond the immediate life of a project, are expensed when incurred.

*Depreciation, Depletion and Amortization* – Depreciation, depletion and amortization of the capital cost of producing properties, both tangible and intangible, are provided for on a unit of production basis. Developed reserves are used in computing unit rates for tangible and intangible development costs and proved reserves for depletion of leasehold costs. In all cases the unit determination is by field. Other plant and equipment are depreciated on a straight line basis over their estimated useful lives. On a cycle basis asset lives are reviewed for propriety of estimated useful life. Changes in depreciation rates, if any, are prospective only. Differing rates or deductions are used for tax purposes.

*Maintenance, Repairs and Retirement of Properties* – Major renewals and betterments are charged to the property accounts while minor replacements, maintenance and repairs which do not improve or extend life are expensed currently. At the time properties are retired or otherwise disposed of in the normal course of business, the cost is charged against the accumulated provision; however, if the retirement relates to a casualty or material obsolescence, the loss or gain is reflected in current income.

*Office Relocation, Employee Relocation and Severance Costs* – The cost directly related to relocating operating and executive offices from New York was amortized over a four year period ending in September, 1973. The cost of consolidating research facilities is being amortized over a four year period commencing in January, 1972. All other office relocation, employee relocation or severance costs are charged to expense when incurred.

*Non-Mineral Leases* – Obligations under noncancellable leases and other contractual commitments are reflected in the Notes to Financial Statements.

*Income Taxes* — Items of income or income deductions are often recognized for payment of income taxes and for book purposes in different time periods; however, tax allocation accounting as prescribed by Accounting Principles Board Opinion No. 11 adjusts book income to eliminate the effect of all material book/tax timing differences.

For those differences pertaining to capital extinguishments, including intangible drilling and development costs deducted currently for tax purposes, tax deferment is computed by applying the current tax rates to the current difference in deduction. The net cumulative effect is reflected in Deferred Credits — Federal Income Taxes in the Balance Sheet.

For other timing differences tax deferment is computed by setting up initial differences at current tax rates and reversing these amounts in the appropriate subsequent period. The net cumulative effect of the latter is reflected in Receivables, Prepayments, Etc. in the Balance Sheet.

Investment tax credits are applied to reduce federal income taxes in the year realized.[2]

The information in the statement of accounting policies is fundamental to understanding, interpreting, and evaluating much of the significant information reported in the financial statements. It is particularly useful in evaluating the *credibility and quality of the reported earnings,* and in comparing data across companies and industries.

## OVERALL EXAMINATION OF THE FINANCIAL STATEMENTS

Following the examination of the accountants' opinion and analysis of the summary of accounting policies used by the company, the interpretation and evaluation process should continue with a careful examination of the financial statements in their entirety. This phase of the analysis involves study of each statement in order to gain overall perspective and to identify major strengths, weaknesses, and unusual changes such as *turning points* in the trend of sales, earnings, asset structure, liabilities, and cash flow.

The overall examination should include careful study of all of the statements included and the *notes* referred to in those statements. Each note should be read and evaluated at the point in the statement where it is referenced. Consideration of the notes as a separate activity is not fruitful; a specific note is helpful primarily in the context of the specific statement item to which it is referenced.

Concurrent with, or subsequent to, the overall examination of the financial statements under review, application of the techniques of proportional analysis, discussed in the next section, are often quite helpful to the analyst.

## APPLICATION OF ANALYTICAL TECHNIQUES

Several techniques are used to enhance communication by financial statements. Techniques commonly incorporated in the financial state-

---

[2] Shell Oil Company, Annual Report, 1973. Extracted from AICPA, *Accounting Trends and Techniques,* 28th ed. (New York, 1975) pp. 17–18.

ments themselves are earnings per share (EPS), subclassifications of information on the statements, comparative statements, and supplementary information in separate schedules and notes to the statements. In addition, numerous analytical techniques often are applied, external to the financial statements, to aid the particular external decision-maker in the evaluation process. Some of the techniques often used are discussed in the paragraphs to follow.

### Comparative Statements

Comparative statements involve the presentation of financial information for the current and one or more past periods in a way that facilitates comparison by the statement user. Basically, comparative statements are of two types, viz:

1. Presentation of financial reports for (a) the current year, and (b) the immediately preceding year.
2. Presentation of selected financial information for a number of years past (usually five or ten years). These are often referred to as *financial summaries.*

Trends in the financial development of a business have particular significance to all users. The comparison of current results with those of one or more prior periods provides the reader wih an added perspective in evaluating the reasonableness of current performance; that is, the period results provide a sound basis for evaluating progress, improvement, or deterioration. In recognition of the importance of presenting comparative financial information, the AICPA Committee on Accounting Procedure, in *Bulletin No. 43*, Chapter 2, stated:

> 1. The presentation of comparative financial statements in annual and other reports enhances the usefulness of such reports and brings out more clearly the nature and trends of current changes affecting the enterprise. Such presentation emphasizes the fact that statements for a series of periods are far more significant than those for a single period and that the accounts for one period are but an installment of what is essentially a continous history.
> 2. In any one year it is ordinarily desirable that the balance sheet, the income statement, and the statement of retained earnings be given for one or more preceding years as well as for the current year. Footnotes, explanations, and accountants' qualifications which appeared on the statements for the preceding years should be repeated, or at least referred to, in the comparative statements to the extent that they continue to be of significance. If, because of reclassifications or for other reasons, changes have occurred in the manner of or basis for presenting corresponding items for two or more periods, information should be furnished which will explain the change. This procedure is in conformity with the well recognized principle that any change in practice which affects comparability should be disclosed.

As a result of this pronouncement, practically all published financial statements include comparative data for the current and prior year. The actual financial statements illustrated at the end of Chapters 4 and 5, and at the end of this chapter, are comparative.

For illustrative purposes, the financial statements for WZ Corporation are used throughout this chapter. Exhibits 24–1, 24–2, and 24–3 present the three comparative statements (condensed for discussion purposes). Observe the form: the current year results in the first column, and single underscores for subtotals to facilitate the presentation in a single column for each period. Placing the various items for the two periods in juxtaposition in the two columns is thought to be preferable to separation as would be necessary for the multiple column approach for each period.

The *long-term summaries* of selected financial information often included in the annual financial report are especially significant. An excellent example of such a summary is presented at the end of this chapter. Observe in particular the nature of the items selected for inclusion in the summary. These vital statistics of the long-term financial performance of the company are particularly relevant to practically all statement users. The annual financial statements for a particular

**EXHIBIT 24–1**

### WZ CORPORATION
### Comparative Income Statements
### For the Years Ended December 31, 1975 and 1976

|  | 1976 | | 1975 | |
| --- | --- | --- | --- | --- |
| *Revenues:* | *Amount* | *Percent** | *Amount* | *Percent** |
| Sales......................................... | $400,000 | | $370,000 | |
| Investment revenue ..................... | 4,500 | | 3,000 | |
| Gain on disposal of investments ... | 500 | | | |
| Total Revenue ................. | 405,000 | 100 | 373,000 | 100 |
| Expenses: | | | | |
| Cost of goods sold ...................... | 265,000 | 65 | 250,000 | 67 |
| Distribution................................ | 67,000 | 17 | 61,200 | 16 |
| General administrative .............. | 30,000 | 7 | 27,000 | 7 |
| Interest...................................... | 7,100 | 2 | 6,200 | 2 |
| Total Expenses .................. | 369,100 | 91 | 344,400 | 92 |
| Pretax operating income ........... | 35,900 | 9 | 28,600 | 8 |
| Income tax expense | 16,155 | 4 | 12,870 | 4 |
| Income before extraordinary item... | 19,745 | 5 | | |
| Extraordinary loss (net of taxes, $3,600) ............................... | 4,400 | 1 | | |
| Net Income............................... | $ 15,345 | 4 | $ 15,730 | 4 |
| Earnings per share: | | | | |
| Income before extraordinary item ................................... | $.40 | | | |
| Extraordinary item .................. | .11 | | | |
| Net Income† ............................. | $.29 | | $.33 | |

\* For illustrative purposes; not usually included on published statements.

† ($15,345 − $2,500) ÷ 44,000 = $.29.
($15,730 − $2,500) ÷ 40,000 = $.33.

**EXHIBIT 24-2**

### WZ CORPORATION
Comparative Balance Sheets
At December 31, 1975, and 1976

| | 1976 | | 1975 | |
|---|---|---|---|---|
| *Assets* | *Amount* | *Percent** | *Amount* | *Percent** |
| Current Assets: | | | | |
| Cash.......................................... | $ 55,000 | 12 | $ 74,000 | 16 |
| Investments, short term ............... | 4,000 | 1 | 10,000 | 2 |
| Accounts receivable (net of allowance for doubtful accounts) | 39,000 | 8 | 30,000 | 6 |
| Inventory (*Fifo,* lower of cost or market) ............................ | 95,000 | 20 | 80,000 | 17 |
| Prepaid expenses ..................... | 200 | | 1,000 | |
| Total Current Assets ......... | 193,200 | 41 | 195,000 | 41 |
| Long-term investments ............... | 55,000 | 11 | 50,000 | 11 |
| Land, plant, and equipment: | | | | |
| Land....................................... | 10,000 | 2 | 10,000 | 2 |
| Plant and equipment ................. | 315,000 | 66 | 290,000 | 62 |
| Less: Accumulated depreciation ... | (97,000) | (20) | (77,000) | (16) |
| Total............................... | 228,000 | 48 | 223,000 | 48 |
| Intangible assets: | | | | |
| Patent (less amortization) ........... | 1,800 | | 2,000 | |
| Total Assets ..................... | $478,000 | 100 | $470,000 | 100 |
| *Liabilities* | | | | |
| Current Liabilities: | | | | |
| Accounts payable........................ | $ 40,000 | 8 | $ 55,000 | 12 |
| Notes payable, short term ............ | 5,000 | 1 | 8,000 | 2 |
| Taxes payable .......................... | 4,555 | 1 | 7,000 | 1 |
| Total Current Liabilities ...... | 49,555 | 10 | 70,000 | 15 |
| Long-Term Liabilities: | | | | |
| Bonds payable (less unamortized discount) ........... | 99,100 | 21 | 99,000 | 21 |
| Total Liabilities ................. | 148,655 | 31 | 169,000 | 36 |
| Stockholders' Equity: | | | | |
| Common stock, par $5, authorized 60,000 shares ......... | 220,000 | 46 | 200,000 | 42 |
| Preferred stock, 5%, par $10, authorized 10,000 shares | 50,000 | 10 | 50,000 | 11 |
| Contributed capital in excess of par, common stock .................. | 14,000 | 3 | 12,000 | 3 |
| Retained earnings ..................... | 45,345 | 10 | 39,000 | 8 |
| Total Stockholders' Equity... | 329,345 | 69 | 301,000 | 64 |
| Total Liabilities and Stockholders' Equity ... | $478,000 | 100 | $470,000 | 100 |

* For illustrative purposes; not usually included on published financial statements.

**EXHIBIT 24–3**

WZ CORPORATION
Comparative Statements of Changes in Financial Position, Working Capital Basis
For the Years Ended December 31, 1975 and 1976

| | 1976 | | 1975 | |
|---|---|---|---|---|
| | Amount | Percent* | Amount | Percent* |
| Sources of Working Capital: | | | | |
| Income before extraordinary items... | $19,745 | | $15,730 | |
| Add (deduct) items not requiring or generating working capital: | | | | |
| Depreciation ............................. | 20,000 | | 18,000 | |
| Amortization of bond discount...... | 100 | | 100 | |
| Amortization of patent .............. | 200 | | 200 | |
| Working capital provided by operations......................... | 40,045 | 66 | 34,030 | 86 |
| Extraordinary loss (net of tax) ......... | (4,400) | (7) | | |
| Total .................................... | 35,645 | 59 | 34,030 | 86 |
| Other sources: | | | | |
| Sale of common stock .............. | 22,000 | 36 | 5,500 | 14 |
| Tax refund (from 1974) .............. | 3,000 | 5 | | |
| Total from Other Sources ......... | 25,000 | 41 | 5,500 | 14 |
| Total Funds Provided ......... | $60,645 | 100 | $39,530 | 100 |
| Uses of Working Capital: | | | | |
| Equipment acquired ..................... | $25,000 | 59 | | |
| Long-term investments ................. | 5,000 | 12 | 10,000 | 56 |
| Cash dividends ........................... | 12,000 | 29 | 8,000 | 44 |
| Total Funds Used............... | $42,000 | 100 | $18,000 | 100 |
| Difference—Net Increase in Working Capital ........................ | $18,645 | | $21,530 | |
| Summary of Changes in Components of Working Capital: | | | | |
| Increase (decrease) in current assets: | | | | |
| Cash ...................................... | $(19,000) | | $ (6,070) | |
| Investments, short term............... | (6,000) | | 10,000 | |
| Accounts receivable (net)........... | 9,000 | | 11,000 | |
| Inventory ............................... | 15,000 | | 12,000 | |
| Prepaid expenses .................... | (800) | | 600 | |
| Total ............................... | (1,800) | | 27,530 | |
| Increase (decrease) in current liabilities: | | | | |
| Accounts payable ..................... | 15,000 | | (2,000) | |
| Notes payable, short term........... | 3,000 | | (3,000) | |
| Taxes payable ......................... | 2,445 | | (1,000) | |
| Total ............................... | 20,445 | | (6,000) | |
| Net Increase in Working Capital...... | $ 18,645 | | $21,530 | |

* For illustrative purposes; not usually included on published financial statements.

year present a very narrow view of the successes and failures of the company. In contrast, the long-term summary provides a broad overview of where the company has been (financially) and where it is apt to go in the future. Clearly, the results of one, or even two, years may give an overly optimistic or pessimistic view of the future potentials of the company. It is for these reasons that experienced analysts always take a careful look at the long-term summary. Its importance is suggested by the current discussions concerning the desirability of subjecting the summary to audit which is not now required.

## PERCENTAGE ANALYSIS OF FINANCIAL STATEMENTS

Financial information expressed in absolute amounts is necessary for practically all purposes; nevertheless, there is a weakness in that proportionate relationships are not clearly revealed. Thus, the expression of relationships in terms of percentages significantly aids the interpretation of financial information. There are two common forms of percentage analyses used on financial statements – vertical analysis and horizontal analysis.

*Vertical analysis* involves the expression of each item on a particular financial statement as a percent of one specific item which is referred to as the base. For example, the component items on the income statement may be expressed as a percent of total revenue as shown in Exhibit 24–1. Note that the base amount representing 100% is divided into each component item to derive the component percentages, and that the percentages may then be summed. Alternatively, the relationships may be expressed as ratios, in which case net sales would represent 1.00 (rather than 100%) and the components likewise would be expressed in terms of this base.

In applying vertical analysis, an appropriate base amount must be selected for each statement. Observe on Exhibit 24–2 that the base amount for the balance sheet is total assets, and total liabilities plus stockholders' equity respectively; and in Exhibit 24–3 the base amounts for the statement of changes in financial position are total funds provided and total funds used respectively. Financial statements expressed in percentages only are referred to as *common-size* statements.

*Horizontal analysis* refers to the development of percentages indicating the proportionate change in the same item over *time*. The conversion of absolute amounts of change to percentages facilitates interpretation and evaluation of trends. For example, horizontal percentages shown on the income statements in Exhibit 24–4 serve to emphasize the trend of each component.

It should be noted in the examples relating to horizontal analysis that in computing the percent as well as the amounts of increase or decrease, the base year usually is the earlier period. The percents may not be added or subtracted as between lines since each separate component percentage has a different base. In this respect, attention should be called to the incorrectness of percentages of increase and decrease

EXHIBIT 24–4

WZ CORPORATION
Comparative Income Statements
For the Years Ended December 31, 1975 and 1976
(horizontal analysis)

| | Year Ended December 31 | | Increase or (decrease) 1976 over 1975 | |
| --- | --- | --- | --- | --- |
| | 1976 | 1975 | Amount | Percent |
| Revenues: | | | | |
| Sales......................................... | $400,000 | $370,000 | $30,000 | 8 |
| Investment revenue ..................... | 4,500 | 3,000 | 1,500 | 50 |
| Gain on disposal of investments ... | 500 | | 500 | |
| Total Revenue ................. | 405,000 | 373,000 | 32,000 | 9 |
| Expenses: | | | | |
| Cost of goods sold ..................... | 265,000 | 250,000 | 15,000 | 6 |
| Distribution................................ | 67,000 | 61,200 | 5,800 | 9 |
| General administrative .............. | 30,000 | 27,000 | 3,000 | 11 |
| Interest...................................... | 7,100 | 6,200 | 900 | 15 |
| Total Expenses ................. | 369,100 | 344,400 | 24,700 | 7 |
| Pretax operating income ............ | 35,900 | 28,600 | 7,300 | 26 |
| Income tax expense.................. | 16,155 | 12,870 | 3,285 | 26 |
| Income before extraordinary item... | 19,745 | 15,730 | 4,015 | 26 |
| Extraordinary loss (net of taxes). | 4,400 | | 4,400 | |
| Net Income ................................ | $ 15,345 | $ 15,730 | $ (385) | (2) |

which are computed from negative or zero base-year amounts. For example, assume a net loss in 19A of $5,000 and a net gain in 19B of $5,000. With an actual increase of $10,000 the ratio of increase appears to be a minus 200% (+10,000 ÷ −$5,000), a computation which may be misleading. Manifestly, percentage figures should not be computed for accounts which for the base year had no balance or a negative balance. The table in Exhibit 24–5 points out the correct procedure for computing percentages resulting from horizontal increases and decreases.

In considering percentage increases or decreases the analyst also should be aware of misleading inferences when the absolute amounts are small. For example, assume a particular expense in 19A was $10 and in 19B, $30. The percentage increase is 200% which appears significant despite the fact that there was only a $20 increase.

When the statements for more than two years are to be compared, the columns may be shown as in Exhibit 24–6. Note that the base year for 19B changes is 19A, while the base year for 19C changes is 19B.

Practically all users of financial statements will benefit significantly from comparative data and percentage analyses. In this respect a word of caution is in order; the accountant, whether industrial or public, should be discriminating in the selection of information to be presented to the several groups of users; for example, an income statement prepared for internal use should be quite different from one prepared for

**EXHIBIT 24–5**
**Computing Differences – Horizontal Analysis**

| | December 31 | | Increase (decrease) | |
| --- | --- | --- | --- | --- |
| | 19B | 19A | Amount | Percent |
| Positive amounts in the base year (19A): | | | | |
| Item No. 1 ..................................... | $ (200) | $800 | $(1,000) | (125) |
| 2 ..................................... | – | 800 | (800) | (100) |
| 3 ..................................... | 200 | 800 | (600) | (75) |
| 4 ..................................... | 1,200 | 800 | 400 | 50 |
| Negative amounts in the base year (19A): | | | | |
| Item No. 5 ..................................... | (1,000) | (800) | (200) | – |
| 6 ..................................... | 200 | (800) | 1,000 | – |
| 7 ..................................... | – | (800) | 800 | – |
| No amounts in the base year (19A): | | | | |
| Item No. 8 ..................................... | 200 | – | 200 | – |
| 9 ..................................... | (200) | – | (200) | – |

external use. Frequently, the quantitative information presented is so voluminous that the user is confused rather than enlightened, or perhaps completely discouraged, thereby precluding serious consideration of the information. It should be realized that large volumes of complex tabulations dismay the average person. Discrimination must be exercised in selecting (a) information relevant to the normal problems of the intended users, and (b) appropriate analyses of data that will shed light on the situations generally confronting expected users.

In interpreting comparative data and the related percentage analyses, the accountant, as well as the user, should recognize unusual or nonrecurring items that are reflected in the data for each of the periods. Nonrecurring items should be omitted in projecting future potentials. In addition, changes in the general price level (value of the dollar) may have a significant monetary effect on financial data covering a long period. In such cases it may be desirable to express data for all periods in terms of dollars of current (or common) purchasing power (see Chapter 25).

**EXHIBIT 24–6**
**Determination of Base Period**

| | December 31 | | | Increase– Decrease* | | Percent of Increase– Decrease* | |
| --- | --- | --- | --- | --- | --- | --- | --- |
| | 19C | 19B | 19A | During 19C | During 19B | During 19C | During 19B |
| Item No. 1 ......... | $200 | $400 | $300 | $200* | $100 | 50.0* | 33.3 |
| 2 ......... | 400 | 300 | 200 | 100 | 100 | 33.3 | 50.0 |
| 3 ......... | 400 | 300 | 400 | 100 | 100* | 33.3 | 25.0* |

## PROPORTIONATE (OR RATIO) ANALYSIS

The relationship between two amounts may be expressed as a fraction, a percent, or a decimal. The analysis of financial statements generally includes one or more forms of proportionate analysis (often called ratio analysis). It involves the selection of two amounts from one statement, such as the income statement, or from two statements, such as the income statement and balance sheet. The amounts may represent the balances of two different accounts, the balance of one account and a classification total (such as total assets), or two classification totals. Proportionate analysis, however expressed, is supplementary information for the decision-maker that often is particularly important in interpreting the information provided directly by the financial statements.

The mode of expression of proportionate analysis is quite varied. To illustrate, working capital has been discussed and referred to in a number of preceding chapters. The *current ratio* is the relationship between current assets and current liabilities. Assume the following:

| | |
|---|---|
| Current assets | $5,000,000 |
| Current liabilities | 2,000,000 |
| Difference — Working Capital | $3,000,000 |

The amount of working capital, $3,000,000, standing alone is a useful figure; however, proportionate analysis adds insight to this relationship, viz:

Current Ratio (or working capital ratio) = $5,000,000 ÷ $2,000,000 = 2.5

Alternatively, this ratio may be expressed as 250%; 2.5 to 1; or for each $2.50 of current assets there was $1 of current liabilities.

Proportionate analysis is significant only when the relationship between the selected factors, when expressed as a proportionate relationship, sheds additional light on the interpretation of the individual absolute amounts. In view of the large number of ratios that could be computed it is important that the accountant select for analysis only those related amounts that appear to have significance. In determining significance, consideration must be given to the purposes for which the ratios are to be used. Investors, managers, and creditors have essentially different interests and problems; consequently, they would have somewhat different needs with respect to ratio analyses. Since a complete study of proportionate analysis is outside the scope of this text, only representative ratios having general application are discussed. The analyses selected for discussion will be explained under the following general headings:

1. Proportionate measurements of current position.
2. Proportionate measurements of equity position.
3. Proportionate measurements of operating results.

## PROPORTIONATE MEASUREMENTS OF CURRENT POSITION

The proportionate measurements in this category focus on working capital; they are supplementary to the statement of changes of financial position, working capital basis. The ratios relate to selected elements of working capital and are designed to help the statement user evaluate the short-term liquidity and the ability of the business to meet its maturing current liabilities. Seven measurements of current position are summarized in Exhibit 24-7. Observe that they are variously expressed as a percent, decimal, fraction, or turnover figure. The analysis of current position involves (a) tests of overall liquidity, and (b) movement of current assets (turnovers).[3]

### Current Ratio

The current or working capital ratio has long been recognized as an index of short-term liquidity—the ability of the business to meet the maturing claims of the creditors plus the current operating costs. The amount of working capital and the related ratio have a direct impact on the amount of short-term credit that may be granted. Traditionally, as a rule of thumb, a working capital ratio of 2 to 1 has been considered to be adequate. However, analysts in recent years have tended to disavow simplistic decision rules such as this one in favor of a more enlightened approach. The working capital ratio tends to be unique to the industry in which the business operates and even to the business itself in the light of its operating and financial characteristics. For example, a ratio of 2 to 1 may be realistic in one situation, but it may be too low or too high in another situation. The peculiarities of the industry in which the firm operates and other factors, such as methods of operations and seasonal influences, also should be taken into account in evaluating the current ratio.

The working capital ratio is only one measure or index of solvency and ability to meet short-term obligations, and it has certain weaknesses. A high working capital ratio may be the result of overstocking of inventory; a business may have a high current ratio while at the same time it may have a cash deficit. In addition, an extremely high working capital ratio may indicate excess funds which should be invested or otherwise put to use. As with all ratios there is a delicate balance between a ratio that is too high and one that is too low. The determination of the most desirable ratio varies from firm to firm, and the determination of the optimum ratio for a particular firm is a complex problem.

---

[3] The reader should be cautioned that there is no single "generally accepted" method of computing specific ratios or of determining the values to be substituted in the formulas. Generally the precise computation should be determined by (1) the data available, and (2) the use and interpretation expected in the particular situation. The formulas given herein are indicative of the general approach.

## Acid-Test Ratio

Cash, accounts receivable, short-term notes receivable, and short-term investments in marketable securities generally represent funds which may be made readily available for paying current obligations,

**EXHIBIT 24–7**
**Ratios that Measure Current Position**

| Ratio | Formula for Computation | Significance |
|---|---|---|
| *Ratios that measure short-term solvency:* | | |
| 1. Current or working capital ratio. | $\dfrac{\text{Current Assets}}{\text{Current Liabilities}}$ | Primary test of short-term liquidity indicates ability to meet current obligations from current assets as a going concern. Measure of adequacy of working capital. |
| 2. Acid-test or quick ratio. | $\dfrac{\text{Quick Assets}}{\text{Current Liabilities}}$ | A more severe test of immediate liquidity than the current ratio. Tests ability to meet sudden demands upon current assets. |
| 3. Working capital to total assets. | $\dfrac{\text{Working Capital}}{\text{Total Assets}}$ | Indicates relative liquidity of total assets and distribution of resources employed. |
| *Ratios that measure movement of current assets(turnover):* | | |
| 4. *a.* Receivable turnover. | $\dfrac{\text{Net Credit Sales}}{\text{Average Receivables (Net)}}$ | Velocity of collection of trade accounts and notes. Test of efficiency of collection. |
| *b.* Age of receivables. | $\dfrac{365 \text{ (Days)}}{\text{Receivable Turnover (computed per [a] above)}}$ | Average number of days to collect receivables. |
| 5. Inventory turnover. *a.* Merchandise turnover (retail firm). | $\dfrac{\text{Cost of Goods Sold}}{\text{Average Merchandise Inventory}}$ | Indicates liquidity of inventory. Number of times inventory "turned over" or was sold on the average during the period. Will exhibit tendency to over- or under-stock. |
| *b.* Finished goods turnover (manufacturing firm). | $\dfrac{\text{Cost of Goods Sold}}{\text{Average Finished Goods Inventory}}$ | Same as 5*(a)*. |
| *c.* Raw material turnover. | $\dfrac{\text{Cost of Raw Materials Used}}{\text{Average Raw Materials Inventory}}$ | Number of times raw material inventory was "used" on the average during the period. |
| *d.* Days' supply in inventory. | $\dfrac{365 \text{ (Days)}}{\text{Inventory Turnover (computed per [a], [b], or [c] above)}}$ | Average number of days' supply in the ending inventory. Indicates general condition of over- or understocking. |
| 6. Working capital turnover. | $\dfrac{\text{Net Sales}}{\text{Average Working Capital}}$ | Indicates adequacy and activity of working capital. |
| 7. Percent of each current asset to total current assets. | $\dfrac{\text{Each Current Asset}}{\text{Total Current Assets}}$ | Indicates relative investment in each current asset. |

hence they are referred to as *quick assets*. Inventories, on the other hand, must be sold and collection made before cash is available for paying obligations. In many cases, particularly where there are raw materials and work in process inventories, the time element as well as marketability involve considerable uncertainty. In view of these considerations the quick ratio (quick assets divided by current liabilities) has come into general usage as a significant test of immediate solvency. Traditionally, an acid-test ratio of 1 to 1 (a rule-of-thumb standard) has been considered to be desirable. As with the current ratio, the acid-test ratio for a particular company must be evaluated in light of industry characteristics and other factors.

## Working Capital to Total Assets

The ratio of working capital to total assets often is considered to be an important ratio in that it is a generalized expression of the distribution and liquidity of the assets employed after current liabilities have been deducted from the current assets. An excessively high ratio might indicate excess cash and/or overstocking of inventory, whereas a low ratio would indicate a definite weakness in the current position.

A related analysis involves a *vertical* percentage analysis of current assets employing *total current assets* as the base (100%). This analysis has particular significance in that (*a*) the relative composition of the current asset structure is revealed, and (*b*) when compared with similar data from prior periods, important trends may be revealed.

## Evaluation of Movement of Current Assets

The usual operating cycle for a trading business is from cash to inventory to receivables and back to cash. The analysis of the movement of inventory and receivables is significant in that efficiency of use of these individual items of current assets has a direct bearing on the current position and the overall efficiency with which operations are conducted. Receivable turnover (collections) and inventory turnover are critical in respect to cash flow and funds invested.

## Receivable Turnover

In some businesses cash sales predominate, whereas in others credit sales predominate. In either case the amount of trade receivables on the average should bear some relationship to the sales for the period and the terms of credit. The application of the receivable turnover in these respects may be illustrated by referring to WZ Corporation financial statements (Exhibits 24–1 and 24–2):

$$\frac{\text{Receivable}}{\text{Turnover}} = \frac{\text{Credit Sales, \$345,000}}{\text{Average Receivables, } \dfrac{\$30,000 + \$39,000}{2}} = 10$$

$$\text{Age of Receivables} = \frac{365 \text{ Days}}{10} = 36.5 \text{ (average number of days to collect)}$$

If we assume the terms of sale are 1/10, n/30, it appears that collections are lagging terms by six days or more on the average—a reflection of lack of care and inefficiencies with which (a) credit is granted, and (b) collections are made.

The above simplified illustration also points up several technical aspects of the computation, viz:

1. Should the total of cash and credit sales, or credit sales only, be used in the computation? A more stable and meaningful ratio will result if credit sales only are used; otherwise a shift in the proportion of cash to credit sales will affect the ratio although collection experience is unchanged. For internal use credit sales should be used (since the figure is available or may be reconstructed readily); however, for comparison with other firms the total of cash and credit sales generally must be used since published data seldom provide the credit sales figures for other businesses.

2. Should the ending balance of receivables or average receivables be used? The average *monthly* receivables balance generally should be used in order to smooth out seasonal influences. The average should be determined by adding the 13 monthly balances (January 1, January 31, and through December 31) of trade accounts and trade notes receivable, then dividing by 13. In the absence of monthly balances the average of the annual beginning and ending balance or only the ending balance may be used. For comparison with other firms the ending balance may, by necessity, have to be used.

3. Receivables should be net of the allowance for doubtful accounts.

4. Trade notes receivable should be included in averaging receivables.

Whether to express the receivable movement as a "turnover" or as "number of days to collect" is principally a matter of personal preference. It is appropriate to note that if the company uses a "natural" business year, the receivables reported on the balance sheet normally will be quite low which would cause the turnover to look better than is actually the case on the average.

### Merchandise Turnover

Merchandise turnover is the ratio between the cost of goods sold (or used) and the average inventory balance. The procedures for determining the average inventory balance are similar to those discussed above for average receivables. For comparisons with other firms the analyst may have to use *sales* rather than cost of goods sold. Obviously, such a ratio would at best represent an approximation since the markup in the sales amount (but not in the inventory amount) would distort the ratio. This error may be minimized by restating the inventory to retail.

The merchandise inventory turnover may be expressed as a "turnover" or as "days' supply"; the latter appears more often in current usage.[4]

---

[4] Some analysts prefer to use 250 (5-day workweek) or 300 (6-day workweek) days, as the case may be, as an approximation of the number of business days in the year.

The turnover or days' supply figure has significance in that the amount of inventory on hand normally should bear a close relationship to cost of goods sold. The relationship necessarily will vary from industry to industry – a grocery store normally should expect a high inventory turnover, whereas an antique dealer may expect a comparatively low turnover. Also, the ratio represents an average – a generalization that does not reflect how fast particular items are moving, but rather how fast all items on the average are moving. For example, a grocer may have a turnover of 15, yet may have items on the shelves that have not turned over at all during the entire year.

Inventory turnover is directly related to profitability. To illustrate, assume that the inventory turnover is 12 (cost of goods sold, $1,200,000; average inventory, $100,000) and that the entrepreneur realizes a profit of $1,000 each time the $100,000 investment in inventory turns over. A $12,000 profit is indicated. Now assume another firm identical in every respect except that the inventory turnover is 6 indicating a $6,000 profit on a similar $100,000 inventory investment.

Work in process inventory turnover is computed by dividing cost of goods manufactured by the average work in process inventory. With respect to all inventories, turnover computations based on appropriate unit data, when practicable, will provide more reliable results than when based on dollar amount data.

## PROPORTIONATE MEASUREMENT OF THE EQUITY POSITION

The balance sheet reports the two basic sources of funds used by the business: (a) owners' equity, and (b) creditors' equity. The relationships between these two distinct equities often are measured because they tend to reflect the financial strengths and weaknesses of the business; in other words, the long-term solvency of a business and its potential capacity to generate and obtain investment resources. Exhibit 24–8 summarizes eight ratios that are commonly used measures of equity position.

### Equity Ratios

These three ratios reflect essentially the same relationship; that is, the proportion of total assets provided by (a) the owners, and (b) the creditors. The three equity ratios for WZ Corporation (Exhibit 24–2) for 1976 are:

1. $\dfrac{\text{Owners' Equity, \$329,345}}{\text{Total Assets, \$478,000}}$ = 69% of the assets were provided by owners

2. $\dfrac{\text{Creditors' Equity, \$148,655}}{\text{Total Assets, \$478,000}}$ = 31% of the assets were provided by creditors

    $\underline{100\%}$ total assets provided

3. $\dfrac{\text{Creditors' Equity, \$148,655}}{\text{Owners' Equity, \$329,345}}$ = $\underline{45\%}$ – the creditors' equity is 45% of the owners' equity

**EXHIBIT 24-8**
**Ratios that Measure Equity Position**

| Ratio | Formula for Computation | Significance |
|---|---|---|
| *Equity ratios:* | | |
| 1. Owners' equity total assets. | $\dfrac{\text{Owners' Equity}}{\text{Total Assets}}$ | Proportion of assets provided by owners. Reflects financial strength and cushion for creditors. |
| 2. Creditors' equity to total assets. | $\dfrac{\text{Total Liabilities}}{\text{Total Assets}}$ | Proportion of assets provided by creditors. Extent of "trading on the equity." |
| 3. Owners' equity to total liabilities. (Sometimes computed as total liabilities to owners' equity.) | $\dfrac{\text{Owners' Equity}}{\text{Total Liabilities}}$ | Relative amounts of resources provided by owners and creditors. Reflects strengths and weaknesses in basic financing of operations. |
| *Other ratios related to equity position:* | | |
| 4. Fixed assets to long-term liabilities. | $\dfrac{\text{Operational Assets (Net)}}{\text{Long-Term Liabilities}}$ | Reflects extent of resources from long-term debt. May suggest potential borrowing power. If the fixed assets are pledged — degree of security. |
| 5. Fixed assets to owners' equity. | $\dfrac{\text{Fixed Assets (Net)}}{\text{Owners' Equity}}$ | May suggest over- or under-investment by owners; also weakness or strength in "trading on the equity." |
| 6. Fixed assets to total equities. | $\dfrac{\text{Fixed Assets (Net)}}{\text{Total Liabilities and Owners' Equity}}$ | May suggest overexpansion of plant and equipment. |
| 7. Sales to fixed assets (plant turnover). | $\dfrac{\text{Net Sales}}{\text{Fixed Assets (Net)}}$ | Turnover index which tests roughly the efficiency of management in keeping plant properties employed. |
| 8. Book value per share of common stock. | $\dfrac{\text{Common Stock Equity}}{\text{Number of Outstanding Common Shares}}$ | Number of dollars of equity (at book value) per share of common stock. |

Although the three equity ratios sometimes are computed, usually only one of the three is used because each one reflects the same relationship (but in a somewhat different way).

The balance between resources provided by debt versus owners' equity is considered critical by expert analysts; however, there is no rule of thumb that can be pointed to as a guide for evaluation. Clearly, a company that has 80% debt and 20% owners' equity usually would be considered to be in an overborrowed (overextended) position; interest payments must be made whether there are profits, and the debts must be paid at the fixed maturity dates. In contrast, if debt and owners' equity are 20% and 80%, respectively, the creditors' position is better and interest payments lower. However, owners' equity usually is more costly than debt capital, particularly since interest paid on debt is deductible for income tax purposes, whereas dividends are not. On the other hand, equity capital does not have maturity dates.

Debt financing also is an important avenue for most businesses because of a favorable effect known as *trading on the equity* or *financial leverage*. These are common terms that refer to the advantage to be gained for the stockholders' by borrowing funds, say at 8%, when the business is earning 12% on *total assets*. This topic is discussed later in the chapter in respect to return on investment.

In computing the equity ratios, it is important that all components, such as the appropriated retained earnings and unrealized capital, be included in owners' equity. Some analysts prefer to subtract the carrying value of intangible assets thereby using *tangible capital* for owners' equity. The authors see no basic reason for this approach since we assume the intangibles are accounted for properly and, as a consequence, are not carried at more than the appropriate value.

Three of the other ratios listed on Exhibit 24–8 (4 through 6) focus in general on measurement of the relationships of the long-term committments of resources to fixed assets and the sources of capital that provided them. They are viewed as rough measures of over- or underexpansion of fixed assets in relation to the sources of long-term capital. Because of their general nature, they are not widely used. The sales to fixed assets ratio, sometimes called the *plant turnover ratio*, attempts to measure over- or underexpansion of plant (i.e., fixed assets) in relation to sales. A high plant turnover rate is favorable because it reflects the effeciency of the plant to produce goods; however, it does not reflect the cost factors—the plant volume may be high, but the costs or production may be prohibitive.

## Book Value per Share of Capital Stock

Although it is often computed, book value per share of capital stock has limited usefulness. It has little, if any, correspondence with the market value per share. Some investors are particularly impressed with stock that has a book value in excess of the market price because, under the cost, matching, and conservatism principles, the assets are apt to be carried at amounts significantly less than their fair market value; they should never be reflected in the accounts at more than their fair value (recall that a loss is recognized when it occurs even though there has been no transaction to measure it). Book value per share is also used for comparative purposes with other companies.

Book value per share is computed by dividing total common stockholders' equity by the number of common shares outstanding. When there is more than one class of stock outstanding, total stockholders' equity must be apportioned between the various classes in accordance with the legal and statutory claims that would be effective in case of liquidation of the company. Since additional classes of stock typically are preferred stock, the usual situation requires allocation based upon the preferential rights of the preferred stock. Liquidation, cumulative, and participating preferences must be in the computation.

To illustrate a typical allocation, assume the Stone Manufacturing Corporation balance sheet reflected the following at a specific date:

Stockholders' Equity:

| | |
|---|---:|
| Preferred stock, 6%, cumulative, nonparticipating, par value $100 per share, 1,000 shares outstanding | $100,000 |
| Common stock, $100 par value (2,000 shares issued) | 200,000 |
| Contributed capital in excess of par, preferred | 10,000 |
| Contributed capital in excess of par, common | 15,000 |
| Retained earnings | 75,000 |
| Treasury stock—common (100 shares at cost) | (17,000) |
| Total Stockholders' Equity | $383,000 |

Preferred preferences—liquidation value $105 per share—two years' dividends in arrears, this includes the year just ended.

## Computation of book value per share:

| | | |
|---|---:|---:|
| Total stockholders' equity | | $383,000 |
| Allocation to preferred stock: | | |
| Liquidation value—1,000 shares @ $105 | $105,000 | |
| Cumulative dividends—$100,000 × 6% × 2 (two years in arrears at 6% including current year just ended) | 12,000 | 117,000 |
| Allocation to common stock (1,900 shares outstanding) | | $266,000 |

Book value per share of preferred:

$$\frac{\$117,000}{1,000} = \$117$$

Book value per share of common:

$$\frac{\$266,000}{1,900} = \$140$$

## RATIOS MEASURING OPERATING RESULTS

In recent years increasing attention has been given to the ability of a business to earn a satisfactory income and return on investment, rather than to the value of the assets. Although ratios relating to income are perhaps of somewhat more interest to investors than to creditors, the latter are giving increasing attention to profitability. A creditor may be unwilling to make loans or grant merchandise credit if an unhealthy profit picture exists in the prospective borrower's business, even though adequate collateral is available. Management and investors are particularly concerned with evidences of the earnings potential of a business. The principal ratios that measure operating results are summarized in Exhibit 24–9.

**EXHIBIT 24–9**
**Ratios that Measure Operating Results**

| Ratio | Formula for Computation | Significance |
|---|---|---|
| 1. Profit margin. | $\dfrac{\text{Net Income}}{\text{Net Sales}}$ | Indicates net profitability of each dollar of sales. |
| 2. Return on investment:<br>  a. On total assets. | $\dfrac{\text{Net Income Plus Interest Expense*}}{\text{Total Assets}}$ | Rate earned on *all resources* used. Measures earnings on all investments including both owners and creditors. |
|   b. On owners' equity. | $\dfrac{\text{Net Income}}{\text{Owners' Equity}}$ | Rate earned on resources provided by owners (excludes creditors). Measures earnings accruing to the owners. |
| 3. Investment turnover. | $\dfrac{\text{Net Sales}}{\text{Total Investment}}$ | Number of times total investment (total assets) turns. Indicative of efficiency with which total resources are utilized. |
| 4. Earnings per share. | $\dfrac{\text{Income Accruing to Common Stock}}{\text{Common Shares Outstanding}}$ | Profit earned on each share of common stock. Indicative of ability to pay dividends and to grow from within. See Chapter 17. |

*Market Tests*

| Ratio | Formula for Computation | Significance |
|---|---|---|
| 5. Price-earnings ratio (the multiple). | $\dfrac{\text{Market Price per Share}}{\text{Earnings per Share}}$ | Earnings rate based on cost of share of stock on the market. Indicates profitableness of firm related to market value of stockholders' equity. |
| 6. Payout ratio. | $\dfrac{\text{Market Price per Share}}{\text{Dividends per Share}}$ | Measures the length of the cash payout period for the investor. |
| 7. Dividend ratio. | $\dfrac{\text{Dividends per Share}}{\text{Earnings per Share}}$ | Measures the proportion of income (before extraordinary items) paid out in dividends on the average. |

* Adjusted for tax savings.

### Profit Margin

The ratio of net income to net sales, generally referred to as the *profit margin*, is widely used as an index of profitability; however, one significant factor related to profitability—investment—is given no consideration in the ratio. To illustrate, assume the accounts of the Conway Company showed the following data: net income, $20,000; net sales, $2,000,000; and total assets, $100,000. In this case the profit margin is 1% whereas the 20% return on total investment appears to be satisfactory. Thus, the profit margin appears inadequate as a measure of profitability. The profit margin has value primarily for evaluation of trends and for comparison with industry and competitor statistics.

**Return on Investment**

This ratio is considered by many accountants to be the single most important ratio because it incorporates the two basic factors that should be considered in measuring profitability: (1) earnings, and (2) investment. Fundamentally, return on investment is computed by dividing *income by investment.* Return on investment is referred to variously as capital yield, return on assets employed, return on capital, rate of return, or simply ROI. Return on investment has two important applications in business situations:

1. Evaluating proposed capital additions (not discussed herein).[5]
2. Measuring profitability in relation to investment.

As a measure of profitability, return on investment may be computed on the basis of either:

1. Owners' equity; that is, net income divided by owners' equity ($ROI_o$).
2. Total assets; that is, net income (adjusted for interest expense) divided by total assets ($ROI_t$).

Most analysts compute both ratios and compare them to measure the effect of *financial leverage* (i.e., trading on the equity). The following data are used to illustrate return on investment:

XY COMPANY

Balance Sheet Data:

| | |
|---|---:|
| Total assets | $100,000 |
| Total liabilities | 40,000 |
| Stockholders' equity | 60,000 |
| Total Equities | $100,000 |

Income Statement Data:

| | |
|---|---:|
| Operating income | $ 20,000 |
| Interest expense | 3,200 |
| Pretax income | 16,800 |
| Income taxes ($16,800 × 40%) | 6,720 |
| Net Income | $ 10,080 |

Return on investment for a business is computed as follows:

1. Return on owners' equity:

$$\frac{\text{Net Income}}{\text{Owners' Equity}} = ROI_o$$

XY Company (data above):

$$\frac{\$10,080}{\$60,000} = 16.8\% \ ROI_o$$

---

[5] For an excellent discussion, see Harold Bierman, Jr. and Seymour Smidt, *The Capital Budgeting Decision* (New York: The Macmillan Co., 1960).

2. Return on total assets (i.e., total investment):

$$\frac{\text{Net Income} + \text{Interest Expense, Net of Tax}}{\text{Total Assets}} = \text{ROI}_t$$

XY Company (data above):

$$\frac{\$10,080 + (\$3,200 - \$1,280)}{\$100,000} = \frac{\$12,000}{\$100,000} = \underline{12.0}\ \text{ROI}_t$$

Difference: Financial Leverage Factor......     4.8%

In computing return on total investment, interest expense (net of income taxes) is added to net income because it is a part of the return earned on total assets which includes the liabilities on which the interest was paid. Interest expense (net of tax) was deducted in determining net income (as reported on the income statement). Also, the denominator includes the resources provided by both creditor and owners; therefore, the numerator must include the return to both sources (net income plus interest).

*Return on total assets* measures the profitability of the total resources available to the business. It indicates the efficiency with which management used the total resources available to them.

*Return on owners' equity* is used to measure the return that accrues to the stockholders *after* the interest payments to the creditors are deducted to derive net income. It does not measure the efficiency with which total resources were used, but rather the *residual* return to the owners on their total investment in the business (i.e., the original investment plus retained earnings).

## Financial Leverage

In a prior paragraph, the concept of financial leverage, sometimes called trading on the equity, was briefly defined. More comprehensively, financial leverage is the effect on return on investment of borrowing versus investment by owners; it may be either positive or negative as regards the interest of the owners. If the interest rate on debt is lower than the rate earned on total assets, financial leverage will be positive; if the interest rate is higher, financial leverage will be negative. Financial leverage can be measured by subtracting return on total assets ($\text{ROI}_t$) from return on owners' equity ($\text{ROI}_o$).

For XY Company, the financial leverage effect was (+) 4.8% (positive) because the return on owners' equity was greater than the return on total assets. The 4.8% positive effect in favor of owners' equity was due to the fact that the company earned a greater rate of return on total assets than the rate of interest, net of tax, paid for borrowed resources. This can be demonstrated for XY Company, assuming interest expense averages 8% on the total debt, as follows:

Earnings on resources provided by debt ($40,000 × 12%*)............... $4,800
Cost (net of tax) of resources provided by debt
($40,000 × .08 × .60) ................................................................. 1,920
Net Gain on Resources Provided by Debt............................ $2,880
Financial leverage factor ($2,880 ÷ $60,000) ............................... 4.8%

* The 12% $ROI_t$, as computed, is net of tax.

Obviously, had there been no debt, return on investment on total assets and return on owners' equity would be identical. In contrast, when there is debt, and the interest rate on the debt and the rate of return on total assets are different, there will be a financial leverage effect causing the two ROI percentages to be different.

The computations for XY Company, when compared, show three separate factors that cause financial leverage, viz.:

1. Investment differential—the difference in investment as between all investors and the owner-investor only. The denominator in computing $ROI_o$ was $60,000 whereas the denominator in computing $ROI_t$ was $100,000.
2. Rate differentials—the difference between the rate earned on total assets and the interest rate paid for debt capital.
3. Income tax differential—the cost of resources obtained by incurring debt (i.e., interest expense) is deductible by the company for income tax purposes whereas dividends paid to owners are not.

The cause and measurement of financial leverage may be diagrammed as follows:

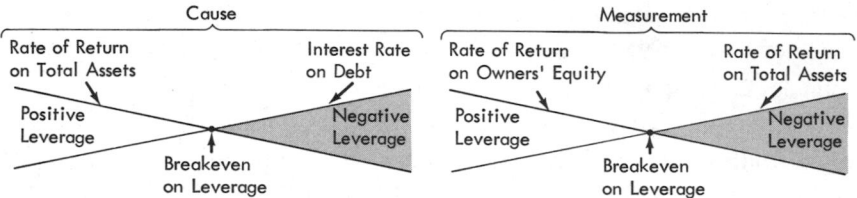

Financial leverage is an important aspect of financial planning in a business because of the greater returns (leverage) that can accrue to the owners. However, excessive debt has the disadvantages of (1) cash interest payments each period must be made whether or not earnings and cash flow are satisfactory, and (2) maturity payments on principal must be made on the specified dates.

The analysis of financial statements should always include *return on investment* and *financial leverage* evaluations. A comparison of the rates of return on owners' equity and total assets provides a particularly realiable measure of the degree and effect of financial leverage. Expert analysts look at this relationship very closely.

Return on investment has gained wide acceptance in the last few years as an important tool of managerial control. The measure has the distinct advantage of directing management attention clearly and forcefully to a combination of the three principal factors affecting profit — sales, expense, and total assets employed. Many accountants believe that the APB in *Opinion No. 15* (see Chapter 17) did not best reflect the long-range needs of the users in recognizing earnings per share as a fundamental measure of the success or failure of a business. Earnings per share, among other weaknesses, gives little attention to the total amount of investment (resources) used in the process of creating net income. Many accountants believe, because of its fundamental characteristics, that return on total investment and return on owners' equity should have been selected as the fundamental measures of profitability and financial leverage. They recognize that profitability fundamentally is the relationship between investment and earnings on that investment.

### Investment Turnover

This ratio, also called the asset turnover, is computed by dividing net sales by average total assets for the year. It measures the effectiveness with which management used the total resources at their disposal. It is similar in concept to inventory turnover. Sales is considered the principal activity of the business, and the lower the amount of investment needed in relation to sales the greater earnings should be. However, this ratio does not include the effect of expenses. A company may have a high asset turnover, viewed as a favorable condition, in the face of a substantial net loss.

### Market Tests

Several different market tests are often used by investors and analysts to measure the relationship between investment by the stockholders (i.e., the purchase price of the shares owned) and the return from the shares (i.e., dividends). Three market tests are listed in Exhibit 24–9. The price-earnings ratio, generally called the *multiple*, is a widely used market test of profitability because it relates the earnings of the business to the current market price of the stock. For this reason, it is of particular interest to the potential investor. Of course, this ratio changes each time the market price of the stock changes. Several years ago, multiples of 50 or more were not unusual; however, multiples in the range of 10 to 20 are more common currently. The multiple generally should be computed on the basis of earnings per share before extraordinary items. To illustrate, assuming the common stock of WZ Corporation is selling at $6.50 per share, on December 31, 1976, the multiple would be:

$$\frac{\text{Market Price per Share, \$6.50}}{\text{EPS (Exhibit 24–1), \$.40}} = 16 \text{ (i.e., the stock was selling at 16 times the earnings per share)}$$

The *payout ratio* is used as a rough measure of the length of time that it may take the investor to recover the cash investment. For example, if the dividends per share have been averaging $.65 per year and a market price of $6.50 per share, the payout period would be 10 years. This ratio is not given much weight because of its imprecision and theoretical weaknesses (tax effects and the interest factor for the investor are ignored).

The *dividend ratio* also is a rough measure of potential return to the investor. It is computed by dividing dividends per share by earnings per share. Preferably, averages covering the past several years should be used. It is a market test that investors consider along with other data; however, it is relatively insignificant in situations where dividends are unstable.

## USE AND INTERPRETATION OF RATIO ANALYSES

In evaluating the financial position of a business, the relationships indicated by both the absolute amounts and the ratios, it is especially important that the limitations of the data be realized. Significantly, ratios represent average conditions; therefore, they must be interpreted broadly. In addition, changes in the accounting system and classification of data may significantly affect a ratio. One writer has suggested that the idea of their use may be conveyed by a comparison with the interpretation of a thermometer reading by a doctor—beyond a certain range the fever reading indicates *something* is wrong with the patient, but not exactly what it is. An unfavorable ratio can be thought of as a red flag—the matter should be investigated. Additionally, one ratio or even several ratios standing alone, whatever their values, may be insignificant. Consequently, a primary problem confronting both the analyst and the statement user relates to the evaluation of a specific ratio. For example, is it good or bad that the inventory turnover for a company is 12? In determining what constitutes an unfavorable or favorable ratio for a particular business the following comparisons are suggested:

1. Comparison of ratios for the current year with those of preceding years for the company. The trend of certain ratios may be highly significant.
2. Comparison of the company's ratios with those of leading competitors (when available from published financial statements).
3. Comparison with ratios of the industry within which the company operates. Industry statistics may be obtained from the following sources:
   a. Industry trade associations—practically all industries support one or more trade associations that generally collect and publish financial statistics (averages) relating to the industry. The National Retail Merchants Association is a good example.
   b. Bureaus of business research of universities—the University of Texas prepares comparative data on approximately 100 Texas retail stores, and other universities perform a similar function.
   c. U.S. Department of Commerce, Washington, D.C.

   *d.* Publications of Robert Morris Associates.

   *e.* Dun & Bradstreet, Inc., in the magazine *Modern Industry* and separate booklets.

4. Comparison with budgeted or standard ratios developed by the company.

Because differences in product lines, methods of operation, size, geography, accounting methods, and variations in the method of computing the ratios may significantly influence the results caution should be exercised in comparing ratios with those from other sources. When comparing ratios over a period of several years, price-level changes also assume considerable significance (see Chapter 25). Despite the shortcomings mentioned above, ratio analysis is a useful tool in interpreting financial statements and in evaluating the financial strength of a business. The accountant, both public and industrial, should employ this useful tool to the extent consistent with the situation and the needs of the statement users.

The presentation of ratio analyses is an important aspect of financial reporting. The accountant should report the results of the analyses in a manner that is consistent with the problem at hand. A special report involving a tabulation of specific data often is required for creditor purposes. External annual financial statement usually include a limited number of ratios, although it is fairly common to include some graphical representation based on ratios such as a pie chart indicating the "disposition" of the sales dollar; that is, a graphic representation of a vertical percentage analysis of the income statement.

## THE SEARCH FOR ADDITIONAL INFORMATION

The serious investor should search for information to supplement that provided by the financial statements. Hearsay is hazardous; the investor should seek hard data on the company—its operations, policies, competitive position, the quality of the management, and other nonquantitative information. Brokerage firms and security analysts typically gather and disseminate relevant information. Periodic reports, by listed companies, to the SEC are available; and in some respects, they provide information not included in the published financial statements.

The financial media often is a rich source of information on companies and industries. In addition to news items; they generally carry special well-researched articles. Examples of financial publications include Fortune, Barrons, The Wall Street Journal, Business Week, Forbes, and various industry publications; such publications are available in most libraries on a current basis.

## OVERVIEW

This chapter presented a wide range of techniques for analysis of financial statements. The purpose of these techniques is to glean from the statements particularly relevant information for the statement user.

We re-emphasize that each decision by the statement user tends to be unique and therefore has somewhat different information needs. Not all of the techniques (and specifics) are relevant to all decisions; the statement user must use sound judgment in deciding what information is relevant to the decision at hand.

However, for most important decisions, when the statement user has completed an analysis of the financial statements along the lines suggested in this chapter, a major input to most important decision models exists. Consideration of other relevant factors such as the trend of the industry, the global situation, and the impact of governmental regulation is essential. When such considerations are coupled with the results of the analysis of the financial statements sufficient basis usually exists to support a sound decision by the statement user.

The appendix to follow presents a complete set of actual statements for an interesting situation. Observe that the summary of financial results covers the entire life span of this company. This case is presented as a supplementary device for studying and applying the analytical techniques discussed in the chapter.

# Appendix: Financial Statements, Earth Resources Company

## HISTORICAL CORPORATE PROFILE

Development and marketing of mineral and energy resources of the earth to benefit its shareholders and the nation is the mission of Earth Resources Company. Major operations include a petroleum refinery at Memphis, Tennessee; retail gasoline stations throughout the mid-South, a copper mine in New Mexico, a marine transportation system on the Mississippi River, and a majority interest in a silver and gold mine being developed in Idaho. Through Energy Company of Alaska, a subsidiary, the company is also engaged in supplying roadbuilding and paving materials, and plans to build a petroleum refinery to serve the Alaskan Interior. The company also conducts an active mineral exploration program, and owns a coal mine in Alaska. Earth Resources Company common stock is traded on the American Stock Exchange and the Pacific Coast Stock Exchange, with the symbol **ERC.**

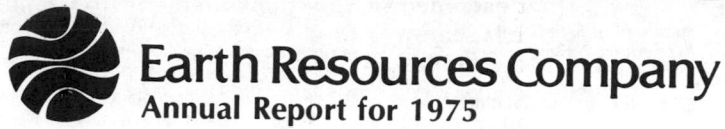

# Earth Resources Company
### Annual Report for 1975

## Financial Highlights

|  | 1975 | 1974 | % Increase |
|---|---|---|---|
| Revenues | $230,859,000 | $141,874,000 | 63% |
| Income before taxes | 20,068,000 | 14,366,000 | 40% |
| Net income | 10,380,000 | 7,392,000 | 40% |
| Earnings per common and common equivalent share | $2.31 | $1.68 | 38% |
| Cash flow (before exploration, interest and taxes on income) | 24,255,000 | 19,387,000 | 25% |
| Dividends on common stock | 3,092,000 | 1,843,000 | 68% |
| Dividends per share | $ .70 | $ .42 | 67% |
| Total assets | 90,081,000 | 70,850,000 | 27% |
| Shareholders' equity | 31,663,000 | 24,286,000 | 30% |

## Corporate Profile

The diversified resource development activities of Earth Resources Company offer a broad scope of service to America's needs. Major operations include a 44,000 BPD petroleum refinery; retail gasoline operations throughout the mid-South; marine and surface transportation; silver, gold, and copper mining, and an active mineral exploration program. Energy Company of Alaska, a subsidiary, manufactures roadbuilding materials, provides contracting services, and plans to build the Alaskan Interior's first refinery, near Fairbanks. Earth Resources Company common stock is traded on the American Stock Exchange and the Pacific Stock Exchange with the symbol ERC.

## Summary of Significant Accounting Policies
EARTH RESOURCES COMPANY AND SUBSIDIARIES

### Principles of Consolidation:

The consolidated financial statements include the accounts of all subsidiaries. All intercompany balances and significant intercompany transactions have been eliminated. The cost of investments in subsidiaries has been assigned to the acquired assets based on the fair value of such assets.

### Inventories:

Inventories are valued at the lower of cost or market. Effective September 1, 1974, cost of the petroleum products and crude oil of the company's refinery are determined on a last-in, first-out (LIFO) basis. The cost of other inventories is determined on a first-in, first-out basis.

### Exploration, Research and Development Expenditures:

The company charges all exploration, research and development expenditures to income as incurred. Exploration costs previously expensed on properties on which commercial development is later undertaken are capitalized and assigned to the related mine investment.

### Property, Plant and Equipment:

Property, plant and equipment is stated at cost. Depreciation other than for mining facilities is based on the straight-line method over estimated service lives from three to twenty years. Depreciation, depletion and amortization of mining facilities, including development costs, is based substantially on the units of production in relation to total estimated units of reserve.

Expenditures for general property maintenance and repairs are charged to earnings as incurred. The company capitalizes major replacements and betterments and relieves the asset and the related allowance for depreciation accounts of the cost and accumulated depreciation in respect to items replaced, retired or otherwise disposed of. The gain or loss on property, plant and equipment items sold or retired is included in current earnings.

### Income Taxes:

Deferred income taxes are provided to the extent of the benefit received from timing differences between financial and taxable income. The timing differences relate primarily to mine development costs, depreciation methods and income recognition. The allowable investment tax credit is applied as a current reduction of income tax expense.

### Pension Plans:

Pension costs are provided for and funded at amounts not less than actuarially determined estimates. Unfunded past service costs are being amortized over a thirty-year period.

**Opinion Of Independent Accountants**

The Board of Directors
Earth Resources Company
Dallas, Texas

We have examined the consolidated balance sheet of Earth Resources Company and Subsidiaries as of August 31, 1975 and the related consolidated statements of income and retained earnings and changes in financial position for the year then ended. Our examination was made in accordance with generally accepted auditing standards, and accordingly included such tests of the accounting records and such other auditing procedures as we considered necessary in the circumstances. We previously examined and reported upon the consolidated financial statements of the company for the year ended August 31, 1974.

In our opinion, the aforementioned financial statements present fairly the consolidated financial position of Earth Resources Company and Subsidiaries at August 31, 1975 and 1974 and the consolidated results of their operations and changes in financial position for the years then ended, in conformity with generally accepted accounting principles applied on a consistent basis, except for the change, with which we concur, to the last-in, first-out method of determining costs of certain inventories as discussed in Note 1 to the notes to consolidated financial statements.

Dallas, Texas
October 10, 1975     *Coopers & Lybrand*

**Consolidated Statement of Income and Retained Earnings**
EARTH RESOURCES COMPANY AND SUBSIDIARIES
For the years ended August 31, 1975 and 1974

|  | 1975 | 1974 |
|---|---|---|
| Net sales and other income | $230,859,000 | $141,874,000 |
| Costs and expenses: | | |
|    Cost of sales (Note 1) | 195,265,000 | 114,568,000 |
|    Selling expenses | 8,140,000 | 5,866,000 |
|    Exploration, research and | | |
|      development expenses (Note 3) | 596,000 | 740,000 |
|    General and administrative expenses | 5,868,000 | 5,562,000 |
|    Interest expense | 922,000 | 772,000 |
| | 210,791,000 | 127,508,000 |
|      Income before income taxes | 20,068,000 | 14,366,000 |
| Provision for federal and state | | |
| income taxes (Note 7): | | |
|    Current | 8,483,000 | 7,739,000 |
|    Deferred | 1,205,000 | ( 765,000) |
| | 9,688,000 | 6,974,000 |
|      Net Income | 10,380,000 | 7,392,000 |
| Retained earnings, beginning of year | 9,204,000 | 3,655,000 |
| Dividends declared on common stock (Note 6) | ( 3,092,000) | ( 1,843,000) |
| Retained earnings, end of year | $ 16,492,000 | $ 9,204,000 |
| Earnings per common and common | | |
|    equivalent share (Note 8) | $2.31 | $1.68 |
| Dividends declared per share of common stock | $ .70 | $ .42 |

The accompanying summary of significant accounting policies
and notes are an integral part of the financial statements.

**Consolidated Balance Sheet**
EARTH RESOURCES COMPANY AND SUBSIDIARIES
August 31, 1975 and 1974

| ASSETS | 1975 | 1974 |
|---|---|---|
| Current assets: | | |
| Cash .................................. | $ 9,357,000 | $ 4,158,000 |
| Temporary cash investments ............... | 15,175,000 | 15,550,000 |
| Accounts receivable, trade ................. | 11,455,000 | 9,398,000 |
| Other accounts and notes receivable ........ | 1,525,000 | 1,826,000 |
| Inventories, primarily crude oil and | | |
| petroleum products (Note 1) ............. | 9,526,000 | 8,563,000 |
| Prepaid expenses ........................ | 825,000 | 670,000 |
| Future income tax benefits ................. | | 434,000 |
| Total current assets ................... | 47,863,000 | 40,599,000 |
| Property, plant and equipment: | | |
| Land and mineral leases .................. | 6,939,000 | 6,973,000 |
| Refinery facilities ....................... | 22,288,000 | 16,896,000 |
| Mining facilities and development costs ...... | 12,357,000 | 12,413,000 |
| Other property and equipment ............ | 17,760,000 | 11,147,000 |
| | 59,344,000 | 47,429,000 |
| Less allowance for depreciation, | | |
| depletion and amortization .............. | 21,279,000 | 19,311,000 |
| | 38,065,000 | 28,118,000 |
| Other assets .............................. | 4,153,000 | 2,133,000 |
| | $90,081,000 | $70,850,000 |

| LIABILITIES AND CAPITAL | | |
|---|---|---|
| Current liabilities: | | |
| Current portion of long-term debt (Note 4) ... | $ 1,515,000 | $ 1,602,000 |
| Accounts payable, trade .................. | 19,513,000 | 16,179,000 |
| Accrued expenses ....................... | 14,028,000 | 11,903,000 |
| Federal and state income tax payable (Note 7) | 2,586,000 | 7,442,000 |
| Total current liabilities ................. | 37,642,000 | 37,126,000 |
| Long-term debt (Note 4): | | |
| Banks ................................. | 12,284,000 | 1,945,000 |
| Other ................................. | 4,726,000 | 5,964,000 |
| | 17,010,000 | 7,909,000 |
| Less current portion ..................... | 1,515,000 | 1,602,000 |
| | 15,495,000 | 6,307,000 |
| Deferred federal and state income | | |
| taxes (Note 7) .......................... | 4,973,000 | 3,014,000 |
| Minority interest in consolidated subsidiary ..... | 308,000 | 117,000 |
| Commitments and contingencies (Note 5) | | |
| Capital (Notes 4 and 6): | | |
| Common stock, no par value .............. | 14,992,000 | 14,904,000 |
| Paid-in capital ......................... | 290,000 | 289,000 |
| Retained earnings ....................... | 16,492,000 | 9,204,000 |
| Less 7,407 common shares in treasury, | | |
| at cost ............................. | (   111,000) | (   111,000) |
| | 31,663,000 | 24,286,000 |
| | $90,081,000 | $70,850,000 |

The accompanying summary of significant accounting policies
and notes are an integral part of the financial statements.

**Consolidated Statement of Changes in Financial Position**
EARTH RESOURCES COMPANY AND SUBSIDIARIES
For the years ended August 31, 1975 and 1974

| | 1975 | 1974 |
|---|---:|---:|
| Working capital provided: | | |
| From operations: | | |
| Net income .......................... | $10,380,000 | $ 7,392,000 |
| Items not affecting working capital in the current period: | | |
| Depreciation, depletion and amortization ...................... | 2,669,000 | 3,509,000 |
| Noncurrent portion of deferred income taxes (credit) ............... | 771,000 | ( 331,000) |
| Other, net ......................... | 236,000 | 11,000 |
| Working capital provided from operations ................. | 14,056,000 | 10,581,000 |
| Issuance of long-term debt ................ | 11,000,000 | 7,868,000 |
| Noncurrent income tax payable ........... | 1,188,000 | |
| Proceeds from disposal of property, plant and equipment ................... | 791,000 | 664,000 |
| Proceeds from issuance of common stock .... | 88,000 | 447,000 |
| Other ............................... | 270,000 | 304,000 |
| | 27,393,000 | 19,864,000 |
| Working capital applied: | | |
| Additions to property, plant and equipment .. | 13,644,000 | 6,489,000 |
| Property, plant and equipment of company acquired .................... | | 4,458,000 |
| Reductions of long-term debt .............. | 1,812,000 | 8,624,000 |
| Dividends declared on common stock ....... | 3,092,000 | 1,843,000 |
| Increase in other assets ................... | 2,097,000 | 943,000 |
| Other ............................... | | 97,000 |
| | 20,645,000 | 22,454,000 |
| Increase (decrease) in working capital ......... | $ 6,748,000 | ($ 2,590,000) |
| | | |
| Changes in components of working capital: | | |
| Increase (decrease) in current assets: | | |
| Cash and temporary cash investments ..... | $ 4,824,000 | $ 9,881,000 |
| Receivables .......................... | 1,756,000 | 6,144,000 |
| Inventories .......................... | 963,000 | 4,473,000 |
| Prepaid expenses ...................... | 155,000 | 271,000 |
| Future income tax benefits .............. | ( 434,000) | 434,000 |
| | 7,264,000 | 21,203,000 |
| Increase (decrease) in current liabilities: | | |
| Current portion of long-term debt ......... | ( 87,000) | ( 627,000) |
| Accounts payable and accrued expenses ... | 5,459,000 | 17,861,000 |
| Federal and state income taxes payable .... | ( 4,856,000) | 6,559,000 |
| | 516,000 | 23,793,000 |
| Increase (decrease) in working capital ......... | $ 6,748,000 | ($ 2,590,000) |

The accompanying summary of significant accounting policies
and notes are an integral part of the financial statements.

**Notes to Consolidated Financial Statements**
EARTH RESOURCES COMPANY AND SUBSIDIARIES

### 1. Inventories:

Prior to 1975, petroleum products and crude oil costs for the company's refinery had been determined on the latest three-month average cost method. As of September 1, 1974, the company adopted the LIFO method of determining cost for these inventories. The new method is considered preferable because it more closely matches current costs with current revenues in periods of price level changes. This change had the effect of reducing inventory by $1,802,000 and net income for the year ended August 31, 1975 by $881,000 or $.20 per share. There is no cumulative effect on retained earnings as of August 31, 1974 for this type of accounting change.

### 2. Company Acquired:

On October 16, 1973, the company's majority-owned subsidiary, Energy Company of Alaska ("ECA"), acquired all of the outstanding capital stock of Rogers & Babler, Inc., of Anchorage, Alaska for the purchase price of $6,000,000. The acquisition was accounted for by the "purchase method." The results of operations of Rogers & Babler, Inc., have been included in the consolidated statement of income of the company since the date of acquisition. The pro forma effect on the 1974 consolidated statement of income prior to the date of acquisition is not material.

### 3. Mining Operations:

The company has entered into an operating joint venture with others providing for the commercial development of the DeLamar Silver Mine. The company has a 52½% interest and is manager of the joint venture. Under the terms of the agreement the company will provide up to $9,700,000 as its share of the estimated costs required to place the mine and mill in operation. At August 31, 1975, the company's investment is $1,115,000 including prior year's exploration costs of $369,000 capitalized during the year.

In February 1975, the company suspended operations at its Nacimiento Copper Mine since the United States producer price for copper did not permit an adequate return of investment. At August 31, 1975, Nacimiento Copper Mine total assets were $10,393,000. Management is of the opinion that the mine's potential remains undiminished and there has been no diminution in the carrying value of the assets. Management intends to resume operations when the price the company will receive for its copper concentrate will yield a sufficient rate of return after deducting operating and other costs.

### 4. Long-Term Debt and Credit Agreements:

During 1974 and 1975, the company entered into long-term credit agreements which provide up to $12,500,000. As of August 31, 1975, $12,053,000 was outstanding under these agreements which amount bears interest at rates ranging from ½ of 1% over bank prime rate (7¾% at August 31, 1975) to 9¾%. The notes have various maturities through 1980.

In connection with the acquisition of Rogers & Babler, Inc., ECA issued notes payable to the selling stockholders of which $3,408,000 was outstanding at August 31, 1975. The notes are payable in four equal annual installments bearing interest at bank prime rate (7¾% at August 31, 1975) with the final payment due in October 1978. During 1974, ECA entered into a 9¾% bank loan agreement of which $1,213,000 was outstanding at August 31, 1975. The bank notes are due in quarterly installments through 1979. The company has guaranteed these ECA notes.

Other long-term debt aggregating $336,000 at August 31, 1975 bears interest at rates ranging from 5% to 9¼% and are payable in installments to 1986.

Maturities of long-term debt are scheduled as follows:

Years ending August 31:

| | |
|---|---|
| 1976 | $ 1,515,000 |
| 1977 | 7,545,000 |
| 1978 | 3,578,000 |
| 1979 | 3,144,000 |
| 1980 | 1,026,000 |
| After 1980 | 202,000 |
| | $17,010,000 |

The terms of certain long-term loan agreements contain covenants, the most significant of which requires the maintenance of certain working capital amounts, limits future borrowings and prohibits "unreasonable" dividend rates. Retained earnings of $12,837,000 were available for the payment of dividends at August 31, 1975.

The company has short-term bank lines of credit of $6,500,000 which stipulate compensating balances of $650,000 on the loan commitments and increasing amounts when funds are drawn. The compensating balances are not legally restricted and are available for the company's use on a temporary basis. No amounts were outstanding at August 31, 1975.

The company has received approval of a $30,000,000, 15-year loan from two insurance companies. The terms of the loan include an average interest rate of 11-3/8% and warrants to purchase 200,000 shares of the company's common stock at a price of $14 per share. Notes payable to banks totaling $12,213,000 at August 31, 1975 will be repaid from the proceeds of the loan. The funds will become available to the company upon conclusion of a satisfactory loan agreement.

### 5. Commitments and Contingencies:

The board of directors of the company has approved a capital expenditure program estimated at $45,000,000 largely for the construction of a refinery and development of the DeLamar Silver Mine of which approximately $21,000,000 is expected to be expended during 1976.

The company is obligated under long-term lease agreements primarily for land used in petroleum product marketing. Minimum lease rental payments total approximately $6,773,000 over the lives of the leases and are due as follows:

Years ending August 31:

| | |
|---|---|
| 1976 | $ 675,000 |
| 1977 | 638,000 |
| 1978 | 618,000 |
| 1979 | 593,000 |
| 1980 | 574,000 |
| Five-year periods thereafter: | |
| 1981 to 1985 | 2,151,000 |
| 1986 to 1990 | 956,000 |
| 1991 to 1995 | 351,000 |
| After 1995 | 217,000 |

These leases extend for varying periods of time, generally 10-15 years and in most cases contain renewal options equal to the original term of the lease. There are no material noncapitalized financing lease agreements.

The company has several pension plans covering substantially all employees. Such plans provide retirement benefits through investments, insurance and trust funds. The expense of the pension plans for 1975 and 1974 was approximately $404,000 and $290,000, respectively. The impact of the Employees Retirement Income Security Act of 1974 (ERISA) on future provisions for pension expense and funding pension costs has not been determined at this time. In management's opinion no significant liability will result from complying with ERISA.

Certain sales made by the company are subject to the Renegotiation Act of 1951, as amended. The company's reports have been filed through 1974 and accepted through 1972. Management is of the opinion that refunds, if any, would not result in any material adjustment of net income as reported.

The company has a stock redemption agreement, presently fully funded with life insurance, with the president and another stockholder of the company in the event of one or both of their deaths. The terms of the agreement provide that the funds necessary to effect such redemption must be provided from insurance, for which the cost is not material.

## 6. Capital:

The company's charter authorizes 5,000,000 shares of $10 par value preferred stock, none of which has been issued. During 1975, the charter was amended increasing the authorized common stock from 5,000,000 to 8,000,000 shares. A summary of common stock activity for the two years ended August 31, 1975 follows:

|  | Common Stock | |
| --- | --- | --- |
|  | Shares | Amount |
| Balance, August 31, 1973 | 4,313,476 | $14,457,000 |
| Issued on exercise of employee stock option and stock purchase agreements (plan terminated in 1974) | 100,597 | 447,000 |
| Balance, August 31, 1974 | 4,414,073 | 14,904,000 |
| Issued on exercise of employee stock options | 17,224 | 88,000 |
| Balance, August 31, 1975 | 4,431,297 | $14,992,000 |

The company has qualified and nonqualified stock option plans. The plans cover 550,000 shares of common stock which includes an increase of 200,000 shares under the nonqualified plan approved by the board of directors in 1975, subject to stockholders' approval. The plans provide that option prices for the qualified and nonqualified stock options shall be not less than 100% and 85% of market value at the date of grant, respectively. Options for the purchase of 178,428 shares were available for grant under the plans at August 31, 1975. Options to purchase 185,754 shares, at prices ranging from $4.04 to $10.94 per share, were outstanding at August 31, 1975, of which 101,804 shares were exercisable. The company makes no charges to income in connection with the stock option plans.

The company's equity in the capital of ECA in excess of its cost therein has been credited to paid-in capital.

On September 15, 1975, the board of directors declared a $.25 per share cash dividend totaling approximately $1,100,000 on the company's common stock payable October 10, 1975 to stockholders of record on September 30, 1975.

## 7. Income Taxes:

Deferred federal and state income taxes include $1,188,000 representing taxes not currently payable related to a change in the tax basis of valuing inventory. The provision for federal and state income taxes is summarized as follows:

|  | 1975 | 1974 |
| --- | --- | --- |
| Current: | | |
| Federal | $7,321,000 | $6,889,000 |
| State | 1,162,000 | 850,000 |
|  | $8,483,000 | $7,739,000 |
| Deferred: | | |
| Federal | $1,011,000 | ($ 767,000) |
| State | 194,000 | 2,000 |
|  | $1,205,000 | ($ 765,000) |

The federal provisions for 1975 and 1974 have been reduced by investment tax credits of $1,160,000 and $66,000, respectively.

The provision for deferred federal and state income taxes for the years ended August 31, 1975 and 1974 relates to timing differences between financial and tax reporting as follows:

|  | 1975 | 1974 |
|---|---|---|
| Depreciation | $ 478,000 | $   59,000 |
| Inventory pricing | ( 1,386,000) | 1,126,000 |
| Income recognition | 1,689,000 | ( 1,736,000) |
| Mine development costs | 595,000 | ( 232,000) |
| Other | ( 171,000) | 18,000 |
|  | $1,205,000 | ($ 765,000) |

Following is a reconciliation of the statutory federal income tax rate with the effective income tax rate for the years ended August 31, 1975 and 1974:

|  | 1975 | 1974 |
|---|---|---|
| Statutory income tax rate | 48% | 48% |
| State income taxes, net of federal income taxes | 3 | 3 |
| Investment tax credit | ( 6) |  |
| Statutory depletion |  | ( 3) |
| Other | 3 | 1 |
| Effective income tax rate | 48% | 49% |

### 8. Earnings Per Share:

Earnings per common and common equivalent share have been computed on the basis of the weighted average number of common and common equivalent shares outstanding during the year, 4,495,520 shares in 1975 and 4,411,027 shares in 1974. Options to purchase common stock have been considered to be common stock equivalents.

### Management's Discussion and Analysis of the Summary of Operations

#### Fiscal 1975 Compared with 1974

Financial results benefited from increased refinery processing of 10,500 BPD. Refinery sales volume increased 55%. Higher crude costs of 30% were offset by refinery price increases of 26%. The number of retail gasoline stations in operation was increased by 37. Gasoline costs and related selling expense increased 15% and 39% respectively. However, these increases were offset by volume gains of 37% and price increases of 8%. During the year, the U.S. producer price of copper declined 27%, and mining operations were suspended pending an increase in prices.

#### Fiscal 1974 Compared with 1973

Crude oil and other raw material costs increased 72% and refinery expenses by 14%. Prices for petroleum products escalated by 70% offsetting the higher costs and expenses. Retail gasoline operations are included in the financial results for a full year in 1974 — 8½ months in 1973. Forty stations were also added during the year. Higher gasoline selling prices of 33% and a sales volume gain of 44% offset increased costs of operation. Record high copper prices prevailed throughout a large part of fiscal 1974 and were reflected in an increase in mining revenues of 33%. General and administrative expenses were up over the prior year due to G&A costs associated with new operations such as retail gasoline, paving materials and general corporate expenses.

**Summary of Operations** Years Ended August 31 (In thousands of dollars except per share amounts)

|  | 1975 | 1974 | 1973 | 1972 | 1971 |
|---|---|---|---|---|---|
| Net sales and other income .......... | 230,859 | 141,874 | 88,203 | 66,587 | 57,295 |
| Costs and expenses: | | | | | |
| Cost of sales and operating expenses ..................... | 209,273 | 125,996 | 81,429 | 63,438 | 54,986 |
| Exploration expense .............. | 596 | 740 | 846 | 719 | 1,167 |
| Interest expense ................. | 922 | 772 | 875 | 1,014 | 242 |
|  | 210,791 | 127,508 | 83,150 | 65,171 | 56,395 |
| Income before taxes ............... | 20,068 | 14,366 | 5,053 | 1,416 | 900 |
| Provision for federal and state income taxes ................ | 9,688 | 6,974 | 2,625 | 747 | 501 |
| Net income ...................... | 10,380 | 7,392 | 2,428 | 669 | 399* |
| Earnings per common and common equivalent share ......... | $2.31 | $1.68 | $.61 | $.20 | $.12* |
| Dividends per share ............... | $.70 | $.42 | $.06 | | |
| Weighted average common and common equivalent shares (000 omitted) ............. | 4,496 | 4,411 | 4,007 | 3,384 | 3,376 |

**Summary of Financial Data** August 31

|  | | | | | |
|---|---|---|---|---|---|
| Working capital .................... | 10,221 | 3,473 | 6,062 | 2,557 | 545 |
| Capital expenditures ................ | 14,390 | 10,947 | 3,776 | 2,204 | 8,263 |
| Total assets ....................... | 90,081 | 70,850 | 42,206 | 32,107 | 31,503 |
| Long-term debt .................... | 15,495 | 6,307 | 7,063 | 9,146 | 8,577 |
| Shareholders' equity ................ | 31,663 | 24,286 | 18,311 | 13,849 | 13,039 |
| Book value per share ............... | $7.16 | $5.51 | $4.25 | $4.09 | $3.87 |

*1971 net income is before $147,000 and $.04 per share reduction for an extraordinary item.

**Lines of Business**

The following information summarizes the approximate contributions to sales and income of ERC's lines of business for the five years ended August 31, 1975:

| Sales: | 1975 | 1974 | 1973 | 1972 | 1971 |
|---|---|---|---|---|---|
| Petroleum Refining ..................... | 78% | 65% | 65% | 94% | 99% |
| Retail Petroleum Operations ............ | 46% | 51% | 34% | | |
| All Others (1) ......................... | 5% | 9% | 8% | 9% | 4% |
| Intercompany sales eliminated .......... | (29%) | (25%) | (7%) | (3%) | (3%) |
|  | 100% | 100% | 100% | 100% | 100% |
| Income (2): | | | | | |
| Petroleum Refining ..................... | 60% | 51% | 65% | 90% | 82% |
| Retail Petroleum Operations ............ | 23% | 34% | 30% | | |
| All Others (1) ......................... | 17% | 15% | 5% | 10% | 18% |
|  | 100% | 100% | 100% | 100% | 100% |

1 Includes marine transportation, paving materials, construction and copper mining. Each of the individual lines of business contributed less than 10% of sales and income during 1975 and 1974.
2 Income is before exploration, corporate administrative expenses, income taxes and extraordinary items.

**Market and Dividend Information**

ERC's common stock is traded on the American Stock Exchange. High and low sales prices and dividends per share of common stock for the years ended August 31, 1975 and 1974 are shown below:

|  | Sales Price of Common Stock | | | | Dividends Per Share | |
|---|---|---|---|---|---|---|
|  | 1975 | | 1974 | | 1975 | 1974 |
|  | High | Low | High | Low | | |
| 1st Quarter ............ | 11 7/8 | 7 5/8 | 9 3/4 | 5 5/8 | $.15 | $.03 |
| 2nd Quarter ........... | 10 1/4 | 8 3/4 | 10 3/4 | 7 | $.15 | $.03 |
| 3rd Quarter ............ | 14 3/4 | 9 1/4 | 10 1/8 | 6 3/4 | $.15 | $.09 |
| 4th Quarter ............ | 16 1/2 | 12 1/8 | 9 1/4 | 6 7/8 | $.25 | $.27* |

*Includes a special dividend of $.15 per share declared in August and paid in September 1974.

## QUESTIONS

1. Why is the past financial track record of a company important to the investor? What is meant by a turning point?

2. Explain why expert financial analysts, in analyzing a set of financial statements, first examine the auditors' report and the summary of accounting policies.

3. Explain why the notes to the financial statement should be carefully read in the process of analyzing a set of financial statements. Why are long-term summaries considered to be particularly important to the statement user?

4. Distinguish between vertical and horizontal analyses. Briefly explain the importance of each.

5. What is meant by proportionate ratio analysis? Why is important in the analysis of financial statements?

6. Distinguish between the current ratio and the quick ratio. What purpose does each serve?

7. Current assets and current liabilities for two companies having the same amount of working capital are summarized below; evaluate their relative solvency.

|  | X Company | Y Company |
|---|---|---|
| Current assets | $200,000 | $900,000 |
| Current liabilities | 100,000 | 800,000 |
| Working capital | $100,000 | $100,000 |

8. X Corporation has an accounts receivable turnover of 15; interpret this value. What would be the age of the receivables? What does it reveal?

9. Y Corporation has an inventory turnover of 9; interpret this value. What would be average number of days of supply?

10. Explain and illustrate trading on the equity.

11. Compute and explain the meaning of the book value per share of common stock of the Pride Manufacturing Company assuming the following data are available:

| | |
|---|---|
| Preferred stock, 6%, cumulative, nonparticipating, 200 shares outstanding | $ 20,000 |
| Common stock, par value $100, 1,000 shares outstanding | 100,000 |
| Retained earnings | 7,000 |
| (Three years dividends in arrears on preferred stock including current year.) | |

12. Explain the circumstances where a company has debt financing and the leverage factor is (a) positive, (b) negative, and (c) zero.

13. Explain the ROI concept. Why is it a fundamental measure of profitability?

14. What is meant by "the multiple"? Why is it considered to be important?

15. What are the principal limitations in using ratios?

## DECISION CASE 24-1

Scott Corporation needs additional funds for plant expansion. The board of directors is considering obtaining the funds by issuing additional short-term notes, long-term bonds, preferred stock, or common stock.

*Required:*

1. What primary factors should the board of directors consider in selecting the best method of financing plant expansion?
2. One member of the board of directors suggests that the corporation should maximize trading on equity, that is, using stockholders' equity as a basis for borrowing additional funds at a lower rate of interest than the expected earnings from the use of the borrowed funds.
   a. Explain how trading on equity affects earnings per share of common stock.
   b. Explain how a change in income tax rates affects trading on equity.
   c. Under what circumstances should a corporation seek to trade on equity to a substantial degree?
3. Two specific proposals under consideration by the board of directors are the issue of 7% subordinated income bonds (secured only by the general credit of the issuer with interest paid each year only if there is net income equal to the interest charge) or 7% cumulative, nonparticipating, nonvoting preferred stock, callable at par. In discussing the impact of the two alternatives on the debt to stockholders' equity ratio, one member of the board of directors stated that he felt the resulting debt-equity ratio would be the same under either alternative because the income bonds and preferred stock should be reported in the same balance sheet classification. What are the arguments (a) for and (b) against using the same balance sheet classification in reporting the income bonds and preferred stock?

(AICPA adapted)

## EXERCISES

### Exercise 24-1

Baker Trading Company income statements (condensed) for two quarters are shown below. Prepare a multiple-step comparative income statement including a vertical percentage analysis. (Round to even percents).

|                                                        | *First Quarter* | *Second Quarter* |
| ------------------------------------------------------ | --------------- | ---------------- |
| Gross sales                                            | $221,000        | $242,000         |
| Returns and allowances                                 | (1,000)         | (2,000)          |
|                                                        | 220,000         | 240,000          |
| Cost of goods sold                                     | (110,000)       | (130,000)        |
|                                                        | 110,000         | 110,000          |
| Expenses:                                              |                 |                  |
|   Selling expenses                           | (62,000)        | (63,000)         |
|   Administrative expenses (including         |                 |                  |
|     income taxes)                  | (30,000)        | (31,000)         |
|   Financial expenses (net of financial       |                 |                  |
|     revenue)                       | (3,000)         | 2,000            |
| Net income before extraordinary items                  | 15,000          | 18,000           |
| Extraordinary items, net of tax                        | 5,000           | (3,000)          |
| Net Income                                             | $ 20,000        | $ 15,000         |
| Shares of common stock outstanding                     | 10,000          | 10,000           |

**Exercise 24–2**

Prepare a single-step comparative income statement including horizontal percentage analysis for Baker Trading Company using the data given in Exercise 24–1. (Round to even percents.)

**Exercise 24–3**

The following data were taken from the financial statements of the Ralston Company. Based on these data compute (a) the working capital, (b) the current ratio, and (c) the acid-test ratio (carry to even percents). Evaluate each change.

| Current Assets: | 19A | 19B |
|---|---|---|
| Cash ................................................... | $ 30,000 | $ 40,000 |
| Short-term investments........................... | 10,000 | 10,000 |
| Trade accounts receivable (net)............... | 60,000 | 70,000 |
| Notes receivable .................................... | 6,000 | 2,000 |
| Inventory ............................................. | 150,000 | 170,000 |
| Prepaid expenses ................................. | 4,000 | 2,000 |
| Current Liabilities ................................. | 90,000 | 120,000 |

**Exercise 24–4**

The condensed financial data given below were taken from the annual financial statements of Foster Corporation:

| | 19A | 19B | 19C |
|---|---|---|---|
| Current assets (including inventory) ... | $ 200,000 | $ 250,000 | $ 270,000 |
| Current liabilities ............................. | 150,000 | 180,000 | 130,000 |
| Cash sales ...................................... | 800,000 | 780,000 | 820,000 |
| Credit sales...................................... | 200,000 | 280,000 | 250,000 |
| Cost of goods sold .......................... | 560,000 | 600,000 | 600,000 |
| Inventory ......................................... | 120,000 | 140,000 | 100,000 |
| Quick assets ................................... | 80,000 | 90,000 | 85,000 |
| Accounts receivable (net) ................. | 60,000 | 58,000 | 64,000 |
| Total assets (net) ............................ | 1,000,000 | 1,200,000 | 1,400,000 |

*Required:*

1. Based on the above data, calculate the following for 19B and 19C (round to even percents):
   - a. Current ratio.
   - b. Acid-test ratio.
   - c. Working capital to total assets.
   - d. Receivable turnover.
   - e. Age of receivables.
   - f. Merchandise turnover.
   - g. Days' supply in inventory.
   - h. Working capital turnover.
2. Evaluate the results of each computation including trends. Use 360 days for computation purposes.

**Exercise 24–5**

The following data were taken from the financial statements of the Action Company:

|  | 19A | 19B | 19C |
|---|---|---|---|
| Sales—cash ....................... | $190,000 | $200,000 | $220,000 |
| Sales—credit ....................... | 100,000 | 120,000 | 130,000 |
| Average receivables.............. | 25,000 | 34,000 | 50,000 |
| Average inventory................. | 60,000 | 70,000 | 80,000 |
| Cost of goods sold .............. | 180,000 | 190,000 | 200,000 |

*Required:*

What conclusions may be made relative to *(a)* inventories and *(b)* receivables? (Use 300 business days in year; credit terms are 90 calendar days.)

## Exercise 24–6

The balance sheet for two similar companies reflected the following:

|  | Company A | Company B |
|---|---|---|
| Current liabilities ...................................... | $ 30,000 | $100,000 |
| Long-term liabilities .................................... | 70,000 | 300,000 |
| Stockholders' Equity: | | |
| Common stock, par $5................................ | 220,000 | 46,000 |
| Preferred stock, par $10 ............................ | 100,000 | 20,000 |
| Contributed capital in excess of par ............ | 20,000 | 4,000 |
| Retained earnings ...................................... | 60,000 | 30,000 |
| Net Income (less taxes, 45%)....................... | 49,500 | 33,000 |

*Required:*

1. Compute the three equity ratios that measure equity position.
2. Interpret and evaluate each situation. The average interest rate is 10% (on total liabilities).

## Exercise 24–7

Basey Manufacturing Corporation balance sheet showed the following as of December 31, 19A:

| | |
|---|---|
| Preferred stock, 7%, par value, $50 per share ......................... | $200,000 |
| Common stock, nopar, 30,000 shares outstanding .................. | 360,000 |
| Contributed capital in excess of par, preferred stock.............. | 40,000 |
| Retained earnings ............................................................. | 80,000 |

*Required:*

Compute the book value per share of preferred and common stock assuming:

a. None of the preferred shares have been issued.
b. Preferred is noncumulative and nonparticipating.
c. Preferred is cumulative and nonparticipating (three years' dividends in arrears including current year).
d. Preferred has a liquidation value of $60 per share and is noncumulative and nonparticipating.
e. Preferred has a liquidation value of $60 per share and is noncumulative and nonparticipating, and the Retained Earnings account shows a *deficit* of $40,000.

## Exercise 24-8

The financial statements for Weston Corporation for 19C reported complete comparative statements. The following data were taken therefrom:

|  | 19A | 19B | 19C |
|---|---|---|---|
| Sales revenue | $12,000,000 | $13,000,000 | $14,000,000 |
| Net income | 100,000 | 120,000 | 100,000 |
| Interest expense, net of tax | 10,000 | 12,000 | 9,000 |
| Stockholders' equity | 1,400,000 | 1,450,000 | 1,460,000 |
| Shares of common stock outstanding | 20,000 | 20,000 | 24,000 |
| Total assets | 3,500,000 | 3,500,000 | 3,700,000 |
| Market value per share | $66.00 | $72.00 | $70.00 |

*Required:*

1. Based on the above financial data, compute the following ratios for 19B and 19C: (*a*) profit margin; (*b*) return on investment, total assets; (*c*) return on investment, owners' equity; (*d*) the leverage factor; and (*e*) the earnings per share. (Carry computations to two decimal places.)
2. What ratios would you prefer as a measure of profitability? Why?
3. Explain any significant trends that appear to be developing.

## Exercise 24-9

The following data relate to the Wallace Printing Company:

|  | 19A | 19B | 19C | 19D | 19E |
|---|---|---|---|---|---|
| Net income | $ 12,000 | $ 15,000 | $ 25,000 | $ 30,000 | $ 40,000 |
| Interest expense, net of tax | 1,000 | 1,200 | 2,000 | 2,200 | 3,000 |
| Sales | 120,000 | 140,000 | 180,000 | 230,000 | 260,000 |
| Total assets | 50,000 | 72,000 | 110,000 | 160,000 | 190,000 |
| Total liabilities | 25,000 | 30,000 | 40,000 | 70,000 | 80,000 |

*Required:*

Evaluate the company in terms of the (*a*) profit margin, (*b*) ROI, and (*c*) leverage factor.

## PROBLEMS

### Problem 24-1

The following pretax data of Knox Corporation was provided by the accounts:

| | For Year Ended December 31 | |
|---|---|---|
|  | 19A | 19B |
| Sales revenue | $400,000 | $450,000 |
| Return sales | (5,000) | (3,000) |
| Cost of goods sold | (236,000) | (265,000) |
| Selling expenses | (90,000) | (95,000) |
| Administrative expenses | (70,000) | (73,000) |
| Extraordinary items (loss) | 2,000 | (5,000) |
| Pretax net income | $ 1,000 | $ 9,000 |
| Shares of common stock outstanding | 20,000 | 20,000 |

*Required:*

1. Prepare a single-step income statement including a vertical percentage analysis. Assume an income tax rate of 40% on all items. Round to even percent.
2. Prepare a multiple-step income statement including a horizontal percentage analysis (amounts and percents). Round to even percents.
3. Evaluate the results and pinpoint items that you think need further investigation. Explain what further investigation should be considered.

## Problem 24–2

The following condensed data (rounded to even $1,000) for Royal Manufacturing Company financial position are available for two years:

|  | Year Ended December 31 | |
|---|---|---|
| *Assets* | *19A* | *19B* |
| Cash | $ 476,000 | $ 451,500 |
| Trade receivables | 184,000 | 220,000 |
| Allowance for doubtful accounts | (8,400) | (8,800) |
| Inventories | 640,000 | 682,000 |
| Prepaid expenses | 16,000 | 11,000 |
| Bond sinking fund | 320,000 | 120,000 |
| Long-term investments | | 176,000 |
| Land | 48,000 | 48,000 |
| Plant and equipment | 400,000 | 673,000 |
| Accumulated depreciation | (120,000) | (176,000) |
| Goodwill | 40,000 | |
| Deferred charges | 4,400 | 3,300 |
| Total | $2,000,000 | $2,200,000 |
| *Liabilities and Stockholders' Equity* | | |
| Accounts payable | $ 300,000 | $ 310,000 |
| Income taxes payable | 30,000 | 44,000 |
| Accrued wages | 10,000 | 15,400 |
| Bonds payable | 500,000 | 300,000 |
| Capital stock | 1,000,000 | 1,200,000 |
| Retained earnings | 160,000 | 210,600 |
| Reserve for bond sinking fund | | 120,000 |
| Total | $2,000,000 | $2,200,000 |

*Required:*

1. Prepare a classified balance sheet including a vertical analysis. Round to even percents.
2. Prepare a classified balance sheet including a horizontal analysis (Note: Requirements 1 and 2 can be combined if you prefer). Round to even percents.
3. Evaluate the results and pinpoint items that you think need further investigation. Explain what areas warrant further investigation.

## Problem 24–3

The following data were taken from the annual financial statements of Mason Corporation:

|                                     | 19A        | 19B        | 19C        |
|-------------------------------------|------------|------------|------------|
| **Current Assets:**                 |            |            |            |
| Cash                                | $   10,000 | $    5,000 | $    8,000 |
| Trade receivables                   | 180,000    | 170,000    | 190,000    |
| Less: Allowance for doubtful accounts | (5,000)  | (6,000)    | (8,000)    |
| Notes receivable (nontrade)         | 110,000    | 125,000    | 100,000    |
| Short-term investments              | 45,000     | 30,000     | 20,000     |
| Inventories                         | 298,000    | 355,000    | 387,000    |
| Prepaid expenses                    | 12,000     | 11,000     | 13,000     |
| Total                               | $ 650,000  | $ 690,000  | $ 710,000  |
| **Current Liabilities:**            |            |            |            |
| Trade payables                      | $   70,000 | $  158,000 | $  196,000 |
| Notes payable                       | 90,000     | 72,000     | 60,000     |
| Accrued wages payable               | 72,000     | 46,000     | 52,000     |
| Income taxes payable                | 19,000     | 23,000     | 24,000     |
| Deferred rent revenue               | 2,000      | 2,000      | 2,000      |
| Accrued liabilities                 | 17,000     | 19,000     | 16,000     |
| Total                               | $ 270,000  | $ 320,000  | $ 350,000  |
| **Additional Data:**                |            |            |            |
| Cash sales                          | $3,300,000 | $3,500,000 | $3,200,000 |
| Credit sales                        | 1,500,000  | 1,700,000  | 1,800,000  |
| Cost of goods sold                  | 2,500,000  | 2,900,000  | 2,800,000  |
| Total assets (net)                  | 6,600,000  | 7,200,000  | 7,200,000  |

*Required:*

1. Compute the ratios for each year that measure current position. Round to even percents.
2. Evaluate the current position as indicated by the statements and the ratios. What additional information would you need to buttress your evaluation?

### Problem 24–4

The financial statements of Staley Manufacturing Company for a three-year period showed the following:

|                                   | 19A        | 19B        | 19C        |
|-----------------------------------|------------|------------|------------|
| Total assets                      | $2,000,000 | $2,040,000 | $1,940,000 |
| Total current assets              | 368,000    | 450,000    | 480,000    |
| Total current liabilities         | 230,000    | 150,000    | 150,000    |
| Fixed assets (net)                | 1,248,000  | 1,257,600  | 1,260,000  |
| Total liabilities                 | 1,090,000  | 1,110,000  | 900,000    |
| Common stock (par value $100)     | 600,000    | 600,000    | 700,000    |
| Retained earnings                 | 310,000    | 330,000    | 340,000    |
| Sales (net)                       | 6,600,000  | 7,000,000  | 7,100,000  |
| Net income (after tax)            | 50,000     | 70,000     | 40,000     |
| Interest expense (net of tax)     | 34,000     | 38,000     | 30,000     |

*Required:*

1. Based on the above data, calculate the following ratios to measure the current

position for each year (round to even percents, or if a decimal, to two places):
   a. Current ratio.
   b. Working capital turnover.
   Evaluate the current position. What additional significant information do you
   need to adequately evaluate the current position? Explain.
2. Based on the above data, calculate the following ratios to measure the equity
   position (round to even percents):
   a. Creditors' equity to total assets.
   b. Book value per share of common stock.
   Evaluate the equity position. What additional significant information do you
   need to adequately evaluate the equity position? Explain.
3. Based on the above data, calculate the following ratios to measure operating
   results (round to even percents):
   a. Profit margin.
   b. Return on investment on total assets.
   c. Return on investment on owners' equity.
   d. Earnings per share.
4. Evaluate the operating results. What additional significant information do you
   need to adequately evaluate operating results? Explain.
5. Evaluate the financial leverage factor.


## Problem 24-5

The following annual data was taken from the records of Grant Trading Corporation:

|  | 19A | 19B | 19C | 19D | 19E |
|---|---|---|---|---|---|
| Sales | $400,000 | $420,000 | $450,000 | $440,000 | $490,000 |
| Net income | 15,000 | 16,000 | 20,000 | 5,000 | 40,000 |
| Total assets | 200,000 | 220,000 | 230,000 | 240,000 | 250,000 |
| Owners' equity | 100,000 | 110,000 | 120,000 | 115,000 | 140,000 |
| Market price per share | 60 | 62 | 55 | 50 | 60 |
| Dividends per share | 4 | 4 | 4 | 1 | 5 |
| Capital stock outstanding (shares) | 4,000 | 4,000 | 4,000 | 3,900 | 3,800 |
| Interest expense (net of tax) | 4,000 | 4,500 | 4,600 | 5,000 | 4,100 |

*Required:*
1. Compute the ratios that measure operating results.
2. Compute the market test ratios.
3. Evaluate the profitability of the company; pinpoint indicated strengths and
   weaknesses. What additional significant information do you need? Explain.
4. Compute the financial leverage factor.


## Problem 24-6

The following summarized data were taken from the published statements
of two companies that are being compared:

|  | (in thousands) | |
| --- | --- | --- |
|  | Company A | Company B |
| Sales | $3,000 | $ 9,000 |
| Cost of goods sold | 1,900 | 6,942 |
| Operating expenses | 400 | 1,600 |
| Interest expense (net of tax) | 8 | 108 |
| Extraordinary items (loss), after tax | (22) | 550 |
| Income taxes (on income before extraordinary items) | 240 | 300 |
| Current assets | 1,000 | 4,000 |
| Fixed assets | 5,000 | 19,000 |
| Accumulated depreciation | 2,000 | 7,000 |
| Investments, long term | 400 | 100 |
| Other assets | 600 | 7,900 |
| Current liabilities | 900 | 2,000 |
| Long-term liabilities | 100 | 1,800 |
| Capital stock ($10 par value) | 3,000 | 18,000 |
| Retained earnings | 1,000 | 2,200 |
| Current market value per share | $16.75 | $1.50 |

Compute the one ratio that would best answer each of the following questions (show computations). Justify your choice.

a. Which company probably has the best current position?
b. Which company has the best working capital turnover?
c. Which company is earning the best rate on total resources available to the management? On resources provided by the owners?
d. Which company has the advantage in "trading on the equity"?
e. Which company has the best profit margin?
f. Which company has the highest book value per share?
g. Which stock is the best buy?


## Problem 24–7

Fulger Corporation is considering building a second plant at a cost of $600,000. The management is considering two alternatives to obtain the funds: (a) sell additional common stock or (b) issue $600,000, five-year bonds payable at 8% interest. The management believes that the bonds can be sold at par (for $600,000) and the stock at $30 per share.

The balance sheet (before the new financing) reflected the following:

| Liabilities | None |
| --- | --- |
| Common stock, par $10 | $200,000 |
| Contributed capital in excess of par | 100,000 |
| Retained earnings | 120,000 |
| Average net income for past several years (net of tax) | 30,000 |

The average income tax rate is 45%. Average dividends per share have been $.50 per share per year. Expected increase in pretax net income (excluding interest expense) from the new plant, $100,000 per year.

*Required:*

1. Prepare an analysis to show (a) expected net income after the addition and (b) cash flows for the new capital, and (c) the leverage advantage or disadvantage to the present shareholders of issuing the bonds to obtain the financing.

2. What are the principal arguments against issuing the bonds (as opposed to selling the common stock)?

## Problem 24–8 (based on the Appendix)

This problem focuses on an actual set of financial statements. Assume you are a prospective investor and are in the process of analyzing several sets of financial statements with a tentative decision to invest $10,000 in common stocks.

*Required:*

1. Examine the auditors' report. Does it present any problems to you as a potential investor? Explain.
2. Examine the summary of accounting policies. Does it present any problems to you as a potential investor? What particular items does it pinpoint where you should be cognizant of the accounting policy? Explain.
3. Examine the financial statement in overall context, noting comparative amounts and percentage increases:
    a. Income statement—What is the amount of net income? Did it increase from last year? Do you observe any particular items that should be carefully watched during your analysis to follow? Explain.
    b. Balance sheet—What are the amounts of (1) cash, (2) total assets, (3) long-term liabilities, and (4) stockholders' equity? Do you observe any particular items that you should watch during your analysis to follow? Explain.
    c. Statement of changes in financial position—Is the statement on a cash or working capital basis? Did cash and working capital increase or decrease? What was the primary source of working capital? What was the primary use of working capital?
4. Examine the long-term financial review. What strengths and weaknesses do you observe? Explain.
5. Analytical—Develop ratios for 1974 and 1975 as follows:
    Measurements of current position:
    a. Current ratio.
    b. Quick ratio.
    Measurements of equity position:
    c. Creditors' equity to total assets.
    d. Book value per share.
    Measurements of operating results:
    e. Profit margin.
    f. Return on total assets.
    g. Return on owners' equity.
    h. Earnings per share (already computed).
    i. Leverage factor.
6. On the basis of your response to the above requirements:
    a. Evaluate the current position.
    b. Evaluate the equity position.
    c. Evaluate the profitability and leverage effect.
7. What specific additional information about this company, other than that reported in the financial statements and your analysis, would you urgently need prior to a decision to invest or not?

## Problem 24–9 (based on the Appendix)

The chapter Appendix presents a complete set of financial statements for a medium-sized company. This problem focuses on those statements. The objective is to develop an analysis of them.

*Required:*

1. Examine the auditors' report. What significant information (favorable and un-favorable) is provided?
2. Examine the summary of significant accounting policies. What important information (favorable and unfavorable) is provided?
3. Examine the overall financial report:
   a. What titles are used for the three required statements?
   b. How many notes are included? What is the topic of each?
   c. Is there a statement of retained earnings? Explain.
   d. Is there a long-term financial summary? How many periods does it encom-pass?
   e. Income statement—What are the amounts for each year and the changes in net sales, net income, dividends, EPS, extraordinary items, and income tax expense? Did you observe any unusual items? Explain.
   f. Balance sheet—What are the amounts for each year and the changes for cash, inventory, current assets, fixed assets, total assets, current liabilities, long-term debt and stockholders' equity? Do you observe any unusual items other than those above? Explain.
   g. Statement of changes in financial position—On what basis was it prepared? What were the two largest sources of funds for each year? What were the two largest uses of funds each year? Did funds increase or decrease during each year? By how much? Did you observe any unusual items? Explain.
4. Explain the long-term financial summary. What strengths and weaknesses do you observe? Explain.
5. Analytical—Develop ratios for 1974 and 1975 as follows (show computations and carry to even percents, or if a decimal, to two places):
   Measurements of current position:
   a. Current ratio.
   b. Acid test ratio.
   c. Receivable turnover.
   d. Inventory turnover.
   Measurements of equity position:
   e. Creditors' equity to total assets.
   f. Plant turnover.
   g. Book value per share.
   Measurements of operating results:
   h. Profit margin.
   i. Return on total assets.
   j. Return on owners' equity.
   k. Earnings per share (already computed).
   l. Leverage factor.
6. On the basis of your responses to the above requirements:
   a. Evaluate the current position.
   b. Evaluate the equity position.
   c. Evaluate the profitability.
   d. Evaluate the leverage effect.
7. Assume you have $25,000 cash to invest and are interested in acquiring com-mon stock. What specific information about this company, other than that reported in the financial statements and your analysis, would you urgently need prior to making a decision to invest, or not invest, in this company?

# Chapter 25

## Price-Level and Fair Value
## Accounting and Reporting

Each of us is aware, almost daily, that prices of most things we buy have been rising sharply. While this fact may have unpleasant personal consequences, the focus of this chapter is to analyze the accounting consequences and to describe various proposals designed to cope with them.

When the unit-of-measure assumption was discussed in Chapter 2, it was noted that the conventional accounting model, based on historical cost, either assumed a stable monetary unit or assumed that changes in the value of money were not material. At some eras in the history of the U.S. economy such assumptions were valid; and even today, for a limited category of entities, there may be some validity to the assumption that changes in the value of money are not significant.[1] For the vast majority of businesses and other entities, however, changing prices are quite important in accounting and financial reporting as will be shown in the section "The Impact of Inflation on Financial Statements."

### PRICE CHANGES AND HOW THEY ARE MEASURED

Since the early years of the Great Depression of the 1930s, prices of virtually all goods and services in the United States (and in most of the world) have been rising almost without interruption. Stated another way, the general purchasing power of the dollar (and other monetary units) has been falling almost continuously. General purchasing power is the power of the monetary unit to purchase real goods and services. When there is a general increase in prices (i.e., the general purchasing power of the monetary unit decreases), the condition is referred to as

---

[1] For example, financial institutions, whose obligations consist primarily of debts, the dollar amount of which can be determined with precision and whose assets consist of cash, receivables, bonds, lease contracts and the like can be less seriously concerned with the effects of inflation.

*inflation.* When there is a general decline in prices (i.e., when the general purchasing power of the monetary unit rises), that condition is called *deflation.* Because inflation has been so pervasive, our discussions, illustrations, and assignment material will be primarily in the context of rising prices; however, the concepts discussed apply to deflation as well. It should be borne in mind, of course, that "purchasing power losses" which are reflected under conditions of inflation would become "purchasing power gains" should similar holdings prevail under conditions of deflation.

Because we use the dollar as the unit of measure or common denominator to express many diverse kinds of assets and claims and because each business entity is likely to own many kinds of assets and owe diverse types of claims and also because statement users are interested in making interfirm comparisons, it is both logical and necessary that measures be devised to express the degree of change in the prices of assets and the purchasing power represented by various claims. These measures of changes in prices are known as *index numbers.*

A price index has been defined as "a series of measurements, expressed as percentages, of the relationship between the average price of a group of goods and services at a succession of dates and the average price of a similar group of goods and services at a common date. The components of the series are price index numbers. A price index does not, however, measure the movement of the individual component prices, some of which move in one direction, and some in the opposite direction."[2] There are several index numbers which purport to measure changes in prices in the United States on a general basis. The three most widely known measures of general price changes in the United States are the Gross National Product Implicit Price Deflator (GNP Deflator), the Consumer Price Index, and the Wholesale Price Index. The GNP Deflator has been recommended in connection with the preparation of price-level adjusted financial statements successively in an AICPA *Research Study,* an *APB Statement* and in an FASB exposure draft.[3] It is accurate to say that the three indices move roughly in parallel. In other words when there is a sharp rise or persistent upward movement of prices, all will show increases, but not the same relative change. However when prices are comparatively stable, it is not uncommon for two of the indices to move in one direction while the other moves in an opposite direction.[4]

---

[2] AICPA, *Accounting Research Study No. 6,* "Reporting the Financial Effects of Price-Level Changes" (New York, 1963), p. 63.

[3] Successively, see footnote 2, also AICPA, "Financial Statements Restated for General Price Level Changes," *APB Statement No. 3* (New York, 1969); and "Financial Reporting in Units of General Purchasing Power" Exposure Draft (Stamford, Conn.: FASB, December 31, 1974).

[4] Reasons for preference of the GNP Deflator over the other measures are to be found in the following quotations in Appendix A of *Accounting Research Study No. 6,* "The only index currently compiled that is a measure of the general level of prices in the United States is the GNP Implicit Price Deflator. It is the only price index compiled in this country whose 'universe' encompasses the entire economy" (p. 111).

It is important to recognize that a price index is an average or composite; therefore, it measures the average trend of a group of prices over time. Not all of the prices in the group change at the same rate; in a period of inflation some will increase faster than others, and while the overall index is rising some prices included in the set may be falling.[5]

## HOW MUCH HAVE PRICES CHANGED?

Because the GNP Deflator has been preferred by three authoritative studies as a basis for preparing price-level adjusted financial statements, it is pertinent to indicate the extent to which prices have changed according to this index. Currently, 1958 serves as base year and is assigned a value of 100. This index dates back to 1929 when the average value was 50.6; it fell steadily to an all-time low of 39.3 in the depression year of 1933, then rose continuously thereafter except for three years. The years in which it fell were 1938, 1939, and 1949; in none of these was the percent of decrease more than 1.6% from the level of the preceding year. "Double-digit" inflation was experienced in four years. The years and their rates of increase over the preceding year were: 1942, 12.3%; 1946, 11.7%; 1947, 11.8%; and from the first quarter of 1974 to the first quarter of 1975, 10.8%. By the first quarter of 1975 the index had risen to an all-time high of 181.4.

Stated one way, the price-level change implies that what would have cost $100 in 1929 cost more than $358 in early 1975, but this is not altogether a valid statement or comparison. In 1929 one could not buy TV sets (much less color sets), cars with automatic transmissions, air-conditioned homes, electronic computers, clothing made of synthetic fibers, open-heart surgery, and a host of other products and services accepted as fairly commonplace in 1975. Further, people were spending different proportions of their incomes for shelter, food, recreation, communication, and medical care in those days than they are today. These kinds of change present some of the major problems in constructing an index number and keeping it valid over an extended period of time—technological factors change, quality of goods and services improves, and the proportions of goods and services people buy do not remain constant.

## IMPACT OF INFLATION ON FINANCIAL STATEMENTS

The impact of inflation on financial reports, prepared in accordance with the conventional accounting model, varies considerably from one entity to the next depending upon a number of factors. One factor is

---

[5] From 1965 to 1972, for example, wholesale prices of commodities in the United States generally rose over 23% (the index changed from 96.6 to 119.1). During this same period wholesale prices of the following items were showing these percentage drops: home electronic equipment, 10.1%; floor coverings, 6.7%; crude rubber, 6.0%; and plastic resins, 10.7%.

In the area of communications it is rather startling to note that most long-distance telephone calls are cheaper in 1975 than they were in 1951, while it costs eight times more to mail a postcard in the United States in 1975 than it did in 1951.

that by selecting from the array of alternative accounting procedures which comprise current GAAP, the impact of inflation on some elements of the financial report may be lessened or postponed. The financial statements of businesses which are *capital intensive* (i.e., they commit a relatively large proportion of their resources to investment in fixed assets) are likely to be affected by inflation more than those whose capital is largely committed to short-term assets. At the same time businesses which borrow heavily on a long-term basis (and this is likely to include the capital intensive ones) are in a better position to gain from inflation than those which do not. Also, some businesses can serve their customers with little or no investment in inventory, while others must make large investments in inventory which often have a low turnover. The latter type of businesses are affected by inflation more than the former, though they may be able to reduce the impact on financial statements by selecting *Lifo* rather than *Fifo* for inventory purposes.

During a period of inflation, the conventional accounting model reflects a matching of dollars of different "size" on the income statement. Revenues are usually expressed in current dollars, but many of the expenses matched against them frequently are not. For example, depreciation and similar cost expirations may reflect cost levels which prevailed years ago when the dollar had a vastly different purchasing power. Depending on the inventory flow method in use, *cost of goods sold* may represent an amount in current dollars or it may not. If there is a relatively high correspondence between the volume of purchases and the volume of sales, and if selling prices are based on current costs, use of *Lifo* will tend to give a reasonable matching of current costs against current revenues.[6] The conventional accounting model ignores the fact that an entity which maintains large balances of cash and receivables during periods of inflation loses purchasing power as a result, while one that is heavily in debt gains because it has borrowed dollars with greater *buying* power than the ones it is likely to repay. Conventional accounting defers all gains (or losses) from the holding of an asset until it is sold; no recognition is given to the price-level effect on that gain (or loss).

When there has been marked inflation and comparative statements for two or more successive periods are prepared on a conventional basis, they can be quite misleading. Suppose, for example, the sales amount on the current income statement is 15% higher than on the income statement of four years ago. If prices of the company's product and prices generally have risen 50% in the interval, there has been a material decline in *physical volume* of goods sold. On a common-dollar (i.e., price-level adjusted) basis the change in volume would have been evident. Conventional financial statements also obscure the comparability of financial statements of two or more entities whose accounts consist of items that were bought in different years.

---

[6] At the same time, use of *Lifo* during a period of sustained inflation will ultimately result in unrealistically low balance sheet valuation of inventories.

## DEPRECIATION AND RISING REPLACEMENT COSTS

The purpose of depreciation accounting, as traditionally viewed, is to allocate the original cost of depreciable property over its economic useful life. Other things being equal, recording depreciation holds back an amount of assets equal to the investment in the depreciable property, thereby facilitating its replacement if the replacement cost remains constant (i.e., no inflation). Since depreciation is an expense that must be recovered, it is included in pricing decisions on products and services sold by the entity. Therefore, the management of an entity must be concerned with the adequacy of depreciation charges in (a) asset replacement, and (b) current pricing policy. Because present GAAP permits depreciation charges to be based only on historical cost, extensive attention is being accorded some form of price-level accounting or current-value accounting (both discussed later in this chapter) because under conditions of inflation they would afford means of recording depreciation charges that (a) in total can approximate replacement costs, and (b) are appropriate to realistic financing policy.

Illustrated simply, suppose Jones bought a new automobile in 1972 and put it in service as a taxi in a small town. Jones and a hired driver comprise the entire staff of the enterprise. All expenses except depreciation of the cab are incurred on a cash basis; as a consequence, except for depreciation, the excess of receipts over payments is regarded by Jones as pretax income. Because the cab cost $3,600 and is expected to trade in for $600 after five years of use, Jones decided to set aside $600 each year to replace the cab. The $600 depreciation expense is deducted on the tax return. Aside from the $600 set aside, Jones spends the remaining cash receipts from the business for living expenses and income taxes. By 1976 the cheapest comparably equipped car had risen in cost to $5,500, and it likely will cost $6,000 if Jones replaces the cab on schedule in 1977. Where will Jones get the extra $2,400 that will be needed? The $3,000 saved back plus the $600 trade-in allowance will not buy even the smallest comparably equipped compact car by 1977, besides such a vehicle would be obviously unsuited to use in the enterprise. Is it not logical to say Jones has overstated the income from the enterprise by $2,400? Has Jones paid income taxes on what amounts to both income and a return of capital? Has Jones priced the taxi services on the basis of economic reality if the additional cost of replacing the taxi when worn out was disregarded?

One may ask whether this example is relevant to a large corporation. The answer must be that it is relevant. Profitable corporations generally pay taxes at a rate of 48% on most of their income and, in addition, their shareholders pay another income tax on dividends received. Therefore, to the extent that what is taxed as income is really a return of capital, the problem exists. Corporations have essentially the same fixed asset replacement and pricing problems as sole proprietors. In an era of sustained inflation a hotel chain, a factory, or a local business which does not include in its pricing of products and services an amount sufficient to cover the future replacement cost of facilities now in use will be unable to maintain its present scope of operations when the existing facilities must be replaced unless it is willing and able (a) to incur added debt, or (b) obtain additional equity capital, and perhaps to dilute the equity of existing owners. Obviously, the adoption of either price-level or current-value accounting will not solve the capital replacement and pricing problems of an entity, but it may add more economic realism in financial reports on which these decisions, in part, are made.

## PIECEMEAL ACCOUNTING APPROACHES
## UNDER CONDITIONS OF INFLATION

One piecemeal accounting approach focuses on *inventories*. The *Lifo* inventory method has been cited as a means of achieving a closer matching of current costs against current revenues when prices are changing. This is true, of course, only to the extent that there is some correspondence between the physical volume of goods purchased and sold during the period. Also, if prices have doubled after *Lifo* was adopted (as they have between 1955 and 1975), and physical volume remains constant, the inventory value reported on the balance sheet would be about one half its cost. Thus, this piecemeal solution is totally inadequate because (a) it does not attain effective reporting on the financial statements, and (b) it deals with only one problem area—inventories.

Another accounting approach focuses on *depreciation* and similar cost allocations. The use of accelerated depreciation in the accounts and reports has been cited as a means of solving the problem of *understatement* of depreciation during inflation. Accelerated depreciation is effective only when property, plant, and equipment items subject to depreciation are relatively new and also the compensating effect generally is during the first half of their useful lives. Over their total useful life, the aggregate amount of the depreciation charges cannot exceed what it would under straight-line or any other allowed alternative. This piecemeal solution is singularly deficient because (a) it deals only with the short run, (b) focuses only on one aspect of the problem—depreciable assets, and (c) tends to cause arbitrarily determined effects.

Still another piecemeal accounting approach which has some balance sheet impact, but does not affect reported net income, is the technique of appropriating retained earnings (i.e., replacement costs) for excess plant designed to notify statement users that the management is cognizant of inflationary effects on asset replacement and that dividends must be restricted. The implication is that there are no adequate means of coping with the problem within the purview of present GAAP. This piecemeal approach is deficient on all counts.

Another piecemeal approach, not accorded general acceptability, is the proposal that an extra expense charge be made in the income statement to compensate for the understatement of depreciation, cost of goods sold, and other expired costs likely to be too low because of inflation during the period. The proposal has a number of obvious difficulties. First, such a charge is likely to be arbitrarily estimated instead of being objectively and systematically measured; second, it does not consider the balance sheet impact; and, third, it does not deal with the broader problem of inflationary impacts.

The piecemeal approaches are subject to numerous objections. They ignore replacement costs. In some situations they may achieve a reasonably desirable short-run result (from a standpoint of counteracting the effects of inflation) on one financial statement but they either ignore or worsen the reporting on another statement. They make it unrealistic to attempt to compute meaningful rates of return for the entity (partly because of the lack of consistency between the balance sheet and income statement). They may lull many users of the financial statements into a false sense of security that the inflation problem is adequately accounted for and reported by the entity or that it is not serious enough to cause concern. Finally, they do not deal with the broad area of inflationary effects and as a result cause inconsistent measurements of assets, liabilities, and net income.

## COMPREHENSIVE ACCOUNTING APPROACHES

Three of the four piecemeal approaches to cope with the major changes in the price level have serious deficiencies. Primarily, they do not comprehensively deal with the problem. The two major alternatives that deal with the price-level problem comprehensively are discussed and illustrated in the paragraphs to follow.

## GENERAL PURCHASING POWER (INDEX NUMBER) APPROACH

Fundamentally, the general purchasing power or index number approach uses a selected index, such as the GNP Deflator, to restate on a *current basis* those elements of the financial statements which are out of date in terms of most recent price levels. This general explanation requires demonstration of its application. Therefore, after a review of the background of the index approach, the application steps will be explained. This will be followed by a simple example and then a more complex illustration.

### Background

Dr. Henry W. Sweeney introduced the index approach in a series of *Accounting Review* articles in the 1920s and 1930s. The concept and its application were presented in his book *Stabilized Accounting* which first appeared in 1936 and was republished as an accounting classic in 1964. Sweeney's thinking was heavily influenced by experience and practice in Germany following World War I when that nation experienced drastic and ruinous inflation. Although academicians were aware of the techniques involved in the index approach (also called general purchasing power or price level approach), they were largely ignored by the world of accounting practice. The first significant attention by practitioners to the deficiencies of conventional accounting when prices change rapidly came in the late 1940s—not a surprising development in view of the fact that in 1946, 1947, and 1948 prices rose 11.7%, 11.8%, and 6.7%, respectively, as measured by the GNP Deflator.

### AICPA and the Price-Level Problem

In December 1947 the AICPA's Committee on Accounting Procedure, in *ARB 43*, Chapter 9A, (which at the time had responsibility for determination of accounting principles) considered the problem, which they designated as "Depreciation and High Costs"; they concluded:

1. At that time it would not be satisfactory to increase depreciation charges against current income to reflect higher replacement costs of plant or to recognize such costs by recording appraisals.
2. In considering depreciation in connection with product costs, prices, and business policies, management must take into consideration the likelihood that replacement costs of plant assets then in use would greatly exceed their historical costs.
3. Periodic appropriation of net income or retained earnings in contemplation of replacement of plant at higher costs was a proper managerial action.

This basic position was reaffirmed by the same committee the next year in a letter addressed to the AICPA membership.

In 1953 the same committee again considered the problem and reaffirmed its earlier position. The vote was 14 to 6, whereas in 1947 it had been 20 to 0, with one member not voting and another voting favorably but with qualification.

The Committee on Accounting Procedure was replaced in 1959 by the Accounting Principles Board. Initially the APB commissioned research studies on six problem areas; one dealt with price-level accounting. *Accounting Research Study No. 6*, "Reporting the Effects of Price-Level Changes," was published in 1963. After considering reactions to this study the APB developed *Statement No. 3*, "Financial Statements Restated for General Price-Level Changes," published in 1969. In the process of developing the statement, the techniques recommended in it were experimentally applied over a two-year period to the financial records of 18 cooperating businesses. Results of this experiment were reported in the *Journal of Accountancy* (June 1969).

Timing of the issuance of *Statement No. 3* was fortunate in one sense, but unfortunate in another. The *Statement* was timely in that it appeared when prices were again rising sharply. Concurrently, though, business profits began to fall in 1969 and continued to decline in 1970. As a consequence, business managements were loath to adopt the recommended procedures of *Statement No. 3*. The statement recommended preparation of a set of supplemental statements to accompany the regularly prepared balance sheet, income statement, and retained earnings statement. The supplemental statements would reflect the application of a price index reflective of general price changes to specific statement items and amounts. Given the long inflation which preceded 1969 and the sharp acceleration of prices in that year and in 1970, and given the drop in reported profits as compared with 1968 and earlier, one can understand the reluctance of the typical company management to adopt on a voluntary basis an accounting procedure which may worsen their already deteriorating profit picture. As a consequence, almost no adoptions of supplementary price-level adjusted statements occurred and interest in the subject outside academic circles largely disappeared.

### FASB and the Price-Level Problem

When the FASB was created early in 1973, it initially placed six topics on its agenda; none of them related to inflation accounting. This is understandable because up to that time it was the view of many that inflation was not a serious problem in this country. Throughout the 1960s the rate of inflation as measured by the GNP Deflator had been well below 3% per year. The rate began to accelerate in the late 1960s. By year-end 1973 it was found the highest rate of increase experienced for a quarter of a century had been attained; 1973 was 5.6% higher than 1972 in terms of average prices for the year. At the December 1973 meeting of the FASB's Advisory Council action was taken to get the subject on the Board's agenda. Thereafter, events unfolded swiftly; a Discussion Memorandum issued on February 15, 1974, led to a two-day public hearing in April 1974. By December 1974, based on testimony gathered at the hearing and from other sources, the FASB issued a proposed accounting standard on the subject. The Discussion Memorandum and the proposed accounting standard both relied heavily on earlier work done by the AICPA's research staff and the APB. The principal provisions of the proposed standard are summarized, and two illustrations show application of its provisions. The proposed standard uses index numbers and many of the techniques first introduced by Sweeney.

The preceding background review provides a sound basis for considering the two basic accounting approaches that depart significantly from the traditional, or conventional, historic cost model, viz:

1. Financial statements restated on purchasing power or price-level bases.
2. Current fair value accounting and reporting.

Each will be discussed and illustrated in this order.

### APPLICATION OF THE INDEX NUMBER APPROACH TO RESTATE FINANCIAL STATEMENTS

Financial statements under current GAAP are prepared on the traditional historical cost basis. The historical cost basis amounts on the financial statements are restated in terms of *units of general purchasing power*. The FASB clearly does not view restatement by using index numbers as a departure from the historical cost basis; rather there is a change in the *measuring unit* but not in the attribute (i.e., the cost of the asset) being measured.[7]

The restatement of historical cost basis amounts on traditional financial statements to units of general purchasing power, by using index numbers, involves the following steps:

1. Obtain the complete set of financial statements prepared under current GAAP.
2. Select the appropriate index to use and obtain the index numbers for each period covering the life of the *oldest* item on the financial statements. The FASB stated that "The Gross National Product Implicit Price Deflator shall be the index of the general purchasing power of the dollar used in preparing general purchasing power financial information."
3. Each statement item is classified as monetary or nonmonetary. *Monetary items* are defined as cash and claims to cash that are fixed in terms of numbers of dollars regardless of change in prices. Thus, cash, receivables, and most liabilities are monetary items. All other items are classified as *nonmonetary* items. Thus inventories, fixed assets, and common stock equity are nonmonetary items. Exhibit 25–1 presents more details on the classification of items as monetary or nonmonetary.
4. Restate each nonmonetary item in terms of its current general purchasing power for financial statement purposes. This involves computation of a *conversion factor* which is the index number that prevailed when the nonmonetary item was originally recorded in the accounts divided into the current year index number. The cost of the item as reported on the traditionally prepared financial statement is multiplied by the conversion factor to derive the restated amount. Example: Land was acquired for $22,000 when the GNP Deflator figure was 110; and on the date statements are being prepared it is 132. The conversion factor is: $132 \div 110 = 1.20$. On the general purchasing power adjusted statements, computation of the Land restated amount to be reported would be $22,000 \times 1.20 = $26,400.[8] Significantly, the *monetary items are not restated* because the amount of dollars they will command (assets) or demand (liabilities) is fixed.[9]
5. Compute the *general purchasing power gain or loss* (sometimes called *price-level gain or loss*) on the monetary, but not the nonmonetary, items. Recall that purchasing power gains and losses occur *only* on monetary items because the number of dollars to satisfy them is fixed—they are constant in amount, although these dollars are changing in real value. The change in their real value is the purchasing power gain or loss. To compute the purchasing power

---

[7] An alternative procedure, *current value accounting* (discussed in the next section) is significantly different conceptually, procedurally, and as to results. *Fair value* accounting is a conceptual departure from the historical cost concept.

[8] Arithmetically this is $22,000 \times {}^{132}/_{110} = $26,400.

[9] FASB Exposure Drafts (see footnote 3).

**EXHIBIT 25–1**
**Classification of Items as Monetary or Nonmonetary**

|  | Monetary | Nonmonetary |
|---|:---:|:---:|
| Cash on hand and in banks[1] | x | |
| Foreign currency on hand and claims thereto | | x |
| Marketable securities: | | |
|   Stocks (nonmonetary because prices can change) | | x |
|   Bonds (expected to be held to maturity) | x | |
|   Bonds (expected to be sold before maturity) | | x |
| Receivables | x | |
| Allowance for doubtful accounts | x | |
| Inventories[2] | | x |
| Prepaid expenses | | x |
| Property, plant, and equipment | | x |
| Accumulated depreciation | | x |
| Cash surrender value of life insurance | x | |
| Deferred charges (including income taxes) | | x |
| Intangibles | | x |
| Accounts and notes payable, accrued expenses | x | |
| Advances received on sales contracts[3] | | x |
| Bonds payable and other long-term debt | x | |
| Unamortized premium or discount on debt | x | |
| Obligations under warranties | | x |
| Deferred income tax credits (and debits) | | x |
| Preferred stock[4] | | x |
| Common stockholders' equity | | x |

[1] All claims are assumed to be payable in U.S. dollars unless specifically stated otherwise.

[2] An exception would be inventories produced under fixed price contracts accounted for at the contract price. Such inventories would be monetary.

[3] This obligation will be satisfied by delivery of goods or services that are nonmonetary because their prices can fluctuate.

[4] Preferred stock carried at an amount equal to its fixed liquidation or redemption price is monetary because the claim of the preferred shareholders on assets of the entity is in a fixed number of dollars. In other instances preferred stock would be nonmonetary.

gain or loss, the monetary items are restated in the computation, but not on the price-level financial statements. The restated amount is compared with the reported historical cost to determine the purchasing power gain or loss. In contrast, the nonmonetary items, by their characteristics, change in the number of dollars they will command. Thus, no purchasing power gain or loss is recognized on them in price-level accounting. Nonmonetary items are not included in the computation of purchasing power gains or losses; they are restated on the price-level adjusted statements.

The gain and loss effects of holding monetary items may be summarized as follows:

| | General Price Level Rising | | General Price Level Falling | |
|---|:---:|:---:|:---:|:---:|
| Item | Gain | Loss | Gain | Loss |
| Monetary assets | | ✓ | ✓ | |
| Monetary liabilities | ✓ | | | ✓ |

Computation of the purchasing power gain or loss on monetary items involves a series of sub steps, viz:

a. Determine excess of monetary assets over monetary liabilities (or vice versa) at the start of the period.

b. Restate the excess of the monetary items described in step (a) to its end-of-the-period purchasing power equivalent. Assume cash and payables (both monetary) at the start of the period were $20,000 and $8,000, respectively, and the starting and ending index numbers were 140 and 151.2. The excess of the monetary assets over monetary liabilities of $12,000 would be restated as: $12,000 × 151.2/140 = $12,960. Since there is an *asset excess* there is a potential purchasing power *loss* of $960 for the period.

c. Identify all transactions during the year which *increased monetary items;* restate them to the year-end basis and add the total restated amount to the restated balance derived in step (b). Example: Sales for cash and on account occurred evenly throughout the year and amounted to $728,000. The average index value for the year is 145.6; the year-end value is 151.2. The increase in monetary items due to sales would be restated to $756,000 ($728,000 × 151.2/145.6) which would be added to (b).

d. Identify transactions which *decreased monetary items;* restate them to the year-end basis and subtract the total restated amount from the sum of (b) + (c). Examples: Purchases for cash and on account occurred evenly throughout the year and amounted to $436,800. The restatement of the decrease in monetary items due to (a) purchases, and (b) equipment would be computed as follows: $436,800 × 151.2/145.6 = $453,600. Equipment was bought at the start of the year for $28,000. The restatement would be $28,000 × 151.2/140 = $30,240.

e. Derive a total of the price-level adjusted net monetary items as above, and a total of the carrying value of the monetary items as of the end of the period; subtract the latter from the former to determine the *purchasing power gain or loss*. Using the foregoing figures we have the following:

| | Monetary Items | |
| --- | --- | --- |
| | Carrying Values (historical cost) | Restated Amount (end-of-period purchasing power) |
| From step (b) ........................................ | $ 12,000 | $ 12,960 |
| From step (c) ........................................ | 728,000 | 756,000 |
| Subtotal ................................................ | 740,000 | 768,960 |
| From step (d) ........................................ | 464,800 | 483,840 |
| Totals—per Step (e) ............................. | $275,200 | 285,120 |
| Deduct historical carrying value.............. | | −275,200 |
| Purchasing Power Gain (Loss) .............. | | $ (9,920) |

The comprehensive procedures recommended by the FASB will now be illustrated; first with a simplified example, followed by a more complex and realistic example.

## SIMPLIFIED ILLUSTRATION OF PRICE-LEVEL ACCOUNTING

To illustrate all aspects of the accounting process, including price-level restatement, this example will include the following:

1. Beginning trial balance (dated December 31, 19C) for XY Company (given in the first two columns of Exhibit 25–2).
2. Transactions for 19D including relevant price index data:
   a. Sold merchandise for cash and on credit, $400,000.
   b. Bought merchandise on credit, cost $290,000 (assume periodic inventory system).
   c. Payments on current liabilities, $340,000.
   d. Declared and paid a $12,000 cash dividend at year-end.
   e. Various expenses paid at an approximately uniform rate throughout the year, $55,000.
   f. Depreciation expense on fixtures recorded at year-end, $20,000. The fixtures, acquired on January 1, 19A, when the price index stood at 116, have an estimated ten-year life and zero residual value. The future plant site also was acquired on this date.
   g. Income tax expense of $20,000 was accrued uniformly throughout the year.
   h. Ending inventory, $105,000.
   i. Relevant price index data:

|  | Index Numbers | Conversion Factor (%) |
|---|---|---|
| January 1, 19A | 116 | 159.5/116  = 137.5 |
| December 31, 19C | 145 | 159.5/145  = 110.0 |
| December 31, 19D | 159.5 | 159.5/159.5 = 100.0 |
| Average for 19D | 151.9 | 159.5/151.9 = 105.0 |

3. Worksheet for 19D to derive traditional cost basis income statement and balance sheet (Exhibit 25–2).
4. Application of conversion factors to convert traditional cost basis statements to purchasing power basis, that is, price-level conversion (Exhibit 25–3).

### Application of Conversion Factors

The preceding summary of steps to develop price-level adjusted statements indicated that cost basis amounts are restated (by using the conversion factors) for two purposes, viz:

EXHIBIT 25-2

XY COMPANY

Worksheet to Develop Income Statement and Balance Sheet—Traditional Cost Basis

Year Ended December 31, 19D

| | Balances December 31, 19C | | 19D Transactions and Adjustments | | | | Income Summary – 19D | | Balance Sheet, December 31, 19D | |
|---|---|---|---|---|---|---|---|---|---|---|
| | Debit | Credit | Debit | | Credit | | Debit | Credit | Debit | Credit |
| Cash and receivables | 145,000 | | (a) | 400,000 | (c) 340,000<br>(d) 12,000<br>(e) 55,000 | | | | 138,000 | |
| Inventory | 90,000 | | | | | | 90,000 | 105,000* | 105,000 | |
| Future plant site | 50,000 | | | | | | | | 50,000 | |
| Fixtures | 200,000 | | | | | | | | 200,000 | |
| Accumulated depreciation | | 60,000 | | | (f) | 20,000 | | | | 80,000 |
| Current payables including taxes | | 60,000 | (c) | 340,000 | (b) 290,000<br>(g) 20,000 | | | | | 30,000 |
| Long-term note payable | | 50,000 | | | | | | | | 50,000 |
| Capital stock, par $10 | | 300,000 | | | | | | | | 300,000 |
| Retained earnings | | 15,000 | (d) | 12,000 | | | 30,000† | | | 33,000 |
| Sales | | | | | (a) | 400,000 | | 400,000 | | |
| Purchases | | | (b) | 290,000 | | | 290,000 | | | |
| Expenses (except depreciation and income taxes) | | | (e) | 55,000 | | | 55,000 | | | |
| Depreciation expense | | | (f) | 20,000 | | | 20,000 | | | |
| Income tax expense | | | (g) | 20,000 | | | 20,000 | | | |
| | 485,000 | 485,000 | | 1,137,000 | | 1,137,000 | 505,000 | 505,000 | 493,000 | 493,000 |

* Ending inventory.

† Net income transferred to retained earnings.

1. To compute the purchasing power gain or loss on *monetary items.*
2. To develop price-level adjusted financial statements by restating the nonmonetary items.

### Computation of the 19D Purchasing Power Gain or Loss

If this were the first year of operations for XY Company, the purchasing power gain or loss could be directly computed by applying the conversion factors to each monetary item. However, in subsequent periods the computation becomes more complex. Therefore, restatement steps 5(*a*)–(*e*) page 1073 must be completed for XY Company (as is the usual case). These restatement steps are reflected in Exhibit 25–3. Observe that first the beginning restated net amount of monetary items (i.e., carried over from 19C) is determined by using the 19C conversion factor of 110, viz: $35,000 × 110% = $38,500. The transactions during 19D that

**EXHIBIT 25–3**

XY COMPANY
Calculation of General Purchasing Power (Price-Level) Gain or Loss
Year Ended December 31, 19D

|  | Cost Basis Amount (per books) | Conversion Factor | Restated at December 31, 19D |
|---|---|---|---|
| Net monetary items at December 31, 19C: |  |  |  |
| Cash and receivables................................ | $145,000 |  |  |
| Current payables, including income taxes ... | (60,000) |  |  |
| Long-term payable.................................... | (50,000) |  |  |
| Net (assets) .................................... | 35,000 | 110 | $ 38,500 |
| Add sources of net monetary items during 19D: |  |  |  |
| Sales ................................................. | 400,000 | 105 | 420,000 |
| Subtotal........................................... | 435,000 |  | 458,500 |
| Deduct uses of monetary items during 19D: |  |  |  |
| Purchases .............................................. | 290,000 | 105 | 304,500 |
| Operating expenses (except depreciation) ... | 55,000 | 105 | 57,750 |
| Income taxes ........................................ | 20,000 | 105 | 21,000 |
| Dividends paid at year-end ....................... | 12,000 | 100 | 12,000 |
| Total Uses........................................ | 377,000 |  | 395,250 |
| Net monetary items restated at December 31, 19D ($458,500 − $395,250) .................... |  |  | 63,250 |
| Net monetary items at December 31, 19D, not restated: |  |  |  |
| Cash and receivables............................... | 138,000 |  |  |
| Current payables including taxes .............. | (30,000) |  |  |
| Mortgage payable .................................. | (50,000) |  |  |
| Total ............................................ | $ 58,000 |  | 58,000* |
| Purchasing Power Gain (Loss) in 19D on Monetary Basis ...... |  |  | $ (5,250) |

* This amount can be calculated directly as $435,000 − $377,000 = $58,000, or detailed as reflected here.

increased (i.e., sources) and decreased (i.e., uses) monetary items are identified and restated. Deduction of the 19D ending balances of the monetary items from the net of these amounts gives the purchasing power gain or loss. For XY Company there was a $5,250 loss because the losses on monetary assets held exceeded the gains on the monetary liabilities owed during 19D. This loss is reported on the restated income statement shown in Exhibit 25–5.

### Restatement of Balance Sheet Amounts

When steps in the application of the index number approach were summarized, it was pointed out that *only nonmonetary items* are restated in terms of their current general purchasing power for financial statement purposes. As to balance sheet items, this means taking the end of the period index value as a numerator and the index value which prevailed, when the nonmonetary item was first recorded in the accounts, as a denominator and multiplying this fraction by the historical cost (book carrying amount) of each nonmonetary item. For example, as to Future Plant Site and Fixtures acquired on January 1, 19A, when the index was 116, for arriving at the purchasing power equivalent of those assets at the end of 19D when the index is at 159.5, one would multiply the book value of these items by the conversion factor of 137.5 (i.e., 159.5/116). As to ending inventory, under a *Fifo* flow assumption, the inventory came from purchases made during the period, so the inventory needs an upward adjustment only by the amount which pur-

**EXHIBIT 25–4**

XY COMPANY
Restatement of Balance Sheet – Price-Level Basis

| Assets | Cost Basis Amount | Conversion Factor | Restated Amount |
|---|---|---|---|
| Cash and receivables ............................ | $138,000 | 100 | $138,000 |
| Inventory............................................ | 105,000 | 105 | 110,250 |
| Future plant site ................................. | 50,000 | 137.5 | 68,750 |
| Fixtures ............................................. | 200,000 | 137.5 | 275,000 |
| Less: Accumulated depreciation ............ | (80,000) | 137.5 | (110,000) |
| Total Assets ............................... | $413,000 | | $482,000 |
| *Liabilities* | | | |
| Current payables, including taxes ......... | $ 30,000 | 100 | $ 30,000 |
| Long-term payable ......................... | 50,000 | 100 | 50,000 |
| Total Liabilities ........................... | 80,000 | | 80,000 |
| *Stockholders' Equity* | | | |
| Capital ............................................... | 300,000 | | |
| Retained earnings ............................. | 33,000 | | |
| Total Stockholders' Equity............ | 333,000 | | 402,000* |
| Total Liabilities and Stockholders' Equity ............ | $413,000 | | $482,000 |

* This is a balancing figure; Total Assets, $482,000 – Total Liabilities, $80,000 = Stockholders' Equity, $402,000.

chases lagged the end-of-the-period index value. Since purchases were assumed to have occurred evenly over the period and since the average index number for the period was 151.9 (as compared with the ending index number of 159.5), an upward adjustment for 19D of 5% (i.e., 159.5/151.5 = 1.05) is needed to restate the inventory. If the company had been using *Lifo* for some period of time the degree of inventory adjustment would have been much larger because the lag would be much longer.

Recall monetary items on the current statements *are not restated* on the price-level statements because the amounts of cash, receivables, and payables are fixed; they do not change in dollar amount because of a change in the price level. As to common stock equity, the FASB recommended that a lump-sum restated amount be shown because separate historical cost figures for capital stock, premium on capital stock, and retained earnings generally would not have much significance. The view is that attempting to preserve such a separation on price-level adjusted statements would be meaningless from a legal standpoint and involve far more effort than the benefit would warrant.

The restated 19D balance sheet for XY Company is shown in Exhibit 25–4.

### Restatement of the Income Statement

The revenue and expense items on an essentially current basis (such as sales, purchases, and expenses, but not depreciation and similar items) require upward adjustment only to the extent average prices for

**EXHIBIT 25–5**

XY COMPANY
Restatement of Income Statement—Price-Level Basis

|  | Cost Basis Amount | Conversion Factor | Restated Amount |
|---|---|---|---|
| Sales.................................................. | $400,000 | 105 | $420,000 |
| Inventory, January 1, 19D ...................... | 90,000 | 110 | 99,000 |
| Purchases ......................................... | 290,000 | 105 | 304,500 |
| Goods available.................................... | 380,000 | | 403,500 |
| Inventory, December 31, 19D ............... | 105,000 | 105 | 110,250 |
| Cost of goods sold ............................. | 275,000 | | 293,250 |
| Gross margin...................................... | 125,000 | | 126,750 |
| Expenses* ......................................... | 55,000 | 105 | 57,750 |
| Depreciation expense .......................... | 20,000 | 137.5 | 27,500 |
| Total Operating Expense ............. | 75,000 | | 85,250 |
| Income before taxes  .......................... | 50,000 | | 41,500 |
| Income taxes ..................................... | 20,000 | 105 | 21,000 |
| Net Income......................................... | $ 30,000 | | 20,500 |
| Purchasing power loss  ......................... | | | 5,250 |
| Net Income Restated  .......................... | | | $ 15,250 |

* Excluding depreciation and income taxes.

the period lag the level of prices at the end of the period. In the example, as explained above, this requires an upward adjustment of 5% for 19D.

*Depreciation expense* is restated by relating it to the price-level restatement of the assets involved. To illustrate, in the example for XY Company the fixtures cost $200,000 and were depreciated on a cost basis of 10% or $20,000 for 19D. The $200,000 asset cost is restated to $275,000 by application of the 137.5 conversion factor. The restated depreciation expense is: $20,000 × 137.5 = $27,500.

Cost of goods sold is derived as beginning inventory plus purchases minus ending inventory. Restatement of this amount requires restatement of each of these three component amounts. To illustrate, for XY Company the beginning inventory was restated at the end of 19C when the price level was 145, hence it is subject to the conversion factor of 110 (i.e., 159.5/145). Both purchases and ending inventory are subject to the 105 conversion factor, (i.e., 159.5/151.9) as explained above.

The restated 19D income statement for XY Company is shown in Exhibit 25–5.

## PREPARATION OF COMPARATIVE PRICE-LEVEL STATEMENTS

The preceding discussion and illustrations focused on the development of price-level adjusted statements for the current year (i.e., 19D for XY Company). An additional problem is posed when *comparative* price-level statements are needed, which is the usual situation. The problem is due to the fact that the price-level statements reported for the *prior* year are no longer appropriate; they must be restated again, but on the current year price-level basis. The restatement procedures are similar to those discussed above.

To illustrate, assume comparative statements are required at the end of 19D for XY Company. The balance sheet reported at December 31, 19C, on a price-level basis, was as follows:

XY COMPANY
Restated Balance Sheet—Price-Level Basis
At December 31, 19C

| | | | |
|---|---|---|---|
| Cash and receivables | $145,000 | Current payables | $ 60,000 |
| Inventory | 90,000 | Long-term note payable | 50,000 |
| Future plant site | 62,500 | Stockholders' equity | 362,500 |
| Fixtures | 250,000 | | |
| Accumulated depreciation | (75,000) | | |
| | $472,500 | | $472,500 |

Since this balance sheet is no longer relevant at December 31, 19D, the 19C cost basis statement must again be restated using 19D conversion factors as reflected in Exhibit 25–6. The price-level adjusted amounts shown in Exhibits 25–4 and 25–6 would be reported in juxtaposition on the 19D comparative price-level balance sheets.

**EXHIBIT 25-6**

XY COMPANY
Data for Comparative Balance Sheet—Restatement of Prior Year, 19C
For Comparative Statement, 19C and 19D
(stated in terms of 19D price level)

| Assets | Cost Basis Amount | Conversion Factor | Restated Amount |
|---|---|---|---|
| Cash and receivables ......................... | $145,000 | 110 | $159,500 |
| Inventory ........................................... | 90,000 | 110 | 99,000 |
| Future plant site ............................... | 50,000 | 137.5 | 68,750 |
| Fixtures ........................................... | 200,000 | 137.5 | 275,000 |
| Less: Accumulated depreciation ............ | (60,000) | 137.5 | (82,500) |
| Total Assets ........................... | $425,000 | | $519,750 |
| | | | |
| *Liabilities* | | | |
| Current payables, including taxes ......... | $ 60,000 | 110 | $ 66,000 |
| Mortgage note payable ....................... | 50,000 | 110 | 55,000 |
| Total Liabilities .......................... | 110,000 | | 121,000 |
| | | | |
| *Stockholders' Equity* | | | |
| Capital Stock ..................................... | 300,000 | | |
| Retained earnings ............................. | 15,000 | | |
| Total Stockholders' Equity............ | 315,000 | | 398,750* |
| Total Liabilities and | | | |
| Stockholders' Equity ............ | $425,000 | | $519,750 |

* This is a balancing figure:
Total Assets, $519,750 − Total Liabilities, $121,000 = Stockholders' Equity, $398,750.

Preparation of a comparative income statement would require the same approach. Since 19C revenue and expense data were not provided for XY Company, development of the comparative income statement is not illustrated at this point. However, the basic procedure which would be followed can easily be described. Assume sales for 19C on a historical cost basis were $340,000 and had been restated to $350,000 on the 19C price-level statement because the year-end index number was almost 3% higher than the average index value for 19C. Now assume the year-end index number for 19D is 10% higher than the year-end value prevailing at 19C year-end. Consequently, the original $350,000 sales amount would be raised to $385,000 (i.e., $350,000 × 159.5/145) when the 19C amounts are restated to 19D year-end equivalent purchasing power. Consider another item, depreciation expense. On the 19C price-level statement, this expense would have been $25,000 (i.e., $20,000 × 145/116). It would be again restated for the 19D comparative income statement to $27,500, which is the same amount as on the 19D price-level statement (because straight-line depreciation was used).

## PROOF OF RESTATEMENT

When comparative balance sheets are prepared as illustrated above, a proof of the accuracy of the price-level adjustment process can be developed as follows:

December 31, 19C stockholders' equity at December 31,
19D price level (Exhibit 25–6) ................................................. $398,750
Add: Net income including purchasing power gain or loss
(Exhibit 25–5)......................................................................... 15,250
Total .............................................................................. 414,000
Deduct: Dividends adjusted to price-level basis (Exhibit 25–3) ......... 12,000
December 31, 19D stockholders' equity at December 31, 19D,
price level (Exhibit 25–4) $402,000

## COMPLEX ILLUSTRATION OF PRICE-LEVEL ACCOUNTING

This illustration is more realistic than the preceding one because revenue and expense data are given on a quarterly rather than on an annual basis. It also involves the acquisition of fixed assets and payment of a dividend during the year. Since GNP Deflator data are released on a quarterly basis, quarterly application is realistic. This illustration will focus on the development of price-level statements for AB Company for the year ended December 31, 19F. The assumed data are as follows:

1. Relevant price index numbers (see also transactions C and D):

|  | Index Number | Conversion Factor |
|---|---|---|
| December 31, 19E (when beginning inventory was acquired)...................... | 147 | (159/147) = 108.2 |
| End of – |  |  |
| First quarter, 19F ................................. | 150 | (159/150) = 106.0 |
| Second quarter, 19F............................. | 153 | (159/153) = 103.9 |
| Third quarter, 19F................................ | 156 | (159/156) = 102.0 |
| Fourth quarter, at December 31, 19F ...... | 159 | (159/159) = 100.0 |

2. Trial balance, cost basis, December 31, 19E: As reflected on Exhibit 25–7.
3. Transactions for 19F: As reflected at the bottom of Exhibit 25–7.
4. Additional information: Assume a *Fifo* basis for inventory (therefore the ending inventory was from purchases made during the fourth quarter). Sales, purchases, general expenses, and income tax expense are restated from historical cost amounts to price-level amounts on a quarterly basis.

Based on these data, development of price-level statements for 19F is illustrated as follows:

1. *Exhibit 25–7.* Worksheet to develop traditional cost basis income statement and balance sheet for 19F.
2. *Exhibit 25–8.* Restatement of quarterly revenues and expenses. Completion of this schedule requires application of the 19D *quarterly* conversion factors to the cost basis amounts. The annual total for each revenue and expense is transferred to the restated annual income statement.
3. *Exhibit 25–9.* Calculation of purchasing power gain or loss. The purchasing power loss of $2,195 is carried to the income statement.

**EXHIBIT 25-7**

## AB COMPANY
### Worksheet to Develop Income Statement and Balance Sheet—Traditional Cost Basis
### For Year Ended December 31, 19F

| | Dec. 31, 19E Balances | | 19F Transactions and Adjustments | | 19F Income Summary | | Dec. 31, 19F Balance Sheet | |
|---|---:|---:|---|---|---:|---:|---:|---:|
| Cash | 36,000 | | (f) 115,000 | (e) 12,000<br>(g) 80,000<br>(h) 10,000<br>(i) 20,000 | | | 29,000 | |
| Receivables | 24,000 | | (a) 120,000 | (f) 115,000 | | | 29,000 | |
| Inventory | 20,000 | | | | 20,000 | 25,000* | 25,000 | |
| Building | 100,000 | | | | | | 100,000 | |
| Accumulated depreciation, building | | 20,000 | | (c) 4,000 | | | | 24,000 |
| Fixtures | 40,000 | | (i) 20,000 | | | | 60,000 | |
| Accumulated depreciation, fixtures | | 20,000 | | (d) 4,000 | | | | 24,000 |
| Accounts payable | | 35,000 | (g) 80,000 | (b) 85,000 | | | | 40,000 |
| Income taxes payable | | | | (j) 10,000 | | | | 10,000 |
| Capital stock | | 100,000 | | | | | | 100,000 |
| Retained earnings | | 45,000 | (h) 10,000 | | | 10,000† | | 45,000 |
| | | | | | | | | |
| Sales | | | | (a) 120,000 | | 120,000 | | |
| Purchases | | | (b) 85,000 | | 85,000 | | | |
| Depreciation expense, building | | | (c) 4,000 | | 4,000 | | | |
| Depreciation expense, fixtures | | | (d) 4,000 | | 4,000 | | | |
| General expenses | | | (e) 12,000 | | 12,000 | | | |
| Income tax expense | | | (j) 10,000 | | 10,000 | | | |
| | **220,000** | **220,000** | **460,000** | **460,000** | **145,000** | **145,000** | **243,000** | **243,000** |

\* Ending inventory.

† Net income transferred to retained earnings.

Transactions during 19F (summarized):

(a) Sales of $30,000 were made each quarter (assume all on credit).

(b) Purchases of $20,000 were made each of the first three quarters and $25,000 the last quarter (assume all on credit).

(c) The building is depreciated 4% per year with no residual value; when bought in 19A, the price index was 127.

(d) Fixtures are depreciated 10% per year with no residual value; when the original fixtures were bought in 19B, the price index was 138.

(e) General expenses of $3,000 were paid each quarter.

(f) Collections on receivables, $115,000.

(g) Payments on accounts payable, $80,000.

(h) At mid-year, a $10,000 cash dividend was paid.

(i) New fixtures costing $10,000 were bought at year end.

(j) Income taxes in the amount of $2,500 were accrued each quarter.

**EXHIBIT 25-8**

AB COMPANY
Conversion Schedule of Quarterly Revenues and Expenses
For Year Ended December 31, 19F

|  | First Quarter | Second Quarter | Third Quarter | Fourth Quarter | Year Total |
|---|---|---|---|---|---|
| Conversion factor ................. | 106 | 103.9 | 102 | 100 |  |
| Sales .................................... | $30,000 | $30,000 | $30,000 | $30,000 | $120,000 |
| Restated sales....................... | 31,800 | 31,170 | 30,600 | 30,000 | 123,570 |
| Purchases............................. | 20,000 | 20,000 | 20,000 | 25,000 | 85,000 |
| Restated purchases .............. | 21,200 | 20,780 | 20,400 | 25,000 | 87,380 |
| General expenses ................. | 3,000 | 3,000 | 3,000 | 3,000 | 12,000 |
| Restated general expenses...... | 3,180 | 3,117 | 3,060 | 3,000 | 12,357 |
| Income tax .......................... | 2,500 | 2,500 | 2,500 | 2,500 | 10,000 |
| Restated income tax.............. | 2,650 | 2,598 | 2,550 | 2,500 | 10,298 |

**EXHIBIT 25-9**

AB COMPANY
Calculation of Purchasing Power Gain or Loss
For Year Ended December 31, 19F

|  | Cost Basis Amount (per books) | Conversion Factor | Restated at Dec. 31, 19F |
|---|---|---|---|
| Net monetary items at December 31, 19E: |  |  |  |
| Cash ............................................... | $ 36,000 |  |  |
| Receivables....................................... | 24,000 |  |  |
| Accounts payable................................ | (35,000) |  |  |
| Net............................................... | 25,000 | 108.2 | $ 27,050 |
| Add: Sources of net monetary items during 19F: |  |  |  |
| Sales................................................. | 120,000 | * | 123,570 |
| Subtotal ........................................... | 145,000 |  | 150,620 |
| Deduct: Uses of net monetary items during 19F: |  |  |  |
| Purchases ......................................... | 85,000 | * | 87,380 |
| General expenses (except depreciation)... | 12,000 | * | 12,357 |
| Income tax expense............................. | 10,000 | * | 10,298 |
| Dividends paid at mid-year ................. | 10,000 | 103.9 | 10,390 |
| Fixtures purchased ............................. | 20,000 | 100 | 20,000 |
| Total Uses .................................... | 137,000 |  | 140,425 |
| Net monetary items at December 31, 19F, restated ($150,620 − $140,425)............ |  |  | 10,195 |
| Net monetary items at December 31, 19F, not restated: |  |  |  |
| Cash ............................................... | 29,000 |  |  |
| Receivables....................................... | 29,000 |  |  |
| Accounts payable................................ | (40,000) |  |  |
| Taxes payable ................................... | (10,000) |  |  |
| Total ............................................ | $ 8,000 |  | 8,000 |
| Purchasing power gain (loss) in 19F on monetary items .......................... |  |  | $ (2,195) |

* See Exhibit 25-8.

**EXHIBIT 25-10**

AB COMPANY
Restatement of Balance Sheet—Price-Level Basis
At December 31, 19F

|  | Cost Basis Amount | Conversion Factor | Restated Amount |
|---|---|---|---|
| Cash | $ 29,000 |  | $ 29,000 |
| Receivables | 29,000 |  | 29,000 |
| Inventory | 25,000 | 100(a) | 25,000 |
| Building | 100,000 | 125.2 | 125,200 |
| Accumulated depreciation, building | 24,000 | 125.2 | 30,048 |
| Fixtures | 60,000 | (b) | 66,080 |
| Accumulated depreciation, fixtures | 24,000 | 115.2 | 27,648 |
|  | $195,000 |  | $216,584 |
| Accounts payable | 40,000 |  | 40,000 |
| Taxes payable | 10,000 |  | 10,000 |
| Capital stock | 100,000 |  |  |
| Retained earnings | 45,000 |  |  |
| Balancing amount |  |  | 166,584 |
|  | $195,000 |  | $216,584 |

(a) Since the ending inventory was entirely from purchases during the fourth quarter, no price-level adjustment on statement should be made.

(b) Old asset acquired for $40,000 in 19B when index was 138; therefore, restatement is:

$40,000 \times 159/138$ (i.e., 115.2) =        $46,080
New asset acquired for $20,000 on
December 31, 19F; therefore, no
restatement needed ........................  20,000
       Total Restated Amount...............  $66,080

**EXHIBIT 25-11**

AB COMPANY
Restatement of Income Statement—Price-Level Basis
For Year Ended December 31, 19F

|  | Cost Basis Amount | Conversion Factor | Restated Amount |
|---|---|---|---|
| Sales | $120,000 | (b) | $123,570 |
| Inventory, January 1, 19F | 20,000 | 108.2 | 21,640 |
| Purchases | 85,000 | (b) | 87,380 |
| Goods available for sale | 105,000 |  | 109,020 |
| Inventory, December 31, 19F | 25,000 | 100 | 25,000 |
| Cost of goods sold | 80,000 |  | 84,020 |
| Gross margin | 40,000 |  | 39,550 |
| General expenses | 12,000 |  | 12,357 |
| Depreciation expense, building | 4,000 | 125.2(a) | 5,008 |
| Depreciation expense, fixtures | 4,000 | 115.2(a) | 4,608 |
| Total Expenses | 20,000 |  | 21,973 |
| Income before taxes | 20,000 |  | 17,577 |
| Income tax | 10,000 | (b) | 10,298 |
| Purchasing power loss | — | (c) | 2,195 |
| Net Income | $ 10,000 |  | $ 5,084 |

(a) See restated balance sheet, Exhibit 25-10.
(b) See Exhibit 25-8.
(c) See Exhibit 25-9.

4. *Exhibit 25-10*. Restatement of 19F balance sheet. Observe that only the nonmonetary amounts are restated and that restated stockholders' equity is a plug figure.
5. *Exhibit 25-11*. Restatement of 19F income statement.
6. *Exhibit 25-12*. Data for comparative balance sheet—restatement of 19E balance sheet at 19F price level.
7. *Exhibit 25-13*. Proof of restatement—December 31, 19F.

**EXHIBIT 25-12**

AB COMPANY
Data for Comparative Balance Sheet—Restatement of Prior Year (19E)
At December 31, 19E and 19F
(stated in terms of December 31, 19F, price level)

|  | Cost Basis Amount | Conversion Factor | Restated Amount |
|---|---|---|---|
| Cash | $ 36,000 | 108.2 | $ 38,952 |
| Receivables | 24,000 | 108.2 | 25,968 |
| Inventory | 20,000 | 108.2 | 21,640 |
| Building | 100,000 | 125.2 | 125,200 |
| Accumulated depreciation, building | (20,000) | 125.2 | (25,040) |
| Fixtures | 40,000 | 115.2 | 46,080 |
| Accumulated depreciation, fixtures | (20,000) | 115.2 | (23,040) |
|  |  |  | $209,760 |
| Accounts payable | 35,000 | 108.2 | $ 37,870 |
| Stockholders' equity | 145,000 | * | 171,890 |
|  |  |  | $209,760 |

* Balancing amount.

**EXHIBIT 25-13**

AB COMPANY
Proof of Restatement
December 31, 19F

| | |
|---|---|
| December 31, 19E, stockholders' equity at December 31, 19F, price level (Exhibit 25-12) | $171,890 |
| Add: Net income, including purchasing power gain or loss (Exhibit 25-11) | 5,084 |
| Total | 176,974 |
| Deduct: Dividends adjusted to price-level basis (Exhibit 25-9) | 10,390 |
| December 31, 19F, stockholders' equity at December 31, 19F, price level (Exhibit 25-10) | $166,584 |

Some brief explanation of the conversion of fixtures from the historical cost amount of $60,000 at December 31, 19F, to its price-level equivalent may be in order. Recall $20,000 of fixtures were added at year-end. For practical purposes, therefore, we are concerned only with conversion of $40,000 of fixtures held during an interval over which prices changed.

The $40,000 acquisition took place when the index was at 138; at December 31, 19F, it is at 159, so the adjustment applied to the $40,000 and to the related accumulated depreciation of $24,000 is 115.2 (159/138).

The discussions and illustrations of the development of financial statements restated on a price-level basis have focused on the underlying concepts and basic computational procedures. It encompasses the proposed FASB *Statement* and should provide an adequate understanding of the problems and their resolution. Price-level adjusted statements do not report "fair value" except by occasional coincidence. The next section will consider fair-value accounting.

## HIGHLIGHTS OF THE FASB STATEMENT ON REPORTING IN TERMS OF GENERAL PURCHASING POWER

Now that the procedures for implementing price-level restatement of financial statements have been illustrated, it is appropriate to highlight the following salient points of the proposed FASB *Statement* on the subject.

1. Conventional financial statements prepared at the close of a fiscal year shall be accompanied by information stated in units of general purchasing power. The information shall be based upon comprehensive rather than piecemeal restatement of the financial statement items. General purchasing power information is not required to accompany financial statements for interim periods such as a month or a quarter.
2. The same accounting principles used for the conventional cost-basis statements shall be used in preparing the general purchasing power (price-level restated) information. Only the measuring unit is changed. The GNP Deflator shall be used for restatement purposes.
3. General purchasing power information shall be stated at the most recent statement date. The most recent quarterly GNP Deflator numbers will serve as an acceptable approximation of the general purchasing power at the balance sheet date.
4. The net gain or loss of general purchasing power from holding monetary assets and liabilities shall be included in determining income in units of general purchasing power; there shall be no deferrals to future periods.
5. The amount of income tax expense included in determining net income in units of general purchasing power shall be based on the amount of income tax expense included in determining net income in units of money. No added taxes shall be accrued for income taxes that may be paid in the future because of the nondeductibility for tax purposes of the excess amounts of nonmonetary assets revalued over their amounts as conventionally stated.
6. It is permissible to present less than a complete income statement;

but, at a minimum, the following elements must be presented in units of general purchasing power:
  *a.* Total revenues.
  *b.* Depreciation of property, plant, and equipment.
  *c.* Net purchasing power gain or loss.
  *d.* Income from continuing operations (includes *c* above).
  *e.* Net income.
  *f.* Net income per common share.
  *g.* Cash dividends per common share.
7. It is permissible to present less than a complete balance sheet, but the following elements must be presented in units of general purchasing power:
  *a.* Inventories.
  *b.* Working capital.
  *c.* Total property, plant, and equipment (net of depreciation).
  *d.* Total assets.
  *e.* Total common stockholders' equity.
8. A "normal" presentation presumably should set out details of the computation of purchasing power gain or loss rather than Item 6(*c*) as one line.

## CURRENT FAIR-VALUE ACCOUNTING

Current fair value (hereafter called current-value or fair-value accounting), although significantly different conceptually, is akin to price-level accounting in some respects. For example, it draws the same distinction between monetary and nonmonetary items. On the other hand, a major difference is that it substitutes fair or current dollar values for the general index restatement of nonmonetary items. Fair value accounting has not been definitely described, and no authoritative guidelines have been developed, much less agreed upon. There are numerous proponents of fair value accounting, and a variety of views of the basic concepts that should prevail. Proponents of current-value systems are less well agreed as to the implementation guidelines that should be followed. Significantly, there are numerous ways of arriving at fair values. Aside from this problem, some advocates of fair value accounting would also separately identify the effects of general price-level changes while others would not.

### Measuring Current Values

Several ways of measuring current values have been proposed, and some have limited application under the historical-cost based accounting model. Means of measuring current values include:

Entry values:
1. Replacement cost
2. Reproduction cost

Exit values:
3. Realization value

Special:
4. Discounted cash inflows
5. Specific price-index numbers
6. Appraisals

*Replacement cost* is the estimated cost of acquiring new similar items at current prices after allowing for comparable physical and functional depreciation that has already occurred on the items being valued. If the property would serve the same function, it need not be identical.

*Reproduction cost* is the estimated cost of producing new essentially identical property in kind adjusted for physical and functional depreciation to date.

*Realization value* is the amount that could be realized from the current sale of the item assuming no forced or distress sale is implied. It is recognized that many of the assets of an entity are not ordinarily up for sale.

*Discounted cash inflows* are the present value of the future estimated net cash inflows, or cost savings, of an item being valued. The future cash inflows are discounted at a realistic rate of interest. The concepts discussed in Chapter 6 are used.

*Specific price-index numbers* are regularly developed and published for various types of construction, kinds of machinery, equipment, and vehicles, and for hundreds of commodity groups. Some larger companies have found it feasible to develop their own index numbers to value specific assets, such as plant assets. Specific index numbers are to be distinguished from general index numbers such as the GNP Deflator which measures changes in a broad range of prices. Whereas, general index numbers can be used, as discussed in the preceding section, to measure changes in general purchasing power, specific index numbers tend to measure the change in value of single or groups of similar items. Thus, specific index numbers are often viewed as a realistic way to measure fair value.

*Appraisals* are estimates developed by professionally competent and independent individuals of the current fair value of an item in its present condition.

### Measurement of Current Fair-Value Costs of Specific Assets

The measurement of the current fair value of each kind of asset at each financial statement date presents complex inplementation solutions. Let's consider a few.

1. Inventories.  Price lists or catalogs from suppliers adjusted for discounts and transportation and handling costs often would provide realistic fair values for purchased inventories. As to manufactured inventories, the cost accounting systems usually provide past unit cost amounts for material, labor, and overhead; and these can be modified, for known changes, to a current basis. Standard costs can be used, provided they are frequently revised. Some inventories are, of course, subject to quotations in established markets (e.g., commodities, precious metals).

2. Investments.  Market quotations often can be used for marketable securities which would not be sold in such large quantities as to materially affect the quotations. If market quotations are not available, or if the blocks are apt to be too large, satisfaction of this criterion is much more difficult.

3. Property, plant, and equipment.  The current fair value of some fixed assets can be measured on the basis of price data from supplier's catalogs. In some instances there is a well-established market for used property. Another approach is to determine the reproduction or replacement cost of new similar property and consider the remaining service life of the property being valued against the new cost as a starting point. In the case of land and buildings, it may be possible to determine recent sales prices for property with a similar location and function. Appraisals represent another approach particularly appropriate for fixed assets.

4. Natural resources.  Valuation of natural resources on a current fair value basis often must be made by technical experts, such as geologists, forestry specialists, or engineers. Their valuations are based on careful estimates of what is economically recoverable and marketable from the resource. Realistic current sales prices of variable grades of the product are often available and can be used for future projection. If recoverable assets, future sales prices, and removal costs can be determined with reasonable accuracy, discounted cash flow techniques can be applied to measure the current fair value of the natural resource. There are often well publicized sales prices to leases and other mineral rights which may afford useful guidelines to the valuation of a natural resource.

## COMPARATIVE EFFECTS OF ACCOUNTING ALTERNATIVES

Criticisms of traditional cost-basis accounting include (1) gains are recognized only in the periods in which a sale takes place, and (2) the amount of gain recognized is the difference between the original cost (carrying value) of the asset sold and its sale price.[10] Both price-level

---

[10] Except for the softening effect of allowing possible capital gains treatment, income tax laws tend to do the same thing. There are some tax exceptions, as for example when the disposition of the asset was an involuntary conversion and the gain is reinvested soon after the sale.

and fair-value accounting report gains differently as to both amount and timing than conventional cost-basis accounting. To illustrate, assume that in 19A an entity paid $4,000 for oil for resale when the general price level index number was 154. In 19B, the price index was 10% higher at 169.4, and the replacement cost of oil was $6,000. In 19C the oil was sold for $7,500. The gain (ignoring income taxes) would be reported under conventional cost basis accounting, price-level accounting, and current-value accounting for 19A, B, and C as follows:

| | Profit Reported (before monetary gains and losses) Assuming — | | |
| --- | --- | --- | --- |
| | Conventional Cost Basis | Price-Level Basis | Current Fair Value Basis |
| 19A (period of purchase).................. | $ 0 | $ 0 | $ 0 |
| 19B (period of price change): | | | |
|   Increase in income due to increased ending inventory valuation ............................... | 0 | 400 [a] | 0 |
|   Fair-value adjustment ($6,000 − $4,000) ..................... | | | 2,000 |
| 19C (period of sale): | | | |
|   Increase due to sale: | | | |
|     ($7,500 − $4,000) ..................... | 3,500 | | |
|     ($7,500 − $4,400) ..................... | | 3,100 | |
|     ($7,500 − $6,000) ..................... | | | 1,500 |

(a) The inventory is restated on the price-level basis to: $4,000 × 169.4/154 = $4,400.

In the case of the current fair-value example the $2,000 gain in 19B can be separated into two effects as follows:

| | |
| --- | --- |
| Current replacement cost .............................. | $6,000 |
| Deduct acquisition cost ................................. | 4,000 |
| Total gain ..................................................... | 2,000 |
| Price-level adjustment ($4,000 × 10%).............. | 400 |
| Holding gain ................................................ | $1,600 |

A holding gain is viewed as a real value increase (i.e., the amount of the gain which exceeds inflation) which accrues to the entity by holding an asset while specific prices rise (i.e., the inventory price), as opposed to a rise in the general price level.

### Sale of Fixed Assets

Similar differences result in respect to fixed assets. To illustrate, assume a business bought equipment for $20,000 when the price index was at 105. The equipment is depreciated on a straight-line basis with no residual value and a 20-year life. At the end of the eighth year, the general price-level index was 147 and the equipment had a current fair value of $14,000. Early in the ninth year, the equipment was sold for $15,000. The results would be as follows:

| | Gain (Loss) Reported Assuming — | | |
|---|---|---|---|
| | Conventional Cost Basis | Price-Level Basis | Current Fair Value Basis |
| First eight years: | | | |
| Depreciation expense ................. | $(8,000) | | |
| Price-level restatement ............... | | $(11,200)*(a)* | |
| Fair value adjustment | | | |
| ($20,000 − $14,000) ................. | | | $(6,000) |
| Year of sale: | | | |
| $15,000 − ($20,000 − $8,000)......... | 3,000 | | |
| $15,000 − ($28,000 − $11,200) ...... | | (1,800) | |
| $15,000 − $14,000...................... | | | 1,000 |

*(a)* The asset and accumulated depreciation, as nonmonetary assets, would be restated as follows:

| | Restated Amount | Change |
|---|---|---|
| Equipment  $20,000 × 147/105 = | $28,000 | $8,000 |
| Accumulated depreciation $8,000 × 147/105 = | (11,200) | (3,200) |
| Net effect*........................................... | $16,800 | $4,800 |

* The $4,800 net restatement increase in this nonmonetary asset would not be reflected as a gain on the income statement, but rather it is reflected in the restatement of owners' equity.

## Long-Term Capital Gains

The combined inflation and income tax effects of long-term gains are reported differently under conventional cost basis accounting, price-level account, and current fair value accounting. To illustrate, assume a taxpayer is subject to a long-term capital gain tax rate of 25%. The taxpayer bought land for $20,000 in 1946 when the GNP Deflator number was at 66.7. The land was sold in 1973 when the GNP Deflator was 156.7 (approximately 135% higher) for $56,000 when its fair value recorded in the fair-value accounts was $50,000. The reported gain or loss for 1973 would be as follows:

| | Gain (Loss) Reported Assuming — | | |
|---|---|---|---|
| | Conventional Cost Basis | Price-Level Basis | Current Fair Value Basis |
| Sales price (1973)......................... | $56,000 | $56,000 | $56,000 |
| Deduct carrying value .................... | 20,000 | 46,987*(a)* | 50,000*(b)* |
| Gain before income tax ................. | 36,000 | 9,013 | 6,000 |
| Deduct income taxes at 25% | | | |
| (per tax return) ........................... | 9,000 | 9,000 | 9,000 |
| Gain (loss) after tax ...................... | $27,000 | $   13 | $ (3,000) |

*(a)* $20,000 × 156.7/66.7 = $46,987. The price-level restatement does not create a gain; since this is a nonmonetary asset the restatement change is reflected in owners' equity.
*(b)* During the prior year a gain of $50,000 − $20,000 = $30,000 was recognized.

Regardless of the accounting basis, the taxpayer has $47,000 cash after paying income taxes and, therefore, has the same *purchasing power* in general price-level terms as when the original $20,000 investment was made in 1946. Under price-level accounting no gain would have been reported, but successive price-level adjusted balance sheets would have shown the land (and owners' equity) at increasingly higher amounts. On fair-value statements, as increments in fair value occurred, they would have been reflected both on balance sheets and on the income statements of the periods in which the increments were recorded for an aggregate increase in income of $30,000 over the 27-year period.

Situations and problems often are encountered where the required sales price (i.e., target proceeds) to stay abreast of inflation must be computed. In solving for *target proceeds* to enable an investor to stay abreast of inflation, the basic formula is as follows:

$$X = \text{Target Proceeds (i.e., necessary sales price)}$$

$$\text{Cost} \times \frac{\text{Index at Date of Sale}}{\text{Index at Date of Purchase}} = \text{Cost} + (1.0 - \text{Tax Rate}) \times (X - \text{Cost})$$

In the preceding example, substituting —

$$\$20,000 \times \frac{156.7}{66.7} = \$20,000 + .75\,(X - \$20,000)$$
$$\$47,000 = \$20,000 + .75X - \$15,000$$
$$X = \$56,000$$

### Summary of Dollar Effects of Accounting Alternatives

In an era of inflation, what would be the comparative dollar effects that one could ordinarily expect the balance sheet and income statement to reflect under the various techniques? The tabulation below gives a general indication of the comparative effects using conventionally prepared statements as the base. Amounts on the conventional statements are designated "Base"; if these would be the same on statements prepared under either of the two alternative accounting approaches discussed in this chapter (i.e., price level, and fair value), "Base" is repeated. If the amount would be higher than base *a*, + appears; if it would likely be still higher under yet another alternative, ++ appears. If the amount would be lower than base *a*, – appears; if it would likely be still lower under yet another alternative, —— appears. In case an item is irrelevant to a particular alternative, a 0 appears.

In respect to the following summary, a qualifying comment is in order. It is likely that for most companies the replacement cost of plant and equipment, and hence the current fair value, will exceed a valuation derived by application of a general index such as the GNP Deflator. This assumption is reflected in respect to "property, plant, and equipment," "cost of goods sold," and "depreciation" in the tabulation above. In respect to net income, because such expenses as depreciation and cost of goods sold will be higher for most entities under each of the alternative techniques than under historical cost, a – sign was shown

| | Inflationary Effect Assuming — | | |
| --- | --- | --- | --- |
| | Conventional Historical Cost Basis | General Price-Level Basis | Current Fair-Value Basis |
| **Balance Sheet:** | | | |
| Cash and receivables......................... | Base | Base | Base |
| Inventories...................................... | Base | + | + |
| Property, plant, and equipment ......... | Base | + | ++ |
| Monetary liabilities ........................... | Base | Base | Base |
| Common stock equity ...................... | Base | + | ++ |
| **Income Statement:** | | | |
| Sales ............................................ | Base | + | Base |
| Cost of goods sold (if manufacturing)............................. | Base | + | ++ |
| Depreciation.................................... | Base | + | ++ |
| Purchasing power gain (or loss)......... | 0 | + | 0 |
| Increase in value of nonmonetary assets ......................................... | 0 | 0 | + |
| Net income (assuming profits)............ | Base | − | − |

for net income as compared to "Base." It should be pointed out, however, that the reduction occasioned by these foreseeable increases might be more than offset by purchasing power gains if the company were heavily in debt or by increases during the current period of the value of nonmonetary assets. If *Lifo* inventory is used, the adjustment of cost of goods sold would tend to be minimal compared with *Fifo* and average inventory techniques.

Usage of current replacement values for external reporting purposes received important official support in March, 1976. This impetus came with the issuance of Accounting Series Release No. 190 by the SEC requiring that specified replacement cost information be disclosed in the annual financial statements of certain listed corporations. All companies with inventories and gross plants aggregating more than $100 million and amounting to more than 10% of their total assets must disclose, either in footnote or in a separate section of their financial statements, the current costs of replacing inventories and productive plant, and the amount of cost of goods sold and depreciation as if these costs had been computed on the basis of current replacement costs. This disclosure requirement takes effect for fiscal years ending on or after December 25, 1976. (For mineral resource assets of registrants in the extractive industries and all assets located outside North America or the Common Market, the effective date is one year later.)

The replacement cost disclosures may be labeled "unaudited" although the auditor will be deemed to be associated with the information. It has been estimated these new rules may apply to the largest one thousand nonfinancial corporations in the nation. It is expected (not now required) that the affected companies will include the same information in annual reports to stockholders. The SEC expects the requirement to be extended to smaller companies in two or three years.

## FUTURE TRENDS

For internal management uses, it is generally believed current fair-value accounting has more relevance than does price-level accounting. Fair-value accounting also is considered to be more relevant for external reporting purposes as well, assuming reasonably objective and consistent implementation is possible. In the view of many accountants, objectivity and realism in applying fair-value concepts is not possible. Therefore, its use would bring about such wide variation in valuation of virtually identical assets as to render attempts at comparison on a value basis almost meaningless. Price-level accounting, on the other hand, preserves whatever comparability now exists on traditional cost basis statements on an intercompany basis because it adjusts cost basis amounts by using a common set of index numbers.

Current fair-value accounting is relevant for internal reporting purposes for a number of reasons. One of the most significant reasons relates to capital preservation and asset replacement. A management concerned with asset replacement is interested in the cost of particular kinds of assets—those in need of replacement, not in how much the general price level had changed. If the price level had doubled since a major fixed asset was acquired and is now fully depreciated, but the cost of replacing that particular asset has trebled, management would have been better served by basing pricing decisions and financing plans on current-value rather than on price-level accounting information.

As we have seen, current value accounting may or may not be implemented in such a way as to reflect purchasing power (price-level) gains or losses. On the other hand, price-level accounting always reflects such gains but does not reflect holding gains and losses. Up to a point, it is "favorable" to be in debt when prices are rising; one retires debt with dollars of lower purchasing power. The most important thing, however, is to be able to pay maturing obligations when they fall due. The idea of running up debt to profit by doing so can be dangerous. It is, however, a fact that price-level accounting makes some of the least solvent companies look good because of the large gains based on excessive debt.

Abandonment of historical cost accounting, or the substitution of price-level accounting or current fair value accounting for it, in this country is not likely in the foreseeable future. It appears that for the foreseeable future the historical cost model will continue to survive and coexist with price level accounting. In time this may be followed by dual usage of historical cost and current fair-value accounting.

## QUESTIONS

1. What is the price phenomenon known as *inflation*? What is the opposite condition called?

2. What indices measure changes in the general purchasing power of the U.S. dollar? What index has been preferred for preparation of price-level adjusted financial statements?

3. In general terms, how much have prices changed in the United States between 1933 and 1975? Why may it be inaccurate to say that prices have changed as much as the percentage of rise in the index between these dates?

4. "When prices are going up, they all go up; when they drop, they all drop." Comment on this statement.

5. As between sales, cost of goods sold, salaries, and depreciation expense, during an era of rapidly changing prices, which would be on the most current cost basis under conventional accounting procedures and which would be on a least current cost basis? Give reasons for your response.

6. When prices are changing rapidly, why are financial statements prepared on the conventional cost basis likely to be deficient in some respects?

7. When prices are rising and depreciation expense is computed in the conventional manner, what is likely to be true insofar as replacement of the depreciable assets is concerned?

8. Several "piecemeal" procedures have been employed or proposed to cope with the inadequacies of cost basis accounting under conditions of rapidly changing prices. Briefly describe them. Indicate which ones are acceptable in the framework of generally accepted accounting principles.

9. Under the index number approach, financial statement items are classified as monetary or nonmonetary. Briefly, by what criteria can these two categories be distinguished?

10. Indicate, with explanations where necessary, whether the following items are monetary or nonmonetary: (a) stocks held as investments; (b) bonds held as investments; (c) deposits in domestic banks; (d) deposits in foreign banks; (e) allowance for doubtful accounts; (f) machinery and equipment; (g) accounts payable; (h) preferred stock; (i) retained earnings; and (j) deferred credit related to income taxes.

11. During its most recent fiscal period, XY Company had a larger balance of cash and receivables than liabilities; prices rose steadily. Would this condition give rise to a purchasing power gain or a loss?

12. If prices rise steadily over an extended period of time, indicate whether the following items would give rise to a purchasing power gain, a purchasing power loss, or neither purchasing power gain nor loss:
   a. Maintaining a balance in             c. Owning land.
      a checking account.                  d. Amortizing goodwill.
   b. Owing bonds payable.                 e. Holding common treasury stock.

13. If data are available on a quarterly basis rather than on an annual basis, how would this alter the preparation of price-level adjusted statements at the end of a year?

14. How would statements prepared on a restated price-level basis differ from those prepared on a current fair value basis? In what respects would they be similar?

## DECISION CASE 25-1

In this situation, restated price-level statements, as supplements to the conventional cost basis statements are presented (inflation has been near double-digit rates). Knowing that you have accounting training, a friend, who owns common stock in several companies, drops their latest annual reports before you with a look that hovers between dismay and bewilderment.

Your friend begins, "I used to think that I understood a little about these reports, but now that the companies have all gone to this price-level accounting, the only things clear to me are the nice pictures of company employees and products!" Upon your inquiry, it develops that the following points bother your friend most of all:

a. Most of the companies reported higher net income on their conventional cost basis statements than on their price-level statements while at the same time, the latter statement showed the assets to be larger in amount.

b. Some of the companies reported purchasing power gains concurrent with operating gains; other reported purchasing power losses concurrent with operating gains; yet all of the companies were subject to the same degree of inflation.

c. The comparative statements, prepared on a restated price-level basis, showed that even the amount of cash reported for last year had changed. Your friend wonders whether the companies discovered overages or shortages of cash or are somehow "juggling the figures."

d. Your friend realizes that the prices of most things are rising and wonders whether the increased values of certain assets on the restated price-level statements represent what the items are worth. At the same time, your friend noticed that some assets are carried at identical amounts on both sets of statements.

*Required:*

1. Explain the specifics that are confusing your friend in such a way that a sophisticated layman (who is not an accountant) can understand them.
2. To cope with inflation (or deflation), aside from price-level statements, what alternative accounting techniques could be used? Describe them briefly and cite some of their pros and cons.
3. What is your assessment of the usefulness of price-level adjusted financial statements? Give reasons for your answer.

**EXERCISES**

**Exercise 25-1**

Select the best answer in each of the following. Items are independent of one another except where indicated to the contrary. Give the basis, including computations, for your choice.

The following information is applicable to items 1 through 4:

Equipment purchased for $120,000 on January 1, 19A, when the price index was 100, was sold on December 31, 19C, at a price of $85,000. The equipment originally was expected to last six years with no salvage value and was depreciated on a straight-line basis. The price index at the end of 19A was 125; 19B, 150; and 19C, 175.

1. Price-level financial statements prepared at the end of 19A would include:
   a. Equipment, $150,000; accumulated depreciation, $25,000; and a gain, $30,000.

    *b.* Equipment, $150,000; accumulated depreciation, $25,000; and no gain or loss.

    *c.* Equipment, $150,000; accumulated depreciation, $20,000; and a gain, $30,000.

    *d.* Equipment, $120,000; accumulated depreciation, $20,000; and a gain, $30,000.

    *e.* None of the above.

2. Price-level comparative statements prepared at the end of 19B would show the 19A financial statements' amount for equipment (net of accumulated depreciation) at:

    *a.* $150,000.                        *d.* $80,000.

    *b.* $125,000.                      *e.* None of the above.

    *c.* $100,000.

3. Price-level financial statements prepared at the end of 19B should include depreciation expense of—

    *a.* $35,000.                        *d.* $20,000.

    *b.* $30,000.                        *e.* None of the above.

    *c.* $25,000.

4. The general price-level income statement prepared at the end of 19C should include:

    *a.* A gain of $35,000.           *d.* A loss of $5,000.

    *b.* A gain of $25,000.           *e.* None of the above.

    *c.* No gain or loss.

5. If land were purchased at a cost of $20,000 in January 19A when the general price-level index was 120 and sold in December 19F when the index was 150, the selling price that would result in no economic gain or loss would be:

    *a.* $30,000.                        *d.* $16,000.

    *b.* $24,000.                        *e.* None of the above.

    *c.* $20,000.

6. If land were purchased in 19A for $100,000 when the general price-level index was 100 and sold at the end of 19G for $160,000 when the index was 170, the general price-level statement of income for 19G would show:

    *a.* A price-level gain of $70,000 and a loss on sale of land of $10,000.

    *b.* A gain on sale of land of $60,000.

    *c.* A price-level loss of $10,000.

    *d.* A loss on sale of land of $10,000.

    *e.* None of the above.

7. If the base year is 19A (when the general price index = 100) and land is purchased for $50,000 in 19C when the general price index is 108.5, the cost of the land restated to 19A general purchasing power (rounded to the nearest whole dollar) would be:

    *a.* $54,250.                        *d.* $45,750.

    *b.* $50,000.                        *e.* None of the above.

    *c.* $46,083.

8. Assume the same facts as in Item 7. The cost of the land restated to December 31, 19G, general purchasing power when the general price index was 119.2 (rounded to the nearest whole dollar) would be:

    *a.* $59,600.                        *d.* $45,512.

    *b.* $54,931.                        *e.* None of the above.

    *c.* $46,083.

                                               (AICPA adapted)

**Exercise 25–2**

Select the best answer in each of the following. Give the basis for your response.

1. In preparing price-level financial statements, a nonmonetary item would be:
   a. Accounts payable in cash.          d. Allowance for doubtful accounts.
   b. Long-term bonds payable.           e. None of the above.
   c. Accounts receivable.
2. In preparing price-level financial statements, monetary items consist of—
   a. Cash items plus all receivables with a fixed maturity date.
   b. Cash, other assets expected to be converted into cash and current liabilities.
   c. Assets and liabilities whose amounts are fixed by contract or otherwise in terms of dollars, regardless of price-level changes.
   d. Assets and liabilities classed as current on the balance sheet.
   e. None of the above.
3. An accountant who recommends the restatement of financial statements for price-level changes should not support this recommendation by stating that—
   a. Purchasing power gains and losses should be recognized.
   b. Historical dollars are not comparable to present-day dollars.
   c. The conversion of asset costs to a common-dollar basis is a useful extension of the original cost basis of asset valuation.
   d. Assets should be valued at their replacement cost.
4. When price-level balance sheets are prepared, they should be presented in terms of—
   a. The general purchasing power of the dollar at the latest balance sheet date.
   b. The general purchasing power of the dollar in the base period.
   c. The average general purchasing power of the dollar for the latest fiscal period.
   d. The general purchasing power of the dollar at the time the financial statements are issued.
   e. None of the above.
5. During a period of deflation, an entity usually would have the greatest gain in general purchasing power by holding—
   a. Cash.                              d. Mortgages payable.
   b. Plant and equipment.               e. None of the above.
   c. Accounts payable.
6. The restatement of historical-dollar financial statements to reflect general price-level changes reports assets at—
   a. Lower cost or market.
   b. Current appraisal values.
   c. Costs adjusted for purchasing power changes.
   d. Current replacement cost.
   e. None of the above.
7. An unacceptable practice for reporting general price-level information is:
   a. The inclusion of general price-level gains and losses on monetary items in the price-level income statement.
   b. The inclusion of extraordinary gains and losses in the general price-level income statement.
   c. The use of charts, ratios, and narrative information.
   d. The use of specific price indices to restate inventories, plant, and equipment.
   e. None of the above.
                                                         (AICPA adapted)

**Exercise 25-3**

Whatley Company is preparing financial statements on the purchasing power basis. Selected data are as follows:

1. Price-index data:

| | |
|---|---|
| January 1, 19A ................. | 95 |
| December 31, 19A.............. | 100 |
| June 30, 19B ..................... | 105 |
| December 31, 19D.............. | 140 |
| Average for 19E................. | 145 |
| December 31, 19E.............. | 150 |

2. Property, plant, and equipment acquisition and depreciation data:
   a. Land acquired January 1, 19A, at a cost of $80,000.
   b. Building acquired December 31, 19A, at a cost of $120,000; by year-end, 19D and 19E respectively, accumulated depreciation on the building amounted to $44,000 and $48,000.
   c. Equipment costing $168,000 was acquired June 30, 19B; by December 31, 19D, accumulated depreciation amounted to $109,200; depreciation recorded for 19E was $8,400.
   d. New equipment added during 19E at a time when the index was at an average value for the year cost $58,000; depreciation recorded on this new equipment for 19E amounted to $4,350.
3. Monetary items:
   At the start of 19E, total monetary assets amounted to $112,000, while total monetary liabilities amounted to $180,000. At the end of 19E, total monetary assets amounted to $120,000 while total monetary liabilities were $190,000.

*Required:*

Use the numbers below for identification and compute the amounts for each numbered item. Round to nearest dollar.

A. On the price-level balance sheet as of December 31, 19E, carrying values for each would be:
   1. Land.
   2. Building (gross amount).
   3. Accumulated depreciation – building.
   4. Original equipment (gross amount).
   5. New equipment (gross amount).
   6. Accumulated depreciation – equipment (original).
   7. Accumulated depreciation – equipment (new).
   8. Total monetary assets.
   9. Total monetary liabilities.
B. On the price-level income statement for the year ended December 31, 19E, amounts reported would be:
   10. Depreciation expense (original equipment).
   11. Depreciation expense (new equipment).
   12. Depreciation expense (building).
   13. Sales (if sales of $290,000 were made evenly throughout 19E).
C. If, as of December 31, 19E, comparative balance sheets were being prepared on a price-level basis, and the amounts related to the December 31, 19D, balance sheet were being restated, the amounts would be:
   14. Land.
   15. Equipment (gross amount).
   16. Building (gross amount).
   17. Accumulated depreciation – building.
   18. Monetary assets.
   19. Monetary liabilities.

### Exercise 25–4

Some items on conventional cost basis financial statements are expressed in current period dollars (or nearly so), while other items are normally expressed in dollars of prior periods.

*Required:*

1. Name the principal balance sheet items which likely would not be expressed in current period dollars. If any part of your answer depends on the accounting procedures employed, explain.
2. Name the principal items in the income statement which likely would not be expressed in current period dollars (or nearly so). If any part of your answer depends on the accounting procedures used, explain.
3. Name the principal items in the statement of changes in financial position which likely would not be expressed in current period dollars. If any part of your answer depends on the accounting procedures used, explain.

(AICPA adapted)

### Exercise 25–5

DE Company is completing its fifth year of operations (19E). Comparative balance sheets (historical cost basis) at year-end 19D and 19E appear below.

|  | December 31 | |
|---|---|---|
|  | *19D* | *19E* |
| Cash and receivables....................... | $250,000 | $325,000 |
| Inventories..................................... | 187,500 | 162,500 |
| Future plant site ............................. | 62,500 | 62,500 |
| Fixtures ......................................... | 210,000 | 270,000 |
| Accumulated depreciation .............. | (50,000) | (74,000) |
|  | $660,000 | $746,000 |
| Current liabilities............................. | $ 75,000 | $137,500 |
| Long-term liabilities ........................ | 150,000 | 125,000 |
| Capital stock................................... | 400,000 | 400,000 |
| Retained earnings ........................... | 35,000 | 83,500 |
|  | $660,000 | $746,000 |

The income statement (historical cost basis) for the year ended December 31, 19E, follows.

| | | |
|---|---|---|
| Sales ............................................................... | | $1,000,000 |
| Cost of goods sold: | | |
| Beginning inventory ......................................... | $187,500 | |
| Purchases....................................................... | 625,000 | |
| Goods available .............................................. | 812,500 | |
| Ending inventory.............................................. | 162,500 | |
| Cost of goods sold........................................... | | 650,000 |
| Gross margin ................................................... | | 350,000 |
| Expenses: | | |
| Operating expenses except depreciation.............. | 120,000 | |
| Depreciation.................................................... | 24,000 | 144,000 |
| Income before taxes ......................................... | | 206,000 |
| Income taxes .................................................. | | 87,500 |
| Net Income ..................................................... | | $ 118,500 |

A dividend of $70,000 was paid at year-end. In mid-year added fixtures costing $60,000 were bought. The annual rate of depreciation on fixtures is 10% of cost. Inventories are on a *Fifo* basis. When the original fixtures and the future plant site were acquired during the first year of operations the relevant price index was at 105. Other price index data and conversion factors are as follows:

|  | Index | Conversion Factor |
|---|---|---|
| December 31, 19E | 136.5 | 100 |
| December 31, 19D | 125 | 109.2 |
| Average for 19E | 131.25 | 104 |

Assume the beginning inventory was acquired at 19D year-end prices. Purchases, sales, operating expenses, and income taxes occurred or accrued ratably throughout the year.

*Required:*

1. Prepared a price-level balance sheet as of December 31, 19E, and a price-level income statement for 19E. Determine the price-level (purchasing power) gain or loss and present a separate schedule detailing its computation.
2. Indicate the gross and net carrying values of the fixtures and of the future plant site for a price-level balance sheet as of December 31, 19D.

### Exercise 25–6

The items reflected in the trial balance below were acquired when the relevant price index was 105.

| | | |
|---|---|---|
| Cash | $57,235 | |
| Land | 79,500 | |
| Liability | | $   2,570 |
| Capital stock | | 100,000 |
| Retained earnings | | 34,165 |

The following transactions took place during the first quarter of the current fiscal year:

| Date | Index | Data |
|---|---|---|
| Oct.  1 | 110 | Purchased machinery costing $8,500 on account. |
| Oct. 15 | 120 | Paid for machinery purchased on October 1. |
| Oct. 31 | 135 | Billed customers for services rendered, $7,500. |
| Nov. 15 | 140 | Paid $1,230 of the initial liability balance. |
| Nov. 30 | 145 | Collected half of the billed revenue. |
| Dec. 10 | 150 | Paid general expense of $5,700. |
| Dec. 31 | 160 | Accrued three months' depreciation on machinery which has a five-year life with no scrap value. |

*Required:*

1. Enter the initial balances, and then record the transactions for the first quarter directly in ledger accounts; also include, in parentheses, the index number values prevailing when each transaction occurred.

2. As of the close of the quarter, prepare both balance sheets and income statements on both conventional cost basis and price-level basis using the index number procedures illustrated in the chapter. Show calculation of the price-level (purchasing power) gain or loss. Since no average index value for the period is given, it will be necessary to apply to each transaction, a specific conversion factor. For example, if a $360 transaction occurred when the index was 120, in December 31 terms, this would convert to: $360 × 160/120 = $480. Round all calculations to the nearest dollar.

### Exercise 25–7

An investor bought land for $60,000 in 19A when the index measuring general purchasing power of the dollar was 110. Assuming a gain on sale of the land is taxable at a capital gains rate of 25%, at what price would the land have to be sold on each of the following dates for the investor to maintain the equivalent purchasing power after taxes? In each instance the index number on the date of sale was:

| Date of Sale | Index |
|---|---|
| a. October 1, 19B | 121 |
| b. May 1, 19C | 129 |
| c. July 1, 19D | 143 |
| d. December 1, 19E | 154 |

Round answers to nearest dollar.

### Exercise 25–8

The controller of the Robinson Company is discussing a comment you made in the course of presenting your audit report.

"... and frankly," L. Fisher continued, "I agree that we, too, are responsible for finding ways to produce more relevant financial statements which are as reliable as the ones we now produce.

"For example, suppose the company acquired a finished item for inventory for $40 when the general price-level index was 110. And, later, the item was sold for $75 when the general price-level index was 121 and the current replacement cost was $54. We could calculate a 'holding gain.'"

*Required:*

1. Explain to what extent and how current replacement costs already are used *within* generally accepted accounting principles to value inventories.
2. Calculate in good form the amount of the holding gain in Fisher's example.
3. Why is the use of current replacement cost for *both* inventories and cost of goods sold preferred by some accounting authorities to the generally accepted use of *Fifo* or *Lifo*?

(AICPA adapted)

### PROBLEMS

### Problem 25–1

MR Company is preparing financial statements on the purchasing power basis. Selected data are as follows:

1. Price level numbers:

January 1, 19A ................. 90
December 31, 19A.............. 95
June 30, 19B ...................... 100
December 31, 19B.............. 106
December 31, 19D.............. 145
Average for 19E................. 150
December 31, 19E.............. 155

2. From historical cost statements—property, plant, and equipment acquisition and depreciation data:
   a. Land acquired January 1, 19A, at a cost of $45,000.
   b. Building acquired December 31, 19A, at a cost of $380,000; by year-end 19D and 19E respectively, Accumulated Depreciation—Building account reflected balances of $22,800 and $30,400.
   c. Fixtures costing $77,000 were acquired June 30, 19B; on these accumulated depreciation recorded by year-end 19D and 19E amounted to $19,250 and $26,950.
   d. Additional fixtures were bought in mid-year 19E for $30,000 when the index was 150; by year-end depreciation recorded on the newest fixtures amounted to $2,250.

3. Monetary assets:
   At the start of 19E, total monetary assets were $87,000 and total monetary liabilities were $31,900. At the end of 19E, total monetary assets were $96,400, and total monetary liabilities were $33,800.

*Required:*

Use the numbers given below for identification and compute the amounts that would appear on price-level financial statements. Round to nearest dollar.

A. On the price-level balance sheet as of December 31, 19E, the carrying values would be:
   1. Land.
   2. Building (gross amount).
   3. Old fixtures (gross amount).
   4. New fixtures (gross amount).
   5. Accumulated depreciation—building.
   6. Accumulated depreciation—old fixtures.
   7. Accumulated depreciation—new fixtures.
   8. Total monetary assets.
   9. Total monetary liabilities.

B. On the price-level income statement for the year ended December 31, 19E, amounts reported would be:
   10. Depreciation expense (building).
   11. Depreciation expense (new fixtures).
   12. Depreciation expense (old fixtures).
   13. Purchases (assume purchases of $285,000 were made evenly throughout 19E).
   14. Price-level gain or loss (based solely on starting and ending monetary items).

C. If, as of December 31, 19E, comparative balance sheets were being prepared on a price-level basis and amounts related to the December 31, 19D, balance sheet were being restated, the restated amounts would be:
   15. Land.

16. Fixtures (gross amount).
17. Monetary assets.
18. Monetary liabilities.
19. Building (gross amount).
20. Accumulated depreciation—fixtures.

## Problem 25-2

Barden Corporation, a manufacturer with large investments in plant and equipment, began operations in 1938. The company's history has been one of expansion in sales, production, and physical facilities. Recently, some concern has been expressed that the conventional financial statements do not provide sufficient information for decisions by investors. After consideration of proposals for various types of supplementary financial statements to be included in the 1976 annual report, management has decided to present a balance sheet as of December 31, 1976, and a statement of income and retained earnings for 1976, both restated for changes in the general price level.

*Required:*
1. On what basis can it be contended that Barden's conventional statements should be restated for changes in the general price level?
2. Distinguish between financial statements restated for general price-level changes and current-value financial statements.
3. Distinguish between monetary and nonmonetary assets and liabilities, as the terms are used in general price-level accounting. Give examples of each.
4. Outline the procedures Barden should follow in preparing the proposed supplementary statements.
5. Indicate the major similarities and differences between the proposed supplementary statements and the corresponding conventional statements.
6. Assuming that in the future Barden will want to present comparative supplementary statements, can the 1976 supplementary statements be presented in 1977 without adjustment? Explain.

(AICPA adapted)

## Problem 25-3

CTZ Company prepared the following comparative balance sheets (historical cost basis) at the close of its fourth year of operations (19D).

|  | December 31 | |
| --- | --- | --- |
|  | 19C | 19D |
| Cash | $ 29,000 | $ 40,320 |
| Receivables | 75,000 | 100,000 |
| Inventory | 21,000 | 35,000 |
| Land | 100,000 | 100,000 |
| Building | 320,000 | 320,000 |
| Accumulated depreciation—building | (38,400) | (51,200) |
| Fixtures | 90,000 | 120,000 |
| Accumulated depreciation—fixtures | (40,500) | (58,500) |
| Total | $556,100 | $605,620 |

| | | |
|---|---:|---:|
| Current liabilities ........................................... | $ 50,000 | $ 75,000 |
| Bonds payable ............................................. | 50,000 | 50,000 |
| Common stock............................................. | 250,000 | 250,000 |
| Retained earnings ....................................... | 206,100 | 230,620 |
| | $556,100 | $605,620 |

The income statement (historical cost basis) for 19D was:

| | | |
|---|---:|---:|
| Sales ...................................................... | | $950,000 |
| Cost of goods sold: | | |
|     Beginning inventory ................................ | $ 21,000 | |
|     Purchases ............................................... | 584,000 | |
|     Goods available ....................................... | 605,000 | |
|     Ending inventory ...................................... | 35,000 | |
| Cost of goods sold ...................................... | | 570,000 |
| Gross margin............................................... | | 380,000 |
| Expenses: | | |
|     Operating expenses ................................. | 125,000 | |
|     Depreciation—building ............................. | 12,800 | |
|     Depreciation—fixtures ............................. | 18,000 | |
|     Salaries ................................................. | 100,000 | 255,800 |
| Income before taxes ..................................... | | 124,200 |
| Income tax................................................. | | 49,680 |
| Net Income................................................. | | $ 74,520 |

A $50,000 dividend was paid at year-end. Fixtures costing $30,000 were bought on January 2, 19D. Fixtures are depreciated 15% per annum on cost. Inventories are on a *Fifo* basis; the ending inventory can be assumed to have been acquired at the average level of prices prevailing during 19D. When the land, buildings, and original fixtures were acquired the price index was 103. Other price index data and conversion factors are:

| | Index | Conversion Factor |
|---|---|---|
| December 31, 19D.............. | 127 | 100 |
| December 31, 19C.............. | 119 | 106.7 |
| Average for 19D................. | 124 | 102.4 |

The beginning inventory can be assumed to have been acquired at 19C year-end prices. Purchases, sales, operating expenses (which include interest), salaries, and income taxes accrued evenly throughout 19D. The building is depreciated over a 25-year life; no residual value, straight-line basis.

*Required:*

1. Prepare a price-level balance sheet as of December 31, 19D, and a price-level income statement for 19D; show computation of the purchasing power gain or loss for the year.
2. Indicate the gross and net carrying values of fixtures and building for a price-level balance sheet as of December 31, 19C.

**Problem 25–4**

Dolphin Company prepared the comparative balance sheets (historical cost basis) which appear below at the close of its tenth year of operations (19J).

|  | December 31 | |
|---|---|---|
|  | *19I* | *19J* |
| Cash | $ 75,000 | $101,000 |
| Receivables | 215,000 | 195,000 |
| Inventory | 135,000 | 127,000 |
| Land | 150,000 | 150,000 |
| Building | 240,000 | 240,000 |
| Accumulated depreciation – building | (56,000) | (64,000) |
| Machinery | 225,000 | 280,000 |
| Accumulated depreciation – machinery | (115,000) | (137,500) |
| Total | $869,000 | $891,500 |
| Current liabilities | $124,000 | $137,000 |
| Long-term liabilities | 75,000 | 81,000 |
| Bonds payable | 60,000 | 60,000 |
| Common stock | 350,000 | 350,000 |
| Retained earnings | 260,000 | 263,500 |
|  | $869,000 | $891,500 |

The land was bought in 19A when the price index was 104. The building was acquired early in 19C when the index was 107; it has an estimated 30-year life and no salvage value and is depreciated on a straight-line basis. Machinery is depreciated 10% per annum on cost with no salvage value. The first machinery was bought in 19B when the price index was 106 at a cost of $50,000; a second machine was acquired for $100,000 in 19D when the index was 108.5; a third machine was bought in 19H when the index was 117. A full year's depreciation is taken in the year of acquisition unless the purchase is at year-end. At year-end 19J machinery costing $55,000 was acquired.

On January 2, 19J, an $85,000 dividend was declared and paid. The beginning inventory can be assumed to have been acquired when the index was 107; the ending inventory should be converted on the assumption the index was 125 when it was bought.

Sales, operating expenses, income taxes, and purchases accrued ratably during 19J. Relevant price index data (aside from that already given) are as follows:

|  | Index | Conversion Factor |
|---|---|---|
| December 31, 19J | 127 | 100 |
| December 31, 19I | 121 | 104.96 |
| Average for 19J | 125 | 101.6 |

The income statement (historical cost basis) for the year 19J was as follows:

| Sales............................................... | | $1,275,000 |
|---|---|---|
| Cost of goods sold: | | |
| Inventory, January 1..................... | $135,000 | |
| Purchases ............................... | 850,000 | |
| Goods available......................... | 985,000 | |
| Inventory, December 31 .............. | 127,000 | |
| Cost of goods sold ....................... | | 858,000 |
| Gross margin ............................... | | 417,000 |
| Expenses: | | |
| Operating expenses.................... | 210,000 | |
| Depreciation, building.................. | 8,000 | |
| Depreciation, machinery.............. | 22,500 | 240,500 |
| Income before taxes....................... | | 176,500 |
| Income tax ................................... | | 88,000 |
| Net income ................................... | | $   88,500 |

*Required:*
1. Prepare an income statement for 19J and a balance sheet as of December 31, 19J on a price-level adjusted basis. Show computations of the purchasing power gain or loss.
2. Compute the gross and net carrying values of machinery and the building for the December 31, 19I price-level balance sheet.

## Problem 25–5

When items in the following trial balance were acquired, the price index was 150.

| | | |
|---|---|---|
| Cash............................................. | $ 7,500 | |
| Equipment ................................... | 10,000 | |
| Accumulated depreciation.............. | | $2,000 |
| Liability ....................................... | | 1,900 |
| Capital stock ............................... | | 8,000 |
| Retained earnings ....................... | | 5,600 |

Transactions during the first half of current fiscal year were as follows. Index values prevailing at the time are indicated parenthetically.

Jan. 10   A payment of $800 on the liability balance is made (160).
Feb. 15   Revenue for services is billed to customers, $2,500 (175).
Mar.  1   Four fifths of the revenue billed is collected (180).
Apr. 20   Land is purchased for $8,000 cash (190).
May   5   General expenses are paid, $500 (185).
June 30   Accrued six month's depreciation on the equipment which has a ten-year life and no scrap value (200).

The index at June 30 was 200.

*Required:*

1. Enter the initial balances, then record the six months' transactions directly in ledger accounts; also enter the date and the index number parenthetically.
2. At the close of the six-month period, prepare both a conventional and price-level balance sheet and income statement using index number procedures illustrated in the chapter. Calculate the purchasing power gain or loss. Since no average for the six-month period is given, it will be necessary to apply to each transaction and balance, a specific conversion factor. For example, if a $660 transaction occurred when the price index was 165, in June 30 terms (when the index was 200), the restatement would be calculated as: $660 × 200/165 = $800. Round all calculations to nearest dollar.

**Problem 25-6**

Published financial statements of United States companies are currently prepared on a stable-dollar assumption even though the general purchasing power of the dollar has declined considerably because of inflation in recent years. To account for this changing value of the dollar, many accountants suggest that financial statements should be adjusted for general price-level changes. Three independent, unrelated statements regarding general price-level adjusted financial statements follow. Each statement contains some fallacious reasoning.

*Statement I*

The accounting profession has not seriously considered price-level adjusted financial statements before because the rate of inflation usually has been so small from year-to-year that the adjustments would have been immaterial in amount. Price-level adjusted financial statements represent a departure from the historical-cost basis of accounting. Financial statements should be prepared from facts, not estimates.

*Statement II*

If financial statements were adjusted for general price-level changes, depreciation charges in the earnings statement would permit the recovery of dollars of current purchasing power and, thereby, equal the cost of new assets to replace the old ones. General price-level adjusted data would yield statement-of-financial-position amounts closely approximating current values. Furthermore, management can make better decisions if general price-level adjusted financial statements are published.

*Statement III*

When adjusting financial data for general price-level changes, a distinction must be made between monetary and nonmonetary assets and liabilities, which, under the historical-cost basis of accounting, have been identified as "current" and "noncurrent." When using the historical-cost basis of accounting, no purchasing-power gain or loss is recognized in the accounting process, but when financial statements are adjusted for general price-level changes, a purchasing-power gain or loss will be recognized on monetary and nonmonetary items.

*Required:*

Evaluate each of the independent statements and identify the areas of fallacious reasoning in each and explain why the reasoning is incorrect. Complete your discussion of each statement before proceeding to the next statement.

(AICPA adapted)

**Problem 25-7**

AB COMPANY
Balance Sheet
At December 31, 19E

| | | | |
|---|---|---|---|
| Cash and receivables | $105,000 | Current liabilities | $ 60,000 |
| Inventory | 75,000 | Capital stock | 250,000 |
| Land | 20,000 | Retained earnings | 93,000 |
| Building | 200,000 | | |
| Accumulated depreciation— | | | |
| building | (20,000) | | |
| Fixtures | 40,000 | | |
| Accumulated depreciation— | | | |
| fixtures | (17,000) | | |
| | $403,000 | | $403,000 |

AB COMPANY
Income and Retained Earnings Statements
For Year Ended December 31, 19E

| | | |
|---|---|---|
| Sales | | $850,000 |
| Inventory, January 1 | $ 90,000 | |
| Purchases | 640,000 | |
| Goods available for sale | 730,000 | |
| Inventory, December 31 | 75,000 | |
| Cost of goods sold | | 655,000 |
| Gross margin | | 195,000 |
| Operating expenses | 136,000 | |
| Depreciation—building | 4,000 | |
| Depreciation—fixtures | 5,000 | |
| Total Expenses | | 145,000 |
| Income before taxes | | 50,000 |
| Income tax expense (40%) | | 20,000 |
| Net income | | 30,000 |
| Retained earnings, January 1 | | 83,000 |
| Total | | 113,000 |
| Dividend, paid at mid year | | 20,000 |
| Retained Earnings, December 31 | | $ 93,000 |

The foregoing statements, prepared on the conventional historical cost basis, are for the most recent year. Land, buildings, and $30,000 of fixtures were acquired January 1, 19A, when AB Company was formed and began operations. Fixed assets are depreciated on a straight-line basis with assumed zero salvage values. The building is assumed to have a 50-year life and the original fixtures, a 10-year life. An added $10,000 of fixtures bought in January, 19E, have a five-year life.

Inventory is accounted for on a *Fifo* basis. Sales and purchases and expenses (including income tax) occurred or accrued uniformly throughout the year.

Relevant price index data are:

| Date | Value | Conversion Factor |
|------|-------|-------------------|
| January 1, 19A .................. | 121.3 | 1.20 |
| January 1, 19E .................. | 136 | 1.07* |
| Average for 19E.................. | 140 | 1.04 |
| December 31, 19E.............. | 145.6 | 1.00 |

* Use this value to restate the beginning inventory.

Balances of working capital elements at January 1, 19E, were:

Cash and receivables............... $100,000
Current liabilities.................... 79,000

*Required:*

1. Prepare a price-level balance sheet and an income statement as of December 31, 19E. Show computations of the purchasing power gain or loss.
2. Show computations of the gross and net carrying values of buildings and fixtures on the price-level statements dated January 1, 19E.

## Problem 25–8

When the items reflected in the trial balance below were acquired, the relevant price index was 120.

| | | |
|---|---|---|
| Cash........................................... | $5,800 | |
| Equipment ................................... | 3,000 | |
| Accumulated depreciation............... | | $ 600 |
| Liability ...................................... | | 900 |
| Capital stock ............................... | | 5,000 |
| Retained earnings ....................... | | 2,300 |

Transactions during the first quarter of the current fiscal year were as follows. Index values prevailing at the time are indicated parenthetically.

Jan. 15  A payment of $480 on the liability balance is made (125).
Jan. 31  Revenue for services is billed to customers, $1,300 (130).
Feb. 15  Half of the revenue billed is collected (140).
Mar. 10  Land is purchased for $5,200 cash (130).
Mar. 20  General expenses are paid, $700 (140).
Mar. 31  Accrued three months' depreciation on the equipment which has a six-year life and no scrap value (150).

The index at March 31 was 150.

*Required:*

1. Enter the initial balances, then record the transactions directly in ledger accounts; also enter dates and the index number data (parenthetically).
2. As of the close of the quarter, prepare both conventional statements and price-level statements using the index number procedures described in the chapter. Show calculations of the purchasing power gain or loss. Since no average for the period is given, it will be necessary to apply to each transaction, a specific conversion factor. For example, if a $650 transaction occurred when the index

was 130, in March 31 terms, this would be restated as follows: $650 \times 150/130$ = $750. Round calculations to the nearest dollar.

## Problem 25–9

Skadden, Inc., a retailer, was organized during 19A. Skadden's management has decided to supplement its December 31, 19D, historical dollar financial statements with general price-level financial statements. The following general ledger trial balance (historical dollar) and additional information have been furnished:

SKADDEN, INC.
Trial Balance
December 31, 19D

| | Debit | Credit |
|---|---|---|
| Cash and receivables (net) ................................. | $ 540,000 | |
| Marketable securities (common stock).................. | 400,000 | |
| Inventory ....................................................... | 440,000 | |
| Equipment...................................................... | 650,000 | |
| Equipment—Accumulated depreciation .............. | | $ 164,000 |
| Accounts payable ........................................... | | 300,000 |
| 6% first mortgage bonds, due 19V....................... | | 500,000 |
| Common stock, $10 par ................................... | | 1,000,000 |
| Retained earnings, December 31, 19C .................. | 46,000 | |
| Sales ............................................................ | | 1,900,000 |
| Cost of sales.................................................. | 1,508,000 | |
| Depreciation................................................... | 65,000 | |
| Other operating expenses and interest .............. | 215,000 | |
| | $3,864,000 | $3,864,000 |

a. Monetary assets (cash and receivables) exceeded monetary liabilities (accounts payable and bonds payable) by $445,000 at December 31, 19C. The amounts of monetary items are fixed in terms of numbers of dollars regardless of changes in specific prices or in the general price level.

b. Purchases ($1,840,000 in 19D) and sales are made uniformly throughout the year.

c. Depreciation is computed on a straight-line basis, with a full year's depreciation being taken in the year of acquisition and none in the year of retirement. The depreciation rate is 10%, and no salvage value is anticipated. Acquisitions and retirements have been made fairly evenly over each year and the retirements in 19D consisted of assets purchased during 19B which were scrapped. An analysis of the equipment account reveals the following:

| Year | Beginning Balance | Additions | Retirements | Ending Balance |
|---|---|---|---|---|
| 19B | – | $550,000 | – | $550,000 |
| 19C | $550,000 | 10,000 | – | 560,000 |
| 19D | 560,000 | 150,000 | $60,000 | 650,000 |

d. The bonds were issued in 19B and the marketable securities were purchased fairly evenly over 19D. Other operating expenses and interest are assumed to be incurred evenly throughout the year.

*e.* Assume that Gross National Product Implicit Price Deflators (1958 = 100) were as follows:

|  | | Index | Conversion Factors (19D 4th Qtr. = 1.000) |
|---|---|---|---|
| *Annual Averages* | | | |
| 19A | | 113.9 | 1.128 |
| 19B | | 116.8 | 1.100 |
| 19C | | 121.8 | 1.055 |
| 19D | | 126.7 | 1.014 |
| *Quarterly Averages* | | | |
| 19C | 4th | 123.5 | 1.040 |
| 19D | 1st | 124.9 | 1.029 |
| | 2nd | 126.1 | 1.019 |
| | 3rd | 127.3 | 1.009 |
| | 4th | 128.5 | 1.000 |

*Required:*

1. Prepare a schedule to convert the Equipment account balance at December 31, 19D, from historical cost to general price-level adjusted dollars.
2. Prepare a schedule to analyze in historical dollars the Equipment—Accumulated Depreciation account for the year 19D.
3. Prepare a schedule to analyze in general price-level dollars the Equipment—Accumulated Depreciation account for the year 19D.
4. Prepare a schedule to compute Skadden, Inc.'s general price-level gain or loss on its net holdings of monetary assets for 19D (ignore income tax implications). The schedule should give consideration to appropriate items on or related to the balance sheet and the income statement.

(AICPA adapted)

## Problem 25–10

The Melgar Company purchased a tract of land as an investment in 19D for $100,000; late in that year the company decided to construct a shopping center on the site. Construction began in 19E and was completed in 19G; one third of the construction was completed each year. Melgar originally estimated the costs of the project would be $1,200,000 for materials, $750,000 for labor, $150,000 for variable overhead, and $600,000 for depreciation.

Actual costs (excluding depreciation) incurred for construction were:

| | 19E | 19F | 19G |
|---|---|---|---|
| Materials ........................... | $418,950 | $434,560 | $462,000 |
| Labor ............................. | 236,250 | 274,400 | 282,000 |
| Variable overhead.............. | 47,250 | 54,208 | 61,200 |

Shortly after construction began, Melgar sold the shopping center for $3,000,000 with payment to be made in full on completion in December 19G. One hundred and fifty thousand dollars of the sales price was allocated for the land.

The transaction was completed as scheduled, and now a controversy has developed between the two major stockholders of the company. One feels the company should have invested in land because a high rate of return was earned on the land. The other feels the original decision was sound and that changes in the price level which were not anticipated affected the original cost estimates.

You were engaged to furnish guidance to these stockholders in resolving their controversy. As an aid, you obtained the following information:

a. Using 19D as the base year, price-level indices for relevant years are: 19A = 90, 19B = 93, 19C = 96, 19D = 100, 19E = 105, 19F = 112, and 19G = 120.
b. The company allocated $200,000 per year for depreciation of fixed assets allocated to this construction project; of that amount $25,000 was for a building purchased in 19A and $175,000 was for equipment purchased in 19C.

*Required:*

1. Prepare a schedule to restate in base year (19D) costs the actual costs, including depreciation, incurred each year. Disregard income taxes and assume that each price-level index was valid for the entire year.
2. Prepare a schedule comparing the originally estimated costs of the project with the total actual costs for each element of cost (materials, labor, variable overhead, and depreciation) adjusted to the 19D price level.
3. Prepare a schedule to restate the amount received on the sale in terms of base year (19D) purchasing power. The gain or loss should be determined separately for the land and the building in terms of base year purchasing power and should exclude depreciation.

                                            (AICPA adapted)

# Appendix—List of Official Pronouncements

This appendix is included to help students (a) gain an overview of the official pronouncements, and (b) identify appropriate source documents for numerous accounting issues discussed in this book. Further study of these issues in the source documents often is desirable.

**Accounting Research Bulletins (ARBs), Accounting Procedures Committee, AICPA (ARBs discontinued in 1959)**

| ARB No. | Contents | Status, January 1, 1976 | Chapter Citations in this Book |
|---|---|---|---|
| 43. | Restatement and Revisions of Accounting Research Bulletins Nos. 1–42, June, 1953 | Continued in force by APB Opinion No. 6 (as amended) | 1, 4, 5, 7, 8, 9, 11, 14, 16, 17, 24 |
| | Chapter 1. Prior Opinions | Amended | |
| | Chapter 2. Form of Statements | Amended and partially superseded | 5, 24 |
| | Chapter 3. Working Capital | Amended and partially superseded | 7 |
| | Chapter 4. Inventory Pricing | Amended | 8, 9 |
| | Chapter 5. Intangible Assets | Amended and partially superseded | 14 |
| | Chapter 6. Contingency Reserves | Superseded by FASB Statement No. 5 | |
| | Chapter 7. Capital Accounts | Amended and partially superseded | |
| | Chapter 8. Income and Earned Surplus | Superseded by APB Opinion No. 9 | |
| | Chapter 9. Depreciation | Amended and partially superseded | 25 |
| | Chapter 10. Taxes | Amended and partially superseded | |
| | Chapter 11. Government Contracts | Amended | |
| | Chapter 12. Foreign Operations and Foreign Exchange | Amended | |
| | Chapter 13. Compensation (Pension Plans) | Amended and partially superseded | 17 |
| | Chapter 14. Disclosure of Long-Term Leases in Financial Statements | Superseded by APB Opinion No. 5 | |
| | Chapter 15. Unamortized Discount, Issue Cost, and Redemption Premium on Bonds Refunded | Amended and partially superseded | |
| 44. | Declining-Balance Depreciation; Revised July 1958 | Amended | 13 |
| 45. | Long-Term Construction-Type Contracts; October 1955 | Unchanged | 10 |
| 46. | Discontinuance of Dating Earned Surplus; February 1956 | Unchanged | |
| 47. | Accounting for Costs of Pension Plans; September 1956 | Superseded by APB Opinion No. 8 | |
| 48. | Business Combinations; January 1957 | Superseded by APB Opinion No. 16 | |
| 49. | Earnings per Share; April 1958 | Superseded by APB Opinion No. 9 | |
| 50. | Contingencies; October 1958 | Superseded by FASB Statement No. 5 | |
| 51. | Consolidated Financial Statements, August 1959 | Amended and partially superseded | |

**Accounting Terminology Bulletins, Committee on Terminology, AICPA (Bulletins discontinued in 1959)**

| ATB No. | Contents | Status January 1, 1976 | Chapter Citations in this Book |
|---|---|---|---|
| 1. | Review and Resume (of the eight original terminology bulletins), June 1953 ......... | Partially superseded | 1, 5, 10, 15, 16 |
| 2. | Proceeds, Revenue, Income, Profit, and Earnings ......... | Amended | |
| 3. | Book Value ......... | Unchanged | |
| 4. | Cost, Expense, and Loss ......... | Amended | |

**Accounting Principles Board (APB) Opinions, AICPA (Opinions discontinued in 1973)**

| APB No. | Contents | Status, January 1, 1976 | Chapter Citations in this Book |
|---|---|---|---|
| 1. | New Depreciation Guidelines and Rules, November 1962 ......... | Unchanged | |
| 2. | Accounting for the "Investment Credit," December 1962 ......... | Unchanged | 13 |
| | Addendum to Opinion No. 2—Accounting Principles for Regulated Industries, December 1962 ......... | Unchanged | |
| 3. | The Statement of Source and Application of Funds, October 1963 ... | Superseded by APB Opinion No. 9 | |
| 4. | Accounting for the "Investment Credit" (Amending No. 2), March 1964 ......... | Unchanged | 13 |
| 5. | Reporting of Leases in Financial Statements of Lessee. September 1964 ......... | Partially superseded | 23 |
| 6. | Status of Accounting Research Bulletins, October 1965 ......... | Amended and partially superseded | 5, 17 |
| 7. | Accounting for Leases in Financial Statements of Lessors, May 1966 ......... | Partially superseded | 23 |
| 8. | Accounting for the Cost of Pension Plans, November 1966 ......... | Unchanged | 22 |
| 9. | Reporting the Results of Operations, December 1966 ......... | Partially superseded | 4, 14, 15, 16, 18, 20 |
| 10. | Omnibus Opinion—1966, December 1966 ......... | Amended and partially superseded | 4, 15, 16, 17 |
| 11. | Accounting for Income Taxes, December 1967 ......... | Amended and partially superseded | 4, 11 |
| 12. | Omnibus Opinion—1967, December 1967 ......... | Amended and partially superseded | 4, 5, 13, 16 |

| # Title | Status | Beyond scope of this book |
|---|---|---|
| 13. Amending Paragraph 6 of APB Opinion No. 9, Application to Commercial Banks, March 1969 | Amended | 4, 17 |
| 14. Accounting for Convertible Debt and Debt Issued with Stock Purchase Warrants, March 1969 | Unchanged | |
| 15. Earnings per Share, May 1969 | Unchanged | 18 |
| 16. Business Combinations, August 1970 | Amended | 14, 18 |
| 17. Intangible Assets, August 1970 | Unchanged | |
| 18. The Equity Method of Accounting for Investments in Common Stock, March 1971 | Amended and partially superseded | 18 |
| 19. Reporting Changes in Financial Position, March 1971 | Unchanged | 5, 21 |
| 20. Accounting Changes, July, 1971 | Unchanged | 2, 4, 7, 9, 11, 12, 13, 17, 20 |
| 21. Interest on Receivables and Payables, August 1971 | Unchanged | 2, 11, 19 |
| 22. Disclosure of Accounting Policies, April 1972 | Unchanged | 5, 13, 24 |
| 23. Accounting for Income Taxes—Special Areas, April, 1972 | Amended | Beyond scope of this book |
| 24. Accounting for Income Taxes—Equity Method Investments, April 1972 | Unchanged | |
| 25. Accounting for Stock issued to Employees, October 1972 | Unchanged | 17 |
| 26. Early Extinguishment of Debt, October 1972 | Unchanged | 19 |
| 27. Accounting for Lease Transactions by Manufacturer or Dealer Lessors, November 1972 | Unchanged | 23 |
| 28. Interim Financial Reporting, May 1973 | Partially superseded | 2 |
| 29. Accounting for Nonmonetary Transactions, May 1973 | Unchanged | 12, 21 |
| 30. Reporting the Results of Operations, June 1973 | Unchanged | 4, 8, 12, 15, 18, 19 |
| 31. Disclosure of Lease Commitments by Lessees, June 1973 | Unchanged | 23 |

**Financial Accounting Standards Board (FASB), Statements of Financial Accounting Standards (1973 to date)**

| FASB No. | Contents | Status, January 1, 1976 | Chapter Citations in this Book |
|---|---|---|---|
| 1. | Disclosure of Foreign Currency, December 1973 | Unchanged | Beyond scope of this book |
| 2. | Accounting for Research and Development Costs, October 1974 | Unchanged | 5, 14 |
| 3. | Reporting Accounting Changes in Interim Financial Statements, December 1974 | Unchanged | 20 |
| 4. | Reporting Gains and Losses from Extinguishment of Debt, March 1975 | Unchanged | 19, 21 |
| 5. | Accounting for Contingencies | Amended | 8, 11, 16 |
| 6. | Classification of Short-Term Obligations Expected to be Refinanced, May 1975 | Unchanged | 5, 7, 11, 19 |
| 7. | Accounting and Reporting by Development Stage Enterprises, June 1975 | Unchanged | 14 |
| 8. | Accounting for the Translation of Foreign Currency Transactions and Foreign Currency Financial Statements, October 1975 | Unchanged | Beyond scope of this book |
| 9. | Accounting for Income Taxes—Oil and Gas Producing Companies (an Amendment of APB Opinions Nos. 11 and 23), October 1975 | Unchanged | 11 |
| 10. | Extension of "Grandfather" Provisions for Business Combinations (an Amendment of APB Opinion No. 16), October 1975 | Unchanged | 18 |
| 11. | Accounting for Contingencies—Transition Method (an Amendment of FASB Statement No. 5), December 1975 | Unchanged | 11 |
| 12. | Accounting for Certain Marketable Securities, December 1975 | Unchanged | 5, 7, 15, 18 |

# Index

*This book has been set in 9 and 8 point Primer, leaded 2 points. Chapter numbers are 18 and 36 point Helvetica italic and chapter titles are 16 point Helvetica. The size of the type page is 27 by 45½ picas.*